ENDICOTT COLLEGE
19
39
BEVERLY, MASSACHUSETTS

1

A — SAI

116

ITI. Vth Dynasty Egyptian Songstress (ca. 2450 B.C.)
The first woman composer in the record of music history
with female harpist Hekenu. (Relief in the Necropolis of Saqquârah.)
Photo: Cairo Museum.

International Encyclopedia of Women Composers

AARON I. COHEN

Second Edition
Revised and Enlarged

Volume 1

A — SAI

Books & Music (USA) Inc.
NEW YORK LONDON

Published by BOOKS & MUSIC (U.S.A.) Inc.
P.O. Box 1301, Cathedral Station, New York, NY 10025

UK and European Distributors
Books and Music UK, 25/26 Poland Street, London WI

Printed and bound by National Book Printers, 1987.

Printed in South Africa

ISBN 0-9617485-0-8 (Vol. 1)
ISBN 0-9617485-1-6 (Vol. 2)
ISBN 0-9617485-2-4 (Set.)

Library of Congress Cataloging in Publication Data
Library of Congress Catalog Card Number: 86-72857
COHEN, Aaron I.
International Encyclopedia of Women Composers
(Second Edition)

1. Women Composers - Biography
2. Music - Bibliography 1. Title

British Library Cataloguing in Publication Data
COHEN, Aaron I.
International Encyclopedia of Women Composers
2nd ed.

1. Women Composers - Biography
I. Title
780'.92'2 ML390

PRINTING HISTORY

First Edition
International Encyclopedia of Women Composers
Copyright © 1981 by Aaron I Cohen
Pp. XVIII + 597. New York NY. R. R. Bowker Co.
ISBN 0-8352-1288-2

First Edition
International Discography of Women Composers
Copyright © 1984 by Aaron I. Cohen
Pp. XXII + 254. Westport CT. Greenwood Press.
ISBN 0-313-24272-0

Contents

VOLUME 1

VOLUME 2

Contents

VOLUME 1

The Editor acknowledges with deep appreciation
the gift of a grant in aid
toward the completion of this edition
by
H. Spencer Clark, C.M., B.A. Sc., LL.D.
of Toronto, Canada
in memory of his wife
Rosa Breithaupt Hewetson Clark
A talented musician
and sponsor of the Arts
to whom this book is dedicated

Foreword

The International Encyclopedia of Women Composers as published in 1981, was the brainchild of a retired town-planner, Aaron I. Cohen. It was a 'labour of love'.

Cohen is the first and only person whose international curiosity and love of music led, without fanfare or publicity of any kind, to a crusade around the world to find all the women composers, living or dead, formerly known or unknown. He succeeded in locating some 6000 over 70 countries. He amassed a collection of 7500 records, which included the world's largest collection of the recorded works of women composers. His research took eight years to produce the first edition and four more years to produce this second edition.

Unaware of Cohen's activity, the Arts/Letters/Music Committee of the International Council of Women, at its 22nd Triennial in Kenya in 1979, was challenged to attempt a much smaller task - that of finding all the women composers, living or dead, in its own 74 member countries. An added directive was to try to enlist program planners and the media in each country to publicize these musical works, not only of their own countrywomen but of women composers of other countries as well.

After two years, 1979 to 1981, of fascinating and rewarding communications we had collected some 1200 names and received printed music, tapes and records from 32 of our member countries. A few names were accompanied by biographical material and photos. Needless to say, we had no intention of publishing a book!

It came as a complete surprise when the publication of Cohen's International Encyclopedia of Women Composers was announced in December 1981, and no group or individual anywhere was more appreciative of that marvelous (and I use the word advisedly) book! Mr. Cohen had succeeded in collecting biographical material, photographs and other information far beyond our imagination, and he had listed his 3700 names not only alphabetically but by country and by century, with an added list of 1200 names needing more information.

Our work had been done for us and in a much more scholarly way than we had ever envisioned. However, we had some names he did not have since some of our member countries were ones he had not included. We offered our lists to Mr. Cohen for inclusion in a second edition and asked only that he give the International Council of Women a line of credit. He generously agreed and immediately undertook the great task of contacting all those of our listed composers that he did not have, or their country's representative, to secure photos and biographies. Then suddenly, world financial conditions changed, and Mr. Cohen found that he could not, alone, finance a second volume. He had underwritten the first volume at a cost of some C$220,000 and he had so far spent another C$190,000 on this second edition.

There was no available money in the ICW treasury, and no individual woman volunteered financial support. However, two men were willing to help, my own husband Ralph S. Mills Q.C., D. Litt.s. and H. Spencer Clark C.M., B.A.Sc., L.L.D. As international convener of Arts/Letters/Music I appreciated the cooperation I had received from my national conveners and felt their work should not be forgotten. I asked Mr. Cohen if I might try to raise the sum needed to finish the manuscript and I found the late Mr. Spencer Clarke who helped out.

I have related these financial details purposely, because although women are being recognized for their abilities in many fields notably in raising money for cultural projects, and have new opportunities in the business and professional world beyond the fondest dreams of our grandmothers, and although there are many independently wealthy women in many countries, their support of women's cultural achievement is comparatively insignificant. There is as yet no women's monetary fund internationally or even nationally of major standing, contributed to and controlled by women to promote women's projects.

At any rate, it was a man, Aaron I. Cohen, not a woman, who initiated, researched and produced the first International Encyclopedia of Women Composers. The new edition has several unique features – making it even more valuable for researchers, performers, libraries and the media. Despite his not being allowed to enter countries 'behind the Iron Curtain' Mr. Cohen located 643 women composers there, a listing which is the only one, even in the countries concerned!

Another important piece of research was the discovery of the sequence of over nine centuries of Arabian women songstress-composers – all before the writing of music.

A noteworthy and unique feature of this Encyclopedia is Cohen's inclusion of numbered references. These indicate the sources of information of every fact that has been given – another first! There are so many new interesting and informative features in this book that appear in no other publication anywhere and in addition the complete and up-to-date discography of the women composers is a further endorsement of Cohen's meticulous and scholarly research. Twenty-five hundred years ago Sappho cried out on behalf of all women in the Arts:

"Someone, I tell you, will remember us,
We are oppressed by fears of oblivion".

That someone has been Aaron I. Cohen. He has rescued these thousands of women composers from that oblivion, most of whom would otherwise still be in utter obscurity, kept there by the unrelenting prejudice that exists in large measure even today. Since the publication of the first volume, the list of 'unknowns' has been reduced by over 500 and there has been a noticeable increase in acceptance of women's compositions by program planners in several countries.

Cohen has given his complete music library and all his working papers to the Institute for the Study of Women in Music at California State University (Northridge Campus) where they will be housed in a new building being erected for the purpose.

A pebble has been dropped in the water and the ripples are spreading widely.

Thora McIlroy Mills C.M., B.A.
International Convenor, Arts/Letters/Music
International Council of Women, Toronto

Preface – 2nd Edition

In a reference book of this nature, the preface is generally a stark raison d'être of the work, sometimes a basic resumé, generally didactic and always impersonal. However, since some twelve years of the winter of my life have gone into the research relative to the production of the first and second editions of this book, I feel that I can claim the privilege of an octogenarian to the injection of a personal note in this preface.

I have encountered surprise that this book was produced by a male town planner who was neither a musician nor a musicologist but merely a collector of phonograph records of classical music and whose musical expertise lay in the lowering and raising of the phonograph tone-arm, as well as the listening to some 7500 records.

But truth is, I am and have always been concerned with research in one discipline or other. However this one seems to have been quite successful, whilst not financially, but certainly in its reception by the musical world, since the first edition went out of print within fifteen months of its publication. I am told that it has since become a collector's item.

The first edition, which took eight years of research and preparation, drew a comparatively large number of reviews which in the main were good, constructive and encouraging. A few were chauvinistically disparaging and nit-picking, and one was vicious and insulting, about which the less said the better. I have been taken to task by some reviewers for the non-inclusion of certain women composers. The answer is simple, I just did not get the information. The project was no 'armchair job' although I sat in more than seventy major libraries in 18 countries. I cannot even estimate how many university and minor libraries and antiquarians I visited. There were limits to the amount of time I could spend because time and money were against me. I must thank those reviewers who were kind enough to give constructive advice which I was happy to use in this second edition. One question however did emerge in most of the reviews - "Why women?", they asked, the general implication being that either such a subject was of rather negligible importance or rather that there should have been no segregation of sexes. It is significant that, except for one, all the reviewers who raised the question were male.

"Why not women?" I reply – "a fascinating subject whose music history had been deliberately denigrated and neglected and had not been previously systematically researched on a fully international scale". But, when I started on the research I became appalled at the amount of prejudice that existed and still exists against the mental creative powers of women in general and the work of women composers in particular. It was this, more than anything that spurred me on towards completing the Encyclopedia and also towards finding out how this prejudice arose and developed. "And again, why not women composers?" Ask any musician, conductor or program director to give the names of women composers, and one would be lucky to find any who, off-hand could give the names of more than a half dozen. This book in its two editions constitutes the first and only listing that so many of the women composers have ever had, even in their own countries, let alone the outside world. This Encyclopedia is, in essence, a catalogue of the women composers who have survived the persistence of male prejudice for some two thousand years.

All in all, the project has been difficult, extraordinarily expensive and at times extremely frustrating.

Difficult because I lived 6000 miles away from the nearest centers of musical research and because of the many languages encountered and I am no linguist. Difficult too because of the discrimination by publishers et al against the women composers, and the search for references to bridge the wide gap in music literature relating to them.

Expensive because of the high cost of air travel and accommodation which I had to bear, since no institution or foundation was prepared to offer any grant-in-aid to the project because of its distaff connotation. Expensive too because of the necessity to build up a large library of books, reference works and other pertinent music literature because of my distance from the major music research centers and libraries. At this point I must express my thanks to the late Mr. Spencer Clark of Toronto, Canada who timeously gave me a sufficient grant to enable the very last lap of the manuscript to be completed (see dedication).

Frustrating because of the modern tendency towards the use of unisex names, as well as the use of men's names by women composers and conversely the use of women's names by men composers. In fact, even at the last stages towards typesetting by the printers, several names, their biographies, cross references in all of the relative appendices had to be deleted, because of last minute discoveries that the composers were men. This reduced my total of women composers to 6195. Frustrating too because of the large number of women who will not disclose their dates or even their countries of birth, and whose frequent residential mobility inhibited contact for further information.

But the publication of the first edition had in no small measure achieved its purpose. It did shake the almost completely masculine world of music into the realisation that there really were women composers and that there were quite a number of them too – 4900 in the first edition and now 6196 in the second – despite Sir Thomas Beecham's declaration that there were no women composers. What is more, some of them were very good and – shocking to the male musical ego – as good as, if not better than many of their male contemporaries, and increasingly so within the last thirty years.

Suddenly I began to get the defensive remark – "Why are there no female Bachs and Beethovens?" – a really stupid question. There are about 70,000 classical music composers (past and present) and nearly 92% are men. With all their superior advantages in learning, practise, research, development and opportunity, one wonders why there never have been any more B & B's amongst the men. One prejudice that still manifests itself is in the deliberate attempt to expunge information about the women composers. How else can I describe the practice whereby, even to this day and age, women composers' names in earlier editions of biographical dictionaries are deleted in later editions? That does not happen to the male composers. Surely if a composer is of sufficient importance to be included in a biographical dictionary why then should she be omitted in a later edition? I have been persuaded to prepare a lecture series on the subject of the history and growth of the prejudice against women in general and the women composers in particular. I expect to complete this soon after the appearance of this second edition.

Despite the good reviews that I received, few if any of the reviewers seem to realize the demoralising difficulties facing women composers, the virtually complete disinclination by publishers to handle their music, their non-recognition by program directors etc. The greatest desire of all composers male or female, is firstly to hear their music performed and secondly to have it published. That I have managed to collect as many women composers as I have, is a tribute to those writers in the centuries gone by who kept the names alive. I have frequently stated that the ubiquitous composer called "Anon" must for the most part be feminine.

The fame of any composers could be measured by the number of entries about them that appear in the international music reference literature. The one composer who did more for recognition of her country's music than anyone in her time was the American - Amy Marcy Beach (Mrs. H.H.A.). Even today she has more references than any other American composer. I have so far listed 52, in half a dozen languages at least.

This 1230 page book contains all of the information about the listed women composers that was available to me by the cut-off date (February 1987) before processing for the printer. The information relates only to the musical history of the composer, her education, her achievements and compositions. Any other information is contained in the numbered references at the end of her biography, which are the sources of every item of fact in the book.

This edition is more than likely to be my 'swan song' as my entire reference library, my phonograph records and albums and all the working papers of this Encyclopedia have been donated to the International Institute for the Study of Women in Music at the California State University, Northridge, Los Angeles, CA.

It would be appreciated therefore if all corrections, up-dates and relative information be referred there. It is my earnest hope that this edition will advance the impact created by the first edition towards the recognition of the growing number of women composers in the world of music today. The one regret that I do have is that the entries on the living composers did not include their residential or postal addresses. From my own experience I have found that the woman composer is probably the most mobile person I have ever known. From a purely selfish point of view, however, this research project has been the most satisfying that I have ever undertaken and I give thanks that at this time of my life when most of my contemporaries have passed on, I have gained a vast number of friends and acquaintances in each of the eighteen countries in which I have been privileged to visit and work, apart from pen friends in the Iron Curtain countries.

''Nos ignoremus quid sit matira senectus,
Scire aevi meritum, non numerare decit''.
Ausonius. (Poems).*

AARON I COHEN.

*''Let us not know what old age will bring, but accept only its rewards''.

Preface - 1st Edition

This book is an international biographical Encyclopaedia of women composers from ancient times to the present. The principal aim of this volume is to fill a significant gap in the history of music and the history of women's lives regarding the contributions of these creative women. The *International Encyclopaedia of Women Composers* represents the first time that research in this long neglected field has been attempted on an international scale. It contains 5000 women composers from nearly 70 countries, with complete biographies of 3700 composers.

One of the unfortunate facts of the history of music is the non-recognition of women composers. Although the performance of music has been regarded as a genteel avocation for women throughout the centuries, and many female performers have attained professional renown, there are few women composers whose works have survived. Notable exceptions include sixteenth-century Italian composer, Francesca Caccini, who composed madrigals and dramatic works and was the first woman to compose an opera; nineteenth-century German composer Clara Schumann, whose numerous works included a piano concerto; and French composer Germaine Tailleferre, who in the early part of this century became the only female member of the exclusive group of Parisian composers known as *the Six*. However, as this book documents, women have composed music throughout the ages – in large numbers and in nearly every country of the world. Indeed, they have contributed to the survival and growth of music before the time that music was first written down through the passage of song from generation to generation.

Women's traditional nurturance of the musical world has continued into this century. In the United States, women are the greatest fund raisers for orchestras and other musical purposes. Women are also estimated to form the majority of the 600,000-member constituency of the 8000 senior and junior music clubs in the United States. Fortunately, the past 20 years have seen a great surge in the number of women composers. Two-thirds of the composers included in this book are living today and one-third are from the United States. More important, perhaps, is the fact that a number of women composers of this century have been able to command serious critical attention and recognition, among them Claude Arrieu of France, Grazyna Bacewicz of Poland and Thea Musgrave of Scotland.

The recent rise to prominence of some women composers is especially noteworthy in view of how they have been handicapped by the neglect of orchestra conductors and program directors to include their compositions in their programs and the reluctance of publishers to accept their works for publication. Only six percent of the concert music composers in this book have had their compositions recorded. Among the interesting problems encountered in the compilation and verification of data for this book has been that many women composers used male pseudonyms in hope of getting their compositions published. This practice was fairly common in the past and two composers born in the nineteenth century who used it extensively were the French pianist and composer Augusta Mary Anne Holmes and the American composer Carrie William Krogmann, who is reputed to have composed over 1000 works under various men's names. More recently, the noted American music historian and composer Edith Borroff has experienced the rejection of her compositions when submitted to publishers under her own name, only to have them accepted when subsequently submitted under a man's name. Furthermore, in the welter of music that has been composed over the ages, one must pause to consider how much of it must consist of works that were performed once and never heard again. And how many surviving anonymous compositions are the work of women composers?

The International Encyclopaedia of Women Composers is the culmination of eight years of research, most of which took place in the major music libraries of many countries and through gratifying contacts with historians around the world. Librarians and music authorities from Cuba to Japan and from Finland to New Zealand freely gave information and assistance even though in many cases it meant much time-consuming endeavor on their part. Regrettably, no information could be elicited from the U.S.S.R.; all the information regarding composers from this country and their works was obtained indirectly from the countries of Eastern Europe, West Germany and the United States. Whenever possible, the composers themselves were contacted by questionnaire for detailed information on their activites and compositions.

In view of the extensive time frame covered in this book, the criteria for inclusion necessarily varied in application from age to age. In all periods, however, the effort was to be liberal and inclusive, rather than overly discriminating. Within the twentieth century, the composers included are known to have composed at least one work of serious instrumental music. Thus, popular songwriters of this century are the only general classification of composers that have generally been excluded. Exceptions to this rule include songwriters who composed for instruments other than voice and, in a few instances, songwriters whose compositions achieved worldwide recognition.

It should be noted, however, that as one goes back in time, from the nineteenth century, songs and ballads gain increasingly greater significance in musical and cultural history, as does the role of the songwriter and female singer who sang her own compositions. Among the most fascinating discoveries made in the research for this book was the identification of the Egyptian songstress Iti (ca. 2450 B.C.) as the first woman composer to have been mentioned by name in musical history. The important contribution of the long sequence of Arabian songstresses who carried the torch of music through the dark ages must not be underestimated and all that is known about the lives of these early composers has been unstintingly recorded here. In general, however, the information contained in these biographies relates to the musical side of the composer's life.

It is hoped that this book will contribute both to the revival of interest in the forgotten composers of the past as well as to the dissemination of knowledge regarding the works and lives of the many women composers active today. There is a wealth of literature on the history and nature of the prejudices against women in music; readers seeking additional information on this topic are referred to the bibliography entitled Further Reading that concludes this volume. There is no doubt that if the women composers of recent years were given the same exposure in the musical world as men, through the publication, performance, recording and broadcasting of their works, then the creative abilites of women composers would receive the full acclaim they justly deserve.

Acknowledgments

Once again I have the pleasant duty of affirming my sincere thanks to those who in one way or another have helped towards the creation of this second edition of the record of women composers, more especially to my secretary Prue Seels for her untiring and efficient attention to detail and to my current and former staff members, Judy van Aswegen, Esme Saraev, Peni Nel, also Shirley Brumage and multilingual Verity Hoff who carried on from the first edition of this book.

Special thanks are due to Dr. James Sabin of Greenwood Press for allowing me to reprint, with up-dates, my International Discography of the Women Composers. I am also grateful to Mr. Gideon Roos Snr. of SAMRO for his permission to print the complete list of the Performing Rights Societies of the world, together with extracts from SAMRO's brochure "Music in Hotels, Restaurants and Cafes" which appear in Appendix 13.

I am especially beholden to Thora Mills and her husband Ralph of Toronto, for their successful efforts in regard to the very welcome grant by the late Spencer Clark and also to Mrs. Mills for my obtaining the addresses of the affiliated members of the International Council of Women (Appendix 11). My thanks too to Dr. Julia Smith, Mrs. Thelma Robinson and Mrs. Antonia Winter for giving me the addresses of the constituent senior clubs of the National Federation of Music Clubs (Appendix 14).

The preparation of this edition has evolved the help of so many people, chief amongst whom was the late Dr. Merle Montgomery, whose friendship and advice I sadly miss. Once again my thanks go to all those people who, helping out in the first edition, have continued their assistance in this one, and they are Rev. Harold Bacon and Robert Dearling of Skipton and Spaulding respectively, England; Patricia Adkins Chiti - Rome; Susan Kagan - New York; Christine Wallbaum - London; Caroline D. Lomax - Toronto; Hilda Holbaeck-Hanssen - Oslo; Judith Rosen - Los Angeles; Jan O. Ruden - Stockholm; Elizabeth Hayden Pizer - Three Mile Bay, NY; Sister Nancy Fierro - Los Angeles; Dr. Peter Gradenvich - Tel Aviv; Kathe Kirk - Copenhagen; Alan Pedigo - Booneville, AR; Dora Sowden - Jerusalem; Nancy Van De Vate - Vienna; Ann Carr Boyd - Strathfield, Australia; Anna van Steenbergen - Brussels; Rocio Sanz-Quiros - Mexico City; David Nelson and Joe Cooper - Goleta, CA; Emma Lou Diemer - Santa Barbara, CA. Prof. R. Musiker - Johannesburg.
Thanks also to Bolivar de Figueredo - Rio de Janeiro; Elizabeth Yeoman - London; Ann Basart - Berkeley, CA; Nicolas Slonimsky - Los Angeles; Wanda Bacewicz - Warsaw; Marnie Hall - New York; Margaret Nabarro - Johannesburg; Catherine A. Dower - Holyoke, MA; Judy Tsou - Ann Arbor, MI; Deborah Hayes - Boulder, CO; Elsa Puccinelli - Buenos Aires; Perry Roth - Tel Aviv; Dr. John Ledec - Prague; Kristin Sveinbjarnardottir - Reykjavik; Heidi M. Boenke - Eugene, OK; Annette di Medio - Philadelphia; Ellen Shipley - Fayetteville, AR; Ray Reeder - Hayward, CA; Deborah Richardson - Washington, DC; Dean W. Corwin - Houston, TX; Donemus - Amsterdam; Odean Long - Victoria, BC. Thanks too, to the librarians of so many music libraries and the representatives of so many societies and institutions all over the world who patiently answered by letters.

Also a thank you to Charles Whitcombe and Malcolm Anderson, who on so many occasions came to our rescue in putting to rights the irritating vagaries of our very fractious computer.

Finally, whilst it is one thing to have carried nearly all the cost of the 12 years of research etc. involved in the compilation of a work of this nature, it is quite another endeavour to get it published and to this extent my sincere gratitude goes to one of my oldest friends, Barney Jacobson, for assisting me with the enormous cost concerned with the printing and binding of these volumes.

Notable facts about the women composers

These notes on the lives and accomplishments of women composers have been extracted from the biographies for general information and interest.

The Prix de Rome, awarded annually by the Académie des Beaux-Arts of Paris, has for a long time been regarded as a pinnacle of music achievement. The following women composers have received it:

Else Barraine	Odette Gautenlaub
Renate Birnstein	Rosa Granje
Lili Boulanger	Ginette Keller
Nadia Boulanger	Barbara Kolb - first American woman
Therese Brenet	Edith Lejet
Nina Bulterijs (twice)	Jeanne Leleu
Monic Cecconi-Botella	Susan Owens
Adrienne Clostre	Eveline Plicque
Fanou Cotron	Lucie Robert
Yvonne Desportes	Henriette Roget
Tamar Diesendruck	Jeanine Rueff
Helene Dolmetsch	Rose Thisse-Derouette
Rolande Falcinelli	Henriette Van Den Boorn-Coclet
Helene Fleury	Berthe di Vito-Delvaux
Jacqueline Fontyn	
Jeanne France	

Lili BOULANGER (1893-1918) of France, was the first woman to win the Prix de Rome with her cantata *Faust et Helene* in 1913 at the age of 19. In 1918 she was disqualified from receiving the Prix de Rome, which she had won with an anonymous composition in the section for unmarried men under the age of 30.

The following composers had one affliction in common - they were all blind:
Fannie Crosby (1820-1915) (U.S.A.)
Elizabeth Garnett (20th-century) (U.S.A.)
Florence Golson-Bateman (b. 1891) (U.S.A.)
Louise Haenel de Cronenthal (1839-1896) (Austria)
Ruth Maedler (b. 1908) (Germany)
Frances McCollin (1892-1960) (U.S.A.)
Jean Miller (20th-century) (U.S.A.)
Sachie Murao (b. 1945) (Japan)
Maria Theresa von Paradis (1759-1824) (Austria)
Jeannine Vanier (b. 1929) (Canada)

Agathe Backer-Groendahl (1847-1907) of Norway lost her hearing and so did Marie Duchamp (b. 1789) of France.

Two women composers passed their centenary. They were **Margaret Ruthven LANG**, an American who died in 1972, aged 105 and **Eloisa d'Herbil DE SILVA** of Cuba, who died in 1944 aged 102.

Three queens, all composers, were beheaded. **Anne BOLEYN** (1507-1536) of England and **Mary STUART** (1542-1587) of Scotland by the axe and **Marie ANTOINETTE** (1755-l793) of France by the guillotine.

Sister M. Rosalina ABEJO (b. 1922) of the Philippines, was the first nun to have papal dispensation to undertake the direction and conducting of symphony orchestras and other musical activities.

Raffaela-Argenta ALEOTTI (ca.1570-ca.1638) of Italy, composed the earliest printed collection of sacred music by a woman, with her *Sacrae Cantiones* in 1595.

Josephine AMANN (1848-1887) of Austria, founded and directed the first European female orchestra in Vienna.

Ruth ANDERSON (b. 1928) of America, was the first woman admitted to Princeton University Graduate School in 1962.

Elfrida ANDREE (1841-1929) of Sweden, was the first woman to compose an organ symphony. She was also the first woman telegraphist in Sweden and a pioneer of women's rights.

Violet ARCHER (b. 1913) of Canada, was the first woman composer chosen by the Canadian Music Council to be Composer of the Year in 1984. In 1958 she was the first Canadian composer to represent Canada at the 1st Inter-American Music Festival, with her *Trio No. 2*.

Nora ARQUIT (b. 1923) of America, was the first woman guest conductor of the United States Air Force Band in Washington, DC.

Florence AYLWARD (b. 1862) of Britain, became the organist at Brede Church at the age of nine.

AZZA AL-MAILA (7th cent.) of Arabia, was the first singer of Hejaz to sing in rhythmic cadences.

Tekla BADARZEWSKA-BARANOWSKA (1834-1861) of Poland, composed a song at the age of 22 that became the world's best-seller at that time. *La priere d'une vierge*, had over 140 editions and reprints throughout the world, and is still on sale.

BADHL (ca. 820) an Arabian songstress, was reputed to have a repertoire of over 30000 songs.

Esther BALLOU 1915-1973) was the first American composer to have a work premiered at the White House. This was her *Capriccio for violin and piano* (1963).

Alexandrine BAWR (1773-1860) of France, worked to support herself and was one of the first women in music to make a conscious effort to alter 19th-century attitudes to women.

Amy BEACH (1867-1944) composed *Symphony in E-Minor, op. 32*, which was the the first major symphony to be composed in America as well as the first by an American woman.

Marie BIGOT DE MOROGUES (1786-1820) of France introduced Beethoven's music to the Parisians.

Victoria BOND (b. 1945) of the United States, was the first woman to be awarded a D.Mus. (orchestra conducting) from the Juilliard School of Music and the first woman appointed as assistant conductor to the Pittsburgh Symphony and music director of Pittsburgh Youth Symphony.

Nadia BOULANGER (1887-1979) of France, was the first woman to conduct the Boston Symphony Society Orchestra, in London in 1937, the New York Philharmonic Orchestra in 1939 and the Halle Orchestra in 1963. She was the person who wielded the greatest influence on the course of music composition in America. She was probably the world's greatest composition teacher and it is calculated that from 1934 she had over 600 American pupils.
The following 83 women composers mentioned in this Encyclopedia studied under Nadia Boulanger:

Marcelle Aaron
Yvonne Aaron
Sister M. Rosalina Abejo
Esther Alejandro-de Leon
Ruth Anderson
Grażyna Bacewicz
Ruth Bampton
Susana Baron Supervielle
Marion Bauer
Suzanne Bloch
Lili Boulanger
Joanna Bruzdowicz
Maggie Burston
Katherine Davis
Sharon Davis
Elvira De Freitas
Rachel Eubanks
Beatriz Ferreyra
Cecily Foster
Dorothea Freitag
Lila-Gene George
Elizabeth Gest
Peggy Glanville-Hicks
Victoria Glaser
Ida-Rose Gotkovsky
Marian Grudeff
Rebekah Harkness
Andree Honegger-Vaurabourg
Mary Alberta How
Bonnee Hoy
Anna Kamien
Sharon Kanach
Ginette Keller
Dorothea Kelley
Tomoko Kusunoki
Charma Lepke
Maria Linnemann
Helen Lipscombe
Joan Littlejohn
Ellen Lorenz
Shirley Mackie
Carin Malmloef-Forssling
Marcelle de Manziarly
Marilyn Mason
Bernadetta Matuszczak
Margaret Meachem
Joyce Mekeel
Elizabeth Meloy
Merle Montgomery
Dorothy Moore
Thea Musgrave
Frances McKay
Barbara Niewiadomska
Anne-Marie Oerbeck
Blythe Owen
Muriel Parker
Julia Perry
Alina Piechowska
Evelyn Pittman
Leila Pradell
Dorothy Priesing
Marta Ptaszynska
Priaulx Rainier
Wendy Reid
Julie Reisserova
Ann Riley
Eugenie Rocherolle
Q'Adrianne Rohde
Hedy Salquin
Verdina Shlonsky
Ruth Slenczynska
Marcelle Soulage
Dana Suesse
Sarah Sumner
Rodica Sutzu
Erzsebet Szoenyi
Louise Talma
Michiko Toyama
Jeanne Vignery
Grety Voellmy-Liechti
Elinor Warren
Edith Woodruff
Mirjana Zivkovic

Dora BRIGHT (1863-1951) of Britain, was the first woman to have a work *Fantasia in G*, performed at a London Philharmonic concert in 1892. In the same year she became the first person to give a recital of purely English music in a historical concert from Bryd to Cowen.

Radie BRITAIN (b. 1903) of America was the first woman to receive the Juilliard publication award in 1945 for her *Heroic poem*.

Jadwiga BRZOWSKA-MEJEAN (1830-1886) was the first Polish woman to concertise in America and the first to play Chopin's *E-Minor concerto* outside Poland.

Dorothy BUCHANAN (20th-century) of New Zealand, was the first person to be appointed a composer-in-schools by the government.

Francesca CACCINI (1587-1640) of Italy, was the first woman to compose an opera *La liberazione di Ruggiero dall'isola d'Alcina*, performed on February 2, 1625. It was also the first opera to cover a subject unrelated to antiquity. Published in 1618, her *Primo libro* was the most extensive collection of songs by a woman to appear in print.

Mlle. CAMPET DE SAUJON (18th-century) of France, was one of the earliest composers of piano music.

Dinora de CARVALHO (b. 1905) of Brazil, was the first woman to become a member of the Brazilian Academy of Music.

Maddalena CASULANA (16th-century) of Italy, composed four madrigals which were the first compositions by a woman to be published (Venice, 1566).

CHRISTINE DE PISAN (1363-1441) of France, was the authoress of *Dit de la rose* in 1401, which was probably the first feminist book ever published.

Florence CLARK (1891-1977) of Canada, was the first person to be awarded an honorary membership of the Royal Canadian College of Organists, in 1976.

Avril COLERIDGE-TAYLOR (b. 1903) of Britain, was the first woman conductor of the band of H.M. Royal Marines.

Ruth CRAWFORD SEEGER (1901-1953) of the United States was the first woman to receive a Guggenheim fellowship, to study in Paris and Berlin, in 1930.

Lucille CREWS (1888-1972) of the United States, was the first woman to be awarded the Pulitzer travelling scholarship in 1926, for her symphony *Elegy* and her *Sonata for viola and piano*.

Fannie CROSBY (1820-1915) of the United States, wrote 8500 hymns although she had been blind from the age of six weeks.

Nancy DALBERG (1881-1949) was the first Danish woman to compose a symphony.

Ruby DAVY (1883-1949) was the first Australian woman to receive a D.Mus.

Elisabetta DE PATE (20th-century) of Uruguay, was the first woman in South America to conduct an orchestra and to have her works included in the repertoire of the Pan-American Union Band.

Lucia DLUGOSZEWSKI (b. 1925) of the United States, was the first woman to win the Koussevitzky prize of the International Record Critics' award.

Amy DOMMEL-DIENY (b. 1894) of France, won the first international prize for a composition by a woman in the GEDOK competition in Mannheim, 1950.

Louisa DULCKEN (1811-1850) of Germany, numbered Queen Victoria of Great Britain among her piano pupils.

Louise DUVAL (d. 1769) wrote the music for the ballet *Les genies*, which was the first work by a woman to be performed at the Paris Opera, ca. 1736.

Katharine EGGAR (b. 1874) was the first English woman to perform her own chamber works at a public London concert.

Lillian EVANTI (1890-1875) was the first black American woman to sing an operatic role in Europe. She made her debut in Delibes' *Lakme* in Nice, 1925.

Rolande FALCINELLI (b. 1920) of France was the first woman to receive the Prix Rossini, 1941. The following year she won the Prix de Rome.

Louise FARRENC (1810-1875) was the only woman musician in 19th-century France to hold the important position of professor of the piano at the Paris Conservatoire in 1842. She was succeeded in 1875 by **Louise MASSART** (1827-1887).

Carlotta FERRARI (1837-1907) of Italy, completed her first opera *Ugo* at the age of 20 and had to pay the entire expense of the first performance herself, because of objections to the fact that she was a woman. The performance was a huge success, but it is not known whether she ever received a refund.

Helene FLEURY (20th-century) of France was the first woman to be accepted as a candidate for one of the grand prizes for French artistes, a three year stay at Villa Medici, Rome.

Kay GARDNER (b. 1941) of the United States, founded the New England Women's Symphony in Boston in 1978, which performs works composed and conducted by women.

Roberta GEDDES-HARVEY (b. 1849) was probably the first Canadian composer to write and publish a sacred oratorio.

Abbie GERRISH-JONES (1863-1929) wrote *Priscilla* in her early twenties and it was the first complete opera, libretto and score to have been written by an American woman.

Teodore GINES (16th-century) a black Dominican, was the first woman composer of the Americas.

Ruth GIPPS (b. 1921) of Britain published and performed *The fairy shoemaker* at the age of eight. She was also the first woman to conduct her own symphony, *Symphony No. 3* in a BBC broadcast.

Chiquinha GONZAGA (1847-1935) of Brazil, was the first woman to conduct a theatre orchestra there, in 1885.

Angelique GRETRY (1770-1790) of France, wrote her first opera *Le marriage d'Antoine* at the age of 14. It was successfully performed at the Theatre Comedie-Italienne, Paris, in 1786.

Maria GREVER (1885-1951) was the first Mexican woman to achieve fame as a composer.

Ann-Elise HANNIKAINEN (b. 1946) of Finland was the first woman composer to participate in the Young Scandinavian Composers' Festival in 1968.

Eva HARVEY (1900-1984) is the only South African to have written full-scale grand opera.

HEKENU (25th-century B.C.) of Ancient Egypt, was the first harpist in the record of music history.

Saint HILDEGARD (1098-1179) of Bingen was the earliest composer whose mass has survived to this day. Her book *Materia medica* is still referred to today for information on medieval medicine.

Najla JABOR (b. 1915) was the first Brazilian composer of a piano concerto.

Marie JAELL-TRAUTMANN (1846-1925) of France, was the first person to play all Beethoven's 32 sonatas, in the course of six concerts given in Pleyel's rooms, 1893.

JAMILA (8th-century) an Arabian songstress, conducted the first touring orchestra, which consisted of 50 Arabian women musicians and regularly made the pilgrimage from Medina to Mecca.

Vitezslava KAPRALOVA (1915-1940) of Czechoslovakia, conducted an orchestra playing her *Piano concerto* at the age of 19.

Ivy KLEIN (b. 1895) of Britain, composed the song *She walked in beauty* which was performed at the coronation of Queen Elizabeth II, in 1952.

Dorothy KLOTZMAN (b. 1937) of the United States, was the first woman to conduct the Goldman Band.

Elisabeth-Claude Jacquet de LA GUERRE (1664-1729) of France, was the first major female composer of instrumental work and her opera *Cephale et Procris* was the first by a woman to be performed at the Académie Royal de Musique, in 1694. She wrote double stopping into music for the first time in her two sonatas in 1695. After her death, a medal was struck in her honor.

Margaret LANG (1867-1972) was the first American woman to have a work performed by an American orchestra. This was *Dramatic overture* played by the Boston Symphony, conducted by Artur Nikisch on April 7, 1893.

Maxine LEFEVER (b. 1931) of the United States, was the first and to date, the only woman to be made an honorary member of the United States Navy Band.

Ethel LEGINSKA (1890-1970) of Britain, was the first woman to write for and conduct in a major opera house, when she premiered her opera *Gale* at the Chicago City Opera, November 1935.

Liza LEHMANN (1862-1918) was the first woman in England to be commissioned to write a musical comedy *Sergeant Brue*. She was also the first English woman to enjoy success with her songs with a large proportion of the public and set the vogue for the song cycle in England.

Queen LILIUOKALANI (1838-1917) of Hawaii, was the most prolific composer of her country. She composed over 100 songs, including the Hawaiian National Anthem, despite being imprisoned for treason.

Jenny LIND (1820-1887) of Sweden, was the first woman to be represented in Poets' Corner, Westminster Abbey, London.

Ivana LOUDOVA (b. 1941) of Czechoslovakia, was the first female student of composition at the Prague Academy of Arts, in 1961.

Elisabeth LUTYENS (1906-1983) of Britain, was a pioneer of 12-tone music and with Humphrey Searle introduced this concept in 1939.

Gertrud MELL (b. 1947) of Sweden, is also a master mariner.

Dolores MERTENS (b. 1932) of West Germany, composed the song *Moon mission* which was transmitted to the first astronauts to land on the moon.

Marian MILLAR (19th-century) of Britain, became the first woman to receive a Mus.Bac. from Victoria University, Manchester, in June 1894.

Marquise de la MIZANGERE (1693-ca.1779) was the first French woman to compose piano music.

Ida MOBERG (1859-1947) was the first recognised Finnish woman composer.

Tarquinia MOLZA (16th-century) of Italy, was the first conductor to use a wooden stick to beat time, although batons as such were not used until the 19th-century.

Mary CARR MOORE (1873-1957) of the United States, was the only woman to lead an orchestra of 80 men at the San Francisco Exposition 1915, when they played some of her compositions. Her opera *Narcissa or The cost of Empire*, in 1912, is believed to be the first grand opera by an American woman composer.

Christina MORISON (b. 1840) was the first Scottish woman to compose an opera.

Johanna MUELLNER (b. 1769) of Austria, inspired Beethoven to write his only harp composition in *Die Geschoepfe des Prometheus*.

Alice NAMAKELUA (b. 1892) was named by the Hawaiian Music Foundation in 1972 as the person who had contributed most to Hawaiian music.

Denise NARCISSE-MAIR (b. 1940) was the first woman invited to conduct the Ontario Youth Choir, for the 1981 to 1982 season.

Alicia NEEDHAM (1875-1945) of Ireland, won a prize for the best song in celebration of the coronation of King Edward VII of England.

Dika NEWLIN (b. 1923) of the United States, was awarded the first Ph.D. (musicology) to be given by Columbia University, New York, for her *Bruckner, Mahler, Schoenberg*, in 1945.

Elizabeth OLIN (1740-1828) of Sweden, was the first prima-donna at the Royal Theatre, from 1773 till the mid 1780s.

Daphne ORAM (b. 1925) of Britain, was the first person to compose an electronic sound track for a BBC television play.

Marion OSGOOD (20th-century) of the United States, founded the Marion Osgood Ladies' Orchestra, the first such professional orchestra in America.

Maria Theresia von PARADIS (1759-1824) of Austria, although blind from early childhood, composed a wide range of works from piano concertos to operas.

Annie PATTERSON (1868-1939) of Britain, was the first woman to receive a D.Mus. from the National University of Ireland.

Dora PEJACEVIC (1885-1923) of Croatia, was accredited with the foundation of modern Croatian chamber and concert music.

Mary PERRY (b. 1928) of the United States, received an Outstanding Educator of America award in 1974.

Mary POWNALL (1751-1796) was an English lady who emigrated to America. Her song *Jenny in the glen* was one of the first published by a woman in America, in 1778.

Florence PRICE (1888-1953) was the first black woman in the United States to win recognition as a major composer. Her *Symphony in E-Minor* was played by the Chicago Symphony Orchestra and conducted by Frederick Stock in 1933. It was the first time that a symphony by a black woman was performed by a major orchestra.

Marietta PRIOLI MORISINA (17th-century) of Italy, wrote *Baletti et correnti a due violini* in 1665, the earliest known instrumental work by a woman.

Alice PROCTOR (b. 1915) of the United States was the first woman to receive a Ph.D. (composition) from the Eastman School of Music.

Yelena PUCIC-SORKOCEVIC (19th-century) was the first recognized Croatian woman composer.

Marie QUINAULT (1692-1793) of France, had a number of her compositions performed at Versailles and was decorated with the order of St. Michael by the King of France, the first time such a distinction was awarded to a woman.

Alba QUINTANILLA (b. 1944) of Venezuela, premiered her *Tres canciones* conducting the Venezuelan Symphony Orchestra; being the first woman to conduct it.

Fanny RITTER (1840-1890) wrote *Woman as a musician,* which was the first historical study on women in music to be published in the United States, 1876.

Constance RUNCIE (1836-1911) organized the Minerva Club at New Harmony, IA, said to be the first women's club in America.

Hedy SALQUIN (b. 1928) of Switzerland, was the first woman to be admitted to the orchestra conducting classes at the Paris Conservatoire, ca. 1951.

Margherita SANFILIPPO (b. 1927) of America, plays 11 instruments; the cello, the clarinet, the double-bass, the flute, the horn, percussion, the piano, the saxophone, the tuba, the violin and the viola.

June SCHNEIDER (b. 1939) of South Africa, was the youngest person to graduate with a Ph.D. (music) from the University of the Witwatersrand.

Clara SCHUMANN (1819-1896) of Germany, considered one of the most important pianists of her time, was one of the first to perform and make known Chopin's work. Clara was the first foreigner to be honored by the Empress in Vienna, with the title 'Kammermusikerin' in 1837.

Philippa SCHUYLER (1932-1967) a black American, began composing at the age of three. When she was 12, her award-winning symphony was played by the Detroit Symphony Orchestra. Two years later she made her debut with the New York Philharmonic Orchestra.

Verdina SHLONSKY (20th-century) was Israel's first recognised woman composer.

Dame Ethel SMYTH (1858-1944) of Britain, was the first woman composer to have an opera performed at Covent Garden, with *The Wreckers* in 1910. She was a suffragette who went to prison for her feminist activities.

Joanidia SODRE (1903-1975) of Brazil, was the first South American woman to conduct the Bonn Philharmonic Orchestra, in Germany.

Emma STEINER (1852-1929) of the United States, conducted over 6000 performances of more than 50 operas and operettas.

Florence SUTRO (1865-1906) was the first woman in the United States to receive a Mus.D. She was the founder of the National Federation of Music Clubs.

Iwonka SZYMANSKA (b. 1943) created the piano sonnet, a new musical form, in 1969 .

Maria SZYMANOWSKA (1789-1831) was the first recognised Polish woman composer and after John Field, was the second person to compose the piano nocturne.

Louise TALMA (b. 1906) of the United States, was the first woman to win two Guggenheim fellowship awards, in 1946 and 1947. Her opera *The Alcestiad* was the first work of an American woman produced by one of Europe's leading opera houses, Frankfurt am Main.

Ivana THEMMEN (b. 1935) of the United States, was the first woman to compose a guitar concerto, premiered on October 28, 1981 in Minneapolis.

Adelaide THOMAS (19th-century) of Britain, passed her exams for her B.Mus. at Oxford in 1893, but was refused her degree because she was a woman.

Diane THOME (b. 1942) of the United States, was the first woman to earn a Ph.D. from Princeton, in 1973 and the first woman to compose computer synthesized music.

Vittoria VANZO (b. 1862) of Italy, was one of the leading conductors of Wagnerian music in Italy.

Slavka VORLOVA (1894-1973) was the first woman to receive a doctorate in composition in Czechoslovakia.

Atala WARTEL (b. 1811) of France, was the first woman instrumentalist engaged by the Société des Concerts, Paris.

Grace WHITE (b. 1896) was the first woman composer of a violin concerto in the United States.

Jeanne ZAIDEL-RUDOLPH (b. 1948) was the first woman in South Africa to receive a doctorate in composition, in 1979. In 1987, she was commissioned to compose the score for a new ballet called "The River People". At the rehearsals she was so disillusioned by the off-handedness of the orchestra and their inability to maintain the special tempo and rhythms of the music, that she refused to use their recorded tapes for the rehearsals and final performance. Instead she created her own synthesized tape of the score. The new ballet was a success and the rhythmic complications of the music were brilliant in their electronic reproduction which had all the splendour and realism of a major live orchestra.

Ellen Zwilich (b. 1939) of the United States, was the first woman to be awarded the Pulitzer prize for music, in 1983, for her *Symphony No. 1*.

The following are black composers:

Amanda Aldridge
Marianne Bahmann
Lettie Beckon
Anna Blackwell
Margaret Bonds
Shirley Caesar
Alice Coltrane
Margaret Douroux
Shirley Dubois
Vivian Ellis
Lillian Evanti
Teodora Gines
Emma Hackley
Helen Hagan
Jacqueline Hairston
Ethel Harris
Margaret Harris
Jeraldine Herbison
Irene Higginbotham
Nora Holt
Marylou Jackson
Eva Jessye
Betty King
Tania Leon
Constance Magogo Ka Dinizulu
Delores Martin
Lena McLin
Augusta McSwain
Dorothy Moore
Undine Moore
Camille Nickerson
Julia Perry
Zenobia Perry
Evelyn Pittman
Florence Price
Philippa Schuyler
Nina Simone
Nellie Uchendu
Mary Williams
Ariel Witbeck

Quotations

ARCHIV. SEG. VAT ARMADIO V. VOL LX NO. 240 4/5/1686
On May 4, 1686, Pope Innocent XI issued an edict which declared that; "Music is completely injurious to the modesty that is proper for the (female) sex, because they become distracted from the matters and occupations most proper for them". It carries on to state that "no unmarried woman, married woman or widow of any rank, status or condition, even those for reasons of education or anything else, are living in convents or conservatories, under any pretext, even to learn music, in order to practice it in those convents, may learn to sing from men, either laymen or clerics or regular clergy, no matter if they are in anyway related to them and to play any sort of musical instrument". This edict was renewed in 1703 by Clement XI.

BADINTER, Elisabeth *(Le Rapport des Sexes: Egalite Difference, Alterite.* Unesco Seminar, Athens, 1985)
The dawn of the third millenium is coinciding with an extraordinary reversal in the power structure. Not only will the patriarchal system be dead and buried in most of the industrialised west, but we shall see the birth of a new imbalance between the sexes, this time exclusively to woman's advantage.

BEECHAM, Sir Thomas
There are no women composers, there never have been and possibly, there never will be.

BOND, Victoria (quoted in *Women at Work,* by B. Medsger, 1975)
The conductor traditionally has been anything but a mother figure. The conductor is much more like a general than a mother or teacher. It's a kind of enforced leadership, the kind of leadership more likely to be expected of men than women. A woman conductor, because of these traditions, must rely completely on being able to transmit authority on the grounds of her musical ability.

BUTLER, Samuel *(Note Books)*
If man is the tonic and God the dominant, the Devil is certainly the sub-dominant and woman the relative minor.

CALDWELL, Sarah (in *The Flamboyant of the Opera,* by Jane Scovell)
If you approach an opera as though it were something that always went a certain way, that's what you get. I approach an opera as though I didn't know it.

CLARK, Edward (*Sex in Education,* 1908)
Women might be able to equal or even outstrip men intellectually, but since biology had dictated that such intellectual development would be at the cost of their reproductive functions, it was to be condemned on biological grounds.

CLEMENT, A. (*The Troubadour as Musician,* ca. 1920)
The Musicians' Company of London, as first established under letters patent and the great seal of Edward IV, in 1472, was not only a fraternity but also a sisterhood of minstrels – a minstrel being a musician qualified to sing or play in public. (The present charter, granted by James 1, in 1604, dispenses with the sisterhood.)

DE BEAUVOIR, Simone. (*The Second Sex,* 1949)
Women have never constituted a closed and independent society, they form an integral part of the group, which is governed by males and in which

they have a subordinate place. They are united only in a mechanical solidarity from the mere fact of their similarity, but they lack that organic solidarity on which every unified community is based, they are always compelled to band .together in order to establish a counterservice, but they always set it up within the frame of the masculine universe.

DRINKER, Sophie (*Music and Women,* 1948)
But the music that women do create is of a quality and type entirely satisfactory to them and to their men, and is the highest that their culture knows. It requires for its composition, moreover, the same germ of emotional and artistic potency – the same capacity for symbolic thinking – that is required for the development of musical imagination at any time.

.....(Ibid)
Everything that we can deduce by working backward to these rock paintings suggest that the art of music may have begun in the singing of magic by women, and that women were the first musicians, and perhaps for some time the only ones.

.....(Ibid)
Unless a girl attains the rank of a successful virtuoso, she has far less chance for a profitable and interesting career as an instrumentalist than if she were a man of equal native talent and proficiency.

ELSON, Arthur (*Women's Work in Music,* 1904)
The Hindoo musical system of today is likewise ascribed largely to female sources. The scale consists of seven chief tones, which are represented by as many heavenly sisters. The names of tones (sa, ri, ga, ma, pa, dha, ni, corresponding to our do, re, mi etc.) are merely abbreviations of the names of the nymphs who preside over them.

HEINE, Susanne (*Women and Early Christianity,* 1987)
The suppression of a woman from an academic sphere of activity is a characteristic example of a way of proceeding which is matched by many more serious violations: The oppressive extent of violence against women, open and hidden, practised by strangers or by husbands, fathers and other close relations, against adult women, and also against children, is only now slowly coming into public view.

HENDERSON, Robert (*The Arts:* Daily Telegraph, January 1987)
Music, like poetry or drawing may have been a proper adornment for a cultivated young lady, but to attempt to go beyond that into the world of the professional musician, whether as composer or performer, immediately carried that taint of something unnatural and suspiciously unfeminine. Mostly debarred from adequate, and essential sources of education, the wonder is that they yet managed to achieve so much.

HENSEL, Fanny Caecelia (nee Mendelssohn)
Her family's attitude to women is expressed in the words of her grandfather:
"Moderate learning becomes a lady, but not scholarship. A girl who has read her eyes red deserves to be laughed at."

KORAN SURA. *4.31*
Men have authority over women, because God has made them the one superior to the other.

LANDOWSKA, Wanda (*Letter to a former pupil,* 1950)
The most beautiful thing in the world is, precisely, the joy of learning and inspiration. Oh, the passion for research and the joy of discovery!

LANIER, Sidney (*The Orchestra of Today – Music and Poetry,* 1898).
Let our young ladies .... address themselves to the violin, the flute, the oboe, the harp, the clarionet, the bassoon, the kettledrum. It is more than possible that upon some of these instruments, the superior daintiness of the female tissue might finally make the woman a more successful player than the man.

LAURENCE, Anya (*Women of Notes,* 1978)
Creative people all have a light that shines ahead of them, beckoning them to follow its glow, taunting sometimes, teasing sometimes, infuriating and frustrating at other times, but always there urging the fulfilment of that spark of genius within them.

LEHMANN, Lotte (The singing actor, from *Players at Work,* by Morton Eustis, 1937)
But to me the actual sound of the words is all important; I feel always that the words complete the music and must never be swallowed up in it. Tsic is the shining path over which the poet travels to bring his song to the world.

LUTYENS, Elisabeth
The Cowpat School of English Music. Term coined by Elisabeth Lutyens who was critical of the English type of countryside folk song, based on music typified by Vaughan Williams et al.

NAVARETTA, Cynthia (*Guide to Women's Art Organisations and Directory for the Arts* - 1982)
Women's music has played a role in development

in the political forces of the last decade. Of all the arts, it is the only one that has developed its own industry based on an alternate music movement.

NEULES-BATES, Carol (*Women in Music,* 1982)
Women's work in composition in the past was directly related to the restrictions placed on them as singers and instrumentalists, for it must be remembered that until the nineteenth century the roles of composer and performer were totally intertwined.

RAYNOR, Henry (*A Social History of Music,* 1972)
Music can come to life only in society, it cannot exist, any more than a play can exist, merely as a print on a page, for it pre-supposes both players and listeners. It is, therefore, open to all influences that society and the changes in social beliefs, habits and customs, can exert.

SAPPHO (630-570 B.C.)
Someone, I tell you, will remember us
We are oppressed by fears of oblivion
Yet are always saved
By judgement of good men

SIRA, Ben (*Book of Wisdom,* ca. 190 B.C.)
Consort not with a female musician lest thou be taken in by her snares.

SPENCER, Herbert (*Principles of Biology,* p. 485, 1895)
.... the deficiency of reproductive power among upper-class girls may be reasonably attributed to the overtaxing of their brains - an overtaxing which produces a serious reaction on the physique. This diminution of reproductive power is not shown only by the greater frequency of absolute sterility; nor is it shown only in the earlier cessation of child-bearing; but it is also shown in the frequent inability of such women to suckle their infants.

SMYTH, Dame Ethel (in the foreword to her *Female Pipings in Eden*)
The legend relates that one afternoon while Adam was asleep, Eve, anticipating the great god Pan, bored some holes in a hollow reed and began to do what is called 'pick out a tune'. Thereupon Adam spoke: "Stop that horrible noise", he roared, adding, after a pause, "Besides which, if anyone's going to make it, it's not you but me". (Ref. 645)

TENNYSON, Lord Alfred *(Locksley Hall)*
Woman is the lesser man
And all thy passions
Match'd with mine
Are like moonlight and sunlight
And water and wine

TRISTOAN, Flora (*Peregrinations d'une Paria,* Paris, 1838)
The level of civilization attained by the different human societies is proportionate to the independence enjoyed by women in these societies.

VAN DE VATE, Nancy (*Women in Music,* by Carol Neuls-Bates, 1982)
I would have to say the future of women in composition depends very much upon the future of the overall women's movement. But beyond that, I think the future of women in composition is as promising as women themselves choose to make it.

VAN DYKE, Dick *(Faith, Hope and Hilarity)*
Agnes Dei is a woman composer of music.

WAGNER, Richard (*Opera and Drama,* 1851)
Music is a woman .... she must be loved by the poet, must surrender herself to him, in order that the new art-work of the future may be born .... the begetter must be the artist.

ZHANG, Jue (In interview for *The Art of a Chinese Writer*)
If a woman is to be successful, she has to exert more effort than men. She has to deal with two different worlds. Besides the world that men deal with, we also have to deal with the world that men dominate. I hope my books can show women that they should not just blame society or blame men for their inequality. The correction of this inequality lies in their own hands, in realizing their own self-respect, their own values. And then, in this way, their existence will command respect from men.

BIBLICAL QUOTATIONS

CORINTHIANS 11:3
For the man is not of the woman but the woman of the man. Let the women keep silence in the churches for it is not permitted unto them to speak, but they are commanded to be under obedience, so saith the law.

ECCLESIASTES
All the daughters of music shall be brought low.

EXOD. 34:13
Ye shall destroy their altars, break their images ("goddesses?") and cut down their groves, for thou shalt worship no other god.

TIMOTHY 2:11-12
Let the woman learn in silence with all subjection. But I suffer not a woman to teach or to usurp authority over the man, but to be in silence.

Statistics

FOR THE STATISTICALLY MINDED, the following figures will be of interest.

The total number of women composers listed is 6196, spread over a time span of 44 centuries. Their continental distribution is as follows:

Europe	2997
North America	2164
Central & South America	181
Asia	103
Asia Minor	75
Australasia and Pacific	150
Africa	71
Ancient Near East, 2500 B.C. to 10th-century A.D.	82

Not included in these totals are a few women of ancient times who were not composers but were of significant importance musically to be mentioned in the biographies. The remainder are those composers whose *nationalities* had not been determined at the time of going to press. The detailed comparative distribution of the women composers over the centuries is set out in Appendix 3.

The greatest number of women composers is in the United States of America - 2009 the next is in the United Kingdom, which has 587. Then comes France with 447, Germany (East and West) follows with 423 after which is Italy with 314, whilst in all of the countries which are regarded as being behind the Iron Curtain, there are 648 (Appendices 3 and 4).

Most of these women were occupied as teachers – 1158, professors or assistant professors – 264 and lecturers – 438. There were 72 musicologists and 148 poetesses. There were 47 who were royals and some 123 were ecclesiasts. There were 543 writers, 12 playwrights, 27 actresses, 43 critics, 14 librarians and archivists and 83 publishers and editors (Appendix 9).

Taking the 18th-century as the base for their first real surge towards musical recognition and continuing to the present century, 271 women composed symphonies, 391 composed piano concertos, 129 composed violin concertos, 41 composed cello concertos, 891 composed operas and operettas and 593 wrote incidental music for the theatre, the films, the radio and the television and 302 for the ballet and the dance. 2612 wrote music for the piano, 754 for the violin, 525 for the cello, 283 for the viola, 59 for electronic instruments, 46 for the tuba, 15 for the synthesiser and 2 even wrote for the musical saw and 1 for the bagpipes. (Appendix 8).

It should be noted that some composers' names listed under Operas and under Operettas in Appendix 8 do not appear in Appendix 6. This is due to the fact that the titles of their operas were not available when this book went to print.

Of the women composers who were performers, 1858 were pianists, 462 were singers, 376 were organists, 196 were violinists, 37 were cellists, 51 played on electronic instruments, 11 were percussionists and 1 was a handbell ringer (Appendix 10).

There are 572 photographs of the women composers. Unfortunately a few hundred more could not be used, owing to the fact that for various reasons, the consents to reproduce them could not be obtained.

Guide to Use

ACCENTS. Owing to serious computer problems, the *umlauts* had to be eliminated and after consultation with the language authorities in the various countries, the letter *e* was added to all the characters concerned. The French, Spanish and Portuguese accents had to be added by hand and dealt with by the Optical Character Reader. This illustrates the difficulties facing the International Performing Rights Societies in their endeavour to set up a standard computerised program to cover the composers' names throughout the world.

BIOGRAPHIES of women composers are arranged alphabetically by name, with cross-references from variant names, pseudonyms and maiden names to the main entry. As the information applies, entries have been divided into five main parts: (a) biographical information; (b) compositions; (c) publications; (d) bibliography; (e) references.

a. *BIOGRAPHICAL INFORMATION* includes the composer's name, variant names, current nationality, instrument specialization, occupational activities, place and date of birth and death, a description of her musical career with emphasis on her music education, commissions, awards and distinctions. The word DISCOGRAPHY indicates that some of her works have been recorded and that the listing appears in the *Discography* at the end of this book. The word PHOTOGRAPH indicates the inclusion of her picture in the *Photographs* section immediately following the biographies.

b. *COMPOSITIONS* is a listing of the composer's works, grouped under the categories: orchestra; chamber; solo instrument; vocal; sacred; ballet; opera; theatre; electronic etc. The instruments for which a particular work was composed are listed in parenthesis after the title; names of instruments etc. are given in abbreviated form which are explained in the list of *Abbreviations*. Other information provided for individual compositions includes where available, the date of composition, the publisher and date of publication, dedicatory and commissioning information.

c. *PUBLICATIONS* is a listing of books and articles written *by the composer*.

d. *BIBLIOGRAPHY* is a listing of books and articles written *about the composer*.

e. *REFERENCE* concludes each entry, with a list of reference numbers which are keyed to consecutively numbered sources in the *Bibliography* section of the book. In instances where the composer herself supplied the information for the entry, the word 'composer' precedes the list of reference numbers. The names of individuals who supplied information also precede the reference numbers.

BIBLIOGRAPHY is divided into three sections viz (a) numerical, which relates to the reference numbers at the foot of each biography; (b) the alphabetical listing of these books by author; and (c) the alphabetical listing of the books by title.

PHOTOGRAPHS of women composers appear alphabetically by name following the bibliographical section.

Appendix 1. Information Wanted. This is a list of women composers about whom little or nothing is known. It would be appreciated if readers having knowledge of any item would communicate with the

Director, International Institute for the Study of Women in Music, California State University, Northridge, Los Angeles, CA 91330, USA.

Appendix 2. Music Key Signatures in 25 Languages. This has been provided as an aid towards the identification of the works of the women composers when performed, published or recorded in different countries.

Appendix 3. Comparative Distribution of Composers by Century. This tabulation illustrates the century-wise growth in the number of the women composers in each of the countries. Unfortunately there are quite a number of composers whose nationality and period of activity were not available at the time of going to press.

Appendix 4. Composers by Country and Century. This is a list of composers arranged alphabetically by country and, within each country, chronologically by century. Composers' names appear under their country of birth or subsequent nationality and within the century in which their creative musical abilities were most manifest. Changes in the names and boundaries of countries were taken into consideration in the classification of composers by country. The retention of a country's earlier name was usually influenced by the number of composers, as in the case of Bohemia under which 18 composers are listed. Croatian and Serbian composers are assigned to Yugoslavia; composers from England, Scotland, Northern Ireland and Wales to the United Kingdom and biblical composers to Israel, etc.

Appendix 5. Pseudonyms of the Women Composers. This is a list of pseudonyms used by the women composers in order to get their works published.

Appendix 6. Operas and Operettas by Women Composers. This is a list of the operas and the operettas which were composed by the women.

Appendix 7. Composers influenced by Shakespeare. This is a list of the women composers who were influenced by Shakespeare and lists the resultant works and their music form.

Appendix 8. Composers by Instrument and Music Form. This is a list of composers arranged alphabetically and chronologically by century under the instrument and form or type of music for which they composed.

Appendix 9. Composers by Calling, Occupation and Profession. This is a list of composers arranged alphabetically by occupation, profession or calling and within each category, chronologically by century.

Appendix 10. Composers by the Instruments they Play. This is a list of composers arranged alphabetically and chronologically by century under the musical instrument on which they were proficient.

Appendix 11. International Council of Women and Affiliates. This gives details about this important world wide organization and the addresses of the constituent affiliations in each country throughout the world.

Appendix 12. International Music Societies (selection) and other music organizations pertinent to women composers, and includes national information centers.

Appendix 13. International Performing Rights Societies. This is the most recent listing of all the performing rights societies and their addresses throughout the world.

Appendix 14. National Federation of Music Clubs. This is a listing of the affiliated bodies and senior music clubs of the National Federation of Music Clubs in the United States.

DISCOGRAPHY. This is a fairly complete listing as at the time of going to press, of the albums and recordings of the women composers (classical and serious music only). Where available the performers are listed, otherwise they are substituted by a series of asterisks (* * *). Record labels are indicated by five letter codes which are listed against the actual label names and their relative recording companies or distributors and their addresses where available.

Abbreviations

MUSICAL
A alto voice
a-cap a cappella
a-cl alto clarinet
a-fl alto flute
a-rec alto recorder
a-sax alto saxophone
acc accompaniment
acdn accordion
amp amplified
arr arranged for or by

B bass voice
B-Bar bass baritone voice
b-cl bass clarinet
b-dr bass drum
b-rec bass recorder
b-trb bass trombome
Bar baritone voice
bar-sax baritone saxophone
bsn bassoon

c-bsn contra bassoon
c-fl contra flute
ca circa
cel celeste
ch chorus
cham chamber
chil children
cl clarinet
clav clavichord
comm commissioned by or for
cond conductor
cong congregation
Cont contralto voice
cor cornet
cym cymbals

d-b double bass
ded dedicated to
dir director
diss dissertation
dr drum

elec electronic
ens ensemble
euph euphonium

fl flute

glock glockenspiel
gtr guitar

har harmonica
hn horn
hon honorary
hons honours
hp harp
hpcd harpsichord

inaug inauguration of
inst instrument

lib libretto by

m men's
m-Cont mezzo contralto voice
m-S mezzo soprano voice
man mandolin
mar marimba
med medium
mix mixed
mvt movement

n/a not available
narr narrator
no number

ob oboe
obb obbligato
op opus
opt optional
orch orchestra
org organ

perc percussion
perf performer/performed
pf piano

picc piccolo
prep prepared

qnt quintet
qrt quartet

rec recorder
rev revised

S soprano voice
sax saxophone
s-rec soprano recorder
str string
sym symphony
syn synthesizer

T tenor voice
t-rec tenor recorder
t-sax tenor saxophone
t-trb tenor trombone
tam tamborine
tba tuba
timp timpani
trad traditional
trans translated by
trb trombone
tri triangle
trp trumpet

unacc unaccompanied

var various
vce voice
vib vibraphone
vir virginal
vl viol
vla viola
vlc violoncello
vln violin

w women
ww woodwind

xy xylophone

OTHER
A.B. Bachelor of Arts
A.M. Master of Arts
ABC American/Australian Broadcasting Corporation
ACA American Composers Alliance
ACE American Composers Edition
A.T.C.L Associate of Trinity College, London
ACUM Society of Authors and Composers in Israel
AEFM Association Européenne des Festivals de Musique
AGAC American Guild of Authors and Composers
AIBM Association International des Bibliotheques Musicales
AMC American Music Center Inc./Australian Music Center
AMEB Australian Music Examination Board
A.R.A.M. Associate of Royal Academy of Music, London
A.R.C.M. Associate of Royal College of Music, London
A.R.C.T. Associate of Royal College of Music, Toronto
ARSC Association for Recorded Sound Collections
ASCAP American Society of Composers, Authors and Publishers
ASUC American Society of University Composers
AWC American Women Composers Incorporated

B.A. Bachelor of Arts
B.M. Bachelor of Music
B.M.E. Bachelor of Music Education
B.S. Bachelor of Science
B.Sc. Bachelor of Science
BBC British Broadcasting Corporation
BMI Broadcast Music Incorporated
BMIC British Music Information Center
BPAM Bicentennial Parade of American Music

CAPAC Composers, Authors and Publishers Association of Canada
CAPS Creative Artists Service
CBC Canadian Broadcasting Corporation
CeBeDeM Centre Belge de Documentation Musicale
CFE Composers Facsimile Edition
CGGB Composers Guild of Great Britain
CIF Conseil International des Femmes
CLC Canadian League of Composers
CMAA Church Music Association of America
CMC Canadian Music Center
CMIC Czech Music Information Center
CMS College Music Association
CUNY City University of New York

D.M. Doctor of Music
D.M.A. Doctor of Musical Arts
D.M.E. Doctor of Music Education
D.M.S. Doctor of Music
D.Mus. Doctor of Music
D.S.M. Doctor of Sacred Music
DALRO Dramatic, Artistic and Literary Rights Organization
Dip.Ed. Diploma in Education

F.R.A.M. Fellow of Royal College of Music
F.R.C.O. Fellow of Royal College of Organists, England
F.T.C.L. Fellow of Trinity College, London
FCIM Fédération des Concours Internationaux de Musique
FIJM Fédération Internationale des Jeunesses Musicales
FIM/IFM Federation Internationale des Musiciens
FMIC Finnish Music Information Center
F.R.C.C.O. Fellow of the Royal Canadian College of Organists

GEDOK Society of German and Austrian Women Artists
GMW Gesellschaft der Musikfreunde in Wien

IAML International Association of Music Libraries
IASA International Association of Sound Archives
ICTM International Council for Traditional Music
ICW International Council of Women
ICWM International Council of Women in Music
IIVMD Internationales Institut fuer Vergleichende Musikstudien und Documentation
ILWC International League of Women Composers
IMC International Music Council
IMD Internationale Musikinstitut Darmstadt
IMI Icelandic Music Information Center Israeli Music Institute
IMZ/IMC Internationales Muzikzentrum
ISBN International Standard Book Number
ISCM International Society for Contemporary Music
ISME International Society for Music Education

L.G.S.M. Licentiate of the Guildhall School of Music
L.R.A.M. Licentiate of the Royal Academy of Music
L.R.C.M. Licentiate of the Royal College of Music
L.R.C.T. Licentiate of the Royal College of Music, Toronto
L.R.S.M. Licentiate of the Royal School of Music
L.T.C.L. Licentiate of Trinity College, London
L.U.C.T. Licentiate of the University of Cape Town

M.A. Master of Arts
M.F.A. Master of Fine Arts
M.M. Master of Music
M.M.E. Master of Music Education
M.Music Master of Music
M.S. Master of Science
M.S.M. Master of Sacred Music
MEDIA CULT International Institute for Audio Visual Communication and Cultural Development
MLA Music Library Association
M.M.A. Master of Musical Arts
M.S.M. Master of Sacred Music
MTA Music Teachers Association
MTNA Music Teachers National Association
Mus.D. Doctor of Music

NAACC National Association for American Composers and Conductors
NFMC National Federation of Music Clubs
NME New Music Edition
NMI Norwegian Music Information Center
NMN New Music Newspaper

OGM Oesterreichische Gesellschaft fuer Musik
OKB Oesterreictischer Komponistenbund
ONDA Office National du Droit d'Auteur
ORTF Organisation de la Radio-Diffusion Television Française
OUP Oxford University Press

PWM Polskie Wydawnictwo Muzyczne

R.C.C.O. Royal Canadian College of Organists
RAM Royal Academy of Music
RCM Royal College of Music
RILM International Repertory of Music Literature
RISM Repertoire Internationale des Sources Musicales

SABAM Society of Belgian Composers
SABC South African Broadcasting Corporation
SACEM Société des Auteurs, Compositeurs et Editeurs de Musique
SAMRO South African Music Rights Organization
SARRAL South African Recording Rights Association Limited
SPAM Society for the Publishing of American Music
STIM Swedish Music Information Center

U.P.L.M. University Performers Licentiate in Music
U.T.L.M. University Teachers Licentiate in Music
UCLA University of California, Los Angeles
UM University Microfilms
UNESCO United Nations Educational, Scientific and Cultural Organization

WLP World Library Publications

Addendum

A number of biographies were omitted in the computerised typesetting. Unfortunately, these could not be subsequently included because the pagination of the book had been completed. In consequence, these biographies are set out below and their cross-references have been inserted in the biographical section without disturbing the page numbers.

DAVIES, Margaret K.

20th-century British composer. She gained a B.Sc. in physiology from London University, 1948, a B.A. (hons.) in fine arts from York University, 1973 and became an A.R.C.T. (hons.), 1977. She studied composition under S. Dolin, 1973 to 1980. She resides in Canada.

Compositions

ORCHESTRA

Eastern temple chimes (1978) (1st prize, 1979)

CHAMBER

Brass quintet (2 trp, hn, trb and tba) (1978) (1st prize, Composers' Festival, 1981)

Trio (fl, vla and vlc) (1978)

VOCAL

Songs:

Echoes of Eden (1977)

Six haiku (1977)

Water music (1978)

SACRED

Christ's passion according to Luke, in modern speech (soli, narr, mix-ch, junior ch, spoken ch, perc and org) (1977)

Just as I am, hymn (mix-ch) (1979, rev 1981)

ARRANGEMENTS

Modal tunes (1978-1981)

Ref. Assoc. of Canadian Women Composers, *"Music Magazine"* Nov/Dec 1980

FERRE, Susan Ingrid

American harpsichordist, concert organist, lecturer and composer. b. Boston, September 5, 1945. She received her B.A. and B.Mus. from the Christian University, TX, in 1968; her diploma in the organ from the Schola Cantorum, Paris in 1969; M.Mus. from the Eastman School of Music in 1971 and D.M.A. from North Texas University, 1979. She has appeared in concerts, workshops and lecture-recitals in the United States and Europe; lectured at North Texas University and in philosophy and engineering at Paris University and been performer, musical director and composer for the French Theatre Company.

Ref. 457

GAMBARO, Alceste

19th-century Italian composer.

Compositions

OPERA

Alceste, in 3 acts (1882)

La Perla del Villaggio, in 2 acts (1882)

Ref. 108

HOOVER, Carolyn

20th-century composer.

Compositions

SACRED

God Is, oratorio (1974)

Job, oratorio (1975)

Ref. 465

HUND, Alicia

19th-century German composer. To the horror of the men in the orchestra and audience, Alicia conducted a performance of her own symphony.

Ref. 415

KARR Y DE ALFONSETTI, Carmen (pseud. L. Escardot)

Spanish playwright, writer and composer. b. Barcelona, 1865. She was the niece of the writer Alfonso Karr and married another writer, Jose Maria de Lasarte. From 1907 to 1918, Carmen collaborated in journals, including "Juventut" and "Illustracion Catalana", where she started a campaign to aid the development of the cultural life of the Catalonian women. In 1913, she founded La Llar, a home for teachers and students, the first one of its kind in Spain. Her plays included Caritat; El Idols and Raig de Sol. She composed Catalonian songs under her pseudonym.

Publications

"Boves". 1906.

"Cliches". 1906.

"La Vida de Joan Franch.

Ref. 268

KHANNA, Usha

20th-century Indian composer of film music.

Ref. National Council of Women, India

KIM, Kwang-Hee

20th-century Korean lecturer and composer. She received a B.A. in 1972 and M.A. in 1975 from Seoul National University and an M.A. (theory and composition) from the University of Minnesota, U.S.A., 1978. She returned to Korea to lecture at Seoul National University and Han Yang University. Her works are presented by the Society for Contemporary Music, Seoul.

Compositions

ORCHESTRA

Prayer

CHAMBER
Music (7 perf)
Interchange (2 vln)
A child's afternoon, suite (pf)
Ref. Korean National Council of Women

KNOWLES, Alison
American artist, writer and composer. b. New York, April 29, 1933. She studied art at Pratt Institute and graphics and photography at the Manhattan School of Printing. She has had many one-woman and group shows, had works performed at the New York Avant-Garde Festivals and on the Experimental Intermedia Foundation's radio series 'Concerts by Composers' and in other performances in the United States and Europe. She won a Guggenheim fellowship in 1968 and from 1970 to 1972 was director of the Graphics Laboratory at California Institute of the Arts.
Compositions
ELECTRONIC
Computer poems incl.:
Proposition IV (Squid)
Publications
"Women's Work". Co-edited with Annea Lockwood (q.v.).
Ref. Experimental Intermedia Foundation, 633

KOMIAZYK, Magdelena
Polish concert pianist, teacher and composer. b. Gdansk, October 2, 1945. She made her debut as a composer at Cracow in 1971 and as a pianist, in Warsaw in 1973. She tours as a concert pianist and teacher and is currently living in Italy.
Ref. 645

MAHLER, Hellgart
20th-century Tasmanian composer. Her compositions have been performed by the Melbourne Symphony Orchestra.
Ref. IWC - Australia

MARGLES, Pamela
20th-century Canadian composer. She received a B.A. (hons.) in philosophy from the University of Toronto and is an A.R.C.T.
Compositions
CHAMBER
The same river (pf) (1978)
VOCAL
Tombeau d'Empedocles (mix-ch) (1980)
Pause (m-S, cl, vlc and acdn) (1979)
Ref. Assoc. Canadian Women Composers

MARKS, Selma
20th-century American composer.
Composition
FILM MUSIC
Feelings (1977)
Ref. 497

MENDOZA, Anne
20th-century British composer.
Compositions
MISCELLANEOUS
A festival for autumn
The monkey's hornpipe
Ref. 263

MRASECK, Fraulein
German composer. b. 1802. She composed arias and songs.
Ref. 465

PODGORSKA, Ewa
20th-century Polish composer. In 1979, she received a citation for her entry into the "From Young Musicians to a Young Town" composition competition in Stalowa Wola.
Ref. "Polish Music"

POZZONE, Maria
19th-century Italian composer.
Compositions
VOCAL
Vibrazioni, album of songs incl.:
Pasqua di Risurrezione (A. Negri)
Quiete meridiana nell' Alpe (A. Fogazzaro)
Sogno (G. Pascali)
Storia breve (A. Negri)
Ultima rosa (A. Fogazzaro)
Voce dall'alto (E. de Marchi)
Ref. Ricordi, 502

PRUNEDER, Frau
20th-century composer of two masses.
Ref. 465

PULER, Clara P.
Composer of an opera.
Ref. 465

REED, Mrs. Wallace
20th-century American composer.
Composition
VOCAL
Swing low, sweet chariot (Bar, trb and pf)
Ref. Bicentennial Parade of American Music

REGAN, Sarah Wren Love
American pianist, violinist, lecturer and composer. b. Kosiusko, MS, September 12, 1916. She received a Mus.B. cum laude (1937) from Judson College, Marion, AL, and did post graduate summer studies at Chicago Music College. She taught the piano, the violin and voice privately, as well as the piano in schools and then lectured at the American College of Musicians. She came first in a state composition competition run by the Federated Music Clubs of Alabama.
Ref. 475

ROGERS, Emmy Brady
20th-century American pianist, critic and composer. Her compositions were included in a concert by Colorado composers, held at the Kennedy Center in August, 1976.
Compositions
VOCAL
Songs:
The fairy lake
Hush song
Sea wrack
MISCELLANEOUS
Nocturne
Ref. Bicentennial Parade of American Music

SAROVA, Dagmar
B. 1926.
Composition
ORCHESTRA
Scherzo (Hawkes)

SCHIAVO DE GREGORIO, Maria
Italian composer.
Compositions
MISCELLANEOUS
Improvviso (Milan: Carisch)
Nocturne (Carisch)

SCHULTZOWA, Barbara
20th-century Polish composer.
Composition
PIANO
Polonaise

SCOTT, Molly
American lecturer, soprano and composer. b. Wellsville, NY; January 11, 1938. She obtained her B.A. from Smith College, where she studied voice under Dorothy Stahl, Gretchen d'Armond, Rodney Geisick and Marlene Montgomery. She was a member of the faculty of music and healing at Omega Institute, Lebanon Springs, NY, during summers after 1980 and at the New England Institute of Healing Arts and Sciences, Amherst, MA. She received grants from Meet the Composer in 1981 and 1982.
Compositions
VOCAL
Honor the earth (1980) (Sumitra Music)
Poisin treasure (1980) (Sumitra)
This is our home (1982)
SACRED
Jesus of the colors (1980)
THEATRE
The Dragon (1981)
Ref. 625

SIMONE, Nina (Eunice Waymon)
Black American organist, pianist, arranger, singer, teacher and composer. b. February 21, 1933. She started playing the piano by ear at the age of six and the organ three years later. She studied the piano privately and then the piano and theory at the Juilliard School of Music. She then worked as an accompanist in vocal studios, gave piano lessons and studied at the Curtis Institute of Music. Her first singing engagement was at an Atlantic City night club in 1954, two years later she started recording and soon reached the best seller lists.
Compositions
VOCAL
To be young, gifted and black (mix-ch) (Ninandy Music)
Songs:
Compensation (P. Dunbar) (Rolls Royce Music)
Nobody (Sam Fox, 1964)
Real-real (Rolls Royce)
Revolution (with Weldon Irvine Jnr.) (Ninandy)
Ref. 136

SPRAGG, Deborah T.
20th-century American composer.
Composition
VOCAL
As imperceptibly as grief (Emily Dickinson) (ch and pf) (1979)

STINSON, Ethelyn Lenore
American pianist, violinist, lecturer, music therapist and composer. b. Harrisburg, PA, June 7, 1904. She obtained a violin diploma from Williamsport Dickinson Seminary, 1927 and a teacher's piano diploma from Coombs College of Music, Philadelphia, 1938. She headed the music department at Woods School, Langhorn, 1929 to 1946 and ran a private piano studio from 1946 to 1950, before specializing in music therapy for the mentally handicapped, working in hospitals in Philadelphia. After 1950 she taught the piano in Phildelphia and lectured on music therapy.
Composition
PIANO
Climbing the jungle gym (1938)
Publications
How To Teach Children Music. 1942.
Ref. 475

STOBAEUS, Kristina
Swedish singer and composer. b. 1942. DISCOGRAPHY.
Composition
Den gamba faageln
Ref. STIM

URGEL, Louise
19th-century French composer of melodies.
Ref. 465

VERNAELDE, Henriette
20th-century composer.
Composition
CHAMBER
Berceuse (vln and pf)
Ref. Frau und Musik

WALKER, Shirley
20th-century American arranger, conductor and composer. She has arranged, orchestrated, conducted and composed for feature, industrial and television films.

WEINREICH, Waltraut
German composer. b. 1909.
Compositions
SACRED
Drei Adventslieder (ch a-cap) (Berlin: Merseburger)

WOHL, Maria Viktoria
Austrian musician, nun and composer. b. ca. 1676; d. Graz, August 16, 1755. She belonged to the Ursuline Convent, Graz and was acknowledged as an outstandng musician and composer.
Bibliography
Mingotti, R. Aus dem Musikleben des Steirerlandes. Ed. Hey, A.J. Graz, 1924
Ref. 500

WOLCOTT, Ellen
20th-century American teacher and composer.
Composition
VOCAL
Man on Earth (ch and org)
Ref. Bicentennial Parade of American Music

Biographies of Women Composers

A.L. See LEHMANN, Amelia

AARNE, Els (pseud. of Elze Janovna Paemurru)

Soviet-Estonian pianist, lecturer and composer. b. Makeyevka, Ukraine, March 30, 1917. She studied at the Tallinn Conservatory completing her piano studies under T. Lemba and graduating with distinction in composition in 1942. She studied composition with K. Eller and A. Kapp in 1946. During World War II she taught music at teachers' seminars in Tallinn and later the piano and theoretical subjects at the conservatory. DISCOGRAPHY.

Compositions

ORCHESTRA

Symphony No. 1 (1961)
Symphony No. 2 (1966)
Double bass concerto (1968)
Horn concerto (1958)
Piano concerto (1945)
Ballad (pf and wind orch) (1955)
Adagio for wind orchestra (1955)
Baltiskoye more, more mira (wind orch) (1958)
Overture (1969)
Overture for wind orchestra (1959)
Suite druzya malle (1959)
Other symphonic poems

CHAMBER

Quintet for wind instruments (1965)
Trio (1946)
Two Estonian dances (2 vln and pf; also pf) (1954)
Improvisation (vln and pf) (1952)
Nocturne (vlc and pf) (1970)
Poem (vlc and pf) (1941)
Recital (vln and pf) (1952)
Runo (vlc and pf) (1969)
Waltz (vln and pf) (1952)
Meditatsia (hn) (1970)

PIANO

Ballad (4 hands) (1962)
Pionerski pokhod, cycle (1949)
Eight etudes for beginners (1953)
Four contrasts (1966)
Improvisata (1967)
Seven polyphonic sketches (1961)
Sonatina (1961)
Twelve variations on a theme by A. Vedro (1939)

VOCAL

An die Heimat, cantata (1939)
Meie paevade, laul, cantata (1965)
Nasha poberezhe, cantata (D. Vaarandi) (ch a-cap) (1959)
Obogatitel uglya, cantata (Y. Kross) (m-ch a-cap) (1963)
Poi, svobodnyi narod, cantata (D. Vaarandi) (ch a-cap) (1949)
Rodine, cantata (E. Tarum) (ch and orch) (1939)
Valuoja, cantata (ch and orch) (1956)
Kolybelnaya (K. Korsen) (ch and orch) (1953)
More-nashi polya (M. Kesamaa) (ch and orch) (1953)
S siloi molodosti (K. Korsen) (soloists, ch and orch) (1953)
Kto eto? (M. Veetam) (ch a-cap) (1953)
Pesnya koshki (R. Parve) (ch a-cap) (1954)
Solovei (M. Veetam) (ch a-cap) (1954)
Arrival of Spring (S)
Das Lied unserer Tage (1965)
Guess who we are (Bar and pf)
Songs incl. some with violoncello and piano

INCIDENTAL MUSIC

Music for plays

Publications

Textbook of Solfege. 1959.

Ref. 21, 70, 79, 87, 563, 580

AARON, Marcelle

French composer. b. Paris, September 6, 1894; d. Paris, February 7, 1956. She and her sister Yvonne (q.v.) studied at the Paris Conservatoire and together composed about 200 chamber and symphonic works, which were performed at major concerts throughout the world.

Compositions

ORCHESTRA

Visages de Paris, symphony (with Yvonne) (1938)
Prière rituelle (with Yvonne)
Prière sans paroles (with Yvonne)

CHAMBER

Numerous pieces (with Yvonne)

Ref. Yvonne Aaron

AARON, Yvonne

French composer. b. Paris, June 28, 1897. She and her sister Marcelle (q.v.) studied at the Paris Conservatoire under Xavier Leroux, Andre Gedalge, Maurice Emmanuel, Jean Gallon, Nadia Boulanger (q.v.) and orchestration under Philippe Gaubert. Together they composed about 200 chamber and symphonic works, which were performed at major concerts throughout the world. In 1964 Yvonne was nominated a Chevalier de l'Ordre National des Arts et Lettres and in 1975 was awarded the SACEM Annual Grand Prize. She was the vice-president of the Union of Women Teachers and Composers in France (U.F.P.C.). PHOTOGRAPH.

Compositions

ORCHESTRA

Visages de Paris, symphony (with Marcelle) (1938)
Reflets sur un même thème (pf and orch) (1965)
Ecoute Israel
Prière rituelle (with Marcelle)
Prière sans paroles (with Marcelle)

CHAMBER

Numerous pieces

VOCAL

C'est l'ame de Paris
Tableau d'autrefois

BALLET

One ballet

OPERETTA

One operetta

INCIDENTAL MUSIC
Music for films
Ref. composer

AARUP, Caia
Late 19th-century Swedish composer who spent her later years in America.
Compositions
PIANO
Pieces
VOCAL
Songs incl.:
At dawn
In explanation
Life
The summer wind
To be alone
Ref. 276, 433, 465

AAS, Else Berntsen
20th-century Norwegian composer.
Compositions
CHAMBER
Evening hymn (trp and org; also cor and pf) (1984) (Oslo: Norsk Musikforlag, 1885)
VOCAL
Balladen om birkebeinarne og Kong Sverre (mix-ch)
Julesanger fra mange land (ch and insts)
Julvisa (Bo Setterlind) (ch)
Ref. Otto Harrassowitz (Wiesbaden)

ABBOTT (Bingham Abbott), Jane
English composer. ca. 1894.
Compositions
VOCAL
Songs incl.:
Just for today
My soul what hast thou done
Ref. 276, 347

ABE, Kyoko
Japanese electronic instrumentalist and composer. b. Tokyo, 1950. She studied composition under Saburo Takata at Kunitachi Music College, Tokyo. After 1976 she studied at the Vienna Musikhochschule under Erich Urbanner and Roman Haubenstock-Ramati. She also studied electro-acoustic music in Vienna, under Dieter Kaufmann. She won several prizes in international composition competitions.
Compositions
ORCHESTRA
Three pieces (1976) (Vienna: Ariadne, 1980)
CHAMBER
Quartet (fl, trp, vln and d-b) (Ariadne, 1980)
Dream of the cherry blossoms (mar) (Frankfurt: Zimmermann, 1984)
Rund um die Uhr: zwoelf Mobile (pf) (1980)
Six small pieces for violin (Ariadne, 1980)
Solo for harpsichord (Ariadne, 1980)
VOCAL
Die Jahreszeiten (mix-ch a-cap) (Ariadne: 1979)
Tekona (Bar, fl, hp, vln, vlc and perc)
ELECTRONIC
Metamorphose I (rec, hpcd and tape) (1977)
Ref. *Ariadne* 1981, Otto Harrassowitz (Wiesbaden), 622

ABEJO, Sister M. Rosalina, SFCC
Philippine pianist, conductor, lecturer and composer. b. July 13, 1922. She studied at Lourdes College, St. Scholastica's College and Philippine Women's University, where she received a M.Mus. (composition, 1957). At the Labunski School of Composition, Cincinnati, she studied under Felix Labunski; at the Eastman School of Music she studied composition under Wayne Barlow and at the Catholic University of America, Washington, DC, she continued her composition studies under George Thaddeus Jones (1963 to 1964). Other teachers were Fritz Mahler and Franco Ferrara (conducting), Nadia Boulanger (q.v.) and Marinus Jong (composition), Jose Echaniz and Rosa Mellignani (piano) and Allen McHose (theory). She was Dean of the School of Music, Lourdes College, Cagayan de Oro City, (1957 to 1960); of the Immaculate Conception College, Davao City, from 1960 to 1962 and from 1964, of St. Mary's College, as well as lecturer in the piano, conducting, composition and theory. By permission of Pope John XXIII, she became the first nun in the world to undertake the conducting of symphony orchestras. She became a permanent resident of the United States in 1977 and lectured on music education at Kansas University, whilst attending master courses in music therapy. Sister Abejo founded the symphony orchestras of Cagayan de Oro City (1957) and Davao City (1960). In 1978 she became head and music director of the Pius X Seminary in Kentucky. In 1979 she became music director and teacher of voice, the piano, organ theory and composition at the Holy Spirit Church in Fremont, California. She received the Republic Cultural Heritage Award in music and in 1975 the Tangang Sora Award, awarded to launch the International Women's Year, for her leadership in music. She conducted the following orchestras: the Cultural Center Philharmonic Orchestra, the Manila Symphony Orchestra, the Community Symphony Orchestra, the Filipino Youth Symphony Orchestra, the National Philharmonic Orchestra and the U.P. Symphony Orchestra. DISCOGRAPHY. PHOTOGRAPH.
Compositions
ORCHESTRA
Beatriz, symphony
Dalawang Pusong Dakila, symphony (1975)
Fortaleza, symphony (1977)
Guerilla, symphony (1971)
Hold high the torch, 4th symphony (1981)
Jubilee symphony (1984)
Pioneer symphony (1954)
Thanatopsis symphony
Mangima canyon (2 pf and orch) (1969)
Aeolian, piano concerto (also 2 pf) (1956)
Golden fountain, piano concerto (1959-1960)
Imelda, marimba concerto
Jubilee, piano concerto
Recuerdos (vlc and orch)
Recuerdos de Manila, guitar concerto (1972)
Violin concerto No. 1 (1978)
Death and victory, symphonic poem (1976)
Iberian promenade, symphonic poem (1979)
Vespers in a convent garden, symphonic suite in 4 mvts (1957)
The blood compact of 1561
Bukidnon tone poem
A Filipino in Paris, humoresque (1964)
Grand pontifical march for Pope Paul VI
Gregoria (1950)
In memoriam (of Benjamin Tupas) (1974)
In remembrance (of John D. Rockefeller) (str orch) (1978)
Kaleidoscope '70' (1956)
Leyte chimes
Malacanang gardens
Ode to a statesman (in memory of D. Quinton Paredes) (1973)
Overture 1081 (1974)
Sinfonietta for organ and strings (comm inauguration of St. Mary's Cathedral, San Francisco) (1970)
Strings on the dignity of man (1980)
Sumasayaw and Tikbalang (1981)
Thirteen variations (1957)
Thirty school marches
Three projections (1966)
The trilogy of man, in 3 mvts (1971)
Valle de Los Caidos (1964)
CHAMBER
Nineteenth-century style (10 insts, strs and ww ens)
Twentieth-century style (10 insts, strs and ww ens)
Liturgical serenade for winds and strings
Octet for winds and brasses (comm Philippine Music Festival, 1970)
Octet for winds and strings (1970)
Piano quintet (1966)
Academic festival quartet
Maranaw trail (2 mar, pf and perc) (1971) (comm Philippine Music Festival, 1972)
Three string quartets (1949-1954)
Three violin pieces with piano (1959)
Short pieces for various instruments
Ten instrumental pieces of 20th-century idiom (1961)
PIANO
Imelda (3 pf)
Allegro scherzando (2 pf)
Fantasia (2 pf)
Mangima Canyon trail (2 pf)
Mindanao festival (2 pf)
Five pieces (Boston: McLaughlin and Rilly)
Twenty-five pieces for beginners (1952)
Twenty-five pieces for beginners and advanced (1959)
Over 100 other pieces
VOCAL
Pag-ibig Sa Tinubuang Bayan, choral symphony (1974)
Buhay, song cycle (S and orch) (1969)

Pamuhat Buhat (B, native insts and orch) (comm Philippine Music Festival, 1973)
Woman (S and orch) (1975)
Hating Gabing Tahimik
Larawan Ng Isang Babaye, song cycle (1965)
Marian year, Jubilee songs (1954)
Mother song, song cycle (1951)
Panahon, 4 part song cycle (comm inauguration of the CCP, 1969)
Philippine folk songs
Villancico Filipino
SACRED
Pagtutubos, oratorio (1969)
Advent, cantata (ch and orch) (1957)
The conversion of King Humabon, cantata
He cometh, cantata
Jubilee cantata (Rejoice! Give Thanks!) (soloist, ch and orch) (1984)
Christmas carols
Fifty liturgical songs (1950)
Fifty songs, praises to the Lord (1945)
Hymns (1979, 1981)
Masses (1979, 1981)
Sinfonya Ng Mga Salmos, psalms
BALLET
Muslim Wedding (1974)
MISCELLANEOUS
The lady in black
The man named Hans George Koch
Tragedy of the birds
Travelogue
Publications
Grader's workbook in music. Manila: Catholic Trade School.
Learning to read and write music. 7 vols. Manila: Bustamante Press.
Let's play the piano. Manila: Alemar Phoenix Press.
Music for Philippine high schools. Manila: Catholic Trade School.
Music in our lives. 2 vols. Manila: Coronet Publ.
Our own choruses. Manila: Foundation Printers.
Ref. composer, 77, 265, 465, 563

ABESON, Marion

American composer. b. 1914.
Composition
OPERA
Hansel and Gretel
Ref. 465

ABLAMOWICZ, Anna

American composer. ca. 1852.
Composition
VOCAL
The Vale of Avoca
Ref. 465

ABORN, Lora (Busck)

American organist, pianist, teacher and composer. b. New York, May 30, 1907. She gave her first public performance at the age of ten, playing her own compositions. She received her musical education at the Effa Ellis Perfield Music School, New York, the Oberlin Conservatory (organ) and the American Conservatory of Music, Chicago, studying under Van Dusen and graduating with honors and a gold medal for composition. For over forty years she was organist and music director at Frank LLoyd Wright's Unity Temple, composing songs and choral numbers for the services. She taught the piano, the organ and theory privately. Her work *Ethan Frome* won an honorable mention in the national competition for composition, Chicago. She received a commission from the Chicago Grand Opera Ballet to compose the music for *American Women.* Her works have been performed in most of the major concert halls in America. PHOTOGRAPH.
Compositions
ORCHESTRA
Symphony in A-Minor (Birdsong symphony)
Rhapsody for two pianos and orchestra
The mystic trumpeter
Tone poem after Ethan Frome
CHAMBER
Canons for strings
Quintet for brass
Adagio (qrt)
Trio for piano, violin and cello, in 4 mvts
Sonatina in F-Major (fl and pf)
Threnody (org and fl)
Two Prairie tone poems: Prelude to summer; Prairie twilight (vln and pf)
ORGAN
Chorale – prelude
Chorale and variations
Toccata (from Greatest of these)
Canons, preludes and fugues
PIANO
Capriccio fantastico (2 pf)
Fugue in yellow (2 pf)
Jazz toccata (2 pf)
Etudes I and II
Four pieces for children
Fugue in blue
Fugue in yellow
Lament
Parade (satire of French street band)
Poetic music
Preludes and fugues
Toccata
Two-voice etude
VOCAL
Chicago, prairie gem of Illinois (cham-ch)
Harp of the north (m-ch)
Hiawatha's childhood (S, T, ch and ens)
The mystic trumpeter (Bar, org and trp)
Songs incl.:
How do I love thee
My country is the world
To music
SACRED
Choral works incl.:
All creatures of our God and King
Bless Jehovah O my soul
Bow down Thy ear, O Lord
Canticle of spring
Canticle of the bells
Christmas night
Creation
Give us new dreams for old
The glory of the spring
How far is it to Bethlehem
If ye love me
In the lonely midnight
The kings of the east
Little children, wake and listen
Lo, the day of days is here
Song of life (Bar, ch and ens)
When the herds were watching
Sacred songs
BALLET
American ditties, 4 dances
American women
Boston John (Shaker)
Casey at the bat
The critic, solo dance
Hot afternoons in Montana (Lament)
In my landscape
The lawyer, solo dance
The lonely ones
Nostalgia
Punch drunk, parade
Reunion
Strange new street
Strawberry roan
OPERA
Gift of the Magi, in one act
Mitty, in one act
Ref. composer, *Pan Pipes* Winter 1984

ABOULKER, Isabelle

French concert pianist, accompanist, professor and composer. b. Boulogne-Sur-Seine, October 23, 1938. She studied the piano under Jacques Fevrier, harmony under Maurice Durufle, orchestration under Pierre Wissmer and accompaniment under Henriette Puig-Roget. She was assistant to the singer Jeanine Micheau at the Paris Conservatoire; professor of accompaniment at the Conservatoire of Amiens and in 1982 professor at the Paris Conservatoire. She received first prize for piano accompaniment at the C.N.S.M.
Compositions
VOCAL
Leçons de français aux etudiants americains (3 vces and pf) (1983)
Trois melodies sur des poèmes de Robert Sabatier (m-S and pf) (1982)

OPERA
La lacune, chamber opera (E. Ionesco) (3 vces and pf) (1979)
Les surprises de l'enfer (4 vces and 15 insts) (1981)
OPERETTA
Jean de la Fontaine parmi nous, for children (3 vces and pf) (1980) (Paris: Rideau Rouge)
Ref. composer

ABRAMOVA, Sonia Pinkhasovna
Soviet pianist, lecturer and composer. b. Tashkent, June 2, 1930. At the Tashkent Conservatory she studied composition under G.A. Mushel and Y.N. Tulin and graduated in 1954. From 1953 to 1957 she taught at a nursery school and the following four years taught the piano and theory at a school for gifted children. From 1961 she lectured on piano teaching in Tashkent.
Compositions
ORCHESTRA
Clarinet concerto (1953)
CHAMBER
Concert scherzo for trumpet and piano (1956)
Concert scherzo for violin and piano (1954)
Intermezzo (trp and pf) (1956)
PIANO
Album of pieces (1961)
Concert piece (1961)
Dance fantasy (1954)
Five pieces (1956, 1969)
Six sonatinas (1964)
Sonata (1956)
Twelve children's pieces (1969)
Waltz-humoresque (1971)
VOCAL
Oda druzhbe (V. Arutiunian, trans G. Registan) (mix-ch and orch)
Twenty romances (various poets) (1968)
Twenty-six songs
Two romances (O. Tumanian) (1969)
Choral arrangements
OPERA
Tamara (1954)
INCIDENTAL MUSIC
Theatre music
Ref. 21

ABRAMS, Harriet (Henriette)
English singer and composer. b. London, 1760; d. London, ca. 1825. She was a pupil of Dr. T.A. Arne and made her debut in his opera *May Day* at Drury Lane on October 28, 1775. She and her sister Theodosia were popular London singers and sang at the Handel Commemoration in Westminster Cathedral (1784) and in subsequent concerts. She was often accompanied by Haydn.
Compositions
VOCAL
The Ballad of William and Nancy (vce and pf or hp) (London: Lavenu, 1799)
Collection of Scottish songs (2 or 3 vces and pf or hp) (London: J. Dale, 1800)
Crazy Jane
Eight Italian and English canzonets (1 or 2 vces and pf or hp) (Lavenu, 1780)
The emigrant (M.P. Andrews) (Lavenu, 1800)
Female hardship (M.P. Andrews) (vce and pf or hp) (Lavenu, 1800)
Friend of my heart (M.P. Andrews) (vce and pf or hp) (Lavenu, 1799)
If silent oft you will see me pine (Lavenu, 1800)
O memory thou fond deceiver (O. Goldsmith) (vce and pf or hp) (London: Longman and Broderip, 1790)
Orphan's Prayer (vce and pf or hp) (Lavenu, 1800)
Second set of Italian and English canzonets (1-3 vces and pf or hp)
The shade of Henry (M.P. Andrews) (vce and pf or hp) (Lavenu, 1800)
A smile and a tear (1800)
The soldier's grave (M.G. Lewis) (vce and pf or hp) (Lavenu, 1800)
Tom Halliard (Peter Pindar) (vce and pf or hp) (Lavenu, 1800)
Ye silvan pow'rs that rule the plain (2 vces and pf or hp) (Lavenu, 1800)
The white man, ballad (Mr. Park's Travels) (vce and pf or hp) (Dublin: Hime, 1800)
Ref. 8, 65, 74, 276, 347, 361, 405, 622

ABRAMS, Henriette. See ABRAMS, Harriet

ABRANTES, Duchess of
19th-century French composer.
Compositions
VOCAL
La derniere rose de l'été
Une larme au fils de Napoleon (P. Pacini) (ca. 1822)
La premiere heure de 1833
Ref. H. Baron catalog (London), 128, 465

ABRECHT, Princess of Prussia
19th-century German composer.
Composition
BAND
Parade-march for infantry (Schlesinger)
Ref. 297

ABREU, Julieta Licairac
Dominican composer. b. 1890; d. 1925. She was the sister of Lucila Abreu (q.v.) and composed for the piano.
Ref. 54

ABREU, Lucila
Dominican composer. b. February 21, 1895; d. November 21, 1901. She was a child prodigy and sister of Julieta Licairac Abreu (q.v.). Her naive improvisations were collected and published by her family.
Ref. 54

ACCART (Accart-Becker), Eveline
French concert pianist and composer. b. Laires, February 13, 1921. She studied at the Lycee Nice under Albert Ribollet (piano) and Albert Tadlewski (harmony and counterpoint). She appeared in concert and gave recitals from 1937 to 1940. From 1941 to 1948 she studied counterpoint and fugue at the Paris Conservatoire under Noel Gallon, composition under Roger Ducasse and Tony Aubin and history of music under Norbert Dufourcq. She married Hugues Becker, a cellist. She was awarded first prize for fugue (1944), composition (1945) and history of music (1947). She was employed by Radio France as a mixer musician.
Compositions
ORCHESTRA
Symphony (1951-1953)
Concerto for flute, trumpet, piano and strings (1974)
Concerto for wind instruments and strings (1974) (State comm) (Editions françaises de musique)
Piano concerto (1945)
Concertino for viola and chamber orchestra (1955)
Divertissement sur thèmes alsatiens (1954) (comm Radio Strasbourg)
CHAMBER
Quartet (fl, vla, vlc and hp) (1943)
Sequences for 4 cellos
String quartet (1949)
Sonata for viola and piano (1941)
Suite (vln and pf) (1950)
Variations breves (vlc and pf) (1972)
Viola sonata (1952) (Editions françaises de musique)
PIANO
Nocturne (1941)
Variations sur un thème de Rameau (1945)
INCIDENTAL MUSIC
Ubi-Roi (orch) (Alfred Jarry, 1947)
Ref. composer

ACCART-BECKER, Eveline. See ACCART, Eveline

ACE, Joy Milane
20th-century American writer and composer. b. Helena, MT. She attended McGill University.
Compositions
VOCAL
Songs incl.:
The biographical life of Ludwig van Beethoven
A conflict divine
Immortal lover
OPERETTA
The man from the moon
Ref. 84

ACHARD, Marguerite
French harpist and composer.
Compositions
CHAMBER
Prière, op. 8 (hp and vln)
Receuillement, op. 9 (hp; also pf and org) (Noel, Mustel)

HARP
Meditation, op. 2 (Du Wast)
Melancolie, op. 6 (4 recreations) (Du Wast)
Menuet, op. 4 (4 recreations) (Du Wast)
Methode de harpe, op. 7 (Du Wast)
Pastorale, op. 12 (Lemoine)
Prière, op. 3 (Du Wast)
Reproches, op. 1 (Du Wast)
VOCAL
Chanson de la cavaliere, op. 13 (ch and hp) (Jerlane)
Fleurs cheries, op. 11 (ch and hp) (Jerlane)
Nature, op. 10 (ch and hp) (Jerlane)
Ref. 297

ACHMATOWICZOWA, Helena
Polish composer. b. 1839; d. 1920.
Composition
PIANO
Polonaise
Ref. W. Pigla (Warsaw)

ACKERMANN, Dorothy
20th-century American composer.
Composition
SACRED
God speaks to me
Ref. 465

ACKERNLEY, Mabel
Composition
VOCAL
Dream Song (vce and pf) (Chemet)
Ref. 63

ACKLAND, Jeanne Isabel Dorothy
Canadian organist, pianist, violinist and composer. b. Calgary, Alberta, 1914. She studied privately under Gregori Garbovitski and Jessie Ackland (q.v.) and at Columbia University, New York. She was a member of the Calgary junior symphony orchestra for seven years and from 1948 composed music for radio plays and documentaries.
Compositions
ORCHESTRA
Piano concerto in C-Minor, 1st movement
Sonata in C-Minor (also pf) (1935)
Sonata in G-Minor (also pf) (1935-36)
PIANO
Danza cubana (1 or 2 pf) (1938)
Tango tzigane (1 or 2 pf) (1940)
Berceuse
Buster Brown
California
Camille (also org) (1948)
The chimes
Chinese suite
Country dance
Dedication
Flight
Humoresque
In sunny Spain
Minuet
Morocco
Nautical sketches
Reminiscing
Sleigh ride
Song my fiddle plays
Tango d'amour (also org) (1945)
Trois petites valses
Valse Barbara (also org) (1948)
Valse Grace (also org) (1945)
Valse triste
VOCAL
Songs incl.:
Dawn in Vienna
A fairy ship
A prayer
Scottish love song
Sister o'mine
Two lullabies
OPERETTA
Tut (1951)
THEATRE
Lavender, lace and love, musical comedy (1950)
Music for plays
Ref. 85, 133, 347, 477

ACKLAND, Jessie Agnes
20th-century Canadian pianist, teacher and composer. b. Ontario. She studied under Annie Glen Broder in Calgary and Ernest Hutcheson and Rossiter G. Cole in New York. She specialized in the teaching of the piano, harmony and history of music. She is an L.R.S.M.
Compositions
CHAMBER
Pieces for violin, piano and cello
VOCAL
Songs incl.:
Bluebirds
By night, by day
Cottage of dreams
Lullaby of flowers
Theme song
Ref. 85, 133, 347

ACOCK, Gwendolyn
20th-century English composer.
Composition
CHAMBER
Serenade (vln and pf) (London: Paterson's Publ.)
Ref. 409

ACOSTA, Josefina, Baroness
Colombian pianist, professor and composer. b. Bogota, June 12, 1897. She studied at the Academy Beethoven under Professor Santos Cifuentes and later under Eliseo Hernandes, Honorio Alarcon and Guillermo Uribe Holguin. In 1917 she founded the Centro Musical de Chapinero which she directed until 1929. She taught music at the Instituto Nacional Pedagogico of Bogota from 1926 to 1929. In 1931 she moved to Barcelona in order to perfect her piano studies and study harmony under Mas and Serracant. On her return to Colombia in 1936 she became a professor at the Conservatory of Ibague. She married Baron Acosta.
Compositions
ORCHESTRA
Grand March
PIANO
Bolero
Las estaciones, suite
Impromptu
Preludio y fuga en do menor
La rosa deshojada
Serenata espanola
Vals romantico
Valses nocturnos
VOCAL
Various works (3-part ch)
Ref. 100

ACQUA, Eva Dell'. See DELL'ACQUA, Eva

ACQUAVIVA-D'ARAGONA, Sofia
19th-century Italian composer.
Compositions
VOCAL
Songs incl.:
M'abbandonasti (Ricordi)
Pensa a te!
Quando piega il sol, romanza (Ricordi)
Torna a me! melodia
Ref. 297

ADAGIO, Mlle. See MILANOLLO, Teresa

ADAHVSKA, Ella. See ADAJEWSKY, Ella

A'DAIR, Jeanne
American concert pianist, singer and composer. b. New York City, January 16, 1907. She studied voice under Townsend Fellows from 1921 to 1922, Mme. Bertha Vaughn from 1932 to 1935 and Leon Ardin from 1935 to 1939. She studied the piano and voice under Homer Samuels from 1940 to 1946 and composition under Julius Seyler from 1945 to 1948. She made a number of stage and radio appearances as a singer and pianist.
Compositions
VOCAL
Songs incl.:
Balboa bay
Fifteen songs for once upon a summertime (Eleanor Roberts)
Hymn to California
Mother's lullaby
The river
Where the South Seas gleam
INCIDENTAL MUSIC
Star in Darkness (E. Roberts)
Ref. 496

ADAIR, Dorothy
20th-century American composer.
Composition
VOCAL
A Christmas wreath (ch and orch)
Ref. 280

ADAIR, Mildred
American pianist, teacher and composer. b. Clayton, AL,; d. 1943. She composed piano pieces.
Ref. 347

ADAIR, Yvonne Madeleine
20th-century British pianist, teacher and composer. b. Guernsey. She was an A.R.A.M. In London she taught music teachers and specialised in rhythmic and aural training and the piano.
Compositions
VOCAL
Andante and Vivace (vces and perc)
MISCELLANEOUS
The golden isle
Handelesques
Little dog tales
Sketches from Hans Andersen
Ref. 467

ADAJEWSKY, Ella (Elizabeth) (nee von Schultz) (Adahvska, Adajewski-Schultz, Schultz-Adajewsky)
Russian concert pianist and composer. b. St. Petersburg, January 29, 1846; d. Bonn, Germany, July 26, 1926. She studied under Henselt and then spent several years touring and giving concerts. She returned to St. Petersburg to attend the conservatory from 1862 to 1866 where she studied the piano under Rubinstein and Dreyschock and theory and composition under Zaremba and Famintsin. She made a special study of Greek music. In 1882 she went to Italy, living mainly in Venice and collecting and writing about folk music. She became an authority on the waltz songs of the Rhaetians. She left for Germany in 1909 and lived at Neuwied on the Rhine and later in Bonn.
Compositions
CHAMBER
Greek Sonata (cl and pf) (1880)
PIANO
Air rococo avec doubles (Cologne: Tischer and Jagenberg)
Serenade (1913)
Three rondos (1880)
Twenty-four preludes
Other pieces
VOCAL
Songs incl.:
Horatian ode (S, Bar and pf)
Vierundzwanzig Praeludien (B. Geiger) (vce and pf) (Leipzig: C.F. Kahnt, 1921)
Duets
Four songs (Simrock)
Vocal chamber music
SACRED
Chorale for the Russian Orthodox Church
Four liturgical songs for the Russian Orthodox Church
OPERA
Neprigoshaya ili Solomonida Saburova, in 1 act (1873)
Sarya svobody, in 4 acts (1881)
Publications
La Berceuse populaire, essai d'etude rhythmique et ethnologique. Vol. 1, 1894, Vol. 2, 1897, Vol. 4, 1897. Turin: RMI Revista Musicale Italiana.
Chanson et airs de dance de Rescia. St. Petersburg, 1895.
Du Chant populaire de la Boheme. Vol. 16, Turin: RMI Revista Musicale Italiana, 1909.
Folklore celte. Quelques mots a propos d'un nouveau recueil de chant celte. Turin: RMI Revista Musicale Italiana. 1925.
Die Kirchenlieder des Orients. Turin, 1901.
Napevy i teksty, zapisannye u terskikh slavyan. SPB Russkaya Muzykalnaya Gazeta, 1904.
Ueber die Beziehungen der slawischen Lieder zur altgriechischen Musik. Venice, 1883.
Ref. 7, 15, 17, 23, 74, 105, 193, 297, 330

ADAJEWSKI-SCHULTZ, Ella. See ADAJEWSKY, Ella

ADAM, Margie
20th-century American pianist and composer. DISCOGRAPHY.
Compositions
PIANO
Naked keys
Under the influence (1982)
Ref. Kay Gardner Publ.

ADAM, Maria Emma
Organist, pianist, violinist and composer of Cuban parentage. b. Madrid, September 24, 1875; d. Paris, 1957. She studied at the Real Conservatorio de Musica, Madrid. She studied the organ, the piano and the violin and won a first prize for piano playing at the age of 13. She lived in Cuba for a number of years and went to Paris in 1930.
Compositions
ORCHESTRA
Serenade andalouse (pf and orch)
Dos danzas cubanas
En el campo de Waterloo
L'enfance, suite
VOCAL
Songs incl.:
A une femme
Antonio y Cleopatra
Ars longa
Aubade
Ballade guerriere ecossaise
La cahier des souvenirs, 3 songs
Harmonie du soir
Recueil de l'adolescent
OPERA
La vida es sueño (Calderon)
Ref. Edgardo Martin (Havana)

ADAMOVICH (Adamowitsch), Elisabeth
19th-century Russian composer.
Compositions
PIANO
Berceuse (ded Her Imperial Majesty the Empress Alexandra Theodorovna) (Idzikowski)
Cortège triomphal du courronnement (ded His Imperial Majesty the Emperor Nicolas II) (Idzikowski)
Elegie (ded Her Imperial Majesty the Empress Maria Theodorovna) (Idzikowski)
Mazurka (ded Her Imperial Highness the Grandduchess Xenia Alexandrovna Michailovich) (Idzikowski)
Mazurka melancolique (ded Her Imperial Highness the Princes Eugenie Maximilianovna) (Idzikowski)
Le Ruisseau, étude de concert (Idzikowski)
Ref. 297

ADAMS, Carrie Bell (nee Wilson)
American organist, conductor, teacher and composer. b. Oxford, OH, July 21, 1859; d. 1940. She conducted large works including *The Messiah* and directed the Treble Clef and Rose Polytechnic Glee Clubs.

Compositions
VOCAL
Songs incl.:
Into the silent land (Palmer) (ch)
The lone river (Enzdry) (ch)
The wondrous story (Kohler)
SACRED
Over 100 anthems
OPERA
The national flower (Cincinnati: J. Church, 1921)
Ref. 141, 260, 292, 297, 347

ADAMS, Elizabeth Kilmer
American organist, choral director and composer. b. Oconto Falls, January 8, 1911. She studied voice with Alexius Bass and the organ with Robert Hays, Erna Lau Landt and Clarence Shepard. She was choir director and organist at several churches in Wisconsin.
Compositions
ORGAN
Dedication
They have taken away my Lord
PIANO
Navajo sunset
Wind in the fir tree
VOCAL
Songs incl.:
The window
SACRED
Songs incl.:
Moonlight on Gethsemane
Unto the hills
Ref. 347, 496

ADAMS, Julia Aurelia (nee Graves) (Mrs. Crosby)
American organist, pianist, lecturer, music critic, writer and composer. b. New York, March 25, 1858; d. November, 1951. She studied music under Mrs. C.S. Cary and the piano under Claude Crittenden, both of Rochester and theory under Adolf Weiding of Chicago. She was awarded an honorary D.Mus. by Converse College in 1932 and by the Women's College of the University of North Carolina in 1945. She taught in Leroy, Buffalo, NY, and Kansas City from 1880 to 1892, Chicago from 1892 to 1913 and then Montreal. She composed mainly for children.
Compositions
PIANO
Album of 9 duos
Three duets in unfamiliar keys
The Angelus
Barcarolle
Bourree antique
Circling the Christmas tree
Dance of the marionettes
Doll's miniature suite
Five tone sketches
Hymn tune in F-Major
Like an Aeolian harp
Studies, op. 7
Tone picture
Trumpet flowers
VOCAL
The Doll's music festival, cantata
Songs
SACRED
A little requiem
Publications
An American genius of world renown: Mrs. H.H.A. Beach. Etude, Jan. 1928, p. 34.
Studies in hymnology. Cokesbury Press, 1938.
Days in a doll's life. Asheville, NC. Inland Press.
Ref. 40, 276, 292, 347, 433, 496

ADAMS, Mrs. Crosby. See ADAMS, Julia Aurelia

ADAMS, Sarah
English composer. b. Harlow, East Anglia, February 22, 1805; d. London, August 14, 1848. Her elder sister was Eliza Fowler (q.v.).
Composition
SACRED
Nearer, my God, to Thee, hymn (1840)
Ref. 572

ADDI, Renee d'
19th-century Italian composer.
Composition
OPERA
Isolda (1881)
Ref. 225, 291, 307, 431

ADELINE
11th-century English glee-maiden. She lived in the reign of William the Conqueror, who awarded an estate to her.
Ref. 260

ADELINE L'ANGLOIS
14th-century French minstrel. She was a signatory to the famous charter dated September 14, 1321, that established the Chappelle Saint-Julien-des-Menestriers, a corporation for jongleurs and minstrels.
Ref. 343

ADELUNG, Olga
19th-century German zither player who composed numerous works for that instrument.
Ref. 226, 276

ADERHOLDT, Sarah
American cellist and composer. b. North Carolina, 1955. She studied the cello and composition at the University of North Carolina under Roger Hannay, Thomas Brosh, Annette LeSiege, Dominick Argento and Eric Stokes. She then studied for her M.Mus. at the same university. Her *String Quartet* won first prize in the Search for New Music, sponsored by the International League of Women Composers, 1979. DISCOGRAPHY.
Compositions
ORCHESTRA
Piece
CHAMBER
String quartet (1978) (1st prize, Search for New Music, 1979)
Other works
VOCAL
Songs
Ref. 563, 622

ADRIEN, Atala Theresa Annette. See WARTEL, Atala Therese

AESCHLIMANN-ROCHAT, Andree. See ROCHAT, Andree

AESCHLIMANN-ROTH, Esther
Swiss double-bassist, pianist, teacher and composer. b. Rorschach, April 1, 1953. Her first music teacher was Anne-Marie Boeninger. Esther then attended the Winterthur Conservatory and studied the piano under Klaus Wolters. She then studied the double-bass under Gerd Frank in St. Gallen and received her piano teacher's diploma in 1978. She played the double-bass in the Swiss Youth Orchestra, taught in schools in Ticino and began studying composition under Francesco Hoch. In 1984 she won first prize in the International 'Klangmaschinenwettbewerb', Dornbirn and in the same year attended the international summer courses in Darmstadt. She lives and works in Bellinzona, Ticino. PHOTOGRAPH.
Compositions
PIANO
Quadratur, graphic composition (1982)
VOCAL
Musik fuer 30 Stimmen und 18 Instrumentalisten (1985)
ELECTRONIC
Dialog fuer zwei Spieler (pf and stereo set) (1982)
MULTIMEDIA
Die Zeiten aendern sich, 7 audiovisual pieces (pf, d-b and tape) (1984)
Spektakulum, musical-theatrical street spectacle (20 actors, fanfares, 20 insts, tapes and transparencies) (1985)
Commedia (uniformed band, Guggenmusik players in costume and insts) (1985)
Raum und Zeit I (200 school chil) (1982)
Raum und Zeit II (50 passers-by) (1984)
Flickenteppich (iron objects, b-cl, har, vln, vlc and d-b) (1983)

Audioma (rhythmic sound sculpture with 12 Turkish and Chinese cups of different sizes, played by bicycle) (1984)
Gwindonia, sound sculpture (1984)
Ref. composer, 651

AFARIN
Persian songstress at the court of the Sassanid King Bahram III, ca. 293.
Ref. 305

AFFELDT, Marjorie Jean. See ZIPRICK, Marjorie Jean

AGABALIAN, Lidia Semyenovna
Soviet composer. b. Leninakan, October 7, 1933. In 1957 she graduated from the Gnesin Music School in Moscow, having studied composition under N.I. Peiko.
Compositions
ORCHESTRA
Suite (1956)
CHAMBER
Piano quintet (1955)
String quartet (1954)
Trio for harp, flute and viola (1953)
Pieces for violin and piano (1951)
PIANO
Children's pieces (1950)
Variations (1951)
Ref. 21

AGNES DE NAVARRE-CHAMPAGNE, Comtesse de Foix
14th-century French composer. She was the daughter of Jeanne de France and Phillip d'Evreux. She composed songs.
Ref. 465

AGNESI-PINOTTINI, Maria Teresa d'
Italian harpsichordist and composer. b. Milan, October 17, 1720; d. Milan, January 19, 1780. She was the sister of the mathematician Maria Gaetana Agnesi (1718 to 1799). She lived and studied in Milan, where she attracted attention both for her playing of the harpsichord and her compositions. She married Pietro Antonio Pinottini in 1752. She dedicated a volume of her compositions to Empress Maria Theresa and the music of her opera *Sofonisba* to Emperor Joseph II and *Ciro in Armenia* to Friedrich August I. Her opera *L'insubria consolata* was performed to celebrate the engagement of the Archduke Ferdinand to Princess Maria Ricciarda Beatrice of Modena. Three of her dramatic works were performed in Milan and various airs, keyboard pieces and concertos are extant in manuscript, but none of her works were published. A collection of cantatas in her honor by Pier Domenico Soresi appeared in 1756.
Compositions
CHAMBER
Concerto in F (pf or hpcd, 2 vln and d-b or str qrt)
Two concertos (hpcd, 2 vln and d-b) (1766)
Two concertos (pf, 2 vln and d-b)
PIANO
Allegro ou presto (also hpcd)
Sonatas (also hpcd)
Two fantasies
Other pieces (also hpcd or hp)
VOCAL
Il ristoro di Arcadia, pastoral cantata
Twelve arias (vce and inst)
Various airs (vce and hp)
Cantatas and choral works
OPERA
Ciro in Armenia, in 3 acts (composer or G. Manfredi)
L'insubria consolata, in 2 acts
Nitocri, in 3 acts
Sofonisba, in 3 acts (G.F. Zanetti)
THEATRE
Il re pastore, 3-act music drama
Ulisse in Campania, serenade in 2 parts (4 vces and cham orch)
Ref. 8, 15, 17, 44, 74, 100, 102, 105, 107, 108, 128, 129, 132, 155, 181, 182, 193, 225, 226, 276, 307, 347, 350, 400, 404, 502

AGOSTINO, Corona
16th-century Italian composer.
Composition
SACRED
Beati omnes (1592)
Ref. 465

AGRENEVA, Olga. See SLAVYANSKAYA, Olga

AGUDELO MURGUIA, Graciela
Mexican pianist, singer, teacher and composer. b. Mexico City, December 7, 1945. She was the daughter of the pianist J. Murguia Nunes. In 1951 she began her musical education under Homero Valle. She gained a degree in the piano from the Escuela Nacional de Musica de la UNAM and a fellowship in composition from the National Conservatory in 1970. She was president of the Cultural Music Center in Monterrey from 1965 to 1967, taught the Ensenanza Musical Yamaha System in 1967 and was active in the first seminar of electronic music in Mexico in 1974. PHOTOGRAPH.
Compositions
CHAMBER
Ad Diatessaron (cl, bsn, vln and vlc) (1973)
String quartet (1971)
Variaciones (fl, vla and pf) (1974)
Elegia (vln and pf) (1971)
PIANO
Andante (1970)
Seventeen preludes (1973)
Sonata (1970)
VOCAL
Cancion antiqua, song (1969)
ELECTRONIC
Cancrizante (vln, gtr, vib, pf and trb) (1972)
Ref. composer

AGUDIEZ, Eliza
Spanish composer. b. October 17, 1720; d. Madrid, June 19, 1795.

AGUIRRE, Diana V.
American singer and composer. b. San Diego, June 5, 1941. She graduated from the University of Southern California with a B.Mus. She took part in festivals and concerts of Renaissance music and in 1960 won the Award for Outstanding Madrigal Singer of the Year of San Diego City College. She collects Renaissance instruments.
Compositions
VOCAL
The bait
Nymph's reply to the passionate shepherd
Ref. 457

AHLEFELDT, Marie Theresia, Countess
Danish pianist and composer. b. Ratisbon, February 28, 1755; d. Prague, Czechoslovakia, November 4, 1823. She was the daughter of Prince Alexander Ferdinand of Thurn und Taxis and married the Danish diplomat Count Ferdinand Ahlefeldt. During the 1780s she belonged to the literary and musical circle surrounding Lady Craven (later the Margravine) at Ansbach.
Compositions
VOCAL
To Harmony, cantata (2 S, B and cham ens) (1792)
Romance de Nina (S and cham ens)
Klage (vce, fl and pf) (1788)
OPERA
La Folie, ou Quel Conte, in 2 acts (1789)
Telemachus and Calypso, opera-ballet in 4 acts (1792) (Copenhagen: S. Sonnichsen, ca. 1795)
INCIDENTAL MUSIC
Vaeddemalet, play (P.H. Haste) (1793)
Bibliography
Memoires de la Margrave d'Ansbach. Ecrits par elle-meme. Paris: Gerber NTL, 1825.
Ref. 8, 15, 65, 105, 125, 129, 225, 226, 276, 307

AHMES-NEFRETERE, Queen
Egyptian songstress. She is reputed to have been one of the first leaders of the Amon songstresses at the start of the XVIII dynasty. The songstresses' role seems to have been limited to the recitation of liturgical

responses, but as a member of royalty, Queen Ahmes-Nefretere probably received a musical education.
Ref. 207

AHRENS, Peg
American clarinetist, horn player, pianist, dancer, singer and composer. b. Clinton, OH, July 21, 1950. She studied voice, the clarinet, the horn, the piano and dance in precollege years. In 1973 she graduated from Ohio State University with a B.Mus. in voice performance, having studied singing under Irma Cooper and composition under Jay Huff and Ron Pellegrino. She went on to Mills College, Oakland, CA, where she studied composition under Robert Achley, video under Keith Walker and T.J. McHose, voice under Donna Petersen and Indian raga singing under Terry Riley. In 1975 she obtained an M.F.A. in electronic music and recording media. From 1975 to 1976 she was a member of the San Francisco Opera Chorus. At present she is a recording engineer at Kent State University.
Compositions
ORCHESTRA
Mean Proportion (84 or 56 strs) (1973)
CHAMBER
Repackaged Art, rewriting an orchestra piece (wind insts and strs) (1975)
String quartet (1971)
Stravinsky loved bassoons (3 bsn) (1972)
Wendung (vla and pf) (1972)
Agnus Dei
VOCAL
And then you laughed . . . (vce, fl, a-rec and d-b) (1974)
Did Marconi ever hear the Sermon on the Mount? (vce and fl) (1976)
The French don't care what they do, as long as they pronounce it correctly (1976)
Sorrow (vce, vla and vlc) (1970)
Together again (vce, fl and d-b) (1971)
THEATRE
Babe Didrikson vs Godzilla, for theatre of tennis (live elecs) (1976)
Excuse me, but are there any protozoa in this pond? (live elecs) (1974)
Five vignettes
Italian graffiti (vce and pf) (1974)
You too could be an opera star (live elecs) (1973)
ELECTRONIC
Bobby Clicks/bass rubber band (elec tape) (1973)
Charlemagne backwards (elec tape) (1973)
Electronic improvisations (1972)
Ergodic zoo (concrete tape) (1973)
Fat babyseal (quad tape) (1974)
Fontana mix (concrete tape) (1973)
Jar song (concrete tape) (1973)
Minako (modified vce and elecs) (1973)
Seal rock (seal music) (1975)
Tini sparrow, 3 versions (1974)
Vocalise (concrete tape) (1973)
Walrus and the carpenter (graphic score for any number of performers) (1972)
Wood (concrete tape) (1973)
Woofle, 4 versions (1975)
MULTIMEDIA
Blurp, 2 versions (vce, quad tape and video) (1974)
The definitive atatement on Martian art (video) (1975)
Free space, silent film (1973)
I love you Dylan Thomas, if but vicariously (1974)
In which Tigger comes into the forest and has breakfast (narr and effects) (1974)
A little be-faked Sappho never hurt anybody (1975)
Liza's song (elec tape and video of oscillographics) (1972)
Louisville Lou (video) (1975)
Maestro (video) (1975)
Mama Bear, Papa Bear and Baby Bear (video) (1975)
Night sport (video)
Photosynthesis (1973)
Real time (video) (1975)
Sappho (video) (1975)
Women (video) (1976)
Ref. composer

AHRENS, Sieglinde
German organist, professor and composer. b. Berlin, February 19, 1936. She studied the organ under her father Joseph Ahrens and Marchal and composition under Blacher, Messiaen, Milhaud and Rivier. In 1962 she became organist and professor at the Folkwangschule, Essen.
Compositions
CHAMBER
Sonata (vln and org) (Mueller, 1957)
ORGAN
Fantasie (Mueller, 1958)
Suite (Mueller, 1959)
VOCAL
Three songs (B and org)
Publications
Die Orgelwerke von O. Messiaen. Translation.
Technique de mon langage musical.
Ref. 81, 236

AIN, Noa (formerly Susan)
American composer. b. 1941. She graduated from the Juilliard School of Music in 1965 and gained a diploma from L'Ecole des Beaux-Arts, Fontainebleau, France. She studied composition privately under Hall Overton, Stefan Wolpe and Miriam Gideon (q.v.) and won a CAPS grant for composition in 1972. DISCOGRAPHY.
Compositions
THEATRE
Mourning pictures (with Honor Moore)
Nightwalk
ELECTRONIC
Used to call me sadness: a portrait of Yoko Matsua
Ref. 563

AIN, Susan. See AIN, Noa

AINLEY, Julie
20th-century English composer.
Composition
PIANO
Prelude in G-Minor (1975)
Ref. 230

AINSCOUGH, Juliana Mary (Julie)
English organist, pianist, choral conductor, teacher and composer. b. London, April 25, 1957. She studied the piano, the organ and composition at Trinity College of Music from 1975 to 1979 and from 1981 to 1984 studied part-time at Goldsmith's College, University of London for her M.Mus. in composition. She gained her L.T.C.L. (piano teaching); G.T.C.L. 1st class hons., F.T.C.L. (composition) and A.R.C.O. In 1980 she was a visiting piano teacher at the Francis Holland School, London; from 1981 to 1983 organist and choirmistress at St. Margaret's Church, Putney and since 1983, director of music at Sts. Peter and Paul Church, Putney. She won a John Halford composition prize (1977) and Royal Philharmonic composition prize (1978). PHOTOGRAPH.
Compositions
CHAMBER
Concertino for nine instruments (fl, trp, hn, trb, 2 vln, vlc, pf and perc) (1984)
Quintet (pf, fl, ob, cl and bsn) (1976)
Visions of five (cl and str qrt) (1984)
Alright for Saturday night? three dance movements (ob, cl and bsn) (1984)
Sonata (cl and pf) (1980)
Passacaglia (org) (1982)
PIANO
Sonata (2 pf) (1978)
Six pieces (1982)
VOCAL
Five songs (S, cl and pf) (1975)
Five poems of Gerard Manley Hopkins (Bar and pf) (1979)
Glass, setting of Song of the Degrees (Ezra Pound) (S, fl, hn, vlc and gtr) (1984)
Six poems of Emily Bronte (S, fl and pf) (1983)
SACRED
De profundis (mix-ch and orch) (1978)
Super flumina Babylonis (mix-ch a-cap) (1980)
Hymn to the Virgin (S, S, A and org) (1974)
Cantus Vernalis (S, fl, ob and gtr) (1977)
Ref. composer, 643

AKERS, Doris Mae
American choral conductor, singer and composer. b. Brookfield, MS, May 21, 1922. She wrote her first gospel song at the age of ten. She conducted several choirs including the Skypilot Choir, Los Angeles.

Compositions
SACRED
Lead me, guide me
There's a sweet, sweet spirit in this place
Other Gospel songs epitomizing the Afro-American religious experience in the United States
Ref. 646

AKHUNDOVA, Shafiga Gulam

Soviet composer. b. Nukha, Azerbaijan, January 22, 1924. She studied composition under B. Zaidman and Azerbaijanian music under U. Hadjibekov at the Baku Conservatory, graduating in 1953. DISCOGRAPHY.

Compositions
ORCHESTRA
Dance for orchestra of folk instruments (1964)
Na khlopkovykh polyakh, symphonic poem (1948)
CHAMBER
Scherzo (wind qrt) (1947)
Two pieces for trio (1946)
Sonatina (pf) (1946)
VOCAL
Romance V. Zhizni (Nizami) (S and orch) (1947)
In Memory of U. Hadjibekov (M. Pagim) (ch a-cap)
Two choruses (Nizami)
Approx. 40 romances and songs (Pushkin, Nizami and Soviet poets)
OPERA
Skala Nevest (1972)
OPERETTA
Dom nash taina nasha
INCIDENTAL MUSIC
Music for theatre
Ref. 21, 87, 563

AKIYOSHI, Toshiko

Japanese pianist and composer. b. Dairen, Manchuria, December 12, 1929. She studied at the Dairen Music Academy and won a scholarship to the Berklee School of Music, Boston, where she was a pupil of Margaret Chaloff. She majored in composition and became the only Japanese certified to teach the Schillinger System. As a pianist she performed with three Japanese symphony orchestras, then turned her interest to jazz and formed her own group in 1952. She was founder member of the Personal Aspect Quartet (Lew Tabackin-Toshiko Akiyoshi) and the Toshiko Akiyoshi-Lew Tabackin Big Band, formed in 1972. She has made numerous jazz recordings and concert appearances both as a soloist and a member of the instrumental groups she has formed. In 1980, she received the New York Jazz Award for the best arranger and in 1981 Downbeat magazine listed her as the best jazz composer and arranger of the year. She was also cited, for the third year running, as having the best big jazz band.

Compositions
ORCHESTRA
Double Exposure (1970)
Fool (1970)
A Jazz for strings and woodwinds (Ten Women of the Year, Mademoiselle Award)
My elegy (1958)
Silhouette (1958)
Sumie (1967)
Tuning up (1973)
CHAMBER
Instrumental and piano pieces
VOCAL
Songs
Ref. composer, 280, 347, 622

AKSYANTSEVA, Ninel Moiseyevna

Soviet pianist, lecturer and composer. b. Kazan, June 15, 1933. At the Kazan Conservatory she studied the piano under G.M. Kogan and composition under A.S. Leman, graduating in 1969. She taught the piano at the Kazan Music School from 1959 to 1970 and the Kazan Conservatory from 1967 to 1970. The following two years she lectured at a music school in Moscow and from 1972 taught ensemble music at the Gnesin School.

Compositions
ORCHESTRA
Concerto for flute, chamber orchestra and percussion (1968)
CHAMBER
Sonata (vln and pf) (1965, rev 1970)
Sonata (vlc and pf) (1973)
VOCAL
Chelovek, cycle (B, S, mix-ch and orch)
Cycle (V. Mayakovsky) (1968)
Cycles (R. Rozhdestvensky, M. Lvov, S. Kirsanov, I. Saltkov) (1970)
Ref. 21

A.L. See LEHMANN, Amelia

ALAIN, Marie Claire

French organist, teacher and composer. b. 1926. She studied harmony and counterpoint at the Paris Conservatoire under M. Durufle and the organ under M. Dupre. She won first prize in organ competitions in Geneva and Paris in 1950 and 1951. She taught the organ and recorded all of J.S. Bach's works.

Compositions
CHAMBER
Suite facile (themes of François Campion) (Paris: Billaudot, 1978)
Light organ works
VOCAL
Les chansons espiegles (vce and gtr) (Schott)
Les nouvelles chansons enfantines (vce and pf) (Schott)
Ref. 20, 360, 375

ALAIS

12th-century French troubadour. Together with Iselda (q.v.) and Carenza (q.v.) she wrote the song *Na Carenza al bel cors avinen . . .*; (Lady Carenza of the lovely, gracious body . . .).
Ref. 303

ALAMANDA

French troubadour. ca. 1130 to 1177, who came from Gascoigne, southern France. Alamanda was also referred to as 'Una domna de Gascoina' . . . 'N'Alamanda d'Estacs'. She is reputed to have composed the song *S'ie, us quier conseill, bell'ami Alamanda* . . . with Guiraut de Bornelh.
Ref. Dr. Margaret Nabarro (Johannesburg), 303

ALARCO, Rosa

Peruvian music teacher and composer. b. Lima, November 3, 1911. At the National Conservatory of Music in Lima, she earned a teacher's diploma and studied composition under Andre Sas and Rodolfo Holzmann. She taught vocal music at a school in Lima.

Composition
ORCHESTRA
Amor Ladron (1949)
Ref. 496

ALAZAIS D'AUTIER. See AZALAIS D'ALTIER

ALBANI, Mme. or Dame. See LAJEUNESSE, Emma

ALBRECHT, Elise

Compositions
PIANO
Friedliches Stilleben
Muttergruss in die Ferne
VOCAL
Gute Nacht, lieb' Muetterlein (Callier)
Versage nicht (Callier)
Ref. 297

ALBRECHT, Lillie

19th-century composer.

Compositions
PIANO
Amour inquiet, idylle
Gavotte in D-Major
Gigue in G-Major
La Fête des roses, valse de salon
Grand galop de concert
Lament, on the death of Prince Leopold, Duke of Albany
The maiden's sigh, reverie

The maiden's tear, second reverie
The maiden's dream, third reverie
Marche des heros
Le reveil du rossignol
The streamlet, etude de salon
VOCAL
Tis years since I beheld thy face, song
When all is hushed (To my mother), song
Ref. 297

ALBRIGHT, Janet Elaine
American harpsichordist, pianist, violist, teacher and composer. b. Ardmore, Penn, March 26, 1933. She studied the piano at Beaver College, Pennsylvania and obtained her B.Mus. She received an M.A. (music theory) from Colorado College and at the Conservatory of Geneva she studied the harpsichord under Isabel Nef. At the New School of Music, Philadelphia, she studied the viola under Max Aronoff. She was principal violist of the Alexandria Symphony Orchestra and taught the piano and the harpsichord at North Virginia Community College.
Compositions
ORCHESTRA
Textures I (str orch)
THEATRE
'Twas the Night before . . . A Christmas Fantasy (puppets and orch)
Ref. 457

ALBRIGHT, Lois
20th-century American composer.
Composition
OPERA
Hopity (New York, 1955)
Ref. 141

ALCALAY, Luna
Austrian pianist, teacher and composer. b. Zagreb, Yugoslavia, October 21, 1928. She studied the piano under Seiderhofer and composition under A. Uhl at the Musikhochschule, Vienna from 1951 to 1957, graduating with a prize. In 1958 the Austrian Academy of Sciences awarded her a scholarship to ROM, the Austrian Cultural Institute. She made her first contact with avant-garde music at Darmstadt in 1962. She taught the piano at the Musikhochschule, Vienna. DISCOGRAPHY. PHOTOGRAPH.
Compositions
ORCHESTRA
Dedicazione No. 2 (1971)
Fluides (1962)
Identifications (str orch) (1970)
Image de balance (1964)
Perpetuums (1970)
CHAMBER
Attachi (cham ens) (1962)
Demontage No. 2 (cham ens) (1963)
New point of view (cham ens) (1972)
Object trouvé (cham ens) (1967)
Signals (cham ens) (1964)
The T-factor (cham ens) (1980)
Perceptions for twelve players (1965)
Demontage No. 3 (wind insts, strs and perc) (1963)
Identities (wind insts and strs) (1962)
Three serenades (winds, perc, vln and vla)
In tre condizioni (rec ens) (1980)
Gliederungen (fl, ob, cl, bsn, trp, hn and trb)
Revaluations 2 (fl, cl, vln, hn, vla, c-bsn and perc) (1971)
Three static images for seven players (1964)
Beaute homogene (wind sextet) (1967)
Night club pieces (jazz qnt) (1966)
Interwoven movements (str qrt) (1961)
Many dreams formation (str qrt) (1973)
Revaluations (pf, vln and vlc) (1971)
Trio (a-sax, c-bsn and d-b) (1964)
Trio (fl, ob and cl) (1971)
Organisation for four groups (1972)
Aspects
PIANO
Mechanical systems (1967)
Piece (1961)
Triple fusion (1964)
VOCAL
Human rights, cantata (1968)
Blasphemes ouvertures I-II (News, News) (speaker and cham ens) (1979)
Delicate songs (S and cham ens) (1966)
En dialogue (S, Bar and cham ens) (1970)
For voice and percussion (1966)
Homo sapiens (acoustic scenes for speaker, ch and orch) (1977)
In memoriam Ossip Mandelstam 1891-1938 (narr and orch) (1973)
Picture book (S and cham ens) (1963)
Platitudes en occasion (vces, str qnt and perc) (1972) (won Preis der Stadt Wien) (1973)
Tre canzone semplice (ch and strs) (1978)
Una strofa di Dante (ch a-cap) (1965)
BALLET
Numerotage actionne
THEATRE
Cartographic perspective, musical picture scheme (up to 10 players) (1965)
Jan Palach, dramatic musical work (1982)
ELECTRONIC
Trois poèmes (pf, elec org and drs) (1978)
Ref. composer, 563

ALDEN, Blanch Ray. See DUTTON, Theodora

ALDEN, Zilpha May
American organist, pianist, choral director and composer. b. Sebec, March 2, 1893. She was a pupil of Mrs. Elmer Jenkins at the University Extension Conservatory, before becoming the organist and choir director at the Park Street Methodist Church in Milo, where she lived for a number of years.
Compositions
PIANO
Melody bells (Hatch Music Co. 1928)
Oak leaves reverie (Evan Music Co. 1923)
Ref. 374

ALDERMAN, Pauline
American pianist, professor and composer. b. Lafayette, OR, January 16, 1893; d. Los Angeles, June 22, 1983. She studied at the University of California, Berkeley from 1916 to 1917, at the Juilliard School of Music from 1923 to 1924; the University of Washington in 1933; the University of Strasbourg in 1939 and in 1946 received her Ph.D. from the University of Southern California. She studied the piano in Portland under Alfred Klingenberg, in New York under Abby Whiteside and theory under Carolyn Alchin in Los Angeles. She was a member of the faculties of the Ellison White Conservatory, Portland, from 1920 to 1923; Pomona College from 1924 to 1928 and the University of Washington from 1928 to 1930. She then became associate professor and chairlady of the department of music history and literature at the University of Southern California. She was honored at the 2nd International Congress of Women in Music, April 1982, for her outstanding contributions to the field of music and women in musicology.
Compositions
VOCAL
Songs
OPERA
Bombastes Furioso (1938)
OPERETTA
Come On Over (1941)
Ref. 141, 496

ALDRIDGE, Amanda Ira (pseud. Montague Ring)
Black English pianist, teacher and composer. b. London, March 16, 1866; d. London, March 5, 1956. After attending a convent school in Belgium she studied at the Royal College of Music, London. Her teachers included Jenny Lind (q.v.) and George Henschel (voice), Madge Kendal (elocution), Frederick Bridge and Francis Gladstone (harmony and counterpoint). She turned to teaching after a permanent injury to her voice.
Compositions
DANCE SCORES
Carnival suite of five dances (1924)
Three African dances (1913)
Three Arabian dances (1919)
Ref. 74, 87, 549

ALEGRE, Gracieuse
15th-century Spanish troubadour. She was one of the musicians of the household of Isabeau, Queen of Bavaria.
Ref. 315

ALEJANDRO-DE LEON, Esther

Puerto-Rican composer. b. New York, March 10, 1947. She began her musical studies at the Escuela Libre de Musica and then attended the Conservatory of Puerto Rico, where she obtained her B.Mus. (music education and composition). In 1972 she attended a summer course in theory of music given at the American School of Arts in Fontainebleau, France, where she studied under Nadia Boulanger (q.v.). With the assistance of the Patenring Scholarship awarded to her by the German government, she participated in the 31st International Summer Course for new music, Darmstadt, Germany. In 1977 she received the Jose Ignacio Quinton music prize. In 1979 she was active in the organization and co-production of a young composers' concert and in 1981 was similarly concerned with the 1st Concert-Forum of women composers. She also attended the 2nd Biennial of Contemporary Music in 1980 and in 1981 took part in the 10th Course of Latin-American Comtemporary Music. She received a certificate of merit for participation in the XVth Feast of Puerto Rican music and a certificate of merit from the Lion's Club for the organization and conducting of a vocal ensemble.

Compositions

ORCHESTRA

Autobiografia de Trapo (1977-1978)
The great game (1982)
Hecatombe (1978)

PIANO

Offering (1979)
Pegueno preludio (1971)

VOCAL

Glory (ch and orch) (1982)
Lares 1868 (ch and orch) (1979)
The prodigious shoemaker (narr and orch) (1980)
Madrugada (mix-ch) (1981)
Clues to an obsession (vce, pf and bsn) (1980)
Almost dawn (vce and pf) (1982)
Five Galician songs (vce and pf) (1979)
Minga's syringe (vce and pf) (1978)
Song without shoes (vce and pf) (1982)
With its deaf murmur (vce and pf) (1979)

SACRED

Our Father (mix-ch) (1981)

Ref. composer, 549

ALEKSANDROVA. See KOCHETOVA, Aleksandra Dorimedontovna

ALEOTTI, Raffaela-Argenta (pseud. Rafaele)

Italian organist, prioress and composer. b. Argenta, Ferrara, ca. 1570; d. after 1646. The eldest of five daughters of the architect Giovanni Battista Aleotti, she was a pupil of Alessandro Milleville and Ercole Pasquini. She entered the Augustinian Convent of San Vito, famous for its fine musical education. She first played the organ and in 1593 became director of vocal and instrumental ensembles and finally prioress. The quality of performances during her tenure was praised by contemporary writers and composers. Under her direction the nuns of San Vito gave concerts for Pope Clement VIII and Margaret of Austria. Her madrigals and motets were widely praised, but few survived. D. Lorenzo Agnelli Olivetano dedicated a book of motets to her. The Rafaele Aleotti sometimes referred to, is the deliberate use of the masculine equivalent. According to Eitner, Raffaela and Vittoria were not sisters but the same person, Raffaela being the name she assumed on entering the convent; but the weight of evidence from most of the references makes it clear that Raffaela was the elder sister. Besides the listed compositions, she also composed church music, madrigals and motets under the name Rafaele.

Compositions

SACRED

Sacrae cantiones, first book (5, 7, 8 and 10 vces) (Venice: Ricciardo Amadino, 1593)

Bibliography

Faustini, Lib. delle historie ferraresi....di G.Sardi com le aggiunte di A. Faustini. Ferrara, 1646.
Guarini, M.A.Compendio historico delle chiese die Ferrara. Ferrara, 1621.

Ref. 8, 15, 26, 105, 125, 126, 128, 129, 216, 332, 335, 347, 361, 389, 653

ALEOTTI, Vittoria (Vittorio)

Italian harpsichordist, nun and composer. b. Argenta, Ferrara, ca. 1575. She was the second of five daughters of the architect Giovanni Battista Aleotti. When she was four or five years old, she began listening to the harpsichord lessons given to her elder sister, Raffaela (q.v.). A year later, to the amazement of her parents and her sister's teacher, she began to play the harpsichord. Then she had lessons from Pasquino for two years; he recommended that like her sister she be sent to the Augustinian Convent of San Vito in Ferrara, famous for its musical learning. At the age of 14, against the will of her parents, she took the veil. She composed madrigals from the age of 14, her father publishing 21 of them in 1593, dedicating them to Ippolito Bentivoglio.

Compositions

VOCAL

Ghirlanda di madrigali a 4 voci de Vittoria Aleotti (verses by G.B. Guarini) (Venice: Giacomo Vincenti, 1593)
Di pallide viole, madrigal for 5 voices, in Il Giardino de musici ferraresi (under name Vittorio) (Venice: Vincenti, 1591)

Bibliography

Bottrigari, E. *Il Desiderio overto de concerti di vari strumenti musicali*. Venice, 1594.
Faustini, A. *Lib. delle historie ferraresi.... di G.Sardi con le aggiunte di A.Faustini*. Ferrara, 1646.
Guarini, M.A. *Compendio historico delle chiese di Ferara*. Ferrara, 1621.

Ref. 8, 15, 26, 105, 126, 128, 129, 216, 226, 335, 347, 653

ALESSANDRA, Caterina

Italian composer. b. ca. 1772. She composed songs. She is frequently confused with another composer of the same name, who was also known as Catterina Assandra (q.v.) and who composed sacred motets.

Ref. 157

ALESSANDRA, Catterina. See ASSANDRA, Catterina

ALESSI, Antonietta

19th-century Italian composer.

Compositions

PIANO

La bizzarria (Ricordi)
La capricciosa, op. 4, mazurka (Ricordi)
La fantastica, op. 8, mazurka (Ricordi)
La fata del Tevere, op. 9, polka (Ricordi)
La folgore, op. 6, waltz (Ricordi)
La sirena, op. 10, mazurka (Ricordi)
Variazioni supra due motivi di un valze di Strauss, op. 2 (Ricordi)

Ref. 297

ALEXANDER, Leni

Chilean electronic instrumentalist, lecturer and composer. b. Breslau, Germany, June 8, 1924. She lived in Hamburg until 1939, then emigrated to Chile and studied under Free Focke. She studied at the Paris Conservatoire under Messiaen and privately under Leibowitz. After further studies with Maderna and Nono she returned to Chile in 1955. In 1959 she was commissioned by Jean Cebron to write a ballet for the Metropolitan Opera. From 1960 to 1963 she was a teacher of music at the State University and the Goethe Institute, Santiago. From 1969 to 1970 she worked in the electronic studio of Columbia University.

Compositions

ORCHESTRA

Aconteceres (29 insts) (1965)
Aulicio (1968)
Divertimento ritmico (1956)
Equinoccios (1962)
Musica para orquesta (1951)
Sinfonia triptico (1954)
Five Epigrams (1952)

CHAMBER

Concierto de camera (1959)
Time and consummation (9 insts and perc) (1960)
String quartet (1957)
Trio (fl, cl and bsn) (1952)

PIANO

Adras (2 pf) (comm Aloys and Alfonse Kontarsky) (1969)
Mandals, 8 pieces (1962)
Suite (1950)

VOCAL

De la muerte a la mañana, cantata (Bar, w-ch and orch) (1958)
Tessimenti, cantata (Leonardo da Vinci) (S, A and cham orch) (1964)
Pour quoi, a quoi, par quoi (w-ch, ch, vces and inst ens) (1970)
Impressions, 4 songs (O. Wilde) (S and pf) (1953)
Tres cantos (Rainer Maria Rilke) (vce and pf) (1953)

BALLET
Las tres fases de la luna (1966)
THEATRE
Divertimento ritmico (1956)
Música para el teatro de niños, pantomime (1955)
INCIDENTAL MUSIC
Film music
Ref. 17, 90, 190

ALEXANDER, Mrs. Cecil Frances (nee Humphreys)
British composer. b. Redcross Parish, Ireland, 1818; d. Londonderry, Northern Ireland, October 15, 1895. She married Dr. Alexander, Archbishop of Armagh in 1850. Her *Hymns for little children* was so popular that it reached a 69th edition in 1896.
Compositions
SACRED
400 hymns, incl.:
All things bright and beautiful
The golden gates
Jesus Calls us
Once in Royal David's city
There is a green hill far away
Publications
Burial of Moses.
Verses for Holy Seasons. 1846.
Hymns for Little Children. 1848.
Hymns Descriptive and Devotional. 1858.
The Legend of the Golden Prayers. 1859.
Ref. 369, 646

ALEXANDRA, Liana (Saptefrati, Liana Alexandra)
Rumanian lecturer and composer. b. Bucharest, May 27, 1947. She studied composition at the Ciprian Porumbescu Academy in Bucharest from 1965 to 1971, when she was awarded the Ciprian Porumbescu scholarship. In 1973 she attended international courses in Weimar and in 1974, 1978 and 1980 took part in composition courses in Darmstadt. She has a master's degree in music and is a member of the Union of Rumanian Composers and lectures on orchestration and musical analysis. She won the prize of the Rumanian Academy in 1980; the prize of the Union of Rumanian Composers in 1975, 1979 and 1981; the first Carl Maria von Weber prize in Dresden in 1979 and the prize of the Gaudeamus Foundation, Bilthoven, in 1979 and 1980. She received a scholarship to study in America in 1983. Her works have been performed in Eastern and Western Europe, the United States and at international festivals. DISCOGRAPHY. PHOTOGRAPH.
Compositions
ORCHESTRA
Symphony I, in 2 mvts (1971)
Symphony II, hymns (1978)
Symphony III
Symphony IV (1983-1984)
Symphony V (1985-1986)
Concerto (cl and orch) (1974)
Concerto for flute, viola and chamber orchestra (1980)
Resonances (pf and orch) (1974)
Music for five soloists and orchestra (cl, vln, vla, vlc, pf and orch) (1975)
Valences, symphonic movement (1973)
CHAMBER
Collages (2 trp, hn, trb and tba) (1977)
Incantations II (vln, vla, vlc, cl and pf) (1978)
Incantations III (str qrt)
Sequence lyric (cl, trp and pf) (1974)
Consonances I (4 trb) (1978)
Music for clarinet, harp and percussion (1972)
Consonances II (cl and pf) (1979)
Sonata (fl) (1973)
ORGAN
Consonances III (org) (1979)
Consonances V (org) (1980)
VOCAL
Cantata I (w-ch and orch) (1974)
Cantata II (S, Bar, mix-ch and orch) (1977)
Cantata IV, two images (chil-ch and orch) (1978)
Incantations I, (m-S, fl, perc and hpcd) (1978)
OPERETTA
The Snow Queen, for children (after H.C. Andersen) (1979)
ELECTRONIC
Consonances IV (cl and tape) (1980)
Ref. composer, 457, 563, 643

ALEXANDRA JOSEPHOWNA, Grand Duchess
19th-century Russian composer.
Compositions
ORCHESTRA
Several pieces
PIANO
Bolero (4 hands) (Cranz)
Defilier-Marsch (4 hands) (Cranz)
Koeniglicher preussischer Armee Marsch fuer Kavallerie, No. 73 (Bote)
Nocturne (Johansen)
Olga Polka (1851)
Regimentsmarsch des Ulanen-Regiments Koenig Karl (Bote)
SACRED
Psalms (vce, mix-ch and orch) (St. Petersburg, 1886)
Church music
Ref. 226, 276, 297, 413

ALEXANDRE, Claire
18th-century French composer.
Composition
MISCELLANEOUS
Jeune Flore a l'amour (Paris: Mercure de France, 1777)
Ref. 65

ALEXANDROVA, A.
Russian pianist, operatic and concert singer and composer. b. St. Petersburg, 1835. She composed several sets of songs.
Ref. 276, 433

ALIJZIJA, Slavka. See ATANASIJEVIC, Slavka

ALINGTON, Charlotte. See BARNARD, Charlotte

ALIOTH, Marguerite
Swiss pianist and composer. b. Arlesheim, near Basle, March 22, 1874; d. 1962. She was a pupil of Alfred Volkland and Teresa Carreño (q.v.) (piano) and Friedrich Klose, Hans Huber and Hermann Suter (composition).
Compositions
ORCHESTRA
Overture
PIANO
Trois morceaux
VOCAL
Songs
Publications
Eine Studie ueber Martin Vogt. Sontagsblatt Nr. 7-12 des Tageblattes fuer das Birseck, 1922.
Ref. 101, 651

ALLAIN, Edmee J.
French composer. b. 1894.
Compositions
VOCAL
Les chansons de Mamie, 6 songs (1 or 2 vces and pf)
Ref. SACEM

ALLAN, Esther
American pianist and composer. b. Suvalke, Poland, April 28, 1914. The daughter of Cantor Rubin Bouarsky, she graduated from the Royal Academy of Music, London in 1927 and the Scottish National Academy of Music in 1930. She is a member of ASCAP. DISCOGRAPHY.
Compositions
ORCHESTRA
Norman concerto (pf and orch)
Romantic concerto (pf and orch)
Bethie's theme (pf and orch)
Enchantment (pf and orch)
Freddie's running (pf and orch)
Interlude (pf and orch)
Meditation (pf and orch)
Ocean rhapsody (pf and orch)

Summer waltz (pf and orch)
Trailing (pf and orch)
CHAMBER
Autumn nocturne (pf and hp)
PIANO
Karen's butterflies
Nancy's waltz
Ref. composer, 84, 563

ALLBRITTON, Florence Ziegler
20th-century American organist, concert pianist, assistant professor and composer. b. Clarks, LA. She received her B.Mus. in 1936 and M.Mus. in 1945 from the Chicago Music College. Her teachers included Lula S. Gardner, John Thomas, Moissaye Boguslawski, John Carre, Rudolph Ganz and Mollie Margolies. She appeared as a concert pianist and taught at the Northeast Junior College of Louisiana State University. After 1937 she was a church organist in Monroe. She composed with Blanche Olivier (q.v.).
Compositions
ORCHESTRA
Acadie (1932)
Flood (1932)
Ref. 496

ALLEMAND, Pauline L'
20th-century American composer.
Composition
OPERETTA
The Cape of Confucius (Richard Edon) (1904)
Ref. 431

ALLEN, Denise
20th-century British script writer, singer and composer. b. London. She went to South Africa in 1940, returning to England in 1946 to study at the Royal Academy of Music. After settling in South Africa, she appeared in operas and operettas and collaborated with Richard Cherry in script writing and composition. She prepared programs of folk songs for radio and television.
Compositions
VOCAL
In Praise of South Africa (ch) (1949)
City of Gold, march (1950)
Approx. 28 other songs
OPERETTA
Swiss Interlude (1961)
Ref. 377

ALLEN, Judith Shatin (Shatin, Judith Allen)
American assistant professor and composer. b. Boston, November 21, 1949. She studied at Douglass College under Robert Noevs and received her A.B. in 1971, Phi Beta Kappa. In 1974 she received her M.M. from the Julliard School, studying under Hall Overton and Otto Luening. She continued her music studies at Princeton University, studying under J.K. Randall, Peter Westergaard and Milton Babbitt and obtaining her M.F.A. in 1976 and Ph.D. in 1979. She received the Julia Carlie memorial prize, the Abraham Ellstein award and Aspen Music Festival awards in 1971 and 1972. In 1978 she won a prize in the East and West Artists composition competition and several grants and in 1981 a scholarship to the music and dance program at the American dance festival. Since 1979 she has been an assistant professor at the University of Virginia. DISCOGRAPHY. PHOTOGRAPH.
Compositions
All published by ACA
ORCHESTRA
Arche (vla and orch) (1976)
A toute les heures (1974)
Aura (1982)
Chrysalis (1973)
CHAMBER
Tombeau des morts (vla, vlc, d-b, hp and pf)
Werther (fl, cl, pf, vln and vlc) (comm Montclair State College) (1983)
Wind songs (ww qnt) (1975)
Constellations (str qrt) (1979)
Legends (fl, ob, vlc and perc)
Quatrain (vln, vla, cl and b-cl) (1979)
Lost angels (trp, bsn and pf) (1979)
Rhymes (trp, trb and perc)
Gazebo music (fl and vlc) (1981)
Glyph (vla and pf) (1984)
Nightshades (vlc and pf) (1977, rev 1979)
Study in black (fl and perc) (1981)
When the moon of wild flowers is full (fl and vlc) (1973)
L'Etude du coeur (vla) (1983)
Limericks (fl)
Partials (hp) (1976)
Passages (vla)
Postlude (org) (1975)
Soundspecs (1981)
PIANO
Scirocco (1981)
Sphinx (1982)
Widdershins (1983)
VOCAL
Grave music (S, str trio, d-b and perc)
Love song (Marlowe) (S and cor anglais) (1978)
Soundscreams (1981)
Wedding music (Marlowe) (S and vla; also cor anglais)
SACRED
Psalm XIII (mix ch and org) (1978)
Sursum corda (vlc) (1981)
OPERA
Follies and Fancies, chamber opera based on Moliere's *Les Precieuses Ridicules* (5 vces and pf or ens) (1981)
Job, opera oratorio (10 singers and pf) (1983)
Ref. composer, 142, 474, 563, 622, 624, 625

ALLEN, Marie Townsend. See TOWNSEND, Marie

ALLEN, Mary Wood
19th-century American composer.
Composition
VOCAL
Breaking the day in two
Ref. 465

ALLEN, Mimi
American harpist, teacher and composer. b. July 30, 1925. She graduated from Stephens College, DC, where she studied under Isidor Philipp and Carlos Salzedo. She toured with the latter and appeared as a soloist with various major orchestras.
Compositions
HARP
The happy harp
Strings of my heart
There goes my harp
VOCAL
Carols of four seasons (ch and hp)
Ref. 77

ALLEN, Mme. de Renaud a'. See RENAUD-D'ALLEN, Mme. de

ALLEOTTI, Vittorio. See ALEOTTI, Vittoria

ALLIK, Kristi
Canadian composer of Estonian origin. b. Toronto, 1952. She graduated from the University of Toronto in 1975 with a B.Mus., having studied under Oskar Morawetz, Lothar Klein, John Weinzweig, Gustav Ciamaga and John Beckwith. From the Princeton University she received an M.F.A. for composition in 1971. At the University of Southern California, she completed a doctorate in composition. She received several fellowships and scholarships and was commissioned to compose several works by the Ontario Arts Council.
Compositions
ORCHESTRA
Piano concerto (1975)
Lend me your harp (1979)
CHAMBER MUSIC
Quartet for winds and percussion (1975)
String quartet (1974)
Piano trio (1979)
Trio for flute, clarinet and cello (1976)
Duet for flute and piano (1973)
Guitar duo
PIANO
Etude (1973)
Etude and pastorale (1972)

Fragments (1977)
Piece (1973)
VOCAL
Something (ch and perc) (1973)
Three songs for Marie Under (1972-1973)
Duet (fl and vce) (1973)
OPERA
Loom, Sword, River, in 3 acts, based on Estonian mythology (P. Such) (1975)
INCIDENTAL MUSIC
Woods of Tontla (elec insts) (1977)
Slide shows (elec insts) (1975)
ELECTRONIC
L.A. '79 (brass, perc, ampl fl, pf and d-b)
Trio for flute, violin and vibraphone (1973)
Tape compositions
Ref. composer

ALLINOWNA, Stefania
Polish concert pianist, professor and composer. b. Lodz, November 19, 1895. From 1910 to 1917 she studied the piano under M. Surzynski at the Warsaw Academy. She attended the Chopin School of Music from 1918 to 1919 and studied composition under F. Szopski. She then went to Berlin until 1928, furthering her piano studies under F. Petri and theory and composition under H. Leichtentritt. From 1929 to 1939 she taught the piano at the Silesian Conservatory. During this period she toured Poland, Germany and Czechoslovakia as a concert pianist, often playing with the pianist Wladislawa Markiewiczowna. She was co-editor of the journal *Popular Silesian Music*. In 1945 she left for Breslau and then for Katowice, where she became professor of the piano at the State Music School.
Compositions
PIANO
Ballad
Caprice
Etude in D-Minor (1951) (Warsaw: Czytelnik)
Prelude
Three etudes
Variations in D-Minor
Variations in F-Sharp Minor
Publications
In memory of Professor Alexander Michalowski. 1939. Popular Silesian Music.
On the Piano Teaching of Professor Edwin Fischer. Popular Silesian Music.
Ref. W. Pigla (Warsaw), 118

ALLITSEN, Frances (Mary Frances Bumpus)
English singer, teacher and composer. b. 1849; d. London, October 2, 1912. She studied at the Guildhall Music School, London and appeared as a singer in 1882, but later lost her voice. She was known in the United States for her songs.
Compositions
ORCHESTRAL
Overture Slavonique
Overture Undine
VOCAL
For the Queen, cantata (1900)
Songs incl.:
Absence
After long years
Apart for evermore
Die Botschaft
Break, diviner light (duet)
Come not when I am dead
Du hast Diamanten und Perlen
Eight songs (Heine)
False or true
Give a man a horse
In times of old
Katherine
King and slave
Like violets pale
Love is a bubble
Mary Hamilton
Six songs (Tennyson)
Other songs (Browning, Longfellow, Shelley)
SACRED
Christmas songs
The Lord is my light, duet
A psalm of thanksgiving
INCIDENTAL MUSIC
L'Interieur
Ref. 6, 8, 85, 142, 260, 276, 347, 353

ALLOUARD CARNY, Odette
French organist, pianist, painter and composer. b. Paris, December 30, 1914. She was taught painting by her father and the piano by her mother. She studied under Victor Fumet and became the chief organist of the renowned organ of Sainte Anne de la Maison Blanche, Paris. In 1968 she created the original spectacle *Vitrail* (stained glass window) which incorporated music, painting and poetry. She is a member of SACEM. PHOTOGRAPH.
Compositions
ORCHESTRA
Offering symphony (str orch) (1955)
Symphony for a concert (1951)
Symphony of the royal priesthood (1968)
Scenes of children (1965)
ORGAN
Aurore (1982)
Preludes, fugues and pieces (1968)
Symphony of light (1966)
PIANO
Melodies and pieces (1940)
VOCAL
O vulnera!
Wake up! (4 vces, workmen's ed)
SACRED
Mystery of Christmas, oratorio (soloists, ch and org)
Sebastien under the arrows, oratorio (Pierre Hebert) (soloist, ch, org and sym orch) (1952)
Picture of the passion (ch and org) (1953)
Poem of the Cross (solos, ch and org) (1958)
MULTIMEDIA
A ta recherche, ou les degrés de la Joie (audio-visual) (1980)
Vitrail; music, painting and poetry
Ref. composer

ALMEN, Ruth
Swedish pianist, teacher and composer. b. 1870; d. 1945. She studied the piano under R. Andersson in Stockholm, K. Baeck in Goeteborg, H. Barth in Berlin and R. Lortat in Paris. She studied harmony under G. Haegg in Stockholm, modulation under Professor Malling and counterpoint and fugue under W. Stenhammar in Goeteborg. She also studied composition under K. Jeppesen in Copenhagen and instrumentation under K. Westmeyer in Berlin.
Compositions
ORCHESTRA
Piano concerto
CHAMBER
String quartet
Sonata in A-Minor, op. 3 (vl and pf) (Ries and Erler, 1923)
Violin sonatas
PIANO
Sonata
Other pieces
VOCAL
Songs
Ref. 41, 226, 642

ALMESAN, Irma
American concert pianist, conductor, teacher and composer of Hungarian origin. b. Budapest, September 30, 1891. She studied at the Budapest Academy, obtaining a performance and teaching diploma under the tuition of Agoba Rennebaim, a pupil of Liszt. She played in concerts in Europe, New York, Jersey and Maine and in chamber music groups, some of which she conducted.
Compositions
ORCHESTRA
Hungarian fantasia
CHAMBER
Hungarian melody (vln and pf)
Russian waltz (vln and pf)
Spanish waltz (vln and pf)
PIANO
Modern melodia
Music box
Scherzo
VOCAL
Songs incl.:
Do you know why . . .
Far away
I remember
Little bird flew away
On a bright sunny morning

SACRED
Everlasting peace, anthem
Ref. 374

ALMODIS DE CASENEUVE. See ALMUCS DE CASTELNAU

ALMONDIS DE CASENEUVE. See ALMUCS DE CASTELNAU

ALMUCS DE CASTELNAU (Lady Almucs of Luberon)
French troubadour. b. Castelnau, ca. 1140. She was possibly the same person as Almodis de Caseneuve, who married Guiraut I de Simaine, Lord of Caseneuve, Apt and Gordes, in 1152. A wealthy lady, she became a patron of troubadours, one of them being her own son, Raimbaut, later Raimbaut d'Agould, who also became a patron of the troubadours.
Composition
VOCAL
Dompna n'Almucs, si. us plages . . . song (with Iseut de Capio q.v.)
Ref. Dr. Margaret Nabarro (Johannesburg), 303

ALONSO, Julia
Mexican organist, pianist, teacher and composer. b. Oaxaca, 1889. She studied at the National Conservatory where she later became a teacher of the organ, the piano and composition. She achieved success with her compositions before the age of twenty-one.
Compositions
ORCHESTRA
Two symphonies
CHAMBER
Two quartets
Two suites
Variations
OPERA
Tonantzin
Ref. 361

ALOTIN, Yardena
Israeli pianist, teacher and composer. b. Tel-Aviv, October 19, 1930. She studied at the Tel-Aviv Music Teachers' Seminary under Kestenberg and at the Israeli Academy of Music under I. Vince (piano), receiving her piano teacher's diploma in 1952. She then studied for 12 years with Oedoen Partos. In 1952 she received the Nissimov Prize for her work *Yefei Nof* and was composer-in-residence at Bar-Ilan University from 1975 to 1976. She is a member of the Israeli Music Institute and the Hanerkaz Letarbut Ulechinuch, Tel Aviv, both of which publish her works. PHOTOGRAPH.
Compositions
CHAMBER
String quartet
Fugue for string trio
Piano trio
Six duets (vln)
Sonata (vln and pf) (1960)
Sonatina (fl and pf)
Sonatina (vln and pf)
Sonata (vlc)
PIANO
Passacaglia on a Bukharian theme
Prelude, intermezzo and variation
Six pieces for children
Suite
Three preludes (1962)
VOCAL
Cantata (ch a-cap)
Algola devuya (vce and orch)
Hinei matov (ch a-cap)
Eight songs for children (vce and pf)
Misirei hanachal (Leah Goldberg) (m-S and pf)
SACRED
Yefei nof (ch a-cap; also fl) (1952) (Nissimov prize)
Ref. composer, 94, 189, 205, 206, 379, 457, 501, 643

ALOYSIA, Luise. See WOLFF, Luise

ALPERT, Pauline Edith
American concert pianist and composer. b. New York, December 7, 1912. She studied at the Eastern School of Music under Selim Palmgren. She appeared on the radio and in concerts throughout America and played at the White House for Presidents Roosevelt and Truman.
Compositions
PIANO
Dream of a doll (Mills)
March of the blues (Mills)
The merry minnow (Mills)
Night of romance (Mills)
Perils of Pauline (Mills)
Piano poker (Mills)
Ref. 496

ALSCHANSKY, Serafine
20th-century German composer.
Composition
CHAMBER
Im Walde (hn and pf) (Heilbron: C.F. Schmidt)
Ref. 291

ALSOP, Frances
British composer. d. 1821.
Compositions
VOCAL
Last New Year's day
The poor Hindoo
William and Mary
Ref. 465, 622

ALSTED, Birgitte
Danish violinist, teacher and composer. b. 1942. A conservatory educated violinist, she performed and taught the violin until 1972, when she started composing. She allied herself to the Gruppen for Alternativ Musik, a group of young composers and musicians interested in the composition and performance of new and experimental music and who consider the restraints of conventional music tyrannical and limiting. She takes part in collective improvisation in large and small groups.
Compositions
ORCHESTRA
Lyden Paa Rejse
CHAMBER
String quartet in CD (1977)
Stykke (1973)
Stykke to (1973)
PIANO
Gentagne gange II (2 pf)
Gentagne gange (also theatre, 1980)
Phasing moon facing changing
VOCAL
Haiku (mix-ch) (1979)
Solen og jeg (chil-ch and inst ens)
Solen paa Noddigen (B, lute, vln, d-b, acc, pf and perc)
ELECTRONIC
Antigone (tape)
Brahms, collective work (1974)
Kollektiv komposition (1978)
Kontakte (elec vln) (1971)
Konkurrence (1979)
Musikere paa Muzak (1974)
Zoophus III, collective work (1975)
Zoophus IV, collective work (1976)
THEATRE
Klumpe (1972)
Jorden rundt i 80 dage (collective work)
Peer Gynt (collective work)
Smedierne i Granada (1975-1976)
Timileshoven (d-b, perc and dance)
Tredje tilstand
Ref. composer, 622

ALT, Hansi
American pianist, lecturer and composer. b. Vienna, February 25, 1911. After graduating from the Vienna Conservatory she continued

her studies in theory and composition. She taught the piano and theory at several private and music schools in New York and at the Los Angeles Conservatory. She ran her own studio in Washington, DC, and judged for the National Guild of Piano Teachers.
PHOTOGRAPH.
CHAMBER
Pieces for flute
Pieces for piano
Pieces for violin
VOCAL
Songs
TEACHING PIECES
Numerous pieces incl.:
Let's go by car (pf) (OUP, 1982)
Three games (pf) (OUP, 1982)
Ref. composer, 347, 624

ALTER, Martha

American pianist, assistant professor and composer. b. New Bloomfield, PA, February 8, 1904; d. CT, June 3, 1976. She was a graduate of Vassar College and obtained her M.A. (musicology) at Columbia University and her M.Mus. (composition) at the Eastman School of Music. She studied composition under Seth Bingham, Bernard Rogers, Rubin Goldmark and George Gow and the piano under Kate Chittenden and Jere Hutcheson. She frequently performed her own works. Her awards included the Kendrick-Ryland Fellowship, Associate Alumnae Fellowship (two years), Salmon Fund for Research Award and Vassar 75th Anniversary Publication award. She taught at Vassar, held a teaching fellowship at Eastman School of Music and in 1942 became assistant professor of music at Connecticut College. Her works have been broadcast by national radio networks, played by leading orchestras and performed at colleges throughout the U.S.A.
Compositions
ORCHESTRA
Bric-a-brac suite
Music for Bicentennial Pageant for Perry County (1976)
Rhythmic dance
Sinfonietta (1932)
CHAMBER
Sextet (fl, ob, cl, trp, hn and bsn) (1933)
Suite (vln, pf and perc) (1932)
Suite of three dances (vln, pf and perc) (1928)
Trio (cl, vlc and pf) (1927)
Trio (vln, vlc and pf) (1925)
Wedding music (ob, vlc and pf) (1937)
Americana suite (hpcd) (1940)
Sonata (hpcd) (1941)
PIANO
Suite of songs and dances (2 pf) (1936)
Sonata (1927)
VOCAL
Bill George: march and song (Bar and orch) (1932)
Two Plato settings; Country gods and Country music (1942) (w-vces, fl and pf) (Galaxy Music)
Blackout (Bar, 2 trp, perc and pf) (1941)
Simon Legree, A negro sermon (V. Lindsay) (Bar and 2 pf) (1938)
Emily Dickinson, song cycle (1968)
A prayer for my daughter (comm Connecticut College 50th Anniversary) (1969)
Peace (Bacchylides) (1940)
SACRED
Let God be magnified, cantata (w-ch and pf or org) (1947)
BALLET
Anthony Comstock, or A Puritan's Progress (1934)
OPERETTA
Groceries and Notions, in 3 acts (Gertrude Brown) (1931)
THEATRE
Music for Christmas pageant (vce, dance and org) (1942)
Music of the stratosphere; Through space, Through time and beyond (dance and orch) (1946)
A dimensional fantasy (dance, pf and perc) (1946)
Ref. 13, 124, 140, 141, 168, 465, 496, 622

ALTIER, Azalais de'. See AZALAIS D'ALTIER

ALTMAN, Adella C.

20th-century American composer of Miami, FL. She composed choral works, operettas and musical plays.
Ref. 142, 347

ALULI, Irmgard Keali'iwahinealohanohokahaopuamana (nee Farden)

Hawaiian composer. b. Lahaina, Mani, October 7, 1911. She graduated from the University of Hawaii in 1933 and performed with the Annie Kerr Vocal Trio and the Farden-Poepoe Orchestra, an 11 piece band. She began composing in 1935.
Compositions
VOCAL
Approx. 350 popular, folk and children's songs, the latter written in collaboration with her sister, Edna Bekeart (q.v.)
Songs incl.:
Baby Kalai
Boy from Laupahoehoe
Down on Maunakea street
E Maliu Mai
Ke Kali Nei Au
Ku'u Pete
Lu'au Feet
Nahoe He'e Nalu
Puamana
Punalu'u Alona
SACRED
My Hawaiian Madonna
Hymns incl.:
For a peaceful world
Joseph the beloved Father
Thanksgiving
To the sacred hearts of Jesus and Mary
Other sacred songs
Ref. 438

ALVARES-RIOS, Maria

Cuban pianist, singer, teacher, translator and composer. b. Trunicu, near Sancti-Spiritus, June 5, 1919. She studied at Michigan University and the Havana University under Luisa Chartrand and composers Harold Gramatges and Enrique Bellver. She translated Italian and French opera librettos into Spanish and was active as a music teacher.
Compositions
VOCAL
Abrazame amor
Anda di, corazon
Cinco canciones de Jose Marti (1957)
Cinco canciones de Omar Khayyam (1956-1960)
Como me duele
Diecineuve canciones de Lorca (1955-1969)
Dieciseis canciones de Nicolas Guillen (1971)
Diez canciones de Felix Pita (1971)
La rosa y el ruisenor
Seis canciones de varios autores (1955-1965)
Trece canciones artisticas (composer)
Trece canones cubanos (1960)
Veintiocho canciones de Gabriela Mistral (1956)
Ya no me llamas
Over 200 popular songs, ballads, etc.
INCIDENTAL MUSIC
Music for 4 films by Instituto Cubano de Arte e Industria Cinematografica
Ten works for theatre (some earned national prizes)
Publications
Twenty educational volumes.
Ref. Edgardo Martin (Havana), 604

ALVES DE SOUSA, Berta Candida

Portuguese pianist, conductor, lecturer, music critic and composer. b. Liege, Belgium, April 8, 1906. Her family came from Oporto and returned there when Bertha was very young. She studied at the Oporto Conservatory under Moreira de Sa, Luis Costa, Lucien Lambert and Claudio Carneyro and graduated in the piano. In Paris from 1927 to 1929, she studied the piano under Wilhelm Backhaus and Theodore Szanto, composition under George Migot and improved her piano technique with Vianna da Mota in Lisbon. She studied conducting under Clement Krauss in Berlin and Pedro Freitas Branco in Lisbon and later attended interpretation courses under Alfred Cortot for the piano and studied the teaching of music under Professor Edgar Willems. She was music critic for the press after 1939. She taught chamber music and the piano at the Oporto Conservatory and performed in numerous recitals and concerts as a soloist, accompanist and conductor. She experimented in sound symmetry together with its creator, composer Fernando Correia de Oliveira and received many prizes and awards, including the Moreira de Sã Prize in 1941. PHOTOGRAPH.

Compositions
ORCHESTRA
Vasco da Gama, symphonic poem (1936)
Bolero (1961)
Canto lamatico (also vln and pf) (1953, 1960)
Cançao marinha (also vce and pf) (1965)
Dança exotica (also pf) (1965)
Pavana (also vln and pf) (1943, 1948)
Scherzo-marcha (also 2 pf) (1969)
Tremor de terra (1949)
MILITARY BAND
Porto heroico, march (1951)
CHAMBER
Quinteto de sopro (fl, ob, cl, bsn and hn) (1971)
Dueta para violoncellos (2 vlc and pf) (1965)
Prelude et fugue (3 vlc)
Tema e variações (2 vlc and pf) (1964)
Trio com piano (vln, vlc and pf) (1974)
Variações sobre uma cantiga alentejana (trio) (1950)
Cantilena (vln and pf) (1934)
Lamento (vlc and pf; also vln and pf) (1964, 1949)
Poeme (vlc and pf)
Variações sobre um tema a Beira Baixa (vlc and pf) (1967)
Variações sobre um tema do Algarve (vlc and pf; also vln and pf) (1957, 1956)
PIANO
Esboço elegiaco (2 pf) (1974)
Toccata modal (2 pf) (1974)
Duolo (in memory of C. Carneyro) (1963)
Fauna em música, 8 pieces for children (1976)
Transparencias (1947)
Tres Preludios (1953)
VOCAL
A rivedere i stelle (Dante) (mix-ch and sym orch; also mix-ch a-cap) (1968, 1966)
O jovem rei (O. Wilde) (w-ch and sym orch; also str qrt and pf) (1932, 1949)
Oração a luz (G. Junqueiro) (mix-ch and str orch) (1972)
A noite (vce and orch)
Desejo (mix-ch a-cap) (1948)
Mas porém a que cuidados (Camoes) (mix-ch a-cap) (1971)
Nocturno (A. Lousada) (mix-ch a-cap) (1947)
O Virgens que andais no sol poente (A. Nobre) (mix-ch a-cap)
Rosa da Alexandria (mix-ch a-cap; also vce and pf) (1946, 1949)
Sonho (mix-ch a-cap) (1956)
As rosas (A. Lousada) (2 w-vces a-cap) (1940-1948)
Canção (A. Lousada) (2 w-vces a-cap)
Porquê não fui dancar na boda (A. Gil) (3 w-vces a-cap) (1947)
Silêncio (composer) (3 w-vces a-cap)
Songs:
A fonte dos amores (Camoes) (1965)
De amor escrevo (Camoes) (1965)
Dobadoira (1946)
Le gong a sonné (1966)
Há no meu peito uma porta (J.A. Albano) (1949)
Incêndio (G. Guerreiro) (1965)
Joguei às cartas contigo (1941) (hon mention Jogos Florais, 1944)
Mormaço (M. Bandiera) (1950)
Sete anos de pastor (Camoes) (1966)
Sete canções (prize)
Singra o meu barco (H. Heine) (1944)
Arrangement of tres canções populares harmonizades (vce and pf) (1937)
SACRED
Eia mater, fons amoris (3 vces, hp and str orch) (1950)
Stabat Mater (ch)
Ave Maria (4 vces a-cap) (1946)
Pai nosso (3 m-vces a-cap and pf) (1946)
Salve Regina (2 vces a-cap) (1932)
Ref. 96, 107, 268

ALYA
8th-century Arabian songstress. She was the daughter of Caliph al-Mahdi and the slave singer Macnuna and received a thorough religious training, which included the reading of the Koran. She was a great artist and composer and was said to have composed between 50 and 72 songs.
Ref. 170

AMACHER, Maryanne
American electronic instrumentalist, teacher and composer. b. Kae, PA, February 25, 1942. She studied at the Philadelphia Conservatory of Music from 1955 to 1962 and received a B.F.A. in 1964 from the University of Pennsylvania, having studied under George Rochberg and K. Stockhausen. She taught in the experimental music studio at the School of Engineering, University of Illinois from 1964 to 1966 and was creative associate at the Center of Creative and Performing Arts, State University, New York from 1966 to 1967. She received a multi-media award from the New York State Council of Arts from 1978 to 1979, a composition award from the National Endowment of the Arts, 1978 to 1979 and the Beards Arts Fund in 1980.
Compositions
MULTIMEDIA
Close up
Intelligent life (comm Stichting de Appel, Amsterdam, 1982)
Intercept (comm Kitchen Center Video and Music, 1983)
Lecture on the weather (with John Cage) (C.F. Peters)
Living sound (comm Walker Art Center, 1980)
Music for the Webern car (comm Galerie Naechst St. Stephan, Vienna, 1981)
Remainder (comm Merce Cunningham Dance Co, 1975)
Bibliography
Christina Kubisch. *Time into Space/Space into Time*. Flash Art, 3/79.
Alberto Dentice. *Concerto per Idraulico e Pettiroso*. L'Expresso, 3/80.
Tom Hight. *Music, the Arts*. Omni Mag, 11/81.
Ref. 625

AMALIE, Marie Friederike Augusta, Princess of Saxony (pseuds. Amalie Heiter, Amalie Serena)
German harpsichordist, singer, writer and composer. b. Dresden, August 10, 1794; d. Dresden, September 18, 1870. She was the sister of King John of Saxony and wrote comedies under the pseudonyms Amalie Heiter and Amalie Serena. She spent her whole life in the castle of Pillnitz, Dresden.
Compositions
CHAMBER
Violin sonata
SACRED
Stabat Mater
Other church music
OPERA
L'Americana (1820)
La casa disabitata (1835)
Elisa ed Ernesto (1823)
Elvira (1821)
La Fedelta alla prova (1826)
Il figlio perduto (Il figlio pentito) (1831)
La forza dell'amor
Der Kanonenschuss (1828)
Il marchesino (1833)
Le nozze funeste (1816)
Il prigioniere (1817)
Die Siegesfahne (1834)
Le tre cinture (Antonio) (1817)
Una donna (1816)
Vecchiezza e gioventu (1826)
OPERETTA
A l'honneur de Nancy (1819)
Bibliography
Fuerstenau, M. *Die musikalischen Beschaeftigungen der Prinzessin Amalie*. Dresden, 1874.
Ref. 17, 44, 81, 102, 105, 132, 193, 226, 307, 431

AMALIE HEITER, See AMALIE, Marie Friederike Augusta

AMALIE JULIANE, Countess of Schwarzenberg
German composer. b. 1637; d. 1706.
Compositions
VOCAL
Songs incl.:
Drei Sammlungen Lieder (1683)
Wer weiss, wie nahe mir mein Ende
One cycle
Ref. 465

AMALIE SERENA, See AMALIE, Marie Friederike Augusta

AMANN, Josephine (nee Weinlich)
Austrian pianist, violinist, conductor, teacher and composer. b. Vienna, 1848; d. Lisbon, January 9, 1887. She received her first lessons from her

father Francisco Weinlich and then studied under Clara Schumann (qv). As a violinist she gave recitals throughout Austria. She founded and conducted the first European women's orchestra in Vienna in which her daughter was a soloist and which specialised in the works of Strauss and toured Europe. In January 1879 she went to Lisbon with her husband and became the conductor of an orchestra. Subsequently she turned to piano teaching. Some of her compositions were published in the journal *Gazette Musical*, which was owned by her husband. She died of tuberculosis at the age of 38.

Compositions

PIANO

Impromptu, op. 20
March with trio
Pieces

Ref. Frau und Musik, 104, 226, 268, 276, 347

AMATI, Orlanda (Elinor Barbara d'Amato)

20th-century American pianist, lecturer, poetess and composer. b. New Jersey. She made her debut in a joint recital with her brother at Steinway Hall, New York, at the age of 11. She graduated from the Juilliard School of Music in 1951 and studied the piano privately under Alberta Masiello, Carl Friedberg, Lonny Epstein and David Saperton; ensemble under Robert Mann and composition under David Bannett. She received her M.A. from Columbia University in 1961. She lectured at the Manhattan School of Music from 1962 to 1963 and then at the American College of Musicians, Austin.

Composition

PIANO

The paper piazzetta, suite

Publications

Transcriptions of Italian Renaissance Music. 1959.
Girandola, Wheel of Light. Collection of poetry. 1972.

Ref. 77, 643

AMBUBAJAE

From the third millenium and down the centuries towards the Christian era, every large city in the Mediterranean basin in the near East, was flooded by girls of poor families, mainly Phoenician - Syrian whose only hope of earning a living was from their bodies and prostitution was virtually a social necessity. Those of a better class were recruited by the Phoenician temples of the goddesses Ashera and Astarte, where they became *Kedeshot* dedicated women who practised religious prostitution and whose earnings were part of their offerings to the goddesses. These kedeshot sang and played the flute. It is probable that the great predominance of girls in Phoenician society may have been the result of the institution of the regular and widespread sacrifice of young boys to the god Moloch. This perhaps, could have been behind the sacredotal desire to provide for an uninterrupted supply of girls for religious prostitution whose earnings were a large contribution to the resources of the temples – a fanciful assumption worth investigating.

Most of the girls in the cities became prostitutes who sang and played the short flute the *Abub* and all over the Middle Eastern world this became their trademark. The Romans called them *Ambubajae* and since they generally assembled in the basements of the Roman circuses - these areas were termed *Ambubajarum Collegia*. In Greece these flute playing girls were called *Auletrides* and in the Arabian countries some of them were even called *Quaina*. Because of the harsh treatment meted out to them in Greece and Rome by tax collectors, they preferred to be in captivity as slaves where they were given better treatment.

It is quite probable that they were the forerunners of the itinerant singers and songstresses who, during the later centuries gradually spread to the west and north of Europe, eventually becoming the glee singers, the troubadours and the minnesanger.

Bibliography

Baudot, Alain. *Musiciens Romains de l'Antiquite*. Paris: Lincksieck, 1973.
Cumont, Franz. *Etudes Syriennes*. Paris: Auguste Picard, 1917.
Sendrey, Alfred. *Music in the Social and Religious Life of Antiquity*. New Jersey Assoc. University Presses, 1974.

Ref. Christian Poche (Paris), 151

AMENDOLA, Mariannina

Italian composer.

Composition

VOCAL

La Tradita, romance

AMERSFOORDT-DYK, Hermina Maria

Dutch pianist and composer. b. Amsterdam, June 26, 1821; d. Amsterdam, July 26, 1892. She studied the piano and composition under Bertelman and instrumentation under several masters.

Compositions

ORCHESTRA

Piano concerto
Two overtures

CHAMBER

Quartets

PIANO

Salon pieces
Sonatas
Variations
Other pieces

VOCAL

Floris V, songs
Lieder, op. 40 (Cramer, Gleim and others) (Amsterdam: J.H. and G. Van Heteren, 1871)

SACRED

Gottes Allgegenwart, cantata (Leipzig: F. Hofmeister)
Psalm XXII (ch and pf)
Anbetung
Other cantatas

THEATRE

Music for Willen Bardes

Ref. 44, 70, 105, 123, 226, 276, 400

AMES, Mary Mildred

English composer. b. June 20, 1867. She was taught by her brother John Carlowitz Ames and then studied instrumentation under F. Corder at the Royal Academy of Music, where she won the Charles Mortimer prize for composition in 1894. She continued her studies in Berlin.

Compositions

CHAMBER

Andante and rondo (cl and pf)
Andante in G (vln and pf)
Barcarolle (vln and pf)
Other pieces (vln and pf)

Ref. 6

AMES, Mrs. Henry

19th-century English composer.

Compositions

VOCAL

Arias and part-songs incl.:
Goodbye to winter
When the rosy morn

Ref. 276

AMON SONGSTRESSES

Amon was the protecting god of the Theban metropolis at the beginning of the New Kingdom and songstresses there were known as Amon songstresses. They were initially recruited from the higher classes and led by a high personage, such as the wife of the high priest and were subordinate to the queen or another female member of the royal family. Queen Ahmes-Neferteri is supposed to have been one of the first leaders of the Amon songstresses at the beginning of the XVIII dynasty. Queen Hatshepsut also held this position before ascending to the throne in 1529 B.C. In time songstresses were recruited from a less elevated class. The songstresses were termed *Musicians of God*. At one time it was believed that songstresses took a vow of chastity, but it is now known that some were married; at least one songstress was married to a common officer garrisoned in Nubia. The extent of the musical education of the songstresses is uncertain; their role seems to have been limited to the recitation of liturgical responses. Some are known to have been professional musicians at the palace, but generally they were amateur temple-songstresses, who, due to their social position were wealthy. Evidence of this can be found on richly decorated papyri, on grave memorials, sarcophagi and on statues. In fact, on a pedastal of one such statue of a woman in Herdes, the following inscription is found:

Every priest, who comes into this temple,
and every woman, who follows the priestess
in the daily service or to a festival of the gods
To, All who see me
As I stand with my necklace and mirror,
Pray for me and give me flowers
Remember and honor my beautiful name
and that of my husband and children
as well as the great gods of Mendes.
I was a songstress of their priestess

and a beautiful woman, sweet in love
praised and a cherished member of their temple

A listing of the more famous songstresses can be found in Appendix 2 under the title SONGSTRESS.

ANACLETO, Aurea

Brazilian composer. b. Recife, August 24, 1886; d. Rio de Janeiro, 1965. She composed waltzes for the piano.

Ref. Inter-American Music Review, 1980 Vol III No. 1

ANCELE, Sister Mary

American pianist, teacher and composer. b. February 20, 1931. She studied under Sister Angelus and Mr. Dosogne. She is a member of ASCAP.

Ref. 137

ANCONA, Solange

French composer. b. 1943. She is a member of SACEM.

Composition

VOCAL

Slantze III (Dante, Paradiso) (S and orch) (Rome, 1975)

Ref. Radiotelevisione Italiana Program, July 12, 1975

ANDERSEN, Helen Somerville

American pianist and composer. b. New York, April 3, 1892. She studied at the American Conservatory, Chicago and received her B.M. in 1907 and M.M. in 1908. She studied the piano under Tina Mae Haines and theory and composition under Arthur Olaf Andersen, whom she later married.

Compositions

PIANO

Circus suite
Suite
Other pieces

VOCAL

A book of children's choruses (1947)

Ref. 496

ANDERSON, Avril

20th-century British composer.

Compositions

CHAMBER

Gershwin suite (fl and gtr)
The grass harp (1979)

VOCAL

Black eyes in an orange sky (S and pf) (1979)

Ref. *Composer* (London)

ANDERSON, Beth (Barbara Elizabeth)

American pianist, accompanist, singer, teacher and composer. b. Lexington, KY, January 3, 1950. She studied at the universities of Kentucky and California and at Mills College. Her teachers included John Cage, Robert Ashley, Terry Riley, Larry Austin, Nathan Rubin, Richard Swift, Ken Wright and Helen Lipscomb (q.v.). She gained her B.A.Mus. in 1971, then M.F.A. and M.A. In 1976 she taught at the New School for Social Research in a series about women composers. The following year she taught courses of listening skills for music theory and other programs at New York University and at Martin Luther-King High School. At the College of La Rochelle she taught music appreciation and theory from 1978 till 1980. During the same period she was an accompanist for dance at the American Dance Studio; Martha Graham School of Dance, New York; New York University; Ballet Hispanico; Performing Arts High School; Harlem School of the Arts and Clark Center. Her compositions frequently make use of text as the sounding medium. She received the following grants and awards: Biggerstaff grant, 1971; Alumni fellowship, 1972; Elizabeth Mills Crothers award, 1972 and 1974; National Endowment for the Arts, 1975; Foundation for Performing Arts, 1975. She won the U.C.D. Concerto contest in 1970 and 1971 and the Composers Forum Competition New York, 1975. She teaches at the College of New Rochelle. DISCOGRAPHY. PHOTOGRAPH.

Compositions

ORCHESTRA

Revel (cham orch) (1985)
Revelation (cham orch) (1981)

CHAMBER

Becoming/being (cham ens) (1969)
Valid for life (perc and strs) (1973)
He said (cl and ens) (1976)
Dactylology (ww qrt) (1967)
Music for Charlemagne Palestine (str qrt) (1973)
Wonder (vla and hpscd) (1969)
Preparation for the dominant: outrunning the inevitable (ocarina) (1979)

PIANO

Manos inquietas (1982)
Quilt music (1983)

VOCAL

Beauty runs faster (vce and orch)
Black/White (audience and pf) (1976)
If you have a thought (vces, audience and 2 pf) (1978)
Alleluia (vces and vlcs) (1978)
An argument (Cont, B and tuba) (1969)
Crackers and checkers (1977)
He says he's got (vce and gtr) (1977)
I wish I were single again (1977)
If I were a poet
Kitchy kitchin (1979)
Network (S, 2 A, T and ens) (1982)
Ocean motion mildew mind (1979)
Paranoia (vce and 2 fl) (1969)
Shakuhachi run (S)
Skate suite (vce, vln, cl and d-b) (1979)
Time stands still (vce and pf) (1978)
Twinkle tonight (vce and pf) (1978)
Women rite (vce and pf) (1972)
Yes Sir Ree (vce, pf and perc) (1978)

DANCE SCORES

Taking sides part one (1984) (comm Daniel McCusker Dance Co.)

OPERA

Queen Christina (1973)

ELECTRONIC

Goodbye Brigitte Bardot (vlc and tape) (1974)
Peachy Keen-O (org, gtr, vibes and perc) (1971)
The people rumble louder (text and elec sounds) (1975)
Promised church beautiful river (tape) (1977)
Recital piece (pf and tape) (1973)
Ode (tape) (1976)
She wrote (Gertrude Stein and composer) (vce and 2 amp vln) (1974)
They did it (W.H. Auden) (pf and tape) (1976)
Thus spake Johnston (text and elec sounds) (1973)
Torero piece (text and elec sounds) (1973)
Tower of power (org and tapes) (1973)
Tulip clause and Buchla Bird hiss down the road of life (tape) (1973)

THEATRE

Elizabeth Rex, A gay new musical (Jo Kreston) (1983)

MULTIMEDIA

A day (1967)
Hallophone (vce, sax, gtr, tapes, visuals and dancers) (1973)
I am uh am I (2 strs and 2 light technicians) (1973)
I can't stand it (1976)
Incline thy ear to me (group performance) (1975)
The Messiah is come (sculpture and ens) (1974)
Morning view and maiden spring (vce, tape and lights) (1978)
Music for myself (vib, vce and visuals) (1973)
Nongovernmental process (1976)
Zen piece (1976)

MISCELLANEOUS

Net work (1983) (comm Montclair State College)
Tidal Pool (1983) (comm Montclair State College)

Ref. composer, 142, 206, 228, 301, 347, 403, 563, 622, 624, 625, 633, 647

ANDERSON, Elizabeth D.

Composition

BAND

The Dartmouth, march (Thompson)

Ref. 297

ANDERSON, Florence. See DU PAGE, Florence Elizabeth

ANDERSON, Jay

American pianist, violinist, singer, teacher and composer. b. New Haven, CT, September 9, 1920. She began playing the violin when she was ten years old and had piano lessons from the age of 13, although she had been teaching herself since she was six. At the Longy School of Music, Boston, she studied solfege, harmony, counterpoint, composition and choir directing. After 1950 she composed and sang light songs and taught music writing and the music and culture of other lands. She settled in

Hawaii in 1968. Most of the manuscripts of her compositions were destroyed by floods in Hawaii in 1969. DISCOGRAPHY. PHOTOGRAPH.

Compositions

VOCAL

Songs incl.:
Bye bye good friend (Domino, 1960)
Dawn by the river
Echo below (J. Fischer and Bros.)
Evening star
Reflections (1942)
Softly, softly fell the snow (1942) (Schmitt, Hall and McCleary)
Song in the mist (Domino, 1967)

SACRED

Christ my refuge (M.B. Eddy) (Domino, 1943)
Music chorale set to 23rd psalm (1949)
Music chorale set to 91st psalm (1939)

Ref. composer, 563

ANDERSON, Julia McKinley

Australian pianist, teacher and composer. b. Melbourne, March 13, 1952. She studied the piano under Ada Corda and Ronald Farren-Price and composition under Warren Burt and Keith Humbel. She gained her B.A. hons. in composition at Le Trobe University in 1978.

Compositions

CHAMBER

Tree images (8 4-part str-ens pieces) (1982) (NMN)
Myths (fl, mar, cel, pf, vlc and perc) (1981) (NMN) (special commendation from ILWC, 1982)
Interiors – exteriors (vln and pf) (1983) (NMN)

VOCAL

Price rite (w-vces) (NMN)
Vocal additions # 1 (w-vces) (1977) (NMN)
Birthdayfication (S and hp) (1980) (NMN)
Reverie (S and pf) (1979) (NMN)

FILM MUSIC

Tommy's world, documentary (1980) (NMN)

ELECTRONIC

The B.H.P. man (pf and tape delay) (1981) (NMN)
Four programme pieces (synthesized on analog syn) (1978) (NMN)
Moatal response to tube enbubblement (group improvisation) (1976) (NMN)
Setting # 4 (cornet and synth tape) (1978) (NMN)

TEACHING PIECES

Calm and scared, for schools (pf) (1983)
Fifteen short documentaries, for children (pf) (1983)

Bibliography

New Music Newspaper, October-November 1977, p. 13.

Ref. composer

ANDERSON, Laurie

American electronic instrumentalist and composer. b. Chicago, IL, June 5, 1947. She received a B.A. magna cum laude from Barnard College and an M.F.A. (sculpture) from Columbia University. She worked with film-sound-talking pieces for several years, performing at the Museum of Modern Art, the Whitney Museum, the La Jolla Museum, CA, the Berlin Festival in October, 1976, the Akademie der Kunst and various other museums and universities in the United States and Europe. She invented the tape-bow violin. DISCOGRAPHY.

Compositions

VOCAL

United States parts I to IV, song cycle: Big science; Born, never asked; Close circuits; Drums; Example # 22; For electronic dogs; From the air; It tango; Let X=X; Sweaters; Walking and falling

ELECTRONIC

Blue lagoon
Dr. Miller
Excellent birds
Gravity's angel
If you can't talk about it, point to it
It's cold outside
It's not the bullet that kills you – it's the hole
It was up in the mountains
Kokoku
Langue D'amour
Ludwig Wittgenstein
Mister heartbreak
New York social life (1977)
O Superman
Sharkey's day
Sharkey's night
Structuralist film-making
Time to go (for Diego) (1977)

Publications

Notebook. A collection of scores and photographs of composer's performances. The Collation Center, 1977.

Ref. *Helicon Nine* No. 12/12 1985, 269, 563, 622

ANDERSON, Olive Jennie Paxton

Australian composer. b. 1917.

Compositions

CHAMBER

Elegy, op. 42 (wind ens and strs) (1975)
Gavotte (2 recs, vln and pf) (J. Albert & son, 1975)
My love's an arbutus (str trio; also fl, cl and gtr; also recs and pf)
A little sandwich (2 rec and pf)
Sport street, op. 39 (cl) (J. Albert, 1968)
Elementary chamber music, op. 37

THEATRE

Song of Freedom, musical play in 3 acts (1975)

Ref. 442, 444, 445.

ANDERSON, Pauline Barbour

American librarian, teacher and composer. b. January 27, 1945, Richmond, Virginia. She studied at Shenandoah Conservatory from 1963 to 1966 and graduated from the Luther Rice College in 1969. From the Catholic University of America, she received her B.Mus. cum laude in 1971. She taught voice and music history at Luther Rice College, was librarian of Fairfax Symphony Orchestra, 1969 to 1970, and taught voice and strings privately.

Compositions

ORGAN

Organ fugue for Easter (1973)
Other pieces

SACRED

Calvary, cantata (1973)
Vocal works (1978)

Ref. 475

ANDERSON, Ruth

American flautist, authoress, conductor, professor and composer. b. Kalispell, MT, March 21, 1928. She graduated from the University of Washington with a B.A. (flute, 1949) and M.A. (composition, 1951). She studied chamber music and composition at the Music Academy of the West in 1950; solo orchestral flute and composition at the Aspen Institute of Music in 1951 and 1953, the Manhattan School of Music, 1952 to 1953, and the Mannes College of Music from 1953 to 1955; composition at the Ecole de Musique, Fontainebleau in 1958; musical analysis at Princeton University Graduate School (first woman admitted, 1962 to 1963); computer synthesis at New York University in 1967; electronic music and composition at Columbia-Princeton Electronic Music Center of Columbia University in 1966 and at Columbia University, 1969. She studied composition under Darius Milhaud at intervals between 1951 and 1960 and Nadia Boulanger (q.v.) from 1958 to 1959. She was graduate assistant in musical analysis and conductor of the Composers Orchestra at the University of Washington from 1949 to 1951; taught the flute at Westchester Conservatory from 1951 to 1952 and was visiting professor of the flute and chamber music at the University of Iowa in 1965. Besides academic and professional honors, she won a number of grants, including: Huntingdon Hartford grant in 1951; Martha Baird Rockefeller Foundation for Music grant-in-aid in 1957; two Fulbright awards to study in Paris, 1958 to 1960; Princeton University graduate grant from 1962 to 1963; Ingraham-Merill composition grant in 1963 and the Research Foundation CUNY grant in 1974. From the MacDowell Colony she was awarded five fellowships, 1957 to 1973; from 1975 to 1976 she was a member of CAPS composition awards panel. From 1969 she was director of the Hunter College Electronic Music Studio and responsible for the design and installation of it (1968 to 1969) and from 1970 she served as electronic music studio consultant to various New York colleges and universities. As an orchestrator and choral arranger she worked for NBC-TV from 1960 to 1966 and Lincoln Center Theatre in 1966 and freelanced. Ruth continued her professional activities in the fields of composition, psycho-acoustic research, acoustic design, orchestration and as a flautist. Her works have been performed at music festivals in Vienna, New York, Bonn and Lund. She received composition awards from the Creative Artists program service in 1979; the National Endowment for the Arts in 1980; a recording award from New York State Council on the Arts and the Alice M. Ditson award of Columbia University in 1981. DISCOGRAPHY.

Compositions

ORCHESTRA

Symphony for small orchestra (1952)
String suite (1951)
Two movements for strings (1985) (ACE, 1979)
Two pieces for strings (1957) (ACE, 1979)

CHAMBER
Prelude and allegro (ww qnt) (1952)
String quartet
Two movements (str qrt)
Two pieces (str qrt)
Sonata (fl and pf) (1951)
Sonatina (fl and pf) (1951)
Cards, whist, hearts, baccarat (gtr)
Fugue (pf) (1948) (ACE, 1979)
VOCAL
Feather song (w-ch; also mix-ch) (1957) (Warner Bros., 1958)
Death be not proud (T and pf)
Impression IV (e.e. cummings) (S, fl and str qrt) (1950)
The merchant's song (Coombs) (Cont and pf) (1951) (ACE, 1979)
Richard cory (w-vces and pf) (G. Schirmer, 1960)
Sonnet (Donne) (T and pf) (1951)
Three children's songs (C.J. Fox) (S and pf) (1952) (ASCAP Index, 1964)
To a young child (Hopkins) (Cont and pf) (1952)
SACRED
Awake my soul (mix-ch) (1959) (Carl Fischer, 1960)
Carol of peace (mix-ch) (1957) (Warner Bros. 1958)
The holly carol (mix-ch) (1959) (G. Schirmer, 1960)
Lamp of liberty (w-ch) (1957) (Warner Bros. 1958)
Morning prayer (mix-ch) (1959) (Boosey and Hawkes, 1960)
Motet, psalm XIII (mix-ch) (1952) (Boosey, 1960)
Passiontide carol (mix-ch) (1959) (G. Schirmer, 1960)
Sing Noel, Merry Noel (mix-ch) (1958) (G. Schirmer, 1959)
Song to my Father (w-vces and pf) (1959) (C. Fischer)
Song to the Holy Child (w-vces and pf) (1959) (Boosey, 1960)
DANCE SCORES
Fantasy (cl, vlc and pf) (1954)
Prelude and rondo (fl and strs) (1956)
ELECTRONIC
Conversations (tape) (1974)
Dump (2-channel tape) (1970) (ACE, 1979)
EF (tape) (1979) (ACE)
ES II (tape) (1969) (ACE, 1979)
I come out of your sleep
LL (Bogan) (tape) (1979) (ACE)
Ma Belle (tape collage)
Pieces No. 1, No. 2, No. 3, ES II (tape) (1970)
Points (tape) (1974) (ACE, 1979)
The pregnant dream (Swenson) (tape) (1958) (ACE, 1979)
Sappho (Lardos) (tape) (1975) (ACE, 1979)
So what No. 1, No. 2 (tape) (1971)
Sound environment (elec sound games, bio-feedback installation)
Studies No. 1, No. 2, No. 3, (tape) (1970-1971)
SUM (State of the Union Message) (tape) (1973) (ACE, 1974)
Veils (pf and 4-channel tape)
INCIDENTAL MUSIC
A long sound; Naming; Dress rehearsal; Text (1976)
Sound portraits I-II, text piece (1977) (New Wilderness Anthology, Hawkes ed.)
Silent sound, text (1978) (Ja. 1978 Foldout, Knowles-Lockwood, eds.)
MULTIMEDIA
Christmas oratorio (Auden) (ch, actors, dancers, 4 portable audio speakers and small orch)
Wheel on the Chimney (slide film score) (orch) (1965) (Demeter Music, 1965)
Centering (dance and live elecs) (ACE, 1979)
MISCELLANEOUS
Communications, text piece (ACE, 1980)
Greetings from the Right Hemisphere, text piece (T. Petri) (1979)
ARRANGEMENTS
Annie Get Your Gun (orch) (1974) (Carl Fischer)
Choral arrangements (1960-1962) (Chappell)
In excelsis (junior ch and pf) (Warner Bros.)
Rounds from many countries (1960) (Chappell)
Rounds from many countries, compilation-adaption of 50 (1978) (Silver Burdett)
Rounds from many countries, extracts (1977) (Macmillan)
Serenade (Hanson) (orch) (1974) (C. Fischer)
The Sound of Music (small orch) (1962) (Richard Rodgers Publ.)
Ref. composer, 40, 142, 269, 347, 563, 622, 625

ANDERSON-WUENSCH, Jean Mary

Canadian pianist, teacher and composer. b. Bradford, England, December 5, 1939. She received a B.M. from the University of Nottingham in 1960 and M.M. (composition) from the Eastman School of Music in 1969. She also has a diploma in education from the University of Leeds and is an L.R.A.M. (piano teachers). She taught in England, the United States and Canada. PHOTOGRAPH.

Compositions
ORCHESTRA
Concerto for horn and strings (1960)
The Langdales, overture (1970)
Sinfonia for string orchestra (1968)
BAND
Celebration I (1980)
CHAMBER
Quintet (fl, bsn, trp, vln and vlc) (1967)
Quartet (cl, vla, vlc and hp) (1972)
String quartet (1973)
String trio
String music for children
Five viola duets
Five violin duets
Five violoncello duets
Six sketches for harp and flute (1978)
Sonata (vla and pf) (1976)
Suite (fl and cl) (1972)
Polygon (a-fl and fl, one player) (1975)
Rhapsody (pf) (1979)
VOCAL
Afton Water (m-ch) (1973)
Green owls and others, cycle (S. Cooperman) (S, T, cl, hp and vlc) (1970)
Three songs (e.e. cummings) (S, Cont, T and B, fl, ob, bass cl and hp) (1968)
SACRED
I thank you God for most this amazing day (e.e. cummings) (mix-ch) (1972)
Russian hymn (m-ch) (1978)
Ref. composer

ANDERSSON, Ellen

Danish concert pianist and composer. b. October 17, 1884. She studied at the Copenhagen Konservatorium under Matthison Hansen and Bondesen. She moved to Berlin, where she studied under Breithaupt and Krause and became a concert pianist. She composed piano pieces.
Ref. 113

ANDREE, Elfrida

Swedish organist, teacher and composer. b. Visby, February 19, 1841; d. Stockholm, January 11, 1929. She had her first music education from her father and W. Sohrling in Visby, then she studied composition at the Stockholm Conservatory under L. Norman and H. Berens. She became the first woman telegraphist in Sweden and a pioneer of women's rights. In Copenhagen she studied under N. Gade, then taught singing at a teachers' training college, whilst waiting for a change in the law forbidding women to be organists. She was appointed organist of the Finnish Reform Church from 1861 to 1867 and of the French Reform Church in Stockholm from 1862 to 1867, when she was elected cathedral organist in Goteborg and took over the direction of people's concerts there. She directed 800 such concerts. She was elected a member of the Swedish Academy of Music in 1879. She was the first woman to write an organ symphony and her *Swedish Mass* was frequently performed. DISCOGRAPHY.

Compositions
ORCHESTRA
Organ symphony in B-Minor (London: Augener)
Symphony in A-Minor (1893)
Symphony in C-Major (1869)
Concert-Overture in D (1873)
MILITARY BAND
Piece
CHAMBER
Quintet in E-Minor (Stockholm: A. Hirsch, 1865)
Piano quartet (1865)
String quartet in A (1861)
String quartet in D-Minor (1895)
Trio in C-Minor (1860)
Trio in G-Minor (Stockholm: Musikaliska Konstfoereningen, 1887)
Sonata in B (vln and pf) (1872)
Sonata in E-Flat (vln and pf)
Tva romanser (vln and pf) (A. Hirsch, 1887)
Organ pieces
PIANO
Fem Smarre tonbilder, op. 7 (Stockholm: Huss and Berr, 1880)
Sonata in A, op. 3 (Copenhagen: Hansen, 1873)
Tonbilder, op. 4 (Hansen)
VOCAL
Snoefrid, cantata (V. Rydberg) (ch and orch) (Musikaliska Konstforeningen, 1884)
Ur Droemlif (V. Rydberg) (ch a-cap) (1882)

Songs incl.:
April visor
En vacker hoestdag (Warmuth)
I templet
Sang till naektergalen (Hansen)
Skogsraet (V. Rydberg) (Goteborg: T. Hedlund, 1878)
Vi ses igen (Warmuth)
Visa en varmorgon (Warmuth)
Arrangement of folk songs

SACRED
Psalm 20 (1908)
Psalm 56 (1911)
Svensk maessa No. 1 (Copenhagen: Nordisk Musikforlag, 1903)
Svensk maessa No. 2 (Nordisk Musikforlag, 1907)
Choral arrangements

OPERA
Fritiofs Saga (S. Lagerlof) (1899)

Bibliography

Larson, Margareta d' Hermelin, Carin. *Elfrida Andrée organiste et compositrice (1841-1929). L'Orgue* 157, January-March, 1976. Andrée's life as organist and difficulties in presenting compositions as a woman.

Stuart, E.M. *Elfrida Andrée.* Stockholm, 1925.

Scholander-Hedlund M. *Elfrida Andrée: en pionjar.* Hertha, 1929.

Ref. 1, 2, 8, 15, 17, 20, 22, 23, 41, 44, 70, 74, 95, 100, 103, 113, 167, 204, 226, 276, 297, 347, 361, 563, 622

ANDREE, Fredrika. See STENHAMMAR, Fredrika

ANDREOTTI, Marianna. See BOTTINI, Marianna

ANDREOZZI, Marianna. See BOTTINI, Marianna

ANDREWS, Jenny (nee Constant) (alt. name Mrs. John Holman Andrews)

English singing teacher and composer. b. 1817; d. London, April 29, 1878.

Compositions

CHAMBER
Nocturne (pf)
instumental pieces

VOCAL
Songs incl.:
Adieu
Autumn's golden leaf
Go lovely rose
Prince Charley's farewell to Scotland

Publications

A set of *Two-part vocal exercises.*

Ref. 6, 206, 276

ANDREWS, Mrs. Alfred Buritt. See VAN ETTEN, Jane

ANDREWS, Mrs. George H.

19th-century American composer.

Composition

VOCAL
Where ere I see those smiling eyes

Ref. 465

ANDREWS, Mrs. John Holman. See ANDREWS, Jenny

ANDREWS, Virginia

20th-century American who composed piano pieces.

Ref. 40, 347

ANDREYEVA, Elena Fedorovna

Soviet editor, musicologist, teacher and composer. b. St. Petersburg, June 15, 1914. In 1935 she graduated from Voroshilovgrad Mechanical Technical College and in 1945 graduated cum laude from the Kiev Conservatory, where she studied composition under L. Revutsky. From 1939 to 1941 she taught music and from 1944 to 1948, amateur musical activities and theoretical subjects in the higher music schools. After 1960 she became editor of several Soviet musical journals.

Compositions

ORCHESTRA
Solemn Overture (1945)

CHAMBER
Etude (str qrt and pf) (1936)
Quartet (1940)
Pieces (vln and pf) (1971)
Polka (bayan) (1945)

PIANO
Etude (1949)
Fantasies on a theme from the opera Taras Bulba (N. Lysenko) (1943)
Mazurka (1936)
Preludes (1937, 1940)
Three children's pieces (1950)
Two suites (1938, 1943)

VOCAL
Glory to the Women-Toilers, cantata (Marunich)
Naimichka (Shevchenko) (ch) (1939)
Tri shlyakhi (Shevchenko) (ch) (1937)
Klyatva (Dzhambul) (1949)
Novyi god (Yashin) (1952)
Oi, yak stalo zeleno (Bichko) (1947-1948)
Radostno nam zhit (traditional words) (1938)
Raduites, Karpaty! (T. Masenko) (1949)
Songs (Soviet poets)
Two Latvian harvest songs (Bazhenov and Ivano) (1947-1948)
Vesna otchizny (Yushchenko) (1949)
Vesnyanka (Lutsenko) (1947-1948)
Zastolnaya (Solodar) (1947-1948)
Arrangements of folk songs

Publications

Theory of Music. In Ukrainian. 1946.
School manuals on music theory.

Ref. 21, 87, 465

ANDREYEVA, M.

20th-century Soviet composer.

Compositions

ORCHESTRA
We're all musicians here (chil-orch)

VOCAL
Concertina-tina-tina, collection of songs
Friendship of children the world over, songs (vce and pf)
Let's play, songs (vce, pf and bayan)
Raindrops sing little songs

INCIDENTAL MUSIC
Our Merry-Go-Round, songs for films, radio and TV (pf)

Ref. Collett's catalog (Northants, UK)

ANDRIESSEN, Caecilia

Dutch clavichordist, organist, pianist, choral conductor, teacher and composer. b. Haarlem, February 12, 1931. She is the daughter of the composer Hendrik Andriessen. At the Royal Conservatory in The Hague she studied the piano under Leon Orthel and Jan de Manz and the organ under Adriaan Engels. She spent some time studying in Italy on a bursary from the Italian government. She formed a piano duo with her brother and for several years they appeared in various places in the Netherlands and also on radio. She taught the piano at the Rotterdam Music School and conducted the choir of the Russian Catholic Church in The Hague.

Compositions

PIANO
Mini and modern, 15 small pieces, simple settings of well known Christmas carols

VOCAL
Beestebende (Dolf Verroen) (cham ch and pf) (Donemus, 1972)

Ref. Donemus (Netherlands)

ANDRIEVSKAYA, Nina Konstantinovna

Soviet editor, musicologist and composer. b. December 20, 1928. She studied historical theory at the Kiev Conservatory, and graduated in 1954. She continued with postgraduate studies in history of music. She became an editor in 1955 and head editor of music of Ukrainian radio in 1970. She wrote musical articles and composed vocal cycles, pioneer songs, choruses and vocal ensembles of a patriotic nature, light songs and set to

music works of Ukrainian, Russian and White Russian poets as well as of her own texts.
Ref. 21

ANDRUS, Helen Josephine
American organist and composer. b. Poughkeepsie, NY,; d. 1927. She was a pupil of Dr. F.L. Ritter and a B.Mus. graduate of the Vassar College School of Music. She composed pieces for the organ, the piano, strings, anthems, songs, duets and a cantata.
Ref. 226, 276

ANDRZEJOWSKA, Alina
Polish composer.
Compositions
PIANO
Three polonaises

ANDUZA, Clara d'. See D'ANDUZA, Clara

ANGELI-CATTINI, A. de
20th-century Italian composer of solo harp music.
Ref. 344

ANGELICA FEDELE, Sister. See MASINI, Giulia

ANGELINI, Maria Vittoria
17th-century Italian composer. b. Rome. Her verses and songs are to be found in the *Vita della venerabile Suor Maria Vittoria Angelini Romana Teziaria dell'Ordine de' Servi*. They were described by Abbott G. Battista Pacichetti (Rome, 1670) and were dedicated to the Grandduchess Vittoria of Tuscany.
Ref. 327

ANIDO, Maria Luisa
Argentine concert guitarist and composer. b. Buenos Aires, 1909. She studied under Domingo Prat and Miguel Llobet and made her debut at the age of nine. She won international recognition as a guitarist and performed in Europe, the United States and Japan. DISCOGRAPHY.
Compositions
GUITAR
Aire de vidalita
Aires nortenos
Argentine melody
Canto de la llanura
Catamarquena
Chacarera
Dance of the North Argentine Indians
De mi tierra
Estilo
Misachico
Song of Yucatan
Ref. 390, 563

ANIMUCIA (Animuccia), Giovanna
Italian composer. b. Florence; d. Rome, 1571. She composed sacred madrigals, masses, motets and psalms.
Ref. H. Baron (London)

ANIMUCCIA, Giovanna. See ANIMUCIA, Giovanna

'ANKH-AMENARDAIS
Egyptian songstress in the harem of Amon in the XXV Dynasty (8-7th century B.C.). She is known from her tomb, now in the Berlin Museum.
Ref. 428

'ANKH-SHEPENWEPT
Egyptian songstress in the harem of Amon in the XXV-XXVI dynasty, ca. 650 B.C. She is known from her tomb at Medinet-Habu.
Ref. 428

ANLEY, Charlotte
19th-century British composer.
Composition
VOCAL
The harp of Bendemeer (1826)
Ref. 465

ANNA, Duchess of Mecklenburg-Schwerin
German composer. b. April 7, 1865; d. February 8, 1882. She was the daughter of the Grand Duke Friederich Franz II and Anna, daughter of Prince Carl of Hessen.
Composition
PIANO
Gruss aus der Heimath, waltz (Ihrer lieben Schwester Marie, gewidmet, Weihnacht, 1875)
Ref. Frau und Musik

ANNA AMALIA, Duchess of Saxe-Weimar
German pianist and composer. b. Wolfenbuttel, Brunswick, October 24, 1739; d. Weimar, April 10, 1807. A niece of Frederick the Great and daughter of Charles I, Duke of Brunswick, Anna Amalia was a highly talented and cultured personality. She studied music under Friedrich Gottlob Fleischer, court musician and composer. After her marriage in 1756 to the 18 year old Duke Ernst August Konstantin of Saxe-Weimar, she studied the piano and composition under Ernst Wilhelm Wolf, the court concertmaster and conductor. After the death of her husband, Anna Amalia was regent until her son, later the Grand Duke Charles Augustus, Goethe's patron, ascended the throne. In 1788 Anna Amalia went to Italy for a few years where she met Giovanni Paisello and was much impressed by both him and the Italian vocal style. In Weimar she surrounded herself with musicians and men of letters, such as Herder, Wieland and Goethe. DISCOGRAPHY.
Compositions
ORCHESTRA
Symphony
CHAMBER
Concerto (12 insts and hpcd obb)
Sonatinas (pf or hpcd, 2 hn, 2 fl, 2 vln, vla, bsn and d-b)
Piano quartet with clarinet
Divertimento (pf, cl, vla and vlc) (Weimar: Ambrosius und Zahn)
VOCAL
Se perdesti la Germania, cavatina (m-S and orch)
Duetti di Azima e Diamantina e di Rosalba e Ubaldo
Auf dem Lande (T and pf)
Sie scheinen und spielen (T and pf)
Some songs attributed to Ernst Wilhelm Wolf
SACRED
Oratorio (1758)
Alma Redemptoris (4 vces and orch)
Regina Coeli (4 vces and orch)
Salve Regina (4 vces and orch)
Sieh mich Heil'ger (S and pf)
OPERA
Adolar und Hilaria
OPERETTA
Erwin und Elmire (Goethe) (1776)
THEATRE
Jahrmarktfest zu Plundersweilen (Goethe) (1778)
Die Zigeuner, ein Walddrama nach K.S. von Einsiedel
Bibliography
Abert, A.A. *Anna Amalie von Sachsen-Weimar*. MGG I, 1951.
Bode, W. *Amalie Herzogin von Weimar*. 3 vols. Berlin, 1908.
Heuschele, O. *Herzogin Anna Amalia*. Munich, 1947.
Munnich, R. *Aus der Musikaliensammlung der Weimarer Landesbibliothek, besonders dem Nachlass der Anna Amalie Jubilaere Festschrift der Landes-bibliothek*. Jena, 1941.
Ref. 8, 12, 15, 17, 20, 22, 44, 65, 86, 100, 102, 105, 107, 116, 119, 125, 128, 132, 200, 201, 204, 226, 276, 347, 502, 563, 622

ANNA AMALIA, Princess of Prussia
German harpsichordist, organist, pianist, violinist and composer. b. Berlin, November 9, 1723; d. Berlin, September 30, 1787. She was the youngest sister of Frederick the Great and spent almost her entire life in Berlin

Castle. She became Abbess of Quedlinburg in 1744. At the age of 17 she studied the harpsichord and the piano under Gottlieb Hayne, the cathedral organist. She began to compose at the age of 21 and at 30 commenced the study of the organ and the violin. At 35 she studied counterpoint under Johann Philipp Kirnberger. Her fondness for Bach led her to establish a large and valuable library of his manuscripts, which she bequeathed to the Joachimstalsches Gymnasium in Berlin. It is still on loan to the Berlin Library. DISCOGRAPHY.

Compositions

BAND

March for the Regiment of Count Lottum (1767)
March for the Regiment of General Buelow (1767)
March for the Regiment of General de Moellendorff (1778)
March for the Regiment of General von Saldern (1768)

CHAMBER

Sonata for trio in D-Major
Trio for organ
Sonata in F-Major (fl or vln and hpcd)
Sonata (fl or vln and basso continuo)

VOCAL

Serenata fatta per l'arrivo della Regina Madre a Charlottenburg, per la prima volta, arias (ch and orch) (1774)
Freu' dich, o meine Seele (1778)
Vor die zwei junge Printzen, on text An den Schoepfer
Dich soll mein Lied erheben (1780)
Duetto, Der Bruder und die Schwester, von Gleim: Ich will mit Cloris mich vermaehlen (1778)
Auf! tapfre Krieger, war song

SACRED

Der Tod Jesu, cantata (Ramler)
Chorales incl.:
Christ, alles was dich kranket (4 or 5 vces)
Man lobt dich in der Stille (4 or 5 vces)

Bibliography

Blechschmidt, E.R. *Die Amalien-Bibliothek-Berliner Studien zur Musikwissenschaft VIII*. Berlin. 1965.
Bose, F. *Anna Amalie von Preussen und J.P. Kirnberger*. MF 10: 1957.
Eitner, R. *Katalog der Musikalien-Sammlung des Joachimstalschen Gymnasiums zu Berlin*. Berlin. 1884.
Kopke, F. C. *Geschichte der Bibliothek des Joachimstalschen Gymnasiums*. Berlin. 1831.
Sachs, C. *Prinzessin Amalie von Preussen als Musikerin*. Hohenzollern Jahrbuch, 1910.

Ref. 2, 12, 15, 17, 22, 24, 44, 74, 79, 100, 102, 105, 119, 121, 128, 129, 132, 162, 177, 193, 201, 226, 231, 276, 297, 307, 347, 433, 563, 622

ANNAPURNA, Devi

20th-century Indian composer, who plays her own compositions on the sitar.
Ref. Nat. Council of Women, India

ANOKA, Freddie. See BAGANIER, Janine

ANSBACH, Elizabeth, Margravine of. See ANSPACH, Elizabeth

ANSINK, Caroline

20th-century composer.

Compositions

CHAMBER

Shades of silence (str qrt) (Amsterdam: Donemus, 1985)
Melodie fuer Giulia (fl and pf)
Three dances (fl and pf) (Domemus, 1985)

Ref. Otto Harrassowitz (Wiesbaden)

ANSPACH (Ansbach) Elizabeth, Margravine of (nee Berkeley) (Mrs. Craven)

English composer. b. London, December 17, 1750; d. Naples, Italy, January 13, 1828. She was the daughter of Augustus, fourth Earl of Berkeley. At the age of 17 she married William Craven, but separated from him in 1783. She settled in Ansbach in Franconia and after the death of her husband married the Margrave Christian Frederick. With the incorporation of the Ansbach principality into Prussia in 1792 she and her husband went to live in England.

Compositions

VOCAL

Setting of Shakespeare's *O Mistress Mine* as a madrigal (London: Preston and Son, 1795)

OPERA

The Princess of Georgia (1794)
The silver tankard (1780)

THEATRE

The miniature picture, play (London, 1780)
Music for French plays (1788-1790)

Publications

A Journey through the Crimea to Constantinople. 1789.

Ref. 8, 65, 125, 347, 645

ANSPACH, Wilhelmina Caroline of. See WILHELMINA, Caroline of Anspach

ANSTEY GUTHRIE, Mrs. T. See AUSTEN, Augusta Amherst

ANTHONY, Evangeline

English violinist and composer. b. Hereford, November 28, 1885. She studied under August Wilhelm and made her debut with the London Symphony Orchestra in 1904. She composed pieces for the violin and the piano.
Ref. 226

ANTHONY, Gina

20th-century Canadian composer. She attended the Berklee College of Music, Boston, majoring in composition. Some of her works have been performed in Boston.

Compositions

ORCHESTRA

Piece for Orchestra

CHAMBER

Motivation #1 (3 trp, 3 trb and b-tba) (1980)
Four part fugue (fl, 2 cl, b-cl and pf) (1980)

PIANO

Study in Chromaticism (1981)
Three part fugue (1979)

VOCAL

Four part motet (mix-ch) (1979)

Ref. Assoc. of Women Composers

AOKE, Haruna

Japanese pianist, singer and composer. b. Odawara, 1958. She began studying the piano at the age of four at the Kawai Music School. She was a pupil of Takasi Amatchi at the Nihon University of Performing Arts in Tokyo, where she graduated with a B.A. She performed as a pianist and singer and went to the United States in 1981. She studied for a master's degree at California State University.

Compositions

VOCAL

Bonsho I, II, III (vce and ens)

Ref. ICWM program of Festival of Music

AORENA, Mme. See LILIUOKALANI, Queen of Hawaii

APALA

25th-century B.C. Indian composer. She composed Vedic hymns in the Sanskrit language.
Ref. Nat. Council of Women, India

APPELDOORN, Dina van (Mrs. Koudijis)

Dutch pianist, lecturer and composer. b. Rotterdam, February 26, 1834; d. The Hague, December 4, 1938. She studied under Johan Wagenaar at the Royal Conservatory in The Hague and became a piano teacher there.

Compositions

ORCHESTRA

Symphony
Pecheurs d'Islande, symphonic poem
De Noordzee, symphonic poem
Waldsproke, symphonic poem

Hollandse suite
Jubileumslied
Pastorale
Twee hollandse dansen (str orch: also pf) (Mainz: Schott)
Volksfeest
PIANO
Sonatina
VOCAL
Four duets
Three songs (Vondel)
Ref. 44, 74, 81, 110, 169, 226, 361

APPIANI, Eugenia
19th-century Italian composer.
Compositions
PIANO
Ballatta nell Rigoletto (Ricordi)
Brezze d'autunno, waltz
Fantasie Profeta (Ricordi)
Fantasie Rigoletto (Ricordi)
Melodia di Bellini (Ricordi)
Scherzo
VOCAL
Album di canto (Ricordi)
Nine songs (vce and pf) (Ricordi, 1850)
Partenza, romance
Ref. 105, 226, 276, 297

APPLETON, Adeline Carola
American pianist and composer. b. Waverley, IA, November 29, 1886. Her mother was her first teacher and at 12 Adeline started to compose. Her early advanced studies in the piano and harmony were at Wisconsin College in Milwaukee. Later she studied composition under Dr. Benjamin Blodgett and Carl Seppert.
Compositions
CHAMBER
Piano
VOCAL
Pieces
OPERA
The Witches' Well, prologue, 1 act and 2 scenes (with Percy Davis) (1926)
Ref. 141, 304

ARAGO, Victoria
19th-century French composer. During the reign of Louis Philippe (1830 to 1845) she lived in Paris and published a number of ballads in the vein of Clapisson, Masini and Henrion. Her songs were extremely popular.
Compositions
VOCAL
Albums de romances et chansons, published annually (Paris: Meissonier)
Ref. 26, 105, 276

ARANCIBIA, Francisca
19th-century Peruvian pianist and composer.
Compositions
PIANO
La lluvia de Oro
Las islas de Chincha, waltz (1871)
Ref. 403

ARAUCO, Ingrid Colette
American violinist, lecturer and composer. b. Washington, DC, September 6, 1957. She gained her B.A. hons. in the violin from Goucher College, 1977, had private composition study with Robert Hall Lewis of Peabody Conservatory from 1978 to 1980, gained her M.A. in composition from the University of Pennsylvania in 1983 and was a Ph.D. candidate. Her teachers included George Crumb, George Rochberg, Richard Wernick and C. Jane Wilkinson. She lectured in the music department of University of Pennsylvania. Her compositions have been performed on radio and at music conventions and she won an American Guild of Organists award for organ composition in 1983.
Compositions
CHAMBER
Variations (vln) (1981)
Organ pieces
VOCAL
Three sonnets of Gerard Manley Hopkins (1982)
What seraphs are afoot (1982)
Ref. 643

ARAUJO, Gina de (Araujo Regis d'Oliveira)
Brazilian singer and composer. b. Rio de Janeiro, April 3, 1890; d. Rio de Janeiro, 1960. She studied voice in Paris under Jules Massenet, Andre Gedalge, Dubelle and J. Reszke. She sang in concerts in Paris and was the first Brazilian to become a member of the Societe des Auteurs et Compositeurs de Musique in 1906. In 1922 she wrote the music for the Festival of Flowers.
Compositions
ORCHESTRA
Evocação, symphonic poem
Cega Rega, 14 pictures set to music (Rio, 1943)
PIANO
Automne
Berceuse
Gavotte
Nocturno
VOCAL
Songs incl.:
Bigarreaux
Cloches plaintives
Une larme
Les rêves
Rosée
Voyage dans le bleu
SACRED
Ave Maria
Missa de requiem (for husband Ambassador Regis d'Oliveira)
Bibliography
De Melo, G.A Musica no Brasil. Rio, 1908.
Ref. 8, 94, 106, 268, 333

ARAUJO REGIS D'OLIVEIRA, Gina. See ARAUJO, Gina de

ARAZOVA, Izabella Konstantinovna
Soviet lecturer and composer. b. Rostov-on-the-Don, September 25, 1936. She studied composition under O.A. Yevlakhov at the Leningrad Conservatory in 1959 and two years later went to the Gerivan Conservatory where she continued her composition studies under E.M. Mirzoyan, graduating in 1967. She lectured on theoretical subjects at the Armenian Teachers' College.
Compositions
ORCHESTRA
Concerto for orchestra (1967)
CHAMBER
Variations (vlc) (1961)
PIANO
Fantasia (2 pf) (1964)
Sonatina (1960)
Three preludes (1958)
Three sketches (1966)
Two preludes (1960)
VOCAL
Triptych (Armenian poets) (ch and orch) (1971)
Polyphonic chorus (S. Kaputikian) (1964)
Cycle (V. Grigorian) (vce and pf) (1970)
Other works
Ref. 21

ARBEL, Re Chaya
20th-century Israeli pianist, violinist and composer. She received early lessons in the violin and the piano and started composing at the age of seven. At the age of 15 she moved from Germany to Palestine. She later studied under the composer Professor Leon Shidlovsky. Her generally avant-garde music is influenced by Schoenberg, Bartok, Ligeti and Penderecki.
Compositions
CHAMBER
Violin Fantasia (1982)
SACRED
The sayings of Amos the Prophet
MISCELLANEOUS
Dry tears
Ref. Perry Roth (Israel)

ARBUCKLE, Dorothy M. (Fry)

American pianist and composer. b. Illinois, January 23, 1910. She studied the piano under Professor Carson, attended Northwestern University and the University of Illinois and was president of the Arbuckle Oil Company. DISCOGRAPHY.

Compositions

ORCHESTRA

Elegy to grief (1962)
Evening nocturne (1957)

VOCAL

Approx 200 songs incl.:
Beware of love (1965)
I never knew

SACRED

The tall cathedral windows (w-ch) (1955)
The church wherein I worship (1955)
Jerusalem (1963)
My Saviour came back in my life today (1963)

BALLET

Hear the bells (1959)

Ref. composer, 563

ARCANGELA-MARIA, Sister

18th-century Portuguese composer, from the convent of Marvilla.

Composition

SACRED

Pastorale on the nativity of Jesus Christ (Lisbon, 1737)

Bibliography

Brenet. *La musique dans les couvents des femmes. Schola Cantorum*, No. 4, April, 1898.
Vasconcellos. *Os musicos portugueses*, t. 1, p. 16.

ARCHER, Violet Balestreri

Canadian pianist, professor and composer. b. Montreal, April 24, 1913. She studied at the McGill Conservatory under Claude Champagne and Douglas Clarke. After a short period of private study under Bela Bartok in 1942, she was awarded scholarships from the Province of Quebec and McGill University, which enabled her to study at Yale University under Paul Hindemith from 1948 to 1949. She obtained her M.Mus. in 1950 and then lived in the United States for three years as a resident composer at North Texas State College. She was professor of composition at the University of Oklahoma from 1953 to 1961, then professor and chairlady of the division of music theory and composition at the University of Alberta, Canada. In 1949 the Ladies' Morning Musical Club awarded her a travel bursary and she won the Woods-Chandler prize in composition. In 1958 she was commissioned by the International House of New Orleans to write a work for the First Inter-American Music Festival held in Washington, DC. She was thus the first Canadian composer to represent Canada at the festival, where her *Trio No. 2* was premiered. She was given a citation for her distinguished service in music by the Alumnae of Yale University in 1968. In 1970 she received a merit award from the Government of Alberta and in 1971 was made an honorary doctor of music at McGill University. In 1972 she received the Creative and Performance award from the City of Edmonton. The annual award for Outstanding Success in the Concert Music Field was conferred on her by the Performing Rights Organization of Canada in 1981. Her *Trio No. 2* was extensively performed abroad in 1982 (Rome, Israel, London, Leningrad, Riga, Gomel, Minsk and Moscow), the tour being sponsored by the Alberta Foundation for the Performing Arts. She was professor emeritus of theory and composition at the University of Alberta. In 1984 she became the first woman composer to be chosen as Composer of the Year, by the Canadian Music Council. DISCOGRAPHY. PHOTOGRAPH.

Compositions

ORCHESTRA

Symphony No. 1 (Berandal, 1945)
Capriccio (hand timp and orch)
Clarinet concerto in A (1971)
Concertino (cl and orch) (Berandal, 1946)
Concerto (hand timp and orch) (1939)
Piano concerto (Berandal, 1959)
Violin concerto (Berandal, 1959)
Ballade
Britannia, a joyful overture (1941)
Divertimento (Berandal, 1957)
Fanfare and passacaglia (Berandal, 1949)
Fantasia concertante (fl, ob, cl and str orch) (Berandal, 1941)
Fantasy (cl and str orch) (1942)
Fantasy on a ground (Berandal, 1946)
Intermezzo (small orch)
Miniature suite (small orch)
Poem (Berandal, 1940)
Prelude-incantation (Ricordi, 1964)
Scherzo and andante (str orch)
Scherzo sinfonico, a symphonic jest (Berandal, 1940)
Sinfonia (1969)
Sinfonietta (1968)
Suite (str orch)
Three sketches (Berandal, 1961)
Variations on A la claire fontaine

CHAMBER

Fantasy in the form of a passacaglia (10 brass insts and timp) (CMC, 1951)
Introduction, dance, finale (2 trp, hn, trb, tba, hp or fl, dr and timp) (1963)
Divertimento (brass qnt) (Berandal, 1963)
Divertimento (sax qrt) (1979)
Fugue-fantasy (str qrt) (1949)
Quartet (fl, ob, cl and bsn)
String quartet No. 1 (1940)
String quartet No. 2 (1949)
String quartet No. 3 (1981)
Suite (4 vln) (CMC, 1972)
Variations on an original theme (str qrt)
Divertimento (ob, cl and bsn) (1949)
Divertimento No. 2 (ob, vln and vlc) (CMC, 1957)
Sonata (fl, cl and pf) (CMC, 1946)
Sonata (vla, vlc and pf) (1976)
String trio No. 1 (CMC, 1953)
String trio No. 2 (CMC, 1957)
Trio No. 1 (vln, vlc and pf) (1954)
Trio No. 2 (vln, vlc and pf) (CMC, 1957)
Trio No. 3 (vln, vlc and pf) (1977)
Capriccio (vlc and pf) (1981)
Dance (vln and vlc) (1970)
Fantasy (vln and pf) (1946)
Four duets (vln and vlc) (1979)
Suite (vln and vlc or cl and bsn) (1947)
Twelve miniatures (vln and pf) (1981)
A simple tune (rec and pf) (CMC, 1975)
Little suite (trp and pf) (CMC, 1975)
Prelude and allegro (vln and pf) (CMC, 1954)
Six pieces (pf and timp) (1939)
Sonata (a-sax and pf) (Berandal, 1972)
Sonata (bsn and pf) (1980)
Sonata (cl and pf) (1970)
Sonata (hn and pf) (CMC, 1956)
Sonata (ob and pf) (CMC, 1973)
Sonata (vlc and pf) (1956)
Sonata No. 1 (vln and pf) (1956)
Sonatina (bsn and pf) (1978)
Sonatina (ob and pf) (1976)
Three little studies (vln and pf) (CMC, 1970)
Three duets (2 vln) (1955, 1956, 1960)
Fantasy on Blanche comme la neige (gtr) (1978)
Soliloquys (cl) (1982)
Sonata (vlc) (1981)
Suite (fl) (CMC, 1976)
Two pieces (fl) (1947)

ORGAN

Aeterna Christi mundi, chorale prelude (1940, rev 1976)
Chorale improvisation on O worship the King (CMC, 1967)
Dominus regit me, chorale prelude (CMC, 1948)
Durch Adams Fall ist ganz verderbt, chorale prelude IV (1948, rev 1976)
Festive fantasy based on Pange lingua (1979)
Henlein, chorale prelude (CMC, 1948)
Ibant Magi, chorale prelude III (1948, rev 1976)
Prelude and allegro (1956)
Sonatina (Chanteldair Music, 1944)
Vom Himmel hoch, da komm' ich her, chorale prelude V (1948, rev 1976)
Other chorale preludes

PIANO

Birthday fugue a la Weinberger (2 pf) (1946)
Three sketches (2 pf) (1947)
Ten folk songs (4 hands) (1953)
Black and White (CMC, 1971)
Capriccio fantastic
Eight little canons (1978)
Eleven short pieces (Peer, 1960)
Fantasy for Rose Goldblatt (1947)
Four bagatelles (1977)
Four contrapuntal moods (1978)
Four little studies
Here and Now, 10 pieces (1980)
Holiday (CMC, 1971)
Improvisations (1968)
Little prelude

Lydian mood (1971)
Miniatures: 3 (1965), 2 (1970)
A Quiet chat (1971)
Rondo (peer, 1955)
Six preludes (CMC, 1947)
Sonata (CMC, 1945) (rev. 1957)
Sonata No. 2 (1979)
Sonatina No. 1 (Boosey and Hawkes, 1945)
Sonatina No. 2 (Boosey and Hawkes, 1946)
Sonatina No. 3 (Boosey and Hawkes, 1973)
Suite (1947)
Theme and variations on La-bas sur ces montagnes (1952)
Theme and variations on La-Haut (1963)
Three scenes, Habitant Sketches (Presser, 1945)
Three inventions (CMC, 1974)
Three two-part inventions (1948)
Two miniatures (CMC, 1970)
Variations on Isabeau s'u promene (1941)

VOCAL
Apocalypse (S, mix-ch and orch) (CMC, 1958)
The bell (John Donne) (mix-ch and orch) (1949)
Choruses from The Bacchae (Euripides) (w-ch and orch) (1938)
Lamentations of Jeremy (mix-ch and orch) (1947)
Leaves of grass (Whitman) (mix-ch and orch) (1940)
Centennial springtime (mix-ch and pf) (1967)
Four Newfoundland folk songs (m-ch) (1975)
Harvest (ch and pf) (1967)
Landscapes (mix-ch) (1950)
Paul Bunyan (mix-ch and pf) (1966)
Proud horses (mix-ch) (1953)
Sing the muse (Shakespeare, Marston, Drummond and Raleigh) (ch) (1964)
Some one (ch and pf)
Three French Canadian folk songs (mix-ch) (1953)
Three sailors from Groix (w-ch and pf) (1975)
April weather (vce and pf) (1976)
Caleidoscope, cycle (S and pf) (1981)
Cradle song (m-S and pf) (1950)
Daffodils (m-S and pf) (1972)
Four Canadian folk songs (vce and pf) (1958)
Green jade, cycle (Bar, ob and pf)
The Gulls (vce and pf)
Irradiations (vce and pf) (1955)
Life in a prairie shack (vce and pf) (1966)
Northern landscape (A.J.M. Smith) (vce and pf) (1978)
Prairie profiles, cycle (B, hn and pf) (1980)
Primeval, cycle (T and pf) (1980)
A sprig of flowers, cycle (T, fl and pf) (1979)
Together and apart (m-S and pf) (1978)
Two songs (W. Blake) (1958)
Under the sun (S and pf) (1949-1978)
Other songs (vce and pf)

SACRED
Cantata sacra (composer) (5 solos and small orch) (1967)
Amens for church use (mix-ch and orch) (1968-1974)
Psalmody (mix-ch and orch)
Christmas (w-ch, ob, and hp or pf) (1955)
The glory of God (w-ch) (1971)
I will lift up mine eyes (mix-ch and org) (1967)
Introit and choral prayer (mix-ch and org) (1961)
Mater admirabilis chapel (w-ch, ob and hp or pf) (1955)
O Lord thou hast searched me and known me (mix-ch and org) (1968)
O sing unto the lord, psalm 96 (w-ch, 2 trp or org) (1968)
Offertory acclamations (mix-ch)
One Corinthians, 13 (m-S and pf) (1976)
Psalm 145 (ch a-cap) (1981)
Psalm 150 (mix-ch and org) (1941)
Shout with joy (mix-ch and org) (1976)
A simple anthem, psalm 100 (mix-ch and org) (1969)
Sing a new song to the Lord (mix-ch and org) (1974)
Songs of prayer and praise (mix-ch) (1953)
Souls of the righteous (S or T and mix-ch) (1960)
Sweet Jesu King of bliss (mix-ch) (1967)
To rest in Thee, motet (mix-ch) (1981)
Two songs of praise (w-ch) (1978)
Psalm 23 (S and pf) (1952)
Three biblical songs (1950)

OPERA
The Meal (Rowland Holt-Wilson)
Sganarelle, in 1 act (Moliere) (1973)

FILM MUSIC
Someone cares (1976)
Whatsoever things are true, documentary (1980)

ELECTRONIC
Episodes (tape) (1973)

Publications
Alberta and its Folklore. Canadian Music Society Bulletin, July, 1967.
Ref. composer, C. Lomax (Toronto), 236, 329, 563, 622, 624, 631

ARCHILEI, Vittoria (nee Concarini) (pseud. La Romanina)

Italian lutenist, singer and composer. b. Rome, 1550; d. Florence, after 1618. In 1584 she sang at the wedding of Eleonora de Medici and Vincenzo Gonzaga and in 1589 sang her husband's compositions at the famous Intermedi et Concerti for the wedding of Ferdinando de Medici and Cristina di Lorena. She sang in concerts and social events until 1610, when her rival singer Adriana Basile arrived in Florence and overshadowed her.
DISCOGRAPHY.

Composition
VOCAL
Dalle piu alte sfere

Bibliography
Gandolfi, R. *La cappella musicale della corte di Toscana*. Vol. 16. Turin: *RMI Revista Musicale Italiana*. 1909.
Lozzi, C. *La musica e specialmente il melodramma alla Corte Medicea*. Vol. 9. Turin: *RMI Revista Musicale Italiana*. 1902.
Zanetti, E. *Archilei. Enciclopaedia dello Spettacolo I*. Rome, 1954.
Ref. 3, 5, 135, 563.

ARCHINTA, (Archinto), Marguerite (Margherita)

Italian composer. b. ca. 1520. A member of an aristocratic Milanese family, she wrote both words and music for several songs and madrigals.
Ref. 119, 502.

ARCHINTO, Margherita. See ARCHINTA, Marguerite

ARENA, Iris Mae

20th-century American organist, pianist, teacher and composer of Louisiana. She studied the piano under Carmen Marechal and taught the piano.

Compositions
PIANO
Goblin's frolic
Grasshopper's parade
Gypsy lament
Theme and variations on baa baa black sheep
Piano method for the left hand

Ref. 347, 448

ARENS-ROGER, Adelia

American organist, pianist and composer. b. Detroit, October 11, 1880. She was a pupil of Franz Apel.
Ref. 226

ARETZ, Isabel (Aretz de Ramon y Rivera)

Argentine-Venezuelan pianist, ethnomusicologist, folklorist and composer. b. Buenos Aires, April 13, 1909. She studied the piano and composition under Rafael Gonzalez and Athos Palma at the National Conservatory, Buenos Aires and later took advanced training in orchestration under Heitor Villa-Lobos in Brazil. At the Museum of Natural Sciences in Buenos Aires she studied folklore and musicology under Carlos Vega. She received her Ph.D. (musicology, summa cum laude, 1967) from the Pontificia Universidad Catolica Argentina and obtained scholarships from the National Commission of Culture of Argentina and from the Guggenheim Foundation. After 1952 she lived in Venezuela and became founder-director of the Inter-American Institute of Ethnomusicology and Folklore of the National Institute of Culture and Fine Arts. She married Jose Felipe Ramon y Rivera, Venezuelan ethnomusicologist. She published numerous books on ethno-music and folklore themes and with her husband carried out extensive research in Latin America. Her compositions were influenced by the indigenous and Afro music of South America. She received many honors and awards.
DISCOGRAPHY.

Compositions
ORCHESTRA
Danzas con interludio (pf and orch) (1933-1936)
Chimiterias (orch of Latin American indigenous insts) (1959)

Constelacion espectral (comm Ateneo of Caracas)
Dos acuarelas (str orch) (1939)
Punenas, suite (1937) (pf reduction, 1935-1936) (Ricordi)
Segunda serie criolla (str orch) (1950)
Serie criolla (small orch) (1949)

CHAMBER
Movimentos de percussion (40 perc – 11 performers)
Tres en sonata (vln, vla and pf) (1966)
Habitat No. 1 (acc) (1954)
Suite para clave (hpcd) (1967)

PIANO
Alma curu (1932) (Buenos Aires: M. Calvello) (1933)
Commentarios musicales a tres poemas de Andres Eloy Blanco (1961)
De mi infancia (1935) (M. Calvello) (1935)
Por la senda de Kh'Asana (1935)
Segunda serie criolla (1942)
Serie de mi infancia (1935)
Sonata (1965) (Festival de Primavera Indiana)
Sonata en mi mayor (1931-1932)
Tres preludios (1939, 1950)
Tres preludios negros (1954)

VOCAL
Simiente, cantata (Juan Liscano) (S, m-S, T, B, rec and orch) (1964)
Tocuyana (vces, ballet and orch) (1957) (comm Ministry of Labor, Venezuela, 1957)
Poema angaite (vce and orch) (1949)
Poema aracuano (vce and orch) (1950)
Serie infantial (vce and orch) (1938)
Carnavalito (vce and pf) (1938)
Cinco fulias sobre melodias folkloricas venezolanas (1966) (Ricordi Americana, Buenos Aires)
Danzas criolas (vce and pf) (1938-1940)
De mi infancia
La imilla (vce and pf) (1938)
La luna se llama Lola (vce and pf) (1938)
Primera seleccion de canciones y danzas tradicionales argentinas, 22 pieces (1942)
Primera serie criolla (vce and pf) (1937-1940)
Suite Altipampa (vce, fl and pf) (1936)
Tres cantos indios (vce and pf) (1962)
Arrangements of over 2000 folk songs

SACRED
Soneto de la Fe en Cristo (S and cham ens) (1956)

BALLET
Ahonaya (comm Ministry of Labor, Venezuela, 1958)
El llamado de la tierra (1954)
Movimientos de percusion (comm Ministry of Labor, Venezuela, 1960)
Paramo (comm Ministry of Labor, Venezuela, 1961)

ELECTRONIC
Padro Liberador (speaker, soloists, ch, tape and orch) (1982)
Gritos de una ciudad (2 speakers, tape and small orch) (1979)
Yekuana (vces, 5 tapes and orch) (1974)
Birimbao (mag tape and timp) (comm J. Kregal National Festival of Merida, 1968)
Kwaltaya (S and tape) (1980)

MULTIMEDIA
Argentino hasta la muerte (speaker, tapes, slides and cham orch) (1975)

Publications
La artesania folklorica de Venezuela. 1967.
Cantos navidenos venezolanos. 1962.
Costumbres tradicionales argentinos. Buenos Aires: Ricordi Americana, 1953.
Folk Songs of the Americas. With A. Lloyd. 1965.
El folklore musical argentino. Buenos Aires: Ricordi Americana.
El folklore en la escuela. (1953-1955).
Folklore tachirense. With L.F. Ramon y Rivera. 3 vols. Caracas, 1961-1963.
Instrumentos musicales de Venezuela. Cumana, 1967.
Manual de folklore venezolano. 1957; 3rd. Ed. 1972.
Musica tradicional Argentina. Tucuman, 1946.
Musica tradicional de la Rioja. Caracas, 1978.
El sistema tonal de los Incas. 1939.
El tamunangue. 1970.
El traje del Venezolano. 1976.
Estudios del folklore en America Latina. Revista INIDEF (Venezuela: Cinsejo Nacional de la Cultura) 2 (November, 1976): 44-58.

Bibliography
Stevenson, R.L. *Isabel Aretz: Composer, A Birthday Tribute*. Inter-American Music Review, No. 2, 1983.

Ref. 8, 9, 15, 17, 44, 54, 67, 94, 100, 189, 332, 359, 371, 390, 563, 524

ARETZ DE RAMON Y RIVERA. See ARETZ, Isabel

ARHO, Anneli

Finnish flautist, lecturer and composer. b. 1951. She studied the flute and composition at the Sibelius Academy under Jukka Tiensuu from 1972 to 1977. She continued her composition studies at the Staatliche Hochschule fuer Musik in Freiburg im Breisgau, under Brian Ferneyhough and Klaus Huber until 1979 and continued her studies in baroque and contemporary music at various international summer courses. Since 1979, she has lectured on theory at the Sibelius Academy. Her works have been performed in Finland and abroad.

Compositions

ORCHESTRA
One work

CHAMBER
Woodwind quintet (1979)
Minoa (hpcd) (1978)

VOCAL
Answer (vce, hn and str qrt) (1978)

Publications
Webern's Micro Cosmos. Musiiki, 1979: 1.

Ref. FMIC

ARIB. See ORAIB

ARIMA, Reiko

Japanese professor and composer. b. Tokyo, May 5, 1933. She studied at Tokyo University of Fine Arts, where she completed a composition course in 1962. She is a professor at Tokyo Music College. DISCOGRAPHY. PHOTOGRAPH.

Compositions

ORCHESTRA
Gathering and scattering (1968)

BRASS BAND
Mon-yo (1974)

CHAMBER
As baroque foster, 6 pieces (ens) (1973)
Four seasons of Japan, 12 pieces (ens) (1971)
Utage (8 insts) (1973)
Projection (6 insts) (1973)
Situation (ob, mar, cym and perc) (1975)
String quartet (1968)
Arioso violett (vln and pf) (1976)
Ru-sen (bamboo fl and pf) (1969)
Ballade (org) (1977)

PIANO
Fairy Tales (duet) (Ongaku-no-Tomosha, 1977)
Ballet of the sylphs, 21 pieces (Ongaku-no-Tomosha, 1977)
Children's yard, 18 pieces (Ongaku-no-Tomosha, 1968)
Four pieces for children (Zen-on-galsufu, 1972)

VOCAL
Memories of love, choral suites (Ongaku-no-Tomosha, 1977)
Ochiba no yoni, choral suites (1975)
Sono hi no 2 ji no tame ni (ch) (1977)
Songs with Japanese Poems, 20 pieces (Ongaku-no-Tomosha, 1968-1979)
Children's songs, 10 pieces (Ongaku-no-Tomosha, 1977)
Waves of leaves, choral piece (Ongaku-no-Tomosha, 1974)
Le concert de Noel, arrangement of 13 pieces

OPERETTA
Kaire Dancho, for children (1968)

MISCELLANEOUS
Look back
Spring, summer, autumn, winter (1968)
Trois mouvements pour tout ce qui a disparu (Shunju-sha, 1971)

Ref. composer, 563

ARIZTI SOBRINO, Cecilia

Cuban pianist, teacher and composer. b. Havana, October 28, 1856; d. Havana, June 30, 1930. She began her studies with her father, the pianist and composer Fernando Arizti and then with Nicolas Ruiz Espadero and Francisco Fuentes. She gave piano recitals in the United States at the Carnegie and Chickering Halls and later taught the piano in Havana.

Compositions

CHAMBER
Melodia romantica (vln and pf)
Trio (vln, vlc and pf)
Pieces (vln and pf)

PIANO
Album of 6 pieces (Biblioteca Nacional, Havana) Ballada
Barcarolles (Schirmer)
Berceuses

Capricho brillante
Dances
Impromptu in F-Minor, op. 12 (Schirmer)
Mazurkas
Reverie
Romances
Scherzo in F-Minor, op. 10 (Schirmer)
Technical studies
Three scherzi
Two nocturnes
Waltzes
VOCAL
Romantica, song (vce and pf)
SACRED
Ave Maria
Ref. Edgardo Martin (Havana), 17, 100, 107, 347, 361

ARKWRIGHT, Marian Ursula

English composer. b. Norwich, January 25, 1863; d. Highclere, near Newbury, March 23, 1922. She studied at Durham University, receiving her B.Mus. in 1895 and D.Mus. in 1913. Her symphonic suite *Winds of the World* won a prize offered by the English magazine *The Gentlewoman* for an orchestral work composed by a woman.

Compositions
ORCHESTRA
Winds of the world, symphonic suite (prize, The Gentlewoman)
Suite for strings (1907)
CHAMBER
Pieces (ww)
VOCAL
Last rhyme of true Thomas (ch and strs)
The Dragon of Wantley, ballad (3 treble vces)
Songs and part songs
SACRED
Requiem mass (Cary, 1915)
OPERETTA
The Water-babies (Charles Kingsley)
Ref. 8, 15, 23

ARKWRIGHT, Mrs Robert (nee Kemble)

English actress and composer. d. 1849. She was the sister of the poetess Felicia Hemans and composed songs that enjoyed considerable popularity.

Compositions
VOCAL
Ballads incl.:
Beloved one
Beth Gelert
The messenger birds
Pirate's farewell
Repentance
Sabbath bell at sea
Sailor's grave
Set of six ancient Spanish ballads (London, 1832)
Second set (1835)
Set of six songs (Mrs. Hemans, Mrs. Opie, Sir Walter Scott)
Other similar sets
Treasures of the deep
Zara's earrings
SACRED
Six songs (1866)
Ref. 6, 226, 276, 347

ARLEN, Jeanne Burns

American authoress and composer. b. New York, February 18, 1917. She studied at the New York University and the Malikin Conservatory.

Compositions
PIANO
San Francisco sketches
VOCAL
American women's marching song (official song of the Women's Volunteers, U.S. Treasury)
Songs incl.:
Lady with the fan
To my beloved
Ref. 39

ARLT-KRUSE, Lotte. See KRUSE, Lotte

ARMER, Elinor Florence

American pianist, lecturer, writer and composer. b. Oakland, CA, October 6, 1939. In 1961 she graduated from Mills College with a B.A. (composition). After a period of teaching in schools she resumed graduate studies at the University of California, Berkeley from 1966 to 1968 and then in 1972, graduated from California State University, San Francisco with an M.A. (composition). Her teachers included Darius Milhaud, Leon Kirchner, Roger Nixon and Alexander Liberman. She lectured on musicianship, harmony, counterpoint, the piano and composition at San Francisco Conservatory and the University of California, Berkeley. She received the Norman Fromm Composers' award and a fellowship at the MacDowell Colony.

Compositions
CHAMBER
The gift of tongues (hpcd and 17 insts)
Pieces for the mind's eye, in 3 mvts (10 insts)
Three sonnets for woodwinds (fl, cor anglais, ob, bsn and 2 cl)
Are you sleeping? (six perc incl. vib) (1977-1978)
Recollections and revel, in 2 mvts (vlc and pf) (1978)
The secret (hp and hpcd)
Thaw (pf) (1975)
Variations on Mein junges Leben hat ein End (hpcd) (1975)
VOCAL
Denim Blues – cabaret cantata (m-S, fl, picc, cl, sax, trp, trb, pf, perc and d-b) (1978)
Spin, Garth (mix-ch and pf or org)
The golden ring, 5 songs for California (T, acc, fl, cl, hn, trb, pf, perc, vln, vcl and bucket) (1978)
Five songs on Indian poems (m-S, fl, picc, cl, vln, vlc, pf and perc)
Lockerbones/airbones, 5 poems (Ursula Le Guin) (m-S, fl, pf and perc) (1984)
Pogo cantabile, 5 poems (Walt Kelly) (S and pf, bottles, one-string ukelele and wash-tub) (1975)
The flea, and O thou, poems (John Donne, e.e. cummings) (S, reader and vir) (1975)
Golden years (vce and pf)
Proportions (1981)
Songs
THEATRE
Mowgli, for children (Kipling)
TEACHING PIECES
Work for violin
Ref. composer, 625, 643

ARMSTRONG, Annie

19th-century English composer.

Compositions
VOCAL
Songs incl.:
Just a song
Litle lays for little lassies
True hearts
The weaver's daughter
Ref. 276, 433

ARNIM, Bettina von (Elisabeth) (nee Brentano)

German singer, writer and composer. b. Frankfurt, April 4, 1785; d. Berlin, January 20, 1859. She was the sister of the poet Clemens Brentano and the wife of the poet Achim von Arnim. She met both Goethe and Beethoven, the latter dedicating his *Neue Liebe, neues Leben* to her after her visit to Vienna from 1809 to 1810. In earlier years she sang and from 1810 to 1812 was a member of the Voice Training Academy in Berlin. She made literary history in 1835 with her fictitious *Goethes Briefwechsel mit einem Kinde* (Goethe's correspondence with a child). DISCOGRAPHY.

Compositions
VOCAL
Gesaenge zum Faust: No. 2, O schaudre nicht (1843), No. 5, Herbst Gefuehl (Leipzig: Breitkopf and Haertel)
Liederheft No. 1 (vce and pf) (Leipzig, 1843)
Sieben Gesangstuecke

Publications
Dieses Buch gehoert dem Koenig.
Der echte Briefwechsel mit Goethe. Leipzig, 1927.
Goethes Briefwechsel mit einem Kinde. Berlin, 1835.
Ludwig van Beethoven's saemtliche Briefe. Leipzig, 1912.
Saemtliche Werke. 11 Vols. Berlin, 1853.

Bibliography
Leitzmann, A. *Beethoven und Bettina.* Deutsche Revue, 1918.
Oehike, W.B. *Von Arnims Briefromane.* 1905.
Ref. 17, 26, 121, 129, 202, 276, 347, 563

ARNIM, Elisabeth. See ARNIM, Bettina

ARNOLD, Mrs. E. See HOFFMANN, Peggy

ARNOLD, Rose. See ARNOLD, Rosanna Luisa Swann

ARNOLD, Rosanna Luisa Swann (Rose)

South African pianist and composer. b. East London, August 23, 1868; d. Arnoldton, September 16, 1940. She grew up on a farm near Arnoldton where she had little opportunity to study music. However, she became a competent pianist although unable to read music fluently. Her compositions were written down by her friend, Margaret Gately.

Compositions

PIANO

Amalinda, dance (East London: Franz Moeller)
Amalinda, march (Moeller)
Cheeky, dance (Moeller)
The golden star of the veldt (Moeller)
Manzi Kanya, waltz (Shining Waters) (Moeller)
The motor girl (Moeller)
Somlanga, waltz (Moeller)

Bibliography

Van der Merwe, F.Z. *Suid-Afrikaanse Musiekbibliografie 1787-1952.* Pretoria: J.L. van Schaik, 1958.

Ref. 377

ARQUIT, Nora Harris

American clarinetist, conductor and composer. b. Brushton, NY, June 30, 1923. She studied at a number of colleges and universities in the United States, including Harvard and Rutgers. She toured Europe conducting her own bands and was a guest conductor in the United States, Canada and Europe. She was the first woman guest conductor of the USAF Band in Washington, DC. She was student laureate for her orchestral works and also composed symphonic marches and pieces for an instrumental trio.

Ref. 77

ARRIEU, Claude (pseud. of Louise Marie Simon)

French composer. b. Paris, November 30, 1903. She studied at the Paris Conservatoire under Marguerite Long, Caussade, Roger Ducasse, N. Callon and Paul Dukas and in 1932 won first prize for composition. She also received the Prix Ambroise Thomas, Prix Lepaulle, Prix de Gouy d'Arsy and the Legion of Honor. She was one of the first composers to participate in P. Schaeffer's Musique Concrete. A large number of her works were commissioned by French radio and television. DISCOGRAPHY. PHOTOGRAPH.

Compositions

ORCHESTRA

Symphony in C-Minor (1940)
Concerto (2 pf and orch) (1938) (Presser: Billaudot)
Concerto (fl and orch) (1946) (Kerby: Amphion E.C.)
Concerto (pf and orch) (1932)
Concerto in E (vln and orch) (1938) (Amphion)
Concerto No. 2 (vln and orch) (1949) (Presser: Heigel)
Concerto (trps and str och) (1965) (Amphion)
Concerto (wind qnt and str orch) (1962) (Ricordi)
La Boite à malice (1934)
La Conquête de l'Algerie, suite (1935)
Divertissement (1946)
Fête galante (1947) (Amphion)
In Memoriam (ob, trp and str orch) (1969) (Amphion)
Jeux (pf, vlc, perc and str orch) (1961) (E.F.M.)
Les jongleurs (pf, vls, perc and str orch) (1962) (E.F.M.)
Mascarades, suite (1929) (Presser: Heugel)
Meneut vif (pf, hp, perc and str orch) (1961) (E.F.M.)
Partita (1934) (Amphion)
Petite suite, in 5 parts (1945) (Henmar: Choudens)
Prélude pour un conte de fees (1947) (Amphion)
Scherzo valse (pf, cel, perc and str orch) (1961) (E.F.M.)
Suite for strings (1959) (Ricordi)
Suite funambulesque (1961) (E.F.M.)
Tarantelle (1970) (E.F.M.)
Variations classiques (str orch) (1970) (Amphion)

CHAMBER

Dixtour pour instruments à vent (1967) (Billaudot)
Two pieces (str qrt, hp, hn and perc) (1966) (E.F.M.)
Brass quintet (1962)
Wind quintet in C-Major (fl, ob, cl, bsn and hn) (1955) (Billaudot)
Deuxieme quatuor de clarinettes (Paris: Amphion, 1984)
Quatuor pour clarinettes (1964) (Billaudot)
Suite en quatre (fl, ob, cl and bsn)
Variations, Interlude et final (fl, cl, vla and pf) (1932)
Suite en trio (S-pipe, A-pipe, B-pipe) (Scarabee, 1955)
Trio (pf, vln and vlc) (Amphion, 1957)
Trio d'anches (ob, cl and bsn) (Amphion, 1936)
Capriccio (cl and pf) (Amphion, 1970)
Le coeur volant (hn and pf)
Concertstueck (trp and pf) (Amphion, 1964)
Duo, in 4 mvts (2 fl) (Amphion, 1964)
La fête (cl and pf)
Impromptu (ob and pf) (Leduc, 1954)
Un jour d'été (cl and pf)
Lectures pour divers instruments: Comptine (trb and pf) (1966): Dialogue (vlc and pf) (1966): Intermede (trp and pf) (1966): Menetrier (trp or hn and pf) (1965); Passe-pied (vlc and pf) (1966); Pastorale (ob and pf) (1964); Prelude (fl and pf) (1964) (Chappell)
Mouvements (trb and pf) (Amphion, 1966)
Petit choral (cl and pf)
Pièce bréve (trp and pf) (Lemoine)
Prelude and scherzo (vlc and pf) (Amphion, 1967)
Scherzo (vln and pf) (Enoch, 1946)
Sonata (vln and pf) (Leduc, 1948)
Sonatina (2 vln) (Amphion, 1937)
Sonatina (fl and pf) (Amphion, 1943)
Trois duos faciles (fl and bsn)
Valse et mouvement perpetuel (vln and pf) (Amphion, 1949)
Toccata (hpcd or pf) (Leduc, 1963)

PIANO

Suite pour Melodyne (4 hands) (Amphion, 1946)
La Bôite à malice, 8 pieces (Lemoine, 1939)
Caprice (Enoch, 1945)
Lectures, suite of 8 pieces (Billaudot, 1968)
Marche, étude, choral (Heugel, 1929)
Mouvement perpetuel (Amphion, 1948)
Musique (Salabert, 1939)
Le petit canard (Enoch, 1928)
Les petites filles modeles (Amphion, 1975)
Prelude, forlane et gigue (Enoch, 1940)
Quatre études-caprices (Ricordi, 1954)
Quatre pièces (Choudens, 1946)
Sarabande (1946) (Chant du Monde)
Tendresse (Jardin d'enfants) (1946) (Lemoine)
Trois improvisations (Amphion, 1948)
Les contemporains, valse (Billaudot, 1948)

VOCAL

Cantate des sept poèmes d'amour en guerre (P. Eluard) (S, B and orch) (Ricordi, 1946)
Ballade pour le Paix de Charles d'Orleans (soloist, ch and orch)
Songs incl.:
A claires voix, for children (Y. Lacote) (Enoch, 1957)
A l'Hirondelle (R. Belleau) (2 or 3 equal vces) (1934) (Salabert)
Ah! si j'étais un oiseau (Samivel) (2 or 3 equal vces) (E.F.M., 1946)
Brave Homme
Chanson de la côte (C. Cros) (1954) (Ricordi)
Chanson de Maurice (M. Fombeure) (1959) (Ricordi)
Chanson de la patience (1959)
Chanson de l'ours (2 or 3 vces) (Samivel, 1946)
D'un vanneur de blé au vent (ch of 2 or 3 equal vces) (J. du Bellay, 1934)
Le diable blanc (Samivel) (2 vces) (1946) (Inedit)
Dépêche-toi de rire (Jean Tardieu) (1959)
Espèce de comptine (M. Fombeure) (1959) (Ricordi)
L'Ete (S, vces and pf) (Lemoine, 1932)
L'Eau vive (Claude Roy) (4 mix-vces)
Un fiacre (P. Devaux) (1936) (Enoch)
Il a neige dans les plaines (2 or 3 vces) (Samivel, 1946)
Michka (P. Castor)
Nathalie (A. Mella) (1940)
L'Orgue (C. Cros)
Par la-haut (Samivel) (2 vces) (1946) (Inedit)
Pauvre Jean (J. Cocteau) (1945)
Qu'avez-vous vu, Bergers? (2 or 3 vces) (D. Rimaud, 1950) (Inedit)
Le Roi qui ne pouvait pas eternuer (P. Castor)
Sixty songs (Lorca, Max Jacob, P. Schaeffer, J. Giraudoux, Mallarmé, Verlaine, J. Cocteau, Aragon and others)
Trois rondeaux de Clement Marot (E.F.M., 1957)

SACRED

Mystère de Noël, oratorio (soloists, ch and orch) (L. Masson, 1951)
Requiem (ch a-cap)
Noël de neige (Samviel) (2 equal vces) (1946)

BALLET

Commedia umana, after the Decameron (1960)
Fête galante (Amphion, 1947)
La Maison de la courtisane
La Statue (1968)

OPERA

Balthazar, ou le mort vivant, opera-bouffe in 1 act (P. Dominique) (E.F.M., 1966)

La Cabine telephonique, opera-bouffe in 1 act (M. Vaucaire) (Amphion, 1958)
Cadet-Roussel, opera-bouffe in 5 acts (A. de la Tourasse and J. Limozin) (Ricordi, 1938-1939)
Un Clavier pour un autre, opera-bouffe (J. Tardieu) (Amphion, 1969-1970)
La Coquille à planetes, radio opera (Pierre Schaeffer) (1943-1944)
Cymbeline, in 2 acts (J. Tournier and M. Jacquemont, after Shakespeare) (Amphion, 1958-1963)
Les deux rendez-vous, opera-comique in 1 act (P. Bertin after G. de Nerval) (R.T.F., 1948) (comm French government, 1947)
Noe, imagerie musicale in 3 acts (A. Obey) (E.M.F., 1932-1934)
La princesse de Babylone, opera-bouffe in 3 acts (P. Dominique after Voltaire) (Amphion, 1953-1955)
Resurrezione (Milano: Ricordi)
Zoroastre, lyric tragedy in 5 acts (Jean-Philippe Rameau, adapted and arr composer) (1964)

OPERETTA
Le Chapeau à musique, in 2 acts, for children (A. de la Tourasse and P. Dumaine) (editions de l'Amicale, 1953)

INCIDENTAL MUSIC
Theatre:
Le bourgeois gentilhomme (Moliere) (1969)
Capucine (M. Barbulee) (1944)
Le chateau du carrefour (O. Joyeux) (1953)
Les deux Orphelines (Grenier-Hussenot) (1944)
La farce enfantine de la Tête du dragon (V. Inclan) (1946)
Les gueux au paradis (Martens and Obey) (1945)
L'ile au trésor (Stevenson) (1953)
Liliom (Molnar) (1947)
Loire (A. Obey) (1934)
Le mal court (Audiberti) (1947)
Le marchand de Venise (Shakespeare) (1961)
La tempête (Shakespeare) (1955)
Les trois mousquetaires (Dumas) (1953)
Le village des miracles (Martens) (1952)
Radio:
L'ane culotte (Henri Bosco) (1947)
L'anniversaire (Ribemont-Dessaigne) (1968)
L'aura d'Olga (P. Schaeffer) (1962)
L'aventure de Walter Schnapps (Schilovitz after Maupassant) (1969)
La belle au bois (J. Supervielle) (1962)
Candide (Jean Tardieu, after Voltaire) (1945)
Carte blanche (M. Fombeure) (1948)
Cendrillon (J. Morel) (1952)
Un chapeau de paille d'Italie (A. Sallee and J. Morel after Labiche) (1948)
La Charade flamande (A. Vidalie) (1949)
Comédies italiennes (E. Fuzelier) (1948)
Cornelius (B. Hecht) (1957)
La Dame de l'aube (A. Casona) (1957)
L'Ecureuil du bois bourru (Maurice Genevoix) (1963)
Evocation sur Appolinaire (1947)
Fables de Samivel (1951)
Fait-divers (Meilhac and Halevy) (1952)
Faust (Ribemont-Dessaigne) (1951)
Frédéric Général (J. Constant) (1949) (Prize Italia)
Le huron (J. Comos after Voltaire) (1963)
Indiscretions (Henri Monnier) (1952)
La jalousie du Barbouille (Moliere) (1948)
Jonathan Swift (1954)
Leur coeur (A. Salmon) (1950)
Lorsque cinq ans seront passes (Lorca) (1949)
L'Impossible aventure (Blaise Cendrars) (1947)
La Matrone d'Ephese (G. Sion) (1950)
Mon coeur dans les Highlands (Sorayan) (1957)
Le Monstre Turquin (M. Arnaud) (1954)
La pantoufle perdue (Lucien Jacques) (1966)
La Perruche (J. Grimod) (1957)
Peter Pan (Andre Puget) (1957)
Le pique-nique (Jacques Perret) (1968)
Poètes de Paris (J. Follain) (1953)
Rue des Ormeaux (Claude Roy) (1953)
Salavin (G. Duhamel) (1954)
Sylverie (1948)
Tous les bruits sont dans la nature (A. Lanoux) (1957)
Le voyage à trois étioles (1948)
Television:
Flore et Blanchefore (F. Dumayet) (1961)
Le square des miracles (Jean-Jacques Vierne)
Films:
A belles dents (D. Lecomte) (1960)
Classe enfantine (V. Vicas) (1947)
Comme si le coeur battait (Lamy) (1947)
Les coulisses de la radio (1941)
Crève-coeur (Jaques Dupont) (1956)
L'Enfant au fennec (Jacques Dupont) (1955)
Le fleuve blanc (D. Lecomte) (1947)
Les gosses mènent l'enquête (Labro) (1946)
Haute tension (D. Lecomte) (1956)
Invisible link (V. Vicas) (1948)
Jérusalem (V. Vicas) (1948)
Jours de peine (V. Vicas) (1949)
Lettres de Paris (Roger Leenhardt) (1946)
Lutte éternelle (V. Vicas) (1947)
Malgovert (D. Lecomte) (1953)
Marchands de rien (D. Leconte) (1957)
Montelimar (D. Lecomte) (1958)
Niok (1956)
Noces de papier (Pierre Fabre) (1966)
Le Pain de Barbarie (R. Leenhardt) (1947)
La petite République (V. Vicas) (1947)
De Pierre et de bronze (D. Lecomte) (1954)
Pour les pieds nus d'Hélène (Pierre Fabre) (1968)
Prepare for tomorrow (V. Vicas) (1948)
Routier du desert (J. Dupont) (1953)
Simple conte des causses (Regnier) (1954)
Le tombeur (production Desurmont) (1957)
Le travaux d'Hector (D. Lecomte) (1957)

ELECTRONIC
Fantaisie lyrique (ondes Martenot and pf) (Chappell, 1959)

ARRANGEMENTS
Works by Mozart and Pugnani (Ricordi)

Ref. 8, 13, 17, 94, 96, 193, 206, 280, 524, 563

ARSEYEVA, Irina Vasilievna

Soviet lecturer and composer. b. Saratov, September 21, 1941. She studied music theory at the Saratov Conservatory, graduated in 1967 and studied composition at the Music Teachers' Institute in Rostov-on-the-Don, graduating in 1970, having taught at an Arts school in the same city from 1967 until 1968. She then lectured on theory at the Music Teachers' Institute in Rostov.

Compositions

ORCHESTRA
Symphonic poem (1969)

CHAMBER
String quartet (1969)
Variations (vlc and pf) (1961)

VOCAL
Concertino for soprano (1967)
Cycles (D. Erseyev, 1968; K. Balmont, 1969; O. Khayyam, 1970)
Romances (Pushkin, Lermontov, Blok, Bunin and other poets)
Choruses
Songs

OPERA
Varshavskaya melodia (based on work by L. Zorin) (1970)

Ref. 21

ARTEAGA, Genoveva de

20th-century Puerto-Rican organist, pianist, conductor, editor, teacher and composer. She received her first music lessons from her parents at the Academia Arteaga, Santurce, which she attended from 1907 till 1920. From 1909 till 1923 she was a student at the Colegio Universitario del Sagrado Corazon in Santurce, teaching the piano at the same institute from 1917 till 1920. In 1921 she studied at the New York College of Music, graduating with honors in 1922 and at the Guilmant Organ School. At the Pius X School of Liturgical Music of Manhattan College she studied Gregorian chant and accompaniment under Dom Mocquereau and Dom Desroquettes. In Puerto Rico she taught at the Academia Catolica in San Juan and later founded the Academia de Musica. She was the first woman in San Juan to direct an opera – *Cavalleria Rusticana* – in 1935. In New York she was named judge adjudicator and then chairlady of the National Guild of Piano Teachers. Throughout her career she gave organ and piano recitals and performed in chamber music ensembles. She dedicated herself to serving the Puerto-Rican community in New York, for whom she edited a music journal *Revista Euterpe*.

Compositions

PIANO
Puerto-Rican dances
Other pieces

VOCAL
Songs (Spanish texts)

SACRED
Misa Obispo Jonathen para la Communidad de habla espano

Ref. Prof. Catherine A. Dower, 278

ARTHUR, Fanny. See ROBINSON, Fanny

ARVEY, Verna

American concert pianist, authoress and composer. b. Los Angeles, February 16, 1910. She studied music privately and performed in concert in the States and Latin America and on radio.

Compositions

VOCAL
Highway 1, USA (ch)
Those who wait (ch)
Wailing woman (ch)
Songs incl.:
Lament
Song for the lonely
Up there

BALLET
Miss Sally's party

OPERA
A Bayou legend
Costaso
Mota
A Southern Interlude

MISCELLANEOUS
Lennox avenue (comm CBS)

Ref. 39

ASACHI, Elena

Rumanian singer, teacher, translator and composer. b. Vienna, October 30, 1789; d. Iasi, May 9, 1877. She studied theory, solfege, harmony and counterpoint under her father, Anton Teyber, in Dresden. In Vienna she studied singing under Domino Donzelli. She was a teacher of music in Iasi from 1815 to 1817 and translated songs, arias and scientific and social articles into Rumanian, including a young people's encyclopedia which she translated from the French. She married the writer Gheorghe Asachi.

Compositions

VOCAL
La Tente, cantata (vce and pf) (Iasi, 1834)
Ballade moldave (vce and pf) (1841)
Filomele (vce and pf)
Intre văile (G. Asachi) (2 vces) (1862)
Se il fato barbaro (vce and pf) (1837)
Sie starb, sagst du (ded Terezei Czihak) (1841)
Tăranul (G. Asachi) (2 vces) (1862)

SACRED
Luceafăr lin, hymn (G. Asachi) (unison ch and pf) (1837)

THEATRE
Contrabantul, comedy-vauderville in 2 acts (G. Asachi) (Iasi, 1837)
Dragoş întîiul don suveran al Moldovii, heroic drama with music (G. Asachi) (Iasi, 1834)
Idilă moldovenească, pastorale with songs and dances (G. Asachi) (1837)
Petru Rareş-Vodă, serious drama in 2 acts (G. Asachi) (Iasi, 1837)
Serbarea păstorilor moldoveni, pastorale with songs and dances (G. Asachi) (1834)
Tiganii, idyll with songs (G. Asachi) (1856)
Voichiţa de Romania, historic melodrama (G. Asachi) (1863)

Bibliography

Poladian-Ghenea, Meline. *Elena Asachi*. Stud. Muzicol. Bucuresti, No. 5. 1969.
Viorel, Cosma. *Prima compozitoare româncă: Elena Asachi (1789-1877)*. Magazin. Bucharest. No. 127, 1960.

Ref. 196

ASHFORD, Emma Louise (nee Hindle)

American guitarist, organist, singer, teacher and composer. b. Newark, DE, March 27, 1850; d. 1930. She was taught by her father, a music teacher. She was a church organist at St. Peter's Church, Seymour, CT, and later in charge of music at two churches in Nashville, TN.

Compositions

CHAMBER
Over 200 organ voluntaries
Piano pieces

SACRED
Cantatas incl.:
The Prince of peace
Hymns incl.:
Evelyn (Methodist Hymnal, 1911)
Sutherland (Methodist Hymnal, 1911)
Fifty solos
Gospel songs
Over 250 anthems
Twenty-four duets and trios

Publications

Ashford's Organ Instructor.

Ref. 228, 347, 646

ASHMORE, Grace Flournoy

American pianist, singer, teacher and composer. b. De Funiak Spring, FL, April 20, 1904. At Florida State University, she studied for her voice certificate in 1925, obtaining her B.Mus. (voice and piano) in 1926 and M.A. in 1950. She taught singing and the piano at her own studio.

Compositions

PIANO
Pieces

VOCAL
America my own
Other songs

Ref. 496

ASPRI (Asperi), Orsola (Ursula) (pseud. of Adelhaide Appignani)

Italian pianist, conductor, singer, teacher and composer. b. Rome, 1807; d. Rome, September 30, 1884. The step-daughter of Andrea Aspri, the well known violinist, Orsola received a thorough music education and was a pupil of Fioravano. She taught voice and conducted in Florence, in 1839. She married Count Girolamo Cenci-Bolognetti.

Compositions

ORCHESTRA
Pjeces

VOCAL
La redenzione di Roma, cantata (1871)

OPERA
Le Aventure di una Giornata (1827)
Francesca da Rimini (1835)
I Pirati (1834)
I Riti Indiani (1834)

Ref. 102, 105, 129, 225, 226, 276, 307, 347

ASSANDRA, Catterina (Caterina) (alt. name Alessandra, Caterina)

Italian musician and composer. b. Pavia, ca. 1580. Confusion exists between Catterina and another person of this name who appeared in 1772. Catterina became a nun in the cloister of Sant' Agata in Lomello, diocese of Pavia. She studied counterpoint under Benedetto Re. Her fame as a composer and performer in keyboard instruments during the first half of the 17th-century, extended beyond the borders of Italy. Two of her motets were included in a collection published in Munich by A. De Berg in 1616, titled 'Siren coelestis' and in another collection 'Promptuarium musicum', published in Strasbourg by P. Ledertz in 1622. Her teacher Benedetto Re paid her homage by including her work *Salve regina* in his 'Integra psalmodia', published in Venice in 1611.

Compositions

SACRED
Cantus/Motetti a due e tre voci, per cantar nel organo con il basso continuo, op. 2 (vces, org and basso continuo) incl.:
Audite coeli
O Bone Jesu
O dulcis amor Jesu
O quam sauvis
Duo seraphim
Ecce confessor magnus
En dilectus meus
Factum est silentium
Haec dies
Hodie Christus
Impetum fecerunt in Stephamum
Imple os nostrum
Jubilate Deo
O Salutaris hostia
Veni dilecte mi
Veni Sancte Spiritus
Veni sponsa Christi
Canzone a 4 (Benedetto Re)
Litanie della Beata Vergine (Benedetto Re) (Milan: Per l'Herede di Simon Tini and Filippo Lomazzo, 1609)
Two motets in the collection Siren coelestis (Munich: A. de Berg, 1616) and in the collection Promtuarium musicum (Strasbourg: P. Ledertz, 1622)
Salve Regina (8 vce polychoral setting) in Benedetto Re's collection Integra Psalmodia (Venice: A. Vincenti, 1611)
Organ pieces (in manuscript, Library Regensburg, Germany)

Bibliography

Brenet, M. *La Revue Musicale* 5: 488.
Gaspari, G. *Catalogo della Biblioteca del Liceo Mus. di Bologna*. Bologna, 1892.
Kroyer, T. *Denkmaeler deutscher Tonkunst in Bayern*. Anno X, vol. 1.
Sartori, C. *Bibliografia della musica strumentale italiana stampata in Italia fino al 1700*. Florence, 1952.

Ref. 15, 26, 74, 85, 105, 127, 128, 214, 226, 260, 276, 335, 347, 563

ASSUNÇÃO, Sister Arcangela Maria de
18th-century Portuguese nun and composer. b. Sacavem; d. Marvila, 1737. She took her vows on October 22, 1730, in the convent of Santa Brigida in Marvila. She published a mystic poem for which she composed the music, entitled *Festivo Aplauso em Que Uma Religiosu como Pastora e os Anjos como Musicos . . . celebraram o Nascimento do Menino Jesus.*
Ref. 268

ASTLE-ALLAM, Agnes Mary
English organist, pianist, singer and composer. b. Reading, 1857. She studied under Francis Pritchard, Adolf von Holst, F. Atkins, Dr. Scott, Mr. Aylward and Dr. Haydocks. She played the piano and the organ and became well-known as a singer in South Wales, Manchester and London.
Compositions
VOCAL
Songs incl.:
The Doctor
Morningtide
Nell's Doll
Ref. 467

ASTORGA, Emmanuelle d'
Early 18th-century composer.
Compositions
VOCAL
Songs
SACRED
Cantata (1726)
Stabat Mater (1707)
Ref. 465

ASTROVA, V.
20th-century Soviet composer.
Composition
VOCAL
Strana Liubvi, song cycle (R. Gamsatov) (Sovietski Kompozitor, 1982)
Ref. Collett's catalog (Northants, UK)

ATANASIJEVIC, Slavka (Alijzija)
Croatian pianist, violinist, singer and composer. b. Osijek, November 2, 1850; d. Vienna. In Osijek she studied singing under I.N. Hummel, the piano under D. Trisler and the violin under T. Mahulka. She also studied in Vienna under Kietkowski. She toured in Austria, Hungary and Yugoslavia. Her compositions are mostly variations on national themes, inspired by the virtuoso style of Liszt and Dreyschock.
Compositions
PIANO
Chansonette slave, variations on theme Ustaj, ustaj rode
Fantasie de concert, variations on theme Na te mislim
Fantasies on Slav songs
Reflets du printemps
Ref. 109, 193

ATHERTON, Grace
19th-century American composer of songs.
Ref. 276, 347

ATHOLL, Duchess of. See RAMSAY, Lady Katherine

ATKINSON, Dorothy (pseuds. Valerie D'Orme, Duncan Fife, Beryl Langham)
English poetess, writer and composer. b. London, 1893.
Compositions
PIANO
The cloak of night, suite
In my garden, suite
March
Old China, suite
Summer sketches, suite
To a Flanders poppy, reverie
Valse caprice
VOCAL
A gift of the desert, cycle
An Idyll, cycle
Phases, cycle
Songs incl.:
A heavy dragoon
Here's to life
O! Golden dawn
Ref. 467

ATRE, Prabha
20th-century Indian singer and composer, who sings many of her compositions on the radio. She has also given concerts outside India.
Ref. Nat. Council of Women, India

AUBER, Chantal
20th-century pianist and composer.
Composition
PIANO
Triades (Paris: Hortensia, 1982)
Ref. Otto Harrassowitz (Wiesbaden)

AUBERT, Pauline Louise Henriette
French harpsichordist, pianist, professor and composer. b. Paris, September 1, 1884. She studied the piano, the harpsichord and composition in Paris under Charles Rene, Jean Hure and Arnold Dolmetsch. She was professor of the harpsichord at the Amsterdam Conservatory and worked in national libraries in Paris and Italy. She reconstructed works of the 17th and 18th-centuries.
Compositions
CHAMBER
Two melodies (d-b) (1912) (Senart)
Ref. composer

AUBIGNY VON ENGELBRUNNER, Nina d'
German singer, writer and composer. b. Kassel, 1777; d. Bombay. She was taught by Sales in Koblenz.
Compositions
VOCAL
Songs incl.:
Weep No More
The Woodland Hallo
German, Italian and French songs (vce and pf)
Publications
Briefe an Natalie ueber den Gesang. Leipzig, 1803.
Various essays in the Leipziger Musikalische Zeitung.
Ref. 128, 129, 622

AUBREY, Mrs. Henry Harris. See BEACH, Amy Marcy

AUBUT-PRATTE, Françoise
20th-century Canadian organist, pianist, lecturer and composer. She began her studies at the age of eight, under Eugene Lapierre. She studied the piano in Boston under Sanroma before entering the Paris Conservatoire and then performed in Versailles and Paris. She taught at the Quebec Conservatory and lectured at the University of Montreal and the Nazareth Institute. She was organist at Saint-Edouard. Her awards included several first prizes from the Paris Conservatoire, the first of which she won at the age of 19. Her compositions included an organ mass.
Ref. 355

AUENBRUGG (Auenbrugger), Marianna von
Austrian harpsichordist, singer and composer. d. 1786.
Composition
CHAMBER
Sonata per il clavicembalo o forte piano . . . con ode di A. Salieri (Vienna: Artaria and Co., 1787)
Ref. 119, 125, 128

AUENBRUGGER, Marianna von. See AUENBRUGG, Marianna von

AUENHEIM, Marianna

Early 19th-century Austrian singer, teacher and composer. She was the daughter of Josepha von Aurenhammer (q.v.) and sang at the Kaerntnertor theatre.
Ref. 15

AUFDERHEIDE, May

20th-century American composer. DISCOGRAPHY.
Compositions
CHAMBER
Dusty (pf, perc and d-b)
The Thriller (pf, perc and d-b)
Pelham waltzes (pf)
Ref. 563

AUERHAMMER, Josefa Barbara von. See AURENHAMMER Josefa

AUFDIENER, Caroline. See WUIET, Caroline

AUFFDIENER, Caroline. See WUIET, Caroline

AUGUSTA MARIA LOUISE, Queen of Prussia

German pianist and composer. b. Weimar, September 30, 1811; d. Berlin, January 7, 1890. She was Princess of Saxe-Weimar and the consort of William I. She was taught by Goethe and learned the piano from Hummel. After her marriage she completed her studies in music theory and composition under the court composer Hermann Schmidt and the music director Albrecht Agthe in Berlin.
Compositions
ORCHESTRA
Overtures
BAND
Military marches incl.:
Armeemarsch 102 (Schlesinger)
BALLET
Die Maskerade
Ref. 105, 121, 129

AUGUSTENBURG, Caroline Amelia of

Danish composer. b. 1792; d. 1866. She was the consort of King Christian VIII of Denmark and composed piano pieces.
Ref. 177

AULIN, Laura Valborg

Swedish pianist, teacher and composer. b. Gavle, January 9, 1860; d. Orebro, January 11, 1928. She was the sister of the violinist, conductor and composer Tor Aulin. In 1873 Laura began harmony studies under Albert Rubenson. Three years later, at the Stockholm Conservatory she studied counterpoint under the same teacher and instrumentation under Herman Berens and Ludvig Norman. After receiving the Jenny Lind (q.v.) grant (1885 to 1887) she studied under Gade in Copenhagen and Godard and Massenet in Paris. She also studied composition under S.A. Lagergren and the piano under Hilda Thegerstroem and E. Bourgain in Paris. She taught the piano and music theory in Stockholm and after 1903 in Orebo.
Compositions
ORCHESTRA
Suite
CHAMBER
Two string quartets
PIANO
Sonata
Pieces
VOCAL
Herr Olof, ballad (Bar, ch and orch)
Procul este (vce, ch and orch)
Part songs (w-vces) (1895) (3 won prizes, Copenhagen)
SACRED
Christmas Hymn (mix-ch and org)
Ref. 8, 20, 44, 95, 226, 642, 646

AURELIA, Sister

18th-century German composer.
Composition
VOCAL
Wie's hergieng bey der hoechst schauervollen Exekution, welche im Monath Hornung dieses Jahrs an einigen Hundert eingesperrten Schwestern, 'und besonders an der ehrwuerdigen Mutter Anastase, die nun schon vor Gram gestorben seyn wird, in Wien vollzogen worden, song (vce and pf) (Leipzig, 1782)
Ref. 125

AURENHAMMER (Auerhammer), Josefa Barbara von (Mrs. Boesenhoenig or Bessenig)

Austrian concert pianist and composer. b. Vienna, September 25, 1758; d. Vienna, January 30, 1820. She studied the piano under Richter and the Bohemian pianist L. Kozeluh, before becoming a pupil of Mozart, who was enthusiastic about her ability and often played with her in concerts. In 1781 he dedicated six violin sonatas to her, K. 296 and K. 376-380. The piano variations on *Ah, vous dirais-je, maman*, K. 265, were not dedicated to her by Mozart but by the publisher Toricelli. She was an expert at extemporizing and varying a given theme. From the 1790s till 1813 she gave concerts at the Burg Theatre in Vienna. She occasionally appeared in concert with her daughter Marianne Auenheim (q.v.). DISCOGRAPHY.
Compositions
CHAMBER
Sonata (vln and pf)
HARPSICHORD
Six minuets
Six variations (ded Countess Rumbeke)
PIANO
Duo varie (4 hands)
Sei Variazioni sopra la contradanza del ballo intitolato La figlia mal custodita (also hpcd) (S. Vigano) (Vienna: Artaria and Co., 1794)
Sei variations on Der Vogelfaenger bin ich ja (Mozart) Offenbach: Johan, Andre and Artaria)
Sei variazioni per il fortepiano (Vienna: Tranquillo Mollo and Co.)
Six variations on Nel cor piu from La molinara (Paisello) (Leipzig: B.and H., 1790)
Six variations sur un thème hongrois pour le piano-forte (Vienna: Chemische Druckerey)
Ten variations on A. Salieri dediées à Madame la Baronne de Braun, op. 63 (Vienna: Hoftheater Musik Verlag, 1799)
Ten variations on the theme of the ballet Les folies amoureuses
Two sonatas
Variations on a march from Deux journées (Cherubini) (Vienna Cappi, 1803)
Variations pour le piano-forte, dediées à Madame la Comtesse de Migazzi, née Comtesse de Thuerheim (Vienna: Ludwig Maisch)
VOCAL
Six German songs (vce and pf) (Vienna: L. Lausch, 1790)
Ref. 15, 85, 102, 125, 129, 155, 200, 226, 269, 347, 563

AUS DER OHE, Adele. See OHE, Adele aus der

AUSPITZ-KOLAR, Augusta

Bohemian concert pianist and composer. b. Prague, March 19, 1844; d. Vienna or Prague, August 23, 1878. She was the daughter of the actor and dramatic poet J. Georg Kolar and the actress Anna Kolar. She showed remarkable musical talent in her early years and became a pupil of Bedrich Smetana and later Joseph Proksch. In 1862 she went to Paris to study under Mme. Clauss-Szarvady. There she began her concert career as a virtuoso pianist, which took her all over Europe.
Compositions
PIANO
Concert etude, op. 4
Dans le forêt, op. 6
Etudes
Scherzo fantastique, op. 2
Tarantella, op. 1
Waldstueck, op. 5
VOCAL
Songs
Ref. 70, 129, 238, 276, 347, 433

AUSTEN, Augusta Amherst (Mrs T. Anstey Guthrie)

English organist and composer. b. London, August 2, 1827: d. Glasgow, August 5, 1877. She studied at the Royal Academy of Music. She was

organist at Ealing Church from 1844 to 1848 and then at Paddington Chapel. She composed hymns.
Ref. 6, 85, 276, 347

AUSTER, Lydia Martinovna

Soviet-Estonian, pianist, editor and composer. b. Petropavlovsk, Northern Kazakhstan, May 30, 1912. She studied the piano and composition under M.N. Nevitov at the Omsk Technical School of Music, graduating in 1931. She continued her studies in composition from 1931 to 1935 at the Leningrad Conservatory under M. Yudin and then V. Shebalin at the Moscow Conservatory. After her graduation in 1938 she became musical editor for Turkmen Radio and completed a postgraduate course in composition under V. Shebalin in 1945. In 1949 she was appointed music supervisor of the Estonian Television and Radio Committee. She was head of the Musical Foundation of the Union of Composers of the Estonian SSR. In 1955 she was awarded the title of Merited Artist of the Estonian SSR. DISCOGRAPHY. PHOTOGRAPH.

Compositions

ORCHESTRA
- Lyrical concertino (vln and orch) (1972)
- Piano concerto (1952)
- Violin concerto (1966)
- Estonia, symphonic poem (1945)
- Estonian suite (1948)
- Fantasia Estonia, overture (1945)
- Festive prologue (sym orch) (1976)
- Four Russian folk tunes (1940)
- Glory to Soviet Estonia, overture (1950)
- Music for string orchestra (1973)
- Two pieces (str orch) (1974)

CHAMBER
- Pieces (Russian and Turkmen folk inst ens) (1937-1943)
- Prelude and fugue (wind qrt) (1936)
- Suite on Estonian themes (wind qrt) (1945)
- Three string quartets (1937, 1939, 1945)
- Pieces (vln and pf)

PIANO
- Suite (2 pf) (1947) (1947)
- Lento (duet)
- Spring preludes (1950)
- Three dances (1939)

VOCAL
- Anchar, cantata (Pushkin) (1937)
- The First Day of Peace, cantata (S, mix-ch and orch) (1957)
- Laulad, cantata (1960)
- Four pieces (mix-ch and orch of Turkmen insts) (1941-1943)
- Autumn in Tallinn
- Romances (Yesenin, Lermontov and Soviet poets)
- Mass songs

BALLET
- Nochnaya molotba (1967)
- Romeo, Julietta i tma (1969) (1970)
- Severni son, children's ballet (1960) (1960)
- Tiina (1955) (1955)

OPERA
- Maiskoye utro, in 1 act (1970) (1970)

INCIDENTAL MUSIC
- Children's plays (1947-1950)

Ref. composer, 17, 21, 63, 85, 87, 223, 330, 465, 563

AUSTIN (Austin-Banner), Dorothea

American assistant professor and composer. b. Vienna, July 22, 1922. She was educated at the Vienna Conservatory of Music on a scholarship and at the Royal College of Music, London. She became an A.R.C.M. (performer) in 1941 and L.R.A.M. (teacher) in 1946. At Queens College she received an M.A. (composition) in 1969. She was invited to investigate the compositional possibilities of a new electronic instrument, the timbron. She was assistant professor of music at Queensborough Community College. PHOTOGRAPH.

Compositions

CHAMBER
- Cantore (wind qrt) (1968)
- Opus 1-1/2 (wind qrt) (1969)
- Reflections (wind qrt) (1969)
- Monody (fl) (1968)

PIANO
- Excursion in tritones (1966)
- Images (1966)
- Major 3rds, Minor 3rds (1966)

VOCAL
- The lad I used to be (Thomas Jones Jr.) (ch a-cap) (1967)
- This is my letter to the world (Emily Dickinson) (ch a-cap) (1967)
- Heart of hearts
- Music
- Song cycle (vce and pf) (1966)
- The tranquil blossoms
- True love

ELECTRONIC
- Flowers too (pf and tape) (1971)
- Transformation (vla d'amore, pf and tape) (1973)
- Van Diemen's land (vce, pf, wind, banjo and timbron) (1976)

Ref. composer, 137, 206

AUSTIN, Grace Leadenham

20th-century American pianist and composer. She studied the piano at the Virgil Piano Conservatory, New York and under private teachers; voice under Oscar Saenger and Romano Romani and composition under William Reddick and Dr. M. Richardson.

Compositions

VOCAL
- At eventime (ch) (1935)
- Let us sing a new song (ch) (1974)
- O whistle a song (ch) (1934)
- Rain at night (w-ch and pf) (1934) (J. Fisher and Bros.)
- Songs incl.:
- The old white goose (1947)
- The silver dream ship (1946)
- The sleeping swan (1941)
- Your tears (1940)

Ref. 190, 347, 496

AUSTIN-BANNER, Dorothea. See AUSTIN, Dorothea

AUTENRIETH, Helma

German pianist, teacher and composer. b. Frankfurt, December 6, 1896. Her father was Dr. Carl Scheussner, who together with W. Roentgen invented the first X-ray photographic plate. She studied the piano and composition at the Hochsches Conservatory, Frankfurt from 1914 to 1918, her composition teacher being Bernhard Sekles. Her first public success was *Variations on an Original Theme* in 1918. In 1923 she became a piano teacher at the Music School in Mannheim. The war years and marriage intervened until, at the age of 70, encouraged by her son-in-law, she performed her *Piano Suite*, with so much success that she resumed composing. Professor Richard Langs performed her later compositions. DISCOGRAPHY.

Compositions

ORCHESTRA
- Sinfonietta mit dem Trauermarsch (str orch) (1968)

CHAMBER
- Sonata (2 vlc and pf) (Glockensonate) (1969)

PIANO
- Variations on an original theme (2 pf) (1918)
- Klaviersonate (1968)
- Suite (1951)
- Works for children

VOCAL
- Songs (S and strs)

INCIDENTAL MUSIC
- Works for the stage (1955)

Ref. composer, 563

AUZEPY, Michele

French composer. b. 1931. She composed music for films and television and songs.
Ref. composer

AVAZARALA

20th-century Indian composer of light and folk music.
Ref. 414

AVETISIAN, Aida Konstantinovna

Soviet choral conductor, teacher and composer. b. Erivan, April 7, 1932. She studied under E.M. Mirzoyan at the Erivan Conservatory, graduating in 1955. After 1956 she taught composition and theoretical subjects and conducted choirs at the Korovakan Music School.

Compositions

ORCHESTRA

Piano concerto (1955)
Violin concerto (1968)
Exprompt (cham orch)

CHAMBER

Razmyshlenie, romance (vlc and pf)
Sonata (vln and pf) (1952)

PIANO

Pieces for youth (1971)
Preludes
Sonata (1959)
Variations

VOCAL

Nasha partiya (with M. Isakovsky) (ch and orch) (1970)
Choral works
Romances and songs

Ref. 21, 223

AVRIL, Mireille

20th-century composer.

Composition

SACRED

Messe de requiem (soloists, mix-ch, org and orch) (BMI)

Ref. 403

AXTENS, Florence

20th-century British composer. b. London. She emigrated to Australia and studied aboriginal music. She composed a violin sonata, piano pieces and two sets of part songs on themes from Australian folk songs.

Ref. 85, 226, 347

AYARZA DE MORALES, Rosa Mercedes

Peruvian pianist, folklorist, singer and composer. b. Lima, July 8, 1881. She studied the piano under her aunt, Maria Beingolea and made her debut in 1889. She performed in concert and also sang with C. Rebagliati. She later dedicated herself to the collection and arrangement of folk music, promotion of shows and organisation of several zarzuelas.

Compositions

ORCHESTRA

La Penicholi

VOCAL

Pregones limenos, folk album
Folk pieces (vce and pf)

Ref. 280, 403

AYLOTT, Lydia Georgina Edith (Mrs. Thomas)

English teacher and composer. b. Finningham, Suffolk, January 28, 1936. She studied music at Weymouth College of Education. She lived in Sydney, Australia from 1959 to 1970 and taught in primary schools and after 1968 in secondary schools. She studied harmony from 1968 to 1969 under Muriel King in Sydney and composition in 1973 under Richard Arnell at Trinity College, London. She began to compose in 1967, writing mostly for school children. PHOTOGRAPH.

Compositions

CHAMBER

Piano trio

VOCAL

Songs (ch) (1967)
Three French songs

SACRED

Know the Lord, cantata (Bar, ch and ballet) (1974)
English mass (ch and org) (1973)
Fitzherbert school mass (1972)

OPERETTA

Sir Gawain and the Green Knight, for school children (1974)

Ref. composer

AYLWARD, Florence

English organist, pianist, writer and composer. b. Sussex, March 10, 1862. She began piano studies at the age of five and organ studies three years later. When she was nine, she became organist at Brede Church and continued her studies under Dr. John Abram. In 1876, she attended the Guildhall School of Music and studied the piano under Theodore Trekell, London. She made numerous appearances as an organist and pianist and was a church organist at St. Leonard's-on-Sea till 1946. She began to compose at the age of twelve. She contributed articles and stories to several periodicals.

Compositions

CHAMBER

Love's coronation (org and vln or vlc; also vce, 1897) (Chappell)

VOCAL

More than 200 songs incl.:
Beloved, it is morn (solo, ch and pf) (Chappell and Boosey)
Wake not! (mix-ch) (Chappell and Boosey)
An anthem of love (org or har ad lib) (Chappell and Boosey)
Day dawn (1888) (Chappell and Boosey)
Further on (Chappell and Boosey)
Garland of ivy (Chappell and Boosey)
Love me little, love me long (1887) (Chappell and Boosey)
My love, my crown (1899) (Chappell and Boosey)
My white rose o'Killarney (Chappell and Boosey)
Not mine to ask (org) (Chappell and Boosey)
Song of the bow (1898) (Chappell and Boosey)
The thrush to his love (1900) (Chappell and Boosey)
World of praise (org or har ad lib) (Enoch and Sons)

INCIDENTAL MUSIC

Hospital blues, play
Lessons in love, play
Narcissus, play
Pearl of the night, play
Vassilissa the fair, play

Ref. 433, 467, 496

AYLWIN, Josephine Crew

20th-century American composer.

Composition

OPERA

The Strike, comic opera (San Francisco, 1919)

Ref. 431

AZADA. See AZADE

AZADE (Azada)

Greek harpist and songstress. Persia, ca. 430. She was the beloved of Bahram Gur, Sassanid king, A.D. 420-438, who was famous for his love of music and singers. Azade is portrayed on a 13th-century plate hunting with Bahram Gur on a camel. He aims an arrow and she carries her harp. The picture refers to a legend in which he takes her out hunting and ends by throwing her off the camel and trampling her to death.

Ref. 305

AZALAIS D'ALTIER (Alazais d'Autier)

11th-century French troubadour, known only from one source, her letter to Clara d'Anduza in the St. Mark Library in Venice.

Composition

VOCAL

Tanz salutz e tantas amors (Razo No. 457)

Ref. 117, 222

AZALAIS D'AUTIER. See AZALAIS D'ALTIER

AZALAIS DE PORCAIRAGUES

French troubadour. b. Portiragnes, near Beziers, ca. 1140. She came from a distinguished family in Montpellier and loved Gui Guerajat, son of Guillaume VI. She wrote many successful songs in Gui Guerajat's honor. She sent a jongleur with one of her songs to Ermengarda of Narbonne, who reigned from 1143 to 1192. DISCOGRAPHY.

Composition

VOCAL

Ar em al freg temps ventent (narr, S, vielle, dulcimer, rebec and drum)

Ref. 117, 120, 129, 213, 220, 221, 222, 563

AZARCON, Minda
20th-century composer.
Compositions
FILM MUSIC
Insiang (1978)
Three, two, one (1975)
Ref. 497

AZZA AL-MAILA
Arabian songstress and composer. d. ca. 707. A Christian freed woman of Medina and one of the first important professional woman musicians in Islam. She was given the name Maila (Swaying) for her distinctive gait; although according to other sources, the name came from 'milaye' meaning the cloak in which she sometimes disguised herself as a man and indulged in her inclination to drink. She was taught the music of older days by Ra'iqa and later learned Persian airs from Nashit and Sa'ib Khathir and composed many songs in the Persian idiom. She accompanied herself on the mizhar (skin-bellied lute), the mi'zafa (psaltery) and the oud (wood-bellied lute) and was the first singer from Hejaz to sing in rhythmic cadences. She employed the device of rhythmic symmetry independent of the metrical structure of the verse. At the weekly concerts at her house, which attracted a large number of musicians, the greatest propriety was observed. Her influence was felt even in Mecca, but her popularity scandalized the stricter Muslims, who accused her of leading the populace into moral degeneration, since at that time music was a pleasure forbidden to Muslims. They complained of her to the governor of Medina during the reign of Caliph Mu'awiya, 661 to 680. Their complaints would probably have been upheld were it not for the intervention of the great art patron Abdallah ibn Ja'far. The singer Na'ila bint al-Maila was probably her daughter.
Ref. 170, 171, 234

BAADER-NOBS, Heidi
Swiss violinist and composer. b. Delemont, December 5, 1940. She studied the violin in her home town and then music theory and composition under Jacques Wildberger and Robert Suter at the Basle Conservatory. Her compositions are influenced by the works and theories of Pierre Boulez and Iannis Xenakis.
Compositions
ORCHESTRA
Musique (vln and cham orch) (1969)
Musique de fête (picc, brass and str orch) (1981)
Variations sur un thème connu (str orch) (comm Musikkredit der Stadt Basel, 1980)
CHAMBER
String quartet (1980)
Grande étude chromatique (3 fl) (1983)
Pièce (vla and 2 pf) (1970)
Pièce pour alto et 2 pianos (1970)
Quatre pièces (hp and fl) (1966)
PIANO
Jeux inoffensifs pour pianiste pacifique (1976)
Quatre pièces (1965)
VOCAL
Cinq histoires breves (ch a-cap) (1968)
Cinq pièces (S, fl, cl, vib and hp) (1967)
Lamento y protesto (16 vces a-cap) (1985) (comm Pro Helvetia fuer Basler Madrigalisten)
ELECTRONIC
Pièce (fl, elec org, gtr, d-b and perc) (1967)
Ref. composer, 651

BABAYEVA, Seda Grigorievna
Soviet lecturer and composer. b. Ashkhabad, June 1, 1922. She studied composition under G.A. Musheli at the Tashkent Conservatory, graduating in 1950. After 1964 she lectured on theoretical subjects at the same conservatory and then became a director of Uzbek radio and television.
Compositions
ORCHESTRA
Suite (1948)
CHAMBER
Pieces for violin and piano and cello and piano
PIANO
Eight preludes
Sonatina (1946)
VOCAL
Pesni pro kuiptsa Kalashnikova (Lermontov) (vce and pf) (1944)
Romances (Pushkin, Lermontov and Uzbek poets)
OPERA
Zarema, based on Bakhchisaraiski Fontan by Pushkin (1968)
THEATRE
Light stage works
Music for spectacles
Ref. 21

BABITS, Linda
American pianist, teacher and composer. b. New York, July 28, 1940. She graduated from the Manhattan School of Music with a B.Mus. and won a scholarship to study with Roger Sessions at the Oberlin Conservatory. She has been a guest pianist with symphony orchestras and teaches the piano.
Compositions
ORCHESTRA
Western Star, piano concerto
Clinton Corner Delancey
ELECTRONIC
Vocalise (vce and tape) (1964)
Ref. 39, 142

BABNIGG (Mampe-Babnigg), Emma
German singer, teacher and composer. b. Dresden, ca. 1820. She was the daughter of the tenor Anton Babnigg, who trained her as a singer. Her fame on the stage in Hamburg and Breslau earned her the nickname 'Silesian Nightingale'. While working at the Breslau Town Theatre she married the director Dr. Mampe and left the stage, but still sang frequently in concerts and music festivals. She taught singing in Breslau.
Compositions
VOCAL
Three songs, op. 6: Die Traene; Wie Mondschein so golden; Trockene Traenen (Schuberth, Jr.)
Three songs, op. 7 (Ries und Erler)
Two songs, op. 3: Keine Antwort; Botschaft (Ruhle)
Two songs, op. 4: Sie haben dir viel erzaehlt; Bleib bei mir (Ruhle)
Other songs, ops. 1 and 2
Ref. 129, 297

BACEWICZ, Grażyna
Polish pianist, violinist, concert mistress, lecturer, writer and composer. b. Lodz, February 5, 1909; d. Warsaw, January 17, 1969. Music was cultivated in her parents' home and the Bacewicz family quartet enjoyed much popularity among friends. At the age of ten, Grażyna began her instruction in the piano and the violin at the conservatory in Lodz. At the Warsaw Conservatory she studied composition under Kazimierz Sikorski, the violin under Jozef Jarzebski and the piano under J. Turczynski, graduating with diplomas in the violin and composition (1932). For two years she attended the University of Warsaw department of philosophy. She then went to Paris to continue her composition studies under Nadia Boulanger (q.v.) and to improve her violin technique under Carl Flesch and A. Touret. She returned to Poland to play first violin in the Polish Radio Orchestra under Grzegorz Fitelberg and before World War II she was already known as a brilliant violinist and promising composer in France, Spain, the Baltic States, the USSR, Czechoslovakia, Rumania, Hungary and her own country. In 1955, at the peak of her career as a violinist, she left the concert stage to devote herself to composition. She had already achieved recognition as a composer with her *String Concerto* which used the style of concerto grosso without sacrificing any of the contemporary characteristics of the composer. Grażyna wrote works in almost all the existing forms and her life's work was impressive in quantity and diversity; yet attempts to label her work or divide it into periods have not succeeded. She was drawn to serial technique not as a capitulation to a new trend, nor as an attempt to rejuvenate her music, but because she expected to learn a new vigor of form from it. She enlarged her composing technique with new elements, but discarded what she considered routine. The compositions of her last years show that she was able to adapt and synthesize new elements without losing her individuality. Grażyna taught harmony and counterpoint at Lodz Conservatory from 1934 to 1935 and in 1945 and composition at the State Academy in Warsaw from 1966 till her death and for many years was vice-president of the Union of Polish Composers. She received numerous awards including: Prize Musician of the City of Warsaw for artistic activity in 1949; three State awards for artistic accomplishment in 1950, 1952 and 1962; first prize at the Liege competition in 1951 and 1956; first prize at the Festival of Polish Music in 1951; two prizes of the Ministry of Culture and Arts in 1955 and 1962; distinction from the Tribune Internationale des Compositeurs UNESCO, in 1960; the annual award of the Union of Polish Composers in 1960; award of the Committee for Radio and Television Affairs in 1960 and a prize from the Belgian Government and a gold medal in 1965. In 1966 she won an award in Belgium for her *Violin Concerto No. 7*. She was twice decorated with an Order of Poland's Revival, from 1953 to 1955 and twice with an Order of the Banner of Labour, 1949 to 1959. She was a member of the juries during musical competitions in Poland (she was twice chairlady of the jury of the Henryk Wieniawski International violin competition, Poznan) and in Paris, Liege, Moscow, Naples and Budapest. DISCOGRAPHY. PHOTOGRAPH.
Compositions
ORCHESTRA
Symphony (1938)
Symphony No. 1 (1942-1945)

Symphony No. 2 (1951)
Symphony No. 3 (1952) (PWM, 1954)
Symphony No. 4 (1953) (PWM, 1955)
Symphony for string orchestra (1946)
Concerto (2 pf and orch) (1966) (PWM, 1968)
Concerto (pf and orch) (1949) (PWM, 1949)
Concerto (vla and orch) (1968) (Curci, 1970)
Concerto (large orch) (1962) (PWM)
Concerto No. 1 (vlc and orch) (1951) (PWM, 1972)
Concerto No. 2 (vlc and orch) (1963) (PWM, 1972)
Concerto No. 3 (vln and orch) (1948) (PWM)
Concerto No. 4 (vln and orch) (1951) (PWM)
Concerto No. 5 (vln and orch) (1954) (PWM)
Concerto No. 6 (vln and orch) (1957)
Concerto No. 7 (vln and orch) (PWM)
Easy pieces (cl and orch) (1949)
Rapsodia polska (vln and orch) (1969)
Concerto (str orch) (1948) (PWM, 1974)
Contradizione (cham orch) (Moeck, 1967) (PMW)
Convoi de joie, poem (1933)
Divertimento (str orch) (1965) (PWM, 1968)
Groteska (1949)
In una parte (1967) (PWM, 1969)
Introduction and caprice (1947)
Krakowiak (1950)
Mazur (1944)
Music (trp, perc and str orch) (1958) (PWM)
Musica sinfonica in tre movimenti (1965) (PWM, 1966)
Oberek noworoczny (also vln) (1959)
Overture (1943) (PWM, 1947)
Partita (1955) (PWM, 1959)
Pensieri notturni (1961) (PWM, 1961)
Pod strzecha, suite (1946)
Polish dance No. 2 (1948)
Polish overture (1954)
Serenade (1950)
Sinfonietta (cham orch) (1929)
Sinfonietta (1932)
Sinfonietta (str orch) (1935)
Songs for children (1959-1960)
Suite (str orch) (1931)
Suite of Polish dances (1950)
Szkice ludowe (1948)
Three caricatures (1932)
Variations (1957) (PWM, 1960)
Waltz (1949)
Ze starej muzyki, suite (1946)

CHAMBER
Incrustations (hn and cham ens) (1965) (PMW)
Piano quintet No. 1 (1952) (PMW)
Piano quintet No. 2 (1965) (PWM, 1975)
Vivat (cl and str qrt) (1950)
Wind quintet (fl, ob, cl, bsn and hn) (1932) (PMW)
Double fugue (str qrt) (1928)
Five pieces (4 fl) (1929)
Quartet for four violoncellos (1964) (PMW)
String quartet (1930, 1931)
String quartet No. 1 (1938)
String quartet No. 2 (1942)
String quartet No. 3 (1947) (PWM, 1948)
String quartet No. 4 (1950) (Liege: Tyssens, 1952)
String quartet No. 5 (1955) (PWM, 1964)
String quartet No. 6 (1960) (PWM, 1964)
String quartet No. 7 (1965) (PWM, 1965)
Andante sostenuto (vln, vlc, and org) (PWM, 1945)
Trio (ob, cl and bsn) (1948)
Trio (ob, hp and perc) (1965) (PWM, 1973)
Trio (ob, vln and vlc) (1935)
Sonata (ob and pf) (1937)
Sonata da camera No. 1 (vln and pf) (1945) (PWM, 1951)
Sonata (vln and pf) (1929)
Sonata for violin and piano No. 2 (1946)
Sonata for violin and piano No. 3 (1947) (PWM, 1950)
Sonata for violin and piano No. 4 (1949) (PWM, 1965)
Sonata for violin and piano No. 5 (1951) (PWM, 1954)
Sonatina (ob anf pf) (1955)
Andante and allegro (vln and pf) (1934)
Berceuse (vln and pf) (PWM, 1952)
Three caprices (vln and pf) (1932, 1934, 1949) (PWM, 1970)
Concertino (vln and pf) (1945) (PWM, 1969)
Dances (vln and pf (1949-1953) (PWM, 1971)
Danse masovienne (vln and pf) (1951) (PWM, 1952)
Easy pieces (vln and pf) (1950-1960)
Easy pieces (cl and pf) (1949) (PMW)
Humoreska (vln and pf) (1953) (PWM, 1959)
Legenda (vln and pf) (1945)
Lullaby (vln and pf) (1952)
Melody (vln and pf) (1949) (PWM, 1975)
Oberek (cl and pf) (1949)
Oberek No. 1 (vln and pf) (1949) (PWM, 1952)
Oberek No. 2 (vln and pf) (1951)
Partita (vln and pf) (1955) (PWM, 1957)
Une piece (vln and pf) (1931)
Piesn litewska (vln and pf) (1934)
Polish dance No. 1 (1948)
Songs (vln and pf) (1927)
Taniec antyczny (vln and pf) (1934)
Variations (vln and pf) (1934) (PMW)
Witraz (vln and pf) (1932)
Polish caprices (cl) (1952)
Esquisse (org) (1966) (PMW)
Allegro (1936)

PIANO
Adagio and fugue (1931)
Adante and allegro (1932)
Allego (1929)
Children's suite (1933) (PMW)
Four preludes (1921)
Krakowiak koncertowy (1949)
Little triptych (1965) (PMW)
March (1920)
Preludium (1928)
Preludium and fugue (1927)
Scherzo (1934)
Six concert etudes
Sonata (1930, 1935, 1938, 1942)
Sonata No. 1 (1949)
Sonata No. 2 (1953) (PWM, 1973)
Sonatina (1934)
Sonatina (1955) (PMW)
Study in thirds (1952)
Ten concert studies (1956) (PWM, 1957)
Theme and variations (1924)
Three burlesques (1935)
Three etudes (1949, 1952, 1955)
Three preludes (1941)
Toccata (1932)
Trois pièces caracteristiques (1932)
Two miniatures (1931)

VIOLIN
Quartet (1949) (PWM, 1973)
Easy duets on folk themes (2 vln) (1946) (PWM, 1968)
Suite (2 vln) (1945) (PWM, 1971)
Two caprices (1950, 1952) (PMW)
Four caprices (1968) (PMW)
Polish caprice (1949) (PMW)
Scherzo (1945)
Sonatas (1929, 1932, 1941, 1958) (PMW)

VOCAL
Cantata after the drama Acropolis by Wyspianski (mix-ch and orch) (1964)
Olympic cantata (Pindar) (mix-ch and orch) (1948)
Three songs (T and orch) (Arabic words from 10th-century, trans Polish)
Fugue (double ch; also 4 vces) (1928, 1931)
Zaloti (Adam Mickiewicz) (m-ch) (1975)
Songs:
Bell and little bells (1955) (PWM)
Here is the night (1947)
Lips and fullness (1949)
Little magpie (1956) (PWM)
My head aches (1955)
Oh, mother (1930)
Over the wide, clear water (1955)
The parting (1949)
Pink, trailing wild flowers (1929)
Speak to me, my beloved (1936)
Three roses (1934)
Trail of shadow (1949)

SACRED
De profundis, cantata (soloists, ch and orch) (1932)

OPERA
Przygoda krola Artura, comic opera (1959)

BALLET
Esik w Ostendzie (1964)
Pozadanie, in 2 acts (Desire, after Desire trapped by the tail by Picasso) (1968) (PMW)
Z chlopa krol (1953)

INCIDENTAL MUSIC
Balladyna (Slowacki) (1965)
Farfarello, radio (Stefa Zeromski) (1945)
Konrad Wallenrod (Adam Mickiewicz) (1950)

Macbeth (Shakespeare) (1960)
Mazepa (Slowacki) (1965)
Nieboska komedia (Zygmunt Krasinski) (1959)
O Janku co psom szyl buty (Juliusz Slowacki) (1945)
Sprawa (Suchowo-Kobylin) (1965)
Troilus and Cressida (Shakespeare) (1960)
Music for children's films (1957, 1959, 1960)

ARRANGEMENTS
Capriccio No. 17, transcription (Campagnoli) (vla and pf) (1950) (PWM)
Caprice No. 24, transcription (Paganini) (vln and pf) (1946)
Harnasie (Szymanowski) (pf) (1938)
Nocturne in C, transcription (Grieg) (vln and pf) (1950) (Czytelnik)
Prelude No. 1, transcription (Szymanowski) (vln and pf) (1948) (PWM)

Publications

Jerzyki albo Nie jestem ptakiem (Swifts or I'm Not a Bird). Stage skit.
Znak szczegolny (A Distinctive Mark). Short stories.

Bibliography

Maciejewsk, Boguslaw M. *G. Bacewicz.* Twelve Polish Composers. Croydon, Allegro, 1976.
Kisielewski, S. *Grażyna Bacewicz i jej czasy* (Grazyna Bacewicz and Her Time). Cracow, 1964.
Marek, Tadeusz. *Grażyna Bacewicz.* Polish Music Year IV, no.1 (12), 1969.
Rosen, Judith. *Grażyna Bacewicz - her life and works.* Polish History Series. University of Southern California, Los Angeles, 1984.
Shuttleworth, Anne. *Grażyna Bacewicz: A Stylistic Analysis.* M.Mus. Thesis. University of Witwatersrand, Johannesburg, 1986.
Thomas, Adrian. *Grażyna Bacewicz.* Polish History Series. University of Southern California, Los Angeles, 1985.

Ref. composer's sister Wanda Bacewicz, 1, 2, 4, 5, 8, 15, 17, 22, 52, 70, 74, 94, 96, 109, 118, 177, 189, 220, 258, 524, 563, 622

BACH, Maria

Austrian concert pianist and violinist, artist and composer. b. Vienna, March 11, 1896; d. Vienna, February 26, 1978. Her genealogy dates from the time of Martin Luther, when one of two Bach brothers, a Catholic, fled to Austria. The other, who became a Protestant, stayed in Germany and it is from his line that Johann Sebastian Bach descended. Maria's mother, Leonore, was a well-known oratorio soprano and concert singer in Vienna and her father, Dr. Juris Robert Freiherr von Bach, worked for the ministry until he began to concentrate seriously on his violin playing. Maria, one of four daughters, grew up in a musical atmosphere; her sister Henriette became an accomplished cello soloist who premiered a number of Maria's compositions. Maria began her career at the age of six when she attended the Grimm Piano School, Baden. Here she won five of the school's established prizes. At the age of ten she gave her first concert. In 1910 she was sent to study the violin under Arnold Rose but returned to the piano in 1912 when she studied under Paul de Conne, a renowned piano virtuoso and teacher. At the age of 19 she wrote a piano grotesque *Flohtanz* which attracted the attention of the critic Dr. Julian Korngold. She then went to study composition under Josef Marx in 1919 and instrumentation under the conductor Ivan Boutnikoff. She made her first impact in Vienna, with her *Narrenlied* in 1924. In 1962 she won the Premio Internationale para Compositores Buenos Aires, receiving a gold medal and a first class diploma for her *String Quartet No. 1* in 1935. She set to music the poems of Hesse, Rilke, Rimbaud, Nietzsche and others. She was also a collage artist whose works were exhibited in Austria and Italy. L. Doblinger of Vienna published most of her works.

Compositions

ORCHESTRA
Piano concerto
Giacona und Tanz (1941)
Marcia funebra (perc and wind orch) (1968)
Silhouetten, symphonic suite (1938)
Vier orchesterstuecke (1941)

CHAMBER
Piano quintet (1930)
String quintet (1936)
Piano quartet (1936)
String quartet No. 1 (1935) (gold medal, first class diploma)
String quartet No. 2 (1937)
Klagegebet (vlc and pf) (1932)
Sonata (vlc and pf) (1924)
Sonata (vlc) (1922)

PIANO
Capriccio (1930)
Caravelle (1957)
Etude (1930)
Flohtanz (1929)
Glockenspiel (1957)
Heimweh (1929)
Holztanz (1957)
Idylle (1930)
Sequedilla (1944)
Sirenen (1944)

VOCAL
Arabische Naèchte (deep vce and orch) (1934)
Acht Orchesterlieder (S or T and orch) (1952)
Altdeutsche Lieder (S, Bar and str orch) (1969)
Drei Orchesterlieder (Hamsun, Werfel, Wildgans) (T and orch) (1929)
Drei Orchesterlieder (F. Nietzsche) (B and orch) (1963)
Drei Ritornelle (4 vces and vln or ch and orch) (1932)
Stratosfera (ch and orch) (1939)
Vier Hafislieder (T and orch) (1940)
Drei Orchesterlieder (Franz Csokor) (B) (1962)
Narrenlied (1924)
Japanischer Fruehling (T or S) (1930)
Songs

SACRED
An den Gekreuzigten, cantata (anon) (S, B and orch) (1967)
Das Marienleben (S, B, strs and orch) (1952)

BALLET
Bengele, ballet pantomime (1937)
Suite (1935)

Ref. composer, 70, 96, 105, 194, 206, 622

BACH, Maria Barbara

German songwriter. b. 1684; d. 1720.
Ref. 465

BACHE, Constance

English writer and composer. b. Edgbaston, March 11, 1846; d. Montreux, Switzerland, June 28, 1903. She composed songs.
Ref. 85, 347

BACHELLER, Mildred R. Thomas

American teacher and composer. b. Richmond, IN, January 10, 1911. She obtained her B.A. from Earlham College and M.Mus.Ed. from the University of Michigan. She studied composition under Eric DeLamarter and Cecil Burleigh and taught stringed instruments for 39 years. She was orchestra director of the Year, Michigan Band and Orchestra Association and String Teacher of the Year, Michigan String Teachers' Association (1971).

Compositions

ORCHESTRA
Suite for string orchestra (1947)

VOCAL
Nocturne (D.J. Hayes) (mix-ch a-cap) (1944)

Ref. 347, 395

BACHMANN, Charlotte Caroline Wilhelmine (nee Stowe)

German harpsichordist, singer and composer. b. Berlin, November 2, 1757; d. Berlin, August 19, 1817. The daughter of the chamber musician, W.H. Stowe, she married another chamber musician Karl Ludwig Bachmann in 1785. She was one of the first members of the Berlin Sing-Akademie, founded in 1791 and one of the great virtuoso harpsichord players of Berlin. She instituted annual performances of Graun's *Death of Jesus* on Good Friday from 1797 to 1806.

Compositions

VOCAL
Songs incl.:
Maedchen, wenn dein Lacheln winket (Rellstab)

Bibliography

Erinnerungen an C.K.W. Bachmann. Hartung und Klipfel.

Ref. 8, 26, 105, 121, 128, 347, 622

BACHMANN, Elise

German pianist and composer. b. Naumberg, May 23, 1838. She studied music under G.C. Lobe in Leipzig, where she achieved fame as a pianist. Her compositions enjoyed much popularity in her time.

Compositions

CHAMBER
Piano pieces

OPERA
Die Macht der Musik, op. 30 (Bay)

Ref. 105, 226

BACHMANN, Judith
17th-century Austrian pianist and composer from Vienna. She composed numerous organ fugues.
Ref. 226, 347

BACHMAN, Virginia Catherine. See KENDRIK, Virginia Catherine

BACKER-GROENDAHL (Groendahl), Agathe Ursula
Norwegian pianist, teacher and composer. b. Holmestrand, December 1, 1847; d. Ormoen, near Oslo, June 4, 1907. She was the most important Scandinavian woman composer of her time. She had her first music lessons from a Miss W. in Christiania and then studied the piano under Otto Winter-Hjelm and Halfdan Kjerulf and music theory under L.M. Lindeman. She continued her piano studies in Berlin under T. Kullak from 1865 to 1867 and composition under Wuerst. For a short time she was also a pupil of Hans von Buelow in Florence, who spoke very highly of her and of Liszt in Weimar from 1871 to 1873. She made her concert debut in Oslo at the age of 17 and eventually toured all over Europe. In 1875 she married O.A. Groendahl, a singing teacher, conductor and composer and had two sons - Anders, who became a music publisher and Fridtjof, a pianist and composer. She received the Literis et Artibus award in 1885 and exerted great influence as a teacher. Unfortunately she lost her hearing later in life. DISCOGRAPHY. PHOTOGRAPH.
Compositions
ORCHESTRA
Andante (pf and orch)
Scherzo
PIANO
Etudes de concert, ops. 11, 22, 32, 47, 57 and 58 (1881-1903)
Fantasistykker, ops. 36, 39, 45 and 55
Klaverstykker, ops. 15, 25, 35, 53 and 59
Menuet
Prelude et grand menuet, op. 61 (1904)
Romance
Serenade, op. 21
Skizzer, op. 19
Suite in 5 movements, op. 20
Toccata
Tre ungarske studier, op. 38
In the blue mountains, suite
VOCAL
Songs for voice and piano in Norwegian, Swedish and German, incl.:
Ahasverus: 6 sange, op. 56 (Warmuth)
Barnets vaardag, sangcyclus, op. 42 (Hals)
Blomstervignetter, op. 23 (Warmuth)
Chant des noces, op. 28 (Warmuth)
Norwegian folk songs, op. 18
Norwegian folk songs, op. 34 (Warmuth)
Sange ved havet, op. 17 (Norske Musikforlag)
Sommer, op. 50, cycle (S.) (Hals)
Stig Ribbing
Tre sange, op. 1: En Bon; Gud give, Til min hjertes dronning (Hansen)
Fem sange, op. 2: Agnes, min deilige sommerfugl; Naar Bolgen; I skovens hoisale; Longsel; Jeg ser dig (Hansen)
Two duets, op. 40 (S and Bar)
Tolv folkeviser paa melodier fra fremmede lande, op. 51 (Warmuth)
Ti Sange til digte af Vilhelm Krag, op. 31 (Hals)
ARRANGEMENTS
Norwegian folk songs and dances, op. 30 (pf)
Bibliography
Sandvik, O.M. *Agathe og O.A. Groendahl*. Oslo, 1948.
Ref. 2, 8, 15, 17, 20, 22, 23, 26, 44, 63, 67, 74, 86, 95, 105, 113, 132, 140, 177, 226, 276, 297, 361, 398, 563, 622

BACKER-GRØNDAHL, Agathe. See BACKER-GROENDAHL, Agathe

BACKES, Lotte
German organist, pianist and composer. b. Cologne, May 21, 1901. She was given her first music lessons by her mother, who came from a musical family and had herself written some minor compositions. Later she attended the conservatories in Strasbourg and Duesseldorf, where she studied the piano and the organ. Her earliest compositions; songs and piano pieces, drew the attention of various radio stations and she was given a bursary for further study at the Academy of Arts in Berlin, where she became a pupil of Georg Schumann and Max Trapp. During the war, her compositions were destroyed, but after 1947 she produced chamber music, piano and organ works, oratorios and songs. DISCOGRAPHY.
Compositions
ORCHESTRA
Sommerliche Wanderung (1947)
Symphonic poems
CHAMBER
Walk in the summer (fl, ob, vln, vlc, perc, hp and cel)
Sprazzo di luce (inst qrt, hp and perc) (1974)
Reisebilder (str qrt) (1980)
Ballade (fl, hp and pf) (1974)
Concertante (vlc and pf) (1966)
Concerto (vln and org) (1970)
Episodio (trp and org) (1972)
Movimenti improvisati (hp and perc) (1973)
Serenata (vln and hp) (1965)
Sonata (trp and org) (1972)
Sonata I (vln and org) (1972)
Spielmusik (ob and pf) (1958)
Intermezzo (hp) (1972)
Pieces (vlc)
ORGAN
Capriccio (1959-1960)
Dein Lob Herr, partita (1970)
Erschienen ist der herrliche Tag, partita (1961)
Impressioni divertimenti (1980)
Improvisation (1959-1960)
Introduction and passacaglia (1962)
Marche nuptiale (1967)
Meditationen (1959-1960)
Mysterium Dei: Cyprus meditation (Heinrichshofen, 1978)
Organ Fantasie No. 1 (Chromatische Fantasie) (1958), No. 2 (1963), No. 3 (1964)
Praeludium and Toccata 1 in E (1945)
Reminisci in perpetuum
Toccata II (1960)
Toccata III (1963)
Toccata ritmica (1970)
Veni Creator (1959-1960)
Wie mein Gott will ......, partita (1969)
PIANO
Concertino (2 pf)
Fantasie (1958)
Impressionen (1956)
Konzertstueck (1953)
Laendliche Miniaturen (1948)
Suite (1947)
Three pieces
VOCAL
Blume, Baum, Vogel (Hesse) (m-ch) (1958)
Das Lied vom Sturmvogel (Gorky) (m-ch) (1951)
Die Liebenden (soloists and ch) (1947)
Hymne und Wiederkehr (T, ch and wind insts) (1950)
Over 30 songs
SACRED
Die letzte Vision, oratorio (speaker, soloists, mix-ch, and org) (1953)
Ave Maria gratia plena (ch a-cap) (1950-1951)
Domus mea (ch a-cap) (1950-1951)
Five motets (4 part ch a-cap)
Messe (ch) (1947)
O sacrum Convivium (ch a-cap) (1950-1951)
O salutaris (ch a-cap) (1950-1951)
Psalm 24 (mix-ch and org) (1949)
Psalm 47 (w-ch and org) (1953)
Psalm 100 (w-ch and org) (1957)
Requiem (ch) (1949)
Te Deum (ch) (1948)
Ad Te, Domine (vce and org) (1952)
Confiteor tibi Domine (vce and org) (1952)
Cantiones sacrae (vce and org) (1962)
De ascencione Domini (1961)
De invocatione Spiritus Sancti (1968) (Wilhelmshaven: Heinrichshofen/Sirius, 1973)
Der Gerechte freut sich (1958-1959)
Die Himmel ruehmen (1958-1959)
Et repleti sunt omnes Spiritu Sancto (1963)
In sacratissima nocte (1967)
In tempore adventus (1967)
Et spiritus Dei ferabatur super aquas (1963)
Laudate Dominum (vce and org) (1952)
Psalm 8 (vce and org) (1960)
Psalm 67 (vce and org) (1961)
Tulerunt Jesum
Voll der Barmherzigkeit (1958-1959)
Ref. composer, 70, 105, 200, 226, 236, 563

BACON, Viola Ruth Orcutt

American pianist, lecturer and composer. b. Gillespie, IL, January 29, 1900. She was educated at the Kroeger School of Music (artist's diploma, 1916). The Forest Park College for Women (B.Mus., 1921), the Chicago Music College (M.Mus., 1928) and the University of Kansas (B.A.). She made her debut as a pianist in 1927 at the Fine Arts Recital Hall, Chicago. From 1928 to 1946 she worked at the University of Kansas Music Faculty and from 1946 to 1955 at the Punahov School of Music, Honolulu. She played with the Kansas City Philharmonic Orchestra and the Honolulu and Chicago Symphony Orchestra. She composed a number of piano pieces.
Ref. 77, 84

BADALLA, Rosa Giacinta

17th-century Italian composer. She described herself as *Monaca di S. Redegonda in Milano*. She wrote 12 motets for solo voice (Venice: G. Sala, 1684). Two unpublished secular cantatas of hers are known.
Ref. 125, 128, 653

BADARZEWSKA-BARANOWSKA, Tekla

Polish pianist and composer. b. Warsaw, 1834; d. Warsaw, September 29, 1861. She was known to her small circle as a good pianist and good luck brought her fame, at the age of 22, as the composer of *La Prière d'une vierge*. In 1859 it appeared as a supplement to the Revue et Gazette Musicale, Paris and immediately became the world's best seller, with over 140 editions and reprints, covering hundreds of thousands of copies all over Europe, the United States and Australia. Apart from two, four and eight-hand piano arrangements, it was transcribed for almost every instrument and even full orchestra. Despite its success, it was strongly criticized by such people as Louis Moreau Gottschalk, who composed a parody and invariably played it as an encore at his concerts. DISCOGRAPHY.

Compositions

PIANO

Acción de gracias (Dotesio)
Bayonne, mazourka brillant (Orpheus)
Carollings at Morn (Gordon)
Chants des vendangeurs (Ashdown)
Chough and Crow
Dance revêrie
L'Echo des bois (Schott)
Ecoutez-moi
L'Espérance (Jurgenson)
La Foi (Jurgenson)
The Ghost Melody (Augener)
Harmonies du matin (Constallat, Ricordi)
Hymn to the Virgin (companion to Maiden's Prayer) (Brainard)
Je t'ai écouté (résponse à Ecoutez-moi) (Rozsavolgyi, Costallat, Ricordi)
Lilian Mazurka (Weekes)
Magdalena, mélodie sacrée
The Maiden's Dream, revêrie (Orpheus)
Maiden's Evensong (Donajowski)
Mazurka (Andre, Bauer, Benjamin, Bote, Cranz, A. Fischer, and 29 other publishers)
Trois morceaux de salon (Schott, Mariani, Ricordi)
The orphan's prayer (Brainard, Gordon, Williams)
Prière de la mère (Gordon, Novello, Willing, Ricordi)
La prière d'une vierge, salon piece (1856) (Andre, Bachmann, Bauer, Bellman, Benjamin and 138 other publishers)
La Prière exaucée, ou Reponse de la Prière d'une vierge (Andre, Bellman, Bosworth, Bote and 37 other publishers)
Rêve d'un ange (Hansen, Lundquist)
Sailor's prayer (Donajowski)
Seconde prière d'une vierge (Ferberg)
Soldier's prayer (Donajowski)
Souvenir à ma chaumière (Rozsavoelgyi, Siegal, Joubert, Lundquist, Jurgenson)
Der traum
Vision (Hansen, Leuckard, Rozsavoelgyi, Hirsch, Jurgenson)
Beliebte stuecke (Steingraber)
Sympathie (Hansen, Schott, Ellis, Schott Frères, Guimaraes, Jurgenson)

Ref. 8, 15, 17, 20, 22, 26, 44, 70, 79, 95, 107, 118, 129, 135, 177, 276, 297, 400, 524, 563, 579, 622

BADHL

Arabian lutenist and songstress. ca. 820. She was born in Medina, brought up in Basra and became famous at the court from the time of al-Amin (809 to 813) to the time of al-Mamun (813 to 833). Her repertoire was reputed to consist of 30,000 songs and she compiled a book of 12,000 of them for Ali, the son of Hisham, from whom she received 10,000 pieces of silver. She was a pupil of Ibrahim al-Mosuli, the distinguished music theorist and of Ibn Jami. As a slave, she belonged first to Ja'far ibn al-Hadi, but after hearing her sing, Mohammed al-Amin bought her for a great sum. She accompanied herself on the lute with great skill. Once she sang a hundred songs of the same rhythmic and melodic type to the Prince Ibrahim al-Mahdi, which, although he was a connoisseur of music, he had never heard. She died during an evening's entertainment for the Caliph al-Mamun, when a barbarian from Tabaristan struck her on the head with her lute. Her pupils included Dananir al Barmakiyya and Mutayyam al-Hashimiyya (q.v.)
Ref. 170, 171, 234

BADIAN, Maya

Rumanian composer. b. Bucharest, April 18, 1945. She studied at the Ciprian Porumbescu Conservatory, Bucharest from 1962 to 1968 under Tiberiu Olah (composition), Aurel Stroe (orchestration), Zeno Vancea (counterpoint), Florin Eftimescu (harmony) and Tudor Ciortea (musical form). She is a member of the Union of Rumanian Composers and took part in the International Music Course in 1972 and the Seminary of Contemporary Music, Vicenza, Italy in 1973. DISCOGRAPHY. PHOTOGRAPH.

Compositions

ORCHESTRA

Diptych symphony
Guitar concerto
Piano concerto
Violin concerto
Sinfonietta
Symphonic movement (1968)

CHAMBER

Movimento (wind qnt)
Accents (str qrt) (1973)
Dance (str trio) (1971)
Trio (ob, cl and bsn)
Chamber music concert (cor anglais and perc)
Dialogues (trp and d-b) (1973)
Capriccio (bsn)
Harmonics (fl)
Incantation (cl)
Monodies (ob)
Monologue (vln)
Profiles (trb)
Rumanian dance (vlc)

PIANO

Sonata
Pieces (1963-1968)

VOCAL

Vers les Cîmes, poem (A. Blandiana) (S and orch) (1973)
Nous, les petits, song cycle for children (1972)

Ref. composer

BADYE, Dyeliba

20th-century composer.

Composition

FILM MUSIC

Babatu (1976)

Ref. 497

BAER, Louisa

19th-century German composer of songs.
Ref. 347

BAGA, Ena Rosina

20th-century British organist, pianist and composer. b. London.

Compositions

ORGAN

Riverside reverie

ARRANGEMENTS

For piano and organ

Ref. 490

BAGANIER, Janine (pseud. Freddie Anoka)

French pianist, violinist, authoress, poetess and composer. b. Cosemes, La Nayenne, January 16, 1924. Her father started teaching her the violin and solfege and she took piano lessons at school. She took a course in harmony under the composer Panella. She received first prize for the piano from the Paris Conservatoire. PHOTOGRAPH.

Compositions
CHAMBER
Trio (vln, vlc and pf) (1971)
Hungaria (vln and pf)
PIANO
Over 60 pieces incl.:
Les Alsaciennes
Bonne-Maman raconte (1960)
Butterflies (1968)
Les farfadets
Les feux follets (1962)
Le jardin du Paradis (1963)
Le lutin capricieux (1962)
La mort du loup (1960)
Noël sur la Steppe (1961)
Praha (1968)
La Rêve de Minouchka (1960)
La vieux route de ma Grand-mère
VOCAL
Mina, monologue
Twenty-six songs
THEATRE
Three sketches: Les Yéyés de mon coeur-yéyé; L'Ange-Demon; Mon ami l'indien
Le Prince-Avion, story
L'Histoire de canet, sketch for children
Publications
A qui la faute?'' Novel.
Twenty poems.
Ref. composer

BAGLIONCELLA, Francesca
16th-century Italian composer. b. Perugia. She wrote a large number of madrigals and secular songs.
Ref. 26, 128, 129, 335

BAHINABAI
Indian Marathi poetess and composer. b. 1629; d. 1700. She composed devotional songs.
Ref. 414

BAHMANN, Marianne Eloise (nee Schneider)
American pianist, accompanist, singer, teacher and composer. b. McKeansburg, PA, December 1, 1933. She studied at Drake University under Francis J. Pyle, obtaining her B.Mus. and M.Mus. in voice, piano and composition. She was awarded a year's Fulbright study at the Staatliche Hochschule fuer Musik, Stuttgart from 1954 to 1955. From 1957 to 1958 she did vocal and operatic study under Rose Bampton and Wilfred Pelletier. She was three times winner of the Des Moines Symphony Young Artist award (composition, voice and piano) and won the Chapel Choir competition contest for an anthem in 1961 and the Christ Church carol competition in 1978. She taught at Drake University preparatory department and the Chicago Evangelistic Institute, Oskaloosa, IA. She was an accompanist and singer in New York from 1957 to 1958 and from 1959 a free-lance performer, voice and piano teacher. From 1978 to 1982 she was music reference specialist at Stanford University library. PHOTOGRAPH.
Compositions
ORGAN
Behold, a Host (1978) (Arvon Pub. 1978)
In heavenly love abiding (1984) (Broadman Press)
Meditation for chimes (Abingdon Press, 1977)
Pastorale on Greensleeves (1970) (Broadman, 1970)
Voluntary on a theme of Tschaikovsky (1972) (Hope Publ. Co., 1972)
SACRED
Magnificat (vce and orch)
The Altar of God (mix-ch) (1961) (Carl Fischer Inc. 1962)
Christ Church carol, hymn (mix-ch) (1978)
Take my life (mix-ch) (1984) (Neil A. Kjos Music Co.)
A Service of Commitment, music and liturgy
A Setting of the Lutheran Liturgy, based on spirituals (cong, cantor and org)
Ref. 142, 625, 643

BAIKADAMOVA, Baldyrgan Bakhitzhanovna
Soviet teacher and composer. b. Alma-Ata, November 2l, 1945. She graduated in composition from the School of Arts, Kurmangazy in 1971. The following year she taught theoretical subjects at the K. Baiseitova Music School in Alma-Ata. In 1972 she occupied the chair of polyphony and analysis at the Kurmangazy School of Arts.
Compositions
ORCHESTRA
Symphony (l971)
Concertino for trumpet and orchestra (1969)
CHAMBER
Zolotoya dombra
Pieces for violin and piano and cello and piano
PIANO
Sonata (1968)
Other pieces
VOCAL
Asiatic pictures, cycle (O. Suleimanov) (vce and pf) (1965)
Vocal choreographic work (1973)
Ref. 21

BAIL, Grace Shattuck
American organist, pianist, violinist, musicologist, poetess, singer, teacher and composer. b. Cherry Creek, NY, January 17, 1898. As a small child she studied the piano and singing and first sang in public at the age of three. She later took up the violin. In 1919 she graduated from the Dana Musical Institute in Warren, OH. She also studied the violin under Michael Banner and composition under John Christopher at the Meadville College of Music and the piano, the violin and harmony at Darlington Seminary, West Chester, PA. From 1916 she taught the piano in a school as well as the piano, the organ and the violin privately. She received many awards and medals and was a member of the International Poetry Society of England. DISCOGRAPHY. PHOTOGRAPH.
Compositions
ORCHESTRA
Gypsy dance (str orch)
CHAMBER
String quartets
String trios
Organ and violin pieces
PIANO
Three Mexican waltzes
Trios, duets and solos
VOCAL
Choral pieces
Songs, incl.:
Autumn love
A bird sings in May
Brotherly love
Five little love songs
Harbour song
Hushabye
Remember to dream of Colleen
Restless wings
Sleepy song
Sweet little lotus flower
SACRED
Anthems
Four hundred and sixty five oratorios, cantatas and songs (Biblical themes)
Publications
Piano book.
Ref. composer, 142, 347, 643

BAILEY, Freda
20th-century English composer.
Compositions
PIANO
Nocturne
Rooftop ballet
Ref. 263

BAILEY, Judith Margaret
British clarinetist, pianist, conductor, lecturer and composer. b. Camborne, Cornwall, July 18, 1941. She studied composition, conducting, the clarinet and the piano at the Royal Academy of Music, London. She conducted the Petersfield Orchestra, the Southampton Concert Orchestra and the Haslemere Orchestra. She is a music lecturer for the Open University of Great Britain and taught woodwind instruments in various schools and seminars in Britain. Most of her works have been commissioned. PHOTOGRAPH.
Compositions
ORCHESTRA
Symphony No. 1, op. 21 (1980)
Symphony, No. 2, op. 24 (1982)
Concertino (cl and orch)

Penmorvah, overture (1965)
Gwaynten music (cham orch)
Sinfonietta (15 wind insts)
Trencrom
Two Hampshire pictures (1967)
CHAMBER
Concerto for ten winds (comm Southampton Orchestra, 1979)
Wind octet, op. 26 (2 ob, 2 cl, 2 bsn and 2 hn) (1983)
Septet for woodwind
Wind quintet, op. 25 (fl, ob, cl, bsn and hn) (1982)
Music for four clarinets, op. 22 (1981)
Saxophone quartet
String quartet
Three diversions for brass
Trio (vl, vla and pf) (1961)
Sonata (cl and pf) (1963)
Sonata (vlc and pf) (1963)
Sonata (vln and pf) (1962)
Three diversions (pf) (1966)
VOCAL
Seascape, op. 27 (w-vces, ww trio and str orch) (1983)
SACRED
Praise, my soul, anthem (1967)
From East to West and lighten our darkness, op. 23, anthems (mix-ch, pf or org) (1982)
INCIDENTAL MUSIC
Caucasian Chalk Circle (Brecht) (vces and brass) (1968)
Ref. composer, Donne in Musica 1982

BAILEY-APFELBECK, Marie Louise
American pianist and composer. b. Nashville, October 24, 1876; d. Minneapolis, January 12, 1927. She studied at the Leipzig Conservatory under Carl Reinecke from 1890 to 1896 and under Theodor Leschetizky and Malwine Bree in Vienna from 1896 to 1900. She made her debut at the Leipzig Gewandhaus in 1893. She toured the United States and Europe in 1900.
Compositions
PIANO
Menuet de concert
Piano fantasy on American songs
Other pieces
Ref. 70, 111, 226, 448

BAILIN, Harriett
American authoress and composer. b. Bridgeport, CT, November I, I923. She studied at the University of Connecticut and the Juilliard School of Music. She composed musicals for community theatre groups and non-profit institutions, some in collaboration with Fay Tishman (q.v.) and Elisse Boyd. She is a member of ASCAP.
Ref. 39

BAILLY, Colette
French pianist and composer. b. Lyons, August 27, 1930. She studied at the conservatoires of music in Lyons and Paris. Her piano tutor was Jeanne Loriod. Later she studied composition and dodecaphonic technique under Max Deutsch. PHOTOGRAPH.
Compositions
ORCHESTRA
Chamber symphony (1968)
Ko-hi-nhor (large orch) (comm French government, 1974)
CHAMBER
Oscillations (8 insts) (1969)
Chamber trio (1968)
Spirales (vln, fl and pf)
Piano pieces
VOCAL
Three choruses (ch a-cap) (Max Jacobs)
ELECTRONIC
Grappes (hn, vib and pf) (1970)
Six etapes (trp, perc and elec gtr)
Murs (tape) (1971)
Ultimo-tziem (tape) (1971)
Ref. composer

BAILY, Margaret Naismith Osborne
Scottish singer and composer. b. Cupar, Fife, 1878. She studied privately and at the Guildhall School of Music. She was the first singer in the British Isles to sing the role of Solveig in Grieg's *Peer Gynt*.
Compositions
VOCAL
Songs
INCIDENTAL MUSIC
Antigone (Sophocles)
Dark brown is the river (R.L. Stevenson)
The Emperor and the Galilean (Ibsen) (1924)
Hippolytus (Euripides) (1921)
Ref. 467, 490

BAILY, Mrs. James S.
I9th-century British composer of songs and two song cycles.
Ref. 465

BAINBRIDGE, Beryl
Australian composer. b. 1919.
Compositions
CHAMBER
Little suite five, op. 54 (ob, 3 rec and hpcd or 4 rec and 6 hpcd) (1969)
The rocking boat, op. 23 (vln and pf) (1957)
Romany, op. 25 (vln and pf) (1957)
Seascape, op. 55
PIANO
Dance of the crabs, op. 40 (1965)
Dawn rhapsody, op. 30 (1960)
Rondo, op. 8 (1952)
Seascape, op. 53 (1969)
The thrush in the maple tree, op. 6 (1950)
Transition sonata, op. 20 (1955)
VOCAL
David (vce and orch)
Drifting sands (vce and orch) (1957)
I've never been lonely before (vce and orch) (1956)
The secret of wisdom (vce and orch) (1956)
Way back! Bluey (vce and orch) (1956)
Above renown, op. 28 (unison ch and pf) (1960)
Fisherman's round (ch and pf) (1960-1968)
The droner's wife (vce and pf) (1969)
Fog bound (vce and pf) (1966)
Forest fire (Bar or Cont and pf) (Allans Music 1954) (also 4-part song, 1960-1968)
I called to the breeze, 2 part song (1960-1968)
Nine children's songs (1958-60)
On the river, 2 part song (1960-1968)
Song of the sea, 3 part song (1960-1968)
When all was young (Charles Kingsley) (vce and pf) (1963)
William McPhew (vce and pf) (1969)
SACRED
I dreamt I saw de Lord, op. 27 (1957)
A long way home, op. 29 (Bar or Cont and pf) (Chappell & Co. 1957)
Take my hand, spiritual (1963)
Yes, Lord, op. 26, spiritual (1957)
THEATRE
The lost ring, children's musical (B. Bainbridge) (1967)
Sparrers, children's musical (Bainbridge) (1969)
Tom and the Waterbabies, children's musical (Bainbridge) (1966)
Ref. 440, 442, 444, 446

BAINBRIDGE, Katharine
American authoress and composer. b. Basingstoke, England, June 30, 1863. She studied in Australia and at the University of South Carolina.
Compositions
VOCAL
Songs incl.:
A friend or two
Love came calling
Where the long trail winds
SACRED
Songs incl.:
God answers prayer
Keep close to God
The Lord of life
Songs of the Ten Commandments
Thanksgiving song
Ref. 39, 465

BAIRD, Edith Anna
British professor and composer. b. London, 1889. She studied under W. Harding Bonner, Katherine Bird, Mrs. A.J. Curwen, Dr. T.H. Yorke Trotter

and Frederick Moore. She was a L.R.A.M. and an A.L.A.M. and a professor at the Metropolitan Academy of Music from 1908 till 1920. She composed piano works.
Ref. 467

BAIRD, Irene
20th-century English composer.
Composition
MULTIMEDIA
Blow Spirit, theatre piece based on Eskimo legend (ch, perc, projections, lighting and tape)
Ref. 301

BAIRD, Lorine Chamberlain
20th-century American composer of piano pieces and songs.
Ref. 347

BAJEROWA (Bayerowa), Konstancje
19th-century Polish pianist, teacher and composer. She studied in Moscow, Vienna, Kiev and St. Petersburg, where she taught the piano.
Composition
PIANO
Fantasia for 2 pianos, on a theme by Dabrowski
Ref. Pigla (Warsaw), 118

BAKA-BAITZ, Irma
19th-century Hungarian composer.
Compositions
CHAMBER
Abbazia-walzer, op. 16 (gypsy orch)
Automobil-induló, op. 33 (gypsy orch)
Gyöngyvirág, op. 14, polka-mazurka (gypsy orch)
Havasi rózsa, op. 24, polka-mazurka (gypsy orch)
Margit-keringö, op. 61 (gypsy orch)
Pompeji: Elmul a hév, op. 31 (gypsy orch)
Rococo-Schnellpolka (gypsy orch)
Secessio-induló, op. 26 (gypsy orch)
PIANO
A forrás tündére, op. 20, fantasy
Arvaleanyhaj, op. 7
Aurora, op. 6 polka-mazurka
Bohéme-induló, op. 32, march
Ezer és egy éj, op. 12
Nefelejts-Csárdás, op. 21, Hungarian dance
Postillon d'amour, polka
Rózsa és pillangó, op. 19, polka
Sonnenblume, op. 43, polka-mazurka
Zephir, op. 37, French polka
VOCAL
A tenger Oh! mélységes mély tengerek (Rozsavölgyi)
Bácskai noták, 3 songs; Csillagos éj....Ah, ez az ej, op. 22; Szomorufüz árnyékában, op. 34; Vadviragok, ops. 28-30 (Rozsavölgyi)
Ref. 297

BAJON, Mlle. See LOUIS, Mme.

BAKER, Gertrude Tremblay
20th-century American composer. She composed piano and choral works and songs.
Ref. 347

BAKER, Joanne J.
American pianist, lecturer and composer. b. Kansas City, MO, October 18, 1923. She gave her first full length piano recital at the age of five. She gained her B.Mus. in 1947 and M.Mus. in 1948 from the University of Michigan. In the same year she joined the music faculty of the University of Missouri, becoming chairlady of the keyboard division in 1974. She won the Mu Phi Epsilon prize for composition in 1950 and the Standard Oil award for Outstanding Teacher of Undergraduates in 1969.
Composition
PIANO
Sonata
Ref. 643

BAKER, Mary Winder
20th-century American composer.
Composition
MISCELLANEOUS
Simfony for Frank (experimental ens) (1981)
Ref. AMC newsletter

BAKER, Maude
19th-century American composer of songs.
Ref. 465

BAKIT
Ancient Egyptian harpist and songstress at the time of Thutmosis III (1504 to 1450 B.C.) of the XVIII dynasty, New Kingdom. She is portrayed on the grave of Amenemhet, in the Theban necropolis (grave 82) together with other musicians; a man playing a long-necked three-stringed lute and a woman playing a double oboe. Bakit is shown playing a light shoulder eight-stringed harp in the shape of a ladle, which was particularly popular at the beginning of the New Kingdom. PHOTOGRAPH.
Ref. 309

BAKKE, Ruth
Norwegian organist and composer. b. Bergen, August 2, 1947. She studied at the universities of Bergen and Oslo, the Conservatory of Bergen, the University of Redlands, CA, and Washington State University, graduating with an M.A.Mus. She has given organ recitals in the United States and on radio and television in Norway. She is a member of the Society of Norwegian Composers.
Compositions
ORCHESTRA
Chromocumuli (large orch)
SYMPHONIC BAND
Passacaglia on Draumkvedet, Norwegian folk tune (1969)
CHAMBER
Into the light (vln and org) (1982)
In memoriam (pf)
ORGAN
Dette er dagen, prelude (1983)
Himlens Konge, toccata (1983)
Hjelp meg o, prelude (1983)
Praise the Lord! He is near, prelude
Sonata
VOCAL
A dance of death (S, Bar, fl, elec gtr, hp and perc) (1983)
Development (2 S, 2 A and w-ch) (1982)
Women's fight for peace (w-ch)
The girl in the elf's dance (S, fl and vln)
SACRED
Psalm 100 (mix-ch, perc and brass) (1977)
Three religious folk tunes (vce and vln) (1983-1984)
MULTIMEDIA
The break (org and slides) (1982)
Ref. NMI, 206

BAKLANOVA, Natalia
20th-century Soviet teacher and composer of Moscow.
Compositions
CHAMBER
Concertino (vln and pf)
Etudes (vln and pf)
Pieces from Soviet composers (vln and pf)
Spinning wheel, Russian folk song (Mezhdunarodnaya Kniga) (vla and pf)
Virtuoso pieces (vln and pf)
Teaching pieces (vlc and pf)
The young violinist, for beginners
Ref. 68, 277

BAL, Rosita (alt. name Rosa BAL y GAY)
20th-century Mexican composer.
Composition
PIANO
Preludio: Mexicanas
Ref. 189

BAL Y GAY, Rosa. See BAL, Rosita

BALCKE, Frida Dorothea

German pianist, choir conductor, singer, teacher and composer. b. Warsaw, July 1, 1886. In Berlin she studied harmony and composition under Reinhold Kurth, the piano under Martin Grabert and singing under Olga Bock and Arthur Barth. In 1918 she became a choral director and singing teacher in Berlin.

Compositions

VOCAL

Two lullabies (soloists, ch and org or pf)
Women's and children's choruses
Songs

SACRED

Wir haben hier keine bleibende Stadt, cantata (soloists, mix-ch, org and str orch)
Weihnachtskantate (W. Balcke) (S, mix-ch, chil-ch and org) (1926)
Christmas songs (w-ch)
Motets

Ref. 70, 111, 226

BALDACCI, Giovanna Bruna

Italian pianist, teacher and composer. b. Pistoia, November 19, 1886. She studied at the Royal Institute of Music, Florence under Del Valle del Paz and F. Boghen and composition under Cilea and Moretti. She obtained her piano teacher's diploma at the age of 15 and a year later qualified as a singing teacher. She gave piano concerts in Italy and Switzerland and contributed articles to music journals.

Compositions

PIANO

Piccoli pezzi caratteristici:
Burlesca
Gavotta
Tarantella
Tempo di mazurka

VOCAL

I mesi dell'anno, 12 choral pieces for schools
Madrigal (3 vces in old style with pf) (1st prize, Italian Lyceum, 1910)
Notte di stelle (Nando Vitali) (solo and 3 equal vces) (Florence: Mauri)
Thirty-six choral pieces (one or more vces and pf)
Songs incl.:
Apparizione
Guardami ancor
Madrigale
Pallida viola
Si vous saviez
Vecchia canzone

SACRED

Ave Benito (E. Nessi) (ch)

ARRANGEMENTS

L'anello rapito (3 vces and ch) (from Scherzo by Scarlatti)
Antologia corale, collection of 33 choral pieces from old and modern composers (Maurri)
Raccolta di solfeggi, didactic

Ref. 86, 105, 502

BALDWIN, Esther Lillian

20th-century American concert pianist, teacher and composer. b. Chicago. She studied under Dr. Francis Hemington in Chicago. She graduated from the Columbia School of Music and Art with a B.Mus. in 1946 and a D.Mus. in 195I. She became a teacher and director of the Baldwin Music Studios in Columbia, SC, in 1927 and was a concert pianist after 1946.

Compositions

PIANO

Sonata in C-Major
Sonata in D-Major

Ref. 475

BALEN, Joan

20th-century composer.

Composition

VOCAL

Liebesklange, op. 80 (S or T and orch) (1960)

Ref. 465

BALENOVIC, Draga (pseud. Sonja Goldberg)

Austrian singer, writer and composer. b. Vienna, September 12, 1947. She studied at the Wiesbaden Conservatory and has composed and written texts for radio, television and stage.

Ref. 70

BALL, Frances de Villa

American pianist, teacher and composer. b. Schenevus, NY, 1875.

Ref. 347

BALL, Ida W.

American pianist and composer. b. Dallas, AL, 1851. She was educated at the Judson College, Marion, AL. She was described as an excellent pianist and was the composer of a number of instrumental and vocal works.

Ref. 276

BALL, Rae Eleanor

Compositions

CHAMBER

Creole serenade (vln and pf)
Rufus on the Old Kent Road (vln and pf)

Ref. 63

BALLANDS, Etta

American pianist, accompanist, teacher and composer. b. London, March 29, 1899. She was a L.R.A.M. and an A.T.C. and received a D.Mus. She studied the piano and voice under Signor Boraldi amongst others. She followed a distinguished career as a pianist and accompanist to Kreisler, Kubelik, Casals and Melba in Europe, before going to Canada and the United States after the war. She ran a music school in England for 25 years and in Canada for 11 years. She composed more than 500 works, mainly for the piano.

Compositions

CHAMBER

Cello sonata
Two flute sonatas
Violin sonata
Other works for violin, flute and cello

PIANO

Sonata (2 pf)
Danse exotique
Kaleidoscope
Nineteen preludes
Rhapsodie
Signs of the zodiac
Tone poems
Etude in A-flat for left hand
Etude in A for right hand

VOCAL

Johnny Appleseed, cantata (narr, ch and pf) (1962)
Songs in English and French

SACRED

Easter cantata (Bar and mix-ch)
Other works

Ref. 374

BALLASEYUS, Virginia

American teacher and composer. b. Hollins, VA, March 14, 1893; d. Berkeley, CA, 1969. She received her early musical training from her father, the founder of the Honolulu Symphony Orchestra and she later went to the University of California. She studied under Louis Persinger, Hugo Korschak and Darius Milhaud and taught at the Merritt School in Oakland, CA, for many years. She wrote music for California Centenary productions.

Compositions

ORCHESTRA

Pieces

CHAMBER

Piano pieces

VOCAL

Songs incl.:
America's trust
California

THEATRE

Glory in the land
Gold to spare

Hola amigo, television
Mother Goose on parade, television
Song of the city
Ref. 39, 40, 142, 347

BALLIO, Hilda

19th-century Italian composer.
Compositions
VOCAL
Viver vorrei con te (E. Fattini) (Ricordi)
SACRED
Ave Maria (vce and pf) (A. Fusinato) (Ricordi)
Ref. 297

BALLOU, Esther Williamson

American pianist, professor and composer. b. Elmira, NY, July 17, 1915; d. Chichester, England, March 12, 1973. She studied at Bennington College, VT, (B.A.), Mills College, CA (M.A.) and the Juilliard School of Music, where she obtained a degree in composition under Bernard Wagenaar. She also studied privately under Otto Luening and Wallingford Riegger. Her awards included a MacDowell Fellowship, an honorary doctorate from Hood College and an ASCAP award in 1969. She taught at the Juilliard School and at a Catholic University and from 1959 to 1973 was professor of music at the American University, Washington, DC. In 1963 she achieved the distinction of being the first American composer to have a work premiered at the White House *Capriccio for Violin and Piano*, in 1963. Her papers and original manuscripts are kept in the Esther W. Ballou Memorial Collection at the American University in Washington, DC. DISCOGRAPHY.
Compositions
ORCHESTRA
Concerto (gtr and cham orch) (1964) (ACA, 1966)
Piano concerto (1964) (ACA, 1965)
Konzertstuecke (vla and orch) (1969) (ACA, 1962)
Adagio (bsn and str orch) (1960) (ACA, 1962)
Allegro (str orch) (ACA)
Beguine (forty finger beguine) (tim, perc, acdn and str orchs; also 2 pf, 4 hands; also 4 pf, 8 hands) (ACA, 1960)
Concertino, op. 1 (ob and str orch) (1953) (ACA, 1953)
In memoriam (ob and str orch) (ACA, 1962)
Intermezzo (3 trp and str orch) (ACA, 1942)
Intermezzo for orchestra (pf and str orch) (ACA, 1943)
Prelude and allegro (pf and str orch) (1951) (ACA, 1952) (also titled music for string orchestra and piano) (1957)
CHAMBER
Suite for ten winds (double wind qnt) (ACA, 1957)
Sextette for brass and piano (2 trp, 2 hn in F, 2 trb and pf); also titled brass sextette with pianoforte (ACA, 1962)
Fantasia brevis 1 (pf, ob and str trio) (1950) (also titled Fantasia brevis for oboe and strings) (ACA, 1952)
Fantasia brevis 2 (pf, ob and str qrt) (ACA, 1952)
Divertimento for string quartet (1958) (ACA, 1958)
Trio for violin, cello and piano (ACA, 1956)
Prism for string trio (1969)
Dialogues (pf, ob and gtr; also ob and gtr) (1966)
Capriccio for violin and piano (1963) (comm NFMC) (ACA, 1963)
Elegy (pf and vlc) (1968)
Lament (vlc and pf) (ACA)
A plaintive note, and a cheerful note (vlc and pf) (1951) (ACA, 1952)
Romanza (pf and vln) (1969)
Suite for violoncello and piano (1945-1951) (ACA, 1952)
ORGAN
Impromptu (1968)
Passacaglia and toccata (ACA, 1962)
PIANO
Sonata (2 pf) (New York: Merrymount Music, 1949)
Sonata No. 2 (2 pf) (ACA, 1959)
Berceuse (1946)
Blues
Brown orchids (1942)
Capriccio (1963)
Country dances (1937)
Dance suite (1937)
For Art Nagle on his birthday (1968)
Galliard (ACA, 1956)
Gigue (ACA, 1956)
Jazz theme and variations (1936)
Preludes nos. 1-5 (1939)
Quest for the dance
Sonatina (under maiden name Williamson) (ACA, 1941)
Toccata
Variations, scherzo and fugue on a theme by Lou Harrison (ACA, 1959)
Variations for Gail (1964)
VOCAL
Bag of tricks (mix-ch and pf) (1956)
O the sun comes up-up-up in the opening (2 S, A and ch) (ACA, 1966)
Bride (S and org) (1962) (ACA, 1963)
Early American portrait (S and cham ens) (also titled Five songs) (S and pf) (1961) (ACA)
A song (vce and pf) (1967)
Street scenes (S and pf) (ACA, 1960)
What if a much of a which of a wind (S, Bar, B and ww qnt) (ACA, 1959)
5-4-3 (e.e. cummings) (vce and hp) (ACA, 1966)
SACRED
Beatitudes (ch, mix-ch and org) (1953) (ACA)
Hear us! (mix-ch and org; also mix-ch and brass; also soloists and mix-ch) (1969)
May the words (mix-ch a-cap) (ACA, 1967)
INCIDENTAL MUSIC
A passing word (Yeats) (ob, vlc and pf) (1960)
Tree of Sins (vce and pf)
TEACHING WORKS
Eleven piano pieces (ACA, 1962)
Ref. 22, 52, 94, 138, 142, 190, 195, 228, 322, 347, 371, 477, 563, 622

BALSHONE (Balshone-Becze), Cathy S.

American pianist, librarian, teacher and composer. b. Columbus, OH, April 1, 1946. She received her B.A. from the Sarah Lawrence College in 1968, having studied composition under Meyer Kupferman. She studied school library service at the Columbia University, MS, in 1970 and kindergarten music with Minuetta Kessler (q.v.), receiving her certificate in 1970. She held several librarian and curator posts and taught instrumental music in a school and the piano privately. She received the Sarah Parker Award from the American Symphony Orchestra League, 1976.
Compositions
VOCAL
Androcles and the Lion, cabaret song (1967)
BALLET
Nikstlitslepmur (1967)
OPERA
Echo and Narcissus (1968)
MISCELLANEOUS
Eleanor (Benjamin Balshone) (1982) (Ohio State University)
For You (jazz trio) (1982) (Hyatt Regency)
Sarah Lawrence College: Invitation to a Concert (1974) (Broward Co.)
Ref. 625

BALSHONE-BECZE, Cathy S. See BALSONE, Cathy S.

BALTEIRA, Maria Perez. See PEREZ, Maria

BALTHASAR, Florence

French composer. b. 1844.
Compositions
ORCHESTRA
Concerto (vln and orch) (Schott)
CHAMBER
Aimer, melodie (vln, pf, org and vlc ad lib) (Heugel)
Romance (vln and pf) (Schott)
PIANO
Badinage, romance no. 2 (Katto)
Berceuse (Heugel)
Ne parle pas, melodie (Heugel)
Si l'amour prenait racine, melodie (Heugel)
SACRED
Cantique au Saint-Sacrement (B, m-S and org or orch)
A Jesus, short canticle (1 or 2 vces ad lib and org or orch)
Messe breve (3 equal vces, ch and org or pf or orch)
Pater noster (ch and org or orch ad lib)
Quid retribuam, psalm (S, T, 3 equal vces and org or orch)
Tantum et genitori (3 equal vces and org or orch ad lib; also 2 equal vces and org or orch; also 3 equal vces; also 5 mix-vces and org or orch)
Adeste (vce and ch ad lib) (Schott-Freres)
Au Saint-Coeur de Marie (vce or unison ch)
Ave Maris Stella (T, S and ch ad lib)
Du beau nom de Marie (vce or unison ch)
O Filii (B and ch)
A Marie, canticle
Au Sacre Coeur, canticle
Ave Verum (org)

Chants sacres, collection of 25 religious pieces (solo or vces)
Ecce quam bonum (2 equal vces with T and S)
Jesus Salvator (B, Cont, vlc or org)
Lacrymosa (Katto) (B and org)
Mater misericordiae (B and m-S)
O Salutaris (B or Cont and vlc ad lib)
Tota pulchra (B and Cont)
BALLET
Berceuse du ballet, La Vision d'Harry
Ref. 297

BALUTET, Marguerite
20th-century French composer.
Compositions
CHAMBER
Ave Maria (org or pf, vlc and har)
Rhapsodie, op. 10 (vln and pf) (Loret)
Sonata in G-Minor (pf and vlc or vln) (Baudoux, 1897)
PIANO
Première joie (4 hands) (Loret)
Rose, valse (4 hands) (Evette)
Suite caractéristique (2 pf) (Noel)
Après la Moisson (Evette)
Boutons d'or (Demets)
Cinq pensées musicales (Demets)
Entrée triomphale (Evette)
Etoiles filantes (Hamelle)
Impromptu fantaisie (Baudoux)
Pastorale (Baudoux)
Prélude et bourrée (Baudoux)
Première mazurka (Loret)
Scabieuse (Demets)
Souffrance, op. 27 (Hamelle)
Vingt-quatre feuilles d'album, op. 15 (Bourlant)
Ref. 41, 297

BAMBERGER, Regina
German composer.
Composition
PIANO
Vier Klavierstuecke (Leipzig: Breitkopf)
Ref. Frau und Musik

BAMPTON, Ruth
American organist, choir conductor, professor and composer. b. Boston, MA, March 7, 1902. From the New England Conservatory of Music she obtained a diploma with advanced honors in 1927. In 1931 she attended Boston University (B.Mus.) and in 1933 the Union Theological Seminary, from which she obtained a master of sacred music. She studied at the Eastman School of Music and was a pupil of Nadia Boulanger (q.v.) and Marcel Dupre in Paris in 1928 and 1930. She taught at Vermont College from 1928 to 1930 and was an associate professor of music at Beaver College, Glenside, from 1935 to 1943 and director of music at the Polytechnic School, Pasadena from 1943 to 1964. From 1928 she was an organist and choir conductor and is a member of the American Guild of Organists. She contributed articles to various musical journals and published about 100 works.
Compositions
CHAMBER
Blow golden trumpets (1946)
Piano pieces
VOCAL
Come and play (1948)
In honor of Mother (vce and keyboard) (H.W. Gray Co.)
Singing for fun (1947)
Choral works (mix-ch and w-ch)
Songs
SACRED
A Celtic prayer (S, A, Bar and pf or org) (H.W. Gray)
A Christmas antiphony (S, Bar and pf) (H.W. Gray)
Homage to the Christ Child (1938)
Songs of Bethlehem (1949)
Choral responses (1949)
Anthems
INCIDENTAL MUSIC
Children's plays incl.:
The magic handbill (Vivian Young) (1950)
The miracle of Jean the juggler (V. Young) (1949)
The selfish giant (V. Young) (1948)
MISCELLANEOUS
Life has loveliness to sell (1949)
Lullaby (1948)
Ref. composer, 142, 190, 359, 496

BANAN
Arabian songstress at the court of al-Mutawakkil (847 to 861) in Samarra, near Baghdad. She was the slave of Muhammad Ibn Hammad and often sang for the caliph. She was considered a finely trained songstress and was the confidante of the brother and chief advisor of the vizier Suleiman Ibn Wahb Hasan.
Ref. 224

BANCER, Teresa Barbara
Polish composer. b. Warsaw, March 15, 1935. She studied at the Warsaw Secondary School of Music and the Warsaw High School of Music with Professors Boleslaw Woytowicz and Tadeusz Szeligowski. In 1961 she moved to Katowice, to continue her studies with Professor Woytowicz, who by then had left Warsaw and in 1963 she graduated with a diploma in composition and an M.A.. From 1963 she worked for Warsaw television as a music illustrator and composer. She is a member of the Union of Polish Composers. PHOTOGRAPH.
Compositions
ORCHESTRA
Symphony (1963)
Concertino for orchestra (1960)
Film etudes (1961)
PIANO
Six preludes (1959)
Sonata (1961)
VOCAL
A symphonic lyric (A and orch)
Arabesque (S, cl, b-cl, a-sax, 2 hp, pf, vln, vla, vlc and perc) (1960)
Music for string instruments, percussion and choir (1974)
The visit (m-S, fl, bsn, vln, vla and pf) (1959)
Ref. composer

BANDARA (Bandara-Hofland), Linda
B. Kendal, Java, May 15, 1881. She was a composer of Austrian parentage, who lived jointly in Vienna and Yogyakarta, Java. She studied with her mother, Antonia Leber (q.v.).
Compositions
ORCHESTRA
Symphony for orchestra (1910, rev 1937)
Fanatica (1908)
Ferne Heimat (1951)
Flirt (1906)
Laendliche Stimmungsbilder (1912)
Tropennacht (1898)
VOCAL
Fruehlingslied (1937)
Naechtliche Frage (1951)
Sommer (1951)
Three old Javanese songs (ch and 2 pf)
THEATRE
Die gestoerte Siesta, pantomime (1923)
Waldkoenigs Sohn, pantomime (1927)
Ref. 94, 105, 111, 189, 226

BANDARA-HOFLAND, Linda. See BANDARA, Linda

BANDT, Rosalie Edith
Australian lecturer, musician and composer. b. Geelong, August 18, 1951. She received her B.A. Dip.Ed. from Monash University. In 1976 she studied performance practice in America and at the Schola Cantorum, Basle. She researched experimental music in Illinois, France, Germany, Switzerland and California. In 1975 and from 1978 to 1980 she taught improvisation and community music at Latrobe University. In 1981 she built Australia's first permanent sound playground, funded by the Schools' Commission and the Australia Council. She gave solo performances of her own music on glass and clay instruments and performed with L.I.M.E. (live improvised music events) and La Romanesca, an early music group. PHOTOGRAPH.
Compositions
RECORDER
Drifts in sand (1976)
Meditation (1976)

ELECTRONIC
Environments 4 (1982)
High altitude grabs (1978)
Homemade
I.C.U. Quadrophonic tape piece of hospital environment (1977-1979)
Improvised pieces for L.I.M.E.
Loops (1981)
Minus one
Nuts
O rose
Phoenix
Series 1-6
Silo pieces: Dog, Sweat, Germinal Wheat, Distant Polyphony, Mating Call, Silo Song (for performance in wheat silos)
Soft and fragile glass and clay music, incl.: Ocean Balls, Passacaglia, Shifts, Piece of Eight, Feed the Flagong (1979-1982)
Tank pieces 1-10 (performance in cement water tanks) (1979)
Variations II, 2 realisations of John Cage's score (fl, gtr and syn) (1974)
5 + 5
5 + 4
Ref. composer

BANG, Sophy
20th-century Danish composer.
Compositions
PIANO
Oscar Marsch (1916)
VOCAL
Three songs: Hvorfor? Her skal vaere Fest; Serenade (vce and pf)
Two songs: Ronnebaer; Foraar (vce and pf)
Ref. 331

BANKOVA-MARINOVA, Angelina
Bulgarian mezzo-soprano and composer. b. Plovdiv, 1905. She graduated from the Sofia Conservatory and became well-known as a singer. Her songs were composed in Bulgaria for the Russian baritone Kiril Saraev.
Compositions
VOCAL
Esenni motivi (Yavarov)
Mene, mome, ne lyubi (Yavarov) (1964)
Ovcharska pesen (Yavarov) (1964)
Songs
Ref. composer

BANKS, Hilda
American pianist and composer. b. Boston, MA, 1927. She studied the piano under Leonard Shure in Boston from 1935 to 1940 and Artur Schnabel from 1940 to 1947 and composition under Bohuslav Martinu in New York from 1946. She composed her first piano work when she was eight and made her piano debut at the age of 12. As a concert pianist she toured America, Canada and Europe.
Composition
PIANO
Tom Sawyer suite
Ref. 496

BANNISTER, Mary Jeanne Hoggard
American pianist, accompanist, teacher and composer. b. Brooklyn, NY, March 14, 1932. She studied music at the Oklahoma City University (B.Mus. 1952) and the University of Illinois (M.Mus. 1954). She did graduate study at the University of Illinois, where she was a staff accompanist from 1956 to 1958. She made concert appearances as a pianist, composer and accompanist in the midwestern and eastern states. From 1959, she taught the piano and composition in Rochester. She won the Silver Letzeiser medal in 1951 and the L.C. Mersefelder award in 1952.
Compositions
ORCHESTRA
Suite for orchestra No. 1
CHAMBER
Piano quintet
Three string quartets
Trio (cl, vlc and pf)
Violin duo
PIANO
Four sonatas
Other pieces
VOCAL
Numerous works for organ and choir

Publications
Modal Music for Piano. 1974.
Ref. 77

BAPTISTA, Gracia
17th-century Italian composer. DISCOGRAPHY.
Composition
SACRED
Conditor alme, hymn (vces and hpcd)
Ref. 563

BARADAPRANA, Pravrajika (Doris Ludwig)
American organist, pianist, violinist, choral conductor, ecclesiastic and composer. b. Los Angeles, April 22, 1923. After studying the violin and the piano as a child, she proceeded to Los Angeles City College to study harmony and counterpoint. She studied voice, the organ, choir directing and composition under Dr. Norman Wright. She entered the convent of the Vedanta Society of Southern California when she was 21 and became an ordained nun of the Ramakrishna mission. Her music incorporates Indian themes. DISCOGRAPHY. PHOTOGRAPH.
Compositions
CHAMBER
Trio (vln, vlc and cl) (1975)
Three preludes (org) (1960)
VOCAL
Ten folk songs (S and gtr) (1970)
SACRED
Ramakrishna cantata (w-ch) (1958)
All my sorrow has been lifted (w-ch, vlc and org) (1973)
Be still (mix-ch, vlc and org) (1956)
Fifty songs from the Gita (w-ch) (1955-1957)
Give me thy grace (w-ch, vlc and org) (1972)
May there be peace (w-ch) (1959)
May we meditate (w-ch and org) (1958)
Meditate (w-ch, vlc and org) (1972)
Office for the Dead (w-ch and org) (1960)
Swaniji (w-ch, gtr and vlc) (1970)
Ten peace chants (mix-ch and org) (1956-1958)
Thou shalt love the Lord (w-ch and org) (1958)
You shall know the truth (w-ch and org) (1958)
Fifteen devotional songs (S and org) (1956-1978)
The Lord's prayer (S) (1958)
Radha's song (S, org and fl) (1957)
Other songs (ch)
Ref. 563

BARAMISHVILI, Olga Ivanovna
Soviet pianist, assistant professor and composer. b. Tbilisi, November 30, 1907; d. Tbilisi, September 25, 1956. She studied composition under S. Barchudarian and the piano under A.I. Tulashvili. In Leningrad she studied under Shcherbachev from 1931 to 1933. After graduating from the Tbilisi Conservatory in 1933 she became assistant to Shcherbachev and Kushnarev in Leningrad and from 1939 was assistant professor of harmony at the Tbilisi Conservatory, becoming assistant professor of general solfege in 1943.
Compositions
ORCHESTRA
Symphonic suite
Story of a little deer (1946)
Happy youth, suite (1934)
Waltz from music of Optimistic Tragedy (1953)
Waltz of youth (wind orch) (1952)
CHAMBER
Duos
PIANO
Spanish dance (1953)
Story (1950)
VOCAL
The happiness of the people is in peace, cantata (1951)
Cycle (H. Heine) (m-S and orch) (1940)
K polukhinoi (Lermontov) (Bar and orch) (1940)
Liricheski, cycle (vce and orch) (1935)
Song of the Petrel (M. Gorky) (vce and orch) (1942)
Zhelanie (Lermontov) (Bar and orch) (1940)
Flower
Kavkaz (Lermontov)
Kazhdye imeyet lyubov svoiu (Tabidze)

Kolybelnaya (Margian)
Landslide
On the Georgian hills
Romances and songs (Pushkin and others)
Song cycles (Yesenin, A. Prokofiev and Doronin) (1935)
Two song cycles: War for the Fatherland
Zhdi meniya (Simonov)
INCIDENTAL MUSIC
Romeo and Juliet (1955)
Music for 26 plays
Ref. 87, 94, 458

BARAT (Barat-Pepper), Eliane

French composer. b. 1915.
Composition
VOCAL
Chant de L'Initie (w-ch, fl and perc) (1983)
Ref. Otto Harrassowitz (Wiesbaden)

BARATI, Ruth

Composition
BAND
The Waters of Kane (with George Barati) (1966)
Ref. 594

BARATTA, Maria M. de

El Salvadorian pianist, folklorist, teacher and composer. b. Barrio del Calvario, February 27, 1894. Her great-grandfather was the last Indian chief of the Lencas tribe and her mother was Spanish. Maria studied at the National Conservatory under Maria Zimmermann and A. Gianoli; at the Conservatory of Music, Bologna, Italy and later in San Francisco, under V. Arrilaga (1926) and the piano privately under A. Roig. She taught at the National Conservatory in El Salvador and gave concerts in her country and Guatemala. She spent over 18 years collecting and researching Indian music. Her major work *Nahualismo* is based on old Indian rituals. All the orchestrations of her works are included in the Fleisher Collection, Philadelphia.
Compositions
PIANO
Ofrenda de la elegida, ritual dance
Profession hieratica
VOCAL
Songs:
La campana lhora
Can-calagui-tunal (composer)
Los tecomatillos (composer)
BALLET
Danza del incienso, or Fuego nuevo, or En un templo maya, native ballet (pf) (comm government of El Salvador)
Nahualismo, Diabolus in musica (pf) (1934)
Publications
Cuzcutlan Tipico - Ensayo sobre Etnofonia de El Salvador. Folklore, 2 vols. El Salvador; Ministerio de Cultura, 1951.
Recopilacion de materiales folkloriciso salvadorenos.
Ref. 16, 17, 45, 54, 70, 84, 100, 173, 322, 361

BARBER, Gail Guseman

American harpist, editor, assistant professor and composer. b. New Iberia, LA, February 23, 1937. She studied music at the Eastman School of Music (B.Mus) and at the University of Rochester, New York. She performed in concert and on television throughout the United States and appeared as a soloist with orchestras in the United States, Canada and Mexico. She taught at Furmon University, SC, and Baylor University, TX. She is assistant professor of harp and music theory at Texas University in Lubbock. She received a citation from the American Harp Society for outstanding work for the harp. She is a member of the board of directors of the American Harp Society and the southwestern regional director. She is also editor of the *American Harp Journal*.
Compositions
HARP
Duets (1976, 1983)
Concerto (1980)
Improvisation on a familiar melody
Poem (1976)
Sonata (1983)
Windmill sketches
Visions
ARRANGEMENTS
Bach's prelude in E-Minor (2 hp)
Ref. 77, 625

BARBERIS, Mansi

Rumanian violinist, lecturer and composer. b. Iasi, March 12, 1899. She studied at the Iasi Conservatory from 1918 to 1922 under Sofia Teodoreanu (solfege, theory), Ion Ghiga and Gavriil Galinescu (harmony), Antonin Ciolan (counterpoint), Enrico Mezzetti (singing) and Athanasie Theodorini (violin). In 1922 she went to Berlin to study under Wilhelm Klatte and Lula Mysz-Gmeiner and in 1926 to Paris, where she studied composition and orchestration under Noel Gallon, whilst continuing with her singing and conducting classes. She then studied composition under Jozef Marx in Vienna. She taught singing from 1934 to 1950 and opera from 1941 to 1950 at the Iasi Conservatory and was also a violinist there with the Moldova symphony orchestra from 1942 to 1944. She taught singing at the Theatre Institute I.L. Caragiale in Bucharest from 1950 to 1951 and at the Conservatory of Bucharest from 1951 to 1956. She won the third prize in the George Enesco Composition Competition in 1942, the prize for composition of the Union of Composers in 1955 and the Order of Cultural Merit in 1969. DISCOGRAPHY. PHOTOGRAPH.
Compositions
ORCHESTRA
First symphony (1941)
Concerto in D-Major (pf and orch) (1954)
Pièce concertante (cl and orch) (1972)
Pièce de concert (vla and orch) (1981)
Poème concertante (vln and orch; also vln and pf) (1953, 1952)
Visions, symphonic poem (1934)
Espace (1972)
Les épis (1949)
Pages symphoniques (1930)
Réalisation (1977)
Symphonic variations (1971)
Trois tableaux (1975)
First suite, pastorale (1936)
Second suite, trois moments descriptifs (1951)
CHAMBER
Quartettino (strs) (1976)
String quartet (1976)
Dance (vln and pf) (1952)
Dance bien mon ours Martin (bsn and pf) (1982)
En plaisantant (vla and pf) (1981)
Filles et garçons (vln and pf) (1949)
Par plaisanterie (vln and pf) (1936)
Sonata (vln and pf) (1957)
Caprice (hp) (1965)
PIANO
Obsession (1969)
Prelude (1956)
Scherzando (1934)
Six fables (1949)
Une soirée (1920)
Suite of folk dances (1949)
Valse de concert
VOCAL
La liberation, cantata (D. Corbea) (vce and orch) (1950)
Pintea le brave, cantata (D. Stanca) (B, ch and orch)
Calin (M. Eminescu) (S, m-S, T, Bar and orch) (1947)
La chasse, ballad (M. Dumitrescu) (Bar and orch) (1955)
Conte au coin de feu (D. Miga) (vce and orch) (1949)
La dragonne (S. Losif) (S, T and orch) (1969)
Petit chien et petite chatte (Daniela Miga) (reciter and orch) (1949)
A la campagne (O. Cazimir) (chil-ch and pf) (1948)
Le Cochevis (O. Cazimir) (chil-ch and pf) (1948)
Les enemis succombent en masses! (M. Eminescu) (m-ch) (1952)
La plaine (folk words) (w-ch) (1923)
Suite of five folk songs (vocal qrt, str qrt, wind qnt and perc) (1972)
C'est maman qui m'a envoyée cueillir du raisin (folk text) (S, vln, vlc and pf) (1951)
Destin de poete, cycle of 10 songs (Eminescu) (1981)
Foret, feuille ronde (folk text) (S, cor anglais, cl and pf)
Mai la deal de casa noastra (1950)
Quartet doina (C. Cirjan) (vce, ob, cl and hp) (1969)
Songs (Verlaine, Lesnea, Cazimir, Boldici) (vce and pf) (1918-1951)
Sur un bonjour (O. Cazimir) (2 vces and str qrt) (1972)
Two songs (M. Eminescu) (T, Bar and pf)
OPERA
Apus de Soare
La Charette aux Paillaces (A. Ionescu-Arbore) (1980)
Domnița dind Epartari, in 3 acts (1948, rev. 1971)
Kera Duduca, in 3 acts (A. Ionescu-Arbore) (1963, rev. 1969)
THEATRE
A l'appareil, le Taimir! (Isaev, Galici) (1948)

The Merchant of Venice (Shakespeare) (1934)
Revolution au couvent (Martinez) (1934)
Ref. composer, 148, 457, 563

BARBI, Alice

Italian violinist, linguist, poetess, singer and composer. b. Modena, 1862; d. Modena, 1948. She studied the violin under her father and then turned to singing, which she studied under various masters in Bologna. She made her debut in 1882 and enjoyed a successful career. Brahms wrote some songs for her and accompanied her in a performance in 1893.

Compositions
VOCAL
Collections of ancient airs
Ref. 502

BARBILLON, Jeanne

French pianist, violinist and composer. b. Paris, October 12, 1895. She started to learn solfege and the piano at the age of four and later studied the violin. At eight she entered the Schola Cantorum, where she studied orchestration under Vincent d'Indy, who took particular interest in her. She also studied the violin under Armand Parent and Berthe Duranton and took a composition course with d'Indy in 1912. In 1927 she received the Diplôme Supérieur de Violin et de Composition de la Schola Cantorum. She was awarded the Prix Marmontel from the Société des Compositeurs as well as a medal from the Salon de Musiciens Français. She was a member of SACEM.

Compositions
ORCHESTRA
Cortège funèbre (cor anglais and str orch)
Symphonic study
Two symphonic movements
CHAMBER
Poème d'été (fl, ob, cl, bsn and pf)
Variations on old carols (str qrt and org)
Quartet (pf, vln, vla and vlc)
String quartet
Trio (pf, vln and vlc) (Fortin) (Prix Marmontel, 1928)
Ile de France, 2 pieces (fl and pf) (Fortin)
Poème (vlc and pf)
Sonata in D (vln and pf) (Fortin)
Cadenza to Beethoven's violin concerto (Roudonez)
PIANO
En forêt, suite (4 hands)
Scènes champêtres, 6 pieces for children (4 hands)
Impression maritime
Provence, 2 pieces (Senart-Salabert)
Sonata
VOCAL
Jeanne d'Arc à Rouen, cantata (soloists, ch and orch)
Les Erinnyes (S, T and orch)
Aurore (m-ch)
Dedicace (S, w-ch and pf)
Hymne sylvestre (m-S and mix-ch) (1972)
Les Mouches (w-ch)
La tristesse de Pan (B, fl, hp and qrt)
Automne (vce and pf) (Fortin)
Hymne dorienne (A and chromatic hp)
Nocturne (vce and pf) (Fortin)
Songs
ELECTRONIC
Chorale et pastorale en roundeau (ondes Martenot, org and strs)
Ref. composer, 41, 70, 81, 105, 226

BARBLAN-OPIENSKA, Lydia

Swiss pianist, singer, teacher and composer. b. Morges, April 12, 1890; d. January 3, 1983. She was the daughter of Otto Barblan, composer and organist. She first studied the piano and harmony under Georges Humbert and then attended the Conservatory of Freiburg im Breisgau from 1908 to 1911, where she studied singing under L. Schulze von Korff. She also studied under Clericy-Du Collet in Paris in 1914 and Emma de Beauck in Brussels. She studied composition under H. Huber and Karl Henrich David in Basle in 1911 and later under August Serieyx. She taught singing at the Conservatory of Freiburg, Breisgau from 1911 to 1914, the Ecole de Musique, Basle from 1911 to 1921, the National Polish Conservatory, Poznan in 1921 and 1927 and from 1926 at L'Institut de Ribaupierre, Lucerne. She married Henryk Opienski, a musicologist and violinist and in 1916, together with her brother, Julia Demont and Alexander Kurz, founded the 'Barblan Vocal Quartet' and with her husband, the vocal ensemble 'Motet et Madrigal'. From 1948 to 1960 she was a member of the central committee of the Societe Suisse de Pedagogie Musicale. She was awarded the Palmes Academique (France), the Gold Cross of Merit (Poland) and the Bourgeoisie d'Honneur (Morges).

Compositions
PIANO
Minuet
Petit suite
Scherzo
Variations and fugue on an original theme
Variations sur un theme populaire de l'Engadine
VOCAL
Cantata (Novalis)
Les roses de Saadi (vces and insts or orch)
Choeur des vaudoises
Melodies (Uhland, Heine, Geibel, Hesse, Nietzsche, Novalis, Ronsard, Desbordes-Valmore, Van Lerberghe and others)
Children's songs
SACRED
Agnus Dei
Ave Maria
O quam suavis est
Trois chants pour Noël
Publications
Paderewski tel que je l'ai connu. 1924, 1941.
Ref. composer, 59, 70, 94, 101, 105, 552

BARBOSA, Cacilda Campos Borges

Brazilian pianist, choir conductor, lecturer and composer. b. Rio de Janeiro, May 18, 1914. She was a pupil of the Instituto Nacional de Musica in Rio in 1928, where she studied theory under Lima Coutinho, harmony under L. Fernandes, counterpoint and fugue under P. Silva, composition under F. Braga, conducting under F. Mignone and the piano under P. Chaves. She studied voice under M. Figuero Bezerra and V. Janacopulos. At the National Institute of Music she also studied different forms of music expression and instrumentation under E. Widmer. She worked with the composer Villa-Lobos in the supervision of artistic and music education at the organisation SEMA and conducted its youth orchestra. She was active as a teacher in state schools and universities and was director of the Instituto Villa-Lobos. She directed a students' choir of 40,000 voices in the festival Semana da Patria in 1971. She travelled worldwide, promoting new methods of music teaching and is considered a pioneer in electronic music in Brazil. DISCOGRAPHY.

Compositions
ORCHESTRA
Chibraseando (20 perc) (1973)
Uirapiranga, dance (1955)
CHAMBER
Quatro estudos brasileiros (pf)
VOCAL
Cota zero (ch, perc, fl, vib and vlc) (1969)
Lamentacoes onomatopaicas (ch) (1966)
Procissao da chuva (school ch)
SACRED
Missa em fugas (1971)
Segunda missa brasileira (1968)
Publications
Estudos brasileiros para canto e piano. Sao Paulo.
Estudos brasileiros para piano. Sao Paulo.
Ref. 333, 563

BARBOUR, Florence Newell

American pianist and composer. b. Providence, August 8, 1866; d. Providence, July 24, 1946. She was educated in the United States and traveled through Europe and the Far East. She appeared as a solo pianist with orchestras and chamber groups and gave recitals of her compositions on the radio.

CHAMBER
Reverie (pf and strs)
PIANO
Nature pieces (2 pf)
Melodic etudes (2 pf)
A day in Arcady
All in a garden fair
At Chamonix
Forest sketches
Holland
Venice
VOCAL
Anthems
Choruses (w-vces)
Songs
Publications
Child-Land, songs and rhythms. 1921.
Ref. 22, 714, 226, 292

BARCROFT, E. Dorothea
20th-century English composer. b. Wolverhampton. From 1924 to 1935 she organised children's programs for the BBC.
Compositions
ORCHESTRA
African suite
PIANO
Concert studies
Liebeslied in E
VOCAL
My Book, 8 children's songs
Over the garden wall, 6 songs
Songs of Elfin town
Ballads
Ref. 467

BARD, Vivien
20th-century American composer of piano pieces. b. Terre Haute.
Ref. 347

BARDEL, Germaine
French authoress, poetess, singer and composer. b. Sallanches, January 27, 1910. She started music lessons at the age of eight under Mlles. Marin and Mabon until 1923 and continued her studies under Mlle. Grandjean in Annecy until 1926. She studied under Sister Marie de Chantal at the School Menagere de Sallanches from 1927 to 1930 and had singing lessons under Mme. Bosonett from 1929 to 1931. She is a member of SACEM.
Compositions
CHAMBER
Chant d'instruments (1980)
Point d'orgue (org) (1981)
PIANO
Adagio
Air de fête (1979)
Amusement (1981)
Carillon-Ritournelle-Sur la montagne
La chanson de l'echo-Au pays chinois
Le chant de la cloche-Voici la nuit
Ciel d'orage, soirée de l'opéra
Confidence-Fleurs de neige
Consolation (1979)
Dialogue (1979)
Fantaisie (1980)
France Savoie-Tango sérénade
Imploration (1979)
Jeux de flutes-Alleluia-Cortège
Les jongleurs-Vision du désert
Marche Funébre (1979)
Moment de prière-Crepuscule-Musette
Noël
Pastorale (1981)
Premier refrain-notes joyeuses
Recit (1980)
Refrain nostalgique-Esquisse
Valse des saisons
Valse d'automne-Valse des papillons
Valse du souvenir-Valse des feuilles
Valsons sur la glace, minuet
VOCAL
L'automne
Beau village
Caroline
C'est bonheur dans la vie
Chanson du bonheur
Une chanson pour toi Ninon
Le chant de l'étoile (1981)
J'ai gagné la belle poupée
Jacqueline
Je vous offre la rose
Jeu de lumiere zur vitrail (1980)
Mon Coeur de poète est à vous
Nicole
Paroles lamartine
Pays que j'aime
Ramoneur; Je marche dans la nuit
Soutils finistons les beaux jours (1981)
Les voiles
SACRED
Twenty-two carols incl.:
A Sa Saintete J. Paul II (1980)
C'est Noël chez nous
Caritas (1979)
Le chant des bergers
L'Etoile de Noël
Mariage (1979)
Meditation sur le Cromorne (1979)
Mystère pascal (1979)
Noël de la Vierge
Noël revient (1980)
Noël savoyard
Noël sur les Alpes
Nuit de Noël
Pater Noster
Solennite (1980)
Three Ave Marias
Ref. composer

BARIL, Jeanne (Sister M. Louise-Andree)
Canadian teacher and composer. b. St. Tite, Quebec, February 26, 1913. She composed piano pieces and choral works.
Ref. 133

BARIONA, Madelka Simone
16th-century German composer, from Oppeln.
Compositions
SACRED
Canticum beatissimum (4 vces) (Prague: 1581)
Septem psalmi poenitentiales (5 vces) (Altdorf: 1586) (in Royal Library of Munich)
Ref. 226, 276, 335

BARKER, Laura Wilson (Mrs. Tom Taylor)
English violinist, teacher and composer. b. Thirkleby, Yorkshire, 1819; d. Coleshill, 1905. She was the sixth daughter of the Reverend T. Barker, vicar of Thirkleby. She studied music first under her parents and later under Cipriani Potter. She was a talented violinist and taught music at the York School for the Blind. In 1855 she married Tom Taylor, a playwright and wrote the incidental music for many his plays. She harmonized original melodies for a book he translated and published in 1865. After his death in 1880, she retired to Coleshill, specializing in the composition of songs.
Compositions
CHAMBER
String quartets
A country walk, sonata (vln and pf) (1860)
Other pieces
PIANO
Pieces incl.:
Allegro animato and Introduction
VOCAL
Enone, cantata (1850)
A prophesy (ch and orch) (1899)
Sleep gentle lady (ch) (Curwen)
Seven romances (vce and gtr) (1836)
Six songs (Ashdown)
Madrigals
Solo songs and duets (vce and pf)
THEATRE
Overture and entr'acte for Joan of Arc (Taylor)
As you like it (Shakespeare) (1879)
Ode to the passions (Collins) (1846)
Ref. 6, 8, 177, 226, 276, 297

BARKER, Patricia
20th-century Australian composer.
Compositions
INCIDENTAL MUSIC
The good life (1972)
Two hundred thousand reasons (1973)
Music for documentary films
Ref. 442

BARKER, Phyllis Elizabeth (Mrs. Kent)
South African organist, teacher and composer. b. Durban, January 27, 1920. She was a pupil of Sister Mary Gabriel at the Maris Stella Convent, Durban from 1926 to 1938 and obtained her university performer's licentiate and became a L.T.C.L.. After 1963 she taught music in schools and was organist at St. Elizabeth's Church, Westville.

Compositions
CHAMBER
Sonata in F-Minor (vln and pf) (1956)
PIANO
Coronation march (1953)
Eastern slave dance (1931)
Frustration (1955)
Gnomes and fairies (1931)
March of the empire (1931)
Mountain fantasy (1954)
Musical box (1939)
Nero and the flea (1937)
Prelude (1952)
Puck's frolics (1952)
Scherzo (1933)
VOCAL
Songs incl.:
I saw a stranger yestreen
Indian wayside sketch (1938)
Jolly miller
Lullaby (1937)
The monkey and the crocodile (1951)
The travellers (1964)
School songs
SACRED
As Mary appeared, Christmas oratorio (Una Hooper)
Christ was born on Christmas Day (1952)
Christmas anthem (Una Hooper, 1956)
Come love ye God, carol (Oxford, 1962)
Dedication anthem for St. Elizabeth's Church, Westville (1960)
God's garden, song (1951)
Hold Thou my hands, hymn (E. & H., 1963)
In the bleak mid-winter, hymn (E. & H.)
Little drops of water, hymn (1961)
Lord Jesus hath a garden, carol (Oxford, 1962)
Monday prayer (1962)
Mother's prayer, song (Una Hooper, 1960)
O day of calm and heavenly peace (Una Hooper)
Praise the Lord of heaven, hymn (E. & H., 1961)
Repent ye (1963)
Ref. 377

BARKIN, Elaine (nee Radoff)

American pianist, professor and composer. b. Bronx, NY, December 15, 1932. She studied composition under Karol Rathaus at Queens College. She obtained her B.A. and studied under Irving Fine, Harold Shapero and Arthur Berger at Brandeis University, where she obtained her M.F.A. in 1956 and Ph.D. in 1971. On a Fulbright grant she studied under Boris Blacher at the Hochschule fuer Musik in Berlin (certificate in piano and composition, 1957). She held faculty positions at Queens College from 1964 to 1970, Sarah Lawrence College from 1969 to 1970, the University of Michigan from 1970 to 1973 and Princeton University, as a Humanities Council junior fellow, in 1974. From 1974 she was professor of music at the University of California, Los Angeles. She won the International Society of Contemporary music commission in 1974 and the National Endowment for the Arts grant in 1974 and 1976. In 1980 she was awarded a residency at the Rockefeller Foundation's Bellagio Study Center. She is co-editor of Perspectives of New Music and has written articles and reviews for the major music journals. DISCOGRAPHY.
Compositions
ORCHESTRA
Essay (1956)
CHAMBER
Inward and outward bound (large cham ens) (New York: Composers Facsimile Ed., 1975)
Plus ca change (4 vln, 2 vla, 2 vlc, mar, vib, xy and d-b) (C.F.E., 1973)
Refrains (fl, ob, cel, vln, vla and vlc) (C.F.E., 1967)
Mixed modes (cl, or ob, vln, vla, vlc and pf) (comm League of Composers-International Society for Contemporary Music, New York) (1976)
Prim cycles (fl, ob, vln and vlc) (1976)
String quartet in one movement (1974)
String quartet in two movements (New York: ASUC, 1974)
Woodwind quartet (1956)
NB suite (fls and d-b) (1982) (Association for Promotion of New Music)
Impromptu (vln, vlc and pf) (1981) (ACE)
String trio (vln, vla and vlc)
Triode (vln, vla and vlc)
Ebb tide (2 vib) (1977)
For suite's sake (hpcd) (C.F.E., 1975)
Plein chant (a-fl) (1977)
Sound play (vln) (1974) (1977)
PIANO
At the piano (1982) (APNM)
Brandeis, 4 short pieces (1955)
Six piano pieces or six compositions for piano (1968) (C.F.E., 1969)
VOCAL
Three Dickinson choruses (1976)
OPERA
De amore, chamber opera (4 w and 4 m speaker-singers and ens) (1980) (ACE)
ELECTRONIC
Concerning women or An assembly (4 w-vces and tape) (1983)
MULTIMEDIA
Media speak, theatre piece (9 speakers, sax, tape, slices, fls and cb) (1981) (ACE)
Publications
A View of Schoenberg's op. 23/1.
Bibliography
Eleanor Cory: *Elaine Barkin: String Quartet*'. Musical Quarterly. 1976.
Ref. composer, 94, 137, 142, 206, 228, 397, 563, 622, 624, 625

BARKLUND, Irma L.

Swedish organist, pianist, recorder player, teacher and composer. b. Dala-Jarna, April 5, 1909. She studied literature and history of art, then took the organ and precentor examinations in Uppsala in 1951. She studied at the Conservatory of Stockholm under Alf Linder and H. Lindroth (organ) and Sven Brandel (piano). In 1960 she obtained a certificate in church music and went on to study composition under H. Lindroth and Werner Wolf Glaser. She attended several courses at the Mozarteum, Salzburg. From 1948 she was a teacher of the piano, the recorder, the organ and music theory at the community music school in Vasteras. PHOTOGRAPH.
Compositions
ORCHESTRA
Fata morgana (str orch) (1971)
Hav (1972)
Lento (1978)
Regio incognito (20 insts) (1970)
CHAMBER
Fyra dofter (wind insts, pf and perc) (1970)
Adagio and allegro (5 cl) (1967)
Okenstad (wind qnt) (1972)
Days, 3 pieces (fl, cl and vlc) (1976)
Katedral-pieta-horologium mirabile (vln, vlc and pf) (1969)
Mediterranea (ob, gtr and pf) (1970)
Andante atonale (vlc and pf) (1977)
Pieces for flute and piano (1970)
Chorale preludes and partitas (org) (1954-1958)
Pieces for guitar (1972)
Solo pieces for wind instruments (1949)
PIANO
Nat (1970)
Steg (1949)
Ten short pieces (1966)
VOCAL
Morgonens fagel sjunger (Tagore) (vce and orch) (1950)
Consolatio (R. Enckell) (mix-ch, fl, vlc, vln and hpcd) (1973)
Two songs with piano (1949)
Ref. composer

BARLOW, Betty

20th-century American composer.
Compositions
OPERA
The case of the Missing Part of Speech, a melogrammar
OPERETTA
The Rabbit who Wanted Red Wings
Ref. 141

BARLOW, Sylvia

Compositions
PIANO
Two scenes from a fairy tale: A knight on horseback; The sad little spinner
Ref. 473

BARNARD, Caroline. See RICHINGS, Caroline

BARNARD, Charlotte (nee Alington) (pseud. Claribel)
English poetess and composer. b. London, December 23, 1830; d. Dover, January 30, 1869. She was taught composition by W.H. Holmes and published about 100 ballads from 1858 and 1869, most of which enjoyed great popularity in their time, especially *Come back to Erin*. She derived her pseudonym, Claribel, from letters in her names; Charlotte, Alington, Barnard, adding the el to round off the name.
Compositions
CHAMBER
Piano pieces
VOCAL
Duets, trios and quartets
Songs incl.:
All along the valley
Answer to the dream
Bell's whisper
Blind Alice
By the blue Alsatian mountains
Come back to Erin
Maggie's secret
Sailor boy
When I was young and fair
Publications
Thoughts, verses and songs. 1877.
Fireside Thoughts. Ballads. Nisbet. 1865.
Ref. Rev. H. Bacon (Yorks, UK) 6, 8, 22, 26, 129, 177, 276, 361, 653

BARNEKOW, Deborah
B. 1949.
Composition
ORCHESTRA
Once again the ice cometh (b-fl and orch) (1980)
Ref. 594

BARNES, Bertha L.
19th-century English composer.
Compositions
PIANO
The Arago, op. 3
Pensee fugitive, op. 4
Traeumerei, op. 2
Tyrolienne, op. 5
Ref. 276

BARNES, Mildred. See ROYSE, Mildred Barnes

BARNES-WOOD, Zilpha
American choral conductor, teacher and composer. b. Killbuck, OH, December 5, 1877. She studied and later taught at the Cincinnati College of Music. She then went to New York, where she taught music and conducted choral groups.
Ref. 226

BARNETT, Alice (Mrs. George Stevenson)
American pianist, teacher and composer. b. Lewiston, IL, May 26, 1886. She studied the piano under her father and then at Chicago Musical College under Felix Borowski, Rudolph Ganz and Heniot Levy. Later she studied at the American Conservatory in Chicago and in Berlin under Hugo Kaun. In 1917 she settled in San Diego, teaching at the San Diego High School from 1917 to 1926. She helped found the San Diego Civic Symphony and Opera Guild.
Compositions
VOCAL
Settings for poems incl.:
A caravan from China comes
Chanson of the bells of Oseney
Cycle of Browning's poems
Harbour lights (Boston Music, 1927)
Home coming hour
In a gondola
In May (P.L. Dunbar) (Boston: O. Ditson, 1925)
Merry, merry lark (C. Kingsley) (Summy, 1909)
Music, when soft voices die (Shelley) (G. Schirmer, 1926)
Serenade (C. Scollard)
Three songs of musing (G. Schirmer, 1923)
Tryst (C. Scollard) (G. Schirmer, 1919)
Two even-songs (G. Schirmer, 1921)
Ref. 22, 39, 40, 53, 94, 142, 292

BARNETT, Carol Edith
American pianist and composer. b. Iowa, May 23, 1949. She studied at the University of Minnesota where she obtained her B.A. in 1972 and her M.A. (theory and composition) in 1976. Her teachers included Bernard Weiser (piano) and Dominick Argento and Paul Fetler (composition). She received two commissions from the Minnesota composers' commissioning program in 1979 and 1982 and a commission from the Minnesota Music Teachers' Association in 1981.
Compositions
ORCHESTRA
Adon Olam variations (1976)
Allusions, in 3 mvts (1978)
Arabesques, concert band (1976)
Overture to the Midnight Spectacle (cham orch) (1978)
Nocturne for chamber orchestra (fl or picc, 2 ob, cl, 2 bsn, 2 hn, perc and strs) (1980)
CHAMBER
Music for Immix (str qrt, 2 trp, hn, tba and perc) (1980)
Dragons (pf, 4 hands) (1981) (Belwin Mills)
Memorium (vla and pf) (1975)
Romanza (fl and pf) (1974)
Sonata (hn and pf) (1973)
Suite for two flutes (1977)
Alma del Payaso (acc) (1978)
Four chorale meditations (vln) (1982)
Ich halte treulich still prelude (org)
VOCAL
Cinco poemas de Becquer (mix-ch, rec, gtr and wind chimes)
Voices, song cycle (S and gtr) (1983) (comm performers and Jerome Foundation)
SACRED
Adonai, Adonai (mix-ch) (1979)
Ma Tovu (mix-ch) (1973)
Meciendo, Christmas carol (mix-ch) (1978)
Silent Amidah (mix-ch) (1974)
Requiem for treble voices (2 S and A) (1981)
ELECTRONIC
Three vocalises (mix-ch and vib) (1976)
Suite vibes in F (vib) (1978)
Ref. composer, 625

BARNETT, Clara Kathleen. See ROGERS, Clara Kathleen

BARNETT, Emma
19th-century English pianist and composer. b. London. She was the daughter of a professor of singing and studied the piano under her brother, John Francis Barnett and made her debut in London in 1874 playing Beethoven's *Piano Concerto in G*, thereafter giving many recitals.
Compositions
PIANO
Pieces incl.:
Gavotte in A
VOCAL
Songs
Ref. 6, 276

BARNETT, Wally
Composition
CHAMBER
A horse of a different colour (snare dr and pf) (Melville, NY: Belwin Mills)
Ref. Frau und Musik

BARNEY, Nancy
20th-century composer.
Composition
CHAMBER
Thirteen ways of looking at a blackbird (fl)
Ref. Frau und Musik

BARNS, Ethel
English pianist, violinist and composer. b. London, 1880; d. Maidenhead, December 31, 1948. She studied at the Royal Academy of Music under Sauret (violin), Prout (composition) and Westlake (piano) and made her debut in 1896 at the Crystal Palace, London. She toured England and the United States and married Charles Phillips, a baritone, in 1899. Her *Violin Sonata No. 2* was played by Joachim in Germany in 1903, while her *Fantasy Trio* was frequently played by Emile Sauret.
Compositions
ORCHESTRA
Concert piece for violin and orchestra
Violin concerto
L'escarpolette (F. Louis Schneider) (str orch: also vln and pf) (Schott, 1908)
CHAMBER
Fantasy trio for 2 violins and piano, op. 26 (comm W.W. Cobbett)
Two trios
Humoresque (vln and pf)
Mazurka (vln and pf) (Landy)
Polonaise (vln and pf) (Ashdown)
Romance (vln and pf) (Schott)
Swing song (vln and pf)
Tarantella (vln and pf) (Schott)
Valse caprice (vln and pf) (Schott)
Piano pieces
VIOLIN
Sonata No. 2 in A-Major, op. 9 (Schott, 1909)
Sonata No. 4 in G-Minor, op. 24 (Schott, 1911)
Three other sonatas
Numerous small pieces
VOCAL
Songs incl.:
Berceuse (Leonard)
Come then (Forsyth)
A fancy (Leonard)
The humble swain (Forsyth)
My charming fair (Lloyds)
My love (Forsyth)
O Tsuri San, a Japanese lament (Forsyth)
Waiting for thee (Leonard)
Ref. 8, 17, 41, 44, 63, 70, 105, 226, 297, 322, 361

BARON SUPERVIELLE, Susana
Argentine composer. b. Buenos Aires, 1910. In Buenos Aires she studied under Gilardo and Juan Carlos Paz; in Sao Paulo, Brazil, under Furio Francheschini and Hans Koellreuter and in Paris under Nadia Boulanger (q.v.) and Vera Vaurabourg. She is the niece of the poet Jules Supervielle.
Compositions
CHAMBER
Composition 57 (10 insts and perc) (1957)
Divertissement serial (str qrt, ww qrt and trp) (1952)
String quartet (1947)
PIANO
Cancion de cuna (1941)
Etude (1949)
Preludio (1935)
Sonatina en trois mouvements (1949)
Valse
VOCAL
Tres pequenos coros (mix-ch and pf) (1932)
Un homme va et vient (vce and 8 insts) (J. Supervielle)
Poeme (vce and 8 insts) (H. Michaux) (1962)
Sonnet (vce and 7 insts) (J. Supervielle) (1960)
Songs incl.:
La belette (J. Renard) (1940)
Caracola (G. Lorca) (1954)
Cuatro canciones (G. Lorca)
Cuatro poemas (J. Supervielle) (1950)
Dos melodias criollas (F.S. Valdes and anon) (1928)
Dos poemas con musica (composer) (1966)
L'escargot (J. Renard) (1940)
A Irene Garcia (G. Lorca) (1954)
La mer secrète (J. Supervielle) (1945)
Nueve canciones (G. Lorca) (1954)
La pluie et les tyrans (J. Supervielle) (1945)
Poema (P. Lecuire)
Le pont (P. Lecuire)
Sonnet (J. Supervielle) (1958)
Various melodies (1934)
Ref. 390

BARONI, Eleanora (pseud. L'Adrianetta)
17th-century Italian composer. She was the daughter of Andriana Baroni Basile (q.v.).
Ref. 465, 502, 524, 653

BARONI BASILE, Adriana (Andreana)
Italian guitarist, harpist, lyre player, singer and composer. b. Posillipo, ca. 1580; d. 1640. She was called to the court of the Duke of Mantua by Monteverdi in 1610 and remained till 1616. She also sang at the courts of Venice and Naples and accompanied her daughters Eleonora and Caterina, both singers. Although she is known to have improvised and composed, none of her works have survived.
Ref. 226, 502

BARONI-CAVALCABO (Baroni-Cavalcabo-Castiglioni), Guilia (Julie)
Italian pianist and composer. b. Lvov, October 16, 1813; d. Graz, July 3, 1887. She was a pupil of Franz Wolfgang Mozart, son of Wolfgang Amadeus Mozart. She published her first work at the age of 17. Schumann had a high opinion of her abilities as a pianist and a composer and dedicated his *Humoreske, op. 20* to her. In 1830 she accompanied Karol Lipinski on a tour. She organised weekly concerts in Lvov, at which symphonic and chamber works and oratorios were performed.
Compositions
PIANO
Adieu et le retour, op. 25 (Kistner)
Allegro di bravuro, op. 8 (Hofmeister)
Au bord du lac, op. 26 (Haslinger)
Caprice in F-Minor, op. 2 (Breitkopf)
Caprice no. 2, op. 12 (Haslinger)
Deux morceaux de salon, op. 28 (Haslinger)
Introduction et rondo, B-Major, op. 5 (Cranz)
Nocturne, op. 27 (Haslinger)
Phantasie in C-Minor, op. 4 (Breitkopf)
Sonata in E-Major (Breitkopf)
VOCAL
Songs:
Abschied, op. 20
Es segelt sanft auf Silberwogen, op. 17 (Hoffmann)
Five German songs (Hofmeister)
Grabesrose, op. 6 (Hoffmann) (Bar)
Lebe wohl, op. 9 (Hoffmann)
Zwist und Suehne (Hoffmann)
Ref. 118, 129, 226, 276, 297

BARONI-PASOLINI, Silvia
19th-century Italian composer.
Compositions
VOCAL
Che bella luna! barcarolle (S. Busnanti) (Ricordi)
Disperata (Sul caval de la morte) (G. Carducci) (Ricordi)
Passa la nave mia, melody (A. Heine) (Ricordi)
Sogni e canti (E. Pansacchi) (Ricordi)
Vignetta (G. Carducci) (Ricordi)
Ref. 105

BARRADAS, Carmen (Maria del Carmen Perez Gimenez)
Uruguayan pianist, teacher and composer. b. Montevideo, March 18, 1888; d. Montevideo, May 12, 1963. She studied in Montevideo under M. Lopes Vicente and A. Pablo. She went to Spain in 1915 and gave a recital of her own compositions at the Ateneo in 1917. She returned to Montevideo in 1928 and became active as a choir teacher, giving her last public recital in 1937. She started a children's magazine *Andresillo* in 1940. Most of her compositions have been lost. DISCOGRAPHY.
Compositions
CHAMBER
El molinero (vln and pf)
PIANO
Fabricacion (1 or 2 pf) (ded H. Balzo) (1924)
Aserradero (1916-1922)
Cabalgata de reyes (1916-1922)
Estudio (1949)
Estudios tonales (1943)
Hilvanes
Oracines: La Novicia, Rosarito, La noche, Aurora
Piratas
Taller mecanico (1926)

VOCAL
Mar, Tragedia, Misterio, triptych (based on the tragedy by S. Storni) (w-vces and pf)
Songs for children (vce and pf)
Ref. 100, 361, 563

BARRADAS, Maria del Carmen Perez. See BARRADAS, Carmen

BARRAINE, Elsa
French professor and composer. b. Paris, February 13, 1910. Her father was a cellist in the Grand Opera Orchestra and her mother a singer. Elsa attended the Paris Conservatoire where she studied under Paul Dukas (composition), Caussade (fugue), Estyle (score reading) and J. Gallon (harmony). She won first prizes for harmony in 1925 and fugue and score reading in 1927. In 1929, she won the First Prix de Rome for *La Vierge Guerriere*. In 1932 she composed the comic opera *Le Roi Bossu* which was performed a dozen times that year. From 1936 to 1939 she was Chef du Chant for French Radio. From 1953 she was composer and professor of musical analysis at the Paris Conservatoire. PHOTOGRAPH.
Compositions
ORCHESTRA
Symphony No. 1 (1931)
Symphony No. 2 (Paris: Chant du Monde, 1938)
Symphony No. 3
Fantaisie concertante (pf and orch) (1933)
Harald Harfagar, symphonic variations (1945)
Pogromes, symphonic poem (1933)
Le fleuve rouge (1945)
Les jongleurs (1959)
La mise au tombeau (Presser)
Trois esquisses (1931)
Trois ridicules (1955)
Les Tziganes (1959)
CHAMBER
Atmosphere (ob and 10 insts) (1966)
Ouvrage de dames (5 ww and 5 strs) (Southern Music Co.)
Chiens de paille (tba, t-trb, b-trb and bsn or ondes Martenot) (1966)
Wind quintet (1931)
Musique rituelle, after the Tibetan Book of the Dead (org, gongs and xylorimba) (1968)
Andante et allegro (sax and pf) (Paris: Salabert)
Aria (trp and pf) (1938)
Crepuscule et fanfare (hn and pf)
Fanfares de printemps (hn and pf) (Schott)
Improvisation (a-sax and pf) (1947)
Nocturnes (vln and pf)
Suite juive (vln and pf) (Schott)
Variations (pf and perc) (Paris: Costallat, 1950)
ORGAN
Prelude and fugue No. 1 (Durand, 1928)
Prelude and fugue No. 2 (Durand, 1930)
PIANO
Aria (3 pf) (1938)
La boite de Pandore (1954)
Fantaisie (also hpcd) (1961)
Hommage à Paul Dukas (1936)
Marche du printemps sans amour (1946)
Nocturne (1938)
La nuit dans les chemins du rêve
Prélude (Durand)
VOCAL
Cantate du Vendredi Saint (Pierre Emmanuel) (soloists, ch and orch)
Heracles à Delphes, cantata (1928) (2nd Prix de Rome, 1928)
Avis (Eluard) (ch and orch) (1944)
Christine (J. Supervielle) (soloists, ch and orch) (1959) (Presser)
Les cinq plaies (M. Manoll) (soloists, ch and orch) (1952)
La Nativité (L. Masson) (soloists, ch and orch) (1951)
Les paysans (A. Frenaud) (soloists, ch and orch) (1958) (Presser)
La poèsie interrompue (Eluard) (3 vces and orch) (1948) (Paris: Costallat)
Songs incl.:
Dans la sable (A. Camus, 1938)
Il y a quelqu'un auquel je pense (1931)
Je ne reclamais rien de toi
Je suit ici pour chanter des chansons (Tagore) (1931)
La lumière (Borraine, 1932)
Le march du monde (A. Reizine, 1946)
Pastourelle (A. Fouche, 1931)
BALLET
La chanson du mal aime (1950)
Claudine à l'ecole (1950)
Le mur (1947)
OPERA
Le Roi Bossu, in one act (A. Carre) (1932)
INCIDENTAL MUSIC
Ars (1960)
Brand (H. Ibsen) (1949)
Elisabeth d'Angleterre (F. Bruckner) (1949)
Jeanne d'Arc (P. Bost, 1948)
Madame Bovary (G. Flaubert) (1948)
Megaree (M. Druon) (1946)
Pauvre Jérusalem (R. Pillaudin) (1962)
Penthesilea (H. von Kleist) (1955)
Printemps de la liberté (J. Gremillon) (1948)
Rainer Maria Rilke (1956)
Le Roi Lear (Shakespeare, trans A. Jolivet) (1945)
La tragédie des bonnes intentions (P. Ustinov) (1957)
Varsovie (1956)
Films:
Coeur d'amour épris (1951)
La flute magique (with M. Delannoy) (1947)
Pattes blanches (1948)
Le saboteur du Val de Loire (J. Depry) (1956)
Vercors (1916)
MISCELLANEOUS
La Vierge Guerriere (Premiere Prix de Rome, 1929)
Radio music
Bibliography
Carre, A. *Souvenirs de theatre*. Paris, 1950.
Ref. 8, 9, 15, 17, 20, 22, 52, 70, 73, 76, 94, 96, 105, 107, 172, 193, 200, 236, 280, 347, 580, 622

BARRATT, Carol Ann
English composer. b. 1945.
Compositions
ORCHESTRA
Canzona, op. 17 (a-fl and str orch) (1969) (London: Performing Rights Society)
Passaglia (str orch) (1964) (Perf. Rights Soc.)
CHAMBER
Fanfare for a friend (3 trp) (London: Chester Music)
Episodes, op. 12 (pf and tba) (1968)
Etude, op. 5 (pf and cl) (1964)
Introduction and allegro, op. 5 (pf and cl) (1964)
Invention, op. 4 (2 fl) (1964)
Sonatina, op. 15 (ob and pf) (1969)
Two divertissements, op. 6 (2 ob) (1964)
Series, op. 14 (a-fl) (1969)
Five inventions, op. 16 (b-trb) (1969)
Suite, op. 10 (1967)
PIANO
Burlesca (4 hands) (1968)
Paradigm (4 hands) (1973)
Ref. Otto Harrassowitz (Wiesbaden), 280

BARRELL, Joyce Howard
English organist, pianist, violinist, teacher and composer. b. Salisbury, November 26, 1917. She studied at Leicester University under Dr. Ben Burrows (piano, organ and composition) and Grace Burrows (violin). She also studied privately under Harold Craxton. She held various teaching posts.
Compositions
ORCHESTRA
Norfolk music, op. 17 (str orch) (1961)
Saturday music, op. 13 (1956)
Five Ukrainian sketches, op. 32 (str orch; also str qrt) (1974, 1967)
CHAMBER
Fury, fancy and finale, op. 19 (fl, cl, and 3-part vlc ens) (1961)
Sextet for the Hall family, op. 67 (rec, str qrt and pf)
Quintet, op. 27 (2 cl, bsn and 2 vlc) (1965)
Movement for string quartet, op. 2 (1942)
Sketch No. 1 for string quartet, op. 21 (1963)
String quartet, op. 15 (1960)
Ukrainian Impressions for Woodwinds, op. 37 (1968)
Movement for string trio, op. 6 (1952)
Strata, op. 40 (3 gtr)
String trio, op. 36
Trio for clarinet, viola and piano, op. 44 (1970)
Trio for flute, harp and viola da gamba, op. 24 (1965)
Trio for recorders, op. 10 (1955)
Aerial op. 65 (fl and pf)
Duets, op. 26 (trp and ob) (1965)
Duets for two recorders, op. 5 (1950)
Duets for two recorders, op. 8 (1954)

Duo, op. 25 (vln and vlc) (1964)
Elegy, op. 12 (2 vln) (1956)
In orbit (fl and pf) (1969)
Music for handbells, ops. 61 and 62
One movement for violin and viola, op. 7 (1953)
Partita, op. 73 (pf duet)
Sonatina, op. 38 (vln and pf) (1968)
Three dialogues, op. 20 (fl and viola da gamba) (Thames, 1960)
The three inns (2 gtr)
Four soliloquies op. 64 (gtr) (1981)
Light studies, op. 31 (gtr)
Partita (vib)
Prelude, op. 23 (hp) (1963)
Shapes, op. 72 (gtr)
The fires, op. 51 (1973) (Anglican New Music Series, 1977)
Four contrasts, op. 52 (1973)
Fragments, op. 28 (1965)
Tanzmusik, op. 33 (1967)
Three keyboard pieces, op. 4 (1948)
Two-part inventions, op. 11 (1956)
VOCAL
What am I? op. 68 school cantata, (Jean Pressling) (ch and pf)
Be welcome in this house, op. 56 (anon) (mix-ch) (1976)
Four Canadian poems, op. 70 (mix-ch)
The song, op. 9 (Stephen Coates) (mix-ch) (1955)
Are they shadows? op. 69a (Samuel Daniel) (S and pf)
Think no more lad, op. 18 (A.E. Housman) (1961)
Slow, slow, fresh fount, op. 69 (Ben Jonson) (S and pf)
Tim's hoop (narr and fl) (1963)
Two epitaphs, op. 3 (vce and pf) (1968)
When to her lute Corrina sings, op. 1 (1938) (Thomas Campian)
SACRED
A child is born in Bethlehem (w-ch and hp)
A child of our time, op. 43, carol
Ref. composer, 457, 585

BARRETT-THOMAS, N.
20th-century American composer.
Compositions
ORCHESTRA
Chikona (1973)
CHAMBER
Posauna in the highest (18 trb, timp, perc and xy) (1970)
Refractions (fl, ob, cl, bsn and pf) (1969)
Perpetuum mobile, (fl, bsn, vln and vla) (1969)
Gregarious chants II (vla and cl) (1974)
Gregarious chants III (fl and perc) (1975)
Sonata (vla and pf) (1976)
VOCAL
From the land of the caribou (S, w-ch, ww ens, perc and mar) (1975)
Boston: alone (w-ch) (1977)
Songs to a handsome woman (S, w-ch and pf) (1977)
Boston: reflected (S and pf) (1976)
Songs of singing (A, pf and vlc) (1970)
SACRED
Three psalms (T, vla and pf) (1977)
Ref. 228

BARRIENTOS, Maria
Spanish pianist, violinist, conductor, coloratura soprano, teacher and composer. b. Barcelona, March 10, 1884. d. St. Jean de Luz, France, August 8, 1946. As a child prodigy she conducted her own symphony. She commenced singing at the age of 14 and a year later made her debut in Barcelona in the role of Selika. At 17 she toured the major cities of Germany. She was a famous prima donna in Italy, New York, Paris and South America until 1939, when she taught singing in Buenos Aires. She composed a symphony.
Ref. 2, 8, 44, 74, 323, 345, 361, 425

BARRIERE, Françoise
French pianist and composer. b. Paris, June 12, 1944. She studied the piano and composition at the Paris Conservatoire from 1962 to 1969 and from 1968 to 1969 completed a course on ethnomusicology at the Ecole Pratique de Hautes Etudes. In 1970 together with Christian Clozier she founded the Bourges Group of Experimental Music. Under their direction the group performed many musical works, including a musique concrete opera *A Vie* by Christian Clozier. They also instituted and organized the annual Bourges Festival of Experimental Music. DISCOGRAPHY. PHOTOGRAPH.
Compositions
ELECTRONIC
Au paradis des assassins (1973)
Le code penal (1969)
Cordes-ci, cordes ça (medieval fiddle, vln and tape) (1971)
Fanfares de printemps (hn and pf)
Javarosa (Printemps des Saisons) (1972)
Le mesel et la harpe (1973)
Ode à la terre marine (1970)
Ritratto di Giovane (pf and tape) (1972-1974)
Variations hydrophilusiennes (1971)
Les végétaux, la nuit (A. Beaujean) (1969)
INCIDENTAL MUSIC
Pieces for radio and stage
Ref. composer, 563

BARROWS, Margaret Bentley Hamilton
American poetess and composer. b. New York City, September 6, 1920.
Compositions
SACRED
Easter carol
The Promised Land
MISCELLANEOUS
Living with the arts
To the month of June
Ref. 475

BARRY, Emilie de
Composition
PIANO
Romance sans paroles (Ricordi)
Ref. Ricordi (Milan)

BARTALOTTI, Signora
18th-century Italian composer. She composed ballet music for the opera *Dario* in 1764.
Ref. 226, 260, 276, 347

BARTH, Elise
Bohemian pianist, teacher and composer. b. Prague, ca. 1800. She showed exceptional talent for the piano at a very young age and was accepted as a pupil by Dionys Weber. She travelled in Central Europe as a pianist and later taught the piano at the Prague Conservatory. She composed for the piano.
Ref. 129, 276

BARTHEL, Ursula (nee Wegener)
German guitarist, organist, pianist, recorder player, violinist, choral conductor and composer. b. Demmin, Pomerania, January 30, 1913; d. December 22, 1977. The daughter of a school music teacher, she received her first piano instruction from her father and played in public at the age of seven. She also studied the recorder, the violin and the guitar. She attended the Evangelical Church Music School, Aschersleben and after four semesters graduated in 1934 as organist and choir leader. From 1935 to 1939 she was an organist in Wolfen/Bitterfeld and until 1941 studied teaching in Schneidemuhl. She married the music lecturer Dagobert Barthel. During the war she worked in Berlin and in 1949 settled in Minden, Westphalia, where she organized concerts and composed choral music for the Minden children's choir and the choir and orchestra of the Bellel Gymnasium. DISCOGRAPHY. PHOTOGRAPH.
Compositions
ORCHESTRA
An der Krippe (man and orch) (1973)
Gruss an Amerika (man and orch) (1974)
Kleine Hirtenmusik (man and orch) (1971)
Kleines Weihnachtskonzert (man and orch) (1972)
Weihnacht in aller Welt (man and orch) (1976)
Auf froher Fahrt (wind orch) (1970)
Kleine Tanzsuite nach Kirnberger (1973)
Spielmusik nach altfranzoezischen Tanzweisen (1962)
Suite nach Rameau (1964)
Taenzerische Musik Nr. 1-7 (1967-1974)

Variationen ueber ein Thema von Purcell (1961)
Schuetzenmarsch
Westfaelische Suite fuer Jugendorchester (1969)
CHAMBER
Variationen ueber ein altdeutsches Lied (str qrt) (before 1939)
Variationen ueber ein eigenes Thema (3 viola da gamba) (1937)
Concertina (trb and pf) (1975)
Kleine Suite (t-gamba and hpcd) (before 1939)
Sonata (vln and pf)
ORGAN
Thirty choral preludes
Toccata and fugue
PIANO
Capriccios (1924-1939)
Humoresques (1924-1939)
Intermezzos (1924-1939)
Polonaises (1924-1939)
VOCAL
Der alte Kakadu (mix-ch)
Die Ameisen (In Hamburg lebten zwei Ameisen) (solo and ch)
Der Esel (Es stand vor eines Hauses Tor) (ch)
Festliches Lied (Goethe) (w-ch) (ERES)
Frisch auf warm weht der wind (w-ch)
Frohsinn (ch)
Gute Reise (mix-ch)
Ihr Freunde in der Runde (mix-ch)
Die Musik, allein (ch)
Sonne leuchte mir ins Herz hinein (mix-ch and pf)
Tenga lavo (Calyos) (mix-ch) (ERES)
Wenn ich zum Tanze geh (m-qrt) (ERES)
Heut' wandern wir ins Blau
Musikalischer Kalendar
Neue Kinderlieder
SACRED
Mein Mund, der Singer (mix-ch)
Waldweihnacht (ch)
Weihnacht ist gekommen (ch)
Das Christkind kommt
Es kam ein Engel vom hohen Himmel (Schott)
Stille Nacht, heilige Nacht
BALLET
Ballet music
Ref. composer, 563

BARTHELEMON, Cecilia Maria (Mrs. Henslowe)

English harpist, harpsichordist, singer and composer. b. 1770. She was the daughter of a French violinist and composer, François Hippolyte Barthelemon and Mary Barthelemon (q.v.).

Compositions

CHAMBER
Two sonatas, op. 2 (pf or hpcd and vln, German fl and vlc) (London: Vauxhall, 1729)
Sonata, op. 3 (pf or hpcd) (ded J. Haydn) (John Brand, 1794)
Sonata, op. 4 (pf or hpcd and vln) (Longman & Broderip)
Three sonatas, op. 1 (pf or hpcd and vln) (Vauxhall, 1786)
VOCAL
The capture of the Cape of Good Hope (pf or hpcd) (Lavenu, 1795)

Publications

Henslowe, C.M. Memoir of her father, pub. as a preface to his oratorio *Jefte in Masfa*.
Ref. 8, 65, 85, 123, 125, 150

BARTHELEMON, Mary (Maria, Polly) (nee Young)

English singer and composer. b. London 1749; d. London, September 20, 1979. A member of a large musical family, she married François Hippolyte Barthelemon, violinist and composer in 1766, with whom she travelled and performed. Their only child, Cecilia Maria Barthelemon (q.v.) was a harpsichord player and composer.

Compositions

CHAMBER MUSIC
Six sonatas (hpcd or pf and vln) (London: W. Napier 1776)
VOCAL
An ode on the late providential preservation of our Gracious Sovereign, op. 5 (1795)
Six English and Italian songs, op. 2 (Vauxhall, ca. 1790)
The weaver's prayer (London: Preston and Son., ca. 1790)
SACRED
Three hymns and three anthems, op. 3 (for the Asylum and Magdalen Chapels) (London, J. Bland, ca. 1794)
Ref. 8, 65, 123, 125, 405, 477

BARTHELOMON, Polly. See BARTHELOMON, Mary

BARTHELSON, Joyce Holloway (Mrs. B.M. Steigman)

American pianist, conductor, lecturer and composer. b. Yakima, WA, May 18, 1908. She attended the University of California, Berkeley and studied under Nicholson (voice), Dr. Antonia Brico (conducting), Otto Cesana, Julius Gold and Roy Harris (theory and composition), Katz (counterpoint) and Cesana and Flagello (orchestration). She worked as an ensemble coach and pianist for the National Broadcasting Company, San Francisco and the Arian Trio and went on concert and lecture tours to many universities including Columbia, Indiana, Stanford, Pennsylvania, Alfred and West Virginia. From 1935 to 1940 she worked as an assistant conductor for the New York Women's Symphony Orchestra. She was the composer-in-residence at Western Maryland College from 1942 to 1944, then a choral conductor in New York City and Westchester County until 1960. In 1944 she was co-founder and co-director of the Barthelson Music School in Scarsdale, NY. In 1967 she received first prize from ASCAP and the National Federation of Music for an opera. PHOTOGRAPH.

Compositions

ORCHESTRA
Concerto for 2 pianos
Concerto for oboe and chamber orchestra
Savannah overture
Suite, based on Of time and the river (Wolfe)
Weather report, suite
CHAMBER
Piano pieces
VOCAL
The forty-niners (soloists, ch and orch)
The bagpipe carol (w-ch and pf)
I'm only nineteen (w-ch and pf)
Over 200 choral octavos and folk music
SACRED
Choral series (N.B. Turner & V. Hoff) (mix-ch)
Christmas 1620 (w-ch)
The first Palm Sunday (soloists, nar, ch, org and cham ens)
The pilgrims (mix-ch)
Traditional hymns
OPERA
Chanticleer, comic fantasy (Carl Fischer, 1967)
Devil's disciple (Shaw) (1977)
Feathertop, opera buffa with overture
Greenwich village, 1910 (O. Henry) (1969)
The king's breakfast (Baring) (C. Fischer, 1973)
Ref. 141, 280, 295, 347, 474, 594, 622, 625

BARTHOLOMEW, Ann Sheppard (nee Mounsey)

English organist, pianist, teacher and composer. b. London, April 17, 1811; d. London, June 24, 1891. She became a pupil of Logier in 1817 and was noticed by Spohr on his visit to Logier's institute in 1820. Her harmonization of a melody was subsequently printed in his autobiography. She later studied under Samuel Wesley and Thomas Attwood and in 1828 was appointed church organist in Clapton. She became organist at St. Vedast's in 1837 and remained there for nearly 50 years. In 1834 she became an associate of the Philharmonic Society and in 1839 a member of the Royal Society of Musicians. She gave regular concerts of sacred classical music, at which she introduced several of Mendelssohn's smaller pieces.

Compositions

CHAMBER
Organ pieces
PIANO
Last rose of summer (4 hands) (Ascherberg)
Allegro vivace (Ascherberg)
Andante gracioso (Ascherberg)
Anxiety (Ascherberg)
The blind harper (Ascherberg)
Entreaty (Ascherberg)
Festival march (Ascherberg)
Hope (Ascherberg)
Infancy (Ascherberg)
Prelude and gigue (Ascherberg)
Summer evening (Ascherberg)
Three bagatelles (Ascherberg)
Whirligig (Ascherberg)
VOCAL
Over 100 songs, incl.:
Charming maiden
Days gone by
Dreaming and waking
Flow, murmuring stream
Six duets in canon (1836)
Six four-part songs, op. 36
The young vocalist (arr from classical anthems) (1867)

SACRED
The Nativity, oratorio (1855)
Supplication and thanksgiving, cantata (ded H.R.H. The Princess of Wales)
Holy thoughts, juvenile sacred songs (1875)
Hymns of prayer and praise
Sacred harmony
Thirty-four original tunes set to favourite hymns (1883)
Ref. 2, 6, 8, 74, 226, 276, 297

BARTHOLOMEW, Mrs. M.
19th-century British composer.
Compositions
PIANO
The Sydenham march (6 hands)
Britons! Strike home (variations from Bonduca, after Purcell)
La jeunesse, rondino à la valse (Ashdown)
La Napolitaine, second tarantella (Novello)
O hills, O vales, 6 variations (after Mendelssohn) (Novello)
Rousseau's dream, fantasy with variations (Williams)
La Sicilienne, rondoletto (Ashdown)
Three studies (Ascherberg)
Les trois amis, waltz (Ashdown)
VOCAL
Gentle Spring (mix-ch) (Novello)
The lark now leaves his wat'ry nest (mix-ch) (Novello)
Song of Spring (unison ch)
Take care, take care (mix-ch) (Ashdown)
Approx. 10 songs incl.:
O the merry merry spring, ballad
Six four-part songs
To daffodils (Williams)
SACRED
A wreath for Christmas (mix-ch) (Novello)
I heard the voice of Jesus (Novello)
Te Deum, 3 settings to nine chants (Novello)
Ref. 297

BARTLETT, Agnes
Late I9th-century English composer.
Composition
OPERETTA
Florette, the Goose Girl (1893)
Ref. 431

BARTLETT, Ethel Agnes
20th-century English harpsichordist, pianist and composer. b. Essex. She studied at the Royal Academy of Music under Frederick Corder, Artur Schnabel and Frederick Moore and later became a fellow of the academy. She toured in Europe, the United States and Latin America as part of a piano duo.
Compositions
CHAMBER
Folk tunes for cello and piano
PIANO
Fantastic dance of Delius (2 pf)
Two series
Ref. 467

BARTLETT, Floy Little
American violinist and composer. b. Burlington, IA, 1883. She studied at Knox College Conservatory, Galesburg and later under Gustav Dannreuther in New York and Susan Ghaigneau in Paris.
Compositions
CHAMBER
Barcarolle (2 vln and pf)
Bolero (2 vln and pf)
Caprice (2 vln and pf)
Marionettes (2 vln and pf)
VOCAL
Songs incl.:
At dusk
If I but knew
My fidil is singing
Sweet little woman o'mine
Songs for children
ARRANGEMENTS
Works of Handel, Bach, Haydn, Mozart, Beethoven and Mendelssohn, as historical miniatures for children
Ref. 292

BARTLETT, Nancy Nicholls. See GUSTAVSON, Nancy Nicholls

BARTON, Ann
20th-century American composer.
Composition
INCIDENTAL MUSIC
No Vacancy, music play (with Connie Thomas q.v.) (3 soloists and chil-ch) (Flammer, 1978)
Ref. MLA *Notes*

BASBAS (Caress)
Arabian songstress of Medina, of the Abbasid period. b. ca. 750. She was a slave belonging to Yahya ibn Nafis, whose concerts in Medina were famous. The Caliph al-Mansur (754 to 775) was charmed by her singing and the Caliph al-Mahdi (775 to 785) bought her from Yahya, while he was still a prince for 17 000 pieces of gold. She bore him a daughter, Aliya. Her beauty and voice were praised by contemporary poets and at Medina she was the idol of the Quraish.
Ref. 171, 234, 305

BASSANO, Mlle.
17th-century Italian composer. She was the daughter of Domenico Bassano, ca. 1645. She composed vocal works.
Ref. 465

BASSETT, Beth. See BASSETT, Henrietta Elizabeth

BASSETT, Henrietta Elizabeth (pseud. Beth Bassett)
American organist, pianist, teacher and composer. b. Dallas, March 25, 1932. She studied the piano and the organ at Baylor University, Waco, receiving her B.A. in 1952. She first made radio appearances as a piano soloist in 1944 and from 1945 was organist and pianist in Baptist churches in Mesquite, TX. From 1948 she taught the piano, the organ, theory and composition privately and in schools and directed plays and musicals. From 1948 to 1973 and in 1974 she was music administrator in Mesquite and from 1972 to 1978, chairlady of the national piano and organ auditions. She was three times winner, in 1946, 1947 and 1948 of the national piano auditions sponsored by the National Guild of Piano Teachers and won the International Annual Composition Contest sponsored by the National Guild of Piano Teachers and American College of Musicians (1965 to 1976). She received the National Guild of Piano Teachers' highest award, the Piano Guild's Hall of Fame in 1972.
Compositions
PIANO
Name that tune (3 pf, 12 hands) (lst prize, American College of Musicians, 1975)
Fireworks (1972) (Miklas Press)
Sleepy (1972) (Miklas)
Stepping high (1972) (Miklas)
The water wheel (1977) (Willis Music)
VOCAL
Ten little Indians (2 pf and 10 performers) (1975) (Miklas)
SACRED
The first Christmas, cantata (lst prize, American College of Musicians, 1965)
Girls' auxiliary allegiance (vce and ch) (1972)
Girls for Jesus (vce and ch) (1972)
Publications
Contributions to *Clavier*, *Piano Quarterly*, *The Organist* and *American Home Organist*.
Three theory workbooks, incl. *Listen...then do*. Workbook 1. 1975.
Rudiments of Music, 1978.
Ref. composer, 77, 359, 457

BASSETT, Karolyn Wells
American pianist, singer and composer. b. Derby, CT, August 2, 1892; d. New York, June 8, 1931. She composed choral works and songs.
Ref. 142, 347

BASSOT, Anne-Marie (Nanine)
French composer. b. Paris, December 5, 1901. She studied counterpoint and fugue under Maitre Paul le Fleur. PHOTOGRAPH.

Compositions
PIANO
Deuxieme suite de pieces enfantines (4 hands) (Heugel, 1955)
First suite
Other pieces
VOCAL
Choral works
THEATRE
Based mainly on stage works by Georges Dobbelaere:
Amal (R. Tagore)
Aucassin et Nicolette
Le clerc
Le coq d'or
Des cinq compagnons, for children
Foucauld
L'habit du Grand'Duc, for children
Jeanne d'Arc
Les jeunes filles
Merlin et Vivianine
Mermoz
Noël des hommes
Noël en Flandres
L'oiseleur
Le pont
La rose bleue, for children
Saint François d'Assise
Saint Hilaire
Saint Martin
Saint Paul
Vol de nuit (St. Exupéry)
Ref. composer, 189

BASSOT, Nanine. See BASSOT, Anne-Marie

BATCHELOR, Phyllis
Australian pianist, teacher and composer. b. Healesville, Australia, February 1, 1920. She was taught the piano from the age of three by her mother and then by M. Fritzhart. She studied at Melbourne University (A.Mus.A.), the Melba Conservatory and in London where she became an L.R.A.M.. At 17 she began playing for the Australian Broadcasting Commission and by her 20's was one of ABC'S most frequently heard artists, often performing her own works. She was also a soloist with the Melbourne Symphony Orchestra and taught at the Melbourne Conservatory. She married a Russian violinist, Ivan Pietruschka.
Compositions
CHAMBER
Andante and allegro (vln and pf)
Sonata (vln and pf)
Sonata (fl and pf) (1972)
Suite in three movements (fl and pf)
Three pieces for violin and piano
PIANO
Chorale prelude (2 pf) (1950)
The ballet dancer
City scenes
Four pieces
Nocturne
Prelude and fugue
Sonatina
Variations on an original theme
Variations on a theme in F-Minor
VOCAL
Songs incl.:
Autumn (vce and pf)
The awakening (S and pf)
Cradle song (vce and pf)
For a child (vce and pf)
The green singer (vce and pf)
Jenny kissed me (vce and pf)
The leaves are falling (vce and pf)
Light (vce and pf)
Lyrics from the Chinese (S, fl and pf)
The moon is jealous of the flowers (vce and pf)
Spring light (vce and pf)
When I was one and twenty (S and pf)
The wind (vce and pf)
SACRED
Isaiah 55 (solo, w-ch and 2 pf)
Ref. composer, ABC, Thora Mills (Toronto), 446

BATE, Jennifer
English organist and composer. b. 1944. DISCOGRAPHY.
Compositions
ORGAN
Toccata on a theme of Martin Shaw
MISCELLANEOUS
Introduction and variations on an old French carol (Novello, 1983)
Ref. 563, 585

BATES, Anna Craig
20th-century American composer of piano pieces and songs.
Ref. 347

BATES, Augusta. See CECCONI-BATES, Augusta

BATES, Katherine Lee
20th-century American composer.
Composition
VOCAL
America the Beautiful (with Ethel Hier) (mix-ch and orch) (1919)
Ref. 594

BATTA, Clementine
19th-century Germany composer.
Composition
SACRED
Mélodie religieuse (vce, pf, vlc and org) (Mayence)
Ref. 226, 276

BATTAGINI, Guiseppina
19th-century Italian composer.
Composition
VOCAL
Il canzoniere del giardino, in 54 parts (Ricordi)
Ref. 297

BAU, Elise
19th-20th-century German composer.
Compositions
CHAMBER
Feentaenze zwischen Himmel und Erde (2 vln, fl and pf)
Efeuranken, zither serenade, op. 9
PIANO
Abschied von der Elgesburg, op. 16
Alpenglocken, Salonstueck, op. 10
Auf der schwedischen Eisbahn, waltz, op. 3
Auf hoher See, Salonstueck, op. 12
Auf Wiedersehen, Salonstueck, op. 25
Ein Weihnachstraum, waltz, op. 19
Eisblumen, polka-mazurka, op. 21
Erinnerung an Schloss Elgersburg, op. 16
Fruehlingsblueten, Salonstueck, op. 4
Geburtstags-Straussen, Rheinland polka, op. 13
Gedenke mein, phantasie, op. 26
Die Glocken im Eichwalde, Salonstueck, op. 4
Glueck auf, Salonstueck, op. 8
Leny, polka, op. 24
Leuchtkuglen, polka, op. 7
Lindenblueten, Rheinlander, op. 23
Loviziana, polka-mazurka, op. 14
Martha-Walzer, op. 18
Moosrosen, waltz, op. 29
Schneeflocken, polka-mazurka, op. 11
Sonnenstrahlen, Salonstueck, op. 2
Die Spieluhr, idyll, op. 20
Sternfunkeln, Salonstueck, op. 1
Vergissmeinnicht, Salonstueck, op. 27
Waldesgruen, Salonstueck, op. 6
Wellenspiele, Salonstueck, op. 22
Der Winter, op. 28
Ref. 297

BAUDISSIN, Sofie, Countess Wolf

19th-century German pianist and composer. She was a pupil of Henselt and Pixis.

Compositions

PIANO

Variations on an original theme, op. 8 (2 pf)
Impromptu (Fuerstner)
Six songs without words
Small pieces, ops. 3 and 9
Three etudes
Three nocturnes (Breitkopf)
Traumereien, op. 11 (Challier)
Two mazurkas (Breitkopf)
Valse brillante

VOCAL

Der Wald wird dichter
Die Nachtigall auf meiner Flur
Es schleicht ein zehrend Feuer
Ich fuhr von Sankt Goar, op. 6
Mein Herz ist wie die dunkle Nacht
Ueber die Berge wandelt
Und wenn die Primel
Voeglein, wohin so schnell?
Wenn hinabgeglueht die Sonne
Songs, op. 7 (pf and vlc)
Abschied
An die Laute
Nun ist der Tag geschieden
Sehnsucht
Spielleute
Staendchen

Ref. 226, 276, 297

BAUER, Charlotte

19th-century German composer.

Compositions

PIANO

Sechs Klavierstuecke, op. 24 (E. Stoll)
Trois morceaux de salon, op. 22 (Litolff)

VOCAL

Fuenf Lieder, op. 20 (E. Stoll)
Sechs Kinderlieder, op. 16 (Andre)

Ref. 276, 297

BAUER, Emilie Frances (pseuds. Francesco Nogero, Francisco di Nogero)

American pianist, critic, editor, teacher and composer. b. Walla Walla, WA, March 5, 1865; d. New York, March 9, 1926. Her younger sister was the composer Marion Bauer (q.v.). Emilie studied with Miguel Espinosa and at the Paris Conservatoire. She taught the piano and voice in Washington and Portland, OR, where she was music critic for the *Portland Oregonian*. In 1896 she moved east, teaching and writing in Boston before moving to New York. At one time she was on the staff of the *Musical Courier* and from 1902 to 1903 she edited a women's page in *Etude*. She also wrote for many years for the *Musical Leader*, *Concertgoer* and other periodicals.

Compositions

VOCAL

Songs incl.:
My love is a muleteer
Seville love song

Ref. 347, 433, 415

BAUER, Katharine

German harpsichordist and composer. b. Wurzburg, 1785. She was a child virtuoso and became a pupil of Sterkel in the harpsichord and composition.

Compositions

HARPSICHORD

Airs varies (Leipzig: Offenbach)
Twelve variations, (Offenbach 1798)
Twelve variations on Lieschen nur wollte, op. 2
Twelve variations, op. 3
Two collections of allemandes and waltzes (1785) (Munich: Falter)

Ref. 128, 226, 276, 477

BAUER, Marion Eugenie

American pianist, authoress, critic, editor, professor and composer. b. Walla Walla, WA, August 15, 1887; d. South Hadley, August 9, 1955. She was the youngest of seven children of French parents and was first taught music by her eldest sister, Emilie Frances (q.v.). She was educated at St. Helen's Hall, Portland. She went to New York to study the piano and harmony under Henry Holdenhuss and the piano and theory under Eugene Heffley. In 1905 the French pianist Raoul Pugne and his family visited New York. Marion taught them English and was invited to Paris in 1906. There Nadia Boulanger (q.v.) taught her harmony in return for English lessons. She also studied under Campbell-Tipton and Pierre Monteux. She returned to the United States in 1907 and published her first song *Light*. In 1910 she went to Berlin where she studied counterpoint and musical form under Dr. Paul Ertel. In 1912 she again returned to the United States and studied composition under Walter Rothwell. In 1921 she became a founder member of the American Music Guild and in May 1923 went to Paris where she studied under Professor Andre Gedalge at the Paris Conservatoire. While in France she wrote a string quartet and a second sonata for violin and piano, which was later published as *Fantasia quasi una sonata*. Back in the United States in 1926, after the death of her sister Emilie, she took over as editor and critic of the *Musical Leader*. In 1932 an honorary M.A. was conferred upon her by Whitman College, Walla Walla. From 1930 to 1951 she was an associate professor at New York University, where she taught composition, form and analysis and lectured on musical aesthetics and history. She was visiting professor at the Teachers' College of Columbia University. She taught at Mills College, CA, in 1935, at the Carnegie Institute of Technology in Pittsburgh in 1936 and 1939 and at the Cincinnati Conservatory. She joined the faculty of the Institute of Musical Arts at the Juilliard School of Music in 1940. From 1928 she lectured annually at Chautauqua, NY. In 1950 she received the award of the Society for the Publication of American Music. In May 1951 the Phi Beta Fraternity of Music, of which she was a national honorary member, sponsored an entire program of her work at the Town Hall, New York. In June of that year she was awarded an honorary doctorate of music from the New York College of Music. Her *Symphonic Suite* for String Orchestra won an honorable mention in the Sigma Alpha Iota Contest for compositions by women. Marion was an active member of the Board of the League of Composers, the American Composers Alliance, and the Society for the Publication of American Music. She was on the board of directors of the International Society for Contemporary Music (U.S. section) and a member of the American Musicological Society. She was also a member of the American Music Society, the Chautauqua Society of Greater New York, of which she was vice president from 1948 to 1949 and a member of the MacDowell Colony Association. She was a contributor to the *International Encyclopaedia of Music* and to *Great Modern Composers*. She was also editor of *Etude*. DISCOGRAPHY.

Compositions

ORCHESTRA

Symphony, op. 45 (1945-1950)
Piano concerto, American youth (G. Schirmer, 1943)
Aquarelle, op. 39, no. 2 (cham orch or double ww ens) (1948)
A lament (str orch) (1935)
Indian pipes (1927)
Patterns, op. 41, no. 2 (cham orch or double ww ens) (1968)
Prelude and fugue, op. 43 (fl and str orch)
Sun splendor (also 2 pf) (1934)
Symphonic suite, op. 34 (str orch) (1940)

CHAMBER

Allegretto giocoso (11 insts) (1920)
Concertino (ob, cl and str qrt) (Arrow Music, 1944)
Six little fugues (ww qnt)
Woodwind quintet, op. 48
Five pieces for string quartet, op. 18 nos. 1-5
Trio sonata, op. 40 (fl, vlc and pf) (1944)
Second trio sonata (fl, vlc and pf) (1951)
Duo, op. 25 (ob and cl) (1932)
Fantasia quasi una sonata (vln and pf) (G. Schirmer, 1928)
First violin sonata, op. 14 (vln and pf) (1921)
Second violin sonata (vln and pf) (1925)
Prelude, improvisation, pastoral dance (ob and cl)
Sonata, op. 22 (vla or cl and pf) (SPAM, 1935)
Sonatina, op. 32a (ob and pf) (1939)
Suite for oboe and clarinet (1932)
Five Greek kyries for flute alone (1938)
Up the Ocklawaha, op. 6 (vln) (A.P. Schmidt, 1913)
Meditation and toccata for organ (1951)
Violin sonata, op. 18

PIANO

Anagrams, op. 48
Aquarelle, op. 39, no. 1
Arabesque (1909)
Dance sonata (1935)
Eight divisions (Chappell)
Elegy (1909)
A fancy (Axelrod)
Four pieces, op. 21 (Arrow Music, 1930)
From New Hampshire woods, 3 pieces (G. Schirmer, 1923)
In the country op. 5 (A.P. Schmidt; Summy Birchard)
Moods
Parade (New York: Mercury Music, 1948)

Patterns, op. 41
Pine trees, op. 12, no. 3 (G. Schirmer, 1923)
Quietude (1924)
Six preludes (A.P. Schmidt, 1922)
Six preludettes (G. Schirmer, 1923)
Sonata (1932)
Spring day (Mercury Mus. 1948)
Summertime suite (New York: Leeds Music Corp., 1953)
Three impressions (1918)
Tumbling Tommy (Mercury Mus. 1948)
Turbulence, op. 17, no. 2 (E.B. Marks)
Two easy pieces (1942)
VOCAL
China (mix-ch and orch) (J. Fischer & Bro. 1943-1944) (W.B. Todrin)
Faun song (ch and orch) (1934)
At the New Year, op. 42 (mix-ch and pf) (New York: Associated Music, 1950)
Death spreads his gentle wings (mix-ch a cap) (1951) (Eunice P. Crain)
A foreigner comes to earth on Boston Common (ch) (Horace Gregory, 1951)
A garden is a lovesome thing, op. 28 (mix-ch a-cap) (G. Schirmer, 1938)
Fair daffodils (trio w-vces)
Light, song
SACRED
Three Noels, op. 22 (w-ch) (Boston: A.P. Schmidt)
Wenn Ich rufe an dich, Herr, Mein Gott, op. 3 (Psalm 218) (w-ch and org or pf)
THEATRE
Prometheus bound (2 pf and fl) (1930)
Three moods for dance (1950)
FILM MUSIC
Pan Syrinx, choreographic sketch (fl, ob, cl, str qrt and pf) (1937)
TEACHING PIECES
A new solfeggietto (after C.P.E. Bach) (1948) (Mercury)
Publications
How music grew. With Ethel Peyser. 1926. Putnam.
Music through the ages. With Ethel Peyser. 1932.
Twentieth century music. 1933.
How opera grew. With Ethel Peyser. 1956.
A summary of 20th-century music (as distinct from 20th-century music mentioned in Vol. 1).
Copland. In *New Book of Modern Composers*; David Ewers 3rd rev. edition New York: Knopf 1961. 141-147.
The Music of Mack Brunswick, ACA Bulletin, Vol.II/1/2, Vol.II 4.
Antonio Lora's songs. ACA Bulletin, Vol.II 4.6.
Ref. 8, 17, 22, 40, 44, 52, 53, 68, 70, 71, 73, 79, 81, 94, 96, 100, 106, 107, 109, 177, 226, 292, 361, 228, 415, 433, 477, 496, 524, 556, 560, 610, 611, 622

BAULD, Alison

Australian actress, lecturer, writer and composer. b. Sydney, 1944. She first attended the National Institute of Dramatic Art from 1961 to 1962. After composing incidental music for a N.I.D.A. production of Brecht's *Exception and the Rule* and for a Trust production of *As You Like It*, she studied for her B.Mus. at the University of Sydney from 1964 to 1967. Following a performance of two of her *Three Songs of Love*, she was awarded the Sydney Moss Scholarship enabling her to study under Elizabeth Lutyens (q.v.). She also studied analysis under Hans Keller. Most of her work has been performed at the Cockpit, an experimental workshop under the musical direction of Graham Dudley, an Australian composer. In 1971 she joined the music department of York University.
Compositions
CHAMBER
Piece for unaccompanied violin (1971)
PIANO
Concert (1974)
Piece (1971)
VOCAL
In a dead brown land (composer) (T, S, ch, vln, vlc, a-melodica, fl, picc, pipe and dr) (1971)
Van Diemen's land, choral fantasy (composer) (m-S, B, 2 T or Bar, male speaker and ch a-cap) (1976)
Three songs of love (S, fl, ob, bsn, vln, vlc and perc)
Piece (S, speaker, fl and ob) (1971)
Humpty Dumpty (T, fl and gtr) (1971)
One pearl (S or counter-T, grt and maracas) (Novello, 1973)
Mad Moll (S) (1971)
THEATRE
As you like it (Shakespeare)
Dear Emily (William Blake & A. Bauld) (S and hp) (Novello, 1973)
Egg (S or T, fl, vlc and perc) (Novello, 1973)
Exception and the rule (Brecht)
Exiles (medieval Latin legend) (soli, mix-ch, ens and actors) (Novello)
On the afternoon of the pigsty (pf, perc, mime and tape) (Novello, 1973)
Pumpkin (2 dancers, 2 actors and ens) (Novello, 1973)
ELECTRONIC
Withdrawal 1 (S, vln, vlc, pf, vib, perc, narr and tape of animal vces) (1968)
Withdrawal 11 (S, vln, vlc, pf, vib, perc, narr and tape of animal vces) (1970) (comm Ars Nova of Malmo, Sweden)
Inanna (tape) (Novello, 1975)
Ref. 203, 442, 444, 622

BAUM, Katherine

19th-century German composer.
Compositions
VOCAL
Ballade, op. 9
Four songs, op. 6
Two songs, op. 7
Two songs from Scheffel's Trompeter, op. 3
Ref. 276

BAUMGARTEN, Chris

East German conductor, lecturer and composer. b. Berlin-Zehlendorf, December 16, 1910. She studied at the Berlin Charlottenburg Musikhochschule from 1937 to 1941 and conducted chamber and children's choirs until 1947. From 1948 to 1961 she lectured at the German Theatre Institute, Weimar and at the Theatre School, Leipzig. She founded and developed the subject, *music for actors*. After 1961 she ran her own studio for singing performers, both singers and actors. Working free-lance she gave courses at theatres and schools in East and West Germany, Holland and Sweden.
Compositions
INCIDENTAL MUSIC
Beaumarchais (Wolf)
Der eingebildete Kranke (Moliere)
Die Farce von Advokaten Pathelin
Die chinesische Nachtigall (Anderson)
Hans Herzenstod (Shaw)
Komoedie der Irrungen (Shakespeare)
Der Feigling (Dudow)
Turandot (Schiller)
Publications
Contributions to *Musik und Gesellschaft* and *Theater der Zeit*.
Hallo Du. Collection of literary chansons, songs and lieder, for voice, keyboard and guitar. Henschel, 1971.
Mit heller Stimme. 2 vols. of choral works.
Three hundred settings of literary works to music. 1932-1983.
Ref. Frau und Musik

BAUMGRAS or BAUMGROS, Irene. See HALE, Irene

BAUR, Constance Maude de

18th-century German composer.
Ref. 347

BAWR, Alexandrine Sophie (pseuds. Mme. de Baur; M. François; Saint-Simon, Comtesse de)

French pianist, authoress, singer and composer. b. Stuttgart, October 8, 1773; d. December 31, 1860. The daughter of the Marquis Goury de Champgrand, she went to Paris when young and received an excellent education studying under Gretry (composition) and Boieldieu, Elleviou and Garat (singing). In 1789 she married Claude-Henry de Rouvroy, Comte de Saint-lSimon, philosopher and founder of the Saint-Simonien sect. The marriage ended in divorce after a year and she married the Russian officer Baron de Bauer, who died in 1809. Compelled to earn her own living, she composed romances, comedies and melodramas under the names of Mme. Saint-Simon and Mme. de Bawr and literary works under the pseudonym M. François. An opera and melodrama of hers were successfully performed in Paris and her romances were popular in the salons. She was one of the first women in music to make a sustained effort to alter 19th-century attitudes towards women.
Compositions
VOCAL
D'aimer besoin puissant (vce and pf)
J'etais heureux (vce and pf)
O, Toi qui ne peux plus entendre (vce and pf) (in Le Souvenir des Ménestrels no. 20, Paris, 1814)

THEATRE
Leon ou le chateau de Montaldi melodrama in 3 acts (original text) (1811)
Other comedies with music, performed in Paris
Publications
Mes Souvenirs. Paris: Passard, 1853.
Novels, short stories, children's stories in Bibliotheque Rose, Paris: Hachette.
Bibliography
Gagne, Elise. *Madame de Bawr, Etude Biographique*. Paris: Didier 1861 Hauberstricker. *Cours de litterature ancienne* and *Histoire de France* Encyclopedie des Dames. Paris, 1823.
Ref. 15, 128, 129, 312, 335, 347

BAYER, Karoline
Austrian violinist and composer. b. Vienna, 1758; d. Vienna, 1803. She was the daughter of the court trumpeter and traveled widely in the German Federation as a violinist from 1775 to 1800.
Ref. 105, 126, 128, 129, 276

BAYEROWA, Konstancje. See BAJEROWA, Konstancje

BAYEVA, Vera
Bulgarian choir conductor and composer. b. Burgas, March 18, 1930. At the Bulgarian State Conservatory she studied composition under Professor Marin Goleminov. After graduating, she worked as choir mistress of an ensemble performing on Bulgarian radio and television.
Compositions
CHAMBER
String quartet
Sonata (vln and pf)
Instrumental pieces
PIANO
Sonata (2 pf)
Sonata
VOCAL
Ten choral pieces
More than 50 solo songs
Ref. 217

BAYLIS, Lilian Mary
English violinist, philanthropist, teacher, theatre manager and composer. b. London, May 9, 1874; d. London, November 25, 1937. She studied the violin at the Royal College of Music and the Royal Academy of Music, under John Tiplady Carrodus, to whom she attributed her love of opera. She made her first appearance in London as a child prodigy. At the age of sixteen she went with her parents to South Africa. Besides performing and teaching, she founded a ladies' orchestra in Johannesburg. She was invited back to England to take over the management of the Old Vic Theatre and was instrumental in the founding of a permanent Shakespeare repertory company there. She also played a key role in the reconstruction and opening of the Sadler's Wells Theatre in 1931. She was made an Associate of the Royal College of Music, London.
Compositions
PIANO
Caprice
Lyddon
VOCAL
Songs incl.:
Goodnight
Was that somebody you?
Ref. 8, 347, 377, 467

BAYON, Mlle. See LOUIS, Mme.

BAZIN, Mlle.
French composer.
Compositions
VOCAL
Premier recueil de romances et d'ariettes avec accompagnement de clavecin ou piano-forte (Paris: Guenin)
Ref. 125

BEACH, Alden. See BEACH, Priscilla A.

BEACH, Amy Marcy (nee Cheney) (Mrs. Henry Harris Aubrey)
American concert pianist, writer and composer. b. Henniker, NH, September 5, 1867; d. New York, December 27, 1944. She came from a musical home and showed an early talent for music. She started to play the piano at the age of four and at seven made her first public appearances playing some of her own waltzes. She studied under Ernst Perabo in 1873 and Carl Baermann in Boston and made her debut as a professional pianist playing Moscheles' *G-Minor Concerto* at the age of 16. She studied harmony under Julius W. Hill, but was self-taught in counterpoint, composition and orchestration. She translated Berlioz and Gevaert's treatise on instrumentation for her own use. She appeared frequently with the Boston Symphony Orchestra and other major orchestras, the Kneisel Quartet and in piano recitals. After her marriage to Dr. Beach in 1885 she insisted on being known by his name and devoted herself largely to composition. Her orchestral composition *Symphony in E-Minor, op. 32* was the first symphony to be composed by an American woman. It was performed by the Boston Symphony Orchestra in 1896. She was commissioned to write several works, including *Festival Jubilate*, which she composed for the Women's Building at the Chicago World's Fair in 1892. She made a major contribution to ornithological science by her transcription of bird calls into musical form. After her husband's death in 1910 she spent four years in Europe giving concerts in Rome, Paris and Berlin. She then returned to the United States and spent the rest of her life composing, interrupted from time to time by recital tours. DISCOGRAPHY. PHOTOGRAPH.
Compositions
ORCHESTRA
Symphony in E-Minor, op. 32, 'Gaelic' (1896) (Boston: APS)
Concerto in C-Sharp Minor, op. 45 (pf and orch) (1899) (APS)
Festival jubilate op. 17 (1892) (comm Women's Building, Chicago World Fair)
CHAMBER
Pastorale for woodwind quintet (New York: Composers Press, 1942)
Piano quintet in F-Sharp Minor, op. 67 (APS, 1909)
Theme and variations, op. 80 (fl and str qrt) (New York: G. Schirmer, 1920)
String quartet in one movement, op. 89 (1929)
Trio, op. 150 (pf, vln and vlc) (CP, 1939)
Invocation for the violin, op. 55 (vln and pf) (APS, 1904)
Romance, op. 23 (vln and pf) (APS, 1904)
Sonata for violin and piano, op. 34 (1898) (APS)
Three pieces for violin and piano, op. 40 (APS, 1898)
Two songs for violin and cello, op. 100 (APS, 1924)
Prelude on an old folk tune: O the fair hills of Eire (org; also pf) (New York: H.W. Gray, 1943)
PIANO
Suite for two pianos, op. 104 (JC, 1921)
Summer dreams, op. 47, six duets (APS, 1901)
Bal masque, op. 22 (also orch) (APS, 1894)
Ballad for the pianoforte, op. 6 (APS, 1894)
A bit of Cairo (Bryn Mawr, PA: Theodore Presser, 1928)
By the Still Waters, op. 114 (1925)
Cadenza, op. 3, to the first movement of the Third Concerto for the pianoforte (C-Minor, op. 37) by Ludwig van Beethoven (APS, 1888)
Children's album, op. 36, nos. 1-5 (APS, 1897)
Children's carnival, op. 25, six pieces
A cradle song of the lonely mother, op. 108 (Boston: Oliver Ditson, 1924)
Dreaming (New York: Dover Pub.)
Eskimos, op. 64, nos. 1-4, four characteristic pieces (APS, 1927)
Fantasia fugata, op. 87 (TP, 1923)
Fire flies (Dover)
Five improvisations for piano, op. 148, nos. 1-5 (1938)
Four sketches, op. 15, nos. 1-4 (APS, 1892)
From blackbird hills, op. 83 (an Omaha tribal dance) (APS, 1922)
From Grandmother's garden, op. 97, nos. 1-5 (APS, 1922)
From six to twelve, op. 119, six pieces for children (OD, 1932)
Gavotte fantastique, op. 54, no. 2 (APS,1903)
A hermit thrush at eve, op. 92, nos. 1 and 2 (APS, 1922)
A hermit thrush at morn, op. 92, no. 2 (APS, 1922)
A hummingbird (1932)
Nocturne, op. 107 (Cincinnati, John Church Co., 1924)
Old chapel by moonlight, op. 106 (JC, 1924)
Out of the depths, op. 130 (APS, 1932)
Piano composition, op. 102, nos. 1-2 (OD, 1924)
Prelude and fugue, op. 81 (GS, 1918)
Les rêves de Colombine, op. 65, nos. 1-5
Scherzino
Suite française pour le pianoforte, op. 65 (APS, 1907)
Scottish legend, op. 54, no. 1 (APS, 1903)
Three pianoforte pieces, op. 128, nos. 1-3 (1932)
Trois morceaux caracteristiques, op. 28, nos. 1-3 (APS, 1924)

Tyrolean valse-fantaisie, op. 116 (OD, 1926)
Valse-caprice, op. 4 (APS, 1889)
Variations on Balkan themes, op. 60 (also orch; also 2 pf, 4 hands) (APS, 1906)

VOCAL

The chambered nautilus, op. 66, secular cantata (S, choral 2 S, A, org or pf) (originally for vces and orch) (APS, 1907)
Peter Pan, op. 101, secular cantata (choral 2 S, A and pf) (TP, 1923)
The rose of Avon-Town, op. 30, secular cantata (S, A, mix-ch and pf) (originally for vces and orch) (APS, 1896)
The sea-fairies, op. 59, secular cantata (S, A, ch; also S, A and pf) (APS, 1932)
Sylvania, op. 46, secular cantata (solos, mix-ch and pf) (originally for vces and orch) (APS, 1901)
Ah, Love, but a day! op. 44, no. 2 (Robert Browning) (w or mix-ch and pf) (originally vce and pf, in Three Browning songs, op. 44) (APS, 1927)
The candy lion, op. 75, no. 1 (w-ch) (1915)
Come unto these yellow sands, op. 39 (w-ch and pf) (APS, 1897)
Dolladine, op. 75, No. 3 (w-ch) (GS, 1915)
Drowsy dream-town, op. 129 (vce, w-ch and pf) (APS, 1932)
Dusk in June, op. 82 (w-ch) (GS, 1917)
Fairy lullaby, op. 37, no. 3 (w-ch and pf) (APS, 1907) (originally for vce and pf, in Three Shakespeare songs, op. 37)
Far awa'! op. 43, no. 4 (w-ch and pf) (originally vce and pf in Five songs) (R. Burns)
The greenwood, op. 110 (mix-ch) (Boston: C.C. Birchard & Co., 1925)
A hymn of freedom, op. 52 (mix-ch and pf or org) (APS, 1903)
An Indian lullaby (w-ch and pf) (New York: H.K. Johnson & F. Dean, 1899)
June, op. 51, no. 3 (w-ch and pf; also mix-ch and pf) (originally vce and pf) (APS, 1917)
The little brown bee, op. 9 (w-ch) (APS, 1891)
One summer day, op. 57, no. 2 (w-ch and pf) (APS, 1904)
Only a song, op. 57, no. 1 (w-ch) (APS, 1904)
Over hill, over dale, op. 39, no. 1 (w-ch) (APS, 1897)
Panama hymn, op. 74 (mix-ch, org or pf) (comm Panama Pacific Exposition, 1915) (GS, 1915)
Sheena Van, op. 56, no. 4 (mix-ch and pf; also m-ch and pf; w-ch and pf) (originally vce and pf) (APS, 1919)
Song of welcome, op. 42 (mix-ch and org) (for opening ceremonies of the Trans-Mississippi Exposition, Omaha, 1898) (APS, 1898)
Three flower songs, op. 31 (w-ch) (APS, 1896)
Through the house give glimmering light, op. 39, no. 3 (w-ch) (APS, 1897)
When the last sea is sailed, op. 127 (m-ch) (APS, 1931)
Wouldn't that be queer, op. 26, no. 4 (w-ch and pf) (originally vce and pf) (APS, 1919)
The year's at the spring, op. 44, no. 1 (w-ch and pf; also mix-ch and pf; also arr F. Moore for m-ch and pf) (originally for vce and pf, in Three Browning songs, op. 44) (APS, 1909)
Over 150 songs and part songs incl.:
Across the world, op. 20, Villanelle (APS, 1894)
After, op. 68 (F.E. Coates) (APS, 1909)
Alone, op. 35, no. 2 (APS, 1897)
Ein altes Gebet, op. 72, no. 1 (GS, 1914)
Anita, op. 41, no. 1 (C. Fabbri) (APS, 1886)
Ariette, op. 1, no. 4 (Shelley) (APS, 1886)
The artless maid, op. 99 (L. Barili) (TP, 1923)
Autumn song, op. 56, no. 1 (H.H.A. Beach) (APS, 1904)
Baby, op. 69, no. 1 (MacDonald) (APS, 1932)
The blackbird, op. 11, no. 3 (W.E. Henley) (APS, 1889)
A Canadian boat song, op. 10 (T. Moore) (APS, 1890)
Canzonetta, op. 48, no. 4 (A. Sylvestre) (APS, 1902)
Chanson d'amour, op. 21, no. 1 (V. Hugo) (APS, 1893)
Come, ah come, op. 48, no. 1 (composer) (APS, 1902)
Dark garden, op. 131 (L. Speyer) (APS, 1932)
Dark is the night, op. 11 (APS, 1890)
Dearie, op. 43, no. 1 (R. Burns) (APS, 1899)
Deine Blumen, op. 72, no. 2 (L. Zacharias) (GS, 1914)
Ecstasy, op. 19, no. 2 (composer) (APS, 1892)
Eilende Wolken, Segler der Lufte, op. 18 (Schiller) (APS, 1892)
Elle et moi, op. 21, no. 3 (F. Boret) (APS, 1893)
Empress of night, op. 2, no. 3 (composer) (APS, 1891)
Extase, op. 21, no. 2 (V. Hugo) (also vce and orch) (APS, 1892)
Fire and flame, op. 136 (A.A. Moody) (APS, 1933)
Five songs, op. 43, nos. 1-5, (R. Burns) (APS, 1899)
For me the jasmine buds unfold, op. 19, no. 1 (F.E. Coates) (APS, 1892)
Forget me not, op. 35, no. 4 (composer) (APS, 1897)
Forgotten, op. 41, no. 3 (C. Fabbri) (APS, 1898)
The four brothers, op. 1, no. 2 (Schiller) (APS, 1897)
Give me not love, op. 61 (F.E. Coates) (APS, 1904)
Golden gates, op. 19, no. 3 (APS, 1892)
Good morning, op. 48, no. 2 (A.H. Lockhart) (APS, 1902)
Good night, op. 48 no. 3 (A.H. Lockhart) (APS, 1902)
Grossmuetterchen, op. 73, no. 1 (L. Zacharias) (GS, 1914)
Haste, o beloved, op. 29, no. 4 (W.A. Sparrow) (APS, 1895)
The Host, op. 117, no.2 (M. Lee) (JC, 1925)
Hush baby dear, op. 69, no. 2 (A.L. Hughes) (arr H. Norden for w-vces and pf) (APS, 1908)
Hymn of trust, op. 13 (O.W. Holmes) (APS, 1901)
I know not how to find the spring, op. 56, no. 3 (F.E. Coates) (APS, 1904)
I, op. 77, no. 1 (C. Fanning) (GS, 1916)
I send my heart up to thee, op. 44, no. 3 (R. Browning) (APS, 1900)
I shall be brave, op. 143 (K. Adams) (APS, 1932)
Ich sagte nicht, op. 51. no. 1 (E. Wissman) (APS, 1913)
In blossom time, op. 78, no. 3 (GS, 1917)
In the twilight, op. 85 (Longfellow) (APS, 1922)
Je demande a l'oiseau, op. 51, no. 4 (A. Sylvestre) (APS, 1903)
Jephthas's daughter, op. 53 (I. Martinez) (originally vce and orch) (APS, 1903)
Jeune fille et jeune fleur, op. 1, no. 3 (Chateaubriand) (APS, 1887)
Just for this, op. 26, no. 2 (C. Fabbri) (APS, 1894)
Little brown-eyed laddie, op. 99, no. 2 (A.D.O. Greenwood) (TP, 1923)
The Lotos Isles, op. 76, no. 2 (Tennyson) (GS, 1914)
May eve, op. 86 (SB, 1933)
May flowers, op. 137 (A.M. Moody) (APS, 1933)
Meadowlarks, op. 78, no. 1 (I. Coolbrith) (GS, 1917)
Message, op. 93 (S. Teasedale) (TP, 1922)
Mine be the lips, op. 113 (L. Speyer) (OD, 1921)
Moon boat, op. 118 (SB, 1929)
The moon-path, op. 99, no. 3 (K. Adams) (TP, 1923)
My lassie, op. 43, no. 5 (R. Burns) (APS, 1899)
My love is like a red, red rose, op. 12 (APS, 1889)
My star, op. 26, no. 1 (C. Fabbri) (APS, 1894)
Night, op. 35, no. 1 (C.F. Scherenburg) (APS, 1897)
The night sea, op. 10, no. 2 (H.P. Spofford) (APS, 1890)
Night song at Amalfi, op. 78, no. 2 (S. Teasdale) (GS, 1917)
O mistress mine, op. 37, no. 1 (Shakespeare) (APS, 1897)
O sweet content, op. 71, no. 3 (T. Dekker) (APS, 1910)
Oh, were my love you lilac fair, op. 43, no. 3 (R. Burns) (APS, 1899)
An old love story, op. 71, no. 2 (B.L. Stathem)
Prayer of a tired child, op. 75, no. 4 (A.F. Brown) (GS, 1914)
A prelude, op. 71, no. 1 (composer) (APS, 1910)
The rainy day (OD, 1883)
Rendezvous, op. 120 (L. Speyer) (OD, 1928)
Scottish cradle song, op. 43, no. 2 (R. Burns) (APS, 1899)
Sea fever, op. 126 (APS, 1931)
Sea song, op. 10, no. 3 (W.E. Channing) (APS, 1890)
Le secret, op. 14, no. 2 (J. Resseguier) (APS, 1901)
Separation, op. 76, no. 1 (J.L. Stoddard) (GS, 1914)
The singer, op. 117, no. 1 (M. Lee) (JC, 1925)
Sleep, little darling, op. 29, no. 3 (APS, 1895)
Song album (A), A Cyclus of 14 Selected Songs (APS, 1886)
Song album (B), A Cyclus of 13 Selected Songs (APS, 1891)
Song in the hills, op. 117, no. 3 (M. Lee) (JC, 1925)
Song of liberty, op. 49 (APS, 1894)
Songs of the sea, op. 10, nos. 1-3 (APS, 1890)
Spirit divine, op. 88 (A. Read) (TP, 1922)
Spring, op. 26, No. 3 (C. Fabbri) (APS, 1894)
Springtime, op. 124, (S. Merrick) (GS, 1929)
Sweetheart, sigh no more, op. 14, no. 3 (T. Bailey) (APS, 1891)
Take, o take those lips away, op. 37, no. 2 (Shakespeare) (APS, 1897)
A Thanksgiving fable, op. 75, no. 2 (O. Herford) (GS, 1914)
Three songs, op. 79 (GS, 1914)
Thy beauty, op. 41, no. 2 (H. Prescott Spofford) (APS, 1898)
To the one I love, op. 135 (APS, 1932)
Der Totenkranz, op. 73, no. 2 (GS, 1914)
Twilight, op. 2, no. 1 (composer) (APS, 1887)
The wandering knight, op. 29, no. 2 (APS, 1895)
The western wind, op. 11, no. 2 (W.E. Henley (APS, 1889)
We who sing, op. 140 (OD, 1933)
When far from her, op. 2, no. 2 (composer) (APS, 1889)
When mama sings, op. 99, no. 1 (composer) (TP, 1923)
When soul is joined to soul, op. 62 (E. Browning) (APS, 1905)
Who has seen the wind, op. 118 (SB, 1930)
Wind o' the Westland, op. 77, no. 2 (D. Burnett) (GS, 1916)
Wir drei, op. 51, no. 2 (H. Eschelbach) (APS, 1903)
With thee, op. 35, no. 3 (APS, 1897)
With violets, op. 1 no. 1 (K. Vannah) (APS, 1885)
Within thy heart, op. 29, no. 1 (APS, 1885)
Wouldn't that be queer, op. 26, no. 4 (E.J. Coley) (APS, 1894)

SACRED

The canticle of the sun, op. 123 (St. Francis of Assisi) (originally vces and orch) (APS, 1928)
Lord God of Israel, op. 141 (mix-ch and org)
Hearken unto me, op. 139 (mix-ch a-cap; also mix-ch and org) (for the 100th anniversary of the founding of St. Bartholomew's Church, New York) (APS, 1934)
Mass in E-Flat (Major), op. 5 (mix-ch a-cap; also mix-ch and org) (originally for vces and orch) (APS, 1890)
Service in A (Major), op. 63 a-e, op. 121, 122 (solo, mix-ch and org) (APS, 1906-1928)

Te Deum, op. 63a (solo, mix-ch or mix-ch and org) (APS, 1905)
Christ in the Universe, op. 132, (A, T, mix-ch and org) (originally vces and orch) (A. Meynell) (Gray, 1931)
Let this mind be in you, op. 105 (S, B, mix-ch and org) (JC, 1924)
Lord of the worlds above, op. 109 (S, T, B, mix-ch and org) (I. Watts) (OD, 1925)
The minstrel and the king, op. 16 (Rudolph von Habsburg) (T, B, m-ch and pf) (originally vces and orch) (APS, 1894)
Thou knowest, Lord, op. 76, no. 2 (T, B, mix-ch and org) (GS, 1915)
Benedictus...Domine, op. 103 (B, mix-ch and org) (OD, 1924)
Bonum est, confiteri, op. 76, no. 1 (S, mix-ch and org) (GS, 1916)
Evening hymn, op. 125, no. 2, the shadows of the evening hours (S, mix-ch and pf) (originally vce and pf) (APS, 1936)
Te Deum in F-Major, op. 84 (T, m-ch and org) and in B-Major (T, m-vces, and org) (APS, 1905)
Around the manger, op. 115 (mix-ch and org or pf) (also w-ch and org or pf; also vce and org or pf) (R. Davis) (OD, 1925-1929)
Benedicte omnia opera Domini, op. 121 (mix-ch and org) (APS, 1928)
Help us, O God, op. 50 (mix-ch and org, for rehearsal only) (APS, 1903)
I will lift up mine eyes, op. 98 (ch a-cap) (TP, 1923)
O Lord... God arise, op. 52 (mix-ch and org or pf) (originally pub with a different text as, A hymn of freedom, op. 52) (APS, 1924)
Lamb of God, communion service, op. 122 (APS, 1928)
Last prayer, op. 126 (APS, 1931)
Anthems incl.:
All hail the power of Jesus' name, op. 74, Panama hymn (E. Perronet) (mix-ch and org) (GS, 1915)
Alleluia! Christ is risen, op. 27 (Easter)
Bethlehem, op. 24 (Christmas) (mix-ch and org) (APS, 1898)
Constant Christmas, op. 95 (TP, 1922)
Four canticles, op. 78
Four choral responses (JF, 1932)
I will give thanks, op. 147 (APS, 1939)
I sought the Lord, op. 145 (APS, 1935)
Jesus my Saviour, op. 112 (TP, 1925)
The Lord is my shepherd, op. 96 (TP, 1923)
Lord of all beings, op. 146 (HWG, 1937)
Nunc Dimittis, peace I leave with you, with prayer and supplication
Peace on Earth, op. 38 (Christmas)
Praise the Lord, all ye nations, op. 7 (mix-ch and org) (for the consecration of P. Brooks, D.D. as Bishop of Massachusetts) (APS, 1891)
Responses, op. 8 (APS, 1891)
Teach me thy way, op. 33
Though I take the wings, op. 152 (psalm 139) (last work)

OPERA
Cabildo, op. 149 (1946)

Bibliography

Adams, Mrs. Crosby. *An American genius of world renown: Mrs. H.H. Beach*. Etude, January 1928, p. 34. Biographical sketch.
Among the Composers. Etude, January 1944, 11-12. Biographies of Mrs. H.H. Beach and Ada Richter.
An American composer-pianist with world-wide recognition. Etude, November 1922, p. 746. On Mrs. H.H. Beach.
Apthorp, W. Sketch of Mrs H.H.A. Beach's life and analysis of the Gaelic Symphony. Boston Symphony Orchestra Programmes 16 (1896-1897): 77.
Bean, H.J. *Woman in musichouse*. American Music Teacher, March-April 1957, p.5. On Mrs. H.H.A. Beach.
Brooks, B. *How of creative composition*. Etude, March 1943, p. 151f. Mrs H.H.A. Beach talks about the process of musical composition (and its relation to herself).
Browne, C.A. *Girlhood of famous women in music*. Etude, July 1909, pp. 488-489. On Mrs. H.H.A. Beach.
Cooke, James Francis. *A short sketch of music in America*. Etude, July 1910, pp. 443-444. Includes biographical sketch of Mrs. H.H. Beach.
Eden, Myrna G. *A comparative study of two women*.
Representative of the American Cultivated Tradition in the Arts: Individuality and energy in the Works of Anna Hyatt Huntingdon, sculptor, and Mrs. H.H.A. Beach, pianist and composer.
Famous Women Composers. Etude, April 1917, pp. 237-238. Paragraphs on Beach, Chaminade, Lehman, Smyth; other names given in list.
Freed, Richard. *The piano works of Mrs. H.H.A. Beach: Demonstrating the irrelevance of gender*. Stereo Review 35 (December 1975), pp. 82-83.
Hackett, Karleton. *Some American songwriters*. Negro Music Journal 1, July 1903: 213-217. Discusses ten American composers separately as songwriters (three women– Beach, Gaynor, Lang).
Merril, E. Lindsey. *Mrs. H.H.A. Beach: Her life and music*. Ann Arbor, MI: University Microfilms, 1963. Thorough study of Beach, with statistical breakdown of the theoretical aspect of her music.
Tuthill, Burnett C. *The works of Mrs. H.H.A. Beach*. Music Quarterly 26, 1940: 297-310. Includes lists of works by medium with publisher and date of composition.
Wilson, A. *Mrs. H.H.A. Beach: A conversation on musical conditions in America*. Musician 17, January 1912: 9-10.

Ref. 2, 8, 22, 23, 41, 44, 53, 70, 74, 79, 81, 89, 100, 105, 109, 124, 138, 141, 144, 173, 177, 191, 226, 228, 236, 266, 276, 280, 292, 297, 335, 352, 369, 375, 415, 433, 461, 465, 477, 484, 496, 502, 560, 563, 579, 590, 597, 610, 611, 622, 637, 646, 653

BEACH, Priscilla A. (pseud. Alden Beach)

20th-century American composer. b. Rome, NY.

Composition

ORCHESTRA
City trees, op. 5 (also pf) (1928)

Ref. 322

BEAHM, Jacquelyn Yvette

American pianist, teacher and composer. b. Cherryvale, Kansas, April 7, 1930. She began playing the piano at the age of five. At the University of Kansas she studied the piano under Jan Chiapusso and received her B.Mus. 20 years later she resumed piano study under Angelica Morales von Sauer and obtained her M.Mus. PHOTOGRAPH.

Compositions

PIANO
Christmas carol combinations (2 pf) (Boston Music Co. 1982)
Polish Christmas carols (1 or 2 pf) (Boston Music Co. 1982)
Hannukah songs (1 or 2 pf) (Elkan-Vogel, 1979)
Births, 3 pieces (1981)
Sounds from summer nights, suite (1980)
Suite (1971)

VOCAL
Good bye, Liza Jane (mix-ch and pf) (Elkan-Vogel, 1976)
Haydn seek (mix-ch and pf) (Theo Presser, 1981)
I'm sad and lonely (w-ch and pf) (1975)
Katy cruel (mix-ch, pf and perc) (Elkan-Vogel, 1980)
Three poems by William Blake (deep vce, fl and pf) (1971)

SACRED
From heaven on high (mix-ch and pf or gtr) (1976)
Ringing, singing (Elkan-Vogel) (w-ch and bells) (1977)
Three songs (Mary Baker Eddy) (1960-1964)
Service music on a single theme (org) (1970)

Ref. composer

BEAMER, Helen Desha

Hawaiian dancer, singer and composer. b. Honolulu, September 8, 1881; d. September, 1952. She was educated at Kamehameha High School and Columbia University.

Compositions

VOCAL
Kaahumanu
Keawaiki
Moani ke ala
Pua wa'awa'a

MISCELLANEOUS
Na hula O Hawai'i (1976)

Ref. 438

BEAMISH, Sally

20th-century composer.

Composition

VOCAL
Variation on Berkeley's Reapers' Chorus

Ref. BMIC

BEAN, Mabel

20th-century American composer. She composed piano pieces, works for narrator and orchestra and sacred solos.

Ref. 142

BEARD, Katherine K.

20th-century American composer.

Compositions

PIANO
Nature pieces (1980) (Boston Music)

Ref. MLA *Notes* June 1980, 624

BEARDSMORE, Mrs.
19th-century British songwriter.
Ref. 465

BEARER, Elaine Louise
American conductor, musicologist, assistant professor and composer. b. Morristown, NY, April 1, 1947. She graduated from the Manhattan School of Music with a B.Mus. in 1970 and obtained her M.A. and her Ph.D. from New York University. She taught at San Francisco State University from 1973 to 1975 and was assistant professor at Lone Mountain College in San Francisco from 1973 to 1974.
Compositions
CHAMBER
Five pieces for organ (1974)
VOCAL
Three songs of innocence (1974)
Ref. 206, 457, 625

BEAT, Janet Eveline
Scottish lecturer, music critic and composer. b. Streetly, December 17, 1937. She graduated from Birmingham University with a B.Mus. and received the University's Cunningham award in 1962. She went to Italy to study source material for her thesis 'The development of the orchestra and orchestration in Italian opera, ca. 1600-1750'. She lectures in harmony and counterpoint and history of music at the Royal Scottish Academy of Music and Drama, Glasgow and is a music critic for several newspapers. PHOTOGRAPH.
Compositions
ORCHESTRA
Iter temporis (small orch) (1970)
CHAMBER
Inventions (ww) (1965-1966)
Le tombeau de Claude (fl, ob and hp) (1973)
After reading lessons of the war (vln and pf) (1976)
Dancing on moonbeams (vla and pf)
Noctuary (cl and pf) (1979)
Cadenzas for Mozart's oboe concerto K. 314 (1974)
Circe (vla) (1974)
Dialogue and burlesque (vlc) (1974)
Essay for oboe No. 1 (1968)
Essay for oboe No. 2 (1974)
Five projects for Joan (vlc) (1974)
Mestra (fl)
Pentad (pf) (1969)
Seascape with clouds (cl) (1978)
Vincent sonata (vln)
VOCAL
Hide-and-seek (singer/reciter, w-ch and insts) (1970)
The fiery sunflower (vces and insts) (19723)
Landscapes (T and ob) (1979)
The leaves of my brain (T and gtr) (1974)
Premiers desires (S and pf) (1979)
Study of the object No. 3 (1970)
Summer poem No. V (1970)
DANCE SCORES
The gossamer web, dance drama (S, pf, perc and tape) (1975)
THEATRE
Alice in Wonderland (1973)
Three entractes for Uncle Vanya (1971)
ELECTRONIC
Apollo and Marsyas (cl and tape) (1972-1973)
Cybalis No. 1 (tape) (1969)
Hunting horns are memories (hn and tape) (1978)
Pastore d'aria (ob, ob d'amore, cor anglais and tape) (1980)
Piangram (pf and tape) (1979)
TEACHING PIECES
Works for children
Publications
An edition of Carissimi's 'Jephte'. London, 1974.
An edition of Carissimi's 'Nisi Dominus'. London, 1974.
An edition of Handel's 'Let God Arise', 1975.
An extension of vocal accompaniment to dance. *The Laban Art of Movement Guild Magazine*, November 1970.
Monteverdi and the opera orchestra of his time. *The Monteverdi Companion*, London, 1968.
A scarlatti suite for recorders. London, 1975.
Two problems in Carissimi's oratorio Jephte. *The Music Review*, August-September, 1973.
Ref. composer, 77, 206, 457, 643

BEATH, Betty
Australian pianist, accompanist, teacher and composer. b. Bundaberg, Queensland, November 19, 1932. She began piano lessons at the age of three. In 1948 and 1949 she was a finalist in the Australian Broadcasting Commission's concerts and vocal competitions. The following year she was awarded a Queensland University music scholarship and at the Sydney Conservatory of Music she studied under Frank Hutchens, graduating in voice and the piano. She spent some years in New Guinea, which aroused her interest in the music of Australia's northern neighbours. She resumed her studies at the Queensland Conservatory in 1965, graduating in 1969. In 1975 she and her husband, writer and illustrator David Cox were granted a fellowship by the Australia Council to carry out research in Indonesia, Java and Bali. Her compositions drew much from the music of these countries. Her works for children have been performed extensively by amateur and professional theatre and opera companies, many of them having been commissioned by Australian education authorities. PHOTOGRAPH.
Compositions
CHAMBER
Piccolo victory (images of colonial Australia) (picc, fl, hpcd, vlc, rhythm sticks and side drum) (1982)
Trio, incorporating elements of folk music (fl, hpcd and vlc) (1982)
Black on white (pf, left hand) (1983)
VOCAL
The cry (Tadashi Amano) (vce and ens or cham orch)
Riddles, cycle of 4 songs (T and orch) (1974)
Askesis (Guenter Grass) (vce, vlc, pf and perc) (1975)
The fairy tree (w-ch, recs and perc)
Fire's song (D. Cox) (J. Albert & Son, 1974)
I saw you smile (B. Stellmach) (vce and pf) (1965)
In the Carnavon Ranges, song on an Aboriginal theme
In this garden, cycle of 5 songs (D. Cox) (med-vce and pf) (J. Albert & son, 1976)
Indonesian triptych (Goenawan Mohamed) (vce and ens, incl. Indonesian insts; also med vce and pf) (1975)
Little song (1981)
Manusia pertama di angkasa luar (S. Sastrowardojo) (T and pf) (1983)
NawangwWulan (S. Sastrowardojo) (S and pf) (1980)
Poems from the Chinese, cycle (S, cl, vlc and pf) (Arsis Press, 1979)
Seawatcher (D. Cox) (vce and pf) (J. Albert & Son, 1974)
Song (1981)
Songs from the Beast's Choir, cycle of 5 songs incl. The starfish (Carmen Bernos de Gasztold, trans Rumer Godden) (1977)
Three cautionary songs, op. 13 (D. Cox) (1975)
Yungamurra, river spirit (P. Wrightson) (high vce, fl and vlc) (1984)
Walking in sunshine (6 2-part vocalises with pf) (Asmuse, 1981)
SACRED
Three psalms, nos. 23, 121, 150 (high vce, fl, hp and vlc; also vce and pf) (1981)
OPERA
Francis, based on St. Francis of Assisi (1979) (Amuse, Brisbane)
Marco Polo (D. Cox) (1977) (comm Queensland Opera Co.) (J. Albert & Son)
INCIDENTAL MUSIC
School music dramas:
Abigail and the bushranger, op. 8
Abigail and the mythical beast (D. Cox) (1976) (comm 1981)
Abigail and the rainmaker, op. 14 (D. Cox) (chil-vces and perc) (1976)
Fire and fiddel (1975) (comm Twelfth Night Theatre)
Joan of Arc (w-ch, recs and perc) (1975)
Procession, a march of celebration .....The march of the bunyip (musical event for untrained musicians) (1983)
The Raja who married an angel, based on an Indonesian folktale (D. Cox) (vce and inst ens) (1979) (Playlab Press, 1979) (Leichardt Reprographics, 1979)
Publications
Reflections from Bali. With D. Cox. Allison-Wesley Publ., Sydney, 1981.
Spice and magic. An illustrated account of experiences in Java and Bali. With D. Cox. Boolarong Publications, 1981.
Articles about travel in Indonesia. With D. Cox in *Australian Women's Weekly*, 1976.
Article on school operas, in *Innovations in Australian Secondary Education*. McGraw-Hill, 1977.
Ref. composer, 440, 442, 457, 474, 643

BEATON, Isabella
American pianist, violinist, teacher and composer. b. Grinnell, IA, May 20, 1870; d. Mt. Pleasant, IA, January 19, 1929. She studied the piano in Berlin under Moszkowski from 1894 to 1899 and Emma Koch from 1893 to 1894 and composition under O.B. Boise. She studied the violin in Paris under Berthelier in 1899. She taught piano history and composition at the Cleveland School of Music from 1899 to 1910 whilst taking her M.A. and Ph.D. at Case Western Reserve University. In 1910 she established the Beaton School of Music, Cleveland.

Compositions
ORCHESTRA
Symphony
Scherzo
CHAMBER
String quartets in A-Minor and C
Romanza (vln, pf and org)
PIANO
Norwegian dances
Sonata in G-Minor
Ten fugues
Other pieces
VOCAL
Setting of Keats' Eve of St. Agnes
Songs
SACRED
Ave Maria (Cont and orch)
OPERA
Anacoana
Ref. 22, 74, 81, 89, 141, 142, 226, 292

BEATRICE, Mary Victoria Feodore, Princess of Battenberg

B. 1857; d. 1944. She was the youngest and best-loved child of Queen Victoria. On Beatrice's marriage to Prince Henry of Battenberg, Victoria insisted that she stay in England, so she and her husband settled on the Isle of Wight, where the prince and after his death Beatrice, was the governor. PHOTOGRAPH.
Compositions
ORCHESTRA
Quick march (Schott)
VOCAL
Retrospection (Elliott) (Ascherberg)
The blue-eyed maiden's song (Disraeli) (Ascherberg)
The green cavalier's song (Disraeli) (Ascherberg)
The sunny month of May (Heine)
SACRED
Hear, Holy Father, baptismal hymn (Novello)
Some church responses
Ref. 123, 226, 262, 276, 297

BEATRICE DE DIA (Die), Contessa

B. ca. 1160; d. 1212. She was one of the first troubadours. Much controversy surrounds her identification as the wife of William of Poitiers, Count of Valentinois and the mistress of Rambaud of Orange, also a troubadour. The old biographer of the troubadours, Nostre Dame, speaks of Beatrice as the mistress of Guillaume Adhemar, who pined away in grief when she married the Count of Ambrunois. This story was romanticized by Charier, whose character Alix ended her life in celibacy in the convent of Tarascon; the story was reproduced seriously in the *Histoire litteraire de la France*. However, accounts of Beatrice's life by Father Millet, the Dauphin's biographer and a historic court notice found in one of the old manuscripts of troubadours' verses, confirm that she married William of Poitiers but loved Rambaud of Orange, for whom she wrote her ballads. These ballads, of which four are known today, are regarded as prime examples of love elegies. They identify her difficult role as a lady and a poetess and dispel any myths about the purity of morals in earlier centuries. Having mistaken Rambaud's reserve for infidelity and indifference, she wrote of her unrequited and passionate love for him. Her first ballad *Ab ioi et ab joven m'apais* appears in a precious Vatican manuscript (no. 3204) and has a colored miniature picture of Beatrice on a gold background. In this ballad Beatrice congratulates herself on having found in Rambaud a knight of such honor. In later years Rambaud seems to have abandoned Beatrice, who then wrote her most widely acclaimed ballad *Plang*. Raynourd, who published the songs of the troubadours, compared this ballad to those of Sappho for its tenderness and warmth and ignored the licentiousness sometimes present in Beatrice's ballads. According to Henry Vaschalde in *Histoire des troubadours*, Sappho's verses contained nothing as passionate and as sensual as some of the sentiments expressed in *Plang*. In 1888, Le Cigale (society in the south of France) together with the Felibres of Paris (literary society of Provençal writers) organized a festival in the southern provinces of France. During this event a medal was bestowed on the composer of the best poems in the language of Old Provençal and she was the Contessa Beatrice de Dia. At an exhibition of women composers held in October 1975 by the Public Music Library of Amsterdam, of the twenty compositions available for public listening, *Plang* together with one other piece - Clara Schumann's *Klaviertrio, op. 17* - was most frequently requested by the public. DISCOGRAPHY.
Compositions
VOCAL
Ballads:
Plang
Ab ioi et ab joven m'apais (I thrive on youth and joy)
A chantar m'er de so qu'eu no volria (Plang) (Of things I'd rather keep silence I must sing)
Estat ai en greu cossirier (I've lately been in great distress)
Fin ioi me don' alegranssa (Fine joy brings me great happiness)
Amics, en gran consirier (attributed to both Beatrice and Rambaud of Orange, but more likely Rambaud's work alone)
Bibliography
Charier. *Histoire général du Dauphine.*
Larousse. *Dictionnaire du XIX siecle.*
Millet, L'Abbe. *Histoire littéraire des troubadours.*
Nostre Dame, Jean. *Les vies des plus célèbres et anciens poetes provençaux qui ont Floury du temps des anciens comtes de Provence.*
Raynourd. *Choix des poèsies originales des troubadours.*
Rochas. *Biographie du Dauphine.*
Wellner, Franz. *Die Troubadours, Leben und Lieder.*
Ref. 117, 120, 213, 218, 220, 221, 237, 264, 279, 303, 366, 563, 622, 653

BEAUCE, Delfine. See UGALDE, Delphine Beauce

BEAUCHEMIN, Marie (Soeur St. Marie Cécile du Sacre-Coeur)

Canadian teacher and composer. b. Quebec, 1892. She composed sacred music.
Ref. 347

BEAUHARNAIS, Hortense. See HORTENSE, Queen of Holland

BEAUMESNIL, Henrietta Adelaide Villard de

French singer and composer. b. Paris, August 31, 1758; d. Paris, 1813. She married the actor Philippe of the Comedie-Italienne. She was a pupil of C.F. Clement and became one of the foremost singers of the Grand Opera, Paris, from 1760 to 1774. When her voice began to fail, she turned to composition. In 1784 her first opera *Tibulle et Delie, ou les Saturnales* was performed and enthusiastically received.
Compositions
OPERA
Anacreon (1781)
Les fêtes grecques et romaines (1792)
Les Israelites poursuivis par Pharaon (1784)
Les Législatrices (1792)
Plaire, c'est commander! (1792)
Tibulle et Délie, ou les Saturnales (Fuzelier) (1784)
Ref. 8, 44, 102, 105, 108, 125, 126, 129, 276, 307, 347, 653

BEAUMONT, Vivian

20th-century American composer of piano works and songs.
Ref. 142

BEAUTIFUL BLONDE. See MEGALOSTRATA OF SPARTA

BECK, Martha Dillard (Mrs. G. Howard Carragan)

American lecturer and composer. b. Sodaville, OR, January 19, 1902. She studied at the Oberlin Conservatory of Music (B.Mus. 1924) and at the American Conservatory of Music in Chicago (M.Mus. 1927). She was awarded a Juilliard external scholarship, which enabled her to study at the Juilliard School of Music from 1927 to 1929. She studied in Germany, where her teachers included Frances Frothingham, Adolf Weidig, Silvio Scionti, George Andrews and Hugo Leichtentritt (composition). She received the Adolf Weidig Gold Medal in 1927 and in the same year won two first prizes in the Mu Phi Epsilon National Contest. In 1927 and 1928 she received first prize for composition in the Maxine Schreiver Competition. She taught at North Central College, Naperville and the American Conservatory of Music from 1924 to 1929 and from 1933 to 1948, at the Emma Willard School, Troy.
Compositions
ORCHESTRA
Fantasy for chamber orchestra (1960)
Prelude for orchestra (comm Albany Symphony Orchestra) (1977)
CHAMBER
Piano quintet (1927) (1st prize, Mu Phi Epsilon National Contest)
Suite for violin and piano

PIANO
American Pageant (2 pf)
Suite in 5 movements
Other works
VOCAL
A Legend of Tamarac, cantata (mix-ch and small orch) (1966)
Michael and Cornelia, cantata (A Saga of the Hudson Valley Dutch) (1975)
SACRED
Psalm 122 (ch, org, brass qnt and perc) (1976)
Publications
The Martha Beck Rhythm Rule Method. 1961.
Ref. 84, 142, 280, 347, 625

BECKER, Eveline. See ACCART, Eveline

BECKER (Becker-Pagel), Ida
Late 19th-century Swiss composer. She was a pupil of Albert Becker and Friedrich Kiel, who insisted on the publication of her children's songs when the manuscript was shown to him. Her intimate music for the home and family circle was particularly successful in her time.
Compositions
VOCAL
Drei Balladen (Fuerstner)
Drei Lieder, op. 11 (Fuerstner)
Doerfertanzweise: Den Finken des Waldes die Nachtigall ruft, op. 9 (S and Bar) (Bote)
Kleine Bilder, op. 6 (Fuerstner)
Lieder aus der Kinderwelt, op. 7 (Fuerstner)
Lieder aus der Maerchenwelt (Fuerstner)
Luarin, op. 5 (S and T) (Ries and Erler)
Ostseelieder, op. 12 (Fuerstner)
SACRED
Die heilige Nacht, op. 4, cantata (soloist, ch and pf) (Ries and Erler)
Weihnachtslied (Fuerstner)
Ref. 226, 276, 297

BECKER-PAGEL, Ida. See BECKER, Ida

BECKMAN, Ellen Josephine
American choral conductor, teacher and composer. b. Chicago, March 19, 1909. She received her B.A. from Marietta College in 1934, M.A. from the University of Chicago in 1940 and M.Mus. from the Catholic University in 1956. She also studied at Northwestern University from 1946 to 1947 and the American Conservatory of Music, Chicago, from 1948 till 1950. She taught music, directed bands and conducted choirs at public schools till 1974 and then taught music privately in Hyattsville, MD.
Compositions
ORCHESTRA
Sonata No. 7
MISCELLANEOUS
Down the river 1955
Ref. 475

BECKON, Lettie Marie
Black American clarinetist, electric organist, guitarist, organist, pianist, xylophone player, teacher and composer. b. Detroit, April 13, 1953. She attended the Bailey Temple School of Music, where she studied music history and theory, the piano, the organ, the xylophone and the guitar. She studied under William Wise (pipe and electric organ), under Al Green (clarinet) and Lesley Fishwick (piano). Entering Wayne State University in 1971, she studied with Professor Frank Murch and Mischa Kottler (piano) and under Professor James Hartway (composition), and graduated with a B.A. (piano and composition, 1976). In 1978 she obtained her M.A. (piano and composition) from Wayne State. She taught in several private schools and studios from 1975. She won the Ida K. Smokler Award in 1976. PHOTOGRAPH.
Compositions
ORCHESTRA
Symphony No. 1 in A (MCA and Belwin-Mills, 1966)
Integrated concerto (pf and orch) (1978)
Symphonic essay (str orch and perc) (1977)
Head a woe 11 (str orch) (1978)
Piece (small orch) (1977)
CHAMBER
Composition 1, 12 tones (cl ens) (1976)
Effigy (ob, pf and perc) (1976)
Head a woe I (str trio) (1975)
Visions (pf and mar) (1977)
Moods (pf) (1976)
Pulsations (vln) (1975)
Three implied jesters (cl) (1975)
VOCAL
Help (w-ch and str qrt) (1976)
MISCELLANEOUS
Captain Jinks of the Horse Marines (1975)
Dr. Heidegger's fountain of youth (1978)
Hello out there (1954) (Belwin-Mills)
Lizzie Borden (1965) (Boosey & Hawkes)
My heart's in the highlands (1970)
The sweet bye and bye (1957)
Ref. composer, 625

BECLARD D'HARCOURT, Marguerite
French ethnomusicologist and composer. b. Paris, February 24, 1884; d. Paris, August 2, 1964. She studied at the Schola Cantorum and was a pupil of Decaux, Vincent d'Indy and Maurice Emmanuel. With her husband Raoul d'Harcourt she traveled through Equador, Peru and Bolivia, where she collected the popular melodies of those countries and harmonized over 200 of them.
DISCOGRAPHY.
Compositions
ORCHESTRA
Three symphonic movements, lst symphony (1932)
Les saisons, 2nd symphony (1951-1952)
Chant d'espérance, symphonic poem (1943)
Concerto grosso (str orch) (1956)
CHAMBER
Eclogue (fl, vln and strs) (1949)
En regardant Watteau (fl, vln, vla, cl and hp) (1932)
Quintet
String quartet (1930) (Fortin)
Enchantments (pf, vln and vlc) (1947)
Rapsodie peruvienne (ob, cl and bsn) (1945)
Sonata à trois (vln, vla and vlc) (1938) Paris; (Salabert)
Piano trio
String trio
Creoles (vln and hp) (1939)
Peruvian songs (fl and hp or pf) (1981)
Sonatine (fl and pf) (1946) (Salabert)
Suite (hpcd)
PIANO
Suite française (1946)
Thème varié sur un thème dorien (1951-1952)
VOCAL
Seventy two songs incl.:
Les enfants dans l'enclos (Paris: Fortin, 1934-1935)
La flute de jade (1951-1952)
Marguerite (1951-1952)
Mariposaca, Ninaca
Trois sonnets de la Renaissance (Paris: Salabert, 1930)
Trois poèmes de la mer (1951-1952)
BALLET
Raimi ou la Fête du soleil (1925-1926)
OPERA
Dierdane (after Synge's Deirdre of the Sorrows) (1937-1941)
Publications
Chansons populaires françaises du Canada: leur langue musicale, Paris, 1956.
Mélodies populaires indiennes.
La musique des Incas et ses survivances. Paris, 1925.
Vingt-quatre chansons populaires du vieux Quebec. 1936.
La musique des Aymara sur les hauts-plateaux boliviens. 1959.
Ref. composer, 9, 13, 22, 25, 70, 94, 96, 105, 163, 347, 461, 625

BEDFORD, Mrs. Herbert. See LEHMANN, Liza

BEDINI, Guendalina
19th-century Italian composer.
Compositions
HARP
Andante quasi fantasia in E-Minor (extract from Sonata in C-Minor) (Ricordi)
Rimembranza sul-l'Aida, fantasia, op. 4 (Ricordi)
Ref. 297

BEECROFT, Norma Marian

Canadian flautist, pianist and composer. b. Oshawa, Ontario, April 11, 1934. She studied the piano privately and then at the Royal Conservatory of Toronto from 1950 to 1958, under Aladar Acsedy, Gordon Halett and Weldon Kilburn; from 1957 to 1959 she studied the flute with Keith Girard and from 1952 to 1958, composition under John Weinzweig. On a scholarship from the Berkshire Music Center in Tanglewood she studied composition under Lukas Foss and Aaron Copland from 1952 to 1958. Her postgraduate studies took place in Europe; she attended the Corso di Perfezionamento at the Academy of St. Cecilia, Rome, from 1959 to 1961 and studied the flute under Severion Gazelloni and composition under Goffredo Petrassi, graduating in 1961. In the summer of 1960 she studied composition under Bruno Maderna at the Internationale Ferienkurse fuer Neue Musik in Darmstadt, Germany and at the Darlington School of Music in Devon, England. She received a Canada Council Scholarship (1961 to 1962) and a senior arts fellowship (1962 to 1969). On her return to Canada in 1962 she attended the seminar on electronic music at the University of Toronto, directed by Myron Scheffer and in 1964 worked at the Electronic Music Studio in New York under the direction of Mario Davidovsky. She was script assistant and program organizer for the Canadian Broadcasting Corporation and producer for the National Music Department. She is director of the Association of Composers, Authors and Publishers of Canada. DISCOGRAPHY. PHOTOGRAPH.

Compositions

ORCHESTRA

Improvisazioni concertanti No. 1 (fl and orch) (1961) (MCA, 1970)
Improvisazioni concertanti No. 2 (medium orch) (comm National Arts Centre Orchestra)
Improvisazioni concertanti No. 3 (fl, 2 timp and orch) (1973) (Canadian Music Center)
Fantasy for strings (str orch) (1958) (CMC)
Piece concertante No. 1 and/or No. 2 (1966) (comm Charlotteton Festival, Atlantic Symphony Orchestra)
Two movements for orchestra (1971) (CMC)

CHAMBER

Rasas 1 (fl, hp, vln, vla, vlc, perc and pf) (1968) (comm Societe de musique contemporaine du Quebec) (CMC)
Contrasts for six performers (ob, vla, xylorimba, vib, perc and hp)
Tre pezzi brevi (fl and hp, or gtr or pf) (1960-1961)

VOCAL

The hollow men (T.S. Elliot) (ch a-cap) (1956)
Three impressions (Wayne Keon) (m-ch, pf and perc) (1973) (CMC)
Twelve o'clock chant

SACRED

The living flame of love (St. John of the Cross, trans composer) (m-ch a-cap) (1967) (comm Waterloo Lutheran University Choir)

BALLET

Hedda (orch and tape) (1981) (comm National Ballet of Canada)

ELECTRONIC

Cantorum vitae (fl, vlc, 2 pf, perc and tape) (1980-1981)
Collage '76 (fl, ob, hn, vlc, d-b, pf, hp, 3 perc and tape) (1976)
Collage '78 (bsn, pf, 2 perc and tape) (1978) (comm Music Inter Alia, Winnipeg)
Consequences for 5 (pf, syn, live elec, 3 brass and tape) (1977) (comm Canadian Electronic Ensemble)
Quaprice (hn, perç and tape) (1980-1981)
Elegy and two went to sleep (L. Cohen) (S, fl, perc and tape) (1967) (comm Ten Centuries Concerts)
Eleven and seven for five plus (brass qnt and channel tape) (1975) (CMC)
From dreams of brass (narr, m-ch, orch and tape) (1963-1964) (CMC)
Piece for Bob, one player (fl and perc and 2-channel tape) (1975)
Rasas 11 (various texts) (Cont, fl, hp, gtr, electric org or pf, 2 perc and 4-channel tape) (1972-1973) (CMC)
Rasas 111 (S, 4 musicians and 2-channel tape) (1973-1974) (CMC)
Undersea phantasy (2-channel tape for a puppet show) (1967)
11 & 7 for 5+ (brass qnt and tape) (1975) (comm CBC)

Publications

Two musical adventures in Italy: A Canadian Composer Reports Back. CanCo. No. 76, January, 1973.

Bibliography

A Conversation with Norma Beecroft. The New World of Electronic Music *CanCo*. No. 22. October, 1967.
From Dreams of Brass. CBC Times, February 19-25, 1966.
Miss Norma Beecroft: Well-Travelled Composer. *CanCo*. no. 9. May 1966.
Norma Beecroft-A Portrait. *Mu*. no. 19. May 1969.
Stone, Kurt. *Review of Records*. July 1967.
Such, Peter. *Soundprints*. Toronto: Clarke, Irwin, 1972.
Winters, Kenneth. *A Composer Who Doesn't Wear Music Like a Straightjacket*. *CanCo*. No. 64. November, 1971.
Eight Composers Speak about Their Works for the Future. *CanCo*. no. 56, January, 1971

Ref. 1, 4, 5, 81, 94, 189, 329, 347, 402, 563, 622

BEEKHUIS, Hanna

Dutch pianist and composer. b. Leeuwarden, September 24, 1889; d. February 26, 1980. She had her first piano lessons from her mother and then studied harmony and counterpoint under Peter van Anrooy. At the Cologne Conservatory she was a pupil of Professors Uzielli, Strasser and Bolsche from 1908 to 1911. In 1912 she continued her piano studies in Amsterdam under Dirk Schafer and for a short time in 1913 studied the piano at the Geneva Conservatory under Bernhard Stavenhagen and composition under Barblan. She had lessons in composition from the conductor Frits Schuurman. She traveled in Corsica, Catalonia and Morocco; the influence of the music of those countries can be heard in some of her compositions. During the war she lived in Switzerland and many of her works were performed in Zurich. In 1945 she returned to Amsterdam but in 1952 moved into the country to specialize in vocal music, particularly the setting of her favorite poetry to music and critically revising her earlier works. PHOTOGRAPH.

Compositions

ORCHESTRA

Catalonia, suite (1937)
Djamaa el Fnaa, suite (1930)
Five miniatures, suite (1937)
Demonendans, ballet music (strs) (1930)
Lentedans (1946)

CHAMBER

Wind quintet (1939)
Elegie and humoresque (wind qrt) (1939)
Rondo capricciosо (fl and pf) (1948)
Sonatine (bsn and pf) (1948)

PIANO

Corsica: Zee en rotsen (1935)
Oude sage (1945)

VOCAL

Chi-King, Chinese song (vces and orch (1939)
Three serenades (vce and orch or pf) (1939)
Five old Dutch melodies (vce and orch) (1939)
Schouburg-hdichten (J. van den Vondel) (soloists, ch and orch) (1933)
Zwei lieder nach Gottfried Keller (ch) (1942)
Petite suite: Il a un mois (C. de Pisan); Pour oublier melancholie (A. Chartier) (ch) (1948)
Ach wat heerlijkheid (5 mix-vces)
Les deux flutes (Li-Tai-Po) (m-S, 2 fl and pf) (1928)
Dormeuse (S, w-ch, pf or strs) (1948)
Drie Liederen (Gezelle) (S, A and pf) (1949)
Ik heb gedwaald (A, Bar and org)
Kwatrijnen en nachtstilte (P.C. Boutens) (A and str qrt) (1950)
Liederen (B. Aafjes): Sonnet; Nieltje in het aquarium (S) (1950)
More groet's morgens se dingen (m-S and pf) (1947)
Nachtegesange (N. Bolt): Der sterbende Held; Der Trommler (m-S) (1963-1968)
Nocturne from Natuurindrukken en Stemmingen (E.B. Koster) (S, A, Bar and pf) (1940)
Reflets du Japon (A and vla) (gold medal, Buenos Aires, 1961)
Verrassing (m-S, fl and pf) (1928)
Vier Liederen (P.C. Boutens) (A and pf or str qrt) (1946-1966)
Een Oud-Hollandsche melodie en 2 vrije composities (med vce, fl and hp or pf) (1949)
Cupido-tje (Adema van Scheltema) (vce and pf) (1951)

SACRED

Verkondiging en aanbidding, Christmas cantata (soloists, ch and small orch) (1938)
O et O et Gloria (2 soloists, ch and cham ens) (1945)
Die arme Seele vor der Himmelstur (ch) (1935)
Kleine Kantate: Blueh auf! Geistliches Hirtenlied (Angelus Silesius) (m-ch) (1944)
Lied van de Herdertjes in Bethlehem (fl, vln and chil-ch) (1945)
Vier Kerstliederen (S, vlc and pf) (1946)
Apokalyptischer Advent (Toni Wolff) (A) (1943)

BALLET

De Zeven boeren (A. Verwey) (recitation and cham ens) (1949, rev. 1965)

Ref. composer, 44, 110, 283

BEESON, Elizabeth Ruth

20th-century American organist, pianist and composer. She studied the piano and composition at the University of Houston and began composing at the age of sixteen. The next year, four of her piano works were broadcast over Houston radio. She is organist at the Fairbanks Methodist Church in Houston.

Compositions

CHAMBER

Pieces (small ens)
In green meadows (vln and pf)
Other pieces (vln and pf)

PIANO
The bold chevalier
The days in New England
The fantastic suite
In green meadows
Journey through the darkness
A land of fortune
The new birth
Tear drops of a flower
A time to remember
The Utopian road
Why did you leave me?
VOCAL
A tribute (mix-ch and pf) (ded composer's father)
The dead (S, vln, fl and pf)
The wave (S, vln, fl and pf)
Songs incl.:
Anita
Faraway love
Ref. 474

BEGO-SIMUNIC, Andelka
Yugoslav (Bosnian) composer. b. Sarajevo, October 23, 1941. She studied composition under Professor Miroslav Spiler at the Music Academy, Sarajevo.
Compositions
ORCHESTRA
Symphony (1966)
Allegretto scherzoso (1964)
CHAMBER
String quartet No. 1 (1965)
Sonatina in E (pf) (1963)
VOCAL
Song cycle (Kastelan) (vce and pf) (1965)
Ref. 145

BEHR, Louise
19th-century German composer.
Compositions
VOCAL
Hunter's song (mix-ch)
Terzetto (vce and pf)
Other songs
Ref. 276

BEHREND, Emilie
20th-century Danish composer.
Composition
CHAMBER
Berceuse (vln and pf)
Ref. 331

BEHREND, Jeanne
American pianist, lecturer, writer and composer. b. Philadelphia, May 11, 1911. She graduated from the Curtis Institute of Music in 1934, where she studied the piano under Hoffman, Saperton and Landowska (q.v.) and composition under Scalero, Chasins and Toch. In 1936 she won the Columbia University Bearns Prize. She taught at the Curtis Institute, Western College, OH, the Juilliard School of Music, the Philadelphia Conservatory, the Temple University and from 1969 at the New School of Music, Philadelphia. She appeared as a soloist with leading orchestras. She gave a number of lecture-recitals on Latin American music and was sent by the U.S. State Department on a South American tour as a goodwill ambassador. PHOTOGRAPH.
Compositions
ORCHESTRA
From dawn until dusk, suite (also pf) (Elkan-Vogel, 1934)
Festival fanfare (1959)
Prelude to The star spangled banner
CHAMBER
String quartet (1937-1940)
Lamentation (vla and pf) (1944)
Three dialogues (vla d'amore and pf) (1940)
PIANO
Dance into space (also fl) (Shawnee Press, 1933)
Quiet piece (also fl) (Shawnee, 1932)
Sonata (1935)
Sonatine (1935-1942)
VOCAL
Fantasy on Shostakovitch's Song of the United Nations (w-ch, S and 2 pf) (Shawnee Press, 1923)
The old scissors grinder (1923) (Presser)
Song cycle (Sara Teasdale) (1936)
Twelve songs (1932-1944)
SACRED
Easter hymn (S, w-ch, hp, perc and org) (Housman, 1940-1941)
Publications
Edited *Notes of the Pianist* by Louis Moreau Gottschalk. Knopf, 1964.
Choral Music of the American Folk Tradition. Elkan-Vogel.
Piano Music by Louis Moreau Gottschalk. Presser.
The Unknown Fosters. Songs.
Ref. composer, 100, 138, 142, 191, 228, 280

BEKEART, Edna
20th-century Hawaiian school teacher and composer.
Compositions
VOCAL
Children's songs (with her sister, Irmgard Aluli q.v.) incl.:
Baby has a big lu'au
Humuhumunukunukuapua'a
Ref. 438

BEKMAN-SHCHERBINA, Elena Aleksandrovna Kamentseva
Soviet pianist, professor and composer. b. Moscow, January 12, 1882, d. Moscow, September 30, 1951. She studied under V. Safonov and graduated from the Moscow Conservatory in 1899. She taught the piano at a music school from 1912 to 1918 and lectured at the Moscow Conservatory from 1921 to 1930. From 1940 she was a professor of music harmony. DISCOGRAPHY.
Compositions
CHAMBER
Three children's pieces: Lullaby; Minuet; Waltz (2 pf)
VOCAL
Olyenka-Pevunya, lullaby (L.K. Bekman)
Verochkin pesenki, lullaby (L.K. Bekman)
Ref. 330, 519, 563

BELCHER, Mary Williams
20th-century American composer.
Composition
OPERA
The Legend of Ronsard and Madelon (Cleveland, 1918)
Ref. 141

BELINFANTE-DEKKER, Martha Suzanna Betje
Dutch pianist, poetess, singing teacher, voice therapist and composer. b. Amsterdam, August 12, 1900. Her talent for singing was discovered by J. van Tussenbroek when she was a child. Her singing teachers were Ida v. Ybergen-Santhagens-Waller, J. Dresden-Dhont, B. Seroen, R. Schonberg and I. Mollinger and she studied the piano and composition under Paul F. Sander and D. Belinfante, whom she married in 1923. After losing her voice as a result of repeated attacks of bronchitis and asthma and being declared incurable, she began to find a means to cure herself. The result was her Total System Belinfante ZD, a plastic and conscious use of the breathing and sound organs. She was also the authoress of many singing and declamation games for children, adults and class teaching. In 1933 she won the first prize for the best children's poem. From 1945 she was director of the Watergraafsmeer Music School, Amsterdam. PHOTOGRAPH.
Compositions
VOCAL
De dansers
De wethouders van waterweelde
De zangers
Little rain song (Amsterdam: Alsbach, 1960)
Dieren ABC (books 1, 11 and 111)
Pretjes
FOLK MUSIC
Aan de stilte, song (Alsbach)
Daarom is het Oranje boven! song (Alsbach)
Nu! Dat is wat ons Holland mint, song (Alsbach)
De hemel...nu! song (Alsbach)
Helpt de wereld bouwen! song (Alsbach)
Kerstsproke, song (Alsbach)

Publications

Zo geneest u zelf uw astma en bronchitis. 3 vols. Amsterdam: De Driehoek.

Ref. composer, 110

BELL, Carla Huston

American guitarist, pianist, violinist, actress, singer, teacher and composer. b. Montana, November 5, 1944. She studied the violin, voice, the piano and the guitar and graduated from Montana State University with a B.A. and from Columbia University with an M.A. and M.Ed. in 1975 and a D.Mus. in 1977. She played leading roles on the stages of New York, Los Angeles and San Francisco and performed in concert as well as with the New York City Opera Company. She was a consistent award winner for her compositions. She teaches music theory and musical theatre in New York. She is a member of ASCAP.

Compositions

VOCAL

Suite for a Greek festival (w-ch, 2 vln, 2 vla, 2 vlc, perc, pf and 2 rec) (1964-1965)
Love is the colour (mix-ch) (1967)
Ode to Martin Luther King (w-ch, vlc and d-b) (1976)
Anticipation (vce and pf) (1968)
Katanga (1964)
Let the rain fall on me (vce and pf) (1967)
Reflection (vce and pf) (1969)

Ref. composer

BELL, Elizabeth

American pianist, teacher and composer. b. Cincinnati, December 1, 1928. She began her piano study at the age of six with Dorothy Stolzenbach Payne and later with Robert Goldsand at the Cincinnati Conservatory. She obtained her B.A.Mus. from the Wellesley College in 1950. In 1953 she obtained her B.S. from the Juilliard School of music, where she studied composition under Peter Mennin and Vittorio Giannini. In New York City she continued with the study of composition privately under Paul Alan Levi. She gave performances of her music throughout the United States and from 1971 to 1976 was a music critic for the *Ithaca Journal*, New York. She was a recipient of Meet-the-Composer grants. PHOTOGRAPH.

Compositions

ORCHESTRA

Symphony No. 1 (1971)
Concerto for orchestra (small orch) (1976)

CHAMBER

First string quartet (1957)
Fantasy, sonata (vlc and pf) (1971)
Soliloquy (vlc; also vln) (1980)

PIANO

Arecibo sonata (1968)
Second sonata (1972)
Summer suite (1982)

VOCAL

Loss (S and pf) (1983)
Songs of here and forever (S and pf) (1970)

Ref. composer, 643

BELL, Judith

20th-century American composer.

Composition

FILM MUSIC

The Serpents of the pirate moon (1973)

Ref. 467

BELL, Lucille Anderson

20th-century American pianist and composer. b. St. Louis, MO. She studied at Chicago Music College with Alexander Raab and in New York with Paul Creston. She received ASCAP awards and performed on radio in Chicago and New York.

Compositions

CHAMBER

Three moods (fl and pf)
Lead us on, Thomas Paine, march (pf)

VOCAL

Runaway slave, song cycle

Ref. 142

BELLAMANO, Marietta

Italian composer. She was the sister of the lutenist Franceschina.

Ref. 128

BELLAMY, Marian Meredith

American pianist and composer. b. Woodbury, NJ, March 17, 1927. She graduated from Western Maryland College with a B.A. (1948) and went on to Drexel University, where she studied composition under John Davison and the piano under Stafford Newhall.

Compositions

CHAMBER

Three offices (brass qnt) (1973)
Serenade (str qrt) (1968)
Capricorn suite (hp and vlc) (1971)
Pisces suite (ob and pf) (1970)

PIANO

Asia, sonata (1973)
Four preludes (1967-1968)

Ref. 142

BELLANI (Belloni), Caroline

19th-century composer from Potsdam, Germany.

Compositions

CHAMBER

Grande Fantasia, on themes of Norma by Bellini (hp)
Marietta, polka (pf)

VOCAL

Sechs Lieder, op. 1 (S and pf) (Potsdam, 1849)

Ref. 121

BELLAVANCE, Ginette

Canadian composer. b. Levis, Quebec. She studied under Serge Garant at the University of Montreal and received an M.Mus. (composition). She also studied at the University of Quebec. From 1970 she directed a popular music research group and composed for a number of theatres.

Compositions

ELECTRONIC

Auguste, Auguste, Auguste (Pavel Kohout) (1973)
Bobby Boom (Jean Apostolides) (1972)
CLAC (1971-1972)
La cocufieur cocufié (Ruzante) (1972)
Cyrano de Bergerac (Edmond Rostand) (1973-1974)
Don Juan (Molière) (1972)
Fifteen songs (electric insts, vce, perc, sax, cl and fl) (1970-1974)
Hop theatre (1973)
Julien, Julien (Marcel Godin) (1973)
Match en coordonées (2 perc, 2 elec gtr and tape) (1971)
La moscheta (Ruzante) (1973)
Quand le chat n'est pas lá (Vanderbergue) (1973)
Sonorisation (vce and elec) (1973)
Teresa (Nathalie Ginzburg) (1974)
Le timide au palais (Tirso de Molina) (1971)
Tit-Jean, Margoton et le mauvais génie (1973)

FILM MUSIC

22 Films de l'ONF (1971-1972)

Ref. 329, 402

BELLCHAMBERS, Julliet

19th-century American composer.

Composition

VOCAL

The spell is broken (vce and pf) (New York: Attwell, 1842)

Ref. 228

BELLE, Marie-Paule

20th-century composer.

Compositions

FILM MUSIC

Go to Mama (1978)
Surprise sock (1978)
Thomas (1975)

Ref. 497

BELLEROSE, Sister Cecilia, C.S.C.

American lecturer and composer. b. Suncook or Pembroke, NH, November 8, 1897. She studied at Laval University, Quebec, under Arthur Letondal, Georges Tanquay, C. Morin, Isabel Delorme (q.v.) and O. Pelletier, gaining her B.M. and M.M. She received her Ph.D. from the University of Montreal. She was composer-in-residence and chairlady of the music department of Notre Dame College, Manchester, from 1950 to 1973.

Compositions

PIANO

Pieces

VOCAL

Concert d'oiseaux, cantata
The burning babe
Dieu nous voit
La fontaine
Graduations
Lux
Notre Dame, college song
Playful friskies (Squirrels)
Roller skates
Sayez bin
Motets

Ref. 137, 142, 347

BELLET, Mlle.

Early 19th-century French composer. Her operetta was performed in Hamburg in 1901.

Composition

OPERETTA

Les tribulations d'un reserviste (Croissot) (1901)

Ref. 431

BELLEVILLE-OURY, Anna-Caroline. See BELLEVILLE-OURY, Emilie

BELLEVILLE-OURY, Emilie (Anna-Caroline)

German pianist and composer of French parentage. b. Landshut, Bavaria, June 24, 1808; d. Munich, July 22, 1880. She was the daughter of a French nobleman, Belleville, director of the Munich Opera. She studied with Czerny in Vienna and made her debut there in 1819. Then she traveled in Germany, France and Italy and in 1832 went to London and married the violinist Oury. Together they toured Europe until 1846. Her playing was distinguished by brilliance and spirit. Robert Schumann in 'Music and Musicians' compared her playing to Clara Schumann's (q.v.) saying that Mme. Belleville's playing was technically the finer but Clara's was more passionate. After 1846, Emilie devoted herself to composing. Over 200 of her compositions appeared in print.

Compositions

PIANO

Air de l'ombre (Dinorah) (Boosey)
Andante capriccioso (Williams)
Annie Laurie (Boosey)
Auld Robin Gray (Boosey)
Bluebells of Scotland (Boosey)
Bohemian girl (Boosey)
Bridal, polka (Cramer)
Brighton galop (Boosey)
Britannia, polka (Cramer)
Chant du patriot, Garibaldi's hymn (Williams)
Chasse de compiegne, fanfare (Ashdown)
Consolation (Paterson)
Devonshire, polka (also for 4 hands) (Williams)
Dites-lui (Grande Duchesse) (Boosey)
Don Giovanni, fantaisie de salon (Ashdown)
Duke of York's march (Williams)
Ernani, fantasia (Boosey)
Favorite mazurka (Sheard)
Galop de bravura (Williams)
Gigue et gavotte de Corelli (Williams)
Grande fantaisie sur L'Africaine (Rozsavolgyi)
Highland echoes, melody (Ashdown)
Home sweet home, polka (Cramer)
I montanari, melodies styriennes (Ashdown)
I'm alone, from Benedict's Lily of Killarney (Chappell)
Jessie the flower of Dumblane, fantasia (Williams)
Kathleen Mavourneen, fantaisie irlandaise (Ashdown)
Lily of Killarney, fantasie on Benedict's opera (Chapell)
Marche ecossaise (Ashdown)
Martha, fantaisie (Boosey)
Oberon, polka de salon (Ashdown)
Other fantasies incl. Puritani, Rigoletto, Robert la Diable, Traviata, Trovatore, Un Ballo in Maschera, Sicilian Vespers, Masianello, Merry Wives of Windsor, Nozze di Figaro, Faust, 11 barbiere di Siviglia
Rosalie the prairie flower, impromptu (Williams)
Sigh of the South wind (Pitman)
Souvenir d'Edinbourg (Boosey)
Souvenir de Paris, valse (Ashdown)
Sunshine, valse de salon (Ashdown)
Valse brillante (Ashdown)

ARRANGEMENTS

Transcriptions from Haydn and other composers

Ref. 22, 70, 74, 129, 132, 297

BELLINA, Madonna

16th-century Italian instrumentalist, singer and composer. She lived in Venice around 1566 and was famous as an instrumentalist, singer and composer.

Ref. 25

BELLINCIONI, Gemma

19th-century Italian composer.

Compositions

VOCAL

Songs

OPERA

Eros (1895)
La Sorelle di Mark (1896)

Ref. 465

BELLMAN, Helene M.

20th-century American composer.

Composition

ORGAN

Meditation on altar windows

Ref. 142

BELLONI, Caroline. See BELLANI, Caroline

BELOCH, Dorotea

20th-century Italian composer. She attended the Scuola Nazionale di Musica and studied harmony, counterpoint and fugue under R. Storti from 1905 to 1907 and composition and instrumentation under P. Mascagni from 1907 to 1908.

Compositions

ORCHESTRA

Bozzetto sinfonico (large orch)
Suite

CHAMBER

Various pieces for violin and piano

VOCAL

Orfea (soloists, ch and orch)
Various pieces (soloists and ch)
Approx. 50 songs with orchestral accompaniment

OPERA

I cinque nani della montagna blu, fairy opera (L. Teodoro) (1932)
Il dono della fata, fairy opera (L. Teodoro) (1932)
Il fiore incantato, fairy opera (E. Frontera) (1932)
Liana, dramatic opera in 1 act (V. Zorawsky) (1925)
Il principino smarrito, fairy opera (E. Frontera) (1932)

THEATRE

Assodelo or Asfodelo, medieval legend in 2 acts (L. Okeloy Romiti) (1935)
La figlia del Salci, lyric fantasy in 2 scenes (M. Beloch)
Ynga, Nordic legend

Ref. 86, 105, 108

BELOVED. See MAHBUBA

BELOW-BUTTLAR, Gerda von

German pianist, violinist and composer. b. Saleske, November 9, 1894. She studied the violin, the piano and composition privately at the Weimar Lyceum in Berlin and under Wilhelm Klatte from 1917 to 1920. She composed 20 songs with lute accompaniment.

Ref. 219

BEMBO, Antonia

Italian singer and composer. b. Venice, ca. 1670. She probably belonged to the noble Venetian family of the name of Bembo. She may have been taught by Legrenzi, maestro di cappella at St. Mark's and director of one of the Venetian conservatories. She went to Paris between 1690 and 1695. Her singing talent came to the notice of Louis XIV who offered her a stipend. Lodged at the Convent Notre-Dame des Bonnes Nouvelles, she devoted herself to composing. Her works were dedicated to the King and to the Duchess of Burgundy. A collection of her compositions is preserved in the Bibliothèque Nationale, Paris.

Compositions

SACRED

Te Deum, with dedication (ch and str orch)
Divertimento, for the birth of the prince (5-part ch and str orch)
Te Deum and Exaudiat (vces and str orch)
Produzioni armoniche, collection of 40 pieces offered to Louis XIV and consisting of 3 works written for the marriage of Louis, Duke of Burgundy and Maria Adelaide of Savoy (1967)
Les sept Psaumes de David (vces and insts)
Arias

OPERA

L'Ercole Amante, tragedy (Cavalli, Italian verses by Abbe Buti) (1707)

Bibliography

Rokseth, Yvonne. *Antonia Bembo, Composer to Louis XIV. Musical Quarterly* April, 1937.

Ref. 22, 105, 622

BENARY, Barbara

American violinist, ethnomusicologist, assistant professor, singer and composer. b. Bay Shore, NY, July 4, 1946. She gained her B.A. from Sarah Lawrence College (1968) and after studying the violin, she extended her abilities to include the karnatic violin of India, the erh-hu of China and the gadulka of Bulgaria. She gained her M.A. (1971) and Ph. D. (1973) in ethnomusicology from Wesleyan University and was assistant professor at Livingstone College, Rutgers University, NJ, from 1973 to 1980. She has composed for chamber and ethnic ensembles, two dance companies and a puppet company, as well as opera and theatre music. She also holds workshops on Gamelan related topics. The Gamelan Son of Lion Ensemble was formed in 1976 and functionally duplicates the form and sound of the traditional Javanese village gamelan. The instruments for this ensemble were made by Ms. Benary in America in 1974 and were tuned to non-western scales of slendro and pelog, although she includes other instruments such as the flute, the zither and the drum as well as voice for her compositions. Since the inception of this ensemble she has concentrated mainly on writing repertoire for it. She has received ten Meet-the-Composer sponsorships since 1979. DISCOGRAPHY.

Compositions

Gamelan Son of Lion Ensemble:

Backtracking braid (1979)
Braid (1975)
Cantor's row (1980)
Convergence (1975)
Counterbraid (1979)
Deena's rag (1982)
Dragon toes (1979)
The falls of Richmond (1982)
Gamelan N.E.A. (1982)
Gong fanfare (1978)
Hells bells (1978)
Hot rolled steel (1984)
In scrolls of leaves (1980)
Macrame (1979)
Omnivorous (1979)
O'Rourke in New York (1980)
Sleeping braid (1979)
Tock (1980)
Woodstock (1982)
The Zen story (1979)

THEATRE

The Gauntlet, or The moon's on fire (Braswell) (1976)
Gong of Java, Javanese shadow puppet play (1978)
The interior castle (Braswell) (1979)
A new pantheon (1981)
Night shadow (1982)
The only jealousy of Emer (Yeats) (1970)
Ramayana Parts I and II (1979, 1980)
Sanguine (Braswell) (1976)
Scores for Hudson Vagabond Puppet Theatre, Laura Powel Dance Co., Balinese-American Dance Co.
The story of Hanuman (1983)
The Tempest (Shakespeare) (1981)
Three sisters who are not sisters (Stein) (1967)

Ref. composer, 563, 622, 633

BENAULT (Benaut), Mlle.

18th-century French pianist and composer. She was a child prodigy and composed her first two volumes of pieces at the age of nine, her third volume at age ten. All her listed compositions are in the Bibliotheque Nationale, Paris.

Compositions

HARPSICHORD

Le deuxieme recueil d'airs avec variations
Le premier recueil d'airs avec variations (ca. 1785)
Le quatrieme recueil d'airs avec variations
Le troisieme recueil d'airs avec variations (ca. 1786)

ORGAN

Magnificat
Pièce d'orgue, books 1-9 (ded Mme. de Schodt)

Ref. 128

BENAVENTE, Regina

Argentine pianist and composer. b. Buenos Aires, January 22, 1932. She is the daughter of the composer Manuel Jose Benavente from whom she received her first music lessons. In 1952 she went to the State Conservatory in Buenos Aires, where she studied harmony under Jurafsky, the piano under Rafael Gonzalez and composition under Ginastera.

Compositions

ORCHESTRA

Violin concerto (1956)
Sinfonietta (1954)
Sinfonia de primavera (1951)
Chamber concerto (1955)
Kronos (1968)
Pastorale and dance
Musica para orquestra da cuerda (strs)

CHAMBER

Musica V (cl, vln, vla, vlc, perc and pf) (1966)
Musica (str qrt) (1963)

PIANO

Galaxias (2 pf) (1967)
Musica VI (1967)

ELECTRONIC

Composicion I (1968)
Musica concertante (tape and cl) (1968)

Ref. 17, 70, 280

BENAVIDES, Elena

19th-century Peruvian composer.

Compositions

PIANO

Le cubana, polka (ded Club de Progreso)

Ref. 403

BENDA, Juliana. See REICHARDT, Juliane Benda

BENEDICENTI, Vera

Italian pianist and composer. b. Milan, May 19, 1913. She studied the piano under Gaspare Scuderi at the A. Boito Conservatory, Parma (diploma, 1939). She also studied harmony, counterpoint and instrumentation under Cesare Rossi Oldrati, Gino Marinuzzi, Jr. and Gaspare Scuderi and composition under C.R. Oldrati, Enrico Giachetti and Gino Scuderi. DISCOGRAPHY. PHOTOGRAPH.

Compositions

ORCHESTRA

Per sopravvivere, fantasia (1972)

PIANO

Piccola suite (Milan: Carisch S.p.A., 1957)
Otto bozzetti musicali (Milan: Carisch S.p.A., 1960)
Nostalgia, waltz (1966)
Serenata sui Tetti, waltz (1966)
Three pieces: Silhouette priolettante; Sonia; Sua eccellenza

VOCAL

Lontana (Pascoli) (1936)
Speranze e memorie (Pascoli) (1937)
Ninna-nanna (15th-century author) (pf and vce) (Milan: Carisch S.p.A., 1948)
Quindici canoni a due parti (1967) (Milan: Carisch S.p.A., 1976)
Tu eri il mio unico fiore (Sandor Petofi)

SACRED
Inno a Guiseppe Verdi (for Parish of S. Michele Arcangelo at Roncole Verdi) (1965)
Publications
Contributor of articles to *Rassenga Italiana*, Milan and *Bollettino Musicale di Vita e Cultura Muisicale*, Milan.
Ref. composer, 563

BENES, Jara
20th-century composer of an operetta, in 1936.
Ref. 465

BENFEY-SCHUPPE (Shuppe), Anna
Austrian composer. b. Landeck, 1831; d. Weimar, May 27, 1903.
Compositions
CHAMBER
Pieces
OPERA
Adelheid, Gemahlin Ottos des Grossen (1836)
THEATRE
Overture to Goetz von Berlichingen (Goethe)
Philippine Welser (Dresden: Breslau, Coburg)
Romeo and Juliette
Ref. 226, 276, 307, 431

BENINGFIELD, Ethel
19th-century British composer.
Compositions
ORCHESTRA
Selection of old English airs (man or banjo, gtr and orch) (Turner)
CHAMBER
Melodie espagnole (2 man; also man and pf) (Ricordi)
Reverie (man and pf) (Turner)
MANDOLIN
Selection of Scottish airs (Turner)
Selection of Irish airs (Turner)
Songe d'Avril (also man and pf) (Turner)
VOCAL
Come, live with me (Chappell)
For the Empire and our Queen (Weekes)
A hunting morning (Keith)
I love thee (Chappell)
A lament (Chappell)
Love's meeting (Chappell)
Only waiting (Chappell)
Unless (Chappell)
Ref. 297

BENJAMIN, June. See SCHNEIDER, June

BENNETT, Emma Marie. See MacFARREN, Emma Marie

BENNETT, Claudia
20th-century American composer.
Compositions
VOCAL
Three improvisations (composer) (mix-ch, 2 pf and cham ens)
Ref. 142

BENNETT, Elsie M.
American accordionist, authoress, teacher and composer. b. Detroit, March 30, 1919. She studied at the Ganapol School of Music, Wayne University, where she obtained her B.M. and at Columbia University Teachers' College where she obtained her M.A. Her teachers included Ethel Mendelsohn, Mischa Kottler, George Cailotta and Joe Biviano. She was director and teacher of the Bennett Accordion Studios, Brooklyn, and a vice-president of the American Accordionists' Association.
Compositions
ACCORDION
Easy solos
American home album
Melodies for the accordion
Teaching works
VOCAL
Hebrew-Jewish songs and dances
Ref. 39

BENNETT, Mimi
19th-century American composer.
Compositions
VOCAL
Land of dreams (S, m-S and A) (Boston Music Co.)
Love's reverie (Ricordi)
Ref. 297

BENNETT, Wilhelmine
American writer, lecturer and composer. b. Carmi, IL, June 14, 1933. She studied at the Jordan Conservatory (B.M.) and under Anthony Donato at Northwestern University (M.Mus. and D.Mus.) She undertook postdoctoral study at Columbia University under Chou Wen-chung and won a Fulbright Fellowship in 1964 to study under Wolfgang Fortner at the Freiburg Hochschule fuer Musik from 1965 to 1966. She received the William T. Farley award for creative writing in 1963 and a National Council of the Arts award in 1966. In 1971 she lectured at the University of California in Santa Cruz. She is a director of the International League of Women Composers.
Compositions
ORCHESTRA
Symphony No. 1 (1964)
Symphony No. 2
Colors (1970)
Enola Gay (1966)
Thumbelisa (1949)
CHAMBER
Synura (wind insts) (1964)
Woodwind quintet (1961)
Beyond the quiet (1974)
Crusades (1968)
Five quick visions of the Apocalypse (1971)
Hieroglyphics (1975)
Hyperbolex (1962)
Seven seals (1963)
Suite absurdite (1967)
VOCAL
Songs (A) (1952)
Ref. composer, 142, 457

BENNO, Mrs. See RABINOF, Sylvia

BEN-OR, Mary. See EVEN-OR, Mary

BENOIT, Francine Germaine Van Gool
Portuguese pianist, choral conductor, music critic, teacher, writer and composer. b. Perigueux, France, July 30, 1894. She settled in Portugal in 1906 and took Portuguese nationality in 1929. She studied the piano and composition at the National Conservatory in Lisbon under Rey Colaco and Costa Ferreira and won first prize for harmony. In Paris she studied at the Schola Cantorum from 1917 to 1918 under Vincent d'Indy. She taught from 1920 and was choir conductor and teacher at the Academia dos Amadores de Musica from 1955. Because of her interest in fostering musical culture and education she was instrumental in forming the Conservatory of Music of Coimbra, Portugal. She was a music critic for the daily newspaper *Diario de Lisboa* for many years from 1926. She took an active part in conferences and contributed articles to many journals.
Compositions
ORCHESTRA
Piano concerto
Partita (cham orch)
Tres canções tristes (cham orch)
CHAMBER
Sonata (vln and pf)
Other pieces
PIANO
Four pieces (2 pf)
Enfantines
Nove peças enfantis

VOCAL
Cantata infantil (vln and 10 insts)
Songs (A. Sardinha, E. de Castro, A. de Sousa and A. Serpa)
Publications
Beethoven. Book for the young.
Dos acordes na arte e na escola.
Ref. 8, 70, 94, 96, 100, 268

BENSON, Berenice. See BENTLEY, Berenice Benson

BENSUADE, Jane
20th-century French composer.
Compositions
VOCAL
Songs
OPERA
Gentil Mignon
Ref. 465

BENTLEY, Berenice Benson
American teacher and composer. b. Oskaloosa, IA, January 2, 1887; d. Claremont, CA, April 2, 1971. She studied at Grinnell College, Iowa and then under Mary Wood Chase, Chicago, where she later taught.
Compositions
PIANO
Four northern sketches
Sonatina
VOCAL
Woodland vignettes, 5 songs
Ref. 142, 292

BENTZON, Karen Johanne
20th-century Danish composer.
Compositions
VOCAL
Fem kanons (1942)
Ref. 331

BENZON, Julie
Early 20th-century Danish composer.
Compositions
PIANO
Alfeleg (Wilhelm Hansen Inc.)
Aux yeux fermés (1906) (Hansen)
Denne lille mandolinspiller (1921) (Hansen)
Djoevletrille (1903) (Hansen)
Ellens vuggesang (1908) (Hansen)
Elvertans (Hansen)
Foraar (Hansen)
Klaverstykker 1-11 (1912-1924) (Hansen)
Koncert-etude, op. 16 (1908) (Hansen)
Little skojteloberdans (1919) (Hansen)
Mazurka (1924) (Hansen)
VOCAL
Du funklende Jukstjerne (vce and pf)
Ref. 331

BERAN-STARK, Lola Aloisia Maria
Bohemian pianist, teacher and composer. b. Prague, December 13, 1879. She studied at the Burgschule, Prague, under Augustin Vyskocil from 1892 to 1895 and at the Prague Conservatory from 1895 to 1900. She took the state examination in 1899. From 1889 to 1900 she studied counterpoint at the same conservatory under K. Knittl; In 1901 she studied the piano in Paris under L. Gregh ; from 1904 to 1906 she studied singing in Prague under Maria Petzok; in 1906 she continued her piano studies under Teresa Carreno (q.v.) in Berlin; from 1909 to 1913 and again from 1921 to 1923 she studied composition in Prague under Vitezslav Novak and from 1910 to 1912 she studied the piano under A. Mikes and in Prague. From 1900 to 1906 she went on tour until her marriage to Jaroslav Stark.
Compositions
CHAMBER
Sonata (vln and pf)
PIANO
Concert waltzes (1898)
Im Walde und Felde, cycle (1909)
Piano suite with fugue and double fugue
Variations and fugue on a theme in Aeolian mode (1913)
Other piano works
VOCAL
Lieder
Ref. 70, 111

BERBERIAN, Cathy
American actress, lecturer, singer and composer. b. Attleboro, MA, July 4, 1925; d. Rome, March 6, 1983. She studied at New York University and Columbia University before going to the G. Verdi Conservatory, Milan. She studied voice under Georgina del Vigo in Milan and acting under H. Graf and Peter Brook. In 1950 she married the composer Luciano Berio. She appeared at La Scala and at Covent Garden and the Royal Festival Hall in London, as well as in Germany, Holland, Sweden and France. She taught at the Kolnische Musikschule from 1964 to 1965, the University of Vancouver in 1965, the Royal Conservatory of Toronto in 1971, the Milan Conservatory and La Scala Opera School in 1974 and the Musik Hochschule Freiburg in 1975. She also taught master classes at Berkshire Music Center and many other world-wide centers. She was awarded a Fulbright scholarship from 1950 to 1951 and won the Wiesbaden Festival prize in 1970. She received Grammy nominations in 1971, 1973 and 1974. In 1972 she won the Grand Prix du Disque. She composed for voice and piano and because of her extraordinary vocal range and ability she was able to develop and use vocal techniques appropriate to the music that many famous composers wrote especially for her. DISCOGRAPHY.
Compositions
VOCAL
Awake and read Joyce (1972)
Anathema con VarieAzioni (1972)
Morsicat(h)y (1971)
Stripsody (vce and vln) (1966)
Publications
Anthology of songs composed by women. G. Schirmer, 1982.
Ref. composer, 84, 94, 189, 199, 206, 457, 563, 622

BERCKMAN, Evelyn
American pianist, teacher, writer and composer. b. Philadelphia, October 18, 1900. She taught herself composition. A temporary paralysis caused by too fervent piano practice hampered her career for seven years. Her works have been widely performed and broadcast. She taught and wrote articles for magazines and program notes for the Philharmonic Symphony Chamber Orchestra.
Compositions
ORCHESTRA
The return of song, after a fable of Lord Dunsany (ca. 1927)
CHAMBER
Archangels, suite (3 hp)
Incantations: Percussion; The web; Circus day (hp, fl and vlc) (1934)
VOCAL
Punch and Judy dances (ch and orch) (1937)
Aboard the morning star (vce and orch) (1932)
Die Nebelstadt (S and orch) (Paris: M. Senart, 1924)
Sorbonne (vce and orch) (1937)
Sturm (S and orch) (M. Senart, 1924)
Swans (vce and orch) (1925)
Tours, XVIIth-Century (vce and orch) (1936)
The far land (S and 7 insts) (1930)
The soldier's trade (S and 7 insts) (1930)
The quiet pool (S and str qrt) (1929)
Springtime in the orchard (S and str qrt) (1929)
Dr. Johnson's tour to the Hebrides (S and fl) (1936)
BALLET
From the Odyssey (w-ch and 7 insts) (1931)
Country fair (orch) (1937)
Ref. 44, 53, 94, 124, 142, 191, 226, 228, 322

BERG, Lily
20th-century Hungarian pianist, teacher and composer. She studied at the Budapest Academy of Music under Bela Bartok, Koessler and Weiner and then taught at the Fodor Music School. She gave concerts in Hungary and on foreign radio stations.
Compositions
ORCHESTRA
Suite (pf and orch)
CHAMBER
String trio
Piano pieces
VOCAL
Songs
Ref. 375

BERGE, Irénée
French composer. b. Toulouse, February 1, 1867; d. Jersey City, July 30, 1926.
Compositions
CHAMBER
Nocturne (str qrt, hp and fl)
PIANO
Capriccio (Baudoux)
Le Cyprin, étude fantaisie (Baudoux)
Danse hongroise (Baudoux)
Dormez, ma mie (Baudoux)
Ecoutez chanter les Pinsons (Weiller)
En Mai, valse de salon (Baudoux)
Eté (Hachette)
Les fleurs et l'aimée (Hachette)
Gerbe des roses, mazurka (Weiller)
Impressions d'été (Baudoux)
Impromptu-valse (Baudoux)
La machine à coudre, morceau caractéristique (Fromont)
Mazurka de concert (Leduc)
Mes baisers sont des papillons (Baudoux)
La mouche, fantaisie (Baudoux)
La nuit descent des cieux (Baudoux)
Le papillon, méditation (Joubert)
Rêve d'amour (Baudoux)
Réveil (Baudoux)
Sérénade espagnole (Baudoux)
Six dances anciennes (Baudoux)
Sonnet (Baudoux)
Valse de l'abeille (Ricordi)
Vous, souvenez-vous (Fromont)
VOCAL
Les Nymphes d'Artémis (3 w-vces) (Baudoux)
La gente meunière (B and T) (L. Gregh)
Le joyeux pêcheur (B and T) (L. Gregh)
Berceuse bretonne (Leduc)
Chanson de mousse (Baudoux)
Chanson de vendanges (Fromont)
Chansons des champs, 8 songs (Baudoux)
Le chanson du chevalier (Ondet)
OPERA
Corsica (1910)
Ref. 297, 322, 556

BERGEN, Sylvia
20th-century American composer.
Composition
CHAMBER
Festival frolic (vln, vla, vlc and d-b)
Ref. 80

BERGER, Jean
American composer. b. 1909.
Compositions
PIANO
Country sketches
Sonatina
Ref. *Clavier* April 1984

BERGERSEN, Marie Christine
American pianist and composer. b. Chicago, IL, May 15, 1894. As a child she studied the piano under Louise Robyn in Chicago and with Leopold Godowsky in Vienna (1912 to 1914). At the American Conservatory of Music, Chicago, she studied composition under Adolf Weidig. She played in concerts in the Chicago area and in the 1920s demonstrated an electromagnetic instrument in a series of concerts. She later performed on radio in solos and duos with M. Stapleton in New York, besides composing for several radio stations. She retired in 1954. She was the mother of Edith Borroff (q.v.), musicologist and composer.
Compositions
CHAMBER
String quartet
Piano trio
PIANO
Theme and variations (1911)
Three silhouettes
Numerous other pieces
VOCAL
Songs
SACRED
Anthems
Ref. composer

BERGMAN, Ellen
Swedish organist, teacher and composer. b. 1842; d. 1921. She was a pupil at the Stockholm Conservatory from 1864 till 1869 and took organist examinations in 1867. From 1870 till 1899 she taught singing at the conservatory and in high schools in Stockholm. Her teaching methods for schools, together with those of Anna Bergstrom (q.v.), laid the basis for the teaching of singing in Swedish schools which has prevailed to the present day.
Compositions
VOCAL
Numerous songs incl.:
Den ofvergifna (Malmstrom, 1869)
Blomman (Malmstrom, 1869)
Naktergalen (Atterbom, 1869)
Ref. 167, 642

BERGMANN, Valentina Semyenovna. See SEROVA, Valentina

BERGSTROM, Anna
Swedish organist, teacher and composer. b. 1853; d. 1937. She took the organist examinations at the Conservatory in Stockholm in 1876 and was a pupil of Ellen Bergman (q.v.). She first taught in Filipstad and after 1880 in Stockholm. In the 1890s she studied singing abroad. She published essays on the teaching of singing in schools. Her methods, with those of Ellen Bergman, laid the basis for the teaching of singing in Swedish schools which has prevailed to the present day. She composed songs.
Publications
Saangkurs foer skola. 1905-1908.
Essays on teaching.
Ref. 642

BERK, Adele
American lecturer and composer. b. New York, November 25, 1927. She studied at Hunter College (B.A.), Columbia University (M.A.) and composition at the Berkshire Music Center. She attended graduate level courses at the Juilliard School of Music and studied under David Diamond, Edgard Varese, N. Lockwood and Irving Fine (composition). Her compositions have been performed at the Berkshire Music Center, Columbia University and Hunter College. She was composer-in-residence for the Wantagh Community Arts Program and the Wantagh Public Schools (1972 to 1974). She lectured in music at Dowling College, New York, and was a faculty member at Nassau Community College. PHOTOGRAPH.
Compositions
ORCHESTRA
Air and march (pf and elementary str orch) (1972)
BAND
Festival fanfare (1966-1967)
Wantagh overture (1972-1973)
CHAMBER
Divertimento (cl, vla, bsn and pf) (1980)
Rx for three (cl, vla and pf) (1983)
Three pieces (cl and pf) (1949) (Timbrel Music)
Sonata (vln and pf) (1949-1950)
Duo (pf and snare dr) (1950)
VOCAL
Questions (mix-ch) (1972)
Night song at Amalfi (S and pf) (1949)
Sigh no more, ladies (S and pf) (1981)
Song (S and pf) (1975)
SACRED
O praise the Lord (treble ch) (1963)
Psalm 150 (mix-ch and pf)
He will give his angels charge over thee (mix-ch and pf) (1982)
The Lord bless thee and keep thee (mix-ch and pf) (1980)
O ye gates (ch) (1969)
Alleluia is our song (w-ch and pf) (Belwin-Mills)
Holy, holy, holy, is the Lord of hosts (w-ch and pf) (1981) (Plymouth Music)
Sing praises to God (w-ch and pf)
With my voice I call unto the Lord (mix-ch and pf)
I will lift up mine eyes (vces and pf) (1978) (Belwin-Mills)
Lift up your heads
O sing unto the Lord a new song (S and pf) (1975) (Timbrel Music)
Ref. composer, 77

BERKELEY, Elizabeth. See ANSPACH, Elizabeth

BERL WEINFIELD, Christine
American pianist, lecturer and composer. b. New York, July 22, 1943. She began her piano studies with her father and then studied harmony, counterpoint and Schenkerian analysis under Ernst Oster. After studying composition under Hugo Weisgall and George Perle at Queens College, she obtained her M.A. in 1970 and continued her composition studies under Yehudi Wyner. From 1967 to 1968 she was the private coach of the soprano Pilar Lorengar during her appearance at the Metropolitan Opera. Since 1974 she has taught the piano, composition, 20th-century techniques and orchestration at Mannes College of Music.
Compositions
CHAMBER
Three pieces for chamber ensemble (1975)
Two movements, In Memoriam, incl. Elegy, 2nd movement (pf) (1974)
VOCAL
Ab la dolchor, cantata (S, ch and orch) (1979) (comm Susan Davenny Wyner)
Ref. composer, 625, 643

BERLINER, Selma
German pianist and composer. b. Danzig, October 6, 1860; d. Berlin, December 7, 1930. She lived in Berlin.
Compositions
PIANO
Walzer, op. 11 (4 hands) (Glas)
Bilder aus den Kindertagen, op. 10 (Glas)
Etude mignonne, op. 9 (Challier)
Menuett und Gavotte, op. 6 (Haslinger)
VOCAL
Gruss, op. 8, songs (Leipzig: Preiser)
Ref. 81, 105, 297

BERMAN, Ruth. See HARRIS, Ruth Berman

BERNARD, Eulanie
19th-century French composer.
Composition
PIANO
Souvenirs de L'Etanche, quadrille brillant, op. 6 (1860)
Ref. Philip Martin (London)

BERNARD, Jeanne
20th-century French composer.
Composition
CHAMBER
Les Cigales de Murcie (vlc and pf)
Ref. Billaudot

BERNARD, Vincenzia
German organist, pianist, teacher, writer and composer. b. Krischanovitz, Moravia in 1840. She received her first musical education from her father, a village teacher and organist. She was a well-known organist and piano teacher in Brunn, Austria (now Brno, Czechoslovakia) and Austerlitz. She wrote a treatise on piano technique.
Compositions
PIANO
Pieces incl: Hilfsbuch fuer den Klavierunterricht
Ref. 226. 276, 433

BERNARDI-BELLATI, Eleonora
16th-century Italian composer. b. Lucca.
Compositions
VOCAL
Canzone, song (page 50, Part 1, of 'Scelta di rime di diversi moderni autori' by Pietro Partoli, Genoa, 1591).
SACRED
Canzoni sacre, songs (page 21, 'Viaggio alla S Casa di Loreto, distinto in dodici giornate' by Father Cesare Franciotti, Venice, 1627)
Ref. 327

BERNARDONE, Anka (pseud. of Sister Mary Ann Joyce)
American pianist and composer. b. Champaign, IL, October 3, 1937. She composed piano pieces and choral works.
Ref. 347

BERNOUILLY, Agnes
German composer. b. Berlin, 1825.
Compositions
ORCHESTRA
Works
PIANO
Fruehlingsklange, waltz (Berlin, 1851)
Nocturne (Berlin, 1856)
VOCAL
Motet for the commemoration of the Elisabeth Foundation, Pankow (Fanny Hensel q.v.) (1854)
Ref. 121, 226, 276

BERNOUX, Leon. See PERRONNET, Amelie

BERROA, Catalina
Cuban guitarist, harpist, organist, pianist, violinist, choral conductor and composer. b. Trinidad, February 28, 1849; d. November 23, 1911. She organised and conducted a church choir and trio in Trinidad.
Compositions
VOCAL
Songs
SACRED
La Trinitaria, mass
Salves
Other masses
Hymns
Ref. 604

BERRY, Margaret Mary Robinson
Canadian pianist, choir conductor and composer. b. Drumheller, Alberta, January 30, 1918. She studied the piano under Weldon Kilburn at Toronto Conservatory; composition and arranging under Leo Smith at Chicago Music College and composition under Robert Mann and C. Waal. She became an A.R.C.M. and L.R.S.M. She composed piano, vocal and choral works.
Ref. 133

BERRYMAN, Alice Davis
20th-century American pianist, teacher and composer. b. North Platte, NE. She studied the piano under August Borglum in Omaha, Wager Swayne in Paris and Rudolph Ganz in Switzerland. After studying musical analysis under Cecil Berryman, whom she married in 1916, she studied theory, harmony, composition and orchestration under Emile Schwartz at the Paris Conservatoire. As a concert pianist she performed alone and with her husband, in New York, Paris and midwestern America. In Omaha she taught the piano at the Berryman Piano Conservatory from 1916 till 1960. She was the recipient of several honors and awards including that of the Hall of Fame Piano Guild in 1968.
Compositions
PIANO
Works incl.:
Alice in Wonderland suite (Melody Music Co.)
Birds in the linden tree
The dragon with the one green eye
Slumber song for little dragons
Spanish dance
Swinging on the high trapeze (Lavell)
Ref. 457, 475, 643

BERTACCA, Uberta
20th-century Italian composer.
Composition
FILM MUSIC
Rome wants another Caesar (1974)
Ref. 497

BERTELLI, Clotilde

Late 19th-century Italian composer of chamber and vocal music.
Ref. 502

BERTHE (Bierthe), Mme. (nee Offhuis)

B. ca. 1750. She is known only from a mention in the register of the *Decrets et ordonnances de la Cathedrale de Liege* in 1770; *The production of a musical catechism dedicated to this illustrious chapter by the musician, Mme. Berthe.* The *Gazette de Liege* of November 10, 1769, stated that 'Amateur women are informed that Madame Bierthe, composer and celebrated player of the theorbo and lute, mandolin, guitar, both Polish and Italian, for which she has composed some pieces and some principles in order to facilitate the learning of how to play them also for the sistrum, composed some symphonies, trio duo and solo for the violin, etc., having a 10-year-old daughter, who had difficulties mastering the lute and the mandolin'. In 1775 the same newspaper said that 'Madame Bierthe, born Offhuis, obtained permission to give, together with her daughter, concerts every Wednesday, on payment of half a carolin for each representation'.
Ref. 30

BERTIN, Louise Angelique

French pianist, poetess, singer and composer. b. February 15, 1805; d. Paris, April 26, 1877. She was the daughter of Louis François Bertin, editor of the *Journal des Debats*. This gave her an easy entry into the musical world and enabled her to enlist the support of Berlioz, who was attached to that paper as a critic. She studied music under Fetis and won fame as a composer of opera. Her collection of poetry *Les Glanes*, published in Paris in 1842, was awarded a prize by the French Academy. Victor Hugo wrote the libretto based on his Hunchback of Notre Dame for her opera *Esmeralda* but this was a failure. She achieved success later with her instrumental trios and quartets. DISCOGRAPHY.

Compositions

ORCHESTRA

Five chamber symphonies

CHAMBER

String quartets
Trio (pf, vln and vlc)

VOCAL

La chasse et la guerre (ch)
Les chasseurs (ch)
Le depart du comte (ch)
L'enfant des fées (ch)
Les esprits (ch)
Hymne à Apollon (ch)
Les Juifs (ch)
Prière (ch)
Retour d'Agamemnon (ch)
Ronde de jeune filles (ch)
Songs incl.:
Les derniers adieux (Katlo)
La fleur (Girod)
Le matelot (Girod)
La muse (Girod)
Ninna-nanna
Le page (Girod)
Le soir, ballad

OPERA

Esmeralda, ou Notre-Dame de Paris, in one act (V. Hugo) (Paris 1836)
Faust, in 3 acts (J.W. Goethe) (Paris, 1831)
Guy Mannering
Le loup garou, in 3 acts (A.E. Scribe and E.J.E. Mazares) (Paris, 1827)

Publications

Les Glanes, collection of poetry. (prize, French Academy) Paris, 1842.
Nouvelles Glanes, 2nd vol. Paris: Charpentier, 1876.

Bibliography

Landowski, W.L. Propos du centenaire de La Esmeralda.
Le Ménestrel 98.

Ref. 2, 8, 13, 17, 26, 44, 102, 108, 129, 132, 225, 226, 276, 297, 304, 335, 361, 376, 394, 400, 563

BERTINOTTI, Teresa

Italian singer, teacher and composer. b. Savigliano, Piedmont 1780; d. 1852. She had her first musical education from La Barbiera in Naples and began her stage career at the age of 12. She became famous in Milan, Venice, Vienna, Munich, The Hague, London and Lisbon for her beauty as much as for her voice and was called 'L'Angelo del Canto'. After 1814 she went back to Bologna with her husband, Radicati, a violinist and music teacher and after his death in 1823 she taught singing and composed arias.
Ref. 129

BERTOLAJO-CAVALETTI, Orsola

17th-century Italian composer. She lived in Ferrara.

Compositions

VOCAL

Madrigals (in book called *Il gareggiamento poetico del confuso accademica ordito*. Venice; Barezzo Barezzi, 1611)

Ref. 327

BERTRAM, Madge

Scottish pianist and composer. b. Edinburgh, November 8, 1879. She was the daughter of James Bertram, a well known musician. She studied harmony under Grieve and the piano under Mme. Kruger, a pupil of Clara Schumann (q.v.). She taught herself composition and wrote lieder and piano music. Some of her works were orchestrated for public performances.
Ref. 105

BERTRAND, Aline

French harpist and composer. b. Paris, 1798; d. March 13, 1835. She studied the harp at the Paris Conservatoire under Nadermann, then from 1815 with Bochsa. She made her debut in 1820 and was an immediate success, touring extensively in Europe. In 1828 she met Paganini in Vienna and took part in some of his concerts.

Compositions

HARP

Variations for harp on Nel cor piu non mi sento, op. 1 (Ricordi)
Fantasia sulla Polonese di Oginsky, op. 2 (Ricordi)
Fantasia sulla romanza del Guiseppe di Mehul, op. 3 (Ricordi)

Ref. 105

BERTRAND, Ginette

Canadian pianist and composer. b. Montreal, June 8, 1949. She studied at the Ecole Vincent d'Indy from 1968 to 1970, concentrating on the piano. From 1970 to 1975 she studied composition at Laval University under Jacques Hetu.

Compositions

ORCHESTRA

Eclosion (str orch) (1973)

CHAMBER

Octet for woodwinds (1972)
String quartet (1971)
Elegy (cl and pf) (1970)
Piece for solo flute (1971)

PIANO

Four pieces (1967)
Sonata (1973)
Theme and variations (1970)

VOCAL

Scherzo (ch and str orch) (1972)

BALLET

Le long sommeil de Franz (1973)

ELECTRONIC

La fugitive (inst ens and tape)

Ref. CMC

BERZON, Asya Yevseyevna

Soviet composer. b. Odessa, June 15, 1917. She graduated from the Odessa Conservatory in 1938 and studied composition under B. Mochanov from 1938 to 1941 and after 1944 at the P. Stoliarsky music school.

Compositions

ORCHESTRA

Symphony (commemorating the 20th anniversary of the Comsomol) (diploma composition, 1938)
Armenia Suite (1943)
Scherzo (1938)
Four Ossetian folk dances (orch of folk insts) (1942)

PIANO

Ten preludes (1938)
Three sonatas: 1 (1947) 2 and 3 (1949)
Variations (1940)
Collection of children's pieces (1952)

VOCAL

Romances (Puskin and Lermontov) (1938-1944)
Romances, 5 songs (Shevchenko) (1946)
Songs (Ukrainian poets)
Arrangements of Armenian folk melodies (vce and pf)

Ref. 87

BESSEM, Saar
Dutch lecturer and composer. b. Tiel, March 13, 1907. She attended the conservatory in Rotterdam, where she studied singing under Berthe Seroen and Aaltje Noordewier-Reddingius and composition under Willem Pijper. She became principal teacher at the same conservatory and taught music at the Montessori Lyceum. Her compositions were influenced by the Montessori method of teaching. She wrote her own texts.
Composition
PIANO
Danssuite naar Oud-Hollandse kinderwijze (4 hands) (1948)
VOCAL
De Zee (mix-ch and orch) (1952)
Nixe (G. Eggink) (1947)
Rondeel (G. Smit) (1947)
BALLET
Van het prinsesje, dat niet dansen wilde, in 3 acts (pf, 4 hands) (1947)
OPERA
Floris en Blancefloer
OPERETTA
Assepoester, for young children
Doornroosje, for young children
De nieuwe Kleren van de Keizer (chil-ch)
De Prinses op de Erwt (chil-ch)
Reinaard (chil-ch)
De Varkenshoeder (chil-ch)
Zwaan Kleef aan (chil-ch and pf) (1944-1946)
Ref. 283

BESSENIG, Josefa Barbara von. See AURENHAMMER, Josefa Barbara von

BESSON, Maria
Composition
PIANO
Piccolo album di danse (Ricordi)
Ref. Ricordi (Milan)

BETHEA, Kay
20th-century American composer.
Composition
OPERA
The Little Princess (University of Kansas)
Ref. 141

BEUSCHER, Elisabeth
German composer. ca. 1930. She composed an opera and songs.
Ref. 465

BEYDALE, Cecile
Polish composer of songs. d. 1854.
Ref. 465

BEYER, Johanna Magdalena
German-American secretary and composer. b. Leipzig, 1888; d. New York, 1944. She went to the United States after the turn of the century and took up composition studies under the experimentalist Henry Cowell. She lived for the most part in Lower Manhattan and became secretary and assistant to her teacher during the late 1930's. Her compositions number over 50 and are housed in the library of the American Music Centre in New York. DISCOGRAPHY.
Compositions
ORCHESTRA
Symphonic movement No. 1 (1939)
Symphonic movement No. 2 (1941)
Symphonic opus, 3 (1939)
Symphonic opus, 5 (1940)
Fragments (cham orch)
Other orchestral pieces using special sound effects such as lion's roar, metal bowls, Chinese blocks, thunder sheet and rice bowls
CHAMBER
Movement for woodwind quintet (fl, ob, cl, bsn and d-b) (1938)
Quintet for flute, oboe, English horn, clarinet and bassoon (1933)
String quartet (1934)
String quartet No. 2 (1936)
Movement for string quartet (1938)
Dance for violin, viola, violoncello and double bass
Trio for woodwinds (1939)
Suite 11 for bass clarinet and bassoon
Suite for oboe and clarinet or viola or English horn (1939)
Double movement for double bass and piano (1936)
Suite to Szigeti and Magaloff for violin and piano (1937)
Sonata for clarinet and piano (1936)
Duet for oboe and piano (1939)
Three pieces for oboe and piano (1939)
Three more pieces for oboe and piano (1939)
Six pieces for oboe and piano (1939)
Suite for clarinet 1
Suite 1 for B-Flat clarinet (1932)
Suite 2 for B-Flat clarinet (1932)
Suite for violin and piano (1937)
PERCUSSION
March for 30 percussion (1939)
Percussion suite in 3 movements (tri, woodblock, tam, snare dr, kettle drs and gongs)
IV for percussion (1935) (New Music Orch. Series C 1936)
Percussion, op. 14 (1939)
Three movements (1939)
Waltz (1939)
VOCAL
Ballad of the Star Eater (S and cl) (1934)
Summer grass (S and cl) (1934)
Have faith (S and fl) (1936-1937)
Three songs for soprano and clarinet (1934)
Three songs for soprano, percussion and piano (1933) (Carl Sandburg)
OPERA
Status Quo
ELECTRONIC
Music of the Spheres for strings or electrical instruments, *Soundings Magazine*, no. 7-8, 1973.
Ref. 13, 190, 269, 322, 563, 622

BEYERMAN-WALRAVEN, Jeanne
Dutch pianist and composer. b. Semarang, Indonesia, June 14, 1878; d. Arnhem, September 20, 1969. She received her first piano lessons from her mother and later studied composition at The Hague under Koeberg. She originally composed in a traditional style, but then developed her own style, influenced by modern French music and Schoenberg.
Compositions
ORCHESTRA
Concerto Overture (1910)
Orkeststuk (1921)
CHAMBER
Sonata (vla and pf) (1909-1952) (Brockmans & von Poppel)
Koraal (org or pf) (1911)
PIANO
Andante espressivo con molta emozione (1950) (Brockmans)
Two pieces for piano solo (1929) (Brockmans)
VOCAL
De zieke buur (from Fantomen by F. Pauwels) (vce and orch) (1922)
Mere, 3 poems (Maurice Caleme)
Ref. 81, 282

BEZDEK, Jan or Julia Derleth. See BEZDEK, Sister John Joseph

BEZDEK, Sister John Joseph (Julia Derleth) (pseud. Jan Bezdek)
American pianist, lecturer, music therapist, writer and composer. b. St. Louis, MO, August 29, 1896. She studied composition under Burrill Philips, Wesley La Violette and Borowski and obtained her B.A. from Fontbonne College in Missouri; B.Mus. and M.Mus. from Chicago Music College and Ph.D. from the Eastman School of Music. She was awarded the Eastman research fellowship. She lectured at Fontbonne College from 1930.
Compositions
VOCAL
Three and four-part songs
Arrangements of folk songs
SACRED
Two English masses
Credo
Four responsories
Lamentations for Good Friday
Motets
Hymns

INCIDENTAL MUSIC
Music for The Little Juggler, miracle play
TEACHING PIECES
Twelve piano pieces
Publications
Basic Harmony. 1925.
Detailed Course Outline for Piano Teachers. 1950.
Harmonic and Contrapuntal Style of Orlando Lasso. 1957.
Articles in *Musart*, 1955-69.
Reviews of new piano material.
Ref. composer, 137

BIALKIEWICZOWNA-ANDRAULT DE LANGERON, Irena

Polish pianist, lecturer, singer and composer. b. Niezyn, Ukraine, February 6, 1891; d. Warsaw, April 14, 1957. At the Warsaw Conservatory she studied composition under P. Rytel, Z. Noskowski and R. Statkowski, the piano under A. Michalowski and singing under Nieborski. She continued her singing studies in Italy under G. Battistini. From 1920 to 1924 she sang in Verdi's operas in Italy and from 1924 to 1931 traveled in the United States. During World War II she taught singing at the Warsaw Conservatory.
Compositions
ORCHESTRA
First symphony (1931)
Second symphony (1955)
Piano concerto (1914)
Violin concerto (1914)
CHAMBER
Violin sonata in D-Minor (1914)
PIANO
Miniatures
Sonata
VOCAL
Approx. 100 songs, mostly in Italian (vce and pf)
Ref. W. Pigla (Warsaw), 23, 226

BIANCHERA, Silvia

Italian composer. b. 1943.
Composition
CHAMBER
Tre movimenti (cl and pf) (Milan: Suvini Zerboni, 1979)
Ref. MLA *Notes* Sept 1981, Otto Harrassowitz (Wiesbaden)

BIANCHINI, Emma

Italian pianist, teacher and composer. b. Venice, 1891; d. Milan, September 14, 1929. She studied the piano, harmony and composition under M. Agostini, G. Tagliapietra and F. de Guarnieri at the Liceo B. Marcello, graduating in 1914 and obtaining her piano teacher's diploma in 1916.
Compositions
ORCHESTRA
Concerto (pf and orch)
Amleto, symphonic poem
Regia solis, symphonic poem
Sirenetta (prize, L. Marcello, 1919)
PIANO
La bella umilta (Ricordi)
Bellina e il mostro, 7 pieces (Ricordi)
Biondina, 6 pieces (Ricordi)
Il califfo, cicogna, 7 pieces (Ricordi)
Cappuccetto rosso, op. 11, 5 pieces (Ricordi)
Danse della mia bambola, ops. 7, 8, and 9, 8 pieces (Ricordi)
Il gatto con gli stivali, 7 pieces (Ricordi)
La giornata di bebe, suite, op. 5, 6 pieces (Ricordi)
Morrome, op. 6 (Ricordi)
Natale, small suite, op. 4, 4 pieces (Ricordi)
Puccettino, op. 10, 5 pieces (Ricordi)
Rosapina, 6 pieces (Ricordi)
Il suonatore di piffero, op. 12, pieces (Ricordi)
La suite di Cirillino, 8 pieces (Sonzogno)
VOCAL
Songs
Ref. 105

BIANCHINI, Virginie

French organist, pianist and composer. b. Geneva, Switzerland, September 28 1896. She was a cousin of Giancarlo Menotti the opera composer. She started piano lessons at the age of five with her mother. At 12 she began studying the organ under Marcel Dupre and continued for many years. In 1932 she studied composition under Olivier Messiaen and gave many organ recitals in Paris and New York during the years 1936 to 1957.
PHOTOGRAPH.
Compositions
ORCHESTRA
Poème symphonique: Messages de l'Ile sous le vent (1963)
ORGAN
Chant de joie (Paris: Costallat, 1952)
The mourning dove (New York: St. Mary's Press, 1956)
Sept chansons pour les moins de 10 ans (Paris: Durand, 1956)
VOCAL
Montagne o ma joie (Milano: Riccordi, 1958)
Petite fille qui n'a peut de moi, fantasy for children (ch and fl) (1957)
Sept chansons pour mes enfants (Paris: Costallat, 1951)
Over 30 songs
SACRED
Conte de Noël et le petit Jesus (ch and fl) (1957)
ARRANGEMENTS
Rejouir toi mon ame (Cantata 147 of J.S. Bach) (Paris: Costallat, 1953)
Ref. composer

BIASINI, Marcelle

Early 20th-century French composer. Her ballets were performed in Arcachon and her operettas in Nice.
Compositions
BALLET
Au bord de l'eau (1900)
Mariage bohemien (1900)
Neva (1900)
OPERETTA
Cyr à Nice (1904)
La Reine des Reines (1904)
Ref. 431

BIBBY, Gillian Margaret

New Zealand pianist and composer. b. Lower Hutt, August 31, 1945. She was educated at Otago University, where she obtained a B.A. in 1967, B.Mus. in 1968 and M.A. (musicology) in 1970. She studied at the Hochschule in Berlin from 1971 to 1972 under various teachers, including composition under Karlheinz Stockhausen and Frank Michael Beyer and the piano under Zoltan Pesko and Rolf Kuhnert. From 1972 to 1973 she studied the piano and elecronic music under Aloys Kontarsky at the Hochschule in Cologne. She was a pianist for and co-founder of Ensemble, a chamber group for new music, in Cologne. She obtained an M.Mus from Victoria University, New Zealand in 1973. She made radio and TV performances and worldwide piano and song recitals with her husband, Roger Wilson, from 1973 to 1976. In 1976 she became a Mozart Fellow at the University of Otago, New Zealand. She received various scholarships during 1964 to 1974 and won the Kranichsteiner music prize for composition, Darmstadt for the music of *Drei Hoerer*.
Compositions
ORCHESTRA
Amongst (cham) (1973)
Amongst II (cham) (1973-1974)
CHAMBER
Five Miniatures (pf) (1975)
Tropus (org) (1972)
Anacrocosmos I (1971)
Anacrocosmos II (1972)
Incident I and II (1974)
Space
Musik fuer eine Aula (1974)
Musik fuer drei Hoerer (1972)
Musik fuer drei und einige Hoerer
VOCAL
Beneidenswert (ch) (1974)
BALLET
Lest you be my enemy (tape)
OPERETTA
Sanctuary of spirits, for children (Alistair Campbell)
ELECTRONIC
AIE! A conversation piece (tape) (1975)
Bibliography
Burt, Gordon. *Bibliography of major New Zealand composers and their music.* Victoria University of Wellington, New Zealand.
Ref. 77, 189, 206

BIBER, Maria Anna Magdalena von

17th-century Austrian composer. There is a manuscript of her songs, dated 1694, in the Benedictine Library in Salzburg.
Ref. 128

BICKNELL, Mrs. See YOUNG, Eliza

BID'A
Arabian songstress. b. 856. d. June 22, 915. She was the most famous pupil of Oreib (q.v.) and one of her favorites. When she was offered 100,000 dinars for Bid'a, Oreib asked her whether she wished to be sold. Bid'a preferred to stay with Oreib who was so moved by this that she gave Bid'a her freedom. She mainly accompanied Oreib and sang her songs although she also composed some of her own. She became famous in her own right singing at the circumcision festival of the Prince al-Mutazz. She enjoyed the favor of the Caliph al-Mutamid (870 to 892) being richly rewarded by him so that she was extremely wealthy when she died. Such was her popularity that at her funeral the son of the Caliph al-Muhtadi Abu Bakr led prayers for her.
Ref. 224

BIDART, Lycia de Biase. See DE BIASE BIDART, Lycia

BIDDER, Helen
20th-century composer.
Compositions
PIANO
Four little pieces
Ref. 473

BIEHLER, Ludmilla
19th-century German composer.
Compositions
PIANO
Letzte Rose, op. 20
Serenade, op. 19
Other pieces
Ref. 226, 276

BIEIRIS DE ROMANS
French troubadour. b. Romans. ca. 1121. Her song *Na Maria, pretz e fina valors*... (Lady Maria, in you merit and distinction...) is addressed to an unknown woman, a fact that has caused contention among scholars as to the actual writer of the song. Many believe this troubadour was a man who adopted a woman's name, whilst others maintain that she was a jongleur who tried to make the grade as a troubadour. In old French the name Bieris is a diminutive for the male name of Alberico as well as for Beatrice.
Ref. Dr. Margaret Nabarro (Johannesburg), 303

BIELEFELD, Ljuba
Lithuanian composer. b. Kovno, June 24, 1884. She studied under Jedliczka, Bussler and Mannstadt in Wiesbaden, then moved to Aachen.
Compositions
ORCHESTRA
Orchestral suite
CHAMBER
String quartet
Romance (vlc)
PIANO
Burlesque
Sonatas
Suite
Other works
Ref. 70, 226

BIELICKA, Eugenia
19th-20th-century Polish composer.
Composition
PIANO
Polonaise
Ref. W. Pigla (Warsaw)

BIENVEIGNANT, Liegart
14th-century French minstrel. She signed the famous charter dated September 14, 1321, that established the Chappelle Saint-Julien-des-Menestriers, a corporation for jongleurs and minstrels.
Ref. 343

BIENVENU, Lily
French pianist, professor and composer. b. The Hague, Holland, April 22, 1920. She was the daughter of Marcel Bienvenu, a Belgian violinist and Alice Jourdain, a French pianist. She studied the piano at the Conservatory of Nantes and when at the Paris Conservatoire, studied the piano under Magdalena Tagliaferro, composition under Tony Aubin, history of music under Norbert Dufourcq and counterpoint and fugue under Simone Ple-Caussade. In 1948, when she left the conservatoire, she was engaged by the Jeunesses Musicales de France. She traveled around France and North Africa in the service of ORTF. She received various state commissions. She was professor of the piano at Franconville Conservatory. She is a member of SACEM. PHOTOGRAPH.
Compositions
ORCHESTRA
Piano concerto (1957)
Symphonie concertante (vla or sax and orch) (1960)
Triptyque hippique (pf and orch) (1981)
Arc-en-ciel, suite (str orch)
La Vague et le Goeland, lyric work (Editions Françaises, 1964-1966)
CHAMBER
Pastorale sur le nom de Francis Poulenc (fl, hp, and vlc) (1964)
Alternances (vlc or cl and pf)
Complainte (vlc and pf) (1944)
Esquisse orientale (vla and pf) (1948)
Ritournelle (vlc and pf) (1951)
Sonata (vlc and pf) (1949)
Sonata Hommage à Corelli (vln and pf) (1952)
Sonatine (fl and pf) (1947)
PIANO
Essai de fugue de trois voix (1947)
Les aventures de pianette, 6 children's pieces (Editions Eschig, 1962)
Les cinq sens, suite (1950)
Petite Czernite, 3 pieces inspired by Czerny (1981)
Rêverie au bord de l'eau (1940)
Suite dynamique, 4 parts (1978)
Thème et variations sur le mode romantique (1943)
Touches d'aquarelle pour piano (Max Eschig) (1979)
VOCAL
Correspondances, cantata (S, B, fl, and str qrt) (1974)
Si simple et sans façon, 5 poems (Maurice Careme) (chil-ch a-cap) (1979)
Mere, cycle of 9 poems (Maurice Careme) (S, B and pf; also orch) (1953)
Crepuscules d'Honolulu (Jose Bruyr) (vce and pf) (1956)
Destin (Maurice Careme) (vce and pf) (1953)
Il est midi (Paul Claudel) (vce and pf) (1949)
Invitation à la promenade (L. Bienvenue) (vce and pf) (1941)
La Bise se rue (Verlaine) (vce and pf) (1950)
Le livre fermé (P. de Nolhal) (vce and pf) (1953)
Mignonne, levez-vous (Ronsard) (vce and pf) (1945)
Nocturne (Albert Samain) (vce and pf) (1945)
Prière pour qu'un enfant ne meure pas (Francis Jammes) (vce and pf) (1946)
Sais-tu? (Andre Burgaud) (vce and pf) (Max Eschig) (1962)
Trois chansons de Victor Hugo (vce and pf) (1951)
Une allée du Luxembourg (Gerard de Nerval) (vce and pf) (1955)
Approx. 20 songs and vocal music for choirs
Ref. composer, 76

BIERTHE, Mme. See BERTHE, Mme.

BIGOT DE MOROGUES, Marie (nee Kiene)
French pianist, teacher and composer. b. Colmar, Alsace, March 3, 1786; d. Paris, September 16, 1820. She was the daughter of the violinist Joseph Kiene and the pianist Catherine Leyer. When she married Paul Bigot de Morogues in 1804 she was already an established pianist in Alsace. Her husband was appointed librarian in Vienna where Mme. Bigot de Morogues's reputation as a pianist brought her into contact with Haydn, Beethoven and Salieri. Beethoven presented her with an autographed copy of his *Sonata Appassionata* as a tribute to her interpretation of the copy of the work. She gave an all-Beethoven concert with the Vienna Orchestra in December, 1808. The circumstances of the 1809 war necessitated her move to Paris where her salon soon became the centre of musical activity. Her circle consisted of Cherubini, Auber, Baillet and Lamare and it was from Cherubini and Auber that she gained a knowledge of composition. She was the first person to introduce Beethoven's compositions to the Parisian public. After her husband was taken prisoner during the war, financial problems forced her to turn her musical talents to teaching. She soon had a large class of pupils, one of whom was Felix Mendelssohn on his first Parisian visit in 1816. The unaccustomed strain of her educational work aggravated a chest complaint, from which she died in 1820.

Compositions
PIANO
Andance varié (Vienna: Artaria)
Rondo (Paris: Erard)
Suite d'études, book 1 (Erard)
Ref. 105, 361

BILBRO, Anne Mathilde

American pianist, teacher and composer. b. Tuskegee, AL, 1880. She studied the piano under Kurt Muller in Atlanta and harmony under Oscar G. Sonneck in New York. After graduating from the Women's College of Alabama in 1896, she studied music teaching and composition. She taught master classes throughout the south and east, including New York. She composed theatre works, operettas, music for plays, songs and published more than four hundred works, mainly for the piano.
Publications
The Middle Pasture. Boston: Small; Maynard.
Ref. 292, 496

BILLINGTON, Elizabeth (nee Weichsel) (later Fellisent)

English harpsichordist, pianist, soprano and composer. b. London, 1765; d. near Venice, August 25, 1818. She was the daughter of Carl Weichsel, for a time principal oboist and clarinetist at the King's Theatre, London. Her mother, who had been a pupil of J.C. Bach, sang at Vauxhall Gardens. Elizabeth also studied under J.C. Bach until his death in 1782 and J.C. Schroeter (piano) and had singing lessons with James Billington, a double-bassist whom she married in 1783. She was largely recognized for her singing, having performed in major productions in Dublin, London and Italy. She took lessons with Mortellari in London in order to improve her technique and continued her bel-canto studies under Sacchini in Paris. She sang at the Teatro San Carlo in *Inez de Castro* which was written especially for her. After her husband's death, she remained in Naples, appearing in operas composed for her by Paisiello, Paer and Himmel. She befriended Lord Nelson's Emma and was received by Josephine Bonaparte in Milan. In 1799 she married Monsieur Felican or Felissent, but she left him because of his brutality towards her. She returned to England in 1801. She retired in 1811, Felissent returned to her and she left England with him in 1817. She died the following year at her property near Venice, possibly as a result of injuries inflicted on her by Felissent.
Compositions
CHAMBER
Three sonatas (vln and pf) (Gaulding, 1792)
Favourite lessons for the pianoforte
Six progressive lessons for the harpsichord or pianoforte, op. 2 (London: John Bland)
Six sonatas for the pianoforte or harpsichord (1778)
Three lessons for the harpsichord or pianoforte (1775) (London, Welcker)
Publications
An Answer to the Memoirs. A reply to James Ridgway's *Memoirs of Mrs. Billington from her birth*. 1792
Bibliography
Angelo, Henry. *Reminiscences*. London, 1828.
Edgecumbe, Lord. *Musical Reminiscences of an Old Amateur*. London, 1834.
Hogarth, George. *Memoirs of the Musical Drama*. London, 1834.
Kelly, Michael. *Reminiscences*. London, 1826.
Pasquin, Anthony. *The Children of Thespis*. London, 1792.
Pohl, C.F. *Mozart and Haydn in London*. Vienna, 1867.
Ridgway, James. *Memoirs of Mrs. Billington from Her Birth*. London, 1792.
Ref. 6, 8, 65, 126, 129, 132, 645

BILLSON, Ada

20th-century American composer. She composed choral works.
Ref. 347

BILSLAND, Ethel

20th-century composer.
Compositions
PIANO
The birthday party, six pieces
Ref. 473

BILTCLIFFE, Florence

20th-century English pianist, teacher and composer. b. Yorkshire. She studied the piano under Blanche Smith in Bristol and attended summer school at Queen's University, Kingston, from 1944 to 1945 and at Chautauqua, NY, in 1946, 1947 and 1949. She taught music in private schools in Canada and England.
Compositions
CHAMBER
Andante and rondo (vln and pf)
Berceuse (vln and pf)
Variations on, O dear, what can the matter be (vln and pf)
PIANO
Miniature suite
Prelude in D-Flat Major
Prelude in G-Minor
Sonata
Three impromptus
Other small pieces
VOCAL
To arm! To arm! (ch)
Choral works
Songs
SACRED
The Lord's Prayer (ch)
God is our hope
Sweet was the song the virgin sang
Carols
Ref. 95, 133

BINET, Jocelyne

Canadian pianist, violinist, lecturer and composer. b. East-Angus, Quebec, September 27, 1923; d. Quebec, January 13, 1968. She studied theory and composition under Claude Champagne at the Ecole Superieure de Musique d'Outremont and the piano under Jean Dansereau and Jean Beaudet. At the Paris Conservatoire she studied counterpoint and fugue under Noel Gallon, composition under Tony Aubin and analysis under Olivier Messiaen. In 1946 she won a CAPAC award for composition and received bursaries from the French and Quebec governments from 1948 to 1951. She taught formal analysis and counterpoint at the Ecole Vincent d'Indy from 1952 till 1958 and then at Laval University for the next ten years.
Compositions
ORCHESTRA
Evocation, symphonic poem (1948)
Un Canadien à Paris (1951)
Danse (1949)
CHAMBER
Suite (fl and pf and strs) (1946)
Poème oriental (vln and pf) (1946)
Trio (vln) (1945)
VOCAL
Nocturne (w-ch and pf) (1948)
Petite suite, in 4 movements (w-ch and pf) (1948)
L'adieu (Apollinaire) (vce and pf) (1949-1950)
La captive (V. Hugo) (vce and pf) (1949-1950)
Songs
Ref. 133, 347, 485

BINFIELD, Hanna R.

English harpist, organist, teacher and composer. b. Reading, 1810; d. Reading, May 2, 1887.
Compositions
CHAMBER
Duncan Gray (hp) (Williams)
Organ pieces (Williams)
PIANO
Marion and Edith, caprice (4 hands) (Williams)
Scottish melody, Duncan Gray with variations (3 hands) (Williams)
La Cascatella (Williams)
Little Mary's own, polka (Williams)
Rosalbina, caprice (Williams)
Wintergruen, second caprice (Williams)
VOCAL
Children visiting the fairies (treble vces) (Williams)
Ref. 226, 276, 297

BINGEN, Hildegarde von. See HILDEGARDE, Saint

BINGHAM, Judith

British singer and composer. b. Nottingham, June 21, 1952. She studied composition and singing at the Royal Academy of Music from 1970 to

1973 and was awarded the Principal's prize for composition in 1972. She studied privately with Hans Keller, and pursued a career as a singer and composer. She wrote extensively for the voice, including works for The Finchley Children's Music Group, the BBC Singers, as well as four works for the Songmaker's Almanac. She has been commissioned by several private singers. She composed chamber works for the New London Consort, the Omega Guitar Quartet, Anton Weinberg and John Whitfield and instrumental music for radio and television. Her works have been performed in Britain and abroad. PHOTOGRAPH.

Compositions

CHAMBER

Light fantastic (qrt)
Hallmarks (cl and pf) (comm Anton Weinberg)
The divine image (hpcd) (1975)
Into the wilderness (org) (1982)
An enigma variation (1977)

PIANO

Chopin (1979)
Pictured within (1982)

VOCAL

Book of Hours, on 14th-century (ch) (in prep, 1985)
Chamonix (mix-ch) (1982)
The Ruin (mix-ch) (1981)
Playing with words (vocal qrt and pf) (1977)
Cocaine 'Lil (S and pf) (1975)
A fourth universe (m-S and hpcd) (1976)
A falling figure (Bar, cl and pf) (1979) (comm BBC)
Iago, a study (B-Bar and pf) (1980)
Mercutio, a study (Bar and pf) (1980)
Clouded Windows (m-S and pf) (1980)
A Midsummer Night's Dream (m-S and pf) (1981)
Snow songs (T and pf) (1981)
Ferrara (T and pf)
The old man's road (m-S and pf) (1983)

OPERA

Flynn (1978)

Ref. composer, 263, 555

BINGHAM ABBOTT, Jane. See ABBOTT, Jane

BINNS, Jacqueline

Composition

CHAMBER

Farmyard suite (wind ens) (1981)

Ref. 585

BIRCH, Ernestine

20th-century composer.

Composition

PIANO

The milkmaid's delight

Ref. 473

BIRCHER-REY, Hedy

Swiss composer. b. Basle, January 3, 1900. She was a pupil of Joseph Lauter at the Geneva Conservatory and of Suter in Basle. Most of her works were composed between 1918 and 1930.

Compositions

ORCHESTRA

Small symphony (large orch)
Fugue (str orch)

CHAMBER

Violin piece, in 3 mvts
Pieces (vlc)

PIANO

Suite, 6 pieces
Three etudes

VOCAL

Lullaby
Three songs (m-S)
Three songs in folk style
Trinklied
Numerous other songs

Ref. composer

BIRCSAK, Thusnelda

20th-century American organist, pianist, teacher and composer. b. Chicago. She moved to Phoenix, AZ, in 1939. She studied the piano under Sol Albert and Mrs. Busch and theory, fugue, instrumentation and composition under Dr. Carl Busch. After a year at the Vienna Academy of Music, she studied composition under Viktor Labunski and the piano under Ann St. John. She played the organ in churches in Kansas City and taught the piano, the organ and theory. PHOTOGRAPH.

Compositions

CHAMBER

Prelude and scherzando (vlc)

PIANO

Chinese lullaby
Highland country dance
Hummingbird
Viennese dance (1940)

VOCAL

Brook in the forest (w-ch and pf) (Neil A. Kjos)
Clouds (w-ch)
Desert nostalgia (w-ch)
Fields of grain (w-ch)

SACRED

Lullaby of the Christ child (w-ch)

Ref. composer, 190

BIRD, Sister Mary Rafael

American pianist, teacher and composer. b. Marcus, IA, 1887. She studied at the Mary Wood Chase School of Musical Arts in Chicago until 1914 and graduated with a B.M. from the American Conservatory of Music, Chicago in 1925. At the same Conservatory she obtained an M.Mus. in 1929. She also studied at the University of Iowa in 1941. She studied the piano with Mary Wood Chase (q.v.) and Silvio Scionti and voice with David Clippinger. She taught at schools in Wichita, Sioux City, Chicago and Lead, SD, from 1907 till 1929. In 1930 she joined the faculty of Mundelein College and taught the piano, theory and composition, later becoming head of the music department.

Compositions

SACRED

Benedictus es tu (1934) (Boston: McLaughlin)
Ecce sacerdos (1941) (McLaughlin)
Exult in the Lord (1943) (McLaughlin)
Hymn of the little flower (1934) (McLaughlin)
Mass (cong and ch) (1934) (McLaughlin and Reilly)
O Light of the world (1934) (McLaughlin)
To Christ the King (ch) (1934) (McLaughlin)

Ref. 496

BIRKETT, Gwenhilda Mary

English cellist, teacher and composer. b. Chiswick, 1892. She studied under Professor W.E. Whitehouse at the Guildhall School of Music and taught the cello at schools in Bramley and Guildford. She composed for the cello and the piano and music for a mystery play.

Ref. 94, 467

BIRNIE, Patie

Scottish violinist and composer. b. Kinghorn, ca. 1635; d. ca. 1710.

Composition

VOCAL

The auld man's meer's dead, song

Ref. 572

BIRNSTEIN, Renate Maria

German pianist, violinist and composer. b. Hamburg, November 17, 1946. She commenced violin lessons at the age of seven and piano lessons at 13. She received her diploma in composition and piano in 1973 from the Hochschule fuer Musik, after studying composition under Diether de la Motte and Gyorgy Ligeti. From 1973 to 1980 she lectured at the Hochschule fuer Musik, Luebeck and from 1979 taught at the Hamburg Hochschule fuer Musik. Her *Four pieces for Clarinet, Trombone and Cello* is composed with strict limitations in intervals; using only the intervals of the sixteenth, eighth and fourth. She is the recipient of a number of prizes and scholarships including the Prix de Rome from the 'Villa Hassimo' in 1983, enabling her to study in Rome for 12 months.

Compositions

ORCHESTRA

Imagination (1972) (Hamburg: Sikorski)
Scatola (1979) (Sikorski)
Fuenf Stuecke fuer Streichorchester (1980) (Sikorski)

CHAMBER
Sextet for six ensembles (1981) (Sikorski)
IDEM (fl, cl, vln, vla, vlc and a-fl) (1974) (Sikorski)
Inter pares (fl, vn, vlc, pf and vib) (1975) (Sikorski)
String quintet (1982) (Sikorski)
Peram (fl, gtr and vib) (1976) (Sikorski)
Variationen (vln, vla and vlc) (1977) (Sikorski)
Vier Stuecke (cl, trb and vlc) (1971) (Sikorski)
Duo Concertante (vlc and cl) (1980) (Sikorski)
Ribambelle (cl and perc) (1972) (Sikorski)
Bibliography
Beruf Komponistin.
Ref. Musikhandel 1977, 126

BIRSCH, Charlotte. See PFEIFFER, Charlotte Birsch

BISH, Diane
20th-century American composer. DISCOGRAPHY.
Compositions
ORCHESTRA
Organ concerto (1974)
VOCAL
Passion symphony (narr and org)
Ref. 142, 563

BISHOP, Dorothy
20th-century American composer.
Compositions
PIANO
Pieces
VOCAL
Hoe down (vce and pf)
Song of the wind (vce and pf)
Choral works
Other songs
Ref. 40, 347

BISLAND, Margaret Cyrilla
American pianist and composer. b. Brooklyn, NY. September 30, 1839. She composed piano pieces.
Ref. 347

BISOZIA, Mengia. See VIELANDA, Mengia

BISSET, Elizabeth Anne
English harpist and composer. b. 1800. She was the younger daughter of Robert Bisset, the author of 'Life of Burke' and other works, and the younger sister of Catherine Bisset, a pianist. She studied the harp under F. Gizi.
Compositions
HARP
Ballade
Fantaisie brillant (1840)
Fantasias
The sailor's adieu (1842)
Arrangements
PIANO
Pieces
Ref. 6, 226, 276

BITGOOD, Roberta
American organist, violist, conductor and composer. b. New London, CT., January 15, 1908. She studied at Connecticut College for Women, Guillmant Organ School (gold medal) and Columbia University were she obtained her master's degree in music education. She gained a doctorate and master's degree in sacred music from Union Theological Seminary, New York and was organist and choirmistress at Holy Trinity Lutheran Church, Buffalo, NY; the First Presbyterian Church, Riverside, CA.; Redford Presbyterian Church, Detroit, MI.; First Presbyterian Church, Bay City, MI.; and First Congregational Church, Battle Creek, MI. She was a violist in several orchestras and was the first woman president of the American Guild of Organists. DISCOGRAPHY. PHOTOGRAPH.
Compositions
CHAMBER
Awake, thou wintry earth (org and brass qrt)
Rejoice, give thanks (org and brass) (Hope, 1969)
ORGAN
At Eventide
Chorale prelude on God Himself is with us (St. Cecilia Series 793) (H.W. Gray)
Chorale prelude on Jewels (St. Cecilia Series 746) (H.W. Gray)
Chorale prelude on O Master, let me walk (Sacred Music Press)
Chorale prelude on Siloam (St. Cecilia Series 778) (H.W. Gray)
Meditation on Kingsfold (1976)
Noël (Carol of the Birds) (H.W. Gray)
Offertories from afar (Flammer, 1964)
On an ancient Alleluia (St. Cecilia Series 894) (H.W. Gray)
Prelude on Convenanters' tune (Flammer, 1958)
Postlude on an old Spanish hymn (Sacred Music Press)
Arrangements of works by Bach and other composers (Buxtehude)
SACRED
Job, cantata (H.W. Gray, 1948)
Joseph, cantata (H.W. Gray, 1966)
Let there be light, Christmas cantata (chil-vces) (Dayton: Lorenz, 1965)
Choral benedictions (Nashville: Abingdon, 1965)
Alleluia! Christ is risen (Broadman, 1964)
Altogether joyfully sing (Dallas: Choristers Guild, 1971)
Be still and know that I am God (vce and pf or org) (H.W. Gray, 1952)
Christ the Lord is born (New York: Galaxy Music, 1952)
Christ went up into the hills alone (Choristers Guild, 1974)
Christmas candle (H.W. Gray, 1935)
Closing responses and amends (Glen Roc, NJ. J. Fischer, 1964)
Except the Lord build the house (Flammer, 1956)
Give me a faith (vce and pf or org) (H.W. Gray, 1947)
Glory to God (H.W. Gray, 1943)
Good thing it is to give thanks (Galaxy Music, 1945)
Grant us Thy peace (H.W. Gray, 1940)
The greatest of these is love (vce and pf or org) (H.W. Gray, 1936)
Holy Spirit hear us (Lorenz, 1976)
How excellent Thy name (Flammer, 1965)
Joy dawned again on Easter day (H.W. Gray, 1965)
Let us now praise famous ones (Hanover, PA: Stone Chapel, 1970)
Lord, guard and guide the men who fly (Glen Rock, NJ. J. Fisher, 1963)
Lord, guard our thoughts (Choristers Guild, 1963)
Lord, may we follow (New York: McAfee Music, 1974)
New meanings for our age (Flammer, 1967)
Now a new day opens, now a new year opens (J. Fisher, 1967)
The power of music (New York: McAfee Music, 1972)
Prayer is the soul's sincere desire (H.W. Gray, 1956)
Rejoice, give thanks (Carol Stream, IL: Hope, 1971)
Rosa mystica (H.W. Gray, 1963)
Sixteen amens from the oratorios (Flammer, 1957)
The sons of God (Lorenz, 1973)
That we might find him still (Choristers Guild, 1968)
Ref. composer, 39, 190, 228, 477, 563, 646

BIXBY, Allene K.
American organist, teacher and composer. d. 1947. She composed piano and choral works and songs.
Ref. 347

BIZONY, Celia
German harpsichordist, singer, professor and composer. b. Friedenau, Berlin, 1904. She studied at the Lyceum and the Stern Conservatory in Berlin, the New Conservatory in Vienna and Columbia University, New York. She taught at the New Conservatory in Vienna; McGill University, Canada and Queen's University, Ontario. She was professor of voice at Mount Allison University, Frayn in 1955. She lectured at Morby College, London from 1956 to 1959. She was the co-founder, director and a performer of the Musica Antica e Nuova Ensemble, U.K. and received the Gustav Hollander medal from the Stern Conservatory.
Compositions
CHAMBER
Violin and harpsichord pieces
VOCAL
Part Songs (cham ch)
Song cycle (vces, str, grt and hpcd)
Various works (vce, strs and hpcd)
Part songs for chamber choir
Duets (vces and insts)
Ref. 77, 490

BJELKE-ANDERSON, Olga

Norwegian pianist and composer. b. 1857; d. 1940. She studied the piano, theory and orchestration in Oslo.

Compositions

ORCHESTRA

Suite for the music festival in Oslo, 1914

PIANO

Bjelke, Festmarsch (Oluf Bey)
Skovblomster, 4 pieces (Warmuth)
Four pieces (Hansen)

VOCAL

Cantata for the opening of the Camilla Collet Monument in Oslo (1911)
Trondhyem (m-ch and qrt) (Warmuth)
Skogen (m-ch) (Oluf Bey)
Songs (w-ch)
Floitende Staer (vce and pf) (Oluf Bey)
Landskab (vce and pf) (Oluf Bey)
Four songs (Warmuth)

THEATRE

Oestenfor sol og vestenfor maane
Prinsesse Rosenroed

Ref. Norsk Musikkinformasion, 20, 297

BLACK, Jennie Price

Late 19th-century American composer.

Compositions

VOCAL

Songs incl.:
Cynthia
In May
Misgivings
Regrets
Slumber song
A song of love

Ref. 276, 433

BLACKWELL, Anna Gee

American organist, pianist, business woman, choir conductor, music administrator, teacher and composer. b. Springfield, OH, December 24, 1928. She attended several universities including Sinclair Community College from 1976 to 1979 and Wright State University from 1970 to 1973. She was a recipient of several awards. She was the chairlady and director of the National Guild of Piano Teachers (Springfield Chapter) and budget analyst and financial manager at Aeronautical Systems Division for 32 years. DISCOGRAPHY. PHOTOGRAPH.

Compositions

CHAMBER

Let everything that hath breath praise the Lord (pf and org) (1977)

PIANO

Because you're you (1953)
Because you have said we're through (1954)
Boogie woogie breakdown (1944)
Ebony waters (1955)
There's a new world coming (1979)
They'll come back someday (1944)

SACRED

He is my all and all (1983)
Psalm 150
But they that wait upon the Lord shall renew their strength

Publications

Twenty-Two Days of Music in Europe.

Ref. 276, 433, 643

BLAHETKA, Marie Leopoldina

Austrian physharmonica player, pianist, teacher and composer. b. Gunstramsdorf, near Vienna, November 15, 1811; d. Boulogne, North France, January 12, 1887. Her first piano teacher was her mother. At the age of five Leopoldine's playing so impressed Beethoven that he suggested she become a pupil of Joseph Czerny. Later, she studied the piano under Kalkbrenner and Moscheles, composition under Sechter and physharmonica under Hieronymus Payer. After successful tours in Germany, Holland, France and England in 1840, she settled in Boulogne, where she taught and composed. She became a virtuoso performer on the physharmonica, a small reed organ that was the predecessor of the harmonium. A reference in Schumann's *Gesammelte Schriften* testified to the outstanding quality of her playing.

Compositions

ORCHESTRA

Souvenir d'Angleterre, op. 38 (pf and orch or str qrt) (Hofmeister)
Variations brillantes (pf and orch; also pf) (Hofmeister)
Variations brillantes sur un thème hongrois, op. 18 (orch or str qrt or pf) (Haslinger)
Variations sur la chanson nationale autrichienne *Gott erhalte Franz den Kaiser*, op. 28 (orch or str qrt or pf) (Kahnt)
Variations brillantes sur un thème de Gallenberg, op. 29 (orch or str qrt or pf) (Simrock)

CHAMBER

First quartet in A, op. 43 (pf, vln, vla and vlc) (Hofmeister)
Variations sur la Muette de Portici, op. 26 (str qrt; also pf) (Haslinger)
Fantaisie sur des motifs du Chalet, op. 40 (fl and pf) (Lemoine)
Grande polonaise, op. 9 (vlc and pf) (Hofmeister)
Variations, op. 39 (fl and pf) (Hofmeister)

PIANO

Grand duo, op. 47 (4 hands) (Hofmeister)
Erinnerungen an Holland: Fantasie und Variationen ueber hollaendische Volkslieder, op. 33 (Schott)
Polonaise, op. 19 (Cranz)
Quadrille des patineurs dans le prophète, varié, op. 56
Variations brillantes sur Ah come nascondere, op. 2 (Haslinger)
Variations brillantes, intrade et code sur une valse, op. 4 (Cranz)
Variations brillantes sur le siège de Corinthe, op. 20 (Rossini) (Cranz)
Variations sur une tyrolienne, op. 27 (Cranz)
Six valses favorites de Vienne, op. 35 (Joubert)
Trois rondeaux elegants, op. 37 (Hofmeister)

VOCAL

Songs

SACRED

Pater Noster, op. 58 (4 vces and pf or org) (Lemoine)
Ave Maria, op. 57 (vce and pf or org) (Lemoine)

OPERA

Die Raeuber und der Saenger (1830)

Ref. 8, 15, 22, 70, 76, 102, 105, 109, 129, 132, 193, 225, 226, 276, 297, 361, 367, 375, 400, 524, 622

BLAIR, Kathleen (Kathleen Blair Clark)

20th-century American composer. b. San Antonio, TX.; d. Louisiana. She studied under Olga Samaroff, J.M. Steinfeld in San Antonio, Vianna da Motta in Berlin, G. Ackley Brower and Rubin Goldmark in New York. Her songs were also published under the name Kathleen Blair Clark.

Compositions

PIANO

A whim

VOCAL

In the falling snow
Little rose of May
Love me, kiss me
My heart's country
My sweetheart's face
Springtime joy

SACRED

Love never faileth (high or med vce and keyboard) (H.W. Gray)
Thou wilt light my candle (high or med vce and keyboard) (H.W. Gray)
Requiescat
He restoreth my soul
Songs

Ref. 190, 347, 448

BLAIR-OLIPHANT, Lilian

Composition

ORCHESTRA

Suite in G-Minor (str orch)

Ref. 322

BLAKE, Dorothy Gaynor

American pianist, authoress, teacher and composer. b. St. Joseph, MO. November 21, 1893; d. Webster Groves, MO. She studied the piano under her mother, Jessie Gaynor (q.v.) and theory with Thomas Tapper and Rudolph Ganz. During the seasons 1929 to 1930 and 1933 to 1934 she was educational director of the St. Louis Symphony Orchestra. She was the authoress of many educational books.

Compositions

ORCHESTRA

Irish dance (also 2 pf)
Suite

CHAMBER

Arabesque (vln)

PIANO

Four feathered folk
Heroes of childhood
Portraits from American history
Three winter sketches

Three bits of sunshine
Two water scenes
Teaching works
VOCAL
Hurry little wave (ch)
Mother song (w-ch)
Oriental night (ch)
Part songs (w-vces)
Spirit of Spring (ch)
Spirit of Winter (ch)
An explanation, song
Bye my baby Bunting, song
Evening of life, song
June, song
OPERETTA
The blue belt
A get-acquainted party
Ref. 22, 142, 292, 460

BLAKE, Mary

19th-century American composer.

Composition

Beautiful star of the twilight (S, A and pf) (Boston: Ditson, 1857)

Ref. 228

BLANC DE FONTBELLE, Cecile (pseud. Hugues Waldin)

French conductor and composer. b. Saint Remy de Provence, December 23, 1892. She studied at the Geneva Conservatory, then under Gedalge at the Paris Conservatoire and d'Indy at the Schola Cantorum and the School of the Louvre. She was founder and director of the mixed choir La Provence and director of the orchestra of French Radio. Her compositions included symphonic poems, chamber music, a violin sonata, piano and harp works and songs for choruses.

Ref. 70, 81

BLANCHE DE CASTILLE (Roine Blance)

French queen and troubadour. b. 1188; d. Paris, 1252. She was the daughter of Alphonse III, King of Castille, whose wife Eleanor, was the daughter of Eleanor of Aquitaine (q.v.). Blanche married Louis VIII of France and bore him 12 or 13 children of whom only seven eventually survived. Upon the death of her husband she became Regent of France from 1226 to 1234 and then again from 1248 to 1252. Her son Louis eventually succeeded to the throne as Louis IX against all odds and with tremendous effort on her part. She displayed real resolution and energy and by all accounts was a strong and imperious character, much like her grandmother, Eleanor of Aquitaine. Blanche had a great friend in Thibaut of Navarre, the most important of the troubadours. Blanche was a fine poetess but only one of her songs exists. DISCOGRAPHY.

Composition

VOCAL
Amours, ou trop tard me suis pris

Ref. Dr. Margaret Nabarro (Johannesburg), 206, 268, 563, 622, 637, 653

BLANCHE-FLEUR, Flandrine de. See FLASSAN, Flandrine de

BLANCK, Olga de

Cuban teacher and composer. b. Havana, March 11, 1916. Her father was Hubert de Blanck, a pianist and composer who started a conservatory of music in Havana that later became the National Conservatory. Olga studied under her father and also privately under the composer Amadeo Roldan from 1935 to 1936 and the conductor Pedro Sanjuan from 1937 to 1938. She went to New York in 1938 and studied counterpoint and fugue under Burle Marx. In Mexico she studied under Julian Carrillo and Jimenez Mabarak from 1943 to 1944. In 1945 she became deputy director at the National Conservatory and together with the composer Gisela Hernandez-Gonzalo (q.v.) became active in musical education. Her first works were collections of Cuban songs, which became extremely popular. Together with the writer M. Julia Casanova, she created modern musical comedies, which have been performed on radio and in the theatre. In 1948 she won the first national prize for songs. She became state advisor on music education. She has composed over 300 works.

Compositions

ORCHESTRA
Bohio, suite (1964)
CHAMBER
Danzas de Ignacio Cervantes (strs)
Homenaje a la danza cubana (pf) (Budapest: Edito Musica, 1981)
VOCAL
Cantata Guajira (soloists, ch and orch) (E. Ballagas) (1967)
Cuentos musicalizados, for children (1967)
Diez canciones, for children (National Prize) (1966)
Mi guitarra guajira (1948)
Nuestras vidas (1944)
Over 100 songs (1933-1960)
Seventy-eight songs (1966-1968)
OPERA
Cuento de Navidad, in 3 acts (1950)
THEATRE
Bohio (1964)
Encunetro (A. Alonso) (1962)
Esperancita (1964)
Fifty-four musical comedies for radio , each 1 act (1943-1944)
Mujeres (1958)
Hotel tropical (1950)
El mago de Oz (1967)
Nosotras y ellos
Rendez-vous de tres (1943)
Vivamos hoy (1943)

Publications

Pedagogical works and analyses of Cuban classics with Gisela Hernandez-Gonzalo.

Ref. 14, 20, 70, 107, 361

BLAND, Dora or Dorothea. See JORDAN, Mrs.

BLAND, Maria Theresa

13th-century singer and composer. b. Italy, 1769; d. London, England, January 15, 1838.

Composition

VOCAL
'Twas in the solemn midnight hour

Ref. 125, 347

BLANGINI, Mlle.

Italian violinist, choral conductor and composer. b. Turin, 1780. She was the sister of Guiseppe Blangini, a composer of operas and symphonies. She received her first violin lessons from the celebrated Pugnani, then studied under Puppo and Boucher. She also studied composition under Barni. She gave concerts in Turin, Milan, Vienna and Paris and some years later became choir conductor at the Court of Bavaria.

Compositions

CHAMBER
Three serenades (2 fl, pf and vlc ad lib) (Leonard)
Trio (2 vln and vlc) (Paris: Hanry)
Duetto (org) (Patey)
PIANO
Overtures (4 hands) (Costellat)
Boleros
Nocturnes
Romances
VOCAL
Two chamber trios (treble vces) (Ashdown)
Songs incl.:
Les adieux (Noël)
L'assiette à musique (Sulzbach)
Lei baiser (Lesigne)
On vient, chut! chut! (Heugel)
Approx. 30 other songs
SACRED
Ave Maria (2 vces with org or hpcd) (Castil-Blase)

Ref. 12, 119, 226, 297

BLANGY, Caroline. See GRANDVAL, Marie Felicie

BLASIS, Teresa de

Italian pianist, teacher and composer. b. Naples; d. Florence, April 20, 1868. She came from a musical Neapolitan family, her father and brother both being composers of note and her sister, Virginia, a poetess. She published a number of works for the piano.

Ref. 26, 105, 226, 276

BLAUHUTH, Jenny
German professor and composer. b. Leipzig, April 30, 1862. She studied under Reinecke and Rust and held a professorship at the Karlsruhe Conservatory.
Compositions
PIANO
Lied ohne Worte
Serenata
Other pieces
Ref. 226, 276, 433

BLAUSTEIN, Susan Morton
American pianist, lecturer and composer. b. Palo Alto, CA, March 22, 1953. She received her B.A. in 1975 from Pomona College, having studied the piano and composition under Karl Kohn. She studied at the Royal Liege Conservatory, Belgium, under Henri Pousseur, winning first prize in 1976. She studied composition under Seymour Shifrin at the Brandeis University in 1977 and under Jacob Druckman and Betsy Jolas (q.v.) at the Yale School of Music (M.M. 1979, M.M.A. 1980). She was one of six winners of the 1980 National Composers' Competition of the League of Composers' International Society for Contemporary Music and a winner of a Charles Ives Scholarship in 1979 and in 1979 she won a BMI student composition prize. She lectured on composition at Yale College and School of Music from 1980 to 1981.
Compositions
ORCHESTRA
Concerto (vlc and cham orch) (1984) (comm Joel Krosnick and Fromm Music Foundation)
Song of Songs (1985)
CHAMBER
Sextet (vlc, vln, pf, cl, fl and perc) (1983)
String quartet No. 1, ricercate (1981) (comm Group Contemp Music)
PIANO
La espoza de Don Garcia
Fantasia (1980)
VOCAL
To Orpheus, four sonnets (Rilke) (mix-ch a-cap) (1982)
Due madrigali di Torquato Tasso (vce and perc ens) (1979)
The moon has nothing to be excited about, canzona (1977)
The moon has nothing to be sad about, six poems (S. Plath)
MISCELLANEOUS
Commedia (8 players) (1980)
Ref. AMC newsletter 1985, 625, 643

BLAUVELT, Bula Caswell
20th-century American organist, teacher and composer. b. Jersey City. She studied at the Institute of Musical Art and the Guilmant Organ School, New York.
Ref. 226

BLEITER, Rosa. See BLEITNER, Rosa

BLEITNER (Bleiter), Rosa
Late 19th-century Bohemian pianist, lecturer and composer. She taught singing for many years at the Prague Conservatory. A series of her songs was published in Prague.
Compositions
ORCHESTRA
Funeral march, op. 36
VOCAL
Songs incl.:
Es muss ein Wunderbares sein, op. 32 (Weiner)
Sie liebten sich beide, op. 34 (Weiner)
Zwei Lieder, op. 33: Das Blatt im Buche; Ja, du bist elend (Weiner)
Ref. 226, 276, 297

BLEWIT, Gionata
Irish composer. b. 1782. Her operas were performed in Dublin.
Compositions
OPERA
Il Corsaro (1812)
Il Mago (1813)
Isola dei Santi (1814)
Ref. 225

BLEWITT, Lorna
20th-century English composer.
Composition
CHAMBER
Fantasia on a Cornish song (cor anglais)
Ref. BMIC

BLEY, Carla
American electronic organist, pianist and composer. b. Oakland, CA. 1938. Her father, Emil Borg was a choir director and organist. She was instrumental in forming the the Jazz Composers' Orchestra in 1964. She works in a variety of milieus, including jazz, pop, folk music, rock and electronics. She plays with an 11-piece band that performs her works and was the recipient of a Ford Foundation grant that enabled her to record one of her compositions. DISCOGRAPHY.
Compositions
ORCHESTRA
Three-four (cham orch)
BAND
Beast blues
Bent eagle
Gloria
Los quatros generales
New hymn
Oh say can you do
Paper airline
Sideways in Mexico
Totem
Jesus Maria and other Spanish strains (jazz band)
Musique mecanique I (jazz band)
Musique mecanique II (At midnight) (jazz band)
Musique mecanique III (jazz band) (1978)
VOCAL
Escalator over the hill (Paul Haines)
Heavy heart
Tropic appetites
Live!
ELECTRONIC
Dinner music
Social studies
Untitled piece in 8 layers for harpsichord (2 hpcd on tape) (1968)
Bibliography
Weller, S. *Carla Bley and All Her Jazz*. August 1975: 35-3. Biographical essay.
Ref. 346, 347, 403, 440, 518, 563, 622

BLIESENER, Ada Elizabeth Michelman
American cellist, assistant professor and composer. b. Quincy, IL. October 9, 1909. She studied composition under Ernst Krenek, Ben Johnson and Stella Roberts and received a B.Mus. (cello) in 1931 and M.Mus. (composition) in 1933. She studied at the American Conservatory of Music in Chicago, obtaining an M.Mus. (cello) in 1963 and M.Mus. (composition) at the University of Illinois in 1966. She was a cellist with several symphony orchestras, including the Birmingham Symphony Orchestra. She was a private piano and cello teacher from 1927 and an assistant professor of the cello and theory at Bethany College, Lindsberg, from 1966 to 1970.
Compositions
ORCHESTRA
Children's wartime suite (early 1940's)
CHAMBER
Three movements (str qrt, ob and 2 cl) (early 1940's)
Music (vlc and several insts) (1965)
Quintet (str qrt and pf) (1929-1931)
Cello solo (vlc with 2 vln, vla and d-b) (1963-1964)
A Trip to Itesoa, eight short inventions (str qrt) (early 1940's)
Four movements (str qrt) (1930)
Piece (qrt) (1941)
String quartet No. 1 (1935-1939)
String quartet No. 2 (1952-1955)
Two movements (str qrt) (1930)
Serenade (vln, vlc, and pf) (1941)
Evening song (vlc and pf) (1929)
Four etchings (vlc and pf) (1950)
Serenade (fl and pf) (early 1940's)
Small suite (fl and pf) (early 1940's)
Sonata (vlc and pf) (1931-1933)
Theme with variations (vlc and pf) (1931-1933)
Two movements (vlc and pf) (1955)

PIANO
Caprice burlesque (1929-1933)
Dance in olden style (also orch) (1931)
Free variations (1964)
Largo (1929-1933)
Melody (1929-1933)
Mountain lake (1929-1933)
Parade (1929-1933)
Prelude (1962)
Presto (1929-1933)
Six short inventions (1955)
Sonata (1977)
Spring song (1929-1933)
Suite, five miniatures (1963)
VOCAL
Cirquains (Adelaide Crapsey) (vce and pf) (1931-1933)
The fairies (vce and pf) (1929)
Five canons (2 vces)
From a sonnet by Shakespeare (vce and pf) (1930)
Lullaby (Harriet Monroe) (vce and pf) (1931-1933)
Fugue (3 vces)
SACRED
I, John (ch a-cap) (1950)
Jesus prays for the Church (1950)
Psalms: No. 54 (1930); No. 86 (1930); No. 91 (1950)
Rejoice (1950)
Ref. composer, 84, 94, 137, 206

BLISA, Alice
20th-century American composer.
Compositions
OPERETTA
The Music Club (1966)
The School Board
Ref. 141

BLISS, Marilyn S.
American flautist, editor and composer. b. Cedar Rapids, IA, September 30, 1954. She studied composition under Jerry Owen and Harvey Sollberger at Coe College, Cedar Rapids, graduating magna cum laude in 1976, majoring in composition, the flute and voice. At the University of Pennsylvania she studied composition under George Crumb, George Rochberg and Richard Wernick and theory under Robert Morgan and David Burge. She obtained her M.A. in 1978 and was awarded a Crofts Fellowship in composition at Tanglewood the same year enabling her to study under Jacob Druckman. She received a Charles Ives prize from the American Academy/Institute of Arts and Letters and an ASCAP grant in 1979. She studied for her doctorate at the City University of New York from 1979 to 1980 and held the position of Index Editor of RILM Abstracts of Music Literature from 1979. She was made a Fellow at the Composers' Conference, VT, in 1979 and received a commission from the Philadelphia Art Alliance in 1979 and a Meet the Composer grant in 1981.
Compositions
CHAMBER
Symphony (wind ens) (1975-1976)
Tapestry (str qrt) (1976)
Chameleon (fl, vlc and pf) (1980-1981)
Trio (vln, vlc, and pf) (1978-1979)
Piece (ob and pf) (1974)
Encounter (fl) (1975) (Zalo Publ.)
Evocations (tba) (1981)
Fantasies (pf) (1977)
Three short movements (trb) (1976)
VOCAL
Huatzu Hill (S and cham ens)
Shadowflowers (S, T, and cham ens)
Three farewells (S, fl, vla and hp)
Celestial greetings (S and pf) (1982-1983)
Three songs (S and pf) (1972-1973)
ELECTRONIC
Cape Cod (tape) (1976)
Ref. composer

BLISS, Mrs. J. Worthington. See LINDSAY, Miss M.

BLISS, Pearl
20th-century American composer.
Composition
OPERA
The Feast of the Red Corn (1955)
Ref. 141

BLISS, Tamara
20th-century American composer.
Compositions
VOCAL
Pity the poor spiders, from Archie and Mehitabel (S, S or A and Bar or T and B) (1961)
Come away Death, from Twelfth Night (vce and pf)
Infant joy (S and pf)
The tyger (vce and pf)
Ref. 190

BLOCH, Suzanne
Swiss/American lutenist, virginal and recorder player, singer, teacher and composer. b. Geneva August 9, 1907. She was the daughter of composer Ernest Bloch with whom she commenced her study of music. She then studied under Roger Sessions and in Paris under Nadia Boulanger (q.v.). At the age of nineteen she won first prize in a Paris competition for women composers. She researched the history and playing of old musical instruments. As an authority on lute tablature she restored and transcribed much forgotten music. She performed throughout America, playing the lute, virginal and recorder and singing to her own lute accompaniment. She taught at the Juilliard School of Music and at the College of the City of New York.
Composition
CHAMBER
Lachrymae (strs)
Ref. 496

BLOCK, Isabelle McKee
19th-century American pianist and composer. She composed piano pieces.
Ref. 347

BLOCKSIDGE, Kathleen Mary
English pianist, teacher and composer. b. Hither Green, 1904. She was a L.R.A.M. and an A.R.A.M. and a teacher of the piano and for the Pipers' Guild.
Compositions
PERCUSSION
Nell Gwynn suite
Song of the reeds
MISCELLANEOUS
First glimpses in music Land
Publications
The Children's Percussion Band Book.
Ref. 467

BLOM, Diane
Australian composer. b. 1947.
Compositions
OPERETTA
The Pied Piper, for children (1974)
INCIDENTAL MUSIC
Daisy Bates, T.V. series (1971)
Three farewells (S, fl, vla and hp)
Invocation to Earth (speakers, soli, mix-ch and orch) (1971)
Ref. 442

BLOMENFELD, Fannie. See BLOOMFIELD-ZEISLER, Fannie

BLOMFIELD-HOLT, Patricia (Holt, Patricia Blomfield)
Canadian pianist, lecturer and composer. b. Lindsay, Ontario, September 15, 1910. She studied at the Royal Conservatory, Toronto under Noah de Kresz and Norman Wilkes, the piano under B.H. Carman and composition under Healy William. She taught the piano, theory and composition at the Royal Conservatory, Toronto. Her works have been performed in Europe, the Soviet Union, the United States and Canada. In 1938 her *Suite for Violin and Piano* was awarded the Vogt Society Award for the best Canadian composition.
Compositions
ORCHESTRA
Pastorale (1940)
Short sketch on a theme (1940)
Sonata (str orch)

CHAMBER
String quartet No. 1 (1937)
String quartet No. 2 (Canadian Music Centre, 1953)
Lyric piece No. 1 (vln and pf) (1937)
Lyric piece No. 2 (vlc and pf) (1938)
Pastorale and finale (vln and pf) (1935)
Suite No. 1 (vln and pf) (F. Harris) (1936) (Vogt Society Award)
Suite No. 2 (vln or vla and pf) (BMI, Canada) (1939)
Dirge and dance
Processional (CMC, 1954)
PIANO
Greensleeves (Berandol 1971)
Impromptu (BMI) (1968)
March of the penguins (1971)
Processional (1961)
Riding a bicycle, scherzo (1962)
A sauntering tune (1966)
Skating, scherzo (Harris 1971)
Study No. 1, Touch; No. 2, Imitation (1966)
The promenade
Teaching pieces
VOCAL
Songs of Early Canada (low vce, hp, hn and strs) (CMC 1950)
Songs of my country (B or A, hp, hn and strs) (1950)
Three songs (B, hp, hn and strs) (1949)
The birds, songs (Waterloo, 1971)
Quiet (Pickthall) (m-S and pf) (1966)
Three songs of contemplation (Pratt, Adeney, Lowell) (vce and pf) (1970)
A lake memory, song (Waterloo)
The lost cause (1948)
Diedre (1948)
THEATRE
Sister Beatrice, play (1936)
Ref. composer, 477, 622

BLOOD, Esta Damesek

American pianist, teacher and composer. b. New York, March 25, 1933. Her father Abbe Damesek and mother Sally Kempler Damesek, were both musicians. She attended the Manhattan School of Music, 1942 to 1947 and then studied with Malke Gottlieb and Anita Meyer in Schenectady. Her composition teachers were Henry Brant in 1977, Vivian Fine (q.v.) in 1977 and 1979 and Louis Calabro in 1977 and 1979. She taught the piano from 1950 and began composing in 1966. Her *Bulgarian Trio* was awarded first prize in the International Wind and String Chamber Music Composition Competition, 1979. PHOTOGRAPH.

Compositions
ORCHESTRA
Mirrors, suite (fl, perc and str orch) (1978)
CHAMBER
Cycle, 2 trios (fl, cl, pf, fl, cl and gtr) (1978)
Six traditional songs (fl, vln, vla, bsn, and pf)
Variations on an Armenian theme (str qrt) (1974)
Bulgarian trio (fl, vln and pf) (1972) (1st prize, Int. Wind and String Chamber Music Composition)
Fusions (ob, cl and pf) (1979)
Perceptions (fl, cl and bsn) (1979)
Two designs (vlc and perc) (1977)
Nine Balkan folkdances (vln and pf) (1974)
Nocturne (vln and pf) (1969)
If (gtr) (1977)
Sculpture dance (hp) (1977)
PIANO
Three variations (2 pf, 8 hands) (1977)
Balkan suite (G. Schirmer) (1966-1967)
Five-legged spider (Pro Art Publ., 1968)
Folkdances from the Balkans (1971)
Seven dances in Aksak rhythms (1973)
Variations on a duality (1980)
VOCAL
Antonio (Laura Richards) (narr, 2 winds and 2 strs) (1973)
Five American folksongs (S, fl and gtr) (1977)
Happy birthday to U.S., theme and variations (S, 2 winds and 2 strs) (1976)
The house that Jack built (narr, 2 winds and 2 strs) (1975)
Improvisations on Shaker tunes (S, fl, vln, and vla; also ch) (1975, 1961)
Jack and the beanstalk (narr, 2 winds and 2 strs) (1973)
Variations on Yankee Doodle (S, 2 winds and 2 strs) (1975)
Fall (Carl George) (S and pf) (1972)
Starsong (Tagore) (S and pf) (1970)
Recipe: How to preserve a spouse (narr and pf) (1979)
The three sillies (narr, hp and vlc) (1978)
SACRED
A psalm of David (cantor, ch and pf) (1973)
Ref. composer, 142, 206, 624

BLOOD, Lizette Emma. See ORTH, Lizette Emma

BLOOM, Jane Ira

American saxophonist and composer. B. Newton, M.A., January 12, 1955. She received her B.A. (music, magna cum laude) and her M.M. (composition) from Yale University, after studying under David Mott and Robert Moore. She studied the saxophone privately with Joseph Viola, at the Berklee College of Music and under Donald Sinta at the Hartt College of Music. She was the recipient of several grants and won the Downbeat International Critics Poll award 5 times. She composed music for the Pilobolus Dance Theatre, the New York City Women's Festival and the New Music America Festival. All her compositions are published by Outline Publishers. DISCOGRAPHY.

Compositions
CHAMBER
Braxton BOP (sax, b-viol and 20 piece ens) (1980)
Latin trance (sax, b-viol and 20 piece ens) (1980)
Magic (20 piece ens) (1980)
A unicorn in captivity (b-viol, vib, perc and sax) (1982)
Desert (b-viol, pf, vib and sax) (1981)
The man with glasses (b-viol, perc, pf and sax) (1982)
Noema (b-viol, pf, vib and sax) (1982)
Oshumare (b-viol, vib and sax) (1982)
The race (b-viol, dr, trp and sax) (1983)
Starry night (b-viol, pf, vib and sax) (1982)
Change-up (b-viol, perc, pf and sax) (1982)
Hannifin (b-viol, pf and sax) (1980)
Jackson Pollock (b-viol, vib and sax) (1980)
Mighty lights (b-viol, perc and sax) (1982)
Shan Dara (b-viol, vib and sax) (1980)
Varo (b-viol, perc and sax) (1980)
Electric (b-viol and sax) (1980)
White Tower (b-viol and sax) (1980)
Moonblind (sax) (1980)
VOCAL
II-V-I (vce, 15 piece ens or b-viol, pf, perc and sax) (1980)
Ivy (vce, b-viol, pf, perc and sax) (1981)
Ref. composer, 622

BLOOM, Shirley

American composer. b. 1931.

Composition
CHAMBER
Quintet (fl and str qrt) (1962)
Ref. Working Papers on Women in Music No. 1 1985

BLOOMFIELD-ZEISLER (Blomenfeld), Fannie (alt. name Fannie Zeissler)

American pianist and composer. b. Bielitz, Austria, July 16, 1863; d. Chicago, August 20, 1927. She studied under Carl Wolfsohn and Bernard Ziehn (piano) and made her debut in Chicago in 1875. She went to Vienna, where she studied with Leschetizky from 1878 to 1883, then for the next 30 years toured the United States and Europe. She made her farewell appearance in Chicago in 1925. She generally performed her own works as encores at her concerts. She composed piano pieces and songs. PHOTOGRAPH.

Bibliography
Cole, Rossetter G. *Fanny Bloomfield-Zeisler. Proceedings.* Music Teachers' Association, series, 22, 1927, pp. 76-83.
Mathews, W.S.B. *A Great at Home. Music* 9, October 1895-April 1896: 1-10.
Ref. 276, 347, 352

BLOOM OF YOUTH. See RAIQ

BLUNETT, Emma Marie. See MacFARREN, Emma Marie

BOBROW, Sanchie

American violinist, film and music director, teacher and composer. b. Brooklyn, NY, October 3, 1960. She received her B.A.Mus. (composition and violin) from Douglass College at Rutgers University in 1981, having studied under Noel daCosta and Rolv Yttrehus and graduating magna cum laude in music. She then studied at the Aaron Copland School of Music under Hugo Weisgall, George Perle, Henry Weinberg, Saul Berkowitz and Carl Schachter, receiving her M.A. (composition) in 1983.

She was elected to Pi Kappa Lambda. In 1983 she studied composition privately under Bruce Saylor and in 1984 studied the violin under Ruth Waterman. She worked as a studio musician and music producer and director for film and theatre productions and for a short time taught music appreciation and rudiments at the Aaron Copland School of Music. She was composer and music director for *Henry V*, at the Riverside Shakespeare Company, NY, 1984.

Compositions

CHAMBER

Three Frames of Mind (fl) (1979)

VOCAL

My heart will heal someday (mix-ch a-cap) (1983)
Sounds and silences (mix-ch a-cap) (1983)
Cradle song (2 S, A and pf) (1984)
Three songs to a lost love (composer) (S, fl and vla) (1982)
Memories and time, 3 songs (m-S and vlc) (1980)

SACRED

Three psalms (mix-ch a-cap) (1983)

THEATRE

As you like it (Shakespeare) (gtr, rec, vces and vln) (1982)
Beauty and the beast (after La Fontaine) (vln, 2 gtr, 3 rec and perc) (1982)
Henry V (Shakespeare) (2 trp, vces and perc) (1984)
Life song, for Passover (str trio, fl, gtr and vces) (1981)
Little black fish, children's musical (composer) (1981)
Our town (Thornton Wilder) (vln and gtr) (1982)
Parables and parodies in Pantomime: The Tree of sorrows; Noah's ark; Looney tunes (1983)

FILM MUSIC

Dream Willow (vce and cham orch) (1984-1985)

ARRANGEMENTS

Hebrew melodies

Publications

The Art of Orchestration, Music.....Alive! Cherry lane Music Pub.
The Composers' Recording. *AMC newsletter.*
Music? What Music? Staten Island Advance, Newhouse Publ. 1984.
Program notes for the Queens College Choral Society.

Ref. composer, AMC newsletter, 625

BOCARD, Sister Cecilia Clair

American composer. b. New Albany, 1899. She composed piano, organ and choral works.

Ref. 347

BOCKHOLTZ, Anna. See BOCHKOLTZ-FALCONI, Anna

BOCHKOLTZ-FALCONI (Bockholtz), Anna

German singer, teacher and composer. b. Frankfurt, 1820; d. Paris, December 24, 1879. She first appeared in Brussels in a concert in 1844; the next year she went to Paris and sang in 'Concerts de Musique Ancienne'. She remained in Paris until the end of 1848, when she fled to London to escape the revolution. She returned in 1856 and established herself as a teacher of singing.

Compositions

VOCAL

Es faellt ein Stern herunter (vce and pf) (Cranz)
Frisch gesungen (vce and pf) (Cranz)
Fruehlings Verkuendung
Geisterstimmen
Romances

Ref. 105, 276, 297, 433

BOCK, Anna

19th-century German composer.

Composition

PIANO

Habanera graziosa, Brazilian dance

Ref. 448

BOCK, Bertha

Rumanian pianist, teacher and composer. b. Hermannstadt, March 15, 1857. From 1892 to 1896 she studied the piano under Karl Philp, Victor von Heldenberg and Albert Geiger, singing under Rosa Pfaff and theory under Wilhelm Weiss.

Compositions

VOCAL

Das verlassene Maegdlein, op. 8 (vce and pf)
Five songs, op. 5: Botschaft; Ich weiss einen Namen; Im Sommer; Mahnen; Vaganterliedchen (vce and pf)
Songs, ops. 6, 7, 9 and 10

BALLET

Das erste Veilchen (1906)
Klein Elschens Traum (1905)

OPERA

Die Pfingstkrone (1925)

Ref. 219, 297

BOCQUET, Anne (Marguerite)

17th-century French lutenist and composer. d. Paris. She shared a famous salon in Paris with Mlle. de Scudery from 1653 to 1659, which was a meeting place of artists and some of the founders of the Academie Française. Her compositions constituted a thorough exploration of the tonalities of the lute.

Compositions

LUTE

Dix-sept préludes marquant les cadences
Prélude sur tous les tons
Other pieces with French, German and English manuscripts

Bibliography

Rollin, M. and Souris, A. *Oeuvres des Bocquet*. Paris, 1972.

Ref. M. Rollin

BOCQUET, Marguerite. See BOCQUET, Anne

BODENSTEIN-HOYME, Ruth E.

East German pianist, teacher and composer. b. Wurzen, near Leipzig, March 13, 1924. She studied for the state examination in 1950 at the Hochschule fuer Musik in Leipzig with the piano as her principal subject. Her piano teachers were O. Keller and Rudolf Fischer and her theory teacher was P. Scherk. After 1953 she taught the piano at Carl Maria von Weber Hochschule fuer Musik in Dresden. She undertook a further examination in 1971 with composition as her major subject. Her manuscripts are in the Sachsischen Landesbibliothek, Dresden. PHOTOGRAPH.

Compositions

ORCHESTRA

Im grossen Garten, suite
Music for strings

CHAMBER

Festliche Musik (7 brass insts)
Brass quintet
Five miniatures (vln and vla) (comm Hochschule fuer Musik, Dresden) (Hofmeister-Verlag, Leipzig, 1963)
Tierfabeln fuer Klavier und Schlagzeug (1977)
Variations on a Vietnamese children's song (trp and pf)

PIANO

Kleiner Klavierzyklus
Sonatina
Sonatine in D (comm Hochschule fuer Musik, Dresden) (Peters, Leipzig, 1970)

VOCAL

Il progresso esemplificato, cantata (A, T, Bar, vln, vla and vlc) (1979)
Gespraech mit dem Genossen Lenin (Majakowki) (B, speaker, trp, pf and small perc)
Dem Frieden (A. Schweitzer: Die Lehre der Ehrfurcht vor dem Leben) (1979)
Liederzyklus – Die kleinen Weisheiten (S, A, T and pf) (1976)
Impressionen nach Gedichten von Ho Chi Minh, (aus dem Gefaengnistagebuch) (Bar and pf) (1981)
Song cycle (Georg Maurer) (m-S and pf)
Die vier Jahreszeiten, song cycle (S and pf)

SACRED

Meditation and Fugue after Two Psalms (mix-ch)

Ref. composer, Dr. G. Kumpan

BODOM, Erica

Norwegian pianist, teacher and composer. b. 1861; d. 1942. She studied in Oslo and then Berlin under F. Kullak and C. Becker. She returned to Oslo as a piano teacher. She composed piano pieces and songs.

Ref. 20

BODOROVA, Sylvie

Czech pianist, lecturer and composer. b. Ceske Budejovice, December 31, 1954. At the Bratislava Conservatory she studied the piano under Alzbeta Hirnerova and composition under Juraj Pospisil. Then she attended the Janacek Academy of Arts and Music in Brno where she studied composition under Ctirad Kohoutek, graduating in 1979. Whilst a post-graduate student at the Prague Academy of Arts, she held the position of assistant lecturer in the department of composition and conducting at the Janacek Academy. She lives in Prague and lectures at the Institute of Music Theory and History of the Czechoslovak Academy of Sciences. She won several prizes for her compositions.

Compositions

ORCHESTRA

Plancti (vla and orch) (1982)
Concertino doppio con eco (2 vln, vlc and str orch) (1977)
Canzone da sonar (gtr and str orch) (1980)

CHAMBER

Metamorphosae terrae (fl, ob, vlc and pf) (1975)
Fairytales just so (fl and gtr) (1980)
Musica dedicata (b-cl and pf) (1980)
Scent of summer (fl and pf) (1976)
Plays for Thomas and Martin (vln and vlc) (1980)
Baltic miniatures (gtr) (1979)
Cat paintings (pf) (1974)
Gila, Roma! (vla) (1978)
Musica per due (org)
Saluti da Siena (cl) (1981)

VOCAL

Canto di lode (vce and orch) (1981)
Fight with an angel (m-vce and str orch) (1982)
Two miniatures (chil-ch) (1978)
Strawberry night (w-reciter, S, fl, hn, vln and hp) (1979)
Warning (S, B, bsn and str qrt) (1974)
Bohemia song (1977)

BALLET

Small pool, ballet opera (1976)

ELECTRONIC

To you (w-reciter and tape) (1976)

Ref. CMIC

BOECE, Dame Elpis de. See ELPIS DE BOECE, Dame

BOEHN, Liselotte

German pianist, recorder player, teacher and composer. b. Bielitz, Poland, February 22, 1928. She had her first piano lessons at the age of seven and later studied the recorder and music theory. In 1945, fleeing the Russian Army, her family moved to Offenbach/Main, West Germany. She attended the Staatliche Hochschule fuer Musik in Frankfurt and wrote the state examination. She studied under Professor Leopolder and began a long career of teaching. She played in concerts as a soloist and an accompanist.

Compositions

RECORDER

Kinderlieder in leichten Saetzen (2 S-rec) (Nagel, 1975)
Spiel im Duett (Mainz: Schott Soehne, 1972)
Volkslieder in leichten Saetzen (Nagel, 1975)
Weihnachtslieder in leichten Saetzen (Nagel, 1975)

Publications

Four volumes of compositions for teaching. Schott & Barenreiter.

Ref. composer

BOERNER-SANDRINI, Marie

19th-century German pianist, voice teacher and composer. Her mother, L. Sandrini, was a soprano.

Compositions

VOCAL

Songs

SACRED

Ave Maria (A and pf)

Ref. 226, 276

BOESE, Helen

Canadian pianist and composer. b. Toronto, 1896. She studied under Frank Wrigley, John M. Williams and Doris MacLean. She was chairlady of the Composition Committee for the Canadian Federation of Music Teachers, Alberta and on the board of directors of the Calgary Symphony Orchestra. She was official pianist for the Calgary Symphony Orchestra and accompanied many well-known singers.

Compositions

VOCAL

Two Sketches: The family breakfast; A quick rubber (ch)
Affinity
Song of the weaver

Ref. 133

BOESENHOENIG, Josefa Barbara. See AURENHAMMER, Josefa Barbara

BOESGAARDOVA-SCHMIDTOVA, Lydie

Czech pianist, concert singer and composer. b. Rokycany, February 18, 1890. She studied the piano and singing at the Music College in Plzen and theory under O. Bradac. From 1914 she lived in Italy. As a concert singer, she popularized Czech works and folk songs, appearing mainly with the Bulgarian baritone, Dr. B. Vasiliev.

Compositions

PIANO

Nina-nana del cucu (Hansen, 1952)
Osvobozeni brahy (1945)
Una volta in primavera (Hansen, 1952)

Ref. 197

BOESING, Martha

20th-century American composer.

Composition

OPERA

A Ballad of Now

Ref. 141, 142

BOESSER, Dagmar

German organist, pianist, recorder player, teacher and composer of Bremen. d. 1984. She was particularly successful as a performer of avant-garde recorder music, performing in concerts and on radio. She won a prize in the Gaudeamus competition and attended composition courses in Darmstadt.

Compositions

RECORDER

Animo interno-innere Seele (4 rec)

ELECTRONIC

Radio 3 und 4 (T-rec, contact microphone and shortwave band)

Ref. Frau und Musik 7/84

BOETSELAER, Josina. See BOETZELAER, Josina

BOETZELAER (Boetselaer), Josina Anna Petronella (Baroness Giustina)

Compositions

VOCAL

Arie sciolte, e coro con sinfonia, op. 4
Raccolta d'arie sciolte con sinfonie, op. 2
Sei ariette e canto e cembalo

Ref. 125

BOFILL, Anna

Spanish pianist, architect and composer. b. Barcelona, 1944. She studied architecture at the University of Barcelona, obtaining a doctorate in 1974. She studied the piano and music theory under J. Albareda at the Caminals Academy from 1950 to 1959 and composition under J. Cercos and Xavier Montsalvatge from 1960 to 1961. She then became a pupil of J.M. Mestres Quadreny.

Compositions

CHAMBER

Esclat (fl, ob, cl, pf, perc, 2 vln, vla and vlc) (1971)
Septet de set sous (fl, cl, gtr, pf, perc, vln and vlc) (1978)
Quartet (gtr, hpcd, pf and perc) (1976)
Poema (pf) (1974)
Suite de Tamanrasset (gtr) (1977)

ELECTRONIC

Espai sonor (perc and tape)

Ref. Internazionales Musikinstitut, Darmstadt

BOFILL LEVI, Anna. See BOFILL, Anna

BOGUE, Christina. See MORISON, Christina W.

BOHMANN, Hedwig

20th-century German composer.

Composition

SACRED

Deutsche Messe (1938)

Ref. 465

BOHN, Liselotte. See BOEHN, Liselotte

BOHUN, Lyle de. See BOONE, Clara Lyle

BOISEN, Elisabeth

Early 20th-century Danish composer.

Compositions

CHAMBER

The Americas trio (fl, cl and bsn)

VOCAL

Songs of estrangement (S and str qrt)
Serenade (Runeberg) (vce, org and hp or pf)
Ak, I snefnug!
Efter Sejren
Fra Lunden, 3 songs (1923)
Fred paa Oord
Fremad! (1904)
Frem over hede
Gammel fransk Romance: oversat af Thor Lange, Der skulde to Sostre til Kilden gaae
I Lunder er der fuglesang
Kirkeklokkerne
Lojet (Runeberg)
Naar det er morkt
Raadhusklokkernes sang
Tre folkeviser
Vuggesang til lille solstraale
Other songs (Rosnorn and Runeberg) (1903-1918)

SACRED

Det glade budskab, Christmas songs
Hjaelp mig, min Gud og Herre!
Tre religiose sange (1909)

Ref. 331

BOLEYN, Anne, Queen of England

English lutenist and singer. b. London, ca. 1507; d. London, May 19, 1536. (Some historians put her date of birth at 1501 or 1502.) She was the wife of Henry VIII. She is reputed to have composed several ballads, the most famous being *O death, rock me asleep* believed to have been composed in the Tower of London as she awaited her execution. This song is regarded as a milestone in 16th-century English music because of the independence of the passacaglia-like accompaniment, which is the first example of parts completely separate from the vocal line. DISCOGRAPHY. PHOTOGRAPH.

Compositions

VOCAL

Alas what a wretched life, madrigal (vces and fiddles)
O Death, rock me asleep, madrigal (vces and fiddles)
O fairest maid (vces and fiddles)
Sweet Amarillis stay (vces and fiddles)

Bibliography

Bruce, Mary Louise. *Anne Boleyn*. 1972.
Chapman, Hester. *Anne Boleyn*. 1974.
Friedman, Paul. *Anne Boleyn; A Chapter in English History*. 2 vols. 1884.

Ref. 105, 177, 208, 262, 563, 645

BOLL, Christine E.

East German accordionist, teacher and composer. b. Woltersdorf, January 7, 1931. She studied at the Musikhochschule, Berlin and went on a concert tour of the Soviet Union, Poland, Indonesia, India and Iraq from 1954 to 1964. She taught in East Berlin.

Compositions

ORCHESTRA

Capriccio (vlc and orch)
Partita piccola (str orch)

CHAMBER

Piano and accordion works

Ref. 70

BOLOGNESE, Isabella

16th-century Italian lutenist and composer of songs.

Ref. 465, 128

BOLZ, Harriet (Mrs. Harold A.) (Hallock)

20th-century American pianist, choir conductor, lecturer, writer and composer. b. Cleveland, OH. She attended Case Western Reserve University, where she obtained a B.A. (music) in 1933. At Ohio State University she obtained her M.A. (composition). She studied privately under Leo Sowerby and Paul Creston. She taught the piano and composition, conducted adult and junior choirs, accompanied singers and instrumentalists and played for church services. She lectured and wrote articles on contemporary music. She was chosen as Outstanding Artist of 1962 and one of the Ten Outstanding Women of the Year in Columbus, by a newspaper. She received a National Federation of Music Clubs award in 1965 and first prize in the Sacred Choral Category, National League of American Pen Women Biennial Competition (1970). She received additional awards from this group in 1972 and 1974.

Compositions

ORCHESTRA

Impromptu

CHAMBER

Sonata (str and ww septets) (1962)
Lyric sonata (2 vln, vl, vlc, fl, cl and bsn) (1980)
Linear trilogy (ww trio, fl, cl and bsn)
Pageant, prelude, interlude and postlude (ww qnt) (1970)
Form, fantasy and fugue (str or ww qrt)
Sonata for piano quartet (vln, vla, vlc and pf) (1980) (1st prize Nat. League of American Pen Women, 1983)
Vis-a-vis, 2 short pieces in invention style (fl, cl and bsn) (1965)
Poem cantare (fl, vlc and pf)
Poem capriccio (fl, vlc and pf)
Duo scherzando (b-flat trp and pf) (1959) (Harold Branch)
Polychrome patterns, sonatine (cl and pf) (1963)
Canto lyric (fl and pf) (1983)
Sonata (vlc and pf) (1958)
Narrative impromptu (hp) (1974)

ORGAN

Andante con moto, allegro and fugue
Break forth in joy (1964, rev. 1974)
Episode (1979) (Arsis Press)
Sonic essay and fugue (1981)

PIANO

Capitol pageant (4 hands) (Sisra Publ.)
Floret, a mood caprice (1965)
Two profiles (1974)

VOCAL

Day and dark, cantata (George Cabot Lodge) (Bar, mix-ch and orch)
Star over star, cantata (B, ch and orch) (1958)
Autumn legend (S, A, T, B, ch, vln, vla, vlc and pf) (Naomi C. Maimsohn Award)
Carol of the flowers (w-ch) (Choral Art)
How shall we speak? (mix-ch and pf or org) (Sisra)
Not by words alone (mix-ch)
Nowness (w-ch)
That I may sing (Michelangelo, trans Wordsworth) (w-ch and org) (1970) (Sam Fox)
Who am I (w-ch)
Invocation (S and str qrt) (1960)
Ode to Autumn (S and pf qrt) (1973)
Splendour of the sea and splendour of the seasons (high vce and pf) (1974)
Such be the thought (med-vce, fl, vlc and pf) (1976)
Winds of heaven and winds of the waters (high vce and pf) (1960)

SACRED

Flower of love, Easter anthem (w-ch and pf or org)
Four Christmas songs (m-ch)
Joy to all our hearts (w-ch and pf or org)
Sweet Jesus (m-ch) (Beckenhorst Press)
To love and serve (mix-ch and pf or org)
Two madrigals for Christmas (w-ch) (Sam Fox)
Teach us Thy peace (1972)

Ref. composer, 142, 190, 206, 280, 474, 625, 643

BOLZ, Mrs. Harold A. See BOLZ, Harriet

BON, Anna

Italian composer. b. Venice, 1738. She was a chamber music virtuoso. Her *Sei Divertimenti* were written at the age of 19.

Compositions

CHAMBER

Sei Divertimenti a Due Flauti e Basso, op. 3 (2 fl and d-b) (Nuremberg: Balthasar Schmidts Witwe, 1757) (ded Karl Theodor, Duke of Bavaria)
Sei Sonate da camera, op. 1 (fl, vlc or hpcd) (Nuremberg: Balthasar Schmidts Witwe, 1756)
Sei Sonate, op. 2 (hpcd) (Nuremberg: Balthasar Schmidts Witwe, 1757)
Sei Sonate per il Flauto Traversiere and Basso, in B, C, F-Flat, D, G-Minor and G (Denmark: Egtved)

Ref. 125, 128

BOND, Carrie Jacobs (Jacobs-Bond)

American artist, singer and composer. b. Janesville, WI, August 11, 1862; d. Hollywood, December 28, 1946. She was a pupil of Bischoff. After the death of her second husband in 1895, Carrie moved to Chicago where she lived in poverty with her son. During the next six years she wrote about 32 songs which she published herself and sang in night clubs to augment her income. About 1901 she published her song *I Love You Truly* which sold over one million copies whilst her *A Perfect Day* sold over five million copies. She was entertained at the White House by President amd Mrs. Theodore Roosevelt. With her son she established the shop Carrie Jacobs Bond and Son, which grew from a tiny room to an enormous business. DISCOGRAPHY.

Compositions

PIANO

Betty's music box
The blue flag, military march
Reverie

VOCAL

Crimson breasted bird
Eleven songs (1911)
Half-minute songs (1910-1911)
I love you truly (vce and pf) (pub. ca. 1901)
In the meadow when the roses are in bloom
Just a wearying for you
A little bit of honey
Love and sorrow, song cycle (Bar) (1908)
A perfect day (vce and pf) (1910)
Roses are in bloom
Seven songs, as unpretentious as the wild rose (1901)
The smile songs (1910)
Songs everybody sings (1906)
Ten songs, as unpretentious as the wild rose (1905)
Three songs, as unpretentious as the wild rose (1904)
Twelve songs (1902)

SACRED

Do you remember?

Publications

Jacobs-Bond, Carrie. *The Roads of Melody*. New York: D. Appleton, 1927. *Autobiography*.

Ref. 44, 63, 81, 106, 228, 276, 292, 347, 404, 617, 646, 653

BOND, Victoria Ellen

American pianist, conductor and composer. b. Los Angeles, May 6, 1949. She started composing at the age of five and began her formal training at the Mannes College of Music. She studied composition under Ingolf Dahl at the University of Southern California, where she obtained her B.Mus. hons. in 1968. She was a student at the University of Southern California and of Ellis Kohs. She won a scholarship to the Aspen Music School, where she studied composition under Darius Milhaud in 1968. She received her M.Mus. from the Juilliard School of Music in 1975, studying composition under Roger Sessions and Vladimir Ussachevsky. She obtained a D.Mus. at the Juilliard, where she has been a conducting fellow since 1973 after studying composition under Vincent Persichetti and conducting under Sixten Ehrlung, Jean Morel, Pierre Boulez and Herbert von Karajan. Other teachers included Paul Glass and Jacob Druckman. At the Aspen Music School, she studied under Otto Weiner Mueller and Herbert Blomstedt. She was the first woman to be awarded a D.Mus in orchestra conducting by the the Juilliard. She was assistant conductor at the Cabrillio music festival with Dennis Russell Davies in 1974 and principal guest conductor at the White Mountains Music Festival in 1975. She conducted the American Symphony Orchestra in 1975 and from 1974 to 1978 was assistant conductor to Pierre Boulez and Richard Dufallu of the Contemporary Music Ensemble, 1974 to 1978. She was music director and conductor of the New Amsterdam Symphony Orchestra, New York. In 1975 she won the Victor Herbert award for excellence in orchestral conducting. She was conducting assistant of Pittsburgh Symphony Orchestra and music director of the Pittsburgh Youth Symphony. It was the first time a woman had been appointed to these positions. At the Aspen Music Festival (1975) she was a guest conductor and assistant conductor of the Opera department. She is assistant conductor of the Colorado Philharmonic. She received the Ascap Award in 1978 and 1979. She is a contributor to the International Musician and Parade Magazine. DISCOGRAPHY. PHOTOGRAPH.

Compositions

ORCHESTRA

C-A-G-E-D- (str orch)
Equinox, concert suite
Five preludes (1972)
Interludes (cham orch) (1970)
Sonata (1973)

CHAMBER

Russian suite (cham ens) (1966)
Quintet (ww) (1970)
Ménage à troi (a-fl, B-cl and E-flat sax)
Quartet for clarinet and strings (1967)
Recitative for English horn and string trio (Theodore Front, 1975)
Trio (vln, vlc and pf)
Trio for brass (1969)
Canons (cl and vln) (1970) (Theodore Front, 1975)
Duet (fl and vla) (1969)
Sonata (vlc and pf) (1971) (Seesaw Music, 1975)
Cello sonata (1971)
Pastorale (ww) (1967)
Variations (fl) (1969)
Variations (pf) (1963)
Suite miniature (Theodore Front, 1975)

VOCAL

Birthday cantata (soloists, small mix-ch and pf) (1966)
Cornography, mini-cantata (S and cham ens) (1970)
Tarot (ch and perc orch)
Suite aux troubadours (S and cham ens) (1970) (Theodore Front, 1975)
Margaret (S, fl, vln, vlc and pf) (1984)
From an antique land (Seesaw Music, 1976)
Impressions 5 and Chanson Innocente (vce and pf) (1968) (e.e. cummings)
Aria (S and strs)
La belle dame sans merci (Shelley) (vce and pf) (1964)
Mirror, mirror (vce and cham ens) (1969)
Peter Quince at the clavier (S, pf, perc or vce and perc)
Song cycle (Yeats) (vce and pf) (1964)
Songs (G.M. Hopkins) (1965)
Thirteen ways of looking at a blackbird (Wallace Stevens) (vce and pf) (1968)

BALLET

Equinox (1977) (comm Pennsylvania Ballet) (1977)
Conversation piece (vla and vib) (Seesaw, 1975)
Otherselves

FILM MUSIC

Mirror of nature (1971)

MULTI MEDIA

A woman's journey

Publications

Technical Studies for the Flute. Culver City, CA; Trio Associates.
Closet Composer: A Portrait of Dorian Gray.
International Musician, July 1975.

Bibliography

Medsger, Betty. *Women at Work: A Photographic Documentary*.
MOMA: Women Composers: Summergarden Concert. *High Fidelity Musical America*, 25. December 1975. MA 27-8.
Slayton, Joice. *Careers and Colleges for Young Women*.

Ref. composer, 280, 415, 454, 457, 465, 563, 625, 643

BONDS, Margaret

Black American pianist, historian, lecturer and composer. b. Chicago, March 3, 1913; d. Los Angeles, April 26, 1972. She studied with her mother and composed her first song at the age of five. She studied composition and the piano under Florence B. Price and William Dawson. She graduated from Northwestern University in Evanston, IL, with B.Mus. and M.Mus., then studied under Robert Storer at the Juilliard School of Music. She also studied the piano under Henry Levine and composition privately under Roy Harris and Emerson Harper. In the 1930s she opened a school in Chicago for ballet and music, called the Allied Arts Academy. As a concert pianist, she performed in Canada and the United States, appearing as guest soloist with the Chicago Symphony Orchestra. She also appeared on radio programs in New York and on CBS radio in Hollywood. As a member of duo-piano teams she toured with two of her former students, appearing both in concert and in night clubs. She taught the piano privately in Chicago and New York. She taught at the American Theatre

Wing and was music director at East Side Settlement House and the White Barn Theatre. She lectured on the piano and theory at the Los Angeles Inner City Institute. She won numerous scholarships, fellowships and awards, including the NANM scholarship, Alpha Kappa Sorority scholarship, Rodman Wanamaker award in composition in 1932, Julius Rosenwald Fellowship, Roy Harris Fellowship, Honor Roll of Most Distinguished Negro Women of the Century (IL Centennial Authority) and ASCAP awards from 1964 to 1966. In 1967 she received the Alumni medal, the highest distinction granted by Northwestern University to its alumni members who have achieved eminence in their communities and fields of endeavor. DISCOGRAPHY.

Compositions

ORCHESTRA

Peter and the bells, symphony
The Nile fantasy (pf and orch)

PIANO

Spiritual suite
Troubled water (New York: Sam Fox, 1967)

VOCAL

Credo (ch and orch)
I got a home in that rock (vce and orch; also vce and pf) New York (Beekman Music, 1959)
Children's sleep (Vernon Glasser) (mix-ch and pf) (New York: C. Fischer, 1942)
The Negro speaks of rivers (mix-ch and pf) (New York: Handy Bros. Music Co. 1962)
You can tell the world (mix-ch and pf; also w-ch; also m-ch; also mix-ch a-cap) (Mutual Music Society, 1957)
African dance, art duet song (Langston Hughes) (1956)
Didn't it rain (vce and pf) (Beekman Music, 1967)
Dry bones (Mutual Music Society)
Empty interlude, song (vce and pf) (New York: Robbins Music Co.)
Fields of wonder, cycle (L. Hughes) (m-ch)
He's got the whole world in His hands (Beekman Music)
I shall pass through the world (New York: Bourne Co. 1966)
The pasture (Robert Frost)
Peach tree street (vce and pf) (New York: Dorsey Bros. Music Corp. 1939)
Three dream portraits (L. Hughes) (vce and pf) (New York: G. Ricordi, 1959)
To a brown girl dead (Countee Cullen) (Row Music Co. 1956; also New York: G. Schirmer)

SACRED

The ballad of the brown king, Christmas cantata (L. Hughes) (soloists, mix-ch and pf) (Sam Fox, 1961)
Joshua fit da battle of Jericho (vce and orch; also vce and pf) (Beekman Music, 1967)
Mass in D-Minor (Latin) (ch and orch)
Go tell it on the mountain (mix-ch a-cap; also vce and pf) (Beekman Music, 1962)
Sinner please don't let this harvest pass (S and mix-ch; also vce and pf) (1970)
Standing in the need of prayer (S and mix-ch) (1970)
Every time I feel the spirit (vce and pf) (1970)
Five spirituals (vce and pf) (1946)
I'll reach to Heaven
Lord, I just can't keep from crying
Sit down, servant
This little light of mine

BALLET

Migration
Wings over broadway

THEATRE

Romey & Julie
Shakespeare in Harlem (L. Hughes-Robert Glenn production)
Tropics after dark (American Negro Exposition)
Troubled island (L. Hughes)
U.S.A. (John Dos Passos for ANTA)
Winter Night's Dream

ARRANGEMENTS

I wish I knew how it would feel to be free (S and mix-ch)

Publications

A Reminiscence. In Patterson, Lindsay. *The Negro in Music and Art*. New York: Publishers Company, 1967/1968.

Ref. 136, 142, 335, 347, 415, 523, 549, 563, 610, 622, 646

BONHOMME, Marie Therese

20th-century French conductor and composer of operas.
Ref. 226

BONINCONTRO, Gabrielle

French composer. b. 1878.

Composition

VOCAL

Les yeux (Sais...tu pourquoi) (vce and pf) (Curti)

Ref. 63

BONIS, Melanie. See MEL-BONIS

BONITA, Domina S. Delia

18th-century Italian composer.

Compositions

VOCAL

Songs

SACRED

Cantata
Mass (2 vces) (1723)

Ref. 465

BONNAY, Mlle.

19th-Century French composer.

Compositions

VOCAL

Premier recueil de XII romances ou airs avec accompagnement de piano-forte ou harpe

Ref. 125, 465

BOONE, Clara Lyle (pseud. Lyle de Bohun)

American publisher, teacher and composer. b. Stanton, KY, September 6, 1927. She obtained her B.A. from Center College, KY, where she studied composition under Samuel Sirua. She did graduate studies in music education at Radcliffe College and Harvard Graduate School of Education. At the University of Wisconsin she studied composition under Cecil Burleigh, at Harvard under Walter Piston and at the Aspen Music School under Darius Milhaud. She taught in six states. She owns and directs Arsis Press.

Compositions

ORCHESTRA

Annunciation of Spring (also pf) (1955, 1952)
Motive and chorale (cham) (1962)

CHAMBER

The Americas (fl, cl and bsn) (1960)

PIANO

Excursions (also brass wind ens) (1959)
Petite histoire (1949)

VOCAL

Academic prayer (mix-ch a-cap) (1957)
Alleluia (mix-ch a-cap) (1957)
Meditation (mix-ch a-cap) (1956)
Thou shalt light my lamp (mix-ch) (1955)
Who covets stars (ch a-cap) (1959)
Songs of estrangement (S and str qrt) (1958)
Beyond the stars (1970)
Celestia (1954)
Fantasia (1956)
Goodnight kiss (1955)
Lovely heart (1956)
Mirrored love (1961)
Sea thoughts (1954)
Slumber song (1957)
Sonnet (Shakespeare) (1957)
Time cannot claim this hour (1955)
When songs have all been sung (1956)
Winter song (1968)

Ref. composer, 474, 622, 643

BOORN-COCLET, Henriette. See VAN DEN BORN-COCLET, Henriette

BOOSEY, Beatrice Joyce (pseud. Eustace Phillan)

British pianist and composer. b. Shortlands, 1898. She studied composition under Harry Farjeon and the piano under Evlyn Howard-Jones.

Compositions

PIANO

The brocaded petticoat
Intermezzo
White heather

VOCAL
Evening over the forest
The hungry sea
Songs
Ref. 467

BOOZER, Patricia P.
American teacher and composer. b. Atlanta, March 14, 1947. She studied at Samford University under Newton Strandberg, James Jenson, Bob Burroughs and Philip Landgrave. She taught at the Trusswood School of Music, Birmingham from 1969 to 1971 and the Samford University Preparatory Department from 1971 to 1973 . She composed sacred choral pieces.
Ref. 142

BOPP VON OBERSTADT, Countess
19th-century German composer.
Compositions
CHAMBER
Mein Traum, op. 11 (vlc and pf) (Schmidt)
PIANO
Berceuse, op. 12 (Schmidt)
Butterfly-Marsch, op. 7 (Schmidt)
Passauer Walzer, op. 15 (Schmidt)
Phantastischer Tanz, op. 1 (Schmidt)
Two Melodies, op. 11 (Schmidt)
Valse K.S.W., op. 2 (Schmidt)
VOCAL
Songs incl.:
An die Melancholie, op. 14 (Schmidt)
Bitte, op. 6 (Schmidt)
Der Brief, den du geschrieben, op. 3 (Schmidt)
Der Nebel, op. 5 (Schmidt)
Der Tag ist in die Nacht verliebt, op. 13 (Schmidt)
Im Walde wandl'ich und weine, op. 8 (Schmidt)
Vorwurf, op. 10 (Schmidt)
Vergiftet sind meine Lieder, op. 9 (Schmidt)
Wie sehr ich dein, op. 4 (Schmidt)
Ref. 297

BOR, Modesta
20th-century Venezuelan choir conductor, teacher and composer. b. Juan Griego, Isla de Margarita. She studied in her home town under L.M. Gutierrez and A. Caraballo Reyes and in Caracas at the Escuela Superior de Musica under M.L. Rutundo, E. Arrarte, A. Estevez, V.E. Sojo and J.B. Plaza. She undertook postgraduate studies at the Tchaikovsky Conservatory in Moscow under S. Skripkov, D.R. Levitsky and A. Khachaturian. She was director of the musicology department of the organisation Servicio de Investigaciones Folkloricas Nacionales and the head of the Nucleo de Musica of the Direccion der Cultura de la U.C.V. She was founder of the Grupo Arpegio Choir and a choir-conductor in schools. She taught composition at the Jose Lorenzo Llamozas Music School. She received national prizes for many of her compositions.
Compositions
ORCHESTRA
Genocidio, symphonic poem (1970)
Oberture sinfonica (national music prize, 1963)
Suite para orchestra
CHAMBER
Sonata para violin y piano (vln and pf) (University of Venezuela) (national chamber music prize, 1960, 1963)
Sonata para viola y piano
Suite para violoncello y piano
Various polyphonic arrangements for quintets
PIANO
Quatro fugas
Several easy pieces
Suite criolla
Suite infantil
Waltzes
VOCAL
Jugando a la Sombra de una vieja plaza, cantata (A. Machado)
Himno de la Federacion de Centros Universitarios de la U.C.V., anthem, (prize, 1965)
La Manana Ajena (mix-ch) (municipal vocal prize, 1971)
Manchas Sonoras (mix-ch a-cap)
Primer ciclo de romanzas para contralto y piano (vce and pf) (A.E. Blanco)
Segundo ciclo de romanzas para contralto y piano (vce and pf) (nat. vocal music prize, 1962)
Tres canciones (vce and pf) (Rodriguez, Lezama, Granado) (nat. vocal prize, 1970)
Triptico sobre poesia cubana (Guillen, Ballagas)
Ref. A. Pedigo (Booneville, AK)

BORBOM, Maria dę Melo Furtado Caldeira Giraldes
Portuguese writer and composer. b. 1864; d. 1944. She was well educated in the classics, literature and music.
Compositions
VOCAL
As Minhas Asas (Garrett) (soloists and ch)
No Calvario (soloists and ch)
Auto do Fim do Dia (Antonio Correia de Oliveira)
Nocturno
SACRED
Ave Maria (Teofilo Braga)
Canticos Religiosos
Publications
Alguns Seculos de Musica.
As Nossas Poetisas.
Ecos do Passado.
Melodias Dispersas.
Melodias Portuguesas.
Na Renania.
Os Nossos Concertos.
Os Nossos Poetas.
Vibracoes de Hoje.
Several children's books, incl.:
Fados e Encantos.
Historias de Tia Lilly.
Quem Quer Linhas, Agulhas e Alfinetes?
Ref. 268

BORDERS, Barbara Ann
American organist, pianist, teacher and composer. b. Kansas City, May 9, 1949. After studying the piano and the organ privately she won a scholarship to continue her piano studies at Drake University, IA. She then went to the University of Kansas and received her B.M., M.M. and M.Phil. She teaches the piano and the organ privately in New York. She married William Krusemark, a professional singer and music teacher. PHOTOGRAPH.
Compositions
CHAMBER
Brass quintet (1971)
Three Modnars (ww trio) (1973)
Prisms (pf) (1976)
VOCAL
Epigram (S and str qrt) (1974)
Three songs (S, ob and pf) (1974)
To one in Bedlam (vce and pf) (1973)
SACRED
Words of faith (mix-ch and org) (1972)
Song of the Spirit (S, ob and pf) (1974)
Ref. composer

BORDEWIJK-ROEPMAN, Johanna
Dutch composer. b. Rotterdam, August 4, 1892; d. The Hague, October 6, 1971. She was self-taught and not aware of her talent as a composer until she was about 30. She began by composing little songs to the pictures of her children's books. She then received lessons in instrumentation from Eduard Flipse, conductor of the Rotterdam Philharmonic Orchestra. A visit to North Africa inspired her first suite for orchestra *The Garden of Allah*. After World War II she composed mainly for choir and carillon. In 1946 she was awarded a government prize for her *Piano Sonata*. Some of her works were commissioned by the Dutch government and various municipalities and she was honored with a royal distinction. She married the Dutch author F. Bordewijk. Her works are published by Donemus.
Compositions
ORCHESTRA
Symphony (1942)
Piano concerto (1940)
The Garden of Allah, suite
Three pieces (str orch) (1938)
Epiloog (1943)
CHAMBER
Sonata (vln and pf) (Alsbach)
PIANO
Debout, eveille-toi (1953)
Drie Dansen (1928)
Herfst (1930)

Het vissersdorp (1922)
Impromptu (1959)
Poolse suite (1931)
Sonata (1943) (government prize, 1946)
BELL CARILLON
Prelude and fugue 1950 (prize of the Amsterdam Bell-Ringers Assoc.)
Theme and variations 1950 (prize of the Amsterdam Bell-Ringers Assoc.)
Triptych (Rotterdam Bell-Ringers Assoc.) (1951)
VOCAL
Plato's dood, oratorio (1949)
Bierbaum lieder (soloist and orch) (1941)
De kroaie enden puijt (Don) (S and cham orch)
Holland (Don) (S and cham orch)
Les illuminations (S and orch) (1939)
Oranje may-lied (Don) (S and cham orch)
Ballade au hameau (mix-ch) (1938)
Barque enchantee (mix-ch) (1947)
Boerecharleston: Tulpebollen (P. van Ostayen) (m-ch) (1937)
Cruysiging (mix-ch) (1957)
Deemoed (m-ch) (1947)
De jager van eykhof (m-ch) (1939)
De lentewind (mix-ch) (1939)
De vogelverschrikker (mix-ch) (1940)
The dream-keeper (m-ch) (1947)
Extase (Victor Hugo) (mix-ch) (1938)
High flight (w-ch) (1955)
Ik groet U (m-ch) (1939)
Je maintiendrai (m-ch) (1938)
Le saint cycle (m-ch) (1957)
Les cinq doigts de la main (m-ch) (1951)
Mélopée (mix-ch) (1940)
Moeder des vaderlands (m-ch) (1947)
The moon was but a chin of gold (w-ch) (1962)
Pioniers (mix-ch) (1940)
Reflections (m-ch) (1948)
Ruiters (m-ch) (1938)
Three lyrics (mix-ch) (1948)
Uit het diepst van mijn hart (m-ch) (1944)
Vier puntdichten van Huygens (m-ch) (1951)
Wederopbouw (m-ch) (1954)
Ik wensche u gezelle (S and strs)
Lofpsalm (S, wind insts and perc) (1952)
Dutch, English and French songs (vce and pf) (1925-1950)
SACRED
De heilige cirkel (m-ch) (1950)
Naar Betlehem (m-ch) (1950)
Opstanding (mix-ch) (1957)
Palmendag (m-ch; also w-ch) (1951)
Psalm 136 (mix-ch) (1956)
OPERA
Rotonde, in 1 act (1943)
Bibliography
Paap, Wouter. *Johanna Bordewijk-Roepman. Mens en Melodie* 1. 1946: 1-1-106.
Ref. 44, 50, 52, 81, 169, 189, 280, 283, 465

BORGE, Michele
20th-century American composer of a string quartet.
Ref. Jeannie Pool (Los Angeles)

BORGES, Deolinda Eulalia Cordeiro
19th-century Portuguese composer.
Composition
PIANO
La guirlande de roses, waltz (1892)
Ref. 399

BORGHI, Faustina
Italian cornet player, organist and composer. b. ca. 1569. She was employed in the service of the Duke of Modena in 1596. She is mentioned in Giovanni Battista Spaccini's chronicle of Modenese life.
Ref. 128, 653

BORKOWICZ (Borkowiczowna), Maria
Polish pianist and composer. b. Warsaw, 1896. She studied the piano under S. Urstein.
Compositions
CHAMBER
Daphnis et Chloe (vln and pf)
Romanza e intermezzo boemo (vln and pf)
L'ultimo canto (vln and pf)
PIANO
Ghiribizzo
Idylle champetre
Incantanzione
Miniatures
Plaintes des fleurs
Ref. 8, 17, 23, 105, 107, 110, 118, 226

BORKOWICZOWNA, Maria. See BORKOWICZ, Maria

BORKOWSKI, Marian
B. 1934.
Composition
SACRED
Psalmus
Ref. Otto Harrassowitz (Wiesbaden)

BORON, Marion
20th-century American organist, professor and composer. She gained her B.Mus. from Boston University, M.A. from Smith College and a doctorate from Harvard University. She became professor of music at Boston State University.
Compositions
ORCHESTRA
Organ concerto
CHAMBER
Piano pieces
VOCAL
Pieces
Publications
Study Guide for Music Theory. 1974.
Music Appreciation: Competency-Based Approach. 1976.
Ref. 506

BORRAS I FORNELL, Teresa
Spanish composer. b. Barcelona, July 23, 1930. She studied on scholarships in Italy under Frazzi and Vignanelli. She studied composition under Rudolf Halffter. She composed works for chamber orchestra, a wind quintet, a trio, pieces for the cello, the guitar, the harp and the piano and choral pieces and songs.
Ref. International Council of Women

BORROFF, Edith
American organist, pianist, musicologist, professor and composer. b. New York, August 2, 1925. She was born into a musical family; her mother was Marie Christine Bergersen (q.v.) and her father was a tenor. Edith was educated as a pianist, giving her first public performance of a Mozart sonata in October, 1929. She also studied the piano under Louise Robyn and the organ under Claire Coci. She studied composition under Irwin Fischer in Chicago and obtained her B.Mus in 1946 and M.Mus. (composition) in 1948 from the American University. However, because of the prejudice against women composers in the 1940s and 1950s, she diverted the course of her studies to music history and musicology. In 1958 she received her Ph.D. history of music, at the University of Michigan under Louise Cuyler. She was professor and associate dean for interdisciplinary studies at Hillsdale College, MI, from 1958 to 1962; associate professor at the University of Winsconsin from 1962 to 1966 and professor at Eastern Michigan University. She received an Andrew Mellon postdoctoral award from 1960 to 1961 and a University of Wisconsin summer grant in 1964. In 1973 she became professor of music at the State University at Binghamton. PHOTOGRAPH.
Compositions
ORCHESTRA
Concerto for marimba and small orchestra (1981)
Idyll (vln and orch)
CHAMBER
Suite for percussion: Eight canons for six players (1985)
Christmas prelude on In dulci jubilo (2 fl, 2 hn and pf) (1951)
Game pieces (ww qnt) (1980)
Chance encounters (str qrt) (1974)
Three string quartets

String trio (1943)
Trio (sax, pf and perc) (1982)
Canons (fl and vla)
Sonata (vlc and pf) (1949)
Variations (vlc and pf) (1944)
Sonatina giocosa (vla and pf) (1953)
Voices in exile, canons (fl and vla) (1962)
Ions, 14 pieces in the form of a sonnet (fl and pf) (1968)
Divertimento (fl) (1980)
Horn sonata (1970)
Variations and theme for oboe (1959) (Sam Fox, 1962)
ORGAN
American variations (1982)
Passacaglia (1980)
Prelude in D (1950)
Three chorale preludes (1982)
PIANO
Sonata on English folk tunes (4 hands) (1978)
Fantasy (2 pf) (1985)
Pop's hot bath, rag (1972)
Suite
Tatterdemalion, rag
VOCAL
Monologue (B and orch)
Madrigals for women's voices (1951)
Modern love, song cycle (Keats, Shelley) (1979)
Other songs (Housman, Mew, Browning, Goethe, Stevenson and composer)
SACRED
Anthems (mix or w-ch)
Psalm of praise (1972)
Solo mass (vce and org)
INCIDENTAL MUSIC
Pygmalion (Shaw) (1955)
Madwoman (Giraudon) (1962)
MISCELLANEOUS
An American Olio
Publications
The Arts in the West through History.
Elisabeth Jacquet de la Guerre. Institute of Medieval Music, 1966.
Liberal Education: Past and Future.
Music in Europe and the United States: A History. Prentice-Hall, 1971.
Music in Perspective. With six LPs by Columbia Records with Marjory Irvin of Lawrence University. Harcourt Brace Jovanovich, 1976.
The Music of the Baroque. Wm. C. Brown, 1970. Reprinted, Da Capo, 1978.
Notations and Editions. A book in honor of Louise Cuyler. Wm. C. Brown, 1974. Reprinted, Da Capo, 1977.
Three American Composers.
Women Making Music. Chapter 1. Women and Secular Music in Gothic Europe. Ed. Jane Bowers and Judith Tick. University of Illinois Press, 1980.
Over 70 papers and articles.
Ref. composer, 142, 228, 622, 625, 643

BORRONI, Virginia
20th-century Italian composer of songs and an opera.
Ref. 465

BORTHWICK, Jane Laurie (pseud. H.L.L.)
Scottish translator and hymn writer. b. Edinburgh, April 9, 1813; d. Edinburgh, September 7, 1897. With her sister, Sarah Borthwick Findlater, she made a series of translations from German, calling the work 'Hymns from the Land of Luther' from which the initials of her pseudonym are derived.
Compositions
SACRED
Come labor on, who dares stand idle on the harvest plain
Be still my soul, the Lord is on thy side
Publications
Thoughts for Thankful Hours.
Ref. 79, 482, 646

BORTON, Alice
19th-century English pianist and composer. She was an A.R.A.M.
Compositions
ORCHESTRA
Andante and rondo (pf and orch)
PIANO
Sieg, Lied (4 hands) (Willocks)
Suite de pieces (Ashdown)
Suite in the olden style
Three Scottish pieces (Ashdown)
VOCAL
Songs incl.:
Coleen (ch and military band) (arr E. Sharpe) (Rudall)
Coronation march song, God bless King Edward and Our Gracious Queen (mix-vces) (Novello)
Are all the sweet days o'er (Willocks)
Barbara Deane (Ashdown)
Birds in the high hail garden
Do the next thing (Larway)
Farewell to England's ladies fair, part songs (Curwen)
Go not happy day!
In summer
Margaret to Dolcino (Chappell)
A morning carol (Ricordi)
A voice by the cedar tree (Ricordi)
When summer was! (Ricordi)
SACRED
Sing O daughter of Zion (S and ch) (Novello)
De nobis pacem (Chappell)
ARRANGEMENTS
Irene (from the Minuet in the 18th piano sonata, op. 31, no. 3 by Beethoven adapted to words from Metastasio's Canzonets, with an English translation) (Novello)
Ref. 260, 297

BOSCH, Elisa
19th-century composer.
Compositions
ORCHESTRA
Légère et gracieuse, schottische
PIANO
Le chant des cigales, polka-mazurka (Durand)
Colombine, danse des clowns (Heugel)
Djemma, mazurka (Gregh)
Espère, melody (Labbe)
Gavotte, op. 57 (Durand)
Je veux plaire, polka-mazurka (Durand)
Le Mançanarez, bolero (Durand)
Le myosotis, polka-mazurka (Durand)
Pavane, air de danse du XVII siecle (Durand)
Rêve enchanteur, op. 55 (Durand)
La sensitive, valse (Durand)
Trois pensées melodiques, op. 15 (Heugel)
La villageoise, polka-mazurka (Durand)
VOCAL
Dors, enfant, song (Durand)
Valsons toujours, valse chantée (Labbe)
Ref. 297

BOSCH Y PAGES, Luisa
Swiss-Spanish harpist, lecturer and composer. b. Alstadten St. Gall, Switzerland, ca. 1880; d. Barcelona, 1961. She studied at the Geneva Conservatory under J. Dalcroze, Barblan, Humbert and Tramonti. In Paris she studied the harp under Hasselmans and Verdalle and in Barcelona under Pedrell. She gave concerts in Switzerland, Spain and France. She taught the harp at the Geneva Conservatory in 1916 and in Lausanne and elsewhere. At the International Exhibition of Music in Geneva, 1927, she won a prize for a unique collection of antique musical instruments. She contributed articles to specialized magazines.
Compositions
CHAMBER
Prelude (2 hp and str qrt)
Petit prelude (hp)
VOCAL
Pieces (vce and hp)
Ref. 100, 361

BOSENHOENIG, Josefa Barbara. **See AURENHAMMER, Josefa Barbara von**

BOSHKOFF, Ruth
20th-century composer.
Composition
PERCUSSION
All around the buttercup, for small children (Orff insts) (Schott, 1984)
Ref. Blackwell catalogue (Oxford)

BOSMANS, Henriette Hilda

Dutch concert pianist and composer. b. Amsterdam, December 5, 1895; d. July 2, 1952. She was the daughter of Henri Bosmans, solo cellist of the Concertgebouw Orchestra and Sarah Bosmans-Benedicts, pianist and teacher. Henriette graduated from the Amsterdam Conservatory with honors, at the age of 17. She enjoyed a great reputation as a pianist and played in almost every country in Europe. She began to compose at an early age, showing a preference for her father's instrument, the cello. She studied under Cornelius Dopper and then Willem Pijper in 1927. She was the accompanist of the French singer Noemie Perugia, a partnership that inspired her to write a large number of songs. DISCOGRAPHY.

Compositions

ORCHESTRA

Cello concerto No. 1 (1922)
Cello concerto No. 2 (1924)
Piano concerto (1929)
Concert piece (fl and orch) (1929)
Concert piece for violin and orchestra (1934)
Concertino (pf and orch) (1929)
Poeme (vlc and orch) (1929)

CHAMBER

String quartet (1928)
Trio (1921)
Cello sonata (1919)
Violin sonata (1918)
Impressions (vlc and pf) (1926)
Cadenzas for Mozart's violin concertos in G-Major and A-Major
Six preludes (pf) (1918)

VOCAL

Belsazar (H. Heine) (Cont and orch) (1936)
Doodenmarsch (declamation and orch) (1946)
L'Anneau (vce and pf)
Aurore (vce and pf)
Chanson (vce and pf)
Chansons des escargots qui vont à l'enterrement
La chanson des marins hales
La chanson du Chiffonier
La chanson Fatale
Complainte du petit cheval blanc
Je ne suis pas seul
Een lied vor spanje
Les medisants
Le nafrage
On frappe
Pour toi mon amour
Le regard eternal
Rondel (vce and pf)
Songs of German poems incl.:
Vier liederen (1921-1950)
Drei liederen (1927)

SACRED

Ave Maria (vce and pf)

Bibliography

Elst, Nancy van der. *Henriette Bosmans als liederen Componiste.* Mens en Melodie 7 (1952): 173-175, 197, 198.

Paap Wouter. *De Componiste Henriette Bosmans.* Mens en Melodie 2 (1947): 72-76.

Ref. 8, 13, 15, 22, 26, 40, 74, 79, 96, 100, 110, 169, 183, 280, 283, 433, 563

BOSSER, Dagmar. See BOESSER, Dagmar

BOSTELMANN, Ida

American composer. b. Corning, NY, 1894. She graduated from the Corning Conservatory, founded by her father and the Institute of Musical Art. She also studied under Betsy Culp, Goetschius, Horatio Parker and Rubin Goldmark.

Compositions

CHAMBER

An old fashioned love song (vln)

PIANO

Country dance
The doll's parade
Dream music
Prelude

VOCAL

The harp, song
Love goes as the wind blows, song
The nightingale, song
Sally poses, song

OPERETTA

The Azure Lily

Ref. 292

BOTET, Maria Emma

Cuban pianist, teacher and composer. b. Matanzas, 1903. She studied under pianist-composers Hubert de Blanck and J. Nin and writer Alejo Carpentier. She taught the piano at de Blanck's private school of music and then the State School Amadeo Rolden in Havana. Her compositions are based on Cuban folklore.

Compositions

PIANO

Suite cubana
Cajita de musica que toca una cubana
Over 20 small pieces for piano students (Havana: Diciones de Blanck)

VOCAL

Songs incl.:
Canta la brisa en la rama (vce and pf) (1955)
Duerme a mi cantar (vce and pf)
Opresion (vce and pf) (1954)
Romance criollo (vce and pf) (1951)
Serenata breve (vce and pf) (1949)

Ref. Edgardo Martin (Havana), 604

BOTIANO (Botianu), Helene von (Elena)

German composer.

Compositions

PIANO

Pieces, ops. 5, 6 and 21 (Bremen)

Ref. 276

BOTIANU, Elena. See BOTIANO, Helene von

BOTSFORD, Talitha

20th-century American pianist, violinist, artist, poetess and composer. b. Millport, NY. She graduated from Ithaca College in 1922. She performed as a violinist and pianist at a wide range of concerts from 1922 to 1979. She gave many watercolor exhibitions and contributed poems to newspapers and journals.

Compositions

PIANO

Carnival capers (1946)
Danse de ballet (1925)
Frolic (1946)
Jolly dance (1928)
Whimsical dance (1929)

Ref. 506

BOTTAGISIO, Jacqueline

20th-century Australian composer.

Composition

FILM MUSIC

Pilgrimage of the Devil-Worshippers (Yazidis Series) (1972)

Ref. 442

BOTTELIER, Ina

20th-century composer.

Composition

CHAMBER

Pavane (fl and gtr) (Broekmans & Van Poppel, 1983)

Ref. Blackwell catalogue (Oxford)

BOTTINI, Marianna, Marchioness (nee Andreotti or Andreozzi)

Italian harpist and composer. b. Lucca, November 7, 1802; d. Lucca, January 24, 1858. She studied the harp under Domenico Quilici and showed early talent. Because of her outstanding compositions, she was made an honorary member of the Philharmonic Academy, Bologna.

Compositions

ORCHESTRA

Symphonies for grand orchestra
Piano concertos
Overtures

VOCAL

Pieces for voice, harp and piano

SACRED

Cantata (ch) (ded Orsuici family)
St. Cecile, cantata
Messa da requiem, mass (ch and orch)

Magnificat (4 vces and orch)
Stabat Mater (3 vces)
Vespers (4 vces and insts)
OPERETTA
Elena e Gerardo, in 2 acts
Ref. 2, 105, 129, 226, 276, 307, 347, 361

BOUCHARD, Linda L.

Canadian flautist, conductor, poetess, teacher and composer. b. Val d'Or, Quebec, May 21, 1957. She studied composition under Henry Brant, Vivian Fine (q.v.), Ursula Mamlock (q.v.) and Elias Tanenbaum; conducting under Henry Brant, Neely Bruce and Arthur Weisberg and the flute under Samuel Baron, Linda Chesis, Sue Ann Kahn, Alain Marion, Harvey Sollberger and Ransom Wilson. She received her B.A. (flute and composition) from Bennington College, 1979 and M.A. (composition) from the Manhattan School of Music, New York City in 1982. She taught the flute and music appreciation at high schools in Quebec before becoming a teaching assistant at Bennington College in 1978. She was chosen as the Canadian representative at the First Congress on Women in Music in New York City in 1981.

Compositions
ORCHESTRA
Essay I (cham orch) (1978)
CHAMBER
Before the city set (8 vla, ob, hn and perc) (1981)
Revelling of men (trb sextet and str qrt) (1984)
Quican (3 picc, 4 s-fl, 2 a-fl and b-fl) (1978)
Of a star unfolding (8 perc and prep pf) (1979)
Rocking glances (fl, ob, vln, vla, vlc, man, gtr and perc) (1979)
New paths, aleatory piece (mix ens) (1975)
Icy cruise (picc, trp, vla, vlc, d-b and hp) (1984)
Jeu chromatique (sax qrt) (1976)
Ma lune maligne (fl, vla, hp and perc) (prize NACUSA Composers Contest, 1979)
Stormy light (str qrt) (1981)
Variations (fl, vla, hp and perc) (1980)
Aspects d'un couloir (str trio or 2 antiphonal str trio) (1979)
Five grins (fl, ob, vlc and hpcd) (1984)
Poing de coins (fl, bsn, vln and vlc) (1978)
Quartet for Tafelmusik
Circus faces (fl, vla and vlc) (1984)
Chaudière à traction (fl and pf) (1979)
Le cri-geste (pf) (1977)
Web-trap (1982)
VOCAL
Anticipation of Priscilla (composer) (m-S, fl, vln, vla, vlc, pf and perc) (1980)
A Christmas pot-pourri (S, fl, vln, 2 gtr, pf and perc) (1975)
Tout ça as thought (Genevieve Beaudet) (S, fl, vln, pf and perc) (1977)
L'Homme qui change (G. Beaudet) (B, bsn and vlc) (1978)
ELECTRONIC
Propos (trp and tape) (1984)
Piece hibou (tape) (1981)
MULTIMEDIA
Glances (vlc and dancer) (1980)
Glances II, under water (vlc and dancer) (1981)
INCIDENTAL MUSIC
Triske Lion, concert drama (3 vces and ens) (1982)
Ref. composer, AMC newsletter 1985, LWC newsletter 1984, 624, 625

BOUCHER, Lydia (Sister Marie Therese)

Canadian organist, pianist, violinist, teacher and composer. b. St. Ambroise de Kildare, Quebec, February 28, 1890. She studied under Auguste Descarries (piano and composition), Louis Michiels, Rodolphe Mathieu and Claude Champagne (composition), Raoul Paquet (organ) and J. Dalcourt (violin). She obtained a B.Mus. from the National Conservatory of Montreal (1931) and a licentiate diploma from the Academie de Musique de Quebec. For 41 years she taught music in the various convents of the Soeurs de Sainte- Anne.

Compositions
PIANO
Eclogue
Pastorale
Prelude
Prelude in D-Minor
La ronde des aiguilles (Editions Canadiennes)
VOCAL
Anges gardiens de nos tombeaux (ch and org) (1949)
Cent ans! (ch, pf and str qrt) (1948)
Chant de triomphe et de victoire (ch, str qrt and pf) (1948)
Dans l'urne d'une fleur (Musica Enr.)
Ecoute
Et je t'apporterais des fleurs
Louange à Sainte-Anne
Maman
La messe en cantiques
Nos heures d'aujourd'hui (Belgo-Canadienne)
Notre-Dame de Montréal
O Marie conçue sans perche
Papa
Petite Thérèse
Salut petit Jésus
Sourire de l'an qui s'achève
SACRED
L'Oeuvre d'Esther Blondin, oratorio
Heureux ceux qui sont morts dans la paix du Seigneur (ch and org) (1949)
Noël, chansonette (Editions Canadiennes)
Offertoire (ch and pf) (1950)
Sur le Mont des Béatitudes (soloists, ch and pf) (1950)
A Marie par Sainte-Anne (Belgo-Canadienne)
Ave Maria
Ref. 133

BOULANGER, Lili Juliette Marie Olga

French cellist, harpist, organist, pianist and composer. b. Paris, August 21, 1893; d. Mezy, March 15, 1918. Her paternal grandparents, Frederi and Marie Julie, had received prizes from the Paris Conservatoire. Her father, Ernest, was a composer who taught voice at the Paris Conservatoire for 25 years. Her mother, Princess Raissa, was a singer. Her sister Nadia (q.v.) was a well-known teacher and composer and Lili was a pupil of hers who from a very early age showed exceptional musical talent. At three years old, she accompanied Nadia to her music classes and at six she sight-read Faure's songs to her sister's piano accompaniment. At this time she suffered from a chronic and painful illness that was to hamper her studies throughout her life and eventually cause her death. In spite of her sporadic studies, at 16 she could play the piano, the violin, the cello and the harp. In 1909 she decided to become a composer, being tutored by Georges Caussade in counterpoint, fugue and composition. She also studied composition under Paul Vidal at the Paris Conservatoire in 1912. When she was 19, Lili won the Premier Grand Prix de Rome with her cantata *Faust et Helene*, being the first woman to win this prize. This enabled her to stay at the Villa Medici in Rome, from 1914 until the outbreak of World War 1, when poor health forced her return to Paris, where she worked for a humanitarian organisation helping drafted musicians and their families. In 1916 she returned to the Villa Medici, but illness soon forced her to return to France. She continued to compose, being anxious to complete some major works before her death. Her last compositions were dictated to Nadia from her sick-bed. She composed over 50 works before dying at the age of 25 years. DISCOGRAPHY. PHOTOGRAPH.

Compositions
ORCHESTRA
D'un soir triste, symphonic poem
CHAMBER
String quartet
Cortège (vln, fl and pf) (Paris: Ricordi, 1914)
Harmonies du soir (vln, vlc and pf)
D'un matin de printemps (fl and pf) (1917)
Nocturne (pf and vln or vlc or fl)
Three pieces for violin and piano
PIANO
Dans l'immense tristesse (1916)
D'un jardin clair (1914)
D'un vieux jardin (1914) (Ricordi)
Thème et variations
VOCAL
Faust et Hélène, cantata, lyric episode from Goethe (3 soloists and orch) (1913) (Belwin-Mills; Ricordi) (Prix de Rome)
Baume du fond de l'abime (A, ch and orch) (1914)
Hymne au soleil (solo, ch and orch) (1913)
Pour les funerailles d'un soldat (solo, ch and orch) (1913) (Belwin-Mills and Ricordi)
Soir sur la plaine (S, ch and orch) (1918)
Vieille prière Bouddhique (T, ch and orch) (1917)
Les Sirènes (S, ch and pf) (1912)
Renouveau (vocal qrt and pf) (1912)
Attente (vce and pf) (1910)
Clairieres dans le ciel, 13 melodies (Francis Jammes) (T and pf) (1914) (Paris: Ricordi, 1919)
La Retour (vce and pf) (1924)
Retour d'Ulysse (vce and pf) (Ricordi, 1913)
Reflets (vce and pf) (1912)
La source
Sous bois
SACRED
Psalm 24 (ch and orch) (Durand et Cie, 1916)
Psalm 129 (ch and orch) (Durand et Cie, 1921)

Psalm 130, De Profundis (S or Cont, mix-ch and orch) (Durand et Cie, 1916)
Pie Jesu (m-S, hp and org) (1918) (Durand et Cie)
INCIDENTAL MUSIC
La Princesse Maleine (Maeterlinck)

Bibliography

Chapman, Mary Helen. *The Life and Works of Lili Boulanger*. Indiana Univerity.
Dumesnil, P. *Portraits de musiciens français*. Paris, 1938.
Landormy, P. *Lili Boulanger*. Musical Quarterly, October 1930.
Lebeau, Elisabeth. *Lili Boulanger: 1893-1918*. Paris: Bibliotheque Nationale, 1968. Chronology of Boulanger family, with biography of Lili, including various items surrounding her life and death.
Mauclari, C. *La vie et l'oeuvre de Lili Boulanger*. Revue Musicale, August, 1921.
Palmer, Christopher. *Lili Boulanger, 1893-1918*. Musical Times, March 1968, pp. 227-228. Discusses her achievements in musical compositions.
Reeser, E. *Lili Boulanger*. De Muziek 7 (1933): 5-6.
Rosenstiel, Leonie. *The Life and Works of Lili Boulanger*. Madison, NJ: Fairleigh Dickinson University Press, 1976.

Ref. 22, 44, 173, 214, 246, 280, 347, 431, 433, 524, 563, 609, 622, 637

BOULANGER, Nadia Juliette

French organist, conductor, music critic, lecturer and composer. b. Paris, September 16, 1887; d. October 22, 1979. She came from a family of musicians and was the elder sister of Lili Boulanger (q.v.) and first taught by their mother. At the Paris Conservatoire she studied composition under Gabriel Faure, accompaniment under Vidal and the organ under Widor and Guilmant. She won first prizes in harmony, counterpoint, fugue, the organ and accompaniment. At the age of 21 she won the Second Grand Prix de Rome for her cantata *La Sirene* in 1908. From 1909 to 1924 she was an assistant in the harmony class at the Paris Conservatoire. Nadia's great fame lay in her brilliance as a teacher of composers and she had the advantage of being able to speak English. Paul Dukas, who taught composition at the Paris Conservatoire, recommended her to 16 Americans who arrived in Paris in the 1920s to complete their musical education. She succeeded Paul Dukas at the Ecole Normale de Musique in Paris, where she taught harmony and composition from 1920 to 1939. She taught at the American Conservatory in Fontainebleau from 1921 to 1930, when she became director of the school. In 1924 she appeared as an organ soloist with the New York Symphony Orchestra under Serge Koussevitsky. With the outbreak of World War II Nadia went to the United States, where she taught at Wellesley and Radcliffe College and the Juilliard School of Music. She was the first woman to conduct the Boston Symphony Society Orchestra in London in 1937, the first woman to conduct the New York Philharmonic Orchestra in 1939 and later, the first woman to conduct the Halle Orchestra in 1963. From 1945, she taught a class in accompaniment at the Paris Conservatoire. Nadia was Maitre de Chapelle to the Prince of Monaco and selected and conducted the program performed on the occasion of his marriage to Grace Kelly in 1956. She had many honors bestowed on her, including honorary doctorates from the universities of Oxford, Newcastle and Harvard. She was music critic for the *Monde Musical*, the *Revue Musicale* and the *Spectateur*. She instituted the Societe des Concerts and the Societe Bach and was engaged in training and conducting various choral groups in Paris. Nadia was probably one of the greatest composition teachers of modern times. Among her students were George Gershwin, Jean Francaix, Igor Markevitch, Aaron Copland, Walter Piston, Roy Harris, Roger Sessions, Louise Talma, Elie Siegmeister, David Diamond, Elliot Carter and many others. It was calculated that she had taught some 600 Americans alone. She was a friend of Stravinsky and famous for her interpretation of Faure's *Requiem*. She conducted and taught in England, the United States, Canada and most European countries. DISCOGRAPHY. PHOTOGRAPH.

Compositions

ORCHESTRA
Rhapsody (pf and orch)
CHAMBER
Three pieces (pf and org) (1915) (Hengel)
Impromptu (vlc and pf)
Piece sur des airs populaires flamands (org)
Lux interna
Other organ and instrumental pieces
VOCAL
La Sirène, cantata (Prix de Rome, 1908)
Les heures claires, cycle of songs (W. Verhaeren) (Paris: Hengel, 1909-1912)
Soir d'hiver (Hengel)
Songs
OPERA
La Ville Morte, after La Citta Morta by d'Annunzio (with R. Pugno, 1911)
Driegouchka, lyric scenario

Publications

Kodaly Memorial. Budapest. Musika XV/12. December 1972.
Strecher Festschrift, An Ludwig Strecher. Ed. Dahluis. Mainz: Schott, 1973

Bibliography

Alexandresou. *La aniversarea unei mari muziciene*. Bucharest. Muzica XXII/8, August 1972.
Boulanger-20th Century Music Was Born in Her Classroom. New York Times, September 11, 1977.
Kendall, Alan. *The Tender Tyrant Nadia Boulanger*. London: Macdonald and Jane's, 1976.
Monsaignon, Mlle. Bruno. *Entretiens avec Nadia Boulanger*. (Luynes: Van de Velde 1980).
Monsaignon, Mlle. Bruno. *Mademoielle - Conversations with Nadia Boulanger*. Trans. Robyn Marsack. Paris: Carconet, 1985.
Nadia Boulanger, Teacher of Top Composers Dies. New York Times, October 23, 1979.
Rosenstiel, Leoni. Nadia Boulanger. *A Life in Music*. W.W. Norton & Co. NY.
Russell, Thomas A. *Nadia Boulanger*. Musical Opinion 61: 214-215.
Stevens, Elizabeth M.. *The Influence of Nadia Boulanger on Composition in the U.S.A.*. Thesis. Boston University, 1975.
Valery, Paul. *Nadia Boulanger*. La Revue Internationale de Musique 93, October-November 1938, 607-608.
Walters, Teresa Hietbrink. *Musical Works and Aesthetics of Nadia Boulanger*.

Ref. Peabody Institute, 2, 4, 5, 8, 9, 13, 17, 22, 44, 64, 70, 74, 77, 79, 94, 96, 105, 106, 107, 135, 163, 183, 189, 206, 226, 264, 361, 524, 563, 570, 580, 590, 610, 612, 622, 637

BOULEAU-NELDY, Mlle. A.

19th-century French composer.

Compositions

VOCAL
Songs
SACRED
Messe en do meneur, op. 56
Ref. 465

BOULOGNE, Julia R.C.

19th-20th-century composer.

Compositions

CHAMBER
Bouquet de roses, waltzes (vlns, hn, trp and d-b)
Fado Antoninho (pf)
Ref. 399

BOUNDY, Kate

19th-century English composer.

Composition

CHAMBER
O Lord of Hearts, church music
Ref. 276

BOUQUET, Marie-Therese

French musicologist and composer. b. Dieppe, January 26, 1939. She studied at the Paris Conservatoire, where she won first prizes for music history and musicology. She obtained a doctorate in European studies at the Sorbonne and a diploma from the Music School of Paris. She was a jurist for the Paris Conservatoire. She composed transcriptions of various 17th and 18th-century works from the Savoy region of France and piano pieces.

Publications

La Capella musicale dei duchi di Savoia dal 1450 al 1500 dal 1504-1550. Rivista Italiana di Musicologia (Florence), 1969 and 1972.
Musique et musiciens à Annecy, les Maitrises, 1630-1789. Paris, 1969.
Musique et musiciens à Turin de 1648 à 1785. Paris, 1969.
Ref. 77, 206, 457

BOURGES, Clementine de

French poetess and composer. b. Lyons; d. September 30, 1561. She mastered several instruments and her great learning was acknowledged by her contemporaries. Grove and Mendel have ranked her compositions with those of the great composers of her time. She was married to an officer, Jean de Peyrat, who was killed in a clash with the Huguenots in 1560. A year later she died of grief. She is often confused with Clement de

Bourges, a composer also from Lyons and living approximately the same time, who may also have been the composer of *Da bei rami*. In J. Paix's *Orgeltabulaturbuch*, together with works of Orlandus Lassus, Walther and Senfl, there is a composition attributed to Clementine *Da bei rami* for a four-part chorus, inscribed *Cl. de Bourges*.
Ref. 8, 129, 226, 335

BOURGOGNE, Marie de
French composer. ca. 1450. DISCOGRAPHY.
Compositions
VOCAL
Beaulté, basse-danse, song
La Franchoise nouvelle, basse-danse, song
Dances and songs from the Middle Ages (2 S and a-rec) (Vienna: Universal)
Ref. 563

BOUTRON, Madeleine
French pianist, teacher and composer. b. Chavigni, Vienne, September 1, 1893. She started piano lessons at the age of four with her mother, who was an excellent musician. When Madeleine was 14, her family moved to Mauze, where her mother became a pupil of Falkenberg, a teacher at the conservatory. Madeleine and her sister followed in their mother's footsteps and later Madeleine herself studied under Falkenberg. In 1907 she moved to Nice, where she studied for her teacher's exam at the Lycee and also for the exams of the Monde Musical, which later became the Ecole Normale de Musique. She studied harmony, musical analysis and history of music. She did not pass her exams because of financial difficulties caused by the war in 1914 and her father's illness and death in 1919. Other than encouragement to compose from Ribellet, she was self-taught. She went to Paris in 1920, where she took up music teaching. PHOTOGRAPH.
Compositions
CHAMBER
String quartet (1917-1918)
Trio bref (vlc, vln and pf) (1927-1928)
Action de graces (vln and org) (1947)
De l'aube à la nuit (vln and pf) (1952)
Offertoire (vln and org) (1947)
Poème (vlc and pf) (1924-1925)
Sonata (vln and pf) (1917)
Thrène, evocation, rythme de danse (vlc and pf) (1928-1930)
PIANO
Danses à deux (2 pf) (1928)
Jour de fête (4 hands) (1942) (Lemoine, 1961)
Air de chasse (1928)
Deux Rêveries (1960) (Philippe, 1961)
Kitou veut endormir son chien (1928) (Gallett, 1944)
Methode (Ouvrieres, 1955)
Mouvement de danse (1931)
Le petit berger (1929) (Lemoine, 1954)
Petites esquisses (1913) (Schneider, 1932)
Poème romantique (1913)
Le révérence (1930) (Gallet, 1958)
Sept pensées (1927)
Sonatine champêtre (1919) (Schneider, 1932)
Sur la mer (1930)
Visions (1929)
Quatre caractères de valses (1930-1932)
Trois estampes japonaises (1932)
VOCAL
Elégie (2 vces) (1927) (Schneider, 1932)
Chansons éternelles (vce and pf) (Fortin, 1936)
Deux chansons Ronsard, Verlaine (1915-1916)
Trois nocturnes (vce and pf) (1921, 1922, 1923) (Heugel, 1927)
L'Absence (1917) (Delriue-Nice)
Approx. 10 songs
SACRED
Ave verum (4 vces) (Delrieu, 1951)
Et verbum (2 vces) (Editions Ouvrieres, 1949)
Invidata (4 vces) (1945) (Schola Cantorum, 1950)
Messe 4 voix (1940) (Editions Ouvrieres, 1957)
Tantum ergo (4 vces) (1945) (Editions Ouvrieres, 1949)
Vous qui pleurez (4 vces) (1917) (Editions Ouvrieres, 1949)
O salutaris hostia (1947)
Pater, ave (1937-1938)
Pater noster (1947)
Tota pulchra (1946)
Ref. Marie-Jose Charpentier (Paris)

BOUVARDINSKA, Mlle.
18th-century French composer.
Composition
VOCAL
Le rigueurs de Climene (Paris: Mercure de France, 1740)
Ref. 65, 405

BOVET, Hermine
German pianist and composer. b. Hoxter, January 3, 1842. She studied at Cologne Conservatory under Gustav Jensen, S. de Lange, E. Mertke, Mlle. Schneider, and Elisa Polko. She taught the piano to Schwelm, Barmen, Elberfeld and Honnef.
Composition
VOCAL
Unser Leben in vier Jahreszeiten (composer)
Publications
Anfangstudien in 5 Tonen und getrennten Schluesseln. For piano.
Anregungen in Liedern, Tanzen und Choralen.
Musical Catechism, for Young Voices.
Proben aus Werken alter Meister. Tonger.
School Theory Practice. For piano, 4 vols.
Ref. 105, 276, 297

BOVIA (Bovio), Laura
16th-century Italian instrumentalist and composer in the service of the Court of Mantua. She was educated in the convent of San Geminiano, Modena, although she did not become a nun. She was reputed by Camillo Cortellini to be extremely skilled in both playing and composing.
Compositions
VOCAL
Madrigals (5 vces) (Ferrara: Baldini)
Motets
Ref. 25, 264, 502, 653

BOYACK, Jeanette
20th-century American composer of songs and a dramatic scene.
Ref. 465

BOYCE, Blanche Ula
20th-century American organist, pianist, lecturer and composer. b. Bloomington, IL. She studied music at the Bush-Chicago Conservatory of Music (B.Mus. 1925; M.Mus. 1926) and from 1930 to 1931 went to Paris, where she was a pupil of Marcel Dupre. She was appointed to the music faculty of Bush Conservatory, 1915 to 1918, Chicago Conservatory from 1924 to 1936 and Lake Forest University, 1927 to 1929. She was made dean of the American Guild of Organists in 1935. In 1960 she won first prize for piano composition from the National League of American Pen Women.
Compositions
ORGAN
Marriage service
Sonata
Wedding music
VOCAL
The Sleeping Beauty, song cycle
Ref. 84

BOYCE, Ethel Mary
English pianist and composer. b. Chertsey, Surrey, October 5, 1863; d. 1936. She studied at the Royal Academy of Music under Walter Macfarren (piano) and F.W. Davenport (composition). She won the Lady Goldsmid Scholarship in 1885 and in 1886 was a Potter Exhibitor and winner of the Sterndale Bennett Prize. She received the Lucas medal for composition in 1889.
Compositions
ORCHESTRA
March in E (1889)
CHAMBER
Eight pieces (vln and pf) (Novello)
PIANO
Berceuse (Ashdown)
A book of fancies
By the brook, sketch (Ashdown)
Minuet in C-Minor (Ashdown)
Petite valse (Ashdown)
Songs and dances for the piano (Curwen)
To Phyllis, 4 short pieces (Ashdown)
Valse in F (Ashdown)

VOCAL
Young Lochinvar, cantata (B, mix-ch and orch) (1891)
The sands of Corriemie (w-vces) (1895)
Dream child's lullaby
Love has come, part song
So she went drifting, song (Leonard)
A song of Summer
SACRED
The Lay of the Brown Rosary, cantata (S, A, mix-ch and orch) (1890)
Ref. 8, 226, 276, 297

BOYD, Anne Elizabeth

Australian flautist, pianist, recorder player, lecturer and composer. b. Sydney, April 10, 1946. She spent her childhood on a remote country farm in Queensland and taught herself the recorder at the age of five. She learned to play the piano at the age of 11 and composed a number of small pieces. She won the ABC Children's Hour Commonwealth Music Award for *Air and Variations* at the age of 13. She went to Sydney in 1959 and studied at the N.S.W. Conservatory (harmony and analysis) and the flute under Victor McMahon. In 1963 she enrolled at the University of Sydney, where she studied composition for her B.A.hons. under Peter Sculthorpe. She won the Frank Albert prize for music in 1966. In the same year she made her debut at the Adelaide Festival of Arts. She then joined the orchestra of the Australian ballet and toured with it for the rest of the year. Anne was active in the Australian music world and founded Australia's first contemporary music magazine *Music Now*. In 1969 she received the first Commonwealth overseas grant for composition and went to England to study for a Ph.D. (composition) at the University of York. Her teachers were Wilfred Mellers and Bernard Rands. She became a lecturer in music at the University of Sussex in 1972. She was a finalist for the Radcliffe music award in 1975 with her composition *As I Crossed a Bridge of Dreams*. Her studies of ethnomusicology, in particular her love and knowledge of the Far East, especially Japan and Java, have left their mark on her compositions. Her compositions are all published by Faber Music.

Compositions
ORCHESTRA
L'altro (1964)
Terra australis (1963)
The voice of the Phoenix (1971)
CHAMBER
Greetings to Victor McMahon (12 fl) (1971)
As it leaves the bell (pf, 2 hp and 4 perc) (1973)
The Metamorphoses of the solitary female Phoenix (wind qnt, pf and perc) (1971)
Exegesis No. 1 (4 fl and 2 picc) (1964)
The Creation (5 rec and perc) (1965)
As far as crawls the toad, children's pieces (5 perc) (1970)
Hidden in a white cloud (fls and vlcs or wind qnt) (1970)
Landscape of dreams (qnt) (1967)
The fall of Icarus (fl, vl, vlc and pf) (1966)
String quartet No. 1, Tu dai oan (Vietnamese folk song) (1968)
String quartet No. 2, Play on the Water (1973) (Klee)
Dies non (fl, picc and pf) (1965)
Synchromy No. 1, trio (ob, cl and bsn) (1964)
Trio (fl, vln and pf) (1962)
Trio (ob, vln and vlc) (1967)
Air and variations (fl and pf) (1960)
Goldfish through summer rain (fl and pf)
Rain on Castle Island (Kitahara Hakusko) (perc and pf)
Four studies (fl) (1966)
Pieces (fl) (1966)
PIANO
Angklung (1974)
Infinity (1964)
Three pieces (1965)
VOCAL
La luna asoma (Lorca) (school-ch and orch) (1965)
Summer nights (T, str orch and perc) (1976)
As I crossed a bridge of dreams (ch a-cap) (1975)
My name is Tran (S and ens) (1982)
SACRED
Alma Redemptoris Mater (2 ch and 2 pf) (1968)
BALLET
The stairway (3 insts and perc) (1968)
OPERETTA
The little mermaid, for children (1976)
THEATRE
The rose garden (Robin Hamilton) (1972)
Mr. Fraser (1976)
ELECTRONIC
Chelidiones (fl, picc and magnetic tape) (1965)
MULTIMEDIA
Games (1969)
Nocturnal images (junk insts) (1965)
Prologue for a dinner (1965)
FILM MUSIC
Aurora Australis (1969)
It Droppeth as the Gentle Rain (1963)
MISCELLANEOUS
La tête du mort (1964)
Ref. composer, 70, 77, 203, 206, 412, 442

BOYD, Elisabeth

18th-century English composer.

Composition
OPERA
Don Sancho, or The Student's Whim
Ref. 307

BOYD, Jeanne Margaret

American accompanist, teacher and composer. b. Mt. Carroll, IL, February 25, 1890. She studied under Emil Liebling.

Compositions
ORCHESTRA
Song against Ease, symphonic poem (1940)
Symphonic suite (1922)
Introduction and fugue (1949)
Andante lamentoso
Eleventurous dances, suite (1951)
VOCAL
The Hunting of the Snark, cantata (1929) (Ann Arbor Music Festival) (1929)
Adoration
At morning
Cape Horn Gospel I (1946)
Canzonetta
Have you seen but a whyte lillie grow (1946)
I have a rendezvous with death (1918)
In Italy (1915)
In the cool of the evening (1914)
Invitation (1918)
Invocation (1918)
Mr. Frog (1948)
On a winding way (1914)
Tarantella (Italian folk dance) (1914)
Three sea shanties (1950)
When the Bobolink sings high (1916)
Wind from the South (1916)
THEATRE
My Divinity, musical
Ref. 226, 322

BOYD, Liona Maria

Canadian guitarist and composer. b. London, July 11, 1950. She became a naturalised Canadian in 1975. She studied the guitar under Eli Kassner. After attending the University of Toronto, she went to Paris to continue her studies under Alexandre Lagoya. She took master classes with Julian Bream, Alirio Diaz and Narciso Yepes. After her debut in 1975 at the Carnegie Recital Hall, New York, she toured North and South America, New Zealand and Australia. DISCOGRAPHY.

Compositions
GUITAR
Cantarell
Llanto de Gaviota
Transcriptions of Bach, Beethoven, Cimarosa, Debussy, Satie and other composers
Ref. 485, 563

BOYKIN, A. Helen

American teacher and composer. b. River Falls, AL, November 5, 1904. She studied at Alabama College from 1927 to 1930 and privately in Atlanta from 1933 to 1965. She then taught in Montgomery. In 1971 she received a National Federation of Music Clubs award of merit.

Compositions
ORCHESTRA
Two piano concertos
PIANO
Carnival scenes
En bateau
Geechee dance
Scherzo in B
Seafoam
Ref. 40, 142, 347

BOYLE, Ina
Irish composer. b. 1892; d. 1967.
Compositions
ORCHESTRA
Glencree, symphony (1924)
Elegy from a Virgilian suite (1950)
Pastoral Colin Clout (1936)
Ref. 50, 502

BRAASE, Albertine
19th-20th-century Danish composer.
Composition
GUITAR
Thème varié pour la guitarre (ded Mlle. H. Amnitzboll)
Ref. 331

BRAASE, Sophie
20th-century Danish composer.
Composition
GUITAR
Thème varié pour la guitarre (ded Mlle. Marguerite de Serene)
Ref. 331

BRACQUEMOND, Marthe Henriod
French organist and composer. b. Paris, April 9, 1898. She studied composition under Charles-Marie Widor and the organ under Louis Vierne, Marcel Dupré, and Henri Busser. She was the organist at the Eglise Reformée de la rue Cortembert, Paris from 1937 to 1962.
Compositions
CHAMBER
Sonatine (fl) (Leduc, 1954)
SACRED
Noël avec variation (Schola Cantorum)
Ombres (suite sur la passion) (org) (Leduc)
Ref. 236

BRADLEY, Ruth
American composer. b. New Jersey, 1894.
Compositions
PIANO
Pieces
VOCAL
Abraham Lincoln walks at midnight, cantata (vce or mix-ch and pf) (Lindsay)
Ballad of Mark Twain (mix-ch and pf) (Burton Frye)
Ice cream (mix-ch and pf) (Anthony Euwer) (New York: H. Flammer, 1955)
Prince Toto II (w-ch and pf) (N. Sparlin)
Rain (w-ch)
Bleeker street market (vce with chimes ad lib) (E. Barto)
Budget (vce and pf) (Harry S. Grannatt)
Eight abstractions, series No. 2 (vce and pf) (C. Anderson)
Five abstractions, series No. 5 (vce and pf) (C. Anderson)
Four abstractions, series No. 6 (vce and pf) (C. Anderson)
Nine abstractions, series No. 1 (vce and pf) (C. Anderson)
Procrastination (vce and pf) (E. Pinchard)
Release (vce and pf) (E. Pinchard)
Seven abstractions, (vce and pf) (C. Anderson)
Six abstractions, series No. 4 (vce and pf) (C. Anderson)
Three abstractions, series No. 7 (vce and pf) (C. Anderson)
Two abstractions, series No. 8 (vce and pf) (C. Anderson)
OPERA
The Barren Pines (Dorothy Dix Lawrence) (New York, 1961)
Ref. 141, 142, 190, 228, 347

BRADSHAW, Nellie Shorthill
American organist, soprano, teacher and composer. b. Pineville, MO. June 6, 1874. She was a pupil of William Carl, J. Sauvage, W.W. Wallace and W. Lehman. She concertized and taught in Little Rock, Oklahoma City and Omaha and composed hymns and anthems and teaching pieces.
Ref. 460

BRADSHAW, Susan
English composer. b. 1931. She was educated at the Royal Academy of Music and studied further with Boulez, Max Deutsch and Matyas Seiber.
Compositions
PIANO
Eight Hungarian melodies (J.D.W. Chester Ltd.)
Ref. 52

BRADY, Emma
Composer of an opera.
Ref. 465

BRAGA, Henriqueta Rosa Fernandes
Brazilian organist, pianist, conductor, musicologist, professor and composer. b. Rio de Janeiro, March 12, 1909. She studied at the National Institute of Music of the University of Rio de Janeiro, where she obtained her diploma for piano teaching. She received her maestro diploma at the National School of Music, University of Brazil and her D.Mus. at the Federal University of Rio de Janeiro. She studied under P. Silva (counterpoint and fugue), J. Otaviano (composition, instrumentation and orchestration), F. Mignone (conducting), L. Heitor (national music folklore), A. Sa Pereira (music), A. Silva (organ), and E. Barroso Murtinho (voice). She was a professor at the National Institute of Music from 1936 and the Villa Lobos Institute from 1949. She was professor of history of music at other universities and produced radio programs on that subject. She founded a church choir in 1950 and played the organ for it. She received the Alexander Levy medal in 1964.
Composition
VOCAL
Sonhemos (vce and pf)
Publications
Brinquedos cantados, Sua influencia. With I.P. Marinho and others. Rio de Janeiro, 1955.
Cadernos de folclore, No. 10. Rio de Janeiro, 1970.
Cancioneiro folcloricos infantil brasileiro. Rio de Janeiro, 1966.
Canticos do Natal. Rio de Janeiro, 1947.
Cultura a musical no Rio de Janeiro, em quatro seculos de cultura. Rio de Janeiro, 1966.
Do coral e a sua projeccao na historia da musica. Rio de Janeiro, 1958.
A Musica, como fator educativo. Rio de Janeiro, 1952.
Musica sacra evangelica no Brasil. Rio de Janeiro, 1961.
Peculiaridades ritmicas e melodicas do cancioneiro infantil brasileiro. Rio de Janeiro, 1950.
Ref. 206, 333

BRAGGINS, Daphne Elizabeth
British organist, choral conductor, teacher and composer. b. Bedford, 1916. She obtained her Mus.D. from Dublin and Mus.B. (Cantab) and is a F.R.C.O. and L.R.A.M., having studied at the Royal Academy of Music and Girton College. She taught in schools, trained choirs in Redhill from 1946 to 1954 and gave organ recitals. She composed orchestral suites, organ and piano pieces and songs.
Ref. 490

BRAGGIOTTI, Augusta
19th-century Italian composer.
Compositions
PIANO
La gaite, waltz
Souvenir de Brianza, morceau de salon
Souvenir de Livourne, waltz
VOCAL
Un saluto a Milano
Ref. Ricordi

BRAHE, May. See MORGAN, Mary Hannah

BRAMBILLA, Marietta
Italian contralto, singing teacher and composer. b. Cassano d'Adda, June 6, 1807; d. Milan, November 6, 1875. She studied singing at the conservatory in her home town then made her debut in London in 1827 and performed in Italy and Paris. In 1850 she retired from the stage and settled in Milan to become a highly esteemed teacher of singing.
Compositions
VOCAL
La Capanna, duet (Ricordi)
Lamento, aria (vce and pf) (Cramer)
A perfect day
Raccolta di 5 ariette ed un duettino (Ricordi)
Serenata (Lemoine)
Souvenir des Alpes, collection of 6 Italian melodies (Recordi)
La Tenerezza, romance (Schirmer)
Other songs and romances
Ref. 129, 132, 276, 247, 297, 400, 563

BRANCA, Cirilla. See CAMBIASI BRANCA, Cirilla

BRANCA-MUSSINI, Adele
19th-century Italian pianist and composer. b. Berlin. She was a descendant of the composer Giuseppe Sarti. She studied music in Florence. A number of her piano pieces are published by Ricordi.
Compositions
PIANO
Ballo arabo
Camilla
Capriccio, polka
Dolore, melody
Ecco il tramonto, mazurka
Episodio campestre
Lampo di gioia
Mazurka
Rêve d'un bal
Six Pensées fugitives: Desespoir; Le Calme; Oubli; La Raison; Resignation; Récit du passé
Six Pensées fugitives: Triste pensée; Angoisses; Toujours de même; Distraction; Inquietude; Badinage
Solitudine, gran waltz
Speranza, gran waltz
Tre pensieri sciolti
Ref. 226, 276, 297

BRANCHU, Mme.
19th-century French pianist, singer and composer. She made her debut in the role of Antigone. She composed romances for the piano.
Ref. 119

BRANCOVAN, Princess of
19th-century French song writer.
Ref. 465

BRANDELER, Henriette van den
Dutch pianist and composer. b. The Hague, September 25, 1884. She studied under Johan Wagenaar and Dirk Schaefer and obtained the diploma in the piano of the Nederlandse Toonkunst Vereeniging in 1903. She then studied composition under Bernard Zweers, Amsterdam and Walter Braunfels, Munich. Her choral works were frequently performed in Holland.
Compositions
PIANO
Drie fuga's (1954)
VOCAL
Solomon's song (5 soloists, w-ch and orch) (ca. 1913)
Vijf oud-Nederlandse liederen (vce and orch)
Four volumes of songs (vce and pf) (1906-1916)
Paysages tristes, three songs (Verlaine) (1906)
Settings of poems (P.C. Boutens) incl.:
Laat mij nimmermeer
Oog in oog
Wat is in U
Twenty-five songs (1905-1978)
SACRED
Stabat Mater (S, A, mix-ch and orch) (1913)
Missa Gaudete in Domine (mix-ch and org) (1956)
Wijdingszang, on Old Testament texts (for the opening of a forest chapel near Bilthoven, built by her husband) (w-ch and pf) (1924)
A Christmas Carol (mix-ch a-cap)
Quis est homo (w-ch and pf)
Ave Maria (vce and pf) (1910)
Requiem
Two hymns incl.:
Rector potens (4 vces a-cap) (1956)
Ref. composer, 1, 44, 94, 226, 461

BRANDENSTEIN, Caroline/Karoline. See BRANDENSTEIN, Charlotte von

BRANDENSTEIN, Charlotte von (Caroline, Karoline)
German poetess and composer. b. Schordorf, Wurttemberg, 1754; d. Berlin, 1813. She studied in Mannheim under Abbe Vogler, who praised her abilities as a composer. DISCOGRAPHY.
Compositions
CHAMBER
Sonata for violin and piano in D-Major (1780)
Piano pieces
Ref. 128, 129, 276, 563

BRANDES, Charlotte Wilhelmina Franziska (Minna)
German pianist, singer and composer. b. Berlin, May 21, 1765; d. Hamburg, June 13, 1788. She was the daughter of Johann Christian Brandes, actor and poet. She made her first appearance on the operatic stage in Leipzig at the age of three and four years later sang at the court theatre, Weimar. She studied the piano under Hoenicke in Weimar and later in Dresden. She studied singing under the court singer Muriottini. In 1778 Mara heard her sing and became her teacher. In Berlin (1782) she took lessons in singing from Concialini. Her voice had a range of three octaves. Her life was spent traveling in Germany where she was welcomed at the courts and many songs and operatic roles were composed for her. She was also admired as a pianist. At the time of her death from overexertion, she was the prima donna at the Hamburg Opera.
Compositions
ORCHESTRA
Cavatina
CHAMBER
Largo (strs and ww)
Piano pieces
VOCAL
Duet (2 S, 2 vln and vla)
Collection of Italian and German Canzoni and Arias (vce and pf)
Other Lieder (vce and pf)
Ref. 25, 121, 125, 226, 276

BRANDES, Mina. See BRANDES, Charlotte Wihelmina Franziska

BRANDES, Renée
20th-century composer.
Composition
MULTIMEDIA
She's the best man in my cabinet (musical portrait of Golda Meir)
Ref. ASCAP in Action 1983

BRANDHURST, Elise
19th-century German composer.
Compositions
CHAMBER
Piano pieces
VOCAL
Lieb' Sternlein du, op. 14 (vce and pf)
Other songs
Ref. 226, 276

BRANDLING, Mary
19th-century American composer.
Composition
VOCAL
I pray for thee, or The farewell (S or T and pf) (Philadelphia: G. Hewitt, 1840)
Ref. 228

BRANDMAN, Margaret Susan

Australian accordionist, clarinetist, drummer, guitarist, pianist, teacher, writer and composer. b. Sydney, September 19, 1951. She began studying the accordion at the age of four and then took up the clarinet, the guitar and the piano. At the Sydney Conservatorium she studied the piano, the clarinet, theory, harmony and composition and privately continued studying the accordion, the guitar and the drum. She began teaching when she was 14. She received the diploma of music from the Sydney Conservatorium, and B.Mus. from Sydney University where she studied composition under Peter Sculthorpe. In 1977 she established a monthly column on aspects of keyboard theory and practice for the *Journal of Australian Music and Musicians* and became well-known as one of Australia's leading writers on keyboard matters. She has represented Australia twice at the International Congress of Women in Music in the United States and is involved in compiling programs of Australian compositions for radio stations. PHOTOGRAPH.

ORCHESTRA
I Ching sounds (1974)
CHAMBER
The optimum number (sax, trp, trb, gtr, pf, bass and drs) (Jazzem Music, 1980)
Jazz impressions (pf, 2 sax, d-b and drs) (1976)
String quartet No. 1 (1980)
Saxophone quartet (1976)
Trio (2 cl and bsn) (1969)
Trio (2 cl and vlc) (1971)
Clarinet miniature (cl and pf) (1969)
Antics (fl and pf) (1976)
Music for single swingers (fl and pf; also vce) (1978)
Permutations (cl and pf) (1977) (Jazzem)
PIANO
Allegro and andante (1971)
Animodes 21 pieces (1974)
Badinarie No. 1 (1976) (Jazzem)
Badinarie No. 2 (1976) (Jazzem)
The big band (1971)
Caprice (1967)
Invention (also acdn) (1973) (Jazzem)
Mini-suite (also acdn) (1978) (Jazzem)
Moderato (1971)
Presto (1971)
Rondo (1971)
Sarabande (1971)
Six contemporary pieces (1983)
Sonorities (1981) (Jazzem)
Static ripples (1973) (Jazzem)
Still (1972)
Three sketches (also acdn) (1968) (Waterloo Music)
Variations in a modern style (1971)
VOCAL
For choir (S.T. Coleridge) (1974) (Jazzem)
Images (S, sax and pf) (1976)
Autumn hills (1971)
Find my own place (Marcia Regner) (1979)
Freeze, freeze, thou winter wind (Shakespeare) (1971)
More and more (Cheryl Adlard) (1981) (Jazzem)
Simple things (Linda Hyams) (1971)
ELECTRONIC
Flights of fancy (vce or fl, pf and electric bass) (1963) (Jazzem)
Publications
Contemporary Piano Course, 2 vols. Castle Music, 1982.
Contemporary Chord Workbooks, 2 vols. Castle Music, 1982.
Chord Workbook.
Piano Method.
Ref. composer, 446

BRANDON, Phyllis

20th-century composer.
Composition
PIANO
Valse souvenir (2 pf) (A.H. and C, 1948)
Ref. 473

BRANDT, Dorothea

American pianist, teacher and composer. b. Frewsburg, NY, May 1, 1896. She studied composition under Henry P. Eames and Carl Parrish, Claremont and taught the piano in Yakima, Seattle and Pomona, CA.
Compositions
PIANO
Arietta (1968)
Calico mountain trail (1968)
Chinese woodcutter (1964)
Dancing Japanese marionettes (1963)
Japanese print (1955)
Little donkey in the snow (1964)
Wagon train (1954)
Zapateado (1960)
SACRED
Anthems (ch)
Ref. 142, 347

BRANHAM, Norma Wood

19th-century American composer. b. Brazil, IN. She composed sacred music.
Ref. 347

BRANNING, Grace Bell

American organist, pianist, teacher and composer. b. Washington, DC, October 10, 1912. She studied the piano under Dallmeyer Russell; the piano and composition under Mildred Gardner and voice under Romaine Smith Russell and Conrad Seamen; the organ, the piano and voice under Homer Wickline; composition under Mildred Gardner (q.v.) and Dr. Joseph Jenkins and the organ under Earl Collings. She received her B.M. from the University of Pittsburgh in 1937 and then studied composition under Nicolai Lopatnikoff. She received three awards for composition from the Pittsburgh Piano Teachers' Association. She taught the piano at the Pittsburgh Musicical Institute from 1937 to 1960, the Fillion Studios and privately.
Compositions
CHAMBER
Allegro risoluto (vln)
Arioso and dance (fl)
PIANO
Capriccio, duet
Cardinals, duet
Ballade
Caprice in C
Mazurka
Miniature, suite
Waltz
VOCAL
Barter (vce and pf)
Eternity (vce and pf)
Night song (vce and pf)
Pink dogwood (vce and pf)
Sea love (vce and pf)
Songs of Foo, four Chinese songs (composer)
Virtue (vce and pf)
Wild horses (vce and pf)
SACRED
Psalm 121 (mix-ch)
God's world (w-vces)
Gethsemane (vce and pf)
OPERA
Scene for Icelandic Saga (S, T and ch)
Ref. composer, 142

BRANSCOMBE, Gena (Mrs. John F. Tenney)

American pianist, conductor, lecturer and composer. b. Picton, Ontario, November 4, 1881; d. New York, July 26, 1977. She became a U.S. citizen in 1910. She started to compose before she was five and at the age of 15 won a scholarship to the Chicago Musical College, 1897 to 1904, where she studied the piano under Ziegfeld and Friedheim and composition under Felix Borowski. She also studied the piano with Hans von Schiller and songwriting with Alexander von Fielitz. She obtained her B.Mus. winning the gold medal for composition in 1900 and 1901. She then studied the piano under Rudolph Ganz in Chicago and taught at the Musical College from 1904 to 1907. From 1907 to 1909 she was head of the piano department at Whitman College, Walla Walla, then she went to Berlin and studied composition and orchestration under Humperdinck and the piano, again under Ganz, until 1910. Later she attended conducting classes at New York University under Dr. Chalmers Clifton. She conductd her own music from 1921 to 1931. Gena is chiefly known for her choral works and she composed over 150 songs. In 1934 she founded the Branscombe Chorale, which made a name for itself in New York until it was dissolved in 1954. In 1928 she was awarded the annual prize of the League of American Pen Women for the finest work produced by a woman *Pilgrims of Destiny*. She was president of the American Society of Women Composers from 1929 to 1932 and chairlady of New York State Federation of Music Clubs, 1930 to 1935. In 1932 she received an honorary M.A. from Whitman College. In the 1930s she was vice-president of the National Association of American Composers and Conductors and was a guest conductor of, among many others, the McDowell Chorus of New Jersey. She was conductor of the MacDowell Club Choral, 1931 to 1934; New Jersey State Choral and Contemporary Club Choral, from 1940 to 1946. She was chairlady of American Music and Folksong and received the D.A.R. Award for service to patriotic education. Her works were broadcast over all major American and Canadian radio stations and often conducted by the composer herself. She arranged many works of American composers.

Compositions

ORCHESTRA

Piano concerto (1906)
Baladine (small orch) (1935)
Elegie (1935) (Oliver Ditson)
Festival prelude (1913)
Gailliard (1946)
Just in the hush before dawn (1946)
Maples (small orch) (1935)
Pavane (1946)
Pilgrims of destiny, overture (1937)
Procession (small orch) (1935)
Quebec, suite from The bells of circumstance (Schmidt, 1928)
Valse joyeuse (1946)
Wings (1946)

CHAMBER

Carnival fantasy (fl, hp, pf and strs) (Schmidt, 1920)
Procession (trp, org and pf) (1948)
American suite (hn and pf) (1959)
At the fair; A memory; An old tale; An old love tale, op. 21, nos. 1-4 (vln and pf) (Schmidt, 1911)
Sonata (vln and pf) (1920)

PIANO

A woodsey nymph came dancing (Schmidt, 1925)
Cavalcade (Whaley, Royce and Co. 1902)
Chansonette (Whaley, Royce and Co. 1902)
Four ballet episodes (Schmidt, 1917)
Four miniature sketches (Teller, 1904)
Hill-top dreaming (Schmidt, 1925)
Impromptu (Whaley, Royce and Co., 1902)
In a fairy garden, 4 pieces (Schmidt, 1922)
Miniature suite: In distant lands, op. 2 (Schirmer, 1907)
Two sketches (Schmidt, 1917)
Valse caprice (Whaley, Royce and Co., 1902)
When Joan of Arc was a little girl, 4 pieces (Schmidt, 1922)

VOCAL

Youth of world, cantata (w-vces and orch) (M. Witmark & Sons, 1931)
Phantom caravan (m-vces and orch) (John Church, 1926)
Pilgrims of destiny (mix-ch, soloists and orch) (Oliver Ditson, 1929) (Prize, 1928)
Set him in the bilboes (m-vces and orch) (Oliver Ditson, 1926)
Sun and the warm brown earth (w-vces and orch) (C.C. Birchard & Co., 1934)
A wind from the sea (Longfellow) (w-vces and orch) (Schmidt, 1927)
Into the Light (ch) (1930)
Across the blue Aegean Sea (Galaxy Mus. Corp.)
Afar on the Purple Moor (w-vces or m-vces) (G. Schirmer, 1947)
Ah, love I shall find thee (1927)
At the postern gate (Schmidt)
Blow softly maple leaves (H.W. Gray)
By St. Lawrence water (Eltzin)
Coventry's choir (S, w-vces, pf, org and perc) (W.V. Alvarez) (G. Schirmer, 1944)
The dancer of fjaard (S, A and w-vces) (Schmidt, 1926)
Hail bounteous May (1909)
Hail ye tyme of holiedayes (Schmidt, 1911)
In my heart there lives a song (1936)
Krishna, serenade (I send my heart up to thee) (Schmidt)
Lute of jade, song cycle (Schmidt, 1913)
The morning wind (Schmidt)
Murmur on, sweet harp (w-vces) (G. Schirmer, 1948)
Our Canada, from sea to sea (C.V. Thompson)
With rue my heart is laden (1907) (Canada)
Woodwinds (w-vce) (1949) (H. Fitzsimons)

SACRED

In the manger (ch) (1947)
Mary at Bethlehem (w-ch) (Ricordi, 1934)
A joyful litany (w-vces) (G. Branscombe) (1967)
The Lord is our fortress (Fischer, 1947)
Introit, prayer, response and amen (m-vces) (1973)
Prayer for song (w-vces and pf) (Ricordi, 1944)
Wreathe the holly, twine the bay (J. Fischer & Bros. 1938)

OPERA

The Bells of Circumstance (ca. 1928)

Bibliography

Branscombe, Gena. *The Sound of Trumpets*. Music Clubs Magazine, special issue, 1962.
Elkins-Marlow, Laurine. *Gena Branscombe: American Composer and Conductor, A Study of Her Life and Works*. Ph.D. dissertation, University of Texas, Austin, TX.
Elkins-Marlow, Laurine. *Gena Branscombe: Her Final Years*. Music Clubs Magazine, 1977.

Ref. composer, 8, 17, 22, 44, 53, 70, 71, 74, 89, 94, 96, 100, 105, 107, 110, 124, 133, 141, 142, 168, 177, 191, 226, 228, 280, 292, 347, 361, 415, 433, 496, 560, 594, 611, 653

BRATU, Emma

Rumanian pianist, teacher and composer. b. Ohaba-Bistra, October 11, 1910. She received her B.A. (piano and composition) from the Timisoara Conservatory of Music. She studied the piano and harmony at the Franz Liszt Music Academy Budapest, and orchestration and harmony privately with Sabin Dragoi and Matyas Csany. From 1938 to 1952 she was in Oradea and Bucharest composing and working as a pianist; from 1968 to 1976 she taught the piano and composition in Bucharest and from 1977 onwards she taught the piano and composition in New York.

Compositions

ORCHESTRA

Symphony No. 1, in F-Major (Patria)
Symphony No. 2, in C-Major (Eileen's Dream)
Rivers' cycle, 4 concert waltzes

VOCAL

Songs incl.:
Blossoms of acacia
Blossoms of lime
Rumanian brothers

OPERA

Cosinzeana
Ten Commandments

Ref. 494

BRAUER, Johanna Elisabeth

German pianist, teacher and composer. b. Lahr, Baden, April 27, 1861. She studied composition under Carl Somborn and Hermann Graedener in Vienna in 1898 and Cornelius Rubner in Karlsruhe, in 1905. She traveled widely as a concert pianist and after 1892 was a private music teacher in Lahr.

Compositions

CHAMBER

Suite for violin and piano

VOCAL

Des Saengers Fluch (Uhland) (mix-ch and orch)
Ganymed (Hamerling) (m-ch and orch)
Die im Lichte wandeln (Hirsch) (A and orch)
Elslein, op. 1 (Stieler)
Frauenchiemsee, op. 1 (Stieler)
Im Walde, op. 1 (Heyse)
Die Kindlein wissen's, op. 5 (Hamerling)
Nachtlied (Stieler) (vce and pf)
Treue, op. 5 (Gichendorff)
Wiegenlied, op. 1 (Brauer) (Ries and Erler)
Three songs, op. 4
Arrangements of Minnelieder (Ulrich von Lichtenstein) from the Manesische Handschrift

SACRED

Fuenf Passiongesaenge

Ref. 105, 111

BRAUNSCHWEIG, Anna Maria von, Duchess

German composer. d. 1568. She was the wife of Duke Albrecht I of Prussia and composed psalms and lieder.

Ref. 128, 465

BRAUNSCHWEIG, Elisabeth Christine. See SOPHIE ELISABETH von Braun

BRAUNSCHWEIG, Sophie Elisabeth von, Duchess. See SOPHIE ELISABETH von Braun

BRAY, Anna Eliza

British songwriter. b. 1790; d. 1831.

Ref. 465

BRDLIKOVA, Josefina (nee Mourkova)

Bohemian singer and composer. b. Prague, February 20, 1843; d. Prague, October 21, 1910. She studied music with her brother-in-law, V. Zeleni; her uncle, J. Mourek, the director of the choir in the Mariastern monastery and with J. Kolesovski in Prague. She toured France and England and sang with Prague choirs. She married J. Brdlik in 1865 in Pocatka, but continued her lessons with J. Kaan in Prague. When widowed in 1899 she returned to Prague.

Compositions

PIANO

Aphorismy, waltzes (4 hands) (Urbanek, 1897)
Dva ballady (4 hands) (Urbanek)
V úplňku noci benatskych, nocturne (4 hands) (Urbanek, 1892)
Album Skladel Klavírnich, album of piano pieces (Urbanek, 1897)
Decameron, 12 fantasies in sonata form (Urbanek)
Mazurkas, 10 pieces (Urbanek)
Miniatures, 11 pieces (Urbanek, 1897)
Poeticke preludie (Urbanek)
Poeticke trilogie (Urbanek)
Polní kvítí 2 ceskeho pohori (Urbanek)
Rakosi (Urbanek, 1896)
Three Pilsen serenades (1892)
Variace (Urbanek)
Z davných dob
Z letniho sidla

VOCAL

Six albums of songs (vce and pf) (Urbanek)

Ref. 197, 297

BREASEALE, Jayne

20th-century American composer. She won the composition contest of the Louisiana Federation of Music Clubs (1949).

Ref. 448

BRECK, Carrie Ellis (Mrs. Frank A. Breck)

American poetess and composer. b. Walden, Vermont, January 22, 1855; d. Portland, OR, March 27, 1934.

Compositions

SACRED

Songs incl.:
Face to face with Christ my Saviour (Tullar)
Help somebody to-day (Tullar)
If He abide with me (Tullar)
Nailed to the Cross (Tullar)
Shall I crucify my Saviour (Tullar)
When love shines in (Tullar)

Publications

To Comfort Thee. Poems.

Ref. 39, 40, 347, 433, 646

BRECK, Mrs. Frank A. See BRECK, Carrie Ellis

BREEN, May Singhi

American ukulele player, authoress and composer. b. New York, February 24, 1949. She appeared on radio programmes for 16 years with her husband Peter De Rose, as 'Sweet-hearts of the Air' and on TV and has made recordings. She taught the ukulele, originated the use of ukulele arrangements on sheet music and was known as The Ukulele Lady.

Compositions

VOCAL

Songs incl.:
Bird of paradise
Cross my heart, I love you
Forever and ever
I looked at Norah
Way back home

Ref. 39

BREILH, Fernande

20th-century composer. She married Maurice Decruck, solo saxophonist of the New York Philharmonic Orchestra and collaborated with him in all her compositions.

Compositions

CHAMBER

Chant lyrique, op. 69 (a-sax and pf) (1932)
Huit pièces françaises (a-sax and pf)
Cinquieme chant lyrique (a-sax and pf)
The golden sax (a-sax and pf) (1934)
Rex sax (a-sax and pf)
Sonata in C (a-sax and pf) (1944)
Troisieme chant lyrique (a-sax and pf)

SAXOPHONE

Saxophonie (s-sax, a-sax, t-sax and bar-sax)
Variations symphoniques (s-sax, a-sax, t-sax and b-sax)
Pavane (s-sax, a-sax, t-sax and b-sax)
Printemps (s-sax, a-sax, t-sax and b-sax)
Sicilienne (s-sax, t-sax and b-sax)
Duos (2 sax)
Ecole moderne du saxophone (1932)

Ref. 76

BREITENBACH, Antoinette de

19th-century composer.

Composition

VOCAL

Offender, non so offender (vce and pf)

BREMER, Marie Petronella

Dutch harpsichordist, organist, recorder player, choral conductor, lecturer and composer. b. Texel, May 2, 1933. She studied the organ privately under Piet Kee and Cor Kee from 1951 to 1961. In the latter part of the same period she studied the harpsichord under Gusta Goldschmidt and the recorder under Frans Brueggen at the Amsterdam Music Lyceum. She also studied at the Gehrels Institute and taught the institute's music education method at the Volksmusiek Schools, Amsterdam. She moved to the United States in 1961 and became organist and choral conductor at a church in Washington, DC, for 15 years. At the same time she taught recorder and early music performance, besides performing in early music ensembles. From 1976 till 1977 she studied at the Orff Institute, Salzburg, concentrating on composition study under Wilhelm Keller and dance and percussion study. After obtaining her Orff Schulwerk teacher's certificate she taught at the Music School of the American University in Washington, DC, and private schools. In 1974 Marie began collaborating with Margit Smith (q.v.) in exploring and studying the sounds and characteristics of various instruments from around the world. DISCOGRAPHY.

Compositions

CHAMBER

Chroai (chin, hpcd, pf and kayagum) (with Margit Smith)
Elevensevenseven (kayagum and renaissance b-fl) (with Margit Smith)
Traject I (org, baroque fl and Peruvian fl) (with Margit Smith)
Traject II (org, 2 African fl, gemshorn, b-fl, shakuhachi, Nepalese and Thai fl) (with Margit Smith)

ORGAN

Maqam (with Margit Smith)
Mobile (with Margit Smith)
Ombre (with Margit Smith)

Ref. composer, 563

BREMONT, Countess de

19th-century composer.

Compositions

VOCAL

Golden Africa
Spanish bolero

Ref. 276

BRENET, Thérèse

French pianist, professor and composer. b. Paris, October 22, 1935. She studied under Maurice Durufle, Noel Gallon, Darius Milhaud and Jean Rivier. At the Rheims Conservatory she received first prize for the piano and at the Paris Conservatoire, received first prizes for harmony, counterpoint, fugue and composition, obtaining her diploma with distinction. She won the Grand Prix de Rome in 1965. During the same period she was awarded the Halphen prize for fugue and composition as well as a medal for musicology and a prize from the Coplay Foundation in Chicago. She returned to Paris in 1969 and was appointed professor at the Conservatoire in 1970. She was selected to represent the French section at the UNESCO Tribune of Composers. Since then she has lived abroad, mainly in Italy.

Compositions

ORCHESTRA

Fragor, poem in six movements (2 pf and orch) (comm ORTF Strasbourg, Relations Exterieurs)

Concerto pour un poeme inconnu (pf, ondes martenot and str orch) (1966)
Siderales (comm Mme. Arbeau-Bonnefoy) (1971)
Six pièces breves (Presser, 1971)
CHAMBER
Tetrapyle (4 sax and pf) (1979)
Ce que pensent les étoiles (4 perc) (1980)
Flânerie et autour d'un ré (3 sax) (1964)
Jeu pour cinq instruments (hpcd, fl and 2 vlc)
Six pieces (trp and pf or trp and org)
Accordance (celtic hp and ob) (1981)
Caprice d'une chatte anglaise (2 gtr) (1980)
Inter silentia (trp and pf)
Calligramme (sax) (1981)
Suite fantasque (celtic hp) (1983)
VOCAL
Aube morte, lyric poem (Chants de Maldoror by Lautremont) (vce and orch) (1964)
Le chant des mondes, Evren dile geldi, symphonic poems, in 7 mvts (narr, pf and orch) (from Masnavi by Jalaleddin El Roumi) (comm Ministere des Arts et Lettres, ORTF Strasbourg)
Les mains (Mains du Temps by Michele Saint-Lo) (12 vces and 12 insts)
Sept poèmes chinois (extracts from Flute de jade by F. Toussaint) (B and cham orch) (1967)
Lyre d'étoiles (reciter and str trio) (Paris: Choudens, 1984)
La nuit de Maldoror (S, vlc and pf)
Anamnese (S and vla) (1981)
SACRED
E grido la mia voce, oratorio (after the Book of Job) (narr, S, ch and orch)
Clamavit (Book of Job) (narr, S, ch and orch) (comm ORTF, Relations Exterieurs, 1965)
ELECTRONIC
Hommage à Signorelli (from the Resurrection des Morts by Pierre Jean Jouve) (S, pf, ondes martenot and 2 perc) (comm ORTF for the Biennale de Paris, 1967)
Ref. composer, Otto Harrassowitz (Wiesbaden), 76

BRENNER, Rosamond Drooker
American organist, choral conductor, professor and composer. b. Cambridge, MA, March 23, 1931. She graduated from Radcliffe College in 1953 with a B.A. (teaching). She did postgraduate work as a Fulbright scholar in Vienna at the Academy of Music from 1954 to 1956; gained a professional certificate in the organ from the Geneva Conservatory, 1959, and a Ph.D. from Brandeis University in 1968, where she taught music from 1964 to 1966. She was professor of music history, form and analysis at the Boston Conservatory from 1967 to 1970; professor of musicology at the American Conservatory, Chicago from 1971 to 1975; faculty member at Columbia College, Chicago from 1972 to 1974, organist and choir conductor at Trinity Episcopal Church, Wheaton, 1971 to 1978, and Phillips Congregational Church, MA, from 1969 to 1970.
Compositions
ORCHESTRA
Exhortation (pf and orch) (1976)
VOCAL
The trumpet-pen, oratorio (1977)
The choice, cantata (1975)
Darkness hath fallen
Songs
SACRED
Three meditations: Gratitude, Unidad, Exaltation (Bahai writings) (1981)
Healing prayer (Baha'u'llah) (Esperanto)
Fire tablet (1982)
Prayer for the hands of the cause of God (1982)
O God, refresh and gladden my spirit (1982)
O Thou kind Lord! (1982)
Ref. composer

BRENTANO, Bettina or Elisabeth von. See ARNIM, Bettina

BRES, Dorothy
20th-century American composer.
Composition
PIANO
Elusive quatrads
Ref. 347

BRESCHI, Laura
20th-century Italian painter, poetess, writer and composer. b. Genoa. She studied harmony and composition privately.
Compositions
MILITARY BAND
Gli artiglieri, fanfare
L'Italia chiamo
Dolce oblio (trans M. Ascolese)
Waltz (pour vos beaux yeux) (International Competition Musica Revue award, Paris)
CHAMBER
Compositions (vln, vlc and pf)
Sfumatures (vln and pf)
VOCAL
L'inno alla pace (soloists, 300 vces and orch)
L'inno degli artisti (500 vces and military band)
L'inno degli aviatori, anthem (500 vces and military band)
L'inno dei bombardieri (soloists, ch and orch)
Romances (vce and pf) (many on poems by composer) incl.:
Ella mi disse
Eppur ...
Il mio cuore e con te
Torna l'Aprile
Other songs
SACRED
La Santa delle Missioni (Rosa Vagnozzi) (1932)
Ref. 56, 86, 105

BRESSON (Brisson), Mlle.
French pianist, violinist and composer. b. Paris, 1785. She studied the piano under Adam.
Compositions
CHAMBER
Pieces (hp and pf) (Paris: Leduc)
Pieces (vln and pf) (Leduc)
PIANO
Melange
Theme by Mozart, Nel cor
Ref. 129, 276

BREUIL, Helene
20th-century French composer.
Compositions
CHAMBER
Essai (trb and pf) (Paris: Billaudot, 1978)
Ref. Otto Harrassowitz (Wiesbaden)

BRICE, Jean Anne
South African flautist, teacher and composer. b. Johannesburg, 1938. She studied in Johannesburg, Nairobi and at the Royal Academy of Music. She was music and flute teacher and choir leader at girls' schools in Nairobi until 1960. She composed pieces for the flute and the piano.
Ref. 94, 490

BRICE, Laure
20th-century composer.
Composition
SACRED
Ave Maria (vce and org)
Ref. 399

BRIDGE, Mrs. Frederick A. See STIRLING, Elizabeth

BRIDGET (Saint Bridget of Kildare)
Irish harpist and nun. b. 453; d. 525. She founded several cloisters and was later sanctified.
Ref. 264, 268

BRIDGEWATER, Violet Irene
20th-century Canadian accompanist, teacher and composer. b. Victoria, British Columbia. She studied under Peje Storck at the Brussels Conservatory and under Ludovic Breitner in Paris. She taught at the Webber Douglas School of Singing and Dramatic Art.

Compositions
PIANO
Fantasia
Joie de vivre, waltz
The Maori's dream, waltz
VOCAL
At twilight
Canada for Empire
Ref. 467

BRIGGS, Cora Skilling (Mrs. George A.)

American organist, writer and composer. b. South Paris, ME, May 13, 1859; d. December 12, 1935. She studied under Emery, Kotzschmar and E.W. Hanscom. She was organist of the South Paris First Congregational Church for 48 years.

Compositions
VOCAL
So I can wait, song (1908)
Song of confidence (1911)
SACRED
He knows the way
Hold Thou my hand (1904)
Lead me all the way (1908)
The light of heaven's own day
About 70 other anthems and songs (composer)
Ref. 292, 374

BRIGGS, Dorothy Bell

American pianist and composer. b. St. Louis, 1895. She studied the piano under E.R. Kroeger in St. Louis, Georgia Richardson in Detroit and Jeanette Durno in Chicago and composition under Rossetter G. Cole in Chicago. At the Northwestern University School of Music she was a pupil of Arne Oldberg and Carl Beecher.

Compositions
PIANO
Numerous pieces incl.:
My shadow is a copy-cat (2 pf)
Outdoor sketches
VOCAL
Beautiful, wonderful world, children's cantata (N.R. Eberhart)
The rainbow dream (w-ch) (N.R. Eberhart)
Ref. 292

BRIGGS, Mary Elizabeth

20th-century American composer.

Composition
OPERA
Our Night Out (1952)
Ref. 141

BRIGGS, Mrs. George A. See BRIGGS, Cora Skilling

BRIGGS, Nancy Louise

American pianist and composer. b. St. Paul, MN, June 19, 1950. She received her B.A. from the University of California, Berkeley (1971) and then studied for a year at the Royal Conservatory of Music, the Hague, Netherlands. From 1978 to 1980 she studied electronic and recording media at the Center for Contemporary Music, Mills College and is currently undertaking doctoral studies in music at the University of California, San Diego. From 1964 to 1967 she was the winner of two state-wide composition contests and attended piano master classes. In 1980 she won the Elizabeth Mills Crothers' Prize for excellence in composition and in 1983 an Aspen Music Festival Scholarship. PHOTOGRAPH.

Compositions
ORCHESTRA
Calandria (1983) (Aspen Scholarship)
CHAMBER
Fanfare (sackbutts and shawm qrt) (1978)
Celtica (gtr, fl, vlc and perc) (1984)
Bells (fl, pf and vln) (1957)
Micron (ob, cl and vla) (1982)
River song (pf and ob) (1976)
PIANO
Incidental circus music (1978)
Wishing well (1979)
Other pieces (1957-1975)
VOCAL
Transit, chamber work (3 readers and septet) (1983)
About 50 songs (1957-1975)
THEATRE
Music for the Theatre of Planetary memory, Santa Fe
ELECTRONIC
Box bit (tape) (1978)
Chance chants (1980)
Little song (d-b, pf and vib) (1982)
Rad lab scraps (tape) (1977)
MULTIMEDIA
Analogos (live and pre-taped video, mime, mask and elec music) (1982)
Music for Monstum I (text, paintings and music) (1984-1985)
Improvisations (film, video, slides, lights, movement, live and taped music) (1980)
Ref. composer

BRIGHAM, Helena

19th-century American composer. b. Chicago. She composed songs.
Ref. 347

BRIGHT, Ann

Australian pianist, lecturer and composer. b. Adelaide, November 1, 1943. She studied at Adelaide University (B.A.), the Australian National University (M.A.) and the Southampton University (B.Mus.).

Compositions
CHAMBER
Sonata (fl and pf) (1974)
VOCAL
Recollections of a Latvian song
Ref. 206

BRIGHT, Dora Estella

English organist, pianist and composer. b. Sheffield, August 16, 1863; d. London, November 16, 1951. She attended the Royal Academy of Music, London from 1881 to 1888, studying the piano under Walter Cecil Macfarren and harmony and counterpoint under Ebenezer Prout. She won the Potter and other prizes in 1884 and became the first woman to win the Lucas Medal for composition in 1888. She was also the first woman composer to have her work *Fantasia in G*, performed at a London Philharmonic concert, in 1892. In the same year she gave a historical concert 'From Byrd to Cowen', being the first person to give a recital of purely English music. In 1880 she went on a professional concert tour of Germany, where she played her *Piano Concerto in A-Minor* with Reinecke conducting. She played the organ in England at the Crystal Palace under the direction of August Manns. After her marriage she appeared less in recitals, but continued composing. She wrote several ballets for the dancer Adeline Genee. She was the first English woman to play her own concertos in Leipzig, Cologne and Dresden.

Compositions
ORCHESTRA
Concerto in A-Minor (pf and orch) (1888)
Concerto No. 2 in D-Minor (pf and orch) (1892)
Fantasia in G (pf and orch) (1892)
Suite of eighteenth-century dances (pf and orch)
Suite for flute and orchestra
Theme and variations (pf and orch; also 2 pf)
Air with variations (1890)
Suite of Russian dances
Vienna
CHAMBER
Quartet in D (pf and strs) (1893)
Berceuse (fl and pf)
Liebeslied (fl and pf)
Romance and seguidilla (fl and pf) (Rudall)
Suite (fl and pf) (Rudall and Carte)
Suite (vln and pf) (1890) (Ashdown)
Tarantelle (fl and pf)
Two pieces for violoncello and piano (Elkin and Co., 1934)
PIANO
Variations on an original theme of Sir George Alexander Macfarren (2 pf) (Ashdown)
Three duos (2 pf) (1886)
Berceuse (Ashdown)
Four dances from La camargo, miniature ballet (Elkin & Co., 1912)
Liebeslied (Ashdown)
Romanza and scherzetto (Ashdown)
Tarantella (Ashdown)
Two sketches (Pitman)

VOCAL
Messmates (Bar and m-ch)
The ballad of the red deer (Elkin & Co., 1903)
Colinette, chansonette (J. Williams, 1911)
I know a lady sweet and kind
Jungle songs (Elkin & Co., 1903)
There sits a bird (Leonard)
To blossom (Novello)
To daffodils (Novello)
To music (Novello)
Who is Sylvia (Novello)
BALLET
The Dryad
About 11 other ballets
OPERA
Quong Lung's Shadow
Two other operas
Ref. 2, 6, 8, 41, 74, 276, 297, 307, 467

BRILLON DE JOUY (Juvi), Mme.
18th-century French harpsichordist and pianist. She was praised by Dr. C. Burney in his journal after he heard her perform in a concert in France in 1770. Boccherini and Schubert dedicated some works to her. She composed sonatas and other pieces for the piano and the harpsichord.
Ref. 162, 226, 276

BRILLON DE JUVI, Mme. See BRILLON DE JOUY, Mme.

BRINE, Mary D.
19th-century English composer.
Compositions
VOCAL
One I love
Titania
What is summer made of
Which is the road to Slumberland
Ref. 226, 276

BRINGUER, Estela
American conductor and composer. b. Argentina, June 3, 1931. She went to the United States in 1952. She studied in Argentina under Manuel de Falla, Jaime Pahissa and Clemens Krauss. In 1971 she was named Woman of the Year in Buenos Aires. She was guest conductor of the American Symphony Orchestra and the Philharmonic Orchestra of Buenos Aires. In 1975 she toured the United States and Canada, conducting the Colon Opera House Orchestra of Buenos Aires.
Compositions
ORCHESTRA
Two symphonies
Concerto No. 1 in D, op. 25 (pf and orch) (1963) (F. Colombo)
Candombe, op. 28 (1966)
Carnival in Humahuaca, op. 19, suite from the ballet (F. Colombo)
Cold Spring
El mercader indigena, op. 18, rhapsody (1949) (F. Colombo)
Elegia, op. 24 (1960) (F. Colombo)
Fantasia y danza, op. 13 (1959) (F. Colombo)
Los Bosques de Palermo, op. 21 (F. Colombo)
VOCAL
Ecos de Tupac
Song of my valley
Sueno de luna
Ref. 142, 280, 622

BRINK, Emily R.
American assistant professor and composer. b. Michigan, October 21, 1940. She obtained her B.A. in 1962 from the Culoni College, her M.M. from the University of Michigan (1964) and in 1980 was awarded her Ph.D. (music theory) from the Northwestern University. She taught at both schools and universities and in 1974 was made assistant professor of music theory and composition at the University of Illinois.
Compositions
ORGAN
Four Preludes on Genevan psalm tunes (Geneva Music Press: 1974)
Psalm tunes (org) (1974)
The Composer's Workshop Series II (Culoni College of Music, Grand Rapids, Michigan: 1980)
SACRED
We lift our hearts to God (1976)
Eight songs on texts from the Heidelberg Catechism (board of Publications of the Christian Reformed Church, Grand Rapids, Michigan: 1976)
Ref. composer

BRINK-POTHUIS, Annie van den
Dutch violinist, teacher and composer. b. Amsterdam, March 6, 1906; d. March 10, 1956. She began music study in 1923. She studied the violin under Felice Togni and solfege under Bak. In 1931 she received a diploma from the Amsterdam Conservatory after studying the violin under Togni and H. Rijnbergen and harmony and composition under Dresden, Mulder and Pijper. She then studied privately under Pijper, Professor Smijers and Dresden. She taught the violin in Amsterdam. PHOTOGRAPH.
Compositions
CHAMBER
String quartet No. 1 (1947)
String trio No. 1 (vln, vla and vlc) (1949)
Trio for 3 flutes (1954)
Trio for 3 recorders, op. 41 (1954) (Donemus)
Two trios (ob, cl and bsn)
Sonata (vln and vlc) (1947)
Sonata No. 1 (vln and pf)
Sonata No. 2 (vln and pf) (1936)
Sonata Nos. 1 and 2 (vla) (1953)
Three violin solos
PIANO
Andante (1955)
Sonata No. 1 (1942)
Sonata No. 2 (1944)
Sonata in due parte (1955)
VOCAL
Die klank (S and pf) (1949)
Poème melancolique (vce and pf; also vln and pf) (1940)
Twee momenten (S, A and pf) (1955)
Two songs (A and pf) (1946)
Uit zwarte nacht (Margot Vos) (ca. 1930)
Volkswijze (S, fl and pf) (1955)
SACRED
Worship (S, m-S and A) (1954)
Ref. composer. 44, 81, 94, 110, 478

BRINKMANN, Minna
German composer. b. Osterwieck, Harz Mountains, September 28, 1831; d. Brunswick, ca. 1890.
Compositions
PIANO
Auf Wiedersehen, op. 21 (Brauer)
Baechleins Rauschen, impromptu, op. 3 (Siegel)
Fruehlingslied, op. 16 (Brauer)
Fruelingstraum, op. 28 (Brauer)
Gondelfahrt, op. 29 (Brauer)
Im Tale, Lied ohne Worte, op. 15 (Brauer)
In der Sennerhuette, op. 4 (Siegel)
In die Ferne, op. 1 (also 4 hands) (Brauer, Hansen, Ashdown, Donajowski, McKinley and others)
In stiller Nacht, op. 19 (Brauer)
Indra (Flotow), op. 102 (Brainard)
Kriegers Heimkehr, Karacterstueck, op. 9 (Siegel)
Lebewohl, op. 20 (Brauer)
Der letze Traum, op. 23 (Brauer)
Mutterseelenallein, nocturne, op. 8 (Siegel)
Nach der Heimat, melodie op. 2 (Siegel)
Nach der Heimat, prayer, op. 12 (Brauer)
Nocturne, op. 17 (Brauer)
O frage nicht warum? op. 22 (Brauer)
Schwanenlied, op. 36 (Reinecke)
Silberwellen, etude, op. 13 (Brauer)
Spanische Serenade, op. 11 (Siegel)
Trauermarsch, op. 18 (Brauer)
Undinens Klage, op. 35 (Reinecke)
Wenn's Abendgloecklein klingt, idylle, op. 10 (Siegel)
Die Windsbraut, galop brillant, op. 14 (Brauer)
Ref. 102, 206, 276, 297

BRINKMANN, Wilhelmine

19th-century Austrian composer.

Compositions

PIANO

Abschied von der Alm, op. 72 (Beyer)
Alma's Sehnsucht, op. 18 (Andre)
Alpenklange, op. 70 (Beyer)
Alpners Abendlied, op. 87 (Litolff)
Ballklange, salon waltz, op. 17 (Andre)
Blaue Husaren, galop, op. 71 (Beyer)
Drei Melodien, op. 58 (Schulbuchhandlung)
Feueraugen, polonaise, op. 103
Gestaendnis, op. 51 (Heinrichshofen)
Heimatsglocken, op. 25 (Litolff)
Ich denke dein! op. 73 (Beyer)
Im Nachtigallenhain, waltz, op. 68 (Beyer)
Jaeger-und Schaefermaedchen, op. 100 (Litolff)
Kirmes-Klange, polka, op. 74 (Beyer)
Lachtaubchen, polka, op. 74 (Beyer)
Mein Tirol, op. 32 (Schulbuchhandlung)
O komm!, op. 75 (Litolff)
Prière d'une fiancée, op. 30 (Andre)
Scheiden, op. 24 (Litolff)
So geht's im gruenen Walde, op. 69 (Beyer)
Traum der Liebe, op. 24 (Andre)
Traumende Blumen, op. 54 (Heinrichshofen)
Trauemerei in stiller Nacht, op. 90 (Litolff)

Ref. 297

BRISSAC, Jules. See MacFARREN, Emma Marie

BRISSON, Mlle. See BRESSON, Mlle.

BRITAIN, Radie

American organist, pianist, teacher, writer and composer. b. Amarillo, TX, March 17, 1903. She started piano lessons at the Clarendon Conservatory when she was only seven and graduated with honors at the age of 14. She studied for her B.Mus. (1920) at the American Conservatory, Chicago under Heniot Levy (piano) and Van Dusen (organ). She went back to Clarendon College as a teacher for four years. During this time she attended master classes given by the organist Pietro You in Dallas. She also studied the piano with Joseph Pembauer and Alice Ripper. In 1924 she went to Europe and studied under Isidor Philipp and Marcel Dupre. After a short return to the United States, she went to Berlin. She studied composition under Albert Noelte in Munich, where she made her debut as a composer. In 1938 she joined the faculty of the American Conservatory of Music, Chicago. Many of the compositions were written in a remote canyon in the country where she spent the summers. In 1930 her composition *Heroic Poem* won the international prize given by the Hollywood Bowl and in 1945 the same compositions earned her the Juilliard Publication Award; she was the first woman composer to receive it. Over 50 of her compositions have won international and national awards. *Rhapsodic Phantasy for Piano* and *Barcarola*, received the first national award given by the National League of American Pen Women. An honorary doctorate of music was given to her by the Musical Arts Conservatory of Amarillo. In 1935 her composition *Light* won the first national prize sponsored by the Boston Women's Symphony Orchestra. Her composition *Prison* was performed at the White House in 1936. She was director of the National Society of Arts and Letters of Santa Barbara. The U.C.L.A. has the entire library of her compositions in their music library. PHOTOGRAPH.

Compositions

ORCHESTRA

Southern Symphony (Robert B. Brown Music Co., 1935)
Anwar Sadat (in memory) (pf and orch) (1981)
Phantasy (ob and orch) (1942)
Rhapsodic Rhapsody (pf and orch) (1956)
Rhapsody (pf and orch) (1923)
Alaskan Trail of '98
Angel Chimes (1954)
The Builders (also mix-ch)
Cosmic Mist Symphony (1962)
Cactus Rhapsody (1974)
Canyon (1939)
Chicken in the Rough (1947)
Cowboy Rhapsody (1956)
Drouth (1939)
Heroic Poem (American Music Corp., 1924)
Infant Suite (small orch) (1935)
Jewels of Lake Tahoe (1945)
Kambu (1963)
Prison, lament (1940)
Light (tribute to Thomas Edison) (1935)
Minha terra (Barbaroso netto) (Brazil: Ricordi, 1958)
Mother, A melody of love (1982)
Nocturne (small orch) (1934)
Ontanagon Sketches (perc, cel, hp, str and pf) (R.B. Brown, 1939)
Overture to Pygmalion (1930)
Paint Horse and Saddle (1947)
Pastorale (1939)
Person, lament
Prelude to a Drama (Seesaw Music Corp. 1928)
Pyramids of Giza (1973)
Radiation (1955)
Red Clay (1946)
Rhapsodic Phantasy (1931)
San Luis Rey (also pf) (R.B. Brown, 1941)
Saturnale (1939)
Sea Rhapsody
St. Francis of Assisi (also pf) (R.B. Brown, 1941)
Suite (str orch) (R.B.Brown, 1940)
Symphonic Intermezzo (1928)
This is the Place (1958)
Umpqua Forest (1946)
We Believe (1942)

BAND

Rhumbando (1975)

CHAMBER

Barcarola (8 vlc; also pf and vlc) (1981)
Chipmunks (ww, hp and perc) (1940)
Phantasy (ww-trio, cl, ob and bsn) (1974)
Ode to Nasa (brass qnt)
Epic Poem (str qrt) (1927)
In the Beginning (4 hn) (1962)
Musical Portrait of Thomas Jefferson (str qrt) (1979)
Pastorale (rec, ob, hpcd and hn; also 2 pf) (1967, 1939)
Processional (4 trb) (1969)
Recessional (4 trb) (1969)
String Quartet (1934)
The World Does Not Wish for Beauty (4 tba; also mix-ch) (1977)
Phantasy (ob, hp and pf) (1942)
Casa del sogno (ob and pf; also vln) (1958)
Dance Grotesque (2 fl; also pf) (1960)
Les Fameux Douze (vln and vlc) (1966)
Translunar Cycle (vlc and pf) (1980)
Anima Divina (hp) (Seesaw Music, 1966)

PIANO

Ada Kris (1981)
Adoration (Calui Mus. Co. 1951)
After the storm (1982)
Alaskan inner passage (1983)
Angel chimes (American Music Edition, 1951)
The chateau (also vln) (1938)
Covered wagon (Neil Kjos, 1925)
Cotton fields
Dance of the clown (Summy-Birchard, 1948)
Dreams (1948)
Egyptian suite (1969)
Enchantment (1949)
Ensenada (Brazil: Ricordi, 1956)
Epiphyllum (1966)
Escape (1949)
Geppetto's toy shop (Summy-Birchard, 1942)
Goddess of inspiration (1948)
Hawaiian panorama (1971)
Heel and toe (1949)
Infant suite (1935)
Joy (1953)
The juggler (1951)
Kambu
Kuilimi (1977)
Lakalani (1970)
Le petit concerto (R.B. Brown, 1957)
Lei of love (1978)
Little Spaniard
Little per cent
Mexican weaver (1954)
Prelude (Neil Kjos, 1925)
Riding hard in Texas, 10 pieces (1966)
Serenada del coronada
Serenate sorrentina (1946)
Sonata, op. 17 (1958)
Torillo (1949)
Western suite (Otto Halbriter, 1925)
Wings of silver (Willis Music Co., 1951)
Four sarabandes (1967)

VIOLIN
Legend (1928)
Prison (Neil Kjos, 1935)
Serenade (1944)
VOCAL
Awake to life (Lerae Britain) (mix-ch) (1963)
Baby I can't sleep (1936)
Brothers of the clouds (Kate Hammond) (m-ch) (1964)
The chalice (Alice Halff) (mix-ch) (1951)
Cherokee blessing (mix-ch) (1977)
Dicky donkey (Lester Luther) (mix-ch) (C. Fischer, 1935)
Drums of Africa (Jenkins) (mix-ch) (Witmark & Son, 1934)
Earth Mother (mix-ch) (1975)
Fairy of spring (Butterfield) (w-ch) (A.P. Schmidt, 1935)
Forest procession (Lerae Britain) (mix-ch) (1970)
Haunted (Griffin) (mix-ch) (1935)
Humble me (Lester Luther) (mix-ch) (1941)
Hush my heart (Halff) (mix-ch) (1970)
I found a star (vce and pf) (1980)
In the silence of the temple (Collander) (mix-ch) (1965)
Immortality (F.F. Miller) (ch a-cap) (A.P. Schmidt, 1937)
Lasso of time (Alice McKenzie) (m-ch) (Neil Kjos, 1940)
Little man (Wilton) (w-ch) (1965)
Noontide (Nietzsche) (w-ch) (A.P. Schmidt, 1935)
Open the door (mix-ch) (1939)
Rain (Lester Luther) (w-ch) (R.B. Brown 1935)
Stillness (Lester Luther) (mix-ch) (1941)
Twilight moon (Eberhart) (w-ch) (1938)
Barcarola (S and pf; also 8 vces; also vce and 8 vlc; also pf)
Fulfilment (vce and pf) (1980)
Had I a cave
Lost river (vce and pf) (1982)
Lotusland (vce and pf)
Love song of the Taj Mahal (Halff) (1947)
Nature ushers in the dawn (Harold Skeath)
Overtones (fl and vce) (1970)
We are the wind chimes (vce and pf) (1981)
Withered flowers
Over 50 songs
SACRED
Eternal Spirit (Lerae Britain) (mix-ch) (1964)
Holy lullaby (Halff) (w-ch) (1975)
I'se comin' Lord to you (Alice Mckenzie) (mix-ch) (1940)
Lord God within me (Holmes) (mix-ch) (1977)
Lord have mercy, mass (mix-ch) (1976)
Love still Has something of the sea (mix-ch) (1971)
Prayer (Quarry) (mix-ch) (Ricordi, 1934)
Song of the Joshua (1956) (w-ch) (1938)
The star and the Child (John Lancaster) (mix-ch or w-ch) (1956)
Ten Commandments (mix-ch) (1970)
Venete, felii audite me (Father Fred Consol) (w-ch) (1957)
Christmas story
BALLET
Kambu Ballet (1963)
Shepherd in the Distance (1929)
Wheel of Life (1933)
OPERA
Carillon (1952)
Kuthara, chamber opera (1960)
Lady in the Dark (Shakespearean sonnets) (1962)
Ubiquity, musical drama (Lester Luther) (1937)
Western Testament (1964)
OPERETTA
Happyland (1946)
The Spider and the Butterfly, in 3 acts, for children (1953)
Publications
Major and Minor Moods.
Lasso of Time. Heroica Publications.
Adoration. Heroica Publications.
Composer's Corner.
Bibliography
Goss, Madeleine. *Radie Britain.* Modern Music Makers.
Ref. composer, AMC Newsletters, 22, 71, 142, 185, 361, 415, 454, 457, 474, 477, 560, 594, 610, 611, 622, 624, 653

BRITTON, Dorothy Guyver

American composer. b. 1922. DISCOGRAPHY.
Compositions
ORCHESTRA
Impressions (cham orch) (1957)
Yedo Fantasy (cham orch) (1956)
Ref. 142, 649

BRIZZI-GIORGI, Maria

Italian organist, pianist and composer. b. Bologna, August 7, 1775; d. bologna, January 12, 1812. At the age of 12 she was invited to be the organist of the San Bartolomeo Convent, Ancona. In 1790 she returned to Bologna where she married. She was a member of the Philharmonic Academy and her works and performances were praised by Giordani, Muzio Clementi and Josef Haydn. Most of her compositions were lost, but some extracts have been preserved in the Library of the Liceo Musicale of Bologna.
Compositions
VOCAL
Cantata in honor of the second marriage of Napoleon I to Archduchess Marie Louise (May, 1810)
MISCELLANEOUS
Composition for the arrival in Bologna of the Prince, son of Napoleon Augustus
Other pieces
Bibliography
Bacchetti, A. *Elogio funebre di Maria Brizzi-Giorgi detto nella chiesa delle Muratelle in Bologna nel giorno dei suoi funerali, 22 Genn. 1812.* Bologna: tip. Basi & Co., 1812.
Giordani, Pietro. *Elogio a Maria-Giorgi nelle solenni esequie a lei fatte dall'Accad. Filarm. in San Giov. in Monte di Bologna.* Bologna: tip. D. Franceschi, 1813.
Lozzi, C. *Maria Brizzi-Giorgi.* Gazzetta Musicale, Milan, October 21, 1897.
Scevola, L. *In morte di Maria Brizzi-Giorgi versi ecc.* Bologna, 1812.
Ref. 105, 180, 347

BROADWOOD, Lucy E.

Scottish editor, folklorist, song collector and composer. b. Scotland, August 9, 1858; d. London, August 22, 1929. She was the youngest daughter of Henry Fowler Broadwood of the firm John Broadwood & Sons, piano manufacturers. She studied singing under William Shakespeare and collected songs from the country people of Surrey and Sussex. She edited some of Purcell's works.
Compositions
VOCAL
Annie's tryst
Nae mair we'll meet
Tammy
When trees did bud
Arrangements of Jess MacFarlane, In loyalty (old Scottish airs)
Publications
English County Songs. Edited and arranged with J.A. Fuller Martland. 1893.
Contributions to *Old World Songs.*
Ref. 6, 276, 347

BROCA, Carmen L. de

19th-century Spanish composer.
Composition
OPERA
Perdon Fio! comic opera (1895)
Ref. 431

BROCK, Blanche Kerr

American pianist, singer and composer. b. Greenfork, IN, February 3, 1888; d. Winona Lake, IN, January 3, 1958. She studied at the Indianapolis and American conservatories.
Compositions
SACRED
Beyond the sunset
He's a wonderful Saviour to me
Keep looking up
Men of God awake, arise
O wonderful day
Sing and smile and pray
Some happy morning
We should see Jesus
Ref. 39, 142

BROCKMAN, Jane E.

American professor and composer. b. Schenectady, NY, March 17, 1949. She studied composition under George B. Wilson, Eugene Kurtz, Wallace Benny and Leslie Bassett at the universities of California and Michigan. Between 1975 and 1977 she was awarded the Fulbright Fellowship for study in Paris under Max Deutsch and a Rackham Fellowship for creative work in Vienna. From 1977 till 1978 she was visiting professor and director of the electronic music studio at Rhode Island University and then became assistant professor and founding director of the electronic music studio at the University of Connecticut, Storrs. The subjects she taught were composition, theory, form and analysis, orchestration and music of the Romantic era. She gained her B.Mus., M.Mus., and D.M.A. In 1973 she became the first woman to win the Sigvald Thompson composition award of the Fargo-Moorhead Symphony. Since 1972 she has lectured at the University of Michigan. DISCOGRAPHY.

Compositions

ORCHESTRA

Ballinkeele Music (1977)
Eventail (1973)

CHAMBER

Autumnal contrasts (wind ens)
Labyrinths (ens) (1974)
Two vignettes (ens) (1972)
Two piano quartets (fl, vlc and 2 pf) (1980)
Divergencies (fl, sax and pf) (1975)
String trio (1974)
Music for clarinet and piano
Shadows (cl and pf) (1984)
Horn sonata (1972)
Tower music (carillon) (1974)

PIANO

August thaw (1971)
Finger prints (1971)
Tell-tale fantasy (Arsis Press, 1978)

VOCAL

A Day of summer (ch)

ELECTRONIC

Descent into the maelstrom (tape, timp and vib) (1981)

MULTIMEDIA

Metamorphosis (tape, lighting and dancer) (1981)

Ref. composer, AMC 1985, 142, 477, 563, 624

BRODERICK, Deborah Houstle

20th-century American composer.

Composition

VOCAL

Small town girls (Bar and pf) (1983)

Ref. AMC newsletter

BRODIN, Lena Birgitta Elise

Swedish teacher and composer. b. Gothenburg, June 20, 1941. She obtained her music and piano teacher's diploma at the Royal Academy of Music, Stockholm, in 1966 and her rhythmics teacher's diploma at the Malmo Music Academy in 1969. She attended courses on group teaching in Sweden, Denmark and Finland in 1969 and in 1977 was a member of a Swedish state investigation into group teaching. She composed for the cello, the piano, the violin and small ensembles. PHOTOGRAPH.

Publications

Fela med farg 1 and 2. Violin Book. Nord Musikforlaget, Wilh. Hansen: 1972.
Fritt Fram 1 and 2. Piano Book. Reuter and Reuter: 1974
Spelsugen. Beginners' recorder book. Reuter and Reuter: 1976.

Ref. composer, 457

BROES, Mlle.

Dutch pianist and composer. b. Amsterdam, 1791; d. Paris. She studied under the Dresden court organist, Klegel in 1800 and Fetis in Paris in 1805. In 1814 she returned to Amsterdam and achieved considerable fame as a virtuoso pianist. She composed dances, rondos, sonatas and variations for the piano.

Ref. 129, 226, 276

BROGUE, Roslyn Clara (Henning)

American harpsichordist, organist, pianist, violinist, violist, assistant professor and composer. b. Chicago, February 16, 1919. She played both the piano and the violin at a very early age. She first studied at the University of Chicago, where she obtained a B.A. (language and literature, 1937). She started to study for a Ph.D. in classics but was forced to end her studies in order to support her family. Later she went to Radcliffe College and obtained an M.A. in 1943. She then studied for a Ph.D. in music under Walter Piston from 1942 to 1945. She was a recipient of a graduate honors scholarship from the University of Chicago in 1937, Georgina Holmes Thomas Fellowship from Radcliffe College from 1942 to 1947, Dorothy Bridgman Atkinson Fellowship from the American Association of University Women and Anne Louise Barrett Fellowship from Wellesley College. From 1947 she lectured in music and classics. She was an associate professor of music at Boston University, from 1959 to 1960 and of classics and music at Tufts University, 1964 to 1965. From 1965 she was associate professor of music at Tufts. Many of her harpsichord works have been performed at Carnegie Recital Hall and broadcast over radio stations throughout the United States.

Compositions

ORCHESTRA

Andante and variations (hpcd and orch) (1954-1956)
Suite for Small Orch (1947)

CHAMBER

Quintet (ww) (1971)
Equipoise (a-sax, cl, hpcd and pf) (1972)
Piano quartet (1949)
String quartet (1951)
Suite for recorders (1949)
Quodlibet (fl, vlc and hpcd) (1953)
Sonatina (fl, vlc and hpcd) (1953)
Trio (ob, cl and bsn) (1946)
Trio (vln, cl and pf) (1953)
Allegretto (fl and pf) (1948)
Arabesque (vlc and pf) (1955)
Duo lirico (vln and hpcd) (1952)
Parade (cl and pf) (1954)

VOCAL

Song of Exploration, cantata (S, fl, cl, vlc and hpcd) (1960)
The Baite (T, vlc and hpcd) (1961)
Childing, concert aria (S, fl, vlc and hp) (1957)
Come, lovely and soothing death, duet (S and A or w-ch) (1960)
Darest thou now, O soul (S, cl and vlc) (1959)
Juggler (1962)
Speed, we say (S, fl and hpcd) (1961)
A Valediction: Of weeping (S and hpcd or pf) (1962)
When our two souls (S and pf) (1959)
Four elegies (S and hpcd or pf) (1962)
Five songs of courtly love (S, fl and hpcd) (1958)

SACRED

Adoramus te Christe, motet (ch a-cap) (1938)
Christus factus est, motet (ch a-cap) (1938)
Mass (liturgical ch) (1937-1939)

Ref. composer, 142, 190, 206, 457

BRONDI, Rita Maria

Italian guitarist, editor and composer. b. Rimini 1884. She studied under Luigi Mozzani and Francesco Terrega. She gave concerts throughout Europe, researched on the history of the guitar and the lute, edited articles for the Enciclopedia Italiana and composed for the guitar.

Ref. 502

BRONIKOWSKA, Charlotte von

German composer. She was a member of the 'Sing-Akademie' in Berlin from 1832 to 1846 and a pupil of Rungenhagen.

Compositions

VOCAL

Drei Lieder, op. 1: Der Wald ist stille; Mein Herz; Voeglein mein Bote (Andre) (vce and pf)
Drei Lieder, op. 2: Abendstaendchen (Eichendorff); Traeume (Osterwald) (Schott); Valencias Rose (G. Brandt) (vce and pf)

Ref. 121, 297

BRONSART VON SCHELLENDORF, Ingeborg Lena von (nee Starck)

German pianist and composer. b. St. Petersburg, August 24, 1840; d. Munich, June 17, 1913. Born of Swedish parents, her first teachers were Nicholas von Martinoff and Decker and later Adolf Henselt, Germany. She gave her first public concert at the age of 12, featuring her own composition which was well received. At 14 she played Chopin's *E-Minor Concerto* from memory and when she was 18, on the advice of Henselt, she went to Weimar to become a pupil of Liszt, who soon considered her one of his most talented pupils. He dedicated the re-arrangement of his *Concerto Pathetique* for two pianos into a *Grosses Konzertsolo* to her in 1866. She frequently toured Paris, St. Petersburg and the principal towns of Germany, appearing in Gewandhaus Concerts in Leipzig in 1858 and 1859. In 1861 she married Hans von Bronsart von Schellendorf, whom she had met when a pupil of Liszt. They toured for a few years, but when he became conductor and intendant of the Royal Theatre at Hanover, she was obliged by court rule to retire from public performance. Her opera *Jery und Baetely* was performed repeatedly in Berlin, Weimar, Vienna, Wiesbaden, Koenigsberg and other German cities and was highly praised by critics. *Koenig Hierne* had its first performance in Berlin in the presence of the emperor and the imperial court. In 1887 the von Bronsarts moved to Weimar and eight years later to Munich. DISCOGRAPHY.

Compositions
ORCHESTRA
Piano concerto
Kaiser Wilhelm Marsch (Berlin: Bote & Bock)
CHAMBER
Elegie, op. 14 (vlc and pf) (Leipzig: Breitkopf & Hartel)
Fantasie, op. 21 (vln and pf) (Kahnt)
Fantasie (vlc and pf)
Notturno, op. 13 (vlc and pf) (Breitkopf & Hartel)
Romance (vln and pf) (Weimar: Kuhn)
Romanze, op. 15 (vlc and pf) (Breitkopf & Hartel)
Music for strings
PIANO
Fantasie in G-Minor, op. 18 (Breitkopf)
Fantasie melancolique
Four pieces (Schott)
Fugues
Nocturne (St. Petersburg: Bernard)
Tarantella (Bernard)
Three etudes (Bernard)
Two lullabies (Schott)
Two sonatas
Valse caprice and impromptu (Schott)
VOCAL
Augusta, oratorio
Hurrah Germania (m-ch) (Hannover: Schluter)
Kennst du die rothe Rose nicht (m-ch) (Weimar: Kuhn)
Osterlied: Die Engel spielen noch ums Grab (mix-ch) (Schuberth)
Fuenf Gedichte von E. von Wildenbruch (vce and pf) (Breslau 1883)
Loreley (vce and pf) (Schott)
Six Russian Songs (Lermontov) (St. Petersburg: Johansen)
Three Patriotic Songs (Schott)
Two Swedish Songs (King of Sweden)
Numerous songs (Mirza Schaffy, Fr. Bodenstedt, Otto Jacobi)
OPERA
Die Goettin zu Sais (Weimar, 1867)
Jery und Baetely (after Goethe) (Leipzig: Kahnt, 1873)
Koenig Hierne (Berlin, 1891)
Manfred (after Byron)
Die Suehne (Dessau, 1909)
Ref. 2, 9, 20, 22, 26, 44, 74, 95, 102, 105, 108, 132, 163, 226, 276, 297, 307, 465, 563, 622

BRONTE, Anne

British writer and hymn composer. b. Haworth, January 17, 1819; d. Haworth, May 28, 1849. She was the sister of Charlotte and Emily Bronte.
Compositions
SACRED
Hymns, incl.:
Believe not who say, the upward path is smooth
I hoped that with the brave and strong (1846)
My God, O let me call Thee mine (1846)
Oppressed with sin and woe (1846)
Spirit of truth, be Thou my guide (1846)
Publications
Agnes Grey. 1847.
The Tenant of Wildfel Hall. 1848.
Ref. 482, 502, 646

BROOK, Gwendolyn Giffen

American pianist and composer. b. San Antonio, TX, August 19, 1930. She studied the piano privately under Mrs. R.P. Woodrum, Harold Bauer and Alec Templeton. She obtained the National Piano Guild diploma and then a B.M. (piano and composition) at the Incarnate Word College. She undertook graduate study at Our Lady of the Lake University and Trinity University in San Antonio. She organized a weekly radio program. PHOTOGRAPH.
Compositions
ORCHESTRA
Precis: Piano concerto (1952)
CHAMBER
Tintinnabulation (47 carillons)
Quintet in C-Minor (fl, str trio and pf) (1950)
Prelude (str qrt) (1949)
Four variations on an original theme (vln and pf) (1947)
Les fragments, suite (vln and pf) (1949)
Geburtstagstueck (glock)
PIANO
Dedication (1951)
Impressions from Oscar Wilde (1950)
Martellato (1950)
Paintings of Alexander Brook (1952)
Rhapsody (1952)
Scherzo (1950)
Silver sonata in E-Minor (1950)
Sonatina in E-Minor (1950)
Song without words (1949)
VOCAL
The date (S and pf) (1952)
I sing of brooks (17th-century lyric) (S and pf) (1950)
Three songs (Edna St. Vincent Millay) (1950)
Vittoria mio core (S, fl and pf) (1950)
SACRED
Mary of Magdala, a profile (speaker and orch) (1950)
Service music (org) (1951)
Ref. composer, 206

BROOKS, Alice M.

20th-century American composer. She composed piano and choral works.
Ref. 347

BROOKS, Myra Lou

American pianist and composer. b. Knoxville, TN, January 13, 1933. She studied at the Juilliard School of Music for five years before attending Southern Methodist University, where she obtained a B.M. (piano, 1955) and M.M. (theory and composition, 1956).
Compositions
THEATRE
Make Way for Love; a modern version of Snow White
The Pied Piper of Hamelin, fantasy (narr, soloists, ch and pf) (1956)
Ref. Southern Methodist University, Dallas

BROOMAN, Hanna

Swedish pianist, piano and language teacher and composer. b. 1811; d. Stockholm, 1887. The daughter of Jan Erik Brooman, a dramatic singer, she taught the piano at the Royal Theatrical School in Stockholm as well as the French, Italian, German and English languages. In 1857, at the request of the theatre, she drew up plans for a ballet school.
Compositions
VOCAL
Songs:
Till Laura
Den ensamma Makan
Tanke och Kaensla (Hirsch, 1848)
Norlaenningens Hemlangtan (Elkan, 1862)
Ref. 103, 167, 297

BROUK, Joanna

American radio announcer and composer. b. St. Louis, February 20, 1949. She studied at the University of California, (B.A. 1972) and at Mills College Electronic Music Studio. Since 1972 she has been a radio announcer for KPFA, Berkeley. Her works are mainly electronic pieces using Moog and Buchla synthesizers, although she also composes for the piano, the gong, the flute as well as sound poetry pieces.
Ref. 142

BROUWER, Margaret Lee

20th-century American violinist, teacher and composer. b. Ann Arbor, MI. She received her B.M. (performance) in 1952 and her M.M. (performance) in 1963 from the Conservatory of Music, Oberlin College (1952), having studied under Andor Toth and Stuart Canin. She was first violinist in orchestras from 1972 to 1979 and an associate concertmistress for the Fort Worth Opera Orchestra from 1979. She also taught the violin.
Composition
MISCELLANEOUS
Dream Drifts (1963) (comm Ellen Rose)
Ref. 625

BROWN, Caroline Curtis

19th-century British writer of a song cycle and other songs.
Ref. 465

BROWN, Clemmon May

19th-century American songwriter.
Ref. 465

BROWN, Elizabeth Bouldin (Mrs. J. Stanley)
American composer. b. Halifax, VA, January 11, 1901. She graduated from Cincinnati Conservatory in 1921, where she studied under Edgar Stillman Kelley. She also studied under Eugene Phillips and James Evans in Pittsburgh. She was awarded a first prize from the Pennsylvania Federation of Music Clubs in 1965 and won awards from the National League of American Pen Women in 1967 and 1968. She composed works for strings, the flute and the piano and sacred anthems and hymns.
Ref. 142

BROWN, Elizabeth van Ness
American organist, violinist, choir conductor and composer. b. Topeka, KS, June 12, 1902. She graduated from Kansas State College in 1925 with a B.M. and from the University of Kansas with an M.Ed. in 1945. She also studied at Washburn University, Topeka. She was a public school music supervisor for 30 years, a violinist in the Topeka Symphony Orchestra for ten years and an organist and choir director in several churches. She composed anthems for adult and children's choirs and works for the violin and the piano.
Ref. 142

BROWN, Gertrude M.
American composer. b. Briarcliff Manor, NY, 1907.
Composition
ORCHESTRA
Prelude and allegro (1929)
Ref. 322

BROWN, Gladys Mungen
American pianist, poetess and composer. b. Alexandria, VA, February 21, 1926. She studied voice, the piano and ballet at the Alexandria Institute of Music. She was also a student at the American Academy of Dramatic Arts, The Theatre Guild Drama School, Columbia University, the Sorbonne and La Scala School, Milan. DISCOGRAPHY.
Compositions
VOCAL
Black Tea (S and ens)
SACRED
The Rose of Sharon, a tribute to Israel; official anthem for Earth Day
THEATRE
Homespun Hero, musical based on Johnny Appleseed
Publications
Volumes of poems.
Critical works on poetry.
Ref. 563

BROWN, Harriet Estelle
19th-century composer.
Compositions
MILITARY BAND
Columbo Prize March (Fischer)
PIANO
Cherry Diamond, gavotte (Schirmer)
Ref. 297

BROWN, Katherine. See STEWART, Katherine

BROWN, Mary Helen
American composer. b. Buffalo, NY; d. 1937. She wrote operettas, choral works and songs, some of the latter to German texts.
Ref. 260, 292, 347, 353

BROWN, Mrs. J. Stanley. See BROWN, Elizabeth Boudin

BROWN, Norma
American pianist, choral conductor, musicologist, teacher and composer. b. Cleveland, September 2, 1911. She received a B.A. from the Cleveland Institute of Music in 1962 and M.A. music, from California State University in 1964. She studied musicology under Hans Rosenwald at Schweitzer College, Switzerland. She was music supervisor and choral director in schools and churches and taught the piano privately. She is a member of Mu Phi Epsilon.
Compositions
CHAMBER
Sonata (pf.and vln)
Piano pieces
VOCAL
Pieta and recuerto
Songs
FILM MUSIC
Portrait of a City, documentary
Ref. 643

BROWN, Rosemary
20th-century English pianist, medium and composer. She believed that her compositions were dictated to her by Bach, Brahms, Beethoven, Chopin, Debussy, Grieg, Liszt, Rachmaninov, Schubert, George Gershwin and Fats Waller. When she was seven she had a vision of an old man, whom she later identified as Liszt, who told her he would return later to teach her music. He returned in 1964 to take control of her hands at the keyboard. Critics are divided in their opinion of her work, some thinking that the volume of her works – more than 600 works in less than 15 years – is evidence in her favour. Although she has been the subject of numerous medical and parapsychological investigations there is as yet no agreement as to the source of her compositions. DISCOGRAPHY.
Compositions
PIANO
Over 600 pieces incl.:
Compositions from the other side
Rosemary Brown's music
Publications
Unfinished Symphonies. 1971.
Immortals at my Elbow. 1974.
Bibliography
Parrott. *The Music of Rosemary Brown*. 1978.
Philips 6500 059, record lining.
Ref. Rand Daily Mail – Johannesburg 1979, 502, 563, 637

BROWN, Veronica
English pianist, teacher and composer. b. Nottingham, 1905. She studied at the Royal Academy of Music, where she won a certificate of merit and silver and bronze medals for the piano and aural training. She is an L.R.A.M. and L.T.C.L. She was music mistress at a school in Sussex and taught the piano privately.
Compositions
PIANO
Song of the west wind
VOCAL
Folk song
Ref. 467

BROWN, Zilda Jennings.
American organist, pianist, teacher and composer. b. Farmington, November 27, 1891. She gained her B.Mus. and B.Sc.(Educ.) from Columbia University New York City. She taught the organ, the piano and theory at a school in Chicago and was organist at a church in Farmington. She taught music appreciation at the Farmington State Teachers' College.
Compositions
ORGAN
Berceuse
Fugues
Melody
Responses
SACRED
Hymns
Ref. 374

BROWNE, Augusta (Mrs. Garrett)
American composer. d. 1858.
Compositions
PIANO
The American bouquet (Philadelphia: Osbourn's Music Saloon, 1844)
Angels whisper (Philadelphia: G.E. Blake, 185?)
The Caledonian banquet, op. 33 (New York: C.B. Christian, 1841)
De Meyer grand waltz, op. 73 (New York: Firth & Hall, 1846)
Ethereal grand waltz
The merry mountain horn (also hp) (G.E. Blake, 185?)

VOCAL
The Chieftain's hall (vce and pf) (Boston: H. Prentiss, 1844)
The family meeting (vce and pf) (New York: W. Hall, 1842)
The reply of the messenger bird (vce and pf) (Philadelphia: A. Fiot, 1848)
The volunteer's war song (vce and pf) (New York: C. Holt, 1847)
The warlike dead in Mexico (vce and pf) (C. Holt, 1848)
Other songs
SACRED
Grand vesper chorus (mix-ch and org or pf) (New York: W. Du Bois, 1842)
Hear therefore O Israel (mix-ch and org) (New York: S. Ackerman, 1842)
Ref. 228, 347

BROWNE, Harriet (later Harriet Hughes)
19th-century composer.
Compositions
VOCAL
The captive knight
Music of yesterday (composer's sister Mrs. Hemans) (1836)
Parting gifts (Miss Barber) (1836)
'Tis lone on the waters, duet (Mrs. Hemans, adapted to an Italian air)
Ref. 123

BROWNE, Mrs. Garrett. See BROWNE, Augusta

BROWNING, Bertha Hecker
20th-century Canadian composer.
Compositions
VOCAL
The Chinese Emperor and the nightingale, cantata (1936)
Songs
Ref. 465

BRUCE, Mrs. Walter. See HOWE, Alberta Bruce

BRUCKEN-FOCK, Emilie von
19th-century German composer.
Compositions
ORCHESTRA
Koenigin-Marsch, fantasie (Wagenaar)
CHAMBER
Piano pieces
VOCAL
Songs incl.:
Abendruh: Der schwuele Sommertag verglutet (Kahnt & Noske)
Bitte: Weil'auf mir, du dunkles Auge (Kahnt & Noske)
Friede (Kahnt & Noske)
Herbst (Kahnt & Noske)
Letzte Bitte (Kahnt & Noske)
Sehnsucht (Kahnt & Noske)
Seligkeit: Ich weiss es nicht, wie es gekommen (Kahnt & Noske)
Tod (Kahnt & Noske)
Die Tropfen (Kahnt & Noske)
Zuflucht (Kahnt & Noske)
THEATRE
Seleneia, music drama in 1 act (Noske)
Ref. 276

BRUCKENTHAL, Bertha von, Baroness
18th-century German composer.
Compositions
CHAMBER
Romanza, op. 9 (vlc and pf)
Serenade, op. 19 (vln and pf)
PIANO
Pieces incl.:
Die Thalheimer, op. 16, waltz (Bosworth)
VOCAL
Die Blumen: Entblattre nicht die lieben Rosen, op. 13 (Breitkopf)
Ich steh' am Flussesrand allein, op. 8 (vce and pf) (Bosworth)
Die Sonne huellt in Nebel sich (Gutmann)
Six choruses for men's choir, op. 14 (Breitkopf)
Two songs, op. 20 (Schuberth)
Other songs
Ref. 226, 276, 297

BRUCKSHAW, Kathleen
English pianist and composer. b. Islington, London, January 5, 1877; d. London, October 10, 1921. She studied under Stavenhagen and Busoni and gave her first public performance at the age of 12, when she played Rubinstein's *Concerto in D-Minor* with August Manns. She performed with several English orchestras and the Berlin Philharmonic.
Compositions
ORCHESTRA
Concerto in C-Major (pf and orch)
CHAMBER
Quintet (strs and pf)
Sonata (vln and pf)
PIANO
In remembrance (Edward MacDowell, January 23, 1908)
Moods
Romance No. 1
Wind over a moorland track
Ref. 8, 361

BRUCKNER, Monika. See BRUECKNER, Monika

BRUECKNER, Monika
German composer. b. 1957. DISCOGRAPHY.
Compositions
ORGAN
Variations on Jetzt, Christen, stimmet an (Berlin: Corona R. Budde, 1979)
Ricercare by 3 + 1 tone series (1978)
VOCAL
Im Sommer (vocal ens)
Ref. Bielefelder catalog no. 2 1980, 563

BRUGGMANN, Heidi
Swiss accordionist, pianist and composer. b. St. Gallen, July 23, 1936. At the age of nine she played in her father's orchestra, performing light and folk music. She composed her first waltzes at the age of 11. In 1955 she founded her own orchestra and in 1980 established a trust to promote folk music among the youth. Her compositions have won international prizes.
Compositions
BAND
Laendler (acc, s-sax, pf and d-b)
Marches (acc, s-sax, pf and d-b)
Polkas (acc, s-sax, pf and d-b)
Schottische (acc, s-sax, pf and d-b)
Waltzes (acc, s-sax, pf and d-b, or brass insts)
PIANO
Silber-Jubilaeum (4 hands) (1980)
Zirkuspferdchen (4 hands) (1975)
Die alte Drehorgel (1978)
Beatrice (1980)
Goldener Herbst (1975)
Forellentanz (1979)
Francesca-Elena (1979)
Gluecks-Fontaene (1985)
Lebensfreude (1985)
Schneegloeggli-Polka (1978)
Seiligumpe-Polka (1978)
Tagebuchblaetter (1980)
Wasserspiele (1975)
SACRED
Laendler-Messe: Paxmontana (dialect text, L. Gemperli) (ch and Laendler orch) (1983)
En Tisch mit Brot, Introitus
Heb Erbarme Kyrie
Loblied, Gloria
Glaubesfreud, Credo
Abaettig, Sanctus
Vater unser, Pater noster
Abigmohl, Agnus Dei
Entlassigslied, Ite missa est
Du chlini Schwiz, dialect hymn (1973)
Seid froehlich (1975)
Ref. 651

BRUNDZAITE, Konstantsiya Kazyo

Soviet composer. b. Lithuania, February 6, 1942; d. Vilnius, June 12, 1971. She studied composition under E. Balsis at the Vilnius Conservatory, graduating in 1964. From 1965 to 1967 she worked in the department of literature and art of the central state archives of the Lithuanian SSR. From 1967 to 1970 she was concertmistress at the Vilnius Conservatory. DISCOGRAPHY.

Compositions

ORCHESTRA

White Summits, poem (1964)
Dialogues (org and str orch) (1970)
Simfonietta (str orch) (1963)
Festival Rondo (orch of folk insts) (1965)

VOCAL

S dorozhnym riukzakom (boys' ch and orch) (1964)
Seven enigmas from Lithuanian folklore (mix-ch) (1969)
Romances and songs (vce and pf)
Two Songs (m-S)

Ref. 21, 563

BRUNER, Cheryl

20th-century American composer.

Compositions

CHAMBER

Five Bagatelles (str qrt) (1981)
Woodwind Trio (1980)
Circles (pf) (1980)

VOCAL

Hist Whist (S and pf) (1979)

Ref. AMC Newsletter 22 (3)

BRUNNER, Maria

20th-century Swiss librettist, teacher and composer. She was a school teacher in Thurgau and lived in Basle. She wrote both words and music for 20 lieder for voice and the piano, dedicated to the poet Hans Reinhart.

Ref. 4

BRUSA, Elisabetta

Italian composer. b. 1954. Her work won the Triennial Washington International Competition for String Quartet in 1981.

Composition

CHAMBER

Belsize (str qrt)

Ref. AMC newsletter, Patricia Adkins Chiti (Rome), Otto Harrassowitz (Wiesbaden)

BRUSCHINI, Ernestina

19th-century composer.

Compositions

PIANO

Capriccio (Santojanin)
Minuetto (Santojanin)
Pensiero, waltz (Santojanin)
Il Pescatore, barcarola (Santojanin)

Ref. 297

BRUSH, Ruth Damaris

American organist, pianist, lecturer and composer. b. Fairfax, OK, February 7, 1910. She studied composition at the Kansas Conservatory under Wiktor Lubunski, Gardner Read and David Van Vactor. She received a B.Mus. in 1945. She worked as a studio pianist and accompanist from 1932 to 1940 and joined ensembles in the Midwest from 1938 to 1948. She was head of the piano and organ departments of Frank Phillips College, Borger, TX, from 1951 to 1953 and worked for Radio Station WHB of Kansas City. She was a past president of the MacDowell Music Club and the Texas Music Club. She received a publication award from the Composers' Press in 1959 and awards from the Texas Composers' Guild between 1952 and 1970. She also won awards from the National Federation of Music Clubs. She won first place in the contest for the Oklahoma Heritage Association with her song cycle *Oklahoma Trails* in 1981. She was organist for St. Luke's Episcopal Church in Bartlesville, OK. She received an Ambassador of Good Will Award from the State of Oklahoma in 1983 and was recently appointed State Historian of the Oklahoma Federation of Music Clubs. PHOTOGRAPH.

Compositions

ORCHESTRA

Freedom suite
River Moons, symphonic tone poem (1969)

CHAMBER

Sarabande from Suite (str sextet or orch for 3 vln, vla, vlc and d-b) (1952)
Suite for strings (1968)
Duets (fl and bsn)
The old trail (fl and pf)
Romance sans paroles (vln and pf) (1950)
Silhouette (vln and pf; also pf; also org)
Sketches (vln; also fl and pf) (1967)
Sunset (vln; also fl and pf; also pf or org)
Valse joyeuse (vln and pf) (Composers Press, 1959)
Yucca bells (vln and pf; also bell ch; also pf)

ORGAN

Pastorale (Lorenz, 1956)
Two expressive pieces (J. Fischer & Bro., 1958)

PIANO

American circle (2 pf) (1979)
The night lights (1951)
Osage hills suite (1972)
Playtime pieces (Ontario: Weston)
Rhapsody
Sarabande
Suite (1946)

VOCAL

The harp weaver (w-ch) (1961)
Keep America singing (mix-ch)
Star shined pathetique (w-ch) (1950)
A thing of beauty (w-ch) (1959)
Celebration (w-vce)
Oklahoma trails, song cycle
Songs of Oklahoma
Velvet shoes (vce) (1952)

SACRED

Christmas lullaby (mix-ch)
Christmas story (mix-ch) (1965)
Cradled in a manger (w-ch and pf)
The Lord is my Shepherd (mix-ch)
Praise the Lord, Ye Heavens adore Him, hymn
Praise to the Holiest, hymn
Psalm 138 (1974)
This same Jesus

OPERA

The Fair
The Street Singers of Market Street, folk opera, in one act (1965)

THEATRE

Sing a new song to the Lord, youth musical (1982)

Ref. composer, *Pan Pipes of Sigma Alpha Iota* Winter 1984, 84, 142, 228, 347, 474, 477, 622

BRUSSELS, Iris

American pianist, lecturer and composer. b. Omaha, NE, 1900. She attended New York and Columbia universities and studied under Josef Lhevinne (piano), Rubin Goldmark (harmony), Tom Timothy (orchestration) and Roy Harris (composition). She was a guest music lecturer at the Peabody Institute and the University of Miami. She received the Matthew's Memorial Award and the Trimbel Memorial Award.

Compositions

ORCHESTRA

Symphony
American sketches

TEACHING PIECES

Over 150 piano pieces

Ref. composer, 280

BRUZDOWICZ, Joanna

Polish electronic instrumentalist, pianist, critic, journalist, lecturer and composer. b. Warsaw, May 17, 1943. She was the daughter of Konstanty Bruzdowicz, an architect, engineer, cellist and linguist and Maria Bruzdowicz, a pianist. She began composing at the age of 12 and started her musical studies under Irena Protasewicz and Wanda Losakiewicz at the Warsaw Lyceum of Music, then went on to the higher Conservatory of Music, where she studied composition under Kazimierz Sikorski. In 1966 she graduated with an M.A.. As a pianist she travelled in Poland, Belgium, Austria, and Czechoslovakia. Her works have been played all over Europe and in the Americas, the Far East and Africa. In 1968 she received a scholarship from the French Government and went to Paris to study under Nadia Boulanger (q.v.) and Olivier Messiaen. She also worked in the Groupe de Recherches Musicales of the French Radio, at the same time studying electronic music under Pierre Schaeffer at the Paris Conservatoire. The subject of the thesis for her doctorate at the Sorbonne was 'Mathematics and Logic in Contemporary Music.' In addition to composing, Joanna works as a journalist and critic and lectures in several countries on contemporary electro-acoustic and Polish music. She was one of the founders of Jeunesses Musicales of Poland and is a member and co-founder of the Groupe International de Musique Electroacoustique de Paris. She teaches electro-acoustic music in Vichy and Aix-en-Provence and is a member of SACEM and SACD. DISCOGRAPHY.

Compositions

ORCHESTRA

Symphony (1975)
Impressions, suite (2 pf and orch) (1966)
Piano concerto (1975)
Eclairs (1969)
In Memoriam Serge Prokofiev (1966-1967)

CHAMBER

Episode (pf and 13 strs) (1973)
Tre contra tre (fl, ob, vla and 3 perc) (1979)
Esquisses (fl, vla, vlc and pf) (1969)
Quatuor (vla, ob, trp and trb) (1975)
Variations (str qrt) (1963)
String quartet No. 1, La Vita
Trio (cl, vln and pf) (1975-1976)
Trio dei duo mondi (pf, vln and vlc)
Work for Percussions de Strasbourg (1975-1976)
Fantasia Hermantica sur le theme SABBE (vla and pf) (1979)
Concerto (vib and pf) (1963)
Miniatures (cl and pf) (1963)
Per due, sonata (vln and pf) (1966)
Einklang (hpcd and org) (1975)
Epigrams (vln) (1964)
Ette (cl) (1974)
Mater Polonica (org) (1973)
Pehnidi (hpcd) (1970)
Prelude and fugue (hpcd) (Rideau Rouge, 1980)
Seven miniatures (fl) (1964)
Stigma (vlc) (1969)
Work (fl) (1975-1976)

PIANO

Esistanza (2 pf, 4 hands) (1973)
Election du Pape Jean-Paul II (1978)
Erotiques (1966)
Sonate d'octobre in memoriam 16 X 1978

VOCAL

Jour d'ici et d'ailleurs (P. Cornish-Miguel) (ch, speaker and orch) (1971)
Four songs (Galczynski, Jezewski and P. Lachert) (S and orch) (1965)
Five songs (Galczynski) (ch and cham ens) (1968)
Special etudes, 3 songs (Jezewski) (ch a-cap) (1965)
Niobe, chamber music (K.I. Galczynski) (vce, S, fl, cl, vln, vlc, perc and pf) (1964)
Dessins de Debarcadere (José Gorostiza) (m-S and cham ens) (prize, Union of Polish Composers, 1967)
I have loved thee for so many years (Galczynski) (B and pf) (1965)
Three songs (Galczynski) (B and pf) (1965)
Songs (1975-1976)

OPERA

L'Ane Qui Jouat De La Lyre, radio opera-mysterium of the 20th-century (1975)
Penal Colony, chamber opera (after F. Kafka) (2 vces, 2 actors/mimics and 19 musicians) (1968)
Les Troyennes, musical tragedy (after Euripides) (4 singers, 2 comedians, 12 choristers, 9 musicians and magnetic tape) (1972)

FILM MUSIC

Chita, je t'aime (1974)
Les cyclopes (1973)
Le Hussard sur les toits (1969)

ELECTRONIC

A claire voix (Tetard) (ch, 4 insts and magnetic tape) (1973)
Dum spiro spero (fl and tape)
Le beau Danube bleu (2 pf and tape) (1973-1974)
Le danger (electro-acoustic insts) (1971)
Ek-stasis (electro-acoustic insts) (with E. Sikora q.v.) (1969)
En memoire de mon père (hpcd and tape) (1973)
Epitaph (hpcd and magnetic tape) (1972-1973)
Fabos (1970)
Fas et Nefas (tape and prepared gtr) (1970)
Homo faber (fl and tape)
Marlos Grosso Brasileiras, chant d'amitie (fl, vln, hpcd and tape) (1980)
Salto (magnetic tape and perc) (1970)
La solitude (1972)
Le soufflé (electro-acoustic insts) (1971)
Pieces (fl and tape)

INCIDENTAL MUSIC

La mort de Lord Chatterley, television (1970)

MISCELLANEOUS

Objet à Reflexion (Xenakis) (1970)

Ref. composer, 77, 206, 563, 622

BRYAN, Betty Sue

American organist, pianist, violinist, business woman and composer. b. Madisonville, KY, October 23, 1923. She studied at the Ernest Williams School of Music, New York, from 1941 to 1943 and at New Orleans Baptist Theological Seminary, 1947 to 1949. Besides playing the violin in various orchestras she was pianist and organist at Brookstown Baptist Church from 1973 to 1976 and owned the Betty Bryan Sheet Music Store, Baton Rouge, after 1970. She composed several published works.
Ref. 506

BRYAN, Mrs. M.A.

18th-19th-century English composer.

Compositions

VOCAL

The Bilberry Lass, a pathetic ballad (Miss Wilkinson) (1800)
The Lute of Lisette, an elegiac canzonet (hp, lute and pf) (F. Bryan) (1800)
The Maid of Wooburn, a pathetic ballad (pf or pedal hp) (F. Bryan) (1800)
The Peasant's Prayer, an elegiac canzonet (F. Bryan) (1800)
The Sylvan Scene of Love, arietta a la turca (F. Bryan) (1800)

Ref. 65, 405

BRYANT, Mrs. Charles C. See BRYANT, Verna Mae

BRYANT, Verna Mae (Mrs. Charles C.)

American organist, pianist, teacher and composer. b. Ida Grove, IA, November 1, 1907. She studied at the University of Nebraska and Detroit Conservatory. She studied composition and the piano under Maurice Dumesnil, the organ under Bertha Haggerty and Gordon Young and voice under Ruth Burkholder. She taught the piano.

Compositions

PIANO

Berceuse (4 hands)
Donkey Drag (4 hands)

VOCAL

Slumber song (S and pf or org) (1960)
Time trilogy (S and pf) (1971)

Ref. 395

BRYUSSOVA, Nadezhda Yakolevna

Soviet pianist, editor, musicologist, professor, writer and composer. b. Moscow, November 19, 1881; d. Moscow, June 28, 1951. She studied composition at the Moscow Conservatory under S.I. Taneyev and the piano under Igumnov, graduating in 1904. She became a lecturer at the Moscow People's Conservatory and the Shanyavski University in 1917 and professor at the Moscow Conservatory, 1919 to 1943. From 1948 to 1950 she was editor of the journal, *Sovietskaya Musyka* and *Kolhkozni Teater*. The titles of her compositions are unknown.

Publications

The Music of the Revolution. 1925.
Musicology – Its History and Present. 1910.
The Russian Folk Song in Classical and Soviet Music. 1948.
Scriabin's Rhythmic Forms. 1913.
The Task of Musical Education. 1919.
Vladimir Sakharov. 1949.

Ref. 17, 70, 109, 110, 330

BRZEZINSKA, Filipina (nee Szymanowska)

Polish pianist and composer. b. Warsaw, January 1, 1800; d. Warsaw, November 11, 1886. She was a pupil of Leopold Meyer.

Compositions

ORGAN

Fifteen short preludes (1876)

PIANO

Dzwon, nocturne (Warsaw: A. Brzezina)
Dumanie slepca
Fantazja

Oczekiwanie
Le resignation
W gorach
Six waltzes
VOCAL
Czaty (vce and pf)
Duettino (S and A)
Dwa slowa (vce and pf)
Piesn w utrapieniu do Matki Najswietszej (1861)
Songs (W. Wiktor)
SACRED
Nie opuszczaj nas (K. Boloz-Antoniewicz) (1859)
Archaniol or Ach, powiedz mi, co to jest zycie (N. Zmichowska)
Boze litosny, strzez dzieci swe
Modlitwa
Niebieskiego dworu Pani, Zdrowas Maria (W. Syrokomla)
Piesn do sw Wiktora
Zdrowas Maria (W. Syrokomla)
Ref. 8, 105, 118, 297, 417, 524

BRZOWSKA-MEJEAN, Jadwiga (pseud. Jadwiga Jagiello)
Polish pianist, professor and composer. b. Warsaw 1830; d. Paris 1886. She was the daughter of the composer, cellist, conductor and teacher Josef Brzowski, who was her first teacher. She then studied under K. Kurpinski and in 1844 under Moscheles in Leipzig. She made her piano debut in Warsaw at the age of ten.
Ref. 460, 524

BRZOZOWSKA, U.
Polish composer.
Composition
MISCELLANEOUS
Piesni i tance kujawskie
Ref. *Editions Polonaises de Musique* 1954

BUCHANAN, Annabel Morris
American organist, pianist, choir conductor, folklorist, teacher and composer. b. Groesbeck, TX, October 22, 1889. She studied the organ at Guilmant Organ School under William Carl. She studied composition, the piano and singing at Landon Conservatory, Dallas. She was a music teacher in Texas and Oklahoma. For some time she edited *The Virginia Musician* and together with J. Powell collected, edited and published country songs and dances from the southern United States; she collected more than 2 000 songs. Her other teachers were Charles D. Hahn in Dallas, 1904 to 1907; Hugh A. Clarke in Pennsylvania, 1919 to 1920; William I. Nevins in New York City, 1923, and John Powell in Eastham, VA. She taught at Stonewall Jackson College in Abingdon, VA, and gave piano and organ recitals in the east and southeast. She addressed the First International Music congress in America, New York City, 1939 on 'Modal and Melodic Structure in our Anglo-American Folk Music: introducing a neutral mode'. She compiled, edited and arranged two folksong series for J. Fischer: 'White Top Folksong Series' and 'Early American Psalmody Series' and made numerous transcriptions of folksongs for chorus. She organized many festivals of country music. Her compositions were based predominantly on folklore elements.
Compositions
VOCAL
The moon goes down, choral suite
Come all ye fair and tender ladies (ch)
Song of the Cherubim (ch)
Songs incl.:
An old song
April
The lamp
May madrigal
My candle
Place of dreams
Tonight
Wild geese
Wings
Wondrous love
Wood song
Transcriptions of country songs (ch)
SACRED
Oratorio Rex Christus (soloists and ch)
Anthems, incl.:
The Lord is my Shepherd
O Jesus my Saviour
Break Thou the Bread of Life

Publications
Folk Hymns of America. 1938.
American Folk Music. 1939.
Bibliography
Howard, J.T. *Our Contemporary Composers*. New York, 1941.
Ref. 39, 142, 193, 496

BUCHANAN, Dorothy Quita
New Zealand violinist, teacher and composer. b. Christchurch, September 18, 1946. She studied at Canterbury University, where she obtained a B.Mus. in 1967. She gained a diploma of teaching from the Christchurch Teachers' College in 1975. In 1974 she received second prize from the John Cowie Reid Memorial and in the same year also received a Queen Elizabeth II Arts' Council Grant. She was the first person to be appointed a New Zealand composer-in-schools by the Government. She appeared several times with the Christchurch Symphony and the Canterbury Orchestra.
Compositions
ORCHESTRA
Concertino (cor, trp and school orch) (1976)
BRASS BAND
Prelude (1975)
CHAMBER
Ensemble pieces (beginner cls) (1974-1977)
String quartet (1970)
Trio piece (vln, vlc and pf) (1972)
Air on a ground bass (vlc and pf) (1968)
Elegy (hn and pf) (1966)
Fanfare (2 trp) (1972)
Sonata (vln and pf) (1977)
Sonatine (fl and hp) (1966)
Four duos (vln and pf) (1968)
Three (vln and pf) (1973)
Five pieces (bsn) (1968)
Soliloquy (1970)
VOCAL
Time, rock oratorio (narr, rock group and orch) (1972)
Songs of Wind and Moon (S or T and str orch) (1966)
Three Jacques Prevert settings (narr, T, fl, vln, d-b and pf) (1972)
SACRED
Motet to the Virgin (S or T and str orch) (1974)
Mass in English (w-ch) (1966)
Mass of St. Peter of the Way (cong) (1971)
Song from Ecclesiastes (mix-ch) (1974)
Song of St. Francis (mix-ch and org) (1971)
OPERA
Amazon Grace or The Truth about the Amazons (1975)
THEATRE
Toad of Toad Hall (1971)
Ref. Dorothy Freed (Wellington, NZ), 206

BUCHLEITNER, Therese
19th-century German writer of songs and a song cycle.
Ref. 465

BUCK, Era Marguerite
Canadian organist, pianist, violist, lecturer and composer. b. Manitoulin Island, Ontario, May 2, 1905. She studied at the Regina Conservatory of Music under George Coutts, Edna Marie Hawkin and Lyell Gustin. In Toronto she was a piano pupil of Peter Kennedy and in New York of Howard Brockway. In Banff she studied the viola under Max Pirani and W. Knight Wilson and the organ under Mrs. Stuart, George Coutts and Ernest Moore. She won many composition contests at the Saskatchewan Musical Festival and was a teacher of the piano and the organ at the Regina Conservatory.
Compositions
VOCAL
Good night (F. Harris) (ch)
Can you sew cushions (vce and pf)
The forsaken merman (vce and pf)
A lament (vce and pf)
The plowman (vce and pf)
Slumber song (vce and pf)
The three fishers (vce and pf)
The three poplars, duet
Where dreams are sold (vce and pf)
Where the land lies (vce and pf)
Ref. 85

BUCKLEY, Beatrice Barron

20th-century Canadian pianist, singer and composer. b. Sarnia, Ontario. She studied under George Higginbotham, Karl Keolling, Isabella MacArthur and Joseph O'Donnell. She won a medal for composition at the Saskatchewan Provincial Festival.

Compositions

VOCAL

Songs of Weeny Gopher, 25 songs for children telling of the natural events in the cycle of the year on the western prairies (MacMillan)
My Sanctuary (vce and pf) (Boosey & Hawkes)

Ref. 85, 347

BUCKLEY, Dorothy Pike

American teacher and composer. b. Glens Falls, NY, April 26, 1911. She studied composition at the Eastman School of Music under Burrill Phillips and Wayne Barlow. After 1945 she taught in Rochester. In 1969 she won the annual composition award from the American College of Musicians, Texas.

Compositions

PIANO

Five after five, duet
Adirondack fantasy
Folk theme and variations (1969)
Tarantella
Variphonic suite

VOCAL

The blue waterfall (vce, fl, vlc and pf)
Clouds (vce and pf)
Perception (vce, fl, vlc and pf)

Ref. 142

BUCKLEY, Helen Dallam

American singer, teacher and composer. b. Chicago, October 4, 1899. She obtained her M.M. on a scholarship from the American Conservatory in Chicago, where she taught and obtained her D.Mus. She taught at the Academy of Allied Arts, New York as well as privately in Columbus and Buffalo. She won a number of prizes in contests sponsored by the Chicago News.

Compositions

ORCHESTRA

Camels and land
Exotic dance
Mists of autumn
Oriental suite
Piccaninny lullaby
Scottish air, suite
Sea pictures, suite (1920)
Temple song
Visiting parson

CHAMBER

Two quintets
Quartet (strs and pf)
Trios (strs and pf)
Pieces (vln and pf)
An Indian legend (pf)

VOCAL

Earth in cycle (S, hp and str qrt)
The slave (S, hp and str qrt)
Songs incl.:
After thought
Book of songs
A daily prayer
I shall not care
Love and you
Sweet bird

Ref. 53, 12, 292, 347

BUCKLEY, Olivia. See DUSSEK, Olivia

BUCZEK, (Buczkowna) Barbara Kazimiera

Polish pianist, teacher and composer. b. Cracow, January 1, 1940. She studied the piano under Professor Kazimierz Mirski and completed her studies with distinction in 1959 at the State Music School in Cracow, having studied the piano under Prof. Maria Bilinska-Riegerowa. She continued her piano studies at the State College of Music, Cracow under Professor Ludwik Stefanski, graduating in 1965. After further study under Professor Boguslaw Schaffer she graduated with distinction in 1974. Her *Two Impressions* won a prize in the Grzegorz Fitelberg Composers' Competition in 1970 and her *Violin Concerto* won a special mention in the Nicolo Paganini International Composition Competition in Rome, 1982. She has taught since 1965 and given classes in score reading, aural training, composition and counterpoint at the Academy of Music, Cracow. PHOTOGRAPH.

Compositions

ORCHESTRA

Violin concerto (1979) (mention, Nicolo Paganini competition, 1982)
Anekumena, concerto (89 insts) (1974)
Assemblage (a-fl and str orch) (1975)
Labyrinth (1974)
Metaphonies (1970)
Simplex (1976)
Two impressions (1970) (prize, Grzegorz Fitelberg competition, 1970)

CHAMBER

The darkness of the flame (str duodecet) (1976)
Brass quintet (Ariadne, 1969)
Quintet (sax, fl, hn, vib and vlc) (1971)
String quartet No. 1 (1968)
Composition (fl, pf and vlc for 2 performers) (1970)
Eight easy preludes and eight diatonic canons (2 cl) (1971)
Eidos No. 1 (vln) (Ariadne, 1977)
Eidos No. 2 (tba) (1977)
Eidos No. 3 (bsn) (1979)
Microsonata (vln) (1968)
Sonata breve (pf)
Study (fl) (1968)
Study (vln) (Ariadne, 1970)

VOCAL

Sextet (S, vln, fl, vlc and 2 pf) (1974)
Hypostasis quintet (S, fl, vlc, vib and sax) (1978)
Desunion (vce and d-b)

Ref. composer

BUCZKOWNA, Barbara Kazimiera. See BUCZEK, Barbara Kazimiera

BUECHNER, Margaret

20th-century German composer.

Composition

BALLET

The key, Easter ballet for children (C. Fischer)

Ref. 280

BUENAVENTURA, Isabel (Buenaventura de Buenaventura)

Colombian pianist, painter, poetess, teacher and composer. b. Ibague, December 10, 1903. She obtained a degree from the Colegio del Sagrado Corazon in Bogota and at the Tolima Conservatory, Colombia, studied under A. Castilla, G. Quevedo, J. Bermudez Silva, C.A.A. Ciociano, A. Squarcetta, and D. Haralambia. She taught at the Tolima Conservatory for over 33 years and was nominated assistant director in 1951. She composed symphonies, chamber and organ music and choral works.

Publications

Reflejos del alma. Poems.

Ref. Inst. Nacional de Radio y Television, Colombia

BUENAVENTURA DE BUENAVENTURA. See BUENAVENTURA, Isabel

BUERDE, Jeanette Antonie (nee Milder)

Austrian pianist, singer, teacher and composer. b. Huttleindorf, near Vienna, November 11, 1799. She was educated in Vienna, where her parents mixed with talented artists in all fields. This atmosphere also furthered the career of her elder sister, Ana, who became a famous opera singer in Berlin (1816). Jeanette started piano lessons at the age of seven and then became a pupil of Leon Matzel. She followed these lessons with singing lessons under the imperial court singer Tomaselli and later under the kapellmeister Liverati. She went to Berlin in 1816 where she appeared as a pianist and singer. In 1823 she became a member of the Sing-Akademie, where she learned thorough bass and harmony under Rungenhagen and came into the public eye with about ten songbooks of compositions. Later she married Buerde, an artist and professor at the Academy of Arts. After his death she worked as a singer and piano teacher in Berlin.

Compositions

VOCAL

Abschied
Der Berghirt

Das Heide-Roeslein
Der Jaeger
Liebesgedanken
Das Maedchen und der Totenkopf: Das Schloss am Meer, Hast du das Schloss gesehen
Die Nonne, Im stillen Klostergarten
Was soll ich erst kaufen
Other songs (Heinrichshofen, Trautwein & Schlesinger)
Ref. 121, 129, 276, 297

BUGBEE, L.A. (Mrs. Davis)
American composer. d. 1917. She composed piano works.
Ref. 347

BUGG, Catherine Smiley. See CHEATHAM, Kitty

BUGGE, Magda
19th-century Norwegian composer.
Compositions
PIANO
Tre Karakterstykker, op. 4 (Hansen)
VOCAL
Serenade af A. Munch's Kongedatterens Brudefaerd, op. 3 (vce and pf) (Hansen)
Songs, ops. 1, 2, 5, 6, 8 and 9 incl.:
Aftensang: Den Lyse Dag forgangen er
Hjemoe (Warmuth: Hansen)
Laengtan
Laer mig o Skov
Mai-Sang
Man har et Sagn om Noekken
Soemmeraftenroeden
Sov soedt Barnlille
Spindersken
Vandlilie
Vidste du Vej
Ref. 276, 297

BUIXO, Paulina
19th-century Spanish pianist, poetess and composer. b. Figueras, Catalonia. She was well known in Barcelona around 1865.
Ref. 389

BULLARD-RICH, Carrie or Caryl. See LEWIS, Carrie Bullard

BULLIER, Lea
Composition
PIANO
Fantaisie, sur deux melodies italiennes

BUELOW, Charlotte von
19th-century German composer.
Compositions
VOCAL
Arias (w-vces)
Die Harfnerin, op. 8
Der Lenz ist da, op. 3, no. 2
Nenuphar, die weisse Blume, op. 11
Das Orakel, op. 4
Trost in Tonen, op. 3, no. 1
Verlorenes Glueck, op. 7
Duets
Songs (Breitkopf, Heinrichshofen & Bote)
Ref. 276, 297, 347

BULOW, Charlotte von. See BUELOW, Charlotte von

BULTERIJS, Nina
Belgian pianist, teacher and composer. b. Tamise, November 20, 1929. She studied the piano and staff notation under Jozef D'Hooghe, brother of Clement D'Hooghe. In 1952 she entered the conservatories of Antwerp and Brussels and obtained first prize for harmony, 1955, counterpoint, 1957, and fugue, 1959. As a pupil of Yvonne van den Berghe, she received a diploma with distinction from the Belgian College of Music in 1956. From 1959 to 1962 she studied composition under Jan Louel and fugue under Jean Absil at the Musical Chapel of Queen Elizabeth. Afterward she was appointed teacher of harmony, counterpoint and orchestration at the Lemmers Institute, Louvain. After 1970 she was a teacher of counterpoint and fugue at the Royal Flemish Conservatory, Antwerp. Her cantata *Arion* won the Second Grand Prix de Rome in 1963 and her *Trio* won the Prix E. Doehaerd, 1969. Her *Symphony for Large Orchestra* was the second laureate for the Queen Elizabeth Music Contest in 1965. She is a tone poetess whose work is based on contrapuntal elements within a dodecephonic structure. Her works have been broadcast on Belgian radio stations. DISCOGRAPHY. PHOTOGRAPH.
Compositions
ORCHESTRA
Symphony for large orchestra (1965)
Symphonic movement for large orchestra (1961)
Concerto (2 vlns and orch) (1965)
Piano concerto (1962)
CHAMBER
String quartet (1964)
Sonata (2 vln and pf) (1961)
Trio (pf, vln and vlc) (1962) (prix E. Doehaerd, 1969)
Rondo (vln and pf) (1971)
VOCAL
Arion, cantata (1963) (2nd Grand Priz de Rome, 1963)
De terugkeer van de Krijgsman, cantata
De triomf van het bloed, cantata (1963)
Motet (ch and orch)
God zij geloofd
De yadefluit (T and pf) (1961)
Ref. composer, 1, 188, 563

BUMP, Mary Crane
American marimbist, pianist, trombonist, singer, teacher and composer. b. Monroe, IA, October 13, 1922. She began her piano studies at the age of five with her mother, a piano teacher and then with Mary Phillips Schoettle from 1941 to 1942 and Anthony Koocker in 1947; from 1943 to 1945 she studied the piano at Wheaton College during the summers. She studied voice with Mary D. Liggett from 1941 to 1943 and 1946 to 1947 and Mignon Bole Mackenzie in 1943 and trombone with Geo. W. Unkrich from 1932 to 1938 . She obtained her B.A. cum laude from the Central College in Pella, IA, 1947. She was director of vocal and instrumental music in the public schools of Monroe, from 1943 to 1946. In 1948 she joined the faculty of the Mingo Consolidated Schools as director of vocal and instrumental music. She also pursued a career as a pianist and accompanist, contralto soloist, marimba soloist and a director and member of various vocal and instrumental ensembles.
Composition
CHAMBER
Trombone soliloquy
Ref. 496

BUMPUS, B. Jeannie. See ROSCO, B. Jeannie

BUMPUS, Mary Frances. See ALLITSEN, Frances

BUNCE, Corajane Diane. See WARD, Diane

BUNGE, Jungfer Gertrud
Mid-15th-century German authoress, nun and composer. She was of the Cistercian convent of Wienhausen, near Celle at the time Katherina von Hoya was abbess, from 1422 to 1470. During this time the *Wienhauser Liederbuch* was written by at least five nuns, including Jungfer. This consisted of antiphons and spiritual choral songs; sixteen in Latin, six in a mixture of Latin and German and thirty-seven in Low German. Jungfer was also the authoress and composer of a Responsoriale for the night service.
Ref. 476

BURCHELL, Henrietta Louise

20th-century Canadian organist, choral conductor, lecturer and composer. b. Sydney, Nova Scotia. She obtained a B.Mus. from Oxford University, England and an M.A. from Radcliffe College. She held teaching positions at Mt. Allison University, Wesleyan University, Milwaukee-Downer College and the Halifax Conservatory of Music. She then became organist and choir conductor at Trinity United Church, Windsor, Nova Scotia.

Compositions

CHAMBER

Couperinesque (strs, wws and hns)
Lament (strs)
Variations on St. Anne (org)

PIANO

Acquiescence
Animation

VOCAL

Christmas folk-song (vce and pf)
Griefs (vce and pf)

Ref. 133, 347

BURDE, Jeanette Antonie. See BUERDE, Jeanette Antonie

BURDICK, Elizabeth Tucker

20th-century American composer. She composed operas and songs.

Ref. 347

BURGER, Hester Aletta Sophia.

South African pianist, teacher, writer and composer. b. Worcester, September 30, 1913. She gained her M.Mus. at the University of Pretoria and is an A.T.C.L. and L.T.C.L. She taught the piano in high schools for 34 years and wrote plays for the Republic Festival in the Eastern Cape in 1965 and for the Afrikaans language festival in 1975.

Compositions

SACRED

Christmas oratorio (1972, 1974)
Passion oratorio (1968)

Ref. 457

BURGESS, Brio

20th-century composer.

Compositions

PIANO

Children's dance
Girl on a ball
Toys

OPERA

Rooftops

Ref. Congress of Women in Music

BURGESS, Marjorie

20th-century composer.

Compositions

PIANO

Prisms (Boston, 1979)

MISCELLANEOUS

Mountain laurel

Ref. MLA *Notes* Sept 1980

BURKE, Loretto

American teacher and composer. b. Parkersburg, WV, May 23, 1922. She attended the Catholic University and studied under Conrad Bernier and Thaddeus Jones. She was a high school teacher from 1952 to 1970 and in 1971 became chairlady of the music department of the College of Mount St. Joseph, OH.

Compositions

ORCHESTRA

Symphonic dance suite

CHAMBER

Pastorale (fl, ob and cl)

VOCAL

Valiant Women, cantata (w-vces)

SACRED

Psalm of Praise (mix-ch and brass)

Ref. 142

BURLIN, Natalie. See CURTIS, Natalie

BURNETT, Helen Roth

American pianist and composer. b. Brooklyn, November 11, 1895. Her teachers included Frank Leve, Victor Ehling, Ottmar Moll and Arthur E. Johnstone. She lived in St. Louis.

Compositions

PIANO

Caprice in G
Chant russe
Fantasie in G-minor
Melodie
Spanish sketch

VOCAL

Songs incl.:
Birches
Child songs
Gifts
Nocturne
Pierrot
Things

Ref. Missouri Historical Review, 460

BURNHAM, Georgiana

19th-century American composer.

Composition

SACRED

O worship not the beautiful (vce and pf) (O. Ditson, 1858)

Ref. 228

BURRELL, Dianne

20th-century British composer.

Composition

MISCELLANEOUS

Pavane (1981)

Ref. *Composer* (London)

BURROUGHS, Jane Johnson

20th-century American composer and teacher. b. Martinsville, IL. She composed violin and organ works and songs.

Ref. 347

BURROWES, Katherine

19th-century Canadian pianist, authoress, teacher and composer. b. Kingston, Ontario. She composed piano pieces.

Ref. 347

BURSTON, Maggie

Canadian pianist, poetess, teacher and composer. b. Manchester, England, 1925. She studied the piano at the Royal Academy of Music and won a piano competition set by the Academy for the North of England in 1944. From 1944 till 1955 she lived in Israel and then went to Toronto, Canada. She taught at Hebrew schools till 1959. In 1965 she studied English literature at the University of Toronto and the next year began piano studies under Court Stone. From 1968 till 1972 she studied sight singing, harmony, history of music and composition at the Royal Conservatory where she was a pupil of Gordon Delamont. She continued composition studies under Dr. Dolin until 1978. In 1975 she took a course in 20th-century music and composition at York University and the next year she studied solfege and composition under Nadia Boulanger (q.v.) at Fontainebleau. PHOTOGRAPH.

Compositions

CHAMBER

Reflections (str trio) (1975)
Three moments (vln and pf) (1977)
Ascent (cl and pf) (1979)
Poem (gtr) (1976)
For Christina (pf) (1981)

VOCAL

Haiku, 4 pieces (m-S, hp and fl) cham orch, (1976)
Faces of Summer, 3 poems (mix-ch a-cap) (1978)
Duet (S, T, pf and fl) (1977)
Lament (Cont and pf) (1977)
Lullaby (S and pf) (1975)

Sea's love (S and pf) (1975)
Snow's found (Bar and pf) (1975)
Song of praise (S, pf and fl) (1975)
Summer afternoon (S and cl) (1975)
Were I not weary (Cont and pf) (1975)
SACRED
The Story of Chanukah (narr, ch and pf) (1974)
The Story of Purim (narr, pf, fl and drs) (1973)
MULTIMEDIA
So bless them, bless them (vce, perc, mime and tape) (1981)
Spring song (vce, perc and dance) (1980)
Ref. composer

BURT, Virginia M.
American organist, pianist, choir conductor, teacher and composer. b. Minneapolis, April 29, 1919. She studied under Gerald Bales and Stanley Avery at the Minneapolis College of Music. She taught the organ, the piano and theory.
Composition
VOCAL
Fanfare for a festive day (ch, org and brass)
Ref. 142, 347

BURTIS, Sarah R.
19th-century American composer.
Compositions
PIANO
The Lady's Book polka (T.C. Andrews, 1852)
Morning Star and Evening Star polkas (T.C. Andrews, 1853)
Ref. 228

BURTON, Helen Eugenie Elise. See BURTON, Pixie

BURTON, Pixie (Helen Eugenie Elise) (Mrs. Calburn)
South African pianist and composer. b. Tokai, Cape Town, March 7, 1904; d. Johannesburg, February 4, 1970. She studied the piano at an early age under Caroline Bergman Hodgson and was heard by the visiting Bach specialist Harold Samuel, who greatly encouraged her. She studied composition in Cape Town under Dr. Percy Buck and Professor W.H. Bell and won the overseas scholarship in September, 1926. She studied at the Royal College of Music under John Ireland and Herbert Howells (composition) and Herbert Fryer and Harold Samuel (piano). In 1927 she gave the first performance in South Africa of Mozart's *Piano Concerto No. 20 in D-Minor* with Leslie Heward conducting the Cape Town City Orchestra. In 1930 she obtained a performance A.R.C.M. from the Royal College of Music. She left the world of professional music after her marriage but continued to compose sporadically throughout her life. Her concert appearances were limited by her poor health.
Compositions
PIANO
Allegretto (1954)
Allegro (1932)
Allegro, Aux temps passes (1946)
Assai tranquillo (1954)
Christmas prelude for WWB-Andantino (1940)
Inquietude No. 1, Allegretto, incomplete (1966)
Partita (1965)
Preamble and toccata (1955)
The Simon pieces, suite
Sonata in B-Minor (1926)
Sonatina (1945)
Suite for Sarah, incomplete (1969)
Theme and seven variations (1930)
Three etudes (1954)
Tune on the Chinese-gapped scale (1954)
VOCAL
Where do you hurry (vce and pf)
Ref. R.C. Calburn (Johannesburg)

BURZYNSKA, Jadwiga
20th-century Polish composer.
Composition
VOCAL
Cztery piesni
Ref. 465

BUSCEMI MONTALTO, Margherita
20th-century composer.
Composition
PIANO
Sei acquarelli (Berben, 1983)
Ref. Blackwell catalogue (Oxford)

BUSCK, Lora. See ABORN, Lora

BUSH, Gladys B.
20th-century American composer.
Composition
VOCAL
We give thanks (vce and org) (Canyon Press)
Ref. 190

BUSH, Grace E.
American pianist, lecturer, poetess and composer. b. Ludington, MI, April 25, 1884.
Compositions
PIANO
Lament for a lovely lady (1939)
Other pieces
VOCAL
Songs incl.:
The miracle (high vce and pf) (Composers Press)
Ref. California State University, 142, 190, 347

BUSKY-BENEDETTI, Albina
Italian composer. b. ca. 1869.
Compositions
PIANO
Caprice, op. 2 (Ricordi)
Fantasia on Der Freischuetz, op. 4 (Weber) (Ricordi)
Fantasia on Oberon, op. 3 (Weber) (Ricordi)
Sonata, op. 1 (Ricordi)
OPERA
Clara d'Arta
Ref. 307

BUTCHER, Jane Elizabeth
American pianist, teacher and composer. b. Cleveland, July 7, 1908. She obtained a B.S. (education) from Kent State University, Ohio, and studied the piano, theory and harmony under Hazel L. Hart for 11 years. She studied piano performance for three years under Olga L. Kuehl.
Compositions
PIANO
Hana-Matsuri, Japanese Flower Festival, 5 tone poems in Japanese modes
Ref. 206

BUTLER, Anne Lois
American organist, violinist, conductor, teacher and composer. b. Stockdale, TX, May 25, 1912. She received a B.M. from South Western University (1932) and then a violin scholarship from the Texas Federation of Music Clubs, which she used at the University of Wisconsin, studying composition and the violin under Mr. Burleigh. She studied at the Juilliard School of Music (1936 to 1938) under Louis Persinger and Kathleen Parlow and received an M.M. (violin) from the Peabody Conservatory (1941) where she studied under Dr. Gustav Strube. She was a pupil of Dr. Conrad Bernier and Dr. G.T. Jones at the Catholic University of America, where she received an M.M. in composition in 1956. She was an authorized teacher of the Schillinger System of Musical Composition and granted a B.Mus. equivalent in composition by the Catholic University of America for her work completed at Schillinger House. She studied the violin under Richard Burgin and Dr George Bornoff. Other teachers included Nicolas Slonimsky, Kenneth MacKillop, Lawrence Berk and Mark Gilbert. She played the violin for the Baltimore Symphony Orchestra from 1936 to 1943 and was organist of the First Baptist Church, Silver String, MD, and instructor of string instruments and composer-in-residence with the Washington, DC, public schools. She is a charter member of the International Alban Berg Society and was named composer-in-residence for playing the organ for churches in Texas. She also served as assistant concertmistress for the Juilliard Summer Session orchestra under Peter Wilhousky.

Her *Rondo in E-Minor* won first prize for the Texas Composers' Guild contest; her *Sonnet XLIII* was awarded first place by the Texas Manuscript Society and her violin solo won first place in the Young Artist contest of the Lone Star District. She is a member of A.M.C. PHOTOGRAPH.
Compositions
ORCHESTRA
Symphony of the Hills (1956)
Six mini-pieces (chil-orch)
CHAMBER
Rondo in E-Minor (vln and pf) (1956) (1st prize, Texas Composers' Guild Contest)
Minute pieces (pf)
VOCAL
Sonnet XLIII (Elizabeth Browning) (vce and pf) (1st prize, Texas Manuscript Society)
Songs:
Little boy
Sand castles
Sellers of markers
SACRED
A Christmas carol (mix-ch and org) (Boston Music Co., 1958)
A Christmas story (mix-ch and org) (Boston: R.D. Row)
INCIDENTAL MUSIC
Close to my Heart: A Tale of Three Cities, musical
Ref. composer, 142, 594

BUTLER, Jeraldine Saunders. See HERBISON, Jeraldine Saunders

BUTLER, Mary
English authoress and composer of hymns. b. 1841; d. 1916.
Ref. 502

BUTLER, Patricia Magahay
Canadian composer. b. Toronto, May 3, 1955. She received her B.Mus. and M.Mus (composition) from the University of Toronto. Her teachers included Weinzweig, Ciamaga, Kenins and Hawkins. In 1976 she won a music talent foundation award and in 1977 a Fairclough graduating scholarship. At the Banff School of Fine Arts Composers' Workshop she studied under Mather and Garant.
Compositions
ORCHESTRA
Oboe concerto
CHAMBER
Thoughts for G.B. (ww qnt) (1977)
Trio (1977)
Duo for flute and bassoon (1976)
Beech suite (1979)
Au bord (1978)
Piano pieces
Ref. composer

BUTT, Thelma (nee van Eye)
20th-century American authoress, publisher and composer.
Ref. 347

BUTTENSTEIN, Constanze von
Late 19th-century German composer.
Compositions
CHAMBER
Instrumental pieces
Piano pieces
VOCAL
Songs
SACRED
Ave Maria (A, orch or org and strs) (Vienna)
Ref. 226, 276

BUTTERFIELD, Hattie May
American composer. d. 1969. She composed choral music.
Ref. 347

BUTTIER, Mlle.
18th-century French composer.
Compositions
VOCAL
Vole, amour, dieu vanqueur, an air (Mercure de France, February 1729)
Moments delicieux les plus chers (S and B-continuo) (Paris: Mes-langes de musique, 1727)
Ref. 65, 157

BUTTLER-STUBENBERG, Countess Anna. See STUBENBERG, Countess Anna

BYERS, Roxana Weihe
20th-century American pianist, accompanist, lecturer and composer. b. San Francisco, October 30. She studied music at the American Conservatory under Adolf Weidig and in Vienna from 1927 to 1928. She then studied in Paris under Isidor Philipp, Lazare Levy and Alfred Coret from 1928 to 1931. She was the only woman instructor at the College of Music, AEF University at Beaune, France in 1918 and was founder and director of the department of music for wounded soldiers of the Letterman General Hospital, San Francisco, from 1919 to 1922. She was a soloist for silent films from 1922 to 1923 and for the All Artists Orchestra, New Princess Theatre, Honolulu, from 1923 to 1925. She was founder-director of the Hawaiian Conservatory, Honolulu from 1924 to 1927 and the first soloist with the Honolulu Symphony Orchestra in 1926. In Paris she was assistant teacher to Cortot at the Ecole Normale de Musique from 1929 to 1931. In 1938 she organized and supervised the department of music therapy in the State Industrial Workshop for the Blind, Los Angeles. She was also director of the piano faculty of the Beverly Hills Conservatory from 1943 to 1945 and head of the piano department of Pepperdine University, Los Angeles, 1963 to 1966. She accompanied Efrem Zimbalist and Yehudi Menuhin.
Compositions
CHAMBER
Carols in Fantasy (pf)
Reverie in D-Flat (org) (Boston: Oliver Ditson)
VOCAL
California, gem of the nation's crown (vce and pf)
Mother and I (Fred Books) (vce and pf)
My aim (vce and pf)
When tears flow (Beth Brock) (vce and pf)
A woodland day, five songs (vce and pf)
Ref. composer, 142

BYLES, Blanche D.
20th-century American composer.
Compositions
SACRED
De promis' lan' (mix-ch and pf) (G. Schirmer)
Wood of the Cross
Ref. 190

CABREIRA, Estefania Loureiro de Vasconcelos Leao
20th-century Portuguese musician and composer. b. Lisbon. The daughter of the Viscount of Faro, Estefania graduated from the Lisbon Music Conservatory then worked with her husband on the publications of works for children; he composing the lyrics, she the music. She worked on the Comercio Infantil for 30 years and then directed children's radio programs.
Compositions
VOCAL
Cançãos de amor a terra
Cançãos de gesta
Canteiro de rosas
O Cancioneiro do bebe
Ref. 268

CABRERA, Ana S. de
20th-century Argentine folk song collector and composer.
Compositions
VOCAL
Cantos nativos y danzas del norte argentino (Buenos Aires; Ricordi)
Ref. Ricordi (Buenos Aires)

CABRERA, Silvia Maria Pires
Brazilian pianist, choir conductor, teacher and composer. b. São Paulo, April 4, 1958. She obtained her degree in composition from the São Paulo

University, after studying under Willy Correa di Oliveira (composition), Amilcar Zanni (piano) and Ronaldo Bologna (conducting). Since then, she has attended semesters on conducting at the University and has been a teacher and conductor at the Winter Festivals of Prados since 1979 and conducted other choirs. She composed for various events such as the Winter Festivals and for several vocal groups. PHOTOGRAPH.

Compositions

CHAMBER

Coração selvagem (trp, trb, hn, tba and dr) (1982)
Miragem (pf, fl and ob) (1983)
Limite (pf and perc) (1983)
Memorias (bsn) (1982) (SDP)
Metamorfose (cl) (1984) (SDP)
Assobio (fl) (1982) (Serviço de Difusão de Partituras, ECA-USP)
Sopro (ob) (1983) (SDP)
Variaçãos para piano sobre um tema de Schoenberg (pf) (1982)

VOCAL

Canção dos pastores (4 S, 2 A and ch) (1983) (SDP)
Cançãos (chil-ch) (1980-1983)
Cantar (2 S, A and ch) (1983) (SDP)
Cantavento (2 S, A and ch) (1979) (SDP)

Ref. composer

CACCHIATELLI, Adelina

Compositions

VOCAL

Estasi d'amore
Stornello

Ref. Ricordi

CACCINI, Francesca

Italian guitarist, harpsichordist, lutenist, poetess, singer and composer. b. Florence, September 18, 1587; d. ca. 1640. She was the eldest daughter of composer Giulio Caccini and his wife Lucia, a singer. Francesca studied singing and composition under her father and learned to play the lute at an early age. She made her debut as a singer at the age of 13, appearing with her younger sister Settimia (q.v.) at the Medici Court. By the age of 18 Francesca was an active composer. She also played the harpsichord and the guitar and wrote poetry in Latin and Tuscan. She became the pride of Florence after singing in a number of operas, gaining the nickname 'La Cecchina'. In 1604 to 1605, at the request of Maria de' Medici, the Caccini group traveled to France, where King Henry IV was so impressed with Francesca that he requested her to stay at the French Court. However, she was refused permission to remain by Grand Duke Ferdinando I and in 1605 returned to the Medici Court. In 1607 she married Giovanni Battista Signorini, singer, musician and composer. They had two daughters, who sang at court in their early childhood. Besides her court performances, Francesca also sang in sacred festivals at Pisa and in concerts. In 1616 she traveled to Rome with the entourage of Cardinal Carlo de' Medici, to whom she dedicated her *Primo Libro* in 1618. At the time it was the most extensive collection of songs by a single composer to appear in print. In April 1617 she and her husband toured most of the music centers of Italy. Many of her works composed as entertainments for the Tuscan Court have been lost. The work for which she is best known is an opera that she called a *balletto*, *La liberazione di Ruggiero dall'isola d'Alcina* which was commissioned by the archduchess in honor of the forthcoming visit of the Polish Prince Wladislaw Sigismund and performed with great pomp and ceremony at the Villa Poggio Imperiale on February 2, 1625. It was the first opera to be composed by a woman and the first to take a subject unrelated to antiquity. A medallion of Francesca Caccini was found at the Rospigliosi Palace at Pistoria, Italy. DISCOGRAPHY.

Compositions

VOCAL

Il primo libro delle musichi a una e due voci: 35 madrigals, motets, hymns, canzonets and arias (Florence: Stamperia de Zanobi Pignoni, 1618)
Chi e costei che qual sorgente aurora
Che fai misero core, ecco ch'in croce
Ardo infelice e palesar non temo
Maria, dolce Maria
Nel camino aspro ed erto
Pieta, mercede, aita
Ferma Signor, arresta
Ecco ch'io verso il sangue
Deh chi gia mai potra Vergine bella
Nube gentil che di lucente velo
Io mi distruggo et ardo
Lasciatemi qui solo
O che nuovo stupor mirate intorno
Su le piume de' venti
Giunto 'l di' che dovea 'l cielo
Io veggio i canti verdeggiar fecondi
La pastorella mia fra i fiori e il giglio
Rendi alle mie speranze il verde e i fiori
Dov'io credea le mie speranze vere (also in Constantini's *Ghirlandetta Amorosa*, 1621)
Laudate Dominum de coelis
Haec dies quam fecit Dominus
Regina coeli
Adorate Dominum
Beate Sebastiane
Te lucis ante terminum
S'io men vo'
Non so se quel sorriso
Che t'ho fatt'io
O vive rose
Se muove a giurar fede
Ch'amor sia nudo, e pur, con l'ali al tergo
Fresche aurette
Dispiegate
O chiome belle.
Aure volanti (2 S, A and 3 fl)
Ch'io sia fedele (in Robletti's Le Risonante, 1619)
Canzonettas in Lode della Befana (1620)
Other ariettas and canzonettes in contemporary collections

SACRED

Chi desia di saper che cos e amore
Jesu corona virginum

OPERA

Il ballo delle Zingare (Saracinelli) (1614)
La liberazione di Ruggiero dall'isola d'Alcina (lib from Ariosto's Orlando Furioso by Saracinelli) (Florence: P. Cecconcelli, 1625)
Il martirio di Sant'Agata, sacred drama (with G. Gagliano) (1622)

THEATRE

Festa delle Dame (M. Buonarroti, Jr.)
La Fiera (M. Buonarroti, Jr.) (with G. Gagliano) (1619)
Mascherata di ninfe di Senna (with sister Settimia) (1611)
La stiave (M. Buonarroti, Jr.)

Publications

Books of songs, from the opera La liberazione di Ruggiero dall'isola d'Alcina. (modern reprint ed by Doris Silbert, Northampton, MA, 1945).

Bibliography

Bonaventura, A. *Il ritratto della 'Cecchina. La Cultura Musicale*, 1922.
De La Fage, A. *La prima compositrice di opere in musica e la sua opera. F. Caccini. Gazzetta Musicale di Milano*, 1847.
Ghusi, F. *F. Caccini*. 1952.
Raney, Carolyn. *F. Caccini, Musician to the Medici, and Her Primo Libro (1618)*. Ph.D. dissertation, New York University, 1971.
Raney, Carolyn. *F. Caccini's Primo Libro. Music and Letters* 48, Oct. 1967: 350-357.
Silbert, D. *Francesca Caccini Called La Cecchina*.

Ref. 2, 8, 15, 22, 65, 79, 86, 88, 100, 105, 112, 125, 126, 135, 155, 157, 166, 177, 193, 204, 262, 264, 335, 347, 361, 405, 406, 524, 555, 563, 612, 622, 630, 653

CACCINI-GHIVIZZANI, Settimia

Italian singer and songwriter. b. 1590; d. 1640. She was the daughter of Giulio and younger sister of Francesca Caccini (q.v.) and married A. Ghivizzani. DISCOGRAPHY.

Compositions

VOCAL

Gia Sperai, non spero hor'pui
Madrigals

THEATRE

Mascherata di ninfe di Senna (with sister Francesca) (1611)

Ref. 465, 476, 630, 653

CADDEN, Jill

20th-century Australian composer.

Composition

INCIDENTAL MUSIC

Winslow Boy

Ref. 442

CADORET, Charlotte (Soeur St.-Jean-du-Sacre Coeur)

Canadian pianist, lecturer and composer. b. Newark, NJ, February 29, 1908. She studied music at the Conservatoire National, the Institut Pedagogique and the Schola Cantorum in Montreal. Her teachers were E. Robert Schmitz (piano), Rodolphe Mathieu and Claude Champagne (theory and composition) and Eugene Lapierre, (accompaniment of Gregorian chant). She received her bachelor and licentiate of music degrees from the Ecole Normale de Musique de l'Institut Pedagogique of the University of Montreal, where she taught from 1934 and became director in 1942.

Compositions
SACRED
Cantata in honor of Blessed Marguerite Bourgeoys (m-ch)
Bone Pastor (m-ch)
Ecce fidelis (m-ch)
Parce Domine (m-ch)
Tu verras (m-ch)
Les communiantes
Cradle song (P. Colum) (vce and pf) (G. Schirmer)
Lorsque je mourrai (R. Lasnier) (BMI, Canada)
Messe (3 equal vces and org)
Messe à Notre-Dame (2 equal vces and org) (BMI)
Ref. 133

CADY, Harriette
20th-century American pianist, teacher and composer. b. New York City. She studied under Leschetizky.
Ref. 347

CADZOW, Dorothy Forrest (Hokanson)
Canadian arranger, lecturer, writer and composer. b. Edmonton, Alberta, August 9, 1916. She studied music at the University of Washington, Seattle, where she received a B.A. and a teacher's diploma. In 1942 she was granted a three year fellowship in composition at the Juilliard Graduate School, where she studied under Frederick Jacobi and Bernard Wagenaar. From 1945 to 1949 she taught and did freelance arranging and was a staff writer for *International Musician*. In 1949 she joined the staff of the music department of the University of Washington, teaching theory, orchestration and composition.
Compositions
ORCHESTRA
Northwestern sketches (1945)
Prelude (str orch) (1950)
CHAMBER
String quartet (1944)
PIANO
Heard next door (Elkan-Vogel Co., 1948)
Little bed (Mercury Music, 1944)
Prairie lullaby (Mercury Music, 1944)
Who told you so? (Elkan-Vogel, 1948)
VOCAL
Around a toadstool table, song cycle (1946)
A blackbird suddenly (1949)
Brer Rabbit medley, song cycle (1948)
Golden dawn (BMI Canada, 1949)
Songs to poems, song cycle (M.W. Brown)
SACRED
The Lord's Prayer (Century Music Co.)
OPERA
Undine (1958)
Ref. Working papers on Women in Music, 22, 40, 133, 141, 142, 347

CAESAR, Shirley
American composer. b. Durham, NC, 1939.
Compositions
VOCAL
I'll go (ch)
Stranger on the road (ch)
Ref. 136, 347

CAETANI-RZEWUSKA, Calista, Princess
Polish pianist, artist, linguist and composer. b. Poland, 1810; d. Rome, July 24, 1842. She married Don Michelangelo Caetani, Prince of Teano. She was a woman of great spirit and intelligence who spoke several languages, painted and excelled in music.
Composition
VOCAL
Credo (4 vces)
Ref. 105

CAI, Wen Ji, Princess (Cai, Yan)
Chinese flautist, poetess and composer, who lived at the end of the Han dynasty (202 B.C. to 220 A.D.).
Compositions
CHAMBER
Qin, or 18 Bars on the Hujia (trad Chinese str inst)
Ref. Patricia Adkins Chiti (Rome)

CAI, Yan, Princess. See CAI, Wen Ji, Princess

CAIRN, Anna. See SNEED, Anna

CALAME, Genevieve
Swiss concert pianist and composer. b. Geneva, December 30, 1946. She studied the piano and theory under Lottie Morel and Louis Hiltbrand at the Geneva Conservatory, graduating in 1967. She also studied at the Accademia Musicale Chigiana in Siena, Italy and perfected her piano technique under Guido Agosti in Rome. She studied composition first under Jacques Guyonnet at the Studio de Musique Contemporaine, Geneva and later in Stockholm, Paris and the United States. She won the composition prize of the I. Atelier SMC in Geneva. She has given numerous concerts in Europe, the United States and Latin America and has been president of the Genevan section of the Societe Internationale de Musique Contemporaine since 1975. PHOTOGRAPH.
Compositions
All published by A.R.T., Geneva
ORCHESTRA
Alpha futur (1976)
Les aubes d'Onomadore (African insts and orch) (1977-1978)
Calligrammes (hp and cham orch) (1983)
STEpHAnE mALLArmE (cham orch) (1975)
Je lui dis... (cham orch) (1980)
CHAMBER
Iral desert de metal (4 trp and 4 trb) (1974)
Mandala (7 trp) (1979)
Lude (hp) (1979)
VOCAL
Differentielle Verticale (S and orch) (1974)
BALLET
L'Oiseau du Matin (1972)
ELECTRONIC
Mantiq-al-Tayr (fl, b-fl and tape) (1973)
Le-Son-Qui-Fut-Mille (composed with and for children) (cham orch and tape) (1980)
Le Homme-Miroir (tape and cham orch) (1980)
Oniria (pf and tape) (1981)
MULTIMEDIA
Geometry I, II, III (videotape) (1975)
Le chant remémoré (videotape) (1976)
Videocosme (audiovisual) (1976)
Labyrinthes fluides (videosynthesis) (1976)
Et l'oeil rêve (audiovisual) (1977)
Tableaux video (audiovisual) (1977)
Publications
A la recherché d'un mode de communication. Journal de Genève, 1978.
Base de reflexion pour l'enseignment de la musique à l'école. CO Parents, 1981.
L'utilisation de l'ordinateur comme instrument de creativite et nécessité d'un enseignment interdisciplinaire intègre. 1985.
Ref. composer, 651

CALANDRA, Matilde T. de
Composition
ORCHESTRA
Concerto (4 gtr and orch) (ASCAP)
Ref. 280

CALBRAITH, Mary Evelene
American pianist and composer of Oregon. d. 1972. She was well known in New York as an accompanist.
Composition
VOCAL
My love rode by (m-S and pf)
Ref. Bicentennail Parade of American Music

CALCAGNO, Elsa

Argentine pianist and composer. b. Buenos Aires, October 19, 1910. She studied the piano under E. Melgar and at the Conservatorio Nacional de Musica e Arte Escenica under P. de Rogatis, C. Gaito, F. Calusio, A. Palma, V. Gil, F. Ugarte and R. Rodriguez, as well as musical folklore under Wilkes. She became president of the Cultural Commission of the Sinfonica Feminina Association and founded the El Unisono Association. She was music critic for the journal *La Mujer* and her work also appeared in the *Album de autores argentinos*, published by the National Commission of Culture (vol. 7). She is a member of many South American music associations and gave numerous concerts in Argentina.

Compositions

ORCHESTRA

Symphony (1958)
Sinfonietta (wind insts and double str orch) (1954)
Concerto (2 vln, hp and str orch) (1968)
Concerto (vlc and orch) (1935)
Concerto in C-Minor (pf and orch) (1935)
Fantasía argentina (pf and orch) (1945)
Fantasía y variaciones clasicas (pf and orch) (1942)
Suite sinfonica (1953)
Siete Bocetos sinfonicos de expression (1940)
Orchestral variations (1954)
Plenilunio en un Balneario del Rio de la Plata (1938)
Poema íntimo (1937)
Preludio y cuatro danzas argentinas
Preludio sinfonico
Suite nortena

CHAMBER

Impressiones de las sierras cordobesas (qnt) (1938)
Piano quintet (1942)
Cuarteto breve (qrt) (1938)
Two string quartets
Pieces for piano and guitar
Sonata in E-Minor (vln and pf) (1934)
Tres piezas caracteristicas (vln and pf) (Buenos Aires; Ricordi, 1954)
Sonare y tema con variaciones (1970)
Siete improvisaciones para guitarra (1968)
Sonatina (qrt) (Buenos Aires; Randolph, 1965)

PIANO

Intermezzi, Nos. 1, 2 and 3 (Ricordi, 1962)
Los Naranjales (Aire de Zapateado del Litoral) (Ricordi, 1958)
Milonga estilizada (Danza Argentina) (Buenos Aires; Ricordi Americana, 1952)
Milonga pampaena
Suite infantil (Randolph, 1966)
Twelve preludes
Valle de Zonda Cueca (Ricordi)
Variaciónes clasicas sobre un temade la llanura para le mano izqueirda sola (Ricordi, 1942)
Zambita (Ricordi, 1952)

VOCAL

Sinfonia dramático-coral (soloists, ch and orch)
Nace una nación, symphonic poem (ch and orch) (1966)
Concerto (vce and orch) (1950)
Poema (vce and orch) (1940)
Las manitas del mino (G. Morillo) (w-ch or chil-ch a-cap) (Randolph, 1966)
Tres corales argentinos (ch) (1950)
Campo de Buenos Aires (vce, fl, cl, hp and str qrt) (1950)
Cariñito, para mi madre. Zamba. (R.J. Sanches) (Casa Lottermoser, 1950)
Flor del aire, cancion Argentina (A. Lamberti) (vce and pf) (Casa Lottermoser, 1941)
La parra quebrada (J.B. Grosso) (vce and pf) (Ricordi, 1946)
La Primavera (M.A. Dominguez) (vce and pf) (Casa Lottermoser, 1962)
Lo que yo quiero (P.B. Palacio) (vce and pf) (Editorial Saraceno, 1949)
Madrecita! (A. Capdevila) (vce and pf) (Casa Lottermoser, 1959)
Madre vidalitay (F.S. Valdez) (vce and pf) (Ricordi, 1953)
Siete canciónes escolares (1937)
Six songs (1936)
Three poems (1942)
Umbrales del mar, 9 poems (1939)
Lyrics

BALLET

Postreras visiónes (1938-1939)
El arroyo de las tres hermanas (1942-1943)

THEATRE

El rosal de las ruinas, lyric drama in 1 act (1935-1936)
Boda en el jardín, children's comedy (1939)
Three commissions of children's music for the theatre

Bibliography

Mayer, Otto. *Música y músicos de Latinoamerica*.
Schiuma. *O Músicos argentinos contemporaneos*. Buenos Aires, 1938.

Ref. 16, 17, 70, 100, 361, 390, 477

CALCRAFT, Sharon

20th-century Australian composer.

Composition

FILM MUSIC

On the Ball (1976)

Ref. 442

CALDER, Hattie M.

20th-century American composer.

Composition

ORCHESTRA

Arch Street Polka (small orch) (1977)

Ref. 322

CALDWELL, Mary Elizabeth Glockler (Mrs. C. Philip)

American organist, pianist, choir conductor and composer. b. Tacoma, WA, August 1, 1909. She gained a B.A. (music) from the University of California, Berkeley. She studied composition privately under Richard Schrey in Munich and Bernard Wagenaar in New York and the piano and the organ under Benjamin Moore in San Francisco. She was an organist and choir conductor from 1933. Her *Carol of the Little King* sold some 700 000 copies, whilst her opera *Gift of Song* has been performed over 200 times in the United States, England and Canada.

Compositions

SACRED

Of Time and Eternity, Easter cantata
The Road to Bethlehem, Christmas cantata (Bar and S)
Let us follow Him, cantata (B and S)
Carol for a New-Born King (mix-ch and org) (H.W. Gray & Co.)
Carol of the Little King (w-ch and org) (Gray)
Christus resurrexit (mix-ch and org) (Gentry Publ.)
The crimson drum (mix-ch) (Gray)
The crown (mix-ch and org) (Gray)
Enter this door (mix-ch and org) (Gray)
Gifts (unison ch and keyboard) (Fred Boch Music Co.)
How far to Bethlehem (w-ch and org) (Gray)
I am the one (mix-ch and org) (Boch)
I know a lovely garden (unison ch; also vce and org) (Gray)
In praise of Spring and Easter (unison ch and keyboard) (Boch)
In Spring (unison ch and keyboard) (Boch)
In the fullness of time (mix-ch)
The little lamb (Blake) (mix-ch and org)
May the words of my mouth go forth, O Daniel (unison ch)
The Noel Carol (w-ch) (Gray)
Spring prayer (C.H. Towne) (mix-ch and org)
A little carol (Robert Herrick) (vce and fl or vln)

OPERA

Gift of Song (New York: Boosey & Hawkes, 1963)
The Night of the Star
Pepito's Golden Flower

Ref. 40, 141, 142, 146, 190, 465, 646

CALE, Rosalie Balmer Smith

American pianist, teacher and composer. b. St. Louis, September 24, 1875. She studied under her grandparents, her mother, A.I. Epstein and E.R. Kroeger. She taught in St. Louis for more than 30 years and gave concerts of American compositions. Her operettas were performed in St. Louis and New York.

Compositions

ORGAN

Two Fantasies on Abide with me and Saw ye my Saviour

VOCAL

Masque of Pandora (Longfellow) (w-ch) (1907)
Choral works
Songs

OPERETTA

Four Peeks on a Bushel of Fun, or Cupid's Halloween (1907)
Love, Powder and Patches (1897)

Ref. 460

CALEGARI, Cornelia (Maria Caterina)

Italian organist, nun, singer and composer. b. Bergamo, ca. 1644; d. Milan, 1664. She wrote her first collection of motets at the age of 15. In 1660 she entered the Convent of Santa Margherita in Milan to become a nun and a year later took the veil under the name of Maria Caterina. Her beautiful singing and organ playing in the church of the convent soon drew crowds of music lovers and she was named *La Divina Euterpe*.

Compositions
VOCAL
Madrigali a due voci
Madrigali e canzonette a voce sola
SACRED
Messe a sei voci con instrumenti
Motetti a voce sola (1659)
Vespers
Ref. 74, 101, 105, 126, 128, 212, 264, 276, 335, 347, 361

CALEGARI, Leonarda

17th-century composer. She was a nun at the Convent of St. Ursula in Bologna.
Compositions
SACRED
Masses (4 vces and insts)
Motetti a una, due e tre voci con violini e senza (Bologna, 1687)
Motetti a voce sola (Bologna, 1695)
Motetti concentrati a piu voci (Bologna, 1695)
Vespers
Ref. 502

CALL, Audrey

American violinist and composer. b. April 12, 1905. She studied at Sherwood Music School, Chicago and received her B.Mus. in 1923 and M.Mus. in 1926. After winning two major violin competitions in America she proceeded to Ecole Normale, Paris, where she studied under Maurice Hayot. At the Paris Conservatoire she studied under Edouard Nadand, Firmin Touche and Vincent d'Indy from 1927 to 1929, when she became a laureate of the Conservatoire. She concertised widely as a violinist.
Compositions
ORCHESTRA
American tone poem (vln and orch)
Piece for chamber orchestra
Elegy
VIOLIN
The bishop checkmates
Canterbury Tales
The duke takes the train
Serenade to a cornstalk fiddle
Streamline
To a lady from Baltimore
The witch of Harlem
VOCAL
Songs incl.:
I just telephone upstairs
Indiana lullaby
Ref. 280, 494

CALLAWAY, Ann

American composer. b. Washington, DC, 1949. She studied music under Grace Newsome Cushman at the Peabody Conservatory. At Smith College she became a pupil of Alvin Etler and at the University of Pennsylvania she studied under George Crumb and George Rochberg. Her compositions have been performed by various chamber ensembles including the New York Philomusica. DISCOGRAPHY.
Compositions
CHAMBER
Collections – recollections (pf, fl and vlc)
Easter sequence a tre (1975)
Seven dramatic episodes (fl, vlc and pf) (1976)
Sonata a tre (trp, hn and trb) (1975)
Music (hn and org)
Two elemental pieces: Wind fantasy; Water portrait (hn and pf) (1974)
Compositions (fl) (1975)
Theme and seven variations (pf) (1972)
VOCAL
Night patterns (William Blake) (S, cl, perc, 2 vln, 2 vlc and d-b) (1973)
Besides this May (S, fl and pf)
A dream within a dream (B and pf)
Visions from the natural world, poems, 5 songs (S and perc) (1984)
SACRED
Agnus Dei 1 (S and ch a-cap)
Psalmody (mix-ch and org)
Alleluia, vidimus stellam
Psalm 67 (2 S and 2 A)
Ref. AMC newsletter, 563, 625

CALLINAN, Maureen

Australian composer. b. 1935.
Composition
VOCAL
Socio-voce (7 vces) (1973)
Ref. 442

CALOSSO, Eugenia

Italian conductor and composer. b. Turin, April 21, 1878. She studied at the Conservatory of Leipzig. She conducted her own compositions and toured throughout Europe until 1914.
Compositions
ORCHESTRA
Crepuscolo (large orch)
Suite campestre (large orch)
Suite inglesa (small orch)
Suite araba
Suite mitologica
CHAMBER
Pieces (vln)
PIANO
Danze antiche
Piccole impressioni
Other pieces
VOCAL
Lieder and ballads (vce and large orch)
Choral compositions
Madrigals (3 and 4 vces)
Duets for soprano and contralto
Poemetto lirico (from Horace's Ad fontem bandusiae)
Approx. 50 songs (vce and pf)
OPERA
Vespero (Ernesto Ragazzoni)
Ref. 86, 105, 180, 226

CALPURNIA

1st-century Roman composer. She was the granddaughter of Calpurnius Tabatus, a Roman Knight of Comum. Calpurnia was the third wife of Pliny the Younger (61-113 A.D.) whom she accompanied to Bithyna, where he became governor in 111 A.D. She set Pliny's verses to music, but none exist today.

CALVIN, Susan Heath

20th-century American composer. She obtained an M.A. in 1971 from the University of Texas, Austin.
Compositions
VOCAL
The Half-Moon Westers Low (Housman) (ch)
Words of Comfort (Dorothy Parker) (ch)
SACRED
I will lift up mine eyes (m-ch and org) (H.W. Gray and Co.)
Lamentations (1971)
Ref. 142, 146, 147, 190

CALVO-MANZANO, Maria Rosa

Spanish composer. b. 1944.
Composition
HARP
Retablo de Navidad: el pequeño nacimiento (Madrid: Union Música Espanola, 1975)
Ref. 267, 518

CAMAL. See CAMATI, Maria

CAMALDULI, Sorella

16th-century Italian composer. She was a nun of Bologna and is known to have composed sacred works, but none survived.
Ref. 502

CAMATI, Maria (Camal) (pseud. La Farinetta)

18th-century Italian harpsichordist, singer and composer. She was called *La Farinella* and appeared in Venice in 1729. Her artistic career took her

beyond the borders of Italy and she was famous for her ability at the harpsichord. She composed pieces for her instrument and arias.
Ref. 502

CAMBIASI BRANCA, Cirilla
18th-century Italian pianist and composer. She was the sister-in-law of Felice Romani and studied under Gioacchino Rossini.
Compositions
VOCAL
Choral piece (A. Maffei) (in honor of G. Rossini)
Bibliography
Barbiera, R. *Passioni del risorgimento*. Milan, 1903.
Branca, E. *Felice Romani e i piu reputati maestri di musica del suo tempo*. Turin, 1882.
Ref. 182

CAMERON, Freda. See VAUGHAN, Freda

CAMEU (Cameu de Cordoville), Helza
Brazilian cellist, pianist, musicologist, teacher and composer. b. Rio de Janeiro, March 23, 1903. She studied the piano at an early age under P. Ballariny and later under A. Nepomuceno. At the National Institute of Music she studied under J. Nunes (piano) and H. Richard (theory) and in her final examinations was awarded a gold medal (1919). In 1936 she graduated in composition from the Conservatorio Brasileiro de Musica. She studied under A. Franca (harmony), F. Braga (counterpoint and fugue), Assis Republicano and L. Fernandes (composition), G. Dufriche (voice), N. Padua (cello) and Heitor Villa-Lobos (choral singing). She contributed to the promotion of music in her country and created the program 'Musica e Musicos do Brazil' on radio. From 1950 she worked at the anthropology division of the National Museum on the analysis of indigenous music. She received numerous prizes and awards. DISCOGRAPHY. PHOTOGRAPH.
Compositions
ORCHESTRA
Terra de sol, symphonic poem (after G. Barroso)
Yara poema, op. 7, piano concerto (1936)
Quadros sinfonicos, op. 17 (after G. Penalva) (1937)
Quadros sinfonicos, op. 19 (after E. Doria) (1st prize, competition Orquestra Sinfonica Brasileira (1939)
Seresta Nos. 1 and 2 (1924)
Suite, op. 9 (1st prize, competition Orquestra Sinfonica Brasileira, 1939)
Meditação (also vlc and pf) (1941)
CHAMBER
String quartet, op. 12 (1937)
Suite, op. 3, no. 1 (str trio) (1935), no. 2 (str qrt) (1935)
Cantilena (vln and pf) (1928)
Cidade nova (ob and bsn)
Peça caracteristica (vln and pf) (1950)
Poema (vln and pf) (1959)
Scherzetto (vln and pf) (1928)
Sonata (vlc and pf) (1942)
VOCAL
Liricas (vce and orch) (1941)
Modinha (vce and orch) (1937)
Acalanto (vce and pf)
Amar (vce and pf) (1942)
Ao, op. 8 (vce and pf) (1941)
Eterna incognita (vce and pf) (1928)
Liricas, op. 25 (vce and pf) (1943)
Morena cor de canela (vce and pf) (1934)
Noitinha (vce and pf) (1946)
Querem ver esta menina (vce and pf) (1948)
Saudade (vce and pf) (1928)
Silencio (vce and pf) (1943)
Solidão (vce and pf) (1934)
Tarde (vce and pf) (1943)
Torre morta do ocaso (vce and pf) (1933)
Trovas (vce and pf) (1946)
Vila branca (vce and pf) (1945)
Bibliography
Almeida, Renato. *Historia de Musica Brasileira*. Rio., 1942.
De Bettencourt, Gastao. *Historia da Musica no Brasil*. Lisbon, 1945.
Ref. 100, 106, 333, 563

CAMEU DE CORDOVILLE, Helza. See CAMEU, Helza

CAMINHA, Alda
20th-century Brazilian composer. DISCOGRAPHY.
Composition
CHAMBER
Preludio, op. 16 (vln and pf) (ded Henryck Szeryng and modeled on Kreisler's Prelude and Allegro in C-Minor)
Ref. 563

CAMMACK, Amelia
19th-century American composer.
Compositions
PIANO
Pieces
VOCAL
Songs incl.:
I am waiting
Tears
Ref. 276, 347

CAMPAGNE, Conny
Dutch pianist, recorder player, violist, teacher and composer. b. Amsterdam, August 26, 1922. She was taught her instruments and composition by F. Conrad, J.G.T. Lohmann and F. Buchtger. She lived in Java for 15 years, during part of which period she was kept prisoner in a Japanese camp. She returned to Holland in 1946 to continue her studies and to teach at the Hague.
Compositions
ORCHESTRA
Concerto for alto recorder (also ob and str orch; also str qrt) (1949)
CHAMBER
Totentanz, variations for Renaissance ensemble (1970)
Music for ensemble of six recorders (1980)
Tanzlied aus Ungarn (youth ens) (1982)
String quartet (1950)
Quartet (s, a, t and b-recs) (1957)
Four pieces for youth group (s and a-recs, vln and vlc) (1954-1958)
Three part folk song movements (s and a-recs and vln)
Suite (2 a-rec) (Zurich: Pan, 1953)
Suite for 2 violins (1954)
Theme and Variations (s-rec and hpcd or hp) (1956)
Duettspielbuch (2 rec) (1969) (Stuttgart: Hanssler)
Country Dances (s-rec and hpcd) (Pan, 1958)
Schuelerduette (2 vln) (1959)
Schuelerduette (vln and vlc) (1960)
Sonatine (s-rec and hpcd) (1961)
Polish folk dances (s-rec and hpcd) (1962)
Cantus firmus, movements for 2 recorders (1962)
Sonatina (cl and pf) (1960)
Duette (vln and vlc) (1974)
Trauermusik, 3 pieces (a-rec and vla) (1978)
Eastern European folk song movements (rec and vla) (1979)
Three adagios (vln and vla) (1979)
Tanzbilder (s-rec or ob and hpcd) (Noetzel, 1958)
Three duets (2 a-recs) (Hanssler, 1963)
Slavische Tanzsuite (s-rec or ob and vln) (1966)
Sonata (vln) (1970)
Music (a-rec) (1963)
Variations (a-rec) (1980)
Three themes and variations (a-rec) (1974)
VOCAL
Morgenstern, songs (middle vce and pf or cham orch; also inst ens) (1955)
Guido Gezelle, cycle (ch, recs, gtrs, ob and cl) (1959)
Schuetze, cycle (boys' or chil-ch, strs and recs) (1975)
SACRED
Instrumental movements for church songs (1979)
Ref. composer, 70

CAMPANA, Francesca
17th-century Italian composer from Florence. DISCOGRAPHY.
Compositions
VOCAL
Pargoletta, Vezzosetta (vce and ens)
Arie a una, due e tre voci, op. 1 (Rome: Giovanni Battista Robletti, 1629)
Two madrigals in Robletti's Le Risonanti (1 or 2 vces and acc) (1629)
Ref. 128, 653

CAMPBELL, Aline. See MONTGOMERY, Merle

CAMPBELL, Caroline
English composer. She lived in London, ca. 1787.
Compositions
VOCAL
Two Sonatas and Three English Airs with variations (hp and hpcd) (London, ca. 1787)
Two Sonatas and Six Songs and Some English Airs with Variations, op. 11 (hp and acc) (London, ca. 1788)
Ref. 65, 125, 405

CAMPBELL, Edith Mary
Canadian organist, choral conductor and composer. b. Quebec, September 1, 1912. She studied under Dr. Alfred Whitehead and obtained a F.R.C.C.O. diploma and from 1932 was the organist and choir director of St. James Church, Quebec.
Compositions
ORCHESTRA
Scherzo (str orch)
Theme and variations (1943)
ORGAN
Paraphrase on Jesus Christ is risen (H.W. Gray & Co., 1944)
Prelude and fugue (1947)
SACRED
Kings shall come from Saba (Boston Music Co.)
ARRANGEMENTS
The babe in Bethlehem's manger (org) (A.P. Schmidt, 1945)
Christ has arisen (O. Ditson)
I have called that lovely rosebud (str qrt)
The victor's triumph (org) (O. Ditson, 1974)
Ref. 133

CAMPBELL, Mary Maxwell
Scottish composer. b. Fife, 1812; d. St. Andrews, January 15, 1886. She was the daughter of Sir D.J. Campbell.
Compositions
VOCAL
The march of the Cameron men
The mole and the bat (1867)
Other songs
Ref. 85, 276, 347

CAMPET DE SAUJON, Mlle.
18th-century French composer. She was one of the earliest composers of music for the piano, her works showing great technical ability, but no more seems to be known about her.
Composition
PIANO
Fantaisie et variations (based on Paisello's *Nel Cor piu non mi sento*) (ded Queen of France)
Ref. 502

CAMPMANY, Montserrat
Spanish music teacher and composer. b. Barcelona, March 7, 1901. She studied in Barcelona and moved to Argentina in 1909, studying under J. Aguirre and graduating in 1943 from the Conservatorio Nacional de Musica y Arte Escenico. She worked in Barcelona at the Escuela Blanquerna from 1930 to 1938 and the Escuela del Mar from 1930 to 1940 and taught in Buenos Aires at the Institute of Re-education from 1947 to 1949 and the Bernasconi Institute, 1949 to 1950.
Compositions
ORCHESTRA
La Peri, symphonic poem (1923)
Danza india (ww, pf, perc and orch) (1927)
Vision sinfonica (1929)
La Guspira, sardana (11 folk insts) (1931)
CHAMBER
Música para trompeta metales y timbal (trp, brass and kettle drs) (1969)
Saxophone quartet (1958)
String quartet in E-Major
Trio in F-Sharp Minor (pf, vln and vlc) (1945)
Tres duos para violinas (1941)
Piano pieces
VOCAL
Otonal, symphonic poem in 8 parts (Rube Dario) (1926)
Poemas de Cujo (vce, fl and hp) (1925) (A. Buffano)
Raims y espigues, choral pieces (prize)
Other choral works and pieces (ch a-cap)
Carità del cielo (1959)
Cuatro poemas: Día y noche; Feria de Tunuyan; Patio de Guaymallén; Siesta y Medano
Songs for children
BALLET
Contrapunto final (1968)
THEATRE
Els tres camins, comedy for children
Ref. 17, 107, 361, 390

CAMPOS ARAUJO DE (De Araujo Campos), Joaquina
Brazilian pianist, professor and composer. b. Rio de Janeiro, November 1, 1906. She studied the piano under Francisco Alfredo Bevilacqua and Lois Amabile and composition under Paulo Silva and Francisco Braga at the Music School, University of Brazil, receiving a gold medal in piano playing in 1926 and her doctorate in music in 1936. She was professor of harmony and morphology at the Federal University, Rio de Janeiro and from 1937, music professor at the Lorenzo Fernandez Music Academy. In 1976 she was awarded a prize by the Order of Musicians, Brazil. PHOTOGRAPH.
Compositions
CHAMBER
Um quadro (str qrt) (1944)
Chorinho flauteado (pf and fl) (1965)
PIANO
Abertura Vitoria (1944)
Devaneio (1971)
Estudo em forma e toada (1956)
Estados d'alma (1971)
Interrogação (1944)
Luz que não se apaga (1947)
A noite sonhamos (1947)
O canto do sabiá (1947)
Ode aos que tombaram (1947)
Prece (1947)
Romance (1944)
Romance da Boneca (1947)
To ada sentimental (1947)
Quando eu era criança (1955)
Vale dos reis, fantasy concert
VOCAL
O baile das flores (vce and orch) (1935)
E maravilhoso senhor (vce, ch and pf) (1972)
Brincadeira que fascina (vce and pf) (1973)
Como a luz para o dia (vce and pf) (1966)
Dei-ihe uma flor (vce and pf) (1972)
Enchantement (vce and pf) (1966)
Extase (vce and pf) (1977)
Hino de paracambi (vce and pf) (1974)
Longe (vce and pf) (1967)
Louvor a paracambi (vce and pf) (1974)
Meu Deus (vce and pf) (1977)
Moite de São João (vce and pf) (1966)
Oblata (vce and pf) (1973)
Partita (vce and pf) (1967)
Sublime tourment (vce and pf) (1971)
Teus olnos azuis (vce and pf) (1975)
Trem de ferro (vce and pf) (1972)
Quando ela vieri (vce and pf) (1975)
Publications
Curso de Harmonia e Morfologia Musical. Vol. 1. 2nd Edition, 1965. University of Brazil Press.
Curso de Harmonia e Morfologia Musical. Vol. 2. 2nd Edition, 1977. Grafica Olimpica Editora, Rio de Janeiro.
Ref. composer, 17, 107, 361, 390

CANAL, Marguerite
French professor and composer. b. Toulouse, January 29, 1890; d. near Toulouse, January 27, 1978. She studied at the Paris Conservatoire under Paul Vidal in 1903 and obtained first prizes for harmony, accompaniment and fugue. In 1920 she won the Grand Prix de Rome for her symphonic poem *Don Juan*. From 1919 she was titular professor at the Paris Conservatoire.
Compositions
ORCHESTRA
Don Juan, symphonic poem (1920) (Prix de Rome, 1920)
La flûte de jade (1926)
CHAMBER
Spleen (vlc and qnt) (Paris: M. Jamin, 1926)
Sonata (vln and pf) (1922) (M. Jamin, 1926)
Thème et variations (ob) (1935)
PIANO
Esquisses méditerranéennes (Heugel, 1930)
Pages enfantines (Heugel, 1931)

VOCAL
Over 100 songs incl.:
Amours tristes, song cyle (Baudelaire, Mardus, Toussaint and Verlaine)
SACRED
Requiem (soloists, ch and orch) (1923)
OPERA
Tlass Atka (Jack London) (ca. 1922)
Ref. 22, 23, 96, 105, 110, 556, 622, 637

CANALES PIZARRO, Marta
Chilean violinist, choral conductor and composer. b. 1895. She studied under Professor L. Esteban Giarda. In 1933 she founded the Amalia Errazuriz choir and in 1944 the Ana Magdalena Bach choir. She became well known as a concert violinist and played an important role in Chilean musical life.
Compositions
ORCHESTRA
Elevacion (org, hp and cham orch) (1946)
CHAMBER
Berceuse (vln and pf)
Marche funèbre (vln and pf)
VOCAL
Canteres chilenos, 10 songs from Chilean folklore (ch) (1946)
Cuatro canciones de cuna (ch) (1946)
SACRED
Marta y Maria, oratorio (soloists, ch, org and cham orch) (1929)
Misa de Navidad (mix-ch and cham orch) (1930)
Misa eucarística (soloists, mix-ch and cham orch) (1930)
Doce madrigales teresianos (St. Teresa de Jesús) (mix-ch) (1933)
Villancicos, 50 Christmas songs from South American folklore (mix-ch)
Hymnos y cantos sacros en estilo gregoriano (vces and org) (1936-1940)
Misa en estilo gregoriano (vces and org) (1933)
Ref. 90, 100, 107, 226, 332

CANAT DE CHIZY, Edith
20th-century composer.
Compositions
CHAMBER
Luceat (10 vln) (Paris: Jobert, 1985)
VOCAL
Livre d'heures (4 soloists and orch) (Jobert, 1985)
Ref. Otto Harrassowitz (Wiesbaden)

CANCINO DE CUEVAS, Sofia
Mexican pianist and composer. b. Mexico City, July 29, 1898. She studied the piano under Luis Ogazon and composition at the faculty of music of the National Autonomous University of Mexico, 1932 to 1938. In 1938 she founded an Academy of Opera, which performed the works of Mozart, Pergolesi and Cimarosa in the Palacio de Bellas Artes.
Compositions
ORCHESTRA
Symphony in G
Gallo en Patzcuaro, symphonic poem
CHAMBER
String quartet
Piano pieces
VOCAL
Songs
OPERA
Anette (1945)
Gil Gonzalez de Avil (1937)
Michoacna (1950)
Promessa d'artista e parole di re (1952)
Ref. 17

CANDEILLE, Amelie (Emilie) Julie (F. Simons-Candeille)
French actress, harpist, singer and composer. b. Paris, July 31, 1767; d. Paris, February 4, 1834. She studied under her father, Pierre Joseph Candeille, who was also a composer and the harpsichordist, Holaind. She made her debut in 1782 as Iphigenie in Gluck's *Iphigenie en Aulide* at the Paris Grand Opera. From 1783 to 1796 she worked for the Theatre Francais as an actress, where she produced her own operetta *Catherine ou La Belle Fermiere* and sang the leading role. She wrote both the words and music for the operetta, which had 154 consecutive performances and remained in the repertoire of the Comedie Française for 35 years; it was translated into several languages. In 1798 she married Simons, a carriage builder in Belgium and from then on signed herself F. Simons-Candeille. In 1807 she brought out her comic opera *Ida, l'orpheline de Berlin* which when produced at the Opera-Comique, proved to be a fiasco. She gave some successful concerts under the direction of Viotti and Cramer.
Compositions
ORCHESTRA
Concerto, op. 2 (hpcd or pf and orch) (1787)
CHAMBER
Symphonie concertante (pf, cl, bsn and hn) (1786)
Concerto (pf, hn and fl) (1789)
Three piano trios (Leduc, 1788)
Three sonatas (hpcd, vln and vlc) (Leduc, 1788)
Sonatas (pf or hpcd and vln) (1796)
PIANO
Duo, op. 3 (2 pf) (Paris: Boyer, 1794)
Sonata (2 pf)
Fantasies
Six sonatas, ops. 4, 6, and 8 (pf or hpcd)
Variations sur un thème portugais
VOCAL
Motets (large ch)
Le bain, after *The Seasons* by Thompson (1786)
La bayadere or Le français à Surate (1794)
Chansonettes
Romances
OPERA
Catherine ou La belle fermiere, comic opera (1792)
Bathilde ou Le duc, comic opera (1793)
Ida, l'Orpheline de Berlin, comic opera (1807)
La jeune hôtesse (Paris, 1794)
Publications
Memoirs. In private possession, Nimes.
Souvenirs de Brighton, de Londres et de Paris. Paris, 1818.
Bibliography
Casevitz, T. *Une actrice femme de lettres au XVII, Mlle. Candeille.* Revue Hebdomadaire. Paris, Oct. 1923.
Fusil, L. *Souvenirs d'une actrice.* Paris: Dumont, 1841-1846.
Pougin, A. *Une charmeuse, Julie Candeille.* Le Ménestrel, Oct. 7 1883.
Ref. 2, 8, 15, 17, 41, 91, 100, 105, 119, 128, 129, 132, 218, 226, 307, 335, 361, 368, 400, 404, 406, 431, 653

CANFIELD, Mrs Harold. See TYSON, Mildred Lund

CANNING, Effie I. (pseud. of Effie I. Crockett)
American pianist, actress, poetess and composer. b. Rockland, ME, 1857; d. Boston, January 7, 1940. She studied the piano, harmony and counterpoint under her uncle, Professor A.T. Crockett. At the age of 15 she composed her famous *Rock a bye baby* which was published under her pseudonym. She gave stage performances for 28 years. PHOTOGRAPH.
Compositions
VOCAL
Songs incl.:
Rock a bye baby (1884)
Ref. Dept. American Music, 347, 370, 374, 433

CANNISTRACI, Helen
20th-century composer.
Compositions
SACRED
Ave Maris Stella (3-part ch and orch)
Qui habitat in adjutorio, Psalm 90 (w-ch and str orch)
Ref. BMI

CANTELLO, Annie (Mrs. Henry Cox)
19th-century English pianist and composer. b. Nottingham. She studied at the Royal Academy of Music, London; won the Sterndale Bennett prize in 1881 and was a Lady Goldsmid scholar in 1882. She made her debut in 1882 playing Robert Schumann's *Piano Concerto* in St. James' Hall, London and then gave concerts and recitals in London and Nottingham.
Compositions
PIANO
Sonata in E-Minor
Other pieces
Ref. 6, 276, 347

CANTELO, Anne

18th-century English singer and composer.

Composition

VOCAL

Werter's Sonnet (vce and pf or hp or hpcd) (1790)

Ref. 65

CAPDEVILA I GAYA, Merce

Spanish composer. b. Barcelona, 1946. She studied at the Municipal Conservatory of Music, Barcelona and then worked in the electro-acoustic laboratory, Phonos. She began studying composition under Gabriel Brncic in 1977 and attended a course of new music given by Luigi Nono and Coriun Aharonian.

Compositions

CHAMBER

Eclipsi (12 vlc or 4 vlc or 2 vla and 2 vlc) (1982)
Entre els morats, l'ocre i el blau (fl, ob, bsn, vln and vlc) (1981)
...I noe s'emborratxa de vi (ob, bsn, vib and pf) (1978)
Mene, mene, tekel, upsarin (cl, vla and pf) (1979)
Naturalesa morta (fl and pf) (1980)

PIANO

Diferents Temps i Nivells (1977)
Miratges (1980)

ELECTRONIC

Deshill, Hols, Eamus (tape and hpcd) (1982)
Gramatges (tape and pf) (1983)
Intermezzo (tape) (1981)
Voltes (tape, 2 cl and vlc) (1983)

Ref. ICW

CAPERTON, Florence Tait (Mrs. G.A. Dornin)

American violinist and composer. b. Amherst County, VA, April 21, 1886. She studied the violin under Charles Borjes, conductor of the first Norfolk Symphony Orchestra, of which she became soloist and concertmistress (1902 to 1904). In 1909 she moved to Baltimore where she studied at the Peabody Conservatory. In 1946 she moved to Iowa, studied music at the State University and played in the Symphony Orchestra. She studied harmony and composition under William Critser of Pittsburgh. She moved to Orange, VA, in 1961.

Compositions

CHAMBER

Lullaby (vln and pf) (1948)

SACRED

Bow down Thine Ear, O Lord (m-ch) (1960)
Christ the Lord is risen (m-ch) (1962)
Come, little children (junior ch) (1962)
The little baby Jesus (junior ch) (1962)
Rejoice, give thanks (junior ch) (1966)
Reverie (ch and org) (1970)
Teach me thy way, O Lord (m-ch) (1960)
Give thanks to God (1977)
Sleep, baby, sleep (S with vln obb) (1964)

Ref. composer, 142

CAPERTON, Marilyn Renee. See LEECH, Renee

CAPPELLO, Laura Beatrice

16th-century Italian composer from Brescia.

Compositions

VOCAL

La Ghirlanda della Contessa Angela Bianca Beccaria, madrigals (various authors) (collected by Stefano Guazzi, for the heirs of Girolamo Bartoli, Genoa, 1595)

Ref. 327

CAPPES, Maria Antonia. See NICOLAY, Maria Antonia

CAPPIANI, Luisa

19th-century American singer, singing teacher and composer. b. Trieste, Italy. She studied in Vienna with Ponserdonne and in Italy with Romain and Lampretti (voice). She settled in New York in 1881. She was the only woman elected to the board of 18 professors of the American College of Music in Cleveland in 1883.

Compositions

VOCAL

Songs incl.:
Ave Maria
Darte del canto

Ref. 276, 347

CAPSIR-TANZI, Mercedes

Spanish-Italian opera singer, teacher and composer. b. Barcelona, July 20, 1895; d. Suzzaro, Italy, March 13, 1969. She studied the piano and composition at the Conservatory of Barcelona and voice under V. Nunell and G. Fatuo in Italy. She became an Italian citizen in 1927. She made her debut in Barcelona in 1914 in the role of Gilda in Rigoletto and toured in Europe and Latin America, her greatest successes coming during the 1920s and 1930s. She was acclaimed for her crystal voice, perfect technique and interpretation. She later taught singing in Barcelona.

Compositions

VOCAL

Variations on a theme by Mozart (vce and orch)
La barca grosszanse (after Catalan folk songs)

Ref. 3, 9, 17, 20, 85, 135, 323, 361

CAPUCCI, Lida

19th-century Italian pianist and composer who was acclaimed for her virtuoso playing.

Compositions

VOCAL

Amazzoni
Canzone della fonte
Notte serena, romance
Notturno
Passa la nave mia
Serenata discorde
Sola

Ref. 180

CAPUIS, Margherita Mary. See CAPUIS, Matilde

CAPUIS, Matilde (Margherita Mary)

Italian organist, pianist, violinist, professor and composer. b. Naples, January 1, 1913. She studied the organ, the piano and the violin in Venice and Florence and graduated in composition at the L. Cherubini Conservatory in 1943. Prior to her graduation she undertook postgraduate courses in composition at the Accademia Chigiana of Siena (1941 to 1943 and 1946). She performed in concerts, recitals and on radio and with the cellist Ugo Attilio Scabia formed the Duo Scabia-Capuis, which achieved international recognition. Her symphonic and chamber music pieces have been widely broadcast on European radio and elsewhere and many of her compositions form part of the standard concert repertoire of international artists and orchestras. She was a professor at the State Conservatory Giuseppe Verdi in Turin and received many prizes and awards. DISCOGRAPHY. PHOTOGRAPH.

Compositions

ORCHESTRA

Concentus brevis (ob and str orch) (1975)
Corale (org and str orch) (1942)
Dialogo (str orch) (1948)
Leggenda (str orch) (1948)
Tremomenti (vlc and str orch) (1955)
Sinfonia in G-Minor (1949)
Ouverture (1942)
Variazioni (1941)

CHAMBER

Quintet (1960)
Quintet (vlcs) (1964)
Quartet in A-Minor (1943)
Quartet in C-Sharp Minor (1956) (gold medal prize and hon diploma,
Quartet in D-Minor (1942)
Quartet in G-Minor (1947) (hon mention, quartet competition, Venice, 1948)
International Music Contest Rubinstein, Buenos Aires, 1962)
Collection of pieces (1-3 vlc and opt pf) (Turin: Scomegna)
Animato con passione (vlc and pf) (1959)
Ballata (vlc and pf) (Padua: Zanibon, 1957)
Improvisazione (vlc and pf) (1964)
Introduzione e allegro (vlc and pf) (1959)
Sonata in A-Minor (vln and pf) (1953) (Milan: Curci)

Sonata in C-Minor (vlc and pf) (1952) (Curci) (hon mention, International Competition for Composers, Genoa, 1952)
Sonata in D-Minor (vlc and pf) (1955)
Sonata in F-Sharp Minor (vlc and pf) (1966)
Sonata in G-Major (vlc and pf) (1975)
Sonata in G-Minor (vln and pf) (1950) (Curci)
Sonata No. 5 (vlc and pf) (1980)
Temo variato (vlc and pf)
Canti senza parole (vln) (1976) (Curci)

ORGAN
Fantasia (1974)
Preludio e allegro (1956)

PIANO
Bozzetti (4 hands) (1969) (Curci)
Sei pezzi facili (4 hands) (1966) (Curci)
Fiaba armoniosa (1954) (Forlivesi)
Puppenmaerchen, small pieces
Sette schizzi (Curci)
Six preludes (1972) (Curci)

VOCAL
L'allegro viandante (vce and pf) (Florence: La Nuova Italia)
Canti per bimbi (1-3 vces and opt acc) (Milan: Carisch)
Prima, seconda e terza Desolazioni del poeta (vce and pf) (1945)
Implorazione (vce and pf) (1940)
La nave della vita, ballad (1947) (hon mention, Competition CUC, Bolzano, 1948)
Tre liriche (vce, vlc and pf) (Florence: Forlivesi)
Trilli mattutini, collection of songs for children (1944) (Forlivesi)

SACRED
Pianto della Madonna, oratorio (soloists, ch and orch) (Jacopone da Todi) (1945)
Cantata (w-ch and orch) (1953)
Ave Maria (vce and pf) (1950)
Divagazioni (S and vlc) (Curci) (1979)
Nostalgia dell'Immensita (S, vlc and pf) (1980)

Ref. composer, 563

CAPURSO, Elisabetta
20th-century Italian composer.
Composition
VOCAL
Comprenne qui voudra (S reciter, w-vces, a-fl, cl, sax, pf, vlc and strs) (Padua: G. Zanibon; Peters, 1977)
Ref. MLA *Notes*

CARAFA, Livia
16th-century Italian composer at the Milan court, who composed madrigals and motets.
Ref. 502

CARAFA D'ANDRIA, Anna
Italian composer.
Composition
VOCAL
La mia bambola, song (Schutisch) (Ricordi)
Ref. Ricordi (Milan)

CARBONEL, Cecile Louise Stephanie. See CHAMINADE, Cecile Louise

CARENAS, Countess of. See GARELLI DELLA MOREA, Vincenza

CARENZA
13th-century French troubadour. The only available knowledge of her is from a poem that was presumably written by her and two other women troubadours, Alais (q.v.) and Iselda (q.v.). She might have been a nun at the convent attached to the Abbey de Senanque and was a patron of troubadours.
Ref. Dr. Margaret Nabarro (Johannesburg), 303

CARESS. See BASBAS

CAREW, Lady Henry
19th-century English composer.
Compositions
VOCAL
The bridge (Longfellow)
Other songs
Ref. 347

CAREY, Elena
American pianist, singer and composer. b. Ohio, 1939. She began playing the piano and composing in early childhood and later studied the piano under George Martin at Wagner College faculty; she also trained in classical singing and attended Livingston College. DISCOGRAPHY.
Composition
ELECTRONIC
D.N.A.
Ref. 563

CARISSAN, Celanie
French composer of Creole parentage. b. Nancy, 1859.
Compositions
CHAMBER
Scenes des Alpes (vln and pf)
Deux aires de danse, pavan et rigodon (pf) (Laudy)
Fête montagnarde (Paris: Harquet)
Soir lumieux

VOCAL
Ballade du plongeur (ch) (1895)

SACRED
Rebecca, oratorio
Sonnet à la Vierge, romance (Loret)

OPERETTA
La Fiancée de Gael (1892)
La Jeunesse d'Haydn (1889)

THEATRE
L'Ame de l'amour, lyric drama
La Novice, lyric drama
Séléne, scene antique (dramatic scene for S and orch) (1913)

Ref. 225, 226, 276, 297, 307, 431, 465

CARL, Tommie Ewert
American organist and composer. b. Marion, KS, September 23, 1921. She obtained her M.A. from the American University, Washington, DC. where she studied composition under Dr. Lloyd Ultan. She studied the organ for two years at the Hochschule fuer Musik, Frankfurt, and under Richard Dirksen of the Washington Cathedral for three years. She was founder and is president of AWC Inc. DISCOGRAPHY.
Compositions
CHAMBER
Juxtaposition (ens) (1979)

FLUTE
Anagrams
Reminiscences (1979)

SACRED
Contemporary Mass (mix-ch a-cap) (1972)
Solemn Mass (1970)

ELECTRONIC
Abstraction (1975)
Bells (1976)
Chromosynthesis (1974)
Futurama I (1977)
Futurama II (1977)
Illusions (1976)
Piano ad Lib (1973)
Sands (1975)
Two electronic poems

Ref. composer

CARLOS, Wendy
American electronic instrumentalist, organist, pianist and composer. b. Rhode Island, November 14, 1939. She obtained her B.A. (music and physics) at Brown University in 1962 and her M.A. (composition) at Columbia University in 1965. She studied the piano from 1946 to 1958 and the organ from 1956 to 1957. She worked with Robert A. Moog in developing the Moog synthesizer, from 1965 to 1973. Some of her works were composed as Walter Carlos, before a sex-change operation and the legal changing of her name to Wendy on February 14, 1979. DISCOGRAPHY.

Compositions
ORCHESTRA
Sphera (pf and orch) (1962)
CHAMBER
Sextet (cl, ob, hn, vln, vlc and d-b) (1965)
String quartet (1964)
Sonata (vlc and pf) (1966-1967)
Variations (pf)
OPERA
Noah, in 3 acts (1964-1965)
ELECTRONIC
Variations on a plainsong (synth and orch) (1980) (Tempi Music)
By request
Cosmological impressions (syn)
Dialogues (pf and 2 loudspeakers) (1963)
Episodes (pf and elec sound) (1964 and 1975)
Geodesic dance (1971-1972) (Tempi Music)
Pompous circumstances (1974-1975) (Tempi)
Sonic seasonings (1971)
Timesteps (syn) (1970-1971)
Variations on favorite things (1970) (Tempi; BMI)
Well tempered synthesizer
Variations (fl and elec sound) (1964)
Pieces (pf, elec insts and orch)
FILM MUSIC
A Clockwork Orange (1971) (Tempi; Warner Bros.)
Remember Me (1979)
The Shining (with Rachel Elkind) (1978-1980) (Tempi; Warner Bros.)
ARRANGEMENTS
Bach - Brandenburg Concertos (Moog syn)
Switched-on Bach (Moog syn)
Ref. composer, 142, 559, 563

CARMEN MARINA (pseud. of Carmen Manteca Gioconda)
Spanish guitarist, singer, teacher, writer and composer. b. Santander, July 17, 1936. She was taught the basics of music by her father and later attended the Santander Conservatory, where she studied under R. Saez de Adana and won two scholarships that enabled her to continue her studies at the Royal Conservatory of Music in Madrid. She graduated in classical guitar (first prize) under R. Sainz de la Maza; in harmony, counterpoint, fugue and composition under Rafael Brubeck de Burgos and in orchestration and folk music. She gained honorable mention for her opera *The Old Man and the Sea* based on the Hemingway novel. She won a fellowship at Andres Segovia's annual master class in Siena, Italy, in music appreciation and conducting and later spent two summers at the maestro's course at Santiago de Compostela, where she also studied chamber music under the Spanish composer Gaspar Canado. In 1979 she received a grant from the committee for educational exchange between the United States and Spain to compose music about Spain and its cities. The premiere of this work took place in New York City. She has appeared as a soloist in concerts and on radio and television in Europe, Japan and North Africa. After 1971 she lived in the United States, where she was invited to premiere her composition *First American Impression* in New York. She has also contributed articles to musical magazines in Spain and the United States.
Compositions
ORCHESTRA
Oriente-occidente, fantasy (1961)
Suite amatoria (1960)
CHAMBER
Trio (gtr, fl and vlc) (1963-1975)
Canzoneta (vln and pf)
Jazz duet (cl and gtr) (1977)
Six bagatelles (gtr and vla) (1958)
GUITAR
Fugue (4 gtr) (1959-1975)
Counterpoint and folk (2 gtr) (1976)
Prelude and fugue (2 gtr) (1976)
Choral (1976)
Primera impression americana
Romanza (1974)
Seagulls, suite
Sombras y luces (1973)
Sonata (1975-1976)
Sonatina (1959)
Suite No. 3, Goya (1980)
Suite sobre una fabula infantil
Toccata (1975)
Tonada (1980)
Tremoleando (1980)
Triptice: Conversation; Rag; Nocturne
Zapateado (1974)
VOCAL
Seis caprichos (m-S, gtr and cham orch) (1976-1977)
Cantos a Compostela (S and str qrt) (1965)
Danza de los amorios locos (S, T, mix-ch, pf and perc) (1962)
Oracion (composer) (S, mix-ch and pf) (1976)
Anoche cuando dormia sone (1977)
Adivinanze de la guitar (vce and gtr) (1976)
Cycle of four songs (Rafael Alberti) (vce and gtr) (1981)
Endechas (Gerado Diego) (vce and gtr) (1979-1980)
Four American songs (R. Field) (vce and gtr) (1979-1980)
God's vacation (vce and gtr) (1980)
Lyric (vce and gtr) (1976)
Madre la mi Madre (vce and gtr) (1979-1980)
Segovia (vce and gtr) (1974)
Skyscrapers (R. Field) (vce and gtr) (1977)
Song of Segismundo (vce and gtr) (1980)
Songs (Spanish Poets) (vce and gtr)
Sunday morning in New England (vce and gtr) (1976)
Three American songs: The four little foxes; I can't sleep with two pillows any more; Spring in the season (vce and pf) (1976)
Three enchanted cities: Granada, Cordoba, Sevilla (m-S, fl, vlc and gtr) (1979-1980)
Three songs (Miguel de Unamuno): Nocturnal; Las cuevas de Altamira; La sombra de Don Quijote (vce and gtr) (1979-1980)
Tiromichanta (vce and gtr) (1974)
Tres anas (vce and gtr)
Two songs (R. Montesinos) (vce and gtr) (1967)
Two songs for Georgia: The red eye; Take away the moon (B. Dekle) (vce and gtr) (1981)
La vida es sueno (vce and gtr) (1971)
Y despues de todo que (vce and gtr) (1974)
You are my man aren't you? (vce and gtr) (1977)
Where are you from? (vce and gtr)
SACRED
Dos Canciones de Navidad (vce and gtr) (1964)
Christmas carol (1972)
OPERA
The Old Man and the Sea (Hemingway) (1962-1964) (hon mention)
Ref. composer, 206, 457, 625

CARMICHAEL, Anne Darling
19th-century American pianist and composer. b. Portland. She founded the Brunswick-Topsham Musical Association.
Compositions
PIANO
Idyll (1899)
Remembrance (1899)
Ref. 374

CARMICHAEL, Mary Grant
English pianist and composer. b. Birkenhead, 1851; d. London, March 17, 1935. She was a pupil at the Academy for the higher development of piano playing, where her teachers were Oscar Beringer, Walter Bache and Fritz Hartvigson. She studied harmony and composition under E. Prout and Dr. Porges. She became well known as an accompanist at popular concerts.
Compositions
PIANO
Duet (1880)
Suite (4 hands)
Smaller piano pieces
VOCAL
Daybreak
The flower of the vale
A May song
A poor soul sat sighing, duet
Sing song
The stream, song cycle (1887)
The tryst
Who is Sylvia?
SACRED
Mass in E-Flat (m- and boys' vces)
OPERETTA
The Snow Queen or The Frozen Heart
Publication
Translation of H. Ehrlich. *Celebrated Pianists of the Past and Present.* London, 1894.
Ref. 6, 22, 74, 276, 347

CARMON, Helen Bidwell
20th-century American composer. She composed an anthem and an opera.
Ref. 347

CARNECI, Carmen
20th-century composer.
Compositions
CHAMBER
Cogita, ergo sum (vlc)
D'amore (ob)
Ref. Frau und Musik

CARNO, Zita
20th-century American composer. DISCOGRAPHY.
Composition
PERCUSSION
Sextet for 6 players
Ref. 142, 146, 347

CAROLINE, Mlle.
18th-century French composer. Her opera was performed at the Beaujolais Theatre, Paris on August 19, 1786.
Compositions
OPERA
L'Heureux Stratageme, comic opera
Ref. 26

CAROLINE, Queen of England. See WILHELMINA, Caroline of Anspach

CARON-LEGRIS, Albertine
20th-century Canadian pianist and composer. b. Louiseville, Quebec. She received her first musical education from the sisters of the Assumption and studied under R. Pelletier and Michel Hirvy (piano), under Rodolphe Plamondon (singing) and under C.E. Panneton and Eugene Lapierre (harmony). She obtained a B.M. from the University of Montreal. She won second prize in the Abbe Gadbois competition, has appeared as an accompanist and performed in the radio.
Compositions
PIANO
Danse rustique (BMI Canada, 1947)
Poème pastorale (1948)
VOCAL
Anne, ma soeur Anne
La berceuse de Donalda (Musica Enr., 1947)
La chanson du ber
Chanson pour Don Quichote
Soir d'hiver (BMI Canada, 1948)
Twenty-one French Canadian songs harmonized, incl.:
Ceux qui s'aiment (Passe-Temps, 1947)
SACRED
Cantique à St. Joseph
C'est le mois de Marie
Cor Jesu
Ref. 133

CARP, Susan
20th-century American composer.
Composition
CHAMBER
Uncle Bunk loves Monk (str qrt) (AMC)
Ref. AMC newsletter vol 21 no 1

CARPENTER, Imogen
20th-century composer.
Composition
FILM MUSIC
The Young Guns (1956)
Ref. 326

CARR, Bess Berry
20th-century American composer.
Compositions
SACRED
Works incl.:
Morning Prayer (w-ch and pf) (H.W. Gray Co.)
Ref. 190, 347

CARR, Wynona
20th-century American composer of gospel songs describing the Afro-American religious experience in the United States.
Composition
VOCAL
I Just Rose to Tell You
Ref. BPAM

CARR-BOYD, Ann Kirsten
Australian lecturer, writer and composer. b. Sydney, July 13, 1938. She studied at the University of Sydney graduating in 1960 with a first class B.Mus. In 1963 she obtained her M.A., first class. She was the holder of the Sydney Moss scholarship from 1963 to 1965, awarded by the University of Sydney, which enabled her to study composition in London for two years. She first studied under Peter Racine Fricker and later under Alexander Goehr. She was a tutor and lecturer at the music department of the University of Sydney from 1969 to 1973 and contributed to various Australian music magazines. Her report on Australian women composers was presented at the 2nd International Congress on Women in Music, Los Angeles, 1982. She also wrote entries for the *New Grove Dictionary of Music and Musicians* and a report on the development of Australian composition for the Asian Composers League Festival, Hong Kong, 1981. She has been commissioned to write orchestral, harpsichord and mandolin works. In 1975 she won the Albert H. Maggs Composition Award. PHOTOGRAPH.
Compositions
ORCHESTRA
Symphony in 3 movements (1964)
Textures and variations (cham orch) (1972)
Theme and variations (cham orch) (1965)
Festival (1980)
Gold (1976)
CHAMBER
Two themes and variations (double wind qnt) (1967)
Travelling (massed recs and pf) (1981)
Fanfare for Aunty (brass and perc) (1974)
Patterns (str qrt and org) (1973)
Dance suite (ww qnt) (1984)
String quartet No. 1 (1964)
String quartet No. 2 (1966)
Australian baroque (man ens) (1984)
Fandango (man ens) (1982)
Combinations (vln, vlc and pf) (1973)
Dance (vlns and pf)
Music for Sunday (fl, vln and hpcd) (1982)
ITT, humorous composition (hpcd and org)
Nadir (vln and hpcd) (1973)
Lullaby for Nuck (hpcd) (1972)
Music for Narjade (vlc) (1975)
Suite for Veronique (hpcd) (1982)
Listen! 18 pieces (1981)
Mandolin music
ORGAN
The Bells of Sydney Harbour
Woodford Bay, a fantasy (1974)
PIANO
Duets (1967)
Ten duets (1970)
Look at the stars, 14 pieces
Mandolin music
Six piano pictures (1962)
Stars
Suite for children
VOCAL
A composition of place (mix-ch and pf) (1977)
Catch 75 (vce and cham ens) (1975)
Couperin, op. 16 (speaker, org, hpcd and perc) (1974)
Folk songs 76, 7 songs from France, Greece, Mongolia and Canada (vce and ens) (1976)
The boomerang chocolate cake (S and hpcd) (1974)
Three songs of love (e.e. cummings) (S and pf or hpcd) (1974)
Trois leçons (S, hpcd and chimes) (1974)
SACRED
Dixit Dominus, Psalm 110 (mix-ch, str qrt, d-b and pf) (1971)
Ref. composer, 206, 440, 444, 446, 457

CARREÑO, Teresa
Venezuelan pianist, conductor, operatic singer, teacher and composer. b. Caracas, December 22, 1853; d. New York, June 12, 1917. She was born of Spanish parents and was the granddaughter of the Venezuelan composer Jose Cayetano Carreno and the grandniece of Simon Bolivar. She first studied with her father, who was Venezuela's Minister of Finance and also a pianist. She then studied for a short time under Julius Hoheni. After civil

upheaval in Venezuela the family settled in New York in August 1862. When Teresa was nine years old, she gave her first public piano recital at Irving Hall in New York. A year later, in January 1863, she caused a sensation in Boston, where she gave 20 concerts and was a soloist with the Boston Philharmonic Society Orchestra. In that year she also played several of her own compositions. She studied the piano under L. Gottschalk, who recommended that she study further in Paris. She left for Paris in 1866 where she studied under George Matthias and later under Arthur Rubinstein. She traveled extensively through Spain and England and in 1872 appeared as the queen in the opera *Les Huguenots* in Edinburgh. She returned to America in 1875 and studied singing in Boston under Mme. Rudersdorff. She followed an operatic career until 1882, but her triumphant success in Berlin in 1889 established her as one of the greatest pianists of her time and she was described as the 'Valkyrie of the piano'. She wrote more than 40 compositions. She is reputed to have written the Venezuelan national anthem but actually wrote a hymn commissioned by the Venezuelan government for the Bolivar centenary celebrations in Caracas on October 29, 1885. Her first composition was written at a very early age and her string quartet and piano compositions have been highly praised. She was married four times: first to the violinist Emile Sauret in 1873 and then the baritone Giovanni Tagliapietra. She had one daughter with him - Teresita, who became a well-known pianist. In 1892 Teresa married the composer and pianist Eugen d'Albert and then in 1902 married Arturo Tagliapietra, Giovanni's younger brother. For some time she was a conductor and leader of an Italian opera company and she toured Scandinavia and Australia as a pianist. For a short time she taught MacDowell and was the first person to play his pieces in public, in 1875. He dedicated his *Second Piano Concerto* to her. She made her last appearance with an orchestra, The New York Philharmonic, in 1916 and gave her last recital in Havana in 1917. DISCOGRAPHY.

Compositions

ORCHESTRA

Petite danse tsigane

CHAMBER

String quartet in B-Minor (1896)

PIANO

Ballada, op. 15
Corbeille des fleurs, op. 9
Deux esquisses italiennes: Reverie-Barcarolle, Venise; Cantilene, Florence, op. 33
La fausse note, op. 39
Gottschalk waltz
Intermezzo scherzoso, op. 34
March funèbre
Mi Teresita, waltz
Partie (Secunda elegia) op. 18
Pequeno valse
Plainte (primera elegia) op. 17
Le Printemps, op. 25
Un rêve en mer, op. 28
Une revue à Prague, op. 27
Le ruisseau
Scherzo-caprice
Le sommeil de l'enfant, op. 35
Un val en rêve, op. 32
Valse gayo, (last published composition)
Thirty concert pieces and etudes

VOCAL

Entiendase (ch) (ded Simon Bolivar) (1883)

Publications

Possibilities of Tone Colour by Artistic Use of Pedals Individuality in Piano Playing. Etude, 1909, p. 805.

Bibliography

Burgess, Ruth Payne. *Reminiscences of Teresa Carreño.* Etude, November 1930.
Chapin, Victor. *Giants of the Keyboard.*
Inter-American Music Review, No. 2, 1983.
Marciano, R. *Teresa Careño.* 1966.
Marques Roderiguez, A. *Esbozo Biografie de Teresa Carreño.* 1953.
Milinowski, Marta. *Teresa Carreño: By the Grace of God.*
Pena, J. *Teresa Carreño.* Caracas, 1953.
Plaza, Juan Battista. *Teresa Carreño.* Caracas, 1928
Stevenson, R.L. *Carreño's 1875 California Appearances.*

Ref. 8, 9, 12, 13, 15, 20, 22, 41, 44, 48, 70, 74, 89, 95, 100, 102, 105, 107, 113, 130, 132, 226, 228, 264, 276, 477, 524, 563, 622

CARRILLO, Isolina

Cuban pianist, choir conductor and composer. b. Havana, 1907. She worked for the Cuban radio and television.

Compositions

VOCAL

Songs incl.:
Cancion sin amor
Dos gardenias
Increible
Sombra que besa

Ref. 604

CARRINGTON-THOMAS, Virginia

American organist, teacher and composer. b. Briston, CT, October 27, 1899. She composed organ works.

Ref. 347

CARRIQUE, Ana

Argentine folklorist and composer. b. Buenos Aires, 1895. She studied at the National Conservatory under Athos Palma and Alberto Williams. She received numerous prizes for her original works based on folklore.

Compositions

PIANO

Impromptu
Mazurca
Preludio criollo
Sonatas
Sonatina in E-Flat
Suite

VOCAL

Songs incl.:
Caminito de la Sierra
Canción de Cuna
Canción serrana
Coplas puntanas (1937)
Idilio
Presentimiento
Other songs

Ref. 100, 390

CARRIVICK, Olive Amelia

British organist, percussionist, pianist, teacher and composer. b. Newquay, 1905. After private education she became an L.R.A.M. and A.R.C.M. She taught the piano, theory, percussion and singing at local county schools for 12 years and was a church organist.

Compositions

CHAMBER

Fantasia (vln and pf)

PIANO

Colville Hall, suite
Lullaby in a Bethlehem Stable, fragment

Ref. 467

CARROL, Ida Gertrude

20th-century English composer.

Compositions

CHAMBER

Three pieces (d-b) (London: Forsyth Bros.)
Five easy pieces (d-b) (Doblinger)

Ref. 80

CARROLL, Barbara (Coppersmith)

American pianist and composer. b. Worcester, MA, January 25, 1925. She composed instrumental works and songs.

Ref. 347

CARSON, Ruby B.

American composer. b. Cowan, IN, August 15, 1892. She composed piano pieces.

Ref. 347

CARSON, Zeula Miller

American organist, singer and composer. b. Littleton, June 12, 1883; d. September 16, 1956. She played the organ and sang in the choir at the United Baptist Church, Houlton.

Compositions

VOCAL

Are Heaven's gates in the West, ballad
Don't forget Mother, ballad (London: Laurie and Co., 1932)
Down the path of yesterday (Irving Pub. Co., 1932)

In the Autumn when the leaves begin to fall, ballad
Wanted a pal by the name of Mary (J. McDaniel Music Co.)
Ref. 374

CARSWELL, Francis
English composer. b. Croydon, 1876. She studied under Professor Joseph Beckwith, R. Harvey and Lieutenant O. Hume.
Compositions
PIANO
Anglofranco, march
Betty Demure, waltz
VOCAL
Songs, incl.:
The flower seller
I call it Summer
Summer's waning
Spring's triumph
Tender twilight
When Mummy's ship comes home
Ref. 467

CARTER, Buenta MacDaniel
American organist, pianist, teacher and composer. b. Golden City, MO, 1883. She studied the piano under Albert Sickner of the Sickner Conservatory, Wichita, and the organ under Thomas Kelly of the First Methodist Church, Omaha. She was an organist in Wichita before turning her entire attention to the piano and composition, which she studied under Simon Bucharoff and Adolf Weidig in Chicago at the American Conservatory, where she received her master's degree. She taught the piano and composition in Chicago.
Compositions
ORCHESTRA
Pagan silhouettes (large orch)
Pierrot suite (small orch)
CHAMBER
Trio
PIANO
The Legend of the Moat, dance play
Numerous pieces for one and two pianos
Teaching pieces incl.:
Advanced keyboard harmony
Keyboard harmony
VOCAL
Choral works
Songs
Ref. 292

CARTER, Christine Nordstrom
19th-century American composer of songs.
Ref. 465

CARTER, Dorothy
20th-century composer.
Composition
MISCELLANEOUS
Troubadour (with Sally Hilmer, q.v.)
Ref. Frau und Musik

CARTER, Rosetta
English pianist, choral conductor, teacher and composer. b. London, 1912. After receiving her early education in England, Canada and New York, she became a L.R.A.M. She taught the piano and strings and conducted choirs at various schools in England.
Compositions
ORCHESTRA
Pieces for amateurs
CHAMBER
Clarinet quintet
Two string quartets
Violin sonatina
Sonata (pf)
INCIDENTAL MUSIC
Music for Shakespeare and other plays
Ref. 490

CARTER PAULENA, Elizabeth
American pianist and composer. b. San Francisco, May 6, 1930. She began studying the piano at the age of three. Her later teachers included James Woodward King, Allison R. Drake and Olga Samaroff Stokowski. She attended the Philadelphia Conservatory from 1939 to 1941 and was a pupil of Raissa Kaufman in Los Angeles for the next three years. She furthered her piano studies in Los Angeles under Max Rabinowitsh until 1950 and during that period she studied harmony, counterpoint, canon and fugue, composition and orchestration under Mary Carr Moore (q.v.). Her career as a concert pianist began at the age of seven and included numerous appearances with orchestras in the United States. At the age of thirteen she performed with the Los Angeles Philharmonic Orchestra.
Compositions
ORCHESTRA
California Centennial Fantasy (1948)
PIANO
Cinderella suite
Fantasy
Ref. 496

CARTIER, Marguerite. See RHENE-JAQUE

CARTWRIGHT, Mrs. Robert
19th-century English composer.
Compositions
VOCAL
Songs incl.:
Break, break, break (Tennyson)
Ref. 433, 276

CARTWRIGHT, Patricia
Composition
VOCAL
There is sweet music here (2 vces a-cap) (London: Boosey & Hawkes)
Ref. Frau und Musik

CARUTHERS, Julia
19th-century composer.
Compositions
VOCAL
Songs incl.:
My pansies
Ref. 276

CARVALHO, Dinora de (Dinora Gontijo de Carvalho Murici)
Brazilian pianist, conductor, professor and composer. b. Uberaba, Minas Gerais, June 1, 1905. The daughter of the musician Vicente Gontijo, she was only six when she was admitted to the Sao Paulo Conservatory to study the piano under Maria Lacaz Machado and Carlino Crescenzo (diploma, 1916). She gave her first piano recital at the conservatory at the age of seven and in 1912 made her first attempts in composition with the valse *Serenata ão Luar* and a piano *Nocturne*. She studied under Francesco Franceschini (harmony and counterpoint) and her success as a concert pianist won her a European scholarship with which she improved her piano technique under Isidor Philipp. After a series of concerts in France and Italy she returned to Brazil in 1929 and studied harmony, counterpoint, fugue and composition under Lamberto Baldi and in 1931 took courses in orchestration under Martin Braunwieser and Ernst Mehlich. In 1939 she was nominated federal inspector for advanced music education at the Sao Paulo Conservatory and she founded and directed the Women's Orchestra of Sao Paulo, the first in South America. In 1954 she received a gold medal at the IV Centenary of Sao Paulo for her work in promoting music education of children. In 1960 the Municipal Theatre of Sao Paulo launched the Dinora de Carvalho Festival, in which the Municipal Symphonic Orchestra conducted by Maestro Sousa Lima performed many of her works. She traveled to Europe on assignments from the Ministry of Education and Culture. She was the first woman to become a member of the Brazilian Academy of Music and received numerous prizes and honors. DISCOGRAPHY.
Compositions
ORCHESTRA
Arraial em festa, symphonic suite
Three Brazilian dances (pf, perc and str orch)
Contrastes (pf and orch) (1930)
Fantasia brasileira (pf and orch)
Two piano concertos
Four piano and orchestra pieces (1930)
Procissão do Senhor morto (1954)
Serenada da Saudade (1930)

CHAMBER
Cantiga de ninar (fl and pf)
Pieces (vlc, hp, vln, fl, cl and ob)
Toada chorosa (fl and pf)
Pobre Cega (vln)
Sonata (1968)
Guitar pieces
PIANO
80 pieces incl.:
Epithalame, op. 12 (Bevilacqua) (4 hands)
Premiere valse (Bevilacqua) (4 hands)
O que noite bonital (1961)
Festa na vila (hon mention, Sao Paulo, 1936)
Jogos no jardim
Sonata No. 1
Ballade
Conte de la grand'maman
Mazurka-caprice
Nocturne (1912)
Pipoqueiro (A. Napoleao)
Au printemps
Rêverie
Santo Rei
Serenade (Bevilacqua)
Serenata ão Luar
Solidão
VOCAL
Boi Tungão (ch)
Caramuras de Bahia (ch) (1936)
Ou-le-le-le (ch)
Procissão de cinzas em Pernambuco (ch) (1936)
Two chorals (Gregorio de Matos) (mix-vces)
Over 60 songs incl.:
Acalanto (C. de Campos)
Coqueiro
Menina preta que buscava Dues, folk song (vce and pf) (1960)
Pau Pia
SACRED
De Profundis, mass
Psalm 23 (Bar and octet) (1970)
BALLET
Four ballets
THEATRE
Moema, melodrama in 1 act (Italian text)
Noite de São Paulo, fantasia in 3 acts
Bibliography
Cernicchiaro, Vicenzo. *Storia della Musica nel Brasile*. Milan, 1926.
De Sa, Moreira. *Historia da Evolução Musical*. Porto, 1925.
Ref. 17, 54, 94, 100, 106, 189, 206, 268, 297, 333, 361, 457, 563

CARVER, Miss
18th-century English composer of songs.
Compositions
VOCAL
Patty the milk maid (1790) (Liverpool: J.B. Pye)
The queen of flowers (1790) (Pye)
SACRED
Free from bustle, noise and strife, cantata (1790) (Pye)
Ref. 65, 125

CARWITHEN, Doreen
English composer. b. Haddenham, 1922. She studied at the Royal Academy of Music, London, under W. Alwyn. She is an L.R.A.M. and A.R.A.M..
Compositions
ORCHESTRA
Concertino for piano and orchestra
Concerto for piano and strings
Bishop Rock, overture
CHAMBER
Wind quintet
String quartet
Sonatina (pf)
Violin sonata
FILM MUSIC
Odtaa (1946) (OUP)
Ref. 96, 177, 490

CASADESUS, Regina
French harpsichordist and composer. b. Paris, 1866. She came from the musical Casadesus family, orginally from Figueras, Catalonia. She composed piano pieces, songs and an opera.
Ref. 3, 9, 14, 94, 347

CASAGEMAS, Luisa
Spanish pianist, violinist, singer and composer. b. Barcelona, December 14, 1863. She studied harmony and composition under Sanchez Gavanyach, the violin under Torello and singing under Mrs. Bardelli. She began composing at an early age and in 1893 made her debut with her symphonic poem *Crepusculo* which was performed by the Orchestra Catalana de Conciertos. The following year she gave a concert at the Royal Palace in Madrid before the royal family, performing a number of her own vocal and piano compositions and her opera *Schiava e regina* which she composed at the age of 18. Her compositions were performed in concerts at the Conservatory of Barcelona.
Compositions
ORCHESTRA
Crepusculo, symphonic poem (1893)
CHAMBER
Seventeen instrumental compositions
Twelve pieces
VOCAL
Echi di primavera, 15 melodies (Ayne)
One hundred and one pieces
SACRED
Ave Maria (org) (Dotesio)
OPERA
I Briganti
Schiava e Regina, in three acts (1881) (prize, Chicago Exhibition, 1892)
Ref. 100, 297

CASELLA, Felicita (Felecite) (nee Lacombe)
19th-century Italian pianist, singer and composer. She studied the piano and singing at the Paris Conservatoire. She sang the main role in the presentation of her opera *Haydee* but only a revised and improved version, completed in 1852, was successful.
Compositions
VOCAL
L'arpa flebile, romance (Ricordi)
L'automne, romance (Ricordi)
La mer montait toujours (Ricordi)
SACRED
Ave verum (vce and pf) (Ricordi)
OPERA
Cristoforo Colombo (Felice Romani) (1865)
Haydee (Luiz Felipe Leite) (performed in Porto Delgardo, 1849; rev and performed in Lisbon, 1853)
Ref. 105, 226, 268, 276, 347, 431

CASIA, See KASIA

CASOLANI, Maddalena. See CASULANA, Maddalena

CASPERS, Agnes B.
19th-century English composer of songs, including one cycle.
Ref. 465

CASSEL, Flora Hamilton
American composer. b. Otterville, IL, 1852. She composed songs.
Ref. 347

CASSIA. See KASIA

CASSIAN, Nina
Rumanian poetess, translator and composer. b. Galati, 1924. She studied at the University and Conservatory of Bucharest. She won many prizes for her books and translated Molière, Heine, Becher and Brecht into Rumanian.
Compositions
PIANO
Scherzo
Publications
Children's books.
Ref. 464

CASSON, Margaret
English harpsichordist, singer and composer. b. London, ca. 1775. She wrote her first song *Attend Ye Nymphs Whilst I Impart* at the age of seven. It is not known whether the Miss E. Casson who wrote *The Pearl* a favorite glee for three voices, is Margaret Casson.
Compositions
VOCAL
Attend Ye Nymphs Whilst I Impart (ca. 1782) (Longman & Broderip, ca. 1795)
The Cuckoo, or Now the Sun is in the West (acc or pf or pedal hp) (London: G. Goulding, ca. 1790)
God Save the Queen
Noon, rondo (Cobbold) (ca. 1800)
Snowdrop
Ref. 65, 85, 276, 347, 405

CASTAGNETTA, Grace Sharp
American pianist, arranger, teacher, writer and composer. b. New York, June 10, 1912. She studied under Professor N. Elsenheimer at the Cologne Music Conservatory and then at the Hochschule fuer Musik in Berlin and the Curtis Institute of Music in Philadelphia. She gave her first recital at the age of four and later toured throughout America, appearing with the New York Philharmonic Symphony Orchestra and National Symphony Orchestra of Washington amongst others.
Compositions
PIANO
Music for glad tidings (1941)
Prelude (Boston)
Sonata
VOCAL
Robin Hood ballads (1947)
ARRANGEMENTS
Bach and Gershwin
Numerous well-known songs and carols
Ref. 40, 268, 347, 490, 496

CASTEGNARO, Lola
Costa-Rican conductor and composer. b. San Jose, May 17, 1905. She had her first music lessons from her father and then went to the Verdi Conservatory, Milan and the Philharmonic Academy of Bologna. After living in Paris for some time she returned to Costa Rica in 1940. After 1945 she lived in Mexico. DISCOGRAPHY.
Compositions
ORCHESTRA
Suite
VOCAL
Lasciate amare
Seventy songs
OPERETTA
Mirka
Ref. 100, 563

CASTELLANOS, Tania (formerly Zoila)
Cuban metallurgist and composer. b. Regla, June 27, 1920. She changed her name from Zoila to Tania for political reasons. She received elementary music tuition. After 1975 she received various political appointments and also distinctions in the musical field. She works for the Cuban radio and television.
Compositions
VOCAL
Songs incl.:
Canción a mi Habana
Canción de los niños
Cuba, corazon de nuestra America
Desde hasta la Sierra
En nosotros
Evocacion
Immensa melodia
Me encontraras
Me niego
Por Angela
Por los Andes del orbe
Prefiero sonar
Recordare tu boca
Soldado de mi patria
Vuelvete a mi
Ref. 604

CASTELLANOS, Zoila. See CASTELLANOS, Tania

CASTELLI, Adele
19th-century composer.
Compositions
BAND
Elisina, military march (Ricordi)
PIANO
I fiori d'Aprile (Ricordi)
Gaeta, marcia polka (Mariani)
Il giorno dei morti, marcia funebre (Ricordi)
Kein Sternlein am Himmel, waltz (Michow)
Magenta (Mariani)
Una mascherata al Carlo Felice (Ricordi)
La mascherina (Ricordi)
Parisina (Ricordi)
Un pensiero (Mariani)
Solferino (Mariani)
La tradita (Mariani)
Violetta mia! (Ricordi)
Ref. 297

CASTELLOZA, Dame
French troubadour. b. ca. 1200. She came from Auvergne, in the region of Le Puy. She was the wife of Turc de Mairona, probably a nobleman who fought in the Fourth Crusade, but was in love with Armond de Breon, for whom she wrote four songs.
Compositions
VOCAL
Songs incl.:
Friend, if you had shown consideration ...
God knows I should have had my fill of song ...
You stayed a long time, friend ...
Ref. 120, 220, 221, 303

CASTRO, Alice, de. See DE CASTRO, Alice

CASTRO, Maria, de. See DE CASTRO, Maria

CASTRO, Maria Guilhermina de Noronha E.
Brazilian composer. b. Rio de Janeiro, 1820; d. Rio de Janeiro, 1880.
Composition
PIANO
Passagem de humaita, polka (ded Artur Silveira da Mota, officer of the Brazilian fleet) (Filippone e Tornaghi, 1868)
Ref. 332, 349

CASTRO GUIMARAES, Floripes de
Brazilian writer and composer. b. Bahia, Salvador, 1830; d. Salvador, 1890.
Composition
VOCAL
Bela Eulina, que tens que andas triste? (1864)
Ref. 349

CASULANA (Casolani), Maddalena (nee Mezari) (known as La Casulana)
Italian madrigalist. b. Casulae, Siena, ca. 1540; d. ca. 1583. It is assumed the name Casulana originates from the fact that she was born in Casulae (Casole d'Elsa) in the province of Siena; other famous artists who were born there during the same period were also called Casolani. The 17th-century author Giulio Piccolomini, in his *Siena illustre per l'antichita* also mentions her as Sienese. A.W. Ambros, F.J. Fetis and M. Minghetti say she came from Brescia and R. Eitner states Vicenza. (These references, according to Pescerelli [see below], are wrong). The errors are probably based on her First Book of Madrigals, which was reprinted in Brescia in 1583 although on the frontispiece is printed *Vicenza, 1583.* She was an acclaimed singer who accompanied herself on the lute and appeared in the main cities of Italy, such as Milan, Verona, Florence and Venice. She was made an honorary citizen of Vicenza. In the records of the Olympic Academy, there is the annotation *18 Gennaio 1583 – musica et M. Casulana* and it is assumed she gave a concert at the famous Teatro

Olimpico of Vicenza prior to its inauguration in 1585. Most of her compositions were dedicated to aristocrats and influential personalities of her time and because of her fame some of her works were also included in collections of compositions by male composers. She taught the art of composition to the poet Antonio Molino and he later dedicated to her, his collection of *Dilettevoli madrigali* (printed in Venice, D. da Coreggio, 1568). Many other famous poets and artists dedicated their works to her. She was the first woman composer ever to have her works published, when four of her madrigals appeared in the anthology *Il Desiderio* in 1566.

Compositions

VOCAL

Il primo libro di madrigali a quattro voci (ded D. Isabella de' Medici, wife of P.G. Orsini, Duke of Bracciano) (Venice: G. Scotto, 1568)

Il secondo libro di madrigali a quattro voci (ded D. Antonio Londonio, patron of the arts in Milan) (Scotto, 1570)

Il primo libro di madrigali a cinque voci (ded Count Mario Bevilacqua, patron of the Academy of Music in Verona) (Vicenza: Angelo Gardano, 1583)

One madrigal inserted in the collection Il Gaudio by various famous musicians (Venice: Heirs of G. Scotto, 1586)

Four madrigals in the collection Il Desiderio, Book I, by various musicians of G. Bonagionta (G. Scotto, 1566)

OPERA

One opera

Publications

Two books of madrigals (spiritual) in the collection of Vicenti.

Bibliography

Pescerelli, Beatrice. *Maddalena Casulana*. Doctoral thesis, University of Bologna, 1973-1974.

Ref. 2, 13, 74, 105, 125, 126, 127, 128, 129, 216, 226, 253, 264, 267, 276, 335, 347, 653

CASWELL, Bula. See BLAUVELT, Bula Caswell

CATALANI, Angelica

Italian singer and composer. b. Sinigaglia, May 10, 1780; d. Paris, June 12, 1849. She managed the Theatre des Italiens in Paris from 1814 to 1817. She was the last of the great prima donnas of the age of bel canto and was billed as *Prima Cantatrice del Mondo*. She had a voice of great volume, strength and remarkable agility, a regal bearing and a fantastic wardrobe. She eventually returned to Florence and then to Paris, where she died of cholera.

Compositions

VOCAL

Aria with variations

Airs favorits (S)

Airs favorits varies (S)

La bella molinara, variations on Nel cor piu non mi sento by Paisiello (Ricordi)

Four Italian ariettas and a duet

Il Furbo contra il Furbo (1813)

Questo palpito soave, cavatina (1806)

Sul margine d'un rio (S)

Papa non dite, song (4 vcs) (Kuhnel)

Ref. 20, 22, 128, 135, 276, 297, 323, 347, 421, 423, 433

CATERINA

16th-century Bavarian composer. She was the niece of Adrian Willaert. On the wedding day of Duke William of Bavaria, Orlando di Lasso arranged the performance of two operas, one by Maddalena Casulana (q.v.) and the other by Caterina.

Ref. 264

CATLEY, Anne

18th-century English composer.

Composition

MISCELLANEOUS

Cease Gay Seducers (ca. 1770) (London: Longman; Johnston, 1775)

Ref. 65

CATO, Janet Dickson

20th-century American composer. She wrote pieces for the organ.

Ref. 347

CATUNDA (Katunda), Eunice do Monte Lima

Brazilian pianist, conductor, lecturer and composer. b. Rio de Janeiro, March 14, 1915. She studied the piano under M. Oswald and B. Bilhar from 1920 to 1927, under O. Guanabarino from 1928 to 1936 and under M. Lion in Sao Paulo, 1936 to 1946. She gave her first recital at the age of 12. She studied counterpoint, harmony and music analysis from 1942 to 1943 under F. Franceschini, composition and Brazilian music under Camargo Guarieri from 1942 tò 1945; modern harmony and composition under H.J. Koellreuter from 1946 to 1950 and orchestration under Guerra Peixe in Rio in 1947. In Europe she studied conducting under H. Scherchen, 1948 to 1950, and serial technique under Bruno Maderna. In Brazil she studied choir conducting under I. Karabtchewsky in 1969 and attended seminars on electronic music in Salvador, under J.V. Asuar. She performed internationally in concerts and on radio in Europe, North and South America and the USSR. She was part of the Group Musica Viva (1946) with C. Santoro and Guerra Peixe and conductor of the National Radio Orchestra of Sao Paulo from 1955 to 1956. She contributed to musical activity in Brazil; promoting concerts and organizing conferences and panel discussions and was lecturer at the University of Brasilia in 1973. She wrote articles for numerous publications.

Compositions

ORCHESTRA

Concerto (pf and orch) (1955)

Quatro cantos a morte (1948)

Quatro momentos de Rilke (str orch; also pf) (1958)

CHAMBER

Hommage a Schoenberg (2 cl, vla, vlc and pf) (1949)

Quintet (vla, vlc, cl, b-cl and pf)

Seresta (4 sax) (1956)

Cantiga de cego (vla and pf) (1966)

Duas serestas (1972)

PIANO

Momento de Lorca (1957)

Sonata de Louvação (1960)

Sonatine (1947)

Other pieces

VOCAL

Cantata do soldado morto (ch and small orch) (1965)

O negrinho do pastoreio, cantata (1946) (prize)

A negrinha e yiemanja, suite (ch and orch) (1955)

Seresta a musica, in 4 movements (Oneyda Alvarenga) (ch and small orch)

Trois lyriques grecques (ch and orch) (1949)

Songs

Ref. 17, 22, 70, 96, 206, 218, 333, 457

CAUDAIRENCA (Gaudairenca)

13th-century poetess and troubadour. She was the wife of Raimond of Miraval (ca. 1200), whose vida mentions that his wife could compose and that she made dances (songs). Raimon, himself a poet, discarded her on the pretext that one poet in the house was enough - she then married her lover, Guillaume Bremon.

Ref. 243, 449

CAVENDISH, Georgiana (Spencer) (Duchess of Devonshire)

English composer. b. June 9, 1757; d. London, March 30, 1806.

Composition

VOCAL

I Have a Silent Sorrow Here (The favorite song ...in, The Stranger) (R.B. Sheridan) (adapted by Mr. Shaw)

Ref. 65, 125, 297, 347, 405

CAWTHORN, Janie M.

American authoress and composer. b. Mt. Carmel, SC, November 27, 1888; d. May 21, 1975. She was educated at Harbison College and became a member of ASCAP in 1959.

Compositions

SACRED

Call heaven

Call Him anytime

I see Him

In that beautiful home above

Somebody He can use

Won't you come and see the man?

Ref. 39, 646

CAZATI, Maria
18th-century Italian composer.
Compositions
SACRED
Nisi Domino aedificav. (3 vces, 2 vln and basso continuo)
OPERA
Il Carnevale Esigliato
Nilteti
Orlando
Ref. 128, 307

CECCHINA, LA. See CACCINI, Francesca

CECCONI-BATES, Augusta
American organist, conductor, professor and composer. b. Syracuse, NY, August 9, 1933. She obtained a B.A. from Syracuse University (1956) and an M.A. in musicology (1960) from Cornell University, where she undertook special studies in composition from 1976 to 1977 under Joseph J. McGrath, Brian Israel and Robert Palmer. As music director she ran the Scuola Italiana at Middlebury College in Vermont in the summer of 1956. From 1961 to 1964 she was organist and choir conductor at St. Michael's, Central Square, NY. She held a professorship at the Maria Regina College in Syracuse from 1964 to 1965. From 1968 she was music specialist for the Syracuse School District and from 1976 until the present, a private music teacher. She received an honorable mention in the Stowe Institute Composition Contest in 1976 and was the featured composer at the Norman Rockwell Festival in Dewitt, NY. In 1977 she was the featured composer and director for a concert of her own works sponsored by the Cherubini Society of Rochester, NY. In 1982 she toured Austria with Music International, as assistant conductor of some of her own band music. She made several radio and TV appearances. She is a member of ASCAP and AMC.
Compositions
ORCHESTRA
Pasticcio for symphonic band (1978)
Ten plus one (cham orch) (1980)
CHAMBER
Pasticcio (wind ens) (1980)
From the Tug Hill Plateau (ob, fl, vln, vla and vlc) (1979)
Quartet brevis (1976)
Sonatina (4 fl) (1980)
Seven variations on Terra tremuit (fl, ob, cl and bsn) (1977)
Sonatina (hn, vlc and pf) (1978)
Due pezzi (cl, pf and vlc) (1979)
Two movements (fl, ob, cl and bsn) (1977)
Two movements for 2 trumpets and piano (1977)
Rhapsodic sonata (vln and pf) (1975)
Sonata No. 1 (vln and pf) (1975)
Sonata No. 2 (vln and pf) (1977)
Sonata for French horn and piano (1978)
Sonatina 1981 (vlc and pf)
Cembalo lucido (hpcd) (1980)
Pieces for clarinet, flute and trumpet
PIANO
Four preludes (1962)
Petite ragtime rhapsody (1978)
Piano pasticcio (1978)
Three pieces about piano (1978)
Two suites
VOCAL
We have a dream, cantata (soloists, ch and orch) (1974)
War is kind (S. Crane) (S, Bar and concert band) (1980)
Menagerie, 4 songs (R.W. Archer) (T or mix-ch and various insts) (1978)
Willie was different (N. and M. Rockwell) (narr, ww qnt and pf) (1973-1975)
Street cries of old York (chil-ch) (1983)
The touch of Christmas (chil-ch)
Cynical cycle (S, T and pf) (1980)
Five songs (A. Poliziano) (T, S and pf) (1976)
Four early songs (T, S, pf, vln, vlc and fl) (1956-1962)
The ship of the world (B and m-S) (1980)
Six solos from poet Stephen Crane (vce and pf) (1980)
Some cheese for Charles (H. Buckley) (narr and pf) (1963)
Something songs unrelated (R.W. Archer) (S, cl and pf) (1976)
Summer songs (Emily Dickinson) (S, B, cl, pf and perc) (1979)
Three serious songs (Walter de la Mare, Phillip Agree) (S, cl and pf) (1977)
SACRED
Two English masses
Two Latin masses
MISCELLANEOUS
For Ilya
Ref. composer, 206, 359, 457, 474, 622, 625

CECCONI-BOTELLA, Monic (Monique Gabrielle)
French pianist and composer. b. Courbevoi, September 30, 1936. She studied the piano under Yvonne Lefebure and composition at the Paris Conservatoire under Jean Rivier and Henry Dutilleux. In 1966 she won the First Grand Prix de Rome for composition. Her *Megarythmies* was based on the architect Bernard Schoebel's *Megarythmies*, an architectonic structure using Kandinsky's color theory. Together Cecconi-Botella and Schoebel explored the possibility of uniting the diverse arts of music, sculpture, painting and architecture. DISCOGRAPHY. PHOTOGRAPH.
Compositions
ORCHESTRA
Concerto pour piano et orchestre
Instants (cl and str orch) (1970) (comm ORTF, 1973) (Billaudet)
Mosaiques (perc and str orch)
Aura (cham orch) (1971)
Megarythmies (comm ORTF0, 1968)
Correspondances, a polychrome ballet (Paris: Editions Françaises de Musique)
URRP (Françaises de Musique, 1974)
Cento brani celebri (Zanibon, 1976)
CHAMBER
Anonymes, 2 short pieces (ens) (1972)
Nova (ens) (1972)
Alpha (6 classical gtr and 4 perc)
Hommage à....(2 str qrt and 1 wind qrt) (1974)
Composition pour cinq instruments (1967)
Imaginables, Imaginaires IV (4 perc) (1970) (Paris: Leduc, 1977)
Silences (wind qrt) (1973)
Aubade et danse (3 sax) (1964)
Ariette (a-sax and pf) (1962)
Solitaires I (trb) (1974)
Tuba I (tba) (1971) (Rideau Rouge)
Botella (Françaises de Musique)
PIANO
Courtepointes, 3 short pieces
Ellipseis
VOCAL
La Muse qui est la Grace, cantata (Paul Claudel) (S, B and orch) (1966)
Les Visions prophétiques de Cassandre, cantata (Aeschylus) (S, B and orch) (2nd Grand Prix) (1965)
Fait divers (ch) (1972)
Trois motets à capella (w-vces)
Recit (A. Daudet) (narr, vce and 8 insts) (1967)
Chansons du jour et de la nuit (Philippe Soupault) (S and pf) (1967)
Chansons (Rutebeuf and C. d'Orleans) (S and pf) (1968)
Paroles (1970) (comm Chorale E. Bresseur)
Quatuor (Philippe Soupault) (vce, vln, vlc and pf) (1968)
Trois méditations sur le temps de Pâques (S and pf) (1967)
Vocale (S and 2 perc) (1969)
OPERA
La Méprise, chamber opera in 1 act (Pierre Gripari) (1969)
THEATRE
Prière d'inserer, musical (1975)
ELECTRONIC
D'ailleurs...(2 ondes Martenot, electric gtr and perc) (1973)
Castafior-itures (ondes Martenot) (Brussels: Zephyr, 1983)
MULTIMEDIA
Imaginaires (6 perc and 1 dancer) (1968) (Leduc)
Ref. composer, 76, 276, 347, 563

CECILE, Jeanne
18th-century French composer.
Composition
CHAMBER
Concerto pour forte piano con due violini, due oboe, due corni, violetta et basso (1783)
Ref. 125

CECILE REGINA, Sister
20th-century writer of songs and one cantata.
Ref. 465

CECILIA, Saint
Patron saint of music and legendary inventor of the pipe organ. There are conflicting sources as to her dates of birth and death. According to one group she lived from 154 to 207. Another group gives her birth as 177 and death 230; the only common factor between these is that she lived for 23 years. Another group maintains that she never even existed. The accepted legend is that she was a member of a noble Roman family who became a Christian and was reputed to have asked Pope Urban to convert

her house into a church, where it was said some 400 converts were baptised. In order to avoid her betrothel to the pagan Valerianus she took a vow of chastity and converted him and his brother to Christianity. She, Valerianus and his brother were martyred in Rome for refusing to make a sacrifice to the Roman god Jupiter. When Cecilia did not die by drowning in boiling water she was decapitated. She was identified with the 4th-century church of St. Cecilia in Trastevere, where her body was said to have been placed in the 9th-century. However in 1599 a coffin was opened there and found to contain the bones of a young woman who was promptly identified as being those of St. Cecilia - *strange wanderings indeed for the skeletal remains of a 2nd-century virgin*. She was canonised in the 16th-century. Innumerable paintings show her with the organ, the viola, the pedal harp, the clavichord, the virginal spinet and the viol, but rarely with the lyre with its pagan associations, or with wind instruments and percussion because of their Dionysiac character. She lent respectability to instrumental music which up to the time of her canonization had been condemned by the church and she inspired a vast number of compositions by composers from Purcell onwards. She lent her name to innumerable music academies and schools although she herself was not a composer. From the 5th-century onwards, women were severely prejudiced as far as music (inter alia) was concerned and the prejudice although much reduced, exists to this day. Consequently the choice of St. Cecilia in the 16th-century as the symbol of women's participation in music was somewhat deceptive. Her elevation of the status of the presiding spirit of music is one of the mysteries of music of the Church that has never been explained. The slow inhibited development of music by women and the almost complete domination of the man in the composition of music should rather have resulted in the selection of a masculine saint as its patron. Perhaps in retrȯspect, the musical woman can derive a vicarious satisfaction in the creation of St. Cecilia as the patron saint of music, because after all, it was the woman who created music and fostered its growth so many millenia before the birth of Christ.

Bibliography

Bikle, Charles Henry. *The Odes for St. Cecilia's Day in London between 1683 and 1703*. Ph.D. dissertation, University of Michigan.

Bondini, G. *Di Santa Cecilia, della basilica di Santa Cecilia in Trastevere, di quella ad Sanctam Caeciliam in via Tiburtina*. Rome, 1855.

Bosio, Ant. *Historia Passionis beatae Caeciliae virginis, Valeriani, Tiburtii et Maximii martyrum, necnon Urbani et Lucii pontificum et martyrum*. Rome, 1900.

Brignole, G. L. *Dissertazione sulla basilica di Santa Cecilia in Trastevere*. Rome, 1847.

Cascioli, G. *Sainte Cécile et ses Actes*. Le Monde Catholique Illustré, vol. 4. Rome, 1902.

Crostarosa, P. *Scoperte in Santa Cecilia in Trastevere*. Nuovo Bullettino di Archologia Cristiana. Rome, 1899-1900.

de Cavalieri, Pio Franchi. *Recenti studi intorno a Santa Cecilia*. Note agiografiche, Studi e Testi, vol 24. Rome 1912.

de Santi, P.A. *Santa Cécilia e la musica*. Civilta Cattolica, 1921.

Delehay, H. *Les legendes hagiographiques*. Brussels, 1905.

Dubois. *La vie de sainte Cécile*. Paris, 1694.

Erbes, C. *Die heilige Caecilia in Zusammenhang mit der Papskrypta sowie der altesten Kirche Roms*. Zeitschrift fuer Kirchengeschichte. Gotha, 1888.

Gueranger, P. *Histoire de sainte Cécile vierge et martyre*. Paris, 1853.

Kirsch, J.P. *Die heilige Caecilia in der roemischenkirche des Altertums*. Studien zur Geschichte und Kultur des Altertums, vol. 4. Paderborn, 1910.

Kirsch, P.A. *Das wahrscheinliche Alter der heiligen Caecilia*. Theologische Quartalschrift. Tuebingen, 1903.

Laderci, J. *Sanctae Caeciliae virginis et martyris Acta et Transtiberina Basilica*. Rome, 1722-1723.

Leclerq, H. *Crypte et basilique de sainte Cécile*. Dictionnaire d'archeologie chretienne et de liturgie. Paris, 1924.

Martin. *Die heilige Caecilia*. Mainz, 1878.

Mirimonde, A.P. de. *Sainte Cecile: Metamorphoses d'un theme musical*. Geneva, 1974.

Mohr, J. *Beitraege zu einer kritischen Bearbeitung der Maertyrerakten der heiligen Caecilia*. Rom. Quartalschrift, Freiburg, 1889.

Poiree, E. *Sainte Cécile*. Paris, 1926.

Quentin, H. *Sainte Cécile*. Dictionnaire d'archeologie chretienne et de liturgie, vol. 2. Paris, 1924.

Thiesson. *Histoire de sainte Cécile, vierge et martyre, patronne des musiciens*. Paris, 1870.

Wilpert, J. *La cripta dei Papi e la cappella di Santa Cecilia nel Cimitero di Callisto*. Rome, 1910.

Ref. 8, 15, 95, 103, 105, 107, 132, 135, 151, 164, 244, 391

CENTA DELLA MOREA, Vincenza. See GARELLI DELLA MOREA, Vincenza

CEPPARELLI, Suora Costanza

17th-century Italian composer. She was a nun of San Vincenzo at Prato. She composed a musical comedy on the theme of chastity.

Ref. 502

CERCADO, Mlle. le Senechale de. See KERCADO, Mlle. le Senechale de

CERINI, Geronda

18th-century Italian composer of Perugia.

Compositions

VOCAL

Canzone in Componimenti Poetici, collected by Luisa Bergalli (Venice, 1726)

Ref. 327

CERRINI DE MONTE-VARCHI, Anna von

Swiss composer. b. Geneva, July 14, 1833. She studied under Lysberg.

Compositions

PIANO

Album leaves

Impromptu

Pensee fugitive

Other pieces

Ref. 260, 276, 347

CERUTTI, Paolina

Italian composer. Her works include two romances for soprano and harpsichord.

Ref. 25

CERVANTES, Maria

Cuban pianist and composer. b. Havana, 1889. She was the daughter of the pianist and composer Ignacio Cervantes. Upon the death of her father in 1905 she continued her musical studies under Gonzales Nunes and Enriqueta Garcia de Pujol. She performed several times in the United States.

Compositions

PIANO

Criollita

Ignacio

Josefina

No me toques

Os lunares

Seis danzas cubanas

Tomasa

VOCAL

Fusion de Almas (I. Cervantes, completed by composer)

Ref. 107

CERVONI, Isabella di Colle

17th-century Italian composer.

Compositions

VOCAL

Three songs: The first to Maria de' Medici, Queen of France and of Navarre, in honor of her wedding; The second to Henry IV; The third to Maria de' Medici (Florence: Giorgio Marescotti, 1600)

Ref. 327

CESIS, Sister Sulpizia (Sulpitia)

16th or 17th-century Italian lutenist and composer. A nun of the Order of St. Augustine, she lived in the Convent of San Geminiano in Modena. Her *Motetti Spirituali* were dedicated to the Reverend Mother Superior Anna Maria Cesis, sister of Santa Lucia in Selci in Rome and appeared in print on April 25, 1619. They were reputed to have been performed at the doors of San Geminiano during a religious procession in 1596.

Compositions

SACRED

Motetti spirituali, collection of 23 motets (ded Rev. Mother Superior Anna Maria Cesis) (Modena: Giulian Cassiani Stampator Episcopale, 1619)

Ref. 105, 157, 405, 653

CHACON LASAUCA, Emma

Spanish pianist and composer. b. Barcelona, 1888. She studied the piano, harmony, composition and counterpoint under Enrique Granados and Jose Ribera Miro. In her youth she was active as a pianist, but later dedicated herself to composing concert and sacred music. Her works were frequently performed in Spain and by the Philharmonic Society of Bilbao.

Compositions

ORCHESTRA

Preludio en la bemol (small orch)

CHAMBER

Evocaciones españolas, trio

Plegaria, trio

Rasgueos, trio

Sonata en do menor, trio

Romanza (vln and pf)

Seis estudios (pf)

SACRED

Cantate Domino

Ref. 100, 107

CHADBOURNE, Grace. See WASSALS, Grace

CHALITA, Laila Maria

Brazilian pianist, writer and composer. b. 1943. She gave her first concert at the age of four and at the age of seven was acclaimed a child prodigy. She composed piano and classical works from an early age. In 1953 she was awarded the Merit of Honor medal and diploma.

Ref. 268

CHALLAN, Annie

French harpist and composer. b. 1940. DISCOGRAPHY.

Compositions

HARP

Ballade

Cadcatelle (celtic hp)

Laura (celtic hp)

Magique, boite à musique

Promenade à Marly

Teaching pieces

Ref. 563

CHALLINOR, Alice Maud. See HART, Alice Maud

CHALOIX, Erny. See SCHORLEMMER, Erna von

CHAMBERLAINE, Elizabeth. See VON HOFF, Elizabeth

CHAMBERLAYNE, Edith A.

19th-century English composer. She studied under Professor Prout and H.C. Banister at the Royal Conservatory. Her *Scherzo* was performed at the Crystal Palace in February, 1895.

Compositions

ORCHESTRA

Two symphonies

Overtures

CHAMBER

Scherzo (hp, fl and strs)

Two sonatas

CHAMBER

Organ pieces

Piano suite

VOCAL

Songs

OPERA

One opera

Ref. 6, 276, 347

CHAMBERS, Wendy

20th-century composer. She studied at Barnard College under J. Beeson, Charles Wuorinen and Nicholas Roussakis and thereafter at the State University, New York under David Lewin and the University of California.

Compositions

CHAMBER

Busy Box quartet

Miniatures (pf, 4 hands)

Car horn organ performances

MISCELLANEOUS

Real music for 9 cars

Music for choreographed rowboats

One world percussion

Solar diptych

The village green

Ref. *Composers' Forum* Fall 1985, 625

CHAMINADE, Cecile Louise Stephanie (Mme. Carbonel)

French pianist, violinist, conductor and composer. b. Paris, August 8, 1857; d. Monte Carlo, April 13, 1944. She came from a non-musical family, yet her early musical talent developed rapidly. She composed sacred pieces at the age of eight and Georges Bizet advised her parents to give her a sound musical education. She studied under Le Couppey (piano), under Savard (counterpoint, harmony and fugue) and under Marsick (violin) and later under Benjamin Godard (composition). She made her debut as a pianist at the age of 18 and went on a concert tour of France and England, performing her own works. Soon her salon-style compositions became the vogue in France, England and the United States. In 1892 she was appointed by the French government to the post of Officer of Public Instruction. In 1908 she made her American debut with the Philadelphia Orchestra playing her *Concertstueck*. She composed more than 350 works in almost every musical form, most of which enjoyed an amazing popularity during her lifetime. The French government awarded her the title of Chevaliere of the Legion of Honor. DISCOGRAPHY. PHOTOGRAPH.

Compositions

ORCHESTRA

Concertino for flute and orchestra, op. 107 (Paris: Enoch & Cie, 1905)

Concertstueck, op. 40 (pf and orch) (ca. 1896) (Enoch, 1905)

Deux pièces, op. 79 (Enoch, 1925)

La Lisonjera, op. 50 (also pf) (Fischer)

Plaisirs champetres (Noel)

Première suite d'orchestre: 1. Marche (Litolff); 2. Intermezzo; 3. Scherzo; 4. Choral (Grus)

Six pièces romantiques, op. 55 (orch and pf) (Litolff, Church, Napoleao)

Suite d'orchestre: 1. Prelude; 2. Pas des echarpes; 3. Scherzettino; 4. Pas des cymbales

CHAMBER

Trio No. 1 in G-Minor, op. 11 (pf, vln and vlc) (Durand)

Trio No. 2 in A-Minor, op. 34 (Enoch)

Caprice de concert (vln and pf) (1905)

Trois morceaux, op. 31: Andantino; Romanza; Bohémienne (vln and pf) (Hainauer; Fischer; Schott)

Chant du nord, op. 96 (vln and pf) (Litolff)

Danse orientale (vln and pf) (Fischer)

Concertino (fl) (1902)

Meditation (org)

Pièce romantique (fl) (Durand)

PIANO

Air espagnol, op. 150 (4 hands)

Duo symphonique pour deux pianos, op. 117 (4 hands) (Enoch, 1905)

Air de ballet, op. 30 (Enoch)

Album des enfants, op. 126, 1st and 2nd series

Andante et scherzettino, op. 59

Arabesque, G-Minor, op. 61

Automne, concert etude, op. 35, no. 2 (Enoch)

Autrefois in A-Minor, op. 87

Caprice espagnole, op. 67

Chanson d'orient, op. 157 (Enoch, 1919)

Danses anciennes, op. 95: 1. Passepied; 2. Pavane; 3. Courante (Enoch, 1923)

Etude symphonique, op. 28 (1895)

Gavotte in A-Minor, op. 9, no. 2

Intermède, op. 36

Pas de cymbales, op. 36, no. 2 (Enoch)

Pastorale, op. 114 (1904)

Pianoforte album (Church; McKingley; White)

Piece in old style, E-Minor, op. 74

Pierrette in E-Flat Major, air de ballet, op 41

Preludes, op. 84 (Enoch, 1896)

Scherzando, op. 10 (Enoch)

Serenade espagnole, op. 24

Serenade in D-Major, op. 29

Six études de concert, op. 35 (Enoch, 1924)

Six feuillets d'album, op. 98: Promenade; Scherzetto; Elégie; Valse arabesque; Chanson russe; Rondo allegre (Enoch, 1900)

Songs without words, op. 76

Sonata in C-Minor, op. 21 (1895)

Valse brillante, op. 80 (Enoch, 1898)
Valse caprice, op. 33 (1886)
Over 200 other pieces (Toronto: Anglo Canadian Music Pub. Ass.; London: Arcadia Music Pub. Co.; Paris: Enoch; London: Enoch & Sons; London: Hutchings & Romer; London: J. Williams; others)

VOCAL
Les Amazones, op. 26, choral symphony (Charles Grandmougin) (Paris: Enoch Frères & Costallat, 1890)
Les noces d'or (ch) (1910)
Approx. 100 songs incl.:
Album of songs (Vol. 1)
L'Angelus, op. 69, duet (m-S and B) (A. Silvestre) (Enoch & Sons, 1893)
Le beau chanteur (R. Myriel) (Enoch, 1900)
Berceuse (S and pf)
C'etait en avril (E. Pailleron) (Enoch, 1900)
Chanson espagnole, two-part song (E. Haydon) (Enoch, 1934)
Chanson slave
Contralto album of five songs (Enoch, 1922)
Ode to Bacchus (H. Jacquet) (Enoch, 1899)
Golden memories (D. Freer) (J. Williams, 1929)
L'idéal (S. Prudhomme) (Enoch, 1893)
Invocation (V. Hugo) (Enoch, 1894)
Little silver ring
Madrigal, song (French and English words, G.C. Bingham) (Enoch, 1888)
Melodies, 12 pieces (J. Williams, 1893)
Nocturne pyrenéen, duet (R.H. Elkin)
On silvery waves, two-part song (R.H. Elkin) (1896)
Les papillons (T. Gautier) (J. Williams, 1898)
Portrait, valse chantée (P. Reynel) (Enoch, 1904)
La reine de mon coeur (French version, C. de Bussy; English, R.H. Elkin) (Enoch, 1908)
Ronde d'amour (C. Fuster; English version, R.H. Elkin) (Enoch, 1895)
Soprano album of five songs (Enoch, 1922)
Serenata (E. Guinand; English version E. Oudin) (Enoch, 1893)
Un soufflé à passé (French version P. Reynell; English, H. Hammond-Spencer)
Villanelle (E. Guinand, English version, D. Freer) (J. Williams, 1929)

BALLET
Callirhoe, op. 37, symphonic ballet: Pas des echarpes, pas des amphores; danse pastorale (orch; also pf)

OPERA
La Sevillane, comic opera in 1 act (1882)

Bibliography

Famous Women Composers. Etude, April 1917, pp. 237-238. Paragraphs on Beach, Chaminade, Lehman, Smythe; other names given in list.
Johnson, Thomas Arnold. *The Pianoforte Music of Chaminade. Musical Opinion* 59, 1936: 678-679.
The New Etude Gallery of Musical Celebrities. Etude, July 1929, pp. 511-512. Portraits of musicians with biographies on the back of the portraits, featuring Chaminade as one of the musicians.

Ref. 2, 13, 17, 20, 22, 26, 41, 44, 52, 63, 74, 88, 100, 105, 112, 138, 166, 183, 226, 276, 296, 297, 307, 347, 361, 369, 370, 406, 518, 524, 563, 622, 649

CHAMPION, Constance MacLean

20th-century American composer. b. Independence, KS. She composed piano works, choral works and songs.
Ref. 347

CHAMPION, Stephanie

20th-century German composer.

Compositions

CHAMBER
First suite (2 rec and str qrt) (London: Schott, 1940)
Choral und trio (4 fl) (London: Dolmetsch, 1940)
Vier Kurze Stuecke (s or a-rec, vln and pf) (Schott)
Trio (rec) (Schott)
Fantasie (s or t-rec and pf) (Schott)
Tuneful tunes, 16 pieces (rec) (Schott)

Ref. Schott catalogue

CHANCE, Nancy Laird

American pianist, teacher and composer. b. Cincinnati, OH, March 19, 1931. She studied at Bryn Mawr College from 1949 to 1950 and part-time at Columbia University, 1959 to 1967, when she studied theory and composition under Viadimir Ussachevsky, Otto Luening and Chou Wen-Chung. She studied the piano under Lilias MacKinnon and William R. Smith. Her *Daysongs* was performed at the Carnegie Recital Hall, New York. She taught the piano privately from 1973 and lived and taught in Kenya from 1974 to 1978. DISCOGRAPHY.

Compositions

ORCHESTRA
Liturgy
Lyric essays (Seesaw, 1972)

CHAMBER
Ritual sounds (brass qnt and 3 perc) (1975) (Seesaw)
Woodwind quintet
Ceremonial (perc qrt) (1976) (Seesaw)
Declamation and song (pf, vib, vln and vlc) (1977) (Seesaw)
Movements (str qrt) (1967) (AMC)
Daysongs (a-fl and 2 perc) (1974) (Seesaw)
Duos II (ob and cor anglais) (Seesaw)
Duos III (vln and vlc) (1980)
Exultation and lament (a-sax and timp) (1981)

VOCAL
Motet (double ch a-cap) (1969) (Seesaw)
Dark song (S, 2 fl, 2 cl, 2 hn, hp, gtr, pf and 5 perc) (Seesaw)
Edensong (S, fl, cl, vlc, hp and 3 perc) (1973) (Seesaw)
Four prophetic songs
Three Rilke songs (S, fl, cor anglais and vlc) (1967) (Seesaw)
Duos I (S and fl) (1975) (Seesaw)
Songs

MULTIMEDIA
Bathsabe's Song (a-sax, live and pre-recorded, speaker and dancer) (1972) (Seesaw)

Bibliography

Museum of Modern Art, Women Composers: Summergarden Concert. *High Fidelity/Musical America* 25. December 1975: 27-28.

Ref. composer, 142, 347, 474, 563, 622, 625

CHANDLER, Mary

British oboist, lecturer and composer. b. London, May 16, 1911. She obtained her M.A. from Oxford and is an L.R.A.M. and an A.R.C.M. She was the principal oboist for the City of Birmingham Symphony Orchestra from 1944 to 1958 and area director of the Kent Music School, 1960 to 1971. In 1968 she won the W.W. Cobbett Prize for Women Composers and in 1979 was the winner of the Society of Women Musicians Prize for Women Composers. She was chairlady of the Association of Wind Teachers from 1965 to 1970 and contributed to *Making Music*, *Music Teacher*, *Composer* and the *Times Educational Supplement*. She was an examiner, adjudicator and lecturer in music in the United Kingdom and overseas.

Compositions

ORCHESTRA
Celebration suite (youth orch)
Concerto (ob d'amore and str orch) (Novello)
Concerto (trp, perc and str orch) (1959)
Suite (ww and str orch)
Diversion (str orch)

CHAMBER
Concertantino (strs) (1983)
Sinfonietta (brass sextet) (1956)
Masquerade (wind qnt) (1980)
Pas de quatre (ww qrt) (1981)
Trio (ob, cl and hn)
Sonata (cl and pf)
Sonata (cor anglais and pf)
Sonata (ob and pf)
Suite from Purcell's Orpheus Brittanicus (ob and pf) (Chester)

VOCAL
Trumpet and drum carol (w-ch and pf and opt side drum)
Recollections (S, str trio and hp) (1976)
Part songs (Novello)

SACRED
Nativity Ode, cantata (w-ch) (Novello)
Tobits' Hymn of Rejoicing (ch) (Novello)

Ref. composer, 77, 94, 457, 622

CHANG, Li-Ly

Chinese concert pianist, professor and composer. b. 1952. She gained her B.A. from the National Taiwan University in 1974 and M.M. from West Texas State University in 1977. She studied the piano under S. Potter, B. Evans, W. Hautzig, R. Reyers, F. Laires, S. Gorodnotzki; composition under J. Nelson, J. Pozdro and H. Mitchel and orchestration under M. Cotel. In 1979 she became professor of the piano at Tunghai University and Theological Baptist Seminary before returning to the United States, where she and her husband, saxophonist James Cunningham have performed in concert on tour in Taiwan and on radio as the Cunningham Duo. She founded and directs the Young Artist Piano Competition in Baltimore, MD, which featured two of her latest works in 1985. In 1979 she won first prize for composition from the Phi Mu Alpha fraternity of Peabody Conservatory. Her compositions relate to the folk music, stories and history of China.

Compositions
CHAMBER
Fantasia (a-sax and pf) (1979)
Songs for a barbarian reed flute (a-sax and pf) (1984)
PIANO
Dragon boat festival (1978)
Drum song (1986)
Knick-knack suite (1975)
Variations on a Chinese folk tune (1978)
A visit from the Monkey God (1985)
VOCAL
Locus girl (1975)
Yellow flower (1975)
Ref. composer

CHAPIRO, Fania

Dutch pianist and composer. b. Surabaja, Indonesia, 1926. Her father was of Russian origin and her mother Dutch. She received her first music lessons from her father, a violinist, when she was three years old. At five she began piano lessons under Johan Madlener and at seven played Mozart's *'Coronation Concerto'* in public. She studied under Lazare-Levy in Paris for five years. She also studied theory and solfege at the Paris Conservatoire, under Sem Dresden (harmony and counterpoint) and in New York, under Jerzy Fitelberg (composition and instrumentation). She traveled in Europe and the United States as a pianist and appeared on Dutch, Belgian and American television.
Compositions
CHAMBER
Trio (ob, cl and bsn)
Sonatina (fl and pf) (1962)
Other woodwind works
PIANO
Suite (4 hands)
Sonatina
Other pieces
Ref. Donemus

CHARBONNIER, Janine Andree

French pianist, teacher and composer. b. Paris, June 8, 1936. She married the writer Georges Charbonnier. She studied under Barbaud at the Paris Conservatoire. She furthered her piano studies at the conservatoire and took part in numerous broadcasts as a soloist. She taught the piano for several years. In 1960, mathematics seemed to offer her new possibilities for composition and she utilized methods based on mathematical logic. Her compositions have been played at music festivals in Warsaw, Avignon, Saint-Nectaire and Orleans and several of her works on mathematical music have been commissioned by O.R.T.F. and Radio-France.
Compositions
ORCHESTRA
Automatisme I (1970)
Filtres (cham) (1974)
Métathèses (hommage à Galilee) (1964)
0.11 (hommage à Leibnitz) (1966)
0.11.110 (hommage à Leibnitz) (1967)
Trajets (hommage à J.L. Borges) (1964)
71 (cham) (1960)
CHAMBER
Generateur I and II (hommage à Pascal) (vln, d-b, pf and 4 perc) (1962)
Réseaux aériens (pf and hpcd) (1962) 240 jours Meteo (trb, d-b and perc) (1982)
1 Systematiques (2 perc) (1979)
2 Hommage à Vera Molnar (perc) (1980)
VOCAL
Crible II (vce and trb) (1969)
THEATRE
Circus (1973)
Conditionnement (1968)
Dichotomie (1971)
Montagnes rocheuses (1971)
Polyarchos (1970)
ELECTRONIC
Crible I (2 vln, vla, vlc, d-b and ondes Martenot) (1968)
Systems (cl, b-cl, trp, trb, d-b, pf, ondes Martenot and 2 perc)
Homotopies (tape and trp) (1970)
INCIDENTAL MUSIC
Works for music theatre
MISCELLANEOUS
Hommage à Evariste Galois (1982)
550 (1982)
Ref. composer, 70, 80

CHARLES, S. Robin

Canadian poetess and composer. b. New Westminster, October 2, 1951. She attended the University of Toronto for three years and studied music at the Royal Conservatory of Music in Toronto where she was awarded four composition scholarships and several bursaries. In 1975 she became a music copyist for the Canadian Music Center, The Royal Conservatory and various private organizations and composers. In 1981 she gave two teaching courses on 'How to copy music' and, 'Composition and children' at the summer school of the Royal Conservatory, Toronto. She was also awarded the Archimedes award from the University of Toronto, 1981. She is a member of the Toronto Musicians Union and the Performing Rights Organization of Canada and became an A.R.C.T., in 1981. PHOTOGRAPH.
Compositions
ORCHESTRA
But I'm only twelve years old (str orch)
BAND
Band piece No. 1, A fanfare (1980)
CHAMBER
Uhuru (Graphic) (any inst or inst ens) (1981)
VOCAL
A choral rosary (m-ch and cham orch)
The circle (Markham) (vce and pf) (1976)
Reality (3 vces a-cap) (1977)
SACRED
Blessed is the man (ch a-cap) (1981)
Responsorial psalm (vce, perc, fl, picc and pf) (1977)
Ave Maria (composer) (vce and pf) (1977)
OPERA
The Little Match Girl, radio opera (1979)
Publications
The Resurrection 1975. Poetry. The Grammeteion, Spring Edition, 1979.
Ref. composer, 457

CHARLOTTE, Friederike Wilhelmine Louise, Princess of Saxe-Meiningen

Prussian pianist and composer. b. Berlin, June 27, 1831; d. March 30, 1855. The daughter of Prince Albert of Prussia, she married George, Crown Prince of Meiningen. She studied under Kullak, Stern and Taubert and was an accomplished pianist.
Compositions
BAND
Infantry march (Bote and Bock)
Two cavalry marches (Bote and Bock)
Other works
PIANO
Pieces
VOCAL
Wie ist mir denn geschehen (Bote and Bock)
Other songs
Ref. 121, 226, 276, 347

CHARLOTTE, Princess of Saxe-Meiningen

German composer. b. July 24, 1860. She was the daughter of Emperor Frederick III of Prussia. She married Bernard, Crown Prince of Meiningen.
Compositions
BAND
Defilier Marsch (Haslinger)
Geschwindmarsch (Bote)
Marsch zur Geburtsfeier des Prinz von Preussen (Haslinger)
Parademarsch No. 2 (Bote)
Prussian army march (Bote)
CHAMBER
Cradle song (vln and pf)
Ref. 226, 276, 297, 347

CHARMAY, Countess of. See MONTGEROULT, Helene de Nervode

CHARRIERE, Isabella Agneta Elisabeth de

Swiss librettist, writer and composer of Dutch origin. b. Zuylen, near Utrecht, October 20, 1740; d. Colombier, Neuchatel, December 27, 1805. She was the daughter of Diederik Jacob van Tuyll, Marshall of Montfort and became known as Isabella van Tuyll van Serooskerken. She spent her first thirty years at the castle in Zuylen and became known as Belle van Zuylen. In 1771 she married Charles Emanuel de Charriere, Squire of Penthaz in Colombier. She wrote her first opera *L'Incognito* in Paris with the help of Florito Tomeoni and at her invitation Nicolo Antonio Zingarelli stayed a year in Colombier to help with her other operas. The works were never produced, perhaps never completed and only fragments remain. Besides composing, she wrote novels, opera librettos and several hundred letters; her correspondents including James Boswell, Benjamin Constant and Madame de Stael. Her compositions usually appeared anonymously. In the catalogue of the Biblioteque Nationale in Paris she is mistakenly referred to as Sophie de Charriere. DISCOGRAPHY.

Compositions

CHAMBER

Three sonatas (hpcd or pf) (The Hague: B. Hummel et fils)
Six minuets (2 vln, vla and d-b)

PIANO

Allegros
Andantes
Rondeau
Instrumental opera piece for Polypheme
Six sonatas

VOCAL

Airs and romances (hpcd) (Paris: M. Bonjour)

OPERA

Le Cyclope (composer)
Les Femmes, comic opera (composer)
L'Incognito (with Tomeoni) (1786)
Julien et Juliette
Olimpiade
Les Pheniciennes (1788)
Zadig

Publications

Le Noble, novel.

Ref. Marius Flothuis, 101, 177, 563

CHARRIERE, Sophie de. See CHARRIERE, Isabella Agneta Elisabeth de

CHARTAINE, Marcella La (Vicountess de Chartres)

14th-century French minstrel. She was a signatory to the famous charter dated September 14, 1321, that established the Chapelle Saint-Julien-des-Menestriers as a corporation for jongleurs and minstrels.

Ref. 343

CHARTRES, La Vidame de

12th or 13th-century French troubadour. She married Guillaume de Ferrieres, Vicomte de Chartres.

Compositions

VOCAL

D'amours vient joie de amours ensement
Chascuns me semont de chanter
Combien que j'aie demoure
Desconsilliez plus que nus hom quio soit
Li plus desconfortes du mort
Quant foillessent li boscage
Quant la saison du dous tans s'asseure
Tant ai d'amours qu'en chantant m'estuet pliandre

Ref. British Library catalog

CHARTRES, Vivien

English-Italian violinist and composer. b. Italy, 1896. She studied under Sauret and Sevcik and toured Europe. She composed songs.

Ref. 226

CHASE, Mary Wood

American composer. b. 1868. She composed piano pieces and songs.

Ref. 269

CHASTENAY, Victorine de

19th-century French pianist and composer. Formerly a canoness, she cultivated the arts in general and music in particular with considerable success. She was considered a competent pianist and composed piano pieces.

Ref. 119

CHAVES, Laura da Fonseca

Portuguese poetess, writer and composer. b. Lisbon, 1888. She wrote poetry from the age of eleven. She later wrote children's books, fables and plays, several of the last in conjunction with the poetess Virginia Lopes de Mendonca.

Compositions

THEATRE

Maria Migalha

Publications

A Tentação do Menino Jesus.
Do Amor. 1922.
Esbocos. 1919.
História da Raposa Raposeca e do Favo de Mel. 1928.
Memórias de Uma Galinha da India.
O Anão.
Poeira. 1957.
Trovas Simples. 1921.
Vozes Perididas. 1924.

Ref. 268

CHAVES, Mary Elizabeth

American cellist, pianist, trombonist, tuba player, violinist, teacher and composer. b. Boston, August 24, 1957. She studied under Karen Mumma Palmer (violin) and then under Marian Manahan and Karen La Salle (piano). She played the trombone and tuba at high school and studied under George Perrone (theory). She graduated from the University of Lowell with a B.Mus. and M.Mus. (theory, composition and cello) having studied under Dr. Vaclav Nelhybel, Dr. Artin Arslanian, Maryan Poietropaulo, Ruth Davidson, Seth Carlin and Michael Kramer. Through her works she endeavours to promote an understanding of women's issues. She teaches the cello, the piano, solfege and theory privately. She was founder director of the Circle of Creative Arts.

Compositions

ORCHESTRA

Variations on an old Gaelic tune (str orch) (1979)

CHAMBER

Brass quintet (1974)
Trio No. 1 (fl, cl and pf) (1975)
Trio No. 2 (hn, vln and vlc) (1978)
Trio No. 3 (cl, vln and vlc) (1981) (Dorn Publ. 1982)
Three inventions (ob and vla) (1979)
Five variations on a theme by Schubert (fl and vln) (1978)
Song of the soul (fl and vln) (1978)
Voice out of the whirlwind (fl and pf) (1974)

VOCAL

Women's breath (M. Marcoux) (m-S and cham orch) (1982)
Silentium (m-vce, cl or b-cl, d-b and perc) (1979)
Three songs (M. Marcoux) (vce and pf) (1980)
Turdus migratorius (Thoreau) (vce; also vln or vlc and pf) (1978)
The stream (vce and pf; also vlc or vln and pf) (Thoreau) (1977)

Ref. composer

CHAZAL, Mrs. Elisabetta. See DE GAMBARINI, Elisabetta

CHEATHAM, Kitty (Catherine Smiley Bugg)

American authoress, lecturer, singer and composer. b. Nashville, 1864; d. Greenwich, 1946. She attended school in the United States, then went to France and later studied at the University of Berlin. Her recitals related mainly to the literature and songs of childhood. She led gatherings in community singing and lectured on her travels in Europe, Russia and Iceland.

Compositions

VOCAL

Anthems
Choral works
Songs

Publications

America Triumphant under God and His Christ.
Children and the Bible.
The Discovery of America by Leif Ericson. Early Voyages of the Norsemen.
Jenny Lind.
Kitty Cheatham - Her Book.
A Nursery Garland.
Spiritual Music.
Adaptation of Hoffmann's Fairy Tales. With Walter Pritchard Eaton.

Ref. 74, 347, 353

CHEBOTARIAN, Gayane Movsesovna

Soviet pianist, musicologist, professor and composer. b. Rostov, November 8, 1918. In 1943 she graduated from the Leningrad Conservatory where she studied composition under Kushnarev and the piano under M. Khalfin. From 1947 she lectured at the Erivan Conservatory in general and special polyphony, becoming a professor in that subject in 1977.

Compositions
ORCHESTRA
Kartini, prazdnestovo, symphony (1952)
Piano concerto (1980)
CHAMBER
Trio (1945)
PIANO
Concert etudes (1963)
Polyphonic album for young people (1972)
Sonata (1943)
Six preludes (1948)
Variations on the theme of an Armenian folk song (1939)
VOCAL
Poema cantata (O. Ovanesian and V. Arutunian) (ch and orch) (1947)
Armenian folk songs: Uvidel tebya; Yar dzhan; Gde ona
Unaccompanied choral songs
Ref. 87, 330

CHEN, Nira
20th-century Israeli pianist, teacher and composer. She received her formal education and first piano lessons from the Kibbutz Ein Harod and then studied for one year at the Kibbutz Teachers' Seminary. After three years study at the Jerusalem Conservatory, she graduated in the piano and music education. She teaches music in Ein Harod.
Compositions
PIANO
Pieces
VOCAL
Songs incl.:
Do di li (1948)
Children's choruses, songs and plays
SACRED
Iti Milhvanon, lyrics from The song of songs (1948)
Ref. composer

CHENEY, Amy March. See BEACH, Amy March

CHENOWETH, Vida
20th-century American marimba player, pianist and composer. b. Enid, OK. She studied at William Woods College in Fulton, MO, the American Conservatory and Northwestern University. She studied the piano and having a special interest in the marimba, was determined to establish it as a concerto instrument. She was given a grant to study the marimba in Guatemala where it is the national instrument. She became the composer-in-residence at the University of Wisconsin in 1954 and in 1957 became the advisor in the marimba for the National Federation of Women's Clubs. Composers including Villa-Lobos, Jorge Sarmientos, Robert Kuruka, Bernard Rogers, Paul Creston and Darius Milhaud have written works for her.
Ref. 74

CHERBOURG, Mlle.
French composer.
Compositions
CHAMBER
Six menuets en duo (2 gtr)
VOCAL
Collection of chansons (vce and gtr)
Ref. 125

CHERTKOVA, A.
19th-century Russian composer.
Compositions
VOCAL
Songs for children:
The boy and the bird
Collection of 30 songs (Jurgenson)
The cuckoo
Green grass
Greetings, little friends
Little bird
Little puppets
SACRED
Legend of Christ
Song of resurrection
Ref. 297

CHERTOK, Pearl
American harpist, lecturer and composer. b. Laconia, NH, June 18, 1919; d. August 1, 1981. She studied the harp at the Curtis Institute of Music under Carlos Salzedo and was an instructor at several universities. She was staff harpist at CBS for 25 years and taught at several New York colleges: Manhattanville; Purchase; Kings College, Briarcliff, and Sarah Lawrence. She gave premiere performances of harp compositions by Hindemith, Piston, Francaix, Mondello, Mourant, Tedesco and several other composers. DISCOGRAPHY.
Compositions
HARP
Around the clock, suite (1948)
Baroque
Beige nocturne
Blue smoke
Driftwood
Morning after
Strings of pearl, suite (1958)
Seafoam
Ten past two
Opaque
INCIDENTAL MUSIC
Background music for NBC and Ford Theatre
Tales of a Black Cat for Raven Productions
Theme music for TV dramas
Ref. composer, 142, 563

CHERUBIM, Sister Mary Schaefer
American organist, choral conductor and composer. b. Slinger, WI, January 11, 1886. She joined the Sisters of St. Francis in 1903, was the organist and choir conductor of St. Lawrence's Church in Milwaukee from 1904 to 1909 and director of music at St. Joseph's Convent, 1909 to 1924. She obtained her B.Mus. from Marquette University in 1922. She founded and directed the St. Joseph Conservatory from 1924 to 1933 and then devoted herself entirely to the composition of sacred works.
Compositions
CHAMBER
Sacred organ pieces
VOCAL
Choral works
Songs
Publications
Liturgical Choir Books. 1939.
The Organist's Companion. 1945.
Ref. 347, 415

CHESTER, Isabel
20th-century American hymn composer.
Ref. 347

CHESTER, Mrs. E. See HARRIS, Ethel Ramos

CHESTNUT, Lora Perry
American organist, teacher and composer. b. Beloit, KS, February 23, 1888. She studied at the Harrisburg Conservatory, receiving her diploma in 1908. From 1939 to 1940 she studied the organ under Mary Lyman and William Leonard Hofer in Manhattan, Percy Shaul Hallet in Pasadena and Alexander Schreiner in Los Angeles. In the same city she studied orchestration and composition under Dr. Mary Carr Moore (q.v.) and James H. Rogers. She was an organist at several churches in Kansas, Oregon and Pasadena.
Compositions
ORGAN
Pieces
VOCAL
Sons (solo and ch) (1933)
The wind song (James H. Rogers) (ch) (1935)
Songs
SACRED
Easter Cantata
Ref. 496

CHEVALIER, Charlotte Bergersen
American concert pianist, lecturer and composer. b. Chicago, September 14, 1926. She gained her B.M. (piano, 1949); M.M. (piano, 1952); B.M. (theory, 1970) and B.M. (composition, 1970) from the American Conservatory

and Northwestern University and the University of Chicago. She followed a career as a solo and duo pianist and chamber music player. From 1949 she lectured at the American Conservatory. She won a Cordon Club Young Artist Award (1953).

Compositions

PIANO

Passacaglia and fugue (1970)
Sonata (1970)
Three little dances (1974)

Ref. 643

CHEVALIER DE BOISVAL (Chevallier), Mme.

19th-century French composer.

Compositions

OPERA

Les Anneaux de Marinette (1895)
Assant de Valets (1896)
Le Jeu de l'Amour et du Hasard (1895)
Pierrot Pince (1895)

OPERETTA

Le Champagne (1894)
Faim d'Amour, mystery (1893)
La Leçon Imprevue (1903)
Marivaudage (1895)
La Paise Universelle, comedy (1904)
Pan! Pan! c'est l'ésprit (1898)
Pepita l'Andalouse (1896)
Les Visites d'Yvonette (1897)

Ref. 431

CHEVALIER DE MONTREAL, Julia

French poetess and composer. b. Paris, April 20, 1829. She published a number of poems, odes and other literary works.

Compositions

VOCAL

Three collections of romances, album (vce and pf) (Paris: Challiot)

Ref. 26, 347

CHEVALLIER, Mme. See CHEVALIER DE BOISVAL, Mme.

CHEVALLIER SUPERVIELLE, Marie Louise

Franco-Spanish accordionist, pianist, teacher and composer. b. Madrid, 1869; d. Madrid, 1951. She showed a talent for music at a very early age and her mother, a pianist, became her first teacher. Marie studied the piano at the Real Conservatorio de Musica y Declamation Madrid under Reventos and Compta and later harmony under Karl Beck and R. Hernanda, composition under Arriela and the accordion under Lopez Almagro. She was an accompanist-pianist to the Polish cellist Mirecky and later formed part of the Sociedad de Cuartetos with Jesus Monasterio and Isaac Albeniz. From 1875 to 1897 she toured France and Spain and in 1889 won the Grand Prize at the International Exhibition in Paris from Mustel Accordions. She was a music teacher at the Real Conservatorio but after her marriage to the poet and professor, Eduardo Del Palacio Fontan she retired from public life. She composed 28 works for the piano, the violin, the viola and voice and wrote a comedy on a French text.

Ref. 107

CHICHERINA, Sofia Nikolayevna

Soviet pianist and composer. b. St. Petersburg, November 10, 1904. After school, she entered the Petrograd-Leningrad Conservatory in 1923 and studied the piano under Zagorny and composition under Shcherbachev, graduating in 1931. From 1928 to 1942 she was the pianist and composer at the Theatre for the Proletarian Actor, the Theatre Oktyabrienka and other amateur theatres. During the Siege of Leningrad she wrote for radio and for the Front. In 1942 she collected and recorded songs on collective farms in the Novosibirsk area. She was awarded several medals for her work.

Compositions

ORCHESTRA

Symphony (1954)
Piano concerto (1945)
Russian suite (1952)
Scherzo (1950)
Two pieces (orch of folk insts) (1935)

CHAMBER

String quartet No. 1, op. 27 (Sovietski Kompozitor, 1978)
String quartet No. 2 (Sovietski Kompozitor, 1981)
Three pieces (vln and pf) (1952)

PIANO

Preludes (1954)
Sonata (1947)
Two children's pieces (1940)

VOCAL

Children's songs (Ravin, Marshak and others)
Romances (Pushkin, Lermontov, Belyavsky) (1929-1955)
Songs of Siberian Cossacks, arrangements

THEATRE

Le Médécin par force (Moliere) (1934)
Threat (A. Ostrovsky)
Zaika-Zaznaika, folk tale about a wise rabbit, puppet theatre (S. Mikhalkov) (1952)

Ref. 87

CHICKERING, Mrs. Charles F.

American composer. d. January, 1912.

Compositions

VOCAL

Songs incl.:
In the night she told a story

Ref. 433, 276

CHIERICATI, Lucrezia

16th-century Italian singer and composer. She was a performer on several instruments. Her compositions have not survived.

Ref. 502

CHIEVRE DE REINS, La

French minstrel of the 12th-13th-century. She married Robert de Reins.

Compositions

VOCAL

Songs incl.:
Bien s'est amours honie
Jamais pour tant con l'ame el cors me bate
Ki bien veult amors descrivre
Pleindre n'estmet de la bele en chantant

Ref. British Library

CHILD, Marjorie

20th-century Australian composer.

Composition

FILM MUSIC

Portrait (1973)

Ref. 442

CHILDS, Mary Ellen

20th-century American composer.

Composition

DANCE SCORE

Chorines (comm American Dance Festival, 1983)

Ref. AMC newsletter

CHITCHIAN, Geguni Oganesovna

Soviet pianist, lecturer and composer. b. Leninakan, Armenian SSR, August 30, 1929. In 1949 she graduated from the Erivan Conservatory where she studied the piano. In 1953 she studied composition under G. Yegiazarian and from 1953 taught solfege and composition at the K. Saradzhev Music School. In 1971 she became a lecturer at the Erivan Conservatory.

Compositions

ORCHESTRA

Violin concerto (1976)
Kartinky, children's symphony (1969)
Zdrastvuji utro, overture (1967)
Ballet suite (1953)

CHAMBER

Fugue (str qrt) (1950)
String quartet (1949)
Ballad (vln and pf) (1951)
Sonata (trp and pf) (1979)
Sonatas (vlc and pf) (1951, 1958)

PIANO

Children's album (1954)
Prelude and fugue (1950-1951)

VOCAL
Vremena goda, cantata (ch a-cap) (1972)
Armiyananskiye bareliyefi, cycle (vce and orch)
Children's songs
Romances, cycle (O. Shiraz) (1954-1955)
Six cycles (Armenian poets) (1960-1979)
Ref. 87, 330

CHITTENDEN, Kate Sara
Canadian organist, pianist, lecturer, writer and composer. b. Hamilton, Ontario, April 17, 1856; d. New York, September 16, 1949. She obtained her musical education in London and Ontario. From 1892 to 1900 she was Dean of the American Institute of Applied Music, head of the piano department at Vassar College and head of the Katherine Aiken School in Stanford, CT. She was the organist at the Calvary Baptist Church in New York and a charter member of the American Guild of Organists. She also studied the piano under Lucy Clinton and Jules Fossier and at Hellmuth College, London, Canada. She collaborated with Albert R. Parsons on the *Synthetic Method for the Piano*.
Compositions
PIANO
Children's pieces
Teaching works
SACRED
Synthetic Catechism
Arrangements of sacred music
Bibliography
Canadian Music and Trades Journal, February 1901, vol. 2, No. 3.
Etude, November 1929, p. 805.
Ref. 433

CHKHEIDZE, Dali Davidovna (Tinatin)
Soviet pianist, lecturer and composer. b. Tbilisi, December 26, 1927. After studying composition under I. Tuskia, she graduated from the Tbilisi Conservatory in 1949. In 1951 she studied the piano under V. Shiukashvili. From 1949 she lectured on the piano at the First Music School in Tbilisi.
Compositions
ORCHESTRA
Piano concerto (1949, 1955)
March (orch of wind insts) (1953)
CHAMBER
Humoresque (vln and pf) (1953)
Melody (vln and pf) (1952)
Romance (vln and pf) (1954)
PIANO
Musical moment (1950)
Poem (1955)
Preludes (1951)
Sketches (1953)
VOCAL
Vis gardo (D. Guaramishivili) (soloist, mix-ch and pf) (1955)
Children's round dances (L. Ukrainka; Georgian translation I. Mosashvili; Russian translation I. Arakishvili) (w-ch and pf) (1954)
Fly my swallow, song (V. Zhuruli) (1953)
Ref. 87

CHKHEIDZE, Tinatin. See CHKHEIDZE, Dali

CHLARSON, Linda
20th-century American composer.
Composition
OPERA
Maximilian's Dream (1983)
Ref. AMC newsletter

CHODKIEWICZ, Comtesse
19th-century Polish harpsichordist and composer of a song dedicated to the "immortal glory" of Hetman Chodkiewicz. She is mentioned in the Leipzig Zeitschrift fuer Musik of 1818 as being an accomplished musician and excellent harpsichordist.
Ref. 35

CHOISY, Laure
Compositions
PIANO
Pour l'adolescence, 5 pieces (Geneva: Henn, 1954)
Ref. Frau und Musik

CHOUQUET, Louise
19th-century French composer.
Compositions
PIANO
Beviamo choeur (4 hands) (Ditson)
Attila, caprice, op. 10 (Ditson)
Les Chants du pays, op. 6, fantasie on 2 melodies of Puget (Schott)
Ernani, scene de bal, mazurka et galop (Ditson)
Macbeth, caprice, op. 8 (Ditson)
Mariquita, valse brillante, op. 7 (Ditson)
Le Prophete, divertissement, op. 9 (Ditson)
Terpsichore, air de danse, op. 15 (Ditson)
Ref. 226, 276, 297

CHRETIEN-GENARO, Hedwige
French professor and composer. b. 1859; d. 1944. She was a pupil of Guiraud and in 1881 won the first prize for harmony and fugue at the Paris Conservatoire where she later became a professor.
Compositions
ORCHESTRA
Danse rustique (pf and orch)
Soir d'automne, song (vln, pf and orch; also vlc, pf and orch; also vlc and pf or vln and pf) (Gallet)
Source (pf and orch; also pf) (Enoch)
Escarpolette, waltz (also pf) (Leduc)
CHAMBER
Allegro appassionato (vln, fl, cl, trp, sax, ob or cor anglais; also pf; also a-sax and pf) (Millereau)
Berceuse (vln, fl, cl, sax, ob or cor anglais; also with pf; also for a- sax and pf)
Grand solo (cl, fl, trb, sax, hn or bugle, ob or cor anglais; also pf) (Milleraeau)
Quintet (Millereau)
Confidences (fl, cl, ob or cor anglais; also pf) (Millereau)
Scherzettino (fl, ob, or cor anglais; also pf) (Millereau)
Duo (a-sax and fl)
Esquisse matinale (vlc and pf; also vln and pf) (Leduc)
Grand Solo, andante et allegro (a-sax or t-sax and pf)
Ideal esquisse (vln and pf) (Leduc)
Pastorale (fl and pf; also fl) (Millereau)
Polonaise (cl and pf; also cl)
Romance (vln ob or cor anglais; also fl)
Sérénade pathetique (fl and pf; also fl) (Millereau)
Scène rustique (pf and ob) (Evette & Schaeffer, 1921)
Point d'orgue du menuet (Baudoux)
Ronde de nuit (vlc) (Baudoux)
Sérénade (vln) (Baudoux)
Vers l'infini (vln) (Baudoux)
PIANO
Pastels (4 hands) (Baudoux)
Asphodeles, waltz (Joubert)
Canzonetta (Heugel) (Leduc)
Hirondelle, etude-caprice (Gallet)
Hongrois (Leduc)
Naiades, waltz (Gallet)
Nocturne (Leduc)
Pensées fugitives (Heugel)
Qui vive? morceau de genre (Leduc)
Sérénade japonaise, caprice (Noel)
Scherzo valse (Leduc)
Speranza, slow waltz (Gallet)
Styrienne (Enoch)
Trilby, galop (Gallet)
Valse berceuse (Leduc)
Valse-mazurka (Enoch)
VOCAL
Fanatisme (vce, pf and vlc) (Leduc)
Villanelle (vce, pf and fl) (Millereau)
Bonne chance (Millereau)
Pour ceux qui aiment, melody (vln) (Leduc)
Approx. 25 songs incl.:
Aubade (Leduc)
Chanson pour la bien-aimée (Enoch)
Dueto barcarolle (m-S and Bar) (Baudoux)
Prismes lunaires (Leduc)
BALLET
Ballet oriental
Ref. 72, 226, 276, 297

CHRIST, Fanny
19th-century German zither player and composer.
Compositions
ZITHER
Antonien-Quadrille

Erinnerung an Hohenschwangau, waltz (Hoenes)
Erinnerungs-Klange, waltz
Erinnerung an Neuburg, waltz
Gruesse aus der Ferne, Laendler
Heiterer Sinn, 6 Laendler and Schottish
Hochzeits-Laendler
Immer froehlich, 10 Laendler
Immergruen, 6 Laendler
Immortellen-Walzer
Marienbluemchen, 9 Laendler
Marienlieder-Transcriptions: Segenlied
Mathilden-Walzer
Neujahrs-Wuensche, Laendler
Pensez à moi, waltz (Hoenes)
Die schoensten Augen, transcription (zither and pf) (Hoenes)
D'Schwarzblaett'ln, Laendler
Sehnsuchts-Schwingen, waltz
Vergissmeinnicht, Laendler
Verschiedene Musikstuecke: Tautropfen
Wilhelminen-Laendler

VOCAL

Beliebte Stuecke (vce and pf)
Ein Blumenstrauesschen fuer Zitherfreunde
Potpourri ueber beliebte Lieder u. verschiedene Opernthemen

Ref. 226, 276, 297

CHRISTENSEN, Anna Mae Parker

American pianist, teacher and composer. b. Alexandria, VA, April 15, 1899; d. 1976. She studied at the Institute of Musical Art, New York College. She taught the piano privately in Omaha, NE. She had one of her compositions buried in a time capsule to be opened in 2076.

Compositions

PIANO

Birthday candles
Chinese tinkle glass
Dream castles
Loneliness
Mazurka
Persian chant
Silver ship
Slumber song
Snow fairy
Swedish dance
Tyrolean holiday
Yankee shuffle

Ref. 475

CHRISTIANE. See VERGER, Virginie Morel du

CHRISTIANSEN, Cecilie

19th-20th-century Danish composer.

Compositions

VOCAL

Norge, Norge, du stolte, stejle Land
Aften (A. Berntsen) (vce and pf)
Den lyse Nat (H. Rode) (vce and pf)
Forund mig (H. Rode) (vce and pf)
Kys mig paa Oejnene, Sol! (L. Holstein) (vce and pf)
Morgen (A. Berntsen) (vce and pf)

Ref. 331

CHRISTINE DE PISAN

French poetess, writer and composer. b. Venice, 1363; d. Poissy, France, 1431. Her father was chief physician and astrologer to Charles V of France and she grew up at the French Court. Her father fostered her extraordinary capacity for learning and she spent much time studying in the libraries of the Louvre and of the University of Paris. She particularly admired Aristotle's Ethics. She was married at the age of 15 to the king's notary and secretary, Etienne de Castel and widowed ten years later. To support herself and her three children she turned to songwriting, poetry and literature. She had 20 major works published, five of which dealt with feminist topics. She was renowned as a philosopher and her writings were much in demand. She introduced the works of Dante to the French intelligentsia and wrote treatises on military tactics and on justice. As her fame spread, Henry IV of England and Gian Galleazo Visconti, the Duke of Milan, invited her to their courts, but she chose to remain in France, probably for patriotic reasons. After Agincourt (1415) she retired to the convent of Poissy. For 14 years she wrote nothing, but when inspired by the deeds of Joan of Arc, she wrote a final hymn of praise to her.

Compositions

VOCAL

Ballades and rounds mourning her husband incl.:
Ce mois de mai tout se resjoie
Ha! Le plus doulz qui jamais soit forme
Se souvent vais au moustier
Seulete sui et seulete vueil estre

Publications

Avision Christine. Autobiography. 1406.
Cité des Dames. Feminist Utopian work. 1405.
Le Débat de deux amants.
Dit de la pastoure. 1403.
Dit de la rose. 1401.
The Duke of true lovers.
L'Epistre au dieu d'amours.
Le Livre de la paix.
Le Livre des faits d'armes et de chevalerie. Translated and printed by Caxton as the *Book of Faytes of Arms*. 1489.
Le Livre de trois vertues.
Le Livre du dit de poissy.
La Mutation de fortune.

Bibliography

Kemp-Welch, A. *Of Six Medieval Women*. Massachusetts: Corner House Publishers, 1979.
Varty, K. *Christine de Pisan*. Leicester, 1965.

Ref. *Helicon Nine* Nov. 9 1983, 179, 279, 315, 353, 404, 478, 575

CHRZASTOWSKA, Pelagia

19th-century Polish pianist and composer.

Composition

PIANO

Fantasy

Ref. 118

CHUDOBA, Blanka

Yugoslav pianist, librettist and composer. b. Zagreb, December 5, 1896. She acquired her musical education both privately and at the Zagreb Music Institute, where she studied the piano, theory and voice. She won prizes for popular song lyrics and for her librettos.

Compositions

VOCAL

Songs in free dance rhythm (composer)

INCIDENTAL MUSIC

Children's and young people's plays (composer)

Publications

Pjesma o cvijecu. Libretto for M. Mottl's musical comedy.
Tipkacica. Libretto.

Ref. 145

CHUDOVA, Tatiana Alekseyevna

Soviet lecturer and composer. b. Moscow, June 16, 1944. She graduated from the Moscow Conservatory in 1968 and in 1970 became a lecturer there.

Compositions

ORCHESTRA

Suite from Russian Fairy Tales, symphony (1969)
Two piano concertos (1970, 1971)

CHAMBER

Sonatas (trb and pf) (1980)
Pieces (cham ens)
Violin sonatas (1980)
Concert toccata (1979)

VOCAL

Bogatery, cantata (Vekshegonov, 1975)
Cantata on Moscow (chil-ch and pf) (1975)
Zodchiye, cantata (D.B. Kedrin, 1976)
Volya-Volnaya (E.A. Gulin) (vce and orch of folk insts) (1975)
Perepery-Perepliasy, song cycle (L.G. Serostanov) (m-S and pf) (Sovietski kompozitor, 1981)
Skazy O Stenkye Razinye (trad words) (1981)
Song cycle (trad words) (1969)

OPERA

Skazka o myortvoi Isarevne i semy Bogateriyach (1968)
Russkiye zhenshchiny (after N.A. Nekrakov) (1975)
Na derevhiyu dyeduvke (after A. Chekov) (1978)

Ref. 330

CHURAI, Marusya (Maria Gordeyenva)

Ukranian folk singer and songwriter. b. Poltava, 1620. d. 1650. She was said to be the authoress of a series of popular Ukranian songs, based on her love of Cossack history. Many of her songs are still sung today and her themes have inspired several modern composers.

Compositions
VOCAL
Songs incl.:
Chto dze ti milii, ne prikhodish
Klonilis gustiye lozy
Otchego ne shumyat buyinye vetri
Otchego voda mutnaya
Prile telya kukushechka
Shol milii goroyu
U plotini shumyat Berbi
V ogorodye khmelinushka
V ogorodye verba gustaya
Zelyonyenkii barvinochek
Ref. 330

CHURCHILL, Beatrice

20th-century American composer.
Composition
OPERA
The Christmas Secret (based on Gracia Caines)
Ref. 141

CIANCHETTINI, Veronica Elisabeth

19th-century British composer. She was the daughter of Veronica Rosalie Dussek (q.v.) and the sister of Pio Cianchettini, a composer. She composed overtures, rondos, sonatas and waltzes.
Ref. 6

CIANCHETTINI, Veronica Rosalie. See DUSSEK, Veronica Rosalie

CIANI, Suzanne Elizabeth

American electronic instrumentalist, pianist and composer. b. Indianapolis, June 4, 1946. She was the daughter of a Boston physician and began studying the piano at the age of six. In 1968 she obtained a B.A. in music from Wellesley College and in 1970 an M.A. in composition from the University of California at Berkeley. She was the first person to write a digital composition for pinball machine. She is a player of electronic music using a buchla synthesizer. She lives in New York. DISCOGRAPHY. PHOTOGRAPH.
Compositions
ELECTRONIC
A live electronic environment (1971)
Live electronic performance composition (1974)
Kodesh-Kodeshim (buchla syn)
New York, New York (buchla syn) (1973)
New waves
Paris, in conjunction with the Harold Paris retrospective
Pieces
Seven waves (various syns)
A variety of electronic dances (1968-1972)
INCIDENTAL MUSIC
Lixiviation, film (1972)
The Stepford Wives, film
Help, Help, the Gobolinks
Have a Coke and a Smile
The Incredible Shrinking Woman
Ref. composer, 494, 622, 625

CIBBINI, Katherina (nee Kozeluh)

Austrian pianist and composer. b. Vienna, 1790; d. Vienna, August 12, 1858. She was the daughter of the Bohemian Imperial Kapellmeister, Leopold Kozeluh and first studied under her father and later completed her studies under Muzio Clementi. She married the advocate, Cibbini in 1812, but continued to compose and established herself as a pianist. She became lady-in-waiting to Empress Caroline Auguste and then ceased her musical activities. Her name appeared in 1848 in connection with the political upheavals of the time. DISCOGRAPHY.
Compositions
CHAMBER
La Rimembranza: grand trio, op. 10 (2 pf and vlc) (Vienna: Artaria)
PIANO
Impromptu in E
Impromptu on a theme of Clary di Zentner, op. 7
Introduction and polonaise, op. 9
Introduction and variations in E, op. 5
Introduction et variations brillantes, op. 2
Marche et trio
Six valses, op. 6 (Vienna: Haslinger)
Due divertimenti brillanti, op. 3
Bibliography
Universitni Knihovna v Brne; *Ceske Hudebni Skladatelky*. 1957.
Ref. 13, 102, 105, 109, 129, 276, 563

CIERA, Hippolita

16th-century Italian composer.
Composition
VOCAL
Hic est beatissimus (5 vces) (1554)
Ref. 127

CIMAGLIA DE ESPINOSA (Cimaglia-Espinosa), Lia

Argentine pianist, lecturer and composer. b. Buenos Aires, August 31, 1906. She studied at the Buenos Aires Conservatory under Alberto Williams and Celestino Piaggio and later Jorge de Lalewicz. She made her debut in 1920 and gave her first European performance in Paris at the Salle Pleyel (1939). She taught at the Conservatory founded by Williams and at the Conservatorio Nacional de Musica y Arte Escenico. In 1939 she moved to Paris, where she received lessons from Philipp, Yves Nat and A. Cortot and gave numerous concerts.
Compositions
CHAMBER
Leyenda (vlc and pf) (1920-1928)
Nocturno (vlc and pf) (1940)
Poema (vln and pf) (1940)
Serenata (vln and pf) (1928)
PIANO
Cajita de musica (1912)
Improvisacion (1911)
Recuerdos de mi tierra, suite (1940)
Suite argentina (1937)
Tres preludios, in homage of Debussy (1938)
Triste y danza (1940)
VOCAL
Over 40 songs
THEATRE
Egloga de Nochebuena (Juan Oscar Ponferrada) (1934)
El carnaval del diablo (Juan Oscar Ponferrada) (1943)
El trigo es de Dios (Juan Oscar Ponferrada) (1949)
Ref. 86, 100, 390

CINTI, Mlle. See DAMOREAU-CINTI, Laure

CINTI-DAMOREAU, Laure. See DAMOREAU-CINTI, Laure

CINTOLESI, Liliana

Italian composer. b. 1910.
Compositions
PIANO
Alla marcia (Ricordi)
Alla mazurka (Ricordi)
Andantino (Ricordi)
Berceuse (Ricordi)
Intermezzo (Ricordi)
Tarantella (Ricordi)
Ref. Ricordi (Milan)

CIOBANU, Maia

Rumanian pianist, professor and composer. b. Bucharest, May 5, 1952. She studied at the George Enescu Music Academy in Bucharest from 1959 to 1971 and till 1975 at the Ciprian Porumbescu Conservatory, where she studied under Dan Constantinescu and Myriam Marbe (composition), Mircea Chiriac (harmony), Stefan Niculescu (analysis of musical forms), Emilia Comisel (folklore), George Leahu (aesthetics), Nicolae Beloiu (instrumentation), Aurora Ienei (piano), Dinu Petrescu (electronic music) and O.L. Cosma and A. Sachelarie (history of music). In 1981 she won an honorable mention in the competition for women composers GEDOK in Mannheim, West Germany and her compositions have been performed on American, French and Rumanian Radio. From 1975 to 1976 she taught the piano in Buzao and then became professor of the piano, history of ballet and ballet music at the George Enescu Art Academy in Bucharest. DISCOGRAPHY. PHOTOGRAPH.

Compositions
ORCHESTRA
Violin concerto (1980)
The Earth must live, symphonic movement (large orch) (1975)
CHAMBER
Ballet music (pf and str qrt) (1976-1982)
Three sculptures (str qrt) (1981)
Preludio (cl, gtr and trb) (1978)
Sonata (cl, pf and perc) (1973-1980)
Decor (cl and pf)
Da suonare (pf) (1976)
Teaching pieces (vln and pf or fl and pf)
ELECTRONIC
Meeting with another melody (perc and tape) (1978)
VOCAL
Pean, cantata (Nichita Stanescu) (mix-ch and orch) (1977)
Riddles, cantata (Rumanian folk text) (mix-ch and orch) (1975)
Ref. composer

CITATI-BRACCI, Clelia

Italian composer. b. ca. 1895.
Compositions
PIANO
Two Italian songs, folklore: Danza Siciliana; La Gondoleta (6 hands) (Ricordi)
Pieces for children
Tre Pezzi per due piccoli concertisti (Edizioni Curci)
VOCAL
Eight easy songs (vce and pf) (Ricordi)
ARRANGEMENTS
Two popular German pieces: Es tanzt ein Bi-Ba-Butzemann; Stille Nacht (6 hands) (Ricordi)
Bibliography
Estratto de Catalogo General. Edizioni Curci, 1976.
Ref. Edizioni Curci (Milan)

CLAIRE, Paula

20th-century composer.
Compositions
ELECTRONIC
Astound, concrete canticle (1971)
Breeze, concrete canticle (1971)
Energygalaxy, concrete canticle (1971)
Ref. 406

CLAMAN, Dolores Olga

Canadian pianist and composer. b. Vancouver, July 6, 1927. She studied at the Juilliard School of Music under Rosina Lhevinne (piano), Bernard Wagenaar and Vittorio Giannini (orchestration and composition) and Edward Steuermann (piano and composition). She appeared as a pianist on the radio and in concert. In 1953 she went to London where she married Richard Morris, the writer and composed music for television and was co-writer of songs for West End revues. She returned to Toronto in 1958 where she and her husband won many international awards between 1962 and 1978 for jingle-writing. They also wrote musicals, themes for the CBC network programs and the scores for feature films.
Compositions
ORCHESTRA
Prèlude (1951)
Le rêve fantasque, ballet (small orch) (1950)
PIANO
Primitive dance (1945)
VOCAL
Three songs (James Joyce) (1948-1950)
THEATRE
Graffiti, musical (1979)
In the Klondike, musical (1968) (with M. Leighton)
Timber, musical comedy (1952)
INCIDENTAL MUSIC
Captain Apache, film (1972)
The man who wanted to live forever, film (1970)
A Place to Stand, film (1967) (Oscar winner)
Hockey night in Canada, television
House of Pride, television
Bibliography
Caroll, Joy. *Claman & Morris. CanComp*, 51, June 1970.
Ref. 133, 485

CLARA D'ANDUZA. See D'ANDUZA, Clara

CLARA da Monaco. See MARGARITA da Monaco

CLARIBEL. See BARNARD, Charlotte

CLARISSE DE ROME, Sister

16th or 17th-century Italian composer. Her 12 twelve works are in the collection *Philomela Angelica* by Daniel Speer.
Bibliography
La musique dans les convents de femmes. La Tribune de St. Gervais, Bulletin Mensuel de la Schola Cantorum No. 2. February 1898.

CLARK, Florence Durrell

Canadian organist, pianist, violinist, violist and composer. b. Rochester, NY, April 29, 1891; d. Hamilton, Ontario, December 24, 1977. Her father was a tenor. In 1895 the family moved to Hamilton, Canada. Her musical education began at nine and at 12 she began studying the violin and accompanied her father on the piano. She also played the organ and viola in the Hamilton Symphony Orchestra. At the Royal Conservatory in Toronto she studied under Sir Ernest MacMillan (organ and composition) and under Ella Howard and Luigi von Kunits (violin). She obtained her B.Mus. and in 1941 was the third woman in Canada to be made a fellow of the Canadian College of Organists. In August 1976 she was made an honorary member of the R.C.C.O. the first time that distinction had ever been awarded. PHOTOGRAPH.
Compositions
ORCHESTRA
Minuet sketches (str orch)
Sarabande (str orch)
CHAMBER
Fantasy on a French-Canadian tune (str qrt)
Sketch: Placid lake; Aeolian harp (str trio)
ORGAN
Carillon
Pastorale in A
Prelude on a second mode melody (1938)
Preludes (1940-1970)
Procession
Transcriptions from Bach (also pf duo)
VOCAL
Carol for all seasons, song
National song for Centennial
Now the joyful bells
Ode for St. Cecilia
Other songs
SACRED
Hymns
Ref. composer, 94, 133

CLARK, Jane Leland

20th-century American composer.
Compositions
CHAMBER
Pieces (vln and pf)
VOCAL
Moonlight deep and tender
Other songs
Ref. 292, 347

CLARK, June

British pianist, authoress, teacher and composer. b. St. Albans, Hertfordshire, June 3, 1933. She was educated at St. Albans' Grammar School and the Royal Academy of Music, London. She studied the piano under Cyril Smith and composition under Alan Bush and made her debut as a duo-pianist in Bayreuth, Germany becoming joint-winner of the International Competition for interpreters of Contemporary Music in Utrecht in 1967 and prize-winner for the best performance of a contemporary Dutch work. She teaches piano master classes. PHOTOGRAPH.
Compositions
PIANO
Holiday in the Holy Land (Chappell & Co. 1969)
King Arthur suite (Chappell, 1963)
March of the astronauts (Chappell, 1963)
A pony ride (Chappell, 1963)
VOCAL
Og, unison song (Chappell, 1963)
O where is young Christopher, song (Chappell, 1963)
The dell (Chappell, 1963)

SACRED
The hill of flowers, cantata (1979)
Missa brevis (mix-ch and org) (1966)
Let us light a candle, carol (Chappell, 1966)
O Saviour Christ, anthem
Publications
Music and Musicians in the British Isles. 1981.
Ref. composer, 457

CLARK, Kathleen Blair. See BLAIR, Kathleen

CLARK, Mary Elizabeth
American composer. b. Placerville, CA, 1917.
Compositions
ORCHESTRA
Larghetto (cor anglais and orch) (1941)
Little concerto (fl and orch) (1938)
Ref. 322

CLARK, Mary Margaret Walker
American pianist, teacher and composer. b. McComb, MS, March 24, 1929. She graduated from Louisiana State University in 1951 with a B.Mus. (music education). She won national recognition in a music contest sponsored by the National League of American Pen Women. In 1980 she performed her own piano compositions in a concert honoring women composers. PHOTOGRAPH.
Compositions
VOCAL
Connecticut, state song for children (composer) (1982)
OPERETTA
Will Jack be here for Christmas? in 3 acts, for children (Eldridge Publ. 1973)
The Doll with the Blue Bonnet, in 3 acts (Eldridge, 1976)
Publications
Classical melodies for children to sing. Collection of songs from music of great composers. New York: Paulist Press, 1976.
Jesus lives. Collection of plays and songs for children. New York: Paulist Press, 1977.
Ref. composer, 474

CLARK, Mrs. W. See ROOBEIAN, Amber

CLARK, Ruth Scott
20th-century American composer. She composed choral works and songs.
Ref. 40, 347

CLARKE, Emily
English composer. b. 1927.
Compositions
CHAMBER
Sincerity (vln and pf) (Southgate)
VOCAL
Mine host (E. Teschemacher)
Ref. 63

CLARKE, Helen Archibald
19th-century American editor, lecturer and composer. b. Philadelphia. She composed piano works and songs.
Ref. 292, 347

CLARKE, Jane
18th-century English organist and composer.
Compositions
SACRED
Select portions of psalms and hymns, set to music as sung at Oxford Chapel (1808)
Ref. 226, 276

CLARKE, Jessie Murray
19th-century English vocal teacher, writer on music and song composer.
Publications
How to Excel in Singing. 1884.
Ref. 226, 276

CLARKE, Mary Gail
American teacher and composer of piano pieces. b. Berlin, Germany, 1914.
Bibliography
Barrel, Edgar. *Notable Musical Women*. Etude, November, 1920.
Ref. 347

CLARKE, Phyllis Chapman
20th-century Canadian organist, pianist, teacher and composer. b. Yorkshire, England; d. Calgary, Canada. She studied under Beatrice Chapman (piano and organ), Annie Glen Broder (harmony) and Dr. H.A. Fricker (organ and voice). She gained a B.A. hons. and is an L.R.S.M. and an A.R.C.T.
Ref. 133

CLARKE, Rebecca (Friskin) (pseud. Anthony Trent)
English violinist, violist and composer. b. Harrow, August 27, 1886; d. October 13, 1979. She came from a musical background and started to play the violin at the age of eight. At the Royal Academy of Music she studied the violin under Hans Wessely and then attended the Royal College of Music where she studied composition under Sir Charles Stanford, being his only female student and the viola under Lionel Tertis. She took up the viola professionally and was one of the founders of the famous 'English Ensemble', an all-women's piano quartet. She also became a member of a quartet comprising Adela and Jelly d'Aranyi (violins) and Guilhermina Suggia (cello). In 1916 she left for the United States where she established herself as a composer and soloist. In 1919 she won second prize at the Berkshire Festival for her *Sonata for viola and pianoforte*. In 1921 she again won second prize for her most important work *Trio for violin, cello and pianoforte*. Mrs. F.C. Coolidge commissioned her to write a work for the Pittsfield Festival in 1923. She returned to London that year and toured Europe with the English Ensemble in 1928. Later her concert tours took her around the world. After her marriage to the pianist James Friskin in 1944, she settled in New York. She wrote the entry on the viola in Cobbett's Cyclopedic Survey of Chamber Music (1929). DISCOGRAPHY.
Compositions
CHAMBER
Combined carols, or Get 'em all over at once (str qrt; also str orch) (1941)
Dumka (pf trio) (1941)
Trio (pf and strs) (1921) (London: Winthrop Rogers, 1928)
Chinese puzzle (vln and pf) (1922)
Epilogue (vlc and pf) (1921)
Grotesque (vla and vlc) (1918)
Lullaby (vla and vlc) (1918)
Midsummer moon (vln and pf) (1924)
Passacaglia on an Old English tune (vla and pf)
Prelude, allegro and pastorale (cl and vla) (1941)
Rhapsody (vlc and pf) (1923)
Sonata for viola and pianoforte (2nd prize, Berkshire Festival, 1919)
Sonata (vln and pf) (1909)
Suite (cl and vla) (1942)
Two pieces (vla or vln and vlc) (OUP, 1920)
Cortege (pf)
VOCAL
Daybreak (vce and str qrt) (1940)
Songs incl.:
The aspidistra
The cherry blossom wand
The cloths of heaven (Yeats)
Color of life
Cradle song
The donkey
Down by the Salley Gardens (Yeats)
A dream (1926)
Eight o'clock
Greeting (1928)
Infant joy
June twilight (1925)
Lethe
The Old English songs (vce and vln) (Winthrop Rogers, 1925)

The seal man (1922)
Shy one
Three Irish country songs (vce and vln) (1924)
Tiger, tiger (1933)
SACRED
Psalm (ch a-cap) (1920)
God made a tree
Psalm (vce and pf) (1920)
Bibliography
Rebecca Clarke, violinist and composer. Stradivarius 77, December 1966: 297.
Ref. 2, 8, 9, 17, 22, 23, 41, 44, 68, 74, 94, 96, 142, 155, 172, 191, 226, 228, 622

CLARKE, Rosemary

American professor and composer. b. Daytona Beach, FL, June 23, 1921. She obtained her B.Mus. at Stetson University where she studied composition under Robert Bailey in 1940. She studied under Rollo Maitland at the Philadelphia Musical Academy and received a diploma and her M.Mus. from 1941 to 1942. She has a Ph.D. in composition from the Eastman School of Music where she studied under Bernard Rogers and Herbert Elwell from 1944 to 1950. She was an associate professor of music at Stetson University from 1942 to 1957, the founder and director of the Rosemary Clarke Conservatory, Florida, 1949 to 1957, and in 1962 was appointed professor of music at the University of Wisconsin, where she was composer-in-residence from 1969 to 1975.
Compositions
ORCHESTRA
Two piano concertos
Two elegies
BAND
Fantasy (pf and band)
CHAMBER
Nonet (4 brass, 4 ww and perc) (1978)
Sieben (7 trbs) (1978)
Butter/duck/squiggle (fl, a-sax and tba) (1972)
Continuum (hn, a-sax and vib) (1977)
Gravadante (3 cl) (1973)
Meenet mit diferencias (rec, fl and pf; also hpcd) (1974)
Piano trio
Scherzando (3 cl) (1960)
Trio for brass (trp, hn and trb) (1978)
Trio sonata (trp, vla and vlc)
Happening (fl and d-b)
Sngof roh sn Goffog (sax and pf) (1972)
ORGAN
Chorale prelude on Te Deum (1973)
Lullaby (1973)
Prelude on the tune Elton (1973)
Procession to the Manager (1973)
PIANO
The North and the South (2 pf)
Fantasy on A little star (1973)
Miniature toccata (1973)
VOCAL
Wrath (S and orch)
Cynthia, madrigal (1974)
Suite of changes (vce, perc and 6 insts)
SACRED
A man of sorrows, oratorio (1965)
OPERA
The Cat and the Moon
ELECTRONIC
Fors a tre (tape and 2 hn) (1969)
Grass (arp 2500 syn) (1978)
9 x 2 and 6 x 2 (tape) (1972)
MULTIMEDIA
Circus caricatures (pf and dancers) (1946)
Reflexions on Void's progeny (tape, speaker, visuals, brass, projectionist and dancer) (1972-1973)
Serpents-soldiers (fl, d-b and dancers) (1969)
To beat or not to beat (tape, visuals and dancer) (1972-1973)
MISCELLANEOUS
N.f.t.Pr.Sch. (1979)
October's party (1945)
Party, No. 2 (1979)
Sets (1971-1979)
Sphinx (1980)
Ref. 137, 141, 142, 185, 465, 625

CLARKE, Urana

American writer and composer. b. Wickliffe-on-the-Lake, OH, September 8, 1902. She obtained her diploma at Mannes Music School, New York, (1925) and her Dalcroze certificate at the School of Music, New York (1950). She also received her B.S. (1967) and M.S. (1970) from Montana State University. She was music editor of *The Book of Knowledge* from 1949 to 1961 and director of the International Society of Music Research. She directed weekly radio programs and contributed to magazines on music, navigation and astronomy. She was the inventor and builder of the Clarke adjustable piano stool. She composed five chorale preludes for the organ and two piano pieces.
Ref. 475

CLARKSON, Jane

Late 18th-century English composer.
Compositions
PIANO
Major General Drummond of Strathallan's march and quick step... and the original march of the Hessian Guards and a favourite allemande (London: Corri, Dussek & Co., ca. 1795)
Two marches composed for the Right Honorable Lord Napier and George Baillie Esq. (Corri, Dussek, ca. 1795)
Possibly also The loyal Borrowstounness volunteers slow and quick march (published ca. 1800 and written by a Miss A. Clarkson, who may have been Jane Clarkson)
Ref. 65, 125

CLAUDE, Marie

French pianist, teacher and composer. b. Paris, August 17, 1895. She studied at the Paris Conservatoire under Marguerite Long (piano) and A.G. Cortot. She received the first medal for the piano and the first prize cum laude for harmony and history of music.
Compositions
CHAMBER
PIANO
pieces incl.:
Courants d'air, 14 pieces
Teaching works (1982)
ARRANGEMENTS
Works for piano (Handel, Burgmuller)
Popular French folksongs
Ref. composer

CLAY, Melesina

19th-century English composer.
Composition
VOCAL
The faded bouquet (Mrs. Robinson) (ca. 1800)
Ref. 65

CLAYTON, Laura

American pianist and composer. b. Lexington, KY, December 8, 1943. Her grandmother was a singer, her mother a pianist, and Laura started piano lessons at the age of four. She later attended Rollins College, then Ohio State University, where she obtained her degree in piano performance and studied under Darius Milhaud. She moved to Boston and studied privately before entering the New England Conservatory to obtain her M.Mus. in composition in 1971, studying under Charles Wuorinen and D.M. in composition at the University of Michigan in 1983. Her *Cree Songs for the Newborn* won the National Composers' Competition (1979) and was chosen to represent the United States in the International Rostrum of Composers in Paris. She won numerous endowments, grants and awards. DISCOGRAPHY.
Compositions
ORCHESTRA
Piano concerto
CHAMBER
Sagarama (pf)
VOCAL
Cree songs for the Newborn, 4 creole poems (prize, National Composers' Composition, 1979)
Herself the tide
DANCE SCORES
Panel (fl, cl, vlc, perc and pf) (comm American Dance Festival, 1983)
OPERA
Series of interrelated chamber operas, based on works of Guimeraes Rosa
ELECTRONIC
Simichai-ya (sax, echo-plex and tape)
Ref. AMC newsletters, Pan Pipes Winter 1984, Helicon Nine, 622, 625

CLAYTON, Susan

English harpsichordist, pianist, lecturer and composer. b. Sheffield, October 12, 1950. She gained her B.A. hons (French, 1974) and B.Mus. hons (1976) from the University of Sheffield; a diploma in French language and literature from the Sorbonne (1973) and her A.Mus. (1970) and L.Mus. (1972) from Trinity College, where she is currently studying for her F.T.C.L. She lectured in music at Rotherham College of Arts and Technology from 1979 to 1980 and then at the Open University. She has given concerts as a harpsichordist and piano accompanist and composed orchestral and chamber music and solo songs.
Ref. 643

CLEMENS, Margaret

Canadian pianist, accompanist, arranger, lecturer and composer. b. Toronto, 1908; d. Toronto, January, 1983. She studied at the Royal Conservatory, Toronto and in 1932 became musical director of the Boris Volkoff School of Ballet and for twenty years worked on Promenade concerts involving the ballet school and the Toronto Symphony Orchestra. She was the first pianist for the National Ballet of Canada and musical director of the Canadian Ballet Festivals, 1948 to 1954. In the 1940s she joined the Ontario College of Education and for 30 years was musician and lecturer at the University of Toronto's School of Physical and Health Education.
Ref. *Globe and Mail* - Toronto

CLEMENT, Mary

German composer. b. Stettin, 1861. She studied under Professors Stern, Gernsheim and Radecke in Berlin.
Compositions
CHAMBER
Sonata for violin and piano
PIANO
Aphorismen, 3 pieces, op. 4 (Simon)
Schattenbilder, 6 pieces, op. 8 (Stern)
Serenade, op. 2 (Stern)
VOCAL
Numerous songs incl.:
An Lethe (Stern)
Ein Jaeger (Stern)
Schmetterlingslied (Stern)
Three duets, op. 16 (S and A) (Bote)
OPERETTA
Kinder der Puszta, Zigeuner-Auffuehrung, mit Tanz (3 soloists and small ch with pf; also pf, 4 hands, chil-insts, 2 vln and vlc ad lib) (Bloch)
Ein Schaeferstuendchen, op. 15, musikalisches Rokokospiel (vce and pf) (Bloch)
Ref. 226, 276, 297

CLEMENT, Sheree

20th-century American composer. In 1983 she was awarded a Guggenheim Fellowship in composition.
Compositions
ORCHESTRA
Chamber concerto
CHAMBER
String quartet
Prelude No. 5 (pf) (1981)
ELECTRONIC
Glinda returns (1979)
MISCELLANEOUS
Belladonna dreams (1980)
Ref. AMC newsletter, 622, 625

CLERAMBAULT, N.

B. 1676; d. 1749.
Compositions
OPERA
Le Depart du Roi
Le Soleil Vanguer des Nuages
Ref. 307

CLERCK, Albertine de. See COLIN, Jeanne

CLEREMBAULT, Mme. de

Late 18th-century French composer. She composed romances for the harpsichord.
Ref. 25

CLEVE, Cissi

Norwegian ballerina, opera singer and composer. b. Oslo, December 17, 1911. From 1918 to 1932 she was a ballet dancer, then studied opera in Vienna from 1932 to 1936. She sung in main roles for the Vienna (1936) and the Nuremberg Opera (1936 to 1939). After the war she toured Finland, Holland, Belgium and Sweden. She won prizes and scholarships for her compositions, including the Franz Lehar Medallion in 1938 and her *Symphonisk Poem* was played on the Norwegian radio in 1983. She is a member of the Norwegian Artists' Association. PHOTOGRAPH.
Compositions
ORCHESTRA
Aquarelle (sym orch; also pf) (1980) (Oslo: Musikk-Huset)
Droemmen (sym orch, 1979; also str qrt, 1978; also pf, 1979) (Musikk-Huset)
Kjaertegn (pf and sym orch; also str qrt; also pf) (1981) (Musikk-Huset)
Legende (ob, pf and sym orch; also pf) (1983) (Musikk-Huset)
Maanesoelv (sym orch; also pf) (1979) (Musikk-Huset)
Nocturne (sym orch, 1978; also ob and orch, 1979; also pf, 1978) (Musikk-Huset)
Solglatt (pf and sym orch; also pf) (1981) (Musikk-Huset)
Symphonisk poem (sym orch) (Musikk-Huset) (Franz Lehar Medallion)
Soljevalsen (sym orch, 1977; also pf, 1975) (Musikk-Huset)
Tema con variazione (sym orch, 1955; also pf, 1953) (Norsk Nohestikk)
Valse lyrique (sym orch, 1935; also pf, 1933) (Norsk Nohestikk)
Valse romantique (pf and sym orch) (1980) (Musikk-Huset)
Vemod (sym orch; also pf) (1980) (Musikk-Huset)
Ref. composer, Frau and Musik, NMI

CLIFFORD, Anne

17th-century British composer. She was a pupil of Samuel Daniel.
Ref. 150

CLINGAN, Judith Ann

Australian bassoonist, recorder player, conductor, singer, teacher and composer. She studied the recorder, the bassoon, singing and composition at the Canberra School of Music, and singing and conducting at the Kodaly Institute of Music, Kecskemet, Hungary. Her studies in Hungary were made possible by a Hungarian government scholarship and an Australian government grant. She was the founder and conductor of the Canberra Children's Choir for nine years, for which many of her compositions were written. She was the founder and director of the Young Music Society summer music schools and taught music privately and in schools. She was awarded the composition prize at the Hobart Festival in Tasmania in 1972 and many other prizes at various Australian music competitions for singing and conducting. PHOTOGRAPH.
Compositions
VOCAL
Songs of Middle Earth (Tolkien) (solo, w-ch and orch) (1967-1971)
Peter Pandemonium (chil-vces and chil-orch) (1979)
Witches' Trio (w-vces and perc) (1980)
The Lorax (Dr. Seuss) (2 S, A, fl, cl, vlc and perc) (comm National Eisteddfod Society for International Year of the Child) (1979)
Chanson (m-S, cl, vla and vlc) (1971)
Several choral pieces and arrangements (prizes in Eisteddfods) (1968-1980)
SACRED
A Canticle of Light (S, chil-ch, mix-ch, rec qrt, str sextet and perc) (1974-1976)
Hymn to the Virgin (mix-ch) (1967)
Puer natus (2 S, A, recs, strs and perc) (1963-1965)
INCIDENTAL MUSIC
Under Milk Wood (Dylan Thomas) (vces, str qrt, fl and perc) (1981) (comm Canberra Church of England Girls' Grammar Schools)
Androcles and the Lion (Bernard Shaw) (1969)
Images, for film Into the Darkest Night (m-S, fl, cl and gtr) (1977)
Ref. composer

CLOSTRE, Adrienne

French pianist and composer. b. Thomery, Seine-et-Marne, October 9, 1921. She studied at the Paris Conservatoire under Y. Nat (piano), J. and N. Gallon (harmony, counterpoint and fugue), D. Milhaud and J. Rivier (composition) and O. Messiaen (musical analysis and aesthetics). In 1949 she won the Grand Prix de Rome and in 1954 the Grand Prix for music from the City of Paris for *Raissa ou la Sorciere*. DISCOGRAPHY.
Compositions
ORCHESTRA
Symphony for strings (1949)
Concerto for oboe and chamber orchestra (Presser)
Concerto for trumpet, timpani and string orchestra (1954) (Presser)

Concerto for violin, flute and orchestra (1972) (Presser; Theodore Front)
Concert pour le souper de Roi Louis II (1957)
De patribus deserti (1957)
CHAMBER
Sonata (2 pf, trp and perc) (1951)
Le combat avec l'ange (trp and org) (Choudens, 1983)
Kalamar (s-sax and pf) (1954)
Brother Blue, suite (celtic hp)
Variations italiennes, 4 interludes (pf) (Choudens, 1985)
VOCAL
Songs
SACRED
Tre fioretti di S. Francesco d'Assisi, cantata (6 vces and 10 insts) (1953)
OPERA
Ennuis de l'existence, chamber opera (Chekhov)
Nietzsche
Sie waren so schoen und herrlich...., chamber opera (E.T.A. Hoffmann) (Cont and orch) (1966)
THEATRE
Julien l'apostat, lyric drama (Henrik Ibsen)
Raissa ou la sorciere, lyric drama (Chekhov) (1952)
Le chant du cygne, lyric scene (Chekhov) (1961)
Les musiciens de Breme, lyric tale (Grimm) (1957)
Ref. 9, 12, 76, 94

CLOTILDE, Teresa. See DEL RIEGO, Theresa

CLOUGH-LEIGHTER, Mrs. Henry. See MARSCHAL-LOEPKE, Grace

COATES, Gloria Kannenberg

American actress, lecturer, music director, singer and composer. b. Wausau, WI, October 10, 1938. She showed musical talent at an early age, singing on radio at the age of six and beginning piano studies at eight and voice at 12. She then began composing and at 14 won a superior rating in the National Federation of Music Clubs Composition Contest. She studied composition under Alexander Tcherepnin (1962), Helen Gunderson (1963 to 1964), Dr. Kenneth Klaus (1964 to 1965), Jack Beeson (1966 to 1967) and Otto Luening (1967 to 1968). She obtained a B.A. (theatre and ballet) and a B.Mus. (composition and voice) from Columbia University. She received her M.Mus. (composition and musicology) from Louisiana State University (1965) and continued postgraduate study at Columbia University. In 1962 she attended the Mozarteum in Salzburg. She worked in New York and Los Angeles as a composer, singer, actress, director and writer. She settled in Munich, Germany in 1969 and produced and organized the German-American Contemporary Music Series. She received a grant from the German Ministry of Culture (1971) and was awarded the Alice Ditson Grant from Columbia University (1974 to 1977). She was director of Music Today, Lenbach Gallery, Munich (1973 to 1974) and is currently director of Evening Concert, Munich American House. She is the European representative for the League of Women Composers and was a guest of the Polish Government at the First Jeunesse Musicale Camp. As a member of the International League of Women Composers, she helped build up the European section until the German women split to form their own organization, Frau und Musik. In 1979, she was the first American and non-socialist composer to have works performed at a festival in East Berlin, with her piece *Between*. In 1981 she was invited to the World Music Days in Budapest and in 1982 to the First International Festival for New Music in Moscow. In 1982 she toured India lecturing on her life and music. Her compositions have been performed at international festivals and broadcast. She was the recipient of numerous honors, grants and awards. She contributed articles to German music journals, 1975-1981. DISCOGRAPHY. PHOTOGRAPH.

Compositions
ORCHESTRA
Implorare (str orch) (1977)
Planets, three movements for chamber orchestra: Horizontal, Diagonal, Back and Forth (1976)
CHAMBER
Counterpoint counter (cham ens) (1973)
Music on open strings, or The three ages of the Samurai (7 vln, 2 vla, 2 vlc and d-b) (1978)
Nonett, in 3 mvts (2 vln, vla, vlc, d-b, fl, ob, bsn and hn) (1978)
We have ears and hear not (solo and str qrt) (1978)
Farben canon (str qrt) (1972)
Five abstractions for woodwind quartet (also pf, 1962)
Five abstractions from poems of Emily Dickinson (ww qrt) (1976)
Five pieces for four wind players
Six movements (str qrt) (1980)
String quartet No. 1 (1967)
String quartet No. 2 (1972)
String quartet No. 3 (1976)
String quartet No. 4 (1978)
Mobile for string quartet (1972)
Valse triste (pf, trb, vlc and cl) (1980)
Variations on Lo how a rose (org, tri, alternating vln and vla) (with Blendinger) (1975)
Trio for 3 flutes
My Country 'Tis of thee (pf, 4 hands and 2 other insts)
Fantasy on How beautiful shines the morning star (org and vla) (1974)
Overture to St. Joan (org and timp) (1963)
May the morning star rise (org and vla)
Interlude (org) (1965)
Tones in overtones (pf)
VOCAL
Cantata to Leonardo da Vinci (1974)
Leonardo, parts I, II (soli, ch and orch) (comm, 1984)
Voices of Women in Wartime, cycle (S, 3-8 vlc, pf and timp) (1941-1945)
Aus dem Poesie (Alben) (vce, hp, vlc and perc) (1977)
Five poems of Emily Dickinson (m-S and pf) (1973)
Mathematical problems (I. Rubin) (S and pf) (1963)
Ophelia Lieder (1965)
SACRED
The Beatitudes (mix-ch and org) (1979)
Kyrie, Gloria, Toccata, Agnus Dei (ch and org)
Sing unto the Lord a new song (mix-ch) (1965)
Mass (treble vces and org) (1964)
Missa brevis (1965)
BALLET
Machine man (1982)
THEATRE
Everyman, morality play (1961)
Hamlet (1965)
St. Joan (Shaw) (1964)
Thieves' carnival (1961)
ELECTRONIC
Between (2 tape, perc and vce) (1979)
Ecology I (tape) (1979)
Ecology II (tape, insts and vce) (1979)
Eine Stimme ruft elektronischen Klang auf (live elec, modulator, vce and laser) (1973)
Live electronic (vce and laser) (1973)
Natural voice and electronic sound (1973)
Neptune odyssey (tape) (1975)
Spring morning at Grobholz (3 fl and tape) (1975)
Textures and moods of Emily Dickinson (vce and tape) (1976)

Bibliography
An American Composer in Germany. Music Clubs Magazine, 1977 special.
Ref. composer, AMC newsletters, 142, 185, 190, 206, 359, 465, 610, 622, 625

COATES, Kathleen Kyle

19th-century American composer of piano pieces.
Ref. 276, 347

COBB, Hazel

American teacher and composer. b. Groesbeck, TX, July 15, 1892; d. Dallas, TX, September 8, 1973. She studied at the American Conservatory where she obtained a B.Mus. (1922) and M.Mus. (1924).

Compositions
PIANO
Pieces
VOCAL
The mission bell (ch)
Duets
Songs
OPERETTA
Daughter of Mohammed
Lamps trimmed in burning
Ref. 142

COBBE, Linda

Composition
VOCAL
Oh cast that shadow from thy brow, song (London: T. Holloway)
Ref. H. Baron (London)

COCCIA, Maria Rosa
Italian composer. b. Rome, January 4, 1759; d. Rome, November, 1833. She was a pupil of Sante Pesci and at the age of 16 passed the examination of the Accademia di Santa Cecilia with her composition *Hic vir despiciens mundum*, which was widely acclaimed. The next year she was given the title of Maestra di Capella from the Accademia Filarmonica di Bologna. Her works achieved great fame but very few are still in existence. Tributes to her were published in letters by Padre Martini, Metastasio and Carlo Broschi. PHOTOGRAPH.
Compositions
VOCAL
Il trionfo di Enea, oratorio
Qualche lagrima spargete
SACRED
Daniello nella fossa d'leoni, oratorio (4 vces) (1772)
Cantata (4 vces) (1783)
Dixit Dominus (8 vces, vln, vla, ob, fl and hn)
Hic vir despiciens mundum (4 vces and org) (Rome, 1774)
Magnificat (4 vces and org) (1774)
OPERA
L'isola disabitata
Publications
Treatise on harmony.
Bibliography
Elogio storico della Signora Maria Rosa Coccia, Romana, maestra publica di capella, Accademia Filarmonica di Bologna, etc. Rome, 1780.
Ref. 2, 8, 65, 74, 105, 128, 158, 159, 210, 216, 276, 361, 502, 622, 646, 653

COCHRANE, Peggy
20th-century composer.
Compositions
PIANO
Four tweenies
Irish blarney (1944)
Petits sabots
The playbox
Rock-a-bye
Le ruisseau
Ref. 473

COCKING, Frances M. Hefford
English pianist and composer. b. Kirkheaton. She is an L.R.A.M.
Compositions
PIANO
Sonata
Thoughts on Jenny Jog
Three nocturnes
VOCAL
Christmas song for children
A little sunbeam
Three little autumn thoughts
Three little may songs
SACRED
On sorrow-weep no more, anthem
Ref. 467

COCQ, Rosina Susanna de
Dutch concert pianist and composer. b. Den Helder, May 10, 1891. With the death of her mother at her birth, she was brought up by her grandmother, a soprano who was a pupil of Pauline Viardot-Garcia (q.v.). Rosina received her first music lessons from her grandmother and then Henri Polak and Mme. Clement-de Witt. In 1908 she entered the Royal Conservatory at the Hague, to study the piano under Carel Oberstadt and made her debut as a concert pianist at Zeist. She studied composition under Henri Viotta and left the conservatory in 1913 with the highest honors and the Nicolai prize for composition. In 1923 she received the Maillochon Prize in Paris. She gave innumerable piano recitals. She composed some songs together with Queen Elisavita of Rumania and had some 700 compositions to her credit. She was a member of SACEM. PHOTOGRAPH.
Compositions
ORCHESTRA
Concert ouverture poétique (1913)
L'adieu (1928)
La fête d'hiver, ballet suite (1941)
Marche funèbre (1915)
Marche héroique (1964)
Meditation (1928)
Mimosa (1941)
Nocturne (1924)
Sonatine (1923)
Suite (cham) (1964)
Thème et variations (1928)
CHAMBER
Idylle (str qrt)
Invocation (str qrt)
Quartet (4 vln) (1965)
Thème et variations (str qrt) (1940)
Three minuets (str qrt)
Six pieces (vln, vlc and pf)
Suites, minuets and other pieces for cello and piano and violin and piano
PIANO
Iolanda Vladimiro, Spanish dances (2 pf, 4 hands)
Minuets
Pieces for children
Preludes
Sonatinas
Theme and variations
Other pieces
VOCAL
Works (2, 3 and 4-part choirs and pf)
Children's songs
Numerous songs in Dutch, French, German, Italian, English (vce and pf)
OPERA
La Rose Blanche (1925)
De Spotvogels (1955)
OPERETTA
Sneeuwbruid, for children (1951)
Ref. composer, 77, 110

CODY, Judith
20th-century American lecturer and composer. b. Troy, NY. She studied Japanese music from 1968-1969 and is the recipient of various awards.
Compositions
CHAMBER
Sonata, op. 22 (fl and gtr)
Flute poems, op. 19
Theme and variations, op. 27 (pf)
GUITAR
City and country themes in G-Major (1976)
Concert etudes, ops. 11, 13, 14, 15, 18
Dances, op. 8 (1978)
Etude No. 1 (1976)
Firelights in C-Major (1977)
Firelights in G-Major (1977)
Nocturne, op. 9 (1978)
OPERA
Looking under Footprints (1983)
Ref. 228, 625

COELHO, Ernestine Leite
Early 20th-century Portuguese pianist and composer of piano pieces.
Ref. 398

COEN, Anna
19th-century Italian composer.
Compositions
VOCAL
Nina-nana: Andemo vissere, sera i to oceti (Selvatico) (Ricordi)
Non amo! Voi che salite questo verde monte, romance (L. Stecchetti) (Ricordi)
Spes, ultima Dea: Ho detto al core, al mio povero core, romance (Stecchetti) (Ricordi)
Voi partite! song (Brocco)
Ref. 297

COEN, Augusta
Italian pianist and composer. b. Rome, March 8, 1896. She studied at the Liceo di Santa Cecilia under Alfonso Rendano in 1904 and in 1909 made her debut in Naples as a concert pianist and then performed elsewhere in Italy and in London in 1913.
Composition
PIANO
Afrique, suite d'airs nord-africains (1931)
Ref. 105

COFFMAN, Lillian Craig

American organist, pianist, teacher and composer. b. New London, IA, February 28, 1875. She obtained her B.Mus. from Iowa Wesleyan College in Mt. Pleasant and became an associate of the American Guild of Organists in 1914. She studied under Alexander Rommel (piano, harmony and composition) at Iowa Wesleyan College and with Dr. E.R. Kroeger (composition) at St. Louis. She was organist at the Mellow Memorial Methodist Church, St. Louis, from 1907. She made several appearances as a recitalist, including a performance of her own compositions in 1948.

Compositions

CHAMBER

By the brook (pf) (1914)
The hour of worship (org) (1933)

VOCAL

And you away (1910)
A caprice (1912)
Flowering stars (1937)
Happy hearts (1910)
June roses (1911)
Lullaby (1910)
The passing year
Romany dance (1938)
These three (1941)

SACRED

Abide with me
Jubilate Deo
Nearer my God to Thee

Ref. 460, 496

COGAN, Morva

20th-century Australian composer.

Compositions

VOCAL

Carra barra wirra canna, Aboriginal lullaby (adapted by Morva Cogan and Rolf Harris) (Castle Music, 1965)

BALLET

The truant stars, Aboriginal ballet

OPERETTA

Billarni

FILM MUSIC

Jimmy my boy (Walkabout)

Ref. 442, 440

COHEN, Dulcie M.

20th-century Australian composer.

Compositions

ORCHESTRA

Chanson d'Eviradnus, tone poem
Zuleika

CHAMBER

Pieces

VOCAL

Cantatas
Songs

TEACHING WORKS

Piano pieces

Ref. 23

COHEN, Harriet C.B.E.

British pianist, professor and composer. b. London, December 2, 1901; d. London, November 13, 1967. She studied at the Royal Academy of Music and became a professor at the Tobias Matthay Piano School. She traveled widely in Britain and Europe, both as a soloist with major orchestras and as a chamber music performer. She was awarded the C.B.E. for her services to music in 1938. Works were dedicated to her by Bela Bartok, Ernest Bloch and Moeran. Arnold Bax wrote *Symphonic variations* for her and *Concerto for left hand and orchestra* for her after she injured her right hand in 1948. Vaughan Williams composed his *Piano concerto* for her.

Compositions

PIANO

Russian impressions: The old church at Wilna; The exile; Sunset on the Volga; The Tartars (Augener, 1915)
Arrangements of Bach organ chorale preludes

Publications

Music's Handmaid. 1936.

Bibliography

Brook. *Masters of the Keyboard*. London: Rockcliff, 1946.
Lyle. *Dictionary of Pianists*. London: Hale, 1985.

Ref. 74, 645

COHEN, Marcia (nee Spilky)

American composer. b. Chicago, August 20, 1937. She studied composition under Leslie Bassett at the University of Michigan in 1955 and graduated from Roosevelt University, Chicago in 1958 with a B.A. in education. She continued her composition studies at De Paul University, Chicago, from 1965 to 1967 and in 1968 obtained her M.Mus. from Northwestern University where she was a pupil of Alan Stout. From 1970 to 1971 she was composer-in-residence of the Columbia Dance Troupe; from 1972 to 1976 a faculty member of the Young Artists Studios, School of the Art Institute of Chicago and from 1974 to 1977 guest artist and concert co-ordinator at the same school. In the same period she originated and co-ordinated a series of New Music from Chicago.

Compositions

ORCHESTRA

Prism (cham orch) (1967)

CHAMBER

String quartet (1967)
Trio (hn, cl and bsn) (1956)
City dances (vln and pf) (1976)
A mazement (perc) (1974)

VOCAL

Shir shel Shirim (S, ob, gtr, vib and 2 perc) (1967)
Song (S and pf) (1955)

ELECTRONIC

A*R*P* (tape) (1972)
Beginning (S and tape) (1974)
Changes (vln and tape) (1974)
Chess set (perc and tape) (1971)
Devonshire air (3 tapes) (1973)
Finnegan's wake (Joyce) (1968)
Music for my sister (fl, ob and tape) (1975)
Santa Rosa sound (tape) (1978)
Zodiac cast (fl and tape) (1969)

MULTIMEDIA

Double play (2 dancers and tape) (1970)
Journey of doors (2 actors and tape) (1977)
Stopgo (dance troupe, sculpture and tape) (1971)

Ref. composer, 474, 622

COLACO OSORIO-SWAAB, Reine

Dutch translator and composer. b. Amsterdam, 1881; d. Amsterdam, April 14, 1971. She studied melodic construction under Ernest W. Mulder and Henk Badings. She began composing after the death of her husband. She was interested in psychology and philosophy and translated various books on philosophical subjects. PHOTOGRAPH.

Compositions

ORCHESTRA

Dramatic overture (1953)

CHAMBER

Suite (brass and ww) (1948)
Quartet No. 1 (fl, vln, vla and vlc) (1952)
Quartet No. 2 (str qrt) (1955)
Cavatine (bsn, vlc and pf) (1942)
Suite (fl, vln and vla) (1940)
Trio (1941)
Trio No. 3 (2 vln and vla) (1950)
Trio No. 4 (cl, vlc and hp) (1956)
Fantasia (fl and hp) (1950)
Four short pieces (fl and pf) (1958)
Jesaja spraak, fantasia for harp (1949)
Sonata (2 vln) (1947)
Sonata (cl and pf) (1958)
Sonata No. 3 (vla and pf) (1952)
Theme and variations (2 rec) (1957)
Tsaddiek, intermezzo (vla and pf) (1953)
Five pastorales (fl) (1959)
Sonata (cl) (1947)
Sonata (ob) (1959)
Sonatine (ob) (1964)
Twee gavottes in oude stijl (pf)

VOCAL

Het ezeltje (2 w-vces or ch) (1952)
Wijzang (Tagore) (S, A or 2 part w-ch and fl) (1937)
Avond (with C.S. Adama van Scheltema) (1931)
Dansende duiven Aafjes (1957)
Dorpsdans (J. Perk) (m-S, A and pf) (1931)
Fetes galantes: En sourdine (Verlaine) (1932)
Laat de luiken gesloten zijn (J.H. Leopold) (1951)
Mein Volk (Lasker-Schuster) (1948)
Moeder en kind (2 w-vces) (1956)
Das Roseninnere (Rilke) (m-S and pf) (1932)
Saenge eines fahrenden Spielmanns (S. Georg) (1935)
Zij komt (J. Perk) (S and pf) (1931)

SACRED
Esechiel 37 (1948)
Jesaja 40 (1951)
Jesaja 60 (1950)
John 10 (1950)
De opwekking van Lazarus (speaker and pf) (1954)
De tocht door de hemelen (M. Buber) (speaker and pf) (1974)
Genezing van den blinde (1950)
Ref. Helen Metzelaar (Amsterdam), Donemus (Netherlands)

COLBRAN, Isabella Angela (Mrs. Gioacchino Rossini)

Italian singer and composer. b. Madrid, February 2, 1785; d. Bologna, October 7, 1845. Her father was a musician in the Spanish court orchestra. Her talent for music became evident at an early age and before she was six she began studying under Pareja. At the age of nine she began advanced singing studies under Marinelli and received her final education from Crescentini. From 1809 to 1815 she sang as a contralto in Spain and Italy. In Naples she met the composer Rossini whom she married in 1822. She retired from the stage. Rossini's *Elisabetta*, *Cenerentola* and *Barbiere* were dedicated to her. She composed four collections of canzone and other songs.
Ref. 129, 276, 323, 347, 361, 622

COLE, Charlotte

19th-century English soprano, teacher and composer. She composed songs and ballads.
Ref. 85, 276, 347

COLE, Elizabeth Shirk

American song composer. b. Peru, IN, June 6, 1859; d. October 7, 1927.
Ref. 347

COLE, Ulric

American pianist, music editor, teacher and composer. b. New York, September 9, 1905. Her father, George Cole, was a cellist. She started her musical education at the age of five under her mother, Emilie Cole, a concert soprano. She studied under Homer Grunn in Los Angeles and Percy Goetschius (advanced counterpoint) and George Boyle (piano) at the Institute of Musical Art, New York, 1922 to 1923. She was awarded two fellowships and attended the Juilliard School of Music, where she studied the piano under Josef Lhevinne and composition under Rubin Goldmark. In 1927 she left the Juilliard and went to Paris where she studied for six months under Nadia Boulanger (q.v.). She made public appearances as a pianist and composed from the age of ten. She received awards from the Society for the Publication of American Music in 1931 and 1941. She taught at the Masters School, Dobbs Ferry, from 1936 to 1942 and was on the staff of the New York Philharmonic Young People's Concerts, 1943 to 1945. She was on the editorial staff of Time Magazine for eight years before traveling around the French Islands in the South Pacific and since that time has been living outside the United States. Her works have been performed in many countries. PHOTOGRAPH.

Compositions
ORCHESTRA
Concerto No. 2 (pf and orch) (1941)
Divertimento (2 pf and str orch) (1932)
Divertimento for string orchestra and 2 pianos: Toccata, Intermezzo; Finale; Fantasia (1934-1935)
Divertimento for string orchestra and piano (1938) (J. Fischer, 1939)
Nevada, tone portrait (1948)
Sunlight channel (1949)
Two pieces (str orch) (1937) (SPAM, 1930)
CHAMBER
Quintet (1936) (SPAM, 1941)
String quartet No. 1 (1932)
Suite (str qrt) (1937)
Suite (vln, vlc and pf) (1931)
Sonata (vln and pf) (1926-1927)
PIANO
Concerto (2 pf) (1924)
Divertimento for two pianos (1972) (comm Allan McIlvaine)
Fantasy Tchaikovsky (2 pf) (1943)
Man-about-town (2 pf) (Schirmer, 1947)
Prelude and fugue (2 pf) (1924)
Above the clouds (Cincinnati: J. Church, 1924)
Fantasy sonata (1933)
Metropolitones, 3 pieces (1941) (G. Schirmer, 1943)
The prairie hobgoblins (1925)
Purple shadows (1928)
Six tunes and sketches in black and white (1927)
Three vignettes (Fisher, 1936)
Valse, op. 48, transcription of Tchaikovsky (2 pf) (1971)
Ref. composer, 22, 74, 81, 142, 168, 228, 280, 477

COLEMAN, Ellen

English composer. b. 1893; d. London, 1973. She composed piano music, songs and masses.

Compositions
CHAMBER
Sonata (vlc and pf)
Ref. 70, 177, 347

COLERIDGE-TAYLOR, Avril Gwendolen

British pianist, conductor and composer. b. South Norwood, March 8, 1903. The daughter of the composer Samuel Coleridge-Taylor, she wrote her first composition at the age of 12 and won a scholarship for composition and the piano at the Trinity College of Music in 1915. She studied orchestration and composition under Gordon Jacob and Alec Rowley and conducting under Sir Henry Wood, Ernest Read and Albert Coates. She was the founder and conductor of the Coleridge-Taylor Symphony Orchestra, 1946 to 1951, and founder of the Coleridge-Taylor Musical Society and Choir in 1945. She was the first woman conductor of the band of H.M. Royal Marines and a guest conductor of the BBC Symphony Orchestra and the London Symphony Orchestra. In 1971 she founded and conducted the Malcolm Sargent Symphony Orchestra. She was musical director and conductor of T.C. Fairbairn's production of Hiawatha and his ballet *The Fire Spirits*. She also founded and directed the New World Singers, a male voice ensemble. PHOTOGRAPH.

Compositions
All published by Boosey & Hawkes
ORCHESTRA
Piano concerto in F-Minor (1938)
African forest song (1936)
Ceremonial march for independence of Ghana (1957)
Comet prelude (1952)
From the hills (1936)
The golden wedding, ballet suite
In memoriam
Pastoral suite (str orch)
Spring magic
Sussex landscape
To April, poem (1933)
Valse caprice (1936)
CHAMBER
Crepuscule de nuit d'été (fl and pf)
Fantaisie pastorale (fl and pf)
Idylle (Rudall Carte) (fl and pf)
Impromptu (fl and pf)
Romance (vln and pf)
Melody (In Memoriam) (org)
Threnody (org)
PIANO
All lovely things
Concert etude
Caprice
Four characteristic waltzes
Historical episode
Just as the tide was flowing, berceuse and nocturne
My garden
Rhapsody, op. 174
Two short pieces
VOCAL
Wyndore (wordless ch and orch) (1936)
Symphonic impression (mix-ch) (1942)
April
The dreaming water lily
The entranced hour
Goodbye butterfly
Mister sun
The rustling of grass
Silver stars
Who knows?
Songs
SACRED
God's remembrance (S, hp, vln, vla and vlc)
Ref. composer, 2, 8, 77, 94, 96, 407, 467

COLGAN, Alma Cecilia
American organist, pianist and composer. b. Little Rock, AR, July 13, 1894. She studied under Ernest Hutchinson and toured as a concert virtuoso. She wrote piano music.
Ref. 226

COLIN, Jeanne (nee Albertine de Clerck)
Belgian teacher and composer. b. Brussels, January 9, 1924. She studied at the Royal Conservatory of Music in Brussels but taught herself composition. She taught at the Music Academy in Anderlecht. Her works were broadcast over Belgian radio stations.
Compositions
ORCHESTRA
Violin concerto, op. 22 (1974)
Concerto, op. 17 (fl and orch) (1972)
Matiere habitée, op. 9, 4 symphonic movements (1968)
CHAMBER
Three miniatures op. 2 (3 groups of Celtic hps and leading harp) (with Georges Colin, 1975-1976)
Divertissement op. 13 (11 strs) (1970)
Trois suggestions, op. 23 (9 strs; also str orch) (1974)
Quatour, op. 3 (fls) (with Georges Colin) (1976)
String quartet op. 8 (1968)
Trio, op. 10 (fl, vln and d-b) (1969)
Tryptique, op. 4 (reeds) (1966-1967)
Caprice, op. 14 (vln and pf; also orch) (1970)
Concertati movimenti, op. 24 (vln and pf) (1975)
Deux pièces, op. 4 (fl and hp) (with Georges Colin) (1979)
Sonate, op. 1 (a-fl and pf) (1966)
Sonate, op. 7 (fl and pf) (1966-1967)
Trois pièces faciles, op. 20 (fl and pf) (1974)
Fantaisie, op. 25 (hp) (1975)
Fantaisie, op. 27 (a-sax) (Paris: Billaudot, 1978)
Quatre pièces, op. 18: Lento; Allegro giocoso; Andante; Allegro con fuoco (fl) (1972)
Quatuor, op. 28 (sax) (1976-1977)
Improvisation, op. 11 (fl) (1969)
Pour Corine, op. 16 (1971)
Séquence, op. 12 (vln) (1970)
Sonate, op. 2 (s-fl or t-fl) (1966)
PIANO
Le tombeau d'Andre Jolivet, op. 1 (2 pf) (with Georges Colin, 1975)
Leitmotiv, op. 29
VOCAL
Choeurs sans paroles, op. 15 (mix-ch a-cap) (1971)
Maehlich durchbrechenade Sonne, op. 6 (A. Holz) (mix-ch a-cap) (1967)
Ou gît la nuit, op. 21 (A. Doms) (mix-ch a-cap) (1974)
Dialogue, op. 5 (A. Doms) (vce, vln and perc) (1967)
Forêt, op. 3 (A. Lepage) (vce and pf) (1966)
Nocturne, op. 26 (vce and pf) (1975)
Ref. composer, 77, 188, 206, 457

COLLARD, Marilyn
20th-century American composer. She was a pupil of Robert Manookinar Brigham Young University, Provo, UT.
Composition
PIANO
Theme and variation for piano solo (hon mention, National Music Club's young composers competition, 1977)
Ref. Music Clubs Magazine Autumn 1977

COLLETT, Sophia Dobson
English composer. b. London, 1822; d. Highbury Park, London, March 27, 1894. She composed vocal works, including choruses and part songs as well as church music.
Ref. 6, 85, 226, 276, 347

COLLEY, Betty
20th-century composer.
Composition
PIANO
Reflections at the piano (Kjos, 1983)

COLLIER, Elizabeth Mary
Composition
SACRED
O rest thee in thy green turf grave (Rev. R. Montgomery)
Ref. H. Baron (London)

COLLIN, Helene
19th-century French pianist and composer. She studied under Rety and LeCouppey. She composed piano pieces (Paris: Grus).
Ref. 226, 276

COLLINET, Clara
19th-century French composer.
Compositions
VOCAL
Songs
SACRED
Send out Thy light
OPERA
Le Fauteuil de Mon Oncle
Ref. 276, 307, 347

COLLINS, Janyce
20th-century American composer.
Composition
CHAMBER
As in a twilight of roses (hp and cham ens) (1980)
Ref. AMC newsletter

COLLINS, Laura Sedgwick
19th-century American pianist, actress, dancer, singer and composer. b. Poughkeepsie, NY. She graduated from the Lyceum School of Acting, New York. She was a pupil of Dvorak.
Compositions
CHAMBER
Pieces (vln and pf)
VOCAL
Endymion, dramatic scene (B and S)
Songs incl.:
Foolish little maiden
Where art thou
INCIDENTAL MUSIC
Music to Pierrot
Ref. 226, 276, 433

COLLVER, Harriet Russell
American pianist and composer. b. Clyde, OH, 1871. She studied at the Cleveland Conservatory of Music and was a student under J.H. Rogers and Charles L. Capen in Boston. She studied for a concert career and later turned to composition. Her works have been widely performed and often featured on concert programs.
Compositions
PIANO
Pieces incl.:
Arabian dance
Berceuse
Caprice
Charis
Dexter prelude
Emanov
Impromptu
Kimball prelude
A memory
Le papillon
Pipes of India
Preludes
Romance
Serenade
The toy shop, ballet suite
VIOLIN
Inspiration
Meditation
Whims
VOCAL
The lute unstrung (Oscar Wilde) (w-ch)
Music in the seashell (Oscar Wilde) (w-ch)
Songs incl.:
Birds have told
Chinese legend (Katherine Gunn Dame)
Dancing daffodils
Day and I
Heart's delight
I wandered lonely as a cloud (Wordsworth)
Love among the clover

Many years ago
Morning song
Nocturne
One ray of love
Sleep, my flower
Sometimes I dream
Song without words
The sugar plum tree (Field)
SACRED
Be not afraid
He leadeth thee
Lift up thy voice
Little town of Bethlehem, carol
What Child is this, carol
Ref. 374, 433

COLOMA-SOURGET, Eugenia de. See SANTA-COLONA-SOURGET, Eugenie de

COLOMBARI DE MONTEGRE. See FERRARI, Gabriella

COLOMER BLAS, Maria
20th-century composer.
Compositions
PIANO
Chanson florentine (Ricordi)
Papillons d'or, caprice-ballet (Ricordi)
Ref. Ricordi (Milan)

COLONNA, Vittoria, Duchess of Amalfi and Marchioness of Pescara
Italian poetess and composer of sacred music. b. Marino, 1490; d. Rome, February 25, 1547. She was the daughter of Fabrizio Colonna, Grand Constable of Naples and betrothed at the age of five to Ferdinand Pescara, also aged five, marrying him in 1509. Ferdinand went to war and was taken prisoner at the battle of Ravenna in 1512. He was ransomed and rejoined his wife. In 1525 he died of wounds received at the battle of Pavia. For a while Vittoria entered the convent at Marino, where she began her life as a poetess. She was persuaded to return to her home in Ischia in 1527. Her 117 sonnets became very popular and she became the most famous woman of her day. Some of these sonnets she set to music. She lived a life of great purity and was the friend and confidante of the great intellectuals of the day. Notwithstanding her Roman Catholic background she became influenced by Protestantism and tended to embrace that faith. Nevertheless in 1544 she took up residence in the convent of St. Anne and died there three years later. She composed hymns and sonnets. PHOTOGRAPH.
Publications
Rime Spirituali. Poems and hymns. ca. 1540.
Ref. 268, 347, 626, 637, 646, 653

COLTELLANI, Celeste
Italian operatic singer and composer. b. Livorno, 1764; d. 1817. She made her debut at Naples in 1781 and was engaged by Emperor Josef II for the Vienna Opera. She composed arias and songs.
Ref. 433

COLTRANE, Alice McCleod
Black American harpist, organist, pianist and composer. b. Detroit, August 27, 1937. She started piano lessons at the age of seven. She married the jazz saxophonist John Coltrane. Her music combines African and Asian mysticism with Western sounds. DISCOGRAPHY.
Compositions
CHAMBER
Bliss: The eternal now (pf, hp and gtr)
A monastic trio
Journey in Satchidnanda
Universal consciousness
Ref. 136, 549, 563

COMALE. See WINKEL, Therese Emilie Henriette aus dem

COMBIE, Ida Mae
American composer.
Composition
CHAMBER
A musical calendar (vln and pf)
Ref. 292

COME, Tilde
20th-century Belgian composer.
Compositions
CHAMBER
Bagatelle (cl or s-sax and pf) (1973) (J. Maurer)
Elegy (cl and pf) (1973) (Maurer)
Sarcasme (cl or a-sax and pf) (1973) (Maurer)
Capriccio (fl or ob or cl or a-sax and pf) (1974) (Maurer)
Melopee et danse (fl or a-sax and pf) (1974) (Maurer)
Humoresque (trp or trb and pf) (1975) (Maurer)
Ref. 188

COMPOSER, Mrs. See FINLEY, Lorraine Noel

CONCARINI, Vittoria. See ARCHILEI, Vittoria

CONFORTINI-ZAMBUSI, Lucietta
19th-century Italian composer of Vicenza.
Compositions
VOCAL
Canova, song for the wedding Baggio-Gosetti (Padua: Tipografia del Seminario, 1824)
Canzone, song for the wedding Correr-Zeno (Tipografia del Seminario, 1849)
Canzone ed Anacreontica, song for the wedding Canneti-Confortini (lib ded to Count Giulio Capra)
Ref. 327

CONRAD, Laurie M.
American concert pianist, teacher and composer. b. Manhatten, July 5, 1946. She received her B.M. and M.M. from the Ithaca College, having studied composition under Karel Husa, theory under Malcom Lewis and the piano under George King Driscoll. She has received several grants, including Meet the Composer grants. She is a member of ASCAP.
Compositions
CHAMBER
Clarinet concerto I (cl and cham insts) (1984)
The gates of dawn (fl, cl and vlc) (1982)
Pas à deux (2 cl) (ded Stanley and Naomi Drucker) (1982)
Two pieces (vla and gtr) (1984)
Prelude and solo (vlc) (1981)
Pensées (vlc) (1981)
For solo violin (1982)
Etoiles (1981)
PIANO
For two pianos, in 3 mvts (1984)
Nocturne (1984)
For the left hand (1983)
VOCAL
Apparition (Bar, m-S, fl, cl, pf, vla and vlc) (1983)
Chansons du monde (soloists, ch, pf and orch) (1981)
Japanese songs of separation (m-S, Bar, cl, fl and vlc) (1983)
Preludes (m-S and insts) (1982)
Two volumes of songs (m-S and insts) (1978, 1980)
Volume III, songs (m-S, Bar and insts) (1983)
BALLET
Seaglass (m-S, pf and orch) (1980)
Voiles (1979)
Bibliography
Garden concert. Ithaca Video Project. 1980.
Ref. composer, 625

CONSEY, Jill. See FELIX, Margery Edith

CONSTANCE OF AUSTRIA, Queen of Poland
17th-century Polish composer. She married Sigismund III in Cracow in 1602.
Composition
SACRED
Alleluja (vce) (with A. Parcelli)
Ref. 35, 105

CONSTANS. See DRDOVA, Marie

CONSTANT, Jenny. See ANDREWS, Jenny

CONSTANT, Rosalie de
Swiss guitarist and composer. b. Lausanne 1758; d. 1835. Mme. de Stael praised her compositional talents to the composer Zingarelli.
Compositions
GUITAR
Pieces and arrangements
VOCAL
Sentiments secrets, aria
Ref. 502

CONSTANTIN. See DRDOVA, Maria

CONSTANTINESCU, Domnica
Rumanian pianist, choral conductor, lecturer, musicologist and composer. b. Bucharest, August 24, 1930. At the Ciprian Porumbescu Conservatory, Bucharest, 1949 to 1955, she studied under Ioan Chirescu (theory and solfege), Ion Dumitrescu (harmony), Martian Negrea and Nicolae Buiciliu (counterpoint), Alfred Mendelsohn (composition), Theodor Rogalski (orchestration), Zeno Vancea and Radu Negreanu (history of music), Tiberiu Alexandru (folklore), Ovidiu Drimba (piano) and Dumitru D. Botez (choir conducting). At the Sorbonne, she studied for her doctorate under Jacques Chailley. After obtaining her B.Mus. and licentiate in music (1955) she became an assistant lecturer in the history of music, counterpoint and harmony at the conservatory. In 1971 she was made a lecturer. Since 1969 she has been a member of the board of examiners of the Regional Conservatory in Nice. PHOTOGRAPH.
Compositions
ORCHESTRA
Symphony 1907, op. 1 (1955)
Symphony Victoria (1955)
Piano concerto, op. 4 (1963)
CHAMBER
Quintet, op. 2 (pf and strs) (1959)
Instrumental pieces (1955-1974)
PIANO
Constellations (1969)
Suite, op. 5 (1971)
VOCAL
Dans le forêt (soli, 2 chil-ch, perc and orch) (1983)
La danse roumaine (soli, 3 chil-ch, perc and orch) (1983)
Sol invictus, suite (soli, ch, perc and orch) (1983)
Symphonic legend (A. Drimba) (narr and sym orch) (1958)
Publications
Cours de contrepoint et fugue. For students. 1971.
Cours d'histoire de la musique roumaine. For students. 1959.
D.A. Dinicu. Monograph. 1960.
La musique dans les chroniques du moyen-age roumain. L'Union des Compositeurs Roumains, 1958.
La fonction dans les modes musicaux roumains. Cahiers de Musicologie Vol. XVII. Union des Compositeurs de Roumanie, Edition Musica, Bucarest, 1983
Permanences et innovations dans le folklore des pays de l'Europe du Sud-Est. 1972.
Receuil des oeuvres polyphoniques composées par les etudiants instrumentistes et chanteurs à la classe de contrepoint et fugue. Presses du Conservatoire, Bucharest 1983.
Ref. composer, 196

CONTAMINE, Mlle. de
18th-century French composer who lived in Paris. She composed a volume of airs with guitar accompaniment (1780).
Ref. 126, 128

CONTIN, Mme.
19th-century Italian composer.
Compositions
CHAMBER
Variations for piano with string accompaniment (Vienna: Artaria)
Ref. 226, 276

CONTINI ANSELMI, Lucia
Italian pianist, writer and composer. b. Vercelli, October 15, 1876. She was a pupil of Sgambati (piano) and A. Parisotti (composition) at the Liceo di Santa Cecilia in Rome, from which she graduated in the piano. She toured as a pianist and because of her fame was personally received by Italy's Queen Margherita.
Compositions
ORCHESTRA
Alla patria (large orch)
Cogitata (large orch)
Danza romena (large orch; also small orch)
Sybilla Cumaea (large orch; also 2 pf)
Deliciae (small orch)
Gavotta (str orch)
Minuetto (str orch)
Preludio (str orch)
CHAMBER
Alla mazurka (vln and pf)
Moeror (vln and pf)
Ninna nanna (vln and pf)
PIANO
Aus dem Carneval
Bauernmarsch
Berceuse
Ludentia (gold medal, International Competition, 1913)
Sonata in C-Minor
Thirteen other pieces
SACRED
Salve Regina (vce and orch)
OPERETTA
La Sponda Magica, fairy opera in 3 acts
BALLET
Driadi e satiri
Ref. 56, 105, 180, 465

CONVERT, Josephine
19th-century composer.
Composition
CHAMBER
Marie, grande valse (pf or hpcd) (ded Princess Marie of the Netherlands) (Amsterdam, Wahlberg, ca. 1850)
Ref. H. Baron (London)

CONWAY, Olive
20th-century American composer. She composed choral works and songs.
Ref. 40, 347

COOK, Eliza
English poetess, writer and composer. b. London, ca. 1818. She contributed to literary magazines and wrote words and music for numerous ballads, which were popular in her time and published by W. Blockly, Dempster and Glover.
Ref. 226, 276

COOK, Mrs. Joseph Tottinham. See POOLE, Anna Ware

COOKE, Edith
English composer; d. London, January 28, 1927.
Compositions
ORCHESTRA
I dream'd a dream (Gordon)
PIANO
Etude de concert (Bosworth)
Gavotte romantique (Ashdown)
Valse impromptu (Bosworth)

VOCAL
- Two marionettes (mix-vces)
- The broken story (Cramer)
- Don't forget me, Robin (Chappell)
- Don't quite forget, C and E-Flat (Boosey)
- Dorothy, waltz (Hopwood)
- The dreamers (vce and org) (Cramer)
- I'll watch o'er thee (Ditson)
- In thy presence (Ditson)
- In the twilight grey (Cramer)
- Jackdaw of Rheims (Ascherberg)
- The king's jester
- Loved voices (Ashdown)
- Love's goal (Cramer)
- Many mansions (Cramer)
- Meadow sweet (Cramer)
- Once in the golden past (Cramer)
- Path that leads to you (Patey; Reynolds)
- River of Dart (Chappell)
- Shadows (Cramer)
- Spring and love (Boosey)
- The story of a life (Cramer)
- Sweet lavender (Cramer)
- This green lane (Chappell)
- When this old world was young (Cramer)
- Why must we say good-bye (Cramer; Schirmer)
- Why not today (Cramer)
- Wooed and won (Willcooks)
- Wooing (Williams)
- World of shadows (Cramer)
- Yours for evermore (Cramer)

Ref. 105, 276, 297, 347, 433

COOKE, Marjorie Tibbets

20th-century American carillonneur, pilot, teacher and composer. She studied the carillon under Lowell Smith at the University of California, Riverside and is a member of the Guild of Carillonneurs in North America.

Compositions

CARILLON
- North Idaho Woods

Ref. First Presbyterian Church (Santa Barbara, CA)

COOLIDGE, Elizabeth Sprague

American pianist and composer. b. Chicago, October 20, 1864; d. Cambridge, November 4, 1953. She was a patron of music festivals in Pittsfield, and later in Washington, DC. She established the Elizabeth Sprague Coolidge Foundation at the Library of Congress for concerts and festivals, donating the auditorium of the library and its organ. She gave awards of prizes and medals to composers and aimed to encourage contemporary composers of all countries. Many universities conferred honorary degrees on her in recognition of her work towards the encouragement of music. She also received many foreign decorations and honors.

Compositions

CHAMBER
- Sonata (ob and pf) (C. Fischer, 1947)

VOCAL
- Songs

Ref. 8, 22, 74, 96, 347, 524, 622

COOLIDGE, Lucy

20th-century composer.

Compositions

VOCAL
- Contemplations (Walt Whitman) (Bar and pf) (1984)
- Etchings

FILM MUSIC
- Old Fashioned Woman (1974)

Ref. 622

COOLIDGE, Peggy Stuart

American pianist, conductor and composer. b. Swampscott, MA, 1913; d. May, 1981. She started piano lessons at the age of five and composed her first song when she was nine. Later she studied under Heinrich Gebhard (piano) and Raymond Robinson and Quincy Porter (composition) of the New England Conservatory. Several of her earlier works were introduced by the Boston Pops Orchestra under Arthur Fiedler. Her *Cracked Ice* was the first ballet written specifically for ice skating. In 1963 she was invited to Vienna and Budapest for performances of her music and appeared as a soloist in one of her works. Two years later she was invited to Moscow and Warsaw for similar events and conducted symposiums on the overlap of serious and popular music in American composers' works. After visiting Tokyo, she was invited by Khachaturian to return to Moscow in 1970. A concert consisting of only her works was given, an honor that had not been accorded to any other American composer. She was also awarded the Medal of the Union of Soviet Workers in Art. Thereafter performances of her symphonic works spread throughout Europe. In 1973 she composed a symbolic musical theme to complement the World Wildlife Fund's symbol, which became the basis for her orchestral work *The Blue Planet*. DISCOGRAPHY.

Compositions

ORCHESTRA
- Out of the night, rhapsody (pf and orch)
- Rhapsody (hp and orch) (1965)
- Twilight city, rhapsody (pf and orch)
- American mosaic (comm R.A. Boudreau)
- The island
- New England autumn, suite (cham orch)
- Night froth
- Pioneer dances (1970)
- Smoke drift
- Spirituals in sunshine and shadow (1969)
- The voice
- Dublin Town, suite

CHAMBER
- String quartet
- Solo piece for harp
- Piano pieces

VOCAL
- The Blue Planet (J. Coolidge) (narr and orch)
- Vocalize (vce and orch)
- Suite of songs

BALLET
- Cracked Ice (1937)
- An evening in New Orleans

INCIDENTAL MUSIC
- American reflections
- Red roses for me (Sean O'Casey)
- The silken affair
- Voices (with R. Lortz)

MULTIMEDIA
- The angel's Christmas (with R. Lortz)

Ref. 39, 142, 280, 347, 465, 563, 610

COOMBS, Mary Woodhull

American composer.

Compositions

VOCAL
- Lamentation
- The secret
- With thee

Ref. 292

COONEY, Cheryl Lee

Canadian teacher and composer. b. Alberta, May 30, 1953. She was educated in Edmonton and studied at the University of Alberta, where she obtained her B.Mus. in 1974. She received her performance diploma in chamber music from the Mozarteum Hochschule fuer Musik und darstellende Kunst in 1977 where she studied under Erika Frieser, Kurt Prestel and Cesar Bresgen. From 1977 she taught and directed music in Canada. Between 1979 and 1980 she worked on her master's degree in composition under Elliot Weisgarber.

Compositions

ORCHESTRA
- Spielzeug fuer Orchester (1980)

CHAMBER
- String quartet No. 1 (1977)
- String quartet No. 2 (1980)
- Suite for solo cello (1976)
- Variations for flute and piano (1979)

VOCAL
- Secular cantata (T, ch and cham ens) (1977)
- Slow, slow fresh fount (Echo's song) (1976)

SACRED
- Kyrie eleison (w-ch, fl and rec)

Ref. composer

COOPER, Esther Sayward

American pianist, dancer and composer. b. Boston, May 4, 1897. She was a pupil of Dr. Brinkler, Samuel Wills, Harriet Ware (q.v.) and Harvey Gaul. She also studied dancing at the Gilbert, Dalcroze and Chalif schools of dance, New York. In 1945 she won two awards from the Pennsylvania Federation of Music Clubs.

Compositions
VOCAL
Choral: High flight (Johan Magee) (w-ch)
Songs incl.:
Against the rush of time (H. Williams)
Another April (Williams)
Before you came (Williams)
Blackberry Hill (Williams)
Enough (Teasdale)
Humility (Williams)
Images (Williams)
Negro sketches
O willow in my garden (1st prize, PA, Fed. of Music Clubs contest, 1944)
Why must I dream? (Williams)
SACRED
Did a great bell ring?
In the covert of thy wings
Ref. 347, 374

COOPER, Rose Marie

American composer. b. Cairo, IL, February 21, 1937. After studying under Warren Angell, she graduated in 1959 from Oklahoma Baptist University (B.Mus.) and in 1960 from Teachers College, Columbia University (M.A.) where she studied under Henry Cowell (music and music education). She received seventeen ASCAP awards and the Outstanding Young Woman of North Carolina Award (1971). She was on the faculty of Greensboro College from 1965 to 1967 and in 1976 received a Ph.D. in child development at the School of Home Economics, University of North Carolina. DISCOGRAPHY.
Compositions
CHAMBER
Suite (1971)
VOCAL
An old-fashioned meeting (1982)
Night is a lullaby (1970)
Settings of 5 haiku (1974) (Byron Douglas)
Sing with me, one and three (1970) (Julian Assoc.)
Songs to share (G.V. Thompson) (1964)
This is the land that I love
Trilogy (1969)
Way to go
SACRED
Lord most holy, cantata (1964) (Broadman)
Morning star, cantata (1970) (Carl Fischer)
Plain songs and carols (ch)
Three anthems for junior choir (1967) (Concordia)
Christ Child come below
Chorale-introit (Christ is risen) (1969)
Collection of melodies with descants (1965)
Collection of plain songs and carols (1965) (Flammer)
Crown of thorns (1961) (Fischer)
Hymns to the Trinity (1964) (Fischer)
Hymn of truth (1970) (Julian)
I heard the bells on Christmas day (1969)
Lord speak to me (1971)
Once in Royal David's City (1962)
Praise to the Lord, the Almighty (1968) (R.D. Row; Fischer)
Psalm 93, The Lord reigneth (1961) (Shawnee)
Psalm 145, great is the Lord (1960) (Shawnee)
Psalm 146 (1973) (Brodt Music)
Psalm 150 (Broadman)
Rock a my soul (1956) (Signature Press)
The search for God (1982) (Fischer)
Tell the blessed tidings
This is the day (1959) (Fischer)
THEATRE
Oh, Penelope! bicentennial play (with Susan Graham Erwin) (1975)
Ref. composer, 142, 228, 563, 622

COOPMAN, Rosalie

20th-century British composer.
Composition
MISCELLANEOUS
L'aigle a deux tetes (1981)
Ref. Composer (London)

COPLAND, Berniece Rose

20th-century American teacher and composer. b. Lynnville, IA. She composed piano pieces.
Bibliography
Etude, July 1940, p. 498.
Ref. 347

COPLEY, Maria Kriel (Quinsie)

South African composer. b. Johannesburg, December 13, 1915; d. October, 1980. She studied music in Pretoria under Professor Pieter Croze and received her B.A. from Pretoria University. She was a classical pianist until she lost most of the use of her right hand, when she started to play and compose jazz. PHOTOGRAPH.
Compositions
PIANO
Classical study in A-Minor
Jacaranda waltz (1939)
A little bit of Liszt (1975)
VOCAL
Afgee (studente jare)
Blouberge van Noord Transvaal
Drie beertjies
Hello (aan Bobbie)
Jane
Kersfeesboomliedjie
Kom na my plaas toe
Lyttleton se trein
Net vir jou (aan Ria)
Outeniqua Pas (aan Petra)
Sakkie, Sakkie, Zebedelia lemoene
Sweet sad memories
Waarom (aan Bobbie)
Die waterval
Ref. composer

COPPERSMITH, Barbara. See CARROLL, Barbara

COQUET, Odile Marie-Lucie

French organist, pianist and composer. b. Lyon, October 3, 1932. She was the daughter of the director of the Lyon Ecole Nationale des Beaux-Arts. She graduated from the Lyon Conservatory in the piano, the organ, solfege, harmony and fugue. She also studied at the Paris Conservatoire under O. Messiaen. In Italy she studied under Vito Frazzi (composition) and F.A. Lavagnino (film music). She was placed in the Concours International de Musique in May 1960 with her piano work *Nocturne No. 1: Ete*. She received a bursary to study at St. Jacques de Compostelle Institute of Spanish Music in 1960. She transcribed several old works for orchestra and her compositions have been broadcast. PHOTOGRAPH.
Compositions
ORCHESTRA
Fantasie-impromptu (vln and orch) (1970)
First orchestral suite (1963)
Ode a Cassandre, melodie
Romantic waltz (sym orch)
CHAMBER
Wind trio (ob, cl and bsn)
Deux episodes: Elegie; Fantasie (vln and pf) (1956)
Petite suite (acdn)
PIANO
Gentil cocquelicot (1966) (Lemoine, 1971)
Nocturne No. 1: Ete (prize, Concours International de Musique, 1960)
Ref. composer, 77, 206, 457

CORDULA, Sister M. (Sister of the Holy Cross)

20th-century American teacher, writer and composer. She composed piano pieces.
Ref. 347

CORINA. See CORINNA

CORINNA (Corina)

6th-century B.C. poetess-musician of Tanagra or Thebes, Boeotia, Greece. She was Pindar's teacher and defeated him five times in poetry competitions. She was taught her art by Myrtis and Antipater considered her songs so lovely that he named her one of the nine women whom he selected as earthly Muses. Her works consisted of five volumes of epigrams, lyric poems and choruses for women. She sang of native myths and legends, heroes and more specially of heroines. Little of her poetry and none of her melodies have survived. She was often called the Lyrical Muse.
Ref. 162, 264, 268, 281

CORKER, Marjorie
Composition
CHAMBER
In Ireland (vlc and pf) (London: Schott)
Ref. Frau und Musik

CORMONTAN, Theodora (Dora) (Thodora Nicoline)
Norwegian publisher, teacher and composer. b. 1840; d. ca 1920. She owned a publishing house and music shop in Arendal. She later moved to America and taught music in Iowa. DISCOGRAPHY.
Compositions
CHAMBER
Aftendaemring
VOCAL
Blandt fjeldene, op. 3
Fire sange, op. 1 (vce and pf)
Fire sange, op. 2
Fred til bod for bittert savn, op. 41
Honnoer-Marsch for norske turnere, op. 44
Kjaerlighed er livets kilde, op. 42
Norske turneres nationalfestmarsch
Tre sange, op. 4 (vce and pf)
SACRED
Herre Jesu Christ, op. 36
Hoeyt fra det himmelske hoeje
Til kirke, op. 8
Tre religioese sange, op. 5 (S, A and pf)
Ref. Norwegian Music Info. Center

CORNEA-IONESCU, Alma
Rumanian pianist, lecturer and composer. b. Budapest, May 21, 1900. At the Fodor Conservatory in Budapest (1912 to 1916) she studied under Siklos Antal (theory, solfege and harmony and under Dr. Kovacs (piano)). At the Cluj Conservatory (1924 to 1927) she studied under Traian Vulpescu (theory and solfege), Martian Negrea (harmony, counterpoint and musical form), Augustin Bena (theory, solfege, acoustics and music aesthetics), Ana Voileanu (piano) and Jean Bobescu (chamber music). In Vienna (1929 to 1931) she studied at the Akademie fuer Musik und darstellende Kunst, the Konservatorium fuer Musik, the Internationales Pianistenseminar and the Internationale Hochschulkurse der Universitaet Wien. Other teachers included Paul de Conne (piano), Anton Ruzitska (chamber music), Dr. Roger (harmony and music history) and Anton Webern (musical form). She taught the piano at the Municipal Conservatory of Timisoara (1922 to 1946) and at the Hungarian Gymnasium, the Institute of Art and the Music School. She gave concerts, recitals, concert-lectures and radio performances. She wrote articles for journals and in 1957 received the Workers' award.
Compositions
CHAMBER
Small suite for string quartet (1961)
PIANO
Rondo in A-Minor (1953)
Sonatina (1948)
Songs and dances of the Banat (1963)
Suită de dansure bănăţeneşti (1921)
Suite (1952)
Ten pieces (1965)
Ten variations on a Rumanian theme (1943)
Three bagatelles (1951)
Two pieces in Rumanian style (1930)
VOCAL
Cîntec de pace (mix-ch and pf) (1952)
Lupta noastră (C. Pavelescu) (mix-ch and pf) (1951)
Cîntece pe versuri de Agripina Foreanu (vce and pf) (1968)
De-aş avea (M. Eminescu) (vce and pf) (1955)
Din bătrîni (O. Goga) (vce and pf) (1955)
Două cîntece de dor, folk words (1952)
Şase doine pentru voce şi pian, six doinas (vce and pf) (1964)
Şi dacă (M. Eminescu) (vce and pf) (1954)
Was will die einsamen Traeume (H. Heine) (vce and pf) (1954)
TEACHING PIECES
Albums and pieces for children (1931-1964)
Publications
Organizarea invatamintului muzical din Romania. Timişoara, Moravetz, 1938.
Pianul, arta si maestrii lui. Timişoara, Moravetz, 1938.
Problema muzicii romanesti. Brasov, Astra, 1940.
Tiberiu Brediceanu. Brasov, Astra. 1939.
Bibliography
Bogdan, Elena. *Portrete, Alma Cornea.*
Braun, D. *Cornea Alma új zongora kompozicioi.* Temesvári Hirlap, 1932.
Braun, D. *Zenei arcképek: Ionescuné Cornea-Alma.* Temesvári Hirlap, 1936.
Bumbaru-Basu, C. *O compozitoare banateana: Alma Cornea.* Fruncea. Timişoara, no. 33, 1935.
Gîrneată, Ecaterina. *Valori femenine: Alma Cornea. Curierul muzical.* Bucharest, 1932.
Ref. 196, 300

CORNEILLE
20th-century composer.
Composition
VOCAL
Sleep and forget (vce and pf)
Ref. Frau und Musik

CORNING, Karen Andree
20th-century American composer.
Compositions
CHAMBER
Duo for violin and piano (1958)
VOCAL
Piece (mix-ch, fl, ob and pf)
Ref. 190

CORRER, Ida, Countess
Italian musician and composer. b. Padua, 1855. She was the daughter of Luciano Fornasari and studied harmony and composition under Melchiore Balbi, P. Alessandro Capanna and Alfonso Sommi in Padua.
Compositions
CHAMBER
Due romanze senza parole (vln and pf) (Ricordi)
PIANO
Ma!
Perche!
VOCAL
Two romances: Lontananza; Ricordo d'amore (Ricordi)
Songs
SACRED
Mass
Kyrie (3 vces)
Ave Maria
OPERA
Il Gondoliero, in 3 acts
Una Notte a Venezia
Ref. 105, 180, 225, 226, 297, 309

CORRI, Ghita (Mrs. Neville Lynn)
20th-century British concert and operatic vocalist, teacher and composer. b. Edinburgh. She was the daughter of Henry Corri, the leading baritone at Covent Garden and the founder of the Corri Grand Opera Company. She first appeared at Crystal Palace as an operatic and ballad vocalist and then joined the Carl Rosa Company, making her first appearance in London as Marguerite in *Faust* (1899). She toured with Sir Charles Halle, Foli, Joachim, Hollman and Janotha. She was engaged by Charles Morton to sing her own song *Coronation* at the Palace Theatre in 1902. She had a repertoire of thirty-five operas in English, French, German and Italian.
Compositions
VOCAL
Coronation
Fight, fight, fight
Have faith
The land of light
Love dreams
Say yes
OPERETTA
Coleen's Eviction
Ref. 467, 488

CORRI-DUSSEK, Sofia Giustina (later Moralt)
Scottish harpist, pianist, singer, teacher and composer. b. Edinburgh, May 1, 1775; d. London, 1847. The daughter of Domenico Corri, she was taught by her father and performed publicly on the piano at a very early age. In 1788 she moved to London where she appeared with success as a singer. She studied under Marchesi, Viganoni and Cimador. in 1792 she married the composer J.L. Dussek, under whose instruction she became adept as a pianist and harpist. She performed with her husband in con-

certs in England but later dedicated herself to teaching. After her husband's death she married J.A. Moralt and moved to Paddington, where she founded an academy of music. She had a daughter, Olivia (q.v.) who became a pianist, harpist, organist and composer.

Compositions

CHAMBER

Sonata for the pianoforte or harpsichord with an accompaniment for a violin or German flute, op. 1 (London: Corri, Dussek & Co.)

Six sonatas for the harp, op. 2 (London and Edinburgh: Corri, Dussek)

Three sonatas (B, C, D) for harp or piano with violin accompaniment, op. 9 (Paris: Sieber)

New German waltz, adapted as a rondo (hp or pf) (London: Corri, Dussek)

Nous nous aimons, rondo for harp (London: Pleyel; Corri, Dussek, 1797)

Ref. 8, 9, 15, 65, 74, 100, 125, 126, 226, 276, 347, 405

CORY, Eleanor

American editor, lecturer and composer. b. New Jersey, September 8, 1943. She studied composition under Chou Wen-Chung, Charles Wuorinen, Bulent Ariel and Meyer Kupferman. She holds a B.A. from Sarah Lawrence College; M.A. from Harvard Graduate School of Education, M.M. from New England Conservatory and D.M.A. from Columbia University. She received awards from Composers' Forum and Composers' Conference and grants and awards from the National Endowment for the Arts, the New York State Council on the Arts (CAPS), the Frederick Hilles Fund of Yale University and a Norlin Fellowship at the MacDowell Colony. She lectured at Yale, Columbia and Hofstra universities, the New England Conservatory and Brooklyn College. After 1973 she was at Baruch College, City University of New York. She was an editor of Contemporary Music Newsletter from 1972 to 1977. In 1981 she received the ACA recording award. DISCOGRAPHY.

Compositions

CHAMBER

Concertino (pf and 18 insts) (1970)

Concertino II (winds, perc and man)

Tempi (ww, brass and strs)

Octagons (fl, cl, bsn, pf, vib, gtr, vln and vlc) (1975)

Septet (fl, ob, bsn, hn, vln, vla and vlc) (1971)

Counterbrass (hn, trp, trb, pf and perc) (1978)

Modulations (2 perc and strs) (1972)

Klangfarben three for six (fl, ob, vlc, d-b, pf and hp) (1965)

Morsels (brass qnt)

Adagio quartetto (str qrt) (1964)

Quartet (ob, trp, vlc and vib) (1968)

Designs (vln, vlc and pf) (1979)

Trio for clarinet or bass clarinet, cello and piano (1973)

Trio for violin, bass clarinet and piano (1969)

Trio (fl or picc, ob or cor anglais and pf) (1977)

Ehre (vln) (1984)

Epithalamium (fl) (1973)

PIANO

Apertures (1984)

Caroline's concert, 3 short pieces

Combinations (1970)

Piece for Rebecca (1979)

Suite a la Brecque (1980)

VOCAL

Aria viva (T, fl, ob, cor anglais, bsn and gtr) (1977)

Liebeslied (m-S, fl, b-cl, vla, vlc and d-b) (1969)

Surroundings (vce and pf)

Waking (S, bsn, trp, t-sax, pf, perc, vln, vla, vlc and d-b) (1974)

Words (S and pf) (1967)

SACRED

Agnus Dei and Libera me (w-ch) (1964)

ELECTRONIC

Pieces (pf, fl, cl and tape)

Tempi (cl and tape) (1971)

Publications

Articles in *Perspectives of New Music*. 1973.

Contemporary Music Newsletter.

Ref. composer, 137, 142, 228, 347, 457, 563, 622, 625

CORYELL, Marion

American composer.

Compositions

VOCAL

Songs incl.:

The lamplighter

When cherries bloom

Ref. 292

COSNARD, Mlle.

17th-century French composer. b. Paris.

Composition

THEATRE

Les chastes martyrs, a Christian tragedy (Paris: Nicolas et Jean de la Coste, 1650)

Ref. 218

COSSOUL, Genoveva Virginia

Portuguese composer. b. ca. 1800; d. February, 28 1879.

Composition

MISCELLANEOUS

Homenagen a Camoes, triumphal march (Neuparth)

Ref. 104, 297

COSTA, Maria Helena da

20th-century Brazilian composer. DISCOGRAPHY.

Compositions

PIANO

Etude in counterpoint (prize, University of Salvador Bahia National competition)

VOCAL

Atencao (ch a-cap)

Ref. 563

COSWAY, Maria Cecilia Louise

Late 18th-century English composer.

Compositions

CHAMBER

Two sonatas (hpcd and vln) (London: Birchall and Andrews, 1787)

VOCAL

Songs and duets (hp and vce)

Ref. 65, 128, 347, 405

COTE, Hélène (Soeur Marie-Stéphanie)

Canadian organist, pianist, nun, teacher and composer. b. St. Barthelemy, January 9, 1888. She studied in Montreal under Romain-Octave Pelletier (piano) and after two years received the Diplome Superieur de Piano from the Academie de Musique of Quebec; studying under Alfred Laliberte (piano), Claude Champagne (composition, fugue and counterpoint) and Raoul Paquet (organ). In Paris (1935 to 1936) she studied under Guy de Lioncourt (composition and orchestration). She holds a doctorate in music, summa cum laude (Montreal, 1936) and is a licentiate of the Conservatoire National de Musique, Montreal. In 1908 she became a nun of the congregation of the Saints Noms de Jesus et de Marie and took the name of Soeur Marie-Stéphanie. At Outremont she founded the Ecole Superieure de Musique, which in 1933 became affiliated to the faculty of arts of the University of Montreal. She was director of musical studies at the Institut des Soeurs de Saints Noms de Jesus et de Marie for 30 years and director of the Ecole Superieure de Musique Vincent d'Indy, Outremont for 18 years.

Compositions

CHAMBER

Andante (str qrt)

Fugue (org)

VOCAL

Je n'ai qu'un seul ami (ch)

SACRED

Fugue vocale à 4 voix (based on the Song of Solomon) (4 vces)

Cantique au Sacre Coeur (Montreal: Archambault)

Salut du Saint Sacrement (Archambault)

Publications

Manuals of harmony and analysis.

La Musique au point de vue educatif. Montreal, Fides.

Theòrie de la musique. Ecole Vincent d'Indy.

Ref. 85, 133, 355

COTRON, Fanou

French pianist and composer. b. Chamalieres, July 7, 1936; d. Paris, September 16, 1975. At the age of eight she interpreted Honegger's *Concertino* under his direction and at 12 won first prize for the piano at the Paris Conservatoire. She also won first prize for chamber music under Gaston Poulet. She studied composition under Darius Milhaud and in 1959 won the Grand Prix de Rome for her work *Armide*. She married Jean-Claude Henry, professor of counterpoint at the Paris Conservatoire. PHOTOGRAPH.

Compositions
ORCHESTRA
Fantasie
Suite concertante, choreographic theme (pf and orch) (1959) (1st prize, Pasdeloup Assoc. de Concerts competition, 1960)
CHAMBER
Sonata (pf and vln)
PIANO
Histoire d'un quart d'heure de sommeil (2 pf)
Mystère joyeux and Seance a Guignold, children's pieces
Toccata
VOCAL
Armide, cantata (S, T, B and orch) (1959) (Grand Prix de Rome)
La Loreley, lyric poem (dramatic S, T and orch) (1961)
Trois poèmes de Ronsard (Cont and orch)
Quatre choeurs (vce and 12 insts)
Pic et Pic et Colegrum (reciter and 6 insts)
Melodies (vce and pf)
Lamentations de Jérémie (1957)
Nous sommes (Paul Eluard)
SACRED
Psaume 97 (ch, org and brass)
THEATRE
L'Innocent, ballet, on a theme by Marcel Brumaire
Ref. composer

COTTA, Anastasia

16th-century Italian Kapellmeister and composer at the Court of Milan. She composed madrigals and motets.
Ref. 502

COTTON-MARSHALL, Grace. See MARSCHAL-LOEPKE, Grace

COULOMBE SAINT-MARCOUX, Micheline

Canadian electronic instrumentalist, lecturer and composer. b. Lac-Saint-Jean, Quebec, August, 1938; d. Montreal, February 2, 1985. She studied under Francois Brassard (composition) in Jonquiere and then became a pupil of Claude Champagne at the Ecole Vincent d'Indy, where she obtained a B.Mus. (1962). She also studied at the Montreal Conservatory of Music under Gilles Tremblay and Clermont Pepin. She received the first prize in composition from the conservatory and in 1967 won the Prix d'Europe in composition for *Modulaire*. She studied composition under Tony Aubin in Nice in the summer of 1965 and in 1968 went to Paris for three years on a bursary from the Canadian Council of Arts. She first worked with the French radio-television network Groupe de Recherches Musicales. She performed at the Avignon Music Festival in 1969. In November 1969 she founded a new music group with composers from five other countries, the 'Groupe Electroacoustique de Paris', which toured throughout Europe and broadcast over many radio stations. A bursary from the French government in 1971 enabled her to continue her composition studies under Gilbert Amy and Jean-Pierre Guezec. In 1971 she returned to Montreal and commenced work with three Montreal percussionists: Guy Lachapelle, Pierre Beluse and Robert Leroux. She organized an electro-acoustic conference in 1972 with the Montreal critic Jacques Theriault, during which many of the works of the Groupe Electroacoustique were played. In 1979 she was invited to the 8th Curso Latinoamericano de Musica Contemporanea in Brazil to lecture on instrumental and electronic music in Canada and in 1981 to the Dominican Republic to give similar courses. She organised a week of new music from Latin America in Montreal in February 1982. She was frequently interviewed on Canadian television and wrote numerous articles for music periodicals. DISCOGRAPHY. PHOTOGRAPH.
Compositions
ORCHESTRA
Héteromorphie (1969-1970) (comm Montreal Symphony Orchestra)
Luminance (1978)
CHAMBER
Evocations doréanes (picc, 3 fl, ob and cl) (1964)
Genesis (wind qnt) (1975)
Mandala I (fl, ob, vlc, pf and perc) (1979-1980)
Quatuor à cordes (str qrt) (1965-1966)
Episode II (3 perc) (1972)
Sonata (fl and pf) (1964)
Equation 1 (2 gtr) (1968)
Horizon I (fl)
Composition I (hn) (1982)
Horizon II (ob) (1982)
Intégration I (vlc)
Intégration II (vln) (1982)
PIANO
Assemblages (1969)
Doréanes (1969)
Kaleidoscope (left hand) (1964)
Mandala II
VOCAL
Makazoti (8 vces and small inst ens) (1971)
Moments (S and ens)
Chanson d'automne (Paul Verlaine) (vce and pf) (1963)
ELECTRONIC
Modularie (pf, hp, ondes Martenot and orch) (1967)
Sequences (2 ondes Martenot and perc) (1968)
Ishuma (S, inst ens and syn) (1974)
Episode II (3 perc and audiomixer) (1972)
Regards (elec ens)
Miroirs (hpcd and tape) (1976)
Trakadie (tape and perc) (1970)
Arksalalartôq (tape) (1971)
Bernavir (tape) (1970)
Constellation I (tape) (1981)
Contrastances (electro-acoustic insts) (1971)
Moustières (tape) (1971)
Zones (1972)
MULTIMEDIA
Alchera (m-S, inst ens, tape and lights) (1972-1973)
FILM MUSIC
Tel qu'en Lemieux (electro-acoustic insts) (1973)
Publications
Reflections d'une jeune compositeur. *Vie Musicale*, No. 8, 1968. Reprinted in English in *Canadian Composers*, October 1968.
Bibliography
Coulombe Saint-Marcoux... a Young Composer of Great Talent. Canadian Composers, No. 51 (June 1970).
News from Paris. *Canadian Composers*, No. 49. April 1970.
Ref. composer, 85, 199, 329, 347, 485, 563

COULTHARD, Jean

Canadian pianist, professor and composer. b. Vancouver, February 14, 1908. She received her early musical training from her mother, Jean Robinson Coulthard, pianist and organist. She wrote her first composition at the age of nine and studied under Jan Cherniavsky (piano) and Frederick Chubb (theory). She became an A.R.C.T. In 1928 she won a scholarship from the Vancouver Woman's Musical Club, which enabled her to study at the Royal College of Music in London. Her teachers were Kathleen Long (piano), R.O. Morris (theory) and Ralph Vaughan Williams (composition). She obtained her L.S.R.M. diploma in composition. In 1930 she returned to Canada where she became head of the music departments of St. Anthony's College and Queen's Hall School. She studied under Arthur Benjamin (1939), Darius Milhaud (1942), Bela Bartok (1944), Bernard Wagenaar (1945, 1949), Nadia Boulanger (q.v.) (1955) and Gordon Jacob (1965 to 1966). Among her awards are CAPAC awards (1945 and 1947), the McGill University Chamber Music Award (1949) for her composition *Three Shakespeare Sonnets* and in 1951 the Albert Clement Memorial Prize. In 1953 she won a Royal Society fellowship for a year's study in France. She has also received awards from the XIV Olympiad (London), the XV Olympiad (Helsinki) and the Australian Broadcasting Corporation. From 1947 to 1973 she held positions in the department of music at the University of British Columbia, becoming Professor Emeritus. For the following three years she was composer-in-residence at the Shawnigan Lake Summer School. DISCOGRAPHY. PHOTOGRAPH.
Compositions
ORCHESTRA
Symphony No. 1 (BMI, 1950)
Symphony No. 3 (bsn and cham orch)
Concerto for piano and orchestra (1961-1967)
Concerto for violin and orchestra (1959)
Aegean sketches (also pf) (BMI)
Ballade (str orch) (1942)
Burlesca (pf and str orch)
Canada mosaic (large orch) (comm CBC, 1974)
Canadian fantasy (1939)
Endymion, poem (1964)
Excursion (1940)
Fantasie (pf, vln and cham orch) (1960)
Kalamalka (1973) (comm CBC)
Serenade meditation and 3 dances (1961)
Music for St. Cecilia (str orch) (1954)
Music on a quiet song (fl and str orch) (1946)
A prayer for Elizabeth (str orch) (BMI, 1953)
Rider on the sands, prelude (1953)
Sea Chanty, overture (Song to the Sea) (1942)
Symphonic ode (vlc and orch) (1965)
Symphonic ode (vla and orch) (1976)
Ballade 'Of the East Coast' (pf and cham orch) (1982)

CHAMBER
The bird of dawning singeth all night long (vln, hp and 9 strs) (1962)
Twelve essays on a cantabile theme (str octet)
Octet, 12 songs on a cantabile theme (2 str qrt) (1972)
Divertimento for five winds and piano (1966)
Piano quintet (1932)
Lively (str qrt) (1948)
Piano quartet (1957)
String quartet No. 1 (1948)
String quartet No. 2 (1953, rev 1969)
String quartet No. 3 (1981)
Legend (Legend of the snows) (trio) (1971)
Lyric trio (1968)
Music on a Scottish folk song (vln, hp and gtr) (1964)
Correspondence (vln and pf) (1964)
Where the Trade Winds blow, suite (fl and pf) (1982)
Ballad of the North, theme and variations (vln and pf) (1965-1966)
Day dream (vln and pf) (1964)
The devil's fanfare (vln and pf) (1958)
Duo sonata (vln and pf) (1952)
Fanfare sonata (trp and pf) (1978)
The frisky pony (vln and pf) (1964)
Lyric sonatina (bsn and pf, 1969; also cl and pf, 1976; also fl and pf, 1971)
On the march (vln and pf) (1964)
Pas de deux, sonatina (fl and bsn) (1980)
Poem (vln and pf) (1947)
A quiet afternoon (vln and pf) (1964)
Six bizarre dances (vln and pf) (1958-1960)
Shizen: three sketches from Japan (ob and pf) (1979)
Sonata (vlc and pf; also ob and pf; also ob and fl, 1947; also vln, 1979)
Sonata No. 2 (vln and pf) (1964)
Sonata No. 3: A la jeunesse (vln and pf) (1979)
Sonata-fantasy (hn and pf) (1983)
Sonata rhapsody (vla and pf) (1962)
Two sonatinas (vln and pf) (1945)
When music sounds (vlc and pf) (1970)
Where music sounds (vln and pf; also vln, vlc and pf) (1982)

PIANO
Of the Universe, sonata (2 pf) (1979)
Sonata (BMI, 1948)
Sonata to Jane (1954)
Dare Devil (1964)
Early pieces, teaching manual (1960)
Four variations on Good King Wenceslas (1933-1934)
Four etudes (BMI, 1945)
Image Astrale (1981)
Noon siesta (1964)
Twenty-four preludes (1954-1964)
Rondo (BMI, 1954)
Sketches from the Western Woods (1970)
Theme and variations on B.A.C.H. (1951)
Other dances and pieces

VOCAL
This land (solo, mix-ch and orch)
Vancouver lights (Earle Birney) (S, Bar, mix-ch and orch) (1980)
Night wind, cycle of 4 songs (m-S and orch or pf) (1951)
Two songs of the Haida Indians (S and orch) (1981)
Auguries of innocence (Blake) (mix-ch) (1965)
Axe of the pioneer (J.V. Crawford) (mix-ch) (1958)
Canadian carol (mix-ch a-cap) (1941)
Flower in the crannied wall (Tennyson) (unison ch and pf) (1963-1965)
More lovely grows the earth (mix-ch a-cap)
Quebec May (mix-ch and 2 pf) (1948)
Romance (T, B, boys' ch and pf) (1970)
Sea gulls (E.J. Pratt) (w-ch and pf) (1954)
Soft fall the February snows (m-ch and pf)
Stopping by woods on a snowy evening (R. Frost) (unison ch) (1954)
Three Ballads from the Maritimes (ch) (1979)
To blossoms (w-ch and pf)
Walk softly in the springtime (unison ch and pf or org) (1967)
The white lily flower (composer) (unison ch and pf) (1967)
Wild thorn apple tree (C. Sandburg) (mix-ch) (1978)
Chanson du cour (M. Guimont) (S and pf) (1979)
Cradle song (S, A and pf) (BMI, 1928)
Cycle of three love songs
First song of experience (Blake) (m-S and pf) (1968)
Five love songs (E. Dickinson) (Bar) (1955)
Five part songs
Four prophetic songs (E. Gourlay) (Cont, fl, vlc and pf) (1975)
Gulf of Georgia (E. Birney) (1953)
Lean out of the window
The May tree, three songs (S and pf) (1962)
Pines of Emily Carr (journals of Emily Carr) (narr, A, str gtr, pf and timp) (1969)
Songs from the Distaff Muse, set 2 of cycle of duets (S, A and pf) (comm Nona Marie and Kathleen Fearn)
Spring rhapsody, 4 songs for Maureen Forrester (1958)
Five medieval love songs
Six Irish songs for Maureen (A and pf)
Songs of a dreamer (S and vla) (1982)
Three Shakespeare sonnets (S, str gtr or vlc solo and 8 vlc) (1947) (McGill University choral music award, 1949)
Three Shakespeare sonnets (Cont, gtr and strs) (1977)
Three songs (m-S or B and pf or strs) (1954)
Two French songs (E. Milligan) (B) (1957)
Two idylls from Greece (J. Braddock) (Bar and pf) (1980)
Two night songs (H. Monro, H. Belloc) (B, str qrt and pf) (1960)
Two songs for midsummer (Shelley, L. Abercrombie) (S, vla and pf) (1970)
Two visionary songs (H. Monro, Walter de la Mare) (vce, fl and str qrt) (1968)
Duets (S, T and pf) (1960)
Other songs (vce and pf)

SACRED
Pastorale cantata (psalms) (S, Cont, narr, mix-ch, 2 trp, hn, trb and org) (1967)
A child's evening prayer (M.L. Duncan) (unison ch and pf) (1967)
Hymn of creation (Rig-Veda) (mix-ch and perc) (1975)
Lullaby for Christmas (unison ch and pf) (Jay, 1967)
On Easter (S. Banigan) (unison ch and pf) (OUP, 1964)
Threnody (mix-ch a-cap) (BMI, 1961)
The signature of God (S, A and pf)
The star shone down (composer) (unison ch and pf) (Jay, 1967)

OPERA
The Return of the Native, in 3 acts (after Thomas Hardy) (with Edna Baxter)

ELECTRONIC
The Birds of Landsdowne, or The bird sanctuary
Fantasy (vln, vlc, pf and tape of bird songs) (1972)

Bibliography
W.V. Rowley. *The Solo Piano Music of the Canadian Composer Jean Coulthard*. Dissertation. Boston University, Boston. 1973.
Ref. composer, 22, 31, 52, 70, 77, 96, 133, 140, 329, 371, 402, 477, 563, 622

COUPER, Mildred

American pianist, teacher and composer. b. Buenos Aires, December 10, 1887. She studied at the Williams Conservatory of Music in Buenos Aires (1902) and became an American citizen in 1910. She graduated from Karlsruhe-Baden Conservatory, then studied under Moritz Moszkowski in Paris, Sgambati in Rome and Alfred Cortot in New York. From 1918 to 1927 she taught at the Mannes School of Music, New York and from 1927 to 1940 at the Music Academy of the West, Santa Barbara.

Compositions
ORCHESTRA
Irish washerwoman variations (pf and orch)
Seven more
We are seven

CHAMBER
Piano quintet
Dirge (2 pf) (New Music Editions, 1937)

VOCAL
Barnyard cogitations (Radiana Pazmor)
Fur and feathers (Radiana Pazmor)
Two sets of songs (Ogden Nash)

Ref. 142, 347, 496

COUPERIN, Louise

17th-century French composer. She was a cousin of Francois Couperin and composed for Louis XIII (1601-1643), showing her ability in the contrapuntal style.
Ref. 433

COURMONT, Countess von (alt. name Mme de Siesley)

18th-century French singer and composer. She was a pupil of the famous singing teacher David and became well known in Vienna, St. Petersburg and Moscow. She was engaged as a singer at the Royal Opera in Berlin in 1796. She composed a number of piano pieces and songs.
Ref. 129

COURRAS, Jeanne

Compositions
PIANO
Heure cointaire, op. 2, melodie
La charmeuse, op. 6, valse lente
Colibri, op. 3, mazurka

COUTURE, Priscilla
20th-century American composer. She composed band pieces and choral and vocal works.
Ref. 40, 347

COVERT, Mary Ann Hunter
American harpsichordist, pianist and composer. b. Memphis, September 24, 1936. She received a diploma from the Memphis Conservatory of Music (1954), a B.M. from Oklahoma Baptist University (1957), a diploma from the National Guild of Piano Teachers (1958) and an M.A. from Memphis State University (1965). She made her debut in 1974 at Carnegie Hall, New York. She appears with chamber ensembles and orchestras.
Compositions
PIANO
Sonatina
VOCAL
Love came down (ch)
Other choral works
Ref. 206

COWL, Doreen
English pianist, singer and composer. b. Plymouth, 1904. She studied under Dr. Harold Lake and Septimus Webb. She is an L.R.A.M. and an A.T.C.L.
Compositions
PIANO
Daffodils
Devon boys
Down to Downderry
Impromptu
Love
Prelude
The road
Ref. 467

COWLES, Cecil Marion
American pianist and composer. b. San Francisco, January 14, 1898; d. New York, March 28, 1968. She made her piano debut at the age of nine. She attended the Von Einde School in New York and then the Von Meyernick School in California. She studied the piano under Stojowski and Mansfeldt and composition under Carl Deis.
Compositions
ORCHESTRA
Beyrouth bazaar
PIANO
Cubanita
In a rickshaw
Nocturne
Oriental sketches
Shanghai bund
VOCAL
Songs incl.:
La charme
Persian dawn
SACRED
Jesu Bambino, mass
Ref. 22, 96, 142, 347, 353

COWLES, Darleen
American lecturer and composer. b. Chicago, November 13, 1942. In 1966 she graduated from De Paul University, having studied under Leon Stein; she obtained her M.M. (composition) in 1967 from Northwestern University where she studied under Anthony Donato and Ralph Shapey and studied for her Ph.D. at the University of Chicago. She won the Faricy award for creative composition in 1967 and was a lecturer at Northwestern University in 1967, at Elmhurst College in 1970 and at De Paul University, 1972. In 1980 she created, organised and taught a course at De Paul University on a historical and analytical approach to women composers from the medieval period till the 20th-century. She was director of an improvisational multi-media group, the Marcel Duchamp Memorial Players, which performed extensively throughout the mid-west. She is a member of the theory and composition faculty of the American Conservatory of Music. She has read theoretical papers before the American Musicological and other societies and organised and performed in early music concerts. DISCOGRAPHY.
Compositions
ORCHESTRA
Chamber symphony No. 1 (1965)
BAND
Sonata (1964)
CHAMBER
Translucent unreality No. 1, op 33 (fl, pf and wind chimes) (1978)
Translucent unreality No. 2, op. 35 (fl, cl and pf) (1978)
Translucent unreality No. 4, op. 34 (hn, vlc and 2 pf) (1978)
Translucent unreality No. 6, op. 30 (hn, pf and glock) (1976)
Translucent unreality No. 7, op. 36 (fl, cl, hn, vlc, pf and glock) (1978)
Processional and recessional for an ordination (brass qnt)
Estampie (str qrt) (1974)
String quartet (1966)
Love letters (cl and vlc)
Sonatine (hn and pf)
Dichotic sounds, op. 37 (a-fl) (1981)
Liaisons, op. 38 (org) (1981)
Suite (pf) (1965)
VOCAL
From the King's chamber, op. 31 (T, speaker, sax and cham orch) (1979)
Like strangers (vce and cham orch) (1975)
O sweet spontaneous (ch) (1972)
SACRED
Offering for peace, oratorio (T, ch and orch) (1967)
Be adored, God (a-cap)
ELECTRONIC
Continuum (trp, vibra-hp, mar and pf) (1968)
Fragile walls, op. 32 (org and tape) (1977)
Translucent unreality No. 3 (cl, hn and amp pf) (1974)
Translucent unreality No. 5 (vlc and amp pf) (1975)
Ref. composer, 142, 563

COWLEY, John. See DAVIS, Katherine Kennicott

COX, Alison Mary
British composer. b. London, February 15, 1956. Educated at the Royal Northern College of Music, Manchester, she was awarded the Cecil Fifield prize for composition in 1974, the Leo Grinden prize for composition in 1978 and a bursary from the Vaughan Williams Trust to study film music in Australia.
Compositions
ORCHESTRA
Trilithon
Five pieces for chamber orchestra
CHAMBER
String quintet
Trio for strings
Three pieces (pf)
VOCAL
Two songs (A, counter-T, fl and vla)
Two songs of death (Bar)
OPERA
The Time Killing
INCIDENTAL MUSIC
Chien-Tang, music for a Chinese puppet play
Music for the Caucasian Chalk Circle
The Outing, film music
Ref. 457

COX, Sally
20th-century English composer.
Composition
ELECTRONIC
Dreams (tape)

COZETTE, Cynthia
20th-century American composer.
Compositions
CHAMBER
Nigerian treasures (fl)
OPERA
Adea, exerpts
MISCELLANEOUS
The Steps of the Art Museum
Ref. AMC newlsetter

COZZOLANI, Chiara Margarita
Italian singer and composer. d. 1653. She is said to have been a singer of some renown before entering the Benedictine Convent of St. Radegonda, Milan, in 1620. Between 1640 and 1650 she published four volumes of religious music for one or more voices.
Compositions
SACRED
Concerti sacri a una, due, tre et quattro voci con una messa a quattro voci, op. 2 (Venice: Alessandro Vincenti, 1642)
Salmi a otto voci concertati et due Magnificat a otto con un Laudate pueri a quattro voci et doi violini et un Laudate Dominum omnes gentes a voce sola et doi violini; motetti, et dialoghi a due, tre, quattro, e cinque voci, op. 3 (Alessandro Vincenti, 1650)
Primavera di fiori musicali (1-4 vces) (Milan, 1642)
O dulcis Jesu, melody with basso continuo (1649)
Scherzi di sacra melodia a voce sola, op. 3 (Alessandro Vincenti, 1648)
Ref. 13, 97, 102, 105, 128, 129, 197, 215, 216, 226, 260, 335, 389, 653

CRAIB, Doris
South African cellist, professor and composer. b. Bristol, England, 1906. She received an Associated Board scholarship when she was 17 and studied at the Royal Academy of Music where she was a pupil of Herbert Walenn (cello) and Dorothy Howell (composition). She won awards and prizes for the cello and also gained the performer's licentiate. She taught at the Royal Academy, first as an assistant and from 1931 as an associate professor. In England she gave many concerts and recitals. After settling in South Africa she played in concert and on radio.
Compositions
CHAMBER
Chanson sans paroles (vlc and pf) (1929)
Elegy (vlc and pf) (1929)
A lullaby (vlc and pf) (1925)
Intermezzo (pf) (1929)
Ref. 377

CRAMENT, J. Maude
19th-century English composer of songs.
Compositions
VOCAL
Endymion
Love's seasons
Spells
Ref. 276, 433

CRANE, Helen
American pianist, conductor and composer. b. New York, September 5, 1868. A pupil of both Scharwenkas in New York, she later lived in Berlin from 1906 to 1917.
Compositions
ORCHESTRA
Symphonic poems
Symphonic suite
Four sonnets
CHAMBER
Trio for violin, viola, cello in G-Minor, op. 21 (Leipzig Vetter) (1908)
Trio for violin, cello and piano in E, op. 20 (1907)
Elegy, op. 57 (vlc and and pf) (1919)
Violin pieces
PIANO
Fruehlingslied, G-Major, op. 13 (Breitkopf)
Zwei Novelletten, op. 3 (Breitkopf)
Ref. 41. 70, 142, 292, 297

CRANE, Joelle Wallach. See WALLACH, Joelle

CRAVEN, Mrs. See ANSPACH, Elizabeth, Margravine of

CRAWFORD, Beatrice. See PARKYNS, Beatrice

CRAWFORD, Cynthia D. See DODGE, Cynthia

CRAWFORD, Dawn Constance
American lecturer, writer and composer. b. Ellington Field, TX, December 19, 1919. She holds a B.A. (1939) from Rice University, Houston and B.M. (1940) from Houston Conservatory. After studying composition under Bernard Rogers and Herbert Elwell at the Eastman School of Music, Rochester in 1941, 1946 and 1947, she obtained an M.A. in 1954 and Ph.D. from Columbia University. From 1942 to 1949 she was assistant director at the Houston Conservatory and from 1964 was on the faculty of the Dominican College music department, becoming chairlady in 1972. She gave public lectures on aspects of Brahms' Intermezzi, songs by contemporary American composers and old Italian art songs.
Compositions
ORCHESTRA
The Chinese nightingale (large orch) (1962)
Love possessed Juana (small orch) (1946)
CHAMBER
Quintet 3-70 (3 vln, vla and vlc) (1970)
Woodwind quintet (1979)
Amforsam one, chorale prelude (org and trp) (1980)
Campion suite (fl) (1978-79)
VOCAL
On her dancing (2 T, 2 B and ch a-cap) (1955)
A gamut of badinages, 7 songs (S and pf) (1980)
I'm nobody (vce and pf) (1948)
Ueber Nacht (2 S and pf) (1955)
SACRED
Vermont Requiem (w-ch, fl, ob, cl and 2 bsn) (1977)
Requiescat (vce and pf) (1946)
OPERA
The Pearl, chamber opera in 3 acts (1972)
Publications
Article on Mary Parker Follett in *Notable American Women, 1607-1950*. Harvard University Press, 1971.
Guide to the Music of the Sacramentary. 1976.
Scale Fingering Patterns for Keyboard Instruments. 1981.
Ref. composer, 141, 142, 347, 457

CRAWFORD, Dorothy Lamb
American singer, teacher and composer. b. New York, April 3, 1933. She studied composition under Henri Lazarof, UCLA; Walter Piston, Harvard University and Robert Middletan, Vassar. She received her B.A. cum laude in music and M.A. in composition from Vassar College; and M.F.A. from the University of California, Los Angeles. She furthered her studies at the New England Conservatory, Tanglewood, Vienna Akademie fuer Musik, the Mozarteum, Salzburg, Dartmouth College Congregation for the Arts, and the school of the Performing Arts, University of Southern California. She gave numerous concerts as a lyric soprano and taught music at primary, secondary and college levels at music schools and privately. She received a commission from the Women of the Episcopal Church to compose a work for their triennial meeting in 1985. PHOTOGRAPH.
Compositions
CHAMBER
Heroes (fl, vln, trp, sax, trb, vib and perc) (1979)
Trio for woodwinds (fl, ob and bsn) (1959)
Dialogue (vlc and pf) (1973)
Dance between death and life (vln) (1980)
VOCAL
A song of hope (mix-ch, brass qnt and opt org)
Three rain madrigals (mix-ch and w-ch) (1981)
Portrait of Ann Bradstreet (S, recs, vln and hpcd) (1980)
Songs (Dickinson) (S and pf) (1960)
SACRED
St. Francis, cantata (Bar, w-ch, ob and strs) (1955)
OPERA
The Nightingale, in 1 act (Andersen) (1954)
MULTIMEDIA
Tierschicksale (vln, pf, dancers and audience) (1981)
Ref. composer

CRAWFORD, Louise
20th-century American composer.
Compositions
CHAMBER
Canzonetta (vln and pf)
Legend (vln and pf)
VOCAL
Songs
Ref. 142, 347

CRAWFORD SEEGER, Ruth (Porter)
American pianist, teacher and composer. b. East Liverpool, OH, July 3, 1901; d. Chevy Chase, MD, November 18, 1953. The daughter of a Methodist preacher, she studied and taught the piano at the School of Musical Art,

Jacksonville and then went to the American Conservatory where she studied under H. Levy, Louise Robyn and Djane Lavoie-Herz (piano), and Adolf Weidig and John Palmer (harmony, counterpoint, composition and orchestration). She taught at the Elmhurst College of Music, Chicago and the American Conservatory from 1925 to 1929. In 1930 she became the first woman to win a Guggenheim Fellowship, for study in Paris and Berlin. In 1931 she married Charles Seeger, chief of the music division of the Pan-American Union and then lived in Washington, DC. From 1937 onward she made several thousand transcriptions of American folk music from recordings at the Library of Congress and composed piano accompaniments for some 300 of them. She developed teaching methods for children, using folk music. In 1933 her *Three Songs* was chosen as one of two works to represent the United States at the International Festival of the International Society for Contemporary Music in Amsterdam. DISCOGRAPHY.

Compositions

ORCHESTRA

Suite for small orchestra (1926)
Two movements for chamber orchestra (1926)

CHAMBER

Rissolty Rossolty (10 wind insts, drs and strs) (1941)
Four diaphonic suites (fl, ob, 2 cl and 2 vlc) (1930)
Three movements (winds and pf) (1928)
Suite (fl, ob, cl, hn, bsn and pf) (1927)
Quintet (4 strs and pf) (1927)
Second suite for string quartet and piano (1927)
Suites (wind qnt) (1941 and 1952)
String quartet, a 12-tone work (1931)
Sonata (vln and pf) (1926)

PIANO

The adventures of Tom Thumb (1925)
Etude in mixed accents (1930)
Five preludes (1924-1925)
Four preludes (1927-1928)

VOCAL

Three chants (w-ch) (1932)
Three songs (Cont and 17 insts) (1932) (rep. the U.S.A. at the Int. Fest. of the Int. Soc. for Contemp. Music in Amsterdam)
American folk songs for Christmas
Animal folk songs
Chant (1930)
Five songs (Carl Sandburg) (vce and pf) (1929)
Songs for children
Two ricercari (H.T. Tsiang): Sacco-Vanzetti; Chinaman, Laundryman (1932)

Bibliography

Gaume, Mary Matilde. *Ruth Crawford Seeger: Her Life and Works*. Ph.D. dissertation, Indiana University, 1974, UM 74-6022.
Feminist Art Journal, Spring 1977, pp. 13-16.

Ref. 4, 5, 8, 22, 74, 96, 124, 142, 146, 152, 168, 228, 266, 371, 397, 415, 560, 563, 610, 611, 622, 653

CREES, Kathleen Elsie

British clavichordist, harpsichordist, pianist, lecturer and composer. b. Tollesbury, Essex, October 22, 1944. She is a F.T.C.L.. She also studied in Cologne. She has given recitals of piano and early keyboard music in the United Kingdom and Australia as well as on film, TV and radio. She has lectured in London and made recordings of harpsichord and clavichord compositions. She composed film, television and library music, published by Weinberger, Parry Music, Essex Music and De Wolfe.

Publications

Jonathan and the Magic Clavichord. Children's book with music.

Ref. composer, 457

CRENDIROPULO, Anna G.

Compositions

PIANO

La coquette, polka
Due notturni
L'étoile de Bethléem, polka
Un fiore redowa
Mazurka
Souvenir de Luchon
Vorn, romance

CRESCIMANO, Fiorita

19th-century Italian composer.

Compositions

OPERA

Angiola di Ghemme
Filippo
Maria Tiepolo

Ref. 307

CRETI, Marianna de Rocchis

19th-century Italian harpist and composer.

Compositions

CHAMBER

Terzetto (fl, vlc and hp)
Duetto (pf and hp)
La mia letizia, op. 7 (hp and vln)

HARP

Ernani (2 hp)
Rondo brillanta, op. 6 (2 hp)
Six small preludes, op. 12 (Ricordi)
Souvenir dei, op. 2 (Ricordi)
Solos, op. 3, 4, 9, 10, 11, 16, 17, and 18
Transcriptions (1 and 2 hp) (Ricordi)

Ref. 226, 276, 297, 433

CREWS, Lucille (Marsh, Lucille Crews)

American singer and composer. b. Pueblo, CO, August 23, 1888; d. San Diego, November 3, 1972. She composed a nocturne at the age of seven. She studied at the New England Conservatory, Northwestern School of Music, Redlands University (B.Mus. 1920) and the American Conservatory, Chicago. She later spent one year in Berlin under the instruction of Hugo Kaun (composition), Moratti (singing) and von Fielitz (orchestration) which was followed by one year of study under Nadia Boulanger (q.v.) (orchestration) in Paris. She taught singing in Berlin and toured Germany as an accompanist. In 1926 she received a Pulitzer Traveling Scholarship for her *To an Unknown Soldier* and *Sonata for viola and piano*, the first time this distinction had been awarded to a woman. She also received the prize offered by the California Federation of Music Clubs for a one-act opera and the prize for chamber music for her *Suite* at the Festival of Allied Arts, Los Angeles.

Compositions

ORCHESTRA

To an Unknown Soldier, symphonic elegy (1926) (Pulitzer Traveling Scholarship)

CHAMBER

Suite (ww and strs)
Sonata for viola and piano (Pulitzer traveling scholarship)
Pieces (pf)

VOCAL

La Belgique, cantata (soloist, ch and orch)
Songs

OPERA

Ariadne and Dionysus, miniature opera (1935)
The Call of Jeanne d'Arc, in 1 act (adapted from first act of Percy Mackaye's Joan of Arc) (1923)
The Concert (1959)
Eight Hundred Rubles, grand opera in 1 act (John G. Neidhardt) (1926)

Ref. 22. 70, 141, 142, 292, 304, 556, 622

CRISP, Barbara

20th-century American composer.

Compositions

CHAMBER

Concert trio in D
Three pieces for viola and piano

Ref. 142

CRISWICK, Mary

English guitarist, music copyist, singer, teacher and composer. b. Southend, 1945. From 1963 to 1967 studied for a B.A. hons. in music at Bristol University. From 1967 to 1968 she attended a postgraduate course in singing and the guitar at the Guildhall School of Music, London. She taught the guitar at City University and St. Paul's Girls' School from 1970 to 1974, then moved to France. She is a singer with 'Florilegium Musicum de Paris', an early music group and contributes regularly to musical publications.

Compositions

GUITAR

Ragtime for guitar ensemble (Chappell)
Trios (Chester)
Duets (Chester)
Another ten for guitar (Breitkopf)
Cinq morceaux du Fitzwilliam Virginal Book (Max Eschig)
Danses du 18e siècle (Eschig)
Guitar tutor for young children (Breitkopf)
Ten for guitar (Breitkopf)

VOCAL

Elizabethan and Jacobean songs (vce and gtr) (Stainer and Bell)

Ref. composer

CROCHET, Sharon Brandstetter

American flautist, business woman and composer. b. March 15, 1945. She was a recipient of the University of Houston music scholarship in 1963. She obtained her B.A. in 1967 and her M.Mus. in 1975.

Compositions

VOCAL

Children's songs (1964)
Christmas Ayre (1971)
March for Miki (1980)
Arrangements (ch and orch)

FILM MUSIC

Mother (1979)

Ref. 457

CROCKETT, Effie. See CANNING, Effie

CROFF PORTALUPI, Maddalena

19th-century Italian composer.

Compositions

PIANO

Album di danze:
Celere, mazurka
Fronde di lauro, waltz
Margherita, schottisch
Scintilla, quadrille
Spiritismo, galop
Violetta, polka
Album da ballo:
Concordia, quadrille
Entusiasmo, galop
Flaminia, mazurka
I lancieri, quadrille
Plebiscito, waltz
Roma, polka
Trasteverina, schottisch

VOCAL

Gloria al desio, duet

SACRED

Salve Regina (3 vces)

Ref. Ricordi

CROFTS, Inez Altman

20th-century American contralto, organist, teacher and composer. b. Portsmouth. She obtained her B.Mus. in 1958 and her M.Mus. in 1960 at Chicago Conservatory. She toured with the New York City Opera Company as Bertha in *The Barber of Seville* in 1957.

Compositions

CHAMBER

Pieces

VOCAL

Choral pieces
Songs

OPERA

Mission in Burma (1970)

Ref. 347, 475

CROIX, Sister M. Henry de la. See MILETTE, Juliette

CROKER, Catherine Munnell

American cellist, organist, pianist and composer. b. Canonsburg, PA, November 3, 1897; d. Canonsburg, May, 1958. She studied at the Pittsburgh Musical Institute under Dr. Charles N. Boyd (piano and theory), Hubert Conover and Frantisek Rybka (cello) and Dr. T. Carl Whitmer (composition). She later studied composition and the organ under Dr. Harvey Gaul. In 1947 she was awarded the State Prize by the Pennsylvania Federation of Music Clubs for her composition *Expectation*. She received three other first place awards from the Tuesday Music Club of Pittsburgh. In 1921 she became organist of the first Presbyterian Church of Canonsburg. PHOTOGRAPH.

Compositions

CHAMBER

Introduction and scherzo (vln)
Reminiscence (vln)

ORGAN

Blessings (Pittsburgh; Volkwein Bros.)
A child's prayer (Volkwein)
The dawn of peace (Volkwein)
Dedication
Devotion
The gentle one
Lenten meditation (Lorenz, 1950)
May morning song

VOCAL

Cradle song (S and pf)
Expectation (S and pf) (Volkwein)
Friendship (S and pf)
Spring (S and pf)

SACRED

Lighten our darkness (mix-ch) (H. Flammer)
My soul longeth for Thee (mix-ch) (Lorenz, 1951)
Our Lord and comforter (mix-ch) (Volkwein)
Psalm 48 (mix-ch) (New York: Edwin H. Morris & Co.)
A Christmas song (w-trio) (BMI)
Little Jesus at your birth (w-trio) (Volkwein)
Evening supplication (Bar)
God, let me be aware (S)
My trust in God (Cont)
The tidings, Christmas song
Vesperale (S and pf) (New York: H.W. Gray)
The world's wanderers (S)

Ref. Mrs. W.L. Jenkins, 190

CROMIE, Marguerite Biggs

20th-century American composer.

Composition

VOCAL

Just turn around (2 vces or unison ch, pf and opt perc)

Ref. AMC newsletter December 1976

CRONENTHAL, Louisa Augusta. See HAENEL DE CRONENTHAL, Louise Augusta

CROSBY, Fannie (Mrs. Frances Jane van Alstyne)

American poetess, teacher and composer. b. Putnam County, NY, March 24, 1820; d. Bridgeport, February 12, 1915. Through illness, she became blind at the age of six weeks. She studied music at the School for the Blind, New York, under George F. Root and became a teacher there. She wrote poetry and hymns, the latter totalling over 4000.

Compositions

SACRED

Hymns incl.:
All the way my Saviour leads me
Blessed assurance, Jesus is mine
Do not kill me, oh my glorious Saviour
For me the Saviour is more than life itself
Jesus, keep me near the Cross
One day the silver cord will break
Pass me not, O gentle Saviour
Saved by the grace
Saved in Jesus' arms

Publications

Eighty Years of Memories. 1906.
Fanny Crosby's Life. 1903.

Ref. Music Clubs Magazine Winter 1979, 268, 646

CROUCH, Anna Maria

English singer and composer. b. April 20, 1773; d. Brighton, October 2, 1805.

Compositions

CHAMBER

Say, was it love (ca. 1800)
Go, you may call it madness (hp and pf) (ca. 1800)

Bibliography

Young, J.J. *Memoirs of Mrs. Crouch, including a retrospect of the stage during the years she performed*. London, 1806.

Ref. 128

CROWE, Bonita

20th-century American organist, pianist and composer. She composed orchestral works, choral works and songs.

Ref. 347

CROWNINGSHIELD, Mary Bradford
American authoress and composer. b. Geneva, NY; d. October 14, 1913. She was a descendant of Governor William Bradford of Plymouth Colony.
Compositions
VOCAL
There is a land mine eye hath seen
Thy heart shall know me
SACRED
Carols
Other religious music
Ref. 276, 292, 433

CRUMB, Berenice (nee Wyer)
American pianist and composer. b. North Windham, CT, 1875. She studied under Ernest R. Kroeger, Franz Rummel, Carl Baerman, Adolf Weidig and Heinrich Barth. She gave numerous piano recitals.
Compositions
CHAMBER
Serenade (vln and pf)
Spring fantasie (vln and pf)
Twilight in the garden (vln and pf)
ORGAN
Lento assai
Meditation
Postlude in D-Major
PIANO
April
Ballade in C-Sharp Minor
Concert etude in D-Flat
Legende in A-Flat
A madrigal
Serenade
Two poems: Of chivalry; Of romance
Accompaniments for poetry readings
VOCAL
Songs incl.:
I have a rendezvous with death
The Mockingbird
Remembrance
Requiescat
To ships
SACRED
Chants
Responses
Ref. 433, 460

CRUVELLI, Sofia
Italian composer. b. 1826; d. 1907.
Composition
VOCAL
Variations sur une tyrolienne connue (Ricordi)
Ref. Ricordi (Milan)

CUBONI, Maria Teresa
18th-19th century Italian composer. At the age of 12 she composed *Introduction and variations*. She was a pupil of the Modena School.
Compositions
PIANO
Si, si, verro, ma paventate (Milan: Francesco Lucca)
Introduction and variations, theme from the opera L'Orfanella di Ginevra (ded Franz IV, Archduke of Austria and Duke of Modena)
Ref. 157

CULLEN, Trish
Canadian keyboard instrumentalist and composer. b. 1951. She started playing keyboard instruments at the age of five and later studied under George Delamont. She composes her music by converting sounds on an emulator synthesiser. In 1985 she won the award of Film Composer of the Year from the musicians' publishing association, Pro-Can.
Compositions
INCIDENTAL MUSIC
Care Bears, film
Ewoks, television cartoon
Droids, television cartoon
Ref. Globe and Mail - September 21 1985

CULP, Paula Newell
American percussionist, timpanist and composer. b. Fort Smith, April 9, 1941. She obtained her B.A. at Oberlin College Conservatory, and her M.A. at Indiana University, Bloomington. She also studied at the Mozarteum in Salzburg. She won a special performance award at Indiana University and has received various honors and scholarships. She was the principal timpanist with the Metropolitan Opera National Company from 1965 to 1967 and from 1968 was a faculty member at the University of Minnesota.
Compositions
CHAMBER
Theme and variations for four kettle drums (1973)
Night speech
Ref. 77

CUMAN, Harriet Johanna Louise
Danish pianist and composer. b. Copenhagen, December 26, 1851. She studied under Neupert and caused a sensation by her skill on the piano. She composed piano pieces.
Ref. 276, 433

CUMBERLAND, Mrs. William
18th-century English composer.
Composition
VOCAL
Ten canzonets (vce and hp or pf) (1797)
Ref. 125

CUNIBERTI, Janet Teresa
American pianist and composer. b. San Francisco, March 12, 1949. She obtained her B.A. (1976) and M.A. (1978) from Mills College. She studied under Peggy Salkind, Bernard Abramovitch, Katrina Krimsky and Terry Riley. She attended graduate school on a fellowship sponsored by the Mills College music department and was recipient of the Elizabeth Mills Crothers Award and the Robert Maas Memorial Scholarship.
Compositions
PIANO
Blues for McCoy
Circle
Crystal dancer
If I could
Op. 1, no. 1
Untitled
Ref. composer

CURRAN, Pearl Gildersleeve
American librettist and composer. b. Denver, June 25, 1875; d. New Rochelle, April 16, 1941. She studied at Denver University and with Otto Pfeffercorn, Flora Smith Hunsicker and Martha Miner. She wrote all the words of her secular songs and her song *Life* was sung by Caruso. She had her own internationally broadcasted radio show. DISCOGRAPHY.
Compositions
VOCAL
Nocturne (w-ch)
Other choral works
Songs incl.:
Dawn (1917)
Life
Rain
Sonny boy
SACRED
The Crucifixion
Hold Thou my hand
Bibliography
Pearl Curran, 65, author, composer. Obituary. *New York Times*, April 17, 1941.
Ref. 40, 142, 228, 292, 347, 563

CURRIE, Edna R.
American organist, teacher and composer. b. Brooklyn, January 13, 1913. She obtained a B.A. from Brooklyn College and an M.A. from Columbia University and the Juilliard School of Music. She received an M.S.M. from the School of Sacred Music, Union Theological Seminary, New York. She taught music theory and appreciation at Brooklyn College and at high schools in New York and Pennsylvania. She was organist-director in St. Albans and Hollis, NY, and Easton, PA, for 30 years and taught the piano and the organ privately. PHOTOGRAPH.

Compositions
SACRED
Be strong (mix-ch and org) (Canyon Press, 1954)
Church bells (w-ch) (1954)
Gracias, an anthem based upon Old Hundredth and a traditional Welsh melody (mix-ch, youth-ch, handbells and org) (1975)
Ref. composer, 190

CURRIER, Marilyn Kind
20th-century American composer.
Composition
CHAMBER
String quartet No. 2, theme and variations (1970)
Ref. B.P.A.M.

CURTIS, Elizabeth
20th-century American composer.
Composition
OPERA
Christmas Eve
Ref. 141

CURTIS (Curtis-Burlin), Natalie
American pianist, folklorist, writer and composer. b. New York, April 26, 1875; d. Paris, October 23, 1921. She studied in New York under Arturo Friedheim and later under Busoni in Berlin, Giraudet in Paris, Wolff in Bonn and Kniese in Bayreuth. She returned to America as a pianist and developed an interest in the music of the Indians and blacks of the United States and Africa.
Compositions
VOCAL
Dearest, where thy shadow falls (vce and pf) (Schirmer)
Seven songs from A Child's Garden of Verses (R.L. Stevenson) (1902)
Publications
The Indian's Book. 200 songs of 18 tribes. 1907.
Negro Folksongs. 4 vols. 1918-1920.
Songs and Talks from the Dark Continent. 1920.
Songs of Ancient America. 1905.
Ref. 44, 105, 110, 228, 266, 297, 347

CURTIS-BURLIN, Natalie. See CURTIS, Natalie

CURTWRIGHT, Carolee
20th-century American composer of choral works.
Ref. 40, 347

CURUBETO GODOY, Maria Isabel
Argentine pianist, teacher and composer. b. 1904. At the age of 12 she composed a quartet and several sonatas and at the age of eight she was heard in two concerts by G. Puccini and A. Berutti and later studied the piano at the Conservatory of Cordoba, winning a scholarship to study in Europe. She studied composition under G. Sgambati in Rome and Theodor Leschetizky in Vienna. For many years she studied at the National University of La Plata.
Compositions
CHAMBER
Quartet
Other pieces
PIANO
Dolora
Ensueno y plenitud
Estudio melodico
Evocando a Beethoven
Llamamiento
Passan las mascaras
Sonatas
Two nocturnes
OPERA
Pablo y Virginia, in 3 acts (Adamo y Simoni) (1946)
THEATRE
Fedra (Euripides) (1925)
Ref. 85, 100, 361, 390

CURZON, Clara-Jean
American pianist, teacher and composer. b. Hemet, CA, August 29, 1924. She obtained her B.M. (1946) and M.M. (1947) at the University of Redlands, having studied under Halsey Stevens, Paul Pisk and Rowland Leach. She studied with John Crown at the University of Southern California and George McKay at the University of Washington.
Compositions
PIANO
Fireflies
Humbug wizard
March of the astronauts
Saturn's rings
INCIDENTAL MUSIC
Music for films and radio
Publications
Discovering Music Through Theory. Harmony text.
Ref. 494

CUSENZA, Maria Giacchino
Italian pianist, lecturer and composer. b. Palermo, 1898; d. Palermo, 1979. She studied at the V. Bellini Conservatory in Palermo, graduating in the piano at the age of 17. She continued her piano studies under Alice Baragli, Alberto Fano and Pilati. She performed in Italy and abroad and founded the Quintetto Femminile Palermitano in 1933. She pioneered the performance of contemporary music in Italy. For 49 years she taught at the Palermo Conservatory.
Compositions
CHAMBER
Works for small groups of instruments
PIANO
Basso ostinato (1936)
Other pieces
VOCAL
Songs
TEACHING WORKS
Piano pieces
Ref. Donne in Musica, 1982

CUTLER, Mary J.
20th-century American composer of choral works.
Ref. 40, 347

CUZZONI, Francesca (alt. names Cuzzoni Sandoni, Cuzzoni Sandoni San-Antonio Ferre)
Italian singer and composer. b. Parma, 1700; d. Bologna, 1770. She began her musical studies under Pietro Lanzi and made her debut at the age of 16 in Parma. This was followed by appearances in Bologna, Venice and in England, where she sang at the Haymarket Theatre under the direction of Nicola Porpora. In spite of her success she spent time in Britain in a debtors' prison and returned to Bologna to die in poverty.
Compositions
VOCAL
Il Palladio Conservato, chamber duets and terzets (1742)
Ref. 502

CUZZONI SANDONI, Francesca. See CUZZONI, Francesca

CUZZONI SANDONI SAN-ANTONIO FERRE, Francesca. See CUZZONI, Francesca

CZANY. See SCHMITT, Alois

CZARTORYSKA, Izabela de, Princess
18th-century Polish composer.
Compositions
VOCAL
Arias in Recueil d'ariettes choisies, collection fait par Castella de Bertena (1781)
Romance de Roland, song (1780)
Ref. 35, 65, 118

CZETWERTYNSKA, Marie, Princess (nee Plater)
Polish pianist and composer. b. June 15, 1825; d. Florence, Italy, 1863. She was a pupil of Renner in Vilna. She composed several fugue-like piano pieces in the Polish style.
Ref. 36

CZETWERTYNSKA-JELOWICKA, Janina, Princess
Polish singer and composer. d. Kiev, 1866. The daughter of Princess Kazimira Czetwertynska, she studied singing in Italy and was well received on her return to Poland.
Compositions
PIANO
Bagatela: Chant sans paroles (Kiev: Idzikowski)
Wezwanie do mazura (Kiev: Kocipinski)
VOCAL
Nie zapominaj mnie (vce and pf)
Powrot bocianow (vce and pf)
Rekawiczka (F. Schiller)
Spiewnik, 6 songs (Opacka, Witwicki, Zbyszewski, Mickiewicz) (vce and pf)
Spojrzyj na mnie (vce and pf)
Two Romances (vce and pf) (Kiev: Idzikowski)
SACRED
Religious songs
Ref. 35, 118, 297

CZICZKA, Angela
Slovak pianist, teacher and composer. b. Selmecbanya, 1888. Her father was her first teacher and she began composing as a child. She studied at the Budapest National Conservatory and under Tomka and Istvan Laub. She taught music at primary schools in Timisoara, Transylvania and Eger.
Compositions
CHAMBER
Flute sonata
PIANO
Children's pieces
Teaching pieces
Twelve sonatas
BALLET
A medve, a rak es a csalogany, for children
INCIDENTAL MUSIC
Music for radio
Ref. 375

DA SILVA, Adelaide
20th-century Spanish composer.
Composition
GUITAR
Ponteio No. 1 (Ricordi)
Ref. Frau und Musik

DABROWSKA, Konstancja
19th-century Polish composer.
Composition
VOCAL
Duma O Zolkiewski, in T. Klonowski's Songs and School Songs and Melodies (2, 3 and 4 vces) (1860)
Ref. 118

DABROWSKA, Waleria
19th-century Polish composer.
Compositions
PIANO
Kujawiak
Mazurek
Polka
Schottische
Souvenir de Carnaval Polonaise, op. 4 (Berlin: Bote and Bock)
Ref. 118, 297

DAHL, Emma (nee Freyse)
German singer and composer. b. Ploen, April 6, 1819. She was the adopted daughter of Baroness von Natorp who had appeared in the musical world as Marianne Sessi. In her honor Emma sang under the name of Freyse-Sessi. She appeared with the Royal Opera in Berlin and under the patronage of Bettina von Arnim and von Spontini, sang in Breslau, Leipzig and Schwerin. She was the first dramatic singer of the Copenhagen Court Theatre and appeared as successor to Jenny Lind in Stockholm. She lived in Norway after her marriage except for a short study visit to Paris to familiarize herself with E. Garcia's song method.
Compositions
CHAMBER
Margretes vuggevise af Kongsemnerne (pf) (Warmuth)
Saeterjenten (vlc) (Oluf By)
VOCAL
Jaegerkor: Lyngen bag os staar i Rog (4 or 5 m-vces)
The dream of home (Warmuth)
Eremitens Bon, op. 21 (Oluf By)
Farvel (Warmuth)
Fem digte, op. 10 (Warmuth)
Fire digte, op. 8 (Oluf By)
Fire digte, op. 11 (Warmuth)
Fyra sanger, op. 10 (Hirsch)
Han tvaer over Baenkene hang (Warmuth)
Margaretes vuggesang (Oluf By)
Sangovelser, op. 17 (Oluf By)
Taylors sang af Maria Stuart (Oluf By)
Tre digte, op. 18 (Oluf By)
Two serenades (Warmuth)
Zigeunerskan, op. 19 (Oluf By)
Zwei deutsche Lieder, op. 2 (Oluf By)
Ref. 129, 276, 297

DAHL, Vivian
Danish pianist, violinist, choral conductor, priest and composer. b. 1938. As a child she learnt the piano, the violin and theory, but taught herself composition. She began studying theology at Helsingoer in 1957. In 1968 she became choir conductor at the Vor Frue Kirke in Odense and in 1972, parish priest in Jersie-Kirke-Skensved.
Compositions
CHAMBER
Elegy (vlc and pf)
VOCAL
Songs (T and pf) (1978-80)
Ref. Dansk Komponistforening

DAHMEN, Mona Scholte
Dutch pianist and composer of German origin. b. Haarlem, 1894. She studied at the Conservatories of Berlin and The Hague.
Ref. 9

DAIGLE, Sister Anne Cecile
American pianist, professor and composer. b. Seattle, June 25. 1908. She received her B. Mus. from Marylhurst College in 1936 and M.Mus. from DePaul University in 1949, having studied under Leon Stein, Czerwonky and Lieberson. In 1960 she received her D.M.A. from the University of Southern California, having studied under Halsey Stevens, Ingolf Dahl and Muriel Kerr. She taught composition and the piano at the Holy Names College from 1945 to 1955 and was professor of composition, theory and the piano at Marylhurst College from 1962. She was voted the woman composer of the year in 1972, by the Oregon Music Teachers' Association and in 1973 by the National Federation of Music Clubs.
Compositions
ORCHESTRA
Chronicle of Creation (1953)
Violin concerto (1980)
CHAMBER
Quintet for piano and strings (1959)
Trumpet sonata (1960-1967)
American folk tune suite (pf and vln) (1976)
PIANO
Black is the colour
Country reel
Dance concertino (1970)
The lone
Skip to my Lou
Sonata No. 2 (1971)
Wild bird
ELECTRONIC
Four temperaments: Arioso; Hoe down; Preludium; Scherzo (2 hp and tape) (comm Oregon Music Teachers' Assoc. 1973)
Ref. 228, 625

DAIKEN, Melanie
20th-century English conductor and composer.
Compositions
ORCHESTRA
Attica I
PIANO
Capriccio (1975)
Lorca pieces
OPERA
Mayakovsky and the Sun (1972)
Ref. 141

DAILLY, Claudine
20th-century Belgian guitarist, singer and composer.
Compositions
VOCAL
Numerous songs
Children's songs (composer)
THEATRE
Do re mi pas folle, one-woman show (1979)
Solo sur l'air de rien, musical (1980)
Voyage du train, children's musical (1978)
Ref. composer

DALBERG, Nancy (nee Hansen)
Danish composer. b. Bodstrup, near Slagelse, July 6, 1881; d. Copenhagen, September 29, 1949. The daughter of Councillor of State, Chancellor D.A. Hansen, she was a pupil of Ove Christensen, J. Svendsen and Carl Nielsen. She was the first Danish woman to write a symphony, the first performance of which was conducted by Carl Nielsen. She also assisted Nielsen in the instrumentation of *Aladdin* and *Fynsk Forar*. Her chamber compositions were played by the leading chamber ensembles of her time.
Compositions
ORCHESTRA
Symphony
Andante sostenuto
Capriccio (1918)
Rondo vivace
CHAMBER
String quartet No. 1 (1915)
String quartet No. 2 (1922)
String quartet No. 3 (1928)
PIANO
Fantasie piece (1918)
Scherzo grazioso, op. 8 (1918)
VOCAL
Two songs (m-S and orch) (1937)
Der sidder en munk i bure (1919)
Nit hjem (1917)
Svanerne (1935)
To romancer og zigeunersang (1922)
Duets
Songs (1911, 1914, 1918)
Ref. Dansk Komponistforening 96, 331

DALBERT, (Roth-Dalbert), Anny
Swiss pianist, choral conductor, singer and composer. b. St. Moritz, October 12, 1900. She began piano studies in Zurich under Czeslaw Marek, then from 1917 to 1921 she studied singing, the piano, theory, counterpoint and conducting at the Zurich Conservatory. She conducted the choir of the Evangelical Church in St. Moritz for three years.
Compositions
CHAMBER
Das Geruest (fl, 1-2 vln, vla and vlc) (1983)
Kleine Romanze (str qrt) (1937)
PIANO
Reigen/Impromptu (1983)
Vierzehn kleine Stuecke fuer junge Pianisten (1958)
VOCAL
Romanische Choere (1942, 1977, 1982)
Deutsche gemischte Choere (1958, 1980, 1982, 1983)
German dialect songs (Wettstein, Frey, Haemmerli-Marti) (pf) (1942, 1952, 1958)
German songs (Schneiter, Storm, Scheitlin, Wettstein) (pf) (1943, 1948, 1960, 1983)
Romanish songs (Caflisch, Stupan) (pf) (1935, 1962, 1982)
Men's choruses
Mixed choruses
Children's choruses
INCIDENTAL MUSIC
Die verbrannte Erde, play
Ref. 6, 651

DALE, Kathleen (nee Richards)
English pianist, authoress, lecturer, musicologist and composer. b. London, June 29, 1896; d. Woking, March 3, 1984. She studied the piano privately under York Bowen (1914 to 1916 and 1919 to 1920) and Fanny Davies (1924 to 1926) and composition under B.J. Dale (1914 and 1919 to 1921). She attended the University College, London, where she studied Swedish (1926 to 1928) and in 1928 became an A.R.C.M. in accompaniment. She was a teacher of harmony and theory of music at the Tobias Matthay Piano School (1925 to 1931) and tutor and lecturer on musical appreciation of the Workers' Educational Association (1945 to 1947, 1958). She contributed to numerous musical journals. She served on the Council of the Society of Women Musicians (1920 to 1925, 1946 to 1949) and was appointed musical executor for the late Dame Ethel Smyth (q.v.) in 1944. She performed as a soloist and accompanist and in 1938 was awarded the Elsie Horne Prize by the Society of Women Musicians.
Compositions
CHAMBER
Pastoral (vln and pf) (1920)
Wayfaring (vln and pf) (1939)
PIANO
Music for Two (2 pf) (1934)
Frozen landscape (1948)
Greek myths (1921)
Versailles (1920)
VIOLIN
Six duets (2 vln) (1940)
Two divertimenti (2 vln) (1940)
VOCAL
The flight, part song (1949)
The horn, part song (1947)
The window, part song (1947)
Winter, part song (1949)
Publications
Brahms: A Biography. 1970.
Essays on the piano music of Schubert (1946), Grieg (1948), Schumann (1952) and Handel (1954).
Translations from the Swedish of Hans Redlich's *Claudio Monteverdi: Life and Works*. Oxford, 1952. R. Reiflings's Piano Pedalling. 1962.
Nineteenth Century Piano Music. 1954.
Edited Schubert's *E-Minor Piano Sonata* and *Star Songs*.
Ref. 8, 9, 84, 94

DALE, Phyllis
English pianist, choral conductor, teacher and composer. b. Wolverhampton, 1914. She is an A.R.C.M., A.L.C.M. and L.L.C.M.. She studied at the Royal College of Music and under Frank Merrick. She teaches theory and harmony and trains choirs.
Compositions
ORCHESTRA
Piano concerto in C
PIANO
Two waltzes
Music for dancing and keep fit classes
VOCAL
Songs
SACRED
Carols
Ref. 490

DALL, Miss
English singer and composer. b. 1776; d. 1794. Her father, Nicholas Dall, was a scenery artist at Covent Garden. She studied singing under Joseph Mazzinghi and made her debut at Covent Garden at the age of 14 in Handel's *Messiah*. She published her first songs when she was 16.
Compositions
VOCAL
Songs incl.:
A linnet just fledg'd
Ref. 465, 502

DALL'AQCQUA, Eva. See DELL'ACQUA, Eva

DALLAM, Helen. See BUCKLEY, Helen Dallam

D'ALTIER, Azalais. See AZALAIS D'ALTIER

DALTON, Mrs. Charles. See DEYO, Ruth Lynda

DALY, Julia
19th-century American composer.
Composition
VOCAL
Dying Camille (vce and pf) (Philadelphia: Lee and Walker, 1856)
Ref. 228

DAMASHEK, Barbara
20th-century American actress, teacher and composer. b. New York. She graduated from the Yale School of Drama after studying acting. She taught music at the Hartman Theatre Conservatory in Stanford. PHOTOGRAPH.
Compositions
INCIDENTAL MUSIC
Grimm's fairy tales
Part of The Great American Dream Machine
Unlikely Heroes
Ref. BMI

D'AMATO, Elinor Barbara. See AMATI, Orlanda

DAMCKE, Louise
19th-century German composer.
Compositions
PIANO
Nocturne, op. 1 (Kistner)
Zigeuner caprice, op. 5
Ref. 226, 276, 297

DAMON, Frances Brackett
American composer of songs. b. 1857; d. 1888.
Ref. 465

DAMOPHILA
Ancient Greek poetess and composer. b. Lesbos, 7th-century B.C.. She was the wife of Pamphilos and a friend of Sappho (q.v.). According to Philostratos, she composed hymns to Artemis, which were frequently sung. Like Sappho, she held gatherings where the most beautiful young girls came to hear her poetry and music. She also composed many love songs.
Ref. 116, 129

DAMOREAU-CINTI, Cynthie or Cinthie. See DAMOREAU-CINTI, Laure

DAMOREAU-CINTI (Cinti-Damoreau) (nee Cinti), Laure (Laura) (Cynthie Cinthie) (nee Montalant)
French pianist, lecturer, singer and composer. b. Paris, February 6, 1801; d. Chantilly. February 25, 1863. She studied the piano, singing and composition at the Paris Conservatoire from the age of seven and in 1819 joined the Theatre-Italien, making her first appearance as Cherubino in Mozart's *Figaro*. In spite of her fine voice and dramatic ability, she received the acclaim due to her only after Rossini and later Meyerbeer made use of her talents. She traveled in Holland, England, Russia and together with the violinist Artot, visited America in 1843. From 1834 to 1856 she taught singing at the Paris Conservatoire, then retired to her estate in Chantilly. Her daughter, Marie, also a singer, married the composer Weckerlin.
Compositions
VOCAL
Album de romances, (vce and pf) (Paris: Troupenas)
Methode de chant (ded her pupils) (1849)
Vocalises et points d'orgue pour les operas de Rossini
Bibliography
Escudier, L. *Etudes Biographies*. 1840.
Raugel, F. *Laure Damoreau*. MGG 2, 1952.
Soubies, A. *Le Theatre Italien*. 1913.
Ref. 8, 15, 26, 109, 129, 276, 361, 406

DANA, Lynn Boardman
American pianist and composer. b. Middleport, NY, October 15, 1875. She composed a piano concerto, piano pieces, a secular oratorio and songs.
Ref. 70

DANA, Mary S.B.
19th-century American composer.
Compositions
SACRED
The Northern harp, 33 songs (1 or more vces and pf) (New York: Dayton & Saxton, 1842)
The Southern harp, 43 sacred and moral songs (1 or more vces and pf) (Boston: Parker & Ditson, 1941)
Flee as a bird to your mountain (composer) (pf and vce) (Ditson, 1857)
Ref. 228

DANANIR AL BARMAKIYYA.
Late 8th to early 9th-century Arabian songstress. She was sold by a man of Medina to Yahya ibn Khalid al-Barmaki. The Barmak family was of Persian origin. Many members were given high administrative positions during the reign of Al-Mansur, 754 to 775. Dananir was taught music; her teachers included Ibrahim and Ishaq al-Mausuli, Ibn Jami, Fulaih, and Badhl (q.v.). It was said that she brought her art to such perfection that there was no difference between her and Ibrahim al-Mausuli. The Khalif Harun al-Rashid fell in love with her, giving her great gifts of money and gold, which aroused the jealousy of his wife, Zobeida, who imprisoned her. Yahya freed Dananir and in gratitude she said that after his death she would never sing again. The court musician Aqil wished to marry her, but she refused, saying she could not be allied to a second-rate performer. Dananir was the authoress of a *Kitab mujarrad al-aghani* (Book of Choice Songs).
Ref. 170, 171, 234

DANCLA, Alphonsine Genevieve-Lore (Mme. Deliphard)
French teacher and composer. b. Bagneres-de-Bigorre, June 21, 1824; d. Tarbes, March 22, 1880. She composed piano pieces and songs.
Ref. 85, 347

D'ANDUZA, Clara
13th-century French troubadour. She came from Anduze, one of the most important towns in Languedoc and was probably the wife or daughter of Bernard D'Anduze (d. 1223), lord of the town. She is said to have loved Uc de Saint Circ, the 13th-century biographer.
Composition
VOCAL
En greu esmai et en greu pessamen ...
Ref. 117, 213, 218, 221, 303

DANEAU, Suzanne (pseud. Luc Lalain)
Belgian pianist, lecturer and composer. b. Tournai, August 17, 1901; d. Tournai, November 29, 1971. She was the daughter of Nicolas Daneau, director of the Conservatories of Tournai and Mons, and her first teacher. She then became a pupil of Paul Gilson in Brussels. Her music was greatly influenced by him and she dedicated her *Prelude Elegiaque* to him. She was editor of the *Gazette Musicale de Belgique* and president of the International Jury of Musical Studies in Brussels. She was made an honorary member of SABAM in 1964 and in 1967 received a plaque of honor from her birth town Tournai. She lectured in history of music at the Tournai Conservatory.
Compositions
ORCHESTRA
Variations, lied et finale (vln, pf and orch)
Poeme du rosaire (pf and orch) (1939)
La barque d'or de Karnak, symphonic legend
Serenade traditionelle en six mouvements (fl and cham orch)
Ouverture badine
Prelude elegiaque en hommage a Paul Gilson (1942)
Allegro rhapsodique

Fantaisie
Le forgeron mythique (poem by St. Eloi)
Quadrige planetaire
La legende de Saint Eleuthere
La ronde perpetuelle
Les tournaisiens sur la tombe de Saint Eleuthere
Suite dans le style archaique (after Sonneries et Airs du Cortege)
CHAMBER
Variations pour quatuor d'altos
Invenzioni a quattro voce (fl, ob, cl and bsn)
Hommage a Rubens (str trio) (1967)
Divertimento (vln and pf)
Mausolees d'Italie (vln and pf)
PIANO
Triptique (2 pf)
La danseuse de Kerlouan
Menuet
Nocturne
Tout un serie de morceaux
Other pieces
VOCAL
Melodies and songs

Bibliography

Beatrice, L.J. *Daneau, histoire d'une famille d'artistes*. Brussels, 1927.
Landowski, W.L. *Suzanne Daneau* in L'Annee musicale, 1937. Presses Universitaires de France.

Ref. Belgian Center for Music Documentation, 9, 12, 30, 44, 70, 79, 105, 201, 234

DANFORTH, Frances A.

American clavichordist, harpsichordist, pianist, teacher and composer. b. Chicago, June 28, 1903. She took her B.A. and B.Mus. (piano) at the University of Michigan, her M.A. (music literature and composition) at Eastern Michigan University in 1973. She attended pedagogy classes at Michigan State University for 15 years. She studied composition under Dr. David Stewart, Dr. Anthony Iannaccone and privately under George Cacioppo. She did graduate study under Otto Sturmer at the Toledo Conservatory of Music, then Joseph Brinkman at the University of Michigan. She was a private student of David Renner at East Lansing. She taught the piano, the clavichord and the harpsichord privately for over 45 years and was voted The Piano Teacher of the Year (1978), by the Michigan Music Teachers' Association. She gave workshops to students, organised professional groups and in Ann Arbor started the local chapter of the National Guild of Piano Teachers and a local piano teachers' group. She received several honorable mentions.

Compositions

CHAMBER
Rain forest (mar, perc and tim) (1978, rev 1982)
Theme and variations for wind trio (fl, cl and bsn) (1973) (hon mention, Mu Phi Epsilon competition)
Cloistered walls (hpcd, vlc and perc; also vla, hp, small perc and tape) (1979)
PIANO
Karelian light (1979)
Suite (1972) (1st prize, Mu Phi Epsilon competition)
ELECTRONIC
Into the vortex (dialogue for timp and elec tape) (1981, rev 1982)
Ref. composer, 395, 622

DANIELA, Carmen

Austrian pianist, lecturer and composer of Rumanian origin. b. Fagaras, Rumania, October 15, 1951. She began playing the piano at the age of five and composing at the age of seven. During her studies at the Bucharest Music Lyceum No. 1, she appeared regularly on television and radio. After winning a scholarship to the Vienna Conservatory she studied the piano under Professor Raupenstrauch and composition under Professor Burkhard. Other piano teachers included Professors Thern, Iliev and Puchelt and Paul Badura-Skoda, Jorg Demus and Stanislav Neuhaus in Vienna and Guido Agosti in Siena. From 1973 to 1975 she taught the piano at the Vienna Conservatory. In 1978 she won a silver medal at the International Piano Competition in Vercelli, Italy and the following year was awarded an honorary diploma at a piano competition in Finale Ligure, Italy. Carmen has given numerous concerts in Germany, Austria, Rumania and Italy and prepared a piano course for television for which she received a grant from the City of Vienna.

Compositions

ORCHESTRA
Concertino for piano and orchestra in Rumanian folk style, op. 8 (1969)
CHAMBER
Metamorphosen - theme with variations, op. 6 (2 vln and pf) (1967)
PIANO
Suite, op. 13 (4 hands) (1977)
Chinese toccata, op. 3 (1964)
Klavierschule
Little piece with 12 tones, op. 7 (1968)
Prelude and four fables, op. 5 (1966)
Theme with variations in Rumanian folk style, op. 4 (1965)
Three children's pieces, op. 1 (1961-1963)
VOCAL
Three pieces for children's choir, op. 2 (1964)
Songs, op. 10 (Karl Heinrich Waggert) (1971)
Songs, op. 11 (Rumanian folk texts) (1971)
Two songs from Bonn, op. 14 (1978)
THEATRE
Denke daran! melodrama, op. 12 (speaker, mix-ch, pf, tubular bells and vib) (1972)
Ref. composer

DANIELS, Mabel Wheeler

American pianist, conductor, singer and composer. b. Swampscott, MA, November 27, 1878; d. Cambridge, MA, March 10, 1971. From a musical family, she started piano lessons at an early age and at ten wrote her *Fairy Charm Waltz*. She graduated from Radcliffe College (B.A., 1900) magna cum laude and then studied composition under George W. Chadwick at the New England Conservatory, Boston. She also studied composition and orchestration under Ludwig Thuille in Germany. She was awarded a prize in singing upon completion of the regular course at the Munich Conservatory. She was director of the Glee Club at Radcliffe, 1911 to 1913. From 1913 to 1918 she was music director of Simmons College and then devoted herself to composition. In 1931 she was awarded a McDowell Fellowship. In 1933 she received an honorary M.A. from Tufts College and in 1939 an honorary D.M. from Boston University. She also received a D.M. from Wheaton College (1953) and the New England Conservatory (1958). In 1954 she was given an honorary citation by Radcliffe College. She won awards from the National Federation of Music Clubs (1911), the National League of American Pen Women (1926) and the National Association of American Composers and Conductors (1958). She is an honorary member of Phi Beta Kappa and in 1945 was elected trustee of Radcliffe College. Her compositions have been performed by major orchestras in the United States and Europe. DISCOGRAPHY.

Compositions

ORCHESTRA
Overture (1951)
Pastoral ode op. 40 (fl and str orch) (1940)
Deep forest, op. 34, no. 1, prelude (1931, 1934) (New York: J. Fisher)
Digressions, op. 41, no. 2 (str orch) (1947)
In memoriam (1945)
A night in Bethlehem (1954)
Suite for strings (1910)
CHAMBER
Four observations for four strings (1945)
Three observations op. 41 (ob or fl, cl and bsn) (1943) (New York: C. Fisher, 1953)
Sonata (vln and pf)
Two pieces (vln and pf) (1947)
PIANO
Fairy charm waltz (1888)
Fairy scherzo (1914)
In the Greenwood, suite (1908)
VOCAL
Choral work for mixed voices (S, ch and orch) (Fisher, 1937)
The Desolate City, op. 21 (B and orch) (A.P. Schmidt, 1914)
Eastern song op. 16, no. 1 (ch and orch; also pf and 2 vln) (Boston: A.P. Schmidt, 1911)
Holiday fantasy, op. 31, no. 2 (mix-ch and orch) (Schmidt, 1928)
Peace in liberty, op. 25 (Peace with a sword) (mix-vce and orch) (Schmidt, 1917, 1929)
Songs of Elfland, op. 28 (w-ch, S, fl, hp, perc and strs) (A.P. Schmidt, 1924)
Carol of a rose (w-ch) (New York: G. Schirmer, 1958)
Christmas in the wood, op. 35, no. 1 (mix-ch) (Fisher, 1934)
Collinette, op. 4 (w-ch) (Schmidt, 1905)
Dream song, op. 6, no. 2 (ch) (Schirmer, 1905)
Dum Dianae vitrea, op. 38, no. 2 (w-ch) (Fisher, 1942)
Flower wagon, op. 42, no. 1 (w-ch) (Fisher, 1945)
In Springtime, cycle (w-ch) (1910)
June rhapsody, op. 20, no. 1 (w-ch) (Schmidt, 1914)
Mavourneen, op. 12, no. 1 (ch) (Schmidt, 1906)
Midsummer, op. 10 (ch) (Schmidt, 1906)
O'er brake and heather, op. 18 no. 1 (ch) (Schmidt, 1909)
On the road to Mandalay (w-ch) (Thompson Music)
Piper, play on, op. 49 (mix-ch) (Boston: E.C. Schirmer, 1961)
Secrets, op. 22, no. 1 (m-ch) (Schmidt, 1913)
The wild ride (m-ch) (prize, National League of American Penwomen) (Schmidt, 1926)

Choruses for the dedication of the Radcliffe Graduate Center, 1966
Songs incl.:
Awake my heart (Thompson)
Meet me in the lane (Thompson)
Song of the Persian captive, op. 24, no. 2 (Schmidt, 1915)
Villa of dreams (prize, NFMC) (Schmidt, 1911)
Duets and part songs
SACRED
Song of Jael, op. 37, cantata (S, ch and orch) (Fisher, 1937)
Exultate Deo, op. 33 (ch and orch, or org and pf) (for 50th-anniversary of Radcliffe College) (Schmidt, 1929)
The holy star, op. 31, no. 1 (ch and orch) (Schmidt, 1928)
A Psalm of praise, op. 46 (m-ch and str orch: also ch, 3 trp, perc and strs or orch) (for 75th-anniversary of Radcliffe College) (New York: H. W. Gray, 1955)
Canticle of wisdom (w-ch and pf) (Gray, 1958)
The Christ Child, op. 32, no. 2 (mix-ch a-cap) (Schmidt)
Christmas in the manger, op. 35, no. 2 (mix-ch) (J. Fisher, 1934)
A night in Bethlehem (ch) (Gray, 1953)
O God, of all our glorious past (ch) (C.C. Birchard, 1930)
Salve festa dies, op. 38, no. 1 (mix-ch a-cap) (J. Fisher, 1939)
Through the dark the dreamers came, op. 32, no. 1 (w-ch or mix-ch) (E.C. Schirmer 1961)
Veni, Creator Spiritus (w-ch and pf) (Schmidt, 1912)
The voice of my beloved, op. 16, no. 2 (w-ch, pf and 2 vln) (prize, NFMC, 1911) (Schmidt)
In a manger lowly, Christmas song (S, vln, ob or pf and vln) (G. Schirmer, 1915)
BALLET
Pirates' island, op. 34, no. 2 (orch) (1935)
Two movements of three observations, op. 41 (1945)
OPERETTA
Alice in Wonderland continued (w-vces) (1902, 1904)
The Court of Hearts, comic operetta (w-vces) (Boston: White Smith, 1901)
The Legend of Marietta, in 1 act (w-vces) (1909)
THEATRE
A copper complication, musical comedy (w-ch and orch) (White Smith, 1900)
Publications
The American Girl in Munich. 1905.
Ref. 22, 40, 44, 53, 71, 74, 81, 94, 109, 124, 141, 142, 168, 177, 190, 191, 197, 226, 228, 307, 415, 560, 563, 594, 597, 611, 622, 646, 653

DANIELS, Nellie

20th-century English pianist, teacher and composer. b. Rochester. She studied under Joseph Norman; gained her A.Mus T.C.L. and became an L.R.A.M. and F.T.C.L. She was a winner of the McClure memorial prize for composition. She composed a string quintet and a string trio.
Ref. 467

DANIELSON, Janet Rosalie

New Zealand composer. b. Devonport, July 27, 1950. She obtained her B.Mus. from the University of Victoria, 1972 and M.F.A. from the California Institute of Arts, 1975. She studied composition privately under Cornelius Cardew in London in 1973 and currently resides in Canada. Several of her compositions have been performed on television and radio. In 1975 she produced a radio series for KPFA on Canadian women composers and has been composer-in-residence at the Pioneer Music Camp, British Columbia. She contributes to several music publications.
Compositions
CHAMBER
Parabole (wind qnt) (1978)
A Selah (hn and fl) (1983)
Other pieces, mainly for small ensembles
DANCE SCORES
Works for modern dance incl.:
Messenger of fire (1977)
Strange loop (1982)
Ref. 643

DANILEVSKAYA, V.

19th-century Russian composer.
Compositions
VOCAL
Bozhe, tsarya spasi! (mix-ch) (1888) (Jurgenson, Inc.)
Dni i nochi (Jurgenson)
Evreiskaya melodia (Jurgenson)
Matushka milaya (Jurgenson)
Ni otsyva, ni slova (Jurgenson)
Schastie (Jurgenson)
Twenty two romances (Sokolov) (Jurgenson)
SACRED
Khristos s toboi, cantata (solos and ch) (Jurgenson)
Ref. 297

DANOWSKI, Helen

American authoress, librettist, singer and composer. b. New York, January 27, 1932. She studied at the Eastman School of Music, University of Rochester from 1950 to 1954 and then privately under Joseph Castaldo from 1960 to 1962. At the Coombs College of Music she studied composition and orchestration under Romeo Cascarino from 1963 to 1966. She was also a soprano member of the Vox Humana Choral in 1962. In 1950 she received the Arion National Foundation music award.
Compositions
VOCAL
April (chil-ch and cham orch)
The frost king (chil-ch and cham orch)
The solitary reaper (T, 3 S and pf)
The daffodils (T and pf)
O nightingale (T and pf)
ten songs, collection of ancient Chinese folk songs (vce and pf) (pf part comm, 1968)
SACRED
He writes his mystic name (chil-ch and cham orch)
A shepherd is born (T and cham orch)
Benediction (Latin text) (mix-ch of 12 vces and pf or org) (1967)
O salutaris hostia (mix-ch of 8 vce and pf or org) (1967)
Songs from The pet lamb incl.:
All glories of my King (S and pf)
Beautiful thou art (S and pf)
Dost thou know who made thee? (S and pf)
BALLET
Legend of the lotus (orch)
Ref. 190, 494

DANZI, Franziska Dorothea. See LEBRUN, Franziska Dorothea

DANZI, Maria Margarethe (nee Marchand)

German pianist, singer and composer. b. Frankfurt, 1768; d. Munich, June 11, 1800. She was the daughter of the Munich Theatre Director Theobald Marchand and played child roles in the theatre at a very young age. In 1778 she had her first singing lessons from her future sister-in-law, Franziska Danzi. From 1781 to 1784 she lived with her brother Heinrich at Leopold Mozart's home in Salzburg and he taught them the piano and composition. In Mozart's letters she is frequently referred to as Gretl. After her return to Munich, she sang in the Hofoper and in 1786 was made court singer. She was particularly famous for her interpretation of the women in Mozart's operas. In 1790 she married the court musician and composer Franz Danzi and accompanied him on concert tours. Her compositions were influenced by Mozart and her husband, but nonetheless, according to Carl Cannabich her work was the breath of an original thinking and deep-feeling soul. Her *Sonata, op. 1* shows early signs of romanticism. Nearly all of her piano works were lost. DISCOGRAPHY.
Compositions
CHAMBER
Three sonatas, op. 1 (vln and pf) (Munich: Falter, 1799)
Andante with variations, op. 2 (pf)
Ref. 26, 41, 85, 125, 128, 347, 563, 622

DANZIGER, Rosa (van Embden)

20th-century German composer.
Compositions
OPERA
Die Dorfkomtesse (1909)
Ulanenstreiche (1916)

DANZINGER, Laura

19th-century American composer. She studied under Bussler and Gernsheim.
Compositions
CHAMBER
Sonata (vlc and pf)

PIANO
Gypsy life
In the Spring
In Venice, barcarolle (Church)
Little treasures (Church)
Mazurka
TEACHING PIECES
Eight easy pieces (Church)
Ref. 226, 276, 297, 433

DARABAN, Mrs. Michael. See THOMAS, Mary Virginia

DARE, Margaret Marie
Scottish cellist and composer. b. Newport-on-Tay, February 4, 1902; d. Edinburgh, 1976. She studied at the Guildhall School of Music under J.E.R. Teague and in Paris under Paul Bazelaire. She made her debut at the Aeolian Hall, London.
Compositions
ORCHESTRA
Highland ballade (str orch)
Sonatina, 2 mvts (str orch)
Three Highland sketches (str orch)
Two pastorales (str orch)
CHAMBER
Phantasy (2 vln, 2 vla and vlc)
Elegie (4 vlc)
Le lac (vlc and vln or vla and pf)
Menuet (d-b and pf)
Rhapsody (vlc and pf) (1970)
VOCAL
A widow bird sat mourning, part-song (mix-vces)
Ref. 68, 77, 229

DARGEL, Maud
20th-century French composer who studied under Raoul Pugno. She composed symphonic works, a suite and operettas.
Ref. 226

DARUWALA, Zarine
20th-century Indian concert sarod player and composer.
Ref. Indian Council of Women

DASCALESCU, Camelia
Rumanian pianist, conductor, editor, singer and composer. b. Iasi, January 22, 1921. From 1939 to 1940, she studied at the Iasi Conservatory, harmony under Alexandru Zirra, singing under Vasile Rabega, conducting under Antonin Ciolan and the piano under Eliza Ciolan. From 1942 to 1944, she studied at the Bucharest Conservatory, theory and solfege under Ioan Chirescu and musical form and aesthetics under Dimitrie Cuclin. She was musical editor for the record producers Electrecord, Bucharest from 1957 to 1961 and artistic director and conductor of the Grigore Preoteasa student cultural establishment, Bucharest, 1957 to 1959. PHOTOGRAPH.
Compositions
ORCHESTRA
Timiditate (1957)
VOCAL
Melodii, melodii (A. Felea) (1960)
Nu-ţi fie teamă de-un sarut (V. Burlacu) (1966)
Ploua mărunt şi ne plimbam (G. Astalos) (1967)
Să-ntrebi răsăritul de lună (G. Gheorghiu) (1964)
Să nu crezi că-mi pare rău (F. Buref) (1969)
Un tren întro gară (A. Storin) (1972)
Vorbe, vorbe (F. Buref) (1970)
Numerous other light compositions (Viki Dabrescu, Eugen Mirea, Aurel Storin, Velriu Filimon and others) (vce and pf)
Bibliography
Scripca, G. Interviu cu C. Dăscălescu, in *Magazin*. Bucarest, 1968.
Ref. 148, 196

DASHKOVA, Ekaterina Romanovna, Princess
18th-century Russian composer.
Compositions
A Collection of Airs (Edinburgh: Jacques Johnson, 1777)
Ref. 65, 125

DASI, Jani. See JANABAI

D'AUTIER, Alazais. See AZALAIS D'ALTIER

DAUNCH, Mrs. See OBENCHAIN, Virginia

DAVENPORT, Anne Bridges (Mrs. Charles W.)
American pianist, accompanist and composer. b. Old Town, ME, March 30, 1886. She studied the piano under Abbie Cooper Milliken in Old Town, Knut A. Ringwall in Bangor and the Bangor Piano School with Frederick Mariner and harmony with Abbie Nickerson Garland.
Compositions
PIANO
Jink's rag
VOCAL
Circus day
Ref. 374

DAVENPORT, Mrs. Charles W. See DAVENPORT, Anne Bridges

DAVENPORT GOERTZ, Gladys
English violinist, conductor and composer. b. Croydon, October 11, 1895. She studied the violin and composition under W. Sutcliff and L. Favels at the Croydon Conservatory of Music. She also studied composition privately with C.W.G. Goodworth. She conducted St. Leonard's String Players' Club in England for three years. She later moved to Canada.
Compositions
CHAMBER
Short suite (vln and pf) (Bosworth and Co.)
Will o' the wisp (vln and pf) (Bosworth)
VOCAL
Songs:
Above the timber line
Black Bess
Cherry time in Chilliwack
Comes now my sweeting
Cool and silent is the lake (Western Music)
The dogwood tree
Down by the water willows
England awake (Western)
Fraser river
Gather ye rosebuds
Ladner ferry
London
Precious freight
Sea rapture
Ships
Song of the mad prince
The storm
The sunken isle
Sweetly sings the thrush
When music sounds
Ref. 85, 94, 133

DAVID, Louisa. See DULCKEN, Louisa

DAVIDOVA, V.
20th-century Soviet composer. She composed a vocal chamber cycle of Russian romances and their historical development
Ref. 441

DAVIDSON, Muriel
Compositions
PIANO
The fair
First day of the holidays
Hush-a-bye
Once upon a time
Summer days
Ref. 473

DAVIDSON, Tina

American pianist, lecturer and composer. b. Stockholm, NJ, December 30, 1954. She started piano lessons at the age of five. She received a B.A. from Bennington College (piano and composition) in 1976, having studied composition under Henry Brant, Vivian Fine (q.v.) and Louis Calabro and the piano under Lionel Nowak. She then studied composition privately under Clifford Taylor in 1978. She also studied the piano under Walther Wollman at the State College of Oneonta, H. Schultz-Thierbach at the Conservatory of Wurzburg, West Germany, Karol Klein at the Tel-Aviv School of Music and under Sylvia Glickman at Wynnewood. In 1982 she received the National League of American Pen Women's music award and has received many commissions and grants. From 1976 she was medical draftsperson at the University of Pennsylvania and from 1978 associate director of Relache (Ensemble for Contemporary Music) and their project director for the Emerging Composer's Concert Series, 1981 to 1983 and the piano lecturer at Drexel University from 1981.

Compositions

ORCHESTRA

Piano concerto (1981) (CAP grant, 1982)
Dancers (1980)

CHAMBER

Complex (wind ens) (1976) (comm Hartwick College Wind Ensemble, 1976)
Quintet (a-fl, b-cl, vla, vlc and d-b) (1981)
Lazy afternoon music (2 vln, fl, cl and bsn) (1981) (comm Chamber Music Conference and Composers' Forum of the East, 1981)
Deathdreams (2 b-sax and d-b) (1983)
Recollections of darkness (str trio) (1975)
Other echoes (2 vln) (1982)
Snapshots, six pieces (vlc and pf) (1980)
Company (acc) (1980)
Piece (vlc) (1975)

PIANO

Inside and out (duet) (1974)
Seven macabre songs (1979)

VOCAL

Two beasts from the Forest of imaginary beings (narr and orch) (1975) (comm Sage City Symphony, 1976)
Man-faced-scarab (S, fl, cl and ob) (1979) (comm Dromas Quintet, 1977)

ELECTRONIC

Graffiti (S, electric gtr, fl, and pf) (1980)
Shadow grief (m-S and pre-recorded tape) (1983)
To understand weeping (vce and tape) (1980)
Unicorn/tapestry (m-S, vlc and tape) (1982) (1st prize, NACUSA Young Composers' competition, 1983)
Witches' hammer (S and perc) (1979)

THEATRE

The juniper tree, children's play (1975)

MULTIMEDIA

The game of silence (S, narr, mime and dance) (1976)

Ref. composer

DAVIES, Dotie. See TEMPLE, Hope

DAVIES, Eiluned (Doris)

20th-century British concert pianist, teacher and composer. b. Walthamstow, London. She won an open piano scholarship to the Royal College of Music, where she studied the piano under Kathleen Long and composition and orchestration under Gordon Jacob. She later studied the piano privately with Frida van Dieren. She taught in various adult education centres in London from 1945 to 1979. She also taught privately and contributed to the journal *Welsh Music*. She gave recitals at the Wigmore Hall, for the BBC and appeared as a soloist with the BBC Symphony Orchestra, the Liverpool Philharmonic and the BBC Welsh Orchestra. She also gave concerts in Germany, Spain and Holland. Many of her works were publicly performed. She is an A.R.C.M.. PHOTOGRAPH.

Compositions

PIANO

Three folk dances for piano duet (1979)
Cacak kolo (1976)
Setnja (1976)
Sociable pieces (1969)
Three folk dances for piano solo (1979)
Tropanku (1976)
Wir lieben die Stuerme (1976)
Folk dances arrangements (6 hands)

VOCAL

Cygnus (Margaret Rosalie Taylor) (w-ch) (1981)
Jaegerlied (Ludwig Uhland) (m-ch) (1963)
Lob des Fruehlings (L. Uhland) (m-ch) (1963)
Seagull ballet (M. Taylor (w-ch) (1981)
Shadows (M. Taylor) (w-ch) (1981)
For Ann Gregory (Yeats) (Bar and pf) (1965)
Will you be as hard? (Lady Gregory) (Bar and pf) (1964)

SACRED

Requiem (ch and orch) (1969-1970, rev 1971)
No room at the Inn, carol (mix-ch) (1961)
Agnus Dei
Introit and kyrie
Lully, lullow, carol (words from British Museum) (S, A and pf) (1980)
Offertorium
Sanctus
There is no rose, carol (words from parchment in the Library of Trinity College, Cambridge) (S, A and pf) (1980)

Ref. composer

DAVIES, Llewela

19th-century Welsh pianist and composer. b. Brecon. She entered the Royal Academy of Music in 1887 having won the John Thomas Scholarship. She studied the piano under Walter MacFarren and harmony and composition under Stewart MacPherson. She won the MacFarren scholarship in 1892 and the Lucas medal in 1894, for composition. In 1893 she was awarded the medal of the Worshipful Company of Musicians.

Compositions

ORCHESTRA

Three sketches

CHAMBER

String quartet
Violin sonata in E (vln and pf) (1894)

VOCAL

Four songs incl.:
Briar rose (Williams)
Drip, drip o rain (Williams)

Ref. 6, 226, 276, 297, 347

DAVIES, Margaret K. See ADDENDUM

DAVIS, Eleanor Maud

American teacher and composer. b. Hannibal, MO, February 21, 1889; d. Hannibal, October 29, 1973. She studied music in New York under Anne David, Gwlyn Miles, Edward Marzo, William Call and C. Whitney Coombs. She was the pupil and protegee of Lucien G. Chaffin. She taught at the Davis Studio in Hannibal, founded by her mother Tully Murphy Davis. She gave a recital of her own compositions in the Metropolitan Opera House in 1922. She composed over 80 works. PHOTOGRAPH.

Compositions

CHAMBER

Chanson d'amour op. 56 (vln or fl and vlc; also 2 vln and pf or org) (1923)
Elegy, op. 39 (Over in France) (vla and org or pf) (1918)
Duo classique op. 43 (vln and vlc; also org and fl; also org) (1919-1923)
Trio in F-Minor
The eagle's mate, op. 27 (org and pf) (1950)
Pieces for harp and cello
Teaching works for violin and piano

ORGAN

Berceuse, op. 3 (1907)
Woodland suite, op. 65 (1924)

PIANO

Orientale ballet, op. 73 (duet) (1928)
Fantasie, op 74
Prelude classique, op. 20 (1916) (Davis Studio)
Waltz in F-Sharp Minor, op. 35 (1918)

VOCAL

Who is Sylvia, op. 68 (w-ch; also 3 vces) (1929)
Because I love, op. 14, no. 18, 5 works (1916-1957) (Boston Music)
The call of the sea, op. 19 (3 w-vces) (1916-1956)
Expectancy, op. 18
The last parting, op. 13 (1916)
Woodland birds, op. 55 (1923)
Numerous songs (vce and pf)

SACRED

Come, risen Lord, episcopal communion hymn (mix-ch) (1941)
Episcopal Communion Service in E-Flat Major, op. 46 (1921)

Ref. Mrs Floyd W. LaDue, 40, 347, 460

DAVIS, Eva May

American pianist, singer, teacher and composer. b. Barnard, MO, October 14, 1883. She was educated at Stephens College, Columbia and the University of Missouri. She studied under Alice Dixon, T.C. Whitmer and P.O. Landon. She composed piano pieces and songs.

Ref. 460

DAVIS, Fay Simmons

American pianist, teacher and composer. b. Cambridge, MA; d. Glen Ridge, NJ, February 3, 1943. She composed anthems.

Bibliography

Etude. Oct. 1932, p. 686.

Ref. 347, 353

DAVIS, Genevieve

American pianist, singer and composer. b. Falconer, NY. December 11, 1889; d. Plainfield, NJ. December 3, 1950. She studied the piano under Adolph Frey at Syracuse University.

Compositions

PIANO

The shepherd and the echo

VOCAL

Caprice
Children of light
Eventide
I am joy
Love at dusk
A maid and the moon
The river in spring

Ref. 39, 142, 347

DAVIS, Hazel E.

American authoress, publisher and composer. b. Bucklin, KS, February 14, 1907. She was educated at the Kansas State Teachers' College.

Compositions

SACRED

America, America, return to God, hymn
Through God, hymn

Ref. 347, 646

DAVIS, Hilda Emery (Mrs. Meyer)

20th-century American composer.

Composition

ORCHESTRA

The last knight (1938)

Ref. 226

DAVIS, Jean Reynolds (Mrs. H. Warren, Jr.)

American pianist, authoress, teacher and composer. b. Cumberland, MD, November 1, 1927. She received her B.M. at the University of Pennsylvania after studying under Robert Elmore and William R. Smith. She taught the piano privately and in school. She was a recipient of the Thornton Oakley Medal, the Benjamin Franklin Medal, the Cultural Olympics Award of Merit and an ASCAP award.

Compositions

ORCHESTRA

Two symphonies

CHAMBER

Woodwind quintet

VOCAL

Choral works and songs

SACRED

Adoremus (S, A and gtr)
Blessed art thou
Carol of a new day
Chorale for Easter
Christmas Alleluia

OPERA

The Elevator
The Mirror

BALLET

Shenandoah holiday, for children

TEACHING PIECES

Pet silhouettes (pf)
Tunes for dessert (pf)

MISCELLANEOUS

Yankee Doodle Doodles (1962) (Presser Music Co.)
Slick Tricks (1962) (Witmark & Sons)

Ref. 39, 142, 190, 347, 625

DAVIS, Katherine Kennicott

American pianist, teacher and composer. b. St. Joseph, MO, June 25, 1892; d. Concord, MA, April 20, 1981. She studied the piano under Clarence Hamilton and Wesley Wyamm and composition under H.C. McDougal, Stuart Mason and Nadia Boulanger (q.v.). She was awarded the Billings prize for composition at Wellesley College in 1914, where she also taught the piano and theory, 1916 to 1918. She was given an honorary doctorate by Stetson University, FL, and won an ASCAP award in 1969. She taught at the Concord Academy from 1921 to 1922 and Shady Hill School, Philadelphia, 1923 to 1930. DISCOGRAPHY.

Compositions

ORCHESTRA

The burial of a queen, symphonic poem

CHAMBER

Six collections (pf)

VOCAL

Over 1000 choral works and arrangements incl.:
I have a fawn
The lamb (Blake)
Nancy Hanks (New York: Galaxy Music, 1941)
The tyger (Blake)
A wonderful thing

SACRED

This is Noel, cantata (S, B, mix-ch and insts)
Easter is a song
Fanfare for Palm Sunday
Hail His coming, King of Glory
Let all things now living (Boston: E.C. Schirmer, 1938)
The little drummer boy
The raising of Lazarus (T and org)
Road to Galilee
Sing Gloria

OPERA

Cinderella
The unmusical impressario (Heddie Root Kent) (G. Schirmer, 1956)

Bibliography

Dr. Harrison Broughton. *Katherine K. Davis*. Thesis. University of Missouri, Kansas City. 1974.

Ref. composer, 94, 141, 142, 190, 228, 347, 510, 563, 622, 646

DAVIS, Margaret Munger

American organist, teacher and composer. b. Spencer, IA, July 22, 1908. She studied at Northwestern University and the American Conservatory as well as privately under August Maekelberghe in Detroit. She was a teacher and accompanist from 1931 to 1947 and after 1965, an organist for the Trinity Episcopal Church in Detroit.

Compositions

VOCAL

Autopsy on Aberfan (S and pf)
Haiku (S and pf)
Water music (S and pf)

SACRED

Choral works
Songs

Ref. 142, 347

DAVIS, Marianne (Mrs. Gabriel)

English composer. d. Littlemore, Oxfordshire, July 18, 1888.

Compositions

PIANO

Gavotte in C (Weekes)

VOCAL

Songs incl.:
By the river
Consolation (Weekes)
Dame Trot
Dame Wiggins of Lee
If to love you (Weekes)
King Carnival
Three stars
Zingara

Ref. 6, 226, 297

DAVIS, Mary

20th-century American composer.

Composition

OPERA

Columbine, in 3 acts

Ref. 141

DAVIS, Miss

19th-century English composer.

Compositions

VOCAL

Duets
Songs incl.:
The blind girl to her mother (Dublin: Marcus Moses)

Fair as the summer flower (1 or 2 vces) (Moses)
Footsteps of angels
Glad Summer, fare thee well (Mrs. Hemans) (Moses)
If thou hast crushed a flower (Mrs. Hemans) (Moses)
Passing away (Mrs. Hemans) (Moses)
Ruth (Marcus Moses)
When Spring unlocks the flowers
SACRED
Songs incl.:
Lead, kindly light (2 vces) (Moses)
The Lord of might from Sinai's brow (Moses)
Let there be light (Moses)
My Father's at the helm (Moses)
Night hymn at sea
Ref. 276, 433

DAVIS, Mrs. L.A. See BUGBEE, L.A.

DAVIS, Mrs. Gabriel. See DAVIS, Marianne

DAVIS, Mrs. Meyer. See DAVIS, Hilda Emery

DAVIS, Sharon

American harpsichordist, pianist, violinist, lecturer and composer. b. Los Angeles, September 30, 1937. She began studying the piano at the age of five and the violin when she was seven. After studying the piano under Lois Skartvedt Drew and John Crown, she received a B.M. from the University of Southern California. At the Juilliard School of Music she earned her M.S. under Rosina Lhevinne. She was awarded a Fulbright grant for piano study in Paris, where her teachers were Yvonne Lefebure and Nadia Boulanger (q.v.). She taught at East State University for two years, then returned to Los Angeles to marry the composer and publisher William Schmidt. From 1964 to 1966 she was principal piano instructor at the East Texas State University. She frequently appeared as a solo pianist on tours with large and small ensembles and on the radio. DISCOGRAPHY.

Compositions
PIANO
Cocktail etudes (1979)
VOCAL
Suite of wildflowers (S and insts) (Western International Music, Inc.)
Three moods of Emily Dickinson (S, pf, vln and vlc) (Los Angeles: Avant Music, 1981)
Though men call us free, op. 2 (S, cl and pf) (after Oscar Wilde's The Young King) (Western Int.)
Three poems of William Blake (S and cl) (Avant Music, 1977)
Six songs set to poems of William Pillin (high vce and pf) (1982)
Ref. AMC newsletter, 185, 228, 563, 624, 622, 625

DAVISON, Martha Taylor

20th-century American composer.
Compositions
PIANO
Pieces
VOCAL
Brasilia (ch) (Paragon)
Ref. 40, 347

DAVISSON, Genevieve

Composition
VOCAL
Monotone (low vce and pf)
Ref. 190

DAVITASHVILI, Meri Shalvovna

Soviet pianist and composer. b. Tbilisi, March 13, 1924. After graduating from the Kutais Music School in 1941, where she studied the piano, she entered the Tbilisi Conservatory. She studied composition under A. Balanchivadze and graduated in 1946. From 1946 to 1948 she was concertmistress at the Tbilisi Conservatory. In 1956 she was made a member of the board of the Union of Soviet Composers in the Georgian SSR and in 1968 became secretary of that board.

Compositions
ORCHESTRA
Piano concerto (1946)
Fantasia (pf and orch) (1956)
Overture in the name of peace (1951)
Pioneer suite (1954)
Suite (1946)
Utro v Bakurianskom lesu, symphonic poem (1966)
CHAMBER
String quartet
Piano trio
Aria (vln and pf) (1950)
Poem (vln and pf) (1955)
PIANO
Nocturne
Scherzo
Sonatina (1962)
Three preludes
VOCAL
Evening in the Tbilisi Sea (Abashidze) (ch) (1951)
Fly in my swallow (Shirili) (ch) (1951)
Song for Lese Ukrainka (1952)
Ballad of the Samgorski flower (Gachyechiladze) (1950)
Romance (Khoshtariya) (1952)
Song cycle (A. Kalandadze) (1964)
Songs for pre-school children and pioneers (M. Mrevlishvili) (1951)
Song of the Fatherland (1965)
Romances (W.R. Margiani, S. Chikovan, Sadzhaya and Pushkin)
BALLET
The Son's Marriage (1954)
OPERETTA
Kadzhana, for children (1966)
Natsarkekia, for children (1972)
INCIDENTAL MUSIC
Eight theatrical productions
Ref. 21, 87, 330, 458.

DAVY, Ruby Claudia Emily

Australian pianist, conductor, lecturer and composer. b. Salisbury, South Australia, November 22, 1883; d. Melbourne, July 12, 1949. She studied at the University of Adelaide and was a F.T.C.L. She was the first Australian woman to receive a D.Mus. She lectured and gave recitals in Australia, Britain and the United States.

Compositions
ORCHESTRA
Piano concerto
Symphonic overture
CHAMBER
String quartet
Piano trio
Sonata (vln and pf)
VOCAL
Australia, fair and free, cantata
Other large-scale choral works
Ref. 8, 74

DAWE, Margery. See FELIX, Margery Edith

DAWSON, Alice

20th-century American composer.
Composition
VOCAL
I am the wind (mix-ch) (Neil A. Kjos)
Ref. 190, 347

DAWSON, Nancy

18th-century English composer.
Composition
VOCAL
Of all the girls in our town (1760)
Ref. 91

DE, Li, Princess

Ancient Chinese flautist and composer. As a child she accompanied her father on his travels and received an European education, becoming well versed in literature and music. None of her many compositions can be found in the archives of modern China.
Ref. Patricia Adkins Chiti (Rome)

DE ARAUJO CAMPOS, Joaquina. See CAMPOS DE ARAUJO, Joaquina

DE ARTEAGA, Genoveva. See ARTEAGA, Genoveva de

DE BERIOT, Maria Felicite Garcia. See MALIBRAN, Maria Felicitas

DE BIASE BIDART, Lycia

Brazilian pianist, violinist, conductor, teacher and composer. b. Vitoria, Espirito Santo, February, 18, 1910. She received her musical education in Rio de Janeiro under Giovanni Giannetti, 1927 to 1934. She studied the piano, the violin, instrumentation, harmony, composition, counterpoint and fugue and improved her piano technique under Magdalena Tagliaferro, 1946 to 1949. She made her composer's debut in 1930 under the direction of Francisco Braga at the Municipal Theatre in Rio and as a conductor in 1931. She performed her own compositions in Italy in 1948 and on Radio Roquete Pinto, Brazil, 1953. PHOTOGRAPH.

Compositions

ORCHESTRA

Andante e allegro cantabile (pf and orch) (1969)
Concerto Rio 70 (pf and orch) (1970)
Interludio (pf and orch) (1969)
Adagio improviso (1971)
Anchieta, symphonic poem (1934)
Angelus, symphonic episodes (1934)
Canto sinfonio: A cidade de Colonia (1977)
A catedral de Colonia (1977)
Serie germanica (1977)
Serie: O momento sugere (1974)
Symphonic fantasy on dance rhythms (1976)
Symphonic variations (1970)
Numerous works (str orch)

CHAMBER

Nonada e toada (fl, ob, bsn, hn, 2 vln, vla, vlc and d-b) (1976)
Mefisto (wind ens)
Andante (org, strs and fl) (1938)
Pensamentos poeticos (cl, bsn, hn, vln, vla, vlc and d-b) (1976)
Canto praieiro (fl, ob, cl, hn, bsn and pf) (1971)
Intervalos musicais, 6 pieces (fl, ob, cl, hn, bsn and pf) (1971)
Canto amerindo brasileiro (fl, ob, cl, bsn and hn) (1974)
Elegia (fl, ob, cl, bsn and trp) (1966)
Serie danças (fl, ob, cl, bsn and hn) (1970)
Albatroz (str qrt)
Canção de barauna (2 cl and 2 hn) (1975)
Dedicando, 11 pieces (various combinations of fl, cl, hn and hp) (1974)
Serenga (fl, cl, bsn and hn) (1976)
Serie brasilia (hn qrt) (1975)
Cantos tupis (fl, cl and trp) (1975)
Dedicando, 8 pieces (fl, cl and hn) (1975)
Ecos indigenas (hn and 2 cl) (1975)
Five piano trios (1973-1976)
Sombras (fl, vln and pf) (1976)
Trio som esquecido (vln, hn and pf) (1975)
A bailarina (2 fl) (1974)
Adagio cantabile (ob and pf) (1971)
Adulto e crianca (fl and d-b) (1975)
Allegretto gioioso (hp and pf) (1966)
Andante e cantabile (vlc and pf) (1932)
Canção (vlc and pf) (1969)
Concertino (fl and hp) (1973)
Concerto (trp and pf) (1977)
Crianca e adulto (ob and bsn) (1975)
Danca amerindia brasileira (vln and vla) (1974)
Duas rosas (hp and fl) (1966)
Duo matinale (2 cl)
Estrelas (ob and pf) (1971)
Estudo (cl and pf; also vln and vla) (1974, 1976)
Estudos expressionistas (2 hn) (1975)
Flor de madrugada (ob and pf) (1971)
Jogral (vln and pf) (1971)
Uma canção para Renata (fl and pf) (1976)
Uma rosa (ob and pf) (1971)
O cavalinho (2 fl) (1974)
O lago (vla or vlc and pf) (1965)
Rosal (vln and pf) (1975)
Serenata (vla and pf) (1974)
Solidao (ob and pf) (1975)
Sonata (vln and pf) (1974)
Sonata fantasia (vlc and pf) (1974)
Viola do ceu (vla and pf) (1974)
Cantabile (fl) (1974)
Estudo (fl) (1976)
Evocando *Marie Lach* and *Kreuzberg* (org) (1977)
Musica, 4 pieces (hp) (1974)

PIANO

Noite em Salamanca (2 or 1 pf) (1950)
Andante cantabile e allegro cantabile (1969)
Apelo (1977)
Bruma, evocando Claude Debussy (1961)
Canto breve (1971)
Canto breve No. 2 (1976)
Devaneio (1949)
Dilema (1975)
Estudos (1976)
Interludio catabile (1969)
Interludios (1969, 1971)
Matinal (1951)
Noite, evocando Maurice Ravel (1961)
O caminho (1960)
O passeio (1943)
Outonal evocando Ottorino Respighi (1961)
Sonata ao mar (1961, 1975)
Soneto *Santo Bambino de Aracoeli* (1950)
Tarde (1967)
Veleiro dois irmaos (1966)
Poema ignoto (1972)
Preambulo e Epigramas para tres anjos (1976)
Prismas do Dragão de sete cabeças caroadas (1976)
Som esquecido (1972)
Sonata fantasia No. 2 (1975)
Sonata fantasia No. 3 (1976)
Sons musicais dos sinais graficos (1979)
Numerous teaching works

VOCAL

Canaan, symphonic poem (ch and orch) (1932)
Cantos amerindos brasileiros (ch and orch) (1973)
Rio de Janeiro (ch and orch) (1969)
Canto da noite (Cont, Bar and orch) (1977)
Poema (T or Bar and orch) (1976)
As flores do jambeiro estao caindo (A.F. Schmidt) (mix-ch a-cap) (1977)
Brauna (C.D. de Andrade) (mix-ch a-cap) (1975)
Cantiga de roda (M. Quintana) (mix-ch a-cap) (1977)
Canto de louvação, song in 4 movements (ch)
Convite tribal, Amerindian Brazilian song in 4 movements (ch)
El burro flautista (B. Iriarte) (mix-ch a-cap) (1956)
Ladainha do mar (A.F. Schmidt) (mix-ch a-cap) (1977)
Lamento (A.F. Schmidt) (mix-ch a-cap) (1971)
Paremia de cavalo (composer) (mix-ch a-cap) (1974)
Paredao (C.D. Andrade) (mix-ch a-cap) (1974)
Serenga: canto dos remadores do Rio Tiete (L. da Camara Cascudo) (mix-ch a-cap) (1976)
Tres cantos tupis (W. Pinto) (mix-ch a-cap) (1975)
Quero possuir o azul (vce and ens) (1976)
Numerous songs (vce and pf or other insts)

SACRED

Missa pro sposi (org, fl and strs) (1938)
Mensagem de Natal (mix-ch a-cap) (1976)
Panis Angelicus (mix-ch a-cap) (1938)
Ave Maria (vce and pf) (1927)

BALLET

Simbolismo e Vivencia do Jardim Botanico do Rio de Janeiro (1976)
Som e Cor (1971)

OPERA

A Noiva do Mar (from the novel, A Noiva do golfinho, by Xavier Marques)

Ref. composer, 206, 333

DE BLANCK, Olga. See BLANCK, Olga de

DE CALANDRA, Matilda T. See CALANDRA, Matilda T. de

DE CARDENSAS, Countess. See GARELLI DELLA MOREA, Vincenza

DE CASTRO, Alice

Brazilian pianist and composer. b. Rio de Janeiro, 1840; d. Rio de Janeiro, ca. 1900.

Composition

PIANO

Jo'-Jo' Carlinhos, habanera

Ref. 349

DE CASTRO, Maria
16th-century aristocrat, musicologist and composer. She was skilled in music, philosophy, theology and mathematics. After her marriage she lived in Paris, where she studied at private academies. She left several works in manuscript.
Ref. 13, 99, 232

DE CASTRO LIMA, Kilza Setti. See SETTI, Kilza

DE CEVEE, Alice
American teacher and composer. b. Harrisburg, PA, February 25, 1904. She studied at the Harrisburg Conservatory and at the Juilliard School of Music under Ernest Hutcheson. She taught at the Harrisburg Conservatory and was the recipient of National Federation of Music Clubs awards and commissions.
Compositions
ORCHESTRA
Memorabilia
PIANO
Holland tunnel (2 pf)
Boogie woogie goes high hat
VOCAL
Anniversary (vce and pf) (C. Fischer)
Down by the Salley Gardens (vce and pf) (C. Fischer)
The old river road (vce and pf) (Studio and Concert Music Publ.)
The owl and the pussycat (vce and pf) (C. Fischer)
Slow Boat (C. Fischer)
Other songs
BALLET
Coney Island
THEATRE
Love in a bottle, music drama
Ref. 142, 190

DE CHAMY, Berthe de
20th-century French composer.
Composition
VOCAL
Au Temps Jadis, air de dance ancien (Ricordi)

DE CHARRIERE, Sophie. See CHARRIERE, Isabella

DE CLERCK, Albertine. See COLIN, Jeanne

DE-ESIHEBSED
6th-century B.C. Egyptian singer of the harem of Amun. She was the daughter of Esptah, known from her tomb in the temple of Queen Shepenwept II at Medinet-Habu in the XXVI dynasty, ca. 660 B.C.
Ref. 428

DE FAZIO, Lynette Stevens
American arranger, choreographer, dancer, teacher and composer. b. Berkeley, CA, September, 1929. She studied at the University of California and San Francisco State College. She was a dancer, ballet mistress and choreographer in California and other states from 1938 till 1977.
Compositions
THEATRE
Le ballet du cirque (1964)
The ballet of Mother Goose (composer) (1968)
Publications
Basic Outlines for Dance Classes. 1960.
Other books on dancing.
Ref. 475

DE FREITAS, Elvira Manuela Fernandez
Portuguese pianist, conductor, professor and composer. b. Lisbon, June 8, 1927. She was the daughter of composer Frederico de Freitas, who was her first teacher. She studied composition and the piano under Lourenco V. Cid, Jorge Croner de Vasconelos, Antonio E. da Costa Ferreira, Fernando Lopes Garcia and her father at the Lisbon Conservatory. In 1959, on a Gulbenkian scholarship, she proceeded to the Ecole Normale and the Paris Conservatoire, where she studied composition under Nadia Boulanger (q.v.) and Olivier Messiaen. She was conductor of the National Orchestra at the National Theatre and at the National Broadcasting Company, Lisbon. She was professor at the Lisbon Conservatory until 1978, when she became professor at the Gregorian Institute, Lisbon. Among the prizes she won are the Carlos Seixas National Composition Prize, 1971 and the Camara Municipal de Lisboa prize, 1955. PHOTOGRAPH.
Compositions
ORCHESTRA
O comboio, op. 4 (pf and orch) (1956)
O natal dos meus meninos, op. 5 (1956)
O passeio publico, op. 6 (1956)
CHAMBER
Sonata, theme and variations, op. 13 (vlc and pf) (1969)
Bagatelles, op. 27, 6 pieces (ob and bsn) (1982)
Four easy pieces, op. 26 (fl) (1982)
Pieces for 2 clarinets, op. 19 (1979)
Para gostar de clarinete, op. 17 (1977)
Recordações de Azurara, op. 18 (fl) (1979)
Sonata, op. 2 (pf) (1950)
VOCAL
Cantata Cenica 'O Iluminado, op. 9 (J.B. Portugal) (soli, ch and orch) (1960)
As Profecias do Bandarra, op. 12 (Almeida Garrett) (soli, ch and orch) (1967)
Bartolemue Marinheiro, op. 10 (Vieira) (3 vces and orch) (1969)
...E as Caravelas de Cabral, op. 14 (O. Mariano, R. Couto) (3 vces and orch) (1971)
A Heranca, op. 11 (J.B. Portugal) (vce, pf, ob, bsn, trp and perc) (1966)
A passagem estreita, op. 25 (F. de Castro) (m-ch a-cap) (1981)
Quadras, op. 24 (F. de Castro) (m-ch a-cap) (1981)
A amizade, op. 3 (C. Queiroz) (vce and pf) (1951)
Andaluzia, op. 20 (Lorca) (vce and gtr) (1979)
Cantigo sagrada de folia, op. 3 (16th-century canon) (vce and pf) (1951)
Lirio de Sao Damião. op. 28 (F. de Castro) (vce and fl) (1982)
Se tu viesses Poesia, op. 29 (S. da Gama) (vce and pf) (1982)
Os enamorados, op. 1 (A. Serpa) (vce and pf) (1946)
Os insectos, op. 8, cycle (A. Alves) (vce and pf) (1959)
Numerous light and children's songs
SACRED
Gloria, op. 22 (mix-ch a-cap) (1981)
Pieces for a Requiem, op. 15 (mix-ch a-cap) (1971)
Requiem, op. 16 (mix-ch a-cap) (1975)
Two psalms, op. 23 (m-ch a-cap) (1981)
THEATRE
A Floresta encantada, op. 7, for children (composer) (1957)
Ref. composer, 643

DE GAMBARINI, Elisabetta (Mrs. Chazal)
British organist, conductor, soprano and composer. b. England, 1731. On May 14, 1764, she conducted a concert in London that included six of her own compositions.
Compositions
ORCHESTRA
Organ concerto
CHAMBER
Forest scene (hns and tim)
Lesson for the harpsichord, intermixed with Italian and English songs, op. 2, (1748)
Overture for French horns
Six sets of lessons for the harpsichord (1748)
Piano solo
Violin solo
VOCAL
Ode for chorus
Twelve English and Italian songs, op. 3 (German fl and thorough bass)
Ref. 65, 125, 128, 226, 276, 347

DE JONG, Sarah
20th-century Australian composer.
Composition
THEATRE
Sleezee, cabaret (1976)
Ref. 442

DE KLUIS, Annie. See TACK, Annie

DE LA GUERRE Elisabeth-Claude. See LA GUERRE, Elisabeth-Claude Jacquet de

DE LA MARTINEZ, Odaline

Cuban pianist, conductor and composer. b. 1947. She lived in America from the age of 12 and then moved to England. Her music is influenced by the Voodoo music she heard as a child in Cuba. She graduated with honors in mathematics and music from Tulane University in 1972 and was selected as the outstanding Alumnus in 1983. She won a scholarship to the Royal Academy of Music, London and studied under Paul Patterson (composition) and Elsa Cross (piano). In her postgraduate year she also studied at the University of Surrey, gaining her B.Mus. (composition), studying under Reginald Smith Brindle and worked on her Ph.D. (computer music). She was a founder member of Lontato, a contemporary music ensemble in 1976, of which she is currently musical director. She founded and conducts the Contemporary Chamber Orchestra. Her interests include computer music and the development of new sounds in music. She composed an opera based on the life of the evangelist Amy MacPhearson.
Ref. *Music* October 1983

DE LACKNER, Mrs.

English composer. ca. 1800.
Compositions
PIANO
Second set of six original German waltzes, adapted for the piano forte (London: E. Riley, ca. 1800)
Ref. 65

DE LARA, Adelina (pseud. of Adelina Tilbury)

English pianist, teacher and composer. b. Carlisle, Cumberland, January 23, 1872; d. Woking, November 25, 1961. She gave a command performance before King Edward and Queen Alexandra and King George and Queen Mary. She gave recitals as a child prodigy throughout Great Britain and Ireland until 1884 and then went to the Hoch Conservatory, Frankfurt, for six years. Iwan Knorr taught her theoretical subjects, and she studied the piano under Clara Schumann (q.v.). On her return to England she gave concerts in London and with the Halle Orchestra, Manchester. She gave recitals in Australia, USA and South Africa. She was one of the last upholders of the Clara Schumann tradition and trained many distinguished pianists from 1891 until her retirement in 1938.
Compositions
ORCHESTRA
Two piano concertos
Concerto for strings (1938)
In the forest, suite (str orch) (1949)
PIANO
Nocturne (Heller)
VOCAL
Idyll (T and orch)
Numerous ballads (vce and pf)
Rose of the world, song cycle
Two song cycles
Publications
Finale. Autobiography. Burke Publishing Co., 1955.
Ref. 8, 96, 297, 572

DE LEATH, Vaughn

American pianist, singer and composer. b. Mt. Pulaski, IL, 1897. She studied under Ellen Beach Yaw, Anthony Carlson, Caroline Alchyn and Robert Hosea.
Compositions
ORCHESTRA
Arabian carnival
VOCAL
Songs incl.:
The blue bowl
God bless thee love
In the arms of the night
Madonna's lullaby
My lover comes a-riding
Old glory
Rosemary
Sea chair
Sometimes in the early evening
Wild geese
Ref. 292

DE LISLE, Estelle

19th-century American composer.
Composition
PIANO
Cape cottage waltz (Philadelphia: J.E. Gould, 1856)
Ref. 228

DE LYLE, Carlyon (Maud Wingate)

British composer. b. Hamilton, Scotland, 1877. She is an L.R.A.M. Her recording *Dedication* was accepted by H.M. Queen Elizabeth in 1937.
Compositions
CHAMBER
La Russie, sonata (pf and vln)
Nine suites (pf)
VOCAL
Popular ballads
Folk songs
INCIDENTAL MUSIC
Programme music
Ref. 467

DE MICCO, Lora

19th-century Italian composer.
Compositions
PIANO
Minuetto (Ricordi)
VOCAL
Ninna-nanna a Maria Pia, lullaby (L. Cavelli) (vce and pf)
Ref. Ricordi (Milan)

DE MOL, Josephine

Belgian singing teacher and composer. b. December 19, 1873. She wrote piano pieces and music for children; mainly dances, ballets and songs.
Ref. SABAM

DE MONET, Antoinette Paule. See DUCHAMBGE, Pauline

DE MONTEL, Adalgisa

Italian pianist and composer. b. Florence, February 25, 1875. She studied the piano privately under Babuscio, composition under M. Cappelli and M. Bagnoli and orchestration under V. Doplicher. She toured for several years giving concerts and from 1910 dedicated herself to the composition of religious music. She made her debut in 1917 at the Duomo with the mass *Missa Sanctae Mariae Floris*. Her works have been performed in Europe and Egypt.
Compositions
ORCHESTRA
Notte di Wagram, poem
Suite pastorale (strs)
CHAMBER
Zingaresca
Piano pieces
VOCAL
Fourteen romances
SACRED
Missa Regina Pacis (4 vces and orch) (1920)
Missa Sanctae Mariae Floris (3 vces and orch) (1917)
L'ora della Desolata, sacred poem (3 vces and orch)
Le Sette Parole di Cristo in Croce, parts of mass (3 vces and orch) (1918)
Stabat Mater Speciosa (3 vces and orch)
Victimae Paschali, sequence (3 vces and orch)
Ecce Panis Angelorum, mass (2 vces)
Responsori dei Tre Mattutini delle Tenebre, parts of mass
Six motets for Mass (2 vces)
Litany: Ave Maria and others
Ref. 86, 105

DE MONTET, Antoinette Paule. See DUCHAMBGE, Pauline

DE PATE, Elisabetta M.S.

20th-century Uruguayan pianist, writer and composer. b. Montevideo. From the age of six she was a pupil of Signor Giuffra and Felicite and Joanna Baumgarten. She was considered a child prodigy and at the age of 11 composed military marches and concert waltzes. She was the first woman in South America to conduct an orchestra and the only woman to have works included in the repertoire of the Pan-American Union Band. Later she moved to New Orleans. She wrote articles on South American folklore.

Compositions
ORCHESTRA
Un sogno (str orch)
PIANO
Caprice Uruguay - Italy
Claveles
Don Bosco
The flag
The gypsy
Pensieri d'affetto
Second chasseurs
Viva el parvenir
Welcome
SACRED
Elegie
Gloria, on the life of Carlos Herrera
Ref. 448

DE PURY, Marianne
Swiss/American composer. b. St. Gall, Switzerland, April 3, 1935. She studied at the Conservatoire de Musique, Geneva. She was composer, director and performer for the Open Theatre, the Omaha Magic Theatre and the Santa Fe Theatre. PHOTOGRAPH.
Compositions
INCIDENTAL MUSIC
Music for theatre, films and television incl.:
America hurrah (G.C. van Itallie)
Bums (A. Sze, T. Thompson)
The firebugs (M. Frisch)
Kegger (M. Terry)
Viet rock (M. Terry)
Ref. composer

DE SCHAETZEL, Pauline. See DECKER, Pauline

DE SIESLEY, Mme. See COURMONT, Countess von

DE SIVRAI, Jules. See ROECKEL, Jane

DE SOUSA HOLSTEIN, Donna Teresa
Portuguese singer and composer. b. 1823; d. 1865. She was the daughter of Don Pedro de Sousa Holstein, first Duke of Palmela and married the Count of Alcacovas. She lived in Rome for some time and her compositions revealed an Italian inspiration, with Italian lyrics.
Compositions
VOCAL
Chamber romances (1 or 2 vces)
Ref. 502

DE VALDES, Sylvia Soublette. See SOUBLETTE, Sylvia

DE VILLA, Frances. See BALL, Frances de Villa

DE VILLIERS, Justina Wilhelmina Nancy
South African organist, pianist, soprano, teacher and composer. b. Paarl, January 21, 1871; d. Parys, September 19, 1957. She was the twelfth child of Stephanus de Villiers, a prominent church musician and composer of Paarl. From 1899 to 1902 she studied the piano, the organ, composition, singing and elocution at the Berlin Conservatory. In 1903 she and her sister, Mrs. von Wielligh, founded the Villieria School of Music in Stellenbosch and two years later established the Stellenbosch Conservatory, together with F.W. Jannasch and Hans Endler. She taught there until her marriage in 1910.
Compositions
CHAMBER
Lied ohne Worte
Romanza
PIANO
Mazurka in A-Major
Moment musical in E-Major
Op die moment, improvisation
Rondo in B-Major
Rondo in F-Major
VOCAL
Lied van vroue-landbouvereniging, Kaapprovinsie (E.H. Nellmapius)
Seitdem die Mutter heimgegangen ist, op. 2, no. 2
Der stille Thal, op. 2, no. 1
Ref. 377

DE WEYRAUCH, Anne. See WEYRAUCH, Anna Julie

DE ZUBELDIA, Emiliana. See ZUBELDIA, Emiliana de

DEACON, Mary Connor
American organist, pianist, authoress, teacher and composer. b. Johnson City, TN, February 22, 1907. She studied at East Tennessee State College and under Frank LaForge, William Stickler and Carl Deis. She taught at the Royal Conservatory, Toronto.
Compositions
PIANO
Pieces
SACRED
Choral works and songs incl.:
Beside still waters (H.W. Gray)
Call of the sea
Follow the road
Hear my prayer
Little Holy Jesus
Ocean lore
I will lift up mine eyes
Your Cross
Ref. 39, 142, 190

DEAN, Laura
American choreographer and composer. b. Staten Island, NY, December 3, 1945. She studied under Lucas Hoving at the American School of Ballet. She is the head of the Laura Dean Dance Company. Among her awards is a Guggenheim Fellowship.
Compositions
BALLET
Changing (comm American Dance Festival, 1974)
Circle dance (1972)
Dance
Drumming (with Steve Reich)
Music
Night
Song
Spiral (comm Brooklyn Academy)
Square dance (with Steve Reich)
Tympani
Walking dance (with Steve Reich)
Bibliography
Music Journal, March 1978.
Ref. *Newsweek* Dec. 7, 1981, 633

DEAN, Mrs. B.H. See HARKNESS, Rebekah West

DEAN PAUL, Lady. See WIENIAWSKA, Irene Regina

DEBARO, Charlotte. See ROZMAN, Sarah

DEBORAH
12th-century B.C. Hebrew judge, poetess, prophetess and songstress. She composed the famous song of triumph that related to that period of the final battle with Sisera and his hosts. The oldest existing fragment of Hebrew literature gives Deborah's song of triumph and tells of the death of Sisera.

Bibliography
Stanton, Elizabeth Cady. *The Woman's Bible*. Edinburgh: Polygon Books. 1985.
Who's Who in the Bible. Comay and Browrigg. New York: Bonanza Books. 1980.
Ref. 264, 576, 598

DEBRASSINE-PRIJAT, Laure
Belgian conductor, professor and composer. b. October 31, 1890. She was a professor of music and composed works for the piano and the violin or the violoncello and the piano with voice accompaniment.
Ref. SABAM

DECAIX, Marianne Ursula
French composer. b. 1715; d. 1751. She composed sacred songs.
Ref. 465

DECARIE, Reine (Sister Johane d'Arcie)
Canadian pianist, singer, teacher and composer. b. Montreal, January 4, 1912. Her parents were singers and musicians and she learnt to play the piano at a very early age. She studied at the Vincent d'Indy School of Music and obtained a B.M. in singing in 1941. She received an M.M. in singing from the University of Montreal in 1944 and a diploma in composition in 1948. She studied the history of medieval music and composition of the Renaissance at Boston University and psychophony at Cap Rouge in Quebec. Among her teachers were Claude Champagne (composition), Rodolphe Plamondon, Roger Filiatreut, Alfred Laliberte, Bernard Diamant and Dr. Harry Seitz. She sang on television and radio. She taught singing at the Vincent d'Indy School and one of her pupils was Louise Lebrun. PHOTOGRAPH.
Compositions
ORCHESTRA
Fugue instrumentale, op. 70 (1947)
Poème symphonique, op. 87 (1953)
PIANO
Sonatine, op. 74 (1948)
VOCAL
Chanson de mon pays, op. 86 (France Decarie) (1952) (Ed. Bonne Chanson)
Four seasonal poems (1956)
Le jeu de ma subconscience, op. 75, 4 poems (1948)
SACRED
Cantate à Ste-Cecile, op. 31 (soloist and ch) (1944)
Cantate jubilaire, op. 111 (1960)
Psalm 90, op. 15 (soloist and ch) (1970)
Chante, ma joie, op. 155 (ch)
Messe solennelle en l'honneur de Marie, op. 76 (ch a-cap) (1948)
Mass of the Annunciation, op. 142 (1971)
Messe complete en l'honneur de St. Pie X, op. 109 (1958)
Messe française, op. 115 (1960)
Te Deum! Reconnaissance! op. 160 (1975)
Psalms (1955)
Chants liturgiques pour une messe de mariage, op. 118 (1965)
Afferentur virgines post eam, op. 120 (1968)
Dies est laetitiae, op. 102 (1956)
Elevation à i'Immaculee, op. 90 (1954)
Jam sol recedit, op. 72 (3 vces a-cap) (1947)
Magnificat jubilaire, op. 89 (1954)
Palinods, op. 35, nos. 1 and 2 (1950)
Quem vidistis, op. 103 (1956)
Regina virginum, op. 153 (1974)
Songs
Ref. composer, 133

DECKER, Pauline (nee de Schaetzel)
German operatic singer and composer. b. Berlin, 1812. She made a brilliantly successful debut at the Berlin Opera in the role of Agathe in *Der Freischutz*. She sang in a number of operas and was acclaimed for her youth, beauty, fine diction and purity of voice. She retired from the theatre after her marriage.
Compositions
VOCAL
Duet for two sopranos, op. 5
Ten songs, ops. 6-15
Two duets for soprano and alto, op. 17
Ref. 26, 276, 347

DEDEKAM, Sophie
Norwegian pianist, singer and composer. b. Arendal, 1820; d. 1894.
Compositions
VOCAL
De to Drosler (C. Winther) (1 or 2 vces and pf) (Hansen)
En Aften ved Alsteren (vce and pf) (Warmuth)
Sympathier (Warmuth)
Romances and songs, 3 vols (1 or 2 vces and pf) (Hansen) incl:
Den gamle Mester
Det gamle Arnested
Hvad jeg elsker
I Skogen Smaagutten gik Dagen lang
Naar solen ganger til Hvile (W. Thisted)
Sang af Arne
Taaren
Ungbirken
Vaarbebudelse
Vi modes i Himmelen
Ref. Oslo University Library, 20, 276, 297, 331

DEDERICH, Hilda
Early 20th-century composer.
Compositions
PIANO
The land of Nod
Laughing water
Moonlight through the cedar tree
Moths
The old fair
A question
Ref. 473

DEDIEU-PETERS, Madeleine
French composer. b. 1889.
Compositions
CHAMBER
Septet (pf, fl, trp and strs)
Three small preludes (tim, perc, hp and strs)
Piano quintet (Prix Halphen)
Three pieces (str qrt) (1920) (Serart, 1922)
Second string quartet (1925) (Marmontel Prize) (Serart, 1927)
Ref. 41

DEE, Margaret. See DIEFENTHALER, Margaret Kissinger

DEICHMANN, Julie
19th-century German composer.
Compositions
VOCAL
Grundlos (vce and pf)
Meerfrau (vce and pf)
Was bleibt (vce and pf)
Ref. 276, 347

DEJAZET, Hermine
French composer. b. 1829; d. 1880.
Composition
OPERETTA
La Diable Rose, in 1 act (1859)
Ref. 226, 276, 307

DEL CARRETTO, Cristina
20th-century Italian composer.
Compositions
PIANO
Canzonette (Ricordi)
Capriccio
La gratudine
Norvegienne
Polka
Romanza
Three mazurkas
Valzer melodico
SACRED
Ave Maria (vce and pf)
Ref. Ricordi (Milan)

DEL RIEGO, Theresa (Teresa Clotilde) (Mrs. Leadbetter)

English pianist, violinist singer and composer of English-Spanish parentage. b. London, April 7, 1876; d. London, January 23, 1968. She studied singing under Marie Withrow and Francesco Tosti. She studied the violin, the piano and singing at West Central College, London and received Trinity College certificates for the same subjects. She began writing music at the age of nine and composed over 250 works.

Compositions

CHAMBER

Air in E-flat (vlc and 2 pf; also orch)

VOCAL

Invocation (solo, ch and orch) (1944)
Gloria, song cycle
Homing, duet
Songs incl.:
L'amour
Eloge du rive
A garden is a lovesome thing
Harmony
Heart my heart
Little red-coat
Love is a bird
My gentle child
Oh, dry those tears
Red clover
Scotch love song
Slave song
Spring gardens
A star was his candle

SACRED

Ave Maria
The Madonna's lullaby

Bibliography

Etude, November 1932, p. 762.

Ref. 142, 276, 347, 433

DELABORDE, Elie Miriam

French pianist, teacher and composer. b. February 7, 1839; d. December, 1913. She was a pupil of Charles-Henri Alkan and Ignaz Moscheles and taught at the Paris Conservatoire.

Compositions

ORCHESTRA

Attila, overture

CHAMBER

Pieces

OPERA

La reine dort

VOCAL

Songs

Ref. 465, 505

DELAHAYE, Cecile

French composer. b. Paris, September 20, 1931. She studied at the conservatoires of Versailles and Paris under N. Dufourcq and at the Schola Cantorum under D. Lesur. After 1959 she studied under A. Jolivet. She won a prize for music history and worked for the Revue Musicale Suisse. She is of Breton origin and her music shows Celtic influence.

Compositions

CHAMBER

Piano quartet (1966)
Flute sonata (1966)
Violin sonata (1966)

PIANO

Deux intermezzi (1960-1963)
Dialogues (1959)
Légendes marines (1962)
Portrait (1962)
Preludes (1966)
Sonate (1965)

VOCAL

Poèmes de la brise (1964)

Ref. 1

DELANDE, Jo. See RAMAKERS, Christiane Josee

DELAVAL, Mme.

French harpist and composer. ca. 1794. She was extremely popular in London for her virtuoso harp playing.

Compositions

CHAMBER

Prelude and Divertimento for the Harp and Pianoforte, with accompaniment for 2 French Horns, ad libitum, op. 3 (London: Birchall, 1795)
Three Sonatas for the Harp or Pianoforte, with an Accompaniment for the Violin, op. 1 (Birchall, 1790)
Other pieces

VOCAL

Les adieux de l'infortune Louis XVI à son people, cantata (1794)
Songs

Ref. 66, 125, 226, 260, 276, 347, 405

DELBOS, Claire (pseud. of Louise Justine Delbos)

French violinist and composer. b. 1910; d. April, 1959.

Compositions

ORGAN

Deux pièces (Herelle) (Lemoine, 1935)
L'offrande à Marie (Herelle) (1935)
Paraphrase pour la fête de tous les saints, le jour des morts, les dimanches .... (Lemoine)

Ref. 172, 236

DELBOS, Louise Justine. See DELBOS, Claire

DELIPHARD, Mme. See DANCLA, Alphonsine Genevieve-Lore

DELIRE, Alice

Belgian pianist, singing teacher and composer. b. October 10, 1890. She composed ballet music, light music and songs.

Ref. SABAM

DELIZ, Monserrate

20th-century Puerto Rican pianist, teacher and composer. She taught music and the piano at the Boston Conservatory and was active in the research, collection and compilation of folk music of her native country, whilst working at the University of Puerto Rico.

VOCAL

Renadio del cantar folklorico de Puerto Rico (1951; 2nd edition, 1952); collection of folk songs, games, ballads and choruses
ABC de cantos infantiles, educational songs for children.

Publications

El himno de Puerto Rico. 1957. A study on the anthem of Puerto Rico.
Translated into Spanish: Libro primero de piano, John Thompson.

Bibliography

Negron Munoz, Angela. *Mujeres de Puerto Rico desde el periodo de colonizacion hasta e primer tercio del siglo XX*. San Juan: Imprenta Venezuela, 1935.
Salgado, M.C. *In Memoriam of M. Deliz*.

Ref. 278, 523

DELL'ACQUA, Eva (Acqua, Eva Dell') (Dall'Acqua)

Italian-Belgian singer and composer. b. Brussels, February 25, 1856; d. Ixelles, February 12, 1930. She was the daughter of a distinguished Italian painter, Cesare Dell'Acqua. Her song *Villanelle* achieved worldwide fame and her opera and operettas were frequently performed in Belgium. She was also a fine singer. DISCOGRAPHY.

Compositions

ORCHESTRA

Chanson provencal

CHAMBER

Aveu romance (vln and pf) (Schott)

PIANO

Aline, polka (Georges Ortel)
Gavotte
Tirailleurs

VOCAL

Menuet (vce and orch)
Miguarde (vce and orch)
Prière d'amour (vce and orch)
Songes, valse chantée (vce and orch)
Vision (vce and orch)
Songs incl.:
Serenade joyeuse, duet
Amour defunt (Schott)

Bonjour Guzon
Chanson due rouet
Demade
Ein Traumbild
J'ai vu passer l'hirondelle
L'hirondelle
Je donnerais
Ne cherchez pas
Orphan's Christmas
Quand les pommiers sont fleuries (Schott)
Springtime (Williams)
Valse tendre
Villanelle
Virelai

OPERETTA
Zizi (1906)
La Bachelette (1896)
Le Feu de Paille (1888)
Les Fiancailles de Pasquin (1888)
L'Oeillet Blanc (1889)
L'Oiseau Bleu
Une Passion (1888)
Le Prince Noir (1882)
Quentin Metzys (1884)
Une Ruse de Pierette (F. van der Elst) (1903)
Le Secret de l'Alcade (1888)
Tambour Battant, comic operetta (orch) (1900)
Le Tresor de l'Emir (1884)

THEATRE
Au Clair de la lune, pantomime (1891)

Ref. 105, 226, 276, 297, 307, 347, 563

DELLE GRAZIE, Gisella (pseud. Gisella Raedzielg)

19th-century Italian composer.

Compositions

OPERA
Atala or I Pelli Rosse (under pseudonym) (1894)
Il Passaporto del Droghiere, or Passaporto (1896)
La Trecciaiuola di Firenze (1895)

Ref. 307, 502

DELMOULY, Marie Mathilde (Rica)

Greek pianist and composer. b. Athens, 1904. Her mother was an eminent pianist. Marie showed an early interest in music and at the age of 12 entered the Royal Conservatory in Brussels. After four years of study under Professors C. Guericks and E. Bosquet, she won a prize with distinction; four years later she won a prize for virtuosity. In Athens, she continued her piano studies under Woldemar Freeman and gave concerts at the Athens Conservatory, Parnassus, the French-Greek Lyceum, the Hellenic American Union and the French Institute. PHOTOGRAPH.

Compositions

ORCHESTRA
Piano concerto

CHAMBER
Elegie (vln and pf) (1958)
Three humoresques (vln and pf) (1956)
Two caprices (vln and pf) (1962)

PIANO
Arabesques
Etudes
Humoresques
Impromptus
Intermezzos
Marches
Poème
Printemps
Scherzos
Toccatas

VOCAL
Forty melodies or poems (vce and pf)

Ref. composer

DELMOULY, Rica. See DELMOULY, Marie Mathilde

DELORME, Isabelle

Canadian violinist, lecturer and composer. b. Montreal, November 14, 1900. She studied the piano under Sister Madeleine-Marie and Arthur Letondal, the violin under Albert Chamberland and Agostino Salvetti and theory under Claude Champagne. She became an licentiate of the Quebec Academy and taught at the Quebec Provincial Conservatory in Montreal.

Compositions

ORCHESTRA
Berceuse dans le style ancien (pf and str orch)

CHAMBER
Andante (str qrt)
Fantasy, chorale, fugue (str qrt)
Prelude and fugue (str qrt)
Suite (str qrt)

ORGAN
Chorale in A-Minor on a Bach theme
Chorale in G-Major on a Bach theme
Chorale varié sur un thème de Bach
Prelude

SACRED
Ave Maria, motet (ch a-cap)
Gloire à toi maison neuve (ch)
Prière du soir (ch)
Cor Jesu, motet
O salutaris, motet
Prière à la Vierge
Tantum ergo, motet

Ref. 85, 133, 347

DELYSSE, Jean. See ROESGEN-CHAMPION, Marguerite Sara

DEMAR (Demars), Therese

French harpist and composer. b. 1801. She was the daughter of the composer Sebastian Demar. She studied the harp under Francois Nadermann at the Paris Conservatoire and in 1808 or 1809 gave a spiritual concert for the Empress of France, who called her a chamber virtuoso. DISCOGRAPHY.

Compositions

CHAMBER
Pot-pourri d'airs connus (hp and pf) (Paris: Benoit Pollet; Orleans: Demar; Wurzburg: Demar)
Six nouvelles romances (hp and pf) (Benoit Pollet)

HARP
Cavatine variée d'apres Di tanti Palpiti de Tancredi de Rossini (2 hp)
Theme favori de Mysta tagoju uk raschennyil, variations (Demar)
Il est parti, romance

VOCAL
Hercule et Omphale (vce and orch)
Les Avantages du buveur (vce and orch)

Ref. 125, 128, 129, 226, 276, 312, 347, 563, 653

DEMAREST, Alison

20th-century American composer.

Compositions

SACRED
Easter introit (mix-ch and org) (Canyon Press)
He is not here, but is risen (Canyon)
Little lamb (Canyon)

Ref. 190

DEMAREST, Anne Shannon

American pianist, editor, teacher and composer. b. Waldron, AR, November 26, 1919. She studied at Oklahoma College for women, Ballard School, New York University, Hunter College and Denver University. She was assistant editor of children's publications for the Friendship Press, New York from 1938 to 1943 and then taught the piano in Denver and Arvada. She was director of the Arvada Recorder Consort.

Compositions

ORCHESTRA
Banff panorama symphonic suite (also pf) (1973)

PIANO
Children's pieces

VOCAL
Jungle cruise, suite (narr and pf) (1979)

Publications

Bobby Lee's Keys, eight-book piano course. 1969.

Ref. 475

DEMAREST, Victoria

Composition

SACRED
Hymn of the last supper

Ref. ILWC

DEMARQUEZ, Suzanne

French critic and composer. b. Paris, July 5, 1899; d. Paris, October 23, 1965. She studied under Robert Lortat and at the Paris Conservatoire, where she won first prizes for history of music and score reading (1921 to 1922). DISCOGRAPHY.

Compositions

ORCHESTRA

Sonatine pour orchestra (1932)

CHAMBER

Suite de valses (strs) (1931)
Variations, interlude et tarantelle (qnt) (1938)
String quartet, op. 10 (1927)
Pièces breves (fl, vlc and perc) (1946)
Petite suite (vln and pf) (1941)
Rapsodie lyrique (vln and pf; also orch) (1930)
Sonata (vln and pf) (1923)
Sonatine for flute and piano (1953)
Bosphore (vlc) (1957)
Deux pièces (hp) (1929-1930)
Sonata pour violoncelle, op. 6 (1923)
Variations sur un thème oriental (fl) (1957)

PIANO

Barcarolle (2 pf)
Two sonatines (1927-1928)

VOCAL

Songs with string quartet (1943)
Quatre contrerimes (vce, fl and hp) (1932)
Vocal quartets a-cappella
Deux poèsies d' A. de Musset (1948)
Deux sonnets de Gerard de Nerval (1942)
Quatre poèmes (D. Cools) (1930)

OPERA

Thesée à Marseille

Publications

Purcell. Biography. Paris, 1951.
A. Jolivet. Biography in *Musiciens d'aujourd'hui.* Paris, 1958.
M. de Falla. Biography. 1963; trans. into English, 1968.
H. Berlioz. Biography in *Musiciens de tous les temps*, Vol. 42. Paris, 1969.

Ref. 8, 9, 13, 17, 20, 44, 52, 70, 85, 94, 96, 109, 347, 649

DEMARS, Therese. See DEMAR, Therese

DEMBO, Royce

American pianist, teacher and composer. b. Troy, NY, March 19, 1933. She studied composition and the piano at the Eastman School of Music, Syracuse University and Ithaca College. After her marriage in 1953 she lived in Taiwan for two years where she taught music at Chinese and American schools. On her return to the United States she took composition courses at UCLA and in 1970 received her M.M. (composition) from the University of Wisconsin. Since then she has taught privately. Her works have been performed in Taiwan, Indonesia, Scotland and the United States. PHOTOGRAPH.

Compositions

CHAMBER

Sextet (fl, ob, cl, bsn, hn and pf) (1980)
Woodwind quintet (fl, ob, cl, bsn and hn) (1974)
Suite (2 t-rec, b-rec and vla da gamba) (1973)
Woodwind trio (1976) (1st prize Nat. Fed. Music Clubs)
Piano trio (1974)
Trio (fl, cl and pf)
Dance (cl and pf) (1970)
Hebraic reflections (fl and pf) (1977)
Humoresque (fl and pf) (1972)
Humoresque (ob and pf) (1968)
Pastorale (treble rec and pf) (1970)
Three pieces (bsn and pf) (1975)
Two twelve tone sketches (cl and pf) (1971)
Suite (fl) (1965)

PIANO

Triptych (4 hands) (1978)
Metamorphosis, 3 pieces (1976) (1st prize, State Contest)
Dance No. 1 (1968)
Haiku No. 1 and 2

VOCAL

Gems (Wilfred Owen) (mix-ch) (1980)
The little ghost (E.S. Millay) (w-ch and pf) (1974)
Songs of Pan (James Joyce) (S, fl and hp) (1979)
Four poems (Emily Dickinson) (reader and fl) (1974)
Four songs (Elinor Wylie) (S, hn and pf) (1979)
Song cycle (Anna Akhmatova) (S and pf) (1978)
Three songs (E.S. Millay) (S and pf) (1972)
Three songs from the Chinese (S and pf) (1975)

SACRED

Concord hymn (mix-ch and org) (Emerson) (1973)

OPERA

The Audience, chamber opera (1981)

OPERETTA

Beowulf, drama for children (early insts) (1979) (comm WI, Art Board)

Ref: composer, 474

DEMESSIEUX, Jeanne

French organist, pianist, lecturer and composer. b. Montpellier, February 14, 1921; d. Paris, November 11, 1968. She studied at the Paris Conservatoire under Tagliaferro and Dupre and won first prize for harmony in 1937, the piano in 1939, fugue in 1939 and the organ in 1941. She was organist for the Church of the Saint-Esprit in Paris from 1933 to 1962 and at the Madeleine from 1962. She taught the organ at the Conservatory of Nancy from 1950 to 1952 and at the Royal Academy of Liege, 1953 to 1968. She toured Europe and made a highly successful debut in the United States in 1953. She was a member of the jury for the International Organ Contest held at Haarlem. DISCOGRAPHY.

Compositions

ORCHESTRA

Poeme pour orgue et orchestre. op. 8 (1952) (Durand, 1952)

ORGAN

Prélude et fugue en ut, op. 13 (Bornemann)
Réponse pour le temps de Pâques (Durand)
Sept meditations sur le Saint-Esprit (Durand, 1947)
Six études, op. 5 (1946) (Bornemann, 1973)
Triptyque, op. 7 (1949) (Durand)
Twelve chorale preludes on Gregorian themes (Boston: McLaughlin and Reilly, 1951)

VOCAL

La Chanson de Roland (m-S, ch and orch)

SACRED

Te Deum, op. 11 (1965) (Durand, 1971)

Bibliography

Denis, P. *Les Organists français d'aujourdhui: Jeanne Demessieux. L'Orgue* no. 75, 1956.
Paap, W. *In Mens en Melodie*, 24, 1969.
Trieucolleney, Christine. *Jeanne Demessieux: une vie de luttes et de gloire.* Paris: Les Presses Universelles, 1977.

Ref. 1, 7, 9, 15, 22, 26, 44, 74, 79, 94, 177, 236, 347, 400, 406, 490, 524, 563

DEMILLIERE, Marthesie

18th-19th-century American composer. She lived in or near New York between 1812 and 1818.

Compositions

PIANO

Pieces incl.:
Malbrook with four variations in C-Major (4 hands) (1812)

Bibliography

Richard J. Wolfe. *Secular Music in America 1801-1825.* Vol. I. New York Public Library. 1964.

Ref. Susan Kagan (New York), Jeannie G. Pool (Los Angeles)

DEMING, Mrs. L.L.

19th-century American composer.

Compositions

VOCAL

I cannot sing tonight (vce and pf) (Boston: H. Tolman, 1854)

Ref. 228

DENBOW, Stefania Bjornson

American organist and composer. b. Minnesota, December 28, 1916. She studied at the University of Minnesota, where she obtained a B.A. in 1937 and an M.A. in 1939. She studied composition under Karl Ahrendt and later under James Stewart from 1971 to 1974 at Ohio University. She was a church organist from 1949. She won the MU Phi Epsilon composition award in 1973 and 1977 and the NFMC special award of merit, 1976. PHOTOGRAPH.

Compositions

CHAMBER

String quintet
Surtsey string quartet (Seesaw Music Corp., 1974)
Trio Islandia, 3 mvts (pf, vln and vlc) (Seesaw, 1976)
The interior life, 3 cantilenes (hp) (1980)
Three Hellenic stanzas (pf)

ORGAN
Anthem for two seasons (1983)
Exultatio (Seesaw, 1975)
Suite: chorale; chorale prelude; fugue; passacaglia (1971)
Six interludes (1973)
Portrait
VOCAL
By the willows, song cycle (S, vln, ob and hp)
Four songs of the Eremite Isle
SACRED
All glory for this blessed morn, cantata (soloists, ch and org) (Seesaw, 1976)
Christ is risen, cantata (soloists, ch and cham ens) (Seesaw, 1972)
Contemporary mass
Magnificat (m-S, ch and cham ens) (1976)
Ref. composer, 142, 185, 228, 347, 477, 624

DENEUVILLE, Irene
Belgian composer. b. June 21, 1946. In France, in 1981, she received first prize at the 'Festival d'Evreux' and was laureat of 'Jeunes Talents'. She set the works of many Belgian poets to music.
Compositions
THEATRE
Les mots, les sons et les rythmes, for children (1975)
Les trois coups (1977)
VOCAL
Poèsie et chanson contemporaines (1975)
Ref. Belgian Music Info. Centre

DEPECKER, Rose
19th-century composer.
Compositions
PIANO
Chrysalide (Enoch)
Two fugues: Fugue à quatre parties sur un sujet de Charles Gounod; fugue à trois parties sur un sujet de Alphonse Duvernoy (Schott)
Reveuse (Enoch)
Ref. 297

DEPPEN, Jessie L.
American pianist, teacher and composer. b. Detroit, July 10, 1881; d. Los Angeles, January 22, 1956. She studied at the American Conservatory in Chicago under Adolph Weidig and Leopold Godowsky and taught the piano in Cleveland, OH. She made her debut at Steinway Hall, New York, 1896.
Compositions
PIANO
Pieces
VOCAL
Songs incl.:
Eleanor
In the garden of tomorrow
Japanese sunset
Oh, Miss Hannah
Ref. 142, 292, 347

DERBYSHIRE, Delia
British composer. b. 1937.
Compositions
ELECTRONIC
Potpourri
FILM MUSIC
The Legend of Hell House (1973)
Ref. 497

DERHEIMER, Cecile
French soprano and composer. d. Paris, August 5, 1896. She composed sacred organ pieces and masses.
Ref. 226

DERING, Lady Mary (Harvey)
English composer. b. 1629; d. 1704. She was the wife of Sir Edward Dering and a pupil of Henry Lawes.
Compositions
VOCAL
And This Is All? What, One Poor Kiss
In Vain, Fair Chloris, You Design (vce and pf) (London: Staine & Bell)
When First I Saw Fair Doris's Eyes (pub. in Second Book of Ayres & Dialogues by Henry Lawes)
Bibliography
Kerr, Jessica. *Mary Harvey-Lady Dering. Music and Letters*. Jan. 23, 1944.
Ref. 8, 91

DERLETH, Julia. See BEZDEK, Sister John Joseph

DERLIEN, Margarete
German composer. b. 1900.
Compositions
VOCAL
Von Fruehling und Floetenblasen, cantata (chil-vces and fls) (Barenreiter)
Ich trag mein Licht (chil-vces and inst) (Barenreiter)
Von Sonne und Regen (chil-vces and fls) (Barenreiter)
Ref. Barenreiter catalogue

DES ROCHES, Gilbert. See LEGOUX, Julie, Baroness

DESCAT, Henriette
20th-century French composer.
Composition
OPERA
Les Menhirs de Carnac (1914)
Ref. 431

DESCHAMPS, Jacqueline
French composer.
Composition
PIANO
Doudou chien savant
Ref. Billaudot (Paris)

DESFOSSES, Elisabeth Françoise, Countess
18th-century French composer. She composed three sonatas for the piano with optional violin or cello accompaniment.
Ref. 119, 125

DESHAYES, Marie (Mme. la Popliniere)
19th-century French singer and composer.
Compositions
CHAMBER
Quintette No. 1, grand format (Jobert)
Quintette No. 2 (fl, ob, cl, hn and bsn) (Jobert)
Ophicleide (Jobert)
PIANO
Brises du parc, waltz (2 pf) (Jamin)
Cake-Walk (Hamette)
Chambon (Pinatel)
Confidences de Marguerite, waltz (Ploix)
Patrouille espagnole (Hachette)
Stella-Waltz (Grus)
VOCAL
Bienfaisance (Billaudot)
Commençons nos chansons (Billaudot)
Credo du travail (Benoit)
Il se croit banni de mon coeur! (Giroud)
Nuit (Billaudot)
Prix (Billaudot)
Qui donne vite donne deux (vce and pf) (Benoit)
Reveil des moissonneurs (Billaudot)
Sort de l'hirondelle (Billaudot)
Travail (Billaudot)
Ref. 129, 297

DESPORTES, Yvonne Berthe Melitta

French pianist, lecturer and composer. b. Coburg, Saxony, July 18, 1907. She was the daughter of the composer Emile Desportes. She studied at the Paris Conservatoire under Jean and Noel Gallon, Paul Dukas, and Marcel Dupre and won first prizes in harmony in 1927, counterpoint and fugue in 1930, composition in 1930 and piano accompaniment. She received the Grand Prix de Rome in 1932 and lived in Rome from 1933 to 1937. After 1943 she lectured at the Paris Conservatoire, in solfege until 1959 and then in counterpoint and fugue. She also taught piano accompaniment at the Lycee la Fontaine. She was made a Chevalier of the National Order of Merit. PHOTOGRAPH.

Compositions

ORCHESTRA

Symphony No. 1 (1958)
Symphony No. 2 (1964)
A batons rompus (2 perc and orch) (1957)
Caprice champêtre (vln and orch) (1955)
L'exploit de la coulisse, ballad (trb and orch) (Presser)
Piano concerto No. 1 (1957)
Piano concerto No. 2 (1960)
Symphonic variations (pf and orch) (1946)
Hercule et les geants, symphonic poem
Rondeau du voyageur ou Resurrection, symphonic poem
Une libellule dans les violettes (cl and str orch) (1980)
Et on dansera à toujours (1980)
Hommage à la Duchesse Anne (1980)
Si on chantait le Poitou (1980)
Si on chantait la Normandie (1980)
Three suites (1934-1938)

CHAMBER

Autour de pan, 10 pièces (ens) (Leduc, 1975)
Bach-annales (fl, gtr and str qrt) (1981)
Imageries d'Antan (2 trp, hn, trb and b-trb or tuba) (Billaudot, 1979)
La maison abandonée, sextet
Piano quintet
Ceux du village (4 cl) (Billaudot, 1980)
Les feux ardents de la Saint Jean (4 acdn) (1981)
Conversations (ob, cl and bsn) (1981)
Les ménéstriers du ciel (fl, gtr and hp) (1981)
La complainte de Quasimodo (bells) (1980)
The star (bells and pf) (Schott)
Baboum pan-pan (perc and pf) (Billaudot, 1981)
Une batterie rechargée (perc and pf) (Billaudot, 1981)
Branlebas de combat (perc and pf) (Billaudot, 1981)
Chansons percutants (perc and pf) (Billaudot, 1981)
Un choix difficile (a-sax and perc) (1980)
Cocktail percutant (perc and pf) (Billaudot, 1981)
Le coeur battant (perc and pf) Billaudot, 1981)
Des chansons dans la coulisse (b-trb and pf) (Billaudot, 1980)
En cueillant les lauriers (perc and pf) (Billaudot, 1981)
L'homme des cavernes (b-cl and acc) (1981)
L'horloge jazzante (a-sax and gtr) (Billaudot, 1984)
Les marionettes (xy and pf) (Schott)
Un méchant tambour (perc and pf) (Billaudot, 1981)
Un petit air dans le vent (b-trb and pf) (Billaudot, 1980)
Un petit concert pour lutins (perc and pf) (Billaudot, 1981)
Le petit echiquier (cl and pf) (Billaudot, 1981)
Petite pièce (perc and pf) (Schott)
Prélude, intermezzo et fugato (perc and pf) (Schott)
Six danses pour syrinx (fl and gtr) (Billaudot, 1980)
Six variations (vln and pf)
The Spanish dancer (castanets and pf) (Schott)
Un soufflé profond (b-trb and pf) (Billaudot, 1981)
Tambour battant (perc and pf) (Billaudot, 1981)
Tim xy tam (perc and pf) (Billaudot, 1981)
Timpano et xylonette (perc and pf) (Billaudot, 1980)
Eglises de Paris (org)
La naissance du papillon (cl)
Pièce melodique (trb) (Billaudot, 1981)
Pièce technique (trb) (Billaudot, 1981)
Vingt petites pièces en forme d'études (xy)
Vision celeste (cl)
Vision cosmique

GUITAR

Pot pourri folk (2 gtr) (1981)
Coctail français
En schumannisant (Billaudot, 1981)
Guitare mozartienne (Billaudot, 1981)
Histoires d'arbres (Billaudot, 1980)
Modes d'antan (Billaudot, 1980)
Play Bach dances (Billaudot, 1981)

PIANO

Danses d'autrefois (Salabert)
La Foire aux croutes, 12 small pieces
Hommage à Maurice Emmanuel (Billaudot, 1984)
Idoles au Rebut (Puteaux, 1980)
Potagers sous la grele (Puteaux, 1980)
Other pieces

VOCAL

Discordances (solo, ch and orch) (1966)
Seven abstract poems (mix-ch and perc) (1959) (Eschig)
Eight vocal pieces (mix-ch) (1959)
Choral pieces (ch a-cap and opt perc)
Concerto for ten instruments, percussion and voice quintet (1965)
Octet (vocal qrt and str qrt)
Sonate pour un baptême (S, fl, a-sax, perc, hpcd and pf) (1959)
Le bon vin (Bar and pf) (1980)
La lettre T. (Bar and pf) (1980)
Polka, duet (vce and pf) (Schott)

SACRED

Et Jesus calma la tempête, oratorio
Une nuit dans la Cour des Miracles, cantata (1945)
La paix du Christ

BALLET

Eternel renouveau (1942)
Le Rossignol et l'orvet (with song and ch) (1936)
Les Sept Péchés capitaux (1938)
Symphonie, mechanical ballet (1961)
Trifaldin (1934)

OPERA

Chanson de Mimi Pinson (1952)
La Farce du carabinier (1943)
Le Forgeur de merveilles (after O'Brien) (1965)
Maitre Cornelius (after H. Balzac) (1940)

ELECTRONIC

The Old Fashioned Dolls (vib and pf) (Schott)

Publications

Comment former l'oreille musicale. 1970.
Initiation au langage musical, 3 vols. Billaudot, 1981.
Guide servant d'apprendre aux traites d'harmonie. 1960.

Ref. composer, 8, 12, 13, 17, 44, 76, 81, 84, 94, 96, 109, 172, 280, 477, 574

DEVISME (Devisme da Valgay), Jeanne-Hippolite Moyroud

French pianist, singer and composer. b. Lyons, 1765; d. 1808. She married the theatre and opera director Anne Pierre Jacques Devisme.

Compositions

OPERA

Praxitele ou la Ceinture, in 1 act (Paris, 1802)
La Double Recompense (Paris, 1805)

Ref. 128, 129, 162, 225, 263, 307

DEVISME DA VALGAY, Jeanne-Hippolite. See DEVISME, Jeanne-Hipollite

DEVONSHIRE, Georgiana, Duchess of. See CAVENDISH, Georgiana

DEWEY, Mrs. W. See THOMPSON, Mary Frances

DEWITZ, Hildegard. See KAZORECK, Hildegard

DEYO, Ruth Lynda (Mrs. Charles Dalton)

American pianist and composer. b. Poughkeepsie, NY, April 20, 1884; d. Cairo, Egypt, March 4, 1960. She studied the piano under William Mason and Teresa Carreno and composition under MacDowell. She first appeared in concert at the age of nine at the World Columbian Exposition in Chicago, 1893, then performed in Berlin in 1904, played with orchestras in the United States and Europe and in recitals with Kreisler and Casals. She settled in Egypt in 1925 and concentrated upon composition. She wrote *Diadem of Stars* (an attempt at a reconstruction of ancient Egyptian music) to be performed on the occasion of the marriage of King Farouk of Egypt, which was an attempt at a reconstruction of ancient Egyptian music. The prelude was performed by Stokowski and the Philadelphia Orchestra in 1931.

Compositions

ORCHESTRA

Orchestral suite

PIANO

Pieces

OPERA
The Diadem of Stars (Charles Dalton)
Ref. 22, 70, 85, 142, 226, 228, 347

DEYTON, Camilla Hill
American clarinetist, pianist and composer. b. Raleigh, NC, September, 23 1952. She studied the piano and the clarinet at Southern Park Music School in Charlotte, NC,. Later she studied the clarinet, the piano, theory and voice at the Brevard Music Center, North Carolina, in 1968 and at Canon Music Camp at the Appalachian State University, in 1969. She obtained her B.Mus. (composition and piano) at Converse College, Spartansburg, SC, in 1974 and her M.Mus. (theory) at the University of North Carolina, 1978. One of her compositions was selected for performance at the University of South Carolina New Music Festival in Columbia, in 1974. PHOTOGRAPH.
Compositions
ORCHESTRA
Andante and allegro (1974)
CHAMBER
The wasp, in 3 mvts (2 cl, 2 hn and tba) (1974)
Saturday blues, in 2 mvts (b-flat cl) (1972)
Reminder, op. 7, in 3 mvts (pf) (1974)
VOCAL
Do I believe? (vce and pf) (1972)
Once when I died (vce and pf) (1972)
Songs for Monday (vce and pf) (1974)
Songs for Thursday (vce and pf) (1974)
Ref. composer, 457

DEZEDE, Florine
18th-century French composer. She was the daughter of Nicholas Dezede (Dezaides) a composer of popular operas. The dates of birth and death usually assigned to her are really those of her father, 1740 and 1792.
Compositions
PIANO
Barbier et Seville: Je suis Lindor, transcription (Gallet)
Blaise et Babet, overture (also vln) (Le Boulch)
Couplet (Gallet)
OPERA
Lucette et Lucas, comedy in 1 act (Paris; Forgeot, 1781)
Ref. 26, 128, 297

D'HARCOURT, Marguerite Beclard. See BECLARD D'HARCOURT, Marguerite

D'HARDELOT, Guy. See HARDELOT, Guy d'

D'HORVOST. See GOUBAU D'HAVORST, Leopoldine

DI NOGERO, Francisco. See BAUER, Emilie Frances

DI TINGOLI, Cesarina Ricci di. See RICCI, Cesarina di Tingoli

DIA, Beatrice de. See BEATRICE DE DIA, Countess

DIAKVNISHVILI, Mzisavar Zakharevna
Soviet composer. b. Tbilisi, October 27, 1938. She studied composition under A.D. Machavarian and graduated from the Tbilisi Conservatory in 1963.
Compositions
ORCHESTRA
Kartina mogilshchik (1960)
Heroic poem (1963)
Little suite (str orch) (1968)
CHAMBER
String quartet (1968)
Sonata (vln and pf) (1956)
Improvisation (fl and pf) (1961)
Andante expressivo allegro molto (gtr) (1970)
PIANO
Two sonatas (1957, 1963)
Sonatina (1970)
Variations (1957)
Six pieces (1968)
VOCAL
Lyrical songs (Bar and orch) (1971)
Three miniatures (G. Tabidze) (vce and pf) (1968)
Cycle of children's songs
Light songs
Ref. 21

DIAMOND, Arline
American teacher and composer. b. New York, January 17, 1928. She obtained a diploma from the Juilliard School of Music and then studied at the Eastman School of Music, where she obtained a B.M. under Bernard Rogers. Her composition teachers were Ralph Shapey, Benjamin Boretz, Stefan Wolpe, Felix Greissle and Bernard Wagenaar. She received her M.A. from Columbia University. She teaches privately. DISCOGRAPHY.
Compositions
ORCHESTRA
Florida symphony (1954)
CHAMBER
Cantata (wind insts) (1969)
Composition (vlc qrt) (1976)
Small fugue (str qrt)
String quartet No. 1 (1950)
String quartet No. 2 (1965)
String quartet No. 3 (1968)
String quartet No. 4 (1969)
String trio (1980)
Student trio (cl, trp and fl) (1979)
Trio (fl, vlc and pf) (1981)
Duo (cor anglais and vla) (1979)
Duo (vln and vla) (1976)
Duo (vln and vlc) (1975)
Duo (2 vlc) (1977)
Eight pieces (vlc and pf) (1981)
Eight pieces (vln and pf) (1981)
Perambulation (vln and vla) (1972)
Sketch (tba and pf) (1981)
Composition (cl)
Flute pieces (1980)
Harp solo (1980)
PIANO
Seven pieces on Greek modes (1981)
Three pieces (1974)
Three pieces (1976)
VIOLIN
Composition (1964)
For Beth (1981)
In celebration of (1979)
Sonata (1980)
VOCAL
Rites de passages (Marie France) (8 vces and 8 perc) (1975)
Afternoon on a hill (Edna St. Vincent Millay) (vce and pf) (1982)
Bobolink (E.S. Millay) (vce and pf)
Let the winds roar (Tennyson) (vce and pf) (1979)
The rabbit (E.S. Millay) (vce and pf) (1981)
Songs (vce and pf; also vce and fl)
Ref. composer, 137, 190, 562, 563

DIANDA, Hilda
Argentine conductor, musicologist, professor and composer. b. Cordoba, April 13, 1925. She studied composition in Buenos Aires under Honorio Siccardi from 1942 to 1950. She was awarded a fellowship from the General Direction of Culture of Argentina. She studied conducting under Hermann Scherchen in Venice, 1949 to 1950. In 1958 she was invited by the French Government to join Pierre Schaeffer's Groupe de Recherches Musicales. In 1959 Italian Radio-Television invited her to study electronic music in the Studio di Fonologia, Milan and in 1961 she received a fellowship from the Kranichstein Music Institute. The Italian Government honored her with the Medal of Cultural Merit in 1964 for her work in Italy. From 1967 to 1970 she was professor of composition, instrumentation, orchestration, technical and orchestral conducting at the School of Fine Arts of the National University of Cordoba, Argentina. She was also titular conductor of the Chamber Orchestra of the School and toured extensively in Argentina, Latin America, and Europe and participated in a number of international festivals, including the Internationale Ferienkurse fuer neue Musik held in Darmstadt, Germany, in 1960 and 1961. DISCOGRAPHY. PHOTOGRAPH.

Compostions
ORCHESTRA
Ludus-1 (vlc and orch) (1965) (Schott)
Resonancias-3 (vlc and orch) (1965) (Schott)
Nucleos (2 pf, 10 perc and str orch) (1963)
A Copernico (1973)
Canto (1972)
Diptico (1962) (Buenos Aires: Argentina de Musica)
Impromptu (1970) (Schott)
Ludus 2 (1969)
Musica para arcis (str orch) (1951) (Argentina de Musica)
Obertura concertante (1957)
Obertura para titeres (1948)
Scherzo-adagio-final (1950)
CHAMBER
Concertante (vlc, winds, d-b and perc) (1952) (Argentina de Musica)
Percussion-11 (11 perc) (1962) (Argentina de Musica)
Andante allegro-scherzo (wind qnt and str qrt) (1947)
Ode a Heine (2 trp, 3 trb and 3 perc) (1974)
Divertimento A-6 (6 perc) (1969-1970)
Concierto (vln and str qnt) (1955) (comm Asociacion de Conciertos de Camara de Buenos Aires) (Argentina de Musica)
Quintet (fl, ob, cl, bsn and hn) (1957)
Resonancias (cl, trp, vlc and 2 perc)
Resonancias-1 (5 hn) (1964) (Argentina de Musica)
Rimas (fl, trp, c-bsn and perc) (1963) (Argentina de Musica)
String quartet No. 1 (1947) (1st prize, Interamerican chamber music competition, 1953)
String quartet No. 2 (1959-1960)
String quartet No. 3 (1962) (Argentina de Musica)
Ida-nda (3 perc) (1969)
Trio (fl, ob and bsn) (1953)
Adagio-allegro (vlc and pf) (1952) (Ricordi Americana)
Celebracions (vlc and pf) (1974)
Estructuras nos. 1-3 (vlc and pf)
Diedros (fl) (1962) (Argentina de Musica)
Figuras sonoras-3 (bandoneon) (1962)
Ludus-3 (org) (1969)
PIANO
Resonancias-2 (1964)
Three sonatas (1956) (Ricordi Americana)
VOCAL
Dos brumas y luces (ch and perc) (composer) (Argentina de Musica)
Resonancias-5 (ch a-cap) (1967-1968)
Canciones (vce, gtr, vib and perc) (Rafael Alberti-Canciones del Litoral) (1962) (Argentina de Musica)
La flauta de jade, five songs on Chinese text in French translation (1954) (Ed. Argentina de Musica)
Tarde, La (Antonio de la Torre) (vce and pf) (1949) (Argentina de Musica)
ELECTRONIC
'a, 4' (vlc and magnetic tape) (1962)
A-7 (vlc and magnetic tape) (1966)
Dos estudios en oposicion (1959)
Publications
Musica en la Argentina de Hoy. Buenos Aires: Proartel Ed. 1966.
Ref. composer, 4, 17, 20, 45, 52, 94, 109, 189, 322, 371, 390, 406, 524, 563

DIBDIN, Isabelle Perkins

English soprano and composer. b. Southwold, Suffolk, January 19, 1828.
Compositions
VOCAL
Sweetly the birds were singing (London: Goulding)
Tambourines (London: J. Longman, Clementi and Co.)
Ref. 85, 347

DICHLER-SEDLACEK, Erika (pseud. M.T. Spenger)

Austrian pianist and composer. b. Vienna, June 23, 1929. She studied at the Vienna Musikhochschule under J. Dichler and gave many concerts on radio and television. She composed piano pieces.
Publications
Leitfaden fuer den Klavierunterricht.
Ref. 70

DICK, Edith A.

19th-century English composer.
Compositions
CHAMBER
Piano pieces
VOCAL
Sweet slumber (vce and pf)
When daffodils unfold (vce and pf)
Ref. 276, 347

DICK, Ethel A.

20th-century English composer of piano pieces and songs.
Bibliography
Barrel, Edgar A. *Etude*, November 1929, p. 805.
Ref. 347

DICKISON, Maria Bobrowska

American composer of Polish origin. b. Warsaw, March 16, 1902. She was a member of ASCAP.
Ref. 39

DICKONS, Mrs. Maria. See POOLE, Maria

DICKSON, Ellen (pseud. Dolores)

English composer. b. Woolwich, 1819; d. Lyndhurst, July 4, 1878. She lived in Lyndhurst and was an invalid from youth. Her songs acquired great popularity in her day.
Compositions
VOCAL
Songs incl.:
All yesterday I was spinning
Clear and cool
Destiny
Goldilocks
The land of long ago
O my lost love
Pack clouds away
The racing river
She walked beside me
Tell her not when I am gone
Unchanged
Ref: 6, 85, 276, 653

DIE, Beatrice de, See BEATRICE DE DIA, Contessa

DIECKMANN, Jenny

West German composer.
Composition
VOCAL
Wanderlied aus Schweden (3 w-vces)
Ref. Eres catalog 1976

DIEFENTHALER, Margaret Kissinger (pseud. Margaret Dee)

20th-century American pianist, teacher and composer. She composed piano pieces and songs.
Ref. 40, 347

DIEHL, Paula Jespersen

Contemporary American composer.
Composition
ELECTRONIC
In the field and groundwater (sounds, pf ens, elec keyboard, gtr, elec gtr, elec d-b and perc) (1984)
Ref. AMC newsletter

DIEMER, Emma Lou

American harpsichordist, organist, pianist, professor and composer. b. Kansas City, MO, November 24, 1927. She studied under Richard Donovan and Paul Hindemith at the Yale School of Music, where she obtained a B.M. in 1949 and an M.M. in 1950. Other teachers included Ernst Toch, Roger Sessions, Bernard Rogers and Howard Hanson at the Eastman School. She won a Fulbright Scholarship in composition and the piano and studied at the Royal Conservatory in Brussels, 1952 to 1953. She was a composition student at the Berkshire Music Center in the summers of 1954 and 1955 and in 1960 obtained her Ph.D. from the Eastman School of Music. She received several composition awards. In 1959 she won the Arthur Benjamin award and in 1959 to 1961 a Ford Foundation-National Council Young Composers Project Grant, which enabled her to become composer-in-residence at Arlington, VA. Since 1962, she has received the American Society of Composers, Authors and Publishers Standard Award annually. She was assistant professor of theory and composition at the University of Maryland from 1965 to 1970 and since 1971 has been professor of theory and composition at the University of California, Santa Barbara. In 1977 she received the Yale School of Music certificate of merit and in 1981 the Standard award from ASCAP for publications and performances. DISCOGRAPHY. PHOTOGRAPH.

Compositions

ORCHESTRA

Symphony No. 2 (American Indian themes) (1959) (Seesaw Music Corp., 1981)
Symphony No. 3 (Symphony Antique) (1960) (Belwin Mills)
Chamber concerto (hpcd and small orch) (1959) (Seesaw, 1979)
Concert piece (org and orch) (1985)
Fairfax, festival overture (pf and orch) (1967)
Flute concerto (1977) (Texas Southern Music Co.)
Harpsicord concerto (1958) (Seesaw, 1979)
Piano concerto (1954)
Suite for orchestra (1954) (Seesaw, 1981)
Festival overture (1961) (Philadelphia: Elkan-Vogel, 1968)
Youth overture (1959) (Belwin Mills, 1962)
Rondo concertante (1960) (Boosey & Hawkes, 1971)
Pavane (str orch) (1961) (Carl Fischer, 1962)

BAND

The brass menagerie (1960) (Belwin Mills, 1967)
La eag, symphonic band (1981)

CHAMBER

Toccata (fl ch) (1968) (C. Fischer, 1972)
Sextet for winds and pianoforte (1962) (Seesaw, 1976)
Woodwind quintet No. 1 (1960) (Boosey, 1962)
Music for woodwind quintet (OUP, 1976)
Movement (fl, ob, cl and pf) (Seesaw, 1976)
Music for woodwind quartet (OUP, 1976)
Quartet (vln, vla, vlc and pf) (1954) (Seesaw Music, 1976)
Movement (fl, ob and org) (1974) (C. Fischer, 1976)
Serenade (fl and pf) (1954)
Sonata (fl and hpcd or pf) (1958) (Southern Music, 1973)
Sonata (vln and pf) (Seesaw, 1976)
Suite (fl and pf) (1947)
Summer of 82 (vlc and pf) (1983)
Echo space (gtr) (1980)
Solo trio (one player with xyl, vibes and mar) (for Marta Ptaszynska, 1980) (Ft. Lauderdale, FL: Music for Percussion, 1982)
Toccata (mar) (New York: Music for Percussion, 1957)

CARILLON

Bellsong (1983)
Interlude
Three pieces (1972) (Michigan: Carilloneurs Guild, 1976)

ORGAN

Elegy (2 players) (1983)
Celebration, 7 hymn settings (Minneapolis: Augsburg, 1976)
Contrasts (1976)
Declarations (Seesaw, 1976)
Fantasie (OUP, 1976)
Fantasy on O sacred head (Boosey, 1972)
He leadeth me, hymn setting (OUP, 1976)
Improvisation on a drawing by Ann Skiold (1981)
Jubilate and contrasts (Augusburg, 1976)
Little toccata (1978)
Pianoharpsichordorgan (1974) (Seesaw, 1976)
Seven hymn preludes (1965)
Ten hymn preludes (1960)
Three fantasies on Advent - Christmas hymns (1978)
Toccata and fugue (1969) (Seesaw, 1976)
Toccata (1964) (OUP, 1967)
Other pieces

PIANO

Homage to Cowell, Cage, Crumb and Ezerny (2 pf) (Ft. Lauderdale: Plymouth Music, 1983)
Suite (2 pf)
The bells (E.A. Poe) (4 hands) (Boosey, 1961)
Four on a row (Scribner's Sons, 1972)
Encore (1982) (Arsis Press, 1983)
Seven etudes (C. Fischer, 1972)
Sound pictures (Boosey, 1971)
Time pictures (Boosey, 1962)
Toccata (1979) (Arsis, 1979)

VOCAL

As a heart longs (mix-ch and opt acc) (1956) (H.W. Gray)
At a solemn music (Milton) (mix-ch and pf) (Boosey, 1970)
Away, delights (m-ch) (1979)
Before the paling of the stars (C. Rossetti) (mix-ch, pf or org) (1957) (Elkan-Vogel)
California madrigals (mix-ch, pf or org) (1976)
Dance, dance my heart (mix-ch, org and perc) (1967) (C. Fischer, 1973)
Laughing song (mix-ch, pf and hn) (1974)
A little song of life (mix-ch, pf or org) (1964)
Love is a sickness, full of woes (mix-ch) (1974)
A musical instrument (w-ch and 2 pf) (1979)
O to make the most jubilant song (Whitman, Tennyson) (mix-ch and pf) (C. Fischer, 1972)
Romance (mix-ch and pf) (1974)
Shepherd to his love (Marlowe) (mix-ch, pf and fl) (Marks Music, 1963)
So I have seen a silver swan (ch) (1974)
Spring (mix-ch and pf) (1965)
Three madrigals (Shakespeare) (mix-ch and pf or org) (1960) (Boosey, 1962)
Three poems (Ogden Nash) (m-ch and pf) (Harold Flummer, 1965)
Verses from the Rubaiyat (Omar Khayyam) (mix-ch) (Boosey, 1970)
Weep no more (w-ch) (1979)
When in man's music (mix-ch and pf) (1978)
Wild nights! Wild nights! (mix-ch and pf) (1978)
Your friends shall be the tall wind (ch) (1960)
Four poems (Alice Meynell) (S and cham ens) (C. Fischer, 1976/1977)
Four Chinese love poems (S and hp or pf) (Seesaw, 1976)
Madrigals three (Campion, Donne, Shakespeare) (C. Fischer, 1972)
A miscellany of love songs (vce and pf) (1972-1973)
Songs of reminiscence, song cycle (Dorothy Diemer Hendry) (S and pf) (1980) (Seesaw, 1981)
Tell me dearest, what is love? (1979)
Three mystic songs (S and Bar) (Seesaw, 1976)
Choral works
Song cycles

SACRED

Palm Sunday, cantata (1963)
St. Chrysostom, cantata (1956)
A service in music and poetry, cantata (1967)
Anniversary choruses (mix-ch and orch) (C. Fischer, 1970)
Alleluia (w-ch) (C. Fischer, 1962)
The Angel Gabriel (mix-ch and pf or org) (1959)
Anthem of faith (mix-ch and pf or org) (1966)
For ye shall go out with joy (mix-ch and pf) (C. Fischer, 1968)
Four carols (Christmas) (w-ch) (Elkan-Vogel, 1962)
Fragments from the Mass; Kyrie, Gloria, Credo, Sanctus, Agnus Dei (w-ch) (Marks Music, 1961)
Honor to Thee (mix-ch, pf and org) (1957)
How majestic is Thy name (ch and pf or org) (1957)
I will give thanks (mix-ch and pf or org) (1959)
The Lord is my light (mix-ch and pf or org) (1977)
Noel: Rejoice and be merry (mix-ch and pf or org) (1959)
Now the spring has come again (St. Piae Cantiones, 1582) (mix-ch and pf) (Boosey, 1970)
O come, let us sing unto the Lord (mix-ch and pf) (C. Fischer, 1961)
Praise the Lord (mix-ch, brass qnt and org) (C. Fischer, 1975)
The prophecy (w-ch) (Boosey, 1974)
Psalm 134 (mix-ch) (Seesaw, 1976)
Sing, O heavens (mix-ch) (C. Fischer, 1975)
Strong Son of God (mix-ch and pf or org) (1976)
Thine, O Lord (ch and pf or org) (1961)
Carols for organ (1979)
Celebration - such hymn settings (1970)
I stand beside the manger stall (1960)
Magnificat (S, A and opt pf or org) (Marks, 1963)
Mary's lullaby (Helen Barkley) (vce and pf) (Boosey, 1960)
Men are fools that wish to die (1974)
O to make the most jubilant song (mix-ch and pf or org) (1970)
O to praise God again (1972)
Outburst of praise, Latin hymn (trans Dryden) (mix-ch and pf)
Praise of created things (St. Francis of Assisi) (vce and org or pf) (Belwin Mills, 1964)
Psalm 121 (vce and org) (1980)
A Spring carol (William Blake and the Song of Solomon) (vce and pf) (C. Fischer, 1962)
Three Advent/Christmas fantasies (1980)
Three hymn anthems (ch, brass, org, perc) (1980)
To Him all glory give (D.D. Hendry) (Elkan-Vogel, 1962)

ELECTRONIC

Add one (elec pf and tape) (1980)
Of the past (tape) (1980)
Lightly stepped a yellow star (computer tape) (1983)
Patchworks (tape) 1977
Presto canon (tape) (1980)
Quartet (fl, vla, vlc, hpcd and tape) (1974) (Seesaw, 1976)
Scherzo (tape)
Trio (fl, ob, hpcd and tape) (1974) (Seesaw, 1976)

Bibliography
Notes, vol. 35, no. 4, June, 1979.
Ref. composer, AMC newsletter, 39, 40, 77, 94, 142, 146, 190, 206, 228, 280, 347, 397, 415, 457, 474, 563, 574, 622

DIESENDRUCK, Tamar
20th-century composer. She won the Prix de Rome in 1983.

DIETRICH, Amalia
German pianist and composer. b. Dresden, May 2, 1838. She first performed in public at the age of eight.
Compositions
CHAMBER
Piano pieces
VOCAL
Songs incl.:
Schneegloeckchen (Hoffarth)
OPERETTA
Les amours de my lord
Ref. 276, 307

DILAL
Pre-Islamic Arabian musician and composer. She was the legendary inventor of the lyre.
Ref. 502

DILCARO, Mrs.
17th-century Irish composer.
Composition
VOCAL
O! Had I been by fate decreed (Dublin: Hime, 1800)
Ref. 65

DILLER, Angela
American pianist, teacher and composer. b. Brooklyn, New York, August 1, 1877; d. May, 1968. She studied under MacDowell, Goetschius and Shreyer and held a Mosenthal Scholarship at Columbia University in 1900. She was head of the department of theory at the Music School Settlement for seventeen years and then became director of the Diller-Quaile School in New York. She was co-founder of the 'Adeski Chorus' and 'A Cappella Singers' of New York.
Compositions
PIANO
Air and dances from the 19th-century
Gigue in B
Off we go
Teaching works
VOCAL
Numerous songs
Publications
Diller and Quairle Piano Book.
Ref. 276, 292, 433

DILLER, Saralu C.
American violinist, actress and composer. b. Ohio, June 3, 1930. She received her B.M. from the Baldwin-Wallace Conservatory and her M.M. from the University of Maryland. She also studied at the University of Colorado where she was staff accompanist, from 1966 to 1968 and under Carlisle Floyd at Florida State University, 1969. She was director-actress of the Nomad Playhouse in Boulder from 1959 to 1972 and director of the Vail Summer Theatre, Vail, CO, 1973. She was a violinist with the Akron Symphony Orchestra, Akron, OH, 1956 to 1959.
Compositions
CHAMBER
The bad quartet (brass) (1970)
Three sketches (pf) (1966)
VOCAL
Ship of death, two poems (ch and orch) (1971)
Format #1, #2, #3 (6 players; vce and 2 perc) (1970)
Songs:
The feast (1968)
In that strange city (1968)
Lonely (1968)
Outside in (1969)
OPERETTA
The Little Prince, folk operetta for children (1972)
INCIDENTAL MUSIC
Cave Dwellers, play (1963)
A Child Is Born, play (1962)
ELECTRONIC
Ding-an-sich (3 players; 1 perc, 1 tape and 3 vces)
Ref. 142

DILLON, Fannie Charles
American pianist, teacher and composer. b. Denver, CO, March 16, 1881; d. Altadena, CA, February 21, 1947. She studied at Claremont College, then in Berlin under Kaun and in New York under Rubin Goldmark. She studied the piano under Godowsky. Other teachers included Urban, Grainger and Edwin Hughes. She taught privately, at Pomona College from 1910 to 1913 and after 1918 in Los Angeles schools. DISCOGRAPHY.
Compositions
ORCHESTRA
A Western concerto, in A-Flat Major, op. 117 (pf and orch)
In a mission garden, symphonic pastorale, op. 52 (timp, perc, hp and str orch)
The Alps (1920)
Celebration of victory (1918)
The cloud (1918)
Letter from the Southland
Prince Su Wing Wong
CHAMBER
String quartet
Trio (pf, vln and vlc)
Pieces (vln)
Woodland flute call (org)
PIANO
At the chickadee's nest, op. 54, no. 1
A song of life, op. 108, fantasy sonata (1939)
Birds at dusk
Brooklets
Eight descriptive compositions, op. 20: April moods; Birds at dawn; The desert; Evening; Forest mourning dove; Ocean depth; A song of the Sierras; Under the pines (Cincinatti: J. Church, 1917)
From the Chinese, op. 93: Butterfly wings; Winter moonlight; Chinese temple scene (New York: Composer's Press, 1944)
Harp of the pines
Heights sublime
Heroic etude, op. 6 (J. Church, 1917)
Kleine suite, op. 1 (Stahl)
The legend of Finn MacCool, ballade
Melodic poems of the mountains
Menuett, op. 3 (Stahl)
Quiet pools
Six preludes, op. 8 (J. Church, 1908)
Sonata in C-Minor
Songs of the seven hills, op. 65: Panorama; On the Olive Hill; Shimmering pool (G. Schirmer, 1927)
Zwei Stuecke, op. 2: Scherzo; Sommerturm (Stahl)
VOCAL
Dawn, cantata
Hellas, cantata
Sunset, cantata
An April day (New York: Hardy Brothers, 1949)
Message of the bells, op. 38 (Los Angeles: C.R. Foster, 1917)
Songs incl.:
Aroma of the pines
I will lift mine eyes unto the hills
The spirit
Temple of trees
Time sweeps on
ELECTRONIC
Chinese symphonic suite, op. 96 (tim, 2 perc, vib, 2 hp and strs)
Bibliography
Musical Courier, LXXIII/20, Nov. 16 1916, 45. California's brilliant composer-pianist, Fannie Dillon.
Ref. 39, 70, 74, 142, 226, 228, 260, 280, 292, 297, 347, 353, 562, 563, 597

DIMENTMAN, Esfir Moiseyevna
Soviet pianist, conductor, folklorist and composer. b. Penza, July 6, 1908. From 1925 to 1928 she was pianist and concertmistress of the state entertainment enterprise in Penza. For the next four years she conducted choirs in schools and factories in Leningrad and in 1936 graduated as a choir conductor from the Leningrad Conservatory. At the same time she worked as a folklorist, collecting folk songs of various peoples of the Soviet Union. From 1936 to 1950 she was choir conductor of the Ashkhabad opera and ballet and also directed children's operas. She moved to Moscow in 1950. She received the Artistic Award of the Turkmen SSR in that year.

Compositions
PIANO
Polka
Three children's pieces on Turkmen themes
VOCAL
Choruses in Turkmen language (Muzgiz)
Kak khorosho, duet (N. Fatyanov)
Schastlivaya zhizn, duet (Kerbabayev)
Songs (A. Keshokov, F. Balkarova) (1955)
Two volumes of Turkmen folk songs (1948)
FILM MUSIC
Svadebnyi podarok
Ref. 87

DIMITRIU, Florica

Rumanian pianist, conductor, librarian, professor and composer. b. Iasi, December 8, 1915. She studied at the Conservatory of Iasi from 1935 to 1938 and 1940 to 1942. Her teachers included Sofia Teodoreanu (theory and solfege), Alexandru Zirra (harmony), Antonin Ciolan (conducting), Eliza Ciolan (piano) and Radu Constantinescu (chamber music). She was pianist-accompanist at the Iasi Opera from 1940 to 1941 and music librarian at the conservatory, 1942 to 1944. She taught choral singing at the conservatory and conducted choirs and orchestras in Iasi. She occupied various positions in Rumanian radio, becoming musical director of Rumanian Radio-Television in 1954. From 1964 to 1968 she was professor of chamber and orchestral music at Music School No. 1 and 2 in Bucharest. She toured Rumania as a pianist, as a soloist and with chamber groups and as a conductor of symphony orchestras. In 1968 she was awarded the Order of Merit for Culture.

Compositions
ORCHESTRA
Dans moldovenesc, Nos. 1 and 2 (1956)
Five miniatures (small orch) (1950)
Romanta, lyric piece (1955)
Triptic simfonic (1971)
CHAMBER
Dance (ob and pf) (1956)
Sonata in E-Minor (vln and pf) (1960)
PIANO
Five miniatures (1953)
Suite for children (1948)
Suite in Rumanian style (1949)
VOCAL
Cintec pentru viata noua, cantata (C. Teodori) (soloists, ch and orch) (1951)
Partidului, cantata (soloist, chil-ch and small orch) (with Florin Dimitriu) (1948)
Ancearul (Pushkin) (B and orch) (1956)
Ecou de romantă (G. Bacovia) (vce and orch) (1957)
Intrebare (O. Goga) (vce and orch) (1957)
Somnul rozelor (M. Codreanu) (vce and orch) (1958)
Prisaca, suite of songs (T. Arghezi) (chil-ch and pf) (1960)
De pe-o bună dimineată (O. Cazimir) (vce and pf) (1955)
Gospodina (O. Cazimir) (vce and pf) (1954)
Jocul anotimpurilor, small suite of songs (D. Miga) (vce and pf) (1951)
Other songs (Pushkin, Topirceanu and other Rumanian poets) (vce and pf)
INCIDENTAL MUSIC
O poveste cu ursuleti, film (with Florin Dimitriu) (1952)
Ariciul răutăcios (with Florin Dimitriu) (1955)
Ref. 81, 94, 148, 195

DINESCU (Dinescu-Lucaci), Violeta

Rumanian teacher and composer. b. Bucharest, July 13, 1953. Educated at G. Lazar Lyceum and the Gheorghe Enescu School of Music. From 1973 she studied music and composition at the Ciprian Porumbescu Music Academy, graduating with distinction, 1978. She began teaching at the Enescu School in 1978. In 1984, she studied for a doctorate in musicology at Heidelberg. She participated in International Youth Festivals of Bayreuth and attended the modern composition course at Darmstadt, 1980. In the same year she became a member of the Union of Composers of Rumania. She is a member of NACUSA. She has won several composition prizes: In 1965, 1976 and 1980, she won prizes from the Union of Rumanian Composers; in 1982, second prize in the Mannheim International competition; in 1983, third prize in the Canadian Okanaglan Music Festival and third prize in the Women and the Arts Festival in the United States. In 1984 she received a bursary from the City of Mannheim. PHOTOGRAPH.

Compositions
ORCHESTRA
Akrostichon (1983)
Anna Perenna (1979)
Memories (str orch) (1980)
Verwandlungen (1978)
CHAMBER
Auf der Suche nach Mozart (ens) (1983)
Aion (cl, bsn, vlc, 2 d-b and perc) (1982)
Septett von 1984
Alternanzen (wind qnt)
Melismen (rec qnt)
Satya V (bsn, cl, vln and d-b) (1981)
String quartet (1974)
Three miniatures (sax qrt) (1982)
Trio (ob, cl and bsn) (1982)
Arabesken (fl and perc) (1980)
Echos I and II (pf and perc) (1982)
Echos III (org) (1982)
Elogium (trp and trb) (1981)
Sonata (ww and pf) (1973)
Immagini (fl) (1982)
Intarsien (vlc) (1983)
Para quitara (gtr) (1982)
Prelude (hpcd) (1982)
Satya I (vln) (1981)
Satya II (bsn) (1981)
Satya III (d-b) (1981)
Satya IV (cl) (1981)
PIANO
Pieces (1970)
Story (1977) (Editura Musicala)
VOCAL
Change me into a silver bird, cantata (ch and orch) (1975)
Game (chil-ch, perc and orch) (1978)
Apagic (ch) (1981)
Ballade (ch) (1980)
Country of songs (ch) (1978) (Editura Musicala)
Flowers (ch) (1979)
In meinem Garten (ch) (1981)
Latin sentences (ch) (Editura Musicala, 1977)
Lied in einer Floete (ch) (1980)
Lied durch Blumen (ch) (1980)
Liederland (ch) (1980)
Sonnenuntergang (ch) (1980)
Tamina (ch) (Editura Musicala, 1979)
Euraculos (m-S and cl)
Mondlicht (m-S and org) (1981)
Stalactites (vce and pf) (1972)
BALLET
Die Historie von der schoenen Lau (Eduard Moerike)
OPERA
Hunger und Durst, chamber opera after play by Eugene Ionesco (Roland Hess)
Ref. composer, Frau und Musik

DINESCU-LUCACI, Violeta. See DINESCU, Violeta

DINIZ, Thereza da Fonseca Borges

Brazilian composer. d. Recife, September 7, 1911.

Composition
PIANO
Barcarola
Ref. International American Musical Revue vol. III 1980

DINIZULU. See MAGOGO KA DINIZULU, Constance, Princess

DINN, Freda

English composer. b. Herne Hill, 1910.

Compositions
(All published by Schott)
VOCAL
Four folk songs (1-2 S, recs, pf ad lib and strs)
TEACHING PIECES
Several pieces (vln, rec and pf)
ARRANGEMENTS
Sonata in D-Minor (Johann C. Pepusch) (rec and continuo)

Publications
Early Music for Recorders. Schott, 1974.
The Recorder in the School. Schott.
Teaching Material. Schott.

Bibliography
The Quarterly Journal of the Music Library Association, vol. 35, no. 4, June 1979.
Ref. Schott, *Notes*, Otto Harrassowitz (Wiesbaden)

DINO, Janita. See TAJANI MATTONE, Ida

DIRKS, Jewel Dawn
American assistant professor and composer. b. Lovell, WY, November 16, 1951. She studied under Joseph Schwantner, receiving her M.M. in 1975 and then under Warren Benson, gaining her D.M.A. in 1977. She received her B.M. from Columbia State University. She was an assistant professor at Radford University from 1979.
Compositions
MISCELLANEOUS
Aus dem Handbuch (1982)
Ear-bird (1983)
Ecliptic (1976)
Elegy for Kathy's harp (1977)
My sister's recipes (1982-1983) (comm Radford Foundation)
Ref. 625

DISAPPEARING PIANIST. See LEGINSKA, Ethel

DITMARS, Elizabeth
20th-century American composer.
Composition
ELECTRONIC
Small rain (tape, bsn and pf) (1977)
Ref. International Congress of Women Composers

DITTENHAVER, Sarah Louise
American authoress, teacher and composer. b. Paulding, OH, December 16, 1901; d. Asheville, NC, February 4, 1973. She studied at the Oberlin Conservatory and at the Cosmopolitan Conservatory, Chicago, then taught privately and in schools. In 1961 she was made a Fellow of the International Institute of Arts and Letters, Switzerland. She has won a number of composition awards. In 1969 she received an honorable mention in the ASCAP award for piano teaching material.
Compositions
PIANO
Let's play duets (2 pf) (1947)
My pony and I (2 pf) (1949)
Sailing the rainbow (2 pf) (1949)
Among the daffodils (1947)
Carolina cakewalk
The children's parade
Lyric to the moon
Mardi gras
Night wanderer (1950)
Robin in the pine tree (1943)
Sleepy wind (1941)
Pied Piper's tune
Purple pansy (1944)
Toccata in D
Tumbling creek
Where go the clouds?
Witches ride
VOCAL
Songs incl.:
Hurdy-gurdy playing in the street
Lady of the amber wheat
Once more, beloved
Passage
Concert songs
SACRED
Alleluia, Jesus Child (mix-ch)
Bless the Lord, O my soul (mix-ch)
Light of the lonely pilgrim's heart (youth ch)
Trust in the Lord (unison choir)
Anthems
MISCELLANEOUS
March of the astronauts
Street fair
Sunrise canter
Publications
Pick a Tune. Books 1 and 11.
Ref. 39, 40, 142, 646

DIVINE ADELINA. See PATTI, Adelina

DIXIE BLUEBIRD. See WALLACE, Mildred White

DIXON, Esther
20th-century American composer. She composed choral works and songs.
Ref. 40, 347

DLUGOSZEWSKI, Lucia
American pianist, poetess, teacher, writer and composer. b. Detroit, June 16, 1925. The only child of Polish parents, she began writing poems and songs and playing the piano at the age of three. She commenced studying the piano at the Detroit Conservatory of Music at the age of six, under Agelageth Morrison. Whilst there, she gave a solo recital, playing both Bach and her own compositions. She studied medicine at Wayne State University from 1946 to 1949 then changed to the arts, moving to New York to study the piano under Grete Sultan. Lucia attended the Mannes School of Music, 1950 to 1951. She also studied composition privately under Felix Salzer and Edgard Varese. In 1947 she received the Tompkins literary award for poetry and in 1966 won the National Institute of Arts and Letters award. In 1972 she was given a BMI-Thorne Fellowship. She was the first woman to win the Koussevitzky Prize of the International Critics' Award. From 1960 she taught periodically at New York University and the New School for Social Research. She taught and composed for the Foundation for Modern Dance, Erick Hawkins' Dance Company, New York. She invented over 100 percussion instruments made of glass, metal, plastic and wood. The best known of these is her timbre piano which has bows and plectra in addition to a keyboard. She has performed her own music in Europe, Canada and America. DISCOGRAPHY. PHOTOGRAPH.
Compositions
ORCHESTRA
Amor new tilting night (1978)
Arithmetic points (1955)
Beauty music 2 (invented perc and cham orch) (1965)
Beauty music 3 (timbre pf and cham orch) (1965)
Four attention spans (1964)
Hanging bridges (also str qrt) (1968)
Instants in form and movement (timbre pf and cham orch) (1957)
Kireji: Spring and tender speed (cham orch)
Orchestra structure for the Poetry of everyday sounds (1952)
Orchestral radiant ground (1964)
Skylark concert, an evening of music (cham orch) (1969-1970)
CHAMBER
Abyss and caress, concerto (trp and 17 insts) (1975)
Angels of the inmost heaven (trps, trbs and horn) (1972)
Rates of speed in space (ladder hp and qnt) (1959)
Naked quintet (brass qnt) (1970)
Flower music (str qrt) (1959)
Pure flight (str qrt) (1970)
Transparencies 4 (str qrt) (1952)
Transparencies 3 (hp and vln)
Music for left ear in a small room (vln; also pf)) (1965)
Sabi music (vln) (1970)
Sonata (fl) (1950)
Space is a diamond (trp) (1970)
Transparencies 1 (hp)
Transparencies 2 (fl)
PERCUSSION
Kitetail beauty music (vln, timbre pf and invented perc orch) (1968)
Naked swift music (vln, timbre pf and invented perc orch) (1968)
Quick dichotomies (2 trp, cl and invented perc orch) (1965)
Suchness concert (invented perc orch) (1958-1960)
Archaic aggregates (timbre pf, ladder harps, tangent rattles, unsheltered rattles and gongs) (1961)
Beauty music (cl, timbre pf and perc) (1965)
Concert of man rooms and moving space (fl, cl, timbre pf and 4 unsheltered rattles in various locations) (1960)
Delicate accidents in space (unsheltered rattle qnt) (1959)
Leap and fall, quick structures (2 trp, cl, 2 vln and perc) (1968)
Percussion airplane hetero (1965)
Percussion flowers (1965)
Percussion kitetails (1965)
Suchness with radiant ground (cl and perc duo) (1965)
Suite from nine concerts (vln, cl, perc timbre and pf)
Swift diamond (timbre pf, trp and invented perc) (1970)
Velocity Shells (timbre pf, trp and invented perc) (1970)
PIANO
Swift music (2 timbre pf) (1965)
Archaic timbre piano music (1953-1956)
Melodic sonata (1950)
Music for small centers (1958)

Music for left ear (1958)
Sonata No. 1 (1949)
Sonata No. 2 (1950)
Sonata No. 3 (1950)
White interval music (timbre pf) (1961)
VOCAL
Fire fragile flight (vce and orch) (1973)
John Ashbery poetry (vces and cham orch)
Parker Tyler language (vces and cham orch)
Silent paper spring and summer friends songs (1953-1970)
OPERA
The Heidi Songs (John Ashbery) (1970)
Tiny Opera (1953)
DANCE SCORES
Agatholon algebra (timbre pf and orch) (1968)
Black lake (timbre pf and invented perc orch) (1969)
Cantilever 2 (pf and orch) (1964)
Dazzle on a knife's edge (timbre pf and orch) (1966)
Eight clear places (100-piece invented perc orch) (1958-1961)
Geography of noon (invented perc orch) (1964)
Here and now with watchers (timbre pf) (1954-1957)
Lords of Persia (2 trp, cl and invented perc orch) (1965)
Lords of Persia 2 (cham orch) (1968)
Lords of Persia 3 (cham orch) (1971)
Of Love .... or he is a cry, she is his ear, (brass qnt and invented perc orch) (1971)
Openings of the eye (fl, perc and timbre pf) (1952)
Tight rope (cham orch) (1968)
To everyone out there (orch) (1964)
THEATRE
Desire, theatre structure (Picasso) (vce and timbre pf) (1952)
Moving space theater piece for everyday sounds (1949)
Tender theatre flight nageire (sound and movement of cl, timbre pf and perc orch) (1970)
Ubu Roi, for the Living Theatre (Jarry) (orch of everyday sounds) (1952)
INCIDENTAL MUSIC
Guns for the trees, film (cham ens) (1961)
Variations on Noguchi, film (vces and sounds) (1953)
Women of Trachis, Ezra Pound's translation of Sophocles (1960)
A Zen in Ryoko-In, film (Ruth Stephan) (invented perc orch) (1971)
MISCELLANEOUS
Amor elusive April Pierce (1980)
Do not go gentle into that good night (D. Thomas) (1977)
Everyday sounds for e.e. cummings with transparencies (1951)
Strange tenderness of naked leaping (1978)

Publications

A New Folder. Poetry. 1969.
Article on philosophical aesthetics in *Main Currents*. With F.S.C. Northrup. 1970.
Composer/choreographer. Choreographer/composer. Dance perspectives 16. With Vivian Fine (q.v.). 1963.
Notes on New Music for the Dance. *Dance Observer*, Nov. 1957.
Other articles on modern dance.

Bibliography

Gruen, John. L.D. *Surfacing in Vogue*. Oct. 1970.
Hughes, Allen, And Miss D.. Experiments - A lot. *Time Magazine*, March 7, 1971.
Musician of the Month. *Hi Fidelity/Musical America*. June 1975.
Ref. 5, 142, 152, 153, 173, 228, 347, 397, 403, 415, 560, 563, 594, 610, 611, 622, 625

D'ORME, Valerie. See ATKINSON, Dorothy

DOANE, Dorothy

20th-century American pianist, authoress, publisher and composer. b. Leesburgh, IN. She composed instrumental works and songs.
Ref. 39, 40, 347

DOBBINS, Lori

20th-century American composer.

Compositions

CHAMBER
String quartet
VOCAL
Four songs (S and cham ens)
Ref. ILWC

DOBIE, Janet

Australian guitarist, pianist, teacher and composer. b. Armadale, Perth, 1936. She studied the piano under Rex Hobcroft and Edward Black and became a Licentiate . She taught the piano, the guitar and class singing at a school, then took up composition studies under James Penberthy, leaving teaching to concentrate on composing. DISCOGRAPHY.

Compositions

ORCHESTRA
Dimensions for strings
CHAMBER
Wind quintet
VOCAL
The restless Earth (ch and pf)
The child (S and pf)
Ref. composer, 563

DOBSON, Elaine

Australian pianist, lecturer and composer. b. England, 1945. Her family emigrated to Brisbane, Australia when Elaine was five and there she commenced piano lessons. She studied at the Newcastle Music Conservatory, NSW, for four years and then commenced a teaching career as a music specialist in the Outback. She then studied at the Queensland University, graduating in composition and completing an honors year. She lectured in composition at the Queensland Conservatory. She was awarded a Young Composer's Fellowship allowing her to work with symphony orchestras in each of the six states and to become composer-in-residence with the Australian Youth Orchestra.

Compositions

ORCHESTRA
Emersion (1969)
Kinesis (1970)
Music for flute and chamber orchestra (1973)
CHAMBER
9 (9 insts) (1971)
Now (6 insts) (1974)
Piece of Eb (str qrt) (1973)
Something to do with the moon (fl and perc) (1972)
Twice (cl and vln) (1972)
PIANO
Despite straight lines
Sets (1972)
Torn (1973)
VOCAL
Two Ruthies (narr, or cl, d-b and perc) (1971)
All in green (narr, fl, cl and hn) (1969)
Sh! (S, A, B, strs and perc) (1970)
The sun turning round: Oh don't mistreat the fly; At the butterflies; Traditional counting rhyme; The sunflower; Army; From the wheat of the peasants; There was an old man
SACRED
Five psalms of common (Christopher Middleton) (B, mix-ch and org) (1969)
OPERETTA
The Facemen
ELECTRONIC
Image & emotion (fl, cl and prep elec and concrete tape) (1969)
Ref. 440, 442, 443, 444, 445, 446

DOCKHORN, Lotte

19th-century German composer of songs.
Ref. 465

DODD, Dorothy

20th-century Australian composer.

Composition

THEATRE
Leading Lady, musical
Ref. 442

DODGE, Cynthia (Cynthia D. Crawford)

20th-century American composer.

Composition

OPERA
College Days
Ref. 141, 260, 347

DODGE, May Hewes
20th-century American pianist, violinist, teacher and composer. b. Wisconsin. She composed several operas.
Bibliography
Etude, June 1933, p. 4.
Ref. 347

DOETE
13th-century French troubadour of Troies, France. ca. 1260. She was a jongleur who sang her own compositions.
Ref. 218

DOLAN, Hazel
20th-century American composer. She composed piano pieces and songs.
Ref. 40, 347

DOLE, Caroline
19th-century American composer.
Composition
VOCAL
Answer to the messenger bird (S, A and pf) (Boston: C.H. Keith, 1848)
Ref. 228

DOLLEY, Betty Grace
20th-century American composer. She composed piano pieces, choral works and songs.
Ref. 40, 347

DOLMETSCH, Helene
French cellist, viola da gamba player and composer. b. Nancy, April 14, 1880; d. 1924. She was the daughter of the instrument maker Arnold Dolmetsch and educated in London and Germany. She performed from an early age. She composed for the cello.
Ref. 483

DOLORES. See DICKSON, Ellen

DOLORES, Maria Francisca de los
18th-century Mexican composer of songs.
Ref. 178

DOMANGE, Mrs. Albert. See MEL-BONIS

DOMBROWSKY, Maria
20th-century German composer. Between 1921 and 1929 she was a pupil of Hans Pfitzner.
Composition
VOCAL
Herbstweh (Eichendorff) (Fuerstner, 1929)
Ref. 189

DOMINIQUE, Monica
Swedish pianist, arranger, teacher and composer. b. July 20, 1940. She graduated from the Stockholm Conservatory in 1961 and qualified as a music teacher two years later. She played the piano in theatres and taught in Malmo.
Compositions
INCIDENTAL MUSIC
Storklas och lilleklas (with husband Carl-Axel) (1971)
Music for films and television
Ref. 20

DOMMEL-DIENY, Amy
French musicologist, professor and composer. b. Beauvais, June 21, 1894. She studied at the Schola Cantorum, Paris, where she obtained diplomas in harmony, counterpoint and Gregorian chant. She received the first international prize for composition by a woman in the GEDOK competition, Mannheim, Germany in 1950. She was assistant professor at the Sorbonne; professor at the Strasbourg and the Fresnes Conservatories and the Conservatory of the 6th District, Paris.
Compositions
VOCAL
The story of my dolls, duets (chil-vces)
THEATRE
Two musical plays for children
Publications
Harmonie Vivante. 6 parts. 18 vols. 1953-1976.
Ref. 206

DOMNA DE GASCOINA, Una. See ALAMANDA

DOMNA H.
13th-century French troubadour; thought by many to be the pseudonym of a male troubadour as the subject of the poem was believed to be too effeminate for a man to compose.
Composition
Rosin, digatz m'ades de cors (Rosin, tell me from the heart ...)
Ref. Dr. Margaret Nabarro (Johannesburg), 213, 303

DONAHUE, Bertha Terry
American composer. b. New York, June 3, 1917. She attained her B.A. (composition) from Smith College and received a certificate from the Dalcroze School of Music, New York. She received several commissions.
Compositions
CHAMBER
String quartet
String trio
Suite (ob, vla and hpcd)
Piano suite
VOCAL
Three elegies (Bar and str qrt)
The castle yonder, song cycle (S and pf) (Arsis Press)
Choral pieces
SACRED
Laude delle creature a dio, cantata (1973)
Make we joy, 15th-century carol (ch)
Christmas motet (Associated Music)
OPERETTA
Two operettas
Ref. composer, 142, 147

DONALDS, Belle
19th-century American composer.
Compositions
PIANO
Pieces
VOCAL
Songs incl.:
Bonny bride
My love
Ref. 276, 347

DONALDSON, Elizabeth
19th-century composer of instrumental music and songs.
Ref. 276, 347

DONALDSON, Sadie
American organist and composer. b. New York, July 2, 1909. She studied at Hunter College and the New School for Social Research. In 1970 and 1972 she won prizes in the hymn contests of the American Guild of Organists.
Compositions
VOCAL
Art songs
Ballads

SACRED
Hymns:
Hallelujah! Christ was born
Have you not known?
Thanksgiving hymn
OPERETTA
Horse Opera
Ref. 142, 347

DONATOVA, Narcisa
Slovak composer. b. Maratice, Uherske Hradiste, May 8, 1928. She studied composition privately under Desider Kardos, then at the Bratislava Conservatory and the High School of Musical Arts under Alexander Moyzes, graduating in 1952. She worked in the department of music at the Czechoslovak Television in Bratislava. Her compositions are influenced by folklore motifs.
Compositions
ORCHESTRA
Two symphonies
Dances of Eastern Slovakia
Overture 1921
Scherzo (small orch)
VOCAL
The Slovak land of mine, cantata
Eight children's choirs a cappella
Songs for community singing
For eternal glory, 3 patriotic songs
Liberty to all peoples, 6 revolutionary songs
Three lyric songs (T and pf)
Arrangements of folk songs
BALLET
The Weiner case, in 1 act
OPERA
The Forester's Wife
Inez
Ref. 32, 70, 197

DONCEANU, Felicia
Rumanian pianist, conductor, lecturer and composer. b. Bacau, January 28, 1931. She studied at the Bucharest Conservatory from 1949 to 1956, where her teachers were Ioan Chirescu (theory and solfege), Paul Constantinescu (harmony), Nicolae Buicliu (counterpoint), Mihail Jora (composition), Theodor Rogalski and Mircea Basarab (orchestration), Zeno Vancea (history), Tiberiu Alexandru (folklore), Dumitru D. Botex (choir conducting) and Eugenia Ionescu (piano). From 1956 to 1965 she was musical director of Editura Musicala of Bucharest. She has written studies and articles in *Muzica*, verses and texts for choral works and lectured and performed on radio. In 1961 she was mentioned at the International Composition Competition in Mannheim. DISCOGRAPHY. PHOTOGRAPH.
Compositions
ORCHESTRA
Three symphonic sketches: Inserare; Marele Grohotis; Istorioare vinatoresti
Mesterul Manole, symphonic poem (1956-1958)
Piatra craiului (1962)
CHAMBER
Concertino (wind and perc) (1968)
Trio (ob, cl and bsn) (1960)
Andante cantabile (vlc and pf) (1959)
Sonata in D-Minor (vln and pf) (1955-1957)
PIANO
Five choreographic pretexts (1973)
Sonatina (1958)
Two miniatures (1968)
VOCAL
Bujorul (folk words) (soloists, m-ch and orch) (1966)
Apărătorii patriei (m-ch) (1969)
Decor (G. Bacovia) (mix-ch) (1973)
Grivita, triptique (V. Sirbu) (mix-ch and perc) (1969)
Matinale (G. Bacovia) (mix-ch) (1973)
Monotonie (G. Bacovia) (mix-ch) (1973)
L'Oiseau bleu (S, mix-ch, 2 fl, hn and perc) (1971)
Sub steagurile țării (composer) (mix-ch) (1969)
Three love songs (folk words) (w-ch) (1974)
Trei inscriptii (T. Archezi) (ch a-cap) (1968)
Trois images (A. Voitin) (mix-ch and perc) (1973)
Il y a encore des roses (Alexandru Makedonski) (S, 2 fl, vlc, pf and perc) (1972)
Jadis, seven songs (G. Bacovia) (vce and pf) (Edit Musicala, 1959)
Ponti Euxini (Publius Ovidius Naso) (S, ob, cl and hp) (1971)
Three poems (Lucian Blaga) (1969)
Two serenades (A. Baconsky) (vce, fl and hp) (1973)
Other songs (Rumanian poets, incl. Arghezi, Eminescu, Dragomir, Calinescu) (vlc and pf)
Numerous songs (Rumanian poets) (vce and pf)
THEATRE
Cyrano de Bergerac (Edmond Rostand) (1965)
Measure for Measure (Shakespeare) (1965)
Tartuffe (Moliere) (1965)
Twelfth Night (Shakespeare) (1964)
Music for plays (Gorbatov, Stoenescu, Voitin, Delavrancea, Eftimiu and other Rumanian playwrights)
Ref. Union des Compositeurs Roumains, 81, 148, 196, 563

DONI, Antonia
18th-century Italian composer.
Composition
VOCAL
Song in Componimenti Poetici (L. Bergalli) (1726)
Ref. 327

DONIACH, Shula
British pianist and composer. b. Samara (now Kuibishev), Russia, 1905. She came to England when she was only a few months old and wrote her first compositions at the age of ten. She studied the piano at the Royal Academy of Music and then in Berlin, Vienna, Budapest and Switzerland. She returned to England in 1934.
Compositions
CHAMBER
Rhapsody (vln and pf)
VOCAL
Voices of Jerusalem (composer, S. Levi, I. Ezra, A.L. Yaron and S.S. Shalom) (S, Bar, ob, str qrt and pf)
Rhymes from Carmel (2-3 vces and opt pf) (A.L. Yaron)
Songs (English poems)
Ref. 94, 139, 177

DONOVAN, Eva Noel. See HARVEY, Eva Noel

DOORLY, Dorothy Whitson. See FREED, Dorothy Whitson

D'ORSAY, Maria Luisa. See PONSA, Maria Luisa

DOR, Daniela. See KAUFMAN, Barbara

DORABIALSKA, Julia Helena
Polish pianist, musicologist, professor and composer. b. Sosnowiec, May 22, 1895; d. Wolomin, July 20, 1944. She studied the piano at the Warsaw Conservatory under K. Jaczynowska and at the Moscow Conservatory under A. Borowski. In 1924 she received her doctorate from the Jagellan University, Cracow. In 1925 she completed her course in composition under R. Statkowski at the Warsaw Conservatory and from 1922 to 1927 was assistant to P. Rytel, the teacher of harmony. From 1929 to 1939 she was professor of harmony, musical form and history and the piano.
Compositions
ORCHESTRA
Concert-opera intermezzo, in 1 act
CHAMBER
String quartet
Fugue (3 vln)
Arietta (vln and pf)
Canzonetta (vln and pf)
Kolysanka (vln and pf)
Melodia (vln and pf)
PIANO
Barcarole
Capriccio
Chorale
Four preludes (Warsaw, 1930)
Lilie
Triptych
Rondo
Sonatina
Toccatina
Two etudes

VOCAL
Piesni robotnicze (m-ch)
Byl skrzypek (A. Dzieciolowski) (vce and pf)
Deszcz jesienny (L. Staff) (vce and pf)
Jak to býc moze (L. Staff) (vce and pf)
Kolysanka (E. Szelburg-Zarembina) (vce and pf)
Na Aniol Pánski (K. Tetmajer) (vce and pf)
Preludium (L. Rydel) (vce and pf)
SACRED
Mass (T, ch and pf or org)
Cién, Swiety Boze (vce and pf)
OPERA
Dewaki (Schure)
Hanusia, in 1 act (G. Hauptmann)
Publications
Cziczenia praktyczne z harmonii. Warsaw, 1927.
Jozef Damse i jego komedie muzyczne. 1925.
Polonez przed Chopinem. Warsaw, 1938.
Ref. 118, 431, 524

DORIA, Claria. See ROGERS, Clara Kathleen

DORIGNY DENOYERS, Mme.
19th-century French composer.
Composition
GUITAR
Romance sur la mort de Mazet (1822)
Ref. 312

DORISI, Lina
19th-century composer. Her work was performed in London in 1896.
Composition
THEATRE
A Japanese Lamp, musical comedy (1896)
Ref. 431

DORNIN, Mrs. G.A. See CAPERTON, Florence

DOROTHEA SOPHIA, Duchess
17th-century Italian composer. She married Prince Edoard, Duke of Parma. She composed an opera and songs.
Ref. 465

DOROW (Dorow-Bell), Dorothy
20th-century English singer, teacher and composer. She lived in Sweden after 1963. She studied singing under Maggie Teyte. She led a course at Opera Studio 67 in Stockholm and taught master classes in Amsterdam and at The Hague. She appeared in Europe and the United States as a concert singer. DISCOGRAPHY.
Compositions
VOCAL
Songs incl.:
Lo! Here the gentle lark (S, fl and pf)
The Russian nightingale (S, fl and pf)
Dream
Pastourelles/Pastoureux
THEATRE
Hands and Fate, 8 songs (2 hn, 2 perc, vlc and strs) (1972)
Ref. 282, 524, 563

DOROW-BELL, Dorothy. See DOROW, Dorothy

DORTCH, Eileen Wier
20th-century American composer. She composed sacred anthems and vocal duets and solos.
Ref. 142, 347

DOUGAN, Vera Warnder
American composer. b. Chicago, July 7, 1898. She composed piano pieces and songs.
Ref. 40, 347

DOUROUX, Margaret Pleasant
American choral director, teacher and composer. b. 1941.
Compositions
(All published by Rev. Earl Pleasant Publ. Co.)
SACRED
Deep water (1975)
Give me a clean heart (best song award, James Cleveland Academy of Gospel Music)
God is not dead (1973)
God is passing out blessings
God made a man (1975)
I'm glad
I'm gonna take my burdens
An instrument for Thee (1975)
The Lord is speaking
The Lord lifted me (1975)
Love song (1975)
My help cometh from the Lord
Only God (1974)
Show me the way (1973)
Strengthen me
Teach me how to love
There is God (1973)
We're blest
What have you done for Jesus
What shall I render (1975)
Ref. 136

DOWNEY, Mary
American organist, pianist, choral conductor and composer. b. St. Paul, MN, 1897. She began playing the piano at the age of four and published her first piano composition at the age of nine. In 1911 she entered the St. Paul College of Music and studied composition, harmony and the piano under Enrico Sansone. After graduating she went to New York to study under Theodore Haeck. In 1916 she returned to St. Paul to study the organ with particular attention to church music, Gregorian chant and liturgical form. She studied the organ and composition under Pietro Yon and travelled throughout the United States, Canada and Newfoundland, giving organ concerts and holding master classes in liturgical form and the organ. She directed boys' choirs.
Compositions
ORGAN
Crinolina
Florete flores
Irish rhapsody
VOCAL
You are love, song
SACRED
Missa in honor nativitatis B.V.M. (vces, hns and str orch)
Come ye shepherds, pastorale
Missa De profundis
Missa in honor S.S. Sacramenti (vces)
Missa in honor St. Francis de Sales
Several hymns (ch and part singing)
Ref. 292, 347

DOYLE, Beth
20th-century Australian composer.
Composition
INCIDENTAL MUSIC
Indians
Ref. 442

DRAKE, Elizabeth Bell
20th-century American composer.
Compositions
CHAMBER
First string quartet (1958)
Fantasy sonata (vlc and pf) (1971)
PIANO
Arecibo sonata (1968)
Second sonata (1972)
Variations and interludes (1952)

VOCAL
Songs of here and forever, song cycle (S and pf) (1970)
Ref. 228

DRAPER, Mrs. J.T.
19th-century American composer.
Compositions
VOCAL
Just as I am
The shadows of the evening hour
Other songs
SACRED
Deum laudamus
Magnificat
There is a fold whence none can stray
Ref. 276, 292, 347

DRASCHE-WARTINBERG, Luisa, Countess. See ERDOEDY, Luisa

DRATTELL, Deborah
20th-century American composer. She studied at Pennsylvania State University.
Compositions
CHAMBER
Homonymous (1978)
VOCAL
Plexus solar (S and ens)
Ref. AMC

DRDOVA, Marie (pseud. Constans, Konstantin)
Czech composer. b. Blansko, September 9, 1889; d. 1970. She studied music privately in Vienna from 1905. She studied theory and composition under V. Novak from 1927 to 1928, at the Sorbonne, Paris from 1923 to 1925 and in Rome under Respighi, 1925 to 1926.
Compositions
ORCHESTRA
The Spring, concert waltz (1930)
Overtures
CHAMBER
Quartets
Piano pieces
VOCAL
Choruses
Songs
BALLET
Klice
OPERA
Six part cycle: Zeme; Indrani; Drahomira; Ohen; Vzpoura; Vzlet
Cil
Vestalka
Ref. Music Info. Center of Czech Music Fund, 197, 431

DREGE-SCHIELOWA, Lucja
Polish pianist and composer. b. Warsaw, February 13, 1893; d. Lodz, January 26, 1962. She studied at the Music College of the Warsaw Music Society under F. Szopski (composition) and M. Wasowicz-Badowsla (piano). She graduated in 1915.
Compositions
ORCHESTRA
Polish dance suite (1951)
CHAMBER
Partita (fl, vlc and pf) (1953)
Sonata (vln and pf) (1917-1918)
PIANO
Thirty miniatures, some for 4 hands incl. 2 Krakowiaki (1952); Polkas; Kujawiaki
Ballad (1916-1918)
Etude (1952)
Scherzo (1916-1918)
Sonata (1917)
Toccata and fugue (1917)
Two etudes (1916-1918)
Two sonatinas (1954)
VOCAL
Five songs (L. Krzemieniecka and J. Czechowicz) (vce and pf) (1959)
Six songs (vce and pf) (1958)
Songs (L. Staff and Z. Debicki) (Gebethner & Wolff, 1917-1918)
Songs (K. Galczynski, J. Ficowski and J. Tuwim) (vce and pf) (1952)
Three songs about Lodz (vce and pf) (1954)
Youth march (H. Rajter) (1950)
Entertainment songs
Mass songs
THEATRE
Music for puppet shows and children's radio
Ref. 8, 118, 524

DREIFUSS, Henrietta
19th-century German composer.
Compositions
VOCAL
Eight songs, op. 1
Six songs, op. 2
Russian song
Ref. 347, 433.

DRENNAN, Dorothy Carter
American lecturer and composer. b. Hankinson, ND, March 21, 1929. She studied under Clifton Williams and Alfred Reed at the University of Miami, receiving her B.Mus.Ed. in 1969, M.M. in 1971 and Ph.D. in 1975. From 1972 she was a lecturer there. She received Sigma Alpha Iota awards in 1971, 1972 and 1973.
Compositions
CHAMBER
Turn (vln, cl, trb and 2 perc)
VOCAL
Here is the rose (Dance thou here), concerto (ch and trb)
Seashores (Tagore) (ch and wind qnt)
Songs of William Blake, song cycle (1974)
SACRED
The Word, cantata for Pentecost
Kyrie eleison (1981)
Ref. 142, 347, 625

DRETKE, Leora N.
American arranger, conductor, singer, teacher and composer. b. Canton, OH, October 17, 1928. She obtained her B.M. at Mt. Union College and her M.A. at Western Reserve University. She was music supervisor in Canton public schools and head of the vocal department at Louisville High School. She won the Ohio Authors and Composers award and is a member of ASCAP.
Compositions
SACRED
In praise and adoration
Sing alleluia! Christ is born
Sing we now for Christ is King
Ref. 39, 142, 347

DREVJANA, Anna (nee Kozlova)
Czech composer. b. Janovice, Frydek-Mistek, May 26, 1905.
Compositions
VOCAL
To janovske Hradisko (Ostrava, 1956)
Forty-three songs (composer)
Ref. 197

DREYFUS, Francis Kay (nee Lucas)
Australian celeste player, pianist, lecturer, music critic and composer. b. Ballarat, Victoria, May 26, 1942. She studied at the Conservatory at the University of Melbourne from 1960 to 1963, graduating with a B.M. in the piano, composition, and music history and an M.M. hons. in 1966. She was awarded a Commonwealth overseas scholarship to study at York University, England, 1966 to 1967. A Fulbright travel grant enabled her to study aesthetics and the philosophy of art criticism under Professor M.C. Beardsley at Temple University, PA, 1969. She obtained her Ph.D. from the University of Melbourne in 1972. She was a part-time lecturer in music at the University of Melbourne from 1968 to 1975 and lecturer in music at the University Women's College, Melbourne, 1969 to 1973. She contributed to numerous music journals and was deputy music critic of the *Melbourne Herald* in 1969 and *The Australian*, 1972. At present she is working in the archives department of Melbourne University collecting material relating to Percy Grainger. She married the composer George Dreyfus. PHOTOGRAPH.

Compositions
ORCHESTRA
Overture (1964)
CHAMBER
Sonata (fl and pf) (1963)
PIANO
Come and play, suite of 12 pieces for children (1962)
VOCAL
Three songs from Towards the Source (Christopher Brennen) (Bar and pf) (1963)
Songs from Goethe's Faust (1964)
SACRED
A hymn to God the Father, anthem (J. Donne) (mix-ch) (1964)
Missa brevis (mix-ch) (1964)
BALLET
Thumbelina (with Margaret Crawford) (1964)
INCIDENTAL MUSIC
Leonce und Lena (G. Buchner) (1966)
Songs for Australia Felix, film (1964)
Ref. composer

DRIEBURG, Louise, von (nee von Normann)

German poetess, singer and composer. b. Stolzenau, Hanover, January 4, 1801; d. Protzen, February 8, 1843. She married a composer and musicologist. Without formal training, she enjoyed some success as a song composer.
Compositions
VOCAL
Gruss an die Ostsee, six songs (S or T and pf) (Berlin: Trautwein, 1842)
Huldigungslied der Ritterschaft: Gott segne unser theures Vaterland (S or T and pf) (Berlin: Bock, 1840)
Six songs, op. 2 (S or T and pf) (Berlin: Lischke, 1840)
Six songs, op. 5 (S or T and pf) (Bock, 1843)
Songs, op. 1 (vce and pf) (Lischke, 1840)
Ref. 121, 276, 347

DRING, Madeleine

English pianist, actress, librettist, scriptwriter, singer and composer. b. London, September 7, 1923; d. London, March 26, 1977. She won a scholarship to the junior department of the Royal College of Music at the age of ten and a second college scholarship allowed her to study composition under Herbert Howells and Vaughan Williams. She was known as an actress, singer and pianist. She married Roger Lord, principal oboist of the London Symphony Orchestra. DISCOGRAPHY.
Compositions
ORCHESTRA
Dance suite: Italian dance; West Indian dance; American dance; Waltz finale (also har, hp and pf; also 2 pf) (Arcadia Music Co.)
Festival scherzo (pf and str orch)
CHAMBER
Dance gaya (ww ens and gtr or pf and ob; also 2 pf)
Paste panache (inst ens)
Shades of Dring (inst ens)
Trio (ob, bsn and hpcd) (1971-1972)
Trio (fl, ob and pf) (1967) (Weinberger)
Polka (ob and pf) (1962) (Arcadia)
Polka (pf and fl) (1962)
Three piece suite (ob and pf) (Nova Music, 1984)
Three pieces (fl and pf) (Cambia Pub., 1982)
PIANO
Caribbean Dance (2 pf) (1958) (Inter-Art Music Co.)
Sonata (2 pf) (1951) (Lengnick)
Tarantelle (2 pf) (OUP, 1948)
Three fantastic variations on Lilliburlero (2 pf) (1951) (Lengnick)
Valse Française (2 pf)
Four duets (1964)
Colour suite (1963) (Arcadia)
Fantasy sonata (1948) (Lengnick)
Jig (1948) (Lengnick)
March for the New Year
Moto perpetuo
Prelude and toccata (1948) (Lengnick)
Spring (1952) (Lengnick)
Three dances, suite (Cambria, 1981)
Three for two (1970)
Up and away, 12 pieces
Other dances and waltzes
Teaching pieces
VOCAL
Fair Queen of Yueh (vces, ob, str qrt and hp)
Away Princess (Aitken) (vce and pf)
Dedications (vce and pf)
Four night songs
Five songs (John Betjeman) (1976-1977)
Melisande the Fair
Three Shakespeare songs (Lengnick)
Other songs
OPERA
Cupboard Love
MISCELLANEOUS
Deserted city
Galop (Lady Luck)
Spring romance, theme music (Joseph Weinberger)
Bibliography
Royal College of Music Magazine, vol. 73, nos. 2 and 3. Oct. 1977.
Ref. Roger Lord, 94, 189, 431, 477, 563, 574, 622

DROBYAZGINA, Valentina Ivanovna

Soviet assistant professor and composer. b. Lvov, May 24, 1947. She studied composition under J.T. Borisev at the Institute of Arts in Kharkov, graduating in 1971. The next year she lectured on theoretical subjects at a music school in Voroshilovgrad and then taught theory in Kharkov. After 1973 she was assistant to the professor of composition at the Institute of Arts in the same city.
Compositions
ORCHESTRA
Humoresque concerto (pf and orch) (1974)
Piano concerto (1971)
Simfonietta (1968)
Divertimento (cham orch) (1969)
CHAMBER
Variations (str qrt) (1967)
Five pieces (vln and pf) (1967)
PIANO
Rondo
Other pieces
VOCAL
Six songs (S. Marshak) (chil-ch) (1973)
Two ballads (Lorca) (vocal qrt and jazz trio) (1969)
Songs (Soviet poets) (vce and pf)
THEATRE
Incidental music
OPERA
One opera
Ref. 21

DROSTE, Doreen (Mrs. Gerard J.)

American composer. b. Tacoma, WA, May 29, 1907. She studied privately under George Tremblay and at the University of California, Los Angeles under Henry Leland Clarke and obtained her M.A. In 1958 she won first prize in a national anthem contest.
Compositions
VOCAL
The happy heart (ch)
The ship of state (ch)
Song of wandering Aengus (ch a-cap) (1973)
To drive the cold winter away (ch a-cap)
Sixpence in her shoe, Elizabethan tale (Richard Corbet) (S, A and pf)
SACRED
Hear my prayer (ch) (1958)
The hymn of St. Columba (ch)
Ride on in majesty (ch)
Ref. 142, 147

DROSTE-HUELSHOFF, Annette Elise von, Baroness

German poetess and composer. b. Hans Huelshoff, near Muenster, Westphalia, January 14, 1797; d. Meersburg am Bodensee, May 24, 1848. She became the most famous German poetess of her century. She received an excellent musical education in her childhood from her father, Baron Clemens August II, a violinist and composer and her uncle, Maximilian Friedrich von Droste-Huelshoff, some of whose compositions were produced in Vienna. She set texts of Byron, Goethe and Brentano to music as well as her own poems and translations. Some of her songs were inspired by the old lieder. She arranged songs from the Lochamer Liederbuch and other folk songs. She planned three operas but wrote no more than sketches and fragments. She dedicated herself to poetry rather than singing as a result of a chest complaint. DISCOGRAPHY.
Compositions
VOCAL
Dass ihr euch gegen mir so freundlich thut beweisen, from the Lochamer Liederbuch (Bar and pf) (1877)
Wenn die Sonne weggegangen (Brentano) (Bar and pf) (1877)

Wenn ich traeume (Byron) (Bar and pf) (1877)
Wer nie sein Brot mit Thraenen ass (Goethe) (Bar and pf) (1877)
Lieder mit Klavierbegleitung (Muenster: C.B. Schlueter, 1877)
Other songs
Publications
Der Schlacht im Loener Bruch. Poem. 1838.
Das Hospiz auf dem Grosse St. Bernard. 1938.
Das festliche Jahr, nebst einem Anhang religioser Gedichte. 1852.
Gedichte. 1838.
Bibliography
Fellerer, K.G. *Musikerin Annette von Droste-Huelshoff*. Muenster, 1954.
Schulte-Kemmingshausen. *Die Briefe der Annette von Droste-Huelshoff*. Jena, 1944.
Ref. 9, 12, 15, 44, 268, 347, 353, 406, 563, 653

DRYE, Sarah Lynn
20th-century American composer of choral pieces.
Ref. 347

DRYNAN, Margaret
Canadian organist, percussionist, choirmistress, journalist, singer, teacher and composer. b. Toronto, Ontario, December 10, 1915. She gained her B.Mus from Toronto University in 1943 and was awarded her ARCT in 1975 and became an F.R.C.C.O. Her teachers included Arthur Benjamin, Madeline Bone, Michael Head, E. Kelvin James, Campbell McInnes, Molly Sclater and Healey Willan. She sang with various choirs in Toronto and was organist and choirmistress at the Holy Trinity Church in Oshawa from 1950 till 1953. She then founded and for 15 years conducted, the Canterbury Singers of Oshawa. She was the national president of the R.C.C.O. from 1982 to 1984. For 21 years she was music consultant for the Durham Board of Education and taught the piano and music theory privately and was percussionist with the Oshawa Symphony Orchestra. In 1983 she was awarded the title of Woman of Distinction of the Year in the Arts, by the Y.W.C.A.. She was the Canadian editor of *Diapason* magazine and contributed articles to music periodicals. PHOTOGRAPH.
Compositions
CHAMBER
Prelude and fugue in C-Minor (org)
String works
VOCAL
Fate of Gelbert Gim
Including me
Rainy day song
Songs for Judith
Numerous children's songs
SACRED
Missa brevis in F-Minor
To Mary and Joseph
Why do the bells of Christmas ring?
Carols
Plainsong arrangements
OPERETTA
The Canada Goose
Other operettas
Ref. composer, 85, 93, 347, 485

DU PAGE, Florence Elizabeth (nee Anderson)
American organist, pianist, choral conductor and composer. b. Vandergrift, PA, September 20, 1910. She studied privately under Rubin Goldmark (harmony), Aurelio Giorni (counterpoint), Tibor Serly (composition), Ignace Hilsberg (piano), Dr. Thomas Richner (organ) and her husband Richard du Page (orchestration). She was musical director of the Advent-Tuller Schools, Westbury and Sag Harbour, NY, for 12 years, choral conductor of the Cathedral School of St. Mary, Garden City, NY, for three years and organist and choir conductor in various churches. PHOTOGRAPH.
Compositions
ORCHESTRA
Oh, Varmeland, Symphony on a Swedish folk tune
Alice in Wonderland, ballet suite (sym orch) (1951) (Carl Fischer)
Concerto for piano and strings (1985) (Porter Press)
Figurations (pf and str orch) (1984) (Porter)
Jumping Jack (str orch) (1946)
Lost valley (1946) (New York: B.V.C.)
The pond (1948) (award, Boston Women's Symphony Orchestra)
Two sketches for string orchestra (1946) (Philadelphia: Elkan-Vogel)
CHAMBER
Figuration (brass qnt) (1948) (Porter)
Humpty Dumpty (4 tba)
Von Himmel hoch (brass qrt) (New York: Andre M. Smith Music Co.)
Fantasy (vln and pf) (Porter, 1985)
Rondo (trb and pf) (1956) (Andre M. Smith)
ORGAN
Three chorale preludes (1961) (Porter)
Prelude to a quiet evening
PIANO
Double variations upon two southern tunes (1985) (Porter)
From morn 'til night
Misty morning
OPERA
Contemporary mass (ch, trp, perc and org)
New world for Nellie, ballad opera (R. Emett) (2 soli, ch, perc, timp, vib or xy and orch) (Porter)
Trial universelle, sacred chamber opera (Sister Jean) (1963) (Church of the advent)
OPERETTA
Alice in Wonderland, for children (Lewis Carroll) (1957)
Ching Foo and the Emperor, for children
THEATRE
Squanto, pantomime
Whither, an allegorical music drama (Sister Jean) (Porter, 1964)
Ref. composer, 39, 40, 77, 94, 141, 142, 228, 280, 494, 625, 643

DUBANOWICZ, Wanda
Polish composer. b. 1928.
Composition
CHAMBER
Musical pictures (3 cl)
Ref. PWM

DUBOIS, Dorothea
Irish authoress and composer. d. Dublin, 1775. She was the illegitimate daughter of the Earl of Anglesea.
Composition
THEATRE
The Divorce, musical comedy (1771)
Publications
Theodora. Novel, in 2 volumes. 1770.
Ref. 433

DUBOIS, Mrs. W.E.B. See DUBOIS, Shirley Graham

DUBOIS, Shirley Graham (Graham, Shirley Lola) (Mrs. McCanns, Mrs. W.E.B. Dubois)
Black American authoress, lecturer and composer. b. Indianapolis or Evansville, November 11, 1904; d. September 6, 1978. She had special training under many private teachers and completed courses of study at Oberlin College, OH; Howard University, Washington, DC; the Institute of Musical Art, New York City and the Sorbonne, Paris. For three years she was musical director at Morgan College of Baltimore, MD, and she frequently lectured on black music.
Compositions
VOCAL
I promise (New York: Handy Bros., 1934)
Songs
OPERA
Little Black Sambo (1938)
The Swing Mikado
Tom-Tom (composer) (500 singers, dancers and orch) (1932)
Publications
Booker T Washington. New York: Messner, 1955.
Cool Dust. Play.
Elijah's Ravens. Play.
George Washington Carver. New York: Messner, 1944.
His Day is Marching On: A Memoir of W.E.B DuBois. Philadelphia: J.B. Lippincott, 1971.
It's Morning. Play.
John Baptiste DeSable. New York: Messner, 1953.
Julius K. Nyerere. Teacher of Africa. New York: Messner, 1975.
Spirituals to Symphonies. Shirley Graham. Etude, November 1936, p. 691-692.
The Story of Paul Robeson. New York: Messner, 1967.
The Story of Phillis Wheatley: Poetess of the American Revolution. New York: Messner, 1949.

There Was Once a Slave: Heroic Story of Frederick Douglass. New York: Messner, 1966.
Track Thirteen. Play.
Tribute to Paul Robeson, Freedomways. First quarter 1971, pp. 6-7.
Your Most Humble Servant: The Story of Benjamin Banneker. New York: Messner, 1949.
Zulu Heart. New York: Okpaku Communications, 1974.

Bibliography

Hare, M.C. *Negro Musicians and Their Music*. Washington Assoc. Pub., 1936. P. 345.
Matney, W.C., ed. *Who's Who Among Black Americans*.

Ref. 136, 141, 304, 347, 353, 549

DUCELLE, Paul. See KROGMANN, Carrie William

DUCHAMBGE, Pauline (Antoinette Paule de Montet)

French composer. b. Martinique, May 1778; d. Paris, April 23, 1858. She was born to a noble and wealthy family and studied music at the convent under L.B. Desormery. She married the Baron Duchambge and regarded music as a diversion until her divorce, when she studied seriously under Auber, Cherubini and Dussek and started composing romantic music. She was praised by Empress Josephine and in 1815 met Marceline Desbordes-Valmore, who introduced her to the musical and artistic life of Paris. Chateaubriand, Hugo, Lamartine and Vigny wrote verses for her. Her melodies, with their melancholic character and emotional overtones, are illustrative of French romanticism at the beginning of the 19th-century.

Compositions

Approx 400 romances incl.:
Album musicale
Le Bearnais
La brigantine ou le depart

Bibliography

Boulanger, J. *M. Desbordes-Valmore*. Paris. 1926.
Boyer d'Agen, ed. *Oeuvres manuscribes de M. Desbordes-Valmore*. Albums à Pauline. Paris, 1921.
Hedouin, P. *Mme. Pauline Duchambge. Le Ménéstrel*. June-July 1858.
Pougin, A. *La jeunesse de M. Desbordes-Valmore*. Paris, 1898.

Ref. 9, 17, 85, 116, 128, 260

DUCHAMP, Marie Catharine

French singer, teacher and composer. b. Paris, May 14, 1789. She attended the Paris Conservatoire where she studied under Plantade and later Garat. She completed her studies in 1807 and appeared in major concerts, 1813 to 1817. Increasing deafness forced her to dedicate herself to teaching. She composed romances with harpsichord accompaniment.
Ref. 129

DUCHESS OF AMALFI. See COLONNA, Vittoria

DUCOUREAU, Mme. M.

20th-century French composer. She was director of the Société Charles Bordes at St. Jean-de-Luz (Pyrenées) and a pupil of the Schola Cantorum.

Compositions

CHAMBER
Trio (pf, vln and vlc) (Rouart Lerolle)
Rapsodie Basque (vln and pf)

PIANO
Gigue (Baudoux; Bellon)
Nocturne (Bellon)
Sarabande (Bellon)
Suite, 4 short pieces on Basque themes (Mutuelle)

VOCAL
Songs incl.:
Enfant malade et la lune (Schola)
Orage (Baudoux)
Trois melodies espagnoles (Baudoux)

SACRED
O salutaris (Bourlant; Bellon)

Ref. 41, 297

DUCZMAL-JAROSZEWSKA, Agnieszka

Polish flautist, pianist, conductor and composer. b. Krotoszyn January 7, 1946. She holds diplomas for the piano, the flute and conducting from the State Higher Musical School, Poznan, 1971. She is the founder and conductor of the chamber orchestra, Jeunesses Musicales, which has given concerts throughout Poland. She has made recordings on Polish radio and television and given concerts in East and West Germany and Bulgaria and conducted symphonies and oratorios with various Polish philharmonic orchestras. She is the conductor at the Moniuszko Opera House, Poznan. She composes theatre music.
Ref. 206, 643

DUDLEY, Majorie Eastwood

American professor and composer. b. South Dakota, November 6, 1891; d. June 13, 1963. She was stricken by polio at the age of six and left physically handicapped for life. She earned her B.Mus. and M.Mus. in composition from Chicago Musical College; a D.Mus. in composition from the University of Toronto and a certificate in composition from the American Conservatory, Fontainebleau. She studied under Peter C. Suskin, Andre Bloch and Felix Borowski. She was professor of music at the College of Fine Arts, University of South Dakota, 1920 to 1956.

Compositions

ORCHESTRA
Piano concerto
Andante
Tone poem

CHAMBER
Octet (fl, ob, cl and strs)
In the cotton garden (ob, cl, vla, vlc and pf)
String quartet No. 1
String quartet No. 2
Andante cantabile (vln, vla and hp)
Fantasy and fugue (vln and pf)
Rhapsody in G-Minor (cl and pf; also pf)
Sonata in D-Major (vln and pf)

PIANO
After the war, suite in 3 parts
Dakota wind
Dear lambs among the primrose meadows sleeping
Fantasy
Fragments from a broken mosaic
Pierrette
Pierrot
Russian dance
The sea
Sonata
Spanish dance
Teaching pieces

VOCAL
Songs:
Awake
Behold a rose of beauty
By starlight and candlelight
Evensong
Fairest regions
For Alice
Hero to Leander
Keramos
Lone wandering
My garden
Only the wind knows
Pastels
Pastorale
Peace
Songless
To a waterfowl
To Constantia singing
Tristan in the wood
Two Chinese songs
Unrest
Wild bird
Wind elegy

Ref. 40, 142, 347, 433

DUFFENHORST, Irma Habeck

20th-century American composer of piano pieces.
Ref. 347

DUFFERIN, Lady Helen Selina, Countess of Gifford (nee Sheridan) (pseud. Impulsia Gushington)

Irish composer. b. 1807; d. June 13, 1867.

Compositions

VOCAL
A set of ten songs and two duets (1833)
Sets of twelve and seven songs (1833-1839)
Ten songs (Cont or m-S and pf) (1861)

O bay of Dublin (Chappell)
Katy's letter (Brainard)
Lament of the Irish emigrant
Terence's farewell to Kathleen
Songs, poems and verses set to music by composer and others (ed. Marquess of Dufferin, 1895)
Ref. 6, 74, 85, 260, 276, 297, 347

DUFRESNOY, Mme.
18th-19th-century French composer.
Compositions
CHAMBER
Sonata for the Harp or Piano, Arranged with Accompaniment for 2 French Horns (ca. 1800) (London: Robert Birchall)
Two Sonatas for the French Pedal Harp with ad libitum Violin Accompaniment, op. 1 (ca. 1800)
Ref. 65, 405

DUGAL, Madeleine
Canadian pianist and composer. b. Chicoutimi, Quebec, June 3, 1926. She studied at Quebec Provincial Conservatory under August Descarries and in Chicoutimi under Eliane Saucier (piano). In 1944 she won the CAPAC composition prize and in 1950 the second medal in solfege at Quebec Provincial Conservatory. She played in concert in Montreal and on Chicoutimi radio.
Compositions
PIANO
Après l'orage
Les Arbres
Au petit galop
Etude en double tierces
Etude en doubles notes
Fête champêtre
Mazurka
Menuet et trio
Nocturne
Petite valse
Sonata No. 1, in G-Major (1947)
Sonata No. 2, in C-Major (1948)
Sonatinas
Souvenir de voyage
Sports d'hiver
VOCAL
La grenouille (1944)
Pour être un vrai marin (1946)
Souvenez vous (1946)
Ref. 85, 133

DUGGAN, Beatrice Abbott
American pianist, musicologist, teacher and composer. b. New York, June 22, 1911. She obtained a B.A. (1933) from Vassar College, Poughkeepsie and then studied musicology at Columbia University until 1936. She taught the piano privately and was music consultant at the Princeton Day School, NJ. She contributed articles to many publications.
Compositions
CHAMBER
Violin sonata (1933) (music prize, Vassar College)
VOCAL
Songs (1932) (music prize, Vassar College)
Ref. 84

DUHAMEL, Mlle.
18th-century French composer.
Composition
OPERA
Agnes, divertissement in 1 act, with ballet (1763)
Ref. 218

DUHAN, Mme.
19th-century French music writer and composer. She lived in Paris.
Compositions
PIANO
Rondos
Variations

Publications
Methode ou Alphabet pour apprendre le doigté et posseder en peu de temps d'Aplomb du Pianoforte, renfermant 102 planches, qu'il suffit d'exercer à la muette.
Trent-et-un leçons de musique doigtées et relative aux exemples, qui sont autant des Claviers. Paris: Duban.
Ref. 66, 226, 276, 312

DULCKEN, Louisa (nee David)
German pianist, teacher and composer. b. Hamburg, March 20, 1811; d. London, April 12, 1850. A younger sister of Ferdinand David, a violinist, she studied under Willy Grund and C.F.G. Schwenke and made her debut in Hamburg at the age of ten. She performed in Berlin and Leipzig, leaving Germany for London after her marriage in 1828. She became extremely well known in London musical circles. She was an excellent teacher and Queen Victoria was one of her pupils.
Compositions
PIANO
Valse de la cour
Second set of 6 waltzes and trios
VOCAL
Choral pieces
Ref. 8, 22, 75, 123

DULCKEN, Sophie (nee Lebrun)
German pianist and composer. b. London, June 20, 1781; d. ca. 1815. She was the daughter of Ludwig August Lebrun, an oboist and composer and Franziska Lebrun (q.v.). After studying under Knecht, she studied the piano under Streicher and harmony under Schlett. She married Dulcken, a pianoforte maker of Munich in 1799 and made successful concert tours in France, Italy and Germany. She composed piano sonatas and other pieces.
Ref. 8, 26, 85, 109, 226, 276

DUMESNIL, Evangeline Lehman. See LEHMAN, Evangeline Marie

DUMONT, Jeanne-Louise. See FARRENC, Louise

DUMUR, Mme.
18th-century French harpist, pianist and composer. She settled in St. Petersburg in the latter half of the 18th-century. She composed for the harp and the piano.
Ref. 156

DUNFORD, Nancy Ridenhour
20th-century American composer. She received her M.M. from the University of Texas, 1950.
Composition
ORCHESTRA
Essay (1950)
Ref. 147

DUNGAN, Olive
American pianist, teacher and composer. b. Pittsburgh, PA, July 19, 1903. She studied at the Pittsburgh Institution of Musical Art, the University of Miami and the University of Alabama. Her teachers included Charles N. Boyd, Anton Koener, Emily Byrd and Franklin Harris. She was a piano recitalist and teacher and the first recipient of the Chi Omega Bertha Foster award.
Compositions
ORGAN
Pieces
PIANO
The Everglades
Fun and fancies, 7 pieces
Impression of the Argentine
The peacock
Pieces
Tropic night suite

VOCAL
Choral pieces
Songs incl.:
Can these be gone?
Character studies for young folks
Down the wild wind
Eternal life
Fish seller
Fleeting things
Let me go remembering
Stranger
Tropical tunes for tiny tots
White jade
Wind song
You
Your hands
SACRED
Be still and know that I am God
The Christ Child
Eternal life
I will lift up mine eyes, anthem
I will love thee
OPERETTA
The Mysterious Forest
Ref. 39, 40, 142, 190, 292, 347, 477, 494, 622, 646

DUNLOP, Isobel (pseud. Violet Skelton)
Scottish violinist and composer. b. Edinburgh, March 4, 1901; d. Edinburgh, May 12, 1975. She studied under Tovey and Dysan and gave concerts of her own works. She was concert organizer for the Scottish Arts Council from 1943 to 1948 and music secretary of the Saltire Society in 1949. With Hans Oppenheim she founded the Saltire Singers, an internationally famous vocal quartet.
Compositions
CHAMBER
Suite (vlc and pf) (1946)
Ardkinglas suite (d-b and picc) (1967)
Sonata (vla)
Three solos (fl) (1967)
PIANO
Le petit Noël
Preludes from A Brittany sketch book (1958)
Theme and variations
VOCAL
The Stevenson triptych
Choral pieces
Songs and part songs
SACRED
Beatus Colomba, cantata (4 vces and pf)
Sancta Caecilia, cantata (4 vces and pf)
Michael the Archangel, cantata (Bar and pf)
Gabriel, cantata (Bar and pf)
OPERA
The Silhouette
OPERETTA
The Scarecrow, for children
BALLET
The Moon Maiden
Bibliography
Composer. No. 55, summer, 1975.
Ref. 8, 22, 85, 94, 177, 347, 490, 572

DUNN, Rebecca Welty
American pianist, authoress and composer. b. Guthrie, OK, September 23, 1890. She studied at Washburn and Southwestern colleges and under Otto Fischer at Friends University. She is a member of ASCAP.
Compositions
VOCAL
Choral pieces
Songs incl.:
Sunflower song (Hoffman)
Tick tock (Hoffman)
SACRED
As channels of Thy grace
Halleluiah rain
OPERETTA
Purple on the Moon (prize, Kansas Authors' Club)
Sunny (national prize)
Seven children's operettas
Ref. 8, 39, 40, 142, 347

DUPORT, Marie
19th-century Russian composer. b. Tartu, Estonia. She composed piano pieces.
Ref. 276

DURAND, Jean. See ROCHAT, Andree

DURAND, Nella Wells
20th-century American organist, pianist, teacher and composer. b. Oakfield, WI. She studied at Wayland College, 1903 to 1904 and then in Chicago under Mrs. E.P. Fitzgerald to earn the artist degree in the piano. She studied the organ under Mrs P.B. Whitman, A.C. Shepard and Dr. Minor C. Baldwin. She played the organ in churches in Wisconsin, Florida and South Dakota. She started teaching the organ, voice, the piano and theory in 1906 and opened her own studio in Tampa in 1934. From 1909 till 1910 she lived with the Sioux Indians in South Dakota studying their music and was later adopted by both the Sioux and the Blackfoot tribes.
Compositions
BAND
Impetus
The Tampa march
PIANO
Pieces for children incl.:
Elegy to a robin
Squirrels at play
Ref. 496

DURAND DE FORTMAGNE, Baroness de. See FORTMAGNE, Baroness de

DURAS, Marguerite
20th-century composer.
Composition
FILM MUSIC
Nathalie Granger (1972)
Ref. 326

DUSCHEK (Dusik, Duskova), Josefina (nee Hambacher)
Bohemian pianist, operatic singer and composer. b. Prague, 1754; d. Prague, January, 1824. She studied the piano and singing under František Xaver Duschek, a pianist and composer whom she later married. As an opera singer she performed in Prague, Vienna, Dresden, Weimar and Leipzig. Mozart, when visiting Prague in 1787, 1789 and 1791, stayed with the Duschek family and after Mozart's death, his eldest son Carl lived with them for a long time as their foster son. Josefina Duschek died in poverty. She composed piano pieces and songs.
Ref. 20, 109, 276, 524

DUSCHEK, Veronica Rosalie. See DUSSEK, Veronica Rosalie

DUSHKIN, Dorothy Smith
American composer. b. Chicago, July 26, 1903. She graduated from Smith College in 1925 with honors in music and then went to study composition under Nadia Boulanger (q.v.) in Paris. In 1931, with her husband, Dorothy founded the Dushkin School of Music in Winnetka, IL, later named the North Shore Music Center. From 1953 she was co-director of the Kinhaven School of Music, Weston. Her works were performed in England and the United States. PHOTOGRAPH.
Compositions
ORCHESTRA
Concerto (pf and orch) (1960)
Kinhaven concerto for orchestra (1955; rev 1970)
Morris dance fantasy (small orch) (1940)
Tapestry suite (str orch) (1966)
CHAMBER
Chorale (antiphonal brass choirs) (1968)
Octet for woodwinds (1973)
Four plus four, suite (4 strs and 4 ww) (1963)
Eight voices, short piece (8 strs)
Septet for brass (1974)
Sextet (ww, pf and hn)
Retrospective (fl, ob, cl, hn, bsn and pf) (1966)

Claviquint, No. 1 (pf, fl, ob, cl and bsn) (1970)
Claviquint, No. 2 (pf, fl, ob, cl and bsn) (1971)
Claviquint, No. 3 (pf, vl, fl, hn and vlc) (1973)
Diversion (4 hands and perc) (1976)
Pour s'amuser, suite (mar and 4 ww) (1975)
Quintet (fl and strs) (1962) (London: '71 Musica Rara)
Quintet (hn and strs) (1974)
Quintet (ob and strs) (1956) (Northampton, MA: Valley Music Press, 1956)
Quintet for Amanda (Valley Music Press, 1956)
Quartet in D-Minor (ww or recs) (1962)
Quick-step-quartet (4 strs or 4 winds) (1954)
Three short flights for four flutes (1975)
Fantasy for three (fl, mar and d-b)
Four episodes, short pieces for trio
Percussion plus, suite (perc, fl and d-b) (1973)
Sonata (2 vlc and pf) (1968; expanded 1971)
Trio (pf, vln and vlc) (1976)
Suite for three (2 fl or rec and vla or cl) (1955)
Sonata (bsn and pf) (1975)
Sonata (hn and pf) (1975)
Sonata (2 hpcd) (1948)
Suite (2 fl or a-rec) (1956)
Time out, suite (perc and pf) (1972) (Shawnee Press, 1976)
Three moods (fl and pf) (1950)
Precision patterns, suite (perc) (1971)
Sonata (fl)

PIANO
Toccata (1 or 2 pf) (1925, 1934)
A gay set

VOCAL
Canaan bound, cantata (ch and orch) (1947; revised 1965)
Interpretations, cantata (2 solo, narr, ch and orch)
The light of man (mix-ch and orch) (1967)
The old soldier (de la Mare) (w-ch and ww) (C. Fischer, 1952)
On Paumonok shore (narr, w-ch, fl and pf) (1958)
The prince of sleep (w-ch and ww) (de la Mare) (C. Fischer, 1952)
The ship of Rio (w-ch and 3 ww) (de la Mare) (C. Fischer, 1952)
Ten poems in a filigree (w-ch, fl, str qrt and pf) (1976) (comm Lehigh University)
Songs of the bards of Bengal (w-ch, fl, vl, vlc and perc) (1972)

Ref. composer, 94, 142, 146, 347

DUSIK, Josefina. See DUSCHEK, Josefina

DUSIK, Veronica Rosalie. See DUSSEK, Veronica Rosalie

DUSKOVA, Josefina. See DUSCHEK, Josefina

DUSMAN, Linda

Composition

VOCAL
Nightwatch (S and pf) (1983)

Ref. AMC newsletter

DUSSEK, Olivia (Buckley)

English harpist, organist, pianist, writer and composer. b. London, September 29, 1801; d. London, 1847. The daughter of a Bohemian composer, Johann Ladislav Dussek and an Italian singer and composer, Sophia Guistina (q.v.), Olivia studied the piano and the harp under her mother and became an excellent performer. She was the organist at Kensington Parish Church from 1840.

Compositions

HARP
God save the King, rondo (Chappell)
Home, sweet home, rondo (Chappell)
St. Patrick's day, rondo (Chappell)
Scots, wha hae wi' Wallace bled, rondo (Chappell)

PIANO
Pieces

VOCAL
Two books of fairy songs and ballads for the young (1846)

SACRED
Fragments of sacred song (Ruth, St. Luke and Solomon) (1845)
The sacred musical volume, or Sabbath recreation (1845)

Publications

Musical Truths. 1843.

Ref. 6, 8, 123, 226, 276, 297, 347, 572

DUSSEK (Duschek, Dusik), Veronica Rosalie (Katerina Veronica Anna) (Mrs. Cianchettini)

Bohemian pianist, teacher and composer. b. Caslav, March 8, 1779; d. London, 1833. The daughter of Jan Josef Dussek, teacher, organist and composer of sacred music, and sister of Jan Ladislav Dussek, an organist, conductor and composer, she began piano studies under her father at an early age and soon became a virtuoso player. In 1797 she joined her brother in London, where she married the Italian musician Francesco Cianchettini and became a well-known teacher. Her son, Pio Cianchettini (b. 1799), was called the English Mozart as a child and later published some compositions. Her daughter, Veronica Elizabeth Cianchettini, became a pianist.

Compositions

ORCHESTRA
Two piano concertos

PIANO
A Sonata for Pianoforte, with or without Additional Keys in Which Is Introduced the Portuguese Hymn Adeste Fideles, op. 2 (ca. 1800) (London: Goulding, Phills and D'Almaine)
Viscountess Sudley's Favourite Waltz, with Variations for the Piano (ca. 1797) (London: Corri, Dussek & Co.)
Other sonatas

Ref. 6, 8, 65, 102, 108, 125, 129, 135, 226, 276, 361, 405, 524

DUTTON, Theodora (pseud. of Blanch Ray Alden)

American pianist and composer. b. Springfield, MA,; d. Northampton, MA, November 14, 1934. She composed violin and piano pieces, teaching pieces and songs.

Ref. 40, 105, 347, 353

DUVAL, Louise

French singer and composer. d. Paris, 1769. She was a member of the Paris Opera from 1720 to 1760 and composed the music for the ballet *Les Genies*, which was the first work by a woman to be performed at the Opera. She was extremely popular as a singer.

Compositions

VOCAL
Tout ce que vois me rappelle (Paris: Mercure de France, 1776)

BALLET
Les Genies, or Les Caracteres de l'amour, prologue and 4 acts (Paris: Ballard, 1736)

Publications

Methode agreable et utile pour apprendre facilement à chanter juste et avec gout. Paris, 1741.

Ref. 65, 85, 125, 129, 226, 276, 307, 347, 404

DUVOSEL, Seraphien Lieven

Belgian composer. b. Ghent, December 14, 1877, d. St. Martens-Latem, April 20, 1956.

Compositions

ORCHESTRA
Leie cycle, symphonic poems: No. 1, The morning (1918); No. 4, Christmas Eve (1925)

Ref. 94, 322

DVORKIN, Judith

American pianist and composer. b. New York, 1930. She received her B.A. from Barnard College and her M.A. from Columbia University, where she studied under Roger Sessions. DISCOGRAPHY.

Compositions

CHAMBER
Suite (ob, bsn and pf)

VOCAL
Three letters: John Keats to Fanny Brawne (Bar and orch) (1960)
The Eden tree (mix ch)
Maurice, a modern madrigal (mix-ch and pf) (1955)
Moments in time (B and cham group) (1961)
Six zoological considerations (vce and pf)
Song cycle (m-S) (1980)

OPERA
Blue Star (composer) (1983)
The Crescent Eyebrow, legend (1955)

MISCELLANEOUS
Cyrano (1965)
Four women (1981)

Bibliography

John Tasker Howard. *Our American Music*. Cromwell. 1954.
Miriam Green. *Women Composers' Works*. University of Arkansas Press. 1980.

Ref. 141, 142, 190, 347, 563, 622, 625

DYBERG, Ella. See HEIBERG, Ella

DYCHKO, Lesya (Ludmila) Vasilevna

Soviet composer. b. Kiev, September 24, 1939. She began her studies under K. Dankievic and graduated from the Kiev Conservatory, where she studied composition under B.N. Lyatoshinski. In 1971 she did postgraduate work under Lyatoshinski and N.I. Peiko. In 1968 she was active in the Ukrainian Government and in 1970 was a laureate of the Komsomol of the Ukrainian SSR.

Compositions

ORCHESTRA

Morning of the soldier's execution, symphonic fantasy (1962)
Ukrainian songs (1972)
Vesianki (1972)

CHAMBER

Dialogue, 6 pieces (vln) (1965)
Pieces (vln) (1970)
Pisanki (fl) (1972)

PIANO

Polyphonic variations (1972)
Sonata (1964)

VOCAL

The Carpathion, cantata
Good day, cantata (Audienko)
Lenin cantata (Soviet poets) (ch and orch) (1964)
Spring, cantata for children
Sun circle, cantata for children
Chervona Kalina, motifs from Ukrainian folk songs (vces and orch) (1970)
Pasteis (P. Tychina) (m-S and orch) (1967)
Rhapsody (Shevchenko) (S, m-ch and orch) (1965)
Symphony (S, B, strs, fls, hp, pf and perc) (1970)
Diptych (Japanese poets) (soloists, ch, pf and wind insts) (1972)
Two Japanese haiku (ch a-cap) (1969)
Cycle of romances (M. Rylski, C. Ukrainka) (vce and pf)
Enharmonia (M. Rylski) (S and pf)
Choruses (N. Voroni)

BALLET

Predrassvetniye Ogni, in 1 act (1968)
Metamorfozi, in 1 act (1963)

Ref. 21, 87, 420, 456

DYCHKO, Ludmila Vasilevna. See DYCHKO, Lesya Vasilevna

DYER, Susan

American composer. d. 1923. DISCOGRAPHY.

Composition

CHAMBER

Outlandish suite (vln and pf)

Ref. 292, 563

DZHAFAROVA, Afag Mamed kyzy

Soviet editor, lecturer and composer. b. Baku, April 22, 1943. She studied composition under K. Karaev at the Baku Conservatory graduating in 1969. Until 1972 she was an assistant lecturer at the same conservatory. For two years she was concertmistress at a music school in Baku. From 1966 till 1970 she was music editor for radio and television in Baku and after 1972 she lectured on composition at the Baku Conservatory.

Compositions

ORCHESTRA

Polyphonic symphony (1972)
Concerto (str qrt and orch) (1969)

CHAMBER

Pieces (wind insts)
Piano pieces

VOCAL

Cycle (Fizul and R. Rza) (1971)

Ref. 21

DZIELSKA, Jadwiga

20th-century Polish composer.

Compositions

PIANO

Etudes (PWM, 1979)

Ref. Frau und Musik

DZIEWULSKA, Maria Amelia

Polish conductor, musicologist, professor and composer. b. Warsaw, June 1, 1909. In 1933 she completed her studies at the State Music Conservatory in Warsaw, having studied under K. Sikorski and J. Turczynski. In 1936 and 1937 in London, she specialized in children's works and film music. From 1945 she taught theoretical subjects, composition and conducting at the State Musical College in Cracow; in 1956 she was made assistant professor. In 1961 she was appointed the head of the department of aural training. Since 1966 she has been professor at the State Music College in Warsaw. Her compositions for children earned her the Prize of the Prime Minister in 1958.

Compositions

ORCHESTRA

Kujawiak i oberek, folk dances (chil inst ens) (1947)
Partita (school orch) (1957)
Sinfonietta (small orch) (1957)

CHAMBER

Stravaganza (cl, vln, vla, 2 vlc and 2 tam-tams) (1966)
String quartet No. 1 (1954)
String quartet No. 2 (1960)
Dances and songs (2 vln or 2 groups of vlns) (1955)
Flute duets (1970)
Melody (vln and pf) (1951)

ORGAN

Spotkania, 5 pieces (1968)

PIANO

Folk melodies (2 pf, 4 hands)
Canon (1967)
Inventions
Pieces for children (Prime Minister's prize, 1958)
Three little pieces for children (1952)
Three preludes (1955)

VOCAL

Triptyque (folk texts) (mix-ch and orch) (1952)
Sobotka (mix-ch and folk band) (1952)
Wysla na pole (w-ch and folk band) (1950)
Cyrwona rutka, folk tune from Kurpie (mix-ch a-cap) (1948)
First Lower Silesian suite, 5 folk songs (mix-ch a-cap) (1953)
Folk songs (2 and 3-part chil-ch) (1952)
Mazowsze suite, 5 folk songs (mix-ch a-cap)
Pelnia (L. Staff) (mix-ch a-cap) (1969)
Second Lower Silesian suite, 5 folk songs (mix-ch a-cap)
Songs from Kurpie region (chil-ch and pf) (1951)
Two Kurpie songs (mix-ch and folk band) (1949)
Winnie the Pooh's songs (A.A. Milne and I Tuwim) (vce and pf)
Wszystko (A. Slonimski) (mix-ch a-cap) (1968)
Wysli chlopcy, folk tune from Kurpie (mix-ch a-cap) (1948)
Wzloty (A. Slonimski) (S and pf) (1958)
Za zedowskim mlynem, song (1954)

SACRED

Holy mass, Missa in honorem Sc. Vincenti (mix-ch and ww insts or org) (1958)

THEATRE

Music for puppet theatre

Publications

Metodyka ksztalcenia sluchu. PWM, 1951.
Materaily do ksztalcenia sluchu. Cracow, 1963.

Ref. 70, 118, 206, 457, 524

E.T.P.A. See Maria Antonia WALPURGIS

EAGAR, Fannie Edith Starke (nee Webb)

South African pianist, teacher and composer. b. Cape Town, August 4, 1920. She studied at the South African College of Music from 1938 to 1940, under Doris Lardner (piano) and Professor W.H. Bell (composition), receiving her L.U.C.T. and U.T.L.M. diplomas. From 1941 to 1945 she taught, whilst studying under Dr. Alban Hamer. She holds the U.T.L.M. (harmony and counterpoint, 1944), L.T.C.L. (1963), F.T.C.L (1964) and U.P.L.M. (1964) diplomas. She taught in several high schools and gave piano recitals in South Africa.

Compositions

VOCAL

In die wonder van die berge (J. de V. Krynauw) (3 part ch) (1958)
Laetitia (A. Visser) (mix-ch) (1954)
Unielied (J. de V. Krynauw) (3 part ch) (1960)
Hermanus school song (A. van Vyk) (1954)
Die pêrel se klokkies (A.G. Visser) (1954)
Seën huis Naudè (2 S and A) (1956)
Vreugdelied (1954)

SACRED

Church anthem (St. Francis of Assisi) (mix-ch) (1954)
Psalm 121 (2 part ch) (1962)

OPERETTA

As die reënnimfe verdwyn, for girls (I. Krynauw, 1959)

Publications

For Eager Fingers. 2 vol. course for beginners. 1967.

Ref. 377

EAGER, Mary Ann
20th-century American poetess and composer. b. Ireland.
Compositions
VOCAL
Glory train (mix-ch)
Songs incl.:
Bloomfield, fair and free
Blue-eyed Kathleen from Killarney
I invoke thee Ireland
I planted a rose in a garden
June
Mother's love
Ode to Thomas More
Oh happy the skylark and I
Painting piano pleasures
When the world smiles again
SACRED
God's will be done
Hitch a ride with the Lord
Let's worship together
The light of God
Thank God for a new-born day
Publications
Poems incl.: *I Stand Accused* and *Open Your Eyes*.
Ref. 8, 190

EAGLES, Moneta M.
Australian organist, concert pianist, singer and composer. b. Concord, 1924. She studied the piano, the organ, singing and composition at the Sydney Conservatorium of Music from 1943 to 1950 and composition privately under Matyas Seiber in London in 1951. She appeared as a piano soloist with the Sydney Symphony Orchestra in 1949 and was a piano recitalist for the Australian Broadcasting Commission from 1946 to 1961. She was director of music for the Australian Delegation to the Edinburgh Film Festival in 1960. She received numerous honors and awards for her compositions.
ORCHESTRA
Autumn rhapsody (pf and orch) (1964)
Diversions for piano and orchestra (1950)
Essay
Illilliwa, 2 preludes (1965)
Soliloquy (1953)
Short orchestral works
CHAMBER
Conversation (cl and pf) (1961)
Two sketches (cl and pf) (1962)
Scherzino (cl)
Lullaby (cl in A) (1956)
PIANO
Aquarelles (1962)
Arabeske (1952)
Mirage (1950)
Sonatina (1954) (Allan and Co.)
VOCAL
The singing of the stars (ch) (1953)
I will lift up mine eyes (1967)
Spring on the plains (1967)
FILM MUSIC
Twenty-one documentaries
Ref. 94, 142, 206, 412, 457

EAKIN, Vera O.
American organist, pianist and composer. b. Emlenton, August 6, 1890. She studied under Ernest Hutcheson at the New England Conservatory, privately under the organist Hugh Giles and at the Juilliard School of Music. She was staff pianist for CBS and for over 30 years was an organist in the New York area. She received several awards from the National Federation of Music Clubs. Her songs have been sung by Laurence Tibbet, James Melton and Eileen Farrell.
Compositions
VOCAL
Songs incl.:
Ay, gitanos
Blind eyes
Christmas morn
Flamenco gypsy moon
Sand stars
To love and dream
Wind and girl
SACRED
The place prepared for thee
Ref. 142, 347

EAKLOR, Vicki
20th-century American composer.
Composition
CHAMBER
Short 'n suite (3 perc) (Music for Percussion, Inc.)

EAMES, Juanita. See MASTERS, Juan

EARLEY, Judith
20th-century British composer.
Composition
CHAMBER
Celone (vlc) (1982)
Ref. *Composer* (London)

EASTES, Helen Marie
American composer. b. Galesburg, April 21, 1892. She obtained her B.Mus. from Knox College. PHOTOGRAPH.
Compositions
CHAMBER
Trio (trb)
Instrumental pieces
PIANO
Aquarelle
Arabesque
Deep blue water
La fille bleu
Impromptu
Reflections
Remembrance
Rondeau
Silhouette
VOCAL
April came across the hill (w-ch)
Can you sing A song (w-ch)
Show lovely spring (w-ch)
Numerous songs
SACRED
God grant us peace (mix-ch)
Numerous religious anthems (ch)
Numerous sacred songs
Ref. composer

EATON, Frances
19th-century English composer.
Compositions
CHAMBER
Piano pieces
VOCAL
The fire slave, cantata (soli, ch and pf)
Choral works
Songs
Ref. 226, 276

EBERLIN, Anna Margrethe
19th-century Danish composer.
Compositions
VOCAL
Mine Gutter (Copenhagen: Carl Allers Forlag, 1899)
Sommer (composer) (Forlag, 1899)
Ref. 331

EBERLIN, Maria Barbara Caecilia
Austrian composer. b. Salzburg, November 17, 1728; d. December 14, 1766. The eldest daughter of the Salzburg Hofkapellmeister Johann Ernst Eberlin, she was a close friend of the Mozart family. In 1751 she married the court singer Joseph Nikolaus Meissner.
Compositions
VOCAL
Four religious songs (German text) (vce and insts) (1750, 1751)
Ref. 128

ECHENFELD, Katharina

German nun and composer. ca. 1521. She belonged to the Tangendorff convent in the Naumburg diocese and composed a mass.

Ref. 128

ECKHARDT-GRAMATTE, Sophie-Carmen

Canadian pianist, violinist, professor and composer of Russian and French parentage. b. Moscow, January 6, 1902; d. Stuttgart, December 2, 1974. She spent her childhood in England and France and had her first piano lessons from her mother, who was a pupil of Anton Rubinstein and teacher of Tolstoy's children. She later studied the violin and the piano at the Paris Conservatoire and was examined by Debussy, Ravel and Moszkowski. At the age of 11 she made her debut in Berlin and studied at the Preussische Akademie, Berlin under Jacques Thibaud and Bronislaw Hubermann (violin). She toured Europe as a pianist with Edwin Fischer and after her marriage lived in Barcelona from 1924 to 1929. In 1928 Leopold Stokowski invited her to the United States to play her own compositions with the Philadelphia Symphony Orchestra. She returned to Germany and attended the composition master classes of Max Trapp. In 1939, she went to live in Vienna, where she enjoyed great success as a composer. In 1948 and 1949 she was awarded the composition prize of the Musikverein and in 1948 received the prize of the IGNM (Austrian section of the International Society for Contemporary Music) for her *Concerto for piano and orchestra, No. 2.* 1949 she won the Austrian State prize for her *Triple concerto.* In 1953 she left Vienna to settle in Winnipeg, where her husband was appointed director of the Art Gallery. She shared first and second prizes for orchestral works at the GEDOK World Competition for Women Composers in Mannheim, Germany (1961, 1966); received an honorary doctorate from Brandon University and the title of professor from the Austrian government (1970). Between 1965 and 1967 she received four commissions for compositions. Her work has been performed and broadcast in the United States, Canada, Austria and Germany. She had a large number of pupils and was a member of the Canadian League of Composers, CAPAC and the Oesterreichische Gesellschaft fuer zeitgenossische Musik. DISCOGRAPHY. PHOTOGRAPH.

Compositions

ORCHESTRA

Symphony in C (1939)
Symphony No. 11, Manitoba (1969-1970)
Markantes Stueck (2 pf and orch; also pf) (1946-1950)
Concerto for bassoon and orchestra (1950) (CMC)
Concerto for orchestra (1953-1954) (CMC)
Concerto for piano No. 1 (1925)
Concerto for piano and orchestra No. 2 (1946) (IGNM prize)
Concerto for violin and orchestra II (1948-1952) (CMC, 1952)
Grave funèbre (vln and orch)
Symphonic concerto for piano and orchestra (CMC, 1967)
Triple concerto (trp, cl, bsn, timp and str orch) (1949) (Austrian State prize, 1949)
Trumpet concerto
Capriccio concertante (1940)
Concertino for strings (1947)
Passacaglia and fugue (also pf) (1937)
Ziganka, ballet suite (1920)
Konzertstueck (vlc and cham orch) (1974)
Molto sostenuto (str orch) (1952)

CHAMBER

Nonet (ww qnt and str qrt) (CMC, 1967)
Fanfare for 8 brass instruments (1971)
Woodwind quintet (CMC, 1963)
String quartet No. 1 in C-Sharp Minor (1938)
String quartet No. 2, Hainburger (1943)
String quartet No. 3 (CMC, 1964)
Wind quartet (1946) (CMC)
Nicolas trio (vln, vla and vlc) (CMC, 1947)
Piano trio (CMC, 1967)
Trio for winds (1947)
Triotino (vln, vla and vlc) (1947)
Woodwind trio (fl, cl and bsn) (CMC, 1967)
Concerto (vla da gamba and hpcd) (1971)
Berceuse (fl and pf)
Berceuse and presto in old style (fl and vln) (1922)
Duo (fl and vln)
Duo (vla and vlc) (1944)
Duo (vlc and pf)
Duo concertante (fl and vln) (CMC, 1956)
Duo concertante (vlc and vln; also vlc and pf) (1959)
Duo No. 1 (2 vln) (1944) (Oesterr. Bundesverlag, 1949)
Duo No. 2 (2 vln) (Oesterr. Bundesverlag, 1949)
February suite (vln and pf)
Der geiger (vln and pf)
Improvisation (fl and pf)
Lacrima (vla or vlc and pf)
Ruck-ruck sonata (cl and pf) (CMC, 1947)
Prestos I and II (fl and pf)

PIANO

Arabeske
Danse de nègre (N. Simrock, 1924)
Etude de concert II
Fourteen alphabet pieces
Introduction and variations
Kosak
Petite danseuse à la corde
Six caprices (1936)
Sonatas I-4
Sonate No. 5, Klavierstueck (1950)
Suite No. 1, Sonata (1923) (Simrock, 1924)
Suite No. 2, Biscaya (1924)
Suite No. 3 (1924)
Suite No. 4 (1928)
Suite No. 5 (1950)
Suite No. 6, Drei Klavierstuecke (1928-1952)
Trepak
Tune for a child
Arrangements (Paganini, Chopin)

VIOLIN

Concerto for violin solo (1925)
Suite for violin solo No. 1, Sonata I (Simrock, 1924)
Suite for violin solo No. 2, Partita II (Simrock, 1924)
Suite for violin solo No. 3, Mallorca (Eschig, 1929)
Suite for violin solo No. 4, Pacific (CMC, 1969)
Ten caprices (1924-1934) (Simrock, 1929)

VOCAL

Christmas songs (mix-ch and cham insts) (1953-1954)

Bibliography

Canadian Composer. Sept. 1969, pp. 9-11.
Sangwine, Jean. *S.C.E-G. Composer. Chatelaine*. Canada, Sept. 1967. p. 43.
Sophie Carmen Eckhardt-Gramatte: A Portrait. Musicanada, Oct. 1969, pp. 8-9.
Winters, Ken. *The Same Moon and Start: E-G. in Profile. Winnipeg Free Press*. Feb. 17, 1962.

Ref. composer, 5, 8, 17, 22, 41, 52, 63, 70, 74, 77, 93, 94, 96, 105, 189, 194, 226, 280, 329, 347, 371, 402, 563

EDELMANN, Mme.

18th-century French composer. She married the German composer Johann Friedrich Edelmann (1749 to 1794) who was guillotined in Paris.

Ref. 177

EDELSBERG, Philippine von

German pianist, singer and composer. b. Munich, 1835. She made her name as a pianist, then turned to singing and until 1867 sang in the Berlin Opera. From 1870 to 1872 she was at the Royal Theatre in Brussels and after 1873 sang at La Scala in Milan. She later moved to the United States. She composed piano pieces and songs.

Ref. 129

EDGERLY, Cora Emily

American organist, soprano and composer. b. Portland, 1865; d. June 2l, 1956. She studied the organ under Latham True and Alfred Brinkler and voice under M. Bowdoin, Ernest Hill and Elizabeth Brown.

Compositions

MISCELLANEOUS

Roses in bloom
Military hesitation waltz
General pershing march

Ref. 374

EDICK, Ethel Vera Ingraham

Early 20th-century American pianist, music teacher and composer. She made her piano debut in 1913, then gave concerts and taught at Portland, OR,. She composed piano pieces and songs.

Ref. 226

EDWARDS, Bella

Compositions

PIANO

Pierrot valse (Hansen)
Rosenvalsen (Hansen)

Ref. Willem Hansen catalog

EDWARDS, Clara (pseud. Bernard Haigh)

American pianist, singer and composer. b. April 18, 1887; d. New York, January 17, 1974. She studied at the Cosmopolitan School of Music and in Vienna. DISCOGRAPHY.

Compositions

VOCAL

Choral works
More than 50 songs incl.:
All thine own (C. Fischer, 1935)
At twilight (G. Schirmer, 1944)
Awake beloved (Schirmer, 1925)
A benediction (Schirmer, 1927)
Birds
By the bend of the river (vce and pf) (Schirmer, 1927)
Clementine
The day's begun (Schirmer, 1930)
The fisher's widow (Schirmer, 1929)
Into the night (vce and pf) (Schirmer, 1939)
Lady Noon (O. Ditson, 1927)
Ol' Jim
Stars of the night, sing softly
With the wind and the rain in your face (Schirmer, 1930)

SACRED

Dedication
Psalm 27
When Jesus walked on Galilee

INCIDENTAL MUSIC

Music for marionettes (Tony Sarg)
Film music

Ref. 39, 40, 85, 94, 142, 190, 228, 292, 347, 563, 622

EDWARDS, Jessie B.

20th-century American composer of choral works and songs.

Ref. 142

EFREIN, Laurie

20th-century American composer.

Composition

CHAMBER

Attraction (fl)

Ref. 142

EGEBERG, Anna

Norwegian composer. b. 1843; d. 1914.

Compositions

(All published by Warmuth)

CHAMBER

Skizze (pf and vln)
Piano pieces

VOCAL

Three songs (mix-ch)
Digte af Henrik Wergeland
En vaarnat
Five songs
Five new songs
Tre sange af arne
Tre sange med tysk text
Serenade: Toer ikke daempet og sagte
Til Overlaerer Knudsen paa 80-aarige Foedselsdag
Wasserflut: Manche Traen' aus meinen Augen

SACRED

Kirkesange af Kingo, Oldenburg, Grundtvig
Lyksalige pinse
Four songs
Tre Julesange

Ref. NMI, 297

EGEBERG, Fredrikke Sophie

Norwegian composer. b. November 23, 1815; d. May 6, 1861.

Compositions

PIANO

Marsch (4 hands)
Carlsmarch
Four Norwegian songs for piano
Six songs without words

VOCAL

Didtets aand
Asylbarnets farvel til generalinde Wedel-Jarlsberg
Tre digte af B. Bjornson
Engelske digte med norsk oversettelse
Jacob Peter Mynster
En moders boen
Tre norske sange
Tredje quartetter for mandsstemmer
Svenske og danske digte af Boettiger og Hauch

SACRED

Gud give mig det at laere
Guds fred

Bibliography

Anna Lindhjem: *Women Composers and Music Teachers in Scandinavia.* 1931.
J.G. Conradi: *Music's Development and Present Position in Norway.* 1878.

Ref. NMI

EGERT, Nina

20th-century American composer of vocal works, some of which were performed at the Mills College Chapel in 1980.

Ref. AWC newletter

EGGAR, Katharine

English pianist and composer. b. London, 1874. She was the first English woman to perform her own chamber works at a London public concert.

Compositions

CHAMBER

Piano quintet
Idyll (fl and pf)
Sonata for violoncello

PIANO

Tarantella
Two sketches (Chester)

VOCAL

Songs

SACRED

Hymns

Ref. 41, 105, 226, 297

EGGELING-SPIES, I.

Composition

CHAMBER

Rondo D-Moll (vln and pf)

Ref. Frau und Musik

EGGLESTON, Anne E.

Canadian pianist, teacher and composer. b. Ottawa, September 6, 1934. She studied under Robert Fleming in Ottawa (piano and composition) and from 1953 at the Royal Conservatory in Toronto under Pierre Souvairan (piano) and Oskar Morawetz, Godfrey Ridout and John Weinzweig (composition). She received her artist diploma in 1956 and obtained her M.Mus. at the Eastman School of Music (1957 to 1958) after studying under Emily Davis, Orazio Frugoni (piano) and Bernard Rogers (composition). She was winner of the CAPAC Composers' Competition in 1953 and 1954 and won the Arthur Comeau Scholarship for composition in 1965 and the Canada Foundation Trophy of the Ottawa Music Festival in 1953. From 1958 she taught the piano, theory and composition privately in Ottawa. DISCOGRAPHY. PHOTOGRAPH.

Compositions

ORCHESTRA

Variations on a theme by Bela Bartok (1972)
Fanfaron for orchestra (1966)
Interlude for small orchestra (1957)
On Citadel Hill (str orch) (1964) (comm Canadian Music Center)
Suryanamaskar (1972) (comm Merivale High School Concert Band)
Three pieces (1955-1956)

CHAMBER

Quartet for piano and strings (1954-1955)
String quartet (1956-1957)
Antique suite (2 a-rec and pf) (1967)

PIANO

Hurry, hurry, hurry (1973)
Seven variations (1975)
Sketches of Ottawa (1962)
Sonatine (1964)

VOCAL

Autumnal clouds (J.C. Fletcher) (Bar and orch) (1958)
I never shall forget (D. Lachman) (w-ch and pf)
My lonely heart, Quebec City (w-ch and pf) (1963)

Autumn wind (vce and pf) (1952)
Armenian lullaby
Five lullabies of Eugene Fields (1960)
Jewish lullaby
Norse lullaby
Songs from Deep Wood (1955)
Three songs (1967) (comm CAMMAC)
To the lute players (vce and pf) (1952)
Other songs and lullabies
SACRED
The Christ Child's lullaby (ch and pf)
Christmas song (B. Carmen)
OPERA
The Wood Carver's Wife (Pickthall) (1961)
ARRANGEMENTS
Five French Canadian folk songs (S, A and T recs) (1954) (comm CAMMAC)
Ref. CMC, 94, 329, 347, 402, 457, 477, 563

EGNOS, Bertha
20th-century South African producer and composer.
Compositions
THEATRE
Ipi Tombi
FILM MUSIC
Dingaka (1965)
Ref. 326

EGOROVA, Maria
Soviet composer. d. 1951. She earned the title of Honored Worker in the Arts of the Kazakh SSR.
Composition
VOCAL
Dudar-ay!
Ref. 453

EHRHARDT, Else
20th-century German composer.
Composition
CHAMBER
Fuenf Flotenspruenge (rec) (Celle: Moeck, 1943)
Ref. Frau und Musik

EHRMANN, Rosette
French composer. b. 1887. She studied under Vincent d'Indy.
Compositions
CHAMBER
Fantaisie (2 vln and pf)
Sonatas
Ref. 41, 226

EICHENWALD, Sylvia
Swiss flautist, pianist, conductor, lecturer and composer. b. Basle, March 17, 1947. Her father was her first piano teacher. She then studied the flute under Joseph Bopp and the piano and singing in Basle and Vienna. She studied theory under Hans Ulrich Lehmann, Robert Suter, Jacques Wildberger, Thomas Kessler, Wolfgang Neininger and Juerg Wyttenback. She graduated in 1978 and continued conducting studies. From 1970 to 1975 she was assistant conductor for opera at the Basle Theatre. After 1980 she taught theory at the Basle Music Academy, becoming assistant principal in 1982. She conducted various orchestras and from 1984 lectured at the Volkshochschule.
Compositions
ORCHESTRA
Passacaglia (str orch) (1984)
CHAMBER
Spielstudie: Capriccio (3 fl, 2 ob, 2 cl and 2 bsn) (1980)
Liebeslied (2 fl) (1981)
VOCAL
Kinderlieder (chil-ch) (1984)
Es loest der Mensch nicht (Schiller) (m-S, Bar and cl) (1982)
Sie erlischt (H. Heine) (narr, vln, trp, d-b and dr) (1977)
Ref. composer

EICHHORN, Hermene Warlick
American organist, choir director and composer. b. Hickory, NC, April 3, 1906. She studied music privately and earned a B.A. at the University of North Carolina. From 1926 she was organist at the Holy Trinity Episcopal Church, Greensboro and from 1932 was choir director there. From 1928 to 1951 she wrote the music column for the *Greensboro Daily News*.
Compositions
CHAMBER
Organ pieces (Brodt Music Co.; T. Presser)
Piano pieces (Brodt; T. Presser; Summy)
VOCAL
Chansonette
SACRED
Corinthians 1, cantata
Mary Magdalene, cantata
Song of the highest, cantata
Ref. 40, 142, 347

EICHNER, Adelheid Marie
German pianist, singer and composer. b. Mannheim, 1762; d. Potsdam, April 5, 1787. She was the daughter of Ernst Eichner, bassoonist and oboist. Her first teacher was an aged Italian castrato in Mannheim. In 1773 she went with her father to Potsdam, where she was engaged by the Crown Prince for his private orchestra. She also sang in the opera in Potsdam.
Compositions
VOCAL
Deux chansons (vce and pf) (1784)
Lieder fuer eine Singstimme mit Clavier (Potsdam: Horvath, 1780)
Lieder in Musikalischer Blumenstrauss (Berlin, 1792)
Mach mir vom Volk, in Andres Lieder, Arien und Duette
Ref. 8, 26, 121, 128, 347

EILERS, Joyce Elaine
American teacher and composer. b. Mooreland, July 28, 1941. She received her B.Mus. from the University of Oregon. She taught in schools from 1963 and after 1972 lived in Corvallis, OR,.
Compositions
VOCAL
Choral works
Other published works
SACRED
Born today
The gift
A star shone bright
Tiny King
Ref. 142

EIRIKSDOTTIR, Karolina
Icelandic teacher and composer. b. Reykjavik, January 10, 1951. She graduated from the Reykjavik College of Music in 1974 and gained her M.Mus. (music history and musicology) from the University of Michigan in 1976 and in composition in 1978. She is currently teaching at the Reykjavik College of Music. Her works have been performed in the United States, Iceland and elsewhere in Scandinavia. PHOTOGRAPH.
Compositions
ORCHESTRA
Five tunes (cham orch) (1983)
Notes (1978)
Sonans (1981)
CHAMBER
Nabulations (2 fl, 2 trp, 2 trb, 2 per, vln and d-b) (1978)
Brot (fl, ob, cl, hn, perc, hp, vln, vla and vlc) (1979)
Six movements (str qrt) (1983)
IVP (fl, vln and vlc) (1977)
In vultu solis (vln) (1980)
Rondo (pf) (1984)
VOCAL
Six poems from the Japanese (m-S, fl and cl) (1977)
Sumir dagar (S, fl, cl, vlc and pf) (1982)
Two tunes for choir (1983)
Ref. composer

EISENSTEIN, Judith Kaplan
20th-century American composer.
Composition
SACRED
The Sacrifice of Isaac, liturgical drama (1972)
Ref. 142

EISENSTEIN, Stella Price

American organist, pianist, violinist, teacher and composer. b. Glasgow, MT, February 16, 1886; d. Moberly, MT, March 28, 1969. She studied the violin and the piano at Goetz Conservatory in Moberly and the Cincinnati Conservatory. She later studied composition under Felix Borowski at the Chicago Musical College and organ under Hans Feil in Kansas City. In 1928 she became an Associate of the American Guild of Organists. She toured as a violinist and after she married, settled in Moberly as a violin, piano and organ teacher.

Compositions

CHAMBER

Memories of the South (vln and pf)
Organ works
Violin works

VOCAL

Anthems and other choral works

Ref. 40, 142, 347

EISENSTEIN DE VEGA, Silvia

Argentine pianist, conductor, ethnomusicologist, teacher and composer. b. Buenos Aires, January 5, 1917. She studied under E. Drangosch and made her debut at the age of nine. Later she continued her studies under J. de Lalewicz and at the Conservatory and University of Buenos Aires. She researched throughout South America in collaboration with musicologist Carlos Vega and was active as a teacher.

Compositions

ORCHESTRA

Andinas, suite
Surena, symphonic suite

CHAMBER

Piano pieces

VOCAL

Choral works
Ten songs

BALLET

Supay, in one act, based on a native legend

ARRANGEMENTS

Folk tunes and dances

Ref. 81, 361, 390

EKIZIAN, Michelle

20th-century American composer.

Compositions

CHAMBER

Midnight voices (ob and 5 insts) (1984)

VOCAL

Hidden crosses (vces and ens)

Ref. Frau und Musik

EKSANISHVILI, Eleonora Grigorevna

Soviet pianist, lecturer and composer. b. Tbilisi, February 11, 1919. She graduated from the conservatory there in 1940, having studied the piano under A. Tulashvili. In 1945 she completed her composition studies under P. Ryazanov and A. Balanchivadze. She also studied the piano under E.V. Cherniavsky. In 1950 she completed postgraduate study in the piano at the Moscow Conservatory under A. Goldenweiser. From 1944 to 1946 and after 1950, she lectured on the piano at the music school in Tbilisi and after 1953 at the conservatory. After 1944 she was a soloist with the Philharmonic Orchestra of the Georgian SSR.

Compositions

ORCHESTRA

Piano concerto No. 1 (1943-1944)
Piano concerto No. 2 (1953-1955)

CHAMBER

Piano quintet (1945)
String quartet No. 1 (1944)
String quartet No. 2 (1948-1949)

PIANO

Etudes (1944)
Partita (1947-1948)
Preludes (1944)
Sketches
Teaching works

VOCAL

Kakhetinskie nochi (I. Mosashvili) (vce and pf) (1947)
Klyatva (G. Abashidze) (vce and pf) (1944)
Noch (A. Abasheli) (trans E. Aleksandrova) (vce and pf) (1950)
Posvyashchenie akademiku Aleksandru Dzhavakhishvili (M. Kavtaradze) (vce and pf) (1955)
Sovietski pogranichnik (V. Gabeskiriya) (vce and pf) (1944)
Zhaloba Davida (D. Gulamishvili, trans. E. Zabolotski) (vce and pf) (1955)

INCIDENTAL MUSIC

Kovarstvo i lyubov, theatre (Schiller) (1945)

Ref. 87, 458

EL RUISENOR MEXICANO. See PERALTA CASTERA, Angela

ELCHEVA (Yelcheva), Irina Mikhailovna

Soviet composer. b. 1926.

Compositions

ORCHESTRA

Pechorskie stariny, suite (Leningrad: Sovietski Kompozitor, 1981)

VOCAL

Rural scenes on folk poems (15 m-vces and w-ch a-cap) (1979)
Lebed belaia, cycle (m-S and pf) (Muzyka, 1982)
Zhanrovye zarisovki (S, Bar and pf) (Sovietski Kompoz., 1985)

Ref. Otto Harrassowitz (Wiesbaden)

ELDESE, Renee

19th-century composer.

Compositions

CHAMBER

Andantino (vln) (Girod)
Attendu (vlc) (Pfister)
St. Jean (vln) (Hachette)
Apaisement (Pfister)

PIANO

Aurore (Pfister)
Caresse d'avril, impromptu (Lemoine)
Fête au village (Lemoine)
Mai (Pfister)
Matinale (Girod)
Neige (Pfister)
Prelude (Heugel)
Printemps, prelude (Heugel)
Quatre saisons (Heugel)
Ronde de papillons (Lemoine)
Sounds and sweet airs (Pfister)
Sur la fleure (Pfister)
Te souvient-il? (Heugel)
Variations sur un thème de Schumann (Heugel)
Vergeu del'aurore (Heugel)

Ref. 297

ELEANOR OF AQUITAINE

French troubadour and Queen of France and England. b. 1122; d. April 1, 1204. She was the granddaughter of William IX, Duke of Aquitaine and one of the earliest patrons of the troubadours. Eleanor, who inherited his musical tastes, married Louis VII of France and became the greatest patroness of the troubadours. She was said to have introduced the art into northern France, where they were called trouvères. She encouraged the poets there to emulate the skills of their southern counterparts. She accompanied her husband on crusades and enjoyed many romantic episodes in the name of chivalry. In 1511, despite their three daughters, the marriage was annulled and Eleanor married Henry of Anjou, who succeeded to the English throne in 1154. Her attempts to introduce the troubadour movement met with little success owing to the prevalence and popularity of the glee-singers and glee-maidens. Eleanor was the mother of King John of Magna Carta fame and of King Richard who was the subject of the minstrel Blondin's famous search. She was also the grandmother of Blanche de Castille (q.v.) also a famous troubadour. PHOTOGRAPH.

Ref. 208, 260, 565, 653

ELENA

Archaic Greek singer and composer who lived prior to the period of Homer. She was famous for the quality of her voice and compositions. She is mentioned in Book 4 of Ptolemy's History, as preserved by Photius.

Ref. 162

ELIAS, Graciela Morales de

Mexican violinist teacher and composer. b. Mexico, October 28, 1944. She studied the violin under H. Novelo, L. Samuel Saloma and J.R. Vasca and at the Escuela Nacional de Music de Universidad Nacional Autonoma de

Mexico, gaining her B.A. and B.Sc. in the violin and composition. She attended a seminar on avant-garde music under Jean Etienne Marie in 1968 and undertook courses on the works of Karlheinz Stockhausen under the composer himself. She founded the University Group of Composition X-1, took part in numerous conferences and participated in popular concerts (Diploma Award by the Federal District Departments, 1970). She was teacher of solfege, harmony and violin at the Instituto Mexicano de Musica, 1967 to 1970.
ORCHESTRA
Tangente (3 soloists and orch) (1973)
CHAMBER
Rapsodia (fl and str qrt) (1971)
Policromia (fl, cl, hp, bsn and perc) (1970)
Quartet (strs) (1965)
Nine preludes (pf) (1967)
VOCAL
Fantasia (w-ch and cl) (1969)
Soneto (mix-ch) (Fray Miguel de Guevara) (1967)
Dos poemas (S, cl and vlc) (1973)
Ref. composer

ELIDORA, Donna. See WUIET, Caroline

ELIODD. See ODDONE SULI-RAO, Ėlisabetta

ELIZABETH, Margravine of. See ANSPACH, Elizabeth, Margravine of

ELIZABETH I, Queen of England and Ireland
English Queen and composer. b. Greenwich Palace, September 7, 1533; d. March 24, 1603. She was the daughter of Henry VIII and Anne Boleyn (q.v.). Elizabeth was a woman of high educational standards, being well versed in the Greek and Latin classics and fluent in French, Spanish and Italian. She ascended the throne of England on November 17, 1558. She set to music the psalms of Margaret of Navarre in 1549 and these were published in 1845. She composed some songs and hymns.
Ref. 465, 637, 645, 646

ELKAN, Ida
American pianist, teacher, writer and composer. b. New York City, December 25, 1894. She studied at Hunter College from 1912 to 1914 and at the Teachers' College of Columbia University. Her principal music teacher was violinist Israel Rudolph Katz, with whom she made her debut in 1915 and whom she married the following year. She taught adult piano classes at the Cass Technical High School and at the Institute of Musical Art in Detroit. She opened her own studios in New York City in 1935 and contributed articles to music periodicals, including a regular column for *Music Forum and Digest*.
Compositions
CHAMBER
Moods major and minor (pf) (1949)
VOCAL
Our family piano suite with words, songs (1942)
The United Nations song (1943)
Other songs
OPERETTA
Several children's operettas
ARRANGEMENTS
A piano part to the Partita in E (vln) (J.S. Bach)
Let's sight read at the piano, 25 Russian folk songs
Publications
Piano Sight Reading Can be Taught. 1948.
Practical Piano Playing Manual. 1933.
Technical Work in Ear Training for the Piano. 1926.
Theory Writing Book. 1939.
Ref. 433, 496

ELKIND (Elkind-Tourre), Rachel
American record producer, singer and composer. b. Hong Kong, September 22, 1937. She went to the United States in 1946 and received the B.A. from the University of California, Berkeley (1959). Her arrangement of *Switched-on-Bach* won the Grammy Award of the National Academy of Recording Arts and Sciences in 1969, the National Association of Record Merchandisers award for the best-selling classical record in 1969 and 1972 and was the Schwann Readers' Poll winner in 1969 and 1970. DISCOGRAPHY.
Compositions
FILM MUSIC
A Clockwork Orange (with Wendy Carlos q.v.) (1971)
Remember Me, for Unesco Year of The Child (1979)
The Shining (with Wendy Carlos) (1980)
ARRANGEMENTS
Switched-on-Bach
Ref. 506, 563

ELKIND-TOURRE, Rachel. See ELKIND, Rachel

ELKOSHI, Rivka
Israeli pianist, teacher and composer. b. Radauz-Bokovina, Rumania, July 17, 1949. She left Rumania for Israel when she was two years old. She received her B.Mus. in piano performance from the Rubin Music Academy, Jerusalem in 1973 and her M.A. in music education at New York University (1976). She studied musicology at the Hebrew University, Jerusalem from 1970 to 1976 and for a Ph.D. in music education and composition at the University of California, Los Angeles, 1983 to 1984. She taught the piano at the Rubin Conservatory, Jerusalem from 1972 to 1981 and then for a year in an American school. She won several study awards, in Israel and the United States. PHOTOGRAPH.
Compositions
CHAMBER
Six postcard pictures (fl and pf) (1981) (Israel Music Publ.)
PIANO
Five invented dances (4 hands) (1979) (Israel Music)
Frames and Forms, 6 aleatoric pieces (1981) (Tel Aviv: Israel Music Institute)
Moving Structures, 5 aleatoric episodes (1979)
Stories in Sounds (1980) (Israel Music Inst.)
VOCAL
Fifty Israeli pieces for an Orff ensemble (songs, calls, poems and insts) (1984)
SACRED
Fruits of Heaven, youth cantata (1982-1983) (Israel Music Inst.)
OPERA
Intervals and Intrigues (chil-vces, improvised perc and pf) (1980) (Israel Music)
TEACHING PIECES
Let's Play Dissonances, 16 pieces for early graders (1978) (Tel Aviv: Or Tar)
Ref. composer, Dr. Peter Gradenwitz (Tel Aviv)

ELL. See LOUD, Emily L.

ELLEN, Mary
Belgian pianist and composer. b. August 27, 1910.
Compositions
PIANO
Berceuse (1954)
Musique legere (1939, 1952)
Ouverture (1939)
Suite de valses (1938)
Waltzes and tangos
Ref. Belgian Music Info. Center

ELLERMAN, Helen
American composer. b. 1925.
Composition
ELECTRONIC
Invensartita (with Ray Ellerman) (hpcd and tape)
Ref. 346

ELLICOTT, Rosalind Frances
English pianist and composer. b. Cambridge, November 14, 1857; d. London, April 5, 1924. She was the daughter of the Reverend Charles John Ellicott, the Bishop of Gloucester and Bristol and began to compose at the age of six and at 18 entered the Royal Academy of Music until 1881. Later she studied form and orchestration under Thomas Wingham, 1885 to 1892. She was commissioned to write works for the Gloucester and Cheltenham festivals.

Compositions
ORCHESTRA
Fantasia in A-Minor (pf and orch) (1895)
Concert overture (1886)
Dramatic overture (1886)
Festival overture (1893)
CHAMBER
Quartet in F
Piano trios in G and D-Minor
Sonata (vla and pf)
Sonata (vlc and pf)
Piano pieces
VOCAL
The birth of song, cantata
Elysium, cantata (1889)
Henry of Navarre, cantata (1894)
Radiant sister of the dawn, cantata
Choral songs incl.:
To the immortals (1803)
Duets
Part songs incl.:
Bring the bright garlands (1890)
Songs
Ref. 6, 8, 22, 44, 70, 85, 100, 105, 107, 110, 124, 160, 226, 276, 347, 369

ELLIOTT, Charlotte
English composer. b. Clapham, March 17, 1789; d. Brighton, September 22, 1871. She was an invalid for most of her life. She edited the *Christian Pocket Book* from 1834-1859 and her hymns have appeared in Hymnals thoughout the English-speaking world.
Compositions
SACRED
Approx 150 hymns incl.:
Just as I am, without one plea
My God, my Father, while I stray
O Holy Saviour, friend unseen
Thy will Be done
Publications
Hymns for the Week.
The Invalid's Hymn Book.
Ref. 369

ELLIOTT, Janice Overmiller
American composer. b. Atchison, KS, February 5, 1921. She studied composition under Howard Hanson and Bernard Rodgers. She obtained a B.Mus. from Southwestern College, KS, and an M.Mus. from the Eastman School of Music. She received first and second prizes for composition from the Kansas State Federation of Music Clubs.
Compositions
ORCHESTRA
Viola concerto
PIANO
Pieces
VOCAL
Cantata (mix-ch and str qrt)
Songs
Ref. 137

ELLIOTT, Marjorie Reeve
American authoress, choir conductor, teacher and composer. b. Syracuse, NY, August 7, 1890. She came from a musical background and showed talent for composing at an early age. She studied under Adolph Frey at Syracuse University where she received a B.Mus. and an honorary D.Mus.. She founded the Settlement Music School, Syracuse, in 1916 and the Settlement Music School, St. Louis, in 1921. She was choir conductor of the Baptist and Presbyterian churches from 1942 to 1968 and the head of Elliott Studio of Music, Oneida, from 1942 to 1973. She won an award from the National League of American Pen Women in 1968 and 1972 and received the George Arents Medal from Syracuse University for achievement in music in 1973. She also received the Centennial Award from the City of Syracuse in 1948. She was active as a teacher and published over 40 choral and piano works.
Compositions
PIANO
Numerous pieces incl.:
I want to be a pilot (1983)
March on America (1934)
VOCAL
Songs incl.:
Give me a song to sing (solo and mix-ch)
Gremlins (ch)
Jolly farmer (ch)
Joy of life (mix-ch and pf) (1983)
On a lovely summer evening (ch)
The storm king (ch)
Three little maids (w-ch) (R.A. Hoffman) (sold more than 50,000 copies)
Where willows bend (ch) (1946)
Your song (ch) (1946)
Awake it's spring!
Beloved, did you come to me?
Brother's lament
The drum (Hoffman)
The gift (S and pf) (Harold Flammer, 1983)
I flew with the wind
I love a windy day (Gail Brook Burnet)
Lament
Looking at the sky with you
The moon lends a hand
Spring gossip (B.F. Wood)
Springtime lullaby and fairy parasols
Starlight (Hoffman)
Tattered veil (1st prize, National League of American Pen Women, 1968)
Numerous fun songs
SACRED
A better world (mix-ch and pf) (1983)
An understanding heart (soli and ch) (Hoffman)
God gave us love (mix-ch and pf) (Flammer)
Christmas eve (mix-ch and pf) (1983) (Montgomery Co.)
Easter and other anthems for church choir incl.:
Blessed Saviour
Father of mankind (J. Spratt)
He hath great understanding (Broadman)
Know ye the Lord
Unto God let praises ring (Hoffman)
OPERA
Gypsy Moon
OPERETTA
Big Sister's Wedding (Hoffman)
The Happy Scarecrow (Willis Music Co.)
Medics and Merriment (Hoffman)
A Strange Adventure, for elementary students
Publications
The Red Geranium. Novel.
Ref. composer, 84, 141, 142, 190, 496, 624

ELLIOTT, Mary Sims
American writer and composer. b. Summit, NJ, May 22, 1890. She studied at Dr. Frank Damrosch's Institute of Musical Art, New York from 1911 to 1912 and composed music mainly for the Women's Federation Clubs.
Publications
Land of My Father's Pride. 1964.
Songs of Life and Love. 1965.
Speak Lord. 1963.
Ref. 84

ELLIS, Cecil Osik
American composer. b. Chicago, 1884. She composed choral works and songs.
Ref. 347, 353

ELLIS, Vivian
English pianist, authoress and composer. b. London, 1904. She studied the piano under Dame Myra Hess.
Compositions
OPERETTA
Big Ben
Bless the Bride
Tough at the Top
Water Gypsies
INCIDENTAL MUSIC
Jill Darling
Listen to the Wind
Mister Cinders
Revues
Under your Hat
MISCELLANEOUS
Coronation Scot
Ref. 295, 490

ELMORE, Cenieth Catherine
American professor and composer. b. Wilson, NC, July 4, 1930. She obtained her B.Mus. in theory at the University of North Carolina in 1953, where she studied composition under Elliott Weisgarber, Edgar Alden, Wilton Mason and Roger Hannay. She studied at the University of North Carolina, Chapel Hill and received a M.A. in composition in 1962, M.A. in musicology in 1963 and a Ph.D. in musicology in 1972. From 1963 she was associate professor of music at Campbell College.
Compositions
CHAMBER
Fugue in G (str qrt) (1960)
PIANO
Five pieces (1967)
Sonatina (1953)
VOCAL
Secular cantata (1962)
O world (mix-ch) (1961)
Publications
Some stylistic considerations in the piano sonatas of Nikolai Medtner.
Ref. composer, 137, 347

ELPIS DE BOECE, Dame
5th-century French composer. Her two Latin hymns were incorporated into the Roman breviary. Guy Lefevre translated the first hymn into French.
Compositions
SACRED
Aurea luce, hymn
Felix per omnes, hymn
Ref. 218

ELSCHNIG, Marietta
Austrian teacher and composer of songs. b. Trieste, May 1, 1860.
Ref. 226

ELSSLER, Fanny
Austrian composer of songs. b. 1810; d. 1884.
Ref. 502

ELST, Nancy van der
Dutch choral conductor, critic, musicologist, professor, writer and composer. b. Utrecht, May 9, 1919. She was the daughter of campanologist Wijnandus van der Elst. Her compositions were influenced by her teacher Catharina van Rennes (q.v.). She studied musicology at the Rijksuniversiteit in Utrecht under A. Smijers and E. Reeser. She was awarded a doctorate from the Sorbonne in Paris in 1972, having studied singing under Noemie Perugia and musicology under Jacques Chailley. She took final diplomas in singing at the Utrecht Conservatory and the Ecole Normale in Paris. She was professor of singing, history of music and choir conductor at Rotterdam Conservatory. She was music critic for the *Utrechts Nieuwsblad*.
Compositions
ORGAN
Twee koraalvoorspelen in Barokstijl
VOCAL
Cantata in honorem Reginae Julianae (ch, brass and org) (1973)
Wat wilt gij? (K.H.R. de Josselin de Jong) (2 S) (1975)
Songs and works for female choirs
SACRED
Drie kerstliederen op Oud-Hollandse tekst (1949)
Three Christmas Carols (w-vces) (1973)
Preghiera semplice (vces and org) (1979)
Publications
Gelukskind. Life of Mendelssohn. 1953.
Henri Duparc, l'homme et son oeuvre. 1972.
Contributions to *Mens et Melodie*, *Ouverture* and *Revue Musicale de Suisse Romande.*
Ref. 77, 283, 461

ELVYN, Myrtle
American pianist and composer. b. Sherman, TX, 1886. She studied under Godowsky and made her debut in Berlin in 1904. She performed with some of the major European orchestras and composed piano pieces.
Ref. 226

ELWYN-EDWARDS, Dilys
20th-century Welsh accompanist, lecturer and composer. b. Dolgellau, Gwynedd. She was educated at Dr. William's School, Dolgellau. She was awarded the Turle Music Scholarship in composition to Girton College, Cambridge and the Dr. Joseph Parry Scholarship to University College, Cardiff. Accepting the latter she read for her B.Mus. at University College, then for three years taught at her old school. She was awarded an open scholarship to the Royal College of Music in London where she studied composition under Herbert Howells. From 1946 to 1972 she taught at the Central Foundation School for Girls, the Canton High School for Girls, Cardiff and the Grammar School for Girls, Bangor. She was visiting lecturer in the piano at University College, North Wales, Bangor from 1955 to 1956, 1966 to 1972 and the Normal College, Bangor from 1973. She is an adjudicator at the Eisteddfod and other major musical festivals. She is also well known as an accompanist. Her works are frequently broadcast and performed at music festivals and recitals and her songs have been described as reflecting the influence of the English Renaissance and of the first half of the century on Welsh Music. DISCOGRAPHY. PHOTOGRAPH.
Compositions
VOCAL
All that's past (mix-ch a-cap) (1957) (Novello; Gwynn Publishing Co.)
Tre saith (mix-ch a-cap) (1970) (University of Wales Press)
Cadwyn O Wyldd, song cycle (m-S, S, T and pf) (1977)
Song cycle (S, cl and pf) (1980) (comm Academi Sant Teilo)
Caneoun Natur, 3 songs (T, S and pf) (1977) (comm North Wales Music Festival, 1973)
Caneuon y Tri Aderyn, 3 songs (T, S and pf) (1963) (University) (comm BBC Wales, 1961)
Eirlysian (S and pf) (1979) (comm Royal National Eisteddfod, Caernarfon)
Hwiangerddi y Dref Wen, 8 settings of Welsh nursery rhymes (S and pf) (Gwynn, 1983) (comm North Wales Music Festival, 1982)
In Faery, cycle of 3 songs (1955) (University)
Pedair Can Serch, 4 love songs (T and pf) (comm BBC Wales, 1975 St. David's Festival)
Tymhoran, cycle of 4 songs (m-S and pf) (comm Guild for the Promotion of Welsh Music for the Swansea Music Festival, 1978)
Y Wong (T and pf) (1979) (comm Royal National Eisteddfod)
Three songs (W.H. Davies) (S) (comm Welsh Arts Council for W.H. Davies's Centenary)
Merry Margaret (1959) (University)
Sweet Suffolk owl (1959) (University) (comm BBC Wales, 1965)
Six songs for children (1967) (University) (comm BBC Wales, 1965)
Sound the flute (1955) (Edward Arnold Ltd. Gwynn)
Spring, the sweet spring (1955) (Edward Arnold; Gwynn)
SACRED
The bird of Christ (1948) (Swansea: Hughes and Son, now Christopher Davies)
Ref. composer, 563

ELY, Carroll
Composition
CHAMBER
Epitaph to Barney (strs) (G. Schirmer)
Ref. 280

EMANUEL, Pauline. See ROSENTHAL. Pauline

EMERY, Dorothy Radde
American pianist and composer. b. Cleveland, 1901. Her father, Carl A. Radde, was choral conductor in Cleveland. She began to study the piano under James H. Rogers and in 1922 graduated from Oberlin College, where she studied under Dr. George Whitfield Andrews. She later studied under Ernest Hutcheson. Her compositions were performed in New York, Washington, Pittsburgh, Cleveland, Chicago, San Francisco and other cities.
Compositions
CHAMBER
Romance (pf qnt)
String quartet in A-Minor
String quartet in F
Trio in E-Minor, in 3 mvts
Trio in F, in 3 mvts (fl, vlc and pf)
Organ pieces
PIANO
The city, suite
The seasons, suite

VOCAL
Flower cycle, suite (S, vln, vlc and pf)
Tropic suite (S, Bar, fl, vln, vlc and pf)
Anthems
Choruses (H. Flammer)
Thirty songs
SACRED
Part songs (mix-ch or w-ch or m-ch)
Saviour, like a shepherd
Ref. 40, 190, 292, 347

EMIDIO TAVORA, Florizinha
20th-century Brazilian composer. DISCOGRAPHY.
Compositions
PIANO
Saudosinho ão Violão
Ref. 563

EMIG, Lois Irene
American organist, pianist, librettist, teacher and composer. b. Roseville, OH, October 12, 1925. She obtained a B.Sc. in music education with distinction from Ohio State University in 1946, where she also did post- graduate work in composition. She studied piano teaching at the Peabody Conservatory of Music. She taught in schools and privately, was a librettist of over 150 compositions and a church organist.
Compositions
SACRED
Cantatas:
Beautiful Saviour (1962)
The children's alleluia (1960)
Come to Bethlehem (1962)
The greatest blessing (1957)
The herald angels sing (1958)
Let everything praise the Lord
The shepherd's carol (1966)
Song of Bethlehem (narr, w-ch and acc) (1963)
The wonder of Easter (w-ch, org and narr) (1970)
Choral works:
A merry Noël (1958)
All my heart this night rejoices (1957)
All the earth is singing (unison ch, handbells and org) (1967)
Around for Christmas (1954)
Candles, candles
Carry candles to the manger (1970)
Children's hosanna (1958)
Christmas comes to our school (narr and ch) (1961)
Come we that love the Lord (1961)
Come ye blessed (1957)
God is great (1959)
He took a child (1957)
Hosanna to the King (1968)
Like birds at eve (1958)
O sing Noël (1967)
O come and mourn with me awhile (1958)
Pin a star on a twinkling tree (1963)
Shepherds I can see you (1973)
Soft is the night (1962)
Spin, little Dreidel (1972)
Thank Thee, O Lord (1957)
Ref. composer, 40, 77, 142, 347, 457, 625

EMINGEROVA, Katerina
Czech concert pianist, professor, writer and composer. b. July 13, 1856; d. September 9, 1934. She studied the piano at the J. Jiranek Institute, then with K. Slavkovsky, L. Prochazka and K.H. Barth in Berlin from 1882 to 1883. She studied composition privately under Z. Fibich and V. Novak. She was a concert pianist and later became a professor at Prague Conservatory, turning her attention to music pedagogy, theory and composition. She wrote a number of articles about music teaching in Czech musical and women's journals and revised and published singing exercises and arrangements for the piano, of the music of old Czech masters.
Compositions
CHAMBER
Czech sonatinas (pf) (Prague, 1943)
Melancholic polka, sonata (vln) (1881)
Pieces (vln and pf)
VOCAL
Songs (ch)
Four vocal quartets (Prague, 1910)
Publications
Bedrich Smetana. Prague, 1923.
Obrazky ze stare hudebni Prahy. Prague, 1924.
O klavirnich skladbach starych ceskych mustru. Prague.
Ref. 238, CMIC

ENDE, Amelia (Amalie) von (nee Kremper)
American pianist teacher and composer. b. Poland, 1856. She went to the United States in childhood and studied in Milwaukee and Chicago and taught in New York. She wrote articles for European and American publications.
Compositions
CHAMBER
Piano pieces
VOCAL
Songs incl.:
Four songs, op. 2 (Eisoldt; Raabe)
Ref. 226, 297

ENDRES, Olive Philomene
American organist, pianist, teacher and composer. b. Johnsberg, WI, December 23, 1898. She began studying the piano at the age of four and studied the organ under her father's tuition at the age of 12. She graduated in the piano at the Wisconsin School of Music and in composition with honors at the American Conservatory, where her teachers were Adolph Weidig and Leo Sowerby. She attended a summer course at the Juilliard School of Music. Some of her compositions were awarded prizes in the Wisconsin composer contests. She taught at the Wisconsin School of Music and at Milton College.
Compositions
ORCHESTRA
Divergent moods, 12-tone composition (str orch)
Prelude and fugue, theme and variations (str orch)
Romana, 12-tone composition (str orch)
CHAMBER
Prelude (2 trp and 2 trb)
Cradle song (pf trio)
Poem (vln and pf)
Summer night (vln and pf)
Chorale and variations (cor anglais)
Violin sonata
Prelude (org)
VOCAL
The canticle of Judith (m-S and w-vces)
Other choral works
SACRED
Magnificat (S, mix-ch, trp and strs)
Ref. 142

ENGBERG, M. Davenport
American violinist, conductor, music teacher and composer. b. Spokane, WA, February 15, 1880. She studied in Europe, made her debut as a violinist in Copenhagen in 1903 and appeared as soloist with several American orchestras. She founded and directed the Davenport Engberg Orchestra of 85 players at Bellingham, Washington.
Ref. 226, 353, 415

ENGELBRETSDATTER, Dorthe
Norwegian poetess and composer of Bergen. b. 1634; d. 1716. She composed a collection of religious songs for the most important religious festivals, which was published in Copenhagen in 1677 and republished in 1685, together with a collection of religious songs for teaching. Of the songs contained in the work, 11 are sung to church melodies and the other 31 to foreign melodies for which descants are given.
Compositions
SACRED
Siaelens sang-offer (1681)
Ref. 97

ENGER, Nelly
Norwegian pianist, music teacher and composer. b. 1873. She studied in Kristiania (later Oslo) and composed about 50 piano pieces.
Ref. NMI

ENHEDUANNA
Sumerian high priestess and poetess. She was the daughter of Sargon, first king of Sumeria. In 2350 B.C. she wrote the words and music of her famous *Exaltation* a hymn to the goddess Inanna describing the destructive forces of the mountains; *Oh mistress, when you roar, the countries bow down.*
Ref. 502, 637

ENTHALLER, Sidonia
Austrian organist, nun and composer. b. ca. 1607; d. Graz, June 23, 1676. She was a Dominican nun, of whom it was written *she was mainly an excellent mistress of the organ, at the same time a good composer, who by her diligence and composition advanced and lifted up the religious service.* She composed sacred works.
Ref. 500

EPEN-DE GROOT, Else-Antonia van. See VAN EPEN-DE GROOT, Else

ERARD, Mlle.
19th century French composer of ariettes and one song cycle.
Ref. 465

ERDELI, Xenia Alexandrovna
Soviet harpist, pianist, choral conductor, teacher, writer and composer. b. Kirovograd, February 8, 1878; d. May 27, 1971. From 1891 to 1899 she studied the harp under Walter Kuehn and in 1921 graduated from Smolin Music School with distinction, after studying the piano, singing and choir conducting. She was a soloist for various orchestras, including the Bolshoi Theatre from 1899 to 1907 and 1918 to 1938. She also taught at music schools including the Gnesin, 1944 to 1954. She was a founder member of the Soviet school of harpists and her virtuoso performances promoted the development of the harp in the USSR. She organized a harp ensemble for 20 harps and founded the only professional harp quartet in the world.
Compositions
HARP
Ukraina, fantasia
Forty etudes
Ten pieces in the Russian folksong style
Three preludes in memory of Glinka
Publications
Arfa v moyei zhezni.
Moya zhizn v muzike.
Zamyetki ob arfe.
Ref. 330

ERDING, Susanne
20th-century West German composer. She won first prize at the 23rd International Competition for Symphonic Music, a second prize in a competition of the Wurtemberg State Opera of Stuttgart for her opera *Joy* and second prize from the City of Trieste in 1984 for her *La Mia Isola Vera*.
Compositions
CHAMBER
Rotor (4 vla)
El sueno (fl, cl and gtr)
Grotesques arabesques (vlc and pf)
Cadeau cosmique (1982)
VOCAL
La mia isola vera (H. Kromer) (Bar, mix-ch and large orch)
Pirotizgo (m-S) (1983)
OPERA
Joy, chamber opera (Roy Kift) (1983)
Ref. Frau und Musik

ERDMANNSDOERFER (Erdmannsdorfer-Fichtner), Pauline (nee Oprawnik) (called Fichtner after her adoptive father)
Austrian concert pianist and composer. b. Vienna, June 28, 1847; d. Munich, September 24, 1916. She studied the piano under Liszt and played with great success in concerts. She was appointed court pianist to the Grand Duke of Weimar. In 1874 she married Max Erdmannsdoerfer, composer and Kapellmeister.
Compositions
CHAMBER
Zwei Phantasiestuecke (vln and pf) (Ries)
Piano pieces
VOCAL
Brautlied
Des Saengers Wunsch
Sechs tuerkische Liebeslieder (Ries)
Songs
Ref. 85, 226, 260, 276, 297, 347

ERDMANNSDORFER-FICHTNER, Pauline. See ERDMANNSDOERFER, Pauline

ERDODY, Luisa, Countess. ERDOEDY, Luisa, Countess

ERDOEDY, Luisa, Countess (nee Drasche-Wartingerg) (pseud. Lios)
Austrian pianist and composer. b. Vienna, 1853. She studied the piano under Moritz Zweigelt and played the works of Liszt and Schumann in concert. Her career was interrupted by her early marriage, but after the death of her husband, she married Count Erdoedy and resumed her artistic activities. Her songs were favorably received.
Compositions
CHAMBER
Romance (vlc)
VOCAL
Songs
Other vocal works
Ref. 105

ERHART, Agnes Alice. See ERHART, Dorothy

ERHART, Dorothy (Agnes Alice)
English harpsichordist, conductor, teacher and composer. b. London, January 5, 1894; d. April, 1971. She studied under Dr. H.A. Harding and then at the University of Birmingham, where she obtained a B.Mus. in 1916. She studied composition under Granville Bantock and conducting under Adrian Boult and at the Salzburg Mozarteum. She studied the harpsichord under Alice Ehlers and was on the staff of the Webber-Douglas School of Singing from 1930 until her death. She founded the Erhart Chamber Orchestra in 1926 and was its conductor until 1938. She was a musical advisor for various institutes and committees between 1934 and 1951. She conducted and played the harpsichord for the Chanticleer Opera Company. She wrote articles for various music journals.
Compositions
ORCHESTRA
Variations for pianoforte and orchestra (1929)
The Emperor's new clothes, overture
CHAMBER
Piano quintet in D-Major (1916)
Quintet (ob, hp, vln, vla and vlc)
Miniature trio (vln, vla and pf)
Trio (vln, vla and pf)
Sonata (vln and pf)
VOCAL
Ode to a nightingale (T, pf and strs)
The spotted cow (1935)
Choral duets
Part songs
Songs
Two part songs (m-vces)
ARRANGEMENTS
Little Gaddesden May song
Ref. 8, 41, 81, 85, 226, 347, 467, 490

ERICKSON, Elaine M.
American composer. b. 1941.
Compositions
PIANO
Sonata
SACRED
Holy, Holy, Lord God of Sabaoth
Christmas songs
MISCELLANEOUS
Trifles
Vignettes

ERINA. See ERINNA

ERINNA (Erina)
Poetess and composer of ancient Greece. ca. 7th-century B.C.. She was also known as Lesbia, coming from the island of Lesbos and Mitilena. She studied poetry and music in the art school founded by Sappho (q.v.) on the island of Lesbos. She was said to be the most gifted of Sappho's pupils and her mother was purported to have chained her to the spinning wheel to make her spin rather than sing, or at least to make her spin whilst she was singing. By the time she died at the age of 19 her poems were already known and admired; some maintained that her hexameters were better than Sappho's. The only known fragment of her work is a lyric sung in honor of a dead girl singer, Baucis. Later incorrectly titled *The Distaff* the poem is a lament written in hexameter with recurring cries of sorrow.
Ref. 264, 268

ERNEST, Sister M.
20th-century American lecturer and composer. She was head of the music department of the Dominican College in Houston, TX. She composed instrumental and vocal music.
Ref. 40, 347

ERNEST, Sister O.P. See SCHWERDTFEGER, E. Anne

ERNST (Ernst-Meister), Siegrid (Adelheid)
German pianist, violinist, lecturer and composer. b. Ludwigshafen/Rhein, March 3, 1929. She began studying the piano at the age of seven and the violin at the age of 11; she studied in Heidelberg, Mannheim, Frankfurt and Vienna. Her piano teachers included Else Rehberg, August Leopolder and Richard Hauser. She studied composition under Gerhard Frommel in Heidelberg and attended the Darmstadt Summer courses. She gave piano recitals and concerts with orchestras. From 1968 she lectured at music high schools in Heidelberg and Mannheim and after 1970 in Bremen, her subjects being piano composition, the theory of music and avant-garde composition. In 1981 she won a composition scholarship at the Cite Internationale des Arts in Paris. PHOTOGRAPH.
Compositions
ORCHESTRA
Three pieces for orchestra (large orch) (1984)
Bacchanal und Huldigung (large orch) (1981)
Dance and hymn
Recitativo appassionato e salto (str orch) (1985)
Variations (1965)
CHAMBER
Sextet (ww insts) (1956)
Progressions (str qrt)
Mutabile (3 players with 11 recs) (1977)
Trio (1955)
Concertantes duo (pf and perc) (1966)
Play for pedal and register (org) (1980)
PIANO
Quattro mani dentro e fuori (4 hands) (1975)
Fantasie and toccata (1954)
Small suite (1963)
VOCAL
Damit es anders anfaengt zwischen uns allen ..., cantata (Hilde Domin) (ch and org) (1982)
Wohin, 3 groups (Ingeborg Bachmann) (screaming, speaking and whispering) (B, ch, str qrt, org and orch) (1972)
Fifteen new tunes for children (from The Ants, by Ringelnatz) (chil-ch, players and audience) (1983)
Kleine Hand in meiner Hand, 12 songs (S and pf) (1966)
Seven miniatures after Japanese haiku (deep vce and pf) (1961)
MISCELLANEOUS
Circle of sounds for youth
Ref. composer, 70

ERNST-MEISTER, Siegrid. See ERNST, Siegrid

ERPACH, Amalia Katharina, von, Countess
German poetess and composer. b. 1640; d. January 4, 1696. She was the daughter of Count Philipp Dietrich von Waldeck in Eisenberg and in 1664 married Count Georg Ludwig von Erpach.
Compositions
SACRED
Andaechtige Sing-Lust: Morgen-Lieder; Abend-Lieder; Tage-Lieder; Beth-Lieder; Buss-Lieder; Klag-und Trost-Lieder; Lob-und Danck-Lieder; Lehr-Lieder (Hildburgshausen: Samuel Wentzel, 1692) (ded Duke Ernst of Saxony)
Ref. 105, 128

ERTIS. See ESTERHAZY, Alexandrine, Countess

ERVIN, Karen
20th-century composer.
Compositions
CHAMBER
Tracks for woodwind quintet
Five little pieces (ob and hp)
Anthem (org and perc)
Ref. *Best in Contemporary Music* Catalog, 1980

ESCAMILLA, Manuela de
Spanish actress, singer and composer of Galician origin. d. 1695. She was the daughter of Antonio, a playwright and performed in one of her father's comedies at the age of seven. Later she was acclaimed as a singer at the Royal Palace, where she sang her own works before Charles II of Spain. Her compositions included two romances for the comedy *Orfeo y Euridice*.
Ref. 100

ESCARDOT, L. See KARR Y DE ALFONSETTI, Carmen

ESCHBORN, Georgine Christine Maria Anna (Nina) (alt. name Nina von Koenneritz)
German harpist and composer. b. Mannheim, May 13, 1828; d. Hohen-Lubbichow, 1911. Nothing is known of her childhood except that in 1837 she sang in Amsterdam in Mozart's *Magic Flute* as one of the three Genies, with her brother and sister. Like her sister Nathalie and brother Karl, she probably received her musical education from her father. She was the most prolific composer in her family, but few of her works were ever performed. In 1865 she married Gotthelf von Koenneritz, a Saxon aristocrat who fell in the battle of Tauber-Bischofsheim in 1866.
Compositions
ORCHESTRA
Elegie, op. 45
Emilien-Polka, op. 3
Prinz Eugen Marsch, op. 1
Natalia Nocturne, op. 44
Olga-Laendler, op. 2
Pazzarella-Galoppade, op. 5
Sommernacht, op. 71 (small orch)
Sophienwalzer, op. 62
Souvenir de Mont Saint-Jean, op. 4
CHAMBER
Fantasie, op. 64
Sonata
Pieces (hp)
PIANO
Four nocturnes
Four waltzes
Polka
Rhapsodie
Saltarello, op. 74
Two marches
Two salon pieces
Zwei Galoppaden
Zwei Laendler
VOCAL
Aria with variations
Der Liebesbote, op. 120 (vce and pf) (Bauer)
Drei zweistimmige Lieder, op. 97 (Sulzbach)
Drei Lieder, op. 101 (Wernthal)
Duo (4 vces and org)
Eighteen quartets
Ein Lied (vce and ww)
Fuenf Alpenlieder (vce and pf)
Sechs zweistimmige Lieder, op. 96
Sommernacht, kein kosendes Lueftchen, op. 71 (vce and pf) (Bauer)
Traum der Mutter (vce, hp and pf)
Twenty duets (vce and pf)
Wiegenliedchen, Schlaf mein holdes Kind, op. 113 (vce and pf) (Bauer)
Numerous songs, lullabies, marches, canzonets (composer, Schiller, Uhland, von Schwarzkoppen, Grimminger and other poets) (vce and pf)
SACRED
Church aria (vces and inst qrt)
OPERETTA
Alpenrose, op. 86
Ref. 192, 226, 276, 297

ESCHBORN, Nina. See ESCHBORN, Georgine Christine Maria Anne

ESCOBAR, Maria Luisa (nee Gonzalez-Gragirena)
Venezuelan pianist and composer. b. Valencia, Venezuela, December 3, 1908. She commenced playing the piano at the age of four and composed her first song at the age of six. She was taught at the Colegio de Welgelegen, Curaçao and studied singing, harmony and composition under Estevez in Venezuela and Roger Ducasse in Paris. Her speciality was the study of the indigenous tribal music and folklore of Venezuela. In 1931 she became artistic director of Radio Caracas and founded the Ateneo de Caracas, of which she remained president until 1942. In 1943 she founded the Venezuelan Association of Authors and Composers and was its president until 1972. She regularly represented Venezuela at international music conferences and received nearly 90 honors, medals, diplomas and plaques. She married J.A. Escobar Saluzzo. DISCOGRAPHY.
Compositions
ORCHESTRA
Vals sentimental, concerto in 2 mvts (pf and orch) (New York: CBS, 1949)

CHAMBER
El pajaro de los siete colores, legend (vln and pf)
PIANO
Preludio (2 pf)
Barcarola (1928)
El encuentro (Homage to Liszt)
Nana (1940)
Noche de luna en Altamira, nocturne
Valses
VOCAL
Canciones sentimentales
Canto Caribe
Costa Montana y Llano
Desesperanza, song
Naranjas de Valencia (Caracas)
Ternura (Caracas)
BALLET
Las Cinco Aguilas Blancas
Guaicaipuro, in 3 acts (1951)
Kanaime, choreo-drama, in 3 acts (composer) (1964)
Murachi (Cacique de la Sierra Nevada) (1959)
Orinoco, symphony-ballet, in 2 acts
Orquideas Azules, symphony-ballet (based on Venezuelan folklore) (Lucila Palacios) (1941)
Ruptura de Relaciones, satire
Tiuna (1955)
OPERA
Blanca Nieves, in 2 acts
Cuento Musical, in 3 acts
El Rey Cuaicaipuro, in 3 acts
OPERETTA
La Princesa Girasol
THEATRE
Cenicienta, musical comedy in 3 acts
ARRANGEMENTS
Numerous Venezuelan popular melodies, songs, dances, incl.:
Dos Danzas Aborigenes Venezolanas
Canto Caribe
Bibliography
Ritjmo y melodia nativos de Venezuela. Boletin Latino-Americano de Musica, vol. 3.
Ref. composer, 17, 20, 54, 74, 77, 79, 96, 107, 226, 361, 563

ESCOT, Pozzi

American professor, writer and composer. b. Lima, October 1, 1933. She studied composition under Andres Sas at the Sas-Rosay Music Academy in Lima, 1949 to 1953, and under William Bergsma at the Juilliard School of Music, New York, where she obtained a B.Sc. in 1956 and M.Sc. in 1957. She then studied composition under Philipp Jarnach in Hamburg, Germany. She was the recipient of four MacDowell Fellowships and of grants from the German government. She was a Fellow at the Radcliffe Institute from 1968 to 1969 and in 1956 named as laureate composer of Peru. She received grants from the Ford Foundation and participated in international festivals in Europe and America. In 1972 she was advisor and lecturer by invitation of the United States State Department and the Ministry of Culture of Peru. She taught theory and composition at the New England Conservatory of Music (1964 to 1972) and in 1972 became assistant professor at Wheaton College, Norton, MA. Her works have been performed by major orchestras and her lectures on contemporary composers have been acclaimed by the composers themselves. She married the composer Robert Cogan. DISCOGRAPHY.
Compositions
ORCHESTRA
Sinfonie No. 1 (1953)
Sinfonie No. 2 (1955)
Sinfonie No. 3 (1957)
Sands.... (International Festival of the Avant-Garde, 1969)
CHAMBER
Cristos (a-fl, c-bsn, 3 vln and perc) (1963)
String quartet No. I (1953)
String quartet No. 2 (1954)
String quartet No. 3 (1956)
Tres movimientos (vln and pf) (Cambridge, MA: Pub. Contact International, 1957)
Eure pax (vln) (1980)
Neyrac lux (gtr) (1978)
Thirteen preludes (org) (1968)
PIANO
Diferencias I and 2 (1963) (1975)
Piezas infantiles, I (1942) II (1947)
Sonatina No. I (1950)
Sonatina No. 2 (1951)
Sonatina No. 3 (1952)
VOCAL
And here I rest, cantata (1958)
Ainu, epilogue (20 vces) (1969) (1975)
Lamentos (S, 2 vln, pf and perc) (1962)
Visione (1964)
Credo (S and str qrt) (1958)
Three poems of Rilke (narr and str qrt) (1959) (1975)
Canciones de mi Paris (1954)
Dos lamentaciones, songs (1950)
Songs of wisdom (1955)
SACRED
Missa triste (w-ch) (1981)
ELECTRONIC
Fergus Are (org and tape) (1975)
In Memoriam (tape)
Interra 2 (pf, left hand and pre-recorded pf) (1980)
Pluies (alto-sax and pre-recorded sax) (1981)
BALLET
Metamorphosis (1951)
FILM MUSIC
Razapeti, television (1973)
MULTIMEDIA
Interra, overture (1968)
Publications
Music in America, Bloomington, IN. Indiana University Press.
Perspectives of New Music, Princeton, NJ. Princeton University Press.
Sonic Design: The Nature of Sound and Music. With R. Cogan, Englewood Ciffs, NJ. Prentice-Hall, 1976.
Sonic Design: Practice and Problems. With R. Cogan. Prentice-Hall, Inc. 1981.
Twentieth Century Sound: Techniques and Vision. University of California Press, Berkeley.
Ref. composer, 45, 173, 206, 228, 347, 371, 465, 563, 622

ESCRIBANO SANCHEZ, Maria

Composition
VOCAL
Visibilité imparfaite (vce and ens) (1975)
Ref. Darmstadt Catalog 1976/77

ESSEX, Margaret

18th-century English composer.
Compositions
CHAMBER
The amusement of a leisure hour (pf or hp) (ca. 1800) (Robert Birchall)
Beautiful eyes (pf or hp) (ca. 1795) (Birchall)
Good humour's my motto (pf or hp) (ca. 1795) (Birchall)
Three sonatas for the pianoforte with an accompaniment for violin ad libitum, op. 1 (1795)
VOCAL
Songs incl.:
Absence (ca. 1795) (Birchall)
The lover's address (R.A. Davenport) (Birchall)
The olive branch (vce and pf) (Birchall)
Select songs Nos. 1-7 (ca. 1795-1800) (Birchall)
The silent admirer (Birchall)
Ref. 65, 125, 128, 405

ESTABROOK, G.

19th-century American composer.
Compositions
VOCAL
Over 40 songs
OPERETTA
The Joust, or The Tournament
Ref. 260, 276, 347

ESTERHAZY, Alexandrine, Countess (pseud. Ertis)

Austro-Hungarian composer. b. ca. 1849; d. Vienna, April 17, 1919. Her opera was performed in Bratislava.
Composition
OPERA
Pamaro (Xaver, Gayrsperg and Schwertner) (1907)
Ref. 431

ESTRELLA, Blanca

Venezuelan pianist, teacher and composer. b. San Felipe, September 5, 1915. From 1940 to 1948 she studied the piano under Elena Arrarte and Moleiro and composition under Sojo at the Escuela Nacional de Musica y Declamacion in Caracas. From 1950 to 1953 she continued her studies under Primo Casale and in 1969 under Ioannidis. In 1962 she founded the Escuela Experimental de Musica Blanca Estrella.

Compositions
ORCHESTRA
Maria Leonza, symphonic poem (1950)
Imagen de Barquisimeto romantico
Symphonic ballet (1968)
CHAMBER
String quartet (1952)
Yuribi (str qrt) (1971)
Piano trio (164)
PIANO
Danza (2 pf) (1954)
Suite (1953)
VOCAL
Four albums of children's songs
Other songs
Ref. 17, 81, 94

ETHRIDGE, Jean

Canadian pianist, teacher and composer. b. Rossland, British Columbia, January 31, 1943. She studied the piano under Helen Dahlstrom and Boris Roubakine in Canada; Denis Dahlstrom and Boris Roubakine in England and composition under Jean Coulthard (q.v.), Murray Adaskin, Bernard Stevens, Violet Archer (q.v.), Oskar Morawetz, Gilles Tremblay, Serge Garant and Joel Spiegelman. In 1962 she completed her A.R.C.T. diplomas in teaching and solo performance. She gained her B.M. in composition from the University of British Columbia in 1967. From 1967 to 1968 she did postgraduate study in the piano and composition at the Royal College of Music, London. She has had several of her compositions broadcast in Canada and has given piano performances. She teaches the piano, theory and composition and organised workshops and adjudicated at the Okanagan Music Festival for Composers in 1975 and the Vancouver North Shore Music Festival, 1977. She has won many awards, including the Heintzman trophy in 1961, the Women's Musical Club of trail scholarship in 1962, the Vancouver Women's Centennial Committee award for composition for voice in 1967, the Koerner Foundation and Canada Council study grants in 1967, the Jean Coulthard scholarship and Women's Committee to the Vancouver Symphony Society scholarship for composition in 1968, a Canada Council grant in 1968, the Gladys and Merrill Muttart foundation scholarship in 1978 and the Banff Centre School of Fine Arts scholarship in 1979. She is a member of the Association of Canadian Women Composers and a past president of the Registered Music Teachers' association. PHOTOGRAPH.
Compositions
ORCHESTRA
Dialogues for chamber orchestra (1969)
CHAMBER
Three pieces for woodwind quintet (1979)
Seven miniatures for brass (1971)
Sonata for violin and piano (1967)
Variations (t-rec and a-rec) (1974)
Calumet (acc) (1971)
Dialogues two (acc) (1970)
PIANO
Londrems (1969)
Reflections
Sonatina (1965)
Suite (1976)
Sunday morning (1966)
Three contemporary epigrams (1975)
Three pieces for children (1974)
VOCAL
Childface (1967)
Dialogues
Forestness (1973)
Go to the shine that's on a tree (1967)
Kaleidoscope (1973)
Offering and rebuff (1967)
SACRED
Mass of St. Joseph (1972) (comm Christ Church Cathedral, Victoria)
Publications
A La Jeunesse. 8 graded books for violin and 4 teachers' manuals with piano accompaniments. With Jean Coulthard and David Duke. Waterloo Music Co. Ltd. 1983.
Ref. Carolyn Lomax (Toronto)

ETOILE, Mme. de L'

18th-century French composer. b. Rouen. Her works were honored by the Academy of the Immaculate Conception of Rouen in 1770 and 1771.
Compositions
SACRED
Cantique de Moise, an ode (1772)
Le Reveil d'Abel, an idyll
Ref. 218

ETPA (Ermelinda Talea Pastorella Arcada). See MARIA ANTONIA WALPURGIS

EUAN-SMITH, Lady
19th-century composer.
Compositions
CHAMBER
Lady Carmelita (pf and vlc obb) (Metzler)
Lady Fortune's wheel, waltz (Metzler)
Rosette No. 1, in E
Rosette No. 2, in G (Novello)
VOCAL
Age and love (Boosey)
At even ere the sun was set (Novello)
Come ye yourselves apart (Novello)
Down the stream (Boosey)
Where do they sleep (Boosey)
SACRED
Benediction service: O Salutaris, litany and Tantum ergo (Novello)
Hark my soul (Novello)
Office for the Holy Communion in G (Novello)
Two flower service hymns (Novello)
Thirty original tunes to popular hymns
Ref. 297

EUBANKS, Rachel Amelia

20th-century American pianist, lecturer and composer. b. San Jose. She received her B.A. (music theory) from the University of California in 1945 and M.A. (composition) from Columbia University in 1947 and her D.M.A. (composition) from Pacific Western University in 1980. Her composition teachers were Charles Cushing, Seth Bingham, Norman Lockwood, Douglas Moore, Roger Sessions and Nadia Boulanger (q.v.). She also attended the Eastman School of Music. She taught theory and composition and was head of the music department at Wilberforce University from 1949 to 1950 and the founder and president of Eubanks Conservatory of Music and Arts from 1951. She is a member of the Alpha Mu Honor Society and received a Mosenthal Fellowship.
Compositions
CHAMBER
Three songs (d-b, pf, 7 tuned gongs, vibes, gamelan and fl; d-b, pipe and pf; d-b and pf) (1984)
Trio (cl, vln and pf) (1977)
PIANO
Five interludes (1982)
Prelude (1942)
VOCAL
Songs
SACRED
Cantata (ch and orch) (1947)
Symphonic requiem (4 vces and orch) (1980)
Other choral works
Ref. composer, 457, 624, 625

EUGENIE, Charlotte Augusta Amalia Albertina, Princess of Sweden

B. 1830; d. 1889. She was the daughter of Oscar I and Queen Josephine. Like her brother the 'singing prince' Gustaf, she inherited her musical talent from her father and from childhood showed interest in music and composing. She was one of the first members of the Royal Music Academy (ca. 1859). She devoted her life to charitable works and the arts. DISCOGRAPHY. PHOTOGRAPH.
Compositions
PIANO
Sorg-marsch (4 hands) (in memory of Queen Louise of Sweden and Norway) (1871)
Drottning Josephinas polonaise (1854)
Louisa-vals
La prière (1844)
Tullgarns-galopp (1853)
VOCAL
Afontankar (4 m-vces)
Afsket fran flyende aret (1878)
Andalusisches Staendchen (Henkomsten) (duet) (1864)
Blick pa tidens tecken
Farewell of the sailor (duet) (1865)
Farvel (4 m-vces)
Die Glocken (S and T) (1862)
Guds frid
Hjertats hem (duet)
In schaukelnder Gondo (duet) (1864)
Korsvagen (vocal qrt) (1879)
Morning hymn of the birds (S and Cont) (1865)

My only care (S, Cont, T and B) (1886)
Novemberkvaellen (vce and pf) (1862)
Quiet (vocal qrt) (1878)
Solnedgangen
En sommardag (S and Cont)
Til vaagen (S and T)
SACRED
Den gode herden (1879)
Den troende brundens pilgrimsang (1883)
Four sacred songs (4 w-vces) (1878)
Four sacred quartets (S, Cont, T and B) (1879-1883)
Bibliography
Hagen, E. *Prinsessan Eugenie, Konstnarinna och filantrop.*
Ref. 20, 563

EUNICE DOMONTE LIMA. See CATUNDA, Eunice

EUTENEUER-ROHRER, Ursula Henrietta
West German pianist, teacher and composer. b. Karlsruhe, April 26, 1953. In 1969 she entered the Badisches Konservatorium in Karlsruhe, where she was a pupil of Reinhold Weber. At the same time, she took piano lessons from Irmgard Keller. In 1970 she entered the Karlsruhe Staatliche Hochschule fuer Musik where she studied the piano under Professor Valentin Rybing and Herbert Seidemann and composition under Professor Eugen Werner Velte. She completed her composition studies in 1981. In 1974, 1976 and 1982 she attended the Darmstadt Summer School for New Music. Since 1980 she has taught theory and the piano at the Gaggenau Music School. DISCOGRAPHY.
Compositions
ORCHESTRA
Two pieces for accordion, percussion and chamber orchestra (1983-1984)
CHAMBER
Two pieces for 10 instruments (1977)
Klanggewebe (gtr ens, trb, acc, d-b and perc) (1984)
Nebensonnen (pf, fl, vla and vlc) (1974)
Three pieces for percussion and accordion ensemble (1982)
Five pieces for percussion and accordion ensemble (1983)
Two pieces for string quartet (1974)
Percussion quartet (1983)
Five pieces (perc and pf) (1979)
Five trios (acc, perc and pf) (1980-1983)
Zwei Stuecke fuer das Knopfgriffakkordeon (1983)
Surrealismen I (vln and pf) (1972)
Surrealismen II (vln and pf) (1978)
Selbstgefaellig droht die vermeintliche Ordnung das scheinbare Chaos zu vernichten... (2 players, perc and pf) (1983)
Two pieces for accordion (1981)
Two pieces for violin (1971)
PIANO
Zwoelf Geraeusche (1978)
Surrealismen III (1983-1984)
VOCAL
In diesem Amethyst (Nelly Sachs) (S and pf) (1976)
Quetschuli Fresk (vce and pf) (1976)
Ref. composer

EVANS, Patricia Margaret
English pianist, lecturer and composer. b. Bristol, August 26, 1935. She obtained her teacher's diploma in music with distinction from Newton Park College of Education, 1953 to 1955. She studied the piano at the Leschetizsky School from 1961 to 1964 and under Peter Katin, 1970. She has given many piano recitals and since 1969 worked as a free-lance composer, pianist and lecturer for the Open University, Worker's Educational Association and Cambridge University Board of Extra-mural Studies.
Compositions
PIANO
Variations (2 pf) (1962)
Fantasy for St. Cecilia (1954)
Five studies (1974)
Prime minuet (1950)
Rondo in G (1950)
Sonatina (1974)
Suite (1953)
VOCAL
Songs incl.:
At daybreak (1973)
Dirge (1973)
Five songs of mysticism (1974)
Four songs (1973)
The garden of love (1974)
Nowell (1973)
Song cycle (1970)
Song cycle for Battle of Hastings (1962)
Songs for the nursery class (1963) (Doric Music)
Ref. composer

EVANS, Sally Hazen. See HAZEN, Sara

EVANS, Winsome
20th-century Australian composer.
Compositions
OPERA
L'Amfiparnaso (5 soli, miming actors and renaissance inst ens) (1974)
Play of Herod, 12-13th century liturgical drama (soli, ch and medieval inst ens) (1974)
Slaughter of the Innocents, 12-13th century liturgical drama (soli, ch and medieval inst ens) (1974)
Son of Getron, 12-13th century liturgical drama (soli, ch and medieval inst ens) (1972)
FILM MUSIC
27 A (1974)
Ref. 442

EVANTI, Lillian
Black American singer and composer. b. Washington, DC, August 12, 1890; d. Washington, DC, December 7, 1967. She graduated from Howard University, Washington and studied in Europe. She made her debut in Nice, France, in Delibes' *Lakme* being the first black American to sing an operatic role in Europe. She sang in a number of operas in Europe, before continuing her career in the United States and South America. She was co-founder of the National Negro Opera Company.
Compositions
VOCAL
Songs and anthems incl.:
Dedication (G.D. Johnson) (New York: Handy Bros. 1948)
Forward march to victory (1943) (trans into various languages)
Hail to fair Washington (G.D. Johnson) (1953)
High flight (J.G. Magee, Jr.) (Handy) (1948)
Himno pan-americano (Edward B. Marks Music, 1941)
I'm yours for tonight (Colombia Music)
Tomorrow's world (G.D. Johnson) (1948)
United nations (mix-vces) (1953)
Victory in defeat; The Mighty Rapture (E. Markham) (Handy, 1948)
SACRED
My little prayer (Bruce Evans) (med-vce and pf) (Handy, 1948)
Speak to Him Thou from the higher pantheism (Tennyson) (med-vce and pf) (Handy, 1948)
Psalm 23 (med-vce and pf) (Handy, 1947)
Ref. 136, 285, 287, 335, 523, 549

EVEN-OR (Ben-Or), Mary
Israeli conductor and composer. b. September 8, 1939. After studying law for three years at Tel-Aviv University she changed to music and obtained her B.A. in musicology from the same university. She then studied at the Tel-Aviv School of Music and the Rubin Academy of Music in Tel-Aviv, graduating with a B.Mus. in composition and conducting and an M.Mus. with distinction in composition in 1983. PHOTOGRAPH.
Compositions
ORCHESTRA
Ad infinitum (str orch) (1982) (comm, Israel)
Music for strings (Israel Music Inst. 1979)
Musikinesis (sym orch) (1983) (ACUM prize)
CHAMBER
Cardioyda (brass qnt) (prize, Germany, 1982)
Dances (fl, vln, d-b and perc) (1961)
Reflections (4 rec) (1979)
Dreams (gtr, fl and cl) (1978)
Melos (fl, vln and vlc) (1980)
A piece for three (ob, vln and vlc) (1977)
Centrifuga in G (2 vln) (1984)
Duo (cl and vlc) (1978)
A piece for two (trp and pf) (1978)
Contrasts (fl) (1962)
Elegy (vlc) (1980)
Small piece (fl)

PIANO
Songs for Adi (1979)
Three small pieces (1980)
Tone-Colours (1981)
Tunes (1981)
VOCAL
Espressioni musicali (chil-ch) (1981) (Israel Music)
Love songs (mix-ch) (1983)
Lullaby (mix-ch) (1980)
Melos (mix-ch, fl, vln and vlc) (1980)
Poem (David Fogel) (A or S, fl and vlc or b-cl) (1979)
SHIKA (ch a-cap) (1979)
SACRED
Holy curtain (chil-ch) (1983)
Prayer (mix-ch) (1983)
Ref. composer

EVERAERTS-ZLICA, Mme.

20th-century Belgian Composer.
Compositions
ORCHESTRA
Marche du centenaire
Two suites
Walzes and gavottes
VOCAL
Songs
Ref. Belgian Music Info. Center

EVERETT, Alice

19th-century Hawaiian song composer. Her first listed song became a favorite of Berger and the singers Walanika and Nani Alapai.
Compositions
VOCAL
Ua Hiki No Me A'u (ca. 1882) (Wall Nichols Co.)
Ua Like No A Like (ca. 1882) (Nichols)
Ref. 438

EVERETT-SALICCO, Betty Lou

American pianist, professor and composer. b. Milwaukee, WI, April 9, 1925. She gained her B.Mus. and M.Mus. from the University of Houston in Texas and her D.M.A. from North Texas State University in Dallas, with an emphasis on electronic music. She taught the piano and orchestration at Agnes Scott College for one year, was visiting professor at Emory University for four years and theory and chorus at Mercer University in Atlanta, GA, for three years. She was then music director at Brunswick Junior College in Brunswick, GA.
ORCHESTRA
A set of three (1967)
CHAMBER
Quintet for woodwinds (1970)
Two woodwind trios (1969) (1972)
PIANO
Three bagatelles (1st prize, Delius contest, 1977)
Ballade (comm) (1978)
VOCAL
Johnny, I hardly knew ye (Richard Sale) (B, ch and orch) (1972)
Eight songs for contralto (Whitman and Frost) (1969-1978)
Four songs for soprano (Whitman and Frost) (1969-1977) (ded Janet Stewart)
Trilogy for three Americans (Bar and pf) (1970)
MULTIMEDIA
Variations 2-4-6 (dancer, ch, fls and tape) (1969)
Ref. composer, 147

EVERSOLE, Rose M.

19th-century American composer of songs.
Ref. 276, 347, 433, 465

EZELL, Helen Ingle

American pianist and composer. b. Marshall, OK, May 18, 1903. She received degrees in music education and in the piano from Oklahoma City University (1947) and did postgraduate work at the Juilliard School of Music (1949 to 1951). She studied composition under Otto Luening and Henry Cowell at Columbia University. She did music research in Europe and conducted a number of workshops for piano teachers, including some sponsored by colleges in Oklahoma and North Carolina. She is a member of ASCAP. PHOTOGRAPH.

Compositions
CHAMBER
Quintette (1959)
Trio (vln, vlc and pf) (1958)
VIOLIN
Nocturne (1975)
Viennese waltz (1975)
PIANO
We two, duets (Boston)
Alpine serenade (Belwin)
Bound for Birmingham (Brodt)
Cinderella (Cole)
Drowsy afternoon (Associated)
Echo (Carl Fischer)
April (OUP)
Arab riders (Belwin)
Bayou nights (Boston)
By a quiet stream (Fischer)
The clown (Willis)
Cock o the walk (Summy-Birchard)
Creole lullaby (Willis)
Day in spring (OUP)
Flower girl in Paris (Willis)
Flying bird (Fischer)
Gazelle (Willis)
Ghost town (Fischer)
Hilda and Hans (Boston)
Igor is captain (Willis)
Little buckaroo (Brodt)
Lively dance (Willis)
Louisiana levee (Boston)
A lovely day (Boston)
Moonlit garden (Sam Fox)
My Uncle Willie (OUP)
Next week Terry and I (OUP)
Nine preludes (1974)
Oklahoma windmill (Summy-Birchard)
Parade of the dwarfs (Willis)
Peasant dance (Willis)
Petite ballerina (Willis)
Plantation party (Summy-Birchard)
Pollyanna (Boston)
The posse (Cole)
Proud Mr. Gobbler (Belwin)
Quite contrary (Schirmer)
Restless brook (Schirmer)
River boat (Schirmer)
See-saw (Brodt)
Shepherd boy (Cole)
Snips and snails (Boston)
Soft little breeze (Brodt)
Square dance (Belwin)
Susanne (Melody)
Tiresome raindrops (Fischer)
Toccatina (Willis)
Travelin' west (Schirmer)
Two pigeons (Music Publishers Holding Corp.)
Village square (Summy-Birchard)
Wagon train (Boston)
When we went to Liza's house (OUP)
Wintry day (Boston)
Wishing (Willis)
Witches' party (Belwin)
In the forest (1 hand) (Boston)
VOCAL
Songs incl.:
A blue eyed phantom
The clouds have left the sky
The drifter
Gray day
I cannot mind my wheel
I have loved flowers that fade
I praise the tender flower
Lilac violet
My windows of the world
Riders (hon mention)
Seashell
She dwelt among the untrodden ways
Song for you
So sweet love seemed that April morn
Velvet shoes
When I am dead, my dearest
SACRED
I know that mind unfolds (R.D. Rowe; C. Fischer)
Psalm 139

Publications
Sam Fry and we two. Music books for beginners. Boston.
Piano Party. Easy solos. C. Fischer.
Ref. composer, 39

FABRE, Marie
19th-century French composer.
Compositions
PIANO
Pieces incl.:
Mouches et Papillons
Résponds moi
Ref. 226, 276, 347

FADL (1)
Arabian poetess and songstress. d. 870 A.D. According to one source, she was born in Basra, the daughter of a slave woman originally from Yamama and brought up by her mother's master, of the tribe of the Abd al-Qais and finally sold. According to another version, confirmed by Fadl herself, her mother, a slave pregnant by her master, was sold by his son on his father's death. In a third version her father was alive at her birth and recognized her as his legitimate daughter, but on his death, his legitimate sons sold Fadl as a slave to cheat her of her inheritance. She changed owners several times and was finally given to the Caliph al-Mutawakkil of Baghdad. He was delighted with her beauty, her talents as a poetess and singer and her ready wit. She became a favorite of his and would entertain him with her impromptu verses. She became known as the most talented poetess of her time and gathered around her a circle of writers, musicians and poets. Although she was famous primarily for her poetry, one source stresses that she was an excellent singer and lutenist who set her verses to her own music. However, many of her verses were also set to music by other women singers, including Oreib (q.v.). Fadl was given her freedom by Caliph al-Mutawakkil. She dedicated many poems to the poet Sa'id Ibn Humaid, whom she later left for the favored court singer Bunan Ibn Amr. After the Caliph's death Fadl enjoyed as much favor from his successors, first from Caliph al-Muntasir (861 to 862), whose murder she commemorated in an elegy, and then from Caliph al-Mutamid (870 to 892), for whom she wrote a song on the death of a favorite slave.
Ref. 224

FADL (II)
Arabian songstress at the court of Caliph Abd-al Rahman II (822 to 852) in Andalusia. She was a slave of a daughter of Harun al-Rashid (786 to 809) at the court in Baghdad. She learned her art in Baghdad and Medina and then with her companion, Alam, traveled to Andalusia. They were both bought by the Cordobese monarch and with Qalam became the main singers at court.
Ref. 171, 244

FAGET, Zelie. See SAUGEON, Zelie

FAHRBACH, Henrietta
Austrian choir conductor, teacher and composer. b. Vienna, January 22, 1851; d. Vienna, February 24, 1923. In 19th-century Vienna the Fahrbach family was as well known as the Strauss family. All members played in the family dance orchestra or other orchestras and sang or taught. Henriette conducted a touring women's choir and was a music teacher in Vienna.
Compositions
PIANO
Characterstueck, op. 11
Idylls, op. 7 and 12
Reverie, op. 9
Waltzes
VOCAL
Songs incl.:
Three songs, op. 50
OPERETTA
Several operettas
Ref. 9, 226, 276, 335

FAHRER, Alison Clark (Mrs. G. William Fahrer)
American pianist, authoress, educational administrator, music publisher and composer. b. Washington, March 29, 1923. She studied at the University of Washington, Seattle from 1939 to 1940. She was the founder of Canyon Press Inc., NJ, in 1951 and the president in 1972. She was a member of the Music Educators' National Conference and director of the Music Publications Association, 1958 to 1962. She was also a member of the Music Industrial Council and the International Society of Music Education. She composed various piano and choral works and edited the *Canyon Hymnal for Boys and Girls* in 1958.
Publications
Elements of Music. 1970.
Ref. 475

FAHRER, Mrs. G. William. See FAHRER, Alison Clark

FAIRCHILD, Helen
20th-century American composer.
Compositions
VOCAL
Songs
SACRED
The Son of the Highest, Christmas cantata (4 soloists, ch and orch) (Flammer)
Ref. 280, 347

FAIRLIE, Margaret C.
American pianist, writer and composer. b. Atlanta, March 27, 1925. She obtained her B.S. from the Juilliard School of Music in 1948 and M.M. from the Converse School of Music in 1955. She studied privately under Edwin Gerochefski from 1953 to 1955 and Wallingford Riegger until 1957. She was awarded scholarships to attend the Bennington Composers' Conference in 1958, 1961 and 1962 and the MacDowell Colony, 1963 and 1967. She obtained fellowships from the Converse School of Music in 1954 and 1955 and Bennington College, 1957 and 1958.
Compositions
ORCHESTRA
Piano concerto (1959-1969)
Festival overture (comm Bennington College)
CHAMBER
Four structures (cham ens) (1963-1964)
Suave (cham ens) (1967)
Score for percussion and brass (1960)
Wind quintet (1962)
Music for string quartet and percussion (1959)
Trio for violin, clarinet and piano (1957)
Designs for flute and clarinet (1963)
PIANO
Suite (4 hands) (1953)
Set of four (1962)
THEATRE
Wedding on the Eifel Tower, television film (orch) (1967)
Electra, dance-drama (cham orch) (comm Agnes Scott College)
Ref. composer, 40, 94, 142, 347

FAISST, Clara Mathilde
German pianist and composer. b. Karlsruhe, June 22, 1872; d. Karlsruhe, November 22, 1948. She studied under Rudorff, Kahn and Bruch.
Compositions
CHAMBER
Sonata, op. 14 (vln and pf) (Simrock, 1912)
Piano pieces
VOCAL
Altdeutsches Lied (vce and pf)
Ingeborgs Lied (vce and pf)
Viel tausend Bluemlein (vce and pf)
Wiegenlied (vce and pf)
Choral works
Ref. 41, 44, 70, 105, 226, 276

FALCINELLI, Rolande
French organist, pianist, lecturer and composer. b. Paris, February 18, 1920. She commenced studying the piano at the age of five and at seven gave her first concert. She studied at the Paris Conservatoire under Samuel-Rousseau, Simone Ple-Caussade and Estyle and obtained first prizes in harmony, fugue and piano accompaniment. She studied composition under H. Busser. She obtained first prize for the organ and improvisation under Marcel Dupre in 1942. In the same year she won the Grand Prix de Rome and was the first woman to receive the Prix Rossini. In 1945 she became organ mistress of the Sacre Coeur de Montmartre. She taught at the American Conservatory in Fontainebleau and then at the Ecole Nor-

male de Musique. In 1955 she succeeded Marcel Dupre as teacher of organ and improvisation at the Paris Conservatoire. She performed in a number of concerts in Europe and North America. DISCOGRAPHY. PHOTOGRAPH.

Compositions

ORCHESTRA

Over 50 compositions incl.:

D'un âme, poème en dix chants, op. 15 (pf and orch)

Choral et variation sur le kyrie de la messe Orbis Factor, op. 12 (org and orch)

Mausolée, op. 47, à la gloire de Marcel Dupré (org and orch)

Polska suite, op. 8, on popular Slavic themes (pf and orch)

Soleil couchant, melodie orchestrée (T.L. Gautier)

CHAMBER

Nocturne féerique, op. 23 (org, 2 pf, 2 hp, cel and perc)

Fantastique op. 9 (str qrt)

Berceuse, op. 33 (bsn or vlc and pf) (Leduc)

Aphorismes, op. 64 (pf and org) (1979)

Azan, op. 61 (fl and org) (1977)

Chant de peine et de lutte, op. 53 (vln and org) (Transatlantiques)

Suite, op. 6 (vln and pf)

Tetrade, op. 60 (vla and org) (1976)

Chant d'ombre et de clarte, op. 56 (vlc) (1975)

Krishna Gopala, variations (fl) (1920)

Inventions, op. 58 (Ed. Ouvrieres)

Resonnances romantiques, op. 54

Chant d'ombre et de clarite

Prelude and scherzo, op. 3

ORGAN

La mystère de la sainte messe, op. 59 (2 org) (1976)

Cinq chorales d'orgue sur l'antienne du magnificat du saint-sacrement, op. 28 (Bornemann)

La cathedrale de l'Ame, op. 39

Cor Jesu Sacratissimum (Transatlantiques)

Cortège funèbre, op. 41 (Schola Cantorum)

Epigraphe funèbre, op. 21

Esquisses symphoniques en forme de variations, op. 45

Mathnavi, op. 50 (Bornemann)

Messe pour la fête de Christ-Roi, op. 38 (Schola Cantorum)

Miniatures persones, op. 52

Poème, op. 31

Poèmes-études, op. 26

Prelude à l'introit de la messe de Sacre-Coeur

Prophétie, op. 42 (Transatlantiques)

Rosa mystica sur 7 thèmes gregoriens à la Vierge, op. 29 (Schola Cantorum)

Salve Regina (Bornemann)

Triptyque, op. 11

Variations-études sur un berceuse, op. 48

PIANO

Jeux d'un Biquet, op. 30

Harmonies et lignes, op. 32 (Leduc)

Memorial Mozart, op. 35, suite (also hpcd)

Pochades, op. 44

Resonnances poetiques, op. 40, 8 pieces

VOCAL

Cavalier op. 13 (St. Georges de Bouhelier) (mix-ch and orch)

Danse de nymphes, op. 19 (Trisian Derene) (w-vces and orch)

Ophelia, op. 16 (A. Rimbaud) (w-vces and orch)

Affinites secretes, op. 49 (T. Gautier) (vce and pf)

Canzon per sonar, op. 57 (vce and org)

Eight popular songs, op. 4

Prélude et fugue sur le nom de Jean-Sebastien Bach, op. 27 (vce and pf or hpcd)

Quand sonnera la glas, op. 62 (vce and org) (1968)

Quargla op. 18 (Pierre Bertin)

Quatrains d'Omar Khayyam, op. 51 (vce and str qrt)

Soleil couchant (T. Gautier), op. 7

Trois chants profanes, op. 55 (vce and org)

Three melodies, op. 1 (Paul Fort)

Three melodies, op. 5 (T. Gautier)

Two songs, op. 2 (S and T)

SACRED

Oratorio

Psautier, op. 65 (S and orch) (1980)

Messe de Saint-Dominique, op. 25 (mix-ch a-cap)

Quatre motets à la Vierge, op 37 (vce and org)

Le Sermon sur la Montagne, op. 46, mystic poem after St. Matthew

Petit livre de prières, op. 24 (Bornemann)

Psaume XIII, op. 63 (Bar and org) (1978)

BALLET

Cecca, la bohémienne ensorcelée, op. 22, in 1 act

OPERA

Icare, op. 17

Louise de la Misericorde, op. 20

Pygmalion Delivre, op. 14

Publications

Anthologie des Maitres classiques de l'orgue. Bornemann.

Ecole de la technique moderne de l'orgue.

Initiation à l'orgue. Bornemann.

Transcription pour orgue de l'Offrande Musicale de Bach. Schott.

Ref. composer, 9, 12, 44, 563

FALL, Ethel. See NORBURY, Ethel

FALLADOVA-SKVOROVA, Anezka

Czech harpist, professor and composer. b. December 24, 1881. After completing her harp studies at Prague Conservatory she toured and then became professor of the harp at the Conservatory in Kiev and the harpist for the Kiev Orchestra. Whilst there, she married the distinguished Czech cellist, Max Skvor. During her time in Kiev she was influenced by foreign, particularly Russian, composers. She returned to Czechoslovakia to become professor at the Brno Conservatory.

Compositions

CHAMBER

Pieces (hp and vlc)

Pieces (pf)

HARP

Pieces (1 or 2 hp)

Etudes

Fantasies of Czech and Russian folk songs

Suites

Teaching works

Bibliography

Universitni Knihovna v. Borne. Ceske Hudebni Skladatelky. 1957.

FALTIS, Evelyn

Bohemian composer. b. Trautenau, February 20, 1890; d. Vienna, Austria, May 19, 1937. Evelyn was brought up in a convent in Paris and studied music at the Vienna Academy under Robert Fuchs, Eusebius Mandyczewski, Richard Heuberger and Hugo Reinhold. She studied under Felix Draeseke and Eduard Reus at the Dresden Conservatory where she received a composition prize for her *Fantastic symphony*. She also studied under Sophie Menter in Munich. She was a prompter at the Stadtheater, Nuremberg, the Royal Theatre, Darmstadt, the German Opera, Berlin and at Bayreuth (1914).

Compositions

ORCHESTRA

Fantastic symphony, op. 2a

Piano concerto, op. 3

Hamlet, op. 26, symphonic poem

CHAMBER

String quartet, op. 13a

String quartet, op. 15

Piano trio in G-Minor, op. 4

Piano trio No. 2

Adagio (vln and pf)

Andante and Slav dance, op. 5 (pf and vln)

Sonata in D-Minor, op. 6 (vln and pf) (Ries and Erler, 1923)

Fantasy and double fugue on Dies irae, op. 12 (org)

VOCAL

Gipsy songs, op. 12a

Invocation, op. 9 (mix-ch)

Songs, ops. 7, 8 and 10

SACRED

Mass with organ, op. 136

Sacred song, op. 11

Ref. 17, 23, 70, 74, 100, 105, 111, 226

FARE, Florence

19th-century English composer of dances.

Ref. 276, 347

FARGA PELLICER, Onia

Spanish pianist, violinist, conductor and composer. b. Barcelona, November 25, 1882. She studied the piano and composition at the Municipal School of Music under Rodrigues Alcantara and Crikboom. At the age of 15 she won all the prizes awarded by the school, including the composition prize for a *Grand march for orchestra and organ* which she herself conducted at the Palacio de Bellas Artes. To facilitate her studies in orchestration she studied the violin. She performed extensively in Spain, France and Switzerland. She founded and directed the academy in Barcelona that bears her name and founded and conducted the musical ensemble *Musica pro Amore Artis*.

Compositions
ORCHESTRA
Grand march (orch and org) (prize, Municipal School of Music, 1897)
CHAMBER
Flabiolejant (vln and pf)
Sonata (vln and pf)
Piano pieces
VOCAL
Numerous songs (Spanish texts)
Teaching material
SACRED
Misa de requiem, mass (ch, orch and org)
OPERA
La bella Lucinda (Pujola Valles, 2nd version by Martinez Bello)
Ref. 100, 107

FARIDA
Arabian songstress. b. ca. 830. She was a slave of the singer Amr Ibn Bana and with other slave girls was brought up and educated by him. Amr Ibn Bana made a gift of her to the Caliph al-Watiq (842 to 847), who was much taken with her. At his court she made the acquaintance of Shariyya (q.v.). For a while she was Shariyya's pupil but a great rivalry arose between the two and thereafter Shariyya took no more pupils, or at least, none likely to threaten her position. Another reason for their dissent may have been that as a pupil of Amr Ibn Bana and Shariyya, Farida was expected to follow the romantic school of Arabic music; but she was in fact a great admirer of the classicist Ishaq al-Mausili. Like most Arabian women singers, Farida belonged to the Caliph's harem, but as she was the favorite of al-Watiq she exerted considerable influence over him. She was better treated by him than by his brother, al-Mutawakkil, who succeeded him. However, an incident is related in which, while she was playing her lute and singing for al-Watiq, he was seized by jealousy at the thought that after his death she would play as sweetly for his brother, so he kicked her from her seat and threw her to the ground, shattering her lute. Such sadistic treatment was not unusual at the courts of the caliphs. After al-Watiq's death, Farida passed into the hands of al-Mutawakkil, who was enraged with jealousy when she sang only mournful songs for her late master. However, he later married her, but beyond the fact that she bore him a son, no more is known of her.
Ref. 224

FARINELLA, La. See CAMATI, Maria

FARLEY, Marion
19th-century American composer.
Compositions
VOCAL
Songs incl.:
Coming of the song
Night song
To a rose
Ref. 226, 276, 347

FARMER, Emily Bardsley (Mrs. Arthur W. Lambert)
19th-century English composer.
Compositions
CHAMBER
Trio (vln, vlc and pf)
Barcarolle (vln and pf; also vln and hp)
Quatuor No. 1 in E-Flat (har or org; also vln, vlc and hp)
Quatuor No. 2 in A (har or org; also vln, vlc and hp)
Queenie minuet (vln and pf)
Restless wavelets (pf and hp)
Solitude (vln and pf; also vln and hp)
Stray thought (vln and pf; also vln and hp; also org or har)
Fairy revels (hp)
Muriel waltz (hp)
VOCAL
Action song book
Aglaia (Looking for light) (vce, vln and vlc)
Songs incl.:
Dancing lesson (vce and pf)
Falling, falling, softly falling (vce and pf)
For you and me (vce and pf)
Hunting song or The morning is breaking (vce and pf)
If I might choose (vce and pf)
Last words (vce and pf)
Old letters (vce and vlc)
Snowdrops (vce and pf)
Shall I wear a white rose (vce and pf)
Wert thou like me in life's low vale (vce and pf)
OPERA
One opera
Ref. 85, 297, 347

FARNINGHAM, Marianne (real name, Marianne or Mary Ann Hearn)
English teacher, writer on religion and hymn composer. b. Farningham, Kent, December 17, 1834; d. Barmouth, Wales, March 16, 1909. She taught in schools (1852 to 1896) and edited the *Sunday School Times*. Her collected works were published in 20 volumes. Her hymns appear in many hymnals.
Ref. 479, 502, 646

FARR, Hilda Butler
20th-century American composer of two operas and songs.
Ref. 465

FARRENC, Louise (nee Jeanne-Louise Dumont)
French pianist, professor and composer. b. Paris, May 31, 1804; d. Paris, September 15, 1875. She came from an artistic background and her talent for music became apparent very early. She commenced her piano and theory lessons at the age of six, studying the piano under Moscheles and Hummel, and at 15 went on to study composition and orchestration under Antonin Reicha, professor of counterpoint and fugue at the Paris Conservatoire. She interrupted her lessons when she married the flautist and composer Aristide Farrenc in 1821, resuming studies under Reicha in 1825. Her originality and inventiveness were not recognized by the public although Schumann, after hearing her *Air russe varié* praised it for its logic and melody. Her outstanding contribution to musical scholarship was her chamber music, which included two piano quintets scored for double bass. In 1842, she was appointed professor of the piano at the Paris Conservatoire, a post she held until her retirement in 1873: Louise was the only woman musician of the 19th-century to hold such an important position. She was appointed music instructor for the household of Louis Philippe's eldest son, the Duke of Orleans, in 1841. The Academie des Beaux-Arts awarded her the first Prix Chartier in 1861, an honor she received again in 1869. After her husband's death in 1860, she completed the last 15 volumes of their 23 volume magnum opus *Le tresor des pianistes*, a collection of keyboard music over 300 years, edited and annotated by both Farrencs. This work was published after her death by Leduc, who also reissued her etudes and other didactic works in the collection *L'école du pianiste*. *Le tresor des pianistes* has been described as a remarkable and valuable work and Louise is considered a fore-runner of the French musical renaissance of the 1870s. Her daughter, Victorine Louise (q.v.) was also a pianist and composer. DISCOGRAPHY. PHOTOGRAPH.
Compositions
ORCHESTRA
Symphony No. 1 (1841)
Symphony No. 2 (1845)
Symphony No. 3 in G-Minor (1847-1849)
Grand fantasie et variations, sur un thème du comte Gallenberg, op. 25 (pf and orch; also pf and qnt)
Piano concerto in B-Minor
Overture No. 1
Overture No. 2, op. 24
Overture No. 3 (1834)
CHAMBER
Nonet in E-Flat, op. 38 (winds and strs)
Sextet, op. 40 (strs)
Piano quintet No. 1, op. 30 (1839) (Costallat, Hofmeister, 1842)
Piano quintet No. 2, op. 31 (1840) (Farrenc)
Trio, op. 44
Trio in E-Minor, op. 45 (Leduc, ca. 1850)
Trio No. 1 in E-Flat, op. 33 (pf, vln and vlc) (Leduc)
Trio No. 2 in D-Minor, op. 34 (pf, vln and vlc) (Farrenc, ca. 1850)
Sonata in B-Flat, op. 46 (vlc and pf) (Leduc, ca. 1851)
Sonata No. 1 in C-Minor, op. 37 (vln and pf) (Leduc, ca. 1848)
Sonata No. 2 in A, op. 39 (vln and pf) (Leduc)
Pieces for flute and piano, ops. 15, 16, 19, 20, 21 and 22
Serenade (vln and pf) (Fromont)
Troisieme rondelette (fl and vln)
Variations sur un air suisse, op. 20 (vln and pf)
Sonata (vlc)
PIANO
Air martial de Bellini, op. 29 (Capuleti) (4 hands)
Bouquet, quadrille (4 hands) (Lemoine)
Souvenirs des Huguenots, op. 19 (2 or 4 hands) (Lemoine)
Air russe varié, op. 17 (1836)

Les Allemandes, de melodies allemandes verses, op. 16
Deuxieme valse brillante, op. 51
Douze etudes brillantes de dexterite, op. 41
Etudes, op. 26
Etudes, op. 40
Etudes progressives, op. 50
Exercise du pianiste sur les modulations
Grand'mère, rondoletto (Hansen)
Hymne russe varié, op. 27
Iris, valse de concert (Fromont)
Italiennes, 3 cavatines favorites de Bellini et Caraffa, variées, op. 14 (Simrock, Hirsch)
Jours heureux, 4 rondinos, op. 21
Laissez-moi vous revoir (Benoit)
Melodies, op. 43
Nocturne, op. 49 (Leduc)
Nuit (Heugel)
Pastorale (Fromont)
Premiere Nocturne, op. 49
Promenade champêtre (Fromont)
Romanesca, air de danse du XVIe siècle (also fl) (Choudens)
Ronde de nuit (Fromont)
Rondeau sur un chant d'Il Pinato, op. 9
Rondeau sur un thème de Zelmira de Carafa, op. 13
Rondeau sur des thèmes d'Eurianthe, de Weber, op. 11
Six fugues
Scherzo, op. 47
Souvenir d'Orient (Fromont)
Sur l'eau (Benoit)
La Sylphide, rondo-valse sur un motif de Masini, op. 18
Trois petits airs variés (Fromont)
Trois rondeaux originaux, op. 8
Trois Rondinos (Fromont)
Variations sur l'air: O ma tendre, musette, op. 6 (Leduc)
Variations brillantes sur la cavatine d'Anna Bolena, Nel veder la tua constanza, op. 15 (Simrock)
Variations brillantes sur le Colporteur, op. 10 (Simrock)
Variations brillantes sur un thème d'Aristide Farrenc, op. 2 (1825)
Variations for piano on an original theme ... op. 5
Variations for piano on an original theme by A. Farrenc, op. 4
Variations sur une galopade hongroise, op. 12
Variations on different themes
Vingt études de genre et de mecanisme, op. 42 (Hofmeister)
Other romances, rondos and variations

VOCAL
Chanson de bergeres (1 or 2 vces) (Rouart)
Je me taisais, romance
La Tourterelle, romance

Publications
Methode de piano. Paris: Leduc.
Traite des abreviations (signes d'agrements) employees par des clavecinistes des XVII and XVIII siècles. Paris, 1895.
Le Tresor des pianistes. Paris: Leduc.

Bibliography
Friedland, Bea. *Louise Farrenc (1804-1875): Composer, Performer, Scholar*. Ann Arbor, MI. UMI Research Press. 1980.
Hall, Marnie. *Women's Work*. Booklet in record album, Gemini Hall R.A.P. 1010.
Louise Farrenc: A Revival. *Music Heritage Review*, vol. 2, no. 3, March 20.
Mermontel, A. *Les Pianistes célèbres*. Paris, 1878.

Ref. 2, 8, 12, 15, 17, 26, 41, 102, 103, 105, 109, 129, 173, 216, 260, 276, 297, 347, 361, 394, 476, 518, 563, 593, 622

FARRENC, Victorine Louise

French concert pianist and composer. b. Paris, February 23, 1826; d. Paris, January 3, 1859. The daughter of Louise Farrenc (q.v.) Victorine studied under her mother at the Paris Conservatoire from 1843 to 1844 and won a first prize for piano playing, 1844. She was extremely talented and at the age of 14 played works by Mozart and Beethoven, subsequently becoming a popular concert pianist. At the age of 20 she became ill with consumption.

Compositions
PIANO
Romance, in *Beethoven Album*, album issued by a group of artists, to commemorate the inauguration of the Beethoven Memorial in Bonn, 1845
Etudes
Melodies
Romances
Salon pieces

SACRED
Choruses

Ref. 8, 15, 85, 102, 103, 260, 276, 347, 394

FAUCHE, Marie

19th-century composer. Her opera was first performed at the London Lyceum in 1823.

Composition
OPERA
The Shepherd King, or The Conquest of Sidon

Ref. 431

FAULKNER, Elizabeth

British composer. b. 1941.

Composition
PIANO
Five ideas (1971)

Ref. Orchestral Music by Living British Composers Catalog

FAUNT LE ROY, Constance. See RUNCIE, Constance Owen Faunt Le Roy

FAUTCH, Sister Magdalen

American organist, pianist, concert violinist, lecturer and composer. b. Seattle, WA, May 9, 1916. She obtained her B.M. at Marylhurst College, OR, and her M.M. (composition) at the University of Southern California where she studied with Ingolf Dahl, Ernest Kanitz and Halsey Stevens. She also studied with John Verral and George Frederick McKay at the University of Washington. She was founder and then president for two years, of the Seattle Archdiocesan Commission on Sacred Music and founder and editor of *The Canticle*, official bulletin of the Music Commission. She won first place for composition in the Spokane Music Festival and in the Mu Phi Epsilon National Competition. She is a member of the National Association of Composers. Her compositions have been performed on radio and at local colleges and she published articles on liturgy in the *North-West Progress*. She was a music lecturer at Marylhurst College of Life-Long Learning and played the violin in the Marylhurst Symphony Orchestra.

Compositions
ORCHESTRA
Prelude and dance (str-orch) (1956)

CHAMBER
Adagio for string quartet (1956)
String quartet (1959)
Lyric sonata for violin, cello and piano (comm, 1965)
Gigue for violin and cello (1957)

ORGAN
Anamnesis and great amen (WLP, 1976)
Celebration, postlude (1974)
Eight gospel acclamations (WLP, 1969)
Four gospel acclamations (The Minstrel, New Catholic Press, 1970)
Holy, holy, holy (Minstrel, 1975)
I will thank Thee, psalm (WLP, 1970)
Organ prelude No. 1 on Mass XI (WLP, 1958)
Organ Prelude No. 2 on Mass XI (WLP, (1960)
Praise you servants, psalm (WLP, 1970)
Proper for Requiem Mass (1962)
Wedding meditation/Alleluia (Minstrel, 1971)

PIANO
Prelude and two-part invention (1964)
Sonata (1958)
Three miniatures on a row (1964)

VOCAL
Les joies (3 poems by Victor Hugo) (S and orch) (1963)
Trois melodies dans la nuit (m-S and orch)
Gitanjali, No. 23 (Tagore) (vce and pf) (1982)
Invitatory (S, A and org) (1964)
My song (S and pf) (Tagore) (1980)
Three poems (Paul Claudel) (1959)

SACRED
Missa brevis (w-vces a-cap) (1959)
All creation sing (S, A and org) (WLP) (1969)
Proper for midnight mass (S, A and org) (1960)
You are a priest forever (S, T, B and A, tmp, fl, gtr, org and perc) (1969)

Ref. 148, 477, 624

FAXON, Nancy Plummer

American composer. b. 1914. DISCOGRAPHY.

Composition
CHAMBER
Adagio espressivo (org)

Ref. 563

FAY, Amy
20th-century American composer.
Composition
SACRED
Hasten, sinner, to be wise (mix-ch and pf) (New York Singing Society, 1917)
Ref. 228

FAYEL, La Dame du
12th-13th century French troubadour.
Composition
VOCAL
Chanterai pour mon courage (manuscript in British Library, London)
Ref. British Library (London)

FECHNER, Paulina (Pauline)
Polish pianist, writer and composer. b. Plock, 1817; d. Plock, November 23, 1874.
Compositions
PIANO
Caprice, op. 8
Fantaisie-impromptu, op. 29
Hommage au génie, op. 20 (Gebethner)
Lucia di Lammermoor, fantaisie and variations, op. 9 (Gebethner)
Polonaise, op. 28
Premier caprice, op. 8 (Gebethner)
Rêvèrie
Salut au rossignol, waltz (1857) (ded Pauline Viardot Garcia)
Valse brillante, op.7
Variations brillantes sur une cracovienne favorite, op. 7 (Hofmeister)
VOCAL
Bratek (vce and pf)
Listek (vce and pf)
Roza (vce and pf)
Zyczenie (vce and pf)
Publications
Kilka slow o muzyce judowej. 1870.
Opera wloska i francuska i jej kompozytorowie. Klosy, 1868.
Romantyzm w muzyce i jego kaplani: Weber i Chopin. Klosy, 1868.
Ref. 26, 35, 118, 226, 276, 297

FEDELE, Diacinta
17th-century Italian composer.
Composition
VOCAL
Scelta de villanelle napolitane bellissime con alcune ottave siciliane nove, con le sue intavolature di guitarra alla spagniola (Vicenza: Francesco Grossi, 1628)
Ref. 65, 125, 405, 653

FEDERHOF-MOLLER, Betty
Early 20th-century Danish guitarist, pianist, teacher and composer. b. Copenhagen. She was a pupil of Professor Malling (theory) and taught the guitar, the piano and singing.
Compositions
VOCAL
Jeg elsker dig som havet, af det hvide hus (H. Bang) (vce and pf) (W. Hansen, 1912)
SACRED
Allesjaelesnat (Johannes Jorgensen, 1912)
Davids 1ste Psalme (deep voice) (W. Hansen, 1915)
Sange om Israel (vce and pf)
Ref. 331

FEHRS, Anna Elisabeth
German pianist, conductor, teacher and composer. b. Holstein, September 18, 1875. She was the daughter of the poet Johann Hinrich Fehrs. She studied music in Ikehoe under H. Junge till 1892 and then under Hassler-Lubeck. At the Royal Academy of Music in Berlin she was a pupil of von Petersen, Franz Schultz and Adolf Schulze. She returned to Ikehoe to teach the piano and after 1908 conducted the combined women's choirs of Ikehoe and Neumunster.
Compositions
VOCAL
Holsteinische Lieder (Garding: Luhr & Diercks)
Lieder im Volkston (Garding: Luhr & Diercks)
Ref. 393

FEIGIN, Sarah
Israeli pianist, teacher and composer. b. Dvinsk, Latvia, July 1, 1928. She attended the Musical Institute in Riga, Latvia from 1946 to 1950 and obtained her M.A. (composition), 1959. She was a composer and musical consultant at the Choreographical Institute and Opera, Riga from 1959 to 1972 and then settled in Israel. She was a piano teacher at the Conservatory of Kiron, for one year and in 1973 founded the Conservatory in Holon and was director until 1980. After 1959 she was active as a concert pianist and appeared on both radio and television and after 1980 did freelance piano teaching, playing and composing. PHOTOGRAPH.
Compositions
CHAMBER
Fantasy (cl and pf) (1979)
Prayer (vln and pf) (1972)
Sonata (vln and pf) (1968)
PIANO
Sonata (1968)
Toccata (1971)
Over 100 other pieces
VOCAL
Listen, symphonic poem (vce and orch) (1972)
Children's Carnaval, cycle of 5 songs (vce and pf) (1979)
Approx. 50 songs (1958-1981)
BALLET
My Bright Day (1965)
Three choreographical miniatures (1965-1966)
OPERETTA
Cats' House, for children (1959)
TEACHING PIECES
Group teaching (pf)
Ref. composer, 457

FEININGER, Leonore Helene
German pianist and composer. b. Berlin, December 14, 1901. She began studying the piano under her mother's guidance and then studied at a folk music college in Berlin-Charlottenburg and privately. In 1978 she won a prize for her lyrics in Berlin. Her music has been played on television and by a dance orchestra in Southern Germany. PHOTOGRAPH. DISCOGRAPHY.
Compositions
ORCHESTRA
Numerous pieces
BAND
Im leichten Schritt, march
Lasst uns immer vorwaerts gehen! march
PIANO
Erinnerung Tango (1960)
Hochzeitsglocken (1957)
Rondo (1976)
Slavische Weisen (1976)
Sternen Blues (1960)
Valse de soir (1960)
Valse musette (1960)
Vorspiel
Zur Begruessung, march (1968)
VOCAL
Bleibt der Platz leer? (1975)
Das Wohlbefinden (1975)
Jubilee for a Club Romantique
Marilyn
Paules Pech-Chanson
Schicksals-Lied : Murre nicht
Schoenes Heimatland (soli and ch)
Sprich doch leise
Weihnachtsglocken
Other songs
MISCELLANEOUS
Abendgedanken I and II
Ref. composer, 563

FEIRING, Bertha. **See TAPPER, Bertha**

FEIST-STEINHAUSEN, Alwine
German pianist and composer. b. Cologne, March 8, 1873; d. Berlin, October 13, 1924. She completed her studies at the Conservatory of Brussels. She composed piano pieces and chamber songs.
Ref. 105

FEJARD, Simone
French composer. b. 1911.
Composition
ORCHESTRA
Le Khene enchanté, six sketches

FELDMAN, Joann Esther
American professor and composer. b. New York, October 19, 1941. She obtained her B.A. from Queens College, New York, where she studied composition under Hugo Weisgall. She also studied under Seymour Shifrin, Arnold Easton and William Denny at the University of California, Berkeley, where she received an M.A. in 1966. She won the composition prize at Queens College in 1962 and in 1966 received the University of Redlands' orchestral composition prize. She was an assistant at the University of California from 1965 to 1966 and a faculty member of California State College, 1966 to 1972. In 1972 she became an associate professor at California State College.
Compositions
ORCHESTRA
Antiphonies (1965)
Homage to Stravinsky (1974)
CHAMBER
Woodwind quintet (1966)
More music from the magic theatre (vln and pf) (1980)
Twenty-five graded pieces (Associated Bd.)
The Western Isles (Bagley & Ferguson)
Other pieces (Freeman; E.M.I.; Weinberger; Galliard)
VOCAL
A pastoral, madrigal (4 vces)
Songs incl.:
Day by day
A gracious duet
In the days of long ago (1 or 2 vces)
In my country garden
Little songs and dances (Freeman; E.M.I.)
London town
Scenes from Holland
Things I remember
Two part songs (Boosey & Hawkes)
Windmill land
Unison songs
Ref. composer, 457
Two songs without words (vln and pf) (1974)
Variations for viola and piano (1963)
PIANO
The ill-tempered Cavalier, rhapsody (2 pf) (1974)
Variations (1973)
VOCAL
The three peoples (ch)
Songs
Ref. composer, 40, 137, 142, 347

FELIX, Margery Edith (pseuds. Margery Dawe, Jill Consey, Carol Medway)
English teacher and composer. b. London, 1907. She studied composition at the Guildhall School of Music under Harry Farjeon. She was principal of the Nottingham School of Music from 1947 and music teacher for a number of London schools from 1955.
Compositions
ORCHESTRA
Miniature symphony
CHAMBER
Playing together (str trios and pf)
Rhapsody string quartet
PIANO
Pieces, solos and studies
VOCAL
Thy voice
Duet
THEATRE
Bremen Town Musicians, children's play
Publications
Clarinet Tutor.
New Road Series of Educational Music. 6 books for piano; 9 books for strings.
Theory of Music. 6 books.
Travel Tunes series. 3 books.
Ref. 77

FELLISENT. See BILLINGTON, Elizabeth

FELLOWS, Mrs. Wayne Stanley
American pianist, violinist, choir conductor, soprano, teacher and composer. b. Hugo, OK, August 8, 1908. She studied at Putnam Hall, Poughkeepsie from 1926 to 1927, Southeastern State College from 1927 to 1928 and obtained her B.A. in 1930 and M.A. in 1932 at Mechanical College, Stillwater. She studied with Mae Brannon, Zeta Collins, Amelita Galli-Curci, Celeste Chamblee, Gladys Dunkleberger, Noble Cain, Berniece Webb, G. M. Patterson, Faye Musgrove, H. G. Ridgeway, Julia Stout, Lillian Opal Kent, Paul Klingstedt, Frank Hladky and Daniel Huffman. In 1931 she was a teacher at the Sand Springs Consolidated Schools, band conductor at the Hugo High School in 1941 and conductor of the Hugo High School Federated Mixed Chorus in 1946.
Compositions
VOCAL
A clubwoman's prayer
A ship sailing (S)
Chorale in C-Minor
Has you made up your mind, negro spiritual
The heart of a rose (S)
Kindergarten volume of songs
SACRED
Christmas suite (mix-ch)
Glory to Jesus, Son of God, anthem
I wondered at such a birth (B)
Oh Great and Glorious Lord, anthem
Ref. 496

FELSENTHAL, Amalie
German composer. b. Iserlohn, 1841.
Compositions
PIANO
Pieces
VOCAL
Children's songs, incl. ops. 8 and 9
Fifty songs (publ. as *Dorothy's Songs*)
Ref. 226, 276

FEMININE FIELD. See SZYMANOWSKA, Maria Agata

FEMININE HOMER. See SAPPHO

FENASCI, Dorothy
20th-century American composer. She won the composition contest of the Louisiana Federation of Music Clubs in 1954 and 1955.
Ref. 448

FENGER, Johanne
19th-century Danish composer.
Compositions
VOCAL
Digte af Helen Nyblom (W. Hansen)
Fem sange (M. Rosing, Hansen)
Freias guldsmykke (vce and pf)
Lyriske sange (m-S or Bar) (Hansen)
Menneskets engle (vce and pf)
Sex sange til texter af Ingemanns Ahasverus (Hansen)
Ref. 331

FENNER, Beatrice
American poetess and composer. b. Los Angeles, April 15, 1904. She studied at the Juilliard School of Music and the Master Institute of United Arts, Roerich Museum, New York. She also studied under Tertius Noble.
Compositions
VOCAL
Songs and children's songs incl.:
Night song
Reciprocation
Weep little Mary
SACRED
Setting of the Lord's Prayer
When children pray
Publications
Blue Laughter. Poems.
The Sacred Tree.
Ref. 39, 226

FENSTOCK, Belle
American pianist, artist and composer. b. New York, April 21, 1939. She studied music under Joseph Schillinger. She collaborated with other composers in several works.
Compositions
ORCHESTRA
American rhapsody (pf and orch) (with Clarence Cox) (Ditson)
VOCAL
Cafe society
Calypso man
Holiday in Venice
Mexican fiesta
Simonetta
Song of the refugee
Stranger in the dark
MISCELLANEOUS
Assorted ladies
Safari
Ref. 39, 280

FERGUS-HOYT, Phyllis
20th-century American composer. b. Chicago. She studied under Henry Dyke Sleeper at Smith College in Northampton, MA, and at the American Conservatory in Chicago, where she took an M.A. in 1918. She specializes in story poems with a musical background for the piano. The piano part is recorded on a roll and she recites the poem during the playing of the roll, which is then re-recorded.
Compositions
ORCHESTRA
The Highwayman (A. Noyes)
CHAMBER
Solos (pf) (Presser, Summy)
Solos (vln) (Presser, Summy)
VOCAL
Choral (w-vces) (Birchard)
Songs (S and vln) (Presser)
Over 50 story poems (narr and pf)
Other songs
OPERA
One opera
Ref. 40, 226, 292, 323, 347, 353

FERNANDES, Maria Helena Rosas
20th-century Brazilian composer. She was a prize winner at the 1978 to 1979 Brazilian competition of classical piano music. DISCOGRAPHY.
Compositions
PIANO
Cycle
Ref. Records International

FERNANDEZ, Helen Lorenzo
Brazilian lecturer and composer. b. Aracaju, 1915. She is the director of the Music Academy Lorenzo Fernandez, Rio de Janeiro and a member of the Vienna Music Academy and the Santa Cecilia Academy, Rome.
Ref. 268

FERNANDEZ, Terresita
Cuban guitarist, singer and composer. b. Santa Clara, December 20, 1930. She sang her own compositions, accompanying herself on the guitar in concerts in Havana and gave radio and television performances.
Compositions
VOCAL
Bola de nieve
Canta pajarito
La gaviota
Ismaelillo
Pinares de Mayari
Rondas
Tia jutia
Ref. 604

FERNANDEZ DE LA MORA, Pilar
Spanish pianist, teacher and composer. b. Seville. She studied in Seville under O. de la Cina and in Madrid under Guelbenzu; later in Paris under Mme. Masart and Ambroise Thomas, director of the Paris Conservatoire. She gave concerts in Paris and Madrid and became a well-known piano teacher. Among her pupils was the pianist Jose Cubiles.
Compositions
PIANO
Pieces
VOCAL
Three poems (Jacinto Verdaguer)
TEACHING PIECES
Una hora de mecanismo (pf)
Adaptation of foreign piano teaching methods
Ref. 361

FERNANDO, Sarathchandra Vichremadithya
Sri Lankan oboist, conductor and composer. b. Colombo, July 22, 1937. She made solo oboe appearances and conducted orchestras and chamber ensembles in Sri Lanka.
Compositions
ORCHESTRA
Fantasia on a folk tune (1973)
CHAMBER
Three pieces for strings (1974)
VOCAL
Songs
FILM MUSIC
Several films
Ref. 457

FERRA, Susana
16th-century Italian lutenist and composer. She lived in Ferrara ca. 1545.
Ref. 128

FERRAND-TEULET, Denise
French pianist and composer. b. Montreal, Canada, July 28, 1921. She studied the piano under Marguerite Long and Jacques Fevrier at the Marguerite Long-Jacques Thibaud School and composition under Arkady Trebinsky, director of the Russian Conservatory in Paris. She performed as a pianist in Munich, Frankfurt, Baden-Tuebingen and throughout France. In 1957 she won a Pas de Loup prize for her *Concerto for Piano and Chamber Orchestra*. She is a member of SACEM.
Compositions
ORCHESTRA
Concerto for piano and chamber orchestra (1957) (Pas de Loup prize)
Concerto for trumpet and string orchestra (1972) (Transatlantiques)
CHAMBER
Octet for winds (1972)
Trilogue (pf, vln and vlc) (1972)
Trio for piano, violin and saxophone (1964) (A.P. Pazcille)
Movements for piano and percussion (1957)
Sonata for violin and piano (1969)
VOCAL
Sonatina for saxophone and piano (1960)
Sonatina for trumpet and piano (1960)
Refraction 73 (ch, pf and perc) (1973) (Transatlantiques)
Album for Mary-Ann, for children (1965) (Transatlantiques)
Ref. composer, 9, 76

FERRARI, Carlotta
Italian pianist, poetess, singer, writer and composer. b. Lodi, January 27, 1837; d. Bologna, November 23, 1907. She studied the piano and voice under Strepponi and Panzini and composition under Mazzucato at the Milan Conservatory from 1844 to 1850. When she completed her first opera *Ugo* at the age of 20, she had to pay the entire expense of the first performance herself, because of objections that she was a woman. However, it was a success and later her works were in great demand. She was commissioned by the Turin government to write a cantata for a Roman deputation at Turin and a Requiem mass for the anniversary of the death of King Charles Albert (Turin, July 22, 1868). She was considered one of the great masters of the canon form; Pougin spoke of her talent as being remarkable. Carlotta also wrote poems, sonnets, three volumes of prose and an autobiography.
Compositions
PIANO
Ai fratelli napolitani, tarantella (Mariani)
Garibaldi in pace e in guerra, waltz (Mariani; Ricordi)
Rondinella pellegrina (also vce and pf) (Ricordi)
Spensieratezza, mazurka (Ricordi)
Vezzi e carezze, waltz (Ricordi)

VOCAL
Cantata
Il canto in morte di Felice Romani
La fioraia (Ricordi)
Six canons (3 vces and pf)
Six melodies in canon form (Ricordi)
Twelve canons (3 vces) (Breitkopf & Hartel)
Other songs and canons
SACRED
Grand Mass (comm government for Cathedral of Lodi, 1868)
Requiem (comm anniversary of the death of King Charles Albert, 1868)
Te Deum
Hymns
OPERA
Eleonora d'Arborea (composer) (1870)
Sofia (composer) (1866)
Ugo (composer) (1857)
Publications
Nuove Liriche. Poetry. 1858.
Le Prime Poesie. Poetry. 1853.
Rime Sculte. Poetry. 1891.
Verse e Prose. 1878.
Autobiography.
Ref. 9, 17, 22, 26, 44, 100, 102, 105, 107, 108, 129, 225, 226, 268, 276, 297, 301, 335, 369, 433

FERRARI, Francesca Jessie

19th-century composer.
Compositions
PIANO
Caprice in E-Minor (1876)
VOCAL
Herbstklage (J. Troutbeck, 1881)
Left alone (W.H. Wills, 1881)
Ref. British Library (London)

FERRARI (Ferri), Gabriella (nee Colombari de Montegre)

French-Italian pianist and composer. b. Paris, September 14, 1851; d. Paris, July 4, 1921. She appeared as a child prodigy at the age of 12. Later she studied at the Milan Conservatory under G. Martini (piano) and E. Ketten (piano and composition); under P. Serrao (counterpoint) and G. Minceli (composition) in Naples and composition under Charles Gounod and Alfred Apel in France. She was greatly encouraged in her work by T. Dubois and F. Leborne and her works were featured in the concerts of Leborne and Lamoureux, where she also appeared as a pianist.
Compositions
ORCHESTRA
Lontan dagli occhi (gold medal, Bellini Competition)
Suites symphoniques
Rhapsodie espagnole
Valse des guirlandes (Bertram)
CHAMBER
A une fiancée (gtr) (Schirmer)
PIANO
Album: In memory of Vincenzo Bellini (Ricordi)
Aspiration, Caprice, op. 74 (Paris: Durand & Schoenewerk, 1887)
A franc étrier, étude de concert, op. 64 (Durand & Schoenewerk, 1887)
Menuet (Ricordi)
Quasi, waltz (Gebethner)
Spanish rhapsody
Romance sans paroles, op. 68 (Paris: Richault et Cie, 1886)
Le ruisseau
The stream
The swallow
Tarantelle, op. 11 (1884)
Trois pièces poetiques: Feuille morte; Par le sentier; Ciel radieux (Ricordi)
VOCAL
Songs and romances incl.:
L'Aimée
Ad una stella
Berceuse
Le berger de Blandy, in old style
La boucle blonde, op. 57
Chanson de la poupée, op. 31 (1884)
Chant d'amour
Chant d'exil
Chansons espagnoles (1884)
O Fior della pensosa sera, serenade (Ricordi)
J'ai tant de choses à vous dire (1885)
Larmes en songe
Lazarone
Rest (Williams)
A Sylvanire, Air dans le style ancien, op. 38 (A. d'Albert) (Richault et Cie, 1886)
Smiling eyes, op. 55 (T. Moore) (London: J. Williams, 1901)
Sogno d'un poèta, romance (ded Gounod)
Sous bois
Sylvaine
Tarantella
Those evening bells (Williams)
Je veux quitter la vie (Ricordi)
Whene'er I see those (Williams)
SACRED
Cantata
Ave Maria
OPERA
Sous le Masque, in 1 act (1898)
Dernier Amour, comic opera (P. Berlier) (1895)
L'Ame en Peine, in 2 acts (A. Bernede) (1896)
Le Cobzar, in 1 act (Princess E. Vacaresco and P. Milliet) (1908)
Le Captif (Russian text)
Le Tartare, in 2 acts (1906)
MISCELLANEOUS
J'ai tant de choses à vous dire
Ref. 13, 14, 17, 22, 44, 74, 86, 108, 109, 128, 183, 226, 268, 276, 297, 347, 477

FERRE, Susan Ingrid see Addendum

FERRER OTERO, Monsita Monserrate

Puerto Rican concert pianist and composer. b. San Juan, 1882; d. 1966. At the age of six she commenced piano studies with Rosa Sicardo and then Ana Otero. She studied harmony with Julio Carlos De Arteaga and later with Aristides Chavier Arevalo. She continued her piano studies with Gonzalo Nunes in New York and from 1961, with Jesus Maria Sanroma at the Conservatorio de Musica de Puerto Rico. She participated in a number of concerts. In 1906 she performed at the Ateneo Puertorriqueno with Ana Otero in four-handed works and also accompanied the violinist Angel Celestino Morales.
Compositions
CHAMBER
String quartet
Other pieces
PIANO
Capricho brillante
Estudio en Do
Nocturno in E-Flat Major (prize, 1913)
Nocturno en el tropico
Polonaise in A-Flat Major
Ten variations on a theme by Aristides Chavier, waltzes
Two marches in festive style
Two minuets
Vals ideal (prize, 1908)
VOCAL
Fuga a cuatro voces
Amanecer (Llorens Torres)
Canciones escolares
Canciones populares
SACRED
Marcha pontificia (1st prize, 1940)
Sanctus y Benedictus (2 vces)
Christmas carols
FOLK MUSIC
Collection of three Antillan dances
Dances of Latin-American origin
Divagacion, dance
El cuatro de majo, dance
Ensuenos de Gloria (honorable mention, 1913)
La Carcajada, dance
Popular songs
MISCELLANEOUS
Apolo, two-step (hon mention, 1910)
Bibliography
Monserrate Ferrer Otero. *Puerto Rico Illustrado*, November 24, 1945.
Pardo de Casablanca, Coloma. Composicion musical puertorriquena.
Veray, Amaury. *Monsita Ferrer, Sonatina Puertorriquena, Para Canto y Esperanza*.
Ref. Prof. C. Dower (Holyoke, MA), 278

FERREYRA, Beatriz

Argentine electronic instrumentalist, pianist, violinist and composer. b. Cordoba, June 21, 1937. She studied the piano and the violin in Cordoba from 1943 to 1950 and the piano in Buenos Aires, under Celia Bronstein. From 1962 to 1963 she studied harmony and musical analysis under Nadia Boulanger (q.v.) in Paris and electroacoustic and electronic music in Paris and Milan under Edgardo Canton. She joined the Groupe de Recherches Musicales of French Radio in 1963 under the direction of Pierre Schaeffer and in 1968 attended a composition course in Darmstadt, Germany, under G. Ligeti, K. Stockhausen, and E. Brown. In 1969 she became the representative responsible for seminars on audio-visual music at the Paris Conservatoire. She was active in initiating courses on electro-acoustic music and collaborated in a number of publications. She researched the use of music therapy in France and elsewhere. DISCOGRAPHY.

Compositions

ELECTRONIC

Musicotherapie (5 tapes) (1973)
Tobogan (pf, perc and tape) (1966)
Vol final (elec org and tape)
Canto del loco (tape) (1974)
Demeures aquatiques (tape) (1967)
Echos (tape)
Etude aux iterations (tape) (1965)
Etude aux sons flegmatiques (tape) (1971)
Jeu (tape) (1966)
Medisances, dance recital (tape) (1968)
Mirage for the ballet, A la lueur de la lampe (Susan Birge) (1973)
L'Orvietan (tape) (1970)
Le recit (vce and tape) (1971)
Siesta blanca (tape) (1972)
Solfege de L'Object Sonore

INCIDENTAL MUSIC

Antartide, television (1971) (prize, National Cinema Center, 1972)
Un certain regard, television (1969)
Etude 65 (1965)
Faux visage du vrai (1967)
Les arbres (1965)
La fenêtre (1969)
Mutations (1972)
Pour les pieds nus d'Hélène (1968)

Publications

Rapport entre la hauteur et le Fundamentale d'un son musical: d'Henri Chiarucci. Revue Internationale d'Audiologie. France, March 1966.

Ref. composer, 563

FERRI, Gabriella. See FERRARI, Gabriella

FERRIERES, Mme. de

18th-century French composer.

Compositions

VOCAL

Songs incl.:
Chanson poitevines

Ref. 218

FERRIS, Isabel D.

20th-century American composer. She composed choral works.

Ref. 40, 347

FERRIS, Joan

20th-century American composer.

Compositions

VOCAL

Six songs (James Joyce) (ch)

Ref. 142, 146

FICHTNER, Pauline. See ERDMANNSDOERFER, Pauline

FIELD, Miss A.

18th-century Austrian song composer.

Ref. 465

FIFE, Duncan. See ATKINSON, Dorothy

FILIPOWICZ, Elise-Minelli (nee Mayer)

Polish violinist and composer. b. Rastadt, 1794; d. England, 1841. She studied under Spohr. She performed in several German towns and later worked for the family of Count Starzenski in Poland. In 1831 her husband joined the army and she went to France, where her violin playing was in great demand. In 1835 she left France for London.

Compositions

ORCHESTRA

Warsovienne (vln and orch)

CHAMBER

Trois valses (vln, vla and pf)
Divertimento, scherzoso on Polish themes (vln and pf)
Fantasia on Polish airs (vln and pf)
Introduction and rondo on Polish themes (vln and pf)
Rondo alla polacca (vln and pf)
Variazioni capricciosi (vln and pf)

Ref. 35, 129

FILIPPONI, Dina

Italian pianist and composer. b. Rome, February 1903; d. Resina, Naples, September 14, 1926. She composed piano pieces.

Ref. 70

FILZ, Bogdanna

20th-century Soviet-Ukrainian composer. She studied at the Conservatory of Lvov under Stanislav Liudkievich, graduating in 1959.

Compositions

ORCHESTRA

Symphonic works

VOCAL

To youth, cantata
Romances
Settings to poems (T. Shevchenko, I. Franko and L. Ukrainka)

Ref. 223, 465

FINCH, Miss

18th-19th-century English composer.

Composition

PIANO

Captain Campbell of Shanfield's March (Edinburgh: J. Hamilton, ca. 1800)

Ref. 65

FINE, Sylvia

American authoress, librettist and composer. b. New York, August 29 19?. She married Danny Kaye and was his librettist. She became a member of ASCAP in 1948.

Compositions

VOCAL

Anatole of Paris
Bali bogie
Delilah Jones
Eileen
Five pennies saints
Happy ending
Happy times
Life could not better be
Lobby number
Lullaby in ragtime
Melody in 4
Molly O
Pavlova
Spec songs
Stanislavsky vonschtickfitz monahan

INCIDENTAL MUSIC

Films:
Bway Show, score
Let's Face It, score
The Man with the Golden Arm, score
Straw Hat Revue, score
the Moon is Blue, songs
On the Double, songs
Up in Arms, songs
Television:
The Court Jester
Inspector General
Knock on Wood
On the Riviera
The Secret Life of Walter Mitty

Ref. 39, 494

FINE, Vivian

American pianist, lecturer and composer. b. Chicago, September 28, 1913. At the age of five she was awarded a scholarship to attend the Chicago Musical College, 1919 to 1922. She studied under Silvio Sconti from 1923 to 1924 and then Djane Lavoie-Herz. At 13 Vivian attended the American Conservatory, Chicago where she studied harmony and composition under Ruth Crawford Seeger (q.v.) and counterpoint under Adolf Weidig, until 1925. In 1931 she moved to New York and studied composition, counterpoint and orchestration under Roger Sessions from 1934 to 1942, the piano under Abby Whiteside from 1937 to 1945 and orchestration under George Szell in 1943. She also attended the Dalcroze School in New York from 1935 to 1936. She taught at New York University from 1945 to 1948, the Juilliard School of Music in 1948 and the State University Teachers' College at Potsdam, NY, in 1951. In 1963 she taught at Connecticut College School of Dance and from 1964 taught composition and the piano at Bennington College, Vermont. She was founder of the American Composers' Alliance and vice-president from 1961 to 1965. She was director of the Rothschild Foundation from 1953 to 1960 and gave lecture-recitals at various American universities, 1965 to 1968. In 1968 she was composer-in-residence at the Panorama of the Arts at the University of Wisconsin, Oshkosh and held the same position at Skidmore College, Saratoga, NY, in 1976. In 1966 she received the Dollard Award. Her "Drama" was nominated for the Pulitzer Prize. She received grants from the Ford Foundation in 1970 and the National Endowment for the Arts, 1974. In 1980 she was awarded a John Simon Guggenheim Memorial Fellowship for composition and became a member of the American Academy and Institute of Arts and Letters. DISCOGRAPHY.

Compositions

ORCHESTRA

Concertante for piano and orchestra (1944) (New York: ACA)
Poetic fires (from the Greeks) (pf and orch) (1984) (comm Koussevitsky Foundation)
Concerto for piano, strings and percussion for one performer (1972) (Shaftsbuy, VT: Catamount; Facsimile, 1973)
Dance suite (1938)
Drama (comm San Francisco Symphony)
Prelude and elegiac song (str orch; also str qrt) (1937) (ACA; Montevideo: Instituto Interamericano de Musicologia)
Race of life (1937) (ACA)

CHAMBER

Dreamscape (perc ens, 3 fl, vlc and pf) (1964)
Chamber concerto (vlc and 6 insts) (1966)
Concertino for piano and percussion ensemble (1965) (Catamount)
Quintet for string trio, trumpet and harp (1967) (Catamount)
Capriccio for oboe and string trio (1946) (ACA)
Composition for string quartet (1954) (ACA)
Quartet for brass (1978) (Catamount)
String quartet (1957) (ACA; Catamount, 1972)
Music for flute, oboe and violoncello (Catamount, 1980)
Trio for strings (1930) (ACA; Catamount, 1974)
Trio for violin, cello and piano
Three pieces for flute, bassoon and harp (1961)
Divertimento for violoncello and percussion (1951) (ACA; Catamount, 1972)
Duo for flute and viola (1961) (C. Fischer, 1976)
Fantasy for violoncello and piano (1962) (Catamount, 1972)
Four pieces for two flutes (1930) (ACA; Catamount, 1974)
Lieder (vla and pf) (1980)
Lyric piece for violoncello and piano (1937) (ACA)
Sonata for violin and piano (1952) (ACA; Catamount, 1972)
Sonatina for oboe and piano (also vln and pf; also vlc and pf) (1939) (ACA)
Suite for oboe and piano (award, Music Guild, PA, 1943)
Teisho (vln and pf)
Three Buddhist evocations for violin and piano (Catamount, 1977)
Three pieces for violin and piano (1940) (ACA)
The flicker (fl)
Melos (d-b) (1964)
Second prophet-bird (fl) (1972) (Catamount, 1973)
Variations for harp (1953) (hon mention, Northern California Harpists' Assoc. contest, 1954) (ACA)
Second solo for oboe (1947) (ACA; Catamount, 1972)
Solo for oboe (1929) (ACA; Catamount, 1974)
Song of persephone (vla) (1964) (Catamount, 1972)
Divertimento (1933) (ACA)

PIANO

Chaconne (1947) (ACA)
Four pieces (1966)
Four polyphonic pieces (1931-1932) (ACA; Catamount, 1974)
Five preludes (1939-1941) (ACA; Catamount)
Momenti (1978)
Music for study, Nos. 1-5 (nos. 1-2, E. H. Morris)
Rhapsody on a Russian folk song (1944) (ACA)
Sinfonia and fugato (1952) (New York: Lawson-Gould, 1963)
Small sad sparrow (1963)
Suite in E-Flat Major (1940) (ACA; Catamount, 1972)
Variations (1952) (ACA)
(1952) (ACA)
Teaching pieces

VOCAL

Cantata (m-S, Bar, narr, ch and orch) (1975)
Meeting for equal rights, 1866, cantata (S, B, ch, timp and perc incl. glock and strs) (Catamount, 1976)
Three multilined textures, cantata (1960)
Paean, cantata (T, narr, w-ch and brass ens) (1969)
Epitaph (mix-ch and orch) (1967) (Catamount, 1972)
Cherry-ripe (T. Campion) (mix-ch and pf) (1947) (ACA)
Morning (Thoreau) (narr, mix-ch and org or pf) (1962) (Catamount, 1972)
Sonnet, to a cat (J. Keats) (mix-ch) (1934) (ACA)
Sounds of the nightingale (S, w-ch and cham) (1971)
Teisho (8 soloists or small ch and str qrt) (1975) (Catamount, 1976)
Passionate shepherd to his love and her reply (C. Marlowe and W. Raleigh) (w-ch a-cap) (1938) (ACA)
Valedictions (J. Donne) (S, T, mix-ch and 10 insts) (1959)
The confession (Racine) (S, fl, vln, vla, vlc and pf) (1963) (Catamount, 1972)
Epigram and epitaph (W. Jones, H. Wotton) (m-S) (1941) (ACA)
Five songs (anon, E. Dickinson, J. Joyce, J. Keats, Whitman) (m-S) (1933-1941) (ACA)
Four Elizabethan songs (J. Donne, J. Lyly, W. Shakespeare, P. Sidney) (S) (1937-1941) (ACA; Catamount, 1972)
Four songs (anon, R. Herrick, J. Joyce) (m-S, vln, vla and vlc) (San Francisco: New Music, 1933)
Great Wall of China (F. Kafka) (New York: New Music, 1947-1948)
A guide to the life expectancy of a rose (S. R. Tilley) (S, T, fl, vln, cl, vlc and hp or pf) (ACA; Catamount, 1972) (comm Rothschild Foundation, 1956)
Romantic ode (1976)
She weeps over Rahoon (vce and strs)
Songs of our time (B. Brecht, J. Wittlin) (S) (1943) (ACA)
Tragic exodus (B and pf) (1939) (ACA)
Two Neruda poems (vce and pf) (1971) (Catamount, 1972)
The nightingale (vce and perc)
Songs

SACRED

Psalm 13 (mix-ch and pf or org) (1953) (ACA)
For a bust of Erik Satie, mass (S, m-S, narr and 6 insts)

BALLET

Alcestis (orch) (1960)
My son, my enemy (1965)
Opus 51 (pf and perc) (1938-1940)
The race of life (pf and perc; also orch) (1937, 1938)
They too are exiles (pf and perc) (1940)

OPERA

The Women in the Garden, chamber opera (1978)

INCIDENTAL MUSIC

Dollars and Cents, play (vces and pf) (1941)

ELECTRONIC

Missa brevis (4 vlc and tape) (1972)
Transformations (vlc and tape)

MISCELLANEOUS

Momenti (1978)

Publications

Untitled article on composers and choreographers. "Dance Perspectives" 16. 1963:8-11.
Fine, Vivian; Composer/choreographer. Choreographer/composer. "Dance Perspectives" 16. 1963. With Dlugoszewski, Lusia.

Bibliography

Humphrey, D. *Music for an American Dance*. "Bulletin of the ACA". Vol. 8, no. 1. 1958.
Riegger, W. *Music of Vivian Fine. Ibid.*, pp. 2-3.

Ref. 3, 4, 5, 6, 13, 17, 20, 22, 40, 52, 53, 70, 74, 81, 85, 94, 124, 138, 141, 142, 146, 152, 185, 189, 190, 206, 226, 228, 353, 397, 415, 457, 465, 468, 475, 494, 560, 563, 569, 594, 610, 611, 622

FINK, Emma C.

20th-century American composer. She composed chamber and band music, piano and organ pieces.
Ref. 347

FINLEY, Lorraine Noel (Mrs. Theodore F. Frank)

American pianist, violinist, authoress, singer and composer. b. Montreal, December 24 1899; d. Greenwich, CT, February 13, 1972. She went to school in Canada, Switzerland and Germany and continued her education at Wellesley College, the Juilliard School of Music and Columbia University. Her teachers were J.J. Goulet, Ada Richardson, Louise Heritte-Viardot

(q.v.), Frank La Forge, Percy Goetschius and Rubin Goldmark. She received numerous awards in national competitions and traveled extensively. She specialized in translating lyrics of compositions by well-known composers into English. Her translation for Milhaud's *Le Pauvre Matelot* was used for the Broadway premiere of that opera. She and her husband, Theodore appeared in recitals as Mr. and Mrs. Composer.
Compositions
ORCHESTRA
Symphony in D
Three theatre portraits, suite
CHAMBER
Clarinet sonata
Two violin sonatas
Three other instrumental pieces
VOCAL
Trees of Jotham, cantata
Brave horse of mine (m-ch)
Thirteen songs
BALLET
Persian miniatures
Ref. 39, 40, 142, 347

FINZI, Graciane
French pianist, teacher and composer. b. Casablanca, Morocco, July 10, 1945. She came from a musical background and entered the Conservatory in Casablanca at the age of ten. At the Paris Conservatoire she studied harmony under Henri Challan, counterpoint under Marcel Bitch, fugue under Yvonne Desportes (q.v.), the piano under Joseph Bonvenuti, sight reading under Elsa Barraine (q.v.) and composition under Tony Aubin. She obtained four medals, for solfege, history of music, the piano and sight reading and four first prizes, for harmony, counterpoint, fugue and composition. She taught solfege, harmony and musical analysis in Casablanca and was artistic advisor for the Musique à la Defense festival in France, 1975 to 1976. She is responsible for organizing concerts for young performers at the Paris Conservatoire. DISCOGRAPHY. PHOTOGRAPH.
Compositions
ORCHESTRA
Symphony (perc and str orch) (1967)
Edifice (vln and orch) (1976)
Concerto (vln and cham orch) (comm Radio France)
CHAMBER
Concordances (perc and 12 strs)
Juxtaposition (12 strs) (1975)
Dionyme et Jocante (wind qnt) (1970)
Cinq sequences pour quatour de saxophones (Billaudot, 1983)
Libre-parcours (4 gtr) (1975)
Quartre études (str qrt)
Trio (pf, vln and vlc) (1975)
De l'un à l'autre (a-sax or cl and pf) (Paris: Leduc, 1977)
Sonata pour hautbois et piano (1969)
Sonata pour violon et piano (1969)
Toujours plus (org and hpcd) (1975)
Structure contraste (vla and pf) (1972)
Structures sonores 1 and 2 (vlc and pf) (1972)
Rythmes et son (hp) (Paris: Transatlantiques, 1983)
HARPSICHORD
Profil sonore (1971) (Chappell)
Progression (Leduc, 1978)
ORGAN
Etudes (1976)
Graphique sonore
PIANO
Prelude et final (1969)
Schema sonore (1972)
VOCAL
Ertnoc (narr and orch) (1972)
Prophèties d'Isaie (narr, ch and orch)
Poème (R. Tagore) (m-S and str qrt) (1968)
Processus (vce, fl, vlc and pf) (1972)
Songs (1975)
Ref. composer, SACEM, 199, 267, 563

FIRESTONE, Elizabeth
20th-century American composer.
Compositions
ORCHESTRA
Concertino (pf and orch) (G. Schirmer)
FILM MUSIC
Once more my darling (1949)
That man from Tangier (1933)
Ref. 280, 326

FIRESTONE, Idabelle
American composer. b. 1874, d. 1954. DISCOGRAPHY.
Compositions
VOCAL
Bluebirds (vce and orch)
If I could tell you (vce and orch)
In my garden (vce and orch)
You are the song in my heart (vce and orch)
Ref. 563

FIRNKEES, Gertrud
West German pianist, teacher and composer. b. Passau, October 22, 1925. She began a nursing career, but in 1947 changed to piano study at the Hochschule fuer Musik und Theater in Heidelberg. In 1953 she graduated from the Akademie fuer Musik und darstellende Kunst, Salzburg. She has taken part in several international piano and composition classes and numerous piano recitals. She began teaching in 1960. PHOTOGRAPH.
Compositions
PIANO
Vierhaendige Anfaengerstuecke (Zurich: Moseler; Wolfenbuettel, 1964)
Aleatorik (Bote & Bock, 1972)
Polymetrika, study in 5 parts (1976)
VOCAL
Songs (vce and pf) (1942)
Publications
Introduction into the music of our days by improvisation.
The various kinds of improvisation.
Piano lessons with Schoenberg, op. 19.
Piano tutor in seven books.
Studies for piano in 7 volumes. Zurich: Moseler, Wolfenbuttel, 1960.
Miniaturen fuer Klavier zur Einfuehrung in Dodekaphonik und Aleatorik.
Ref. composer

FIRSOVA, Elena
Soviet composer. b. Leningrad, March 21, 1950. The daughter of an atomic physicist, she studied composition under A. Pirumov and analysis under Y. Kholopov in Moscow. Influenced by Alban Berg, Elena's work is characterized by a strong awareness of form and calculated use of tone color. She was commissioned to write a composition to commemorate the 100th anniversary of Stravinsky's birthday. She married the composer Dmitri Smirnov. DISCOGRAPHY.
Compositions
ORCHESTRA
Cello concerto
Chamber concerto (fl and str orch)
Postludium (hp, cel, bells, glock and str orch)
Violin concerto
Stanza
Other orchestral works
CHAMBER
Elegie (pf) (1979)
Sonata for clarinet solo (1976)
VOCAL
Sonnets of Petrarch (trans Ossip Mandelstam) (vce and pf) (1976)
Setting of poems (Boris Pasternak, Ossip Mandelstam)
OPERA
The Feast during the Plague, chamber opera (Pushkin)
MISCELLANEOUS
Tristia
Ref. Neue Zeitschift fuer Musik

FISCHEL, Marguerite
19th-century American song composer.
Ref. 465

FISCHER, Edith Steinkraus
American violinist, professor, singer and composer. b. Portland, OR, January 9, 1923. She studied at the University of Minnesota (B.A.) and took the artist diploma in singing at the Juilliard School of Music in 1947. She studied opera under Goldovsky at the New England Conservatory, Boston from 1948 to 1950. She was vocal soloist of the Montclair Operetta Club, the Chautauqua Opera Company, the Fred Waring Trio, Temple Emanuel

in New York, the Minneapolis Symphony Orchestra from 1942 to 1947, Brown University Orchestra, Rhode Island Philharmonic Orchestra from 1947 to 1966 and the Newman Congregational Church, Rumford, RI. She was adjunct professor of voice at Brown University and at Rhode Island Junior College, Providence, RI. In addition to being a violinist in the Brown University Symphony Orchestra, she performed leads in her own operas and gave recitals and concerts with the symphony orchestra. She married Martin Fischer, a conductor and violist. PHOTOGRAPH.

Compositions

ORCHESTRA

Fugue (str orch)

CHAMBER

Five string quartets
Woodwind and viola trio
Four pieces for oboe and piano
Prelude (org)
Viola solos
Violin solos

PIANO

Improvisations, four pieces
Improvisation II

VOCAL

Five canonic movements (1970)
Book of children's songs
Over 100 songs

SACRED

Anthems incl.:
Everywhere, Christmas tonight (1978) (Providence Music Press)
O Lord, rebuke me not (S, A, T, B and org)
Our God, our help (1978) (Providence)
Why art thou cast down, my soul?
Songs:
For God alone (Bar and S)
God is our refuge (S, A and org)
Trust in the Lord (S, T and org)
Two books of sacred choral responses

OPERA

Several operas

ARRANGEMENTS

Trio arrangements of Christmas carols
Vouchsafe, O Lord (vce and fl or vln)

Ref. composer, 84, 185

FISCHER, Emma Gabriele Marie von, Baroness

Austrian pianist, teacher and composer. b. Vienna, May 2, 1876. She studied the piano under Emma Klenner and Julius Epstein and theory under Cyril Wolf and Robert Fuchs. She was a concert pianist from 1895 to 1907, then taught the piano and theory privately. She was an honorary member of the Austrian Music Teachers' Association and the Viennese Music Teachers' Society.

Compositions

ORCHESTRA

Piano concerto

CHAMBER

Easy sonata in C (vln and pf) (1942)
Sonata (vln and pf) (1907)

PIANO

Andantino and scherzo, op. 1, in range of 5 notes (4 hands)
Romance, impromptu and etude, op. 2
Song without words
Variations on a theme (1908)
Teaching pieces

VOCAL

Songs

Ref. 111

FISHER, Charlotte Eleanore (Carlotta)

20th-century English pianist, violinist, editor and composer. b. London. She studied in Vienna, London, Leipzig and Toronto, her teachers being Leschetizky and Lutz (piano), Toeving (violin), Heynsen and Ettore Mazzoleni (harmony and composition) and Lindner (singing). She served in the British Intelligence in France during World War I and later became editor of the *Toronto Symphony Orchestra News*. She is a member of CAPAC.

Compositions

PIANO

Baroque (Bosworth & Co., 1941)

VOCAL

Bells of Montreal (1949)
By the deep blue Saguenay (Bosworth, 1944)
Canada - my home (1949)
Christmas chant (Bosworth)
Invitation to Quebec (Bosworth, 1941)
One perfect rose (Bosworth, 1942)

Ref. 85, 133, 347

FISHER, Doris

American authoress, producer, singer and composer. b. New York, May 2, 1915. The daughter of composer Fred Fisher, she studied at the Juilliard School of Music. She sang with the Eddie Duchin Orchestra in 1943, then formed her own group.

Compositions

VOCAL

Songs incl.:
Amado mio
Angelina
Courage was the fashion then
Into each life some rain must fall
Whispering grass
You always hurt the one you love

FILM MUSIC

Down to earth
Gilda
Thrill of Brazil

Ref. 39, 40, 142, 347

FISHER, Gladys Washburn

American professor and composer. b. Klamath Falls, OR, May 16, 1900. She studied composition at Mills College (B.A. and B.M.) under W.J. McCoy, D. Brescia, D. Milhaud, H. Gaul and R. Leich. She taught from 1921 and was assistant professor at Mills College, 1924 to 1925. She won a number of awards in the Pennsylvania Federation of Music Clubs' contests.

Compositions

CHAMBER

Days of '49 (brass sextet)
Contrasts (vlc trio)
A hike in the woods (vlc trio)

ORGAN

Joy of Heaven, chorale prelude on 'Beecher'
Prayer (Bourne Music)
Psalm prelude (Bourne)
Psalm 31
Shepherd's psalm

PIANO

Three waltzes (duet)
Caprice
Clown dance (Willis Music)
Gossip (Willis)

SACRED

Choral works incl.:
Music, I yield to thee
Sing ye with gladness
To us in Bethlehem, hymn
Wake my heart
What child is this?

Ref. 40, 142, 347, 477, 475

FISHER, Jessie

American violinist, authoress, teacher and composer. b. Brielle, NJ, July 16, 1909. She was educated at the Philadelphia Conservatory and the Trenton State University. She studied under Boris Koutzen and helped establish community choral and symphony groups. She was the first violinist for the Riverhead Friends of Music. She was a member of ASCAP.

Compositions

VOCAL

Dance of the wooden shoes
Have you ever seen a star?
I want to play the glockenspiel
Joyous tidings
Mysterious forest
Nocturne
Shades of song

Ref. 39

FISHER, Katherine Danforth

American pianist, conductor, lecturer and composer. b. Cleveland, OH, April 29, 1913. She obtained her B.A. from Oberlin College and Conservatory in 1936. She studied composition at the Eastman School of Music under Burrill Phillips, Wayne Barlow, Bernard Rogers and Alan Hovhaness. She was resident of the Oberlin College Glee Club from 1933 to 1936 and director of music at the Harley School, Rochester, 1936 to 1939. She taught music appreciation at the Columbia School from 1953 to 1960 and was a visiting instructor at the University of Rochester's School of Education, 1958 to 1961. For ten years she taught the piano privately. She conducted several youth and women's choruses. DISCOGRAPHY. PHOTOGRAPH.

Compositions

ORCHESTRA

Folk tune fantasy (vln, hp and str orch) (1948)

CHAMBER

Rondo (vln and pf) (1948)

Sonatina for flute and piano (1950, rev 1957)

PIANO

Conversation pieces (2 pf) (1953)

In memoriam, pieces

March for puppets (1946)

Music for Judy, 6 short pieces (1945)

Preludes to outer space (1956)

VOCAL

Song of Summer, cantata (Walt Whitman and Richard Hovey) (treble vces)

The lamp on the stream, cantata (soli, w-ch and pf) (1954) (Drinker Lib. of Choral Music)

Songs of the seasons, on Japanese Tanka poetry (w-ch, fl and pf) (to Mildred Kimbell) (comm Hansdale Music Club, 1967)

How shall I know (Millay)

John French Wilson songs (high or med-vce)

Little fir tree

May it all be a wonder to you (solo or treble vces and pf) (Eleanor West Haupt)

Old English rhyme (treble vces) (comm Shirley Cooman for Penfield O Music Festival, 1968)

Perfect love, wedding song

Song at Amalfi (S. Teasdale)

Sonnet (Shakespeare) (1952)

Spring madrigal

Wisdom (S. Teasdale)

The years are wise

Three songs (T and str qrt) (F. McLeod)

SACRED

The Beatitudes (B, mix-ch and org) (1948)

A grateful heart, benediction (mix-ch a-cap) (1941)

How excellent Thy name (Psalm 8), anthem (mix-vces with pf or org) (1947)

Magnificat (St. Luke) (w-ch and org) (1955)

Maimonides' prayer (B, m-vces and org) (1962) (comm J. Baldwin, Hamilton College)

No coward soul (Emily Bronte) (mix-ch and org) (1953)

Praised be my Lord, motet (St. Francis of Assisi) (ch) (1947)

Serve the Lord with gladness (2 chil-ch) (comm Ethel Rider, Downtown The United Presbyterian Church, 1974)

The spirit of God (Isaiah 61: 1 and 3) (ch and org) (1952)

Transfiguration (Matt. 17) (B and mix-ch a-cap) (1974)

Wings of the morning, on Psalm 139 (T and mix-ch a-cap) (1981)

How great is His beauty (vce and pf) (1947)

In a walled garden

New things do I declare (after Isaiah) (1961)

A Gaelic blessing

Christmas carols (1971)

MISCELLANEOUS

Music for friends

Ref. composer, 563

FISHER, Renée Breger

20th-century American double-bassist, organist, pianist, vibraharpist, lecturer, writer and composer. b. New York. She holds an M.A. from Columbia University. She is currently on the faculty of the University of Bridgeport, CT,.

Ref. 77

FISHER, Susan

American lutenist and composer. b. Pittsburgh, Pa, 1952. She studied the lute under Murray Panitz and composition under Lawrence Widdoes and Vincent Persichetti and gained a masters degree in composition from the Juilliard School of Music. She was awarded an ASCAP Foundation grant for young composers in 1979.

Compositions

ORCHESTRA

Pieces

CHAMBER

Pieces

THEATRE

Last of the Ice Age

Ref. AMC newsletter, ICWM

FISHMAN, Marian (Marion)

American teacher and composer. b. Brooklyn, December 7, 1941.

Compositions

ORCHESTRA

Adagio (1964)

CHAMBER

Six studies in sonorities for four woodwinds (fl, ob, cl and bsn) (1972)

Glimpses (1969)

VOCAL

The hollow men, cantata (T.S. Eliot) (1966)

Ref. 190, 280, 347

FITZGERALD, Lady Edward

19th-century Irish composer.

Compositions

VOCAL

Songs incl.:

I remember how my childhood fleeted

Ref. 433

FITZGERALD, Sister Florence Therese

20th-century American teacher and composer. b. Chicago. She composed choral works.

Ref. 347

FIUZA, Virginia Salgado

Brazilian conductor, lecturer and composer. b. Fortaleza, August 5, 1897. She studied in Rio de Janeiro at the National Institute of Music in 1916 under Nicia Silva (voice) and Alfredo Richard (theory) and in 1921 under Arnaud Gouveia and Angelo Franca. She improved her technique under Paulo Silva (harmony, counterpoint and fugue). She studied folklore under Luis Heitor, composition and orchestration under J. Otaviano and conducting under Francisco Mignone. She was active as a teacher from 1919 and became deputy director of the Brazilian Conservatory of Music in 1948, where she taught harmony and composition until 1967.

Compositions

CHAMBER

Ecce sacerdos

Quadro brasileiro (1949)

Rio abaixo (1949)

PIANO

Divertimento (1948)

Sonata in D-Minor (1940)

Suite classica (1939)

Suite infantil (1950)

Suite romantica (1949)

Vissungo (1951)

VOCAL

Songs incl.:

Adormecer (1942)

Ambição de ventura (1943)

Canção dramatica (1947)

Canção triste (1964)

Cantiga, song (1943)

Enganos do coração (1949)

Publications

Analise musical.

Harmonia instrumental e estruturação musical.

Harmonia e polifonia instrumental para classe de harmonia superior.

Ref. 333

FLACH, Elsa Anna Clara (nee Wolde) (alt. name Wolde-Flach)

German pianist, choral conductor, singer, poetess and composer. b. Hamburg, December 22, 1891. She studied at the Bernuth Conservatory, Hamburg, where her teachers included James Kwast (piano), Max Loewengard and Richard Barth (composition), Walter Wilmar and Julius Spengel (singing) and Max Fiedler. After 1916 she toured in Germany and Belgium and formed a women's choir in Hamburg as well as the Hamburg Society of Women Composers of New Music.

Compositions

ORCHESTRA

Ungarische fantasie, op. 23 (vln and orch) (1913)
Elegie, op. 24, no. 1 (1913)
Rosenwalzer, op. 62 (1919)
Valse, op. 24, no. 2 (1913)
Walkueren, op. 36, poem (1915)

CHAMBER

Bardengesang, op. 13 (vln and hp) (1912)
Capriccio, op. 51, no. 3 (vln and pf) (1916)
Gondellied, op. 51, no. 2 (vln and pf) (1916)
Menuett, op. 51, no. 1 (vln and pf) (1916)
Pieces for harp

PIANO

Fruehlingsreigen, op. 11, no. 1 (1909)
Heideblumen, waltz, op. 4 (1907)
Kleiner Tanz, op. 11, no. 3 (1909)
Launen, waltz, op. 3 (1907)
Liebeswunsch, op. 53 (1916)
Two minuets, op. 11, no. 2 (1910)

VOCAL

Eilidt Seidenhaar, op. 66 (vocal qrt, m-ch and orch) (1917)
Am Wiesenbach, op. 46, no. 4 (Himmelbauer) (w-ch) (1916)
Die deutsche Flagge, op. 31 (Ompteda) (m-ch) (1914)
Fruehling, op. 46, no. 5 (Baehr) (w-ch) (1916)
Gartengespraech, op. 50, no. 1 (Wildenbruch) (duet) (1916)
Hollunderbaum, op. 25 (Roquette) (mix-ch) (1913)
Hunnenritt, op. 30 (after Krell) (m-ch) (1913)
Im Fruehling, op. 56, no. 1 (Knoop) (w-ch) (1917)
Im Walde, op. 46, no. 1 (Bauer) (w-ch) (1913)
Reiterlied, op. 45, no. 1 (Hyan) (m-ch) (1915)
Reiterlied, op. 42, no. 1 (Volker) (m-ch) (1915)
Rosenzeit, op. 46, no. 3 (Seiffert) (w-ch) (1916)
Schwalbenlied, op. 47 (Collani) (solos, w-ch and pf) (1916)
Schwert aus der Scheide, op. 35 (Goldfeld) (m-ch) (1915)
Soldatenlied, op. 42, no. 2 (Rommel) (w-ch) (1915)
Soldatenlieder, op. 44, folk songs (m-ch or w-ch) (1915)
Steht eine Maedel am Weg, op. 46, no. 2 (Stangen) (w-ch) (1916)
Um die 50 Gulden, op. 26, folk song (m-ch) (1913)
Wanderer, op. 46, no. 6 (Muller) (w-ch) (1917)
Ein Dialog, op. 50, no. 2 (Goldfeld) (duet) (1916)
Es ist nicht gut allein zu sein, op. 60, no. 2 (duet) (1918)
Das sind die schwuelen Sommernaechte, op. 34, no. 1 (Ritter) (vce and hp) (1913)
Numerous lieder for voice and piano incl.:
Abendlied
Aus deinem lieben Munde
Es schauen die Blumen alle
Im Felde
Jugend
Maedchengebet
Oft in der stillen Nacht

SACRED

Deutsche Christnachtlegende, op. 68 (Fliegel) (S, A, Bar, w-ch and orch) (1925)
Glaube, op. 49 (Lienhardt) (w-ch and org) (1916)
Psalm 53, op. 61 (Klopstock) (S, A, w-ch and org) (1918)
Jesus klagt, op. 40 (Morgenstern) (vce and org) (1915)
The Mother's hymn

BALLET

One ballet

Ref. 70, 111

FLAGG, Mary Houts

American singing teacher and composer. b. Texas, June 20, 1881. She studied at Hardin College, Mexico and the Warrensburg School of Music and privately in Kansas City and Chicago. She was the music supervisor at the Kansas City Public School for 18 years and taught at the Kansas City Conservatory for five years.

Compositions

ORCHESTRA

On a spring morning

VOCAL

Approx. 20 songs incl.:
Joy in spring

SACRED

The Child Jesus, children's cantata

OPERETTA

The Land of Manana

Publications

Wisht I was a Soldier and other Verses. Kansas City, 1918.

Ref. 460

FLASSAN, Flandrine de (alt. name Blanche-Fleur)

14th-century French poetess, troubadour and song composer.

Ref. 218

FLEISCHER-DOLGOPOLSKY, Tsipporah (Tsippi)

Israeli lecturer and composer. b. Haifa, May 20, 1946. She received a B.Mus. (theory of music) from the Rubin Academy of Music, Jerusalem in 1969 and an M.A. (music education) from New York University in 1975. From 1968, she lectured on the theory of music at the Tel Aviv College of Music Teachers, from 1979 at the department of musicology, Tel Aviv University and from 1984 at the department of musicology, Bar-Ilan University. Some of her compositions have been performed on Israeli radio and television. PHOTOGRAPH.

Compositions

ORCHESTRA

A girl named Limonad, symphonic poem (1983) (Tel Aviv: Israel Music Institute)
Fantasia concertante (cham orch) (1983-1984)

CHAMBER

Resuscitation, 5 miniatures (vlc) (Holot: Israel Brass Woodwind Publ.)
To the fruits of my land, suite (gtr) (Israel Music)

VOCAL

Ha-shaon rotse lishon (chil-ch) (1984) (Jerusalem: Israel Music Publ.)
Visions of Israel, 6 madrigals (mix-ch) (1981-1984)
Girl-butteı fly-girl, cycle of 4 songs (S or T and acc) (Israel Music)

Ref. composer

FLEITES, Virginia

Cuban lecturer and composer. b. Havana, July 10, 1916. At the Conservatory of Music she studied under F. Carnicer and A. Roldan (harmony) and later under Jose Ardevol (counterpoint, fugue, instrumentation, history and aesthetics of music). She taught privately and at the Municipal and National Conservatory and the Hubert de Blanck Conservatory. She was a founder member of the Grupo de Renovacion Musical and took part in numerous conferences.

Compositions

CHAMBER

Ricercar (qrt) (1943)
Invencion (fl, ob and bsn) (1943)
Sonata a tres (2 vln and vlc) (1942)
Suite (fl, ob and bsn) (1943)
Pastoral y allegro (fl and pf) (1945)
Sonata (vlc and pf) (1944)

PIANO

Pequena suite (1943)
Preludio y fuga (1942)
Sonata en un tempo (1942)
Sonata in D (1942)
Sonatina (1941)
Tres pequenas piezas (1942)
Variaciones, on a theme by Frescobaldi (1944)

VOCAL

Fugas (3-4 vces and pf) (1943)
Invenciones (2-4 vces and pf) (1941)
Soneto de Dante (2-3 vces and pf)
Soneto de Petrarca (4 mix-vces)
Songs (E. Ballagas) (2-3 vces) (1943)

Ref. 9, 12, 13, 54, 72, 94, 100, 189, 361

FLEMING, Lady

18th-century English composer.

Compositions

PIANO

Lady Fleming's Favourite Minuet (later arr J. Dietz as *Six Variations on Lady Fleming's Favourite Minuet*)

Ref. 65

FLEMING, Shari Beatrice

20th-century American lecturer and composer. b. St. Johnsbury, VT. She graduated from the Peabody Conservatory. She won the Gustav Klemm prize in 1957 and 1958 and joined the faculty of the University of Vermont in 1970.

Composition

SACRED

Break forth into joy (ch) (1963)

Ref. 142, 347

FLEMMING, Elsa
American composer. b. Brooklyn, 1880; d. 1906. She showed musical talent at an early age and learnt much from her father.
Compositions
CHAMBER
La fête des fleurs, waltz
La jeune débutante, waltz
Nocturnes (pf)
BALLETS
Several ballets
Bibliography
The World's Best Music. New York: University Society, 1909.
Ref. California State University

FLEMMING, Martha (nee Harnig)
German pianist and composer. b. Berlin, April 29, 1872. She was a pupil of Theodor and Franz Kullak. She played chamber music, mainly with the wind sextet of the Berlin State Opera Orchestra. She composed chamber compositions for wind instruments and piano pieces.
Ref. 70, 226

FLEUR, M. See FLOWER, Amelia Matilda

FLEURY, Helene
20th-century French pianist and composer. She studied the piano and composition at the Paris Conservatoire under Planchet, Dallier and Widor. She won the Prix de Rome in 1904. She was the first woman to be admitted as a candidate for one of the grand prizes for French artists, which was a three-year stay at the Villa Medici in Rome. She composed several works.
Ref. 105

FLICK-FLOOD, Dora
American pianist, authoress, teacher and composer. b. Cleveland, OH, August 3, ca. 1895. She studied at the Sanster Music School and the Baldwin-Wallace College under Carleton Bullis and James Rogers. She also studied under A. Gehring and Sigismund Stojowski and held five piano scholarships. She taught at the Tucker School and public schools in Cleveland. She toured the United States and Europe as a pianist. DISCOGRAPHY.
Compositions
BAND
Tango del Prado (Ludwig)
PIANO
Huajilla
Theme and variations
Waterfall
VOCAL
Choral works (Ricordi; Schroeder)
Bethlehem (mix-ch and keyboard) (Boston Music)
Songs
Publications
Cross-Country Silhouettes.
The Relative Tale of Triad and Scale.
Universal Flag.
Ref. 39, 40, 94, 142, 190, 563, 594

FLONDOR, Florica. See RACOVITZA-FLONDOR, Florica

FLORING, Grace Kenny
20th-century American pianist, teacher and composer. b. Tipton, IN. She composed chamber music, piano pieces and songs.
Ref. 347

FLOTOW, Marthe von
19th-century German composer. She was the daughter of the famous opera composer Fredrich von Flotow. Marthe composed numerous songs published in Berlin by Sulzbach.
Ref. 226, 276

FLOWER, Amelia Matilda (pseud. M. Fleur)
20th-century English pianist, teacher and composer. b. London. She was an L.R.A.M., Associate of the Guildhall School of Music and member of the Royal Society of Teachers. She studied at the Guildhall School of Music and taught the piano at King Edward's School, London.
Compositions
PIANO
By meadow and stream, album
By the still lagoon
In lakeland
Impromptu
In springtime
Song in the desert
Ref. 467

FLOWER, Eliza
English poetess, singer and composer. b. Harlow, Essex, April 19, 1803; d. London, December 12, 1846. She was the daughter of the political writer Benjamin Flower.
Compositions
VOCAL
Fourteen musical illustrations of the Waverley novels (Sir Walter Scott) (ch) (1831) (Novello)
Flower from Mother's grave (Hopwood)
The gathering of the unions (1832)
Songs of the seasons (1834)
Part songs
SACRED
Now pray we for our country (ch) (1842) (Curwen; Bayley; Novello; Church)
Nearer my God to thee, original music setting (Sarah Flower)
Sixty-two hymns in *Hymns and Anthems* (Fox, 1841)
Ref. 6, 8, 85, 105, 226, 276, 297, 347, 361, 645, 646

FODY, Ilona (pseud. Helen Jacob)
American pianist, poetess, teacher and composer. b. Elizabeth, NJ, July 13, 1920. She took a degree in the piano at St. Mary's Convent. She wrote poems for the *Passaic Citizen Weekly*.
Compositions
VOCAL
Songs incl.:
Angel face
Green is the colour
Till eternity
A woman
INCIDENTAL MUSIC
Ask for me
Legend of the cowboy saint
Ring of virgin gold
You are my Love
Music and songs for films, television and radio
Ref. 494

FOLKESTONE, Susan. See SPAIN-DUNK, Susan

FOLKESTONE, Viscountess. See RADNOR, Helen, Countess of

FOLVILLE, Eugenie-Emilie Juliette
Belgian pianist, violinist, conductor, professor and composer. b. Liège, January 5, 1870; d. Dourgne, France, October 28, 1946. She studied the piano under her father and the violin under Malherbes in Liège and later under O. Musin and Cesar Thomson. She studied composition under J.T. Radoux at the Liège Conservatory and soon distinguished herself as a composer and concert violinist. At the age of 17 her work *Chant de Noël* was performed at the Liège Cathedral. She made her debut as a concert violinist in 1879. She was professor of the piano at the Liège Conservatory from 1898 until the outbreak of the war, when she settled in Bournemouth, England and taught. She returned to the continent several years later.
Compositions
ORCHESTRA
Esquisse symphonique, concerto
Piano concerto (1924)
Triptyque (vlc and orch; also vln and pf)
Violin concerto
Oceano nox, symphonic poem

Scènes champêtres, suite (1885)
Scènes d'hiver, suite
Scènes de la mer, suite
CHAMBER
Piano quartet
Mazurka (vln and pf)
Poème (vlc and pf)
Suite poètique (vln and pf)
Berceuse (vln)
Morceau de concert (vlc)
ORGAN
Twenty-four organ works incl.:
Verset sur le thème du Tantum (Joubert)
PIANO
Esquisses
Sonata No. 1 (1881)
Sonata No. 2 (1882)
VOCAL
Eva, cantata (S, ch and pf)
Noce au village, cantata (soloists, ch and orch)
SACRED
Chant de Noël (ch and orch) (1887)
Offertoire sur le thème de Lauda Sion (Liège: Muraille)
Motets (ch a-cap)
OPERA
Atala (1892)
Publications
Les Maitres contemporains de l'orgue III. 1912.
Two books of songs: *Rappelle-toi* and *Berceuse*. Chants printaniers, 1883.
Bibliography
Gregoir, E. *Les artistes-musiciens belges au XVIIIe et au XIXe siècle*. Bruxelles, 1885-1887.
Ref. 7, 15, 17, 22, 23, 44, 83, 85, 100, 105, 107, 109, 225, 226, 307, 347, 361, 398

FONDER, Sister Mary Teresine

American organist, professor and composer. b. March 23, 1897. She obtained her B.M. from Marylhurst College, OR, in 1933 and her M.M. from the University of Seattle, WA, in 1935. She did postgraduate study at De Paul University, Chicago, The University of Southern California in 1947, the Juilliard School of Music in 1949 and St. Johns University, MN, 1957. At a summer workshop in Tacoma in 1953 she did concentrated study under Arthur Howes, Ernest White and Carl Weinreich. She taught music in Portland, Eugene and Seattle from 1917 to 1933 and became lecturer and then professor of the organ, harmony, counterpoint and composition at Marylhurst College, 1935 to 1971. In 1965 she gave a concert of her works for the Regional American Guild of Organists' Convention.
Compositions
SACRED
Mass in honor of St. Ann
Mass in honor of St. Edward (1965) (comm Oregon Liturgical Commission)
Gregorian masses
Magnificat (w-ch)
Cantemus Domino
Hymns and motets incl.:
A new song
Two hymns to St. Joseph
Twenty-six miniatures for organ suites
Four recessionals and processionals, based on Gregorian masses
It is a good thing (4-part ch)
Propers: Immaculate Conception, Holy Name of Jesus and others
Suite from proper of St. Joan of Arc (vce and org)
Publications
Liturgical Music in Contemporary Idiom. Master's thesis. University of Seattle. McLaughlin and Reilly, 1936.
Bibliography
Notable Americans of Bicentennial Era. Vol. 1. 1976.
Ref. composer, 84, 359

FONSECA, Ida Henriette da

Danish composer. b. Copenhagen, 1802; d. Copenhagen, 1858.
Compositions
VOCAL
Vokalnumre, Hefte 1 (vce and pf) (1848)
Vokalnumre, Hefte 2 (1853)
Ref. 413

FONTYN (Schmit-Fontyn), Jacqueline

Belgian pianist, professor and composer. b. Antwerp, December 27, 1930. She studied the piano under Ignace Bolotine and Marcel Maas and harmony, counterpoint, fugue, orchestration and composition under Marcel Quintet in Brussels. She attended Max Deutsch's composition classes in Paris and on a state scholarship studied at the Academy for Music and Arts in Vienna. She then worked for three years at the Chapelle Musicale Reine Elisabeth. From 1963 to 1970 she was a professor of counterpoint at the Antwerp Royal Conservatory and after 1971 was professor of composition at the Royal Brussels Conservatory. She married the composer Camille Schmit. Jacqueline won several composition prizes throughout Europe and the United States, including the silver medal at the International Composition Contest held in Moscow, 1957; the Grand Prix de Rome in 1959; the first prize for chamber music at the International Contest for Women Composers held in Mannheim, 1961; the Prix International de Composition Oscar Espla in Spain, 1962, for her work *Psalmus tertius* and first prize in the International Halifax competition, Canada, 1973. She was founder and director of a mixed choir 'Le Tympan' and was a member of the jury for the Concours de Composition. Her works have been performed on radio and in concert throughout the world. DISCOGRAPHY. PHOTOGRAPH.
Compositions
ORCHESTRA
Piano concerto (1967)
Violin concerto (1975)
Danceries (1956)
Deux estampies (1961)
Digressions (vlc and str orch) (Brussels: CeBeDeM, 1964)
Divertimento (str orch) (1953)
Creneaux (student orch)
Evoluon (1973) (London: Chappell)
Frises (1975)
Frises II (1976)
Petite suite (1951)
Per archi (large str orch) (1973) (Chappell)
Piedigrotta, ballet suite (also w-ch and orch) (1958)
Prèlude et rondo (1957)
Six èbauches (Jobert, 1964)
Variaties op een vlaams volkslied (1952)
CHAMBER
Galaxie (17 insts) (Jobert, 1965)
Halo (hp and cham ens) (1978)
Colloque (wind qnt and strs) (1969)
Mouvements concertants (2 pf and strs) (CeBeDeM, 1957)
Pour 11 archets (1971) (Chappell)
Nonetto (ww qnt, vln, vla, vlc and d-b) (1969)
Rhumba (2 trp, hn, trb and tba)
Wind quintet (1954)
Zones (fl, cl, vlc, perc and pf) (1979)
Horizons (str qrt) (1977)
Mosaiques (4 cl; also cl and pf) (1965)
Musica a quattro (vln, cl, vlc and pf) (Paris: Choudens, 1966)
String quartet (1958)
Piano trio (1956)
Sept petites pieces (ob, cl and bsn) (1956) (Schirmer)
Agami (trp and pf) (1974) (Choudens)
Anacleta (2 vln) (1982)
Controverse (b-fl or b-cl or t-sax and perc) (1983) (Berlin: Bote & Bock, 1984)
Danceries (vln and pf) (1953) (Schirmer)
Dialogues (sax and pf) (Choudens, 1969)
Digressions (vlc and pf) (1964) (New York: Seesaw)
Filigrane (fl and hp) (Jobert, 1969)
Fourgères (vla and hp; also sax and hp; also sax and pf)
Mime 1 (fl and hp) (Schirmer)
Mime 2 (cl and pf) (Schirmer)
Mime 3 (sax and pf) (Schirmer)
Six climats (vlc and pf) (1972) (Chappell; Schirmer)
Sonata (fl and pf) (CeBeDeM, 1952; Schirmer)
Strophes (vln and pf) (Choudens, 1972)
Digitale (hpcd) (1973) (Chappell)
Intermezzo (hp) (Chappell)
Shadows (hpcd)
Digressions (1964)
PIANO
Spirales (2 pf) (New York: Peer Southern Organization, 1971)
Aura
Ballade (CeBeDeM, 1964; Schirmer)
Bulles, 6 short pieces (1980)
Capriccio (1954) (Schirmer)
Flakes (1980)
Gong (1980)
Mosaici (Antwerp: Metropolis, 1964)
Rosée, 5 improvisations (1971)
Two impromptus (1980)
VOCAL
Ephemeres (m-S and orch) (1979)
La trapeziste qui a perdu son coeur (m-S and orch) (1955)
Madrigale e canzone (mix-ch a-cap) (1968)

Quatre rondeaux (mix-ch a-cap) (1958)
Alba (Vincenzo Cardarelli) (S, cl, vlc, perc or hp and pf)
Deux rondels de Charles d'Orleans (vce and pf) (CeBeDeM, 1956)
SACRED
Psalmus tertius (Bar, mix-ch and orch) (1959)
Het was een maghet uitvercoren (mix-ch a-cap) (1955)
Ref. composer, AMC, CeBeDeM, 1, 15, 17, 20, 26, 70, 77, 94, 185, 188, 457, 461, 477, 563

FOOT, Phyllis Margaret
Canadian pianist, teacher and composer. b. London, October 15, 1914. She studied at the Royal Academy of Music, London from 1931 to 1934 and taught music in schools, 1934 to 1937. She then moved to Canada, where she played her own works over station CKUA, Edmonton and taught at schools in St. Helen's, Quebec and Rupertsland, Winnipeg.
Compositions
PIANO
Birds in the cherry orchard (1950)
Book of ancient classical dances (1950)
Canadian cities, suite (1950)
Dover beach (1933)
Holiday suite (1949) (Western Music)
The little Dutch boy, dance for children (1950)
Moment musical (1950)
Our forest friends, for children
Tziganka, a Russian fantasy (1949)
Publications
Jolly Beginners' Book. Piano method. Waterloo Music, 1950.
Ref. 133

FORD, Mrs. Raymond C.
20th-century American composer of an opera and several songs.
Ref. 465

FORD, Nancy
20th-century American composer.
Compositions
OPERA
Shelter
FILM MUSIC
Last sweet days of Isaac
Ref. 295

FORD, Olive Elizabeth
American pianist, authoress, teacher and composer. b. Big Spring, TX, September 2, 1918. She studied at the Life Bible College in Los Angeles till 1949 and then studied the piano under Stella Champagne and Kathleen Blair Foster. She continued her piano studies on the West Coast. She taught the piano and singing.
Compositions
VOCAL
Blow gentle breeze
I didn't know
In the meantime
More than a bridge
One look that day
Through the heat of summer
SACRED
Thanks be to God, cantata
The theme of my song, cantata
Because of Calvary
For God and country
The Gospel according to Mother Goose
He silently plans for me
His Majesty, Jesus
My yesteryears
Oh, praise the Lord
Waters are flowing from Shiloh
ARRANGEMENTS
Works (ch)
Ref. 494

FORMAN, Addie Walling (Mrs. R.R.)
American organist, pianist and composer. b. Brooklyn, NY, August 1, 1855; d. Hightstown, NJ, December 10, 1947.
Compositions
VOCAL
Rose streams, cantata
Songs
OPERETTA
The pirate's umbrella
Ref. 226, 347, 465

FORMAN, Ellen
American choreographer, dancer and composer. b. New York, September 21, 1945. She gained her B.A. from Brooklyn College, City University of New York and M.A. from University of Wisconsin. Since 1974 she has been director and resident choreographer of South Street Company, Philadelphia. She received grants from the Pennsylvania Council for the Arts and the National Endowment for the Arts.
Compositions
BALLET
Close quarters (1983)
Concord cafeteria (1976)
Correspondences (1979)
Dream of Genesis (1975)
Pageant (1982)
Ref. 643

FORMAN, Jeanne
American teacher and composer. b. Los Angeles, March, 3, 1916. She studied at the Bush Conservatory, De Paul University, Redlands University and the U.C.L.A. where her compositions were later performed.
Ref. 467

FORMAN, Joanne
American playwright, writer and composer. b. Chicago, June 26, 1934. She studied at Los Angeles City College, Los Angeles State College, the University of California, Merritt College and the University of New Mexico. She studied composition under Carolyn Trojanowski Chean, 1953 to 1957. She was director of The Migrant Theatre from 1966 and vice-president of El Centro Cultural y Museo del Barrio from 1973. She was co-director of Apple House Gallery from 1961 to 1965 and an assistant for the New Mexico Composers' Guild. She worked as an arts editor, playwright, journalist and puppeteer. DISCOGRAPHY.
Compositions
ORCHESTRA
Goya
The last beautiful days of autumn
Overture for a modern novel
Winter songs
CHAMBER
Satie's shoes (fl, ob and vlc) (1983)
Sonatina for viola and piano (1982)
VOCAL
Blessed is the match
Dragonsongs, song cycle (1983)
Haiku (S and ww qnt) (1975)
In time of daffodils/Who know (e.e. cummings) (S, hp and org)
Maggie and Milly and Molly and May (e.e. cummings) (S, hp and org)
Noche (Lorca)
Punch and Judy
Rilkelieder, song cycle (1978)
Three songs (e.e. cummings) (1973)
Three songs for Rachel (Lorca) (1973)
Walden songs
Weather report
SACRED
Ave beata dea (ch a-cap) (1976)
I thank you God for most this amazing (e.e. cummings)
Kaddish
O come thou child of David
Psalm 137, by the waters of Babylon
BALLET
La brava
The little match girl, for children (H.C. Andersen) (1975)
OPERA
The Blind Men (1978)
Ikarus
The Little Tin Soldier (H.C. Andersen)
Polly Baker (1977)
THEATRE
My Heart Lies South, musical (1963)
North Star, music drama (composer and Avis Worthington)

INCIDENTAL MUSIC
Beauty and the Beast, mime for children (1974)
The Dancing Princess, mime for children
The Innocents (1960)
The Scarecrow (1960)
Three Sisters (1963)
Skipper and the Witch (narr, mix-ch and pf) (1975)
Twelfth Night (Shakespeare) (1964)
The Ugly Duckling (H.C. Andersen) (narr, 2 ob, 2 bsn and 2 elec hp) (1983)
Ref. composer, 142, 185, 347, 563, 624, 625, 643

FORMAN, Mrs R.R. See FORMAN, Addie Walling

FORREST, Margret
English composer. ca. 1800.
Compositions
CHAMBER
Six Sonatas for the Harpsichord or Pianoforte with Accompaniments for a Violin and Bass, op. 1 (London: William Napier)
Ref. 125

FORREST, Sidney. See STAIRS, Louise E.

FORSTER, Charlotte
20th-century composer. Her operetta was performed in London.
Composition
OPERETTA
Queen Nada and the Wood Nymphs (1912)
Ref. 431

FORSTER, Dorothy
English pianist and composer. b. Carshalton, February 20, 1884; d. December 25, 1950. She studied at the Royal Academy of Music under W. Macfarren, F. Corder and F. Arnold. She toured Great Britain as a concert pianist.
Compositions
CHAMBER
Rose in the bud (vln and pf)
VOCAL
Dearest, I bring you daffodils
I wonder if love is a dream
In fair arcadia
Myfanwy
Perhaps
A psalm of love
Some day soon
When I think on happy days
Ref. 39, 63, 297, 347, 353

FORSYTH, Josephine (Mrs. P.A. Meyers)
American poetess, singer and composer. b. Cleveland, OH, July 5, 1889; d. Cleveland, May 24, 1940. She studied under Elandi and Sembrich and made her debut in musical comedy in New York in 1919. From 1924 to 1927 she gave concerts of original songs and poetry. Her best known composition, a setting of *The Lord's Prayer* was written as a wedding gift for her husband.
Compositions
VOCAL
Coming home to you
SACRED
Joy cometh in the morning
The Lord's Prayer (hp obb)
New Year carol
Precious Wee One
Ref. 40, 85, 292, 347

FORTENBERRY, Myrtis
20th-century American composer. In 1958 she won the competition contest of the Louisiana Federation of Music Clubs.
Ref. 448

FORTEY, Mary Comber
English pianist and composer. b. ca. 1860. She studied at the Royal Academy of Music, London.
Compositions
VOCAL
Songs incl.:
Castles in Spain
Going to sleep
Love, the truant
Other songs
Publications
How to Teach the Pianoforte to Young Beginners. London: Hughes, 1883.
Ref. 6, 85, 226, 276, 347

FORTI, Elsa
Late 19th-century Italian composer.
Composition
CHAMBER
Capriccio (Ricordi, 1904)
Ref. Ricordi (Milan)

FORTMAGNE (Fortmague), Baroness de (alt. name Baroness Durand de Fortmagne)
19th-century French composer.
Compositions
ORCHESTRA
Barcarolle (vln and str orch) (New York: Manus Music, ca. 1926)
OPERA
Bianca Torella (1897)
Folies d'amour (1894)
Idylle
Le Sergent Larosse (1903)
Ref. 226, 276, 307, 322, 347

FORTMAGUE, Baroness de. See FORTMAGNE, Baroness de

FOSIC, Tarzicija
Yugoslav organist, singer, teacher and composer. b. Molve, October 7, 1895; d. Osijek, November 11, 1958. She studied composition and the organ under Franjo Dugan and solo singing under N. Eder-Bertic. She graduated from the Music Academy of Zagreb in 1924 and taught music in high schools.
Compositions
ORGAN
Prelude
SACRED
Latin, Old Slavonic and Croatian masses
Motets
Ref. 109

FOSTER, Cecily
20th-century English pianist, teacher and composer. b. Florence, Italy. She studied the piano and harmony in Rome under Alfredo Casella, harmony under Paul Gilson in Brussels, counterpoint under Nadia Boulanger (q.v.) in Paris and Charles Kitson in London and the piano under Tobias Matthay. She was a teacher of counterpoint in several London institutions including the Matthay School. She lived in Mallorca for many years and was a close friend of Manuel de Falla and pianists Nin-Culmell and George Copeland. A large number of her compositions were produced during this period.
Compositions
ORCHESTRA
Concertino (pf and orch)
Orchestral works
CHAMBER
Piano pieces
VIOLA
Sonata
Toccata de Buxtehude, transcription (London: OUP)
VOCAL
Variaciones on Cant des ocells (ch and orch)
La fontaine, poem (mix-ch and pf)
Choral works
Lieder

SACRED
Psalms (mix-ch)
BALLET
Fiesta, on popular themes
Jack in the Green
The Trees
Ref. 107

FOSTER, Dorothy Godwin
20th-century American conductor, teacher and composer. She studied at the London Academy of Music and she is an A.T.C.L.
Compositions
VOCAL
Songs incl.:
The weaver of dreams
Within your hands
SACRED
Moses, oratorio
Mass in honour of Our Lady of Buckfast
Emmanuel, a nativity play
INCIDENTAL MUSIC
The Blessed Thomas More, play
Philip of Arundel, play
The Three Kings, play
Ref. 94, 292, 467

FOSTER, Fay
American organist, pianist, teacher and composer. b. Leavenworth, KS, November 8, 1886; d. Bayport, NY, April 17, 1960. She studied at the Chicago Conservatory under W.H. Sherwood, Gleason and Mme. Boitte; at the Munich Conservatory under H. Schwartz and at the Leipzig Conservatory under A. Reisenauer and S. Jadassohn. Other teachers were Moritz Rosenthal, Carl Preyer and Sophie Menter. She taught at the Ogontz School, Rydall and in New York, San Francisco and Berlin. She is a member of various societies, including the Society of American Women Composers. She was the recipient of many awards and prizes.
Compositions
CHAMBER
Violin pieces
PIANO
Etude de concert
Prairie flowers, waltz (prize, International Waltz Competition, 1910)
Three other pieces
VOCAL
Women's choruses
More than 100 published songs incl.:
The Americans come
Are you for me or against me
Dusk in June
In the carpenter shop
The King: Call of the trail
My journey's end
My menagerie
One golden day
The place where I worship
Russian doll
Spinning wheel
Your kiss
OPERA
The Moon Lady, Chinese theme
The Honorable Mme. Yen, Chinese theme
OPERETTA
Blue Beard
The Castaways
The Land of Chance
Ref. 39, 40, 44, 70, 85, 142, 226, 228, 260, 292, 347, 353

FOURNIER, Alice
19th-century French composer.
Composition
OPERA
Stratonice (1892)
Ref. 225

FOWLER, Eliza
English composer. b. Harlow, East Anglia, April 19, 1803; d. London, December 12, 1846. She was the elder sister of Sarah Adams (q.v.) and an early love of the poet Browning and said to be the inspiration for his *Pauline*.
Ref. 572

FOWLER, Jennifer Joan
Australian teacher and composer. b. Bunbury, Western Australia, April 14, 1939. She graduated from the University of Perth in 1960 with a B.A. hons in music, and received her Dip. Ed. from the University of Perth in 1962. Whilst teaching in schools in Western Australia, she continued studying composition under Dr. John Exton and in 1967 completed a B.M. In 1968 she went to study in Holland on a Dutch Government scholarship. At the University of Utrecht she completed a course at the Studio for Electronic Music under G.M. Koenig. In 1969 she moved to London and divided her time between composing and teaching. She is a member of the Fellowship of Australian Composers. Some of her compositions have been awarded prizes in international competitions, including first prize for chamber music in the International Contest for Women Composers, GEDOK, Mannheim in 1975. DISCOGRAPHY. PHOTOGRAPH.
Compositions
ORCHESTRA
Chant with garlands (Universal Edition, 1974)
Fanfare (brass and str orch) (1968)
Look on this Oedipus (Universal, 1973)
Ring out the changes (bells and str orch) (1978)
Sculpture in four dimensions (1969)
CHAMBER
Chimes, fractured (2 fl, 2 cl, 2 bsn, org, bagpipes and perc)
Ravelation (str qnt) (2nd prize, Radcliffe Trust Award, 1971) (Universal, 1971)
String quartet (1967)
PIANO
Piece for an opera house (1 or 2 pf; also pf and tape) (Universal, 1973)
Ascending and descending (1980)
Piece for E.L. (1981)
VOCAL
Hours of the day (4 m-S, w-ch, 2 cl and 2 ob) (prize, International Composers' Competition, Berlin, 1970)
Letter from Howarth (m-S, cl, vlc and pf) (1984)
Voice of the shades (S, ob, cl and vln) (1977)
SACRED
Veni Sancte Spiritus, Veni Creator (cham ch) (Universal Edition, 1971)
Tell out, my soul: Magnificat (S, vlc and pf) (1980)
ELECTRONIC
The arrows of St. Sebastian II (B, cl, vlc and tape) (1981)
MISCELLANEOUS
By a pool reflected
Bibliography
Composer, No. 58, 1976
Composer, No. 83, 1984,
Ref. composer, 1984, 77, 206, 412, 457, 563, 622

FOWLER, Marje
American violinist, choir conductor, teacher and composer. b. New Haven, CT, January 8, 1917. She studied under Morris Ruger and David Ward-Steinman. She studied the violin under Hugo Kortschak at Yale University and Vera Barstow in Los Angeles. She obtained her B.A. and M.A. at California State University and was violinist with the Stockton Symphony Orchestra, 1951 to 1960.
Compositions
ORCHESTRA
Introduction and fantasia (also org)
ORGAN
Elegie
VOCAL
Cante jondo, setting of Romance de la luna (Lorca) (m-S, perc and hpcd) (1973)
Deux ballades sombres (Villon) (T, vla and pf) (1967)
SACRED
All praise to Thee (ch a-cap)
Service (liturgist, 3 part ch and org)
Ref. 94, 142, 347

FOWLES, Margaret F.
19th-century English organist, pianist, choral conductor and composer. b. Ryde, Isle of Wight. She studied harmony, the piano and counterpoint under Chalmers Masters, the organ under Dr. Hopkins and singing under Emil Behnke, Alberto Randegger and W. Shakespeare. She was appointed organist of St. James' Church, Ryde, at the age of 15. She founded the Ryde Choral Union and conducted it for 20 years, retiring in 1894. She composed sacred oratorios, anthems, hymns and songs.
Ref. 6, 85, 226, 276, 347

FOX, Erika
20th-century English composer. She won the 1983 Gerald Finzi Composition Award for her work, *Kaleidoscope*.

Compositions
VOCAL
Jeder Engel ist schrecklich (1979)
Voices (1979)
MISCELLANEOUS
Kaleidoscope
Duo
Epitaph for Cathy
Paths where the mourners tread (1980)
Spirals
Ref. BMIC, Tempo No. 148

FOX, Gyul Reginald. See LVOVA, Julia Fedorovna

FOX, Kalitha Dorothy
English composer. b. 1894; d. Windsor, August 11, 1934. She composed a viola sonata.
Ref. 41, 105, 226

FRACKER, Cora Robins
American guitarist, teacher and composer. b. Iowa City, August 11, 1849. She composed piano and guitar pieces.
Ref. 347

FRAJT, Ludmila
Yugoslav composer. b. Belgrade, December 31, 1919. In 1946 she completed studies in composition at the Music Academy of Belgrade, where her teachers were Miloje Milojevic and Josip Slavenski. From 1946 to 1952 she was head of the music section of Avala Film and from 1952 to 1958 was deputy editor-in-chief of the music program of Radio Belgrade. From 1958 to 1972 she was secretary of the music commission of Yugoslav Radio-Television. She attended a course in modern music in Darmstadt in 1961 and since 1972 has devoted herself to composition. She is a member of the Association of Composers of Yugoslavia. Several of her works have been awarded prizes in Yugoslavia. DISCOGRAPHY. PHOTOGRAPH.
Compositions
ORCHESTRA
Symphony in C (1946)
Svirač i ptice, rhapsody (cl and orch) (1966)
CHAMBER
Srebrni zvuci (str qrt) (prize, Assoc. of Serbian Composers) (1972)
Preludes I and II (hp) (1953)
Preludes III and IV (hp) (1965)
VOCAL
Kres, cantata (mix-ch and perc) (1st prize, Belgrade Radio-Television Competition) (1973)
Pesme noci, cantata (w-ch, pf, hp and str orch) (2nd prize, Yugoslav Radio-Television) (1970)
Neobični svirač (Desanka Maksimovic) (vce and sym orch) (1965)
Pesme rastanka, cycle (mix-ch a-cap) (1969) (prize, Assoc. of Serbian Composers; 2nd prize of Stevan Mokranjac; 1st prize, Yugoslav Radio-Television for choral music) (1969)
Tuzbalica (w-ch a-cap) (1973) (prize, Assoc. of Serbian Composers, 2nd prize of Stevan Mokranjac)
Uspavanka (w-vce and toy insts) (1971)
Songs incl.:
Baloni (1961) (prize, Yugoslav Radio-Television)
Hajd na more (1960) (prize, Yugoslav Radio-Television)
Mali rak (1960)
Mladi narastaj (1961) (prize, Yugoslav Radio-Television)
Moj narod 91961)
Pesma suncu u maju (1965)
Prica o zimi (1961)
Prvi maj (1962)
INCIDENTAL MUSIC
Music for documentary films and radio plays incl.:
Bata laza (1964)
Deca naroda (1948)
Gilda, zove me Vest (1965)
Konavoka (1961)
Majstor Hanus (1965)
Muve (1963)
Opstinsko dete (1952)
Ponesi me masto (1962)
Prica o razmazenoj carici (1969)
Te nemoguce zimske veceri (1961)
Ugalj i ljudi (1949)
Umetnicke skole (1951)
Il kongres KPS (1950)
ELECTRONIC
Asteroidi (tape) (1967)
Ref. Union of Yugoslav Composers, 94, 145, 206, 457, 563

FRANCE, Jeanne Lelen
French composer. b. 1898. She won several prizes as a student at the Paris Conservatoire and the Prix de Rome in 1933. She composed a piano concerto, three symphonic suites and two ballets.
Ref. 72

FRANCESCHINI, Petronia
Italian composer. d. Bologna, 1683. She was much celebrated as a composer of operas.
Ref. 400

FRANCHERE-DESROSIERS, Rose de Lima
Canadian pianist, teacher and composer. b. Montreal, January 6, 1863. She studied under Paul Letondal and R.O. Pelletier (piano), Alcibiade Beique and M. Dussault (harmony). In addition to teaching the piano and singing in schools, she was a church organist in Montreal.
Compositions
ORGAN
Piece (1940, 1945)
PIANO
Bric-a-brac (1941)
La brise, fantasy (1939)
Chorale (1941)
Le dodo du rossignol (1897)
Petite pastorale (1940)
Promenade (1940)
VOCAL
Etudiants et copains (ch) (1940)
Cantique de mariage (1898)
Les oiseaux ont des coeurs d'enfants (1897)
SACRED
Ave Maria (1898)
Ref. 133, 347

FRANCHI, Dorothea
20th-century New Zealand composer.
Compositions
ORCHESTRA
Concertina (har, hp and small orch)
Rhapsody (vln and small orch)
Ref. 280

FRANCHINO, Raffaela
20th-century composer. Her operas were performed in Limoges and Chateaudun.
Compositions
OPERA
Babet et Colin (1905)
Le mariage par ruses (1899)
Ref. 431

FRANCIS, Mrs. See RALPH, Kate

FRANCISCO DI NOGERO. See BAUER, Emilie Frances

FRANCK, Elsbeth
German composer. ca. 1599. She composed Latin lieder.
Ref. 465

FRANCK, Philippine
Belgian professor and composer. b. November 14, 1885. She was professor of harmony at Liege Conservatory.

Compositions
CHAMBER
Berceuse (pf trio)
Pastorale (fl and pf)
Remembrance (fl and pf)
VOCAL
Pieces (vce and org)
Ref. Belgian Music Info. Center

FRANCO, Clare
20th-century American pianist and composer. From 1962 to 1964 she studied at Bennington College, VT, where she was a pupil of Louis Calabro (composition), Lionel Nowak (piano), Orrea Pernel (chamber music) and Paul Boepple (music history). At the Aspen Music Festival (1963) she studied composition under Darius Milhaud, winning a grant to enable her to continue her studies with him in 1964, when she also studied counterpoint and orchestration under Charles Jones. For the next four years she attended the Juilliard School of Music, majoring in composition and also studying privately under Vincent Persichetti, Luciano Berio, Leonard Stein and Stefan Wolpe. She received her B.M. in 1967 and her M.S. (composition) in 1968. She also won the Elizabeth Sprague Coolidge (q.v.) Chamber Music Prize. She spent the summers of 1967 and 1968 at the Internationales Musikinstitut and the Composition Studio of Karlheinz Stockhausen in Darmstadt.
Compositions
ORCHESTRA
Double concerto (2 vlc and str orch) (1968) (Joseph H. Bearns Prize in Music, Columbia University)
Variations for orchestra (1967)
CHAMBER
Within (10 insts) (1975)
Nonet (1964) (Fromm prize, 1964)
Fantasie (pf)
VOCAL
Inscriptions at the City of Brass (5 part antiphonal mix-ch a-cap) (1956) (BMI student composers' award, 1967)
Light breaks (T, fl, vla, hp and perc) (1964, rev 1965)
Three songs (Robert Frost) (S) (1964-1966) (M. Freschl Prize, 1967)
The wind sprang up at four o'clock (T.S. Eliot) (m-S) (M. Freschl prize) (1967)
ELECTRONIC
Voices (m-ch and tape) (1969)
Bibliography
Internationales Musikinstitut. Darmstadt, July, 1979.
Ref. composer, 40, 94, 142, 189, 347, 594

FRANÇOIS, Emmy von
19th-century German composer. She composed marches for military bands and piano pieces.
Ref. 276, 347

FRANÇOIS, M. See BAWR, Alexandrine Sophie

FRANGS, Irene
20th-century South African pianist, ethnomusicologist, music producer, teacher and composer. b. Bethlehem, Orange Free State. She graduated from the University of Cape Town in the piano and singing. Her teachers there included Professors Gregorio Fiasconaro, Robert Mohr and Bill Smuts. She studied ethnomusicology in London, Rome, Paris and Athens. She teaches singing and is particularly involved in promoting and aiding black artists.
Compositions
VOCAL
Song cycle (comm Yannis Negroponti)
INCIDENTAL MUSIC
Some sequences of King Solomon's Mines, film
Music for art exhibitions and happenings in Athens and other European cities
Ref. composer

FRANK, Jean Forward
American composer. b. Pittsburgh, PA, August 13, 1927. She studied at Chatman College with Louis P. Coyner, Russell Wichmann, Roland Leich and Joseph Wilcox Jenkins.
Compositions
ORCHESTRA
Scatterpunctus (str orch)
PIANO
Pieces incl.:
Afternoon street noise
Chimera
Contemplation
Melodic mood
Sonata
Thoughts before dawn
VOCAL
Into the woods my master went (ch)
SACRED
The Christmas story (ch)
If God be for us
So answereth my soul
OPERETTA
Princess of a Thousand Moons
Time of our Lives
Ref. 142, 347, 625

FRANK, Mrs. Theodore. See FINLEY, Lorraine Noel

FRANKEL (Frankl), Gisela
19th-century German composer.
Compositions
PIANO
Auf Fluegeln des Tanzes, polka, op. 28 (Cranz)
Gavotte
Herzensfrage, Lied ohne Worte (Rose)
Mazurka de salon, op. 39
Meeres-Sagen, Tonstueck
Mes adieux, melodie (Bosworth)
Nocturne
Romanze
Sommernacht-Staendchen
VOCAL
Hochzeitshymne (mix-ch)
Other choral compositions
Ref. 226, 276, 297

FRANKL, Gisela. See FRANKEL, Gisela

FRASER, Shena Eleanor
Scottish pianist, violinist, lecturer and composer. b. Stirling, May 26, 1910. She studied at the Royal College of Music, London, under Henry Wilson (piano), Maurice Sons (violin) and Herbert Howells (composition). She obtained A.R.C.M.s for piano performance and violin teaching. She worked as a freelance adjudicator, lecturer and accompanist. In 1982 she formed a music publishing partnership with Yvonne Enoch known as Fraser-Enoch Publications specializing in piano and choral music.
Compositions
CHAMBER
Prelude and scherzino (ob and pf) (1954) (Boosey & Hawkes)
PIANO
Hornpipe and jig for two pianos (1948) (United Music Publ.)
The drunken sailor (duet) (Fraser-Enoch Publ.)
Strathspey and reel (duet) (Fraser-Enoch)
Three maritime folk songs (duet) (Fraser-Enoch)
VOCAL
Full fathom, cantata (1972) (comm Talbot Lampson School for Conductors)
A ring of jewels, cantata (1974) (Fraser-Enoch)
The valleys of delight (ch) (1973)
Boating (vces and pf)
Grannies to sell (vces and pf)
A highland lad (S and A) (Banks)
Part songs
SACRED
Carillon, Christmas cantata (1957) (Curwen)
To Him give praise, choral suite (w-ch) (1959-1960)
Carols for the accompanist (1965)
Child of bliss, carol cycle (1966) (Curwen)
Three psalms (1967) (comm Westminister Choral Society)
MISCELLANEOUS
Five pairs (1963) (Chappell)
Hebridean lullaby (1963) (Associated Board)
Minuet for a modern grandmother (1960) (Assoc. Bd.)

Bibliography
Composer, spring 1975, no. 54.
Publications
Sing at Sight. Patersons Publ.
Ref. composer, 77, 84, 230

FRASER-MILLER, Gloria Jill

American electronic instrumentalist, teacher and composer. b. Cincinnati, OH, October 11, 1952. She received her B.M. (1974) from the East Carolina University, having studied composition under Dr. Otto Henry and Dr. Gregory Kosteck. At the California Institute of the Arts she obtained an M.A. in 1977. Her teachers of composition included Morton Subotnik and Earle Brown and her subjects included computer-assisted electronic music, electronic circuit design and video synthesis. At the University of North Carolina, she studied composition under Dr. Roger Hannay. She has worked and taught in various electronic music studios in California and North Carolina. She is a member of the 'Electronic Synthesizer Ensemble', a live electronic performance group devoted to performing music by contemporary composers and developing electronic music performance techniques.

Compositions
ORCHESTRA
Park parallel (1977)
CHAMBER
Walking music (3 vln) (1974)
Woodwind trio (1971)
Fanfare for two trumpets (1970)
Sweet firebird (2 pf) (1974)
ELECTRONIC
Diamonds (B, cl and tape) (1974)
EBB tide (audience and tape) (1975)
Four Tese (1977)
Goldminds part 1 (tape) (1977)
Nightlights (tape) (1975)
Pie a la Moog (tape) (1972)
Study for live Moog synthesizer (1972)
Surfaces (perc and elecs) (1974)
Tape piece 1 (1972)
Tape piece 2 (1972)
INCIDENTAL MUSIC
The Empire of Ants, film (1977)
Holiday, children's television (1975)
Twilight's Last Gleaming, film (1976)
Windows, experimental film (1976)
Zardoz, film
Bibliography
AMC Newsletter, vol. 20, no. 3.
Ref. composer

FRASIER, Jane

American clarinetist, conductor, library assistant, teacher and composer. b. Loveland, CO, September 24, 1951. She graduated from the University of Northern Colorado in Greeley in 1972 with a B.A. in music education. Until 1977 she was band and choir leader and music teacher in Lyman, WY, and then returned to the University of Northern Colorado to study theory and composition. She received her M.M. in 1977. She continued her teaching career at public schools in Ovid, CO, and taught woodwind instruments privately. She is a library assistant at the University of Northern Colorado in Greeley and plays the clarinet in the Loveland Municipal Band and the Northern Colorado Concert Band. PHOTOGRAPH.

Compositions
ORCHESTRA
Connection (1983)
BAND
Chorale/canon (1978)
Introduction and fantasy (1978)
Minor moods (1978)
Resolution (1979)
Trumpet march/Woodwind tune (1978)
CHAMBER
Woodwind quintet II (1975)
Flute quartet I (1979)
Trio (fl, vibes and vlc) (1973)
Woodwind trio I (ob, cl and bsn) (1972)
Woodwind trio II (ob, fl and bsn) (1975)
Sixty-second trio (ob, cl and bsn) (1976)
Recital collection (cl and pf) (1981)
Three short sketches (cl) (1973)
PIANO
Festivous sonata (Arsis Press, 1976)
Sonata (1980)
VOCAL
Your eyes (mix-ch and pf) (1977)
Pacific fantasy (S and wind ens) (1984)
SACRED
An American requiem (mix-ch and orch) (1976)
Christmas story (narr, ch and pf) (1976)
God is love (w-ch, cl and pf) (1977)
Joy, peace and singing (w-ch and fl) (Studio PR, 1979)
Publications
Women Composers - A Discography. 1984.
Ref. composer, 474, 475, 622

FRAZER, Mrs. Allan H.

19th-century songwriter.

Compositions
VOCAL
Cupid in the garden
Hush thee
Ref. 276

FREED, Dorothy Whitson (nee Doorly)

New Zealand librarian and composer. b. Dunedin, February 10, 1919. She graduated from the Victoria University, Wellington with a B.M. in 1959 and in the same year received a diploma from the New Zealand Library School. She studied composition under David Farquhar from 1953 to 1958 and Peter Racine Fricker, 1964 to 1965. She published a number of articles, mainly on music in New Zealand libraries and contributed to Grove's Dictionary of Music and Musicians. From 1970 she was vice-president of the Australia-New Zealand branch of the International Association of Music Libraries. She won three major local composition prizes. DISCOGRAPHY. PHOTOGRAPH.

Compositions
ORCHESTRA
Suite for string orchestra (1961)
Variations on a fanfare (1962)
BRASS BAND
Aquarius march (1971)
CHAMBER
Diversion for 10 brass instruments (1967)
Woodwind quintet (fl, ob, cl, bsn and hn in F) (1959)
Barrel organ piece (4 rec) (1963)
String quartet No. 1 (1968)
String quartet No. 2 (1970)
Woodwind quartet (ob, 2 B-flat cl and bsn) (1971)
Variations (4 B-flat cl) (1958)
Woodwind trio (ob, B-flat cl and bsn) (1957)
Siciliana (B-flat cl and vlc)
Theme and variations (B-flat cl and vla) (1966)
Rondo (pf) (1973)
VOCAL
A penny for a song (vce and pf) (1969)
SACRED
Whence comes this rush of wings (w-ch a-cap)
Songs and carols (mix-ch or w-ch a-cap)
THEATRE
Suicide deferred, farce (composer) (S, 2 pf, perc and mime) (1965)
INCIDENTAL MUSIC
Faust (Goethe) (1967)
The Good Woman of Szechuan (vce, pf, fl and perc) (1958)
ARRANGEMENTS
Four Jewish songs (vln and pf) (1962)
Let all that are to mirth inclined, carol (mix-ch and org) (1963)
Old Hungarian song (1958)
Ref. composer, 206, 563

FREEHOFF, Ruth Williams

American pianist, singer, teacher and composer. b. Waukesha County, WI, April 9, 1893. She studied voice under Mrs. Beth Williams of Wales, WI, and Kathryn Clark and Verna Lean at the Wisconsin Conservatory, Milwaukee and Alexius Baas at Carroll College. At the same college she studied harmony under Mary Gamble and composition under Reuel Lahmer. At the University of Wisconsin she studied composition under Cecil Burleigh. She also studied the piano under Frances Harland at the Wisconsin School of Music in Milwaukee. She sang contralto in the Presbyterian Church of Waukesha after 1937. Her hymn *Take me, O my Father* was chosen as the Wisconsin state hymn for the centennial year.

Compositions
VOCAL
Order of the Eastern Star Book of Songs; songs, marches and other compositions (1941, rev 1945)
Song of our democracy (1941)
Choral works
Songs
SACRED
By the waters of Babylon, psalm 137 (1st prize, Wisconsin Federation of Music Clubs, 1949)
The Lord's prayer (1947)
Praise the Lord (1958)
Press ye, ever forward (1946)
Take me, O my Father (1948)
Anthems
Ref. 496

FREER, Eleanor Warner Everest

American lecturer, singer and composer. b. Philadelphia, May 14, 1864; d. Chicago, December 13, 1942. She was the daughter of the singer Cornelius Everest. She showed musical promise at the age of four and at seven received regular musical instruction from her father. At 14 she sang the part of Josephine in a semi-professional performance of *HMS Pinafore*. At 18 she went to Paris and studied voice under Mathilda Marchesi, composition under Benjamin Godard and the teaching of voice under Massenet, Widor and Remberg. On her return to Philadelphia she became the first certified American teacher of the Marchesi Method and was teacher of voice at the National Conservatory of Music, New York, 1889 to 1891. She studied in Leipzig for seven years, where she sang for Verdi, Gerster and Liszt; the last named accompanying her in two of his own songs at a soirée in the studio of Count Munkacsy. She returned to Chicago in 1902 and commenced five years of study under Bernhard Ziehn. She founded the American Opera Society of Chicago and was awarded a D.Mus. in 1934 by the Boguslawski College of Music. She was decorated for her war work between 1914 and 1919 by the French and Belgian governments and the French Red Cross.

Compositions
CHAMBER
Numerous pieces
PIANO
Pieces incl.:
Andante
Four modern dances
Lyric intermezzo
Lyric studies for the pianoforte, op. 3, Nos. 1-8 (Milwaukee: W.A. Kaun Music, 1904)
Rhythmic harmonic etude
Rondo
Souvenir
VOCAL
Part songs incl.:
Be true, op. 4, no. 5 (H. Bonas)
Trios and quartets (m-ch or w-ch)
Approx. 150 songs incl.:
Five songs to spring, op. 6, nos. 1-5, incl. An April pastoral (A. Dobson, W. Watson) (mix-ch and pf)
Six songs to nature, op. 10, nos. 1-6, incl. My garden (T.E. Brown) (mix-ch and pf) (Kaun, 1907)
Apparitions, op. 9, no. 2 (R. Browning) (Kaun, 1906)
A book of songs, op. 4 nos. 1-9 incl. When is life's youth, no. 3 (A. Freer) (Kaun, 1905)
The dancers, op. 12, no. 2 (M. Field) (Kaun, 1907)
Galloping song, op. 12, no. 3 (S.H. Birchel) (Kaun, 1907)
Golden eyes, op. 15, no. 2
I have done, put by the lute, op. 14, no. 2 (D. C. Scott) (Kaun, 1907)
The nights of spring, op. 29, no. 1 (B. Ochsner) (Kaun, 1923)
The old boatman, op. 23, no. 1 (H. Weedon) (Cincinnati: W. Willis, 1910)
She is not fair to outward view, op. 14, no. 1 (Coleridge)
The shepherdess, op. 5, no. 1 (A. Meynell) (Kaun, 1905)
Songs from the Greek
Sonnets from the Portuguese, op. 22, song cycle of 44 songs (Chicago: Music Library, 1939)
Sweet and twenty, op. 25, no. 1 (Shakespeare) (Willis, 1912)
A vagabond song, op. 9, no. 1 (B. Carmen) (Kaun, 1906)
Other poems (R. Browning, Coleridge, Donne, Crashaw, Herrick, Longfellow, Lowell, Milton, Shelley and Tennyson)
SACRED
Choral pieces (mix-ch and pf) incl.:
A Christmas carol, op. 13, no. 4 (A.G. Foster)
Lord, when the sense of Thy sweet grace, op. 8, no. 3 (R. Crashaw)
Unto us a son is born, op. 13, no. 3 (A. Meynell)
OPERA
The Brownings go to Italy, op. 43, in 1 act (G.A. Hawkings-Ambler on poetry of R. and E.B. Browning) (Chicago: Music Library, 1936)
The Chilkoot Maiden, op. 32, in 1 act, Alaskan legend (composer) (Kaun, 1926)
A Christmas Tale, op. 35, in 1 act (Maurice Bouchor; trans Barret H. Clark) (Kaun, 1928)
Frithiof, op. 40, in 2 acts, Norse legend (Esaias Tegner; trans. Clement B. Shaw) (Kaun, 1929)
Joan of Arc, op. 38, in 1 act (Kaun, 1926)
The Legend of Spain, op. 35, in 1 act (composer) (Kaun, 1931)
The Legend of the Piper (South Bend, IN, 1924)
The Masque of Pandora, op. 36, in 1 act (Longfellow) (Kaun, 1930)
Massimilliano/The Court Jester/The Love of a Caliban, op. 30, in 1 act (Elia W. Peattie)
Preciosa/The Spanish Student, op. 37, in 1 act (Longfellow) (Kaun, 1928)
Scenes from Little Women; op. 42 in 2 acts (composer) (Music Library, 1934)

Publications
Recollections and Reflections of an American Composer. New York: Musical Advance Pub. Co., 1929. Autobiography.

Bibliography
Eleanor Everest Freer's Songs. *Musical Courier*, January 3, 1906, p. 2.
Foster, Agnes Greene. *Eleanor Everest Freer - Patriot and Her Colleagues*. Chicago: Musical Art Publ. Co., 1927.

Ref. 22, 40, 44, 74, 81, 85, 141, 168, 226, 228, 292, 304, 347, 353, 415, 465, 611, 653

FREGA, Ana Lucia

Argentine professor, writer and composer. b. Buenos Aires, November 25, 1935. She obtained a scholarship to the Buchardo National Conservatory and graduated as Profesora Nacional Superior de Piano, 1954. She is the director of the Institute of Higher Studies at the Teatro Colon and since 1967 has lectured pedagogics, didactics, methodology and teaching practice at the National Conservatory of Music. Since 1979 she has also been honorary director of the Music Education Center of the Institute of Research in Education. She is a member of several societies relating to education in music and is currently doing research into the professional profile of Argentine music teachers. She has had many books and articles published and is an active lecturer on her topic.

Compositions
VOCAL
Songs
TEACHING MUSIC
Haciendo musica con los mas chiquitos
Haciendo musica con los mayorcitos
Musica viva

Publications
Guia de musica para escuchar. 1971.
Musica y educacion. 1972.
Planeamiento y evalucacion de la ensenanza de la musica. 1973.

Ref. 77

FREITAG, Dorothea Hackett

American pianist, arranger, teacher and composer. b. Baltimore, December 2, 1914. She studied at the Curtis Institute from 1930 to 1933 and took her teacher's certificate at Peabody Conservatory in 1934. She attended the Ecole Normale in Paris from 1934 to 1936 and was a pupil of Alexander Sklarevski, Nadia Boulanger (q.v.), Bohuslav Martinu and Mario Castelnuovo-Tedesco. She was the pianist in a number of light musical productions.

Compositions
BALLET
Windy city (1946)
Dance music
MISCELLANEOUS
Jazz in five movements (1950)
Veracuzana (1950)

Ref. 84

FREIXAS Y CRUELLS, Narcisa

Spanish choral conductor, teacher and composer. b. Barcelona, 1860; d. Barcelona, 1926. She began her musical studies at the age of 17 under J.P. Pujol, Pedrell and Granados. She founded the organization 'Cultura Musical Popular' aimed at the promotion of cultural music among the young and also founded several choirs in Madrid and Barcelona. She took part in the formation of a theatre and founded a juvenile library. She composed mainly for children and young people. An illustrated volume of over 115 of her compositions was published in 1928.

Compositions
PIANO
Llibre des nines
Piano infantil
Melodies and other pieces
VOCAL
Cançons amoroses
Cançons catalanes
Cançons d'infante, 3 series
FOLK DANCES
Danses catalanes
Dolca catalunya, sardana
A Sant Medi, sardana
THEATRE
La Cova del Mar
Festa Completa
La Pastoreta
Rodamon
TEACHING PIECES
Perfeccionamiento de los cantos de las escuelas, conference course. 1917.
Ref. 100, 226, 268, 361

FRENCH, Tania
20th-century American composer.
Compositions
CHAMBER
Trio (ob, cl and bsn) (1985)
Variations (vln and pf) (1985)
VOCAL
Oread (Williams, Whitman, Lowell, Sandburg, Crane) (soli, ch, gtr and cham orch) (1984)
SACRED
Psalm 100 (w-ch, org, timp and opt trp) (1985)
Ref. AMC newsletter

FRENSEL-WEGENER, Bertha. See WEGENER-KOOPMAN, Bertha

FRENSEL-WEGENER, Emmy. See WEGENER-FRENSEL, Emmy

FRERICHS, Doris Coulston
American concert pianist, lecturer and composer. b. Edgewater, NJ, April 20, 1911. She gained an M.A. from the Juilliard School of Music and made her concert debut in 1943, thereafter touring the United States, Europe and the USSR and appearing on radio and television in America. She was a member of the piano faculty at the Juilliard School from 1934 to 1948, the Teachers' College of Columbia University from 1948 to 1955 and taught at Barrington Girls' School, 1934 to 1942.
Compositions
PIANO
From my jewel box
The land of tempo-marks
Piano compositions USA
A royal suite
Ref. 457

FRESON, Armande
Belgian composer. b. Liege, November 29, 1896. She studied at the Ecole de Musique and at the Royal Conservatory of Liege, where she obtained two first prizes. She then studied under Paul Vidal at the Paris Conservatoire. In 1932 she was placed first at the Franco-Belgian contest organized by the Society of French Musicians under the direction of Maxime Thomas. She gave numerous concerts of her works, which were also broadcast on the French radio.
Compositions
ORCHESTRA
Piano concerto (1963)
CHAMBER
Quintet (pf and strs) (1964)
Berceuse (vln and pf) (1915) (Paris: Schneider)
Elegy (vlc and pf) (1922)
Gigue (vln and pf) (1915)
Sonata (vln and pf) (1972)
Badinerie and rondeau (hpcd) (1961)
Passe-pied and gavotte (hpcd) (1959)
Triptyque (org) (1927)
PIANO
First and second ballade (1942)
Impromptu (1921) (Schneider, 1925)
Scherzo and waltz, (1921) (Schneider, 1925)
Scherzo (1972)
Sonata (1965)
VOCAL
Dream (1916) (Schneider)
Four melodies (1973)
May song (1918) (Schneider)
Poème lyrique (1930) (Scuart)
Three melodies (vce and pf) (1955)
Two melodies: Oh, laisse frapper à la porte; Viens, lentement t'asseoir (1932) (Scuart)
SACRED
Jeanne d'Arc, oratorio (S, ch and orch) (1929)
La voix du Christ, cantata (T, ch and orch) (1967)
Poème évangelique (ch and orch) (1938)
Noël (T, ch and org) (1924)
Le Crucifix (vce and hp) (1916)
Je vous salue, Marie (vce and org) (1922) (Schneider, 1929)
Notre Père (vce) (1917) (Philips, 1925)
Ref. composer

FREYSE, Emma. See DAHL, Emma

FREYSE-SESSI, Emma. SEE DAHL, Emma

FRICKER, Anne (Mogford)
English poetess and composer. b. ca. 1820. Many of her songs, the first of which was published in 1839, achieved considerable popularity.
Compositions
CHAMBER
Britannia overture (org) (Williams)
Piano pieces
VOCAL
Songs incl.:
Angel of peace
Autumn breezes
The bird of the sunbeam (Ascherberg)
Consolation
Dear voices of home
Fading away (Gordon-Leonard)
Gentle Clare
A harvest hymn
Phyllis fair
Regret
To thee alone
Ref. 6, 226, 276, 297

FRIEDBERG, Patricia Ann
English authoress and composer. b. London, May 4, 1934. She studied journalism in London and then attended the Marguette University from 1969 to 1971. She wrote for television and theatre in Zimbabwe, South Africa and America, collaborating with Sylvia Bernstein and Goldie Kossow and was authoress of the plays *Is Today Tomorrow* and *The Masquerade*.
Compositions
OPERA
Simcha 73, with ballet
Twenty-one Aldgate, with ballet
MISCELLANEOUS
The return
Ref. 494

FRIEDRICH, Mrs. Johann. See EDELMANN, Mlle.

FRISKIN, Rebecca. See CLARKE, Rebecca

FRITSCH, Magda von
20th-century German composer.

Compositions
CHAMBER
Die Weihnachtsfloete (s-rec and a-rec) (Heidelberg: Suddeutscher Musikverlag, 1942)
Ref. Frau und Musik

FRITSCHER, Eleonore Sophie. See WESTENHOLZ, Eleonore Sophie Marie

FRITTER, Genevieve Davisson
American violinist, concertmistress and composer. b. Clarksburg, WV, December 13, 1915. She received her B.M. from Judson College, Alabama, and did postgraduate study at the Juilliard Summer School, the Birmingham (Alabama) Conservatory of Music, and the Cincinnati Conservatory of Music. She studied composition privately under Esther Williamson Ballou (q.v.). She received awards from the Alabama Federation of Music Clubs in 1938, the National Federation of Music Clubs in 1939 and the Mu Phi Epsilon National Competition, 1946. In 1966 she was awarded the Outstanding Alumna achievement award from Judson College. She was concertmistress of the National Ballet Orchestra for five years and music director of the Montgomery Ballet Company for 17 years, where she composed most of its repertoire.
Compositions
ORCHESTRA
Inflections (cham orch) (1976)
Theme and variations (str orch) (1968)
CHAMBER
Woodwind quintet
Woodwind trio
Suite for flute and piano (1958)
Solos for flute
Solos for violin
Piano pieces
VOCAL
Monotone (1937) (Schirmer) (Nat. Fed. of Music Clubs award)
Other songs (vce and pf)
SACRED
Judaean hills are holy, anthem (1958) (J. Fischer)
BALLET
Ballets for children (1960-1972) incl.:
Alice
Adventures in Oz
Hansel and Gretel
Peter Pan
Snow White
Ref. composer, 77

FRITZ, Sherilyn Gail
Canadian teacher and composer. b. Princeton, September 19, 1957. She studied under Cortland Hultberg, Stephen Chatman, Elliot Weisgarber, Jean Coulthard (q.v.), Violet Archer (q.v.), Malcolm Forsyth, Alfred Fisher and Theo Goldberg. She obtained her B.M. and teaching qualifications at the University of British Columbia. She won numerous awards for her compositions. DISCOGRAPHY.
Compositions
BAND
Elephants and unicorns (1980)
Fantasy in fifths (1974)
CHAMBER
Marriage suite (trp, hn, trb, b-trb and tba) (1982)
Music for Hamlet (trp, timp, rec, hpcd and viola de gamba) (1978)
Confrontation (2 trp and perc) (1977)
Titan Moons (trp, hn and trb) (1981)
Audition (pf and perc) (1980)
Meditation II (fl) (1982)
PIANO
Eleventh hour (1979)
Haunted house suite
Mindscape (1980)
Relaxation techniques (1979)
VOCAL
Love poems (ch) (1977)
The suicide (ch, vln and perc) (1980)
Uncommon women (girls' ch) (1981)
Chanson innocentes II (vocal ens) (1978)
A midsummer night's dream (vce and inst ens) (1980)
Nine nursery rhymes (vce and inst ens) (1981)
The skin of our teeth (vce and inst ens) (1980)
The bedtime concert (narr and fl) (1979)
Childhoods ago (narr, d-b and perc) (1978)
Love songs (vce and perc) (1981)
Observances (vce and gtr) (1979)
Vancouver collection (Bar and pf) (1977)
SACRED
Genesis (ch and cham orch) (1976)
Alleluia (boys' ch) (1980)
Mass of the morning sun (ch and inst ens) (1979)
Requiem Mass (ch and perc) (1981)
OPERA
Deck, rock opera (solo, ch and stage band)
ELECTRONIC
Brecht on Brecht (vce, perc, elec gtr, gtr and keyboards) (1981)
Chimericon (amp-fl and org) (1982)
King Lear electronic suite (1982)
Song of the killer whales (concrete music) (1981)
Third planet from the sun ... and beyond (elec tape) (1978)
10-63 (concrete music) (1974)
Ref. composer

FROHBEITER, Ann W.
American organist and composer. b. Evansville, IN, September 27, 1942. She studied the organ at Indiana University and received her B.M.. At Southern Methodist University she received an M.M. She also studied choral arranging under Lloyd Pfautsch. She was organist in Dallas, from 1964 until 1966 and thereafter in Houston.
Composition
SACRED
Blow ye the trumpet, blow (ch, trp and org) (1972)
Ref. 142

FROMM-MICHAELS, Ilse
German pianist, professor and composer. b. Hamburg, December 30, 1888. d. Detmold, 1986. She studied at the Hochschule fuer Musik, Berlin, under Professor Bender and H. van Eyken; at the Stern Conservatory, Berlin, under J. Kwast and C. Friedberg: and at the Cologne Conservatory under H. Pfitzner and F. Steinbach (composition). As a virtuoso pianist she played under the baton of Nikisch, Fuertwangler and Arnold Schoenberg. In 1957 she became professor of the piano at the Hamburg Musikhochschule.
Compositions
ORCHESTRA
Symphony in C-Minor, op. 19 (1938) (Berlin: Ries & Erler)
CHAMBER
Musica larga (str qrt and cl) (1944)
Suite for wind quintet
Sonata, op. 10 (vln and pf)
Stimmungen eines Fauns, op. 11 (cl) (Tischer & Jagenberg)
Suite, op. 15 (vlc) (1931)
PIANO
Acht Skizzen, op. 5 (1908)
Passacaglia in F-Minor, op. 16
Sonata in E-Minor, op. 6 (1917)
Variations on an original theme, op. 8 (1919)
Vier Puppen, op. 4 (1908)
Walzerreigen, op. 7 (1917)
Twenty cadenzas to Mozart's piano concertos
VOCAL
Drei Rilke-Gesaenge (Bar and orch) (1949)
Marien-Passion, op. 18 (ch a-cap, 3 trp and cham orch) (1933)
Canoni (3 vces)
Fuenf Lieder aus Des Knaben Wunderhorn, op. 9a
Vier winzige Wunderhornlieder, op. 9b (1921)
Ref. 15, 17, 23, 44, 70, 94, 105

FRONDONI LACOMBE, Madalena
Portuguese writer and composer. b. Lisbon, 1857, d. 1936. She was a spiritualist who wrote mainly on metaphysical themes.
Compositions
OPERA
Pif-Paf
Publications
Dernières lettres d'un poitrinaire à sa fiancée.
Merveilleux phénomènes de l'au-dela.
Segredo da Morte.
Une visite au Pantheon. 1908.
Ref. 268

FRONMUELLER, Frieda
German organist, conductor, teacher and composer. b. Lindau/Bodensee, September 8, 1901. She studied at the Musikhochschule, Leipzig and the Conservatories of Nuremberg and Wurzburg. She was organist, choir conductor, private music teacher and chamber music conductor in Furth and Nuremberg. DISCOGRAPHY.

Compositions
CHAMBER
Festliche Musik (3 trp and 4 trb)
Christ ist erstanden, Intrade (trbs) (1971)
Ruf Intrade (trbs) (1973)
Violin sonata
Piano pieces
VOCAL
Songs
SACRED
Busstagskantate 1947 (T, B, ch and orch)
Jerusalem, du hochgebaute Stadt, cantata (ch and wind insts)
In Wald und Flur
Herr, wie sind deine Werke so gross und viel, psalm motet
Christe, du Beistand
Du, meine Seele singe (mix-ch, cong, 2 trp and 2 trb)
Jesus Christus herrscht als Koenig
Nun bitten wir den heiligen Geist (mix-ch, cong, 4 trp, 2 trb, trp and wind insts)
Geschichte vom verlorenen Sohn
Ref. 50, 70, 563

FRONMULLER, Frieda. See FRONMUELLER, Frieda

FRONTIERA, Mary Jo
20th-century composer.
Composition
FILM MUSIC
Sticks and Stones (1970)
Ref. 326

FROST, Mary. See PLUMSTEAD, Mary

FROST WARREN-DAVIS, Betsy. See WARREN, Betsy

FROTHINGHAM, Eugenia
B. 1908.
Composition
ORCHESTRA
Soliloquy (cor anglais and orch)
Ref. 594

FRUGONI, Bertha
19th-century Italian composer. She composed piano pieces and songs.
Ref. 226, 276

FRUMKER, Linda
American horn player, pianist, lecturer and composer. b. Geneva, OH, December 11, 1940. She studied the piano under Arthur Loesser, the horn under Martin Morris and composition under Marcel Dick. She obtained her B.M. and M.M. at the Cleveland Institute of Music, where she taught from 1964 to 1967. Later she taught at the Cleveland Supplementary Education Center. She won the Ernest Bloch award three times and received an award at the Aspen Music Festival in 1962.
Compositions
ORCHESTRA
Symphony (1964)
Anniversary overture (1973)
CHAMBER
Four for Fred (cl qrt)
Music for friends (str qrt)
Two string quartets
Wind quartet
VOCAL
Octet (S and insts) (1962)
Like Noah's dove (S and inst ens) (1972)
Songs incl.:
Angel songs (1973)
Four Aspen songs (1962)
Three songs of love (1960)
Ref. 142, 347

FRY, Dorothy M. See ARBUCKLE, Dorothy

FRYDAN, Kamilla
20th-century Austrian composer.
Compositions
OPERETTA
Liebesmagazin (1926)
THEATRE
Baron Menelaus, vaudeville (1919)
Die grosse Trommel, revue (1925)
Madame Napoleon, historical musical (1933)
Ein Maerchentraum, musical play for children (1919)
Ref. 431

FRYXELL, Regina Holmen. See FRYZELL, Regina Holmen

FRYZELL (Fryxell), Regina Holmen
American organist, pianist, teacher and composer. b. Morganville, KS, November 24, 1899. She received her B.A. and B.M. in 1922 and Litt. B. in 1961 from Augustana College, Rock Island, IL. She also studied at the Juilliard School of Music under Wallingford Riegger and A. Madeley Richardson. She obtained a diploma for the organ in 1927 and studied privately with Leo Sowerby. She taught the organ and the piano privately and at Augustana College, the Juilliard School of Music, Knox College and Black Hawk College. DISCOGRAPHY.
Compositions
CHAMBER
Ensembles
SACRED
Christmas wish, carol (J.K. MacKenzie) (mix-ch) (Gray, 1957)
Heaven, peace and joy (mix-ch) (Gray, 1957)
O come, Creator Spirit, come (mix-ch and org or pf) (Gray, 1959)
Praise to the Lord (J. Neander; trans C. Winkworth) (mix-ch and org or pf) (Gray, 1953)
To the Christ Child (F.N. North) (ch and org or pf; also S or T and org or pf) (Gray, 1953)
To the hills I lift mine eyes (mix-ch and org or pf)
The unseen presence (F.L. Hasmer) (mix-ch and org or pf)
Praise, my soul, the King of Heaven, on a melody by J.S. Bach (S and A or T and B and org or pf) (C. Fisher, 1963)
Psalm 67 (S or T and org or pf) (Gray, 1954)
A vision, 15 English carols (S and org or pf) (Gray, 1956)
Other choral works
Songs
Ref. 40, 142, 190, 228, 341, 563, 646

FUCHS, Lillian
American violist, teacher and composer. b. New York, November 18, 1910. She studied at the Institute of Musical Art and made her debut with her brother, the violinist Joseph Fuchs in 1945, when they performed as soloists in Mozart's *Symphonie concertante* with the National Orchestral Association. Lillian played with major orchestras in the United States and Europe and was the first person to perform and record the six Bach *Suites for viola solo*. She received the Morris Loeb Memorial prize from the Institute of Musical Art and for three consecutive years won the Isaac Newton Seligmon prize for composition. She taught in New York at the Manhattan School of Music. DISCOGRAPHY.
Compositions
CHAMBER
Jota (vln and pf)
Three pieces (vln)
VIOLA
Twelve caprices
Sixteen fantasy etudes
Fifteen characteristic studies
Sonata pastorale
Numerous arrangements
Ref. 63, 68, 74, 77, 146, 148, 206, 457, 563, 625

FULCHER, Ellen Georgina (Nelly)
20th-century English violinist, violist, critic, teacher and composer. b. Whitchurch, Salop. She studied under Edith Knocker and at the Royal Academy of Music. She was orchestra leader of the London Coliseum from 1916 to 1919, the Bournemouth Municipal Orchestra from 1924 to 1925 and other orchestras. She taught the violin and the viola at schools in

Winchester, Twyford and West Downs and was music critic for a newspaper after 1945. She also gave lecture recitals and adjudicated. She is an A.R.A.M. and an L.R.A.M.

Compositions

ORCHESTRA

Testament of many, concerto (vln and str orch)

CHAMBER

Quintet (ob and strs)

Sonata (vln and pf)

Theme and variations (vln and pf)

Violin pieces

VOCAL

Song cycle

INCIDENTAL MUSIC

Music for plays

Ref. 490

FULCHER, Nelly. See FULCHER, Ellen Georgina

FULLER, Jeanne Weaver

Canadian professor and composer. b. Regina, Saskatchewan, October 23, 1917. She obtained her B.A. from Pomona College in 1937 and her M.A. from the California State University in 1964, having studied under Halsey Stevens. She lectured at the El Caino College.

Compositions

CHAMBER

Fugue for woodwinds

PIANO

Jeux aux douze tons (4 hands)

Dorian rondo

VOCAL

At the window (Sandburg)

Maggie and Milly and Molly and May (e.e. cummings) (w-vces)

Now (More near ourselves than we) (vce and pf)

When young hearts break (Heine)

SACRED

Exultate Justi, Psalm 32 (ch)

The praise of Christmas (ch)

Three motets

Ref. 142, 146, 347

FULLER-HALL, Sarah Margaret

American composer. b. March 11, 1959, South Boston, VA. She studied composition at the Appalachian State University under Scott Meister, Max Smith and Robert Ward. She began composing at the age of 13. Her *Three movement suite* was her first work to be publicly performed. She is a member of the American Women Composers, League of Women Composers and the Music Educators' National Conference. She is also the vice-president of the Epsilon Theta chapter of Sigma Alpha Iota music fraternity for women.

Compositions

ORCHESTRA

Trumpet concertino (trp and orch) (1979)

BAND

Minor distraction march (wind ens and perc) (1979)

Round trip ticket (jazz band) (1977)

Scherzo (symphonic band) (1975)

Three movement suite

CHAMBER

Overture of hymns (brass qnt, org and timp) (1979)

Jazz impromptu (1978) (brass qnt, 1979)

Six movements (4 tba, or 2 tba and 2 euph) (1979)

Abbreviated duet (2 cl) (1976)

Adagio (vln and pf) (1974)

Bravura (2 trp) (1978)

Controversy (hn) (1978)

VOCAL

Sephestias' lullaby (1978)

Ref. 474

FUNK, Susan

20th-century American composer.

Composition

SACRED

Vision of the Cross: psalm 22 (S, A, T and B)

FURGERI, Bianca Maria

Italian organist, pianist, choral conductor, teacher and composer. b. Rovigo, October 6, 1935. She began her piano studies at an early age and at 16 took private lessons in composition. She studied the piano under G. Giuseppe Piccioli at the Milan Conservatory in 1954, choir conducting and choral music in 1958 under B. Coltro and the organ under Wolfango della Vecchia at the Padua Conservatory in 1962 and postgraduate courses in composition under G.F. Ghedini. Since 1962 she has been active in teaching and has worked with the national teaching center. She is the recipient of prizes and awards and her works have been performed throughout Europe.

Compositions

ORCHESTRA

Antifonie (pf and orch) (1975) (hon mention, Treviso, Italy)

CHAMBER

String quartet

Juvenilia (pf, 4 hands) (Padua: Zanibon, 1983)

ORGAN

Pezzi

Sonata (1964) (3rd prize, Ex-aequo Magadino, Switzerland) (Zanibon, 1964)

VOCAL

Guatimozimo, cantata (Nello Gaspare Vetro) (1976-1977) (soli, ch and orch)

Discanto (4 vces and mix-ch) (1974) (Ungaretti and Baudelaire) (hon mention, Guido d'Arezzo, 1975)

Raccolta di composizioni polifoniche sacre e profane (mix-ch) (1958) (Bologna: Bongiovanni, 1958)

Ode a Leuconoe (Horatio) (4 w-vces) (1976)

Voci del tempo (E. Montale) (4 w-vces) (hon mention Guido d' Arezzo, 1975)

Piccoli musici, vols. 1 and 11, collection of popular songs for children (ch and insts) (Zanibon, 1969)

SACRED

Messa dei S.S. Apostoli Pietro e Paolo (mix-ch and org) (1973) (Milan: Ricordi, 1975) (1st prize, A. Conti Varese)

Piccola messa di fanciulli, for children (1977)

Publications

Didattica della musica. Treviso: Canova, 1976.

Il libro dei ritmi e dei suoni. Padua: Zanibon, 1972.

Ref. composer

FURZE, Jessie

English pianist, teacher and composer. b. Wallington, Surrey, February 4, 1903. She studied at the Royal Academy of Music, specializing in piano and chamber music. Many of her educational pieces were composed for the Associated Board of the Royal School of Music. She is the recipient of awards for both piano and composition.

Compositions

PIANO

Grandpa's diary (Robertson Publ.)

Hansel and Gretel (Ashdown)

In time of spring (Robertson)

Isle of Sark (Robertson)

A merry suite (Ashdown)

Six little pieces

Ten little ditties (Robertson)

Twenty-five graded pieces (Associated Bd.)

The Western Isles (Bagley & Ferguson)

Other pieces (Freeman; E.M.I.; Weinberger; Galliard)

VOCAL

A pastoral, madrigal (4 vces)

Songs incl.:

Day by day

A gracious duet

In the days of long ago (1 or 2 vces)

In my country garden

Little songs and dances (Freeman; E.M.I.)

London town

Scenes from Holland

Things I remember

Two part songs (Boosey & Hawkes)

Windmill land

Unison songs

Ref. composer, 457

G****** See HAXTHAUSEN, Aurore M.G.Ch. von**

GABASHVILI, Nana

Soviet composer. b. 1962. She was a student of the Tbilisi Music School. By the age of 14 she had completed over 300 works. She composed sonatas, marches, a children's operetta and nearly 300 songs.

Ref. 177

GABLER, Jeanette
B. 1820. She composed songs.
Ref. 465

GABRIEL, Mary Ann Virginia
English pianist and composer of Irish parentage. b. Banstead, Surrey, February 7, 1825; d. London, August 7, 1877. She studied the piano under Pixis, Dohler and Thalberg and harmony and composition under Molique. She married George E. March, who wrote most of the librettos for her operettas.
Compositions
CHAMBER
Hoila! Hoila! (gtr) (Boosey)
PIANO
La gondola (Chappell)
Het roode kruis (Bolle)
In memoriam (Chappell)
Long ago, musical sketch (Novello)
Luna, waltz song (Ditson; National Music Co.; Novello)
Moonbeams (Chappell)
Murmures eoliens (Chappell)
Old memories (Williams)
Only (also vce and pf) (Ashdown; Brainard; Church; Ditson; Gordon; Schirmer; Williams)
Pavonia, waltz (Hopwood)
Pensier dolente, 2 melodies (Ricordi)
Polka de concert (Ashdown)
Un sourire, nocturne (Ashdown)
Sunshine, valse elegante (Williams)
VOCAL
Dreamland, cantata (1870)
Evangeline, cantata (based on Longfellow) (1873)
Graziella, cantata
A carol round the fireside (mix-ch) (Novello)
Avevo una compagna, stornello (Ricordi)
Giovane bella, stornello (Ricordi)
Passo ripasso, canto popolare (Ricordi)
Songs incl.:
Across the sea (Boosey; Brainard; Ditson; Gordon)
Alone (Williams)
Alone in the twilight
Arden towers
Ariel (Ashdown)
Asleep
At her wheel the maiden sitting (Ashdown)
At my feet
At rest
Brighter hours (Ashdown)
Bye and bye (Church)
Corra Linn (Ashdown)
Dawn of springtide (Brainard; Church)
Echo (Ashdown)
A fisher's wife
Forsaken, she sat beside the mountain spring (Brainard; Gordon; Hammond; Schirmer; Turner)
Golden wedding day
Happy days
Hawking song
Lady of Kienast Tower
Little blossom
A mother's song, lullaby (Ashdown)
Ruby (Brainard; Church; Ditson; Ellis; Gordon; Metzler; Schirmer; Williams)
Servian ballad
Think of me when far away (Fischer)
Three roses
Wake my beloved
When sparrows build (Brainard; Church; Ditson; Gordon; Metzler; Schirmer; Williams)
Part songs
SACRED
Our Father waits over the May (ch and pf) (Fischer)
Dormi Jesu, melodia (Ricordi)
Sacred vows (vce and pf) (Boosey)
OPERETTA
The Follies of a Night, in 2 acts (J.R. Plauche) (1860) (Cramer)
The Grass Widows, in 1 act (G. Marsh) (Metzler, 1873)
Lost and Found (Marsh) (1860)
A Rainy Day, in 1 act (H. Sewith) (Ascherberg)
Shepherd of Cornouailles
Who's the Heir? (Marsh)
Widows Bewitched (Marsh, A. Hamilton) (Metzler, 1867)
Ref. 6, 8, 22, 74, 85, 102, 226, 260, 276, 297, 307, 347, 353, 361, 431

GABRIELLE, Monic. See CECCONI-BOTELLA, Monic

GABRYS, Ewa Lucja Maria
Polish harpsichordist, translator and composer. b. Cracow, November 5, 1936. She received a diploma in the theory of music from the State College of Music, Cracow in 1964, composition in 1966 and in postgraduate music editorship in 1976. She gave harpsichord concerts in her own country and abroad and recorded for Polish television and radio. She won several awards including the first prize at the Old Music Festival for the harpsichord in Lodz. She translated books on music from English into Polish.
Compositions
ORCHESTRA
Concerto (hpcd and orch) (1965-1966)
Overture (sym orch) (1964)
Over-abundance contra reduction (1967)
CHAMBER
Concertino per undici strumenti (1967)
Miniatures (ww qrt) (1962)
String quartet (1965)
Contrasts (fl and hpcd) (1968)
Sonatina (trp and pf) (1959-1960)
Miniatures (hpcd) (1962-1963)
Miniatures (pf) (1960)
Toccata for Landowska (hpcd) (1979)
VOCAL
Triptych (vce and a-sax) (1963)
Ref. composer

GABURO, Elizabeth
20th-century composer.
Composition
ELECTRONIC
Pygmy pipes under fallen leaves (vce and tape) (1980)
Ref. 227

GABUS, Monique
French pianist, lecturer and composer. b. Cambrai, March 15, 1924. At the age of eight she studied harmony under Victor Gallois in Douai. In Paris she studied the piano under Magda Tagliaferro and entered the Paris Conservatoire at the age of 17. She won prizes for harmony and composition in the classes of Jean Gallon and Tony Aubin. She studied fugue and counterpoint under Noel Gallon and music analysis under Olivier Messiaen. She taught at the Schola Cantorum of Paris but ill health interrupted her work. PHOTOGRAPH.
Compositions
ORCHESTRA
Légende, symphonic poem (1948)
CHAMBER
Automne (ob and pf) (1970)
L'école des oiseaux (fl and picc) (1971)
Sans Souci (cl and pf) (1970)
Sonate (vln and pf) (1946)
Etude (a-sax) (A.G. Gourdet)
La harpe de Graziella
Pièces pour harpe, for children (1960)
Stèle pour une jeune indienne (gtr) (Paris: Lemoine, 1977)
PIANO
Weekend musical (4 hands) (1968)
Le clavier de Pierre et Françoise, pieces for children (Lemoine)
Images indiennes, 14 pieces
Jeunes artistes au clavier (1966)
Le livre des animaux, 14 pieces (1974)
Three pieces for children (1962) (Lemoine)
Pièce de piano pour la main droite (1960)
VOCAL
La nuit obscure, cantata (St. Jean de la Croix) (ch and orch) (1950)
A Janek (Ronsard) (mix-ch a-cap)
Melodies to poems by André Gide (1949) (Mus. Transatlantiques)
Quatre esquisses grecques (S and fl) (Lemoine)
Quatre vocalises pour voix de basse (vce) (1973)
Tantas, Japanese melodies (1963)
Trois vocalises pour soprano (Chappell)
Vocalises (vce and pf) (Lemoine)
Popular melodies
SACRED
Alleluia (ch a-cap) (1961)
Laudate Dominum (ch a-cap) (1961)
Noël (4 mix-vces) (1965)
Offertoire pour tous les temps (4 vces and org) (1968) (Desdée)
Quatre répons pour les funerailles (1968)
Ref. composer, 70, 76

GADE, Margaret
19th-century English song writer.
Compositions
VOCAL
Forgotten
When hearts grow old
Ref. 276, 433

GAERTNER, Katarzyna
Polish composer. b. Myslenica, February 22, 1942. She received an award from the Polish Ministry of Culture in 1975. Her songs have been performed at music festivals in Poland, Ostende and Las Palmas.
Compositions
VOCAL
Zagrajcie nam dzisiaj wszystkie srebrne dzwony, oratorio (E. Bryll) (1975)
Eurydyki tanćzaçe
Malgośka
Na skle malowane (1970)
Zakwitne róza
SACRED
Msza beatowa (1967)
THEATRE
Rumcajs, children's musical (1974)
Ref. 504

GAIGEROVA, Varvara Andrianovna
Soviet pianist concertmistress and composer. b. Oryekhovo-Zuyevo, October 4, 1903; d. Moscow, April 6, 1944. From 1917 to 1923 she was a pianist and concertmistress. In 1927 she graduated from the Moscow Conservatory, having studied the piano under G. Nuhaus and composition under N. Myaskovsky and G. Katuar. From 1936 to 1944 she was concertmistress at the Bolshoi Theatre. She was particularly interested in the musical folklore of the southeastern people of Soviet Russia. DISCOGRAPHY.
Compositions
ORCHESTRA
Symphony No. 1 (1928)
Symphony No. 2, on Kalmuk themes (1934)
Symphony No. 3 (1936)
Symphonic suite on Caucasian themes
Suite on Udmurt themes (domra orch) (Muzgiz, 1933)
Two suites on Kazakh themes (domra orch)
CHAMBER
String quartet (1926-1927)
String quartet on Yakuts themes (Muzgiz, 1947)
Suite for viola and piano, op. 8
PIANO
Four Sketches (Muzgiz, 1929)
Sonata
Sonatina on Buryat-Mongolian themes (Muzgiz, 1949)
VOCAL
Dnevnik frontovnika, cantata (soloists, ch and orch) (1943)
Monolog Bertrana, cantata (Blok) (soloists, ch and orch) (1928)
Rastsvet Turkmenistana, cantata (S. Bolotin) (soloists, ch and orch) (1934)
Solitse sotsialisma, cantata (A. Zharov) (soloists, ch and orch) (1932)
Elegiya (1950)
Five romances (Pushkin) (1937)
Kolonialnaya pesnya (S. Gorodetsky) (Muzgiz, 1932)
Stepnoi gigant (S. Bolotin) (vce and pf) (1932)
Vesna, song cycle (J. Kolas) (vce and pf)
Arrangements of Russian, Kalmuk, Bashkir, Byelorussian, Buryat, Kazakh, Kirghiz, Udmurt, Tatar and Uzbek songs
OPERA
Krepost u kamennogo broda (composer, based on Lermontov and some Caucasian poets) (1937-1940)
Ref. 2, 9, 44, 70, 74, 87, 96, 100, 109, 172, 226, 330, 379, 563

GAIL, Edmée-Sophie (nee Garre)
French singer and composer. b. Paris, August 28, 1775; d. Paris, July 24, 1819. She started composing at the age of 15 and studied under Mengozzi. She then went on a concert tour through southern France and Spain, returning to Paris, where she studied harmony and counterpoint under Fetis. She studied under Perne and Neukomm in Brussels. In 1816 she sang in London and in 1818 toured Germany and Vienna with the actress Mme. Catalani. Her operas were extremely successful; her last work *La Serenade* had a long run in Paris in 1818.
Compositions
VOCAL
A mes fleurs (3 vces and pf)
Celui qui sut toucher mon coeur, tyrolienne (with pf) (Costallat)
Deux nocturnes françaises (2 vces and pf)
Les devoirs du chevalier
Dimanche dans la plaine, nocturne (2 vces with pf or hp) (Paris: Naderman)
Honneur et patrie (Salut au vaillant)
N'est-ce pas elle
O pescator dell'onda, barcarolle (3 vces and pf) (Simrock; Schott)
Romances and melodies incl: La charmante Isabelle; Heure du soir; Le souvenir du diable (Ashdown)
Viens écouter ce doux serment
Vous qui priez pour moi
Part songs
OPERA
Angela, ou L'atelier de Jean Cousin, in 1 act (Monscloux d'Epinay) (with F.A. Boieldieu) (1814)
Les Deux Jaloux (Dufresny and J.B.C. Vial) (1813)
Mademoiselle de Launay à la Bastille, in 1 act (A.F. Creuze de Lesser, J.F. Roger and Mme. Villiers) (1813)
Medée
La Meprise, in 1 act (Creuze de Lesser) (1814)
La Sérènade, in 1 act (Sofia Gay) (1818)
Two arias for Montoni ou Le chateau d'Udolphe (A. Duval) (Paris: 1797)
Ref. 9, 13, 15, 17, 70, 85, 100, 102, 103, 105, 108, 128, 132, 225, 226, 260, 276, 297, 347, 353, 361, 400, 431

GAINSBORG, Lolita Cabrera
American concert pianist and composer. b. 1896; d. Danville, NJ, May 23, 1981. She made her New York debut at the age of 14 in the Mendelssohn Hall. After 1924 she was a featured pianist on the NBC radio network and gave concerts until her marriage. DISCOGRAPHY.
Composition
PIANO
Lullaby for the right hand alone
Ref. *New York Times* 5 June 1981, 563, 622

GAJDECZKA, S.
Polish composer.
Composition
MISCELLANEOUS
Naprzod, zolnierze wolnosci
Ref. Editions Polonaises de Musique, 1954

GALAJIKIAN, Florence Grandland
American concert pianist, accompanist, lecturer and composer. b. Maywood, IL, July 29, 1900; d. 1972. She studied under Albert Noelte at the Northwestern School of Music and received a B.M. in 1918. She also studied at the Chicago Music College and under Oldberg, Borowski, Saar, Lutkin, Beecher and Raab. Later she studied under Rubin Goldmark in New York. She was coach-accompanist with Saenger and taught the piano and composition at the Chicago Conservatory. She toured as a concert pianist and soloist with the Chicago Symphony Orchestra. Her works were played by major symphony orchestras.
Compositions
ORCHESTRA
Symphonic intermezzo (1932) (Nat. Broadcasting award)
Tragic overture (1936)
Transitions, ballet suite (1937)
CHAMBER
Andante and scherzo (str qrt)
String quartet
Fantaisie (vln and pf)
Hillbilly's dance (vlc and pf) (C. Fischer, 1940)
The girl with the Spanish shawl (vln)
Magical land of triads (pf)
Piece (org)
VOCAL
Song of joy (w-ch and pf) (Fischer, 1941)
A lilt of spring (L. Gard) (vce and pf) (1924)
Other choral works
Songs
Ref. 9, 70, 74, 94, 142, 226, 228, 292, 361, 403

GALBRAITH, Nancy Riddle
American pianist and composer. b. Pittsburgh, January 27, 1951. She obtained her B.Mus in 1972 and her M.Mus. from the Ohio University. She studied composition under Leonardo Balada and the piano under Nelson Whitaker. In 1984 she was director of music at the Christ Lutheran Church, Pittsburgh.

Compositions
CHAMBER
Nonet
Dance (comm Renaissance City Woodwind Quintet, 1982)
Fantasy (pf) (1979)
Ref. AMC newsletter, 625

GALEOTTI (Galetto), Margherita

Italian concert pianist and composer. b. Mauern, Bavaria, ca. 1867. She studied the piano in Florence under G. Buonamici and composition under G. Bellio. She received her diploma under G. Martucci at the Liceo di Bologna. As a concert pianist she performed with the Cherubini Society, the Philharmonic in Florence and in France and Switzerland. She gave nine consecutive performances at the classical concerts in Monte Carlo under the baton of Leon Jehin.
Compositions
CHAMBER
Trio in D-Minor (vln, vlc and pf) (1914)
PIANO
Two suites
Other pieces
VIOLIN
Canzonetta (Milan: Carisch & Janichen)
Gavotta
Madrigale introduzione
Sonata
VIOLONCELLO
Allegro capriccioso
Andantino con moto
VOCAL
Tre ariette in old style
Ref. 70, 86, 105, 226

GALIKIAN, Susanna Avetisovna

Soviet pianist, accompanist, lecturer and composer. b. Tbilisi, April 5, 1894; d. Erivan, February 20, 1963. She studied the piano under Davidov from 1907 until 1912 and singing under U. Spendiarov from 1917 to 1919. In 1917 she graduated from Petrograd Conservatory having studied the piano under V. Ossovsky, A. Polyetik and N. Posiyakovsky. She went to Erivan in 1922 and taught the piano and singing and accompanied singers until 1930. From 1930 she taught pre-school children various instruments and after 1944 taught at a teachers' training institute.
Compositions
PIANO
Eight marches for children
Twenty-one dances for children
VOCAL
Armenian songs (composer and Armenian poets)
Azerbaijanian songs (composer) (1930-1952)
Russian songs (Russian poets)
Approx. 150 songs for children
Other song collections
MISCELLANEOUS
Seven musical games and eurhythmic exercises for children
Ref. 21, 87

GALINNE (Gluchowicz), Rachel

Israeli pianist, musicologist and composer. b. Stockholm, 1949. She began studying the piano in Stockholm in 1958 and in 1969 entered the Stockholm University to study musicology, film science and pedagogics. She graduated in 1974 and the next year went to Tel Aviv University where she studied musicology until 1978, and then began composition studies at the University's music academy. She studied theory and electronic music under Sadai and composition under L. Schidlowski. In 1984 she received her bachelor's degree in composition and then began studying for her master's degree. In 1980 she participated in a composition course in France, led by Witold Lutoslawski, and in 1984 studied at the Darmstadt seminar of contemporary music and took part in the Gaudeamus Festival in Amsterdam. In 1986 she attended the ISCM festival in Budapest.
Compositions
ORCHESTRA
Piece for orchestra 1983
Concerto for chamber orchestra
Cycles
CHAMBER
De profundis (6 wind insts and d-b)
Breaking the bonds of ice (2 pf and 2 perc)
VOCAL
Gluehende Raetsel (Nelly Sachs) (mix-ch a-cap)
Ref. composer

GALLI, Signora

Italian singer and composer. She settled in England where she was a popular singer for many years. She was frequently employed in male parts and appeared at Covent Garden in 1797, more than 50 years after her debut.
Compositions
VOCAL
Conservati fedele, arietta (S, vln, vla and d-b)
Se son lontana (London: Philips, ca. 1750; The Gentleman's Magazine, 1760, 1763)
Twelve duets (J.A. Hasse)
Ref. 65, 91, 161, 226

GALLI-CAMPI

20th-century American coloratura soprano and composer. She studied in the United States and Europe and made her operatic debut in Cincinnati. She toured the United States as a recitalist and appeared on radio.
Composition
OPERA
Air Castles (composer)
Ref. 226

GALLINA, Jill

20th-century composer.
Compositions
THEATRE
Santa and the Snowmobile, musical play (vce and tape)
The Wackadoo Zoo, musical play (1982)
Ref. MLA *Notes*

GALLOIS, Marie

19th-century French composer of piano pieces, ballets and songs.
Ref. 226, 276

GALLONI, Adolfa

Italian composer. b. ca. 1861.
Compositions
CHAMBER
Instrumental works
VOCAL
Songs
OPERA
I Quattro Rustici
Ref. 226, 276, 307

GAMBARINI, Costanza

Italian composer. b. ca. 1951.
Compositions
CHAMBER
Sonatinas (rec and gtr) (Milan: Ricordi, 1976)
ARRANGEMENTS
Recorder and guitar pieces
Ref. Otto Harrassowitz (Wiesbaden)

GAMBARINI, Elisabetta de. See DE GAMBARINI, Elisabeth

GAMBARO, Alceste. See Addendum

GAMBOGI, Federica Elvira

19th-century Italian composer.
Compositions
PIANO
Album, 6 pieces (Augener)
VOCAL
Child-land, cycle of songs and duets (Boosey)
Coronation song (Metzler)
Cupid's message (Boosey)
The dearest May (Ricordi)
Flowers of spring (In Italian: Weekes) (In English: Leonard)
If in some meadows fair? (also in French) (Chappell)
If it could be (Cramer)
Stray memories (Boosey)
Thy remembrance, to please my bonnie belle, in D and F-Sharp (Leonard)
Winter blossoms
Ref. 297

GAMBOGI, Luigia
Italian composer.
Compositions
CHAMBER
Mai se di lui (man and vln)
Marche brillante (J. Scott-Burne) (man and pf) (Ashdown)
Should love for him (man and vln)
Valse (Scott-Burne) (man and pf) (Ashdown)
PIANO
Beautiful flowers, bolero
Un fiore, fantasie brillante
VOCAL
Songs incl.:
Amore
Aveu
Child of the butterfly
Daisy (Ashdown)
A dream of life (Weekes)
Il ne sait pas
Il Rosignolo
So dear, so very dear to me
Ref. 297

GAMILA. See JAMILA

GAMILLA, Alice Doria
Philippine pianist, teacher and composer. b. Philippines, September 20, 1931. At the age of six she was given music lessons by her mother. She obtained a B.S. (education) magna cum laude from the National University in 1965. She studied the piano at the University of Santo Tomas Conservatory and composition under Professor Felipe Padilla de Leon. From 1951 she taught the piano in schools. She was featured in a radio program in 1973 in acknowledgment of her contribution to music in the Philippines. She received many prizes and awards. DISCOGRAPHY. PHOTOGRAPH.
Compositions
ORCHESTRA
Concerto No. 1 in E-Minor (pf and orch) (1972)
PIANO
Forever love (1960)
My dreams (1960)
My first etude de concert (1957)
VOCAL
Takip silim at bukam liwayway (S and cham ens) (1970)
Songs incl.:
Ballade I (1974)
Ikaw agn iahat sa aking buhay (S or T) (1956-1957)
Ina (B) (1973)
Magpahanggang langit (S or T) (1956-1957)
My wonderful world is you, ballad
You're my beloved (1954)
SACRED
I give you my heart on Christmas
I pray so hard (Dalangin) (S and cham ens) (1970)
My Christmas love affair
Church hymns, songs and Christmas carols
OPERETTA
Pasko'i Pag-Ibig (1975)
SA Lahat NG Oras, in 2 acts (1974)
Sumpaan Ng Puso, zarzuela, in 1 act (1975)
Zarzuelas on family planning, 5 sequels (1974-1975) (comm Asian Foundation and Zarzuela Foundation of the Philippines)
THEATRE
Of Songs that Spring from Love, musical (1971)
Kundi Lang SA Tio (1972)
INCIDENTAL MUSIC
Dearest One, film
A Million Thanks to You
MISCELLANEOUS
Aliw ng tugtagan
Ref. composer, 563

GANNON, Helen Caroll
American pianist, lecturer and composer. b. Baltimore, MD, April 13, 1898; d. December, 1939, Greensboro, NC. She studied at the Musical Academy in Philadelphia and at the Hyperion School of Music. In 1921 she studied under Harold Henry and Annette Middelschulte in Chicago. She received a diploma in the piano and voice from Averett College, Danville, VA, and was director of music from 1916 to 1935. She also studied at the Miessner Institute of Music and the Chicago Music College under Aronson, Ganz, da Violette and Putman. She performed in concerts and composed piano works and songs.
Ref. 461, 433

GANNON, Ruth Ellen
American teacher and composer. b. San Francisco, December 4, 1894. She obtained her B.M. in 1943 from the Chicago University Extension Conservatory. She was a member of the National Academy of Music, New York and wrote over 150 compositions.
Compositions
ORCHESTRA
Leisure moments, symphony
BAND
The President's march
VOCAL
Tribute to music and song (ch)
I'll stand by our grand old U.S.A. (1944)
Love hold me in your arms (1944)
My soul entwined (1949)
A red red rose (1947)
The right partner (1944)
SACRED
The Lord was seen in His glory, hymn
OPERA
Druscilla and Orestes
Egretta
Untried
Ref. 496

GANUKAM DSCHEMILET. See JAMILA

GARCIA, Maria Felicitas. See MALIBRAN, Maria Felicitas

GARCIA, Eduarda Mansilla de (pseud. Daniel)
Argentine singer, critic and composer. b. Buenos Aires 1835; d. 1892. She was music critic of *La Gaceta Musical* from 1879. Her son, Eduardo Garcia Mansilo was a composer.
Compositions
PIANO
Brunette, ballad
VOCAL
Songs incl.:
Cantares
October, romance (vce and pf)
Se alquilla, bolero
Yo no se si te quiero
Ref. 390

GARCIA ASCOT, Rosa
Spanish pianist, accompanist and composer. b. Madrid, 1906. She studied the piano under Enrique Granados, and the piano and composition under Manuel de Falla. She was the piano accompanist to Manuel de Falla on his debut in Paris. She settled in Mexico and composed piano pieces.
Compositions
ORCHESTRA
Concerto (pf and orch)
Suite
Ref. 9, 60, 100, 107, 354, 361

GARCIA DE BERIO. See MALIBRAN, Maria Felicitas

GARCIA MUNOZ, Carmen
Argentine pianist, lecturer, musicologist and composer. b. Buenos Aires, March 3, 1929. She studied at the Conservatorio Nacional de Musica y Arte Escenico and obtained a doctorate in composition and musicology under Rafael Gonzalez. She was a faculty member of the same institution. DISCOGRAPHY.
Compositions
ORCHESTRA
Concert in A-Minor (pf and orch)
El ruisenor, symphonic poem (2nd prize, Fabian Sevitzky competition)
CHAMBER
Pieces
VOCAL
Cathedral (2 S and cham orch)
Numerous songs
BALLET
La noche encantada

MISCELLANEOUS
Una montana pasando
Publications
Un Archivio Musical Americano. With Roldan Waldemar Axel. Buenos Aires: Eudeba, 1970
Ref. 70, 390, 563

GARCIA ROBSON, Magdalena (Magda)

Argentine pianist, lecturer and composer. b. Buenos Aires, January 28, 1916. At the Conservatorio Nacional de Musica y Arte Escenico she studied the piano under Corina H. de Lima and G. Kolischer, harmony under Athos Palma, counterpoint under J. Gil, fugue under A. Luzzatti, composition under R. Rodriguez and orchestration under C. Gaito. She taught at the conservatory and later became its director.
Compositions
ORCHESTRA
La cenicienta, symphonic poem (1939)
Tres bocetos sinfonicos (1951)
CHAMBER
Variaciones breves (fl, ob, bsn, cor anglais and pf) (1948)
Homenaje a César Franck (vln, vlc and pf)
Sonata criolla (vln, cl and pf) (prize, National Commission of Culture, 1942)
PIANO
Sonatina
Suite
Surena (1946)
VOCAL
Cancion de cuna (vce and pf) (1940)
Copla festiva (vce and pf) (1947)
Coplas de amores (S, vla, vlc and pf) (1947)
Coplas de soledad
Tres canciones infantiles (1944)
THEATRE
Escenas liricas on *Senor Corregidor* (B. Roldan)
Ref. 100, 390

GARDINER, Mary Elizabeth

Canadian pianist, choir conductor, teacher and composer. b. Toronto, August 23, 1932. She studied the piano under her mother and later with Elsie Bennett and composition under Samuel Dolin. Having graduated in the piano with honors in 1953 she became an A.R.C.T. and the following year graduated from the University of Toronto with honors in music. She also qualified as a high school teacher of English and vocal music but later resigned to give piano recitals, to accompany and to conduct church choirs and compose. She was president of a branch of the Registered Music Teachers' Association and of the Alliance for Canadian New Music Projects which sponsors festivals of contemporary music. She conducts workshops on contemporary Canadian piano music for teachers. DISCOGRAPHY. PHOTOGRAPH.
Compositions
ORCHESTRA
Concerto (pf, perc and str orch) (1977)
CHAMBER
Trilos (2 fl and pf) (1979)
Other works
PIANO
Footloose (Frederick Harris, 1955)
Modicums (1978)
Mosaic (1984)
Short circuits (1982)
VOCAL
What's in a name (ch) (1977)
Love is ... (vce and pf) (1982)
A pot of gold (vce and pf) (1982)
The rose (vce and fl) (1976)
SACRED
Gloria (ch; also w-ch) (1976, 1981)
Hosanna (ch) (1977)
Deck thyself, my soul (vce and pf) (1978)
Lazarus (vce, fl and pf) (1977)
Ref. composer, CMC

GARDNER, Kay

American flautist, conductor, lecturer and composer. b. Freeport, NY, February 8, 1941. She studied conducting at the University of Michigan from 1958 to 1961 and under Elizabeth Green. She researched and performed the flute and women's music and then played in symphony orchestras after studying under Nelson Hauenstein. In 1968 she founded the Norfolk Chamber Consort, with herself as the flautist and which gave concerts of avant-garde and contemporary music. She taught at the Norfolk State and the Old Dominican Universities. She entered the State University of New York at Stony Brook in 1972 and studied the flute under Samuel Baran. She received her M.Mus. in 1974. In 1977 she studied conducting under Antonia Brico in Denver and made her debut as a conductor at the National Women's Music Festival, Champaign, IL, in 1978. In the same year she founded the New England Women's Symphony in Boston which performs works composed and conducted by women.
Compositions
ORCHESTRA
Rain forest (1977)
BAND
The Victoria Woodhull march (1974)
CHAMBER
A rainbow path (fls, ww, small perc, hp and str ens) (1980)
Winter night, gibbous moon (3 picc, 3 fl, 3 a-fl, 2 bass fl) (1980)
Sailing song (fl or picc, vln, vla, 2 vlc, or ww qnt) (1978)
Prayer to Aphrodite (a-fl and str ens) (1975)
Crystal bells (fl, gtr, vlc and random insts) (1976)
The rising sun, variations on an American Blues Theme (fl or a-fl, ob or cor anglais, cl or b-cl, vlc, pf or hpcd)
Romance (fl or a-fl, vla or vlc and gtr) (1975)
Energies (fl, ob and vla) (1973)
Touching souls (a-fl, gtr and small perc) (1975)
Innermoods (fl or a-fl and gtr) (1975)
Seven modal improvisation studies (pf and bass or treble inst) (1978)
Moonflow (fl; also vce and pf) (1975)
Song studies (pf) (1979)
VOCAL
When we made the music (w-ch and pf) (1977)
The cauldron of Cerridwyn (w-vce, rec, lute, 2 vla da gamba, Baroque vln and small perc) (1978)
Changing (m-S and gtr) (1974)
The rootwoman (1982) (comm Kansas City Women's Chorus)
Sea chantress (vce, fl and cimbalom) (1978)
Sea gnomes music
The seasons (1982) (comm Arcady Chamber Players)
Thirteen songs, collection (m-S and gtr or autoharp) (1974)
Three Mother songs (m-S and gtr) (1977)
ELECTRONIC
Atlantis rising (fl or a-fl, vln or vla, vlc, prep pf, wood chimes and tape) (1975)
OPERA
Ladies' Voices (comm Southwest Chamber Opera)
A Short Opera (1981)
Ref. *Woman Artists News* Vol 8 No. 3, 474, 622, 625

GARDNER, Mildred Alvine

American pianist, accompanist, lecturer and composer. b. Quincy, IL, October 12, 1899. She studied under Edgar Stillman Kelley at the Cincinnati Conservatory from which she graduated with honors in the piano and composition and received a two-year graduate fellowship from the conservatory. She studied the piano under Marion Bauer (q.v.) in New York and Sigismund Stojowski. She was an accompanist and teacher in Cincinnati and New York from 1920 to 1933 and taught privately in Pittsburgh from 1935 to 1939 and at Fillion Studios from 1940 to 1968. She was on the faculty of Carlow College after 1969 and responsible for organizing composers' forums from 1939 to 1942. She received four Yaddo fellowships, two Pennsylvania Federation of Music Club awards and a NFMC award.
Compositions
CHAMBER
String quartet
Woodwind quartet
Sonata (2 pf)
VOCAL
The daisies
Madonna
September separation, song cycle
Ref. 142

GARELLI DELLA MOREA, Vincenza (Countess de Cardenas) (pseud. Centa della Morea)

Italian pianist and composer. b. Valeggio, Pavia, November, 1859. She received her musical training from Carlo Pedrotti, Giovanni Bolzono and Giovanni Sgambati. She wrote her *Ave Maria* when very young and it was successfully performed at the Carignano Theatre in Turin and later in Catania and Rome in 1888.
Compositions
ORCHESTRA
La ballata d'Arlecchino
CHAMBER
String quartet

PIANO
Berceuse (Turin: Bianchi)
Minuetto
Three piano pieces
VOCAL
Ballad (ded Queen Margherita) (Giudici; Strada)
Barcarola veneziana (vce and pf) (Turin: Allione)
Canzonette toscane (London: Augener)
Romances
SACRED
Ave Maria (4 vces and orch)
OPERA
Le nozze di Leporello, farce (1924)
OPERETTA
Incantesimo (G. Drovetti) (1915)
Il viaggio dei Perrichon, in 3 acts (Drovetti, after a comedy by Labiche)
THEATRE
L'esultanza della stirpe, pantomime (Count Gloria)
Idilio pastorale, pantomime (Princess Ruffo)
Ref. 85, 86, 347, 465

GARLAND, Kathryn
20th-century American composer.
Composition
OPERA
Ruth (1952)
Ref. 141

GARNETT, Louise Aires
20th-century American writer and composer. Her compositions included lyrical dramas and cantatas.
Publications
The Incidental Music. 1916.
Master Will of Stratford.
A Midwinter Night's Dream.
The Muffin Shop. 1908.
Ref. 268

GARR, Wieslawa
Polish composer. b. 1953.
Compositions
ORCHESTRA
Violin concerto
CHAMBER
Epilogue (4 perc) (Baudelaire) (1980)
VOCAL
N'importe ou hors du monde (S, hn, perc, hp, pf, 2 vla and 2 vlc) (1979)
SACRED
Liturgical mass
OPERA
Kominek zgasl
Ref. 465

GARRETT, Mrs. William
19th-century American composer.
Composition
PIANO
Emily polka (Boston: Russell & Richardson, 1857)
Ref. 228

GARRETT BROWNE, Mrs. See BROWNE, Augusta

GARRIGUES, Malvina. See SCHNORR VON CAROLSFELD, Malvina

GARSCIA-GRESSEL, Janina
Polish pianist, conductor, lecturer and composer. b. Cracow, March 12, 1920. She graduated with honors from the Wladyslaw Zelenski Higher School of Music in 1945, having studied the piano under Professor Olga Stolfa. At the Higher School of Music in Cracow she studied composition under A. Malawski and conducting under S. Wiechowicz. From 1946 she taught the piano at the W. Zelenski Higher School of Music and from 1951 at the State School of Music No. 1 in Cracow. She composes music mostly for children, from easy pieces for piano to combinations of other instruments. She lectured on music all over Poland and received the award of the Minister of the Board of Education, the gold cross of merit, the gold medal of Cracow City and the award of the Prime Minister. PHOTOGRAPH.
Compositions
CHAMBER
Impressions (4 vlc) (1973)
Song (ob, vlc and pf) (1966)
Trio (1967)
Miniatures (vlc and pf) (1971)
A magic drumstick (chil-perc) (1974)
Rhythmical world (pf and chil-perc) (1974)
Two sonatinas (vlc and pf) (1968)
Miniatures (d-b) (1970)
Oddments, 7 pieces (ob or bsn) (1969)
Trifles, op. 42
PIANO
Carols (4 hands) (1947)
Jas and Malgosia (4 hands) (Cracow: PWM, 1977)
Let's play piano duet, Parts I, II, III (1968-1976)
Hania, 6 pieces (1946)
Musical pictures (1955)
Winterliche Spiele fuer Klavier fuer Kinder
Numerous etudes, preludes, variations, sonatinas and other pieces mainly for teaching
VOCAL
Early Sunday morning (ch and folk band) (1951)
Folk are wondering (ch and folk band) (1951)
ELECTRONIC
The pensive pony (pf and tape)
Slushy weather (pf and tape)
THEATRE
Plays (Czechowicz and St. Wyspianski) (1944-1947)
Ref. composer, 52, 80, 118

GARSENDA, Countess of Provence
12th-century French troubadour. She was the granddaughter of Count Guilhelm de Forcalquier, who gave her in marriage to Alphonse II of Provence in 1193 as a token of the Forcalquiers' subjection to the house of Provence. The court of Alphonse II was a thriving cultural center and Garsenda became the patron of several poets. After Alphonse's death in 1209, Garsenda became Regent of Provence, later retiring to the Abbey of la Celle, near Brignoles.
Composition
VOCAL
Vos qui.m. semblatz dels corals amadors
Ref. 117, 213, 221, 303

GARSTKA, Ewa
20th-century Polish composer. She made her debut at the second all-Polish festival of contemporary music for children and youth, Lodz, 1979.
Ref. Polish Music 4/79

GARTENLAUB, Odette
French pianist, professor and composer. b. Paris, March 13, 1922. She was a brilliant young pianist and was awarded a first prize for the piano at the Paris Conservatoire when she was 14. She studied composition and won the Premiere Grand Prix de Rome for harmony, fugue and counterpoint in 1948. From 1959 she taught at the Paris Conservatoire where she became a professor. She performed as a piano soloist with major French and foreign orchestras. She married the teacher and composer Bernard Haultier and is a member of SACEM. PHOTOGRAPH.
Compositions
ORCHESTRA
Symphonie (Eschig)
Concerto (fl and orch)
Concertino (pf and orch) (Leduc)
Ouverture, symphonic movement
In memoriam, suite (hp and orch) (in memory of Jacqueline Ibert-Gillet)
Trois Caractères (trp and orch)
Illustrations musicales pour Horace et Polyeucte (Disque Bordas)
Illustrations musicales de Goupil à Margot d'Al (Pergot)
Quatre pièces d'orchestre pour le petit Prince
CHAMBER
Sextour (wind insts and perc)
Environnement (5 hp)
Quintet à vent (wind qnt)

Trio (fl, ob and bsn) (Leduc)
Chant (cl and pf) (Otto Harrassowitz)
Essai (b-trb and pf) (Rideau Rouge)
Paralleles (2 hp)
Pièces faciles (fl and hp) (Paris: Hortensia)
Pour le cor (hn and pf) (Rouge)
Profils (bsn and pf) (Transatlantiques)
Rite (1977) (trb and pf) (G. Bilaudot)
Silhouette (ob and pf) (Rouge)
Sonatine (bsn and pf) (Transatlantiques)
Sonatine (vln and pf) (Leduc)
Suite No. 1 and 2 (vlc and pf) (Leduc)
Three short pieces (trp and pf) (Eschig)
Improvisation (trb) (Hortensia, 1983)
Jell (Celtic hp)
Ponctuations (gtr) (Rouge, 1976)
Six pieces pour flute à bec (also fl and pf) (Rouge)
Sonata (hp)

PIANO
Mécanique (4 pf)
Zigzag (2 pf)
Petites études
Pièces faciles (Hortensia)
Sept petites Etudes
Trois pièces (Leduc)
Trois préludes (Leduc)
Variations (Leduc)

VOCAL
Espace sonore (2 vces and small orch)
La Cassandre d'espoir (mix-ch) (Leduc)
La danse de fous (mix-ch) (Leduc)
Melodies (vce and pf) (Leduc)

SACRED
Psaume No. 162 (soloist, ch and orch) (Eschig)

THEATRE
Genovefa, lyric scene

TEACHING PIECES
For piano (Rouge)

Publications
Preparation au dechiffrage instrumental pour tous les instruments avec initiation au graphisme contemporain. Paris. Rideau Rouge.

Ref. composer, 96, 457, 514

GARUTA, Lucia Yanovna

Latvian-Soviet pianist, lecturer and composer. b. Riga, May 14, 1902. After graduating in 1924 from the Conservatory of Riga where she studied composition under Wihtol and the piano under L. Goman she continued her piano studies under Ludmilla Gomane-Dombrowska in 1925, then in 1926 and 1928 under Isidor Philipp and Alfred Cortot in Paris and took lessons in theory from Paul Dukas. On her return to her homeland she gave concerts and taught. After 1940 she was lecturer in composition and theory at the Riga Conservatory. Her *Piano Concerto* was at first condemned by critics for offending the principles of Soviet art, but five years later it was applauded for its poetic beauty. DISCOGRAPHY.

Compositions

ORCHESTRA
Piano concerto (1951)
Meditacija, symphonic poem (1934)
Teika, symphonic poem (1932)
Zelta zirgs, symphonic poem (1960)
Mana dzimtene, variations (1936)

CHAMBER
Piano trio (1948)
Sonata (vln and pf)
Meditation (org)
Pieces (vln)
Pieces (vlc)

PIANO
Etudes
Preludes
Variations on Latvian folk themes (1933 and 1951)
Other pieces

VOCAL
Dziva kvele, oratorio (m-S and Bar) (Y. Rayinis) (1967)
Pavasara vejos, cantata (vces and orch) (1959)
Vins lido! cantata (to commemorate flight of Yuri Gagarin) (1961)
Pieces (ch and mix-ch)
Latvian folk songs
Living flame (m-S and Bar)
Romances, trios, duets

OPERA
Sudrabotais putns (1938)

Ref. 14, 17, 21, 70, 87, 223, 330, 420, 563

GARWOOD, Margaret

American pianist, lecturer and composer. b. New Jersey, March 22, 1927. She received an M.A. from Philadelphia Music Academy after studying composition under Miriam Gideon (q.v.) and orchestration under Romeo Cascarion. She received a Whiteside Foundation grant from 1965 to 1968 and a National Endowment for the Arts grant from 1973 and 1977. She taught the piano at the Philadelphia Music Academy from 1953 to 1969 and at the Settlement Music School from 1960 to 1969. She was the pianist and composer for Young Audiences, Inc. from 1965 to 1970 and resident composer at the MacDowell Colony.

Compositions

CHAMBER
A joyous lament for a gilly-flower (cl and pf)

VOCAL
Song cycles:
The cliff's edge (S and pf) (1969)
Love songs, 6 songs (e.e. cummings) (S and pf) (1964)
Six Japanese songs (vce, cl and pf)
Spring songs, 5 songs (e.e. cummings) (S and pf) (1970)

BALLET
Aesop's fables (comm Young Audiences) (1970)

OPERA
The Nightingale and the Rose, in 1 act (Oscar Wilde) (1973) (comm Franklin Concerts) (C. Fischer)
Rappaccini's Daughter
The Trojan Women, in 1 act (1967) (comm Suburban Opera Co.)

Ref. *Music Clubs* summer 1978, 40, 141, 142, 228, 347, 415, 494, 625

GARY, Marianne

Austrian professor and composer. b. Vienna, July 19, 1903.

Compositions

ORCHESTRA
Cello concerto (1957)
Piano concerto (1966)
Orchestral sonata in D (1967)
Orchestral sonatina (1967)
Dance suite in old style (1967)

VOCAL
Vom Lied und Heldentum der Ungenannten, oratorio (soloists, ch, org and orch) (1961)
Vorfruhling im Gebirge, cantata (composer) (soloists, ch and str orch) (1967)
Drei Agnes-Miegal-Lieder (vce and orch) (1962)
Sieben Weinheber-Lieder (soloists, ch and orch) (1964)
Seven Japanese love songs (composer) (soloists and orch) (1964)
Vier Goethe-Lieder (vce and orch) (1962)
Vier Weinheber-Lieder (vce and orch) (1963)
Lieder nach Gedichten von Fritz Stuber

Ref. 194, 457

GARZTECKA-JARZEBSKA, Irena

Polish pianist and composer. b. Kiev, May 31, 1913; d. Skarzysko Kamienna, November 14, 1963. She completed her piano studies at the State Conservatory, Warsaw, under the direction of M. Klimantt-Jacynowa and received her diploma in 1941. She studied composition under K. Sikorski, Warsaw, in 1942 and continued under his tuition at the State Music College in Lodz from 1947 to 1951.

Compositions

ORCHESTRA
Cztery portrety, symphony (1949)
Piano concerto (1952)
Violin concerto (1960)
Symphonic poem (1956)
Concertino (vln and orch) (1943)
Grafika (1962-1963)
Symphonic overture (1958)

CHAMBER
Adagio (vln and pf) (1941)
Andante (vln and pf) (1940)
Chamber sonata (vln and pf) (1950)
First burlesque (vln and pf) (1940)
Nocturne (vln and pf) (1941)
Second burlesque (vln and pf) (1949)
Suite of preludes (vln and pf) (1956)
The young violinist, 10 folk songs and dances (vln and pf) (1952)

PIANO
Obrazki na szkle, suite (2 pf) (1957)
Fantasy (1941)
Polish dances (PWM, 1954)
Prelude (1942)
Rondo (1942)
Short pieces for children (Czytelnik, 1943)

Six etudes (1958)
Suite (PWM, 1952)
Variations (1947)
VOCAL
Ptasie radio, cantata (J. Tuwim) (soloists, ch and orch) (1951)
Concerto (S and small sym orch) (1960)
Piesni julii, suite (m-S and cham ens) (1962)
Song cycle (M. Bialoszewski) (S and cham ens) (1960)
Chamber suite (S, str qrt and hp)
Mass songs
Ten children's songs (vce and pf) (1951)
Variations (folk texts) (S and pf) (1948)
Arrangements of folk songs for voice with piano
TEACHING PIECES
Pieces for various instruments and ensembles
Ref. 70, 118

GASCHIN-ROSENBERG, Fanny, Countess
German pianist and composer. b. Thorn, March 9, 1818. She studied the piano under Liszt, Thalberg and Henselt and was a distinguished performer. Several of her piano pieces imitated Chopin's style.
Compositions
PIANO
Bourache musicale, op. 11 (Bote)
Causerie musicale, op. 22 (Bote)
Charme brisé, poème harmonique in G-Major, op. 9 (Bote)
Emilie, Polka-Mazurka, op. 18 (Leuckart)
Hohenzollernmarsch, op. 25 (Furstner)
Mazurka in A-Major, op. 10 (Bote)
Pamela-Polka, no. 2, op. 15 (Heinrichshofen)
Papelitos, waltz, op. 24 (Furstner)
Poème harmonique, op. 10
Reverie, romance (Bote)
Schmetterlinge, waltz (Bote)
Souvenir de Lazienki, mazurka, op. 19 (Leuckart)
Steeple-chase-Polka, op. 21 (Leuckart)
Wanda-Polka, no. 1, op. 14 (Heinrichshofen)
Ref. 129, 276, 297, 347, 433

GASCOINA, Domna de. See ALAMANDA

GASPARINI, Jola
Italian pianist and composer. b. Genoa, March 4, 1882. She studied under her father Angelo Gasparini and Perosio Falconi.
Composition
ORCHESTRA
Works
CHAMBER
Piano pieces
Other pieces
VOCAL
Songs
SACRED
Three masses
OPERA
Ester (1908)
Lisia (1905)
OPERETTA
L'amour non e cieco
Come ando
Cose d'America
L'ultima beffa
Ref. 226, 502

GASTON, Marjorie Dean
20th-century American composer. She wrote chamber and organ music and songs.
Ref. 347

GATELY, Francis Sabine. See ROSE OF JESUS, Sister

GATES, Alice Avery
19th-century American composer.
Compositions
VOCAL
Bitter sweet
June slumber
Ref. 276, 292, 347

GATLIN, Mrs. Denby. See STANLEY, Helen Camille

GAUDAIRENCA. See CAUDAIRENCA

GAUTHIER, Brigitte (nee Choufour)
French composer. b. Paris, August 31, 1928.
Composition
CHAMBER
Improvisation et final (d-b) (Peters)
Ref. 80

GAUTHIEZ, Cecile
French lecturer and composer. b. Paris, March 8, 1873; d. France. She studied composition under Leon Saint-Requier, G. Bret and V. d'Indy at the Schola Cantorum in Paris where she taught harmony from 1920. She became Maitre of the Chapel of Notre Dame d'Auteuil in 1926 and mainly wrote church music.
Compositions
CHAMBER
String quartet
Sur les chemins, suite (pf)
Organ solos
VOCAL
Choral works
Lieder
Songs
SACRED
Ancilla Domini, mass (2 part chil-ch) (Schola Bureau Ed.)
Motets incl.:
Benedicta es tu (Paris: Schola Cantorum)
Communione calicis
Hodie Christus natus est
In me gratia omnis viae (Paris: Herelle)
Publications
Leçons pratiques de culture musicale. 1926.
L'harmonie au clavier. 1924.
Methode elementaire pour l'enseignement de l'ecriture musicale. 1919.
Ref. 9, 17, 23, 44, 100, 105, 347, 417

GAY, Sofia Maria Francesca (Marie Sophie)
French pianist, poetess, writer and composer. b. Paris, July 1, 1776; d. Brussels, March 5, 1852. She studied the piano under Steinbelt and composition under Candeille.
Compositions
PIANO
Goodbye, waltz (Gordon)
VOCAL
Cantata with orchestra
I am dreaming (Hopwood)
Moeris, romance (Durand: Gregh)
Chamber romances
Publications
Comedies and dramas incl.:
Laura d'Estela, novel.
Maria o la povera fanciulla.
Serenade.
Ref. 26, 105, 226, 260, 268, 276, 297, 347

GAYNOR, Jessie Love (Lovel) (nee Smith)
American pianist, teacher and composer. b. St. Louis, MO, February 17, 1863; d. Webster Groves, MO, February 20, 1921. She studied the piano, theory and harmony under Cady, Weidig, Goodrich and Louis Maas and taught in Chicago, St. Louis, and St. Joseph. She was the mother of Dorothy Gaynor Blake (q.v.).

Compositions
ORCHESTRA
When love was young, song (Coleman)
PIANO
Annie-an-Louise, waltz (4 hands)
Etudes
Reverie (also org) (Keller)
Teaching pieces
VOCAL
Quartets (m-vces and w-vces)
Approx. 50 songs incl.:
Album of seven songs
Cradle song
Fireflies
Five songs (Church)
Rose song collection
Songs and scissors
Songs of the child world
Songs to little folks
SACRED
Birth and the Resurrection
Christ Child in art, story and song (Hofer)
Christmas carols
Star of Bethlehem
Hymn, in 3 parts (w-vces) (Summy)
OPERETTAS
Seven Operettas incl.:
The First Lieutenant
The House that Jack Built
Pierre the Dreamer
Princess Bo-Peep
The Toy Shop
Publications
Elements of Musical Expression. 1907.
Bibliography
Hackett, Karleton. *Some American Songwriters. Negro Music Journal*. 1 July 1903: 213-217. Discusses 10 American composers separately as songwriters.
Ref. 8, 17, 40, 85, 105, 276, 292, 297, 307, 347, 353, 415

GAZAROSSIAN, Koharik

Armenian composer. b. Istanbul, 1908. She attended the Paris Conservatoire as a child. Her teachers were L. Levy, P. Fauchet, Paul Dukas, R. Ducasse and in America, E. Weiss. Her first works were performed in Paris in 1940.
Compositions
CHAMBER
Quintet
String quartet
PIANO
Album
Preludes
Suite
VOCAL
Symphonic work with soprano solo
Armenian poem
Thirty melodies
ARRANGEMENTS
Folk songs (R.P. Komitas)
Ref. 163

GEBUHR, Ann Karen

American pianist, professor and composer. b. Des Moines, IA, May 7, 1945. She received her B.M. (piano) in 1968 after studying under Alfonso Montecino and Dr. Joyce Gault; her M.M. (music theory) in 1971 and her Ph.D. (music theory) in 1983 from Indiana University. She studied composition under Dr. Frederick Fox and orchestration under Dr. Juan Orrego-Salas. She taught the piano and theory at the Indiana University from 1967 to 1969 and was assistant professor of music at the Northern State College, SD, from 1969 to 1976. She held the position of associate lecturer at Indiana University for two years and in 1984 became associate professor of music and chairlady of the department of theory and composition at the Houston Baptist University. She received several commissions and awards including first prize at the Contemporary Music Festival in Indiana in 1981.
Compositions
ORCHESTRA
Fanfare, variations, and fugue (1980)
CHAMBER
3 for 5 (fl, cel, timp, gong and tri) (1981)
Synthesis for three flutes
Prelude on Ein feste Burg (pf and org) (1983)
Floejtespil (fl) (1980)
Parodies on shapes (hpcd) (1982)
VOCAL
Ichabod (vce and orch) (1983)
SAI symphony (w-ch and inst trio)
Cycle of duets (Tennyson) (S and pf) (1973)
Helas (T and org) (1980)
A prairie sunset (S, fl, cl, trp, cel, timp and perc) (1977)
There is a lady sweet and kind (bar, fl and pf) (1982)
SACRED
Cantata for Good Friday (mix-ch, 2 fl and org) (1979)
Advent carol (w-ch)
Alleluia: Angelus Domini (mix-ch and handbells) (1983)
Bidding prayer (ch and org)
Canticle (mix-ch, 2 ob, 2 bsn, 2 timp and bells) (1973)
Lord, God of Love (mix-ch and org) (1969)
Psalm 8 (T, B, mix-ch, 2 fl and org) (1979)
Te Deum (soloists, ch, brass and tim)
Psalm 103 (S)
Two sacred songs (S)
OPERA
Brian Boru
Ref. 142

GEDDES-HARVEY, Roberta (Anne Catherine)

Canadian organist and composer. b. Hamilton, December 25, 1849. Her sacred oratorio was probably the first to be published by a Canadian composer. She was appointed organist at St. George's Parish in 1876, a post she held for 50 years. She graduated from Trinity College, Toronto in 1899 with a B.M. at the age of 50. Her contribution in music to her church, the city of Guelph and to Canada was unique for a woman of her time.
Compositions
ORCHESTRA
Pieces
PIANO
May Day, minuet
Swing song (Toronto: Whaley-Royce, 1908)
VOCAL
Bayonet (soloist and ch)
Lullaby (w-trio)
Round the camp fire (soloist and ch)
A baby's evensong (vce and pf)
Canada first (John H. Bernard) (Winnipeg: Bulman Bros., 1897)
The Canadian scout (vce and pf)
The daisy's answer (vce and pf)
Deux chansonnettes (Silver Clouds and the Noble Life) (vce and pf) (Boston: C. W. Thompson)
Good bye my summer (Richard Scrace) (Thompson, 1908)
Hurrah for the Union Jack (Bernard) (Bulman Bros. 1899)
Jessie McCrae (vce and pf)
Little maid from Germany (vce and pf)
Love quest (Thompson)
Our own (vce and pf)
Parting, duet (Thompson)
Queen Autumn (vce and pf)
Song of hope (Scrace) (Thompson, 1919)
The song of the leaves (Thompson)
Two little heads, duet
Victoria, the Rose of England, Canada's greeting to the Queen on her Diamond Jubilee (vce and pf) (Whaley-Royce, 1897)
A war song (ded Canadian contingent) (vce and pf) (Whaley-Royce, 1900)
Wayfarers (Scrace) (Thompson, 1908)
The wild North Sea (Thompson)
SACRED
Hymns: Hazelmere; Herberton; Kangra
Salvator (The Saviour) (Thompson, 1908)
Singing softly, A Christmas Song (A. Klugh) (Whaley-Royce)
We have kept faith, an answer to Lieut. Col. McCrae (Edna Jacques) (Thompson, 1919)
OPERA
La Terre Bonne or Land of the Maple Leaf (A. Klugh) (ca. 1903)
Ref. 307

GEERTSOM, Joanne van

17th-century Dutch composer.
Compositions
SACRED
XIV Motetta duarum vocum sive bicinia sacra Liber secundus, Vox I (Vox II: Basso continuo) 3 part (Rotterdam: Henrici de Bruyn, 1661)
Ref. 65

GEIGER, Constanze

Austrian pianist and composer. b. Vienna, 1836. She was the daughter of Joseph Geiger, composer of the opera *Wlasta*. She was a child prodigy, performing in public at the age of six.

Compositions

PIANO
Nocturnes
Romanze, op. 15
Waltzes, ops. 3, 8 and 9
VOCAL
Duettino (T, B and pf)
Lieder (vce and pf)
SACRED
Ave Maria, op. 4 (S, ch and org)
Other choral works
Ref. 226, 276, 347

GEIGER-KULLMAN, Rosy Auguste

German pianist and composer. b. Frankfurt-am-Main, June 20, 1886; d. Monterey, United States, January 4, 1964. She studied the piano under Carl Friedberg and later harmony and counterpoint under Iwan Knorr. She studied composition under Bernhard Sekles from 1910 to 1920 and orchestration under Carl Schuricht. In 1910 she became a member of the Frankfurter Tonkuenstlerverein, which performed 15 of her songs in 1911. Before World War II she left Germany and settled in New York, U.S.A. Her works were performed on radio and some of her songs sung by the tenor John Garris.

Compositions

ORCHESTRA
Symphony No. 1
Symphony No. 2
Concerto grosso (1967)
Variations (1916)
CHAMBER
String quartet
Violin, cello and piano sonatas
VOCAL
Drei Tagore Lieder (vce and orch) (Ries & Erler)
Orchestra songs from the Chinese flute
Five choruses (w-ch a-cap)
Sechs alte Minnelieder
Three song cycles
Vier Eichendorff-Lieder
Approx. 500 other songs
SACRED
Moses, oratorio (1931)
Jacob and Esau, cantata (1934)
Ruth and Boas, cantata (1934)
Two memorial cantatas for composer's mother and husband
OPERA
Columbus
Emanuela
Der Hut
Ritter Lancelot
Vogel Fuss (1936)
THEATRE
Tischlein deck dich, fairy tale
Ref. Ruth Engel - composer's daughter, 70, 111, 226

GENET, Marianne

American organist, teacher and composer. b. Watertown, NY, 1876. She studied under Hermann Korthewer, Guiseppe Ferrata, Isidor Philipp and Andre Bloch. She was the organist at St. Stephen's Church, Pittsburgh and taught privately.

Compositions

VOCAL
The simoon, desert drama (Bar and orch)
Blow, bugle, blow (m-ch)
God save the people (mix-ch and pf) (Broadcast Music Inc.)
Sea love (m-ch)
Songs incl.:
The Canton boat woman
First love, song cycle
Heigh O!
Invocation of Isis
Lotus blossom
My love is a blossom
At night on the terrace
SACRED
Hymn to the Night (1908)
Anthems
Songs
OPERETTA
The Green Sybil
Ref. 142, 190, 292, 465

GENGLIS (Genlis), Stephanie Felicité, Countess of Saint-Aubin

French harpist, writer and composer. b. Champcerie, January 25, 1746; d. Paris, December 31, 1830. She studied the harp under Goepffert and was considered a brilliant virtuoso. She composed mainly for the harp.

Publications

Methode de harpe. Paris, 1802.
Over 200 literary works including memoires and romances.
Ref. 276, 266

GENNAI, Emanuela

Italian composer. b. 1886.

Compositions

OPERA
Berta alla Siepe (Milan, 1908)
Cinderella (1910)
Ref. 431

GENTEMANN, Sister Mary Elaine

American organist, pianist, professor and composer. b. Fredericksburg, TX, October 4, 1909. She obtained her B.Mus. from Our Lady of the Lake College, San Antonio and M.Mus. from the American Conservatory, Chicago and at Columbia University she did the doctoral equivalent in composition under Otto Luening. She also studied at the Juilliard School of Music and at Teachers College in New York. In 1963 and 1968 she was named composer of the year by the Texas Music Catholic Music Educators' association. The National Guild of Piano Teachers cited her as a composer of distinction in 1967. From 1929 she was on the faculty of Our Lady of the Lake College, later becoming professor of the piano and the organ.

Compositions

PIANO
Duets
Solos
VOCAL
Fifteen chant melodies
Meine lieder (German text)
Mes chansons (French text)
Le mie canzoni (Italian text)
Mis canciones (Spanish text)
Thirty-one familiar Christmas tunes
Unison choruses
SACRED
Suscipi, Domini, motet
Anthems
Fifteen well-known hymns
Hymnals
Masses

Publications

Piano books.
Recorder teaching material.
Teachers' manual.
Ref. 77, 137, 142, 347, 625

GENTIL, Alice (Mrs. Lea Alice Lambert-Gentil)

Swiss composer. b. La Chaux de Fonds, September 7, 1872.

Composition

PIANO
Nocturne (1896) (in Album des compositeurs neuchatelois, La Chaux de Fonds, Willie & Cie, 1896; also Lausanne: Foetisch
Ref. 101

GENTILE, Ada

Italian pianist, lecturer and composer. b. Avezzano, L'Aquila, July 26, 1947. She studied at the Conservatory of San Pietro a Majella of Naples (piano diploma, 1970) and at the Conservatory of Santa Cecilia in Rome from where she graduated in composition under Irma Ravinale in 1974. She did postgraduate studies under Goffredo Petrassi at the Academy of Santa Cecilia from 1975 to 1976. She taught at the conservatories of Trieste and Frosinone. After a series of piano concerts she decided to concentrate on composition. Her works have been performed on national and Vatican radio and in festivals of international contemporary music. One of her compositions for orchestra won a prize in the 1976 G. Marinucci composition competition in San Remo. She teaches at the Conservatory of Santa Cecilia. PHOTOGRAPH.

Compositions

ORCHESTRA

Veraenderungen (1976)

CHAMBER

Composizione No. 3 (cham ens) (1974)
Episodi (cham ens) (1974)
Sintesi (cham ens) (1975)
Diaeresi (str qrt) (1981)
Similarity (cl and str trio) (mention, Filarmonica Umbra chamber music competition)
Trio (vln, vla and vlc) (1968)
Adagio (fl and pf) (1968)
Together (vlc and cl) (1978)
Come dal nulla (cl) (Ricordi, 1984)
Trying (pf) (1980)

Ref. composer, Donne in Musica 1982, 622

GENTY, Mlle.

French composer. ca. 1800.

Compositions

VOCAL

Songs incl.:
Receuil de chansons avec accompagnement de guitarre par musique et par tablature (Paris: Le Chevardiere)
Receuil de chanson avec un accompagnement de guitarre (Paris: Mlle. Vendome)

Ref. 125

GEORGE, Lila-Gene

American pianist, teacher and composer. b. Sioux City, IA, September 25, 1918. She studied at the University of Oklahoma, where she obtained a B.A. in 1939 and a D.Mus. in 1940. She did postgraduate study at Northwestern University in 1950, Mills College from 1950 to 1953 and at Columbia University under Otto Luening and Vladimir Ussachevsky. She studied the piano privately under her mother, Lila Plowe Kennedy and also under Egon Petri, Herbert Ricker, Silvio Scionti and Edward Steuermann. She studied composition under Nadia Boulanger (q.v.) in France during the summers of 1971 to 1974. In 1969 she received a Sigma Alpha Iota composer's award. She was a solo pianist with the Oklahoma City Little Symphony Orchestra from 1935 to 1937 and with the Houston Symphony Orchestra in 1956. She taught the piano privately in South America from 1948 to 1952, New York from 1961 to 1965 and Houston from 1955 to 1966, and in 1971. From 1971 she adjudicated contests in Oklahoma and Houston.

Compositions

CHAMBER

Trio (vln, hn and pf) (1963) (Award, 1969)
Quest (fl and pf) (1979)
Quintad, suite (vln and vlc)
Sonata (vln and pf) (1964)
Introduction and dance (fl) (1971)
Preludes and postludes (1965, 1973, 1974)

PIANO

L'étang
Jeux d'esprit (1973)
Suite (1980)
Three adjectives (1973-1975)

VOCAL

For winter's rains and ruins are over, madrigal (1965)
Merry-go-round for Christmas, madrigal (1965)

Ref. composer, 84, 142, 190, 477, 625

GERARD, Miss

19th-century American composer.

Composition

MISCELLANEOUS

Fire polka (1854) (New York: Dressler & Clayton)

Ref. 228

GERARD, Mrs. J. See DROSTE, Doreen

GERCHIK, Vera Petrovna

Soviet choir conductor, editor, teacher and composer. b. Yekaterinoslav, Dnepropetrovsk, December 6, 1911. She studied composition under N. Miaskovsky at the Moscow Conservatory, graduating in 1937. She was musical director of the Moscow Radio from 1937 to 1938 before teaching theoretical subjects at a children's music school. From 1942 to 1948 she taught theoretical subjects at the M. Ippolitov-Ivanov Music School and from 1953 to 1955 at the music school of the Timiryazev region. She conducted a children's choir and was editor for the Central Music Publishing Company.

Compositions

ORCHESTRA

Symphony (1937)

CHAMBER

Fantasy on Russian themes (vln and pf) (1944)

PIANO

Five pieces (1937)
Fugue (1931)
Poema (1933)
Sonata No. 1 (1934)
Sonata No. 2 (1943)
Sonata No. 3 (1946)
Two children's pieces (1953)

VOCAL

Chetyre cheloveka (Z. Lyubarskaya) (ch and pf) (1938)
Cycle of romances (Pushkin, Lermontov, Tiutchev) (ch, vln and vlc) (1943)
Druzhba (S. Ostrovogo) (ch and pf) (1939)
Kazachya pesnya (ch and pf) (1937)
Molodost strany (P. Kudryavtsev) (ch and pf) (Muzgiz, 1948)
My yug rodimyi zashchitim (Z. Lyubarskaya) (ch and pf) (1942)
Pesnya molodykh bortsov za mir (Martynov) (ch and pf) (Muzgiz, 1950)
Pokhod zenitchikov (T. Solodarya) (ch and pf) (1942)
Polyarnaya vakhta (Ryzhov) (ch and pf) (1939)
Sovietski prostio chelovek (V. Levedev Kumach) (ch and pf) (1937)
Vyshla v pole molodezh (Y. Tereshchenko) (ch and pf)) (Muzgiz, 1951)
Zolstaya Ukraina (ch and pf) (1938)
Other works (ch and pf)
Pesnya o Raimonde Dien
Pesnya shkolnykh druzei
Romances (Pushkin, Lermontov, O. Fadeyeva, O. Vysheslavtseva and other Soviet poets) (vce and pf) (1937-1955)

OPERETTA

Lesniye Chudessa (1967)

Ref. 21, 87, 330, 441

GERE, Florence Parr. See PARR-GERE, Florence

GERENYI, Ilse

B. 1929.

Composition

PIANO

Hommage (Doblinger)

Ref. Blackwell catalogue (Oxford)

GERING, Karoline

19th-century Swiss composer.

Composition

VOCAL

Fritzchens Morgenlied (vce and pf) (1812)

Ref. 101

GERLACH, Clara Anna. See KORN, Clara Anna

GERMANO, Vittoria

Composition

OPERA

Il governatore ed il ciarlatano (1897)

Ref. 431

GERRISH-JONES, Abbie

American organist, pianist, critic, writer and composer. b. Vallejo, CA, September 10, 1863; d. Seattle, WA, February 5, 1929. Her father, Samuel Howard Gerrish, was a flautist and her mother, Sarah Jane Rogers, an opera singer. Abbie studied voice, the piano, harmony, the organ and later theory and composition. Her teachers were Charles Winter, Hugo Mansfeldt, Daniel Ball, Humphrey J. Stewart and Wallace Sabin. She also studied languages, psychology, philosophy, writing and verse. *Priscilla,* her first work for the stage, was written when she was in her early 20's and is the first complete opera, libretto and score to have been written by an American woman. She was music critic and correspondent for several journals and received prizes and awards.

Compositions

PIANO

Barcarolle
Marguerite waltz
Prelude (1906) (prize, J. Hofmann)
A psalm of life (after Longfellow)
Tarantelle

VOCAL

Five song cycles (one after R.L. Stevenson's Child's Garden of Verses)
Over 100 songs

SACRED

Quartet for mixed voices (Sarah Jane Rogers)

OPERA

Abou Hassan or The Sleeper Awakened, in 3 acts (based on an Arabian Nights tale)
The Andalusians, in 3 acts (Percy Friars Valentine)
The Aztec Princess
The Milk-Maids Fair, in 1 act (composer)
Priscilla, in 4 acts (1885-1887)
Sakura-San, Japanese (Gerda Wismer Hofmann)
The Snow Queen, music drama (Gerda Wismer Hofmann, based on H.C. Andersen's fairy tale)
Two Roses (based on Grimm's fairy tale)

TEACHING PIECES

Rhythmic songs, rhythmic games and rhythmic dances (in the curriculum at the University of California)

Ref. 292, 304, 353, 415

GERSTMAN, Blanche Wilhelminia

South African double bassist, pianist, accompanist, lecturer and composer. b. Cape Town, April 2, 1910; d. Cape Town, August 11, 1973. Of English parentage, she adopted the name of her foster parents at the age of 12. At the same time she commenced lessons in harmony under Victor Hely-Hutchinson. She studied at the South African College of Music from 1928 where she became the first student to obtain a B.Mus. She studied under W.H. Bell and received piano lessons from Colin Taylor. She was the official accompanist and pianist of the SABC in Cape Town for ten years, after which she lectured on harmony and counterpoint at the South African College of Music, until she was appointed principal double bassist in the Cape Town Municipal Orchestra. In 1950 a scholarship from the South African Performing Rights Society enabled her to study under Howard Ferguson at the Royal College of Music in London. On her return from London in 1952, she resumed her position in the orchestra, remaining a member until 1961, when she was appointed lecturer in harmony and counterpoint at the new department of music at the University of Pretoria. In June 1963 she resigned to become double bassist in the Durban Civic Orchestra. She returned to Cape Town in 1964 to resume her position as lecturer in harmony and counterpoint at the College of Music.

Compositions

ORCHESTRA

Serenade to starlight (pf and orch)
Orchestrations of Don Quixote (Meinkes); Andenken (Beethoven); In questa tomba oscura (Beethoven)
Melody (str trio; also school orch) (1957)
Minuet (str trio; also school orch) (1957)
Fear in my heart, waltz
Paraphrase of Grieg's Ich liebe dich (1937)
Prelude (1949)
A Story (str trio; also school orch) (1957)
Table Mountain overture (1958)

CHAMBER

Fanfare for Jan van Riebeeck Festival (1952)
Vorausnahme, song prelude (vln and strs) (1938)
Out of the Christmas Stocking, suite (strs; also pf) (1947) (composition prize)
Romanze (vln and pf) (1929)
Serenade and minuet (strs)
Serenade and scherzo (1951)
Sonata (vln and pf) (1951-1952)
Bagatelle (vln; also vln and pf) (1928 or 1929)

PIANO

Ballade
Caprice (1929)
Intermezzo in D-Flat Major (1947)
Intermezzo in D-Major (1932)
Intermezzo in F-Major (1947)
The pink faced monkey with the big ears
Prelude and fugue in A-Minor (1928)
Scherzo (1932)
Study (1928)
Variations on a theme by Rignini: Vieni amore (1950)

VOCAL

Branders (J. Celliers) (orch or pf and S or m-S) (1936)
The country faith (N. Gale) (Bar and orch or m-S) (1943)
Drie liedere (C. Weich) (S and orch) (1934-1935)
Epitaph (Walter de la Mare) (S and orch) (1928)
Have you seen but a white lily grow? (B. Jonson) (S and orch) (1928)
Hellas (Shelley) (S, w-ch and orch) (1928)
Ode to South Africa (I.D. du Plessis; trans G. Roos) (S, vce qrt, mix-ch and orch) (1947)
Only in dreams (W. Leftwich) (S and orch) (1942)
Vaalvalk (W.E.G. Louw) (S and orch) (1934) (1937)
Voice in the night (J. Galsworthy) (S and orch) (1942)
Fareweil my lute (T. Wyatt) (Bar, ww and strs; also Bar, ww, perc and strs) (1937)
Fruehlingslied (L.H.C. Holty) (S and strs or pf) (1930)
Hoor jy my? (J. Malan) (vce, hp and strs)
Die lied van die stem (Malan) (vce, hp and strs)
Thuismarsch (Heurkes) (double vce qrt and pf)
Songs incl.:
Ariel's songs from The Tempest (Shakespeare) (S and cel) (1946)
As those we love decay (J. Thomson) (m-S or Bar and pf)
Blow, blow thou winter wind (Shakespeare) (S and pf) (1933)
The donkey (G.K. Chesterton) (m-S or Bar and pf)
How sweet the moonlight sleeps upon this bank (Shakespeare) (m-S or Bar and pf)
Huweliksgebed (Weich) (m-S or Bar and pf or org)
Kontras, song cycle No. 2 (X. Haagen) (m-S and pf)
Kruger song 1968 (Celliers) (Bar and pf)
Die lied van 'n vrou, song cycle (E. Eybers) (S and pf) (1958)
May sweet oblivion lull Thee (anon) (m-S and pf) (1938)
Nagrit (N.P. van Wyk Louw) (S and pf) (1948)
Ontmoeting, song cycle No. 1 (Haagen) (m-S and pf)
Swayeth my linden (F. Strindberg from Marriage with Genius) (S and pf) (1937)
Die waterjaarlied (G.A. Watermeyer)

SACRED

Uit die Passie, Easter cantata (Louw) (mix-ch and orch) (1941-1946)
Come ring the merry bells (composer) (unison ch and pf; also mix-ch and orch)
Maria (Eybers) (m-S and orch)
Maria (Louw) (m-S and orch) (Bosworth)
Requiem (R.L. Stevenson) (m-S and orch) (1928)
Die boodskap aan Maria, Christmas cantata (van Wyk Louw) (m-S, mix-ch and org) (1945)
Bethlehem's Star, carol (T. Holloway) (w-ch)
Heilige nag (Eybers) (w-ch, hp and strs)
The Lord's Prayer (w-ch a-cap; also m-S or Bar and pf) (1934) (1957)
Psalm 8 (mix-ch) (1970)
Book of choruses for Sunday school (composer) (vce and pf) (1951)
Did the Wise Men know?, carol (2 w-vces and pf)
The Little Babe of Bethlehem, carol (with J. Ross) (vce and pf)
O Lord God of Israel (2 or 3 S and org) (1953)
Psalm 23 (Cont or B-Bar and pf) (1957)
A Song for St. Cecilia's Day 1687, (J. Dryden) (w-vces and pf) (1956)

BALLET

Pieces for ballet, children's pieces (1953)
We shall endure (2 pf)

THEATRE

The Ox and the Ass at the Crib, for radio (strs)

Ref. composer, 22, 26, 44, 70, 81, 175, 184, 377, 622, 646

GERTRUDE OF HELFTA, Saint

German nun of Helfta in Saxony. b. 1256; d. 1302. She spent her whole life in the convent at Helfta, composing sacred music and revising some of the liturgy.

Ref. 502

GERZSO, Angela

19th-century Hungarian composer.

Compositions

VOCAL

Arra kérlek kis madárka (vce and pf) (Rózsavölgyi)
Azt mondják, szépek a pesti lányok (vce and pf) (Nador)
Ha Félnezek a csillagos égre (vce and pf) (Rózsavölgyi)
Hamar, hamar, ide ezt a kulacsot (vce and pf) (Rózsavölgyi)
Ha te tudnád (vce and pf) Rózsavölgyi)
Kelö napnak aranyos sugára (vce and pf) (Rózsavölgyi)
Minket sirat Kossuth Lajos (vce and cimbalom) (Nador)
Most ismerem csak az igaz banátot (vce and pf) (Nador)
Nincsen annyi rózsabokor (vce and pf) (Rózsavölgyi)

Ref. 297

GESELSCHAP, Maria

Pianist, teacher and composer. b. Batavia, Dutch East Indies, December 15, 1894. A pupil of L. Ehlert in Wiesbaden, then of Scharwenka in Berlin, she continued her studies under Ferruccio Busoni in Boston and in New York. She studied composition under A. Reuss. As a concert pianist she was widely applauded. She lived in Munich and passed Busoni's teachings on to her pupils. She composed piano sonatas, other piano works and lieder.
Ref. 70, 105

GESSLER, Caroline

American teacher and composer. b. Indiana, PA, March 7, 1908. She studied at Indiana University, privately under Harvey Gaul and at the Fillion Studios in Pittsburgh. From 1929 to 1970 she taught in public schools, but between 1944 and 1949 she also taught at Fillion Studios. From 1970 she taught privately. She won three first prizes in Pennsylvania Federation of Music Clubs contests.

Compositions
ORCHESTRA
Creation for strings, 3 mvts
VOCAL
I wait alone beside the sea (w-ch and pf)
Cycle of children's songs
SACRED
Bless the Lord, O my soul (mix-ch)
Give ear to my prayer (ch)
God is our hope (ch)
O let the nations be glad (mix-ch and keyboard)
Psalm of the harvest (mix-ch and keyboard)
A psalm of trust (ch)
Songs of praise (mix-ch)
OPERA
Le Diable à Yvetot
Ref. composer, 40, 142, 190, 307, 347

GEST, Elizabeth

20th-century American arranger, teacher and composer. She studied at the Peabody Institute, Baltimore, the Institute of Musical Art, New York and under Nadia Boulanger (q.v.) in Paris. She gave piano courses at the Women's College of the University of North Carolina and similar institutions and gave numerous concerts.

Compositions
ORCHESTRA
North American tunes for rhythm orchestra
CHAMBER
Jubilee (vln and pf)
PIANO
Duos
Solos
Teaching pieces
VOCAL
Songs incl.:
Down to the sea
I'm not weary yet
The Lighthouse (Longfellow)
ARRANGEMENTS
Londonderry Air; Morris dance on old English tunes; Song of India (pf, 4 hands) (Rimsky-Korsakoff)

Publications
Betty and the Symphony Orchestra.
What Every Junior Should Know About Music.
Ref. 40, 292, 341, 353

GEYER, Marianne

Austrian composer. b. Vienna, February 20, 1883. She lived in Berlin. She composed songs with guitar accompaniment.
Ref. 226

GEYER, Stefi (nee Schulhess)

Hungarian violinist and composer. b. Budapest, June 23, 1888.

Composition
CHAMBER
A cadenza to Mozart's third violin concerto (Budapest: Harmonia, 1911)
Ref. 7, 226

GEYMULLER, Marguerite Camille-Louise de (Mrs. Sarasin)

Swiss pianist and composer. b. Le Havre, France, March 5, 1897. She studied the piano under Ludovic Breitner and harmony, counterpoint and composition under Alexander Denereaz at the Lausanne Conservatory. She was advised in composition by H. Swarowsky, Max Conrad and Walter Rehberg. In 1951 and 1952 she attended seminars and lectures given by Hindemith in Zurich. In 1958 she married Hans Franz Sarasin, president of the Chamber of Basle. She was a member of the Association des Musiciens Suisses and her works were performed on Swiss radio, at the Mozarteum, Salzburg and in concerts in Switzerland. PHOTOGRAPH.

Compositions
CHAMBER
Sonata (2 cl and pf) (1928)
PIANO
Fugue
Morceaux faciles (1961-1966)
Le moulin (poem by Verhaeren) (1918-1919)
Petite fantaisie (1918)
Sonata (1919)
VOCAL
Deux fables de La Fontaine (1948)
French songs (1930-1960)
German songs (1930-1960)
Le heron (vce, fl and str qrt) (1971)
Italian songs, incl. Tre Liriche di R. Bacchelli (1939)
Rilke Lieder (1964)
Six morceaux pour enfants (1960)
Ref. composer, 101, 206, 457

GEYRING, E. (pseud.)

19th-20th-century Austrian composer.

Compositions
CHAMBER
Quintet (cl and strs)

Bibliography
Musical Times, 67: 173.
Ref. 41

GHANDAR, Ann

Australian lecturer and composer. b. Adelaide, November 1, 1943. She obtained an M.A. (English) at the Australian National University, Canberra in 1970. Then, having studied under Lance Dossor and Righard Meale at Elder Conservatory, Adelaide, and under Larry Sitsky at Canberra School of Music and at Southampton University, she obtained a B.Mus. in 1974. She has been a lecturer in music at the University of New England, Armidale, New South Wales. PHOTOGRAPH.

Compositions
ORCHESTRA
Serein (1974)
CHAMBER
Haloes (pf qrt) (1975)
Six pieces (str trio) (1975)
Sonata (fl and pf) (1973)
PIANO
The Earth sings MI-FA-MI (1973)
Paraselene (1973)
...uncertain comets chance-drafting...(1973)
VOCAL
The prisoners (S, fl, vlc and pf) (1975)
Recollections of a Latvian song (1973)
Ref. composer, 457

GHARACHE-DAGHI, Sheyda

20th-century composer.

Composition
FILM MUSIC
Downpour (1972)
Ref. 326

GHERTOVICI, Aida

Israeli teacher and composer. b. Cetatea-Alba, Rumania, 1919. She graduated from the Bucharest Conservatory. She gave performances with orchestras in Rumania and abroad.

Compositions
VIOLIN
I postasi on a Hebrew theme, 12 studies of modern virtuosity (1972) (OR-TAV Music Publ.)

MISCELLANEOUS
Hypostasis
Publications
Dont and Gavinies Studies.
Revision of Paganini Caprices.
Tartini Sonata in G-Minor. (1960-1962).
Ref. 457

GHIGLIERI, Sylvia
American harpsichordist, pianist, professor and composer. b. Stockton, CA, March 13, 1933. She studied the piano under Egon Petri and Alexander Liebermann at Mills College, CA, from 1949 to 1951, and obtained a B.Mus. from Dominican College, San Rafael in 1954. She studied the piano under Gyorgy Sandor at the Music Academy of the West, Santa Barbara, and then under Robert Casadesus and Jean Casadesus at the Ecole de Beaux Arts, Fontainebleau, France. In 1961 she received an M.Mus. from the University of the Pacific, where she studied under Stanworth Beckler. She did postgraduate study at the Eastman School of Music in 1969 and Northwestern University in 1971. She studied the harpsichord under Laurette Goldberg in Oakland, CA, in 1972. She gave piano concerts in San Francisco and Europe from 1954 to 1955 and appeared as a soloist with the Modesto and Stockton symphony orchestras from 1950 to 1969. From 1973 she also performed as a harpsichord player. She joined the faculty of California State College in 1961, became an associate professor in 1970 until 1975 and in 1975 became professor of music.
Compositions
PIANO
Sonata
Three Irish pieces (1959)
VOCAL
Pieces (ch and orch)
SACRED
Psalm 56 (ch and orch) (1963)
Ref. 40, 84, 142, 206, 341

GHIKA-COMANESTI, Ioana
Rumanian composer. b. Bolintin, Ilfov, June 6, 1883. She studied theory, solfege and harmony under Dimitri Kiriac and harmony and counterpoint under Constantin Brailoiu in Bucharest.
Compositions
VOCAL
Cîntare de sărbătorirea maestrului D.G. Kiriac (composer) (mix-ch)
Colinda (folk words) (mix-ch and pf; also 3 vces)
Marşul Văii Trotuşului (composer) (mix-ch)
Vara (unison ch)
A venit un lup (G. Cosbuc) (vce and pf)
Acul (G. Castriseanu) (vce and pf)
Anotimpuri (3 vces)
Cel mai bun vin (G. Dudu) (vce and pf)
Cercul (G. Haju) (vce and pf)
Cîntecul păstorului (E. Ravent) (2 vces and pf)
Craciunul (L. Dans) (2 vces and pf)
Marş de primăvară (Anton Pann) (2 vces and pf)
Oita (S. Dimitriu) (vce and pf)
Păsărica şi cuibul (Dudu) (vce and pf)
Pe cimpea verde (Dimitriu) (2 vces and pf)
Primavara (Rusescu-Focsani) (2 vces and pf)
Rîndunelele (Dudu) (vce and pf)
Sint roman (2 vces and pf)
Sosirea berzelor (Dimitriu) (vce and pf)
La vie (Dimitriu) (2 vces and pf)
SACRED
Cîntările Liturghiei Sf. (Ioan Gura-de-Aur) (mix-ch) (Bucharest: Ed Socec)
Imn închinat Crucii roşii (Horia Furtuna) (mix-ch) (Bucharest: Ed Caraianu)
Pre tine te lăudăm (mix-ch)
Sfinte Dumnezeule (mix-ch or m-ch)
Ref. 44, 196

GHILARDI, Syra
Italian pianist, choral conductor, teacher and composer. b. Lucca, November 9, 1888. She studied the piano under Maestro de Luca and composition under Luporini. She was active as a choral conductor and director of the Choir Piccole e Giovani Italiene and as a teacher at the School of Music in Livorno, Italy. She married Maestro Giuseppe Rapallo Cianetti.
Compositions
ORCHESTRA
Pieces
CHAMBER
Piano pieces
VOCAL
In barca (m-ch) (1924)
Inno delle piccole, anthem
Ref. 105

GHOSHA
Legendary Indian character, singer and composer of hymns of invocation to the Asvins, demi-gods who were the forerunners of dawn. The revelation of the Veda is attributed to her. Living the ideal spiritual life, she performed religious rites, sang hymns and discussed the problems of death and God with the great philosophers. Reference to her is found in the Rigveda.
Ref. 414

GIACCHINO CUSENZA, Maria
Italian organist, concert pianist, lecturer and composer. b. Palermo, 12 October 1898; d. Palermo 6 August 1979. 1898; d. 1979. She came from a musical family and her father was her first teacher. She gave her first public performance at the age of five. She graduated from the Regio Conservatory of Palermo after studying the piano under Alice Ziffer and under the organ and organ composition under Guido Alberto Fano. She also studied under Alice Baragli and Alfredo Casella and composition under Favara and Pilati. In 1933 she founded the Quintetto Femminile Palermitano, which performed contemporary compositions. She toured throughout Italy as a concert pianist and formed the Trio Siciliano with violinist Teresa Porcelli and cellist Giuseppe Martesano. She founded a piano school in Palermo where she taught her own methods. She also taught at the Liceo Cherubini and the Regio Conservatory of Palermo.
Compositions
CHAMBER
Pieces (small ens)
PIANO
Allegretto con sussiego
Basso ostinato (1936)
La canzone di giugno
Piccola serenata
Sei personaggi in cerca di esecutori, album of easy pieces
TEACHING PIECES
Arpeggi per pianoforte
Esercizi tecnici pianistici (2 vols)
Ref. composers sister, 56, 94, 502 (also see ADDENDA)

GIACOMELLI, Genevieve-Sophie Bille
French soprano and composer. d. 1819. She composed and sang her own chamber songs.
Ref. 465, 502

GIBBS, Prue
20th-century Australian composer.
Compositions
THEATRE
The French Revolution (2 vces, fl, cl, gtr, pf, dr and vlc)
INCIDENTAL MUSIC
Hamlet on Ice (1973)
Ref. 442

GIBSON, Isabella Mary (nee Scott)
Scottish harpist, singer and composer. b. Edinburgh, 1786; d. Edinburgh, November 28, 1838. She was related to Sir Walter Scott and ran a boarding school for young ladies in Edinburgh. R.A. Smith consulted with her in the composition of his songs and duets.
Compositions
VOCAL
Loch-na-gar, song (R.A. Smith's Scottish Minstrel)
SACRED
Psalm tunes in Dr. Andrew Thomson's Sacred Harmony, (1820) and in Steven's Church Music (Turnbull, 1833)
Ref. 6, 85, 347

GIBSON, Louisa
English writer and composer. b. London, 1833. She composed songs.
Publications
A First Book on the Theory of Music Applied to the Pianoforte. London, 1876.
Ref. 226, 433

GIBSON, Mrs. Henry. See SPAIN-DUNK, Susan

GIDEON, Miriam

American pianist, professor and composer. b. Greeley, CO, October 23, 1906. She studied the piano under Hans Barth in New York and Felix Fox in Boston. She obtained a B.A. in 1926 from the College of Liberal Arts, Boston University and an M.A. (musicology) from Columbia University in 1946. She studied composition privately in New York under Lazare Saminsky from 1931 to 1934 and Roger Sessions from 1935 to 1943. In 1970 she received her doctorate in sacred music and composition from the Jewish Theological Seminary of America. She was a lecturer in the department of music of Brooklyn College from 1944 to 1954 and from 1955 on the music faculty of the Jewish Theological Seminary. In 1971 she was appointed professor of music at City College, City University, New York. In 1948 she was awarded the Bloch prize for choral work and received the National Federation of Music Clubs and ASCAP award for contribution to symphonic music in 1969. In 1974 she was given a National Endowment of the Arts grant for an orchestral work with voice and was elected to the Collegium of Distinguished Alumni of Boston University. She was on the board of governors of the AMC, the AMA, the League of Composers and the ISCM. Her compositions have been performed in the United States, Europe and South America and by the London, Prague, Tokyo and Zurich symphony orchestras. DISCOGRAPHY. PHOTOGRAPH.

Compositions

ORCHESTRA

Symphonia brevis (comm City College Orchestra of New York, 1953) (ACE)
Allegro and andante (1940)
Epigrams (1941)
Lyric piece for string orchestra (comm City College Orchestra of New York 1941) (ACE, New York)
Two Movements (1953)

CHAMBER

Divertimento for woodwind quartet (1948) (ACE)
Lyric piece for string quartet (1941) (ACE)
Quartet for strings (1946) (ACE)
Three cornered piece (fl, cl and pf) (1936)
Trio (cl, vlc and pf)
Air (vln and pf) (1950) (ACE)
Fantasy on a Javanese motive (vlc and pf) (1948) (ACE)
Incantation on an Indian Theme (vla and pf) (1940)
Sonata (fl and pf)
Sonata (vla and pf) (1948) (ACE)
Sonata (vlc and pf) (1961) (ACE)
Suite (bsn and pf)
Suite (cl and pf) (1972) (ACE)
Allegro (ww) (1948) (New York: Independent Music Pub., 1972)
Fantasy on Irish Folk Motives (ACE)

PIANO

Suite (4 hands)
Dances (2 pf)
Hommage a ma jeunesse (2 pf)
Sonatina (2 pf)
Canzona (New Music)
Of shadows numberless, suite (after Keat's Ode to a Nightingale) (1966) (CFE; ACE)
Piano suite No. 3 (1951) (Lawson)
Seven suites, solos
Six cuckoos in quest of a composer, suite (1953) (ACE)
Sonata (ACE)
Walk (1955)

VOCAL

Songs of youth and madness (Friedrich Hoelderin) (S and orch) (1977)
Slow, slow fresh fount, madrigal (Ben Jonson) (mix-ch) (1941) (Merrymount Music)
Sweet western wind (Herrick) (ch a-cap) (Merrymount Music)
The Adorable Mouse, French folk tale (General Music Corp., 1960, 1971)
Bells (William Jones) (low vce and pf)
The condemned playground (Horace, Milton, Baudelaire) (S, T, fl, bsn and str qrt) (1963) (ACE)
Epitaphs (R. Burns) (vce and pf) (1957) (ACE)
Farewell tablet to Agathocles (vce and pf)
The hound of heaven (Francis Thompson) (vce, ob and str trio) (1945) (ACE)
Jubal trio (vce and cham ens) (comm, 1984)
Lockung (Eichendorff) (S and pf)
Mixco (Asturias) (vce and pf) (1957) (ACE, 1959)
Morning star, a song cycle in Hebrew on poems of childhood (1981)
Nocturnes (Shelley, Untermeyer, F. Sherman) (S and cham ens) (1975)
Questions on nature (Adelard of Bath) (vce, ob, pf and perc) (1965) (ACE)
The resounding lyre (vce and lyre)
Rhymes from the hill, song cycle (Galgenlieder of Christian Morgenstern) (vce, cl, vlc and mar) (1968) (ACE)
The seasons of time, song (ancient Japanese Tanka poetry) (vce, fl, vlc and pf alternating with cel) (1969) (ACE)
Several cycles (S and cham ens)
Songs of voyage (vce and pf) (1961) (ACE)
Sonnets from fatal interview (Millay) (vce, vln, vla and vlc) (1952) (ACE)
Sonnets from Shakespeare (vce, trp and str qrt) (1950) (ACE)
Spirit above the dust (vce and cham ens) (Edition, Peters 1982)
Spiritual airs (T and seven insts) (1980)
To music (Herrick) (vce and pf) (1957) (ACE, 1964)
Vergiftet sind meine lieder (Heine) (S and pf)
Voices from Elysium (on ancient Greek poetry) (1979)
Wing'd hour (vce and 5 insts) (comm, 1984)

SACRED

The habitable earth, cantata (Book of Proverbs) (soloists, mix-ch, ob and pf) (1965) (ACE, 1966)
Adon Olom (ch, ob, trp and strs) (1954) (ACE)
Sacred service (Saturday Morning Service) (mix-ch, soloists, org, fl, ob, bsn, trp, vla and vlc) (1971) (ACE)
Shirat Miriam L'Shabbat (Albert Weisser) (cantor, mix-ch and org) (1974) (New York: C.F. Peters, 1978)
How goodly are thy tents (3-part w-vces, pf or org) (1947) (Merrymount Music, 1951)
Spiritual madrigals (Rilke, Heine, von Trimperg) (m-vces, vla, vlc and bsn) (1965)
Three biblical masks (vln and pf; also org) (ACE)

OPERA

Fortunato, in 3 scenes (Serafin and Joaquin Quintero) (1958) (ACE)

Publications

The Music of Carlos Chavez. New Book of Modern Composers, New York, 1961.
The Music of Mark Brunswick. ACA Bulletin. 13/1: 1-10.

Bibliography

Ewen, D. *Composers Since 1900*. New York, 1969.
Fertig, J. P. *An analysis of selected works of the American composer Miriam Gideon in light of contemporary Jewish musical trends.*
Perle, G. *The Music of M.G.* ACA Bulletin. 7/4: 2-9.
Stevens, D. *A History of Song*. 1961.
Weisser, A. *Interview with M.G. Dimensions in American Judaism*. New York, 1970.

Ref. composer, 4, 5, 17, 20, 22, 40, 52, 68, 70, 74, 77, 81, 84, 85, 94, 96, 137, 138, 141, 142, 146, 163, 179, 189, 190, 191, 195, 228, 397, 403, 415, 560, 563, 594, 609, 610, 622, 624, 625

GIFFORD, Helen Margaret

Australian pianist and composer. b. Melbourne, September 5, 1935. She began studying the piano at the age of eight and entered the University of Melbourne Conservatorium in 1953. She was awarded a Commonwealth scholarship and studied the piano under Roy Shepherd, harmony under Dorian Le Gallienne and gained an M.Mus. in 1958. In 1965 she became the first recipient of the Dorian Le Gallienne award. She turned her interest to Asian music and the influence of the music of India and Polynesia can be found in some of her works. In 1970 she became resident composer of the Melbourne Theatre Company and in 1974 was the recipient of a Senior Fellowship from the Australian Council for the Arts. DISCOGRAPHY. PHOTOGRAPH.

Compositions

ORCHESTRA

On reflection (2 vln and str orch) (1972)
Canzone (cham orch) (1968) (for ABC program Hommage to Stravinsky)
Chimaera (1967)
Imperium (1969)
Phantasma (str orch) (1963) (J. Albert & Son)

CHAMBER

Play (picc, fl, cl, hn, trp, bass trb and perc, 4 players) (1979)
Septet (fl, ob, bsn, hpcd, vln, vla and vlc) (1962)
Company of brass (comm ABC for the Australian Brass Choir, 1973)

VOCAL

Foretold at Delphi, a collection of proverbs in ancient Greek (S, picc, ob, Arabian drum and pre-recorded krumhorn) (1978)

THEATRE

Regarding Faustus (T, cham ens and pre-recorded choric effect)

INCIDENTAL MUSIC

The Double Dealer (W. Congreve) (1975)
Electra (Sophocles) (1978)
Equus (P. Shaffer) (1974)
The Merchant of Venice (Shakespeare) (1977)
Othello (Shakespeare) (1976)
The Revenger's Tragedy (C. Tourneur) (1975)

Ref. Australian Music Centre, 442, 444, 457, 563

GIGNOUX, Jeanne
19th-century French composer.
Composition
OPERA
La vision de Jeanne d'Arc, lyric drama (1890)
Ref. 226, 260, 276, 347, 433

GILBERT, Florence
19th-century English composer. She was the sister of W.S. Gilbert and studied harmony and composition under Stainer and Prout.
Compositions
VOCAL
Ballads incl.:
Message to Phyllis
Ref. 260, 433

GILBERT, Janet Monteith
American cellist, assistant professor and composer. b. New York, August 6, 1946. She studied the cello at the Naples Conservatory from 1966 to 1968 and obtained her B.A. (music) in 1969 from the Douglass College, New Brunswick, NJ. In 1972 she obtained her M.A. (composition) at Villa Schifanoia, Florence and her doctorate of musical arts (composition) in 1979 at the University of Illinois, Urbana. She studied composition with Ben Johnston and Salvatore Mortirano, and computer music with Pietro Grossi, Charles Dodge and John Melby. She was a founder and member of the St. Olaf verbal workshop, a group of six musicians devoted to exploring the possibilities of verbal improvisation controlled by musical and poetic structures. She is director of the St. Olaf Contemporary Music Ensemble and a member of the ACA, American Society of University Composers and the Minnesota Composers' Forum. From 1979 to 1980 she was assistant professor at the St. Olaf College. She also founded the Champaign Living Newspaper in 1979. Her compositions have been performed at many colleges and symposiums. PHOTOGRAPH.
Compositions
CHAMBER
Solo for clarinet (1972)
VOCAL
Circumflexions on Mallarme (S) (1977)
Lorca (S)
Mallarme (S)
SACRED
A Psalm of Penitence, psalm 51 (1982)
THEATRE
Metalogue (1977)
ELECTRONIC
Drone (fl and tape)
Mass for dancers (tape) (1972)
The orange book (S, sax and tape) (1974)
Out of the looking glass (tape) (1975)
Paisaje con dos tumbas (S and tape)
Timelapse (tape) (1977)
Tracings (tape) (1977)
MULTIMEDIA
Un coup de des (readers, mix-ch, tape and visuals) (1979)
Fusions (dance, tape, computer visuals and film) (1981)
Oenone (tape and visuals) (1975)
Revelation (tape and film) (1981)
Ref. composer, 474, 622, 624, 625

GILBERT, Marie
American pianist, teacher and composer. b. New Haven, CT, 1845. She studied the piano under Professor Barbar and at the Leipzig Conservatory from 1861 to 1866. She then settled in New York as a music teacher. She composed piano pieces and songs.
Ref. 129

GILBERT, Pia
American professor and composer. b. Germany, June 1, 1921. She studied at the New York College of Music and from 1947 was composer-in-residence and professor of music and dance at the University of California, Los Angeles. DISCOGRAPHY.
Compositions
CHAMBER
Spirals and interpolations (ob, a-sax, perc and pf)
Interrupted suite (cl and 3 pf)
Transmutations (org and perc)
VOCAL
Food (S, B, trp, perc and pf) (New York: Peters, 1981)
BALLET
Game of gods
Metamorphoses
THEATRE
The Deputy
The Devils
Murderous Angels
Publications
Music for the Modern Dance.
Ref. 142, 347, 474, 563, 622

GILBERT DES ROCHES. See LEGOUX, Julie, Baroness

GILENO, Jean Anthony
American music therapist and composer. b. Philadelphia, PA, October 11, 1941. She received her M.M.E. from Temple University in 1973 and in 1979 became a registered music therapist. She then studied for her Ph.D. under Regina Therese Unsinn.
Compositions
CHAMBER
Austerity (gtr) (1981)
VOCAL
The rustic alleluia (ch, org and gtr)
Ref. 624

GILLES, Yvette Marie
French pianist and composer. b. Berty, June 2, 1920. She studied at the Jean Titelouze Institute and under Lazare Levy, Jean Gallon and Emile Passani. PHOTOGRAPH.
Compositions
ORGAN
Elegie (1953)
Marche funèbre (1953)
PIANO
Caprice (1952)
VOCAL
Eveille-toi ma lyre (vce and pf) (1952)
Lassitude (vce and pf) (1952)
SACRED
Ave Maria (vce and org) (1952)
Ref. composer

GILLICK, Emelyn Mildred Samuels
American accompanist, arranger, music consultant and composer. b. Brooklyn, NY, November 13, 1948. She obtained a B.S. in music from Skidmore College and an M.A. in related arts from New York University. She studied composition at the Juilliard School of Music under Stanley Wolfe and Laurence Widdoes. She worked as a music calligrapher and arranger then became accompanist and music consultant for the Memphis Ballet Company. PHOTOGRAPH.
Compositions
CHAMBER
Sonatina (fl and pf) (1977)
Suite (pf) (1977)
THEATRE
Caucasian Chalk Circle (Brecht) (1977)
Sound environment for Macbeth (1977)
Sound environment for The Revenger's Tragedy (1975)
ELECTRONIC
Cages (gtr and tape) (comm Ballet South)
Ref. composer

GILLUM, Ruth Helen
American pianist, lecturer and composer. b. St. Louis, 1907. She received her B.Mus. (piano) and M.M. (piano) from the University of Kansas and then did post-graduate study at Indiana University. She was chairlady of the music department at the Prairie View State College, the Philander Smith College and North Carolina Central University from 1944 to 1971.
Compositions
VOCAL
Choric dance (mix-ch and pf)
Roll, Jordan, roll (mix-ch and pf)
There's no hiding place (mix-ch and pf)
Ref. 523

GIMENEZ, Maria del Carmen Perez. See BARRADAS, Carmen

GINDLER, Kaethe-Lotte

German pianist, teacher and composer. b. Brunswick, November 17, 1894. After studying at the Brunswick Conservatory she studied theory under Dr. Besuch and Georg Bottcher from 1921 to 1924, and instrumentation under Otto Leonhardt from 1924 to 1927. She taught the piano at the Beethoven School, Wolfenbuettel from 1921 to 1923 and after 1923 was a teacher in Brunswick.

Compositions

CHAMBER

String quartet in G, op. 16
String quartet in 1 movement, op. 13 (1925)
Barcarole and Marche grotesque, op. 12 (vln and pf)
Scherzo and Traeumerei, op. 11 (fl and pf)
Variations on a theme by Melchior Franck, op. 3 (vln and pf)
Violin sonata, op. 7 (1923)

PIANO

Five pieces, op. 9
Three pieces, op. 14
Two fugues, op. 1
Variations, op. 4 (1922)

VOCAL

Symphonic poem with choir, op. 15 (1926)
Drei lieder, op. 8 (1923)
Mein gedenken, op. 6 (S)
Vier kinderlieder, op. 2
Vier lieder, op. 10 (S) (1924)
Zwei lieder, op. 5 (S)
Zwei lieder, op. 18 (A)

Ref. 111

GINES, Teodora (Ma Teodora)

16th-century black Dominican minstrel. b. Santiago de los Cabelleros, Dominican. Teodora was the first recognised woman composer in the Americas. She and her sister Micaela were sisters who lived in Santiago de Cuba. They formed part of a small orchestra with two shawm players and a Sevillan violist, Pascual de Ochoa and played at public gatherings and in church. Later the group moved to Havana, but Ma Teodora remained in Santiago where she became famous for her songs. Her *Son de la Ma Teodora* is considered reminiscent of the Cuban popular music of that period. It was strummed on a bandora or mandola (a type of mandolin) and was still in vogue in San Juan and Santiago during the 19th-century.

Compositions

VOCAL

Songs incl.:
Son de la Ma Teodora (vce and bandona)

Ref. 306

GIPPS, Ruth (M.B.E.)

English oboist, pianist, conductor, professor and composer. b. Bexhill-on-Sea, Sussex, February 20, 1921. She studied privately and at the Bexhill School of Music from 1925 to 1936 where her mother, Helene Gipps, was principal. She made her first public appearance at the age of four and had *The Fairy Shoemaker* published and performed when she was eight. She became an A.R.C.M. for piano performance in 1936 and then went to study composition, the piano and the oboe at the Royal College of Music from 1937 to 1942 under R.O. Morris, Gordon Jacob and Vaughan Williams, Arthur Alexander and Kendall Taylor and Leon Goossens. She obtained her B.Mus. (Dunelm) in 1941. She studied under Matthay at his piano school and in 1948, at the age of 27, became one of the youngest doctors of music in Great Britain (D.Mus. Dunelm). Her conducting career included positions as director of the City of Birmingham Choir from 1948 to 1950, conductor of the Co-op Orchestra and Listeners' Club Choir from 1949 to 1954, founder and conductor of the London Repertoire Orchestra from 1955 and founder and conductor of the Chanticleer Orchestra from 1961. She was chairlady of the Composers Guild of Great Britain in 1967 and a professor at Trinity College, London from 1959 to 1966. She was the first woman to conduct her own symphony, her *No. 3* on a BBC broadcast, and her tone poem *Knight in Armour* was conducted by Sir Henry Wood on the last night of the 1942 Promenade Concerts. She won five composition prizes, including the Cobbett Prize in 1957 and the Caird Traveling scholarship. She became an honorary member of the Royal Academy of Music in 1966 and a F.R.C.M. in 1972. In 1981 she was invested as an M.B.E. by HM Queen Elizabeth. She was commissioned to write *Military March* for an unknown country. She married the clarinetist Robert Baker.
PHOTOGRAPH.

Compositions

ORCHESTRA

Symphony No. 1 in F-Minor, op. 22 (Joseph Williams, 1942)
Symphony No. 2 in B, op. 30 (Williams, 1945)
Symphony No. 3, op. 57 (1965)
Symphony No. 4, op. 61 (1972)
Symphony No. 5
Clarinet concerto with small orchestra, op. 9 (1940)
Horn concerto, op. 58 (1968)
Oboe concerto with small orchestra, op. 20 (Williams, 1941)
Piano concerto, op. 34 (1948)
Violin concerto in B-Flat, op. 24 (1943)
Concerto for violin and viola with small orchestra, op. 49 (1957)
Chanticleer, an overture, op. 28 (1944)
The Chinese cabinet, op. 29, suite for full orchestra (Williams, 1945)
Coronation procession, op. 41 (1953)
Cringlemire gardens, op. 39 (str orch) (1952)
Death on a pale horse, op. 25 (Williams, 1943)
Jane Grey fantasy, op. 15 (vla and str orch) (1941)
Knight in armour, op. 8 (1940)
Leviathan, op. 59 (bsn and cham orch) (1969)
The rainbow, op. 40, pageant overture (Williams, 1954)
Song for orchestra, op. 33 (1948)
Variations on Byrd's Non Nobis, op. 25 (small orch) (1943)

BAND

Military March

CHAMBER

Seascape, op. 53 (10 wind insts) (Sam Fox, 1958; Keith Prowse)
Quintet, op. 16 (ob, cl, vln, vla and vlc) (1941)
Rhapsody, op. 23 (cl and str qrt) (1942)
Brocade, op. 17, 1 movement (pf qrt) (1941)
Sabrina, op. 13, 1 movement (str qrt) (1940)
String quartet, op. 47 (1956)
Billy Goats Gruff, op. 27 (ob, bsn and hn) (1943)
Chamois, op. 3 (2 vln and pf) (1939)
Flax and Charlock, op. 21 (cor anglais and str trio) (1941)
Trio, op. 10 (ob, cl and pf) (1940)
Elephant God, op. 12 (cl and dr) (1940)
Evocation, op. 48 (vln and pf) (1956)
Honey-coloured cow, op. 3 (bsn and pf) (1939)
The Kelpie of Corrievreckan, op. 5 (cl and pf) (Hinrichsen, 1939)
Kensington Gardens suite, op. 2 (ob and pf) (1938)
Lyric fantasy, op. 46 (vla and pf) (Fox, 1955)
Pixie caravan, op. 3a (fl and pf) (1939)
Rhapsody, op. 27 (vln and pf) (1943)
Rowan, op. 12 (fl and pf) (1940)
Sea shore suite, op. 3 (ob and pf) (1939)
Sea weed song, op. 12 (cor anglais and pf) (1940)
Sonata in G-Minor, op. 5 (ob and pf) (1939)
Sonata, op. 42 (vln and pf) (1954)
Sonata, op. 45 (cl and pf) (1955)
Sonatina, op. 56 (hn and pf) (Fox, 1950)
Suite for two violins, op. 12 (1940)
A tarradiddle for two horns, op. 54 (Galliarde, 1959)
The piper of dreams, op. 12b (ob) (1940)
Prelude, op. 51 (b-cl) (Williams, 1958)

PIANO

Conversation, op. 36 (2 pf) (1950)
The fairy shoemaker (Forsyth, 1929)
Theme and variations, op. 57 (1965)

VOCAL

The cat, op. 32 (Cont, Bar, double-ch and orch) (Joseph Williams, 1967)
Goblin market, op. 40 (Christina Rossetti) (2 S, w-ch and str orch) (Novello, 1953)
Mazeppa's ride, op. 1 (w-ch and small orch) (1937)
The Prophet (Kahlil Gibran) (orator, Bar, S, ch, small chil-ch and orch)
Rhapsody without words, op. 18 (S and small orch) (1941)
Ducks, op. 19 (S, fl, vlc and pf) (1941)
Four baritone songs, op. 4b (1939)
Heaven, op. 4a, (Rupert Brooke) (S and pf) (1939)
In other worlds, op. 43 (Noyes) (m-S and strs) (1954)
Porphyria's lover, op. 26 (T or Bar and pf) (1943)
The song of the Narcissus, op. 37 (S and pf) (1951)
Songs of youth, op. 11 (Brooke) (1940)
Two songs, op. 11 (Winifred Holtby) (1940)

SACRED

The Temptation of Christ, op. 6 (S, T, ch and small orch) (1939)
An Easter carol, op. 52 (mix-ch and pf or org) (Williams, 1958)
Gloria in excelsis, op. 62 (unison vces and org) (1972)
Magnificat and Nunc dimittis, op. 55 (mix-ch and org) (Fox, 1959; Keith Prowse)
Safety, op. 11, Psalm 91 (1940)
Three incantations, op. 50 (S and hp) (1957)

BALLET

Sea Nymph, op. 14 (small orch; also or 2 pf) (1941)
Virgin Mountain, op. 38 (1952)

Ref. composer, 2, 8, 17, 22, 68, 70, 74, 77, 84, 94, 109, 172, 177, 206, 359, 457, 622, 646

GIROD-PARROT, Marie Louise

French organist and composer. b. Paris, October 12, 1915. She studied the organ at the Paris Conservatoire under Henriette Puig-Roget and Marcel Dupre. She received first prizes for improvisation, history of music, fugue and counterpoint. She was director of the Academie d'orgue de St. Die and in 1940 became organist of the oratoire of The Louvre. She was president of the organ section of the Protestant Federation of France. DISCOGRAPHY.

Compositions

ORGAN

Complainte
Cortège, procure du clerge (1958)
Fugue sur un thème de Claude Le Jeune
Fantaisie sur un psaume de Claude Le Jeune (1954)
La goutte d'eau
Interlude sur le psaume 47
Noël, procure du clerge (1959)
Paraphrase sur choral *Jese une joie*
Prelude, choral et fantaisie
Psaume 137
Suite sur le psaume 23
Tryptique sur le noël, Dans une étable obscure, Procure du clerge (1963)

Ref. composer, 236, 563

GITECK, Janice

American pianist, lecturer and composer. b. Brooklyn, June 27, 1946. She studied at Mills College, Oakland and received a B.A. (music) in 1968 and an M.A. (composition) in 1969. From 1969 to 1970 she attended the Paris Conservatoire where she was a pupil of Oliver Messiaen. She was a student of Darius Milhaud from 1963 to 1970, and attended various summer schools for music from 1963 to 1977. Her other composition teachers were Barney Childs, Morton Subotnick, Leonard Klein, Charles Jones and Lowell Cross. She studied the piano with Bernhardt Abramowitch, Rebecca Weinstock, Russell Sherman and Morton Estrin. From 1964 she worked with numerous dance companies and was director and co-ordinator of various music groups from 1973 to 1979. She was lecturer in the piano and theory at the Frankfurt American community, Germany, 1970 to 1971; guest lecturer at the California State University at Hayward on composition, theory and analysis of Schoenberg, Webern and Berg, in 1974; lecturer in harmony and musicianship, University of California, Berkeley, 1974 to 1976; composer-in-residence at summer camps in 1974 and 1977, and has held the position of lecturer in composition and theory at the Cornish Institute, Seattle since 1984. She was a founder member of the Port Costa Players and served as music director of the Oakland Museum and KPFA Radio. She received commissions and awards, among them the Copley Fellowship, Aspen Music School in 1964, the Francis J. Hellman Talent Award, Mills College from 1964 to 1968 and first prize in composition, Mills College in 1968 and 1969. She has participated in radio program discussions on music and contributed to musical periodicals.

Compositions

CHAMBER

Helixes (fl, trb, vln, vlc, gtr, pf and perc) (1974)
Breathing songs from a turning sky (fl, cl, bsn, vlc, pf and perc) (1979)
String quartet (1967)
Primaries, dance music (fl and perc) (1977)

VOCAL

Sun of the center, cantata (R. Kelley) (m-vce, fl, cl, vln and pf) (1970)
Far north beast ghosts the clearing (Swampy Cree Indian text, trans. H.A. Norman) (ch) (1978)
Magic words to feel better (mix-ch a cap) (1974)
Le ange Heurtebise (J. Cocteau) (m-vce and pf) (1971) (1st prize Concorso Internazionale di Musica e Danza, G.B. Viotti) (Vercelli, 1973)
Callin home coyote burlesque, (L. MacAdams) (T, steel dr and b-strs) (1978)
Eight sandbars on the Takano River (G. Snyder) (5 vces, fl, bsn and gtr) (1976)
Magic words (North American Indian poems) (T, S and pf) (1973)
Matinée d'ivresse, monody (Rimbaud) (high vce) (1976)
A new (L. Zukofsky) (m-vce and pf) (1969)

OPERA

A'Agita, ceremonial opera (Pima/Papago Indian mythology) (3 singing actors, dancing actor and 8 instrumentalist/actors) (1976)
Messalina, mini opera (m-vce, vlc and pf) (1973)

THEATRE

A Picture of Dorian Gray (O. Wilde) (theatre/dance adaptation) (1974)
Trans (12 players)

INCIDENTAL MUSIC

Five pieces for museum collections, television

ELECTRONIC

Peter and the wolves (trb, actor and tape) (1978)
Study I and II (tape) (1969)

MULTIMEDIA

Thunder, like a white bear dancing (ritual performance based on the Mide picture songs of the Ojibwa Indians) (S, fl, pf, hand perc and slide projections) (1977) (comm San Francisco Chamber Music Society)

MISCELLANEOUS

Carnival
Chaconne
Open house
Summerspace (chil-ens)
Tree air

Bibliography

AMC Newsletter, Vol 21, No. 3.
Commanday, Robert. *An engrossing Opera. San Francisco Chronicle*, April 26, 1976.
Hamilton, Mildred. *Old sources for new music. San Francisco Examiner*, November, 1977.
J-M-F. *Tomita joue en coulisse du tuyau d'arrosage. Le Monde de la Musique*, Fevrier, 1979.
Peterson, Melody. *Indian-inspired Opera at Theatre Vanguard. Herold Examiner*, Los Angeles, January, 1977.
Shere, Charles. *Bay Composer's Successful New Opera. Oakland Tribune*, April 28, 1976.
Tucker, Marilyn. *Giteck's mysterious themes lovingly set to music. San Francisco Chronicle*, November 30, 1977.
Ulrich, Allan. *Indian Opera faces Acid Test. Los Angeles Times*, January 14, 1977.

Ref. composer, 622

GIOCONDA, Carmen Manteca. See CARMEN MARINA

GIULIANI-GIULELMI, Emilia

19th-century Italian composer.

Compositions

GUITAR

Six preludes, op. 46 (Schott)

ARRANGEMENTS

Belliniana, op. 2, (Bellini) (Ricordi; Schott)
Variations on the theme, Ah perche non posso odiarti, in the Sonnambula, op. 3
Non piu mesta accanto al fuoco in the Cenerentola, op. 5

Ref. 297

GIURANNA, Elena Barbara

Italian harpist, pianist, teacher and composer. b. Palermo, 18 November 1902. She studied the piano and the harp under G.A. Fano at the Conservatory of Palermo graduating with a diploma in 1919 and composition under C. De Nardis and A. Savasta at the Regio Conservatory of Naples, graduating with a diploma in 1921. She improved her instrumental technique in Milan under Giorgio Federico Ghedini and made her piano debut with the Naples Symphonic Orchestra in 1923. She was the first Italian woman composer invited to participate in the International Festival of Music in Venice in 1935 and the Festival of International Music in Brussels in 1938. She taught harmony, counterpoint, fugue and composition at the Santa Cecilia Conservatory in Rome after 1937. She was music consultant to the National Radio and the recipient of many prizes and awards. She married the conductor Mario Giuranna.

Compositions

ORCHESTRA

Musica per Olivia, small symphony (1970)
Concerto (1942)
Concerto per orchestra (1966) (prize, Trieste, 1966)
Il miracolo delle rose, symphonic poem (1923)
Patria, symphonic poem (1939) (Ricordi)
Apina rapita dai nani della montagna, symphonic suite (Anatole France) (1924)
Episodi (pf, perc wind and brass insts) (1947) (Ricordi)
Marionette, scherzo (1925)
Notturno (1935)
Poema eroico (X. Legio) (1936) (prize Rome, 1937) (Ricordi)
Toccata (1938) (Ricordi)

CHAMBER

Adagio e allegro da concerto (9 insts) (1935) (Ricordi)
Sonatina (pf) (prize, Rome 1932)
Sonatine (hp) (1942) (Ricordi)
Viola for Aura (vla)

VOCAL

Allegreze (ch and small orch)
Canto di nozze (ch and small orch)
Ninna nanna degli angeli (ch and orch)
Addio bella sora (Ricordi)
Augurio (1936) (Ricordi)
Canto arabo (vce and orch) (Ricordi)
Canto di guerra (3 m-vces)
Canto storico (1928) (Ricordi)

Dienai (3 m-vces)
Due quartine popolari greche (w-vces) (Ricordi)
Due strofe siciliane (1936) (Ricordi)
Las astrellas del cielo (Ricordi)
Freccecarella mia (old Neapolitan text) (1945) (Ricordi)
La guerriera (vce and orch) (1934) (Ricordi)
I canti del Dnipro (1946) (Ricordi)
Milano (Ricordi)
Mi madre se mi date Giovannino (1928) (Ricordi)
Ninna nanna (1928) (Ricordi)
Quattro canti fanciulleschi (Ricordi)
Stornello (1928) (Ricordi)
Suonno viene, O (old Neapolitan text) (1945) (Ricordi)
Tre coretti (w-vces and five insts) (1932) (Ricordi)
Tre cori (m-vces) (1935) (Ricordi)

SACRED
Tre canti alla vergine (solo, ch and small orch) (1950)
Gloria in Excelsis Deo (3 vces) (1950)

BALLET
Trappola d'oro (1929)

OPERA
Hosanna, lyric opera in 1 act (C. Pinelli)
Jamanto, lyric opera in 3 acts (Bergamo, 1914) (prize, 1937)
Mayerling, lyric opera in 3 acts (V. Viviani) (Naples, 1961)

ARRANGEMENTS
Le astuzie femminili, opera (Cimarosa)
Concertos for viola d'amore (Vivaldi)
I due baroni di Roccazzura, opera (Cimarosa)
La molinara, opera (Paisiello)
Re Teodoro in Venezia, opera (Paisiello)

Ref. composer, 8, 16, 17, 44, 70, 72, 74, 75, 85, 94, 96, 100, 105, 107, 109, 110, 135, 165, 166, 189, 226, 347

GIUSTINA, Baroness. See BOETZELAER, Josina Anna Petronella

GIZYCKA-ZAMOYSKA, Ludmilla, Countess

Polish pianist and composer. b. Trnava, 1829; d. Baden, September 15, 1889. She lived in Slovenia and then in Vienna where she studied under J. Herback, Hellmesberger, F.A. Wolf, E. Naumann, G. Nottebohm and Robert Fuchs. She was prominent in the musical life of Bratislava and Vienna.

Compositions

ORCHESTRA
Pieces

PIANO
Ballade polonaise, op. 11
Petite valse, op. 12
Polish melodies, op. 1
Roccoco gavotte, op. 18
Sarabande and gavotte, op. 10
Three serenades, op. 3
Two mazurkas, op. 14 (1885)

VOCAL
Conseil, op. 13 (Alfred de Musset)
Eight songs, op. 2
Marie, romance for soprano and piano, op. 7
Petite romance pour soprano avec accompagnement de piano, op. 17
Zwei Lieder fuer Tenor (1885)

Ref. 197, 226, 276, 297

GLANVILLE-HICKS, Peggy

American pianist, conductor, music critic and composer. b. Melbourne, Australia, December 29, 1912. She started lessons in composition under Fritz Hart at the Melbourne Conservatorium when she was 15 years old. In 1931 she won the Carlotta Rowe Open Scholarship to study at the Royal College of Music, London from 1932 to 1936. Her teachers were Vaughan Williams (composition), Arthur Benjamin (piano), Constant Lambert and Sir Malcolm Sargent (conducting), R.O. Morris and C. Kitson (harmony and counterpoint) and Gordon Jacob (orchestration). In 1936 the Octavia traveling scholarship enabled her to study in Vienna under Egon Wellesz and in Paris under Nadia Boulanger (q.v.) from 1936 to 1938. In 1938 her *Choral Suite* was conducted by Sir Adrian Boult in the ISCM Festival in London. This was the first time Australia was featured in this festival and it was represented again in 1948 when her *Concertino de Camera* was performed at the ISCM Festival held in Amsterdam. Together with Stanley Bate she founded the ballet company Les Trois Arts in 1940 and in 1942 settled in America. In 1953 she was awarded a grant from the American Academy of Arts and Letters and she received two Guggenheim Fellowships in 1956 and 1958. In 1959 she settled in Athens. She received a Fulbright Fellowship from 1961 to 1963 for research in Aegean demotic music and a Rockefeller grant in 1961 for travel and research in the Middle and Far East. This resulted in her opera *Nausicaa* which was presented by the Greek Government in the Athens Festival of 1961. Her next opera was *Sappho*, commissioned by the Ford Foundation for the San Francisco Opera House. She introduced Carlos Surinach, the Spanish composer-conductor and Nicanor Zabaleta, the Spanish harpist, to American audiences. She produced Lou Harrison's opera *Rapunzel*, which was awarded the 20th-century Masterpiece prize in Rome. Together with Carleton Sprague Smith she was co-founder of the International Music Fund which helped re-establish European artists after World War II. She was the music critic of the New York Herald Tribune from 1948 to 1958 and director of the Composers' Forum from 1950 to 1960. She wrote the essay entries for Scandinavia and the United States in the current edition of Grove's Dictionary of Music and Musicians and with Yehudi Menuhin was joint music consultant to the concerts of Indian music given at the Museum of Modern Art in 1955. She married the English composer Stanley Bate. DISCOGRAPHY. PHOTOGRAPH.

Compositions

ORCHESTRA
Etruscan concerto (pf and cham orch) (1956)
Flute concerto (1937)
Piano concerto (1938)
Sinfonia da pacifica (1953)
Sinfonietta No. 1
Sinfonietta No. 2
Spanish suite (1936)
Concerto romantico (vla and cham orch) (1957)
Gymnopedie No. 1 (ob, hp and str orch) (ACA, 1953)
Gymnopedie No. 2 (hp, cel and str orch) (ACA, 1953)
Gymnopedie No. 3 (hp and str orch) (ACA, 1953)
Mediatation
Prelude and scherzo (1937)

CHAMBER
The Masque of the wild man (hp, pf, perc and strs)
Musica antiqua No. 1 (2 fl, hp, mar, perc and timp)
Concertino antico (hp and str qrt)
Concertino de camera (fl, cl, bsn and pf) (Paris: Lyre Bird Press, 1945)
String quartet (1938)
Sonata (hp, fl and hn) (1950)
Sonata (pf and perc) (ACA, 1952)
Sonata for harp (Weintraub Music Co., 1951)
Sonatina (fl or rec and pf) (London: Schott & Co., 1940)

PIANO
Prelude for a pensive pupil (1963)
Sonatina (1939)

VOCAL
Dance cantata (Navaho text) (T, narr, spoken ch and orch) (1947)
Aria concertante (Mario Monteforte-Toledo) (T, w-ch, ob, pf and gong) (1945)
Poem (ch and orch) (1933)
Song in summer (John Fletcher) (ch and orch) (1935)
Choral suite (John Donne) (w-ch, ob and strs) (Lyre, 1937)
Pastoral (Tagore) (w-ch and cor anglais) (Weintraub, 1937)
Ballade, songs (P. Bowles) (vce and pf) (Hargail, 1947)
Be still you little leaves (vce and pf) (Lyre)
Come sleep (vce and pf) (Lyre)
Frolic (A.E. Housman) (Lyre, 1931)
In Mid-wood silence (S and pf) (1935)
Last poems (Housman) (vce and pf) (1945)
Letters from Morocco (Bowles) (T and cham orch) (ACA, 1949)
Profiles from China (E. Tietjens) (vce and pf) (1945)
Rest (A.E. Housman) (L'Oiseau Lyre, 1931)
Sidi Amar in winter, 3 songs (P. Bowles) (1947)
Thirteen ways of looking at a blackbird (W. Stevens) (S and pf) (1947)
Thomsoniana (V. Thomson) (S and cham ens) (ACA, 1949)
Other songs

BALLET
Hylas and the Nymphs (1937)
Jephthah's Daughter (1966)
Killer-of-Enemies (narr, ww and perc) (1946)
The Masque of the Wild Man; also orch version as Tapestry (1958)
Postman's Knock (after *The Wedding Group*, painting by Henri Rousseau) (1940)
Saul and the Witch of Endor (trp, perc and strs; also orch; also drama)
A Season in Hell (Rimbaud) (1965)
Tragic Celebration (1966)
Triad (1958)

OPERA
Caedmon (composer) (1933)
The Glittering Gate, in 1 act (Lord Dunsany) (1959)
Nausicaa, in 3 acts (Robert Graves) (1961)
Rapunzel (Lou Harrison) (1958)
Sappho (Lawrence Durrell) (comm Ford Foundation of San Francisco Opera) (1963)
The Transposed Heads, in 6 scenes (Thomas Mann) (1950) (New York: Schirer, 1953) (comm Louisville Orch, KY)

FILM MUSIC
The African Story from All Our Children for the United Nations (1956)
Clouds (1938)
Glacier, documentary (1938)
The Robot, abstract cartoon film (1937)
A Scary Time, for UNICEF (1958)
Tel, cartoon (1950)
Tulsa (1949)

Bibliography

Bulletin of the ACA, vol. 4, no. 1, 1954.
Composer for Theatre. P. Glanville-Hicks. *Composers of the Americas*. Vol. 13.

Ref. composer, 2, 4, 5, 8, 15, 17, 22, 44, 68, 70, 74, 75, 84, 96, 141, 142, 172, 190, 193, 195, 203, 228, 412, 440, 442, 444, 560, 563, 594, 610, 622, 637

GLASER, Victoria Merrylees

American flautist, pianist, lecturer and composer. b. Amherst, MA, September 11, 1918. She graduated with a B.A. cum laude in 1940 and an M.A. from Radcliffe College in 1943 where she studied composition under Walter Piston, Nadia Boulanger (q.v.), Tillman Merrit, Otto Gombosi and Archibald Davison. She studied the flute under Georges Laurent, the piano under Fredrick Tillotson and voice under Bernard Barbeau. She was a lecturer at Wellesley College from 1943 to 1958 then until 1982 was chairlady of the music theory department of the Adult Extension and Preparatory Division of the New England Conservatory. In 1961 she received an honorable mention in the GEDOK Competition, Mannheim, Germany.

Compositions

ORCHESTRA
Birthday fugue (1961)
Question and answer (1960)
Two movements (1964)

CHAMBER
Sonata (3 pf) (1975)
Sonatina (fl and vl)
Harpsichord suite

VOCAL
Homeric hymn (w-ch) (1956)
An idyll song (w-ch) (1954)
La musique (ch) (1973)

SACRED
Three carols (mix-ch, handbells, rec and hpcd) (1974)

ARRANGEMENTS
Choral and instrumental works

Publications

Third Concord Anthem Book. E.C. Schirmer.
Training for Musicianship. Extension tests.

Ref. composer, 39, 142, 646

GLASS, Jennifer

B. 1944.

Composition

CHAMBER
Sonatine (pf and tba) (Emerson; Ampleforth)

Ref. Frau und Musik

GLATZ, Helen Sinclair

English lecturer and composer. b. South Shields, Durham, March 13, 1908. She studied under Dr. W.G. Whittaker at Armstrong College, Newcastle-upon-Tyne. She was the first woman from the North to win an open scholarship for composition to the Royal College of Music, where she studied under Vaughan Williams and Gordon Jacob. In 1933 on a traveling scholarship for composition, she went to Vienna, Italy and Budapest where she studied under Kodaly. She was also a Cobbett prize winner. She lived in Hungary and returned to England as a refugee. From 1953 she was a member of the music staff of the Dartington College of Arts in South Devon. PHOTOGRAPH.

Compositions

ORCHESTRA
Concertino (fl and str orch) (1948)
Concertino (trb, timp and str orch) (1965)
Dance rhapsody (hp and orch) (1967)
Elegy (str orch) (1951)
Five carols (str orch) (1951)
Scherzo and trio (1932)
Theme and variations (1949)

BAND
Essex suite (brass) (1935)

CHAMBER
Septet (1932)
Suite of Hungarian folk songs (brass septet) (1964)
Suite (brass qnt) (1968)
Four miniatures for string quartet (1930)
Phantasy string quartet (1934)
Quartet for brass instruments (1963)
String quartet No. 1 (1929)
String quartet No. 2 (1936)
Suite (fl, ob, cl and hn) (1954)
String trio (1933)
Suite (3 rec) (1958)
Elegy (vlc and pf)
Prelude and dance (rec and vla) (1962)
Sonata (hpcd and vln) (1968)
Sonata (vla and pf) (1928)
Suite (vln and vla) (1950)
Suite (vln and hpcd) (1968)
Two pieces (vln and vla) (1950)
Five pieces (ob) (1966)
Sonata (vln) (1972)
Three Studies (rec) (1966)
Two pieces (rec) (1966)
Prelude and scherzo (fl) (1958)

PIANO
Suite, based on 7 Hungarian folk songs (duet) (1963)
Harlequin, based on French traditional tunes (1934)
Suite of children's pieces (1952)
Theme and variations (1928)

VOCAL
Cella alcuni: In memoriam Dorothy Elmhirst (mix-ch and wind orch) (1969)
Five Herrick pictures (w-ch and str orch) (1950)
Three-part songs (mix-ch a-cap) (1930)
Two Latin poems (w-ch and 2 fl) (1962)
Four songs by German poets (1959)
Song cycle (Keats) (S and pf) (1933)
Three songs on cats (S and cl) (1962)
Three winter songs (Walter de la Mare) (S, fl and vla) (1958)
Two songs (S and fl) (1966)

SACRED
A Christmas carol (mix-ch a-cap) (1953)
Psalm 104 (mix-ch a-cap) (1931)
Two carols (w-ch, fl and vla) (1956)

THEATRE
Dr. Knock (1956)
The Giant's Christmas, play for children (1954)
The Merchant of Venice (Shakespeare) (1957)
The Merry Wives of Windsor (Shakespeare) (1955)
Much Ado about Nothing (Shakespeare) (1957)
Polka (1970)
Rashomon (1966)
Romeo and Juliet (Shakespeare) (1956)
Sacrifice to the Wind (ww and pf) (1959)
St. Joan (G.B. Shaw) (1965)

FILM MUSIC
Henry and I (fl, vla and pf) (Shakespeare) (1962)

ELECTRONIC
Hall sands (narr, taped vce, spoken and sung ch, perc and wind insts) (1971)

MULTIMEDIA
Cemen, allegory (narr, ch, orch and dancers) (1967-1968)

Ref. composer, 280

GLAZIER, Beverly

American teacher and composer. b. Syracuse, NY, May 8, 1933. While teaching she studied humanities and music at Wayne State University and obtained her B.Sc. (elementary education) from Syracuse University. She studied composition under Bette Kahler, Howard Boatright, Brian Israel, Dr. Selden and Joseph McGrath. Her liturgical music won a prize for two consecutive years in The Temple Sinai Composers' contest. PHOTOGRAPH.

Compositions

CHAMBER
Prayers of a dreamer (ww qnt)
Currents (fl, vlc and pf)

VOCAL
Screaming eagle (mix-ch and pf)
Sing out hadassah
A woman of valor
A woman of vision (S, cl and pf)

SACRED
Come to us in peace (Boachem Sholom) (mix-ch and pf)
In freedom rejoice (mix-ch and pf)

Kedushah (mix-ch and pf; also mix-ch and org)
A new song unto the Lord (2 part m-and w-ch and pf; also mix-ch and org)
Sh'ma (high vce, low vce and pf)
Shavuous (S and pf)
V'shomru (mix-ch and org)
Ref. composer, 625

GLEN, Irma

American organist, pianist, actress, authoress and composer. b. Chicago, August 3, 1902. She attended the Sherwood Music School, the Illinois Institute of Technology and graduated from the American Conservatory in the piano, the organ and composition. She was organist and composer for the National Broadcasting Company for 15 years before moving to California in 1946. She obtained her D.Mus. and doctorate in religious studies. DISCOGRAPHY. PHOTOGRAPH.

Compositions
CHAMBER
Organ pieces
Piano pieces
SACRED
A bridge to higher consciousness, song
Christmas miracles now
Don Blanding's vagabond's house, song
Prayer therapy
The promises of Christ Jesus
Songs (1949-1950)
Story book lady, song
Twenty-one hymns in Religious Science hymnal, 1954.
Hymns (1954)
INCIDENTAL MUSIC
This Thing Called Life, television
Publications
Awakening.
Contemplation.
The Church of Religious Science and its Music.
Fall upon Your Knees.
The Masters Touch.
Music Ecology and You.
Ref. composer, 39, 347, 563, 646

GLENN-COPELANN, Beverly

20th-century composer.
Composition
FILM MUSIC
Montreal Main (1974)
Ref. 497

GLICK, Henrietta

20th-century American composer.
Composition
ORCHESTRA
Paris 1927, symphonic suite (1931)
Ref. 168

GLICK, Nancy Kay

American harpist, pianist, teacher and composer. b. Findlay, OH, December 22, 1941. She gained her B.S. (education) at Bowling Green State University, OH. As a graduate student she studied the harp under Ruth Inglefield. She was the pianist and the harpist with the Lima Symphony Orchestra and teaches music in Findlay city schools.

Composition
CHAMBER
Fantasia (hp)
Ref. 77

GLICKMAN, Sylvia

20th-century composer.
Composition
VOCAL
The hollow men (T.S. Eliot) (S, ch and pf) (1965)
Ref. 465

GLOVER, Mrs. Frank. See HARRADEN, R. Ethel

GLOWACKA, Ludwika

19th-century Polish composer.
Compositions
PIANO
Obertasa, folk dances, in Zbior mazurow roznych autorow (Warsaw: A. Dzwonkowski, 1859)
Ref. 118

GLUCHOWICZ, Rachel. See GALINNE, Rachel

GLYN, Margaret Henriette

English musicologist, writer and composer. b. Ewell, Surrey, February 28, 1865; d. Ewell, June 3, 1946. She studied under Henry Frost and Yorke Trotter in London.

Compositions
CHAMBER
Organ pieces
PIANO
Six overtures
Six suites
Six symphonies
VOCAL
Songs
Publications
About Elizabethan Virginal Music and Its Composers. London: Reeves, 1924.
Analysis of the Evolution of Musical Forms. 1909.
The National School of Virginal Music. 1917.
Theory of Musical Evolution. 1934.
Editions of virginal and organ music by Byrd, O. Gibbons, John Bull, Farnaby.
Ref. 8, 9, 12, 70, 85, 347, 360

GNESINA, Yelena Fabianovna

Soviet pianist, professor and composer. b. Rostov-on-the-Don, May 31, 1874; d. Moscow, June 4, 1967. She was the sister of the composer Mihail Fabianovitch Gnesina. In 1893 she graduated from the Moscow Conservatory with a silver medal. Her teachers in the piano were V. Safanov, L. Langer, F. Busoni and P. Schletzer. In 1890 she started teaching the piano and after a period of concert tours, she and her sisters Evgenia and Maria, founded the Gnesina school of music in Moscow in 1895. After the Russian Revolution the state took over the running of the school and in 1944 the sisters founded another such school which she directed. She remained a professor of the piano until 1935 and director until 1953. In 1935 she became a member of the Committee of Artistic Workers; from 1940 to 1948 she was a deputy of the Moscow City Council. She was awarded the titles of Artist of the Russian Soviet Federated Socialist Republic in 1925 and of Activist in Art, Russian Soviet Federated Socialist Republic in 1935; the Order of the Red Banner for Laborers in 1937 and the Order of Lenin in 1945.

Compositions
PIANO
Miniatures, 11 pieces (1927)
Piano ABC (1937)
Seventeen-piece pictures (1943)
TEACHING PIECES
Album of children's pieces (1940)
Little etudes for beginners (1923)
Methodical manuals for teachers and pupils (1940)
Preparatory exercises for different techniques
Bibliography
Articles and Memories. Selected and edited by M. Rittikh.
Ref. 15, 17, 20, 70, 74, 87, 109, 277, 330

GNUS, Ryta

Polish pianist, teacher, writer and composer. b. Warsaw, 1881. She studied the piano in Kiev under Puchalski and taught at music schools in Kiev and Warsaw. She wrote numerous articles in Polish musical journals on Chopin, Schumann and particularly on teaching methods for pre-school and school children.

Compositions
PIANO
Miniatures
Sonata
VOCAL
Spiewnik dla mlodziezy
Trzydziest piosenek dla przedszkola
Other songs for children (vce and pf)
Ref. 118

GODDARD, Arabella (Davison)

English pianist, critic, teacher and composer. b. Saint-Servan, Brittany, January 12, 1836; d. Boulogne-sur-Mer, April 6, 1922. She played the piano from a very early age. At the age of eight she played for Queen Victoria and made her debut in London at the age of 14. She studied in Paris under Kalkbrenner; in London under Thalberg; harmony and composition under Anderson, Macfarren and J.W. Davison, whom she married in 1859. She gave recitals in Italy and Germany in 1854 and 1855, and toured the United States, Australia and India between 1873 and 1876. In 1880 she retired from public life and settled in Tunbridge Wells, where she taught the piano.

Compositions

PIANO

Ballade (1853)
Piano album (Boosey)
Six waltzes

ARRANGEMENTS

Bijoux perdus (4 hands) (Mozart, Steibelt and Dussek) (Chappell)

Ref. 24, 44, 74, 85, 105, 60, 268, 276, 297, 307, 361

GODDESS OF THE DATE PALM. See INNANA

GODLA, Mary Ann

20th-century American guitarist, arranger, teacher and composer.

Composition

CHAMBER

Concerto primero (gtr and str ens)
Collection of eight short pieces (gtr, 2 vln, vla and vlc)

ARRANGEMENTS

Pieces (Carcassi, G. Sanz, de Visée, F. Sor and J.S. Bach)

Publications

Music through the Guitar. Series with Fred Nance. 18 vols.

Ref. 77

GODWIN-FOSTER, Dorothy

English composer. b. 1889.

Composition

CHAMBER

Violin sonata

Ref. 41, 226

GOEBELS, Gisela (nee Behrend)

German cellist, pianist, violist and composer. b. Magdeburg, December 3, 1903. She came from a musical family and was mainly self-taught.

Compositions

CHAMBER

Sinfonietta (5 strs) (Mannheim: Musik Verlag, 1960)
String quartet (1961)
Piano trio (1957)
Serenade (cl, vla and pf) (1965)
Sonata (vlc and pf) (1961)
Sonata (vlc) (1959)
Sonata (pf) (1958, 1964)

VOCAL

Quartet
Two terzets (1965)
Over 100 songs (1955-1968)

Ref. composer

GOERRES, Maria Vespermann. See VESPERMANN, Marie

GOERSCH, Ursula Margitta

German flautist, teacher and composer. b. March 4, 1932. She studied music teaching and graduated from the Conservatory in Karlsruhe in 1969. She studied the flute and composition privately under Hermann Klemeyer and Albert Barkhausen and took courses in techniques of 20th-century composition. Since 1975 she has been chairlady of a nationwide competition for young musicians in Bremen. PHOTOGRAPH.

Compositions

ORCHESTRA

Anatolische suite (1974)

CHAMBER

Rondo (Orff insts) (1972)
Diarium fuer Querfloeten (1983)
Variationen ueber ein tuerkisches Liebeslied (fl and pf) (1983)
Miniaturen fuer Schlagzeug (perc) (1976)

VOCAL

Heitere Tierkantate, cantata (chil-ch and Orff insts) (1973)
Die stumme Uhr von Horsten, cantata (chil-ch and orch) (1981)

SACRED

Sie kamen durch die Wueste, cantata (chil-ch and orch) (1982)

Ref. composer

GOETSCHIUS, Marjorie

American cellist, pianist, scriptwriter, singer and composer. b. Raymond, NH, September 23, 1915. She attended Georgian Court College and Tufts University and studied composition under her grandfather, Percy Goetschius. She also studied the piano at the Juilliard School of Music under James Friskin, composition under Bernard Wagenaar and Joseph Schillinger. She studied voice under her grandmother, Maria Stefany. She worked for the radio as a singer, cellist, pianist and scriptwriter.

Compositions

CHAMBER

Lament (vln and pf)
Tango del ensueno (vln and pf)
Nebuleuses (vln)
Valse burlesque (vln)

PIANO

Berceuse
Poetique
Rhapsody in G
Rondo
Scherzo in thirds
Sonata in B-minor
Suite
Theme and variations

VOCAL

Songs incl.:
The Magic of Christmas, 12 songs
Reminiscence (S)

THEATRE

Background music for CBS Theatre

Ref. 39, 94, 142

GOETZE (Gotze) Auguste (pseud. Auguste Weimar)

German singer, teacher and composer. b. Weimar, February 24, 1840; d. Leipzig, April 29, 1908. She was the daughter of the vocal teacher Franz Goetze and considered a highly talented singer. She started an opera school in Dresden in 1875. Her pupils included von Kotzebue and Fanny Moran-Olden.

Compositions

VOCAL

Set of vocal studies
Songs

OPERA

Eine Heimfahrt
Magdalena
Susanna Monfert
Vittori Accoramboni

Publications

Ueber den Verfall der Gesangskunst. 1884.
Vocal Method.

Ref. 269, 276, 291, 347, 433

GOKHMAN, Elena Vladimirovna

Soviet lecturer and composer. b. Saratov, November 19, 1935. In 1962 she graduated from the Moscow Conservatory where she studied composition. After 1962 she lectured at the Saratov Conservatory.

Compositions

ORCHESTRA

Piano concerto (1968)

CHAMBER

Piano quartet (1970)
Piano trio (1969)
Sonata (vln and pf) (1969, 1971)

PIANO

Easy sonata (1961)
Other pieces

VOCAL

Gloria, suite (w-ch and cham ens) (1974)
Cycle on verses (N. Khikme) (vce and pf) (1964)

Ref. 21

GOLDBERG, Sonja. See BALENOVIC, Draga

GOLDFOOT, Mrs. Sybil. See MICHELOW, Sybil

GOLDSCHMIDT, Lore

German pianist and composer. b. Hanover, February 28, 1908. She studied theory under Otto Leonhardt from 1923 to 1927, the piano under Emil Taegener and composition at the Stern Conservatory in Berlin under Wilhelm Klatte in 1927.

Compositions

ORCHESTRA

Symphony (1926)

CHAMBER

String quartet (1928)

Ref. 70, 111, 226

GOLDSTEIN, M. Anna

19th-century composer.

Compositions

PIANO

The Cruiskeen lawn
Garibaldi's hymn
Giulia gentil
Golden reign, waltz (Williams)
Jerusalem the Golden
New and popular tunes (Williams)
Santa Lucia
Turluretta

Ref. 297

GOLDSTON, Margaret Nell Stumpf

American pianist, choral conductor, teacher and composer. b. Havana, Cuba, November 28, 1932. She began her piano study at the age of four at the University of Havana and between the ages of 13 and 17 studied the piano and theory at Loyola University, the New Orleans Baptist Seminary and Newcomb College under Walter Goldstein. She obtained her B.Mus. (piano) from the Louisiana State University where she studied under Rowena Dickey. In 1982 she studied composition under Robert Ward on a scholarship received from the Independent Music Teachers' Association. PHOTOGRAPH.

Compositions

PIANO

Adventures of an African boy (Galaxy Music Corp)
The magic typewriter (Galaxy, 1982)
Windows (Galaxy)

Ref. composer

GOLETTI, Nelly

20th-century composer.

Composition

FILM MUSIC

One Too Many (1950)

Ref. 326

GOLIA, Maria

20th-century Italian composer.

Compositions

PIANO

Cinque piccoli pezzi (Ricordi)
Favola
In morte di un canarino
Passeggiata
Piccola danza
Preludietto

Ref. Ricordi

GOLLAHON, Gladys

American composer. b. Cincinnati, April 8, 1908.

Compositions

VOCAL

Songs incl.:
Old Lady of Fatima

SACRED

Songs

Ref. 39, 142

GOLLENHOFER-MUELLER, Johanna, Josephine. See MUELLNER, Johanna

GOLOVINA, Olga Akimovna

Soviet teacher and composer. b. Sverdlovsk, May 26, 1924. She studied composition at the Ural Conservatory under B.D. Gibalin, graduating in 1948. The following year she began teaching theoretical subjects at the Sverdlovsk Music School.

Compositions

ORCHESTRA

Symphony (1948)
Razdumya, symphonic poem (1970)
Ural tales, symphonic poem (1957)
Cycle with pictures of V. Vasnetsov (1956)
Youth overture (1971)

CHAMBER

Quintet (fl, 2 vln, vla and vlc) (1968)
Adagio (str qrt) (1969)
String quartet (1947)
Dance (vln and pf) (1944)
Scherzino (fl and pf) (1968)
Three miniatures (vln and pf) (1970)

PIANO

Sonata (1947)
Sonatina (1958)
Three sketches (1963)

VOCAL

Ballada shestoi (A. Surkov) (vce and orch) (1964)
Vsegda v puti (Soviet poets) (vce and orch) (1967)
Proshchanie s yunostyu, song cycle (Soviet poets) (T and str qrt) (1971)

BALLET

Vozmutitel spokoistviya (1961)

OPERA

Zolotoi Lotos (1971)

Ref. 21

GOLSON-BATEMAN, Florence (Mrs. W.W. Bateman)

American lecturer, singer and composer. b. Fort Deposit, AL, December 4, 1891. She studied at the Eilenberg Conservatory, Montgomery; the Tennessee School for the Blind, Nashville from 1913 to 1915 and Woman's College (now Huntingdon College), Montgomery from 1916 to 1917. She graduated from the Cincinnati Conservatory, Ohio in 1921 with a diploma in composition and an artist's diploma in voice. She studied voice under Ferri Lulek and Dan Beddoe and composition under Edgar Stillman Kelly and Ralph Lyford. She did postgraduate work and studied voice privately under Walter Golde and composition and orchestration under Frederick Jacobi from 1921 to 1922. She worked with Roy Harris on contemporary trends and composition and sang in joint concerts with Dwight Anderson. She gave numerous lecture-recitals in the United States from 1923 to 1967. In 1974 she was one of 13 Alabama composers chosen by the NFMC to participate in a nationwide broadcast of American music. She was the first Alabama musician to have her portrait unveiled in the Music Room of the Alabama Department of Archives and History in the War Memorial Building, Montgomery. PHOTOGRAPH.

Compositions

CHAMBER

The banjo (vln and pf) (1922)
Solitude (vln and pf) (1922)
Moods, suite (pf) (1922)

VOCAL

A spring symphony, cantata (S, w-ch and pf) (1921) (New York and London: J. Church)
Night, cantata (P.L. Dunbar) (w-ch and pf) (1922) (J. Church)
The bird with the broken wing (1918) (J. Church)
A kiss from Columbine (1923) (G. Schirmer)
Little boy blue (1920) (J. Church)
A message (1920) (J. Church)
Rest (1921) (J. Church)
Songs (vce and pf)

Ref. composer, 40, 142, 347, 353

GOLUB, Marta Naumovna

Soviet composer. b. New York, April 9, 1911. She studied composition under B. Asafiev and B. Arapov at the Leningrad Music School. She was also a pupil of Maria Gnesina.

Compositions
ORCHESTRA
Concerto (pf and strs) (G. Schirmer, 1962)
Oboe concerto (1965)
Yunosheski kontsert (pf and orch) (1960)
CHAMBER
Intermezzo (str qrt) (1950)
Five preludes (vln and pf) (1962)
Rondo, poema (vla and pf) (1966)
Sonata (3-stringed domra and pf) (1965)
BAYAN
Ballada (1961)
Etudes
Ten lyrical pieces (1966)
Toccata (1961)
Twelve preludes (1964)
Two sonatas (1963, 1966)
VOCAL
Choruses (I. Gruzdev) (1968)
Romances, folk songs (A. Blok, A. Grasha)
Veselo (L. Ozerov) (1968)
Zimniy les (V. Tikhomirov) (1968)
Ref. 21, 280

GOMEZ CARRILO, Maria Ines

Argentine concert pianist and composer. b. Santiago del Estero, 1918. The daughter of the composer Manuel G. Carillo, she studied the piano under R. Gonzalez, making her debut at the age of 12. She studied composition at the Conservatorio Nacional del Musica y Arte Escenico Athos Palma and was awarded a grant to study in the United States where she studied the piano under Edward Steuermann and composition under Jerzy Fitelberg. She performed with major orchestras in Europe and North and South America. She composed a string quartet, piano pieces and songs.
Ref. 54, 361, 390

GOMM, Elizabeth

British pianist, violinist, violist and composer. b. Henley-on-Thames, March 12, 1951. She began to study the violin and to compose at the age of seven. She studied at Dartington College of Arts and the Guildhall School of Music and Drama, where she was a pupil of Alfred Nieman and P. Standford. She is an L.R.A.M. and plays the violin and the viola in the Lyra Ventura Dance Theatre Commune. In 1974 she was awarded the Composer of the Year award by the Greater London Arts' Association in the Young Musician series. PHOTOGRAPH.
Compositions
CHAMBER
Piece for 12 strings (1973)
Moonraking (vln) (1971)
VOCAL
Clytemnestra's argument (w-ch) (1973)
Orestes' argument (mix-ch) (1974)
Four songs (T and pf) (1973)
Songs of the bull (1972)
SACRED
Agnus Dei (1973)
Ref. composer, 206, 457

GONTARENKO, Galina Nikolayevna

Soviet lecturer and composer. b. Rostov-on-the-Don, August 24, 1946. She studied composition under V.N. Salmanov at the Leningrad Conservatory, graduating in 1971. She began lecturing theoretical subjects in the same year, returning to Rostov in 1972 to lecture at the Music Teachers' Training College.
Compositions
ORCHESTRA
Russian suite (1971)
CHAMBER
Piano quintet (1967)
Five pieces (str qrt) (1965)
Ballade (vln and pf) (1968)
Dance (trb and pf) (1965)
Sonata (vln and pf) (1970)
Sonatina (fl and pf) (1966)
Waltz-scherzo (vln and pf) (1968)
VOCAL
Lobnaya ballada, cantata (A. Vosnesensky) (1975)
Choruses (M. Tsvetaeva) (1967)
Cycle (V. Sosnora) (1973)
Five romances, Russian folk texts (1970)
Other romances (Russian poets)
Ref. 21

GONTIJO DE CARVALHO MURICI, Dinora. See CARVALHO, Dinora de

GONZAGA, Chiquinha (Francisca Hedwiges Neves Gonzaga)

Brazilian pianist, writer and composer. b. Rio de Janeiro, October 17, 1847; d. Rio de Janeiro, February 28, 1935. She studied the piano under E. Alvares Lobo and Artur Napoleao. She wrote her first piece at the age of 11 and became one of Brazil's most popular and prolific composers, writing over 2 000 works. She was the first woman to conduct a theatre orchestra in her country in 1885 and from 1885 to 1933 she wrote the score for 77 plays. Her *Forrobodó* had over 1 500 performances although her *Maria* was considered her best classical theatre work. She was active in the slave freedom movement and through the sale of one of her scores bought freedom for the slave musician, Jose Flauta. She traveled in several countries in Europe from 1902 to 1910 and when in Portugal set several Portuguese plays to music. She was a founder member of the Sociedade Brazileira de Autores Teatrais. DISCOGRAPHY.
Compositions
ORCHESTRA
Ary, waltz (grand orch)
Cananeia, waltz (pf and orch)
Dança No. 2
Estrella d'Alva
Forrobodó
Habanera
Meditação
Os mineiros
BAND
O abre-alas, carnival march (1899)
A memória do General Osorio, funeral march
Duquesne (pf and band)
Marcha do Cordão, march
Palaciana (pf and band)
CHAMBER
Manha de amor (cham ens)
Musiciana (cham ens)
Plangente (cham ens)
Tim tim (cham ens)
Balada (pf and vln)
Choro (fl and pf)
Linda Morena (fl and pf)
Meditação (vlc and pf)
Serenata (vln and pf)
Paraguaçu (sax)
Bionne
Em guarda
PIANO
Ballads, marches, polkas, serenades incl.:
Carlos Gomes, waltz
Dança No. 1, in minuet style
E enorme, polka
Foi um sonho, barcarolle
Grata esperança, waltz
Harmonias do coração, concert-waltz
Iara, concert-waltz
Juraci, waltz
Laurita, mazurka
Maria, waltz
A noite
O padre amaro
Radiante, polka
Sonhando, habanera
Toujours et encore, polka
Valquiria, waltz
Yo te adoro
VOCAL
A morena (S and cham ens)
Atraente (1877)
Ai, que bruma (E. Matoso)
Amor (João de Deus)
A baiana dos pasteis, canzonet
Barcelona, barcarolle (composer)
Canção dos pastores (1858)
Desejos (Esculapio)
Espanha e Brasil (J. do Patrocinio Filho)
Gonza (Manobras do Amor, Osorio Duque Estrada)
Ha alguma novidade (Moreira Sampaio)
Iaia fazenda ... (Almeida Junior)
A jandira (R. Gil and A. Breda)
Juriti (Fogo Foguinho, Viriato Correia) (1919)
Lua branca (S and cham ens)
Macucha (S and cham ens)
O mar, ballad (Holanda Cunha)
Menina faceira (composer)

O namoro (Frederico Junior)
O perdão, romance (A. Quintiliano)
O que e simpatia, modinha
Os namorados da lua (S and strs)
A republica
Santa (A. de Oliveira)
A trigueira (Julio Diniz)
SACRED
Songs (vce and pf) incl.:
L'age du seigneur
Agnus Dei
Ave Maria
Prece a Virgem
Vamos a missa
Vinde, vinde
OPERETTA
A corte na roca (Francisco Sodre)
Forrobodó, in 3 acts (L. Peixoto and C. Bettencourt) (1912)
Maria (Viriato Correa) (1933)
THEATRE
Music for about 77 plays incl.:
A bota do Diabo (A. Andrade)
As três graças (L. Galhardo)
Corta-Jaca (O Gaucho)
Festa de S. João (composer) (1883)
A sertaneja (1915)
Viagem ao Parnaso (A. Azevedo)

Bibliography

Almeida, Renato. References in *Historia da Musica Brasileira*. Rio de Janeiro: F. Briguet & Ca, 1942.
Cernicchiaro, Vincenzo. *Storia della musica nel Brasile*. 1926.
Chase, Gilbert. *A Guide to Latin American Music*. 1943.
Correia de Azevedo, L.H. *150 anos de musica no Brasil*. 1800, 1950, 1956.
Lira, Mariza. *C. Gonzaga, grande compositora popular Brasileira. Rio de Janeiro*. 1939.

Ref. 17, 19, 106, 297, 333, 349, 563

GONZAGA, Margherita
15th-century Spanish musician and composer. She was a member of the concerto of ladies, a group who played woodwind instruments and viols and were led by a concertmistress.

GONZALEZ-GRAGIRENA, Maria Luisa. See ESCOBAR, Maria Luisa

GONZALEZA, Dona Paz
19th-century composer.
Composition
OPERA
Cambio de clima, zarzuela (Santander, 1866)
Ref. 431

GOODE, Blanche
American pianist, lecturer and composer. b. Warren, IN, March 26, 1889. She studied under Alexander Lambert and Theodore Leschetizky and later taught at Smith College, Northampton, MA. She made her debut in New York in 1914 and was a soloist with the New York Philharmonic. She composed piano pieces and songs.
Ref. 226

GOODEVE, Mrs. Arthur (also Mrs. William)
19th-century English composer.
Compositions
VOCAL
Donald Graeme
Fiddle and I (vce and pf) (Jacobson-Zimbalist)
If thou must love me
In the silver years
Ref. 63, 226, 276, 433

GOODMAN, Lillian Rosedale
American pianist, authoress, lecturer, singer and composer. b. Mitchell, SD, May 30, 1887. She was educated at Columbia University and the Juilliard School of Music. She studied under Alexander Lamber, Percy Gretchin, Julius Gold, Buzzi-Peccia, Mme. Jandenzi and Emil Fuchs. She was awarded an honorary D.Mus. by the Boguslawski College and was head of the vocal department there. She sang in vaudevilles, operettas, theatres, concerts and on radio. She started her own musical booking agency in Chicago. She became the vocal teacher for the Desilu Workshop, Hollywood in 1958. She did most of her work with Anton Bilotti and her husband Mark Goodman. She was a member of ASCAP.
Compositions
VOCAL
Cherie, I love you
If I could look into your eyes
I say you can sing (vocal exercises)
Just a bit of dreaming
The sun goes down
You have my heart
SACRED
Ecstasy
I found you
Let there be peace
My shepherd is the Lord
Our prayer
Ref. 39, 63

GOODSMITH, Ruth B
American pianist, professor and composer. b. Chicago, IL, September 27, 1892. She studied under Arne Oldberg and Carl Beecher at Northwestern University where she obtained a B.M. in 1922. She studied the piano under Josef Lhevinne in 1921, Isidor Philipp and Mme. Helene Chaumont in Paris in 1927 and Tomford Harris in Chicago from 1938 to 1940. She also studied under Andre Bloch in Fontainebleau in 1927, Alfred Rossi in Milan in 1930 and Adolf Weidig and Leo Sowerby at the American Conservatory, where she received her M.M. in 1939. She was on the faculty of Stephens College from 1920 to 1928 and visiting professor at the University of Redlands from 1952 to 1953. In 1954 she won first prize in a Mu Phi Epsilon contest and in 1967, third place in a contest organized by the NFMC.
Compositions
ORCHESTRA
Cello Concerto (1938)
CHAMBER
String quartet (1938)
Lullaby (hp; also pf)
Piano pieces
VOCAL
And in the hanging garden (ch and orch)
SACRED
God's rider (ch and orch) (hon mention, Juilliard composition contest, 1939)
OPERA
Lolita, chamber opera (1953)
Ref. 142, 347, 496

GOODWIN, Amina Beatrice
English pianist, teacher and composer. b. Manchester, December 5, 1867; d. East Moseley, March 10, 1942. She received her first lessons from her father, the violinist and conductor John Lawrence Goodwin. She studied under Reinecke and Jadassohn in Leipzig; Delaborde in Paris; Liszt; and Clara Schumann (q.v.). She was considered one of the leading pianists of her day. In 1901, together with Achille Simonetti the violinist and William Edward Whitehouse the cellist, she formed the London Trio. She founded the Pianoforte College for Women in London in 1895.
Compositions
PIANO
Toccata (Augener)
Other pieces
Publications
Practical Hints on Technique and Touch: Practical Hints on the Technique of Pianoforte Playing. Augener, 1892.
Ref. 6, 8, 85, 226, 260, 276, 297, 347

GOOLKASIAN-RAHBEE, Dianne Zabelle
Armenian-American pianist, lecturer and composer. b. Somerville, MA, February 9, 1938. She began studying music with Antoine Louis Moeldner, a pupil of Paderewski and Helen Hopekirk (q.v.). She then studied the piano at the Juilliard School of Music, working with the composers Hugo Weisgall, Vittorio Giannini, Robert Starer and Arnold Fish; and privately with David Saperton and at the Mozarteum in Salzburg. She later studied composition with John Heiss and the piano with Lily Dumont, Russel Sherman and Veronica Jochum. She gave lectures for musical organisations and workshops in Boston. DISCOGRAPHY. PHOTOGRAPH.

Compositions
CHAMBER
Fragments, op. 14, short pieces (fl, ob, cl and bsn)
Pages from my diary (str qrt) (1984)
String quartet, op. 2a
String quartet improvisation, op. 6
Discourse (vla and pf) (comm)
PIANO
Tarantella, duet (Carousel)
Abstracts, op. 7
Essay No. 1, op. 1 (Carousel)
Essays, op. 4, 12 short pieces
Expressions, op. 8, 9 short pieces
Phantasie variations, op. 12
Question, op. 11
Pictures, op. 3 (Boston Music)
Preludes, op. 5, 3 pieces
Ref. composer, 625

GOOSENS, Marie Henriette
English harpist, arranger and composer. b. London, August 11, 1894. She was the sister of conductor Eugene Goosens and studied at the Royal College of Music. From 1912 she was principal harpist for the Convent Garden Opera, Diaghilev Ballet Seasons, Queen's Hall Orchestra from 1920 to 1930, London Philharmonic Orchestra from 1932 to 1939 and the London Symphony Orchestra from 1940 to 1959.
Compositions
THEATRE
Mrs Dale's Diary, radio (hp)
ARRANGEMENTS
Fourteen Tunes (Celtic harp)
Ref. 77, 457

GORDON, Hope
Compositions
PIANO
Daphne, Lied ohne Worte (Bosworth)
Welcome home, march (Leonard)
Ref. 297

GORE, Blanche
Compositions
CHAMBER
Gavotte in D (vln and pf) (Leonard)
OPERETTA
Invisible maiden (Leonard)
Ref. 297

GORE, Katharina (nee Francis)
English writer and composer. b. Nottingham, 1799.
Compositions
VOCAL
Of the Highlandchurch, song
And ye shall walk in silk attire (Burns)
Ref. 129

GORELLI, Olga
American lecturer and composer. b. Bologna, Italy, June 14, 1920. She became an American citizen in 1945. She studied under Gian Carlo Menotti and Rosario Scalero at the Curtis Institute, under Quincy Porter and Paul Hindemith at Yale University, Werner Josten and Alvin Etler at Smith College and under Darius Milhaud. She was a teaching fellow at Smith College from 1948 to 1950, lecturer at Hollins College from 1950 to 1954 and faculty member at Trenton State College from 1954 to 1957. She won the Fatman Prize at Smith College in 1949 and 1951.
Compositions
ORCHESTRA
Works
CHAMBER
Pieces
VOCAL
Songs
SACRED
Mass (English)
OPERA
Between the Shadow and the Dream
Dona Petra
THEATRE
Two dance dramas
Incidental music
Ref. 142

GORODOVSKAYA, V.
20th-century Soviet composer. She composed many pieces for the domra which the talented domra player and folk singer Y. Shishakov included in his repertoire.
Compositions
CHAMBER
Concert pieces for the domra
Ref. 441

GORONCY, Emilie
19th-century German singer and composer. She entered the Singakademie in Berlin in 1826 and sang the soprano role in *Tod Jesu* in 1826 and 1827.
Compositions
VOCAL
Six songs incl.:
Die Friedensgesellschaft in West-Preussen (vce and pf) (Danzig: Ewert, 1832)
Wanderers nachtlied (vce and pf) (Berlin: Wagenfuhr)
Ref. 121

GORTON, Karen
Composition
CHAMBER
Folk Suite (ww qnt)
Ref. 624

GORYAINOVA, A.
19th-century Russian composer.
Compositions
PIANO
Chad zhizni, op. 6, waltz (Seywang)
Chic de Varsovie, op. 2, mazurka (Seywang)
Dans noble, pas de quatre, op. 11 (Seywang)
Dvenattsits mraka k svit, waltz, op. 2 (Seywang)
Gvardeiskaya, mazurka, op. 21 (Seywang)
Igra v lyubov, waltz, op. 7 (Seywang)
Magnit polka, op. 3 (Seywang)
Neugodno la vam, polka, op. 1 (Seywang)
Ne uprekai, waltz, op. 14 (Seywang)
Pas de quatre, op. 16 (Seywang)
Pod tremya orlami, polka, op. 17 (Seywang)
Quadrille on themes from operettas Martin Rudokop and Probnyi Potsielyi, op. 12 (Seywang)
Regatta valse, op. 4 (Seywang)
Tsaritsa bala, minuet, op. 19 (Seywang)
Vysh subdy, waltz, op. 18 (Seywang)
Zhivye tsviety, waltz, op. 20 (Seywang)
Zhizi khokhochet, waltz, op. 13 (Seywang)
Ref. 297

GOSSLER, Clara von
19th-century German composer. She composed piano pieces and songs.
Ref. 226, 276

GOTKOVSKY, Ida-Rose Esther
French pianist and composer. b. Calais, August 26, 1933. She is the daughter of the violinist Jacques Gotkovsky and sister of the violinist Nell Gotkovsky. She studied at the Paris Conservatory under Ciampi, Hugon, N. Gallon, Tony Aubin, Messiaen and Nadia Boulanger (q.v.). Her prizes included the Prix Blumenthal in 1958; Prix Pasdeloup in 1959; Prix de Composition du Concours International de Divonne les Bains in 1961; Medaille de la Ville de Paris in 1963 and Prix Lily Boulanger (q.v.) in 1967. DISCOGRAPHY.
Compositions
ORCHESTRA
Concerto lyrique, pour clarinette et orchestre (1968)
Concerto pour deux violins et orchestre (1962)
Concerto pour orchestre (1971)

Concerto pour saxophone et orchestre (1966)
Concerto for trombone and orchestra (Harrassowitz, 1978)
Concerto pour trompette et orchestre (1972)
Concerto pour violoncelle et orchestre (1974)
Symphonie pour cordes et timbales (1958)
Symphonie pour orchestre d'harmonie
Symphonie pour quatre-vingts instruments à vent (Holland: Molenaar, 1960)
Musique en couleurs (1966)
Scherzo (1956)
Variations concertantes pour basson et orchestre (1970)

CHAMBER
Suite pour dix instruments (1957):
Quatuor à cordes (1956)
Trio à vent (1955)
Baladins (tba and pf) (Robert Martin, 1983)
Brillance (sax and pf) (1974)
Caractères (vla and pf) (1974)
Concerto (hn and pf) (Billaudot, 1984)
Eolienne (fl and hp) (1976)
Lied (trb and pf) (Martin, 1983)
Romance (trb and pf) (Martin, 1983)
Ritournelle (trp and pf) (Martin, 1983)
Piano pieces

VOCAL
Invocation lyrique (A and pf)
Songs

BALLET
Rien ne va plus

OPERA
Le Rêve de Makar (W. Korolenko) (1964) (1st prize, Ville de Paris, 1966)

INCIDENTAL MUSIC
Escapades
Funambulesques
Jeux
Jongleries

Publications
Traite d'orchestration de D. Dondeyne.
Ref. composer, 76, 84, 85, 94, 206, 304, 347, 563, 622

GOTTSCHALK, Clara

English composer. b. October 4, 1837.
Compositions
PIANO
Echo de la Floride
Joyous Spring (Williams)
Minuit à Venise, reverie barcarolle (Novello)
Pixies' merry-making, petite caprice de genre (Ashdown)

VOCAL
Wake thee, my dear (mix-ch) (Novello)
Love thee? (Novello)

ARRANGEMENTS
Cradle song (Taubert) (pf) (Schott)
In seclusion (Franz R) (pf) (Schott)
Ref. 297

GOTZE, Auguste. See GOETZE, Auguste

GOUBAN D'HORVOST, Mme. See D'HAVORST, Leopoldine

GOUBAU D'HAVORST, Leopoldine

Early 19th-century Austrian composer.
Compositions
PIANO
Sonata in A-Flat (2 pf) (Vienna: Haslinger)
Caprice, op. 2 (Vienna: Maisch, 1813)
Ref. 433

GOUGELET, Mme.

Late 18th-century French composer. She wrote a method for piano accompaniment.
Ref. 226

GOULD, Doris

20th-century English composer.
Composition
OPERA
Love's a Gamble (London: OUP, 1961)
Ref. 141

GOULD, Elizabeth Davies

American pianist and composer. b. Toledo, OH, March 9, 1904. She studied at the University of Toledo, Oberlin College and Conservatory, and the University of Michigan under Artur Schnabel and Guy Maier (piano). She obtained a B.A., a B.M. and an artist's diploma. In 1965 she won the Delta Omicron first prize. She was named one of ten leading women composers by the National Council of Women of the United States in 1963. She received the Arthur Shepherd award in 1969 and won six first prizes and two special citations in Mu Phi Epsilon contests.
Compositions
ORCHESTRA
Mini-symphony with an introduction to the instruments (1973)
Concerto for piano and orchestra (1953)
Concerto for trumpet and strings (1959)
Concertino for clarinet, trumpet and strings (1959)
Escapade, overture (1960)
Flashes of our time (comm Toledo Symphony)
Games, for orchestra and very young pianists (1962)
Music for a celebration (1971)

CHAMBER
Suite for woodwinds, brass and percussion (1965)
Six affinities (brass qnt) (1962)
Flute quartet (1963)
Free forms for four flutes (1973, 1976)
The kitty-cat bird (fl, ob, cl and bsn) (1964)
String quartet (1960) (award, Mannheim, 1961)
The acrobatic winds (ob, cl and bsn) (1963)
Disciplines (ob, cl and bsn) (Presser, 1963)
Fantasy and passacaglia, string trio
Trio (vln, vlc and pf) (1964)
Andante (trp and pf) (Presser, 1959)
Fantasy and fugue (bsn and pf) (1965)
Fifteen easy pieces (vlc and pf) (1965)
Figments (fl and marimba) (1972)
Music for viola and piano (1964)
Sonata (vla and pf) (1963)
Sonata (vln and pf) (1951)
Sonata (vlc and pf) (1959)
Triadic suite (fl and pf) (1974)

ORGAN
Celebration fantasy (1970)
Sonatina No. 1 (1962)
Sonatina No. 2 (1971)
Toccata and four preludes (1950)

PIANO
Rhythm (2 pf) (1955)
Scintillations, ballet music (2 pf) (1969)
Tarantella (2 pf) (1969)
Three effects (4 hands) (1958)
Bits and bites
Five ideas
Four preludes, set 2 (1973)
Guidelines
Marches
Prelude (1947)
Reflector, prelude
Rhythm (1971)
Sonata No. 1 (1958)
Sonata No. 2 (1961)
Sonatina (1962)
Smog
Speed
Three stylistic effects (1969)
Toccata (1950)
Tranquilizer

VOCAL
Declaration for peace (ch and orch) (1955)
Ballad for an Indonesian feast (comm Masterworks Chorale)
The barber's song (w-vce) (1982)
The drum of morning and the flute of night, madrigal cycle (1964)
Fiddle songs (w-vce and pf) (1971)
Personal and private, song cycle (1969)
Prologue to men are naive (narr, pf, fl and vln) (1955)
Reflections at dawn (3 S and pf) (1971)

SACRED
Halleluia, anthem (ch, org, timp and cym) (1969)
Hymn of the Ascension (ch, chil-ch and org) (1975)

Transformation, a song of hope, anthem (ch, chil-ch and org) (1970)
Christmas (S and org) (1969)
OPERA
Ray and the Gospel Singer, comic opera
Ref. composer, 40, 94, 142, 147, 228

GOULD, Janetta
Scottish harpsichordist, pianist, lecturer and composer. b. Kilsyth, August 19, 1926. She attended the University of Glasgow where she obtained an M.A. She studied music for two years under Sir Ernest Bullock and the piano under Bernard Stevens. Her works were accepted for inclusion in the Scottish Music Archives Glasgow University. Together with her husband she founded the Glasgow Harpsichord Society in 1981. She was a lecturer in Glasgow University's Extra-Mural Department and a private piano teacher. PHOTOGRAPH.
Compositions
CHAMBER
Fils (vl, cl, vlc and pf) (1973)
Duo for clarinets in B-Flat (1967)
Sontag II (vlc and pf) (1978)
Suite for horn and piano (1958)
Abbey suite (org) (1969)
Fun fairs (hpcd)
Introduction and allegro (cl) (1970)
September (vla) (1976)
Les dix, two short studies (hpcd) (1982)
VOCAL
Saltire suite (ch and org) (1977)
Country lass, song cycle (1967)
Fifteen Burns songs (1966-1976)
My heart is overflowing (S and vla) (1973)
Two dialogue songs (1969)
Publications
Harpsichord playing for pianists. 1980-1981.
Collection of short pieces for harpsichord. 1982.
Composition *studies for harpsichord*. 1983.
Ref. composer

GOULD, Octavia R.
Composition
OPERA
A Real Merry Christmas
Ref. 465

GOVEA, Wenonah Milton
American harpist, organist, pianist, lecturer and composer. b. Modesto, CA, January 19, 1924. She studied composition under Fred Fox at the California State University where she obtained her M.A. and taught.
Compositions
VOCAL
Soletas (Lorca) (ch and 2 hp)
Indian day cycle (vce and hp)
Opus felinus (T.S. Eliot) (vce and pf)
SACRED
Sing we now of Christmas (Walton, 1981)
OPERETTA
A Jigger o'Scotch
Ref. California State University

GOWER, Beryl. See ATKINSON, Dorothy

GRAB, Isabella von
19th-century German composer.
Compositions
PIANO
Deux marches funebres, op. 1
Dramatisches Fantasiebild, op. 3
Impromptu, op. 2
Songs without words, op. 4
Ref. 226, 276, 347

GRABOWSKA, Clementine, Countess
Polish pianist and composer. b. Poznan, 1771; d. Paris, 1831. She was a talented pianist and settled in Paris in 1813 and gave concerts. Her compositions were published in Warsaw and Poznan.
Compositions
ORCHESTRA
Piano concerto
PIANO
Grande polonaise
Notturno, op. 3 (Heinrichshofen)
Sonata, op. 1
Sonata, op. 2
Two polonaises
Variations on the air Narguons la tristesse
Ref. 8, 35, 105, 128, 129, 226, 276, 297

GRAD-BUCH, Hulda
Israeli pianist, teacher and composer. b. Haifa, September 30, 1912. She studied at the Paris Conservatoire. DISCOGRAPHY. PHOTOGRAPH.
Compositions
PIANO
A sweet for youth (1974) (Israel Music Edition)
Cultivation for piano music (1965) (Israel Music)
Other pieces
Publications
Piano First Book. 1940. Israel Music.
Books of Exercises and Etudes. 1975-1980. Israel Music.
Ref. composer

GRAEFIN (Grafe), Sophia Regina
18th-century German poetess and composer. She was the daughter of a priest and lived near Leipzig. According to Wetzel in his 'Liederhistorie', vol. 1, she set the church services for holidays and Sundays to music. These were printed without her knowledge under the title *Eines andachtigen Frauenzimmers S.R.G. ihrem Jesu im Glauben dargebrachtes Liebes-Opfer*. (Leipzig, 1715).
Ref. 126, 129

GRAEVER, Madeleine
Dutch concert pianist, teacher and composer. b. Amsterdam, ca. 1830. She studied under Bertelsman, D. Koning and Moscheles and later under Litolf. She was a highly successful concert pianist and performed in Paris, Belgium, Germany, England and New York. In 1861 she settled in New York as a pianist and teacher. After the War of Succession she returned to Europe and in 1863 became court pianist to the Queen of Belgium.
Compositions
PIANO
L'Attente
Le réveil de printemps
La ronde des fantomes
Other pieces
Ref. 26, 129, 276, 400

GRAFE, Sophia Regina. See GRAEFIN, Sophie Regina

GRAFF, Maria Magdelena. See KAUTH, Maria Magdalena

GRAFIN, Sophia Regina. See GRAEFIN, Sophia Regina

GRAHAM, Janet Christine
English pianist, violist, teacher and composer. b. Consett, Durham, June 4, 1948. She began playing the piano at the age of two but had little professional training until she was 14, when she wrote her first compositions. She played the viola in the Durham Youth Orchestra. From 1966 to 1971 she studied composition at the Royal College of Music under James Iliff and the piano under Virginia McLean and George Rogers. She won several awards for composition and after graduation taught the piano and composition at the Mid-Hertfordshire Music Centre. She continued her study of composition under Elisabeth Luytens (q.v.) for another year and a half. She married the organist Philip Deane. PHOTOGRAPH.
Compositions
ORCHESTRA
The sons of Cronos
CHAMBER
Septet (fl, ob, cl, vln, vla, vlc and perc)
Quartet (fl, vln, vla and vlc)

String quartet (1976)
String quartet No. 4
Circulus (vlc and pf)
Crux (fl and pf) (1976)
Three pieces for bass clarinet and piano (comm Nottingham Festival, 1978)
Evening flights (fl)
Soliloquium (ob)
Atque in perpetuum (1974)

PIANO
Diversitas (2 pf) (1974)
Five pieces (1977)
Hecate
Persephone
Sonata (1972)

VOCAL
Cras amet (S) (1973)
The dream (S and str qrt) (1977)
Four songs (S and pf)
This great and wide sea (S, cl, pf and perc)
When we two walked (S, cl, b-cl and pf)

Ref. composer

GRAHAM, Shirley Lola. See DUBOIS, Shirley Graham

GRAHAM, Sybil
20th-century Australian composer.
Compositions
THEATRE
But I Wouldn't Want to Live There, musical (1969)
A Cup of Tea, a Bex and a Good Lie Down, musical
Hail Gloria Fitzpatrick, musical (1970)
Is Australia Necessary, musical (1965)

Ref. 442

GRAINGER, Ella Viola Strom-Brandelius
American painter, writer and composer. b. Stockholm, Sweden, May 1, 1889; d. July 17, 1979. After attending school in Liljeholmen she spent two years at the Bjoerstedska Handels-Institut in Stockholm and in 1906 studied art at the Slade School in London. After her marriage to the composer and concert pianist Percy Aldridge Grainger she became involved in music and composing. DISCOGRAPHY. PHOTOGRAPH.
Compositions
PIANO
Bigelow march (1940)

VOCAL
Farewell to an Atoll (S, mix-ch and orch; also vce and pf) (1944)
Heartless (m-S and mix-ch) (1947)
Love at first sight (S, w-ch and opt Bar; also S, mix ch; also vce and pf) (G. Schirmer, 1946)
Playing on the heartstrings (mix-ch or w-ch) (1950)
Crying for the moon (Cont, perc; also Cont and pf) (1946)
Honey pot bee (m-S, strs, hp, pf, harm and vibraharp; also vce and pf) (1947)
The mermaid (m-S, a-sax; also vce and pf) (1947)
There's a thing you never knew (1946)
To echo (vce and pf) (1945)

SACRED
Sussex Mummer's Christmas Carol

MISCELLANEOUS
Carman's whistle
Children's march
Chinese - beautiful fresh flower
Immovable 'Do'
Irish tune from county derry
Lullaby from tribute to Foster
Molly on the shore
Nell, après un rêve
Walking tune

Ref. Stewart Manville, 433

GRAMATTE, Sonia Friedman. See ECKHART-GRAMATTE, Sophie-Carmen

GRAMEGLIA-GROSSO, Emma
Italian composer. b. 1908.
Compositions
CHAMBER
Nine pieces for the harp (trans from compositions for lute)
Pieces (lute)

Ref. Ricordi (Milan)

GRAMMONT, Mme. de. See RENAUD-D'ALLEN Mme. de

GRANDVAL, Marie Felicie (Felice) Clemence de Reiset, Vicomtesse de (pseuds. Caroline Blangy, Clemence Valgrand, Maria Felicita de Reiset and Maria Reiset de Tesier)
French composer. b. Chateau de la Cour-de-Bois, Saint-Remy des Monts, Sarthe, January 20, 1830; d. Paris, January 15, 1907. One of the most active members of the French musical school, she began to study music at the age of six and later studied composition under Flotow. Her education was left incomplete when her tutor left France. Later she studied under Camille Saint-Saens for two years and received instruction from Chopin. She was said to be one of the foremost woman composers of her time.
Compositions
ORCHESTRA
Amazones, lyric symphony
Ouverture (grand orch)
Divertissement hongrois
Esquisses symphoniques
Le matin
Le soir

CHAMBER
Gavotte (vlc, d-b and pf) (Costallat)
Trios, No. 1, op. 7, and no. 2 (Paris: Lemoine)
Andante con moto (vlc and pf) (Costallat)
Chanson suisse (vlc and pf)
Chant serbe (vlc and pf) (Costallat)
Concertino (vln and pf)
Concerto, op. 7 (ob and pf) (Heugel)
Musette (vln and pf) (Schott)
Prélude et variations (vln and pf)
Serenade (vlc and pf) (Costallat)
Sonata, op. 8 (vln and pf) (Lemoine)
Suite de morceaux (fl and pf) (Costallat)
Two Pieces: Andantino; Bohemienne (vln and pf)
Two Pieces: Lamento; Scherzo (d-b and pf)
Valse mélancolique (fl and hp)

PIANO
Mazurka du ballet (2 pf)
Attente (Durand)
Barcarolle
Chanson d'hiver (Fromont; Durand)
Cloche (Durand)
Consolatrix (Durand)
Grillon (Durand)
Menuet (Fromont)
Nocturnes, op. 5 and op. 6 (Lemoine)
Paquerette (Durand)
Transcriptions for piano

VOCAL
La Forêt, lyric scene (soloists, ch and orch) (1875)
Marche, choeur triomphale: Gloire a toi (mix-ch and pf)
Ronde des songes (ch and pf)
Fleur du matin (ch and pf; also pf) (Durand; Fromont)
Heures (ch and pf)
Adeon (1876)
Album de sept melodies
Chanson d'autrefois
Chanson de la coquille
Chanson laponne (Fromont)
Délaissee
Jeanne d'Arc, grand scène
Les Lucioles, révèrie (m-S, vln, pf and org)
Nimes (1902)
Rapelle-toi
Regrets
Rose et violette (S)
Si jetais Dieu
Si tu m'aimais (Heugel)
Solitude (Fromont)
Stalactites
Trilby
Vilanelle

SACRED
La fille de Jaire, oratorio (Rossini Prize, 1879) (P. Collin)
St. Agnes, oratorio
Benedictus (3 vces or mix-ch, org and pf)

Kyrie, duet (ch) (Durand)
Mass No. 2 (soloists, ch and orch)
Stabat Mater (soloists, ch, pf and org) (Durand) (1870)
Agnus Dei (S and T) (Durand)
Ave Verum
Gratias (vces, pf and org)
Lauda anima mea Dominum (Durand)
March to Calvary and Juxta Crucum
Messe breve (Durand)
Noël (Fromont)
O Salutaris (S) (Durand)
Offertoire (vce and insts)
Pater Noster (S, pf and org)
Tarry with me O my Saviour (3 vces) (Ditson)

BALLET
Callirhoe, ballet-symphonie

OPERA
Atala (1888)
Le Bouclier de Diamant
La Comtesse Eva, opera comique in 1 act (1864)
Donna Maria Infanta di Spagna, in 3 acts (with Langert) (Leiser) (1865)
Les Fiancées de Rosa, opera comique in 1 act (C.A. Choler) (as Clemence Valgrand) (Paris, 1863)
Mazeppa (Bordeaux, 1892)
Il Mugnaio di Marlinac (La Mugnaia di Marly) (1863)
La Penitente, opera comique in 1 act (E. Meilhac and G.B. Busnach) (1868)
Piccolino, in 3 acts (A. De Lauzieres) (1869)
Salli Ventadour (1875)

OPERETTA
Le Sou de Lise, in 1 act (as Caroline Blangy) (1859)

Bibliography
Buffenoir, Hippolyte. *Madame de Grandval.* Paris: Mirabeau.

Ref. 17, 22, 26, 44, 70, 74, 85, 105, 108, 110, 129, 132, 183, 225, 226, 260, 276, 296, 297, 347, 369, 394, 415, 465, 646

GRANJE, Rosa

Belgian lecturer and composer. b. Antwerp, November 23, 1907. She studied composition, counterpoint and fugue at the Royal Flemish Conservatory under Flor Alpaert. In 1934 she won the A. de Vleeschouwer prize and in 1935 received an honorable mention in the Prix de Rome. In 1942 she became assistant teacher and in 1954 teacher of harmony at the Antwerp Conservatory. She was also music teacher at the Royal Girls' Lyceum in Antwerp.

Compositions

ORCHESTRA
De oude soldaat (1935)
Sir Haelewijn (1936)
Somerindruk (1934)

VOCAL
Lieder (vce, orch or pf) (1937-1953)

Ref. CeBeDeM, 44, 94

GRANT, Louise (Louisa)

20th-century American composer.

Compositions

VOCAL
Love's calendar (mix-vces) (Novello)
Walk the world (mix-ch and pf) (Neil A. Kjos)
When I am dead, my dearest (vln obb) (Paterson)
Unionist march (Weekes)

Ref. 190, 297

GRAU, Irene Rosenberg

American pianist, professor and composer. b. New York, October 12, 1927. She was a professor of music at Missouri University for Women and contributed articles to various musical publications. In 1965 she received a grant for composition from the University; she also received other local awards. She is a member of ASCAP.

Compositions

ORCHESTRA
Passacaglia and fugue for strings

SACRED
Hear us O Lord from heav'n, Thy dwelling place
Hymn of praise
Unto Thee do we cry

Publications
A comparison of three methods for improving intonation in the performance of instrumental music. 1963.

Ref. 206

GRAUBNER, Hannelore

East German composer. b. Erfurt, June 7, 1924. She studied in Graz at the Hochschule fuer Musikerziehung from 1941 to 1943 and in Weimar at the Hochschule fuer Musik Franz Liszt from 1947 to 1949, where her teachers were Karl Marx, Johann Cilensek and Ottmar Gerster.

Compositions

ORCHESTRA
Chamber concertino, op. 12, 1 movement (vln and str ens)

CHAMBER
String quartet, op. 18
Wind trio, op. 15 (fl, cl and bsn)
Sonata, op. 8 (vln and pf)
Sonata piccola capricciosa, op. 5 (a-rec and pf)
Compositizione con mono proposta, op. 17 (org)
Sonata, op. 7 (pf)

VOCAL
Small chamber choral cycle, op. 4 (Lori Ludwig) (w-vces)
Die Igelei, op. 9 (speaker and pf)
Three love songs, op. 16 (w-vce and pf)
Totenlieder, op. 14 (vce and pf)
Two children's songs, op. 10 (S and pf)

Ref. composer

GRAUMANN, Mathilde. See MARCHESI, Matilde de Castrone

GRAVES, Julia Aurelia. See ADAMS, Julia Aurelia

GRAY, Dorothy

20th-century American composer. She composed choral works and songs.

Ref. 40, 347

GRAY, Judith

20th-century American composer. She studied under Stefan Grove at the Peabody Conservatory.

Composition

PIANO
Convocation, No. 3 (1967)

Ref. 142

GRAY, Louisa (Mrs. Abingdon Compton)

19th-century English composer.

Compositions

PIANO
Addio, waltzes
At eve (Chappell)
Fiorita (Chappell)

VOCAL
Songs incl.:
Evening star
Jeanette (A and B) (Brainard)
Jenny's wedding (m-S) (Brainard; Cramer; Williams)
The thread of the story
Under the lamplight (A) (Brainard; Williams)
What an angel heard

OPERETTA
Between Two Stools (ca. 1860)

Ref. 6, 85, 226, 276, 297, 307

GRAY, Victoria Winifred

Canadian pianist and composer. b. Victoria, British Columbia, July 27, 1959. She obtained her B.Mus. (composition) at the University of Regina. She studied at the Shawnigan Summer School of the Arts under Malcolm Arnold and Rudolf Kamorus and composition under Dr. Murray Adaskin and Dr. Thomas Schedel. She has performed extensively. PHOTOGRAPH.

Compositions

CHAMBER
Woodwind quartet No. 1 (fl, ob, cl and bsn) (1980)
Soliloquy in waltz time (pf and vln) (1974)
Pan (fl) (1976)
Puck (fl) (1974)

PIANO
The old stone wall, suite of 9 pieces (1969)
Fantasia (1970)
Hallowe'en suite (1972)
Theme and variations (1971)
Ref. composer

GRAZIANA
French composer.
Compositions
PIANO
A batons rompus (Givre)
Carmen, mazurka (Givre)
Coco, polka (Ascherberg)
Etoile des amours, waltz (Ascherberg)
Langage du coeur (Ascherberg)
Lever de l'aurore, waltz (Ascherberg)
Moscovite, polka (Ascherberg)
Parade écossaise, march (Ascherberg)
Polka hongroise (Ascherberg)
Valse russe de Michel Strogoff (Ascherberg)
Voeux de bonheur, waltz (Ascherberg)
VOCAL
Faut que j'travaille, song (la chanson joyeuse)
Ref. 297

GRAZIANINI, Caterina Benedicta
Early 18th-century Italian composer. Her music was performed at the Vienna Court and in Modena.
Compositions
SACRED
Oratorio di San Gemignano vescovo e protettore di Modena, in 2 parts (1705)
Santa Teresa, in 2 parts (4 vces and insts)
Ref. 105, 128

GRAZIE, G delle. See DELLE GRAZIE, Gisella

GREATEST STAGE NAME OF THE NORTH. See HEIBERG, Johanne Louise

GREATOREX, Martha
19th-century British composer.
Compositions
THEATRE
Midas, vaudeville (1824)
MISCELLANEOUS
Cease your funning, air
Ref. 431

GRECA, Antonia La (Fardiola)
Italian composer. b. Palermo, ca. 1631; d. Palermo, May 8, 1668.
Compositions
SACRED
Armonia sacra a 2, 3, 4, e 5 voci, op. 1, libro 1 (1647)
Ref. 128

GREEN, Lydia
20th-century composer.
Composition
OPERA
Exit the Villain (Harriet Lyons)
Ref. 141

GREEN, Martha. See STAIR, Patty

GREEN, Mary Thompson
American singer and composer. b. Portland, July 30, 1823; d. January 1924. She ran an entertainment bureau in Portland for several years and sang with the Savage Opera Company.
Composition
VOCAL
Dear old Maine (State song)
Ref. 374

GREEN, Miss
Compositions
VOCAL
The Pimpernel (ded Mrs. W.C. Long) (Cramer, Beale and Co.)
Life is a summer's day (ded Mrs. W.C. Long) (Cramer, Beale and Co.)
Ref. H. Baron (London)

GREENE, Diana
20th-century composer.
Composition
MISCELLANEOUS
Rigorisms II (comm Pittsburgh New Music Ensemble)
Ref. AMC newsletter

GREENE, Edith
19th-century English composer.
Compositions
ORCHESTRA
Symphony (1895)
CHAMBER
Sonata (vln and pf)
Other works
Ref. 226, 260, 276, 347

GREENE, Genevieve
American pianist, violinist, lecturer and composer. b. Winfield, KS, February 26, 1924. She studied at Southwestern College, Ohio University and the Juilliard School of Music. She was the musical director of the Parkersburg Actors' Guild, a faculty member of Marietta College, OH, and concertmistress of the Civic Symphonette, Marietta.
Compositions
CHAMBER
Duo violin sonata in F-Minor
Four preludes (pf)
BALLET
Ballet music
THEATRE
Eden on the River, musical drama
Ref. 206

GREENE, Margo Lynn
American pianist, accompanist, secretary, teacher, writer and composer. b. Brooklyn, NY, June 10, 1948. She had her first piano lessons at the age of five. After attending Bennington College for two years, she studied the piano privately under Edna Golandsky and composition under Louis Calabror while completing her B.A. in music at Barnard College. She obtained her M.A. (composition) in 1972 at Columbia University, where her principal teachers were Mario Davidovsky, Vladimir Ussachevsky, Charles Wuorinen and Jack Beeson. In 1977 she studied composition privately under the composer Bulent Arel. She was recording assistant to Vladimir Ussachevsky and secretary to Julius Rudel. She contributed to numerous American journals and performed in concerts. PHOTOGRAPH.
Compositions
CHAMBER
Suite from Coo-me-doo, they're only made of clay (whistles, 3 rec, perc, hpcd and/or pf) (New York: Associated Music, 1977)
Quintet (fl, ob, cl, vln and vlc) (1977)
Movement for string quartet (1969)
Study for solo clarinet (1971)
Variations for clarinet solo (Assoc. Music, 1972)
Letting go (vln)
Shortcut (pf) (1975)
VOCAL
Five songs (m-S and orch) (1973)
ELECTRONIC
Targets (elec tape) (1973)
Ref. composer, 228, 625

GREENE, Pauline
20th-century British composer.
Compositions
VOCAL
Four songs
MISCELLANEOUS
Brass dance
The human orchestra
The opus
Ref. 422

GREENFIELD, Lucille
American teacher and composer. b. New York, February 24, 1938. She graduated with a B.S. (music) from Columbia University in 1959.
Compositions
ORCHESTRA
The alienated ones (cham orch) (1st prize, Composer, Author and Artists Chamber Orchestra Competition, 1983)
VOCAL
Three songs for children
MISCELLANEOUS
Drifting on by
Follow your fading star
How many miles must I run
Life's rolling sea
Ode to my windows
Walk with love
Wrong side of the street
Ref. ASCAP in Action Fall 1983, 625

GREENFIELD, Marjorie
20th-century Scottish composer. She is a L.R.A.M.
Compositions
PERCUSSION
Sixteen percussion band songs for little children
Drums and triangles
Three pieces for percussion band
VOCAL
Simple songs with percussion
Folk songs, for children
Ref. 467

GREENOUGH, Lilly. See MOULTON, Mrs. Charles

GREENWALD, Jan Carol
American composer. b. New York, July 12, 1952. She obtained her B.A. from the California Institute of the Arts and attended the Darmstadt Ferienkurse in 1974 and 1976. She studied composition under James Tenney, Stephen Mosko and Morton Subotnick. She was a founder member of the Los Angeles Symposium of Women Composers. Her works have been performed in Germany, Holland, France, Denmark and the United States. DISCOGRAPHY.
Compositions
ORCHESTRA
Dissolution (1974)
Duration 'Perseverance Furthers' (1975)
CHAMBER
Mobile 1, sculptural score (8 mid-range insts) (1974)
Mobile 2, sculptural score (4 insts) (1975)
Mobile 3, sculptural score (3 nonpitched perc insts) (1976)
VOCAL
Plainsong (m-ch) (1974)
ELECTRONIC
Duration 2 (computer-generated syn or tape) (1976)
Mobile 4 John Cage (5 players with 5 radios) (1977)
MULTIMEDIA
Sidewalk sound (approx. 20 musicians and actors) (1977)
Ref. composer, 563

GREGER, Luisa (Luise) (nee Sumpf)
German composer. b. Greifswald, December 27, 1862.
Compositions
VOCAL
Tramonto, characteristic piece (man and pf)
VOCAL
Songs incl.:
Ich wollt'ich waer des Sturmes Weib
Das letzte Kaennchen: Gib mir, trautes Aennchen
Lied des Barden am Trollhattan: Hast du ein Leib, halt's fest
Nun steigt aus blauen Tiefen
Spielmanns Lied: Musikanten muessen wandern
Ueber die Berge weit zu wandern
Ueber die Heide hallet mein Schritt
Waldtrauts Lied: Glockenblumen, was lautet ihr?
Wiegenlied: Schlaf, mein liebes Kind, schlaf ein!
Liederalbum
THEATRE
Gaenseliesel, op. 170
Melodramas
Ref. 105, 297

GREGORI, Nininha
Brazilian composer. b. Sao Paulo, January 20, 1925. She studied under Koellreutter. Her compositions are written mostly in the 12-tone technique.
Compositions
CHAMBER
Trio (fl, vln and vla)
Three pieces
VOCAL
Four old Greek poems (S, cel and 4 winds) (1951)
Lieder
Ref. 22, 70, 94, 189

GREGORY, Else
German lutenist and composer. b. Berlin, January 16, 1872. She was a pupil of Leporello Muller, Therese Schnabel-Behr, W. Schutt, P. Scharwenka and Heinrich Scherrer.
Compositions
VOCAL
Avanti, avanti, granatieri! march
Five songs (Harnisch)
Songs (lute)
OPERA
Haschisch (R. Delli Ponti) (1911)
Ref. Ricordi, 141, 226, 297

GREIF, Marjorie. See GRIEF, Marjorie

GRERICHS, Doris
20th-century composer.
Compositions
PIANO
The Land of Temp Marks, 8 short pieces (Willis, 1979)
Ref. MLA *Notes*

GRESHAM, Ann
20th-century American composer.
Composition
CHAMBER
Baroque Lament (4 sax)
Ref. 142, 146

GRETL. See DANZI, Maria Margarethe

GRETRY, Angelique Dorothee Lucie (Lucille)
French composer. b. Paris, December 1, 1770; d. Paris, March 1790. She studied under her father, the Belgian composer Andre Ernest Modeste Gretry. She wrote *Le Mariage d'Antoine* at the age of 14 and it was successfully performed at the Comedie-Italienne in Paris. She married an amateur musician, Pierre Marin de Champcourt, but died soon after her marriage.

Compositions
OPERA
Des les Premiers Jour du Printemps
Des Oncles, les Paris (1805)
Le Mariage d'Antoine, in 1 act (1784) (A.L.B. Ronineau and Mme. Besumier)
La Méprise Volontaire
Toinette et Louis, in 2 acts (J. Patrat) (1787)
Ref. 2, 8, 30, 51, 65, 105, 108, 177, 225, 226, 307, 335, 404

GREVENKOP CASTENKIOLD, Olga

Early 20th-century Danish composer.
Compositions
CHAMBER
Aveu (vln and pf)
Narcose, op. 1 (vln and pf) (W. Hansen, 1918)
Kompositioner, ops. 2-3 (pf) (Hansen, 1918)
VOCAL
Budskab, op. 5
Fire sange, op. 4 (Hansen, 1918)
Invocation, op. 7
Langsel, op. 9 (1918)
Sct. Johannes Klokker, op. 8
Syn, op. 6
Ref. 331

GREVER, Maria

Mexican composer. b. Leon, Guanajuato, September 14, 1885; d. New York, December 15, 1951. She studied in Paris under Debussy. She became the first Mexican woman to achieve fame as a composer. DISCOGRAPHY.
Compositions
CHAMBER
Piano pieces
VOCAL
Jurame (T and cham orch)
Te quiero, dijiste (T)
Ref. 81, 226, 563

GREY, Edith

20th-century American composer.
Composition
CHAMBER
Prelude in D, op. 9 (In Memoriam) (strs) (Galaxy)
Ref. 280

GRIEBEL WANDALL, Tekla (Thekla)

Danish choir conductor, novelist, poetess and composer. b. Rander, February 25, 1866; d. June 28, 1940. She had her first lessons with her composer father, Theodor Griebel and later studied at the Copenhagen Conservatory and in Germany. She began composing at the age of 16 and in 1933 produced a catalogue of over a hundred compositions. She wrote the music for Henrik Ibsen's play *Naar vi Doede vaagner*.
Compositions
CHAMBER
Ernster lander (vln, vlc and pf) (Grueninger)
Romanze (vln, vlc and pf) (Grueninger)
PIANO
Dannebrogs-Marsch (Nordisk Musikforlag)
Festgalop (Hansen)
Fremandskriedende smaastykker for de foerste begyndere (Nordisk Musikforlag, 1888)
Pianoskola for barn (Gehrmann)
Sommernatsdroemme, waltz
VOCAL
Cantata for the jubilee of the Women's Industrial Drawing and Art School (1901)
Cantata for the reunion festival for women of soenderjysk (1920)
Second peace cantata (191)
Uddrag af B. Bjoernsons oratorium, cantata (2 soloists, w-ch and pf) (Nordisk Musikforlag, 1899)
Leonore, recitation (ch and pf)
Aftensang: Hvor soedt i aftenstunden (vce and pf) (Hansen)
Berces par la nuit (vce and pf) (Nordisk Musikforlag)
Drei lieder fuer eine tiefe Stimme (Nordisk Musikforlag)
Fem sange af Oscar Madeens Den flyvende Hollaender (Nordisk Musikforlag)
Le rossignol, nocturne (S and pf) (Hansen)
Slesvig, dine kirkeklokker (S and pf)
To sange (Nordisk Musikforlag)
Tre sange: O glem det ej; Silde vid nat hin kolde; Flyveren (Hansen)
BALLET
I Rosentiden (pf) (Nordisk Musikforlag)
OPERA
Don Juan de Marana (1885, revised 1931)
Skoen Karen, in 1 act (Einar Christiansen) (Nordisk Musikforlag, 1895)
INCIDENTAL MUSIC
Naar vi Doede vaagner (Ibsen)
Sizoejnerhumoer, radio play (V. de Stampe) (1932)
Theatre music
Publications
Musikteori for Sangere.
Musikteori i korte Traek, Hjaelpmiddel ved Sangundervisningen. Nordisk Musikforlag.
Ref. 20, 226, 276, 297, 307, 331, 347

GRIEBLING, Karen Jean

American bassoonist, pianist, violist, singer and composer. b. Akron, OH, December 31, 1957. She came from a musical family and took her early training with her father who was a self-taught composer, pianist, violinist and clarinetist. She studied at the Eastman School of Music and majored in the viola, the piano and composition at the Cleveland Institute of Music and at the Cleveland Music School. From 1971 to 1972 she studied voice and the bassoon privately under Betty Dornan, under Marian Bahr in 1975 and with Jeanne Werner from 1970 to 1972. Her other teachers included Marie Martin, Al Metz, Margaret Ann Griebling (q.v.), Grace Newsom Cushman, Dr. Starling A. Cumberworth, Dr. Howard Whittaker, Arnold Thomas, Dr. Joseph Schwantner and Dorothy S. Payne-Penn. She was awarded first prize in 1971 and second prize in 1972 in the NFMC competitions and the Fred Waring Award for Choral Writing in 1973, the Cavalcade for Creative Youth String Award in 1974, Charles Ives Scholarship, Indian Hill in 1975 and 1976 and a Special Excellence Award in 1976. As recipient of honors from the Akron Scholastic Composer's contest since 1968, she won 21 first prizes. In addition, she was awarded the Cleveland Music School Settlement Charles M. Rychlic scholarship for composition study from 1975 to 1976 and a scholarship from the Eastman School of Music from 1976 to 1980. Other honors include National Parent and Teachers Association three-year Best of Show-Encyclopaedia Britannica; Ohio Parent and Teachers's of Music Clubs six-year superior publication; two gold cups; and Ohio Music Educators Association three-year first rating. She was awarded the Dror Fellowship by Milton Katims at the University of Houston in Texas for the study of composition and the viola. She performed as principal bassoonist and singer with orchestras, bands and choirs in New York, Ohio and London. She was the violist in the University's Graduate String Quartet at Houston. Her works have been performed in the United States and Europe. PHOTOGRAPH.
Compositions
ORCHESTRA
Overture (1979)
Simple suite (1973)
CHAMBER
Sound piece for 12 violas (1979)
Sonata for viola and wind ensemble (1978)
Quintet (ob, 2 vln, vla and vlc) (1977-1978)
Quintet I (2 vln, vla, vlc and pf) (1974)
String quartet I (1970)
String quartet 2 (1971)
String quartet 3 (1972)
String quartet 4 (1973)
Elegie (fl, vla and hp) (1976)
Trio I (2 vln and vla) (1973)
Trio II (fl, cl and bsn) (1976)
Five little viola pieces (vla and pf) (1971)
Five miniatures (fl and bsn) (1976)
Five sketches for viola and piano (1975)
Four pieces (ob and cl) (1976)
Meditation and humoresque (ob and tba) (1976)
Melodie (fl and pf) (1971)
Musica doloris (vla and pf) (1973)
Sonata for viola and piano (1976)
Three viola pieces (vla and pf) (1972)
Two etudes (2 cl in B-Flat) (1974)
Prelude (org) (1971)
Sonata for unaccompanied English horn (1979)
Sonata for unaccompanied violin (1979)
Theme and variations (org) (1971)
PIANO
March (1975)
Nocturne (1971)
Ode to Debussy (1973)
Seven short pieces (1977)
Sonata V
Variations on Come all ye faithful (1977)

VOCAL
Arsis, cantata (S, mix-ch, ob and str orch) (1975)
Prediction (Tolkien) (mix-ch and cham orch) (1973)
Anguish, feast (Millay) (m-S and B-ch) (1977)
Five songs (Millay) (m-S and B-ch)
The reed (Browning) (w-ch, ob and pf) (1971)
Three love poems, 1860 (Whitman) (w-ch, hp and perc) (1977)
Afternoon on a hill (Millay) (T and pf) (1975)
Departure (Millay) (m-S and pf) (1972)
Forbearance (Emerson) (m-S and cl) (1977)
Four songs for (high-vce and pf) (1978)
July 4 in New England (S, m-S and org) (1976)
Maid of Orleans (Millay) (T and pf) (1972)
Memory of Cape Cod (Millay) (m-S, Bar, cymbal and prepared pf) (1974)
Nuit blanche (Millay) (m-S, bar and pf) (1973)
Renascence (Millay) (m-S and pf) (1971)
Rubies (Emerson) (m-S and cl) (1977)
Sea songs (Millay) (m-S and pf) (1970)
Sonnet (Millay) (m-S and pf) (1974)
The struggle (Hopkins) (m-S and pf) (1977)
To a young poet (Millay) (m-S, rec, 2 vla and 2 vlc) (1973)
Five Tzu-Yeh songs
SACRED
Psalm 61 (S, mix-ch and orch) (1974)
Psalm 31 (1978)
Three carols (1978)
Two anthems for Church
BALLET
Johnny Appleseed
INCIDENTAL MUSIC
Music for Richard III (orch) (1976)
Film music (orch) (1975)
Ref. composer, 625

GRIEBLING, Margaret Ann

American oboist, conductor and composer. b. Akron, OH, November 17, 1960. She began studying music at the age of six and three years later studied the oboe under Patricia Grutzmacher, Harvey McGuire, Ernest Harrison and John Mack, principal oboist of the Cleveland Symphony Orchestra. She studied theory and composition under Marie Martin of the Cleveland Institute of Music. She studied composition with Dr. Douglas Borwick at the Eastman School of Music, Rochester, graduating with a B.M. in 1982. She held the position of principal oboist in the Heidelberg Opera Orchestra in 1981 and from 1982 to 1983 in the Blossom Music Centre Festival Band. Among other honors were a BMI grant for conductors under 26 years of age and the Lancaster Summer Arts Festival award in its first annual National Orchestral Composers' Contest. She is currently studying at the San Francisco Conservatory.

Compositions
ORCHESTRA
Atalanta, symphonic tone poem (pf and orch) (winner, 1st Annual National Orchestral Composers Contest, NFMC)
Trees (LSAF award, 1978, 1979)
CHAMBER
Two bagatelles (bsn and ob)
MISCELLANEOUS
Goldsmith's pasticcio
Bibliography
AMC Newsletter, vol, 21, nos. 1 and 2.
Music Clubs Magazine, summer 1978.
Ref. 625

GRIECO, Ida

20th-century Italian pianist and composer. She showed musical ability at a very early age and wrote three pieces before studying composition. She studied the piano under E. Lanciano and A. di Lorenzo and harmony and composition under C. De Nardis and Ancona. Her works have been performed on radio.

Compositions
ORCHESTRA
Visione dell'antica Roma (catacombe romane), symphony
Risveglio di primavera, symphonic poem
Danza orientale
Serenata spagnola
CHAMBER
Barcarolla (vln and pf)
Romanza alla antica (vlc and pf)
PIANO
Minuetto
Romanza senza parole
Scherzo di nuvole
Scherzo in C-Major
Suite
Suonata quasi una fantasia in re minore, sonata
Ref. 56

GRIEF (Greif), Marjorie

20th-century American composer.

Compositions
ORCHESTRA
Variations
CHAMBER
Composition for String Quartet
VOCAL
Songs incl.:
April morning (vce and pf)
Death (vce and pf)
A glass of beer (vce and pf)
The gull (vce and pf)
I shall Not Care (vce and pf)
Julia's room (S and pf)
Ref. 40, 190, 347

GRIFFINS, Vashti Rogers

American artist, musician and composer. d. San Diego, CA, 1961.

Compositions
VOCAL
Songs incl.:
America first
California moon (m-qrt)
Dawn
Every girl can be a Joan of Arc to the soldier boy she loves
Grandma's spinning wheel
If daisies won't tell, ask a rose
Meet me at the San Diego fair in 1936
Moonlight waltz song
My stairway of dreams
Oklahoma my home town
Poinsettia; you are San Diego's pride
San Diego waltz
Sleep, dear soul, sleep
Sweetheart o'mine
Vibrant with life
You're the girl of my heart, senorita
You were never meant for me
SACRED
The Lord's prayer
Ref. San Diego Public Library

GRIGSBY, Beverly (nee Pinsky)

American professor and composer. b. Chicago, January 11, 1928. She studied medicine at the University of Southern California, before attending the Southern California School of Music and Arts, where she studied theory and composition from 1947 to 1949. From 1949 to 1951 she was a composition pupil of Ernst Krenek. In 1961 she graduated with a B.A. from the San Fernand Valley State College. She received her M.A. (composition) at California State University, Northridge in 1963 and her D.M.A. at the University of Southern California in 1969. She studied computer music at Stanford University in 1976. She was professor of theory, composition and music history at California State University, Northridge and in 1976 founded a computer music studio there. She is co-chairlady of the Western Region of the ASUC. She received various grants and awards for her work on computer music.

Compositions
CHAMBER
The two faces of Janus (str qrt) (1963)
Dithyrambos (vln and vlc) (1974)
Movements for guitar: prelude; serenade; dance (1982)
VOCAL
Dialogues (T and gtr) (1973)
Love songs (T and gtr) (1974)
Sonnet XI (vce and pf) (1949)
Songs (m-S) (1949)
SACRED
Fragments from Augustine, the Saint, cantata (T, ob, hp and perc) (1971)
OPERA
The Mask of Eleanor, chamber opera (S and ens)
Moses
FILM MUSIC
Ayamon the Terrible (elec tape) (1964)

ELECTRONIC
Concerto (pf, tape and orch) (1978)
Five studies on two untransposed hexachords (1971)
Morning at seven for flute and computer generated sounds incl.: Sunbird (picc); Sunbow (b-fl); Sunrise (a-fl) (1981)
The awakening (tape) (1963)
Shakti (fl and tape)
A little background music (computer tape) (1976)
Preludes (T.S. Eliot) (m-S and elec tape) (1968)
Ref. composer, 40, 142, 347, 622, 625

GRILLI GALEFFI, Elvira
Italian composer.
Compositions
CHAMBER
Fissando il cielo, nocturne (man and pf)
Gioconda (man and pf)
PIANO
Piu non verra, piccola fantasia
Il ritorno, notturnino
VOCAL
La lontananza, romanza
Ref. 297

GRIMANI, Maria Margherita
18th-century Italian court musician and composer of Venetian origin. She may have been related to the aristocratic Venetian family Grimani, owners of the Theatre San Giovanni Crisostomo. Her *Sinfonie* probably served as an introduction to a longer work such as a cantata or other vocal piece which has been lost. She lived at the Viennese Court from 1715 to 1718 and was the last of a line of women composers of oratorios at the court. DISCOGRAPHY.
Compositions
ORCHESTRA
Sinfonie (1713)
SACRED
La decollazione di S. Giovanni Battista, oratorio (1715)
La visitazione di Santa Elizabetta, oratorio (1713)
THEATRE
Pallade e Marte, dramatic cantata (ded Emperor Charles VI)
Ref. Women's Orchestral Works, 9, 15, 85, 105, 347, 563, 622

GRIMAUD, Yvette
French ondes Martenot player, pianist and composer. b. Algiers, January 29, 1920. She studied the piano in Algiers and then entered the Paris Conservatoire where she studied under J. Gallon, O. Messiaen, L. Levy and J. Gentil and graduated with a first prize in 1941. From 1932 she performed in Germany, Brussels and London. She studied the Martenot under M. and G. Martenot and ethnomusicology under C. Brailoiu. She researched the music of the Bushmen and the Pygmies.
Compositions
CHAMBER
Pieces (vlc and pf)
Preludes (pf)
ELECTRONIC
Aum sur le nom de Jean-Claude Touche (vce, ondes Martenot and timp) (1945)
Chant de courbes (2 ondes martenot and timp; also 2 pf) (1946-1948)
Quatre chants d'espace (vce, ondes martenot and perc) (1944-1947)
Ref. 12, 22, 70, 74, 85, 96, 347

GRIMES, Doreen
American accordionist, clarinetist, guitarist, organist, pianist, teacher and composer. b. Weatherford, TX, February 1, 1932. She studied under Jack Frederick Kilpatrick at the Southern Methodist University where she obtained a B.M. and an M.M. (piano). She obtained her Ph.D. in 1966 from North Texas State University, where she studied under Samuel Adler and George Morey. In addition to performing, she was director of her own music school from 1950 to 1962 and head of department of theory at Eastern New Mexico University, Portales from 1962 to 1971. In 1966 she was named Woman of the Year by Eastern New Mexico University. From 1971 she was music co-ordinator at Angelo State University. She was president of District II Texas Federation of Music Clubs from 1974 to 1976.
Compositions
ORCHESTRA
Seventeen compositions
CHAMBER
Twenty-three chamber works, incl.:
Prelude and allegro (2 pf)
Piece for harpsichord (1963)
Suite for harpsichord (1970)
Americana
VOCAL
The canyon (mix-ch)
Season of peace (mix-ch)
It satisfies my longing
One hundred and fifty solos
SACRED
Come in adoration
Mass of the Good Shepherd
Sing a joyful song
OPERA
Drugstore Panorama, in 1 act
MISCELLANEOUS
The face of a pioneer woman
Vermillion red
Ref. 77, 142, 625

GRISI, Mme.
Polish composer. b. 1835. She wrote songs which were sung by Countess Anna Grabowska.
Ref. 465

GRISWOLD, Gertrude
19th-century American composer of songs.
Composition
VOCAL
What the chimney sang
Ref. 276, 433

GRO, Josephine
19th-century American composer.
Compositions
PIANO
Dances
Other pieces
VOCAL
Songs incl.:
Something more
La tambourine
With shy brown eyes
Ref. 260, 276, 292, 347

GROBENSCHUTZ, Amalie. See GROEBENSCHUETZ, Amalie

GRODZICKA-RZEWUSKA, Julia
19th-century Polish singer and composer. She lived in Cracow from 1818 to 1831.
Compositions
VOCAL
Songs
OPERA
Malzonek wszystkich kobiet, comic opera in 1 act (1825)
Obiadek z Magdusia, comic opera in 1 act (A.F. Desaugiers; trans L.A. Dmuszewski) (1821)
THEATRE
Malwina i Ernest, vaudeville (1825)
Ref. 118

GROEBENSCHUETZ, Amalie (nee Seiler)
German pianist, teacher and composer. d. Berlin, 1845. She was the wife of the royal chamber musician and the violist at the court and opera in Berlin and had a son who also composed. She gave many concerts in Berlin between 1809 and 1816.
Compositions
PIANO
Dances (Berlin: Groebenschuetz)
Rondos (Hamburg: Schuberth; Groebenschuetz)
Two waltzes (Groebenschuetz)
Ref. 121, 129

GROH, B. Jeannie. See ROSCO, B. Jeannie

GRONDAHL, Agatha Ursula. See BACKER-GROENDAHL, Agatha Ursula

GRONOWETTER, Freda

Canadian cellist, teacher and composer. b. Toronto, Ontario, February 10, 1918. She received a scholarship to the Royal Conservatory, Toronto in 1930 for cello study under Serge Stupin. She then studied under Emanuel Feuermann, Joseph Schuster and Alfred Wallenstein as a scholarship student. She was a cellist in the Toronto Symphony Orchestra, the American Symphony Orchestra, the New York City Opera Company Orchestra, the Ballet Theatre Orchestra and soloist with the Markova-Dolin Ballet Company.

Composition

ORCHESTRA

In a sacred mood (vlc and orch; also pf) (Marks, 1941)

Ref. 496

GROOM, Joan Charlene

American composer. b. Cameron, MO, February 4, 1941. She obtained a Ph.D. from the University of Rochester, New York, in 1973.

Compositions

ORCHESTRA

Variations (1963-1964)

VOCAL

Four songs of the air (T and orch) (in memory of Roger K. Louden)

Ref. 322

GROOM, Mrs. (nee Wilkinson)

English singer and composer. d. May, 1867.

Compositions

VOCAL

Songs incl.:

By the waters of Babylon

Fairy's reveil

Over the sea, Jacobite song

Ref. 276, 297, 347

GROSSMAN, Deena

American flautist and composer. b. Fairfield, CA, January 31, 1955. She obtained a B.A. in music composition from the University of California and then continued with graduate studies at the Shepherd School of Music, Rice University, Texas. She studied with composers Paul Cooper, Thea Musgrave (q.v.), Lou Harrison, Peter Fricker and Marta Ptaszynska (q.v.) and studied music and dance in Bali and India. She also studied the flute with Yaada Weber of the San Francisco Conservatory of Music. She was a member of the music staff of radio station KPFA (California) and produced the program *Focus on Women in Music*. From 1982 to 1985 she was awarded a graduate fellowship in music composition from The Shepherd School of Music. She is a member of the ILWC. PHOTOGRAPH.

Compositions

CHAMBER

Music of spaces: Asunder; Expanses; Ellipse; Unfolding; (vln, cl, d-b, cl and pf) (1983)

Sea cliff hands quartet (ob, vln, banjo and d-b)

For shadows and roses (Sandburg) (a-sax, hp and vib)

So clear a puzzle (cl, vlc and American gamelan) (1979)

Trio (fl, hp and vlc) (1983)

Aria and dance (fl and prep pf)

Dialogue, deep changing blue (fl duet)

Blue tides (ob)

Morning raga (fl)

Red (ob)

Three colors (ob)

That yellow hat

VOCAL

Leopard flowers, four songs (S and pf) (1983)

The world is round (1982)

THEATRE

The story, play (Carol Lashof) (fl and ob)

ELECTRONIC

Ibiza (vce, shakuhachi, fl, clay whistles, timp, gtr, pf and tape)

Screen play (fl, elec pf, banjo and perc) (1980)

Wildwood (elec tape) (1983)

Ref. composer, 622, 625

GROTTGEROWA, Krystyna

Early 19th-century Polish composer.

Compositions

CHAMBER

Marsza pogrzebowego na 31 lipca 1874, march

VOCAL

Patriotic songs

Ref. 118

GROTTOLO, Vera. See BENEDICENTI, Vera

GRUDEFF, Marian

Canadian pianist, arranger, lecturer, lyricist, music director and composer. b. Toronto, April 18, 1927 of Bulgarian parents. Her first piano teacher was her mother. At the age of eight Marian became a pupil of Mona Bates and at the age of 11 she played Liszt's *Hungarian Fantasy* with the Toronto Symphony Orchestra. She subsequently appeared with the New York Philharmonic in 1946 and in 1948 commenced her teaching career. Later she studied the piano under Eduard Steuermann in New York and composition under Nadia Boulanger (q.v.) in Paris. She performed in concerts in Europe and in the 1950s and early 1960s was associated with the Toronto revue 'Spring Thaw' as rehearsal pianist, arranger, music director and she finally collaborated with Ray Jessel on lyrics and music. She and Jessel then collaborated on other musicals. In 1972 Marian returned to teaching at the Royal Conservatory, Toronto and gave a series of concerts with the Royal Conservatory Trio from 1976 to 1977. PHOTOGRAPH.

Compositions

THEATRE

Baker Street, on Sherlock Holmes (with Ray Jessel)

Life can be like wow (with Ray Jessel) (1969)

Spring Thaw (with Ray Jessel)

Ref. Royal Conservatory of Music, Toronto

GRUNBAUM, Theresa

Austrian composer. b. 1791; d. 1876. She composed songs.

Ref. 465

GRUNBERG, Janeta (Negrano-Schori, Jenny)

Rumanian composer. b. Bucharest, 1926. She graduated at the Bucharest Conservatory and went to Israel in 1950.

Compositions

VOCAL

Songs

MISCELLANEOUS

British Legion March (medal, British Legion, Tel Aviv)

Ref. 379

GRZADZIELOWNA, Eleonora

Polish pianist, teacher and composer. b. Murchi, Pszczyna, January 31, 1921. She studied the piano at the State Music College in Katowice under M. Furmanikowa and composition under L. Rozycki and B. Woytowicz, receiving her diplomas in 1951 and 1955 respectively. In 1951 she began teaching in the Music Secondary School in Katowice.

Compositions

ORCHESTRA

Concerto (pf and orch) (1969)

Concertino (pf and orch) (1951)

Concerto (2 hp and str orch) (1959)

Five miniatures (trp, pf and str orch) (1965)

Dialogues (cham orch) (1968)

Divertimento (ww and str orch) (1961)

Intermezzo (1956)

Ondraszek, ballet suite (1964)

Polish suite (small sym orch) (1962)

Toccata (1948)

CHAMBER

Concertino (pf, 9 wind insts and perc) (1963)

Lullaby (ob, 2 cl and bsn) (1948)

Sonata (2 vln and d-b) (1966)

Sonata (fl and pf) (1953)

Sonata (vla and pf) (1957)

Thème variée (vln and pf) (1948)

Two duets (vln and pf) (1967)

Two miniatures (cl and pf) (1948)

PIANO
Fairy tales for children (4 hands) (1955)
Bulgarian suite (1958)
Three characteristic pieces (1957)
VOCAL
Brzask, cantata (Mieczslaw Jastrun) (ch and orch) (1950)
Concerto for soprano and orchestra (R. Tagore) (1963)
Triptiyque (A. Slonimski) (ch and orch) (1967)
Plainsong preludes (C. Aiken) (boys'-ch, str qrt and org) (1970)
Piesn o urodzaju (T. Sliwiak) (vce and pf) (1954)
Three songs (Pushkin, Galczynski and Zegladlowicz) (S and pf) (1956)
ARRANGEMENTS
Silesian folk songs
Ref. 70, 94, 118

GUBAIDULINA, Sofia Asgatovna

Soviet pianist and composer. b. Chsistopol, Tataria, October 24, 1931. She studied theory under Nazib Zhiganov at the Kazan Music Academy from 1946 to 1949 and the piano under Maria Piatnitskaya. She continued her studies at the Kazan Conservatory from 1949 to 1954 where her piano teachers were Leopold Lukomsky and Grigory Kogan and composition teacher was Albert Leman. From 1954 to 1963 she studied composition at the Moscow Conservatory under Nikolai Peiko and Vissarion Shebalin and from 1963 to 1964 she was an accompanist at the Moscow Theatre Institute. She was a composer with the Studio of Documentary Films from 1963 to 1967, the Studio of Art Films, Odessa from 1964 to 1969, the Theatre on Taganka in Moscow in 1966, the Studio of Animated Cartoons from 1968 and the Moscow Soviet Theatre after 1970. From 1968 she worked at the Electronic Music Studio in Moscow. DISCOGRAPHY.

Compositions
ORCHESTRA
Symphony (1958)
Concerto for two orchestras (jazz and symphony)
Concerto (bsn and low strs) (1975)
Concerto (pf and orch) (1959)
Offertorium: Concerto for violin and orchestra
Introitus: Concerto for piano and chamber orchestra
Adagio and fugue (vln and str orch) (1960)
Fairy tale poem
Overture triumph (1963)
Stupeni (1972)
CHAMBER
Intermezzo (8 trp, 16 hp and perc) (1961)
Concordanza (cham ens) (1971)
Detto (vlc and cham ens; also org) (1972)
Piano quintet (1957)
Quartet (1971)
Variations (str qrt) (1956)
Five etudes (d-b, hp and perc) (1965)
Garden of joy and suffering (fl, vla and hp) (1980)
Quattro (2 trp and trb) (1974)
Allegro rustico (fl and pf) (1963)
In croce (vlc and org)
Muzika (hpcd and perc) (1977)
Pantomime (d-b and pf) (1966)
Rumore e silenzio (hpcd and perc) (1974)
Light and dark (org) (1976)
Misterioso (perc) (comm W. Shteyman)
Sonata (perc) (1966)
Ten etudes (vlc) (1974)
PIANO
Chaconne (1962)
Eight preludes (1955)
Sonata (1965)
Sonatina (1952)
Variations on a Tartar song Epipe (1946)
Children's pieces (1969)
VOCAL
Laudazio pazis, oratorio (Y.A. Kamenski) (1975)
Noch v Memfis, cantata (m-ch and cham orch) (1968)
Sowjetische Meister der Balladenkunst, cantata
Fatselia, cycle (M. Prishvin) (S and orch) (1956)
Percussio di Pekarski, concerto (perc, m-S and orch) (1976)
Poema chas dushi (Cont and wind orch) (1974)
Rubayat (B and orch) (1969)
Rozy, cycle (G. Aigi) (vce and pf) (1972)
SACRED
De profundis (ch)
BALLET
Begushchaya po volnam (A. Grin) (1962)
Flute of Tania (1961)
Volshebnaya svirel (1960)
ELECTRONIC
Vivente-non vivente (tape) (1969-1970)
Ref. Neue Zeitschrift fuer Musik, 4, 5, 21, 94, 223, 277, 563, 622

GUBITOSI, Emilia

Italian pianist, conductor, lecturer and composer. b. Naples, February 3, 1887; d. Naples, January 17, 1972. She married the composer Franco M. Napolitano. She studied the piano at an early age under A. Roche and B. Cesi and later attended the San Pietro a Majella Conservatory in Naples. She received her piano diploma in 1904 after studying under Simonetti and improved her piano technique under C. Palumbo. She was the first woman to apply to study composition at the conservatory and was initially admitted on an experimental basis. She graduated in 1906 having studied harmony under De Nardis and composition under M. D'Arienzo. In 1918 she founded the Alessandro Scarlatti Society with its own orchestra and choir which she conducted. Together with her husband she promoted concerts in Naples and taught at the Conservatory of Naples from 1914 to 1957. PHOTOGRAPH.

Compositions
ORCHESTRA
Allegro appassionato (vln and orch; also vln and pf) (Curci)
Concerto (pf and orch) (Carisch)
Corale sinfonico (org and orch; also org and pf) (Carisch)
Fantasia (pf and orch; also hp)
Cavalcata grotesca
Notturno (Ricordi)
CHAMBER
Colloqui (fl, hp and vlc or vla) (Curci)
Adieu, romantic suite (vlc and pf)
Dialogo (vlc and pf) (Curci)
Dittico (vln and pf) (Curci)
Due pezzi (vlc and pf) (Curci)
Elegia (vlc and pf) (Curci)
Notturno (vln and pf) (Ricordi)
Leggenda (hp)
PIANO
Pieces incl.:
Di notte (4 hands)
Disperata (4 hands)
Due piccoli pezzi (4 hands)
A briglia sciolta (Curci)
Chagrin d'amour
Dormire
Due liriche (Carducci)
Favoletta russa (Curci)
Mais pourquoi?
Mattino di Pasqua
Nostalgia
Pagliaccetto
Pastore e pastorella (Curci)
Piccola danza
Souvenir di concerto (Curci)
Souvenir triste
Stravaganze
Studio per mani alternate (Curci)
Suite mignonne (Curci)
Tema con variazioni (Curci)
Umoresca (Curci)
VOCAL
Ninna nanna (S, w-ch and orch) (Curci)
Notte lunare (soloist, ch and orch)
Sonata in bianco minore, symphonic poem (soloist, w-ch and orch) (Carisch)
Il flauto notturno, symphonic piece (S, fl and orch)
Songs incl.:
L'Aquila di Roma
Chanson, in old style (De musset)
Di notte (m-S or Bar and pf) (Curci)
Dialogo di marionette
Disperata (Carducci)
Dormire (Ricordi)
Giovinezza (Fucini)
Le illusioni (Corazzini)
Mattinatta
Mattuttino (Betti) (1936)
Nera Nerella (Ravasio)
Ninna nanna cosacca (Curci)
Non aspettar (Ogor)
Notturnino (S and pf) (Curci)
Notturno (Graf)
La premiere (Coppee)
Saluto a primavera (Curci)
Serenata (Buja) (Ricordi)
Songs for children (Carisch)
Ultimo sogno (S and pf) (Curci)
SACRED
Cantata sacra (S, ch and small orch)
Redemisti-nos (2 vces and org) (Carrara)
OPERA
Ave Maria, in 1 act (Naples, 1906)
Fatum, in 4 acts

Gardenia Rossa, in 1 act
Nada Delwig, in 1 act (F. Verdinois and A. Menotti-Buja) (1910)
ARRANGEMENTS
Orchestration and revisions of works by Aldora, Arne, Cherubini, Del Cavaliere, Durante, Purcell, Pergolesi, Scarlatti and others
Publications
Compendio di teoria della musica. With F.M. Napolitano. Curci, 1930.
Esercizi preliminari. Ricordi.
Guida per il dettato melodico ed il solfeggio cantato. Curci, 1932.
Il libro di canto corale. With G. Napoli. Curci.
Metodo fondamentale per lo studio del pianoforte.
Suono e ritmo. Curci, 1919.
Bibliography
Tebaldini, G. 'Emilia Gubitosi' in *Il pensiero musicale.* Bologna, 1926.
Ref. 14, 47, 56, 70, 85, 86, 94, 100, 105, 108, 110, 129, 135, 166, 189, 226, 347, 622

GUCHY, Gregoria Karides. See SUCHY, Gregoria Karides

GUDAUSKAS, Giedra
American pianist, teacher and composer. b. Kaunas, Lithuania, July 10, 1923. She became a U.S. citizen in 1952. She studied voice and the piano at Kaunas State Conservatory from 1933 to 1940 and composition under Karel Jirak at Roosevelt University, receiving a B.Mus. in 1952. She studied film scoring and jazz improvisation at the University of California from 1962 to 1964 and taught privately.
Compositions
CHAMBER
Lithuanian suite (2 vlc and pf; also xyl, elec gtr and pf) (1967, 1969)
Impressions on three proverbs (pf and perc) (1969)
PIANO
Rondo
Variations
VOCAL
Four songs for Soprano
I'm alone (vce and pf)
The journey (vce and pf)
Little girl and the hope clover (vce and pf)
Love dream (vce and pf)
Melody of Lithuanian folk songs
The swallow (vce and pf)
SACRED
Requiem for my friends (vce and pf)
The world of God (vce and pf)
ELECTRONIC
Lithuanian suite (xyl, elec gtr and pf) (1969)
Ref. 142, 625

GUEDON DE PRESLES, Mlle.
18th-century French composer.
Compositions
VOCAL
L'Amour d'un air doux et flateur, chansonette (1742)
La bergère indifferente, musette (1742)
C'est en vain qu'on veut se defendre, ariette (1744)
Le Dieu du mystère, rondeau (1742)
D'un tendre amant, l'objet qui regne, air serieux (1742)
Petits oiseaux, qui sous ces verds feuillages, air serieux (1742)
Le retour du printemps, musette (1742)
Ref. 65, 125

GUELL, Elizabeth
Spanish composer.
Compositions
ORCHESTRA
Minuet (str orch) (Novello)
CHAMBER
Serenata (vln, vlc and pf) (Novello)
SACRED
Ave Maria (S, vln, har and org)
Ref. 297

GUELL, Maria Luisa
Spanish composer.
Compositions
CHAMBER
Balada (org and str qrt) (Novello)
Elizabeth, gavotte (str qrt) (Novello)
Una floreta de Sant Francesch, introduction to a Catalan poem (vln, org and pf) (Novello)
Ref. 297

GUENIN, Helene
French composer. b. Amiens, 1791. Her opera, composed when she was 16 was very successful.
Composition
OPERA
Daphnis et Amenthée (1807)
Ref. 226, 276, 307

GUERIN, Alipson (Guillot)
14th-century French minstrel. She signed the famous charter dated September 4, 1321, that established the Chappelle Saint-Julien-des-Ménéstriers, a corporation for jongleurs and minstrels.
Ref. 343

GUERINI (Guerini-Wilberforce), Rosa
19th-century Italian composer.
Compositions
CHAMBER
Pensée fugitive (vln and pf)
Six bagatelles, op. 4: Ecoute; Pensée; Berceuse; Bourée; Mazurka; Rêvèrie (vln and pf)
Romance (vln and pf)
PIANO
Foglie d'album, six pieces incl.: Preludio; Romanza senza parole; Improvviso
Six pensées musicales, op. 3: Etude; Pensée fugitive; Pourquoi; Romance sans paroles; Souvenir; Scherzo
VOCAL
Close thine eyes and rest secure (Augener)
Enfant! si j'etais roi! (V. Hugo) (Ricordi)
Je t'aime tant! (F. d'Eglantine) (Ricordi)
Quando cadran le foglie (Ricordi)
Spes, ultima dea: Ho detto al core
Widow bird (Augener)
Ref. 297

GUERRE, Elisabeth-Claude. See LA GUERRE, Elisabeth-Claude Jacquet de

GUERRANT, Mary Thorington
American pianist, assistant professor and composer. b. Taft, TN, May 7, 1925. She received her B.A. from Austin College, Texas in 1946; her M.Mus. (applied piano) in Texas and graduated from the Texas Technical University, Lubbock with a Ph.D. in fine arts (music). She also studied the piano under Bomar Cramer, Rosalyn Tureck, Mary Jeanne van Appledorn (q.v.) and Louis Catuogno. She taught the piano at Austin College from 1957 to 1958 and gave solo recitals there and at the University of Dallas during the same period. From 1976 to 1977 she was an associate professor in composition and the piano at the Tunghai University, Taiwan.
Compositions
CHAMBER
Pecos ruins (ww octet)
Passacaglia (pf)
OPERA
The Shepherd, chamber opera (orch)
Publications
Auth; who says your hands are too small? Clavier.
How secure is your memory? Piano Quarterly, summer 1979.
What constitutes a compelling piano performance? Art and Reality.
The culmination of a concept in Beethoven's last works. American Music Symposium.
Three aspects of music in Ancient China and Greece. J. Collins Music Society.
Ref. 457, 625

GUEST, Jeanne Marie (Miles)
English harpsichordist, pianist, teacher and composer. b. Bath, ca. 1769. She was the daughter of Ralph Guest, a well-known organist and composer. She studied under her father and gave piano and harpsichord reci-

tals in concerts in London in 1783. She was music teacher to Charlotte, Princess of Wales and dedicated sonatas to her after Charlotte became Queen of England.
Compositions
CHAMBER
Concertos for piano or harpsichord
Six sonatas for harpsichord or piano, op. 1 (with vln or German fl) (1783) (ded Queen Charlotte)
Four sonatas for harpsichord or piano (with vln) (1786)
Pieces and voluntaries (org)
Piano pieces
VOCAL
The Afflicted African, cantata
Ref. 17, 65, 276

GUIDI LIONETTI, Teresa (Huidi)
19th-century Italian conductor and composer. b. ca. 1861. She lived in Naples and her brother was the poet Achille Guidi. She was praised by Ferdinando Villani in his conference La Musica (Naples, 1885).
Compositions
PIANO
Gardenia, mazurka (Izzo)
Mughetto, galop (Izzo)
Myosotis, waltz (Izzo)
Nuptiae, waltz (Izzo)
Olga, mazurka (Martinenghi)
The rose, polka (Izzo)
Salut militaire (Pisano)
VOCAL
Angelo e demone, melodia (Izzo)
Dolce riscatto, melodia (Izzo)
Fior di neve (Izzo)
Occhi ladri (Izzo)
Tra il dire e il fare! proverbio, stornello (Izzo)
OPERA
Don Cesar di Bazan
Estrella
Le Nozze di Fiorina
Rosa di Perona
Susinette
Ref. 180, 276, 297, 307

GUIDICCIONI, Laura
18th-century Italian composer of an oratorio and songs.
Ref. 465

GUILBERT, Christiane
Canadian composer. b. 1936.
Compositions
VOCAL
Le petit Gregoire (Botrel) (w-ch)
Ref. Catalog of Canadian Choral Music 1978

GUILBERT, Yvette
B. 1865; d. 1944.
Compositions
VOCAL
Mme. Arthur
Ten songs of Paul de Kock (1927) (Heugel, 1984)
Ref. 622

GUILLELMA DE ROSERS
13th-century French troubadour. She probably came from Rougiers, near Monaco, on what is now the Côte D'Azur. She exchanged a tenson with Lanfrancs Cigala, her troubadour lover, a lawyer from Genoa.
Compositions
VOCAL
Na Guillelma, à cavalier arratge ...
Ref. 213, 303

GUILLELMA (GUILLAUMETTE) OF MONJA
French jongleuse. ca. 1200. She was the wife of Gaucelm Faidit, a would-be troubadour who, according to his vida, "sang as badly as possible. He took Guillelma to the courts of the great. She was very beautiful and informed and became as big and fat as he was".
Ref. 449, 243

GUINEVERE, Queen
According to legend, Queen Guinevere and the knights of the Round Table (ca. 500) rejoiced when two of their company were married, singing songs of Guinevere's composition.
Ref. 264

GUITTY, Madeleine
19th-20th-century French composer. Her works were performed in Paris.
Compositions
OPERETTA
Il n'y à plus d'enfants (1897)
Mominette (1906)
Passez Muscade (1897)
INCIDENTAL MUSIC
Conte blanc (1894)
Pages intimes (1898)
Ref. 431

GULESIAN, Grace Warner
American pianist, authoress, teacher and composer. b. Lawrence, MA, May 16, 1884. She studied the piano under Agide Jacchia and composition under Karl Weigl and Frederick Converse. She studied at Pinkerton Academy under Mme. Prescott and Carl Faelton and at Radcliffe College.
Compositions
PIANO
In a Hong Kong garden
VOCAL
Choral works
Songs incl.:
Brittany love song
Hymn to America
Songs of the East
Summer night
BALLET
Ballet of Bacchus
Ballet of Nubi
OPERETTA
Cape Cod Ann
Dick Whittington and his Cat
A Honeymoon in 2000
Princess Marina
Ref. 39, 141, 142, 347

GUMMER, Phyllis Mary
Canadian instrumentalist and composer. b. Kingston, Ontario, March 12, 1919. She studied at Queen's University, Kingston, where she received her B.A. She obtained a B.Mus. from the Royal Conservatory, Toronto and also studied at the Juilliard School of Music. In 1940 she won a CAPAC scholarship. She worked for the National Film Board.
Compositions
CHAMBER
Four string quartets
Trio (vln, vlc and pf)
Trio, non gravius (fl, cl and vla)
Sonata (fl and pf)
Sonata (vlc and pf)
Pieces (fl and cl)
PIANO
Sonata in A-Major (CAPAC prize)
Sonata in C-Major
Other pieces
VOCAL
Choral (ch and org)
Songs
Ref. 85, 133

GUNDERSON, Helen Louise
20th-century American pianist, conductor, professor and composer. b. Vermilion, SD. She obtained her B.M. from the University of South Dakota in 1914 and her M.M. from Yale University. She studied the piano under Carl Faelton in Boston, Fraeulein Sabbatini in Vienna, Tobias Matthay and Marion Snowdon in London, Frank Mannheimer in 1967 and Bruce Simonds in 1968 in the United States. She studied theory under Paul Corder and Cecile Foster in London. She was a lecturer at the University of South Dakota and the University of Wisconsin from 1915 to 1923 and then went to Peking where she was initially a lecturer at Yenching Women's College, Tsing Hua University, and then director of the music department at the Peking Institute of Fine Arts from 1926 to 1928. She became professor of

music at Louisiana State University in 1930 and head of department and then professor emeritus of theory and composition in 1963. She was founder and chairlady of the Louisiana Festival of Contemporary Music from 1944 to 1963 and national chairlady of American Music, and NFMC from 1944 to 1948.

Compositions

ORCHESTRA

Symphonic fantasy

PIANO

Sonata for piano

Ref. 84

GURAIEB KURI, Rosa

Mexican concert pianist, professor and composer of Lebanese origin. b. Matias Romero, May 20, 1931. She became a piano teacher in 1948 and in 1949 studied the piano, theory and harmony under Michel Cheskinoff at the National Conservatory, Beirut. She studied harmony under Juan Pablo Moncayo and the piano under Salvador Ordones Ochoa at the Conservatory of Mexico in 1950. In 1954 she studied with Professor Simmonds at the Yale University School of Music and between 1962 and 1965 under Carlos Chavez in composition workshops at the National Conservatory. In 1972 she studied composition and the piano under Gerhart Muench and Alfonso de Elias at the Mexico Conservatory and in 1977 took part in composition and investigation workshops under Mario Lavista and Daniel Catan. She appeared as a soloist with the National Symphony Orchestra of Mexico and had works presented at music forums and festivals.

Compositions

CHAMBER

Cuarteto II, Homenaje a Gibran (str qrt) (1982)
Reminiscencias (str qrt) (1978)
Canto a la paz (ob, bsn and pf) (1982)
Sonata para violin y piano (1978)
Impresiones para guitarra (1983)

PIANO

Espacios (1983)
Pieza ciclica (1977) (Ediciones de la Liga de Compositores de Mexico)
Scriabiniana (1981)

VOCAL

Arias olvidadas (S and pf) (1983)
Lyrica (S and pf) (1980)
La yarde, song (S and pf) (1969)
Tus ojos, song (S and pf) (1984)
Vida, song (S and pf) (1969)

Ref. composer

GUSEINZADE, Adilia Gadzhi Aga

Soviet lecturer and composer. b. Baku, Azerbaijan, April 28, 1916. In 1939 she completed a course at the Industrial Institute. From 1943 to 1948 she studied Azerbaijanian folk music at the Conservatory of Baku under U. Hadjibekov. In 1953 she graduated from the conservatory, having studied composition under B. Zaidman and then taught composition at the same conservatory.

Compositions

ORCHESTRA

Poem dedicated to heroes of Socialist labor (1951)

CHAMBER

String quartet (1952)
Two pieces for string quartet (1948)
Sonatina (vlc and pf) (1949)

PIANO

Piece in harmony (1944)
Sonatina (1946)
Suite (1947)

VOCAL

Golos mira, cantata (T. Mutallibov) (1953)
Moya rodina (S. Burgin, M. Pagim, B. Bagabzade) (vces and orch)
Gazeli (Nizami, I. Sultan) (vce and pf)
Solovei (A. Jamila, I. Rafibeili) (vce and pf)
Tsvetok (A. Pushkin) (vce and pf)

Ref. 87

GUSHINGTON, Impulsia. See DUFFERIN, Lady Helen Selina

GUSTAVSON, Nancy Nicholls (Bartlett)

American harpist, pianist, lecturer and composer. b. Oakland, CA, January 30, 1921. She studied at the University of California, Berkeley, where she obtained a B.A. in 1942 and an M.A. in 1944. In 1965 she received a B.A. from San Jose State University. She studied the piano under M. Guiselmann from 1928 to 1937 and the harp under Marjorie Chauvel from 1958 to 1965. She was the solo harpist with the Santa Clara Philharmonic Orchestra and the San Jose Symphonic Orchestra and soloist in many concerts in California, Arizona and the Netherlands. She was on the faculty of San Jose State University from 1962 to 1972.

Compositions

HARP

The magic road (1972)
Pacific sketches (1971)
Songs without words (1973)
Sparklers, five pieces (1975)

Ref. composer, 77

GUY, Helen. See HARDELOT, Guy d'

GUYVER, Dorothy. See BRITTON, Dorothy Guyver

GVAZAVA, Tamara Davidovna

Soviet pianist, lecturer and composer. b. Tiflis, September 20, 1927; d. Tbilisi, May 13, 1972. She studied composition under A.M. Balanchivadze at the Tbilisi Conservatory, graduating in 1951. The following year she studied the piano under V.K. Kuftina. From 1951 to 1956 she lectured at a music school in Tbilisi and then became concertmistress of the Georgian State Theatre.

Compositions

ORCHESTRA

Symphony (1955)
Concert piece (pf and orch) (1943)
Three pictures: Morning, In the mountains, Rustavi (1949)

CHAMBER MUSIC

Quintet (pf, hp, vln and 2 fl) (1958)
Romance (vlc and pf)

PIANO

Sonata (1947)
Variations (1959)
Pieces

VOCAL

Romances (vce and pf)

Ref. 21

GWILY-BROIDO, Rivka

Israeli pianist, conductor, teacher and composer. b. Sziget, Hungary, August 23, 1910. She began composing as a child and studied the piano under Hilda Stern and took lessons in harmony and counterpoint. She left the New Vienna Conservatory at the age of 18 with honors having acted as an assistant teacher. In 1930 she settled in Israel and specialized in conducting. She later taught the piano, harmony and musical appreciation. PHOTOGRAPH.

Compositions

VOCAL

Songs incl.:
Ey Sham Al Gevulot Hamidbar (S. Shalom) (General Committee for Jewish Soldiers, 1942)
Hachilazon, for children (R. Saporta) (Inter-Kibbutz Commitee for Musical Education)
Hayareach Hatzahov, lullaby (Lea Goldberg) (Sifrey Zabar)
Kadima (Y. Cohen) (vce and pf) (Merkaz Letarbut)
Yakinton (vce and pf) (Merkaz Letarbut Ulechinoch)
Yom Yafe (Lea Goldberg) (vce and pf) (Subar)

FILM MUSIC

Hora, for 'The juggler' (pf) (New York; Ludow Music Inc.)

TEACHING PIECES

Yom Aviv (cham music)
Instrumental pieces and songs

Ref. composer, 205

GYANDZHETSIAN, Destrik Bogdanovna

Soviet pianist, lecturer and composer. b. Baku, September 23, 1923. She studied the piano at the Azerbaijanian Conservatory under A.S. Baron and graduated in 1945. She graduated from the composition class of B.I. Zaidman in 1954 and then lectured in the piano at a music school in Baku.

Compositions

ORCHESTRA

Piano concerto (1958)
Ballet suite (1952)
Three pieces (1956)
Variations (1951)

CHAMBER MUSIC
Piano quintet (1954)
Fugue (ww qrt) (1953)
Piano quartet (1953)
Three pieces (str qrt) (1953)
Piano trio (1949)
Pictures from a child's life, 8 pieces (vln and pf) (1966)
Poem in memory of Lenin (vlc and pf) (1969)
Lively games, 12 pieces (vln and pf) (1971)
Sonata (vlc and pf) (1960)
Sonata (vln and pf) (1960)
Sonatina (bsn and pf) (1951)
Sonatina (vln and pf) (1966)
PIANO
Six Children's pieces (1951)
Twenty-four preludes (1971)
VOCAL
Ballad, Klyatva (A. Prokofiev) (ch and orch) (1954)
Ballad, Za spinoi Moskva (A. Surkov) (ch and orch) (1968)
Ballada o semnadtsatom, cycle (vce and pf) (1967)
Romances
Arrangements of folk songs
Ref. 21

GYDE, Margaret

19th-century English pianist, violinist and composer. b. London. She studied the piano and composition under Walter Cecil and Sir George Alexander Macfarren and the violin under F. Ralph. She won the Sterndale Bennett prize in 1879, the Potter prize in 1880 and the Lady Goldmid and Thalberg scholarships in 1881 and became an A.R.A.M. in 1884. She gave a number of concerts and recitals and in 1895 established the Kensington Music Academy.

Compositions
CHAMBER
Pieces incl.:
Chansonette (vln and pf) (Ashdown)
Dances (vln and pf)
Idylls of summer, suite (vln and pf)
Menuet fantastique (vln and pf)
Reverie (vln and pf)
Romanza (vln and pf)
Scherzo (vln and pf)
Sonata in G-Minor (vln and pf)
Sonata in C-Minor (vln and pf)
Suite de pieces (vln and pf)
Suite of Norwegian airs and dances (vln and pf)
ORGAN
Prelude and fugue in G-Minor (org)
PIANO
Dainty dot
Impromptu
Minuet
Sabina, minuet and trio
Tarantella
Other pieces
VOCAL
Songs incl.:
The bridge of tears
Love's greeting
Seas apart
Ref. 6, 226, 276, 297

GYLDENKRONE, Clara

20th-century Danish composer.

Composition
VOCAL
Seks sange til tekster af Heine, Lenau, Stuckenberg og Herman Bang (W. Hansen, 1914)
Ref. 331

GYLLENHAAL, Aurore. See HAXTHAUSEN, Aurore M.G.Ch. von

GYLLENHAAL, Matilda Valeriana Beatrix, Duchess of Orozco in Spain (pseud. Montgomery)

Swedish singer and composer of Spanish origin. b. Milan, June 14, 1796; d. Stora Ekeby, Sweden, October 19, 1863. She married the Marquis B. Conami and was widowed before she was 20 years old. In 1817 she married J. Montgomery-Cederhjelm in Vienna and was again widowed in 1825. After 14 years she married Baron K.A.F. Gyllenhaal. In the 1820s she became known for her popular romances which she herself often sang in the salons of Stockholm.

Compositions
VOCAL
Axels monolog (vce and pf)
Jeg aldrig det for Vellyst kender (Frankenau) (vce and pf) (1805)
Rings drapa (Tegner) (vce and pf)
La serenata contadinesca (vce and pf)
Stjernsaangen (vce and pf)
Tank naagon gaang (vce and pf)
Vid julbrasan foer naagra aar sedan (vce and pf)
MISCELLANEOUS
Husarmarsch
Other marches
Ref. 20, 95

GYRING, Elizabeth

American composer. b. Vienna, Austria, 1906; d. United States, 1970. She received her early music training in Vienna and her earlier pieces were performed in concert and on the radio by members of the Vienna and Berlin Philharmonic Orchestras. In 1939 she went to live in New York and became an American citizen. Her works have been widely performed in America. DISCOGRAPHY.

Compositions
ORCHESTRA
Symphony (New York: ACA)
Concerto (vln and orch) (ACA)
Concerto (ob and str orch) (ACA)
Sinfonietta No. 1 in D-Minor (ACA)
Sinfonietta No. 2 in B-Minor (ACA)
Andante (ob and str orch) (ACA)
Scherzo No. 3 (str orch) (ACA)
Suite (str orch) (ACA)
Adagio (ACA)
Divertimenti Nos. 1, 2, 3 (ACA)
Furioso (ACA)
Introduction and fugue (ACA)
Larghetto (ACA)
Orchesterstuecke Nos. 1-4 (ACA)
Rondo (ACA)
Scherzo Nos. 1 and 2 (ACA)
Two military marches (ACA)
CHAMBER
Nonet
Sextet fantasy (fl, cl, hn, vln, vla and vlc) (1955)
Concertino quintet (1960)
Quintet for winds and horn
Capriccio (4 cl)
Fugues Nos. 1-16 (cl and str trio)
String quartets Nos. 4, 5, 6 and 7 (1953)
Two marches (2 pf, timp and tri)
Ten canons (2 and 3 ww) (1950)
Trio (cl, bsn and pf; also cl, pf and vla)
Trio fantasy (vla, vlc and pf) (1954)
Concert piece (d-b and pf)
Largo (d-b and pf)
Little serenade (cl and pf) (1963)
Sonata (cl and pf) (1963)
Two duos (cl and vla)
Arabesque (bsn) (1963)
Scherzando (cl) (1963)
ORGAN
Allegro
Fantasies Nos. 1-16
Happy birthday, a little joke on a familiar theme
Prelude
Prelude and fugue Nos. 1-3
Sonata No. 1
Theme and variations
Theme, variations and fugue
PIANO
Sonata No. 1
Sonata No. 2 (1957)
Two pieces
VOCAL
My country, cantata (m-ch, soloists and orch) (ACA)
The secret of liberty, cantata (m-ch, soloist and orch) (ACA)
The reign of violence is over, cantata (mix- or m-ch, pf or orch) (1943)
Enoch (F. Nemans) (w-ch and orch) (ACA)
Heresy for a classroom (w-ch and pf)
New York (mix- or w-ch and pf)
Three easy choruses for schools (mix-ch and pf)
Andante Cantabile (excerpt from Night at Sea and Day in Court) (vce and pf)
Blissful Eden (vce and pf or org) (1955)
Daffodils (Wordsworth) (S and pf)

Fable (Emerson) (S and pf)
Hymn (Addison) (S and pf)
Song from Henry the Eighth (S and str qrt) (1951)
Song from The Tempest (S and str qrt) (1951)
SACRED
Kyrie, Sanctus, Agnus Dei and Gloria (mix-ch and org) (1955)
OPERA
Night at Sea and Day in Court (ACA)
Ref. 40, 94, 141, 190, 322, 403, 563, 594

H.H.L. see BORTHWICK, Jane Laurie

HAAPASALO, Kreeta von
Finnish kantele player, rune singer and composer. b. 1813; d. 1893. She was famous for the clarity of her voice and sincere interpretation of Finnish folksongs with the kantele (a zither type instrument) accompaniment. She remained in her East Bothnian homeland till 1853, when she traveled to Helsingfors and later to Viborg, St. Petersburg and Stockholm. She composed songs with kantele accompaniment.
Ref. 20

HAASS, Maria Catharina
German writer and composer. b. Ottweiler, February 29, 1844. She studied under Friedrich Lux and was editor of a children's journal *Musikalische Jugendpost*. She composed duets, pieces for two and four hands for the harmonium and the piano and songs.
Publications
Kuenstlerleben.
Musikanten Geschichten.
Ref. 226, 276

HABAN, Sister Teresine M.
American professor and composer. b. Columbus, OH, January 15, 1914. She studied composition under Bernard Dieter at the College of St. Francis, IL, (B.A. and B.Mus.); took her M.Mus. at the Chicago Musical College and finally studied under Wayne Barlow at the Eastman School of Music, graduating with a Ph.D. She received an award from the Outstanding Educators of America and was professor and from 1958, chairlady of the music department at the College of St. Francis.
Compositions
ORCHESTRA
Piece (cham orch) (1970)
CHAMBER
Sonata-allegro (trp and pf) (1970)
Prelude (pf) (1966)
SACRED
Mass in honor of St. Ambrose (1959)
Mass in honor of St. Francis
Hymn of praise (w-ch and org) (1965)
Hymns, antiphons and psalms
Music for services (org)
Ref. 137, 142

HABBABA
Arabian songstress. d. Medina, 724. One of the four outstanding songstresses of the Umayyad period, she was taught her art by Azza al-Maila (q.v.), Jamila (q.v.), Ibn Muhriz, Ibn Suraij, Ma'bad and Malik. She was bought by Yazid II when he was a prince, from Ibn Rummana (or Ibn Mina) of the Banu Lashik, for 4 000 gold pieces. When Yazid became Caliph in 720, she became his constant companion until her death; he died of grief a week later. Like other famous songstresses of this period, Habbaba often sang with an orchestra of 50 singing women with lutes, hidden behind a curtain. She was as famous for her charm and beauty as for her art and is said to have exerted considerable political influence over Yazid II.
Ref. 171, 234

HABICHT, Mrs C.E.
19th-century American composer.
Composition
VOCAL
Sun is in the West (vce and pf) (1848) (Boston: G.P. Reed)
Ref. 228

HACKETT, Marie (Maria)
English authoress and composer. b. November 14, 1783; d. London, November 5, 1874. She wrote about cathedral choir schools, composed many songs and encouraged the composition of church music. She founded the Gresham prize in 1831.
Publications
A brief account of Cathedral and Collegiate Schools. London, 1827.
A popular account of St. Paul's Cathedral. London, 1816.
Ref. 226, 433

HACKLEY, Emma Azalia Smith
Black American authoress, singer, teacher and composer. b. Murfreesboro, TN, June 29, 1867; d. Detroit, December 13, 1922. She graduated from the University of Denver, CO, (B.Mus.) in 1900. She was active in educating black communities in the appreciation of black folk songs and helped to advance the careers of many black musicians.
Composition
VOCAL
Carola, song (New York: Handy Bros., 1958)
Publications
A Guide to Voice Culture. Ca. 1909.
Bibliography
Davenport, M. Marguerita. *Azalia: The Life of Madame E. Azalia Hackley*. Boston: Chapman and Grimes, 1949.
Ref. 136, 347, 549

HADDEN, Frances Roots
American pianist, teacher and composer. b. Hankow, China, August 24, 1910. She was the daughter of the Episcopal bishop of Hankow. She attended Mount Holyoke College where she obtained a B.A. She received an Otto Kahn scholarship for music study and also studied with E. Robert Schmitz. She taught in China from 1932 to 1934. She toured the United States, Europe and the Far East as a pianist and also as a duo-pianist with her husband, Richard Hadden. Premier Chou En-lai invited them to return to China in 1972 to present the first performance of her *Lu-Shan suite*.
Compositions
PIANO
Lu-Shan suite (2 pf)
VOCAL
Songs incl.:
Change in a home on the range
I'm the luckiest girl alive
It's been quite a party
Look to the mountains
Spin those propellers
Sweet potato pie
Twicklehampton School for Girls
Weaver of life
We're all the same underneath
THEATRE
The Crowning Experience, musical
The Good Road, revue
The Hurricane, play
Jotham Valley, musical
A Statesman's Dream, dramatic fantasy
Take It to the World, revue
Turning of the Tide, Asian musical
Ref. 39, 142, 347

HADELN, Nancy von
19th-century German composer.
Compositions
ORCHESTRA
Legende, op. 41 (vlc and orch) (Ries and Erler)
Eine Romanze, op. 38 (Schmidt)
CHAMBER
Praeludium, op. 32 (pf and org) (Gries)
VOCAL
Bin ich die gift'ge Pflanze, Liebeslied, op. 36 (2 S, A and pf)
Approx 30 songs incl.:
Kleine Bitte: Moechte euch in Liedern sagen, op. 1 (Gries)
Meine Lieder in Wort und Ton, 16 Lieder (Ries and Erler)
Pappeln im Winde, op. 47 (Ebner)
Traumvergessen: Das ist nun wied'rum ein Tag, op. 25 (Gries)
Wie frischer Tau faellt's, op. 4 (Gries)
THEATRE
Treue Liebe: Es rastet ein Wanderer am Erlenbach, op. 23, melodrama (pf) (Gries)
Ref. 297

HADEWIJCH OF BRABANT
13th-century Flemish poetess and composer. It is thought that she belonged to an informal group of women called Beguines, dedicated to the religious life, but without permanent vows. They were known first in Liège

and Flanders and later in the Rhineland and throughout northern Europe. Continuing the work of Hildegard von Bingen, they cared for the sick and led a contemplative life. The influence of popular troubadour and trouvere songs is apparent in Hadewijch's songs, but they are more spiritual than the earlier secular poems and songs of the chivalric love tradition that swept over Europe and marked the first softening of the harsh and suspicious medieval attitude toward women.
Ref. 335

HADLER, Rosemary. See LORENZ, Ellen Jane

HAENDEL, Ida
Polish violinist and composer. b. Chelm, January 15, 1923. She studied at the Chopin School, Warsaw, winning a gold medal at the age of seven. She studied under Mikhaelowitsch, Carl Flesch, George Enesco and Joseph Szigeti. She made her debut at Queen's Hall, London, playing Brahm's *Violin concerto* under Sir Henry Wood. She toured throughout Europe and America.
Compositions
ORCHESTRA
Piano concerto in A-Major
PIANO
Fantasy
Sonatina
ARRANGEMENTS
Saltarello, for Mendelssohn's Italian Symphony (vln and pf)
Ref. 84, 206, 434

HAENEL DE CRONENTHAL, Louise Augusta Marie Julia (Marquise d'Hericourt de Valincourt)
Austrian composer. b. Graz, June 18, 1839; d. Paris, March 9, 1896. She came from an aristocratic family and at the age of 17 went to Paris to study music. She studied composition under T. Franchomme, Demerssemann, M.M. Tariot, Camille Stamaty and Eugene Prevost. She specialized in the transcription of Chinese national airs and ancient Asiatic music and in 1867 received a medal at the Paris Exhibition for her work. Nearly 100 of her pieces were published.
Compositions
ORCHESTRA
Symphony No. 1, La cinquantaine villageoise
Symphony No. 2, Salut au printemps
Symphony No. 3, La fantastique
Symphony No. 4, Appolonia
Symphony No. 5, Bonheur pastorale
CHAMBER
Cremone (str qrt)
Ophelia, romance dramatique (vlc and pf)
PIANO
Fantasies incl.:
La cloche du soir
Romances sans paroles incl:
Au bord de la mer
Fragilité de la vie
Le naufrage du bonheur
Rondos incl.:
Joyeuse humeur; Musettes gasconnes
Six nocturnes incl.:
Filius dolorosus
Nocturne
La patrie absente
Regrets et souvenirs
Twenty-two sonatas incl.:
Bonheur pastorale
La dramatique
L'enfance de Beethoven
Gaieté classique
Heureux jour
Leonicia
Maestosa
Naïveté
La pathetique
La simplicité
Vieux style
Other pieces incl.:
Alla militare
Scherzo capriccioso
L'elegante, polonaise
La pastorale
Bluette
La source, impromptu
VOCAL
Songs
SACRED
Noël, Christmas carol
OPERA
La nuit d'epreuve (1867)
ARRANGEMENTS
Mazurkas, polkas, varsoviennes and waltzes (large orch)
Old Chinese airs incl.:
La chanson du thé
Chatumeau de Niou-Va (pastorale by Ta-Joun)
La danse des plumes, ballet (Jang-Cheu)
Descente de l'hirondelle (after Confucius)
La grande tournante, danse
Joueuse de flute de Sou-Tchou-Fou; La tasse d'or
Ref. 22, 41, 44, 85, 102, 105, 129, 132, 226, 269, 276, 347, 400

HAGAN, Helen Eugenia
Black American organist, pianist, librarian, teacher and composer. b. Portsmouth, NH, January 10, 1893; d. New York, 1964. She graduated (B.Mus.) from the Yale University School of Music in 1911 and made her debut in New Haven, CT. She was awarded the Samuel Simmons Sanford Fellowship which enabled her to study abroad for two years. She entered the Paris Schola Cantorum where she studied under Blanche Selva and Vincent d'Indy and earned a diploma in 1914. She promoted programs for black soldiers overseas and played in numerous concerts. She was dean of the school of music at Bishop College in Marshall, TX, and coached professional singers.
Compositions
ORCHESTRA
Concerto in C-Minor (pf and orch)
CHAMBER
Piano pieces
Ref. 85, 136, 226, 347, 549

HAGEMANN, Virginia
20th-century American composer.
Compositions
OPERA
The Bird's Christmas Carol (Eleanor Jones) (Bryn Mawr: Theodore Presser, 1957)
A Christmas Carol (Eleanor Jones)
Ref. 141

HAGER-ZIMMERMANN, Hilde
Austrian composer. b. Rosenthal im Boehmerwald, April 17, 1907. She studied at the Bruckner Conservatory, Linz and under Professor Alfred Uhl at the Music Academy, Vienna. In 1973 she received the Cult Prize of the City of Passau. Amongst her composition were 870 choral works and songs, of which about 400 were published by the composer in 108 albums, including 16 albums of choral works. DISCOGRAPHY. PHOTOGRAPH.
Compositions
CHAMBER
Romance (str qrt)
Serenade (str qrt)
Prelude (vlc and pf)
Romantic suite (vln and pf)
Traumwandeln, impression (vlc and pf)
PIANO
Klangspiele
Other pieces
MISCELLANEOUS
Fruehlingsgeschenk
Meditation
Bibliography
Zamazal, Franz. *Komponistin H. Hager-Zimmermann.* Linz, Sept. 1977.
Ref. composer, RILM X1/3 5176, 70, 206, 563

HAGUE, Harriet
English pianist and composer. b. 1793; d. 1816. She was the daughter of Charles Hague, a composer and organist and she composed songs.
Ref. 347

HAHN, Sandra Lea

American pianist, lecturer and composer. b. Spokane, WA, January 5, 1940. She studied under William Brandt at Washington State University and Robert Crane at the University of Wisconsin. She was a pianist with the Milwaukee Symphony Orchestra from 1966 to 1967 and from 1970 a piano lecturer at the University of Idaho.

Compositions

CHAMBER

Quartet (fl, cl, bsn and pf)
Piano trio
Sonorities (fl, hpcd and perc)
Five miniatures (fl and pf)
Variations (fl and pf)
Sonata (vlc) (award, Wisconsin State Music Teachers' competition)
Sonatina (hp)

PIANO

Fantasy
Scherzo
Toccata

THEATRE

The Cave Dwellers (comm Washington State University)

Ref. 142, 625

HAHR, Emma

19th-century American pianist, teacher and composer. b. Fayetteville, NC. She studied in Germany with Karl Klindworth and in Weimar with Liszt.

Compositions

VOCAL

Goodnight song
Lady in the moon
Lullaby
Song from Browning's Pippa Passes

Ref. 433

HAIGH, Bernard. See EDWARDS, Clara

HAIK-VANTOURA, Suzanne

French organist, musicologist, teacher and composer. b. Paris, July 12, 1912. She studied at the Paris Conservatoire, where she was a student of Roger Ducasse and Marcel Dupre and received two first prizes, one for harmony and one for fugue. DISCOGRAPHY.

Compositions

ORCHESTRA

Visages d'Adam, concerto (sax and orch)
Rapsodie israelienne (pf and str orch)

CHAMBER

String quartet
Un beau dimanche (trio) (Paris: Internationale Transatlantiques)
Adagio (sax or inst and org) (Paris: Billaudot)

SACRED

Psalms, Nos. 3, 6, 8, 15, 19, 23, 24, 27, 29, 93, 96, 122, 123, 130, 131, 133, 137
Temoinage, liturgy (S and str qrt)

Publications

La Musique de la Bible revelée, deux recueils. Paris: Choudens, 1978.

Ref. composer, 347, 563

HAIMSOHN, Naomi Carrol

American pianist, poetess and composer. b. Worcester, MA, April 15, 1894. She studied under her father and made her debut at Carnegie Hall at the age of eight. She was a concert pianist for 73 years. In 1974 she gave a concert in Tennessee, becoming the oldest woman classical composer to perform an entire program of her own works. In the early 1930s she was designated Poet Laureate of the Piano. In 1974 she was appointed chairlady of Tennessee State Music. She was dean of the Central Academy of Music, Tennessee from 1921 to 1948.

Compositions

PIANO

Concerto No. 2 in C-Minor (1966)
Concerto religioso in A-Minor (1963)
Gypsy rhapsody in D-Minor (1967, 1974)
Nine concert etudes (1963-1977) (Etude No. 4, National award, 1977)
Reverie in E-Minor (1967)
Revolutionary echoes in E-Major (1976)
Waltz carole in C-Minor (1966)

VOCAL

Boy Scouts of America (G. Schirmer, 1933)
Democratic National Anthem (1932)
Reality (1961)
Song of the Legionnaire (1927)
Starlight (1974)

SACRED

Cry of David, song (1969)
Oh Lord, song (1974)

Publications

The happy tree and other poems. Milwaukee, WI: Peacock, 1974.

Ref. composer, 206

HAINES, Julia Howell

American pianist and composer. b. Montclair, NJ, November 2, 1952. She started to play the piano at the age of five and studied music throughout school and college. She received a B.A. in music from Smith College, Northampton, MA. She was a freelance composer at the Bregman Electronic Music Studio, Dartmouth College, Hanover, from 1974 to 1977. She studied improvised and notated contemporary forms with the Creative Music Studio.

Compositions

VOCAL

EA (hp, dr, rec and vce) (1976)
First memory (fl, perc and vce) (1977)
No nuke woman blues (1976) (Lebanon, NH: New Victoria Printers)

ELECTRONIC

EV 1975 (tape) (1975) (comm Smith College, Northampton, MA.)
Witch (tape) (1975)

Ref. composer, 227

HAIRSTON, Jacqueline Butler

20th-century black American arranger, teacher and composer. b. Charlotte, NC.

Composition

SACRED

Nowhere to lay His head (mix-ch) (1971)

Ref. Morgan State University

HAJDU, Julia

Hungarian pianist, teacher and composer. b. Budapest, September 8, 1925. She obtained her piano teacher's diploma from the Hungarian Academy of Music and studied composition under Gyorgy Ranki. She made her debut on Hungarian Radio in 1948. Julia is a member of the Societies of Artists of the Hungarian Republic, of Musical Artists and of Artisjus. Her work won first prize in the song festival of Radio Budapest in 1948, the Hungarian Folk Song Festival in 1950 and special prize of the Hungarian Republic in 1952. She was the first woman composer for the theatre in Hungary, composing for musicals, operettas, revues, vaudevilles and television. She composed over 200 songs and four suites. Her works are published by Zenemukiado, Budapest. PHOTOGRAPH.

Ref. composer, 77, 206

HALACSY, Irma von

Austrian violinist and composer. b. Vienna, December 30, 1880. She was the daughter of Halacsy de Halacsy, a medical doctor and botanist and studied at the Vienna Conservatory under M. Grun. From 1900 to 1912 she toured as a concert violinist. She was a member of the Austrian Authors' Association and Composers' Union.

Compositions

ORCHESTRA

Violin concerto, op. 1 (1905)

CHAMBER

Divertimento, op. 52 (2 vln, vla and pf) (1927)
String quartet, op. 4 (1906)
Trio in D, op. 43 (pf, vln and vla) (1926)
Paraphrase on Aida (vln and pf; also orch)
Cadenza for Brahms's violin concerto, op. 2 (1904)
Paraphrase on An der schoenen blauen Donau by Strauss, op. 3 (vln)
Two piano pieces, op. 44 (1927)
Violin sonata, op. 7 (1909)
Paraphrase on 3 etudes by Paganini

VOCAL

Here, op. 14, after Homer's Iliad (soloists and orch)
Lieder with orchestra, ops. 17, 18, 28, 34, 35
Quartet, op. 15 (w-vces)
Abbé Mouret, op. 21 (A.G. Swoboda) (vce and pf)
Herz à tout, op. 29 (Swoboda) (vce and pf)
Der Puppen Sper, op. 27 (Swoboda) (vce and pf) (1922)
Schelmenerbschaft, op. 32 (Swoboda) (vce and pf) (1924)
Numerous Lieder

SACRED
Jesushymne, op. 38 (soloists, ch, org and strs)
Psalm 128, op. 47 (S and org) (1927)
BALLET
Spuk, op. 33, mime (Swoboda) (1924)
OPERA
Antinoos, op. 5 (1908)
FILM MUSIC
An der schoenen blauen Donau, op. 37 (Swoboda) (1925)
Die Lore von Tore, op. 36 (Swoboda) (1925)
ARRANGEMENTS
Carmen fantasie (1917)
Ref. 70, 219, 226

HALE, Irene (nee Baumgros, Baungros or Baumgras) (pseud. Victor Rene)
19th-century American composer. b. Syracuse, NY. She was the wife of Philip Hale, an eminent Boston music critic. She studied at the Cincinnati Conservatory, where she was awarded the Springer gold medal in 1881 and under Oscar Raif and Moszkowski in Berlin. She published a number of piano compositions under her pseudonym.
Compositions
PIANO
Pieces incl.:
Quatre pensées poetiques, op. 16, incl.:
Chansonette
Valse impromptu
Morceaux de genre, op. 15
VOCAL
Songs incl.:
Five little white heads
Maise
Mystery
An opal heart
We'll go no more a-roving
Ref. 226, 276, 292, 297, 347

HALL, Beatrice Mary (Marie)
English composer. b. Hamar, Norway, August, 1890; d. Strasbourg, 1961. She studied at the Oslo Conservatory.
Composition
CHAMBER
Sonata (pf and vln) (Senart)
Ref. 41, 81, 226

HALL, Frances
American composer.
Composition
VOCAL
Go to the well
Ref. 142

HALL, Pauline
Norwegian pianist, music critic, translator and composer. b. Hamar, August 2, 1890; d. January 24, 1969. She studied the piano under Backer and Lunde and composition under Catharinus Elling, 1910 to 1912. She continued her studies in Paris from 1912 to 1913, where she became acquainted with the music of Stravinsky and French Impressionism, both of which influenced her early compositions. Later compositions revealed neo-classical elements. She was a harmony pupil of E. Kauffmann-Jassoy in Dresden, 1913 to 1914. She made her debut as a composer in Oslo in 1917. She translated several opera texts, among them Milhaud's *Le Pauve Matelot*, Stravinsky's *L'Histoire du Soldat*, Poulenc's *La Voix humaine* and Mozart's *Don Giovanni*. She also translated Einstein's History of Music. From 1926 to 1932 she was music and theatre correspondent in Berlin for the Norwegian *Dagbladet*; from 1934 to 1942 and from 1945 to 1963 she was music critic for the same newspaper. In 1938 she was instrumental in setting up the Norwegian chapter of the International Society for Contemporary Music and under her presidency from 1938 to 1960 the motto was Look to Europe. She strongly opposed reactionary nationalism in Norwegian music. In 1932 she founded the Pauline Hall Quintet of women's voices, which she led until she received a State Artist's salary. She was an honorary member of the International Society for Contemporary Music. She was awarded the King's Gold Medal of Merit in Norway. DISCOGRAPHY. PHOTOGRAPH.

Compositions
ORCHESTRA
Circus pictures (1933)
Poeme elegiaque (1920)
Verlaine suite (1929)
CHAMBER
Suite for 5 wind instruments (fl, ob, cl, bsn and hn) (1945)
Sonata (str qrt)
Sonatina (str qrt)
Little dance suite from As You Like It (Shakespeare) (ob, cl and bsn) (1960)
Variations on a classical theme (fl) (1961)
VOCAL
Pieces (vce and orch)
Smeden og bageren (ch) (1932)
Fire tosserier (S, cl, bsn, hn and trp) (1961)
Orneland (vce and pf)
Songs
BALLET
The Marquise (1964)
THEATRE
Agilulf den vise
Blodet ropar under almarna (O'Neill)
Caligula
Camus
Familien Turbin (Bulgakov)
Hamlet (Shakespeare)
Hendrik og Pernille
Jarlen
Julius Caesar, suite (1950)
Kongsemnerne (Ibsen) (1958)
Lysistrata (Aristophanes)
Mord i Katedralen (T.S. Eliot)
Piraten (Achard)
Raskolnikov
Sa tuktas en arbigga
The Taming of the Shrew (Shakespeare)
INCIDENTAL MUSIC
Film music
Ref. 4, 5, 15, 17, 20, 22, 23, 44, 67, 70, 94, 95, 96, 105, 113, 130, 163, 226, 563, 622

HALLOCK, Harriet. See BOLZ, Harriet

HALPERN, Stella
American pianist, lecturer and composer. b. Austria, May 18, 1923. She became an American citizen in 1949. She obtained her B.A. from Columbia University and her M.A. in theory and composition from Queens College, NY. She then studied composition under Leo Kraft. She was a lecturer at Queens College from 1968 to 1971 and a teacher at Queensborough Community College, 1971 to 1975. She was involved in a doctoral program at Columbia Teachers' College. She studied the piano under Hedda Ballou, performed on radio and gave recitals in New York. PHOTOGRAPH.
Compositions
CHAMBER
Music for eleven players (1970)
Movement for five players (ob, cl, vln, vlc and perc) (1972)
Three brevities (trp and 4 perc; also cl and 4 perc; also pf and 4 perc) (1969)
Caprice for five tones (cl, trp, pf and temple blocks) (1973)
Pentagram (cl, vlc and blocks) (1972-1973)
Ovoid (ob, B-flat cl and hn) (1975)
Rondo (B-flat cl and pf) (1974)
Two pieces (pf) (1974)
VOCAL
Ozymandias (T, perc and winds)
Two songs (vce and pf) (1975)
Ref. composer, 137, 142, 347

HALSTED, Margo
American carillonneur, organist, lecturer and composer. b. Bakersfield, CA, April 24, 1938. She obtained her B.A. (music) and M.A. (education) at Stanford University and her M.A. (music) at the University of California, Riverside. She was an organ lecturer, carillonneur and faculty member at the University of California, Riverside and an associate carillonneur at Stanford University, 1967 to 1977. She gave carillon recitals in all parts of North America and Europe and is active in the Guild of Carillonneurs. PHOTOGRAPH.

Compositions
CARILLON
Desert wind
Morning song
Nocturne
Petite Suite: Prelude; Sarabande; Rondeau; Toccata
Shepherd boy
Ref. composer, 5, 14

HAMAN, Elizabeth
19th-century composer.
Compositions
VOCAL
Songs incl.:
Barbara Fritchie
Ref. 276

HAMBACHER, Josefina. See DUSCHEK, Josefina

HAMBLEN, Suzy
American film producer and composer. b. Gage, OK, May 9, 1957. She produces films with her husband, Stuart.
Compositions
VOCAL
Songs incl.:
Be happy today
Come unto me
You'll always be mine
SACRED
Songs incl.:
Help Thou my unbelief
There's a place in God's heart
Ref. 39

HAMBROCK, Mathilde
19th-century German composer.
Compositions
CHAMBER
Three pieces for violin and piano, op. 12
A set of four-hand pieces, op. 11 (pf)
VOCAL
Two songs, op. 6
Ref. 226, 276

HAMER, Janice
20th-century English composer.
Compositions
PIANO
Pieces incl.:
Two morning asanas
Ref. *Tempo* No. 127

HAMILL, Roseann
20th-century American composer.
Composition
OPERA
The Blessed Event (Diane Ward) (Interlochen Press, 1958)
Ref. 141

HAMILTON, Gertrude Bean (Mrs. Donald L.)
American pianist, poetess, writer and composer. b. Katahdin Iron Works, 1872; d. Attleboro, MA, January 11, 1951. She studied under Nina Darlington, Thomas Tapper and F.H. Shepard of Orange, NJ. She was a contributor to Etude and a writer of verse and short stories.
Compositions
PIANO
Pieces
VOCAL
Songs incl.:
Twilight songs
Ref. 374

HAMILTON, Marcia
20th-century American librettist and composer.
Composition
OPERA
To Please Mr. Plumjoy (composer) (1957)
Ref. 141

HAMILTON, Mrs. Donald L. See HAMILTON, Gertrude Bean

HAMMANN, Rebecca
American composer. b. Philadelphia, 1964.
Composition
VOCAL
Tide (S and pf) (IBM award, 1980)
Ref. *AWC newsletter* IV/1980

HAMMARBERG-AKESSON, Sonja
20th-century Swedish composer.
Composition
ELECTRONIC
Fragar du vad vi haller pa med (with Jarl Hammarberg) (1968)
Ref. 406

HAMMER, Marie von
19th-century American composer. She was the daughter of Albert H. Wood, a pianist and composer.
Compositions
CHAMBER
Romanza (vlc and pf)
Cello pieces
PIANO
Chasse au papillon
Mumet
Poème d'amour
Two moments musical
VOCAL
Cradle song
A fair, good man
Gondellied
Good night
Heliotrope
If I were thou
Lend me thy fillet, love
Love's doubt
Remember (French and English)
A rose once grew
A valentine
Ref. 226, 276, 292, 297

HAMMOND, Fanny Reed
20th-century American pianist, teacher and composer. b. Springfield, MA. She composed pieces for the violin and songs.
Ref. 347, 353

HAMPDEN, Elizabeth
19th-century English song composer.
Ref. 128

HAMPE, Charlotte
German violist, violinist, professor and composer. b. Heidelberg, August 1, 1910. She studied the viola and the violin at the Hochschule fuer Schulmusik, Berlin. She gave recitals for many years with Hermaine Diener and then became solo violist with the Rias Chamber Orchestra. In 1955 she became a lecturer at the State Conservatory, Berlin and then at the State Hochschule fuer Musik from 1967 to 1969, becoming a professor in 1969.
Compositions
CHAMBER
Variations for viola and viola pomposa
Variations on various chorales (vln and vla)
Seven short baroque dances (vla) (1937) (Berlin: Ries and Erler)
Sonata (vln)

VOCAL
Lieder zum Trostbuch (insts)
ARRANGEMENTS
Petits airs (vln and vla; also vln and vlc or 2 vln) (1951)
Ref. composer

HANCHETT, Sybil Croly
20th-century American composer of an opera.
Ref. 347

HANEFELD, Gertrud
German violinist, teacher and composer. b. Wuppertal-Elberfeld, February 10, 1936. After working for ten years as a nursery school teacher she commenced music studies at the Bergisches Conservatory, Wuppertal-Elberfeld in 1967. In 1972 she took her state examination in the violin. Since 1974 she has taught the violin and elementary music in Siegen. She studied precentorship under Helmut Kahlhofer for five years and was interested in the musical structure of church services.
Compositions
VIOLIN
Erwartung (Erfuellung) (1976)
Fruehlingsbilder (1983)
Hoffnung, meditation
Sehnsucht (1976)
Improvisations
VOCAL
Katz jau jau jau (Hanefeld and Zoller) (1981)
Sternensinger (Hanefeld) (1979)
Treckerlied, children's song (Hanefeld)
SACRED
O Haupt voll Blut und Wunden, cantata (speaker, T, org, vln and ob) (1977)
Christ ist erstanden (ch and inst ens; also T and vln) (1977)
Gott liebt diese Welt (ch and inst ens) (1979)
Ein heller Stern in dunkler Nacht (ch and inst ens) (1979)
Helle Naechte (Hanefeld) (ch, ob, vln and vlc) (1977-1979)
Nun danket all' und bringet Ehr (ch and inst ens) (1979)
Siehe, ich bin bei euch (ch, vln and vlc) (1979)
Stern ueber Bethlehem (ch and inst ens) (1979)
Geboren Jesus Christ, canon (Hanefeld) (1983)
Lobe den Herrn (S, vln and vlc) (1978)
Magnificat (Dorothee Soelle) (speaker and S) (1983-1984)
Nun lob mein Seel' den Herrn (Bar and 2 vln) (1979)
Passionskantate (Keppler) (speaker, T, ob, vln and org) (1977)
Ref. composer, *Frau und Musik*

HANIM, Durri Nigar
Turkish composer. b. 1840. She composed a mazurka, a polka and a valse for the piano.
Ref. Nat. Council of Turkish Women

HANIM, Leyla (Leyla Saz)
Turkish pianist, poetess, writer and composer. b. Istanbul, 1850; d. Istanbul, December 6, 1936. The daughter of the court doctor, vizier and governor, Ismail Pasha, Leyla grew up at the Ottoman Court and after her marriage to the governor, Shiri Pasha, lived in various provincial capitals before returning to Istanbul, where her husband later became Prime Minister. From the age of seven she received piano lessons from an Italian pianist and after 1876 studied Turkish music under Medini Aziz Efendiu and Astik Aga. She played both Turkish and Western music with the palace orchestra. She was fluent in Greek, French and Arabic and extremely well educated for a woman of her time and country. She was at the center of an artistic circle in which both Turkish and western music and literature were cultivated. She wrote articles on the lives of Turkish women for journals. She received her nickname Leyla Saz, for her unceasing interest in the saz instruments, which is a general name given to stringed instruments in Turkey. She composed about 200 instrumental and vocal compositions including a collection of 50 for which she wrote the lyrics (Istanbul: Samli Iskender, 1923).
Ref. Nat. Council of Turkish Women, 17, 430

HANIM, Tanburi Faize
Turkish composer. b. Istanbul, 1894; d. 1959. Her teachers included Tanburi Cemil, Ismail Hakki and Enderunlu Hafiz Husnu. Her husband wrote some of her lyrics.
Compositions
FOLK MUSIC
Devr-I Hindi (Turkish insts)
Sedd-i Araban (Turkish insts)
Ref. Nat. Council of Turkish Women

HANKS, Sybil Ann
American composer. b. Madison, WI, March 5, 1908.
Compositions
ORCHESTRA
Concertino, op. 16 (4 sax and orch; also pf)
CHAMBER
Pieces (pf and sax)
VOCAL
Choral works
Songs
Ref. 76, 347

HANNIKAINEN, Ann-Elise
Finnish pianist and composer. b. Hango, January 14, 1946. She began to improvise on the piano at the age of five and later studied the piano in Poland, Finland, Sweden, the United States, Peru and Spain. From 1967 to 1972 she attended the Sibelius Academy in Helsinki studying the piano under Tapani Valsta and composition under Einar Englund. She was the first women composer to participate in the Young Scandinavian Composers' Festival in 1968. From 1972 she lived in Spain, studying under the Spanish composer Ernesto Halffter. In 1976, her *Concierto*, composed for the centenary of the birth of Manuel de Falla had its world premiere at the inaugural concert of the Helsinki Festival, with the composer at the piano and Ernest Halffter conducting the Helsinki Philharmonic Orchestra.
Compositions
ORCHESTRA
Concierto (pf and orch) (1976)
Anerfalicas, tema y II variaciones (1973)
Cosmos (1977)
CHAMBER
Sextet (wind insts and pf)
Chactiara (fl and pf) (1980) (1st prize, international music competition, Barcelona) (Fazer)
PIANO
Pensamientos (1974) (Fazer)
Theme and 2 variations (1968)
Theme and 4 variations (1966)
Toccata fantasia (1975) (Fazer)
Ref. composer, FMIC

HANS, Lio (pseud. of Scheidl-Hutterstrasser, Lili)
20th-century Austrian composer.
Compositions
ORCHESTRA
Symphonic poems
VOCAL
Sturm-Zyklus (S, Bar and orch)
OPERA
Maria Magdalena, op. 3 (1921)
Other operas
Ref. 70, 108, 431

HANSEN, Hanna Marie
French organist, pianist, teacher and composer. b. Trondheim, Norway, 1875; d. France, 1954. In 1927 she became a French citizen. She was a child prodigy, making her debut in Paris and Oslo in 1882 and studying at the Ecole Normale in Paris from the age of five. She graduated from the Paris Conservatoire with highest honors in 1894 and in 1896 won the Grand Prix. She studied composition in Berlin and gave concerts in Germany, England and Norway. She was also an organist in the Scandinavian Church and later a piano teacher in Paris.
Compositions
ORCHESTRA
Noces norvegiennes
CHAMBER
String quartet
Clair de lune (vln and pf)
Elegie (vln and pf)
Légende (vln and pf)
Romance (vln and pf)
PIANO
Fantaisie
Romance sans paroles et air de ballet, op. 4
Valse populaire

VOCAL
Songs
OPERA
Kleon
Ref. NMI

HANSEN, Joan

20th-century Canadian pianist, teacher and composer. b. Mission, British Columbia. She studied at the universities of British Columbia and Victoria. She taught in North Vancouver and wrote primarily for the keyboard.

Compositions
PIANO
Four pieces, suite
Sonata
Publications
Music of Our Times. With Jean Coulthard (q.v.). Series of teaching books. Waterloo.
Ref. Carolyn D. Lomax (Toronto)

HANSEN, Nancy. See DALBERG, Nancy

HANSEN, Renée

20th-century French harpist and composer. She married the harpist Pierre Jamet and composed solo pieces for harp.
Ref. 344

HANSEN, Thyra

Danish composer. b. October 15, 1891.
Compositions
ORGAN
Firti salme-forspil i kirkestil (1938)
Other pieces
Ref. 331

HANSON, Fay S.

20th-century American composer. She composed for brass instruments.
Ref. 40, 347

HARA, Kazuko (1)

Japanese librettist, professor, singer and composer. b. Tokyo, February 10, 1935. She studied composition under Professor Tomijiro Ikenouchi at the Tokyo Teijutsu Daigaku, faculty of music, from which she graduated in 1957. In 1962 she entered the Ecole Normale in Paris, where she studied under Henri Dutilleux and then studied composition under Tcherepnin at the L'Academie International d'Ete in Nice in 1963. At the Bernedetto Mercello Music Academy in Venice she studied voice under I.A. Carradetti before returning to Japan to study Gregorian chant under Father R.F.J. Mereau. She was awarded the second prize of the NHK and Mainichi Music Contest in 1955; the Takei prize in 1974 and a scholarship, the Ataka prize, from 1953 to 1957 and a scholarship from L'Academie International d'Ete in Nice, 1962 to 1963. From 1968 she was a professor at the Faculty of Music, Osaka University of Arts and from 1970 she lectured at Tokyo Geijutsu Daigaku. She married the composer Hiroshi Hara. PHOTOGRAPH.

Compositions
ORCHESTRA
Frammento per orchestra-jyo (1969)
Concertino for flute, harpsichord and strings (1966)
CHAMBER
Concerto da camera per 8 strumenti (1955)
Sextuor (2 vln, vla, vlc, d-b and pf) (1956)
Quintet (2 vln, vla, vlc and hpcd) (1962)
Quintetto for oboe, horn and strings (1970)
Introduction and allegro for guitar trio (1981)
Sonata for violin and piano (1954)
Monogramme – La fête japonaise (fl) (1962)
Preludio, aria e toccata (gtr) (1973)
PIANO
Children's picture book (ZOG, 1971)
Composition (1971)
Gavotte
Pieces for children: Gioco; piccola danza; aria antica (Yamaha, 1971)
Sonatine (1957) (Tokyo: OGT, 1957)
VOCAL
Airs and duet for concert: Kotaro and Chieko, Love (K. Takamura, from Chieko-Sho) (S, Bar and orch) (1972)
Psyche: ballade (2 vces and orch) (Kimura) (1979)
Yugato-Eika (S or S and T, vln, vla, vlc and fl or picc) (1966)
Canto lacrimoso (Bar, fl, cl, vln and pf) (1975)
Trois ballades – élègie du pierrot (composer) (vce, cor anglais and pf) (1956)
The age of innocence (composer) (vce and pf) (1971)
Composition on the theme of summer: The gloomy season; hell's angels
The letter from lunatic (composer) (vce and pf) (1958)
OPERA
The Case Book of Sherlock Holmes - The Confession (Jun Maeda after A. Conan Doyle) (1981)
Chicko-Sho (Maeda)
On the Merry Night (composer and I. Kikumura) (1982-1983) (prize of encouragement to creative work)
MISCELLANEOUS
Flower of native town
Ref. composer

HARA, Kazuko (2) (pseud. of Kazuko Yamaguchi)

Japanese composer. b. December 25, 1949.
Compositions
VOCAL
My heart touched
Paper carp
Ref. Japanese Phonograph Record Society

HARCOURT, Marguerite Beclard d'. See BECLARD D'HARCOURT, Marguerite

HARDELOT, Guy d' (nee Guy) (Mrs. W.L. Rhodes) (pseud. of Helen Rhodes)

French composer. b. Chateau d'Hardelot, Boulogne-sur-Mer, 1858; d. London, January 7, 1936. She studied at the Paris Conservatoire under Maury, Gounod and Maurel. She traveled in the United States with Emma Calve in 1896 and then settled in London, where her songs were extremely popular and performed in concerts by Calve, Melba, Plancon and other singers. DISCOGRAPHY.

Compositions
VOCAL
Songs incl.:
Avec toi
Because
Big lady moon
Chanson de ma vie
La fermiere
I know a lovely garden
Mignon
Say yes
Serenade
Sous les branches
Three green bonnets, ballad (A.L. Harris)
Tristesse
OPERETTA
Elle et lui
Ref. 8, 22, 27, 41, 85, 96, 177, 226, 260, 276, 307, 347, 563

HARDIMAN, Ellena G.

Canadian pianist and composer. b. 1890; d. 1949. She studied at the Toronto College of Music and in 1918 became an A.T.C.M. She studied the piano under Cyril R. Hoff and theory under W.E. Fairclough in Winnepeg.

Compositions
ORCHESTRA
Symphonic poem of global war
Sonata of the sea
CHAMBER
The rushing wind (str qrt)
Coronation march suite (pf)
VOCAL
Distaff (vce and pf)
Go to I (vce and pf)
Our memorial in France (vce and pf)
That's that (vce and pf)
Twenty-four other songs
OPERA
Isti and Beau Vingt (1945)
Ref. 133, 347

HARDING, Elizabeth
18th-century English composer.
Compositions
HARPSICHORD
Six lessons (1770)
VOCAL
Amintor's choice: Would kind fate bestow a lover, song (1767)
Ref. 65, 91, 125

HARDING, Mildred Thompson
American pianist, violinist, teacher and composer. b. Pittsburgh, PA, June 10, 1910. She received her B.Ed. from the University of Toledo in 1940 and her M.A. from the University of Michigan in 1942. She studied privately with Professor J. Schmitt in Pittsburgh in 1914, with U.G. Marks in Denver in 1918; with Otto Sturmer at the Toledo Conservatory in 1925 and with Jean Parre in 1927 and Charlotte Rugger at Toledo, 1940. She made numerous public appearances as a performer after her debut as a violinist in 1927. She taught the violin in schools in Toledo for eight years and then founded the Harding Music School in 1935. She also taught the piano privately.
Compositions
ORCHESTRA
The immigrant, symphonic poem (1942)
CHAMBER
Sonata italiana (vln and pf) (1939)
VOCAL
Fugue (4 vces) (1941)
Ref. 496

HARDY, Helen Irene
Canadian pianist, lecturer and composer. b. Thunder Bay, Ontario, May 9, 1943. She became an A.R.C.T. in 1963, and an L.R.C.T. in the piano in 1966. In 1984 she was working for her fellowship in composition at Trinity College, London. As a student she received scholarships and awards for her piano performances, which specialized in contemporary works. She teaches the piano, theory and composition and adjudicates and examines for the Royal Conservatory of Music. PHOTOGRAPH.
Compositions
ORCHESTRA
Symphony No. 1, in 3 mvts (classical orch) (1983)
CHAMBER
Four movements for woodwind quintet (fl, ob, cl, bsn and hn) (1982)
Four states of mind: jest; sorrow; contemplation; bewilderment (vln and vlc) (1982)
PIANO
Child's play, 4 pieces based on children's games (1980) (composer)
Three preludes (1980) (composer)
Uhuru, on a drawing by S. Robin Charles (1982)
VOCAL
Three songs: The golden glove; The wreck of the Atlantic; Prospect Harbour (Canadian maritime poetry) (m-S and pf) (1982) (composer)
Ref. composer

HARDY, Mrs. Charles S.
19th-century American composer.
Compositions
VOCAL
Songs incl.:
A child's complaint
Fir tree
Ref. 276, 433

HARKNESS, Rebekah West (Mrs. B.H. Dean)
American composer. b. St. Louis, MO, April 17, 1915. She studied orchestration under Lee Hoiby, composition privately under Nicholas Stein and Frederick Werle at the Mannes College of Music; under Nadia Boulanger (q.v.) in Paris and at the Jacques Dalcroze Institute, Geneva. She received honorary doctorates from Franklin Pierce College in 1968 and Lycoming College, 1970. She furthered the development of ballet in the United States and was sponsor for Jerome Robbins' Ballets USA and the ballets of Robert Joffrey. In 1964 she founded her own company, the Harkness Ballet Company of New York and in 1965 opened Harkness House, which contained a ballet school and gallery. Her company toured successfully in Europe, performing her own music. In 1965 she donated a new stage to the East Room of the White House and in 1972 acquired a theatre in New York which is administered by the Harkness Ballet Foundation. Her awards included the bronze medal of appreciation for her many cultural contributions to the City of New York, 1965; New York's Handel award; a Congressional record citation, Marques de Cuevas prize from Universite de la Dance in Paris and Ballet de Jeunes Annual award. In 1966 she was named an Officier Merite Culturel et Artistique, France. She was a member of the board of directors of the John F. Kennedy Center for Performing Arts, Washington, DC, and served on the President's Council for Youth Opportunity, Washington. *Journey to Love*, written for the Marquis de Cuevas, was performed at the Brussels World Fair in 1957. DISCOGRAPHY.
Compositions
ORCHESTRA
Gift of the Magi, in 4 mvts (1958-1959)
Letters to Japan (1961)
Mediterranean suite (1957)
Musical chairs (1958)
Safari in Africa, tone poem (1955)
VOCAL
Songs incl.:
My heart tells me
Theme of the jewel
Tulips in springtime
When love is new
Windy day
BALLET
Aiyoku (1971)
Barcelona suite (1985)
Dreams of glory (1962)
The elements (1965)
Journey to love (1958)
Macumba (1966)
The palace (1963)
Zealous variations (1967)
MISCELLANEOUS
Il Palio (1957)
Music with a heartbeat
The seasons (1956)
ARRANGEMENTS
Works by Schubert, Schumann and Rachmaninoff
Ref. 17, 39, 94, 142, 347, 475, 625

HARLAND, Lizzie. See HARTLAND, Lizzie

HARLEY, Frances Marjorie
American pianist, singer, teacher and composer. b. Park Ridge, IL, September 24, 1914. She received her B.Mus. from Mundelein College, Chicago and her M.Mus. from the American Conservatory, Chicago. Her post-graduate study was carried out at the UCLA. She was the director of several choirs and taught singing, the piano and theory both privately and at a school. She sang on radio programs and contributed to several journals. She composed and arranged 38 choral works.
Ref. 457

HARLOW, Barbara
20th-century American choir conductor and composer.
Composition
SACRED
Magnificat (ch and pf) (1980)
Ref. 10

HARLOW, Clarissa
18th-century English composer.
Composition
VOCAL
Ode to wisdom (The solitary bird of night) (Elizabeth Carter) (1748)
Bibliography
Richardson, Samuel. *Clarissa: Or, The history of a young lady*. Vol 2, pp. 50-51, part of Letter IX.
Ref. 91

HARMS, Signe
20th-century Danish composer.
Compositions
CHAMBER
Chanson triste (vla and pf)
Fire praeludier (org or pf)

VOCAL
Aladdins vuggevise (vce and pf)
Altid frejdig, naar du gaar (vce and pf)
Ref. 331

HARNDEN, Ethel. See HARRADEN, Ethel

HARNIG, Martha. See FLEMMING, Martha

HARP OF THE HOLY SPIRIT. See HILDEGARDE, Saint

HARPER, Marjorie

American pianist and composer. b. St. Paul, MN, April, 26 1902. She studied the piano under Alexander Lambert and theory under Rubin Goldmark. She toured the United States with Tito Guizar, performing her own compositions and was vice-president of the Concert Piano League, New York. PHOTOGRAPH.

Compositions

PIANO
By the Alhambra (1951)
Una calle en Granada (1955) (Remick)
El campo gitano (1949) (G. Schirmer)
Cuevas da Granada (1951) (Belwin Pub.)
Echoes of Sevilla (1951) (Carl Fischer)
Fiesta in Aragon (1951) (Schirmer)
La fiesta gitana (1951) (Belwin)
The floating gardens (1955) (Boston)
La flor de Valencia (1949) (Oliver Ditson)
A flower market in Spain (1964) (Belwin)
Guitarras de Sevilla (1953) (Boston)
In a Hindustani market (1959) (Belwin)
In a Syrian bazaar (1961) (Belwin)
Memories of Malaga (1964) (Belwin)
Noche de fiesta (1948) (Ross Jungnicole)
Noches flamencas (1948) (Jungnicole)
Ole Gipsy (1954) (Boosey & Hawkes)
On the rancho (1961) (Belwin)
Pancho's serenade (1954) (Boosey)
La plaga de Malaga (1953) (Boston)
Serenade to Mercedes (1951) (Schirmer)
Serenata flamenca (1955) (Remick)
Under the crescent moon (1952) (Belwin)
A visit to Argentina (1952) (Belwin)
A visit to Brazil (1953) (Belwin)
A visit to Mexico (1959) (Belwin)
A visit to Puerto Rico (1953) (Belwin)

VOCAL
In my lonely caravan (1941) (Harold Flammer)
Santa Rosa de Luna (1953) (Whalen Music)
Senora de Guadalupe (1953) (Lawrence Welk)
Other songs

SACRED
Blessed is He (St. Mark) (ch) (1961) (Theodore Presser)
Deliver us (1st Chronicle) (ch) (1957) (Presser)
Great and marvellous are Thy works (ch) (1957) (Bourne)
We have a strong city (Isaiah) (ch) (1970) (Presser)
Ref. composer, 39

HARPER, Mrs. Sidney. See WRIGHT, Ellen

HARRADEN, R. Ethel (Mrs. Frank Glover)

Late 19th-early 20th-century English composer. Her opera *The Taboo* was successfully produced at the Trafalgar Square Theatre, London, 1895.

Compositions

CHAMBER
Gavotte (vln and pf) (Ashdown; Augener)
An idyll (vln and pf; also pf) (Forsyth)
Legende (vln and pf) (Forsyth)
Moto perpetuo (vln and pf) (Forsyth)
Six characteristic pieces (vln and pf) (Ashdown)
Six pieces for violin and piano (Forsyth)
Tristesse, romance sans paroles (vlc and pf) (Schott)
Two Melodies (vln and pf) (Ashdown)

VOCAL
Pearl, cantata (w-vces) (Forsyth)
Birth of Flora (w-ch) (Forsyth)
Over the sea our galleys went (ch) (1884)
Songs incl.:
As we love today (vce and pf) (Boosey)
Bird let loose (vce and pf) (Chappell)
Castanets, Spanish duet
A flower lullaby (2-part equal vces) (Forsyth)
Go tell the flowers (vce and pf) (Leonard)
Great book (2-part equal vces) (Forsyth)
A laddie is coming to woo me (vce and gtr) (Ashdown)
Listen to the wind (2-part equal vces) (Forsyth)
Sky (2-part equal vces) (Forsyth)
Violet and the snowdrop (vce, vln and vlc ad lib) (Ashdown)
Waves (2-part equal vces) (Forsyth)

OPERA
Agatha's Doctor
All about a Bonnet
The Taboo (London, 1895)

OPERETTA
His Last Chance, in 1 act (1891)

ARRANGEMENTS
Andante (Glueck) (vln, vlc and pf) (Donajowski)
Largo (Handel) (vln, vlc and pf) (Ashdown)
Ref. 6, 226, 276, 297, 307, 431

HARRHY, Edith

20th-century Australian composer.

Compositions

PIANO
Maori sketches: On the Wanganui; Lullaby; Love song; War dance; Poi dance; Lament (Boosey & Allan)

VOCAL
Colette (Allan)
Elizabeth (Allan)
Mother England (Allan)
Pierrot's cradle song (Allan)
The thrush (Allan)
Two songs of the sea (F. Harris)
Children's songs (Allan)

SACRED
Requiem in C and B-Flat (Boosey & Hawkes)
Ref. 490

HARRINGTON, Amber R. See ROOBENIAN, Amber

HARRIS, Dorothy

English pianist, accompanist and composer. b. Ilford, 1895. Her teachers were Frederick Moore, Elsie Horne and Harry Farjeon.

Compositions

PIANO
After sunset
Among the reeds
In Arcadia
Nocturne
Old country dance
Rippling brooklet
Song without words
Valse mignonne

VOCAL
Songs incl.:
Boat song
By the rustic gate
Evensong
The waterfall
Ref. 467

HARRIS, Ethel Ramos (Mrs. Chester E.)

Black American pianist, authoress, lecturer, singer and composer. b. Newport, RI, August 18, 1908. She studied at the New England Conservatory under Charles Dennee and Warren Storey Smith; at Carnegie-Mellon University under Nikolai Lopatnikoff; under Isidor Philipp in New York and Aaron Copland at Tanglewood. She received two scholarships; one to study under Harvey Gaul and one from the American Palestine Committee, to study in Israel. She won a Delta Sigma Theta award in 1959 and 1973 and in 1971 won the National Association of Negro Women's Outstanding Musician award. In 1972 she received the Martin Luther King, Jr. award. She was a pianist with the National Negro Opera Company.

Compositions
PIANO
Pieces
VOCAL
Choral works incl.:
I've been in the storm so long
Stan' ready
There'll be a jubilee
When I reach the other side
Songs
Ref. 142, 347

HARRIS, Letitia Radcliffe

20th-century American pianist and composer. b. Germantown, PA. She composed chamber music, piano pieces and songs.
Ref. 347

HARRIS, Margaret R.

Black American pianist, conductor, teacher and composer. b. Chicago, September 15, 1943. She was a child prodigy, playing in public at the age of three and performing a Mozart concerto at the age of ten. She studied at the Curtis Institute in Philadelphia and obtained her B.S. in 1964 and her M.S. in 1965 from the Juilliard School of Music. She was a music director and a teacher and in 1970 made her debut as a pianist, playing some of her own compositions. She conducted orchestras and musicals extensively, being conductor and musical director of *Hair* and frequently conductor, pianist and composer of productions. She appeared on television and radio. In 1972 she received an award from the National Association of Negro Musicians.
Compositions
ORCHESTRA
Concerto No. 2 (pf and orch)
MISCELLANEOUS
Collage one (1970)
Dear love (1970)
Grievin (1970)
Tonite's goodbye (1970)
Bibliography
Women in the Pit. Newsweek, Aug. 21, 1972.
Ref. 136, 347, 549

HARRIS, Ruth Berman (Ruth Berman)

American harpist and composer. b. New Haven, CT, November 3, 1916. She attended the Albert Magnus College in 1934, New York University in 1935 and the Institute of Musical Art, preparatory division, from 1932 to 1934. From 1934 to 1937 she was a student at the Institute of Musical Art (now the Juilliard School of music) and then attended the State University of New York at Purchase for Continuing Education, 1978 to 1981. She studied the harp privately under Marie Miller, Carlos Salzedo, Lucille Lawrence and Caspar Riardon and composition and orchestration under Ronald Herder. She performed extensively as orchestral harpist and soloist for the National Broadcasting Company, the Columbia Broadcasting System and the ABC radio and TV networks. She won the Musical Society's 1933 Madrigal award and a Meet the Composer grant in 1982. She was guest of honor to the Eighth International Harp Contest, Israel, in 1982 and 1985. She judged many competitions. PHOTOGRAPH.
Compositions
CHAMBER
Woodwind quintet (ob, fl, cl, bsn and hn) (1984)
Rhapsody (fl, cl, vlc and hp) (1979)
String quartet No. 1 (1982)
Winter (1982) (hp, fl and cl) (Sumark Press)
Nocturne (1978) (hp and vlc) (Sumark)
HARP
Song of Guadalajara (1981) (2 hp) (Sumark)
Miniatures, 5 solos, 2 original and 3 transcriptions (1976) (Sumark)
Miniatures II, 6 solos, 5 original and 1 transcription (1978) (Sumark)
PIANO
Passacaglia (2 pf) (1980)
The prizefighter (1981)
Rhapsody (1979)
VOCAL
Night song (4 vces, 2 fl, cl, vlc and pf)
SACRED
Requiem for Mark Sumner Harris (vces and cham orch) (1980)
Prayer (1977) (vce and pf or hp) (Sumark)
ARRANGEMENTS
Silent Night (Franz Gruber) (with S. Harris) (vln, pf and hp)
O Holy Night (Adolphe Adam) (with S. Harris) (hp) (1982) (Sumark)
Ref. composer, 625

HARRISON, Annie Fortescue (Lady Arthur Hill)

English composer. b. 1851; d. 1944.
Compositions
PIANO
Pieces
VOCAL
In the gloaming, cantata (vce and pf) (1877)
We meet again, cantata (vce and pf)
At noontide
I want to be a soldier
In the moonlight
Let me forget thee
Yesteryear
OPERA
The Ferry Girl (1883)
The Lost Husband (1884)
Ref. 226, 307, 347, 370, 653

HARRISON, Pamela

English pianist and composer. b. Orpington, November 28, 1915. At the Royal College of Music she studied the piano under Arthur Benjamin, accompaniment under Harry Stubbs, harmony and counterpoint under Herbert Howells and composition under Gordon Jacob.
Compositions
ORCHESTRA
Concertante (pf and str orch) (1958)
Brimstone down (small orch) (1960)
An evocation of the weald (1959)
A suite for Timothy (str orch) (1948)
CHAMBER
Octetto pastorale (2 ob, 2 cl, 2 bsn and 2 hn) (1981)
Septet (cl, bsn, hn, vln, vla, vlc and d-b) (1980)
Quintet (cl and strs) (1958)
Quintet (fl, ob, vln, vla and vlc) (1947)
Quartet (fl, vln, vlc and pf) (1973)
Quartet (ww) (1943)
Piano Trio (1970)
String Trio (1942)
Badinage (fl and pf) (1950) (Chappell)
Drifting Away (cl and pf) (1976) (Josef Weinberger)
Faggot dance (bsn and pf) (1950) (Galliard)
Five pieces (fl and pf) (1976)
Lament (vla and pf) (1950) (Galliard)
Sonata (cl and pf) (1954)
Sonata (vla and pf) (1956)
Sonata (vlc and pf) (1947)
Sonnet (vlc and pf) (1950) (Chappell)
Two pieces (vlc and pf) (1950) (Joseph Williams)
PIANO
Six dances for Fanny Simmons (duets) (1977)
Anderida (1950) (Chappell)
Six eclogues of Portugal (1962)
VOCAL
The dark forest, song cycle of 6 poems (Edward Thomas) (vce and str orch) (1960)
Eight songs with recorder (Walter de la Mare) (1968)
Five poems of Ernest Dowson, song cycle
The kindling of the day, 10 poems (Robert Herrick) (1952)
The lonely landscape, song cycle of 6 poems (Emily Bronte) (1954)
A present for Paul, 6 poems (Walter de la Mare) (1950)
Six poems of Baudelaire, song cycle (1957)
Ref. composer

HARRISON, Susan Frances (Susie) (pseuds. Seranus, Gilbert King)

Canadian pianist, poetess and composer. b. Toronto, February 24, 1859; d. Toronto, May 5, 1935. She was considered an authority on French Canadian folk material.
Compositions
CHAMBER
Piano pieces
VOCAL
Songs
OPERA
Pipandor
Ref. Nat. Library of Canada, 347

HARROD, Beth Miller

20th-century American composer. She composed instrumental, piano and choral works.
Ref. 40, 347

HARSHMAN, Margaret B.

20th-century American composer of Louisiana. Her composition was preserved in a time-capsule in the cornerstone of the new Louisiana State Archive Building in Baton Rouge.

Composition

MISCELLANEOUS

Made in America, march

Ref. ASCAP Fall 1983

HART, Alice Maud (Alice Maud Challinor)

South African pianist, singer, teacher and composer. b. Kent, England, May 17, 1859; d. Durban, South Africa, August 28, 1944. At the age of 17 she became an L.R.A.M. and in 1880 was appointed music teacher at Miss L. Hall's establishment for Young Ladies at Graaff-Reinet, Cape Province, South Africa. In 1881 she moved to Durban, where she continued her career as a teacher by opening her own music school and teaching the piano, singing, part-singing, composition and harmony. She also taught at the Ladies' College, Durban. She spent much time stimulating interest in classical music with pupil concerts, by singing in a ladies' choir and giving song and piano recitals with her sister Carrie. She also introduced Tableaux Vivants, a combined musical and visual experience, which proved very popular.

Compositions

PIANO

Minuet and trio in F-Sharp Minor
O! Wonder (Cecil Loraine)
South African dance (ded Mrs. F.W. Frank)
South African march
Twelve finger exercises

Bibliography

Henning, C.G. *Graaff-Reinet, A Cultural History, 1786-1886*. Cape Town: T.V. Bulpin, 1975.
Jackson, George. *Music in Durban, 1850-1900*. Johannesburg: Witwatersrand University Press, 1970.

Ref. 184, 297, 377

HART, Dorothy

Compositions

VOCAL

Songs incl.:
Dance of dreams (D.M. Beeman)
The garden of the world (composer)
I already knew (Beeman)
Without you (Beeman)

Ref. Ricordi (Milan)

HART, Elizabeth Jane Smith

American composer. b. Rockwell City, IA, September 4, 1913. She obtained a B.S. from the Juilliard School of Music in 1938 and an M.A. from Columbia Teachers College in 1958. She was head of the music department at the Horace Mann-Barnard School, Riverdale, 1971 to 1977. She was director of Young Artists New Rochelle Annual Concert from 1964 to 1977, director of composer musical productions for the Horace Mann-Barnard School and president and program chairlady of the Music Teachers' Council of New Rochelle, 1965 to 1969.

Compositions

CHAMBER

Music notes on greetings (tba, vln and pf) (1974)
Sonata (vln and pf) (1960)

PIANO

Variations on spirituals (4 hands) (1961)
Rondo (1977)

VOCAL

Spirit's truth (4-part ch) (1964)
Stopping by woods (Frost) (4-part ch) (1964)
Song cycles (Emily Dickinson and Edna St. Vincent Millay) (S) (1967)
Song for Zapalya (Coleridge) (1976)

SACRED

Everytime I feel the Spirit (4-part ch) (1964)

THEATRE

Nevada (1971)
Message to Valley Forge (1975)

Ref. composer

HART, Imogine

19th-century American composer.

Composition

VOCAL

Gaily smiles the earth before me (vce and pf) (Boston: O. Ditson) (1859)

Ref. 228

HARTER, Louise C.

20th-century American composer. She composed piano pieces, choral works and songs.

Ref. 40, 347

HARTER, Mrs. See RAIGORODSKY, Leda Natalia Heimsath

HARTLAND (Harland), Lizzie

19th-century English pianist, conductor, teacher and composer. She came from a family of musicians and was accompanist to the West Bromwich Choral Society before commencing teaching.

Compositions

PIANO

Pieces

VOCAL

Coeur de lion, cantata
Queen of the roses, cantata (w-ch)
Bow down thine ear (Ashdown)
Britain, the land of freedom (Ashdown)
Idylle (Augener)
Other songs and part songs

SACRED

Christmas bells (Ashdown)
A Christmas song (Ashdown)

Ref. 6, 226, 276, 297, 347

HARTMANN, Emma Sophie Amalie (nee Linn) (pseud. F.H. Palmer)

Danish composer. b. Copenhagen, August 22, 1807; d. March 6, 1851. She married the composer J.P.E. Hartmann. Six of her ten children survived; one, Emil, became a composer and another, Sophie, married the composer Niels W. Gade. For many years Emma composed songs secretly, sometimes on texts of her friend Ernst Weis. When her husband discovered her compositions he helped her to publish them.

Compositions

PIANO

Pieces (4 hands) (Hansen)
Danse (Hansen)
Deux rondeaux brillants et non difficiles, op. 6

VOCAL

Danske sange, 2 volumes (1851)
Romancer og sange med accompagnement af pianoforte, 5 vols (vce and pf) (1849-1854) (Horneman & Erslevs, 1851)
Samtlige romancer og sange (Hansen)

Bibliography

Kvindelig komponist, gamle Hartmanns hustru. i. Politiken. 10-5. 1955.

Ref. Dansk Musik, 13, 20, 331

HARTZER-STIBBE, Marie

Dutch pianist, teacher and composer. b. Semarang, Dutch East Indies, January 29, 1880; d. November 9, 1961. She studied the piano in Amsterdam under Sarah Bosmans and at the Frankfurt Conservatory under Carl Friedberg in 1901. In Berlin she studied theory under Friedrich Gernsheim and Georg Schumann. From 1904 to 1906 she taught the piano at the Bernuth Conservatory, Hamburg. She traveled on concert tours with Hans Hermans, whom she married in 1901 and who died in 1909. In 1910 she married Richard Hartzer, a violin teacher and lived in Berlin until 1926, when they emigrated to the United States.

Compositions

ORCHESTRA

Piano concerto

CHAMBER

Piano trio, op. 30

PIANO

Chaconne
Round melodies, op. 25
Small pieces

VOCAL

Children's songs
Im weissen Mondlicht (vce and pf)
Sechzehn Lieder
Terzetten

SACRED

Psalm 130 (vce and org)

Ref. 70, 105, 111

HARVEY, Ella Doreen

20th-century English pianist, teacher and composer. She studied privately and at the Bexhill School of Music. She became an L.R.A.M. She was music teacher at a school in Rye, Sussex, accompanist for the Rye String Players and a member of the local operatic Society.

Compositions

ORCHESTRA

Valse de concert (str orch)

PIANO

Suite of four pieces

Other pieces

OPERETTAS

Various

Ref. 467

HARVEY, Eva Noel (nee Donovan)

South African pianist, violinist, painter, poetess, singer and composer. b. Swaziland, October 30, 1900; d. Johannesburg, December 12, 1984. She was the first South African to write an opera and the only South African to have written grand opera. At the Johannesburg Conservatory she studied the piano under Maud Harrison and the violin under Violet Jamieson and Ethel Mann. She concentrated on the violin, studying for two years under Ellie Marks of Cape Town, then joined Johannesburg's first symphony orchestra under John Connell. For 25 years she gave a first hearing in the concert room of her home to any South African showing musical promise. She won several SABC composition competitions. She composed over 400 songs and many of her works were performed in Holland, Ireland and the United States as well as in concerts and on the radio in South Africa. Eva also painted and wrote poetry. PHOTOGRAPH.

Compositions

CHAMBER

Chanson de soir

Suite (celtic hp)

Suite (fl and pf)

Suite (ob and pf)

Suite (vln and pf)

PIANO

Suite (2 pf)

African tone pictures

African suite: The song of the Ntombazana; The corngrinder's lullaby; The Old warrior, Mdala (also orch) (prize, SABC competition)

VOCAL

Gipsy jingle (m-S and orch)

Go bind thy dark red berries (m-S and orch)

Joan (A. Neyse) (m-S and orch)

Over 400 songs incl.:

Aftermath

And beauty came (Siegfried Sassoon)

Arise, shine (vce and pf or org)

Bokmakierie (Ourmeister) (Studio Holland)

Chinese lanterns

A Chinese proverb (Studio Holland)

Drake's drum rolls again

Fain would I waken (Studio Holland)

Japanese song cycle (prize, SABC song contest)

Kom dans met my (Leipoldt)

Krulkop (Leipoldt) (Studio Holland)

Laat winter dag (van Heerden)

The loom

My tears will gently fall

O diep rivier (Eugene Marais)

Oktober (Louw)

Ontwaak

Salute d'amore (Visser) (Studio Holland)

Sing vinkie, sing (Leipoldt)

Song cycle: Francesca; The white stag; Dance figure (Ezra Pound)

Three songs from Venus legends: Birth of Venus; Echo and Narcissus; Marriage of Bacchus and Ariadne

Toeral loeral la (Leipoldt)

Tranquility (Burmeister)

Windswael (Leipoldt)

SACRED

Lift up thine eyes, oratorio

To the glory of God, cantata

Christmas carol

I know that my Redeemer liveth (Jennens) (vce and pf or org)

A little child shall lead them (vce and pf or org)

Praise ye the Lord

Six carols

The wisdom carol (vce and pf) (Studio Holland)

With His truth, psalm 96 (vce and pf)

BALLET

The Silver Slipper

OPERA

Esther, grand opera in 3 acts (1965)

Ruth and Naomi, biblical opera in one act (1966)

Yugao, miniature opera in one act (1966)

Ref. composer, 184, 377

HARVEY, Mary. See DERING, Lady Mary

HARVEY, Roberta

B. 1873.

Composition

OPERA

La Bonne Terre

Ref. 307

HARVEY, Vivien

20th-Century American composer.

Composition

VOCAL

Summer (mix-ch) (B.M.I.)

Ref. 190

HARWOOD, Mrs. Waldo E. See HARWOOD, Sylvia Rowell

HARWOOD, Sylvia Rowell (Mrs. Waldo E. Harwood)

American violinist and composer. b. Portland, 1913. She studied the violin under David Fisher and also under Paul Taylor White at the Eastman School of Music, Rochester. She studied composition under Berniece Preston. She was staff violinist with the studio orchestra at the WCSH Radio Station for two years and worked for theatre, concert and radio for 25 years.

Compositions

CHAMBER

Violin solos

VOCAL

I'm only pretending, ballad (Dixon Pub., 1931)

Life without you (Sylvan Publ., 1931)

Where the Saco river flows, ballad (Sylvan, 1931)

Songs (vce and vln)

MISCELLANEOUS

A musical reading

Ref. 374

HASHIMOTO, Kunihiko

20th-century Japanese composer.

Compositions

VOCAL

Kuhihiko Hashimoto album (2 part w-ch a-cap)

Zen-on Gakufu Shuppan-sha (2 part w-ch a-cap) (1962)

Ref. Library of Congress catalog

HASKELL, Doris Burd

20th-century American violinist, teacher and composer.

Compositions

VIOLIN

Solo in Old Dorian mode

Other pieces

Ref. 347, 448

HASWIN, Frances R.

American poetess and composer. b. Ripon, WI, May 14, 1852. She composed instrumental and vocal works.

Ref. 433

HATCH, Edith

American organist, pianist, lecturer and composer. b. Aberdeen, MI, April 16, 1884. Her mother, a pupil of Leopold Godowsky, was her first piano teacher. Edith then studied under Louise Sims and won scholarships to

Cincinnati and Stern Conservatories, accepting the former. She taught at the Cincinnati Conservatory and then became director of the Music Departments of All-Saints' Episcopal College in Vicksburg, MI, from 1910 to 1912 and of the Dillon unit of the Montana State Normal College, 1913 to 1919. She was a church and recital organist and opened her own studio in 1936.

Compositions

PIANO

The clown's dance
Etudes in double notes and octaves
Mountain spirits
Queen of the May
Rambles in Melody Land, suite
Spanish carnival
Spirits at play
Summer comes again

TEACHING PIECES

Essential rudiments
Seven special descriptive studies

Publications

The Edith Hatch class piano method.

Ref. 496

HATCH, Mabel Lee

20th-century American composer.

Compositions

PIANO

April blossoms
Gay butterflies

Ref. 292

HATSHEPSUT, Queen

Egyptian songstress of the XVIII dynasty. Before ascending to the throne in 1520 B.C. she held the position of leader of the Amon songstresses, a position traditionally held by a high personage at that time. The role of the songstress seems to be little beyond the recitation of liturgical responses, but some were professional musicians who composed sacred songs. (See Songstresses).

Ref. 473

HATTON, Anne

American composer.

Composition

OPERA

Tammany, comic opera

Ref. American Music, Summer 1983

HATZLERIN, Sister Clara

15th-century composer. Her vocal works included a song cycle.

Ref. 465

HAUSMAN, Ruth Langley

American pianist, arranger, teacher, writer and composer. b. Philadelphia, October 4, 1897. She attended New York University and studied the piano, theory and composition privately. She was supervisor of music in Philadelphia public schools from 1924 to 1961.

Compositions

VOCAL

Danny Boy, adapted from an old Irish air (Fred Weatherly) (w-ch)
Sing and Dance with the Pennsylvania Dutch (vce and pf or auto-harp) (E.B. Marks Music Corp. 1953)

SACRED

Suffer the little children (vce and pf) (Schirmer)

Publications

Australia: Traditional Music and Its History. Christopher House, 1975.
Hawaii: Music and Its History. Tokyo: C.E. Tuttle Co., 1968.

Ref. composer, 190

HAVERGAL, Frances Ridley

English poetess and composer. b. Astley, December 14, 1836; d. Oystermouth, Wales, June 3, 1879. She was the daughter of the Reverend William Havergal Astley, a composer of sacred music. She studied in Duesseldorf.

Compositions

SACRED

Hymns incl.:
I could not do without Thee
Jesus, Master, whose I am
Master speak
Take my life and let it be

Publications

Poetical works. 1884.

Ref. 369, 572, 646

HAVEY, Marguerite

American organist, choir conductor, teacher and composer. b. New York City, December 16, 1910. She studied at the Juilliard School of Music in 1933 and was a student at the American Conservatory of Music in Chicago from 1948 till 1949. She was founder director and organist of the professional Choir of Epiphany in New York from 1939 till 1957; guest conductor of the Greenwich, CT, Choral Society in 1967 and after 1976 a freelance organist and choir conductor. She taught at Brearley School, New York from 1957 to 1976, becoming chairlady of the music department in 1973.

Compositions

SACRED

In praise of Mary's Son (mix-ch) (H.W. Gray Co.)
Carol of the Adoration
Noël
O Spirit, who from Jesus came

Ref. 190

HAWAII'S SONGBIRD. See MACHADO, Lena

HAWES, Charlotte W.

19th-century American pianist, lecturer and composer. b. Wrentham, MA. She studied in New York and Boston and later studied the piano under Friedrich Wieck in Dresden.

Compositions

VOCAL

Cradle song
God bless the soldier (1890) (comm National Encampment, Boston)
Greeting
Nannie's sailor lad

Publications

Famous Themes of Great Composers.

Ref. 433

HAWES, Maria (Billington)

English contralto and composer. b. London, April, 1816; d. Ryde, Isle of Wight, April 24, 1886. She studied under her father, William Hawes.

Compositions

VOCAL

Ballads incl.:
Oh! chide me not, my mother! (W.H. Bellamy) (ded Felix Mendelssohn-Bartholdy)

Ref. 8

HAWLEY, Carolyn Jean (nee Bowen)

American pianist, choral and orchestral conductor, teacher and composer. b. Terre Haute, IN, May 18, 1931. She received her B.A. from Hamline University, St Paul, MN, and M.A. from Mills College, Oakland, CA, where her teachers included Darius Milhaud and Leon Kirchner (composition) and Egon Petri (piano). Her other teachers were Glenn Glasow (composition), Tom Nee and Elizabeth Green (conducting) and Edith Byquist-Norberg. She taught at Laney College, Oakland, in schools and privately. In California she conducted church and contemporary choirs and the Berkley Community Orchestra and Chorus in 1978. She gave numerous piano concerts in Northern California. She was the founder and is currently seasonal conductor and musical director of the Ukiah Symphony Orchestra. PHOTOGRAPH.

Compositions

ORCHESTRA

Pieces

CHAMBER

500 quintet (ww and pf) (1973)
Cricket, string quartet No. 1 (1965)
Quartet No. 2 (ob, gtr, vlc and hpcd) (1961)
Quartet No. 3 (fl, vlc, pf and perc) (1962)

Quartet No. 4 (fl, ob, bsn and pf) (1973)
String trio (1956)
Trio partita (fl, vln and pf) (1958)
Sheep trio (fl, bsn and pf) (1972)
Land of heart's desire (fl, bsn and pf) (1974)
Music for cello and viola (1952)
Romance (fl and bsn) (1974)
Shades of grey, 12 pieces (pf)
VOCAL
Russian river Mass, based on six Russian folksongs (soli, mix-ch and orch) (1976, revised 1980)
Story of the world, epic (ch and orch)
Sonnets to Orpheus (Bar, gtr, fl, pf and strs) (1959)
Auccassin et Nicollet (narr, gtr, fl and vlc) (1959)
Six songs (chil-ch and pf) (1978)
Four songs the night nurse sang (soli, mix-ch and pf) (1967)
Six haiku (S and pf) (1970)
Six love songs (A and pf) (1975)
Three bird songs (S and pf) (1965)
Nay, loose no flame (S and pf) (1952)
SACRED
Eli, Eli (mix-ch) (1971)
I heard a great voice (mix-ch) (1971)
Publications
New Age Music Manual. 1967.
Ref. composer

HAXTHAUSEN, Aurore M.G.Ch. von (nee Gyllenhaal) (pseuds. Clara Kuhlman, G******)**
Swedish writer and composer. b. Stockholm, 1836; d. Stockholm, February 7, 1888. In the 1870s she was well-known in the larger Swedish cities and published many pieces under her pseudonym G********.
Compositions
PIANO
Fest-Polonaise (4 hands) (Lundquist)
En avant, galop (Hansen)
En stilla stund, tonstyck (Hansen)
VOCAL
Songs
Ref. 95, 167, 297

HAY, Louisa. See KERR, Louisa

HAYAKAWA, Kazuko
Japanese composer. b. October 31, 1944. DISCOGRAPHY.
Composition
FLUTE
Insistence II
Ref. Japan Federation of Composers

HAYES, Mrs.
19th-century English composer.
Composition
PIANO
The Princesses of England, set of waltzes (ded Her Most Gracious Majesty) (London: T.C. Bates & Son)
Ref. H. Baron (London)

HAYS, Doris Ernestine
American pianist, lecturer, singer and composer. b. Memphis, TN, August 6, 1941. She studied under Harold Cadek at the University of Chattanooga where she obtained a B.M. in 1959. She attended the Munich Hochschule where she studied under Friedrich Wuehrer and received an artist's diploma in 1966. She studied under Paul Badura-Skoda at the University of Wisconsin (M.M.) in 1968 and composition under Richard Hervig at the University of Iowa in 1969. She was soloist with the Residence Orchestra of The Hague and appeared in many concerts in the Netherlands, Germany, Italy and Yugoslavia. She was on the faculty of the University of Wisconsin from 1967 to 1968 and Cornell College, Iowa in 1969. She was a special consultant in contemporary music from 1972 to 1980 and artist-in-residence to the Georgia Council for Arts, 1975 to 1976. She won a performance award in the Wisconsin State Composition contest in 1968 and first prize in the International Competition for Interpreters of Contemporary Music, Rotterdam, 1971. From 1975 she promoted women's music and organised an eleven-concert series in 1976 which won her a citation of merit from the National Federation of Music Clubs. In 1980 she co-ordinated the first conference on string quartets by women. She compiled and produced 'Expressions', a radio series of the ILWC. She won composer grants from the National Endowment for the Arts in 1977, 1979 and 1982 and several Meet the Composer Grants. From 1976 to 1983 she won a yearly ASCAP award. Her *Southern voices for orchestra* was the subject for an American television documentary. She is currently specializing in tape based musical multi-media combinations. DISCOGRAPHY.
Compositions
CHAMBER
Pieces from last year (16 cham insts, ocarina and pf) (1975)
Juncture dance (5-8 insts) (1974)
Sensevents for Lincoln Center (vln, vla, vlc, fl, ob and hn) (1977)
Sound piece I (cham ens)
Sound Piece II (cham ens)
Scheveningen beach (fl qnt) (1972)
Characters, harpsichord concerto (hpcd, str qrt and 3 winds) (1978)
Windpipes (5 fl)
Harmony (in die bleierne Zeit) (strs) (1982) (Tallapoosa Music)
Lullaby (fl, vln and pf)
Tunings (bsn, cl and fl, 1979; also vla, 1980; also d-b, 1978; also S, vln, cl and fl, 1979; also vln, pf, vlc and S, 1981; also str qrt, 1982) (Tetra Music)
Segment/junctures (vla, cl and pf) (1978)
Fanfare study (trp, trb and hn) (1980)
Homing (vln and pf) (1981)
For A.B. (cl and pf) (1977)
Tommy's trumpet (trp duo) (1979)
Breathless (b-fl) (1976)
For my brother's wedding (org) (1974)
Winded (picc) (1978)
PIANO
Chartres red (1972)
Sunday nights (1977)
Sunday mornings (1982) (Tetra Music, A.B.I. Inc.)
Etude base basses (1979)
Past present (1979) (Tallapoosa)
VOCAL
Southern Voices for Orchestra (S and orch) (1982) (Henmar Press; C.F. Peters)
Juncture dance II (mix-ch and inst ens)
On the way to ...... (mix-ch and inst ens)
Rest song (mix-ch) (1982) (Tetra; A. Broude)
Brian Swan's versions of American Indian ritual songs (Bar and pf) (1981)
Circling around, 4 songs (Bar, pf and fl) (1982) (Tallapoosa)
Delta Dad (vce and pf) (1979)
Did Sid and Busy Lizzie (chil-vces) (1979)
Duet (audience and pf) (1970)
For women, 5 songs (S) (1976)
Four against three (4-part spoken chorus) (1973)
Help compose (audience and pf)
Hush (vce, reco-reco and sand block) (1981)
In-de-pen-dance (chantor and nylon strs) (1979)
Lookout, 3-part canon for children (1974)
Lullago (Bar and scat singer) (1982) (Tallapoosa)
Make a melody, make a song (vce and pf) (1973)
Ol' Clo' (vce and pf)
Set of cheeky tongues (S and pf) (1976)
Song for bringing a child into the world; You, where have you fallen from; Just by sitting; Song of the sky: Brian walkin' talkin' blues (vce and opt d-b) (1973)
ELECTRONIC
Arabella rag and twenty-one other electronic music shorts (1971)
Awakening, poem (Paul Romsey) (tape) (1979)
City cedar, pink turtlehead (buchla and pf) (1979)
Certain: Change (bass fl, picc and tape) (1978)
Ex-, Rock-, In-, Re- (tape and chant) (1982) (Tallapoosa)
Exploitation (S and tape) (1981)
Fire pink (buchla and pf)
Glub (b-fl, picc and tape)
The gorilla and the girl (tape for dance) (1981)
Hands full (w-ch, tam-tams and tape) (1975)
The high and low of it and the long and short of it (tape for dance) (1974)
If (pf and 4 tapes) (1970)
PAMP (amp pf, tape and bird calls) (1973)
Passion flower, sunflowers, orange butterfly weed (buchla and pf) (1978)
Peace camps tapes (1983)
Pipsissewa, trailing arbutus (buchla and pf) (1973)
Saturday nights (pf and tape) (1980)
Sensevents for Lenox Square (5 cham insts and tape) (1976)
Star busic (ch, tape and bells) (1974)
Syn rock; Bleep M; Creepy Street; 13th Street beat; Giraffe round around; Merry grate round; Grim carnival; Carnibell; Somersault beat, short elec pieces (1971)

Translations and comments (pf, tape and improvising insts) (1974)
Uni-music, for a ballet suite (narr, fl, tape and str qrt)
Wildflowers (buchla and pf)
MULTIMEDIA
Celebration of NO (tape, or tape with vln, vlc, prep pf, film, slides and chanters) (1983) (Tallapoosa)
Flowing quilt; Creeks and bathtubs; Waterfalls (S, vln, tape, slides, film, water pool and pump) (1982) (Tallapoosa)
For four, graph notation (4 players)
Hands and lights (pf, photocells and flashlights) (1971)
M.O.M.'n P.O.P., Music only music, piano only piano (1 or 2 pf, film, slides, tape and mime) (1982) (Tallapoosa)
Only (pf, 2 tapes, slides and film) (1981)
Reading Richie's paintings (syn, fl and slides) (1979)
Rocking (fl, vln, vla and opt light patterns) (1983) (Tallapoosa)
Round around (plastic sculptures, lights and tape) (1974)
Spectrum, graph piece for several players (1974)
Water music (S, tape, water pump and slides) (1981)
Sensevents wildflower music (9 insts, sculpture, lights and tape)
Spectrum, graph notation (6 players)
FILM MUSIC
The Invasion of the Love Drones (1975)
Publications
Sound Symbol Structures: An Introduction to New Keyboard Notation.
Ref. composer, ILWC newsletter, 142, 206, 228, 474, 563, 625

HAYWARD, Mae Shepard

20th-century American composer. She composed three piano trios, other piano works and songs.
Ref. 142, 347

HAZELRIG, Sylvia Jean Earnhart

Canadian composer. b. 1934.
Composition
CHAMBER
Trio (S, A and T recs) (Toronto: BMI, 1964)
Ref. Blackwell catalog (Oxford)

HAZEN, Sara (Sally Hazen Evans)

American pianist and composer. b. Sarasota, FL, July 14, 1935. She studied under John Carter at Rollins College and obtained a B.A. from Duke University in 1957. She studied under Roland Leich and Leonardo Balada at Carnegie-Mellon University from 1972 to 1973 and the piano under Ferguson Webster.
Compositions
CHAMBER
Delta suite (brass ens) (1973)
City serenade (sax qrt) (1972)
PIANO
Fantasy (1972)
Festival (1964)
Omega alpha variations (1973)
SACRED
Alleluia, we live in Thee (1967)
Christ is born (1964)
Ref. 142

HEALE, Helene

English pianist and composer. b. London, February 14, 1855. At Queens College, London, she obtained the Maurice Scholarship. She studied music under John Hullah and in 1876 won a scholarship to the National Training School. She was also a pupil of Ernest Pauer, J.F. Barnett, E. Prout and Sir Arthur Sullivan. In 1877 she won a royal scholarship, which she held until 1881. She played before the Queen at Windsor Castle in 1880.
Compositions
CHAMBER
Polacco (3 vln and pf)
PIANO
Six characteristic pieces, duet
Piano Method
VOCAL
Epithalamion, cantata (Edmund Spenser) (T, ch and orch) (1893)
The watersprites, cantata (w-ch) (1885)
Jubilee, ode (ch and orch) (1887)
Adieu! Adieu! My native shore, barcarole (mix-ch) (Augener)
Mourn, oh rejoicing heart (prize, Madrigal Society, 1882)
A spring song (w-ch) (Augener)
Two part choruses (w-ch)
Cradle Song
SACRED
Eleven Christmas carols (qrt) (Ditson)
Six Christmas songs (mix-ch) (Novello)
ARRANGEMENTS
Numerous works by Rossini, Handel, Haydn, Gretry, Mozart, Moszkowski and others
Numerous arrangements for women's duets
Publications
Class Singing School. Four books.
Songs for Female Voices. Editor and arranger.
Songs for the Young.
Ref. 6, 276, 297

HEARN, Marianne or Mary Ann. See FARNINGHAM, Marianne

HEATON, Eloise Klotz

American organist, pianist, teacher, writer and composer. b. Baldwinsville, NY, June 1, 1909. She obtained her B.Mus. from the University of Syracuse in 1933 and M.A. in 1960. In 1950 she obtained a certificate in choir teaching at the Royal Conservatory of the University of Toronto. She taught the piano and voice privately and at schools in Syracuse, Peterboro and Fultan from 1933.
Compositions
CHAMBER
Invocation (vln) (1956)
VOCAL
Lady at the harpsichord, song (1945)
The springtime is my mother, song (1930)
SACRED
Christ in Gethsemane, cantata (1944)
Law of the harvest, cantata (1946)
Hear me when I call, O Lord, song (1965)
The Lord is merciful, song (1937)
My soul is athirst for God, song (1948)
One prayer, song (1946)
Psalm 91 (1962)
OPERETTA
The Queen's Garden (1938)
TEACHING PIECES
First piano duets (1961)
Play-time music for kindergarten (1953)
Publications
Around the Sun. 1948.
Contributions to Anthology of American Lyricists. 1954.
Ref. 506

HEBER, Judith

Norwegian pianist and composer. b. Gol Hallingdal, June 27, 1880; d. Christiania (later Oslo), October 7, 1919. She studied under Agathe Backer-Groendahl (q.v.) and Dagmar Walle-Hansen in Christiania and under Jedliczka and Scharwenka in Berlin. She made her debut as a pianist in Christiania in 1907.
Compositions
CHAMBER
Romance, op. 3 (vln and pf) (1915)
Sonata, op. 7 (pf)
VOCAL
Songs
Ref. 20, 23, 44, 113, 226

HECHLER, Ilse

20th-century German arranger and composer. She arranged music of Telemann, Gabrieli, Praetorius, Graun and other masters, particularly of the 17th and 18th-centuries, for the recorder and other instruments.
Compositions
VOCAL
Lieder und Spielstuecke fuer Sopran Blockfloete und andere Instrumente, 2 volumes (Spielbuch fuer den Anfaenger)
Ref. Moeck Verlag, 92

HECKSCHER, Celeste de Longpre (nee Massey)

American pianist and composer. b. Philadelphia, February 23, 1860; d. Philadelphia, February 18, 1928. She studied the piano under Zerdahal, composition under H.A. Land and orchestration under Vassily Leps. She was president of the Philadelphia Operatic Society.

Compositions
ORCHESTRA
Dances of the Pyrenees, suite (1911)
CHAMBER
Pastorale (vlc and pf)
To the forest, fantasy (vln and pf) (1902)
Romance (vlc)
PIANO
Impromptu
Passecaille
Valse bohème
Other pieces
VOCAL
Out of the deep, anthem
L'ange gardien (vce and pf)
The folded rose (vce and pf)
Gypsy lullaby (vce and pf)
Music of Hungary
The Norse maid's lament (vce and pf)
Pourquoi je t'aime (vce and pf)
Serenade
OPERA
The Flight of Time
Rose of Destiny, prelude and 3 acts (1918)
Biography
Hipsher E.E. *American Opera and Its Composers*. Philadelphia, 1927. Pp. 256-258.
Ref. 22, 89, 141, 292, 304, 415

HEDOUX, Yvonne

French pianist, teacher and composer. b. Paris, 1890. She studied at the Paris Conservatoire, where she obtained first prize for the piano in 1908 and first prize for harmony in 1913. She received a teacher's diploma from the Ville de Paris in 1908. Her teachers were M. Auguste Capuis, Henri Busser, Charles Widor, Roger Ducasse and Georges Caussade. She was president of the Union of Women Teachers and Composers, France. PHOTOGRAPH.
Compositions
ORCHESTRA
Le fantôme
Faune au miroir
La femme obéissante
Les guerriers noirs
La grotte enchantée
Moise sauvé des eaux
CHAMBER
Cascade Stabheim (vln, vlc and pf)
Angoisse (vln and pf)
Danse chaldéene (hp or pf)
Fantaisie (vln and pf)
Légende (vln and pf)
Pastorale (fl and pf)
Prélude et berceuse (vln and pf)
Rhapsodie (vlc and pf)
Seconde berceuse (vln and pf)
Sonate libre en 3 parties (vln and pf)
Prélude et fugue (org)
PIANO
A Bocognano
A Formentor ... unde chanson s'élève
A Grenade dans les bois de l'Alhambra
A Istanbul
A l'Alcazaba e Malaga
A Piana
A Stersa sur le lac majeur
Au jardin botanique de Puerto de la Cruz
Ballada
Barcarolle
Barque sous les pins
Castelest de Lisbonne
Chant populaire à Granna
Couronnement
Crepuscule
Dans à Selva
Dans le Bosphore et Ste. Sophie
Dans le fjord et la ville d'Oslo
Dans le jardin
Dans le parc de Bilbao
Dans le temple de Karnak
Dans les ruines de Pompeii
Dans un jardin des Anges à Nice
Danse à la taverne gitane
Danse à Seville
Danse creatoise à Candie
Danse espagnole à Santa Cruz de Teneriffe
Danse gitane à Grenade
Danse gitane à Madrid
Danse turque à Istanbul
Desert du Teide dans l'Ile de Teneriffe
En mer ... vers Corinthe
Fête a Kena
Forêt d'Alingsas
Forêt de Bussaco
Forêt de Rold
La fort Vizzavona et la cascade
Images d'Algerie
Images d'Espagne
Images de Sicile
In entend une fête au loin
Jour de paques à Santa Cruz de Teneriffe
Kristiansund en Norvege
Marche funebre
Matin
Le Matin à Venise
Meditation
Meditation sur le musée Fesch à Ajaccio
Messuguiere
Parc de Santa Cruz à Coiembra
Parc du Retiro à Madrid
Partinho da Arrabida
Pièce en mi
Places es palmiers à Ajaccio
Port de Bonifacio et L'eglise St. Dominique
Pour un rêve
Prèlude
Prelude in C-Major
Prelude in C-Minor
Prelude in E-Flat Major
Prelude in G-Major
Partinho da Arrabida
Rayons de soleil sur la mer
Ruines de Cologne
Scherzo
Soir sur le sognefjord
Soir sur la mer à Granville
Sous le palmiers
Sur l'Acropole d'Athens on entend les cloches de paques
Sur la mer de Marmara ... les mouettes volent
Sur le bateau vers Larwick
Sur le Nil
Tango d'amour
Theme and variations in A
Variations sur un thème dans la mode Dorien
VOCAL
Medora, cantata (3 vces and orch)
Hymne à la Rose (adaptation); Je vous aime Marie (vce and orch)
Sous l'parapluie
Dans le clairiere (w-ch)
Songs incl.:
Ah je l'attends
Aupres de ma blonde
SACRED
Ave Maria (vce and org)
Je vous salué, Marie (vce and org)
Pater Noster (vce and org)
FILM MUSIC
Chanson des fontaines
Ref. composer

HEDSTROEM, Ase

Swedish electronic instrumentalist, teacher and composer. b. Moss, Norway, April 17, 1950. She received a degree in instrumental pedagogics from the Norwegian State Academy of Music in 1975 and a diploma in composition in 1980. She studied composition and electronic music under Dr. Werner Kaegi and G.M. Koenig at the Institute of Sonology, Utrecht, Holland, 1975 to 1976. She was president of Ny Musik from 1976 to 1978 and is currently part-time music co-ordinator at the modern museum Hoevikodden Art Center, Oslo.
Compositions
ORCHESTRA
Anima (sym orch) (1983-1984)
Faser (sym orch) (1980)
CHAMBER
Close by (fl, cl or b-cl, vln and vlc) (1980)
Chain (pf) (1983)
VOCAL
Krets (T, fl, perc and tape) (1982-1983)
Krets, second version (m-S, T, perc and tape) (1983-1985)
Through (m-S, T, perc and tape) (1983)

ELECTRONIC
Distances (perc and tape) (1981)
Ref. composer, NMI

HEDWIG, Sister
Polish nun and composer. d. 1243. She composed a cycle of songs.
Ref. 465

HEGELER, Anna
German violist and composer. b. Oldenburg, 1896. She studied under Petri, Marteau and Flesch and composition under M. Schillings. She became a violist in the Oldenburg orchestra in 1923. She composed violin pieces and songs.
Ref. 70, 226

HEGGE, Mrs. M.H.
20th-century American composer. b. Stoughton, WI. She composed choral works.
Ref. 347

HEGNER, Anna
Swiss violinist, teacher and composer. b. Basle, March 1, 1881. She studied the violin under A. Stiele and H. Heermann. From 1904 to 1908 she taught the violin at the Hochschen Conservatory, Frankfurt. She then taught for three years in Basle before founding a string quartet in Freiburg-im-Breisgau in 1911. P. Hindemith was among her numerous pupils. She enjoyed an excellent reputation as a violinist. She composed numerous violin pieces, mainly for her pupils, and songs.
Ref. 17, 70

HEIBERG, Ella (nee Dyberg)
Swedish singer and composer. b. Uppsala, November 3, 1897. She studied at the Stockholm Conservatory and made her debut in 1913. She lived in Copenhagen. She appeared in cabaret, singing songs of her own composition.
Compositions
CHAMBER
Romance in G-Minor (vln) (1915)
PIANO
Koebenhavnervalsen (1939)
Wienervals (1928)
VOCAL
Anemoner i November (S and pf)
Aus Irrgarten der Liebe, 5 Gedichte von Otto Julius Bierbaum (Hansen, 1914)
Der hviler en duft (Josias Bille) (Hansen, 1915)
Eventyr till Ellen (H. Wildenvey) (Hansen)
For dig var det kun smaating (S and pf)
I, som er gamle af dage, children's songs
Jeg oensker ikke roser (S and pf)
Kildevalsen (S and pf)
Moedes og skilles (S and pf)
Naar kastanjen staar i Blomst (S and pf)
O jeg vil ha' en hjertenskaer (S and pf)
Sol og regn (S and pf)
Other songs
BALLET
Ballet suite (1950)
INCIDENTAL MUSIC
Music for plays and radio
Ref. 96, 331

HEIBERG, Johanne Louise
Danish actress, authoress, ballerina, teacher and composer. b. Copenhagen, November 22, 1812; d. Copenhagen, December 21, 1890. From 1820 to 1875 she was employed at the Royal Theatre, as a dancing pupil and then as a teacher. She was best known as an actress, being called the 'Greatest Stage Name of the North'. Although she received no training in composition her vaudevilles enjoyed success at the Royal Theatre in 1848 and 1849.
Compositions
VOCAL
Aprilsnarrene
De Danske i Paris
De uadskillelige
Emilies hjertebanken
Ja
Kjoege Huskors
Kong Salomon og Joergen Hattemager
Nej
Recensenten og dyret
Songs for Vaudeville (Hansen)
THEATRE
Abekatten
En Soendag paa Amager
Ref. 297, 331

HEIDENREICH, Henrietta
19th-century German composer.
Compositions
CHAMBER
Duo concertante, op. 2 (2 vla)
Duo brillante, op. 3 (2 vln)
Ref. 276, 347

HEIDRICH, Hermine Margaret
German poetess and composer. b. Dresden, July 2, 1884. She lived in Berlin. She composed chamber music, choral works, songs and opera.
Ref. 70, 226

HEILBRON, Valerie
American composer. b. Meridan, CT, April 25, 1948. She studied literature and critical writing at San Francisco State University and while completing her B.A. began to study music, receiving her M.A. (composition) in 1982. She received the Peter Frampton award for excellence in contemporary music in 1982.
Compositions
ORCHESTRA
Tricot (1982)
CHAMBER
Argument in E (brass qnt; also cham orch) (1981, 1983)
Duet for violin and piano, on a theme by T.S. Eliot (1972)
VOCAL
American suite: Thoughts from a young man's collection (Clifford Johnson) (S, m-S, 2 T and cham orch) (1983) (comm Trinity Arts)
In Memoriam Adam Hess (mix-ch a-cap) (1982)
Susie Asado (Gertrude Stein) (2 S a-cap) (1975)
THEATRE
Ladies' Voices (Gertrude Stein) in 4 acts (3 S and 1 A a-cap) (1973)
MISCELLANEOUS
Blue, green and white
Ref. composer

HEIMERL, Elizabeth
American organist, pianist and composer. b. Jefferson, WI, June 4, 1906. She studied the piano privately in Milwaukee and composition under Carl Eppert, graduating from Milwaukee-Downes College in 1928. She took courses in the organ and theory at the Wisconsin Conservatory in Milwaukee and continued her organ studies under Dr. Roger Nyquist of the University of California, Santa Barbara.
Compositions
ORCHESTRA
Renascence, tone poem (1938)
CHAMBER
Suite for string quartet (1937)
PIANO
Children's suite (1944)
Four meditations (1965)
Four short pieces (1965)
Sonatina in C-Minor (1934)
Theme and variations (1934)
Two preludes (1944)
VOCAL
Approx. 25 songs (Whitman, Reese, Hansman, Robert Farren and others) (1934-1972)
SACRED
Feed my sheep (Mary Baker Eddy) (1968)
Two Christmas songs (1935)
Ref. composer

HEIMLICH, Florentine
20th-century American teacher and composer. b. Calumet, MI. She composed operas and songs.
Ref. 347

HEINDRICH-MERTA, Marie. See HENDRICH-MERTA, Marie

HEINE, Eleanor
20th-century Danish composer.
Composition
PIANO
Skovcyclus, op. IV-XI (W. Hansen, 1920)
Ref. 331

HEINEMANN, Jenny
19th-century German singer and composer. She was a pupil of Rellstab at the Berlin Sing-Akademie from 1835 to 1836.
Compositions
VOCAL
Liederspenden incl.:
Und als ich aufstund frueh (Berlin; Buero fuer Literatur und Kunst)
Bin ein-und ausganga (Berlin: Buero fuer Literatur und Kunst)
Sechs Lieder und Gesaenge (vce and pf) (Berlin: Challier) (ded L. Rellstab)
Ref. 121

HEINKE, Ottilie
19th-century German composer. b. Breslau.
Compositions
CHAMBER
Two romances, op. 17 (vlc and pf)
PIANO
Kindermaskenball, op. 12
Nine pieces in dance form, op. 16
Ref. 276

HEINRICH, Adel Verna
American harpsichordist, organist, conductor, professor and composer. b. Cleveland, OH, July 20, 1926. She obtained a B.A. magna cum laude in 1951 from Flora Stone Mather College, an M.S.M. in 1954 from the Union Theological Seminary and an A.Mus.D. from the University of Wisconsin in 1976. She studied the organ under Hugh Porter, John Harvey, E. Power Biggs, Andre Marchal and Jean Langlais. She studied conducting under Robert Shaw and Robert Fountain and the harpsichord under Eugenia Earle. She was a church organist from 1954 to 1964, guest organist in New York under Margaret Hillis and gave many recitals. She received the Clemens award in music and won two scholarships. In 1969 she received an award of merit from the National Federation of Music Clubs. She received a Maximum Humanities travel grant in 1978 to 1979 to study and perform on historical organs in Europe; a Mellon grant in 1978 to 1979 to develop a course on Shakespeare and music and a humanities grant in 1979 to 1980 for further research on Shakespeare and music.
Compositions
ORCHESTRA
Concerto No 1, for organ and orchestra, op. 20 (1983)
CHAMBER
Sonata in F-Major, for flute and harpsichord or piano, op. 18
Fantasy-variations on paired subjects for flute and harpsichord, op. 27 (1982)
Humours of harlequin, op. 15 (fl) (1979)
Rondo-variations on B-A-C-H for unaccompanied flute, op. 8 (1978)
Concerto for solo harpsichord, op. 26 (1982)
Liturgical suite for unaccompanied soprano recorder, op. 30 (opt 2nd and 3d rec) (1983)
ORGAN
Festive sonata in E-Major, op. 25, A Host of Alleluias (1982)
Four chorale preludes on hymns of praise, op. 5 (1977)
Prelude and fugue in F-Minor, op. 1 (1954)
Three partitas on American hymn tunes, op. 7 (1977)
Variations and toccata on a theme of Mendelssohn, op. 10 (1978)
PIANO
Sonata in B-Major, op. 24, For those who mourn (1981)
Sonata in B-Minor, op. 22, The cosmos (1981)
Sonata in F-Sharp Minor, op. 23, For the joyous (1981)
VOCAL
Seasons in song, books I-II (w-ch) (Boston Music, 1963)
Spring sketches, books I-II (w-ch and pf or org) (Boston Music)
Birches, op. 9, song cycle (Robert Frost) (S, vln and vla; also S and pf) (1978)
Five nocturnes, op. 21 (Robert Frost) (S and pf) (1980)
Five Shakespearean sonnets, op. 14 (narr and vln) (1979)
New Hampshire poems of Robert Frost, op. 6, song cycle (S and pf) (1977)
SACRED
The Nazarene, op. 19, oratorio (3 T, mix-ch, timp and org) (1980)
Cantata on Ah, Dearest Master, op. 2 (mix-ch and org) (1954)
Alleluia, Alleluia, op. 4 (S, w-ch, mix-ch, pf or org, vln, modern dance choir) (1968)
A carol is born, op. 3, no. 1 (w-ch, fl, pf or org and drama) (Boston Music, 1962)
Choric-dance, Christ has been risen, op. 29. no. 2 (mix-ch, 2 trp, opt org or pf and modern dance ch) (1983)
Choric-dance, Hallelujah, praise our God, op. 28, no. 2 (mix-ch, 2 fl, hp and modern dance ch) (1983)
Choric-dance, Hosanna!, op. 2, no. 1 (mix-ch, 2 fl, hp, modern dance ch and org or pf) (1983)
Choric-dance, lo I tell you a mystery, op. 29, no. 1 (mix-ch, trp, org or pf and modern dance ch) (1983)
Christmas in England, op. 3, no. 3 (mix-ch, handbells and org) (1963)
Christmas in Germany, op. 3, no. 2 (mix-ch, vln and org) (1962)
Christmas in Mexico, op. 3, no. 4 (w-ch and perc) (1963)
Litany of faith, op. 13 (S, trp and org) (1979)
Sacred song cycle on Isaiah texts, op. 12 (S and org) (1979)
DANCE SCORES
Dramatic banquet: Shakespearean men, op. 17 (vln, 2 fl, picc, trp, snare dr, pf and modern dance)
Romeo and Juliet, duologue, op. 16 (2 fl, vln and 2 dancers)
Shakespearean women, op. 11 (2 vces, 2 fl, picc, vln, pf and modern dance)
MISCELLANEOUS
America the Free (1964)
Publications
Articles in *Perspectives*, *Choral Journal* and *Music*.
A Collation of the Expositions in *Die Kunst Der Fuge of J.S. Bach*. pp 28-140 of Bach, vol. XII, No. 2, April, 1981.
Bach's Die Kunst Der Fuge: A living Compendium of Fugal Procedures. 380 pp. University Press of America. 1982.
Ref. composer, 142, 347, 474

HEINRICHS, Agnes
German pianist, lecturer and composer. b. Cologne, July 26, 1903. She was a pupil of Paul Heinrich, Konstantin Wassenhaven, Josef Streiffeler, August Forstmann, Lazzaro Uzielli, Hans Heinrich, Willi Kahl, Heinrich Lemacher, F.W. Franke and Paul Mania from 1916 to 1925. She was a music teacher at the Engelbert-Haas Conservatory, Cologne from 1923 to 1924 and at the Cologne-Nippes Music Academy from 1924 to 1925, when she taught music privately.
Compositions
CHAMBER
Vortragsstuecke (vln and pf)
Characterstuecke (pf)
Violin pieces
SACRED
Herz-Jesu Messe (1924)
Das Leiden Christi (1925)
Marienmesse (1925)
Mysterienspiel
Sakramentsgesaenge
Sechs Marienlieder
Vincenzmesse (1926)
A cappella choruses
Choruses with organ
Ref. 70, 111, 347

HEINSIUS, Clara
German composer. b. Berlin, 1801; d. Berlin, March 11, 1823. She was the daughter of Theodor Heinsius, a historian of literature and a grammarian. She studied composition under Rungenhagen.
Composition
VOCAL
Lieder und Balladen (1819)
Ref. 129, 276

HEINY, Margaret Harris
American organist, concert pianist and composer. b. Amarillo, TX, October 16, 1911. She obtained her music teaching certificates from the St. Louis Institute of Music and Sherwood Music School, Chicago and taught the organ and the piano for 30 years. She was a church organist for many years and gave organ and piano concerts.

Compositions
ORGAN
Devotional (1975)
SACRED
My eyes are unto Thee, song (1975)
Ref. 457

HEITER, Amalie. See AMALIE, Marie Friederike Augusta, Princess

HEITMANN, Mathilde
19th-century German composer.
Compositions
VOCAL
Ein- und zweistimmige Melodien. Solfeggien nach Volksweisen, op. 2 (Cranz)
Ein- und zweistimmige Kinderlieder, op. 20 (Ebner)
Er isch, er isch (Ebner)
Gebet, op. 14 (Ebner)
Gesang der heiligen drei Koenige an der Wiege des neugeborenen Himmelsknaben, in Morgenlanden der Weisheit fern, op. 7 (Hamburg: Meyer)
Marienwuermchen: Marienwuermchen, setze dich auf meine Hand, op. 18 (Zumsteeg)
Schlummerliedchen: Schlaft mir all zusammen ein, op. 16 (Zumsteeg)
Vergueckt (Ebner)
Das verlassene Maegdelein, op. 17 (Zumsteeg)
Wenn es hatt, op. 11 (Ebner)
Wer isch? Mit dem Schnabele nippt's, op. 10 (Ebner)
Ref. 226, 276, 297, 433

HEKENU
Egyptian harpist, b. Old Kingdom, V Dynasty (2563 to 2423 B.C.). She was the first harpist in the record cf music history. In the frontispiece to this book she is shown as the accompanist to Iti (q.v.).
Ref. 207

HELASVUO, Elsa
20th-century Finnish composer.
Composition
FILM MUSIC
Poor Little Maria (1927)
Ref. 326

HELBLING, Elsa
Swiss pianist, recorder player, teacher and composer. d. 1967. She studied in Zurich and Stuttgart and taught the piano and the recorder in Uznach.
Compositions
RECORDER
Canti populari ticinesi, collection of folk songs from Ticino
Ein Ferientag
Heiterkeit, Gueldene, komm
Von Himmel hoch, 15 old and new Christmas songs
VOCAL
Kindersymphonie (chil-vces and orch)
Ref. 4

HELLER, Ottilie
19th-century German composer.
Compositions
CHAMBER
Piano pieces
VOCAL
Fischerbraut
Rittersabschied
Sehnsucht
Ref. 276

HELLER, Ruth
20th-century American pianist, arranger, authoress, music editor, singer and composer. b. Chicago. She received her B.M.Ed. in 1942 and M.M.Ed. in 1943 from Chicago Musical College, having studied voice under Mme. Nelli Gardini, the piano under Elizabeth S. Guerin, musicology under Hans Rosenwald, music education under Mary Strawn Vernon and composition under Max Wald. She was music editor and arranger for the Hall and McCleary Company, Chicago. She composed treble choir responses and arranged choral works.
Ref. 496

HELLER-REICHENBACH, Barbara
German pianist, lecturer and composer. b. Ludwigshafen am Rhein, November 6, 1936. She studied in Mannheim at the Staatliche Hochschule fuer Musik und Theater, where she studied composition under Hans Vogt and the piano under Helmut Vogel. After taking state examinations in 1957 she taught the piano at the same institute. In 1962 she resumed piano studies at the Staatliche Hochschule fuer Musik in Munich under Professor Eric Ten Berg and composition studies under Professor Harald Ganzmer. From 1963 she taught the piano in Darmstadt and in 1970 worked in the Hermann Heiss Archive. Her documentation of Hermann Heiss was published in 1975. Her work with piano music by women culminated in the founding of Frau und Musik Internationaler Arbeitskreis, 1978. PHOTOGRAPH.
Compositions
ORCHESTRA
Sinfonietta (str orch) (1959)
CHAMBER
String quartet (1958)
Frueher oder Spaeter (cl and pf)
Ten pieces for recorder and piano, for children (1963)
Three pieces for flute and piano (1960)
PIANO
Eight short pieces (1962)
Lettere Scarlattine
Suite (1956)
VOCAL
Die Lateinarbeit, ballad (3 part girls' ch and pf) (1961)
Five songs (vocal qrt and pf) (1959)
Four songs (S and pf) (1958)
Meine Musca Domestica (S and pf) (1961)
Ref. composer, Frau und Musik

HELLMERS, Ellen
20th-century Danish composer.
Compositions
VOCAL
Sange til Sophie Greums Jul i Kohmandsgaarden
Ref. 331

HELSINGIUS, Barbara
20th-century Finnish editor, singer, teacher and composer. In 1961 she graduated from Helsinki University as a physical education teacher and became interested in American folk music while on a scholarship to Stanford University, CA. On her return she worked as an announcer and editor for the Finnish Broadcasting Company and performed her own and American songs on radio. Her songs are in Finnish, Swedish, Norwegian and English. She is chairlady of the Helsinki chapter of a Scandinavian song society. DISCOGRAPHY. PHOTOGRAPH.
Compositions
VOCAL
Barbara's Blandade, Swedish collection (1982)
Det var en gaeng, Swedish collection (1977)
Fra Barbara med kjerlighet, Norwegian collection (1983)
Kahlaajatyttoe, Finnish collection (Aale Tynni, Aila Meriluoto) (1984)
Olipa kerran, Finnish collection (1978)
Rakkaudella, Finnish collection (1986)
Reflection, English version of Speiling (1984)
Speiling, Norwegian collection (1982)
Vill du visor min vaen, Swedish collection
Ref. composer

HELSTED, Bodil
Danish composer. b. March 23, 1880; d. 1950.
Compositions
CHAMBER
Fest-Praeludium (org or har) (1915)
Zwei Klavierstuecke, op. 54 (pf)
VOCAL
Four songs of Kaj Munk (vce and pf)
Ingers Dag. 6 pieces for children (vce and pf)
Det lakker mod Jul (vce and pf)
Majsol (vce and pf)
Symfoni til lille Lise (vce and pf)
Ref. 331

HELYER, Marjorie

English teacher and composer. b. Hampshire, 1919. She taught at Cranborne Chase Public School for some years, later becoming head of music at Farlington Girls' School.

Compositions

PIANO

Contrasts, duet
Two's company, duet
Two dance duets
Away day
Carol tunes
Down a country lane
Gay pictures
Holidays, 20 easy pieces
Nimble fingers
Over the hills
Plum stones
Polka dot
Ship ahoy

Ref. composer, Novello

HEMENWAY, Edith

20th-century American composer.

Composition

OPERA

The Twilight of Magic (Sarah Hemenway) (1983)

Ref. AMC newsletter

HEMON, Sedje

20th-century Dutch violinist, professor and composer. b. Rotterdam. She studied the violin at the Amsterdam Conservatory under Professor Jewssey Wulf and contemporary music under F. Travis and Iannis Xenakis. She was a professor of integration, painting, music and dance and at one time the only professor of the panpipes in the world. Her compositions were played in several European countries and she appeared on radio and television. She contributed to musical magazines. PHOTOGRAPH.

Compositions

ORCHESTRA

Orchestre symphonique
Violin concerto
Concerto (panpipes and cham orch)
Caprice
Harmony
Mouvement d'un adagio
Never again an Auschwitz
Suite in four movements

CHAMBER

Concerto for oboe and eight wind instruments
Embrasse en vain (org)
Fantaisie (vln)
Pieces (pf)

PANPIPES

L'agreable (5 panpipes)
Jesus, joy of men's desiring (5 panpipes)
Light and dance music
Rumanian music

ELECTRONIC

Lignes ondulatoires (vib and cham orch)

Ref. composer, 206, 457

HEMRE

Ancient Egyptian leader of the court music. ca. 2723 B.C. She was the earliest named musician, male or female, in the record of music history. This was the time of the first appearance of Cheironomy, the regulation of music performance by the movement of the hands.

Ref. 207

HENDERSON, Elizabeth

20th-century American composer. She composed choral works and songs.

Ref. 40, 347

HENDERSON, Moya

New Zealand composer. b. 1941.

Compositions

CHAMBER

Trio for flute, clarinet and piano (1973)

PIANO

Nolle Prosequi (1972)
Prelude I (1969)
Prelude II (1972)

VOCAL

Flame tree in a quarry (Judith Wright) (S) (1970)
Green singer (John Shaw Nielson) (S) (1970)
Nembutal rock (Craig Powell) (1973) (T and pf)
Stubble (S and Bar) (1975-1976)
Tree and river bank (C. Powell) (S) (1970)

THEATRE

And my practice ...
Clearing the air (d-b and 5 ww) (1974)
Conversations for two clarinets
Double take (vce)
Marxisms (vlc) (1975)
Mummy Church (B-Bar, T and dancers) (1975)
Once upon a time in China (John Maguire) (1973)
Vivet academia
Split second: Ear theatre, radio music drama

Ref. 189, 440, 442, 444, 446

HENDERSON, Rosamon (Mrs. P. Stanley)

American composer. b. Shellman, GA, July 13, 1894. She studied at Andrew and Wesleyan Colleges and won awards for choral works in contests of the National League of American Pen Women and the Alabama Writers' Conclave.

Compositions

SACRED

The Lord's day
Sing praises to God
Think on these things
Wave on old glory
Other choral works

Ref. 142

HENDERSON, Ruth Watson

Canadian organist, concert pianist, choirmistress, teacher and composer. b. Toronto, November 23, 1932. She studied the piano under Viggo Kihl at the Toronto Conservatory from 1937 to 1945, graduated as a gold medallist and became an L.R.C.T. and A.R.C.T. She studied the piano further under Alberto Guerrero, Hans Neumann and Karl Schnable and composition under Oskar Morawetz, Richard Johnston and Samuel Dolin, at Mannes College, New York. As a concert pianist, she toured Canada, England and the USSR, appeared on Canadian television and performed with the Winnipeg and other orchestras. She was commissioned to write choral compositions for the Toronto Children's Chorus, The Alliance for Canadian New Music Projects, the Guelph Spring Festival and the Ontario Youth Choir. She was organist and choirmistress in Winnipeg from 1957 to 1961 and then in Kitchener, Ontario, 1962 to 1968. DISCOGRAPHY. PHOTOGRAPH.

Compositions

CHAMBER

Sonata (ob and pf) (1976)
Sonata (ob) (1976)

PIANO

Children's suite (1980)
Suite (1978)

VOCAL

Clear sky and thunder, children's cantata (S, A, fl and pf) (1984)
Five tongue twisters (mix-ch and pf) (1977)
Mary Ann (mix-ch and pf) (1975) (G.V. Thompson)
Les raftsmen (mix-ch and pf) (1975) (G.V. Thompson)
A sequence of dreams, choral suite (mix-ch and pf) (1983)
Through the eyes of children, English and French songs (chil-ch and pf) (1981) (G.V. Thompson)
The ballad of St. George (m-S, B, ch, hp, org and trps) (1982)
Musical animal tales, 9 songs (S, A and pf) (1979) (G.V. Thompson)
Arrangements of folk songs

SACRED

God be merciful unto us (mix-ch) (1968)
I will extol thee (ch) (1965)
Missa brevis (mix-ch a-cap) (1976) (G.V. Thompson)
O King of Kings (mix-ch and org) (1965)
Pater Noster (mix-ch) (1974) (G.V. Thompson)
Three motets (1964-1968)

Ref. composer, Canada Choral Music Festival Singers, 485

HENDRICH-MERTA (Heindrich-Merta), Marie

Austrian musician and composer. b. Salzburg, October 7, 1842.

Compositions

CHAMBER

Trio (vln, vlc and pf)
Piano pieces

VOCAL
Konieg Lenz, Fruehlingshymnus, op. 41 (m-ch)
Endlich doch (vce and pf)
Gruss (vce and pf)
Gute Nacht (vce and pf)
Ref. 226, 260, 276, 297, 347

HENN, Angelica

19th-century German composer. b. Pforzheim. She was a pupil of Kalliwoda.

Compositions

VOCAL
Cantata
Lieder
SACRED
Missa solemnis
OPERA
Die Rose von Libanon
Ref. 226, 276

HENNING, Roslyn Clara. See BROGUE, Roslyn Clara

HENSEL, Fanny Caecilia (nee Mendelssohn)

German pianist and composer. b. Hamburg, November 14, 1805; d. Berlin, May 14, 1847. She was the sister of Felix Mendelssohn and the eldest of four children, the next being Felix who was three years younger. She was a piano pupil of L. Bergen in Berlin. Her family's attitude to women was expressed in the words of her grandfather: *Moderate learning becomes a lady, but not scholarship. A girl who has read her eyes red deserves to be laughed at.* Her father felt that being a housewife and mother was the only occupation befitting a woman and was extremely averse to seeing his daughter perform in public. Stifled by these attitudes limiting her development as a musician and composer, she lived through and for Felix, who often remarked that she was a better pianist than he, and always discussed his compositional ideas with her before writing them down. As the family was strongly opposed to Fanny publishing her early works, they were published under Felix's name. When Felix went to play for Queen Victoria, he asked her to sing. The queen sang *Italien* believing it to be one of his songs; in embarrassment, he told her it had been written by his sister Fanny. It is impossible to say how many other songs published under his name were in fact composed by her. Although her husband, the Prussian court artist Wilhelm Hensel, whom she married in 1829, encouraged her to publish her works, she was unwilling to do so without her family's consent, which was never forthcoming. She revealed in correspondence that she continued to compose, but most of her over 400 works remained unknown and unpublished. DISCOGRAPHY. PHOTOGRAPH.

Compositions

ORCHESTRA
Ouverture in C (1830)
CHAMBER
Piano quartet in A-Flat Major (1922-1924)
String quartet in A-Flat (1823)
String quartet in E-Flat (1834)
Trio in D-Minor, op. 11 (pf, vln and vlc) (Leipzig: Boosey & Hawkes, 1850)
Adagio (vln and pf) (1823)
Capriccio (vlc and pf) (1829)
Praeludium in F-major (org) (1829) (for her wedding)
PIANO
Drei stuecke (4 hands)
Achtzehn Stuecke (1836-1839)
Das Jahr, zwoelf Charakterstuecke (1841)
Dreizehn Stuecke (1824-1827)
Elf Stuecke (1823)
Klavierbuch (Praeludium, Fuge, Allegro, Largo and Toccata)
Pastorella (Berlin: Bote & Bock, 1852)
Praeludium in E-Major (1824)
Prelude in E-Minor (1827)
Prelude in F-Major
Sechs melodien, op. 4 (Berlin: A.M. Schlesinger, 1847)
Sechs melodien, op. 5 (A.M. Schlesinger, 1847)
Sonata in C-Minor (1823-1824)
Sonata in G-Major (1843)
Sonata movement in E-Major (1824)
Siebzehn Stuecke (1846)
Vier Lieder ohne Worte, op. 2 (Bote & Bock, 1846)
Vier Lieder ohne Worte, op. 6 (Bote & Bock, 1847)
Vier Lieder ohne Worte, op. 8 (Leipzig: Boosey & Hawkes, 1850)
Zwei Bagatellen fuer die Schueler des Schindelmeisserchen Musik Instituts (1848)
Zwoelf Stuecke (1823-1824)
VOCAL
Hiob, cantata (A, mix-ch and orch) (1831)
Meine Seele ist so stille, cantata (A, mix-ch and orch) (1831)
Hero und Leander (S and orch) (1832)
Duett und Chor (ch a-cap) (1840-1941)
Einleitung lebenden Bildern (speaker, mix-ch and pf) (1841)
Gartenlieder, op. 3: Hoerst du nicht die Baeume rauschen; Schoene Fremde; Im Herbste; Morgengruss; Abendlich schon rauscht der Wald; Im Wald (mix-lch) (Bote & Bock, 1847)
Neunzehn Choere (ch a-cap) (1846)
Three four-part songs (ch a-cap) (1824-1928)
Vier Gesaenge (ch a-cap) (1836-1939)
Achtundzwanzig Lieder (1823-1824)
An die Ruh (Hoelty)
Du bist die Ruh
Ein Duett und 1 Terzett (1835)
Ein Lied (1838)
Ein Lied, published as no. 4 of Felix Mendelssohn's op. 34
Ein Lied in Album (Berlin: A.M. Schlesinger, 1837)
Es rauschen die Baeume (vocal qrt a-cap) (1829)
Fuendundvierzig Lieder and drei Duette (1824-1827)
Fuenf Lieder, op. 10: Abendbild; Bergeslust; Nach Sueden; Vorwurf; Im Fuenfzehn Lieder (1846)
Fuenfzehn Lieder und zwei Duette (1833-1834)
Herbst (vce and pf) (Leipzig, Boosey & Hawkes, 1850)
Fuenfzehn Lieder (1823)
Das Heimweh; Italien; Die Nonne. Published as nos. 2, 3 and 12 of Felix Mendelssohn's op. 8 (vce and pf)
Das letzte Lied: O Lust, vom Berg zu schauen (Eichendorff) (vce and pf) (1847)
Nachtwanderer
O, dass ich tausend Zungen haette, aria (S and pf) (1831)
Die Schiffende, in Album Original Compositionen (1845)
Schloss Liebeneck, in Rhein-Sagen und Lieder (vce and pf) (Koeln und Bonn: J.M. Dunst, 1839)
Sechs Lieder (1829)
Sechs Lieder op. 1: Gondellied; Mayenlied; Morgenstaendchen; Schwanenlied; Wanderlied; Warum sind denn die Rosen so blass (vce and pf) (Berlin: Bote & Bock, 1846)
Sechs Lieder op. 7 incl.: Dein ist mein Herz; Fruehling; Bitte (vce and pf) (Bote & Bock, 1848)
Sechs Lieder op. 9: Die Ersehnte; Ferne; Die fruehen Graeber; Der Maiabend; Die Mainacht; Der Rosenkranz (vce and pf) (Leipzig, Boosey & Hawkes, 1850)
Sechsunddreissig Lieder, Duette und Terzette (1820-1829)
Sehnsucht; Verlust; Suleika und Hatem, published as nos. 7, 10 and 12 of Felix Mendelssohn's op. 9
Sechzehn Lieder und Neun Duette (1836-1839)
Die Sennin (Lenau) (vce and pf)
Die Spinnerin (Fink)
Vier Lieder (J.W. von Goethe) (1828, 1841)
Zwei Lieder (1824)
Zehn Lieder, zwei Duette und ein Terzett (1840-1841)
Zwei Lieder und ein Duett (1836)
SACRED
Oratorium: Nach Bildern der Bibel (ch and orch) (1831)
Ave Maria (Sir Walter Scott)

Bibliography

Elvers, Rudolf. *Fanny Hensel, geboren Mendelssohn-Bartholdy: Dokumente ihres Lebens*. Berlin, 1972.
Hensel, S. *Die Familie Mendelssohn, 1729-1847*. Berlin, 1879.
Kupferberg, Herbert. *The Mendelssohns: Three Generations of Genius*. Scribner's.
Quin, C.L. *The Musical Life of Fanny Mendelssohn Hensel*. Ph.D. dissertation, University of Kentucky.
Schnapp, F.F. *Mendelssohn-Bartholdy's Briefe an seine Schwester*. 1959.
Werner, Jack. *Felix and Fanny Mendelssohn*. Music and Letters, 1947.

Ref. 2, 9, 15, 17, 20, 22, 41, 44, 70, 74, 100, 102, 103, 105, 106, 110, 113, 121, 132, 177, 211, 226, 276, 282, 297, 347, 361, 400, 476, 563, 570, 622, 653

HENSLOWE, Mrs. See BARTHELEMON, Cecilia Maria

HENUTTAUI

Egyptian songstress of Amon, Late Kingdom XXI dynasty (1085 to 950 B.C.). Her tomb, which was formerly the tomb of Minmosi, XVIII Dynasty, was found at Deir-el-Bahri, in the Hatshepsut temple and is now in New York.
Ref 207, 428

HERBERT, Dorothy

20th-century American composer. She composed opera, choral works and songs.
Ref. 40, 347

HERBERT, Muriel

20th-century American composer.
Composition
OPERA
Candy Floss (composer)
Ref. 141

HERBISON, Jeraldine Sanders (Butler)

Black American violinist, conductor, teacher and composer. b. Richmond, VA, 1941. She graduated with distinction from Virginia State College and did postgraduate work at the Virginia State College and the University of Michigan. She studied composition under Undine Moore (q.v.) George Wilson and Tom Clark. She played the violin in orchestras, taught and conducted orchestras in schools.
Compositions
ORCHESTRA
Promenade (cham orch) (1982)
Suite No. 1 in C (str orch) (1960, rev 1976)
Suite No. 2 in F (str orch)
Suite No. 3 (vln, vla and pf; also fl, cl, ob and str orch) (1972)
Theme and variations (str orch) (1976)
CHAMBER
I heard the trailing garments of the night (fl, vln, vlc and pf) (1976)
Introspection (fl, vln, vlc and pf) (1973)
Little suite in C-Major, op. 1: Gavotte; Sarabande; Gigue (str qrt)
Melancholy on the advent of departure (qrt) (1980)
String quartet, op. 14
Miniature trio, op. 3 (ob, vln and pf) (1961)
Nocturne (ob, vln and pf) (1961)
Intermezzo (vlc and pf) (1976)
Fantasy in three moods (vlc and pf) (1976)
Six duos (vln and vlc) (1976)
Sonata (vlc and pf; also vlc) (1982)
Fugue (vlc)
VOCAL
Christmas Bells (ch)
Destiny (ch)
Little brown baby (S, A, T, 2 vln and pf) (1967)
Love me not (vce and pf)
Nine art songs (vce and pf) (1980)
The rainy day (vce and pf)
Spring, sweet spring, 4 pieces (2 S, A and pf) (1962)
Ref. Nat. Black Music Colloquium, Working papers on Women in Music, 523

HERICARD, Jeanne

20th-century French composer.
Compositions
VOCAL
Domisoldaire, études pour chant seriel (Heugel, 1964)
Zoo et Do, 19 études pour chant seriel (Heugel, 1965)
Ref. 94, 189

HERITTE-VIARDOT, Louise Pauline Marie

French contralto, teacher and composer. b. Paris, December 14, 1841; d. Heidelberg, January 17, 1918. She was the daughter of the famous singer Pauline Viardot-Garcia and the niece of Malibran and Manuel Garcia. She studied with her mother and then taught singing at the Conservatory of St. Petersburg and the Hochschen Conservatory in Frankfurt. She married Heritte, the French consul-general of the Cape of Good Hope, in 1862. After a few years in the Cape and in Paris, they settled in Berlin in 1886 where she continued to teach singing. DISCOGRAPHY.
Compositions
CHAMBER
Quartet, Im Sommer, op. 9 (pf, vln, vla and vlc) (Boosey & Hawkes, 1883)
Spanisches Quartet, op. 11 (pf, vln, vla and vlc) (Peters, 1883)
Four string quartets
Third piano quartet
Two piano trios
Sonata, op. 40 (vlc and pf) (Hofmeister, 1909)
PIANO
Sonata (2 pf)
In Gondola (Novello)
Serenade (Heugel)
VOCAL
Die Bajadere, cantata (ch and orch)
Wonne des Himmels, cantata (soloists, ch and orch) (Kahnt)
Das Bacchusfest, cantata (1880)
Drei lieder fuer eine Singstimme mit Pianoforte: Arme kleine Liebe; Tag und Nacht; Unter'm Machendelbaum (Kahnt)
Listen a minute (vce and pf) (Boosey)
Lullaby (vce and pf) (Leonard)
Praises (vce, pf, vln or cl) (Leonard)
Sechs Lieder fuer eine Singstimme
Shower of blossoms (vce and pf) (Ditson)
Spinning song (vce and pf) (Ditson)
Vers le sud (vce and pf) (Heugel)
OPERETTA
Lindoro, comic opera in 1 act (1879)
Publications
Memoires de Louise Heritte-Viardot. Paris, 1923.
Memories and Adventures. London, 1913.
Une famille de grands musiciens. 1922.
Ref. 2, 8, 20, 22, 26, 41, 107, 132, 135, 193, 225, 276, 282, 297, 307, 347, 361, 394, 563, 622

HERMANN, Miina (Miyna Khyarma)

Estonian organist, choral conductor, singer, teacher and composer. b. Ratshof, near Tartu, January 28, 1864; d. 1941. She attended the St. Petersburg Conservatory from 1883 to 1890 and then gave organ concerts in the Baltic countries and in Germany. In 1894 she founded a choir in Tartu with which she toured. She was active in furthering singing in Estonia, teaching there for most of her life, except for a period from 1904 to 1914, when she taught in Kronstadt. DISCOGRAPHY.
Compositions
VOCAL
Kalew and Linda, cantata (ch)
Childhood song (ch)
Formerly and now (m-ch)
I must not keep silent (mix-ch)
Song of the men (m-ch)
Tulyak (mix-ch)
How beautiful was my flower (T)
When you come bring some flowers (m-S)
Numerous choral songs in the German romantic style
OPERA
Murneide Tytar (Reval, 1904)
ARRANGEMENTS
Choral songs
Ref. 17, 431

HERMANSEN, Gudrun

20th-century Danish composer.
Compositions
PIANO
Drei kleine Klavierstuecke, op. 3
Mark og Eng
Menuetto antico
Zwei Etuden: E-Dur, A-Moll, op. 2
VOCAL
Frejdigt mod (vce and pf)
Ref. 331

HERNANDEZ-GONZALO, Gisela

Cuban pianist, choral conductor, lecturer and composer. b. Cardenas, September 15, 1910; d. August 23, 1971. She began her music studies in Cardenas at the Escuela Santa Cecilia and then at the Conservatorio de Musica y Declamacion of Havana, from where she graduated in the piano and solfege, 1928. She studied under Maria Munoz de Quevedo at the Conservatorio Bach from 1930 to 1935 and resumed her studies of harmony, aesthetics and history of music at the Conservatorio Municipal de Musica of Havana under Jose Ardevol, 1940 to 1944. At the Peabody Institute in the United States she studied composition under Gustabe Strube and choir conducting under Theodore Chandler, 1940 to 1944. She was active as a choral conductor in Cuba, a founding member of the Grupo de Renovacion Musical in 1942 she also taught at the Conservatorio Hubert de Blanck in Havana, 1947 to 1962. She and Olga de Blanck (q.v.) founded Ediciones de Blanck publishers, in 1949. She researched musicological history and after the revolution held a number of official posts with the National Cultural Council and the Ministry of Education. From 1969 she was musical advisor for the Cuban radio. DISCOGRAPHY.

Compositions
ORCHESTRA
Cubanas (1963)
Triptico cubano (1954)
CHAMBER
Pequeña suite (vln, vlc and pf; also pf) (1929, 1941)
Sonatina (vln and pf) (1945)
PIANO
Dos preludios (1939)
Four cubanas (1957)
La habana
Preludio y giga (1943)
Primera suite
Seis preludios (1969)
Sonata en Do (1942)
Tema y variaciones (1930)
Variaciones faciles
Zapateo cubano (1954) (Havana: de Blanck)
VOCAL
Dialogo de Octubre (2 soloists, ch and orch) (Mitra Aguirre) (1969)
Romance antiguo (mix-ch of 7 vces) (Rodrigues Santos) (1942)
Dos canciones (chs of 3 and 6 vces) (J. Ramon Jimenez) (1942)
Como alla (mix-ch of 5 vces) (Jose Marti) (1969)
Soneto coral (mix-ch of 5 vces) (1943)
Triptico cubano (mix-ch of 4 and 6 vces) (Nicolas Guillen) (1967)
Suite coral (mix-ch a-cap) (National Prize, 1944) (Montevideo: Ed. Instituto Interamericano de Musicologia)
Cancion (E. Ballages) (mix-ch a-cap) (1942)
La muchacha de Quang-Nam (mix-ch a-cap) (1969)
Dos villancicos tradicionais (mix-ch a-cap) (1944)
Dos villancicos cubanos (2 and 3 vces) (1948)
Dos cantes al mar (M. Aguirre) (1943)
Five Lieder (F. Garcia-Marruz, A. Gaztelu, Lizama Lima, C. Solis, C. Vitier) (1964)
Forty-five songs for children (1966-1969)
La muñeca negra (1969)
Nine songs (M. Aguirre) (1943-1958)
Romancillo (G. Lorca)
Seis canciones infantiles (1941-1944)
Solo por el rocio (G. Lorca) (1944)
Songs (vce and pf)
SACRED
Salmo davidico (ch and str orch) (1954)
Alleluya (3 mix-vces; also vce and pf) (1948)
Palmas reales
Son de Navidad (1948)
INCIDENTAL MUSIC
El Alcalde de Zalamea
Hamlet
Juana de Lorena
Pedro de Urdemales
Publications
Editions and analyses of Cuban classics. With Olga de Blanck. Havana: de Blanck.
Leonardo da Vinci, musico. Revista Grafos, 1940.
La musica de nuestro tiempo. Boletim del Grupo de Renovacion Musical, 1943.
Volor del disco fonografico en la educacion musical. Boletim bimestral de critica, 1939.
Vida extravagante de Piero de Cosimo. Revista Grafos, 1940.
Bibliography
Carpentier, Alejo. *La musica en Cuba.* Mexico, 1946.
Fuchs, A. *Gisela H. Gonzalo.* 1957.
Ref. 4, 5, 8, 9, 13, 17, 54, 94, 100, 109, 189, 361, 563

HERRERA Y OGAZON, Alba

20th-century Mexican concert performer, music critic, professor and composer. She was a professor at the Mexican National School of Music and Drama and contributed to several journals.
Ref. 268

HERRESHOFF, Constance

19th-century American composer.
Compositions
VOCAL
The beloved stranger, song cycle
Other songs
Ref. 260, 292, 347

HERSCHER-CLEMENT, Jeanne

French composer. b. Vincennes, 1878; d. Givry, 1941. She studied under Koechlin.
Compositions
VOCAL
Melodies (Hoggar)
SACRED
Requiem
Psalm
BALLET
La Farce du Pont-Neuf
MISCELLANEOUS
Suite on Indian themes
Ref. 13

HERTEL, Sister Romana

American violinist, professor and composer. b. Stockbridge, WI, December 3, 1915. She obtained a B.Mus. and M.Mus. from the Cosmopolitan School of Music, Chicago and a Ph.D. from the Catholic University of America, Washington, DC. She did postgraduate study at the University of Michigan and the Eastman School of Music, taught at parish schools in Milwaukee, WI, and at St. John High School, Lima, OH. In 1954 she became professor of music and chairlady of the music department of Cardinal Stritch College, Milwaukee. She performed with the Milwaukee Catholic Symphony Orchestra and directed the Stritch Chamber Ensemble. In 1958 she won the string category of the Wisconsin Composition Contest.
Composition
ORCHESTRA
Tone poem
Publications
The Keyboard Concertos of Johann Wilhelm Hertel, 1727-1789. 1964.
Ref. 77

HERTZ, Hedwig

19th-century German composer. She composed piano pieces, choral works and songs.
Ref. 276, 347

HERZ, Dr. Albert. See HERZ, Maria

HERZ, Maria (pseud. Dr. Albert Herz)

German pianist and composer. b. Cologne, August 19, 1878. She married Dr. Albert Herz and composed under his name. She studied the piano under Max Pauer in Cologne from 1893 to 1910, H.H. Wetzler and Philipp Jarnach in 1925 and instrumentation and theory under August von Othegraven in Cologne, 1921 to 1925. From 1934 she lived in Trier.
Compositions
ORCHESTRA
Piano concerto (1927-1928)
CHAMBER
String quartet (1926-1927)
Four small pieces for string quartet (1927-1928)
VOCAL
Acht Lieder (1921)
Drei Lieder (Christian Morgenstern) (1921)
Drei Lieder (Stefan Georg) (1922)
Lied (Goethe) (1926)
So einer war er (Tonger)
Three songs (Hoelderlin)
Two songs (1925)
Two songs (Friedrich Nietzsche) (1926)
ARRANGEMENTS
Ciaccona (str qrt) (Bach)
Ref. 70, 105, 111, 226, 297

HERZOGENBERG, Elizabeth von (nee von Stockhausen)

German pianist and composer. b. Paris, April 13, 1847; d. San Remo, Italy, January 7, 1892. She married the composer Heinrich von Herzogenberg.
Compositions
PIANO
Eight pieces (Rieter-Biedermann)
VOCAL
Vierundzwanzig Volkskinderlieder
Ref. 85, 276, 286, 347

HESSE, Marjorie Anne, M.B.E.

Australian concert pianist, lecturer and composer. b. Brisbane, November 13, 1911. After obtaining her B.A. from the University of Sydney, she attended the conservatory in the same city and was awarded a doctorate and licentiate of the Royal Academy of Music. She lectured at the Sydney Conservatorium and the University of Sydney, toured Australia and other countries as a pianist and appeared as a soloist with orchestras in Australia and New Zealand. She was an adjudicator and examiner for the Australian Music Examinations Board. Among other honors, she was made a Member of the British Empire. DISCOGRAPHY.

Compositions

CHAMBER

An Irish croon (vln and pf)

PIANO

All suddenly the wind comes soft
At play
The ballerina
Come play with me
Country jig
Curious piano
Eight solos
Growing up
Jollity
La pastourelle
The piper
Playtime
Romance (1937)
Rustic dance
Skipping suite
Suites for children
Ten busy fingers
Twilight
Valse gracieuse
When we are very young

VOCAL

Seven songs for children (Diana Morgan) (vce and pf)
Two Australian songs: In early green summer; O singer in brown (composer)

TEACHING PIECES

Sightreading excursion

Ref. 206, 440, 444, 446, 457, 563

HETRICK, Patricia Anne

American accordionist, pianist, singer and composer. b. Crawfordsville, IN, May 7, 1937. She obtained her B.A. from Lincoln Christian College, IL, and took private lessons in voice, the piano and the accordion.

Compositions

SACRED

All things work together
He watches over me
I love to worship

Ref. 77

HEUBERGER, Jenny

German singer, teacher and composer. b. Kassel, July 13, 1831.

Compositions

VOCAL

Morgenstaendchen
Other songs

Ref. 276, 347

HEUSSNER, Amelie. See NIKISCH, Amelie

HEWITT, Estelle

19th-century American composer.

Composition

PIANO

The snow-drop, waltz (Baltimore: F.D. Benteen, 1847)

Ref. 228

HEWITT-JONES, Anita

20th-century composer.

Composition

ORCHESTRA

Whirligig: Waltz, windmills and ragtime (str orch) (1983)

Ref. Otto Harrassowitz (Wiesbaden)

HEYMAN, Katherine Ruth Willoughby

American pianist, writer and composer. b. Sacramento, CA, 1877; d. Sharon, CT, September 28, 1944. She toured the United States and Europe, playing works by Scriabin. In 1928 she founded the Groupe estival pour la musique moderne in Paris.

Compositions

CHAMBER

Piano pieces

MISCELLANEOUS

Lament for Adonis

Publications

Works on Scriabin.

Ref. 70, 85, 347

HEYNSSEN, Adda

German pianist, singer and composer. b. Hamburg, August 7, 1893.

Compositions

PIANO

Dance suite
Other pieces

Ref. 70, 226

HIBLER, Nellie

American composer. b. Utica, NY, September 10, 1858. She obtained the degree of Associate in Music from the University College of Wales. She composed for the piano and voice.

Ref. 433

HICKS, Marjorie Kisbey

Canadian organist, pianist, teacher and composer. b. London, 1905. She became an A.R.C.T. and Associate of the Ontario Conservatory of Music, where she was awarded a gold medal for the piano. She was on the music faculty of Ontario Ladies' College, Whitby, and then worked privately, teaching and coaching the piano and voice in Prince Albert, Saskatchewan. She won a first prize for piano composition from the Ontario Registered Music Teachers' Association and a first prize for choral composition from the Saskatchewan Jubilee and Centennial Corporation. She was one of five Canadian composers to be included in the International Library of Piano Music, published by the University Society in New York. Many of her piano compositions were teaching pieces. She married the organist and poet John Victor Hicks. Her compositions were published by; BMI, Berandol, Boosey and Hawkes, Frederick Harris, Gordon Thompson, Leslie Music, Saska-Music, Waterloo Music and The University Society publishing companies. DISCOGRAPHY. PHOTOGRAPH.

Compositions

PIANO

Numerous pieces incl.:
Reflection of two pianos
Arguments
Clouds
Cradle song
Hide and seek
Leap-frog
Little black lullaby
March
Pyrotechnics
Sorrow for a sick right hand
Sprains No. 1 and No. 2
Tag, canon
Two indispositions
Two preludes

VOCAL

Icelandic lullaby (ch and pf)
Songs:
The dark wood
Dawn
Ghost hornpipes
How do I love thee?
A piper
Three black crows
Many art song settings of folk songs of different countries

SACRED

The Lord is my Shepherd (ch)
The Mass of St. Alban the Martyr (ch)
Meditation on a man of God (pf)
Psalm 150, festival setting (ch)
Te Deum, festival setting (ch)
The word was made flesh (ch)
O little lambs (vce and pf)
Psalm 23 (vce and pf)

Ref. composer, 77, 563

HIER, Ethel Glen (Glenn)
American pianist, teacher and composer. b. Cincinnati, OH, June 25, 1889; d. New York, January 14, 1971. She studied at the Cincinnati Conservatory of Music, from which she graduated with a B.M. in 1911. She studied composition under Stillman-Kelley and Percy Goetschius and the piano under Marcian Thalberg and later Friedberg at the Institute of Musical Art, New York. She studied privately under Hugo Kaun in Berlin, Malipiero in Italy and Ernest Bloch from 1918 to 1921 and her music was influenced by Alban Berg, Egon Wellesz and Arnold Schoenberg. She received an honorary degree from the Institute of Musical Art in 1917 and from Cincinnati Conservatory in 1922. She was a private teacher in Cincinnati and then New York. She was one of only two women awarded Guggenheim Fellowships in music for the season 1930 to 1931.

Compositions

ORCHESTRA

Carolina, suite (also str qrt and 2 pf) (New York: CFE, 1952)
Christmas, suite (cham orch; also str qrt) (1939)
Asolo bells (1938) (originally for pf as Campane d'Asolo) (New York: Composers Press, 1946)
Badinage (also pf) (Composers Press, 1949)
Scherzo in D-Minor
Three pieces for orchestra (1938) (Composers Press)

CHAMBER

Suite (fl, ob, vln, vla, vlc and pf) (1925)
Poems for remembrance, suite (vln, vla, vlc and pf) (CFE, 1957)
Scherzo (fl, vlc and pf) (CFE, 1952)
Joy of spring (vln and pf) (CFE, 1952)
Poem (vln and pf)
Rhapsody (vln and pf) (1940) (CFE, 1955) (1st prize, NY State Federation of Music Clubs)

PIANO

Study in blue (4 hands) (CFE, 1953)
Ballade (CFE, 1952)
A day in Peterborough Woods (Chicago: Gilbert Music, 1924)
Dragon-Flies, op. 6, barcarole (Cincinnati: Willis Music, 1913)
Prelude (Composers Press, 1938)
Study in thirds, fourths and fifths (CFE, 1953)

VOCAL

Mountain Preacher, cantata (mix-ch, orch and narr) (CFE, 1966; BMI)
America the Beautiful (with Katherine Bates) (mix-ch and orch) (1919)
Suite (vce, fl, vla, vlc and hp) (1935)
Three quintets (vce, fl, vln, vlc and hp) (1936) (CFE, 1965)
Down in the glen (vce, vln, vlc and pf) (Composers Press, 1958)
If you must go, go quickly (vce, vln, vlc and pf)
Three memorial sonnets (vce, vln and vlc) (CFE, 1965)
Songs incl.:
Approach
Avalon ((Composers Press, 1938)
Bacchanal
The bird in the rain (CFE, 1955)
Click of the latch (Composers Press, 1938)
Dreamin' town (Willis Music, 1919)
Dusk in the hill country (CFE, 1953)
The fairy ring (Composers Press, 1938)
Gulls (Composers Press, 1938)
The hour (Composers Press, 1949)
Japanese lullaby (1925)
My kite (Willis Music, 1914)
The return (Composers Press, 1949)
The time to woo (Willis Music, 1914)
La chanson du cordonnier (CFE, 1955)
May song
The song sparrow (CFE, 1955)
Swans
Wind and sun (CFE)

SACRED

Then shall I know (mix-ch)

BALLET

Choreographe (orch) (CFE, 1952)

Ref. 22, 46, 70, 124, 142, 168, 190, 226, 228, 280, 292, 403, 415, 594, 622

HIGGINBOTHAM, Irene (Mrs. Moetahar Padellan) (pseud. Hart Jones)
Black American pianist and composer. b. Worcester, MA, June 11, 1918. She composed instrumental works and songs.
Ref. 347, 549

HIGGINS, Esther S.
American organist, teacher and composer. b. Elmer, NJ, October 29 1903. She played the organ for silent movie pictures and in concert. She also taught the organ.

Compositions

ORGAN

Aria
Elegy
Festival march
In a pensive mood
Melodie
Pastorale
Reverie
Virgin's lullaby

VOCAL

Berceuse
Flute song
Grand chorus
Morning song
Song for Mother's Day
Spring song

SACRED

Christmas reverie
Love is of God
Passiontide
Worship

ARRANGEMENTS

Works of Saint-Saens, Wieniawski and Chaminade (q.v.)

Publications

Introductions, Breaks, Fills and Endings. All Organ Series, No. 18 and 40.

Ref. 494

HILDEGARD VON BINGEN. See HILDEGARDE, Saint

HILDEGARDE, Saint (Hildegard von Bingen)
German musician, mystic, naturalist, writer and composer. b. Bockelheim, near Kreuznach, 1098; d. Rupertsberg, near Bingen, September 17, 1179. Of noble birth, she was educated at the Benedictine nunnery of Disibodenberg from the age of eight, to become a pupil of the recluse, Jutta of Sponheim. On Jutta's death in 1136, Hildegard was elected abbess of the nunnery and in 1148 moved with 18 nuns to the convent of Rupertsberg above Bingen. From her childhood she had seen visions about which she later wrote in Latin in Liber scrivias. She was credited with extraordinary intelligence and her advice was sought and followed by kings and bishops. She claimed to have received her knowledge of music directly from God, calling herself the Zither or Harp of the Holy Spirit, the strings of which were plucked by the Spirit of the Lord. She wrote on theology and natural history, was credited with healing powers and corresponded with Emperors Conrad III and Frederick I and Popes Anastasius IV and Adrian IV. In her morality play 'Ordo Virtutem' the virtues appeared personified and the characters sang plainsong melodies that she had composed. Her music departed from traditional Gregorian style, traces of folk song being apparent in it. Her book 'Materia Medica' is still referred to for information about medieval medicine. This remarkable woman, who became known as the Sybil of the Rhine, was like a primitive priestess, combining in one person the ancient arts of prophesy, healing and music. She composed about 70 hymns, psalms and cantatas. As far as it is known, she was the earliest woman composer whose music composed for the mass has survived. Hildegarde enjoyed a great intellectual friendship with a high-minded and earnest monk named Bernard de Clairveaux and this was to have a far-reaching and startling efect upon the people of Europe. Bernard deplored the sporadic fighting that was going on between the princes and knights of his day. He felt that their warlike impulses should be channelled into a common aim. A few knights from northern France already had an aim - they had gone on a crusade to rescue the Holy Land from the Saracens and Bernard felt that this should become a common aim for all. In the meantime Hildegarde had a series of visions, which she wrote down in fiery words which Bernard felt, came straight from God. He presented these to the Pope who was equally convinced and put his seal of authority on them. She became the officially recognised prophetess of the Crusades and her writings circulated throughout Europe. Hildegarde's burning prophecies which inspired Bernard's passionate preaching, inflamed the people of Europe and gave growth and meaning to the Crusades. She was virtually responsible for this great turning point in European history. From everywhere kings, princes, knights, soldiers and peasants jammed the roads to the ports and to the east. Everyone wanted to go; men, women and even children. Europe was never the same again. Hildegarde was sanctified and music began to assume a new direction. People began to believe that music gave an added power to prayer and this new concept pervaded the whole of Christendom. Hildegarde was canonized in the 15th-century. DISCOGRAPHY.

Compositions

SACRED

Ordo Virtutem, morality play with 85 songs
Symphonia virginum, hymn
Symphonia viduarum, hymn

Symphonia armoniae celestium revelationum, cycle of liturgical songs
Ave generosa, liturgical song
Caritas-castitas, liturgical song
Columa Aspexit
Seven sequences incl. Sequence of Maria
Ten hymns incl. O Ecclesia; O Euchari; O Ignis Spiritus; O Jerusalem; O Presul Vere Civitatis; O Viridissima Virga; O Virga diadema, still sung in Bingen and other convents
Die Glocken der Abteikirche
Nineteen responsoria
Thirty-five antiphons
Kyrie
Other works

Bibliography

Bockeler, M. *Aufbau und Grundgedanke des Ordo Virtutem der heiligen Hildegard.* Benediktinische Monatschrift, 1923.
Bronarski, L. *Die Lieder der heiligen Hildegardis.* Leipzig, 1922.
Eltz, Monika zu. *Hildegard.* Freiburg: Herder, 1963
Fischer, Hermann. *Die heiligen Hildegard von Bingen, die erste deutscher Naturforscherin und Arztin, ihr Leben und Werk.* Muenchener Beitrage zur Geschichte und Literatur der Naturwissenschaften und Medizin, nos. 7-8. Munich: Muenchener Brucke, 1927.
Fuehrkoetter, Adelgundis. *Hildegard von Bingen.* Salzburg: Otto Mueller Verlag, 1972.
Gmelch, Dr. Joseph. *Die Kompositionen der heiligen Hildegard.* Dusseldorf: L Schwann, 1913.
Isti: *Beziehungen des Ordo Virtutum' der heiligen Hildegard zu ihrem Hauptwerk 'Scrivias'.* Benediktinische Monatschrift, 1925.
Krauss, Wilhelmine. *Die Musik der heiligen Hildegard von Bingen.* Gregoriusblatt 61 (n.d.): 17-22.
May, J. *Die heilige Hildegard von Bingen: ein Lebensbild.* Kempten and Munich, 1911.
Quentin, E. *Hildegard von Bingen: A Modern Woman Physician - 800 years ago.* Muenchener Medizinische Wochenschrift 109-147. Nov. 24, 1967: 2509-2510.
Schipperges, H. *Hildegard von Bingen Heilkunder' das Buch von dem Grund und Wesen und der Heilung der Krankheiten.* Salzburg: Mueller, 1957.
Singer, Charles. *The Scientific Views and Visions of Saint Hildegard (1098-1180).* pp. 1-55. London: OUP, 1917.
S. Hildegardis abbatissae opera omnia. Patres Latini, 1855.
Schmelzeis, J.P. *Das Leben und Wirken der heiligen Hildegardis nach den Quellen dargestellt.* Freiburg in Breisgau, 1879.
The Visions of Hildegard of Bingen. From Magic to Science, pp. 199-1239. New York: Dover Publ., 1958.

Ref. Barbara L. Grant, 2, 3, 8, 15, 20, 88, 109, 110, 264, 335, 347, 404, 415, 417, 476, 502, 563, 622, 637, 646, 653

HILDERLEY, Jeriann G.

American percussionist, authoress and composer. b. Saginaw, MI, July 17, 1937. She played percussion instruments as a child and then attended Smith College, University of California (Berkeley) and the University of Michigan. She obtained her M.A. (art and music) and also studied under the sculptor Joseph Goto, the painter Herman Cherry and the composer Denise Hoffman. She was a director of Sea Wave Records and of a women's ritual theatre group and published articles on theatre and music in papers and magazines. DISCOGRAPHY. PHOTOGRAPH.

Compositions

VOCAL
Jeritree's house of many colours (vce, perc, vlc, gtr and wooden fls) (1979)
Songs (Sea Wave, Caw Magazine and Camille) incl.:
Don't tell me it's the rain
Footsteps of Diana
I'm no fool
I poke a seed
I want to live in a beautiful city
In this circle
Mother
Sea wave
Song of the cleaning woman
Sweet lips
Through your blue veil
Turn around sister

Ref. composer, *Heresies Magazine*, 563

HILDRETH, Daisy Wood

20th-century American composer. She composed piano works and songs.
Ref. 40, 347

HILL, Lady Arthur. See HARRISON, Annie Fortescue

HILL, May

American organist, authoress, publisher, singer, teacher and composer. b. Cleveland, OH, August 11, 1888. She won scholarships to Chicago Musical College and the Columbia School of Music. She worked in radio from 1920 to 1923 and in 1933 was a voice teacher in Chicago. She was a member of ASCAP. PHOTOGRAPH.

Compositions

CHAMBER
Piano pieces

VOCAL
Dear old girl
Everybody loves a big brass band
I believe in you
Take me back to dreamland
You'll want me back some day

Ref. composer, 39, 347

HILL, Mildred J.

American organist, pianist, authoress and composer. b. Louisville, KY, June 27, 1859; d. Chicago, June 5, 1916. She trained at Bellewood Seminary and studied music with her father, Calvin Cady and Adolph Weidig. She was an authority on black spirituals. In her children's suite *Good morning to you* is *Happy birthday to you* the most often sung and translated song in the world.

Compositions

CHAMBER
Piano pieces

VOCAL
Apart
Good morning to you, suite for children, incl. Happy birthday to you
How many ways the infinite has (Cale, Young, Rice)
Legacies
Love's paradise
My star
A perfect day
A sleep song
Smiles and frowns
Songs for kindergarten
To Anthea

Ref. 39, 276, 292

HILL, Mirrie Irma. See SOLOMON, Mirrie Irma

HILL, Sister M. Mildred

Australian cellist, pianist, violinist, lecturer and composer. b. Sydney, July 22, 1930. She received her music teaching diploma from the Dominician Training College, Maitland and the Sydney Conservatory and her L.T.C.L. from the Liszt Academy, Hungary, 1973. She taught the piano, the violin, the cello, composition and singing and lectured on music.

Compositions

SACRED
Mass of St. Dominic
Prayers of the ark
Psalm Sunday mass

Publications

Listen. Books 1-3. 1968.

Ref. 457

HILLEBRAND-LAUSSOT, Jessie

Musicologist and composer. b. 1827; d 1905. A great admirer of Liszt, she settled in Florence after a sentimental interlude with Wagner and became a member of the Cherubini Society.
Ref. 361

HILLIER-JASPAR, Jeanne

20th-century Belgian composer. She composed chamber music, a comic opera and pieces for the piano.

HILMER, Sally

20th-century composer.

Composition

MISCELLANEOUS
Troubadour (with Dorothy Carter)

Ref. Frau und Musik

HILSTON, Lucille

20th-century American composer.

Composition

ORCHESTRA

Onghiara (Niagara river) (1962)

Ref. 280

HIND BINT'UTBA

Arabian songstress of the pre-Islamic period. d. 610. Women of this time enjoyed far more liberty than after Mohammed; they played their instruments at family and tribal festivities. Even Mohammed's wedding with Khadiya was 'celebrated with great festivity, mirth, music and dancing'. In 605 the journey of the Quraish was entertained at Uhud by the women, led by Hind Bint'Utba, singing war songs and laments for those killed at Badr. Hind, a poetess and musician, was considered a representative songstress of the jahiliyya, the 'days of ignorance' preceding Mohammed.

Ref. 171

HIND O'MALLEY, Pamela

English cellist, pianist, lecturer and composer. b. London, February 27, 1923. She started composing for the piano at the age of four and began composition lessons under Herbert Howell at 13. She continued to study under him at the Royal College of Music, 1939 to 1943. She studied the cello and the piano under Pablo Casals, Jane Cowan, Imogen Holst (q.v.) and Kathleen Long. She taught the cello and the piano at the Cranleigh School from 1943 to 1945 and then at Darlington College of Arts, 1947 to 1950. From 1962 she was an ensemble coach to the Cambridge University Music Club as well as a part-time cello teacher at King's College School. She gave many solo piano and cello recitals at Wigmore Hall and Purcell Room, London. In 1963 she gave the first London performance of Britten's *Cello sonata, op. 65.*

Compositions

ORCHESTRA

Lament for string orchestra (1939)
Two movements for string orchestra (1943)

CHAMBER

Two movements (ob qnt) (1943)
Cycle of four rounds (4 vln) (1948) (Staines & Bell)
Theme and sixteen variations (str qrt) (1939)
Trio (fl, vla and vlc) (1948)
Three duos (vln and vlc) (1930, 1939, 1948)

PIANO

Chorale and choral prelude (1943)
Passacaglia (1950)
Prelude and fugue in E-Minor (1943)
Variations on an original theme (1943)
Approx. 60 other pieces

VOCAL

Part of Eliot's Wasteland (S and vlc) (1950)
Rounds for voices (1950)
Song (Blake) (1950)
Songs (Shakespeare, Shelley, Bouvillon, Dixon)

SACRED

I sing the almighty power of God, hymn (Isaac Watts)
Two psalms (S) (1950)

Ref. composer

HINDLE, Emma Louise. See ASHFORD, Emma Louise

HINE, Marie M.

20th-century composer.

Composition

SACRED

The Redemption, oratorio (1913)

Ref. 465

HINEBAUGH, Bessie

20th-century American composer. She composed anthems.

Ref. 40, 347

HINKLE, Daisy Estelle

20th-century American composer. b. Bloomington, IN. She composed chamber music and piano pieces.

Ref. 347

HINLOPEN, Francina

Dutch harpist, poetess and composer. b. Amsterdam, August 9, 1908. She studied the harp under Rosa Spier and composition and theory under Anton van der Horst and C. van Erven Dorens. She passed the state examination in music at The Hague. She was solo harpist of several provincial orchestras in the Netherlands and introduced the harp as a principal instrument in churches. She appeared on television and radio, performing her own compositions. In 1945 she received a silver medal from La Société Arts-Sciences-Lettres, France and an award for contemporary achievement, England. PHOTOGRAPH.

Compositions

ORCHESTRA

Fantasy for string orchestra (1964)
March for fanfare orchestra (1960)
Symphony for chamber orchestra (1957)

CHAMBER

Praeludium fuga per quattor corni (4 hn) (1961)
Prelude and fugue on Sh'ma Israel (4 trb) (1962)
Fantasy on a folk song and the song of a blackbird (hp and fl) (1960)
How far is my heath, fantasy (hp and fl) (1963)
In the mountains (hp and fl) (1956)
Praeludium on the old Irish hymn melody, Come Holy Ghost our hearts inspire (hp and org) (1969)
Fantasy on an Easter song, Daar juicht een toon (hp and org) (1967)
Improvisation of Te deum (hp and org) (1967)
Prelude and chorale on Abide with Me (hp and org) (1967)
Prelude and chorale Psalm 42 (hp and org) (1967)
Prelude on Psalm 98 (hp and org) (1967)
Prelude and chorale on Psalm 139 (hp and org) (1968)
Sonatine (org) (1956)
Passacaglia and fantasy on Psalm 150 (1973)
Theme with variations on a song by G. Neumark (1954)

CARILLON

Fantasy (1972)
Fantasy on a theme for Psalm 42 (1975)
Improvisation on C. Kreutzer's evening prayer (1952)
Theme and Variations on Les Lieux et la terre celebrent en choeur (1974)

HARP

Chorale on now thank we all our God (7 hp) (1946)
Accompaniment to the Preface: The great land (1969)
Accompaniment to the Sermon in the field (1969)
Accompaniment to the Sermon on the mountain (1969)
Accompaniment to seven lute songs by John Dowland (1966)
Angel's Dance (1956)
Fantasy on Luther's A safe stronghold our God is still (1950)
Improvisation on Psalm 43 (1961)
Improvisation on Psalm 118 (1952)
Improvisation on the song Rough storms may rage (1966)
Improvisation on Welsh song Men of Harlech
Introduction, improvisation and final apotheosis on Adon Olam (1969)
Prelude, intermezzo, postlude on Kadosh (1969)
Spring Waltz (1974)
Theme and variations on Va-anachnu (1974)
Three variations on a Russian song Ich bete an die Macht der Liebe
Fantasy on C. Kreutzer's Das ist der Tag des Herrn (1958)

VOCAL

Bulb festival (mix-ch and hp) (Amsterdam: Alsbach, 1957)
Two songs (w-ch and hp) (1956)
Harbinger of spring (chil-ch) (1958)
The seasons, song cycle of 4 sonnets (1960)
Seventeen negro spirituals with original harp accompaniment (1965)
The singer's curse, song (1957)

SACRED

Hymn of Psalm 84 (Milton) (m-ch) (Amsterdam: Pijlman, 1967)
Missa antiphonalis (4-part ch, hp and org) (1981) (comm Hilversum Roman Catholic Church, on the 25th jubilee of the pastor)
Psalm of Life (Longfellow) (m-ch and hp) (1970)
Fantasy on Psalm 3 (1956)
Goliath and David (vce and hp) (1952)
Missa sacra (vce and 7 hp) (1969)
Prelude and song on Psalm 23 (1971)
Psalm 60 (S and hp) (1968)

Publications

A Bundle of Poems. 1967.
The History of the Harp and its Significance in the History of Israel. 1971.

Ref. composer, 77, 457

HINRICHS, Marie

German composer. b. 1828; d. Halle, May 5, 1891. Her brother Frederick was an amateur composer and she married Robert Franz, also a composer.

Compositions
VOCAL
Songs:
Blicke zum Himmel, mein Kind (Breitkopf)
Du bist wie eine Blume (Breitkopf)
Eine alte Kunde: Ich weiss eine alte Kunde (Breitkopf)
Hoer ich das Liedchen klingen (Breitkopf)
Ihr Bild: Ich stand in dunklen Traumen (Breitkopf)
Im Mai: Im wunderschoenen Monat Mai (Breitkopf)
Im stillen Klostergarten (Breitkopf)
Du welker Dornenstrauch (Breitkopf)
Wenn du mich lieb hast: Aus meinen Traenen (Breitkopf)
Ref. 105, 226, 276, 297

HIRSCH, Barbara

American electronic instrumentalist, librarian, teacher and composer. b. New York, 1953. She received her B.A. from the University College of Santa Barbara and M.A. (composition) in 1979. In 1978 she became recording technician and music librarian at Santa Barbara City College and after that date taught electronic music.
Compositions
VOCAL
Old trees (ch and pf) (1981)
Works for voices and chamber ensemble
ELECTRONIC
Pieces
MISCELLANEOUS
Music for dance concerts
Ref. University of California (Santa Barbara)

HIRSCHFELDT, Ingrid

20th-century German composer. DISCOGRAPHY.
Composition
SACRED
Wir alle essen von einem Brot (Lothar Zenetti) (ch and cham orch)
Ref. 563

HJORT, Thecla

19th-century Swedish composer.
Compositions
VOCAL
I skog (vce and pf) (1879)
Kolar-Svensvisa (vce and pf)
Skogens kaella (vce and pf)
Vind-sus (vce and pf)
Ref. 167

H.L.L. See BORTHWICK, Jane Laurie

HO, Wai On

British pianist, lecturer, singer and composer. b. Hong Kong, May 26, 1946. She studied language and literature at the Chinese University of Hong Kong and was later awarded a John Swire and Sons U.K. scholarship, which enabled her to study at the Royal Academy of Music from 1966 to 1971. She became an L.R.A.M. in 1969, an A.R.C.M. in 1969, a G.R.S.M. in 1970, gained her professional certificate in 1971 and became an A.R.A.M. in 1984. She studied the piano under Guy Jonson and Max Pirani, singing under Henry Cummings and composition under James Iliff. She is a member of the Composers Guild of Great Britain and the Incorporated Society of Musicians, England. From 1976 she spent much time studying and composing electronic music, receiving a M.A. (electronic and contemporary music) from Cardiff University in 1984, after study under Mike Greenhough and Stephen Walsh. Her works have been performed in concert and on the radio in England, the United States and Hong-Kong, where she has also lectured on music.
Compositions
ORCHESTRA
Fantasy (vla and orch without brass, 1974; also vln and pf, 1979)
Festival overture (sym orch) (1978)
Tze rondo (Chinese insts) (1979)
CHAMBER
Interval (str qrt) (1977)
Saxophone quartet (1974)
Impression of an opera II (ob, B-flat cl, bsn and hn in F) (1983)
Quarry (B-flat cl, vla and perc) (1976)
Trio after Spring river in flowery moonlight (fl, gtr and hp) (1979)
Five variations on Sakura (vlc and hpcd) (1975)
Spring river in flowery moonlight, duo (pipe and hp) (1977)
Tai chi (fl and gtr) (1977)
5, 7, 12 (vln and pf) (1979)
GUITAR
Distance (1975)
Melody (1979)
Study on thirds (1975)
Tremolo (1979)
PIANO
Apollo dancing (1975)
Distance – In memory of Max Pirani (1976)
Pygmalion & Galatea (1984)
The waves (1974)
VOCAL
Shadow's farewell (high vce and str orch, 1975; also high vce and pf, 1975)
Song of Buddha (mix-ch a-cap) (1974)
Four songs in Chinese (high vce and cor anglais, 1974: also high vce and fl, 1979)
Song cycle, poems (MacNiece) (high vce and gtr, 1978; also high vce and pf, 1979)
To you (high vce and pf) (1977)
Wisdom (high vce and gtr) (1974)
3.10 am (speaker, vla and gtr) (1977)
ELECTRONIC
The anxious elements (2 channel tape) (1977-1978)
A piece for modern ballet (2 channel tape and perc) (1976)
Spectrum (2 S, fl, vln, gtr, hp, perc, pf and 2 channel tape)
Tango concertino (2 channel tape and gtr) (1981)
Twenty-part composition (2 channel computer-electronic) (1982)
MULTIMEDIA
Metamorphosis (2 channel tape, 3 instrumentalists, 3 stage persons, 2 dancers, slides, colour and mobile lighting and scenery) (1978-1979)
FILM MUSIC
Three short films
Ref. composer

HODGES, Ann Mary

18th-century English composer.
Compositions
VOCAL
Songs (harmonized and pub Mr. Hullmandel, for the benefit of orphan children, London: 1798)
Ref. 65, 125

HODGES, Faustina Hasse

American organist and composer. b. New York, 1823; d. Philadelphia or New York, February 4, 1895. She was the daughter of the British organist Edward Hodges. She was organist at Brooklyn, NY, and at two churches in Philadelphia. One hundred thousand copies of her song *Rose bush* were sold.
Compositions
CHAMBER
Organ pieces
PIANO
Marigena, 3 reveries by the waterside (New York: Beer & Schirmer, 1863)
Pensées du coeur, nocturne (New York: G. Schirmer, 1873)
VOCAL
Songs incl.:
All in the sunshine (Schirmer)
Amicizia (Schirmer)
Dreary day (Schirmer)
Drifting (Schirmer)
Rose bush (Schirmer)
Yearnings (Ditson)
SACRED
Let your light so shine (vocal qrt) (Schirmer)
Whatsoever ye would (vocal qrt) (Schirmer)
Blessed are the meek (Schirmer)
Ring out the bells, Christmas carols (Schirmer)
Church music
Publications
Memoir of Edward Hodges. 1896.
Ref. 8, 226, 228, 297, 347, 415, 653

HOEGSBRO-CHRISTENSEN, Inge

Danish lecturer and composer. b. Farup, March 14, 1872. She studied under Christian Sinding, Leo Ornstein and Vassili Safonoff and theory under Emil Hartmann. Later she studied under Robert Young in New York and attended the Chittenden School from which she received a teaching certificate. She was a teacher at Hartley House, an East Side settlement house and a director of the Northern Conservatory in 1911.

Compositions

VOCAL

Cradle song

Mona

Mother's song

Serenade

Too late

Publications

Biography of Agathe Backer-Groendahl (q.v.).

Ref. 433

HOEK, Agnes

20th-century German composer.

Composition

CHAMBER

Festliche Sonate (vln and pf)

Ref. Frau und Musik

HOELSZKY, Adriana

20th-century West German composer.

Compositions

ORCHESTRA

Space (1984)

CHAMBER

Innere Welten (str qrt) (prize, competition for young composers)

Intarsien II (fl, vln, hpcd and pf) (1983)

Decorum (hpcd) (1982)

Nouns to nouns (vln) (1983)

Ref. Frau und Musik

HOENDERDOS, Margriet

Dutch pianist and composer. b. Santpoort, May 6, 1952. She studied the piano at the Conservatory of Zwolle and then composition under Professor de Leeuw at the Sweelinck Conservatory in Amsterdam. Since 1982 she has concentrated on electronic and computer music.

Compositions

ORCHESTRA

Het niewe verlaat

CHAMBER

Blue time (2 pf) (1981)

Camilla (fl) (1982)

VOCAL

Coplas (S and perc) (1980)

ELECTRONIC

Bouw (13 wind insts, 5 perc and tape) (1981)

Ref. composer

HOFER, Maria

Austrian organist, pianist and composer. b. July 6, 1894. She studied at the Academy of Music in Vienna and traveled in Europe, playing her own piano and organ works. After 1938 she lived in the Tyrol.

Compositions

ORCHESTRA

Totentanz (1948)

ORGAN

Die Maschine

Toccata

SACRED

Cantabilia spiritualia (sextet and org)

Seven masses

THEATRE

Incidental music

Ref. 94, 96, 189

HOFER-SCHNEEBERGER, Emma

Swiss composer. b. Herzogenbuchsee, near Bern, April 2, 1855.

Compositions

VOCAL

Erinnerungsblumen, 9 songs (3 part chil-ch; also mix-ch and m-ch) (1894)

Ref. 101

HOFF, Regina Clara

German composer. ca. 1620.

Compositions

PIANO

Bassa imperiale

Saltarello del bassa imperiale

Ref. Frau und Musik

HOFF, Vivian Beaumont

American pianist, authoress, choral conductor, teacher and composer. b. Shelby County, IN, December 17, 1911. She studied at the Jordan College of Music and Butler University, Indianapolis. She studied the piano under Bomar Cramer and Thelma Todd; voice under Elma Igleman and harmony and advanced composition under William Pelz. She was a piano teacher and choir director and gave recitals of her own compositions over the radio.

Compositions

PIANO

Suite (1956)

Pieces for children (1969-1970)

VOCAL

Keep the Star-Spangled Banner waving (1962)

SACRED

Be of good courage (1957)

Father in Heaven (1953)

I look to my Lord (1960)

Ref. 84, 475

HOFFERT, Brenda

Canadian composer. b. Toronto, May 25, 1944. She studied at the Toronto School of Drama and the Royal Conservatory. She is vice-chairlady of the Academy of Canadian Cinema. PHOTOGRAPH.

Compositions

VOCAL

Songs for films and television

Children's songs

FILM MUSIC

Wild Horse Hank (with Paul Hoffert) (1979)

Ref. composer, 497

HOFFMAN, Phyllis Sampson

American horn and trumpet player and composer. b. Quincy, MA, May 20, 1918. At the New England Conservatory she studied the trumpet under Georges Mager from 1936 to 1940, the horn under Willem Walkenier from 1940 to 1941 and composition under Warren Storey Smith and Francis Judd Cooke, 1939 to 1950. She played the horn and the trumpet in the Boston Women's Symphony Orchestra from 1938 to 1941.

Compositions

ORCHESTRA

First symphony (1947)

Viola concerto (1948)

CHAMBER

Piano quartet (Paderewski award, 1948)

Horn sonata

Organ suite

Ref. 496

HOFFMANN, Miss J.

Late 18th-century English composer.

Compositions

CHAMBER

Duet (2 hp; also hp and pf) (1795)

PIANO

Six duets (ca. 1798)

Two duets (1795)

VOCAL

In yonder vale, song (C. Rickman) (1795)

The world, song (C. Rickman) (ca. 1796)

Ye Britons be bold, song (Mrs. Duckrell) (1795)

Ref. 65, 125

HOFFMANN, Peggy (Mrs. Arnold E.)

American organist and composer. b. Delaware, OH, August 25, 1910. She studied at Miami University under Edward G. Mead, at the University of Chicago under Cecil Smith and at the University of Akron under Elmer Ende. She was church organist in Raleigh, NC, from 1950 to 1966 and Cary, NC, 1967 to 1973.

Compositions
SACRED
The Cross shines forth, Easter cantata (ch)
God's Son is born, Christmas cantata (ch)
Anthems
Chorales
Organ pieces
Ref. 142

HOFFMANN-BEHRENDT, Lydia

Soviet concert pianist and composer. b. Tiflis, Georgia, September 1, 1890.
Ref. 226

HOFFRICHTER, Bertha Chaitkin (Mrs. Maurice J.)

American composer. b. Pittsburgh, PA, December 8, 1915. She obtained her B.A. and M.A. from Carnegie-Mellon University and studied privately under Joseph Jenkins.
Compositions
CHAMBER
Violin sonata
Piano trio (Composers' Division prize)
PIANO
Sonata (2 pf) (Martin Leisser award, Pittsburgh Art Society)
Suites (1 or 2 pf)
VOCAL
Choral works
Song cycle (James Joyce) (award, PA, Federation of Music Clubs)
SACRED
Psalm 23 (S and ch)
Psalm 24 (ch a-cap)
Ref. 142

HOFFRICHTER, Mrs. Maurice J. See HOFFRICHTER, Bertha Chaitkin

HOGBEN, Dorothy

English composer.
Composition
PIANO
The Punch and Judy show, duet
Ref. 473

HOHNSTOCK, Adele

19th-Century American composer.
Composition
PIANO
Hohnstock concert polka with variations (Philadelphia: A Fiot, 1849)
Ref. 228

HOIJER, Anna Ovena

17th-century Dutch poetess and composer.
Compositions
SACRED
Geistliche und weltliche Poemata (Amsterdam: Ludwig Elzevier, 1650)
Poems with two melodies: Christe Gotts eigner Sohn; Kommet her, mit Fleiss betrachtet
Ref. 128

HOKANSON, Dorothy Cadzow. See CADZOW, Dorothy Forrest

HOKANSON, Margrethe

American organist, pianist, arranger, conductor, professor and composer. b. Duluth, MN, December 19, 1893; d. April 24, 1975. She studied composition under Arthur Andersen at the American Conservatory, Chicago and at the Margaret Morrison School under Josef Lhevinne, Heniot Levy, Marcel Dupre and Wilhelm Middelshulte. She was dean of the organ department of St. Olaf College and founded the Nordic Choral Ensemble, 1939 to 1943. She was associate professor at Allegheny College from 1944 to 1954 and received a National Federation of Music Clubs award for an orchestral work.
Compositions
ORCHESTRA
Four seasons in the north
Nordic reverie, tone poem (also org)
CHAMBER
On the mountain (pf, 4 hands)
Three fleeting impressions (org)
VOCAL
Shepherds at night (mix-ch and keyboard)
Songs:
Come, close the curtain of your eyes
In the primeval forest
Nordic song
Ring dance
Song without words
O summer idyll
SACRED
Bohemian carol (mix-ch and pf)
In dulci jubilo (mix-ch and pf)
O praise Him (mix-ch and pf)
Ref. 39, 40, 142, 190, 280, 347, 646

HOLBERT, Diana Brown

American composer. b. January 30, 1947. She received an M.M.E. in voice from the Southern Methodist University in 1972. Her master's thesis was based on *The Little Prince* by Antoine St. Exupery. PHOTOGRAPH.
Composition
THEATRE
The Musical Prince, musical drama for children in 1 act (Jo Ann H. Snyder) (1972)
Ref. composer, 146

HOLCK, Hansine. See HOLCK, Sine

HOLCK, Sine (Hansine)

Norwegian pianist, singer, teacher and composer. b. February 2, 1868; d. May 9, 1966. She studied the piano and singing in Berlin and Oslo and later worked as a music critic.
Compositions
PIANO
Twelve little pieces (4 hands)
Festival march (1936)
Hjemover fra Schildberg
Med liv og lyst
Til undervisning og selvstudium. Trinn II og III
To stemningsbilleder (1936)
ARRANGEMENTS
Firhendig fronoeyelse
Kimer i klokker, Julens melodier
Sju tre-stemmige sanger
Publications
The First Teaching in Piano Playing. 3 vols.
The Young Pianist. 2 vols.
Bibliography
Anna Lindhjem. *Kvinnelige komponister og musikk-skoleudivere i Skandinavien*. 1931.
Ref. NMI

HOLCOMB, Louanah Riggs

American pianist, lecturer and composer. b. Springdale, AR, November 30, 1913. She received her B.Mus. from the University of Arkansas in 1935, then did postgraduate study at the Southwestern Baptist Theological School of Music from 1936 to 1937, at the St. Louis Institute of Music in 1955 and at the George Peabody College, 1955 to 1956. In 1935 she taught music privately in Springdale; from 1936 to 1937 she was a member of the faculty of the Weaver Conservatory, Tulsa and from 1937 to 1941 she taught at Fort Worth, where she was at the Texas Wesleyan College, from 1939 to 1940. From 1941 to 1945 she taught at Pineville, Baton Rouge; then at Jacksonville, FL, 1945 to 1952 and from 1952 onwards at Nashville, TN. In 1970, she was listed in the Piano Guild Hall of Fame. She contributed to various journals.
Compositions
PIANO
Alleluia
Immortal
Invisible
When morning gilds the sky

VOCAL
Children's songs
Publications
Hymns for the Beginning Pianist. 1971.
Missionary Melodies. 1950.
Ref. 475

HOLDEN, Bernice
20th-century American composer.
Composition
OPERA
The Travelling Musician (Josephine F. Royle)
Ref. 141

HOLLAND, Caroline
19th-century English choral conductor and composer. Her choir premiered works by Grieg, Rheinberger and Tinel in England.
Compositions
VOCAL
Miss Killmansegg and her golden leg, cantata (1883)
After the skirmish, ballad (Sir Alfred Lyall) (ch and orch) (1896)
Part songs
Ref. 6, 226, 276

HOLLAND, Dulcie Sybil
Australian cellist, pianist, lecturer and composer. b. Sydney, January 5, 1913. At the Sydney Conservatorium she studied composition under Alfred Hill, the piano under Frank Hutchens and the cello under Gladstone Bell and privately under Roy Agnew. She later studied under John Ireland at the Royal College of Music, London, where she won the Blumenthal Scholarship and the Cobbett Prize for chamber composition in 1938. She is an L.R.S.M. and has her D.S.C.M. (teacher's diploma) and her A.Mus.A. She was an examiner for the Australian music examination board, gave radio broadcasts and made concert appearances as a pianist. She received many composition awards from the ABC and won the Warringah and Henry Lawson Festival award in 1965. DISCOGRAPHY. PHOTOGRAPH.
Compositions
ORCHESTRA
Symphony for pleasure (1974)
Civic overture (1957)
Festival flourish (1965)
Kambala suite (str orch) (1967)
Secret pool (light concert ens)
Variations on a theme of Alfred Hill (5 composers) (ww, brass, perc and str orch) (1970)
BAND
Stanmore Road
CHAMBER
Night out (2 hn, 2 trp and 2 trbs) (1973)
Serenade for oboe and percussion (ob, cym, timp, side drum, gong and tri) (1968)
Voulez-vous promener avec moi ce soir? (2 trp, hn, trb and tba)
Aria (a-sax and strs)
A Merry Christmas to you (brass qnt)
Conversation a 4 (str qrt) (1981)
Fantasy trio (vln, vla and pf) (1938)
Promenade (2 vln and pf) (1969)
Sonatina (2 rec and pf) (London: Boosey, 1938)
Sonatina for two recorders (2 descant rec and pf) (BMI) (1962)
Sonatina for two soprano recorders and piano (BMI) (1964)
Trio (vln, vlc and pf) (1944)
Trio diversion (fl, vln and vla) (1953)
Alla Marcia (cl and pf) (Allans, 1970)
Autumn piece (vln and pf) (1936)
Autumn sarabande (vln and pf) (J. Albert & Son)
Ballade (cl and pf) (Boosey, 1954)
Caprice No. 1 (ob and pf)
Cradle song (vln and pf) (Boosey & Hawkes, 1952)
Divertimento (vln and pf) (1952)
Elegy (fl and pf) (1954) (Boosey & Hawkes, 1971)
Episode (hn and org) (1975)
Evening hymn (hn and org) (1970)
The fallen leaf (ob or cl and pf) (Allans, 1970)
Holiday piece (vln and pf) (Albert, 1975)
In tribute: H. Brewster Jones (vln and pf) (1955)
Lullaby, my little tiny child (rec or fl and keyboard inst) (Albert, 1974)
Musette & gigue (sax and pf) (1950)
Peter-Paul (vln and pf) (1958)
Sonata (E-flat sax and pf)
Sonata (vlc and pf) (1938)
Sonata (vln and pf) (1936)
Sonatina (vla and pf) (1932)
Sonatina (vln and vla) (1940)
Starlight (rec or fl and keyboard) (Albert, 1974)
Three dialogues (cl and hp) (1969)
Three dialogues (cl and pf)
Prelude on a motive (cl) (Allans, 1970)
Ronolo (B-cl) (1958)
Shy one (sax) (1954)
Three humours (vln) (Albert, 1974)
CARILLON
Capricietto for little bells (1942)
Little suite (1970)
Three cheers for Captain Cook
ORGAN
Complaint
Joy cometh in the morning (1974)
Joyous departure (1975)
Soliloquy (1974)
Twilight piece (1974)
Two salutations (1965)
With a gladsome mind (1974)
PIANO
Numerous pieces incl.:
Two nursery sketches (2 pf) (1966)
Three duets for young Australians (1973)
Asterisk (1965)
Autumn (1947)
Christmas greeting
Country tunes (Paling, 1964)
Dreamy John
Eleven pieces for Grade I (Allans) (1973)
The end of summer
Everyday pieces (Allans)
Flags in the breeze
Green lizards (1936)
Humoresque (1954)
The hunt (Allans, 1973)
In the dreamtime (Allans, 1973)
The lake
Merry fingers (Paling, 1958)
Nocturne (1947)
Over hill, over dale (Allans, 1947)
Picnic races (1964)
The sand man comes (1944)
The scattering leaves
A song remembered (1938)
Suggested by the rain (1954)
Ten study pieces (Allans)
Three easy pieces (Paling, 1955)
Three preludes (1980)
Tribute to Clement Hosking (1965)
VOCAL
College cantata (1951) (mix-ch)
The circle of the year (Kalidasa, trans John Wheeler) (1949) (A, mix-ch and orch)
This land Is mine (Bar and orch) (1959)
This white shell standing (narr and orch) (1973)
Song of the constant spirit (Kathleen Murray) (Bar, mix-ch and pf or org)
Simple shepherd (composer) (mix-ch and org) (1973)
Anzac cove (Leon Gellert) (mix-ch) (1937)
Australia, my country (Dorothea MacKellar) (mix-ch a-cap or S, A and pf) (Allans, 1951)
Be still you little Leaves (Mary Webb) (mix-ch) (1936)
Calliopsis (Joyce Trickley) (w-ch and pf or 2 S, soli or 2 S and pf) (1967)
The cow (Robert Louis Stevenson) (mix-ch) (1936)
Three nursery rhymes, traditional (mix-ch) (1937)
The hirron carol (w-ch) (1972)
Three carols (2 S and pf) (1960)
Happy times (composer) (unison chil-vces) (1972)
The ballad of fair Joanna (Patricia Francis) (S and pf) (1957)
The beryl tree (John Wheeler) (vce and pf) (Southern Music, 1954)
Comin' through the rye (vce and pf) (1969)
Evening walks soft-footed (Kathleen Monypenny) (vce and pf) (1937)
For no reason (anon) (S or T and pf) (1937)
The fountain (J.R. Lowell) (vce and pf) (1931)
Golden stockings (Oliver Gogarty) (vce and pf) (1936)
Happy days, for children (Alberts)
He that is thy friend (Shakespeare) (S and pf) (1936)
The hill pines were sighing (Robert Bridges) (vce and pf) (1936)
Hope in spring (composer) (Paling) (1953)
I contemplate the dawn (K. Monypenny) (vce and pf) (1936)
The light-hearted fairy (George Darley) (S or m-S and pf) (1937)
A lullaby (composer) (S and pf) (Paling) (1956)

Mad Tom (J. Wheeler) (T and pf) (1954)
Mary Gilmore songs (S, m-S and pf) (1950)
Noon (K. Monypenny) (vce and pf) (1936)
Northside vision (Joyce Trickett) (S, Bar and pf) (1963)
O mistress mine (Shakespeare) (S, T and pf)
A pussy-willow pussy (Sonia Hardy) (S and pf) (1936)
Sing-o, for children (Alberts)
Sky roses (vce and pf) (Allans) (1954)
Song to a queen (J. Trickett) (vce and pf) (1954)
That goodly fragrance (S and pf) (1969)
This insignificant meeting (Robert Fitzgerald) (1936)
Time for singing, for children (Palings)
To an infant son (Patricia Francis) (S and pf) (1955)
Young Australia, for children (Palings)
INCIDENTAL MUSIC
Jenolan Adventure, musical play (J. Trickett) (1962)
My Unwritten Play (1975)
More than 40 film scores
Publications
From Beethoven to Brahms. With Alan Bellhouse.
A History of Music. With Alan Bellhouse.
Master Your Theory. Book I. 1981.
Musicianship Course. 1973.
Practice in Musicianship. Books 1-7. 1979-1980.
Senior School Harmony and Melody. With Alan Bellhouse.
Ref. composer, 1, 77, 84, 94, 280, 412, 440, 442, 443, 444, 445, 446, 457, 563

HOLLAND, Ruby
Compositions
PIANO
Eleven pieces
Five Little Pieces (Anglo-French)
Kensington garden (Anglo-French)
Three Impressions (Anglo-French)
Ref. 473

HOLLINS, Dorothea
Early 20th-century English composer.
Compositions
CHAMBER
Sonata in G-Minor (vln and pf)
VOCAL
Dor as thro' the land at Eve we went (Bar) (Novello)
E te lo voglio dire, romance (Carisch)
O mournful mist (Nebel) (Leonard)
A prayer in Thessaly (Novello)
Sechs Lieder, op. 1 (Novello)
Similitudine, romance (Carisch)
Six songs (German and English texts) (Novello)
Ten songs (German and English texts) (Leonard)
With boot and saddle (Church)
Year's at the spring (Novello)
Ref. 226, 297

HOLLIS, Ruby Shaw
20th-century American composer. She composed choral works.
Ref. 40, 347

HOLLISTER, Leona Stephens
20th-century American composer.
Compositions
VOCAL
Meet me at Naples in Maine (1940)
Sebago (1926)
Somewhere in Maine
Ref. 374

HOLLWAY, Elizabeth L.
20th-century American composer. She composed piano pieces and songs.
Ref. 40, 347

HOLMBERG, Betty
20th-century Norwegian violinist and composer.
Compositions
CHAMBER
Andante (vln and pf)
Suite (vln and pf)
Violin pieces
PIANO
Praeludium mit Fuge
Scherzo
Ref. 276, 297

HOLMBERG, Emelie Augusta Kristina
Swedish organist, pianist, singer and composer. b. Stockholm, May 6, 1821; d. United States, March 28, 1854. She published her first songs at the age of 15 and appeared as a singer and pianist when she was 17 years old. In the 1840s and 1850s her settings of poems by Atterbom, Runeberg, Dahlgren, Bottiger and Franzen were very popular. She gave concerts in Stockholm and Paris. In 1841 she founded a music institute in Stockholm. In 1844 she married Peter Hjalmar Hammarskoeld, a patron of the arts. They went to the United States where she continued her career and was acclaimed 'probably the best known Swedish singer in America, after Jenny Lind.' They settled in Charlestown where she became the organist at St. Peter's Church.
Compositions
VOCAL
Goeken gal i lunden (Dahlgren)
Hoek o. Dufva (Dahlgren)
Seven volumes of songs (1845) incl.:
Sof oroliga hjaerta sof (Runeberg)
Till en tonkunstnar: Hoej dina vingar (Hirsch)
Till skogs en liten faagel floeg (Atterbom)
Ufven och Laerkan, till haerkan sade oemt herr Uf (Hirsch)
Ur stormarne ser jag en aflaegsen hamn (Bottiger)
Ref. 90, 95, 103, 297

HOLMES, Augusta Mary Anne (pseud. Hermann Zenta)
French pianist and composer of Irish parentage. b. Paris or Versailles, December 16, 1847; d. Paris, January 28, 1903. She was a child prodigy, excelling at the piano. She conducted an artillery band playing one of her own compositions when she was 11 years old. She studied harmony and counterpoint under Henry Lamber, organist of the cathedral at Versailles. She studied instrumentation under Klose and Saint-Saens and composition under Cesar Franck from 1875. Nearly all her compositions date from 1873. Pasdeloup performed the score of her work *Les Argonautes* at the Concerts Populaires in 1881; her *Ode triomphale* was played at the Paris Exhibition in 1889; *Hymne à la paix* was presented in Florence at the festivities held in honor of Dante in 1890. Cesar Franck dedicated an organ piece to her. On July 13, 1904 a monument to her memory was unveiled in the Saint-Louis Cemetery at Versailles. DISCOGRAPHY. PHOTOGRAPH.
Compositions
ORCHESTRA
Andante pastoral, symphony
Hymne à la paix, symphony
Orlando Furioso (Ariosto), symphony
Au pays bleu, symphonic suite (also 2 pf) (Heugel)
Andromede (Enoch)
Les Argonautes (1880) (Grus)
Hymne à Apollon
Irlande (1885) (Grus)
Lutece (1879) (2nd place 1878, hon mention 1880, in Prix de la Ville de Paris) (Grus)
Pologne (Grus)
CHAMBER
En mer (2 vln, vla, vlc and pf) (Heugel)
La nuit et l'amour (2 vln, vla, vlc and pf: also for pf)
Trois petites pièces (fl and pf)
PIANO
Andromede (4 hands) (Enoch)
Polonaise
Rêverie zigane pour piano (Paris, L. Grus, 1887)
VOCAL
La chanson de la caravane, cantata (ch and orch)
La fleur de neflier, cantata (T and ch) (Grus)
Lutin, cantata
La vision de la reine, cantata (w-soloists and ch) (Heugel)
Ludus pro patria, symphonic ode (ch and orch) (Grus)
Ode triomphale (solos, ch and orch) (Durdilly) (1st prize, 1889)
La vision de St. Therese (S and orch)
Danse d'almées (ch of 4 vces) (Durand)
Retour (ch of 4 vces) (Durand)
Dans les Bois, duet (Grus)

Hymne á Venus (Heugel)
Le Pays de rêve, duet (Durand)
Princesse neige, duet (Heugel)
Songs (vce and pf) incl.:
L'amour (Schirmer)
Asthore Machree (Grus, 1887)
Au dela (Enoch)
Barcarolle (Enoch)
Berceuse (Grus)
Le brick l'esperance (1886)
Chanson catalane (E. des Essarts) (1886)
Chant du cavalier, from Trois melodies (Louis de Lyvron) (G. Flaxland, 1867
Le clairon fleuri, chanson populaire (Grust, 1887)
Contes mystiques (1890)
Dans mon coeur (Enoch)
En chemin (Schirmer; Heugel; Schott)
Les exiles (Enoch)
Le fil du coeur (Heugel; Napoleao)
Garcia Perez (Heugel)
Guerriere (Heugel)
Les Heures: L'Heure rose; L'Heure d'or; L'Heure de poupré; L'Heure d'azur (Heugel)
Hymne à Eros (1886)
Hymne à soleil (Heugel)
Invocation (Durand)
La légende de l'amour
Message d'amour (Durand)
Nocturne (Durand)
Prière (Grus)
Plus loin (Grus)
Le ruban rose
Les sept ivresses (1883)
Les Serenades: Serenade printaniere; Serenade d'été; Serenade d'automne; Serenade d'hiver
Sirene (Durand)
Soir d'hiver
Tirele (Grus)
Ton nom? (Schott Frères; Napoleão)
Trois chansons populaires: Les trois pages; Mignonne; La princesse

SACRED
Contes devins: Les lys bleus; Les moutons des anges; Noël; Le chemin de ciel (Durand)
In exitu Israel, psalm (1973)
Veni Creator, motet (Grus)

OPERA
Astarte
Hero et Leandre (1874)
Lancelot du Lac
La Montagne Noire (Joubert)

Bibliography
Barillon-Bauche. *Augusta Holmès et la femme compositeur*. Paris: Librairie Fischbacher, 1912.
Imbert, H. *Nouveaux profils de musiciennes*. 1892.
Myers, R. *Augusta Holmès: A Meteoric Career*. 1967.
Pichard du Page, René. *Une musicienne versaillaise: Augusta Holmès*. Paris, 1921.
Theeman, Nancy Sarah. *Life and Works of Augusta Holmès*. Ph.D. dissertation, University of Maryland.

Ref. 2, 8, 13, 17, 20, 22, 26, 30, 44, 70, 88, 100, 102, 105, 106, 107, 108, 110, 113, 132, 165, 177, 225, 226, 247, 264, 276, 296, 297, 307, 347, 391, 394, 398, 431, 433, 563, 622, 646, 653

HOLMES, Mary
19th-century English composer.
Composition
PIANO
Songs without words (1850)
Publications
A Few Words About Music. London, 1851.
Ref. 276, 347

HOLMES, Shirlee McGee
20th-century accordionist and composer.
Compositions
VOCAL
Acceptance (vce and ens)
Morning song (vce and ens)
Song of spring (vce and ens)
Ref. AMC newsletter

HOLMSEN, Borghild
Norwegian pianist, music critic, teacher and composer. b. Christiania (later Oslo), 1865; d. Bergen, December 6, 1938. She studied under Reinecke and Jadassohn in Leipzig and Albert Becker in Berlin. She made her debut in Oslo in 1890, playing her own compositions. She taught at the Bergen Conservatory, was a music critic and toured Scandinavia and Germany as a concert pianist.
Compositions
CHAMBER
Sonata for violin in D-Major, op. 10
Piano pieces
Two romances (vln)
Other violin pieces
VOCAL
Songs
Ref. 17, 23, 105, 226

HOLST, Agnes Moller
American composer. b. Pittsburgh, PA, January 29, 1911. She gained her B.Mus. from the Carnegie Mellon University and did graduate work at the same university and at Arizona State University.
Compositions
CHAMBER
Three portraits of old Denmark (strs) (Pittsburgh, Volkweins)
Piano pieces
VOCAL
Four desert scenes (m-S)
Sleep sweetly (m-S)
Three miniatures (m-S)
Ref. composer, 347

HOLST, Imogen Clare
English pianist, authoress, conductor, teacher and composer. b. Richmond, Surrey, April 12, 1907; d. Aldeburgh, March 9, 1984. She was the daughter of the composer Gustav Holst. She began to study under her father and then attended St. Paul's Girls' School, where her father was music master. At the Royal College of Music she won a scholarship in composition in 1927. In 1966 she became a F.R.C.M. and in 1968 was awarded a Ph.D. from Essex University and in 1969 a D.Litt. She was a teacher in several schools and interested in folk song and dance. She was a member of the Royal Music Association. PHOTOGRAPH.
Compositions
ORCHESTRA
New work for viola and orchestra (1976)
Overture
Variations on Loth to depart (str qrt and 2 str orch) (O.U.P.)
CHAMBER
String quintet (1982) (Faber Music, 1984)
Four easy pieces (vla and pf) (Augener)
The fall of the leaf (vla) (O.U.P.)
Piano pieces
VOCAL
The sun's journey, cantata (w-ch, 2 fl, pf, perc and strs) (O.U.P.)
Out of your sleep (mix-ch) (Faber)
Twenty traditional British folksongs (ch)
Welcome joy and welcome sorrow (w-ch and hp or pf) (O.U.P.)
Homage to William (B and d-b)
SACRED
Twenty-four traditional carols (w-ch) (O.U.P.)
ARRANGEMENTS
Folk tunes
Publications
An ABC of Music. 1963.
Britten. 1966.
Byrd. 1972.
Conducting a Choir. 1973.
Gustav Holst: A Biography. O.U.P., 1938.
Henry Purcell: Essays on His Music.
Holst. 1974.
The Music of Gustav Holst. O.U.P., 1951.
Thematic Catalogue of Gustav Holst's Music. 1974.
Tune. 1962.
Bibliography
Composer. No. 58, summer 1976.
Ref. composer, 2, 8, 44, 68, 70, 81, 94, 177, 206, 457, 622

HOLST, Marie Seuel. See SEUEL-HOLST, Marie

HOLT, Nora Douglass
Contemporary black American composer.
Composition
MISCELLANEOUS
A Negro dance (Music and Poetry, ca. 1921)
Ref. Prof. D.R. de Lerma (Baltimore)

HOLT, Patricia Blomfield. See BLOMFIELD-HOLT, Patricia

HOLTHUSEN, Anita Saunders
20th-century American teacher and composer. b. Milwaukee, WI. She composed one piano work and one choral work.
Ref. 347

HOME, Anne. See HUNTER, Anne

HONEGGER-VAURABOURG, Andree
French pianist and composer. b. Toulouse, September 8, 1894. She studied at the Toulouse Conservatory and then under Widor, Dallier, Caussade and Nadia Boulanger (q.v.) in Paris. She studied the piano under Pugno from 1908 to 1913. In 1919 she won the Conservatory prize. She married the composer Arthur Honegger. She and her husband performed with "Les Six".
Compositions
ORCHESTRA
Interieur
Prelude
CHAMBER
String quartet
Sonata (vln and pf)
PIANO
Sonata
Other pieces
Ref. 2, 105

HONG, Sung-Hee
Korean assistant professor and composer. b. January 1, 1939. She graduated from university with a master's degree and thereafter attended the Staatliche Hochschule fuer Musik in Cologne. She is currently the assistant professor of the department of composition at Eqha Womens University. She has composed works for orchestra and vocal works.
Ref. Korean National Council of Women

HOOD, Francis. See HOOD, Helen

HOOD, Helen (Francis)
American pianist, teacher and composer. b. Chelsea, MA, June 28, 1863; d. Brookline, MA, January 22, 1949. She studied in Boston under B.J. Lang (piano), G.W. Chadwick (composition) and J.C. Parker and John K. Paine (harmony). She also studied the piano in Berlin under Moszkowski and Philipp Scharwenka. She obtained a diploma and medal from the World's Columbian Exposition, Chicago.
Compositions
CHAMBER
String quartet
Trio (vln, vlc and pf)
Five pieces (vln and pf)
Novelette in A (pf) (Woolhouse; Schirmer)
Romance, op. 19 (org) (Woolhouse; Schirmer)
Two suites (vln)
VOCAL
Christmas time
Cornish lullaby
The dandelion
A disappointment
Maidens and swans
Message of the rose
The old oak tree
The robin, part song
Shepherdess
Skating
Sleighing
Song etchings, set of 6 songs (Schmidt)
The violet
SACRED
Te Deum in E-Flat
THEATRE
Die Bekehrte (Ries & Erler)
Ref. 22, 70, 102, 276, 292, 297, 347, 415

HOOPER, Carolyn. See Addendum

HOOPER, Mrs. M. See PENNA, Catherine

HOOVER, Katherine
American flautist, lecturer and composer. b. Elkins, WV, December 2, 1937. She studied the flute under Joseph Mariano at the Eastman School of Music where she received a performer's certificate and B.M. (music theory). She received her M.A. (music theory) from the Manhattan School of Music. She also studied the flute under William Kincaid in Philadelphia. She was active as a concert artist with leading orchestras and appeared many times under the auspices of the Concert Artists Guild and in numerous radio and television programs. She received the National Endowment composers' grant and an ASCAP award. She originated the Festivals I, II and III of Women's Music, covering the work of 55 historical and contemporary women composers. Her *Trio* was voted one of the ten outstanding American chamber works of 1978 to 1979 by the Kennedy Center Friedheim Contest judges. She was on the theory and flute faculty of the Manhattan School of Music. DISCOGRAPHY. PHOTOGRAPH.
Compositions
ORCHESTRA
Concerto (fl, perc and str orch) (1980)
Nocturne (fl, perc and str orch) (1977)
CHAMBER
Homage to Bartok (picc, ob, cl, bsn and hn) (1976)
Variations on a Bach theme (brass qnt) (1974)
Divertimento (fl, bsn, vla and vlc) (1975)
Saxophone quartet (1980)
Sinfonia (bsn qrt) (1976)
Trio (pf, vln and vlc) (1978)
Trio for flutes (1974)
Two dances (fl, ob and gtr) (1976)
Duets (fl) (1977, 1979)
Medieval suite (fl and pf) (1980)
On the betrothal of Princess Isabella of France, age six (fl and pf)
Reflections (fl)
Set for clarinet
PIANO
Allegro molto (1978)
Chase (1977)
Forest bird (1980)
Lament (1977)
Three plus three (1977)
VOCAL
Four English songs: Heart's music; Prayer of Mary, Queen of Scots; Sabrina fair (Milton); Some have too much (mix-ch, ob, cor anglais and pf)
Lake Isle of Innisfree (Yeats) (mix-ch and pf) (1973)
Syllable songs (w-ch and woodblock) (1977)
Canons (vces and lengths variable) (1972-1973)
From the testament of Francois Villon (Bar, bsn and str qrt) (1983) (comm Huntingdon Trio)
Lullay, lullay (S and pf) (1971)
Selima, ode on the death of a favorite cat drowned in a tub of goldfishes (S, cl and pf) (1979)
Seven haiku (S and fl) (1973)
To many a well (m-S or S and pf) (1978)
Wings: Acceptance; Proud songsters; Auspex (S, fl, cl, vln and pf) (1974)
SACRED
Psalm 23 (ch of 400 and orch) (comm Episcopal Diocese of New York)
Songs of joy, German carols: Come ye shepherds; Do you hear?; Of a young maid; Rejoice; Run, run all ye shepherds (trans composer) (mix-ch, 2 trp and 2 trb) (1974) (New York: C. Fischer, 1975)
Three medieval carols: Have mercy on me; Now make we mirthe; There is no rose (S, w-ch and fl) (New York: C. Fischer, 1972)
Four carols (S and fl) (1970)
Ref. ASCAP, 190, 228, 563, 625

HOPE, Douglas. See WILSON, Hilda

Hopekirk, Helen

Scottish/American pianist, lecturer and composer. b. Edinburgh, May 20, 1856; d. Cambridge, MA, November 19, 1945. She studied in Edinburgh under G. Lichtenstein and A.C. Mackenzie and then at the Leipzig Conservatory. She studied in Vienna under Leschetizky and made her first appearance at the Gewandhaus, Leipzig in 1878. She appeared in England at the Crystal Palace the following year and settled and lived in Vienna from 1887 to 1891, studying composition under Carl Nawratil and orchestration under Richard Mandl. She taught at the New England Conservatory, Boston from 1897 to 1901 and then in Brookline, MA. She was instrumental in popularizing the works of the modern French composers in America.

Compositions

ORCHESTRA

Concerto in D-Major (pf and orch)
Concertstueck (pf and orch) (1894)
Other pieces

CHAMBER

Melody (vln and pf)
Romance (vln and pf; also vlc and pf)
Sonata in D (vln and pf) (1893)
Sonata in E-Minor (vln and pf) (1891)

PIANO

Bouree (Cary)
Gavotte (G. Schirmer, 1885)
Iona memories, melodies (G. Schirmer, 1909)
Lento and allegro (Cary)
Norland eve (Boston Music, 1919)
Reveil fantaisie (Cary)
Reverie and dance
Robin Good-fellow (Boston Music, 1923)
Romance (Pond)
Serenade (London: Paterson, 1895)
Serenata, suite (Boston Music, 1917)
Shadows and brocade
Suite (Boston Music, 1917)
Sundown (G. Schirmer, 1909)
Tone pictures (Boston: E.C. Schirmer, 1930)
Three fantaisie pieces (Pond)
Three pieces (G. Schirmer, 1915)
Twenty Scottish folk songs
Two compositions (Boston Music, 1924)

VOCAL

My heart's in the Highlands (ch) (Thompson)
Slumber song (w-ch) (G. Schirmer, 1925)
A song of flowers (m-ch and pf) (Boston: A.P. Schmidt, 1887)
Over 100 songs (vce and pf) inc.:
Adieu (M. Wheeler) (A.P. Schmidt, 1887)
Blows the wind to-day (R.L. Stevenson) (G. Schirmer, 1915)
Bonnie wee thing, cannie wee thing (R. Burns) (Boston: O. Ditson, 1897)
Eldorado (M. Wheeler) (Schmidt, 1887)
A face (S and T) (Pond)
Highland baloo (R. Burns) (Ditson, 1897)
Hush-a-by (Ditson, 1905)
Jackie's (Jockie's) ta'en the parting kiss (Ditson, 1897)
A lament (Ditson, 1897)
Love me, love (Schmidt, 1886)
Love's lyric (S and T) (Pond)
Love's trust (S and T) (Pond)
Lullaby (S and T) (Pond)
The minuet (M.M. Dodge) (G. Schirmer, 1915)
My lady of sleep (New York: J.O. von Prochazka, 1885; Pond)
Reconciliation (Whitman) (G. Schirmer, 1915)
Requiescat (M. Arnold) (von Prochazka, 1886; Pond)
Rosebud (M. Wilder) (Schmidt, 1886)
Sleep my babe (E. McAdam) (Ditson, 1899)
Song of the Glen Dun (M. O'Neill) (G. Schirmer, 1915)
Song of early summer (S and T) (Pond)
St. Cecilia (M. Wheeler) (Schmidt, 1886)
Under the still, white stars (M. Wheeler) (vln and ob) (prize, Musical Record contest) (Ditson)
A voice in the night (M. Wheeler) (Schmidt, 1887)
The voice of the mountains (B. Ritchie) (G. Schirmer, 1915)
Five songs (F. MacLeod) (G. Schirmer, 1904)
Six poems (MacLeod) (G. Schirmer, 1907)

SACRED

God is a Spirit
The good Shepherd (H.H. Jackson) (vce and pf) (von Prochazka, 1886; Pond)
I to the hills will lift up my eyes
The Lord is my Shepherd

Bibliography

Cameron, Allan Gordon. *Helen Hopekirk.* A critical and biographical sketch.
Helen Hopekirk, pianist, 89, dead. New York Times, 20 November, 1945.
Helen Hopekirk, 1856-1945. Constance Huntingdon. Hall and Elen Ingersoll, Tetlow. Cambridge, MA,. Privately printed.

Ref. 2, 6, 8, 17, 23, 44, 70, 74, 89, 110, 226, 228, 276, 292, 297, 347, 361, 369, 415, 653

HOPKINS, Sarah

20th-century composer.

Compositions

ELECTRONIC

Cello timbre (amp vlc)
Seasons II (vlc and tape delay)

Ref. *Composer* (London)

HOPPE, Clara

German singer, teacher and composer. b. Samter, Poznan, December 7, 1857. She studied singing under Teschner in Berlin from 1877 to 1879, at the Leipzig Conservatory from 1879 to 1880 and under Adolf Schultze, Blumner and Amalie Joachim (q.v.) in Berlin. She studied composition under Dippe, Wilhelm Berger, Hugo Kaun and Friedrich E. Koch. She taught singing in Merseburg from 1877 to 1883, in Frankfurt from 1883 to 1903 and in Berlin.

Compositions

VOCAL

Achtzehn Lieder, ops. 4-8 (composer) (Berlin: E. Alert)
Aufs wilde Dirndl (composer) (vce and pf)
Deutsche Frauen, op. 10 (composer) (vce and pf) (E. Alert)
Drei Lieder, op. 9 (composer)
Greenhild, die Seherin (composer) (vce and pf)
Lieder, ops. 1-3 (composer) (Leipzig: Ries & Erler)
Zwei Lieder, op. 11 (Manter, Graziella)

SACRED

Zwanzig Kirchenlieder (m-ch) (Breslau: Handel)

Ref, 70, 111, 226, 297

HORAK, Hilda

B. 1914.

Compositions

PIANO

Etudes (Ljubljana: Drzavna Zal. Slov, 1984)

Ref. Otto Harrassowitz (Wiesbaden)

HORI, Etsuko

Japanese composer. b. Kyoto, February 22, 1943. She graduated from the Graduate School of Tokyo University of Fine Arts in 1970, having won second prize in the chamber music section of the 34th Music Competition in 1965. She is a member of the Japanese Association of Contemporary Music. She composes chamber works.

Ref. Yamaha Music Foundation

HORNBACK, Sister Mary Gisela

20th-century American harpist, organist, pianist, choir director, lecturer and composer. She obtained her B.M. in 1928 at the Cincinnati Conservatory, studying composition under George Leighton, orchestration under Peter Froehlich and the organ under Parvin Titus. She received her M.M. in 1930 at the American Conservatory, Chicago, studying composition under Dr. Leo Sowerby and the organ under Dr. William Middelschulte. From 1902 to 1913 she was a music teacher at the Notre Dame Convent in Milwaukee and from 1913 to 1929 director of the Notre Dame Conservatory at Quincy, IL.

Compositions

SACRED

Mass in honor of our Lady (1932)
Puer natus est nobis (J. Fischer, 1942)
The transitus, or Commemoration of the death of St. Francis (1940)
Hymns (Latin and English)

Publications

Mount Mary Hymnal. 1937.
Mount Mary Motet Book. 1947.

Ref. 496

HORROCKS, Amy Elsie

English pianist, teacher and composer. b. Rio Grande-do-Sul, Brazil, February 23, 1867. She studied the piano and composition at the Royal Academy of Music, London in 1882 under A. Schloesser and F.W. Davenport.

She won the Potter Exhibition prize in 1888 and the Bennett prize in 1889. She taught the piano in London and gave chamber concerts in Princess Hall, 1891. She became a F.R.A.M. in 1895. She later returned to Brazil.

Compositions

ORCHESTRA

Undine, legend, op. 16 (1897)

CHAMBER

Variations for piano and strings, op. 11
Eight variations on an original theme (vln, vla, vlc and pf)
Piano trio in B-Flat (1887)
Cradle song and scherzo a la mazurka (vln and pf)
Irish melody and country dance (vlc and pf)
Rigaudon (vln and pf) (Augener)
Sonata (vlc and pf)
Trois pieces faciles: Barcarolle; Elegie; Mazurka (vln and pf) (Schott)

PIANO

Berceuse, op. 4, no. 1
Margory gavotte (Hopwood)
Waltz, op. 4, no. 2

VOCAL

Spring morning, op. 22, cantata
Wild swans, cantata
Two fairy songs (S, w-ch, hp, tri and strs)
Songs incl.:
Album of 12 songs, op. 6
Amoret (Boosey)
Ashes of roses, a love song
Bird and the rose (Boosey; Williams; Church; Ditson; Schirmer)
Blackbird (2 w-vces) (Augener)
Come love, across the sunlit land, duet (Williams)
Dancers (2 w-vces)
Eight vocal canons, op. 15
Fairy cobbler, duet (Augener)
Five vocal duets
Fourteen songs, op. 20
Golden eyes (Boosey)
Harebell curfew, duet (Augener)
Irish love song
July the peddlar (Chappell)
Lady of Shallot recitation (Boosey)
Love's requiem (vce and vlc obb)
A midsummer song (Augener)
Nightingale (Boosey)
Prithee maiden (Boosey)
Rigadoon (Chappell)
Sing heigh-ho! (Boosey)
Six Greek love songs (Boosey)
Six songs, op. 10
Sweet dreams (2 w-vces) (Augener)
To her I love
Tragedy, duet (Augener)
Winds (treble vces)

THEATRE

Idyll on New Year's Eve (1890)

Ref. 6, 226, 297, 347, 465

HORSLEY, Imogene

American musicologist, writer and composer. b. Seattle, WA, October 31, 1931. She composed piano works.
Ref. 347

HORST, Carita von

German composer. b. December 4, 1871. She composed operettas and incidental theatre music.
Ref. 226

HORTENSE DE BEAUHARNAIS. See HORTENSE, Queen of Holland

HORTENSE, Queen of Holland (Hortense de Beauharnais)

B. Paris, April 10, 1783; d. Arenenberg, October 5, 1837. The step-daughter of Napoleon, she married his brother, Louis Napoleon who became king of Holland. The marriage was unhappy and she amused herself with music, drawing and young officers. She wrote songs and romances for which Plantade or Carborel wrote the accompaniment. Her *Partant pour la Syrie* became the national song of France during the reign of her son Napoleon III, although the composer Drouet claimed it as his own. *Le bon chevalier* was used by Franz Schubert as the basis for his *Variations on a French song*. DISCOGRAPHY.

Compositions

BAND

Marche imperiale, fanfare (Tilliard)

VOCAL

Hymne à la gloire, cantata (Belmontel) (ch and orch)
Autre ne sert (vce and pf) (Heugel)
Chant de Berceau (vce and pf) (Heugel)
Devine-moi (vce and pf) (Heugel)
Je l'ai reçu (vce and pf) (Heugel)
Partant pour la Syrie
Romances: Le bon chevalier; N'oublieras-tu; Une larme
Numerous other songs and romances in French and German (Breitkopf; Heugel; Schott)

Ref. 8, 13, 105, 297, 347, 361, 398, 563

HORTON, Marguerite Wagniere

American pianist and composer. b. Florence, September 25, 1875. She studied under Sgambati, the Buonamicis and Reginald de Koven and made her debut in Geneva in 1915. She appeared in recitals in the United States. She composed piano and violin pieces and songs.
Ref. 226

HOSEY, Athena

20th-century American composer.

Composition

FILM MUSIC

A New Life Style (1970)

Ref. 326

HOTCHKISS, Evelyn Dissmore

20th-century American composer. She composed opera and songs.
Ref. 40, 347

HOULLIER, Beatrice. See SIEGRIST, Beatrice

HOUSE, L Marguerite

20th-century American cellist, authoress, choral conductor, associate professor and composer. b. St. Louis, MO. She studied at Cincinnati Conservatory and received her B.A. from Oxford College and M.M. in voice and the cello from Northwestern University. She continued her studies at Columbia University and abroad. She was an associate professor of music education at the Florida State College for Women, 1928 to 1930. She assisted in organizing the Symphony Orchestra of Tulsa, OK, and directed choirs. She is a member of ASCAP.

Compositions

VOCAL

Almost spring (w-ch) (Belwin, 1957)
Burro mio (2-part chil-ch) (Fox, 1963)
Daffodils (w-ch) (Bourne, 1953)
Drowsy tune (ch) (1946)
Jamaica farewell (mix-ch or m-ch or w-ch) (Fox, 1961)
Lonesome road (mix-ch or w-ch or boys' ch) (Hoffman, 1951)
Looking up at the stars (mix-ch) (Kjos, 1969)
On that night (with Jean Cook) (w-ch) (1972)
Recuerdo (mix-ch) (1971)
Remember the day? (w-ch) (Bourne, 1952)
The Russian cavalry song (ch) (1945)
Sea song (w-ch) (Fox, 1968)
Soon we will be free (w-ch) (Kjos, 1973)
This parrot (2-part chil-ch) (Fox, 1963)
Timber (with Phyllis Hoffman) (boys' ch or qrt) (Fox, 1954)
We three (2-part chil-ch) (Warner, 1971)
Who's dancing with me (Papa Haydn's dance) (mix-ch) (Interlochen, 1960)

SACRED

Chimes of Christmas, 2-part cantata (narr) (1975)
God of the Wilderness (mix-ch) (Kjos, 1969)
I never knew how great my word could be (mix-ch) (Bourne, 1956)
A joyous Easter Song (mix-ch) (Hoffman, 1952)
Our Thanksgiving Day (mix-ch) (Frank, 1954)
Prayer for today (with P. Hoffman) (mix-ch) (Schmitt, 1956)
Rise up shepherds (mix-ch or boys'-ch) (Hoffman, 1954)

OPERA

The Tourists, chamber opera (1st prize, MI, Federated Music Clubs competition, 1973)

OPERETTA
A New Dawn (Boston, 1946)
Professor Owl (Hoffman, 1971)
Sliding down a Moonbeam (Hoffman, 1950)
The Stockings Were Hung (Presser, 1958)
Trimming the Christmas Tree (Hoffman, 1972)
Publications
My Music Book. 2 vols. 1936, 1939.
O Say, Can You Hear? Music appreciation books in 3 vols. 1947.
Ref. 141, 347, 397, 496

HOUSMAN, Rosalie

American pianist, lecturer, musicologist and composer. b. San Francisco, June 25, 1888; d. New York, October 28, 1949. She studied in Germany and under Arthur Foote, Ernest Bloch, Oscar Weil, Walter Henry Rothwell. Her works have been performed in concert and over the radio in England and the United States.
Compositions
CHAMBER
Suite (vln and pf)
Piano pieces
VOCAL
Color sequence (S and small orch)
Choral music
Pieces of jade
Songs
SACRED
Synagogue service
Ref. 22, 70, 142, 226

HOVDA, Eleanor

American pianist, choreographer, dancer, lecturer and composer. b. Duluth, MN, March 27, 1940. She did undergraduate work at Randolph-Macon Women's College and at the American University receiving her B.A. (piano, 1963). After graduation she studied composition at Yale University School of Music and at the University of Illinois. She attended Stockhausen's classes at the Cologne Kurse fuer neue Musik and then in New York, and received an M.F.A. in dance at Sarah Lawrence College in 1971. She continued her studies in dance music composition under Lucia Dlugoszewski (q.v.) and studied modern dance technique in the Erick Hawkins and Merce Cunningham Studios. Other teachers of composition and dance music were Esther Ballou (q.v.), Gordon Smith, Mel Powell, Kenneth Gaburo, Allan Thomas, Ruth Lloyd, Norma Dalby, Bessie Schoenberg, Phyllis Lamhut and Don Redlich. She teaches modern dance at the College of St. Scholastica and is an executive director of the Arrowhead Regional Arts Council. She lectured at Sarah Lawrence College and the Wesleyan University. Her work has been performed widely in the United States and recorded and broadcast in Germany, Holland, Sweden, France, Italy and Canada. She was a recipient of one of the 1984 McKnight fellowships. PHOTOGRAPH.
Compositions
CHAMBER
Air moment (33 fl) (1973)
Journeymusic (fl, cl, vln, d-b, pf and perc) (1981)
Waveschart (fl, cl, pf, c-bsn and perc) (1970)
Ondes doubles I (ondes Martenot, hp, vla and fl) (1971)
The Lion's Head (fl, cl, vln and vlc) (1972)
Embermusic (pf with glass and rubber friction mallets) (1978)
Spring music with wind (pf with glass and rubber friction mallets) (1973)
Ondes doubles II (ondes Martenot and gtr) (1972)
Breathing (fls) (1983)
Music from several summers (2 d-b) (1972)
Ariadnemusic (1984)
VOCAL
Char's first songbook (S, fl, 2 bowed flexitones, c-bsn and bowed perc) (1971)
DANCE SCORES
Trails III/crossings (perc, cl, c-bsn and bird chorus) (1983)
THEATRE
Bones, cascades, scapes (perc) (1974)
Butterfly (tape) (1973)
Cymbalmusic/centerflow II (doubled bowed cymbals and audience) (1983)
Earthrunner (fl, d-b and timp) (1966)
Firefall (vce, fl, d-b and perc) (1974)
Folio (vce, pf, perc, rec, cl, dulcimer and tape) (1980)
Greensward (vce and perc) (1976)
Gargoyles (tape and d-b) (1971)
Long-distance (pf, bamboo fl, perc and tape) (1978)
Longrun (vces, fl and glass har) (1976)
Match (vce, gongs, vfl and gtr) (1972)
Movement projects (vce and perc) (1972)
Odoori (vce, glass har, fls and zither) (1972)
Oracles (tape, fl, d-b and perc) (1975)
The proclamation (fl) (1966)
Rashena's tale (rec, pf and perc) (1979)
Regions (tape, fl and perc) (1971)
Season of earth-hush (vce, cym and gongs) (1973)
Smelting song (vce, cl, pf and perc) (1981)
Solo for Anthony (vce, fl, d-b and tape) (1973)
Some of us, most of the time (vce, gtr, fl and perc) (1972)
Sphynx (vce, cym, gtr and Thai mouth org) (1973)
Sphynx's night out (perc) (1974)
Threading the wave (pf and perc) (1976)
Welkwoman (fl, d-b and ceramic perc) (1970)
Whitewave (pf) (1978)
ELECTRONIC
Lady Astor (acoustic gtr) (1975)
Ref. composer

HOVORST, Mme. Gouban d'

19th-century Hungarian composer.
Compositions
PIANO
Sonata in A-Flat (2 pf) (Vienna: Haslinger)
Other pieces
Ref. 226, 276

HOWARD, Beatrice Thomas

American authoress, teacher and composer. b. Eutaw, AL, March 7, 1905. She was a school principal for 20 years and directed local shows for films and TV.
Compositions
VOCAL
Burnt sand
Naughty winds
SACRED
Christ is my pilot
In Bethlehem
Let us all give thanks
Mary, Mother of Jesus
We will come rejoicing
Ref. 39, 646

HOWARD, Helen Willard (Mrs. Nelson W.)

American pianist, authoress, lawyer and composer. b. Auburn, MA, 1872. She was educated at Bates College, Lewiston and Boston University.
Compositions
PIANO
Romance des fleurs (1954)
Southern melodies
Ref. 374

HOWARD, Mrs. Nelson W. See HOWARD, Helen

HOWE, Mary Alberta Bruce (Mary Carlisle Howe) (Mrs. Walter Bruce)

American pianist, singer and composer. b. Richmond, VA, April 4, 1882; d. Washington, DC, September 14, 1964. She studied the piano in Dresden under Richard Burmeister and at the Peabody Institute of Music, Baltimore, MD, under Ernest Hutcheson and Harold Randolph. She later returned to the Peabody Institute to study composition under Gustav Strube, obtaining a diploma in 1922. She undertook further composition study in Paris under Nadia Boulanger (q.v.). She appeared with chamber ensembles and in programs of two piano music and formed a madrigal singing group with her three children. She was national chairlady of orchestras in the National Federation of Music Clubs for four years and served on the board of directors of the Friends of Music at the Library of Congress and the National Symphony Orchestra. Her orchestral works have been played by leading symphony orchestras and over the radio. In 1961 she received an honorary doctorate from George Washington University. DISCOGRAPHY.
Compositions
ORCHESTRA
Castellana (2 pf and orch; also 2 pf) (1935) (G. Schirmer)
American Piece (What Price Glory) symphonic poem (1935) (G. Schirmer)
Paean, symphonic poem (1940) (C. Fischer)

Rock, symphonic poem (1955) (New York: Galaxy Music, 1965)
Agreeable overture for chamber orchestra (1949)
Allegro inevitabile (also str qrt)
Ambience
Attente
Axiom, free passacaglia and fugue (cham orch) (1932)
Berceuse (also pf; also vce and pf)
Coulennes, tableau de genre (cham orch) (1936) (C. Fischer)
Dirge (1931) (G. Schirmer)
Fugue (str orch) (1922)
Mists
Ombrine
Poema (also S, m-S and cham orch) (1924)
Polka, waltz and finale (also as polka and waltz) (1946)
Potomac, suite (1940) (C. Fischer)
Sand (also cham orch; also 2 pf) (1928, 1932) (G. Schirmer)
Scherzo (also pf qnt)
Spring pastoral (also cham orch; also w-ch and orch or pf) (1936, 1938)
Stars (orch or cham orch; also 1 or 2 pf) (1937) (Edition Musicus)

CHAMBER
For four woodwinds and French horn
Four pieces for wind quintet
Suite for piano quintet (1923)
Suite for quintet (1928)
Suite for wind quintet
Fugue (str qrt)
Fugue in A-Minor (str qrt)
Grave piece for strings from a devotion by John Donne (str qrt) (1951)
Cancion romanesca (str qrt) (1928)
Quatuor (str qrt) (1931)
Quatuor II (str qrt)
Quatuor III (str qrt)
Scherzo and fugue for string quartet (1936)
String quartet (Yaddo) (1940)
Three pieces after Emily Dickinson (str qrt) (1941)
Piano trio
Suite mélancolique (1931) (pf, vln and vlc)
Ballade fantasque (vlc and pf) (1930)
Interlude between two pieces for alto recorder and harpsichord (also fl and pf) (1942)
Patria (pf and vlc or vla)
Sonata (vln and pf) (New York: Henmar Press, 1962; C.F. Peters, 1962)
Sonata in D (vln and pf) (1922)
Three restaurant pieces: Melody at dusk; Fiddler's reel; Valse (vln and pf) (Fiddler's reel also pf and orch; also orch)
G string fugue (vln)

ORGAN
Elegy (New York: H.W. Gray, 1948)
For a wedding

PIANO
Three Spanish folk tunes: Habanera de Cinna; Petenera; Spanish folk dance (2 pf) (Boston Music, 1926)
Trifle (2 pf)
Andante douloureux (G. Schirmer)
Blue hills, sketch (1941)
Clog-dance (Possum-a-lah)
Estudio brillante
Intermezzo in B-Flat Major
Intermezzo in E-Flat Major
Nocturne (G. Schirmer, 1925)
Prelude (G. Schirmer, 1925)

VOCAL
Chain gang song (m-ch or mix-ch and pf or orch; also opt S, A and ch a-cap) (G. Schirmer, 1925)
Irish lullaby (H.C. Crew) (vce and pf or orch; also vce, fl or cl, hn and strs) (C. Fischer, 1948)
Liebeslied (Rilke) (vce and orch; also vce and pf)
Song of Palms (O'Shaughnessy) (w-ch and pf or orch) (G. Schirmer, 1938)
To the unknown soldier (N.G. Lely) (T and pf or orch) (G. Schirmer, 1945)
When I died in Berners Street (E. Wylie) (Bar and pf or orch) (1936) (G. Schirmer, 1947)
Catalina (mix-ch and pf) (1924) (C. Fischer, 1948)
Cavaliers (m-ch and pf) (1933)
A devotion (J. Donne) (m-ch a-cap) (1944) (H.W. Gray, 1955)
Drink to me only (mix-ch and pf) (1921) (G. Schirmer)
Great land of mine (mix-ch or vce and org or pf) (New York: Mercury Press, 1955)
Music when soft voices die (Shelley) (ch)
Prophecy, 1792 (W. Blake) (m-ch and pf; also m-ch and wind insts; m-ch and pf, brass and perc) (1943) (H.W. Gray, 1955)
Robin Hood's heart (m-ch and pf) (1936)
Williamsburg Sunday (K.G. Chapin) (mix-ch a-cap) (C. Fischer, 1955)
Yule catch (w-ch) (1940)
Let us walk in the white snow, velvet shoes (E. Wylie) (vce and pf or str qrt) (C. Fischer, 1948)
Little elegy (E. Wylie) (vce and pf or str qrt) (G. Schirmer, 1929)
The little rose (G.H. Conkling) (vce and pf or str qrt) (G. Schirmer, 1939)
Baritone songs (vce and pf) incl.:
The rag picker (1932) (Galaxy, 1959)
English songs, part I (vce and pf) incl.:
The bailey and the bell (1950) (Galaxy, 1959)
Go down, death (J.W. Johnson) (vce and pf)
Needle in the knee: A travesty (vce and pf)
Ripe apples (L. Speyer) (vce and pf) (G. Schirmer, 1939)
English songs, part II (vce and pf) incl.:
Three hokku from the Japanese (Galaxy, 1959)
English songs, part III (vce and pf) incl.:
The horseman (Walter de la Mare) (also w-ch or m-ch and pf)
O mistress mine (Shakespeare) (G. Schirmer, 1925; Galaxy, 1959)
French songs (vce and pf) incl.:
Berceuse cossaque (Galaxy, 1959)
German songs (vce and pf) (Galaxy, 1959) incl.:
Mein Herz
Ueber allen Gipfeln (Goethe) (also vlc and pf)
Seven Goethe songs (m-S and pf) (Galaxy, 1959)
Six songs for children (1941) (Silver Burdett)

SACRED
Poema (S, m-S and cham orch) (1924)
Christmas song (mix-ch and pf or org) (G. Schirmer, 1942)
Laud for Christmas (mix-ch a-cap) (G. Schirmer, 1936)
The pavilion of the lord (Domine Illuminatio) (mix-ch and org)
Song of Ruth (mix-ch and org) (G. Schirmer, 1940)
Hymne (J. Donne) (1943)
The Christmas story (L. Ourusoff) (vce and org or pf) (C. Fischer, 1949)

BALLET
Cards, a game in one trick (orch; also 2 pf and drs) (1936)
Le jongleur de Notre Dame (1959)

Ref. 9, 17, 20, 22, 40, 44, 53, 70, 71, 81, 94, 96, 109, 124, 142, 146, 168, 173, 190, 193, 226, 228, 236, 266, 280, 292, 347, 415, 494, 496, 563, 610, 611, 622

HOWE, Mary Carlisle. See HOWE, Mary Alberta Bruce

HOWELL, Alice

20th-century American composer.

Composition

OPERA
Christmas in Coventry (Boston: C.C. Birchard, 1953)

Ref. 141

HOWELL, Dorothy

English pianist, professor and composer. b. Handsworth, February 25, 1898; d. January 12, 1982. She studied at the Royal Academy of Music, London from 1914 to 1919 under Percy Waller and Tobias Matthay (piano) and J.B. McEwen (composition). She was on the staff of the Royal Academy of Music from 1924 to 1970, first as a lecturer and then as professor of harmony and composition. She also taught at the Tobias Matthay School, London.

Compositions

ORCHESTRA
Concerto in D-Minor (pf and orch) (1923)
Lamia, symphonic poem (Keats) (1919) (Novello)
Divertissements
The rock, overture (1928)
Nocturne (str orch)

CHAMBER
Pieces incl.:
String quartet
Phantasy (vln and pf)
Rosalind (vln and pf)
Sonata (vln and pf) (1954) (Augener)

PIANO
Mazurka (2 pf)
Recuerdos Preciosos, No. 1, in B-Minor or E-Flat (2 pf)
Five studies, in D, F, G, G-Sharp
Hundresque
Pieces for the bairns: The paper boat; follow my leader; Lament for Cock Robin; Leap frog
Prelude in F-Minor
Spindrift
Toccata, in D, F, G, G-Sharp
Teaching pieces

SACRED
Four anthems of our Lady
Masses
BALLET
Koong Shee (1921)
Ref. BBC catalogue, 2, 7, 8, 9, 18, 22, 23, 44, 79, 94, 96, 105, 110, 172, 177, 226, 467

HOY, Bonnee L.
American cellist, clarinetist, flautist, organist, pianist, lecturer and composer. b. Jenkintown, PA, August 27, 1936. She studied the flute, the clarinet, the cello and the organ privately from 1951 to 1965 and had piano tuition under Florenga Decimo Levengood and Gaby Casadesus. She also studied at the Philadelphia Musical Academy from 1948 to 1949, 1954 to 1958 and 1960 to 1962 under Roy Harris and Joseph Castaldo. She won the New Century Club scholarship in 1954 and gold and silver medals in the piano from the Philadelphia Musical Academy, 1949 and 1956. She was awarded the Esther Cowen Hood Memorial scholarship in 1960 and 1961 and studied at the Fontainebleau Conservatory under Nadia Boulanger (q.v.). She obtained her B.Mus. and then did graduate studies at the Graduate School of Music, Temple University, 1967 to 1968. She taught the piano and composition privately and was on the piano faculties of the Philadelphia Musical Academy and St. Basil's Academy, 1962 to 1964. She also taught at the Settlement Music School from 1966 to 1973. In 1973 she arranged the WUHF-FM radio program series on poetry and the arts and was artistic director of the Philadelphia Contemporary Music Committee, 1972 to 1974. From 1975 she was on the board of directors of the National Association of American Composers and Conductors. She received a diploma of merit in the GB Viotti International Competition, Vercelli, Italy, 1974. DISCOGRAPHY.
Compositions
ORCHESTRA
Violin concerto (1963)
CHAMBER
Demmazia quintet (1973)
Piano quintet (1973)
String quartet (1972)
Piano trio (1968)
Lament for solo violin (1947)
PIANO
Piano sonata, op. 11 (1961)
Excursions, vol. 1 (1973)
Preludes (1969)
Storybook suite for children (1970)
Two sonatas (1970, 1971)
VOCAL
The spring of Earth's rebirth, oratorio (4 soloists, 2 ch and orch) (1971)
The Freeman celebration, songs and dances (S, fl, vlc and pf) (1971)
The hour-glass suite (S, T and cham ens) (1966)
Threnody (rec, vlc and drs) (1973)
Verlaine songs (1972)
The winter garden
SACRED
Quartet and gloria (ch a-cap) (1968)
Three sacred motets (ch a-cap) (1963)
BALLET
Pinocchio (1958)
MISCELLANEOUS
Circus music I
Ref. 142, 206, 477, 563, 622

HOYA, Katherina von
15th-century German nun and and composer. She was of noble birth and abbess of the Cistercian convent of Wienhausen, near Celle, from 1420 till 1470. The chronicles of the convent note that in 1470 the abbess had a book completed with antiphons and all kinds of songs for the choir to sing. The book, later known as the 'Wienhauser Liederbuch' was compiled by at least five nuns including Jungfer Gertrud Bunge (q.v.) and contained 37 low German, 17 Latin and six mixed Latin and German songs. One of the best pieces *No. 24* was composed by Katherina and *Nos. 13* and *25* are thought to be her work as well. The Wienhauser Liederbuch includes the oldest known version of the Vogelhochzeit, signed by the abbess.
Ref. 476

HOYLAND, Janet
20th-century American composer. She composed choral works.
Ref. 347

HOYLE, Aline Isabelle (nee van Barentzen)
American pianist and composer. b. Somerville, MA, July 7, 1897. She studied at the Paris Conservatoire and in Berlin. She made her debut in Dieppe in 1906 and after touring Europe made her New York debut in 1913. She composed piano pieces.
Ref. 226

HOYT, Marie Mack
American pianist, authoress, poetess and composer. b. Maine or Beaver Falls, 1893; d. 1965. She studied the piano with Selma Bonner and played with orchestras in New Brunswick and Pennsylvania. She wrote poetry and short stories.
Compositions
VOCAL
Songs incl.:
Beans (A. Guiterman)
Let's go on
Listen to my dream song (ch)
Old log cabin on the Tote road
Song of victory (E. Sprague)
Publications
We Gathered No Moss. Genealogy of the Sager and Cupples families.
Ref. 347, 374

HROSTWITHA (Roswitha) (pseud. of Helene von Rossow)
German poetess, writer and composer. b. 935, d. 1000. She was a nun of the Benedictine Convent of Gandersheim and the earliest German poetess. She wrote legends, dramas and poetry, some of which she set to music. Her works included dissertations on mathematics and music.
Composition
SACRED
Martyrertod einer Heiligen
Ref. 276, 433, 476, 624

HRUBY, Dolores Marie
American pianist, choral conductor, teacher and composer. b. Chicago, May 9, 1923. As a child she studied the piano under Louise Robyn. She gained her B.M. from the American Conservatory of Music where she studied under Leo Sowerby. At Michigan State University she was a pupil of H. Owen Reed and Jere Hutchinson and received her M.M. She conducted church and secular choirs and taught the piano.
Compositions
PIANO
Sailing
Sea gulls
Greek dance
VOCAL
Black is the color of my true love's hair, folk song (w-ch and pf) (Cincinnati: Westwood, 1969)
Peter Piper (w-ch or mix-ch and pf) (Westbury, NY, Pro Art, 1969)
Set down servant (w-ch and pf) (Cincinnati: World Library, 1966)
SACRED
And let us all be merry (ch and perc) (New York: Plymouth, 1970)
Christ the Lord is risen (ch, pf or org) (Minneapolis: Augsburg, 1976)
Come and praise the Lord with joy (mix-ch and perc) (St Louis: Concordia, 1974)
For the least of my brothers (mix-ch, pf or org) (Concordia, 1976
Gather around the Christmas tree (w-ch, pf or org) (Concordia, 1977)
He whom joyous shepherds praised (w-ch and perc) (Concordia, 1969)
The Holy Child (w-ch or mix-ch and org or pf) (Westbury, NY, Pro Art, 1972)
I lift my hands to the Lord most high (ch, pf, perc and fl) (Dallas: Choristers Guild, 1975)
Lord, let your hands
Love thy neighbor, mass (mix-ch, org and cong) (Boston: McLaughlin & Reilly, 1967)
Sweet it is to praise the Lord (w-ch and handbells) (Chicago: Hope, 1969)
Three sacred songs (w-ch, pf and org) (Concordia, 1973)
Your holy Cross (w-ch or m-ch and org) (G.I.A, 1974)
Ref. 228, 494

HSIAO, Shu-Sien (Mme. Scherchen)
20th-century Chinese composer. She was the mother of the composer Tona Scherchen (q.v.).

HSU, Wen-Ying
American cellist, pianist, violist, musicologist, poetess, professor and composer. b. Shanghai, China, May 2, 1909. She became an American citizen in 1972. She studied at Yenching University, Peking from 1930 to

1933 and at the George Peabody College under Philip Slates, 1955. She obtained her M.Mus. from the New England Conservatory, Boston in 1959 having studied under Carl McKinley and Francis Judd Cooke. She studied under John Vincent at the University of California, Los Angeles, 1963 to 1964 and at the University of Southern California under Ingolf Dahl, Harold Owen and Frederick Lesemann, 1965 to 1966. She was professor of music at the National Institute of Fine Arts, Taiwan, 1958 to 1963 and the College of Chinese Culture, Taiwan, 1971 to 1972. She was awarded first prize from the Manuscript Club of Los Angeles in 1969, 1971 and 1980. From old Chinese books in the Yenching Harvard Institute and from the Library of Congress she discovered origins of Chinese music theory from the seven strings of the Ku-ch'in, an instrument known in China since the 29th-century B.C. and from which the seven-tone scales of Western music are derived. This research resulted in her paper, *Origin of music in China*, which was delivered at the annual meeting of the Society of Ethnomusicology in 1970 and approved and published in Taiwan in 1972. Besides composing and doing musicological research, Wen-Ying Hsu translated hundreds of the most famous Chinese poems into English and wrote original poetry in English. Her works have been broadcast in the United States and Taiwan. She received a special award for distinguished service to music from the National League of American Penwomen.

Compositions

ORCHESTRA

Cello concerto (1963)
Concerto for orchestra (1962)
Autumn moon festival (1961)
Dragon boat festival (1981)
March of Chinese cadets (also military band) (1966)
Sky maidens, dance suite (1980) (2nd prize, biennial conference of National League of American Penwomen)

CHAMBER

Percussions east and west (8 players) (1966)
Sonorities of Chinese percussions with tune of three plum blossoms (8 players; also perc) (1971, 1968)
Travelers suite (pf qnt)
String quartet No. 1 (1958)
String quartet No. 2 (1968)
Evening prayer (2 fl and vln) (also vce) (1951)
Light of God (2 fl and vln) (also vce) (1960)
Parting song (2 fl and cl) (also vce) (1956)
Theme and variations (fl, cl and bsn) (1964)
Trio for violin, cello and piano (1955)
Capriccio (fl and pf) (West Babylon, NY: H Branch, 1977)
Violin suite (vln and pf) (1966)
Air on G string (vln) (1956)
Impromptu (cl) (1956)
Impromptu No. 1 (vln) (1956)
Longing (vln) (1951)
Pieces for beginners (vln) (1974)

PIANO

Fantasia (2 pf) (1955)
Little soldier's march (2 pf) (1952)
Etude (1952)
Impromptu (1980) (1st prize, biennial conference of National League of Penwomen)
Jade fountain (1958)
Nocturne
Perpetual momentum (1973)
Piano suite (1967)
Running water (1952)
Scenes in a Chinese village (1958)
Second accompaniments to Spindler's sonatina, op. 157, no. 3 and 4 (1951, 1954)
Sonata (1958)
Sonata No. 1 (1972) (H. Branch, 1977)
Sound of autumn (1974) (Branch, 1977)
Suite (1964)
Swaying willow (1958)
Variations (1956)

VOCAL

Song of old fisherman (B and orch or vln) (1978)
Songs of sung cycle (S and orch) (1972)
Vocal series No. 1 (S and orch) (1972)
Dreams of longing (w-ch) (1974)
Song and sound (S and m-ch) (1966)
Vocal series No. 3 (S, T, mix-ch and pf) (1974)
Prelude to the water tune (S and ens incl. Chinese perc) (1956)
At a glance, in Chinese (vce and pf) (1960)
The founders (vce and pf) (1978)
Let me serve (vce and pf) (1978)
Longing for home (vce and pf)
Regret (vce and pf) (1955)
Ring out Liberty Bell (vce, hp and vibe) (1976)
Song of Ching Hai (vce and pf) (1956)
Songs of nature (S, perc and pf) (1974)

SACRED

Alleluia (1960)
Light of God, in English and Chinese (vce, pf and fl) (1960)
Merciful Father (w-ch and pf; also 3 w-vces) (1974, 1980)
Praise the Lord (hon mention, National League of American Penwomen) ,
Three anthems: Pray our Lord (1951); Jesus our Saviour (1958); Good News for Christmas (1965)

OPERA

Cowherd and Weaving Maiden, in 1 act (composer) (ww, hp, xy, glock, Chinese perc and strs) (1964)

Publications

The Ku Ch'in Theory book. In Chinese.
The Ku Ch'in. In English. Wen Ying Studio, Pasadena, 1978.
Origin of Music in China. Chinese Culture Quarterly, 1972.
The Cat and translations of Chinese poems.

Ref. composer, AMC newsletter, AWC IV 1980, 142, 206, 228, 474

HSUEH T'ao

Chinese poetess and songstress. b. 768; d. 831. The daughter of a government official in Ch'ang An, she became a singing girl at the age of ten and was soon recommended to sing at the imperial court. She served eleven regional commanders of Shu (Szechwan) and was famous for her beauty and talent. She and Yu Husuan-chi were the leading women poets of the T'ang Dynasty.

Compositions

VOCAL

The Chin River Collection, said to contain 500 lyrics, all except 90 had been lost by the beginning of the Ming dynasty (1368)

Ref. 464

HUALALAI. See PARIS, Ella Hudson

HUBER, Nanette

19th-century German writer and composer.

Compositions

PIANO

Variations for 4 hands, op. 5
Other pieces

Ref. 226, 276

HUBICKI, Margaret Olive (pseud. Katharine Lovell)

English pianist, violinist, teacher and composer. b. Hampstead, 1905. She studied the piano, the viola and composition and became an A.R.A.M. and an F.R.A.M. She won several awards for composition. She taught theory, harmony and composition and for a while taught at the Yehudi Menuhin School, London.

Compositions

ORCHESTRA

Irish fantasy (also pf)
Seven Shakespeare sketches (also pf)

CHAMBER

Four Scottish and Irish airs (vln, vlc and pf)
Green London (vln, vlc and pf)
A posy of pieces (vln and pf)
Three summer sketches (vlc and pf)

PIANO

April showers
Holiday music
Sussex pictures

SACRED

Two Christmas carols: By Thy birth Thou blessed Lord; Out of the Orient crystal skies (Bosworth, 1952)

TEACHING PIECES

Colour staff (pf)

Ref. composer, 94, 490

HUBNER, Ilse. See HUEBNER, Ilse

HUBLER, Evelyne

20th-century French composer.

Composition

BALLET

L'accompagne la danse, 2 vols (pf)

Ref. Billaudot

HUDSON, Mary

English organist and composer. b. London; d. London, March 28 1801. She studied under her father, Robert Hudson and was a church organist in London.

Compositions

VOCAL

Applaud so great a guest (set for five voices: The English version of the Latin epitaph on Purcell's gravestone)

SACRED

Hymns

Church music

Ref. 8, 276

HUEBNER, Caroline

18th-century German composer.

Compositions

PIANO

Sechs Polonaisen

Ref. 125

HUEBNER, Ilse

Austrian teacher and composer. b. Vienna, 1898; d. 1969. She composed piano pieces.

Publications

The Modern Pianist.

Musical Therapy Book.

Ref. 347, 433

HUEGEL, Margrit

Early 20th-century German pianist and composer. At the age of eight she was attempting to write polyphonic movements. Until 1914 she studied the piano and harmony under Blumer. She was then a pupil of Lucien Chevaillier and in 1916 began to study under the composer Hans Pfitzner whose influence on her later compositions was evident.

Compositions

ORCHESTRA

Scherzo

CHAMBER

String quartet

Scherzo aus der Sonate f moll (vlc and pf) (Fuerstner, 1929)

Suite (fl and pf)

Two sonatas (vlc)

VOCAL

Numerous songs in German and French

Ref. Strasbourg newspaper, 189

HUENERWADEL, Fanny

Swiss organist, pianist, singer and composer. b. Lenzburg, January 26, 1826; d. Rome, April 27, 1854. She studied the piano under L. Kurz, J.H. Breitenbach and P. Tietz and was a member of the singing institute founded by M.T. Pfeiffer in Lenzburg. She made her debut as a pianist in 1842 in Lenzburg and continued her piano studies after 1846 under Alexander Mueller and G. Rabe. In 1853 she went to Florence to develop her singing, but died of typhus in Rome at the age of 28.

Compositions

PIANO

Introduction, variations and rondo

Phantasie (1854)

VOCAL

Morgenlied (1854)

Sechs hinterlassene Lieder fuer Singstimme und Pianoforte (1855)

Ref. 101, 651

HUGEL, Margrit. See HUEGEL, Margrit

HUGH-JONES, Elaine

20th-century English pianist, accompanist, teacher and composer. b. London. She studied under Dr. F.W. Wadely, Harold Craxton, Julius Isserlis and she later studied composition under Sir Lennox Berkeley. She is an L.R.A.M. and A.R.C.M. She was director of music at Derby High School in 1949, Notre Dame Grammar School, Blackburn in 1952 and Kidderminster High School, 1955. From 1956 she was accompanist for Midland Region B.B.C. She was accompanist and piano teacher at Malvern Girls' College from 1963.

Compositions

CHAMBER

Children's suite (hp and pf trio) (1969)

Reverie (vlc and pf) (1974)

VOCAL

Chanticleer (1973)

Cornford cycle (Cont and pf) (1974)

Four American songs (1975)

Four De la Mare songs

Torches (1974) (OUP)

Two Sandburg songs (T and pf) (1974)

SACRED

Setting of Magnificat and Nunc Dimittis (1974) (comm Precentor of Coventry Cathedral)

The Son of God is born for all, carol (1972)

Sweet was the song the virgin sung, carol (1972)

Ref. composer, 77, 457

HUGHES, Harriet. See BROWNE, Harriet

HUGHES, Sister Martina

American pianist, professor and composer. b. Hibbing, MN, September 2, 1902. She obtained a B.A. from the College of St. Scholastica, Duluth, and a B.Mus. from Bush Conservatory, Chicago. She studied at the University of Michigan, Ann Arbor, under Ralph Doty and Louise Cuyler and received an M.A. in 1939. She then did graduate study at the University of Minnesota and under Bernard Rogers (composition) at the Eastman School of Music. She was head of the music department of the College of St. Scholastica from 1930 to 1951 and also emeritus professor of the piano, theory and composition.

Compositions

ORCHESTRA

April 1943 (1943)

Invocation (1946)

Revelation (1964)

Sounds heard from the shore of Lake Superior (1976)

CHAMBER

Occasional music (pf, vln, vla and vlc) (1947)

Jolie (fl, cl and pf) (1945)

Polytonal puck (fl, cl and pf)

Soliloquy for french horn (hn and pf) (1979)

Diko (pf) (1973)

VOCAL

The highwayman (mix-ch and orch) (1941) (MN, composers' award)

Stars (w-ch or mix-ch) (1972)

SACRED

The Christmas wind (w-ch and pf)

Mass in honor of Christ the King (unison w-ch or mix-ch or m-ch and org) (1964)

One thing I ask of the Lord (w-ch and org) (1979)

Psalm 26 (mix or w-ch and org) (1977)

Rejoice unto God (w-ch and pf) (Cincinnati: Willis Music, 1965)

Ref. composer, 142, 228, 347

HUGHEY, Evangeline Hart

20th-century American composer. She composed choral works and songs.

Ref. 40, 347

HUIDI, Teresa. See GUIDI LIONETTI, Teresa

HUJSAK, Joy Detenbeck (Ruth)

American harpist, organist, pianist, accompanist, lecturer and composer. b. Buffalo, NY, May 13, 1924. She studied the organ privately under Catherine Crozier from 1941 to 1945 and Harold Gleason, 1944 to 1945. She obtained a B.Mus. from the Eastman School of Music in 1945 and then attended the Lamont School of Music, University of Denver and the Schmitz School of Piano, San Francisco. In 1948 she received a scholarship from the Schmitz School of Piano. She studied privately under E. Robert Schmitz from 1947 to 1949 and Leo Smit from 1961 to 1965 and studied the harp under Marjorie Call, 1961 to 1974. She was a piano and harp lecturer at Mississippi University for Women, Columbus from 1946 to 1947; University of California Extension, San Diego from 1968 and San Diego State University in 1970. She also taught privately in Buffalo and was a piano soloist and accompanist. She composed harp pieces.

Ref. 40, 77

HUJSAK, Ruth. See HUJSAK, Joy Detenbeck

HULFORD, Denise Lovona

New Zealand pianist, singer, teacher and composer. b. October 24, 1944. She is an A.T.C.L. (piano performance, 1965); has a B.Mus. from Victoria University, Wellington (1982) and her M.Mus. (composition) from Auckland University. She studied the piano under Jim Powell at Wollongong Conservatory and singing under Joan Howard, Emily Mair and Dorothy Hopkins and sung in several choirs and operas. She taught the piano in Australia and New Zealand, 1968 to 1983. PHOTOGRAPH.

Compositions

VOCAL

Evolution! (T or narr and orch) (1985)

SACRED

The disciple's dream, cantata (S, T, ch, org, fl and vlc) (1985)
Psalm (S, mix-ch and insts) (1983)

ELECTRONIC

Mirage (1984)
Rhythmics (1984)
1985: Forty years plus (1985)

Ref. composer, 643

HULL, Anne

American composer. b. ca. 1888.

Composition

CHAMBER

Ancient ballad (pf ens)

Ref. 142

HULL, Kathryn B.

American pianist, music director, teacher and composer. b. Sanders, ID, June 14, 1928. She received her B.A. (music, 1949) from Pasadena College (now Point Loma College) and studied the piano privately under Elsie Cook Laraia, Sergei Tarnowsky and Frances Jensen Hedman. She taught the piano and theory at Pasadena College, schools and privately from 1949. She directed a video production of *A Christmas Carol* in 1975 and live musicals in Hollywood from 1968 to 1983.

Compositions

PIANO

He ain't done right by Nell (2 pf) (1982)
Soliloquy I, II, III (1985)

VOCAL

Create in me (vce and pf) (1973)
My creed (vce and pf) (1975)
Real to me (vces and pf) (1975)

INCIDENTAL MUSIC

The Lion, the Witch and the Wardrobe, overture (C.S. Lewis) (14 piece ens) (1983)
A Christmas Carol (Dickens) (1968)
Hudson Taylor's spiritual secret, songs (1980)

Ref. composer, 643

HULST, Margaret Gardiner

20th-century American composer. She studied in Washington, DC. She composed pieces for the piano, the organ, the violin and voice.
Ref. 226

HUME, Agnes

17th-century Scottish composer of songs.
Ref. 465

HUME, Phyllis

20th-century English composer.

Composition

THEATRE

Joy Time, musical comedy (London, 1919)

Ref. 431

HUMPHREY, Doris

American choreographer, dancer and composer. b. Oak Park, IL, October 17, 1895; d. New York, December 29, 1958. She helped to found the Juilliard Dance Theatre in 1955.

Compositions

DANCE SCORES

Dance rhythms (perc) (notation by Wallingford Riegger) (comm Bennington School of Dance) (1936)

Ref. 322

HUMPHREYS, Miss. See ALEXANDER, Cecil Frances

HUND, Alicia. See Addendum

HUNDT, Aline

German pianist, conductor and composer. b. Germany, 1849; d. Berlin, 1873. She studied under Liszt and conducted the first performance of her *Symphony in G-Minor* in Berlin, 1871, with great sucess.

Compositions

ORCHESTRA

March for grand orchestra (1871)
Symphony in G-Minor (1871)

CHAMBER

Capriccio à la hongroise, op. 12 (vln and pf) (Bote)
Traumgestalten, op. 6 (vla and pf)

PIANO

Fantaisie, op. 1 (Klemm)
Mazurka-caprice (Challier)
Polka (Challier)
Trois fantaisie-caprices, op. 2 (Klemm)

VOCAL

Champagnerlied (T, m-ch and orch)
Men's choruses
Alle gingen, Herz, zur Ruh (vce and pf) (Challier)
Horch, im Winde saeuseln sacht (vce and pf) (Challier)
Klinge, klinge mein Pandero (vce and pf) (Challier)
Wie waer' ein Maedchen, das Blumen pflueckte (vce and pf) (Challier)

Ref. 50, 129, 226, 276, 297, 415

HUNEEUS, Isidora Zegers de

Chilean composer. b. 1803; d. 1869. She composed songs.
Ref. 465

HUNERWADEL, Fanny. See HUENERWADEL, Fanny

HUNKINS, Eusebia Simpson

American authoress, lecturer and composer. b. Troy, OH, June 29, 1902; d. September 9, 1980. She studied at the Juilliard School of Music under James Friskin, Rubin Goldmark and Albert Stoessel and then Darius Milhaud, Ernest Hutcheson and Ernst von Dohnanyi. She attended classes at Aspen, Chautauqua, Tanglewood and Salzburg. She was a teacher at Cornell College before being appointed project director of Musical World of Ohio Broadcasts from 1972 to 1974. She was an authority on Appalachian folk music and from 1976, a compiler for the National Opera Association.

Compositions

CHAMBER

Dance suite (ww qnt) (1973)
Adagio (str qrt)
String quartet
Violin sonata

VOCAL

Americana (festive ch and orch or band) (1966) (New York: C. Fischer)
Shall I marry? (ch) (1961)
Wisps of smoke (fl, m-S and pf) (1973)

SACRED

Appalachian Mass (narr, S, ch and hps or org or pf) (C. Fischer)
What wondrous love (narr, mix-ch and org or pf) (C. Fischer, 1959)

BALLET

4-H on parade (1973)

OPERETTA

Child of Promise, children's dance opera (1964)
Forest Voices (1958)
Happy Land, our American heritage in story and song, in 1 act (1975)
The Magic Laurel Trees, for children (1974)
Maniian (1956)
Mice in Council, in 1 act (1956)
Reluctant Hero (1956)
Smoky Mountain, folk opera in 1 act (1954)
Spirit Owl, in 2 acts (1956)
What Have You Done to My Mountain? folk opera in 2 acts (1973)
Young Lincoln, folk opera (1956)
Young Lincoln II, folk opera in 1 act (1960)

Ref. MLA *Notes* June 1981, Working papers on Women in Music, 141, 142, 228, 347

HUNT, Gertrude
19th-century song writer.
Ref. 276

HUNTER, Alberta
20th-century American composer.
Composition
FILM MUSIC
Remember my Name
Ref. 497

HUNTER, Anne (nee Home) (Mrs. John) (alt. name Lady)
Scottish poetess and composer. b. Greenlaw, 1742; d. London, 1821. She wrote the words for Haydn's 12 canzonets in 1792, of which the first six were dedicated to her.
Compositions
VOCAL
Ah, could my sorrowful ditty, a favourite song written on Mr. Sheridan's new play of the Stranger (London: W. Rolfe, 1798)
Alknomook, The death song of the Cherokee Indians (New York: G. Gilbert; London: Longman & Broderip)
Bless'd those sweetly shining eyes, song (London: Lady's Magazine, June 1797)
Lady Ann Bothwell's lament
Nine canzonets for two voices and six airs with an accompaniment for the pianoforte (Longman and Broderip, 1782)
Queen Mary's lamentation
Second set of canzonets with an accompaniment for the harp or piano (Preston, ca. 1785)
Six ballads, with an accompaniment for the harp (ca. 1800)
Publications
Poems. 1 vol. 1801.
Ref. 6, 65, 85, 119, 125, 347

HUNTER, Henrietta Elizabeth
Late 18th-century Scottish composer.
Compositions
CHAMBER
The Grenadiers' march for the Edinburgh volunteers (pf and German fl) (Edinburgh and London: Corri Dussek & Co. 1795)
Ref. 65, 125

HUNTER, Hilda
English oboist, pianist, recorder player, lecturer and composer. b. December 6, 1919. She gained a Barber Scholarship to Birmingham University and from there received her B.A. and M.Sc. From the University of Wales she received her M.A. She lectured on the piano, the oboe, the recorder and other woodwind instruments. She composed for the recorder.
Publications
The grammar of music. 1952.
Teaching the recorder. 1977
Music for today's children. Co-author. 1974.
Ref. 457

HUNTER, Mrs. John. See HUNTER, Anne

HUNTINGTON, Mrs. See TURNER, Mildred Cozzens

HUNTINGTON-TURNER, Mildred Cozzens. See TURNER, Mildred Cozzens

HUNTLEY, Helen. See VAN DE VATE, Nancy Hayes

HUNTLEY, William. See VAN DE VATE, Nancy Hayes

HURAIRA
One of the Arabian songstresses belonging to Bishr ibn 'Amr, a dignitary of al-Hira in the pre-Islamic days of al-Numan III (d. ca. 602).
Ref. 171, 305

HURLEY, Susan
American composer. b. Massachusetts, March 30, 1946. She received a B.Mus. summa cum laude (theory and composition) from the University of Massachusetts, Amherst and M.Mus. (composition) from the Eastman School of Music, Rochester, NY. She was a doctoral student in composition at Indiana University, Bloomington. PHOTOGRAPH.
Compositions
ORCHESTRA
Prana (wind orch) (1981)
The Sybilline books, ballet (cham orch) (1977)
CHAMBER
String quartet No. 1 (1972)
String quartet No. 2 (1973)
String quartet (1979)
VOCAL
Visions, mystical poem (ch a-cap) (1980)
The Legend of Weeping Rocks (4 m-vces and ens) (1982)
Brightness (vce and pf) (1979)
ELECTRONIC
Nocturne (amp vln and sax) (1981)
Ref. composer, Working papers on Women in Music

HUSSAR, Malgorzata
20th-century Polish composer.
Compositions
CHAMBER
String quartet (1979) (joint 2nd place, Young Composers' Competition, Poland. 1979)
Ref. *Polish Music* 4/79

HUSTON, Carla. See BELL, Carla Huston

HUTET, Josephine
19th-century American composer.
Composition
PIANO
The sigma waltz
Ref. 228

HUTSON, Wihla L.
American composer. b. East Gary, IN, April 29, 1901. She studied privately and at Wayne University, Detroit. PHOTOGRAPH.
Compositions
ORGAN
Play something quick, 3 voluntaries for services (Harold Flammer)
Hymn tune voluntaries (Flammer)
Quiet spots (Lorenz Corporation)
SACRED
Over 100 choral pieces (Shawnee Press; Plymouth Music; Gray; Canyon Press)
Ref. composer

HUTTON, Florence Myra
New Zealand organist, pianist, violinist, playwright, poetess, singer, teacher and composer. b. March 24, 1931. She studied the piano from an early age and gained her L.T.C.C. in 1948. She obtained her B.Mus. from Auckland University in 1952. She taught in Durham and Leeds, England between 1954 and 1956, becoming teacher in charge of school music in junior schools, then head of the music department at a school in Lower Hutt. She is musical director of local primary school music festivals and theatrical companies. In 1980 she won a playwriting competition in New Zealand. She studied jazz and improvisation. PHOTOGRAPH.
Compositions
VOCAL
Gold fever (vce and pf) (1970)
SACRED
Setting of Psalm 121 (vce and pf) (1973)
THEATRE
Everyone makes Mistakes, musical comedy for children (1980)
James, musical comedy for children, on life of Captain Cook (1978)
Ref. composer

HYDE, Cicely

20th-century English composer.

Composition

CHAMBER

Slumber song (vln and pf)

Ref. 63

HYDE, Miriam Beatrice O.B.E.

Australian pianist, teacher and composer. b. Adelaide, January 15, 1913. She first studied under her mother and at the age of 12 won an Australian Music Examination Board scholarship to Elder Conservatory, Adelaide University. She studied under William Silver and obtained a diploma and then a B.Mus. in 1931. She won the Elder scholarship to the Royal College of Music, London, 1932 to 1935, where she studied the piano under Howard Hadley and Sir Arthur Benjamin and composition under R.O. Morris and Gordon Jacob. She became an A.R.C.M. and L.R.A.M. in the piano and composition. While in London she was soloist in her own two *Piano concertos* with the London Philharmonic Orchestra, conducted by Leslie Heward and the London Symphony Orchestra, conducted by Constant Lambert. She returned to Adelaide in 1936 where her *Adelaide Overture* was conducted at the State Centenary concert by Sir Malcolm Sargent. She moved to Sydney, where she taught at the Kambala School. From 1945 she was an examiner for the AMEB, becoming an advisory board member in 1958. She was councillor of the Music Association of New South Wales from 1960 and was made an honorary life member in 1974. In 1981 she was awarded an O.B.E. for services to music. She won the Sullivan, Farrar and Cobbett prizes for composition at the Royal College of Music in London and was three times winner of the Anzac Song prize. DISCOGRAPHY. PHOTOGRAPH.

Compositions

ORCHESTRA

Piano concerto No. 1, in E-Flat Minor (1934)
Piano concerto No. 2, in C-Sharp Minor (1935)
Fantasy-romantic (pf and orch)
The symbolic gate, symphonic poem
Adelaide overture (1957)
Symphonic overture
Heritage
Heroic elegy (1934)
Kelso overture
Lento in E-Minor (timp, perc and str orch)
Lyric
Prelude and dance
Theme and variations

CHAMBER

String quartet in E-Minor, op. 77
Christmas carol fantasy, op. 100 (fl, pf, vln and vlc)
Fantasia on Waltzing Matilda; op. 40a (1 or 2 pf); op 40b (4 fl); op 40c (vln, vla and pf); op. 40d (vln, vla and pf) (also 1 or 2 pf)
Fantasy quartet in A, op. 31 (2 vln, vlc or vla and pf)
Quartet in B-Minor, op. 10 (2 vln, vlc and pf)
Sailing boats, op. 131 (fl, ob, cl and pf)
Marsden pastorale, op. 46 (fl, hp, vln and opt vlc)
Fantasy trio in B-Minor, op 26 (vln, vlc or vla and pf)
Suite in A-Minor, op. 24 (fl, vla and vlc)
Three Irish folk tunes, op. 52 (vln, vla and pf)
Trio in G-Major (fl, cl and pf)
Trio (fl, ob and pf)
Prelude and scherzo (fl, ob and pf)
Sonata in B-Minor (vla and pf) (ca. 1940)
Sonata in F-Minor (cl and pf) (ca. 1940)
Canon and rhapsody, op. 88 (cl and pf)
The little juggler (fl and pf or fl)
Nightfall and merrymaking (ob and pf) (Chappell)
Sonata (fl and pf)
Dryads' dance, op. 39 (vln or fl)
Beside the stream (fl) (Allans)
Dancing shadows, op. 144, no. 1 (vla)
Evening under the Hill (fl)
Marsh birds (fl)
Minuetto, op. 84a (cl)
On the hillside, op. 12, no. 31 (fl)
Passing thoughts, op. 68, no. 1 (vla)
Scherzetto, op. 112 (sax)
Scherzino, op. 68, no. 2 (vla)
Seashell fantasy, op. 144, no. 2 (fl)
Serenade (vln)
Wedding morn (fl)

PIANO

Gay toccata in F, op. 142 (4 hands)
Cadenza for Mozart concerto in E-Flat, op. 79 (1 or 2 pf)
Along the coast, op. 11, no. 2
Birds in sunlight (1973)
Bourree in E-flat, op. 2, no. 1
Brown Hill creek in spring, op. 55
Burlesque in A-Minor, op. 23
Cadenzas for Beethoven concerto No. 4, op. 34a
Cadenza for Mozart C-Minor concerto (1975)
Cadenza for Mozart concerto in D, op. 74
Cadenza for Mozart concerto in E-flat, K 842, op. 75
Caprice in G-Minor, op. 16, No. 2
Captain Cook sketch book, op. 35 (Allans Music, 1975)
Concert studies No. 1-3, op. 28
Divertimento (1968)
Drought stricken grasses, op. 12a
Earrings from Spain, op. 133, no. 1
Fantasy sonata in C-Sharp Minor, op. 14
Firewheel, op. 19
Forest echoes, op. 12
The forest stream, op. 53
Fugue on F.E.B. op. 81
Humoresque (1974)
Impromptu in E-Flat, op. 21 (Allans Music)
Ivy leaves, op. 133, no. 2
Kaleidoscope, op. 8, no. 1
Lamp with a fringe, op. 132, no. 1
Lengthening shadows, op. 140, (1974)
Long ago in Paris, suite, op. 50 (Allans)
Lullaby for Christine, op. 85 (Chappell & Co.)
Meditation in G-Minor, op. 16, no. 1
Memories of a happy day, op. 47
More small pieces, op. 129 (Allans)
A mountain holiday, op. 71a (Allans)
My favourite days, op. 64 (Chappell & Co.)
The nest in the rose bush, op. 126 (Southern Music)
Pauline, op. 17
Pigeon in the studio (1974)
The poplar avenue, op. 44, no. 1
Preludes in B-Flat, F-Sharp Minor, F-Minor, op. 1, nos. 1-4
Reflected reeds, op. 103 (Allans)
Reverie, op. 2, no. 2 (Allans)
Rhapsody in A-Minor, no. 2, op. 92
Rhapsody in F-Sharp Minor, op. 25 (1935)
A river idyll, breakers, op. 20, nos. 1 and 2
Riverina sketches, op. 71, 8 pieces
Scherzo in G-Major, op. 44, no. 2
The sea shell, op. 11, no. 1
Slow movement concerto no. 1, op. 27a
Slow movement concerto no. 2, op. 32a
Spanish caprice in A-Minor, op. 22
Sonata in G-Minor, op 121 (ca. 1940)
Spring, op. 48
The spring of joy, op. 67
Study in E-Minor
Study in A-Minor
Study in blue, white and gold, op. 132, no. 2
Summer evening and birds in the bush, op. 5
Summer sketches, op. 4
Susan bray's album, op. 63, 12 pieces (Paling)
Tap tune, op. 65 (Schirmer)
Three European sketches (1974)
To a skylark, op. 18
Trends, op. 130
Valley of rocks (1975)
Variations and fugue on a theme by my mother in C-Minor, op. 13
Variations on Waltzing Matilda, op. 127 (Allans)
The village, op. 52, suite
Waltz fantasia, op. 42
Woodland sketch op. 118 (Allans)
Intermezzo for left hand, op. 6
Poem for right hand solo (1973)
Children's pieces incl.:
At the ballet, duet
Autumn stream, duet (Allans)
By the Thames, duet
Grey foreshore
Lullaby for Christine
Magpies at sunrise
On a Swiss lake
Oriental dance
Venetian lullaby (Paling)
Wet night on the highway

VOCAL

The cedar tree, op. 58a (vce and orch) (1944)
Dreamland, op. 15 (C. Rossetti) (S and pf or orch) (1933)
The wind in the sedges, op. 43a (vce and orch) (1937)
Australia land of liberty (composer) (vce and orch or pf)
The Illawarra flame, op. 97 (Patricia Francis) (mix-ch) (1955)
Sea shells (w-ch and pf)

Anzac threnody, op. 87 (D. Dowling) (S and pf) (1951)
Bridal song, op. 123 (V. Barton) (S and fl) (1962)
Elfin fantasy, op. 115 (composer) (S and pf) (1958)
Gay comes the singer (vce and pf) (1948)
The land where the bellbirds call, op. 120 (vce and pf)
Megalong Valley, op. 128 (composer) (C and pf) (1966)
Music, op. 54, No. 1 (W. de la Mare) (S and pf) (1942)
Olympia magnificat, op. 106, No. 3 (J. Harvey) (S and pf) (1956)
The river and the hill, op. 104, No. 2 (H. Kendall) (vce and pf)
Sea fantasy, op. 98, No. 1 (W. Alder Harrison) (S or T) (1954)
Three Latin lyrics (trans H. Waddell) (S and pf) (1944)
Twilight beach, op. 108 (D. Dowling) (S and pf) (1956)
Welcome song to the Queen, op. 91 (K. Murray) (S and pf) (1954)
The apple tree
Four songs, op. 43: A bridal song; Laughter; The wind in the sedges; Unknown (vce and pf) (1937)
My favourite days, children's song (also pf)
Nightfall by the river
Sunrise by the sea (Nicholson)
Thoughts at dusk (Chappell)
Under the Milky Way, children's song (also pf)
Winter willow music (Boosey & Hawkes)

SACRED
Behold now, praise the Lord, op. 9, anthem (mix-ch and pf)
Mary of Bethlehem, op. 57, no. 3 (mix-ch)
Motet for five part unaccompanied chorus, op. 33, psalm 96
Twelve carols (M. & D. Dowling) op. 57, 125 (Southern Music)
Requiem, op. 70 (F. Lisle) (B and pf) (1946)
Six carols (Southern)

BALLET
Village Fair

Publications
Piano Course. Books I & II. A tutor for Australian children. J. Albert & Son, 1976.
Polyphonic Album. 2, 3 and 4-part writing. 8th grade and diploma. Three booklets of verse.
Sight Reading Adventures. Book 1: 1st-5th grades; Book 2: 6th-7th grades.

Ref. composer, 44, 58, 77, 84, 94, 280, 412, 440, 444, 445, 446, 457, 563

HYLIN, Birgitta Charlotta Kristina

Swedish guitarist, pianist, artist, poetess and composer. b. Stockholm, July 24, 1915. She studied the piano privately and at the Wohlfart Piano School, Stockholm. She sang her own songs on the radio and traveled on concert tours in Sweden and the Faroe Islands. She is a specialist in Faroese folklore and a member of the Swedish Society of Music.

Compositions
VOCAL
Sommardansen (1941)
Sommardansen och andra visor (1970)

Ref. 206, 457

HYSON, Winifred Prince

American pianist, teacher and composer. b. Schenectady, NY, February 21, 1925. She studied composition under Esther Ballou (q.v.) and the piano under Evelyn Swarthout and Roy Hamlin Johnson. She obtained her B.A. magna cum laude at Radcliffe College in 1945. She received prizes and awards, including a master teacher's certificate from Phi Beta Kappa. She taught the piano, music theory and composition privately.

Compositions
ORCHESTRA
Partita for string orchestra (also 2 pf) (1970)
Suite for young orchestra (Elkan Vogel) (1964)

CHAMBER
Three night pieces (fl, cl and vlc) (1976)

PIANO
Eight light-hearted variations on The jolly miller (2 pf) (1971)
Fantasy on three English folk songs (2 pf) (1970)
The legend of St. Katherine (2 pf) (1972)
Our British cousins (2 pf) (1976)
A western summer (2 pf) (1976)

VOCAL
Becoming (w-vce and rec) (1968)
Forgotten wars (mix-ch a-cap) (1981)
Gestures (S and cl) (1977)
Memories of New England (S, perc, vln and pf) (1974)
New Hampshire poems of Robert Frost, op. 6 (S and fl)
Songs of Job's daughter, song cycle (S and pf) (1970) (Arsis Press)
Three love songs from the Bengali (A, fl and vlc) (1975)
View From Sandburg (S, cl, vla and pf) (1979)
Winter triptych, fantasy (S, fl, vln and pf) (1972)

SACRED
An Island of content, cantata (S, mix-ch, fl, perc and org)
A hymn to the virgin (S, w-ch and pf) (1967)
Song to the soul of a Child (S and mix-ch) (1978)
A litany of faith, op. 13 (S, trp and org)

Publications
The Keyboard Companion. Hansen House, 1983.

Ref. composer, 228

HYTREK, Sister Theophane

American organist, professor and composer. b. Stuart, NE, February 28, 1915. She studied composition with Bernard Dieter, Samuel Lieberson, Leon Stein and Bernard Rogers. She obtained her B.M. (organ) at Alverno College; M.M. (organ) and B.M. (composition) at Wisconsin Conservatory; M.M. (composition) at De Paul University and Ph.D. (composition) at the University of Rochester Eastman School of Music. She was on the faculty of Alverno College from 1941 and chairlady of the music department from 1956 to 1968 and then professor, 1968 to 1974. She received awards from the National Association of College Wind and Percussion Instructors in 1959, the Wisconsin Federation of Music Clubs in 1962 and the American Guild of Organists, Milwaukee Chapter, 1967.

Compositions
ORCHESTRA
Chamber concerto (winds and orch) (1955)
The hound of heaven, tone poem (also 2 pf)

CHAMBER
Psalms (org and insts) (comm AGO) (1969)
Sonata for piano and violin (1949)
Prelude and allegro for oboe and piano (1955)
Violin sonata (1962)
Holiday at the Vatican (pf) (1963)

ORGAN
Sonata-fantasia (1941)
Paschaltide suite (1953) (McLaughlin & Reilly; Summy-Birchard)
Marche nuptiale and recessional (1956) (McLaughlin & Reilly; Summy-Birchard)
Suite in honor of Mary Immaculate (1956) (McLaughlin & Reilly; Summy-Birchard)
Postlude-partita on the old one hundredth (1967)

SACRED
Pilgrim Mass (cantor, cong, mix-ch and org) (Assoc. Music, 1976)

Publications
Aspects of Style in the Performance of Organ in Developing Teaching Skills in Music. Catholic University Press, 1960.
Facing Reality in the Liturgical Music Apostulate Contained in the Crisis in Church Music. Article, Liturgical Conference, Washington, D.C. 1967.

Ref. 40, 137, 142, 347, 477

IAKHNINA, Yegenia Yosifovna. See YAKHNINA, Yevgenia Yosifovna

IASHVILI, Lili Mikhailovna

Soviet critic, lecturer and composer. b. Tiflis, May 10, 1920. In 1953 she graduated from the Tiflis Conservatory, having studied under I.I. Tuskia (composition). After 1962 she lectured composition at a music school in Tbilisi and from 1970 taught at a theatre school. She received the title of Honored Art Worker of the Georgian Soviet Socialist Republic (1966). She wrote musical reviews for newspapers.

Compositions
ORCHESTRA
Suite (1954)

CHAMBER
Sonata (vln and pf) (1953)

VOCAL
Quartets
Trio
Duets
Children's songs

OPERETTA
Bashmaki Babadzhany, for children (1968)
Irmisa, for children (1971)

Ref. 21

IBANEZ, Carmen

Spanish teacher and composer. b. Mula, Murcia, August 19, 1895. She studied at the Conservatory of Madrid. She taught from 1917 and founded the Orfeon Albacateno.

CHAMBER
Chamber pieces
Piano works
VOCAL
Songs for children
SACRED
Masses
TEACHING PIECES
Metodologia de la musica en las escuelas
Teirian razonada del solfeo
Publications
Biografias de musicos espanoles.
Ref. 361, 465

IBRAGIMOVA, Ela Imamedinovna

Soviet concertmistress, editor and composer. b. Adzhibakul, Azerbaijan, January 10, 1938. She studied composition under K. Karaev at the Azerbaijanian Conservatory, graduating in 1964. From 1957 to 1966 she was concertmistress at a music school in Baku. From 1970 to 1972 she was an editor and set designer for Azerbaijanian radio and television and in 1972 became concertmistress of the M.A. Aliev Institute of the Arts.
Compositions
ORCHESTRA
Piano concerto (1964)
CHAMBER
String quartet (1962)
Piano trio
VOCAL
Songs (A. Alibeil, A. Kiurchaili, S. Muradov, M. Ragim, A. Rasul, Y. Tasambek) (vce and pf)
Ref. 21

IBRAGIMOVA, Sevda Mirza kyzy

Soviet pianist, lecturer and composer. b. Baku, November 28, 1939. She studied the piano under M.R. Brenner and composition under K. Karaev at the Azerbaijanian Conservatory, graduating in 1964. Before graduating she taught at a music school attached to the Conservatory. She became assistant to Karaev in 1965 and started lecturing in composition in 1968.
Compositions
ORCHESTRA
Poema (pf and orch) (1964)
Algerian Reminiscences (cham orch) (1971)
CHAMBER
Two string quartets (1966, 1967)
Bakhadur-Sona, suite (str qrt) (1957)
Piano Trio (1961)
Five pieces (vln and pf) (1957)
Scherzo (vlc and pf) (1959)
Sonata (vln and pf) (1960)
Variations (vln and pf) (1955)
PIANO
Suite (1958)
Two fugues (1966)
VOCAL
Cycle of romances (N. Khazri) (vce and pf) (1966)
Four romances (S. Burgun) (vce and pf) (1954)
Songs
Vocal exercises
OPERA
Koltso Spravedlivovosti (1970)
INCIDENTAL MUSIC
Music for films and theatricals
Ref. 21

ICASIA. See KASIA

ICE, Mary Virginia. See THOMAS, Mary Virginia

IGENBERGA, Elga Avgustovna

Soviet pianist, choral conductor, concertmistress and composer. b. Jelgava, Latvia, February 10, 1921. She studied the piano at the Latvian Conservatory, graduating in 1949. She studied composition under L.Y. Garuta at the same conservatory (1962 to 1967). She was musical consultant at the Galgava Theatre; concertmistress of the Latvian Philharmonia (1945 to 1959) and musical director of vocal ensembles. From 1966 she was musical director of the youth ensemble of the House of Culture of the Latvian S.S.R..
Compositions
PIANO
Choreographic Miniatures: Adagio (1955); Waltz (1955); In Daugavpils (1960)
VOCAL
Korabli prekhodyat domoi, cycle (vce and pf) (1971)
Plechom k plechu, cycle (vce and pf) (1971)
Songs (G. Beilin, L. Bridak, P. Vilips, A. Kruklis, S. Leichuk, T. Melamed, Y. Osmanis, L. Pelmanis, K. Sun, A. Epners)
Choruses
OPERETTA
Annele (1964)
Tretya lyubov (1972)
Ref. 21

IKA. See PEYRON, Albertina Fredrike

ILLIUTOVICH, Nina Yakovlevna

Soviet pianist and composer. b. Petersburg, November 21, 1906; d. Moscow, April 27, 1972. She studied the piano at the Leningrad Conservatory, graduating in 1928. In Moscow she studied under N.A. Roslavts and S.A. Khalatov (composition). After 1924 she worked as a pianist, performing in concerts of light music. She composed pieces for light orchestra, songs and romances.
Ref. 21

INAN

Arabian songstress. ca. 800. She was born and brought up in Yamama, Arabia. Al-Natifi bought her and taught her music and her fame reached the caliph in Bagdad, Harun-al-Rashid, who wished to buy her. Al-Natifi wanted no less than 30,000 pieces of gold for her. According to Al-Asmai, Harun was deeply infatuated with Inan and this aroused great jealousy in his wife. On the death of her master, Inan was publicly auctioned and acquired by the succeeding caliph.
Ref. 171, 234

INANNA

Sumerian goddess. In the Sumerian kingdom (ca. 3000 B.C.) women were able to be priestesses, conduct business, own property and were held in higher regard than was the case later in Mesopotamia. Inanna came to be considered the mother of all creation although originally she was the goddess of the date palm. Her veneration was believed to assure the fertility of the land and the animals. Inanna was said to have composed *The Song of Life and Marriage* and a number of other Sumerian hymns, which were sung at ceremonies in choral form, probably accompanied by flutes, tambourines and cymbals.
Ref. 502

INGBER, Anita Rahel

Israeli pianist, teacher and composer. b. Vienna, Austria, January 25, 1917. She teaches the piano in Israel. She was awarded first prize at the review of Israeli Popular music. DISCOGRAPHY.
Compositions
VOCAL
Am Jisrael (vce and pf) (Illan Melody Press)
Buba Li (vce and pf) (Illan Melody Press)
Horat Hanoar (vce and pf) (Illan Melody Press)
Ilana (vce and pf) (Illan Melody Press)
Merhavim (vce and pf) (Illan Melody Press)
Shalom Lehitraot (vce and pf) (Illan Melody Press)
Shir Eres, lullaby (vce and pf) (Illan Melody Press)
Shir Haaviv (vce and pf) (Illan Melody Press)
Shir Hagalil (vce and pf) (Illan Melody Press)
Shir Haolim (vce and pf) (Illan Melody Press)
Yom Haatzmaut (vce and pf) (Illan Melody Press)
Zeh Dodi (vce and pf) (Illan Melody Press)
Ref. composer

INGEBOS, Louise-Marie

20th-century French composer.
Composition
CHAMBER
Modes (hp) (Paris: Jobet, 1980)
Ref. Otto Harrassowitz (Wiesbaden)

INGLEFIELD, Ruth karin

American harpist, musicologist, professor and composer. b. Plainfield, NJ, November 30, 1938. She obtained her B.A. (1960), M.Mus (1968) and Ph.D. (musicology) at the University of Cincinnati (1973). She studied privately under Marcel Grandjany, New York and Pierre Jamet, Paris. She made her debut in 1953 with the New York Philharmonic Orchestra and made concert, radio and TV appearances in Europe (1960 to 1968) and the Amerian Midwest (1968 to 1970). She was principal harpist with the Toledo Symphony Orchestra, OH, (1970 to 1973) and is professor of the harp and music history at Bowling Green State University. She won the first prize for the harp at the Paris Conservatoire (1960) and was a Fulbright Scholar (1970).

Compositions

HARP

Branie (trio)
Branie and Gaillarde
Danz proficiat
Songs for Sonja
Suite Brunette

Ref. 77

INJADO

German singer and composer. b. Frankfurt, 1937. She studied singing in Freiburg and at the State Hochschule fuer Musik in Munich. She taught herself composition.

Composition

ELECTRONIC

Hauptstadt (vces, sitar and tape) (1973) (Munich: Hans Wewerka)

Ref. Musikverlag, Hans Wewerka (Munich)

INVERARITY, Eliza (Mrs. Charles Martyn)

British soprano and composer. b. Edinburgh, March 23, 1813; d. Newcastle-on-Tyne. She was a popular singer and composed ballads.

Ref. 347

INWOOD, Mary Ruth Brink Berger

American electronic instrumentalist, pianist, lecturer and composer. b. Boston, July 27, 1928. She studied at Yale University College of Music and Queens College, where she received a B.A. music magna cum laude (1975). She studied the piano under Bruce Simons and Harry Knox, composition under Hugo Weisgall, Lee Kraft and Joseph Goodman and electronic synthesis under Hubert Howe. She taught music and theory privately. She was co-winner of the Alter Machlis prize for composition, Queens College in 1972, 1974, 1975 and 1976 and winner of the Edna Mills Prize for choral composition, Queens College. She was nominated to enter the Charles Ives Fellowship Competition by the National Institute of Arts and Letters in 1975 and the composition contest of the American Association of University Composers. She is currently lecturing at the Theory faculty of the Roosa School of Music, Brooklyn, and teaching the piano and theory privately. She is a member of ASCAP.

Compositions

ORCHESTRA

Symphony No. 1 (1976-1977)
Short Overture for Small Orchestra (1974)

CHAMBER

Piece for Symphonic Wind Ensemble (1975)
Bagatelles (ens)
Five Laconic Pieces for Wind Octet (1978)
Three Movements for Brass Sextet (1974) (New York: Seesaw Music Corp. 1975)
Advent Quintet (fl or picc, ob, cl, bsn and hn) (1978)
String Quartet No. 1 (1972)
String Quartet No. 2 (1973)
String Quartet No. 3 (1975) (Seesaw Music Corp., 1975)
Seven Bagatelles for Wind Trio (fl, cl and hn) (1977)
Trio (fl, vlc and pf) (1981)
Trio (ob, hn and pf) (Seesaw, 1983)
Trio (vln, hn and pf) (1982)
Sonata (fl and hpcd) (1975)
Sonata (trp and pf) (1982)
Fragments, Vols I and II, 18 pieces (pf) (1978)

VOCAL

Babel, cantata (ch, wind and perc) (1973)
The Song of Deborah (S, Bar and orch) (1979-1980)
Three Choral Settings from Patulli Veronensis Liber (mix-ch) (1975)
Cheerful and Tender Songs (S, hp and ob) (1979)
Five Songs (S and 3 cl) (Susan Berger) (1975)
The Lamentations of Jeremiah (S and pf) (1981-1982)
The Remembrance (Emile Bronte) (S and pf)

SACRED

Rite II of '79 Prayer Book (m-vces) (1980-1983)

INCIDENTAL MUSIC

The Cenci, play (P. Shelley) (small ens) (1981)

Ref. composer, 185, 457

IORDAN, Irina Nikolayevna

Soviet cellist, editor and composer. b. Saratov, November 22, 1910. She studied the cello at the Moscow Conservatory under G. Pecker (1934 to 1935). The following three years she studied under V. Shebalin (composition) at the Gnesin Music School. From 1948 she edited a range of music by Russian and foreign composers and after 1951 worked for the M.I. Glinka Central State Museum of Music. She was awarded two medals.

Compositions

ORCHESTRA

Symphony in A (1944)
Concerto for Cello and Orchestra (also vla) (1950, 1952)
Concerto for Cello and Orchestra (1971)
Concerto for Violin and Orchestra (1964) (also vln and pf) (Moscow: Sovietski Kompozitor, 1977)
Overture (1939)
Prazdnichnaya uvertiure na khakasskie temy (1955)
Suite (1943)
Uvertiure na temy revoliutsionnikh pesen 1905 (1955)

CHAMBER

Piano Quintet on Tajik themes (with G. Kirkov) (1951)
String Quartet No. 1 (1937)
String Quartet No. 2 (1948)
String Quartet No. 3 (1961)
String Quartet No. 4 (1972)
Easy pieces with variations (vlc and pf) (1950)
Four pieces (vln and pf) (1951-1952)
Poema (vln and vla) (1972)
Scherzo (vla and pf) (1965)
Sonata No. 1 (vlc and pf) (1937)
Sonata No. 2 (vlc and pf) (1951)
Theme and Variations (vlc and pf) (1943)
Two Pieces (vlc and pf) (1935, 1954)
Fantasia (hp) (1963)

PIANO

Three Pieces (1934)
Two Pieces (1951)

VOCAL

Moscow, cantata (with G. Kirkov) (1947)
Six romances (Pushkin, Tyuchev) (1945)
Collection of songs (1951)

INCIDENTAL MUSIC

Films and radio

Ref. 21, 87, 267, 330

IPPOLITO, Carmela

American violinist and composer. b. Boston, July 18, 1902. She first appeared in public at the age of five and studied under C.M. Loeffler at the Juilliard School of Music and E. Zimbalist of the Curtis Institute. She toured in the United States, playing under Monteux, Fiedler and Koussevitzky as well as on radio.

Compositions

CHAMBER

Heaven's Lyre and the Dance, fantasy (vln and pf) (1947)
Sonata (vln and pf) (1949)
Pieces (pf)

Ref. 96

IRFAN

Arabian songstress at the court of the Caliph al-Mutawakkil (847 to 861), in Samarra, near Baghdad. She was a slave of Shariyya (q.v.) and with her mistress took part in a musical competition at the house of the Prince Abu Isa Ibn al-Mutawakkil, competing against Oreib and her singers. At the time there was great rivalry between the classical, conservative school of music, represented by the teacher, composer and theoretian Ishaq al-Mausuli, with the songstress Oreib and her followers and an innovative, Persian influenced romantic school of music, represented by Ibrahim ibn al-Mahdi, with Shariyya and her followers. Irfan is mentioned singing for the guests of Abu-l-'Ubais ibn Hamdun. He may have bought her from Shariyya, or Shariyya may have freed her, for she is also mentioned as singing for al-Mutawakkil at the circumcision festival for his son al-Mutazz and is not referred to as being a slave of Shariyya's.

Ref. 224

IRGENS-BERGH, Gisela, von
20th-century Danish composer.
Composition
PIANO
Festmarsch, til Erindring om den kgl. Livgarde...
Ref. 331

IRMAN-ALLEMANN, Regina
Swiss guitarist, percussionist, pianist, teacher and composer. b. Winterthur, March 22, 1957. She learnt the guitar and the piano as a child and then studied the guitar at the Winterthur Conservatory. Important teachers in her courses of new music were Roland Moser, Peter Streiff and Robert Rudisuli. She taught herself composition and in 1982 received her teacher's diploma. She took up percussion studies in 1985 and teaches the guitar at a music school in Winterthur. PHOTOGRAPH.
Compositions
CHAMBER
Boden (los) (3 vln) (1985)
Huegel bei Ceret II (2 vla and d-b) (1983)
Es ist (immer noch) ein Takt sonst nichts (vla and pf) (1985)
Melodie (quarter tone gtr) (1985)
VOCAL
In Darkness let me Dwell (w-vce, ob, vln, vla and vlc) (1982)
MULTIMEDIA
Vier Lieder nach Christian Morgenstern: Gruselet, Galgenbruders Lied an Sophie die Henkersmaid, Das Mondschaf, Tapetenblume (w-vce, pf, perc, gtr, fl or picc and transparancies) (1981)
Speculum (perc, 4 cl, mirror scenery and sisyphus machine) (1984)
Ref. composer, 651

IRMINGER, Caroline
20th-century Danish composer.
Compositions
CHAMBER
Andante (vln and pf)
VOCAL
Genforeningssangen (vce and pf)
Kaerlighed fra Gud (vce and pf)
Ref. 331

IRVINE, Jessie Seymour
Scottish composer. b. Dunotter, July 26, 1836.
Composition
SACRED
Crimond, hymn
Ref. 572

ISABEL LA LORRAINE
14th-century French minstrel. She signed the famous charter dated September 14, 1321, that established the Chappelle Saint-Julien-des-Ménestriers, a corporation for jongleurs and minstrels.
Ref. 343

ISABELET LA ROUSSELLE
14th-century French minstrel. She signed the famous charter dated September 14, 1321, that established the Chappelle Saint-Julien-des-Ménestriers, a corporation for jongleurs and minstrels.
Ref. 343

ISABELLA (Isabella of Perigord)
Italian troubadour. b. ca. 1180. Isabella exchanged a tenson with Elias Cairel, a troubadour of Perigord, whom she may possibly have married. He may have met her between 1215 and 1225 if she was the daughter of Boniface of Montferrat (b. ca. 1160 and a patron of troubadours) or of Marchesopulo Pelavicini. She may have been the daughter of Guido Marchesopulo, Lord of Bodonitza in Thessaly, who went to Rumania in 1210. Aside from the fact that all three men had daughters named Isabella, little else is known. Isabella may even have been the daughter of a nobleman from one of the Christian empires of the East.
Ref. Dr. Margaret Nabarro (Johannesburg), 117, 213, 220, 313

ISAKOVA, Aida Petrovna
Soviet pianist, lecturer and composer. b. Vladimir-Volynsk, March 23, 1940. She studied piano theory and composition at the local music school, graduating in 1956. At the Moscow Conservatory she studied the piano under E.K. Golubev. After 1964 she lectured at the Kazakh Institute of the Arts, Alma-Ata.
Compositions
ORCHESTRA
Symphony for String Orchestra and Timpani (1964)
Piano Concerto on Kazakh Themes (1969)
Two piano concertos (1963, 1967)
Humoresque (trb and light orch) (1968)
CHAMBER
Sonata (bsn and pf) (1963)
PIANO
Five sonatas (1959, 1961, 1966, 1968)
Suite (1959)
Twenty four preludes (1968)
Variations on Kazakh themes (1966)
VOCAL
Pesnyi Svobody, cantata (1962)
O More, song cycle (I. Bukash) (1962)
Cycles of songs (negro poets, 1961) (R. Burns, 1965)
BALLET
Hamlet (1971)
Sostryanie, choreographic suite (1970)
Ref. 21

ISELDA (Yselda)
12th-century French troubadour who composed a tenson between herself, Alais (q.v.) and Carenza (q.v.); or who, according to Chailley was a singing nun who wrote poetry and sang it to the sisters; the only known piece being *Lady Carenza*.
Composition
VOCAL
Na Carenza al bel cors avinen ...... (Lady Carenza of the lovely, gracious body ....)
Ref. Dr. Margaret Nabarro (Johannesburg), 117, 303

ISEUT DE CAPIO, Dame
12th-century French troubadour, from Provence. She asked Mme. Almois de Chateauneuf to pardon her knight Gui de Tournon in her song *Dompna n'Almues, si us plaques*. She was also probably a partoness of troubadours, as was her son, Raimbaut d'Agoult.
Composition
Dompna n'Almucs, si us plagues .... (Lady Almucs, with your permission..) (with Dame Almucs de Castelnau (q.v.))
Ref. 117, 120, 213, 220, 303

ISIDORA ZEGERS Y MONTENEGRO, D. See ZEGERS, Isadora

ISIS
Egyptian goddess. She was said to have composed the dirges and laments that later became models of their kind. There was also an Isis who was an Amon songstress ca. 1230 B.C. in the reign of Rameses II and yet another Isis was an Amon songstress and sistrum player ca. 1340 B.C.
Ref. 207, 264

ISMAGILOVA, Leila Zagirovna
Soviet pianist, lecturer and composer. b. Moscow, May 26, 1946. At the Kazan Conservatory she studied composition under A.S. Leman from 1965 till 1968. From that year until 1970 she studied composition under V.G. Fere at the Moscow Conservatory and completed her studies at the Gnesin School in Moscow as a pupil of G.I. Litinsky. After 1972 she lectured at the Institute of the Arts in Ufa. DISCOGRAPHY.
Compositions
ORCHESTRA
Piano concerto (1969)
Zemlya Ottsov, cycle (1972)
CHAMBER
String Octet
String Quartet (1973)
Pieces for flute and piano (1967)
Pieces for violin and piano (1966)
PIANO
Sonata (1973)
Variations (1963)
Other pieces

VOCAL
Romances
Songs
Ref. 21

ISSLE, Christa

West German composer. b. 1960.

Composition

CHAMBER
Trio (a-sax, vla and pf)
Ref. Frau und Musik

ISZKOWSKA, Zofia

Polish pianist, teacher and composer. b. Nowy Sacz, November 30, 1911. She studied at the Polish Conservatory in Lvov under H. Ottawowa (piano) and A. Soltys. She obtained her piano diploma in 1938. In Lodz she studied under K. Sikorski (composition).

Compositions

ORCHESTRA
Symphony (1954)
Piano Concerto
Polish Suite (small orch) (1951)
CHAMBER
String Quartet (1948, 1949)
Preludium (vln and pf) (1941)
Sonata (vln and pf) (1941, 1942)
Triptych (fl and pf) (1964)
PIANO
Sonata (1949)
Three virtuoso etudes (1950)
Variations in E-Major and B-Minor (1942)
VOCAL
Fletnia tajemna (vce and orch)
Lecial aniol nad gwiazdami (vce and orch)
Piesn poety (vce and orch)
Dyskobol (m-ch)
Five songs (w-ch and ww) (1965)
Andante (vce and pf)
Czeka (L. Staff)
Do Ciebie (vce and pf)
Jestem plama na podlodze, children's song
Kiedy Jas odjezdzal
Narodziny Chopina (J. Braun)
Nasza noc (J. Braun)
Piesn na Zjednoczenie Partii
Piesn przodownikow (J. Bronowicz)
Piosenka o odbudowie (J. Lan)
Pozegnanie (S. Dobrowolski)
Przed nami (J. Braun)
Smierc snu (M. Gamska)
Tancowala igla z nitka, children's song
W gorze (J. Braun)
Wezwanie (vce and pf)
Wiatr zaniesie ci (L. Staff)
Wykolysalem cie (vce and pf)
Zachod (vce and pf)
ELECTRONIC
Suite for Flute, Vibraphone and Cello (1962)
Ref. 118

ITI

Egyptian songstress. b. V Dynasty (2563 to 2424 B.C.) under the Pharaoh Neferefre. She is believed to have been the first woman songstress in recorded music history. She had a beautiful grave near the Chefren pyramids in the Necropolis of Gizeh. Because of numerous references to her in writing and in pictures, it is assumed that she was a famous personality in her time. In the Necropolis of Saqqarah, which, with Gizeh, belonged to Memphis, the former capital of Ancient Egypt, a noble Egyptian had the picture of this prominent songstress put on his tomb. Such a representation indicated that the deceased wished to enjoy her music in the hereafter and this was a memorial to her art. She is represented with one hand on her ear and the other hand making cheironomic signs to show the accompanist which note she wants. The accompanist is the harpist Hekenu (q.v.). FRONTISPIECE.
Ref. 207

IVANOVA, Lidia

Russian organist, pianist and composer. b. Paris, ca. 1900. She received her diploma in 1920 from the Moscow Conservatory, then studied under Popov (composition). In 1924 she went to Rome and studied at the Santa Cecilia Conservatory under Ottorino Respighi and received her composition diploma (1926). She received a diploma for her organ playing.

Compositions

ORCHESTRA
Poemi sinfonici, symphonic poems
Teme e Variazioni (rorate coeli desuper) (1930)
PIANO
Pieces
VOCAL
Songs (3 w-vces and orch)
Choruses
Ref. 105

IVEY, Jean Eichelberger

American electronic instrumentalist, pianist, lecturer and composer. b. Washington, DC, July 3, 1923. She obtained her B.A. magna cum laude from Trinity College, Washington (1944) and her M.M. (piano) from the Peabody Conservatory (1946). She taught at Trinity College (1945 to 1955), the Catholic University (1952 to 1955) and Misericordia College (1955 to 1957). During part of that period she also studied composition at the Eastman School of Music under Wayne Barlow, Kent Kennan and Bernard Rogers, receiving an M.M. in composition in 1956. From 1960 to 1962 she taught at Xavier University, New Orleans. She was the founder (1969) and then director of the Peabody Conservatory Electronic Music Studio. In 1972 she was awarded her D.M. (composition) by the University of Toronto, where she studied electronic music under Myron Schaeffer and Hugh Le Caine. She won several ASCAP awards and was commissioned to write numerous works. She toured Europe, the United States and Mexico as a concert pianist. She was awarded the distinguished Peabody Alumni Award in 1975. She received a National Endowment for the Arts Fellowship grant for a violoncello and piano composition. DISCOGRAPHY.

Compositions

ORCHESTRA
Forms in Motion, symphony (1972)
Ode for Orchestra (1968)
Overture
Passacaglia (cham orch) (1968)
CHAMBER
Scherzo for Wind Septet (fl, ob, cl, bsn, hn, trp and trb) (1953)
Androcles and the Lion, suite (ww qnt)
Dinsmoor Suite (2 cl, trb, perc and xy)
String Quartet (1960)
Music for Viola and Piano (New York: C. Fischer, 1975)
Ode for Violin and Piano (1965)
Pantomime (cl and xyl)
Six Inventions (2 vln) (1959)
Song of Pan (a-rec or fl and pf) (1954)
Suite (vlc and pf) (1960)
Tonada, duo (vln and vlc) (1966)
Triton's Horn (t-sax and pf)
Sonatina for Unaccompanied Clarinet (C. Fischer, 1972)
PIANO
Magic Circles
Pentatonic Sketches (1967)
Prelude and Passacaglia (1955)
Sleepy Time (1967)
Sonata (1958)
Theme and Variations (1952)
Water Wheel (1967)
Teaching Pieces
VOCAL
Tribute: Martin Luther King (Bar and orch) (1969)
Madrigal (w-ch)
Absent in the Spring (Shakespeare) (m-S, vln, vla and vlc) (1977)
A Carol of Animals (C.G. Rossetti) (m-S, ob and pf) (1976)
Crossing Brooklyn Ferry (W. Whitman) (Bar and pf)
Notes towards Time (J. Jacobson) (comm Baltimore Chamber Music Soc.)
Solstice (S, fl or picc, perc and pf) (1977)
Two Songs (S, pf and cl)
Song cycles and songs
SACRED
Lord, Hear My Prayer (mix-ch) (McLaughlin & Reilly, 1966)
O Come Bless the Lord (mix-ch) (Boston: McLaughlin & Reilly, 1966)
Choral anthems
INCIDENTAL MUSIC
The Exception and the Rule, film
Montage IV, film
Montage V, How to Play Pinball, film
Music for plays
ELECTRONIC
Sea Change (tape and orch) (C. Fischer)
Testament of Eve, monodrama (m-S, tape and orch)

Hera, Hung from the Sky, op. 9 (C. Kizer) (m-S, fl, ob, cl, bsn, hn, trp, trb, timp, perc incl. vib and xy, pf or cel and tape) (C. Fischer, 1974)
Three Songs of Night, song cycle (S, fl, cl, vla, vlc, pf and tape) (C. Fischer, 1973)
Aldebaran (vla and tape) (C. Fischer, 1973)
Continuous Form
Cortege for Charles Kent (tape) (1969)
Enter Three Witches (1964)
Parade Duet (1965)
Pinball, musique concrete (tape) (1967)
Prospero (Bass, hn, perc and tape) (1978)
Skaniadaryo (pf and tape) (C. Fischer, 1975)
Terminus (R.W. Emerson) (m-S and tape) (1971) (C. Fischer, 1972)

Publications

Contributor to Electronic Music: *A Listener's Guide*. Elliott Schwartz, ed. 1973.

Bibliography

AMC Newsletter, vol. 20, no. 3.

Ref. *Pan Pipes* Winter 1984, 40, 52, 84, 94, 137, 142, 146, 185, 190, 228, 397, 415, 454, 475, 494, 518, 563, 611, 622, 625

IWAUCHI, Saori

Japanese electronic organist, pianist and composer. b. 1970. She studied the electric organ and composition with the Yamaha junior advanced course. DISCOGRAPHY.

Compositions

PIANO
Brave Knight
The Hunters
The Milkway Train
Picnic
Twilight Bell

VIOLIN
Violin in a Grassy Plain

Ref. Yamaha Music Foundation

IZATO-L-MILA. See AZZA AL-MAILA

JABOR, Najla (Najla Jabor Maia de Carvalho)

Brazilian conductor and composer. b. Rio de Janeiro, September 25, 1915. A graduate of the Escola Nacional de Musica do Brasil in Rio de Janeiro, she studied under Henrique Oswald, J. Otaviano, A. Franca, A. Gouveia, F. Braga and A. Sa de Brito Bastos. Her compositions were broadcast on Brazilian and English radio. She received national and foreign prizes and was the first Brazilian woman composer of a piano concerto.

Compositions

ORCHESTRA
Piano concerto
A dança do paje, symphonic poem
Tango brasileiro, symphonic poem (also pf) (São Paulo: Ricordi Brasileira, 1958)
Americas - triptico sinfonico

PIANO
Batuquinho classico, humorous piece (São Paulo: Mangione, 1972)
Estudo Alvorada (Sao Paulo: Irmaos Vitale, 1974)
Estudo para 3, 4 e 5 dedos, contendo um samba (Ricordi Brasileira, 1974)
Jongo (Ricordi Brasileira, 1958)
Noturno Nos. 1 and 2 (Mangione, 1961)
Para você, mestre (Rio de Janeiro: Edições Guanabara, 1973)
Somente...... saudade, waltzes 1-5 (Edições Guanabara, 1973)
Suite de 3 peças: O cabritinho e a flauta; Loucura de um polichinelo; Pandemonio (Ricordi Brasileira, 1958)

VOCAL
Hino da Força Aerea Brasileira (vces and orch)
Hino da Marinha Brasileira (vces and orch)
Hino do Exercito Brasileiro (vces and orch) (Hino do Soldado Brasileiro)
Anthems (vces and orch) (comm)
Canção bárbara (O. Mayer) (Ricordi Brasileira, 1971)
Canção do trovador (J.A. Maia de Carvalho) (Ricordi Brasileira, 1971)
Copo de cristal (A. Grieco) (Sao Paulo: Seresta, 1971)
Novo Amor: Berceuse, op. 85 (A. Rivera de Rezenda) (Mangione, 1961)
A Palavra de Deus (S. Dubois) (Edições Guanabara, 1973)
O Sonho (Silveira Peixoto) (Irmaos Vitale, 1971)

Ref. 208, 333

JACKSON, Barbara May

English pianist, violinist, lecturer and composer. b. Monks Risborough, 1926. She is an L.R.A.M. and taught the violin and the piano at Furzedown Teachers' Training College from 1946 to 1949, then in schools.

Compositions

ORCHESTRA
Two movements (str orch)

CHAMBER
Nocturne (fl and strs)
Suite (ob, vla and pf)
Romance (vlc and pf)

Ref. 490

JACKSON, Elizabeth Barnhart

American organist, pianist, lecturer and composer. b. Terre Haute, IN, May 25, 1887. She studied music privately in Indiana and then attended Western College, Oxford, OH, majoring in the piano. She studied at the Indianapolis Conservatory and privately under Leschetizky. She taught the piano and the organ, playing the latter for 22 years in Takoma Park Presbyterian Church. For a few years she was a member of the organ faculty at Guincy, IL. PHOTOGRAPH.

Compositions

ORGAN
Berceuse (1940) (Belwin-Mills)
Consecration (1939)
Tranquility (1939) (Belwin-Mills)
Worship (1938) (Belwin-Mills)

VOCAL
She shall be praised (1944)
A star so bright (w-ch) (1967)

SACRED
Christmas prayer for peace (mix-ch and pf) (Belwin-Mills, 1949)
O God Thou art my God (mix-ch and pf) (Belwin-Mills, 1949)
The beauty of God's world (S and A) (1965)
The boy Jesus (S and A) (1965)
But Mary kept, anthem (1956)
Christmas chimes (1951)
Hast Thou not known, duet (1954)
Magnificat (1946)
Manger lullaby (1959)
O praise the Lord (1968)
Psalm 8 (1960)
Psalm 43 (1975)
Sleep on little babe (1968)
Spring song of praise, anthem (1950)
Watch ye standfast, anthem (1940)
What manner of love, anthem (1964)

Ref. composer, 228

JACKSON, Jane. See ROECKEL, Jane

JACKSON, Mary

20th-century American composer. She composed choral works and songs.

Ref. 40, 347

JACKSON, Marylou I.

20th-century black American composer.

Compositions

SACRED
Negro spirituals and hymns (w-ch and w-vces) (J. Fischer & Bros. New York, 1935)

Ref. Prof. Dominique-Rene de Lerma (Baltimore)

JACOB, Elizabeth Marie

Canadian guitarist and composer. b. Halifax, Nova Scotia, July 7, 1958. She taught herself the guitar and attended Acadia University, Wolfville, on a scholarship to obtain her B.Mus. (composition) in 1979, then her M.M., studying voice under Marie McCarthy and James Sugg and composition under Gordon Callon. PHOTOGRAPH.

Compositions

CHAMBER
Tree breezes (fl, ob, cl and bsn) (1979)
Green music (fl, cl and mar) (1978)
Three watercolours (2 trp and trb) (1979)
Keyboard harmonies, 3 pieces (pf)
Rainbow, variations (vln)

VOCAL
The tortoise and the hare (soli, ch, fl, trb'and perc) (1980)
Canticle of the seasons (T, B, fl, cl and pf) (1978)
Nocturnes (S and pf) (1977)
The waking (vce and pf) (1979)
Ref. composer

JACOB, Helen. See FODY, Ilona

JACOB-LOEWENSOHN, Alice
Israeli musicologist and composer. b. Berlin, Germany, 1895; d. Israel. She wrote Jewish music before World War Two then emigrated to Palestine, where she worked as a musicologist, collected Chassidic melodies and composed for the piano.
Ref. 448

JACOBINA, Agnes Marie
German pianist and composer. b. 1847; d. 1925. She lived in England for most of her life.
Ref. Robert Dearling (Spaulding, UK)

JACOBS-BOND, Carrie. See BOND, Carrie Jacobs

JACOBSON, Henrietta
18th-century Polish composer. She lived in Warsaw from 1778 to 1779.
Compositions
HARPSICHORD
Divertissement (1778)
Polonaises (1778-1779)
Other pieces (in National Library, Warsaw, until 1939)
Ref. 118

JACOBUS, Dale Asher
20th-century American composer. She composed operas, choral works and songs.
Ref. 118

JACQUE, Emilie
French composer.
Compositions
ORCHESTRA
Meditation de Thais (vln and orch) (Heugel)
Frou-Frou, fanfare (Gobert)
Sainte-Cécile Retraites, fanfare (Gobert)
Souvenirs de Tunis, fanfare (Lory)
CHAMBER
Arlequin et Colombine (ob and str qnt) (Enoch)
Barcarolle des Duos pittoresque (R. de Vilbac) (2 vln and pf) (Enoch)
Fantaisie de concert, op. 2 (vln and pf) (Costellat)
VOCAL
Patria (2 vces and pf) (Lory)
Réveil (2 vces and pf) (Lory)
ARRANGEMENTS
Menuet de 42e quatuor de Haydn (vln and pf) (Noel)
Menuet d'un quintet (de Boccherini) (vln and pf) (Costellat)
Nuit étoilée (Schumann) (ob and str qnt) (Enoch)
Pastorale de Bobbrecht (vln and qrt) (Costellat)
Ref. 297

JACQUES (Jacques-Labalette), Charlotte
19th-century French pianist, teacher and composer.
Composition
OPERETTA
La Veillee, in 1 act (1862)
Ref. 26, 226, 276, 307

JACQUES-LABALETTE, Charlotte. See JACQUES, Charlotte

JACQUES-RENE, Sister. See RHENE-JAQUE

JACQUET DE LA GUERRE, Elisabeth. See LA GUERRE, Elisabeth-Claude Jacquet de

JAEGER, Hertha
German pianist and composer. b. Berlin, July 8, 1899. She studied under Sonderburg, Herman Scholtz, Juon and Hindemith.
Compositions
CHAMBER
Pieces
PIANO
Old German Laendler
Polonaise
Works for four hands and two pianos
VOCAL
Songs
Ref. 70, 226

JAELL-TRAUTMANN, Marie
French pianist, teacher and composer. b. Steinseltz, Alsace, August 17, 1846; d. Paris, February 7, 1925. She studied under Hamma and Moscheles in Stuttgart and then under Herz at the Paris Conservatoire, where she won first prize for the piano in 1862. She studied composition in Paris under Franck and Saint-Saens and in Weimar under Liszt, 1882. One of her pupils was Albert Schweitzer. Marie was the first person to play Beethoven's 32 sonatas in the course of six concerts given in Pleyel's rooms in 1893. One of her pupils was Albert Schweitzer. She married the pianist Alfred Jaell.
Compositions
ORCHESTRA
Cello concerto
Piano concerto in C-Minor (Noel)
Ossiane, symphonic poem
Harmonies d'Alsace
CHAMBER
Quartet in G-Minor
Romance for violin and piano
Cello sonata
Violin sonata
PIANO
Valses pour piano à quatre mains (Leuckart; Ricordi; Breitkopf; Sulzbach)
Voix du printemps, 6 pieces (4 hands) (Raabe; Ricordi)
Babillardes, allegro (Heugel)
Bagatelles and sonata (Heugel; Ricordi)
Les beaux jours, small pieces (Heugel)
Impromptu
Les jours pluvieux, small pieces (Heugel)
Mer (Société Nouvelle)
Orientales (Société Nouvelle)
Prisme, problemes en musique (Heugel)
Promenade matinale (Société Nouvelle)
Six esquisses romantiques (Noel)
Six petits morceaux (Breitkopf)
Two meditations (Rieter)
Valses mélancoliques and valses mignonnes (Heugel)
Teaching pieces
VOCAL
Sur la tombe d'un enfant (ch and orch)
Fuenf Lieder (Schott)
SACRED
Psalm (mix-ch)
ARRANGEMENTS
Marcia alla turca des Ruines d'Athenes de Beethoven, op. 113, no. 4 (pf, 4 hands) (Leuckart)
Publications
La Coloration des sensations tactiles. 1910.
L'Intelligence et le rythme dans les mouvements artistiques. 1905.
La Main et la pensée musicale. 1925, posthumous.
Le Mécanisme du toucher. 1896.
La Musique et la psycho-physiologie. Paris: Alcan, 1895.
La Résonance du toucher et la topographie des pulpes. 1912.
Le Rythme du regard et la dissociation des doigts. 1906.
Le Toucher. 1899.
Les Toucher nouveaux principes elementaires pour l'enseignement du piano. 3 vols. Heugel.

Bibliography

Chantavoine, J. *Lettres de Liszt a M. et A. Jaell. Revue Internationale de Musique*. 1952.
Kiener, H. *Marie Jaell. Problemes d'esthétique et de pedagogie musicales*. Paris: Flammarion, 1952.
Laloy L. *M. Jaell*. RM, 1925.
Lang, M.; Kiener, H.; and Klipffel. *A. M. Jaell, pianiste, compositeur, auteur*. Strassbourg, 1967.
Minivielle, E. *M. Jaell, essai sur ses recherches d'esthétique musicale*. La Nouvelle Revue. 1925.
Schweitzer, A. *Selbstdarstellung*. Leipzig, 1929.
La Secrétaire de Liszt, M. Jaell. Mercure de France, 1925.
Van's Gravemoer, J. Bosch. *L'Enseignement de la musique par le mouvement conscient*. Paris, 1938.
Van's Gravemoer, J. Bosch. *L'oeuvre de M. Jaell*. Le Monde Musical. 1925.
Waddington, H. *M. Jaell et la formation musicale*. Revue Triades, 1957.
Ref. 12, 15, 22, 109, 276, 297, 335

JAGGER, Maglona Patricia Bryony. See PHILLIPS, Bryony

JAGIELLO, Jadwiga. See BRZOWSKA-MEJEAN, Jadwiga

JAHNOVA, Bozena (nee Svobodova)

Bohemian pianist and composer. b. Prague, December 4, 1840; d. Prague, May 21, 1902. She studied the piano under Joseph Jiranek, C. Muller and A. Dreyschock. She made her debut as a pianist in Prague and after her marriage moved to Pardubic. She taught at a girls' language school, gave numerous solo recitals of contemporary works and took part in chamber recitals.

Compositions
PIANO
Chanson bohème
VOCAL
Choruses (mix-ch)
Duets (w-vces)
Trios (w-vces)
Songs
THEATRE
Stary bojovnik, melodrama (J.V. Jahn)
Ref. 197

JAMA, Agnes

Dutch composer. b. June 11, 1921.

Composition
VOCAL
Vocation (m-S, cl and pf) (1971)
Ref. 283

JAMBOR, Agi

American pianist and composer. b. Budapest, Hungary, February 4, 1909. She studied composition under Zoltan Kodaly and Leo Weiner at the Budapest Royal Conservatory. She won the Brahaus Prize, Berlin, in 1928 and the Philharmonic Orchestra Prize, International Chopin competition, Warsaw, in 1937, for her piano performances. Agi became an American citizen in 1954 and in 1958, a professor at Bryn Mawr College.

Compositions
PIANO
Preludes
Sonata
SACRED
Psalmus humanus (Albert Szent-Gyorgyi) (vce and pf)
Ref. 142

JAMES, Allen. See LORENZ, Ellen Jane

JAMES, Dorothy E.

American professor and composer. b. Chicago, December 1, 1901; d. December 1, 1982. She studied composition under Louis Gruenberg (Chicago Musical College), Adolf Weidig (American Conservatory of Music), Howard Hanson (Eastman School of Music), Ernst Krenek (University of Michigan) and Healy Willan (Toronto). She obtained her B.M. and M.M. at the American Conservatory of Music, Chicago. She was professor of theory and musical literature at Eastern Michigan University, Ypsilanti, from 1927 to 1968. She received two music scholarships from Adolf Weidig as well as the Adolf Weidig Gold Medal for Composition. She won three first prizes in Mu Phi Epsilon contests and first prize in the Miliken University Choral Clinic contest and the Michigan Composer Club contest. She received four MacDowell Fellowships. In 1971 she was given an honorary doctorate of musical arts on her retirement from Eastern Michigan University as professor emeritus of music.

Compositions
ORCHESTRA
Elegy for the lately dead (1938)
Fun at the fair (A. Rowley) (New York: C. Fischer)
Suite for small orchestra (1940) (New York: AMC)
Three symphonic fragments (1931)
CHAMBER
Three astorales (cl, cel and strs) (1933) (1st prize, 1934)
Recitative and air (str qrt) (1944) (AMC)
Rhapsody (vln, vlc and pf) (1929) (1st prize, 1926)
Ballade for violin and piano (1st prize, 1926)
Morning music (fl and pf) (1967)
Motif (org and ob) (1970)
ORGAN
Autumnal (1934) (New York: H.W. Gray)
Dedication (1958)
PIANO
Dance, Johnny (4 hands)
Dirge (1964) (New York: Pioneer Edition; ACE)
Impressionistic study (1962)
Mitzie polka
Tone-row suite (1962) (Ann Arbor)
Pagoda of exquisite purity
Sevilliana
Two in one (1962)
Two satirical dances (1934)
VOCAL
Cantata (1937)
The golden year (Tennyson) (mix-ch and orch) (1953)
The Jumblies (E. Lear) (chil-ch and orch) (Chicago: H.T. Fitz-Simons Co.)
Mary's lullaby (E. Coatsworth) (4 part w-ch and orch)
Niobe (Alfred Noyes) (w-vces and orch) (1941)
Paul Bunyan (E. Tatum) (chil-vces and orch) (1938)
Tears (Whitman) (mix-ch and orch) (1930)
Envoy (w-ch and pf) (1958) (J. Fischer & Bros.)
The night (Hilaire Belloc) (4-part m-ch and pf) (1950) (New York: J. Fischer & Bros.)
Fifteen songs (Verlaine, A. Lowell, E. Dickinson) (1925-1967)
Four preludes from the Chinese (low vce, str qrt and pf) (1932)
Lacquer prints (A. Lowell) (S and pf) (1924)
Mutability (Shelley) (w-vces, fl, 2 cl and pf) (1967)
So sleeps the night (G. Goff) (m-vce and pf) (1930)
Sonnet after Michelangelo (med-vce, hn and pf) (1967)
The white moon (Verlaine) (med-vce and pf) (1924)
SACRED
Christmas night (E. Tatum) (mix-ch) (H.T. Fitz-Simons, 1934)
The little Jesus came to town (L. Reese) (mix-ch a-cap) (Fitz-Simons, 1935)
Nativity hymn (Milton) (mix-ch, brass qrt and org or pf) (1957) (J. Fischer)
OPERA
Paola and Francesca, in three acts (S. Phillips) (1931)
INCIDENTAL MUSIC
As You Like It (Shakespeare) (1927)
Ref. composer, 17, 20, 22, 44, 53, 70, 94, 109, 124, 142, 226, 228, 403, 415, 477, 611, 646

JAMES, Mrs. See RUNCIE, Constance Owen Faunt Le Roy

JAMES, Vera

20th-century composer.

Composition
PIANO
In dancing mood, suite (OUP, 1948)
Ref. 473

JAMET, Marie-Claire

French harpist and composer. b. 1930.

Compositions
CHAMBER
Three cadenzas to Mozart's flute and harp concerto, K 299 (Paris: Leduc, 1981)
Ref. Otto Harrassowitz (Wiesbaden)

JAMILA (Gamila) (Ganukam Dschemilet)

Arabian songstress, teacher and composer of Medina. d. ca. 725. One of the four great songstresses of the Umayyad era, the others being Sallama al-Qass, Sallama al-Zarqa, and Habbaba (q.v.). She was a freed-woman of the Banu Bahz, a branch of the Banu Sulaim. Saib Khathir, a noted Persian singer, was her neighbor and Jamila memorized songs she heard him sing, surprising her mistress by singing not only his songs but also those of her own composition. After gaining her freedom she married and her house became a center of attraction for the musicians and dilettantes of Medina. She was in great demand as a teacher of singing girls and many artists of later fame, including Mabed and Ibn Aisha. She trained an orchestra of 50 singing women with lutes, which accompanied her and other famous songstresses. Her pilgrimage to Mecca with her 50 singing women in splendid litters was one of the great musical events of the Umayyad period; all the principal musicians, male and female, took part in the event, as well as poets and dilettantes. A series of musical fetes took place on their arrival in Mecca and on their return to Medina, with Jamila singing to the accompaniment of her 50 women playing lutes. Jamila was acclaimed the artistic sovereign of all the first generation of musicians who sang in Arabic. She had an amiable character and her biography is full of charming scenes that show her as a woman of great magnetism.

Bibliography

Yunus al Khatib. *Kitab al-qiyan*. (Book of Singing Girls).

Ref. 170, 171

JANABAI (Saint of Pandharpur) (Maharasthra) (Dasi Jani)

14th-century Indian composer. She commenced a life as a house maid at the age of six and although illiterate, composed religious verses, which are still sung today. She composed sacred abhangs and bhajans.

Ref. Nat. Council of Women in India, 414

JANACEKOVA, Viera

20th-century Czech composer.

Compositions

CHAMBER

String quartet (1985)

Zehn variationen auf ein slowakisches Thema (4 rec)

VOCAL

Abbitte

Ref. Frau und Musik

JANINA, Olga

19th-century Russian pianist, teacher, writer and composer. She lived in Paris, was a pupil of Liszt and active in Parisian musical life. She composed piano pieces.

Ref. 226, 276

JANITA, Dino. See TAJANI MATTONE, Ida

JANKOVIC, Miroslava

Yugoslav teacher and composer. b. Belgrade, August 25, 1943. She studied music at the Music Academy, Belgrade, under Pedrag Milosevic from 1964 to 1970. She taught musical theory in the Stanislav Binicki Music School, Belgrade.

Compositions

ORCHESTRA

Simfonijski stav (1969)

CHAMBER

String quartet (1968)

Sonata (vln and pf) (1966)

Variations (cl and pf) (1967)

Variations (vln and pf) (1974)

Suite (pf)

VOCAL

Cvilila je zelena livada (m-ch a-cap) (1965)

Cycle of songs: Napon; Noc i sunce (Jovan Ducic) (vce and pf) (1965)

Ref. composer

JANKOWSKI, Loretta Patricia

American pianist, professor and composer. b. Newark, NJ, October 20, 1950. She studied the piano under Gustave Robert Ferri and then took composition and theory lessons at the Juilliard School of Music, preparatory division. She studied composition at the Eastman School of Music under Samuel Adler, Warren Berson and Joseph Schwanter and received her B.M. (composition) in 1972. In the following year she studied at the Darlington Summer School of Music, England under Harrison Birtwistle and Morton Feldman. Through a scholarship from the Polish Government, she studied composition at the Higher School of Music, Cracow, under Marek Stachowski, 1973. She received the Bernard Rodgers award for composition in 1972 and was winner of the ABA-Ostwald Band Composition Contest in 1976. She received her Ph.D. (composition, theory and music history) from the Eastman School of Music, 1979. The next year she was assistant professor of theory and composition at California State University, Long Beach and in 1981 became adjunct professor of composition and theory at Kean College, Union, NJ. From 1983 she was assistant professor of theory and composition at the Ball State University, Muncie Indiana. She won the Women's Association for Symphony Orchestras music award in 1977 and a Meet the Composer grant, 1980.

Compositions

ORCHESTRA

Demeanor, suite for children (1974) (comm Hood College, MD)

Lustrations (New York: Alexander Broude, 1978)

OR (cham orch) (1976)

CHAMBER

Todesband (large wind ens) (1973)

Flute sextet (1972)

Praise the Lord, psalm 148 (fl, cl, vla, hp and pf) (Broude, 1981)

Declarations (vlc and 3 perc) (1972)

Four haiku (trp, mar and perc) (1980, revised 1983)

No time to mourn (vln and 2 cl) (1975)

Daguerreotypes (cl and perc) (1979)

Reverie (cl and pf) (Broude, 1982)

Sonata for B-Flat trumpet and piano (1970) (Dorn, 1982)

PIANO

Homage to Chopin (1981)

Three little Chinese girls in bright yellow dresses (1973)

VOCAL

Inside the cube, empty air (30 w-vces and Renaissance insts) (1975)

Icons: Fragments of a poem (S, hp, a-fl, vib and vlc) (1971) (Broude, 1978)

A naughty boy (J. Keats) (S, cl and pf) (Broude, 1978)

Paterson songs (T, fl, cl, vln, vlc and pf) (1983)

Cycles, 5 songs (S and pf) (1969)

SACRED

Jerusalem (mix-ch, B, org and perc) (1983)

Next to of course God (mix-ch, 2 trb and pf) (1976)

Die Sehnsuchten (m-S and org) (Broude, 1982)

ELECTRONIC

Strephenade (tape) (1973)

Ref. composer, 206, 457, 474, 625

JANOTHA, Marie Cecilia. See JANOTHA, Natalia

JANOTHA, Natalia (Marie Cecilia)

Polish pianist, writer and composer of Persian origin. b. Warsaw, June 8, 1856; d. The Hague, June 9, 1932. Her father taught Paderewski at the Moscow Institute of Music. She studied under Rudorff, Clara Schumann (q.v.), Brahms, Princess Czartoryska and F. Weber (piano) and Woldemar Bargiel (harmony). She played at the court of William I when she was 12 years old and later at Buckingham Palace for Queen Victoria and Princess Beatrix, as well as for King Edward VII and Queen Alexandra, King George V, Queen Victoria Ena of Spain and Queen Margherita of Italy. She made her debut at the Leipzig Gewandhaus in 1874. In 1885 she was appointed court pianist in Berlin. During a visit to London in 1916 she was deported because of her connection with the Kaiser and she settled in The Hague. She was Officier d'Academie and a member of the Academies of England, Italy, Germany, Austria and the Royal Academy of St. Cecilia in Rome. She published some of Chopin's works and wrote several books on him, having derived her knowledge of his music from her mother, a friend of Chopin's sister.

Compositions

ORCHESTRA

Deutscher Kaisermarsch, op. 9 (pf and orch) (Schott, 1892)

Infanteriemusik (pf and orch) (1892)

White heather, op. 16 (London: Bosworth)

PIANO

Cadenza to Beethoven's concerto in G-Sharp, op. 58 (Chappell)

Chant sans paroles (Gebethner)

Fleurs des Alpes (Gebethner, 1894)

Gavotte imperiale (Chappell, 1896)

Jubilaeumslied, op. 10 (Boosey & Hawkes, 1892)

Mazurkas, ops. 6, 8 and 14 (Breitkopf; Gebethner, 1898-1900)

Morceaux gracieux, op. 12 (Breitkopf)

Suites written for the Dutch royal family

Tatra, impressions from Zakopan (1891-1892)

Two gavottes, E-Flat and A-Sharp

Mazurkas

VOCAL
Songs incl.:
Jubilaeumslied
SACRED
Ave Maria, in A-Flat and B-Flat (S and orch) (Ashdown)
Other church music (vces and har or org)
Publications
Chopin's Greater Works.
Glimpses of Chopin's Diary.
English edition of Tarnowski's biography of Chopin.
Ref. 8, 118, 123, 297, 335, 433

JAPHA, Louise. See LANGHANS, Louise

JAQUETTI ISANT, Palmira
Spanish pianist and composer. b. Barcelona, 1895. At the Escuela Municipal de Musica, Barcelona and the Conservatorio del Liceo she studied the piano under Goberna, harmony under Sune Sintes and composition under Taltavull. She specialized in folklore and made arrangements of over 10 000 popular songs. She contributed to many anthologies.
Compositions
FOLK MUSIC
Mis canciones
Mis canciones navidenas, over 1500 songs for children
Songs (composer) (vce and fl)
Ref. 107

JARADATAN. See QU'AD and THAMAD

JARRATT, Lita
English bassoonist, violist and composer. b. London, 1879. She studied under Henri Sieffert, Kalma Roth and Dr. Herbert Botting. She played the bassoon in the O'Mara Opera Company and the first Women's Symphony Orchestra at Queen's Hall. In the Carl Rosa Opera Company she played first viola. She composed piano pieces, music for brass band, film music and songs.
Ref. 467

JASTRZEBSKA, Anna
20th-century Norwegian composer.
Compositions
PIANO
Telex to Poland (1982)
VOCAL
Small fairy-tales (ch and Orff insts) (1981)
Ref. NMI

JAZWINSKI, Barbara
American lecturer and composer. b. Chorzow, Poland, May 14, 1950. She obtained her B.A. from the National Academy of Music, Warsaw in 1971 and her M.A. from Stanford University in 1972. She was an adjunct lecturer in music theory and musicology at Brooklyn College from 1980 to 1981, of instrumental theory and ear training at New York University in 1981 and adjunct lecturer in theory at Col Staten Island, City University, New York, 1983. In 1981 she received the Prince Pierre of Monaco composition award.
Compositions
ORCHESTRA
Music for chamber orchestra (1974)
CHAMBER
Music for flute, oboe, clarinet, viola, piano and percussion (1970)
Diachromia (1971)
The seventh night of the seventh moon (1982)
Spectri sonori (1983)
VOCAL
Deep green lies the grass along the river (S, fl, cl, vln, vlc and pf) (1980)
Ref. 624, 625

JEBELES, Mrs. Themos
20th-century American composer.
Composition
OPERA
The Audition (composer) (1979)
Ref. AML newsletter

JEHANE LA FERPIERE
14th-century French minstrel. She signed the famous charter dated September 14, 1321, that established the Chappelle Saint-Julien-des-Menestriers as a corporation for jongleurs and minstrels.
Ref. 343

JENKINS, Susan Elaine
American choral conductor and composer. b. Lewis, DE, April 8, 1953. She obtained a B.S. (music education) from the University of Delaware, 1975 and an M.M. (composition) from Ohio State University, 1979, studying under Thomas Wells. She conducted a choir from 1975 to 1977 and currently works as a computer programmer, analyst and data processor.
Compositions
CHAMBER
String quartet (1975)
The ralley rag (pf) (1982)
VOCAL
Meditations I and II (ch) (1979)
For lovers parted and lovers never joined (B, pf and perc) (1983)
ELECTRONIC
Griqua (tape) (1978) (performance prize, National Conference of Women in Music, 1979)
Music for dancer and tape (1974)
Ref. 625

JENKS, Maud E.
19th-century American composer. She composed piano pieces, sacred music and songs.
Ref. 276, 343, 347

JENNEY, Mary Frances
American organist, pianist, choral conductor, lecturer, writer and composer. b. Benton, IL, November 12, 1911. She gained her Mus.B. from Lindenwood College in 1932 and Mus.M. from the University of Southern California, 1939. She taught in schools from 1932 to 1940, then became assistant to the head of the voice department, University of Southern California, until 1941. She was organist and choir conductor at Pine Shores Presbyterian Church, Sarasota, 1951 to 1960. She taught the organ, the piano and singing privately.
Composition
OPERETTA
Orange Blossom Time
Publications
History of Songs from the Living Past to the Living Present. 1939.
Ref. 643

JENNINGS, Carolyn
20th-century composer.
Compositions
VOCAL
Cat and mouse, 4 poems (John Ciardi) (2 and 3 part ch) (G. Schirmer, 1980)
A menagerie of songs (unison, 2 and 3 part ch) (Schirmer, 1979)
Ref. 624

JENNINGS, Marie Pryor (nee Epton)
American violinist, teacher and composer. b. Spartanburg, SC, December 24, 1893. She studied music at the Edith L. Wynn School of Music, Boston, the Eastman School of Music, Rochester and the University of South Carolina. She taught music in public schools in Spartanburg, was a church violinist for over 60 years and a member of various instrumental groups.
Compositions
PIANO
Dirge (1974)
Prelude, with variations (1974)
VIOLIN
Interlude (3 vln) (1960)
Moods (3 vln) (1950)
Dancer's love affair (1962)

Hopscotch (1962)
Majestic solitude (1974)
Mystic solitude (1969)
Prayer bells (1915)
Quietness (1974)
Reflections (1963)
Soliloquy (1969)
Stolen themes (1961)

VOCAL
Daffodils (1950)
Home (1950)
Love in pigtails (1965)
Music is for everyone (1967)
Ode to mother love (1950)
Oh Lil'lam (1930)
Suite: The daddy bird; De sickle moon; Hush my baby; Just beginning (1934)

SACRED
Christmas story (1970)
Lord's prayer (1968)
My prayer, anthem (1965)
Praise, hymn
Prayer for peace (1970)
Walk with me, hymn (1966)

Ref. composer

JENNY, Marie-Cécile. See JENNY, Sister Leonore

JENNY, Sister Leonore (born Marie-Cécile) (pseud. Benedikt Lopwegen)

Swiss violinist, choral conductor, nun, teacher and composer. b. Grosswangen, December 24, 1923. Her father was organist, choral and orchestra conductor of the town. After qualifying as a primary school teacher in 1945, she took up violin studies at the Lucerne Conservatory, studied composition under Robert Blum and taught music in Baldegg. From 1948 to 1949 she continued violin studies at the Music Academy, Zurich and after 1950 taught music at the Teachers' Seminar, Baldegg. She conducts the choirs of the teachers' seminar and the Baldegg convent. PHOTOGRAPH.

Compositions

CHAMBER
Duet with pentatonic theme (2 vln)
Easy duet (2 vln)
Double fugue (org)
Two inventions (pf)

VOCAL
Al lado de mi caana, Spanish folksong (ch a-cap)
Bemesst den Schritt (C.F. Meyer) (ch a-cap)
Du, Tau, den keine Sonne trinkt (W. Bergengruen) (ch a-cap)
Durch Nebel und Wind (F.A. Herzog) (ch a-cap)
Es treibt der Wind (Rilke) (ch)
Krokus (Waggerl) (ch, pf, vln and perc)
Leise duftend drehn, folk song from Israel (ch a-cap)
Die Sterne (J.h. Voss) (ch, a-fl and Orff insts)
Tagesanfang (G. Kindler) (ch a-cap)
Tausendguldenkraut (ch and Orff insts)

SACRED
Jubelt dem Herrn, small cantata (3-4 vces a-cap) (1966)
Leben muss man (ch, pf, vln, metallophone and xy) (1965)
Benedicite, Benedictus, Magnificat (2-4 vces a-cap or with org) (1970-1985)
Jesus Christus ist unser Gott (3 vces and org) (1970)
Lobet den Herrn (Psalm 135) (3 vces) (1966)
Psalm 22 (3 vces a-cap) (1983)
Psalm 36 (3 vces a-cap) (1983)
Psalm 45 (3 vces a-cap) (1960)
Sanctus Alleluja (2-4 vces a-cap or with org) (1970-1985)
Thirty Latin motets (3-4 vces a-cap or with org) (1964-1969)
Unser Leben ist Jesus Christus (3 vces and org) (1970)
Latin Mass songs (ch a-cap or org)
German Mass songs (ch a-cap or org)
Liturgical choral music
Sacred songs (ch a-cap or org)

INCIDENTAL MUSIC
Dem Kinde im Menschen, scenic collage (Morgenstern) (ch, strs, fl, rec and Orff insts) (1972)
Jedermann (H.v. Hoffmansthal) (ch a-cap) (1962)
Spiel der bunten Dinge (Gryphius) (ch a-cap) (198?)

ARRANGEMENTS
Masses (Mazate, Eberlin, Mozart) (mix-ch)
Violin, cello and organ accompaniment for numerous hymns of the Catholic hymn book

Ref. composer, 641

JENSEN, Helga

20th-century Danish composer.

Compositions

VOCAL
Tre sange for en dybere stemme (vce and pf)
Vaarhilsen, op. 3 (vce and pf)

Ref. 331

JENTSCH, May

German pianist, teacher and composer. b. 1855; d. 1918.

Compositions

SACRED
In Excelsis Gloria, carol
Other works

Ref. 433

JEPPSSON, Kerstin Maria

Swedish conductor and composer. b. Nykoping, October 29, 1948. She studied at the Conservatory of Music in Stockholm, specializing in conducting, harmony and counterpoint and graduating in 1973 and also in 1976 from the Stockholm University. Her composition teachers included Erland von Koch, Maurice Karkoff and Krzysztof Penderecki. She won a scholarship to study composition and conducting in Cracow, Poland under Krzysztof Meyer and Radwan. DISCOGRAPHY. PHOTOGRAPH.

Compositions

ORCHESTRA
Crisis for string orchestra and percussion (1977)
Impossible (vla and cham orch) (1977)
Quatro pezzi (1973)
Tre pezzi minuti (1972)
Tre sentenzi (1971)

CHAMBER
String quartet No. 1 (1974)
Piano trio
Fabian som remlade omkull men kom upp igen (Orff insts for chil)
Tre petitesser (2 fl) (1972)
Voccazione per chitarra solo (ded Magnus Andersson) (1982)
Prometheus per percussione (ded Gert Mortensen) (1983)

PIANO
En droem (ded Rolf Lindblom) (1980)
Fire smaastycken (1972)
October 1974, monologue
Three ironical pieces (1974)

VOCAL
Blomstret i Saron (solo and ch) (1972)
Fem Japanska bilder (ch) (1973)
Tre visor (T and m-ch) (1972)
Tre motetter (Karin Boye) (ch) (1972)
Fem koraler (vce and org or pf) (1979)
Jag vill moeta (Karin Boye) (S and pf) (1981)
Kvinnosaanger (m-S and pf) (1973)
Three Ryska poems (m-S and cl) (1973)
Children's songs

Ref. composer, 563, 622

JEREA, Hilda

Rumanian pianist, lecturer and composer. b. Iasi, March 17, 1916. She studied theory at the Iasi Conservatory under Sofia Teodoreanu. At the Bucharest Conservatory she studied harmony, counterpoint and composition under Mihail Jora from 1929 to 1935, aesthetics, form and composition under Dimitri Cuclin and the piano under Florica Musicescu. She studied composition in Paris under Noel Gallon in 1939 and in Budapest under Pal Kadosa in 1947. She also studied chamber music under Leo Weiner. She taught the piano at the Bucharest School of Art from 1942 to 1944 and then at the Bucharest Conservatory, 1948 to 1949, where she also taught chamber music, 1969 to 1972. In 1966 she founded the chamber music ensemble Musica Nova, which toured extensively. She was secretary of the Union of Rumanian Composers, 1949 to 1952. She received the Robert Cremer prize in 1942, the State prize in 1952, the Order of the 23rd August in 1959, the Order of Cultural Merit in 1969 and the Prize of the Union of Rumanian Composers in 1972, all for composition. DISCOGRAPHY. PHOTOGRAPH.

Compositions

ORCHESTRA
Piano concerto (1945)
Patru recitari (1944)
Suite for string orchestra (1945)

CHAMBER
Dansuri romanesti (vln and pf) (1948)

PIANO
Mici piese (4 hands) (1963)
Patru imagini vesele (4 hands) (1946)
Sonata (1934)
Suita in stil romanesc (1939)
Tabara de munte, suite (Editura Musicala, 1960)
VOCAL
Sub soarele păcii, oratorio (Dan Deslio) (1952)
Băiatul cu povestile (Cicerone Theodorescu) (ch) (1963)
Cintec de intrecere (I. Boldici) (mix-ch) (ESPLA, 1955)
Cintec de leagan (I. Minulescu) (ch) (1970)
Cintec vesel de brigadier (F. Albu) (ch) (1959)
Legàmint de pace (C. Theodorescu) (mix-ch) (1959)
Mai cioban de la mioare (I. Pingu) (B and m-ch) (1959)
Patria ma cheama (I. Banuta) (ch) (1971)
Partid, tu, inimă a țării (Mihai Beniuc) (mix-ch and pf) (Musicala, 1960)
Pui de fag și de stejar (T. Constantinescu) (ch) (1955)
Ramuri inflorite, suite (Veronica Porumbacu) (chil-ch and pf) (1962)
Sase madrigale (popular verses) (2 soloists and w-ch) (1970) (Musicala)
Sus la Murfatlat in vie (Ion Bunea) (mix-ch and pf) (Musicala, 1962)
Veniti cu noi (F. Albu) (ch) (1959)
Choruses (1946-1957) (Musicala, 1958)
Cintece de Lupta (1955)
Cintec Haiducesc (T and pf) (1967)
Dansul spicelor (V. Zamfirescu) (vce and pf) (1963)
Leiduri (M. Isanos) (vce and pf) (1963)
Melancolie (S, pf and fl)
Patru madrigale (I. Minulescu) (Musicala)
Pierda-vara (T and pf) (1967)
Sase madrigale (folk words) (1970)
Songs (Bacovia, Arghezi, Blaga, M. R. Paraschivescu, Labis, Isanos and others) (vce and pf) (Musicala)
Trei cintece (George Bacovia) (vce and pf) (1942)
Trei madrigale (I. Minulescu) (1971)
Tara holdelor bogate (C. Theodorescu) (3 vces and pf) (1957) (Musicala, 1958)
Ulciorul (S, fl and pf)
Unde in cintec este (S, fl and pf)
Veselie (T and pf)
BALLET
Haiducii (Gelu Matei) (1956)
OPERA
Casa Bernardei Alba (G. Lorca) (1966)
Ref. 94, 109, 148, 196, 563

JESI, Ada

Italian pianist, conductor, lecturer, singer and composer. b. Venice, December 12, 1912. She studied at the Music Lyceum Benedetto Marcello in Venice and in Florence at the Cherubini Conservatory, from which she graduated in the piano, singing and composition. From 1937 to 1938 she studied composition in France under Ernest Bloch. In Brazil she taught singing and composition at the Conservatory of Campinas, São Paulo from 1939 to 1947. In Italy she taught the piano from 1949 to 1955 at the Conservatory of Turin and singing at the Conservatory of Milan Giuseppe Verdi in Milan, 1955 to 1977. She performed in chamber concerts in Italy and abroad and in radio concerts in Brazil. PHOTOGRAPH.
Compositions
ORCHESTRA
Concertino per pianoforte e orchestra (1934) (mention, Franco Alfano competition)
Alice's Adventures in Wonderland, suite (1939)
Il cerchio magico, suite (1933)
Sior Todaro Brontolon, prelude (1930)
CHAMBER
Quintetto per pianoforte e quartetto d'archi (1935)
Sonata per violoncello e pianoforte (1954) (Ferraguti prize)
PIANO
La danza attraverso i secoli, for young pianists (Sao Paulo: Ricordi)
Rapsodia biblica (1937)
VOCAL
Scena mistica (3 S, ch, org and orch) (Fogazzaro) (1931)
Cino da Pistoia (A. Orvieto) (vce and pf) (1937)
Due liriche (Diego Valeri) (vce and pf) (1931)
Sei vocalizzi da concerto (vce and pf) (Milan: Suvini & Zerboni; schott, 1974)
SACRED
Salmo 12 (vce, ch and orch) (1965)
THEATRE
I due cinesini e i briganti, musical comedy (Mary Chiesa) (1938)
Ref. composer, 622

JESKE-CHOINSKA-MIKORSKA, Ludmila

Polish singer and composer. b. Poznan, 1849; d. Warsaw, November 2, 1898. At the Warsaw Conservatory she studied theory and composition under M. Zawirski, G. Roguski and Z. Noskowski and instrumentation under A. Munchheimer. She then went to Vienna where she studied singing under M. Marchesi. In Milan she studied under F. Lamberti, Sr., in Paris under A. Revial and in Frankfurt-am-Main under J. Stockhausen.
Compositions
ORCHESTRA
Rusalka, ballad (prize, competition, Chicago, 1893)
PIANO
Dances
Mazurkas
Polkas
VOCAL
Songs
OPERA
Marquise de Crecqui, comic opera (1891)
Zuch Dziewczyna, in 3 acts (also as Filutka) (K. Zaleski) (1885)
Publications
Muzykanci. Novel. Warsaw, 1884.
Bibliography
Tygodnik Illustrowany. Warsaw, 1885, no. 105.
Ref. 8, 118

JESSUP-MILDRED, Marion de (Mrs. W.)

19th-century American composer.
Composition
OPERA
Etelinda (1894)
Ref. 432

JESSYE, Eva

Black American choral conductor and composer. b. Coffeyville, KS, January 20, 1895. She obtained her M.A. from Wilberforce University and D.M. from Allen University. She studied under Percy Goetschius in New York and Will Marion Cook. She founded the Eva Jessye Choir in 1926 and toured with it in the United States, Europe and the Middle East. She was musical director for the film *Hallelujah* in 1929 and choral director of *Porgy and Bess*. She conducted the choir for *Four Saints in three acts* in 1934 and served as American consultant and composer-in-residence at Maryland State College. The City of Ann Arbor Michigan, declared January 19, 1974, Eva Jessye Day in recognition of the Afro-American Music Collection she gave to the University of Michigan. She received awards from the U.S. Treasury; National Negro Musicians; St. Louis Trailblazers; Council of Negro Women Musicians Arts Committee; Detroit Freedom Citation; Martin Luther King Foundation and a Centennial Medal from the Afro-Methodist Episcopal Church.
Compositions
VOCAL
Nobody (4 part m-ch and pf) (New York: Marks, 1956)
When the saints go marching in (ch and pf) (Marks, 1956)
SACRED
Paradise lost and regained, folk oratorio (Milton) (2 narr, ch and org) (1936)
My spirituals, song collection (New York: Robbins-Engel, 1927)
THEATRE
The Chronicle of Job, folk drama (1955)
The Life of Christ in Negro Spirituals
ARRANGEMENTS
Simon, the fisherman, Negro song (narr and mix-ch) (Boston: Birchard & Co.)
An' I cry, song
The Spirit o' the Lord done, song
Who is that yondah? song
Ref. 39, 136, 142, 335, 549

JEWELL, Althea Grant

19th-century American composer.
Compositions
Songs incl.,
In a gondola
Ref. 276, 292, 347

JEWELL, Lucina

American organist, pianist, teacher and composer. b. Chelsea, MA, 1874. She studied the piano at the New England Conservatory and the organ with Parker at Syracuse University and Henry Dunham in Boston. She also studied under Elson, Strong, J.C.D. Parker and Goetschius. She played the organ and then taught theoretical subjects at the Dana Hall School in Wellesley, MA, and at Pine Manor Junior College, Brookline, MA.

Compositions

CHAMBER

Introduction and fugue (org)
A musical calendar (pf)

VOCAL

Arbor vitae
Crossing the bar
The mermaiden
Proposal

Ref. 226, 276, 292

JIJON, Ines

20th-century Peruvian composer.

Compositions

MISCELLANEOUS

Choreographic poems:
Alegria de las cumbres (Quito, 1957)
Despertar de la montana
Nieve en el Chimborazo

Ref. Ricordi Americana

JIRACKOVA, Marta (Martha)

Czechoslovak musical director and composer. b. Kladno, March 22, 1932. She studied at the Prague Conservatory under Emil Hlobil (orchestration, conducting and composition) and after 1958 studied under Alois Haba. From 1959, she worked as musical director for Czechoslovak Radio in Prague. She won the Krasnohorska Prize in a vocal composition competition in 1972. In 1978 she completed postgraduate studies in new methods of contemporary composition at the Janacek Academy of Music, Brno. In the same year she founded a vocal chamber ensemble with conductor and choirmistress Jindra Jindackova, *Laetitia* which has given numerous performances of ancient folk songs and madrigals from Europe, in their original languages. She married Vaclav Jiracek, conductor-in-chief of the State Philharmonic Orchestra, Ostrava. PHOTOGRAPH.

Compositions

ORCHESTRA

Nanda Devi: First symphony, op. 25 (1979)
Homage to Slava Vorlova, op. 8, symphonic sketches (1973)

CHAMBER

Pastel of six colours, op. 14 (fl, ob, vln, vla, vlc and hpcd) (1975)
Two inventions, op. 6 (vln, vlc and pf) (1975)
Fantasia on Otakar Jeremias' theme, op. 27 (gtr) (1981)

PIANO

A child's world, op. 11, 3-part cycle of recital studies (1974)
Five preludes, interludium and postludium, op. 5 (1974)
A few minutes in intervals, op. 1, studies (1972)

VOCAL

Loc Geet, op. 2, cycle (Indian folk poetry) (w-ch) (Krasnohorska Prize, 1972)
Song for Czech children, op. 4 (El Car) (chil-ch, fl, cl and tam) (1972)
What will I be?, op. 6, short songs (chil-ch and pf, 4 hands)
Eight wonders of the world, op. 18 (ch, hp, perc and bells) (1979)
Salut, op. 26 (chil-ch a-cap) (1979)
Three songs without words, op. 21 (S, perc and cham ens) (1976)
Fairy-tale train, op. 15. cycle of songs for children (1975)
I, Charles Lounsbury, op. 7 (composer) (B and pf) (1973)
Just like that, op. 3 (J. Prevert) (S, A and pf) (1974)
Little headscarf game, op. 17
New Christmas songs, op. 12 (Czech poets) (S, A and pf) (1974)
Three Australian folk songs, op. 10 (A.B. Peterson) (vce and pf) (1974)
Two minute melodramas, op. 16 (1975)

ELECTRONIC

The Ship of Fools (on a picture by Hieronymus Bosch) (1977)
Lullaby (1977)

MULTIMEDIA

The dove of peace, with ballet (1978)

INCIDENTAL MUSIC

The Time for Life, TV drama (1981)
The Owl's Nest, TV drama (1981)

Ref. composer

JIRKOVA, Olga

Czechoslovak pianist, conductor and composer. b. Zilina, January 7, 1936. In 1966 she graduated in the piano and composition from the Prague Academy of Music and in 1967, graduated in orchestral conducting. In 1959 she won a silver medal in a state piano competition and in 1977 third prize in a state competition for choir conducting.

Compositions

ORCHESTRA

Violin concerto (1981)
Our army, march (1958)

CHAMBER

Sonata (ob and pf) (1966)
Variation for wind quintet impression (trp and pf) (1967)

PIANO

Cadenza to Mozart's F-Major concerto (1966)
Children's pieces (1960)

VOCAL

Clouds fly; my home (chil-ch) (1958)
All the ways, cycle (T) (1972)
Solemn sonnet (1966)
Vernal wind understands me (old Chinese poetry) (S) (1972)

BALLET

The Hunchback (1975)

INCIDENTAL MUSIC

Scenic music for fairy tales (1965)

Ref. composer

JOACHIM, Amalie (nee Weiss)

Austrian contralto, professor and composer. b. Marburg, May 10, 1839; d. Berlin, February 3, 1898. She made her debut at Troppau in 1853 and was later engaged at the Kaerntnertor Theatre in Vienna. After her marriage to the violinist Joseph Joachim in 1863 she won worldwide fame as a singer of Schumann's and Brahms' songs. She became professor of singing at the Klindworth-Scharwenka Conservatory, Berlin.

Compositions

VOCAL

Aus Gothland
Bei Tag, in meiner Sorg' und Mueh'
Fragen soll feierlich
Die Nixe
Six Swedish folksongs
Wermeland

Ref. Frau und Musik, 8

JOCHSBERGER, Tzipora H.

American pianist, professor and composer. b. Germany, December 27, 1920. She received a piano diploma from the Palestine Academy of Music and a teacher's diploma from the Music Teachers' Seminar, Jerusalem. She obtained a master's degree in Jewish Music Education and a doctorate in sacred music from the Jewish Theological Seminary of America. She became an American citizen in 1956. She lectured in various colleges in Israel and America and from 1947 to 1950 was the founder and a director of the Rubin Academy, Jerusalem and in 1952 founder and director of the Hebrew Arts school for music and dance. She was choral director for The Society of the Advancement of Judaism from 1955 to 1972 and for the Tree of Life Fellowship, 1972 to 1974. In 1981 she founded the American Jewish Choral Festival. She received an honorary mention in the Ernest Bloch Competition, 1968. She appeared on radio and television in the United States. DISCOGRAPHY.

Compositions

CHAMBER

Melodies of Israel, duets and trios (recs and other insts)
Four recorder pieces (S, A and T recs)
Duets (obs)
Fire Island suite (2 rec)
Holiday suite (fl and cl)
Blessings, suite (vln)
Hava N'Halela, on Israeli folk songs (rec)

PIANO

Contrasts
Dancing leaves, for children
Favorite Hassidic and Israeli melodies, for children
Fragments
Hebrew folk melodies
Moods
Ten musical experiences, for children
Variations on a song, for children

VOCAL

Mibershit (Bar, ch and orch)
Song of Moses (B and str orch)
Aphorisms (Rabindranath Tagore) (mix-ch a-cap)
Four Hebrew madrigals (Rahel) (mix-ch a-cap)
Hashamayim Mesaprim, three choral pieces (boys' ch)
Eshet Hayil (vce and fl)
A harvest of Jewish songs (vce and pf)
Shirei Hanagid (T and pf)

Shirei Zelda (m-S, vln and vlc)
Songs of Rahel (vce and pf)
Two Yehuda Halevy songs (vce, fl and vln)
Yearnings (counter-T, rec and viol)
SACRED
Bekol Zimrah, collection (mix-ch a-cap)
Hallel, psalms (cantor, chil-vces and ch)
Lament and Kaddish (m-S, Bar, vln and vlc)
Ref. composer, 142

JOERGENSEN, Christine
20th-century Danish composer.
Compositions
PIANO
Skovsoen
VOCAL
Kaelkebakken eller Rutchebakken (vce and pf)
Ref. 331

JOEST, Emma
20th-century Danish composer.
Compositions
CHAMBER
Menuet (vln and pf)
VOCAL
Blabaer, 7 songs (vce and pf)
Den lille hund, children's songs
Klokker, op. 2 (vce and pf)
Ref. 331

JOHN, Patricia Spaulding
American harpist, editor, teacher and composer. b. Canton, IL, July 16, 1916. She studied at the William Marsh Rice University (B.A. 1941), the Curtis Institute of Music from 1936 to 1937 and Mills College in 1935 and studied the harp under Carlos Salzedo, Anna Louise David, Kathryn Julye and Mildred Milligan. She was a harp teacher from 1950 to 1976 and a harpist with the Springfield Civic Symphony in 1947, Galveston Civic Symphony in 1952 and Houston Symphony Orchestra, 1956. Patricia gave recitals in the United States, British West Indies, Indonesia, Netherlands and England. She was founder of the Houston Chapter of the American Harp Society in 1966 and editor of *Harpist*, New York in 1969. She was president of the San Jacinto Chapter of the American Harp Society in 1975. PHOTOGRAPH.
Compositions
HARP
Tachystos (1 or more hp) (Pantile Press, 1974)
Americana, suite: Preamble; A time of snow; Imago ignato (Pantile, 1978)
Aprille (Pantile, 1969)
Henriette (Un portrait) (Pantile, 1974)
Let's play arithmetic, series (1975)
Let's play canoe, series (1975)
Let's play clown dances, series (non-pedal hp) (Pantile, 1975)
Mnemosyne (Pantile, 1969)
Sea anemones (non-pedal harp) (1982)
Sea changes, suite: Fog off Pelican Spit; Summer squall; Surf (Pantile, 1968)
Serenata (1981) (ded Pierre Jamet)
Ref. composer, 77, 526, 625

JOHNOVA, Slava. See VORLOVA, Slava

JOHNS, Altona Trent
Compositions
PIANO
Barcarolle
There's no hiding place down here
Ref. ILWC

JOHNSON, Elizabeth
American composer. b. 1913. DISCOGRAPHY.
Composition
CHAMBER
String quartet (1938)
Ref. 563

JOHNSON, Eloise Lisle
American composer. b. Holliday Cove, WV, November 15, 1928. She obtained her B.M. from Mount Union College and M.A. from Ohio State University. She studied composition under Arthur Shepherd, Wendell Otey, Walter H. Hodgson and George Wilson and was music consultant for Grand Rapids public schools. She was awarded the Theodore Presser scholarship. PHOTOGRAPH.
Compositions
VOCAL
The Pied Piper of Hamelin (Browning) (unison ch, speaking ch and pf) (1970)
In a manger, song (1952) (New York: Silver Burdett)
Jack-in-the-box, song (1952) (Burdett)
Mike Fink, song (1948) (Burdett)
Paul Bunyan, song (1948) (Burdett)
THEATRE
A Christmas Carol (Dickens) (narr, unison ch, pantomime and pf) (1970)
Johnny Appleseed (unison ch and pf) (1971)
The Land of Pretend (Summy-Birchard, Evanston)
Ref. composer, 395

JOHNSON, Harriet
20th-century American composer.
Compositions
VOCAL
Songs
OPERA
The Pet of the Met
Ref. 142, 465

JOHNSON, Lena. See McLIN, Lena

JOHNSON, J. Rosamond
American composer. b. 1873; d. 1954. DISCOGRAPHY.
Composition
VOCAL
Lit'l gal (vce and pf) (1917)
Ref. 563

JOHNSON, Mary Ernestine Clark
American pianist, poetess, teacher and composer. b. West Alden, NY, July 8, 1895. She studied the piano under Anton Rubinstein and Kullack; under Heniot Levi and Helen Clark Watson at the American Conservatory and William Geist and Dr. Rossiter Cole at the Cosmopolitan Roosevelt University. She studied composition under Arthur Dunham and Dr. Walter Goodell and did postgraduate study at Chicago Conservatory under Walton Perkins. She was a teacher at the School of Piano and Art, Park Manor for five years. She received a special commendation from Rudolph Ganz as well as awards from the National League of American Pen Women. She obtained a bronze medal and diploma from the Centro Studi e Scambi Internazionali, Rome.
Compositions
PIANO
Age of fantasy
Children's suite
Fantasy in A-Minor
Sonatine in C-Major
Staccato caprice
Wimsey
OPERETTA
Thirteen Clocks
Publications
Lacquered Faces. Poems. 1954.
Ref. 84, 141

JOHNSTON, Alison Aileen Annie
English organist, pianist and composer. b. London, September 13, 1916. She studied at the Royal Academy of Music and privately under Maurice Cole. She gave concerts in the London area between 1939 and 1945 and later gave solo concerts and organ recitals. She was a teacher and coach to various ensembles and school orchestras. She composed orchestral pieces, bassoon pieces, string, piano and recorder trios, a viola sonata, organ preludes, bagatelles for the piano and songs. She composed for the Tavistock Theatre productions and had some teaching works published.
Ref. 206

JOHNSTON-REID, Sarah Ruth (Sally)

American professor and composer. b. East Liverpool, OH, January 30, 1948. She obtained a B.M.E. from Abilene Christian University in 1969 and an M.M. from Hardin Simmons University, 1971. She was assistant professor at Abilene Christian University and director of its electronic studio, becoming chairlady of its department of music in 1979. She is a member of the Abilene Philharmonic Orchestra and the San Angelo Symphony Orchestra.

Compositions

SYMPHONIC BAND

New Manchester suite
Wasatch symphony (1971)

CHAMBER

Escape wheel for five (d-b, 3 cl and pf)
Studies (2 ob and cor anglais)
Arioso (hn and pf)
Braxton (pf and perc)

VOCAL

Note the silence (vce, perc, pf and brass ens)
Five haiku (vce and pf)

Ref. composer, 147

JOHNSTON-WATSON, Miss

Early 20th-century English composer. Her opera was performed in London.

Composition

OPERA

The Daughter of Snow (1901)

Ref. 431

JOLAS, Betsy

French organist, pianist, editor, singer and composer of American parentage. b. Paris, August 5, 1926. She spent her childhood in the United States and France, returning to the United States in 1940. She obtained her B.A. from Bennington College in 1946, where she studied composition and theory under Paul Boepple, the organ under Carl Weinrich and the piano under Schnabel. She sang with and accompanied the Dessoff Choir while she was in New York in the 1940s. In 1946 she went to Paris and completed her music studies at the Paris Conservatoire, studying composition under Darius Milhaud, analysis under Olivier Messiaen and fugue under Simone Ple Caussade. After 1955 she edited *Ecouter aujourd'hui*, the periodical of the French Radio-Television Network and was a regular contributor to *Preuves*. She acted as a substitute for Olivier Messiaen at the Paris Conservatoire. She received awards from Besancon International Contest for young conductors in 1953; the Chicago Copley Foundation in 1954; Prix des Auteurs et Compositeurs de Langue Français in 1961; the American Academy of Arts and Letters in 1973 and the Koussevitsky Foundation, 1974. In June 1985 she was named Commandeur des Arts et des Lettres by Maurice Fleuret, director of music and dance. DISCOGRAPHY. PHOTOGRAPH.

Compositions

ORCHESTRA

Symphony (light orch) (1957)
Stancés, piano concerto
Eleven Lieder (trp and small orch) (1977)
Musique d'hiver (org and orch) (1971) (Heugel)
Quatre Plages (str orch) (1968) (Heugel)
Tales of a Summer Sea, tone poem (1977)
Trois rencontres (str trio and orch) (1972) (Heugel)

CHAMBER

Le chant de l'amour triomphant (after Turgenev) (inst ens) (1964)
D'un opéra de voyage (22 insts) (1967)
J.D.E. (14 insts) (1966) (Heugel)
Well met (12 insts) (1973)
Figures (9 insts) (1958)
How now (8 insts) (1972) (Heugel)
Etats (vln and 6 perc) (1969)
Lassus ricercare (brass, hp, 2 perc and 2 vlc) (1970) (Heugel)
O wall (ww qnt) (Heugel 1980)
Points d'aube (vla and wind insts; also 1 performer on 15 sax) (1968)
Quatuor III, 9 etudes (str qrt) (1973) (comm Kindler Foundation)
String quartet No. 1 (1956)
Remember (cor anglais, vla and vlc) (1971) (Heugel)
Sonate à trois (1955)
Quatre pièces en marge (vlc and pf) (Paris: Billaudot, 1984)
Trifolium (fl and pf) (1947)
Trois duos (tba and pf) (Paris: Leduc, 1984)
Auprès (hpcd) (Ricordi, 1980)
Autour (hpcd) (Heugel, 1974)
B for sonata (1973) (Heugel)
Episode (fl) (1964)
Episode troisieme (trp) (1981) (Heugel)
Episode quatrieme (sax) (Leduc, 1984)
Episode sixieme (vla) (Leduc, 1984)
Fusains (picc and fl, 1 player) (1971) (Heugel)
Musique de jour pour orgue (Heugel, 1981)
Scion (vlc) (Heugel, 1974)
Sonata (vla) (1955)
Tranche (hp) (1966) (Heugel)

PIANO

Calling E.C. (Leduc, 1985)
Chansons d'approche
Stancés (Heugel, 1981)

VOCAL

Dans la chaleur vacante, cantata (ch and orch) (1963) (Heugel)
L'oeil égaré dans les plis de l'obeissance du vent, cantata (Victor Hugo) (S, A, B, mix-ch and orch) (1961) (Heugel)
Cinq poèmes de Jacques Dupin (vces and orch or pf) (1959)
Diurnes (mix-ch) (1970) (Heugel)
Everysom sings (double w-ch and brass insts) (1955)
Madrigal (12 vces) (1947)
Motet II (12 mix-vces and cham ens) (Jacques Dupin) (1965) (Heugel)
Musique pour le Cantique des Cantiques (12 mix-vces) (1970)
Pantagruel (mix-ch) (1954)
Sonata à douze (mix-ch) (1954)
Caprice à deux voix (m-S, Cont and pf) (Heugel, 1983)
Caprice à une voix (1976) (Heugel)
Chansons pour Paule (vces and pf) (1951)
Mon ami (Ariettas to sing and play) (1974) (Heugel)
Motet I, To everything there is a season (7 vces)
Mots (5 vces and 8 insts) (1963) (Heugel)
Quatour II (S and str trio) (1964) (Heugel)
Plupart du temps (vces and pf) (1949)

SACRED

Mass (1946)

OPERA

D'un opéra de poupée (11 insts) (Paris, Salabert, 1982)
Le pavillon au bord de la riviere, Chinese chamber opera, in 4 acts (Kua Han Chin) (reciter, vces and inst ens) (1975)

INCIDENTAL MUSIC

Ajax (Sophocles) (1960)
Code génétique, film (1964)
La dernière existence au camp de Tatenberg (A. Gattis) (1962)
Iphigénie (Racine) (1964)
La Tempête (Shakespeare) (vocal and inst ens) (1966)
The Trojans (Euripides) (1961)
Voix premières, radio play (1974)

Publications

Il fallait voter seriel meme si. Preuves 178: 40-42.

Bibliography

Cadieu, Martine. *Entretien avec Betsy Jolas*. Lettres Françaises. Feb. 21, 1968.
Chauvin, M.J. *Entretien avec Betsy Jolas*. Courrier Musical 27, 1969.
Fleuret, Maurice. *La Musique au feminin*. Nouvelle Observateur, 1966: 36.
Genet, Janet Flanner. *Letter from Paris*. New Yorker, May 11, 1968.
Krasteva, I. *Betsy Jolas*. Schweizerische Musikzeitung, 1974: 6.
Biographical sketch of Betsy Jolas. Mens en Melodie 30, Sept. 1975: 273.
Pulido, Esperanza. *Con Betsy Jolas en Paris*. Heterofonia, vol. 11, No. 6.

Ref. composer, *Composers' Forum* Fall 1985, 4, 5, 17, 20, 22, 94, 109, 173, 189, 397, 454, 563, 622, 625

JOLLEY, Florence Werner

American organist, pianist, choral conductor, teacher and composer. b. Kingsburg, CA, July 11, 1927. She obtained her B.A. from California State University and continued with postgraduate study in composition and theory at the Eastman School of Music. She received an M.M. in church music from the University of Southern California in 1957. She was a lecturer and demonstrator of piano improvisation for the Los Angeles Community College District from 1962 and a lecturer at Los Angeles Pierce College from 1962 to 1965. From 1965 to 1966 she studied composition at the University of California, Los Angeles and in 1977 was a doctoral candidate at Nova University. Her composition teachers were Russell Bodley, Lara Hoggard and John Vincent. For more than a decade she served as a professional church organist and multiple-choir conductor and was also a private piano teacher. She is a member of ASCAP.

Compositions

CHAMBER

Recollections (ob and pf) (Innovative Music Studies, 1971)

PIANO

Little suite
Suite

VOCAL

Choral pieces

SACRED
Gloria in excelsis (ch) (Shawnee Press, 1953)
Holy Lord God of Hosts (ch) (Shawnee, 1954)
The light has come (ch, brass and org; also ch, brass and timp)
ELECTRONIC
Journey thru' a rock (org and tape)
ARRANGEMENTS
All people that on earth do dwell (Lawson Gould)
My grandfather's clock (2 pf) (Innovative, 1975)
My old Kentucky home (Foster) (2 pf) (Innovative, 1975)
Oh Suzanna (Foster) (2 pf) (Innovative, 1975)
When love is kind (2 pf) (Innovative, 1975)

Publications

Basic Music Theory and Harmony. 1 400 visuals, 12 tapes. Curriculum development; Instructional Development Department, Los Angeles Community College District, 1974.

The Beginner's Positive Approach to Music Theory. Text, cassettes. Innovative Music Studies, 1976.

The Florence Jolley Piano Method. Text, cassettes, Rev. edition, Innovative Music Studies, 1973. *Braille edition*, Innovative Music Studies, 1974.

The Positive Approach to Music Theory. Musicianship 1. Innovative Music Studies, 1975.

Ref. composer, 137, 142, 347

JOLLY, Margaret Anne

South African organist, violist and composer. b. Marseilles, France, June 4, 1919. She studied at the University of Cape Town College of Music and the organ under Eric Coates. From 1969 she studied harmony, composition and the viola under Walter Swanson. She was assistant organist at various churches in India from 1937 to 1945 and returned to South Africa in 1946, where she was appointed organist at St. Thomas' Church, Rondebosch, Cape Town. In 1973 she joined the Cape Town Philharmonic Orchestra. She wrote over 150 compositions, of which 25 were published. PHOTOGRAPH.

Compositions

CHAMBER
Toccata (str trio)
Trio (vln, vlc and pf)
Air (ob and pf)
Air (vla and pf)
Felicity (vln and pf) (1977)
ORGAN
Concluding voluntary (1971)
Chorale prelude on Tallis (1972)
PIANO
Gigue (1978)
Mazurka
Song without words
Three part invention (1978)
Two part invention No. 1 in F-Major (1979)
Two part invention No. 2 in E-Flat Major (1979)
The haunted house
VOCAL
Loveliest of trees (mix-ch and pf) (1970)
It was a lordling's daughter (mix-ch and pf) (1970)
The poor soul sat sighing (ch a-cap) (1970)
A birthday (vce and pf) (1969)
The Christmas tree (vce and pf) (1977)
Come live with me (vce and pf) (1970)
Farewell to all make-believe (vce and pf) (1975)
I will make you brooches (vce and pf) (1970)
A match (vce and pf) (1970)
Omnia Vincit (vce and pf) (1971)
Stars for breakfast (vce and pf) (1977)
Weathers (vce and pf) (1969)
SACRED
Carol for the southern hemisphere
When morning golds the skies
Hail to the day, carol (1976)
OPERETTA
The Auctioneer (overture and 22 songs linked by continuous music) (1976)
THEATRE
Orange Blossoms, musical play (overture and 12 songs) (1972)
Asylum for the Sane, musical play, (12 songs) (1973)
The Robin's Nest, musical play, (overture and 17 songs) (1974)
Twenty-five songs from When a Smile is Born, children's play and Rough Diamond (Dalro, 1972)
ARRANGEMENTS
Away in a manger (vln, vlc and pf) (1977)
Bethlehem (vln, vlc and pf) (1977)

Ref. composer

JOLY, SUZANNE

French pianist, lecturer and composer. b. Oran, Algeria, March 16, 1916. She began her musical education at the age of four and started composing when she was six. She studied the piano under Lazare Levy and A. Veluard and harmony, fugue, counterpoint and composition under Noel Gallon, Roger Ducasse, Tony Aubin and Olivier Messiaen. After 1946 she gave numerous piano recitals in Paris and Switzerland and over the radio. She studied composition again under Messiaen from 1951 to 1953 and later taught the piano at the Conservatoire of the 14th Arrondissement, Paris, 1960 to 1969. PHOTOGRAPH.

Compositions

ORCHESTRA
Fantaisie concertante (pf and orch) (1946) (Boosey & Hawkes)
Petite suite (1943) (EFM Technisonor)
Petite valse (1948)
Rupestre (after a painting at Tassili) (EFM)
Serenade (1948)
CHAMBER
Passacaille (cl and str qrt) (1976)
Sequence (sax qrt) (1973) (EFM)
Triptyque (str qrt) (1964)
PIANO
Au Luxembourg (1948)
Theme, variations and allegro fugato (1952)
VOCAL
Ode à la jeune fille (young w-vce, reciter and small inst ens) (1968)
INCIDENTAL MUSIC
Cantilene et danse
Deux Mélodies (Verlaine, Chanson d'automne) (1942)
Musique pour un court-metrage (Un ete a Boulouris) (small inst ens) (1963)

Ref. composer

JONAS, Anna

19th-century German composer. She lived in Berlin in 1858.

Compositions

PIANO
Amorosa, polka-mazurka, op. 8 (1859)
Glueckechen, polka-mazurka
Moosroeschen, polka-mazurka (1858)
Glocken, polka-mazurka (1858)
Camelien, waltz, op. 35
Jugendtraeume, waltz
Benefiz, quadrille, op. 34
Lancier, quadrille a la cour, op. 9
Ernestinen, Galop
Rondo (Rouhier)

Ref. 121, 297

JONES, Catherine

American pianist and composer. b. California, 1958. She studied the piano under Peter Yazback, composition under Gordon Crosse and Justin Connolly and graduated from the University College of Santa Barbara in 1980 with a B.A. (music theory and composition).

Composition

CHAMBER
Dialogues (2 fl) (1979)

Ref. University of California, Santa Barbara

JONES, Dovie Osborn

20th-century American composer. b. near Corydon, IN. She composed piano works and songs.

Ref. 347

JONES, Hart. See HIGGINBOTHAM, Irene

JONES, Joyce Gilstrap

20th-century American composer. She obtained her M.S.M. at Southwestern Baptist Theological Seminary, Forth Worth, 1957.

Composition

SACRED
Psalm XVIII, cantata (vce, mix-ch and org) (1957)

Ref. 147

JONES, Marjorie

20th-century American singer, teacher and composer. b. Portland, OR. She studied under Leon Kirchner and graduated from the University of Southern California with an M.A..

Compositions

VOCAL

Choral works and songs, incl.:
It couldn't be done
Little sister Rose-Marie
November night
One seeing weather-beaten trees
Rain
Shine
Song cycle
The songs of Marjorie Jones, 2 vols
Triad

SACRED

Hosanna we sing, cantata (ch)
Two other cantatas
A sense of Him
A study in Colossians
What can I give Him?

Ref. 148, 465, 494

JONES, Sister Ida (O.S.U.)

American harpist, organist, pianist, lecturer and composer. b. Louisville, KY, August 9, 1898. She studied at the Ursuline College and the Cincinnati Conservatory under George Leighton and Carl Hugo Grimm and the piano, the organ and the harp privately. She taught in church schools from 1922 to 1934 and at the Ursuline College from 1934 to 1940 and then until 1966 was chairlady of the music department. In 1961 she won a Composers' Press publication award. From 1968 she was on the staff of the Ursuline School of Music.

Compositions

CHAMBER

Scherzo (fl, cl and bsn) (1961)

SACRED

Mass for the Christ Child (ch) (1972)
Mass in honour of the Prince of Peace (ch) (1970)
Mass in honour of our Lady (ch) (1972)
Ave Maria (ch) (1972)
The benedictus (ch) (1971)
Hodie Christus natus est (w-ch a-cap) (1959)
The Magnificat (ch) (1971)
Supplication (w-ch) (1958)
The immortal, song (S and pf) (1958)

Ref. 142

JONES-DAVIES, Maude

20th-century British pianist, teacher and composer. b. Pencader. She studied privately and at the Royal Academy of Music under Hilda Wright and Victor Booth, becoming an L.R.A.M. and an A.R.C.M. She was a concert pianist and accompanist and taught the piano and singing at a girls' school on the Isle of Thanet. She composed hymns, anthems and songs.

Ref. 467

JORDAN, Alice Yost

American organist and composer. b. Davenport, IA, December 31, 1916. She graduated from Drake University, Des Moines, with an B.M.E. and continued with graduate study in composition under Dr. Francis J. Pyle. She won first prize in the Publication award contest, Composers Press in 1959 and the Contemporary Music award from the Central Iowa Chapter of Chorister's Guild, 1959. In 1970 she received the Alumni Distinguished Service Award from Drake University and the Orah Ashley Lamke Distinguished Alumni Award at the International Convention of Mu Phi Epsilon, International Professional Music Fraternity in 1980. The One-in-a-Hundred, Drake University Centennial award was conferred on her in 1981. DISCOGRAPHY. PHOTOGRAPH.

Compositions

ORGAN

Adoration on a traditional English melody (1976)
All hail the power of Jesus' name (1976)
Cantabile on Hyfrydol (1974)
Elegy on a Norwegian folk melody (Broadman Press, 1956)
Fantasy on foundation (Broadman, 1976)
Four nativity melodies (1976)
Hymns of grateful praise, 11 voluntaries (Broadman, 1980)
Meditation on Penitentia (1974)
Prelude on mercy (Broadman, 1976)
Variations for hymn singing (1977)
Worship service music for the organist (1975)

SACRED

All things are Thine (mix-ch and opt acc) (Composer Press, 1959; now Seesaw Music Corp.)
America the beautiful (mix-ch) (Heritage Music Press)
The beatitudes (mix-ch) (Abingdon Press)
Choral service sentences (mix-ch) (Sacred Music)
Eight reponses (ch) (1978)
Exhortation (mix-ch and org) (McAfee, 1982)
God of mercy, God of blessing (mix-ch and opt acc)
God who touchest earth with beauty (mix-ch) (Belwin-Mills)
In the calm night (mix-ch) (Broadman)
Joyfully we hymn Thy praise (mix-ch) (Belwin-Mills)
Late have I loved Thee (mix-ch) (Harold Flammer)
Name of wondrous love (mix-ch and org) (H.W. Gray, 1982)
Only a manger (mix-ch and opt acc) (Belwin-Mills)
Prayer is the soul's sincere desire (mix-ch) (Canyon)
Psalm 103: Bless the Lord, O my soul (ch) (1970)
A season and a time (mix-ch and pf; also org) (1982)
See the land (Easter and spring) (mix-ch) (Abingdon Press)
Seven responses (mix-ch) (Sacred Music)
Song of praise (mix-ch) (Harold Flammer)
The time for singing has come (ch) (1969)
As Joseph was a-walking (unison vces and acc) (H.W. Gray)
Beloved night (w-vces) (J. Fischer)
Come and dwell with me (unison vces and acc) (Broadman)
God is here on every hand (unison vces and acc) (Belwin-Mills)
God who made the earth (unison vces and acc) (Broadman)
God's lark at morning (w-vces) (H.T. Fitz Simons Co.)
Harvest song of praise (unison vces and acc) (Broadman)
Hymn to joy (unison vces and acc) (Broadman)
Hymn to spring (unison vces and acc) (Broadman)
How softly love was born (mix-ch and org) (McAfee, 1982)
In spring (w-vces) (J. Fischer)
Prayer in winter (unison vces and acc) (Belwin-Mills)
Ring, Christmas bells (unison vces and acc) (Sacred Music)
Sing praises (unison vces and acc) (Broadman)
Song to sing out (unison vces and acc) (Broadman)
Suffer the little children (unison vces and acc) (Hope Publishing)
Touch my life (unison vces and acc) (Broadman)
Choral service sentences (1977)
Hymn of praise (1972)
Psalm 5 (vce and org)
Take joy home (Roger Dean Pub.)

Ref. composer, 142, 190, 228, 359, 475, 563

JORDAN, Frances Elizabeth. See MOSHER, Frances Elizabeth

JORDAN, Mrs. (pseud. of Dorothea/Dora Bland)

British actress, singer and composer. b. Waterford, 1762; d. St. Cloud, near Paris, July 3, 1816. A milliner by trade, she acted on the stage in Dublin, 1777. She never married but had several children and adopted the name of Mrs. Jordan.

Composition

VOCAL

The Bluebells of Scotland, ballad (also pf and hp) (London: Longman, Clementi & Co.; Thos. Jones & Co., 1800)

Ref. 6, 65, 276, 347, 405

JORGENSEN, Christine. See JOERGENSEN, Christine

JOSEPH, Rosa

German composer. b. Hamburg, December 23, 1889; d. Hamburg, May 30, 1928. She composed dances and songs.

Ref. 226

JOSEPHINE, Queen of Sweden and Norway

B. 1807; d. 1876. The daughter of Napoleon's adopted son, Eugene Beauharnais, Duke of Leuchtenberg and granddaughter of King Maximilian I of Bavaria, she married Crown Prince Oscar (later Oscar I) in 1823. From an early age she was interested in music. In her later years she arranged and participated in quartets in her apartments in the Royal Palace of Stockholm. DISCOGRAPHY. PHOTOGRAPH.

Composition

PIANO

Romance islandaise (Xavier Marmier)

Ref. STIM, 563

JOULAIN, Jeanne-Angele-Desirée-Yvonne

French organist, professor and composer. b. Paris, July 22, 1920. She studied at the Conservatory of Amiens from 1934 to 1943, the Ecole Cesar-Franck in Paris from 1941 to 1943 and at the Paris Conservatoire, 1947 to 1952. She studied the organ under Marcel Dupré and composition under Guy de Lioncourt. In 1951 she was a professor at the Lille Conservatory; from 1952 to 1961 professor at the Conservatory in Roubaix; after 1954 organist at St. Maurice de Lille and from 1961 to 1969 professor at the Douai Conservatory.

Compositions

ORGAN

Communion pour tous les temps
Elevation pour le saint jour de Paques sur Victimae paschali
Noël flamand
Paraphrase pour la fête de la Toussaint sur Justorum animae in manu Dei sunt
Postlude
Pour la Fête des Rameaux sur Hosanna Filio David
Other elevations, preludes, introits, offertories, Christmas and Communion music

Ref. 236

JOUVENEL, Germaine de

French composer.

Composition

PIANO

A trois temps

Ref. Frau und Musik

JOY, Margaret E.

20th-century American composer of an opera and songs.

Ref. 465

JOYCE, Florence Buckingham

19th-century American composer.

Compositions

VOCAL

Songs incl.:
The dream tree
Little Boy Blue

Ref. 276, 292, 347

JUDD, Margaret Evelyn

20th-century British teacher and composer. b. Brackley, Northamptonshire. She studied at the Royal Academy of Music and won many first prizes for composition. She taught music for several years.

Compositions

ORCHESTRA

Trieste, slow movement in B-Minor for string orchestra

PIANO

At the court of Louis (Bosworth)
Chinese gardens (1960) (1st prize)
Crinoline dances (1958) (1st prize)
Dance of the Mazurs (Bosworth)
Dance of the shadows (Bosworth)
Dance of the West Wind (1959)
Dawn (Bosworth)
Four little miniatures (1967)
Giga alla ecco (Bosworth)
Hop-along Jenny (Bosworth)
In a gondola (Bosworth)
Into the park a-maying (Bosworth)
Irish hills (Bosworth)
Jane's gavotte (1960) (1st prize)
Jolly Roger (Bosworth)
Music for school assembly, 2 vols (Bosworth)
Papillons (Bosworth)
Passepied (1959)
A path through the wood (Bosworth)
Queen Elizabeth's dances (1972)
Raindrops (1957)
Rondonello (1963)
Scherzino (1961)
Spring dances (Bosworth)
Summer dances (1964)
Swiss sketches (1966)
Told by the firelight (Bosworth)
Two divertimenti
The witches (Bosworth)

VOCAL

To daffodils (w-ch) (1954)
There's a charm in spring, 2 part song (1970)

SACRED

The Babe He lay a-sleeping, unison song (1964)
Magnificat and Nunc Dimittis in E-Flat

Ref. composer, 206

JUENGER, Patricia

Austrian/Swiss organist, pianist and composer. b. in aeroplane, August 6, 1951. She studied composition, the organ and the piano in Vienna, Paris and Frankfurt. In 1979 she won the Theodor Koerner Stiftung Composition Prize and the prize of the Vienna Art Fund. From 1980 to 1983 she won scholarships from the Alban Berg Foundation in Vienna, the Paul Sacher Foundation in Basle, the Austrian government and Aargau, Switzerland. She works as a freelance composer. PHOTOGRAPH.

Compositions

ORCHESTRA

Machine's Party (cham orch) (1985)

CHAMBER

Vibrazioni (37 drums and 4 players) (1981)
Oh you my sweet evening star (6 perc) (1982)
Gesang des Poseidon (org, 2 players) (1981)
Evocations (1 or 2 perc) (1980)
Articulations (cl) (1978)
Fourberie (vln) (1978)
Poem (vln) (1981)

VOCAL

Rappresentazione, homage to Samuel Beckett (speaker, ch, hn, b-cl and vlc) (1979)
The last roundup (Mayroecker) (vce, 3 trp, 11 metronomes and 9 strs) (1980)
Diese Liebe zu Deutschland (Weidacher) (vce, perc and pf) (1985)
Sieg der Weichseln (Enzenberger) (m-S and timp) (1979)
Symphonie vom Tod (m-S, org and vln) (1978)

ELECTRONIC

Alles in Ordnung, alles OK? (1983)
Amok (1983)
Balances (tape and pf) (1981)
Eingebrannt in die Netzhaut (Weidacher) (1985)
Elevator (1983)
Etude on getting crazy (1983)
Images des beaux temps (prep pf, org, perc, spinet and tapes) (1981)
Rien ne va plus (Aragon) (vce, pf, perc and tapes) (1985)
Rosa, du (Weidacher) (1985)
Ruhe ist nicht nur erste Buergerpflicht, Ruhe ist schoen (1983)
Ueber allen Wipfeln ist Ruh' (1984)
Valse fatale (1983)
Vampirella (1984)
Zoll fuer Zoll I and II (Weidacher) (1983)

MULTIMEDIA

Muttertagsfeier oder die Zerstueckelung des weiblichen Koerpers (Jelinek) (1984)
Alban Berg hoert Wimbledon (2 vln, vla, video monitor and 2 loud speakers) (1984)

Ref. composer, 561

JULIEN, Jeanne

French composer. b. 1883.

Composition

OPERA

Le Chien Perdu

Ref. 307

KA DINUZULU, Constance Magogo. See MAGOGO KA DINUZULU, Constance, Princess

KAAD. See QU'AD

KABAT, Julie Phyllis

American singer, teacher and composer. b. Washington, DC, April 17, 1947. She studied composition from the age of 11 under Ron Nelson of Brown University. She obtained a B.A. in philosophy (Phi Beta Kappa) from Brandeis University and then studied voice under Hall Overton from 1971 to 1972, Jacob Druckman from 1972 to 1973 and Karen Ranung. She was a teaching assistant in the critical studies department of the California Institute of the Arts from 1970 to 1971 and a music therapist in N.Y. State Clinic, 1972 to 1973. From 1974 to 1977 she was director of the Composer's Forum in Albany. From 1980 to 1982 she won the National Endowment Humanities award and in 1983, a Creative Artists' Public Service Award. Since 1977 she has worked for the Albany City Arts Office. DISCOGRAPHY. PHOTOGRAPH.

Compositions

ORCHESTRA

Matrix I (cham orch) (1972)

CHAMBER

In return (str qrt) (1974)

Breath-pace (ob) (1973)

VOCAL

A mi hija (vce, pf and saw) (1983)

Chantings (Navajo text) (1973)

Five poems by H.D.: The moon in your hands; Evadne; Oread; Fragment; The helmsman (vce, vln and glass har) (1980)

Homespun (4 vces and perc) (1973)

Invocation in centrifugal form (vce and glass har) (1976)

Kalimba alight (vce and kalimba) (1981)

Lines and sounds (vce, ob and perc) (1978)

The night fisherman (vce, fl and glass har) (1982)

On edge (vce, pf and drs) (1983)

The queen of hearts (vce and syn) (1980)

Tapestry (vce, saw and water jar) (1976)

War and silence (S and 5 insts) (1972)

MISCELLANEOUS

And so, do I like to bang and tootle (1974)

Evadne (1977)

The idea of order at Key West (Wallace Stevens) (1977)

Rounds (1973)

Ref. composer, 625

KABATH, Augusta de

19th-century French composer.

Compositions

PIANO

Un chanson française, polka-march

Douchinka, Russian mazurka

En troika, Russian caprice

Seville, bolero

Valse du petit baiser

VOCAL

Angelus (Pitault & Grazioni)

Berceuse cosaque (Pitault & Grazioni)

Chanson d'un soldat (Pitault & Grazioni)

Fleurs cueillies (Pitault & Grazioni)

Ingenu, chanson XVIII siècle (Pitault & Grazioni)

Je suis la cache dans le bois! (Pitault & Grazioni)

Non chère, ne chante pas (Pitault & Grazioni)

Romance de quatre saisons (Pitault & Grazioni)

Serenade mauresque (Pitault & Grazioni)

Vous l'avec oublié, marquise? (Pitault & Grazioni)

Triste amour (Pitault & Grazioni)

Ref. 297

KABE, Mariko

Japanese composer. b. March 30, 1950. She studied at the Toho-Gakuen University under Sadao Bekku, Akio Yashiro and Akira Miyoshi and graduated in 1974.

Compositions

ORCHESTRA

Nocturne (1972) (1st prize, 41st Mainichi Music Competition, 1972)

Piano concerto (1981)

CHAMBER

Youe (str grt) (1976)

At the time of daybreak (pf and perc) (1978)

VOCAL

Choral work (1977)

The flower's longing for the moon (Takuji Ohte) (m-S, a-fl, vln, hp and pf) (1980)

Other songs (Takuji Ohte)

Ref. Japan Federation of Composers

KABOS, Ilona

20th-century composer.

Composition

FILM MUSIC

The Fake (1953)

Ref. 326

KACZURBINA-ZDZIECHOWSKA, Maria

Polish pianist, choral conductor, lecturer and composer. b. Warsaw, July 30, 1908. She studied the piano under K. Zaska and A. Rytel. From 1926 she studied at the University of Warsaw and from 1927 at the Warsaw Conservatory where her teachers included S. Kazury, P. Maszynski, S. Waljewski, R. Chojnacki, P. Rytel, K. Sikorski and S. Taube. She also studied privately under Z. Bielewicz. From 1929 to 1939 she taught music in schools in Warsaw and later conducted a mixed choir. She then lectured in various music schools and arranged children's programs for the Polish Radio. In 1953 she received the prize of the Ministry of Labor for her compositions for children and youth and in 1954 a Polish radio prize for a song.

Compositions

VOCAL

Dzieci spiewaja, 30 songs (vce and pf) (Czytelnik, 1951-1953)

Fraszki szkolne, 6 songs (H. Pietrusiewiczowa) (vce and pf) (Czytelnik, 1953)

Jestem zuch, 8 songs (H. Kojaczkowska) (1951)

Nowe zabawy dziecizece z piosenkami, 6 songs (vce and pf) (Czytelnik, 1953)

Przedszkole spiewa, 14 songs (vce and pf) (Czytelnik, 1951)

Songs for children and youth

Publications

Nasze pierwsze nutki. PWM, 1959.

Podrecznik umuzykalniena. Articles in Druzyna Harcerska. 1960.

Ref. 118

KADIMA, Hagar Yonith

Israeli composer. b. Haifa, May 23, 1957. She obtained her B.A. (composition and philosophy) from the Rubin Academy of Music, Tel Aviv University, where she studied under Professor Abel Ehrlich. She studied for a doctorate at the University of California, Santa Barbara under Dr. Edward Applebaum. She was the winner of prizes from the Israeli American Foundation for Arts from 1977 to 1980. She has given numerous performances in Israel and broadcast on radio in Israel and Germany.

Compositions

ORCHESTRA

Clusters (pf, hp, cel, xy, vib, mar, tubular bells and str orch) (1982) (Humanities Research Grant, UCSB)

Re-experience (str orch) (1980)

Silences (1982)

CHAMBER

Octet (fl, ob, 2 cl, 2 hn and 2 bsn) (1979)

Six little dots in the air for brass trio to play with (2 timp and trb) (1982)

Autosuggestion (1 or 2 vln) (1979)

Dualism I (vlc) (1980)

Dualism II (ob) (1980)

Dualism III (pf) (1980)

Dualism IV (bsn) (1980)

VOCAL

Forgot what he wanted to say (S and str qrt) (1981) (Shevill C. Coswin award)

Ref. composer

KAESER-BECK, Aida

Swiss dance teacher and composer. b. Aesch, August 3, 1928. She studied languages and music at a teachers' training college and concentrated on teaching dance as a form of self expression.

Compositions

CHAMBER

Three baroque-jazz concert pieces for quartet (1977)

Pieces for clavichord and organ (1975-1984)

PIANO

Pieces for dance (1980-1982)

Musik zu Tanz-Bewegung-Ausdruck (1981)

Spiel-und Tanzbuch (1985)

Tanz des Narren (1983)

Tanzreise (1984)

VOCAL

Inventar der Heimatliebe (1983)

Chanson des choses a partager (1983)

Wir bauen mit am neuen Tag (1983)

Choral works

Songs (Rilke, von Cube, Brecht, Morgenstern) (vce and pf) (1980)

INCIDENTAL MUSIC

Music for theatre (1970-1985)

Ref. 651

KAHANANUI, Dorothy

Hawaiian composer. She was one of a small circle of island composers of children's songs.

Ref. 438

KAHMANN, Chesley

American pianist, teacher and composer. b. New York, August 12, 1930. She graduated from the Moravian Seminary in 1948 and in 1952 from the Eastman School of Music. She did further studies in composition under Bernard Rogers at the Eastman School of Music, Louis Cheslock at the Peabody Conservatory and at the Chautauqua Institution, New York. She studied voice under Mahon Bishop. She ran the music department of Oldfields School from 1952 to 1958 and Brooklyn Friends School, 1958 to 1960. In 1971 she formed a singing group 'The Interludes' which appeared frequently in concert performing her compositions. She teaches the piano, theory and voice.

Compositions

ORCHESTRA

Symphony No. 1 (also pf) (1964)
Piano concerto (1966)
Fugue (1955)
Songs for flute and strings (also pf) (1962)
Suite (1957)
Suite for strings and timpani (1962)
Theme and variations (1955)

CHAMBER

Call for trumpets and trombones (1979)
String quartet No. 1 (1963)
Adagio for organ, violin and viola (1976)
Song for flute, trumpet and piano (1973)
Trio for flute, oboe and bassoon (1965)
Trio for flute, oboe and piano (1973)
Trio for flute, violin and piano (1966)
Sonata for violin and piano (1954)
Sonata for violoncello and piano (1963)
Trumpet I for Ames (1971)
Trumpet II for Ames (1976)

PIANO

Five short pieces (1963)
Little pieces (1965)
Passacaglia (1952)
Sonata (1963)
Sonata-allegro (1955)

VOCAL

Second song cycle (e.e. cummings) (vce and orch or pf) (1964)
Exercise 1 (high vce) (1977)
I have a bird in spring (E. Dickinson) (1965)
Song cycle (e.e. cummings) (high vce and pf) (1954)
The summit songs, 45 songs (composer) (1971-1977)
The voice of my beloved (high vce and pf) (1965)
Without the mercy (e.e. cummings) (high vce and pf) (1965)
Numerous other songs (composer)

SACRED

Amen (mix-ch) (1976)
Angels we have heard on high (mix-ch, keyboard and trp) (1983)
For everything there is a season, anthem (m-ch) (1962)
Mass (soli, mix-ch, orch, org and pf)
We will give thanks to thee (high vce, fl, ob and strs; also pf, org, fl and ob) (1965)
While shepherds watched their flocks (traditional words) (mix-ch or w-ch) (1965)
Agnus Dei (1981)
Angels a'plenty (1983) (Orbiting Clef)
The baby has come (1983) (Orbiting Clef)
Circle of love (1983) (Orbiting Clef)
Credo (1983) (Orbiting Clef)
Gloria (1983)
The father gave (1983) (Orbiting Clef)
Lord, let me know (1983) (Orbiting Clef)
The Lord of all (1983) (Orbiting Clef)
Miracle chief (Orbiting Clef)
O Blessed Saviour (1983) (Orbiting Clef)
Sanctus (1982)

THEATRE

Six musical plays (1952-1958)

Ref. composer

KAHN, Esther

B. London, 1877. She lived in Kensington, Australia and founded the International Society of Musical Therapeutics in 1924.

Compositions

CHAMBER

Sonata (vln and pf)

PIANO

Pieces incl.:
Concert piece (2 pf)

VOCAL

Over 50 songs

MULTIMEDIA

Illuminations (nonmusical piece, for an instrument invented by A.B. Heeld, projecting abstract color in motion)

Ref. 23, 70, 226

KAHRER, Laura Rappoldy

Austrian composer. b. 1853; d. 1925. She composed orchestral works.
Ref. 502

KAIMEN. See STUART-BERGSTROM, Elsa Marianne

KAINERSTORFER, Clotilde

19th-century German composer.

Compositions

SACRED

Bittruf, op. 39 (ch and org)
Salve Regina, op. 51 (6-part ch and org)
Adoratio Salvatoris, op. 40, hymn (A and org)
Marienbild, op. 17 (S, A and org obb)
O Sanctissima, op. 32 (vce and org)

Ref. 226, 276, 433

KALB, Janet

19th-century American song composer.
Ref. 465

KALFA, Dilhayat

Turkish guitarist, singer and composer. b. Istanbul, 1710; d. 1780. She is thought to have received her training in the palace. She wrote about 100 instrumental works and songs, of which only seven have survived.
Ref. National Council of Turkish Women

KALKHOEF, Laura von

19th-century German composer.

Compositions

CHAMBER

Duo (vln and pf)
Piano pieces

Ref. 226, 276

KALKHOF, Laura von. See KALKHOEF, Laura von

KALLEY, Sara Poulton

English choral conductor, teacher and composer. b. Nottingham, 1825; d. Edinburgh, August 18, 1907. She married a church minister and composer, Dr. Robert Reid Kalley. They went to Brazil in 1855 and founded the first Sunday school in Petropolis, Rio de Janeiro. Dedicated to missionary work, she started primary schools and gave free musical instruction. On their return to England in 1868, Sara became choir director of the Fluminense Evangelic Church till 1876. With Robert Reid she published the first collection of hymns in Portuguese of which 169 are her own compositions.

Compositions

SACRED

Hymns:
Luz do mundo! Jesus Cristo!
O Deus, com infinito amor
O Rei! sumblime em majestade e gloria
Salmos e hinos, collection (Rio de Janeiro: 1861)

Ref. 333

KALLOCH, Doley C. (Mrs. William)

American poetess, singer and composer. b. Fort Fairfield, March 30, 1893.

Compositions

VOCAL

On the sunny side of the ocean
There's a star that twinkles on Broadway
When twilight falls

SACRED

Jesus is calling you home

Ref. 374

KALLOCH, Mrs. William. See KALLOCH, Doley C.

KALOGRIDOU, Maria

Greek pianist, teacher and composer. b. Athens, December 29, 1922. She obtained a diploma in the piano in 1950 and then went to Rome to study under Aprea, returning to Athens to study under Mario Laskaris before going to England to study under Harold Craxton. She taught herself orchestration and counterpoint and began composing in 1964. She taught the piano in Athens. Her works were performed over Radio Athens. She published two childrens' books. DISCOGRAPHY. PHOTOGRAPH.

Compositions

ORCHESTRA
- Cello concerto (1968)
- Concerto for trumpet and percussion
- Piano concerto (Byzantine)
- Children's suite for string orchestra (1970)
- Concertino for trumpet (1972)

CHAMBER
- Dutch rhapsody (Anna Frank) (brass insts)
- Piano trio (1972)
- Trio in G (vln, vlc and pf)
- Inventory for violin and cello (1972)
- Sonata (vln and pf) (1968)
- Ten dances for violin and piano

PIANO
- Suite (4 hands) (1972)
- Six preludes and fugues in the Greek modes (1955)
- Sonatina (1972)
- Homage a Charlot, suite
- Suite

VOCAL
- Eleven songs (Yianis Ritsos)
- Numerous children's songs incl.:
- Five children's games (chil-vces, pf, vlc and perc)
- Seven songs for children (vces and inst ens)

BALLET
- Ballet for children (pf, vlc and perc) (1970)

OPERA
- Graft

Ref. composer

KALTENECKER, Gertraud

German organist, pianist, violinist, soprano and composer. b. Regensburg, May 20, 1915. She began her piano studies at the age of seven and her violin studies five years later. She began her singing career in the school choir and from 1930 until recently, sang in the choir of the Herz-Jesu Church of Regensburg. From 1936 to 1940 she studied harmony and composition privately under Max Jobst; from 1943 to 1944 she studied church music and choral singing under Dr. Ferdinand Habert at the Church Music School of Regensburg, where she also studied the organ under Otto Dunkelber, the organist of the Passau Cathedral. From 1946 to 1948 she attended the Musikhochschule in Munich, where her teachers included Gustav Geierhass (counterpoint), Joseph Haas (composition), Franz Theo Reuter (singing), Maria Hindemith-Landes (piano), Heinrich Knappe (conducting) and Hans Mersmann and Gustav Fellerer (music history). She graduated in 1948 as a singer and composer. In 1944 she filled the role of the mother in *Hansel and Gretel* at one day's notice and thereafter sang in concerts and church performances. She began composing in 1936 and some of her songs have been performed on the German radio and as far afield as Japan. PHOTOGRAPH.

Compositions

ORCHESTRA
- Weihnachtspastorale (fl, ob and str orch) (1946)
- Serenade in 5 movements (str orch) (1950)

CHAMBER
- Kinderliedersuite (vlc and pf) (1941)
- Suite (bsn and pf) (1971)
- Suite (vln and pf) (1947)
- Trifolium, 3 small pieces (rec or fl or pf) (1977)

ORGAN
- Choral prelude, variations and fugue on 'Maria breit den Mantel aus' (1954)
- Liturgische Impressionen (1972)
- Partita (1957)
- Partita 'Der Sonnengesang des Heiligen Franz von Assisi' (1977)
- Partita 'Die Toene der Glocken des Regensburger Domes' (1979)
- Partita 'Die Minoritenkirche zu Regensburg' (1982)
- Partita on 'Christ ist erstanden' (1955)
- Partita on 'Es sungen drei Engel' (1966)
- Postludium zur Missa 'Virgo Mater' (1949)

PIANO
- Suite (4 hands) (1947)
- Variationen und Fuge uber ein eigenes Thema (4 hands) (1958)
- Altbayrische Miniaturen, suite (1973)
- Six easy pieces for youth (1949)

VOCAL
- Deutsche Minnelieder, cycle (4 part mix-ch) (1952)
- Leitspruch (G. de Larigandie) (4 part mix-ch) (1967)
- Zwei heitere Gesange (Ringelnatz) (3 part mix-ch) (1949)
- Blast nur, ihr Stuerme, canon (Geibel) (4 vces) (1968)
- Dimensionen (E.L. Biberger) (A and pf) (1978)
- Drei Lieder (Billinger, Jacobi, Carossa) (S and pf) (1937)
- So ruhig geh ich, canon (Eichendorff) (4 vces) (1968)
- Spirale, 7 Lieder (Regensburg poets' group) (Bar and pf) (1978)
- Und inmitten der Mensch, 6 lieder (P. Coryllis) (S and pf) (1984)

SACRED
- Mater Dei, cantata (3 S, chil-ch, 4 part mix-ch, vln and org) (1964)
- Veni creator Spiritus (4 part mix-ch, ob, bsn, trp and str orch) (1959)
- Cum esset desponsata (3 part w-ch and org) (1958)
- Da Jesus in den Garten ging (4 part mix-ch) (1937)
- Deutsche Eigengesaenge (Proprium) zum Passionssonntag (3 part mix-ch a-cap) (1968)
- Gebet zu Maria (F.X. Lehner) (4 part mix-ch) (1965)
- Marienlied (Novalis) (4 part mix-ch, vln and org) (1940)
- Marienlied (H. Erbertseder) (3 part w-ch a-cap) (1959)
- Mass, Virgo Mater (3 part mix-ch) (1949)
- Popule meus (6 part mix-ch) (1947)
- Preisen will ich den Herrn (3 part mix-ch and org) (1972)
- Stetit Angelus, offertory for St. Michael's Feast (4 part mix-ch) (1968)
- Tota pulchra (6 part w-ch and org) (1959)
- Und unser lieben Frauen (3 part w-ch) (1941)
- Ave Maris Stella (S, Cont and org) (1959)
- Benedicta et venerabilis (2 S, Cont and org) (1959)
- Bereit ist mein Herz, O Gott (vce and org) (1959)
- Dem Herrn will ich singen (2 S or 2 T and org) (1968)
- Drei liturgische Gesaenge (S and org) (1957)
- Deutsche Brautmesse (S or T and org) (1968)
- Gegruesset seist du, Maria (S and org) (1954)
- Gloria Patri (S and org) (1962)
- Improperium exspectavit cor meum, liturgical song (S and org) (1966)
- Lauda anima mea, Dominum (S and org) (1962)
- Lobgesang (2 S or 2 T and org) (1968)
- O Virgo pulcherrima (2 S and org) (1959)
- Psalmmeditationen in 5 Saetzen (B-Bar and org or org) (1981)
- Regina Coeli (S and org) (1953)
- Salve Regina (S and org) (1957)
- Virgo mitis (S and org) (1959)

Ref. composer

KAMAR. See QAMAR

KAMIEN, Anna

American pianist, choral conductor, teacher and composer. b. New York, January 29, 1912. She started private piano lessons at the age of five and studied the piano and harmony under August Walther between the ages of ten and 18. She went to Paris until 1935, to study the piano at the Ecole Normale under Mme. Vuilliard, Di Gueraldi and Alfred Cortot and counterpoint under Nadia Boulanger (q.v.). She studied form privately under Annette Dieudonne and the piano under Lazar Levy. She taught the piano for ten years and conducted the Hadassah Chorus for 30 years. PHOTOGRAPH.

Compositions

CHAMBER
- Piano quintet (1958)
- String quartet (1960)
- Sonatina (vln and pf) (1957)

VOCAL
- Chinese odes (ch and orch)
- Memories (Longfellow) (vce and pf) (New York: Lyra Music Co., 1964)

OPERA
- Ruth (1954)

Ref. composer, 142, 622, 625

KAMINSKY, Laura

American composer. b. New York, September 28, 1956. She studied at Oberlin College and the City College of New York, receiving her M.A (composition) in 1980. She was co-founder and artistic director of 'Musicians' Accord' a chamber ensemble specializing in contemporary music. Many of her compositions have won awards and been performed at the Carnegie Recital Hall and Symphony Space. She has received grants from Meet the Composer every year since 1983 and a fellowship from the Tuch Foundation from 1978 to 1980.

Compositions
CHAMBER
Still life for the end of the day (a-fl, ob, cl or b-cl, vlc and hp) (1983)
In memoriam Eleazer (trp, 2 hn and trb) (1980)
Five for three (fl, vlc and pf) (1982)
Remembering August (vln, vla and vlc) (1983)
Triptych (ob, vlc and pf) (1984)
Duo (fl and perc) (1982)
Enkomios (fl and perc) (1980)
Enkomios II (fl and perc) (1983)
Tangents (perc) (1981)
VOCAL
For everything (ch, cl, vlc, perc and pf) (1985)
Deux poémes point et durée (S, cl and vlc) (1978)
Nightpiece and song (T, fl, cl, vlc and pf) (1985)
Night song for Nina (S, vib or mar and hp) (1983)
Para mi corazon (m-S, fl, s-sax or cl, vlc, vib and pf) (1982)
Poems of Tufu (S, cl, vln, perc and pf) (1979)
Sonnet lines (m-S, fl, vib and pf) (1982)
Sonnet lines No. 2 (S and pf) (1982)
Twilight settings (S, str qrt and perc) (1985)
DANCE SCORES
Steepletop dances (dancers, ob and perc) (1984)
ELECTRONIC
A dream revisited (elec fl and perc) (1984)
Ref. composer

KANACH, Sharon E.

American pianist, teacher and composer. b. Flemington, NJ, July 31, 1957. She obtained her B.A. from Bennington College in 1979 and took a course in computer programming in 1981 at IRCAM, Paris. She studied composition with Vivian Fine (q.v.), Otto Luening, Michael Czajkowski, Charles Jones, Oliver Messiaen, Nadia Boulanger (q.v.) and Annette Dieudonne. She also studied the piano, conducting and orchestration with Henry Brant, semiology of music with George Guy and at the University of Paris with Iannis Xenakis. From 1979 to 1981 she was the director of the Atelier Musical Pour Enfants organized by the Association d'education Publique at Montparnasse Rencontre. In 1980 she gave master classes at the International Society of Bassists' Festival, Cincinnati, Ohio, in collaboration with Joelle Leandre (q.v.). She was responsible for concert programming at Galerie Nane Stern, Paris and was artistic co-ordinator for the 'Delegation Francaise de Musiciennes' in collaboration with the Documentation Center for Contemporary Music, Paris. Her *Bal(l)ade* was televised in Germany. She is presently a private teacher in composition, the piano, harmony, solfege and counterpoint. PHOTOGRAPH
Compositions
ORCHESTRA
Aistheton (cham orch) (1977)
Distant light (cham orch) (1981)
CHAMBER
Entelechy I (str insts) (1979)
Entelechy III (wind insts) (1979)
Kismet (brass qnt and perc) (1977)
Bal(l)ade (ww qnt) (1979)
Sonance (ww qnt) (1981)
Patterns (rec qrt) (1979) (comm FABER)
Short movements for string quartets (1979)
String quartet (1975)
Winter trilogy (ww qrt) (1977)
Anlage (fl, vln and vlc) (1979)
Asphodele for wood wind trio (ob, cl and bsn) (1980)
Phusis (str trio) (1979)
Trio (1978)
Haut(e) boisson (ob and bsn) (1978)
Melisma (vlc and pf) (1978)
On (2 gtr) (1981)
Die Altero (gtr) (1976)
Folos (fl) (1978)
Stone II (vla) (1980)
Stone III (vla)
Va (vlc; also bsn; also d-b) (1980)
ORGAN
Elegy (1977)
Etude (1977)
PIANO
Spontaneous dialogue I (2 pf) (1978)
Spontaneous dialogue III (2 pf) (1979)
Directions (1979)
Entelechy II (1979)
VOCAL
Anatomy of monotony (Wallace Stevens) (mix-ch and pf) (1976)
Two songs of Blake (Bar and cham ens) (1977)
Entelechy IV (1979)
Fabliau (T) (1979)
Hong Kong (P. Claudel) (fl and S) (1976)
J'ai tant reve (vce and d-b) (1979) (comm J. Leandre)
To ... (m-S, pf and perc) (1980) (comm la Delegation Francaise de Musiciennes)
THEATRE
Blackout, image play
ELECTRONIC
Offrande (S,-tape and cham orch)
Entre-voir (cl, vlc, pf and tape)
Stone I (bsn and opt tape) (1980)
Publications
The Musiciennes of Paris. Heresies, Vol 10, New York, 1981.
Translation of Iannis Xenakis *Arts/Science: Alliages*. Pendragon Press, New York, 1982.
Trois Mosaiques sur Xenakis. Stock-Musique. Paris, 1981.
Troons. Musical fiction for children. With Elzbieta Violet.
Ref. composer, 468

KANAI, Kikuko

Japanese composer. b. Okinawa, March 13, 1911. She gained a fine arts degree from the University of Tokyo (1938). She was the director of the Japan Association of Folklore Music and a member of the Japan Federation of Composers. She received the Mainichi Award (publication culture) and the Okinawa Times Culture Award.
Compositions
ORCHESTRA
Reminiscences of Okinawa, symphony
Okinawan dance suite
VOCAL
Flower song
Golden lantern
Port
OPERA
Hiren Kara Bune (1967)
Hiren Tosen
A Legend of Okinawa, grand opera
Ref. Yamaha Music Foundation, 465, 622

KANAKA'OLE, Edith Ke-Kuhikuhi-I-Pu'u-one-o-Na-Ali'i-O-Kohala

20th-century Hawaiian chanter, dancer, teacher, entertainer and composer. She was trained in oli-chanting (an unaccompanied chant) as a young girl, first by her mother and then by Akoni Mika, the well-known chanter. She acquired fluency in Hawaiian which allowed her to comprehend the 'kaona', the hidden meaning of a chant. Her numerous chant compositions covered all the major styles of delivery and objectives of the oli and have been performed in many places over the years. For many of her chants she choreographed hulas. She believed the oli formed the foundation for all aspects of Hawaiian cultural history. In 1979 she received the Distinction of Cultural Leadership award.
Ref. 438

KANZLER, Josephine

German pianist and composer. b. Markt-Tolz, near Munich, 1780. She studied under Marcus Falter and Lauska in Munich and under Gratz, Danzi and Abbe Vogler to became a virtuoso pianist. She married the oboist Fladt. She composed a piano quartet, a piano sonata and variations, songs and published a treatise on harmony.
Ref. 102, 128, 226, 276

KAPLAN, Lois Jay

American oboist, conductor, critic, music director, sculptor, teacher, writer and composer. b. Chicago, February 6, 1932. She obtained her B.Mus. from De Paul University, her M.Sc. from the University of Wisconsin and her M.Arts from the Jacksonville State University and studied for Ph.D at the Florida State University; composition with Alexander Tcherepnin and conducting with Paul Stassevitch. She was a professional trombonist, private teacher and technical director, music director and stage manager of the University Theatre, University of Chicago. From 1954 to 1958 she conducted the De Paul University Stadium Band and from 1956 to 1962 was band director and art teacher in Chicago schools.
Compositions
BAND
Salute to the citizen soldiers
This indeed we'll defend
VOCAL
Pallas Athena, marching song
Ref. 457

KAPP, Corinne
American composer. b. November 10, 1955. She studied at the Lawrence University Conservatory of Music, Appleton, WI, and received her B.Mus. in 1977. She studied under William Ferris at the American Conservatory and William Russo of Columbia College, Chicago. She was awarded the Pi Kappa Lambda award in composition.
Compositions
CHAMBER
For TT/CC, selections (vln, ob, fl and pf) (1977)
Two movements for string quartet (1976)
Four pieces (2 fl) (1977)
Two pieces (vln and pf) (1975)
PIANO
Sonata (1980)
Two pieces for students (1976)
VOCAL
Moonsongs, cycle of 5 songs (S, T and str qrt) (1981)
The hermit (m-S and pf) (1979)
The night of the sad women (m-S and pf) (1977)
Ref. composer

KAPRALOVA, Vitezslava
Czech conductor and composer. b. Brno, January 24, 1915; d. Montpellier, France, June 16, 1940. She was the only daughter of the Brno piano teacher and composer Vaclav Kapral. Vitezslava started composing at the age of nine, showed remarkable talent and at 14 entered the Brno Conservatory, where she studied composition under Vilem Petrzelka and conducting under Zdenek Chalabala. When she completed her studies in Brno, she conducted her *Piano concerto*. She then attended master classes at the Prague Conservatory under Vitezslav Novak (composition) and Vaclav Talich (conducting). She left Prague in 1937 on a scholarship to Paris to study composition under Bohuslav Martinu and conducting under Charles Munch. Martinu introduced Vitezslava to the musical world of Paris and helped her develop a post-romantic polytonal technique. In 1937 she conducted the Czech Philharmonic in Prague in her *Military Symphonietta*. She conducted the BBC orchestra performing the same composition at the opening of the ISCM Festival in London in 1938. She returned home in 1938 and won another scholarship to Paris. She developed tuberculosis during the Paris evacuation and died in Montpellier. DISCOGRAPHY. PHOTOGRAPH.
Compositions
ORCHESTRA
Piano concerto in D-Minor, op. 7 (1935)
Military symphonietta, op. 11 (1937)
Concertino, op. 21 (vln, cl and orch) (1940)
Partita for piano and string orchestra, op. 20 (1939)
Suite en miniature, op. 1 (also pf) (1932)
Suita rustica, op. 19 (1938)
CHAMBER
Christmas prelude (cham ens) (1939)
String quartet, op. 8 (1936)
Deux ritornelles, op. 25 (vlc and pf) (1940)
Elegy (vln and pf) (1946)
Legend and burlesque, op. 3 (vln and pf) (1932) (Pazdirek, 1933)
PIANO
April preludes, op. 13 (Hudebni Matice, 1938)
Funeral march, op. 2 (1932)
Six variations on the bells of the Church of Saint Etienne du Mont in Paris, op. 16 (1938)
Sonata appassionata, op. 6 (1933)
Three pieces, op. 9 incl. Groteskni passacaglia (1935)
Two dances, op. 23 (1940)
VOCAL
Ilena, op. 15, ballad (L. Podjavorinska) (unfinished) (soli, mix-ch and orch) (1937-1938)
Sbohem a satecek, op. 14 (V. Nezval) (vce and orch or pf) (1937)
Vezdicka, Potpolis, op. 17 (O. Prikryl) (2 w-ch) (1937)
Jablko s klina, op. 10 (J. Seifert) (vce and pf) (1936)
Jiskry z popela, op. 5 (B. Jelinek) (vce and pf) (1932)
Navzdy, op. 12 (J. Carek and J. Seifert) (vce and pf) (1937)
Two songs (R. Bojko) (vce and pf) (1933)
Vteriny, op. 18, 8 songs (various texts) (vce and pf) (1939)
Zpivano de dalky
Bibliography
Macek, J. *Vitezslava Kapralova*. Knihovna Hudebnich rozhledu 4, Prague, 1958.
Ref. 2, 8, 15, 22, 44, 70, 72, 74, 94, 96, 189, 197, 226, 330, 447, 477

KARASTOYANOVA, Elena
Bulgarian lecturer and composer. b. Sofia, October 1, 1933. At the Bulgarian State Conservatory she specialised in musical theory and graduated in 1958. She studied composition under her father, Professor A. Karastoyanov. After 1965 Elena lectured on harmony and musical analysis at the State music school in Sofia.
Compositions
ORCHESTRA
Sinfonietta (str orch)
CHAMBER
Sonata (vln and pf)
Sonatina (pf)
VOCAL
Choruses
Suite of 4 songs (vce and pf)
Children's songs
Arrangements of folk songs
Ref. 217, 463

KARG, Marga
German composer. b. Munich, July 17, 1903. She composed chamber and piano pieces, women's choruses, masses, sacred cantatas and songs.
Ref. 105, 226

KARGER-HOENIG, Friederike
Composition
PIANO
Toccata, op. 2
Ref. 473

KARGER-HONIG, Friederike. See KARGER-HOENIG, Friederike

KARHILO, Liisa
20th-century Finnish composer.
Compositions
CHAMBER
Sinaa ja minaa: elementary duets (vln and pf; also vlc and pf) (Fazer, 1977)
Ref. MLA *Notes* 35/3 March 1979

KARL. See THIEME, Kerstin

KARL, Anna
19th-century, possibly French composer.
Compositions
ORCHESTRA
Au pays des rêves, waltz (Billaudot)
Bonjour printemps, mazurka
Douce ivresse, mazurka (also cl, fl, vln, man and cor) (Jobert)
Polka des patins (also pf) (Billaudot)
Sac au dos, polka-marche (also pf) (Billaudot); (Gheluwe)
Tout en rose, waltz (also pf) (Billaudot); (Noel)
Tout s'envole, waltz (also pf) (Billaudot); (Noel)
PIANO
Dicksonn, polka (Joubert)
Gervaise, waltz (Lesigne)
Paris-Murcie, waltz (Tilliard)
Primavera, waltz (Chatot)
Souvenir de Pesth, polka (Fromont)
VOCAL
Ami Greluchon (vce and pf) (Rouart)
Baronne de Bellepistache (vce and pf) (Billaudot)
Capote a Manillon (vce and pf) (Billaudot)
Chanson du Merle (vce and pf) (Billaudot)
Chikinska (vce and pf) (Billaudot)
Nachtwaechter, polka, with humorous text (Reinecke)
Approx. 30 other songs (vce and pf)
Ref. 297

KARNITSKAYA, Nina Andreyevna
Soviet pianist, lecturer and composer. b. Kiev, May 5, 1906. She studied composition under B. Karagichev and the piano under M. Pressman at the Baku Conservatory, graduating in 1931. She taught theoretical subjects at music schools until 1938 and then at the Baku Conservatory until 1948, when she became head of the department of theoretical subjects at the Music School of Ordzhonikidze until 1961. She was composer for the Russian Theatre in Baku. From 1941 to 1946 she was a member of the government of the Azerbaijanian Soviet Socialist Republic and was active in the Ossetian government. From 1975 she lived in Novosibirsk. DISCOGRAPHY.

Compositions
ORCHESTRA
Symphony (1942)
Azerbaijanian etudes (vln and orch) (1974)
Double concerto for violin, piano and orchestra (1962)
On the banks of Gizeldon, symphonic poem (1952)
Ossetian etudes (vln and orch) (1952)
Piano concerto No. 1, in D-Minor (1960)
Piano concerto No. 2 (1975)
Poema (vln and orch) (1947)
Elegy to the memory of Kosta Khetagurov (1953-1954)
Fantasia on Ossetian themes (orch of folk insts) (1951)
In the mountains, in the field
Joyful suite (orch of folk insts) (1974)
Lenin, overture (orch of folk insts) (1970)
Nocturne, dance, march (orch of folk insts) (1953)
Overture, druzhba (1969)
Pictures of an Ossetion collective farm (1959)
Poem, Ossetian homeland (1960)
Simfonietta (str orch) (1947)
Suite (orch of folk insts) (1974)
CHAMBER
Little legend (vln ens) (1959)
String quartet (1946)
Trio on Ossetian themes (1951)
Aria (trb and pf) (1966)
Concert fantasy on a theme from Arshin mal alan, opera by Hadjibekov (vln and pf) (1939)
Concert fantasy on a theme from Shakh Ismail, opera by M. Magomayev (vln and pf) (1946)
Lyrical poem (ob and pf) (1948)
Ossetian dances (vln and pf) (1965)
Poem (vln and pf) (1947)
Sailors' dance (trb and pf) (1966)
Sonata I (vln and pf) (1950)
Sonata II (vln and pf) (1968)
Sonata III (vln and pf) (1969)
Sonata-poema (vlc and pf) (1966)
Suite, Za polyarnym krugom (vln and pf) (1938)
PIANO
Azerbaijanian pieces, cycle (1968)
Etude-sketches, cycle (1966)
Little tales, cycle (1957)
Preludes and fugues (Sovietski Kompozitor, 1980)
Sonata (1954)
Sonata II (1967)
Sonata III (1971)
Suite I (1960)
Suite II (1967)
Twelve preludes and fugues (1976)
VOCAL
Ballad of the Komsomol (Gurzhibekova) (vce and pf) (1968)
Docheri (Tushnova) (vce and pf) (1946)
Lenin of the mountains, ballad
Leshi (Bryusov) (vce and pf) (1948)
Nishchii (M. Lermontov) (1940)
Rusalka (M. Lermontov) (1940)
Songs (Kaitukov, Basiev and others)
THEATRE
Music for more than 100 plays
Ref. 87, 94, 420

KARR Y DE ALFONSETTI, Carmen. See ADDENDUM

KARVENO, Wally

B. 1914.
Compositions
CHAMBER
Petite suite enfantine (vln and pf)
PIANO
Passacaille graduée, 18 variations (Paris: Combre, 1980)
Sonatine-minute (Paris: ORTF, 1964)
Twenty-eight variations progressives (Paris: Lemoine, 1966)
Vingt-huit variations romantiques (Combre, 1980)
VOCAL
Interlude (mix-ch a-cap)
Hommage à Francis Poulenc (T duo and pf)
Trois chansons de la Renaissance (B and pf or hpcd)
La voie du tenor (vce, pf, fl and vlc) (1983)
OPERA
La Fiancée du Diable (Pal Stoecklin) (1941)
Ref. Frau und Musik

KASHPEROVA, Leokadia Alexandrovna

Soviet pianist, lecturer and composer. b. Lyubim, Yaroslav district, May 4, 1872; d. Moscow, December 3, 1940. She graduated in 1893 from the St. Petersburg Conservatory and from 1888 to 1901 studied the piano privately under A. Rubinstein and composition under H.F. Solovyov. She performed as a soloist in concerts and ensembles in Russia and abroad. She taught at the Moscow Conservatory.
Compositions
ORCHESTRA
Symphonies
Piano concerto
Overtures
CHAMBER
Two sonatas (vlc and pf)
Other pieces
Piano pieces
VOCAL
Orvasi, cantata
Romances
Songs
Publications
Vospominania.
Vospominania ob A.G. Rubinstein.
Ref. 330

KASIA (Casia, Cassia, Icasia, Kassia)

Byzantine nun, poetess and composer. b. 810. According to the chronicles of the time she was one of a number of girls from whom the Emperor Theophilus was to choose a bride. He stood a long time in front of her and as he was about to hand her the apple indicating that she was his chosen one, he lamented that evil had come to the world through women. Kasia replied that much good had also come through women, referring to the birth of Christ. Theophilus, taken aback, moved on to the next candidate and Kasia was sent to a convent. Her numerous hymns were composed for all the religious festivals and occasions and included four for the festival of the martyr Christina. A sticheron of her composition became part of the liturgy of the Greek Orthodox Church for Holy Week. The words of the hymns she composed were written by Byzantius, Georgius, Cyprianus and Marcus Monachus. Two of her hymns were transcribed in Tillyard's Byzantine Music and Hymnography. She also wrote secular poetry, partially of a biting and sarcastic nature; surprising for a nun of her time.
Compositions
SACRED
Come Christ-bearing people, let us look upon the marvel which confounds thought and holds it bound
Lord the woman fallen in many sins
Stichera for Christmas, Lent and Easter
Bibliography
Great Ages of Man – Byzantium. Philip Sherrard and editors of Time-Life Books.
Ref. 264, 476, 550, 637, 622

KASILAG, Lucrecia R.

Philippine pianist, administrator, professor, writer and composer. b. La Union, August 31, 1918. She received her B.A. cum laude in 1936 at the Philippine Women's University; her music teacher's diploma in 1939 at St. Scholastica College; her B.Mus. in 1949 at the Philippine Women's University and M.Mus. (theory and composition) in 1950 at the Eastman School of Music, University of Rochester. In 1975 she obtained her D.Mus. from the Centro Escolar University and in 1980 her doctor of law from the Philippine Women's University. In 1981 she graduated with her D.F.A. from St. John's University. She held the position of Dean of the College of Music and Fine Arts at Philippine Women's University (1953 to 1977) when she became professor of music. She is the director of the Theatre for Performing Arts of the Cultural Center of the Philippines and president of the National Music Council of the Philippines and the Philippine Society for Music Education. She holds the position of chairlady of the League of Philippine Composers. She headed many Philippine cultural delegations to the United States, Canada, Europe, Africa and Asia and presided over several international music conferences. She received international study grants from the Fulbright Scholar Commission, J.D. Rockefeller 3rd Fund, Colombo Plan, Asia Foundation and the Federal Republic of Germany cultural grant. She received numerous awards, among which were the Presidential award for the Woman Composer of 1956, Republic Cultural Heritage awards of 1960 and 1966, Mu Phi Epsilon citation of merit in 1964 and the Arawing Maynila cultural awards for 1966 and 1973. She wrote several articles and essays on varied aspects of the humanities and research in Asian music. She pioneered the combination of resources of occidental and oriental instruments in East-West compositions. DISCOGRAPHY. PHOTOGRAPH.
Compositions
ORCHESTRA
Concert-divertissement for piano and orchestra (1956)

Concertante (pf, brass, perc and str orch) (comm St. Scholastica's Music Alumn Assoc.) (1960)
Divertissement (pf and orch) (1960)
Legend of the Sarimanok (Philippine insts and cham orch)
Philippine scenes
Amada (cham orch) (1970)

CHAMBER
Essay to CB (fl, pf, perc and strs)
Psalms (org, wind, perc and strs) (1978)
Toccata (perc and wind insts) (1958)
Capriccio and Fantasie (pf qnt) (1963, 1965)
Quintet (pf and str qrt) (1965)
Toccata for percussions and winds (wind insts, orthodox and moslem perc) (1959)
Fantasie on a four-note theme (3 vln and pf) (1957)
Homage to Sr. Baptista Battig (2 pf and trp; also pf) (1960)
Introduction and frolic on a tone row (pf, vln and vlc) (1966)
Whims and repartee (pf, vln and vlc) (1967)
Intermezzo (vln and pf) (1957)
Rondo in F (vln and pf) (1950

ORGAN
Essay to CB: Elegy and eulogy (1971)
Evocative (1965)
Ostinato (1956)
Passacaglia (1950)
Variations of Bahay Kubo theme (1955)

PIANO
Pieces incl.:
April morning (1941)
Ang tagak
Burlesque (1957) (Silliman)
Derivation I, II, III and IV (prep pf)
Elegy (1960)
Lanot-gloria
Nocturne in A-Flat (1941)
Prelude and fugue
Rondeau 1981
Rondo in E-Minor (1950)
Scherzino 1980 (NAMCYA comm contest piece)
Scherzo in D
Sonata in G-Minor (1950)
Sonata orientale (also pf and cham) (1961)
Sonata quasi una fantasia
Theme and variations based on a Filipino folk tune

VOCAL
Numerous songs incl:
Love songs, cycle (S and orch) (1956)
Five Filipino folk songs (w-ch) (1957) (Silliman)
Far meadows (S and mix qrt) (1950)
Muslim trio set (vce, pf and Muslim insts) (1961)
Paruparo at uod (vce and str qrt) (1954)
Sariling awitin, cycle (1961)
Songs of the east I, II and III
Three tagalog serenades (1959)
Two humorous tagalog songs

SACRED
De profundis, requiem (ch and orch) (comm Chorale Philippines) (1977)
Missa brevis (w-ch) (1963)
Filiasana (mix-ch and Asian insts) (1965)
Misang filipino (mix-ch, gtr and org) (1965)
Ave Maria
Heaven-sent
Nuptial prayer
Renunciation
Requiem (Bar) (1956)
The rosary

OPERETTA
Jose, aking anak (1976)

DANCE SCORES
Amanda, ballet (1970)
Salakot na ginto, dance (ch and Asian insts)
Sisa, ballet (chant, syn and orch) (1978)

THEATRE
Dulawaran Golden Salakot (soloists, ch, dancing group and Asian insts)

ELECTRONIC
Five portraits, parody (2 amp pf, gongs, kubing jaw's hp and transistor) (1973)
Trichotomy for solo voice (Asian insts and tape) (1967)

INCIDENTAL MUSIC
Numerous pieces incl.:
Ang kuripot
Ang princesa
Anino ng bukas
Bayan-bayanan
Hamlet
Igkas kayumanggi
Kambal (Plautus)
Macario sakay
May katwiran ang katwiran
Mirandolina
Morolandia
Mother Courage
Negosyante ng Venecia
The onyx wolf
Paano man ang ibig
Putong pula
Quadrilogue
Rizaliana

Ref. composer, 17, 52, 70, 77, 206, 457

KASSIA. See KASIA

KATS, Elena. See KATS-CHERNIN, Elena

KATS-CHERNIN, Elena

Australian pianist, teacher and composer. b. Tashkent, USSR, November 4, 1957. She began her musical studies at the age of six at Yaroslav Music School and later attended the Gnesina Music School in Australia in 1975. She attended the New South Wales Conservatorium in Sydney, where she studied composition under Richard Toop and the piano under Gordon Watson. In 1978 she won the Shadforth Hooper Prize for the most outstanding piano recital of the year. She graduated from the Conservatorium in July 1979 as a teacher, performer and composer. She received a national fellowship for composition grant in 1980 from the Australian Music Board and was awarded a DAAD Scholarship in 1980 which enabled her to study under the composer Helmut Lachemann in West Germany. PHOTOGRAPH.

Compositions

ORCHESTRA
Piano concerto (pf, perc and double str orch) (1979) (Frank Hutchens scholarship, 1980)
Bienie (1980)
Introduction to a dance (1983)
Stairs (1984) (comm Australia youth orch)

CHAMBER
In tension (fl, b-cl, perc, pf, vln and vlc) (1982) (comm Seymour group, Australia)
Pre (fl, trb, vlc, perc and 2 pf) (1985)
Vetyer (fl, vlc and cl) (1977) (Raymond Hanson Memorial prize, 1978)
Chechyotka I (trb and pf) (1979)
Chu (trb and perc) (1978)
Duo I (vln and pf) (1984)
Zeugspiel (vlc and trb) (1981)
Chechyotka II (trb)
Solo January (acc) (1985)

PIANO
Metro (2 pf and 2 metronomes) (1976)
Reductions (2 pf) (1983)
Shestizvuchya (1977)

THEATRE
Ballett-Studio
Behind the scenes (Rhys Martin) (vce, movement, ob and cl – 2 performers) (1984)
Dinosaur, ballet theatre (fairlight computer)
Sketches of an island (Rhys Martin) (1983)

Ref. composer

KATTS, Letty

20th-century Australian composer.

Compositions

PIANO
By the Billabong (4 hands) (Allans Music, 1975)
The gallop (4 hands) (Chappell & Co.)
Pieces for children

VOCAL
A day in the bush, 8 children's songs (chil-vce, pf and inst ens) (J. Albert & Son, 1956)

Ref. 440, 446

KATUNDA, Eunice do Monte Lima, See CATUNDA, Eunice do Monte

KATZ, Elena. See KATS-CHERNIN, Elena

KATZMAN, Klara Abramovna

Soviet composer. b. Surazh, May 31, 1916. She studied composition under M. Yudin at the Leningrad Conservatory and graduated in 1941. From 1943 she lived in Sverdlovsk and from 1945 was artistic director of the radio, becoming musical director in 1953. She studied composition under P.B. Ryazanov and K. S. Kushnarev and instrumentation under M.O. Steinberg.

Compositions

ORCHESTRA
Symphony (1947)
Fresco, bessmertie (1976)
CHAMBER
Sonata (vlc and pf) (1949)
Sem nastroyeni (pf) (1976)
VOCAL
Yunii barabanshchik, oratorio (E. Khorinska) (1953)
Rodina, cantata (N. Ogarev) (1943)
Ural-bogatyr, cantata (1946)
Za mirna zemlye, cantata (M. Matusovsky) (1952)
Lenin Suite (ch and orch) (1959)
Four song cycles (vce and orch)
Romances and songs
BALLET
Kaslinski pavilion (1967)
OPERA
Lyubava (1967)
Malchish-Kibalchish, in 3 acts, with ballet (I. Keller) (1969)
Polovodie (1962)
Rytsarskaya ballada (1973)
OPERETTA
Lyubov buvaet raznaya (1957)
Mark Beregovik (A. Geveksman) (1955)
Nepoferennye (B. Pevzner) (1943-1944)
THEATRE
Cyrano de Bergerac, play (1948)
Domik-pryanik, play
Ivan Rybakov, play
INCIDENTAL MUSIC
Almazy, film (1947)
Anthony and Cleopatra (1956)
Don Khil Zelenie Shtany (1963)
Khrabruy Kikila (1972)
Lope de Vega (1969)
Mera za Meru (1964)
Nakhalenok (1974)
Skazka o tsare Saltane (1969)
Solovennaya shlyapka (1969)
Ukrali konsula (1964)
Uyekhavshi ostalsya doma (1969)
Zakhudaloye korolevstro (1967)
Zolushka (1968)
Zvonok v pustuyu kuartiru (1968)
Ref. 87, 330

KAUFFMAN, Amanda

Compositions

PIANO
Trefle a 4 feuilles (2 pf) (Eulenburg)
Abschied (P. Fischer)
Fantasie-caprice (Fischer)
Flirt, polka internationale, op. 9
Mazurka
Schneeflocken
Sonata in C, op. 28 (Licht)
Souvenir des bords du Rhin (Fischer)
VOCAL
Songs incl.:
Ach! Die Augen sind es wieder, op. 11
Allerseelen, op. 32 (Licht)
Liebeslied und Liebeslust, Ninas Lied, op. 25 (Licht)
Noch sind die Tage der Rosen, op. 29 (Licht)
Trost: Du bist mein Sonnenschein (Fischer)
Ref. 297

KAUFMAN, Barbara (pseud. Daniela Dor)

Hungarian-Israeli violinist and composer. b. Hungary, 1912. She earned a reputation as a violinist in Hungary and Rumania and emigrated to Israel in 1950 and to Paris, in 1956. She wrote popular music and songs under her pen name.

Compositions

ORCHESTRA
Scherzo (1951)
CHAMBER
String quartet (1948)
Short pieces (vln and pf; also pf)
VOCAL
Children's songs
Popular songs
Ref. 94, 205

KAUFFMANN, Mrs. See PHILLIPS, Linda

KAUSITAKI. See LOPAMUDRA

KAUTH, Maria Magdalena (nee Graff)

Late 18th-century German composer, probably from Berlin. Several of her compositions were published in Berlin. Her *Piano concerto* was frequently played by Hummel.

Compositions

ORCHESTRA
Piano concerto (1792)
CHAMBER
Danses de muses, consistant en 3 menuets, 3 anglaises et 3 allemandes à plusieurs instruments (ded Duke of York and Princess Frederique of Prussia)
PIANO
Three menuets
Other pieces
VOCAL
Das Gemaelde der Natur in Form eines Monodram (1789)
Ref. 128, 129, 226, 276, 347, 433

KAVALIEROVA, Marie

Czech pianist, zither player and composer. b. Prague, January 12, 1860; d. Sazava near Prague, December 13, 1933. She studied the zither, the piano and composition at the Wanausova School of Music, Prague. She married Dr. V. Srb, the Mayor of Prague in 1883.

Compositions

PIANO
Polka mazur, op. 2 (Prague: R. Veit)
Sen mladi, op. 7
Other small dance pieces
ZITHER
Czech songs, op. 8 (R. Veit)
Other pieces
VOCAL
Songs (Stary)
Ref. Czech Music Info. Center, 197

KAVARNALIEVA, Konstantina

20th-century Russian composer.

Compositions

ORCHESTRA
Symphony in E-Flat Major, op. 6 (Doiran) (1963)
Idylle sur la mer, in 2 mvts (1950)
Ref. 280

KAVASCH, Deborah Helene

American violinist, archivist, assistant professor, singer and composer. b. Washington, DC, July 15, 1949. She studied the violin and music theory at the Mozarteum, Salzburg, 1969 to 1970. She obtained a B.A. magna cum laude, in German in 1971 and a B.M. magna cum laude in composition theory in 1972, from Bowling Green State University, OH. In 1973 she received an M.M. (composition-theory) and studied for her Ph.D. at the University of California, San Diego. She studied composition under Wallace DePue, Donald Wilson, Burton Beerman, Roger Reynolds, Kenneth Gaburo and Robert Erickson and voice under Richard Mathey, Linda Vickerman, John Large and Beverly Ogdon. She was a lecturer in theory and experimental music at the University of California from 1973 to 1975 and since 1973 has been an archivist and research musician for the Center for Music Experiment, University of California. She taught music at California Community College in 1978 and since 1979 she has held the position of assistant professor of music and theory and voice at California State College Stanislaus. She received numerous scholarships and grants and won first prize in the Ohio Federation of Music Clubs Young Composers' contest, 1972. She has performed as an alto-singer and violinist in numerous concerts. PHOTOGRAPH.

Compositions
CHAMBER
Gestures (cham ens) (1972)
Abraxas (vlc and pf)
Nocturne (cl) (1983)
VOCAL
Abelard (S and vla) (1983)
The Bells, song cycle (4 vces and perc) (1978)
Duo for trumpet and voice (1976)
Medea (2 S)
Miserere (S and cl) (1983) (comm William Powell)
The owl and the pussycat (narr and 6 vces) (1974) (Reimers, 1980)
The philosopher, song cycle (1971)
Sweet talk (w-ch) (1976) (comm University of North Dakota Women's Chorus)
Soliloquy (1981)
Tintinnabulation (3 vces and glock) (1976)
The tortoise and the hare (S, B, cl and b-cl) (1983)
SACRED
I will lift up mine eyes (ch) (1971)
Kyrie eleison (w-ch) (1969)
OPERA
Legends (1971)
ELECTRONIC
Requiem (4 vces and tape) (1978)
Ref. composer, 142, 622, 624, 625

KAWAI, Sawako. See NAKAMURA, Sawako

KAYDEN, Mildred
20th-century American authoress, lecturer and composer. b. New York. She studied at the Juilliard School of Music and Vassar College, where she obtained a B.A. She received her M.A. from Radcliffe College where her teachers were Ernst Krenek and Walter Piston. She taught at Vassar College from 1946 to 1952 and had a radio program on WEVD from 1956 to 1963. She is a member of ASCAP.
Compositions
CHAMBER
String quartet in D
Woodwind trio
PIANO
Sonata in D
Theme and variations
VOCAL
The valley of dry bones, cantata
Green gown (ch)
SACRED
The call of the prophet (T and org)
Psalm 121 (S and org)
THEATRE
The last word, play
Mardi gras, play
The riddle of Sheba, play
The seed and the dream
Strangers in the land, television
FILM MUSIC
Leaven for the Cities
The Procession
The Pumpkin Coach
Ref. 39, 94, 141, 142

KAZANDJIAN, Sirvart
Armenian singer and composer. b. Ethiopia, June 13, 1944. She moved to Switzerland in 1971. One of her first compositions *Les Massacres d'Armenie* appeared in an Armenian magazine in Addis Ababa when she was 16. From 1963 to 1968 she attended the National Conservatory of Erevan and studied composition under Professor Gregor Yeghiazarian, graduating as master of composition and teaching. At this time some of her works were performed on Armenian radio and television. From 1969 to 1970 she was a student of Toni Aubin at the Paris Conservatoire. She obtained a diploma in singing from the Conservatory of Geneva where she studied under U. Mielsch and Claudine Perret and since then she has taken part in recitals and concerts in Switzerland and abroad. In 1973 her *A ma patrie* won her a distinction at the International Composition in Vercelli, Italy. Her works have been performed in Armenia, France, England, Switzerland, the United States, Canada and South America. She produced a series of programs on Armenian music for Radio Suisse Romande, based on her original fieldwork in Armenia. PHOTOGRAPH.
Compositions
ORCHESTRA
Les 40 jours de Moussa Dagh, op. 17 (1968)
Rondo-scherzo, op. 15 (vln and orch)
Aubade, op. 31 (also pf trio) (1980)
CHAMBER
String quartet No. 1, op. 6 (1966)
String quartet No. 2, op. 16
String quartet No. 3, mes sous, op. 36
Pastorale, op. 21 (pf trio) (1980)
Five miniatures, op. 34 (pf trio)
Légendes d'Armenie, op. 35 (ob, fl and pf)
Suite africaine, op. 26 (fl and pf)
Duo, op. 32 (fl and gtr)
Pieces (solo insts)
A ma patrie, 8 pieces (pf) (965-1971)
VOCAL
Cycle of four songs, op. 23 (G. Lorca) (m-S and str orch or pf)
La danse des esclaves, op. 37 (Godel) (mix-ch a-cap)
Vienne la nuit, op 38 (Godel) (mix-ch a-cap)
Cycle of three songs, op. 9 (V. Tekeyan) (S and pf) (1966)
Sept chants d'amour et de fraternité, op. 33, in 7 languages
SACRED
Sept psaumes, op. 29 (S, Bar and orch)
Ref. composer

KAZHAEVA, Tatiana Ibragimovna
Soviet pianist and composer. b. 1950. At the Moscow Conservatory she studied the piano under Tatiana Nikolayeva (q.v.) and composition under T. Khrennikov. She performed her *Chorale and invention* at the 6th International Tchaikovsky Competition. DISCOGRAPHY.
Compositions
ORCHESTRA
Concerto (orch of Russian folk insts)
Symphonic pieces
CHAMBER
Three pieces (bsn and pf) (1976-1978)
Other instrumental pieces
PIANO
Chorale (Sovietski Kompozitor, 1980)
Prelude and invention (Sovietski Kompozitor, 1980)
VOCAL
Lenin, cantata
Romances (Pushkin, Blok and Akhmatova)
Ref. 563

KAZORECK, Hildegard (pseuds. Hildegard Dewitz, Diana Monti)
German composer. b. Berlin, August 25, 1911. She composed music for stage and radio plays and secular and sacred songs.
Ref. 70, 81

KAZURO-TROMBINI, Margerita
20th-century Italian violinist, conductor and composer.
Ref. MLA *Notes* June 1981

KEAL, Minna
20th-century British composer. She studied at the Royal Academy of Music and completed a course in harmony and counterpoint at the Trinity College of Music, but started serious composition later in life.
Compositions
ORCHESTRA
Symphony No. 1
CHAMBER
Wind quintet
String quartet (1979)
Fantasia (vln and pf)
Ref. *The Guardian*, February 13 1984, *Tempo* No. 148

KECK, Pearl
20th-century American composer of Pennsylvania. She composed choral works.
Ref. 40, 347

KEECH, Diana
Composition
CHAMBER
Scherzo rondoso (ob and pf) (Cramer, 1982)
Ref. MLA *Notes*

KEEFER, Euphrosyne

Canadian pianist, violist, singer, teacher and composer. b. England, June 9, 1919. From 1936 to 1941 she studied the piano, the viola, singing and composition at the Royal Academy of Music and became an L.R.A.M. in 1936. She played the viola in the Royal Academy of Music orchestra for three years under Sir Henry Wood. She completed five Royal Academy of Music courses, receiving her bronze and silver certificates in the piano, composition, harmony, singing and aural training. She studied composition under Alan Bush for four years and had works for the viola, the clarinet and voice performed at chamber concerts in London. She studied singing on a scholarship under Frederic Austin and in 1941 was accepted by Sadler's Wells as a soprano soloist. She settled in Canada in 1945 and from 1965 to 1977 taught the piano and theory in Toronto. In 1980 she won the open class at the Okanagan Festival for composers and in 1983 was commissioned to write a flute and piano work for the same festival. PHOTOGRAPH.

Compositions

CHAMBER

Sketch on a sultry day (fl, vln and pf) (1970)
Tower of Aerides (picc, tam and hpcd) (1982)
La dame à la Licorne (cl and pf) (1969)
Four ideas (fl and bsn) (1980)
Three bagatelles (cl and pf) (1941
Chez Jan (fl) (1981)
Lament for Nick (fl) (1981)
Trois hantes (fl) (1969)
Viola sonata (1940)

PIANO

Landscape with trees (1970)
Pieces for young pianists: 6 randoms; 6 problems; 6 brevities; 5 feelings; 5 haphazards (1971)

VOCAL

The clock (1971)
Divertissements (1981)
Haiku, duo (S and fl) (1970)
The nightingale near the house (high vce, pf and fl obb) (1969)
Occasions (med-vce and fl) (1980)
The osprey (1981)
Polar chrysalis (S and pf) (1981)
Two song cycles (S and fl obb) (1969)

Ref. composer

KEETMAN, Gunild

German professor and composer. b. Elberfeld, June 5, 1904. She studied music under Carl Orff at the Guenterschule in Munich, becoming Orff's assistant in music education in 1928, senior teacher at the Guenterschule and a teacher of and composer for dance orchestras. In 1949 she received a professorship for the Orff method at the Mozarteum in Salzburg, where she founded the Orff Institute in 1961. She was responsible for the production of Orff educational methods in the form of records and films.

Compositions

CHAMBER

Rhythmische Uebung (1970)
Spielstueke fuer Blockfloeten und kleines Schlagwerk (1930)
Spielstuecke fuer kleines Schlagwerk (1931)
Spielstuecke fuer Blockfloeten (1932)
Stuecke fuer Floete und Trommel (1956)
Spielbuch fuer Zylophon (1966)

VOCAL

Chansons enfantines (1958)
Japanische Kinderlieder (1973)
Lieder fuer die Schule (1960-1967)

THEATRE

Die Weihnachtsgeschichte, radio play for children (Orff) (1952)

Publications

Elementaria: Erster Umgang mit dem Orff-Schulwerk. Stuttgart, 1970.
Musik fuer Kinder. Co-editor. 1954.
Orff Schoolworks. Co-author. 1930.

Ref. 17, 200

KEIG, Betty

20th-century American composer. She composed piano pieces and songs.

Ref. 40, 347

KELEMEN, Berta Zathureczky

19th-century Hungarian composer.

Compositions

VOCAL

Mikor csend van, dalromanc es Szovatai bucsudal enek es zongorara, songs (vce and pf) (Kloekner)

THEATRE

Hajnal uram! melodrama (Kloekner)
Kevlari bucsu, melodrama (Mery)

Ref. 297

KELEMEN, Mrs. Lajos

19th-century Hungarian composer.

Composition

VOCAL

Kisirtam minden konyom erted (vce and cimbalom) (Nador)

Ref. 297

KELLER, Ginette

French lecturer and composer. b. Asnieres, May 16, 1925. She studied at the Paris Conservatoire under Nadia Boulanger (q.v.), Olivier Messiaen, Tony Aubin and N. and J. Gallon. From 1970 she taught musical analysis at the Paris Conservatoire. She won a Grand Prix de Rome in 1951 and a prize in the Queen Elizabeth of Belgium competition in 1957. Her works have been performed in France, Italy and the United States. PHOTOGRAPH.

Compositions

ORCHESTRA

Symphony fresque (1953)
Piano concerto (1963)
Concertino for violoncello (1955)
Paramorphoses (1969)
Sept mouvements incantatoires (1964)
Sinfonietta (1957)
Variables (cham orch) (1960) (Mannheim prize)

CHAMBER

Six chants de lumiere et d'ombre (double reed qrt) (1965)
Structures (baroque qrt) (1974)
Trio (fl, cl and bsn) (1951)
Trio (hp, vln and vlc)
Chant de Parthenope (fl and pf) (1967)
Girations (pf and perc) (1970)
Incidences poetiques (fl and hp) (1968)
Sonata (pf and trp) (1952)

VOCAL

Cantata (S and orch) (1972)
Chant de la nuit, cantata (after Nietzsche) (1952)
Graphiques (S and small ens) (1971)

BALLET

Nuances (1956)

Ref. composer, 9

KELLER, Lue Alice

American composer. b. Findlay, OH, July 4, 1888. She composed songs and piano pieces.

Ref. 226

KELLEY, Dorothea Nolte

20th-century American violinist, violist and composer. b. Greenwich, CT. She studied the violin, the viola and theory under private teachers in Boston from 1916 to 1923 and in New York City from 1923 to 1929. She attended the Juilliard School of Music from 1929 to 1931 and 1933 to 1936 and spent the summer of 1939 studying in Fontainebleau, France. Her teachers included Barbara Werner Schwaab in Boston, Albert Stoessel, Mischa Mischakoff in New York City, Arnold Schonberg in Chautauqua and Nadia Boulanger (q.v.) in Paris. She played the viola in the Buffalo Philharmonic Orchestra after 1945.

Composition

ORCHESTRA

Episode (1927)

Ref. 496

KELLEY, Florence Bettray

20th-century American teacher and composer. b. Racine, WI. She composed piano pieces.

Ref. 347

KELLEY, Patricia Ann

American electronic instrumentalist, lecturer and composer. b. New Albany, IN, March 17, 1951. She studied music theory, composition and electronic music at Ohio State University and obtained a B.M. in 1972. She then studied at the Center for Contemporary Music, Mills College and obtained an M.F.A. in electronic music and recording media, 1976. In 1976 she was awarded the Elizabeth Mills Crothers Prize for excellence in composition. She lectured at Mills College from 1974 to 1976.

Compositions

ELECTRONIC

Hum (4 channel tape) (1977)
Nightwalk (4 channel tape) (1977)
Syzygy (4 channel tape) (1975)
The auction at your home (2 channel tape) (1975)
This time (jazz pf and vib) (1971)
A public service announcement in four movements

MULTIMEDIA

Cosmic commercial (film and 4 channel tape) (1975)
Daze of phaze (4 channel tape and coloured video) (1976)
Slide show for seven years of crazy love, musical anthology (1977)
A tribute to armed forces day (moog tape and film) (1976)
What's in it for you? (video) (1975)
Upon seeing oneself as a product of television (video) (1976)

Ref. composer

KELLY, Denise Maria Anne

Irish harpist, pianist, lecturer and composer. b. Belfast, April 24, 1954. She studied the Irish harp, singing and the piano at the Royal Irish Academy of Music, Dublin and the concert harp at the College of Music, Dublin, then gained her Mus.Bac. from the University of Dublin. In 1973 she went to London, where she studied privately under Maria Korchinska, the famous Russian harpist and at the Guildhall School of Music under Robert Barclay Wilson (composition). She became an L.G.S.M. at the Conservatory of Music, Brussels. In 1976 she began concert harp studies under Sidonie Goossens at the Guildhall and in 1977 returned to Ireland to be the concert harp teacher at the School of Music, Cork. She performs regularly in Ireland and London. One of her composition prizes was the Alexander Grosz memorial prize from the Guildhall School of Music. She also won two gold medals for the Irish harp and the concert harp at the Dublin Reis Ceoil.

Compositions

CHAMBER

Gog and Magog (str qrt) (1976)

VOCAL

From beginning to end (mix ch) (1976)
Thus it was (S, vlc, pf, hp and cel) (1977)
Sundry notes (S, fl, perc and hp) (1975)
Helas mon dieu (vce, fl and hp) (1974)
Journey of the soul (vce and pf) (1978)
Metaphyscycle (vce and hp) (1978)
Dialogue to unity (1975)
Songs

SACRED

In the beginning (mix-ch) (1975)

Ref. composer, 206, 457

KELLY, Georgia

20th-century American composer. DISCOGRAPHY.

Composition

CHAMBER

Seapeace (1978)

Ref. Kay Gardner Publ.

KELSO, Alice Anne

20th-century American composer. DISCOGRAPHY.

Composition

MISCELLANEOUS

Mournful sounds in memory of Abraham Lincoln

Ref. 563

KEMBLE. See ARKWRIGHT, Mrs. Robert

KEMBLE, Adelaide (Mrs. Sartoris)

English singer and composer. b. 1814; d. August 1879. She composed songs.

Ref. 276, 347

KEMP, Dorothy Elizabeth Walter

American accordionist, horn player, pianist, conductor, professor and composer. b. Cincinnati, OH, November 23, 1926. She studied at the College of Music, Cincinnati (B.S., education, 1948) and the University of Cincinnati. She obtained an M.A. (education, 1949) from Eastern Kentucky State College, Richmond. She did postgraduate courses at Western Kentucky State College and Miami University. In 1946 she obtained a certificate for the French horn and from 1950 to 1954 held the position of professor of horn music, theory, arrangement and music education at the Appalachian State University and from 1959 to 1962 was music educational assistant at the Willis Music Company, Ohio. She studied the French horn on a partial scholarship at the Cincinnati College of Music. From 1972 she was conductor of the Powel Crosley Y.M.C.A adult concert band. She contributes to music publications and is a free-lance musician. PHOTOGRAPH.

Compositions

SYMPHONIC BAND

Circus scene (1977)

CHAMBER

Beginning brass (brass septet) (1972)
The brassy saints (brass septet) (1973)
Dixie-doodle (brass septet) (1972)
La classe chasse (hn qrt) (1963)
Easter fanfare No. 1 (brass qrt) (1962)
Easter fanfare No. 2 (brass qrt) (1962) (Willis Music Co.)
French horn finesse (hn qrt) (1963)
Modern velvet (hn qrt) (1963)

VOCAL

Groundhog day, children's song (1977)
The groundhog rock, children's song (1977)

ARRANGEMENTS

Christmas in brass (brass qrt) (1959) (Willis)
Easter in brass (brass qrt) (1962) (Willis)
Four brass for Christmas (brass qrt) (1960) (Willis)

Ref. composer, 206, 457

KEMP-POTTER, Joan

20th-century British choral conductor, lecturer and composer. b. Chatham. She studied at the Royal College of Music and the Guildhall School of Music. She worked at the Montpellier Music School from 1948 to 1950 and was a music advisor to the Y.W.C.A Central Club from 1950 to 1954 and the Royal Overseas League, 1954 to 1959. She was on the staff of the Royal College of Music, Junior Department from 1950 to 1968 and from 1968, a lecturer at the London College of Music. She conducted a number of choral societies and received a recording prize for conducting.

Compositions

CHAMBER

Pieces

VOCAL

Songs

OPERETTA

Three operettas

INCIDENTAL MUSIC

The Tempest (Shakespeare)

Ref. 84

KENDAL, Sidney. See MASON, Gladys Amy

KENDIKOVA, Zdenka (Mrs. Linhartova, Linhart)

Bohemian pianist and composer. b. Pisek, July 10, 1861; d. Prague, June 17, 1904. She studied the piano in Jindrichov Hradec under V. Chabr and in Prague under Karl Slavkovsky. She studied composition under Fibich in Prague from 1880 to 1890 and collaborated with him in his piano school and arranged a number of his compositions for the piano. She studied under Jindrich Pech and R. Panajotova and appeared in operas of Wagner, Mozart and Smetana. After her marriage to Dr. J. Linhart she retired from artistic life.

Compositions

CHAMBER

Two mazurkas (vln and pf) (1886)

PIANO

Humoresque (1890)
Quatre morceaux (under name Linhart)
Other works

Ref. 197

KENDRICK, Virginia Catherine (nee Bachman) (Mrs. W.D.)

American organist, pianist and composer. b. Minneapolis, MN, April 8, 1910. She studied at the University of Minnesota, 1928 to 1933. She was organist at the First Church of Christ Scientist, Excelsior from 1962 to 1975 and worked in the organ music department of Schmitt Music Co., Minneapolis, 1958 to 1975. In the same period she was a pianist with the Andahazy Ballet Company, Minneapolis. PHOTOGRAPH.

Compositions
PIANO
Concert piece
High sky
VOCAL
From my window (S, w-ch and pf) (1960)
Little Miss Whuffit (w-ch and pf) (1962)
Other works (mixed and m-vces)
Songs incl.:
April whimsy
Before the world was (1973)
A brownie lives with me (1945)
Green is the willow (Schmitt Music Co., 1965)
In this soft velvet night (1977)
Jade summer (pf or hp and vce) (Schmitt, 1971)
Little Goody Two Shoes (S, A and pf) (1956)
The Little Red Hen (Schmitt, 1955)
Music is beauty (1969)
Song about Sue (1943)
Tribute (1970)
Wealth of mine (vce, pf and hp) (Schmitt, 1941)
White sky
SACRED
Brood o'er us with Thy sheltering wing (1975)
Gethsemane (1950)
Hear my cry, O God (Schmitt, 1975)
I will lift up mine eyes (Schmitt, 1976)
Lo, I am with you always unto the end of the world (1976)
Look unto Me, said our God (Schmitt, 1974)
The Lord Omnipotent reigneth (1975)
Mother's evening prayer (1975)
Settings of Mary Baker Eddy hymns
Ref. composer, 142, 328, 457, 474, 475, 622

KENNEDY-FRASER, Marjory

Scottish pianist, folklorist and singer. b. Perth, October 1, 1857; d. Edinburgh, November 21, 1930. She was the daughter of the famous Scottish singer David Kennedy and studied under him and was his accompanist from the age of 12. She later studied under Mathilde Marchesi in Paris, Matthay (piano) and F. Niecks (music history). She became a collector of folk songs and in 1905 visited the Outer Hebridean Isles to research Celtic music and study arrangement of Gaelic folk material. DISCOGRAPHY.
Compositions
CHAMBER
Hebridean suite (vlc and pf)
PIANO
Sea pieces
Lyrics
VOCAL
An Island sheiling song
Scots folk tunes
Songs of the Hebrides, 3 vols incl. An Eriskay love-lilt (vce and pf) (1910, 1917, 1921)
Ten unison songs, for schools
Volume of Lowland Scots songs
Publications
Hebridean Song and the Laws of Interpretation. Glasgow, 1922.
A Life of Song. Autobiography. London, 1928.
Ref. 22, 100, 110, 361, 563, 572, 622

KENSWIL, Atma

Surinam pianist and composer. b. Paramaribo, April 29, 1892. She studied the piano at the Utrecht Conservatory; under Laszloffy at the Liszt Academy in Budapest and Lazare Levy at the Paris Conservatoire. She studied composition under Leo Weiner at the Liszt Academy and de la Presle at the Paris Conservatoire. She lived in the Netherlands.
Compositions
ORCHESTRA
Phantasie orientale
CHAMBER
Fuga (str qrt)
PIANO
Poème d'une flute orientale
Preludium (1946)
VOCAL
Meditation symphonic (mix-ch and orch) (1946)
Kerstmeditatie (mix-ch and pf)
Lentelicht (vce and pf) (1946)
Per tenebras ad lucem (1952)
Wijang, v. Tagore I and II
Ref. 77

KENT, Ada Twohy

Canadian organist, pianist, lecturer and composer. b. Helena, MT, or Denver, CO, February 8, 1888; d. July 23, 1969. She studied under J.E.P. Aldous and at the Royal Conservatory, Toronto, under Dr. Vogt, obtaining her Mus.Bac. (1906) and an L.R.A.M. She was the organist in various churches in Hamilton and Toronto and accompanist to the Mendelssohn Choir. She gave numerous recitals and taught at the Royal Conservatory, Toronto. PHOTOGRAPH.
Compositions
VOCAL
As I pass by (S and mix-ch) (Waterloo Music Co., 1958)
No flower so fair (ch) (Carl Fischer)
Dorothea (England: Stainer & Bell)
Five eyes (Canada: Waterloo Music Co., 1953)
Hey ho for the open road (Stainer & Bell)
The Royal Mounted (Waterloo, 1953)
Sing a song of Canada, children's songs (Toronto: T. Nelson, 1937)
Tip toe turns (Waterloo, 1952)
Twilight town, lullaby (Stainer & Bell)
Two songs of autumn (G.V. Thompson)
When love's afar (Oakville: Frederick Harris)
SACRED
Dominion hymn (vce and ch) (Waterloo)
Peace hymn (vce and ch) (Waterloo)
How near to God, wedding song (Waterloo, 1945)
No flower so fair; O Jesu, may I grow each day (S, Cont, B, mix-ch and org) (C. Fischer, 1939)
At Christmastide (Waterloo)
Long ago, carol (Waterloo)
Ref. Eileen Drake (composer's daughter), 94, 133, 347

KENT, Phyllis Elizabeth. See BARKER, Phyllis Elizabeth

KER, Ann S.

American organist, choral conductor, ecclesiastic, teacher and composer. b. Warsaw, IN, November 10, 1937. She attended De Paul University from 1955 to 1957, Butler University from 1957 to 1958 and obtained her B.M.E. from Indiana University in 1974. She studied for her M.A. at Notre Dame University. She held the position of organist at the First Presbyterian Church, Warsaw, IN, from 1969 to 1979; was choir conductor at the Central Christian Church in 1980; on the faculty at Huntington College from 1976 and from 1980, director of music at the Redeemer Lutheran Church. In 1974 she was awarded first prize at the St. Francis College composition competition.
Compositions
CHAMBER
Christmas fantasy (pf) (1979) (Indiana Music Center)
Christmas trilogy (pf) (1979) (Indiana)
The Creation (org) (1975)
VOCAL
Hear this! (1974) (Neil A. Kjos)
Softly (1982) (Kjos)
Triptych (m-S and pf) (1980) (Indiana)
SACRED
For me O Lord (ch) (1982) (Richmond Music Press)
Soli Deo gloria (ch) (1982) (Richmond)
Ways to praise (ch) (1982) (Richmond)
Three men on camelback (1981) (Harold Flammer)
Ref. composer

KERBY, Caroline

19th-century American composer.
Composition
VOCAL
The thornless rose (vce and pf) (Philadelphia: R.H. Hobson, 1829)
Ref. 228

KERCADO (Cercado), Mlle. Le Senechal de

19th-century French composer. Her operetta was presented at the Paris Opera-Comique on June 5, 1805.
Composition
OPERETTA
La meprisée volontaire, or La double leçon (1805)
Ref. 26, 226, 276, 307, 347

KERCHER, Eleanor

20th-century British composer.

Composition
ELECTRONIC
I say no world (vce and elec insts)
Ref. *Composer* (London)

KERMOR, Mireille

19th-century French composer.
Composition
OPERA
La Mouette Blanche (Rouen, 1903)
Ref. 431

KERN, Frida (nee Seitz)

Austrian professor and composer. b. Vienna, March 9, 1891. She studied music at the Musikhochschule, Vienna, under Franz Schmidt and P. Heger from 1923 to 1927. She lectured in music theory at the University of Vienna from 1943 to 1945 and in 1960 became professor of music and vice-president of the Upper Austrian Artists Union. In 1942 she won a prize in a music competition organized by the City of Linz.
Compositions
ORCHESTRA
Symphony No. 1, op. 46 (1943)
Symphony in one movement, op. 2 (1926)
Cello concerto, op. 28 (1937)
Piano concerto with strings and timpani, op. 36 (1940)
Concertino, op. 60 (trp and orch) (1951)
Variations for small orchestra and piano, op. 7 (1930)
Violin concerto, op. 27 (1937)
Afrikanische Stimmungsbilder, op. 34 (small orch) (1934)
Galgenhumor-Walzer, op. 30 (small orch) (1939)
In memoriam, op. 5 (1929)
Musikalische Zeitwoerter, op. 32 (small orch) (1939)
Orchestral suite, op. 33 (1939)
Orchestral variations, op. 38 (1941)
Passacaglia, op. 45 (1943)
Scherzo, op. 43 (hn and small orch; also pf) (1942)
Sinfonische Radio-Pausenzeichen (1937)
Symphonic march for orchestra, op. 73 (1956)
Symphonic music for orchestra, op. 20 (1934)
Suite for strings, interval studies, op. 12 (1932)
Suite in old style, op. 17 (vln and small orch or pf) (1933)
Taenze, op. 35 (1939)
Waldmaerchen, op. 6 (small orch) (1929)
CHAMBER
Octet, op. 3 (cls, ob, bsn and strs) (1927)
Pieces for youth, op. 67 (2 vln, 4 vln, vln and pf – 4 hands) (1953)
Ernste musik, op. 37 (ww, brass and perc) (1940)
Clarinet quintet, op. 19 (1933)
Four pieces, op. 25 (wind qnt) (1939) (Munich: Grosch, 1979)
Froehliche Impressionen, op. 51 (fl, vln, vla, vlc and hp) (1951)
Rondino, op. 58 (pf and str qrt) (1950)
Staendchen, op. 77 (5 vln) (1958)
String quintet, op. 57 (1950)
Theme and variations, op. 82 (wind qnt)
Wind quintet (Leipzig: Grosch 1956)
Variations, op. 4 (hn qrt) (1942)
Die vier Geigerlein, op. 74 (4 vln) (1956)
Vier Vortragsstuecke fuer die Jugend, op. 74 (4 vln) (Vienna: Doblinger, 1959)
String quartet No. 1, op. 8 (1930)
String quartet No. 2, op. 21 (1934)
String quartet No. 3, op. 39 (Vienna: Europa, 1941)
String quartet No. 4, op. 48 (1948)
String quartet No. 5, op. 72 (1956)
Piano trio, op. 15 (1933)
Sonatine for youth, op. 55 (vln, vlc and pf) (1949)
String trio, op. 42 (1942)
Andalusia, op. 75 (vln and pf) (1957)
Andante lyrica, op. 76 (vln or vlc and pf) (1958)
Ballade, op. 63 (vlc and pf) (1952)
Drei stuecke, op. 26 (2 vln) (1936)
Duo, op. 71 (2 vlc or vln and vlc) (1955)
Flute serenade, op. 62 (fl and pf) (1952)
Larghetto, op. 81 (vla and pf)
Variations, op. 61 (vln and hp) (1951)
Ballade, op. 59 (hp) (1951)
Cello sonata, op. 10 (1931)
Etudes, op. 80, 40 pieces (man) (Doblinger, 1959)
Pieces for violin, op. 47 (1944)
Two pieces, op. 50: Spatz; Nachtigall (vlc) (Doblinger)
Vier cellostuecke, op. 24 (1935)
Violin sonata, op. 9 (1931)
PIANO
Scherzo, op. 13 (2 pf) (1932)
Three pieces, op. 49 (2 pf) (1947)
Capriccio, op. 70 (Europa, 1955)
Five bagatelles, op. 53 (1949)
Five pieces for youth (Landbilder), op. 79
Humoresques, op. 18 (1923)
Introduction and toccata, op. 66 (Europa, 1953)
Klavierfantasie, op. 22 (1934)
Klaviervariationen, op. 14 (1932)
Konzertwalzer, op. 40 (1941)
Maerchenerzahlung fuer die Jugend, op. 67a (1954)
Russische sonate, op. 1 (1926)
Stimmungsbilder, op. 84
Tierbilder, op. 54 (1949)
Elegy and toccata for the left hand, op. 56 (1949)
VOCAL
Chorwerk, op. 23 (T, B, mix-ch and orch) (1935)
Drei Orchesterlieder, op. 41 (Bar and orch) (1942)
Frau Musica, hymn, op. 85 (m-ch and brass)
Hymnus, op. 78 (A and str qrt) (1959)
Kinderchorlieder, op. 52 (1952)
Liederzyklus, op. 65 (A and pf) (1953)
Liederzyklus aus dem Chinesischen, op. 83 (A and pf)
Liederzyklus, op. 69 (m-S and pf) (1954)
Streichquartettlieder, op. 16 (A or m-S and str qrt) (1933)
SACRED
Auferstehungskantate, op. 31 (S, Bar and m-ch) (1938)
Ref. 70, 194

KERN, Louise

19th-century German composer.
Compositions
VOCAL
Songs
ARRANGEMENTS
Das Rheingold (Wagner) (Reminiszenz, op. 40) (pf and harmonium) (Schott)
Grande Fantasie aus Wagner's Tannhaeuser, op. 39 (pf, vln and harmonium) (Furstner)
La toute puissance de François Schubert, Grand Trio, op. 36 (vln, org and pf) (Cranz)
Meditation sur le Requiem de Verdi, op. 32 (vln, org and pf) (Ricordi)
Cavatine (Raff) (harmonium and pf) (Mustel)
Revolver (harmonium) (Evette)
Ref. 226, 297, 433

KERR, Bessie Maude

Canadian pianist, teacher and composer. b. Toronto, June 4, 1888. She studied at the Toronto College of Music in London, Ontario, under Willgoose (harmony, counterpoint and composition) and under Dr. Horwood (composition) at the Royal Conservatory in Toronto. She taught the piano and theory in St. Thomas, Ontario.
Compositions
CHAMBER
Two movements: Night clouds; Morning reflections (str qrt)
PIANO
Capriccio in F-Minor
Fantasy
Miniatures for young pianists
Minute rhapsody
Mirage
Nocturne
Pastorale
Prelude
Two short preludes
VOCAL
Lake of bays, suite
Group of songs
Ref. 133

KERR, Louisa (nee Hay) (Mrs. Alexander)

Early 19th-century English composer.
Compositions
VOCAL
Ballads incl.:
Melodies (composer) (1835)
Part songs
Songs
SACRED
Evening hymn
Ref. 6, 226, 276

KERR, Mrs. Alexander. See KERR, Louisa

KERR, Julia. See KERWEY, Julia

KERSENBAUM, Sylvia Haydee

Argentine pianist and composer. b. Buenos Aires, December 27, 1941. She studied the piano at the Buenos Aires State Conservatory under Esperanza Lothringer from 1953 to 1956 and Scaramuzza from 1956 to 1966 and composition under Gilardi, Bautista and Garcia Morillo. In 1966 she studied at the Accademia Musicale Chigiana in Siena and obtained a diploma from the Accademia Nationale di Santa Cecilia in Rome in 1968. She completed her studies in Geneva under Magaloff and Hans Graf, 1971.

Compositions

VOCAL

Various works

BALLET

La mascara roja

Ref. 17, 70

KERWEY, Julia (nee Weismann) (pseud. of Julia Kerr)

German composer. b. Wiesbaden, August 28, 1898. She lived in Paris from 1933 and studied under W. Klatte.

Compositions

VOCAL

Songs

OPERA

Der Chronplan

Ref. 70, 226, 465

KESAREVA, Margarita Alexandrovna

Soviet lecturer and composer. b. Sverdlovsk, May 21, 1936. She studied composition at the Uralsk Conservatory under V.N. Trambitski, graduating in 1962 and staying on as a lecturer. Her compositions draw on Ural folklore and political themes presented in contemporary style.

Compositions

ORCHESTRA

Simfonietta (1963)
Cantilena, poem (small orch) (1965)

CHAMBER

Cycle (fl, ob, cl and bsn) (1971)
String quartet (1962)
Cycle (ob and pf) (1976)
Sonata (pf) (1962)

VOCAL

Svetloye ozero, oratorio (soli, ch and sym orch) (1972)
The blue snake, choral suite (Kolotushkina) (chil-ch and bayan)
Noch kladoiskatelstva (Kolotushkina) (ch) (1976)
Taganai, poem (Kushtum) (ch) (1966)
Cycle on motives from old Ural songs (vce, ob, bsn and pf) (1968)
Hill digger in the Steppe (ch a-cap)
Khud i Kurgany (ch a-cap) (Sovietski Kompozitor, 1982)
Lesnye legendi, cycle (Pilipenko and Sorokin) (vce and pf) (1965)
Nagovornaya legenda, cycle (folk words) (vce and pf) (1969)
Sibirski, song cycle (Kuznetsova) (vce and pf) (1964)
Skas, cycle (Kolotushkina) (vce and pf) (1975)
Sweet bitterness, cycle (vce and insts)
Zori studenogo kraya, cycle (Danilov) (vce and pf) (1960)
Songs (ch)
Songs (vce and pf)
Arrangements of Ural folk songs

INCIDENTAL MUSIC

Music for plays

Ref. 21, 420

KESHNER, Joyce Grove

American pianist, conductor, musicologist, teacher and composer. b. New Haven, CT, May 24, 1927. She obtained a B.S. in education from Southern Connecticut State College in 1948. She studied the piano at the Juilliard School of Music and Mannes College of Music under Joseph Raiff, Martin Canin, John Goldmark and Francis Dillon. She studied conducting under Abraham Kaplan, Rudolph Thomas and Harold Aks, composition under Edward Murray, Fredric Werle and Mario Davidovsky and voice under Ruth Hand and James McClure. In 1972 she received an M.A. in composition from City University of New York. She was assistant conductor of the Mannes College of Music chorus and conductor of Ars Musica Chorale and orchestra. She was artist-affiliate with Ramapo College, NJ, From 1973 to 1976 and researched into bel canto. In 1971 she won the Harry M. Cohen Award from City College of New York. She teaches the piano, voice, theory and conducting privately.

Compositions

CHAMBER

String quartet (1971)
Monophonic piece (bsn)
Piece (bsn)

SACRED

Lord what is man? (B, ch and small orch)
Waiting born (fl, vce and pf)

Ref. 77, 457

KESSICK, Marlaena

B. 1935.

Composition

CHAMBER

Contrasti (fl and pf) (Milan: Curci, 1978)

Ref. Otto Harrassowitz (Wiesbaden)

KESSLER, Minuetta Schumiatcher

American concert pianist, teacher and composer. b. Gomel, USSR, September 5, 1914. She studied the piano under John M. Williams in Calgary, Canada at the age of five; at ten with Gladys McKelvie Egbert; when she was 13 she won a scholarship with Howard Brockway of New York, while studying in Regina, Canada and at 15 received her L.A.B. and won a scholarship to study with Ernest Hutcheson in New York. She is an L.R.C.M. and an L.R.A.M. and gained her diploma in the piano from the Juilliard School of Music and also her postgraduate teacher's and artist's diploma. Later she was a teacher at the Juilliard. She studied the piano under Ania Dorfman and Mieczyslaw Munz and composition under Ivan Langstroth. She performed as soloist of her own works and in concert in the United States and Canada. She was invited to contribute her *Alberta Concerto* to a time capsule buried in her home town of Calgary. She became an American citizen in 1940. She received Canadian ASCAP awards for composition in 1945 and 1946 and the Chamber Music award by the Brookline Library Music Association in 1957. She received a citation for the best concert of works by a woman composer in 1975 from the National Federation of Music Clubs and was awarded the Key to the City of Calgary in 1951. She was president of the New England Pianoforte Teachers' Association from 1965 to 1967 and president of the Massachusetts Music Teachers' Association, 1979 to 1981, which commissioned her to write a string quartet for their 1981 Convention. In 1981 she received three prizes in the Biennial Composition Contest of the National League of American Pen Women, and in 1982 was appointed music editor of their monthly journal *The Pen Woman*. She was made an honorary member of Sigma Alpha Iota in 1979 and in 1984 won awards at the Biennial Convention of the National League of Pen Women for her works *Trilogy* and *Lake O'Hara Fantasy*. She was appointed chairlady of theory and composition for the eastern division of the Music Teachers' National Association and was awarded a citation for distinguished service from the League of Pen Women. DISCOGRAPHY.

Compositions

ORCHESTRA

Alberta concerto (pf and orch) (1947)
New York suite, op. 21 (pf and orch; also pf) (1942)

CHAMBER

Scherzetta, op. 68 (fl, cl, 2 vln, vlc and pf) (1969)
String quartet No. 1, op. 109 (2 vln, vla and vlc) (1981)
Introduction and allegro, op. 62 (vln, vlc and pf) (1966)
Trio (1955)
Trio No. 1, op. 39 (vln, vlc and pf) (1981)
Trio No. 2, op. 125 (cl, vlc and pf) (1983)
Cello sonata, op. 54 (vlc and pf) (1961)
Fantasies of the night, op. 135 (vlc and pf)
Fantasy (ob and pf)
Lake McArthur fantasy, op. 93 (fl and pf) (1979)
Lake O'Hara fantasy, op. 87 (ob and pf) (1978)
Sonata (cl and pf) (1961) (prize, 2nd annual chamber music competition)
Sonata (vln and pf) (1953)
Sonata concertante, op. 38 (vln and pf) (1956)
To ignite a star, op. 110 (vln and pf) (1981)
Variations on a Jewish lullaby, op. 104 (fl and hp) (1981)

PIANO

Boston red sox, op. 58 (2 pf) (1964)
A day in the park, op. 30 (Willis Music Co., 1981)
Autumn vignette, op. 111, No. 4 (Willis, 1982)
Ballet sonatina (1943)
Bicentennial sonata, op. 78 (1977)
Caprice, op. 71 (1973)
Castles in the sky, op. 120 (1982)

Cat 'n mouse tales, op. 85 (Willis, 1982)
Etude brillante, op. 129 (Hora) (1954) (New York: Transcontinental Music. (1965)
Fantasette, op. 17 (1943)
Four exotic colours, op. 129 (1965)
Frolicking in F-Sharp, op. 108, (Willis, 1981)
The improper grasshopper, op. 97 (Boston Mus. Co., 1979)
The jugglers, op. 99, no. 2 (1980)
Jewish easy piano pieces (Transcontinental, 1981)
Mid-point reflections, op. 100 (1980)
Minuet, op. 53, no. 2 (Willis, 1959)
My toys, op. 117 (Boston, 1981)
Nocturne, op. 99, no. 1 (1980)
Nocturne in blue, op. 50, no. 2 (Willis, 1983)
Playful squirrels, op. 56 (Willis, 1961)
Prelude, op. 15 (1941)
Rustic dance, op. 29, no. 3 (Willis, 1980)
Savory suite, op. 61 (Willis, 1980)
Sharples sonata, op. 20, no. 1 (1946)
Spanish rhapsody (1978)
Spring vignette, op. 111, no. 3 (Willis, 1982)
Suite No. 1, op. 53 (1959)
Summer vignette, op. 111, no. 4 (Willis, 1982)
Tarantella, op. 123 (1982)
Three Christmas carols, op. 40 (1957)
Toccata in red, op. 50, no. 1 (Willis, 1983)
Winter vignette, op. 111, no. 1 (Willis, 1982)

VOCAL
Thought is a bird of space, cantata (4 soloists and ch) (1961)
Victory hora, op. 65 (mix ch and pf) (Transcontinental, 1967)
Alberta, with love, six songs (1979)
The ant and the cricket, op. 25, no. 6 (vce and pf) (1945)
A baby is a precious thing, op. 103 (vce and pf) (1980)
Baby's music box (vce and pf) (1945)
Childhood cameos (S, bar and pf) (Afka Records)
Cholem fraid - will he come? op. 105 (vce and pf) (1981)
Hunting hoodlebabes, op. 14, no. 3 (vce and pf) (1940)
Johnny and the tree, op. 25, no. 4 (vce and pf) (1945)
Kiddy Kidoodle Land, op. 33 (vce and pf) (1950)
Lake O'Hara's magic circle, op. 55 (vce and pf) (1961)
Leave me a leaf, op. 126 (vce and pf) (1983)
Little Red Ridinghood of today, op. 25, no. 2 (vce and pf) (1945)
Love's garland, op. 14, no. 2 (vce and pf) (1940)
The room with a door, op. 124 (S, fl and pf) (1982)
The secret of death, op. 52, no. 5 (S, B and pf) (1975)
The three pigs, op. 25, no. 1 (vce and pf) (1945)
Three songs of Western Canada (1979)
Through mothers, op. 49 (vce and pf) (1960)
Today and tomorrow, op. 115 (vce and pf) (1978)
Trilogy: From Gibran's The Prophet (vce and pf) (1963)
The wolf and the fox, op. 25, no. 3 (vce and pf) (1945)
The wolf and the goats, op. 25, no. 5 (vce and pf) (1945)
You are my lucky four-leaf clover, op. 14, no. 1 (vce and pf) (1940)

SACRED
Peace and brotherhood through music, cantata (Transcontinental, 1960)
Sacrifice of the innocents, cantata (mix-ch, org, brass and perc)
Yom Kippur cantata (1970)
The blessing of the Sabbath candles, op. 37, no. 1 (mix-ch and org) (1955)
Dedication offering, op. 102 (mix-ch, B, Bar, org and fl) (1980)
Grant us peace, op. 76 (mix-ch, B and org) (1975)
Hear my prayer, op. 63 (mix ch and org or pf) (Transcontinental, 1967)
Kol Nidre cantata, op. 70 (mix-ch, org, trp, trb, hn and perc) (1970)
Silent meditation and may the words, op. 74, no. 2 (mix-ch and org) (Transcontinental, 1975)
Victory hora (English and Hebrew) (mix-ch and pf) (Transcontinental)
Am Yisraeil Chai, op. 101, no. 6 (vce and pf or org) (1980)
Confirmation prayer, op. 37, no. 2 (T and org or pf) (Transcontinental, 1957)
Halleluhu, op. 101, no. 2 (vce and pf or org) (1980)
Hamotsi, op. 101, no. 4 (vce and pf or org) (1980)
Psalm 23, op. 122 (vce and org or pf) (1982)
Shehecheyanu, op. 101, no. 5 (vce and pf or org) (1980)
Yerushalayim, op. 101, no. 1 (vce and pf or org) (1980)
Ze Hayom, op. 101, no. 3 (vce and pf or org) (1980)

BALLET
The dancing teapot, op. 112 (1981)
Little Red Riding Hood, op. 94 (1979)
Memories of Tevye (1962)
A world passed by (1954)

OPERETTA
Kiddy City, op. 51, for children (1961)

TEACHING PIECES
Piano is my name, op. 77 (1975)
Staftonia, op. 47 (1958)

Ref. composer, 142, 206, 347, 457, 485, 563, 622, 624, 625

KETTERER, Ella

American writer and composer. b. Camden, NJ, 1889. The daughter of a musician, she studied under Constantin von Sternberg. She was the director of the New Jersey branches of the Sternberg School of Music. She wrote two educational books and composed over 100 pieces, mainly for children.
Ref. 292

KETTERER, Laura

20th-century American composer. She composed choral works and songs.
Ref. 40, 347

KETTERING, Eunice Lea

American professor and composer. b. Savannah, OH, April 4, 1906. She studied at the Oberlin Conservatory of Music where she obtained a B.M. in 1929. She received her master's degree from the School of Sacred Music of the Union Theological Seminary in 1933. She studied composition privately under Norman Lockwood, Felix Labunski, Edwin J. Stringham and then under Bela Bartok in Mondsee, Austria. She was a teacher of music at Madison College, Harrisonburg, VA, from 1929 to 1932 and a lecturer and then professor of music and composer-in-residence of Ashland College, Ashland, 1935 to 1958. From 1959 she lived in New Mexico and composed. The National Federation of Music Clubs awarded her first prize for a choral-orchestral composition in 1943, a special individual award of merit in 1968 and a merit award for outstanding service to other composers, 1970. In 1972 she was awarded first prizes by the National League of American Pen Women for secular choral composition, piano composition and vocal solo-art song. In 1958 the Ashland, OH, Junior Music Club was renamed the Eunice Kettering Music Club and in 1961 she won first prize and a citation from the Annual Institute for Education by Radio and Television. DISCOGRAPHY. PHOTOGRAPH.

Compositions

ORCHESTRA
Affirmato (1961)
A-wearin o' the green o! (1961)
Prelude, toccata and fugue (1962)
Saint Francis, in 3 mvts (org and cham orch; also org, 1967; org and str orch, 1968)

CHAMBER
South of the Border, suite (woodwind quintet) (1966)
String quartet (1960, 1983)
Festive suite (fl, vln and pf) (1963)
Woodwind trio (fl, cl and bsn) (1962)
Suite (vlc and pf) (1982)
Desert canticle (1982)

HARP
Barcarolle (1980)
Biblical miniatures, suite (1950)
Cascades of joy (1980)
Love song (1980)
Nature suite (1981)
Tranquillity (1980)

ORGAN
The House of the Lord (1945)
The Lord into His garden comes (1940) (H. Flammer, 1958)
Paraphrase on an American folk song (1944) (New York, H.W. Gray)
Passacaglia in G-Minor (1929) (Elkan-Vogel)
Praise (1974)
Quietude (1974)
Song of contentment (1980)
Song of love (1979)
Song of praise (1979)
Song of quietude (1979)
Song of rejoicing (1980)
Song of repose (1980)
Song of serenity (1980)
Toward peace (1974)

PIANO
Brigadoon (4 hands) (1934) (G. Schirmer, 1970)
Paddy O'Hara (4 hands) (1960) (G. Schirmer, 1970)
Three Spanish folk dances, etude in F-Sharp Minor (4 hands) (1934)
Cascading waters (1973-1974)
Etude in B-Major (1934)
Heaven is not so far (1974)
Mourning dove song (1974)
My heart's star (1974)
Rain, clouds, wind, suite (1947) (G. Schirmer, 1970)
Sailing toward the moon (1974)
Searching, seeking (1974)
Sketches (1983)
Suite (1979)
What lovers say (1974)

VOCAL
John James Audubon, cantata (1964) (S, T, mix-ch, narr and orch)
Johnny Appleseed, cantata (1943) (mix-ch and orch)
William Holmes McGuffey was the man, cantata (narr, mix-ch and pf) (1963)
Abraham Lincoln walks at midnight (mix-ch a-cap) (1945)
Angels of the night wind (w-vces and hp) (1969)
The donkey (mix-ch a-cap) (1964)
A dirge for a righteous kitten (S and w-ch a-cap)
Drying their wings (w-ch a-cap) (1942)
Factory windows are always broken (mix-ch a-cap) (1942)
Four anthems (youth ch, mix-ch and org) (1970)
Hope (w-ch; also S, w-ch and pf) (1967)
I hear America singing (mix-ch and pf) (1968) (Chicago: Somerset Press)
In the valley of the Rio Grande (mix-ch a-cap) (1967)
The lion (w-ch and pf; also vce and pf) (1942)
The little turtle (w-ch and pf; also vce and pf) (1942)
Lullaby (w-ch and pf; also vce and pf) (1949)
The moon's the north wind's cooky (w-ch a-cap) (1942)
The mysterious cat (mix-ch a-cap) (Willis Music Co.)
Spring journey (w-ch and pf) (1935) (Willis)
The sun (w-ch a-cap) (1951) (Caro; Fischer)
The sun says his prayers (w-ch a-cap) (1949)
Tennessee mountain (m-ch a-cap) (1940)
The three little kittens (S, A and w-ch a-cap)
Two old crows (w-ch a-cap) (1942)
Valley forge (mix-ch a-cap) (H.W. Gray Co., 1942)
While night is young (mix-ch and fiddle) (1950)
XXth century (w-ch and pf; also vce and pf) (1949)
On, and on, and dancing (w-vces and hp) (1969)
Across long-time, we sing, cycle of 7 songs with epilogue (T and pf)
Compensation (low vce, high vce and pf) (1955)
Gifts (vce and pf) (1954) (New York: Galaxy, 1955)
The gull (vce and pf) (1949)
Live alone and like it? (vce and pf) (1956)
Longing (vce and pf) (1938)
Music for two: Blithely; Tenderly; Piquantly (S and T rec) (1980)
Rhyme for Anybody (vce and pf) (1947)
Sea craving (vce and pf) (1947)
Songs of a gypsy girl, song cycle (m-S and pf) (1967)
Songs of the seasons, song cycle of 5 songs (vce and pf) (1950)
Three Spanish folk dances (vce and pf) (1971) (G. Schirmer, 1972)
Trilogy: Day-sunset-night (vce and pf) (1946)

SACRED
David and Jonathan, cantata (1 part chil-ch, narr and pf) (1967)
Song for Tishri, cantata (B cantor, mix-ch and org) (1966)
And above, singing angels (w-ch and org) (1966) (Mills Music, 1969)
The bells of Sunday (double mix-ch, org and chimes) (1954) (H. Flammer, 1959)
Christ, the Christ is risen (mix-ch and org or pf) (1968) (J. Fischer and Bro., 1973)
A Christmas sermon (narr and mix-ch a-cap) (1952) (Chappell and Co., 1955)
God of the dew (mix-ch a-cap) (1951) (H.W. Gray Co., 1956)
Listen, Lord (B and mix-ch a-cap)
A mothering-on-Sunday (girls' ch and pf) (1967)
Psalm 86 (mix-ch a-cap) (1950) (Mills Music, 1955)
Saints of Brittany (m-ch a-cap) (1967)
Silence (mix-ch a-cap) (Associated Music Pub.)
Sing unto the Lord (w-ch and hp; also pf or org, 1967; also vce and hp) (World Library of Sacred Music)
Song from St. Matthew (w-ch and pf or org) (1966) (G. Schirmer, 1968)
A youth's prayer (mix-ch a-cap) (1953)
David's harp (vce and hp) (1966)
Introit (vce and handbells) (1967)
The lamb (mix-ch a-cap)
Penance (vce and pf) (1932)
Portraits from the Holy Scriptures, song cycle (m-S and org) (1965)
Psalm 23 (vce and handbells) (1967)
Psalm 67 (vce and handbells) (1967)
Song of praise (vce and hp; also pf or org)
A story of Mary, meditation (Cont, narr and fl) (1964)
Tower of David (vce and hp) (1967)

OPERETTA
Angel on a holiday, in 3 acts (mix-ch and pf) (1954)
Any man will do, in 3 acts (mix-ch and pf) (1954)
Brimstone, in 3 acts (mix-ch and pf) (1953)

THEATRE
Christopher Columbus, pageant-drama in 1 act, 2 scenes (A, T, B, speakers, mix-ch and cham ens) (1965)
Trails West (Men-in-a-hurry), A grass-roots Singspiel (5 speakers, mix-ch and pf) (1969)

MULTIMEDIA
Let's play zoo (narr, chil modern dance group and 2 pf) (1968)
Navajo prayer (B, fl, 3 American-Indian perc insts, and dancer or dances, opt) (1969)
Pilgrimage in Brittany (mix-ch, narr, org and slides) (1969)
Ruth (men, women, one or more chil and opt dancers)

ARRANGEMENTS
Paddy O'Hara, traditional fiddletunes (G. Schirmer, 1970)
Paraphrase on American folk-hymn Kemath (1944) (H.W. Gray Co., 1951)
The House of the Lord, American folk-hymn (org) (1945)
Folksongs from the Holy Land (handbell ch) (1965)
Folksongs from Mexico and New Mexico (handbell ch) (1965)
Songs from Early Ireland, song cycle of 5 songs (vce and pf) (1965)
Fifteen carols (two treble insts) (1967) (Concordia, 1969)
Cowboy songs, cycle of 6 songs (1969)
American folk-hymns, cycle of 8 songs (org) (1969)

Ref. composer, 40, 84, 94, 142, 190, 228, 236, 563, 594, 622

KHANNA, Usha. See ADDENDUM

KHASANSHINA, D.

20th-century Bashkir Soviet composer.

Composition

VOCAL
Liubliu tsebia, zemlia ottsov, in a collection of songs by Bashkir composers (Moscow: Sovietski Kompozitor, 1980)

Ref. Otto Harrassowitz (Wiesbaden)

KHOSS VON STERNEGG, Gisela

Austrian pianist, teacher and composer. b. Brunn, Moravia, August 17, 1892. She studied the piano under Hilde Schauer and Heinrich Janoch from 1918 to 1924, harmony under Lilly Friedlweigl from 1921 to 1924 and theory and composition under Bruno Weigl. She taught in Vienna after 1928.

Compositions

CHAMBER
Four pieces, op. 4 (org) (1929)

PIANO
Phantasie und Burleske, op. 5 (1928)
Seven pieces, op. 3 (1928)
Sonatina, op. 2 (1928)

VOCAL
An den Sturm (Elsinger-Thonet)
Mit dir (composer)
Narrenlied (M. Susmann)
Vier Lieder (high vce)
Der Wanderer und das Blumenmaedchen (Hermann)

Ref. 219, 226

KHULAIDA (Hulaida) (1)

Ca. 740. She was a contemporary of Jamila (q.v.) and one of the songstresses who sang to the accompaniment of Jamila's orchestra of 50 singing women with lutes.

Ref. 171, 305

KHULAIDA (Hulaida) (2)

Ca. 600. She was one of the songstresses of Bishr ibn 'Amr, a dignitary of al-Hira in the pre-Islamic days of al-Numan III.

Ref. 171, 305

KHYARMA, Miyna. See HERMANN, Miina

KICKINGER, Paula

Austrian pianist and composer. b. Vienna, February 20, 1899. She studied the piano privately and at the Akademie fuer Musik und darstellende Kunst, where she passed the state examination. Before World War II she spent some time in Berlin, studying under Schoenberg. She gave numerous concerts, playing her own compositions, in Vienna and on the radio. PHOTOGRAPH.

Compositions

ORCHESTRA
Piano concerto
Ouverture (1956)
Scherzo (1937)
Sinfonie (1975)

CHAMBER
Piano quintet
String quartet
Wind quartet
String trio
Cello variations
Viola variations
PIANO
Fugues
Preludes
VOCAL
Compositions (M. Zwinz-Breyer) (ch; also 3 w-vces)
Duets (S, m-S and pf)
Numerous songs (vce and pf)
THEATRE
Melodramas (German texts)
Ref. composer, 194

KICKTON, Erika
German pianist, lecturer, writer and composer. b. Berlin-Schoeneberg, May 21, 1896. She studied the piano in Poznan from 1907 to 1914 and then under Otto Becker in Berlin, 1914 to 1916. She studied theory and composition under Wilhelm Klatte, 1917 to 1922. She taught music at the Potsdam Conservatory from 1921 to 1927 and composed piano pieces and songs.
Publications
Was wissen wir ueber Musik? Leipzig: Merseburger, 1976.
Music articles. Potsdam newspaper. 1923-1927.
Music articles for international journals. From 1927.
Ref. 70, 111, 219, 226

KIEK, Bessie
British composer.
Composition
PIANO
Revels in Fairyland, 4 pieces (Anglo-French)
Ref. 473

KIELANOWSKI, Alina
20th-century composer.
Composition
FILM MUSIC
The Epidemic (1972)
Ref. 326

KIENE, Marie. See BIGOT DE MOROGUES

KIERNICKA, Anna
18th-century Polish nun of the Benedictine convent of Staniatka.
Composition
SACRED
Kancjona 1 (3-4 w-vces and continuo) (1754)
Ref. 417

KILBY, Muriel Laura
Canadian marimbist, pianist and composer. b. Toronto, November 5, 1929. She studied at the Royal Conservatory, Toronto, under Hayunga Carman (piano) and Oscar Morawetz (composition). She studied the piano under James Friskin at the Chautauqua Institute, New York on a scholarship from the National Federation of Music Clubs, 1951. She played the marimba with the Toronto Symphony Orchestra. She won CAPAC prizes for composition in 1949 and 1950.
Compositions
CHAMBER
Fantasy (vln and pf) (1951)
PIANO
Ballet suite (1950)
Suite (1949)
VOCAL
First song from Songs of the sea-children (1949)
No. 40 from A Shropshire lad (1949)
The scarecrow (1950)
Young sea (1950)
Ref. 133

KIM, Kwang-Hee. See ADDENDUM

KIMPER, Paula M.
20th-century American composer.
Composition
CHAMBER
Underground dream suite (str qrt) (1979-1980)
Ref. Conference workshop of 20th-century string quartets of women composers

KING, Betty Jackson (Betty Lou)
Black American choral conductor, lecturer and composer. B. Chicago, IL, February 19, 1928. She began composing pieces in early childhood. She received her B.Mus in 1950 and M.Mus in 1952 from the Roosevelt University, Chicago. She also studied at Oakland University, Rochester, The Glassboro College, NJ, the Peabody Conservatory, Baltimore, The Westminster Choir College, Princeton and Bank Street College, New York. She taught at the Dillard University, New Orleans, the Chicago University Laboratory School and in schools in New Jersey. She was president of the National Association of Negro Musicians from 1979 and received many honors from civic and professional organisations.
Compositions
CHAMBER
Nuptial suite: Processional; Nuptial song; Recessional (org)
PIANO
Fantastic mirror
Four season sketches: Spring intermezzo; Summer interlude; Autumn dance; Winter holiday
Mother Goose parade
VOCAL
Dawn (Paul Laurence Dunbar)
A lover's plea (Shakespeare)
SACRED
Simon of Cyrene, cantata
God's trombones (ch)
God shall wipe away all tears, requiem
OPERA
Saul of Tarsus, biblical opera (1952)
Ref. 136, 347, 549

KING, Betty Lou. See KING, Betty Jackson

KING, Gilbert. See HARRISON, Susan Frances

KING, Frances Isabella
19th-century American composer.
Composition
VOCAL
Fly, fly away or The dream (vce and pf) (New York: H. Waters, 1853)
Ref. 228

KING, Mabel Shoup
20th-century American composer.
Compositions
VOCAL
Twilight (w-ch) (Broadcast Music Co.)
SACRED
Lord, now lettest Thou Thy servant (mix-ch and pf) (Broadcast)
Ref. 190, 347

KING, Patricia
20th-century American composer.
Compositions
PIANO
Confrontations (2 pf, 4 hands) (1984)
Theme and variations for forty fingers (2 pf, 4 hands) (1984)
VOCAL
Buchenwald, near Weimar (S, B, vlc and pf) (1984)
SACRED
Give me your hand (S, B and pf) (1984)
Ref. AMC newsletter

KING, Pearl
20th-century American composer. b. Spring Green, WI. She composed a work for band and a piano piece.
Ref. 347

KING, Rebecca Clift

20th-century South African composer. b. Birmingham, England. She studied at the Royal Academy of Music, of which she became a licentiate and an associate honoris causa. She was interested in African music and collected many songs and dances. Some of her works were performed by the Cape Town Orchestra.

Compositions

ORCHESTRA

Bantu suite

In the Garden of the Khalifeh

CHAMBER

Andante cantabile (t-rec and pf) (Society of Recorder Players, 1940)

Badinage (treble and t-rec)

PIANO

Isle of delight, valse caprice (Glasgow: Paterson's Pub.)

Sous les palmiers, danse exotique (London: Goodwin & Tabb)

Three musical sketches (London: Joseph Williams)

Three Old English Scenes (Joseph Williams)

VOCAL

Reflection (vce and pf)

Ref. 184, 467

KING, Thea

20th-century composer. She composed two volumes of clarinet solos (Willem Hansen, 1978).

Ref. William Hansen verlagskatalog 1978/1979

KING, Wilton. See MULLEN, Adelaide

KINGSBURY, Lynn C.

20th-century American composer.

Composition

SACRED

O kind Creator (soloists, mix-ch and org) (H.W. Gray Co.)

Ref. 190

KINGSTON, Marie Antoinette (Baroness von Zedlitz)

19th-century British composer of songs.

Ref. 465

KINKEL, Johanna (nee Mockel)

German pianist, choral conductor, poetess, writer and composer. b. Bonn, July 8, 1810; d. London, November 15, 1858. The daughter of Peter Joseph Mockel, a singing teacher at the Royal Bonn Gymnasium, she was given her first lessons in composition by Franz Anton. In 1832, her marriage to a Cologne bookseller, Johann Paul Matthieux was annulled after a few days. In 1843 she married the poet Gottfried Kinkel and was the cofounder of a literary society in Bonn, the *Maikaeferbund*. In Frankfurt she was encouraged by Mendelssohn to pursue a musical career and she traveled to Berlin to become a pupil of the musician and composer Karl Boehmer and the pianist and conductor Wilhelm Taubert. Back in Bonn after 1840, she was involved with chamber and vocal ensembles and salon performances. In 1848, the year of the revolutions, her literary and musical circles collapsed and her husband was arrested and condemned to death for his political activities. After his escape from Spandau she and her four children followed him to London where they struggled to make a living. She became a choir director and continued writing music, librettos and poetry and supported her husband in his political pursuits. She wrote essays about music, particularly on Chopin, that are still valued today. Suspected of being 'freethinking' by religious circles and accused of being 'emancipated' by the bourgeoisie, she was nevertheless generally considered by most to be a 'grande dame'. After her death by suicide, the words 'Freiheit, Liebe und Dichtung' were inscribed on her tombstone in London. DISCOGRAPHY.

Compositions

PIANO

Flirt, polka (Ditson)

Mountain spring, caprice (Ditson)

VOCAL

Aus meiner Kindheit, Katzen-kantate (chil-ch)

The baker and the mice, cantata (chil-ch)

Jubilaeum des Grossvaters, cantata (composer) (1849)

Maeuse-Kantate (chil-ch)

Die Vogelkantate-ein musikalischer Scherz, op. 1, cantata (Berlin: Trautwein, 1830)

Die beiden Brueder (H. Heine)

Demokratenlied (J. Kinkel) (Bonn: Sulzbach)

Der deutsche Rhein (N. Becker) (Leipzig: Kistner)

Der gefangene Freischaerler (composer) (1850)

Don Ramiro, op. 13, ballad (H. Heine) (A or Bar and pf) (Cologne and Amsterdam: Eck; Leipzig: Hofmeister)

Griechisches Volkslied (G. Kinkel) (Sulzbach)

Koelln (H. Heine)

Liederspiele (G. Kinkel)

Political songs (G. Kinkel): Maennerlied (1846); Der letzte Glaubensartikel (1850)

Der Rheinstrom (H. Heine) (Cologne: Dunst)

Ritters Abschied, Weh dass wir scheiden muessen (German and English)

Der Runenstein (H. Heine) (Trautwein)

Das Schloss Boncourt, op. 9 (Chamisso) (vce and pf) (Trautwein)

Six poems, op. 8 (E. Geibel)

Six Scottish songs

Six songs, op. 6, nos. 1-3 (A. Oppenhoff) (Kistner)

Six songs, op. 7, nos. 1-9 (Bettina von Arnim) (Trautwein)

Six songs, op. 10

Six songs, op. 15 (A or Bar and pf)

Six songs, op. 16 (Hofmeister)

Six songs, op. 17 (deep vce and pf) (Berlin and Breslau: Bote & Bock)

Six songs, op. 18 (Berlin: Schlesinger)

Six songs, op. 19 (A or Bar and pf) (Cologne: Schloss: Berlin: Ries & Erler)

Six songs, op. 21 (G. Kinkel) (deep vce and pf)

Soon ss the morn with roses (m-qrt) (Ditson)

Three duets, op. 11 (w-vces) (Trautwein)

Three duets, op. 12 (w-vces) (Trautwein)

Trinklied (Heine), in musical supplement of *Neue Zeitschrift fuer Musik 1*

SACRED

Hymnus in Coena Domini, op. 14, cantata, 7th-century text (Cologne: Eck, 1840)

Peal, sweet Sabbath bells (men's qrt) (Ditson)

OPERETTA

Die Fuerstin von Paphos

Die Landpartie, comic operetta (composer) (before 1840)

Otto der Schuetz

THEATRE

Das Malztier oder Die Stadt-Boennischen Gespenster, comedy in Bonn dialect with songs and arias on well-known opera melodies (1840)

Die Assassinen (G. Kinkel), in 4 acts (1843)

Humoristische Satyre (G. Kinkel) (1842)

Themis und Savigny oder Die Olympier in Berlin (before 1840)

Vaudeville fuer den Hochzeitstag des Professors von Henning (before 1840)

TEACHING PIECES

Anleitung zum Singen. Uebungen und Liedchen fuer Kinder von 3-6 Jahren, mit Begleitung des Klaviers, op. 20 (1849) (Schott)

Tonleitern und Solfeggien fuer die Altstimme mit Begleitung des Klaviers, op. 22 (Schott)

Publications

Acht Briefe an eine Freundin ueber Klavierunterricht. Stuttgart and Tuebingen: Cotta, 1852

Ein Familienbild aus dem Fluechtlingsleben. Stuttgart, 1860.

Friedrich Chopin als Komponist. 1855.

Musikalische Orthodoxie. Autobiographical novel.

Ueber Erziehungswesen in London.

Essays on Mozart, Beethoven, Mendelssohn and others, also in English.

Stories, poems and memoirs.

Bibliography

Schulte, J.F. *Johanna Kinkel*. Muenster, 1908.

Thalheimer, G. *Johanna Kinkel als Musikerin*. Dissertation, Bonn, 1922.

Ref. 17, 105, 110, 121, 129, 132, 192, 226, 276, 297, 307, 347, 431, 476

KINSCELLA, Hazel Gertrude

American authoress, musicologist, professor and composer. b. Nora Springs, IA, April 27, 1893; d. Seattle, July 15, 1960. She studied under Rafael Joseffy, Tapper and Jessie Gaynor at the University of Nebraska, where she gained a Mus.Bac. in 1916, a B.F.A. in 1928 and B.A. in 1931. After obtaining her M.A. from Columbia University, she received a Ph.D. from the University of Washington in 1941. She also took lessons in composition from Gleason Cale and Howard Brockway. Until 1947 she was a professor of music at Nebraska University and lectured at various summer schools and in 1950 established an American Music Center at Washington University, Seattle. She was the originator of the Kinscella method 'Lincoln Way' of teaching the piano.

Compositions
CHAMBER
American Indian tribal airs (str qrt)
Indian sketches (str qrt) (1935)
Numerous duets, solos and teaching pieces (pf)
VOCAL
Folk tune trio (ch)
Songs incl.:
Daisies
Longing
SACRED
A child is born, cantata
Our prayer (ch a-cap) (1934)
My days have been so wondrous free
Psalm 150
Settings of Christmas carols
Publications
Early American Song Unit. With Mabel Spizzy, 1939.
Essentials on Piano Techniques.
Flag over Sitka. 1946.
History Sings in America. 1940; rev. 1949.
Liberty Island. 1946.
Music and Romance. 1934; rev. 1941.
Music in the Small School. With Elizabeth Tierny. 1939, rev. 1951.
Music on the Air. 1934.
Young Pianists.
Ref. 8, 39, 40, 44, 142, 292, 347, 433, 646

KIP, Yuksel
Turkish conductor, singer, teacher and composer. b. Istanbul, March 31, 1937. She graduated from the music department of Istanbul Municipality in 1957. During 1956 and 1957 she attended the Higher Turkish Music Conservatory where she sang and conducted. In 1959 she won a singing competition organized by the Ankara Radio Station and then worked and sung for Turkish Radio. Since 1977 she has directed the female chorus of Turkish Music and given singing lessons. She composes songs and instrumental pieces.
Ref. National Council of Turkish Women

KIRBY, Suzanne
20th-century American composer. She composed a symphony, organ and piano pieces, an oratorio and songs.
Ref. 40, 347

KIRCH, Irene E.
Compositions
SACRED
Hymns for Handbells (Concordia, 1980)
Ref. MLA *Notes* September 1981

KIRCHER, Maria Bertha
Swiss pianist, teacher and composer. b. Basle, November 29, 1831; d. Basle, January 18, 1903. She was the daughter of pianist and composer Jacques Kircher.
Composition
PIANO
Taenze
Ref. 101

KIRCHGASSNER, Elisabeth
German composer. b. 1864; d. 1941. DISCOGRAPHY.
Composition
SACRED
Mannheimer Kindermesse (chil-ch and inst ens)
Ref. 563

KIRCHNER, Elisabeth
German pianist and composer. b. St. Petersburg, September 4, 1866; d. Halle, Germany, December 12, 1947. She studied under Adolf Henselt and at the Stuttgart Conservatory. She composed chamber pieces, a piano sonata and other piano pieces and songs.
Ref. 70, 105, 226

KIRKBY-MASON, Barbara
British pianist, lecturer and composer. b. London, March 7, 1910. She began to play the piano at four years of age and continued to study, eventually becoming an L.R.A.M.. She trained further under Harold Samuel. She was elected a F.R.A.M. and an honorary F.T.C.L. She traveled widely, giving lectures, master classes, piano recitals and broadcasts. PHOTOGRAPH.
Compositions
PIANO
Modern society, suite (Chappell)
Mood sequence
Sonata fantasy (Island memories incl. In the Orient)
TEACHING PIECES
Adult beginner (Bosworth)
Adult solo album (Bosworth)
At Xmastide, nursery-rhyme land (Bosworth)
For children, books I and II (Keith Prowse)
Growing-up series
Jamaican folk songs: Book I, Easy duets; Book II, Easy solos (1975) (OUP)
Modern course for piano, 21 parts (Bosworth)
Musical beginnings (Bosworth)
Time for music, for young children (Bosworth)
Ref. composer

KIRKMAN (Kirkman-Jones), Merle
20th-century American violinist and composer. b. Kokomo, IN.
Compositions
CHAMBER
Violin pieces
VOCAL
Deep wet moss (med-vce and pf) (Carl Fischer)
Ref. 190, 347

KIRKMAN-JONES, Merle. See KIRKMAN, Merle

KIRKWOOD, Antoinette
English conductor and composer. b. London, February 26, 1930. In 1957 she founded the St. Columba's Orchestra, which she conducted until 1961. She was a member of the executive committee of the Composers' Guild of Great Britain, 1969 to 1973. PHOTOGRAPH.
Compositions
ORCHESTRA
Symphony No. 1, op. 8
Fantasias 1, 2 and 3, ops. 13, 14 and 18
Suite for string orchestra, op. 5
CHAMBER
Largo, No. 1, op. 14 (pf and fl)
Sonata for cello and piano, No. 1, op. 6
Rhapsodie (hp)
Piano pieces
VOCAL
Must she go? (B and str orch)
Songs
BALLET
Alessandro, mime drama
Musa the Saint
THEATRE
Incidental music
Ref. composer, 77

KISCH, Eve (Evelyn Myra)
English flautist, choral conductor, critic, lecturer, musicologist, writer and composer. b. London, March 18, 1912; d. October 15, 1945. The daughter of Sir Cecil Kisch, economist, Eve was a pupil of Gustav Holst at St. Paul's School for Girls in London before attending the Royal Conservatory of Music. In Paris she studied the flute under Marcel Moyse and then went to Somerville College, Oxford, as a senior scholar. She took her B.A. in 1933 and B.Mus. in 1938. She worked for the Arts Council until 1944 when she became music lecturer at Durham University. She played the flute in concerts, specialized in choir training, wrote numerous articles on music, and was music critic for a London newspaper.
Compositions
CHAMBER
Fantasy (fl)
Other pieces

VOCAL
Songs
Publications
Rameau and Rousseau. Music and Literature, April 1941.
Bibliography
Rameau and the Critics. Issued privately by Durham University in her memory.
Ref. 8

KISTETENYI, Melinda

Hungarian organist, pianist, accompanist, lyricist and composer. b. Budapest, 1928. She played the piano from the age of three and at five passed an exam playing Mozart. She studied the organ and composition in Budapest and was a pupil of Zoltan Kodaly. She wrote the lyrics to Kodaly's *Epigrams and Tricinias*. She gave organ recitals in Hungary, appeared on radio and television and was the accompanist to the Hungarian mezzo-soprano Klio Kemeny on a visit to Britain in 1965.
Compositions
CHAMBER
Easy trio (vlc and 2 vln) (1969)
Duets (ob and hp) (1958)
Duets (vlc and vln) (1953)
Suite (bsn and pf) (1950)
Suite (vlc) (Editio Musica, 1963)
Thoughts for violin (Editio Musica, 1973)
ORGAN
Concerto (1963)
Trio sonata, in 2 mvts (1974)
Versetts (1957)
VOCAL
Shakespeare sonnets (vce and ch) (1956)
Songs (chil-ch) (French, Scottish and English) (1964)
Anthem to the night (Anna Hajnal) (vce and pf) (Editio Musica, 1961)
Choruses (Janos Arany and Endre Ady) (1952)
Choruses (Akos Fodor and Weores Sandor) (Editio Musica, 1960)
In praise of the Balaton (Kistetenyi) (mix-ch) (Editio Musica, 1962)
Japanese and Eskimo songs (1965)
Songs (Ady) (1948)
Songs (Rilke and Toth) (1951)
Songs (S. Ptofi) (1954)
Two choruses (Berzsenyi) (Editio Musica, 1961)
SACRED
Psalm of Geneva (mix-ch) (Editio Musica, 1970)
Two psalms of Geneva (mix-ch) (Editio Musica, 1972)
First Hungarian mass (1966)
Second Hungarian mass (Editio Musica, 1971)
BALLET
A halalba tancoltatott leany (1955)
OPERA
The Golden Kerchief
TEACHING PIECES
Easy Pieces for flute beginners (Editio Musica, 1967)
Exercises for the trumpet (Editio Musica, 1963)
Exercises for the violoncello (Editio Musica, 1963)
Ref. composer

KITAZUME, Yayoi

Japanese composer. b. March 26, 1945. In 1971 she graduated from the Graduate School of Tokyo University of the Arts having won first prize in a wind instrument contest in 1970. DISCOGRAPHY.
Compositions
CHAMBER
Prelude (wind insts)
Me (Sprout) (2 syo, 17 str koto and 2 rec) (1974)
Deep blue sky (ob, 2 vln, vla and vlc) (1977)
Indice '72 (2 cl, 2 vla and d-b) (1972)
Enek II (fl, ob, bsn and pf) (1976)
Approach (d-b and 2 bsn) (1975)
PIANO
Inner space (2 pf) (1978)
Enek III (1979)
Sonatine (Billaudot)
VOCAL
Enek I (3 S, 2 trp and perc) (1973)
Ref. 563

KJAER, Kirsten

Danish harpist, organist, pianist, choral conductor, teacher and composer. b. February 26, 1938. She graduated from the Royal Danish Conservatory, Copenhagen, with a distinction in the piano in 1957. Her studies also included the organ, the harp and solfege. After qualifying in 1958 as a piano teacher, she took further piano lessons from Esther Vagning until 1966 and studied conducting under Professor Arne Hammelboe and Ole Schmidt. In Vienna she studied the interpretation of lieder under Professor Eric Werba and in Finland advanced choir technique under Professor Har Andersen. She also took a choir conducting course in Hamburg under Dr. Gottfried Wolters. She has taught since 1953 and been involved in the development of municipal music schools in Denmark. From 1968 to 1974 she was director of music in Koge, where she conducted the town choir and symphony orchestra, before becoming choir director of the Copenhagen Baptist Choir. In the same period she studied under Professor Ericsson in Stockholm. In 1976 her interest in electronic music took her to the New England Conservatory, Boston, where she was a pupil of Professor Robert Ceely and on to Syracuse University, New York. Her work has been mainly in the field of improving teaching methods. Her school is the first in Denmark to include corrective courses and the use of a piano laboratory. She is at present Stadskomponist of the Albertslund Kommune; principal of the town music school and on the artistic advisory board and arranges and composes music for official occasions. PHOTOGRAPH.
Compositions
PIANO
Pieces incl.:
Den ny klaverskole (pf) (1971)
Ref. composer

KLAGE, Marie (Marianne)

German singer and composer. b. Berlin, 1817. The daughter of Charles Klage, a guitarist, pianist and composer, she became known as a singer in 1838 in Berlin and Leipzig.
Compositions
VOCAL
Four songs, op. 1 (vce and pf) (Berlin: Schlesinger, 1846)
Ref. 26, 121

KLEBE, Willemijntje

Dutch pianist, singer and composer. b. Rotterdam, July 8, 1902. She studied the piano and theory at the Rotterdam School of Music under Wouter Hutschenruyter and studied singing privately under Berthe Seroen. After graduating she continued her piano studies under Stefan Askenase, Willem Pijper and Nelly Wagenaar. PHOTOGRAPH.
Compositions
ORCHESTRA
Thema met variaties (1955)
CHAMBER
Prelude en rondo (w-qnt) (1959)
Eclogue (fl, cl and hp) (1954)
Scherzo (cl) (1958)
Strijktrio (1954)
PIANO
Petite suite (2 pf) (1952)
Barcarolle (1953)
Capriccio (1954)
Divertimento (1957)
Fetes (1954)
Invention (1958)
Pantomine (1955)
Prelude (1958)
Saltimbanques, rondo (1953)
Sonatine (1952)
Suite pastorale: Danse; Abandon; Toccata (1952)
Suite: Air caprice; Sicilienne; Danse; Pavane; Mouvement (1951)
Thema met variaties (1951)
Three canons (1953)
Three etudes: Allegro; Andante; Vivace (1953)
Three preludes (1952)
VOCAL
Jerusalem, surge (mix-ch and org) (1957)
Drie Liederen op gedichten van Leopold (1956)
Ein Lied op tekst van Sophia Dupray (1959)
ARRANGEMENTS
Prelude en fuga in A grote terts voor orgel (J.S. Bach) (1955)
Ref. composer

KLECHNIOWSKA, Anna Maria

Polish pianist, professor and composer. b. Volhynia, April 15, 1888; d. Warsaw, August 28, 1973. She studied the piano under K. Jaczynowska and theory under G. Rogski at the Warsaw Conservatory until 1905 and continued her studies in Lvov under Soltys and S. Niewiadomski (composition). From 1906 to 1908 she studied the piano under J. Pembauer and composition under S. Krehl at the Leipzig Conservatory and then under K.

Czop-Umlauf. In 1917 she graduated from the Music Academy in Vienna, where she had been a pupil of F. Schmidt. After her graduation and until 1939 she held her own music courses for beginners. In 1947 she became professor of the piano in the Folk Institute in Lodz and later an inspector of music schools in Warsaw. In 1951 she received the Prime Minister's prize for her children's compositions.

Compositions

ORCHESTRA

Pory roku, symphonic suite (1953)
Uvertura weselna (1942)
Wawel, royal castle in Krakow, symphonic poem (1917)

CHAMBER

Krakow march (wind ens) (1937)
Elegy (vlc and pf) (1924)
Legend (vln and pf) (1925)
Small pieces (vln)

PIANO

Four preludes (1907)
Frolics, 12 short pieces for beginners
Fugues
Lyrical pieces
Preludes
Sailor's vision, triptique (1925)

VOCAL

Little cantata for children (1950)
Uwielbienie matki, cantata (H. Januszewska) (1952)
Four carols (vce and small orch) (1946)
Phantasy of Zaolzie (boys-ch and small orch) (1938)
Lunatyczka (w-vce and pf) (1948)
Sea song (A. Nitschowa) (w-vce and pf) (1953)
Ten songs for children (vce and pf)
Choral songs
Arrangements of folk songs (vce and pf or orch)

OPERA

Bilitis, with ballet (composer, after Greek mythology) (1930)

BALLET

Bazyliszek
Fantasma (large sym orch) (1964)

Bibliography

Barlara. Smolenska. *Ostatnia z Kregu Mlodej Polsi Sylwetka Kompozitorki A.M. Klechniowskiej*. Ruch muzyczny, No. 21, October 13, 1974.

Ref. W. Pigla (Warsaw), 8

KLEES, Gabriele

German pianist and composer. b. Kronstadt, December 12, 1895. She composed a piano concerto, piano sonatas and ballets.

Ref. 70

KLEIN, Ivy Frances (nee Salaman)

English pianist, singer, teacher and composer. b. London, December 23, 1895. The grand-daughter of the pianist and composer Charles Kensington Salaman, she played the piano and composed as a young child. She studied harmony and composition under Dr. A. Pollitt in Liverpool from 1912 to 1915 and published her first songs in 1921. In 1923 she studied composition under Benjamin Dale at the Royal Academy of Music in London and took private singing lessons with Anne Thursfield. She appeared in concerts singing and accompanying herself. Her *She walked in beauty* was performed at the coronation of Queen Elizabeth II in 1952.

Compositions

VOCAL

She walked in beauty (Byron) (w-ch and org or pf) (1952)
Among the roses (E. Blunden) (1949)
A Cyprian woman (M. Widdemer) (1933)
Dirge (R.C. Trevelyan) (1926)
Foolish lover (Heine) (1926)
I had a dove (Keats) (1926)
Music when soft voices die (Shelley) (1928)
Ode on solitude (Pope) (1926)
A pedlar (1926)
The rosebud (William Brown) (1928)
The shepherd boy sings in the valley of humiliation (Bunyan) (1926)
Sister awake, madrigal (W. Bateson) (1926)
A windless day (R. Church) (1946)
Other songs

SACRED

A child's song of Christmas (M. Pickthall) (1937)
A Christmas folksong (Lizette Reese) (1933)
The Corpus Christi carol (1948)
Easter (G. Herbert) (1926)
Triste Noel (L.I. Guiney) (1932)

Ref. 8, 22

KLENZE, Irene von

19th-century German composer. Her songs were published in Berlin by Bote & Bock.

Ref. 226, 276

KLEPPER, Anna Benzia

Israeli teacher and composer. b. Raciu Rashov, Rumania, 1927. She graduated in economics and law and from the Rumanian Academy of Music. Since 1960 she has lived in Israel, where she and her husband, composer Leo Klepper, teach at the Rubin Academy of Music in Jerusalem.

Compositions

PIANO

Suite for four hands
Other pieces

VOCAL

Choral works
Songs (S and pf)

Ref. 94, 379

KLETZINSKY, Adele

19th-century Polish composer.

Compositions

CHAMBER

Barcarolle, op. 34 (vln and pf)
Piano pieces

VOCAL

Songs

Ref. 226, 276

KLIMISCH, Sister Mary Jane

American musicologist, professor and composer. b. Utica, SD, August 22, 1920. She obtained her B.A. from St. Mary-of-the-Woods College, IN, where she studied under Sister Florence Therese. She studied under John B. Egan at St. Joseph's College, IN, and obtained her M.Mus.Ed. from the American Conservatory, Chicago. She studied under Robert Wykes at Washington University, where she received a Ph.D. She studied Gregorian chant under Dom Desrocquettes and Dom Gajard of Solesmes. She taught at Mount Marty High School from 1943 to 1950 and was head of the music department and creative arts division of Mount Marty College from 1950 to 1966, becoming a professor in 1970. She was director of the Sacred Music Resource Center.

Compositions

SACRED

Glory hymn book
Mass to honor Joan of Arc
Nativity antiphon

ELECTRONIC

Threnody (vces and elecs)

Ref. 142, 206, 457

KLINKOVA, Zhivka

Bulgarian pianist, conductor, professor and composer. b. Samokov, July 30, 1924. She studied the piano and composition at the Bulgarian State Conservatory under Professors D. Nenov, P. Khadzhiev and V. Stoyanov. She made her debut as a concert pianist in 1948 and after 1951 conducted the State National Song and Dance Ensemble. She worked for some years in East Germany and furthered her studies under Professors W. Regeny and B. Blacher. Some of her compositions won prizes in festivals in Bucharest and Warsaw.

Compositions

ORCHESTRA

Symphony
Concerto for flute, clarinet and string orch (1966)
Concerto for piano, saxophone and orchestra (1960)
Concerto for trumpet and orchestra (1955)
Concerto for violin and orchestra (1961)
The living icons, in praise of the Sofia crypt (cham orch) (1970)
Pictures from Bulgaria (cham orch) (1971)
Pieces (orch of folk insts)
Two pieces (str orch) (1970)
Sinfonietta (1962)
Symphonic suites and dances
Symphony of timbres (cham orch) (1968)
Variations (str orch) (1952)

BRASS BAND

September 1923 overture

CHAMBER
Bulgarian rhythms (13 trp, hn, trb, tba, d-b and pf)
String quartet
Wind trio (ob, cl and bsn)
Sonata (fl and vla)
Sonata (vln)
Piano pieces
VOCAL
Twenty-three years, cantata
Choruses
Songs
Arrangements of folk songs
BALLET
Gergana
Kaliakra (1963)
OPERETTA
Petko samokhvalko, for children (1959)
Snezhanka, for children
Ref. 217, 463, 466

KLOTZ, Leora. See DRETKE, Leora N.

KLOTZMAN, Dorothy Ann Hill

American conductor, teacher and composer. b. Seattle, March 24, 1937. She received her B.S. from the Juilliard School of Music in 1958 and her M.S. in 1960. She studied composition with William Bergsma, Vincent Persichetti and Darius Milhaud and in 1969 did postgraduate study at the University of Washington. She received the New York Philharmonic composition prize in 1953 and 1954 and 1960 received the Fromm prize from the Aspen Music School and the E. Harris award for gifted teaching from the Danforth Foundation in 1972. Since 1971 she has been head of the department of music at Brooklyn College and conductor of its symphonic band. She was the first woman to conduct the Goldman Band.

Compositions
ORCHESTRA
Concerto (a-sax and orch)
Variations
CHAMBER
Pieces
PIANO
Solos
Sonatina
VOCAL
Four songs (Medieval texts)
Poetical sketches: Rondeau; Chanson; This song wants drink (2 part-ch)
SACRED
Good day, Sir Christmas, cantata
Ref. 40, 280, 347, 475

KNAPP, Mrs. Joseph F. See KNAPP, Phoebe Palmer

KNAPP, Phoebe Palmer (Mrs. Joseph F.)

American composer. b. New York, March 8, 1839; d. Poland Springs, ME, July 10, 1908.

Compositions
VOCAL
Songs incl.:
The bird carol
A happy joyous life
SACRED
Prince of Peace, cantata (mix-ch and org) (1883)
Blessed assurance (Fanny Crosby q.v.)
Open the gates of the temple (F. Crosby)
Over 500 gospel hymns
Ref. 40, 228, 276, 292, 347, 646

KNIGHT, Judyth

20th-century British pianist, accompanist, lecturer and composer. She accompanied and composed music for dance classes and performances in London, New York and Europe from the 1960's. She lectured on improvisation at the Guildhall School of Music and Drama and was head accompanist at the London School of Contemporary Dance. Her own company 'Songscape' performs her vocal works.

Composition
CHAMBER
Aubade (fl and pf)
Publications
Ballet and its Music. 1973.
Articles in *Dancing Times*.
Ref. Schott catalog

KNIGHT, Julia Baylis

19th-century English composer.

Composition
VOCAL
Yes 'tho I'm doom'd to sorrow (composer)
Ref. H. Baron (London)

KNOBLOCHOVA, Antonie

Czech organist, teacher and composer. b. Split, Yugoslavia, June 18, 1905. She studied the organ at the Prague Conservatory under K. Dousa from 1928 to 1932 and composition under O. Sin from 1932 to 1933 and Vitezslav Novak from 1933 to 1936. She continued her organ studies under S. Jakub in Prague from 1937 to 1946. She taught theoretical subjects at a music school in Liberec after 1946.

Compositions
ORCHESTRA
Symphony in C
CHAMBER
Sextet in C (fl, pf, bsn, vln, vla and vlc)
String quartet in G
Trio in F
Suite: Prelude, passacaglia and fugue (org)
PIANO
Children's suite
Lullaby
Scherzo
Suite
VOCAL
Budme, svoji (mix-ch)
Tri duchovni pishé (w-ch)
Tulácká (m-ch)
Liberecka, mass song
Majova, mass song
Rudy prapor, mass song
Polka (w-ch)
Oblaka (J. Wolker) (1951)
Three songs (V.J. Svingr)
Ref. 197

KNOUSS, Isabelle G.

20th-century American pianist, teacher and composer. b. Arendtsville, PA. She composed violin and piano works, choral pieces and songs.
Ref. 347, 353

KNOWLES, Alison. See ADDENDUM

KNOWLTON, Fanny Snow

American composer. b. Cleveland, OH, 1859; d. Ohio, 1926. She studied at the Oberlin Conservatory under Sumner Salter and Wilson G. Smith, privately under Johann Beck and later under Fuchs in Dresden. She was prominent in the musical life of Cleveland.

Compositions
CHAMBER
Instrumental pieces
VOCAL
The mermaid, cantata (w-vces)
Hawthorne and lavender, song cycle (w-vces)
If summer skies were always blue
Last night I heard a bird singing
There little girl, don't cry
Nature songs for children
Approx. 30 other songs for children
Ref. 276, 292, 323, 347, 433

KNUDSEN, Lynne

19th-century American composer. She composed a song cycle.
Ref. 465

KNYVETT, Mrs. Edmund
19th-century English composer.
Compositions
SACRED
Brother thou art gone before us, from Martyr of Antioch (Rev. Henry Hart Milman) (T. Swain)
Distill'd amidst the gloom of night (Penrose) (ded Rev. Arthur Pemberton)
Ref. H. Baron (London)

KOBLENZ, Babette
German authoress, publisher and composer. b. Hamburg, August 22, 1956. She studied theory and composition at the Musikhochschule in Hamburg from 1975 to 1980 and composition privately for two years under Gyorgy Ligeti. PHOTOGRAPH.
Compositions
CHAMBER
Days (brass ens) (Kodasi, 1981)
Grey fire (cl, a-sax, t-sax, trp, pf and perc) (2nd prize, Juergen-Ponto-Stiftung, 1981) (Kodasi, 1981)
Walking on the sun (cl, a-sax, trp, pf and perc) (Kodasi, 1982)
Mysterium Buffo I (vla, d-b and pf) (Kodasi, 1979)
Mysterium Buffo II (vln, vlc and pf) (Kodasi, 1980)
No entry for the Lions Club (2 pf and perc) (Kodasi, 1983)
VOCAL
Madrigal for Hermes Trismegistos (Kodasi, 1983)
Can't explain (Kodasi, 1984)
OPERA
Hexenskat oder der Streit der Hexen (4 vces and 19 insts) (Kodasi, 1980)
Ref. composer

KOCHANOWSKA, Franciszka
Polish operatic singer and composer. b. Warsaw, 1787; d. Warsaw, December 13, 1831. Her historical song about Casimir I was published in J.U. Niemcewicz's *Spiewy historyczne z myzyko i rycinami* (Warsaw, 1818). In 1816 she appeared in concerts of religious and folk music. She appeared in a one act opera written for her by P. Metastasio, *La ritrosia dissarmata*.
Composition
VOCAL
Kazimierz I (vce and pf) (Warsaw, 1818)
Ref. 35

KOCHER-KLEIN, Hilda
20th-century German composer.
Compositions
PIANO
Kobolde, op. 1, 9 pieces
Ref. Frau und Musik

KOCHETOVA, Aleksandra Dorimedontovna (pseud. Aleksandrova)
Russian operatic singer, professor and composer. b. St. Petersburg, October 13, 1833; d. Moscow, November 17, 1902. She studied singing under G. W. Teschner in Berlin and after 1853 under Felice Ronconi in St. Petersburg. She became well known as a singer in Leipzig, Prague and at the Bolshoi Theatre in Moscow, 1865 to 1878. From 1866 to 1880 she was a professor at the conservatory where she trained a number of important singers. She composed several romances for voice and piano.
Ref. 15

KODALY, Emma
20th-century Hungarian composer. She married Zoltan Kodaly.
Compositions
PIANO
Hungarian country dance
Mek, mek, mek, folk dance
Ref. 448

KODHAI
9th-century Indian composer. She composed religious songs in Tamil.
Ref. National Council of Women Composers, India

KODOLITSCH, Michaela
Austrian poetess and composer. b. Graz, 1875. She studied under Camillo Horn. She composed piano pieces, songs, children's and fairy tale operattas and dances.
Ref. 70, 226

KOEHLER, Estella
German pianist and composer. b. Bistritz (now in Czechoslovakia), July 5, 1903. She studied under R. Stohr at the Vienna Academy.
Ref. 226

KOELLING, Eloise
American professor and composer. b. Centralia, IL, March 3, 1908. She studied at Northwestern University and under Bernard Dieter of the Chicago Conservatory College. She received three University of Wisconsin grants and 14 first prizes in Wisconsin composer contests and other awards. Two of her works were performed at the International Society for Contemporary Music, Chicago. She was a professor at the University of Wisconsin, Milwaukee, from 1949 to 1968.
Compositions
ORCHESTRA
Symphony in D-Minor (1958)
Concentrante No. 2 (pf and orch) (1961)
Two piano concertos
Montage (vln and str orch) (1963)
Four portraits of a woman (1960)
Symphonic piece (1966)
Tragic overture (1963)
CHAMBER
Five woodwind ensembles
Four variations (ww qnt) (1968)
Four miniatures (ww)
Impressions of the fairytale age (b-cl and 4 strs) (1965)
Improvisation for timpani and string quartet (1963)
Three moods (ww qnt) (1967)
Four string quartets (1958-1963)
String quartet No. 5 (1964)
Suite (str qrt) (1967)
Three nocturnes (vln, cl and vlc) (1966)
Three variations (fl, cl and vla) (1968)
Fantasy (vlc and pf) (1967)
Sonata (vln and pf) (1952)
Suite (vla and pf) (1957)
Two suites (vln and pf)
Sonata (org) (1957)
PIANO
Teenage sketches (2 pf) (1960)
Creative dance suite (1959)
Fantasy of a city (1965)
Idyll (1959)
Profiles (1963)
VOCAL
Democratic thinking in 18th, 19th, 20th-centuries (ch)
Devonshire rhyme (w-ch) (1965)
Fire (Bar and mix-ch) (1956)
Fuguing tune (mix-ch) (1959)
Grass (w-ch, snare dr and strs) (1968)
Horizon march (m-S and cham ens) (1963)
Can't talk about love (S) (1959)
Five songs about children (1960)
The latch is on the door tonight (1959)
Other songs
SACRED
As long as my saviour reign (ch)
Gradual, alleluia (ch)
I believe (mix-ch) (1945)
In memoriam (w-ch, ww, str qrt and timp) (1965)
Naomi's lament (w-vces and ww)
Prayer of St. Francis (S) (1960)
A song of Christmas (S) (1960)
Anthems
Ref. composer, 40, 142, 347

KOENIG, Marie
19th-century German composer. b. Lobau, Saxony.
Compositions
PIANO
Leichte Potpourris ueber beliebte Opernmelodien und Lieder (4 hands)
Marsch, op. 7
Abschiedsgruess

Melancolie, op. 1 (Brauer)
Rhapsodie a la hongroise
Ungarisher Marsch, op. 8
VOCAL
Ich hab' im Traum geweinet, op. 5 (m-ch and pf)
Heller ward mein inneres Leben (vce and pf)
Ich habe den Fruehling gesehen (vce and pf)
Voegleins Tod (vce and pf)
Other songs
Ref. 226, 276, 297

KOENNERITZ, Nina von. See ESCHBORN, Georgine Christine Maria

KOESTLIN, Josephine. See LANG, Josephine

KOHAN, Celina
Argentine pianist and composer. b. Buenos Aires, January 31, 1931. She studied at the State Conservatory in Buenos Aires and completed her studies under Raul Spivak and Aldo Romaniello (piano) and Gilardi (composition). In 1952 she appeared as a concert pianist in Buenos Aires.
Compositions
ORCHESTRA
Symphony in C-Major (1955)
Violin concerto (1958)
Symphonic suite (1967)
Fantasy and fugue for string orchestra (1967)
CHAMBER
String quartet (1957)
Fantasia y fuga en do mayor (vln and pf)
Violin sonata (1954, 1961)
PIANO
Burlesque (1957)
Suite (1953)
VOCAL
Choral music
Songs
Ref. 31, 79, 390

KOHARY, Marie, Countess of
Hungarian pianist and composer. b. 1769. Her two-movement sonatas in the style of the young Haydn are in a library in Vienna. She is believed to have been related to Janos Kohary, an actor at the French theatre in Vienna.
Compositions
PIANO
Sonata (2 pf)
Set of duets
Ref. 276, 375, 433

KOHLER, Estella. See KOEHLER, Estella

KOKDES, Neveser
Turkish concert pianist, tamborist and composer. b. Drama, Macedonia, 1904; d. 1962. She was the sister of the composer Muhlis Sabahattin and trained in both classical Turkish and Western music. She attended the French school, Dame de Sion and at the age of 12 composed a polka piece and songs. She worked for Istanbul Radio and gave concerts with her brother. She composed about 30 works.
Ref. National Council of Turkish Women

KOLARIKOVA-SEDLACKOVA, Marie
Czech composer. b. Mistek, January 3, 1897. She was the daughter of Frantisek Kolarik a choir director and lived in Mistek until 1961.
Compositions
CHAMBER
Pieces
VOCAL
Motyl (1937)
Nine songs (P. Bezruc)
MISCELLANEOUS
Dance music
Ref. CMIC, 197

KOLB, Barbara
American clarinetist, professor and composer. b. Hartford, CT, February 10, 1939. Her father was a pianist, organist and composer and Barbara began her clarinet studies at the age of 11 under William Goldstein. She studied at the Hartt College of Music of the University of Hartford from 1957 to 1964 where she studied the clarinet under Louis Speyer and composition under Arnold Franchetti. She received a B.M. cum laude in 1961 and an M.M. in composition in 1964. She was awarded a fellowship to Tanglewood, where she studied under Lukas Foss and Gunther Schuller (1960, 1964 and 1968). Between 1964 and 1966 she studied the clarinet privately under Leon Russianoff. She also received a fellowship from the McDowell Colony. She was a clarinetist with the Hartford Symphony Orchestra from 1960 to 1965, assistant professor at Brooklyn College and from 1975, a professor at Wellesley College. She was the first American woman composer to win the Prix de Rome (1969 to 1971). She was awarded a Fulbright Scholarship to Vienna in 1966 and received two Guggenheim awards in 1971 and 1976, which enabled her to spend a year in Paris. In 1973 she won an American Academy National Institute of Arts and Letters award and a Martha Baird Rockefeller grant. She also received a grant from the Ford Foundation to study electronic music at Mills College in Oakland, California. She received commissions from the Fromm and Koussevitzky Foundations. She was a member of the board of trustees of the American Academy in Rome, 1972 to 1975. DISCOGRAPHY.
Compositions
ORCHESTRA
Crosswinds (also a-sax and winds) (1968) (Boosey & Hawkes, 1969)
Grisaille (1978-1979) (Boosey & Hawkes, 1984)
Soundings (also tape) (Henmar)
CHAMBER
Trobar clus (cham ens) (1967) (Carl Fischer) (comm Fromm Music Foundation)
Double woodwind quintet
The point that divides the wind (org and 4 perc)
Crosswinds (a-sax and winds) (Fischer; Boosey, 1968, 1969)
Seguela (strs) (1966) (Fischer)
Figments (fl and pf) (1967) (Fischer)
Rebuttal (2 D-Flat cl) (1965) (Peters; Hawkes)
Three lullabies (gtr)
Appello (pf) (1976) (Boosey, 1978)
VOCAL
Poem (ch a-cap)
Chanson bas (S and cham ens) (1966) (Fischer)
Chromatic fantasy (speaker and cham ens)
Looking for Claudio (S and cham ens) (1975)
The sentences (Pinsky) (vce and gtr) (1976) (Boosey & Hawkes, 1976)
Songs before an adieu (S, grt, fl and a-fl) (1978)
Three place settings (narr and cham ens) (Fischer, 1972)
THEATRE
Vernissage (1979) (Boosey)
ELECTRONIC
Frailties (T, 4-channel tape and orch)
Soundings (13 insts and tape) (1971) (C.F. Peters, 1977)
Spring, river, flowers, moon, night (2 pf, tape and perc ens)
Homage to Keith Jarrett and Gary Burton (fl and vib) (Boosey, 1975)
Percussion quartet (incl. vib and xy)
Solitaire (pf and vib) (1971) (Peters, 1976)
Toccata (hpcd and tape) (Peters, 1976)
MISCELLANEOUS
Mille foglie (Boosey, 1985)
Ref. 4, 5, 142, 173, 179, 228, 280, 397, 415, 563, 622, 625

KOLBE, Caroline Johanna Lovisa. See RIDDERSTOLPE, Caroline

KOLLER-HOPP, Margarete
German composer. b. June 30, 1888. She lived in Liegnitz. Her piano pieces included a sonata and she also composed light music and songs.
Ref. 70, 142, 226, 560, 594, 610, 611, 624

KOLODUB, Zhanna Efimovna
Soviet pianist, violinist, lecturer and composer. b. Vinnitsa, January 1, 1930. She studied the violin and the piano at the Kiev Music School and graduated in 1954. At the Kiev Conservatory she studied the piano under K.N. Mikhailov and later taught the piano there. DISCOGRAPHY.
Compositions
ORCHESTRA
Piano concerto (1972)
Dance suite (with L. Kolodub) (1962, 1965)
Simfonietta (1966)
Suite, pictures from Kiev (1976)
CHAMBER
Melody (trb and pf) (1965)
Nocturne (fl and hp) (1965)
Poem (fl and pf) (1966)
Three pieces (ob) (1976)

PIANO
Exprompt (1969)
Four pieces (1974)
Seventeen piece album (1974)
Three etude pictures (1973)
Three pieces for children (1973)
Six Ukrainian folk songs (1975)
Toccata (1972)
Vesenniye vpechatleniya, cycle (1965)
Waltz and dance (1964)
Zverniets (1966)
VOCAL
Pioneer, cantata (I.L. Muratov) (ch and orch) (1967)
Two Irish folk songs (vce and pf) (1973)
Ukrainian folk songs
Children's songs
Romances
BALLET
Prigodi vesnianki (1969)
THEATRE
Veseli divchata, musical comedy (with L. Kolodub) (1968)
Prigodi na Misisipi, musical comedy based on Huckleberry Finn (with L. Kolodub) (1971)
INCIDENTAL MUSIC
Music for films
Light music
Ref. 21, 87, 330, 563

KOMINZYK, Magdalena. See ADDENDUM

KOMOROWSKA, Stephanie, Countess
19th-century Polish pianist and composer. b. Latvia. She received piano lessons from well-known pianists in St. Petersburg and Paris and was considered a talented performer.
Compositions
PIANO
Fantaisie on a theme from C.M. Weber's Preciosa, op. 1
Mes adieux (andante), op. 2
Pensées fugitives, op. 3
Sonatas
VOCAL
Songs
Ref. 26, 35, 118

KOMPANUETS, Lidia
Soviet composer. b. 1914. She composed an opera and other vocal works.
Ref. 465

KONIG, Marie. See KOENIG, Marie

KONISHI, Nagako
Japanese composer. b. September 16, 1945. In 1971 she graduated from the Tokyo University of Fine Arts Graduate School with an advanced degree. Her teachers included Tomogiro Ikenouch, Makoto Moroi and Akio Yashiro. From 1976 until 1978 she attended the University of California, Berkeley, as a student of the Graduate School. She was a student of Andrew Imbrie and is a member of the Japanese Federation of Composers, International Women Composers and The Federation of Women Composers in Japan. DISCOGRAPHY. PHOTOGRAPH.
Compositions
CHAMBER
Karuna I (shakuhachi, vln, vla, vlc and hp) (1977) (Japanese Federation of Composers)
Five romances (str qrt) (1978)
Kalpa II (vln, vla, vlc and hp)
The ring (also as The circle and blue circle) (2 shakuhachis and futozao) (1974)
Lullaby (fl and pf) (1981)
Sketch for two shakuhachi (also as Sketch for shakuhachi duet) (1979)
The song of night (a-fl and hp) (1982)
Suikoh (2 shakuhachi) (1979)
Transience II (vla and pf) (1982)
Indigo sky (org) (1977)
Kalpa III (shakuhachi) (1979)
Soh (shakuhachi) (1977)
Transience I (vln) (1979)
Tree of love (pf) (1974)
VOCAL
S'radda (chil-ch and org) (1976)
Sinful petals (w-ch) (1975)
The spring (chil-ch) (1982)
Swan (m-ch) (1969) (Kawai Music Pub. Co.)
Grave post (6 w-vces) (1978) (Japan Federation)
Karuna II (6 m-vces) (1980)
Kara (A, hp and perc) (1972)
Moon angel (S, fl and pf) (1979)
Ref. composer, 4, 563

KONNERITZ, Nina, von. See ESCHBORN, Georgine Christine Maria Anna

KONSTANTIN. See DRDOVA, Marie

KOPPEL-HOELBE, Maria
German pianist, lecturer and composer. b. Dresden, July 30, 1894. She studied the piano at the Dresden Conservatory from 1910 to 1920 under Laura Rappoldi-Kahrer and composition, conducting and sight reading under Kurt Striegler and taught these subjects from 1920 to 1923.
Compositions
CHAMBER
Sonata (vlc and pf) (1921)
VOCAL
Totentanz (A, ch and orch)
Trio (w-vces and cham orch)
Pieces (ch a-cap)
Songs
Ref. 219

KOPTAGEL, Yuksel
Turkish concert pianist and composer. b. Istanbul, October 27, 1931. She was the grand-daughter of General Osman Koptagel, an eminent commander of the Turkish War of Independence. She gave her first concerts when she was six years old and studied the piano, theory and composition in Istanbul with the Turkish composer, Cemal Resit and then in Madrid and Paris with Joaquin Rodrigo, Jose Cubiles, Lazare Levy, Tony Aubin and Alexandre Tansmann. She obtained the Diplome Superieur of the Paris Conservatoire with several first prizes and mentions for composition and the piano. She participated in various music festivals including the Santiago festival in 1959 for Spanish music interpretation and composition and has given numerous recitals and appeared as a soloist with many international orchestras. She is a member of the jury of the Schola Cantorum, Ecole Superieur de Musique, Paris and of the Istanbul State Symphony Orchestra. PHOTOGRAPH.
Compositions
CHAMBER
Fossel suite (pf or gtr) (Berlin: Bote & Bock)
Romance de Castille (vlc and pf) (Paris: Max Eschig)
Tamzara (Turkish dance) (pf or gtr) (Bote)
PIANO
Brian's diary, children's album (Eschig)
Danse mélancolique (Eschig)
Danse rustique (Eschig)
Etude (Eschig)
Epitafio (Epitafio de un muchacho muerto en abril) (J.R. Jimenez)
Esquisse turque - tanzara
Pastorale (Eschig)
Sonata menorca (Eschig)
Toccata (Eschig) (1st prize, Radio Paris ORTF, piano composition, 1959)
VOCAL
Deux chansons du pecheur japonais (Hiroshima Lieder) (Eschig)
Terezin Lieder (Eschig)
When we two parted (Byron) (Eschig)
Zwei spanische Lieder (Eschig)
MISCELLANEOUS
Danse rituelle (Eschig)
Der Freiwillige (Horloge du Maitre Janus)
Der Held (Horloge)
Les hueres de Prague (Horloge)
Trois pièces (Eschig)
Veprés de dimanche (Horloge)
Ref. composer

KORD, Mira. See VORLOVA, Slavka

KORHONEN, S. Gloria
American choral conductor and composer. b. Astoria, OR, March 8, 1929. She received her B.Mus.Ed. from the University of Michigan and M.Ed. from Wayne State University. She also studied at the University of Detroit,

Siena Heights College and St. Joseph College, Rensselaer, IN. She studied composition under S. Denise Mainville and Dr. John Egan. She directed church choirs and became liturgical musician at St. Joseph Roman Catholic Church, Port Huron and musical director of the Creative Arts Center. She was one of eight winners in the 1979 Live Hearing Competition of the National Association of Pastoral Musicians in Chicago. PHOTOGRAPH.

Compositions

ORGAN

Four pieces

SACRED

Mass in honor of St. John the Evangelist (vces and org) (Chicago: GIA Publ., 1969)

Come, O long awaited saviour (w or m-ch a-cap) (GIA, 1971)

Alleluia (S and A vces a-cap) (GIA, 1971)

Brief responses and acclamations for the liturgy (chil-vces and insts)

Three-year cycle of gospel acclamations

Twelve motets (w-vces)

Arrangements of Easter and Christmas carols (mix-ch)

THEATRE

Advent, sacred concert (soloists, ch, dancers and small orch)

Ref. composer, 395

KORN, Clara Anna (nee Gerlach or Gerlack)

American pianist, lecturer and composer. b. Berlin, Germany, January 30, 1866; d. New York, July 14, 1940. She went to United States when very young. She won a scholarship to the National Conservatory on Tchaikovsky's recommendation in 1891 and studied under Horatio Parker, Bruno Oscar Klein, C.C. Muller and Dvorak. She taught theory at the conservatory from 1893 to 1898 and then settled in Brooklyn as a private teacher. She wrote articles for musical journals.

Compositions

ORCHESTRA

Symphony in C-Minor

Piano concerto

Violin concerto

Morpheus, symphonic poem

Ancient dances, suite

Rural snapshots, suite

CHAMBER

Violin pieces

Other pieces

PIANO

Gymnasium march (Presser)

Swinging (Presser)

VOCAL

Songs (ch and orch)

OPERA

Our (Their) Last War

ARRANGEMENTS

Tchaikovsky's Overture solenelle (2 pf) (Jurgenson)

Ref. 22, 89, 226, 276, 292, 297, 347

KORNILOVA, Tatiana Dmitrevna

Soviet music editor and composer. b. Moscow, June 4, 1902. She studied composition under M. Gnesin at the Moscow Conservatory, graduating in 1931. After 1951 she was music editor for a studio of documentary films.

Compositions

ORCHESTRA

Cello concerto (1948)

Three pieces for small orchestra (1939-1940)

Two marches (wind orch) (1942)

Waltz (1950)

CHAMBER

String quartet (1931)

Seven pieces (vlc and pf) (1943-1948)

Sixteen pieces (vlc and pf) (1956)

Sonatina (vln and vla) (1933)

Poem (vlc and pf) (1970)

Pieces (trb) (1938)

Waltz (Hawaiian gtr) (1938)

PIANO

Four children's pieces (4 hands) (1930)

Two pieces (4 hands) (1931)

Other pieces

VOCAL

Five songs for children (A. Barto) (1937)

ELECTRONIC

Tango and polka (1968)

Ref. 21, 87

KOSHETZ, Nina

Russian pianist, operatic singer, teacher and composer. b. Kiev, December 30, 1894; d. Santa Anna, CA, May 14, 1965. She studied the piano as a child and later, singing. She was a graduate of the Moscow Conservatory and sang at the Imperial Opera, St. Petersburg and elsewhere in Russia. She toured Russia with Rachmaninoff, of whose songs she was a much admired interpreter. She also toured Europe, the United States and appeared at the Paris Opera, the Chicago Civic Opera and at theatres in Buenos Aires and Rio de Janeiro. She settled in Los Angeles around 1941 and commenced teaching. DISCOGRAPHY.

Composition

VOCAL

To the Sun

Ref. 22, 74, 563, 622

KOSSAKOWSKA, Wanda

Late 19th-century Polish composer.

Compositions

PIANO

Marzenie

Melodia (Hoesick)

Tesknota

Ref. 118, 297

KOSSE, Roberta

American conductor, lecturer and composer. b. May, 1947. She received her B.Sc. in composition from Manne College of Music and her M.M. from the Manhattan School of Music. She chairs a department at the Mannes College of Music. DISCOGRAPHY.

Compositions

CHAMBER

Divertimento (fl, cl and vlc)

Toot suite (fl and cl)

VOCAL

The return of the Great Mother, oratorio (Jenny Malmquist)

Two songs (Olga Broumas, Thetis and Calypso) (m-vce and insts)

MULTIMEDIA

Portraits in concert (music, poetry and dance) (1979)

Bibliography

Astrala Foundation Journal. Spring, 1980.

Music Journal. January, 1979, p. 42.

Ref. AMC newsletter, 563

KOSTAKOVA-HERODKOVA, Marie

Czech harpist, pianist, accompanist, singer, teacher and composer. b. Prague-Vrsovice, August 3, 1900. She studied the harp at the Prague Conservatory and graduated in Brno in 1922. She studied singing in Prague under D. Branbergrove from 1917 to 1923 and E. Fuchs from 1924 to 1926. She toured in Czechoslovakia giving harp concerts and accompanying singers on the piano. She played in orchestras and on the radio and taught the harp.

Compositions

CHAMBER

Piano trio (1950)

Other chamber pieces

Piano teaching pieces

HARP

Fantasie na české nar pišné

Fantasie on motifs from Dvorak's Rusalka (1927)

Kde domov muj (1930)

Variations on folk songs (1928)

Ref. 197

KOTSBATREVSKAYA

19th-century Russian composer. DISCOGRAPHY.

Compositions

VOCAL

Forget all bygone loves and passions

The grove was still (vce and pf trio)

Ref. MLA *Notes*, 563

KOUDIJIS, Mrs. See APPELDOORN, Dina van

KOVALEVA, Olga Vasilevna

Soviet librettist, singer, writer and composer. b. Saratov, August 4, 1881; d. Moscow, January 2, 1962. She became a National Artist of the Soviet Union in 1947. She studied in Saratov and St. Petersburg under S. Loginova and I.P. Pryanishnikov. In 1910 she sang in opera in Rostov-on-the-

Don and after 1912 sang folk songs in Moscow. During 1921 and 1922 she toured Scandinavia and in 1925 became the choral consultant for Russian folk songs on the national radio. She wrote the texts of her songs, arranged folk songs and wrote articles on the performance of Russian folk song.

Compositions

VOCAL

Songs in folk style, incl.:
Cantata
Oi, ty, Volga, Volga-rechenka
Poidu vuydu k bystroi rechke
Oi, tsveti, kudryavaya ryabina
Five childrens' songs (1927)

Ref. 21, 465

KOWALOWSKA (Kowalewska), Wiktoria

19th-century Polish composer.

Composition

ORCHESTRA

Piekne dni maja, waltz (Warsaw: G. Sennewald, 1837)

Ref. 35, 118

KOZAKIEVICH, Anna Abramovna

Soviet pianist and composer. b. Warsaw, October 24, 1914. She studied the piano under G. Beklemishev and A. Lufer in Kiev for five years. From 1932 to 1933 she studied at the I. Lysenko Music-Drama Institute in Kiev under L.N. Revutsky (composition) and then went to the Moscow Conservatory where she became a pupil of V. Shebalin and M.F. Gnesin and graduated in 1938.

Compositions

ORCHESTRA

Piano concerto (1938)
Ballet suite (1949)

CHAMBER

Quintet (1943)
String quartet No. 1 (1937)
String quartet No. 2 (1961)
String quartet No. 3 (1973)
Piano trio (1944)
Piece (vln and pf) (1972)
Pieces for bayan (1949)

PIANO

Pieces for beginners (1952)
Six preludes (1970-1971)
Sonatina (1943)
Three preludes (1963)

VOCAL

Lenin, cantata (Yesenin) (soli, ch and orch) (1970)
Tri palmi, cantata (Lermontov) (ch and orch) (1964)
Burevestnik (Gorky) (ch and orch) (1967)
Razgulyalas viuga (Yesenin) (ch) (1971)
Vo glubine sibirskikh rud (Pushkin) (ch) (1971)
Romances (Lermontov, Shevchenko, Tyutchev, Maikov, Tolstoy) (1938-1947)
Children's choruses (Lermontov, Yesenin, Isakovsky, Avdeyenko, Choshcharin)
Songs (Surkov, Baukov, Tatianicheva, Turkina, Parkhomenko, Avdeyenko, Turgenev and others)

BALLET

Dyadya stepa-militsioner (1963)
Snezhnaya kololeva (1962)
Volshebniy myach (1966)
Za mir (1959)
Zolotoye zerno (1947)

INCIDENTAL MUSIC

Geroi nashego vremeni (1939)
Othello (Shakespeare) (1943)

MULTIMEDIA

Pieces (state choir and folk dance ens) (1947)

Ref. 87

KOZANKOVA, Anna

Czech composer. b. Kromeriz, July 5, 1861; d. Doksy, February 18, 1952. She had her first music lessons from her father and began composing at an early age.

Compositions

CHAMBER

Two string quartets
Tuzba (vln and pf) (1916)

PIANO

Nocturno
Romance
Smutecni pochod
Sonata in C
Venkovske nalady

SACRED

Ave Maria (vce and pf)

Ref. 197

KOZELUH, Katherina. See CIBBINI, Katherina

KOZHEVNIKOVA, Ekaterina Vadimovna

Soviet composer. b. 1954. She studied composition under Khrennikov at the Moscow Conservatory and in 1967 won first prize in the Young Composers' Competition. DISCOGRAPHY.

Compositions

ORCHESTRA

Symphony No. 2 (Soviet Kompozitor, 1984)

VOCAL

Elegie (Krzhizhanovsky) (vce, ch, org and orch)
Triptych: Life, death, immortality (Afanasia Feta) (T and pf; also T and cham orch)
Other vocal cycles (Lorca, Omar Khayyam and Valery Bryusov)

Ref. 563

KOZINOVIC, Lujza (Zorka)

Yugoslav organist, choral conductor, teacher and composer. b. Slimena, near Travnik, March 20, 1897. She studied the organ and composition under F. Dugan at the Music Academy in Zagreb. She taught music and singing at schools in Banja Luka, Sarajevo, Nova Gradiska and Zagreb. In Zagreb she was choir conductor and organist and collected folk songs and old Slavonic liturgical music from the Croatian coastal areas.

Compositions

CHAMBER

String quartet

VOCAL

Rukoveti (mix-ch)
Revolutionary melodies

SACRED

Fifteen Latin, Old Slavonic and Croatian masses
Motets

Publications

Rasprava o starocrkvenom pjevanju u Kraljevici. Discussion of Old Church Singing in Kraljevica.

Ref. 109, 193, 417

KOZLOVA, Anna. See DREVJANA, Anna

KRAEHMER, Caroline (Karol Krahmer) (nee Schleicher)

German clarinetist, pianist, violinist, conductor and composer. b. Stockach, Lake Constance, December 17, 1794; d. 1850. Her father was a musician in the service of the Duke of Wurtemberg and the family followed him to Stuttgart. There Caroline studied the violin under Baumiller. At the age of nine, she was given a clarinet and was tutored by her father. She also studied the violin under Occhernal and Zanaboni. In 1819 she went to Karlsruhe where she studied the piano under Fesca and harmony under Danzi. She married the chief oboist of the Viennese Court, J. Ernest Kraehmer. She made her debut in Vienna in 1822 and then toured with her husband giving many successful concerts. Her name appears as Karol Krahmer in some collections of ecossaises and waltzes for piano edited and published by K.F. Muller in 1825.

Compositions

CHAMBER

Compositions (cl, pf and vlc) (Vienna: Diabelli)
Sonatina (pf and cl) (Vienna: Liedesdorf)
Ecossaises and waltzes (pf) (K.F. Muller, 1825)

VOCAL

Sechs Lieder (vce and pf) (Karlsruhe)

MISCELLANEOUS

Variations

Publications

Autobiography. Auctioned in Berlin, 1922.

Ref. 26, 226, 276, 347, 471, 472

KRAHMER, Karol. See KRAEHMER, Caroline

KRAINSKA, Justyna

19th-century Polish violinist and composer. She completed her violin studies under Joachim Kaczkowski in Warsaw in 1825.

Compositions

PIANO

Two polonaises

Ref. 118

KRALIKE, Mathilde. See KRALIK VON MAYERSWALDEN, Mathilde

KRALIK VON MAYERSWALDEN (Kralike, von Kralik), Mathilde

Austrian pianist and composer. b. Linz, December 3, 1857. She studied in Vienna from 1876 to 1877 under Julius Epstein (piano) and Anton Bruckner (counterpoint). She then entered the Vienna Conservatory, where she studied composition under Franz Krenn, 1877 to 1879. She was a composer for the Women's Choral Society in Vienna and a member of the Vienna Bach Society and the Austrian Composers' Union.

Compositions

ORCHESTRA

Heroische Overture (1906)

CHAMBER

Nonett (str qrt, wind qrt and pf) (1901)
String quartet
Trio in F (vln, vlc and pf)
Sonata (vln and pf) (1877)

PIANO

Five pieces (1881)
Rhapsody
Variations

VOCAL

Auf Goethes Wegen, cantata
Weissblume (R. Kralik) (mix-ch)
Blumenlieder (Irene Zoepf) (1912)
Jugendlieder (1899)
Lieder aus R. Kralik's Buechlein der Unweisheit (1885)
Maia (R. Kralik) (1895)
Mutterlied (1928)
Prinz Eugen (R. Kralik)
Der Rosenkranz (vce and pf)

SACRED

Der heilige Leopold, oratorio (R. Kralik) (soloists, ch and orch)
Der Kreuzweg, cantata (R. Kralik) (soloists, ch and orch)
Weihnachtskantata (R. Kralik) (soloists, ch, orch and org)
Requiem (soloists, ch and orch)
Four masses with organ (1906)
Hymnus der heiligen Hildegardis
Lieder im heiligen Geist
Die Taufe Christi

OPERA

Blum und Weisblume
Der heilige Gral (R. Kralik) (1907)

THEATRE

Amphortas, melodrama
Four melodramas (pf) (1912)
Jeanne d'Arc's Todesweg, melodrama
Karl der Grosse in Wien, melodrama (pf)
Unter der Linde, melodrama (Walther von der Vogelweide)
Zwei Frauen, melodrama

Ref. 70, 105, 111, 226, 276, 297, 347, 465

KRALIKOVA, Hana. See KRALIKOVA, Johanna

KRALIKOVA, Johana (Hana) (nee Slavkovska)

Czech pianist, accompanist, artist, teacher and composer. b. Prague, March 25, 1888. She studied art in Prague and then turned to music, receiving her first piano lessons from her father. She studied composition under V. Novak, piano under L. Urbanova and singing under M. Bogucka. She passed the state examination in singing in 1911 and in the piano in 1913. She taught the piano from 1923, gave concerts and was an accompanist.

Compositions

PIANO

Humoreska (1916)
Kilebava (1916)
Other pieces

VOCAL

Raseni (w-ch)
Slavnostni sbor (m-ch)
Sen lasky, song cycle
Vecerni pisne, song cycle
Other songs

OPERETTA

Two operettas (J. Svab)

THEATRE

Music for puppet theatre and children's theatre

Ref. 197

KRAMER, Caroline. See KRAEHMER, Caroline

KRASNOGLIADOVA, Vera Vladimirovna

Soviet pianist, teacher and composer. b. February 14, 1902. She graduated from the Institute of Rhythm in Moscow in 1924. From 1921 to 1927 she studied the piano under E. Savina-Gnesina, composition under M. Gnesin and fugue and instrumentation under R. Gliere at the Gnesin Institute in Moscow. At the Moscow Conservatory she studied the piano under E. Bekman-Shcherbina (q.v.) and A. Shatskes and composition under M. Gnesin and V. Shebalin, graduating in 1931. For the next few years she taught rhythmics and choir singing in schools and privately. From 1949 to 1955 she was musical director of the radio.

Compositions

ORCHESTRA

Lyrical overture (1944)
Variations on a Ukrainian theme (orch of folk insts) (1934)

CHAMBER

String quartet (1952)
Five pieces (vln and pf) (1940)

PIANO

Waltz (1949)
Five preludes (1946)
Four preludes and fairy tale (1927)
Six pieces for teaching (1938)
Four pieces on Russian folk themes (1968)
Three miniatures (1948)

VOCAL

Lenin zhiv, cantata (Yakuts poets) (soloists, ch and orch) (1947)
Ballada o Garcia Lorca (V. Neishtadt) (soloist and orch) (1936)
Ballada o trekh geroyakh-sibiryakakh (P. Smerdov) (soloists, ch and orch) (1942)
Pionieri michurintsi suite (S. Severtsev) (chil-ch a-cap) (1953)
Bratishki suite (A. Barto) (vce, wind qrt and hp) (1933)
Cycle (Yakuts poets) (vce and pf) (1945)
Gibel Chapayeva, mass song (Z. Alexandrova) (1939)
Gonimi veshnimi luchami, duet (Pushkin) (1939)
Na kholmakh Gruzii, Ty i vy (Pushkin) (vce and pf) (1939)
Pesnya mira i druzhby, mass song (A. Mashistov) (1954)
Three Shakespeare sonnets (S. Marshak) (vce and pf) (1955)
Velyeyet parus odinokii (Lermontov) (vce and pf) (1939)
Children's songs (1931)
Other songs
Arrangements of Folk Songs (vces and pf) (1983)

Ref. 87

KRAUS, Rozann Baghdad

American recorder player, choreographer, dancer, lecturer and composer. b. Ohio, October 7, 1952. She gained a B.A. (psychology) from University of Rochester, 1972; M.F.A. (dance) from Southern Universaty, NY, and an M.A. (theatre and dance) from Goddard College, 1984. Musically, she was self taught. From 1973 to 1975 she was on the faculty of New England Conservatory and artist-in-residence, Clark University Center for Contemporary Performance, 1982 to 1984. She won an Ohio State, an Artist Foundation Fellowship and a Paul Robeson Award.

Compositions

MISCELLANEOUS

Echoes of men, manipulated text
His brother was an only child, sound collage
Jacks and bells

Ref. composer, 643

KRAUSE, Anna

19th-century German composer.

Compositions

VOCAL

Gesaenge, ops. 6 and 7
Drei Lieder, op. 8
Fuenf Lieder, op. 5

Ref. 76, 347

KRAUSE, Ida
19th-century German composer.
Compositions
VOCAL
Lieder, 2 cycles
Ref. 465

KRAUSZ, Susan
20th-century American pianist, professor and composer. b. Stuttgart, Germany. She received a piano teacher's diploma from Stuttgart College of Music in 1933, an M.Mus. from Case Western Reserve University in 1956 and teaching certificates from Columbia University in 1947 and 1948, studying under Raymond Burrows. She did postgraduate study at Columbia University under Dr. Robert Pace and attended master classes with Professors Walter Rehberg, Edwin Fischer and Dinu Lipatti in Switzerland and Thomas Richner and Leonard Shure in the United States. She studied for her Ph.D. Mus. at the College of Jewish studies, Shaker Heights. She was a lecturer at Cleveland Music School Settlement from 1949 to 1955, lecturer in music at the Case Western Reserve University after 1966 and professor of music, Yavne College for Women from 1984. She appeared in concerts in Germany, Switzerland and the United States, with orchestras and in a piano-viola duo with her late husband, Laszlo Krausz and played her own compositions on television. She won second prize in a Mu Phi Epsilon composition contest in 1956. PHOTOGRAPH.
Compositions
PIANO
Pieces incl.:
Piano picture books I, II and III (1960, 1983)
Sonata
Variations
Ref. composer, 643

KREBS, Frau
19th-century Austrian composer.
Compositions
VOCAL
Lieder
Ref. 465

KREBS, Suzanne Eigen
American composer. She received a Ph.D. from the State University of New York in 1975.
Compositions
VOCAL
Sunday morning (Wallace Stevens) (small ch and cham orch)
Ref. State University of New York

KREISS, Hulda E.
American harpist, poetess, teacher and composer. b. Strasbourg, France, December 15, 1924. She became an American citizen in 1933. She studied at San Diego State College, where she received a B.A. in 1946. She studied the harp under Carlos Salzedo and was harpist with the San Diego Country Symphony for nine years. From 1946 she taught in San Diego schools. She received awards for poetry, teaching and community service.
Compositions
CHAMBER
Dream love (hp and vlc)
Fantasie (pf)
VOCAL
Beth's lullaby (vce and pf)
Chorale (vce and pf)
Moonlight reverie (vce and hp)
Publications
Reaching the Exceptional Child Through Music. Winner of a set of States of the Union Commemorative Medals.
Ref. 142

KRIMSKY, Katrina (Margaret Krimsky Siegmann)
American harpsichordist, concert pianist, teacher and composer. b. St. Simon's Island, GA, March 5, 1938. She began her piano study at the age of four with her mother, who was an accomplished pianist. Katrina studied at the Eastman School of Music and obtained her B.M. in 1959. During the mid-sixties she gave numerous performances of contemporary music in Europe and later became involved in jazz improvisation. She taught the piano at Mills College from 1973 to 1979 and currently lives in Switzerland. DISCOGRAPHY.
Compositions
MISCELLANEOUS
Crystal morning (1981)
Duogeny (1981)
Epilogue (with Woody Shaw)
Mial (1981)
Moonbeams (1981)
Song for Hans (1981)
Specs (with Woody Shaw)
Stella Malu (1981)
Villa in Brazil (1981)
Ref. 625

KROFINA, Sharon
20th-century American composer.
Compositions
CHAMBER
String quartet I (1977)
ELECTRONIC
Flotations (elec tape and pf)
Ref. Working papers on Women in Music, 4

KROGMANN, Carrie William (pseud. Paul Ducelle)
American composer. b. Danvers, MA; d. 1943.
Compositions
PIANO
Pieces incl.:
Arcadian lullaby
Zephyrs from melody
VOCAL
Songs
Ref. 292, 347

KRONING, Mlle.
20th-century Algerian or French composer. Her opera was performed in Algiers.
Compositions
OPERA
Bobson et Abdulle (Villa) (1905)
Ref. 431

KROSNICK, Mary Lou Wesley
American pianist and composer. b. Bayonne, NJ, June 11, 1934. She gained her B.Sc. from the Juilliard School of Music, having studied under Rosina Lhevinne; her B.S. from the University of Wisconsin, Madison, having studied under Gunnar Johansen and her M.Mus from Yale University School of Music, where she studied theory and composition under Quincy Porter. She studied the piano under Isabella Vengerova in New York and composition under Bernard Wagenaar and Wolfgang Fortner. She appeared as a soloist with the Boston Pops and on many radio and TV stations. She won the New York Philharmonic Symphony Society's Young Composers' Contest in 1949, first prize in an international piano contest organized by the National Guild of Piano Teachers in 1953 and first prize in the teachers' division in the International Recording Competition in 1972.
Compositions
CHAMBER
Fantasy (vln, wind and perc) (1960)
PIANO
Fugue in romantic style (1978)
The rain comes (1949)
Sonata (1961)
Ref. 77, 625

KRUGER, Catharina Maria (Kate van den Heever)
South African teacher and composer. b. Plankfontein, 1883. She studied music from an early age under Mrs. Werdmuller and then Miss Burke-Taylor. She attended the Albert Academy Teachers' Training College and taught in the Transvaal. Her compositions can be viewed as the first attempts by an Afrikaans woman to compose in the popular Afrikaans idiom.
Compositions
MISCELLANEOUS
Albert waltz (Cape Town: Darter & Sons, 1906)
Orange River reveries (Darter, 1910)
Rooi dagbreek (Johannesburg: MacKay Bros.)
Vastrap (Darter, 1908)
Ref. 377

KRUGER, Lilly Canfield

American authoress, teacher and composer. b. Portage, OH, April 13, 1892; d. 1969. She studied at the University of Toledo, where she received a B.A. and a B.Ed. She studied music with Mary Willing and later taught in schools.

Compositions

PIANO
Rondino
Summer sunset
VOCAL
The Easter Bunny comes hopping to town
SACRED
Christmas pastorale
He lives
Settings of Psalms 1 and 128
Ref. 39, 40, 142, 347

KRULL, Diana (Lilian Diana Victoria)

Swedish teacher and composer. b. Tallinn, Estonia, July 26, 1930. She became a Swedish citizen in 1954 and studied composition under Edvard Tubin and Karl-Birger Blomdahl at the University of Stockholm. In Darmstadt she studied composition under H. Scherchen, P. Boulez and L. Nono. From 1957 she worked as a music teacher. PHOTOGRAPH.

Compositions

CHAMBER
Quartet (cl, 2 vln and vlc) (1955)
Quartet (fl, cl, bsn and pf) (1957)
Four pieces for young pianists (pf) (New York: Estonian Music Fund, 1959)
Varianter Sonat (vln) (1958)
Ref. composer

KRUMPHOLTZ, Anne-Marie (nee Steckler)

German harpist and composer. b. Metz, 1755; d. London, after 1824. She was the daughter of the harp maker Christan Steckler and in his workshop met her future husband, the harpist and composer Jean-Baptiste Krumpholtz. Anne-Marie became a virtuoso harpist and from 1779 played her husband's compositions at the Paris Concert Spirituel. In 1789 she eloped to London with the pianist J.L. Dussek and gave concerts at the Hanover Square Rooms for many years, often appearing with him in a harp-piano duo. She composed light harp pieces. Her daughter Fanny Krumpholtz Pittar (q.v.) also composed for the harp.
Ref. 8

KRUMPHOLTZ PITTAR, Fanny

German harpist and composer. She is possibly the same person as Charlotte Esprit, b. February 28, 1785. She was the daughter of the harpist Anne-Marie Krumpholtz (q.v.) and the harpist, instrument designer and composer Jean-Baptiste Krumpholtz. She composed light harp pieces.
Ref. 8

KRUSE (Arlt-Kruse), Lotte

German pianist, violinist, lecturer and composer. b. St. Gallen or Berlin-Lichterfelde, May 1, 1899; d. Zullichau, April 13, 1930. She studied under Jos Pembours and Hugo Kauns and was director of the Tomasini Conservatory in Zullichau from 1924. She married the violinist Ernst Arlt in 1925. She composed orchestral, violin and piano pieces, choral music and songs.
Ref. 70, 105, 226

KRYSINSKA, Maria

19th-century Polish composer.

Compositions

PIANO
Nocturne (Alleton)
VOCAL
Chanson de Mai (Alleton)
Chanson de route Arya (Alleton)
Mauresque (Rouart)
Prière d'une vierge (Joubert)
Quatre melodies (pf) (Choudens)
Rencontre (Alleton)
Rendez-vous (Choudens)
Sérenade à la lune (Choudens)
Tes yeux (Choudens)
Un peu de musique (Alleton)
Ref. 297

KRZANOWSKA, Grazyna

20th-century Polish composer.

Compositions

ORCHESTRA
With the beat of the kettledrum, symphony (1978)
Concerto grosso (str orch) (1977)
Passacaglia (1976)
... Per orchestra (1976)
CHAMBER
Song without words (4 vln, 2 vlc, fl, ob, trp and vib) (1978)
Trio (1979)
Partita (vln and pf) (1980)
VOCAL
Glade fires (S, A and ens) (1979)
Postlude (m-S, fl, gtr, vln and vlc) (1978)
Ref. Polish Music 4; 1979, 3; 1980

KRZYZANOWSKA, Halina

Polish concert pianist, lecturer and composer. b. Paris, 1860; d. Rennes, January 18, 1937. She was a member of the same Polish family as Chopin. Halina was brought up in Paris and studied the piano under A. Marmontel and composition under E. Guiraud at the Paris Conservatoire, graduating with the first prize in 1880. For some years she toured as a pianist, appearing in Warsaw and Cracow in 1894. From 1889 she taught the piano at the Conservatory in Rennes, combining a teaching career with concert touring in France and Poland.

Compositions

ORCHESTRA
Symphony
Fantasie (pf and orch)
CHAMBER
String quartet in A-Major, op. 44 (Paris: Hamelle, 1925)
Violin sonata in A-Minor, op. 43 (Hamelle, 1924)
Violin sonata in E-Minor, op. 28 (Hamelle, 1915)
PIANO
A la gavotte, op. 11 (Gebethner)
Aria op. 16 (Gregh)
Chanson du soir
Coeur de femme (Lorent)
Dumka (Lorent)
Fée de berceau
Force et beaute
Gavotte (Keith)
Hungaria (Lorent)
Krakowiak (Bellon)
Lune de miel (Keith)
Mazur, op. 15
Mazurek (Lorent)
Minuetto (Lemoine)
Romance (Keith)
Serenada
Seule
Sonata No. 1 in D-Minor
Sonata No. 2
Valse-ballet (Lemoine)
VOCAL
Echa (vce and pf)
Zakochana (vce and pf)
SACRED
Sancta Radegunda, oratorio
THEATRE
Jasyr (S. Duchinska)
Ref. 8, 41, 118, 297

KUBISCH, Christina

German composer. b. Bremen, 1948. She lives in Milan. DISCOGRAPHY.

Compositions

VOCAL
A conversation of cliches so redundant, that they are not consciously noticeable (1975)
Language in progress
ELECTRONIC
Diverso No. 10 tempo liquido (tape and insts)
Divertimento (1 pf, 5 soloists and tape) (1974)
Liquid piece (artificial and natural sounds) (1974)

Bibliography

Musikhandel. No. 3, 1977.
Ref. Frau und Musik, 189, 199

KUBO, Mayako

Japanese pianist, musicologist and composer. b. Hyogo, 1947. From 1966 to 1970 she was a student at the Osaka College of Music and the following two years a pianist in Tokyo. In 1972 she went to the Vienna Musikhochschule to study the piano under Weber, composition under Haubenstock-Ramati and Urbanner and electronic music under Kaufmann and Helmut Lachenmann. Before commencing her musicology studies at Vienna University in 1977 she attended the Darmstadt summer courses of contemporary music.

Compositions

ORCHESTRA

Arachnoidea (1980)

CHAMBER

In und Yo fuer sieben Spieler und einen Dirigenten (fl, ob, cl, pf, vln, vlc and perc) (1979)
Suite Sumi-E (str qrt) (1979)
Aktionen (fl and pf) (1977)
Le mie passacaglie (2 gtr) (Breitkopf & Haertel, 1984)
Am Anfang (vlc) (1977)
Three studies (pf) (1979)

VOCAL

Spinnfaden Ballett-Suite (ch and orch; also tape) (1980)
Yogi (ch a-cap) (1979)

ELECTRONIC

Bach Variationen (8-track tape or 4 stereo tapes) (1980)
Iterum meditemur for Hiroshima (trb and tape) (1978)
Mothers, children, lovers, people (1982)
Piano Piece (2 hands and tape) (Breitkopf) (1984)

Ref. Otto Harrassowitz (Wiesbaden)

KUBOTA, Minako

Japanese pianist and composer. b. 1972. She attended a special junior advanced Yamaha Music Education System course. She has performed in Japan and in 1983 traveled to America with the National Symphony Orchestra. DISCOGRAPHY.

Composition

PIANO

Cheerful dumbo

Ref. Yamaha Music Foundation

KUCEROVA-HERSTOVA, Marie

Czech pianist, choral conductor, teacher and composer. b. Kutna Hora, February 20, 1896. She studied theory under K. Steckar, composition under V. Novak and conducting under F. Spilka at the Prague Conservatory, graduating in 1915. At the same time she studied the piano at the A. Miksa Piano School. She conducted in East Czech theatres and taught at music schools in Tabora and Kutna Hora from 1921 until World War II. She was active in musical life in Kutna Hora, taught in schools and privately and conducted adults and children's choirs.

Compositions

ORCHESTRA

Nove jaro, variations (1947)

PIANO

Polka (6 hands) (1949)
Broučci (1923)
Broučinkovy melodie (1931)
Etudy (1934)
Hurvinek dětem (1931)
Kulihrášek (1930)
O Palečkovi (1934)
Polonéza (1949)
Tri zimni nalady (1927)
Vanočni fantasie (1928)

VOCAL

Songs for children (1925-1931)
V zemi české (J. Carek) (mix-ch)
Krásné město (R. Krupicka) (mix-ch)

BALLET

Kdyz hracky ozivnou (A. Fischerova) (1928)

OPERA

Broučci (1938)
Mlády génius (1938)
Tri tovarysi (1956)
Ulicnik Pericko (1956)

THEATRE

Holubinka, melodrama (1920)
Oznánemi, melodrama for children (1928)

Ref. 197

KUCZOR, Hilda (nee Scheinzer)

Austrian pianist, teacher and composer. b. Vienna, March 7, 1894.
Ref. 226

KUESTER, Edith Haines

19th or 20th-century American organist, pianist, teacher and composer. b. Indiana. She studied in New York, Chicago and Los Angeles and made her debut as a pianist at the age of 12. She composed songs, song cycles and duets.
Ref. 226

KUFFLER, Eugenie

20th-century American flautist, reed player, singer and composer. She lived in Paris.
Ref. AMC newsletter

KUHLMAN, Clara. See HAXTHAUSEN, Aurore M.G.Ch. von

KUHNLOVA, Julie. See REISSEROVA, Julie

KUKUCK, Felicitas (nee Kestner)

German flautist, pianist and composer. b. Hamburg, November 2, 1914. She studied at the Hochschule fuer Musik in Berlin from 1935 to 1939 under P. Hindemith (composition), Jurgen Uhde (piano) and Scheck (flute). Her main compositons are based on the evangelical service. DISCOGRAPHY. PHOTOGRAPH.

Compositions

CHAMBER

Trio (rec, ob and vla da gamba) (Moseler, 1955)
Fantasie (vla and pf) (Moseler, 1963)
Sonata (fl and pf) (Moseler, 1962)
Sonata (a-rec and hpcd) (Moseler, 1951)
Sonata (s-rec) (Moseler, 1968)
Teaching works (vln and pf)
Die Bruecke ueber den Main, variations (pf)

VOCAL

Eichendorff, cantata (Fidula, 1957)
Hoelderlin, cantata (Bar and orch) (1949)
Kuckucke aus aller Welt, cantata (Fidula)
Rilke Motets: Werkleute sind wir (mix-ch) (Moseler, 1951)
Stormlieder (mix-ch) (Moseler, 1951)
Die Bruecke, suite of songs (Chinese text, trans Hans Bethgel) (S, rec and lute) (Berlin: Lienau Verlag, 1956)
Komm, wir wollen tanzen, dances for youth (vce and opt insts)

SACRED

Der Gottesknecht, passion oratorio (Moseler, 1959)
Das kommende Reich, oratorio (1953)
Seligpreisungen, oratorio (Hanssler Verlag, 1953)
Es begab sich, cantata (Fidula, 1961)
Psalm 147, cantata (Moseler, 1955)
Reformation Day, cantata (Hanssler Verlag, 1960)
Wo bleibst du, Trost, cantata (1974)
Osterhistorie (mix-ch) (1956)
Osterkantate (ch and strs) (Moseler, 1947)
Adventskantate (Fidula, 1954)
Dialog zur Auferstehung (1979)
Dreikoenigskantate (Moseler, 1954)
Missa Sancti Gabrieli Archangeli (1968)
Ostermotette (Merseberger Verlag, 1958)
Weihnachtsgeschichte in Liedern (Moseler, 1973)
Weihnachtslieder (Moseler, 1950)

THEATRE

Wo ist der neugeborene Koenig der Juden, Christmas play (Moseler, 1974)

INCIDENTAL MUSIC

Marat (Peter Weiss) (1964)

Ref. composer, 15, 17, 563

KULESHOVA, Galina Grigorevna

20th-century Soviet composer. She composed an opera and songs.
Ref. 465

KULIEVA, Farida Tairovna

Soviet pianist, lecturer and composer. b. Yessentuki, June 12, 1930. She studied the piano under G.G. Sharoyev at the Azerbaijanian Conservatory and composition under D. Gadjiev, graduating in 1953. From 1952 to 1957 she was pianist and concertmistress at the same Conservatory and taught at the Azerbaijanian Music School. After 1958 she lectured at the Azerbaijanian Conservatory.

Compositions
ORCHESTRA
Concert rhapsody (vln and orch) (1968)
Fantasy (pf and orch) (1973)
Piano concerto (1953)
CHAMBER
String quartet (1950)
Sonata (cl and pf) (1954)
Three pieces (fl and pf) (1969)
Three preludes on Azerbaijanian folk songs (pf) (1954)
VOCAL
Azerbaijan, cantata (soli, ch and orch) (1951)
Romances and Songs (vce and pf)
Ref. 21

KUMMER, Clare (Clare Rodman Beecher)

American authoress, playwright and composer. b. Brooklyn, NY, January 9, 1888; d. Carmel, CA, April 21, 1958. She studied music privately.
Compositions
VOCAL
The bluebird
Blushing June roses
Dearie
Egypt
Garden of dreams
Lover of mine
Only with you
The road to yesterday
Somebody's eyes
Sunset
Thro' all the world
Today
THEATRE
Annie dear
Good gracious Annabelle
Her master's voice
Madame Pompadour
Ninety in the shade
One kiss
Pomeroy's past
Rollo's wild oats
A successful calamity
The three waltzes
Ref. 39

KUNEGUNDE, Queen

Polish composer. b. 1234; d. ca. 1292. She composed songs.
Ref. 465

KUNITZ, Sharon Lohse

American pianist, lecturer and composer. b. Williston, North Dakota, March 3, 1943. She studied at the Augsburg College from 1961 to 1963 and then obtained her B.Mus in 1965 from the University of Colorado, Boulder. She attended the University of Washington from 1965 to 1966 and in 1967 obtained her M.A. from the University of Denver. From 1973 to 1975 she taught the piano and theory at the North Mexico Junior College and in 1977 joined the New Mexico State University as a lecturer for the music history department.
Compositions
PIANO
Pretzel prance (2 pf) (1980) (Boulder: Myklas Press)
Sonatine royale (1981)
SACRED
Hallelujah! Sing your praise (1974)
Reformation Sunday (1976)
MISCELLANEOUS
Brown sugar boogie (duet) (Myklas)
Camp Hook (1981)
Concerto for friends (1979)
Crickets came to dance (duet) (1978) (Myklas)
Frisbees (trio) (1979) (Myklas)
I love to swing (duet) (1980) (Myklas)
Legend of Straight Arrow (1979)
My flesh shall rest in hope (1983)
Red Horse Canyon (1981)
Scenes of the Southwest (1977) (Myklas)
Ref. composer, 625

KUNTZE, Olga

German organist, pianist and composer. b Pallau, August 12, 1879. She lived in Stettin and composed chamber, organ, piano and choral works.
Ref. 70, 226

KURIMOTO, Yoko

Japanese composer. b. Aichi, March 11, 1951. She graduated from the Graduate School of Aichi University of Arts in 1976 after studying under Kan Ishii. She entered the first and third composition competitions run by the Japanese Choral Directors' Association. DISCOGRAPHY.
Compositions
CHAMBER
June end songs, in 2 parts (rec and gtr) (1982)
PIANO
Breathing space (1975)
Messages from one pianist (1973)
The red shoes (1979)
VOCAL
Form with a sad face (mix-ch) (1974)
Kumotta Aki (w-ch) (1978)
Message from one 'In Summer' (mix-ch) (1975)
Hana-Mandala (S, vln, vlc and pf) (1981)
Ref. Japan Federation of Composers

KUROKAWA, Manae

Japanese pianist and composer. b. 1966. She graduated from the Yamaha Junior Music Course and then studied in the Junior Special Course at the Nemu Music Academy. She was the recipient of awards in Japan and performed in Japan, Australia, Hungary and Italy. DISCOGRAPHY.
Compositions
ORCHESTRA
Piano concerto in G-Major
PIANO
Cute kitty
Dance of the snowy egret
Festival suite
A Parthenon in my heart
Rainbow fantasy
The spring dew drops
Ref. Yamaha Music Foundation

KURZBOECK, Magdalene von

18th to 19th-century Austrian pianist and composer. Haydn dedicated his *Piano sonata, op. 92* to her. She composed piano pieces and songs.
Ref. 129, 226, 276

KURZBOCK, Magdalene von. See KURZBOECK, Magdalene von

KUSS, Margarita Ivanovna

Soviet composer of German origin. b. Ryazan, October 13, 1921. She studied composition under Shebalin at the Moscow Conservatory, graduating in 1948. Her work combines the influences of late romanticism and Russian folk song. DISCOGRAPHY.
Compositions
ORCHESTRA
Symphony in G-Major (1948)
Chaika, symphonic poem (1950)
Fantasy on a theme of A. Olenicheva (orch of folk insts) (1955)
Festival overture (1953)
Poem on themes of contemporary Russian folk songs (1961)
Sinfonietta (1955)
Two suites (light orch) (1949, 1950)
CHAMBER
Sonata in C (vln and pf) (1974)
Sonata in E (vln and pf) (1963)
Piano pieces
VOCAL
Slavsya, molodost, cantata (Y. Kolas and A. Prokofiev) (soloist, choir and str orch) (1948)
A headache for the young lads and girls (m-S and orch of folk insts)
Ah, thou my night (m-S and orch of folk insts)
I walked in the garden (m-s and orch of folk insts)
Five romances (A. Gmyrev) (1952)
Four romances (N. Khikmet) (1953)
Four romances (E. Nechayev, E. Tarasov, A. Gmyrev) (1955)
Eleven Russian folk songs

Iz poezi mikelandzhelo (vce and pf) (1975)
Lyrical songs of the foothills
Ognennuye gody, poema (vce and pf) (1960)
Russkie pesni (vce and pf) (1983)
Ten Russian folk songs (vce, 3 fl and pf) (1971)
Three romances (O. Shiraz) (1949)
INCIDENTAL MUSIC
Music for films
Bibliography
Rogachev, N. *Margarita Kuss*. 1959.
Ref. 17, 63, 70, 81, 83, 87, 223, 330, 419, 563, 622

KUSUNOKI, Tomoko
Japanese composer. b. Sendai City, April 4, 1949. In 1973 she graduated from Tokyo University of Fine Arts and in 1976 from the Pro Musica Nipponia masterclass. From 1981 to 1982 she studied music, theory and composition at the Padue University Graduate School. Her composition teachers included Nadia Boulanger, T. Ikenouchi, A. Yashiro, S. Sato, M. Nagatomi, H. Hara and J. Orrego-salas. She studied theory under H.L. Riggins. DISCOGRAPHY.
Compositions
ORCHESTRA
Kyoo (pf and orch) (1973)
CHAMBER
Quartet (shakuhachi, biwa, 20 str koto and 17 str koto)
Ren (shakuhachi, 20 str koto and vlc)
The lake (vlc and perc)
En fantement (1980)
VOCAL
Vineyard, cantata (S and B) (1977)
OPERETTA
Kasa-Jido (chil-ch) (1979)
Ref. Japan Federation of Composers

KUYPER, Elizabeth
Dutch conductor, lecturer and composer. b. Amsterdam, September 13, 1877; d. Lugano, Switzerland, February 26, 1953. She studied at the Berlin Hochschule under H. Barth and Max Bruch, then taught theory and composition there from 1908 until 1920. She was the founder and leader of the Berlin 'Tonkuenstlerinnen Orchester' in 1908. She led a few concerts of the London Women's Symphony Orchestra and in 1923 conducted the New York Women's Symphony Orchestra. She was also conductor of the Saenger-Vereinigung of the German Lyceum Club. She worked in New York for a number of years and later returned to Europe, where she lived at Lago Maggiore in Brissago, Switzerland.
Compositions
ORCHESTRA
Symphony
Sonata (vln and orch)
Violin concerto, op. 10 (Simrock, 1910)
Serenade
CHAMBER
Trio in D, op. 13 (pf, vln and vlc) (Eulenburg, 1913)
Ballad (vlc and pf)
Sonata in A (vln and pf)
VOCAL
Cantatas
Choruses (w-ch and mix-ch)
Songs
Ref. 7, 17, 22, 26, 41, 44, 70, 94, 105, 110, 226, 347, 653

KUZMENKO, Larysa
Canadian concert pianist, lecturer and composer. b. Toronto, January 23, 1956. She gained a B.Mus. from Toronto University. Her teachers included Boris Lysenko, Clifford Poole, Samuel Dolin, Kenneth Harrison, Oskar Morawetz, Walter Ruczynski, Dennis Patrick and Gustav Ciamaga. As a pianist she has given solo recitals and concerts and performed in chamber ensembles. She teaches harmony, theory, composition, history and piano at the Royal Conservatory in Toronto. PHOTOGRAPH.
Compositions
ORCHESTRA
Concerto (pf and orch) (1982)
Marah (1976, rev 1982)
BAND
Fantasy (1981)
Ritual (1978)
CHAMBER
Grimoire (brass qnt) (1982)
Movement (pf and wind insts) (1981)
Halloween dance (mar and tba) (1985)
Improvisations (a-sax and perc) (1981)
Mystery (cl and pf) (1976)
Proportions (fl and cl) (1977)
PIANO
Elihia (1974)
Little suite (1982)
Silver birds (1977)
VOCAL
Ukraine (w-ch and pf) (1978)
Elegy and song (S, fl, vib and pf) (1979)
Faust (S and pf) (1985)
Love song (S and pf) (1985)
Nocturne and dance (S, fl and pf) (1980)
Three songs (S and pf) (1980)
Ref. composer

KUZMICH, Natalie
Canadian composer. b. 1932.
Composition
VOCAL
When icicles hang by the wall (Shakespeare) (w-ch) (Waterloo Music, 1966)
Ref. CMC

KUZMYCH, Christina
American pianist, administrator, teacher and composer. b. Perth, Australia, January 25, 1954. She has her B.Mus. in piano performance and her M.Mus. and D.Mus. in composition all from the Indiana University. She was awarded a Pi Kappa Lambda honorary award in music. PHOTOGRAPH.
Compositions
ORCHESTRA
Archipian (pf and str orch) (1978)
CHAMBER
String quartet (1977)
String quartet (1980)
3x3 alternatives (ob, vlc and hpcd) (1980)
Microtrio (str trio) (1974)
Three movements for three flutes (1978)
Trio (vlc, vln and pf) (1980)
Treble fantasies (fl and sax) (1983)
When the distant guns of autumn cease (vlc and timp) (1977)
Fragments (vlc) (1977)
Three movements (cl) (1978)
Geometrics (1975)
VOCAL
Haiku (S, fl and orch) (1975)
Six miniatures (S and cham ens) (1974)
Shapes and sounds I (S, pf and perc) (1976)
Shapes and sounds II (S, cl, vlc and hp) (1979)
Shapes and sounds III (S and vln) (1981)
Shapes and sounds IV (S and sax) (1982)
Ref. composer

KUZNETSOVA, Zhanetta Alexandrovna (pseud. Evgenia Strella)
Soviet composer. b. Irkutsk, July 26, 1937. In 1967 she graduated from the Moscow Conservatory, having studied composition under A.Y. Eshpai and Y. Shaporin.
Compositions
ORCHESTRA
Symphony No. 1 (1967)
Symphony No. 2 (1969-1972)
Symphony No. 3 (1970)
Piano concerto (1968)
Overture (1971)
CHAMBER
String quartet (1967)
Five Russian tunes (vln and pf) (1965)
Russkie napevy (vln and pf) (Soviet Kompozitor, 1984)
Sonata (vlc and pf) (1970)
PIANO
Diatonic ricercare and 12 fugues (1966)
Polyphonic sonatina (1968)
Russian bells (1975)
Sonata No. 1 (1962)
Sonata No. 2 (1968)
Sonata No. 3 (1969)
Sonata No. 4 (1970)
Sonata No. 5 (1971)
OPERA
Don Juan v Egipte (1971)
Khleb ty moi (1978)
Lipaniushka (1976)
Posle bala (Tolstoy) (1959)

VOCAL
Russian cantata (soli, ch and orch) (1974)
Ruskaya diatonika (vce and orch) (1973)
Ruskaya pentatonika (vce and orch) (1971)
Five songs (ch) (1975)
Otdayet menya batiushka zamuzh, cycle (ch) (1971)
Avdotia's dancing song
Baker's song
Fenya's song
Girlyandy slov (vce, vlc and hp) (1972)
Menya milenki brosayet (vce, fl, pf and perc) (1973)
O serdtse, yesli ty gorish, cycle (vce and pf) (1965)
Pripody russkoy khram, cycle (vce and pf) (1964)
Song of the bride
Three songs, folk words (vce and pf) (1977)
Yoye neudachnik zhenitsya, cycle (vce and pf) (1968)
Za polyanym krugom, cycle (vce and pf) (1962)
INCIDENTAL MUSIC
Music for films
Light music
Ref. Otto Harrassowitz (Wiesbaden)

KVERNADZE, Bidzina

Russian composer. b. 1929. DISCOGRAPHY.
Compositions
ORCHESTRA
Violin concerto
Choreographic poem
Dance fantasia
Incident at the weir
BALLET
Berikoaba
FILM MUSIC
The miracle tree (1978)
Ref. 497, 563

KYNTZELL-HAGSTROMER, Louise

Swedish composer. b. 1826; d. 1875.
Compositions
VOCAL
Novisen (vce and pf)
Romans (vce and pf)
Se'n har jag ej fraagat mera (Runeberg) (vce and pf)
Ref. 167

KYROU (Chamass-Kyrou), Mireille

20th-century Greek composer. DISCOGRAPHY.
Composition
MISCELLANEOUS
Etude I
Ref. 94, 563

L'ADRIANETTA. See BARONI, Eleanora

L'ANGELO DEL CANTO. See BERTINOTTI, Teresa

LA BALTEIRA. See PEREZ, Maria

LA BARBARA, Joan (Subotnik) (Lotz, La Barbara)

American concert singer, writer and composer. b. Philadelphia, June 8, 1947. She studied voice under Phyllis Curtin at the Tanglewood-Berkshire Music Center from 1965 to 1968 while studying for her B.Mus. at Syracuse University School of Music. During her studies she transferred to New York University, where she obtained her B.Sc. (music education) in 1970. She also studied voice privately with Helen Boatwright and Marion Szekely-Freschl. She received many grants and awards for composition and multi-media, including CAPS from 1975 to 1978, ASCAP composers' award in 1976 and many others. Joan performs all of her vocal compositions. DISCOGRAPHY.

Compositions
VOCAL
Ides of March Nos. 1, 2, 4, 5, 5a and 7 (vces and strs)
Twelve for five in eight (mix-vces)
Circular song (1975)
Twelvesong (1977)
Voice pieces: One note internal resonance investigation (1974)
ELECTRONIC
Chandra (soloist, m-vces, 17 insts and elecs) (1978)
Thunder (vce, 6 timps and elecs)
Cyclone: A sound sculpture (vce, arp and Moog syns, panning device and tape)
Responsive resonance with feathers (vce tape broadcast inside body of pf and pf)
Vocal extensions (vce and elecs) (1975)
After obervogelsang (S and elecs) (1983)
Autumn signal (vce and quadraphonic sounds) (1978)
Berliner traeume (amp vce and tape) (1985)
Cathing (S and tape)
Electronic solo for voice (S and tape)
Klee Alee (vce and tape) (1979)
Shadowsong (vce and tape) (1979) (comm Radio, Am Sector, West Berlin)
Tapesongs (1977)
Performance piece
Winds of the canon
MULTIMEDIA
She is always alone (video)
MISCELLANEOUS
As lightning comes, in flashes (1981)
Erin (comm VPRO Radio, Holland, 1980)
Executioner's bracelet (1979)
October music
Rayers, for dance
Reluctant gypsy (1979)
Signing alphabet, music for Sesame Street, TV
The solar wind (comm Nat Endowment Comp Programme) (1983)
Star showers and extraterrestrials
Vlissingen harbor (1982)
Voice is the original instrument
Q-uatre petites betes? (1979)
Publications
Los Angeles Times. New music critic.
Musical America. Contributing editor, new music, 1977.
Soho in Berlin. Catalogue of Akademie der Kuenste, Berlin, 1976.
Soho Weekly News. New music columnist, 1974-1975.
Steve Reich and Philip Glass: Two from the Steady State School. Milan: Data Arte, winter issue, no. 13. 1974.
Bibliography
Joan La Barbara Sings Own Works. The New York Times, January 19, 1975.
Joan La Barbara: Une Technique vocal revolutionnaire. Le Provencal, August 13, 1977.
Music: After Satie. The New York Times, April 8, 1977.
Vocale experimenten in het Holland Festival. NRC Handelsblad, June 17, 1977.
Ref. AMC 1985, 228, 299, 494, 563, 622, 625

LA CASULANA. See CASULANA, Maddalena

LA CECCHINA. See CACCINI, Francesca

LA GUERRE, Elisabeth-Claude Jacquet de

French harpsichordist, organist, writer and composer. b. Paris, 1664; d. Paris, June 27, 1729. Her father was an organist and harpsichord maker and her mother, Anne de la Touche, was related to the Dacquins, a Parisian musical family. Elisabeth married the organist of Saint-Severin, Marin de la Guerre. Her early talent for improvisation on the organ and sight reading caused the Paris monthly, *Mercure Galante*, to call her a 'Wonder Child' and the 'Marvel of our Century'. She was five when she came to the attention of Louis XIV, who arranged for her to be educated by Mme. Montespan. Her education was completed by Mme. de Maintenon. She remained in Paris when the court moved to Versailles in 1682, but in 1685 her first theatrical work was performed in Louis's presence at the home of his eldest son. She dedicated many of her compositions to the king. In 1694 her *Cephale et Procris* was the first opera by a woman composer to be performed at the Academie Royale de Musique. After her husband's death in 1704, till 1717 she gave several public harpsichord recitals for which she became famous. Her music was greatly influenced by Italian sonatas and her cantatas were among the first to be published in France.

In 1713 she composed and performed for the Theatre de la Foire. On her death in 1729 a medal was struck in her honor. Elisabeth was the first major female composer of instrumental works. Her *Six sonatas for violin, basso continuo and viola da gamba* and *Sonate a violino* made use of double stopping for the first time in the history of written music. All of her compositions prior to 1691 were lost. DISCOGRAPHY. PHOTOGRAPH.

Compositions

CHAMBER

Six sonatas (2 vln, basso continuo and viola de gamba) (1695)
Trio sonate (vln, viola de gamba and basso continuo)
Six sonatas (vln and hpcd) (1707)
Pièces de clavecin, 14 pieces (ded King Louis XIV) (1687)
Pièces de clavecin qui se peuvent jouer sur le violon (1707)
Sonate a violino, solo e viola de gamba obligata con organo (1965)
Sonata in D (vln) (University of Pittsburgh Press)
Suites: A-Minor, D-Minor, F-Major, G-Minor (hpcd)

VOCAL

Cantatas mondaines (1715)
L'ile de Delos, cantata (1710) (ded Maximillian Emanuel, Elector of Bavaria) (Paris: P. Ribou)
La musette, ou Les bergers de Suresnes, pastoral cantata (1713)
Semele, cantata (1710) (ded Maximillian Emanuel) (Ribou)
Le someil d'Ulisse, cantata (1710) (ded Maximillian Emanuel) (Ribou)
Three books of cantatas (vce, basso continuo and opt sym insts)
Airs (1 or 2 vces)
Les amusements de Monseigneur le Duc de Bretagne, Le Dauphin (1712)
Aux vains Attraits d'une mouvelle ardeur, song (1710)
La ceinture de Venus, comic duet (1713)
Les jeux à l'honneur de la victoire (1693) (also ballet, 1685)

SACRED

Cantates françoises sur les subjects tirez de l'Ecriture, 2 vols incl. Esther; Judith; Samson; Susannem; Jacob et Rachel; Jonas; Le passage de la Mer Rouge (1708-1711) (Paris: Christopher Ballard)
Other cantatas
Te Deum à grand choeur (ch) (1721)

OPERA

Cephale et Procris, lyric tragedy (Christopher Ballard) (incl. inst intermezzos) (1694)
Raccammondement de Pierrot et de Nicole, comic duet stage piece (1708)

Publications

Elisabeth Jacquet de la Guerre: Pièces de Clavecin. Paris: P. Brunold, 1938.
Sonates de violon. 1707.
Three books of cantatas.

Bibliography

Bates, Carol H. *Elisabeth-Claude Jacquet de la Guerre: Les Pièces de Clavecin*.
Bates, Carol H. *The Instrumental Music of Elisabeth-Claude Jacquet de la Guerre: A Transcription with Commentary*. Indiana University, 1975.
Borroff, E. *An Introduction to Elisabeth-Claude Jacquet de la Guerre*. Institute of Mediaeval Music, Brooklyn, Musicological Studies, v. 12.
Brenet, M. *Quatre Femmes musiciennes*. L'Art 59 (1894).
Brunold, P. *Les Maitres françaises de clavecin*. Paris.
Laurencie, I. de la. *L'Ecole française de violon*. 1922.
Piro, A. *Les Clavecinistes*. 1925.

Ref. 2, 12, 14, 15, 17, 22, 26, 44, 51, 52, 65, 70, 100, 102, 105, 125, 128, 138, 140, 149, 177, 225, 226, 231, 276, 282, 347, 361, 391, 396, 404, 405, 415, 417, 476, 555, 563, 622, 637, 646, 653

LA HYE, Louise Genevieve (nee Rousseau) (pseud. Monsieur Leon Saint-Amans Fils)

French organist, pianist, singer, lecturer and composer. b. Charenton, March 8, 1810; d. Paris, November 17, 1838. She was the grand-niece of Jean-Jacques Rousseau. She first studied under her father, Charles Louis Rousseau and then under Saint-Amans. She entered the Paris Conservatoire in 1821 at the age of 11 and studied the organ, the piano and singing. She received an honorable mention for voice in 1825, a second prize for the organ in 1826 and first prize in 1827. She taught harmony at the conservatory on Cherubini's recommendation in 1831. She played her *Fantasia* at the Sociètè des Concerts at the conservatory in 1831 and in 1835 gave a concert at the Hotel-de-Ville, introducing the dramatic opera *Le songe de la religieuse*. Poor health interrupted her career and she died at the age of 28.

Compositions

ORCHESTRA

Fantasia (org and orch) (1831)

CHAMBER

Piano solos with string accompaniment
Variations for piano with string quartet accompaniment
Duos on a motif from Robin Hood (pf and hn)
Twenty pieces (org and pf)
Le muette de Potici, variations on an air (pf) (under pseud)

VOCAL

Collection of six Italian songs
Other songs

SACRED

Several masses

OPERA

Le songe de la religieuse

Publications

Les Deux Justices. La Gazette des Salons. Novelette.
J'ai vue. La Gazette des Salons. Novelette.
Methode d'orgue expressif.
Treatise on Harmony and Counterpoint.
Une methode et des etudes de piano.

Ref. 50, 70, 105, 129, 226, 276, 431

LA MAINA

16th-century Italian composer at the court of Ludovico the Moor in Milan. She composed madrigals and motets.
Ref. 502

LA PEREGO

16th-century Italian composer of Milan. She composed madrigals and motets.
Ref. 502

LA PIERRE, Mme.

17th-century French composer. She composed harpsichord pieces ca. 1680.
Ref. Otto Harrassowitz (Wiesbaden)

LA ROCHE, Rosa

Late 18th-century French harpsichordist, pianist and composer.

Compositions

ORCHESTRA

Piano concerto (Paris: Benout)
Sonatas (pf and orch) (Benout)

Ref. 50, 128, 226, 276, 347

LA ROMANINA. See ARCHILEI, Vittoria

LA VALLE, Deanna

20th-century American composer. DISCOGRAPHY.

Composition

PIANO

Piece (1971)

Ref. 563

LABAULT, Pauline Thys. See THYS, Pauline

LABEY, Charlotte Sohy

French organist and composer. b. Paris, July 12, 1887; d. Paris, December 19, 1956. She studied harmony under George Marty, the organ under Guilmand and Vierne and composition and counterpoint under d'Indy. Three of her works were produced by the Société Nationale.

Compositions

ORCHESTRA

Symphony (1916)
Sinfonia in C-Sharp Major (1916)

CHAMBER

Two string quartets
Petite suite (vln, vlc and pf) (Senart)
Two trios (vln, vlc and pf)
Sonata (vln and pf) (1910) (Senart)
Thème varié (vln and pf) (1922) (Senart)

PIANO

Sonata (1910) (Senart; Rouart; Lerolle)
Other pieces

VOCAL

Poème (vce, ch and orch) (1912)

SACRED
Three masses
OPERA
Astrid, lyrical drama in 3 acts (from Scandinavian legend of Selma Lagerlof)
L'Esclave, lyrical drama (1917-1920)
Ref. 41, 70, 95, 105

LABORI, Marguerite. See OKEY, Maggie

LACERDA, Bernarda Ferreira de (Perreira de Lacerda) (Heroina)

Portuguese noblewoman, poetess, writer and composer. b. Porto, 1595; d. October 1, 1644. She was a prodigy praised by famous authors of her time. She studied philosophy, history and mathematics, was a fine linguist and miniaturist and played musical instruments. She was asked by Phillip II of Spain to educate his children but she declined the offer in order to study. Her vocal compositions are preserved in manuscript at the Royal Library of Madrid.

Publications
Cazador del Cielo.
Hespanha libertada. 2 vols. 1673.
Soledades do Buçaco. Lyrical poem. 1634.
Ref. 226, 232, 268, 276, 338, 465

LACHANTERIE (Lechantre), Elisabeth

18th-century French harpsichordist, organist and composer. She studied under Couperin. She lived in Paris and in 1770 became organist at the Church of Saint-Jacques de la Boucherie.

Compositions
CHAMBER
Two concertos, op. 1 (hpcd or pf with 2 vln and 2 ob)
Ref. 50, 129, 226, 347

LACHARTRE, Nicole Marie

French electronic instrumentalist, musicologist, writer and composer. b. Paris, February 27, 1934. She studied at the Paris Conservatoire where she received first prizes for counterpoint and fugue. She studied composition under Milhaud in 1961 and Andre Jolivet, 1966 to 1968. Her other teachers were P. Schaeffer and J. Rivier (musique concrete) and P. Barband. Later she studied composition by computer under Xenakis and Barbaud. She worked on electronic music with the Groupe de Recherches Musicales of ORTF from 1966 to 1968 and was in charge of research from 1970 to 1973. She was a member of the French Committee of the International Society for Contemporary Music. She wrote several reviews and articles for Grove's Dictionary of Music and Musicians and for the Encyclopaedia Universalis. Many of her compositions are inspired by the works of mystic thinkers and spiritual experiences. Her works have been performed in Europe and the United States. PHOTOGRAPH.

Compositions
BAND
Hommage à Ruysbroeck (1979)
CHAMBER
Music of musicians interrupted by the repetitive words of Kohelet-Ecclesiastes, 5 versions (ww and hpcd; brass qnt; vocal qrt and pf; str qrt and org; and 4 groups together) (1972)
Ana'al Haqq (wind qnt) (1976)
Quintet (cl and strs) (1965)
Sonata (vla and pf) (1964)
Three movements (vln and pf) (1966)
Dix presentations musicales du nom d'Herman Sabbe (fl) (1978)
Pottcho, Nos. 1 and 2 (fl) (1981)
Sonata (pf)
VOCAL
Sonorous textures for the book of 4999 characters (4 solos, m-ch, w-ch, mix-ch and orch) (1969)
Nidaa (B and 3 str gtr) (1975)
ELECTRONIC
Essai I (S, cl, ob and ondes Martenot) (1968)
Essai II (hp, hpcd, gtr and zarb) (1968)
Mundus imaginables (1970)
Mundus sensibilis (1970-1972)
Mundus intellectualis (1973)
Mordre la terre vivante (1973)
Notes for ten musicians (1968)
Piece (ondes Martenot and hp) (1970)
Resonance et paradoxe (ondes Martenot, pf and perc) (1971)
Suicide cosmique (1970)
Suite (vce, ondes Martenot and zarb) (1968)
Transmutation (1968)
Ultimes (ondes Martenot and magnetic band) (1970)

Publications
Les musiques artificielles. Diagrammes du Monde, no. 146. April 1969.
Reviews and articles for Grove's Dictionary of Music and Musicians and the Encyclopaedia Universalis.
Ref. composer, 461, 622

LACHOWSKA, Stefania

Polish pianist, editor, teacher and composer. b. Lvov, August 20, 1898; d. Krakow, May 24, 1966. She studied at the Conservatory of the Music Society in Lvov under J. Lalewicz (piano) and W. Friedmann (composition). She continued her composition studies at the State Music Conservatory in Warsaw under K. Sikorski and received her diploma in 1934. She also studied privately under Karol Szymanowski. From 1924 to 1951 she taught music theory in schools in Krakow and from 1946 to 1958 she was editor with the Polskie Wydawnictwo Muzyczne in Krakow.

Compositions
ORCHESTRA
Variations (pf and orch) (1960)
Concert overture (1956)
Concertino (pf and str orch) (1953)
Dance suite (str orch) (1949)
Overture (1957)
Sinfonietta (1955)
Symphonic music (1958)
CHAMBER
String octet (1951)
String quartet (1947)
Zamkniety krag (vln, vla, vlc and pf) (1962)
Malowanki ludowi (vln, vlc and pf)
Suite (fl, cl and bsn) (1964)
Five characteristic pieces (cl and pf) (1963)
Lyrics (cl and pf) (PWM)
Sonatina (cl and pf) (PWM, 1963)
Ten miniatures (2 vln) (PWM, 1962)
Duets (trp)
PIANO
Music (1959)
Short pieces for children (1946)
Sonatina No. 1 (1953)
Sonatina No. 2 (1956)
Sonatina No. 3 (1961)
Toccata (1957)
Triptique (1952)
Variations (1957)
Polonaises
Six preludes (PWM, 1960)
VOCAL
Kochanie, kochanie (O. Kolberg) (S and orch)
Silesian suite (Kolberg) (S and str orch) (1949)
Skowroneczek spiewa (Kolberg) (w-ch and orch)
Three songs (Kolberg) (S, ch and orch) (1953)
Nie dlalego spiewam (Kolberg) (mix-ch)
Plakala dziewczyna (mix-ch)
Arrangements of folk songs (mix-ch)
Two Kurpie songs
Two Kaszub songs
Ref. 52, 70, 94, 118

LACKMAN, Susan C. Cohn

American pianist, poetess, teacher and composer. b. Tsing Tao, China, July 1, 1948. She began piano lessons at the age of three, composing her first work at the age of eight and from 12 she taught the piano. She graduated from Temple University, Philadelphia in 1970 with a B.M. (piano and voice). From the American University in Washington, DC, she earned an M.A. (composition and theory) in 1971. In 1979 she gained a Ph.D. from Rutgers University. She taught theory in public schools and universities. She became a fellow of Wolf Trap Composer's Forum, 1971. She holds the sword of honor from Sigma Alpha Iota International Music Fraternity and is a member of the Pi Kappa Lambda Music Society.

Compositions
ORCHESTRA
Chamber symphony No. 1
CHAMBER
Woodwind quintet
Brass quintet
String quartet No. 1 (1976)
String quartet No. 2 (1977)
String trio (vln, vla and vlc)
Dinner music (brass trio)
Fragments (fl, vlc and pf)
Game of cards (d-b, pf and perc)

PIANO
Fits
Five little pieces
Rondo
Three characters
VOCAL
Chanson des escargots (mix-ch and pf)
Omen of victory (m-S, fl, ob, cl and vlc)
SACRED
Wedding song
OPERA
Lisa Stratos
ELECTRONIC
Four love songs (Moog syn on tape)
Publications
I Held Out. New Poetry. Palmer Press, 1971.
Music Educators Journal. Book reviews on music theory, composition and general music.
Musicians Are So Insular. Music Journal, July 1974.
Premiere Reactions to Carmen. Opera Journal, Winter 1978.
Woodwind. Primary reviewer of classical and avant-garde concerts and records for arts newspaper in Washington, DC.
Ref. composer, Working papers of Women in Music, 474, 625

LACMANOVA (Latzmannova), Anna
Czech pianist, teacher and composer. b. April 8, 1875; d. Ostroh, April 8, 1930. She attended the music academy in Kromeriz from 1889 to 1891 before going to the Cimrova Music Academy and the conservatory in Prague, 1895 to 1897. She studied the piano under J. Jiranek and took the state examination in 1904. She studied composition under F. Spilka. She taught the piano in Ostroh. Her first compositions appeared in 1905.
Compositions
PIANO
Ciganske tance
Polkas
Romance
Scherzo
Three etudes
Waltzes
VOCAL
Padejte listkya (mix-ch) (1933)
Pisen rolnicka (mix-ch) (1913)
Pozary (mix-ch)
Five songs (mix-ch) (1913)
Fifty songs (V. Halek, J. Vrchlicki, J.V. Sladek, A. Heyduk. H. Longfellow)
Ref. 197

LADEN, Bernice F.
20th-century American composer.
Compositions
VOCAL
Three songs (vce and fl) (1983)
Ref. AMC newsletter

LADY. See HUNTER, Anne

LADY ALMUCS OF LUBERON. See ALMUCS DE CASTELNAU

LAFLEUR, Lucienne (Sister M. Therese-de-la-Saint-Face)
Canadian organist, pianist, teacher and composer. b. Ste. Agatha-des-Monts, Quebec, February 8. 1904. She studied composition, the piano, the organ and voice under Claude Champagne, Alfred Lamoureux, Jean Charbonneau and Auguste Descarries. She obtained the Laureat de l'Institut Musical, her B.Mus. and licentiate from Montreal University. She taught at the Ecole Superieure de Musique d'Outremont.
Compositions
PIANO
Fifteen pieces
VOCAL
A ma mère-à mon père (1945)
Berceuse (1944) (Archambault)
Bluette, Noël (1949)
Bonjour Noël (1936) (Archambault)
Le matin (1944)
Petits oiseaux (1949)
Pinson chanteur (1945)
Le rouet du bonheur (1945)
SACRED
Les cloches du pays natal, cantata (ch and pf) (1948)
Gloire à ton institut, cantata (ch and pf) (1946) (Archambault)
Hymne à Sainte-Anne cantata (ch and org) (1946) (Archambault)
Jublie d'argent, cantata (ch and pf) (1947)
Mai, cantata (ch and pf) (1948)
Pais mes agneux! cantata (ch and pf) (1948)
A nos saints matyrs canadiens (ch and org) (1948)
A Sainte-Anne (ch and org) (1949)
Au coeur immacule de M. (ch and org) (1949)
Chant de ralliement (ch and pf) (1947)
Mon offertoire (ch and org) (1949)
O ma céleste mère (ch and org) (1949)
Offertoire in D (ch and org) (1947)
Par la main d'une femme une lampe s'allume! (ch and pf) (1949)
Par Lui, avec Lui, en Lui (ch and org) (1949)
Trois saluts du T.S. Sacrement (No. 1: Archambault)
Ref. 133

LAGIER, Suzanne
French composer. b. ca. 1835.
Composition
OPERA
Jupiter et Leda
Ref. 307

LAGO (nee Pistolekors) (pseud. of Laura Netzel)
Swedish concert pianist, singer and composer. b. Finland, March 1839; d. March 10, 1927. She went to Sweden at the age of one year. She studied the piano under the German teacher Gisiko and Anton Door in Vienna. She studied singing under Professor Julius Guenther and composition under W. Heintze and C. Vidor in Paris. She made her debut as a pianist in 1836 in Stockholm and thereafter made numerous chamber and soirée appearances. Her first compositions, a-capella choruses for women's voices, published in 1874, were widely acclaimed and she then dedicated herself to composing rather than playing. Between 1894 and 1907 she organised many concerts for workers in Stockholm, for which she became well known.
Compositions
ORCHESTRA
Piano concerto (also 2 pf)
CHAMBER
Preludio e fughetta, op. 68 (vln, vlc and pf) (Paris: A. Noel, 1900)
Serenade, op. 50 (vln, vlc and pf) (Berlin: Simrock, 1895)
Trio in D-Minor, op. 78 (vln, vlc and pf) (Lyon, 1903)
Andante religioso, op. 48 (vln and pf) (Simrock)
Berceuse et tarantelle, op. 28 (vln and pf)
Berceuse, op. 59 (vln and pf) (Simrock, 1896)
Berceuse, op. 69 (vln or fl and pf) (Lyon)
Chanson slave, op. 53 (vln and pf) (Simrock)
Danse hongroise, op. 51 (vlc and pf) (Warmuth)
Gondoliera, op. 60 (vln and pf) (Simrock)
Romance, op. 40 (vln and pf) (Simrock)
Sonate, op. 66 (vlc and pf) (Simrock) (1899)
Suite op. 33 (fl and pf)
Suite, op. 62 (vln and pf) (a-moll) (Simrock)
Tarantelle, op. 33 (vln and pf) (Simrock)
Prelude et fughetta, op. 87 (org) (Lyon)
Cello pieces
Violin pieces
PIANO
Deux etudes de concert, op. 52: 1. Fileuse 2. Inquietude (Simrock, 1895)
Feu follet. Etude de concert, op. 49 (Warmuth)
Humoresker, op. 26 (Lundguist, 1889)
Menuet, op. 48 (Copenhagen: Hansen)
Sonate, op. 27 (Paris, Hamelle)
Three salon pieces: Prelude; Etude; Scherzoso; op. 24 (Warmuth)
VOCAL
Cantata (vce, double ch and hp; also 2 pf) (1st prize, Copenhagen, 1895)
Cantata (vce, ch and org)
Ballad (ch and orch)
Ballade, op. 35 (E. Bogh) (vce and pf)
Blomman (Runeburg) (vce and pf) (Hirsch, 1887)
Colibri (vce and pf)
Edelweiss (Snoilsky) (vce and pf)
Ett barns aftonboen (vce and pf)
Fjaeriln (vce and pf) (Lundquist, 1884)
Four songs, op. 36 (pf) (Warmuth, 1888)
Four French songs, op. 46 (m-S or B and pf) (Warmuth)

Kennst du am Rhein die Glocken mit ihrem tiefen Klang, op. 75 (Cont or Bar and pf)
Swedish and French songs
Three duets, op. 39 (w-vces and pf) (1889)
Three German songs, op. 44 (pf)
Three songs for Augusta Oehstrom (vce and pf) (1889)
Three songs, op. 47 (vce and pf) (Warmuth)
Three trios (w-vces and pf) (ded Mme. L. Heritte Viardot) (1889)
Till en fagel (Runeberg) (vce and pf)
Two songs, op. 20 (vln and pf) (1888)
Voici la brise, op. 55 (Zari) (vce and pf)
Choruses
SACRED
Ave Maria, op. 41 (vce and org or pf) (Warmuth)
David's 146th Psalm (ch and org)
Kyrkoaira (vce and org or pf) (Lundquist, 1884)
Stabat Mater (soloists, ch and orch or org)
Ref. 95, 226, 276, 297, 642

LAIGHTON, Ruth
19th-century American composer. She composed chamber music.
Ref. 347

LAITMAN, Lori
American flautist, teacher and composer. b. Long Beach, January 12, 1955. She obtained a B.A. (music) magna cum laude from Yale College in 1975 and an M.A. in 1976. She taught music at Buxton School, Williamstown from 1976 to 1977 and the flute in New York schools until 1980. She was a flautist with the VT Symphony in 1977. She is a member of the League of Women Composers and the American Federation of Musicians. Her main interest is writing for films and the theater.
Compositions
ORCHESTRA
Catabais (cham orch) (comm Drew University Consort, 1977)
CHAMBER
Suite for flute, harp and cello (1980)
Canons 1 and 2 (2 fl) (1974)
I wrote it last Saturday (2 fl) 91974)
VOCAL
Put out my eyes (w-ch) (1975)
THEATRE
The Taming of the Shrew (1980)
They dance real slow in Jackson (1982)
FILM MUSIC
Camera arts (Dick Roberts) (1980)
Illusions (D. Roberts) (1980)
One (Robert Just) (1978)
Popular photography (D. Roberts) (1981)
Psychology today (D. Roberts) (1979)
The two knights (John Gati) (1977)
Ref. composer, 625

LAJEUNESSE, Emma, Dame (Albani) (Marie Louise Cecile)
Canadian pianist, operatic soprano, singing teacher and composer. b. Chambly, Quebec, November 1, 1847; d. London, April 3, 1930. She was the daughter of a French Canadian professor of the harp. She studied at the Couvent du Sacre-Coeur, Montreal and then went to Paris, where she studied singing under Duprez. She also studied in Milan under Lamperti. She made her singing debut as Anina in Bellini's *Sonnambula* in Milan, 1870. She sang lead roles in several operas in Europe, the United States and Canada. She also toured India, Australia and South Africa. In 1911 she stopped performing publicly and devoted herself to teaching the Lamperti singing method. She was made a Dame of the British Empire in June, 1925.
Compositions
CHAMBER
Variations on Tis the last rose of summer (hp) (ca. 1864)
PIANO
Grand duett, on themes from Sabatier's cantata (2 pf) (ca. 1860)
Grande marche triomphale (ca. 1860)
Grand fantasia on When this cruel war is over (before 1864)
SACRED
Hymn to Pius IX (solo and ch) (ca. 1860)
And must these states now sever (ca. 1864)
Les martyrs (ca. 1860)
O salutaris (ca. 1867) (New York: Hallenson)
Travail de reconnaissance (ca. 1860)
Publications
Forty Years of Song. Memoirs of Emma Albani. London, 1911.
Bibliography
Charbonneau, Helene. *L'Albani*. Biography. Montreal, 1938.
Ref. 8, 133, 347

LAKE, Bonnie
20th-century American composer. b. Waterloo, IA. She composed music for television, films and nightclubs.
Ref. 40, 347

LALAIN, Luc. See DANEAU, Suzanne

LALAUNI, Lila
French concert pianist and composer. b. Athens, Greece, June 9, 1918. She became a French citizen in 1952. She was born into a family of musicians and studied music in Vienna, Berlin and Paris. She studied the piano under Arthur Schnabel and composition under Marcel Dupre. She made her debut as a pianist at the age of ten, playing Beethoven's *First piano concerto* with the Vienna Philharmonic Orchestra at the Grosser Konzerthaussaal. She performed in Paris, London, Athens, Israel, Yugoslavia and Belgium. PHOTOGRAPH.
Compositions
ORCHESTRA
Symphony No. 1
Two piano concertos
CHAMBER
Four Greek dances (fl and pf)
Three impromtus (fl and pf) (1982)
PIANO
Sonata (1980)
Other pieces
VOCAL
Lieder (Goethe, Heine)
Three Lieder
ARRANGEMENTS
Cycle of Lieder (Richard Strauss)
Ref. composer, 44, 96

LAM MAN LEE, Violet
20th-century composer of Hong Kong.
Compositions
ORCHESTRA
Leng die
CHAMBER
Tieh meng (gtr and perc)
FILM MUSIC
The secret (1979)
Ref. 497

LAMB, Myrna
Composition
OPERA
Mother Run

LAMBELET, Vivienne Ada Maurice
20th-century English singer and composer. b. London. She studied at the Royal Academy of Music and in Brussels. She won a scholarship for composition at Trinity College.
Compositions
ORCHESTRA
Spanish intermezzo
VOCAL
Songs incl.:
Cavalier
Daffodil-dell
Derry down
Faint-heart
Idyll
King's messenger
Litany
Yesterday's roses
MISCELLANEOUS
Dance tunes incl.:
Searching the world for love
Straws in my hair
Wonder where the blackbird went
You-fever
Ref. 467

LAMBERT, Agnes

English composer. b. 1860.

Compositions

ORCHESTRA

Valse dorée (Lambert)

PIANO

Bataille des fleurs à Alger, schottische (Bovard)
Marche joyeuse (Lambert)
Neris-les-Bains, valse (Lambert)
Valse des flots (Bovard)
Valse-impromptu (Schirmer)

VOCAL

J'aime les fleurs du printemps (Labbe)
Voila la vie (Lambert)

Ref. 41, 226, 297

LAMBERT, Catherine. See MOSEL, Catherine de

LAMBERT, Cecily

American composer. b. 1915. She later resided in England.

Compositions

CHAMBER

Quartettino, little string quartet (1955) (Market)
Acrobats (vln and pf)
The fisher's horn pipe (vln and pf; also 2 pf)
Rhumba rhythm (vln and pf)
Sonata-fantasy (vln and pf) (Market)

PIANO

Elegy for the drowned
Island pieces: White sails flying; Harbour nocturne; Rooks and sea
Pieces of eight, suite: Cubana, Pastorale; Toccata and finale
Sonata

VOCAL

The devotee (S and keyboard)
Everyone sang (vce and keyboard)
Golden song (S and keyboard)
Home thoughts (B and pf)
Lullaby (vce and pf)
Spring thunder (vce and keyboard)
The summons (S and keyboard)
Sussex summer (vce and keyboard)

Ref. 40, 190, 142, 477

LAMBERT, Mrs. Arthur W. See FARMER, Emily Bardsley

LAMBRECHTS-VOS, Anna Catharina

Dutch organist and composer. b. Rotterdam, June 29, 1876; d. Rotterdam, January 16, 1932. She studied under Schravesandre and Johan Sikemeyer in Rotterdam and later under Bernard Zweers. She then served as organist for the Doopsgezinde church in that city. She received a prize for her *String quartet in C-Minor* in a competition in Trieste.

Compositions

ORCHESTRA

Various works

CHAMBER

String quartet in A-Minor, op. 7, In memoriam parentum (Harmonie)
String quartet in C-Minor, A celui qui m'a sauve la vie
Sonata in F-Sharp Major, op. 9 (vln and pf) (Harmonie)
Suite, op. 5. Nie welkende knoesplein (vln and pf)

VOCAL

Feestzang, cantata (w-ch)
Levensblijheid, cantata (w-ch)
Huwelijkszang (w-ch)
Dingaansdag (J.F. Celliers)
Groot Suid-Afrika, 21 lieder (Transvaal poems) (vce and pf) (1952)

SACRED

Lente-cantate (chil-ch)
Two Christmas cantatas (w-ch)

Ref. 26, 41, 44, 70, 105, 110, 226, 377

LAMEGO, Carlinda J.

Brazilian pianist, poetess, teacher and composer. b. May 20, 1910. She studied the piano under Professor de Vasconcellos, teaching theory under Oscar Lourenzo Fernandez and harmony, counterpoint and fugue under Professor Paulo Silva who persuaded her to compose. In 1959 she won first place in the course 'Language of Music' at the Conservatorio Nacional de Canto Orfeonico. She was active in the teaching of music to young children. Her poems won prizes in Brazil and Portugal. DISCOGRAPHY. PHOTOGRAPH.

Compositions

CHAMBER

Prece (vln and pf) (1965)

PIANO

Ponteio (1 or 2 pf) (1964)
Pequeña valsa (1 or 2 pf) (1965)
Barcarola (1961)
Four preludes (1962, 1963, 1963, 1964)

VOCAL

Trovas (composer) (3 part ch) (1965)
A saudade de voce (Luiz Otavio) (med or high vce and pf) (1966)
Acaso (composer) (med or high vce and pf) (1967)
Andorinha (Manoel Bandeira) (med or high vce and pf) (1972)
Estrela do ceu (Luiz Otavio) (med-vce and pf) (1959)
Eu quero crer (composer) (med or high vce and pf) (1970)
O bem de te querer (composer) (med-vce and pf) (1959)
Se o lobisomen falasse (composer) (med or high vce and pf) (1975)
Songs (Brazilian poets)
Teu nome (composer) (med or high vce and pf) (1972)
Children's songs

SACRED

Noite de Natal (composer) (mix-ch and pf) (1960)
Pão de cada dia (composer) (mix-ch and org) (1975)
Hymns

Ref. composer

LAMSON, Georgie

19th-century American composer.

Compositions

VOCAL

Songs incl.:
Only my love
Twilight town

Ref. 276, 292, 347

LANDOWSKA, Wanda

Polish harpsichordist, pianist, teacher, writer and composer. b. Warsaw, July 5, 1879; d. Lakeville, CT, August 16, 1959. She had her first piano lessons from J. Kleczynski and then studied at the Warsaw Conservatory under A. Michalowski. In 1896 she went to Berlin and studied composition under H. Urban for four years. In 1900 she moved to Paris and married Henry Lew, a writer and expert on Hebrew folklore. She devoted herself to the study of music of the past and the revival of the harpsichord. She took part in concerts organized by the Schola Cantorum and although she was well established as a pianist, she decided to concentrate on the harpsichord. She gave concerts and did much to revive interest in old music. From 1913 to 1919 she gave classes in the harpsichord at the Berlin Royal School of Music and thereafter held master classes in Basle and Paris. In Saint-Leu-la-Foret she founded the Ecole de Musique Ancienne, where she kept her collection of old instruments and gave concerts and lessons. She had a library of more than 10,000 volumes but was forced to leave the school with the arrival of the Nazis in Paris in 1940. She fled to the United States and continued her work there. The modern harpsichord was built by Pleyel to her specifications. DISCOGRAPHY.

Compositions

ORCHESTRA

Fanfare de la Liberation (military orch)
Poème hebreu
Serenata (str orch)
Other works (str orch)

CHAMBER

Bourrées d'Auvergne (hpcd)

PIANO

Variations (2 pf)
Follette
Petite sonata
Querelle
Rhapsodie orientale
Many other pieces

VOCAL

Choir (w-ch and orch)
Piece (w-ch and orch)
Polish popular songs (vce, ww, hpcd and strs; also ch a-cap)
The hop, wedding folk song
More than 100 songs

ARRANGEMENTS

Cadenzas for some of Mozart's piano concertos and Haydn's Concerto in D-Major (pf)

Publications

A Propos du 25e anniversaire de la Société Bach. Guide Musical. 1930.
Les Allemands et la musique française au 18e siècle. Mercure de France. 1911.
Chopin et l'ancienne musique française. Rev. Mus. December 1, 1931.

Comment faut-il interpreter les inventions de J.S. Bach? Monde Musical. July 1921.
Le concerto en mi bemol majeur de Mozart. Tribune de Geneve. January 7-8, 1923.
En vue de quel instrument Bach.... Rev. Mus. December 1, 1927.
Handel, Bach, Scarlatti. L'Art Musical. December 25, 1936.
Les influences françaises chez Bach. Courrier Musical, July 15, 1912.
L'interpretation de Chopin. Courrier Musical. January 1, 1910. Lettre d'Astrahan. 1910.
La musique ancienne. Courrier Musical. January 1, 1910.
La musique d'aujourd'hui. Revue Contemporaine. October 1, 1923.
La nationalite de Chopin. Monde Musical. April 30, 1911.
Note on a Great Neapolitan. New York Times. October 24, 1943.
A Note on Bach. New York Times. February 15, 1942.
Strings Plucked and Struck. New York Herald Tribune. February 28, 1943.
Les suites de clavecin de Handel. Radio Magazine. January 3-10, 1937.
Sur l'interpretation de la musique à deux voix de J.S. Bach. Guide Musical. April 1936.
Sur l'interpretation des oeuvres de clavecin de J.S. Bach. Mercure de France. November 15, 1905

Bibliography

Bittner, C. *Erinnerung an eine epochale Frau Wanda Landowska.* Musica. 1970.
Dufourg, N. *Le Clavecin (Que sais-je).* Paris, 1929.
Dumesnil, R. *Wanda Landowska et les dimanches de Saint-Leu-La-Foret.* La Scala, 1960.
Gavoty, B., and Hauert, R. *Wanda Landowska.* Geneva, 1956.
Schaeffner, A. *Wanda Landowska et le retour aux humanites de la musique.* Rivista Musicale, 1927.

Ref. 8, 9, 14, 15, 17, 22, 44, 70, 74, 94, 96, 100, 105, 107, 118, 135, 201, 226, 330, 347, 361, 433, 563

LANDREE, Jaquenote Goldsteen

American harpist, organist, pianist and composer. b. Stoughton, WI, July 5, 1885. She was a pupil of Caroline Eggleston Sharer, Georgie Martin, Emma Wilkins Gutman, George Enzinger, Ottmar Moll and Wilhelmina Lowe Speyer. She was the organist at several churches and composed organ pieces and songs.

Ref. 460

LANE, Elizabeth

English composer. b. 1964. She began to compose at the age of six. When she was 14 her *Sinfonietta for strings* was premiered by the Royal Philharmonic Orchestra, conducted by Arthur Davison and televised.

Compositions

ORCHESTRA
Sinfonietta for strings (1978)
CHAMBER
Soliloquy (d-b)
VOCAL
Two songs for an occasion (ch) (1981)
SACRED
Magnificat, Nunc dimittis
Psalm 98 (ch a-cap)
Psalm 148 (treble vces and org)

Ref. R. Dearling (Spalding, UK)

LANG, Edith

20th-century American organist, teacher and composer. She studied in Germany and became a church organist at the age of 16.

Compositions

VOCAL
A merry roundelay (w-ch and pf) (Boston Music)
East Indian lullaby (Boston)
Lord, Who through these forty days (duet) (Boston)
ORGAN
Meditation (prelude religieux) (org) (Boston)

Ref. 40, 142, 226

LANG, Josephine (Koestlin)

German pianist, singer, teacher and composer. b. Munich, March 14, 1815; d. Tuebingen, December 2, 1880. The daughter of a Munich court violinist and a singer, Regina Hitzelberger, whom both Louis XVI and Napoleon had tried unsuccessfully to bring to Paris, she showed her musical talent at an early age. She learned to sing and to play the piano from her mother and later from Fraeulein Berlinghof. When she was 15, the 21-year-old Mendelssohn heard her play and sing her own songs and was profoundly impressed by her charm, personality, delicacy and musical gifts. He wrote to friends that he had never heard anyone so gifted at composing and singing songs. A year later, on his return from Italy, he gave her free daily lessons in fugue and theoretical subjects. Among her friends were Ferdinand Hiller, Chopin, Vieuxtemps, Cramer, Clara Schumann (q.v.) and later Brahms, but the music of Mendelssohn remained her ideal. In 1835 she was made a church singer in the royal chapel and in 1840 became a royal court singer. At this time she met her future husband, Christian Rhenhold Koestlin, a lawyer and poet and about the time of her engagement to him, between July 6 and August 12, 1840, she composed no less than 41 songs, some of which she dedicated to Mendelssohn. His immediate response was to write to Koestlin, imploring him not to let marriage interfere with her composing. Nevertheless the birth of her six children and her husband's illness kept her from composing much until his death in 1856, when she resumed teaching and composing. By this time however, the prime of the romantic songs was approaching its end and other German women composers such as Clara Schumann (q.v.), Johanna Kinkel (q.v.) and Emilie Zumsteeg had ceased composing. Within a few years her son Felix died and also her friend, the poet Ludwig Uhland, who, more than her husband had encouraged her to compose. Soon Mendelssohn and two of her other sons also died. Her later sacred songs stem from her years of tragedy. DISCOGRAPHY.

Compositions

CHAMBER
Herz, mein Herz (vlc and pf) (Schlesinger)
PIANO
Apollo marsch (Ditson)
Basler Turnermarsch (Dupre)
Bummler-Marsch, op. 52 (Hoenes)
Dans infernale, op. 46 (Weimar: Kuehn)
Deutscher Siegesmarsch
Die schoene Alpnerin, mazurka, op. 44 (Voigt)
Elegie auf den Tod L. Uhlands, op. 31 (Zumsteeg)
Festmarsch, op. 31 (Ebner)
Fruehlingszauber, op. 52, waltz (Voigt)
Grand impromptu, op. 50 (In the twilight)
Hochzeitsmarsch, op. 42 (Ebner)
In der Daemmerung, op. 50
Lied ..., op. 44 (Ebner)
Maedchentraeume, concert waltz, op. 34 (Voigt)
Rheingolder Schuetzenmarsch (Dupre)
Rosengefluester, gavotte, op. 38 (Voigt)
Touristen-Marsch, op. 33 (Voigt)
Two mazurkas, op. 49
Zwei Charakterstuecke (Zumsteeg)
Zwei Lieder ohne Worte, op. 35
VOCAL
Abschied
Ach, wenn du waerst wie mein eigen (Platen)
Am Morgen
An die Entfernte
Du denkst an mich so selten (Platen)
Fruehes Sterben (Heine)
Fruehlingsahnung
Fruehlingsgedraenge
Lieder der Jahreszeiten
Lieder des Leids, op. 19 (Zeler)
O sehntest du dich so nach mir
Saengers lust
Scheideblick
Schilflied (Lenau)
Sie liebt mich
Sprache der Liebe (Platen)
Traumbild
Der Trompeter von Saechingen, verse-epic (Viktor von Scheffel)
Wehe, so willst du wieder (Platen)
Wie glanzt so heil dein Auge
Numerous Lieder

Ref. 8, 15, 17, 74, 79, 102, 105, 107, 200, 204, 226, 264, 297, 400, 433, 476, 563, 622, 653

LANG, Margaret Ruthven

American pianist, violinist and composer. b. Boston, November 27, 1867; d. Boston, May 29, 1972. The most long lived of all women composers, she died at the age of 105. She was the daughter of Benjamin J. Lang, a noted Boston musician amd composer. She studied the piano under her father and then P. Scharwenka. Later she studied composition in Munich under Drechsler, Abel and Victor Gluth, 1886 to 1897. She returned to America and continued her violin studies under Chadwick, MacDowell, Louis Schmidt, Paine and J. Parker. She stopped composing in 1930. She was the first woman to have a work performed by an American orchestra. This was the *Dramatic Overture* which was played by the Boston Symphony Orchestra and conducted by Artur Nikisch on April 7, 1893. DISCOGRAPHY.

Compositions
ORCHESTRA
Ballade (1901)
Dramatic overture in E-Minor, op. 12 (1893)
Tatila, op. 23, overture (1901)
Witichis, op. 10, overture (1893)
CHAMBER
Quintet, in 1 mvt (pf and strs) (1879)
String quartet
PIANO
Meditation, op. 26 (Boston: A.P. Schmidt, 1897)
Petit roman pour le piano en six chapitres, op. 18 (Schmidt, 1894)
Revery, op. 31 (J. Church, 1899)
Rhapsody in E-Minor, op. 21 (Schmidt, 1895)
A spring idyll, op. 33 (Church, 1889)
Springtime, op. 30 (1889)
Starlight (Boston: J.B. Millet, 1894)
Twilight (Millet, 1894)
VOCAL
The Jumblies, cantata (B, m-ch and 2 pf) (Schmidt, 1890)
Phoebus, cantata (B, ch and orch)
The wild huntsman, cantata
Armida (vce and orch) (1896)
Sappho's prayer to Aphrodite (vce and orch) (1895)
Wind (double mix-ch a-cap)
Alistair MacAlistair (m-ch and pf) (Schmidt, 1901)
Boatman's hymn, op. 13 (m-ch and pf)
Bonnie ran the burnie down, op. 25 (mix-ch) (Schmidt, 1897)
Ghosts (w-ch and pf; also vce and pf) (Schmidt, 1889)
The lonely rose (w-ch and pf) (Schmidt, 1906)
Song of the three sisters (w-ch and pf) (Schmidt, 1906)
White butterflies (opt B, w-ch and pf) (Boston: C.C. Brichard, 1904)
The wild-brier (w-ch and pf) (Schmidt, 1909)
Approx. 200 songs incl.:
April weather, op. 15, no. 3 (Schmidt, 1893)
A bedtime story, op. 6, no. 2 (Schmidt)
Chimes, op. 54, no. 2 (Schmidt, 1915)
Day is gone, op. 40, no. 2 (Schmidt, 1904)
Eros (Schmidt, 1889)
The garden of roses, op. 15, no. 4 (Schmidt, 1893)
The harbor of dreams, op. 7, no. 3 (Schmidt, 1891)
In a garden (Schmidt, 1890)
Irish love song, op. 22
The king is dead (Schmidt, 1898)
Lydia (Church, 1899)
My true love (Schmidt, 1891)
Night, op. 7, no. 1 (Schmidt, 1891)
Out of the past, op. 37, no. 2 (Schmidt, 1901)
A poet gazes on the moon, op. 8, no. 3 (Schmidt, 1892)
Snow flakes (Schmidt, 1912)
A thought, op. 37, no. 1 (Schmidt, 1901)
SACRED
Grant, we beseech Thee, merciful Lord, op. 51 (mix-ch and org) (Schmidt, 1912)
The heavenly noël, op. 57 (m-S, w-ch and pf; also vces and cham ens) (Schmidt, 1916)
In praesepio, op. 56 (mix-ch or w-ch and org) (Schmidt, 1916)
Te Deum (mix-ch and pf) (Schmidt, 1899)
Christmas cycle (vce and gtr)

Bibliography
Hackett, Karleton. *Some American Songwriters. Negro Music Journal 1*, July 1903: 213-217.
Hughes, Rupert. *Women Composers. Century Magazines 55*. March, 1898.
Syford, Ethel. Margaret Ruthven Lang. *New England Magazine* XLVI/I, March 1912. 22-23.
Ref. 14, 17, 22, 23, 40, 44, 89, 94, 105, 226, 292, 297, 347, 415, 563, 622, 653, 646

LANG, Rosemary Rita

American clarinetist, cor anglais player, oboist, saxophonist, woodwind player, arranger, musician, teacher and composer. b. Weisburg, IN, April 29, 1920. She obtained her B.Mus. at the Jordan College of Music and her M.Mus. at Butler University, IN. She played the alto-saxophone, bass clarinet, clarinet, cor anglais, oboe and other woodwind intruments in the Indianapolis Symphony and other orchestras. She taught woodwind intruments and was the director of woodwind ensembles at the Jordan College of Music. She is a woodwind repair expert.

Compositions
CHAMBER
Opus in ebony (cl ch)
Rhapsody (cl ch)
Four pieces (ww qnt)
Chorale (fl qrt)
Humoreske (cl qrt)
Nocturne (cl qrt)
Scherzo (fl qrt)
Tarantelle (cl qrt)
Concert piece (b-cl)
TEACHING PIECES
For woodwind instruments
Ref. 457

LANG-BECK, Ivana

Yugoslav pianist, professor and composer. b. Zagreb, November 15, 1912; d. January 1982. She completed her piano studies at the Music Academy of Zagreb and in 1913 was made assistant to Professor Matz at the Academy where she later became a professor. From 1940 to 1943 she taught at the teachers' college in Zagreb and after 1943 taught the piano at the Vatroslav Lisinski Music Academy there. She attended lectures in theoretical subjects given by Dr. Joseph Marx at the Mozarteum in Salzburg, where some of her compositions were performed. Her works were also performed in Hamburg, Strasbourg, Triest and the Soviet Union and on Yugoslav radio and televison. She devoted much time to the study of Istrian folk music, traces of which are to be found in most of her work. She taught the piano privately. PHOTOGRAPH.

Compositions
ORCHESTRA
Piano concerto (1956)
Four bagatelles (hp and str orch) (1974)
Groteska, op. 11 (1956)
Simfonijski ples, op. 33 (1950)
CHAMBER
Nokturno, op. 84 (vln, vlc and pf) (1974)
Impresije, op. 83, Ljeto-jesen-zima-proljece (Seasons) (hp and fl; also pf) (1973)
Narodna, op. 82 (vln and pf) (1973)
Ples sablasti, op. 6 (vlc and pf) (1967)
HARP
Odisej i Sirene, op. 80 (1972)
Starinska vura, op. 104 (1982)
Tajanstvenim koracima, op. 101 (1982)
Toccatina, op. 77 (1972)
PIANO
Children's march, op. 81 (4 hands) (1973)
Luna park, op. 79 (4 hands) (1972)
Mali saroliki svijet, op. 61 (4 hands) (1969)
Perpetum mobile, op. 106 (4 hands) (1982)
Decimna etida, op. 103 (1982)
Four bagatelles, op. 59 (1962)
Four compositions, op. 50 (1959)
Galop, op. 69 (1968)
Istrian barcarole, op. 31 (1948)
Kvintna etida, op. 66 (1966)
Mali ivicin svijet, op. 59 (1962)
Melodrami, op. 21 (1942)
Na ladanju, op. 62, 3 miniatures (1963)
Nocturne, op. 7 (1942)
Nocturne, op. 29 (1947)
Octave etudes, op. 26 (1947)
Preludes and fugues, op. 43: F-Major; A-Major (1953)
Proljetne radosti, op. 63 (1963)
Ptičice, op. 73 (1970)
Rondino, op. 68 (1968)
Septimna etida, op. 71 (1969)
Sedam krokija, op. 56 (1961)
Six preludes, op. 42 (1952)
Sonatina, op. 24 (1947)
Sonatina, op. 70 (1969)
Suite in three movements, op. 13: Prelude; Intermezzo; Toccata (1942)
Three preludes, op. 25 (1947)
Three waltzes, op. 76 (1972)
Variations, op. 60 (1962)
Dvije minijature, op. 72 (left hand) (1969)
Solfeggietto, op. 74 (left hand) (1970)
VOCAL
Dvije vidricĕve (dramatic S and orch) (1947)
Grijeh, op. 3 (V. Vidric) (vce and orch or pf) (1940)
Jutro, op. 16 (V. Vidric) (vce and orch or pf) (1942)
Three Istrian songs (A and cham orch) (1947)
Slavoniji (A and orch) (1960)
Three Istrian songs, op. 27 (vce and cham ens or pf) (1947)
Five Russian songs, op. 51 (chil-ch) (1959)
Akuarel, op. 9 (N. Neugebauer) (vce and pf) (1942)
Bezimenoj, op. 75, cycle of 4 songs (V. Radaus) (1970)
Bilo vavek veselo, op. 41 (2 vces and pf) (1952)
Črna Maslina, op. 49, song cycle (Vesma Parun) (vce and pf) (1959)
Crni metuli, op. 18 (D. Domjanič) (vce and pf) (1942)

Cvete, op. 19 (D. Domjanič) (vce and pf) (1942)
Dve Domjaniceve, op. 17 (D. Domjanič): Jagode; Jabuke (vce and pf) (1942)
Dvije Istarske iz Pazina, op. 39 (2 vces and pf) (1952)
Dvije Istarske na brajsin zapis, op. 35 (2 vces and pf) (1950)
Durdic, op. 8 (A.G. Matos) (vce and pf) (1942)
Five Istrian songs, op. 32 (vce and pf) (1948) (2nd prize, contest of Radio Zagreb)
Kraj albus, op. 28 (vce and of) (1947)
Lan, op. 20 (D. Domjanič) (vce and pf) (1942)
Lisinskom, op. 65 (V. Radaus) (vce and pf) (1965)
Mak, op. 6 (D. Arnold) (vce and pf) (1940)
Maslinov Gaj, op. 107 (1982)
Mi, op. 47 (V. Nazor) (4 w-vces and pf) (1956)
Misli, op. 102 (vce and pf) (1982)
Murve, op. 1 (D. Domjanič) (vce and pf) (1940)
Neizreceno, op. 45 (N. Brlic) cycle (vce and pf) (1954)
Nepoznatim stazama, op. 54, cycle of 6 songs (F. Valzalo) (vce and pf) (1960)
Oblek gegubi v daljini, op. 2 (D. Domjanič) (vce and pf) (1940)
Otudeni san, op. 57, cycle of 4 songs (F. Valzalo) (vce and pf) (1962)
Plesne skice, op. 23 (vce and pf) (1946)
Prosula Seguncina, op. 85 (V. Radaus) (vce and pf) (1974)
Roblje, op. 105 (vce and pf) (1982)
Ruka bulesnog mladica, op. 12 (F. Alfirevic) (vce and pf) (1942)
Slaviniji, op. 55 (V. Radaus) (vce and pf) (1960)
Two Istrian songs, op. 30 (2 vces and pf) (1948)
Uspavanka, op. 4, (K. Ivoci) (vce and pf) (1942)
Utjeha kose, op. 4 (A. Matos) (vce and pf) (1940)
Vuz put, op. 14 (D. Domjanič) (vce and pf) (1942)
Children's songs
SACRED
Agnus Dei, op. 15 (vce and org) (1942)
BALLET
Lažni Vitez, op. 53, in 2 acts (1960)
Nijeme sjene, op. 52, in 3 acts (1960)
Ples crnaca, op. 36 (pf) (1950)
OPERA
Kastavsk Kapetan, in 3 acts (1955)
INCIDENTAL MUSIC
Kako je vilko postao pionir, op. 48, play in 4 acts (Brmbota) (1957)
Kastavski Kapetan, op. 44, puppet theatre (Tomislav Prpic) (1953)
Pospanko izmaj, op. 37, dance for puppet theatre (J. Buksa) (1951)
Tri tocke za igrokaz Veli Joze, op. 40, puppet theatre (Vojmila Rabadana) (1952)
Ref. composer, 94, 109, 145, 416, 435, 457

LANGE, Anny von
German composer. b. Dresden, June 20, 1887. She composed chamber music, piano pieces including a suite and songs.
Ref. 70, 226

LANGHAM, Guy. See ATKINSON, Dorothy

LANGHANS, Louise (nee Japha)
German pianist and composer. b. Hamburg, February 2, 1826; d. Wiesbaden, October 13, 1910. She studied the piano under Fritz Warendorf, theory and composition under G.A. Gross and Wilhelm Grund and in 1853 under Robert and Clara Schumann (q.v.) in Dusseldorf, where she completed a higher course in piano performance and composition. She married the composer and violinist W. Langhans. In Paris she was regarded as one of the great pianists of her time. She gave several chamber music concerts with her husband.
Compositons
CHAMBER
String quartets
Romanze, op. 25 (vln and pf) (Hoffahrt)
PIANO
Ballade, op. 21 (Schuberth Jr.)
Deux sonatines, op. 18 (Hamelle)
Mazurkas, op. 14 (Schuberth)
Nocturne, op. 20 (Bote: Heugel)
Seven works, op. 36 (Schuberth)
Sicillienne, op. 22 (Schuberth)
VOCAL
Drei Lieder, op. 37: Lied der Voeglein; Morgengruss; Schlaf ein (3 solo, ch and pf) (Schuberth)
Other choral works
Am Ceresio, op. 23
Danse guerriere, op. 19
Drei Lieder, op. 30: Es war einmal ein Knabe; Als ich dir bebend eingestand; Zu Assmannshausen (Schuberth)
Fuenf Gesaenge: Die Gletscher leuchten; Es haucht in's fein Ohr; Sommernacht; Ueber die Berge; Wie dem Vogel sein Gefieder (Kahnt)
Laendler, op. 23 (Schuberth)
Zwei Lieder, op. 33 (Schuberth)
OPERA
One opera
ARRANGEMENTS
Adaptation of the opera Die Koenigin von Saba by Goldmark (pf)
Adaptation from R. Wagner's music drama Das Rheingold (pf) (Schott)
Adaptation from Cherubini's Quatuor (pf) (Cranz)
Ref. 297, 433, 448

LANGRISHE, May Katherine (pseud. Orchard May)
English pianist and composer. b. Barrow-in-Furness, 1879. She studied in Germany and under Arthur Dolmetsch.
Compositions
CHAMBER
Romance in F (vln and pf)
PIANO
I love to love you
Moonlight wanderings
VOCAL
Songs incl.:
Alone with the moon
God's morning
I love life
If I had known
Somewhere in the world
Spinner of dreams
While all the world goes drifting by
Ref. 467

LANKMAR, Helen
German pianist and composer. b. Neresheim, Wuerttemberg, June 23, 1897. She studied under M. Pauer and Josef Haas. She lived in Munich from 1922 and composed chamber and piano works and songs.
Ref. 70, 226

LANNOY, Clementine-Josephine-Françoise-Thérése, Countess (nee Comtesse de Looz-Corswarem)
Belgian pianist, teacher and composer. b. Brabant, June 29, 1764; d. Liege, June 4, 1820. She married Florent Stanislas-Amour, Count of Lannoy in 1789. She left Belgium as an exile when the French Republicans invaded the Low Countries. She exercised her talents as a musician and composer in Berlin in order to earn a living and published a number of songs there. She compiled several collections of Austrian folk songs.
Compositions
CHAMBER
Three sonatas (hpcd or pf and vln or vlc) (ded Prince Ernest Auguste of England) (Berlin: J.J. Hummel)
Three romances (pf or hp) (1801)
Two French romances (pf) (1798)
Sonata, op. 9
VOCAL
Ballads
Folk songs
SACRED
Ave Maria
Mass
Tantum ergo
Ref. 50, 129, 226, 236, 276, 398

LANTI, Teresa
17th-century Italian composer of songs.
Ref. 465

LANUZA Y VAZQUEZ, Agustina
19th-century Spanish soprano and composer. She was well known in Madrid between 1840 and 1860 and held concerts at her house, for which she composed various pieces.
Ref. 389

LANZARINI DE ISAJA, Antonietta
19th-century Italian composer of chamber music.
Ref. 502

LAOUREUX DE GUCHTENAERE, Marguerite
Belgian pianist and composer. b. 1887; d. Ghent, 1934.
Ref. 105

LAPEIRETTA, Ninon de Brouwer
Dominican pianist and composer. b. Santo Domingo, January 4, 1907. She studied the piano under Blanca Mieses and Manual Polanco and after 1940, composition under Enrique Casal Chapi. In 1935 she was founder president of the Sociedad pro Arte and the founder of the Sociedad Dominicana de Conciertos Intarin.
Compositions
ORCHESTRA
Suite de danzas (1963)
Two capriccios (wind orch) (1941)
CHAMBER
Preludio pastorale (1950)
Suita arcaica (1944)
PIANO
Fugues
Inventions
Sonatas
VOCAL
Abominacion de la espera, recitative and aria (S and orch) (1943)
BALLET
La reine del Caribe (1950)
Ref. 17

LAPEYRE, Therese
20th-century American composer.
Composition
CHAMBER
A John Glenn (timp, perc, hp and strs) (Presser)
Ref. 280

LAPIN, Lily
South African cellist, concert pianist, teacher and composer. b. Pretoria, June 26, 1893. Her first piano teacher was her elder sister and at the age of 16 Lily went to Brussels Conservatory, where she studied advanced piano technique under Leopold Wallner, Eumar Maelstrom and Arthur de Greeff, singing and composition under Victor Mercier as well as ensemble playing and the cello. She went on to the Royal Academy in London to continue her piano studies with Charles Reddie and singing under Frederick Keel. She commenced her career as a concert pianist in 1915 in South Africa and taught the piano privately.
Compositions
CHAMBER
Tango, trio (vln, vlc and pf)
PIANO
Capriccio (1942)
Five moods: Prelude; Toccatina, Nocturne; Rhapsody; Allegretto grazioso (1940)
Study in D-Flat (1935)
Two preludes (1939)
VOCAL
Songs incl.:
Evocation (Mary Kennedy)
Klim op
A lament
Lullaby
Rise up my love (from Song of Solomon) (1925)
Slumber song (composer) (London: Peter Derek)
Spring song (Rupert Brooke)
Three French songs: Chanson d'automne: La mort des oiseaux; Romance (1929)
Three songs of loneliness
Two African songs: Drought (D.L. Darlow); The herd boy in the rain (Mary Byron)
Unyielding
Vryheidsgee
Publications
The Art of Singing. 1943.
Bibliography
South African Women's Who's Who. Biographies (Pty). Ltd. Johannesburg. 1938.
Ref. 184, 377

LARA, Catherine
20th-century French composer.
Composition
FILM MUSIC
Dr. Françoise Gailland (1975)
Ref. 497

LARA, Nelly Mele (Mele Lara, Nelly)
20th-century Venezuelan composer.
Composition
CHAMBER
Sonata (vln and pf) (New York: Peer)
Ref. 94

LARCHER, Maria Amalia
19th-century Portuguese composer.
Compositions
PIANO
Bartolemeu Dias, march
Prise de la tour (1860) (manuscript-Biblioteca da Ajuda, Lisbon)
Ref. 399

LAREN, Derek. See VAN EPEN-DE GROOT, Else Antonia

LARHANTEC, Marie Annick
French composer. b. 1947.
Composition
CHAMBER
Mouvements à la corde lisse (Celtic hp) (Paris: Editions Françaises de Musique, 1974)
Ref. 83

LARKIN, Deirdre
English pianist, accompanist, teacher and composer. b. Oxted, Surrey, September 24, 1931. She studied at the Royal Academy of Music, where she became an L.R.A.M. and an A.R.C.M. She obtained a certificate from the London School of Dalcroze Eurhythmics and studied under Claudio Arrau at the Vienna Academy of Music. She gave piano recitals and was an accompanist and music director in Queenswood. She lives in South Africa and composes songs, trios, operettas and instrumental arrangements.
Ref. 77

LARSEN, Elizabeth (Libby) Brown
American lecturer and composer. b. Wilmington, DE, December 24, 1950. She obtained her B.A. (1971), M.A. (1974) and Ph.D. (1978) from the University of Minnesota. Her composition teachers were Paul Fetler, Dominick Argento and Eric Stokes. From 1973 she was a teaching assistant at the University of Minneapolis. From 1983 to 1985 she was composer-in-residence of the Minnesota Orchestra and in 1985 manager-composer of the Minnesota Composers' Forum. She won many grants, awards and commissions and in 1981 was the Minnesota Woman of the Year in Arts and in 1983 voted the Woman to Watch. She received a National Endowment for the Arts Fellowship in 1982 and 1984 and a Minnesota State Arts Board Fellowship in 1980. DISCOGRAPHY. PHOTOGRAPH.
Compositions
ORCHESTRA
Weaver's song and jig (str band and cham orch) (Massachusetts: E. Schirmer)
Three cartoons (5 perc and orch) (Schirmer)
Deep summer music (trp and orch) (Schirmer)
Overture, parachute dancing (3 perc and orch) (comm American Composers Orchestra, 1984) (Schirmer)
Pinions, violin concerto (Schirmer)
CHAMBER
Black roller (fl, cl, bsn, ob, vln, vla, vlc and pf) (Schirmer)
Cajun set (gtr, vln, vla and vlc) (Schirmer)
Air and jig (cl qrt) (Schirmer)
Four on the floor (vln, vlc, d-b and pf) (Schirmer)
Bronze veils (trb and 2 perc) (comm William McGlaughlin) (1979) (Schirmer)
Impromptu (fl, ob and bsn) (Schirmer)
Aubade (fl and pf) (Schirmer)
Canti breve (fl and gtr) (Schirmer)
Circular rondo (fl and gtr) (Schirmer)
Ulloa's ring (fl and pf) (Schirmer)
Jazz variations (bsn) (Schirmer)
Piano suite (Schirmer)
Sonata in one movement on Kalenda Maya (org) (Schirmer)

GUITAR
Argyle sketches (Schirmer)
Istar fantasia
HARP
Theme and deviations (Schirmer)
Triage (Schirmer)
VOCAL
A Creeley collection (mix-ch, T, fl and perc) (Schirmer)
Dance set (mix-ch, cl, vlc, drs and pf) (Schirmer)
Double joy (double mix-ch, org and handbells) (Schirmer)
Everyone sang (mix-ch, 2 hp and 2 perc) (Schirmer)
In a winter garden (T, m-S, mix-ch and orch) (Schirmer)
Ringeltanze (mix-ch, pf and handbells) (Schirmer)
Soft pieces (ch)
Cowboy songs (S and pf) (Schirmer)
Eurydice: Through the looking glass (S and str qrt) (Schirmer)
Rilke songs (T and gtr; also S, fl, gtr and hp) (Schirmer)
Saints without tears (S, fl and bsn) (Schirmer)
Travelling in every season
SACRED
Lacrimosa Christi (soli, ch and orch)
OPERA
Claire de Lune (1985)
Psyche and the Pskyscraper
The Silver Fox, chamber opera in 1 act (Schirmer)
Some Pig (1973)
Tumbledown Dick, in 2 acts (12 singers and orch) (Schirmer)
MULTIMEDIA
The art of love (S, T, hp, ob, perc and dance)
Tom Twist (opt narr, mime or dance and orch) (Schirmer)
Ref. AMC 1985, 141, 142, 494, 622, 625, 646

LARSEN, Libby. See LARSEN, Elizabeth Brown

LARSON, Anna Barbara
American pianist, orchestral conductor, dancer, lecturer and composer. b. Knoxville, TN, November 9, 1940. She obtained her B.A.Mus. (1962) from the Sarah Lawrence College, Bronxville, studying the piano and composition, the latter under Andre Singer. From 1970 to 1977 she studied the piano under Florence Robertson and from 1978 to 1979 under Tamara Djmitrieff. She gained her M.M. (1978) from Virginia Commonwealth University after studying composition under Jack Jarrett and from 1979 to 1980 she studied composition under Robert Ward and conducting under Allen Bone at Duke University. She is currently working towards her doctorate of musical arts, studying composition under Lawrence Moss, conducting under William Hudson and theory under Thomas Delio. From 1962 to 1970 she taught music in junior school and was a guest lecturer at Lynchberg College and a lecturer at George Washington University. She received extensive training as a ballet dancer in England and America and performed and taught ballet and dance. Her debut as a conductor in 1983 came with a performance of her *Dance for Orchestra*.
Compositions
ORCHESTRA
Dance for orchestra (pf and orch) (1977)
PIANO
Impromptu (1976)
Song for piano (1976)
VOCAL
Eternal thou (John Spong, Lucy Boswell) (mix-ch) (1976)
The listeners (Walter de la Mare) (Bar and pf) (1979) (Arsis Press)
When that Aprille (Chaucer) (S and pf) (1976)
Nora! Nora! aria from contemplated opera (S and T) (1980)
ELECTRONIC
Conversation (pf and tape) (1975)
Dirge without music (elec assembled poetry and syn sounds on tape) (1975)
THEATRE
The picnic, children's musical play (1981)
Ref. composer, 625

LARUELLE, Jeanne-Marie
French organist, teacher and composer. b. 1934. She gained her organ and teaching diplomas from the Schola Cantorum, where she was a pupil of Jan Langlais and Gaston Litaize. She is a member of SACEM.
Compositions
CHAMBER
Duettissimo (rec or fl and gtr)
Mouvement de menuet (hpcd or hp)
Printemps (celtic or large hp)
Chateaux (celtic or large hp)
PIANO
Esquisse et toccata
Valse romantique
Ref. composer

LASANSKY, Ada Julia
20th-century composer.
Composition
VOCAL
Cantares de la madre joven, cantata (Tagore) (S and ch)
Ref. 465

LASCHANZKY, Mme.
19th-century composer.
Composition
CHAMBER
Concerto à cinq (ob, 2 vln, vla and basso continuo)
Ref. Frau und Musik

LASDAUSKAS, Jacqueline
20th-century Australian composer of Tasmania. She was a pupil of Wayne Madden.
Composition
ORCHESTRA
Symphonic poem No. 2
Ref. ABC

LASRY-HERRBACH, Yvonne
20th-century French composer. She married the composer Jacques Lasry. She composed and performed for the group named Structures Sonores Lasry-Baschet. She is a member of SACEM.
Ref. composer

LAST, Joan Mary
English pianist, professor and composer. b. Littlehampton, Sussex, January 12, 1908. She studied the piano under Mathilde Verne in York Bowen. She was music director in Rosemead, Littlehampton from 1930 to 1954 and director of music at Warren School, Worthing, 1940 to 1961. In 1959 she was made a professor of the piano at the Royal Academy of Music. From 1960 she was an examiner for the Associated Board and an adjudicator for the British Federation of Music Festivals. She toured extensively in the United States and Canada conducting piano workshops. She became an honorary A.R.A.M. in 1965 and an honorary F.R.A.M. in 1975. PHOTOGRAPH.
Compositions
PIANO
Over 100 albums of piano pieces (OUP)
Publications
Interpretation in Piano Study. OUP, 1961.
The Young Pianist. OUP, 1953.
Ref. composer

LASZLO, Anna von
19th-century Hungarian composer. She lived in Portugal.
Compositions
CHAMBER
Cantilena, op. 13 (vln and pf)
Concertino, op. 40 (fl and pf) (ded King Luis)
Fantasie, op. 1 (vlc and pf)
SACRED
Ave Maria, op. 8 (S and ch)
Ref. 226, 276, 399

LATHAM, Joan Seyler
American composer. b. Cincinnati, April 27, 1921. She gained a B.A. (1943) from the Western College for Women, Oxford and a M.Mus (1945) from the College of Music, Cincinnati. She married the composer William P. Latham.
Compositions
ORCHESTRA
Overture in D-Minor, op. 6 (1945)
CHAMBER
String quartet in F-Minor, op. 5 (1945)
Sketch, op. 4, no. 1 (vln and pf) (1944)
Violin and piano pieces, op. 2 (1943)

PIANO
Piano pieces, op. 1 (1943)
Piano reduction of Fantasy concerto for flute and strings by William P. Latham
Ref. composer

LATHROP, Gayle Posselt
American flautist, guitarist, lecturer and composer. b. Chicago, February 7, 1942. She studied at Indiana University under Thomas Beversdorf and Bernhard Heiger and at California State University, Humboldt, under Leon Wagner. She studied the flute under Pellerite, Houdeshel, Johnson and Peck. She was director of music for schools in Hoopa, CA, from 1968 to 1970 and a guitar lecturer at California State University, Humboldt in 1972. From 1973 she taught the guitar at the College of the Redwoods.
Compositions
BAND
The party
State of the union (1968)
Tish tang
CHAMBER
Pieces 4-5 (qnt)
Joamerdap (fl trio)
Sonatina (fl)
Preludes (gtr)
Triskelion
VOCAL
Black (S and pf)
Ref. 80, 142

LATIMER, Ella May Elizabeth
Canadian composer. b. 1906.
Composition
SACRED
Love came down at Christmas (Christina Rossetti) (mix-ch and pf) (Leeds Music, 1963)
Ref. CMC

LATIOLAIS, Desirée Jayne
American pianist, lecturer and composer. b. Natchitoches, LA, October 28, 1928. She gained her B.A. (music) in 1928 from the Louisiana State University, studying under Helen Gunderson and her M.Mus. in 1950 from the University of Michigan, having studied under Ross Lee Finney, at the Eastman School of Music and at Ohio State University under Marshall Barnes. She was a guest lecturer at Ohio State University from 1971 to 1979 and a part-time faculty member of Denison University, 1973 to 1974. Her compositions have been broadcast on Musical World of Ohio in 1973 and 1974 and her *Clarinet sonata* won the National Federation of Music Clubs Contest in 1973.
Compositions
ORCHESTRA
Passacaglia and double fugue (also 2 pf) (1951, 1973)
Introduction and allegro (1951)
CHAMBER
Piano quartet
Duo (vlc and vln) (1974)
Lithuanian suite (vln and pf)
Movement (vlc and vln)
Sonata (cl and pf) (1971)
Suite (pf) (1973)
VOCAL
Trilogy (ch a-cap)
Salome (vce, vlc, fl and pf) (1980)
Songs from the Chinese
Ref. 142, 347, 625

LATY, Mme.
Polish composer. ca. 1840. Her songs were performed by Countess Anna Grabowska.
Ref. 465

LATZ, Inge
German pianist, teacher and composer. b. Aachen, June 14, 1929. Her mother, a professional musician, taught her music as a child. From 1945 to 1950 Inge studied the piano and composition under Carl Jochims. After school she studied at the Staatliche Musikhochschule, Cologne and was music teacher there from 1954 to 1962. From 1974 she taught both children and adults at a music school in Meckenheim and in various seminars, including those on music therapy. For the past few years she has done freelance work, taught children and youth groups and organized workshops, seminars, song and piano evenings. PHOTOGRAPH.
Compositions
CHAMBER
Freundinnen (pf)
VOCAL
Alte Hexenlieder (mix-ch)
Approx 100 songs (w-ch and insts or pf)
Fifty children's songs, der singende Gummibaum (ch and insts) (1980)
Die Bonner Blaustruempfe singen Protest und Spottlieder
Sing Frau sing (vce and pf) (1980)
BALLET
Improvisationen, for children (1979)
INCIDENTAL MUSIC
Fremdkorper (1981)
Kunstpreis (1981)
Die letzte Suende (1980)
Der weite wilde Westen
Das verlorene Gesicht (1980)
Music for show Schmuck und Skulptur (pf)
Ref. composer, Frau und Musik 5/85

LATZMANNOVA, Anna. See LACMANOVA, Anna

LAUBER, Anne Marianne
Canadian/Swiss pianist, violinist, orchestral conductor, lecturer and composer. b. Zurich, Switzerland, July 28, 1943. She studied the piano privately under Jean Nyder and at the Ribeaupiere Institute in Lausanne, Switzerland from 1953 to 1967 and the violin in Lausanne under Jean-Pierre Chablot from 1959 to 1962. From 1963 she studied harmony, counterpoint and fugue under Andras Kovach at the Music Conservatory of Lausanne, graduating in 1967. In 1965 she met Darius Milhaud, who collaborated with her on some of her works, notably the *Sonatine Burlesque* and *Trio for Strings*. In 1967 she emigrated to Canada. From 1972 to 1973 she studied orchestration under Alexandre Brott at McGill University and then continued her studies in composition and musical analysis under Andre Provost and Serge Garant. In 1982 she received her M.Mus. (composition) from the University of Montreal and was accepted as a Ph.D. candidate. From 1979 to 1980 she attended conducting courses with Jacques Clement and conducted orchestras for broadcasting, recording and films. She received grants from the Swiss government and a subsidy from the Minister of Cultural Affairs in Quebec in 1977 for the composition of a woodwind quintet and a concert piece for piano and orchestra. She lectured in composition at the University of Montreal from 1979 to 1980. Her works have been played in Switzerland and Canada and she participated as an artist in two radio broadcasts. She is a member of the CMC and the CLC. DISCOGRAPHY. PHOTOGRAPH.
Compositions
ORCHESTRA
Symphonic piece No. 1 (1978)
Fantasy on a known theme (pf and orch) (1980) (CMC)
Piece concertante (pf and orch) (1977)
Beyond the sound barrier (1983) (CMC)
Colin Maillard (1982) (CMC)
Concerto quebecois (1976)
Concerto (str orch) (1976)
Divertimento (str orch) (1970)
Osmose (1980) (CMC)
Poème pour une metamorphose (1978)
Waltz for piano and orchestra (1982) (CMC)
CHAMBER
Mouvement (str qrt, pf, 2 fl and ob) (1973)
Five elements (vln, fl, bsn, sax and tba) (1974)
Woodwind quintet (1977)
String quartet (1973)
Music for piano, violin and percussion (1975)
String trio (1967)
Divertimento (fl and gtr) (1978)
Duo (a-sax and pf) (1972)
Mollesiennes (fl and pf) (1978)
Movement for bass and piano (1980) (CMC)
Movement for cello and piano (1980) (CMC)
Movement for clarinette and piano (1980) (CMC)
Movement for flute and piano (1980) (Doberman)
Movement for horn and piano (1980) (CMC)
Movement for violin and piano (1980) (CMC)
Sonata (vla and pf) (1975)
Sonatina burlesque (vln and pf) (1967)
Stadacona (fl and vlc) (1972)
Piece (fl and hp) (1971)
Arabesque (gtr) (1983) (Doberman Music)
Five pieces (org) (1978)

PIANO
Movement, monologue (CMC)
Pour jeunes et vieux enfants, 28 progressively difficult pieces (1960)
Sonata (1976)
Variations (1966)
VOCAL
A tonal work (mix-ch and orch) (1976)
Orchestration of popular songs for the chorus of the Polytechnic School of the University of Montreal on the occasion of its 100th birthday (1973)
Berceuse (mix-ch a-cap) (1970)
Three poems (Monika Merinat) (Bar or m-S and pf) (1976)
La triade d'Hector, 3 melodies (S or T and pf) (1963)
Le joue de la poupée (vce and vlc) (1982) (CMC)
Le petit prince (narr and pf)
Movement for alto and piano (1980) (CMC)
BALLET
Les Jardins d'Anton (1976)
THEATRE
Le Croque-nature, marionettes (1975)
Les Femmes Savantes, play (Molière) (1964)
FILM MUSIC
L'Affaire Coffin (pf and orch)
Ref. composer, 563, 622

LAUER, Elizabeth

American concert pianist, critic, lecturer and composer. b. Boston, December 2, 1932. She received her B.A. from Bennington College, and her M.A. from Columbia University. She received a Fulbright scholarship to study in Germany, at the Staatlich Hochschule fuer Musik, Hamburg where she attended master classes in the piano under Walter Hautzig. She worked for Columbia records from 1957 to 1963 becoming associate producer in masterworks. Since 1963 she has performed as a keyboard soloist and chamber musician and with orchestras. She lectures on keyboard and chamber music and is a music critic and program note writer. In 1984 she won a Pen Woman award and was composer-in-residence at the Chamber Music Center of the East in 1983.
Compositions
ORCHESTRA
Works (orch and cham orch)
CHAMBER
Suite of dances (fls and hn) (1983)
Five miniatures for three winds (1983)
Other works for winds and strings
PIANO
Works incl.:
Sonata
Sonatina
Soundings (1981) (Carl Fischer)
VOCAL
Song cycles (Edna St. Vincent Millay, James Joyce, Ringelnatz)
Choral works
BALLET
Child's play (2 pf)
OPERA
Desire under the dryer, comic chamber opera in one act (Gerald Walter)
INCIDENTAL MUSIC
Music for theatre (small cham ens)
ARRANGEMENTS
Gershwin: 7 songs with introduction
Gottschalk: Grande Tarantelle
Prokofiev: Peter and the wolf (pf, 1 hand) (1983) (San Diego: Kjos)
Ravel: Introduction and allegro (2 pf, fl and cl)
Schubert: Trout quintet, variation (2 pf)
Ref. composer, *Pan Pipes* Winter 1984

LAUFER, Beatrice

American composer. b. New York, April 27, 1923. She attended the Chatham Square Music School and the Juilliard School of Music in 1944 where she studied composition under Roger Sessions and Marion Bauer (q.v.) and orchestration under Vittorio Giannini. She also studied under Nathan Novick. In 1948 her first symphony was performed in Germany and Japan under the auspices of the State Department. Her *Song of the fountain* was commissioned by the American Association of the United Nations and performed by an interracial chorus of 250 voices in 1952. She also received a commission from the State of Connecticut to write a choral work for the 1976 bicentennial year. She is a member of ASCAP. PHOTOGRAPH.
Compositions
ORCHESTRA
Symphony No. 1 (1944)
Symphony No. 2 (1961)
Concerto (vln and orch)
Concertante (vln, vla and orch) (1986)
Concerto (fl, ob, trp and str orch) (1962)
Concerto (cham orch)
Dance festival (1945)
Crucible, overture
Cry, prelude (1966) (New York: Belwin-Mills)
Dance frolic (1945)
In the throes.... (1982)
Orchestral trilogy: Cry, prelude; In the throes ...; Resolution (Theodore Presser)
Prelude and fugue (1964)
CHAMBER
Lyric (str trio) (1966)
VOCAL
And Thomas Jefferson said (B, narr, mix-ch and orch) (1974)
Sergeant's prayer (B, mix-ch and orch or pf) (1943)
Do you fear the wind (mix-ch) (Assoc. Music, 1948)
Everyone sang (mix-vh) (Presser)
Evolution (mix-ch a-cap) (1943)
He, who knows not (mix-ch) (Presser)
People of unrest (mix-ch a-cap) (1943)
Percussion (mix-ch) (Shawnee Press, 1950)
Song of the fountain (mix-ch and pf) (ded United Nations Freedom Fountain)
Spring thunder (mix-ch and pf) (Assoc. Music, 1948)
Under the pines (mix-ch and pf) (Assoc. Music)
New Orleans (w-vces a-cap) (1945)
What is to come we know not (w-vces a-cap) (1945)
Soldier's prayer (B and pf) (Assoc. Music, 1955)
SACRED
Adam's Rib (bible and John Milton) (vces, ch and orch)
BALLET
The Great God Brown (Belwin-Mills, 1966)
OPERA
Ile (Eugene O'Neoll's The long voyage home) (Belwin-Mills, 1958)
My Brother's Keeper, biblical (1968)
Ref. composer, 142, 191, 280, 622

LAUMYANSKENE, Elena. See STANEKAITE-LAUMYANSKENE, Elena Ionovna

LAURENT, Ruth Carew

20th-century American composer. She composed choral works, Christmas carols, children's and other songs.
Ref. 40, 347

LAURIDSEN, Cora

20th-century American composer.
Composition
OPERA
Job (1965)
Ref. 141

LAVATER, Magdalena Elisabeth

Swiss pianist, teacher and composer. b. Zurich, December 2, 1820; d. Zurich, February 7, 1901. She taught the piano in Zurich until 1892 and then later in Hoengg.
Composition
SACRED
Stille Nacht du sinkst hernieder (A. Pfister) (mix-ch) in Heim's Gemischte Choere II (1892)
Ref. 101

LAVIN, Marie Duchesne

Australian composer. b. 1930.
Compositions
VOCAL
Songs from Papua New Guinea, books 1 and 2 (1969) (chil-ch and gtr or pf) (Castle Music, 1973)
SACRED
Lutu: Mass No. 1; Mass No. 2; (2 part ch and traditional Papua New Guinea insts - split bamboo for beating drum with skin head and shell rattle) (1973)
Set of five mass hymns (chil-ch and org or gtr) (1970)

OPERETTA
How Chaleu became chief, for children (folk insts) (Castle, 1975)
TEACHING PIECES
Make and play bamboo flutes
Ref. 440, 442, 444

LAVOIPIERRE, Therese
20th-century South African composer.
Compositions
VOCAL
Happy birthday (vce and pf)
Lalela (vce and pf)
Lullaby (vce and pf)
A malusi (vce and pf)
SACRED
Carol in the sun (w-ch a-cap)
The Lord's Prayer (vce, vlc and pf or org)
Ref. 295

LAVRANS, Elayne
20th-century American composer.
Composition
CHAMBER
Suite (fl and pf)
Ref. 228

LAWHON, Gladys Louise
American pianist, accompanist, teacher and composer. b. Denton, TX. She studied at Texas Women's University where she obtained a B.Mus. (piano), a B.S. (music education) and an M.A. (education). She received a D.Mus. from Texas State University. She also studied at the Juilliard School of Music and Columbia University and attended music workshops under Bernice Frost, Hans Barth, Robert Pace and Frances Clark. She taught the piano and theory at Meredith College, Raleigh and was an accompanist and composer for modern dance groups. For over ten years she was a co-ordinator of student accompanists at North Texas State University. She is an adjudicator for the national board of the National Guild of Piano Teachers.
Ref. 84

LAWRENCE, Elizabeth S.
19th-century English organist and composer. She was the mother and first teacher of Emily M. Lawrence (q.v.) and the organist at Rugby Parish Church from 1842 to 1877. She composed a book of psalmody, hymn tunes and chants.
Ref. 6

LAWRENCE, Emily M.
English organist, pianist, choir conductor and composer. b. Rugby, 1854. She first studied under her mother, Elizabeth (q.v.) an organist and composer and later in London under Sterndale Bennett, Manuel Garcia and Dr. Stegall and then for three years at the Royal Academy of Music. She conducted a ladies' choral society at Rugby and Wembley. She was the organist at St. John's Church, Wembley, from 1889.
Compositions
CHAMBER
Sonata in F-Sharp Minor (vln and pf)
PIANO
Evensong, 4 songs without words (Weekes)
Album of pieces
VOCAL
Bonny Kilmeny, cantata (w-vces) (1890)
The ten virgins, cantata (w-vces) (1893)
Songs incl.:
A book of songs for girls and boys (Weekes)
Come what may (Weekes)
Do I love thee (Weekes)
Dolly and Dick (2 part-ch of treble vces) (Ashdown)
Duets (Weekes)
In a garden (Weekes)
Romance, op. 16
Singing in the rain (Weekes)
Sowing and reaping (Weekes)
SACRED
Anthems
In manus tuas (Weekes)
Ref. 3, 6, 226, 297

LAWRENCE, Mme. See TOWNSEND, Pearl Dea Etta

LAWSON, May
Composition
PIANO
La mascotte
Ref. 473

LAYMAN, Pamela (Quist)
American pianist, lecturer and composer. b. Rhode Island, April 3, 1949. She studied at the Peabody Conservatory of Music under Julio Esteban, Jean E. Ivey and Robert Hall Lewis, gaining her B.M. (piano) and M.M. (composition). She won a composition award from the Friday Morning Music Club, 1975. She was vice-president of the Walden School in 1973; on the music faculty of the State University, New York College, 1974 to 1975 and then a member of the music faculty of Peabody Institute, lecturing in composition, the piano and theory. DISCOGRAPHY.
Compositions
ORCHESTRA
Lazarus (1976)
CHAMBER
Mosaic (vlc and pf) (1978)
Three poems (bsn and cl) (1974)
Gravitation I (vln) (1975)
Meditations (trp) (1977)
Syllogisms (pf) (1979)
VOCAL
Sette canzone d'amore (T, perc and gtr) (1973)
Ref. 563, 622, 625

LAZAR, Ella
Israeli pianist, singer and composer. b. Haifa, September 1, 1954. She commenced music and piano lessons at an early age and gained her B.Mus. (theory and composition) from the Rubin Academy, Tel-Aviv in 1979. From 1974 to 1979 she studied composition privately under Professor Zwi Avni and from 1977 to 1984 studied vocal training and singing with Mrs. Gila Yaron in Israel and Professor Erika Schmidt-Valentin in Germany. From an early age she composed light music and songs and in 1975 started composing classical music. Her *Duo for flute and cello* was played in a concert to celebrate 30 years of Israeli music in 1978. She won an American Israel Foundation scholarship for composition from 1976 to 1977. PHOTOGRAPH.
Compositions
CHAMBER
Divertimento (brass qnt) (1984)
Duo (fl and vlc) (1977) (IMI)
Duo (vln and vla) (1976)
VOCAL
Moodinesc, poem (Rachel) (ch a-cap) (1976)
Poem (H.N. Biolik) (S, cor anglais and pf) (1975)
Poem (P. Yasur) (A, cl, vlc and pf) (1984)
Ref. composer

LE BAS, Gertrude
Compositions
VOCAL
A lament (Shelley) (Ricordi)
The old fashioned bonnet (E.A. Guest) (Ricordi)

LE BEAU, Louisa Adolpha
German pianist, violinist, singer and composer. b. Rastatt, April 25, 1850; d. Baden-Baden, July 2, 1927. She studied the piano under Kalliwoda and Clara Schumann (q.v.), composition and harmony under M.E. Sachs, Franz Lachner and Rheinberger, the violin under Mittermayer and singing under Anton Hainzinger. She was considered one of the most talented women composers of her time and her works were highly praised by the critic Eduard Hanslick. As a pianist, she frequently performed her own compositions in Vienna, Berlin, Cologne, Leipzig, Munich, Frankfurt and Stuttgart. Several of her compositions were selected for performance at the Chicago World Fair.
Compositions
ORCHESTRA
Symphony
Piano concerto No. 1, op. 7
Piano concerto No. 2, op. 37
Symphonic poem
Concert overture, op. 23 (1882)

Fantasie, op. 25 (pf and orch)
Festival Overture
CHAMBER
String quintet
Piano quartet, op. 28 (1883)
String quartet, op.34
Trio, op. 15
Concertstueck, op. 24 (vlc and pf) (1st prize, Hamburg competition)
Romance, op. 35 (vln and pf)
Three solos, op. 26 (vla and pf)
Cello sonata, op. 17
Violin sonata, op. 10
PIANO
Acht Praeludien, op. 12
Cadenzas for Mozart's and Beethoven's piano concertos
Gavotte, op. 32
Konzert-etude, op. 2
Six fugues, op. 21
Sonata
Sonata in A-Minor, op. 8
Sonata in C-Minor, op. 10
Theme and variations, op. 3
Two sonatinas, op. 13
Variations on an original theme, op. 3
Improvisation for left hand, op. 30
Other pieces
VOCAL
Hadumoth, cantata (Scheffel's Ekkehard) (5 soloists, double ch and orch)
Ruth, op. 27, cantata
Im Saengersaal, op. 22, concert aria (Bar or A and orch)
Five choruses a capella, op. 9
Two choral ballads, op. 16 (mix-vces)
Lieder, op. 5 (m-S and pf)
Ballads
Songs
OPERA
Der verzauberte Kalif
Publications
Lebenserinnerungen einer Komponistin. Autobiography. 1910.
Ref. Frau und Musik, 1, 70, 109, 110, 226, 276, 347, 400, 476, 477, 653

LE BORDAYS, Christiane
French guitarist, pianist, musicologist, and composer. b. Le Raincy, July 30, 1937. She obtained her bachelor's degree and then studied the piano under Marcel Ciampi and worked towards her doctorate at the Sorbonne. She also studied the guitar, flamenco dancing and Spanish folklore and adapted flamenco repertoires for the piano.
Compositions
ORCHESTRA
Concerto de azul (gtr and orch) (1970)
PIANO
Zapateado (2 pf) (1970)
Cantares
Ritmos andaluces, suite (1970)
Adaptations of flamenco repertoires
MISCELLANEOUS
Adaptations of Andalusian music: Allegrias; Siguiriya; Soleares; Zambra
Ref. composer, 280

LE CLERE, Victoire
Early 19th-century French composer.
Composition
VOCAL
The virgin's first love, a favorite ariette (vces, hp or pf and German fl) (London: L. Lavenu, ca. 1800)
Ref. 65

LE DENTU, Odette
20th-century French composer.
Compositions
CHAMBER
Pieces classiques pour harpe celtique (4 vols)
Ref. Gerard Billaudot catalog (Paris)

LE ROUX, Nanine
19th-century French composer.
Composition
VOCAL
Sul margine d'un rio, air (Paris: Sieber, ca. 1860)
Ref. H. Baron (London) Cat. No. 109

LE SIEGE, Annette
20th-century American composer. She obtained her Ph.D. from the Eastman School of Music, Rochester in 1975.
Compositions
ORCHESTRA
Montage (perc and str orch) (1975)
Street clowns (symphonic wind orch)
CHAMBER
Four bagatelles (vlc, perc and wind octet)
Ricercare (3 picc, 4 fl and a-fl)
Phidian (2 fl, a-fl, b-cl, vib and pf)
Dialogue (ob, cor anglais and bsn)
Rigaudon (ob and fl)
Suite (sax and pf)
Sonata (pf) (1977)
ELECTRONIC
Ordinary things (vce, fl, sax, vib, vlc and pf)
Outside the frame (vce, vib and pf)
Publications
Analysis of 'Montage'. Images from Mediaeval Montserrat. Dissertation. University of Rochester, Eastman School of Music. New York, ABD75- 20071.
Ref. 280

LEACH, Mary Jane
20th-century American composer.
Composition
ELECTRONIC
Trio for duo (vlc, fl and tape) (1983)
Ref. AMC 1985

LEADBETTER, Mrs. See DEL RIEGO, Theresa

LEAF, Ann (Audrey Lynn)
20th-century American organist, pianist and composer. b. Nebraska. She studied under Sigmund Lansburg, Jean Duffield and at the Juilliard School of Music. She composed piano and organ pieces and popular ballads.
Ref. 40, 347

LEAF, Audrey Lynn. See LEAF, Ann

LEAHY, Mary Weldon
American pianist and composer. b. St. Louis, MO, August 20, 1926. Her mother, Sophia Blake Cotner, was a piano teacher and gave her her first lessons. She studied composition at North Texas State University and privately under Carl Eppert, Norman Lockwood and Dr. Gordon Jacob in England. She won first prize in a Wisconsin state contest for a string quartet and a song in 1949. PHOTOGRAPH.
Compositions
ORCHESTRA
Symphony No. 1
Symphony for strings
Modern dance rhapsody
Spring frolic (perc and str orch) (1983)
Suite (str orch)
BAND
The gypsy trail
The machine age
The march of the zombies
CHAMBER
Swiss folk tune (ww qnt)
Agitation (B-fl cl, ob, bsn and pf)
Coquette (brass qrt)
String quartets 1 and 2
Suite (fl, B-flat cl and bsn)
Suite (perc qrt)
Sunday afternoon (brass qrt)
Little suite (tba trio) (1969)
Piano trio in F-Minor
Reverie, tone poem (vla, vlc and pf)
Suite (a-rec, vlc and pf)
Tone poem (vln, vlc and pf)
Alto recorder or flute and piano sonata
Cello and piano sonata
Duo (3-octave org and pf)
Four short sketches (ob and bsn)

Gay air (S-rec and pf)
Little piece (vla and pf) (1984)
Little suite for recorders
Organ and piano suite
Short suite (ob and pf)
Suite (d-b and pf) (1968)
Suite (vln and pf)
Violin and piano duo
Harp etude
Innovation (vln)
Magic pool (hp)
Moods (vln) (1971)
CARILLON
Carol
Elegy
Nocturne (National Guild of Carilloneurs)
Prelude (Guild of Carilloneurs)
ORGAN
Fantasy
Prelude (1972)
Postlude
Romantic waltz
Toccata
Voluntary
PIANO
Arrangement of America (4 hands)
Frolic (4 hands)
March of the dragons (4 hands)
Suite (4 hands)
Study (duet) (1984)
Animation
Circus
Daydream
Divertimento
Elysium
A little piece
March
Mexican jumping beans
Mimi
Nocturne
The pony and the fly
Rondo capriccio
Sonatas No. 1 and 2
Theme and variations
Three little pieces: Pastorale prelude; Selene on Latmos; Jazz impromptu (1982)
Toccata
Waltz
VOCAL
And so, lost (S)
Annabel Lee (m-S)
Arms and the boy (S)
Bells of time (S)
Between two loves (B)
A brindle cow (T)
Come back again (m-S)
Evening waterfall (S)
Ho Mia Kor (T)
Like the river (m-S)
Love, what wilt thou with this heart (S)
My better half (m-S) (1971)
O death, death, he is come (Cont or m-S)
Of all the arts (m-S)
Play us a tune, song cycle (m-S)
A red, red rose (m-S)
She walks in beauty (T)
Sorrows of Werther (B)
Tears, idle tears (T)
Time (S)
Yesterday, remember (S and pf)
SACRED
Blessed is the man (mix-ch)
Give ear O Shepherd of Israel (mix-ch)
How long wilt thou forget me, O Lord (mix-ch)
How sweet and silent (mix-ch)
In the Lord put I my trust (mix-ch)
Lord, who shall abide in Thy tabernacle (w-ch)
O come let us sing unto the Lord (mix-ch)
Praise ye the Lord (mix-ch)
Praise ye God (mix-ch)
Sing thou my soul (mix-ch)
Sing unto the Lord a new song (mix-ch)
Tall trees and little children, anthem (mix-ch) (1983)
We're building His cathedral, anthem (mix-ch) (1983)
Christmas proper
Clap your hands
Dec. 8th proper, Immaculate Conception
Delta Omicron prayer
English mass for Christian renewal
I will praise Thee, O Lord
Latin mass in honore Dei
O God I love Thee (S) (1976)
The Lord's Prayer (S)
Spanish mass for choir
Spanish mass for congregation
BALLET
The Chinaman and the Senorita (pf)
ARRANGEMENTS
Christmas carol medley
Girl with the flaxen hair (Debussy) (orch)
Tin soldier march (str orch)
Un rêve d'autrefois (str orch)
Ref. composer, 142, 280

LEANDRE, Joelle

20th-century French double-bassist, actress, mezzo-soprano and composer. DISCOGRAPHY.

Compositions
CHAMBER
Les douze sons (d-b and others)
La maison d'Anna (on writings of Anais Nin)
Ref. 563

LEAVITT, Helen Sewall

American organist, pianist, editor, harmonist, teacher and composer. b. Chicago, July 11, 1880. She studied under Arthur Foote, taught harmony and was associate music editor for Ginn and Company.

Composition
ORCHESTRA
Folk-tune symphony
Ref. 226

LEAVITT, Josephina

19th-century German composer. She composed piano pieces and songs.
Ref. 276, 347

LEBARON, Anne (Alice Anne)

American harpist, zither player, lecturer and composer. b. Baton Rouge, LA, May 30, 1953. She obtained a B.A. (composition) from the University of Alabama in 1974 and her M.A. from State University of New York in 1978. She spent the summer of 1974 at the Salzedo Harp Colony studying under Alice Chalifoux. She then studied under Mauricio Kagel at the Hochschule fuer Musik, Cologne and under Gyorgy Ligeti at the Hochschule fuer Musik, Hamburg. She is currently working towards her doctorate at Colombia University, studying under Bulent Arel and Chou Wen-chung. Since 1976 she has taught theory, composition and electronic music at the University Alabama and the State University of New York. She developed unique performance methods for the harp and the plucked zithers from the Orient, which she uses as harp-extenders. She played the harp in concerts in Europe and America in 1981 and 1982. She received many awards and grants including CAPS awards, a GEDOK prize, ASCAP grants and a Fulbright full scholarship, 1980 to 1981. Many of her compositions have been performed in America. DISCOGRAPHY.

Compositions
ORCHESTRA
Three movements for strings and percussion (1973) (ACA)
CHAMBER
Metamorphosis (picc, fl, ob, cl, hn, t-trb, hp and large perc ens) (1977) (Bearns prize, 1978; ASCAP grant, 1979) (APR Publ.)
Extensions: Three movements (hp, pf and large perc ens) (1975) (ACA)
Music for peyote cactus (vla, ob, t-sax, large gong, temple blocks, tam and assorted wind chimes; also perc, vla, b-cl and vibs) (1973) (ACA)
Giuoco piano (picc, fl, 2 trp, 2 trb and d-b) (1971) (ACA)
Memnon (6 hp) (1976) (Lyra Music)
Passacaglia (vln, fl, ob, cl, bsn and vlc) (1971) (ACA)
Fertility (fl, mar, 2 bongos and d-b) (1971) (ACA)
Three motion atmospheres for brass quintet (1974) (Arnold Salop memorial award, 1974; Mu Phi Epsilon award, 1974) (ACA)
Rite of the black sun (Antonin Artaud) (perc qrt and opt dancers) (1980) (Associated Music) (GEDOK award, Germany; hon mention ASUC/SESAC student contest)

Resonances (pf, hp and timp) (1971) (ACA)
Spicebox of strings (vln and pf) (1972) (ACA)
Creamy hands (hp and trb)
Doggone catact (hp)
After a dammit to hell (bsn) (1982) (ACA)
Butterfly collection (cham improvisation)
Drunk underwater koto (cham improvisation)
Jewels (cham improvisation)
Rare sea wolves (cham improvisation)
Siesta (cham improvisation)
Sudden noticing of trees (cham improvisation)
Transparent zebra (cham improvisation)
Ukranian ice eggs (cham improvisation)
VOCAL
Umi (m-S and orch) (1982)
Light breaks where no sun shines (Dylan Thomas) (mix-ch, S, A, T soli, 2 perc, 2 b-dr, Chinese bell tree, tamtam and perc) (1977) (IBM student composer award, 1979) (ACA)
Suite No. 1 (m-S and cham ens)
Euphorbia (with Jon English and Candace Natvig) (vce, hp, vln and trb)
Her cardboard bathroom (Rev. F. Lane) (narr, 2 fl, ob, cl and c-bass) (1976) (ACA)
I saw a man pursuing the horizon (S. Crane) (Bar, pf and hp) (1972) (ACA)
In the desert (S. Crane) (S, fl, mar and temple blocks) (1973) (ACA)
Lamentation/invocation (Edwin Honig) (B, cl, hp and vlc) (1984)
A little left of center (with Jon English and Candace Natvig) (vce, vln, hp and trb)
The sea and the honeycomb (A. Machado) (Cont, S, fl, cl, 2 perc and pf) (1979) (ACA)
DANCE SCORES
Cumuline (tape) (ACA)
Eurydice is dead (tape) (1983) (ACA)
OPERA
Orpheus Lives, chamber opera (4 soli, 2 ch, 12 insts and tape)
ELECTRONIC
Concerto for active frogs (B, mix-ch, t-sax, ob, perc and tape) (1974) (ACA)
Planxty bowerbird (hp and elec tape) (1982) (ACA)
Quadratura circuli (tape) (1978) (ASCAP grant, 1979) (ACA)
Shadows (elec tape)
FILM MUSIC
The Moonbeam Wishbook (org, pf and hp) (1980) (ACA)
Publications
Darmstadt 1980. Perspectives of New Music, 1981.
Ref. composer, 474, 622, 624, 625

LEBEDEVA, A.
20th-century Soviet composer.
Compositions
VOCAL
Muy umeyem urozhai bolshoi rastit (ch)
Other choral works
Songs
Ref. 441

LEBENBOM, Elaine F.
American pianist, teacher and composer. b. Detroit, MI, March 12, 1933. She studied composition under Clark Eastem, Ross Finney, Homer Keller and Ruth S. Wylie and the piano under Karl Haas, James Berry, Benning Dexter and Evelyn Gurvitch. She obtained her B.Mus. (composition) from the University of Michigan and taught at Detroit Community Music School.
Compositions
CHAMBER
Three facets of the dialogue (fl, ob, vlc, cl, pf and perc) (1975)
Quintet for winds (1955)
La journée (cor anglais and pf) (1976)
Suite (ob and pf) (1951)
Sonnets for a solitary oboe
PIANO
Sonata (1957) (1st prize, National Federation of Music Clubs, 1971)
Suite
VOCAL
Mark (mix-ch a-cap) (1954)
Freddie the second fiddle (narr, fl, ob, bsn, 2 vln and d-b) (1962)
Sephardic songs (S, fl, ob and fl) (1972)
Ref. 395, 622

LEBIZAY, Marguerite
Belgian pianist, professor and composer. She composed songs for children with orchestral accompaniment and music for the violin and the cello.
Ref. Belgian Music Info. Center

LEBRUN, Franziska Dorothea (nee Danzi)
German pianist, soprano and composer. b. Mannheim, March 24, 1756; d. Berlin, May 14, 1791. She was the daughter of the cellist Innocenzo Danzi and the elder sister of the composer Franz Danzi. She married Ludwig August Lebrun, an oboist and composer. She was one of the foremost sopranos of her time, making her operatic debut at the age of sixteen, at the Schwetzingen Castle Theater in 1777 and she then traveled to Paris and on to Milan, where she sang in Salieri's *Europe reconosciuta* at the Teatro alla Scala. She returned to London in 1779 for the new season at the King's Theatre and stayed for the following season, working under Giovanni Battista Bianchi, 1780 to 1781. She sang in Munich from 1782 to 1786. She died a few months after her husband. Her daughter was Sophie Dulcken (q.v.). DISCOGRAPHY.
Compositions
CHAMBER
Six sonatas, op. 1 (hpcd or pf and vln) (Paris: Sieber, 1779; London: J. Bland, 1780)
Six sonatas, op. 2 (hpcd or pf and vln) (Bland, 1780)
Piano sonatas
Ref. 2, 8, 14, 26, 41, 65, 70, 105, 109, 276, 347, 400, 405, 563, 622

LEBRUN, Sophie. See DULCKEN, Sophie

LECHANTRE, Elisabeth. See LACHANTERIE, Elisabeth

LECLERC, Michelle
French organist and composer. b. 1939. DISCOGRAPHY.
Compositions
ORGAN
Improvisations
Toccata (1961)
Ref. 563

LECLERCQ, Leila Sarah
20th-century American composer.
Composition
OPERA
Deidre of the Sorrows
Ref. D. Reynes (London)

LEE, Anna Virginia
American organist, pianist, choral conductor, teacher, poetess and composer. b. Jonesboro, TN, May 18, 1909. In 1929 she was a radio performer and in 1930 opened her own piano school. She was a church organist, choir director and originator of the publication *My Music Time* in 1964.
Ref. 475

LEE, Bo-Chas
20th-century Chinese composer.
Composition
OPERA
The Great Campaign (1951)
Ref. 465

LEE, Chan-Hae
Korean assistant professor and composer. b. Seoul, October 8, 1945. She gained her B.A. (composition) from Yonsei University, Seoul and her M.M. (composition) from the Catholic University of America where she did doctorate study in theory. She is assistant professor at the school of Music, Yonsei University.

Compositions
ORCHESTRA
Symphony No. 1 (1974)
Symphony No. 2 (1975)
Symphony No. 3 (1976)
Symphony No. 4 (1977)
Overture for orchestra (1971) (Catholic University)
Chungsombulgok (1983) (20th-century Music)
Gang-gang suele (1980) (20th-cent)
Glory (str orch) (1982) (20th-cent)
CHAMBER
Chung (str qrt) (1972) (Catholic University)
Structure (2 vlc) (1983) (20th-cent)
Dademi (perc) (1983)
Galpiri (cl) (1981) (20th-cent)
Line (vln) (1981) (20th-cent)
VOCAL
Cantata for chamber ensemble (Hooseng) (1978) (20th-cent)
Cantata for chamber ensemble (Choseng) (1979) (20th-cent)
SACRED
Resurrection, cantata (S, A, T and B) (1973) (Catholic University)
Jesus (mix-ch) (1982) (Seoul Music Festival)
Ref. composer

LEE, Hope Anne Keng-Wei
Canadian cellist, electronic instrumentalist, flautist, organist, pianist, trombonist, accompanist, choir director, teacher and composer of Chinese origin. b. Taipei, Taiwan, January 14, 1953. She commenced her music education in 1957 and gave a piano solo on Taiwan television at the age of nine years. She gained her B.Sc. from the University of Toronto (1973), her B.Mus. (1978) and her M.Mus. (1981) from McGill University, Montreal, having studied composition under Brian Cherney, Bengt Hambraeus and Jon Rea; electronic music under Mariano Etkin, Alcides Lanza and Bengt Hambraeus and the piano under Rose Goldblatt and Louis Philippe Pelletier. She won a German exchange scholarship in 1981 for a year's composition study under Klaus Huber at the Staatliche Hochschule fuer Musik, Freiburg. She has worked as a accompanist, organist, choir director and piano teacher, both privately and at the International Music Conservatory, Missisauga and as a piano, theory and ear training teacher at Montreal. She won several scholarships and prizes including the most outstanding and promising young composer prize at McGill University, 1978. She married the composer David Eagle.
Compositions
ORCHESTRA
Onomatopoeia: Chan chan (str orch); Jia Yuan (chil-ch and inst ens); 3. Tiao tiao (cham orch) (1981)
CHAMBER
M-Nabri (fl, cl, man, gtr, hp, vla, cb and mar) (1983)
Nohr (2 hn, 2 trp and 2 trb) (1983)
Initium (str qrt) (1977-1978)
Yeh (fl, vlc and hp) (1977)
Nabripamo (pf and mar) (1982) (1st prize, Okanagan Music Composers' Festival, 1983)
Melboac (hpcd) (1983)
Three pieces (vlc) (1976)
PIANO
Dindle (1979)
Pieces for children (1976)
VOCAL
Lili's dream image of life (Bar, perc and str orch) (1984)
Ballade of endless woe (vocal qrt and perc ens) (1979)
ELECTRONIC
Collaboration chant VI (with David Eagle) (tape) (1979)
La danse des étoiles (tape) (1977)
Study chant IV (tape) (1979)
Study chant V (tape) (1979)
MISCELLANEOUS
Nothing new music (with others at McGill University) (1978)
Ref. composer, 622

LEE, Hwaeja Yoo
Korean harpsichordist, organist and composer. b. Chong Ju, May 25, 1941. She obtained her B.A. from Seoul University, her M.A. and D.M.A. from the University of Oregon, lives in the United States and gives organ and harpsichord recitals.
Compositions
ORCHESTRA
Four movements (cham orch) (1967)
CHAMBER
Woodwind quintet (1962)
String quartet (1961)
Fantasy (ob, vln and 2 vlc) (1967)
Suite (fl, hn and perc) (1967)
Trio (ob, cl and bsn) (1961)
Duo (vln and pf) (1965)
Two pieces (org) (1967)
PIANO
Sonata (1961)
Two pieces (1966)
Publications
Secular Elements in Andre Raison's Organ Masses. 1970.
Ref. 77

LEE, Michelle
English flautist, recorder player and composer. b. London, May 31, 1952. She studied at the Bartok Conservatory, Budapest from 1970 to 1971; Royal College of Music, London from 1971 to 1975; Robert Schumann Institute, Dusseldorf from 1975 to 1978; Franz Liszt Academy, Budapest, 1978 to 1980. She is an A.R.C.M. (flute and recorder). She gives regular recitals in Britain and has recorded for Hungarian and British radio.
Composition
ELECTRONIC
Scarlet runner (fl, perc, 5 syn and tape)
Ref. 643

LEE, Young Ja
Korean professor and composer. b. Seoul, June 4, 1931. She graduated from the Ewha Women's University in 1954 and their Graduate School in 1956. She also studied composition under Tony Aubin and counterpoint under Noel Gallon at the Paris Conservatoire from 1958 to 1961 and from 1969 to 1970 she attended the Royal Music Conservatory at Brussels, studying composition and fugue under Marcel Quinet. Since 1961 she has been professor and chairlady of the composition department of the Ewha Women's University. DISCOGRAPHY. PHOTOGRAPH.
Compositions
ORCHESTRA
Mouvement symphonique (1972) (Munjo)
Mouvements concertants (vln and orch) (1972) (Munjo)
Concerto (pf and orch) (1971) (Munjo)
Ouverture festival (Art Assoc.)
Suite pour petit orchestra (1970)
CHAMBER
Quintet (vln, vlc, ob, bsn and pf) (1966)
String quartet (1956)
Trio (ob, bsn and pf) (1967)
Ballade pour clarinettes et piano (1970) (Chang)
Suite for cello and piano (1967) (Munjo)
Cello sonata (1957)
Suite romantique pour piano (1967) (Munjo)
Violin sonata (1956)
PIANO
Sonatine (1972) (Munjo)
Theme and variations (1960) (Munjo)
VOCAL
Five art songs (1968)
Ref. composer, 563

LEECH, Lida Shivers
American organist, pianist, authoress, teacher and composer. b. Mayville, NJ, July 12, 1873; d. Long Beach, CA, March 4, 1962. She studied under Helen Leaming, Elmer Fink and at Columbia University, Temple University and the Moody Blue Bible Institute. She taught music and was church organist and pianist in Camden, NJ.
Compositions
SACRED
God's morning
God's way, gospel song
I have redeemed thee
No fault in Him
Some day He'll make it plain, hymn
This I would ask from day to day, gospel song
We often grow weary, and lonely, and sad, gospel song
What will it matter then?
When the veil is lifted
Ref. 39, 347, 433, 646

LEECH, Renee (nee Caperton)
Anglo-American pianist, violinist, teacher and composer. b. Los Gatas, CA, October 26, 1942. Her father taught her to play by ear and from the age of five she studied the violin and the piano sporadically. She worked as a

dance improvisation pianist and studied piano and music theory whilst working for a teaching certificate from the California State Universities of San Jose and San Fransisco. She later moved to Novato and studied the Robert Pace and Suzuki piano teaching method.

Compositions

CHAMBER

Quartet No. 1 in 5/4 (str qrt) (1979)

Three twelve-tone reflections on the prevailing wind (rec qrt; also fl or str qrt) (1981)

VOCAL

Three morning songs from youth (Leech, R. Browning) (mix-ch and opt pf; also vce and pf) (1981)

DANCE SCORES

Petaluma river suite, in 6 mvts (cham ens) (1981)

Ref. composer

LEFANU, Nicola Frances

English conductor, lecturer and composer. b. Wickham, Essex, April 28, 1947. She is the daughter of composer Elizabeth Maconchy (q.v.). She commenced her composition studies under Jeremy Dale Roberts whilst at school and obtained her honors degree in music at Oxford in 1968. She studied composition privately under Goffredo Petrassi in Siena, Italy, Earl Kim at Harvard and Thea Musgrave (q.v.) and Peter Maxwell Davies in England. She was director of music at a London school and lectured at Morley and King's Colleges. In 1976 she spent six months in Australia and returned there in 1977 to be joint composer-in-residence at the New South Wales Conservatorium with her husband David Lumsdaine. She has conducted her works in the United States and England, had performances and broadcasts all over the world and directed seminars and workshops for young composers. She was recipient of the Cobbett chamber music prize in 1968 and winner of the BBC National Composers' competition in 1971, the Gulbenkian Dance award, 1972 to 1973, the Mendelssohn composition scholarship in 1973 and the Harkness fellowship, 1973 to 1974. DISCOGRAPHY. PHOTOGRAPH.

Compositions

ORCHESTRA

Columbia falls (1975)

The hidden landscape (1973) (Novello & Co.)

Preludio (cham orch) (1969)

CHAMBER

Deva for solo cello and seven players (vlc and ens) (1979) (Novello)

Collana (a-fl, b-cl, vln, vlc, d-b and perc) (1982) (Novello)

Clarinet and strings quintet (1970)

Variations (ob qrt) (1969) (Novello)

Quartettsatz (str qrt) (1970)

Trio (cl, vln and vlc) (1967) (Novello)

Abstracts and a frame (vln and pf) (1971) (Novello)

Chiaroscuro (pf) (1970) (Novello)

Omega (org) (1971)

Songs and sketches (vlc) (1971) (Novello)

Soliloquy (ob) (1966) (Novello)

VOCAL

The valleys shall sing (mix-ch and wind ens) (1973) (Novello)

But stars remaining (S) (1970)

The old woman of Beare (S and perc) (1982)

Rondeaux, French medieval love poems (T and hn) (1977)

The same day dawns (S and 5 insts) (1974)

SACRED

Christ calls man home (mix-ch) (1971) (Novello)

Stranded on my heart (1983)

Trio II – song for Peter (1983)

BALLET

Anti world, music theatre (1972)

The last laugh (1973)

OPERA

Dawnpath (composer) (2 singers, dancer and 5 insts) (1977)

MISCELLANEOUS

Magic theatre (1973)

SPNM birthday fanfare

Ref. composer, BMIC, *Composer* (London), 22, 69, 77, 79, 94, 141, 177, 206, 422, 457, 461, 563, 585, 612, 622

LEFEBURE, Marguerite (nee Verbrugghe)

Belgian pianist, accompanist, lecturer and composer. b. Ghent, 1871. She taught at the Conservatory of Ghent ca. 1890.

Compositions

PIANO

Concertstueck (2 pf)

Other pieces

Ref. 398

LEFEBVRE, Françoise (Sister Paul du Crucifix) (pseud. Paduci)

Canadian lecturer and composer. b. Valleyfield, Quebec, February 17, 1912. She obtained her B.Mus. from the Ecole Superieure de Musique d'Outremont, having studied under Claude Champagne, Jean Beaudet and Raoul Paquet and then lectured there.

Compositions

ORGAN

Symphony No. 1 (1946) (CAPAC award, 1974) (Ecole Superieure de Musique)

Symphony No. 2 (1950)

Fugue in C-Minor (1941)

Poèmes evangeliques (1950)

PIANO

Sonata (2 pf) (1949)

Theme and variations (1950)

SACRED

Cantata (ch) (1949)

Messe breve à l'unisson (ch) (1944)

Motets (ch)

Salut du Saint-Sacrement, 6 pieces (ch) (1950)

Ref. 133

LEFEVER, Maxine Lane

American band conductor, lecturer and composer. b. Elmhurst, IL, May 30, 1931. She studied under John Noonan at the Illinois Wesleyan University. She obtained her degrees from Western State College, CO, and Purdue University. She taught in public schools and was then assistant director with the Purdue University bands. She lectured throughout the United States and is director of Purdue University's Summer Music Workshops and executive secretary-treasurer of the National Band Associations. She is the president of American Bands Abroad and an honorary member of the United States Navy Band.

Compositions

PERCUSSION

Bandalier (Kendor Music)

Bernalillo (Kendor)

Bluff (Kendor)

Bryce Canyon (Kendor)

DeChelly (Kendor)

Desert (Kendor)

Dolores (Kendor)

Durango (Kendor)

Mancos (Kendor)

Mesa verde (Kendor)

Monticello (Kendor)

Monument Valley (Kendor)

San Luis (Kendor)

Shiprock (Kendor)

Sonora (Kendor)

Summit (Kendor)

Ref. composer, 142

LEFEVRE, Armande

20th-century French composer.

Compositions

PIANO

Villanelle, 2 pieces

Ref. Gerard Billaudot Catalog (Paris)

LEFEVRE, Jeanne

Early 20th-century French composer. She studied under Vincent d'Indy.

Composition

CHAMBER

Sonata in G (vln and pf) (Senart)

Ref. 41, 226

LEGINSKA, Ethel (pseud. of Ethel Liggins)

English concert pianist, conductor, teacher and composer. b. Hull, April 13, 1890; d. Los Angeles, February 26, 1970. Her pseudonym was given to her as a child by Lady Maud Warrender, who believed that a Polish-looking name would help Ethel's artistic career. Ethel first appeared in concert at the age of seven and in 1900 entered the Hochschen Conservatory, Frankfurt, where she studied the piano under Kwast and composition under I. Knorr and Sekles until 1904. She continued her piano studies for another three years in Vienna under Theodor Leschetizky. In 1907 she made her formal debut in London and then toured Europe and the United States where she studied harmony under Rubin Goldmark and composition under Ernest Bloch. She founded the Boston Philharmonic Orchestra of 100 players and later the Women's Symphony Orchestra of Boston. She conducted the Chicago Women's Symphony Orchestra and appeared as guest conductor with various other orchestras. In 1939 she settled in Los Angeles and taught the piano. She was known as the 'disappearing pianist' because of the numerous occasions on which she failed to appear at scheduled recitals. She was the first woman to write for and conduct in a major opera house, when she premiered her opera *Gale* at the Chicago City Opera. DISCOGRAPHY.

Compositions

ORCHESTRA

Beyond the fields we know, symphonic poem
Fantasy (pf and orch)
Quatre Sujets barbares, suite
Two short pieces

CHAMBER

From a life (13 insts)
Triptych (11 insts)
String quartet, 4 poems (Tagore)

PIANO

Pieces incl.:
Cradle song (John Church, 1932)
Dance of the little clown
Dance of the puppet
A dirge
Gargoyles of Notre Dame
Impromptu
Nostalgic waltz
Scherzo
Three Victorian portraits (New York: Composers Press, 1959)

VOCAL

Songs incl.:
Six nursery rhymes (S and cham ens)
In a garden
Four songs

OPERA

Gale (1935)
The Haunting, in one act
Joan of Arc
The Rose and the Ring (1932)

Bibliography

Ethel Leginska directs her Opera. New York Times, November 24, 1935.

Ref. 17, 22, 23, 44, 53, 55, 70, 74, 79, 94, 105, 110, 141, 142, 193, 201, 226, 228, 292, 295, 415, 455, 477, 563, 622, 653

LEGOUX, Julie, Baroness (Mrs. Rudolph) (pseud. Gilbert des Roches)

French composer. b. 1842; d. Paris, January, 1891. Her *Armide et Renaud* was performed at the concerts of the Chateau d'Eau.

Compositions

ORCHESTRA

Armide et Renaud, symphonic poem
Other works

Ref. 105

LEHMAN, Evangeline Marie (Dumesnil, Evangeline Lehman)

American pianist, authoress, singer, teacher and composer. b. Northville, MI, May 16, 1896; d. Highland Park, MI, February 28, 1975. She studied at the Oberlin and Fontainebleau conservatories and later in Paris. Her teachers were Isidor Philipp, Charles-Marie Widor, Marcel Dupre, Maurice Dumesnil and Camile Decreus (piano, voice, composition and instrumentation). In America she received an honorary D.Mus. from the Detroit Institute of Musical Arts, a citation from Port Huron and honors from Sigma Alpha Iota. From the French Government she received the Cross of Chevalier of the Legion of Honor (1962), the Palms of an Officer of the French Government and the Ordre Latin. Many of her compositions were performed in France and America and she appeared in concert with major orchestras in Europe and America. She taught privately and gave many workshops. She married the concert pianist Maurice Dumesnil.

Compositions

CHAMBER

Suite for strings and woodwinds
Trio (vln, vlc and pf)
La rivière verte (vlc and pf) (A. Leduc)
Scene pastorale (vln and pf) (Leduc)
Scherzo caprice (vln and pf)
Valse capricieuse (vln and pf) (Leduc)

PIANO

Numerous pieces incl.;
A juggler in Normandy (2 pf-4 hands; also pf) (Theo Presser)
Armistice Day (Presser)
Autumn sunset (Presser)
Ballet in white (Presser)
Indian flute call (Presser)
Légende (Presser)
Mount Vernon, suite
Musical clock in the antique shop (Presser)
Normandie, suite
Southland frolic
Tumbling clowns
Valse nostaligique

VOCAL

Songs incl.:
The good night star (Presser)
Bois de Boulogne, song cycle
A day's poem: At dawn; At mid-day; At dusk (2 S and A) (J. Fischer)
Golden wedding
Harp and bells (vce and pf) (G. Schirmer)
Minuet in a toy shop (vce and pf) (Presser)
Songs in grey minor

SACRED

St. Thérèse de l'enfant Jesus, oratorio (soli, ch, orch and org) (silver medal Ministere des Affaires Etrangères, France, 1933)
La nuit de noël, cantata (soli, ch, org and orch) (1935) (Presser)
Christmas (ch, org and orch) (Schirmer)
Messe pour la Sainte-France (soli, ch, org and orch (1958)
Agnus Dei (vce and pf) (Oliver Ditson)
Noël noël (vce and pf) (Presser)

Ref. Judy Tsou (University of Michigan), 226, 292, 347, 40, 142, 353

LEHMAN, R.

20th-century English composer. Her opera was performed in London.

Composition

OPERA

A la Watteau (1906)

LEHMANN, Amelia (Mrs. Rudolph) (pseud. A.L.)

19th-century English arranger, teacher and composer. She was the mother of Liza Lehmann (q.v.), to whom she gave her first singing lessons.

Compositions

VOCAL

Songs incl.:
When love is kind

Ref. 8, 74, 347

LEHMANN, Liza (Elizabeth Nina Mary Frederika) (Mrs. Herbert Bedford)

English pianist, soprano, teacher and composer. b. London, July 11, 1862; d. Pinner, September 19, 1918. She was the daughter of the painter Rudolph Lehmann and grand-daughter of the Edinburgh publisher Robert Chambers. Her first singing teacher was her mother, Amelia Lehmann (q.v.) and then Albert Bandegger. She studied composition under Raunkilde in Rome, Freudenberg in Wiesbaden and Hamish MacCunn in London. She made her debut as a singer at the Monday Popular Concerts in November 1885. She appeared in concert throughout the United Kingdom from 1885 to 1894, being encouraged by Joseph Joachim and Clara Schumann (q.v.), who accompanied her at the Philharmonic in 1888. In 1894 she married the painter and composer Herbert Bedford, retiring from singing to concentrate on composing. She was the first English woman to enjoy success with her songs with a large proportion of the public and she set the vogue for the song cycle in England. She was the first woman in England to be commissioned to write a musical comedy *Sergeant Brue*. Sir Thomas Beecham produced her setting of *Everyman* in London, 1916. She taught at the Guildhall School of Music in 1913. DISCOGRAPHY.

Compositions

CHAMBER

Romantic suite (vln and pf) (Keith Prowse)
Romance (vln)

PIANO

Album of 10 sketches
Cobweb castle
Other pieces

VOCAL

Once upon a time, fairy cantata (1903)
Endymion (S and orch) (J. Church Co.)
Molly's spinning (vce and orch) (Boosey)
Young Lochinvar (B, ch and orch)
The golden threshold, song cycle (solo and mix-ch) (Boosey & Hawkes)
Alice in Wonderland, song cycle
At love's beginning, duet
Baby seed song
Bird songs
Blind Cupid

Cautionary tales and a moral, set of 4 song cycles (Hilaire Belloc) (1909)
Come dance the romaika
The cuckoo
Daisy chain, song cycle
In a Persian garden (Omar Khayyam) (4 vces and pf) (1896)
In memoriam, song cycle (after Tennyson)
Mirage
More daisies, song cycle
Prairie pictures, song cycle
Secrets of the heart, song cycle (Boosey)
Songs of love and spring
There are fairies at the bottom of the garden (vce and pf)
Titania's cradle
Two albums of English songs
Two albums of German songs

OPERA
Everyman (1915) (London: Dinhan & Blythe, 1916)
Vicar of Wakefield (after Goldsmith) (1906) (Boosey)

OPERETTA
Sergeant Brue, musical comedy (1904)

INCIDENTAL MUSIC
Good-night, Babette, theatre (Boosey)
The Happy Prince
The Selfish Giant

Publications
The Life of Liza Lehmann. London, 1919.

Ref. 2, 6, 8, 14, 17, 22, 23, 40, 41, 44, 70, 100, 109, 110, 141, 226, 280, 347, 431, 473, 563, 622, 645

LEHMANN, Mrs. Rudolph. See LEHMANN, Amelia

LEHMANN, Nanna. See LIEBMANN, Nanna Magdalene

LEHOTSKA-KRIZKOVA, Ludmila

Czech organist, pianist and composer. b. Kremnica, January 10, 1863; d. May 8, 1946. Although largely self-taught she studied music in Kremnica under F. Janacek. She composed salon piano pieces and songs and accompanied choirs on the piano as a child but after the war played the organ and composed more serious music. She gave concerts in Marina, Kremnica and Bratislava, playing her own compositions.

Compositions

CHAMBER
Slovak dances (vln and pf)

PIANO
Sonata in F
Salon pieces

VOCAL
Choruses
Fifteen songs on folk words (vce, vln and pf) (1935)

Ref. 197

LEIBOW, Ruth Irene

20th-century pianist, lyricist and composer. She graduated from the University of Southern California with a B.Mus. (composition, 1957). She studied the piano under Jakob Gimpel and composition under Darius Milhaud, Ernst Tocj, Leon Kirchner and Ernest Kanitz.

Compositions

ORCHESTRA
Birth of Israel, symphony (also fl, vln, vla and hpcd or pf) (1971)
Two dances of fantasy (also 2 pf) (1949)

CHAMBER
Piano quintet No. 1 (1949)
Piano quintet No. 2 (1956)
String quartet movement (1951)
String trio (1961)
Sonata for cello and piano (1959)
Sonatine for flute and piano (1955)
Duo for violin and piano (1955)
Pieces for woodwinds and strings

PIANO
Pieces (2 pf)
Sonata (1951)
Scherzo (1954)
Theme and variations (1954)
Teaching pieces

VOCAL
Songs incl.:
Enchantment of love (composer) (1981)
How do I love thee (1962)
The Lake Isle of Innisfree (Yeats) (1956)
Let's live for today (composer) (1981)
Love in song (composer) (1979)
My sweet and lovely one (composer) (1954)
On joy and sorrow (Kahlil Gibran) (1961)
Sonnet (William Tarter) (1963)
Sonnet (Joseph Lippe) (1966)
A vagabond song (Bliss Carman) (1954)

SACRED
Silent prayer, chorale (mix-vces and pf or org) (1954)
Bar Mitzvah or Confirmation song (composer) (vce and pf or org) (1950)

Ref. composer

LEITE, Clarisse

Brazilian pianist, professor and composer. b. Sao Paulo, January 11, 1917. She studied at the Conservatorio Dramatico e Musical of Seo Paulo under Z. Leite Rizzo, J. Wancolle, J. Kliass and T. Noguera (composition) and O. Farinello (orchestration). She won a scholarship to study in France in 1930 and two years later won a gold medal in the Gomes Cardin competition. She worked for the Sao Paulo educational radio from 1932 to 1937 and toured for the State Department of Culture and made concert appearances, 1937 to 1959. She gave performances in Austria in 1959 and Hungary and on television. She is a professor at the Academia Internacional de Musica do Rio de Janeiro.

Compositions

PIANO
Impressões de Viena
Intimidade
Minuano
Quilombo dos Palmares
Resurrectio
Suite nordestina
Suite ouro verde
Ten poems: 5 new poems; 5 last poems (1981) (Sao Palo: Editora Ricordi)
Valse eterea

VOCAL
Concert No. 2 in F-Major (ch, org, pf and orch)
Songs

Ref. composer, 206, 333

LEIVISKA, Helvi Lemmiki

Finnish pianist, critic, librarian, teacher and composer. b. Helsinki, May 25, 1902; d. Helsinki, August 12, 1982. She was Finland's most important woman composer. She studied the piano and composition under Erkki Melartin at the Sibelius Academy, Helsinki, graduating in 1927. She continued with composition studies under Professor A. Willner in Vienna from 1928 to 1929 and under L. Madetoja and L. Funtek, 1931 to 1935. She taught the piano and in 1933 became librarian at the Sibelius Academy. From 1957 to 1961 she was music critic of *Ilta-Sanomat*, an evening newspaper. Her symphonies were widely performed in Finland. DISCOGRAPHY. PHOTOGRAPH.

Compositions

ORCHESTRA
Symphony No. 1, op. 23 (1947)
Symphony No. 2, op. 27 (1954)
Symphony No. 3 (1971)
Symphony No. 4
Piano concerto (1935)
Captive eagle (1946)
Child fantasies (1972)
Folk dance suite, op. 4
Four orchestral songs, op. 6
Impromptu energico, op. 24 (1948)
Sinfonia brevis, op. 30, in 1 mvt (1962)
Song of the stars (1946)
The song of the waves (1946)
Song without words, op. 26 (small orch)
Suite I, op. 8 (1934)
Suite II, op. 11 (1938)
Triple fugue, op. 10 (1935)
Two intermezzos, op. 16 (1945)
Variations and finale, op. 2 (1929)
Wild rose (1946)

CHAMBER
Piano quartet (1935)
Cantibile (vlc and pf) (1936)
Sonata (vln and pf) (1945)

PIANO
Capriccio, canto intima, con fuoco, op. 25
Five small children's pieces, op. 5
Sonatine (1939)
Suite antique, op. 3
Two fantasies (1943, 1944)
VOCAL
The lost continent, op. 28, cantata (soli, ch and orch) (1957)
Pimeaen peikko, op. 15, cantata (ch and orch)
Children's fantasies, op. 12, cycle (vce and small orch or pf)
Litania, op. 20 (ch and pf or org)
Nouse ole kirkas (S and pf)
Psalm of morning, op. 9 (vce and pf)
Songs with piano, op. 13
Songs with piano, op. 17
Songs with piano, op. 18
Songs with piano, op. 22
Songs with piano, op. 29
FILM MUSIC
Juha (1937)
Ref. composer, 20, 44, 62, 96, 280, 563

LEJET, Edith

French professor and composer. b. Paris, July 19, 1941. She studied under Rivier and Jolivet at the Paris Conservatoire, where she won first prizes for harmony, counterpoint, fugue, composition and general aesthetics. She taught harmony at the Sorbonnė Institute of Musicology from 1970 to 1972 and then taught a form of solfege at the Paris Conservatoire where she became a titular professor in 1975. In 1968 she won the Second Grand Prix de Rome and in 1967 the Prix de la Vocation. She was awarded the Prix Florence Gould in 1970. She was holder of an artist's scholarship from Casa de Velazquez in Madrid from 1968 to 1970. PHOTOGRAPH.

Compositions
ORCHESTRA
Flute concerto (1979)
Monodrame (vln and orch) (Editions Française de Musique, 1969)
CHAMBER
Fresque (14 insts) (Française, 1968)
Harmonie du soir (13 strs) (1977)
Concert for cello and instrumental ensemble (1978)
Espaces nocturnes (2 fl, cl, b-cl, perc, hp and d-b) (1976)
Musique (trp and wind insts) (Française, 1968)
Musique pour Rene Char (fl, hn, hp, perc, vla and vlc) (1974)
Quatour de saxophones (Française, 1974)
Aube marine (sax qrt) (1982) (Auvidis)
Petits poèmes (fl, vla and hp) (1981)
Musique (trb and cl) (1972)
Commande de l'etat (fl) (1983)
Balance (gtr) (1983)
Geneaux (gtr) (1978)
Triptyque (org) (1979)
Volubilis (vlc) (Paris: Amphion, 1981)
Metamorphoses (hp) (Editions Musicales Translantiques, 1982)
VOCAL
Journal d'Anne Frank (girls'-ch and inst ens) (1970) (Paris: Gerard Billaudot, 1970)
Ref. composer, 17, 280, 457

LEJEUNE-BONNIER, Eliane

French organist, professor and composer. b. Sartrouville, July 17, 1921. She studied at the Schola Cantorum and the Ecole Cesar Franck in Paris. She was titular professor of the organ and score writing at the National Conservatory of Mons. She performed as a soloist of the ORTF and stood in as organist for Marcel Dupre at St. Sulpice, for Bernard Gavoty at St. Louis des Invalides and for Jeanne Demessieux (q.v.) at Le Madeleine. She is a member of the Paris Conservatoire jury and an honorary organist of the great organ at Mons Cathedral. In 1955 she won first prize for the organ and improvisation at the Paris Conservatoire. She was awarded the Vercelli-Viotti prix de composition in 1953, the Ricordi prix de composition in 1954 and the prix de composition Scene Française in 1956.

Compositions
CHAMBER
Jeu et choral varie (fl, cl, vla and pf) (1980)
Sept miniatures (ob or fl, pf or hpcd or org) (1981)
Diptyque (vla and pf) (1975)
Theme and variations (vla and pf) (1981)
Elegie pour harmonie (1965)
Quatour à cordes (1953)
Thème varié (pf, 4 hands, vla and vlc) (1976)
Trio-rhapsodie (fl, vla and vlc) (1976)
Sogno et arabesco (acc) (1954) (Ricordi)
Trois legends (gtr) (1979)
ORGAN
Choral, variations and toccata for the great organ (1965)
Ricercare, In memoriam sur le nom de Marcel Dupre (1979)
PIANO
Fugue en Fa (4 hands) (1979)
Les paradoxes, suite in 5 mvts (1977)
VOCAL
Trois fables de Florian (w-ch or chil-ch a-cap) (1980)
Triptyque La Corbeille des Heures (4 w-ves a-cap) (1953) (Vercelli)
La Vierge à Midi (4 vces)
SACRED
Salve Regina (w-ch or chil-ch and org) (1981)
Ref. composer

LELEU, Jeanne

French pianist, teacher and composer. b. Saint-Michel, December 29, 1898; d. Paris, March 1980. She came from a musical background and entered the Paris Conservatoire at the age of nine. She studied the piano under Marguerite Long and A. Cortot (1913), harmony under Chapius (1917), score reading under Estlye (1918), counterpoint under G. Caussade (1919) and composition under d'H. Buesser and C. Widor (1922). In 1945 she became a teacher of sight reading at the Paris Conservatoire and taught harmony there from 1953. She received first prizes for the piano (1913) and composition (1922) at the Paris Conservatoire and in 1923 was awarded the Grand Prix de Rome for her cantata *Beatrice*.

Compositions
ORCHESTRA
Piano concerto
Croquis de theatre (1932)
Danse nocturne (Paris: Heugel, 1927)
Danse rustique (Heugel, 1927)
Transparencies, symphonic sketches (Paris: Leduc, 1931)
Femmes, suite (1947)
Trois esquisses italiennes (1926) (Leduc)
Suite pour un jour d'été (1941)
Virevoltes, suite (1950)
CHAMBER
Quartet for piano and strings (1922) (Heugel, 1922)
Suite symphonique (pf and wind insts) (Leduc, 1926)
PIANO
Danse nostalgique (a-sax and pf) (1956)
En Italie (Leduc)
Pochades (Leduc)
Other pieces
VOCAL
Beatrix, cantata (1923)
Le cortège d'Orphée (solo, ch and orch)
Six lyric poems after Michelangelo Sonnets (1924)
Songs (Paris: Choudens)
BALLET
Nauteos
Un jour d'ete (1940)
THEATRE
Le cyclope, satirical drama (Euripides) (1928)
Ref. 13, 14, 15, 17, 44, 76, 94, 96, 107, 172, 347

LEMAIRE-SINDORFF, Jeanne

Belgian pianist, teacher and composer. b. Uccle, near Brussels, July 19, 1931. She studied the piano and solfege at the Royal Music Conservatory, Brussels, where as a pupil of Sylvain Vouillemin, she won second prize in harmony. She studied the piano at the Schumann Conservatory, Duesseldorf and at the Mons Conservatory where she won first prize. In composition she is mainly self-taught. During 1962 to 1964 she taught at the Music Academy, Etterbeek. She composed a piano concerto.
Ref. CeBeDeM

LEMCKE, Anna

German composer. b. Elbing, October 4, 1862. She studied at the Conservatories of Berlin and Leipzig and under Robert Schwalm.

Compositions
CHAMBER
Piano pieces
VOCAL
Songs incl.:
Komm mit
Wie man nach einem Stern blickt
Ref. 226, 276

LEMMEL, Helen Howarth
19th-century American composer.
Compositions
VOCAL
Songs incl.:
Pansy and dewdrops
Two dandelions
We two
Ref. 276, 292, 347

LEMMENS, Mrs. Nicholas Jacques. See SHERRINGTON, Helena L.

LEMOINE, Mme. or Loise(a), Louise(a). See PUGET, Loise

LEMON, Laura G.
Canadian composer. b. Guelph, Ontario, October 15, 1866; d. Red Hill, Surrey, England, August 18, 1924. She studied at the Royal College of Music, England.
Compositions
CHAMBER
Pieces (vln and pf)
Columbia, minuet (pf) (Ashdown)
VOCAL
Songs incl.:
As once I saw thee (Boosey)
Glad is the world (Chappell)
Hey nonny no (Boosey)
I envy the bird that sings (Boosey)
In spring (Chappell)
Little songs (Williams)
My ain love and my dearie, Scottish song (Williams)
Nobody knows (Boosey)
Rose garden (Chappell)
Slumber song (Chappell)
There is no star that shineth (Chappell)
Tis now (Chappell)
Two songs (Cramer)
Youth and age (Chappell)
Ref. National Library of Canada, 297

LENNEP, Henrietta van
Dutch ethnomusicologist and composer. b. Surabaya, Java, September 14, 1906; d. June 30, 1972. She studied composition under B. Zweers and at the University of Amsterdam studied ethnomusicology and French literature. In 1948 she founded the Union Internationale des Amis du Bel Canto.
Compositions
ORCHESTRA
Works
CHAMBER
Pieces
VOCAL
Cantatas
Songs
INCIDENTAL MUSIC
De trekschuit, film
Ballet music
Stage music
Publications
De Muziek der Volkeren. 1956.
Ref. Donemus

LEON, Tania Justina
Black American pianist, conductor, teacher and composer. b. Havana, May 14, 1944. She obtained a B.A. (piano and theory, 1963) from Carlos Alfredo Peyrellade Conservatory, Havana; an M.A. (music education, 1964) from the National Conservatory, Havana; a B.A. (accounting, 1965) from Havana University; a B.S. (composition, 1971) and an M.S. (1973) from New York University. From 1973 she was involved in further post-graduate studies. She performed as a piano soloist in Cuba from 1964 to 1967 and with the New York University Orchestra in 1969 and the Buffalo Symphony Orchestra in 1973. She was a guest conductor of the Genoa Symphony Orchestra (1974, 1976), BBC Orchestra (1974, 1976), Halle Orchestra (1972), Buffalo Philharmonic Orchestra (1975) and at Royal Command Performances at the London Palladium (1974, 1976). She was music director for television in Havana (1965 to 1966); founder of the Dance Theatre of Harlem Orchestra in 1975 and of Meniscus and co-founder of The Brooklyn Philharmonic Community Concert Series. Since 1968 she has been staff pianist and conductor of the Dance Theatre of Harlem, becoming music director in 1970. She was awarded the Young Composer's prize by the National Council of Arts, Havana (1966), the Alvin Johnson award by the Council for Emigres in the Profession (1971), and the Cintas award in composition (1974 to 1975). She was a National Endowment for the Arts Fellow in 1975. She won ASCAP and Meet the Composer awards (1978 to 1983). Since 1982 she has been a teaching artist at Lincoln Center Institute. DISCOGRAPHY. PHOTOGRAPH.
Compositions
ORCHESTRA
Tones, piano concerto (1970)
Concerto criollo (pf, 8 timp and orch)
Latin lights (1979)
Pet's suite (also pf and fl) (1980)
CHAMBER
Four pieces for cello (1980)
VOCAL
Namiac poems (vce, ch and orch) (1975)
Spiritual suite (narr, 2 S, ch and mix-ens) (1976)
I got ovah (S, pf and perc) (1980)
BALLET
Dougla, African ballet (1974)
Haiku (1974)
Tones
ELECTRONIC
Voices and piccolo flute (tape)
THEATRE
La Ramera de la Cuena, musical (1974)
Sailor's Boat, musical (1974)
Ref. composer, 494, 549, 563, 625

LEON SAINT-AMANS FILS, M. See LA HYE, Louise Genevieve

LEONARD, Antonia Sitcher de Mendi
Spanish singer, teacher and composer. b. Talavera de la Reina, 1827. She studied in Paris and toured Europe. She taught music in Brussels and married the violinist and composer Hubert Leonard.
Compositions
VOCAL
Songs incl.:
Anne-Rose
Chansons des moissonneurs
La chaumiere dans les champs
Florine
Le pain des pauvres
Quand viendra la saison nouvelle
Ref. 268

LEONARD, Clair
B. 1901. DISCOGRAPHY.
Composition
CHAMBER
Recitativo and abracadabra (sax and pf) (1952)
Ref. 562

LEONARD, Mamie Grace
American pianist, teacher and composer. b. Dallas, TX, January 13, 1909. She began studying the piano at the age of seven under Mrs. George Carsey. She received a scholarship from Parks Goodie, then studied for three years under Frank Renard. She took a course in concert piano performance with C. Boris Grant. She moved to Kansas City in 1950 and studied composition, counterpoint, medieval modes and orchestration under Dr. Francis Buebendorf at the Conservatory of Music, University of Missouri, 1957 to 1963. She taught music. PHOTOGRAPH.
Compositions
CHAMBER
Adagio (vln and pf) (1961)
Canonic suite (1963)
PIANO
Christmas fantasy (1960)
Israel, La Chaim (1960) (3rd place, Otto Preminger competition)
Miniature pieces (1957)
Opus 1, Nos. 1-4 (1957)
Suite (1960)
Two bagatelles (1959)

VOCAL
From fairest creatures, sonnet (Shakespeare) (vce and pf) (1957)
I am going back to Old Erin (high vce and pf) (1960)
Jenny kissed me (L. Hunt) (vce and pf) (1960)
So oft I invoked thee (Shakespeare) (1959)
Spring and fall (G.M. Hopkins) (vce and pf) (1962)
SACRED
Descants for Christmas carols (ch) (1962-1964)
The Lord reigneth, anthem (93rd psalm) (chil-ch) (Volkwein, 1962)
Thanks be to Thee, anthem (chil-ch) (Volkwein, 1962)
Choral responses for church services, one in medieval modes (1960)
Invincible, hymn (vocal and inst descants) (comm 75th anniversary, Community Christian Church, Kansas City) (1965)
ARRANGEMENTS
Fixed in His everlasting seat, from Samson (Handel) (strs and brass octet) (1961)
Bach chorales (strs) (1959)
Minuet (Paderewski) (strs)
Ref. composer

LEONARDA, Sister Isabella (b. Anna Isabella Leonarda) (La Musa Novarese)

Italian composer from a minor noble family. b. Novara, September 6, 1620; d. Novara, 1704. Her date of birth seems uncertain but it appears that she entered the Convent of Sant' Ursula of Novara in 1636 at the age of 16 years and stayed to become mother superior about 1686 and madre vicaria in 1693. She probably studied music under Gaspare Casati, chapel master at the cathedral. Her first composition, two motets for two voices, appears in Casati's Third Book of Sacred Concerts (Venice, 1642). She was the first woman to publish trio sonatas for violins and basso continuo as well as a single solo sonata. She wrote over 200 pieces of sacred music and approximately twenty printed books most of which are preserved in the Biblioteca del Liceo Musicale of Bologna. DISCOGRAPHY.

Compositions
SACRED
Messe a quatro voci concertate con istromenti, et motetti a una, due etre voci pure con istromenti, op. 18 (ded Bishop of Novara, Mons. Gio Visconti) (P.M. Monti, 1696)
Messa e salmi concertati et a cappella con istromenti ad libitum con organo, op. 4 (Milan: Frat, Camagni, 1674)
Motetti a una, due, tre et quatro voci parte con istromenti e parte senza, con le litanie della Beata Vergine, op. 7 (G. Monti, 1677)
Motetti da una a tre voci con violini e senza, op. 13 (G. Monti, 1687)
Motetti a voce sola parte con istromenti e parte senza, op. 6 (ded Archdeacon Lorenzo Leonardi of Novara) (Venice: Gardano, 1676)
Motetti a voce sola parte con istromenti op. 20 (ded Rev. Filippo Avogadro) (M. Silvani, 1700)
Motetti a tre voci, Libro 1, op. 1 (Milan, 1665)
Motetti a due voci (Venice: Magni, 1642)
Motetti a voce sola, op. 10 (G. Monti, 1687)
Motetti a voce sola, op. 11 (ded D. Gaspar Francesco Fernandez Manrique, Governor of Novara) (G. Monti, 1684)
Motetti a voce sola, op. 12 (Milan: Frat. Camagni, 1686)
Motetti a voce sola, op. 14 (ded Ms. Stefano Maria Caccia) (G. Monti, 1687)
Motetti a voce sola, op. 15 (ded Lady Paula Beatrice Odescalchi) (P.M. Monti, 1690)
Motetti a voce sola, op. 17 (ded Dr. Ferrante Nazzari) (P. M. Monti, 1695)
Sacri concerti a una, due, tre et quatro voci con organo, op. 3 (Milan: Frat. Camagni, 1670)
Salmi concertati, op. 19 (psalms with insts) (Silvani, 1698)
Sonate a uno, due, tre e quatro istromenti, op. 16 (ded Mons. Federico Caccia, Archbishop of Milan) (P.M. Monti, 1693)
Vespro a cappela della Beata Vergine e motetti concertati, op. 8 (ded Count Vitaliano Borromeo) (G. Monti, 1678)

Bibliography
Carter, Stewart Arlen. *The Music of Isabella Leonarda.* Ph.D. Thesis. Stanford University, 1982.
Fedeli, F. *Le capelle musicali di Novara.* Instituzioni e Monumenta dell'arte musicale italiana. Milan, 1939.
Frati, L. *Donne musiciste bolognesi.* In RMIXXXVII. Vatican, 1930.
Ref. 8, 9, 13, 15, 26, 65, 72, 79, 85, 105, 125, 128, 129, 135, 163, 214, 216, 276, 335, 347, 361, 563, 622, 646, 653

LEONARDO, Luisa

Brazilian concert pianist, actress, teacher, writer and composer. b. Rio de Janeiro, October 22, 1859; d. Salvador, June 12, 1926. Her father, Vitorino Jose Leonardo, was a piano teacher and she studied under Isidoro Bevilacqua. She gave her first recital before Pedro II at the age of eight. In 1873 she went to France, where she studied for six years at the Paris Conservatoire and received a first prize in the piano in 1879. She studied under A.F. Marmontel (piano), A. Lavignac (harmony and composition) and A. Rubenstein. She performed in concerts in Brazil and Portugal and was the official royal pianist to Louis I in 1880. She returned to Brazil in 1885 but, disillusioned with the musical scene, reverted to acting. In 1900 she retired and settled in Salvador where she taught. Some of her piano pieces were published by the Casa Narciso and Artur Napoleao of Rio de Janeiro.

Compositions
ORCHESTRA
Hino a Carlos Gomes, anthem (1903)
Marcha funebre, march (1892)
CHAMBER
Petites mouches, (vln, fl and cl) (1893)
PIANO
Appassionato, study (1879)
Douleur, elegy (1879)
Flor da noite, waltz (1879)
Grande marcha triunfal (ded Emperor of Brazil) (1877)
Prière à la mémoire de Thalberg (1869)
Sombre désespoir (1904)
Souvenir, waltz (1879)
Teu sorriso (1903)
VOCAL
Songs incl.:
Hier (vce and pf)
Ma mère (vce and pf)
Saudação a estrela do oriente (vce and pf)
Solitude (vce and pf)
Two barcarolles (vce and pf)
MISCELLANEOUS
Habaneras, tangos, waltzes

Publications
Gazel. Rio de Janeiro: Gazeta de Tarde, 1881. Novel.
Ref. 333

LEONCHIK, Svetlana Gavrilovna

Soviet lecturer and composer. b. December 5, 1939. She studied composition under V.G. Fere at the Moscow Conservatory, graduating in 1965. From 1965 to 1973 she lectured at the music school in Petrozavodsk and then at the music school in Novorossiysk. DISCOGRAPHY.

Compositions
ORCHESTRA
Symphony (1965)
Piano concerto (1966)
Trumpet concerto (1964)
Festival overture (1967)
Simfonietta (str orch) (1963)
Poema (vln and str orch) (1973)
CHAMBER
Trio (vln, vlc and pf) (1960)
Sonata (fl and pf) (1962)
Sonata (vln and pf) (1966)
Sonata (vlc and pf) (1968)
PIANO
Preludes (1966)
Sonatina (1962)
VOCAL
Rylenkoy, cantata (soli, ch and orch of folk insts) (1964)
Lyrical songs from Kanteletara (Russian words) (vce and pf) (Leningrad: Soviet Kompozitor, 1975)
Songs (Soviet poets) (vce and pf)
INCIDENTAL MUSIC
Music for theatre
Ref. 21, 78, 563

LEONE, Mae Grace

American organist, pianist, conductor and composer. b. New York, June 17, 1931. She graduated from New York College with a B.A., M.Ed. and Ph.D. She continued with postgraduate studies at Adelphi College, Garden City, NY, and Goddard College, Plainfield.

Compositions
BAND
Pieces
CHAMBER
Pieces incl,:
Guitar ensemble music
Acclamations (org) (1962)
PIANO
Florid melodies (1962)
Pianoforte sonata (1952)
Variations in C

VOCAL
Lovely lady dressed in blue (mix-ch)
Other choral works
SACRED
Alleluia (1969)
Mass for peace
Psalm 100 antiphon 1-10 (1967)
Reception of religions
ARRANGEMENTS
Let there be peace (1975)
The Lord bless you and keep you
See us Lord (1970)
Choral arrangements
Publications
Contributions to Musical Arts.
The Modern Approach to Musicology. 1965.
The Spirit of Music. 1968.
Ref. composer

LEONI, Eva

20th-century American composer.
Composition
OPERA
Mr. Cupid, American Ambassador (New York, 1964)
Ref. 141

LEOPOLD, Mrs. Joseph. See ROECKEL, Jane

LEPEUT-LEVINE, Jeannine

French teacher and composer. b. Champigny sur Marne, May 14, 1934. She studied at the Paris Conservatoire under Mme. and M. Marcel Samuel-Rousseau, Jeanne Leleu (q.v.), Noel Galon, Tony Aubin, Jean Rivier, Darius Millhaud, Olivier Messiaen, Norbert DuFoure and Jean-Jacques Grenenwald. She received first prizes for solfege (1949), fugue (1957) and philosophy of music (1960). In 1971 she received the Medaille de la Ville de Paris. She was a member of Musiki Artis and now teaches music.
Compositions
ORCHESTRA
Mouvement symphonique (str orch) (1961)
CHAMBER
Sextet, in 4 mvts (2 fl, vln, vla, vlc and pf) (1960)
PIANO
Chorale, variations and finale (1955)
Prelude (1960)
Sonatina (1959)
VOCAL
Divers arrangements de chansons folkloriques (equal vces and chil-orch) (1977)
Trois choeurs à voix mixtes (mix-ch) (1960)
Poèmes chinois (2 vces and 4 insts)
Imitation de Notre Dame La Lune: Locutions des Pierrots I and Locutions des Pierrots XVI (vce and pf) (1959)
Je vous salue Marie (vce and org) (1962)
Lune Laune (Henri de Regnier) (vce and pf) (1959)
Ref. composer

LEPKE, Charma Davies

20th-cent. American organist, pianist, lecturer and composer. b. Delavan. She studied the organ under Carl Weinrich at Wellesley College and theory under Nadia Boulanger (q.v.), gaining her B.A. in 1941 and M.A. in 1942. At the American Conservatory of Music she studied the piano under Rudolph Reuter, obtaining her M.Mus. in 1946. She taught the piano and the organ at Fairfax Hall Junior College from 1942 to 1944 and the piano at the University of Nebraska from 1946 to 1950 as well as privately. From 1972 she was a church organist.
Compositions
PIANO
Canzona (1968)
Egoli - in Johannesburg (Lovedale Press, 1956)
Parade & four for five (Hal Leonard, 1983)
SACRED
Call to remembrance (mix-ch) (Mercury Music, 1966)
Great and marvellous (high vce) (Coburn Press, 1976)
Ref. 40, 347, 625

LEPLAE, Claire

Belgian sociologist and composer. b. September 3, 1912. She studied at the Louvain University and between 1964 and 1979 composed over 100 pieces. DISCOGRAPHY.

Compositions
CHAMBER
Pieces for flute, violin, piano, harmonium or organ
PIANO
Pieces (4 hands)
Danses imaginaires
Suite classique
Suite impressloniste
Tableau d'extreme orient
Ref. 563

LESBIA. See ERINNA

LESICHKOVA, Lili

Bulgarian pianist, lecturer and composer. b. Pleven, March 18, 1928. In 1951 she graduated from the Bulgarian State Conservatory, where she studied the piano under A. Stoyanov. Two years later she completed the composition course under Veselin Stoyanov. During this time she worked at the State School of choreography and after 1965 lectured on the piano at the State Conservatory.
Compositions
CHAMBER
Children's carnival (sextet)
Dobroudjana (ww, brass and perc)
Intrumental pieces
PIANO
Scherzo and toccata
Variations
VOCAL
Malka kantata za geroite ot 1878 (mix-ch and orch)
Praznik na mladosta
Other choral songs
Songs (vce and pf)
Light songs
BALLET
Karnaval, for children
Ref. 217, 463, 466

LESSEL, Helena

19th-century Polish composer.
Composition
PIANO
Serenade (1858) (ded J. Nowakowski)
Ref. 118

LESUR, Mme. A.R.

French composer. b. 1881. She was a pupil of Charles Tournemire.
Composition
CHAMBER
Sonata (vln and pf) (medal award) (Rouart, 1917)
Ref. 41, 226

LESZCZYNSKA, Marie, Queen

Polish composer. ca. 1730. She was the wife of King Louis XV and composed songs.
Ref. 465

LEUTNER, Minna. See PESCHKA, Minna

LEVEY, Lauren

American pianist, assistant professor and composer. b. New York, June 20, 1947. She studied at the Sarah Lawrence College under Joel Spiegelman and Mayer Kupferman and at Yale University under Jacob Druckman, Bulent Arel, K. Penderecki and Mario Davidovsky. From 1971 she was an associate on the Sarah Lawrence College piano faculty and from 1973 assistant professor and acting director of Bregman Electronic Music Studio, Dartmouth College.
Compositions
ORCHESTRA
Dissolves (cham) (1973)
VOCAL
A womb (with a view) of one's own (w-ch) (1974)
ELECTRONIC
Study (tape) (1973)
And now a message from our sponsor especially for you ladies (tape) (1974)
Ref. 142

LEVI, Mme.
French violist and composer. b. Brittany, ca. 1715.
Compositions
CHAMBER
Six solos for the viola in folio (Leclair)
Ref. 50

LEVI, Natalia Nikolayevna (Smyslova)
Soviet actress, translator and composer. b. St. Petersburg, September 10, 1901; d. Leningrad, January 3, 1972. In 1924 she graduated from the Russian Drama School and in 1936 from the Leningrad Conservatory, where she studied composition under P. Ryazanov. From 1924 to 1931 she was an actress and head of the Mobile Theater. She moved to Petrozavodsk in 1936 and began collecting folk songs of the northern peoples of the Soviet Union. During World War II she worked in Leningrad as a translator and then as a composer of war songs at the front. She was awarded two medals for songs hailing the defence of Leningrad. DISCOGRAPHY.
Compositions
VOCAL
Dva detstva (soloists, ch and orch of folk insts) (1938)
Karelskaya suita (soloists, ch and orch of folk insts) (1937)
Kliuch zemli (speaker, w-ch and orch of folk insts) (1947)
Nasha rodina (soloists, ch and orch of folk insts) (1938)
Ognevushka-poskakushka (chil soloists, chil ch and orch of folk insts) (1952)
Russkaya (soloists, ch and orch of folk insts) (1940)
Russki sever (soloists, ch and orch of folk insts) (1950)
Zimine kanikuly (soloists, ch and orch of folk insts) (1949)
Zolotoi volos (P. Bazhov) (speaker, 2 soloists and orch of folk insts) (1954)
Seven romances (P. Shubin, B. Likharev, S. Vogelson, A. Pushkin) (1940-1955)
More than sixty romances (A. Surkov, B. Likharev, A. Prokofiev, A. Dykhovichny, N. Shcherbakov and other poets) (1932-1955)
I stroll along the forest path, song
Songs for children
Arrangements of Karelian, White Russian, Ukranian and North Russian songs
OPERA
Karelskaya skaska (V. Chekhov) (1940)
INCIDENTAL MUSIC
Klyatva, play (D. Shcheglov) (1939)
Tam gde sosmy shumyat, play (D. Shcheglov) (1951)
Krasmaya shapochka, play (E. Shvartz) (1954)
Volshebnye tykvy, play (N. Khodza) (1955)
Khibini, documentary film (1947)
Monchetundra, documentary film (1947)
Murmansk, documentary film (1948)
Publications
Songs of the Peoples of the Karelo-Finnish Republic. Co-author.
Bibliography
Rogoshina, V. *Natalia Nikolayevna Levi.* 1962.
Ref. 87, 330, 563

LEVIN, Erma E.
20th-century composer.
Composition
FILM MUSIC
The Projectionist (1970)
Ref. 326

LEVIN, Rami Yona
American oboist, pianist, recorder player, teacher and composer. b. Brooklyn, February 27, 1954. She graduated from Yale University with a B.A. (music, 1975) having studied under Yehudi Wyner and Robert Morris and from the University of California, San Diego with an M.A. (composition, 1978), where her teachers were Bernard Rands, Pauline Oliveros (q.v.), Robert Erickson and Kenneth Gaburo. Her composition teachers also included Miriam Gideon (q.v.) in New York, 1970 to 1971. She persued further composition studies at the Aspen Music School in the summer of 1977 and won first prize in their composition competition. She received private oboe lessons from Bert Lucarelli and Ronald Roseman in New York. She was the oboeist with the Morley Wind Ensemble in London from 1979 to 1980 and teaches the oboe and the piano privately.
Compositions
CHAMBER
And yet again (3 fl and 2 cl) (1977)
Out of the blue (ww qnt) (1976)
Movements (str qrt) (1978)
Dialogue (fl and ob) (1980)
Double exposures (fl and ob) (1975)
Light reflection (fl and ob) (1974)
Exaltation of larks, No. I (ob and vlc) (1976)
Exaltation of larks, No. 2 (ob and pf) (1976)
Connections (ob) (1976)
Ambages (1976)
PIANO
Doubletake (2 pf) (1976)
Half an octopus (4 hands) (1977)
Take a pianist to lunch (4 hands) (1977)
Blues toccata (1973)
Intensities (1984)
Safari sweet (1976)
VOCAL
Becummings 1 and 2, song cycle (e.e. cummings) (1977)
Now we are six, song cycle (S, ob, vlc, vln and vla) (1975)
Rain has fallen (S and vlc) (1973)
MULTIMEDIA
Plugged-in (3 actors and headphones) (1976)
Ref. composer, 624, 625

LEVINA, Zara Alexsandrovna
Soviet concert pianist, teacher and composer. b. Simferopol, Crimea, February 5, 1907; d. Moscow, June 27, 1976. In 1923 she graduated with a gold medal from the Odessa Conservatory where she studied the piano under B. Dronseiko-Mironovich. From 1926 to 1929 she taught the piano to senior classes at the Skriabin School of Music and composition classes at the Moscow Conservatory. In 1932 having studied composition under N. Myashovsky and R. Gliere, she graduated from the Moscow Conservatory. She pursued a career as a pianist, playing works of Liszt, Chopin, Schumann, Prokofiev and Beethoven in the larger cities of the Soviet Union. She contributed numerous articles on music to various Soviet newspapers and journals. She was awarded the title of Honored Artist of the Republic (R.S.F.S.R.) and a number of medals. DISCOGRAPHY.
Compositions
ORCHESTRA
Piano concerto (1945)
Piano concerto No. 2 (1975)
Three pieces for light orchestra (1955)
Three symphonic waltzes (1951)
CHAMBER
Fantasia on Bashkir themes (vln and pf) (1942)
Poema (vla and pf; also vlc and pf) (1928, 1931)
Poema and canzonetta (vlc and pf) (1938)
Sonata (vln and pf) (1928)
Sonata No. 2 (vln and pf) (1948)
Ten pieces (vln and pf)
Toccata in E-Minor
PIANO
Dance in A-Flat Major
Pieces for youth (1972)
Rhapsody: 3 pieces (1940)
Sonata No. 1 (1925)
Sonata No. 2 (1955)
VOCAL
Oda soldatu (soloists, ch, pf, org and orch) (1963)
Poem of Lenin (A. Surkov) (soloists, ch and orch) (1930)
Song of the stormy petrel (M. Gorky) (soloists, ch and orch) (1926)
Album of verse (Lermontov)
Four romances (Lermontov) (1940-1942)
Eight romances (Ysenin)
Fourteen romances (S. Marshak)
Lyrical romances
Romances (A. Isaakian, S. Kaputukian, O. Shiraz and other poets) (1955)
Round year, song cycle (O. Shiraz) (1947)
My fatherland, song cycle (O. Shiraz) (1952)
Songs (G. Rublev, P. Gradov, L. Nekrasova, O. Driz, S. Esenin)
Three romances (Pushkin) (1936)
Two romances (E. Dolmatovksy) (1942-1943)
Two romances (A. Surkov) (1946)
Under a mysterious cold half mask (Lermontov)
Over 80 children's songs incl.:
Children of the world for peace (T. Rublev) (1950)
We are marching to the Kremlin (L. Nekrasova) (1948)
INCIDENTAL MUSIC
Music for dramas and radio plays
ARRANGEMENTS
Russian, Byelorussian, Rumanian, Bulgarian, Polish, Hungarian, French and Icelandic folk songs (vce and pf)
Bibliography
Mikhailovskaya, N. *Zara Levina.* 1960.
Ref. 17, 70, 84, 87, 94, 193, 226, 277, 330, 379, 419, 420, 441, 563, 622

LEVITE, Miriam (Miriam Levite Resnikoff)
Israeli pianist, accompanist and composer. b. Russia, 1892; d. ca. 1970. She studied at the Moscow Philharmonium and went to Israel in 1914, where she performed as a soloist and accompanist.
Compositions
VOCAL
Shir ha-shirim, poem (Bar, A, ch and orch)
Shir erez chafoni (duo and str qrt)
Zemer (duo and ch acc)
Seven songs (vce and pf)
SACRED
Tfilla ahrona (vce and ch)
Song of Rachel
Ref. 94

LEVITOVA, Ludmila Vladimirovna
Soviet concertmistress, editor and composer. b. Romi, Ukraine, December 29, 1926. She studied composition under L. Revutsky at the Kiev Conservatory and graduated in 1950 with distinction. She also studied instrumentation under B.N. Liatoshinsky (1953 to 1962) and was concertmistress at the Kiev opera, 1962 to 1963. She edited the Ukrainian *Sovietski Kompozitor* and later became editor of other Ukrainian music periodicals.
Compositions
ORCHESTRA
Festival overture (1949)
Poem, solntsu navstrechu (1961)
Tantsevalnaya poema (vln and orch) (1951)
CHAMBER
Intermezzo (wind qnt) 91967)
String quartet (1948)
Dance (fl and pf) (1972)
Romance (vlc and pf) (1946)
Ozorniki (balalaika) (1973)
Pieces for bayan and bandura
PIANO
Etude (1944)
Fantasy (1953)
Forest pictures, suite (1942)
Ten pieces (1973)
Three preludes (1944-1945)
Variations (1945)
VOCAL
Glory to the woman toiler, cantata
Slava zhenshchinam-truzhenitsam, cantata (soli, ch and orch) (1960)
Zdravstvue, vesna! vocal-choreographic pictures (soli, chil-ch and orch) (1961)
Zima, suite (soli, chil-ch and orch) (1958)
Zdravstvui Oktyaber (V. Sosyura) (ch) (1948)
Okh kak zhalko (P. Voronko) (ch) (1949)
Three songs on words by Soviet poets
Romances of over 50 songs
Arrangements of folk songs
INCIDENTAL MUSIC
Music for films
Light music
Ref. 21, 87, 465

LEVITSKAYA, Viktoria Sergeyevna
Soviet editor, teacher and composer. b. Kharbin, July 20, 1911. In 1938 she graduated from the Moscow Conservatory, where she studied composition under V. Shebalin. In 1941 she completed her postgraduate studies under R. Gliere whilst teaching composition and harmony. After 1949 she was editor of opera and symphonic works for Muzgiz, music publishers.
Compositions
ORCHESTRA
Symphony (1968)
Symphonic poem (1939)
Suite (orch of folk insts) (1948)
CHAMBER
Five string quartets (1936, 1945, 1946, 1951, 1955)
Pieces (fl and pf, ob and pf, hn and pf) (1948)
PIANO
Prelude and fugue (1933)
Two sonatas (1933)
VOCAL
Otechestvannaya voina, oratorio (1941)
Cantata (M. Raskovaya) (1940)
Cantata (S. Shchipachev) (soli, ch and orch) (1959)
Pesnya sovietskogo naroda (M. Rysky) (mix-ch and pf) (1947)
Three choruses (A. Surkov, S. Shchipachev, N. Aseyev) (ch a-cap) (1947)
Suite moya rodina (S. Shchipaehev) (1946)
Two choruses (A. Prokofiev) (1973)
Cycles (F. Tiuchev, Akhmatova) (vce and pf) (1975, 1976)
Approx. 40 romances (A.K. Tolstoy, M. Lermontov, T. Shevchenko, L. Pervomaisky) (1935-1949)
Eight songs (M. Aliger, S. Bolotin, V. Sayanov, A. Surkov) (1942-1945)
OPERA
Tarasova noch (Y. Galitsky) (1944)
Teni i zemlya dvizhetsya (1938)
Ref. 21, 87

LEVY, Ellen
20th-century American composer.
Compositions
CHAMBER
Brass quintets (hn, trb, 2 trp and tuba) (1967)
Ref. Library of Congress

LEVY, Mrs. I. See PERETZ-LEVY, Liora

LEWANDOWSKA, Janina. See SZAJNA-LEWANDOWSKA, Jadwiga Helena

LEWIN, Olive
20th-century Jamaican Government Director of Art and Culture and composer.
Compositions
VOCAL
Daniel (ch, drs and gtr) (1980)
Run Moses (ch and gtr) (1982)
Zion (ch and drs) (1981)
Ref. composer

LEWING, Adele
German pianist, teacher and composer. b. Hanover, August 6, 1866; d. New York, February 16, 1943. She first played in public at the age of 14 and graduated with honors from the Leipzig Conservatory, where she studied under Reinecke and Jadassohn. She toured Europe and the United States and taught in Chicago and Boston. From 1893 to 1896 she continued her studies in Vienna under Leschetizky (piano) and Fuchs (composition). She settled in New York in 1897. Her compositions won prizes at the Columbian Exposition in 1893 and in Baltimore in 1910.
Compositions
PIANO
Berceuse (Ditson)
Children in the forest
Children's march
Greeting
Legend
Meditations
Old French dance
Romance, op. 17 (Ditson)
Song without words, op. 16 (Ditson)
VOCAL
By the Rhine
Evening rest
Fair Rohtraut (Ditson)
Faithfulness
Legende, op. 15
Liebeslied, op. 14
Love song
Proposal
Springtime
Wanderer's night song
Winter night
Ref. 74, 276, 292, 297, 347, 415, 433

LEWIS, Carrie (Caryl) (Mrs. Bullard-Rich)
20th-century American composer.
Compositions
VOCAL
The captivity, cantata (soli, mix-ch and pf) (1938)
Songs
SACRED
He that dwelleth in the secret place

OPERA
The Rose and the Ring (Boston: White-Smith Music, 1934)
OPERETTA
Carnival of the Flowers
The Fairy Godmother's Lesson
The Methodical Music-master
One Day's Fun
The Queen of the Garden, for children (F.H. Martens)
Ref. 141, 190, 291, 292, 347

LEYLA SAZ. See HANIM, Leyla

LIADOVA, Ludmila Alexseyevna
Soviet pianist and composer. b. Sverdlovsk, March 29, 1925. At the Sverdlovsk Conservatory, she studied the piano under B. Marantz and composition under V. Trambitsky, graduating in 1948. She received numerous awards for her compositions and frequently performed her own works in public.
Compositions
ORCHESTRA
Piano concerto (1965)
Ballet miniatures (pf and orch) (1975)
Concert polka (pf and orch) (1976)
Poem osvobozhdennaya Korea (pf and orch) (1951)
Rhapsodia (pf and orch) (1976)
Kolkhoznaya polka (orch of folk insts) (1950)
Suite Volga-Don (orch of folk insts) (1952)
Three miniatures (orch of folk insts) (1954)
Uralskaya rapsodiya (orch of folk insts)
VOCAL
Dorogami muzhestva, cantata (1970)
Slushai starshii nash bozhatyi, cantata (1971)
Songs incl.:
Chudo-pesenka
Edem c nami
Estafeta novostei
Sibir Sibir
Soldatskaya liricheskaya
Vozhatuy nash
OPERETTA
Atamansha (1972)
Dusha soldata (1963)
Pod chornoi maskoi (I. Lelgant) (1961)
Schastlivay mel (G. Binder)
Ref. 87, 330

LIBBEY, Dee. See ROHDE, Q'Adrianne

LICHT, Myrtha B.
20th-century American composer.
Composition
VOCAL
One thing more (mix-ch and pf) (H.W. Gray Co.)
Ref. 190

LICHTENSTEIN, Olga Grigorievna
Soviet pianist, concertmistress, lecturer and composer. b. Aleksandrovsk, July 22, 1902; d. Moscow, June 1, 1973. From 1909 to 1918 she attended composition classes given by Glazunov at the St. Petersburg Conservatory. In 1928 she graduated from the Moscow Conservatory, having studied the piano under S.E. Geinberg. From 1930 to 1931 she lectured at the October Revolution music school in Moscow. She was then concertmistress of a theatre orchestra and from 1950 to 1960 at the B. Shukin Theatre School.
Compositions
ORCHESTRA
Ballet suite, Ivan da Marya
PIANO
Fantasy tales, Ivan da Marya (2 pf) (1968)
VOCAL
Rhapsody-vocalise (vce, vln, cl, vlc and pf) (1965)
Cycles (vce and pf)
Romances (Lermontov, R. Burns, Tsvetayeva, Mistral, Kvitko and other poets)
INCIDENTAL MUSIC
Music for plays (Moliere, Lermontov, Irasek, Garcia Lorca)
Ref. 21

LIDDELL, Claire (Elizabeth Claire)
British pianist and composer. b. Glasgow, Scotland. She studied at the Royal Scottish Academy of Music, Glasgow and the Royal College of Music, London, where she was awarded a three year scholarship. The original manuscript sketches of her composition *Five Orkney scenes* were bought by the National Library of Scotland in Edinburgh. She was awarded the Ellen Shaw Williams prize for the piano. DISCOGRAPHY.
Compositions
PIANO
Three pieces (Ascherberg, 1960)
VOCAL
Consider the lilies (ch) (Decumuse)
Song remembered (Siegfried Sassoon) (ch) (comm)
Songs incl.:
Affirmations (Emily Bronte poems) (T, hn and pf) (comm Duncan Robertson)
The charm of the kilt (composer) (1978)
Children's songs:
Five Orkney scenes, song cycle (Roberton, 1975)
Garden of love, French-Canadian folk song (trans composer's mother)
Go-to-bed blues (1978)
Impressions, song cycle (1978)
Jubilee (1978)
The kindling fire, 12 songs (Burns) (Roberton, 1974)
My wish (1978)
Orphead: A spell for rain, song cycle (George Mackay Brown) (high vce) (1978)
Rain (1978)
The rhythm of life (Brunton, 1985)
So sweet was the sound (1978)
Some may doubt (1979)
We're learning French (1978)
Where are the joys
SACRED
A Scottish carol (3-part trebles) (Roberton, 1975)
Carols (1977-1978) incl.:
Aud glory know (composer) (mix-ch and org)
Branch bare of leaf (composer) (mix-ch)
No room! No room! (composer) (mix-ch)
THEATRE
Animal talk, children's playlet (1978)
ARRANGEMENTS
Ae fond kiss (choral setting) (Roberton, 1976)
Fine flowers in the valley (Roberton, 1976)
I'l lay ea'in by you rom (choral setting) (Roberton, 1974)
Other Burns settings (choral setting) (1974)
Settings for voice and piano (old Scots songs) (1977-1978)
Settings for choral pieces (1977-1978)
Scots folk song settings
Ye banks and braes (choral setting) (Roberton, 1976)
Publications
The Book of Keyboard Harmony. 1979.
So you want to play by ear. Stainer & Bell.
Ref. composer, 563

LIDGI-HERMAN, Sofia
Bulgarian pianist, conductor, singer and composer. b. Vidim, Sofia, November 15, 1930. After attending the University of Sofia, she went to the Bulgarian Musical Academy in Sofia (1949 to 1954). She conducted provincial opera in Bulgaria (1959 to 1960) and the Turkish opera in Istanbul (1966). She won prizes in international competitions for choir conducting (1948, 1949 and 1953) and in Bulgaria for singing (1948). She now lives in Israel.
Compositions
CHAMBER
Nocturnes (vln and pf or fl and hp)
PIANO
Nocturno, prelude, sonatas and toccata
VOCAL
Romances (S)
OPERETTA
Children's operetta
Ref. 77

LIEBLING, Estelle
American authoress, singer, teacher and composer. b. New York, April 21, 1880; d. September 25, 1970. She was educated at Hunter College and the Stern Conservatory in Berlin. She studied under Nicklass Kempner and Matilde Marchesi. She was awarded honorary degrees by the Boguslawski College of Music and Fairleigh Dickinson College of Music. She made her debut as Lucia in *Lucia di Lammermoor* at the Dresden opera house and her New York debut in 1903. She appeared as a soloist with many orchestras and was decorated by King Edward VII. She settled in New York where she taught singing.

Compositions
PIANO
Canzonetta (Church)
First meeting (Church)
Madeleine, waltz (Church)
Manuela (Church)
Mazurka de concert (Church)
Menuette scherzoso (Church)
Spring song (Church)
Valse poetique (Church)
VOCAL
Faustiana (on the ballet from Gounod's Faust) (New York: Galazy, 1950; Church)
Indian love song (Church)
ARRANGEMENTS
Blue Danube waltz
Carnival of Venice
Invitation to the dance
Ombre legere
Souvenir waltz
Waltz of the flowers
Publications
Estelle Liebling Coloratura Digest.
Ref. 39, 74, 85, 297, 376

LIEBMANN, Helene (nee Riese)
German pianist and composer. b. Berlin, 1796. Her date of birth could well be earlier as her *Sonata for cello and piano, op. 11* was published in 1806. She was a pupil of Lauska from an early age and first performed in public at the age of ten years. By the time she was 13 she was arousing great interest and when her first sonata appeared, Mozart's influence was evident in this work. A second sonata followed soon after and was highly praised by Rochlitz in the *Allgemeine Leipziger Musikzeitung* in 1811. In 1812 or 1814 she married and moved to London - thereafter nothing is known of her. Her last compositions appeared in 1819.
Compositions
CHAMBER
Several string quartets incl. op. 13, in A-Flat (Peters Edition)
Two trios, op. 11 (pf, vln and vlc) (Peters)
Sonata (vlc and pf)
Sonata, op. 9 (vln and pf)
Sonata, op. 14 (vln and pf)
Sonata, op. 11 (vlc and pf) (1806) (Grancino, 1982)
Other pieces (vln and pf)
PIANO
Phantasie, op. 16
Sonatas, ops. 1-5
Sonata, op. 15
Six Laendler
Variations on ballet Figaro
Variations on Cendrillon
Variations on Wenn mein Pfeifchen
VOCAL
Songs incl.:
Kennst du das Land (Goethe) (Berlin: Schlesinger)
Ach, aus dieses Thales Gruenden (vce and pf) (Berlin: Ruecher)
Adieux bergere (vce and pf) (Ruecher)
Ihr Weisen ohne Leidenschaft (vce and pf) (Ruecher)
Im Hain, am Bach (vce and pf) (Ruecher)
Le Matin dans une bruyere (vce and pf) (Ruecher)
Oede war des ersten Menschen Leben (vce and pf) (Ruecher)
Ref. 26, 121, 129, 158, 276

LIEBMANN, Nanna Magdalene (nee Lehmann)
Danish pianist, singer, teacher and composer. b. September 27, 1849; d. May 5, 1935. She studied at the Danish Music Conservatory, Copenhagen and performed as a singer and as a pianist. She also composed works for the piano. She married the composer Axel Liebmann.
Compositions
VOCAL
Der Goldschmiedgesellschaft (Hansen)
Der Rattenfaenger (Hansen)
Five songs (Thor Lange, Ludwig Holstein) (1904)
Lenz (Hansen)
Minnelieder (Gammeltyske kjaerlighedssange) (Nord Musikforlag, 1963)
Seven songs (Goethe, H. Heine, Lenau)
Sommer
Vier Schaeferlieder
Ref. 297, 331

LIECHTI, Grety
Composer, b. 1904.
Compositions
PIANO
La source
Variationen
Ref. Frau und Musik

LIEDBERGIUS, Camilla (nee Rasmussen)
Swedish pianist, singer and composer. b. Kristianstad, June 1, 1914. She studied at the Stockholm Conservatory under O. Wibergh, A. Hagiunius and G. Boon, passing the music teachers' examination in 1938. She worked as a piano soloist and accompanist on the radio and sang with church choirs. In 1940 she married the bass-baritone Sixten Liedbergius. She composed arrangements of folk music for three violins, songs and made arrangements of folk songs.
Ref. 96

LIFFER, Binette
Contemporary American composer.
Composition
CHAMBER
Gavotte for woodwind (fl, ob, cl and bsn) (1982)
Ref. AMC newsletter

LIGGINS, Ethel. **See LEGINSKA, Ethel**

LIGHTFOOT, Mils
19th-century British composer.
Composition
VOCAL
We are sisters beautiful flowers! (ded Mrs. Blamire) (London: R. Mills)

LIKELIKE, Miriam Cleghorn, Princess
Hawaiian guitarist, pianist, ukulele player and composer. b. Honolulu, January 13, 1851; d. February 2, 1887. She was the younger sister of Kalakaua and Liliuokalani, Queen of Hawaii (q.v.). Princess Likelike was raised in Hilo and when she moved to Honolulu in the 1860s was already an accomplished musician. With her sister she shared the leadership of one of the royal clubs, where they played a significant role in perpetuating and encouraging Hawaiian music and musicians. They were both sponsors of concerts and musical pageants in and around Hawaii.
Compositions
VOCAL
Ainahau
Ka 'owe a ke kai
Aia hiki mai
Lei ohaoha
Ref. 438

LILIEN, Antoinette von, Baroness
Late 18th or early 19th-century Austrian pianist and composer. Several of her works were published in Vienna in 1799 and were well received.
Compositions
PIANO
Seven variations on a theme from the ballet Alcine, op. 2
Eight variations on the theme Pria ch'io l'impegno
Nine variations on an original theme
Ref. 26, 128, 129, 226, 276

LILIUOKALANI, Queen of Hawaii (Lidia Kamakaeha Paki) (pseud. Mme. Aorena)
B. Honolulu, September 2, 1838; d. Washington, DC, November 11, 1917. She came from an extremely musical family and was probably the most musically gifted of her class and time in Hawaii. She became Queen in 1891 and reigned for two years, until she was deposed by the Americans under Sanford B. Dole, who became the first and only president of the Hawaiian Republic. Under his orders she was arrested in January 1895 and sentenced to life imprisonment, but she was kept in Iolani Palace until her release in September of the same year. Her Hawaiian National Anthem, composed ca. 1868, was played at official functions for 20 years, until a new anthem was written. In 1898 she wrote that her song compositions ran into the hundreds and she lived and composed for 19 more years; even if her number was only half correct it would make her the most prolific of the Hawaiian composers of that century.

Compositions
VOCAL
Alola oe! song (ch) (1884)
Ahe lau makuni, waltz songs (San Francisco: Pacific Music Co., 1897)
A chant (Pacific, 1897)
Ehehene ko aka, song
He mele lahui Hawaii, national anthem (Pacific, 1897)
He pule, a prayer and a chant (Pacific, 1897)
Hooheno (Pacific, 1897)
Ka oiwi nani (Pacific, 1897)
Ka wai mapuna (Pacific, 1897)
Kauau o 'oe e kealoha, song
Kokohi, song
Kuu pua i paoakalani (Honolulu: J.H. Wilson)
Liliuokalani's prayer and serenade (Washington: Sanders & Stayman)
Nani na pua (Pacific, 1897)
Pau'ahi o kalani, song
A prayer
Puia ka nahele, waltz song (Pacific, 1897)
Puna paia aala, waltz song No. 2 (Pacific, 1897)
The Queen's jubilee (Pacific, 1897)
OPERETTA
Mahailani (incomplete)
Publications
Hawaii's Story by Hawaii's Queen. 1898.
Music of Hawaii. 1898.
Ref. 53, 123, 370, 438, 617

LILLENAS, Bertha Mae

American authoress, minister and composer. b. Hanson, KY, March 1, 1889; d. Tuscumbia, MO, March 13, 1945. She studied music privately and became an ordained minister of the Church of the Nazarene in 1912. She is a member of ASCAP.
Compositions
SACRED
Are you watching this star?
He will not forget
His Grace is my strength and my song
Jesus is always there
Jesus took my burden
Leave your burden at the place of prayer
Saved by the blood
When clouds are hanging Low
Ref. 39, 347, 646

LIMA CRUZ, Maria Antonietta de

Portuguese musicologist and composer. b. Lisbon, November 3, 1901; d. 1957. She revealed early musical talent and studied the piano and composition under Florent Schmitt. She made her piano debut in 1921, performing her own works. She was music critic to the daily *A Voz* and from 1928 contributed articles to French and Portuguese journals and publications. She was curator of the Museum Instrumental and the library of the Conservatorio Nacional and worked for the department of music studies of National Radio, Lisbon.
Compositions
ORCHESTRA
Poemas, op. 19 (pf and orch)
Ritmos lusitanos, op. 26 (pf and orch)
CHAMBER
String quartet, op. 24
Sonata, op. 25 (vlc and pf)
Sonata quasi fantasia, op. 17 (vln and pf)
PIANO
Balada, op. 21
Casa dos brinquedos, op. 1
L'enchanteur, op. 7
Impressoes do campo, op. 4
Jardins, op. 12
Lenda, op. 3
A Lua, op. 2
Mascaras, op. 9
Nocturnos, op. 10 (national composition prize, 1926)
Nevicata (also vce and pf)
Noite de S. Jaoa, op. 5
Santo Antonio, op. 8
VOCAL
Adoração, op. 18 (Gil Vicente) (ch and orch)
Cantares de amigo, op. 13 (vce and pf) (National Composition Prize)
Cantigas de amor, op. 14 (vce and pf)
Cantigas de Escarneo e Maldizer, op. 15 (vce and pf)
Deus Pan, op. 11 (vce and pf)
Dois sonetos de Camoes, op. 20
Publications
Carlos de Seixas. 1941. Biography.
Grandes Musicos. 1939. Collection of biographies of Portuguese musicians.
Historia da musica Portuguese. 1955.
Rodrigues Coelho. Biography. 1948.
Contributions to dictionaries: *Analogico da lingua Portuguese*. Porto, 1949; *Dicionario enciclopedio da musica*. Barcelona, 1948-1949.
Ref. 9, 100, 107, 268

LIND, Jenny (Johanna Maria) (Swedish Nightingale)

Swedish soprano and composer. b. Stockholm, October 6, 1820; d. Malvern Hills, England, November 2, 1887. The daughter of a bookseller, she became a pupil of C.M. Craelius and I. Berg at the Royal Stockholm Theatre. She made her debut at the age of nine years and thereafter appeared with growing success in a number of roles. In 1841 she went to Paris to further her studies; M. Garcia believed that her voice had already been worn out by faculty teaching and overwork, however he gave her lessons for almost a year. She then performed in opera in Sweden, Germany and England and in 1850 traveled to the United States. Everywhere she went she was feted and prices of seats where she was performing rose to incredible heights. Later in her life she preferred to perform in concerts and oratorios rather than in opera and she particularly liked Swedish folk songs. Her voice was very strong and brilliant in the higher register and her cadenzas were usually of her own composition. She gave numerous performances for charity and with the earnings of her American tour founded and endowed art scholarships and other charities in Sweden. She coached the Bach Choir, conducted by her husband Otto Goldschmidt, for the first performance in England of Bach's *B-Minor Mass*. After her death, a plaque of her was unveiled in Westminster Abbey by H.R.H. Princess Christina; Jenny was the first woman to be represented in Poets' Corner.
Compositions
CHAMBER
Serenading polka (vln, gtr and pf) (Ditson)
VOCAL
Norwegisches Schaeferlied, Herbei, ihr munter'n Tiere (Cranz)
Schwedisches Volkslied, Tanzleid aus Dalekarlien (Cranz)
Ref. 8, 20, 297, 572, 637

LIND, Johanna Maria. See LIND, Jenny

LINDEMAN, Anna Severine

Norwegian pianist, teacher and composer. b. October 29, 1859; d. June 24, 1938. The Lindemans were a prominent Norwegian musical family and Anna taught the piano at the Kristiania Conservatory from 1891 to 1895 and 1912 to 1925. She married her cousin Peter Brynie Lindeman and worked to build up the music conservatory that he founded with his father in 1883 and which became the Norwegian State Academy of Music in 1973. DISCOGRAPHY.
Compositions
CHAMBER
String quartet in G-Minor
Three pieces (pf and vln or vlc)
Piece for flute and piano
PIANO
Three small pieces (4 hands)
Eight small easy pieces
Four pieces, op. 5
Six character pieces, op. 3
Six small pieces for beginners
Sorte fugle, op. 7
Three piano pieces, op. 4
Three piano pieces, op. 8
Three piano pieces, op. 9
Publications
Women Composers and Music School Authors in Scandinavia.
Ref. Royal University Library, Oslo

LINDEMAN, Hjelle Signe

Norwegian organist, pianist, teacher and composer. b. July 2, 1895; d. 1981. She had her first music lessons from her organist and music teacher father Peter Lindeman and later studied at the Oslo Conservatory, passing the organ examination in 1916. She studied under K. Straube and P. Graener in Leipzig. She was organist at the Famlebyen church in Oslo and taught the organ, the piano and harmony at the Oslo Conservatory. She gave numerous concerts, sometimes playing her own compositions. PHOTOGRAPH.

Compositions
ORCHESTRA
Halling
Haust pae fjellet
Norsk
Tema med variat
CHAMBER
Suite (vlc and vln)
ORGAN
Fantasifuge
Fantasisonate
Katekismus for organists
Paskemorgen (1928)
Passacaglia and fugue (1927)
Pre- and postludes
Soengadstemninger
Two stemningsbilleder (1929)
Other compositions
PIANO
Et besoek paa landet
Eventyr
Teaching pieces
VOCAL
St. Haward suite (vces and orch)
Fire blix-slamar (vce and orch) (1927)
Pieces (solo, w-ch, vlc, ob and pf)
Ref. composer, 20, 96

LINDEN VAN SNELREWAARD-BOUDEWIJNS, Nelly van der
Dutch composer. b. Breda, January 12, 1869; d. Crowhurst, England, February 8, 1926. She studied at Keulen Conservatory from 1887 to 1890.
Composition
THEATRE
Jantje in Modderstrad (soloists, chil-ch and pf) (Middelburg: A.A. Noske)
Ref. 44

LINDSAY, Miss M. (Mrs. J. Worthington Bliss)
19th-century English composer. b. Wimbledon.
Compositions
VOCAL
Songs incl.:
Airy, fairy Lilian
Alone
Arrow and the song
Danish maid
Excelsior (1854)
Far away (1868)
Hymn of the Moravian nuns (Pulaski's banner) (1854)
Children's songs (1871-1872)
Part songs
ARRANGEMENTS
The bridge (1856)
Home they brought the warrior dead (Longfellow) (1858)
Ref. 6, 226, 276

LINES, Ruth W.
20th-century American composer.
Composition
SACRED
Sanctus (double mix-ch) (H.W. Gray Co.)
Ref. 190

LINEVA, Yevgeniya Eduardovna
Russian composer. b. 1853. She composed two song cycles and other songs.
Ref. 465

LINHARTOVA. See KENDIKOVA, Zdenka

LINN, Emma Sophie Amalie. See HARTMANN, Emma Sophie Amalie

LINNEMANN, Maria Catharina
British guitarist, pianist, violinist, teacher and composer. b. Amsterdam, December 21, 1947. She lived in England from 1948 to 1971 and studied at the Royal Academy of Music, London from 1966 to 1970. She attended master classes under Nadia Boulanger (q.v.), studied conducting under Maurice Miles, the piano under Madeline Windsor and harmony under Margaret Hubicki (q.v.). In 1970 she was awarded the principal's prize and obtained her teaching diploma in 1971. She emigrated to Germany in 1971 and taught music and the piano in schools until 1973. In 1973 she was inspired by Martin Nicolai to study the guitar and in 1976 began to compose for that instrument. PHOTOGRAPH.
Compositions
CHAMBER
Come August and September (fl, cl, vlc and gtr)
Ballad of Belfast (gtr and fl)
Ballad of County Armagh (gtr and fl)
GUITAR
Juliet (2 gtr)
The old church, theme and variations (2 gtr)
To sleep, perchance to dream (2 gtr)
Aus dem Schweigen
Ballad of County Down (Musical New Services, London)
Ballade pour Christine et Richard
Death of a seagull
Der clown (New Services)
Just for my guitar (New Services)
Lady Claire (New Services)
Your name in the sand
Your name in the stars
Ref. composer

LINNET, Anne
Danish pianist, saxophonist, arranger, singer and composer. b. Aerhus, June 30, 1953. She began singing with a rock group in 1970 before beginning composition studies under Per Noergard, graduating in 1976. She then turned to serious music, characterised by a strong sense of rhythm.
Compositions
ORCHESTRA
For symfoniorkester, in 1 mvt (1977)
CHAMBER
Tivoli (qnt) (1976)
Danse brutale, rhythmic chamber music (1978)
Danse solitaire, rhythmic chamber music (1978)
Quatuor brutale, 6 dances (gtr)
VOCAL
Pedros praeludium (3 vces and org) (1979)
Sang til hjertet (A, B and hp) (1976)
Som sand der forsvinder (vce and 2 gtr) (1979)
Music for kvindesind (Tove Ditlevsen) (1977)
SACRED
Hosiannah (mix-ch) (1978)
MISCELLANEOUS
Son of life, rhythmic music
Ref. composer

LINWOOD, Mary
English composer. b. Birmingham, 1755; d. Leicester, March 2, 1845. She gave several exhibitions of her fine needlework.
Compositions
VOCAL
David's first victory, oratorio (1840)
Songs incl.:
Pretty fairy
OPERA
The Kellerin
The White Wreath
Ref. 6, 102, 226, 276

LINZ VON KRIEGNER, Marta
Hungarian violinist, conductor and composer. b. Budapest, December 21, 1898. In Budapest she studied the violin under Jeno Hubay, Carl Flesch, Stephen Thomas and Koessler. She studied composition under Zoltan Kodaly and in 1924 was the first woman to be accepted as a pupil in the conducting class at the Berlin Hochschule fuer Musik. She later graduated from master classes in conducting given by F. von Weingartner in Basle and C. Krauss in Salzburg. After 1924 she lived in Berlin and in the 1930s traveled extensively as a virtuoso violinist and conductor with the Berlin Philharmonic and the Guerzenich Orchestras of Cologne. She married Dr. Kalman von Kriegner, musicologist, jurist and philologist.

Compositions
ORCHESTRA
Hungarian capriccio (vln or pf and orch)
CHAMBER
Dialog (vln and pf)
Rumanian rhapsody (vln and pf)
Sonata (vlc and pf; also vln and pf)
Other violin compositions
PIANO
Capriccio e capriccetto
Don Quixote polka
VOCAL
Works (ch and orch)
Hungarian folk songs
Other songs
SACRED
Koenig Drosselbart
MISCELLANEOUS
Der Rahelose
Film music
ARRANGEMENTS
Humoreske, op. 101, no. 7 (Dvorak) (vln and pf)
Slavischer Tanz, op. 72, no. 2 (Dvorak)
Slavonic dance in E-Minor (Dvorak) (vln and pf)
Der Schottischer (Linz) (pf)
Ref. 17, 44, 70, 105, 110, 189, 226, 231

LIOS. See ERDOEDY, Luisa, Countess

LIPINSKA-PARCZEWSKA, Natalia

19th-cent. Polish pianist and composer. She was the daughter of violinist Karol Lipinski (1790 to 1861) of whom Paganini, when asked who he thought was the greatest violinist, replied, *Without doubt Lipinski is the second greatest.*

Compositions
PIANO
Two mazurkas, op. 1 (ded Chopin) (1838)
Mazurka, no. 2, on the theme Perruquier de la Regence (Paris: Richault)
Ref. 35

LIPSCHUTZ, Lita

Composition
MISCELLANEOUS
Three episodes (New York: C. Fischer)
Ref. Frau und Musik

LIPSCOMBE, Helen

American pianist, lecturer and composer. b. Georgetown, KY, April 20, 1921; d. Lexington, KY, January 4, 1974. She studied at the University of Kentucky where she obtained her B.A. (music hons, 1941) and M.A. (1945). She studied the piano under Mrs. E.A. Cheek, John Richardson, Ford Montgomery and Robert Morgan; composition under Dean Robert Sandess at Bloomington and Nadia Boulanger (q.v.) at Longy School, Cambridge, MA; she also studied under Robert L. Saunders. *To the waters* won first place in the 1947 Kentucky Music Composition contest and she won a prize in the song division of Phi Mu Alpha. She taught the piano and composition at the University of Kentucky for five years and privately for over 27 years and composed for the Modern Dance Group of the University of Kentucky.

Compositions
ORCHESTRA
Chorale, waltz and lullaby for strings (also pf) (Los Angeles: Avant Music, 1965)
CHAMBER
Nocturne and waltz (strs)
Design (cl and str qrt)
Variations (ww qnt)
Three clarinet trios
Two by two (vln and vlc)
Three solos for clarinet and piano
Evensong (vln)
ORGAN
Passacaglia and toccata
Reverie
PIANO
Sonatas
Other pieces
VOCAL
The ballad of William Sycamore (Bar, m-ch and pf)
Anthems
SACRED
Alleluia: Let us sing, 14 hymns (w-ch)
Bethlehem town (w-ch)
MISCELLANEOUS
Child's world (1949)
Double exposure
Lament
The masque of the red death, children's pieces
Soliloquy
Suite for Dorothy Jean
To the waters
Triple play
Ref. 39, 40, 94, 142, 322, 347, 496

LISSONI, Giulia

Italian pianist and composer. b. Novara, 1902. She was a pianist in Parma and composed piano works.
Ref. 70, 226

LISTON, Melba

Jamaican trombonist and composer. b. 1926.

Composition
FILM MUSIC
Smile Orange (1976)
Ref. 497

LITER, Monia

20th-century American composer.

Compositions
ORCHESTRA
Prelude espagnole (pf and orch) (Boosey & Hawkes)
CHAMBER
Mediterranean suite (perc, gtr, hp and strs) (Boosey)
Scherzo transcendent (timp, perc, hp and strs) (Boosey)
Serenade for strings and harp (Boosey)
Ref. 280

LITSITE, Paula Yanovna

Latvian-Soviet singer, translator and composer. b. Riga, August 20, 1889; d. Riga, July 11, 1966. She graduated from the Riga Conservatory in 1923, having studied under Ya Wihtol. She was also a student of P. Yuryan. From 1912 to 1915 she was a soloist at the Latvian opera. She translated the libretti of classical operas and Russian songs and romances into Latvian.

Compositions
ORCHESTRA
Four miniatures (1935)
Noch ligo, poem (1936)
Sarabande and gavotte (1933)
CHAMBER
Piano quintet (1947)
Piano trio (1934)
Larghetto (vlc and pf) (1941)
Melodia (vlc and pf) (1942)
Narodnaya svita (vlc and pf) (1963)
Pesnya (vlc and org) (1964)
PIANO
Children's album (1952)
Sonatina (1955)
Three preludes, 5 pictures (1936)
Variations on a folk theme (1955)
VOCAL
Choruses (Rokpelnis, Saulitis, Baodis, Kruklis, Sils and other Latvian poets)
Over 80 romances and songs incl.:
Kolkhoznyi tsikl (1952)
Soldatskaya kruzhka (1958)
Solnechnaya Gruzia (1950)
Tri pesmi o Lenine (1947)
ARRANGEMENTS
Latvian folk songs (ch)
Ref. 330

LITTLE, Anita Gray

American pianist and composer. b. Portland, OR, June 6, 1966. She studied under Lucy Blanchard and Helen Lamson Elwell. Her compositions have been performed in Portland and Boston.

Compositions

VOCAL

Brave Britain (ch)
Beside the sea
Cradle song
Encore song
Lest we forget
Love
Only wait
Prosperity
We can have peace

SACRED

Song for peace (mix-ch)
The Lord reigneth
Whatsoever God doth

Ref. 374, 433,

LITTLEJOHN, Joan Anne

English pianist, editor, musicologist, teacher, writer and composer. b. London, April 20, 1937. She was a G.R.S.M. and an L.R.A.M. She did post-graduate study under Dr. Herbert Howells (music and poetry, 1961 to 1964) and Sir Lennox Berkeley (1970 to 1971), Nadia Boulanger (q.v.) and Ruth Dyson (composition), gaining her L.F.A.B.I. in 1983. She was on the administrative staff of the Royal College of Music from 1960 to 1983 and from 1972 assistant keeper of the Parry Room Library at the College. She taught the piano at Harrow School from 1972 to 1973 and in 1972 promoted and produced a song and poetry recital 'With my father a-ploughing' at the Purcell Room, South Bank, London. She prepared the full score of Fricker's *Third symphony* in 1960 and was the editor of 'Musicologist'. She contributed to several publications and exhibitions as a writer, photographer, editor and musicologist.

Compositions

VOCAL

The sword and the ploughshare, cantata (1973-1974)
O Brignall banks, part song (mix-ch, fl and opt ints) (1970)
The bonny Earl of Murray (w-ch, pf and pedal timpani) (1975)
A morning of May (S and orch) (1962)
De La Mare songs (vce and pf) (1963)
Four sea songs (vce and pf) (1969)
A garland for De La Mare (1982)
La mascarade de Jean de La Fontaine, song cycle (vce and pf) (1964)
The heights of Haworth, song cycle (Emily Bronte) (vce and pf) (1971)
Poems from Palgrave (vce and pf) (1968)
Robert Herrick song-garland (1971)
Songs of innocence and experience, double song cycle (m-S) (1970)
St. Juliot Cornwall (Rachel Pearse)
Three Shakespeare songs (vce and pf) (1961)
Other songs

Ref. composer, 77

LIU, Tyan-Khua

Chinese composer. b. 1895; d. 1932. DISCOGRAPHY.

Composition

VOCAL

Chinese folk dance

Ref. 563

LIVINGSTON, Helen

American authoress and composer. b. New York, NY, March 26, 1900. Her chief collaborators were Yoshi Aeri and Oscar and Helene Wach. Helen is a member of ASCAP.

Composition

SACRED

Kaddish

Ref. 39, 494

LLANOVER, Lady (nee Waddington)

Welsh composer. b. 1802; d. 1896. She composed songs.

Ref. 465

LLOYD, Caroline Parkhurst

American music director and composer. b. Uniontown, AL, April 12, 1924. She studied under John D. Robb at the University of New Mexico, where she received a B.M. She studied at the Eastman School of Music under Bernard Rogers and at Columbia University (1973) under Donata Fornuto, Arpad Szabo and Charles Wourinen. She taught privately from 1946 to 1973 and acted as musical activities director at the Centro Venezolano Americano in Caracas from 1955 to 1968. Her opera *Dona Barbara* was performed in commemoration of Caracas's 400th anniversary. In 1944 she received a Sigma Iota scholarship and commenced honors work in composition at the University of New Mexico. DISCOGRAPHY.

Compositions

VOCAL

Works for voice, chorus, keyboard and string quartet
Calle de Elvira, for children (vce and pf)
Granada, for children (vce and pf)
Seis canciones de los paises bolivarianos (vce and pf)
Three songs of the Bolivar countries (1965)
Three songs (Garcia Lorca) (1966)
Two songs (Jose Ramon Medina) (1968)

OPERA

Dona Barbara (1967)

Ref. Working papers on women in music, 141, 142, 190, 563

LLUNELL SANAHUJA, Pepita

Spanish pianist, singer, teacher and composer. b. Barcelona, August 4, 1926. She studied solfege, theory, the piano and singing at the Barcelona Conservatory. She continued studies in dramatic art and declamation at the Theatre Institute. She gave recitals of songs and poetry with various theatrical companies and on radio, television and film. Several of her light songs won prizes. She teaches music and declamation. DISCOGRAPHY. PHOTOGRAPH.

Compositions

ORCHESTRA

Suite No. 1 (cham orch) (1982)
Suite No. 2 (cham orch) (1985)

CHAMBER

Dos invenciones transcendentales (str qrt or org) (1985)
Siete piezas cortas en forma de suite (str qrt)
Waltzes (pf)

VOCAL

Coleccion de canciones clasicas (vce and pf)
Coleccion de canciones navidenas (vce and pf)
Numerous light songs
Twelve Sardanas, Catalan folk songs

Ref. composer

LOCKE, Flora Elbertine Huie

American teacher, writer and composer. b. Wilson, NY, June 1, 1866. She studied at the Leipzig Conservatory and under Liszt, Scharwenka, Reinecke, Mason and Leschetizky. She introduced the Locke Primary Plan for teaching young pupils and ran her own school. She composed songs and teaching pieces.

Publications

The Foundation of Music in Rhymes and Songs.

Ref. 226

LOCKSHIN, Florence Levin

American pianist, teacher and composer. b. Columbus, OH, March 24, 1910. She studied the piano under Frank Murphy (1920 to 1935) and orchestration under Morris Wilson at Ohio State University, where she obtained a B.S. in 1931. She graduated with an M.A. (orchestration) in 1953 from Smith College having studied under Alvin D. Etler. She was a private piano teacher and performer from 1924 to 1945 and a member of a four-piano team from 1945 to 1955. In 1951 she was chosen as a composer-performer to represent Ohio for the National Federation of Music Clubs and in the same year was made an honorary life member of the American Federation of Musicians. PHOTOGRAPH.

Compositions

ORCHESTRA

Annie Bradley's tune, fantasy on a Negro folk tune
Aural
Cumbia! (Columbian folk tune)
Paen (Mexican folk song) (New York: Independent Music, 1962)
Scavarr (Independent, 1969)
Song forn (Independent, 1961)
Statement, lament and protest
Virgin of Guadalupe (Mexican folk tune)

VOCAL

Poems of Prospice, trilogy (m-ch, w-ch, mix-ch and orch)
Do not go gentle (Dylan Thomas) (m-ch and orch) (Independent, 1959, rev 1979)
Song (Christina Rossetti) (w-ch)

BALLET

The cycle (comm Smith College)

Ref. composer, 142, 228, 475, 594, 625

LOCKWOOD, Annea Ferguson

New Zealand electronic instrumentalist, pianist, singer, teacher and composer. b. Christchurch, July 29, 1939. She studied at the University of Canterbury, Christchurch from 1958 to 1961, obtaining a B.Mus. (first class honors). On scholarships from the Royal School of Music and the New Zealand Arts Council she studied at the Royal College of Music, London from 1961 to 1963 under Peter Racine Fricker (composition) and E. Kendall Taylor (piano). She became an L.R.A.M. and A.R.C.M. (performance). In 1961 and 1962 she attended the Darmstadt Ferienkurse fuer Neue Musik, with a grant from the Fereinkurs in 1962. From 1963 to 1964 she attended classes at the Cologne Musikhochschule and Bilthoven Electronic Music Studio, Holland, studying instrumental and electronic music composition under Gottfried Michael Koenig on a scholarshp from the German academic exchange service. She studied psychoacoustics with computer scientist Peter Grogono, completing her third year at Southampton University Institute of Sound and Vibration Research, England, 1969 to 1972. She produced a series of programs for BBC radio on 'trance music of many cultures'. She taught at Hunter College, City University of New York and worked as a free-lance composer-performer. She periodically gives workshops at Bedford women's correctional facility in Bedford, New York. Since 1982 she has been director of the Electronic Music Studio, Vassar College, Poughkeepsie, NY, and taught composition and other courses at Vassar. DISCOGRAPHY.

Compositions

ORCHESTRA

Violin concerto (1962)

VOCAL

A Abelard, Heloise, chamber cantata (m-S and 10 insts) (1963)
Aspekte einer Parabel (Kafka) (B and cham ens) (1963-1964)
Malolo, lullaby (3 w-vces a-cap) (1982)
Malaman (one or more vces) (1974)

ELECTRONIC

And sound flew like a bird (tape) (1973)
Bus trip (1971)
Cloud music (tape) (1974)
Consulting musician (live elects and one inst) (1975) (Ear Magazine, vol. 1 [5], 1975)
Deep dream dive (d-b and elects) (1974)
End (with H.M. Matusow) (1970)
Gentle grass (ritual for 6 players) (1970)
Glass concerts 1 and 2 (1960) (British & Continental Music)
Glass water (1969)
Glass world of Anna Lockwood
Glass sound sculpture (1969)
Humm for 70 or more hummers (1971)
Love field (tape)
Pillow talk, love stories and comedies (tape playing into pillow) (1981)
River archive (tape) (1973) (Source Magazine, no. 10)
Singing to earth-singing the air (1976)
Sound map of the Hudson River (2 tapes of river sounds) (1983)
Spirit catchers (live vces amplified) (1975) (Ear Magazine, vol. 1 1975)
Tiger balm (tape and live environmental sound) (1971) (Source Magazine, no. 9)
Windhover and free fall (tape) (1972)
World rhythmns (tapes and gong) (1975)

MULTIMEDIA

Delta run (tape, slide, projection and movement) (1981)
Shone (mixed media)
Dark touch (tactile-aural equipment) (1970)
Eye/ear (1972)
Spirit songs unfolding (tapes and photographs) (1977)
Piano burning, event (1968)
Piano drowning, sound sculpture (1971)
Piano garden, environment (1971)

Publications

Women's Work. Co-edited with Alison Knowles. (q.v.)

Ref. composer, 22, 70, 94, 185, 269, 468, 563, 622, 625

LOCKWOOD, Charlotte Mathewson

American organist and composer. b. Granby, CT, 1903; d. May 19, 1961. She studied at the School of Sacred Music at Union Theological Seminary in New York City; under Widor in Paris and Ramin in Leipzig. She was organist at Crescent Avenue Presbyterian Church, Plainfield, NJ. Her hymn tune was based on an old Hebrew melody.

Composition

ORGAN

Tune for Rock of Ages

Ref. 646

LODER, Kate Fanny (Lady Henry Thompson)

English pianist, professor and composer. b. Bath, August 21, 1825; d. Headley, August 3, 1904. She was the cousin of the composer Edward (James) Loder. She studied under Miss Batterbury and Henry Field and at the Royal Academy of Music from 1839 to 1844 and under Mrs. Lucy Anderson and Charles Lucas. In 1839 she received a King's scholarship. In 1844 she played the adagio and rondo from Mendelssohn's *G-Minor Concerto* in the composer's presence and to his satisfaction. In the same year she was appointed professor of harmony at the Royal Academy of Music. She appeared for the Philharmonic Society, first in 1847 and then in 1854. Brahms's *Requiem* was first performed in England at her house on July 7, 1871. The accompaniments were played on the piano by herself and Cipriani Potter.

Compositions

ORCHESTRA

Overture

CHAMBER

Two string quartets
Trio (pf, vln and vlc)
Sonata (vln and pf)

ORGAN

Second set
Six easy voluntaries (Novello)

PIANO

En Avant, galop (Ashdown)
Little duets for the pianoforte (London, L. Brooks: 1876)
Three duets (1869)
Twelve studies (Ashdown)
Two sonatas

VOCAL

Songs incl.:
The blind boy (J. King) (1873)
My faint spirit (Ashdown)
The victim (1854)
Winter is past (Ashdown)

OPERA

L'Elisir d'Amore

Ref. 2, 6, 8, 72, 102, 226, 276, 297, 347

LOEWE, Auguste

German singer and composer. b. Berlin, 1822. Her contralto voice was frequently praised by Robert Schumann in his writings. She composed songs.

Ref. 226, 276, 347

LOEWY, Irma

Composition

PIANO

Chanson passée, op. 1

Ref. Ricordi

LOGAN, Virginia Knight

American authoress and composer. b. Washington County, PA, May 3, 1850; d. Oskaloosa, IA, November 27, 1940.

Compositions

VOCAL

Songs of Cupid (ch)
Songs incl.:
Fallen leaf
In fancy's bower
Moonlight waltz
O, vision fair
Over the hills
Rose of my heart
A song for you and me
Thru the night

Ref. 39, 40, 347

LOH, Kathy Jean

American pianist, violinist and composer. b. Portsmouth, VA, June 20, 1952. She gained a B.A. (composition, 1976) from the University of California, Santa Barbara and is currently working towards a masters degree in music theory, studying under Joan Smith. She also studied under Peter Fricker and Marta Ptaszynska. She studied the violin as a child but was self taught on the piano. PHOTOGRAPH.

Compositions

CHAMBER

Short song (ww qnt) (1974)
Three short studies (str qrt) (1975)
String quartet, in 2 mvts (1976)

PIANO

Dream (1974)
Reflection (1974)
Study on a 4 note motif (1975)

VOCAL
- Waves (S, perc and orch of 7) (1980)
- Little lamb (T and pf) (1981)
- Sitting in a tree (S and pf)

ELECTRONIC
- Poem (tape) (1976)

THEATRE
- Waves, music for The dream play (soloist, ch, perc and orch) (1980)

Ref. composer

LOHOEFER (Lohoffer), Evelyn (pseud.)

American accompanist, authoress, teacher and composer. b. Clinton, NC, December 28, 1921. She studied at the University of North Carolina (B.S.), at Bennington College on scholarship, and under Sigismund Stojowski, Norman Lloyd and Vittorio Giannini at the Juilliard School of Music. She was an assistant to Norman and Ruth Lloyd, Connecticut College School of Dance, New London (1954 to 1959) and then taught privately in New York and Washington. In 1944 she was accompanist for a USO dance tour of Europe.

Compositions

BALLET
- Bird prince
- Conversation piece
- Frog and the ox
- Madeleine and the bad hat
- Modern fantasy
- Pony trails
- Shakers
- Shoemaker and the elves
- Totem pole
- Wee lee train

Ref. 39, 94, 142

LOHOFFER, Evelyn. See LOHOEFER, Evelyn

LOHR, Ina (Marina)

Swiss violinist, choral conductor, teacher and composer. b. Amsterdam, August 1, 1903. She studied the violin under F. Helman in Amsterdam and in Basle, history of music under H. Rutters and K. Nef, theory under G. Gueldenstein and composition under A. van der Horst and R. Moser. She was musical assistant to conductor P. Sacher of the Basle Chamber Orchestra and from 1959 to 1961 she led the Collegium Musicum of Basle University. From 1968 she directed the choral choir of the Schola Cantorum Basiliensis and taught evangelical church music, school music, method and ensemble work. In 1958 she was awarded an honorary doctorate in theology from Basle University.

Compositions

VOCAL
- Sprechen, lauschen, singen, 120 children's songs (1965)
- Drei lieder (Heinrich von Lauffenberg) (ch and str orch) (1940)
- Ten chansons (vce and pf)

SACRED
- Die Geburt unseres Herrn Jesus Christ (vce, vln and vla) (1948)
- Psalmen, Lobgesaenge und geistliche Lieder der Christenheit (arr W. Fischer, T. Sutter, L. Wieruszowski) (1946)
- Three psalms for one voice and keyboard (1958)
- Deutsche Messgesaenge fuer 16 Sonn- und Festtage (1967) 25 dreistimmige Psalmsaetze zum Singen und Spielen (1967); Laudinella-Reihe (1970)
- Kleine biblische Balladen zum Singen und Sagen (1972)

Publications
- *H. Purcell und seine Bearbeiter*. SMZ 91. 1951.
- *Musik aus der Sprache, Musik aus dem Spiel*. Singt und Spielt 25. 1958.
- *Praktische Arbeit am Kirchenlied*. Musik und Gottesdienst 10. 1956.
- Solmisation und Kirchentonarten. Zurich, 1943.
- Uebungsbuch zur Erlernung der Solmisation und des Kontrapunkts. Basle, 1955.
- *Versuch ueber die melodische Gebaerde*. Singt und Spielt 27. 1960.
- *Von der 'natuerlichen' zu der 'geschaerften und polierten Musica.'*. SMZ 108. 1968.
- *Zur Programmestaltung; Die Kunst der Fuge*. Alte und neue Musik, Das Basler Kammerorchester ... (1962-1951). Zurich, 1952.
- *Zur Wiederbelebung der geistlichen Monodie des Mittelalters im heutigen Chor-Konzert*. Festschrift K-Neg. 1933.

Ref. 17, 70, 461

LOHR, Marina. See LOHR, Ina

LOMAKINA, Fania Filippovna. See NAIKHOVICH-LOMAKINA, Fania Filippovna

LOMBARDA

French minstrel from Toulouse. b. ca. 1190. In the middle ages the name Lombard referred to those who dealt in money and it is therefore likely that she was the daughter of a banker. She is described by Boutiere as 'a lady noble and beautiful, and gracious in her person and accomplished. She knew how to write poems, and she composed beautiful verses about love'. Don Barnat Arnaut, brother of the count of Armagnac, heard tell of her goodness and worth and he went to Toulouse to see her. He lived with her for some time before leaving her to return to his country. She was credited with a fine literary reputation; her tenson with Barnat Arnaut d'Armagnac shows her ability to write in trobar clus, the hermetic closed style of some of the Provencal poets.

Ref. 120, 220, 303

LOMBARDINI, Maddalena. See SIRMEN, Maddalena Laura di

LOMON, RUTH

American pianist, teacher and composer. b. Montreal, Canada, November 8, 1930. She studied at McGill University, the Conservatoire de Quebec and the New England Conservatory. She teaches composition and the piano and coaches chamber music, concentrating on works written by women composers from the 18th-century to the present. She gives lectures and recitals in colleges and on radio and television. She has received various awards for composition: a Yaddo Fellowship (1977); Helene Wurlitzer Grant (1978); an Ossabaw Island Project Fellowship (1979); MacDowell/Norlin Fellowship (1982, 1983); Meet the Composer Grants (1981, 1983) and a National League of Pen Women scholarship for mature women. She was awarded a commission for a harp slide show and received a recording award from American Women Composers. DISCOGRAPHY. PHOTOGRAPH.

Compositions

ORCHESTRA
- Bassoon Concerto (1978-1979)

CHAMBER
- Iatiku ....'bringing to life' (b-cl, vib, mar, hp, pf and hpcd) (1983) (comm Music Teachers' National Assoc)
- Diptych (ww qrt) (1983) (comm Lyricum ens)
- Equinox (2 trp and 2 trb) (1978)
- Shapes (vln, vlc, gtr and pf) (1969)
- Vitruvian Scroll (str qrt) (1981)
- String Quartet (1981)
- Trio (hn, vlc and pf) (1961)
- Dialogue (vib and hpcd) (1964)
- Phase I (vlc and pf) (1969)
- The Furies (Erinnyes) (ob, ob d'amore and cor anglais) (1977)
- Solstice (2 trp and 2 trb) (1978)
- Celebrations (Nimbus and the Sun God) (2 hp) (1978)
- Dust Devils (hp) (1976) (Arsis, 1977)
- Seven Portals of Vision (org) (1982) (Arsis Press)
- Desiderata (1984) (comm Canadian Contemporary Music Festival)

PIANO
- Soundings (duet) (1076)
- Tritych (4 hands) (1976)
- Five Ceremonial Masks (1980) (Arsis)
- Masks (from Yeibichi night chants) (1976) (Arsis, 1982)
- Rondo (1959)
- Toccata (1961)

VOCAL
- Three Zuni Songs (ch, prep pf and vlc) (1982)
- Winnowing Song (mix-ch, pf and vlc) (1982)
- Five Songs on Poems by W. Blake (Cont and vla) (1962) (Arsis)
- Phase II (Walt Whitman poems: Manhattan and Oh Living Always, Always Dying) (S, vlc and pf) (1975)
- Symbiosis (m-S, pf and perc) (1983) (comm National Women Studies Assoc)

SACRED
- Requiem (mix-ch, trps, trbs, S and ww) (1976-1977)
- Song for a Requiem (S, fl, 2 cl, b-cl and bsn) (1977)
- Songs for a Requiem (S and pf) (1982)

OPERA
- Fisherman and his Soul, chamber opera (1969)

Ref. composer, 228, 474, 563, 622, 625

LONG, Eleanor Newell. See NEWELL, Eleanor

LONGWORTH, Helen
20th-century English composer.
Compositions
CHAMBER
String Quartet
Un Mon en Flor (vln) (comm BBC, London, 1978)
MISCELLANEOUS
Une Phase
Ref. *The Composer,* 1980

LONSDALE, Eva
19th-century English composer.
Compositions
CHAMBER
Chant du Soir (vln and pf) (Ascherberg)
Romance (vln and pf)
Souvenir de Belvedere (vln and pf; also pf) (Ascherberg)
PIANO
Alsteriana, barcarolle (4 hands) (St. Cecilia)
Two Little Beauties (4 hands) (St. Cecilia)
Man in the Moon is Looking, waltz (Gordon)
Tommy Make Room for Your Uncle, waltz (also vln and pf) (Brainard)
Wood Nymphs (St. Cecilia)
Four Characteristic Pieces: Au Revoir; Berceuse; Holidays; Little Brook (Ricordi)
VOCAL
Songs incl.:
Ah! Little Flower (F. Ray) (Ricordi)
April's Lady (F. Thorpe) (Ricordi)
At Last (Ricordi)
Blue-Bells (Leonard)
Boys of Dublin Town (Chapell)
Columbine (A. Hancock) (Ricordi)
Four Love Lyrics (Ricordi)
O, Memory Sweet! (E. Lonsdale) (Ricordi)
A River Song (Ricordi)
Snowdrop (B. Fennell) (Cramer)
Ref. 297

LOOTS, Joyce Mary Ann
South African pianist and composer. b. Durban, September 30, 1907. She studied music at the Cape Town College of Music under Professor W. Bell (composition) and Colin Taylor (piano) in 1929. She also studied for a short while under Sir Arnold Bax in London (composition, 1930) and Richard Cherry in Johannesburg (counterpoint, harmony and orchestration, 1940). Many of her works have been performed or broadcast in South Africa and her *Three Afrikaans Songs* were performed in Orlando, United States of America (1982). PHOTOGRAPH.
Compositions
ORCHESTRA
Concertstuk (pf and orch) (SAMRO)
Festival March (1952-1953) (1st prize, SABC competition, 1952)
Festival March II (1982)
South African Lyric Suite, 4 pieces (1st prize, SABC competition, 1952)
Suite for String Orchestra (SAMRO)
Three Orchestral Pieces
CHAMBER
Conversations No. 1 (fl and pf)
PIANO
Three Pieces (2 pf)
Tone Poem (2 pf)
Piet my vrou
VOCAL
The Golden Threshold (S. Naidu) (vce and orch) (1945) (SAMRO) (1st prize SABC competition, 1948)
Lines from Walt Whitman (vce and orch) (1956)
Die Duif (I.D. Du Plessis) (vce and orch) (1957-1963)
Die Lied van die Nagwind (D.F. Malherbe) (vce and orch)
A Widow Bird (Shelley) (vce and orch)
Pathfinders (Vance Palmer) (mix-ch and pf) (1955)
Rejoice and Be Merry (mix-ch)
Aspects of Time, 4 songs (vce, vln, vlc, cl and hp)
Avidar Bird (vce and pf)
The Call (vce and pf)
Chanson de l'automne (Paul Verlaine) (vce and pf) (1957-1963)
The Crescent Moon, song cycle (vce and pf) (1957-1963)
Evening (Sappho) (vce and pf)
Four Wiegeliedjies
Lines from Sappho (vce and pf)
Madonna's Prayer (Lope de Vega) (vce and pf)
Rejoice (Tagore) (vce and pf) (1957-1963)
She Is Near to My Heart (Tagore) (vce and pf)
Spring Goeth All in White (vce and pf) (Bridges)
Three Afrikaans Songs (vce, pf, ob and bsn) (1967)
Time, You Old Gipsy Man (Hodgson) (3 vces)
Two Settings of Pluck This Little Flower (lines from Gitanjali) (Tagore) (vce and pf)
Wonder-Thirst (G. Gould) (vce and pf)
SACRED
Christ is Born, carol (ch)
Death Carol (m-S and orch)
Lute-Book Lullaby, carol (ch) (Society of South African Composers and Studio Holland)
Magnificat (vce, mix-ch and org) (1970)
God Bless Our Land (vce and pf)
Ref. composer, 77, 84, 94, 280, 377, 457

LOOZ-CORSWAREM, La Comtesse de. See LANOY, Clementine-Josephine-Françoise-Therese

LOPAMUDRA (Kausitaki) (Varaprada)
Indian composer. She was the daughter of the King of Vidarbha and the wife of the famous rishi Agastya.
Composition
SACRED
Hymn 179 of the first book of Rigveda
Ref. 414

LOPEZ ROVIROSA, Maria Isabel
Cuban composer. b. Havana, July 8, 1912. She studied harmony and composition under Jose Ardevol, whom she later married.
Compositions
ORCHESTRA
Fanfarria (1934)
Preludio y allegro (1935)
CHAMBER
Suite (fl, ob, bsn, vln, vla, vlc and pf) (1938)
VOCAL
Dos canciones corales (ch)
Other works
Ref. 100

LOPEZ Y PENA, Maria del Carmen
Spanish singer and composer. b. 1885. She studied at the Madrid Conservatory where she founded and directed the 'Sociedad de Amigos de la Musica'. She gave numerous concerts.
Compositions
PIANO
Nocturne on Arabian themes
VOCAL
Two arias (vce and orch)
Cuadros liricos madrilenos
OPERA
One chamber opera
Ref. 361

LOPUSKA-WYLEZYNSKA, Helena
Polish pianist, teacher and composer. b. Warsaw, 1887; d. Moscow, May 4, 1920. At the Warsaw Conservatory she studied the piano under J. Kleczynski and P. Romaszki and counterpoint and composition under Z. Noskowski. She also studied the piano and composition at the Leipzig Conservatory, graduating with a gold medal. She gave concerts in Berlin and Leipzig and married Adam Wylezynski, conductor and director of the Vilna Conservatory. She taught in Vilna and appeared in Moscow in 1914 and 1918.
Compositions
ORCHESTRA
Legenda (pf and orch)
Ballad
CHAMBER
String quartet
Violin sonata
PIANO
Sonata
Variations on a theme
Miniatures incl.:
Crepuscule, op. 3 (Warsaw: Gebethner & Wolff, 1910)
Chanson sans paroles, op. 2 (Gebethner, 1910)

Le soir, op. 4 (Gebethner, 1910)
Matine printaniere, op. 5 (Gebethner, 1910)
Question, op. 6 (Gebethner, 1910)
VOCAL
Smutno mi Boze, cantata (ch and orch)
Pieces (m-ch)
Ref. W. Pigla (Warsaw)

LOPWEGEN, Benedikt. See JENNY, Sister Leonore

LORD, Helen Cooper
American lecturer and composer. b. Rockland, December 10, 1892; d. Rockland, June 28, 1957. She studied at the Bradford Academy and under Mme. French, Dr. Latham True, Dr. Harris, S. Shaw and Mme. Suza Doane. She taught harmony for two years at Washington, DC, College of Music.
Compositions
VOCAL
Choral works
Songs incl.:
Down by the locker of Davy Jones
In de cabin do'
Love's vision (Kenneth P. Lord)
The message of the rose
Old pine
The year's at the spring (Browning)
Ref. 40, 347, 374

LORE, Emma Maria Theresa
American harpist, contralto, music teacher and composer. b. Wilmington, DE, October 15, 1868. She studied in New York and Germany.
Compositions
VOCAL
Ballade
Choruses
SACRED
Children's mass
Choral setting for the 137th psalm
Ref. 226

LORENZ, Ellen Jane (Mrs. Porter) (pseuds. Rosemary Hadler, Allen James)
American handbell ringer, organist, pianist, choir director, editor, lecturer, writer and composer. b. Dayton, May 3, 1907. She studied the piano from the age of eight to 18 and had organ lessons throughout her college career. She had private lessons in harmony and composition under Ira B. Wilson, Hamilton McDougall and Nadia Boulanger (q.v.) (Paris, 1932). She obtained a B.A. (music honors) from Wellesley College in 1929 and attended the Northampton Institute of Music Pedagogy in the summers of 1927 and 1928. From 1932 to 1968 she was editor-in-chief and partner of the Lorenz Publishing Co., Dayton. She was a choir director from 1932 and a handbell director from 1958. She gave many lectures on hymnology, folk songs, the Elizabethan age and handbells. In 1946 she was awarded an honorary Mus.Doc. from Lebanon College, Annville, PA. She received the Billings Prize for excellence in practical and theoretical music from Wellesley College. She was four times winner of the Capital Choir Guild anthem contest and received prizes from Mu Phi Epsilon, Sigma Alpha Iota and the Society of Women in Liberal Professions. She is a member of ASCAP.
Compositions
ORCHESTRA
Appalachian suite
Dayton suite
Five fairy tales
Overture
Three Appalachian tunes
Short works
CHAMBER
Fanfare for nine (1977)
Five flourishes for brass quintet (comm Dayton Philharmonic Orchestra, 1983)
Five elegies (str qrt)
String quartet (as Ellen Jane Porter) (1969)
Nocturne (fl and handbells)
Sonatina (bsn and pf)
Five microstudies (pf)
From an old tune book (org) (Dayton: Lorenz, 1971)
Japanese suite (fl)
Four short movements
HANDBELLS
Bell jubilee (Dallas: Chorister Guild, 1969)
Bell passacaglia
Bell rondelle (prize, American Guild of English handbell ringers, 1983)
The cathedral (Chorister Guild, 1970)
A festive ring
Tintinnabulation (Concordia, 1977)
VOCAL
Paul Bunyan, cantata
Beauty shop quartet (ch)
Stand in awe (ch)
Epitaph for a light love, madrigal
The silver hind, madrigal
SACRED
Carols of Christmas, cantata (mix-ch and org or pf) (Lorenz, 1942)
Alleluia (ch a-cap)
Easter, folk style (mix-ch and org or pf) (under pseud Rosemary Hadler) (1969)
Echo in alleluia (mix-ch) (under pseud Allen James) (Nashville: Abingdon, 1942)
O that our tongues were bells (comm United Theological Seminary Choir, 1984)
Venite adoremus Dominum, church suite (strs)
Candlelight carol
Elect of God
God is here
Gospel song of Easter
Hosanna to the son of David
The love of God
One o'er all the Earth, anthem
OPERETTA
Johnny Appleseed, for children (1974) (Lorenz)
Up on Old Smokey
ARRANGEMENTS
Church music (pf, hpcd and org) (1978)
Publications
Handbell Ringing in Church. Abingdon Press.
The Learning Choir. Abingdon Press.
Ref. composer, Frau und Musik, 40, 77, 94, 142, 185, 228, 280, 457, 465, 477, 496, 625

LORENZ, Petra
20th-century composer.
Composition
VOCAL
Hexenlieder
Ref. Frau und Musik

LORING, Nancy
American singer, writer and composer. b. May 13, 1906. She obtained a B.A. from Radcliffe College in 1929 and studied conducting under Archibald T. Davison at Harvard Graduate School of Education. She studied voice and singing privately under Percy Rector Stevens in New York and with Laura Littlefield and Gertrude Tingley in Boston. She studied repertory and singing under Gerald Moore in London and Coenraad V. Bos in New York. She was director of music at the Sunset Hill School in Kansas City from 1932 to 1939; director of the Bach and Handel Chorus, Kansas City from 1934 to 1938; director of choral music at Concord Academy from 1942 to 1960 and director of the Concord Chorus in Massachusetts, 1945 to 1958. She was soloist with the Choral Society, Harvard Glee Club from 1928 to 1932, Columbia University in 1931 and Wellesley Choir, 1948. She gave solo recitals in New York, Boston and Kansas City and composed several original works and arrangements, including one volume of music for school choirs.
Ref. 359

LORINSER, Gisela von
Austrian pianist and composer. b. Falkburg, near Vienna, September 27, 1856. She studied under Bruehl, R. Fuchs and H. Graedner and composed piano pieces and songs.
Ref. 70, 226

LORIOD, Yvonne
French concert pianist, ondes Martenot player, lecturer and composer. b. Houilles, Seine-et-Oise, January 20, 1924. She studied at the Paris Conservatoire under L. Levy (piano), O. Messiaen (composition) and Caussade, Calvet and M. Ciampi and won eight first prizes. She toured Europe in 1948 and Africa and the United States in 1949. Well known as an inter-

national concert pianist, she gave first performances of Schoenberg's compositions. She participated in the Darmstadt summer courses and taught at the Musikhochschule of Karlshuhe. She was a teacher of the piano, counterpoint and fugue at the Paris Conservatoire.

Compositions

ORCHESTRA

Pièces sur la Sainte-Face

Pièces sur la souffrance (1946)

CHAMBER

Pièces (cham ens)

Pièces (prep pf)

VOCAL

Grains de cendre (S and cham ens)

Other works

ELECTRONIC

Melopées africaines (ondes Martenot, pf, fl and perc) (1945)

Other pieces (ondes Martentot)

Ref. 9, 14, 22, 85, 96, 109, 135, 347

LOROLLE, Annie

20th-century French composer.

Composition

PIANO

Au studio de danse classique et rythmique: Barre; Milieu (Billaudot, 1982)

Ref. MLA Notes (1983)

LORRAINE, La Duchesse de

14th-century French minstrel. She signed the famous charter dated September 14, 1321, that established the Chapelle Saint-Julien-des-Ménestriers, a corporation for jongleurs and minstrels.

Compositions

VOCAL

Songs incl.:

Par maintes fous aurai este requise

Un petit devant le jour

Ref. British Library, 343

LOTTI, Silvana di

Italian pianist, lecturer and composer. b. Aglie Canavese, Turin, 1942. She studied the piano under Giorgio Ferrari at the G. Verdi Conservatory, Turin. She then attended a course given by Kurt Leimer at the Summer Academy in Salzburg and various seminars given by Goffredo Petrassi, Franco Evangelisti, Louis de Pablo and Luciano Berio at the Accademia Chigiana in Siena. She won the Alfano prize at Turin Conservatory and the Ancona Prize in the Tenth International Competition for woodwind instruments in 1980. She lectures at the A. Vivaldi Conservatory in Alessandria.

Compositions

ORCHESTRA

Conversari (sym orch)

CHAMBER

Contrasti (2 cl)

Works for small groups of insruments

Ref. Donne in Musica 1982

LOTTIN, Phedora

Composition

PIANO

Souvenirs du Coudray, op. 6, galop

Ref. H. Baron (London)

LOTZ, La Barbara. See LA BARBARA, Joan

LOUD, Annie Frances

American organist, teacher and composer. b. Weymouth, MA, November 16, 1856. She studied at the Boston Conservatory and wrote about 150 works, including piano and organ pieces, sacred and profane songs and choruses.

Ref. 226

LOUD, Emily L. (pseud. Ell)

19th-century American composer.

Composition

PIANO

Koh I Noor, waltz

Ref. 228

LOUDOVA, Ivana

Czech pianist and composer. b. Chlumec nad Cidlinou, March 8, 1941. She began her piano studies under her mother, Bozena Loudova, a professor of the piano in Chlumec. She began composing when she was 12 years old and when she finished school in 1958 went straight into the third year composition class at Prague Conservatory, becoming a student of Professor Miloslav Kabelac. In the first three years of her studies she composed a number of works, two of which *Suite for solo flute* and *Sonata for violin and piano* have been performed frequently. In 1961 she became the first woman student of composition at the Prague Academy of Arts, under Professor Emil Hlobil. She took part in the holiday courses for new music in Darmstadt (1967 to 1969) and was a guest at festivals in Holland, Kassel and Eger, Hungary. In 1968 she was a postgraduate student at the Prague Academy of Arts and Music under Professor Kabelac. In 1971 she received a grant to study in Paris under O. Messiaen and Andre Jolivet. In 1980 she was composer-in-residence for the American Wind Symphony Orchestra, Pittsburg, for six weeks. DISCOGRAPHY. PHOTOGRAPH.

Compositions

ORCHESTRA

Symphony No. 1 (1965)

Chorale (org, perc and wind orch) (1971)

Chorale (1973)

Concerto breve (fl or vln and orch) (1979)

Concerto (org, perc and wind orch) (1974)

Concerto (cham orch) (1962)

Cadenza (vln, fl and str orch) (1975)

Dramatic concerto (perc and wind orch) (1979) (New York: C.F. Peters)

Fantasy (1961)

Hymnes (wind insts, perc and orch) (Peters, 1972)

Magic concerto (xy, mar, vib and wind orch) (Peters, 1976)

Nocturno (vla and str orch) (1975)

Olympic overture (wind orch) (1979)

Partita in D (fl, hpcd and str orch) (1975)

Spleen, hommage a C. Baudelaire (1971)

CHAMBER

Musica Festiva (3 trp and 3 trb) (1981)

Ritornello (2 trp, hn, tba and perc) (1973)

Flower for Emanuel, in memory of C.P.E. Bach (jazz qnt) (1981)

String quartet No. 1 (1964)

String quartet No. 2, in memory of B. Smetana (1976)

Hukvaldy's suite, in memory of Leos Janacek (str qrt) (1984)

Romeo and Julia, renaissance suite (1974)

Air à due boemi (b-cl and pf) (1972)

Duo concertante (b-cl and mar) (1982)

Ballata antica (trb and pf) (1966)

Ballata eroica (vln and pf) (1976)

Sonata (vln and pf) (1961)

Sonata (cl and pf) (1963-1964)

Sonatine (ob and pf)

Two eclogues, in memory of Vergil (fl and hp) (1982)

Agamemnon suite (perc) (1973)

Aulos (b-cl) (1976)

Per tromba, 5 studies for trumpet (1974)

Solo for King David (hp) (Prague: Panton, 1972)

Suite for solo flute (1959)

Four pieces for clarinet solo (1982)

Variations for cat (vln) (1982)

PIANO

Prelude (1961)

Tango-music (1984)

VOCAL

Fortune, cantata (mix-ch and chil-ch a-cap) (1983)

The little prince, children's cantata in 7 scenes (S, A, speaker, chil-ch and insts) (1967)

Second symphony (A, ch and orch) (1965)

Amor (mix-ch a-cap) (1981)

Ego Sapientia (m-ch a-cap) (1969)

Good night songs, unison songs (chil-ch a-cap) (1966)

The heavenly guilt, song cycle (chil-ch and pf) (1965)

Kuroshyo, dramatic frescoes (S and large mix-ch) (1968)

Little evening music (mix-ch and ob) (1983)

The look round (w-ch a-cap) (1981) (1st prize, Jihlava composers' competition)

Meeting with love (m-ch) (1966)

Merry counterpoints (3 chil-ch a-cap) (1981) (2nd prize, Jirkov vocal composition competition)

Mummy, cycle (chil-ch) (1966)

Occhi lucenti e belli (w-ch a-cap) (1984) (1st prize, XIth Guido d'Arezzo international composers' competition)

Riddles, two-part songs (chil-ch and pf) (1966)
Songs about roses (2 chil-ch a-cap) (1983) (2nd prize, Olomouc composition competition)
Trefoil (ch-ch, tam and tri) (1981)
Gnomai (S, fl and hp) (1970)
SACRED
Stabat Mater (m-ch) (1966)
BALLET
Rhapsody in black (ob and cham orch)
ELECTRONIC
Mobile X (aleatoric qrt for 4 tape recorders)
Ref. composer, Fanfare July 1982, 17, 77, 94, 189, 197, 206, 457, 563, 622

LOUIE, Alexina Diane

Canadian pianist, lecturer and composer, of Chinese descent. b. Vancouver, July 30, 1949. She studied the piano from the age of seven and later theory and acoustic and electronic composition under Cortland Hultberg at the University of British Columbia, where she received a B.Mus. She continued her piano studies with Barbara Custance and Frances Adaskin whilst at University and afterwards studied composition at the University of California, San Diego, under Robert Erickson and Pauline Oliveros (q.v.), obtaining an M.A. She is also an A.R.C.T. (piano performance). She has taught the piano privately since the age of 14 and was a teaching assistant at the University of California from 1970 to 1973, music instructor at Los Angeles City College in 1976, solo pianist in Vancouver from 1966 to 1971 and a copyist in Los Angeles, after 1973. From 1974 she was a music instructor at Pasadena City College and since 1981 has been teaching harmony, theory and composition at the Royal Conservatory, Toronto. She was a member of 'The Ensemble' from 1971 to 1974, a group of eight women who performed under the direction of Pauline Oliveros. She designed Pasadena City College's electronic music studio. She received tuition scholarships from the government of British Columbia in 1967, 1968 and 1969, fellowships and a full-term Canada Council arts grant for composition in 1974. In 1982 she was part of a small delegation of performers, composers and music teachers invited by the Union of Soviet Composers to participate in a music symposium in Erevan, Armenia. Her *Dragon bells* and *Pearls* were performed there.
Compositions
ORCHESTRA
Jasmine (1980)
Lamentation for the Canadian tragedy (cham orch) (1973)
O magnum mysterium: In memoriam Glenn Gould (str orch) (1982)
Songs of Paradise (1983) (comm Thunder Bay Symphony)
CHAMBER
Lotus (cham ens) (1977)
Lotus II (cham ens) (1978)
Piece for nine flutes (3 picc, 4 fl and 2 a-fl) (1975)
New York Times (fl, cl, vln, vla, vlc, c-bass, pf and perc) (1980)
Pearls (fl, ob, pf, vlc and perc) (1980)
Suite of changes (with Marjan Mozetich) (cl, vla, c-bass, pf and perc) (1982) (comm Array Music)
Edges (str qrt) (1981)
String quartet (1975)
Refuge (acdn, hp and vib) (1981)
From the eastern gate (7 mvts) (hp.) (Micheline Coulombe St. Marcoux Prize, 1987.)
PIANO
Afterimages (2 pf) (1981)
Dragon bells (2 pf or prep pf or pre-recorded pf) (1978)
Three coloured fragments (1967)
ELECTRONIC
Incantation (cl and tape) (1980) (comm Music Inter Alia)
Molly (4 channel tape) (1972)
Naked poems (cham ch and elec pf) (1968)
Pale delicates (2 channel tape) (1971)
MISCELLANEOUS
Sanctuary
Ref. composer, *Canadian Composer* September 1984, 206, 622

LOUIS, Mme. (nee Bayon or Bajon)

French harpsichordist, singer, teacher and composer. b. 1746. She was a friend of Diderot and taught his daughter to play the harpsichord.
Compositions
CHAMBER
Six sonatas (hpcd or pf, 3 with vln) (1770)
Overture (arr for hpcd or pf with vln and vlc)
VOCAL
Airs detaches
Ariettas
OPERETTA
Fleur d'epine, in 2 acts (Paris: Huguet, 1776)
Publications
Du doigte, des manieres et de l'esprit de l'execution sur le piano.
Principes de la doctrine de l'accompagnement.
Ref. 13, 26, 119, 125, 128, 129, 143, 276, 307, 347, 404

LOUISE OF SAVOY. See MARIE THERESE OF SAVOY-CARIGNANO

LOUISIANA LADY. See NICKERSON, Camille Lucie

LOUVENCOURT, Mlle. de

French theorbo player, musician, poetess and composer. b. 1680; d. 1712. Her poetical talents were greatly admired and she was esteemed for her modesty and conversation and her voice was praised by her contemporaries. She composed many cantatas, of which M. de Genlis said "There are none in the French language equal to those of Mlle. de Louvencourt."
Ref. 334, 491

LOUVIER, Nicole

French musician, singer and composer. b. Paris, June 23, 1933. She won the Grand Prix de la Chanson in 1953.
Compositions
CHAMBER
Hydre à cinq têtes (sax) (Alphouse Leduc)
VOCAL
Songs incl.:
Chanson pour t'apprivoiser
J'imagine que sur ta naissance
Plus tard j'aurai le temps
Soyons amis
Ref. 51

LOVAN, Lydia

20th-century American composer. She composed works for the piano, the organ and the harpsichord.
Ref. 40, 347

LOVE, Loretta

20th-century American composer.
Composition
OPERETTA
The Stone Princess, fairy tale (Karl Bratton) (Phoenix, 1974)
Ref. 141, 142

LOVELACE, Carey

American ethnomusicologist, journalist and composer. b. Los Angeles, August 21, 1952. She received her B.F.A. (1975) after studying composition under James Tenney and Leonard Stein at California Arts College. She currently lives in Paris.
Compositions
ORCHESTRA
Among windy spaces (1975)
CHAMBER
Four tiny pieces (cl and pf) (1977)
Crotchets and contrivances (1977)
Words carefully chosen (1977)
Ref. composer

LOVELL, Joan

Compositions
CHAMBER
Four country sketches (vla and pf) (London: Augener)
Ref. Frau und Musik

LOVELL, Katharine. See HUBICKI, Margaret Olive

LOWE, Auguste. See LOEWE, Auguste

LOWELL, Dorothy Dawson

20th-century American composer.

Compositions
SACRED
Christ, my master (w-ch or mix-ch)
Come into my heart, Lord Jesus (w-ch)
My life is like a weaving (w-ch or mix-ch)
O what can I give to the Holy Child? (w-ch or mix-ch)
Easter in Heaven (soli and ch)
I need Thee, Heavenly Father (soli and ch)
I know the touch of His Hand (ch)
Thanks be to God (mix-ch)
Love's garden, wedding song
Ref. 40, 347

LOWELL, Edith
American cellist, pianist, poetess and composer. b. Portland, January 2, 1888. She wrote several books of verses and many of her songs and marches were used by junior music clubs.
Compositions
VOCAL
Songs incl.:
Christmas song
Junior choir
Junior marching song
Summer
OPERETTA
Oil from the Deejah's Tail
Ref. 347

LOWENSKJOLD, Hannah. See LOEVENSKJOLD, Hannah

LOWENSTEIN, Gunilla Marike
English teacher and composer of Swedish origin. b. Uppsala, December 21, 1928; d. August 28, 1981. She lived in Lund, Sweden until 1949 and then settled in England. She studied under Alfred Nieman (composition) at the Guildhall School of Music, London from 1954 to 1958 and obtained her L.R.A.M. and A.G.S.M. After being awarded the Guildhall School prize for composition (1958) she continued her studies with Matyas Seiber (1958 to 1960). She was appointed teacher of composition at Watford School of Music in 1960 and moved to Birmingham in 1962, where she was a piano teacher for the Education Department. DISCOGRAPHY. PHOTOGRAPH.
Compositions
ORCHESTRA
Swedish-Hungarian variations, op. 3 (1960)
CHAMBER
Tellus Mater (a-fl, mar and strs) (1980)
Ritornel for 6 instruments, op. 6 (1965)
Sextet, op. 17 (wind insts and pf) (1972)
Music for strings, op. 16 (1972)
String quartet, op. 4 (1961)
Trio, op. 18 (fl, ob and pf) (1973)
Duo, op. 8 (cl and vlc) (1965)
Quinque mobilia, op. 7 (1965)
Triptych, op. 5 (1963)
PIANO
Six fragments, op. 1b (1959)
Sonata No. 1, op. 9 (1964)
Sonata No. 2, op. 12 (1968)
Sonata No. 3, op. 15 (1970)
Soliloquy, op. 10 (1966)
Seriso, op. 11 (1967)
Sonatina, op. 12 (1969)
Transformations, op. 19 (1974)
In tenebris, op. 14 (1969)
Mosaics (1978)
VOCAL
Min laengtan ar inte mon, op. 1a (Paer Lagerkvist) (1959)
SACRED
The morning of creation, song cycle (1976)
To the supreme being, op. 2 (1960)
Ref. composer, 77, 585

LOWTHIAN, Caroline (Mrs. Cyril Prescott)
English composer. b. Penrith, 1860; d. 1943. She studied under Oscar Beringer.
Compositions
PIANO
Pieces incl.:
Bouree
Dance de ballet
Mother Hubbard polka
Myosotis waltz
VOCAL
Songs incl.:
Gates of the west, in D (Chappell)
Rally round the flag, in D (Chappell)
Sunshine
Ref. 6, 226, 268, 276, 473

LU, Yen
Chinese editor and composer. b. Nanking, September 7, 1930. She went to the United States in 1963. She studied at Mannes College of Music under William Sydeman and at City College, University of New York, under Mario Davidovsky. Since 1970 she has been an editor at a music publishing company in New York.
Compositions
ORCHESTRA
Music for orchestra, I and II (1969, 1970)
CHAMBER
Piece for 7 players (fl, cl, hn, trp, vlc and 2 perc) (1967)
Quartet (fl, b-trb, pf and perc) (1968)
Quartet (cl, tba and 2 perc) (1970)
Sonata (vln) (1972)
Dawn (1969)
To a little white flower (1970)
VOCAL
Some days I toss in bed (m-S and cham ens) (1973)
Ref. 142, 280

LUCAS, Blanche
French lecturer and composer. b. Paris, January 8, 1874; d. Chateau-du-Loire, February 9, 1956. She studied under d'Indy and taught at the Schola Cantorum from 1902 to 1914.
Compositions
CHAMBER
Sonata in G (pf and vln) (1919) (Senart)
SACRED
Cantatas
Hymns
Masses
Motets
Ref. 13, 41, 81, 226

LUCAS, Francis Kay. See DREYFUS, Francis Kay

LUCAS, Mary Anderson
English pianist and composer. b. London, May 24, 1882; d. London, January 14, 1952. She studied the piano at Dresden Conservatory (1899 to 1900) and the Royal Academy in London (1900 to 1903). She married in 1903 and retired for a time but later studied composition under R.O. Morris, Herbert Howells and Maurice Jacobson. Many of her orchestral and chamber works were performed in England and the United States. Her ballet *Sawdust* was performed in 1941 in London and Wolverhampton by the Ballet Guild. Before World War II her music aroused opposition for its modern approach and dissonance of texture rather than dynamics; it was more in accordance with the ideals of present-day serious composers than those of her contemporaries.
Compositions
ORCHESTRA
Ballet preludes (cham orch) (1941)
Circus suite (1939)
Concerto (fl and cham orch) (1940)
Variations on a theme of Purcell (str orch) (1938)
CHAMBER
String quartet No. 2 (1933)
String quartet No. 3 (1935)
Rhapsody (fl, vlc and pf) (1946)
Trio (cl, vla and pf) (1939)
Duo (cl and vla) (1941)
Sonata (cl and pf) (1938)
VOCAL
Book of Thel, masque (William Blake) (soloists, narrs, ch and cham orch) (1935)
Numerous songs and part songs
BALLET
Cupid and Death (pf and cham orch) (1936)
Sawdust (small orch) (1941)
Undine (orch) (1936)
Ref. 13, 22, 218

LUCILLA D.
Italian composer. ca. 1820-1886.
Compositions
OPERA
La bella fanciulla di Perth
Il conte di Benzeval
Il conte rosso
L'eroe delle Asturie
Giuliano Salviati
Sindaco di villagio
Il solitario
Ref. 307

LUCK, Maude Haben
American composer. b. Milwaukee; d. Milwaukee, November 27, 1944. She composed choral works and songs.
Ref. 40, 347

LUCKE, Katharine E.
American teacher and composer. b. Baltimore, March 22, 1875; d. Baltimore, May 21, 1962. She studied at the Peabody Conservatory, received her diploma in 1904 and taught there from 1919.
Compositions
ORCHESTRA
Family portrait
CHAMBER
Piano trio
Keyboard harmony (pf or org) (1959)
VOCAL
Choral works and songs
Ref. 142

LUCKMAN, Phyllis
American cellist, teacher and composer. b. New York, September 13, 1927. She studied at Hunter College and obtained her B.A. in 1947. At California State College, Hayward, she studied under Fred Fox and at Mills College under Darius Milhaud, receiving her M.A. in 1973. From 1959 to 1969 she worked as a professional cellist and from 1956 taught the cello.
Compositions
ORCHESTRA
Symphony for massed cellos
CHAMBER
Templates (8-13 performers)
Fantasia (2 fl)
Hart crane poem (perc)
Severity (vlc and pf) (1976)
Five puzzles (cl)
Spirals (hpcd)
ELECTRONIC
Songs from underground (str qrt and tape)
Ref. 142, 229, 625

LUDVIG-PECAR, Nada
Yugoslav professor and composer. b. Sarajevo, May 12, 1929. She completed her third degree in composition at the Music Academy of Ljubljana in 1966, having studied under L.M. Skerjanc. She is professor of theoretical subjects at the Secondary School of Music in Sarajevo. Her children's songs won awards in 1962 and 1964.
Compositions
ORCHESTRA
Simfonietta (1962)
CHAMBER
String quartet in D-Major (1962)
String quartet in D (1966)
Sonatina (vln and pf) (1965)
Suite (vlc) (1965)
Suite (vln) (1965)
PIANO
Prelude and fugue (1953)
Suite in C-Minor (1954)
Two sonatinas (1960)
VOCAL
Uspavanka, u sumi (w-ch) (1955)
Antun-tun
Kisa pada
Rot endan u sumi
Twelve children's songs
Ref. 81, 94, 145

LUDWIG, Doris. See BARADAPRANA, Pravrajika

LUDWIG, Rosa
19th-century German composer.
Compositions
PIANO
Studies incl.:
Etude, op. 3
Nocturne
Le trille et l'octave, op. 2, etude
Ref. 276, 433

LUFF, Enid
British pianist and composer. b. Glamorgan, Wales, February 21, 1935. She received an honors degree in modern languages from Newnham College, Cambridge in 1956. Her first musical training was as a pianist; she was awarded the Birkenhead Borough piano studentship at the age of 15, became an L.R.A.M. in 1965 and continued her studies with George Hadjunikos from 1965 to 1968. She obtained her M.Mus. from the University of Wales in 1974. She was awarded the Welsh Arts Council Bursary for the study of advanced composition from 1975 to 1977, studying in London under Elisabeth Lutyens (q.v.) and later with Anthony Payne. In 1977 she won another bursary to study in Italy under Franco Donatoni. She has a particular interest in composing music for dancers. In 1980, together with Julia Usher (q.v.) she formed the music publishing company Primavera.
Compositions
ORCHESTRA
Symphony (large orch) (1974) (Primavera)
Star trek (youth orch) (1977) (Primavera, 1980)
Three pieces (1975) (Primavera)
CHAMBER
The coastal road (wind qnt) (1980) (Primavera)
String quartet No. 2 (1973) (Primavera)
String quartet No. 3 (1976) (Primavera)
Dream time for bells (fl or a-fl or picc - 1 player, also vib, hp and vlc) (Primavera, 1980)
Tapestries for chamber group (cl, vla, vlc and pf) (1971) (Primavera)
Lament (vla and pf) (1974) (Guild for promotion of Welsh Music)
Midsummer Night's Dream, 7 pieces (fl and pf) (1980) (Primavera)
Swiss interiors (2 fl) (Primavera, 1982)
Canto and doubles (fl) (Primavera, 1980)
The coming of the rain (ob) (1980) (Primavera)
Mathematical dream (hp) (1978) (Primavera)
PIANO
Angry machine (Primavera, 1983)
Four pieces (1973) (Primavera)
Mixed feelings, 5 short mood pieces (1973) (Primavera)
Statements (1974) (Primavera)
VOCAL
Metres and images (Bar, cl, gtr and perc) (1974)
The mermaid in summer (mix-vces, hn and fl obb) (1977) (Primavera)
The bird (mix-vces) (Primavera, 1980)
Swn dwr, song cycle (m-S, fl and pf) (1981) (Primavera)
Three Shakespeare sonnets (vce, vln and pf) (1978) (Primavera)
Counterpoints, song cycle (S and pf) (1974) (Primavera)
Five nocturnes, song cycle (S and pf) (1975) (Primavera)
Lux in tenebris, song cycle (S and pf) (1971) (Primavera)
Marmnad gwentury far, song cycle (S and pf) (1979) (Primavera)
Sheila na gig, song cycle (S and pf) (Primavera, 1985)
Spring bereaved, song cycle (Bar and gtr) (1974) (Primavera)
Three Japanese songs, song cycle (S and pf) (1973) (Primavera)
Vox ultima crucis, song cycle (Bar and pf) (1979) (Primavera)
Weather and mouth music (S and d-b) (1977) (Primavera)
SACRED
Glory be to God on high (ch) (1978) (Primavera)
Y cymun bendigaid (Welsh setting of communion service) (ch and org) (1972) (Primavera)
MULTIMEDIA
A Sabbath's journey (Kevin Yell) (vces, dancers and insts) (1981) (Primavera)
Publications
Articles for *Welsh Music*.
Ref. composer, 422

LUIGI, Mrs. Giuseppe. See TIBALDI, Rosa

LUMBY, Betty Louise
20th-century American organist, professor and composer. She obtained her B.Mus. at the Detroit Institute of Musical Art; her B.Mus. (summa cum laude) at the University of Detroit; her M.Mus. at the University of Michi-

gan and her D.Mus. (sacred) at the Union Theological Seminary, New York. She is an associate and fellow of the American Guild of Organists. She studied under Helmut Walcha on a Fulbright Scholarship at the Staatliche Hochschule fuer Musik, Frankfurt-am-Main. She was a lecturer at the Detroit Institue of Musical Art, assistant professor of the faculty of Samford University and held positions in various churches. She is currently professor of the organ and organist at the University of Montevallo. She toured widely in America and is a consultant for churches and a lecturer on contemporary organ design. PHOTOGRAPH.

Compositions

ORCHESTRA

Four non-objectives (org and orch)

ORGAN

Background for a worshipper (St. Marys Press)

Three sketches

VOCAL

Songs of Sappho (B and pf)

SACRED

Te Deum (ch and org)

Kierkegaard prayer (cham ch a-cap)

TEACHING PIECES

Beginning organ method

Ref. composer

LUNA DE ESPAILLAT, Margarita

Dominican pianist, professor and composer. b. Santo Domingo, July 31, 1921. She commenced her musical studies at the age of ten, studying the piano and solfege under Juan Francisco Garcia. She later studied the piano at the Liceo Musical and composition at the National Music Conservatory, becoming professor of the piano in 1935. She completed her studies under G. Manuel Rueda (advanced piano and music teaching), Manuel Simo (fugue, 1956 to 1962) and in New York under Overton (1964 to 1967). In Santiago she was principal of the Liceo Musical from 1953 to 1963 and taught at the Liceo Musical in La Vega from 1966 to 1971. She became professor of music history and form at the National Music Conservatory in Santo Domingo.

Compositions

ORCHESTRA

Cambiantes (1967)

Orquesta (1970)

Three preludes (str orch) (1964)

CHAMBER

Parametros (double qnt) (1967)

Diferencias (vlc, cl, pf and perc) (1970)

Doce duos y trios faciles, on folk songs (12 duos or trios for various groups of insts) (1972)

Divertimento for five wind instruments (1967)

Sonoridades (fl, ob, cl and bsn) (1970)

Variations (vlc, cl, pf and perc) (1970)

Abstraccion (vln and pf) (1972)

Cuatro estudios (wind duo) (1970)

Fantasia (vln and pf) (1966)

PIANO

Estruturas I and II (1971)

Tres piezas (1964)

Two bagatelles (1966)

Variante VII (1972)

VOCAL

Vigilia eterna, oratorio (soloists, ch and orch) (1967)

Cantata al Padre de la patira (ch, narr and orch) (1976)

Misa quisqueyana (ch and orch) (1966)

Amor secreto (mix-ch) (1971)

Cancion de cuna (2 equal vces and pf) (1967)

Epitafio en el aire (mix-ch, narr and orch) (1970)

Tres cantos (m-S and cl) (1967)

SACRED

Aleluya (mix-ch) (1966)

Publications

For the World of the Orchestra. Teaching Work. 1973.

Translation of *Twentieth Century Harmony*. 1973.

Various articles in periodicals on musical subjects. 1975.

Ref. composer, 17, 371

LUND, Baroness van der

19th-century Dutch composer.

Compositions

PIANO

Allegretto grazioso, op. 4

Arabesque, op. 5

Auf Fluegeln des Gesanges, op. 2

Moment de tristesse, op. 7

Serenade romantique, op. 3

Ref. 226, 276

LUND, Gudrun

Danish pianist, violinist, musicologist, teacher and composer. b. Aalborg, April 22, 1936. She received her B.A. (piano) from the Royal Danish Conservatory in 1953 and her M.A. (musicology) from the University of Copenhagen in 1955. She lived in the United States for the following ten years, teaching music appreciation and playing the piano and the violin. She became an American citizen in 1963 but returned to Denmark in 1966 to study composition under Svend S. Schultz and M. Winkel Holm. In 1983 she received a government grant for a year of study in the United States to experience a different musical atmosphere. Her music has been performed widely in Scandinavia, the United States and Germany. PHOTOGRAPH.

Compositions

ORCHESTRA

Patchwork, op. 63, symphony in 4 colors (1982)

Chamber concerto, op. 18 (ob, vla and orch) (1977)

Divertimento, op. 37 (2 trp and orch) (1979)

Concerto, op. 26 (a-trb and cham orch) (1978)

Concerto, op. 55 (ob and str orch) (1981)

Consequences, op. 32 (1979)

Festival overture, op. 15 (1977)

Scherzo, op. 2 (1976)

Variations and theme, op. 24 (cl and str orch) (1978)

Overture (1979)

SYMPHONIC BAND

Negotiations, op. 76 (wind ens) (1984) (comm Harvard University Band)

CHAMBER

Music for 7 players, op. 22 (hpcd, fl, ob and strs) (1978)

Abstract too, op. 71 (fl, cl, bsn, vla, vlc and d-b) (1983)

Rainbow, op. 81 (fl, vln, vla, vlc, pf and hp) (1984)

Relations, op. 37 (ww qnt and trb) (1978)

Patterns, op. 29 (ww qnt) (1978)

Variations on an innocent theme, op. 49 (ww qnt) (1980)

Quintet, op. 44 (pf and strs) (1980)

Quinteto di bassetto, op. 34 (fl, ob, basset hn, hn and bsn) (1979)

Clarinet quartet No. 4, op. 72 (1983)

Con Anima, op. 73 (fl, vln, vla and vlc) (1983)

Goddag mand, oekseskaft (ob, hn, vln and vlc) (1982)

Three melodic studies, op. 56 (4 vlc) (1981)

Quartet, op. 13 (ob, vln, vlc and vla) (1977)

Quartet, op. 52 (cl and strs) (1981)

String quartet No. 1, op. 8 (1976)

String quartet No. 2, op. 20 (1978)

String quartet No. 4, op. 70 (1983)

String quartet No. 5, op. 77 (1984)

Clarinet trio (1978)

Lonely souls, op. 64 (ob, a-sax and org) (1982)

Piano trio, op. 67 (1982)

Serenata seriosa, op. 42 (str trio) (1980)

Three subjects, op. 68 (3 trb) (1982)

Trio, op. 10 (fl, vln and vla) (1976)

Trio sonata 1978, op. 21 (trp, trb and org) (1978)

Trio, op. 23 (fl, vla and pf) (1978)

Trio, op. 25 (cl, vla and pf) (1978)

Variations, in 4 mvts, op. 30 (pf, vln and vlc) (1978)

Duet, op. 17 (2 ob) (1977)

Duet (fl and d-b) (1977)

Reflections, op. 47 (trb and org) (1980)

Six duets for 2 trumpets, op. 40 (1979)

Sonata for 2 musicians, op. 28 (rec and vln) (1978)

Sonatina, op. 50 (ob and pf) (1981)

Sonata, in 3 mvts, op. 59 (vla and pf) (1981)

A suite in 3 1/2 movements, op. 75 (fl and vla) (1983)

Three canons and a row, op. 79 (2 cl) (1984)

Uneven partners, op. 58 (fl and d-b) (1981)

Abstract, op. 66 (acc) (1982)

Break, op. 74 (ob) (1983)

Continuous, op. 82 (ob) (1984)

Five boys I know, op. 53 (b-trb) (1981)

Seven facets, op. 43 (org) (1980)

Sonata, op. 61 (pf) (1981)

Sonata con forza, op. 54 (vlc) (1981)

Sonata for violin, op. 38 (1979)

A woman's mind, op. 4, suite (pf) (1976)

VOCAL

Elegy, op. 3 (Dylan Thomas) (T, mix-ch and orch) (1976)

Skisma, op. 14 (S and orch) (1977)

A prayer of pain, op. 60 (boys-ch and org) (1981)

Round of the seasons, op. 79 (mix-ch) (1984)

Sorrow, op. 65 (S, mix-vces, ob and pf) (1982)

Thoughts in the dark, op. 35, 3 songs (Ditlevsen) (m-ch) (1979)

About life and nature, op. 46 (Housman) (vce and vln) (1980)

Destruction, op. 69 (S, acc and hammer) (1983)

Eight danish songs, op. 57 (vce and pf) (1981)

The flute (Meyer) (S, fl and pf) (1977)

Four songs for mixed voices, op. 12 (1976)
Four songs about the seasons, op. 7 (vce and pf) (1976)
The princess and the pea, op. 41 (Lund) (1980)
Three on a Line, op. 45 (3 m-vces) (1980)
Three songs about life and death, op. 36 (Risbjerg Thomsen) (S, trb and org) (1979)
Two lieder (1976)
Two songs, op. 6 (Ditlevsen) (vce, pf and vlc) (1976)
Two songs, op. 48 (Ditlevson) (T and org) (1980)
Two worldly hymns, op. 19 (S, vln, ob and strs) (1977)
Why don't they listen? op. 78 (S, T, cl and org) (1984)
Winter sonata, op. 51 (S, vlc and c-b) (1981)
Ref. composer

LUND, Hanna
Danish concert pianist, teacher and composer. b. Herning, October 18, 1904. She studied at the Paris and Vienna Conservatories and made her debut in Copenhagen in 1929. She obtained her Mus.Bac. at the University of Chicago in 1934 and toured Canada, the United States and in 1939 performed in Copenhagen, playing her own compositions.
Compositions
CHAMBER
Suite (vln and pf) (1935)
PIANO
Pieces incl.:
Boernesuite, for children
SACRED
Mass
Ref. 94, 96, 465

LUND, Inger Bang
Norwegian composer. b. September 19, 1876; d. December 26, 1968. She studied at the Bergen Conservatory under J. Halvorsen and at the Rome Conservatory under Casella.
Compositions
CHAMBER
Romance (vln and pf)
PIANO
Mot hoest, op. 14
Mot vaar, op. 15
Nocturnes
Trold, op. 11
VOCAL
Songs (T. Caspari and Sivle) incl.:
Goeym meg, Mor
Ref. 20

LUND, Signe (Lund-Skabo) (Skabo, Singe-Lund)
Norwegian pianist and composer. b. Oslo, April 15, 1868; d. Oslo, April 6, 1950. She studied under E. Nissen, I. Holter and P. Winge in Oslo and under W. Berger in Berlin in 1896. She later spent periods of study in Copenhagen and Paris. From 1902 to 1920 she lived in Chicago. She was awarded a state pension in 1941 for her compositions.
Compositions
ORCHESTRA
Pieces incl.:
Berceuse, op. 28
Music for the Bjoernson centenary in Chicago (1910)
CHAMBER
Barcarolle et chanson (fl or vln and pf) (Zappfe)
Berceuse, in E-Minor (vln and pf) (Hansen)
Other pieces for violin and piano
PIANO
Cinque morceaux lyriques, op. 34 (Zappfe)
Drei lyrische Stuecke, op. 25 (Schuberth; Schirmer)
Fire pianostykker, op. 9 (Hals)
Fire pianostykker, op. 15 (Gehrmann)
Menuet, op. 17 (Schuberth; Schirmer)
Norske smaastyker, op. 15 (Gehrmann)
Petite valse, op. 10 (Hansen)
Souvenir, op. 29, no. 1 (Hals)
Trois etudes poetiques, op. 32 (Zappfe)
Valse brillante (Hals)
VOCAL
Cantata to celebrate the centenary of the Norwegian Constitution (1914)
Norwegian-American cantata (1914)
The road to France, cantata (Daniel Henderson) (on occasion of America entering World War I) (1917)
Fem sange, op. 22 (vce and pf) (Hals)
O Herre; Atter er det sommerveir; Vandraren, op. 26 (vce and pf) (Warmuth)
Wahrhaftig, op. 28 (vce and pf) (Hansen)
Wild briar (vce and pf) (Summy)
Publications
Sol gjennem skyer. Autobiography. Oslo, 1944.
Ref. 2, 20, 22, 70, 94, 105, 110, 226, 297, 331, 622

LUNDBERG, Ada
19th-century Swedish composer.
Compositions
VOCAL
Songs incl.:
All thro' sticking (Reeder)
Coster's Sunday out, or We've got the moke (Ascherberg)
Favoritkupletter: Den med staemped pa (Johns)
Good old mother-in-law (Reeder)
Ref. 297

LUNDQUIST, Christie
20th-century American composer. She composed music for two clarinets and percussion.
Ref. 142, 347

LUND-SKABO, Signe. See LUND, Signe

LUO, Jing-Jing
Chinese pianist and composer. b. 1953. Her father was also a composer. Luo studied the piano and composition at Shanghai Conservatory. Her music represents the new development of the art since the conventional music forms during the cultural revolution in China. DISCOGRAPHY.
Compositions
ORCHESTRA
Piano concerto (1981, rev 1983)
PIANO
Three Dunhuang poems: Acaopup; Tianxianzi; Zhetazhi
VOCAL
Two movements (m-S, pf and orch) (1983)

LUPTON, Belle George
American singer, teacher and composer. b. 1889. She sang leading roles in opera from 1905 to 1911 and taught music and art in schools and studios for over 50 years.
Compositions
VOCAL
Songs:
Marching along
Memories of Idaho
Surrender
Ref. 433

LURGAN, Annie Patterson. See PATTERSON, Annie Wilson

LUSTIG, Leila Sarah
American music broadcaster and composer. b. Louisville, April 30, 1944. She obtained her B.A. (1966) and M.A. (1968) from the University of California, Los Angeles, studying composition and theory under Roy Harris, John Vincent and Roy Travis. She obtained her Ph.D. (1972) from the University of Wisconsin, studying under Bert Levy and Robert Crane. She won a Meet the Composer Award in 1983.
Compositions
CHAMBER
Buffalo prints (brass qnt) (1983)
VOCAL
Vocalissimus (vce and str qrt) (1983)
MISCELLANEOUS
Opposites (1980)
Ossipee (1980)
Six significant landscapes (1979)
Ref. 625

LUTHER, Mary (Molly)

American pianist and composer. b. Cleveland, September 15, 1927; d. 1979. She studied the piano as a child. As her father refused to support her in her desire to pursue a musical career, she majored in religion at Wellesley College at his insistence. She then attended the music department of Columbia University, obtaining her M.A. in 1955. She went to the Royal College of Music, London and studied under Kathleen Long. She studied for her M.M. at the University of Michigan obtaining it eight years later from the Manhattan School of Music.

Compositions

ORCHESTRA

Variants (1971)

CHAMBER

Woodwind quintet (1968)
Movement for string quartet (1960)
Prelude and fugue for brass quartet (1968)
Trio for flute, French horn and harp (1969)

PIANO

Introduction and invention (1969)
Sonata (1959)

VOCAL

Four songs, cycle (1969)

SACRED

Magnificat, (S, mix-ch and orch) (1974)

Ref. composer's daughter

LUTTRELL, Moira

Late 19th-20th-century English composer.

Composition

OPERETTA

The Frozen Princess (1908)

Ref. 431

LUTYENS, Elisabeth

English violist, authoress and composer. b. London, July 9, 1906; d. April 14, 1983. The daughter of the architect Edwin Lutyens she studied composition under Harold Darke and the viola under Ernest Tomlinson at the Royal College of Music, 1926 to 1930. She studied under N. de Manziarly at the Ecole Normale in Paris from 1922 to 1923 and privately under George Caussade, 1930. She helped found the MacNaghten-Lemare Concerts in London in 1931 and founded the Composers' Concourse there in 1954. In the mid-1960s she formed her own publishing company, the Olivan Press. Her first work to gain international recognition was *String quartet No. 2* performed at the ISCM Festival in Warsaw in 1939. She was represented again at these festivals in 1942, 1945, 1948 and 1949. She composed about 2000 published works and was the authoress of a number of books, including an autobiography and many articles. In 1969 she was awarded the C.B.E. and also received the Lord Mayor of London's midsummer award to the arts. She married Edward Clark, a conductor. DISCOGRAPHY.

Compositions

ORCHESTRA

Symphonies, op. 46 (pf, wind, hps and perc) (1961) (Schott)
Concerto, op. 15 (vla and orch) (1947) (Mills)
Lyric piece (vln and orch) (1951)
Music for piano and orchestra, op. 59 (1964) (Schott)
Three symphonic preludes (1942) (Mills)
Music for orchestra, op. 31 (1955) (Mills)
Music for orchestra, op. 48 (1962) (Schott)
Music for orchestra, op. 56 (1963)
Three salutes (brass, strs and perc and/or full orch) (1942)
Bustle for the W.A.A.F.
Chamber concerto No. 2, op. 8 (cl. t-sax, pf concertante and str orch) (1941) (Mills)
Chamber concerto No. 4, op. 8 (hn and small orch) (1947) (Mills)
Chamber concerto No. 5, op. 8 (str qrt and small orch) (1947) (Mills)
Chorale, op. 36 (1956) (Hommage to Stravinsky) (Schott)
Concerto, op. 8, no. 3 (bsn, perc and str och) (Mills)
Divertissement (1944) (Mills)
Echoi, op. 129 (1980)
Eos (small orch) (1975)
En voyage, suite
The English seaside suite (1951)
The English theatre suite (1951)
Fantasy for strings (1937)
Five pieces (1939)
Novenaria, op. 67, no. 1 (1967) (Olivan)
Petite suite (1946)
Proud city, overture (1945)
Rondel (1978)
Salute I and II (timp, perc, hp, pf and str orch) (Mills)
Six bagatelles (cham orch)
Suite gauloise (small orch) (1944) (De Wolfe)
Three pieces, op. 7 (1939) (Mills)
Wild Decembers
Winter of the world, op. 98 (1974) (Olivan)

CHAMBER

Plenum II, op. 92 (ob and 13 insts) (1973) (Olivan)
Divertissement (double wind qnt)
Music for wind, op. 60 (double wind qnt) (1964) (Schott)
Six tempi, op. 42 (10 insts) (1957) (Olivan)
Chamber concerto No. 1, op. 8 (9 insts) (1940) (Mills)
Rape of the moon, op. 90 (wind octet) (1973) (Olivan)
Fanfare for a festival (brass ens)
Concertante for five players, op. 22 (1950) (Mills)
The fall of the leaf (ob and str qrt) (1966) (Olivan)
String quintet, op. 51 (2 vln, vla and 2 vlc) (1963) (Schott)
Wind quintet, op. 45 (fl, ob, cl, bsn and hn) (1950) (Mills)
Mare et minutiae (str qrt)
Plenum III, op. 93 (str qrt) (Olivan)
Quartet, op. 139 (1982)
String quartet No. 1 (1938)
String quartet No. 2, op. 5 (1938) (Mills)
String quartet No. 3, op. 18 (1949) (Mills)
String quartet No. 4 (1952)
String quartet No. 5 (1952)
String quartet No. 6 (1952) (Mills)
Capricci, op. 33 (2 hp and perc) (1955) (Schott)
Fantasie trio, op. 55 (fl, cl and pf) (1963) (Olivan)
Horai, op. 67, no. 4 (vln, hn and pf) (1968) (Olivan)
Kareniani (vla and insts) (for Karen Phillips)
Music for three, op. 65 (fl, ob and pf) (1966) (Olivan)
Nocturnes, op. 30 (vln, gtr and vlc) (1955) (Schott)
Scena, op. 58 (vln, vlc and perc) (1964) (Olivan)
String trio (1939)
String trio, op. 5, no. 6 (Mills)
String trio, op. 57 (1969) (Schott)
Trio (cl, vlc and pf)
Wind trio, op. 52 (fl, cl and bsn) (1963) (Schott)
Baker's dozen, 12 pieces (2 vln)
Chamber concerto No. 6, op. 8 (ob and hp)
Constants (vlc and pf)
The farmstead (2 vlc) (1956)
Five little pieces, op. 14 (pf and cl) (Schott)
Footfalls (fl and pf) (1978-1979)
In the direction of the beginning (d-b and pf)
Madrigal (ob and vln)
Nine bagatelles, op. 10 (vlc and pf) (Mills, 1947)
Partita (2 vln) (1938)
Scroll for Li-Lo, op. 67, no. 3 (vln and pf) (1967) (Olivan)
Sonata (vln and pf)
This green tide, op. 103 (cl or basset hn and pf)
The tides of time, op. 75 (d-b and pf) (1969) (Yorke)
Three duos, op. 34 (hn and pf; also vlc and pf; also vln and pf) (1957) (Schott)
Valediction, op. 28 (cl and pf) (1954) (Mills)
Air-dance-ground (1946)
Aptote (vln) (1948) (Mills)
Driving out the death, op. 81 (1971) (Olivan)
The dying of the sun, op. 73 (1969)
Pieta (hpcd) (1975)
Prelude and capriccio (vlc) (1949)
Presages, op. 53 (ob) (1963)
Sonata (vla) (1946)
Sonata, op. 5, no. 4 (vla) (1958)
Tre, op. 94 (cl) (1973) (Olivan)
Valediction in A (cl) (1958)
Variations, op. 38 (fl) (1957)
6, op. 147, improvisations

ORGAN

What is the wind, what is it? (4 hands) (Olivan)
Plenum IV, op. 100 (1974)
Sinfonia, op. 32 (1955)
Suite (1948)
Temonos, op. 72 (1961)
Three brief pieces (cham org) (1969) (Olivan)

PIANO

Helix, op. 67, no. 2 (4 hands) (1967)
The great seas, op. 132 (4 hands) (1978) (Olivan)
The check book, children's pieces
Five bagatelles, op. 49 (1962) (Schott)
Five impromptus, op. 116 (1977) (Olivan)
Five intermezzi, op. 9 (1941) (Mills)
Holiday diary, children's pieces (1949) (A. Lengnick)
Hommage a la France

Overture (1944)
Piano e forte, op. 43 (1958) (Mills)
Plenum I, op. 87 (1972)
The ring of bone (1976)
Seven preludes
Three improvisations (1948) (Mills)

VOCAL
Catena, op. 47, cantata (S, T and 21 insts) (Phoenix Trust award) (1961) (Schott)
De amore, cantata (S, T, ch and orch) (1957) (Schott)
O saisons, o chateaux, op. 13, cantata (Rimbaud) (S, man, gtr, hp and str orch) (1946) (Mills)
Winter the huntsman, chamber cantata (Osbert Sitwell) (ch, hn, trp, vlc and pf) (1934)
Elegy of the flowers (vces and orch) (1980)
Essence of our happiness, op. 69 (T, ch and orch) (Abu Yasid, Donne and Rimbaud) (1968) (Olivan)
French songs (S and vla or str orch or cham orch) (1938)
Quincunx, op. 44 (after Sir Thomas Browne) (S, B and orch) (1962) (Mills)
Three salutes, no. 3 (Milton) (T, ch and orch) (1942)
To sleep (Keats) (Cont and small orch)
Voice of quiet waters, op. 84 (ch and orch) (1972)
Bienfaits de la lune (Baudelaire) (S, T, ch, perc and strs) (1952)
Counting your steps, op. 85 (ch, fl and 4 perc) (1972) (Olivan)
Ecomion, op. 54 (ch, brass and perc) (1963) (Schott)
Motet, op. 27 (ch)
Sloth (from The seven deadly sins) (mix-ch)
The tyme doth flete, op. 79 (mix-ch a-cap) (1968) (Olivan)
Verses of love (Ben Jonson) (mix-ch a-cap) (1970)
And suddenly it's evening, op. 66 (Quasimodo) (T and 11 insts) (1966) (Olivan)
Akapotik rose, op. 64 (Eduardo Paolozzi) (S, fl, 2 cl, str trio and pf) (1966) (Olivan)
Anerca, op. 77 (trans from Eskimo poetry) (speaker and 10 gtrs) (1970) (Olivan)
Chimes and cantos, op. 86 (Robert Herrick) (B, 2 trp, 2 trb, 4 vln, 2 d-b and perc) (1972) (Olivan)
Four songs (T and str qrt) (1934)
Island, op. 80 (Sophocles) (S, T, narr and inst ens) (1971) (Olivan)
..... Like a window (vces, fl, vlc and drs)
By all these (S and gtr)
Dialogo, op. 88 (Quasimodo) (T and lute) (Olivan)
The egocentric (T or B and pf) (1968) (Olivan)
Epithalamion (S and org)
In the direction of the beginning, op. 76 (Dylan Thomas) (B and pf) (1970) (Olivan)
In the temple of a bird's wing, op. 37 (B and pf) (1956, rev 1965) (Olivan)
Nine songs (vce and pf) (1948) (Olivan)
Ode alla tormenta, op. 78 (Pablo Neruda) (m-S and pf) (1970) (Olivan)
A phoenix, op. 71 (Ovid) (S, vln, cl and pf; also op. 71a, S and pf) (1968) (Olivan)
Refugee blues (vce and pf)
She tells her love while half asleep (S)
Six songs (Housman, Bronte, Bandor and Auden) (vce and pf) (1936)
Stevie Smith songs (vce and pf)
The supplicant (B and pf) (1970) (Olivan)
That sun (Cont and pf)
Three songs (1953) (Olivan)
The valley of Hatsu-Se, op. 62 (Japanese words) (S, fl, cl, vlc and pf) (1965) (Olivan)
Vision of youth, op. 79 (Joseph Conrad) (S and 3 cl) (1970) (Olivan)

SACRED
Nativity (W.R. Rodgers) (S and str orch) (1951) (Olivan)
Requiescat (Stravinsky) (S and str orch) (1971) (Olivan)
Requiem for the living (soli, ch and orch) (1948)
The country of the stars, motet (Boethius) (ch a-cap) (1963)
Excerpta tractatus-logico philosophici, op. 27, motet (ch a-cap) (Schott)
The hymn of man, op. 61, motet (Swinburne) (m-ch) (1965) (rev mix-ch, op. 61a, 1970) (Schott)
Magnificat and Nunc dimittis (ch a-cap) (1965) (Schott)
Si uis celsi lura, motet (1957)

BALLET
Ballet for nine wind instruments and percussion (1949)
The birthday of the Infanta (after Oscar Wilde) (1932)
Midas

OPERA
Infidelio, op. 29, in 7 scenes (composer) (S, T and 7 insts) (1954) (Olivan)
Isis and Osiris, op. 74, lyric drama (composer) (8 vces and small orch) (1970) (Olivan)
The Linnet from the Leaf, op. 89 (composer) (Olivan)
The Numbered, op. 63, prologue and 2 acts (1967) (Olivan)
One and the Same, op. 97 (composer) (1973) (Olivan)
Penelope, music drama with ballet (1948)
The Pit (1972)
Time Off-Not a Ghost of a Chance, op. 68, charade in 4 scenes (composer) (1978) (Olivan)
The Waiting Game, op. 91, in 3 scenes (composer) (1973) (Olivan)

OPERETTA
Everyman, for children

INCIDENTAL MUSIC
Bartholomew Fari, radio (B. Jonson)
Margate, radio (Dylan Thomas)
Oxford, radio (Dylan Thomas)
Blood Fiends, film (1966)
Don't Bother to Knock, film
Eldorado, film
The Skull, film
World without End, film
As You Like It (Shakespeare)
The Bacchae (Euripides)
Enter Caesar (Julius Macneice)
Julius Caesar (Shakespeare)
The Mad Woman of Chaillot (Giradoux)
The Oresteia (Aeschylus)
Sleep of Prisoners (C. Fry)
Volpone (B. Jonson)

ELECTRONIC
Go said the bird (str qrt and elec gtr)

MISCELLANEOUS
Any dark morning (Willis Hall)

Publications

A Goldfish Bowl. Autobiography. Casse & Co.

Bibliography

Bradshaw, Susan. *The Music of Elisabeth Lutyens*. Musical Times, July 1971, pp. 653-656.
Henderson, Robert. *Elisabeth Lutyens*. Musical Times, August 1963.
Murray-Schafer, R. British Composers in Interview. London, 1963.
Weissman, J.J. *The Music of Elisabeth Lutyens*. The Listener, 1950.

Ref. 2, 4, 5, 8, 15, 17, 22, 26, 52, 68, 70, 73, 75, 76, 80, 81, 84, 86, 88, 96, 109, 131, 141, 150, 172, 177, 184, 189, 193, 199, 206, 230, 280, 284, 295, 347, 397, 422, 457, 477, 497, 563, 572, 580, 622, 637, 645, 653

LUTYENS, Sally (Speare)

American lecturer and composer. b. Syracuse, NY, October 31, 1927. She studied under Paul Boepple at Bennington College, VT. She studied composition at the University of Southern California and is head of the music department at Cambridge School, Weston, MA.

Compositions

CHAMBER
Midsummer night's dream (2 fl, 2 vlc and pf) (1969)
Dance technique demonstration (pf, fl and perc) (1972)
Piano trio (1973)
Recorder trio (1973)
Journeys (pf and perc) (1973)
Alice is
Byzantine omelette
The birds (1973)

VOCAL
A parody (S, fl vln and pf)

ELECTRONIC
Antigone (elec tape) (1970)

Ref. 94, 142

LVOVA, Julia Fedorovna (Gyul Reginald Fox)

Soviet pianist, folklorist, teacher and composer. b. Paris, November 30, 1873; d. Leningrad, April 22, 1950. She studied the piano under Vyolfl and Chezya and composition under A. Glazunov and A. Liadov at the St. Petersburg Conservatory (1883 to 1892). From 1890 to 1895 she studied law at St. Petersburg University but returned to music, continuing her piano studies in Vienna under T. Leschetizky. She taught the piano and music theory and from 1889 to 1941 worked as an accompanist and soloist. She was interested in folklore and researched into the simultaneous action of sound and light and their healing properties. Together with O. Karatygin she invented a light-sound piano, Phonophot, in 1930. She took part in the siege of Leningrad in 1943 and was awarded two medals during the defence of Leningrad.

Compositions

ORCHESTRA
Indian cycle
Simfonietta
Spanish suite (str orch) (1937)
Stormy petrel (also vocal) (1934, 1905)

CHAMBER
Spanish dance suite (str qnt; also str qrt) (1937, 1938)
Cycle of twenty pieces (str qrt) (1950)
Indian suite (str qrt) (1933)

Oriental sketches (str qrt) (1935)
Quartet on Turkish themes (str qrt) (1938)
Melody (b-cl and pf) (1928)
Piece (cl and pf) (1928)
Piece (vla and pf) (1928)
Three pieces (vln and pf) (1945)
Three rhapsodies (vln and pf) (1944)
PIANO
Children's pieces on motives from Ukranian songs (4 hands) (1947)
Children's sonatina (1894)
Dance cycle (1926)
Four Indian dances (1940)
Indian sketches, 9 pieces (1937)
Sonata No. I (1899)
Sonata No. II (1901)
Sonata No. III, for children (1902)
VOCAL
Indian fairy tale (vce and orch) (1922)
Polish pastorale (ch and pf) (1949)
Russian nature (ch and opt pf) (1950)
Songs incl.:
Children's songs (A. Barto, N. Vengrov, S. Marshak, K. Chukovsky and others) (1929)
Cycle of six Spanish songs (1931)
Cycle on the constitution of the USSR (1937)
Fatherland (1940)
Jewish songs (Manucharova) (1934)
To women communists (V. Knyazev) (1929)
Romances (Pushkin, 1935-1936; Lermontov, 1940-1941; A.K. Tolstoy, 1895; V. Velichko, 1895, A. Apikhtin, 1899, B. Liska, 1910-1912;, M. Voloshin, 1910-1916; I. Turgenev, 1912; R. Tagore, 1916-1950; O. Vaksel, 1915-1922; N. Shcherbin, 1937-1938)
Songs (M. Dudin, 1943; K. Simonov, 1944; G. Grigorian, 1944; G. Gulyan, 1944; B. Khetagurov, 1944; A. Prokofiev, 1948; B. Likharev, 1948; M. Komissarova, 1948)
Two duets (composer) (1936, 1948)
OPERETTA
Mila and Nelly, for children (1897)
INCIDENTAL MUSIC
Music for plays
ARRANGEMENTS
Sixty Ukranian folk songs (1936-1937)
Songs of the peoples of the USSR (1936-1948)
French songs (1936-1940)
Ref. 87

LYELL, Margaret

Scottish composer. b. 1910.
Compositions
CHAMBER
Barcarollina (fl and pf) (1979)
VOCAL
Love in May, song
Ref. 263

LYLE DE BOHUN. See BOONE, Clara Lyle

LYNN, Cathy

20th-century American composer.
Composition
FILM MUSIC
Toys are not for children (1972)
Ref. 326

LYNN, Mrs. Nevile. See CORRI, Ghita

LYONN LIEBERMAN, Julie

American violinist, authoress, singer, teacher and composer. b. Newark, NJ, July 16, 1954. She gained her B.A. from the Sarah Lawrence College and her M.A. from New York University. She had private study with Samuel Applebaum, Nancy Clarke, Ronald Tecco, Stanley Richie, Bill Henry, Sal Mosca, Ray Evans Harrell, Stanley Walden, Dary John Miselle, Ken Guilmartin, Neil Waltzer and Judar Kataoni. She is a member of ASCAP and contributes articles to several musical journals. DISCOGRAPHY.

Compositions
BAND
Arcturus (vln and band) (1984) (Huiksi Music)
Tune in transit (vln and band) (1978) (Huiksi)
Violinova (vln and band) (1978) (Huiksi)
VIOLIN
Blues fiddle anthology (1981) (Huiksi)
VOCAL
Empathic connections (vce, vln and sruti box) (1981) (Huiksi)
Van Gogh songs (vce, vln and hp) (1985) (Huiksi)
THEATRE
Music for theatre and dance incl.:
Against silence (Emmatroupe)
A girl starts out (Emmatroupe)
Lighthouse (Judy Dubrin)
Van Gogh (Leonard Shapiro)
MISCELLANEOUS
In a dance with Celestana
Seven
Love is all
Polaris
Publications
Blues Fiddle. Oak Publications. 1982.
Improvising Violin in All Styles. Columbia Pictures. 1984.
Ref. composer, 643

LYONS, Ruth

20th-century organist, pianist, authoress, librarian and composer. b. Cincinnati. She was educated at the Universiy of Cincinnati School of Music. Whilst there, she wrote musicals and broadcast on the radio in 1929. In 1933 she was the musical director of a station and in 1942 hostess of her own television show.
Compositions
VOCAL
Songs:
Christmas is a birthday time
Let's light the Christmas tree
The ten tunes of Christmas
This is Christmas
Wasn't the summer short
Ref. 39

LYRICAL MUSE. See CORINNA

LYUBOMIRSKAYA-BOYARSKAYA, Revekka Grigorevna

Soviet pianist, lecturer and composer. b. Rzhishchev, district Kiev, 1893. In 1918 she graduated from the Frebelevski Institute in Kiev, having already graduated in 1917 from the Kiev Music School, where she studied the piano under V. Pukhalsky and theory of composition under Ivanov. From 1919 to 1922 she lectured in singing and rhythmics and in music courses for nursery school teachers in Kharkov and Kiev. In 1922 she moved to Moscow. During World War II she taught pre-school teachers in Chistopol.
Compositions
VOCAL
And so the Red Army entered (P. Markish)
Arbeit, Speil, Gesang, 36 songs
Eight Jewish songs (composer) (1939)
Jewish songs, collections
Klinge gemerlech, 40 children's songs (1925)
A letter to Comrade Voroshilov (L. Kvitko)
Let us sing, 30 songs (1940)
Little builders, 28 songs
Songs about peace (I. Kerler)
Songs about happiness (I. Fefer)
Songs of defence (P. Usenko)
Ref. 87

MAAS, Marguerite Wilson

American concert pianist, lecturer and composer. b. Baltimore, MD, April 17, 1888. She studied at the Peabody Conservatory, Baltimore and the Stern Conservatory, Berlin and appeared in concert in Berlin in 1914 and later in America. She taught at Skidmore College from 1915 to 1916. She composed a piano sonata, other piano pieces and songs.
Ref. 226, 292, 433

MacARTHUR, Fern
20th-century American composer.
Composition
CHAMBER
Moods and tenses (str qrt) (1980)
Ref. Working papers on women in music

MacARTHUR, Helen
American pianist, teacher and song composer. b. La Crosse, WI, 1879; d. 1936.
Ref. 347

MacCOLLIN, Frances. See McCOLLIN, Frances

MacDONALD, Catherine
American conductor, teacher and composer. b. New York, October 22, 1940. She studied at the Sarah Lawrence College under Meyer Kupferman and Ezra Laderman; the Juilliard School of Music under Jaco Druckman and Vittorio Giannini and at Columbia University under Jack Beeson, Otto Luening and Chou Wen-Chung. She was assistant conductor of the Interracial Chorale from 1963 to 1965, conductor of the New York Fellowship Chorus from 1964 to 1965 and teacher of composition and conducting at the New Lincoln School from 1964 to 1970.
Compositions
VOCAL
Madrigals (w-ch)
THEATRE
Enemies
Siamese connections
A Streetcar named Desire
Twelfth Night (Shakespeare)
Ref. 142

MacDONNELL, Lilly
English composer.
Composition
OPERETTA
Vingt-et-un (London, 1914)
Ref. 431

MacFARREN, Emma Marie (nee Bennett or Blunett) (Mrs. John) (pseud. Jules Brissac)
English concert pianist, teacher, writer and composer. b. London, June 19, 1824; d. London, November 9, 1895. She studied under W.H. Kearns and Mme. Dulcken before becoming a composition pupil of Sir George MacFarren. In 1846 she married Sir George's brother. After 1851 she appeared regularly in concerts and recitals until 1883 when she devoted her time to teaching and writing.
Compositions
PIANO
Bonnie Scotland
Operatic fantasies
Valse de bravoure
Ref. 6, 70, 226, 276, 347

MacFARREN, Mrs. John. See MacFARREN, Emma Marie

MacGREGOR, Helen
20th-century American composer of piano pieces.
Ref. 40, 347

MacGREGOR, Laurie
American teacher and composer. b. Minneapolis, 1951. She graduated with her M.A. (composition) in 1977 from Columbia University where she studied under Jack Beeson, Alice Shields (q.v.) and Vladimor Ussachevsky and privately under Meyer Hupferman. She taught theatre and music in schools in New Hampshire, was a MacDowell Colony fellow, a Norlin Foundation fellow in 1979 and received a grant from the Alice M. Ditson fund, Columbia University. DISCOGRAPHY.

Composition
CHAMBER
Intrusion of the hunter (perc ens) (1974) (ded Meyer Kupferman)
Ref. 563

MacINTOSH, Mary
18th-century English composer.
Compositions
VOCAL
Collections of airs (vce and pf) (1785)
Ref. 128

MacKENNA, Carmela
Chilean pianist and composer. b. Santiago, 1879; d. Santiago, January 31, 1962. She was the great granddaughter of General MacKenna of the Chilean Independence and the aunt of the composer Alfonso Leng. She studied music at the age of 50 under Bindo Paoli in Santiago and the piano under Kindrade Ansorge and composition under Hans Mersmann in Berlin in 1930. She won a first prize in the International Competition of Religious Music, Frankfurt. The score of her *Concerto* is in the Fleisher Collection, Philadelphia, PA.
Compositions
ORCHESTRA
Concerto (pf and cham orch) (1934)
Dos movimientos sinfonicos (1935)
CHAMBER
Visiones chilenas (snare dr and strs)
String quartet
Trio (1936)
Trio for flute, violin and viola (1932)
Sonata (vln and pf) (1931)
PIANO
Sonatas and pieces (2 pf)
Chilean suite
Six preludes (1931)
Theme with variations
VOCAL
Album of Lieder
Poema (P. Nureda) (vce and pf)
Spanish and German songs
SACRED
Mass (ch and str orch)
Mass (m-ch a-cap) (1936)
Ref. 54, 81, 90, 100

MacKINLAY, Mrs. J. (pseud. Antoinette Sterling)
American contralto and composer. b. Sterlingville, NY, 1850; d. Hampstead, 1904. She studied singing under Marchesi, Garcia and Pauline Viardot-Garcia (q.v.). After marriage she settled in England. Sullivan's *Lost chord* was written for her.
Compositions
VOCAL
Songs and duets incl.:
Flowers that never die
Now the parting hour
Parting
Remember thee
Ref. 276, 347, 433

MacKOWN, Marjorie T.
20th-century American composer. Her works were performed at the ACA concerts at the Eastman School.
Compositions
ORCHESTRA
Theme and variations for cello and orchestra (1934)
CHAMBER
Piano quintet (1936)
Ref. 168

MacLEOD, Mary
Hebridean authoress and composer of folk songs. b. ca. 1600. Many of the Highland folk songs show strong traces of her influence. Women in Celtic society held a high place and most of the music of that time consisted of passionate songs expressing women's love.
Ref. 149

MacPHAIL, Frances
20th-century American composer.
Composition
SACRED
My Master (high vce and org or pf) (H.W. Gray Co.)
Ref. 190

MACAULAY, Janice Michel
American harpsichordist, organist, pianist, conductor, lecturer and composer. b. Providence, RI, August 19, 1949. She studied at Brown University and graduated with an M.A. (music) in 1977. She studied orchestral conducting under Karel Husa; choral conducting under Thomas Sokol and Robert Molison; the organ and the harpsichord under William Dinneen and composition under Karel Husa, Steve Stucky and Paul Nelson. She studied for a doctorate in musical art at Cornell University. From 1966 to 1979 she was organist and choir director at several churches and gave organ and harpsichord recitals. In the same period she taught music theory at Brown University and was a teaching assistant in musical appreciation and the piano at Cornell University from 1980 to 1982. She won two best of category awards in the Delius Composition Competition, Jacksonville University, 1983.
Compositions
ORCHESTRA
Elegy (1982)
Ithaca, NY (1981)
SYMPHONIC BAND
Concerto (1978)
CHAMBER
Improvisations (4 fl and 4 cl) (1979)
Brass quintet (2 trp, hn, trb and tba) (1979)
Canzona (brass qnt) (1976)
Three pieces (str qrt) (1980)
Sonata (trp and org) (1979)
Six chorale preludes for Lent and Easter (org) (1977)
Tuba contra mundum (tba) (1983)
VOCAL
Three love poems of Emily Dickinson (w-ch, cel and strs) (1981)
Aestivation (O.W. Holmes) (S, Bar, sax, tba, perc and pf) (1983)
Seven love poems of Emily Dickinson (S and pf) (1983)
SACRED
O Lord, You have searched and known me! (mix-ch a-cap) (1978)
ARRANGEMENTS
Da Jesus an dem kreuz stand, 3 chorale preludes (orch) (1977)
Ref. composer

MACEDA, Corazon S.
Philippine lecturer and composer. b. Binan, Laguna, May 10, 1911. She graduated with a B.Sc. (education) in 1931 from the Music Conservatory, University of Philippines and an M.A. from the Eastman School of Music, 1948. She was associate dean of the College of Fine Arts, Philippine University.
Compositions
SACRED
Araw na dakila, Christmas song
Ave Maria
Pangarap
Publications
Pointers for Music Teachers. 1957.
Philippine Choruses for All Occasions.
Workbooks in Music Education. Series.
Ref. 457

MACHADO, Lena
Hawaiian singer, teacher and composer. b. Honolulu, October 16, 1903; d. January 22, 1974. She first sang on the radio at the age of 16 and was later a soloist for the Royal Hawaiian Band and toured America several times. She became known as 'Hawaii's Songbird'. In 1948 she opened a singing and hula studio. She composed in the traditional Hawaiian style, helping to carry the traditional song into the contemporary period.
Compositions
VOCAL
Songs incl.:
E ku'u baby
Ei nei
Holo wa'apa
Ho'onanea
Kaulana
Kauoha mai
Mom
O hilo hanakahi
U'ilani
Ref. 438

MACIEL, Argentina
Brazilian composer. b. Recife, March, 1888; d. Olinda, January, 1970.
Composition
PIANO
Valsas
Ref. Inter-American Music Review Vol. 1, 1980

MACIRONE, Clara Angela. See MACIRONI, Clara Angela

MACIRONI (Macirone), Clara Angela
English concert pianist, professor and composer. b. London, January 20, 1821; d. 1895. She was descended from a noble Roman family and her father was a tenor and her mother a pianist. She entered the Royal Academy of Music in 1839 and studied the piano under W.H. Holmes and Ciprian Potter, composition under C. Lucas and singing under Signor Negri until 1842. She became professor of the piano at the academy and was elected an A.R.A.M. From 1846 to 1964 she gave concerts, frequently playing her own works. After 1864 she devoted her time to teaching and composing. She was head music teacher at Aske's School for Girls from 1872 to 1878 and at the Church of England School for Girls, London. She systemized the teaching of music with successful results; her method was endorsed by such authorities as Sir G.A. Macfarren, Barnby and W. Macfarren.
Compositions
CHAMBER
Suite de pieces in E-Minor (vln and pf)
PIANO
Cantilena
Nacht Rise Lied
Rondino in G
Summer serenade
VOCAL
Part songs incl.:
Autolycus' song
The Avon to the Severn runs
The battle of the Baltic
Echoes
Humptie Dumptie
Jack and Jill
Jog on, jog on the footpath way
Old Daddy Longlegs
Sir Knight, Sir Knight
Soldier's dream
When summer's come at last
Songs incl.:
The Balaclava charge
Cavalier's song
Dreams
Golden grain
Henri de Lagardere
Hesperus
Montrose's love song
My child
Oh hush thee my babie
The recall
Sweet and low
There is dew for the flow'ret
SACRED
Benedictus
By the waters of Babylon, anthem
Jubilate
Te Deum
Other sacred songs
Ref. 6, 102, 226, 276, 347

MACKEN, Jane Virginia
American authoress and composer. b. St. Louis, January 14, 1912. She studied music privately.
Compositions
VOCAL
Tired of being lonely, song
SACRED
The Cross on the hill, anthem
Ref. 39

MACKENZIE, Grace
Late 19th-century American composer.
Compositions
VOCAL
Songs incl.:
The helmsman
Ref. 433, 276

MACKIE, Frances C.

20th-century American composer.

Composition

SACRED

Carol fantasy for Christmas Day (mix-ch and org) (H.W. Gray Co.)

Ref. 190

MACKIE, Shirley M.

American clarinetist, conductor, lecturer and composer. b. Rockdale, TX, October 25, 1929. She attended Louisiana State University on a clarinet scholarship, playing the clarinet with the University Symphony Orchestra. She received a B.Mus. in 1949 and M.Mus. in 1950 and continued her study of composition at Louisiana State University under Helen L. Gunderson from 1951 to 1953 and later under Darius Milhaud in Colorado and Nadia Boulanger (q.v.) in France. She was the founder and conductor of the Chamber Orchestra of Waco from 1966 to 1969 and band conductor for Riesel High School. She taught all levels and phases of music from elementary school through university. She received a number of composition awards.

Compositions

ORCHESTRA

Symphony for the Bicentennial (1975)
Symphonic dances (1962)
Sinfonietta (1963)
Chamber symphony (1954)
Divertimenti (1971)
Gemini's journey (1966)
Passacaglia (1953)
Passacaglia for strings (1968)

BAND

Concertino (cl and band) (1968)
Passacaglia (1969)
Ricerta (1971)

CHAMBER

Dances and departures (7 fl) (1959)
Preludio, cancion y baile (ww qnt) (1962)
Three Latin dances (5 cl) (1964)
Four Trifles (2 fl, cl and pf) (1964)
Fugue (ob, cl and bsn) (1950)
Introduction and allegro (cl, vlc and pf) (1953)
Five vibrations (winds and perc) (1974)
Five dialogues (cl and pf) (1949)
Five tempi (cl and pf) (1949)
Inventions (cl and pf) (1950)
Sonatine (cl and pf) (1952)
Suite breve (fl and pf) (1960)
Five moods (fl) (1966)
Lamentations triology (vlc) (1964)
Three movements for solo clarinet (1968)
The sky is falling (1974)

PIANO

Journey to the moon (6 pf) (1970)
Un poco rara (2 pf) (1957)
Aria (1963)
Berceuse du chien (1963)
Concert piece (1965)
Etude (1968)
Latin duo (1967)
Primitive sarcasms (1962)
Un promenade sur la bicyclette (1960)

VOCAL

Lullaby (w-ch) (1956)
Aria concertata Nos, 1 and 2 (S, cl and pf) (1957)
From the shore (S and cl) (1968)
Goodbye (S and cl) (1968)
The ironwood tree (S and cl) (1968)
It is easy to forget a song (S and pf) (1957)
The leaf (S and pf) (1957)
Light (S and pf) (1956)
Loss (Cont and pf) (1955)
Questions for Americans (S, cl and pf) (1960)
Serenade (Cont and pf) (1955)
There is no time (S, cl and pf) (1960)
The watchdog (S and pf) (1957)

SACRED

Requiem (ch and orch) (1967)
Jesu, priceless treasure (mix-ch) (1960)

BALLET

Chamber ballet (1968)
Dance in the Brazos Brakes (1973)

OPERA

Mister Man (1963)

MISCELLANEOUS

Concatenation (1973)
Projections (1972)
Venus 2071 (1971)

Ref. composer, 77, 84, 206

MACONCHY, Elizabeth

English pianist and composer of Irish parentage. b. Broxbourne, Hertfortshire, March 19, 1907. She is the mother of Nicola Frances Lefanu (q.v.). Elizabeth studied at the Royal College of Music, London from 1923 to 1927 under Charles Wood and Vaughan Williams (composition), C.H. Kitson (counterpoint) and Arthur Alexander (piano). She was awarded a Blumenthal traveling scholarship to Prague where she made her debut as a composer. Her *Concerto for piano* was performed by the Prague Philharmonic Orchestra in 1930. Her works were played at I.S.C.M. festivals in Prague in 1935, Paris in 1937 and Copenhagen, 1947. In 1933 she received a *Daily Telegraph* award for chamber music and in 1970 a medal from the Worshipful Company of Musicians for services to chamber music. She also received Edwin Evans prizes in 1948 and 1969, a Radcliffe award in 1969, Octavia scholarship, Sullivan prize, L.C.C. Coronation prize in 1953 and an GEDOK International prize, 1961. She was the first chairlady of the Composers' Guild, 1959. She was vice-president of the Society of Woman Musicians and of the Workers' Music Association. DISCOGRAPHY.

Compositions

ORCHESTRA

Symphony (1948) (Lengnick)
Symphony for double string orchestra (1952) (Lengnick)
Dialogue (pf and orch) (1940) (Lengnick)
Serenata concertante (vln and orch) (1962) (OUP)
Double concerto (ob, bsn and str orch) (1957) (Lengnick)
Concerto (pf and cham och) (1928) (OUP)
Christmas music
Concertino (pf and small orch) (Lengnick)
Concertino (bsn and str orch) (1951) (Lengnick)
Concertino (cl and str och) (1945)
Concertino (pf and str orch) (1928) (Mills)
Epyllion (vlc and str orch)
An Essex overture (1966) (British & Continental Music Agencies)
The land, suite (Victoria Sackville-West) (1929) (Lengnick)
Nocturne (1951) (Lengnick)
Proud Thames, overture (1953) (Lengnick)
Sinfonietta
Suite (cham orch) (1930)
Theme and variations (str orch) (1942)
Three cloudscapes (1968)
Two dances from Puck Fair (Lengnick)
Variations on a well-known theme (1942)

CHAMBER

Romanza (vla and ens)
Variazioni concertanti (ob, cl, hn and strs) (1965) (Lengnick)
Music for woodwinds and brass (1966)
Quintet (cl and strs) (1963) (OUP)
Wind quintet
Oboe quartet
Sonatina (str qrt) (1963) (Lengnick)
String quartet No. 1 (1933)
String quartet No. 2 (1936)
String quartet No. 3 (1938)
String quartet No. 4 (1943)
String quartet No. 5 (1948)
String quartet No. 6 (1951)
String quartet No. 7 (1956)
String quartet No. 8 (1966)
String quartet No. 9 (1966)
String quartet No. 10 (London: Chester)
String quartet No 11 (1978) (Lengnick)
String quartet No. 12
Tribute (vln and wind insts)
Piccola musica (str trio)
Trio (strs) (1957)
Colloquy (fl and pf) (Chester, 1980)
Divertimento (pf and vlc) (1944) (Lengnick)
Duo (2 vln) (1934)
Duo, theme and variations (vln and vlc) (1951) (Lengnick)
Music (d-b and pf) (1970)
Prelude, interlude and fugue (2 vln) (1934)
Serenade (vlc and pf) (1944)
Sonata (vln and pf) (1944)
Sonata (vlc and cl)
Sonata (vln and pf) (1938)
Three bagatelles (ob and hpcd or pf)
Three pieces (2 cl) (1956)
Three preludes (vln and pf)
Fantasia (cl and pf) (Chester, 1981)

Five sketches (vla)
Notebook (hpcd) (1966)
Sonatina (hpcd) (1965) (Lengnick)
Three pieces (hp) (1977)
Touchstone (ob or org)
Variations on a theme from Job (vlc) (1957) (Lengnick)
Reflections (1962)
PIANO
Preludio fugato e finale (2 pf) (1967) (Lengnick)
Childrens' pieces: Sad story; The bell; Conversation; Cradle song; Nodding; The dancing bear; The sewing machine; Spring waters (Lengnick, 1952)
Contrapuntal pieces (1941)
A country town, children's suite
Impromptu-fantasia on one note (1939) (Hinrichsen)
Sonatina (1965) (Lengnick)
The yaffle and mill race (1962)
VOCAL
Ariadne (S and orch)
The leaden echo and the golden rule (ch and cham orch) (1931)
Siren's song (ch and orch)
Starlight night and peace (S and cham orch) (1964)
Sonnet sequence (Kenneth Gee) (S and str orch) (1946)
Three settings of Gerald Manley Hopkins (S and orch)
Pied beauty and heaven haven (ch and brass)
The Armado (ch and pf) (1962)
Creatures (ch a-cap) (Chester, 1980)
Four miniatures (ch a-cap)
Heloise and Abelard (soli and ch) (1979)
I sing of a maiden this day (w-ch) (1966)
Nocturnal (William Barnes) (mix-ch)
Stalingrad (w-ch) (1946)
The voice of the city (Jacqueline Morris) (w-vces a-cap) (1943)
Witnesses (S, fl, ob, cl, hn, vlc, perc and ukulele or banjo) (1967)
Fly-by-night (w or chil-vces and hp or pf)
A winter's tale (K. Gee) (S and str qrt) (1949)
The garland, song cycle
Have you seen but a bright lily grow (OUP)
A meditation for his mistress (OUP)
Ophelia's song (Shakespeare) (1926) (OUP)
Propheta maidax (1965)
Samson at the gates of Gaza (Chappell)
Seo-heen sho, Irish lullaby (OUP)
Sun, moon and stars (S and pf)
Take, o take these lips away (Shakespeare) (S and pf) (1965)
Twelfth Night (Shakespeare) (OUP)
SACRED
Christmas morning, cantata (1963)
And death shall have no dominion (ch and brass)
Carol Nowell
Hymn to Christ, motet
A hymn to God the Father, motet
BALLET
Great Agrippa (1933)
The Little Red Shoes (1935)
Puck Fair (1940)
OPERA
The Birds, operatic extravaganza (after Aristophanes) (London: Boosey & Hawkes, 1974)
The Departure
The Sofa (Ursula Vaughn Williams)
The Three Strangers (after Thomas Hardy)
To Jesse Tree (Anne Ridler) (1970)
OPERETTA
The King and the Golden River, for children

Publications

A Composer Speaks. Composer 42, Winter 1971-1972: 25-29.

Bibliography

Howes, F. *Elizabeth Maconchy. Monthly Music Record*, July-August, 1939.
Macnaghten, A. *Elizabeth Maconchy*. MT. 1955.

Ref. 2, 8, 14, 15, 17, 22, 44, 68, 70, 75, 77, 80, 84, 86, 94, 96, 141, 150, 172, 177, 193, 226, 280, 347, 422, 563, 572, 622, 637, 646

MACRINA, Saint

Byzantine singer, teacher and composer. b. Caesarea, 327 A.D. She was the deaconess of the church of St. Sophia in Byzantium and the sister of Gregorius of Nyssa. As a child she learnt the art of psalm singing from her mother and after the death of her fiancé founded a convent on the river Iris, in Pontus, where according to her brother, the singing of psalms never ceased day or night. Macrina was singing mistress of the virgins and wrote both the text and music of her songs.
Ref. 476

MADDISON, Adele (Adda) (nee Tindal)

English composer. b. Ealing, December 15, 1866; d. Ealing, June 12, 1929. She studied under A. Debussy. She lived in Berlin before World War I.

Compositions

PIANO
Pieces incl.:
Quintet
VOCAL
Songs
OPERA
Der Talismann (1910)
Ref. 70, 105, 226, 431

MADISON, Carolyn

American composer. b. 1907. DISCOGRAPHY.

Compositions

VOCAL
Bitte (ch and pf) (1966) (ded Arnold Schoenberg)
Weltlauf (ch and pf) (1966)
Ref. 563

MADISON, Clara Duggan

American pianist, teacher and composer. b. Sequin, TX, July 31, 1879. She studied under Fannie Bloomfield-Zeisler (q.v.), Max Spicker and Rafael Joseffy. She composed piano pieces, anthems, sacred works and songs.
Ref. 226

MADLER, Ruth. See MAEDLER, Ruth

MADRIGUERA RODON, Paquita

Spanish concert pianist and composer. b. Igualada, Barcelona, September 15, 1900. She studied the piano under her mother and gave her first recital at the age of five, winning first prize. She later studied the piano under Marshal and theory and composition at the Ganados Music Academy under Mas and Serracant. She gave recitals in Barcelona and Madrid at the ages of 11 and 13 and later appeared in New York and California and toured Central and South America, 1919. Her second marriage was to Andres Segovia, the guitarist. DISCOGRAPHY.

Compositions

GUITAR
L'aplec del l'Ernita
La Boda India
Capuestre d'Istiu
Enyorant la meva terra
Humorada
Pastoral
Serenata aragonesa
VOCAL
El canto del grillo
Non-non
Ref. 100, 107, 563

MADSEN, Florence J.

20th-century American composer.

Compositions

CHAMBER
Chamber pieces
VOCAL
Spirit of spring (w-ch)
Songs
Ref. 40, 142, 347

MADURO, Sarah H.L.

Late 19th-20th-century composer. She was the mother of the violinist and composer Charles L. Maduro. She composed songs.

Bibliography

History of the Jews of the Netherlands Antilles - Cincinnati: American Jewish Archives 1970. 2 vols.

MAEDER, Emily Peace. See MEADER, Emily Peace

MAEDLER, Ruth

German composer. b. Berlin, July 1, 1908. She was blind and composed chamber works, piano sonatas, vocal and sacred works.
Ref. 70, 226

MAGDEBURG, Mechthild von. See MECHTHILD

MAGEAU, Mary Jane

American harpsichordist, lecturer and composer. b. Milwaukee, September 4, 1934. She studied under Leon Stein at DePaul University, where she obtained a B.Mus.; under Ross Lee Finey and Leslie Basset at the University of Michigan, where she obtained an M.Mus. (composition) and under George Crumb at Tanglewood, 1970. She received a Tanglewood Fellowship and won the second prix Gottschalk International Competition in 1970. She was music lecturer at Scholastica College, Duluth from 1969 to 1973, guest lecturer at the University of Wisconsin in 1973 and music lecturer at Brisbane College of Advanced Education, Australia from 1974 to 1978. She is a permanent resident of Australia and a freelance composer working on commissions and is the harpsichordist with the Brisbane Baroque Trio. She received several composition awards, including a Louis Moreau Gottschalk centenary competition silver medal, a commission grant from the Australian Council Music Board in 1980 and an annual ASCAP standard award since 1981. DISCOGRAPHY.

Compositions

ORCHESTRA
Montage (sym orch) (1970)
Variegations (sym orch) (1968) (Gottschalk award)
Concerto grosso (fl, vlc, hpcd, tim, perc and str orch) (1982)
Indian summer (youth orch) (1976)
Pacific portfolio (youth orch) (1983)
SYMPHONIC BAND
Celebration music (1971) (comm University of Minnesota)
CHAMBER
Forensis (fl, ob, cl, bsn and 2 perc) (1973)
Doubles (rec qrt and perc) (1977) (comm Brisbane Recorder Society)
Dialogues (rec qrt) (1977)
Landscape (perc ens)
Concert pieces (vln, vlc and pf) (1985)
Dialogues (cl, vlc and pf) (1979) (comm Aulos Trio, Australia)
Scarborough Fair variations (fl, vlc and hpcd) (comm Brisbane Baroque Trio)
Sonata concertante (fl, vlc and hpcd) (1980) (comm Brisbane Baroque Trio)
Cantilena (fl and perc) (1981)
Fantasy music (vln and pf) (1972) (comm Diane Spognardi Balko)
Winter's shadow (hpcd and chimes) (1983)
Contrasts (vlc) (1976)
Nach Bach (hpcd) (1983)
Statement and variations (vla) (1979) (comm John Curro)
Three movements for violoncello (1968)
Three pieces (org) (1969) (World Library of Sacred Music)
PIANO
March (4 hands) (1980) (Melbourne: Allans Music)
Pacific ports (4 hands) (1979)
Australia's animals, 6 solos (1976) (New York: G. Schirmer)
Cityscapes (1978)
Clouds
Cycles and series (1970) (comm Terence Rust)
Forecasts (1974)
Ragtime (1977)
Soliloquy (1984)
VOCAL
The line always there (w-ch, fl, perc and pf duet) (1981) (Brisbane: Asmuse)
SACRED
A chime of windbells (mix-ch, fl and perc) (1971)
A community mass (mix-ch, cong and org) (1978) (comm Dr. F. Holford)
Lacrimae (mix-ch and perc) (1972)
Mass for our Lady of Victory (unison ch and org) (1967)
A new Lacrimae (ch)
ELECTRONIC
Arches (vln, cl, pf and tape)
I never saw another butterfly, 5 songs (S, cl, vla, pf and 2 channel tape) (1972)
Interaction (cl and magnetic tape)
INCIDENTAL MUSIC
Sound and space adventures
Ref. composer, AMC 1985, 94, 137, 142, 280, 440, 474, 477, 494, 622, 625

MAGENTA, Maria

20th-century South African composer.

Compositions

VOCAL
Annelien gaan trou (vce, vln and pf)
Hul seil na Tafelbaai (vce, vln and pf)
In my drome (vce, vln and pf)
Manuella (vce, vln and pf)
Rosanna, die bruin mot: Rosanna (vce, vln and pf)
Skereraand (vce, vln and pf)
Ref. 295

MAGNEY, Ruth Taylor

20th-century American composer.

Compositions

CHAMBER
Pieces
Piano works
VOCAL
Works
SACRED
Ring, bells of Christmas (w-ch, pf and org)
OPERA
The Gift of the Magi
Ref. 40, 141, 190, 295, 347

MAGOGO KA DINIZULU, Constance, Princess

South African ugubhu player, singer and composer. b. Nongoma, 1900; d. Durban, November 21, 1984. Her father was the Zulu chief Dinuzulu Ka Cetshwayo and her brother King Solomon Ka Dinuzulu. She married Chief Mathole Shenge Buthelezi and their son Chief Mangosutho Buthelezi is the chief minister of KwaZulu. Constance was a great authority on Zulu music; in her youth she had learnt by heart, from her grandmothers, the Zulu musical repertoire that dates back to the 18th-century. She played the ugubhu (musical bow for song accompaniment) and the umakhweyana bow and the European autoharp. She received her early musical training from her mother and grandmother. At her marriage she became the tenth but principal wife of Chief Mathole and moved to Kwa Phindagene on the hills above Mahlabathini. Her songs were intimately connected with the cultural, social and historic life of the Zulus. In addition to songs of a court and ceremonial nature, she sang the more traditional songs of praise and admiration and laments. Her singing was first recorded by Dr. Hugh Tracey in 1939 and in the 1950s other songs were recorded by the SABC. She was consulted by researchers on the subject of Zulu music. She was musical consultant for the film *Zulu*. DISCOGRAPHY. PHOTOGRAPH.

Compositions

VOCAL
Over 100 songs incl.:
Helelel yipiphi leliyana
Laduma ekuseni (1923)
Umuntu ehlobile singemjabise uini tina?
Uyephi na? lullaby
Zulu love song
SACRED
Bambulal' uJesu yama Juda, hymn for Good Friday (1963)

Bibliography

Rycroft, Dave. *The Zulu Bow Songs of Princess Magogo. African Music Society Journal.*
Weman, Dr. Henry. *African Music and the Church in Africa.* Uppsala.
Obituary. *The Times*, London, December 4, 1984.
Ref. 37, 563

MAGUY LOVANO, Marguerite Schlegel

French artist and composer. b. Paris, February 27, 1934. At the Paris Conservatoire she studied music, aesthetics and analysis under Olivier Messaien, composition under Marius Milhaud and Jean Rivier and privately under Max Deutsch. In 1968 she and her husband founded a musical theatre company, 'La Petite Compagnie', which presents mainly avant-garde compositions from around the world. Her paintings have been exhibited in France and Canada.

Compositions

ORCHESTRA
Diamorphose I (cham och) (1973) (Technisonore)
VOCAL
Spirale (6 vces and orch) (1974)
Cinq cris-gestes (vce; also vce and mime) (1964, 1974)
THEATRE
Le chantier (1973)
A corps de mots (1974)
De l'alpha à l'alpha (1966)

Diamorphose II (1973)
Grandes demences en contre-haut (1974)
Quipo (1971)
Resurgence (1968)
Seuphonigraphie for crystal organs (1974)
Solipsismes .... et les emeures incertaines (1970)
Sourdre (1968) (Technisonore)
Ref. composer

MAHARASTHRA. See JANABAI

MAHBUBA (Beloved)
9th-century Arabian lutenist, poetess and songstress. She was born in al-Basra and became the property of a man of al-Taif. She was well educated and became an accomplished lutanist and songstress but achieved fame mainly for her poetry. With many other slaves she was given to al-Mutawakkil (847 to 861) as a gift on his accession to the throne. He became so infatuated with her beauty and talents that he kept her at his side at all times, hidden from view of his visitors behind a curtain. When he was murdered, Mahbuba, along with other court songstresses, passed into the hands of the wazir Wasif al-Turki, chief of the conspirators. He was furious when she continued to mourn for al-Mutawakkil and had her thrown into prison; only the interception of a Turkish captain prevented her from being killed. She was freed on condition that she leave Samarra. She went to Baghdad and nothing more is known of her. Her fidelity to her late master was so exceptional that it became legendary, referred to in serious Arabic references as well as in folklore. She is the only historical songstress mentioned in the most famous of all collections of tales in Arabian literature *The Thousand and One Nights*.
Ref. 171, 224

MAHLER, Alma Maria (nee Schindler)
Austrian pianist, writer and composer. b. Vienna, August 31, 1879; d. New York, December 13, 1964. She was the daughter of the painter Emil Jakob Schindler and studied the piano under Josef and composition under Alexander von Zemlinski. In 1902 when she married Gustav Mahler, who was opposed to her composing, she had written about a hundred songs, but only near the end of his life did he hear them and realise the error of his opposition. He was sufficiently penitent to help her edit and publish many of them before his death. A total of fourteen songs were published but most of the others were lost in the bombing of Vienna during World War II. After Gustav' death Alma married the architect Walter Gropius and later Franz Werfel. DISCOGRAPHY.
Compositions
VOCAL
Fuenf Gesaenge (Weinberger, 1924)
Muetterlieder (vce and pf)
Three volumes of songs (vce and pf) (1910, 1915, 1924)
Vier Lieder (1915)
Publications
And the Bridge is Love. Autobiography. Harcourt Brace & Co. New York, 1958.
Erinnerungen und Briefe. Amsterdam: De Lange, 1940.
Mein Leben. Frankfurt am Main: S. Fischer, 1960. Autobiography.
Gustav Mahler. *Memories and Letters* ed. Donald Mitchell, trans. Basil Creighton. Viking Press, New York, 1969.
Bibliography
Diether, Kack. *The Murderous Marriage of Alma and Gustav Mahler*. *Helicon Nine*, No. 10, 1984.
Mahony, Patrick. *Alma Mahler-Werfel*. *Composer* 45, Autumn 1972. 13-17.
Monson, Karen. *Alma Mahler, A Life*. Collins, 1983.
Monson, Karen. *Alma Mahler, Muse to Genius*. Collins, 1984.
Smith, Warren Storey. *The Songs of Alma Mahler*. Chord and Discord 2, 1930: 74-78.
An extensive collection of material is contained in the Mahler-Werfel Collection in the Charles Pattison Van Pelt Library of the University of Pennsylvania, PA.
Ref. 23, 94, 105, 189, 200, 297, 347, 563, 637

MAHLER, Hellgart. See ADDENDUM

MAIER, Amande. See RONTGEN, Amande

MAIER, Catherine (nee Schiatti)
Late 18th-century Russian composer. She lived in St. Petersburg, Russia.
Compositions
PIANO
Eleven fantasies, trios and variations (1795-1798)
Ref. 26

MAILA. See AZZA AL-MAILA

MAILIAN, Elza Antonovna
Soviet pianist, conductor, lecturer, teacher and composer. b. Tbilisi, October 21, 1926. She studied the piano under G. Sharoyev and theoretical subjects under N. Chumakov at the Baku Music School. At the Tbilisi Conservatory she studied conducting under A. Gauk, composition under S. Barkhudarian and the piano under L. Ginsburg from 1941 to 1942. She also studied conducting at Kiev Conservatory under A.I. Klimov. From 1950 to 1954 she taught theoretical subjects at the Tbilisi Music School. After 1954 she continued studying conducting at the Kiev Conservatory and conducted symphony orchestras in Tbilisi, Borzhomi and Baku and from 1958 to 1960 conducted the Philharmonic orchestra of Altai and for the following five years conducted the orchestra and iectured at the Alma-Ata Conservatory, returning to Baku in 1965 to teach at a music school.
Compositions
ORCHESTRA
Piano concerto (1949)
Violin concerto (1952)
Concertino (cobza and orch of folk insts) (1969)
Heroic overture (1946)
Partisan suite (1945)
CHAMBER
Quartettino (str qrt) (1946)
Piano trio (1951)
Melody (vln and pf) (1950)
Romance (vln and pf) (1950)
PIANO
Fantasia (2 pf) (1970)
Altai suite, 7 pieces (1959)
Five preludes (1948)
Four preludes and fugues (1969)
Theme and variations (1948)
VOCAL
Babochka (A. Feta) (vce and orch) (1945)
Before battle (A. Surkov) (vce and orch) (1948)
Noch (A. Feta) (vce and orch) (1945)
Posmo (A. Surkov) (vce and orch) (1944)
Ptichka (A. Pushkin) (vce and orch) (1937)
Ekh, yan (Nizami) (1945)
Korablik (A. Pushkin) (1937)
Smyelost (S. Spassky) (1946)
THEATRE
Nobii sad (G. Mdivayan) (1947)
Molodaya gvardiya (A. Fadeyev) (1947)
Ref. 21, 87

MAILLART, Aimee
German composer. b. 1817; d. 1871.
Compositions
VOCAL
Songs
OPERA
Das Gloeckchen des Eremiten der liebt mich, comic opera
Ref. 465

MAINVILLE, Denise
20th-century American composer.
Composition
OPERA
The Jig is Up
Ref. 141

MAIRE, Jacqueline
British composer. b. 1912.
Compositions
ORCHESTRA
Algeriana
Concorde
Fugue algerienne
La gavotte des poupées (light orch)
L'homme auz yeux clairs
CHAMBER
Pastorale (2 pf, d-b and perc)
BALLET
I kachle magnifique

INCIDENTAL MUSIC
Pelerinage au lieux saints, film
The Same Door, film (Jospeh)
Sundown in Rabat, film (Francis, Day & Hunter)
Twelve and a Half Percent, film
Baion, jazz band
Bayadepe, jazz band
To-Tem, jazz band
Ref. 280

MAISTRE, Baroness of

French composer. b. Brussels, 1840; d. Cannes, June, 1875. She never recovered from the death of one of her children and thereafter lived in seclusion.

Compositions
SACRED
Stabat Mater
OPERA
Cleopatre, Reine d'Egypte (M. Bogros)
Ninive
Les roussalkas (M. Bogros)
Ref. 108, 150, 225, 226, 276, 307

MAITLAND, Anna Harriet

American concert pianist, choir director, professor and composer. b. Fitchburg, MA, September 8, 1911. She studied privately under Katherine Gibbs in 1931 and gained her B.Mus. magna cum laude from the Olivet Nazarene College in 1943 and M.Mus. from the Texas Technical University. She also studied at the American Conservatory of Music and was a Ph.D. candidate at Northwestern University. She worked as a concert pianist and accompanist from 1929 to 1936 and was professor of the piano and music theory at Chicago Conservatory from 1942 to 1952. She directed several choirs and taught voice and the piano privately.

Composition
VOCAL
Cycle of 17 sonnets (1976)
OPERA
To each his own (1964)
Ref. 475

MAITLAND, S. Marguerite

American composer. b. Philadelphia, 1909.

Composition
OPERA
The Snow Queen, 7 scenes from the fairy tale (H.C. Anderson) (1933) (hon mention, Carl F. Lauber music award, 1933)
Ref. 322

MAIXANDEAU, Marie-Vera

French composer. b. 1929.

Compositions
CHAMBER
Sonata No. 2 (pf) (1965)
SACRED
Cantatas incl.:
Stabat Mater
Ref. 52, 465

MAJLATH, Julia

Hungarian composer. b. 1921. She composed songs and an opera (ca. 1935.)
Ref. 465

MAKAROVA, Nina Vladimirovna

Soviet composer. b. Yurino, Nizhni-Novgorod, July 30, 1908; d. Moscow, January 15, 1976. The daughter of the village schoolmaster, she showed an early interest in Russian and Mari folk song. When she was 15, she began her studies at the Music School in Gorki and proceeded to the Moscow Conservatory in 1925 where she studied under N. Myaskovsky, graduating in 1927. She completed postgraduate studies in 1938. She traveled widely outside Russia and married the composer Aram Khachaturian. DISCOGRAPHY.

Compositions
ORCHESTRA
Symphony in D-Minor, in 3 mvts (1938)
Symphony, in 3 mvts (1958)
Kak sakalyalas stal, suite (1955)
CHAMBER
Melody and scherzo, op. 18 (vln and pf) (1938)
Pieces (ob and pf) (Soviet Kompozitor, 1983)
Sonata (vln and pf) (1934)
Two melodies (ob and pf) (1934)
Two pieces for cello and piano
Two pieces for violin and piano
Two compositions for harp (1964)
Vocalise and a memory (vlc and pf)
PIANO
Pastorale, chorale and prelude (1928)
Six etudes (1938)
Six preludes
Sonatina (1933)
Two children's suites (1955)
VOCAL
Skas o Lenine, cantata (S, ch and orch) (1970)
To Molotov, cantata (Panov) (soloists, ch and orch) (1940)
Children's songs to Stalin
Dreams (m-S)
Drugo (Ketlinskaya) (1945)
Lastochki (Algier) (1948)
Leningradskaya kolubelnaya (Berggoltz) (1945)
Marianna Pineda, fragments (m-S)
My nightingale (S, T and B)
Ogonek (Izakovsky) (1943)
The path (S, T and B)
Pesn o rodine (Berggoltz) (1943)
Polyarnaya (Altauzen) (vce and pf) (1942)
Song cycle (Pushkin)
Song cycle (S. Rustaveli) (1938)
Song of the poplar (S, T and Bar)
To a friend (S, T and B)
Tsveti, tsveti, rodimaya zemlya (Oshanin) (1945)
Two romances (S, T and Bar)
Ty lo mne s pobedoyu pridesh (Lebedev-Kumach) (1942)
Uralskaya (Barto) (vce and pf) (1942)
V dni voyni, song cycle (Kovalkov) (1945)
Vasilki (Firsov) (1955)
Voyevaya podruga (Veselchakov and Flerov) (1942)
OPERA
Muzhestvo (ded builders of Komsomolsk, 1947)
Zoya (1955)
INCIDENTAL MUSIC
Dva kapitana (Kaverin) (1948)
Madlena Godar (A. Speshnev) (1949)
Mariana Pineda (1957)
Pervyi grom (Algier) (1947)
Schastlivaya smena (1936)
Skazka o pravde (Algier) (1946)
Vesennii potok (Chepurin) (1953)
Volodya Dubinin (L. Kassilya) (1951)
Ref. 2, 8, 17, 22, 44, 63, 70, 74, 81, 86, 87, 94, 96, 135, 172, 193, 223, 226, 277, 330, 361, 563, 580, 622

MAKNUNA

8th-century Arabian songstress. She was a slave bought by Caliph al-Mahdi (775 to 785) for 100000 dirhem and renowned for her talent and beauty. With al-Mahdi, Maknuna had a daughter Ulayya (q.v.).
Ref. 171, 234

MALDYBAYEVA, Zhyldyz Abdylasovna

Soviet lecturer and composer. b. Frunze, July 6, 1946. In 1972 she graduated from the Kirgiz Institute of Arts where she studied composition under B.G. Glukhov. She also studied under Karaev at the Azerbaijanian Conservatory. After 1969 she lectured at the Teachers' Training College in Frunze. In 1975 she won the Lenin prize of the Kirgiz SSR.

Compositions
ORCHESTRA
Simfonietta I (1970)
Simfonietta II (1971)
Suite for chamber orchestra (1973)
Suite for string orchestra (1968)
CHAMBER
String quartet (1966)
Piece (ob and pf) (1972)
Piece (vlc and pf) (1967)
Sonatina (vln and pf) (1969)
PIANO
Scherzo (1967)
Sonata (1969)
Sonatina (1973)

Suite (1967)
Ten children's miniatures (1970)
Toccata (1971)
Twenty-four preludes (1966)
Variations (1968)
VOCAL
Cycle (Tokombayev) (ch) (1969)
Songs (vce and pf) (1971)
Arrangements of folk songs
Ref. 21

MALHE, Maria Aparecida
20th-century Brazilian composer.
Compositions
BAND
Folk melodies, 16 pieces (rhythmic band) (San Paola: Irmaos Vitale, 1969)
VOCAL
Folk melodies, 18 songs (chil-ch) (Irmaos Vitale, 1969)
Ref. Ricordi Americana

MALIBRAN, Maria Felicitas (nee Garcia) (Maria Felicia Malibran, Maria Garcia Malibran, Maria Felicite Garcia de Beriot, Maria Felicita Garcia Malibran, Maria Malibran)
Franco-Spanish pianist, mezzo-soprano opera singer and composer. b. Paris, March 24, 1808; d. Manchester, England, September 23, 1836. She was the daughter of the tenor and composer Manuel Garcia, and sister of Pauline Michelle Ferdinande Viardot-Garcia (q.v.). Maria spent her early years in Italy and France and sung an arietta from an opera by Paer at the age of four in a theatre in Naples. She studied the piano under Herold, solfege under Penseron in Naples and later voice with her father. She made her Paris debut in a concert recital in 1924 and her London debut at the age of 12 in the part of Rosina in the opera *Il Barbiere di Siviglia*. At the end of the season the Garcia troupe went to New York, where Maria, as the leading prima donna, became the popular favorite. After an unsuccessful marriage to Malibran she left New York in 1829 and returned to Europe. Her performances were received with enthusiasm both in London and Paris, surpassed only by the reception she received in Italy, where in Venice in 1934 her arrival was announced with a fanfare of trumpets. Her repertoire consisted of 35 operas. She had a voice of unusual beauty and enormous compass and was gifted as an actress. Her gaiety made her irresistible in light opera, although her greatest triumphs were obtained in tragic parts. Rossini was known to have said: 'I have met in my life only three singers of great genius: La Blache, Rubini and that spoiled child of nature, Malibran'. A month after her marriage to the Belgian violinist Charles de Beriot in 1836, she fell from her horse and sustained severe injuries, from which she never recovered. She died later that year while in Manchester for a charity festival. DISCOGRAPHY.
Compositions
VOCAL
Dernières Pensées musicales (vce and pf) (Troupenas; Schott):
La fiancée du brigand, ballad
Le message, romance
Prière à la madone
Hymne des matelots
Les noces d'un marin, chanson
Au bord de la mer
Adieu à Laure
Le montagnard
Les brigants, ballad
Le moribaud
Collection of twelve airs (Schlesinger):
Lève toi
La voix qui, petits rossignols
Le village, l'aube matinal
La tarantelle, le plaisir nos appelle
Les refrains, sur ce rivage
Rataplan
La bayadère
La résignation, sous ce rameaux
Le ménestrel, avec moi j'ai
Enfant, ramez! Les temps est lourd
Le retour de la tyrolienne
L'ecossais
Pensées de Malibran, collection d'airs et de duos, nos. 1-14 (Simrock)
Numerous songs incl.:
Barcarolo (Cottrau)
Belle, viens à moi, duo (Joubert)
Eight romances
Follettino (Cottrau)
Gondoliere (Cottrau)
Indifférence (2 vces) (Costallat)
J'etais sur la rive fleurie (2 vces) (Costallat)
Je fus heureux (Costallat)
Le Beau Page (Cottrau)
Ma mère est morte (Sulzbach)
Deja la nuit sombre, nocturne (Augener)
Molinara, air varié intercale dans Il Barbiere di Siviglia (Costallat)
Pensée (Costallat)
Prendi per me sei libero, da lei introdotta nell' Elisir d'amore d'Donizetti (Cottrau; Ricordi)
Prisonnier (2 vces) (Costallat)
Le ranz des vachers, duet (Schirmer)
Refrains (Cottrau)
Réveil d'un beau jour (Ashdown; Joubert)
Tyrolienne, en soupirant (Cottrau)
Voix qui dit je t'aime (Cottrau)
Bibliography
Barbieri, G. *Notizie biografiche di Maria Malibran*. Milan, 1836.
Bardi, De Lorenzi. *La breve et merveilleuse vie de La Malibran*. Paris. Ed. Tallandier, 1936.
Bielli, D. *Maria Malibran*. Casalbordino.
Bushnellm H. *Maria Malibran*. PA, State University Press, 1982.
Heron-Allen, E. *A Contribution towards an Accurate Biography of C. de Beriot and M. Malibran. De Fidiculis opuscula*, no. 6, 1894.
Lanquine, C. *La Malibran*. Paris, 1911.
Merlin, Comtesse. *Les Loisirs d'une femme du monde*. Paris, 1838. Biography. German translation by G. Lotz, M.M. also Weib und Kuenstlerin. Leipzig, 1839. English translation, London, 1836.
Nathan, J. *The Life of Mme. Maria Malibran de Beriot*. London, 1836. German translation by A. de Treskow, Quedlinburg, 1837.
Pougin, A. *M. Malibran: Histoire d'une cantatrice*. Paris, 1911. English trans., London, 1911.
Viardot, Louise H. *Une famille de grands musiciens*. Paris, 1923.
Ref. 8, 9, 22, 26, 85, 105, 109, 113, 129, 132, 135, 204, 207, 216, 231, 276, 282, 297, 347, 400, 413, 563, 572, 622, 637, 639

MALIUKOVA, Tamara Stepanovna. See SIDORENKO, Tamara Stepanovna

MALLARD, Clarisse
19th-century English composer.
Compositions
CHAMBER
Two pieces (vln and pf)
Two sketches (vln and pf) (Ashdown)
VOCAL
Harvest home (S and 2-part ch) (Schirmer)
Hymn to Diana (2-part ch) (Woolhouse: Schirmer)
In the merry merry May (2-part ch) (Schirmer)
Could I forget (vce and pf) (Woolhouse)
Keramos: The potter's song
Song of love
Violet
Where Claribel low lieth
Ref. 297

MALLEVILLE, Charlotte Tardieu de
19th-century French pianist and composer. She composed piano pieces.
Ref. 276

MALLIA-PULVIRENTI, Josie
20th-century Maltese composer.
Composition
ORCHESTRA
Espressionismo, symphonic poem (1925) (London: Chester)
Ref. 322

MALMLOEF-FORSSLING, Carin
Swedish pianist, teacher and composer. b. Gaevle, March 6, 1916. She studied counterpoint at the Stockholm Conservatory from 1938 to 1940, composition under H.M. Melchers from 1941 to 1943 and the piano under G. Boon. In 1957 she studied under Nadia Boulanger (q.v.) in Paris. She taught the piano in Falun from 1943. Her works were performed in Scandinavia, Iceland, East and West Germany, France, Austria, Rumania, Israel and the United States. DISCOGRAPHY. PHOTOGRAPH.

Compositions
ORCHESTRA
Release (str orch) (1973)
Revival (1976)
CHAMBER
Triptyk (bongos and prep pf) (1965)
Ceremonial prelude (org) (Boston: Arthur P. Schmidt, 1938)
Lalendo (vlc) (1970)
Love-dawn (vlc) (1972)
Sonata svickel (fl) (1963)
Tupp-preludium (ob) (1968)
PIANO
Five small pieces (1947)
Humoristisk miniatyr (Nordiska Musikforlaget, 1948)
Sonata in D-Minor (1944)
Suite (1935)
Viewpoints (1980)
VOCAL
Ecce jubile (m-ch) (1975)
Fruktplockning XXIV (R. Tagore) (mix-ch) (1964)
Inget var som somer 72 (S, mix-ch and pf) (1972)
Liten svit (w-ch a-cap) (1954)
Paus (E. Lindegren) (m-ch a-cap) (1964)
Saengen brinner (mix-ch a-cap) (1953)
Skytisk vaer (E. Lindegren) (m-ch a-cap) (1964)
Tupp som vaerper karamell (C. Larsson) (solo, chil-ch and ob) (1968)
Saeng i regnet (B. Magneli) (3 vces and strs) (1944)
ABC (C. Larsson) (vce and ob) (1968)
Blue (Birgen Norman) (S and fl) (1976)
Bondsyrener (Forsta sommardagen) (vce and pf) (1966)
Daffkaepebyn (B. Bjoers) (S) (1973)
De nakna traedens saenger, song cycle (S. Siwertz) (vce and pf) (1962)
En liten vattenfaegel (R. Lindstroem) (vce and pf) (1966)
Faeglar (B. Anderberg) (vce and pf) (1962)
Flickan och hinden (B. Setterlind) (vce and pf) (1966)
Holmen (1968)
Hui husche, children's song (E. Aehlman) (1963)
Humlan bumle, children's song (1963)
Jag kysser din osynliga vos (Goran Sonneri) (S and fl) (1976)
Lisbeth om du vaeger (C. Larsson) (vce and ob) (1968)
Litania (W. Aspenstroem) (vce and pf) (1967)
Orizzonte (S) (1981)
Pae moerka vinterhimlen
Rymfarden, children's song (1963)
Sex saenger im ljus och moerker till dikter (H. Martinsson) (1975)
Silvermanen, children's song (E. Ahlman) (1963)
Sjung mig saenger (S. Siwertz) (3 vces) (1944)
Sorg (Rune Lindstrom) (S and fl) (1976)
Three experiences (S) (1976)
Tigge tagge, children's song (A. Aehlman) (1963)
Tror du, 5 small pieces (B. Bjoers) (S) (1973)
Vollmond, haiku (vce and pf) (1967)
SACRED
Maria och barnet, cantata (B. Setterlind) (recitation, S and mix-ch) (1971)
Biblia Delcarlica, biblical texts (recitation, S, T, B, mix-ch amd cl) (1971)
THEATRE
Maenvaka, melodrama (E. Lindorm) (declaration and pf) (1963)
Raettan Rikus, children's musical (G. Lejkner) (vce, pf, rec and perc) (1967)
Vaerteeken, melodrama (G. Nasenius) (declamation and pf) (1963)
ELECTRONIC
Nattliga ackord (1978)
Ref. STIM, 20, 563, 642

MALMLOF-FORSSLING, Carin. See MALMLOEF-FORSSLING, Carin

MAMLOK, Ursula

American pianist, assistant professor and composer. b. Berlin, February 1, 1928. She studied the piano and theory in Germany under Gustav Ernest and composition privately under George Szell, Roger Sessions, Stefan Wolpe and Ralph Shapey in New York. She received her B.M. and M.M. from the Manhattan School of Music where she studied from 1955 to 1958. She received awards from the National Federation of Music Clubs and the National School Orchestra Assocation and a grant from the City University of New York Foundation in 1972 and 1973. She was the winner of the ASCAP award to Women Composers for Symphonic and Concert Music in 1969. She lectured at New York University and the Manhattan School of Music from 1968 and became assistant professor of theory and composition at Kingsborough College in 1971. She won the award of the American Academy and Institute of Arts and Letters in 1981 and an award from the National Endowment for the Arts. DISCOGRAPHY. PHOTOGRAPH.

Compositions
ORCHESTRA
Concerto for oboe and orchestra (1976) (ACA)
Concerto for string orchestra (1950) (ACA)
Andante (str orch) (ACA)
Divertimento for young players (ACA)
Festival suite
Grasshoppers, 6 humoresques (1956) (ACA)
CHAMBER
Work for woodwind quintet, strings and percussion (1984)
For seven (trp, cl, b-cl, vln, vlc, d-b and perc) (1963) (ACA)
Sextet (fl, cl, b-cl, vln, d-b and perc) (1977) (ACA)
Festive sounds (ww qnt) (1978) (ACA)
When summer sang (fl, cl, vln, vlc and pf) (1980)
Woodwind quintet No. 1 (1955)
Concert piece for four (fl, ob, vla and perc) (1964) (ACA)
Divertimento (fl, vlc and 2 perc) (1975) (ACA)
From my garden II (ob, hn, pf and crotals) (1983)
String quartet (1962) (ACA)
Temporal interrelations (fl, ob, vln and vlc) (1977)
Variations and interludes (4 perc) (1971) (ACA)
Movements (fl, d-b and perc) (1966)
Music for clarinet, cello and percussion
Panta Rhei (vln, vlc and pf) (New York: Peters, 1982)
Capriccios (ob and pf) (1967)
Designs 1962 (vln and pf)
Eight easy duets (2 cl) (ACA)
Five capriccios for oboe and piano (1967-1968) (ACA)
Music for viola and harp (1965) (ACA)
Sintra (a-cl and vlc) (1969) (ACA)
Sonatina (2 cl) (1957) (ACA)
Composition, in 4 mvts (vlc; also vla) (1962, 1982)
From my garden I (vln)
From my garden III (vla) (1984)
Polyphony (B-flat cl) (1968) (ACA)
Polyphony II (cor anglais) (ACA)
Variations (fl) (1961) (ACA)
PIANO
Children's suite No. 2 (2 pf) (ACA)
Bells (4 hands)
Piano piece (1952) (ACA)
Scherzo (1947)
Sculpture I (1964) (ACA)
Two sets of recital pieces for children (1982)
VOCAL
Mosaics (mix-ch a-cap) (1968) (ACA)
Daybreak (Longfellow) (S or m-S and pf) (1948) (ACA)
German songs (S and pf) (1957)
Haiku settings (S and fl) (1967) (ACA)
Stray birds (S, fl and vlc) (1963) (ded J.F. Kennedy) (ACA)
SACRED
The first Psalm (soli, mix-ch and pf) (1958) (ACA)
ELECTRONIC
Sonar trajectory (tape) (1966)
Bibliography
New Members: *Ursula Mamlock. ACA*, bulletin 12. Spring 1964: 14. Biographical sketch.
Ref. composer, 4, 77, 80, 94, 137, 142, 185, 201, 347, 397, 415, 468, 563, 622, 624, 625

MAMPE-BABNIGG, Emma. See BABNIGG, Emma

MANA-ZUCCA (pseud. of Augusta Zuckermann)

American pianist, operatic singer and composer. b. New York, December 25, 1894; d. March 8, 1981. She was a child prodigy who made her debut with the New York Philharmonic Orchestra in Carnegie Hall when she was seven. She embarked on a continental tour at the age of 13, which lasted for four years. She studied the piano under Alexander Lambert in New York and Leopold Godowsky and Busoni in Berlin. She studied composition in London under Hermann Spielter and singing in London and Paris under Von Zur Muehlen. She was also a singer of light opera and first appeared as lead soprano in Lehar's *Count of Luxembourg* in 1914. She started composing seriously in 1916 and wrote over 1100 published items. She was awarded an honorary D.Mus. from the University of Miami. DISCOGRAPHY.

Compositions
ORCHESTRA
Piano concerto No. 1, op. 49 (Miami: Congress Music)
Piano concerto No. 2 (Congress)
Violin concerto, op. 224 (Congress)
Bickerings (Congress)
Coolie dance (Congress)

Cuban dance (Congress)
Frolic for strings (Congress)
Fugato humoresque (Congress)
Havana nights (Congress)
Novelette (Congress)
Tone poem (Congress)
Zouaves' drill (Congress)
BAND
Brother love (Congress)
CHAMBER
Trio, op. 40 (vln, vlc and pf) (Congress)
Ballade and caprice, op. 28 (vln and pf) (Congress)
Hakinoh (vla and pf) (Congress)
Paraphrase on a Chopin etude (vln and pf) (Congress)
Moment pensif (vla and pf) (Congress)
Novelette (vlc and pf) (Congress)
Serenade (vlc and pf) (Congress)
Serenade (vln and pf) (Congress)
Sonata, op. 132 (vln and pf) (Congress)
Sonatina (vln and pf) (Congress)
Toccata (vln and pf) (Congress)
My musical calendar, 20 pieces (org) (Congress, 1940)
PIANO
Pieces incl.:
The gazelle (2 pf) (Congress)
La poverina (2 pf) (Congress)
Arcadian waltz (Congress)
Bradley waltz (Congress)
Capricietto (Congress)
Day dreaming waltz (Congress)
Etude en hommage (Congress)
Five biblical impressions (Congress)
Hazy moon (Congress)
Interlude (Congress)
Joy waltz (Congress)
Memories (Congress)
Polka comique (Congress)
Prelude (Congress)
Scherzando (Congress)
Sonata No. 1, op. 217 (Congress)
Sonata No. 2, op. 280 (Congress)
Sonata No. 3, op. 281 (Congress)
Valse brillante (Congress)
Valse pastorale (Congress)
VOCAL
Be not afraid (w-ch) (Congress)
The golden rule (mix-ch) (Congress)
I love you so (w-ch) (Congress)
O how amiable (mix-ch) (Congress)
Ode to music (mix-ch) (Congress)
Top of the morning (m-ch) (Congress)
Those days gone by (w-ch) (Congress)
Two little shoes (mix-ch) (Congress)
Unless (w-ch) (Congress)
Songs incl.:
Across the way (Congress)
Because of you (Congress)
Call of love (S) (Congress)
Children's songs (Congress)
Doux plaisirs (Congress)
Eve (Georgeanne Newcombe) (Congress)
Evening (Congress)
First love (Congress)
Glow worm (Congress)
A glowing west, op. 33 (G. Newcombe) (Congress)
Happy times (Congress)
I must away (T) (Congress)
Israel lives (Congress)
It matters not (S and A or T and B) (Congress)
Just you (Congress)
Leaves (Congress)
Madrigal (Congress)
The ocean (Congress)
Piu belo del sole (Congress)
Rachem (Congress)
Shalom alachem (Congress)
Tear drops (Congress)
Unless (Congress)
Whispered vows (high and low vces) (Congress)
White birds (Congress)
Your quest (Congress)
Xmas bells (Congress)
Seventeen songs (Bar and pf)
SACRED
Thy will be done (mix-ch) (Congress)
Duc alma dux (Congress)
God bless you dear (Congress)
God's minute (Congress)
In God we trust (Congress)
Just married, wedding song (Congress)
BALLET
The wedding of the butterlies (Congress)
OPERA
Hypatia (Congress)
The Queen of Ki-lu (Congress)
MISCELLANEOUS
I love life, op. 83

Bibliography

A Great American Lady Honored. Washington, DC: US Govt. Printing Office, November 10, 1975.

Polansky, Hannah: *Manna Zucca. Grande Dame of Miami Music. The Miami Reporter*, April 11, 1971. p A-14.

Ref. composer, 22, 40, 70, 76, 77, 94, 105, 142, 226, 228, 280, 292, 347, 563, 611

MANACIO-GALDI, Elvira

Composition
PIANO
Souviens-toi (Ricordi)
Ref. Ricordi (Milan)

MANCINI, Eleonora

16th-century Italian composer of an opera.
Ref. 502

MANGGRUM, Loretta C. Cessor

American organist, pianist, teacher and composer. b. Gallipolis, OH, July 28, 1896. She started playing the organ at the age of eight and obtained her B.M. from Ohio State University in 1951 and her M.M. from Cincinnati Conservatory in 1953. She taught music in schools in Cincinnati for ten years.

Compositions
VOCAL
Innocent blood
Solos
Watch
SACRED
Five cantatas incl.:
Blessed is the man, psalm 1
Ref. 206

MANIR, Anna. See SICK, Anna

MANKIN, Linda

20th-century American pianist, lecturer and composer. She graduated cum laude from New York University with a B.Mus. (education) in 1949. At the Juilliard School of Music she studied composition under Henry Brant. At Stanford she was a pupil of Leonard Ratner, Harold Schmidt and Leland Smith and received a M.Mus. (composition) in 1964. She did postgraduate work at Berkeley, Indiana, San Jose, San Francisco and San Diego universities. She has lectured in music theory, appreciation, the piano and applied music at Foothill College since 1964.

Compositions
SACRED
Halleluyah, 4 part setting of psalm 50 (Hebrew and English) (ch and pf) (1979)
Other psalm settings

Publications

Prelude to Musicianship: Fundamental Concepts and Skills.

Ref. League of women composers

MANNING, Kathleen Lockhart

American pianist, singer and composer. b. Hollywood, CA, October 24, 1890; d. Los Angeles, CA, March 25, 1951. She studied the piano under Elizabeth Eichelberger in Los Angeles and gave recitals as a child. In 1908 she studied under M. Moszkowski in Paris and in 1911 appeared as a pianist and opera singer with the Hammerstein Opera Company in London. DISCOGRAPHY.

Compositions
ORCHESTRA
Piano concerto
Four symphonic poems
CHAMBER
String quartet
PIANO
In the summer
Three dance impressions
VOCAL
Chinese impressions (vce and pf) (New York: G. Schirmer, 1931)
Five fragments (vce and pf) (Schirmer, 1931)
Shoes (vce and pf)
Sketches of London (vce and pf) (New York: Fischer, 1929)
Sketches of New York (vce and pf) (Schirmer, 1936)
Sketches of Paris (vce and pf) (Schirmer, 1925)
The water lily (vce and pf) (London: Boosey, 1923)
Other songs, some with orchestra
OPERA
For the Soul of Rafael
Mr. Wu (L.J. Milu) (1926)
OPERETTA
Operetta in Mozartian style
Ref. 14, 22, 39, 40, 70, 74, 94, 141, 142, 229, 292, 304, 347, 563, 622

MANNKOPF, Adolphine (nee Polczinska)
19th-century German singer and composer.
Compositions
ORCHESTRA
Overture to the tragedy Corinna (1855)
VOCAL
Mutterliebe (H. Heine) (vce and pf) (Berlin: Bock)
Three songs
Two songs, op. 3 (vce and pf) (ded Johanna Wagner) (Berlin: Trautwein)
SACRED
Three spiritual songs, op. 4 (Louise Hensel, Geibel and Kurmmacher) (mix-ch) (ded Queen Elizabeth of Prussia) (Berlin: Schlesinger)
Sacred quartets (mix-vces)
Ave Maria (vce and pf) (Hamburg: Jowien, 1854)
Ref. 121, 226, 276, 297

MANSFIELD, Hermine. See RUDERSDORF, Erminie

MANTECA GIOCONDA, Carmen. See CARMEN MARINA

MANUKIAN, Irina Eduardovna
Soviet music editor and composer. b. Moscow, August 22, 1948. In 1973 she graduated from the Moscow Conservatory, where she studied composition under S.A. Balasanian. After 1974 she worked as a music editor in Moscow.
Compositions
ORCHESTRA
Concerto for orchestra (1973)
Suite (small orch) (1971)
Simfonietta (str orch) (1970)
CHAMBER
Quintet (fl, ob, cl, hn and bsn) (1971)
String quartet I (1970)
String quartet II (1976)
PIANO
Bagatelle, suite (4 hands) (1974)
Sonata (1973)
Sonatina (1970)
VOCAL
Garcia Lorca, chamber cantata (soli, 2 pf and perc) (1976)
Utro nairi (ch and sym orch) (1972)
Choruses, incl. one in memory of Lenin (Charents) (1974)
Cycle of romances (Kuchak) (vce and pf) (1973)
Songs
Children's songs
INCIDENTAL MUSIC
Music for theatre
Ref. 21

MANZIARLY, Marcelle de
French pianist, conductor, lecturer and composer. b. Kharkov, Russia, October 13, 1899. Her father was French and her mother Russian. Marcelle grew up in Paris and became a pupil of Nadia Boulanger (q.v.) at the age of 12. She composed her *String quartet* when she was 15. She attended a course on conducting given by Felix Weingartner in Basle and later perfected her piano technique under Isabella Vengerova in New York, where she spent several years composing, performing in chamber concerts and lecturing at universities. She was awarded the prize of the Ligue des Femmes de Professions Liberales for her *Violin sonata*. In India she made the acquaintance of Rabindranath Tagore and of Indian scales and rhythms. DISCOGRAPHY. PHOTOGRAPH.
Compositions
ORCHESTRA
Concerto for piano and orchestra (1933)
Incidences for piano and orchestra (1966)
Musique pour orchestre (1950)
Sonate pour Notre Dame de Paris (1948)
Spheres (1974)
CHAMBER
Quintet (fl, hp, vln, vla and vlc) (1943)
String quartet (1943)
Trilogue for flute grave, viola da gamba and harpsichord (1957) (comm Radio Geneva)
Trilogue (vln, vlc and pf)
Trio (fl, vlc and pf) (1952)
Trio (vln, vlc and pf) (1922)
Dialogue (vlc and pf) (1970)
Periple (ob and pf) (1973)
Sonata (vln and pf) (prize, Ligue des Femmes de Professions Liberales) (1920)
Suite (fl and pf) (1937)
PIANO
Sonata (2 pf) (1946)
Impressions de mer (1922)
Six etudes (1951)
Stances (1969)
Trois atmospheres slaves (1922)
VOCAL
Poèmes en trio (Louise de Vilmorin) (A, S, m-S and ch a-cap) (1948)
L'oiseau blessé (vce and inst ens)
Triptique pour une madone de Lorenzo d'Alessandro (S and cham ens) (1934)
Le cygne et le cuisinier (vocal qrt and pf) (Fontaine, 1959)
Chansons pour enfants (2 or 3 vces) (Radio, 1937)
Deux odes de Gregoire de Narek (A and pf) (1955)
Six chants (A and pf) (1923)
Trois chants (S and pf) (1935)
Trois duos (2 S or T and cl) (1953)
Trois fables de la Fontaine (S and pf) (1935)
Trois sonnets de Petrarch (Bar and pf) (1961)
OPERA
La femme en fleche, chamber opera (1956) (comm Radio & Television Française)
Ref. composer, 8, 41, 44, 70, 74, 94, 96, 105, 154, 172, 347, 563, 622

MANZONI, Eugenia Tretti
20th-century Italian composer.
Composition
FILM MUSIC
Power (1971)
Ref. 326

MAQUISO, Elena G.
20th-century Philippine composer.
Compositions
SACRED
Three anthologies of Visayan hymns
Ref. 265

MARA, La (Elisabeth Gertrud) (nee Schmeling-Mara)
German singer and composer. b. February 23, 1749 (or December 11, 1750); d. Reval, Estonia, January 20, 1833. She studied under Paradisi and Hiller and possessed both sensitivity and power of voice and could be heard above choir and orchestra and became famous throughout Europe for her incredible vocal range. Great rivalry existed between her and Luiza Todi of Portugal, which led to brawls between the Maratists and the Todists. Her notorious private life led to her dying penniless in Estonia in the same year as her great rival.

Compositions
VOCAL
Songs incl.:
Ah che nel petto io sento (vce and hp) (1791)
Artaxerxes (P. Hoare) (1797)
High rolling seas that bear afar (Hoare) (1797)
Say you can deny me (Hoare) (1798)
Ref. 65, 128, 323, 622

MARAIS, Abelina Jacoba

South African pianist and composer. b. Potchefstroom, September 14, 1907. She studied the piano at the College of Music, Potchefstroom. PHOTOGRAPH.

Compositions
PIANO
The living fountain (rev for ch and org)
VOCAL
Walsie for Viegie (L. Leipoldt) (ch)
Die feetjielied (vce and pf)
Flieder fladder voeltjie, children's song
Hartenbosch lied Nos. 1 and 2
Klaas Vakie
My sielmaat
SACRED
The Creed, liturgy (ch)
Kers oggend vir Maria, Christmas song
Kers wiegelied
My Vader huis
Rabvoenie
Saggues
OPERA
The Bride of the Cango Caves (composer)
MISCELLANEOUS
Variations on Polly ons gaan Paarl toe
Ref. composer

MARBE, Myriam

Rumanian pianist, music editor, professor and composer. b. Bucharest April 9, 1931. She first studied the piano with her mother, Angela Marbe, a piano teacher. At the C. Porumbescu Conservatory, Bucharest she studied theory and solfege under Ioan D. Chirescu, harmony under Martian Negrea and Ion Dumitrescu, orchestration under Theodore Rogalski, music history under Zeno Vancea and Vasile Popovici, the piano under Silvia Capatina and Florica Musicescu, composition under Mihail Jora and Leon Klepper and folklore under Sabin Dragoi and Emilia Comisel from 1944 to 1954. She was music editor of the cinematographic studio in Bucharest from 1953 to 1954. In 1960 she became assistant professor and in 1972 professor of harmony and counterpoint at the Bucharest Conservatory. In 1961 she was mentioned and in 1966 won second prize at the International Composition Competition in Mannheim; in 1972 she won the prize of the Rumanian Composers' Union and of the Academie des Beaux-Arts de Paris and in 1975 shared the prize for choral music in the Gedok Competition, Mannheim, Germany with Kazuyo Nozawa (q.v.). DISCOGRAPHY. PHOTOGRAPH.

Compositions
ORCHESTRA
Concerto for viola and orchestra (1977)
Concerto for viola de gamba and orchestra (1982)
Les temps inevitable (pf and orch; also pf) (1971)
Divertismentul pentru coarde si suflatori de alama: Musica festiva (brass and str orch) (1961)
Evocara (perc and str orch) (1976)
Parable of the granary II (cham orch) (1977)
Piesa lirica, In memoriam (1959)
Serenada sun music (cham orch) (1974)
Time and space
Time found again (cham orch) (1982)
Trium (1978)
CHAMBER
Concerto for harpsichord and instruments (1978)
Les oiseaux artificiels (cl, vln, vla, vlc and hpcd) (1979)
String quartet No. 1 (1981)
Cyclus (fl, gtr and perc) (1974)
Vocabulaire II, rythme (perc ens) (1974)
Sonata (cl and pf) (1961)
Sonata (vla and pf) (1955)
Sonata (2 vla) (1965)
Piece (pf and hpcd)
Incantation sonata (cl) (1964)
Parable of the granary (cel and hpcd, 1 player) (1979) (Musicale, 1981)
Schaefers pavane mit Voegeln (hpcd) (1981)
Joc secund
Serenata
PIANO
Accents (1971)
Allegro
Cluster studies I and II (1970)
Din lumea copiilor (Bucharest: ESPLA, 1957)
Piese (ESPLA, 1962)
Preludin-choral-final (1959)
Sonata (ESPLA, 1956)
Suita pentru pian
Teaching works
VOCAL
De aducere aminte, cantata (folk words) (ch and inst ens) (1967)
Noapte taraneasca, cantata (C. Theodorescu) (mix-ch and orch) (1958)
Chiuituri (chil-ch and small orch) (1978)
August (I. Constantin) (mix-ch) (1964)
Ce-a vazut vintul (P. Aristide) (unison ch) (1963)
Cine-cine? (P. Aristide) (unsion ch) (1956)
Cintec pentru republica (mix-ch) (1963)
Cintecele ploii (N. Cassian) (chil-ch and pf)
Madrigale (Japanese poets) (w-ch) (1968)
Mica suita pentru cor de femei (T. Arghezi) (w-ch) (1968)
O poveste (P. Aristide) (unison ch) (1963)
Songs of Skei (ch) (1971)
Suita corala (D. Corbea and P. Aristide) (ch) (1969)
Clime (I. Negoitescu) (m-S and cham ens) (1966)
Ritual pentru setea pamintului (folk words) (7 vces, perc and pf) (1968)
Vocabulaire I, chanson (S, cl, pf and bells) (1974)
Anotimp (I. Negoitescu) (vce and pf) (1965)
Balada unui greier mic (G. Topirceanu) (vce and pf) (1954)
Balada a ziselor marunte (F. Villon, trans R. Vulpescu) (vce and pf) (1959)
Balada a doamnelor din vremea de ordnioara (F. Villon trans R. Vulpescu) (vce and pf) (1959)
Colind (T. Arghezi) (vce and pf) (1950)
Denie cu clopote (T. Arghezi) (vce and pf) (1957)
Glas de toamna (A. Maniu) (vce and pf) (1958)
Inscriptie pe un mormint (T. Arghezi) (vce and pf) (1959)
Inscriptie pe un inel (T. Arghezi) (vce and pf) (1959)
The moon passes above the peaks (M. Eminescu) (vce and pf) (1955)
Profilul unu tarm (S.A. Doinas) (vce and pf) (1966)
Sapte lieduri (G. Lorca) (vce and pf) (1961)
Three choruses (folk words) (D. Corbea)
Voice of autumn (A. Maniu) (vce and pf) (1958)
SACRED
Psalm (T. Arghezi) (vce and pf) (1957)
ELECTRONIC
Jocus secundus (ch, vln, vlc, vla, cl, pf, perc and tape) (1969)

Publications
Cvartetul de coarde nr. 2 de G. Enescu. Muzica, no. 8, 1961.
Poezia argheziana si cintecul romanesc. Muzica, no. 6, 1960.
Varietatea tematica si unitatea structurala in luvrari de camera de Enescu. Muzica, no. 5, 1965.
Ref. 17, 70, 148, 196, 563

MARCELL, Florence

American organist and composer. b. Minneapolis, May, 1885. She composed an orchestral piece.
Ref. 347

MARCELLI, Anais. See PERRIERE-PILTE, Anais

MARCHAND, Maria Margarethe. See DANZI, Maria Margarethe

MARCHESA DI PESCARA. See COLONNA, Vittoria, Duchess of Amalfi

MARCHESI, Mathilde de Castrone (nee Graumann)

German singing teacher and composer. b. Frankfurt am Main, March 24, 1821; d. London, November 17, 1913. She studied singing in Vienna under Otto Nicolai in 1843 and in Paris studied solfege under Mlle. Klotz, singing under Manuel Garcia and diction under Samson in 1845. She gave concerts in Europe and in 1852 married Salvatore Marchesi, Cavalier de Castrone, an Italian of noble birth and a singer and teacher. After ten years at the Vienna Conservatory in Vienna, she moved to Paris and became one of the world's foremost singing teachers. Her method was highly recommended by Rossini. She was awarded a gold cross for merit by the Emperor Franz Josef in 1874.

Compositions
TEACHING PIECES
Ecole marchesi, l'art du chant, vocal piece
Vocal exercises
Publications
Erinnerungen aus meinem Leben. 1877.
Ref. 26, 276, 347

MARCHI, Giuliana

Italian composer. b. 1925.
Compositions
PIANO
Piccolo zoo musicale, 5 fantasie pianistiche (Ricordi)
ARRANGEMENTS
Works by Spanish harpsichordists (Padre Vicente Rodrigues, P. Antonio Soler, P.F. Rodrugues, Mateo Albeniz, Cantallos and P.J. Galtes) (Ricordi)
Ref. Ricordi

MARCHISIO, Barbara

Italian guitarist, singer, teacher and composer. b. Turin, 1833; d. Venice, 1919. A contralto, she taught her sister Carlotta, who became a famous prima donna and at the Conservatorio di San Pietro a Majella in Naples. Her guitar is preserved in the museum there. She composed vocal works and miscellaneous variations.
Ref. 502

MARCKWALD, Grace

19th-century American composer. b. Brooklyn. She composed orchestral and piano pieces and songs.
Ref. 226, 276, 292

MARCUS, Ada Belle Gross (Ada B. Marcus)

American concert pianist, teacher and composer. b. Chicago, July 8, 1929. She studied the piano under Sergei Tarnowsky and theory and composition under Samuel Lieberson on a five year scholarship to De Paul University graduating in 1944. In New York she attended piano master classes with Robert Goldsend for three years and then studied composition at the American Conservatory under Leo Sowerby. From 1954 to 1959 she was a composition pupil of Dr. Karel B. Jirak at the Chicago College of Music, Roosevelt University. Returning to De Paul University, she studied electronic music under Dr. Alexander Tcherepnin till 1961 and Philip Winsor till 1974 and conducting under Milton Preves of the Chicago Symphony Orchestra. She was a concert pianist from 1942 and a piano teacher from 1959. Several of her compositions were chosen to be exhibited at the International Society for Contemporary Music World Days, Rotterdam, Holland in 1974. Most of her compositions are self published. She is a member of ASCAP. PHOTOGRAPH.
Compositions
ORCHESTRA
Fantasy, Wheaton symphony (1958)
Symphony of the spheres (1972)
Garden of the gods (symphony orch) (1980)
Concertino (pf and orch) (1963)
Anecdotes (cham orch of vlns, vlcs and pfs) (1982)
Fantasia Nos. 1 and 2 (1954, 1955)
Jazz prelude (school orch) (1969)
Setting to seasons (cham orch) (1975)
Textures, in 4 mvts (pf, fl and str orch) (1981)
Violin concerto (hp and cham orch) (1965)
Zen (1974)
SYMPHONIC BAND
Outward bound
CHAMBER
Piano quintet (1983)
String quartet (1953)
String quartet No. 2 (1981)
A child's day (fl, vln and snare dr or pf) (1975)
Blue flute (fl and pf) (1972) (West Babylon: H. Branch, 1977)
Nocturne (fl and pf) (1955)
Sonata (vln and pf) (1964)
A song for flute (fl and pf) (Chicago: Tempo Music)
Three song poems (fl and pf) (1983)
Toccata (org) (1982)
Sonata, in 3 mvts (1979)
PIANO
A child's day, suite (1957) (Branch, 1977)
A day in New York, suite (1951)
Electronics (1975)
Etude erotique, 12 tone (1963) (Branch, 1977)
Monologue (1973)
Preludes after 1945
Refractions through a prism (1973)
Sonata (1970)
Sonata No. 2 (1981)
Theme and variations (1961) (Branch, 1977)
Youth in orbit (1969)
Three modules (1980)
VOCAL
Christmas bells (Longfellow) (mix-ch, brass and fl) (1967)
The house by the side of the road (Sam Walter Foss) (mix-ch and pf or str qrt)
Setting to seasons (Robert Frost) (w-ch, pf and strs) (1962)
A Shakespearean duo: A consolation; The seven ages of man (mix-ch and pf) (1968)
Four preludes on playthings to the wind (Carl Sandburg) (vce and pf) (1968)
Song cycle (Dylan Thomas) (1971)
Song cycle (Robert Frost) (vce and pf) (1959)
Two, three and four voice fugues (ca. 1945)
Two and three part inventions (ca. 1945)
SACRED
Chorales, psalms (mix-ch and org or pf) (1981)
God, whom shall I compare to Thee! (Halevy) (mix-ch and brass) (1960)
OPERA
Snow, chamber opera (Robert Frost) (1966)
ELECTRONIC
Various tapes
Ref. composer, 40, 84, 142, 206, 228, 347, 474, 475, 622

MARCUS, Bunita

American clarinetist, pianist, conductor, assistant professor and composer. b. Madison, WI, May 5, 1952. She studied composition under Franz Loschnigg from 1968 to 1973 and Morton Feldman, 1976 to 1981. She gained a B.Mus. in music theory, from the University of Wisconsin in 1976 and a Ph.D. in composition, from the State University of New York, Buffalo in 1981. She is currently assistant professor of composition at Brooklyn University. She has received many awards and commissions and her works have been performed in Europe, Japan and the United States.
Compositions
CHAMBER
Parent terrain (cl, b-cl, vln, d-b and 2 perc) (1977)
Oboe, clarinet, bass clarinet, trumpet, trombone (1978)
Quintet (cl, b-cl and 3 perc) (1976)
1975 (Arp 2500, a-sax, b-cl, gtr and steel dr) (1975)
Music for Japan (fl, cl, hp, pf and perc) (1983)
Sleeping women (fl, vln and pf) (1984)
Two pianos and violin (1981)
Apogee four (a-fl and perc) (1978)
Apogee two (d-b and perc) (1977)
Apogee one (gtr) (1976)
Apogee three (cl) (1977)
Solo (fl) (1982)
PIANO
Merry Christmas Mrs. Whiting (1981)
Piece (1979)
Wolpe variations (1980)
VOCAL
Untrammeled thought (vce and pf) (1980)
Valentine (1974)
OPERETTA
Droum (S, m-S, T, fl, d-b, vln, b-cl, gtr and perc) (1975)
ELECTRONIC
The sky is falling (tape) (1974)
Tape piece (1975)
MULTIMEDIA
Perhaps a woman would know (tape, dance, live insts and theatre) (1976)
Visa (tape, film, slides and gtr) (1976)
Ref. composer

MARES, Rosita

Composition
PIANO
Victoria Regina (Viladasau)
Ref. 473

MARESCA, Chiara

Compositions

PIANO

Suite

VOCAL

Ariel (S and 8 insts)

Ref. Frau und Musik

MAREZ-OYENS, Tera de

Dutch harpsichordist, pianist, violinist, conductor, lecturer and composer. b. Velsen, August 5, 1932. She graduated from the Amsterdam Conservatory (piano and conducting) in 1953 having studied the piano under Jan Ode, the harpsichord under Richard Boer, the violin under Camille Jacobs and Jan Henrichs and conducting under Felix Hepla. She then studied composition under Hans Henkemans and electronic composition under Professor Gottfried at the Institute of Sonology of the University of Utrecht, gaining her diploma in electronic music in 1965. She is currently a lecturer at the Conservatory in Zwolle and has given various radio talks on musical education, electronic music and women composers and made television appearances conducting orchestras and choirs. She leads children's groups in musical improvisation and concerts. She is a member of the National Council of Art in The Hague and vice-president of the Dutch Composers' League. She received an honorable mention in Concours Electro-Acoustic, Bourges, France in 1982. DISCOGRAPHY. PHOTOGRAPH.

Compositions

ORCHESTRA

Episodes (ens and orch) (Donemus, 1976)
Adventures in music (school orch)
Divertimento (Donemus, 1964)
In exile, concertino (pf and cham orch) (Donemus, 1977)
Introduzione (Donemus, 1969)
Litany of the victims of war (1985)
Modus I (small orch) (1973)
Partita for David (school orch) (Harmonia, 1960)
Ricercare (1972)
Rynaert tunes (school orch) (Harmonia, 1969)
Shoshadre (str orch) (Donemus, 1976)
Suite for pipers and fiddlers (school orch) (Harmonia, 1971)
Suite de petit prince (school orch) (Harmonia, 1958)
Transformation (1972)
Valentino serenata (small orch) (Harmonia, 1967)
Via octava (1985)
Violin Concerto (Structures and Dance) (1987)

CHAMBER

Starmobile (5 groups of insts) (Donemus, 1974)
Juli (fl, ob, bsn, 2 trp, trb, 2 vln, vla and vlc) (1961)
Octet (wind insts) (1972)
Tre modi (3 vln, vlc and rec qrt) (1973)
Canzone per sonar (2 inst groups) (Donemus, 1972)
Departure time ten to two (variable ens) (1983)
Droompardje (fl, ob, bsn, 2 hn and hp) (1961)
Mahpoochah (Lamentacion II) (7 or more insts)
Polskie miasta (fl, ob, vla, vln, vlc and pf) (1981) (Donemus)
Relaxations (rec ens) (1971)
Lenaia quintet (fl, 2 vln, vla and vlc) (1982) (Donemus)
Two sketches (fl, ob, cl, bsn and hn) (Donemus, 1963)
O, wind (str qrt and perc) (1961)
Second string quartet contrafactus (1981) (Donemus)
String quartet (1959)
Trajectory (sax qrt) (1985)
Yagon (cl, vl, vla and pf) (1984)
Concerto (fl and wind ens) (1983)
Bamboerijntjes (bamboo fls) (1957)
Cantico (org and 2 trb) (1956)
Inter-times (ob, bsn and keyboard) (Donemus, 1976)
Swatches (wind or str trio) (Harmonia, 1975)
Three dansen voor truus (bamboo fls and perc) (1975)
Cellogism (vlc and pf) (1980) (Donemus)
Confluence (vlc and acc) (1985)
Deductives (ob and hpcd) (Donemus, 1964)
Moebius by ear (vla and pf) (1983) (Donemus)
Octopus (b-cl and perc) (1982) (Donemus)
Pearls and strings (gtr and vlc) (1981) (Donemus)
Serenade (vlc and pf) (1964)
Sonata (vln and pf) (1958)
Sonatine (cl and pf) (1957)
Sonatine (ob and pf) (1964)
Hall of mirrors (gtr) (1985)
Johannes, 9 pieces (hpcd) (1962)
Journey (d-b) (1985)
Lenaia for flute solo (1982) (Donemus)
Lamentacion (t-rec) (1965)
Partita over Komm Gott (org) (Schoepfer, 1958)
Parallels (perc) (1984)
Valalan (gtr) (1984)

PIANO

Music book for Valentine (2 pf) (Broekmans & Van Poppel, 1974)
Sonatine (2 pf) (Donemus, 1961)
Ballerina on a cliff (Donemus, 1980)
Nocturne à Chopin joke (Harmonia, 1976)
Seven dances (Harmonia, 1976)
Sonatine (Donemus, 1963)

VOCAL

The odyssey of Mr. Goodevil, oratorio (M.S. Arnoni) (4 soloists, 2 narr, 2 mix-ch and orch) (1981)
The fire and the mountain, cantata (Israel Eliraz) (mix-ch and orch) (1978)
In groene veld, cantata (mix-ch, bamboo fls and perc) (1963)
Oorlog is vrede, cantata (ch and orch)
Schoon lief hoe ligt gij hier, cantata (mix-ch and cham ens) (1962)
Der chineschische Spiegel (T and orch or pf) (Donemus, 1962)
Ode to Kelesh (mix-ch and small orch) (1975)
Het lied van de duizend angsten (2 soli, 2 ch, perc, timp and strs) (1984) (comm Fonds voor de Scheppende Toonkunst)
Abschied (mix-ch) (1983)
Ballade grotesque (m-ch and pf, 4 hands) (1957)
Ballad of Mr. Knox (Bar and mix-ch) (1973)
Bist du bist (mix-ch) (1973)
Bist du bist II (mix-ch) (Donemus, 1973)
Bist du bist III (mix-ch of amateur vces) (Donemus, 1978)
Black (mix-ch) (1981) (Donemus)
Canto di parole (mix-ch) (1966)
Deposuit (mix-ch) (Donemus, 1970)
Lament of the frontier guard (Ezra Poind) (S, Bar and mix-ch) (1965)
The lover (mix-ch a-cap) (Donemus, 1975)
Pente sjawoe koste (7 speakers and mix-ch) (Donemus, 1970)
Roulette of moments (vces, strs and perc ad lib) (1979) (Donemus)
Schoolslag (Bar and mix-ch) (Donemus, 1970)
To Sweden with love (mix-ch) (Donemus, 1974)
Tragoedie (Heine) (mix-ch) (Koneza, 1957)
And blind she remained (vce, keyboard and perc) (Donemus, 1978)
Imploring mother (S, cl, b-cl and pf) (1982)
Ryoanji Temple (A, ob, vln, vla and vlc) (1972)
Takadon (vces, ww, brass, gtr, perc, strs and pf) (De Toorts, 1978)
Tekens bij de tujd (Bar and perc) (1963)
Vier Zuid-Afikaanse liederen (S and pf) (Ars Nova, 1951)
Vignettes (vce and 2 pf) (1984)
Vocafonie (4 m-vces) (1972)
Children's songs

SACRED

Kerstcantate (chil-ch and school orch) (Harmonia, 1960)
Laudent Deum (w-ch) (1966)
Motet on psalm 69 (mix-ch) (Center of Church Music, 1957)
Psalm 115 (mix-ch, trp and org) (1961)
Psalm 148 (Bar, m-ch and brass band) (1958)
Liturgic mass (1961)
Three hymns (m-S and pf) (1979) (Donemus)
Songs
Church music

BALLET

Dances of illusion (Verbosonisch-elektronisch Ballet) (1985)
Delta (Donemus, 1973)

OPERETTA

De kapitein is jarig, for children (1966)
Dorp zonder musiek, for children (1960)
Liedje gezocht, for children (1962)
Van den vos Reynaerde, for children (1966)

THEATRE

Communioation (mix-ch and dancers) (Donemus, 1970)
Sound and silence I and II (Donemus, 1971)

INCIDENTAL MUSIC

Music for radio plays

ELECTRONIC

Human (tape and orch) (Donemus, 1975)
Ambiversion (b-cl and tape) (1983)
Capolinea
Charon's gift (pf and tape) (1982) (Donemus)
Combattimento di cuori (1965)
Combattimento ritmico II (vlc, perc and tape) (Donemus, 1968)
Concerto for horn and tape (1980) (Donemus)
Contrapunctus (1965)
Dialogo (1965)
Etude for piano and technician (1964)
Etude II (1965)
From death to birth (M.S. Arnono) (mix-ch and tape) (Donemus, 1973)
Fusione (1965)
Mixed feelings (4 soundtracks and perc) (Donemus, 1973)
Motivo caustice (1965)
New Babylon impressions (1965)
Perturbazione (1965)
Photophonie, sound and light (Donemus, 1970)

Produzione (1965)
Safed (1967)
Spazio (1965)
Trio (bass insts, perc and tape) (Donemus, 1974)
Valentino serenato (1967)
Vagaries (pf and tape) (1983)
MULTIMEDIA
Anders den Anderson (chil-ch, school orch and pantomime) (1966)
Roulette of Moments (vces, strs and perc ad lib) (1979) (Donemus)
Sound and silence II (actress and 1 or more insts) (Donemus, 1971)
MISCELLANEOUS
Trajectory and Confluence
Ref. composer, Composers' Forum, 1, 70, 77, 185, 206, 461, 518, 563, 622

MARGARET, Queen of Scotland (Saint)

B. 1046; d. 1093. She was the daughter of Edward the Confessor. After the Battle of Hastings in 1066 Margaret fled to the continent, but bad weather drove her ship to the Scottish coast, where she was well received by King Malcolm III. Her feast day is June 10th. She was famous for the ballads she composed and sang with her ladies-in-waiting.
Ref. 264, 268

MARGARET OF AUSTRIA

B. Brussels, January 10, 1480; d. 1530. The daughter of Emperor Maximilian I and Mary of Burgundy, she was married whilst still a child to the future Charles VIII, but he soon divorced her for political reasons in order to marry Anne of Brittany. At the age of 17 Margaret married Juan of Spain, who died during their first year of marriage. In 1501 she married Duke Philibert of Savoy and spent three happy years with him before being widowed again. She decided to remain faithful to his memory and transform the simple Benedictine Hermitage at Brou into a great abbey. The sarcophagi of Philibert, his mother and Margaret are there today. From 1507 Margaret was governor of the Low Countries. She wrote love songs which were melancholy in character. The music album of Margaret of Austria, contains works by Pierre de la Rue, Ockeghem and other composers of the later Netherlands school, written for Margaret. DISCOGRAPHY.

Compositions
CHAMBER
Livres de basses dances
SACRED
Symphonia in laude summi regis (ded Maximilian I)
Ref. 264, 563

MARGARITA (Clara) da Monaco

Ca. 1649.
Composition
SACRED
O dulcis Jesu (counter-T and basso continuo)
Ref. 127

MARGLES, Pamela. See ADDENDUM

MARGRAVINE OF BAYREUTH. See WILHELMINA, Sophie Friederike

MARGUERITE AU MOINE

14th-century French minstrel. She signed the famous charter dated September 14, 1321, that established the Chappelle Saint-Julien-des-Menestriers, a corporation for jongleurs and minstrels.
Ref. 343

MARGULIUS, Myrna Frances. See SCHLOSS, Myrna Frances

MARI, Anne Valerie. See MARI, Pierrette

MARI, Pierrette (Anne Valerie)

French pianist, music critic, musicologist, writer and composer. b. Nice, August 1, 1929. She studied at Nice Conservatory and in 1946 obtained first prizes for the piano, harmony, solfege and history of music. In 1948 she entered the Paris Conservatoire to study under Noel Gallon, Tony Aubin and Olivier Messiaen. She received first prizes for counterpoint in 1953 and fugue in 1954. After an accident to her right hand she gave up instrumental work, taught herself to write with her left hand and entered composition classes. She wrote numerous articles for music journals and was music critic to *Lettres Françaises*. She also worked for the press at the Concours International. In 1946 she won the Prix de la Ville de Nice and in 1961 the Grand Prix de la Melodie Française. DISCOGRAPHY. PHOTOGRAPH.

Compositions
ORCHESTRA
Diverttissement (fl and orch) (1954)
Le sous préfet aux champs, symphonic poem (1959)
Concerto (gtr, perc and str orch) (1971)
Diptyque (1956)
CHAMBER
Three movements (strs) (1954)
Wind quintet, in 2 parts (1965)
Quatour de flutes (1968)
Trio (sax) (1956)
Fantaisie pour un enfant (pf, vln and vlc) (1971)
Au bois de Provence (ob and pf) (1962)
Ciel de bruyere (vla and pf) (Billaudot, 1981)
Jaserie (trp and pf) (1959)
Pièce (a-sax and pf) (1959)
Prière (a-sax and org) (1961)
Pour bercer Mimi (fl and pf) (1965)
Sonatine (bsn and pf) (1956)
Vislane (vln and pf) (1959)
Espagnolette (gtr)
Pastels egrenes (gtr)
Sonata (hpcd) (1967)
PIANO
Barcarole (1954)
Campagnolette
Le chardonet (Billaudot, 1980)
Escalades sur un piano (1955-1970)
Gayle (1958)
Le petit ecrit musical (1971)
Le rouet (1956)
Theme et variations (1955)
ELECTRONIC
Les travaux d'Hercule (ondes Martenot, pf and perc) (1972)
Publications
Bartok. Hachette.
Henri Dutilleux. Hachette.
Olivier Messiaen. Seghers.
Ref. composer, 70, 76, 94, 280, 347

MARIA ANTONIA WALPURGIS, Princess of Bavaria, Electress of Saxony (pseud. ETPA-Ermelinda Talea Pastorella Arcada)

German harpsichordist, pianist, artist, librettist, poetess, singer and composer. b. Munich, July 18, 1724; d. Dresden, April 23, 1780. The eldest daughter of the Elector Karl Albert of Bavaria, later Emperor Karl VII, she showed a talent for music, poetry and art at an early age. She was taught the piano by the chamber music director of the electorate, Giovanni Ferrandini, in Munich. After her marriage to the Elector Friedrich Christian of Saxony in 1747 she studied composition and singing under Nicola Porpora and Johann Adolf Hasse in Dresden until 1752. She played the harpsichord and was said to have a pure but weak voice. She later sang in her own operas. Today she is remembered as a patron of the arts. Many works of music, art and literature were dedicated to her and many of her literary works were set to music by such composers as Graun, Ferrandini, Hasse, Risteri and Naumann. She wrote the words for cantatas, for Hasse's oratorio *La Conversione de St. Agostino* and for some of her own operas under her pseudonym ETPA. As a result of her initiative Glucks' opera *Orpheus and Euridice* was produced in Munich, which marked the beginning of a reform in opera. Between 1763 and 1779 she maintained a lively correspondence with Frederick the Great who supported her in her artistic activities. In Weesenstein many of her paintings, including a self-portrait, can be seen. She was a member of the Arcadian Academy of Rome.

Compositions
ORCHESTRA
Overture in eight parts (ca. 1770)
VOCAL
Intermezzi comiche (S, Bar and insts)
Meditations, in 4 vols (1746)
Pastorale (1740)
Prendi l'ultimo addio
Prologus and chorus, in 4 parts
About 40 arias (vce and acc)
SACRED
Mottetti spirituali per la chiesa (1739)

OPERA
Il trionfo della fedelta (lib with Metastasio and intermezzi by Hasse, Frederick II, Graun and Benda) (1754)
Lavinia e Turno
Talestri, regina delle amazoni (with G. Ferrandini) (Nymphenburg: 1763)

Bibliography

Drewes, H. *Maria Antonia Walpurgis als Komponistin*. Leipzig, 1934.
Fuerstenau, M. *Maria Antonia Walpurgis. Monatschrite fuer Musikgeschichte*. 11, 1879.
Lippert, W. *Correspondence between Frederick the Great and Empress Maria Therese*. 1747-1772.
Preuss. *Correspondence between Frederick the Great and Marie Antonia de Saxe*. Berlin, 1854.
Von Weber, K. *Maria Antonia Walpurgis*. Dresden, 1857.
Yorke-Long, A. *Music at Court. Four Eighteenth Century Studies*. London, 1954.

Ref. 2, 9, 12, 13, 14, 15, 17, 22, 74, 85, 105, 119, 123, 129, 135, 155, 157, 158, 162, 177, 216, 226, 264, 276, 307, 335, 347, 361, 404, 405, 563, 622

MARIA BARBARA D. See MARIA TERESA BARBARA DE BRAGANÇA

MARIA CATERINA. See CALEGARI, Cornelia

MARIA CHARLOTTE AMALIE, Duchess of Saxe-Gotha, Princess of Saxe-Meiningen

Harpsichordist and composer. b. September 11, 1751. The daughter of Ulric, she was considered one of the most talented musicians among the 18th-century aristocracy.

Compositions

CHAMBER
Symphony for ten instruments
Variations (hpcd) (some with Benda, Schweitzer and Scheidler) (1782)
VOCAL
Canzonetti with variations (1781)
Zwoelf Lieder einer Liebhaberin (1786)
Other songs
SACRED
Church music

Ref. 26, 119, 128, 129, 226, 269, 276, 347

MARIA de VENTADORN

French troubadour. b. Limousin, ca. 1165. Her father was Ramon II, Viscount of Turenne, one of the four viscounties of the Limousin. She was married to Ebles V of Ventadorn, a neighboring viscounty, between the age of 13 and 20. Ventadorn was already established as a center of troubadour culture and Maria became the patron of the troubadours Pons de Capdoill, the Monk of Montaudon, Savaric de Mauleon, Guiraut de Calanson, Gaucelm Faidit and Gui d'Ussel, all of whom, as was the custom, dedicated songs to her. There were probably song fests, banquets and dances at her chateau. She is last referred to in 1221, when her husband, two sons and two of her brothers, entered the Cistercian Abbey of Grandmont as monks. Gaucelm Faidit loved Maria for a long time; in one song he said, 'Soon it will be seven years, that she has let me love her above all measure.' When the relationship finally became too onerus to her, Audiart of Malamort helped Maria to part from Faidit. She was frequently called upon to arbitrate in tensons, the dialogue songs between two troubadours. Her tenson with Gui d'Ussel is the only extant sample of her writing. Beginning 'Gui d'Ussel, because of you I'm quite distraught', she provokes Gui, who has long been silent, to sing again of his love for her.

Ref. 13, 117, 120, 213, 222, 303

MARIA PAULOWNA, Grand Duchess of Weimar

Russian pianist and composer. b. February 16, 1786; d. June 23, 1859. The daughter of Tsar Paul I of Russia, she studied under Liszt, who used one of her themes for the fourth of his set of *Consolations*. She tried unsuccessfully to persuade her brother the Tsar, to allow the Polish princess Carolyne of Sayn-Wittgensten to divorce her Russian husband in order to marry Liszt. Maria composed piano pieces.

Ref. 226, 276, 335, 347

MARIA TERESA BARBARA DE BRAGANÇA, Princess of Portugal and Queen of Spain

Portuguese harpsichordist and composer. b. Lisbon, December 4, 1711; d. 1758. The daughter of Joao V of Portugal and Maria Anna of Austria, she married Fernando, who later became king of Spain. An extremely well educated lady, she spoke several languages, had a particular love of music, played the harpsichord and studied under Domenico Scarlatti. Soriano Fuertes, in his *Historia de la musica española* mentions that her orchestral piece was performed by the Royal Chapel Musicians at the Salesias Monastery in Madrid. She was praised by Father John Baptist Martini, who dedicated the first volume of his *Historia de musica* to her and by Manuel de Figueredo, who wrote her eulogy after her death.

Composition

ORCHESTRA
Salve

Ref. 104, 268

MARIANI-CAMPOLIETI, Virginia

Italian harpist, pianist, conductor and composer. b. Genoa, December 4, 1869. She studied under various teachers and in 1883 became a pupil at the Liceo Musicale Rossini in Peraro where she studied under Vitali and Torchi and obtained her piano diploma in 1892. Later she studied composition under Pedrotti, the harp under Cambiano and Gianuzzi, voice under Bocabadati, Bercanovich and Coen and history and aesthetics of music under Yorchi. She was the conductor for her opera performances in Genoa and Modena.

Compositions

CHAMBER
Piano pieces
VOCAL
Apotheosis di Rossini, cantata (S, ch, org and orch) (Bodoira prize)
Cantate bambini, 12 songs (Ricordi)
Cantiamo, 33 songs for children (Ricordi)
Canzioncine, 30 songs (Ricordi)
Raccolta de canzioncine, collection of songs
Songs (Buffa; Nagas; Ricordi)
Two anthems (Ricordi)
OPERA
Dal songo all'vita, in 3 acts (F. Fulgonio) (Vercelli, 1898)

Ref. 86, 105, 225, 260, 276, 347, 622

MARIC, Ljubica

Yugoslav conductor, professor and composer. b. Kragujevac, Serbia, March 18, 1909. She studied under J. Slavenski at the Music School in Belgrade from 1929 to 1931 or 1932 and then studied composition at the Prague Conservatory under Josef Suk and quarter-tone-music under Alois Haba from 1936 to 1937. She studied conducting under Nikolai Malko in Prague and H. Scherchen in Strasbourg. During World War II she joined the partisans in their struggles against the Nazi invaders. From 1938 to 1945, besides conducting, she taught at a secondary school of music in Stankovic. After the war she became junior professor and in 1957 visiting professor of theoretical subjects and composition at the Music Academy of Belgrade. She is a member of the Serbian Academy of Sciences and Art. DISCOGRAPHY.

Compositions

ORCHESTRA
Byzantine concerto (from Musica octoiha cycle) (pf and orch) (1959)
Music for orchestra (1933)
Musica octoiha Nos. 1-3 (1958, 1959, 1962)
Passacaglia (theme on folk tune from Pomoravlje) (sym orch) (1957 or 1958)
Symphonica octoiha (from Musica octoiha cycle) (1964)
CHAMBER
Ostinato on an Octoiha-theme (from octoiha cycle) (str qnt, hp and pf) (1963)
Wind quintet (1932)
String quartet (1931)
Trio in quarter tones (cl, trb and d-b) (1937)
Sonata (vln and pf) (1948)
Sonata (vln) (1930)
PIANO
Pieces incl.:
Brankovo kolo (1947)
Etudes
Sketches (1945)
Suite for quarter-toned piano (1937)
Three preludes
VOCAL
Pesme prostora, cantata (medieval Bogumil tombstones) (mix-ch and orch) (1956) (October prize, 1957)
Prag sna, cantata (Ristic) (2 soli, reciter and cham ens) (1961)
Slovo svetlosti (medieval Serbian poetry) (6 narr, ch and orch) (1965)

Stihovi iz gorskog vijenca (Bar and orch) (1947)
Tri narodne, 3 folk songs (ch)
Carobnica (Virgil) (S and pf) (1964)
Other choruses
Songs

Publications

The Tractate on Monothematic and Monolthic Form of the Fugue. 1964.

Ref. 4, 5, 8, 14, 15, 17, 22, 44, 94, 189, 193, 206, 219, 226, 330, 418, 461, 563, 581

MARIE ANTOINETTE, Archduchess of Austria, Queen of France

Harpist and composer. b. Vienna, November 2, 1755; d. Paris, October 16, 1793. In 1770 she married Louis, Dauphin of France and was crowned Queen in 1775. She studied under Gluck in Vienna and supported his efforts to introduce reforms in opera, against the opposition led by Mme. du Barry. Marie studied the harp under Hinner and two harps were built for her by Naderman. She regularly attended society concerts in Paris. She was guillotined after the French Revolution. PHOTOGRAPH.

Compositions

CHAMBER
Salon pieces
VOCAL
Songs incl.:
C'est mon ami (melody also attributed to Prince Felix Youssoupoff)

Ref. 119, 177, 226, 344, 622

MARIE DE FRANCE

Breton glee-maiden and poetess. b. Brittany, ca. 1140; d. ca. 1200. Her patron was William Longsword, Earl of Salisbury and an illegitimate son of Henry II. Marie lived mostly in England and was familiar with Latin and the Breton tongue. Her first composition was a set of French songs which became popular throughout England.

Publications

L'espurgatoire Seint Patriz. Ca. 1190.
Isopet, 103 translated fables. Ca. 1180.
Lais. Short narrative poems. Before 1180.
Le lai de Lanval.

Ref. 260, 637

MARIE ELIZABETH, Princess of Saxe-Meiningen

19th-century German composer.

Compositions

ORCHESTRA
Einzugmarsch (Leipzig: Kahnt)
CHAMBER
Cradle song (vln and pf)
Romanze (cl and pf)
PIANO
Pieces incl.:
Fackeltanz (pf, 4 hands; also 2 pf)

Ref. 226, 276, 433

MARIE-STEPHANIE, Soeur. See COTE, Helene

MARIE THERESE, Sister. See BOUCHER, Lydia

MARIE THERESE LOUISE OF SAVOY-CARIGNANO, Princess of Lamballe

French composer. b. Turin, September 8, 1749; d. Paris, September 3, 1792. The daughter of Louis Victor of Carignano, she married the Prince de Lamballe. She was Marie Antoinette's (q.v.) companion and confidante and superintendent of the royal household. She was imprisoned at the Temple with Marie Antoinette on August 10, 1792 and after refusing to take the oath against the monarchy, was guillotined.

Compositions

VOCAL
Romance, song (Paris: Bouin, 1791)

Bibliography

Bertin, George. *Madame de Lamballe*. 1888.
Dobson, Austin. *Four Frenchwomen*. 1890.
Hardy, B.C. *Princesse de Lamballe*. 1908.
Lambeau, L. *Essais sur la mort de madame la princesse de Lamballe*. 1902.
Montefiore, Sir F. *The Princesse de Lamballe*. 1896.

Ref. 65, 208, 264, 405

MARINELLI, Maria

19th-century Italian pianist and composer. b. Aquila. She was a talented concert pianist, but retired early from public life. She composed piano pieces.

Ref. 180

MARINESCU-SCHAPIRA, Ilana

Rumanian pianist and composer. b. Bucharest, 1935. At the State Conservatory in Bucharest she studied under Mihail Jora, Martian Negrea and Theodor Rogalski. She studied the piano under Florica Musicescu. In 1956 she won second prize in a competition at the Bucharest Conservatory for vocal music and in 1957, second prize in a piano competition, Bucharest. Ilana lives in Tel-Aviv, Israel.

Compositions

ORCHESTRA
Burlesque (pf and orch)
Piano concerto
CHAMBER
Trio (fl, ob and cl)
PIANO
Etudes
Suites
VOCAL
Choral works incl.:
Fliege, du Lied (ch a-cap) (1st prize, World Youth Festival Moscow, 1957)
Songs

Ref. 280

MARINI, Giovanna

20th-century Italian composer.

Compositions

FILM MUSIC
I belong to me (1978)
If pigs had wings (1977)

Ref. 497

MARINKOVIC, Jelena

20th-century Yugoslav composer.

Composition

CHAMBER
Violin sonata

Ref. 81

MARION, Mrs. W. See JESSUP-MILDRED, Marion de

MARKIEWICZOWNA, Wladyslawa

Polish concert pianist, professor and composer. b. Bochnia, near Cracow, February 5, 1900. At the age of 14 she studied the piano under Eisenberger and composition under Z. Jachimecki at the Cracow Conservatory. After graduating she studied the piano at the Academy of Music, Berlin under Bruno Eisner and composition under Hugo Leichtentritt until 1928. From 1926 to 1929 she gave concerts and recitals in Berlin and many centers in Poland. From 1929 she taught at the Conservatory of Katowice, becoming professor at the State music college, Katowice in 1945. PHOTOGRAPH.

Compositions

CHAMBER
Kolorowe obrazki (fl, ob, cl and bsn) (1937)
Suite (fl, ob, bsn and pf) (1934)
Divertimento, op. 10 (ob, bsn and hp) (1937)
Trio (cor anglais, cl and bsn) (1938)
Sonata (cl, bsn and pf) (1950)
Suite (ob, bsn and pf) (1934)
Burlesque (bsn and pf) (1976)
Sonata (trp and pf) (1954)
Sonatina (bsn and pf) (1950)
Sonatina (ob and pf) (1935)
Toccata, op. 14 (bsn and pf) (PWM, 1946)
PIANO
Sonata (2 pf) (1954)
Suite, op. 9 (2 pf) (1937)
Compendium of 17 pieces (1973)
Humoresque, op. 11 (1933)
Kolorowe obrazki (PWM, 1947)
Miniatures
Preludes

Samuel Zborowski (1944)
Sonatas
Sonatina (PWM, 1942)
Tema con variationi
Variations on a folk theme (1924)
Teaching works
VOCAL
Chamber suite (J. Przechwa) (S and 9 insts) (1957)
Numerous songs (Polish poets) (vce and pf)
Ref. composer, 118

MARKOV, Katherine Lee
American teacher and composer. b. Santa Barbara, August 2, 1948. She gained a B.A. and M.A. (theory and composition) from the University of California and was awarded the Cheny music scholarship. She taught music at Riverside City College and the Compton Conservatory for children. PHOTOGRAPH.
Compositions
CHAMBER
Two movements for string quartet (1977)
Phrygian (ob and pf) (1971)
Sonata on A, in two mvts (vlc) (1972)
PIANO
Four sketches (1981)
Romance and fantasy (1979)
VOCAL
The clear sky (mix-ch) (1973)
For Marshall No. 2 (vce and ww qnt) (1981)
Escapist's song (vce and pf) (1973)
Fertile tears, 7 songs (m-S) (1982)
For Marshall No. 1 (vce and pf) (1981)
Songs for Vivien's wedding, 3 songs (vce, fl and vlc) (1973)
Velvet shoes (vce and pf) (1973)
SACRED
Ecclesiastes (mix-ch) (1972)
Prayers from the Ark, song cycle (4 soloists and mix-ch) (1972)
Ref. composer

MARKOWKSKA-GAROWSKA, Eliza (Elzbieta)
19th-century Polish composer.
Composition
ORCHESTRA
Piano concerto
Ref. V. Pigla (Warsaw)

MARKS, Jeanne Marie
American authoress and composer. b. Wenonah, NJ, February 9, 1919. She studied at Spring Garden College and under Frederick Starke in Philadelphia.
Compositions
SACRED
I gave myself to Jesus
MISCELLANEOUS
Around the clock
On your hand and face
Ref. 494

MARKS, Selma. See ADDENDUM

MARQUES, Fernandina Lagos
20th-century Brazilian pianist, school inspector, singer and composer. b. Curitiba, Parana. She was awarded the Parana Arts Center honorary diploma.
Compositions
VOCAL
A primavera chegou
Brasil amado
Cantiga de ninar
Parana national anthem (composer)
SACRED
Ave Maria
Ref. 268

MARQUES, Laura Wake
Portuguese pianist, singer, writer and composer. b. Lisbon, 1870; d. 1957. She was the daughter of the musician Joaquim Jose Marques. She studied the piano under Rey Colaco at the Lisbon Conservatory, singing under her mother, Vellani and Jane Bensaude and harmony and composition under Ruy Coelho. She gave concerts with symphony orchestras, and unaccompanied, in the theatre and on the radio. In 1924 she organised a series of conferences on the history of Portuguese music, illustrated by concerts.
Compositions
VOCAL
Anthem for the College of Braga
Cantos portugueses (A.L. Vieira, A. de Monsaraz)
BALLET
Figurinhas de Sevres, for children
Publications
Do Meu Lar.
Cronolgia da Opera em Portugal.
Livro de Memorias.
O Canto dem Portugal.
Palestras Musicais.
Ref. 268

MARQUES, Maria Adelaide
Brazilian composer. d. ca. 1955. She composed piano pieces.
Ref. Inter-America Music Review, Fall 1980 No. 1

MARQUISE d'HERICOURT DE VALINCOURT. See HAENEL DE CRONENTHAL Louise Augusta

MARRA, Adelina (Adele)
Italian singer and composer. b. Catanzaro, 1858.
Compositions
VOCAL
Songs incl.:
Occhi veri, romanza (Ricordi)
T'amo, romanza (Ricordi)
OPERA
Sara, in 3 acts (M.V. de Mercurio) (Catanzaro, 1888)
Ref. 225, 307

MARSCHAL-LOEPKE, Grace (pseud. Grace Cotton-Marshall) (Mrs. H. Clough-Leighter)
American pianist and composer. b. Nineveh, IN, 1895. She studied under her teacher and composer husband, Henry Clough-Leighter and composed piano and choral pieces and songs.
Ref. 292, 323, 347, 353

MARSH, Lucille Crews. See CREWS, Lucille

MARSH, Gwendolyn
20th-century American composer of piano pieces, songs and anthems.
Ref. 40, 347

MARSHALL, Florence A. (nee Thomas) (Mrs. Julian)
English conductor, writer and composer. b. Rome, March 30, 1843. She studied under Sterndale Bennett, Goss and Sir G.A. Macfarren at the Royal Academy of Music, London. She conducted the South Hampstead Orchestra and was an associate of the Philharmonic Society.
Compositions
ORCHESTRA
Pieces incl.:
Nocturne for clarinet and orchestra
VOCAL
Cantatas
Part songs
Songs

OPERETTA
Prince Sprite (1897)
Publications
Interval Exercises for Singing Classes. Novello.
Handel. Great Musicians Series. London: Sampson Low, 1883.
Solfeggi Primer. Novello.
Ref. 6, 85, 226, 260, 276, 307, 347, 431, 433

MARSHALL, Jane Manton
American organist, pianist, conductor, professor and composer. b. Dallas, December 5, 1924. She studied the piano, the organ, voice and conducting at the Southern Methodist University and gained her B.Mus. and M.Mus. She lectured there from 1948 to 1950, and from 1968 to 1973 and then became an adjunct professor of church music at Perkins School of Theology. In 1965 she received the Woman of Achievement award from Southern Methodist University, where she was a member of Mortar Board and Sigma Kappa. She held various positions as a church organist and after 1981 was chairlady of the hymn supplement task force of the United Methodist church. She won an American Guild of Organists prize for an anthem in 1957.
Compositions
SACRED
Numerous works incl.:
Awake, my heart (mix-ch and keyboard) (1957) (H.W. Gray)
Blessed is the man, psalms (ch) (1960) (Abingdon Press)
God's own people (I. Peter) (ch) (1965) (Carl Fischer)
Great King of Glory, come (mix-ch and keyboard) (Gray)
He comes to us (Schweitzer) (ch) (1957) (Fischer)
My Eternal King (mix-ch) (1954) (Fischer)
Praise the Lord, psalms (ch) (1969) (Fischer)
Spirit of life (mix-ch and keyboard) (Gray)
Ref. 142, 190

MARSHALL, Kye
Canadian concert cellist, pianist and composer. b. Toronto, October 19, 1943. She studied the cello and the piano at the Royal Conservatory of Music, gained her B.Mus. from the University of Toronto and then studied cello improvisation and jazz performance at York University. She studied arrangement and composition for seven years at the Gordon Delamont studio. She is a concert cellist in Toronto with the Epic String Quartet, National Ballet of Canada, O'Keefe Center Orchestras and the Kye Marshall Jazz Quartet. PHOTOGRAPH.
Compositions
ORCHESTRA
Concerto (b-trb and str orch) (1982)
CHAMBER
String quartet No. 1 (1977)
Duo (fl and pf) (1980)
Elegy (vlc and pf) (1978)
Fantasy (vlc) (1981)
Two pieces: Song; Dance (pf) (1979)
VOCAL
Song (S and pf) (1980)
Ref. composer

MARSHALL, M.E.
Early 20th-century English composer. She was a member of the Society of Women Musicians.
Compositions
CHAMBER
Two string quartets
Trio, dance fantasy (Supplementary Cobbett prize, 1920)
Two violin sonatas
Ref. 41

MARSHALL, Mrs. Julian. See MARSHALL, Florence A.

MARSHALL, Mrs. William
19th-century English composer of songs and ballads.
Ref. 6, 85, 347

MARSHALL, Pamela J.
American horn player, lecturer and composer. b. Beverly, MA, May 31, 1954. She gained her B.M. (composition) in 1976 from the Eastman School of Music and her M.M. from the Yale School of Music in 1980. She attended the computer music workshop at the Massachusetts Institute of Technology in 1979. Her teachers included Samuel Alder, Warren Benson and Joseph Schwantner and she studied the horn under Verne Reynolds, Paul Ingraham and Charles Kavaloski of the Boston Symphony Orchestra. She was a member of several orchestras. She taught at the Yale Music School from 1978 to 1980 and organised a program for gifted children at Milton Academy, MA, 1981. She was awarded a MacDowell College fellowship in 1981.
Compositions
ORCHESTRA
Blessing for a good journey (1976) (Seesaw Music)
CHAMBER
Spindrift (wind ens) (1974) (Seesaw)
Nautilus (ww qnt) (1977) (Seesaw)
Nor brass nor sounding sea (brass qnt) (1974) (Seesaw)
Wander bitter-sweet (hn and str qrt) (1976)
Torrsong (2 cl, vla and xyl) (1976) (Seesaw)
Dances for the morning (hp) (1975)
Miniatures for unaccompanied horn (1973)
VOCAL
Fyr on flode (m-S, ch, 2 ob, 2 hn, perc, 2 vln and vla) (1976) (Seesaw)
A chill wind in autumn, 8 songs (1979)
Watchmen for the morning (vce, hn and pf) (1976)
SACRED
Blessed and holy (mix-ch) (1976) (Seesaw)
Christo Psallat (1974) (Seesaw)
INCIDENTAL MUSIC
As You Like It (Shakespeare) (1982)
Macbeth (Shakespeare) (1982)
Richard III (Shakespeare) (1982)
MISCELLANEOUS
Meadowlarks and shawms (1979)
Toccata armonica (1980)
Ref. composer, 625

MARTENOT-LAZARD (Martenot), Ginette-Genevieve
French ondes Martenot player, pianist, teacher and composer. b. Paris, January 27, 1902. She studied at the Paris Conservatoire and the Faculté des Lettres of the Sorbonne University. She gave her first concert at the age of five and performed as soloist with many orchestras, including the Berlin Philharmonic, the Amsterdam Concertgebouw, the New York Philharmonic and the London Symphonic. She also played the ondes Martenot with leading orchestras. She founded the Ecole d'Art Martenot in Paris which has 272 centers in France and abroad. She composed film music, songs and teaching pieces for the piano.
Publications
L'Etude vivante du piano. 4 vols. Henri Lemoine.
Ref. composer, 490

MARTH, Helen June
American organist, authoress, choir conductor, drama coach and composer. b. Alton, IL, May 24, 1903. She studied the organ and composition under C. Albert Scholin in St. Louis and conducted children's choirs, ran radio programs and worked at the 'Little Theatre' for 30 years. She toured the Chautauqua circuit as an accompanist and drama coach.
Compositions
SACRED
Sing O ye heavens, cantata
The triumph of Christ
Anthems incl.:
You taught me how to pray
Ref. 39, 142, 347, 646

MARTHA
Late 9th-century Byzantine nun. She composed sacred works.
Ref. 502

MARTIN, Angelica
19th-century American teacher and song composer.
Ref. 347

MARTIN, Dolores J.

Black American pianist and composer. b. Los Angeles, July 18, 1943. She began piano lessons at the age of 14 and whilst in high school studied at the University of Southern California's Music School. She then studied at City College, Los Angeles, but gained her B.A. (music theory) from Pepperdine University, studying under Joseph Wagner and received a diploma in composition from the Paris American Academy, France. She is a member of Mu Phi Epsilon. She also composes commercial and popular music.

Compositions

CHAMBER

Sketches (fl and str qrt)
Sounds in a park (str qrt; also vlc)

PIANO

La mer turbulente (2 pf)
The art of Edward Hopper
Circle of dreams
Cities three
Un jour (Seattle: Soundwork, 1979)

Ref. composer

MARTIN, Giuseppina

French concert pianist and composer. b. 1822; d. Paris, July, 1902. She lived in Paris and concert toured from 1840 to 1880.

Compositions

PIANO

Pieces incl.:
Les cloches du couvent, op. 28 (Durdilly)
Danse syriaque
Fantaisie espagñole
Fantarella, op. 17 (Heugel)
La kermesse, fête flamande, op. 13 (Sulzbach)
Menuet
Naples serenata, op. 18 (Heugel)
Nuit etoilée, berceuse (Sulzbach)
Tarantella

Ref. 105

MARTIN, Judith Reher

American organist, pianist, electronic synthesist, singer and composer. b. St. Paul, MN, January 20, 1949. She studied the organ from an early age and won performance awards whilst still at school. She gained her B.A. (electronic media in arts) in 1973 and M.A. (composition) in 1980 from Indiana University's School of Music where she studied under John Eaton, Mary Ellen Solt, Xenakis and Bernard Heiden. She founded the Electronic and New Music Ensembles whilst at university and continued as an electronic music performer and occasionally as a vocalist, pianist or organist. PHOTOGRAPH.

Compositions

ORCHESTRA

Celebration (1972)
Il sole (1980)
Kirlian chorale (1977)
Love brings good fortune (cham orch) (1980) (Gaudeamus prize, 1981)
Pastorale (1977)

CHAMBER

Chorale (str qrt) (1973)
Introit (str qrt)
Sombiage (3 vlc) (1972)
For the funeral of dead certain (trp) (1971)
Inner dialogue (d-b) (1975)
Celebration (carillon) (1977)

VOCAL

The moon dreams her (vce, trp, perc, pf, syn, vln, vlc and d-b) (1983)
The gate (vce and ens) (1972)
Jack and Jill (vce and ens) (1972)
The sick rose (vce and d-b) (1971)
Songs incl.:
Bolt of magic (1981)
Everything is alive (1981)
He said she said (1977)
Incantation for Aquarius (1969)
Joshua's lullaby (pf and vce) (1984)
One (1980)

THEATRE

Bolt of Magic in the Land of Nod (vce, syn, dance and projection) (1981)
A Midsummer Night's Dream (Shakespeare) (readers, mix-ch, recs, syn, perc, pf, trb and English hn) (1983)
Sign (1975)

ELECTRONIC

The big bang (syn, trb, perc and pf) (1983)
Center of the wheel (vce, tape and syn) (1977)
Change fear to the opposite (pf and syn) (1980)
Chorale (vce and syn) (1972)
Creative visions (syns) (1981)
Dream arena (vce and syn) (1981)
Eros flies into a tradition (pf and syn) (1978)
Ex loves (syn) (1980)
First voyage (syn) (1980)
Forsythia (vce and syn) (1972)
Frankenstein (tape) (1976)
GAB CDE (syn) (1980)
Harmonious beings (syn) (1980)
In the heart (syn) (1980)
Kenya night train (syn) (1980)
My one perfect deep blue (2 trb, 2 syn and trb) (1984)
Ocean sides in the well-tempered being (vce, trb, ob, perc and syn) (1981)
Parlour pieces (mini Moog) (1972)
Pastorale (vce and syn) (1976)
Quiet fire (elec vla) (1976)
Release the mighty flame of cosmic peace (vce, drs and syn) (1983)
Song for a new age (S, syn and perc) (1982)
Sonora borealis (syn) (1971)
Syzygy (syn) (1972)
Touch (vce and syn) (1974)
White Alice (syn) (1975)
X's on its eyes (vce and syn) (1980)

MULTIMEDIA

Fantasy space tour
Gradual unlock mystery box (1973)
Hoop (1975)
Predictions: World's end (vce, syn and dancer) (1982)
The secret circuit, for children (narr, ballet, syn and projection) (1982)

Ref. composer, AMC newsletter, 625

MARTIN, Ravonna G.

American pianist, lecturer and composer. b. Jasper, TX, October 18, 1954. She obtained a B.A. (music education) in 1980 and M.A. (music history) from the University of Alaska in 1983. She then lectured at the University of Alaska.

Compositions

VOCAL

Beauty art thou (mix-ch and pf) (1983)
Alaska animal miniatures (Robert McCoy) (1983)
Five meditations from Anne Bradstreet (m-S and pf) (1983)
T'is you that are the music (m-S and pf) (1983)

SACRED

Christmas liturgy (soloist, mix-ch, narr and cham orch) (1984)
Christmas psalm (mix-ch, fl, org and perc) (1982)

THEATRE

Swashbuckler I and II (1983)

Ref. 625

MARTINES, Marianne. See MARTINEZ, Marianne

MARTINEZ, Anna Caterina. See MARTINEZ, Marianne

MARTINEZ (Martines), Marianne (christened Anna Caterina)

Austrian harpsichordist, pianist, singer, teacher and composer. b. Vienna, May 4, 1774; d. December 13, 1812. Her father was a Neapolitan of Spanish origin and master of ceremonies to the Papal Nuncio. Metastasio, a great friend of her father, undertook her general education. He thought of her as a daughter and on his death left her a sum of money, his piano, spinet and music library. She had harpsichord lessons under Haydn when he was young and unknown and studied singing and composition under Porpora, Bonno and Hasse. Burney, who heard her sing in Vienna in 1772, praised her in his *Travel journal*. She also won the admiration of Hasse and Gerbert. Her first attempts in composition were made when she was 12 and were received very favourably. Her *Isacco* was performed by the Tonkuenstler Gesellschaft in Vienna in 1782. She held weekly musical gatherings at her home, which were attended by all the principal artists. On one of these occasions she played a four-hand sonata with Mozart. She later devoted her time to teaching talented pupils. In 1773 she was made an honorary member of the Philharmonic Academy of Bologna. Many of her manuscript are at the Gesellschaft der Musikfreunde, Vienna. Two of her sonatas were reprinted by E. Pauer in his *Alte Meister*. Wurzbach believed that besides sacred music she composed 31 sonatas, 12 concertos and 156 arias. DISCOGRAPHY.

Compositions
ORCHESTRA
Symphony
Two piano concertos
Overture in C (small orch)
CHAMBER
Sonata, op. 4 (hpcd or pf)
Sonata, op. 5 (hpcd or pf)
Sonata No. 3 in E-Minor (hpcd or pf)
Concierto in A-Major (hpcd)
Other sonatas
Motets
VOCAL
Amor timido, cantata (S and orch)
Orgoglioso fiumecello, cantata (S and orch) (1786)
Perche compagne amate cantata (S, 2 vln and basso continuo)
La tempesta, cantata (Metastasio) (S and orch) (1778)
Deh dami un altro core, aria (vce and orch) (1769)
Tu vittime non vuoi, aria (vce and orch) (1769)
Dell'amore i dei momenti, aria (vce and basso continuo)
Twenty-four arias (vce and basso continuo) (1767)
SACRED
Isacco figura del Redentore, oratorio (Metastasio) (soloists, ch and orch) (1781)
Santa Elena al Calvario, oratorio
Kyrie (4 vces and orch)
Mass in C-Major (ch and orch)
Psalm XLI: Quemadmodum desiderat cervus (soloists, ch and orch) (1770)
Psalm L: Miserere (4 vces and orch) (Vienna: Hertel, 1769)
Psalm CXIII: In exitu Israel (4 vces and orch)
Psalm CXII (4 vces and orch)
Six motets (S and orch)
Three litanies (ch and orch) (1760-1765)
Et vita venturi (4 vces a-cap)
Motet (4 vces a-cap)
Psalm CIX: Dixit dominus (5 vces, vlns, ob, trp and drs) (Hertel, 1774)
Regina Coeli (8 vces and insts)
Three masses
Ref. 2, 8, 9, 13, 14, 15, 17, 22, 26, 44, 74, 100, 105, 107, 119, 128, 129, 132, 155,158, 159, 162, 216, 242, 276, 335, 361, 476, 555, 563, 622, 646, 653

MARTINEZ, Odaline de la

American pianist, lecturer and composer. b. Matanzas, Cuba, October 31, 1949. She moved to the United States in 1961 and to England in 1972. She gained her B.F.A. hons. from Tulane University in 1972 and her G.R.S.M. (piano and composition) from the Royal Academy of Music, London in 1976. She obtained her M.Mus. in composition from the University of Surrey in 1977 and her Ph.D. in computer music in 1980. She lectured on 20th-century music at the Royal Academy and in workshops and concerts throughout Britain and is a free-lance musician and musical director of Lontano, a contemporary music ensemble. She received several scholarships and prizes and her compositions are performed widely on the radio.

Compositions
ORCHESTRA
Phasing (cham orch) (1975)
CHAMBER
Litanies (hp, fl and str trio) (1981)
A moment's madness (fl and pf) (1977)
Suite (vlc and cor anglais) (1982)
Colour studies (pf) (1978)
Eos (org) (1976)
Improvisations (vln) (1977)
Little piece (fl) (1975)
VOCAL
Two American madrigals (ch a-cap) (1979)
Absalom (B, Bar, 2 T and counter-T) (1977)
After Sylvia, song cycle (S and pf) (1976)
Five imagist songs (S, cl and pf) (1974)
OPERA
Sister Aimee: An American Legend (1978)
THEATRE
A mind of its own (cor anglais) (1981)
ELECTRONIC
Lamento (amp mix-ch and tape) (1979)
Hallucination (tape) (1975)
Three studies (perc and electronics) (1980)
Visions and dreams (tape) (1978)
Ref. composer, 422, 622

MARTINEZ DE LA TORRE Y SHELTON, Emma

Cuban pianist, lecturer and composer. b. Havana, January 15, 1889. She went to Spain at the age of two and later studied the piano at the Academia de Santa Cecilia under Rafel Toniasi Requena. She completed her studies with a first prize. She settled in Tenerife, Canary Islands, where she continued her harmony and composition studies under Santiago Sabina Corona. She taught the piano privately and in conservatories from 1909.

Compositions
ORCHESTRA
Estampas de siglo XVIII
Marionetas
CHAMBER
Sonata (vln and pf)
VOCAL
Songs
THEATRE
Danzas gitanas, dances
Manana de Abril, incidental music
Tenerife 1942, children's play
Ref. 100, 107

MARTINS, Maria de Lourdes

Portuguese clavichordist, harpsichordist, pianist, professor and composer. b. Lisbon, May 26, 1926. Her mother, Maria Helena Martins was her first piano teacher, then Maria studied the piano under Professor Abreu da Mota at the Conservatory Nacional, graduating in 1944 and composition under Artur Santos and Croner de Vasconcelos, graduating in 1949. She studied the harpsichord and the clavichord under Santiago Kastner. On a grant from the Calouste Gulbenkian Foundation she commenced advanced studies in composition under Professor Genzmer at the Musikhochschule in Munich in 1959 and under K. Stockhausen and Bruno Maderna in Darmstadt from 1960 to 1961. She studied film composition in Siena under Lavagnino and holds the diploma of the Orff-Institut at the Mozarteum in Salzburg. She was invited by the Gulbenkian Foundation to organize a Portuguese version of the scholastic work of Carl Orff, which she introduced and taught at the foundation from 1960 to 1971. She held summer courses in the Orff method in Canada and Brazil and studied the Kodaly method in Kecskemet, Hungary in 1970. She was active in the field of music education, lecturing in Europe, the United States, South America and Japan and taking part in foreign congresses and seminars. She was founder and president of the Associação Portuguese de Educacão Musical and professor of music education at the Conservatorio Nacional from 1971 to 1978 and of composition from 1973. She received prizes and awards, including the Calouste Gulbenkian composition prizes in 1965 and 1971. DISCOGRAPHY.

Compositions
ORCHESTRA
Pezzo grotesco, op. 19, symphonic piece (1959)
Convergencias, op. 27 (cham orch) (1970)
Rondo, op. 34
Suite de dancas tradicionais portuguesas
BAND
III, IV, V, for youth (1965)
CHAMBER
Divertimento para quinteto de sopro, op. 26 (wind qnt) (1967)
Sonatina para quinteto de sopro, op. 20 (wind qnt) (1959)
Esqueletos (fl, bsn, vln and pf) (1962)
Cuarteto de cordas, op. 9 (2 vln, vla and vlc) (1958)
Trio, op. 17 (Carlos Seixas prize, 1959)
Cromos, op. 16, 4 pieces (vln and pf) (1958)
Dois esbocetos, op. 32 (vlc and pf) (1976)
Prelude, op. 10 (vln and pf) (1953)
Sonata, op. 4 (vln and pf) (1948)
Sonatina de oboe, op. 5 (ob and pf) (1949)
Sonorita, op. 28 (pf and perc - 1 performer)
Sonatina de violino, op. 12 (1955) (Juventude Musical Portuguesa prize, 1960)
Suite, op. 13 (hpcd) (1957)
Vamos tocar flauta de bisel (fl) (1965)
PIANO
Dance, op. 7 (2 pf) (1950)
Grotesca, op. 16 (1950)
Peças para crianças, op. 21 (Lisbon: Valentim de Carvaho, 1978)
Sonatina No. 1, op. 3 (1947)
Sonatina No. 2, op. 14 (1957)
Tocatina, op. 13 (1976)
Valsas, op. 33 (1976)
VOCAL
O encoberto, op. 25, choral symphony (narr, soloists, mix-ch and orch) (F. Pessoa) (Calouste Gulbenkian prize, Lisbon, 1965)
O litora, op. 29 (A. Megreiros) (mix-ch and perc) (Calouste Gulbenkian prize, 1971)
Twelve harmonizations of traditional songs, op. 18 (mix-ch a-cap) (1951)

Cantigas de amigo, op. 23 (D. Diniz) (vce and str qrt) (1960)
Cançoes para as escolas (vce and insts) (Bonn: Schott, 1961)
Musica para crianças, I and II (vce and insts) (Schott, 1965)
Musica para jovens, I and II (vce and insts) (Lisbon: Valentim de Carvalho, 1974, 1978)
Tia Anica do Loule, op. 18 (3 vces a-cap) (1959)
SACRED
Cantata de Natal, op. 8 (soloists, w-ch, fl, vln and pf) (1951)
Auto de Natal (vce and insts) (1962) (adapted as Historia de Natal, 1969)
Rapsodia de Natal, op. 35
OPERA
Silencio, aonde estas tu, op. 15, for radio (T. Maria Gersao)
THEATRE
A outra morte de Ines, op. 30 (F. Luso Soares) (1972)
Publications
Creativety in Music Education. Bonn: Schott, 1973.
Musica para jovens. Lisbon: Valentim de Carvalho.
Das Orff-Schulwerk in Verbindung mit der portugiesischen Tradution. Vol. 1. *Rueckblick auf die musikalische Entwicklung.* Vol. 2. *Das portugiesiche Volkslied.* Vol. 3, Das Orff Schulwerk in Portugal. Orff Institut, 1965.
O som e o homem. Lisbon: Audiovisualmente, 1976.
Bibliography
Cage, John. Notations. New York: Something Else Press, 1969.
Cassuto, Alvaro. *A.C. entrevista Maria de Lourdes Martins. Arte Musical.* Lisbon, 1967.
Ref. composer, 12, 70, 77, 189, 563, 622

MARTYN, Mrs. Charles. See INVERARITY, Eliza

MARX, Berthe
19th-century French concert pianist and composer. b. Paris, July 28, 1859. She was the daughter of a musician and was admitted to the Paris Conservatoire at the age of nine without a preliminary examination. Auber took special interest in her studies. She was a pupil of Mme. Retz and won the theory and harmony prizes and medals for piano playing. She then studied under Henri Herz and at 15 won the Conservatoire's first prize. After touring extensively throughout Europe as a concert pianist, alone and with the violinist Pablo de Sarasate she had over 400 performances to her credit. In 1894 she married Otto Goldschmidt, a composer and critic.
Compositions
PIANO
Pieces incl.:
Variations
ARRANGEMENTS
Violin and piano pieces
Ref. 276, 433

MARXHAUSEN, P.F. See SCHATZELL, Pauline von

MARY ANN JOYCE, Sister. See BERNADONE, Anka

MARY BERNICE, Sister
American organist, pianist, violinist, lecturer, nun and composer. b. Hospers 10, July 22, 1891. She graduated from the Ellison-White Conservatory, Portland in 1929, the St. Louis Institute of Music and gained her B.M. and M.M. from the Chicago College of Music in 1932 and 1933 and her B.A. from Loras College, 1936. She studied the piano under David Campbell and Frances Streigl Burke in Portland, under Godfried Galston in St. Louis and Molly Margolies and Rudolph Ganz in Chicago. Her composition and music theory teachers were A.E. Johnstone, Wesley La Violette, Max Wald and W. Glas. Sister Bernice became a member of the faculty of the Immaculate Conception Academy, Iowa and taught the piano, the violin and music theory there and in other colleges from 1902.
Compositions
ORCHESTRA
Symphonic variations
CHAMBER
Four string quartets
Sonata (vln and pf)
Fifty piano pieces
Motets
SACRED
Mass in honor of St. Pascal (1st prize, Nat. Catholic Music Teachers' Assoc. competition, 1947)
Ref. 496

MARY ELAINE, Sister
American pianist, lecturer, nun and composer. b. Fredericksburg, TX, October 4. She received her B.Mus. (piano) from Our Lady of the Lake College, San Antonio in 1933 and her M.M. (composition) from the American Conservatory of Music, Chicago in 1942. Sister Mary joined the faculty of the Lady of the Lake College in 1929 and taught the piano, music theory, harmony, form, analysis and ear training. She studied the music of the Negro and the music and customs of the American Indian. Her compositions won several prizes.
Compositions
PIANO
Numerous pieces incl.:
Cadets on review (1943)
Humoresque (1949)
Keep in step! (1948)
Plantation dance (1942)
Rosita mia (1948)
VOCAL
Arioso (unison ch) (1948)
Fight for freedom (unison ch) (1945)
Flag of our country (unison ch) (1944)
SACRED
Choral works incl.:
Al Nino Jesus (trio) (1947)
Benediction service, set II (1944)
Lullaby (trio) (1945)
Mass in honor of the blessed Martin de Porres (1945)
Mass in honor of the venerable M. Moye (1948)
Prayer for peace (trio) (1945)
Two Ave Marias (1944)
Ref. 496

MARY GABRIEL, Sister. See O'SHEA, Mary Ellen

MARY STUART, Queen of Scots
B. Linlithgow, December, 1542; d. Fotheringay Castle, Northamptonshire, February 8, 1587. She was the daughter of King James V and Mary of Lorraine. She received her musical education in France, where she married the Dauphin but returned to Scotland on his death. She was subsequently convicted of plotting against Queen Elizabeth I of England and executed. Her songs enjoyed great popularity in her time.
Compositions
VOCAL
Las! en mon doux printemps
Monsieur le Provost des Marchands
Bibliography
Antonia Fraser. *Mary, Queen of Scots.* New York Dell 1969.
Ref. 226, 276, 645

MASINI, Giulia (Sister Angelica Fedele)
Italian pianist, nun, teacher and composer. b. Bologna, July 22, 1821; d. 1840. She became a member of the Philharmonic Academy in 1840.
Compositions
PIANO
Variations
SACRED
Laudate Dominum (4 vces and orch)
Tantum ergo (2 S and org)
Antifona
Ref. 242

MASON, Gladys Amy (pseud. Sydney Kendal)
British teacher and composer. b. Wolverhampton, 1899. She studied composition privately under Drs. Edmunds and Rubbra and taught music in schools.
Compositions
ORCHESTRA
Piano concerto
Prelude and fugue (str orch)
CHAMBER
Two vignettes (ww qrt)
Suite (ob and pf)
Prelude and fugue (org; also pf)
VOCAL
Cantata (mix-ch, pf and strs)
Choral pieces
Songs
Ref. 94, 490

MASON, Margaret C.
American harpsichordist, pianist, lecturer and composer. b. New Market, IA, November 19, 1901; d. February 27, 1971. She obtained her D.Mus. from the New England Conservatory. Her teachers included Stuart Mason, conductor of the People's Symphony Orchestra of Boston, whom she married in 1925; Frederick S. Converse (composition); Lazare-Levy (piano) and Georges Caussade (counterpoint), both in Paris. She lectured in the piano, the harpsichord, harmony, counterpoint and music at the New England Conservatory for 40 years and taught harmony at Longy School, Cambridge for 7 years. After her husband's death she moved to Portland, OR.
Compositions
PIANO
Cadenza to the Haydn piano concerto (2 pf, 8 hands)
Three pops pieces (2 pf, 4 hands)
Orientalia, pieces based on Japanese, Korean and Chinese melodies
ARRANGEMENTS
Korea through western ears, Korean folk tunes
Publications
Keyboard Harmony. For piano students.
Ref. 40, 347, 374

MASON, Marilyn May
American organist, teacher and composer. b. Alva, OK, June 28, 1925. She attended the University of Southern California in 1943 and obtained her B.Mus. in 1946 and M.Mus. in 1947 from the University of Michigan. In 1946 she received the Albert A. Stanley medal for outstanding music scholarship and achievement from the University of Michigan. She studied privately under Professor Daniel Huffman at Stillwater in 1942, Dr. Clarence Dickinson at the Union Theological Seminary, New York in 1943 and Dr. Palmer Christian at Ann Arbor from 1944 to 1947. She went to France to study the organ under Maurice Durufle and composition under Nadia Boulanger (q.v.) in 1948. Marilyn made numerous concert appearances as an organist and is a member of ASCAP.
Compositions
CHAMBER
Sonnet and dance (cl and strs) (1946)
String quartet (1948)
Sonatina (pf) (1945)
Three pieces (org) (1946)
Ref. 496

MASONER, Elizabeth L. (Betty)
American percussionist, lecturer and composer. b. Bemidji, MN, May 22, 1927. She studied under Edgar B. Gangware at Bemidji State College, obtaining her B.S. in 1948. She taught in schools until 1973 and then became visiting lecturer in percussion at Bemidji College.
Compositions
CHAMBER
Cymbal solo No. 1 (cmbs and pf)
Trio (perc ens)
Ref. 142

MASSARENGHI (Mazzarenghi), Paola
Italian composer. b. Parma, ca. 1585.
Compositions
SACRED
Quando spiega l'insegna al sommo padre, madrigal in Frater Arcangelo Gherardini, Primo Libro de' Madrigali a 5 voci (Ferrara: Vittorio Baldini, 1585)
Ref. 105, 157, 653

MASSART, Louise Aglae (nee Masson)
French pianist, teacher and composer. b. Paris, June 10, 1827; d. Paris, June 26, 1887. She studied at the Paris Conservatoire under Coche in 1838 and Adam in 1839. She was elected professor as successor to Louise Farrenc (q.v.) at the Conservatoire in 1875. She taught Roger-Miclos and Clothilde Kloberg. She wrote piano pieces and arrangements for the violin and the piano.
Ref. 226, 276

MASSEY, Celeste de Longpre. See HECKSCHER, Celeste de Longpre

MASSON, Carol Foster
20th-century composer.
Composition
CHAMBER
March of the buffoons (fl and pf) (Southern Music, 1978)
Ref. 185

MASSON, Elizabeth
British contralto, teacher and composer. b. Scotland, 1806; d. London, January 9, 1865. She was a pupil of Mrs. Henry Smart in England and of Giuditta Pasta in Italy. She sang at the Ancient Concerts and with the Philharmonic during a career of about 12 years. She revived forgotten works of Purcell, Handel, Pergolesi, Gluck, Mozart and others. In 1839 she founded the Royal Society of Female Musicians in London. After retiring from performing she devoted her time to teaching and composing.
Compositions
VOCAL
Original Jacobite songs (1839)
Set of vocal exercises (1855)
Song (poets incl. Scott and Adelaide Proctor)
Twelve songs by Byron (1843)
Twelve songs for the classical vocalist, in 24 parts (1st series, 1845; 2nd series, 1860)
Numerous arrangements
Ref. 6, 8, 226, 276, 646

MASSON, Louise Aglae. See MASSART, Louise Aglae

MASSUMOTO, Kikuko
Japanese pianist, lecturer and composer. b. Tokyo, February 2, 1937. Her mother was her first piano teacher, later she attended the Toho-Gakuen University, where her teachers were Minao Shibata (composition), Saduo Bekka (harmony and counterpoint), Yoshiro Irino (theory) and Hideo Saito (ensemble). She studied ethnomusicology at the University of Tokyo and then lectured at the Toho-Gakuen School. She is a member of the Contemporary Music Society of Japan and of the Society for Research in Asiatic Music. DISCOGRAPHY.
Compositions
CHAMBER
Chaos (koto, Gagaku-Japanese court music and str ens) (1975)
Iro-Aya (koto and str ens) (1979)
Four scenes (cham ens) (1963)
Kaiko (2 rec and 2 shakuhachi) (1974)
Constellation (mandolin ens) (1977)
Encounter (rec and shakuhachi) (1974)
Trio (rec, vla d'amore and hpcd) (1978)
Twelve tableaux (2 pf, 3 players) (1972)
Improvisation (cimbalom) (1968)
Pastorale (rec) (1973) (Zenon Music)
Roei, ancient Japanese aria (vla d'amour) (1976) (Japanese Federation of Composers)
VOCAL
Songs incl.:
Good night
Parting
Song of Arabia
Three songs from medieval Japan: Aware; Hayashi; Shi-te-ten (S and pf) (1980) (comm Hiroko Asaoka)
Three songs of the seashore (1959)
Vocalise (S and shakuhachi) (1980)
Publications
Gagaku: Court Music in Japan. 1968.
Ref. composer, 622

MASTERS, Juan (pseud. of Juanita Eames)
20th-century American concert pianist, lecturer and composer. b. Chicago, March 15. She showed an early interest in music and played by ear from the age of three. At high school she wrote her class song. She won a scholarship to the American Conservatory and subsequently attended the University of Chicago, studying for her B.M. and then her M.A. She toured for several seasons in Chautauqua during her teens and then made appearances as a soloist. Her first opus was published in 1924. A program of her works was given at the Illinois House Auditorium, Century of Progress, on October 14, 1934, sponsored by professional women of Chicago. She is a faculty member of the American Conservatory, Chicago.

Compositions
ORCHESTRA
Piano concerto
PIANO
Butterfly waltz
By a rippling stream
Chapel bells
Espagnol
In an oriental bazaar
Japanese suite incl.: Little Plum Blossom; Nono-san; Under a Japanese parasol
Teaching method
VOCAL
Numerous songs
Ref. 39, 40, 292, 347

MATES Vega
Chilean composer. b. 1880; d. 1937. She composed folk music.
Ref. 172

MATEU, Maria Cateura
20th-century Spanish pianist, teacher and composer. She taught the piano, theoretical subjects and composition at the Barcelona Conservatory
Compositions
CHAMBER
Trio (vln, vlc and pf)
PIANO
Sonata
Suite
VOCAL
Canciones en forma de canon (vces and pf)
Coleccion de canciones infantiles
Coleccion de canciones populares
Publications
La Formacion Musical. 3 vols. Clivis.
Carrillon, work on pre-school music education. V. Vives.
Musica para Todos los Ciclos. Teachers' and students books.
Ref. ICW

MATEVOSIAN, Ariaks Surenovna
Soviet pianist, lecturer and composer. b. Rostov-on-the-Don, July 31, 1941. In 1964 she graduated from the Moscow Conservatory having studied composition under A.I. Khachaturian and the piano under V.K. Merzhanov. She lectured at the Rostov Institute of Arts from 1964 and at the Teachers' Training College in the same city from 1975.
Compositions
ORCHESTRA
Symphony No. 1 (to commemorate 100th anniversary of Lenin's birth) (1970)
Symphony No. 2 (1974)
Piano concerto (1971)
Overture (1973)
CHAMBER
String quartet No. 1 (1965)
String quartet No. 2 (1968)
Piano trio (1964)
Sonata (vln and pf) (1970)
Sonata (vln) (1976)
PIANO
Chasy staroi ratushi (1965)
Doroga k Shopenu (1965)
Olshanski prelud (1965)
Three miniatures (1960)
Zamok shilion, fonta zeleny, vitrazh (1972)
VOCAL
Odessa of the 20th-century, choral suite (N. Skrebov) (1967)
Ballada o kolokole (A. Rogachev) (vce and pf) (1972)
Romances: Dorogi stranstvii (A. Garnakerian) (vce and pf) (1972)
Smezhnye grani, choral suite (A. Akhmatova, M. Tsvetayeva, S. Kaputikian) (1975)
Arrangements of Armenian folk songs
THEATRE
Vozvyshenie Andreya Rubleva, play (A. Rogachev) (1973)
Ref. 21

MATHEWS (Matthews) Blanche Dingley Moore
20th-century American teacher and composer. b. Auburn ME. She composed piano pieces and songs.
Bibliography
Barrel, Edgar. *Notable Musical Women. Etude*, November, 1929.
Ref. 40, 347

MATHIESON, Ann Emily
British/Australian composer. b. Westcliff-On-Sea, England, June 6, 1919. She moved to Australia in 1949. Her carol was performed at the Sydney Opera House, 1979. PHOTOGRAPH.
Compositions
VOCAL
Songs
SACRED
Jesus Boy was born today, carol (1979)
Other carols
Ref. composer

MATHIEU, Emilie
19th-century French composer. Her operetta was performed in Paris.
Composition
OPERETTA
Une heure de liberte (composer) (1883)
Ref. 431

MATHIS, Judy M.
American percussionist, arranger, band director and composer. b. Bisbee, AZ, October 23, 1939. She holds a B.S. (music education) from McMurry College, Abilene. She played with the Atulene Symphony Orchestra for twelve years from the age of eleven; from 1955 to 1957 she was All-State percussionist and in 1957 All-American percussionist. Her first compositions were published when she was fifteen and she received awards in 1964 and 1973. In 1974 she was awarded a gold medal in Mexico.
Compositions
BAND
Twenty-four pieces
CHAMBER
Impressionato (perc)
Ref. 77, 146

MATJAN, Vida
Yugoslav pianist, teacher and composer. b. Ljubljana, May 6, 1896. She completed her piano studies under E. Hajek at the Music School in Belgrade. Although Vida is Slovenian, most of her music is influenced by the music of Montenegro. She was principal of the Kotor (Montenegro) Music School and also taught at the Music School in Cetinje.
Compositions
PIANO
Miniatures
VOCAL
Klinika lutaka
Vucko
Ref. 109

MATOS, A. de
Brazilian concert pianist and composer. b. Rio de Janeiro, ca. 1820; d. Rio de Janeiro, ca. 1880. She was well known as a pianist in her home town.
Compositions
PIANO
Album de jovem brasileira
Waltz
Ref. 349

MATRAS, Maude
20th-century American composer.
Composition
ORCHESTRA
Ballade, op. 8 (vln and orch) (Galaxy)
Ref. 280

MATTEI, Beatrice
18th-century Italian composer.
Composition
THEATRE
Il gefte, drama (Florence: 1743)
Ref. 128, 431

MATTFELD, Marie
19th-century composer.
Compositions
PIANO
At the festival (4 hands) (Fischer)
SACRED
Mass in honour of St. Cecilia (mix-ch and orch) (Fischer)
Mass in honour of St. Joseph (2 or 4 vces and orch) (Fischer)
Come Gracious Spirit (mix-ch) (Fischer)
O salutaris (mix-ch) (Fischer)
Vespers and magnificat, 5 psalms (mix-ch) (Fischer)
All praise to him (Bar) (Fischer)
Almighty Father (S and vln) (Fischer)
Ave Maria (S and vln) (Fischer)
Come Holy Spirit (vce and pf) (Fischer)
Evening blessing (vce and pf) (Fischer)
God is our refuge (vce and vln) (Fischer)
O God, our help (A and pf) (Fischer)
Salve Regina (S and vln) (Fischer)
Teach us, O Lord (vce and pf) (Fischer)
To a mind worn and weary (vce and pf) (Fischer)
Veni creator (vce and pf) (Fischer)
While Thee I seek (vce and pf) (Fischer)
Ref. 297

MATTHEIS-BOGNER, Helga. See MATTHEISS-BOEGNER, Helga

MATTHEISS-BOEGNER, Helga
20th-century German composer. She studied under Phillippine Schick (q.v.).
Compositions
VOCAL
Songs (composer's father, Josef Boegner, pseud. Irmin Born)
ELECTRONIC
Mystische impressionen (elec org and pf)
Der weg zum meer (elec org and pf)
Ref. 448

MATTHEWS, Blanche Dingley Moore. See MATHEWS, Blanche Dingley

MATTHEWS, Dorothy White
American pianist, violinist, music critic, teacher and composer. b. Yale, OK, June 29, 1918. She was a violinist with the Midland-Odessa Symphony Orchestra. She holds a B.S. from Texas Women's University and a certificate from the National Music Teachers' Association. She had her own weekly radio program in Tyler, TX, in 1936 and reviewed music and books for *American Music Teacher*. She composed several works.
Ref. 77

MATTHISON-HANSEN, Nanny Hedwig Christiane (Mrs. Melbye)
Danish pianist and composer. b. Copenhagen, February 26, 1830; d. 1915. The daughter of the organist and composer Hans Matthison-Hansen, she distinguished herself as a talented performing artist and married the artist Professor Wilhelm Melbye in 1854. She composed songs.
Ref. 20, 95

MATTHYSSENS, Marie (nee Scheywyck)
Belgian pianist, singer and composer. b. Antwerp, 1861. She studied harmony under Ergo and Blockx.
Composition
OPERA
Le Sire de Ducucu
Ref. 307, 398

MATTULLATH, Alice
20th-century American composer.
Composition
VOCAL
Cradle song, based on Kreisler's Caprice Viennois (vce and pf) (1915) (Ball)
Ref. 63

MATUSZCZAK, Bernadetta
Polish pianist and composer. b. Torun, March 10, 1937. She studied the piano under Irena Kurpisz-Stefanowa; theory of music under Z. Sitowski at the State Music College in Poznan and composition under T. Szeligowski and K. Sikorski at the State Music College in Warsaw graduating in 1958 and 1964. In 1968 she studied under Nadia Boulanger (q.v.) in Paris.
DISCOGRAPHY. PHOTOGRAPH.
Compositions
ORCHESTRA
Per strumenti (trp, b-cl, perc and str orch) (1969)
Contrasts (1970)
CHAMBER
Lieder ohne Worte (cham ens) (1978)
Musica da camera (3 fl and perc) (1967) (prize, Competition Jeunesses Musicales, 1967)
Canto solenne per strumenti (1965) (prize, Young Composers, 1967)
Partita (vln and pf) (1979)
Aphorisms (fl) (1975)
Quasi sonata (pf) (1963)
VOCAL
Elegy for a Polish Boy (S, A, 2 w-ch and orch) (1974)
Liebestotenlieder (R.M. Rilke) (Bar and orch) (1971)
Epigrams (J. Kochanowski) (m-ch a-cap) (1980)
Feuer auf der Wladwiese (S, A and inst ens) (1979)
Gitanjali (R. Tagore) (male speaker, S, fl and bells) (1963)
Invocazione (10 vces, fl, d-b, theorbo and gong) (1968)
Poesie de chambre (M. Sabathir-Levegue) (speaker, b-cl, vib, 2 cmb and tam-tam) (1968)
SACRED
Septem tubae (Apocalypse of St. John) (mix-ch, org and orch) (1966) (prize, G. Fitelberg Composers' Competition, 1966)
Canticum canticorum (S, Bar, B and orch) (1979)
Salmi per uno gruppo di cinque, psalms of David (1972)
OPERA
Apocalypsis, radio opera (m-S, Bar, recitors, 2 ch and orch) (1977)
Chamber drama (T.S. Eliot) (Bar, speaker, inst ens and tape) (1965)
Diary of a Fool, monodrama (after M. Gogol) (soloists and cham ens) (1976)
Heloises Mysterium, in 7 scenes (from historical sources of 12th-century) (1975)
Humanae Voces, opera-oratorio in 1 act (composer, from literary fragments) (1971)
Juliet and Romeo, chamber opera in 5 scenes (Shakespeare) (1967)
Prometheus (Aeschylus) (1981)
ELECTRONIC
Canzone (S and S on tape; also 2 S, cor anglais and bongos) (1970)
Ref. composer, 70, 189, 563

MATVEYEVA, Novella
Soviet poetess, singer and composer. b. 1934. She began to compose songs as a child. She wrote her own lyrics and many of her verses and songs were played in concert and on the radio and television.
DISCOGRAPHY.
Compositions
VOCAL
The Adriatic sea (vce and gtr)
Following the gypsies (vce and gtr)
Foot-prints (vce and gtr)
Gypsy-woman (vce and gtr)
The homeless brownie (vce and gtr)
The horizon (vce and gtr)
How long our journey is (vce and gtr)
The little ship (vce and gtr)
Little star (vce and gtr)
Missouri (vce and gtr)
The organ-grinder (vce and gtr)
Red Indian song (vce and gtr)
Road song (vce and gtr)
A soldier rode through the forest (vce and gtr)
Sorceress (vce and gtr)
We dance this song (vce and gtr)
Publications
Collections of poems incl.:
The Little Ship. 1963.
Lyrics. 1961.
Selected Lyrics. 1964.
The Soul of Things. 1966.
The Swallows' School. 1973.
Ref. composer, 563

MATZEN, Margarete (nee Schottensack)
German composer. b. Kaukehmen, August 1, 1887. She composed dance music and songs.
Ref. 226

MAUD DE BAUR, Constance. See BAUR, Constance Maud de

MAUR, Sophie

German pianist, teacher and composer. b. July 10, 1877. She studied the piano under Albert Eibenschuetz and Max van der Sandt in Cologne and theory and composition under Max Regerin Leipzig. She taught in Cologne and was a member of the Reichsverband deutscher Tonkuenstler und Musiklehrer and the Genossenschaft deutscher Tonsetzer. In 1929 she became musical advisor to the government.

Compositions
CHAMBER
Bilder aus Oesterreich (str qrt)
Piano pieces
VOCAL
Songs
Ref. 70, 111, 226

MAURICE, Mrs. J. See HOFFRICHTER, Bertha Chaitkin

MAURICE, Paule

French lecturer and composer. b. Paris, September 29, 1910; d. Paris, August 18, 1967. She studied under the Gallon brothers and H. Busser and taught sight reading at the Paris Conservatoire from 1943. DISCOGRAPHY.

Compositions
ORCHESTRA
Symphony (1937)
Tableaux de Provence (a-sax and orch; also a-sax and pf) (1954)
Two piano concertos (1950, 1955)
CHAMBER
Volio (sax) (1967)
PIANO
Nine pieces (2 pf) (1955)
Melodies (1939)
Preludes (1942)
VOCAL
Cantata (1938)
BALLET
Cosmorama (1954)

Publications
Treatise on Harmony. With her husband.
Ref. 9, 76, 563, 622

MAURICE-JACQUET, H.

French concert pianist, accompanist, conductor, teacher and composer. b. St. Mande, March 18, 1886; d. New York, June 29, 1954. She made her piano debut at the age of nine and later studied at the Paris Conservatoire. She was the founder of the Union des Femmes Artistes Musiciennes, Paris and a teacher at the School of Vocal Arts, New York, the Academy of Vocal Arts, Philadelphia and the American Conservatory of Music, Drama and Dance, New York. She toured Europe as a pianist and conductor and was an accompanist to Grace Moore. She was awarded the French Legion of Honor.

Compositions
ORCHESTRA
American symphony
BALLET
Les danses des chez nous
OPERA
Messaoula
Romanitza
OPERETTA
Le petite dactyl
Le poilu
Ref. 142

MAURY, Renaud (Mme.)

19th-century French composer. She studied at the Paris Conservatoire under Bazin and Cesar Franck, winning first prizes for fugue and composition.

Compositions
ORCHESTRA
Symphonic fantasy (prize, Society of Composers, Paris)
Jeanne d'Arc
Scene lyrique
Ref. 226, 276

MAXIM, Florence

American pianist, playwright and composer. b. Brooklyn, NY, June 4, 1873. She studied the piano at the New England Conservatory, graduating in 1895.

Compositions
OPERETTA
April fool (1898)
Ten teddy bears (1907)
MISCELLANEOUS
Ten little fancies (1901)
The holidays (1902)
Ref. 433

MAXWELL, Elsie

20th-century American composer.

Compositions
CHAMBER
Pieces (vla and pf)
VOCAL
Songs incl.:
Laughing eyes
OPERA
One opera
Ref. 292

MAXWELL, Helen Purcell

American editor and composer. b. Vincenes, IA, December 20, 1901. She obtained her B.M. from De Pauw University School of Music. She was a member of ASCAP and the National League of American Pen Women. From 1952 to 1954 she was chairlady of the fine arts department, Federation of Women's Clubs. She was editor and co-owner of the newspaper *Naperville Clarion*.

Compositions
VOCAL
Songs incl.:
All my love, dear
Autumn ballet
Campus days
Give us a campus
Hawaiian holiday
I am a little Christmas tree
Let's sing to victory
Toast to music (Gamble Hinged)
Wheels a-rolling
Ref. 39, 40, 190, 347

MAXWELL, Jacqueline Perkinson

American pianist, arranger, teacher and composer. b. Denver, September 16, 1932. She studied under George Kuhlman in Brazil; Walter Keller at the University of New Mexico and Max di Julio and George Lynn at Loretto Heights College. She teaches the piano, composition, transcription and orchestration at the Golden Music Studio and the piano and theory privately.

Compositions
ORCHESTRA
Humoreske
BAND
Chipmunks
CHAMBER
Jubilo (2 fl and pf)
PIANO
Autumn suite (2 pf)
Four frustrations
VOCAL
Over 30 art songs (composer)
SACRED
Psalm 121 (mix-ch) (1984)
Psalm 98
Ref. 142

MAY, Florence

English concert pianist and composer. b. London, February 6, 1865; d. London, June 29, 1923. She initially studied the piano under her father, Edward Collett May, organist and composer and then under Clara Schumann (q.v.). Through Clara's influence, Brahms accepted Florence as a pupil and she became a successful interpreter of his music. After some years in Germany she returned to London about 1873 and continued her

harmony studies under her father and Sir George Alexander Macfarren and gave concerts and recitals. She toured as a concert pianist in Germany and Austria between 1890 and 1896 and in Britain. She edited a collection of pieces for the harpsichord by old masters, including Henry Symonds.
Compositions
PIANO
Bouree
Three mazurkas
Waltzes, op. 4
VOCAL
Choruses (w-vces)
Six songs (English and German)
SACRED
Benedictus (1878)
Osanna (1878)
Ref. 6, 276, 347

MAYADAS, Priya

American composer. b. Florida, 1970.
Composition
CHAMBER
String quartet (prize, 28th annual Student Composers' Competition, 1980)
Ref. AWC News IV 1980

MAYER, Elise-Minelli. See FILIPOWICZ, Elise-Minelli

MAYER, Emilie

German sculptress and composer. b. Friedland, Mecklenburg, May 14, 1821; d. Berlin, April 10, 1883. She received her first piano lessons from the organist, Driver and when her talent became apparent she went to Stettin and became a pupil of Carl Loewe. Her first compositions were dances and variations. In 1847 she went to Berlin and studied fugue and counterpoint under B.A. Marx and orchestration under Wieprecht. Three years later she gave the first concert of her own works, consisting of a concert overture; a string quartet; a setting of Psalm 118 for chorus and orchestra; two symphonies and some piano solos, which scored great success. For these and other compositions she was presented with the gold medal of art by Queen Elizabeth of Prussia. In 1886 she traveled to Vienna and was received by Archduchess Sophie. Three months later she returned to Berlin where her instrumental works were frequently performed and acclaimed. In Munich she was made an honorary member of the Philharmonic Society. She later became co-director of the Opera Academy in Berlin. Besides composing, she had some success as a sculptor using the unusual material of white bread. Pieces of her work were in royal collections and she received a gold medal from the Queen of Prussia for a vase.
Compositions
ORCHESTRA
Seven symphonies
Piano concerto
Faust overture, op. 46
Twelve concert overtures (large orch)
CHAMBER
Two quintets
Twelve piano quartets
Twelve string quartets incl. op. 4 (Simrock)
Ten piano yrios incl. op. 13 in D and op. 16 (Challier)
Eight sonatas incl. ops. 17 and 21 (vln and pf)
Nocturne, op. 48 (vln and pf)
Sonatas (vlc and pf) (Bote)
Seven violin solos from the ballet Papillon (Gutheil)
PIANO
Pieces incl.:
Allemande fantastique, op. 29
Impromptu, op. 44 (Bote)
Mazurka, op. 33
Tonwellen, waltz, op. 30 (Simon)
Ungaraise, op. 31 (Simon)
Valse, op. 32 (Simon)
VOCAL
Approx. 40 part songs
Sixty-five songs (4 vces)
One hundred and thirty songs
SACRED
Psalm 118 (ch and orch)
OPERETTA
Die Fischerin
Le Tonnelier de Nuremberg
Ref. 70, 105, 121, 260, 276, 297, 307, 347

MAYER, Lise Maria

Austrian pianist, conductor, professor and composer. b. Vienna, May 22, 1894. She studied the piano under Vera Schapira and Richard Robert, theory under Josef B. Voerster and conducting and composition under Franz Schaik, Franz Schreker and R. Stoehr. She became professor at the New Conservatory in Vienna.
Compositions
ORCHESTRA
Works incl.:
Symphony
CHAMBER
Quintet (pf, vln, vla, vlc and sax)
String quartet
Piano trio
PIANO
Pieces incl.:
Varieté exotique
VOCAL
Fantasia sinfonica (T, mix-ch and orch)
Symphonic poem (mix-ch and orch)
Songs (vces and orch)
Other songs
OPERA
One opera
Ref. 44, 94, 105, 111, 226

MAYFIELD, Alpha C.

20th-century American composer of choral works.
Ref. 40, 347

MAYHEW, Grace (Stults, Grace Mayhew)

20th-century American composer.
Compositions
VOCAL
My little girl (vce and pf)
The shoogy-shoo (vce and pf)
SACRED
Guide me, O Thou Great Jehovah
Ref. 276, 292

MAYSUNAH

7th-century Arabian poetess and songstress. She was the Bedouin wife of Mu'awiyah who was Caliph from 661 to 680 and the mother of the Caliph Yazid I (680 to 683). A song of hers was heard by Sir Richard Burton and described in his 'Personal Narrative to Al-Madinah and Meccah'. It describes her longing for the desert tents and the wilds, to which her husband having overheard her song, sent her with Yazid. She only returned to Damascus after the death of her husband. Her songs were very popular with the Bedouin.
Ref. 171, 491

MAZELL, Helen Roberts

19th-century French composer.
Compositions
VOCAL
Songs incl.:
Le chant du marin
Les deux étoiles
Les lunettes
La rose blanche
Ref. 276, 347

MAZOUROVA, Jarmila

Czech cimbalom player, pianist, recorder player, lecturer and composer. b. Prostejov, December 5, 1941. She studied composition at the Janacek Academy of Arts and Music in Brno under V. Petrzelka and then Ja Kapr, graduating in 1963. In 1965 she graduated from the piano class of the Conservatory of Brno. She teaches the piano at the Brno School of Music. DISCOGRAPHY. PHOTOGRAPH.
Compositions
ORCHESTRA
Symphonic dialogue (pf and orch) (1963)
Four compositions (1962)
CHAMBER
Autumn suite (pf and vln ens) (1966)
Ballad and burlesque (brass qnt) (1973)
Andante e vivo (cl, vln and cimbalom) (1971)
Inventions (fl, vln and cimbalon) (1964)

Summer aquarelles (3 trp; also cl) (1965)
Trio (ob, vlc and pf) (1961)
Two moods (hn, trb and pf) (1967)
Vietnamese ballad (xyl, cimbalom and pf) (1973)
Barcarola and tune (fl in F and pf) (1979)
Duettina (fl in F and vln) (1980)
Fantasy and scherzo (vln and pf) (1965)
Instructive compositions (cl and pf) (1966)
Nocturne and dance (vlc and pf) (1968)
Three capriccios (vln and pf) (1962)
Winter preludes (fl in F and pf) (1984)
Prelude and toccatinas (cimbalom) (1969)
Suite (vla) (1970)
PIANO
Dance (4 hands) (1972)
Miniatures (1970)
Sonata (1961)
VOCAL
The little dead girl (chil-ch) (1961)
Welcome to the world (w-ch and pf) (1962)
Without wings (w-ch) (1966)
Come (M. Prochazkova) (S and gtr) (1982)
Three songs (Jiri Zacek) (S and pf) (1979)
BALLET
The Tale of the Golden Fish, in 9 scenes (1969)
THEATRE
African Pictures, children's musical (1971)
Ref. composer, 563

MAZZUCATO or MAZZUCATO-YOUNG, Elisa. See YOUNG, Eliza

McALISTER, Mabel
Australian composer. b. 1905.
Compositions
CHAMBER
Gavotte (ob and pf) (1963)
Highland sunset (ob and pf) (1963)
PIANO
Copy cat (1960) (Chappell & Co)
Dream waltz (1960) (Chappell)
Holiday in Spain (1960) (Chappell)
Leap frog (1960) (Chappell)
Spooks (1960) (Chappell)
Thistledown waltz (1960) (Chappell)
Trip-toe (1960) (Chappell)
VOCAL
Coronation, anthem (mix-ch) (1963)
The most important guest (Rubina Hay Stephens) (ch; also vce and org or pf) (1963)
Ref. 440, 444, 446

McALLISTER, Rita (Margaret Notman)
Scottish pianist, lecturer, musicologist and composer. b. Mossend, Lanarkshire, March 6, 1946. She studied the piano under J. Wight Henderson of the Royal Scottish Academy of Music and composition under Anthony Hedges from 1960 to 1963 and Frederick Rimmer. She studied music at the University of Glasgow from 1962 to 1966, when she went to Cambridge and obtained a doctorate for her thesis on the operas of Prokofiev. After visiting the Soviet Union for research, her musicological activities were concerned with modern opera and music in Poland and the Soviet Union. She lectured in composition and aspects of 20th-century music at the University of Edinburgh; was engaged in work on a biography of Prokofiev and was a contributor to *The International Encyclopaedia of Music and Musicians*. She composed a string quartet, piano pieces, a cantata, orchestral song cycle and songs.
Ref. 74

McBURNEY, Mona
Composition
ORCHESTRA
A northern ballad (pf and orch) (Novello)
Ref. 473

McCANNS, Mrs. See DUBOIS, Shirley Graham

McCARTHY, Charlotte
20th-century composer. She composed choral works and songs.
Ref. 40, 347

McCLEARY, Fiona
American pianist and composer. b. Sanderstead, England, January 29, 1900. She studied under Myra Hess, Harriet Cohen, Ralph Vaughn Williams and Arnold Bax at the Royal Academy of Music and also at the Matthay Piano School, London. She became a United States citizen in 1932.
Compositions
ORCHESTRA
Overture
Serenata (small orch)
CHAMBER
String quartet
Melody (vlc)
Trois melodies (vlc)
Violin sonata
PIANO
Pieces incl.:
Whispering waltz
Ref. 39, 41, 142, 226, 280, 347

McCLEARY, Mary Gilkeson
American organist, pianist, choral conductor and composer. b. Sellersville, PA, August 17, 1920. She gained her B.Mus., valedictorian, from Westminster Choir College, Princeton in 1941 and is an associate of the American Guild of Organists. For 25 years she was organist and choir director at Naugatuck Congregational Church, United Church of Christ. She won a composition prize from the American Guild of English Handbell Ringers, 1976.
Compositions
CARILLON
Arioso
Ballade in C-Minor
Fanfare for bells
Fantasy
Festival overture
Pastorale and ostinato on Psalm 23
Praise and alleluyas
Psalm 26
Ref. 643

McCOLLIN, Frances (pseuds. Alfred, Atticus, Awbury, Canonicus, Garrett, Karlton, Mayfair, Pastor, Pilgrim, Selin, Wendel, Wheelwright)
American organist, pianist, choral conductor, lecturer and composer. b. Philadelphia, PA, October 24, 1892; d. Philadelphia, February 25, 1960. As a result of an eye infection at birth she became blind at the age of five. Her father, a lawyer and violinist and one of the founders of the Philadelphia Orchestra was her first music teacher. She was educated at the Pennsylvania Institute for the instruction of the blind, where she studied the piano and the organ under Miss Small and David Wood and composition under Drs. William Gilchrist and Alexander Matthews. She wrote 333 compositions of which 93 were published during her lifetime. Her orchestral works were performed by the Philadelphia Orchestra, the Indianapolis Symphony, the Robin Dell Orchestra, the Polish Warsaw Philharmonic and the People's Symphony of Boston. Her works were broadcast on several radio programs and during her lifetime there were over 500 performances of her works and she won nineteen national awards. She lectured at the Philadelphia Orchestra lecture sessions and conducted several girls' choirs. In 1951 she received the Distinguished Daughter of Pennsylvania award. She was a member of the National Federation of Music Clubs, ASCAP and ACA. Her printed scores and manuscripts are housed in the music department and the Fleisher Collection of the free library of Philadelphia. PHOTOGRAPH.
Compositions
ORCHESTRA
Madrigal (fl and orch) (1941)
Variations (pf and orch) (1942)
Christmas poem (1940)
I wonder as I wander, chorale prelude (also org) (1945)
Nocturne (1940)
Nursery rhyme suite (1940)
Scherzo and Fugue in C-Minor (1946)
Suite in F (1934)
Works (school orch)

CHAMBER
Suite in F for string sextet (1932)
Diversion (wind qnt) (1943)
Piano quintet in F-Major (1927)
Theme and variations (ww qnt) (1954)
Ye watchers and ye holy ones, chorale prelude (pf qnt) (1938) (comm Society of Ancient Instruments)
Fantasia for string quartet (1935)
String quartet in F-Major (1920)
Pavane (org and hp)
In fairyland suite (vln) (1929) (Theodore Presser)
Spanish dance (vlc) (1942)

ORGAN
Duetto
All glory laud and honor (1941) (Ricordi)
Berceuse (1916) (O. Ditson)
Canzonetta (1921) (Boston Music)
Cherubs at play (1926) (H.W. Gray)
Christmas fantasia
Fantasia in D-Minor
Now all the woods are sleeping, chorale prelude (1949) (Ricordi)
Pastorale
Prelude and variations on a chorale
Rondo (1920) (Ditson)

PIANO
August (4 hands) (1937)
Cuckoo clock (4 hands)
Duettino (1935)
Letting the old cat die (4 hands) (1937)
May pole dance (4 hands) (1940)
Summer afternoon (4 hands) (1942)
At the court ball, gavotte
Bedtime story (1938)
Berceuse for Barbara
Can't catch me
Chorale prelude on Hatikvah (1952)
Dance for Derek (1946)
Day dreaming (1946)
Doll's ball (1939)
Dripping faucet (1948) (Galaxy Music)
Gigue
Gypsy dance (1904) (G. Schirmer)
Merry Marita (1940)
Minuet (1940) (Harold Flammer)
Prelude in A-Flat-Major
Prelude in A-Minor
Prelude in C-Minor
Prelude in D
Prelude in D-Flat
Prelude in E-Minor (1946)
Promenade
Rain on the leaves (1938)
Rondo (also org)
Sarabande
Sicilienne (1937)
Sonatina (1951)
Springboard (1938)
Water wheel (1939)
What time is it? musical puzzle
Pieces for children

VOCAL
Going up to London, cantata (1935) (C. Fischer)
June, cantata (Lowell) (1922) (Schmidt)
Singing leaves, cantata (Lowell) (1918) (Ditson)
Sleeping beauty, cantata (Tennyson) (1917) (Ditson)
Children's cantata
Ring out wild bells (ch and orch) (Tennyson)
Suburban sketches (ch and orch) (1936)
Echoes of the valley (ch a-cap) (Butting) (1945)
The fly and the flea (ch a-cap) (1932) (C. Birchard)
The four winds (Luders) (m-vces) (1932) (H.W. Gray)
Go not, happy day (ch a-cap) (Tennyson) (1939) (J. Fischer)
God's miracle of May (ch a-cap) (Sherman) (1919) (Schmidt)
Grasshopper green (ch a-cap) (Harrington) (1945) (H.T. Fitzsimmons)
In bleak midwinter (ch a-cap) (Rossitti) (1933)
In the hammock (ch a-cap) (composer) (1949)
It was a lover and his lass (Shakespeare) (ch a-cap) (1951) (Ditson)
Love took me softly by the hand (ch a-cap) (1913)
Mary sat at even (ch a-cap) (1931) (J. Fischer)
May madrigal (ch a-cap) (1926) (Schmidt)
Motto for Philadelphia Music Club (ch a-cap) (Brainerd) (1912)
My garden (ch a-cap) (Parker) (1936) (Birchard)
My sweet Sally (ch a-cap) (Nutting) (Schmidt)
Nights of spring, madrigal (ch a-cap) (1919) (Ditson)
Now is the month of Maying (ch a-cap) (Ditson)
O Robin, little Robin (ch a-cap) (1919) (Ditson)
Pack clouds away (ch a-cap) (Haywood) (1942) (Ditson)
Pixy people (Riley) (ch a-cap) (1942) (Schirmer)
Queen Anne's lace (Newton) (ch a-cap) (1940)
A roundelay (ch a-cap) (Permen) (1925) (Ditson)
Snow flakes (ch a-cap) (Morgan) (1919) (Schmidt; Dodge)
Song of four seasons, madrigal (ch a-cap) (Ditson)
Song of spring, madrigal (ch a-cap) (1934) (Ditson)
Spirit of spring (ch a-cap) (Fabbri) (1892) (Schirmer)
Spring in heaven (ch a-cap) (Driscoll) (1931) (MacMillan)
What care I, madrigal (ch a-cap) (Wither) (1923) (Ditson)
When fairies hide their heads (ch a-cap) (Bayley) (1927) (Schmidt)
Whispering dreams (ch a-cap) (Nutting)
Hunting aong (Scott) (m-vces) (1923) (Schmidt)
Ann Hutchinson's exile (Hale) (1949)
Ahkoond of Sivat (Lanigan) (m-vces)
At eventide (1920) (H.W. Gray)
Come live with me and be my love (Marlowe) (1961) (Boosey & Hawkes)
Coming of June (Brand) (1944) (Summy)
Cycle of 3 songs: With weary steps I loiter on; Wild bird; Dear friend (Tennyson) (1921)
Evening song (Lippincott) (1937)
Into the wood my master went (Lanier) (J. Fischer)
Invitation (La Gallienne)
I walked with you (Miller) (1951)
The optimistic frog (m-vces) (1949)
Persian serenade (Taylor) (m-vces) (Schmidt)
Serenade (1943)
Song at midnight (Balm) (1951)
Things of everyday are all so Sweet (Allen) (1913) (Schmidt)
Thou art like unto a flower (1910)
Vagabond song (Carman) (m-vces) (1926) (Schmidt)
Winds of God (Sealeard) (1915) (1st prize, Philadelphia Society of Arts and Letters)
Approximately 80 songs

SACRED
How firm a foundation, cantata
T'was the night before Christmas, cantata (Moore) (1923) (Schmidt)
All my heart this night rejoices (ch a-cap) (Gerhard)
The beatitudes (ch a-cap) (1949)
Behold the Lamb of God (ch a-cap)
Calm on the listening ear of night (ch a-cap) (Sears) (1928) (H.W. Gray)
The children's friend (ch a-cap) (1942)
Christmas carol (Rossetti) (ch a-cap) (1937)
Come hither ye faithful (ch a-cap) (1927, 1936) (Ditson)
Dear Lord and Father of mankind (ch a-cap) (Whittier) (1938) (Galaxy Music)
Eternal God whose power upholds (composer) (ch a-cap)
For all ye saints (ch a-cap) (Haw) (1949)
He is risen (ch a-cap) (1939) (Gray)
The holy birth (ch a-cap) (1930) (Ditson)
Hymn for the Y (ch a-cap) (composer) (1954)
Laus Deo (ch a-cap) (Sherman) (1908)
My peace, I leave with you (ch a-cap) (Dickinson) (1926) (Ditson)
Now the day is over (ch a-cap) (Baring-Gould) (1926) (Gray)
O come and mourn (ch a-cap) (Faber) (1953) (Ditson)
O love that will not let me go (ch a-cap) (Matheson) (1948)
O master let me walk with thee (ch a-cap) (Gladden) (1953)
Owe no man anything save to love one another (ch a-cap) (1919) (Schirmer)
Peace, I leave with you (ch a-cap) (1942) (C. Fischer)
Praise my soul, the king of heaven (ch a-cap)
Prayer (ch a-cap) (1934) (C. Fischer)
Processional hymn (ch a-cap)
Quest of Mary (ch a-cap) (Evans) (1943)
Rejoice the Lord is King (ch a-cap)
Resurrection (ch a-cap) (Peattie) (1927) (Ditson)
Shepherds had an angel (ch a-cap) (Rossetti) (1938)
Shouting sun, spiritual (ch a-cap) (Turner) (1934) (Presser)
Sing alleluia (ch a-cap) (1934) (Schirmer)
Then shall the righteous shine (ch a-cap) (1920) (Gray)
Way of the cross (ch a-cap) (Bonnell) (Ditson)
Awake my soul
Behold the works of the Lord (1942)
Christmas bells (Longfellow) (1947) (Mill Music)
Christmas lullaby (composer) (1937)
Come, my soul, thou must be waking
The cross was his own
Dedication (1953)
Dream of the Christ Child, madrigal (1957) (St. Mary's Press)
Fairest Lord Jesus (1943)
Fantasia on 'O little town of Bethlehem' (Brooks) (1947) (Boosey)
God is our refuge and strength (1922) (Schmidt)
God so loved the World (1914) (Presser)
Hail to the King of Glory, anthem (Rossetti) (1937) (Gray)
How living are the dead (Coates) (1944) (Ditson)

Jubilate Deo (1916) (Ditson)
The Lord is King (1918) (Gray) (Clemson gold medal)
The Lord is my shepherd (vce and org)
Mass for the feast of St. Mark (1918) (Gray)
A new commandment give I unto you (1916) (Ditson)
Nunc dimittis
O day of rest and gladness
O give thanks unto the Lord (1939)
O lamb of God, Agnus Dei (1907) (Presser)
O sing unto the Lord a new Song (1916) (Boston Music)
Once to every man a nation (Lowell)
Prophecy (1944)
Sleep, Holy Babe (Caswell) (1930) (Ditson)
Te Deum (1950)
Welcome happy morning (1940) (Schirmer)
Ye watches and ye holy ones (Riley) (1940) (Birchard)
Hymns and hymn tunes (assorted)

OPERA
King Christmas (Schirmer)

THEATRE
Musical plays for children

Bibliography
Di Medio, Annette. *Frances McCollin*. Metuchen, NJ: Scarecrow Press, in prep, 1987.
Di Medio, Annette. *The McCollin Catalogue*. Doctoral dissertation, Bryn Mawr College, 1985.
Etude. Nov. 1950, pp. 38-40.

Ref. 142, 146, 168, 226, 228, 292, 347, 646

McCOY II, Mrs. John W. See WYETH, Ann

McDOWALL, Cecilia

Compositions
CHAMBER
Six pastiches (fl or ob and pf)

Ref. Blackwell catalogue (Oxford)

McDUFFEE, Mabel Howard

American organist, choral conductor and composer. b. Portland, January 12, 1870; d. August 23, 1954. She studied under Godowski, William Middleschulte, Adolphe Weidig and E.A. Kraft. She was the organist and choir conductor at churches in the Chicago area.

Compositions
ORGAN
Andantino in D
Barcarolle
Romanza and intermezzo (Gamble Hinged)
Toccatina

VOCAL
My heart is calling (vce and pf) (1936)
Springtime (vce and pf) (1936)

SACRED
Abide with me
Glory to God, anthem
It came upon the midnight clear
The Lord's Prayer, anthem
O for a closer walk with God
Out of the depths
Thy love O Lord (composer)

Ref. 374

McFARLAND, Susan. See PARKHURST, Susan

McFARLANE, Jenny

20th-century Australian composer.

Composition
FILM MUSIC
Two hundred years, documentary (1971)

Ref. 442

McGILL, Gwendolen Mary Finlayson

Scottish cellist, celtic harpist, pianist, arranger, teacher and composer. b. Aye, 1910. She attended colleges in Edinburgh, Vienna, Paris, Salzburg and Prades. She taught the piano, the cello and the celtic harp in Scottish schools and performed on all these instruments in Britain and Europe. She won the Townshend gold medal for piano and strings prize at the Edinburgh Festival. She was an arranger and composer for the celtic harp, the piano and the cello.

Ref. 490

McGOWEN, Beatrice. See McGOWAN SCOTT, Beatrice

McGOWAN SCOTT (McGowen), Beatrice

20th-century American composer. She composed piano pieces and songs.

Ref. 260, 347

McILWRAITH, Isa Roberta

American organist, choral conductor, professor and composer. b. Paterson, NJ, May 17, 1909. She obtained her B.A. from Barnard College, Columbia University in 1931 and her M.A. in 1932, where her teachers included Philip James, Daniel Gregory Mason and Douglas Moore. At the Union Theological Seminary she studied under Seth Bingham and at the Juilliard School of Music under Albert Stoessel, becoming a fellow of that school in 1937 and then continued her studies at the Organ Institute, MA, and privately under Car Weinrich and Ernest White. She was awarded various scholarships and was organist in Brooklyn and New York from 1932 to 1938, assistant professor at Holyoke College from 1937 to 1938 and associate professor at the University of Tennessee at Chattanooga from 1938 to 1974. She worked as an organist, choir director and conductor in New Jersey, New York and Chatanooga and wrote articles on musical subjects for professional journals. PHOTOGRAPH.

Compositions
ORGAN
Fughetta
Fugue in A-Minor
O Jesu Christ
Triptych
Uns ist ein Kindlein

VOCAL
Songs incl.:
Green candles
Here awa', there awa' (vce and pf)
It was the wind
My heart's in the highlands (vce and pf)
Vergissmeinnicht

SACRED
Agnus Dei (mix-ch)
Alleluia, sing of gladness (mix-ch)
Appalachian Christmas carol (mix-ch) (New York: H.W. Gray, 1942)
Behold, what manner of love (mix-ch)
Blessed art thou, O Lord God (mix-ch)
Christ, our passover (mix-ch) (1947)
Christians, all rejoice (mix-ch) (1947)
Hosanna to the son of David (mix-ch) (1946)
I know a lovely angel song (mix-ch)
O god, our help (mix-ch)
Prayer for peace (mix-ch)
Unto Thee, O Lord, will I lift up (mix-ch)

Ref. composer, 142

McINTOSH, Diana

20th-century Canadian concert pianist, lecturer and composer. b. Calgary. She became an A.R.C.T in 1957 and obtained the Licentiate of Music, Manitoba in 1961 and her B.Mus. from the University of Manitoba in 1972. Her teachers included Gladys Egbert, Boris Roubakine, Adele Marcus, Alma Brock-Smith, Leonard Isaacs and Robert Black. She has given numerous chamber music concerts and recitals throughout Canada and the United States, including premier performances of the piano and chamber works by Canadian composers. She teaches the piano privately and lectures on music appreciation at the University of Manitoba and has given workshops and lectures on contemporary music at various centers in Canada. She has organized concerts of music by Canadian women composers, of contemporary music and of multimedia works, mainly in Winnipeg. In 1977 she became founder and artistic director of a series of mixed media concerts called Music Inter Alia, featuring 20th-century and particularly Canadian music. All her compositions have been performed in concerts and most of them on CBC radio and television. In 1984 she was elected Woman of the Year in the Arts in Manitoba. PHOTOGRAPH.

Compositions
CHAMBER
Bagatelle (ww qrt) (1978)
Quartett (fl, vln, cl and vlc)
Gulliver (rec, perc and pf) (1981)
Sonograph (ob, rec and bsn) (1980)
Luminaries (fl and pf) (1979)
VOCAL
Colours (mix-ch and fl) (1980)
Eliptosonics (speaker and pf) (1979)
Music at the center (speaker, cl and pf) (1981)
PIANO
Duo (4 hands)
Gradatim ad summum (duet) (1982)
Greening (1978)
Paraphrase No. 1 (1978)
Paraphrase No. 2 (1978)
Prelude and fugue (1972)
THEATRE
Kivioq, puppet theatre (tape) (1982)
ELECTRONIC
Aiby-Aicy-Aidy-Ai (toy pf and amp mouth perc) (1983)
Doubletalk (amp mouth and vce sounds with elec tape) (1983)
Extensions (pf and tape) (1981).
Sound assemblings (pf and elc tape) (1983)
Tea for two at Whipsnade Zoo (rec and elec tape) (1982)
MULTIMEDIA
A different point of view (tape and projections) (1983)
Ref. composer, 622

McINTYRE, Margaret

20th-century Canadian concert violinist, conductor, teacher and composer. b. England. She studied music at the Royal Manchester College of Music and the Cornish School of Music, Seattle. She started her career as a concert violinist and went to Canada in 1930. She performed on radio and in concerts, taught and trained small orchestras and vocal groups.
Compositions
ORCHESTRA
Song of autumn (1935)
Three nocturnes (1949)
Valse in E-Minor (1930)
VOCAL
Songs of the north (S, w-ch and orch) (1950)
Chinese song (1949)
Four songs (1930-1940)
Lost lagoon (1949) (prize, CBC International Service contest)
Ref. 93, 94, 133

McKANN-MANCINI, Patricia

20th-century American pianist, orchestral conductor, teacher and composer. She obtained her B.A. (French) from Randolph Macon Women's College and her M.A. (music) from the University of California, Berkeley. She then studied music at the Sorbonne, Paris. She conducted orchestras at Mills College and California State University, Hayward, and taught the piano, theory, composition and conducting in Oakland.
Composition
CHAMBER
Terra in F (str qrt) (1981)
Ref. Jeannie Pool (Los Angeles)

McKAY, Frances Thompson

American pianist, lecturer and composer. b. Newport, VA, April 24, 1947. She obtained her B.A. from Mary Baldwin College in 1969; her M.A. (composition) from the University of Virginia in 1972 and her D.M.A. from the Peabody Conservatory in 1982. She studied composition under Robert Hall Lewis at Peabody and Nadia Boulanger (q.v.) in Fountainbleau and Paris, the piano under Carl Broman at Mary Baldwin College and Marjorie Mitchell at Virginia University. She lectured at Georgetown University and the Smithsonian Institute and taught the piano and theory privately. She won several awards, grants and prizes.
Compositions
ORCHESTRA
Currents, concerto (1979)
Echoes from beyond the sound barrier (1980)
CHAMBER
Catacoustics (10 players) (1979)
Elegy in the form of a dream (fl, vln, vlc and pf) (1979)
Filigrane, chaconne (fl, cl and pf) (1982)
Pegasus (fl) (1982) (Arsis Press, 1982)
Rondeau (vla) (1975)
Sonances soneri (hn) (1975)
VOCAL
Portrait of a lady (T.S. Eliot) (T and cham orch) (1975)
Lotus Land: Virginia, 1974 (D. Collingwood) (vce, ob, vln and pf) (1975)
Nursery rhymes (Beatrix Potter) (S, fl, perc, pf and cel) (1980)
MULTIMEDIA
Sea dances (S, fl, perc, tape, opt dance and lights) (1981)
Ref. composer, AMC newsletter, MLA *Notes*

McKEE, Jeanellen

20th-century American composer.
Compositions
OPERA
Dream of an Empire (1959)
MISCELLANEOUS
Collectors' piece (1958)
Ref. 141, 321

McKENZIE, Sandra

20th-century Australian composer.
Compositions
INCIDENTAL MUSIC
Abelard & Eloise (vce and perc) (1975)
Arturo Ui (pf, trp, drs and perc) (1971)
As You Like It (1971)
The Chapel Perilous (elec org) (1973)
Forget-me-not (drs and pf) (1972)
Good woman of Setzuan (cl, perc and elec pf) (1972)
Habeas Corpus (vce, drs and pf) (1976)
How could you believe me when I said I'd be your valet when you know I've been a liar all my life (drs and perc) (1972)
Macbeth (inst ens) (1974)
The Magistrate (actors, 4 part ch and pf) (1969)
The Matchmaker (drs, perc, bsn and strs) (1976)
Much Ado about Nothing (man, acc, elec gtr, perc and pf) (1976)
Of Mice and Men (perc) (1975)
Peer Gynt (b-ob, 3 cl, acoustic gtr, perc and strs) (1974)
Richard II (orch ens) (1973)
Richard III (man, pf, acc, elec gtr and perc) (1976)
Rosencrantz and Guildenstern are Dead (hpcd, vlc, vln, perc, 2 rec and trp) (1976)
The Shoemaker's Holiday (hpcd and rec ens) (1976)
A Streetcar named Desire (jazz ens) (1976)
Taming of the Shrew (trp and mouth org) (1972)
'Tis Pity she's a Whore (fl, flugelhorn, hp, perc, cl and vln) (1973)
A Tooth of Crime
A Trelawney of the Wells (barrel org) (1972)
Twelfth Night (perc and rec ens) (1972)
Uncle Vanya (ob, cl, perc and strs) (1972)
Ref. 442

McKINNEY, Ida Scott Taylor

19th-century American authoress and composer. b. Springfield, IL. She composed songs.
Ref. 347

McKINNEY, Mathilde

American pianist, professor and composer. b. South Bend, IN, January 31, 1904. She studied at Oberlin Conservatory and the Juilliard School of Music. Her piano teachers were Lee Pattison and Josef and Rosina Lhevinne. She taught at Wooster College, OH, at Douglass College and privately in Pittsburgh, OK, New York and Princeton. In 1962 she became associate professor at Westminster Choir College.
Compositions
ORCHESTRA
Elegy for strings (1953, rev. 1958)
CHAMBER
String quartet
Trio (vln, vla and pf)
Seven modes (2 a-rec)
Fantasy toccata (org)
Violin sonata
Piano pieces
SACRED
Christmas, cantata (ch and brass insts) (1957)
The wise men (girls'-ch) (1957)
Ref. 142, 347

McLAIN, Margaret Starr

20th-century American professor and composer. b. Chicago. She studied under Frederick Converse and George W. Chadwick of the New England Conservatory, where she received two Endicott prizes for composition, and at Trinity College, London. From 1924 she was a member of the MacDowell Colony then lectured at Boston University from 1928. She was associate professor from 1949 to 1970 and then emeritus professor.

Compositions

ORCHESTRA

Overture (1937)

CHAMBER

String quintet
Violin sonata

VOCAL

The storke: A Christmas ballad (mix-ch and pf) (C.C. Birchard)
Choral works
Songs

Ref. 142, 190

McLAUGHLIN, Erna

20th-century American composer of Wisconsin. She composed piano pieces.
Ref. 347

McLAUGHLIN, Marian (Mrs. Thomas R. Ostrom)

American clarinetist, lecturer and composer. b. Evanston, IL, November 26, 1923. She received her B.Mus.Ed. from Northwestern University and M.M. (composition) from New England Conservatory, Boston. She studied the clarinet under Robert Lindeman of the Chicago Symphony Orchestra and composition under Dr. Albert Noelte, Carl McKinley, Frances Judd Cooke and Walter Piston. She taught theory and woodwind instruments at Evansville College, IN, and played first clarinet in the Evansville Philharmonic Orchestra. She held a teaching fellowship in theoretical subjects at the New England Conservatory from 1947 to 1948.

Compositions

ORCHESTRA

Night music (1955)
Overture to a comedy (1954)
Sinfonietta (small orch) (1954)

CHAMBER

Six fragments for woodwind quintet (fl, ob, cl, hn and bsn) (1963)
Sonatina for strings (2 vln, vla, vlc and d-b) (1954)
Concertino for string quartet, piece (1966)
Theme and variations (vln, fl, cl and vlc) (1948)
Excursions (fl, cl and bsn) (1955)
Trio (cl, vlc and pf) (1955)
Trio (fl, vla and pf) (1954)
Trio (vln, cl and pf) (1953)
At night (B-flat cl and pf) (1945)
Brevities, first recital pieces (trp and pf) (1970)
Cantilena and variations (handbells and vlc) (1963)
A carol for the Christ Child (org and/or handbells) (1954)
Cassation (fl and hp) (1954)
Cavatina and rondeau (ob and pf) (1954)
Children's march (handbells and hp) (1962)
Divertimento (vla and vlc) (1965) (1st prize, Friday Music Club Composers' Group Competition, 1967)
Elegy and march (hn and pf) (1953)
Habanera for castenets and handbells (1964)
Romantic piece (vla and pf) (1958)
Second sonatina (cl and pf) (1955)
Siciliano (handbells and hp) (1962)
Solemn prelude (handbells and org) (1962)
Sonatina (cl and pf) (1947)
Sonatina (vl and pf) (1970)
Sonatina (vla and pf) (1962)
Third sonatina (cl and pf) (1948)
Three pieces (cl and pf) (1948)
Descants (handbells) (1974)
Nocturne and scherzo (fl) (1954)
Six introits on hymn tunes (handbells) (1966)
Three etudes (cl) (1960)
Three fantasies (org) (prize, American Guild of Organists)
Two carols (hp) (1954)
Two fanfares (handbells) (1964)
Thirty easy solos, arrangements (trp and pf) (1970-1971)

PIANO

Elegy and march (2 pf) (1965)
March of the Turkish Sultan (4 hands) (1954)
The rain that falls at 4 o'clock (4 hands) (1954)
A sad song (4 hands) (1954)
Suite (4 hands) (1954)
Theme and variations (4 hands) (1954)
Waltz of the Queen of Spades (4 hands) (1954)
Tre archaic studies (4 hands) (1973)
November pieces (1970)
Suite (1948)
Other pieces
Teaching pieces

VOCAL

There was a child went forth (mix-ch and orch) (1948)
Autumn fires (w-ch and pf) (1960)
The band of children (unison mix-ch and org) (1964)
Be of good courage (m-ch and acc) (1955)
Blow, blow, thou winter wind (mix-ch) (1959)
The cradle (girls' ch and handbells)
Golden sheaves (mix-ch and org) (1961)
Lullaby to a forester's child (w-ch and pf) (1944)
Lullaby to a seafarer's song (w-ch and pf) (1941)
Moon (w-ch and pf) (1961)
New Year carol (junior mix-ch, opt descant and org)
Song of the ship (junior ch, org and opt handbells) (1962)
Song for an evening (w-ch and pf) (1972)
Torches (w-ch and pf) (1956)
Two birds (w-ch and pf) (Kjos)
Three counting rhymes (w-ch and pf) (1957)
Three young rats (w-ch and pf) (Kjos)
One I love (w-ch)
The wind (w-ch and pf) (1961)
Windy nights (mix-ch, pf and handbells)
Festival set for brass (Bar, B, 2 trp, hn and trb)
Songs incl.:
Lord of the winds (m-S and pf) (1963)
Nine songs from the Greek (vce and pf) (1963)
The wench (vce, fl and pf) (1971)

SACRED

Alleluia, Christ is risen (opt solo, unison mix-ch, handbells and org)
Come where the Christ Child is sleeping (w-ch) (1955)
God be merciful unto us (mix-ch and opt acc) (1955)
In Thee, O Lord (mix-ch and org)
Mary's wandering, the Passion (2 soli, junior ch or unison ch and org)
O give thanks unto the Lord (mix-ch) (1955)
Sleep, Holy Jesus (girls' ch, opt antiphonal ch and org) (1963)
The three wise men (junior unison ch and org) (1963)
Numerous other choral pieces

Ref. composer, 40, 142, 190, 622, 625

McLEAN, Priscilla Anne Taylor (Priscilla Taylor)

American electronic instrumentalist, pianist, lecturer and composer. b. Fitchburg, MA, May 27, 1942. She studied composition under Richard Kent at Massachusetts State College, Fitchburg from 1959 to 1965 and received a B.M.E.. She then studied electronic studio technique under Michael Babcock and obtained her M.M. in 1969 from Indiana University, Bloomington. She also studied composition at Boston University under Hugo Norden, Thomas Beversdorf and Bernard Heiden. She taught composition and theory courses at Indiana University from 1966 to 1969 and theory at Indiana University, 1971 to 1973. From 1973 she was on the faculty of St. Mary's College, Notre Dame, IN, teaching the piano, composition and theory. From 1972 she performed live electronic music and formed the 'McLean Mix' with her husband, which gave concerts throughout the United States. She and her husband co-directed a national radio program series of new music by members of the ASUC. She was composer-in-residence at Indiana University. She received several awards for composition, including a Martha Baird Rockfeller grant in 1975, a MacDowell Colony fellowship from 1979 and 1981, a National Endowment of the Arts grant, 1979 to 1980 and 1981 to 1982. DISCOGRAPHY. PHOTOGRAPH.

Compositions

ORCHESTRA

Variations and mozaics on a theme of Stravinsky (1969)

BAND

Holiday for youth (concert band) (1965) (Bourne, 1966)

CHAMBER

Elan! A dance to all rising things from the earth (fl, vln, vlc, pf and perc) (1981)
Fire and ice (trb and 2 pf)
Interplanes (2 pf) (1970) (New York: Broude, 1978)
Spectra II (perc and prep pf)

VOCAL

Songs incl.:
Candlelight (w-ch and pf) (1967) (Silver Burdett, 1972)
Four songs in season: Chant of autumn; Lullaby of winter; Song to the spring; Summer soliloquy (mix-ch and pf) (1963, rev 1967) (as Taylor)
In the spring the mountains sing (w-ch and pf) (1965) (Bourne, 1966)
In the still of night (w-ch and pf) (1967) (Silver Burdett)
Lights (w-ch and pf) (1967) (Silver Burdet, 1972)
Men and angels share (mix-ch and pf) (1959) (Philadelphia: Elkan-Vogel)
There must be a time (mix-ch, fl and pf) (1970) (Silver Burdett, 1971)

ELECTRONIC
Ah-Syn! (autoharp and syn) (1976)
Beneath the horizon I (tba qrt and whale ens on tape) (1979) (ACA)
Beneath the horizon III (tba and whale ens on tape) (winner, Gaudeamus Festival, Holland, 1979) (Broude)
Dance of dawn (quad tape) (1974)
Fantasies for adults and other children, 8 songs (e.e. cummings) (S and amplified pf) (1980) (ACA)
Invisible chariots (quad tape) (1977)
Night images (2-channel tape) (1973)
Messages (soli, ch, elec and acoustic cham ens and microphones) (1972) (ACA)
Spectra I (perc and syn)
MULTIMEDIA
The inner universe, 8 pieces (pf, tape and slides) (1981)
Publications
Fire and Ice: Query by Priscilla McLean. Perspectives of New Music. 1977.
Interplanes. ASUC Journal of Music Scores, vol. 5.
The McLean Mix. Philosophies and Soliloquies by Barton and Priscilla McLean. *Asterisk: A Journal of New Music 2.* May 2, 1976: 5-7.
Articles in *Musical America*. 1981, 1982.
Ref. composer, 142, 146, 190, 280, 563, 594, 622, 625, 643

McLELLAN, Irene Mary
Canadian concert pianist, conductor, teacher and composer. b. Toronto, February 1, 1928. She studied the piano under E.R. Schmitz and Karl Ulrich Schnabel; voice under Eilene Law, Ernest Vinci and George Lambert and dance under Sabina Nordoff in New York and became an A.R.C.T. She toured as a piano recitalist in Canada, Bermuda and the United States and appeared on the radio. From 1957 to 1963 she was head of music at Rudolf Steiner School, New York, from 1964 to 1967 conducted the Scarborough Light Opera Company and examined for the Royal College of Musicians. She composed music for Sabina Nordoff dance groups, several vocal works and one electronic piece.
Ref. 643

McLEMORE, Dorothy Jean. See PRIESING, Dorothy Jean

McLEMORE, Monita Prine
American pianist, arranger, choral conductor, lecturer and composer. b. Avera, MO, June 7, 1927. She gained her B.Mus. and M.Mus. and certificate from the American College of Musicians. She taught privately and in schools for 20 years and lectured at the University of Arkansas at Little Rock. She conducted choirs and made occasional stage, radio and television appearances. She composed 25 piano pieces and five vocal solos and made numerous arrangements of vocal and instrumental compositions.
Publications
Therapeutic Influence of Music in Cases of Mental Disorder. 1953.
Ref. 77

McLEOD, Evelyn Lundgren
20th-century American pianist, teacher, writer and composer. She received a diploma from the Idaho Technical Institute in 1924, a B.Mus. from Anderson School of Music, Pocatello, ID, in 1930 and pursued postgraduate studies at Chicago Music College, the University of Iowa and under Oscar Wagner in Salt Lake City. She taught the piano and theory at the Anderson School of Music and in Salt Lake City. She composed chamber pieces for small ensembles, the cello, the violin, the piano and vocal works.
Publications
The Homesteaders. 1977.
Numerous professional journal articles.
Ref. 40, 347, 359

McLEOD, Jennifer Helen
New Zealand pianist, poetess, professor and composer. b. Wellington, November 12, 1941. In 1964 she gained her B.Mus. first class hons, from Victoria University, Wellington. She was considered the most gifted student to have passed through Victoria's music department. Before she went to Europe on an Arts Council bursary, she had already received a commission from the Wellington Youth Orchestra and several of her works had been performed. In Europe she continued her studies under Messiaen at the Paris Conservatoire, Stockhausen in Cologne, and under Boulez, Pousseur, Gielen, Berio, Aloys Kontarsky and Christoph Caskel until 1966. In 1967 she was appointed music lecturer at Victoria University and in 1971, professor. She introduced courses of pop and non-Western music into curricula and was attracted to rock music. She retired from academic and musical life in 1976 to work for the Divine Light Mission, resuming her composing in 1981 on her return to New Zealand after the completion of a craftsman's course on making stained-glass windows.
DISCOGRAPHY.
Compositions
ORCHESTRA
Little symphony (cham orch) (1963)
Cambridge suite (cham orch) (1962)
Diversions (1964)
CHAMBER
For seven (fl or cl, vln, vla, vlc, mar, vib and pf) (1966)
Three serial pieces (strs) (1962)
Toccata (brass ch) (1963)
String trio (1964)
Metamorphosis (vln and pf) (1964)
Four profiles (vlc) (1963)
PIANO
Piece (1965)
Six little pieces (1962)
Suite (1961)
VOCAL
Oh what a proud dream horse (ch, wind qrt, hn, trp and perc)
OPERA
Earth and Sky
Under the Sun (1971)
INCIDENTAL MUSIC
Hamlet (1967)
Mr. Brandywine chooses a gravestone (1968)
Troilus and Cressida (1964)
Twelfth Night (1967)
Music for films
Publications
Childhood. 10 short poems. 1981.
Ref. 141, 189, 206, 612, 622

McLIN, Lena (nee Johnson)
Black American pianist, violinist, choral conductor, teacher and composer. b. September 5, 1928. She obtained a B.M. (violin and piano) from the Spelman College in Atlanta in 1951. As a student of Leonora Brown and Willis Lawrence James she studied music theory and composition. Later she began graduate studies in music and voice under Thelma Waide Brown at Roosevelt University, Chicago. She studied music theory and counterpoint under Stella Roberts and the piano under Howard Hanks at the American Conservatory of Music, where she graduated with a M.M. She then studied electronic music at Roosevelt University, where she worked in that medium and later became head of the music department at Kenwood High School, Chicago. She conducted workshops throughout the United States. The influence of the church and use of gospel characteristics is evident in her works, which have been performed in the United States and abroad. She received an honorary doctorate from Virginia Union University in 1975 as well as numerous awards from civic and community groups. She founded a small opera company, the McLin Ensemble and worked with educational films.
Compositions
ORCHESTRA
Impressions No. 1
PIANO
Impressions, 1957
Song in C-Minor
A summer's day
VOCAL
The Johnny Coleman cantata (Bar, narr and mix-ch)
Colors of the rainbow (composer) (mix-ch and pf) (Westbury: Pro Art, 1971)
Down by the river (mix-ch a-cap) (Kjos, 1971)
Friendship, song cycle (mix-ch and pf) (Park Ridge, IL: General Words & Music, 1972)
Gwendolyn Brooks: A musical portrait (composer) (mix-ch and pf) (General, 1972)
In this world, collection of mixed choruses (composer) (General, 1970)
We've just got to have peace all over this world (composer) (mix-ch and pf) (New York: Sildet Music, 1971)
What will you put under your Christmas tree? (composer) (mix-ch and pf) (General, 1971)
And she took a ring and placed it on his finger, art song (1963)
Gay, art song (Paul Dunbar) (Bar)
I cannot believe (composer)
I wish that I could hear you say
I'm gonna make it anyway
If I could give you all I have (composer)
Now that I've come for you

Silence (P. Dunbar)
Song cycle (composer)
Winter, spring, summer, autumn (composer)
The year's at the spring
SACRED
The Advent, Christmas cantata (S, A, T and mix-ch)
The Ascension, Easter cantata (S, T and mix-ch)
The (marriage) agreement, cantata
Free at Last, cantata (tribute to M. Luther King, Jnr.)
All the earth sing unto the lord (mix-ch a-cap) (Kjos, 1967)
Burden Down (mix-ch)
Cert'nly Lord, cert'nly Lord (S or T and mix-ch a-cap) (Kjos, 1967)
The Earth is the Lord's (mix-ch) (Pro Art, 1969)
Eucharist of the soul, liturgical mass (mix-ch and pf or org) (General, 1972) (comm Holy Cross Episcopal Church, Chicago)
For Jesus Christ is born (mix-ch a-cap) (Kjos, 1971)
Glory, glory hallelujah (S, mix-ch and pf) (Kjos, 1966)
I am somebody (narr, mix-ch and pf)
I heard the preaching of the elders (mix-ch)
I'm moving up (composer) (mix-ch and pf) (Pro Art, 1969)
I'm so glad trouble don't last always (mix-ch) (also arr as spiritual) (Kjos)
If they ask you why he came (composer) (mix-ch and pf) (General, 1971)
Is there anybody here (mix-ch and pf) (Pro Art, 1969)
Jesus stayed in the wilderness (mix-ch)
Judas (mix-ch)
Keep silence (mix-ch)
Let the people sing praise unto the Lord (mix-ch, pf or org and B-flat trp) (General, 1973)
Lit'le lamb, Lit'le lamb (S and mix-ch a-cap) (Kjos, 1969)
The little baby (composer) (opt solo, mix-ch and pf) (Kjos, 1971)
Missa Nigra, folk mass
New born King (composer) (mix-ch a-cap) (General, 1972)
O sing (mix-ch)
Out of the depths have I cried unto you (mix-ch)
Psalm 100 (mix-ch a-cap) (Pro Art, 1971)
Psalm 117 (mix-ch and pf) (Pro Art, 1971)
Psalm 124 (mix-ch)
Psalm 133 (mix-ch)
Sanctus and benedictus (mix-ch and pf) (General, 1971)
Steady, Jesus Listening (mix-ch)
When Jesus met the woman at the well (mix-ch)
Who knowest whether thou art comest to the kingdom (mix-ch)
Writ'en down my name (Bar and ch a-cap) (Kjos, 1967)
Done made my vow to the Lord, spiritual
Don't let nobody turn you around, spiritual
Down by the river, spiritual
Give me Jesus
God made us all
Give me that old time religion, spiritual
Gonna rise up in the kingdom, spiritual
Lord, oh hear me praying, spiritual
Low down the chariot let me ride, spiritual
St. Raymond the pinafold, liturgical mass
The torch has been passed (composer, on text by John F. Kennedy) (General, 1971)
Why don't you give up the world? spiritual
OPERA
Bancroft Inc. (m-S, 2 Bar, T, Cont and mix-ch)
Comment, rock opera
The Party
You Better Rise Women, Face the Challenge (for Women's Day Program)
OPERETTA
Humpty Dumpty
Jack and the Beanstalk
Rumplestiltskin
ELECTRONIC
If we could exchange places (composer) (mix-ch, fl, elec pf and elec B-gtr) (New York: Marks Music, 1971)

Publications

Pulse: The History of Music in America.

Bibliography

Winer, Linda. *Kenwood High's Little Lady of Music.* In Lena McLin, *In This World.* 1970.

Ref. 136, 142, 335, 347, 415, 549, 563

McMILLAN, Ann Endicott

American horn player, director, lecturer, writer and composer. b. New York, March 23, 1923. She obtained her B.A. from Bennington College and then studied under Otto Luening and Edgard Varese. She studied the horn under Joseph Singer and was student assistant to Varese from 1953 to 1955. She received Fulbright, Guggenheim and Creative Arts public service grants, a Tanglewood fellowship and numerous commissions. From 1949 to 1955 she was music editor for RCA Victor and Columbia Records; she was program director for French Broadcasting in North America from 1958 to 1964. She also worked as director of an orchestral library, music director to WBAI-FM, manager of an art gallery and a freelance lecturer and writer. DISCOGRAPHY. PHOTOGRAPH.

Compositions

CHAMBER
Strings 1980 (vln; also vln abstracted on tape)
Pieces (hpcd)
Other pieces
DANCE SCORES
Gateway summer sound (1980)
Music for ballet
ELECTRONIC
Amber 76
Animal I (1972)
April-episode (hpcd and tape) (1978)
Carrefours (hpcd, balafo and shell chimes) (1971)
Gateway animal sound (abstracted animal and other sounds)
Glass reflections (glass perc, tape, hpcd, vla and cham ens) (1973)
Gong song I & II (tape) (1969)
A little cosmic dust (pf and tape) (1982)
Piece for live saxophone and tape (1972)
Saxophone trio (sax and tape) (comm Thor Dahl, Norway)
Syrinx
Theater I, music for home or future soap (Megan Terry) (1971)
Whale I (structure of abstracted whale sounds) (1973)
INCIDENTAL MUSIC
Music for choose a spot on the floor, play (Schidman and Terry) (1972)
Sound-silence, film score for Black and White (1973)
Turn of the Year, film score (1973)
MISCELLANEOUS
Earth show I
Human song
Ocean
Thrush song

Ref. 9, 40, 142, 282, 347, 563, 622, 624, 625

McNAIR, Jacqueline Hanna

American pianist, authoress, choral conductor, critic, teacher and composer. b. Norfolk, VA, May 25, 1931. She received her B.A. from Duke University in 1952 and ran a private piano school from 1958 to 1966. She conducted a children's church choir and was a concert columnist for a newspaper. From 1965 she taught music at Macon Junior College and after 1972 was a recital and theatrical accompanist.

Compositions

SACRED
Cantatas incl.:
Hear ye! Be joyful!
Anthems incl.:
Al-le-lu, Hawaiian carol
Come and rejoice with us
God is in his heaven
Jubilate
A thousand hosannas

Ref. 494

McNEIL, Janet L. Pfischner

American professor and composer. b. Pittsburg, PA, March 20, 1945. She graduated from the Baldwin Wallace Conservatory, Berea, OH, with a B.Mus. in 1967; studied under David Diamond and David Burge at the University of Colorado where she obtained an M.Mus. in 1970 and with Ben Johnston, Edwin London and Salvatore Martirano at the University of Illinois from 1973 to 1976. She received several awards and commissions and a MacDowell fellowship. She was appointed guest composer at the Baldwin-Wallace College contemporary festival in 1972. She was professor at the University of South Dakota from 1972 to 1973, graduate assistant at the University of Illinois in 1973 and assistant director of the Fine Arts Center, Clinton, IL, in 1973. She won four first prizes in Mu Phi Epsilon contests from 1967 to 1975 and a MacDowell Colony fellowship in 1970.

Compositions

CHAMBER
Epithet I (ww qnt) (1967)
Epithet II (ww qnt) (1969)
Antiphons II (pf) (C. Fischer, 1975)
VOCAL
Snow gifts (T and large ens) (1969)
Aureate Earth, with 3 preludes (Omar Khayyam) (T, perc and prep pf) (1972)
In soundless grasses (1972)
Opus 10: Songs of commitment (S or T and pf) (C. Fischer, 1975)
Wind song (1972)

THEATRE
Music to Jimmy Shrine, play (1971)
Music for Passion in the library, play (1973)
MULTIMEDIA
Asphodel (1974) (comm Fischer Foundation)
MISCELLANEOUS
Sermon in stone (1975) (C. Fischer)
Ref. 142, 228, 625

McPHERSON, Frances Marie

American pianist, associate professor and composer. b. Tarkio, MO, 1912. She obtained her B.M. from Lindenwood College in 1934 and her M.M. from Michigan State University in 1942. She studied the piano privately under John Thompson in Kansas City and continued her piano and composition studies in Barcelona. For five years she composed music for the Little Theatre, St. Joseph, MO. She taught at Tarkio College and Florida State University and was associate professor at the Eastern Kentucky State College from 1944 until her retirement.

Compositions
CHAMBER
Violin sonata
Piano pieces
VOCAL
My Kentucky (B and ch)
Songs
SACRED
A man named John, cantata (mix-ch)
Psalm 150 (mix-ch)
OPERA
The Snow Queen
Ref. 142

McQUARRIE, Marguerite. See SPENCER, Marguerite

McQUATTIE, Sheila

Scottish pianist, lecturer, singer and composer. b. Edinburgh, March 23, 1943. She is an L.C.T.L. in the piano, singing and class teaching and an A.C.T.L. in singing and piano teaching. She is involved in recital and oratorio work and was the recipient of many awards and two scholarships. She has composed two cantatas and Christmas music, both for children.
Ref. 457

McSWAIN, Augusta Geraldine

Black American concert pianist, professor and composer. b. Omaha, NE, May 4, 1917. She gained her B.A. in 1937 and B.Mus. in 1938 from Bishop College and her M.M. in 1943 from Northwestern University. She studied the piano under Helen Hagan in New York from 1933, Raymond Morris in Hartford from 1937 and Kurt Wanjeck in Chicago from 1939 to 1946. Augusta made numerous appearances as a concert pianist and in 1938 joined the faculty of Bishop College, becoming assistant professor in 1940, associate professor in 1943, acting director in 1943 and dean of the school of music two years later. She composed a string quartet, six piano pieces, three choral works and two songs.
Ref. 496

McTEE, Cindy Karen

American composer. b. Tacoma, WA, February 20, 1953. She obtained her B.Mus. from the Lutheran University in 1975, having studied under David Robbins and her M.Mus. from Yale University in 1978, having studied under Krzysztof Penderecki, Jacob Druckman and Bruce MacCombie. She studied under Marek Stachowski at Cracow Conservatory, Poland from 1974 and then gained her Ph.D. (music composition) from Iowa University, having studied under Richard Hewig, Donald Jenni and Peter Todd Lewis. She won a composition prize at Yale University and a Broadcast music award.

Compositions
ORCHESTRA
Music for 48 strings, percussion and piano (1975)
BAND
Sonic shades (1977)
CHAMBER
String quartet No. 1 (1976)
Capriccio (hpcd and pf) (1978)
Piano percussion piece (1978)
Chord (fl) (1977)
VOCAL
Songs of spring and the moon (S and ens) (1983)
SACRED
Psalm 100 (mix-ch) (1982)
MISCELLANEOUS
A bird came down the walk (1978)
Ref. composer, 624

MEACHEM, Margaret McKeen Ramsey

American flautist, pianist, professor and composer. b. Brooklyn, NY, January 1, 1922. She studied science at Bennington College for a year before changing to music, graduating with a B.A. in 1962. Her teachers were Paul Boepple, Henry Brant and Lionel Nowak. She studied the piano under Henry Holen Huss; the flute under Louis Moyse from 1962 to 1970 and theory under Dr. Robert Barrow at Williams College from 1969 to 1972. At the University of Massachusetts, Amherst she studied under Charles Fussell and Philip Bezanson, gaining an M.A. (music theory) in 1972. She returned to the electronic music studio at Bennington College to study under Joel Chadabe from 1975 to 1976. From 1976 she continued her flute studies under Julius Baker and also studied for a month under Nadia Boulanger (q.v.) in Paris in 1976. She gained her D.M.A. (composition) from the University of Maryland in 1982. She taught the flute and ensemble in schools and privately and played in orchestras and chamber groups. Her compositions were performed in concert and on radio. She received the Charlotte W. Newcombe Fellowship whilst at Maryland University and was elected to the Phi Kappa Phi Society. PHOTOGRAPH.

Compositions
SYMPHONIC BAND
Three Latin dances (1984) (comm Mt. Greylock Friends of the Arts)
CHAMBER
Sunbursts (2 picc, 12 fl and pf) (1979)
Moonshadows (picc, 5 fl and 2 a-fl) (1984)
Trio for winds (fl, cl and bsn) (1972)
Sonata for violoncello and piano (1977)
Variations for two flutes (1970)
Cadenzas for Mozart's G-Major flute concerto (1979)
PIANO
Capricious caper (1983)
Reflections (1983)
VOCAL
In the beginning, cantata (Dylan Thomas) (S, T, mix-ch, double wind qnt, brass qnt and perc) (1972)
Chanson d'automne (mix-ch, ob and xy) (1975)
Haiku kaleidoscope: Dragon fly (Chisaku) (S, trp and vln) (1975, rev 1983 for narr, fl, cl, vln, vlc and perc); In icy moonlight (Buson) (S, fl, perc, vib and glock) (1975, rev 1982 for S, fl, picc, pf, perc and tape); Six gaping beaks (Issa) (S, fl, cl, bsn, trp, hn and perc) (1975, rev 1983 for S, fl, cl, bsn, ob, hn and perc)
Three French songs (Lamartine, La Fontane, Gautier) (S, fl, picc and pf) (1974)
SACRED
Christ in a stranger's guise (mix-ch a-cap) (1950)
THEATRE
Alice in Wonderland (S, T, m-S, dancers, 15 insts and tape) (1982)
ELECTRONIC
Prologue, transition, in 2 scenes: Who am I?; How doth the little crocodile? (S, m-S, T, dancers, elec tape and small orch) (1982)
Fusion for electronic tape, study in timbres (1981)
Kilogram/meters per second squared, study in acceleration and velocity (elec tape) (1977)
MULTIMEDIA
The origin of death, setting of African folk tale (mime and dance)
Ref. composer, 228, 474, 622

MEAD, Catherine Pannill

American critic, singer and composer. b. Norfolk, VA, 1868; d. Milwaukee, WI, 1936. She was educated mainly in England, where her teachers included Henry Altman, Sir Charles Santley, August Halter and William Goldbeck. Before her marriage in 1893 she became known as a singer. She was a music and drama critic for the "Milwaukee Sentinel" for 19 years.

Compositions
VOCAL
Songs incl.:
The little Dutch garden
The log of the good ship Nod
The sandman am comin'
A song of singing
Up with the flag (Berton Braley)
Why I love you
Ref. 292

MEADE, Margaret Johnston
American organist, pianist and composer. b. Dickson, TN, December 15, 1903. In 1928 she received a diploma for the piano and the organ and a B.M. from Cincinnati Conservatory and in 1955 an M.M. from Texas Christian University, where she studied under Dr. Ralph Guenther. She had teaching material published.
Compositions
VOCAL
Breath of love (vce and pf)
Four stages, cycle of 4 songs (1955)
Supplication (vce and str qrt)
SACRED
Everlasting life, song (bible)
On Earth peace, Christmas song (bible)
Ref. composer, 147

MEADER (Maeder), Emily Peace
American pianist and song composer. b. February 5, 1858; d. September 4, 1914.
Compositions
VOCAL
The robin
Soft and gently through my soul
Sweetheart, sigh no more
Ref. 40, 276, 347, 374

MEARS, Caroline
South African lecturer and composer. b. Croydon, England, December 18, 1942. She is an L.U.C.T. From 1963 to 1965 she taught music in Cape Town schools and in 1965 received her B.Mus. from the University of Cape Town. From 1966 to 1967 she taught in schools in Zambia, returning to Cape Town to obtain her M.Mus. (composition) in 1969, having studied under Stanley Glasser, Ronald Stevenson and principally Gideon Fagan. She received the Myer Levinson (Emdin) prize for composition after completing her master's degree. In 1970 she joined the University of Cape Town music department as a harmony and theory lecturer. She wrote the entries on music in South Africa for the sixth edition of Grove's Dictionary of Music and Musicians.
Compositions
CHAMBER
Five movements for wind quintet (1968)
Piece for clarinet and piano (based on Again I hear the sea (S. Quasimodo)
Sonatine (cl and bsn) (1962)
VOCAL
At the round earth's imagined corners (J. Donne) (ch a-cap)
Sonata for bass voice and piano, song cyle (D. Justice, D.H. Lawrence) (1968)
Ref. composer

MECHTHILD (Mechthild von Magdeburg)
German nun, poetess, singer, writer and composer. b. Magdeburg, 1212; d. Helfta, 1282. She was a nun of the Cistercian convent of Helfta, where she was cantrix for 30 years. Her visionary poems and writings, written originally in Low German, are thought to have been one of the inspirations of Dante's *Divine Comedy* and to have been acknowledged by him in the episode where he meets Matilda in the earthly paradise. Many of her compositions consisted of spiritual love songs; Charlemagne had forbidden women to sing love songs or erotic songs as they performed their daily tasks, so the nuns transformed the words into passion for Christ. Mechthild wrote many such songs, but her best works were her settings of conventional ritual texts. Her works were collected and arranged by a Dominican friar Heinrich von Halle and entitled *The Flowing Light of the Godhead.* She composed requiems and spiritual love songs in Latin and Low German.
Ref. 264, 335, 433, 481

MEDA, Sister Bianca Maria
Late 17th-century Italian nun and composer of the convent of San Martino del Leano, Pavia.
Composition
SACRED
Mottetti a 1, 2, 3 e 4 voci, con violini e senza (Bologna: P.M. Monti, 1691) (ded Marchese D. Cesare Pagani, Podesta di Pavia, December 15, 1691)
Ref. 26, 105

MEDECK, Mme.
French pianist and composer. b. Lithuania, 1791. She studied at the Paris Conservatoire under Louis Adam and became known for her piano playing in 1814. She married the cellist Medeck and traveled with her husband to France and Spain and settled in Madrid, where her husband was attached to the royal chapel. She composed piano pieces.
Ref. 26

MEDICI ORSINI, Isabella de, Duchess of Bracciano
Italian musician and composer. b. ca. 1540; d. July 16, 1576. She was the daughter of Cosimo de' Medici and married Paolo Giordano Orsini, Duke of Bracciano. The composers Stefano Rosseto, Maddalena Casulana (q.v.), Pompilio Venturi and Filippo de Monte dedicated works to her. She was strangled by her husband on a suspicion of infidelity.
Composition
VOCAL
Lieta vivo e contenta... (vce and lute)
Bibliography
Memorie e contributi alla musica di Frederico Ghisi. Bologna: University of Bologna Press, 1974.
Vecchi, Guiseppe, ed. *A Solution to a Lute Tablature of Isabella de Medici.*
Ref. 105, 157, 347, 622

MEDWAY, Carol. See FELIX, Margery Edith

MEEK, Ethel Alice
20th-century American organist, pianist, teacher and composer. b. Stamps, AR. She taught the piano, the organ, theory and composition.
Compositions
ORCHESTRA
Rondo
ORGAN
Toccata
PIANO
Sonata (4 hands)
Chaconne and double fugue
VOCAL
My dark chateau (vce and strs)
Ref. 347, 448

MEEKER, Estelle
20th-century American composer.
Composition
SACRED
Sweet Jesus, guide my feet (mix-ch) (Broadcast Music)
Ref. 190

MEERA. See MIRA BAI

MEGALOSTRATA OF SPARTA
7th-century B.C. Greek dancer, poetess, singer and composer. She was called the 'Beautiful Blonde'' and led choirs of Spartan girls and composed the music for their performances. At this time girls' choirs were particularly important in Greek life. Megalostrata's fame as a leader and composer has survived, but none of her songs.
Ref. 264

MEGEVAND, Denise
20th-century French harpist and composer. DISCOGRAPHY.
Compositions
CHAMBER
Le harpe celtique des Iles Hebrides (celtic hp and ens)
Psallere in chordis (lute, hp and hpcd) (Paris: Technisonor-Editions Françaises de Musique)
Ref. 346, 563

MEIGS, Melinda Moore
American harpsichordist, singer, teacher and composer. b. Michigan, November 28, 1953. She gained her B.A. and B.Mus. from Smith College, Massachusetts in 1975 where she studied under Ilse Wolf, Ronald Mur-

dock and Lory Wallfish. She attended master classes with Gustav Leonhardt. She toured as a soprano soloist and a harpsichord soloist and accompanist in Europe, Canada and the United States. She is a member of Phi Beta Kappa.

Composition

ELECTRONIC

Glissando (tape) (1981)

Ref. 643

MEINI-ZANOTTI, Maddalena

20th-century Italian composer. Her operetta was performed in Florence, 1909.

Composition

OPERETTA

La Principessa Iris (composer) (1909)

Ref. 431

MEISTER, Marianne

East German concert pianist, conductor and composer. b. Altburg, Thuringia, September 9, 1914. As a child she received training in the piano and theory and later taught herself. Her first compositions appeared in 1935. She formed an ensemble and from 1945 to 1947 was conductor of the orchestra of a traveling variety troupe. After 1947 she worked as a freelance composer and concert pianist.

Compositions

ORCHESTRA

Ferientag im Thuringer Wald, concert waltzes (large orch; also pf)
Festival overture
Romantic ballet waltzes
Spanische Legende, Fantasie-Tango
Spiel nicht mit dem Feuer, paso doble

PIANO

Klingendes Ungarland (Hungarian impressions)

VOCAL

Vergangenheit (Bar, S and orch)
Songs (vce and orch; also vce and pf)

THEATRE

Music for stage and variety

Ref. Otto Harrassowitz (Wiesbaden)

MEKEEL, Joyce

American harpsichordist, pianist, anthropologist, assistant professor and composer. b. New Haven, CT, July 6, 1931. She studied at the Longy School of Music, Cambridge, AM, from 1952 to 1955. She was awarded a private study grant to the National Conservatory, France, to study under Nadia Boulanger (q.v.) from 1955 to 1957. She studied the harpsichord under Ralph Kirkpatrick from 1957 to 1959 and attended Yale University School of Music on a full scholarship, studying the harpsichord under Gustav Leonhardt in 1957 and theory under David Kraehenbuehl from 1957 to 1960 and graduating with her B.M. in 1959 and M.M. in 1960 in theory and composition. From 1960 to 1962 she studied composition under Earl Kim. She taught the piano and theory privately in Princeton from 1960 to 1964; was awarded fellowships to the MacDowell Colony in 1963 and 1964 and the Ingram-Merrill grant in composition in 1964. From 1964 to 1970 she taught at the New England Conservatory; she received the Inter-American music award in 1965; she composed for the Ina Hahn Dance Company from 1967 to 1969 and was awarded the Radcliffe Institute grant from 1969 to 1970. In 1970 she became assistant professor in theory and composition at Boston University and directed the university's electronic music studio. She was composer and co-director of 'The Ensemble' from 1969 to 1971. She appeared as a harpsichordist with the New Haven Symphony, New Haven Chorale and Princeton Symphony. She was composer for the productions of the McCarter Theatre, Princeton. She organized a series of concerts of baroque music at Berkeley College and Yale University. She spent the summer of 1971 in West Africa studying ethnomusicology. In 1975 she was awarded the National Endowment for the Arts composer assistance grant. DISCOGRAPHY. PHOTOGRAPH.

Compositions

ORCHESTRA

Vigil

CHAMBER

Monotony of absences (picc, a-fl, cl, cor anglais, bsn, vlc and hp) (1968)
Embouchures II (brass sextet) (1972)
Homages (brass qnt) (comm Empire Brass qnt) (1974)
Spindrift (str qrt) (1971)
Rune (fl and perc) (1977)
Planh (vln) (comm Nancy Cirillo) (1975)
Shape of silence (fl) (1969)
String figures disentangled by a flute (1969)

PIANO

Epiphanies (1961)
Gifts of the ebb tide (1967)
Variations (1961)

VOCAL

Toward the source (ch and orch) (1975)
Waterwalk (mix-ch) (1970)
White silence (Haiku of Basho and Joso) (mix-ch a-cap) (1965) (C.F. Peters)
Alarms and excursions (m-S, cl, pf, vln, vlc, perc and cond) (1978)
Corridors of dream (Kandinsky, M.P. Hein, W.D. Schnurre, G. Stamm, H.M. Enzenberger) (m-S, a-fl, b-cl, vlc, vla, hp and cond speaking and playing perc) (comm Goethe Institute, Munich) (1972)
Dark rime (vce and pf) (1961)
Grido (T and prep pf)
Nunc est cantandum (vce and prep pf) (1960)
Phrases (vce and pf) (1961)
Serena (m-S, speaker and prep pf)

THEATRE

Androcles and the Lion (Shaw) (1961)
Fuente ovejuna (1963)
Knight of the Burning Pestle (1962) (Beaumont; Fletcher)
Macbeth (Shakespeare) (1962)
Merchant of Venice (Shakespeare) (1962)
Moveable Feast (1973)
Othello (Shakespeare) (1964)
Richard II (Shakespeare) (1964)

ELECTRONIC

Embouchure I (tape) (1969)
Feast, ceremony (tape and dancers) (1970)
Serena (vce, pf and tape) (1975) (comm Fromm Foundation)
Stop-lights and chains, an environment event (1973)
Yes is for a very young man (Gertrude Stein) (tape) (1965)

MULTIMEDIA

Chains (7 chains and 5 dancers) (1969)
Duet for dancer and percussion
Jaywalk (vla and dancer)
Pleasure of merely circulating
There were two of them

Publications

Harmonic Theories of Kirnberger and Marpurg. Thesis, Yale. The Journal of Music Theory, November, 1960.

Anton Webern. Review by Walter Kolneder. *Perspectives of New Music*, 1969.

Ref. composer, 40, 70, 142, 206, 282, 347, 397, 415, 563, 622, 625, 643

MEL-BONIS (nee Melanie Bonis) (pseud. of Mrs. Albert Domange)

French composer. b. Paris, January 21, 1858; d. Sarcelles, March 18, 1937. She was a pupil of Guiraud and Cesar Franck. Many of her works were well received in concerts of the Society Nationale, Paris and about 200 of them were published.

Compositions

ORCHESTRA

O danse sacrée, symphony
Fantasy (pf and str orch)

CHAMBER

22 works incl.:
Septet (2 cl, pf and strs) (ded Mrs. Coolidge)
Wind sextet
Quartet in B-Flat, 4 movements (vln, vla, vlc and pf) (1905)
Suite oriental (vln, vlc and pf) (1907)
Soir et matin (vln, vlc and pf) (1907)
Suite (fl, vln and pf) (Demets)
Suite, in 4 mvts (fl, hn and pf)
Suite, in 3 mvts (fl, vlc and pf) (1907)
Sonata in A, in 4 mvts (vln and pf) (1907)
Largo in E-Major (vln and pf) (Demets)
Serenade (vlc and pf)
Serenade (vln and pf)
Elevé-toi mon ame (pf and vlc) (Bretonneau)
Meditation (vlc and pf; also pf)
Sonata in C-Minor (fl and pf) (1904)
Sonata in F, in 3 mvts (vlc and pf) (1905)

PIANO

150 pieces incl.:
Scherzo (2 pf)
Variations (2 pf) (Hachette)
Les gitans (4 hands; also pf) (Hammelle)
Suite en forme de valses (4 hands)
Ballabile
Ballade
Balle de piano
Barcarolle-etude
La chanson du rouet

L'escarpolette, waltz
Etiolles, waltz (Grus)
Interlude and slow waltz
Marionettes
Mazurka
Le moustique (Demets)
Orientale, waltz
Pensées d'automne
Pieces for children
Pourriez-vous pas me dire, melody
Prélude
Près du ruisseau
Romance sans parles (Lemoine)
Rondo dans le genre ancien (Grus)
Scherzo-waltz
Sorrente
Tambours et clairons (Baudoux)
Viennoise (Leduc)
Villanelle, romance (also gtr) (Grus)
VOCAL
Madrigal (solo and 2 part ch; also 3 w-vces) (Hachette)
Le moulin (ch; also duo) (Hamelle)
Prière (mix-ch)
Le ruisseau (2 part ch; also duo)
Songs
SACRED
Prière de Noël (mix-ch) (Leduc)
O salutaris (Bar and org or har)
Regina coeli (2 equal vces and pf or hp or org, vln and vlc ad lib)
Carols
Ref. 22, 41, 105, 226, 297

MELBYE, Nanny Hedwig Christiane. See MATTHISON-HANSEN, Nanny

MELE LARA, Nelly. See LARA, Nelly Mele

MELIA, Gabrielle
19th-century Italian composer. Her opera was performed in Rome in 1923.
Composition
OPERA
Matilde nel castello delle Alpi
Ref. 431

MELL, Getrud Maria
Swedish organist, pianist, choral conductor, master mariner, teacher and composer. b. Ed, August 15, 1947. At the age of five she began studying the piano and writing her first compositions. She studied the organ, instrumentation, conducting and music history at the Lund Conservatory from 1965 to 1967 and took the pedagogic precentor certificate in Stockholm in 1968. She made her debut on Swedish television in 1972, playing her own compositions and later had her own radio and television programs. She taught music in schools and conducted three choirs in Bengstfors until 1976. In Ed she founded Mells Musik-institut, a society dedicated to freeing musicians from the chains of counterpoint. She passed her mates' examination in 1979 and her master mariner examination in 1981. Since 1982 she has been the organist at the Pater Noster church, Goteborg. DISCOGRAPHY. PHOTOGRAPH.
Compositions
ORCHESTRA
Symphony No. 1 in A-Major (1964)
Symphony No. 2 in E-Major (1965)
Symphony No. 3 in G-Major (1966)
Symphony No. 4, in 2 mvts
Symphony No. 5
Symphonic poem (1980)
Solvind (small orch) (1984)
CHAMBER
String quartet, No. 1 in C-Minor or E-Major (1969)
Melodie ans Meer (vln and pf) (1967)
Solvind (fl and pf) (1975)
Gloria (org) (1966)
Other organ pieces (1982-1984)
PIANO
Fantasie in A-Minor, Svikna forhoeppningar (1961)
Fantasie in C-Major (1962)
Improvisation in C-Minor (1971)
PT 1972
Vals
Varens alkomst (1963)
Songs (vce and pf)
SACRED
Pater Noster (solo, ch and solo acc) (1983)
Soli Deo Gloria (mix-ch) (1965)
Kyrie Eleison (1968)
Peace (1972)
Ref. composer, 77, 563

MELLISH, Miss
18th-century English composer.
Composition
VOCAL
My Phillida, adieu, love (1790) (Dublin: John & Edmond Lee, 1795; London: Broderip & Wilkinson, 1800)
Ref. 65

MELOY, Elizabeth
American organist, assistant professor and composer. b. Hoopeston, IL, August 7, 1904. She studied under Carl Beecher and Albert Noelte at Northwestern University, Bernard Rogers at Eastman School of Music, Nadia Boulanger (q.v.) in France and Darius Milhaud and Leo Sowerby in Colorado. From 1927 to 1929 she taught in a public school, from 1929 to 1932 at Taylor University and from 1933 to 1969 at Ball State University. She retired as associate professor of the organ and theory.
Compositions
ORCHESTRA
Dance suite (award, Indiana Composers' Guild)
Overture
CHAMBER
String quartet
Piano trio
Trio for flute, oboe and cello
Sonatina (vln and vla)
Pieces (pf)
Preludes (org)
Sonatina (vla)
VOCAL
Heaven and earth and sea and air (mix-ch)
This is my father's world (mix-ch)
Anthems
Songs
Ref. 142

MELVILLE, Marguerite Liszniewska (Melville-Liszniewska)
American pianist and composer. b. Brooklyn, NY, 1884; d. Cincinnati, OH, March 7, 1935. She was a pupil of O.B. Boise and assistant to Theodor Leschetizky.
Compositions
CHAMBER
Piano quintet
Romanza in F (vln and pf)
Sonata in G-Minor (vln and pf)
Other pieces
VOCAL
Songs incl.:
Einkehr
Die Wasserrose
Wehmut
Ref. 276, 292, 347

MELVILLE-LISZNIEWSKA, Marguerite. See MELVILLE, Marguerite

MELY, Marie, Countess Van den Heuvel
19th-century composer.
Compositions
VOCAL
Legend of Narcissus, cantata (Weekes)
I'm a wee fay (vce and pf) (Ricordi)
My mother willed it so (vce and pf) (Ascherberg)
Songs: Longing; Sleep; Love and rest; Coming (vce and pf) (Williams)
When the year was young (vce and pf) (Ricordi)
OPERETTA
Snow White (1869)
Ref. 297, 307

MENA, Carolina
19th-century Spanish composer. Her opera was performed in Madrid in 1904.
Composition
OPERA
Por elevar mismo nombre, zarzuela
Ref. 431

MENDELSSOHN, Erna
German lutenist, singer and composer. b. Berlin, June 13, 1885. She studied under her pianist and composer father, Ludwig Mendelssohn and the pianist and lute singer Helene Bormenamm-Dorn. She married Dr. Bruno T. Saton-Neumann, theory and music writer. She composed duets for the mandolin and lute, concert pieces for the lute and songs with lute accompaniment.
Ref. 111

MENDELSSOHN, Fanny Caecilia. See HENSEL, Fanny Caecilia

MENDELSSOHN, Luise
German singer and composer. b. Ratibor, October 22, 1863; d. September 17, 1923. She composed sacred vocal works.
Ref. 226

MENDOSA, Dot
20th-century Australian composer.
Compositions
THEATRE
Alice in Wonderland, children's pantomine (William Orr from Lewis Carroll) (vces, 2 pf and dr) (1956)
Mistress Money, musical (John McKellar) (vces and orch) (1960)
A Ride on a Broomstick, children's fantasy (John McKellar) (vces, 2 pf and dr) (1959)
The Vatican (John Crane) (narr, actors, ch and orch) (1963)
The Willow Pattern Plate, children's fantasy (J. McKellar) (vces, dr and pf) (1957)
A Wish is a Dream (William Orr) (vces, 2 pf and dr) (1960)
Ref. 442

MENDOZA, Anne. See ADDENDUM

MENEELY, Sarah Suderley. See MENEELY-KYDER, Sarah Suderley

MENEELY-KYDER, Sarah Suderley (Meneely, Sarah Suderley)
American pianist, sarod player, sitar player and composer. b. Albany, NY, February 18, 1945. She gained a B.A. (theory and piano) from Goucher College in 1967, having studied composition under Robert Hall Lewis. She studied under Stefan Grove and Earle Brown at the Peabody Conservatory graduating with an M.M. (composition) and under Robert Morris at Yale University where she obtained her M.M.A. in 1973. Her earlier compositions were influenced by the 12-tone serial technique of Schoenberg, Berg and Webern and later by American and ethnic folk traditions and North Indian sitar music. She contributed to the *Dictionary of Contemporary Music*. PHOTOGRAPH.
Compositions
ORCHESTRA
Piano concerto, in 3 mvts (1967)
Time (2 pf and small cham orch) (1971)
CHAMBER
Buzz (resonating bells, tubular chimes, kalimba and gtr) (1973)
Lament (sitar, resonating bells and drone) (1976)
Music based on North Indian ragas: Baby is lying in the manger (raga Bageshri)
Lament (raga Parameshwari)
Laudate Dominum, 3 circle canons (raga Maru Behag)
Puzzle (raga Miyan ki mallar) (1978) (comm The Early Music Ensemble of Brown University)
Homegrown (pf) (award)
VOCAL
Everywoman: A morality tale, oratorio (N.F-H. Meneely) (w-vces, mix-ch, 15 small and toy insts, gtr and pf) (1973)
Narcissus monologue (Meneely) (T and small cham orch) (1968)
Stereo and discord (mix-ch, brass and ww ens) (1968)
Six pieces for waking and sleeping (mix-ch and pf)
The billion freedoms (K. Patchen) (T and pf) (1971)
Epithets (S and pf) (1968)
Five systems (w-vces, resonating bells, tubular chimes, kalimba and gtr) (1973)
Six songs (S and pf) (1974)
Songs for morning and prayer (medieval and Renaissance consort)
ELECTRONIC
Five widdew pieces (T, toy pf, pf and tape) (1972)
Ref. composer, 142, 347, 465

MENESSIER-NODIER, Marie Antoinette Elisabeth
French composer. b. 1811; d. 1893. She was the daughter of Charles Nodier. She composed songs.
Ref. 465

MENETOU, Françoise-Charlotte de Senneterre
French harpsichordist, arranger and composer. b. 1680. She was the daughter of the Duchess de la Ferte, who was her teacher and possibly a pupil of Couperin. At the age of nine she played the harpsichord and sang some of her own songs for Louis XIV who was reportedly delighted. It is doubtful whether she wrote the texts herself. Her *Airs serieux de Mademoiselle Menetou* contains original songs and harpsichord works among numerous harpsichord transcriptions from operas by Lully, Lambert, Lebegue and d'Anglebert. PHOTOGRAPH.
Compositions
HARPSICHORD
Les folies d'Espagne
Gavottes
Menuets
Les olivettes
VOCAL
Aymez desormais (vce and hpcd)
De toutes les heures (vce and hpcd)
J'ay pour tous bien une musette (vce and hpcd)
Sans crainte dans nos prairies (vce and hpcd)
Other songs
Ref. 573

MENK-MAYER, Florence
Australian composer. b. Melbourne, March 27, 1867.
Composition
OPERA
Victorine (1887)
Ref. 431

MENNECHET DE BARIVAL, Mme.
French pianist and composer. b. Paris, January 15, 1861.
Compositions
PIANO
L'aveu, nocturne
Brises du soir, op. 57
Duchesse de Fontanges, op. 25
La Marquise de Presles, waltz
Mazurka brillante
Two melodies: Guitare; Simple fleur
La prière, melody
Six etudes poetiques
Speranza, op. 26
Ref. 50

MENTER, Sophie
German concert pianist, professor and composer. b. Munich, July 29, 1846; d. Stockdorf, near Munich, February 23, 1918. She was the daughter of the cellist and Munich court musician Joseph Menter and a pupil of Leonhard, Carl Tausig and Hans von Buelow and in 1868 of Franz Liszt, who described her as 'my only legitimate piano daughter'. She traveled widely in concert tours and in 1868 became court pianist to the Prince of Hohenzollern. In 1874 she was appointed pianist to the Austrian court and from 1883 to 1887 was professor at the St. Petersburg Conservatory. She married the cellist David Popper in 1872; they divorced in 1886, when she lived at Schloss Ittel in the Tirol and was visited there by Liszt and Tchaikovsky among others. The piano concerto *Hungarian gypsy songs* originally believed to be composed by Menter, was in fact composed by Liszt and the manuscript given to her to take to Tchaikovsky to orchestrate. Menter told Tchaikovsky it was her score and it is probable he believed that she at least composed the solo piece. In 1892 the piece was performed by Menter, with Tchaikovsky conducting.

Compositions
PIANO
Consolation, op. 10
Etude in A-Flat, op. 9
Mazurka, op. 6
Petit valse, op. 7
Romance, op. 5
Sexten-studie, op. 8
Tarentelle, op. 4
Ref. 8, 22, 23, 44, 74, 98, 113, 347, 361, 455, 477

MENTES, Maria
19th-century Spanish composer. Her zarzuela was performed in Madrid in 1895.
Composition
OPERETTA
El Lucero del alba, zarzuela
Ref. 431

MENTZEL-SCHIPPEL, Elisabeth
German composer. b. 1849; d. 1914.
Compositions
OPERA
Alte Hausmittel, comic opera in 1 act (1901)
Das Puppenspiel vom Erzzauberer Goethe, tragic opera in 4 acts (1901)
Ref. 108

MEREDITH, Margaret
20th-century British composer.
Compositions
ORCHESTRA
Chamber music rhapsody (vln and orch)
VOCAL
Songs:
The debit
If we must part
The immortelle
King's men
Love's benediction
Mother's song
O heart of insatiable longing
Our princess
To our heroes
Unseen companions
The white robe
SACRED
The at-one-ment (ch and orch)
The passing of King Edward VII, requiem (ch and orch)
Sacramentum supremum (ch and orch)
Sursum corda (ch and orch)
He that dwelleth
Hear my prayer
The Lord is my shepherd
Magnificat
Nunc dimittis
The vision of the Cross
OPERA
The Pilgrim's Way or The Garden of Life
The Unseen Lover
Ref. 467

MERELLE, Mlle.
French composer. ca. 1800.
Compositions
HARP
Les folies d'Espagne, avec de nouvelles variations (London: Broderip & Wilkinson, ca. 1800)
Petites pièces (Broderip, ca. 1800)
Ref. 65

MERESAMENT
8th or 9th-century B.C. Egyptian singer of the harem of Amun. She was the daughter of Userken and Sha-amenimes and granddaughter of Takelotis II, XXII Dynasty, 950 to 730 B.C.
Ref. 428

MERIT
Egyptian songstress of the XVIII dynasty under Amenophis II, 1450 to 1425 B.C. Besides priests, cantors, professional choral singers and instrumentalists playing harps, lutes, flutes and trumpets involved in the cult of the gods in the temples, there were groups of women who shook sistra and sang in unison. A statue of Merit in the Rijksmuseum van Oudheden in Leiden, Holland, shows her holding not the usual sistrum but a menat, either a cult object or a decorative piece of unknown significance. PHOTOGRAPH.

MERLI-ZWISCHENBRUGGER, Christina
Swiss pianist, teacher and composer. b. Plans, South Tirol, Italy, May 26, 1954. She studied church music for three years at the Conservatory of Bolzano and then composition for five years under Francesco Valdambrini. After her marriage in 1977 she moved to Zurich.
Compositions
ORCHESTRA
Passacaglia (1977)
CHAMBER
Stimmen (vln and pf) (1980)
Streichduett (vln and vlc) (1981)
VOCAL
An die Nachgeborene (Brecht) (vce, vla and orch) (1976)
Blutwort (Konrad Rabensteiner) (mix-ch, 2 trp, hn and trb) (1983)
Klagelied (Jeremiah) (speaking ch and 2 pf) (1974)
Rondel (Georg Trakl) (m-ch, fl and str qnt) (1975)
Drei Lieder: Sysiphos, Gaeste, Nachtwache (Rabensteiner) (S, 2 cl and bsn) (1973)
Ref. 641, 651

MERMAN, Joyce
Compositions
OPERETTA
Charles, the carousel horse, for children
Sam, the sad circus clown, for children
Two circus stories, for children
Ref. MLA *Notes*

MERO, Jolanda
Hungarian concert pianist and composer. b. Budapest, August 30, 1887; d. New York, October 17, 1963. She studied the piano under Augusta Rennebaum and toured in Europe, the United States and Cuba. She later settled in the United States.
Compositions
ORCHESTRA
Capriccio ungharese (pf and orch)
PIANO
Sonata
VOCAL
Songs
Ref. 461

MERRICK, Maire E. (pseud. Edgar Thorne)
20th-century American composer. Her piano works were frequently performed and the Mendelssohn Glee Club of New York sang some of her male choruses.
Compositions
PIANO
Pieces incl.:
Amourette
VOCAL
Songs incl.:
Forgotten fairy tales (m-vces)
Six fancies (m-vces)
Ref. 226, 433

MERRICK, Mrs. Frank. See SQUIRE, Hope

MERRIMAN, Margarita Leonor
American professor and composer. b. Barcelona, Spain, November 29, 1927. She received her B.M. (piano) from the University of Tennessee in 1948, her M.M. (theory) in 1953 and her Ph.D. (theory) from the Eastman School of Music in 1960, where she was a composition pupil of Herbert Elwell, Alan Hovhaness and Bernard Rogers. From 1948 to 1951 she was

director of music at Shenandoah Valley Academy; from 1951 to 1956 assistant professor at Andrews University; from 1956 to 1958 assistant professor at Southern Missionary College of Music and from 1959 professor at Atlantic Union College. PHOTOGRAPH.

Compositions

ORCHESTRA

Symphony No. 1 (1959)
Symphony No. 2 (1981)
Concertante for horn and chamber orchestra (1976)
Pavane and galliard (1958)
Piece (cham orch) (1957)
1776 (small orch) (1975)

CHAMBER

Quinary (brass qnt) (1976)
Introduction and rondo (4 vlc) (1980)
Lament for the peacekeepers (hp, vln, vlc and pf) (1984)
Two miniatures (pf, cl, hn and bsn) (1952)
Dialogue (vlc and perc) (1976)
Sonata (vlc and pf) (1973)

PIANO

Currents (1969)
Meditations on a college bulletin (1963)
Sonata (1974)

VOCAL

The Millennium, oratorio (mix-ch, soloists and orch incl. timp, perc and hp; also pf reduction) (1973, 1977)
The excluded (S, vln, vlc and pf) (1981)
Songs incl.:
A complaint (1953)
Dearest it is spring (1956)
Expectation (vce and pf) (1965)
Homeward (1953)
I hoed and trenched and weeded (vce and keyboard) (1958)
Music I heard with you (vce and keyboard) (1952)
The night is freezing fast (vce and keyboard) (1953)
To E.M.P. (vce and keyboard) (1953)

SACRED

Behold the Tabernacle of God (mix-ch and org) (1967)
Lord, Thou hast been our dwelling place (mix-ch) (1951)
Psalm 24 (mix-ch and org) (1964)

Publications

A new look at 16th-century counterpoint. University Press of America, 1982.

Ref. composer, 84, 137, 142, 190, 228, 624, 625

MERSANNE, Maddalena

19th-century Italian composer.

Compositions

VOCAL

Six ariettas: Nel silenzio della notte; Tenera Mamoletta; Se il barbar destino; Come posa porporina; No che non e possibile; Mi lusingo amor (vce and pf) (ded Maria Teresa Beatrice, Princess of Modena)

Ref. 157

MERTENS, Dolores

German guitarist, harpist, pianist and composer. b. Berlin, April 2, 1932. She studied the guitar, the harp and the piano as a child and began composing when she was 14. In 1964 she composed light music and later turned to classical music. Her *Moon Mission* was transmitted to the first astronauts to land on the moon. She lives in Germany and the United States where she composes for the Mormon Tabernacle Choir.

Compositions

ORCHESTRA

Works (wind orch)

CHAMBER

Pieces (hp, gtr, pf and har)

VOCAL

Songs incl.:
Don Alfonso
Duello
Journey to the moon
Lucky Luciano
Moon mission
Ray of sun

SACRED

Songs incl.:
A prayer (Fritz Von Opel)
Emita requiem (Von Opel)

THEATRE

Silver Violins, children's play

INCIDENTAL MUSIC

Music for films

Ref. composer

MESNEY, Dorothy Taylor

American mezzo-soprano, autoharpist, dulcimer player, pianist, teacher and composer. b. Brooklyn, September 15, 1916. She obtained her B.A. from Sarah Lawrence College and also studied at Columbia University, Queens College, the New School for Social Research, the Juilliard School of Music and the Manhattan School of Music. She made her debut at Carnegie Hall and then gave numerous performances of American music of all periods and types, sometimes accompanying herself on the autoharp and dulcimer. She is a member of the Metropolitan Opera Guild and the National Federation of Music Clubs. She founded and produced the American Experience Quintet. She taught singing and the piano privately and at Douglaston from 1958.

Compositions

CHAMBER

Quartets
Trios

VOCAL

Songs incl.:
Spread your wings and fly (1960)

SACRED

Song of creation (1974)
Walk into the Promised Land (1964)
Zion's Hill

Ref. 206

MESRITZ-VAN VELTHUYSEN, Annie

Dutch concert pianist, teacher and composer. b. Salatiga, Java, September 2, 1887; d. Amsterdam, March 29, 1965. She studied at the Royal Conservatory of the Hague and graduated with a gold medal for the piano and the Nicolai prize for composition. She continued her studies under Winz and Dopper, Arthur de Greef in Brussels and Dohnanyi in Berlin. She gave concerts in the Dutch Indies and on her return gave a concert of her own compositions in Brussels. Her orchestral works were performed by the Concertgebouw orchestra.

Compositions

ORCHESTRA

Fantaisie (pf and orch) (ded Willem Mengelberg)
Poeme (vla and orch) (1918)
Mars (medal, 650th anniversary of foundation of Amsterdam)
Thema met variaties (1916)

CHAMBER

Twee oude dansen (2 vln, 2 vlc, vla and cl) (1930)
String quintet
String quartet
Piano trio (1936)
Elegie (vlc and pf) (1939)
In memoriam (vln and pf) (1942)
Sonata, canzonetta and capriccio (vln and pf) (1939)
Suite (vlc and pf) (1938)

PIANO

Works incl.:
Kleuren, suite (2 pf, 4 hands) (1938)
Six preludes

VOCAL

Adieu, le bonheur, baroque d'or (S and orch) (1938)
Le lait: L'enfant disait un soir; L'enfant au Paradis (Luka) (m-S, fl, vlc and pf) (1945)
Riwajak kampong (Legende) (T, ob, pf, 2 vln, vla and vlc) (1946)
Die alte Kirche (E. Bjoerne) (A and pf)
Other ensembles (Javanese texts)
Songs (composer)

Ref. 1, 26, 44, 110, 461

MESSAGER, Hope. See TEMPLE, Hope

MESSIAM, Eve

20th-century composer.

Composition

OPERA

Inner City (Helen Miller)

Ref. 227

MESTDAGH, Helene

Belgian pianist and composer. b. November 18, 1899. She composed a piece for the orchestra or the piano, waltzes, sentimental pieces and songs without words for the piano between 1939 and 1955.

Ref. ILWC

METALLIDI, Zhanneta Lazarevna

Soviet concertmistress, lecturer and composer. b. Leningrad, June 1, 1934. In 1960 she graduated from the Leningrad Conservatory where she studied under O.E. Evlakhov. From 1959 to 1963 she was concertmistress at a theatre school and then lectured at a music school in Leningrad.

Compositions
ORCHESTRA
Symphony (1962)
Concertino for flute and orchestra (1960, rev 1965)
Tale of the tin soldier (H.C. Anderson) (1959)
CHAMBER
Excerpt (vln, pf and ens) (1976)
Piano quintet (1958)
Suite (wind qnt) (1971)
Concertino (fl and pf) (Otto Harrassowitz)
Sonata (trb and pf) (1975)
Sonata (vln and pf) (1975)
PIANO
Pieces for children (1968)
Sonata (1969)
VOCAL
Songs (Uitmen, Mayakovsky, Moritz, Elinar) (vce and pf) (1957-1971)
BALLET
The Golden Key (1960)
INCIDENTAL MUSIC
Music for films
Ref. 21

METZGER-VESPERMANN, Clara

German singer and composer. b. Munich, 1800; d. Munich, 1827. The daughter of Charles-Theodore Metzger, she studied singing and composition under Winter, made her debut as a singer in 1817 and was considered an artist of great promise. She married the actor Vespermann and together they visited Vienna, Dresden and Berlin. She returned to Berlin, where her career was cut short by her early death.

Composition
VOCAL
Air variations
Ref. 26

METZLER, Bertha

19th-century American composer. b. New York.

Compositions
PIANO
Alexandra, polka-mazurka (Gordon)
Bells are ringing at fairy dell (Ditson)
A call to arms, march (Presser)
Dreams of home, idylle (Gordon)
Etelka waltz (Ditson)
Gipsy waltz (Ditson)
Heimweh, idylle (Ruehle)
In the time of apple blossoms, waltz (Presser)
Komm an mein Herz, Salon-Walzer (Ruehle)
Little wood nymphs (Ditson)
Once upon a time, in G-Major (Ditson)
Twilight dance of the fairies, in F-Major (Ditson)
Up to the times (Presser)
When the roses bloom again, song without words
VOCAL
Marching song (also pf) (Presser)
Old clock's warning (also pf) (Presser)
Ref. 226, 276, 297

MEYER, Elizabeth

Late 19th-century Danish composer.

Compositions
CHAMBER
Berceuse (vln and pf)
Naar duggen falder (pf)
VOCAL
Cantata (soli, ch and pf) (1895) (prize, Copenhagen, 1895)
Blandede digte: Russisk folkevise; Dansk folkevise (Hansen)
Blomsterne sove (Hansen)
Fire sange (1925)
Foraarssang (Hansen)
Jeg pynted mig saa faur og fin (Hansen)
Laeken (Hansen)
Ridderen drager til hove (Hansen)
Other songs
Ref. 226, 276, 331

MEYER, Ilse

20th-century Danish composer.

Composition
SACRED
In dulci jubilo, baroque music (Wilhelm Hansen, 1951)
Ref. 331

MEYERS, Lois

American composer. b. 1925. DISCOGRAPHY.

Composition
SACRED
Carry candles to the manger (ch)
Ref. 563

MEYERS, Mrs. P.A. See FORSYTH, Josephine

MEYSENBURG, Sister Agnes

American teacher and composer. b. David City, NE, March 3, 1922. She studied composition under Bernard Dieter and Sister Theophane Hytrek (q.v.). She obtained her B.M. from Alverno College and M.M. from Wisconsin Conservatory. She taught at Alverno College from 1947.

Compositions
ORCHESTRA
Festival frolic for string orchestra
Several choreographic pieces
Suite for piano and chamber orchestra
SACRED
Suites for Mass
Ref. 137

MEZARI, Maddalena. See CASULANA, Maddalena

MIAGI, Ester Kustovna

Soviet lecturer and composer. b. Tallinn, January 10, 1922. She studied composition at the Tallinn Conservatory under M. Saar, graduating in 1951. At the Moscow Conservatory she continued with postgraduate studies under V. Shebalin until 1954, when she returned to Tallinn to teach theoretical subjects at the Conservatory. She was awarded a medal in 1972. DISCOGRAPHY.

Compositions
ORCHESTRA
Symphony (1969)
Piano concerto (1953)
Serenade (vln and orch) (1958)
Variations (cl, pf and str orch) (1972)
Work for wind orchestra (1959)
CHAMBER
Melody (vln ens) (1966)
Ostinato (wind qnt) (1962)
Dialogue (fl, cl, vlc and pf) (1976)
String quartet No. 1 (1964)
String quartet No. 2 (1965)
Wind quintet (1962)
Trio (1950)
Ballad (vln and pf) (1955)
Eight pieces (vln and pf) (1969)
Presto (vln and pf)
Six Estonian folk melodies (vln and pf) (1975)
Six little pieces (vlc and pf) (1948)
Six pieces (trp and pf) (1959)
Andante and allegro (org) (1974)
PIANO
Three pieces (2 pf) (1956)
Moscow scene, cycle (1961)
Sonata (1949)
Ten pieces (1957)
VOCAL
Puteshestvie kalevipoyega v Finlandiu cantata (F. Kriezwald) (1954)
Pesnya o Lenine, mass song (1950)
Poem burevestnik (ch and org) (1957)
Six Estonian folk songs (ch) (1974)
Sovietskaya molodezh, mass song (1948)
Three songs for choir
Za mir, mass song (1950)
Na golmakh Gruzii, 4 romances (A. Pushkin) (1948)
Songs (Estonian poets) (vce and pf)
Other choruses, songs

INCIDENTAL MUSIC
Music for theatre incl.:
Kogda prishla vesna (1959)
Ref. 21, 63, 87, 330, 563

MICHEL, Josepha
Belgian composer. b. Liège, December 14, 1847; d. Ostende, September, 6, 1888. Her operas were performed in Liège and Brussels.
Compositions
OPERA
Aux-Avant-postes (1976)
Les Chevaliers de Tolede (1872)
La Meunière de Saventhem (1872)
OPERETTA
M. Canadier S.V.P. (1875)
Ref. 431

MICHELI AGOSTINI, Fausta
Italian composer. b. 1889.
Compositions
PIANO
Impressioni musicali per i piccoli pianisti, 8 pieces for children (Ricordi)
Ref. Ricordi (Milan)

MICHELOW, Sybil (Mrs. Goldfoot)
South African pianist, lecturer, singer and composer. b. Johannesburg, 1925. She obtained her music diploma from the University of the Witswatersrand, Johannesburg in 1945 and commenced private piano teaching. She studied the piano under Franz Reizenstein from 1950 to 1953 and singing under Mary Jarred from 1954 to 1961 and made her concert debut in London in 1968, later appearing in numerous recitals and concerts under conductors such as Sir Malcolm Sargent, Sir John Barbirolli and Bertini, in England and on the continent. She was choral instructor at the Royal Academy of Dramatic Art, London from 1956 to 1957 and from 1958 devoted herself to singing.
Compositions
INCIDENTAL MUSIC
Pop goes the queen, children's play (1944)
Music for two Berthold Brecht plays
Ref. 84, 377

MIDDLETON, Jean B.
20th-century American composer.
Composition
ORCHESTRA
Symphony in C (1942, rev 1962)
Ref. 142

MIER, Countess Anna von
19th-century Austrian composer. Her songs were published in Vienna by Kratochwill.
Ref. 226

MIEROWSKA, Jean
South African organist, teacher and composer. She gained her B.Mus. hons. at Birmingham University then taught in London. She lived in Zimbabwe for eight years before settling in South Africa, where she became director of music at St. Andrews College, Grahamstown. In 1982 she gained first place for two compositions for the horn and the piano in a triennial competition.
Ref. *Grocott's Mail* Friday 21, May 1982

MIGRANYAN, Emma
Soviet pianist, lecturer and composer. b. Erivan, January 4, 1940. In 1968 she graduated from the Erivan Conservatory where she studied composition under G.I. Yegiazarian. After 1967 she lectured at the K. Saradzhev music school in Erivan. DISCOGRAPHY.
Compositions
ORCHESTRA
Den Anushik, suite (1974)
Festival overture (1977)
Glazami detei, suite (1973)
In memory of Erivan (1978)
CHAMBER
String quartet (1962)
Suite (str qrt) (1960)
Six pieces (vln and pf) (1973)
PIANO
Four sonatas (1961, 1964, 1975, 1978)
Children's pieces (1971)
VOCAL
Zelenaya alleya (soli, ch and orch) (1972)
Bolshaya ya ili malenkaya, cycle (Muradian) (vce, fl, vln, baraban and pf) (1972)
Romances and songs (S. Muradian, L. Sarkisian, A. Sagian, G. Sevan, A. Marashian and others) (vce and pf)
BALLET
Bashmaki Abu-Gasan (orch) (1968)
THEATRE
Lgunishka-khvastunishka, musical tale (narr, singers and ens) (1974)
Ref. 21, 563

MIHALITSI, Sophia
20th-century Greek composer.
Composition
FILM MUSIC
Metamorphosis (1973)
Ref. 497

MIKESHINA, Ariadna
Composition
MISCELLANEOUS
Rhapsodie russe, op. 65 (Paragon)
Ref. Frau und Musik

MIKUSCH, Margarethe von
Austrian pianist and composer. b. Baydorf, March 26, 1884. She studied under Kwast, Stefan, Max Loewendgard, Wilhelm Klatte, Friedrich Klose, Stocker and Max Reger. After 1904 she lived in Berlin.
Compositions
ORCHESTRA
Suite (str orch)
CHAMBER
String quartet (1916)
String quartet (1927)
Piano trio
String trio
Sonata in G-Minor (vln and pf) (1923)
Zwei Partiten (vln)
PIANO
Preludes and fugues
Three intermezzi (1925)
VOCAL
Songs
Ref. 41, 70, 111

MILA, Leonora
Spanish concert pianist and composer. b. Villaneuva y Geltru, 1942. She studied under Monserrat Ayarbe and was a child prodigy, entering the Academia Ars Nova when very young. She studied the piano under Maria R. Canals and harmony and composition under R. Llates and gave her first public recital at the Palacio de la Musica de Barcelona in 1950.
Compositions
PIANO
Adagio
Ballet
Cancion española No. 8
Cancion oriental
Homenaje a Chopin
Maria Neus
Preludio-fantasia
VOCAL
Songs incl.:
Cabreta
Encen mon cor

Estrella Dourada
Images from Count Berengeur IV of Catalonia's court, op. 39 (International Music Co., 1982)
Matinada
Meditacio
Rondo brillante, op. 18. no. 1 (International, 1982)
Toccata op. 32, no. 1 (International, 1982)
SACRED
Jesus, song
Ref. 107

MILAM, Lena Triplett

American violinist, violist, lecturer, writer and composer. b. Sweet Springs, MO, October 19, 1884. She graduated in the violin from Rowe College in 1901 and obtained her B.S. from North Texas University in 1936. She studied the violin under Max Firschel in Chicago in 1919 and Alexander Block in New York in 1929 and chamber music and ensemble playing with the Roth Quartet in Austria in 1933 and analysis and partiture reading under Dr. Paul Piske in Vienna in 1933. She was director of music education in the Beaumont schools, TX, from 1917 to 1955 and on university faculties for numerous summer music schools. In 1936 she received an honorary Mus.D. from Southwestern University of Georgetown.

Compositions
CHAMBER
Banjo song (strs) (1937)
Serenade for strings (1947)
VOCAL
Children's songs incl.:
Songs for the zoo (1948)
Ref. 433, 496

MILANOLLO, Teresa Domenica Maria (Mme. Parmentier)

Italian concert violinist, teacher and composer. b. Savigliano, Cuneo, August 28, 1827; d. Paris, October 25, 1904. She studied the violin under G. Ferrero and the Royal Chapel violinists Gebbaro and Morra. She gave her first public recital before the age of seven. She studied under Lafont in France in 1837 and toured with him through Belgium and Holland. While touring England and Wales she received lessons from Mori and on her return to France studied under Habeneck and Beriot in Bologne. She gave violin lessons to her younger sister Maria and together they appeared in France, Germany, Italy and England, where they became famous for their performances. Because of their diverse styles they were called Mlle. Adagio and Mlle. Staccato. In Vienna they gave 25 concerts in 1843 and played before the King of Prussia in Frankfurt-am-Main. After the sudden death of her sister in 1848 Teresa retired for some time but eventually resumed her career. In 1857, after her marriage to Charles Joseph Parmentier she retired, except for playing in the Concerts des Pauvres. In 1891 she taught in Hamburg.

Compositions
CHAMBER
Adagio in memoria della sorella Maria (vln and pf) (1856) (Joubert)
Air de Marlborough, variations (vln and pf) (Hamelle)
Ave Maria de Schubert, op. 4 (vln and pf) (Schott)
Fantasie élégiaque (vln and pf) (1853) (Joubert)
Impromptu (vln and pf) (Hamelle)
Lamento (vln and pf) (Hamelle)
PIANO
Grand fantasie (Vienna: Spina)
March (Brainard)
VIOLIN
Bapteme
Extase
Two romances
SACRED
Ave Maria, op. 2 (m-ch and org or pf; also soloists and ch; also m-ch) (Le Beau) (Ricordi)
ARRANGEMENTS
Variations humoristique sur le Rheinweinlied (vln and pf) (Hamelle)

Bibliography
Clarke, A.M. *Les soeurs Milanollo, études biographiques artistiques et moales*. Lione. 1847.
Pansa, R. Collino. *Le M*. La Scala. 1955.
Pougin, A. *Les soeurs M*. RMI, 1916.
Ref. 8, 14, 17, 26, 41, 135, 183, 260, 276, 297, 347, 415

MILASZEWSKA

Early 19th-century Polish composer.

Composition
OPERA
Aspazja i Perykles, in two acts (J. Mlocka) (Lvov, 1824)
Ref. 118

MILDANTRI, Mary Ann

American pianist, choral conductor, teacher and composer. b. Brooklyn, NY, December 17, 1931. She studied voice, composition and conducting under Ralph Hunter at Hunter College. At the Manhattan School of Music she took the methods course in instrumental music and studied the Orff-Kodaly method under Dr. Lawrence Wheeler. She taught voice and the piano.

Compositions
SACRED
Days of Hanukkah (Kondar Music)
Hanukkah fun (Kondar)
Hanukkah means dedication (Kondar)
Shalom (Kondar)
ARRANGEMENTS
Zarumba, Greek songs (Constantino Alevras) (mix-ch) (Kjos)
Ref. 77

MILDER, Jeanette Antonie. See BUERDE, Jeanette Antonie

MILDMAY, Lady

16th-century English composer. In describing her pastimes to a friend she wrote 'Every day I practice my voice and set songs of five parts to my lute'. The courts at the time were centers of musical activity and daughters of the aristocracy studied, played and wrote music.
Ref. 264

MILDREN, Margaret Joyce

British bassoonist, flautist, organist, pianist, conductor, teacher and composer. b. Cannock, Staffordshire, April 20, 1936. She studied the piano and the flute and is an F.T.C.L.; L.R.A.M.; L.G.S.M.; and A.L.C.M. Her teachers included York Bowen and Harold Craxton (organ) and John Francis (flute). She teaches the bassoon and the flute, is an examiner for the Graduate School of Music, organist at Walsall Central Hall and conductor of the Old Marians Symphony Orchestra. In 1981 she won the Private Music Teacher of the Year inaugural award.

Compositions
FLUTE
Games on a flute
ARRANGEMENTS
World renowned Christmas carols
Ref. 643

MILEVIC, Janice. See THORESON, Janice Pearl

MILENKOVIC, Jelena

Yugoslav pianist and composer. b. Belgrade, February 13, 1944. She attended the Mokranjac Music Academy, where she studied the piano under Professor S. Vranjanin and composition under Professor P. Milosevic. She continued postgraduate studies in composition under Professor Stanojlo Rajcic. PHOTOGRAPH.

Compositions
ORCHESTRA
Symphony
Piano concerto
Tri pokreta, in 3 mvts
CHAMBER
String quartet (1967)
Variations (cl, vla and pf) (1966)
Sonata (fl and pf) (1965)
PIANO
Ekstase in Heses (1967)
Suite (1964)
VOCAL
Zelena livada (m-ch) (1964)
Slusaj ti cudo (V. Popa) (vce and pf) (1964)
Vrati mi moje krpice (V. Popa) (vce and pf) (1964)
THEATRE
Linc
Neces jesti batak (V. Matic)
Ref. composer, 145

MILETTE, Juliette (Sister M. Henri de la Croix)

Canadian organist, pianist, lecturer and composer. b. Montreal, June 17, 1900. At the Ecole Superieure de Musique d'Outrement she studied the piano under Alfred Laliberte, the organ under Raoul Raguet and composition under Claude Champagne. She obtained her D.Mus. magna cum laude in Montreal in 1949. She taught the organ and Gregorian chant at the Ecole Superieure.

Compositions
ORGAN
Chorals variés: G-Minor (1936); B-Minor (1937)
Prélude et fugue (1938)
SACRED
Leur maison, oratorio (ch and org) (1945)
Les cloches d'argent, cantata (2 chil-vces) (1950)
Aubade (ch) (1937)
Aurore printanière (ch) (1935)
Notre Père (ch) (1936)
Marie, o douce souveraine, duet (1940)
Notre Dame du Canada, duet (1950)
O Mere, ton étoille, duet (1940)
Ref. 133

MILFORD, Mary Jean Ross

American choral conductor, teacher and composer. b. Houston, August 14, 1943. She gained her B.Mus.Ed. from Mary Hardin-Baylor College in 1965 and M.A. (theory and composition) from California State University, San Jose in 1969. She taught school music, conducted choirs and composed choral music.
Ref. 77

MILH AL-ATTARA

Arabian songstress at the court of the Caliph al-Mutawakkil in Samarra near Baghdad, 847 to 861. She was given her name, meaning 'the perfumer' because of her excessive use of perfume. Although she was described as an outstanding singer, only one detail of her life is known; once when the great Shariyya (q.v.) performed a song for the caliph, he asked her who had composed it. Shariyya was unable to tell him, but Milh al-Attara related the origin of the song to him.
Ref. 224

MILKINA, Nina

British concert pianist of Russian origin. b. Moscow, January 27, 1919. Her first compositions were published when she was eleven. She studied at the Paris Conservatoire and under Marguerite Long, Harold Craxton, Tobias Mattay and M. Cowes.
Compositions
PIANO
Fête du village (W. Rogers)
Marche-burlesque (Rogers)
My toys, suite (Rogers)
Two fairy tales (Rogers)
Ref. 77

MILKULAK, Marcia Lee

American concert pianist and composer. b. Winston-Salem, NC, October 9, 1948. She studied the piano at San Fransisco Conservatory, receiving her B.M. in 1969 and continued with postgraduate studies at Mills College. She received awards for her performances.
Composition
ELECTRONIC
Piece for dance, improvisation (vce, prep pf, perc and tape)
Ref. 142

MILLAR, Marian

19th-century English pianist, librettist, writer and composer. b. Manchester. In June 1894 she was the first woman to obtain a Mus.Bac. from Victoria University, Manchester.
Compositions
VOCAL
Songs
SACRED
A song of praise (soloists, ch and small orch)
Publications
Librettos for Dr. Hile's *Crusader* and G.J. Miller's *The Armada*.
Ref. 276, 347, 433

MILLARD, Mrs. Philip

English composer. d. ca. 1840.
Compositions
SACRED
Songs incl.:
Alice Gray (1835)
Dinna forget
Forget thee my Susie
Happy New Year
Lament of the Scotch fisherman's widow
Soldiers return
A thousand a year
Ref. 6, 276, 347

MILLER, Alma Grace

20th-century American organist, choral conductor and composer. She was organist and choral conductor at St. Agnes Church, Arlington, VA.
Compositions
SACRED
Three Christmas masses
Other choral compositions
OPERA
The Whirlwind (1953)
Ref. 141, 264

MILLER, Elma

Canadian clarinetist, electronic instrumentalist, pianist, lecturer, librarian, writer and composer. b. Toronto, August 6, 1954. She gained her Mus.Bac. and M.Mus. from the University of Toronto in 1977, studying composition under Professors Lothar Klein, Walter Buczynski, John Beckwith and John Weinzweig and the clarinet under R. Chandler. She studied the piano privately under Dr. Elaine Keillor from 1975 to 1978. She studied electronic music at the University of Toronto electronic music studio under Professor Gustav Ciamaga and computer music under William Buxton from 1976 to 1977 and attended a computer music seminar at Stanford University during the summer of 1978. She won several awards and scholarships, including university scholarships, an Estonian cultural committee in Canada scholarship, an Estonia Orchestra award in 1975, an IBM award in 1977 and an Els Kalhot-Vaarman composition award, Stockholm in 1980. She taught the clarinet, theory, counterpoint, orchestration and 20th-century analysis from 1976 to 1978, was librarian technician in the Toronto University faculty of music library during 1978 and lectured in acoustics at the University of Toronto from 1978 to 1979, when she moved to Hamilton and contributed articles and reviews to *The Silhouette* newspaper. She is a member of CAPAC. PHOTOGRAPH.
Compositions
ORCHESTRA
Scholium, chamber concerto (ens and str orch) (1979) (rev as Genesis, 1980) (bronze winner, Sir Ernest MacMillan award, 1981)
CHAMBER
Margarita Anguisque (cham ens) (1979-1980)
Kriss Kringle's wolka paltz (fl, vla, trb and perc) (1977)
Things are not what they appear (4 French hn) (1981)
Chick (3 perc) (1977)
OHC (ob, hn and vlc) (1976)
Duo (cl and d-b) (1975)
Duo (cl and pf) (1976) (rev as Sleep of reason, 1980)
Le phenix (trb and mar) (1980)
Vinderdi vaenderdi (cl and French hn) (1975)
Kalur (cl) (1976, rev 1979)
Minnemata (pf) (1978) (comm Dr. E. Keillor, 1977)
VOCAL
The dachshund (vce and pf) (1975)
Jabberwocky (Bar, pf and opt page turner) (1980)
ELECTRONIC
Esimene takt (elec tape) (1979)
Farce (concrete tape) (1979)
Joust (computer) (1978)
Le melange (fl, cl, trb and vibes) (1978)
Pink champagne (elec tape) (1976)
Ref. composer, 622

MILLER, Jean

20th-century blind American composer from Colorado. Her works have been performed in concerts.
Compositions
CARILLON
Soliloquy
Three short pieces: Air; Lullaby; Chantey
Other pieces
Ref. Bicentennial Parade of American Music

MILLER, Joan

20th-century American composer.
Composition
VOCAL
Tower of Babel, cantata (1966)
Ref. 142

MILLER, Lillian Anne
American pianist, authoress, teacher and composer. b. North Haddonfield, NJ, May 31, 1916. At the Sternberg School of Music she studied under Constantin von Sternberg and Ella Ketterer and at Rutgers University under Aldred Mann. She also studied under M.B. Moulton, Alexander Alexay and Edwin Bave. She taught at the North Haddonfield Branch of the Sternberg School and was an accompanist for the Philadelphia Light Opera Company. She is a member of ASCAP.
Compositions
VOCAL
Songs incl.:
I take thee
In a Mayan temple
Lullaby of the leaves
Peanut whistle
SACRED
Exult in glory
I will call upon God
O Lord, behold the Earth
TEACHING PIECES
Pieces (pf)
Ref. 39, 40, 347

MILLS, Joan Geilfuss
20th-century American composer. She composed chamber music and piano pieces.
Ref. 40, 347

MILNE, Helen C.
British concert violinist and violist, conductor, teacher and composer. b. London, 1897. She gained her B.Mus. from London Academy of Music and was a L.R.A.M. and M.R.S.T.. She gained her teaching certificate from Marylebone Training College and was a strings teacher and conductor from 1916 to 1930. She played the viola and the violin in Queen's Hall Orchestra and the viola in the BBC and Scottish Symphony orchestras.
Compositions
ORCHESTRA
Aubade (str orch)
Landler and conversation (str orch)
CHAMBER
String quartet
Burletta (vla)
Ref. 94, 467, 490

MILNE, Lorraine
20th-century Australian composer.
Compositions
INCIDENTAL MUSIC
Captain Moonlight
The Les Darcy show
Ref. 442

MIMET, Anne-Marie
French composer. b. 1942.
Compositions
CHAMBER
Ar foreu teg (a-sax and pf or hp) (Billaudot, 1981)
Le coeur lourd (a-sac and pf or hp) (Billaudot, 1983)
Complainte (a-sax and pf or hp) (Billaudot, 1978)
Le depart du roi (a-sax and pf or hp) (Billaudot, 1978)
Ref. *Notes* 3/84. Otto Harrassowitz (Wiesbaden)

MINDINHA. See VILLA-LOBOS, Arminda Neves de Almeida

MINEO, Antoinette
American pianist, choral conductor, publisher and composer. b. Tacma, WA, November 6, 1926. She studied the piano and composition under her father, Joseph Lento and married the composer, conductor and pianist Attilio Mineo, with whom she collaborated in composing. Together they founded the publishing company Mineo Music. She conducted a church choir in Tacoma for 18 years. She is a member of ASCAP.
Compositions
ORCHESTRA
Symphony No. 1, Portrait of Jacqueline in C and A
Piano concerto
Music of Century 21
Rhapsody 21
CHAMBER
Eight Dorian modes (pf) (1968-1972)
VOCAL
The sound of love ballads, jazz songs
SACRED
The mass of the beautiful lady (ch, fl, perc and strs)
Other masses
Ref. composer

MINGHELLA, Aida
Italian composer.
Composition
VOCAL
Pace (2 w-vces)
Ref. Frau und Musik

MIRA BAI (Meera)
Indian Queen of a Rajput state, poetess and songwriter. b. Merta, 1498; d. Dwarka, 1547. She was educated at home and received a thorough religious and musical training. She married Prince Bhoj Raj in 1516 and after his death from battle wounds in 1521, devoted her life to religion and the worship of Krishna and left her palace to travel on foot to the sacred places of Krishna, singing her songs. This religious leaning is evident in her songs and poems. Mira was severely censored for her betrayal of caste in caring for the poor. DISCOGRAPHY.
Compositions
VOCAL
Sacred songs or bhajans (vce, vln and mridangam – folk dr) incl.:
Charit
Git govind ki tika
Miri ni garbi
Narisi ji ro mahera
Narsi mehta ni hundi
Odes
Pada collection of raga soratha
Padas
Raga malar
Raga govinda
Rukmani magal
Satbhama nu rusan
SACRED
Hymns
Bibliography
Nilsson, Usha S. *Mira Bai*. New Delhi. Sahitya Akademi.
Ref. 563, 637

MIRANDA, Erma Hoag
American teacher and composer. b. Planfield, IL. She composed piano and choral works, songs and an opera.
Ref. 40, 347

MIRANDA, Sharon Moe
20th-century American composer.
Composition
BAND
American fanfare (timp and brass ens) (New York: Chappell Music, 1974)
Ref. 622

MEREILLE, Saint Plante
French composer. b. ca. 1934. She composed three operas and a song.
Ref. 465

MIRELLE, Wilma
20th-century American composer.
Composition
SACRED
A Christmas legend (mix-ch and pf) (Broadcast Music)
Ref. 190

MIRET, Emilia

20th-century Spanish concert pianist, teacher and composer. b. Barcelona. She studied at the School of Music, Barcelona and the Conservatory of Brussels, where she won a prize. She returned to Barcelona in 1914 and took part in concerts with the Symphonic Orchestra. She gave numerous recitals on the radio and composed piano works and pieces for voice and the piano.
Ref. 361

MIRIAM

Ancient Hebrew musician, biblical prophetess and songstress. ca. 1290 B.C. She was the sister of Moses and Aaron and the prototype of women singers in early Jewish rites, thought to have gained her musical knowledge from Moses. After crossing the Red Sea, Miriam sang to the Lord to give thanks for their miraculous rescue. According to Exodus (15:20, 21) 'Miriam, the prophetess, sister of Aaron, took a timbrel in her hand, and all the women went out after her with timbrals and with dances. And Miriam sang unto them'.
Bibliography
Who's who in the Bible. Comay and Brownrigg. New York: Bonanza Books, 1980.
Ref. 151, 255, 264, 313, 576, 644

MIRON, Tsipora (pseud. Thelma Moore)

American organist, pianist, authoress, lecturer, librettist and composer. b. Olevsk, Ukraine, July 27, 1923. She received a diploma from the North Balfour College Tel Aviv in 1939 and her B.A. from the Israel Conservatory in 1944. She lectured on the piano at the Israel Conservatory Music Academy and was president of the Star Record Company. She translated from the Hebrew and contributed lyrics to Issachar Miron's oratorios and other songs.
Compositions
CHAMBER
Meditation and dance (cl and inst ens)
Lonely hill (trp and inst ens)
PIANO
Mirages, etudes
Oh riddle
Ref. 494

MIRSHAKAR (Mirshakarova), Zarrina Mirsaidovna

Soviet lecturer and composer. b. Dushanbe, March 19, 1947. She studied composition at the Moscow Conservatory under S.A. Balasanian graduating in 1974, then lectured at the Tadzhik Institute of the Arts. DISCOGRAPHY.
Compositions
ORCHESTRA
Suite (str orch) (1973)
Two Pamir gravures (str orch) (1967)
Two Pamir sketches (1974)
CHAMBER
String quartet (1972)
Three Pamir frescoes (vln and pf)
Other pieces (vln and pf) (1970)
PIANO
Preludes (1964)
Six preludes (1968)
Theme with variations (1969)
VOCAL
Cantata (M. Mirshakar) (ch and cham orch) (1972)
Cycle (M. Mirshakar) (vce and pf) (1969)
Ref. 21, 563

MIRSHAKAROVA, Zarrina Mirsaidovna. See MIRSHAKAR, Zarrina

MISHELL, Kathryn Lee

American pianist, lecturer and composer. b. Los Angeles, June 5, 1940. At the University of Kansas she studied under John Pozdr graduating with a B.M. in 1963. She continued her studies under Ingolf Dahl at the University of Southern California until 1964 and then became the opera coach at Oberlin College. She lectured and taught the piano privately.
Composition
CHAMBER
Duo (trp and pf) (1971)
Ref. 142

MIT SCAPUS. See SCHEEPERS-VAN DOMMELEN, Maria

MITCHELL, Izah Pike

American pianist and composer. b. Norway, ME, December 7, 1888; d. April 2, 1967. She studied theory under Louis Elson and H. Redman and the piano under Charles Anthony.
Compositions
PIANO
Corrida de toris
Gypsy rhapsody
Scherzo appassionata
VOCAL
Songs incl.:
Autumn leaves
The sunset of life
Will o' the wisp
Ref. 40, 347, 433

MITCHELL, Janice Misurell

American flautist, lecturer and composer. b. Newark, NJ, May 3, 1946. She studied the flute and composition at Goucher College where she obtained her B.A. in 1967 and Peabody Conservatory graduating with a M.M. in 1968. She taught the flute and studied composition at Ohio State University School of Music from 1968 to 1971 and 1975 to 1977 and then continued her composition studies. At Northwestern University her flute teachers were Bonnie Lake and Donald McGinis; her composition teachers were Robert Hall Lewis, Stefan Grove, Marshall Barnes, M. William Karlins and Ben Johnston. At the Salzburg Mozarteum in summer 1966 she studied the flute under Karl Heinz Zoeller, at Tanglewood the next year she attended a course of solo and ensemble music, with flute teacher James Pappoutsakis. She teaches the flute and plays the flute in various ensembles. PHOTOGRAPH.
Compositions
CHAMBER
Elisions (18 winds) (1984)
Paradigms (7 fl, perc and d-b) (1977)
String quartet No. 1 (1984)
Transfusions (a-sax, t-sax, trp and trb) (1984)
Vanishing points/quantum leaps (cl, vln, vlc and pf) (1980)
Dream storm (fl and gtr) (1977)
Synchromos (fl and gtr) (1976)
Mobius trip (fl) (1973)
Speechscape (a-sax) (1985)
Untitled I (fl) (1982)
Untitled II (fl) (1985)
Any number can play (open instrumentation) (1976)
VOCAL
Mad song (mix-ch a-cap) (1975)
Elegy for Mrs. Ramsay (S and perc) (1984)
Settings of three poems (Wallace Stevens) (speaker, fl, cl, trp, trb and perc) (1968)
ELECTRONIC
Sub-music and song (amp fl) (1983)
INCIDENTAL MUSIC
Metamorphosis, film (tape) (1969)
Lysistrata (Aristophanes) (fl and perc) (1978)
Ref. composer, 643

MITCHELL, Norma Jean

American organist, pianist, arranger, teacher and composer. b. Dallas, July 20, 1942. She studied for the certificate of piano pedagogy at the Musical Arts Conservatory, Amarillo, TX, graduating in 1972. From that date she has worked as a pianist, organist, accompanist and teacher.
Compositions
VOCAL
I don't mind so it don't matter (revival ch) (1975)
My best friend (S) (1974)
Nothing can take his place (B) (1972)
One day at a time (1973)
The roadway to heaven (1974)
This is the way (T) (1971)
THEATRE
Never Too Young, children's musical (1974)
Ref. composer, 206

MITFORD, Eliza

English composer. ca. 1800.

Composition
VOCAL
Jack Latin, with variations (London, 1800)
Ref. 65

MIYAKE, Haruna (pseud. Haruna Shibata)

Japanese pianist and composer. b. Tokyo, September 20, 1942. She studied at the Music School, Tokyo and then under V. Persichetti at the Juilliard School of Music before returning to Tokyo. DISCOGRAPHY.
Compositions
CHAMBER
Music for piccolo, flute and guitar
Piano pieces
VOCAL
Flower fantasy (S, pf and trp)
Why not my baby?
Ref. 70, 563

MIZANGERE, Marquise de la

French harpsichordist and composer. b. Bourret, February 10, 1693; d. ca. 1779. She was taught to play the harpsichord by Couperin and became a skilled and popular player who made numerous concert tours. She studied accompaniment under Bournonville. After the death of her daughter she took up an administrative post in a parish where she worked for 30 years. She is considered to be the first French woman to have composed piano music.
Compositions
CHAMBER
String quartet
Harp pieces
Harpsichord pieces
Piano pieces
OPERA
Der heimliche Bund
Ref. 226, 231, 276

MIZUNO, Shuko

Japanese composer. b. 1934. DISCOGRAPHY.
Compositions
CHAMBER
Ko no jyumon (2 fl, picc, vln and 5 perc)
Tone (pf)
ELECTRONIC
Maboroshi (mix-ch, picc, elec-b and Japanese perc insts)
Ref. Otto Harrassowitz (Wiesbaden)

MKRTYCHIEVA, Virginia Nikitichna

Soviet lecturer and composer. b. Baku, December 22, 1914. She studied composition under V. Shebalin at the Moscow Conservatory from 1938 to 1941. For the next three years she taught music instrumentation and musical form at the Music School in Baku and then continued her composition studies under B. Zaidman and U. Hadjibekov at the Baku Conservatory, graduating in 1945. In 1951 she moved to Moscow. From 1961 she lectured at a music school in Sverdlovsk.
Compositions
ORCHESTRA
Symphony (1946)
Overture (1942)
Toccata (1970)
March (wind orch)
CHAMBER
String quartet (1968)
Scherzo (vln and pf) (1947)
Sonata (cl and pf) (1961)
Three pieces (vln and pf) (1962)
PIANO
Ballade (1958)
Concert scherzo (1962)
Etude (1947)
Five preludes (1947)
Preludes (1943-1944)
Sonatina (1947)
VOCAL
Ballad, zashchitnik Stalingrada (A. Surkov) (vce and orch) (1945)
Poem (vce and orch) (1946)
The pioneer (A. Pushkin) (vce and pf) (1953)
Romances (Pushkin, Lermontov and Soviet poets) (vce and pf)
Songs on Peace (vce and pf) (1950)
Songs on the Second World War (vce and pf) (1942)
Ref. 21, 87

MOBERG, Ida Georgina

Finnish pianist, conductor, teacher and composer. b. Helsingfors, February 13, 1859; d. Helsingfors, August 2, 1947. She was Finland's first recognized woman composer. She studied theory and composition at St. Petersburg Conservatory from 1883 to 1884, then counterpoint under R. Faltin and composition under Sibelius at the Helsinki Philharmonic Society's Orchestra Schoool. From 1901 to 1905 she studied composition under F. Draeseke at Dresden Conservatory and from 1911 to 1912 studied the Dalcroze method of improvisation in Berlin and in Hellerau in 1914. In 1906 she conducted a concert of her own works. She taught music in schools and privately and sight reading at the Helsinki Music Institute from 1914 to 1916.
Compositions
ORCHESTRA
Symphony (1905)
Kalevala fantasy
The legend
Meditation
Overture to Regina von Emmeritz
Rustic dance
Silence
Song of life
Sunrise, suite
Tone poems I and II
CHAMBER
Pieces (pf)
VOCAL
Awaken (m-ch and orch)
Life's struggle (m-ch and orch)
Before the struggle (ch and strs)
King David (ch and strs)
Michael Scott (ch and strs)
Night of the tyrant (ch and strs)
Choruses
Songs
SACRED
Amor mortis (vce and org)
Amor proximi (vce and org)
Ex Deo (vce and org)
Munificentia (vce and org)
OPERA
Asiens Ljus (V. Rydberg)
Publications
Children's song book. 1919.
Bibliography
Composers of Finland I. 1965.
G. Von Klosse. *Ida Moberg, the first Finnish woman composer. White Magazine*, 1948:7.
Ref. 8

MOCKE, Marie Felicity Denise. See PLEYEL, Marie Felicity Denise

MOCKEL, Johanna. See KINKEL, Johanna

MODRAKOWSKA, M.

20th-century Polish composer.
Composition
VOCAL
Piesn marszowa robotnika polskiego (solo, mix-ch or m-ch and pf) (1950)
Ref. Ed. Polonaises de Musique, 1954

MOE, Benna

Danish organist, pianist, conductor, singer, teacher and composer. b. Copenhagen, January 14, 1897. She studied the piano at Horneman's Conservatory in Copenhagen under Dagmar Walsoe and the organ under O.E. Thuner. She was also a pupil of Peter Cornelius, Villie Hagbo Peterson and Rena Pfiffer. As an organist she gave concerts in Denmark, Sweden, England and the United States and was also a cinema organist in Copenhagen. She had two music schools in Dalarna, Sweden.
Compositions
ORCHESTRA
Hyldestmarch til Gustav
Wedding waltz, for the wedding of Queen Margrethe (1967)
Light music
Marches

CHAMBER
String quartet
Organ pieces
Other pieces
PIANO
Den danske Ungdoms Marsche, op. 1
Dolly vals, op. 2
Erste Bataillons Jubilaeumsmarsche, op. 3
Etudes
Gondoliers serenade, op. 11
Soenderjydsk frihedsmarsch, op. 7
Teaching works
VOCAL
Cantata for the Oddfellow Lodge, Sweden
Elegisk stemning (vce and orch)
Alpesuite (m-ch and org) (1929)
Kongen og folket: I smilet er vor rigsom (ch)
Hendes foerste karneval, op. 10 (vce and pf)
Mindesang, digt af Holger Krusenstjerna-Hafstroem, op. 19
Nu kalder der klokker, op. 4 (vce and pf)
Quartets (m-vces)
To danske sange: Vort daedreland: Folk og flag, op. 20 (vce and pf)
Tre aange af Tornerose, op. 5 (vce and pf)
Tre aange ved Soenderjyllands Genforening med Danmark, op. 8 (vce and pf)
Approx. 200 songs
Children's songs
BALLET
Hybris, in 3 acts (1930)
Ref. 96, 331

MOELLER, Agnes

Danish pianist, teacher and composer. b. Copenhagen, December 5, 1857. She studied under Mrs. Rappoldi of Dresden and taught theory and the piano.

Compositions
PIANO
Pieces incl.:
Rococo, op. 6
Ref. 331

MOELLER, Paulette

20th-century Danish composer.

Composition
INCIDENTAL MUSIC
Den lykkelige bissekraemmer, marionette theatre (vces and pf) (Copenhagen, 1968)
Ref. 331

MOERO (Myro)

Ancient Greek poetess and composer of Byzantium. ca. 300 B.C. She was the wife of Andromachus Philologus and the mother of the grammarian and tragic poet, Homerus. She wrote epic, elegiac and lyric poems.

Composition
SACRED
Hymn to Neptune (Poseidon)
Ref. 334, 382

MOESTUE, Marie

Norwegian teacher and composer. b. Nes, July 28, 1869; d. 1948. She was a pupil of Molly Lammers, Wilma Monti, Desiree Artot de Padilla, Sigurd Lie and Grunicke.

Compositions
PIANO
Capriccio (Warmuth)
Deux pieces: Berceuse; A la mazurka, op. 7 (Hansen)
Mazurka and Menuetto, op. 10 (By)
VOCAL
Baantull huldrelok (w-ch) (By)
Aftenbon (Dr. E.F.B. Horn) (vce and pf) (Warmuth)
Ikvoeld er det Julekvaeld (V. Krag) (med-vce and pf) (Warmuth)
Tam svane (vce, vl and pf) (Warmuth)
Ved vuggen (Norwegian and German) (By)
Other songs

Publications
A History of the Vocal Art. Norway, 1917.
Ref. 70, 226, 297

MOGFORD, Anne. See FRICKER, Anne

MOHNS, Grace Updegraff Bergen

American organist, pianist, choral conductor, teacher and composer. b. Dubuque, IO, November 20, 1907. She obtained her B.A. magna cum laude from the University of Minnesota in 1930 then spent two years on a scholarship at the Juilliard School of Music. She was organist and choral conductor in various churches, taught the piano and religion and was a recitalist after 1945. She composed organ and piano works, secular and sacred vocal works.
Ref. 84, 359

MOKE, Marie Felicity Denise. See PLEYEL, Marie Felicity Denise

MOLA, Corradina

20th-century Italian composer.

Compositions
CHAMBER
Burlesca (1944)
ARRANGEMENTS
Seven sonatas by Pergolesi (hpcd or pf) (1948)

Publications
Method for Harpsichord. Curci, 1941.
Ref. 189

MOLAVA, Pamela May

American/British electronic instrumentalist, pianist, violinist, lecturer and composer. b. Sri Lanka, May 7, 1924. She became an L.R.A.M. in 1948 after studying the piano, the violin and dramatic arts and gained her B.S. in 1956 and M.A. in 1958 from the New York University. She studied at the New School from 1960 to 1961. From 1983 she taught electronic and computer music at Hartford Conservatory of Music and Dance. As artistic director of the Studio of Electronic music she co-ordinates festivals of acoustic, electronic and computer music in Hartford. She gives concert performances in New York and Boston. PHOTOGRAPH.

Compositions
ELECTRONIC
Apostrophe for Beatrice (amp and/or elec vln) (1985) (Simsbury: The Studio)
Cosmic patterns (comm Truda Kaschmann Dance Ens., 1983)
Crumer-om prelude (1981)
EEN (tape and acoustic vln) (Studio) (comm Greater Hartford Arts Council, 1982)
Ref. composer, 625

MOLINARO, Simone

B. 1565; d. 1615. DISCOGRAPHY.

Composition
LUTE
Fantasia nova
Ref. Frau und Musik

MOLINE, Lily Wadhams

Composer of organ pieces.

Bibliography
Barrel, Edgar. *Notable Musical Women. Etude*, November, 1929.
Ref. 323

MOLINOS-LAFITTE, Mlle. A.

French pianist and composer. b. Paris, ca. 1798. She studied the piano under Zimmerman.

Compositions
PIANO
Variations pour le piano sur le pas de Zephir (Paris: Leduc)
VOCAL
Songs (Paris: Catelin)
Ref. 26, 226, 276

MOLIQUE, Caroline

19th-century German composer. She was the daughter of the composer Wilhelm Bernhard Molique.

Compositions
CHAMBER
Bolero (vln and pf)
Melody on an exercise by F. Sor (vlc and pf) (Novello)
Suite (vln and pf)
Other violin pieces
PIANO
Isabella, mazurka (Novello)
Mignonette, impromptu (Novello)
VOCAL
Songs incl.:
Ach waer mein Lied (Zumsteeg)
Ref. 226, 276, 297

MOLITOR, Friederike
19th-century German composer.
Compositions
PIANO
Etude, op. 3
Five marches, op. 2
VOCAL
Songs incl.:
Drei kleine Lieder, op. 18
Two songs, op. 20 (S and vln)
Ref. 226, 276

MOLSA DA MODENA, Tarquinia. See MOLZA, Tarquinia

MOLZA (Molsa da Modena), Tarquinia
16th-century Italian conductor, poetess, singer and composer. b. Modena. She sang with Laura Peperara and Lucrezia Benedidi at the Italian Court. It is said that composers from all over Europe flocked to hear the famous trio. Tarquinia also organised and conducted her own women's orchestra, comprising ladies playing viols and woodwind instruments. When the performers had taken their places, Tarquinia would enter and with a long wooden stick, give the signal to commence. This is interesting because batons were not used by conductors until the 19th-century. Her concerts under the patronage of the Duke and Duchess of Ferrara were praised for both their musicality and performance. It appears that her brilliant career was cut short when the duchess dismissed her as a result of her unhappy love affair with Jacques de Wert. She retired to her mother's country estate from where she had no opportunity to present her works. She wrote the poems 'Nella dolce stagion di primavera' for a madrigal by Pietro Vinci (Bergamo, April 15, 1571) and 'La luce occhi miei lassi' for a madrigal by J. Leonard Primavera (Venice, September 6, 1573). She composed music for the lute, the viol, the harp and voice.
Ref. 216, 264, 415, 433, 563

MOLLER, Agnes. See MOELLER, Agnes

MOLLER, Paulette. See MOELLER, Paulette

MOMY, Valerie
19th-century German composer.
Compositions
PIANO
Rondo, with introduction in F (Schott)
Rondo sur Masaniello (Costallat)
SACRED
Ave verum (vce and orch) (Durand)
Benedictus (2 equal vces) (Durand)
O salutaris (Durand)
Ref. 226, 276, 297

MONACA DI S. REDEGONDA in Milano. See BADALLA, Rosa Giacinta

MONACHINA
Italian composer.
Composition
VOCAL
Bramar di perdere per troppo affeto, aria (S, vln, vla and d-b; also orch) (ded Pazzaglia)
Ref. 161

MONCRIEFF (Moncriff), Lynedock
19th-century English composer.
Compositions
VOCAL
Songs incl.:
Creole love song
Green leaf and blossom
Old church door
The parting kiss
Ripplin' tide
OPERA
Pandora (1898)
Ref. 276, 347, 431

MONCRIEFF, Mrs. L. See MONCRIEFF, Lynedock

MONCRIFF, Miss or Mrs. L. See MONCRIEFF, Lynedock

MONDONVILLE, Mme. de
18th-century French harpsichordist, artist and composer. She married Jean-Joseph Cassanea de Mondonville, a musician and composer. She studied the harpsichord under Rameau and composed a number of pieces for her instrument.
Ref. 119

MONET, Antoinette Paule de. See DUCHAMBGE, Pauline

MONGRUEL, Georgiana Catherine Eugenie Leonard
Belgian poetess, teacher, writer and composer. b. Charleroi, 1861. She completed her studies at Mons College in 1855. After her marriage she lived in Brazil, taught in junior schools and wrote for several newspapers. In 1945, after an accident that left her paralysed, she turned her interests to writing and composing seriously.
Compositions
VOCAL
Avril eternel renouveau (Dario Velozo) (vce and pf)
Canção (Ismael Martins) (vce and pf)
Rosa Alquimica (D. Velozo) (vce and pf)
Um violão que chora (Emiliano Perneta) (vce and pf)
Publications
Le Derniere Chevauchée. Poetry. 1952.
Sous le Charme. Autobiography.
Ref. 268

MONK, Meredith
American pianist, choreographer, dancer, lecturer, singer and composer. b. Lima, Peru, November 20, 1943. She came from a musical family and began studying the piano when she was three. Her teachers were Genshon Konikov and Marcia Polis Kosinsky. At Sarah Lawrence College she studied under Meyer Kupferman, Pal Ukena and Bessie Schoenberg from 1960 to 1964. She studied composition under Richard Averee, Ruth Lloyd and Glen Mack and voice under Vicki Starr, William Horn, Roland Wyatt, Ethel Raim and Gerald Siena. She won Obie awards for outstanding achievement in 1972 and 1976; in 1972 she received a Guggenheim fellowship in choreography; in 1974 a Brandeis creative award in dance; in 1868 she founded *The House*, a company of performers dedicated to an interdisciplinary approach to performance. She taught at Goddard College and lectured at New York University from 1970 to 1972. DISCOGRAPHY.
Compositions
PIANO
Piano music for Paris
VOCAL
Drone for chorus (60 vces) (1969)
Ester's song (vce ens)
View 1 (vocal ens)
View 2 (vocal ens)

Anthology and small scroll (vce and pf) (1975)
Engine steps (vce, org, pf and Moog syn)
Key: An album of invisible theatre (vce and org) (1970)
Our lady of late (vce and wine glass) (1972)
Porch, horizon (vce) (1969)
Raw recital No. 1 (vce and elec org) (1970)
OPERA
Education of the girlchild (1973)
Vesse, an epic (1971)
THEATRE
The beach (1965)
Blueprint (vce and tape) (1967)
Break (1964)
Chacon (25 vces, pf and perc) (1974)
Dolmen music (1979)
Fear and loathing in Gotham (vce and pf) (1975)
Juice, cantata (85 vces, Jew's hps, vln and perc) (1969)
Key (vce, vocal qrt, elec org, Jew's hp and perc) (1971)
Needle-brain Lloyd and the Systems Kid (150 vces, elec org, gtr and fl) (1970)
Plainsong for Bill's Bojo (elec org) (1971)
The plateau series (5 vces and tape) (1977)
Quarry (1976)
Recent ruins (14 vces, tape and vlc) (1979)
Sixteen millimeter earrings (vce and gtr) (1966)
Songs from the hill (4 vces, 2 rec, Jew's hp and pf - 4 hands) (1979)
Specimen days (14 vces, pf, org and trp) (1981)
Tablet (1976)
Tour: Dedicated to dinosaurs (1969)
Turtle dreams (4 vces and 2 elec org) (1981)
Venice/Milan (15 vces and pf - hands) (1976)
Waltz (4 vces and 4 org tracks)
ELECTRONIC
Candy, bullets and moon (vce and elec org) (1967)
Ref. composer, MLA *Notes*, 142, 347, 494, 563, 622, 625, 633

MONNOT, Marguerite Angele

French pianist and composer. b. Decize, Niever, May 26, 1903; d. Paris, October 12, 1961. She studied under her father and then under Alfred Cortot and harmony under Nadia Boulanger (q.v.). She made her debut as a pianist on the eve of a tour to the United States. She received world fame for her *Irma la Douce*. Her songs were sung by Yves Montaud and Edith Piaf among others. DISCOGRAPHY.

Compositions
VOCAL
Songs
OPERETTA
Irma la Douce (based on Alexandre Breffort's book)
FILM MUSIC
Desert de Pigalle
Si le roi savait ça
Ref. 1, 70, 130, 295, 392, 563, 608

MONTAGUE RING. See ALDRIDGE, Amanda Ira

MONTALANT, Laure or Cynthie. See DAMOREAU-CINTI, Laure

MONTESQUIOU, Odette de

D. 1908.
Compositions
HARP
Prelude
Valse humoresque
Ref. 75

MONTGEROULT, Helene de Nervode (Countess of Charnay)

French pianist, teacher and composer. b. Lyon, March 2, 1764; d. Florence, May 20, 1836. She studied the piano under Hullmandel, Dussek and Viotti and then taught at the Paris Conservatoire from 1795 to 1798. She was sentenced to death during the French Revolution but was saved by playing the *Marseillaise* before the Tribunal. She lived in Berlin until after the revolution and in 1835 went to Florence. Two pupils of hers were Pradher and Boely.

Compositions
PIANO
Fantasies Nos. 1, 2 and 3 (Paris: Janet & Cortelle)
Sonata in G-Minor (Berlin: Lischke)
Three sonatas, op. 1 (Paris: Troupenas)
Three sonatas, op. 2 (Troupenas)
Three sonatas, op. 5 (Geneva: Minkoff)
Separate pieces for piano only, op. 3 (Paris: Erard)
VOCAL
Six Italian and French nocturnes, op. 6 (2 vces and pf) (Erard)
Publications
Cours complet pour l'enseignement du forte-piano, conduisant progressivement des premiers elements aux plus grandes difficulties. Paris: Janet & Cortele.
Ref. 9, 26, 66, 105, 128, 226, 276, 312, 347

MONTGOMERY. See GYLLENHAAL, Matilda Valeriana Beatrix

MONTGOMERY, Alicia Adelaide. See NEEDHAM, Alicia Adelaide

MONTGOMERY, Merle (pseud. Aline Campbell)

American pianist, lecturer, writer and composer. b. Davidson, OK, May 15, 1904; d. Arlington, VA, August 25, 1986. She studied at the University of Oklahoma where she obtained her B.F.A. in 1924 and at the Eastman School of Music graduating with an M.M. in 1937 and a Ph.D. in 1948. She also received a diploma from the American Conservatory in Fontainebleau, France in 1933. She studied privately with Isidor Philipp and Nadia Boulanger (q.v.) from 1929 to 1931. She taught the piano and theory at the University of Oklahoma from 1931 to 1933 and was head of the piano and theory department at the Southeastern Institute, Weatherford, OK, from 1938 to 1941 and state supervisor of the Federal Music Project from 1941 to 1943. She lectured in the Schillinger system of music composition from 1945 to 1949 and was the national representative for music publisher Carl Fischer from 1947 to 1954 and then his co-ordinator of symphonic repertory from 1967 to 1971. She was educational consultant for OUP, New York from 1956 to 1966 and president of the National Federation of Music Clubs from 1971 to 1975. From 1975 she was president of the National Music Council. She received the University of Rochester alumni citation in 1960, the Oklahoma University distinguished service citation in 1977 and a citation from the Mu Phi Epsilon international music fraternity in 1983. PHOTOGRAPH.

Compositions
ORCHESTRA
Symphony
They dared to lead (1947)
PIANO
Air for 2 hands (1957) (C. Fischer)
Five elementary pieces
Sonatina (1942)
Six pieces (New York: C. Scribner's Sons, 1972)
Stepping lively (1957) (C. Fischer)
VOCAL
Supplication (ch a-cap or with str orch)
The dark hills (mix-ch) (1969)
Leisure (mix-ch and pf or org) (H.W. Gray)
Madrigal (ch a-cap)
Eight songs for children (Allyn Bacon & Co.)
Let Mrs. Lindy pass (1945)
Seventeen songs for children (Scott-Foresman)
Publications
Cours de composition musicale. V. d'Indy. Translated by M. Montgomery. Durand.
Music Theory Papers. Books 1-5. New York: C. Fischer, 1959.
Ref. composer, 40, 142, 347

MONTGOMERY, Mme. de

19th-century French composer. Her opera was performed in Monte Carlo in 1894.
Composition
OPERA
Arethuse
Ref. 431

MONTI, Diana. See KAZORECK, Hildegard

MONTIJN, Aleida
20th-century Dutch composer.
Compositions
CHAMBER
Musik fuer eine Gruppe
PIANO
Etude mit Stereotypen (3 pf)
Etude
VOCAL
Musiken fuer einen Kindermusizierkreis (ch, fls, metallophone, xy and trp or cl)
Seven songs (Sappho) (vce and insts)
TEACHING PIECES
Die Igel (pf)
Ref. Frau und Musik

MOODY, Marie
19th-century English composer.
Compositions
ORCHESTRA
Concert overture in C-Major
Concert overture in E-Minor
Hamlet, overture
King Lear, overture
Othello, overture
Der sterbende Kreiger, overture
CHAMBER
Adagio and allegretto in D (strs)
Allegro moderato in D-Minor (str qrt)
Piano studies
SACRED
Great Lord of Lords
Anthem
Ref. 6, 226, 276

MOODY, Pamela
20th-century British composer,.
Composition
CHAMBER
Impromptu (vla and pf)
Ref. *Composer* (London)

MOOKE, Marie Felicity Denise. See PLEYEL, Marie Felicity Denise

MOON, Chloe Elizabeth
New Zealand violinist, lecturer and composer. b. Christchurch, January 9, 1952. She gained her B.A. first class hons. from the University of Canterbury and did postgraduate study in the violin at Ghent Conservatorium, Belgium. She has performed with several orchestras and was a member of the resident string quartet at the University of Canterbury from 1975 to 1977 and is currently a lecturer in music at the same university. She received several prizes and scholarships whilst at university. DISCOGRAPHY. PHOTOGRAPH.
Compositions
ORCHESTRA
Concertino (fl and cham orch) (1983)
Episodes (str orch) (1979)
Shadows (str orch) (1979)
Sinfonia (str orch) (1973)
Reflections (str orch) (1980)
CHAMBER
Nonette (2 fl, 2 vln, vlc, 2 cl, ob and bsn) (1982)
String quartet, 3 sketches (1980)
Divertimento (fl, cl and bsn) (1982)
String trio (1980)
Three dances (fl, cl and vlc) (1982)
Three pieces for woodwind trio (fl, cl and bsn) (1982)
Trio (cl, vla and vlc) (1983)
Duo (fl and vla) (1983)
Duo (vln and vlc) (1980)
Duo (2 vln) (1980)
Sonata (fl and pf) (1982)
Caprice (vln) (1982)
Five miniatures (vlc) (1972)
Requiem (fl) (1980)
Soliloquy (vln) (1980) (Otago University Press)
Spring dance (fl) (1982)
PIANO
Plumb-bob (1983)
Silhouette (1982)
Traceries (1982)
VOCAL
A crown of windflowers (treble vces a-cap) (1981)
Dandelion parachutes (S, A, T, and B a-cap) (1983)
Four lyrics from chamber music (S, A, T and B a-cap) (1981)
Lizard on a rock (treble vces a-cap) (1982)
The message of the wind (vocal qrt and pf) (1981)
Songs of a maiden (S, A, T and B a-cap) (1981)
Two songs (Christina Rossetti) (m-S and pf) (1983)
Ref. composer, 563

MOORE, Anita
20th-century American composer.
Composition
CHAMBER
Quintet for brass (1981)
Ref. AMC

MOORE, Dorothy Rudd
Black American lecturer, poetess, singer and composer. b. New Castle, DE, June 4, 1940. She studied under Mark Fax at Howard University, Washington, DC, graduating with a B.A. magna cum laude in 1963 and continuing her studies under Nadia Boulanger (q.v.) and Chou Wen-Chung. She taught at New York University and Bronx Community College and founded the Society of Black Composers. Her cello works have been widely performed by her husband Kermit Moore. DISCOGRAPHY. PHOTOGRAPH.
Compositions
ORCHESTRA
Symphony No. 1
CHAMBER
Lament for nine instruments
Reflections (wind ens)
Modes for string quartet (New York: CFE, 1968)
Trio No. 1 (CFE)
Dirge and deliverance (vlc and pf) (CFE)
Moods for viola and cello
Night fantasy (cl and pf)
Three pieces for violin and piano (CFE)
Baroque suite (vlc)
Dream and variations (pf)
VOCAL
From the dark tower, song cycle (8 poems by black American poets) (1972)
From the dark tower, orchestration of 4 songs from cycle of same name (m-S and orch) (New York: Rudmar)
In celebration (S, B, mix-ch and pf) (CFE, 1977)
Sonnets of love, rosebuds and death (CFE, 1976)
Twelve quatrains from the Rubaiyat of Omar Khayyam (m-S and ob)
Weary blues (B, vlc and pf) (CFE, 1976)
Ref. 136, 228, 287, 347, 549, 622, 625

MOORE, Luella Lockwood
20th-century American pianist, teacher and composer. She composed piano pieces and songs.
Ref. 347, 353

MOORE, Mary Carr
American conductor, lecturer, singer and composer. b. Memphis, TN, August 6, 1873; d. Inglewood, CA, January 9, 1957. She began piano lessons at the age of seven and at 12 studied composition under her uncle John Harraden Pratt and voice under H.B. Passmore. She began composing as a child and published a lullaby at the age of 16. She received an honorary D.M. from Chapman College in 1936, three awards from the National League of American Pen Women and the David Bispham medal in 1930. She sang in concerts, choirs and her own operas, conducted orchestras on the West Coast and after settling in Los Angeles, taught music theory. She was the only woman to lead the orchestra of 80 men at the Panama-Pacific International Exposition of 1915, when they performed some of her compositions. She taught theory and composition at the Olga Steeb Piano School from 1926 to 1942, at Chapman College from 1928 to 1947 and in various conservatories and studios. In 1928 she founded the Manuscript Club, Los Angeles and in 1936, with Cadman and Grunn, founded the California Society of Composers, which was succeeded by the Society of Native American composers. DISCOGRAPHY. PHOTOGRAPH.

Compositions

ORCHESTRA

Piano concerto in F-Minor, op. 94, no. 1
Ia-mi-a-kin, or Totem vision, op. 92
Kidnap, op. 9 (1938)

CHAMBER

Saul, op. 80, no. 2, suite (pf qnt)
String quartet in C-Minor, op. 81, no. 6
String quartet in F-Minor, op. 91, no. 8
Poeme, op. 102, no. 1 (pf trio)
Brief furlough, op. 102, no. 2 (qnt of cl, pf and strs)
Chant d'amour, op. 91, no. 3 (fl and pf)
Message to one absent, op. 87, no. 6 (vln and pf) (W. Webster, 1941)
Nocturne, op. 96, no. 2 (fl and pf)
Sonata (vln and pf)
Other pieces (ob, bsn and pf, vln and pf, vlc and pf, cl and pf, trp and pf)

ORGAN

Prelude and fugue in D-Minor, op. 98, no. 13
Prelude in F, op. 72, no. 4
Prelude in G, op. 72, no. 3

PIANO

Barcarolle, op. 75, no. 8 (Webster, 1935)
Forest sketches, op. 100, no. 1.4: Before the dawn, Dance of the wood sprites, Twilight in the forest, Murmur of pines (C. Fischer, 1939)
March humoresque, op. 91, no. 15 (1955) (Webster)
Revons, op. 85, no. 3 (G. Schirmer, 1931)
Song of a faun, op. 81, no. 13 (Webster, 1922)

VOCAL

Approx. 15 choral works incl.:
The quest of Sigurd, cantata (W. Morris) (w-ch and insts) (1905)
Beyond these hills, op. 86 (G. Moyle) (vces and insts) (1924)
California cycle, op. 84, nos. 1-3: The mountain lake (F. Bruner), Half dome (F. van Norden), The pine of Portsmouth Square (C. Dobie) (Webster, 1932)
Idlese, op. 67, no. 1 (C. Scollard) (M. Witmark, 1922)
Oh, wind from the Golden Gate, op. 61 (V. Harrison) (Witmark, 1910)
There is no death, op. 104, no. 2 (S. Murray)
Approx. 250 songs incl.:
Blue herons, op. 91, no. 2 (Hollywood: R.P. Saunders, 1937)
Brahma, op. 69, no. 2
Cicina mia, op. 85, no. 1 (San Francisco: Sherman, Clay, 1925)
Dweller in my dreams, op. 81, no. 10
Four love songs (vce, fl, vln, vlc and pf, also vce and pf) (Webster, 1933)
Homebound, op. 91, no. 14 (Webster, 1948)
I love thee, op. 58, no. 2 (duet) (Witmark, 1910)
May with life and music, op. 28, no. 1 (Schirmer)
Message, op. 98, no. 6 (Webster, 1947)
My dream, op. 79, no. 3 (Webster, 1935)
Mysterious power, op. 76, no. 1 (Webster)
A road song, op. 63, no. 1 (Witmark, 1910)
Sixteen art songs (S, T and pf)
Song of a faun
Sunset, op. 85, no. 9 (Schirmer, 1927)
Vision, op. 98, no. 11 (Webster, 1948)
You, op. 77, no. 2 (Schirmer, 1921)

OPERA

David Rizzio, op. 89, grand opera in 2 acts (Emanuel Mapleson Browne) (1928) (Webster, 1937, Da Capo, 1981)
The Flaming Arrow, op. 83, no. 1, Indian legend in 1 act (Sara Pratt Moore) (1922)
Legend Provencale or Macabre, op. 90, grand opera in 3 acts (Eleanore Flaig)
The Leper, op. 74, tragedy in 1 act (Dudley Burrows) (1912)
Los Rubios, op. 93, romantic opera in 3 acts (Neeta Marquis) (1931) (comm City of Los Angeles for fiesta celebration)
Narcissa or The Cost of Empire, grand opera in 4 acts (S. Moore) (Witmark, 1912) (David Bispham Memorial Award, 1930)

OPERETTA

A Chinese Legend 'The Immortal Lovers', pantomime (F.H. Bruner)
Flutes of Jade Happiness, op. 95, in 3 acts (Laura Sweeney Moore) (1931)
Harmony, op. 71, no. 10, musical farce in 1 act (Mission High School Students)
Memories, op. 78, no. 1, vaudeville in 1 act (Charles Eugene Banks) (1914)
The Oracle op. 25, in 2 acts (composer)

Bibliography

Hipscher, E.E. "American Opera and its Composers". Philadelphia, 1939. Pp. 328-336.
Smith, Catherine P. "Moore, Mary Carr". In New Grove Dictionary of American Music. 1986.
Smith, Catherine P. and Richardson, Cynthia S. "Mary Carr Moore, American Composer". Ann Arbor: University of Michigan Press, 1987.

Ref. Music Dept. University of Nevada, Manuscript Club of Los Angeles, Sonneck Society newsletter summer 1981, 22, 39, 40, 70, 74, 94, 141, 142, 168, 226, 228, 292, 304, 347, 433, 447, 494, 496, 529, 563, 611, 622

MOORE, Undine Smith

Black American pianist, choir conductor, professor and composer. b. Jarratt, VA, August 25, 1905. She obtained her B.A. and B.Mus. from Fisk University, graduating with highest honors. She was the first Fisk student to be awarded a scholarship to the Juilliard School of Music. She continued her studies there, at the Eastman and Manhattan Schools of Music and Columbia University (M.A. and professional diploma in music). She received an honorary doctorate in music from Virginia State College and Indiana University in 1972. Her teachers included Lillian Allen Darden, Alice M. Grass and Howard Murphy (theory and composition) at Columbia University. In 1927 she became a faculty member of Virginia State College, lecturing there for 45 years and establishing a black music center, of which she was co-director. She also implemented the first course for the integration of the arts at Virginia State College. She taught at Virginia Union University and was visiting professor at the Colleges of St. Benedict, St. John and Carleton College. In 1975 the mayor of Petersburg, VA, proclaimed 13 April as Undine Moore Day. After her retirement she taught privately, traveled extensively, lectured at colleges and universities and took part in seminars, conferences and work-shops. DISCOGRAPHY.

Compositions

CHAMBER

Fugue in F (str trio) (1952)
Afro-American suite (fl or a-fl, vlc and pf) (1969) (comm Trio Pro Viva)
Trio (fl, cl and pf)
Duo (cl and pf)
Introduction and allegro (cl and pf) (1953)
Reflections (org and pf) (1952)
Organ variations on Nettleton (1976)

PIANO

Romance (2 pf) (1952)
Romantic young clown (1952)
Scherzo (1930)
Valse caprice (1930)

VOCAL

Sir Olaf and the Erl King's daughter, cantata (Scandinavian folk poem) (w-ch and pf) (1925)
I would be true (Howard A. Walter) (mix-ch and pf) (1958)
Into my heart's treasury (S. Teasdale) (mix-ch) (1950)
Mother to son (Langston Hughes) (double mix-ch) (1955) (New York: Witmark, 1955)
A time for remembering (composer) (mix-ch and pf) (1976)
When Susanna Jones wears red (Langston Hughes) (mix-ch) (ca. 1958)
Heart, have you heard the news? (Christina Rossetti) (S and pf) (1926)
I am in doubt (Florence Hynes Willett) (S and pf) (1975)
I want to die while you love me (Georgia Douglas Johnston) (Cont and pf) (1975)
Love, let the wind cry how I adore thee (also as Wedding song) (T.W. Wharton after Sappho) (S and pf or org) (1961)
Lyric for true love (Florence Hynes Willett) (S and pf) (1975)
Teach me to hear mermaids singing, 3 part canon (John Donne) (treble vces) (1953)
Uphill (Dante Gabriel Rossetti) (S and pf) (1962)

SACRED

Glory to God, cantata (St. Luke, St. Matthew and Book of Common Prayer) (narr, m-ch, fl, org and pf with opt brass and perc) (1974) (comm male choir, 1st Baptist Church, Petersburg, VA)
Scenes from the life of a martyr (speaking or singing narr, ch and orch) (ded Dr. Martin Luther King)
Alleluia (mix-ch and org) (1975)
Benediction (Donald Jeffrey Hayes) (mix-ch) (1974)
A Christmas alleluia (spiritual text) (w-ch) (1970) (comm Spelman College Glee Club)
Choral prayers in folk style (mix-ch) (1974)
Let us make man in our image (mix-ch a cap)
Lord make us more holy, 2 part canonic treatment of spiritual (ch and pf) (1966)
Lord, we give thanks for Thee (Bible) (mix-ch) (1971) (Warner Bros., 1973)
O Spirit who dost prefer before all temples (John Milton) (unison ch and pf or org) (1966)
Striving after God (Michelangelo) (mix-ch) (Witmark, 1960)
Tambourines to glory (L. Hughes) (mix-ch) (1973)
Thou hast made us for Thyself (mix-ch) (1952)
Who shall separate us from the love of Christ (Bible) (mix-ch and pf or org) (1953)
The lamb, 2 part canon (William Blake) (treble vces) (H.W. Gray, 1958)

ARRANGEMENTS

The blind man stood on the way and cried (m-ch) (1932)
Bound for Canaan's Land (mix-ch a-cap) (Witmark, 1960)
Daniel, Daniel, servant of the Lord (double mix-ch) (1952) (Witmark, 1953)
Fare you well, spiritual (mix-ch) (1950) (Witmark, 1951)
Hail! Warrior! Spiritual (mix-ch) (Witmark, 1958)
How I got over, spiritual (mix-ch) (1966)
I just come from the mountain (mix-ch) (1950) (Witmark, 1951)

I'm going home (mix-ch) (1948)
Is there anybody here? (w-ch) (1949)
Long fare you well (mix-ch) (Witmark, 1960)
No condemnation (m-ch) (1935)
Rise up shepherd and follow (m-ch) (1970)
Set down! (S and pf) (1951)
Sinner, you can't walk my path (mix-ch) (1958) (Witmark, 1960)
To be baptised (S and pf) (1973)
Walk thro' the streets of the city, spiritual (mix-ch) (1966)
Watch and pray (S and pf) (1973)

Publications

A Recorded Supplement to Studies in Traditional Harmony. Work on teaching theory with musical examples.

Bibliography

Rare Treat for Retiree: Adieu by Concert. Clavier II, November, 1972.

Ref. 136, 347, 348, 549, 563, 625

MOORE, Wilda Maurine Ricks

American pianist, teacher and composer. b. Vermillion, KS, November 1, 1908. She studied the piano under her mother and later at Matthews School of Piano, Denver and under Miles Blom, Mollie Margolis, Edith Kingsley Renquist, Elmer Schoettle and Robert E. Schmitz. She attended the Eastman School of Music from 1934 to 1935, obtained her B.A. from the University of Denver in 1937 and M.M. from Lamont College of Music in 1941. She taught the piano at the Renquist School from 1929 to 1932, Denver College in 1936, American College of Musicians from 1963 to 1973 and in her own studio from 1937 to 1973. She was a member of the National League of Pen Women and elected to the Hall of Fame, Piano Guild, 1974.

Compositions

CHAMBER

String quartet (1941) (Belwin)

PIANO

Eight pieces for children (1981)
Etude in D (Belwin)
Impromptu in D (Belwin)
Linda waltz (Belwin)
My prayer (Belwin)
Prelude (1929) (Belwin)
Rhapsody on war and peace (Belwin)
Rhapsodic melody (Belwin)
Rhapsody No. 3 (Belwin)
Romantic reverie (Belwin)
Summer fantasy (1980)
Two suites (Belwin)
Waltz in E (Belwin)
Other pieces (Belwin)

Ref. composer, 142, 347, 475

MOOREHEAD, Consuela Lee

American pianist, arranger, choral conductor, assistant professor and composer. b. Tallahassee, November 1, 1926. She graduated with an A.B. from Fisk University in 1948, an Mus.M. from Northwestern University in 1959 and she took postgraduate study at Eastman School during the summers of 1967 and 1968. She was choral conductor and music teacher in schools and music lecturer at several universities, becoming assistant professor of music at Talladega College in 1964. She was the pianist for a choir, chamber groups and resident jazz artist at Prince Edward County High School, Farmville.

Compositions

VOCAL

Two songs for a boy named Mark (1972)

PIANO

Cam's cradle (1959)
Hambone (1974)
A spirit speaks (1971)
Study in fifths (1958)
Suite for stone (1971)
Arrangements

Ref. 475

MORALT, Sofia Giustina. See CORRI-DUSSEK, Sofia Giustina

MORANDI, Jennie Jewett

American pianist and composer. b. Boston, 1874.

Compositions

PIANO

Pieces incl.:
Danse espagñole

Ref. 374

MORATORI ANGIOLA, Teresa. See MURATORI SCANNABECCHI, Angiola

MORATORI SCANNABECCHI, Angiola. See MURATORI SCANNABECCHI, Angiola

MORE, Isabella Theaker

18th-century English composer.

Composition

VOCAL

The walls of my prison, ballad

Ref. 65, 489

MORE, Margaret Elizabeth

British composer. b. Harlech, June 26, 1903. She studied music for two terms under Edward d'Evry at the Royal College of Music, London. She also received informal help from Josef Holbrooke and Eugene Goossens. After her marriage to a son of Granville Bantock, she learned orchestration from her father-in-law. In spite of domestic repression she began her opera *The Mermaid* in 1920 which was finally produced in Birmingham in 1951 during the Festival of Britain.

Compositions

ORCHESTRA

Summer night in the Austrian Tyrol, symphonic poem

CHAMBER

Matric carmina, suite (pf, ww and strs)
Two trios (vln, vlc ad pf)
Sonata

PIANO

Columbine
Harlequin

BALLET

Celtic Legend
Medium in White

OPERETTA

The Mermaid (Hans Christian Andersen)

INCIDENTAL MUSIC

Snow Queen (H.C. Anderson) (Michael Martin-Harvey)

Ref. 8, 94, 141, 572

MOREA, Vincenza della

Compositions

PIANO

Lavandaie notturne, op. 11, round dance

VOCAL

Due novembre, lament (vce and pf)
Misiva d'amore, song
Prega per me, pensiero (vce and pf)

Ref. Ricordi (Milan)

MOREL, Virginie

18th-century French pianist and composer.

Composition

CHAMBER

Sonata pour piano avec accompagnement de viol ..... (Paris: Composer & H. Lemoine)

Ref. 128

MORETTO, Nelly

Argentine pianist and composer. b. Santa Fe, Rosario, September 20, 1925. She studied at the Musical Professorship School, Rosario and the Conservatorio Nacional de Musica y Arte Escenico under Juan Carlos Paz; attended the Di Tella Institute of High Musical Studies in Buenos Aires and the University of Illinois Music School. She is a member of the Agrupacion Nueva Musica and organized radio programs for the Municipal Radio, Buenos Aires. DISCOGRAPHY.

Compositions

ORCHESTRA

Composition No. 11 (sym orch)

CHAMBER

Composition No. 8 (inst ens)
Composition No. 12, funeral march for a violinist (str qrt)
Composition No. 7 (fl, vla, b-cl and gtr)
Trio (vln, vlc and ob)

ELECTRONIC

Coeri battenti (str qrt and magnetic tape) (1968)
Collage and music for dances (1967)
Composition No. 10 (str qrt and magnetic tape)
Composition No. 14, Bah! I told to time (vce, pf, trp and magnetic tape)

Composition No. 13, in memory of Juan Carlos Paz (trp and magnetic tape)
Composition No. 9B (Gustavo Moretto) (magnetic tape)
Ref. composer, 77, 206, 390, 406, 563

MORFIDA. See RALPH, Kate

MORGAN, Dianne. See MORLEY, Nina Dianne

MORGAN, Hilda
20th-century Canadian composer.
Compositions
SACRED
Christmas morn (Waterloo Music, 1964)
Communion hymn (Waterloo, 1964)
This little babe (Waterloo, 1964)
ARRANGEMENTS
I saw three ships (Waterloo, 1964)
Ref. Catalog of Canadian Choral Music

MORGAN, Lady (nee Sidney Owenson)
Irish harpist, novelist, poetess and composer. b. Dublin, ca. 1783; d. London, April 14, 1859.
Compositions
VOCAL
Irish airs (composer)
OPERETTA
The First Attempt (Dublin, 1807)
Publications
The Lay of the Irish Harp. Poems. 1809.
Novels.
Ref. 6, 226, 307

MORGAN, Mary Hannah (pseud. May Brahe)
Australian composer. b. Melbourne, 1885; d. 1956. She went to England in 1912. DISCOGRAPHY.
Compositions
VOCAL
Over 300 songs incl.:
Bless this house (vce and pf)
I passed by your window (vce and pf)
Two little words (vce and pf)
Ref. 8, 563, 572

MORGAN, Maud
American concert harpist, teacher and composer. b. New York, November 22, 1860; d. Princess Bay, NY, December 2, 1941. She studied the harp under her father, George Washbourne Morgan and under A. Toulmin and K. Oberthur in London. She made her concert debut with the violinist Ole Bull in 1875 and later toured frequently, appeared in concerts of harp and organ music with her father and was harpist at Grace Church, NY, for 19 years. She composed pieces for the harp.
Ref. 85, 347, 433

MORGAN, Nina Dianne. See MORLEY, Nina Dianne

MORHANGE-MOTCHANE, Marthe
20th-century French composer.
Compositions
PIANO
Le petit classique, 22 short pieces
Ref. MLA *Notes*

MORI, Junko
20th-century Japanese composer.
Composition
CHAMBER
String quartet No. 2 (1980)
Ref. I.L.W.C.

MORIN-LABRECQUE, Albertine
Canadian concert pianist, professor and composer. b. Montreal, June 8, 1896; d. September 25, 1957. She studied the piano in Montreal under R.O. Pelletier and harmony and composition in Paris under J. Macaire. She graduated with her Mus.Doc. from Montreal University where she was professor of pedagogy. She gave concerts in the United States, France and Belgium.
Compositions
ORCHESTRA
Concerto (poème sur Jeanne d'Arc) (2 pf and str orch)
Concerto in C-Minor (2 pf and orch)
Jugement dernier, symphonic poem
Marche funèbre
Prelude tragique
Valse de concert
BAND
Comme le dit un vieil adage
Pantomime
Quand on porte l'uniforme
CHAMBER
Légènde (vln and pf) (Parnasse Musical)
Album de six pastels (org) (Archambault)
PIANO
Grande valse brillante de concert (2 pf)
Album de miniatures (Cincinnati: Zimmerman)
Album de 10 études de concert (Archambault)
Album de 24 preludes (Archambault)
Berceuse (Leduc)
Confidence (Leduc)
Grande étude de concert (Paris: Leduc)
Pastorale (Leduc)
Other pieces
VOCAL
Farandole (ch) (Archambault)
La main divine (ch) (Archambault)
Souvenez-vous (ch) (Archambault)
Numerous songs
SACRED
A toi, Sainte Vièrge Marie (ch) (Archambault)
BALLET
Au petit Trianon
Bohemien
Les rives du Danube
Russe
OPERA
Francine, comic opera
Madrini, comic opera
Pas-chu, Chinese opera
Publications
L'Art d'étudier le piano. J.E. Turcot.
Methode de piano. Archambault.
Receuil de modeles. Archambault.
Ref. 85, 93, 133

MORISON, Christina W. (nee Bogue)
Irish composer. b. Dublin, 1840. She studied under S. Glover and John Blockley.
Compositions
PIANO
Pieces
VOCAL
Songs
OPERA
The Uhlans, in 3 acts (W. M'Ivor Morison) (1884)
Ref. 6, 226, 431, 433

MORITZEN, Gunda
20th-century Danish composer.
Compositions
PIANO
Fra C till Ges, small pieces
VOCAL
Dreì Lieder fuer Sopranstimme (S and pf)
Sange (vce and pf)
Ref. 331

MORLEY, Angela
British woodwind player, conductor and composer. b. Leeds, March 10, 1924. She was a woodwind player in orchestras when young and studied harmony, counterpoint and composition under Matyas Seiber from 1947 to 1950 and conducting under Walter Goehr. She has composed a large amount of light music and orchestrated and conducted for film music. DISCOGRAPHY. PHOTOGRAPH.
Compositions
ORCHESTRA
Romance (vlc and orch) (1976)

VOCAL
Tehuantapec (ch and orch) (1965)
FILM MUSIC
Captain Nemo and the undersea city (1969)
La collina dei Comali (1979)
For better for worse (1954) (Chappell & Co.)
Friendships, secrets and lies, TV film (1979) (Warner Bros. Music)
It's never too late (1955) (Chappell)
The Little Prince, adaptation (1973) (Academy award nomination)
The looking glass war (1969)
Madame X, TV film (1981) (M.C.A.)
The slipper and the rose, adaptation (1975) (Academy award nomination)
Watership down (1977) (April Music)
When eight bells toll (1970) (Carlin Music)
Will any gentleman (1953) (Chappell)
The world of Florentine painting (1965)
The world of Florentine sculpture (1964)
Ref. composer, 497, 563

MORLEY, Nina Dianne (nee Morgan)
Canadian pianist and composer. b. Evanston, IL, October 7, 1929. She studied the piano from 1936 and composition under Gardner Reed from 1944 to 1946, then entered the Eastman School of Music, where she studied orchestration under Burril Phillips, Wayne Barlow and Bernard Rogers, 1947 to 1949. In 1960 she studied composition under Jean Coulthard (q.v.). She became an Canadian citizen in 1973 and married the composer and conductor Glen Stewart Morley. PHOTOGRAPH.
Compositions
ORCHESTRA
Creatures of a fantasy, overture (1968)
Old-fashioned flowers suite (str orch) (1971)
BAND
Concerto for trombone and concert band (1972)
CHAMBER
Sonata (vln and pf)
PIANO
Pensive dances, 6 pieces (1972)
Sonata (1972)
Sonatina (1948)
The toy box, suite (1972)
VOCAL
Master of the sea, cantata (Geral Manley Hopkins) (S, T, mix-ch and orch) (1971)
Meditations, cycle (m-S and orch) (1973)
The other world, cycle (m-S and orch) (1972)
The balloon man (e.e. cummings) (w-ch and pf) (1974)
Inversnaid (G.M. Hopkins) (mix-ch)
The song my paddle sings (Pauline Johnston) (mix-ch)
All things in all things (vce and pf) (1973)
Cocoon (S and pf) (1948)
False spring (S and pf) (1949)
Find me a wood (S and pf) (1948)
Margaret (G.M. Hopkins) (S and pf) (BMI, 1955)
Refugee (S and pf) (1948)
The seeker, cycle (G.M. Hopkins) (Bar and pf) (1956)
Walk up the mountain (vce and pf) (1973)
SACRED
God's grandeur, anthem (G.M. Hopkins) (ch a-cap) (1954)
Psalm 8 (ch and org) (1956)
Ref. composer, 93, 622

MORMONE, Tamara
Italian composer. b. 1911.
Compositions
ORGAN
Fantasia e fuga in D-Minor
SACRED
Invocazione
Marcia religiosa
Ref. G. Zanibon (Padua)

MORONEY, Sister Mary Emmeline
Australian organist, pianist, music historian, nun, teacher and composer. b. Melbourne, April 16, 1942. She gained her B.Mus. and M.Mus. from Melbourne University and entered the Monastery of Kew, Victoria, where she was chief organist. She composed liturgical works which included masses and a setting of a four week cycle of the Liturgical Hours.
Publications
The Song of Songs and the Medieval Love Lyric. 1976.
Research papers incl. *Music in Medieval England.* 1975.
Ref. 457

MORPURGO, Irene
19th-century Italian composer. Her opera was performed in Florence.
Composition
OPERA
Maria (1885)
Ref. 225

MORRIGU, Queen
Famous ancient Irish queen who taught battle hymns to her army.
Ref. 264

MORRIS, Mrs. C.H.
American composer. b. 1862; d. 1929.
Compositions
VOCAL
Songs
SACRED
Nearer, still nearer, hymn (composer) (Boston Music)
The stranger of Galilee, hymn (Boston Music)
Ref. 433, 347

MORRISON, Julia Maria
20th-century American critic, poetess and composer. b. Minnneapolis, April 26. She gained her B.A. and M.F.A. from the University of Iowa and her M.A. from the University of Minnesota and also studied at North Texas State University. She was a research fellow in computer documentation study at the University of Minnesota, a resident visitor at Bell Laboratories, New Jersey, made appearances in musical shows and held short term positions in electronic music studios. Her fields of research included contemporary Catholic liturgical music and Mahler's Tenth Symphony. She published many poetry books.
Compositions
ORCHESTRA
The fair is on! symphony in 3 mvts, for young people (1969)
CHAMBER
First thing this morning (perc ens)
Traveling after dark (perc ens) (1981)
Coming around (cl, trb and vlc) (1969)
Jula Street (a-sax, pf and d-b) (1969)
Octobermusic (a-sax, pf and d-b) (1969)
VOCAL
Songs incl.:
Arrogant custodian
As for pacifism
Cold turkey
Faust discovers adolescence
Musta been water here
Newcomber's lament
To Mother on her day
SACRED
Lamentations of Jeremiah I (m-ch and insts) (1969)
Psalm 122 (Bar, a-sax and vlc) (1969)
Psalm 131 (Bar and a-sax) (1969)
OPERA
Smile Right to the Bone (Newlin) (1966)
Ruebezahl!
ELECTRONIC
The man next door (timp, mar, vib and xy) (1969)
Subjective objective (t-sax, trp and electric gtr) (1969)
INCIDENTAL MUSIC
Good old fashioned, film
Say what, dance music
MISCELLANEOUS
Love's greeting on your day (1970)
Sestina for Orion (1973)
Ref. composer, 80, 94, 190, 280, 494, 622, 625

MORRISSEY, Elizabeth
Australian composer. b. 1926.
Compositions
CHAMBER
Comments & conversation piece (2 contrasting insts) (1974)
VOCAL
The seven songs (Stella Turner) (S and pf) (1968)
Ref. 440, 444

MORROW, Jean

20th-century American composer. b. Kansas City. She studied composition under Kenneth Gaburo and George Marshall.

Compositions

VOCAL

The grasshopper, song
The night, song

MISCELLANEOUS

Garden suite
Interlude
Petite suite

Ref. 448

MORTAL MUSE. See SAPPHO

MORTIFEE, Ann

Canadian singer and composer. b. Durban, South Africa, November 30, 1947; naturalized Canadian, 1961. She gained her B.A. (English) from the University of British Columbia in 1968. Whilst at university she started her career as a folk and blues singer in local clubs, later performing in several productions of her own works and her own one-woman shows. DISCOGRAPHY.

Compositions

VOCAL

Numerous songs for her one-woman shows (Valerie Hennell King)

SACRED

Baptism

BALLET

The grey goose of silence
Klee Wyck, for Emily Carr (1975)
Variations pour une souvenance/Yesterday's day (1975)

INCIDENTAL MUSIC

The ecstasy of Rita Joe (George Ryga) (with Willy Dunn) (1976) (also ballet, 1971)
Film and television music

Ref. 485, 563

MORTON, Agnes Louise

American organist and composer. b. Snow's Falls, October 20, 1862; d. June 27, 1952. She studied under Myron Whitney, Cora S. Briggs, Will Stockbridge and W.H. Dennett and was a church organist for 22 years.

Compositions

PIANO

Moonlight march

VOCAL

Summer days are passing by, ballad (composer)
We'er growing old together, you and I, ballad (composer)
When night comes on, ballad (composer)
When the roses bloom, ballad (composer) (1939)

SACRED

O Lord, remember me (composer)

Ref. 374

MOSCOVITZ, Julianne

American composer. b. Oakland, CA, January 18, 1951. She studied under William Hoskins at Jacksonville University and John Fahey privately and obtained her B.A. from California State University, Hayward, in 1972. She was assistant music director at the Berkeley Dance Theatre and Gymnasium from 1972 to 1973.

Compositions

GUITAR

Guitar suite in colors (1968)
Tuesday afternoon in October (1972)

VOCAL

Once there was a worm (vce and gtrs) (1967)

FILM MUSIC

Atlanta, an international city (1973)

Ref. 142

MOSEL, Catherine de (nee Lambert)

Austrian organist, concert pianist and composer. b. Kloster-Neuburg, April 15, 1789; d. Vienna, July 10, 1832. She was a pupil of Schmidt, organist at the local convent and made such rapid progress that she gave an organ concert at the convent at the age of nine. She later took piano lessons from Humme and became a concert pianist.

Composition

PIANO

Variations pour le piano sur une thème de M. le comte de Dietrichstein (Vienna: Haslinger)

Ref. 26

MOSELEY, Caroline Carr

Early 20th-century English composer. She composed pieces for the violin, the cello and toy instruments, part songs for women's voices and songs.

Ref. 226, 276

MOSHER, Frances Elizabeth (nee Jordan)

Canadian painter, writer and composer. b. St. John, New Brunswick, October 23, 1911. She received her music training from private teachers and won a composition contest at the New Brunswick Music Festival.

Compositions

PIANO

Pieces incl.:
At dawn
The march of the dolls
A reverie

VOCAL

Songs incl.:
Fundy folk song (vce and pf)
Goodbye little lamb (vce and pf)
Song of Saint John (vce and pf)

Ref. composer, 133

MOSS, Katie

British composer. b. 1881. DISCOGRAPHY.

Compositions

VOCAL

Songs incl.:
The floral dance
Grey flowers of dusk (H.D. Burning)

Ref. Ricordi (Milan)

MOSSAFER RIND, Bernice

American concert harpist and composer. b. Seattle, January 19, 1925. She made her debut with the Southern California Symphony Orchestra at the age of 11 and later studied eurhythmics, solfege, composition and theory at the Cornish School of Fine Arts, Seattle. She obtained a B.A. (premedieval music) at the University of Washington and continued her music studies at the University of Southern California. She studied theatre arts in Los Angeles and played the harp in the Seattle Philharmonic Orchestra, becoming first harpist in 1945. She won scholarships to New York College of Music in 1936, Peabody College of Music, Baltimore in 1942 and Chicago Musical College. PHOTOGRAPH.

Compositions

HARP

Catena de terle
Rhapsody in F-Minor
Serena sonata

Ref. composer, 77, 206

MOSSMAN, Bina

20th-century Hawaiian choral conductor, lyricist and composer. She conducted her own glee club from 1914 to 1944 and the Kaahumanu Choral Group from 1952 to 1968. She composed in the traditional Hawaiian style, with Hawaiian lyrics.

Compositions

VOCAL

He 'ono
Kapua u'i
Ku'u lei
Lae lae
Niu haohao (1924)
Stevedore hula

Ref. 438

MOSUSOVA, Nadezda

Yugoslav professor of musicology and composer. b. Subotica, August 4, 1928. She studied at the Institute of Musicology from 1950 to 1951 on a scholarship and completed composition studies under Professor Predrag

Milosevic in Belgrade in 1953. The next year she attended the Salzburg Seminar of American Studies, where contemporary American music was studied and analyzed. From 1953 to 1954 she worked as an accompanist at the Bosko Buha children's theatre and in 1955 became professor of theoretical subjects at the Stankovic Music School, Belgrade. In 1959 she became assistant and in 1967 scientific collaborator at the Institute of Musicology in Belgrade. Being interested in Slavonic, especially Russian and Serbian music, she gave lectures on that subject in Vienna at the music academy. She was awarded a D.Mus. by the faculty of philosophy of Ljubljana and is a member of the Institute of Musicology at the Serbian Academy of Science and Art. PHOTOGRAPH.

Compositions

ORCHESTRA

Symphonic prelude (1953)
Introduction and largo (str orch) (1969)
Poema (str orch) (1956)

CHAMBER

Fantasy (pf qrt and cl) (1968)
String quartet in F-Minor (1952)
Trio (1972)
Duettino concertante (2 fl) (1967)
Etudes (cl and pf; also cl) (1969)
Prelude and capriccio (fl and pf) (1961)
Two improvisations (fl and pf) (1957)

PIANO

Meditations (1969)
Variations on the theme Crna Gora (collection of 11th-century songs by S. Mokranjac) (1950)

VOCAL

Jedro (Lermontov) (1949)
Mrtva lutka (Cesaric) (1952)
Njih dvoje (Lermontov) (1949)
Oblaci (Lermontov) (1949)
Pjeni se more (Cesaric) (1952)
Srebrne plesacici (Maksimovic) (1949)
Vece (Lermontov) (1950)
Children's songs (1948-1963)

Publications

The influence of folklore elements on the structure of Romanticism in Serbian music. Ph.D. dissertation, 1967.
The influence of Stevan Mokranjac on the creative work of Petar Konjovic. 1967.
Lyricism of Petar Konjovic.
Monograph on Petar Konjovic. 1969.
The period orientation of Stevan Molranjac.
Petar Konjovic on the stage of Belgrade Opera. 1968.
Petar Konjovic-Portrait of the Artist. 1968.
The place of Stevan Mokranjac among the national schools of European Music.
Studies on Petar Konjovic's opera Kostana (1960) and Otadzbina (Homeland). 1963.

Ref. composer, 109

MOSZUMANSKA-NAZAR, Krystyna

Polish pianist, professor and composer. b. Lvov, September 5, 1924. At the State Music College in Cracow she studied composition under S. Wiecowicz and the piano under J. Hoffman, receiving her diplomas in both subjects in 1955. She is currently professor of composition and vice-rector at the Cracow Music Academy. She was president of the Cracow section of the Union of Polish Composers from 1962 to 1971 before becoming a member of the presidium of that organization. Her compositions have been performed in numerous countries throughout the world and at international festivals of contemporary music, particularly in Warsaw and Avignon. She received numerous awards and distinctions. DISCOGRAPHY. PHOTOGRAPH.

Compositions

ORCHESTRA

Concertino (pf and orch) (1954)
Four sketches (1958)
Hexaedre (1960) (prize, International Competition for Women Composers, Mannheim, 1965)
Overture No. 1 (1954)
Overture No. 2 (1956)
Pour orchestre (1969)
Rhapsody II (sym orch) (1980)
Sinfonietta (cham str orch) (1983)
Symphonic allegro (1957)
Variazioni concertante (fl and cham) (1966) (3rd prize, A. Malawski Competition, 1962)

CHAMBER

Music for strings (1962) (gold medal, International Competition for Women Composers, Buenos Aires, 1962)
String quartet (1955)
String quartet No. 2 (1980) (comm Krzysztof Penderecki)
String quartet No. 3 (1980) (PWM)
Implications (2 pf and perc) (1969)
Trio (vl, vla and vlc) (1961)
Five duets (fl and cl) (1959)
Three miniatures (cl and pf) (1957)
Variante (pf and perc) (1979)
From end to end percussion (1979)
Three concert studies (perc)
Three miniatures (perc)

PIANO

Bagatelle (1971)
Constellations (1972)
Mala etiuda (1975)
Sonatina (1957)
Suite of Polish dances (1954)
Variations (1949)

VOCAL

Intonations (2 ch and orch) (1968)
Madonny polski (ch and orch) (1974)
Challenge (Dylan Thomas) (B and cham ens) (1977)
Bel canto (S, cel and perc) (1972)
The bulrush, song (B and pf) (1982)
Wyzwanie (Dylan Thomas) (B and cham ens) (PWM, 1979)

SACRED

Canticum canticorum Salomonis (S, recitors, ch and inst ens) (1984)

ELECTRONIC

Exodus (tape and orch) (1954)
Interpretations (fl, tape and perc) (3rd prize, A. Malawski Competition, 1966)

Bibliography

Polish Music. February, 1973.

Ref. composer, 77, 118, 189, 206, 563

MOTHER OF ALL CREATION. See INNANA

MOTTA, Giovanna

20th-century Italian composer. b. 1950.

Compositions

CHAMBER

Piece for wind instruments

VOCAL

Song cycle
Songs

SACRED

Judith, cantata (1978)

Ref. 465

MOULTON, Mrs. Charles (nee Lilly Greenough)

19th-century American composer.

Compositions

VOCAL

Songs incl.:
Beware
The brook
Confession
Hilda

Ref. 276, 292, 347

MOUNSEY, Ann Sheppard. See BARTHOLOMEW, Ann Sheppard

MOUNSEY, Elizabeth

English guitarist, organist, pianist and composer. b. London, October 8, 1819; d. London, October 3, 1905. She was the sister of Ann Sheppard Batholomew (q.v.). She was organist of St. Peter's Church, Cornhill from 1834 till 1882. Besides the organ and the piano, she studied the guitar and from 1883 to 1884 made public guitar appearances. She composed works for the guitar, the organ, the piano, voice and hymns in collaboration with her sister.

Ref. 2, 6, 8, 74, 226, 276, 572

MOURKOVA, Josefna. See BRDLIKOVA, Josefina

MOYSEOWICZ, Gabriela
German composer. b. 1944.
Compositions
PIANO
Two piano sonatas: Sonata fortepianowa No. 3 (1963); Noumonon-sonata No. 6 (1976) (Berlin: Ries & Erler, 1979)
SACRED
Ave Maria (2 mix-ch a-cap) (Ries & Erler, 1977)
Ref. MLA *Notes*

MOZART, Maria Anna Walburga Ignatia (Nannerl)
Austrian harpsichordist, pianist, teacher and composer. b. Salzburg, July 30, 1751; d. Salzburg, October 29, 1829. The sister of Wolfgang Amadeus Mozart, she appeared for many years as a virtuoso pianist together with her brother. She taught the piano and in 1783 married Privy Councillor von Berchthold zu Sonnenburg. She became blind towards the end of her life and died in extreme poverty. She composed piano and organ pieces.
Ref. 128, 268, 347

MOZART, Nannerl. See MOZART, Maria Anna Walburga Ignatia

MRACEK, Ann Michelle
American concert pianist, orchestral conductor, singer, teacher and composer. b. November 13, 1956. She studied the piano as a child and later under Herb Drury and singing under Virginia Settle. She gained her B.M. from the University of Kansas in 1979 and studied composition at masters level under Dr. Edward Mattila and George Crumb, voice under Kenneth Smith and orchestral conducting under Dr. George Lawner. She appeared in numerous piano and vocal recitals and musicals and taught the piano and theory. PHOTOGRAPH.
Compositions
ORCHESTRA
Symphony No. 1, Shadow dragon, in 3 mvts (1979)
Heska hulka, concerto (pf and orch)
CHAMBER
Balance (vln, ob, trp, t-trb, b-trb and tba) (1978)
Quartet in 4 parts (f, ob, cl and bsn) (1976)
String quartet No. 1, Water quartet (vln, vla, vlc and d-b) (1977)
Active repose: Deepest sleep; The dream; Awakening (fl and pf) (1983)
Perturbations (pf and trb) (1970)
Design (fl) (1977)
PIANO
Evaporation
Thawing
Sonata, in 3 mvts
Other pieces (1965-1977)
VOCAL
Marigolds (mix-ch) (1975)
Rain (mix-ch) (1971)
Vapors (mix-ch) (1976)
Lullaby (S, pf and fl) (1975)
Now gone (vce, a-fl and pf) (1973)
Three songs (S, fl, 2 vln, hn and pf) (1977)
Numerous songs (vce and pf)
Ref. composer, 622

MRASECK, Fraulein. See ADDENDUM

MRIGANAYANA, Queen
Indian composer. b. 1486; d. 1516. She was the wife of the King of Gwalier and composed songs in mixed ragas.
Compositions
VOCAL
Songs incl.:
Babul gujri
Gujuri
Ref. National Council of Women in India

MSHEVELIDZE, Shalva
20th-century Soviet composer.
Composition
ORCHESTRA
Zviadacory, symphonic poem (Moscow, 1946)

MUCHOVA-THOMSENOVA, Geraldine. See THOMSEN, Geraldine

MUCKLE, May Henrietta. See MUKLE, May Henrietta

MUDDUPALANI
Indian vina player, poetess and composer. A courtesan's daughter in the court of Tanjore, she was highly educated in Sanskrit and Telugu and an expert in dance and music.
Composition
MISCELLANEOUS
Ashtapada
Ref. 414

MUELLER, Charlotte
German composer. b. Berlin, April 30, 1886. She studied under Eduard Moritz and composed operettas.
Ref. 226

MUELLER, Elise
German pianist and composer. b. Bremen, 1782. She was the daughter of Wilhelm Christian Mueller and had her first piano lessons from him. She was known for her interpretation of Beethoven's works.
Compositions
VOCAL
Danklied: Frisch auf! Mein Herz (mix-ch and pf) (Simrock)
Chant de remercement d'Arndt, op. 1 (4 vces and pf) (Simrock)
Sechs Lieder (Breitkopf): Wanderlied; Abschied; Und wuessten's die Blumen, die kleinen; Des Stromes Liebe; Es war einmal ganz andre Zeit; Schlummerlied
Six songs, op. 2 (vce and pf) (Leipzig: Hofmeister)
Ref. 22, 226, 297, 347

MUELLER-BENDER, Mme.
19th-century German pianist and composer. She played her composition with the clarinetist Georg Reinhardt in Frankfurt.
Composition
CHAMBER
Introduction, adagio and variations (cl and pf) (1819)
Ref. 472

MUELLER-HERMANN, Johanna
Austrian lecturer and composer. b. Vienna, January 15, 1878; d. Vienna, April 19, 1941. Her mother was a gifted instrumentalist and singer. Johanna began composing in her childhood and became a pupil of Karl Nawratil and Josef Labor. Later she studied under Guido Adler, Alexander von Zemlinsky and J.B. Forester; whom she succeeded as teacher of music theory at the New Conservatory, Vienna in 1915.
Compositions
ORCHESTRA
Heroische Ouvertuere, op. 21
Symphonic fantasy on Ibsen's Brand, op. 25
CHAMBER
Piano quintet in G-Minor, op. 31
String quintet, op. 7
String quartet in E-Flat Major, op. 6 (1912)
Sonata, op. 5 (vln and pf) (Vienna: Doblinger, 1907)
Sonata, op. 17 (vlc and pf)
PIANO
Sonata, op. 8
Pieces, ops. 3, 12, 19
VOCAL
In Memoriam, op. 30, oratorio (Walt Whitman) (vces and orch)
Von Tod und Gedenken, op. 10, cantata (w-ch)
Deutscher Schwur, op. 22 (ch and orch)
Ode for choir and orchestra, op. 29
Der sterbende Schwann, op. 16 (ch and orch)
Von Minnelob and Glaubenstreu, op. 37 (ch and orch)
Symphony in D-Minor, op. 28 (R. Huch) (soli and ch)
Chorus, ops. 9 and 13 (ch a-cap)
Songs
Two duets, op. 15
Ref. 2, 8, 14, 17, 22, 41, 44, 94, 96, 105, 172, 189, 193, 219, 226, 268, 622

MUELLER-WELTI, Hedwig
Swiss pianist and composer. d. 1968. She studied the piano at the Zurich Conservatory under P.O. Moeckel and singing under Emilie Welti-Hertzog. She married the Zurich composer Paul Mueller.

Compositions
VOCAL
Sunneschy und Regenwetter, children's songs (Rudolph Haegni) (with Paul Mueller)
Ref. 6

MUELLNER-GOLLENHOFER (Muellner-Gallenhofer) (Gollenhofer Mueller), Johanna (Josepha, Josephine)
Austrian harpist, singer, teacher and composer. b. Vienna, 1769. The emperor gave her a harp and a scholarship to study in Italy. In 1798 she toured in Europe and won wide acclaim. Her first compositions appeared in 1805 and from 1811 to 1823 she was harpist in the court orchestra in Vienna and also gave lessons and is said to have taught the Empress Marie Louise. Johanna inspired Beethoven to write *Die Geschoepfe des Prometheus* his only piece for the harp.
Compositions
CHAMBER
String quartet
HARP
Monologue to The Bride of Messina
Monologue to The Bride of Orleans
Other pieces
VOCAL
Fourteen German songs (vce and pf)
Other songs
OPERA
Der heimliche Bund
Ref. 26, 128, 129, 344, 347

MUELLNER, Josefa. See MUELLNER-GOLLENHOFER, Johanna

MUENTZING, Paula
Swedish composer. b. 1890.
Composition
VOCAL
Lucia song: Godmorgon mitt herrskap (old verse from Vaermland) (1924)
Ref. 642

MUG, Sister Mary Theodosia (pseud. H. Maery)
20th-century American organist, singer and composer. b. Attica, IN.
Ref. 347

MUKHAMEDZHANOVA, Mariam
Soviet folk instrumentalist, teacher and composer. b. Tashkent, September 20, 1921. She studied composition at the Tashkent Conservatory from 1939 to 1949 whilst playing in an orchestra of folk instruments. She taught theoretical subjects in Namangan from 1941 to 1951 and at a music school in Tashkent from 1951 to 1953.
Compositions
ORCHESTRA
Fantasy (Uzbek folk insts) (1947)
Suite (Uzbek insts) (1947)
Other pieces (Uzbek insts)
CHAMBER
Piece for cello and piano (1945)
Two pieces for violin and piano (1946)
PIANO
Six variations (1948)
Three pieces (1949)
Twenty-four pieces (1948)
VOCAL
Songs
Ref. 87

MUKLE, May Henrietta
English concert cellist and composer. b. London, May 14, 1880. She studied in London under Hambleton and later under Pezze at the Royal Academy of Music. She was a pioneer of women cellists and toured worldwide. In 1908 she toured with the Maud Powell Trio, with her sister Ann as the pianist and Maud Powell as the violinist. May appeared in the first ever chamber music recital in Honolulu in 1918.
Compositions
CHAMBER
The Hamadryad fantasy (vlc and pf)
The light wind, fantasy (vlc and pf)
Cello pieces
VOCAL
Songs
Ref. 8, 89, 105, 347, 361, 433

MULDER, Johanna Harmina Gerdina
Dutch pianist, choir conductor, lyricist and composer. b. Middelburg, September 28, 1912. She studied choral direction under Jos Vranken, the piano under Bernard Verboom, singing under Mrs. Hermann and composition under Henri Zagwijn. She conducted women's and children's choirs in Holland, Britain, the United States and on radio. She received the golden medal of honor and the Order of Orange-Nassau from Queen Juliana. She is a member of the Nederlandse Dirigenten Organisatie. Johanna wrote her own texts.
Compositions
PIANO
Aschenbroedel, ballet music (1980)
VOCAL
Choral songs
OPERETTA
Children's operettas:
Als herders in de nacht, Christmas play (1959)
Circus del mondo, in 1 act (1971)
Gelukskinderen, in 3 acts (1940)
Marjolijntje in Sprookjesland, in 3 acts (1949) (ded four Dutch princesses)
Prins Rudi en de toverstaf, in 3 acts (1938)
De reis van Harlekino, in 3 acts (1980)
De toverspiegel, in 3 acts (1958)
De verdwenen koningzoon, in 4 acts (1936)
Victor en de gouden bloem, in 3 acts
De wonderstaf, in 3 acts (1963)
Ref. composer, 70

MULDER, Maria Antonia (Marga)
Dutch flautist and composer. b. Bussum, July 23, 1952. She studied the flute and composition privately and sonology at Utrecht State University and the culture of art at Amsterdam University. She is a member of the composers' ensemble for electronic music 'Het Nieuwe Leven.'
Compositions
ORCHESTRA
Spheren de Kand II (large orch) (1982)
ELECTRONIC
Der kus van tuin (1978)
MULTIMEDIA
Megalied (elec sounds and video) (1980)
Neon argon (players, projections and zootrope) (1979)
One hundred and twenty five - One hundred and thirty one to Michalkov-chontsjalovski (musique concrete and film) (1979)
Spheren der Kand I (190 computer-generated sine waves and computer generated graphics) (1981)
De weg (elec sounds and large drawings) (1982)
Wolkenmechaniek (elec sounds, paintings and video) (1978)
Ref. composer

MULLEN, Adelaide (pseud. Wilton King)
19th-century Irish singer and composer. b. Dublin. She studied under J.B. Welsh. She first appeared in concert in Dublin in 1883 and toured England and the United States in opera and concerts. She composed songs.
Ref. 226

MULLER, Charlotte. See MUELLER, Charlotte

MULLER, Elise. See MUELLER, Elise

MULLER-BENDER, Mme. See MUELLER-BENDER, Mme.

MULLER-HERMANN, Johanna. See MUELLER-HERMANN, Johanna

MULLER-WELTI, Hedwig. See MUELLER-WELTI, Hedwig

MULLNER, Johanna. See MUELLNER, Johanna

MULLNER-GOLLENHOFER, Josefa. See MUELLNER-GOLLENHOFER, Josefa

MUNCH, Natalie

19th-century Danish composer.
Compositions
VOCAL
Tre digte af Chr Winther og Welhaven (S and pf) (1847)
Ref. 413

MUNDELLA, Emma

English pianist, teacher and composer. b. Nottingham, 1858; d. February 20, 1896. She studied under Arthur Page from 1873 to 1876 and won the Nottingham scholarship in 1876. She then studied under Ernst Pauer, Sullivan, Dr. Bridge, Dr. Stainer and Prout at the Royal College of Music and was one of the first students to become an A.R.C.M. She was director of music at St. Elphin's Clergy Daughters' School, Warrington and at Wimbledon High School, 1880.
Compositions
CHAMBER
Andante and allegro con brio, 3 sets (vln and pf) (Novello)
PIANO
Twelve elementary duets (4 hands)
Three sketches
VOCAL
The victory of song, oratorio (L. Morris) (w-ch, 3 vln, hp and pf)
Autumn leaves (Indes spes) (treble vces) (Williams)
Dreamland, 2-part song (unacc) (Williams)
Flowers-canon, duet or 2-part song (w-vces or boy's vces)
Holidays (w-vces or boy's vces)
Mad love's song (Leonard)
Song of the mermaids and mermen (S and Cont)
Through wisdom is an house builded, 2-part anthem (S and A)
Up and down, duet
What the birds said, 2-part song
Ye spotted snakes (S and A)
SACRED
Blessed be the Lord God, Christmas carol (mix-ch) (Weekes)
Our God is Lord of the harvest (mix-ch)
Day school hymn book (Novello)
Ref. 6, 226, 276, 297

MUNDINGER, Adele Franziska

German pianist, singer, teacher and composer. b. Tsarskoye-Selo, Russia, May 3, 1890; d. Berge, near Osterburg, East Germany, November 7, 1946. She had piano, harmony, counterpoint and composition lessons as a child and studied singing at the St. Petersburg Conservatory until 1917 when consumption forced her to give this up. Having begun improvising and composing as a child, she now dedicated herself entirely to composition. At the beginning of the Second World War she was repatriated to Germany with her mother and sister and most of her compositions were lost. She taught music and after her death her sister had some of her compositions published and some were performed in concert and on radio in Germany. PHOTOGRAPH.
Compositions
PIANO
Berceuse, op. 59 (Herzenberg: G. Duering)
Impromptu, op. 62
Nocturne, op. 48
Nocturne, op. 51 (Duering)
Phantasie, op. 23
Prelude, op. 25
Prelude, op. 40 (Duering)
Prelude, op. 47 (Duering)
Spanish dance, op. 17
Tema con variazioni, op. 60
Two nocturnes
Valse, op. 8
About 60 lost works
VOCAL
Elegy, op. 50 (Pushkin) (vce and pf) (Duering)
Other lost works
Ref. composer's sister, 502

MUNGAY Y PIZARRO, Dona Carolina

Spanish composer. b. Badalona, near Barcelona, September, 1850. She studied music from early childhood.
Composition
ORCHESTRA
La primera flor, fantasy (1869)
Ref. 389

MUNGER, Annette. See MUNGER, Shirley

MUNGER, Millicent Christner

American organist, pianist, choral conductor and composer. b. Rosamond, IL, September 15, 1905. She studied theory at Milliken University and Northwestern University and the piano and the organ in Chicago and New York. She taught the piano in music schools from 1926 to 1935 and was organist and choir conductor in Spencer, IA, from 1935 to 1969 and Tuscon, 1969 to 1973. She won an award for an anthem from the Congregational Church, Spencer. She composed organ and piano works, songs and anthems, including a processional choral anthem.
Ref. 142

MUNGER, Shirley (Annette)

20th-century American pianist, professor and composer. b. Everett, WA. She studied composition under George F. McKay and John Verrall at the University of Washington, where she obtained a B.A. (music) in 1946. She received her M.A. (music) in 1951 and D.M.A. (composition) in 1963 from the University of Southern California, where she studied under Halsey Stevens and Ingolf Dahl. She also studied the piano at the Paris Conservatoire on a Fulbright grant from 1952 to 1953. She was associate professor of the piano and theory at the University of California, Santa Barbara from 1954 to 1960 and the University of Minnesota, Duluth from 1963 to 1968 and professor of theory at West Chester State College from 1960. She is a member of ASCAP.
Compositions
ORCHESTRA
Piano concerto
BAND
Clementi and friends, elementary (1977) (Shawnee Press)
Other pieces
Arrangements
CHAMBER
Concerto grosso (trp trio and wind ens) (1970)
Partita (vlc qrt) (1962)
Sonata (vln and pf) (1959)
ORGAN
Prelude pastorale (1957)
Solos
PIANO
Four for six (6 hands) (1960) (Galaxy Music)
Ensemble, solos and teaching pieces
VOCAL
Songs of the American Revolution (ch and band or pf) (1975)
Ref. 137, 142, 625

MUNKTELL, Helena Mathilda

Swedish pianist and composer. b. St. Kopparberg, November 24, 1852; d. September 10, 1919. She studied composition in Stockholm under Ludvig Norman and Conrad Nordgvist, counterpoint under Johan Lindegren, instrumentation under Joseph Dente and the piano under Carl Fexer. She was also a pupil of J. Epstein. She went to Paris in 1877 and studied composition under B. Godard from 1885 to 1892. During the nineties she became a private pupil of Vincent d'Indy and remained in close contact with him until she returned to Sweden in 1910. Her opera was performed for three seasons at the Royal Theatre in Stockholm and her other works were frequently played by the Societe National de Musique in Paris. She became a member of the Swedish Academy of Music in 1915.
Compositions
ORCHESTRA
Braenningar, symphonic poem
Symphonic suite (1895)
Valborgseld, symphonic poem
Dalsvit (1910)

CHAMBER
String quartet (incomplete)
Piano trio (incomplete)
Sonata Ess-dur, op. 21 (vln and pf) (1905)
Piano pieces
VOCAL
Isjungfrun, ballad (Bar and orch) (1899)
Polardrottningen, op. 2, ballad (Bar and pf or orch)
Upp till Salem, op. 16 (w-ch and Bar)
Choruses
Quartet, op. 2a and b (mix-vces)
Trio (w-vces)
Solo songs
OPERA
I Firenze (Paris: Choudens, 1889)
Ref. 20, 95, 276

MUNTHE-MORGENSTIERNE, Anna
20th-century Danish composer.
Compositions
PIANO
Tre idyller
VOCAL
Tre romancer (vce and pf)
Ref. 331

MUNTZING, Paula. See MUENTZING, Paula

MURAKUMO, Ayako
Japanese composer. b. Gifu, February 25, 1949. She graduated from the Graduate School of Aichi Prefectural University of Arts in 1982 where she studied under Ishii Kan. In 1985 she was the winner of the composition section of the Nagoya City cultural competition. DISCOGRAPHY.
Compositions
ORCHESTRA
Chronos (1982)
Hisho (1980)
Wave (1982)
CHAMBER
Reflection (fl, cl, vlc and perc) (1982)
Fuha (fl, vlc and pf) (1984)
Chiku-in so-sho (shakuhachi and koto) (1985)
Ko-oh (mar and perc) (1985)
Prelude (gtr) (1985)
VOCAL
Projection (m-S, vlc and pf) (1984)
Ref. Japanese Federation of Composers

MURAO, Sachie
Japanese composer. b. Nara Prefecture, April 6, 1945. She graduated from the advanced course of the music department of the Prefectural Blind School in 1966 and then studied under Michiharu Matsunaga and Yoshiro Irino. DISCOGRAPHY.
Compositions
CHAMBER
7646 (cl, mar, pf and perc) (1976)
7791 (mar and 2 perc) (1977)
7310 (2 perc) (1973)
7465 (pf and perc) (1974)
7561 (pf and mar) (1975)
7519 (fl) (1975)
0078 (ded Jueren Macha)
PIANO
7746 (2 pf)
7290 (1972)
7487 Pieces
Ref. Japanese Federation of Composers

MURATORI SCANNABECCHI (Moratori Scanabecchi), Angiola Teresa
17th-century Italian nun and composer. She was at the Convent of San Lorenzo in Bologna about 1687.
Compositions
SACRED
Cristo Morto, oratorio di S. Maria della Morte (1696)
Ester (1695)
I giuochi di Sansone (1694)
Il martirio di Santa Colomba (1689)
Ref. 105, 128

MURDOCH, Elaine
20th-century English composer.
Composition
OPERA
Tamburlaine (J. Murdoch)
Ref. 141

MURDOCH, Heather
20th-century Australian composer.
Compositions
VOCAL
Songs:
Christmas bells (1976)
Spanish donkey (1976)
Spinning song (1976)
Summer sun (1976)
Tirralee tirralon (1976)
Ref. 440

MURDOCH, Marjolijn
Dutch composer. b. 1943. DISCOGRAPHY.
Composition
CHAMBER
Fantasie in D-Minor (ob and hpcd)
Ref. Openbare Muziekbibliotheek (Amsterdam), 563

MURDOCK, Jane. See ROOBENIAN, Amber

MURILLO CABALLERO, Juliana
Spanish composer.
Composition
ORGAN
Variaciones (Gaspar Sanz)
Ref. 60

MURIO-CELLI, Adelina
Italian teacher and composer. b. Italy; d. New York, 1900. She settled in the United States about 1897. She became a well-known singing teacher, counting among her pupils such famous names as Jennie Dickerson, Marie Groebel, Charlotte Walker and Amanda Fabris.
Compositions
PIANO
Pieces
VOCAL
Songs incl.:
The bells of love
L'echo
Etelka waltz
Glide on
Le lagrime d'un padre
The messenger bird
Mignonette
SACRED
Ave Maria
Ref. 105, 226, 276, 347

MURRAY, Lady Edith
18th-century English composer.
Compositions
CHAMBER
Legende (pf and vln)
PIANO
March
The Prince of Wales, waltz (London: London Music Publ.)
Ref. 128

MURRAY, Margaret
English composer. b. 1921.
Compositions
SACRED
Four Christmas carols (chil-ch, rec, glock, xy and perc)
Ref. Schott

MURRI, Alceste
Italian composer. b. 1856; d. 1925.
Compositions
PIANO
Marcia indiana (Ricordi)
VOCAL
Songs incl.:
A te (Ricordi)
L'abbandono (Ricordi)
Il canto del poeta (Ricordi)
La canzone del marinaio (Ricordi)
Dichiarizione, melody (M. Marcello) (Ricordi)
L'infedele, melody (Marcello) (Ricordi)
Il mar c'invita, barcarolle (Ricordi)
Partenza, romance (Ricordi)
Si, romance (Ricordi)
Sul mar m'fido, Venetian barcarolle (Ricordi)
Tilde, se fossi un fiore, romance (A. Panizza) (Ricordi)
Ref. Ricordi (Milan)

MUSA NOVARESE, La. See LEONARDA, Sister Isabella

MUSES' SISTER. See SAPPHO

MUSGRAVE, Thea
Scottish conductor, professor and composer. b. Edinburgh, May 27, 1928. She studied at Edinburgh University from 1947 to 1950, under Hans Gal (history of music and counterpoint) and Mary Grierson (harmony and analysis). She had four years of postgraduate study under Nadia Boulanger (q.v.), studying accompaniment at the Paris Conservatoire from 1952 to 1954 and composition privately from 1950 to 1954. She also studied composition with Aaron Copland. While still a student she was awarded the Donald Francis Tovey prize and the Lili Boulanger memorial prize. In 1955 she became leader and accompanist of the Saltire Singers. A grant enabled her to attend courses at the Berkshire Center in Tanglewood in 1958. She was lecturer on music for the extramural department of London University from 1959 to 1964 and a visiting professor at the college for creative studies, University of California, Santa Barbara, in 1970. She lectured at many universities in the United Kingdom and the United States; she is a member of the central music advisory panel for the BBC. Her works in Great Britain, Europe and the United States have been performed by major orchestras, some of which she conducted; the New York City Opera performed her work *The voice of Ariadne* and the New York Philharmonic played her *Clarinet concerto*. She received numerous commissions; in 1973 she won the Koussevitzky award and in 1974, 1975 and 1982 the Guggenheim fellowship. Prince Charles presented her with an honorary doctorate from the Council for National Academic Awards in 1976, in 1979 she received an honorary doctorate from Smith College and in 1980 an honorary doctorate from the Old Dominion University in Norfolk, Virginia. She wrote a number of works for her husband, the violist Peter Mark. Most of her works were commissioned. DISCOGRAPHY. PHOTOGRAPH.
Compositions
ORCHESTRA
Concerto (cl and orch) (1968) (London: J & W Chester, 1969; Frankfurt: Wilhelm Hansen Musik-Forlag; New York: G. Schirmer)
Concerto (hn and orch) (1971) (Chester, 1974; Hansen; Schirmer)
Viola concerto (1973) (Novello, 1973)
Concerto for orchestra (1967) (Chester, 1968; Hansen; Schirmer)
Divertimento (str orch) (1957) (Schirmer)
Festival Ooerture (1965) (Chester; Schirmer)
Memento vitae, in homage to Beethoven (1970) (Chester, 1975; Hansen; Schirmer)
Night music (cham orch) (1969) (Chester, 1972; Hansen; Schirmer)
Nocturnes and arias (1966) (Chester; Schirmer)
Obliques (1958) (Chester, 1961; Hansen; Schirmer)
Peripeteia (1981)
Perspectives, overture for strings (1961) (Chester; Schirmer)
Scottish dance suite (1959) (Schirmer)
Sinfonia (1963) (Schirmer)
BRASS BAND
Variations (1966) (Chester)
CHAMBER
From one to another (vln and 15 strs) (1980)
Orfeo II (fl and 15 strs) (Version of Orfeo I) (Novello, 1976)
Chamber concerto No. 1 (ob, cl, bsn, hn, trp, trb, vln, vla and vlc) (1962) (Chester, 1977; Hansen)
Space play concerto (fl, cl, ob, bsn, hn, vln, vla, vlc and d-b) (1974) (Novello, 1975) (Koussevitsky award)
Chamber concerto No. 3 (cl, bsn, hn, 2 vln, vla, vlc and d-b) (1966) (Chester, 1968; Hansen)
Chamber concerto No. 2 (fl, picc or a-fl, cl or b-cl, vln or vla, vlc and pf) (1966) (Chester, 1967; Hansen)
Serenade (fl, cl, hp, vla and vlc) (1961) (Chester, 1962; Hansen)
String quartet (1958) (Chester, 1964; Hansen)
Impromptu No. 2 (fl, ob and cl) (1970) (Chester, 1974; Hansen)
Sonata for three (fl, vln and gtr) (1966) (Novello)
Trio (fl, ob and pf) (1960) (Chester, 1964; Hansen)
Colloquy (vln and pf) (1960) (Chester, 1961; Hansen)
Elegy (vla and vlc) (1970) (Chester, 1971; Hansen)
Impromptu (fl and ob) (1967) (Chester, 1968; Hansen)
Music for horn and piano (1967) (Chester, 1967)
Violin sonata
PIANO
Excursions (4 hands) (1965) (Chester, 1966; Hansen)
Monologue (1960) (Chester)
Sonata No. 2 (1956)
VOCAL
Cantata for a summer's day (Hume and Lindsay) (narr, vocal qrt or mix-ch, str qrt, fl, cl and d-b; also fl, cl and str orch) (Chester; Schirmer; Novello)
The five ages of man (Hesiod, trans Lattimore) (ch and orch or pf) (1963) (Schirmer; Chester, 1965; Hansen
The phoenix and the turtle (Shakespeare) (ch and orch) (1962) (Chester, 1962)
Triptych (Chaucer) (T and orch) (1959) (Schirmer; Chester, 1960; Hansen)
Caro m'e il sonno (Michelangelo) (mix-ch) (1953) (Chester, 1958)
Four madrigals (Sir Thomas Wyatt) (mix-ch) (1953)
John Cook (mix-ch a-cap) (1963) (Novello)
The last twilight (D. H. Lawrence) (ch and brass) (1980) (Novello)
Song of the burn (mix-ch a-cap) (1954) (Chester)
Four portraits (Bar, cl and pf)
Five love songs (R. Parry, J. Marston, T. Middleton) (S or T and gtr) (1955) (Chester, 1970; Hansen)
Primavera (S and fl) (1971) (Chester, 1976; Hansen)
Sir Patrick Spens (T and gtr) (1961) (Chester, 1976; Hansen)
A suite of bairnsongs (M. Lindsay) (vce and pf) (1953) (Chester, 1962; Hansen)
Two songs (Ezra Pound) (Bar and pf) (1951) (Novello)
SACRED
Make ye merry for Him is come (soli, Cont soli, chil-ch and org opt) (1961) (Chester, 1968)
Memento Creatoris (Donne) (ch a-cap and org opt) (Chester, 1967; Hansen)
Rorate coeli (William Dunbar) (ch a-cap) (Novello)
Two Christmas carols in traditional style (N. Nicholson) (S, w-ch or mix-ch; also ch and ob, cl, vln and strs without d-b) (Chester, 1954)
The Lord's Prayer
A song for Christmas (high vce and pf) (Chester, 1963; Hansen)
BALLET
Beauty and the Beast (cham and tape) (1969) (Chester)
Orfeo (dancer, fl and tape) (Novello)
Scorpius (based on Chamber Concerto No. 1)
A tale for thieves (Chaucer) (orch; also pf reduction) (1953) (Chester, 1954)
OPERA
The Abbot of Drimock, chamber opera (1955) (Chester)
A Christmas Carol (C. Dickens) (1979)
The Decision (M. Lindsay, based on The devil and John Brown by K. Taylor) orch; also pf reduction) (J. Curwen, 1967; Chester)
Mary Queen of Scots (composer, based on Moray by A. Elguera) (1977) (Novello)
Occurrence at Owl Creek Bridge (1981)
The Voice of Ariadne, chamber opera (A. Elguera based on The last of the Valerii by H. James) (8 vces, 13 insts and tape) (Novello)
OPERETTA
Mariko the Miser, children's opera (composer, F. Samson and Afanasiev) (Chester)
ELECTRONIC
From one to another (vla and tape) (1970) (Novello)
Orfeo I (fl and tape) (1975) (Novello)
Soliloquy (gtr and tape) (Chester, 1969)
Bibliography
Bender, William. *The Musgrave Ritual*. Time, October 10, 1977.
Heinsheimer, Hans. *Mistress Musgrave*. Opera News, September 1977.
Musical Events. *New Yorker*, December 24, 1979.
Smith, P.J. *Musgrave's 'A Christmas Carol'*. *Hi-Fidelity*, April 1980.
Swan, Annalyn. *Queen Mary in Virginia*. *Time*, April 17, 1978.
Thea Musgrave: A Bio-Bibliography. Greenwood Press, 1984.
Ref. 1, 2, 4, 5, 14, 17, 22, 63, 70, 74, 77, 80, 84, 88, 94, 141, 153, 185, 189, 206, 228, 280, 282, 284, 295, 387, 415, 563, 572, 594, 622, 625, 637

MUSICIANS OF GOD. See AMON SONGSTRESSES

MUSIGNY, Mme. de
Late 18th-century French harpist and composer. She studied under Krumpholtz.
Compositions
VOCAL
Six romances d'Estelle (hp or pf)
Ref. 128

MUSTILLO, Lina
American organist, choral conductor, school principal and composer. b. Newport, RI, October 13, 1905. She studied under Hugo Norden in Boston and Arthur Custer at the University of Rhode Island. She was organist and choir conductor in Attleboro, MA, from 1930 to 1935 and ran her own music school from 1935 to 1960.
Compositions
PIANO
Etude intervalle
Passacaglia
A thought
Triphon
Other pieces
VOCAL
Songs incl.:
Trilogy, 3 song-cycle (S and pf)
Ref. 142

MUTAYYAM AL-HASHIMIYYA
Late 8th-century Arabian poetess and songstress of the Abbasid period. A freed woman, she was born and educated in al-Basra and lived there all her life. She was a pupil of Ibrahim al-Mausili and his son Ishaq, who were the two most eminent musicians of the time and considered to be the personification of classical Arabic music. She was also a pupil of Badhl (q.v.). She became famous for both her music and poetry and was considered at the time to be third in rank after Ishaq and Aluya. She sang at the court of the Caliphs al-Mamun (813 to 833) and al-Mu'tasim (833 to 842) and was eventually acquired by Ali ibn Hisham.
Ref. 170, 171, 234

MUTYUNE(T)
Egyptian songstress of the Theban Triad at Thebes, XXI dynasty. late Kingdom ca. 1000 B.C.
Bibliography
British Museum 8527. (guide, p. 146)
Ref. 428

MYAGI, Ester Kustovna. See MIAGI, Ester Kustovna

MYERS, Emma F.
19th-century American composer.
Composition
PIANO
Capitol march (Philadelphia: Lee & Walker, 1850)
Ref. 228

MYERS, Louise. See SPIZIZEN, Louise

MYGATT, Louise
20th-century American composer.
Compositions
CHAMBER
Duets (vln and vla) (1983)
Chorale-variations (pf) (1982)
Ref. AMC

MYRBERG, Anne Sophie
19th-century Swedish composer.
Compositions
PIANO
Nya albumblad: Scherzo, Romans, Capriccio (1888)
Tre bagateller: Prelude, Caprice, Polska (1895)
Ref. 642

MYRO. See MOERO

MYRTIS
6th-century B.C. poetess and composer of Anthedon, Boeotia, Ancient Greece. According to Suidas, she was the teacher of Pindar and Corinna. She was said to have competed with Pindar for the palm of superiority. There were statues in her honor in various parts of Greece.
Ref. 281, 382

MYSZINSKA-WOJCIECHOWSKA (Wojciechowska-Myszinska), Leokadia
Polish pianist, teacher and composer. b. Lowicz, May 9, 1858; d. Warsaw, September 12, 1930. In Warsaw she studied the piano under R. Strobl, harmony and counterpoint under G. Roguski and W. Zelenski and composition under Z. Noskowski. She won many prizes for her songs.
Compositions
ORCHESTRA
Pieces
CHAMBER
Piano trio
Romance (pf or vlc and pf)
Sonata (vln and pf)
PIANO
Etudes
Gavottes
Krakowiak in A-Major
Mazurek
Nocturnes
Polonaises
Preludes
Variations serieuses in A-Major (1902)
VOCAL
Choruses (m-ch a-cap)
Songs incl.:
Czy mi pozyc?
Dlaczego
Fujarka
Gdybym size zmienil w wstzegze zlocistza
Powiadaliscie matulu
Ref. 8, 118

NAESER-OTTO, Martha
German composer. b. Luckenwalde, March 17, 1860. She studied under her father, the organist Julius Naeser and at the Berlin Hochschule.
Compositions
PIANO
Pieces incl.:
Barcarolle in double passages
Etude in sixths, op. 3
VOCAL
Songs
Ref. 226, 276

NAGAYO, Sueko
Japanese composer. b. Tokyo, January 25, 1950. She studied at the Toho Gakuen University in 1972. She is a member of the Japan Association of Contemporary Music.
Composition
MISCELLANEOUS
Signification
Ref. Yamaha Musical Foundation

NAIKHOVICH-LOMAKINA (Lomakina), Fania Filippovna
Soviet pianist, teacher and composer. b. Ashkhabad, Turkmen SSR, October 30, 1908. She studied the piano under A. Konstantinovsky at the Baku Music School until 1930. In 1934 she graduated from the College of Pet-

roleùm Technology in Baku. At the Baku Conservatory she studied composition under L. Rudolph and B. Zaidman and graduated in 1946. After 1938 she taught theoretical subjects in music schools.

Compositions

ORCHESTRA

Poem to commemorate the heroes of Sevastopol (sym orch) (1942)

CHAMBER

Piano quintet (1946)
String quartet (1943)
Three pieces (str qrt) (1942)
Elegia (hn and pf) (1948)
Pesnya (ob and fl) (1948)
Pesnya pastukha (ob and pf) (1948)
Shutka (fl and pf) (1948)

VOCAL

Dorogaya moya, neizmenni moi drug (A. Surkov) (vces and pf) (1951)
Ballada o Lenine (Surkov) (vce and pf) (1951)
Monolog-ballada golos gneva (P. Voronko) (1952)
Ty pomnish li (M. Lermontov) (vce and pf) (1941)
Zimnyaya doroga, duet (Pushkin) (1947)

Ref. 87

NAIRNE, Carolina, Baroness (nee Oliphant)

Scottish composer. b. Broom of Dalreoch, Tayside, August 16, 1766; d. Broom of Dalreoch, October 26, 1845. She was one of the leading contributors to the revival of Scottish poetry and song of her time, but her works were published anonymously from 1792 and not even her husband knew of her achievements.

Compositions

VOCAL

Numerous ballads incl.:
Bonnie Charlie's now awa'
Caller herrin'
Charlie is my darling
The hundred pipers
The Laird o' Cockpen
The land o' the leal
The rowan tree
Will ye no' come back again

Ref. 572, 645

NAITO, Akemi

Japanese composer. b. Tokyo, January 24, 1956. She graduated from Toho-Gakuen University's Music School in 1978 and from the Graduate School in 1980. She studied under Nobuyoshi Iinuma and Akira Miyoshi. She won composition prizes from *Music Today* and *Takei*. DISCOGRAPHY.

Compositions

CHAMBER

Reflection (mar, 2 fl, cel and viv) (1977)
Maya (vln) (1983)
Secret song (gtr)

Ref. Japanese Federation of Composers

NAKAMURA, Sawako (pseud. Sawako Kawai)

Japanese composer. b. Nagasaki, May 25, 1931. She won third prize in the chamber composition section of the 31st competition in 1962 and first prize in the same section of the 34th music competition in 1975. She is a member of the Japanese Association of Contemporary Music.

Compositions

CHAMBER

Woodwind quintet
Jolly trio

PIANO

Pieces incl.:
The letter to Bach

VOCAL

Song of the clock

Ref. Yamaha Musical Foundation

NAKASHIMA, Jeanne Marie

American pianist, authoress, singer and composer. b. Chicago, September 23, 1936. She studied the piano as a child and gave classical recitals. She attended the Chicago Musical College; studied music, drama and languages at the University of California, received a B.F.A. from the Loyola Marymount University in 1957 and studied education and psychology at the Chicago Teachers' College. She specialized in writing songs for Hawaiian and Far East music markets. She formed the New Child Music Publishing Company and later became president of Makai Records.

Compositions

PIANO

Classic mood
Happy butterfly

VOCAL

Songs incl.:
Ano-ne
Chotto matte kudasai
Some day I'll be with you
Tomorrow's rainbow (inauguration song, Governor George Ariyoshi, Hawaii) (1974)
Wakarimasen

Ref. 494

NAMAKELUA, Alice K.

Hawaiian guitarist, singer, teacher and composer. b. Honolulu, August 12, 1892. She was raised in a musical family and started singing at five and playing the slack key guitar at eight. She composed over 180 songs and taught them to children. In 1972 the Hawaiian Music Foundation named her as the person who had contributed most to Hawaiian music.

Compositions

VOCAL

Songs incl.:
Ahi wela
Hale'iwa paka
Ku'u manu
Ku'u pu'u kau pohaku
Ku'u wa'a
Kuahiwi nani oe
Lei 'ilima
Lele koali
Nani
No tutu
Papale u'i
Ukulele kani

Ref. 438

NARBUT-DEMOWSKA, Constance. See NARBUTOWNA, Constance

NARBUTOWNA (Narbut-Dembowska), Constance (Mme. Dembowska)

Early 19th-century Polish composer.

Composition

VOCAL

Melody for the historical song by Zolkiewski, for Spiewy historycze z muzyko i rycinami (1818)

Ref. 35, 118

NARCISSE-MAIR, Denise Lorraine

Jamaican harpsichordist, pianist, choral conductor, professor and composer. b. Kingston, January 19, 1940. She studied the piano at the Royal College of Music, London, as a royal scholar, becoming an L.R.A.C. in 1960 and graduating in 1961. In 1969 she became an A.R.C.M. (teaching diploma, hons). She taught the piano there from 1961 to 1963 and in secondary schools in London and Kent until 1965. She was assistant conductor of the Rochester Choral Society; head of the music department of Rochester Grammar School from 1965 to 1969, then a lecturer at London University, becoming senior lecturer and co-ordinator of postgraduate studies from 1970 to 1971, when she was awarded a B.Mus. hons in musicology from London University, where she continued study for her doctorate in ethnomusicology. She became assistant professor of the department of music, Queen's University, Kingston in 1972 and associate professor in 1976. She is currently director of the choral program at the Royal Conservatory of Music, University of Toronto. She has conducted numerous choirs and was the first woman invited to conduct the 1981 to 1982 season of the Ontario Youth Choir.

Compositions

THEATRE

Tableau vivant, musical drama

INCIDENTAL MUSIC

Space song for infants (1971) (Boosey & Hawkes)
Music for plays

ARRANGEMENTS

Two Indian spirituals (mix-ch) (1974)

Publications

Buddy Lido. Collection of Indian Folk Songs. OUP.

Ref. 206

NARITA, Kasuko
20th-century Japanese composer. She won a prize in a competition for orchestral works in Paris, 1983.
Ref. Frau und Musik

NARRONE, Claudia
20th-century composer.
Composition
FILM MUSIC
Loving cousins
Ref. 497

NASCIMBENI, Maria Francesca
Italian composer. b. Ancona, 1658. She studied under Scipione Lazzarini.
Compositions
SACRED
Canzoni e madrigali morali e spirituali a una, due e tre voci (e organo) (ded D. Olimpia Aldobrandini Pamphillii, Princess of Rossano) (Ancona: Stamperia Musicale per Claudio Percimineo, 1674)
Sitientes venite (3 vces) in collection of motets by Schipione Lazzarini (Stamperia Musicale per Claudio Percimineo, 1674)
Ref. 8, 44, 65, 74, 105, 128, 216, 226, 361, 653

NASH, Grace Helen
American lecturer and composer. b. Clinton, IA, 1882. She lectured at the Universities of South and North Carolina and at the Juilliard School of Music. From 1931 to 1932 she lectured for G. Schirmer and then taught at the Institute of Musical Art, New York. She taught for many years in schools in the Los Angeles area. Her first composition was published in 1927.
Compositions
PIANO
Gibraltar (2 pf)
Night in Algiers (2 pf)
Tarantella (2 pf)
Other pieces
ARRANGEMENTS
Malaguena (pf, 4 hands) (Lecuona)
Numerous choral works
Publications
Finding. For children.
Music study course. For older beginners.
Ref. 292

NASH, Phyllis V.
English composer. b. London, 1891. She was one of the first to broadcast from Marconi House.
Compositions
PIANO
April
Hide and seek
Je t'adore
Tommy's mail day
VOCAL
Songs incl.:
African dance
Folk tune
Minuet
La mouche
Sleepy tune
Spring song
Ref. 467

NASIB AL-MUTAWAKKILIYA
9th-century Arabian songstress at the court of al-Mutawakkil (847 to 861) in Samarra, near Baghdad. She was famous for her musical talents and intelligence. The fact that she sang a song composed by Ibrahim Ibn-al-Mahdi for the caliph shows that she probably followed Ibrahim's Persian influenced Romantic school of music.
Ref. 224

NASON, Susanna
20th-century American composer.
Composition
FILM MUSIC
They are their own gifts (1979)
Ref. 497

NATHAN, Matilde Berendsen
Norwegian concert pianist and composer. b. August 10, 1857; d. February 22, 1926. Of Danish parents, she commenced her piano studies under Edmund Neupert at the Copenhagen Conservatory at the age of 14. She gave piano recitals in Copenhagen and was awarded a scholarship for further study in Paris. After her marriage she terminated her concert career to concentrate on piano composition.
Compositions
PIANO
Allegretto gracioso, op. 18
Barcarole, op. 8
Capriccio, op. 10
Gavotte, op. 13
I gamel stil, op. 27
I tanker, op. 19
Livsglaede, op. 22
Polka mignon, op. 2
Romance, op. 3
Resignation, op. 21
Romance in B-Dur, op. 20
Scherzino, op. 29
Scherzo, op. 4
Seks melodier, op. 15
Serenade, op. 14
Tre etuder, op.1
Tre klaverstykker, op. 11
Tre praeludier, op. 16
Ungarisch, op. 5
Vaarvise, op. 17
Vemod, op. 28
Vuggevise, op. 12
Ref. NMI

NATHUSIUS, Marie
German novelist and composer. b. Magdeburg, March 10, 1817; d. December 22, 1857. Her numerous novels made her famous throughout Germany. She composed over 100 sacred and secular songs.
Ref. 226, 276, 347

NATIBORS (Mme. Tiberge)
A popular minstrel from Chateau de Seranon, near Grasse, Provence. All that remains of her songs is the verse *Beau doux ami, non je n'ai pas été un movement sans vous desirer, depuis que je vous au reconnu pour amant sincere. Tous mes souhaits ont été de vous voir souvent. Jamais je ne me suis repentie de mon choix. Lorsqu'il vous à fallu me quitter, il m'à été impossible de gouter aucun plaisir, que vous ne fussiez revenu.*
Ref. 221

NATSUDA, Shoko
20th-century Japanese composer. DISCOGRAPHY.
Composition
PIANO
Premiere piece

NATSUME, Kyoko. See WATARI, Kyoko

NATVIG, Candace
American violinist, poetess, singer and composer. b. Los Angeles, 1947. From 1967 to 1973 she studied at the University of Iowa, graduating with a M.F.A. in vocal performance. In 1973 she won a Tanglewood Fellowship for voice. The following year she went to Cologne, Germany. Her main collaborator is Jon English, trombonist and composer. She made recordings for Belgian, Dutch, West German and French radio. DISCOGRAPHY.
Compositions
VOCAL
Chuck Will's widow (vce and birdcalls)
Daddy would've loved a day like this! (vce and vln) (1981)
Euphobia (with Anne Lebaron (q.v.) and Jon English) (vce, vln and hp)
Foursome (with Jon English) (vce and vln or trb) (1979)
A little left of center (with Anne Lebaron and Jon English) (vce, hp, vln and trb)
One, not two (vce and vln) (1979)
Solos (vce and vln)
Travels of dog and cat
Vocal solo (vce and vacuum cleaner hose)

ELECTRONIC
It's cold when you can't move a feather (high vce, vln, trb and tape) (1980)
Dog dreams (vces, vln, trb and tape) (with Jon English) (1982)
Other improvised works
MISCELLANEOUS
Idylle und Katastrophen (with A. Schlippenbach, S. Johansson et al)
Iowa ear music
Ref. composer, 563

NAUMANN, Ida
German singer and song composer. d. Berlin, 1897.
Ref. 85, 347

NAVA D'ADDA, Francesca, Countess
Italian composer. d. Milan, October, 1877. She was a patroness of the arts.
Compositions
CHAMBER
Six trios, ops. 17, 18 and 20 (Ricordi)
Duet (vlc and pf) (Ricordi)
Six sonatas (vln and pf) (Ricordi)
Two duets, ops. 14 and 19 (vln and pf) (Ricordi)
Ref. 105

NAZAROVA, Tatiana Borisovna
Soviet pianist, concertmistress, lecturer and composer. b. Moscow, September 24, 1928. She studied the piano under E. Gnesina and composition under N.I. Peiko at the Gnesin Institute of Music, Moscow, graduating in 1961. She was concertmistress at the same institute from 1952 till 1959 and then taught there till 1963. She took part in folklore expeditions.
Compositions
ORCHESTRA
Symphony (1961)
Concerto on Kazakh folk themes (pf and orch) (1958)
Piano concerto (1976)
Children's suite (1961)
Fantasia on Kazakh themes and Altai folk melodies (pf and orch; also folk insts) (1960)
Six ballet scenes (1968)
Suite for Russian folk instruments (1957)
Two Russian folk songs (folk orch) (1966)
CHAMBER
Quintet (fl and str qrt) (1960, rev 1968)
Duet, romance, humoresque, song without words (hn and pf) (1969)
Concert piece (vln and pf) (1969)
Pieces (vln and pf) (1974)
Poetical pictures (domra and pf) (1962)
Sonatina (vlc and pf) (1974)
Spring morning (domra and pf) (1963)
Suite (ob and hp) (1963)
Romans, kolybelnaya, naigrish (gtr) (1964)
BAYAN
Two sonatines (1971)
Variations (1970)
PIANO
Five Vietnamese folk melodies (1976)
Introduction and toccata (1970)
Prelude and fugue (1960, 1970, 1971)
Polyphonic fragments (1973)
Polyphonic sonata (1967)
Polyphonic variations on Kazakh folk melodies (1974)
VOCAL
Tsar Feodor Ioannovich, cantata (A.K. Tolstoy) (reciters, soli, chs and orch of folk insts) (1977)
Song of Hiroshima (Japanese poets) (vce and orch) (1961)
Three Kazakh folk songs (vce and orch of folk insts) (1967)
Numerous choruses (Drunina, Bromlei, Soloukhin, Mikhailova, Lenin, Orlov, Prokofiev, Vekshegonovak, Belov and others)
Numerous romances (vce and pf) (Japanese and Altai poets and S. Yesenin)
Choral arrangements of folk songs
FILM MUSIC
Films incl.:
Orlenok (1968)
Ref. 21

NAZIROVA, Elmira Mirza Rza kyzy
Soviet pianist, professor and composer. b. Baku, November 30, 1928. She studied the piano at the Baku Conservatory under G. Sharoyev and composition under B. Zaidman, graduating in 1954. After 1951 she taught the piano at the same conservatory, becoming a professor in 1971. She became a member of the government of the Azerbaijanian SSR in 1956.
DISCOGRAPHY.
Compositions
ORCHESTRA
Piano concerto (1954)
Piano concerto on Azerbaijanian themes (1957)
Piano concerto No. 2, on Arabian themes (1957)
Piano concerto No. 3 (1968)
Overture (1953)
Poem-elegy (str orch) (1950)
CHAMBER
String quartet (1953)
String quartet No. 1 (1942)
String quartet No. 2 (1949)
Uzbek suite (str qrt) (1951)
Elegy (vln and pf) (1958)
Romance (vlc and pf) (1940)
Sonata (vlc and pf) (1952)
Sonata (vln and pf) (1946)
PIANO
Suite on Albanian themes (with F. Amirov) (2 pf) (1955)
Azerbaijanian folk songs (1955, 1962, 1963)
Bagatelles, cycle of 14 pieces (1971)
Children's album (1976)
Concert piece (1973)
Five children's pieces (1957)
Four etudes (1947)
Kaleidoscope, cycle (1960)
Nastroeniya, cycle (1969)
Novelletti, cycle (1972)
Six preludes (1947)
Sonata poema (1969)
Sonatina (1954)
Twenty four preludes, 1st cycle (1966)
Twenty four preludes, 2nd cycle (1975)
Two toccatas (1958)
Variations (1946, 1951)
Arrangements of Azerbaijanian folk songs and melodies
VOCAL
V tu noch, poem (Ellyaya) (vce and orch) (1954)
Kartinki prigody, cycle (Pushkin) (vce and pf) (1960)
Maski (A. Blok) (vce and pf) (1970)
Ten poems (Blok) (vce and pf) (1971)
Twelve poems (E. Vinokurov) (vce and pf) (1970)
Twelve poems (S. Shchipachev) (vce and pf) (1966)
Arrangements of folk songs
INCIDENTAL MUSIC
Music for theatre incl.:
Kamennei gost
Skazka o zolotoi rybke
Skupoi rytsar (Pushkin)
Vesna v Moskve (V. Gusev) (1949)
Ref. 21, 88, 223, 330, 563

NEAS, Margaret
American pianist, teacher and composer. b. Elizabethton, TN, February 21, 1920. She gained her concert diploma from the Intermont College, VA, in 1940 and her teaching certificate from the Peabody Institute in 1942. She appeared in radio and television programs and as a soloist for various clubs in Birmingham, AL.
Compositions
PIANO
Pieces incl.:
Cathy
Farewell concerto
Harmony in emerald
Lazy holiday
Portrait in satin
Teatime on Fifth Avenue (1967)
Ref. 506

NEEDHAM, Alicia Adelaide (nee Montgomery)
Irish pianist and composer. b. County Meath, near Dublin, 1875; d. 1945. She studied at the Royal Academy of Music, London, under Arthur O'Leary (piano) and Prout and Davenport (harmony and composition). For six sucessive years she won the song competition prize at the Irish Music Festival Feis Ceoil. She also won a prize for the best song in celebration of the coronation of King Edward VII in 1902.

Compositions
CHAMBER
Husheen (hn and pf) (Boosey)
PIANO
Four sketches (Novello)
Husheen
Scherzo (Boosey)
VOCAL
Over 600 songs incl.:
Box of smiles (Boosey)
Croodlin' doo (Boosey)
Donovans (Boosey)
How dear to me, the hour (Novello)
An Irish Lullaby (No. 1 of 4 lyrics) (w or boys' duet) (Novello)
Kissing time (Boosey)
A last (vce and vln or org ad lib) (Novello)
Maiden' song (w-vces or boys' vces) (Novello)
One nest together (Bosworth)
Sing to me sweetheart, waltz song (National Music)
Songs of our land (mix-ch) (Novello)
Terence (Augener)
Yesterday (Boosey)
SACRED
One sweet hope (Brainard)
Ref. 8, 23, 105, 226, 276, 297

NEEL, Susan Elizabeth
American organist, pianist, teacher and composer. b. Palestine, TX, January 5, 1944. She studied at the Universities of Texas in 1963 and Houston (M.Mus.Ed.) in 1965. She made her debut in Palestine as a pianist in 1962 and an organist in 1966. She made numerous appearances on television, radio and on stage and is a member of the faculty of the Music Academy, Palestine. She is also a member of several teaching associations.
Compositions
VOCAL
Creation chorale (ch)
In the beginning (ch)
Ref. 77

NEELD, Peggy
20th-century American composer.
Composition
OPERA
The Magic Fish
Ref. 141

NEGRAND-SCHORI, Jenny. See GRUNBERG, Janeta

NEGRONE, Luisa
19th-century Italian composer.
Compositions
PIANO
Dans le lamac (Ricordi)
Une pensée à Mendelssohn (Ricordi)
Soleil et nuages, impromptu (Ricordi)
VOCAL
L'acqua del mar ti mantien fresca e bella, stornello (m-S or T) (Ricordi)
Bacio vivo-Conosci il fior sulle nevi sbocia, romanza (Ricordi)
Ref. 297

NEILY, Anne MacAdams
20th-century American organist, pianist, choir director, singer, teacher and composer. b. Alton, IL. She attended Milliken University, was the organist and choir director at St. Albans Episcopal Church, Portland and traveled extensively in concert throughout the United States and Canada. She taught the piano and voice.
Compositions
PIANO
Arabesque
The sea gypsy
Teaching pieces
Ref. 374

NEIT
Egyptian songstress of the House of Amon, XXVI dynasty, 663 to 525 B.C. Her tomb is at Medinet Habu.
Ref. 428

NELSON, Mary Anne
American conductor and composer. b. McPherson, KS, October 10, 1945. She studied conducting and composition in Texas and after 1959 worked at the Holstebro experimental and electronic music studio and high school.
Compositions
CHAMBER
Two string quartets
Reflections of a cellist
ELECTRONIC
Pieces incl.:
On statues
Fremad
MISCELLANEOUS
Improviserio 1 and 2
Meditation music for non-thinkers
Ref. 1

NEMTEANU-ROTARU, Doina
20th-century Rumanian composer.
Compositions
CHAMBER
Incantations (fl, ob, cl, bsn and hn)
Lichtscheide (cl, vln, vla, vlc and pf)
Spiegelspiel (4 fl)
String quartet No. 3
Rascruea macilor (pf) (1983)
Sonata (vlc) (Bucharest: Ed. Muzicale, 1982)
Sonata (vln) (1971)
ELECTRONIC
Nacht der Feen (cl, pf and tape) (1984)
Ref. Frau und Musik

NENCIC, Ivanka
20th-century Yugoslav composer.
Composition
PIANO
Zbirka minijatura za klavir, collection of miniatures (1980)
Ref. Otto Harrassowitz (Wiesbaden)

NEPGEN, Rosa Sophia Cornelia (Mrs. W.E.G. Louw)
South African organist, pianist, lecturer and composer. b. Barkly East, Cape Province, December 12, 1909. She received her first piano lessons from her pianist mother and when the family moved to Pretoria, Rosa studied the piano under Dirk Meerкotter and then Ellen Norburn and the organ, singing and speech under Stephanie Fuare. In 1927 she went to the University of the Witwatersrand, Johannesburg where she studied under Percival R. Kirby and Horace Barton, receiving a B.A. and B.Mus. (music, English and ethics) and a B.Mus. hons in 1931. She also received her licentiate diplomas in the organ and the piano as well as the fellowship of Trinity College. She lectured in the music department at Wits University, then from 1954 to 1955 studied instrumentation under Henk Badings and counterpoint under Ernest Mulder, both in Holland. She lived in Stellenbosch, Cape Province, after 1968. Her *Met hart en mond* was the product of research into the melodies of the Geneva Psalm Book of 1562; in this work she effected a partial restoration of the 16th-century forms.
Compositions
ORCHESTRA
Vroeë aand, tone poem (1937)
CHAMBER
Trio (vln, vlc and pf) (1940)
Drie verhale (vln and pf) (1940)
PIANO
Fugale fantasie (1937)
Sonate (1940)
VOCAL
Die dieper reg, cantata (N.P. van Wyk Louw) (soli, mix-ch and orch) (1943)
Agter die rante (van Wyk Louw) (mix-ch)
Die berggans het 'n veer laat val (Boerneef) (m-ch or mix-ch; also high vce and pf) (1972) (comm King's Singers, Cambridge University)
Boplaas het weer toegeval (Boerneef) (mix-ch) (1972) (comm King's Singers)
Keer 'ie ding (van Wyk Louw) (mix-ch) (1959) (in FAK-Sangbundel, 1979)
Lappiedy, lappieda (Boerneef) (mix-ch) (1963) (in FAK-Sangbundel, 1979)
Rembrandt-selfportret (van Wyk Louw) (m-ch) (1972) (comm King's Singers)
Cinque canzoni, incl. Portami il girasole (Eugenio Montale) (S and pf) (1968)

Hart in die nag, song cycle (van Wyk Louw) (S and pf) (1974) (comm Stellenbosch Farmers' Winery, Oude Libertas)
Op die Flottina, song cycle incl. Êrens in die Kro het ek 'n skerm; Hoe stil kan dit word as sedoos gaan lê (Boerneef) (med vce) (comm Cape Performing Arts Board) (Stellenbosch: T. Wever Boekhandel, 1970)
Twaalf klein metafisiese voorspele, song cycle (van Wyk Louw) (1958) (Johannesburg: Cultura Uitgewers, 1966; Cape Town: Studio Holland)
Twee Liedere (van Wyk Louw) (med-vce) (1960) (Studio Holland, 1963; H. Petrus; Jy't Weggegaan)
Liedere van Rosa Nepgen, Deel I, Vyf Vroeë Liedere (W.E.G. Louw) (Cape Town: Nasionale Boekhandel Beperk; Amsterdam: G. Alsbach & Co., 1956): Aan die strand (med-vce and pf) (1941); Bestendige aanwesigheid-wat ek verloor het (high or med-vce and pf) (1943); Herdenking (med-vce and pf) (1941); Ons is almal sterwelinge (high or med-vce and pf) (1945)
Verbondenheid (high-vce and pf) (1941)
Liedere van Rosa Nepgen, Deel II, Drie Liedere (J.H. Leopold) (Nasionale Boekhandel Beperk; G. Alsbach & Co., 1956): O als ik dood zal zyn (med-vce and pf) (1944); In tere schaduw zilver-blauw (med-vce and pf) (1944); Schepen liggen er (med-vce and pf) (1944)
Liedere van Rosa Nepgen, Deel III, Drie Liedere (Eugène Marais) (Nasionale Boekhandel Beperk; G. Alsbach & Co., 1956): Dieprivier (med or low vce and pf) (1955); Hart-van-die dagbreek (high or med-vce and pf) (1944); Winternag (high vce and pf) (1945)
Liedere van Rosa Nepgen, Deel IV, Drie Liedere (E. Eybers) (Nasionale Boekhandel Beperk; G. Alsbach & Co., 1956) Die antwoord (high vce) (1952); Lied van 'n blinde (high vce and pf) (1952); Verhaal (high or med-vce and pf)
Liedere van Rosa Nepgen, Deel V, 2 lyrics from the Chinese (trans H. Waddell) (Nasionale Boekhandel Beperk; G. Alsbach & Co., 1956); White clouds are in the sky (m-S and pf) (1953)
Liedere van Rosa Nepgen, Deel VI, Twee Liedere (J.C. Bloem) (Nasionale Boekhandel Beperk; G. Alsbach & Co., 1956): Spiegeling (high or med-vce and pf) (1953); Voorjaar (high vce) (1954)
Liedere van Rosa Nepgen, Deel VII, Drie Liedere van die droefheid J.C. Bloem (Nasionale Boekhandel Beperk: G. Alsbach & Co., 1956); Die bevryde (med or low vce and pf) (1954); Een dag (med or low vce and pf) (1954); Kanferfoelie (med or low vce and pf) (1953)
Ek het jou liewer as wind of die water (W.E.G. Louw) (high vce) (1940)
Ignatius bid vir sy orde (van Wyk Louw) (med-vce) (Studio Holland, 1963)
Klara majola (D.J. Opperman) (med-vce) (1969)
Ons nuwe vryheidslied (J.F.E. Cilliers) (med-vce and pf) (Johannesburg: Voortrekkerpers Beperk)
Ou flenterkatiera (W.E.G. Louw) (med-vce and pf) (1941)
Salut d'amour (A.G. Visser) (vce and pf) (1936) (in Sing sag menig'lied) (Johannesburg: Samro, 1978)
Van Verlorevlei (Visser) (med-vce) (1942) (in Sing sag menig'lied) (Samro, 1978)
Winterbome (van Wyk Louw) (high or med-vce and pf) (1943) (Studio Holland, 1963)

SACRED
Die Passie van ons Heer, cantata (W.E.G. Louw) (soloists, mix-ch and orch) (1954)
Jeremia 13:15, 16 (Bible text) (mix-ch and org) (1954)
Jesaja (Bible text) (mix-ch and org) (1953)
Drie korale, Psalms 8, 69, 142 (Totius) (mix-ch) (1954)
Die Lofsang (Loflied) van Maria (Magnificat) (high vce) (Nederduitse Gereformeerde Kerk Uitgewers, 1962)
Onse Vader (mix-ch and org) (1953) (Cape Town: Nederduitse Gereformeerde Kerk Uitgewers, 1962)
Psalmkantata (Totius) (ch) (1961) (comm SABC)
Twaalfe korale (Totius) (mix-ch) (1956): Psalm 28 (SABC Music Library Catalogue); Psalm 18 (SAMRO catalogue); Psalms 37, 45, 50, 57, 64, 76, 80, 94, 109, 146 (Psalm 45 also in FAK Sangbundel, 1979)
Psalm 6 (B and pf) (1953)
Psalm 98 (mix-ch and org) (1953)
Psalm 121 (mix-ch and org) (1953)
Psalm 130 (mix-ch and org) (1943)
Psalm 133 (mix-ch and org) (1965)
Die Boodskap aan Maria (van Wyk Louw) (high vce and pf) (1945)
Die Bloeisels van Jesus (W.E.G. Louw) (med-vce and pf) (1941)
Maria (W.E.G. Louw) (high vce and pf) (1949)
Met hart en mond (Totius) settings and arrangements of 150 Psalms (Psalms 23 mix-ch and org, 45 and 137 of this collection in FAK Sangbundel, 1979) (Nederduitse Gereformeerde Kerk Uitgewers, 1966)
Psalm 8, motet (4 vces) (Nederduitse Gereformeerde Kerk Uitgewers, 1962)
Psalm 13 (med-vce and pf) (1956)
Psalm 19 (Totius) (3 vces) (Nederduitse Gereformeerde Kerk Uitgewers, 1962)
Psalm 127 (med-vce and pf) (1956)
Psalm 137, motet (Totius) (4 vces) (Nederduitse Gereformeerde Kerk Uitgewers, 1962)
Psalm 139 (Totius) (A) (1960)

THEATRE
In Salamis (Euripides, trans T.J. Haarhoff) (mix-ch and orch) (1937)
The three Marys, Coventry mystery play (vces, fl, hp and strs) (1938)

Publications

Ons Kerklied in Die Kerkbode. May 1957.

Bibliography

Bouws, Jan. *Rosa Nepgen as Liederkomponis. Die Burger*, April 13, 1971.
Malan, Prof. J.P. *Vyf nuwe gewyde werke van Rosa Nepgen. Die Burger*, December 12, 1963.

Ref. 17, 26, 44, 70, 175, 184, 377

NEPHTHYS

Ancient Egyptian mother-goddess and sister of Isis (q.v.). The laments attributed to her and Isis became the models for formal and informal dirges.
Ref. 264

NERVI, Marta

Composition

VOCAL
La lune blanche, canzone (P. Verlaine) (Ricordi)

Ref. Ricordi (Milan)

NESTE, Rosane van

Belgian pianist and composer. b. Courtrai, August 21, 1911. She studied at the Brussels Conservatory and toured in Belgium, Holland and England.

Compositions

ORCHESTRA
Suite (also vln and pf)

CHAMBER
Serenade (vln)
Sonatina (pf) (Metropolis, 1983)

Ref. 96

NETZEL, Laura C. See LAGO

NEUMANN, Elizabeth

19th-century South African composer of German origin. b. Cape Town.

Compositions

PIANO
Erinnerung an Kapstadt, op. 2, waltz (4 hands)
Other pieces

Ref. 184, 226, 276, 347

NEUVILLE, Mme. Alphonse de

19th-century French composer. She married the painter Alphonse Marie de Neuville.

Compositions

CHAMBER
Ballade (pf and vln)
Barcarolle (pf and vln)
Fantaisie in C-Major (pf and vln)
Forget-me-not, gavotte (man or vln and pf) (National Music)
Meditation No. 1 (pf and vln)
Meditation No. 2 (pf and vln)
Morceau de concert (pf and vln)
Sweet smiles, nocturne (man or vln and pf) (National Music)
Villanelle (vln and pf)

PIANO
Gladys, étude à la polka (National Music)
Gwendoline, intermezzo (National Music)
Innocence, gavotte (National Music)

SACRED
Marche funebre
Mass: Andante religioso; Pie Jesus; Requiem
O Salutaris

Ref. 226, 276, 297

NEUWIRTH, Goesta

Austrian music director, lecturer and composer. b. Vienna, January, 1937. She studied at the Salzburg Mozarteum. She teaches at the University of Vienna and the Vienna Academy of Music and is a music director of a student theatre.

Composition
CHAMBER
Violin sonata brevis (1955)
Ref. 81

NEWCOMBE, Georgeanne (nee Hubi)

English organist, authoress, lyricist, soprano and composer. b. London, December 18, 1843. She studied under Dr. Hiles and R. Glenn Wesley. She was the organist at Latchford Paris Church for several years. She wrote the lyrics for *Eve* and *A glowing west, op. 33*, set to music by Mana-Zucca (q.v.).

Compositions
PIANO
Ye fancye fayer march
Other pieces
VOCAL
Songs incl.:
Ever faithful
Irish potheen
The miner and his boy (prize)
Ref. 6, 85, 226, 276, 347, 433

NEWELL, Eleanor

20th-century composer.

Composition
OPERA
The Music Hater (with Newell Long) (1969)
Ref. 141

NEWELL, Laura E.

American composer. b. New Marlborough, MA, February 5, 1854. She composed songs.
Ref. 347

NEWLIN, Dika

American pianist, critic, musicologist, professor and composer. b. Portland, November 22, 1923. She gained her B.A. in 1939 from the Michigan State University, East Lansing. From 1938 to 1941 she studied composition privately under Roger Sessions and Arnold Schoenberg. In 1951 she received an M.A. from the University of California, Los Angeles. She continued her piano studies under Ignace Hilsberg, R. Serkin and A. Schnabel and in 1945 was awarded the first Ph.D. in musicology to be given by Columbia University, New York, for her work, *Bruekner, Mahler, Schoenberg*. She taught at Western Maryland College, Westminster from 1945 to 1949 and at Syracuse University, from 1949 to 1951. She was awarded the Fulbright fellowship and studied in Vienna from 1951 to 1952. She was professor of music and head of the music department which she established at Drew University, Madison, from 1952 to 1965. She was awarded the Mahler medal by the Brueckner Society in 1957. She received an honorary doctorate of human letters from Upsala College, New Jersey, in 1964. She was also awarded a silver medal by the French Minister of Foreign Affairs. She became professor of musicology at the North Texas State University in Denton in 1965 and in 1973, director of the electronic music laboratory of Montclair State College in New Jersey. From 1976 to 1978 she devoted herself to writing and composition. In 1978 she accepted an invitation from Virginia Commonwealth University in Richmond to develop a new doctoral program in music and is currently professor of music there. Most of her compositions are in the 12-tone idiom. DISCOGRAPHY.

Compositions
ORCHESTRA
Chamber concerto in F-Major (ob, vln, pf and orch) (ACA)
Concerto for piano and orchestra in C
Cradle song
Triple play (ACA)
CHAMBER
Symphony for twelve solo instruments (1949)
Piano trio, op. 2 (1948)
The last duet (vln and pf)
Sonata (vln and pf) (ACA)
Study in twelve tones (vla d'amore and pf) (1959)
Variations (vln and pf)
Circular thoughts for solo clarinet (Theodore Pressor)
PIANO
Pieces incl.:
Fantasia (1957)
Fantasy on a row (1958) (ACA)
Fido flew away
Lhazebur
Old dog Tweetie
Passacaglia (1941)
Six pieces (1942)
Sinfonia (1947) (ACA)
Sonata da chiesa (also org) (1956)
Variations on a row from Mahler's Tenth symphony (1960)
Variations on a theme from The Magic Flute (1956)
VOCAL
Song of the day and night (Cont and orch) (ACA)
Atone (vces and insts) (1977)
Der Du von dem Himmel bist (Goethe) (med-vce and pf) (ACA)
Haus in Bonn (S. George) (med-vce and pf) (ACA)
I saw in Louisiana a live oak growing (W. Whitman) (med-vce and pf) (ACA)
Lied (S. George) (med-vce and pf) (ACA)
Mein weg geht jetzt vorueber (med-vce and pf) (ACA)
The quidditie (G. Herbert) (med-vce and pf) (ACA)
To Mrs. Anna Flaxman (William Blake) (med-vce and pf) (ACA)
SACRED
Genesis 4 (mix-ch, 3 hn and org) (ACA)
This is the record of John (A, T, mix-ch, brass ch and org) (ACA)
Chorale: Preambulam; Prelude, O Mensch bewein deine Suende gross; Fugue
Five nativity songs (Shakespeare and anon) (S, ob and org)
Psalm 100 (med-vce and pf) (ACA)
Psalm 150 (med-vce and pf) (ACA)
OPERA
Feathertop
ELECTRONIC
Big swamp (vce and tape) (1972)
MISCELLANEOUS
Machine shop

Publications
Brueckner, Mahler, Schoenberg. Analytical study. New York, 1947; rev. ed. New York: Norton, 1978.
The Schoenberg Diaries.
Self-Revelation and the Law: Arnold Schoenberg in His Religious Work. Studies of the Jewish Music Research Center. Jerusalem: Magnes Press, 1968.
Translations: Leibowitz, Rene. *Schoenberg and His School*. New York, 1949; Rufer, Josef. *The Works of Arnold Schoenberg*. London and New York, 1962; Schoenberg, Arnold. *Style and Idea*. New York and Toronto, 1950; Werner, Eric. *Felix Mendelssohn*. London and New York, 1963.
Ref. 2, 14, 17, 22, 70, 74, 94, 137, 141, 142, 189, 297, 415, 465, 477, 563, 622, 625

NEWMAN, Adelaide

South African concert pianist, teacher and composer. b. Johannesburg, December 30, 1908. She started her piano studies at the age of six and later studied the piano under Mrs. W. Bell and harmony under Professor W. Bell. She won a scholarship to the Royal Academy of Music in 1921 and in 1924 was awarded a post-graduate certificate by the South African College of Music and appointed the official college accompanist. For three years she gave concert recitals, returning to London in 1933 to study at the Tobias Matthay Piano School. In 1941 she returned to South Africa and continued her concert career.

Compositions
CHAMBER
String quartet
Short preludes (pf)
VOCAL
Songs
Ref. 377

NEWMAN-PERPER, Elfie

20th-century American composer.

Composition
VOCAL
Lullaby (Whitney Blake) (med-vce and pf)
Ref. 190

NEWPORT, Doreen

English pianist, teacher and composer. b. Manchester, February 24, 1927. She gained a B.A. hons in French from Somerville College, Oxford University in 1947 and an Oxford diploma in music in 1948 and education, 1949. She gained her M.A. in teaching from Manchester University in 1949 and is an L.R.A.M.. She taught music appreciation and the piano in schools and music and movement to infants and currently teaches the piano at Winchester College and the Pilgrims' School.

Compositions
MISCELLANEOUS
Lord, we remember Your people
Think of a world without any flowers
Ref. 643

NEWTON, Adelaide (Emily) (nee Ward) (Mrs. Alexander)

English singer and composer. b. London, 1821; d. December 22, 1881. She was one of Jenny Lind's concert party on her first tour of England. She composed piano pieces and songs.
Ref. 6, 85, 226, 276, 347, 433

NEWTON, Rhoda

American organist, authoress and composer. b. Hudson, NY, June 9. She was educated at Columbia College and studied the organ under R.H. Woodman. She later became an organist at various methodist churches. She is a member of ASCAP.
Compositions
SACRED
Christmas bell carol
Easter bell carol
Give thanks
OPERETTA
Man in the moon
Ref. 39

NGUYEN (Nguyen van Ty), Louise

Vietnamese composer. b. 1915.
Compositions
ORCHESTRA
Feast exchange of vows (pf and orch)
Fêtes du Tet, joyful procession (pf and orch)
Offering at the altar of the ancestors (pf and orch)
Song of hope (pf and orch)
Year of the dragon (pf and orch)
Ref. Robert Dearling (Spalding, UK)

NIAY (Niay-Darrol), Apolline

South African concert pianist, lecturer and composer. b. Sutton Coldfield, England, December 5, 1868; d. Cape Town, January 20, 1920. She received her first piano lessons from her father, Gustave Niay and later studied under Adam Wright and Dr. Swinnerton Heap in Birmingham. She received the senior certificate at the Royal Academy of Music at the age of 14. In 1883 she made her debut as a concert pianist in Birmingham, subsequently touring Scotland and the north of England. She was requested to play at a command peformance for the Prince of Wales, later Edward VII. She entered the Royal College of Music in 1887, studying the piano under Franklin Taylor. She was selected council exhibitioner the following year. She emigrated to Australia with her parents in 1891 and performed in concerts in Sydney and elsewhere, formed the Sydney Quintet Society and organized a Conservatorium in New South Wales. She left for South Africa in 1893. She was responsible for the founding of the South African College of Music, now the faculty of music at the University of Cape Town, in 1910. She was the college principal and taught the piano and other subjects there. She also founded the original Music Teachers' Association of South Africa in 1909. She founded and organized the South African Eisteddfod in Cape Town.
Compositions
ORCHESTRA
Defence Force march (Leipzig: C.G. Roeder)
Exhibition march (Cape Town: R. Mueller, 1902)
PIANO
Etude brillante in F (Mueller; Roeder)
Harlequin (Mueller)
Mazurka
Tarantelle (Mueller)
Ref. Mrs. R. Finch (granddaughter), 184, 377

NIAY-DARROL, Apolline. See NIAY, Apolline

NICCOLINI, Virginia

Compositions
VOCAL
Ed or sei lunghe! romance (G. Targioni) (vce and pf)
Fior dissecato, romance (Nada) (vce and pf)
Mesta canzone (G. Buonomini) (vce and pf)
Perche? Romance (C. Benelli) (vce and pf)
Povero amore, romance (L. Stecchetti) (vce and pf)
Sorrisi ammaliati, romance (G. Buonomini) (vce and pf)
Ref. Ricordi, 297

NICHOLS, Alberta

American composer. b. Lincoln, IL, December 3, 1898; d. Holywood, 1957. She studied at the Louisville Conservatory and under Alfred Calzin and George Copeland.
Compositions
INCIDENTAL MUSIC
Angela, theatre
Gay Paree, theatre
Music for radio and commercials
Ref. 142, 433, 465

NICKERSON, Camille Lucie (Louisiana Lady)

Black American guitarist, pianist, arranger, professor, singer and composer. b. New Orleans, 1888; d. 1982. She studied the piano under her father, a violinist, conductor and music teacher and Rene Salomon. At Oberlin Conservatory she obtained her B.M. in 1937 and M.M. in 1962. She studied at the Juilliard School of Music and at Columbia University Teachers' College, New York. She received awards from the National Association of Negro Musicians. She was a member of the Howard University faculty from 1926 to 1962 and then professor emeritus. She researched into Louisiana creole music and was called the *Louisiana Lady*. She received many awards and honors.
Compositions
VOCAL
Christmas everywhere (ch) (Boston Music)
Go to sleep, creole song (Boston)
Gue-gue solingaie (Lemoine) (4 part ch and pf) (Boston)
Interracial hymn (ch) (Boston)
Mister Banjo, creole song (ch) (Boston)
A precious lullaby (ch) (Boston)
Suzanne, creole song (ch) (Boston)
The women of the USA (ch) (Boston)
Chere, mo lemme teo
Dance baby dance, creole song (Boston)
Dear, I love you so, creole song (Boston)
Lizette, my dearest one, creole song (Boston)
Mam'selle Zi Zi, creole song (Boston)
When love is done (Boston)
Ref. 136, 142, 549

NICOLAY, Maria Antonia (nee Cappes)

German teacher and composer. b. Pfalzburg, Alsace, 1782; d. Aachen, October 24, 1855. In 1823 she was principal of a girls' school in Muenster and in 1829 went to Duesseldorf. For twenty years she was the principal of St. Leonard Girls' High School in Aachen.
Composition
PIANO
Zwoelf Klaviervariationen sur un air connu (Dort oben auf jenem Berg) (Muenster, 1810)
Ref. 192

NIEBEL, Mildred

20th-century American composer.
Compositions
VOCAL
Somebody gave ma a lemon cream pie (vce and pf) (Boston Music)
OPERA
Friendship on Parade
Ref. 141, 190

NIEBERGALL, Julia Lee

20th-century American composer.
Composition
PIANO
Horseshoe rag
Ref. University of California (Santa Barbara)

NIECKS, Christina

20th-century Scottish composer. b. Aberdeen. She studied at Edinburgh University.
Compositions
CHAMBER
Trio
String minuet
Fugue (pf)
SACRED
Psalm 6 (4 part ch a-cap)
Ref. 226

NIEDERBERGER, Maria A.

Swiss violinist, teacher and composer. b. Davos, March 2, 1949. She studied the violin under Herbert Scherz at the Lucerne Conservatory and taught music in Zurich until 1975, when she emigrated to the United States. In 1976 she went to Davis University, CA, and in 1981 graduated with a B.A.. She then attended Brandeis University, Boston where her teachers included Donald Martino, Arthur Berger, Andrew Imbrie, Martin Boykan and Conrad Pope.

Compositions

ORCHESTRA
- Violin concerto (1981)

CHAMBER
- Fission and fusion (vln, vla, xy and pf) (1980)
- Daedaleum (vlc) (1984)

VOCAL
- Combinations (Ingeborg Bachmann) (m-S and str qrt) (1983)
- Hymne an den Unendlichen (Schiller) (S, fl and pf) (1984)

ELECTRONIC
- Inferences (fl or a-fl, cl or b-cl, bsn, glock, xy, vib, mar, pf and str trio) (1985)

Ref. 651

NIEDERSTETTER, Emilie

19th-century German composer.

Compositions

PIANO
- Air sans paroles, op. 2 (Leuckart)
- Berceuse, op. 4 (Leuckart)
- Mazurka de concert, op. 3 (Leuckart)
- Romance (Leuckart)
- Scherzo, op. 5 (Leuckart)

Ref. 226, 276, 297

NIELSEN, Henriette

Danish writer and composer. b. West Hanherred, Jutland, 1815; d. 1900. Her vaudeville was performed 78 times at the Royal Theatre and parts of it were translated into Swedish and German.

Composition

THEATRE
- Slaegningene, vaudeville (1849)

Ref. Dansk Komponistforening

NIELSEN, Olga

Danish composer.

Compositions

ORGAN
- Tolv praeludier, heft II

Ref. 331

NIEMACK, Ilza Louise

American violinist, professor and composer. b. Charles City, IA, April 8, 1936. She studied in Chicago and Minneapolis under Leon Sanetine and Otto Meyer and in New York under Leopold Auer for three years. She studied theory and composition under Felix Borowski and Rubin Goldmark. Other teachers included Francis Pyle and Mario Castelnuovo-Tedesco. Ilza was a faculty member of Iowa State University from 1935, professor from 1970 to 1973 and then professor emeritus. PHOTOGRAPH.

Compositions

ORCHESTRA
- Concerto No. 11 (vln and orch) (1947)
- Two piano concertos
- Minneapolis (1946)

CHAMBER
- Elegie (ww, vla, vlc and vln) (1947)
- String quartet (1980)
- String quartet No. 1 (1947)
- Barcarolle (vln and pf)
- Duo No. 1 (vla and vln)
- Duo No. 2 (vla and vln)
- Short pieces (vln and pf)
- Sonata No. 1 (vln and pf)
- Two sonatinas (1947)

VOCAL
- Five songs (1935)

Ref. composer, 40, 142, 347

NIEMIERZYC, Antonia

Polish song composer. ca. 1821.

Ref. 465

NIEWIADOMSKA, Barbara

Polish composer. b. Lubin, April 7, 1938. She studied theory under A. Dobrowolski and composition under P. Perkowski at the State Music College in Warsaw and received diplomas in 1967 and 1969. From 1970 to 1971 she studied composition in Paris under Nadia Boulanger (q.v.).

Compositions

ORCHESTRA
- Allegro (1968)

CHAMBER
- Alleluia (inst ens) (1970)
- Music in three parts (fl, vlc and perc) (1968)
- Tinta e ritmo (2 pf and perc) (1965)
- Non astrando (fl and pf) (1984)
- Music in three parts (cl) (1971)

PIANO
- Children's miniatures (1964-1972)
- Three rhythmical sketches (1973)

VOCAL
- Podanie (composer) (S and inst ens) (1967)
- Zbakane ptaki (Tagore) (S, fl, ob, cl, hp and perc) (1964)
- Gwiazdy (A. Slonimski) (1967)
- Songs

TEACHING PIECES
- Numerous children's pieces

Ref. Authors' Agency (Warsaw)

NIEWIAROWSKA-BRZOZOWSKA, Julia

Polish concert pianist and composer. b. 1827; d. December 1891. Her brother was the poet Karol Brzozowski and she married the writer Aleksander Niewiarowski. She studied under A. Freyer and appeared in concerts in Warsaw in 1848 and in Berlin.

Compositions

PIANO
- Ballada
- Chant d'amour (Warsaw: A. Friedlein, 1857)
- Diabolic fantasy
- Fantasia
- Four mazurkas
- March
- Morceaux pathetiques (Friedlein, 1857)
- Polonaise (Gebethner)
- Scherzo
- Serenada
- Sylfida
- Three obereks
- Waltz (1859)

VOCAL
- Dwa spiewy (vce and pf) (Vilno: Orgelbrand)
- Przypomnienie (W. Wolski) (vce and pf)
- Spiewak w obcej stronie (B. Zaleski) (Warsaw: G. Sennewald)
- Szatan (Wolski) (Senewald: Friedlein)

Ref. 35, 297

NIGHTINGALE, Barbara Diane

American concert accordionist and composer. b. Long Beach, October 11, 1955. She commenced her accordion studies as a child and later gained her B.M. in 1978 and M.A. from California State University. She received private tuition from La Voy Halle. She won first prize for her accordion playing in the Teachers' Guild Competition, Denver, 1973; five scholarships from the American Business Women's Association and Fine Arts Affiliates and was elected to Pi Kappa Lambda. She has performed in numerous concerts on radio and with many orchestras.

Compositions

CHAMBER
- Fall music (cham ens) (1981)
- Rondo (cham ens) (1978)
- Invention (str qrt) (1977)

ACCORDION
- Divertimento (1983)
- Partita (1982)

ELECTRONIC
- Refractions (synclavier II) (1983)

Ref. composer

NIGHTINGALE, Mae Wheeler

American pianist, violinist, choral arranger, authoress, lecturer and composer. b. Blencoe, IA, December 30, 1898. She studied at the University of California, Los Angeles; the University of Southern California, Fresno State College and Westminster Choir College. She studied the piano under Abby DeAveritt and the violin under Ludvig Kading at Long Beach and voice under Bertha Winslow Vaughn at Los Angeles. She taught privately until 1932, then in schools. She was music training lecturer at the universities of California and Southern California and at Los Angeles State College, 1926 to 1959. She received the Mancini award for distinction in music education from the California Music Teachers' Association and the Kimber Foundation. She was an authority on the adolescent boys' voice and lectured at teachers' colleges.

Compositions

VOCAL

Amer

Folk and fun songs

Heritage songs

Paquita (1937)

The pirate ship (1938)

Sailor song (1938)

Three court jesters (1939)

OPERETTA

Queen of the Sawdust (mix-ch or boys'-vces)

Ride 'em Cowboy (boys'-vces)

ARRANGEMENTS

Numerous choral arrangements incl.:

My child is gone

The nightingale choral series for boys (G. Schirmer, 1938)

Recessional

The troubadour series, 2 vols (Fischer, 1937)

Twelve days of Christmas

Publications

Young singers' choir book.

Ref. 39, 142, 496

NIKISCH, Amelie (nee Heussner)

German poetess, singing teacher and composer. b. Brussels, 1860. She married the conductor Artur Nikisch in 1885.

Compositions

OPERETTA

Daniel in der Loewengrube

Immer der Andere

Meine Tante, deine Tante

Publications

Libretto for *Aebelo*, by Gustav Mraczeck. 1914.

Prinz Adolar und das Tausendschoenchen. 1907.

Ref. 105, 142, 431

NIKOLAYEVA, Tatiana Petrovna

Soviet pianist, professor and composer. b. Bezhitsa, near Bryansk, May 4, 1924. She studied the piano under A. Goldenweiser at the Moscow Conservatory, graduated with honors in 1947 and completed her composition studies under E. Golubev and V. Shebalin in 1950 at the same conservatory. After 1945 she was a soloist with the Moscow Philharmonic Orchestra, performing in the Soviet Union, Europe and the Americas. In 1945 she won the Scriabin piano competition in Moscow: in 1948 the second prize of the first international festival of Democratic Youth in Prague and in 1950 first prize for her playing of Bach's keyboard works at the Bicentennial Bach Festival in Leipzig. In 1953 she visited Iceland as a member of the Soviet delegation and toured Siberia in the same year. Her *First piano concerto* received the Stalin prize in 1951. In 1965 she became a professor of the piano at the Moscow Conservatory. She was on the juries of international competitions in Montreal, Leipzig, Munich, Geneva and Vienna. In 1956 she was awarded the title of Honored Artist of the USSR. In 1971 she was a winner of the International Robert Schumann piano competition. She lectured at the Cologne Conservatory. DISCOGRAPHY.

Compositions

ORCHESTRA

Symphony in F (1955)

Peoma (vlc and orch) (1960)

Piano concerto No. 1 (1950)

Piano concerto No. 2, op. 32 (1976)

Violin concerto (1972)

Waltz-capriccio (vln and orch) (1960)

Fantazia iz Russkoi poezi (1975)

Kartina Borodinskoye pole (1968)

CHAMBER

Piano quintet (1947)

Polyphonic triad (pf and str qrt) (1949)

String quartet (1960)

Trio (fl, vla and pf)

Sonata I (vlc and pf) (1960)

Sonata II (vlc and pf) (1973)

Sonatina (vln and pf) (1953)

PIANO

Children's album: March; Little march: Mazurka; Galop (1959)

Five etudes (1959)

Little variations in the classical style

Polyphonic triad (1949, rev 1966)

Shaldi-Baldi, 12 piece cycle (1974)

Sonata (1949)

Sonata II (1977)

Twenty-four concert etudes (1951-1953)

Variations on a theme of Myaskovsky (1951)

Variations on a theme of Tchaikovsky

VOCAL

Pesn o schastye, cantata (A. Churkin) (soloists, ch and orch) (1949)

Islandia, song cycle (A. Sofronov)

Songs (Pushkin, Lermontov and Baratinsky)

INCIDENTAL MUSIC

Zhenshchina v iskusstva, film (1970)

Music for plays

Ref. composer, 9, 14, 17, 21, 22, 44, 70, 87, 94, 109, 193, 223, 277, 330, 441, 563, 580

NIKOLSKAYA, Lyubov Borisovna

Soviet lecturer, writer and composer. b. Vani, Georgia, May 17, 1909. At the Leningrad Conservatory she studied historical theory and composition under M. Steinberg, graduating with distinction in 1945. She continued with postgraduate studies in historical theory in 1946. From 1944 to 1946 she was Steinberg's assistant, taught solfege and composition and became head of department of theory and composition at the music school of the Conservatory. After 1946 she taught theoretical subjects and composition at the Sverdlovsk Conservatory. She also lectured at the Uralsk Conservatory, becoming a senior lecturer in 1964. She wrote numerous articles on her subjects in Russian musical journals.

Compositions

ORCHESTRA

Concert fantasy (1972)

Concert fantasy on Ukrainian themes (1950)

Concerto for bayan and orchestra (1961)

Concerto for domra and orchestra

Piano concerto No. 1 (1939)

Piano concerto No. 2 (1952)

Dance suite (light orch) (1949)

Suite, Ashik-Kerib (based on Lermontov) (1940)

Two Russian folk melodies (cl and orch of folk insts) (1930)

CHAMBER

Prelude and scherzo (wind qrt) (1949)

Two pieces (wind qrt) (1949)

Variations (wind qrt) (1955)

Fantasy to the memory of P. Bazhov, trio (1951)

Concert fantasy on two Russian themes (domra and pf)

Romantic suite (domra and pf)

Sonata (vlc and pf)

Exprompt (trb) (1950)

Two pieces (ob)

PIANO

Dance suite (2 pf) (1950)

Cycles of preludes I (1938)

Cycles of preludes II (1966)

Sonata (1946)

Sonatina (1957)

Two pieces to commemorate the reunion of the Ukraine with Russia (1953)

Ukrainian suite (1952)

VOCAL

Rodnaya Ukraina, cantata (Ukrainian poets) (1945)

Ukranian folk songs (vce and orch of folk insts) (1951)

My pioneri leintsi (chil-ch)

Po lesnoi tropinke (A. Tkachenko) (chil-ch)

U epokhi yest svoi gornisti (D. Kostiurin) (chil-ch)

Cycle of romances (M. Lermontov) (vce and pf) (1963)

Four duets for children

Four romances (S. Shchipachev) (1949)

Two ballads (E. Khorinska) (vce and pf) (1967)

Two romances (M. Lermontov) (1940)

Uralochka, song (Anchapov) (1953)

Ya devochka boyevaya, song (Klushnikova)

BALLET

Repka, for children (1970)

OPERETTA

Alenkiy tsvetochek, for children (1958)

Devushka-semidelushka, for children (1952)

Olino kolechko (S. Marshak) (1975)

Petukh i Lisa, for children (1954)

Serebryanoye kopitse, for children (1959)

Ugomon, for children (1956)

Zhar-ptitsa, opera-novella (1965)

THEATRE

Eto bylo u morya (1965)

Publications
Almast opera: A. Spendiarova. *Aziatski muzykalnyi zhurnal.*
M.O. Shteinberg. *Zhizn i tvorchestvo.*
Narodyne mastera uzbekskoi muzyki.
Nekotorye osobennosti sovietskoi ukranskoi narodnoi pesni.
Osobennosti polifonii russkikh klassikov.
Polifonicheskie priemy i zhanry v opere N. Rimskogo Korsakova.
Tsarskaya nevesta.
Puti razvitiya uzbekskoi muzyki.
Ref. 21, 87

NIKOLSKAYA, Olga Vasilevna
Soviet lecturer and composer. b. Tbilisi, January 25, 1916. She studied Azerbaijanian music under U. Hadjibekov and composition under L. Rudolf and B. Zaidman at the Baku Conservatory, graduating in 1940. From 1961 till 1971 she lectured at the Byulya Music School in Baku.
Compositions
ORCHESTRA
Piano concerto (1952)
Violin concerto (1956)
Azerbaijanian march (wind orch) (1948)
Children's ballet suite (1949)
Geroyam Azerbaidzhana, march (wind orch)
Heroic poem (1940)
Neftyanikam Azerbaidzhana, march (wind orch) (1950)
CHAMBER
String quartets (1940, 1954)
Sonata (vln and pf) (1975)
PIANO
Ballad on motives of Nizami, Khosrov i Shirin (1947)
Fugue (1948)
Poema (1972)
Sonatina (1948)
Three preludes (1952)
Vospominanie (1973)
VOCAL
Patrioticheskaya, cantata (G. Boryan) (1941)
Veliki pevets naroda, poem song to the memory of U. Hadjibekov (P. Panchenko) (B and orch) (1950)
Hymn of the Fatherland (ch) (1972)
Pesnya bratstva (P. Panchenko) (ch a-cap) (1948)
Rodina-mat (P. Panchenko) (ch and pf) (1947)
Slava Sovietskoi otchizne, cycle (Soviet poets) (vce and pf)
Dvadtsat pyat voyennykh pesen, cycle (Soviet poets) (vce and pf) (1972)
Collection of songs from the Caspian Sea (A. Kurochkina, P. Sako, S. Smernogo-Smelova) (vce and pf) (1973)
Four years of war (P. Saiko) (vce and pf) (1975)
Choruses (P. Panchenko, P. Saiko) (1969)
Romances and songs (Fizuli, Vagifa, Nekrasov, Shchipachev, Ragim, Konstantnova, Kaputikian, Pushkin, Lermontov and Nizami) (vce and pf)
Ref. 21, 87

NIKOLSKY, Mlle.
19th-century Russian composer of songs.
Ref. 465

NILLSON, Christine or Kristina. See NILSSON, Christine

NILSSON (Nillson), Christine (Kristina)
Swedish operatic singer and composer. b. Sjoabol, near Vexio, August 20, 1843; d. Stockholm, November 22, 1921. She studied singing in Stockholm under Frans Berwald and in Paris under Pierre F. Wartel, Masset and Delle Sedie. In October 1864 she made her debut at the Theatre-Lyrique, Paris as Violetta in the French version of the opera *La Traviata*. A highlight in her career was her performance as Ophelia in *Hamlet* by Ambroise Thomas, at the Paris Opera in March 1868. She toured in opera and concerts in France, Russia, Spain, Austria, the United States and Sweden.
Compositions
VOCAL
Five airs suedois: Le bal, le cortège des fiances, jeunesse, les roses, le violom enchanté (vce and pf) (Heugel)
Bibliography
Cammer. *The Great Opera Stars in Historic Photographs*. New York: Dover, 1978.
Ref. 105, 297, 323, 421, 423

NISHIKI, Kayoko
Japanese lecturer and composer. b. Mie, December 5, 1949. In 1973 she graduated from the Aichi Prefectural University of Arts and in 1976 from the Graduate school of that University. She studied composition under Professor Kan Ishii. She is currently lecturing at two women's colleges. She obtained the composition prize from the music competition of Japan in 1971 and 1974 and from the Ministry of Culture's music competition in 1979.
Compositions
ORCHESTA
El amara, symphony (1981)
This world is the festivity of gods, symphony (1974) (prize)
Two dreams, symphony (1974) (prize)
CHAMBER
String sextet (1971) (prize)
Ref. composer

NISHIMURA, Yukie
Japanese pianist and composer. b. 1968. She completed the Yamaha advanced music education course. She has performed with orchestras and in overseas concerts, including an appearance with the Washington National Symphony Orchestra in 1983. DISCOGRAPHY.
Composition
ORCHESTRA
Piano concerto No. 3, in D-Major
Ref. Yamaha Music Foundation

NISHUDA, Yamiko
20th-century Japanese composer. She won first prize in the wind section of the Mannheim International Composition Competition for Women Composers, 1985.
Compositions
CHAMBER
Woodwind pieces
VOCAL
Die Geburt des Goldscheines im Tempel (S and pf)
Ref. Frau und Musik

NISS, Sofia Natanovna
Soviet composer. b. Donetsk, July 8, 1916. She studied composition in Moscow under G.I. Litinsky and V.A. Belogo.
Compositions
CHAMBER
String quartet (1959)
Caravan (vln and pf) (1968)
Gavotte (vln and pf) (1970)
Humoresque (vln and pf) (1968)
Little capriccio (vln and pf) (1976)
Mazurka (vln and pf) (1970)
Melodia (vln and pf) (1963)
Piece (cl and pf) (1959)
Romance (vln and pf) (1976)
Tarantella (vln and pf) (1963)
Theme and variations (vln and pf) (1967)
Three pieces (vln and pf) (1971)
Light music
PIANO
Children's suite (1953)
Classical variations on Russian themes (1966)
Eleven variations (1954)
Five preludes (1952)
Russian suite (1952)
Scherzino (1963)
Sonata (1955)
Suite (1952)
Twelve pieces (1971)
VOCAL
Ballada o medali Ilicha (A. Vorobiev) (solo and ch) (1971)
Choruses (I. Veksegonova, S. Orlov, K. Kostrov and others)
Cycles (N. Gilyen, M. Rulsky) (vce and pf) (1961, 1964)
Five miniatures (V. Korkin) (vce and pf) (1968)
Russian aquarelles (A. Prokofiev) (vce and pf) (1968)
Time (R. Ganzatova) (vce and pf) (1970)
Songs
Ref. 21

NIVELLI SCHWARTZ, Gina
20th-century German librettist, script writer and composer. b. February 14. She studied at the Berlin Conservatory and then lived in England.

Compositions
MISCELLANEOUS
Berlin-concerto
Gipsy tango
L'Heure bleu
Light music
Ref. 70

NIXON, June

Australian organist, pianist, choral conductor, lecturer and composer. b. Boort, Victoria, May 20, 1942. She graduated from the Melbourne Conservatorium with a piano diploma in 1963 and a B.Mus. (organ) in 1965. She became a F.R.C.O. in 1967. In 1968 she won the Australian national organ playing competition and in 1970 the first A.E.H. Nickson scholarship and the Lizette Bentwich scholarship for a year's organ study and concert play in England. She was the first woman to win the John Brooke memorial prize for choral conducting by the Royal College of Organists. She attended Bernard Keefe's master classes in choral conducting and Charles Proctor's conducting technique classes. June lectures at the Melbourne University Conservatorium and is an examiner for the piano and the organ for the Australian music examinations board. She gives organ recitals and is organist and choral conductor of St. Paul's Cathedral, Melbourne. PHOTOGRAPH.

Compositions
SACRED
St. Paul's service (mix-ch and org) (1980)
Thomas, service (mix-ch and org) (1982)
Pieces and responses (boys' vces) (1982)
ARRANGEMENTS
Were you there? Negro spiritual (1981)
Ref. composer

NOBLE, Ann (Virginia)

American flautist and composer. b. Oakland, CA, September 24, 1955. She received her B.Mus. (flute and composition) from the University of Redlands, studying under Barney Childs and her M.A. (composition) from Mills College, studying under Terry Riley and Robert Ashley. She won a composition award from Sigma Alpha Iota, 1979. She is a member of the Improvisers' Orchestra.

Compositions
ORCHESTRA
It's nicer down here or Call on God but row away from the rocks (1976)
A paler shade of soft (1976)
CHAMBER
Dreaming of being taken out and allowed to shine (fl, ob, cl, bsn, hn and sax) (1977)
My last true love (double-reed qrt) (1979)
And I saw her in the water, with shining (trp, c-bsn and pf) (1977)
Percussion trio No. 2 (mar, snare dr and tim) (1975)
This is the celebration of the changing of the light (hn, vln and pf) (1979)
When on the east the sheer bright star arose (fl, b-cl and hp) (1977)
Duo (fl and a-sax) (1975)
In the vagueness of a haze someone breaking glass in a tin box (cl and hpcd) (1977)
One of my other pieces (vln and vlc) (1978)
Percussion trio No. 1 (timp and perc)
In a harsh light, gasping whisper (pf)
This is the passing of your soul upon my lips (vln) (1977)
VOCAL
A child saint (Bar and pf) (1976)
Saved in prisms of honey (S, cl and pf) (1976)
Three art songs for Lysbet and friend (S and pf) (1976)
OPERA
Juniper Tree, chamber opera (1977)
ELECTRONIC
An innocent 3 words (tape) (1976)
The raindrops on the windowpane sparkled (tape) (1979)
There are clouds on the horizon (tape) (1976)
Ref. composer, 228, 625

NOBLE, Virginia. See NOBLE, Ann

NOBLITT, Katheryn Marie McCall

American pianist, authoress, lyricist, teacher and composer. She gained her B.Mus. summa cum laude, in 1930, from Greensboro College. She taught the piano in North Carolina from 1930 to 1948 and then in Roanoke, VA. She wrote her own lyrics. PHOTOGRAPH.

Compositions
CHAMBER
Pieces (ens)
The gypsy in me (pf trio) (1943)
PIANO
The alarm clock (2 pf) (1945)
Parade passing by (2 pf) (1961)
Red pepper (2 pf; also pf and vce) (1948, 1976)
Twinkles from a star (2 pf) (1946)
Bells of Peache, duet (1960)
The frog quartet (Montgomery Music, 1976)
The heart of the piano (1962)
March of the American (Bellwin-Mils, 1961)
The old bell-ringer (Pro-Art, 1975)
Twinkling keys (Belwin-Mills, 1961)
Waltz mood (Willis Music Co., 1957)
Windshield wiper rock (Schaum, 1974)
VOCAL
The banjos memories, suite (narr, vces and acc) (1961)
Day at Greensboro College in song, suite (narr, vces and acc) (1963)
Day in an Indian village, suite (1960)
What I saw from the see-saw (1968)
Wonderful woodland walk, suite (1960)
Numerous songs
SACRED
Praise to our wonderful God, anthem (ch)
Lullaby of peace (1934)
Sacred vocal suite: A springtime prayer (Easter) (1959); Thy best name (thanksgiving) (1930); He came and will come again (christmas) (1936); Wait (and then your heart will understand) (1944)
Ref. composer, 39, 347

NOETHLING, Elisabeth

German singer, teacher and composer. b. Berlin, March 19, 1881. She studied at the Music Academy in Berlin, singing privately under Mathilde Mallinger and composition under Wilhelm Klatte. She taught singing in Berlin.

Compositions
CHAMBER
String quartet
Trio
Duet
VOCAL
Choruses
Duets
Natur Lieder (1927)
SACRED
Weihnachtslieder (1927)
Ref. 70, 111, 226

NOGERO, Francisco di. See BAUER, Emilie Frances

NOHE, Beverly

American organist, choral conductor, teacher and composer. b. East Rochester, NY, September 24, 1935. She received a B.A. from the Eastman School of Music, 1959. She was choir conductor and organist in East Rochester from 1967 to 1973 and after 1967 taught at Rochester School for the hard of hearing.

Compositions
CHAMBER
Playground (fl, vln and vlc)
Poeme capricieuse (cl and pf)
SACRED
Choral works
Ref. 142

NORBURY, Ethel F. (nee Fall)

Canadian pianist, lecturer and composer. b. Liverpool, England, April 20, 1872. She studied history of music and theory under H. Wild in Canada. She taught the piano and theory at Alberta College, Edmonton.

Compositions
VOCAL
Choral pieces
Songs incl.:
Annabel Lee, tone poem (after 1920)
Lullaby (before 1920) (Liverpool: Exchange Press)
The south wind and the sun, tone poem (after 1920)
Will you come back home (before 1920) (Ryalls & Jones)
Duets

OPERETTA
A Dream Fantasy (vces and pf)
Lalapaloo (vces and pf)
Quenilda (vces and pf)
The Vendor of Amulets (vces and pf)
Ref. 133

NORDBLAD, Svea Gota. See WELANDER, Svea Gota

NORDENFELT, Dagmar
Swedish concert pianist, teacher and composer. b. Bofors, January 31, 1908. She studied the piano under Gottfrid Boon, Henrik Knudsen and Hilda Sehested (q.v.) in Copenhagen; under P. Weingartner and P.A. Pisk in Vienna and O. Wibergh, G. Boom and H. Rosenberg in Stockholm, where she made her concert debut. she toured Scandinavia and performed on Swedish, French and Finnish radio, as an orchestral soloist and member of a chamber ensemble. After a break due to arthritis she returned to concert performance in 1975. She composed sonatas, piano pieces and songs.
Ref. 96

NORDENSON, Ruth
Early 20th-century Swedish composer.
Composition
CHAMBER
Elvan, polka (vln or pf) (1910)
Ref. 642

NORDENSTROM, Gladys Mercedes
American composer. b. Pokegama Township, MN, May 23, 1924. She studied music and philosophy at the Hamline University, St. Paul and the University of Minnesota. She married the composer Ernst Krenek and lived in Palm Springs after 1966. DISCOGRAPHY. PHOTOGRAPH.
Compositions
ORCHESTRA
Piano concerto (1947)
El Greco fantasy (str orch) (1965) (comm Gesellschaft fuer neue Musik, Mannheim)
Elegy for Robert F. Kennedy (Barenreiter-Verlag)
Work for orchestra, No. 3 (1975) (Barenreiter-Verlag)
CHAMBER
Palm springs sextet (wind insts) (1969) (Wiesbaden: Otto Harrassowitz)
Wind quintet (1977) (Otto Harrassowitz)
Rondo (fl and pf) (1948) (Darmstadt: Musikinstitut, 1956)
Organ works
PIANO
Sonata (1946)
Variations (1945)
VOCAL
Antitheses (ch and orch) (1946)
This life (R.M. Rilke) (1950)
Zeit, XXIV, song (Renata Pandula) (1975)
Choral works
ELECTRONIC
Blocks and beans (tape)
Signals from nowhere (org and elec tape) (1973)
Ref. composer, 94, 142, 347, 563, 622

NORDRAAK-FEYLING, Gudrun
Norwegian pianist, lyricist, singer and composer. b. Oslo, 1896. She studied the piano, harmony and composition and later singing in Oslo, Paris, Dresden and London. She made her debut as a singer in Olso in 1920 and then traveled extensively in Europe, always including her own compositions in her program. Gudrun composed a piano piece, choral works, two song cycles, eight songs for soprano, six songs for baritone and songs for which she wrote the lyrics, in Norwegian, German, English, French and Italian.
Ref. NMI

NORLING, Signe
Early 20th-century Swedish composer.
Compositions
PIANO
Aftonbris (1910)
Boston royal (1910)
Rouge et noire (1910)
Till bruden (1910)
Ref. 642

NORMAN, Ruth
American pianist and composer. b. Chicago, 1927. She studied at Nebraska University and the Eastman School of Music. DISCOGRAPHY.
Compositions
CHAMBER
Pieces (small ens)
Four piano pieces: incl. molto allegro (1970), prelude IV (1974)
OPERA
The gypsies' reward (1958) (Mills Music)
VOCAL
Choral ensembles
Ref. 141, 563, 622

NORMANN, von. See DRIEBURG, Louise von

NORRE, Dorcas (Dorkas)
Swedish concert pianist, teacher and composer. b. Malmberget, March 31, 1911. Her family moved to Stockholm in 1932, when she began her piano study at the Royal Academy of Music, graduating in 1937 with the Academy's medal. Thereafter she studied the piano under Olov Wiberg and Algot Haquinius, composition under M. Melchers and instrumentation under Ivar Hellman. In 1969 she studied at the Accademia Chigiana in Siena, Italy and in 1970 attended a course in electronic music in Stockholm. After her debut in 1937, she appeared as a pianist in concerts and on Swedish radio, performing solos and duos and including her own compositions. PHOTOGRAPH.
Compositions
ORCHESTRA
Piano concerto (1946)
CHAMBER
Espressioni (vln or vla and pf) (1981)
Sonata (vlc and pf) (1980)
Sonatina (vln and pf) (1960)
Pastoraler (cl) (1955)
Sonat commozioni (vlc) (1977)
PIANO
Concerto (2 pf) (1981)
Aries (1975)
Ballad/ballata (1983)
I variationsstil (1968)
Improvisation (1979)
Profiler (1947) (Nordiska Musikforlaget)
Preludium (1973)
Salonsstycke (1979)
Sonata (1985)
Theme and chromatic variations (1948)
Visioner (1951)
Teaching pieces (4 hands)
VOCAL
Oenskeparken (composer) (vce and pf) (1978)
Som ett spaar (composer) (vce and pf) (1979)
Tre saanger (composer) (vce and pf) (1976)
ELECTRONIC
Ainel (1970)
Sirkas (1970)
Ultevis duoddar (1970)
TEACHING PIECES
Andantino och alla marcia (Ehrlings Musik AB)
Sju smaa kulisser
Ref. composer, 77

NORRIS, Mary
19th-century composer.
Compositions
CHAMBER
Largo, op. 13 (vln, pf and org) (Oertel)
Lobgesang, op. 12 (vln, org and har) (Oertel)
Adagio religioso, op. 16 (har and vln)
Elegie (vln and pf) (Oertel)
In memoriam, op. 18 (har and vln)
Sarabande, op. 17 (har and vln)
Scherzo (vln and pf) (Oertel)
Der Brummer in der Klemme, scherzo for G string, op. 10 (vln) (Oertel)
PIANO
Traumerei am Spinnrad (Oertel)
Vogelgezwitscher (Nagel)
Walzer-Fantasie (Oertel)

VOCAL
Adagio, op. 14 (solo, ch, vln and har)
Air, op. 15 (solo, ch, vln and har)
Andacht; Die Hoffnung; Wiedersehen, op. 19
Dre Lieder, op. 23: Kommen und Scheiden; Letzer Wunsch, Straendchen (Schrieder)
Lied bei der Trauung, op. 21 (vce and vlc)
Meeresabend (Nagel)
SACRED
Psalm 102, op. 20 (vlc)
Ref. 297

NORTHEY, Carrie. See ROMA, Caro

NORTON, Caroline Elizabeth Sarah (nee Sheridan)

English musician, novelist, poetess, singer and composer. b. Huddersfield, 1808; d. London, June 15, 1877. She was the daughter of Thomas Sheridan. She wrote some of her lyrics.

Compositions
VOCAL
Songs incl.:
Blind girl's lament
Duet
Juanita
Love of Helen Douglas
Mother's Lament
Murmur of the shells
Set of seven songs
Set of ten songs (co-composer) (1833)
Song of affection
Voice of music
Ref. 6, 85, 276, 347

NORTON, The Hon. Mrs. (Lady W. Stirling Maxwell)

English composer. b. 1809; d. 1877.

Compositions
VOCAL
Songs incl.:
Fanny Grey (composer)
A set of songs, incl. By-gone hours! (Mrs. Price Blackwod) (ded Duke of Devonshire)
Ref. 369

NORUP, Helle Merete

Danish violinist and composer. b. Hellerup, Copenhagen, June 4, 1947. The daughter of a pianist and a cellist, she studied the violin under Henry Holst at the Royal Danish Conservatory. She also studied music education, history and theory. In 1976 she studied under Kagel and Ligeti in Darmstadt. She won a state bursary in 1979.

Compositions
CHAMBER
Exercises for string quartet (1975)
Den hvide fugl (vln and perc)
VOCAL
Rum 27 (2 vces, fl, str qrt and perc)
At Noerreport (1972)
Feminist songs (1974-1975)
Kvinder paa fabrik
Lesson one (1975)
Handlinger
On a textile factory (1972)
That is excellent (1972)
The revolution that failed (1972)
Ref. composer

NOTHLING, Elisabeth. See NOETHLING, Elisabeth

NOTMAN, Margaret. See McALLISTER, Rita

NOVA SONDAG, Jacqueline

Columbian composer. b. Ghent, Belgium, January 6, 1936. She studied at the Faculdad de Artes de la Universidad Nacional de Colombia under Gonzalez-Zuleta and L.A. Escobar. In 1967 she won a scholarship for a year's advanced composition study at the Instituto Torcuato Di Tella under A. Ginastera, L. Nono, F. Kroepfl, V. Ussachevsky, R. Haubenstock-Ramati, F. von Reichenback and G. Gandini. She took part in many international music festivals and organized courses on electronic music on radio in 1969 and conference-concerts in 1970 and worked under the direction of F. Koepfl at the Laboratorio de Acustica Estudio de Fonologia Musical. She formed the Agrupacion Nueva Musica in Bogota and organized its first concert in 1971. She received many prizes and awards, including first prize in chamber music at the 3rd Festival of Music, Caracas, Venezuela, 1966; first prize at the 5th National Theatre Festival, 1969 and the National composition prize, 1971.

Compositions
ORCHESTRA
Segmentos (ob and orch) (1979)
Ensayos (str orch) (1968)
Metamorfosis III (sym orch) (1966)
Moviles, 12 (pf and str orch) (1967) (international composition prize) (Southern Music, 1967)
CHAMBER
String quartet (1974)
Suite de danzas medievales (fl, vla and perc) (1965)
Asimetrias (fl and perc) (1967)
Mesure (vlc and pf) (1965)
Scherzo en estilo primitivo (vlc and pf) (1965)
Signos (vln) (1965)
PIANO
Fantasia (1965)
Perforaciones, various versions (1974)
Sequencias (1965)
Transiciones
VOCAL
Uerjayas (Invocacion a los Dioses) (S, vces and orch) (Peleo-Tegria) (Tunebo) (1968)
Y el movimiento se detine en el aire... (composer) (4 vocal groups) (1965)
L'adieu (G. Apollinaire) (S and pf) (1965)
L'amour est mort (G. Apollinaire) (S and pf) (1965)
A veces un mo niega (S and pf) (1965)
Cuento tempo fuiste dos (P. Salinas) (vce and pf) (1966)
Les mefaits de la lune (P. Verlaine) (vce and pf) (1965)
Cantos medioevales (1965)
SACRED
Salmo (vces) (1972)
THEATRE
Music for plays incl.:
Julius Caesar (vces and elec insts) (1st national prize, 1969)
Macbeth (cham) (1968)
ELECTRONIC
Ballet (tape and vce) (1972)
Cantos de la creacion del mundo (vce processed electronically) (Tunebo) (1972)
H-K-70 (pf, d-b, perc and taped vces) (1972)
Hiroshima (vces, elec sounds and orch) (1974)
Homaggio a Catullo (vce, perc and elec sounds) (1972)
L.M.A. 11 (vces, strs, perc and elec sounds) (1969)
Musica para las esculturas de F. Bursztyn (tape) (1974)
Oposicion-fusion (elec sounds) (1968)
Pitecanthropus (vces, elec sounds and orch) (national composition prize, 1971)
Proyecciones (projector and orch) (1968)
Resonancias I (pf and elec sounds) (1969)
Signo de interrogacion, electronic experience (1969)
Sinkronizacion (vce, pf, har, perc and elec sounds) (1972)
Sintesis (vces, strs, mime and elec sounds) (1969)
W Z K, radio experience (1969)
14-35 (vces transformed at the laboratory and orch)
FILM MUSIC
Camilo (tape) (1974)
Ref. composer, 17, 45, 70, 94

NOVELLI, Mimi

20th-century Italian composer.

Composition
OPERA
Il coscritto (Casserta) (1900)
Ref. 431

NOVELLO, Mary Sabilla

19th-century English writer on music and composer of songs. She was the daughter of Vincent Novello.

Publications
School of the Voice.
Voice and the Vocal Art.
Ref. 226, 433

NOVELLO-DAVIES, Clara

Welsh pianist, authoress, choral conductor, singer, teacher and composer. b. Cardiff, April 7, 1861; d. London, March 1, 1943. Her father, Jacob-Davies, called her Clara Novello after the celebrated singer of that name and she adopted the combined name professionally. In 1881 she organized a Royal Welsh Ladies' Choir, with which she toured Great Britain, France, the United States and South Africa. The choir was awarded first prize at the World's Fair in Chicago in 1893 and at the Paris Exposition, 1900. She also toured with Adelina Patti (q.v.). She was commended by Queen Victoria in 1894 and King George and Queen Mary, 1928. Her son, Ivor Novello wrote the popular World War I song *Keep the home fires burning* at her request.

Compositions

VOCAL

Songs incl.:
Comfort
The virgil
A voice from the Spirit Land

Publications

The Life I have Loved. Autobiography. London, 1940.
You Can Sing.

Ref. 6, 22, 85, 347

NOVI, Anna Beate (nee Petersen)

Danish concert pianist, violinist and composer. b. Frederiksberg, Copenhagen, March 4, 1883. From the age of three she was a pupil of the court pianist Johanne Stockmarr. At the Royal Danish Conservatory, she studied the piano under Albert Orth, theory under Otto Malling and the violin under Georg Hoeeberg. In Berlin she studied under Martin Krause and after her return to Copenhagen pursued higher studies under Franz Neruda, Alexander Stoffrege and Peder Gram. She made her debut as a concert pianist in Copenhagen in 1907 and thereafter gave many concerts in Copenhagen, the provinces and on the radio.

Compositions

CHAMBER

Elegi (con dolore) (vln and strs)
Six small pieces, op. 5 (2 or more vln)
Elegi in A-Minor (vln and pf)
Serenade (vlc and pf)
Suite (vlc and pf)

PIANO

Canons and other pieces (4 hands) (1937)
Menuet in F
Praeludium
Small pieces for beginners, ops. 7 and 8
Other pieces

VOCAL

Aah! Her ligger jeg (ch)
Angelus (m-ch)
Blomstervise: Danmarks sommer gik sin gang (ch)
Havet (m-ch a-cap)
Stille er det, naar det skumrer (ch)
Four small canons (2 vces and pf)
Liljekonvaller, op. 9 (vce and pf)
Lille kantate
Livets kilde, To sange med texter af Hans Egede Glahn fra Digtsamlingen
Olav Trygvason (recitor and hp)
Three trios (m-S or Bar)
Ve sengeti (vce and pf)
Numerous other songs for mezzo or other voices and piano

SACRED

Songs incl.:
Altid frejdig
Gud skal alting mage
Jesus naadig sig forbarme
Paa Guds Jerusalem det ny
Sta fast, sta fast min sjael

Ref. composer, 331

NOVOSELOVA, Ludmila Alexeyevna

Soviet lecturer, musicologist and composer. b. Yoshkar-Ola, April 30, 1942. She graduated from the Kazan Conservatory in 1973, having studied musicology under Y. V. Vinogradov and composition under A.B. Lupov. From 1961 to 1962 and again from 1970 to 1974 she taught at a music school in Yoshkar-Ola and from 1967 to 1970 lectured at a music institute in the same city. After 1975 she lectured at a teachers' college in Cheboksary.

Compositions

ORCHESTRA

Piano concerto (1973, rev 1975)
Violin concerto (1971)
Simfonietta (1972)

CHAMBER

Pieces (vlc and pf) (1975)

PIANO

Prelude (1968)
Prelude and fughetta on Mari themes (1969)
Sonata (1976)
Toccata (1968)

VOCAL

Poema, glavnaya ulitsa (D. Bedny) (ch) (1970)
Choruses (Y. Akim, R. Gamzatov, M. Getuyev, I. Dvorkin, A. Kattaya, E. Moshkovska, O. Koshevi, G. Gorbovsky, K. Kuliev, L. Oshanin, V. Turkin)
Romances (A. Pushkin, K. Ryleyev, F. Tiutchev, S. Kaputikian, I. Zemnukhov) (vce and pf)
Arrangements of folk songs

Ref. 21

NOWAK, Alison

American composer. b. Syracuse NY, April 7, 1948. She studied under Vivian Fine (q.v.), Lou Calabro and Henry Brant at Bennington College, receiving a B.A. in 1970. She studied under Mario Davidsky, Jack Beeson and Charles Wuorinen at Columbia University, receiving an M.A. in 1972, when she won the Rappaport prize at Columbia University for her *String trio*.

Compositions

ORCHESTRA

Quid pro quo (1972)

CHAMBER

Musica composita (fl, cl, bsn, trp, perc, vln, vlc and pf)
Equinox (cl, bsn, hn, vln, vla and d-b)
Quintet for flute, violin, bassoon, guitar and piano (1973)
Quartet for flute, violin, clarinet and cello (1974)
Four pieces for three clarinets (1970)
Musica composita II (perc incl. mar and vib)
String trio (1970)
Trio for woodwinds (fl, cl and bsn) (1973)
Variations (vln and pf) (1975) (ACA)
Cyclorama (vlc) (1977)
Shifting sands (fl) (1977)
Wedding (org) (1975)

PIANO

Five bagatelles (1973)
Klavierstueck (1973)
Piece, in 3 mvts (1970)
Three short movements (1971)
Toccata (1974)

OPERA

Diversion and division, chamber opera, in one act (1973)

ELECTRONIC

Piece (vln and computer) (1973)

Ref. 142, 190, 228

NOYES, Edith Rowena (Noyes-Green) (Mrs. Porter)

American concert pianist, teacher and composer of Hungarian and English ancestry. b. Cambridge, MA, March 26, 1875. Her mother, Jeannette Noyes, was a prominent alto. Edith started playing the piano at the age of six and at ten played the march for her mother's second wedding. Edith studied the piano under Edward Macdowell in Boston from 1891 to 1896 and theory under George Chadwick, 1890 to 1895. She made her debut as a concert pianist at the age of 18 and from 1899 to 1919 gave concerts of American music throughout Europe.

Compositions

ORCHESTRA

Pieces

CHAMBER

Piano trio in D, op. 73
Violin sonata in F-Sharp Minor, op. 70
Piano pieces

VOCAL

The hunter's call
Thou hast wounded the spirit that loved thee

SACRED

Easter morn (soloists and ch)
Hymn of peace (soloists and ch)
Funeral march

OPERA

Osseok, romantic grand opera (1917)
Waushakum, pageant opera (1917)

OPERETTA

Last summer (1898)

Ref 40, 70, 85, 89, 105, 141, 260, 276, 292, 304, 347, 352, 353, 433

NOYES-GREENE, Edith Rowena. See NOYES, Edith Rowena

NOZAWA, Kazuyo

20th-century Japanese composer. In 1975 she shared the prize for choral music in the Gedok competition in Mannheim, Germany, with Miriam Marbe (q.v.).
Ref. Radio Bremen

NUGENT, Maude Jerome

American actress, authoress and composer. b. Brooklyn, January 12, 1877; d. New York, June 3, 1958. She made her professional vaudeville debut at the age of 13 in Brooklyn. She composed her most famous song *Sweet Rosie O'Grady* at the age of 19. She appeared in various Broadway productions. She married William Jerome.
Compositions
VOCAL
Songs incl.:
The donkey trot
Down among the roses
Down at Rosie Reilly's flat
I can't forget you, honey
Love and you
Mamie Reilly
Mary from Tipperary
My lady Peggy waltz
My pretty little china maid
Somebody wants you
Sweet Rosie O'Grady
There's no other girl like my girl
Ref. 39, 228, 347, 433, 653

NUGENT, Trish

20th-century American composer.
Composition
FILM MUSIC
Word is out (1978)
Ref. 497

NUNES SODRE, Joanidia. See SODRE, Joanidia

NUNLIST, Juli

American poetess, teacher and composer. b. Montclair, NJ, December 6, 1916. She gained her B.A. (English) in 1940 from Barnard College. At the Manhattan School of Music she studied under Vittorio Giannini, Nicolas Flagello and Ludmila Ulehla (q.v.) and obtained her B.M. (composition) in 1961 and M.M. (composition) in 1964. In 1956 she was a composition major at the Manhattan School of Music. She was a member of the faculty of Akron University from 1970 to 1973 and music director of the National Regional Ballet Association. She was a faculty member at Connecticut College, American Dance Festival in 1971 and chairlady of the fine arts department, Hathaway Brown School, Shaker Heights, 1972 to 1977. DISCOGRAPHY.
Compositions
ORCHESTRA
Platero and I, symphonic suite (Juan Ramon Jiminez's poems)
CHAMBER
String quartet (1954)
Sonata (vla and pf)
Suite (fl and pf) (comm Fortnightly Music Club, Cleveland) (1978)
PIANO
Pieces incl.:
Lento and presto (1961) (1st prize, Olivet College contest, 1962)
Piece in serial style
VOCAL
Cantata (soloists, ch and sym orch)
Die Stimmen, song cycle (Rilke) (Bar and orch)
Cycle (school ch and mix-ch)
Spells (ch)
English, French and German songs
Prières dans l'arche (Carmen Bernos de Gasztold poems)
Rilke Lieder: Du gehst mit; Schlaflied; Pfauenfeder; Liebeslied; Lied vom Meer; Mir war so weh; Loesch mir die Augen aus
Sieben Gedichte (Rilke) (1982)
Trois chansons (1974)
Zwei Nachtstuecke: Mondsuechtig; Gnomenreigen (S and pf) (prize)
BALLET
Eight children's ballets
OPERA
The Pardoner's Tale, in one act (Chaucer)
Publications
Poems in *Beloit Poetry Journal*, *New York Times* and *New York Tribune*.
Twofer. Binghampton, NY: Robertson Center of the Arts and Sciences. Selection of poems.
Ref. composer, 142, 563

NUNN, Elizabeth Annie

English composer. b. 1861; d. Manchester, January 7, 1894.
Compositions
VOCAL
Songs
SACRED
Mass in C, op. 4 (soloists, ch and orch)
Ref. 6, 226, 276

NURPEISSOVA, Dina

Soviet dombrist and composer. b. Beketai-Kum, Kazakh, 1861; d. Alma-Ata, January 31, 1955. She was taught the dombra (national instrument of Kazakhstan, a type of lute) by her father and received a prize for her performance of her compositions on the dombra in Moscow in 1936, playing solo and with the mixed National Kazakh Kolkoz Choir. In 1944 she was made a National Artist of the Kazakh SSR. Before the October Revolution, women were not permitted to sing among men and dancing was prohibited to both sexes. Painting of everyday life was forbidden by the religious laws of Islam and so all national art was preserved in the memory of professional musicians, who traditionally sang sitting cross-legged on a rug, improvising their accompaniment on the dombra.
Compositions
VOCAL
Songs with domra incl.:
Baizhuma
Doyarka
Gerouam truda
Karakaska-at
Kerbez
Kogentup
Kyui o partii
Nakaz materi
Otkrytie torzhestva
Pobeda
Prekrasnaya konyr
Shestnyadsaty god
Solovei
Vosmoye marta
Zhiger
Ref. 21, 61, 330, 453

NYMAN, Amy Utting

20th-century American composer of chamber pieces.
Ref. 347

NYQUIST, Morine A.

20th-century American composer of band pieces and choral works.
Ref. 40, 347

NYSTEL, Louise Gunderson

20th-century American composer of Texas. She holds an M.M..
Composition
SACRED
Missa brevis (1970)
Ref. 147

NYSTROEM, Elisabeth

Late 19th-century Swedish composer.
Compositions
VOCAL
Ballad for Anna Nordstedt (vce and pf) (E & S, 1890)
Ref. 642

NYSTROM, Elisabeth. See NYSTROEM, Elisabeth

OBAYASHI, Nobichiko
20th-century Japanese composer.
Composition
FILM MUSIC
Death at an old mansion (1976)
Ref. 497

OBEIDET. See UBAIDA

OBENCHAIN, Virginia (Mrs. Daunch)
American authoress, teacher and composer. b. Ohio, April 26, 1919. She studied at St. Louis Institute of Music and privately. She was president of the Ohio Music Teachers' Association.
Compositions
ORGAN
Originals
Solos (Pro Art)
VOCAL
Songs incl.:
Peppermint candy
OPERETTA
Uncle Billy's candy shop
TEACHING PIECES
Piano pieces (Pro Art)
Ref. 39, 40, 347

O'BRIEN, Drena
American teacher and composer. b. Chicago, September, 1892; d. October 6, 1981. She obtained an M.A. from Chicago Conservatory. She composed piano and organ pieces, songs and teaching works.
Ref. composer, 40, 347

O'BRIEN, Katharine E.
American lecturer, pianist, mathematician, poetess, writer and composer. b. Amesbury, MA, April 10, 1910. She studied at Bates College (B.A.), Cornwall University (M.A.) and Brown University (Ph.D., maths). She studied the piano under Gertrude Buxton, advanced harmony and homophonic forms under Sigismond Stojowski and elementary harmony under Joy Sleeper. She taught mathematics for 31 years at Deering High School and lectured for 12 years at the University of Maine, Portland and for five years of summer sessions at Brown University. She received honorary degrees of Sc.D.Ed. from the University of Maine and L.H.D. from Baudoin College.
Compositions
VOCAL
When I set out for Lyonnesse (w-ch) (1947) (Hall & McCreary)
SACRED
Star of Bethlehem (w-ch a-cap)
ARRANGEMENTS
Adagio (Mozart) (str qrt)
Ase's death (Grieg) (ch)
Ave Maria (Bach) (ch)
Cum sancto Spiritu (Mozart) (ch)
Fairytale (Tchaikovsky) (ch)
Gigue (Mozart) (str qrt)
Morris-dance (Grainger) (ch)
Musical snuff-box (Liadow) (ch)
Wanderer's night-song (Beethoven) (ch)
Publications
Excavation and other verse. Anthoensen Press.
Sequences. Mathematics. 1966. Houghton Mifflin Co.
Articles on mathematics in magazines.
Poems in periodicals.
Ref. composer, 142, 374

OBROVSKA, Jana
Czech pianist, editor and composer. b. Prague, September 13, 1930. Her father was Jakub Obrovsky, a pianter and sculptor and her mother a painter. Jana married the concert guitar virtuoso M. Zelenka. She studied the piano under B. Kabelacova-Rixova and theory under J. Ridky. At the Prague Conservatory from 1949 to 1955 she studied composition under Miroslav Krejci and Emil Hlobil. Her graduation work *Piano concerto No. 1* was acclaimed in the German Democratic Republic in 1957. She is an editor for the Supraphon publishing house. DISCOGRAPHY. PHOTOGRAPH.
Compositions
ORCHESTRA
Concerto (2 gtr and orch) (1977)
Concerto de tasca (pf and orch) (1973)
Concerto facile (vla, hpcd and orch) (1966)
Concerto meditativo (gtr and orch) (1971)
Piano concerto No. 1 (1955)
Piano concerto No. 2 (1960)
Concerto (vln, vla, d-b and str orch) (1980)
CHAMBER
Sextet (wind insts) (1955)
Wind quintet (1968)
String quartet (1976)
Bisbiglii e gridi (b-cl, gtr and pf) (1973)
Musica per tre (vln, gtr and acdn) (1970)
Trio (fl, ob and vla) (1966)
Arabesque (cl and pf) (1965)
Autumn preludes (vln and pf) (1956)
Capriccios (vln and gtr) (1970)
Sonata (vln and pf) (1963)
Suite in old style (fl and gtr) (1972)
Suoni (b-cl and pf) (1974)
Symbioses (fl and hp) (1967)
GUITAR
Due musici (2 gtr) (1972)
Hommage a B. Bartok (1970)
Hommage à choral gothique (1983)
Passacaglia and toccata (2nd prize, Paris, Concours Internationale de Guitare, 1972)
Preludes (1969)
Sonata (Otto Harrassowitz, 1983)
VOCAL
Canzoni in stilo antiquo (A and gtr) (1969)
Five songs, folk words (1955)
Ref. composer, 70, 94, 563

OCHSE, Orpha Caroline
American organist, professor, writer and composer. b. St. Joseph, MO, May 6, 1925. She gained her B.M. in 1947, M.M. in 1948 and Ph.D. in music education in 1953. She was director of music at First Congregational Church, Pasadena. She lectured at the California Institute of Technology from 1960 to 1976, became assistant professor at Whittier College in 1970 and professor in 1977.
Composition
CHAMBER
Prelude and fugue (fl and org)
Chaconne (org)
Publications
The History of the Organ in the United States. Bloomington, IN, 1975.
Ref. 142, 147, 625

OCKLESTON-LIPPA, Katherine
19th-century English composer. She studied under Louis Maas and at the Leipzig Conservatory.
Compositions
PIANO
Album leaves
Nocturne in D
VOCAL
Songs
SACRED
Anthems
Church music
Ref. 226, 276, 433

ODAGESCU (Odagescu-Tutuianu), Irina
Rumanian pianist, editor, lecturer, writer and composer. b. Bucharest, May 23, 1937. She studied at the Bucharest Conservatory from 1957 to 1963 where her teachers were Ioan Chirescu (theory), Paul Constantinescu and Alexandru Pascanu (harmony), Zeno Vancea (music history), Miriam Marbe (q.v.) (counterpoint), Tudor Ciortea (musical form), Alfred Mendelsohn and Tiberiu Olah (composition), Anatol Vieru (orchestration), Vinicius Grefiens (score reading) and Emilia Comisel (folklore). Irina was editor of Editions Musicales de Bucharest from 1964 to 1965, a piano teacher at the Art School No. 5, Bucharest from 1965 to 1967 and assistant to the professor of score reading at the Conservatory from 1967. She published a number of studies and articles on music and participated in conferences. DISCOGRAPHY. PHOTOGRAPH.

Compositions
ORCHESTRA
Batalia cu facle, op. 31, choreographic poem (1977)
Cintec inalt, op. 50, choreographic poem (1983)
Improvizatii dramatice, op. 22, symphonic piece (large orch) (1970)
Momente, op. 22, concertino (str orch) (1974)
Noapte de august, op. 8, symphonic movement (xy, cel, pf and str orch) (1964)
Piscuri, p. 15, symphonic poem (xy, cel, org, pf, hp and str orch) (1970)
Unio, symphonic poem (1968)
Passacaglia, op. 11 (hp, xy and str orch) (1966)
CHAMBER
String quartet, op. 6 (1963)
Music for two pianos and percussion, op. 51 (1983)
Continuum e non stop, op. 43 (pf and perc) (1981)
Improvizatii, op. 45 (org and vlc) (1969)
Improvisations, op. 46 (2 vlc) (1982)
Melos II, op. 45 (fl and pf) (1982)
Sonata, op. 13 (vln and pf) (1967) (medal and diploma, Vercelli International chamber music competition Viotti-Valsesio)
Melos, op. 40, sonata (vla) (1982)
Passacaglia, op. 3 (org) (1962)
Sonata, op. 48 (vla) (1982)
PIANO
Improvizatii II, op. 47 (2 pf) (1982)
Patru piese dedicate copiilor, op. 12 (1966)
Rondo-toccata, op. 9 (1964)
Scherzo-toccata, op. 14 (1968)
Sonata monopartita, op. 5 (1963)
Three preludes, op. 1 (1960-1961)
Toccata (1971) (Council of Culture prize)
Variatiuni pe o tema populara din Bihor, op. 2 (1961)
VOCAL
Chemarea pamintului, op. 55b, oratorio (I. Cringuleanu) (reciter, mix-ch and orch) (1985)
Rugul piinii, oratorio (Cringuleanu) (vces and orch; also mix-ch and perc) (1984, 1977)
Chemarea pamintului, op. 55a, cantata (Cringuleanu) (reciter, mix-ch and orch) (1984)
Tinerete, op. 7, cantata (M. Dutescu) (vces and orch) (1963)
Zi de lumina, op. 26, cantata (M. Negulescu) (vces and orch) (1976)
Cetatea de pamint, p. 54, symphonic poem (P. Ghelmez) (B-Bar and orch) (1985)
Ballad, op. 38 (I. Melinte) (recitor, w-ch and perc) (1980) (medal, Citta di Ibague, Columbia, international choral composition competition, 1981)
Bound by oath, we defend the country (Constantinescu) (B, m-ch and pf) (1972)
Cintec de drumetie, op. 20 (T. Bratu) (2 part chil-ch and pf) (1972)
Cintec eroilor cazuti (mix-ch) (1965)
Cintec in memoria eroilor, op. 10 (Constantinescu) (mix-ch a-cap) (1965)
Cintec tineresc, op. 19 (V. Barna) (2 part-ch and pf) (1972)
Cintind plaiul Mioritei op. 33, poem (Constantinescu) (w or mix-ch and pf) (1977)
De doi, op. 27, folk verse (mix-ch and perc) (1976)
De doua decinii (S. Tita) (vce, mix-ch and pf) (1964)
De pace-i insetat pamintul, op. 49 (I. Melinte) (mix-ch a-cap) (1982)
Fetele din tara noastra, op. 34 (Constantinescu) (w-ch a-cap) (1978)
Imn tarii mele, op. 17 (Negulescu) (mix-ch) (1971)
Imn tineretti, op. 21 (D. Ioan) (mix-ch and pf) (1972)
In noi straluce tineretea, op. 44 (R. Muresan) (B, mix-ch and pf) (1962)
Marea inima a tarii, op. 18 (I. Meitoui) (mix-ch a-cap) (1972)
Mindria muncii, op. 28 (Constantinescu) (2 part ch and pf) (1976)
Numele patriei, op. 36 (V. Nicolescu) (mix or m-ch a-cap) (prize, Composers' Union, 1979; Song to Rumania Festival, 1981)
Ochi de flori, op. 35, folk verse (mix or m-ch a-cap) (1979)
Oglindire, op. 16 (M. Dumitrescu) (ch a-cap) (1970)
Pe nimb de vulturi, op. 39, poem (Nicolescu) (mix ch a-cap) (1981)
Radacini strabune, op. 52 (Cringuleanu) (mix-ch and perc) (1983)
Republica slavita tara, op. 32 (S. Tita) (m-S, mix-ch and pf) (1977)
Rugul piinii, op. 30, poem (Cringuleanu) (mix-ch and perc) (1977)
Si-am pornit in drumetie, op. 29 (Constantinescu) (2 part chil-ch and pf) (1977)
Song of youth (V. Birna) (ch and pf) (1972)
Sta in puterea noastra, oameni (I. Melinte) (mix-ch) (1982)
The spring of life (Constantinescu) (ch and pf) (1974)
Tie, tara, op. 37 (Constantinescu) (w-ch and pf) (1980)
Tineret, Vlastar al tarii, op. 23 (Constantinescu) (2 part ch and pf) (1973)
Urare de Dragoste, op. 53, folk verse (m-ch a-cap) (1984)
Cintind partudulu slava (C. Tevdori) (vce and pf) (1960)
Four lieder, op. 42 (L. Blaga) (2 for S and pf; 2 for m-S and pf) (1981)
Melos I, op. 44 (S, cl, vlc and perc) (1981)
Slavito .... (Negulescu) (vce and pf) (1967)
Wayfarer's song (Bratu) (1970) (mention, National Council of Young Pioneers)
We've just gone out for a walk (Constantinescu) (1977) (prize, Composers' Union)

Ref. composer, Union des Compositeurs Roumains, 81, 94, 148, 196, 300, 563

ODDONE SULLI-RAO, Elisabetta (pseud. Eliodd)

Italian organist, concert singer and composer. b. Milan, August 13, 1878; d. March 3, 1972. She studied music under Professor Mapelli and singing with her mother, Giulia Oddone Gavirati. At the Conservatorio Verdi of Milan in 1898 she studied composition under Gaetano Coronaro and the organ under Luigi Cervi. She collected and published numerous Italian melodies and sung them in concerts thoughout Italy. In 1916 she founded and ran the musical section of the Associazione Frateli d'Italia, aimed at the propagation of Italian music. Together with B. Pratella she founded a theatre for children. She took part in conferences and was a contributor to journals and magazines. She was a member of the Philharmonic Academy of Florence.

Compositions
CHAMBER
Quartetto in Mi Minore (strs) (1911)
Quartetto in Re Minore (pf, vln, vla and vlc) (1900)
Piano pieces
VOCAL
Oratorios
Canti pistoiesi, folk songs (Ricordi)
Cantilene popolari dei bimbi d'Italia (Bergamo: Arti Grafiche)
Melodies, 3 sets of 6 melodies (Ricordi)
La montanina, lyrical poem (L. Anzoletti)
Rosa di Macchia, lyrical poem (C. Zangarini from Tennyson) (prize Amici della musica, 1908)
Si canti e si giouchi, folk songs (vce and pf) (1926)
OPERA
A gara colle rondini
La capanna ardente, in 3 acts (A. Rossato) (1920)
La madia (R. Pezzani) (1936)
OPERETTA
La commedia di Pinocchio, children's operetta in 5 acts (C. Collodi) (1927)
Paravento e fuoco, children's operetta in 1 act (R. Picorzi) (1925)
Petruccio e il cavalo cappuccio, children's operetta
THEATRE
Flemma e furia, for children (G. Fanciulli) (1920)
La Principessa Bom-Bom, children's theatre, in 6 scenes (A. Rosato) (1924)

Publications
Canzoncine per bimbi. 2 vols. Ricordi.
Canzioniere popolare italiano. 2 vols. Ricordi, 1918.
Biografia d Gaetano Coronaro. Florence: Ausonia, 1921.
Il divino parlare. 1925.

Ref. 14, 23, 56, 70, 86, 105, 135, 226, 297, 431, 448

O'DONNELL, Malvine, Countess (nee Tarnoczy)

19th-century composer.

Composition
OPERETTA
Die Maennerfeindin (1856)

Ref. 307, 431

OENNERBERG-MALLING, Berta

Swedish composer. b. 1891. She studied harmony, counterpoint and composition privately in Stockholm. She composed dance pieces for the piano and songs.

Ref. 642

OERBECK, Anne-Marie (ORBECK)

Norwegian pianist and composer. b. Oslo, April 1, 1911. She studied in Norway and Berlin under Sandra Droucker (piano) and Mark Lothar and Professor Paul Hoeffer (composition and instrumentation). In Paris, she was a pupil of Nadia Boulanger (q.v.) and Darius Milhaud. She was a member of the Norwegian Composers' Society. DISCOGRAPHY. PHOTOGRAPH.

Compositions
ORCHESTRA
Symphony in D (1954)
Concertino (pf and orch) (1938)
Melodie (1939)
Miniature suite in three movements (1940)
Pastorale and allegro (fl and str orch; also fl and pf) (1959)
Runemarsjen (1946)

CHAMBER
Melody (vln and pf) (1928) (Oslo: Sverre Scheens Forlag, 1939)
Norsk springar (vln and pf) (1928)
Romance (vln and pf) (1928)
Serenade (vln and pf) (1928)
PIANO
Capriccios
Children's pieces
Humoresques
Lullabies
Marcia indomabile
Melodies
Presto
Sonatina, in 3 mvts (1967)
Valse Piccante
VOCAL
So rodde dei fjorda (vce and orch) (1962)
Vill-Guri (vce and orch) (1962)
Ase liti (H.H. Holm) (w-ch) (Oslo: Norsk Musikforlag, 1952)
Ei malmfuru (Holm) (m-ch) (Norsk Musikforlag, 1946)
Heimhug (Holm) (m or mix-ch) (Oslo: Musikkhuset, 1956)
Ovspel-mesterspill (Holm) (m-ch) (1967)
Salme om kunsten (Louis Kvalstad) (m-ch) (1967)
Sommernatt (Oeverland) (m or w-ch) (Bergen: Tonika, 1956)
Vart land (Oeverland) (m or mix-ch) (1954)
Seven poems (Holm) (vce and pf)
Songs (Norwegian poets) (vce and pf)
Vomir i bloemetid, song cycle (vce and pf) (Norsk Musikforlag, 1945)
SACRED
Setting of psalms
ARRANGEMENTS
Works of William Byrd and J. Stenberg (vln and pf)
Folk songs (pf) (Strauss, Stenberg)
Cadenzas to concertos (Haydn, Mozart)
Ref. composer, 2, 94, 96, 280, 518, 563

OEZDENSES, Semahat

Turkish ud player, singer, teacher and composer. b. Istanbul, September 16, 1913. As a child, she took ud (a type of lyre) and music theory lessons. She won a singing competition held by Instanbul radio in 1936. From 1938 to 1968 she worked as a vocalist for Ankara Radio, then returned to Istanbul and taught music privately. She composes songs.
Ref. National Council of Turkish Women

OFFHUIS, Mme. See BERTHE, Mme.

OFFICER, Bronwyn Lee

New Zealand technician and composer. b. Invercargill, October 7, 1959. She gained her B.Mus. hons. from Otago University in 1981. Since 1982 she has been part-time technician with the School of Music, Univerity of Canterbury. She specialises in electronic and multi-media music and in 1980 received a grant from Alex Lindsay Memorial Scholarship. Her *Prolusion* was highly recommended by the Bank of New South Wales Composition Competition, 1976. PHOTOGRAPH.
Compositions
ORCHESTRA
Prolusion, suite (school orch) (1976)
CHAMBER
4-thought, sound study (fl, cl, vln and pf) (1980)
Argument (bsn and ob) (1979)
Introspection (fl) (1979)
PIANO
Five pieces (1980)
Three studies (1980)
VOCAL
Dejeuner du matin (Cont and pf) (1979)
Moon over towns (m-S and pf) (1981)
DANCE SCORES
Armageddon (tape) (1981)
THEATRE
Amedee or How to get rid of it, play (E. Ionesco) (tape) (1981)
Arabell and the Amazing Wardrobe (M. Forster) (tape) (1981)
ELECTRONIC
Collage (tape) (1979)
Solstice (C. McQueen) (vce and tape) (1983)
Les timbres, they are a-changing (2 vces, pf, cl, perc and syn) (1980)
Winter music (concrete and synthesized tape) (1979)
Ref. composer

OGILVIE, Signe

20th-century Danish composer.
Compositions
PIANO
Maler-marsch koebenhavns malerlaug tilegnet (Copenhagen: Kleinerts Musikforlag)
VOCAL
Ved vuggen: Sov nu ind Bernlille; Laeg mod Puden kinden din (vce and pf) (Berlin: Schlesingersche Buchhandlung)
Ref. 331

OH, Sook Ja

Korean conductor and composer. b. Seoul, May 26, 1941. She graduated from the Kying Hee Music College and then studied electronic music at the Peabody Conservatory and orchestral conducting at the Mozarteum Conservatory. Her *Deaut boe ki* was performed in Australia and her *Mu-ak* selected for the Women Composers' Festival in Rome, Italy. DISCOGRAPHY. PHOTOGRAPH.
Compositions
ORCHESTRA
Deaut boe ki (pf and orch) (1980) (Soo Moon Dang)
Violin concerto (1973) (Soo Moon)
Stone (1971) (Soo Moon)
CHAMBER
A mysterious dawn (trp, timp and 11 strs) (1983)
Asteroid B. 612 (6 insts) (1975) (Soo Moon)
Primagnet (4 insts) (1972) (Soo Moon)
Mu-ak (pf and perc)
Nyeoum I (vlc and perc) (1980) (Soo Moon)
Shaman music (pf and perc) (1976) (Soo Moon)
Nyeoum II (vln) (1980) (Soo Moon)
Nyeoum III (cl) (1982)
VOCAL
A water drop (6 w-vces, m-vce, cel, hp and perc) (1976) (Soo Moon)
An orphant (B and str qrt) (1979) (Kyung Hee)
Spring let it be gone, 10 art songs (1977) (Soo Moon)
OPERA
Won Sul Lang, grand opera (1981)
MISCELLANEOUS
The heaven and the earth (1974) (Soo Moon)
Ref. composer

O'HARA, Mary. See STURE VASA, Mary O'Hara

OHE, Adele aus der (Aus der Ohe)

German concert pianist and composer. b. Hanover, December 11, 1864; d. Berlin, December 7, 1937. She studied the piano under Franz and Theodor Kullak at the Kullak Academy, Berlin from the age of seven and first appeared in concert with an orchestra, at the age of ten. In 1877 she went to Weimar and became a pupil of Liszt for seven years. In 1886 she made the first of 17 tours in America, where she appeared with leading orchestras and in recitals. She also made successful tours in Europe and became a pianist at the Prussian court.
Compositions
CHAMBER
Sonata, op. 10 (vln and pf) (New York: Schirmer)
Sonata in F-Sharp, op. 16 (vln and pf) (1906)
PIANO
Bauerntanz
Berceuse
Bouree
Etude de concert
Four pieces, op. 9 (Berlin: Ries & Erler)
Gavotte
Menuette
Musette
Polonaise
Sarabande
Suite No. 1, op. 2
Suite No. 2 in E, op. 8 (Ries & Erler)
Three pieces, op. 4
Other pieces
VOCAL
Songs incl.:
A birthday song
I begged a kiss of a little maid
I grieve to see these tears (vce and gtr)
Silent, silent are the unreturning
Thistledown
Die waise (Chamisso)
Winds to the silent morn
Ref. 41, 74, 105, 111, 415

O'HEARN, Arletta
20th-century composer.
Compositions
PIANO
Jazz themes and variations (2 pf) (Kjos, 1983)
Three preludes in jazz stylings (Kjos, 1984)
Ref. MLA *Notes*

OHLSON, Marion
20th-century American organist, pianist, accompanist, authoress, conductor and composer. b. Jersey City, NJ. She studied at New York University, New York College of Music, Juilliard School of Music and Guilmant Organ School as well as privately.
Compositions
ORCHESTRA
Little concerto (pf and orch)
PIANO
Pieces
VOCAL
Songs
SACRED
Christ is born, anthem
Christ is risen
Mother-love, anthem
Now is the triumph, Easter anthem
The victory of Easter, song
The vigils of Mary, anthem
OPERETTA
Three Little Pigs, for children
Ref. 39, 40, 142, 280, 347, 494

OIKONOMOPOULOS, Eleni N.
Greek pianist and composer. b. Athens, 1912. She studied the piano, music theory and singing and obtained a diploma in harmony and counterpoint. She is a member of the Christian sisterhood Eusebeia, which performed all of her compositions. DISCOGRAPHY.
Compositions
VOCAL
As tragoudissoume (w-ch and pf) (1962)
Fos ke tragoudi (w-ch a-cap) (1954)
G. Veritis (Chloe Achaiekou) (w-ch and pf) (1958)
To asteri tis avgis (soli, w-ch and pf) (1952)
The kitten
My country
One heart
Pindos
Songs (1947)
Today
SACRED
O koinonikos, oratorio, communion song (G. Veritis) (soli, w-ch and orch) (1956)
O protoklitos, oratorio (ded St. Andrew, patron saint of Patras) (soli, w-ch, narrative ch and orch)
Ta theophania, oratorio (Rhodi Erma) (soli, w-ch and orch)
Christmas songs
Easter selections
Joyous voices
Mass of John Chrysostomos (1943)
Songs (1947)
Towards the light
Ref. composer, 563

OKEY, Maggie (Marguerite) (Mrs. Labori)
Australian concert pianist and composer. b. Mudgee, N.S.W. December 15, 1864; d. Paris, July 3, 1952. She studied at the London Academy of Music and under de Pachmann and later Pachulski. She married de Pachmann in 1884 but later divorced him. She performed in Vienna in 1883, Berlin in 1887, Paris in 1889 and the United States, 1890 to 1891.
Compositions
ORCHESTRA
Piano concerto
CHAMBER
Romance in E (vln and pf)
Sonata (vln and pf)
PIANO
Reverie du lac (Novello)
Theme with variations (Novello)
OPERA
Seleis
Yato
Ref. 6, 9, 110, 226, 276, 297, 347, 431

OKEY, Marguerite. See OKEY, Maggie

OLAGNIER, Marguerite
French composer. b. Paris, 1844; d. Paris, 1906. DISCOGRAPHY.
Compositions
VOCAL
Fantaisie, melody (Leduc)
Habãnera, melody (Leduc)
Il etait près de Damanhour, complainte (Heugel)
Kolybielnaya piesn, song (Heugel)
La nuit constellée, air (Heugel)
Passion, melody (Leduc)
Platonisme, melody (Leduc)
Pourquoi rester close, serenade (Heugel)
Qu'importe ta grandeur, duo (Heugel)
Sais, conte arabe (vce and pf) (1881) (Heugel)
Serenade: Almaz, quant vient le soir, berceuse (Heugel)
OPERA
Le Persan, in 5 acts
Sais
OPERETTA
Lilipa
Ref. 70, 276, 297, 431, 649

OLCOTT, Grace
19th-century American composer.
Compositions
VOCAL
Songs incl.:
Life is but a dream
Swift fly the hours
Ref. 276, 347

OLDENBURG, Elizabeth
20th-century American composer.
Compositions
PIANO
Ensemble
Solo pieces
VOCAL
Dedication (composer) (w-ch and pf) (ded Delta Omicron National Professional Music Fraternity)
Songs
Ref. 40, 347, 518

OLDHAM, Emily S. (or G.)
19th-century English composer.
Compositions
VOCAL
Songs incl.:
Fair is the dawn
Her voice
His ship
Ref. 276, 347

O'LEARY, Jane Strong
American pianist, lecturer and composer. b. Hartford, CT, October 13, 1946. She obtained a B.A. in 1968 from Vassar College and an M.F.A. in 1971 from Princeton University. She attended the Accademia Chigiana in Siena, Italy, 1968. She taught at Swarthmore College, PA, from 1971 to 1972 and after settling in Dublin, at Dublin College of Music, 1974 to 1977. Since 1976 she has been the director and pianist of 'Concorde', a contemporary Irish chamber ensemble. She was awarded the W.K. Rose fellowship in creative arts by Vassar College in 1978 and in 1981 was appointed to Aosdana, an affiliation of creative artists in Ireland.
Compositions
CHAMBER
Concortet (fl, vln, vlc and hpcd) (1979)
Quartet (cl, b-cl, vln and vlc) (1968)
String quartet (1983)
Sinfonia for three (fl, vln and pf) (1980)
Trio (cl, vla and bsn) (1967)
Trio (fl, vlc and pf) (1972)
Trio, homage to Webern (fl, cl and pf) (1978)
Variations (fl and pf) (1984)

PIANO
Piano piece (1974)
Piano piece II (1984)
VOCAL
Begin (Kennelly) (mix-ch and fl) (1974)
Filled wine-cup, a set of 6 songs on Irish poems (Kennelly) (mix-ch) (1982)
I sing the wind around (Roethke) (S, fl and cl) (1977)
Poem from a three-year-old (Kennelly) (S, fl and cl) (1977)
The prisoner (Enzensberger) (Bar, hn and pf) (1969)
Three voices: Lightning; Peace; Grass (Kennelly) (S, ob and pf) (1977)
Time to begin (Roethke) (1968)
Ref. composer, 206, 622

O'LEARY, Mrs. Arthur. See O'LEARY, Rosetta

O'LEARY, Rosetta (nee Vining) (Mrs. Arthur)
19th-century English harpist, pianist, choral conductor, singer, teacher and composer. She showed remarkable talent as a child, singing and playing at concerts when seven. She entered the Royal Academy of Music and won King's Scholarships in 1851 and 1853. She studied under John Thomas (harp), W.H. Holmes (piano) and Steggall and G.A. Macfarren (composition). She was an F.R.A.M. and an associate of the Philharmonic Society. For some years she conducted the South Kensington Ladies' Choir.
Compositions
VOCAL
Songs incl.:
A clasp of the hand (Novello)
Dreams of thee (Ashdown)
Es ist zu spaet
I know my love loves me (S or T)
In vain
My angel lassie
My song is love
She is far from the land (Weekes)
Song of the brook
SACRED
How faithful are thy branches
I am the angel
Ref. 6, 226, 276, 297, 347

OLGA, Grand Duchess
19th-century Russian composer.
Compositions
ORCHESTRA
Parademarsch (Berlin: Schlesinger)
Other works
Ref. 276

OLEIJE. See ULAYYA

OLIN, Elizabeth
Swedish singer and composer. b. 1740; d. 1828. From 1773 till the mid 1780s she was the primadonna at the Royal Theatre.
Composition
VOCAL
Gustaviade, heroic poem (E. Brander) (1768)
Ref. 642

OLIPHANT, Carolina. See NAIRNE, Carolina, Baroness

OLIVE, Vivienne
English harpsichordist, organist and composer. b. London, May 13, 1950. She studied at Trinity College of Music, London; the organ under James Stevens and the harpsichord under Valda Aveling gaining an A.Mus. in 1968. She received a B.A.Mus. in 1971 and D. Phil. from the University of York. She studied under Bernard Rands at York University, Franco Donatoni in Milan from 1972 to 1974 and Roman Hauberstock-Ramati in Vienna, 1974 to 1975. She studied composition under Klaus Huber from 1975 and the harpsichord under Stanislav Heller, both of Freiburg. She currently lives in Nuernberg.
Compositions
ORCHESTRA
Tomba di bruno (fl and orch)
CHAMBER
Lacrimae luschiniae for the victims of Seveso, elegy (8 insts)
Context (7 insts)
The coming of the anchovies (6 insts)
Before they came (vib)
FLUTE
Out of context (3 fl)
Duetting (2 fl) (comm Deutsche Akademischer Austauschdienst)
An die Nachtigall
Text
PIANO
Rondel
Tuareg love song
VOCAL
C (30 vces and 5 perc) (comm York University chamber choir)
At all, at all (3 w-vces and 3 vln)
In dem Nachmittag gefluestert (m-S, perc, hp and vib)
Der Schwan (G. Kolmar) (m-S, fl and pf) (1983)
Songs for school children (vce and pf) (London: Edwin Ashdown)
Ref. composer

OLIVEIRA, Alda de Jesus
20th-century Brazilian composer. She won third prize in a composition competition at the University of Salvador, Bahia.
Composition
VOCAL
Cosme-Damião, in 4 mvts (S and mix-ch) (1974)
Ref. 208

OLIVEIRA, Alexandrina Maciel de
Brazilian pianist and composer. b. Rio de Janeiro, ca. 1840; d. Rio de Janeiro, ca. 1900.
Composition
PIANO
Não creio, polka
Ref. 349

OLIVEIRA, Babi de
20th-century Brazilian pianist and composer. DISCOGRAPHY.
Compositions
PIANO
Caboclo amazonese
VOCAL
Numerous songs incl.:
A estrela do ceu (vce, vln and pf)
Amor de outono
Anda a roda
Cantigia para nani
Inhansa
Rio enamorado
Trovas
Ref. 563

OLIVEIRA, Jocy de
Brazilian concert pianist, professor and composer, of French and Portuguese origin. b. Curitiba, Parana, April 11, 1936. She studied the piano under J. Kliass in São Paulo and Marguerite Long in Paris. She received a fellowship from the Pan American Union, Washington, DC, and obtained an M.A. (composition) in 1968 from Washington University, St. Louis, MO. She appeared as a piano soloist with major orchestras in Europe and the United States. In 1966 she was invited by Igor Stravinsky to perform under his direction his *Capriccio* for piano and orchestra in St. Louis and by John Cage to participate in his Music Circus at Urbana, IL. Composers L. Berio, I. Xenakis, L. Hiller, C. Santoro, B. Johnston and L. Austin dedicated compositions to her. Her own works have been performed in the United States, Europe and South America. Her interest in Brazilian popular music produced a series of advanced sambas, precipitating the vogue of the bossa nova. She taught at seminars and creative workshops in festivals and lectured at universities in Brazil and the United States. She was associate professor at the University of South Florida, music department, 1972 to 1973. She received several honors and awards, including the medal Imperatriz Leopolina, São Paulo. She married the Brazilian conductor Eleazar de Arcalho. DISCOGRAPHY. PHOTOGRAPH.

Compositions
CHAMBER
One player 4 keyboards (pf, cel, hpcd and har) (1968)
Chamber pieces
THEATRE
Polinterações I and II, intermedia of happenings, social and theatrical (Sacramento: Source Music of the Avant-Garde, 1970)
Probabilistic Theatre I, II, III (musicians, actors, dancers, lights, television, public and traffic conductor) (Source, 1968)
ELECTRONIC
Audiobiography (pf and tape) (1975)
Be part of a process (process piece; also tape) (1971, 1974)
Estoria (tape) (1967)
Estoria II (w-vce, tape and perc) (1968)
Estoria III (w-vce, electric gtr and d-b) (1972)
MISCELLANEOUS
Advanced sambas, series (1960)
Treasure hunt, creative game (1973)
Publications
Apague meu Spotlight. São Paulo: Massão Ohno.
O Terceiro Mundo. São Paulo: Companhia Melhoramentos, 1959.
Ref. composer, 17, 22, 94, 206

OLIVEIRA, Sophie Marcondes de Mello

Brazilian pianist, musicologist, professor and composer. b. Guaratingueta, August 23, 1897; d. Sao Paulo, December 16, 1980. She studied the piano under Victoria Pinto Serva Pimenta at the Luigi Chiaffarelli School in Sao Paulo and harmony, counterpoint and composition under Arthur Pereira.
Compositions
CHAMBER
String quartet on Brazilian themes, in 3 mvts
PIANO
Seven easy pieces
Seven preludes
Suite in G-Major
VOCAL
Arvores (Mazza) (ch) (1965)
Cantigas populares, 5 songs (ch)
Dona esperace (Pyrigibe) (ch) (1965)
Exortação (E. Talamo) (ch) (1965)
Je voudrais bien savorr (Dargomyzski) (ch) (1965)
Magôa (V.M. de Moraes Mello) (ch) (1965)
Para uns olhos que me fitam (V.M. de Moraes Mello) (ch) (1965)
Tore (Ascenso Ferreira) (ch) (1965)
Cantigas praianask, 3 songs (V. de Carvalho) (vce and pf)
Simile (vce and pf)
SACRED
Agnus Dei (ch and org or pf)
Auto de Natal (Ribeiro Netto) (ch) (1946)
Ave Maria (ch)
Melodias natainas, 4 songs (ch) (1946)
Canto de Natal (Bandeira) (1956)
Publications
Curso de Musica: Fraseologia e Analise. 10 vols.
Bach a Luz de Analise: A Fantasia Cromatica e Fuga.
O Preludio op. 28, no. 11 de Chopin.
Other works on Phraseology and Analysis.
Ref. composer

OLIVER, Blanche. See OLIVIER, Blanche

OLIVER, Madra Emogene

American organist, authoress, singer, teacher and composer. b. Three Rivers, MI, October 28, 1905. She obtained her B.S.M. from the University of Michigan and her M.A. from Claremont College. She also studied at Oberlin College and Conservatory.
Compositions
PIANO
Two portraits
Other pieces
ORGAN
Nocturne in two moods
Preludio e fughetta
VOCAL
Arise my fair one
Danza giocosa
Danza graziosa
Hark now the bells
Love
Seven songs of youth
Small homes
Spring song
Try again
Whispering Wisconsin
Willows in the snow
Ref. 39, 142, 347, 477

OLIVER, Mary

19th-century English composer.
Compositions
CHAMBER
Liebe wohl! op. 8, romance (vln and pf) (Leuckart)
Bride of the wind waltzes (pf) (Brainard)
VOCAL
Songs incl.:
Dreaming (Jennings)
Lay of the sea-shell (Chappell)
Linger, linger
The watching mother
Ref. 226, 276, 297

OLIVEROS, Pauline

American conductor, professor and avant-garde composer. b. Houston, May 30, 1932. She studied under Paul Keopke at the University of Houston from 1949 to 1952 and at the San Francisco State College from 1954 to 1956, when she received a B.A. She studied privately under Robert Erickson in San Francisco. From 1957, she was involved with group improvisations. In 1961, together with Morton Subotnick and Ramon Sender she formed the San Francisco Tape Music Center and became its director when it moved to Mills College in 1966. She studied briefly under Hugh LeCaine at the University of California, San Diego and is currently associate professor of music and director of the Center for Music Experiment. She was awarded the Pacifica Foundation national prize in 1961, Gaudeamus prize for best foreign work in 1962, grants from the University of California in 1968, 1969 and 1971; a Guggenheim Fellowship in 1973 and an honorary doctorate from the University of Maryland, Baltimore in 1986. DISCOGRAPHY.
Compositions
CHAMBER
Lion's eye (gamelan orch; also syn) (1985)
The grand Buddha marching band
Wings of a dove (2 pf and double wind qnt) (1984)
Double X (2 fl, 2 ob, 2 cl and 2 trp) (1979)
Variations for sextet (fl, cl, trp, hn, vlc and pf) (1959) (Pacifica prize, 1960)
.... Jam (acdn and ens) (1982)
Monkey (cham ens) (1981)
Traveling companions (perc ens) (1980)
One thousand acres (str qrt) (1972)
One sound (str qrt)
Outline (fl, perc and d-b) (1963)
Tree/peace (vln, vlc and pf) (1984)
Trio (trp, acdn and d-b) (1961) (Baltimore: Smith Pub.)
Trio for clarinet, horn and bassoon (1955)
Trio for flute, piano and page turner
The witness (any insts) (1979) (Smith)
Duo for accordion and bandoneon with possible mynah bird obbligato, see saw version (1964)
Go (acdn and vln) (1983)
Mother's day (2 concertinas) (1981)
Theatre piece for two double basses
Time let me play and be golden in the mercy of his means (gtr and hpcd)
The wheel of fortune, theatre piece (cl) (1969)
ACCORDION
Song and dance (acdn orch) (1982)
The wanderer (acdn orch) (1982)
Letting go (acdn ens; also acdn) (1984)
Rattlesnake Mountain (1982)
The receptive (1983)
A secret relationship (1983)
Syracuse meditation (1984)
Three meditations (1982)
Wind whirl (1982)
PIANO
Gathering together (8 hands, 1 pf) (1983)
The autobiography of Lady Steinway
Ode to a morbid marble
VOCAL
Angels and demons (ch and ens) (1980)
Drama of the five families (narr, soloist and ch) (1984)
King Kong sing along (ch) (1977)

The klickitat ride (caller, ch and inst)
Meditations on the points of the compass (12 soli, large ch and audience) (comm Wesleyan University, 1970)
Odyssey (ch)
Rose moon (ch and perc) (1977)
Sound patterns (mix-ch) (J. Boonin, 1964) (prize, Gaudeamus competition)
Music for Expo 70 (3 vces, acdn and 2 vlc) (1970)
Music for Tai Chi (vces, acdn, strs, winds, perc and improvisation) (1970)
A love song (vce and acdn) (1984)
Rain music (vce and acdn) (1985)
Song for the ancestors (vce, shell trumpet and didjeridu) (1984)
Three songs (S and pf) (1957)
The well, preponderance of the great and the gentle (vce, fl, a-cl, cl, acdn, sax, vln and perc; also acdn) (1983)

OPERA
Crow Too, ceremonial opera (comm Creative Assoc., Center for Creative and Performing Art, State University of New York, 1975)

THEATRE
Aeolian partitions (fl, cl, vln, vlc and pf) (1969)
Bonn feier (specialized and non-specialized) (1971)
Cat o'nine tails (mimes and tape) (1965)
Evidence for competing bimolecular and thermolecular mechanisms in the hydrochlorination of cyclohexene (performers, sonic events and audience) (1968)
Festival house (mimes, lights, film slides and orch) (1968)
George Washington slept here (amp vln, tape, projection film and staging) (1965)
Hallo, piece for Halloween (tape, insts, mimes and light) (1966)
Link (1971)
O HA AH (ch, conductor and 2 perc) (1968)
Please don't shoot the piano player, he is doing the best he can (ens of soloists) (1969)
Theatre of substitution: Blind/dumb/director (1 performer) (1977)
Valentine (4 card players and amplified sound) (1968)
Why don't you write a short piece? (1 player) (1970)

FILM MUSIC
Covenant (tape) (1965)
Events (vces, acdn, vlc and insts) (1969)

ELECTRONIC
Aga (vce, concertina, whistle, conch shell, trp, electronic processing and digital delay) (1984)
Alien bog (2-channel tape and electronics) (1968)
The bath (soloist and 4 tapes) (1966)
Beautiful soop (tape) (1967)
Big mother is watching you (tape) (1966)
Bog-road with bird call patch (tape and electronics) (1970)
Breathe in/breathe out (sonic meditations) (1983)
The chicken who learned how to fly (narr, vces and fairlight syn) (1985)
The chronicles of hell (tape) (1965)
The day I disconnected the erase head and forgot to reconnect it (tape and electronics) (1966)
Earth ears (acdn, vib and vln) (1984)
El relicario de los animales (Carol Plantamura and 20 insts) (1979) (Smith)
Five thousand miles (2-channel tape and elecs) (1965)
Legend (ch, amp acdn, perc and effects processing) (1985)
Live electronic piece for Merce Cunningham's dance canfield (comm, 1969)
Mills bog (2-channel tape and electronics) (1968)
Mnemonics III (tape and electronics) (1965)
Mnemonics IV (tape and electronics) (1965)
Mnemonics V (tape and electronics) (1965)
Music for Lysistrata (2-channel tape and electronics) (1968)
Night jar (vla d'amore, tape, film and mime) (1968)
Oh sister whose name is Goddess (vce and digital delay) (1984)
Open circuits om mani padre hum, for 1984 summer Olympics (1984)
Pieces of eight (wind octet, cash register and tape) (1965)
Rock symphony (tape) (1965)
The seventh mansion: From The interior castle (amp acdn and effects) (1983)
Sonic meditations, I-XXV (opt insts) (Smith, 1974)
Talking bottles and bones (vce, effects and digital delay) (1984)
Tasting the blaze (perc, elecs, trb, vlc, cl, 4 acdn and gagaku orch) (1985)
Time perspectives (4-channel tape) (1961)
Theatre piece for trombone player (insts and tape) (1966)
Waking the heart (acdn ens or acdn and digital delay) (1984)
The wandering; A love song (vce and digital delay) (1983)
The wheel of time (str qrt and computer generated tape) (1983)
I of IV (tape) (1966)
II of IV
III of IV
IV of IV
V of IV

MULTIMEDIA
Applebox (1964)
Applebox double (1965)
Applebox orchestra (1966)
Applebox orchestra with bottle chorus (1970)
AOK (acdn, vlns, ch, several conductors, 8 country fiddlers and tape) (1969)
Before the music ends (tape and dancer) (1965)
Bye, bye butterfly (oscillators, amplifiers and assorted tapes) (1965)
The C(s) for once (vces, insts, electric gtrs, lighting or projected images and tape)
Circuitry (5 perc and lights) (1968)
Double basses at 20 paces, intermedia (1968) (Smith)
The dying alchemist (1968)
Engineer's delight (picc and 7 conductors) (1967)
Five (trp and dancer) (1964)
Horse sings from cloud (1977)
The Indefinite integral of psi star psi d tau equals one (insts, reader-singers, tapes, microphones, actors and improvisers)
In memoriam Nicola Tesla, Cosmic Engineer (1968) (comm Merce Cunningham Dance Co.)
Light piece for David Tudor (1965)
Participle dangling in honor of Gertrude Stein (tape, mobile and work crew) (1966)
Phantom fathom, an evening ritual (mixed media events including meditation and an exotic pot-luck dinner) (1972)
Phanton fathom (II), From the theatre of the ancient trumpeter (audience participation) (1973)
Post card theatre (performers, mixed media and post cards) (1972)
Rose moon, ceremonial piece (soli, ch, verbalizing, percussive choral chanting and running feet) (Smith) (comm Wesleyan University, Middletown)
Seven passages (tape, mobile and dances)
What to do (performers, sonic and mixed media) (1972)
Wheel of life (sonic meditation) (1977)
Winter light (2-channel tape, mobile and figure) (1965)
To Valerie Solanas and Marilyn Monroe in recognition of their desperation (ch, orch, electronics and lights) (Smith, 1977)
Willowbrook generations and reflections (mixed winds, brasses and audience participation) (Smith, 1977)

MISCELLANEOUS
Anarchy waltz (1980)
Covenant II (har, garden hose and funnel) (1984)
Lullaby for Daisy Pauline (1980)
Wheel of time (1983)
The witness (solo, duo or inst ens) (1980) (comm Storie Crawford Studio)

ARRANGEMENTS
Theatre piece by Douglas Leedy (with Roger Davis) (org, fl, str qrt, conductor and magician) (1970)

Publications
Don't call them Lady Composers. New York Times. 1970.
Invitation Dream. With Becky Cohen. Los Angeles, Asto Artz.
Karl Kohn: Concerto Mutabile. Perspectives, 22: 87-99.
Many Strands. Numus West, no. 3.
Some sound observations. Source 3.
Tape delay techniques for Electronic Music. The Composer, 2.

Bibliography
Kefaias, Elinor. *Pauline Oliveros: An interview*. High Fidelity-Musical America, June 1975.
The Music of Pauline Oliveros. Heidi von Gunden. Scarecrow Press. 1983.
Subotnik, Morton. *P.O. Trio. Perspectives* 21: 77-82.

Ref. 4, 5, 17, 22, 70, 80, 94, 124, 137, 142, 146, 228, 269, 301, 347, 397, 415, 468, 494, 560, 563, 622, 625

OLIVIER (Oliver), BLANCHE (Mrs. Harry)
20th-century American composer of Louisiana.
Compositions
ORCHESTRA
Acadie (with Florence Allbritton, q.v.) (1932)
Flood (with Florence Allbritton) (1932)
Ref. 347, 448, 496

OLIVIER, Charlotte
19th-century German composer. She composed approximately 135 piano pieces.
Ref. 226

OLIVIER, Madelene. See VAN AARDT, Madelene

OLIVIER, Mrs. Harry. See OLIVIER, Blanche

OLIVIERI SAN GIACOMO, Elsa
Italian composer. b. 1894.
Composition
SACRED
Pianto della Madonna (S, T, mix-ch and orch) (Milan: Ricordi)
Ref. Frau und Musik

OLLER BENLLOCH, Maria Teresa
Spanish pianist, choral director, lecturer and composer. b. Valencia, 1920. She studied at the Valencia Conservatory under Palau and received a first prize in the piano in 1941, composition in 1944 and the final conservatory prize, Victor de Bronce. She performed as a soloist and accompanist and choir director. She was a private teacher from 1943 and lectured at the Conservatory of Valencia from 1948. She was a member of the department of musicology and folklore of the Alfonso el Magnanimo organization.
Compositions
ORCHESTRA
Works
PIANO
Pieces
VOCAL
Cyces of songs (pf and orch)
Choral works
Lieder
SACRED
Music
BALLET
Ballet music
MISCELLANEOUS
Llevantines (prize, Radio Nacional de España, Valencia, 1950)
Publications
Cuaderno que contiene musica, fotografias de danzas y canciones denzadas pertenecientes al autentico folklore valenciano.
Ref. 107

OLSEN, Sophie
20th-century Danish composer.
Compositions
PIANO
Folkedans, op. 3
I automobil, op. 5
Joujou musicale, op. 2
Nisse dans, op. 6
Parlow valse, op. 4
Romantiske stykke, op. 7
The sailor's boy, op. 8, reel
Valse berceuse, op. 9, song
Valse douce, op. 1
Ref. 331

OLSON, Lynn Freeman
American pianist, authoress, lecturer and composer. b. Minneapolis, June 5, 1938. She studied at the Minnehaha Academy, the University of Minneapolis and the New School for music. She studied the piano and pedagogy under Cleo M. Hiner and Frances Clark, theory and composition under Glenn Glascow and David Kraehenbuehl and Dalcroze eurhythmics under Martha Baker. She taught and lectured in piano pedagogy and is the staff lecturer for the National Piano Foundation. She has been a listening consultant for Silver Burdett Music, keyboard education consultant for Carl Fischer and a regular contributor to Clavier Magazine. She originated the radio programme 'It's Time for Music', composing over 200 educational songs for the series.
Compositions
PIANO
Ballad of Don Quixote
Brief encounter
Carribean blues
Festival in Aragon
First sonata
The flamengo
Kites
Make it snappy
Wheels
VOCAL
Songs incl.:
Build that building
Counting
Drum and bugle corps
Ebeneezer Sneezer
Good morning, Mister Sun
Hello there, officer
Milk
Rainbows
Topsy-turvey march
Educatonal songs
Ref. 494

OMER, Helene
American flautist, pianist, accompanist and composer. b. New Brunswick, NJ, January 26, 1920. She studied at the Detroit Conservatory of Music and Wayne County and Henry Ford Community Colleges. Her teachers included Mary Louis Handley (theory), Arvada M. Finn (flute) and Eve Onckken (piano). She worked as an accompanist.
Compositions
CHAMBER
For three (vln, vlc and pf) (1976)
Nocture (fl and pf) (1952)
Three miniatures (fl and pf) (1952)
Two songs (fl and pf) (1952)
Passacaglia (org) (1951)
PIANO
Prelude and fugue (also hpcd) (1951)
Sonata
Theme and variations (1951)
VOCAL
White feather blowing (Cont and pf) (1951)
Ref. 395

ONDISHKO, Denise M.
20th-century composer. Her composition won first prize in the 'The World as Mirror' composition competition, Miami University, 1984.
Composition
MISCELLANEOUS
Without and within
Ref. AMC newsletter

O'NEILL, Selena
American teacher and composer. b. Chicago, March 20, 1899.
Composition
ORCHESTRA
Irish rhapsody
Ref. 39

OOSTERZEE (Osterzee), Cornelia van
Dutch writer and composer. b. Batavia, August 16, 1863; d. Berlin, August 12, 1943. At the Stern Conservatory in Berlin she studied instrumentation under Heinrich Urban. She was also a pupil of R. Radecke, de Lange and W. F. G. Nicolai. In 1890 she moved to Berlin and worked as a newspaper correspondent.
Compositions
ORCHESTRA
Symphony in D-Minor (1900)
Two symphonic poems
Iolanthe
Nordic fantasy
Prelude to Iolanthe
Two scenes from Tennyson's Idylls of the King: Elaine's dream and death; Geraint's bridal journey (1897)
CHAMBER
String quintet
Two string quartets
Zwei phantasiestuecke (Pf trio)
Piano pieces
VOCAL
Choruses
Songs
SACRED
Festive cantata
OPERA
Das Geloebnis, op. 2, music drama in 2 acts (G. Klett and L. van Wittich) (1910)
Ref. 26, 44, 70, 93, 105, 111, 276, 431, 433

OPIE, Mary Pickens
20th-century American composer.
Compositions
SACRED
Communion hymn
Other pieces (mix-ch)
Ref. 40, 347

OPIEWSKA-BARBLAN, Lydia. See BARBLAN-OPIEWSKA, Lydia

OPRAWNIK, Pauline. See ERDMANNSDOERFER, Pauline

ORAIB (Uraib, Arib)

Arabian lutenist and songstress of Baghdad. b. 797; d. July or August, 890. She was an illegitimate daughter of Garaf ibn Yahya al-Barmaki. The Barmak family were of Persian origin, held high administrative positions and were patrons of the arts, particularly music. After the death of her mother and the execution of her father when she was about six, Oraib was sold several times (or stolen, in another version) until she came into the hands of Abdallah Ibn Ismail al-Marakibi, overseer of Caliph Harun al-Rashid's horses. He took her to Basra and had her educated in all the arts required of a singer - calligraphy, grammar, poetry and singing. She learnt to play the lute at this time, excelled in all these arts and in addition was exceptionally beautiful, being tall, elegant and graceful. However, like all her later owners and lovers, her proud owner discovered that she was difficult to please, having an insatiable desire for change and variety in all aspects of her life. None of her owners succeeded in confining her to the harem or court. Al-Marakibi refused to sell her to the Caliph al-Amin, who wished to purchase her since he was crown prince. When al-Amin became Caliph, he had al-Marakibi imprisoned on some pretext, fined him 500 000 dinars and confiscated Oraib. Although al-Amin was delighted with her he wanted an expert's opinion: his uncle Ibrahim Ibn a-Mahdi, one of the foremost musicians of the time, said that she not only possessed outstanding talent, but had not yet reached perfection. Oraib remained with al-Amin until he was murdered in 812, when al-Marakibi forcefully abducted her from the harem. However she escaped from him too, to be with a lover. Al-Mamun, al-Amin's successor, considered Oraib to be part of his inheritance. In spite of being confined to the harem, Oraib still succeeded in meeting her lover Mohammed B. Hamid. When al-Mamun heard of this, he had her thrown into the dungeons, fed on bread and water and whipped. She was unrepentant and al-Mamun, amazed at her spirit, married her to Hamid. In spite of this the Caliph loved her; she bore the surname al-Mamuniya and even accompanied him on his expedition against Byzantium. After al-Mamun's death his brother and succesor al-Matasim inherited her and gave her her freedom. Al-Watiq, who considered himself a musician, suffered from her ability to show up his lesser talents; whenever he set certain poems to music, she would then compose her own melodies for the same poems and each time hers were the better. By the time al-Mutawakki succeeded to the throne in 847, Oraib's reputation was such that she enjoyed the confidence and trust of the Caliph and exerted considerable influence over him. The court of Samarra was at her feet. By this time she had acquired great wealth and had her own school of singing women. At this time too, there existed great rivalry between the old traditional classical school of Arabian music, led by Ibrahim a-Mausuli (d. 804) and his son Ishaq (d. 850), represented by Oraib and the Persian romantic movement led by Ibrahim al-Mahdi and represented by Shariyya (q.v.). As long as Ishaq lived, the classicists held sway, but after his death the principles of the romantic school gained the day. The innovations of the romantic school included an alteration in the rhythmic modes and interference with the old melodic modes, by the introduction of the Khurasani scale, which lent additional color to Arabian music and whose influence has remained to the present day. There were frequent noisy scenes in Samarra at which the public, divided into two factions, would listen to the songs of both Oraib and Shariyya, performed by their respective slave women. Half the public would applaud and the other faction would dispute the merits and originality of the composition. Oraib retained her art even into her old age; at 70 she was still singing at the court of al-Mutass, apparently with no loss of her talents. She died at the age of 96. She was credited with knowing 21 000 melodies and on her death the Caliph ordered the music theoretician Yahya Ibn Ali to make a collection of her songs. She was one of the most brilliant prima donnas of the Abbasid era, a true child of her profession. She survived ten Caliphs and countless viziers and her songs and melodies were performed for years after her death.

Ref. 170, 171, 224

ORAM, Daphne Blake

English electronic instrumentalist, inventor, lecturer and composer. b. Devizes, December 31, 1925. She worked for the BBC in London as a music balancer from 1943 to 1957 and in 1958 was co-founder and director of the BBC's experimental studio, Radiophonic Workshop. She was the first person to compose an electronic sound track for a BBC television play. In 1959 she created her own studio for electronic composition. She evolved a new musical notation, which is read by photoelectric equipment and transduced into sound. She called this system Oramics. She was awarded two Gulbenkian Foundation grants and made numerous television, radio and film appearances. DISCOGRAPHY. PHOTOGRAPH.

Compositions

ELECTRONIC

Bird of parallax (concrete and oramic tape) (1972) (performed as ballet Xallaraparallax, 1972)
Broceliande (1970)
Contrast essonic (with Ivor Walsworth) (pf and elec tape) (1967)
Electronic sound patterns, for schools
Episode metallic (1965)
Four aspects (1959)
Pulse persephone (1965)
Sardonica (pf and oramic tape) (1973)

FILM MUSIC

Snow (1964)

Publications

An individual note of Music, Sound and Electronics. England: Galliard. U.S.: Galaxy Music Corp., 1972.

Ref. composer, 77, 84, 206, 497, 563

ORBECK, Anne-Marie. See OERBECK, Anne-Marie

ORCHARD MAY. See LANGRISHE, May Katherine

ORE, Cecilie

Norwegian concert pianist, authoress, editor, lecturer and composer. b. Oslo, July 19, 1954. She studied composition and sonology at the Norwegian State Academy of Music, under Lasse Thoresen and Olav Anton Thommessen and received a postgraduate piano diploma from the Norwegian State Academy of Music, studying under Liv Glaser, Jens Harald Bratlie and Elisabeth Klein. She also studied the piano for one year in Paris. In 1981 she received a Dutch government scholarship for a year's composition study under Professor Ton de Leeuw at Sweelinck Conservatory, Amsterdam and electronic music study at the Institute of Sonology, Utrecht. Her compositions have been performed in Poland, the Netherlands and Scandinavia. Her *Carnatus* was selected to be performed at the ISCM World Music Day, Canada, 1984. She teaches the piano and theory at a Norwegian conservatory and gives concerts as a pianist. PHOTOGRAPH.

Compositions

ORCHESTRA

Camera lucida (cembalo and str orch) (1983) (NMI)
Strata (str orch) (1982) (NMI)

CHAMBER

Helices (wind qnt) (1984)
Janus (vlc) (1985)

VOCAL

Carnatus (S and ch) (1982) (NMI)
Dream Diary (Jean Arasanayagam) (2 vces, 2 perc and sax) (1983) (MNI)
Le Tombeau des Naiades (Pierre Louys) (S and cham ens) (1981) (NMI)
Calliope (w-vce) (1984)

ELECTRONIC

Circe (computer) (1982) (NMI)

Publications

Norwegian Pianoarama. Anthology of Contemporary Norwegian Piano Music. Norsk Musikkforlag.

Contributed to information booklet on Norwegian musical life: organizations and institutions:. NMI.

Ref. composer, NMI

OREFICE, Olga

Composition

PIANO

Valse capriccioso (Ricordi)

Ref. Ricordi (Milan)

ORENSTEIN, Joyce Ellin

American composer. b. Chicago, March 1, 1939. She obtained her B.A. from Stanford Univerity and M.A. from City University, New York. She also studied at the Universities of California, Los Angeles and Chicago. She studied composition under Leonard Stein and Mario Davidovsky. She received the Mark Brunswick award for composition in 1970 and 1971 and a fellowship to the Bennington Composers' Conference, 1973.

Compositions
CHAMBER
Quintet for strings (1974)
String quartet
Music for flute, viola and percussion (1971)
Trio (2 cl and vlc) (1975)
Dialogue (cl and vlc) (1975)
October 31 (ob and vla) (1975)
For Carlos, In memoriam (fl) (1969)
Piece (fl) (1975)
Piece I (cl) (1971)
Three easy pieces (pf) (1979)
Three pieces (cl) (1971)
Three pieces (fl)
VOCAL
Poppies in October (S and 5 insts)
Ref. 137, 474

ORGER, Caroline (Mrs. Reinagle)

English pianist, writer and composer. b. London, 1818; d. Tiverton, March 11, 1892. She was the daughter of Mary Ann Orger, actress and dramatic authoress and she married the composer Alexander R. Reinagle. She performed her own works at the Hanover Square Rooms in 1843 and the Society of British Musicians performed them in 1844, 1846 and 1847.
Compositions
ORCHESTRA
Piano concerto (1843)
CHAMBER
Piano quartet (1844)
Piano trio (1844)
Sonata in G (vlc and pf) (1844)
PIANO
Sonata, op. 6
Tarantellas
VOCAL
Three songs (R. Browning)
Publications
A few words of pianoforte playing, with rules for fingering passages of frequent occurrence. As Caroline Reinagle. Novello, 1855.
Ref. 6, 74, 226, 276, 653

ORIGO, Iris

20th-century composer.
Composition
OPERA
Merchant of Prado

ORLANDI, Nora

20th-century composer.
Compositions
FILM MUSIC
Johnny Yuma (1967)
The strange vice of Signora Ward (1971)
The sweet body of Deborah (1969)
Ref. 326

ORSINA, Eleanora. See ORSINI, Eleanora

ORSINI (Orsina), Eleonora, Duchess of Segni

16th-century Italian singer and composer. With her husband, she was a member of the court of Francesco De' Medici and Bianca Capello between 1560 and 1580, where there were numerous professional and amateur musicians and singers, Orsini being of the latter group. Her composition is in the Estense Library, Modena.
Composition
VOCAL
Per pianto la mia carne si distilla, canzone (S and lute) (1570)
Ref. Donne in Musica 1980, 157, 653

ORSINI, Teresa

19th-century Italian composer.
Compositions
VOCAL
La tempesta, cantata (Pietro Metastasio) (vce and pf) (ca. 1830) (ded Signora Amalia Astori Duodo)
Caro Dafni, pastoral song (vce and pf) (ca. 1830) (ded Signora Amalia Astori Duodo)
Perche non ho del vento, recitative and romance (vce and pf) (ca. 1830) (ded Signore Amalia Atori Duodo)
Ref. Patricia Adkins Chiti (Rome)

ORTH, Lizette Emma (nee Blood)

American pianist and composer. b. Milford, NH, 1858; d. Boston, September 14, 1913. She was a pupil of the pianist, organist and composer John Orth, whom she later married.
Compositions
PIANO
A dozen and three
A dozen miniatures (1899)
Mother Goose songs without words, 70 easy pieces
On the white keys (1900)
Ten pictures from the land (1899)
VOCAL
Numerous children's songs
OPERETTA
Songs from Mother Goose's Jubilee, for children (1900)
Ref. 22, 260, 276, 292, 347

ORTMANS, Kay (Kathleen) Muriel

English broadcaster, teacher and composer. b. London, September 18, 1907. She studied at the Royal Academy of Music, the Dalcroze School of Eurythmics, Ann Driver School of Movement and Music and at Loheland School, Germany. She was a BBC radio broadcaster from 1941 to 1943 and had her own weekly program on CBC, Canada, 1947 to 1950. She was the founder-director of Well-Springs Foundation, Ben Lomond, CA, for teaching programs for personal growth through the arts. In 1949 she received the Canadian Radio award for an outstanding program and in 1983 the Annual Holistic Health achievement award. DISCOGRAPHY.
Compositions
ORCHESTRA
Garibaldi mountain tone poem (solo inst and orch) (1951)
Let's play suite, for children (1949)
Publications
Music as a Carrier Wave. Journal of Holistic Health, vol. 8. Mandala Society, Der Mar, CA, 1983.
Ref. composer, 77

OSAWA, Kazuko

Japanese composer. b. November 27, 1926. She studied composition at Tokyo University of Arts under Kozabura Hirai, Minao Shibata and Naotada Otaka. In 1959 she was awarded the Ministry of Education prize for orchestral composition and the Japanese National Broadcasting Station prize. DISCOGRAPHY. PHOTOGRAPH.
Compositions
ORCHESTRA
Symphony for modern dance (1952)
Four symphonic movements on one theme (1956)
Music for telecommunication pavilion (1969)
CHAMBER
Octet for woodwind, strings and piano (1953)
Five movements (vln, cl and bsn) (1954)
The tea ceremony (mar, xy and hp) (1972)
Three flowers (ob, vlc and pf) (1953)
Trio (ob, vlc and pf) (1952)
Mon (a-sax) (1979) (Japan Federation of Composers)
Nen (gtr) (1979) (Casa de la Guitara)
Sen (a-sax) (1974)
PIANO
Birds, suite for children (1971)
Dance suite (1955)
Ko (1984) (Ongaku-no-tomo sha)
Poem (1952)
Short pieces, nos. 1-4 (1973)
VOCAL
Monolog, suite (mix-ch) (1965)
Poem on Monday (mix-ch) (1966)
Words from Rose (ch) (1973)
Dream (T. Osada) (T and pf) (1967)
Echo amid mist (S and pf)
Elegie (S. Fukai) (m-S and pf) (1952)
In response (S and pf)
Kazhana (vce and pf) (1981)
Lady Yusuge, cycle (vce and pf) (1980)
A letter from June (vce and pf) (1980)
A season-forgotten flower (vce and pf) (1983) (Ongaku-no-tomo sha)
A song
Song of the nature (vce and pf) (1980)
Soon it will be autumn (S and pf)
Spring (T. Shimizu) (vce and pf) (1970)
Voice (T. Iwasa) (T and pf) (1968)
White plum (m-S and pf)
Wind and light (vce and pf) (1980)
Ref. composer, 563

OSCHATZ, Ruth. See ZECHLIN, Ruth

OSETROVA-YAKOVLIEVA, Nina Alexandrovna
Soviet concert mistress, teacher and composer. b. Petrograd, November 20, 1923. From 1946 to 1948 she studied under Shcherbachiev and in 1952 graduated from the Leningrad Conservatory, having studied under V. Voloshinov. From 1940 she was concertmistress of an amateur orchestra and from 1946 to 1950 of the Leningrad puppet theatre. She then taught music in schools.
Compositions
ORCHESTRA
Piano concerto (1951)
Scherzo (cl and orch; also pf)
Akh, ty step shirokaya (folk orch) (1954)
Festival overture (1969)
Glory to the Russian fleet! (folk orch) (1976)
Krakoviak (folk orch) (1976)
Music (folk orch) (1950)
Nezabyvayemoye, poem (1975)
Overture (Sovietski Kompozitor, 1978)
Polka, waltz for collective farm (1955)
Suite from the ballet Black Rose (1975)
Tales from the Brothers Grimm (1975)
Two songs from Ryazan (folk orch) (1950)
Yermak, fantasy (folk orch) (1953)
Volga, poem (folk orch) (1953)
CHAMBER
Fantasy march (wind ens) (1976)
Russkaya plyaska (wind ens) (1957)
Shestvie (wind ens) (1968)
Woodwind quintet (1947)
Two pieces for string quartet (1949)
Concertino (trp and pf) (1970)
Humoresque (cl and pf) (1970)
Scherzo (vlc and pf) (1976)
Sonata (vln and pf) (1948)
Two pieces (fl and pf) (1970)
PIANO
Prelude (1976)
Seven preludes (1968)
Three miniatures (1947)
VOCAL
October, cantata (N. Gleizarov) (soli, narr, ch and folk orch) (1957)
Utro nashei rodiny, cantata (1952)
Oi, nye tak daleki (A. Prolofiev) (ch a-cap) (1949)
Komsomolskaya (vce and pf) (1949)
Numerous romances (Prokofiev, Tikhonov, Suslov, Matusovsky, Gleisarov, Kuklin and other poets) (vce and pf)
Nye raz na volzhskom beregu, ballad (M. Matusovsky) (1949)
Od severnykh Idov (vce and pf) (1949)
Songs for children
Three romances (Pushkin): Obval; Zimneye utro; Trika
THEATRE
Music for adult's, children's, puppet and amateur theatre
Ref. 21, 87, 277

OSGOOD, Marion
American violinist, conductor, teacher and composer. b. Chelsea, MA, late 19th-century. She studied under Franz Kneisel and Percy Goetschius. She founded the Marion Osgood Ladies' Orchestra, the first professional women's orchestra in America. She taught in Boston for many years. She wrote articles for music periodicals.
Compositions
CHAMBER
Fantasie caprice (vln and pf)
Piano pieces
VOCAL
Songs incl.:
Loving and loved
Ref. 226, 276, 292, 433

O'SHEA, Mary Ellen (Sister Mary Gabriel)
Australian nun, teacher and composer. b. Geelong, June 6, 1887. She received music training from an early age and emigrated to South Africa in 1906. She taught at the Parktown Holy Family Convent, Johannesburg until 1909 when she entered the Congregation of the Holy Family. She gained her U.P.L.M. and U.T.L.M. and then went to London to study under C.F. Reddie, becoming an A.R.A.M.. On returning to South Africa she continued teaching at the convent until she retired, when she taught music and singing to novices and student sisters of the Holy Family until 1964. The manuscripts for her piano and organ compositions have been lost.
Compositions
CHAMBER
Organ pieces
Piano pieces
SACRED
Ave, maris stella, motet
Centennial song, to commemorate the first Sisters of the Holy Family in South Africa (Holy Family)
Haec dies quam fecit Dominus, motet
O sacrum convivium, motet
Regina coeli, laetare, motet
Quid retribuam (Sister Mary Flannagan) (Holy Family)
Salve, Regina, motet
School song of the School of the Holy Family (Order of the Holy Family)
Settings of: Ave Maria; Ave verum; Sub tuum; Benedictus; Salutaris hostia; Tantum ergo
Settings for Mass
ARRANGEMENTS
English hymns
Ref. 377

OSIANDER (Osiander Vogel), Irene
Pianist and composer of Georgian origin. b. Tbilisi, December 9, 1903; d. March, 1980. She studied the piano in Tbilisi and then went to Berlin to study the piano under Else Schmitz-Gohr and composition under Gustav Bemcke at the Stern Conservatory. In Denmark she continued her piano studies under Johanne Stockmarr and composition under S.E. Tarp, Vagn Holmboe, N.V. Bentzon, Emil Reesen and Per Noergard. She made her debut in Berlin in 1932 and in Copenhagen in 1945. She became a Danish national in 1945. Her compositions were performed in Denmark and East and West Germany.
Compositions
ORCHESTRA
Det danske foraer, symphony (1969)
Fatima, op. 96, symphony (1966)
Billeder fra Kaukasus, op. 27 (also pf and vln) (1938)
Danish spring, op. 98 (1969)
I de dybe slive ved kasbaek (balalaika orch) (1944)
Negerdrengens serenade, op. 52 (also vln and pf) (1946, 1950)
Oriental variations on the composer's own themes, op. 48 (1946)
Spanish dance, op. 53 (1951)
Spanish dance, op. 100 (1972)
Tamara, op. 94, ballet suite (1965)
CHAMBER
String quartet, op. 65 (1961)
Pastorale, op. 70 (fl and pf) (1968)
Pieces (vln and pf; fl and pf; cl and pf)
PIANO
Lille suite (1940)
Variations over eget tema, op. 34 (1942)
VOCAL
Songs (Louis Levy) (S and pf) (1943, 1966)
Ref. composer, 77, 331, 499

OSIANDER VOGEL, Irene. See OSIANDER, Irene

OSMANOGLU, Gevheri
Turkish ud, tambur and lavta player and composer. b. Istanbul, 1904. She came from a musical family and her father taught her to play the ud – a lyre, the tanbur – a guitar like instrument and the lavta – a lute, from an early age. Upon the declaration of the Republic of Turkey, her family moved to Paris for 32 years and only on her return to Turkey did Gevheri continue her musical studies, becoming very skilled on the tanbur. Her works are kept in the archives of Turkish Radio and Television.
Compositions
FOLK MUSIC
Six instrumental pieces (tambur, ud and lute) incl.:
Eleven songs
Huzzan saz semaisi
Ref. National Council of Turkish Women

OSTERZEE, Cornelia van. See OOSTERZEE, Cornelia van

OSTIERE (Ostlere), May
19th-century English composer.
Compositions
PIANO
Ariadne
Clytic
Dutch doll, polka
Genesta

Hypatia
Isis
Marches
Only once more
Spirit of the star, waltz
Thistledown
VOCAL
Songs
Ref. 6, 85, 226, 276, 433

OSTLERE, May. See OSTIERE, May

OSTRANDER, Linda Woodaman
American assistant professor and composer. b. New York, February 17, 1937. She gained her B.M. from Oberlin College in 1958, studying under Joseph Wood and Richard Hoffman; her M.A. in 1960 from Smith College, studying under Alvin Etler. She also studied at the University of Illinois under Ben Johnston from 1964 to 1965 and gained her D.M.A. in 1972 from Boston University, studying under Gardner Read. She was a lecturer at Adelphi Suffolk College from 1961 to 1963, Southampton College from 1963 to 1964, music consultant at Lesley College from 1972 to 1973 when she became an assistant professor at Bunker Hill Community College. She received the Settie Lehman Fatman prize in 1960, Gilchrist-Potter prize and numerous scholarships and fellowships.
Compositions
ORCHESTRA
Two concerti grossi (1958, 1964)
Two suites
Quiet music
Time studies
CHAMBER
Cycle for six (1972)
Rounds (brass qnt) (1972)
Fun 'n games (str qrt) (1968)
Variations (str qrt) (1958)
String quartet No. 1 (1956)
Piano trio (1961)
String trio (1971)
Time out for tuba (comm Barton Cummings)
Violin sonata (1956)
Game of chance (1967)
VOCAL
Choral and vocal pieces
THEATRE
Outside in, for children
MULTIMEDIA
Montage (slides and music) (1973)
Tarot (sax, reciter, dancer, slides, lights and tape) (1973)
Ref. Working papers on women in music, International Institute of Women in Music, 142, 625

OSTROFF, Esther
American teacher and composer. b. Odessa, Russia, May 6, 1909. She studied music at Teachers College, Columbia University and received an M.A. (music education). She obtained three diplomas from the Juilliard School of Music and three from the Ecole Americaine, Fountainebleau, France. She also studied Japanese culture at the University of Sophia, Tokyo; African culture at Manhattanville College, New York and music and Russian at Seward Park High School and Stuyvesant Adult Center. PHOTOGRAPH.
Compositions
CHAMBER
Rondo (vln and pf) (1932)
PIANO
Cadenza for Beethoven's G-Major concerto (1932)
Cadenza for Mozart's D-Minor concerto (1932)
Reminiscences (1939)
Theme and variations (1931)
VOCAL
Canon (Cont and S) (1931)
Time you old gypsy, canon (T and S) (1931)
Ref. composer, 77

OSTROM, Mrs. Thomas R. See McLAUGHLIN, Marian

OSTROVSKAYA, T.
20th-century Soviet composer of works for the trumpet and the piano, published by Sovietski Kompozitor, Moscow, 1981.
Ref. Otto Harrassowitz (Wiesbaden)

OTA, Junka
20th-century American composer.
Composition
CHAMBER
String quartet (1979)

OTERO, Mercedes
Venezuelan guitarist, choral conductor and composer. b. Caracas, 1953. She studied classical guitar and won a government scholarship to study in England and Italy. In 1976 she majored in choral conducting and composition at the Scola Cantorum of Caracas, the Conservatory of the Venezuelan National Youth Orchestra and Llamozas Music Schools. She was awarded an M.A. at California State University, Northridge.
Composition
ORCHESTRA
Gravitation
Ref. ICWM

OTIS, Edna Cogswell
American teacher and composer. b. Scranton, PA, November 24, 1886. She composed teaching pieces for the piano and choral works.
Ref. 40, 347

OTTAWOWA, Helena
Polish pianist, professor and composer. b. Lvov, February 6, 1874; d. August 15, 1948. She founded and directed her own music school in Lvov from 1902 to 1914 and in 1912 became a professor at the Lvov Conservatory.
Ref. 118

OVERMAN (Russcher-Overman), Meta
20th-century Dutch composer.
Compositions
ORCHESTRA
The jester, symphonic poem
Suite
Suite of old dance forms (str orch)
Ref. 280

OWEN, Angela Maria
American recorder player, conductor, musicologist, teacher and composer. b. Berlin, July 12, 1928. She obtained an B.Mus. (composition) in 1952 and a certificate of conducting from the Boston Conservatory in 1953. She received an M.Mus. (theory) in 1953 and a Ph.D. (musicology) in 1957 from Boston University. She also studied conducting at L'Ecole Monteux, Hancock Maine, 1953. She taught at Oxford city schools, NC, 1953 to 1954; public schools, Weymouth, MA, from 1956 to 1959 and Community School of Music and Arts Mountain View, CA, 1968 to 1974. She taught the recorder, music history and appreciation at Palo Alto Adult Education Center from 1962, Menlo-Atherton Adult School from 1970 and Foothill College from 1974. She was director of the Mid-Peninsula Recorder Orchestra from 1967. In 1972 she won the recorder composition contest, ARS Miami Chapter. PHOTOGRAPH.
Compositions
CHAMBER
Adagio (str qrt) (1953)
String quartet (1952)
Passacaglia (org) (1952)
RECORDER
Conversations (4 rec)
Variations (3 rec) (1971) (University of Maimi Press, 1972)
Favorite German folksongs (2 rec) (1976)
VOCAL
Five songs
ARRANGEMENTS
Villancicos (2 rec)
Recorder music (Galaxy Music, 1963)
Publications
Johannes Ludwig Bach Cantatas. Concordia Publishing House, 1962, 1964.
Prelude to Musicianship. 1979.
Ref. composer, 77

OWEN, Anita

19th-century American composer.

Compositions

PIANO

Pieces

VOCAL

Songs incl.:

'Neath the flag

Only a litte band, polka fantastique

Sevilla

OPERA

The Great Mogul

Ref. 276, 292, 433

OWEN, Blythe

American cellist, pianist, professor and composer. b. Bruce, MN, December 26, 1898. She made her piano debut in Chicago in 1927. She studied under Max Wald and Louis Gruenberg at the Chicago Musical College, obtaining a B.Mus. in 1941. At Northwestern University she studied composition under Dr. Albert Noelte and received her M.Mus., 1942. She also studied under Nadia Boulanger (q.v.) at the Ecole Americaine, Fontainebleau, Summer 1949. In 1953 she earned a Ph.D. (composition) at the Eastman School of Music, where she studied under Dr. Howard Hanson and Bernard Rogers. Among her piano teachers were Rudolph Ganz and Robert Casadesus and Jean Batalla of the Paris Conservatoire. She taught at Northwestern University from 1944 to 1950, the Cosmopolitan School of Music from 1943 to 1961, Chicago Teachers' College from 1947 to 1950, Roosevelt University from 1950 to 1961 and Walla Walla College, 1961 to 1965. From 1965 she was a professor, chairlady of composition and composer-in-residence at Andrews University, Berrien Springs, MI. She received numerous awards, including six Mu Phi Epsilon biennial awards in 1942, 1951, 1953, 1955, 1957 and 1961; the second Henry Lytton award in 1946; The Delta Ommicron award in 1946; the Lakeview Musical Society award in 1950; the Friends of Harvey Gaul contest award in 1951 and 1970 and awards from the American Pen Women, Chicago Chapter, first prize in 1953, the University of Maryland in 1957, the Composers' press award in 1957 and first prize from the Musicians' Club of Women, Chicago, 1959. She received honorable mentions at the GEDOK Competition, Germany in 1961 and the Pedro Paz award, 1969. She was a life member of the International Institute of Arts and Letters, Switzerland. She made appearances as a soloist in clubs, on radio and with orchestras and chamber ensembles. PHOTOGRAPH.

Compositions

ORCHESTRA

Symphony No. 1, op. 13 (1947)

Concerto grosso, op. 29 (1961) (Mu Phi Epsilon biennial award, 1961)

Piano concerto, op. 24 (1953) (Mu Phi Epsilon biennial award, 1955)

Elegiac poem, op. 19 (1954)

Elizabethan suite, op. 32 (1964)

Pastorale and dance, op. 7 (cham) (1942)

State street, op. 1, suite (1946) (Henry P. Lytton award, 1946)

Suite for strings, op. 4 (1941)

BAND

Chorale and fugue, op. 38 (1966)

CHAMBER

Ballad, op. 10 (org and strs) (1944)

Fanfare and processional, op. 44, no. 1 (brass qnt and org) (1969) (Hall Orion, 1974)

Quintet, op. 8, no. 1 (pf and str qrt) (1944) (Delta Omicron award, 1946)

Quartet for strings, No. 1, op. 8 (1944)

Quartet for strings, No. 2, op. 15 (1951) (Mu Phi Epsilon award, 1951)

Quartet, op. 28, no. 3 (pf, vln, vlc and vla) (1963)

Sarabande and gigue for four tubas, op. 42, no. 1 (Hall-Orion Music, 1974)

Trio, op. 18, no. 1 (ob, cl and bsn) (Mu Phi Epsilon award, 1953) (Hall Orion)

Trio, op. 28, no. 1 (fl, cl and pf) (1959) (Musicians Club of Women prize, 1959)

Trio, op. 28, no. 2 (vln, vlc and pf) (1962) (special merit citation, 1967)

Trio, op. 58 (cl, vlc and pf) (1980)

Concert piece, op. 42, no. 2 (bsn and hpcd) (1967)

Diversion, op. 42, no. 3 (a-sax and pf) (1973)

Sarabande and gigue, op. 42. no. 3 (a-sax and pf) (1973)

Sonata, op. 12 (vln and pf) (1946) (Mu Phi Epsilon award, 1951)

Sonata fantaisie, op. 3 (vlc and pf) (1940) (Mu Phi Epsilon award, 1942)

Two inventions for woodwinds, op. 35, no. 1 (1964) (special merit citation, 1967) (Hall-Orion, 1972)

ORGAN

Chorale prelude on Rothwell, op. 5, no. 1 (1977) (Lorenz)

Fantasy on Of The Father's love begotten, op. 37, no. 2 (1967)

Festival (Festal) prelude, op. 7, no. 1 (1960 or 1966)

Passacaglia on Prout's impossible melody, op. 57, no. 1 (1979)

Processional, op. 48, no. 1 (1973)

PIANO

Air-Handel, recital duos, op. 21b, no. 3 (2 pf) (1960) (Summy-Birchard)

Barcarolle and scherzo, op. 21a (2 pf) (1949)

Ring dance, op. 30, no. 4 (2 pf) (1962) (Summy-Bichard)

Sonatina, op. 21b, no. 1 (from God's Best Time is Best by Bach) (2 pf) (1957) (Summy-Birchard)

The Aeolian acrobat, op. 26, no. 5 (1979)

Black key jig, op. 30, no. 1 (1962)

The Dorian dude, op. 26, no. 1 (1956) (Rochester Music)

Good-morning, op. 36, no. 1 (1955) (Summy-Birchard)

The Ionian imp, op. 26, no. 6 (1980)

A little game, op. 25, no. 1 (1955) ((Summy-Birchard)

The Lydian lady, op. 26, no. 3 (1964)

March of the plastic soldiers, op. 25, no. 2 (1962)

The Mixolydian maiden, op. 26, no. 6 (1980) (Hall-Orion)

Nativity suite, op. 34, nos. 1-5 (1964)

Over the telephone, op. 30, no. 2 (1962)

The Phrygian flirt, op. 26, no. 2 (1963)

Playing games, op. 36, no. 2 (Summy-Richard, 1974)

Serially serious, op. 46, nos. 1-3 (1971) (Hall-Orion, 1973)

Sonata No. 1, op. 14 (1948) (prize, Lakeview Musical Society, 1950)

Sonatina in A, op. 2 (1939) (prize, Mu Phi Epsilon, 1942)

Swinging, op. 36, no. 3 (Summy-Birchard, 1974)

Three little preludes and fughettas, op. 40, nos. 1-3 (1966)

Toccata, op. 21a (1950) (Mu Phi Epsilon award, 1957)

Two little trumpeters, op. 30, no. 3 (1962)

Two nocturnes, op. 41, nos. 1 and 2 (1967)

Variations on American folk song, Old Texas, op. 27, no. 1 (1959)

Variations on American folk song, Sacramento, op. 27, no. 2 (1959)

Whirly skirts, op. 25, no. 3 (1956)

VOCAL

Centennial anthem, op. 50, no. 1 (mix-ch, brass, perc and org) (1974)

Go, lovely rose, op. 9, no. 2; also op. 9, no. 1, madrigal (E. Waller) (mix-ch) (1944) (University of Miami Music, 1970)

An Indian prayer, op. 50, no. 1 (mix-ch, w-ch, fl and dr) (1970) (hon mention, Harvey Gaul contest, 1970)

The man on the white horse, op. 43, no. 2 (narr, ch, brass and perc) (1970)

Songs incl.:

The cloud, op. 16, no. 3 (1958)

I know not why, op. 1, no. 2 (high vce) (1941)

Morning glories at my window, op. 16, no. 2 (high vce)

My heart shall bear no burden, op. 1, no. 3 (high vce) (1942) (Pedro Paz award, 1969)

Out of the depths, op. 10, no. 1 (high and med-vce)

Pierrot, op. 1, no. 1 (high vce) (1940)

Rain, op. 16, no. 1 (high vce) (1951)

Song cycle for solo voice, op. 45 (high vce) (1970)

Songs of the night, op. 22 (med-vce) (1958)

SACRED

I heard Emmanuel singing, op. 20 (ch and orch) (1957)

Festival Te Deum, op. 17, no. 2 (4 vces and org) (1951)

Responses, op. 31, nos. 1-5 (1963) (Hall-Orion, 1974)

Responses, op. 39, nos. 1-4 (1966) (Hall-Orion, 1974)

This is the gate of the Lord, op. 33 (ch, org, brass and perc) (1964)

Blessed be the God and Father, op. 23, no. 4 (4 vces and insts) (hon mention, Friends of Harvey Gaul contest, 1951)

Awake o Zion, op. 17, no. 1 (w-trio, pf and trp) (1953) (prize, American Pen Women, 1953; University of Maryland award, 1957)

Hearken unto me, op. 17, no. 4 (mix-ch and org) (Composers Press award, 1957)

Praise the Lord, op. 23, no. 1 (4 vces and org) (1957)

Song of infinity, op. 43, no. 4 (mix-ch and pf)

The Trinity, op. 17, no. 3 (4 vces and org)

We wish you a merry Christmas (mix-ch and pf)

My soul is an enchanted boat, op. 9, no. 1 (w-ch) (1944)

The rock, op. 23, no. 2 (m-ch) (1954)

O Lord, I have heard the report, op. 55, no. 1 (high vce and org) (1979)

O Lord, I will praise Thee, op. 9, no. 3 (5 vces a-cap) (1944)

O Lord, Thou hast searched me, op. 55, no. 2 (med-vce, org and vlc) (1980)

Easter (Easter song) op. 5, no. 1, anthem (G. Herbert) (mix-ch and opt pf) (1942) (University of Miami Music, 1970)

Let God arise, op. 6, no. 2, anthem (4 vces and org) (1944) (Summy-Birchard)

Little Jesus come to town, op. 23, no. 3, anthem (L.W. Reese) (mix-ch and pf) (1955) (Nashville: Broadman Press, 1960)

Song of the oppressed, op. 6, no. 1, anthem (4 vces) (1942)

Victimae paschale, op. 5, no. 2, anthem (4 vces) (1942)

Peace hymn of the republic (H. v. Dyke) (mix-ch, org and brass) (1976) (Bicentennial commission, Andrews University)

Make a joyful noise, op. 10, no. 3 (high and med vce) (1948)

Blessed be the God and Father, op. 10, no. 4 (high vce) (1956)

Rise, oh my soul, op. 10, no. 2 (high vce) (1942)

Bibliography

D.H.R. *Owen, Blythe: Sarabande and Gigue. Instrumentalist*, XXIX/8. April, 1975, 80.

Ref. composer, 40, 77, 94, 137, 142, 228, 395, 468, 622, 624, 625

OWEN, Morfydd Llwyn

Welsh pianist, singer and composer. b. 1891; d. 1918. She studied at University College, Cardiff and later at the Royal Academy of Music. She composed a number of songs in English but was mainly interested in Welsh folk music. She worked with Lady Herbert Lewis of the Welsh Folk Song Society. DISCOGRAPHY.

Compositions

ORCHESTRA

Nocturne

VOCAL

Songs incl.:

Two Madonna songs (vce and pf)

Ref. 563

OWENS, Priscilla

19th-century composer of hymns. She was better known for her literary works.

Ref. 502

OWENS, Rochelle

American authoress, playwright, poetess and composer. b. Brooklyn, April 2, 1936. She wrote many controversial plays and eight books of poetry.

Compositions

THEATRE

The Joe chronicles part 2, poems (mountain dulcimer)

The Joe 82 creation poems

Music for the Karl Marx play

Shemuel, poems (fl)

Ref. 494

OWENS, Susan Elizabeth

American gamelan player and composer. b. Walla Walla, WA, July 8, 1943. She gained a B.A. (English literature) and an M.A. (music theory and composition) from San Jose State University, where she studied under M. Higo Harada. Her works have been performed in America and she was a 1980 winner of the Eva Thompson award and winner of a Prix de Rome.

Compositions

VOCAL

The lady and the bear (vce, pf and fl) (1982)

MISCELLANAOUS

April (1978)

Circles (1980)

Il pleur (1979)

Innisfree (1981)

Ref. composer

OWENSON, Sydney. See MORGAN, Lady

OZAITA (Ozaites Marques), Maria Luisa

Spanish harpsichordist, pianist, conductor and composer. b. Baracaldo, Vizcaya, 1937. She studied the piano, harpsichord composition and conducting in Spain and then went to the Conservatory of Copenhagen on a state bursary to study under Isaken and Thybo. She also studied in Darmstadt, Nice and Granada. She made regular appearances as a harpsichordist and conductor, in Spain and abroad. In 1981 she represented Spain as a composer and performer at the 'Femina Componens' congress in Vienna. She has composed works for chamber groups and the harpsichord.

Ref. Donne in Musica '82, 622

OZAITES MARQUES, Maria Luisa. See OZAITA, Maria Luisa

OZDENSES, Semahat. See OEZDENSES, Semahat

PABLOS CEREZO, Maria de

Spanish lecturer and composer. b. Segovia, 1904. She studied at the Madrid Conservatory under Fernandes Bordas, Perez Casas and Conrado del Campo and later lectured there. She won first prize in composition in 1927 and a grant from Rome in 1928.

Compositions

ORCHESTRA

Castilla, symphonic poem

CHAMBER

Quartet in A-Minor (strs)

VOCAL

Alabanza senor (soli, ch and orch)

SACRED

Ave Verum, motet (vce, ch and orch)

OPERA

La Infanta Desden, in 1 act (F. Aradavin)

Ref. 100, 105, 107, 361

PACHLER-KOSCHAK, Marie Leopoldine

Austrian pianist and composer. b. Graz, October 2, 1792; d. Graz, April 10, 1855. She was a great admirer of Schubert and Beethoven, who called her 'die wahre Pflegerin seiner Geisteskinder' (the true custodian of his spiritual children). Her son, Faust Pachler, wrote *Beethoven and Marie Pachler-Koschak*, which contains details about the last days of the master. In 1827, Schubert composed a *March for piano, 4 hands* for Marie and her son. Marie composed piano pieces.

Bibliography

Faust Pachler. *Beethoven and Marie Pachler-Koschak*. Berlin, 1866.

Ref. 44, 70, 100, 105, 110

PACK, Beulah Frances

American pianist, teacher and composer. b. Cleveland, OH, June 5, 1896; d. June 9, 1971. She graduated from Bennett College, NY, and studied the piano, harmony and composition under Gertrude Ross in Los Angeles and Mary Carr Moore (q.v.) in San Francisco. She taught in summer camps in Maine, moving there in 1922. Her compositions were presented at Portland and Augusta music clubs. DISCOGRAPHY.

Compositions

CHAMBER

Northeast harbor (vln, fl and pf)

Suite (hp and fl)

PIANO

Bell on the reef

Lilacs in the rain

Morning in Muir Woods

Nine preludes

Two nocturnes

Two squirrels

VOCAL

Autumn glory

My heart is like a singing bird

Moonlight sonata

Red, red rose (Burns)

Sing robin sing

Voices of the night

Art songs

Children's songs

SACRED

Songs

Ref. M.C. McLeod, 40, 60, 347, 563

PADE, Else Marie

Danish producer and composer. b. Aarhus, December 2, 1924. She studied music privately in Aarhus and then at the Royal Danish Conservatory in Copenhagen, 1945 to 1950. She studied composition under Vagn Holmboe and Jan Maegaard from 1952 to 1955 and electro-acoustic music under Holger Lauridsen (M.Sc.) in 1957. She frequently attended the Ferienkurse fuer Musik in Darmstadt. She was employed by Danish radio from 1964 to 1973 and from 1973 to 1977 worked at Rigshospitalet (university clinic) Copenhagen, as a collaborator on a research project for handicapped children, retiring to devote time to composing. She received a scholarship from the Arts Foundation from 1970 to 1973 and a research scholarship from the Research Committee of State Welfare for the mentally handicapped in 1974. She shared second prize in a competition organized by Scandinavian opera companies for a children's opera in 1975.

Compositions

ORCHESTRA

Trumpet concerto (1954)

Parametre (str orch) (1962)

Tullerulle tappenstreg: 7 pieces en couleurs, suite (cham orch) (1953)

CHAMBER
Historien om Skrabelsen (cham ens) (1969)
VOCAL
Vola spa hoc est (w-ch) (1956)
Fire anonyme sange (vce and cl) (1955)
Rode bolde (vce and pf) (1955)
Tullerulle tappenstreg, children's songs
BALLET
The Blade of Grass, poem (El Forman) (prep pf, vln, perc and dancers) (1964)
Immortella (perc, zither and dancers) (1969) (ded Aksel Dahlerup)
OPERETTA
Father, Mother and Children, for children (1974)
INCIDENTAL MUSIC
Den lille havfrue, radio play (1958)
En dag pa dyrehausbakken, TV film (1955)
Musik til 4 radiodigte (1971)
Pjerrots forunderlge dans, radio play (fl and hp)
Seks eventyr, radio plays (1966)
Vikingerne, film (1961)
ELECTRONIC
Et spil for cello (vlc and tape) (1962)
Etude I (1961)
Faust, suite in 6 parts (1962)
The glassbead play (1960)
Lys og lyd (tape) (1960)
Maria (S, speaker, mix-ch and tape) (1975)
Period I, II, III (vln and 3 loudspeaker groups) (1961)
The seven circles (1959)
Symphonie heroica (tape) (1962)
Symphonie magnetophonique (1959)
Twenty-one water-colours of the sea (Georg Soenderlund Hansen) (3 speakers, perc, hp and tape) (1971) (ded Georg and Gerta)
Ref. composer, 1, 94, 130, 206

PADELLAN, Mrs. Moetahar. See HIGGINBOTHAM, Irene

PADUCI. See LEFEBVRE, Françoise

PAEMURRU, El'ze Janovna. See AARNE, El's

PAGH-PAAN, Younghi
Korean composer. b. Cheongju, 1945. She studied at the College of Music and the Graduate School of Seoul National University before proceeding to the Freiburg Musikhochschule on a DAAD scholarship, where she studied composition under Klaus Huber and Brian Ferneyhough from 1974 to 1979. Several of her works were commissioned by German and French radio. She lives in Freiburg.
Compositions
ORCHESTRA
Sori, in 5 mvts (1980) (comm Southwest Broadcasting Co., Germany) (prize, Stuttgart Composition Festival)
CHAMBER
Madi (12 players) (1981)
Man-nam (cl and str trio) (two 1st prizes: Switzerland, 1978; Paris, 1979)
Dreisam-nore (fl) (1975)
Violin solo
VOCAL
Flammenzeichen (w-ch; also w-vce) (1983)
Nuhn (5 w-vces and 18 players) (1979)
Ref. Korean Nat. Council of Women

PAGOTO, Helen (Clara)
American pianist, arranger, choral conductor, singer, teacher and composer. b. Hamtrack, MI, March 22, 1922. She won a scholarship to the Detroit Institute of Musical Art, where she studied the piano and music theory privately under Ethel Green and Margaret Manabach and voice under Dr. William Howland. From 1942 Helen taught music in schools. She appeared in concert, on the radio and conducted theatre and church choirs.
Compositions
PIANO
Gypsy dance
Sarabande
Scherzino
VOCAL
Songs incl.:
Children's songs
Desire
I belong to you
Stars in your eyes
This is my song
OPERETTA
Queen of Hearts
Roam, Gypsies, Roam
Other children's operettas
Ref. 496

PAIGNE, Mme. (pseud. Max Silni)
French composer. b. 1827.
Composition
OPERA
Enfermez-la! (1867)
Ref. 307, 431

PAIN, Eva
20th-century English composer. DISCOGRAPHY.
Compositions
PIANO
Boys and girls come in to play
Lullaby
Reflections
Ruritanian dance
To horse and away
We build tunes
VOCAL
Dunmow Flitch
Ref. 263, 649

PAKHMUTOVA, Alexandra Nikolayevna
Soviet composer. b. Beketovka, near Volgograd, November 9, 1929. She studied under V. Shebalin at the Music School and the Conservatory in Moscow, graduating in 1953. She continued with postgraduate studies in composition under Nikolai Peiko, Vladimir Fere and Shebalin. The influence of Russian folk song is apparent in her work. In 1977 she received the award of Artist of the USSR. DISCOGRAPHY.
Compositions
ORCHESTRA
Concerto (1972)
Concerto in E-Flat Minor (trp and orch) (1955)
Russian festival overture (orch of folk insts) (1967)
Russian suite (1953)
Symphonic suite (1953)
Thuringia suite (1958)
Youth overture (1957)
CHAMBER
Nocturne (hn and pf) (1955)
Prelude and allegro (trp and pf)
Sonata (vln and pf) (1947)
Etude (bayan) (1972)
PIANO
Little variations (4 hands) (1960)
Pernatye tdruziya, album (1969)
Sonatina (1946)
Suite
Toccata
VOCAL
Krasnye sledopyty, cantata (1962)
Lenin v serdtse u nas, cantata (Grebennikov, Dobronravov) (narr, chil-ch and orch) (1957)
Otryadnye pesni, cantata (1972)
Vasily Tyorkin, cantata (A. Tvardovsky) (1953)
Epitafia, in memory of Yuri Gagarin (ch and orch) (1969)
Good-bye, Moscow (Dobronravov) (vces and orch) (for 1980 Olympic Games, Russia)
Ode to the lighting of the Olympic flame (ch and orch) (for 1980 Olympic Games)
A street of peace (chil-ch)
Who'll answer (folk ch)
Ballad of the white carnation (Genina)
Dawn of the cosmic era (Grebinnikov, Dobronravov) (1961)
Do you know the kind of lad he was
Geologi (Grebennikov, Dobronravov)
Glavnoye rebyata serdzem me staret!
Khoroshie devchata

Moscow gives the start (Dobronravov) (for 1980 Olympic Games)
Piesna o treboshnoi molodosti (Oshanin)
Pokhodnaya kavaleriskaya (Drunina)
Putevaya pionerskaya (Naidenova) (1949)
Stary klon (Matusovsky)
Two Russian folk songs (1949)
Numerous other songs
BALLET
Ozaryonnost, in 1 act (pf) (1979)
THEATRE
Music for plays
FILM MUSIC
Devchata (1962)
Po tu storonu (1958)
Semya ulyanovikh (1957)
Tri topolya na plyushchikhye (1967)
Yabloko razdrova (1963)
Zhili-bili starik so starukhoi (1964)
Ref. 17, 21, 22, 70, 87, 223, 277, 420, 441, 563, 622

PAKI, Lydia Kamakaeha. See LILIUOKALANI, Queen

PALAEOLOGINA
Late 14th-15th-century Byzantine nun and probably the founder of the convent of Saint Theodora in Thessalonika. She was described as a cultured and intelligent lady. She composed canons in honor of Saints Dimitri, Theodora and other saints. The manuscripts of her compositions have been lost.
Ref. 502

PALDI, Mari
19th-century American composer. b. Minnesota. Her compositions included piano pieces.
Ref. 323

PALLASTRELLI, Giannina, Countess
20th-century Italian poetess and composer.
Compositions
THEATRE
Dal 700 al 2000, in 3 scenes (composer) (1923)
Le danza della jungle (composer) (Fiorenzuola d'Arda, 1929)
Il gatto stivalato, in 3 acts and 4 scenes (with Countess C. Bartolomei) (1932)
Il gobbo di Paggio Chiomadoro (composer) (1927)
Prezzemolina, in 1 act (composer) (1927)
Ref. 105

PALMER, Catherine M.
Canadian composer. b. 1928. Her composition won the Royal Canadian College of Organists anthem competition, 1963.
Composition
SACRED
Christ, my beloved, which still doth feed (William Baldwin) (S or T, mix-ch and org) (Waterloo Music, 1963)
Ref. Century of Canadian Choir Music, 1978

PALMER, F.H. See HARTMANN, Emma Sophie Amalie

PALMER, Florence Margaret (Peggy) Spencer
English pianist, teacher and composer. b. Thornbury, July 27, 1900. She attended the Tobias Matthay Piano School, London to studied the piano under Vivian Langrish and composition under B.J. Dale and Sir Ivor Atkins. She received a B.Mus. from London University. She was the pianist and secretary to La Marechale (Mrs. Catherine Booth-Clibborn) in evangelistic campaigns, senior music teacher at Clarendon School, Malvern from 1930 to 1948 and private music teacher in Bristol and district from 1948. She received the Chappel gold medal for the piano in 1923 and prizes in Horatio Lumb competitions. She composed piano pieces, songs, hymn tunes and descants, having 16 entries in the Anglican Hymn Book.
Publications
The pianist's book of chimes. 1953.
Simplified sight-reading. 1970.
Ref. 77

PALMER, Jane Hetherington
English composer. b. London, October 29, 1952. She attended Girton College, Cambridge from 1971 to 1974, received an honors degree in music and then attended the advanced composition course at the Royal Academy of Music until 1975. DISCOGRAPHY. PHOTOGRAPH.
Compositions
CHAMBER
String quartet (1973)
VOCAL
A quartet of love songs (vce and orch) (1974)
SACRED
Christe's coming, cantata (ch) (1977)
My beloved spake, anthem (ch) (1974)
The fourteen stations of the Cross (S and org) (1973)
Praise our Lord, 8 junior hymns (1965)
Three modern hymns (Paxton, 1969)
Ref. composer, 563

PALMER, Lynne Wainwright
American harpist, lecturer and composer. b. Cleveland, December 6, 1918. She studied the harp under Carlos Salzedo at the Curtis Institute of Music, graduating in 1940 with the Curtis award for the outstanding graduate. She was chosen by Leopold Stokowski for the All-American Youth Orchestra and toured with them in 1940 and 1941. She was first harpist with the Indianapolis and the Philadelphia Orchestras from 1940 to 1942. She was the harp lecturer at the University of Michigan from 1942 to 1947 and at the University of Washington, 1954 to 1966. She then studied composition under Gerald Kechley at the University of Washington. In 1981 she was awarded honorary membership of the Sigma Alpha Iota Society and later served on the board of directors of the American Harp Society.
Compositions
ORCHESTRA
Concerto for Debbie (hp and orch) (1977)
Conversation piece (2 hp and orch) (1982) (comm Bellevue Philharmonic Orch. Assoc.)
Prelude and dance (1 or more troubadour hp and orch: also troubadour hp and pf) (1967)
CHAMBER
Duet (beginner vlc and troubadour hp) (1967)
Sonata (fl and hp) (1979)
Suite for sweets, easy piece (vln and hp) (1982)
Sonata (pf)
HARP
Air and rustic dance (3 hp) (1972)
Parade (3 troubadour hp) (1967)
Triptych (3 hp) (1975)
Troubadour trek (1 or more troubadour hp) (1966)
Classical suite for harp alone (1972) (Santa Monica, Ca.: Salvi Publ.)
Procession for Janet (1976) (Salvi)
Procession for Rae (1966, rev 1982)
R.S.N.F. waltz (1968)
Shades of blue (1980) (Salvi)
A snatch of jazz (1980)
Sounds I and II (1977)
Theme and whimsical variations (1978)
Toccata (1965, rev 1976)
Arrangements for harp
SACRED
Canticle of praise (narr, speaking ch and hp) (1978)
The gift, Christmas anthem (mix-ch and hp) (1980)
Ref. composer

PALMER, Peggy Spencer
Compositions
PIANO
Festive pieces: Preamble; Country dance
Ref. 473

PANETTI, Joan
American pianist, assistant professor and composer. b. 1941. She toured Europe as a pianist and then became an assistant professor at Yale University, receiving a Morse fellowship in 1969. She obtained student composer awards in 1966 and 1977. She also studied at the Peabody Conservatory.
Compositions
ORCHESTRA
Piano concerto
CHAMBER
Small pieces for Gregory, 4 pieces (vlc and strs)
Cavatina (pf)
VOCAL
Songs
Ref. 94, 142, 146, 403, 622

PANZERA, Magdeleine
French composer. b. 1893.
Compositions
PIANO
Berceuse (BMI)
Bremenons-nous (BMI)
Carillon (BMI)
Habañera (BMI)
Je suis punie (BMI)
Mon beau jouet s'est brisé (BMI)
Pastorale (BMI)
Le petit ruisseau chante (BMI)
Recitals (BMI)
Sicilienne (BMI)
Voici les vacances (BMI)
Ref. 52

PAPARA, Teodozja
Polish composer. b. Lvov, 1797.
Compositions
PIANO
About 40 pieces incl.:
Fantaisie à la polonaise
Grande polka
Marche funèbre
Marche militaire
Polka de salon
Polonaise de concert
Ref. 118

PAPAVOINE, Mme. (nee Pellecier)
18th-century French composer.
Compositions
CHAMBER
Recueil d'airs choisis de theatre ... (1770)
VOCAL
Nous voici donc au jour de l'an, Etrennes (1755)
Reviens, amable Themire (Paris: Tournelle, 1761)
Vous fuyez sans vouloir m'entendre (Tournelle, 1756)
OPERA
Barbacole
Le vieux coquet
Ref. 65, 653

PAPOT, Marie Anne
French professor and composer. b. 1854; d. Paris, September 2, 1896. She was a professor of voice at the Paris Conservatoire and composed songs and vocalises.
Ref. 433

PAPPENHEIM, Marie, Countess
19th-century Austrian composer of songs.
Ref. 465

PAQUIN, Anna
Canadian organist, teacher and composer. b. St. Cuthbert, Quebec, 1878; d. Saint-David d'Yamaska, 1923. She composed sacred pieces.
Ref. 347

PAQUIN, Louisa (Rev. Soeur Marie-Valentine)
Canadian teacher and composer. b. Province of Quebec, 1865; d. 1950. She composed sacred music.
Ref. 347

PARADIS, Maria Theresia von
Austrian organist, pianist, singer, teacher and composer. b. Vienna, May 15, 1759; d. Vienna, February 1, 1824. The daughter of Joseph Anton, an imperial councillor, she was a god-child of Empress Maria Theresa. Although blind from early childhood, she first appeared in concert at the age of 11, singing and playing her own organ accompaniment. She studied the piano under Richter of Holland and Kozeluch, singing under Salieri and Righini and composition under Friberth and the Abbe Vogler. Under the Empress's patronage she performed at the court and the Concerts Spirituels in Paris in 1784. In London she played before the King, the Queen and the Prince of Wales; the last accompanied her in a cello concerto. She performed in professional concerts and then in a concert of her own. After visiting Brussels and the important German courts, she returned to Vienna. She performed twice at the Tonkuenstler-Societaet concerts and then devoted herself to composition. She used a system of notation invented for her by a friend, J. Riedinger. After her father's death she founded a music school for girls and taught singing and the piano until her death. Mozart wrote his *Piano concerto in B-Flat, No. 18* for her. DISCOGRAPHY.
Compositions
ORCHESTRA
Two piano concertos
CHAMBER
Piano trio
Sicilienne (vln and pf; also vla and pf; also vlc and pf; also vln ens)
Sonata for piano and violin (Vienna: Hofmeister, 1800)
PIANO
Fantasie
Four sonatas (1778)
Six sonatas, op. 1 (Paris: Imbault, 1791)
Six sonatas, op. 2 (Imbault, 1791)
Toccata in A
VOCAL
Deutsches Monument Ludwig's des Unglueckl inchen, funeral cantata for the anniversary of the death of Louis XVI (J. Riedinger) (solo, ch and pf) (1793)
Grosse Cantate zum Besten der Kaiserlichen Soldatenwitten (1794)
Trauercantate auf Leopold den Gutigen (1791)
Auch die Damen, welche statt Gold Leinwand zupfen (S and pf)
Leonore, ballad (Burgher) (1791)
Lied auf Maria Theresia Paradis' Blindheit (G. Pfeffel) (1785)
Twelve Italian songs (London: Bland, 1790)
Zwoelf Lieder auf ihrer Reise in Musik gesetzt (Leipzig: Breitkopf, 1786)
OPERA
Ariadne auf Naxos, in 2 acts (composer)
Rinaldo und Alcina (L. Baczko) (1797)
OPERETTA
Der Schulkandidat, mourning cantata (1792)
THEATRE
Ariadne und Bacchus, drama in 1 act (1791)
Bibliography
Komorzynski, E. *Mozart und Maria Theresia Paradis. Mozart-Jahrbuch.* Salzburg, 1952.
Nicks, F. *Maria Theresia Paradis. Monthly Music Record*, January, 1913.
Pollak-Schlaffenberg, I. *Die Wiener Liedmusik von 1778-1789.*
Ullrich, H. *M.T. Paradis and Mozart. Music and Letters*, October 1946.
Ullrich, H. *M.T. Paradis und Mozart. Oesterreichische Musik Zeitschrift.* 4, 1949.
Von Goeckingk, G. *Journal von und fuer Deutschland S. Stueck.* 1789.
Ref. Andrea Maxwell (Helicon Nine), 2, 14, 15, 17, 22, 26, 41, 44, 65, 68, 70, 74, 95, 100, 102, 103, 105, 108, 113, 119, 127, 128, 129, 132, 226, 260, 276, 297, 307, 335, 361, 368, 400, 405, 563, 653

PARASKEVAIDIS, Gracela
Argentine composer. b. 1940. DISCOGRAPHY.
Composition
VOCAL
E desidero solo colori (ch)

PARCELLO, Marie
19th-century American composer.
Compositions
VOCAL
Songs mainly for contralto voice incl.:
Gaelic lullaby
Good night
My garden
You charm me
Ref. 276, 292

PARENTE, Sister Elizabeth
20th-century American organist, pianist, choir conductor, teacher and composer. She studied under Professor Thompson at the Georgia Court College and Leslie Hodgson at the New York College of Music. She also studied at the Catholic University and under William Pollack. She was the head of the music department at Villa Victori Academy, Trenton, teaching the organ, the piano, voice and choir. She conducted choirs on radio, television and in concert.

Compositions
PIANO
Fairyland waltz
Frolic
Mitzie's rendezous
Silver waters
Sunbeams
Waltz with me
SACRED
Ave Maria
Mass in honor of Our Lady of Victory
ARRANGEMENTS
Sunrise, arrangement of Serenade of the Roses
Ref. 494

PARGETER, Maud (pseud. Wyatt Pargeter)
English composer.
Composition
CHAMBER
Quartet in G
Ref. 226

PARGETER, Wyatt. See PARGETER, Maud

PARIS, Ella Hudson (pseud. Hualalai)
Early 20th-century Hawaiian translator and composer. The daughter of missionaries, she was a trained musician, a fluent speaker of the Hawaiian language and translated and composed numerous hymns.
Ref. 438

PARIS (Parys), Salomea
Polish harpist, pianist, singer and composer. b. 1800. She studied at the Warsaw Conservatory and from 1821 gave concerts of her own compositions in Warsaw.
Compositions
PIANO
Variations on a theme from Cherubini's opera Fanisca (1822)
THEATRE
Kazimierz Wielki (J.A. Niemcewicz)
Konstanty ksiaze ostrogski (Niemcewicz)
Zygmunt I (Niemcewicz)
Ref. 35, 465

PARK, Edna Rosalind
19th-century American composer. b. Boston. She studied under Lambert.
Compositions
VOCAL
Songs incl.:
Alone I found it on a vine
The cloistered rose
The clouds came upon a summer day
Love (Enoch)
A memory (Enoch)
My Jean
Nightingale and the rose
Rainbows
Romaika (Ditson)
The rose that grew in the nun's white window
The shamrock
Sprays of heather, 5 songs (Enoch)
Sunset
Tarry with me
Tho' cruel fate should bid us part
Thou art so like a flower
A thought (Enoch)
Through Erin's Isle to sport awhile
With a rose (Enoch)
Young rose
Ref. 226, 276, 292, 297, 433

PARK, Jane
19th-century British composer.
Composition
PIANO
The Ettrick Forest quadrilles and waltz (Edinburgh: Small, Bruce & Co., 1835)
Ref. British Library (London)

PARK, Maria Hester. See PARKE, Maria Hester

PARKE, Dorothy
20th-century British composer.
Compositions
VOCAL
By winding roads
The road to Ballydare (John Irving) (vce and pf) (Roberton, 1939)
Song in exile (Irving) (vce and pf) (Roberton, 1939)
Ref. MLA *Notes* March 1984

PARKE (Park), Maria Hester
English pianist, singer and composer. b. London, 1775; d. London, August 15, 1822. She was the daughter of the oboist John Parke, who taught her singing and the piano. She made her debut as a pianist in 1785 and as a singer in 1790, at the Gloucester Festival.
Compositions
ORCHESTRA
Concerto, op. 4 (also pf or hpcd and strs) (London: 1795)
Concerto, op. 6 (also hpcd or pf) (London: 1795)
CHAMBER
Divertimento (vln and pf) (1811)
Two grand sonatas, op. 3 (vln and pf) (London: 1795)
Two sonatas, op. 4 (pf or hpcd) (London: Longman & Broderip, ca. 1794)
Two sonatas, op. 13 (vln and pf) (1801)
Violin pieces
PIANO
A set of glees .... with the dirge in Cymbeline, op. 3 (London: Birchal & Andrews, ca. 1790)
Sonata, op. 7 (London: L. Lavenu, 1796)
Three grand sonatas, op. 1 (1790)
Two sonatas, op. 2 (1794)
VOCAL
Arias
Popular songs
Ref. 6, 8, 14, 65, 128, 226, 276, 335, 347

PARKER, Alice
American arranger, orchestral conductor, lecturer and composer. b. Boston, December 16, 1925. She studied under Robert Shaw and Julius Herford at Smith College, where she obtained a B.A. in 1947. She studied under Vincent Persichetti at the Juilliard School of Music and received an M.S. in 1949. She taught at several schools from 1968 to 1973 and lectured at Yale and Northwestern Universities. From 1948 to 1967 she was an arranger for the Robert Shaw Chorale and then became artistic director of Melodious Accord. She received an honorary doctorate from Hamilton College in 1979, ASCAP awards from 1968 to 1979, a National Endowment for the Arts composers' award in 1974, an American Music Center Fellow of Macdowell and Millay Colonies award and is an honorary member of Sigma Alpha Iota. She worked as a freelance conductor, teacher and workshop leader. She married the baritone Thomas Pyle. She composes only on commission for performance. DISCOGRAPHY. PHOTOGRAPH.
Compositions
CHAMBER
String quartet in D (1968)
Suite (fl and gtr) (1966)
Cello sonata
Double dances (org) (1972)
PIANO
Sonata (1953)
Suite (1965)
VOCAL
Commentaries, cantata, poems (Emily Dickinson) (vces and orch)
Christopher Dock, cantata (soli, ch, recs and strs) (1966)
The sing-song of Old man Kangaroo, cantata (soli, narr, ch, double-reeds, perc and audience) (1971)
Journeys: Pilgrims and strangers (ch and orch) (Chapel Hill: Hinshaw Music, 1979)
Now glad of heart (Bar, mix-ch and orch or pf) (1959)
Away, melancholy (w-ch and perc) (Boston: E.C. Schirmer, 1973)
Carmine Pu-Ursi (ch) (1967)
Hellos and goodbyes (mix-ch and pf) (Fischer, 1976)
Love songs (mix-ch and pf) (1977)
Play on number (w-ch and pf) (Schirmer, 1973)
Songs for Eve (mix-ch and str qrt) (Hinshaw, 1976)
The true use of magic (Wesley) (mix-ch and pf) (1976)
The true use of music (mix-ch and pf) (Hinshaw, 1977)
Oh! (m-vces and org) (1969)
Brief seasons (4 vces and 5 insts) (1973)

Angels supposedly (Pyle) (S, A and pf) (1974)
Echoes from the hills, 7 songs (E. Dickinson) (S and ens) (1979)
Five fragments (Bar and ob) (1969)
Four songs (Robert Frost) (m-S and pf) (1968)
A Gnasherie: Three springs and a fall, 4 duets (m-S, Bar and hpcd) (1971)
In praise of singing
Of Irlande (Bar and pf) (1979)
Songs for Sunday, collections (S, A and pf)
Three lyrics (T, fl, cl and vla) (1949)
Three play-party songs
SACRED
Christmas music (mix-ch and orch)
Seven carols for Christmas (mix-ch and orch) (1972) (Fischer)
Blessings (mix-ch) (1965) (Lawson-Gould, 1971)
Come, let us join (mix-ch)
An Easter rejoining (mix-ch, perc, hp and org) (Schirmer, 1972)
An English mass (2 part ch) (1974)
The feast of ingathering (A, mix-ch, org and opt perc) (1970) (C. Fischer, 1971)
Gaudete: Six Latin Christmas hymns (mix-ch, timp, hp and strs) (1973) (Schirmer)
The Good Shepherd, anthem (mix-ch)
Grace and glory (ch, org and perc) (1967)
I saw a stable (mix-ch, perc and org) (Schirmer, 1969)
I will sing and give praise (S, mix-ch and org or pf) (1977)
O sing the glories (Watts) (mix-ch) (1978)
Prayer (Watts) (double mix-ch) (1971)
Psalm 136 (Bar and mix-ch) (1962)
Psalms of praise (m-ch and perc) (New York: Lawson-Gould, 1966)
A sermon from the mountain (Martin Luther King) (mix-ch, perc, gtr, strs and opt org) (1969) (Schirmer, 1971)
Six hymns to Doctor Watts (mix-ch) (1975)
Thou shalt call thy walls salvation, anthem (T, ch and strs) (1967)
Let brotherly love continue (2-6 vces and opt acc) (1972)
Sunday rounds (2-6 vces and opt acc) (1974)
OPERA
A Family Reunion, backyard opera (1975)
The Martyr's Mirror, sacred opera (Schirmer, 1971)
The Ponder Heart (Eudora Welty)
ARRANGEMENTS
Over 250 folk songs
Hymns, carols and spirituals
Publications
Music Reference Crammer. *Dictionary of Music*. New York: Doubleday, 1964.
Creative Hymn Singing. A guide to choral arranging through improvisation.
Ref. composer, 142, 146, 228, 280, 433, 468, 474, 494, 563, 622, 625, 646, 643

PARKER, Mrs.
18th-century Irish composer.
Compositions
PIANO
Hornpipe (Dublin: Hime, ca. 1800)
Malibran waltz (Boston: H. Prentiss, 1841)
Selection of Scottish tunes, strathspeys and reels (also hpcd) (Dublin: Edmund Lee, ca. 1800)
Ref. 65, 228

PARKER, Muriel
20th-century American pianist, lecturer and composer. She studied under Nadia Boulanger (q.v.) in Paris and taught at Western College for Women, Oxford.
Compositions
PIANO
Sonata
Toccata, prelude and fugue
Ref. 226

PARKER, Phyllis Norman
Early 20th-century English composer.
Composition
ORCHESTRA
Ballet piquant: Minuet; Sleepy dance; Dance piquant; Dance of the fairies (str orch) (London: Hawkes, ca. 1918)
Ref. 322

PARKHURST, Mrs. A.E. See PARKHURST, Susan

PARKHURST, Susan (nee McFarland) (Mrs. A.E.)
American composer. b. 1836: d. 1918.
Compositions
VOCAL
Patter of the rain (solo, mix-ch and pf) (New York: H. Waters, 1866)
Weep no more for Lily (mix-ch and pf) (Waters, 1864)
Give to me those moonlit hours (S, A and pf) (Waters, 1863)
A home on the mountain (vce and pf) (Waters, 1865)
SACRED
The beautiful angel band (solo, mix-ch and pf) (Waters, 1863)
Angel Mary (vce and pf) (Waters, 1863)
Angels are hovering near (vce and pf) (Waters, 1863)
There are voices, spirit voices (vce and pf) (Waters, 1864)
Ref. Women's music collection - University of Michigan, 228

PARKYNS, Beatrice (nee Crawford)
19th-century English composer. b. Bombay, India.
Compositions
CHAMBER
Pieces incl.:
Berceuse (vln and pf) (Augener)
Mazurka-impromptu (Leonard)
VOCAL
Songs incl.:
Because (Leonard)
In dreams alone (Leonard)
Love, my tears are turned to flowers (Leonard)
A posy of flowers (May Gillington)
A posy of proverbs, 6 songs (Gillington)
Shepherd's love song (Leonard)
Ref. 6, 226, 297, 433

PARMENTIER, Mme. See MILANOLLO, Teresa Domenica Maria

PARPAGLIOLO, Iditta
Italian pianist and composer. b. Rome, 1905. She showed early musical aptitude and composed a piece for a puppet show when still a child. She studied harmony, counterpoint and fugue at the Rome Conservatorio di Santa Cecilia under G. Settaccioli. She graduated in the piano in 1924 having studied under F. Barajardi and in composition in 1927 after studying under O. Respighi.
Compositions
ORCHESTRA
Il risveglio dei fiori
Poemetto
Tema con variazioni, in 8 mvts (1930)
CHAMBER
Pastorale (strs)
Sonata (vln and pf) (Bongiovanni, 1932)
VOCAL
Lyrics (Rome: De Santis)
Other works
Ref. 105

PARR, Patricia
Canadian concert pianist, professor and composer. b. Toronto, June 10, 1937. She made her debut with the Toronto Symphony Orchestra when she was nine. Her teachers included Mana Bates in Toronto, Isabella Vengerova at the Curtis Institute and later Rudolf Serkin. She performed with the New York Philharmonic and the symphony orchestras of Philadelphia, Pittsburgh and Cleveland, with chamber ensembles and as a recitalist. She was a member of the music department at Duquesne University, Pittsburgh and in 1974 became a professor at the University of Toronto. She composed piano pieces.
Ref. 133

PARR-GERE, Florence
20th-century American pianist and composer. She composed orchestral, chamber and piano works and songs.
Ref. 347, 353

PARS, Melahat
Turkish ud player, conductor, singer, teacher and composer. b. Istanbul, 1918. She had a musical education from an early age and studied the ud (a type of lyre) under Fahri Kopuz, later playing her instrument in orches-

tras. In 1944 she won a singing contest held by Ankara radio and worked for them for several years. She conducts the Female Turkish Orchestra on radio and teaches music privately. She composes songs.
Ref. National Council of Turkish Women

PARYS, Salomea. See PARIS, Salomea

PATERSON, Wilma

Scottish broadcaster and composer. b. Dundee, April 24, 1944. She studied at the Scottish Academy of Music and later under Luigi Dallapicolla in Florence. She married the poet and composer John Purser. DISCOGRAPHY.

Compositions

ORCHESTRA

Et in Arcadia ego
Preludio and passacaglia (1979) (comm BBC)

CHAMBER

Quintet (fl, ob, cl, hn and bsn) (1981) (comm Biggar Music Club)
Casida de la rosa (fl, hp and vls) (1977)
Fifies ad Zulus (fl or a-fl, cl and pf or hpcd)
Brueglingen suite (fl and b-cl) (1984) (comm Ian Hamilton Finlay)
Casida de los ramos (vlc and pf)
Casida del llanto (vln and pf)
Preludio, arietta and passacaglia (fl and pf) (1980) (comm Peter Lloyd)
Sonata (fl and pf) (1979)
Ariel (a-fl)
Contexts (fl and perc - 1 player) (1980) (comm David Nicholson)

VOCAL

Secular masque (solos, ch and strs) (1983) (comm John Currie)
From Bermudas (mix-ch and pf) (1980)
Edge (S, hn and pf)
Five poems of Charles d'Orleans (T and hn trio)
Perverse songs (T and pf)
Spring at Wu-Ling (4 vces)
Three poems of Li-Ch'ing-Chao (S, vln and pf)

Publications

A country cup. Drinks prepared with wild plants and herbs. Pelham Books.

Ref. composer

PATINO ANDRADE, Graziela

Argentine pianist, teacher and composer. b. Buenos Aires, February 3, 1920. She studied at the Conservatorio Nacional de Musica y Arte Escenico under J. de Lalewicz and A. Luzzati, the piano under Jorge Fanelli, harmony and composition under Athos Palma, counterpoint under Jose Torre Bertucci and orchestration under Julian Bautista. She graduated in 1945 and taught at various schools until 1962. She was co-founder of the Sociedad Argentina de Educacion Musical.

Compositions

ORCHESTRA

Sinfonia para piano e orquesta
Estados interiores, symphonic suite (1968)
Nieve y fuego, 2 symphonic sketches (1951)
Sinfonia da camera (1955)
Sinfonietta (1954)

CHAMBER

String quartet
Sonata (vln and pf)
Piano pieces

VOCAL

Two song cycles
Songs

Publications

El coro escolar. With Alvano and Valero. Buenos Aires, 1968.
Introduccion a cant coral. Buenos Aires, 1969.
La orquesta escolar. 4 vols. Buenos Aires, 1971.

Ref. 17, 345

PATON, Mary Anne

Scottish harpist, violinist, singer and composer. b. Edinburgh, 1802; d. Chapelthorpe, 1864. She made her operatic debut in London as Suzanna in *Le Nozze di Figaro* in 1822. She composed sacred music.
Ref. 345

PATORNI-CASADESUS, Regina. See CASADESUS, Regina

PATTARINA, Maria

17th-century Italian song composer.
Ref. 465

PATTERSON, Andra

New Zealand composer. b. February 3, 1964. She studied composition at Victoria University, Wellington, 1982 to 1984. She won the New Zealand emergent composers' award in 1984.

Compositions

CHAMBER

Boredom blues (trp, trbs, tba, cl, d-b and pf) (1981)
Wind quintet (1983)
From love to deuce (str qrt) (1981)
Fugue for string quartet (1983)
String quartet (1982)
Humoresque (ob, cl and hn) (1982)
Piece for violin and piano (1984)
The retaliation (vlc and hn) (1981)
Involution (gtr) (1977)
Piece for oboe (1982)

PIANO

Mobile (1982)
Theme and variations (1983)
Two pieces (1983)

VOCAL

Babbling bird (mix-ch) (1983)
Sonnet (S and pf) (1980)
Four songs (S and pf) (1983)

THEATRE

Women of Trachis (ch, fl, trp, vln and vlc) (1983)

Ref. composer

PATTERSON, Annie Wilson (Lurgan, Annie Patterson)

Irish organist, folk-song collector, professor, writer and composer. b. Lurgan, October 27, 1868; d. Cork, January 16, 1939. She studied at Alexandra College, Dublin and the organ under Sir R. Steward at the Royal Irish Academy of Music, obtaining a B.Mus. and a B.A. In 1889 she became the first woman to receive a Doc.Mus. from the National University of Ireland. She was an music examiner from 1892 to 1895 and the organist at various churches in Dublin. From 1904 she was the organist at St. Anne Shandon Church, Cork and in 1924 was appointed professor of Irish music. She founded the Feis Ceoil Irish music festival, held annually since 1897.

Compositions

ORCHESTRA

Irish tone poems
Rallying song of the Gaelic League

VOCAL

An Banban, cantata (soloists, ch and orch)
Finola, Irish cantata (soloists, ch and orch)
The bells of Shandon (ch)
Six original Gaelic songs

SACRED

The raising of Lazarus, cantata (soloists, ch and orch)
St. John's vision, cantata
Psalm 93 (1889)

OPERA

The High-King's Daughter
Oisin

ARRANGEMENTS

Ivernia, Irish airs

Publications

Beautiful song and the singer.
Chats with music lovers. London, 1907.
Great minds in music. London, 1926.
How to listen to an orchestra. London and New York, 1913.
The music of Ireland. London, 1926.
The profession of music. London, 1926.
Schumann. Master musician series. London and New York, 1903.
The story of oratorio. London and New York, 1902.

Ref. 6, 8, 17, 22, 74, 226, 276, 347, 361, 433, 572

PATTI, Adelina (Adela Juana Maria)

Italian operatic singer and composer. b. Madrid, February 10, 1843; d. Craig-y-Nos Castle, Wales, September 27, 1919. Her father was a tenor of Sicilian origin and her Italian mother, Barili, a celebrated singer. Adelina received her first musical education from her sisters and brother. When her family moved to New York she made her first public appearance at the age of seven. She traveled widely in the United States and Europe, singing diverse operatic roles and became known as Divine Adelina. Hanslick described her as the ideal embodiment of Italian music. DISCOGRAPHY.

Compositions
PIANO
Fior di primavera, waltz (4 or 2 hands) (Ascherberg; Gutmann; Joubert; Ricordi; Schirmer)
VOCAL
Songs incl.:
Il bacio d'addio (Byron) (Ascherberg; Ricordi)
Speme arcana, melody (Italian, English, and French) (Ricordi; Schott Frères; Schirmer)
French, English, German, Italian and Spanish arias and melodies incl.:
Espoir secret
Hemmelig Laengsel (Hansen)
Ref. 85, 163, 276, 297, 347, 563, 572, 622

PAUL, Lady Dean. See WIENIAWSKA, Irene Regine

PAUL, Doris A.

American authoress, choral conductor, lecturer and composer. b. Upland IN, August 16, 1903. She received a B.A. in 1926 and a B.Mus.Ed. in 1931 from Taylor University; studied at Northwestern University for three summers and gained an M.M. from the University of Michigan, 1935. She studied at summer workshops under Fred Waring and Olaf Christiansen. She taught in schools and then lectured in voice at Taylor University, 1930 to 1931; was instrumental music lecturer and director of choral groups at Denver University from 1945 to 1947 and lectured at Iowa State Teachers' College. She collaborated with her sister Esther Mary Fuller.

Compositions
VOCAL
Seasonal songs for children
Songs of travel in many lands
SACRED
Christmas bells (ch)
Remember now thy creator (ch)
Thou art my lamp (ch)
Altar of Christmas
Let's sing to God, for children
Of such is the Kingdom of Heaven
Peace
We give thanks
Thirty-eight introits and responses
Ref. 39, 142

PAUL DU CRUCIFIX, Soeur. See LEFEBVRE, Françoise

PAULL, Barberi

American pianist, authoress, conductor, lyricist, psychologist, teacher and composer. b. New York, July 27, 1946. She studied composition at the Manhattan School of Music under Charles Wuorinen, Ludmila Ulehla (q.v.), Elias Tannenbaum and Billy Taylor. At the Juilliard School of Music she studied composition under Hall Overton, Vincent Persichetti and Jacob Druckman and also composition, orchestral and choral conducting. She attended the Berkshire Music Center at Tanglewood in 1972; the Dalcroze School; the Institute of Vocal Arts; Lehman Engel's musical theatre workshop and Herbert Berghof Studios of musical theatre. She studied the classical piano under William Ferruccio, Joseph Prostakoff and Leonid Hambro and the jazz piano under Hall Overton, Billy Taylor and Roland Hanna. In 1975 and 1976 she completed bachelor and master degrees in psychology at New York University; from 1980 to 1982 she pursued studies in theatre and therapy for children at the same university. She uses music theatre techniques working with emotionally disturbed children. She taught children and adults and appeared with her music in interviews and concerts on radio and television. She participates in programs of her own works through the New York State Council of the Arts 'Meet the Composer' program. She founded and directed the Barberi Paull Music Theatre, 1972 to 1975. She received several commissions, fellowships and awards; including the Delius Society composers' award in 1975, the Segall award and ASCAP awards in 1977 and 1979 through 1983; the National Endowment for the Arts composer fellowship in 1982 for outstanding achievement in children's musical theatre. Since 1979 she has been founder and director of Cavu Music Associates; consultants and managers on behalf of other music professionals. PHOTOGRAPH.

Compositions
CHAMBER
String quartet No. 1 (1978)
Interplay I, II, III (fl and pf) (1977)
The man alone (Robert Frost) (pf) (1974) (New York: Alexander Broude)
VOCAL
The Gumdrop Castle village adventure, mini-cantata (mix-ch, elementary perc and pf) (1978)
America, you touch me to my soul (ch and insts) (1979) (Broude)
Christmas Carol (Dickens) (narr, mix-ch, pf and opt insts) (1977) (Broude, 1978)
Christmas go round (ch and insts) (180) (Belwin-Mills)
Every Merry Christmas (mix-ch and pf) (Broude, 1977)
Happy to be me (ch and elec pf) (1974)
My song to sing (ch and insts) (1979) (Belwin-Mills)
Peace and joy and love (mix-ch and pf) (Broude, 1977)
Sheer silver sheen flower sky (mix-ch and pf) (Broude)
Sweet Benjamin (ch and insts) (1979) (Broude)
Welcome to the world (ch and insts) (1981) (Bradley)
Blues for Saeko, 2 songs for dance (1971)
O wind (med-vce and str qrt) (1975) (Broude, 1975) (prize)
Two songs (Bar and pf) (1974)
Two songs (S and pf) (1974)
Numerous songs for children
THEATRE
The Bible, children's musical (1979)
Celebration (music of all idioms and hand-painted projections) (1972)
Close to the sky, children's musical (projections and 12 songs) (1980)
The home of the Gum Drop King, children's musical
In the vast space of the world (m-S, pf or electric pf, perc and projections) (rev with narr, 1974) (Broude, 1975)
The land (Bar, org, pf, perc, lights and projections) (1976)
A song of earth and of the sky (narr, ch, dance, tape, lights and 35mm projections) (1973)
ELECTRONIC
Antifon (pf and tape) (Broude, 1974)
Two songs (trp, pf and elec pf) (1974) (Broude, 1972)
Three lullabies (m-S, gtr and pf or elec pf) (1977)
MULTIMEDIA
Asylum (tape, projections for improvising perf, dancers and players) (1974)
Constellation (processional for soloist, narr, small mix-ch and tape) (1977)
Earth pulse (concrete/elec cantata to be danced) (1971)
A land called the infinity of love (narr, elec tape and strobe lights) (1975)
The mass (concrete tape, 2 perc and projections) (with Professor Art Frank) (1975)
Requiem (tape, perc and projections; also 2 perc) (1975)
Requiem for Greece (elec tape and red light wheel) (1973)
The snow moth (mix-ch, 2 perc and projections) (1974)
Time (concrete/elec ballet and projections) (1971)

Publications
Still a Woman after all these Years: The Life and Times of a Woman Composer.
Contributions to magazines and journals incl. a series of articles in *Serendipity Times*, 1976; also *Songwriter*, 1976.
Ref. composer, 142, 228, 474, 494, 622, 625, 643

PAVIA DE MAGALHAES, Isaura (Maria Isaura Belo de Cavalho)

Portuguese concert cellist, professor and composer. b. 1912. She was the daughter of the musician Eduard Henriques Pavia de Magalhaes. She completed her cello studies at the Lisbon Conservatory by winning the first prize, at the age of fourteen. She studied under Adele Heinz, Jose Henriques dos Santos, Tomaz Borba and Costa Ferreira and later under Professor Maurice Eisenberg and Koechlin in Paris. She worked and toured as a concert cellist and at 21 became professor of the cello at the Lisbon Conservatory. She was later a visiting professor at the London International Cello Center. In 1961 she won the Calouste Gulbenkian Bursary for study in Switzerland and studied under Casals and Eisenberg. She married the singer Jose Eurico Lisbõa.

Compositions
ORCHESTRA
Fantasia arabe, symphonic poem
VOCAL
Fifteen Lieder (Portuguese poets) (vce and pf)
Ref. 268

PAYNE, Harriet

American violinist, concert violist, lecturer and composer. b. Indianapolis, December 31, 1911. She studied the violin under Hugh McGibney at Indianapolis Conservatory from 1924 to 1930, Herbert Butler at Chicago from 1930 to 1932 and Emil Heermann in Cincinnati, 1933 to 1936. She studied composition under Leo Sowerby at the American Conservatory, Chicago and gained her B.M. in 1931 and M.M. in 1932. She also studied composition under Eugene Goossens in Cincinnati and London, 1934 to 1937. She played with leading orchestras from 1937 and was on the faculty of the

Arthur Jordan Conservatory from 1938 to 1943 and the School of Music, University of Southern California, 1944 to 1945. Some of her compositions were performed at the 1937 Saratoga Festival. She composed viola and violin concertos, for chamber ensembles, the viola and piano and the violin and piano.
Ref. 226, 496

PAYNE, Maggi

American flautist, filmmaker, lecturer, photographer and composer. b. Temple, TX, December 23, 1945. She studied the flute at Northwestern University (B.M.) in 1968 and at the University of Illinois (M.M.) in 1970. She received a M.F.A. (electronic music and recording media) in 1972 from Mills College, Oakland. In 1970 she obtained a fellowship and teaching assistantship at Mills College and lectured in recording engineering at their center for contemporary music. She is also the artist-in-residence at the Exploratorium, San Francisco, teaching sound design. She received several grants and fellowships, is a member of Pi Kappa Lambda and was a second prize winner at the 3rd International competition for electroacoustic music in 1982. Her works have been performed in the United States and Europe. DISCOGRAPHY. PHOTOGRAPH.

Compositions

CHAMBER
- Ametropia (fl) (1970)

ELECTRONIC
- Flights of fancy (1985)
- Hum (fl and tape) (1973)
- Noms de plume (tape) (1984)
- Sirocco (fl and tape) (1983)
- Shimmering (1985)
- Subterranean network (1985) (comm Hart College, Hartford University)

MULTIMEDIA
- Allusions (dancers, lighting, video and tape) (1974)
- Blue metallics (tape, film or slides) (1980)
- Circular motions (tape and video) (1981)
- Crystal (tape, video and slides) (1982)
- Farewell (tape and slides) (1975)
- Ling (tape and slides) (1981)
- Lunar dusk (tape and slides) (1979)
- Lunar earthrise (tape and slides) (1978)
- Orion (film) (1973)
- Rising (tape and slides for dancers) (1980)
- Solar wind (tape, video and slides) (1983) (Mellon Grant, 1983; Rocky Mountain film center grant, 1984)
- Spheres (tape and slides) (1977)
- Spirals (tape and slides) (1977)
- Ten (tape and video) (1982)
- Transparencies (tape and slides) (1976)
- VDO (video) (1973)

THEATRE
- Music for Shakespeare's A Winter's Tale (1975)
- Dance music for Carolyn Brown's House Party (1974)
- Dance music for Carolyn Brown's Synerg II (1974)

MISCELLANEOUS
- White night (comm Ed. Tannenbaum)

Ref. composer, 622, 625, 643

PAZZINI, Carolina. See UCCELLI, Carolina

PEACOCK, Mary O'Kelley

American pianist, accompanist, writer and composer. b. St. Joseph, MI, March 8, 1905. She gained her B.A. (piano) from Meredith College in 1926. She did further piano study at Meredith preparatory department and music theory and under May Crawford and Mrs. J.W. Ferrell. Mary made her concert debut at Meredith College in 1926. She was a pianist, accompanist and continuity, script and commentary writer for WPTF radio and then program director for WHK radio from 1935 to 1937. She was voted Woman of the Year in 1960 by the Moorestown service club and won first prize for a hymn in 1978 and for a song in 1978 from the New Jersey Federation of Women Clubs.

Compositions

VOCAL
- Fifty songs (Jack and Jill)
- Popular ballads

MISCELLANEOUS
- Love came my way (1936)
- The cool white stars (1936)
- A wreath of holly (1949)
- Three wishing candles (1950)
- Old Kris Kringle (1950)
- The rising of the star (1983)
- Children's plays
- Children's music

Publications
- Plays and stories in *Arrivals and Departures*. 1957.
- Contributions to:
- *A Treasury of Christmas Plays*. 1958.
- *Lazy Circles*. 1980.
- *The Children's Hymnary*. 1968.

Ref. 643

PEAN DE LA ROCHE-JAGU, E. Françoise

French composer. b. Brest, ca. 1820; d. 1871. She composed from an early age but only studied music later, under Berton in Paris.

Compositions

OPERA
- Les deux novices
- Gil Draze (1844)
- La jeunesse de Lully
- Le mousquetaire or Le jeune militaire, or La trahison
- Nell, or Le gabier d'artimon (1844)
- Paul et Julie
- Le reine de l'onde
- Le retour de Tasse
- Simple et coquette
- Le tuteur dupe (1845)

Publications
- *Memoires artistiques de Mlle. Pean de la Roche-Jago, ecrits par elle même*. Paris: Ledoyen, 1861.

Ref. 50, 108, 210, 225, 307, 480

PEARL-MANN (Perelmann), Dora Deborah

American concert pianist, conductor and composer. b. Leningrad, Russia, January 4, 1905. She studied at the St. Petersburg Conservatory; the State Academy of Music, Vienna; the Mozarteum Academy; the Juilliard School of Music; Curtis Institute, Teachers' College, Columbia University and New York University. She also studied under Felix Blemenfeld and Egon Petri. She was conductor of the New York Ladies' Philharmonic Orchestra and the New York Operatic Society. In 1960 she was composer-conductor at Carnegie Hall and then guest conductor of the National Youth Orchestra, Philadelphia. She toured as a pianist, conductor and composer in Israel, the United States and the Orient.

Compositions

ORCHESTRA
- Symphony concertante (pf and orch)
- Israel, Symphony No. 2
- Piano Concerto (winner, American Composers' contest)

PIANO
- Prelude
- Vision victorieuse

VOCAL
- Tone poem (S and orch)

BALLET
- Night violets dream
- The nightingale and the rose

Ref. 39, 84, 94

PEASE, Jessie L.

19th-century American pianist, teacher and composer.

Compositions

VOCAL
- Songs incl.:
- Spring night
- Winter in spring

Ref. 276, 292, 347, 433

PECHWELT, Antoinette. See PESADORI, Antoinette de

PEEK, Betty

20th-century American composer of sacred anthems.
Ref. 40, 347

PEGELOW, Hanna G.

Swedish organist, teacher and composer. b. 1872; d. 1944. She studied at the Conservatory in Stockholm, where she took organist and teacher examinations in 1894 and 1896. She taught in Stockholm from 1907 to 1932.

Compositions
VOCAL
Dur och Moll, collection of school songs
Sma visor (1944)
Other songs
Ref. 642

PEJACEVIC (Pejacsevich), Dora, Countess

Croatian violinist and composer. b. Budapest, Sepember 10, 1885; d. Munich, March 5, 1923. In Zagreb she studied the violin under V. Huml, theory under C. Junek and instrumentation with D. Kaiser. Later she studied composition and the violin in Dresden under P. Sherwood and H. Petri and in Munich under W. Courvoisier. The foundation of modern Croatian chamber and concert music has been attributed to her. There is little folk-music influence in her work but influences of Schumann, Brahms, Grieg and Tchaikovsky are apparent. Her works, totaling about sixty, were performed more frequently abroad than in her own country. DISCOGRAPHY.

Compositions
ORCHESTRA
Symphony in F-Sharp Minor, op. 41 (1916)
Fantasie concertante in D-Minor, op. 48 (pf and orch) (1919)
Piano concerto in G-Minor, op. 33 (1913)
Overture, op. 49
CHAMBER
Piano quintet in B-Minor, op. 40 (1915)
Piano quartet, op. 25 (1909) (Dresden: H. Bock, 1910)
String quartet, op. 31
String quartet, op. 58
Piano trio in C-Major, op. 29 (Rozsavolgyi, 1913)
Sonata, op. 35 (vlc and pf)
Sonata No. 1 in D-Major, op. 26 (vln and pf) (Bock, 1910)
Sonata No. 2, Slavonic sonata in B-Minor, op. 43 (vln and pf) (1918)
PIANO
Barcarolle, op. 4
Berceuse, op. 2
Berceuse, op. 20
Capriccio, op. 47
Capricious mood, op. 54b
Cvijetni vrtlog, op. 45
Humoresque, op. 54a
Impromptu, op. 32a
Mastanja, op. 17
Minuet, op. 18
Nightfall, op. 32a
Nocturne, op. 50, nos 1 and 2
Romance, op. 22
Sest stavaka
Sjecanje, op. 24
Sonata in A-Major, op. 57 (1921)
Sonata in D-Minor, op. 36 (1914)
Two intermezzos, op. 38
Two sketches, op. 44
Zivot cvijeca, op. 19
VOCAL
Songs
Ref. 14, 41, 57, 70, 74, 105, 109, 193, 226

PEJACSEVICH, Dora, Countess. See PEJACEVIC, Dora, Countess

PELEGRI, Maria Teresa

Spanish pianist and composer. b. Barcelona, 1907. She studied the piano under G. Camins and C. Pellicer and harmony, counterpoint and fugue under J. Poch; 20th-century music under C. Guinovart and composition under J. Soler. Her compositions made frequent use of dodecaphonic series. DISCOGRAPHY.

Compositions
ORCHESTRA
Cuatro ideas en cien compases (1976)
Poeme sinfonico (1978)
Prelude (1979)
Tres piezas para orquesta (1976)
Variaciones para orquesta (1976)
CHAMBER
Dos piezas para viola y 5 instrumentos (vla, cl, ob, bsn, hp and cel) (1978)
Cuarteto para musica XXI (cl, vla, vlc and pf) (1979)
String quartet (Alpuerto, 1974)
Musica para piano, contrabajo y percussion (1977)
Trio (cl, vln and pf) (1977)
Pieza para clarinete (1977)
Praeludium fuer Marimba (Zimmermann, 1978)
ORGAN
Memento (1974)
Praeludium und Tiento (1975)
Triptic Celeste (1977)
PIANO
Impromptus (1978)
Tres piezas
VOCAL
Aria del espejo (S and orch) (1979)
Infant joy; Spring (Blake) (mix-ch) (1976)
Quatre Chançons Sentimentales (Apollinaire, Baudelaire, Supervielle, Verlaine) (S and pf) (1975)
SACRED
Pater Noster (Bar and org) (1976)
Requiem (A, S, T, B, fl, org and vlc) (1976)
OPERA
Herodes und Mariamne (Hebbel) (1979)
Ref. Otto Harrassowitz (Wiesbaden)

PELLECIER-PAPAVOINE, Mme. See PAPAVOINE, Mme.

PELLEGRINI CELONI, Anna

Italian pianist, singer, teacher and composer. b. Rome, ca. 1780. Her teaching work was praised by composers and teachers. Primarily a singing teacher, she also composed songs for teaching.

Publications
Grammatica del bel cantare. Translated into German. Reprinted 1817.
Musica. 1822.
Ref. 502

PENGILLY, Sylvia

British lecturer and composer. b. London, March 23, 1935. She graduated from the Guildhall School of Music, London, then moved to the United States in 1957 and studied under James Waters at Kent State University to gain her M.A. (composition) and under Paul M. Palombo to receive a D.M.A. (composition) from the University of Cincinnati. She lectured at Kent State University from 1971 to 1973 and currently lectures at, and is in charge of the electronic music studio, at the Loyola University, New Orleans. She worked on laser technology in music from 1975. PHOTOGRAPH.

Compositions
CHAMBER
Degrees of entropy (wind ens) (1973)
String quartet (1973)
VOCAL
Hommage to Moebius (mix-ch and inst ens) (1978)
Three poems of Emily Dickinson (vce and pf) (1973)
The windhaven (vce and pf)
BALLET
The pie man (soloists and orch) (1978)
ELECTRONIC
Canon for forty voices (tape)
Lament (w-vces and tape) (1974)
Premonitions (fl, vlc, pf and tape) (1982)
Three movements of agony (b-cl, fl and tape) (1979)
Weep for infinity (vln, vla, vlc and tape) (1977)
MULTIMEDIA
Incantation (perc, syn and laser) (1978)
Sonus fluens (laser and sound)
Ref. composer, AWC newsletter (1980), 142

PENN, Marilyn

20th-century American composer.

Composition
VOCAL
Songs of empowerment (vces and pf) (1983)
Ref. AMC newsletter

PENNA, Catherine (Mrs. M. Hooper)

English soprano and composer. d. June 6, 1894. She was the daughter of the baritone and writer Frederic Penna. She composed organ pieces and songs.
Ref. 6, 85, 347

PENNER, Jean Priscilla

Canadian pianist, violinist, choral conductor, contralto, teacher and composer. b. Scott, Saskatchewan, January 10, 1912. She attended the Eastman School of Music and the University of Vermont. She won a scholarship to study singing at the University of Saskatchewan. In 1948 she moved to Trinidad, where she taught and led a church choir. In 1956 she returned to Montreal, teaching in schools till 1965 and attending McGill University, studying composition and counterpoint under Kelsey Jones. Her husband's career led to her living in several countries until 1973, when she settled in Canada and studied composition under Elliot Weisgarber at the University of British Columbia. She is an A.T.C.M. in teaching and performing (voice, piano and violin.). PHOTOGRAPH.

Compositions

CHAMBER

Clouds (vla and pf) (1980)
Reverie (vln and vla) (1980)
Waltz (vla and pf) (1980)

PIANO

Nine short pieces (1980)
Two studies (1980)

VOCAL

Gai lon la (mix-ch)
I meant to do my work today (w-ch) (1980)
I sing of a maiden (mix-ch) (1979)
The last room (T and ch) (1982)
Solitude (mix-ch and pf) (1981)
Songs incl.:
Drink to me only (1981)
Gentle lady (1979)
My love is in a light (1981)
Nod (1979)
Over the roofs (1981)
Rose of Tralee (T and vln obl) (1982)
To the moon (1979)
Songs for children

ARRANGEMENTS

For the Aeolian singers of Halifax:
Un Canadien errant (1980)
Nova Scotia song (w-ch) (1980)

Ref. composer, Assoc. Canadian Women Composers

PENTLAND, Barbara Lally

Canadian pianist, lecturer and composer. b. Winnipeg, January 2, 1912. She started composing at the age of nine and had her first lessons in theory and composition in Paris under Cecile Gauthiez, 1929 to 1930. She continued her lessons by correspondence from Winnipeg for 18 months. In 1936 she was awarded a fellowship in composition to the Juilliard School of Music, where she studied under Frederic Jacobi and Bernard Wagenaar, graduating in 1939. In 1941 and 1942 she attended the Berkshire Music Center and studied under Aaron Copland (composition) and Eve Clare (piano). She lectured at the Royal Conservatory of Toronto from 1943 to 1949 and the University of British Columbia, Vancouver, from 1949 to 1963. In 1956 and 1957 she attended the Darmstadt Ferienkurse. In May 1956 her *String quartet No. 2* was chosen for the ISCM World Festival in Stockholm. She received a centennial medal from the Canadian Government in 1967 and a bronze medal at the XIV Olympiad, 1948. DISCOGRAPHY. PHOTOGRAPH.

Compositions

ORCHESTRA

Symphony No. 1 (1948)
Symphony No. 2 (1950)
Symphony No. 3 (10 insts) (1957)
Symphony No. 4 (1959)
Symphony for 10 parts (cham orch)
Variations concertante (pf and orch) (1970)
Concerto (baroque org and str orch) (1949)
Concerto (pf and str orch) (1956)
Concerto (vln and small orch) (1942)
Concerto-overture (1935)
Arioso and rondo (1971)
Ave atque vale (1951)
Cine-scenes (cham orch) (1968)
Colony music (pf and str orch) (1947)
Five-plus (str orch) (also pf) (1968)
Holiday suite (str orch) (1955)
Lament (1939)
Res musica (str orch) (1975) (comm Baroque Strings, Vancouver)
Ricercar (str orch) (1938)
Strata (str och) (1964)
Two pieces (str orch) (1964)
Variations on a Boccherini tune (1948)

CHAMBER

Octet (fl, ob, cl, bsn, 2 hn, trp and trb) (1950)
Septet (hn, trp, trb, org, vln, vla and vlc) (1967)
Weekend overture (perc, pf and winds) (1949)
Interplay (free b-acdn and str qrt) (1972)
Quartet (pf and str trio) (1939)
String quartet No. 1 (1945)
String quartet No. 2 (1953)
String quartet No. 3 (1969)
Canzona (fl, ob and hpcd) (1961)
Trio (vln, vlc and pf) (1963)
Trio con alea (vln, vla and vlc) (1966)
The devil dances (cl and pf) (1939)
Duo (vla and pf) (1960)
Mutations (vlc and pf) (1972)
Sonata (vlc and pf) (1943)
Sonata (vln and pf) (1946)
Vista (vln and pf) (1945)
Cavazzoni (d-b) (1961)
Little scherzo (hpcd)
Ostinato and dance (hpcd) (1962)
Phases (cl) (1977)
Sonata (vln)
Sonatina (fl)
Variations (vla) (1965)

ORGAN

Ostinato (1938)
Prelude, chorale and toccata (1937)

PIANO

Sonata (2 pf) (1953)
Three duets (after pictures by Paul Klee) (2 pf) (1959)
Canadian folk songs (4 hands) (1963)
Allegro vivace (1965)
Artica, 4 pieces (1973)
Aria (1954)
Caprice (1965)
Dirge (1948) (Berandol Music)
Echoes 1 and 2 (1964) (Waterloo Music)
Ephemera: Angelus; Spectra; Whales; Choral reef; Persiflages (1978)
Fantasy (1962) (Berandol)
Five preludes (1938)
For Helen (1947)
Freedom march (1963)
From long ago: Lone traveler; Obstinate tune flight (1946)
Hands across the C (1965) (Waterloo)
Interlude (1955) (Waterloo)
Little pieces (1946)
Maze/Labyrinthe, Case-tette/Puzzle (1968) (Waterloo)
Mirror study (1952)
Music of now, books 1, 2 and 3 (1970) (Waterloo)
Promenade (1940)
Puppet show (1964) (Berandol)
Rhapsody (1939)
Sad clown/ Song of sleep (1949)
Shadows/Ombres (1964) (Waterloo)
Signs, 4 pieces (1964)
Six pieces for children (1939)
Sonata (1936, 1945)
Sonata in C-Minor (1930)
Sonata Fantasy (1947)
Sonatina No. 1 and 2 (1951)
Space studies (1967) (Waterloo)
Studies in line (1941) (Berandol)
Suite borealis (1966)
Ten for ten (1967)
Tenebrae (1976)
Three pairs (1964) (Berandol)
Toccata (1958) (Berandol)
Two preludes (1935)
Variations (1942)
Vinicula (1983)
Vita brevis

VOCAL

Ballads of trees and the master (mix-ch) (1937)
Dirge for a violet (mix-ch) (1939)
Salutation of the dawn (mix-ch) (1954)
Three sung songs (mix-ch) (1965)
What is a man? (mix-ch) (1954)
Epigrams and epitaphs (4 vces) (1952)
At early dawn (T, fl and vlc) (1932)
A lavender lady (vce and pf) (1932)
Ruins (vce and pf) (1932)
Song cycle (S and pf) (1945)
Sung songs No. 4 and 5 (med-vce and pf) (1971)
They are not long (vce and pf) (1935)
Unvanquished (T and pf) (1940)

BALLET

Beauty and the beast, ballet pantomime (2 pf) (1940)

OPERA

The Lake, chamber opera in one act (1952)

INCIDENTAL MUSIC
Air bridge to Asia, radio (1944)
Payload, radio (1940)
The wind of our enemy, radio (1941)
The living gallery, film (1947)
Reflections (free b-acdn) (1971)
ELECTRONIC
News (vce, tape and orch) (1970)
MISCELLANEOUS
Tellus (1983)

Bibliography

Composers of the Americas. Vol. 6. Washington, DC: Pan American Union, 1960.
Gillespie, John. *Five Centuries of Keyboard Music: An Historical Survey of Music for Harpsichord and Piano*. Belmont, CA: Wadsworth Pub. Co., 1965.
Eastman, Sheila and McGee, Timothy J. *Barbara Pentland*. University of Toronto Press, 1983.
Kallma, Helmut. *Pentland, Barbara*. Die Musik in Geschichte und Gegenwart 10: 1020-1021.
Pentland, Barbara. 1965 supplement to Baker's Biographical Dictionary of Musicians. 5th ed. p. 101.
Ref. 5, 22, 31, 52, 55, 63, 70, 77, 93, 94, 131, 133, 140, 206, 288, 329, 402, 422, 477, 563, 622, 624, 631, 643

PEPARARA, Laura

15th-century Italian harpist, singer and composer. She was a member of the 'Concerto of Ladies' at the Este court at Ferrara. She often recited verse to her own harp accompaniment. She was a friend of Tasso, the poet, and composed songs.
Ref. 264, 433, 502

PERALTA CASTERA, Angela

Mexican pianist, operatic singer and composer. b. Puebla, July 6, 1845; d. Matzatlan, Sinaloa, August 30, 1883. She was a child prodigy and studied singing under Augustin Balderas, solfege under Manuel Barragan and the piano and composition under Cenobio Paniagua at his academy. She made her debut at the age of 15 in the part of Leonora in Verdi's *Il Trovatore* and in 1861 left Mexico for a European study tour. In Spain she acquired the name of *El Ruisenor Mexicano*. In Italy she studied voice under Francesco Lamperti and made her Italian debut at La Scala of Milan at the age of 17. She toured Europe, North and South America, and Cuba. In Mexico she premiered the operas *Ildegonda* in 1866 and *Gino Corsini* in 1877 by Melesio Morales and *Guatimotzin* by Aniceto Ortega. She organized the Mexican premiere of Verdi's *Requiem* in 1877 in memory of three noble liberators, Juarez, Lincoln and Thiers. She formed her own opera companies in 1872 and 1877.

Compositions

PIANO
Diecinueve canciones de salon, 19 pieces (1875)

Bibliography

Castera, Manuel Peralta. *Biography of Angela Peralta*.
Velasquez, Guillermo Orta. *Breve historia de la musica*. Mexico: Libreria de M. Porrua, 1970.
Ref. 74, 82

PERCHERON, Suzanne

19th-century composer.

Compositions

VOCAL
Marquise jolie, melody (F. de Forban) (Ricordi)
Roses d'amour, melody (J. de la Vandere) (Ricordi)

PEREIRA, Diana Maria

Danish pianist, teacher and composer. b. Colombo, Sri Lanka, February 20, 1932. She was educated in London and in 1954 entered the Royal Danish Conservatory, studying the piano, musical theory and history and composition under Professor Vagn Holmboe. She became the accompanist pianist at the conservatory. She teaches at the Hoersholm Music School, contributes to the *Danish Musical Times* and is a member of the Unge Tonekunstner Selskab and KODA. She received three working scholarships from the Danish National Art Fund. DISCOGRAPHY.

Compositions

CHAMBER
Exercises in metamorphosis III (str qrt) (1967)
PIANO
Exercises in metamorphosis I and II (1966)
I'm still alive: preludio
Sonata No. 1, in 3 phases (1978)
Sonata No. 2, op. 3 (1979)
Sonata No. 3
Ref. Danish Composers' Assoc., 77

PEREIRA DA SILVA, Adelaide

Brazilian pianist, lecturer and composer. b. Rio Claro, 1938. She studied the piano under N. de Sousa and H. Bruch, musical analysis and counterpoint under O. Lacerda and composition under C. Guarnieri. After several years as a pianist she turned to teaching. She lectured on Brazilian music; literature and music structure at the Faculdade de Musica Marcelo Tupinamba; on harmony at the Escola Superior de Musica Santa Marcelina and the Faculdade Santa Cecila, São Paulo. She won prizes and honors.

Compositions

CHAMBER
Acalanto (fl and pf) (1974) (Brazil: Ricordi, 1975)
Sonatina (vln and pf) (1976)
Ponteio No. 1 (vla)
PIANO
Caleidoscopio de rosa e azul
Cantigi ingenua
Ponteio No. 2 (1962) (Ricordi, 1965)
Ponteio Nos. 4 and 5 (Ricordi)
Suite No. 1, 5 pieces (Ricordi, 1966)
Suite No. 2, 4 pieces (Irmãos Vitale, 1966)
Suite No. 3 (1977)
Valsa choro No. 1 (1962)
Valsa choro No. 2 (Ricordi)
VOCAL
Canto palista (mix-ch a-cap) (1963)
Coros infantis brasileiros (ch) (1977)
Ogum Dile, in 4 mvts (ch and perc ad lib)
Reza de Umbanda (mix-ch and perc ad lib) (1971)
Songs incl.:
As dadivas (1976)
Ciclo de 3 cancões
Conceitos (1967)
Marimbond caboclo (1977)
O anel de vidro
Se
Volta
Veio de longe
Ref. A. Pedigo (Booneville, AK), University of São Paulo

PERELLI, Natalie

19th-century composer.

Compositions

OPERA
Il contrabbandiere (1842)
Galeotto Manfredi (1839)
Osti et non osti (1840)
Ref. 465

PERELMANN, Dora. See PEARL-MANN, Dora Deborah

PERERA, Carmen

Compositions

PIANO
Per far l'amor, op. 10, Venetian barcarolle
VOCAL
Canto di amoretti, canzone (Ricordi)
Ref. Ricordi (Milan)

PERETZ-LEVY, Liora

Israeli pianist and composer. b. Tiberias, December 10, 1954. She studied under Professor Leon Shidlowsky at the Rubin Academy, obtaining a B.Mus. in 1976 and M.Mus. (artistic diploma) in 1979. She won a scholarship from the American-Israel Cultural Foundation, SHARETT, 1977. In 1979 she became assistant to the musical manager of Habima Theatre, the National Theatre of Israel. PHOTOGRAPH.

Compositions

ORCHESTRA
Sunrise (cham orch) (1978)
Sunset (cham orch) (1977)
PIANO
Three pieces
VOCAL
Cantata (Lorca)
Cantata (Rilke) (ch and orch)
Enigma (S, fl, b-cl, hp and vib) (1st prize, 1976)
Akara (A, ob and pf) (1974)
SACRED
Psalm 22 (m-S, vlc, pf and perc) (2nd prize Rubin Academy, 1975)
Ref. composer

PEREZ, Maria (Balteira, Maria Perez) (La Balteira)
13th-century Spanish singer and composer. She was at the court of Alfonso the Wise. Her character was completely inconsistant; she was immoral, lewd, dissipated and a gambler, but had moments of great penitence when she wished to retire to a convent. She bequeathed an estate to the Cisterian monks at Sobrado, pledged herself to give service to the monastery and gave instructions that on her death she was to be given the ceremonies prescribed to familiars of the monastery. Her constantly proposed and cancelled pilgrimage to the Holy Land, that never proceeded further than Montpellier, inspired Spanish trovadores to write satirical poems about her. Later she was heard of on the Moorish border, fleecing the king's archers and then on the Murcian frontier, consorting with a Moorish chief. Alfonso used her sexual attractions to secure information about his Moorish enemies and was himself one of her greatest admirers. In her old age she changed her mode of living and took up good works. She composed sacred plainsong.
Ref. 465, 639

PEREZ-GIMENEZ, Maria del Carmen. See BARRADAS, Carmen

PERISSAS, Madeleine
French flautist and composer. b. Paris, 1906. She studied the flute under Vidal and Poland-Manuel. DISCOGRAPHY.
Compositions
ORCHESTRA
Bassoon concerto (1948)
Suite romanesque (ob and orch) (1947)
En Auvergne (1940)
Giboulées de printemps (1935)
Suite à danser (str orch) (1939)
CHAMBER
Suite écossaise (wind qnt) (1938)
Prélude, air et quadrille (fl and pf) (1935)
VOCAL
Songs
Folk song arrangements
SACRED
Sainte-Genevieve, oratorio
Magnificat
Motets
THEATRE
Carol of the village (ch and org)
Diablerie (1946)
Legende des deux amants (1937)
L'opera pour rire (1949)
Le queue du diable
Le tambour et la rose (1942)
Ref. 96, 563

PERKIN, Helen
English concert pianist and composer. b. Stoke Newington, February 25, 1909. She became an A.R.C.M. studying under Arthur Alexander and John Ireland and also Anton Webern and E. Steuermann in Vienna. She performed in England, Vienna, Budapest and Germany. DISCOGRAPHY.
Compositions
BRASS BAND
Burlesque
Carnival, suite
Cordell suite
CHAMBER
Fantasy (str qrt)
Pastorale (fl, cl and cor anglais; also str qrt)
String quartet
String trio
Sonata (vlc and pf)
Spring rhapsody (vln)
PIANO
Ballade (1949)
Eleven impressions (1949)
Episode (1935)
Four preludes
Village fair, suite (1930)
VOCAL
Think not of them, cantata (w-vces)
Part songs
Songs
BALLET
Two television ballets
INCIDENTAL MUSIC
Music for films
Ref. 8, 96, 226, 490, 563

PERONI, Wally
Italian organist, pianist, choral conductor, teacher and composer. b. Cirie-Turin, August 23, 1937. She is the grand-daughter of the composer Francesco Angelo Cuneo and was taught the piano by her mother. She gave her first piano recital in duo with her sister Nerina at the age of six. She graduated from the Conservatorio G. Verdi, Turin with diplomas in piano and organ performance, choral direction, composition and orchestration. She did postgraduate studies in the piano and musicology under N. Magaloff at the Accademia Chigiana, Siena and Geza Anda in Zurich. At the Lucerne Conservatory she studied under Mieczyslaw Horszowski and Rudolf Firkusny. She appeared as a soloist and in duos with her sister and her works have been performed throughout Italy and on the radio. She was the founder of the Gruppo Musicale Francesco Angelo Cuneo in 1968 and of a music school in Cirie-Turin in 1969, which she heads. She teaches the piano at the Conservatorio Statale de Musica G. Verdi and is the organizer of postgraduate courses in the piano in the Toscana region. PHOTOGRAPH.
Compositions
CHAMBER
String quartet (1963) (Sindicato Musicisti national prize, 1968)
Preludio, sarabande e finale (str trio) (1973)
Harmonizations of sonatas (vln and pf; also vlc and pf)
Elaborazione di move elementi in forma di variazione (org) (1969)
PIANO
Passacaglia e fuga (2 pf) (1961)
Breve raccolta d esercizi tecnici l'impostamento della mano (1971)
Pezzi facili per le piccole mani, easy pieces (1971)
Raccolta di brani di media difficolta
Sonatina (1963)
VOCAL
Sei liriche (vce and orch) (1966)
Composizioni per coro a capella (1972)
Lyrics (vce and pf) (1972)
Otto liriche (vce and pf) (1966)
Raccolta di bassi, vanti, temi per lo studio della composizione (1968)
SACRED
Cantatas
Dies Irae (ch and orch) (1969)
Masses (1-3 vces and org)
Songs
Ref. composer

PERREIRA DE LACERDA, Bernarda. See LACERDA, Bernarda Ferreira de

PERRELLI, Giuseppina
19th-century Italian composer.
Compositions
ORCHESTRA
Scherzo pastorale, op. 19
Toccata alla corrente, op. 18
PIANO
Bolero, op. 11 (Ricordi)
Le carillon, étude cantilène, op. 3 (Ricordi)
Danse albanaise, op. 4
Fantasies
Grand galop de bravoure, op. 6
Il n'est plus! élegie, op. 6
Marche, processionelle, op. 25
Nocturne, op. 7
Premier adagio de concert sur La Sonnambula, op. 9
Rêverie, op. 32
Rondo fantastico, op. 35
Valse de concert, caprice, op. 5
Transcriptions
SACRED
L'Angelus, op. 22 (vce and pf)
Cantique de Noël, op. 24 (vce and pf)
Salve Regina, op. 23 (vce and pf)
ARRANGEMENTS
Fantaisie sur Il Barbiere di Siviglia, in classical form, op. 12 (pf and orch; also pf)
Fantaisie elegante sur La Favorite, op. 10, in 2 parts (pf and orch; also pf)
Fantaisie militaire sur La Fille du Regiment, op. 8, in 2 parts (pf and orch; also pf)
Ref. 297

PERRIERE-PILTE, Anais, Countess of (nee Marcelli) (pseud. Marulli Anaide)
French composer. b. Paris, 1836; d. Paris, December 1878. Some of her works were published under her maiden name.

Compositions
OPERA
Le dryade (1870)
La grotto del majo
Merlino
Le talon d'Achille
OPERETTA
Le sorcier (1886)
Jaloux de soi, in 1 act (1873)
Les vasances de l'amour, comic opera (1867)
Ref. 26, 105, 276, 297, 347, 433, 465

PERRONNET, Amelie (pseud. Leon Bernoux)

French librettist, poetess and composer. b. ca. 1831; d. Paris, October, 1903. Her romances and songs gained great popularity after interpretation by the singer Anna Judic.

Compositions
VOCAL
Romances
Songs
OPERA
Je reviens de Compiegne, in one act (composer) (1890)
St. Francois
OPERETTA
La chanson de l'aubepin, comic opera
Pulications
Libretto for *La Cigale Madrilene*, composed by her son, Joanni Perronnet.
Libretto for Henri Kowalski's 4-act opera *Gilles de Bretagne*. 1877.
Ref. 105, 226, 276, 465

PERRY, Julia Amanda

Black American pianist, conductor, lecturer and composer. b. Lexington, KY, March 25, 1924; d. Akron, OH, April 24, 1979. She studied voice, the piano and composition under Switten at Westminster Choir College, Princeton, NJ, from 1943 to 1948, where she received a B.M. and M.M.. She did graduate study under Dallapiccola at Tanglewood in 1951 and also at the Juilliard School of Music. In 1952 she went to Paris to study under Nadia Boulanger (q.v.) and continued her study in Florence from 1952 to 1953, and 1955 to 1956. She studied conducting under Carlo Zecchi and Alceo Galliera at the Academia Chigiana in Siena in summers 1956 to 1958. In 1957 she organised and gave a series of concerts sponsored by the United States Information Service in Europe. In 1967 she taught at Forida State University in Tallahassee and in 1969 was visiting music consultant at the Atlanta Colleges Center. She received two Guggenheim fellowships, and an American Academy and National Institute of Arts and Letters fellowship and the Fontainebleau award and the Boulanger Grand Prix for her *Violin Sonata*, 1952. In 1969 she received honorable mention in the ASCAP awards to women composers for symphonic and concert music. In 1973 she had a series of strokes and became paralysed on her right side. However, she managed to teach herself to write with her left hand and continued to compose. DISCOGRAPHY.

Compositions
ORCHESTRA
Symphony No. 1 (1951)
Symphony No. 2 (1960)
Symphony No. 3 (1962)
Symphony No. 4 (1964)
Symphony No. 5 (1965)
Symphony No. 8 (1969)
Symphony No. 9 (1970)
Simple symphony No. 12, Homage to Vivaldi (1973)
Concerto (vln and orch) (1963) (New York: C. Fischer, 1966)
Concerto No. 2 (pf and orch) (1965) (New York: Southern Music)
Contretemps (1963)
Episodes (1973)
Short piece (1952) (Southern Music, 1962)
Study (1952)
SYMPHONIC BAND
Symphony No. 6 (1966) (C. Fischer)
CHAMBER
Homunculus C.F. (10 perc) (1960) (Southern Music, 1966; C. Fischer, 1969)
The beacon (cor anglais, 2 t-sax, 2 bsn and 2 trp) (Southern Music, 1964)
Pastoral (fl and str sextet) (Southern Music, 1962)
String quartet
Violin sonata (1969) (C. Fischer) (prize)
PIANO
Lament (1947)
Pearls on silk (1947)
Suite of shoes (1947)
Three pieces for children
VOCAL
Chicago, cantata (Carl Sandburg) (narr, Bar, mix-ch and orch)
Three warnings, dramatic cantata
Symphony U.S.A., No. 7 (ch and small orch) (1967)
Carillon heigh-ho (composer) (mix-ch) (C. Fischer, 1947)
Is there anybody there? (w-vces) (1947)
Seven contrasts (Bar and cham ens)
La visita
Approx 10 songs
SACRED
Ruth, cantata
Frammenti dalle lettere de Santa Caterina (Italian text) (S, mix-ch and small orch) (New York: Southern Music)
Stabat Mater (m-S or Cont and str orch or str qrt) (ded composer's mother) (1951) (Southern Music, 1954)
Missa brevis (ch and org)
Our thanks to Thee, anthem (composer) (Cont, mix-ch, and org) (Galaxy Music, 1951)
Song of Our Saviour (mix-ch) (1953) (Galaxy Music, 1953)
Ye who seek the Lord, anthem (T, mix-ch and org) (Galaxy, 1952)
Be merciful unto me, O God; Psalm 57: 1, 2 (S, B, mix-vces and org) (1969) (Galaxy, 1953)
The Lord is risen (m-vces) (1947)
Lord, what shall I do? (S and pf) (Boston: McLaughlin & Reilly)
OPERA
The Bottle, in one act (Southern Music, 1953)
The Cask of Amontillado, in one act (Edgar Allan Poe) (Virginia Card – English, German, Italian texts) (Southern Music)
The Selfish Giant, opera-ballet in 3 acts (Oscar Wilde)
Publications
Compendium in Musical Perspective. 1969.
Forty Studies for Classroom Composition. 1970.
Generation Gap in Popular Music. 1969.
Bibliography
Green, Mildred. *A Study of the Lives and Works of Five Black Women Composers in America*. Ph.D. dissertation, University of Oklahoma, 1975.
Ref. 4, 5, 40, 53, 70, 85, 94, 136, 141, 142, 146, 147, 228, 280, 285, 287, 335, 347, 397, 415, 549, 563, 611, 622

PERRY, Marilyn Brown

American pianist, artist, writer and composer. b. Gloucester, MA, February 21, 1937. She composed classical and country music.
Ref. 475

PERRY, Mary Dean

American organist, pianist, choral conductor, assistant professor and composer. b. Scranton, PA, July 3, 1928. She received a B.Mus. cum laude in 1949 and an M.A. in 1953 from Marywood College, Scranton. She did graduate study at the Eastman, Juilliard and Manhattan Schools of Music and Columbia and Temple Universities. She taught the piano from 1956 to 1966 and was the organist and choir conductor of Our Lady of the Snows Church, Clarks Summit, in 1948 to 1974. From 1949 she was assistant professor of music at Marywood College. In 1974 she received an Outstanding Educator of America award.

Compositions
SACRED
Proper of the mass for Christmas Eve (Latin version, 1962; English, 1966)
Proper of the mass for Easter Sunday (1961)
Proper of the mass for Pentecost (1966)
Ref. 77, 206

PERRY, Zenobia Powell

Black American pianist, lecturer and composer. b. Boley, OK, October 3, 1914. She obtained a B.S. from Tuskegee Institute, Alabama in 1938, an M.A. from Northern Colorado University in 1945 and an M.A. from Wyoming University, studying the piano and composition under Alan Willman and Darius Milhaud (composition). She also studied the piano under R. Nathaniel Dett, Gunnar Johansen and Cortez Reece and composition under Charles Jones. She was a faculty member of Arkansas agricultural, mechanical and normal College from 1946 to 1955 and from 1955 a lecturer and composer-in-residence at Central State University.

Compositions
ORCHESTRA
Ships that pass in the night (1953)
BAND
Prelude and dance (1968)
CHAMBER
Three designs for four players (String Quartet, No. 2) (1964)
Four mynymns for three players (fl, cl and pf)
Clarinet sonatina (1963)
Sonatina (pf) (1962)

VOCAL
Atmospheres, song cycle (S and pf)
Narrative (speaker, fl and pf)
Suites on poems by Thomas Hardy
Threnody, song cycle (S and pf)
SACRED
Mass in F-Sharp (S and B) (1969)
Ref. 142, 206

PERRY-BIAGIOLI, Antoinette
French composer. b. 1847.
Compositions
OPERA
Les heroiques (with her brother Henry) (1876)
Les matelots de formidable (with Henry) (1865)
Ref. 431

PERSCHMANN, Elfriede
German choral conductor and composer. b. Schoppenstedt, Brunswick, January 21, 1888. She studied in Berlin and became a choral conductor in 1924. She composed piano and violin pieces, choruses and songs.
Ref. 70, 226

PERUCHONA, Maria Saveria or Xaveria. See PERUCONA, Sister Maria

PERUCONA (Peruchona), Sister Maria Saveria (Xaveria)
17th-century Italian composer. b. Novara. She was a nun in the convent of Sant' Orsola, Galaite in 1675.
Compositions
SACRED
Sacri Concerti di Motetti a una, due, tre e quattro voci, parte con violini e parte senza, op. 1 (Milan: F. Vigone, S. Sebastiano, 1675)
Ref. 2, 105, 128, 653

PERY, M. See PFERDEMENGES, Maria Pauline Augusta

PESADORI, Antoinette de (nee Pechwelt)
German concert pianist and composer. b. Dresden, March 6, 1799; d. Dresden, September 20, 1834. She made her concert debut at the age of 11 and later studied under Dotzauer and Klengel in Dresden and married Pesadori who was a tenor at the Dresden opera.
Compositions
CHAMBER
Pieces (vlc and pf) (with Dotzauer)
PIANO
Pieces incl.:
Introduction et rondeau agreable (Leipzig: Schubert & Niemeyer)
Ref. 26, 276,

PESCARA, Vittoria Colonna. See COLONNA, Vittoria, Duchess of Amalfi

PESCHKA (Peschka-Leutner), Minna (nee Leutner)
Austrian soprano and composer. b. Vienna, October 25, 1839; d. Wiesbaden, January 12, 1890. She studied under Professor and Mrs. Bockholtz-Falconi. She made her singing debut in Breslau in 1856. She composed songs and a set of vocal studies.
Ref. 276, 347, 433

PESCHKLA-LEUTNER, Minna. See PESCHKA, Minna

PESSIAK-SCHMERLING, Anna
Austrian lecturer and composer. b. Vienna, 1834; d. Vienna, March 14, 1896. She studied under Marchesi and taught at the Vienna Conservatory. Several of her masses were frequently performed in Vienna. She composed piano and teaching pieces, choral works, songs, masses and other large sacred works.
Ref. 226, 276, 347, 433

PETERSEN, Else
German pianist and composer. b. Brunswick, April 29, 1874. She composed chamber pieces and songs.
Ref. 226

PETERSEN, Marian F.
American professor and composer. b. Salt Lake City, UT, July 4, 1926. She studied under Leroy J. Robinson at the University of Utah, where she obtained a Ph.D. She became a professor at the University of Missouri in 1972.
Compositions
SACRED
The Revelation, cantata (ch)
OPERETTA
The Wife of Usher's Well
Ref. 142

PETERSON, Melody
American lecturer, journalist and composer. b. Oak Park, IL, February 5, 1942. She studied under Richard Hofmann and Walter Aschaffenburg at Oberlin College. She was a private teacher from 1965 to 1969 and a lecturer at Oberlin from 1968 to 1969. From 1970 she was a music journalist with the Los Angeles Times. In 1967 she won first prize at a North Carolina Federation of Music Clubs contest.
Compositions
CHAMBER
Twice five for two (vln and vlc) (1967)
Prelude and postlude (org)
PIANO
Variations on an original theme (2 pf) (1958)
Prelude and toccata (1963)
VOCAL
Monuments (B) (1972)
Ref. 142, 347

PETRA-BASACOPOL, Carmen
Rumanian writer and composer. b. Sibiu, Sepember 5, 1926. She studied music at the Bucharest Conservatory from 1949 to 1956 under Iaon Chirescu (theory of music), Paul Constantinescu (harmony), Nicolae Biucliu (counterpoint), Mihail Jora and Leon Klepper (composition), Tudor Ciortea (musical form) and Theodor Rogalski (orchestration). She was an assistant from 1962 to 1966 and then head of the department of musical form at Bucharest Conservatory. She wrote numerous articles on music for the Rumanian press. She received a prize at the international competition of the World Youth Festival, Warsaw, 1955, a diploma of honor at the international competition held at Mannheim-Ludwigshafen in 1961 and the George Enescu Composition prize of the Academy of Socialist Republic of Rumania, 1980. In 1969 she received the Order of Cultural Merit and was a member of the jury of the 7th Jerusalem harp competition, 1979. DISCOGRAPHY.
Compositions
ORCHESTRA
Symphony No. 1, op. 6 (1955)
Concerto for cello and orchestra, op. 50 (1982)
Piano concerto, op. 17 (1961)
Violin concerto No. 2, op. 25 (1965)
Concerto for harp, string orchestra and timpani, op. 40 (1975)
Concerto for string orchestra, op. 49 (1981)
Violin concertino, op. 20 (1963)
Jeu de jeunesse (1949)
Tara de piatra, op. 13 (1959)
Triptic simfonic, op. 19 (1962)
CHAMBER
Concertino, op. 30 (hp, wind qnt, d-b and xy) (1969)
Quartet, op. 43 (fl, vln, vlc and pf) (1978)
Tablouri dacice, trio, op. 46 (panpipes, vib and vlc) (1981)
Trio, op. 11 (vln, vlc and pf) (Editura Muzicala, 1958)
Trio, op. 39 (fl, cl and bsn) (1974)
Imagini din Valea Crisului, op. 16, no. 1 (vln and hp) (1960)
Sonata, op. 4 (vlc and pf) (1952)
Sonata, op. 5 (vln and pf) (1954)
Sonata, op. 6 (vln and hp) (Editura Muzicula, 1960)
Sonata, op. 16, no. 2 (fl and hp) (1960)
Suite, op. 3 (fl and pf) (1950)
Trei schite, op. 7, no. 2 (ob and pf) (1956)
Variationi pe o tema macedo-romana, op. 44 (hp and vlc) (1979)
Improvisations, op. 37 (fl) (1973)

Ode, op. 48, no. 1 (d-b) (1980)
Sase preludii, op. 14, no. 2 (hp) (1960)
Sonata pastorala, op. 14, no. 1 (hp) (1960)
Elegy, op. 35 (1972)
Suite for harp, op. 10 (1958)
Suite for cello, op. 48, no. 2 (1981)

PIANO
Rondo, op. 2 (1949)
Douazecipatru imagini pitoresti, op. 7, no. 1, suite for children (Editura Muzicala, 1956)
Impressii din Muzeul satului, op. 15 (Editura Muzicala, 1960)
Imagini marocane, op. 38 (1973)
Metoda de pian (Editura Muzicala, 1959)

VOCAL
Un cintec despre jertfe mari si despre lumina, op. 27, cantata (M. Dumitrescu) (T, m-ch and orch) (1967)
Crengile, op. 25 (M. Dumitrescu) (ch and orch) (1966)
Moartea caprioqrei, op. 26 (N. Labis) (Bar and orch) (1966)
Omagiu vietii, op. 22 (E. Jobeleanu) (B and orch) (Editura Muzicala, 1963)
Pulsatio vitae, op. 33 (ch, cl, hp, xyl, bells and perc) (1970)
Poeme marocane, op. 42 (R. Boissy) (m-S and wind qrt) (1978)
Acuarele argheziene, op, 41, no, 2 (S and pf) (1977)
Anotimpurile, op. 12, no. 2, cycle (N. Cassian) (1959)
Cinci lieduri, op. 18 (T. Arghezi) (S and pf) (1961)
Cinci lieduri, op. 21 (M. Dumitrescu) (T and hp) (1963)
Cintece haiducesti de don, op. 41, no. 1 (Bar and pf) (1977)
Diptych, op. 31, no. 2 (S, ob, cl and hp) (1969)
Doua lieduri, op. 12, no. 1 (M. Dumitrescu) (m-S and pf) (1959)
Doua lieduri, op. 22, no. 2 (B and hp) (1971)
Flori de mucigai, op. 23, no. 2 (T. Arghezi) (1964)
Greierele, op. 23, no. 3 (T. Arghezi) (1964)
Nostalgii, op. 23, no. 1 (L. Blaga) (Bar and cor anglais) (1964)
Ofrande, op. 28 (M. Dumitrescu) (S and pf) (1968)
Primavara, op. 31, no. 1 (M. Dumitrescu) (S, cl and pf) (1969)
Pro pace, op. 34 (E. Jebeleanu) (S, fl and pf) (1971)
Sapte lieduri, op. 8, no. 1 (G. Cosbuc) (vce and pf) (1957)
Songs of life, op. 53 (S and pf) (N. Stainescu) (1984)
Trei lieduri (L. Blaga) (Bar and cor anglais)
Trei lieduri, op. 8, no. 2 (Z. Stancu) (m-S and pf) (1957)

BALLET
Fata si masca, op. 32, in 1 act (N. Coman) (1980)
Mioritza, op. 47, choreographic poem (O. Danovski) (1980)

Ref. 14, 81, 94, 196, 563, 643

PETROVA, Olga Andreyevna

20th-century Soviet composer.

Composition

VOCAL
Istochnik (S, fl, gtr and strs) (Sovietski Kompozitor, 1984)

PETROVA, Mara

Bulgarian conductor and composer. b. Sliven, May 15, 1922. She studied composition under V. Stoyanov and conducting under M. Goleminov at the Bulgarian State Conservatory, graduating in 1947.

Compositions

ORCHESTRA
Tanz-poema, symphonic poem
Mladezhka suita (timp and str orch) (1969)
Moyata rodina, overture (1959)
Youth suite (1953)

CHAMBER
Sofian suite (ob, cl, bsn and drs)
Prelude and dance (wind trio)
Sonata (vln and pf)
Other pieces

PIANO
Children's album
Sonata
Variations

VOCAL
Khristu Botevu, poem (ch a-cap)
Zimna prikazka, poem (ch a-cap)
Mass songs
Children's songs
Choruses
Detski sviat, song cycle (vce and pf)

OPERETTA
Podranilo, for children

Ref. 217, 463

PETROVA-KRUPKOVA, Elena

Czech pianist, lecturer, translator and composer. b. Modry Kamen, November 9, 1929. She married Hanus Krupka, head of the Smetana Library, Prague. She studied the piano under K. Hoffmeister and theory under F. Spilka and musicology and aesthetics at Charles University, Prague, for four terms. She continued to study the piano at the Academy of Arts and Music in Bratislava and later composition under Jan Kapr at the Janacek Academy of Arts and Music in Brno, from which she graduated in 1970. She worked as a dramatist for Czech television and later as a translator. She taught the piano and improvisation at the Ceske Budejovice Pedagogical College. She received numerous prizes, including awards from the Czech Musical Fund in 1968 and the Czech National Competition for vocal music in 1973. DISCOGRAPHY. PHOTOGRAPH.

Compositions

ORCHESTRA
Symphony No. 1 (1970)
Festive prelude (1967)
Passacaglia (1969)

CHAMBER
Quintet for wind instruments (1960)
String quartet No. 1 (1964)
String quartet No. 2 (1968)
Invocation (b-cl and pf) (1972)
Nocturnes (vln and pf) (1953)
Sonata (vla and pf) (1966)
Sonata (vln and pf) (1962, 1965)
Eclogues (b-cl) (1965)
Pantomine (vla d'amour) (1973)

ORGAN
Inspiration (4 hands) (1973)
Capriccios (1962)
Impromptus (1953)
Lullabies (1954)
Preludes (1957)
Sonata (1960)

VOCAL
Nights, cantata (T, mix-ch and orch) (1969)
Lyoleia, melodrama (speaker and orch) (1961)
Tanbakzan, melodrama (speaker and orch) (1962)
Aquarelles (m-ch) (1973)
Five Slovak songs (m-ch) (1969)
Madrigals (mix-ch) (1966)
Marching songs (chil-ch) (1973)
Melancholic songs (w-ch) (1973)
Azalea, melodrama (speaker and cham ens) (1959)
Songs of the old moon (S and cham ens) (1965)
Three children's choruses (1965)
Adventure of courage, song cycle (Bar and pf) (1964)
Vyzvani, cycle (folk text) (m-ch)
Klytie, melodrama (speaker and nonet) (1972)
Yellow ballads (Bar and pf) (1965)

BALLET
The nightingale and the rose, chamber ballet (after O. Wilde) (1970)
The strange rocket, chamber ballet (after O. Wilde) (1971)
The sunflower (after Ovid) (1972)

OPERA
If the sun were not to return (F.C. Ramuz) (1974)

MISCELLANEOUS
Music for radio and television plays

Ref. composer, 77, 94, 189, 518, 563

PETYREK, Felika

Austrian composer. b. 1892.

Compositions

VOCAL
Songs

SACRED
Litanei, cantata (mix-ch)

Ref. 465

PEY CASADO, Diana

Spanish-Chilean teacher and composer. b. Madrid, March 28, 1922. She began her musical studies in Madrid and later studied composition at the Conservatorio Nacional of Santiago under Amengual, Letelier and Orrego Salas.

Compositions

CHAMBER
Trio (1959)
Sonata a dos pianos (2 pf) (1961)
Sonatina (fl and pf) (1954)

VOCAL
El cantar de los cantares, cantata

Ref. 90

PEYCKE, Frieda

20th-century American lecturer and composer. b. Omaha, NE. She studied under Adolf Weidig and Walton Perkins at the Chicago Conservatory, where she also taught. She composed teaching pieces for the piano and vocal music.
Ref. 226

PEYRON, Albertina Fredrika (pseud. Ika)

Swedish pianist and composer. b. Timra, Vaesternorrland, July 1, 1845; d. 1922. She studied the piano in Stockholm under I. Hallstroem, Boom and A. Andersen and composition under J. Dente and E. Sjoegren. She composed organ pieces, violin pieces, cello and piano pieces, quartets and songs.
Ref. 95, 105, 642

PEYROT, Fernande

Swiss lecturer and composer. b. Geneva, November 21, 1888; d. 1978. She studied at the Geneva Conservatory under Jaques-Dalcroze and Ernest Bloch and obtained a diploma of the Jaques-Dalcroze method. She taught at the Jaques-Dalcroze Institute from its foundation and at the L'Ecole de Vaugirard and L'Ecole Normale de Musique, Paris, from 1919 to 1920. She later studied counterpoint at the Paris Conservatoire under Gedalge and Paul Dukas. She won a prize at the International Competition of Women Composers, Basle, 1950 and an award at the Second International Competition and Congress of Women Composers, Mannheim, 1961. DISCOGRAPHY.

Compositions

ORCHESTRA

Esquisse symphonique op. 4 (1929)
Intrada (2 fl and str orch) (1958)
Marche militaire (1940)
Suite (cham orch) (1965)
Suite (str och) (1953)

CHAMBER

String quintet (1933)
Seven preludes (ob, cl, bsn and hn) (1954)
String quartet (1935)
Fantaisie (fl, vln and vlc) (1959)
Indicatif musical (2 trp and trb) (1958)
Trio (fl, vln and pf) (1936) (Henn)
Trio (fl, vlc and pf) (1966)
Duo (fl and hp)
Duo (hn and pf) (1961)
Duo (vlc and pf) (1964)
Duo (vln and pf) (1968)
Sonata (vln and pf) (1934)
Petite suite (gtr) (Geneva: Menestrel, 1954)
Quatre esquisses (vln) (1931)

PIANO

De toutes les couleurs (1962) (Henn)
Les jours (Henn)
Picorez les moineaux (1963)
Prélude et rondo (1963)
Trois esquisses rythmiques (hommage to Jaques-Dalcroze) (1965)
Trois miniatures (Siècle musical)

VOCAL

Cantata (S, mix-ch and small orch) (1938)
La petite sirène (Cont, T, mix-ch and small orch) (1948)
Ballade (mix-ch) (1942)
Deux chansons (composer) (mix-ch)
L'oiseau bleu (S, w-ch and fl) (1949)
Trois choeurs (w-ch) (Henn, 1930)
Chantez, jouez...... (vce and pf) (Henn-Chapuis, 1953)
Dimanche des rameaux (S)
Deux trios (S, m-S, Cont and hp) (1944)
Les heures de l'été (A. Rudhardt) (3 w-vces) (Henn, 1957)
Huit prières d'animaux (m-S or Bar and pf)
Quatrans portugais, op. 30 (vce and pf) (Henn, 1954)
Ronde à Jaques-Dalcroze (vce and pf) (1945)
Suite, op. 2 (S and str qrt) (1924)
Trois poèmes (Bar and pf) (1962)
Vocalise (S and hp) (1950)
Quartets

SACRED

Latin cantata
Messe, op. 1 (mix-ch, org and orch) (1917)
Deux psaumes, 100 and 142 (mix-ch, brass and org) (1963)
Saint, saint, saint le Seigneur (Cont, ch, str qnt and hpcd) (1953)
Image de Noël (2 vces and pf, 4 hands) (1949)
Psaumes 28 and 71
Psaum 103 (Cont, fl and org) (1942)

THEATRE

The Geneva marionettes

Bibliography

Gattiker, Hermann. *Frauenzeitung*. 1938.
Godet, Robert. *Revue Musicale*. Paris, 1924.
Tappolet, Willy. *RMS*. February, 1935.

Ref. Dr. René Peyrot, 7, 36, 59, 101, 563, 552

PFEIFFER, Charlotte Birsch (Birsch, Charlotte)

19th-century German composer of Munich. Her *Santa Chiara* was performed in Paris in 1988.

Compositions

OPERA

Jean Guetenberg, lyric opera (1836)
Il suonatore delle campane
Santa Chiara (1854) (ded Duke Ernest of Saxe-Colburg Gotha)

Ref. 502

PFEIFFER, Clara-Virginie

French pianist, teacher and composer. b. Versailles, April 1816. She was a student of Kalkbrenner and Chopin.

Compositions

CHAMBER

Duo (pf and vln) (Paris: Aulagnier)

PIANO

Duo, on William Tell (2 pf) (Paris: Brandus)
Esquisses musicales, op. 1, 6 studies (Paris: Chabal)
La Gaetana, tarantelle (Choudens)
Six nocturnes, ops. 2, 3, 4, 8 and 11 (Chabal, Heul, Choudens)
Sonata, op. 9 (Paris: Heul)

Ref. 6, 297

PFEIFFER, Irena

Polish pianist, choral conductor, teacher and composer. b. Szczenin, September 23, 1912. She studied at the State Teachers' College, Cracow and the piano at the W. Zelenski Music School, Cracow under K. Tretorowa. After taking the state examination in music and singing at Katowice Conservatory, she studied composition under A. Malawski and conducting under W. Bierdiajew from 1946 to 1952 at the Higher Music School in Cracow, when she received an M.A. and the diploma of artist musician. She taught music in high schools from 1938 and conducted the women's choir Akord from 1939 to 1968 and the men's choir 'Echo' in Cracow from 1949 to 1957 and later the men's choir 'Bard'. She toured in Poland, Yugoslavia and Hungary, conducting choirs. She won numerous prizes and awards. PHOTOGRAPH.

Compositions

ORCHESTRA

Symphonic variations (1952)
Victory overture (1954)
W Krainie czarow, fantastic suite (1949)

CHAMBER

String quartet

PIANO

Customs and folk dances (PWM, 1958)
Dance suite (PWM, 1949)
From the life of animals
Nine Polish dances
Swiat dziecka, miniatures (1948)
Teaching pieces

VOCAL

Krolowa polski, cantata (Z. Krasnski) (w-ch, m-ch, mix-ch and org) (1960)
Zew ziemy, cantata (Slowacki) (Bar, mix-ch and orch) (1951)
Bajka o smuko (J. Brzechwa) (m-ch) (1966)
Ballado o Janosiku (S and w-ch) (1962)
Do zwyciestwa, suite of partisan songs (m-ch) (PWM, 1969)
Fairy Tales (J. Brzechwa) (chil-ch or w-ch) (PWM, 1969)
For Mother Country (Galczynski) (m-ch) (PWM, 1970)
Impressions (Tuwim) (m-ch a-cap)
Majowy deszcz (L. Staff) (w or boys' ch) (PWM, 1973)
Oh swing, I have sown (w-ch) (PWM, 1952)
Romantic songs (m-ch) (PWM, 1969)
Six Bajek (J. Brzechwa) (w-ch) (1963)
Small children are singing (preschool chil-ch and pf) (PWM, 1967)
Suita goralska (T, Bar and m-ch) (1951)
Ten songs (S. Moniuszko) (w-ch) (PWM, 1958)
Three folk songs (w-ch) (PWM, 1952)
Wesele kujawskie, suite (Bar and m-ch) (1964)
Zaby, pociag, oj taradum (Wiszniewski) (w-ch) (PWM, 1952)
Other songs (ch)
Arrangements of folk songs

SACRED
Pojdzmy wszyczy do stajenki, Christmas carol suite (chil-ch and str orch) (1958)
De Profundis, Psalm 129, fugue (mix-ch)
Testamentum Sanctae Angelae Mericiae (w-ch and org)
Twenty-five Christmas carols and pastorales (mix-ch and org) (1957)
W noc Bozego Narodzenia, triptych (w-ch, m-ch, mix-ch and org) (1958)
Praecepta Matris Nostrae Ursulae (vce and org) (1970)
Przed twym oltarzem, mass (1961)
Seven masses based on motifs from Polish church songs (vce and org) (1968)
Te Deum laudamus (vce and org)
Two Books of Marian and Eucharistic songs
Ref. composer, 77, 94, 118

PFEILSCHIFTER, Julie von
German pianist and composer. b. Mannheim, April 15, 1840. Her ballet and opera were successes in Wiesbaden.
Compositions
PIANO
Pieces
VOCAL
Songs
BALLET
Voegleins Morgengruss
OPERA
Agneta
Ref. 226, 276, 347

PFERDEMENGES, Maria Pauline Augusta (pseud. M. Pery)
German organist, concert pianist and composer. b. Rahmel, East Prussia, March 8, 1872. She studied music privately in Berlin and then the piano under Miss Puttkamme and Miss Pritzsche in Danzig until 1886. For the next three years she continued her piano studies under Albert Eibenschutz in Cologne. From 1889 to 1891 she was at the Cologne Conservatory and from 1898 to 1899, studied counterpoint under Salomon Jadassohn in Leipzig. For the following nine years she was a composition pupil of Felix Draeseke in Dresden. She toured as a pianist in concert in France, England and Russia until 1902 and in 1919 became the organist at the Erloeserkirche, Zoppott, Danzig.
Compositions
ORCHESTRA
Concerto for 2 pianos and orchestra, op. 31
ORGAN
Sonata, op. 71
Sonata, op. 82
PIANO
Albumblaetter, op. 39
Drei Phantasiestuecke, op. 38
Fuenf Bagatellen, op. 44
Phantasie und skizzen, op. 59
Three sonatas, ops. 36, 40 and 61
Zehn Variazionen ueber eine Original-Thema, op. 60
Zwei Stimmungsbilder, op. 42
Teaching works
VOCAL
Songs (mix-ch)
Duets and tercets a cappella
Numerous lieder (Nietzsche, Hacker, G. Keller Bodenstedt, Agelmann, Goethe, Grillparzer, Marike Geibe and other poets)
SACRED
Motets, op. 84 (3 part w-ch; also mix-ch a-cap)
Ostergesang, op. 52, tercet (Jacobil) (ch a-cap)
Psalms 117, op. 69 (mix-ch)
Good Friday Mass, op. 78 (2 vlc and org)
Psalm 110, op. 46
Psalm 46, op. 53
Psalms incl. 24, 29, 47, 93, 103, 126, 133 and 142 (vce and pf)
Spiritual songs
Two Passion songs, op. 77
Wedding song, op. 72
Ref. 105, 111

PFOLH (Pfohl), Bessie Whittington
American organist, pianist, arranger, teacher and composer. b. East End, NC, 1881. She received a B.A. in 1899 from Salem College and a piano diploma in 1898.
Compositions
VOCAL
Choral works
Songs
SACRED
Communion hymn (ch) (Brodt)
D.A.R. hymn (ch) (Brodt)
Other pieces
Ref. 40, 347, 433

PFUND, Jeanne
German composer.
Composition
VOCAL
Gruss an die Kameraden: Seid uns gegruesst, Kameraden (mix-ch; also vce and pf) (Fuerstner)
Ref. 297

PFUND, Leonore (nee Thiele)
German composer. b. Glachau, May 21, 1877. She composed romantic and children's songs.
Ref. 433, 347

PHARRIS, Elizabeth
20th-century American harpist, operatic singer and composer. She appeared in the United States and Europe in operas and solo recitals.
Compositions
VOCAL
Songs incl.:
The joy invocation (vce and hp)
OPERETTA
The First Rainbow, for children
Ref. Music Clubs Magazine, convention issue, 1979

PHILHARMONICA, Mrs. (pseud.)
Early 18th-century English composer.
Compositions
CHAMBER
Sonate a due violini con violoncello obbligato e violone o cimbalo, Parte Prima
Divertimento de camera a due violini, violoncello o cimbalo, Parte Seconda (London: R. Meares, ca. 1715)
Ref. 65, 405

PHILIBA, Nicole
French pianist, professor and composer. b. Paris, August 30, 1937. She studied at the Paris Conservatoire under Henri Dutilleux, Tony Aubin, Andre Jolivet and Olivier Messaien where she won prizes for the piano, chamber music and musical analysis. From 1969 she was a professor at the Conservatoire. She appeared on many radio programs and her works were performed in France, Italy, Belgium and Lebanon.
Compositions
ORCHESTRA
Symphony No. 1 (1960)
Concerto (sax and orch) (1967)
Concerto (trp and orch) (1965)
Concerto (sax, perc and str orch) (1964)
Concerto da camera (cl and str orch) (1965)
La Loreley, lyric poem (1961)
Sinfonietta (str orch) (1958)
Variations choreographiques (1967-1971)
CHAMBER
Quintet (pf and strs) (1960)
Quartet (4 sax) (1958)
Trio (hn, trp and trb) (1969)
Trio (vln, vlc and pf) (1958)
Compositions (trp and pf) (1967)
Mouvements (d-b and pf) (1967)
Profils, 5 small pieces (cl and pf) (Paris: Lemoine, 1979)
Sonata (fl and pf) (1965)
Sonata (sax and pf) (1965)
Five sentences (ob) (1965)
Inventions (gtr) (1977)
Mosaiques (trp) (1977)
Preludes (org) (1969)
Sequences I, II, III, IV and V (gtr)
Sonata (fl) (1979)
Sonata (sax) (1969)

PIANO
Sonata (2 pf) (1964)
Evocations (1976)
Five pieces in the form of a suite (1960)
Quatre mouvements successifs (1967)
Six pieces (1975)
Three inventions (1966)
Visions (1969)
VOCAL
Mouvement concertant (vce and orch) (1965)
Mirage (mix-ch, pf and perc) (1968)
Incantesimi (vce and pf) (1969)
ELECTRONIC
Musique (vce, fl, pf and ondes Martenot) (1964)
Musique nuptiale (vce, trp, pf and ondes Martenot) (1969)
Recit (ondes Martenot and pf) (1971)
MISCELLANEOUS
Etudes rythmiques (1979)
Improvisation on a theme of Monteverdi (1969)
Légendes
Ref. composer, 457

PHILIP, Mrs. C. See CALDWELL, Mary Elizabeth

PHILIPPART, Renée
French composer. b. Paris, March 11, 1905. She began her musical studies at the Institute Normal A. Desir under Louise Dupré and Anita Cartier. She studied composition, counterpoint and orchestration under Charles Koechlin and later musical analysis under Louis Aubert and composition under Henri Busser. She was influenced by Andre Caplet, whom she met in 1923 and who started to prepare her religious ensembles for performance. His unexpected death prevented this, but inspired her *Requiem*. Her works were performed in France and South America and on programs presented by Radio-Television France. She was awarded the Jacques Durand prize. DISCOGRAPHY. PHOTOGRAPH.
Compositions
ORCHESTRA
Three preludes (2 pf and orch; also pf, 4 hands) (1938)
Chant funébre (org and orch) (1935)
Fantasie-pastoral (vln and orch) (1933)
Village de montagne, suite (1945)
CHAMBER
Clarté (hp and st qrt) (1927)
Quintet (fl, ob, cl, bsn and pf) (1927)
La Flute de jade, in G (s-fl and a-fl) (1924)
Rondo concertant (fl and pf) (1976)
Suite breve (vln and pf) (1929)
Three small pieces (vln and pf) (1923)
Sept péchés capitaux (pf, 4 hands) (1937)
Port Royal des champes (1976)
VOCAL
La buche de Noël (vce and orch)
Cantique du soleil (w-ch and orch) (1927)
Four melodies (Paul Verlaine) (vce and orch or pf) (1937)
Hommage à Calet (w-ch and orch) (1926)
Litanies (ch and orch) (1934)
Lullaby (vce and orch or pf)
Noël Canadien (vce and orch)
Noël des neiges (vce and orch)
Noël du zoo (vce and orch)
Noel féerique (soloists, chil-vces and orch or pf) (1959) (Jacques Durand prize)
Triptyque, symphonic poem (Bar and orch) (1934)
Berceuse complainte (4 mix-vces a-cap) (1950)
Four lullabies (vces and insts) (1956-1961)
Ode du printemps (Ronsard) (soloist, w-vces and pf) (1924)
Two choruses (w-vce and insts) (1923)
La violette double (4 vces a-cap)
Des fleurs et des sarments (w-ch) (1980)
Annonciation (vce and pf) (1951)
Dors mon soleil (Spanish words) (vce and hp)
Echo (4 vces a-cap)
Five songs of Alsace (vce and pf) (1939)
La reinette ile de re pas (vce and pf) (1960)
Tempo sept (Cont, perc and pf) (1976)
Ten melodies (1922)
Venise, 2 melodies (T. Gauthier and A. de Musset) (vce and pf) (1927)
SACRED
Psaume de Daniel (A, ch and orch or org) (1934)
Requiem (double-ch, org and str orch) (1925)
Alleluia (4 mix-vces and org) (1937)
Ave Maria (2 vces and org) (1926)
Je vous salue Marie, students' canticle (4 vces and org) (1954)
Kyrie Eleison, Agnus Dei (extracts of Verlaine's Sagesse) (2 vces and pf) (1926)
Messe (4 mix-vces and str qrt or org) (1926)
Salve Regina (4 mix-vces and org) (1934)
THEATRE
Ecce Ancimia Domini, musical tableau (Leon Chancerel)
FILM MUSIC
Eleven film scores
ELECTRONIC
Cevenol (6 ondes Martenot) (1982)
Elevation (ondes Martenot) (1940)
Spirlae (6 ondes Martenot)
ARRANGEMENTS
Works by Liszt and Chopin (orch) (1940)
Ref. composer, 563

PHILIPPINA, Charlotte, Duchess of Brunswick
German composer. DISCOGRAPHY.
Composition
ORCHESTRA
March (wind orch)
Ref. 563

PHILIPS, Magnola Patricia Bryony. See PHILLIPS. Bryony

PHILLAN, Eustace. See BOOSEY, Beatrice Joyce

PHILLIPS, Bryony (Maglona Patricia Bryony) (nee Jagger)
Dual British and New Zealand national, oboist, singer, writer and composer. b. Salford, England, March 10, 1948. She gained her B.A. hons. in 1971 from Cambridge University, studying under Roger Smalley and Patrick Gowes. From 1973 she studied far eastern music, literature and history and returned to Cambridge University to study composition and paleography and gained her M.A. hons. in 1974. She did private study in composition under Earl Kim in Boston. From 1982 to 1983 she studied electronic music and the technical aspects of theater at the University of Auckland, New Zealand. From 1970 to 1971 she was founder and musical director of New Hall Madrigal Group. She played the oboe in orchestras and chamber groups in England and New Zealand, sung in choirs and madrigal groups, appeared on radio and television and her works have been performed on radio and in concert in New Zealand and England. In 1977 she won the Doria Choral Composition competition and in 1983 was awarded a grant from the New Zealand and Japanese exchange program, to travel to Japan to study Noh drama. In Autumn 1984 she was appointed a visiting scholar to New Hall, Cambridge. PHOTOGRAPH.
Compositions
ORCHESTRA
A New Zealand symphony (1980)
Childbirth, tone poem (cor anglais and orch) (1979)
Sinfonia di requiem, tone poem (1979)
Theme and variations (cham orch) (1971)
CHAMBER
Octet (2 str qrts) (1971)
Magnifipuss (fl, 2 ob, 2 cl and bsn) (1983)
Brass quintet No. 1 (2 trp, 2 hn and trb) (1969)
Brass quintet No. 2 (2 trp, 2 hn and trb) (1970)
The mask (fl, cor anglais, cl, hn and bsn) (1983)
On another's sorrow (cl, 2 hn and 2 bsn) (1981)
Gur II (3 dr) (1969)
Hark (org, tamtam and xy) (1971)
Amorosa (2 vln) (1979)
Binary fission (fl and/or ob) (1969)
Canonic duets (fl and bsn) (1973)
Pastorale: philika (2 ob) (1967)
Psalm 88, sonata (2 vlc) (1979)
For Tessa, 7 easy pieces (pf) (1978)
Tawhiri (vln) (1978)
Thyrsus triptych (fl) (1976)
VOCAL
Autumn Floods, oratorio (trans of Basho) (S, ch and orch) (1973)
The expiration (S, T and ch) (1980)
Night cycle of haiku (Issa, Gyodai, Shiki) (Cont and small orch) (1972)
Revelation concerto (T and orch) (1981)
Torn veils (ch, pf and str orch) (1980)
Abortion debate (composer) (3 S and double-ch) (1978)
Calico pie (Lear) (vce or boys'-ch, insts and drs) (1980)
Contentment (Sir Philip Sydney) (mix-ch) (1976)
Eternal rest (T and ch) (1978)
Fragments on Sunday (composer) (mix-ch) (1976)
Great sea (Charles Brasch) (boys'-ch, trp and perc) (1980) (comm Auckland Boys' Choir)

Green waters (composer) (mix-ch) (1976)
Happies (m-ch) (1977)
Jumblies (2 T and mix-ch) (1977)
On another's sorrow (m-ch) (1977)
Orange blossom willow shade (composer) (mix-ch) (1976)
Pastorale: country Gods; (w-ch and ob) (1967)
Poor fly (composer) (mix-ch) (1976)
Silence (composer) (high vce and 2 speaking ch) (1978)
Sunset (composer) (mix-ch) (1973)
Thanksgiving (R. Tagore) (S and w-ch; also double-ch) (1978)
Without contraries (mix-ch) (1979)
Mele Sapphoa (Cont, picc, 2 ob, vln, vla, vlc, timp and perc) (1968)
Have I offended thee, Dread Mother, scene from Sacrifice (R. Tagore) (S, B, ob, cl, hn, timp and drs) (1978)
Te kaminara, song cycle (Keith Sinclair) (Bar, fl, cl, bsn, hn, trp and trb) (1977)
Yongy Bonghy Bo (Lear) (B and pf, with pan, sieve, wooden spoon, tri and jug; also A and Bar) (1980)
La belle dame sans merci (Keats) (2 T and 2 B) (1974)
Siren (Cont and wind qrt) (1970)
Cloudwhisperer (m-S and pf) (1980)
Consider the mountains: Reflect on the Wind, pastorale (speaker, rec, vla or perc and elecs) (1974)
Daddy Long Legs (T, B and pf) (1979)
Delusive trance (S and hp) (1979)
The divine meditations of John Donne (T and pf) (1979)
Early morning despair (composer) (narr and 2 fl) (1969)
Ears in the turrets hear (Dylan Thomas) (high vce) (1983)
Encounter (T and pf) (1980)
First love (S and pf) (1979)
Gitanjali, six songs (R. Tagore) (T and ob) (1976)
I am Chitra, aria (R. Tagore) (S and vlc) (1978)
Kasumi, cycle of haiku (in Japanese) (T and pf) (1978)
Leopards of the moon (Yeats) (S and vln) (1982)
The marriage of true minds (Shakespeare) (S and vln) (1982)
Moments (vce and pf) (1980)
Night hours (m-S and rec) (1979)
Oreti beach (B and pf) (1981)
Piece (3 rec and vce, 1 performer) (1978)
The price of experience (S and hp) (1979)
The shadow of your presence (S and pf) (1980)
Shoriken (S and rec) (1980)
Six Basho haiku (Cont, fl, ob, cl and hp and str trio) (1972)
Songs for Katharine: A Parting; Blue Threads (composer) (vce and pf) (1978)
Songs from the asylum (John Clare) (vce and pf) (1977)
Songs of parting (composer) (S and hn) (1978)
Tanka: reality (composer, after S. Hoshi) (S) (1978)
A tear wiped away (S, T and hp) (1979)
Thirteen Basho haiku (T, B and ob) (1972)
Three Li Po songs (low vce and 2 fl) (1973)
Three Simonides songs (Cont, ob, hp and timp) (1971)
Three tanka (Cont and fl) (1972)
Time long past (Shelley) (S and vlc) (1982)
Was I dreaming, aria (T and vlns) (1978)
You tread on my dreams (Yeats) (S and vlc) (1982)
Will you remember? (m-S) (1980)

SACRED
Virgin Birth, Christmas cantata (soloists, ch, ob and pf) (1983)
Le Martyre de St. Sebastien (S, B, hp and str orch) (1978)
Agnus Dei (2 S and ch) (1977)
A Bethleham star, carol (G.M. Hopkins) (w-ch) (1978)
The glory of God (mix-ch) (1979)
Magnificat (mix-ch) (1976)
The marriage of heaven and hell, 7 pieces (Blake) (T and ch) (1979)
Requiem brevis (soloists and double mix-ch) (1973)
Stabat Mater (ch) (1976)
Three Maori psalm settings (T, B and ch) (1976)
The worship of God (T, S and ch) (1979)
Ave verum corpus (Cont, T and B) (1977)
Eternal rest
Four extracts from Psalm 88 (T and B) (1976)

OPERA
Chitra (S, T, B, hpcd, 2 dancers or film and str orch) (1980)

OPERETTA
Release from Hell (from Dr. Setsuko Ito, trans Esashi Juo) (actor, T, S, ch, rec, gtr, timp and perc) (1978)

THEATRE
Birds of Enlightenment, cantata (composer, based on Uto, by Zeami) (2 S, 2 T, Bar, ch, 2 rec, timp, cym and perc) (3rd New Zealand Asia Conference, 1978)
The Frogs, (Aristophanes) musical comedy
Dreams in the Grass (B. Gregory) (reciter, singer, rec, tri and dancer) (1979)

Ref. composer, RILM *Abstracts*, 457, 622, 643

PHILLIPS, Donna

American pianist, singer, teacher and composer. b. Los Angeles, 1953. She began piano studies with her grandmother Grace Koumrian and continued under E. Reddick and B. Sutherland. She taught the piano and voice in Santa Monica and studied composition at California State University, Northridge.

Compositions

CHAMBER
Three movements for eleven players (hp, pf perc and winds)
Other pieces

VOCAL
Songs

Ref. ICWM

PHILLIPS, Karen Ann

American concert pianist and violist, teacher and composer. b. Dallas, October 29, 1942. She studied the piano in Dallas under Mabel Price from 1948 to 1957 and Bomar Cramer in 1957 and at the Eastman School of Music under Henry Rauch in 1960. She received a B.Mus. in 1967 from the Juilliard School of Music. From 1969 to 1971, through the National Endowment Fund, she was the Sears-Roebuck affiliate artist with the Performing Arts Council of the Los Angeles Music Center. As a violist and composer she received an award of merit from the American Music Department of the National Federation Music Center. She gave recitals in Rome, Strasbourg and the United States and her works were performed on radio. She hosted her own radio series on WNYC from 1975 to 1977. She was a viola teacher at the Vermont Youth Festival. She is a member of ASCAP. PHOTOGRAPH.

Compositions

ORCHESTRA
Symphony in A-Major
Symphony in C-Major (1979)
Symphony in E-Major
Symphony in G-Minor, in 3 movements
Concerto (vlc and orch)

CHAMBER
String quartet (1978)
Little caprice (vln and pf) (1978)
Trio (ob, vla and pf) (1978) (Meet the Composer award)
DVOC (vla and hn)
Lake Wiloughby (vla and pf) (1978) (Meet the Composer award)
Lonely days, misunderstandings (vla and pf) (Meet The Composer award)
Peut être (vla and pf)
Seilferif (vla and pf)
Tsolreverof (vla and pf)
Nosam, Nosamsnetram (org)

PIANO
Dannielli
Deceiving hearts
During
Fireflies
Lingering
Now I lay me down to sleep
Out of place
Page-a-day
Perdu pour six mois de pluie
Retfa spahrep
Star's tears
Washable black
Wondering
You're in my thoughts

VOCAL
Trio (vce, hn and pf)
Forever lost (vce and pf)
Mistress, mistress on the wall (vce and pf)
Wondering now (vce and pf)

INCIDENTAL MUSIC
Deceiving hearts, radio series

Ref. composer, 328, 359, 415

PHILLIPS, Linda, O.B.E. (Mrs. Kauffmann)

20th-century Australian concert pianist, music critic, poetess, teacher and composer. b. Melbourne. At the university and Melba Conservatorium, Melbourne, she studied composition under Fritz Hart, harmony under Dr. J.A. Steele and the piano under Edward I. Goll. She made numerous broadcasts of her own compositions for Melbourne, Sydney and Brisbane radio. She gave public recitals of her own and other artists' chamber music and songs. She was a Melbourne reviewer for the *Australian Musical News* and then a music critic for the *Melbourne Sun* for 27 years. She received various scholarships and was awarded an O.B.E. in 1975. DISCOGRAPHY. PHOTOGRAPH.

Compositions
CHAMBER
Exaltation, on a Chassidic air (ob, vln, vlc and pf) (1939)
Music from Lamentations (vln, vlc and pf)
Tal trio (vln, vlc and pf)
Trio Purim (vln, vlc and pf)
Two trios on old Hebraic themes (vln, vlc and pf)
Rhapsody sonata (vln and pf)
Two moods (cl and pf) (1968)
Other solos (fl, cl, vlc and vla)
PIANO
Butterflies, noon (Augener, London)
Suites
VIOLIN
Bush evening
Serenade
Shadow dance
Sonata
VOCAL
Numerous songs incl.:
Apple trees (James Joyce) (S)
Ash trees (m-Cont)
Bracken brown (m-Cont)
The charioteers (Joyce) (S)
Cherry blossom (Kathleen Dalziel)
Cradle song, plum tree (composer and K. Dalziel) (S and pf)
Dawn message (Ivy Jones)
Daydreams (composer) (vce, vln and pf)
Eastern song (composer) (vce and vln obb)
Four bush lyrics (S and pf) (Allans Music)
Evening canticle (Eric Harrison) (m-S, cl and pf) (1967)
Hands of Jae (composer)
The iris marshes (Lord Dunsaney)
Orchard zephyr (composer) (S)
Three songs of the Outback (composer) (Bar and pf)
When the twilight turns to amethyst (m-Cont)
A wish (Samuel Rogers)
Part songs
ARRANGEMENTS
Australia, anthem (composer) (B, ch and brass band)
Songs (vce, cl and pf: also vce, vln and pf)
Publications
From a City Garden. Book of Verse. 1922.
Ref. composer, 70, 77, 94, 206, 440, 443, 563, 643

PHILLIPS, Lois Elisabeth

English concert pianist, professor and composer. b. London, January 19, 1926. She was a student at the Royal Academy of Music for six years, winning several prizes for her piano performance, including the Elizabeth Stokes open scholarship and the Walter Macfarren gold medal, the highest award for a piano student. She appeared as a soloist with the Oriole Ensemble and gave recitals and broadcasts in Germany, Switzerland and England. She was a professor at the Royal Academy, lecturing in German Lieder and piano teaching.
Compositions
PIANO
Arabesque
VOCAL
Still centre (vce, vla and pf)
Two Scottish songs (T and vln)
SACRED
Emmaus, cantata (ch and 13 insts)
Publications
Billa, Beela and Jocksey Ju. Augener, 1961.
Can You Sight Read? Books I and II. Galliard, 1964.
Little Piano Book. Forsyth, 1970.
Starting Now! Forsyth, 1970.
Ref. composer. 84, 94

PHILLIPS, Vivian Daphne

American organist, pianist, violinist and composer. b. Colby, KS, March 9, 1917. She studied the organ, the piano, the violin and composition at Ottawa University, Kansas from 1934 to 1936, where she studied under Harry Cooper. At Bethany College, Lindsborg from 1936 to 1939 she studied under Hagvard Brase and became interested in building and playing folk instruments. She furthered her studies at Oklahoma Baptist University, Shawnee from 1982 to 1984. She was active in local choirs and symphony and chamber groups. PHOTOGRAPH.
Compositions
ORCHESTRA
Repose
CHAMBER
Nocturne (str qnt)
Shades of Papa Hayden (str qnt)
Alleluia (handbells and org)
VOCAL
Songs incl.:
Amare
An assessment of my figure
Day is done
The fog
The look
The pasture
The sky is low
To electra
Why fear death
SACRED
He is risen (ch)
Holy, Holy Lord, we seek You (1985)
I was glad when they said unto me (1985)
Music for trial liturgy (vce and org)
Praises sing to God the Father and the Son (1985)
Prayer (3 vces)
Wedding service (vce and org)
ARRANGEMENTS
Familiar melodies, hymn and folk tunes (folk hp)
Soft sounds, old melodies (African thumb hp)
Ref. composer, 142

PHILP, Elizabeth

English singer, teacher and composer. b. Falmouth, 1827; d. London, November 26, 1885. She studied singing in Bristol under Mary Carpenter, Manuel Garcia and Mme. Marchesi and harmony and composition under Ferdinand Hiller. She sung many of her own compositions in concert.
Compositions
VOCAL
Chants des lavandieres (from Ruy Blas by Victor Hugo) (London: Cramer & Co., ca. 1855)
Hop-pickers
Inclusions (Elizabeth Barrett Browning)
Love that's never told
Oh! why not be happy
Six songs (Longfellow, James Russell Lowell, Melopayn, Emily Ham) (Cramer, Beele & Co., 1855)
Le soupir (Prudhomme)
Tell me, the summer starts, ballad (Edwin Arnold) (1855)
'Tis wine
Violets of the spring
Wrecked hope
Part songs
Publications
How to sing an English Ballad. London, 1883.
Ref. 6, 8, 102, 123, 226, 276, 433

PHIPPEN, Laud German

20th-century American pianist, teacher and composer. b. Whitewright, TX. She composed piano pieces.
Ref. 347, 353

PICCOLOMINI, Marietta

B. 1834; d. 1899. She composed pieces for the saxophone.
Ref. 76, 347, 502

PICCONI, Maria Antonietta

Italian pianist, teacher and composer. b. Rome, September 23, 1869. She studied the piano under Montignani, Mazzarella and Sgambati; voice under Franceschetti and composition under E. Terziani. She graduated from the Academy of Sainte Cecilia in harmony in 1883, the piano in 1885 and composition in Palermo in 1889. She performed in concerts from 1886 and taught the piano and voice from 1896. She composed vocal music, published by Carisch, Milan.
Ref. 105

PICHE, Eudore

Canadian organist, choral conductor and composer. b. Montreal, February 9, 1906. She composed choral pieces.
Ref. 85, 347

PICKHARDT, Ione

American pianist, music critic and composer. b. Hampstead, NY, May 27, 1900. She won a scholarship to the National Conservatory of Music, New York at the age of twelve and studied there for eight years, mostly under Adele Margulies and Rafael Joseffy. She made her debut as a pianist with the New York Philharmonic Orchestra but family disapproval cut short this career. She eventually joined the *New York Evening Mail* as assistant music critic and turned her attentions to composition.

Compositions

ORCHESTRA
Piano concerto in D-Major
Piano concerto in E-Minor

OPERA
Moira, grand opera in 3 acts, (dramatization of Irish legends) (George Gibbs Jr.) (1930)

Ref. 141, 304, 345, 347

PIECHOWSKA (Piechowska-Pascal), Alina

Polish pianist, conductor, poetess, teacher, writer and composer. b. Vilna, USSR, August 29, 1937. Her parents were musicians. She studied the piano under her mother and then at the Vilna Conservatory under Leokadia Marcinkiewicz-Urbanowicz and M. Silman and conducting under Konrad Kaveckas. At the State Music School, Warsaw she studied teaching and composition under W. Rudzinski from 1959 to 1961. From 1971 to 1972 she studied under Nadia Boulanger (q.v.) in Paris and was later a pupil of Kagel in Darmstadt. She works with the Group of Experimental Music, Bourges.

Compositions

ORCHESTRA
Forme bleue (1974)
Imaginaire (ob and str orch) (1978)
Music for strings, hommage a Nadia Boulanger (1972)

CHAMBER
Histoire du rossignol et l'empereur de Chine (inst ens) (1976)
Anagrams (str qrt) (1966)
Illumination (ondes Martenot, perc and pf)
A due (fl and zither) (1973)
Aura (fl and pf) (1978) (Transatlantique, 1979)
Elégie pour un temp present (ob and hpcd) (1983)
In memoriam (vln and pf) (1983)
Theorgta (vln and pf) (1984)
Trois fresques (vlc and gtr) (1983)
Ambitus sonore (vln) (1972)
Area 83 (cl) (1982)
Area 84 (cl) (1982)
Ecmoi (ob) (1975)
Elégy (ob) (1974)
Fresque (ondes Martenot) (1978)
Indifference (bsn) (1982)
Irsama (fl)
Process (vlc) (1978)
Series (zither) (1973)
Tarantelle (d-b) (1980)
Traces II (hpcd) (1974)
Ylayali (fl) (1975)

PIANO
Elégie pour untendre (1983)
Hommage à Maz Ernst (1976)
Hommage à T. Monk (1982)
Indifference (1982)
Moto perpetuo (1980)

VOCAL
Roza wiatrow, oratorio (I. Iredynski) (actor, soloists, mix-ch and orch) (1970)
Invocationes II (S and orch) (1969)
Katharsis (I. Iredynski) (S and orch) (1969)
Ballade de l'écharpe d'Iris (S, reciter, fl, pf and vlc) (1984)
Comme Shirley (M. Butor) (S and d-b) (1980)
Paysage de reponses (Butor) (S and inst ens) (1982)
Peintures...poèmes...murmures (Butor) (m-S and inst ens) (1982)
Praxis (w-vce, zither and perc) (1974)
Seven songs (Z. Bruder) (1976)
Songs of Bilitis (Pierre Louys) (S and inst ens) (1965)
Vibrations pour une voix

BALLET
Salle Favart-climats (1977)
Sept de coeur (S, pf and perc) (1978)

ELECTRONIC
Ballet music (m-S, tape and cham ens) (1972)
Epitaph (1972)
Illumination (ondes Martenot, pf and perc) (1974)
In Memoriam (fl and tape) (1977)

INCIDENTAL MUSIC
Music for Juliette et Romeo (with Joelle Leandre (q.v.) and Stephane Gremaud) (1978)
Music for Pierrot (1979)

MISCELLANEOUS
Pastels

Ref. composer, 64, 77, 189, 622

PIECHOWSKA-PASCAL, Alina. See PIECHOWSKA, Alina

PIERCE, Alexandra

American concert pianist, professor and composer. b. Philadelphia, February 21, 1934. She gained a B.Mus. (piano) in 1955 from the University of Michigan, a B.Mus. (piano) in 1958 from the New England Conservatory, an M.A. (music history) in 1959 from Radcliffe and a Ph.D. (theory and composition) in 1968 from Brandeis University. She was awarded several grants and fellowships. She lectured on the piano at the University of Redlands from 1968, then became associate professor of theory and the piano and then professor of music and movement. In 1984 she became a faculty research lecturer. Since 1980 she has won an annual ASCAP award and performed both as a soloist and a member of a duo team. DISCOGRAPHY.

Compositions

ORCHESTRA
Behemoth (1976) (comm Redlands University Orchestra)

CHAMBER
After Dubuffet's 'Limbour as a crustacean' (cl, sn dr, 3 tom-toms and mar) (1979)
Quartet, music for dance (prep pf, cl, hn and mar) (1979)
Cambodian dancer (vlc and pf) (1984) (comm)
Concord bridge (carillons) (1976)
Three sketches for Iron Hans (hn, vlc and pf) (1984) (comm)
A common chase (rec and mar) (1979)
Echo and Narcissus (fl and pf) (1980)
Job 22:28 (2 cl)
My Lady Hunsdon's pavane (2 cl) (1975) (Seesaw, 1976)
Norwich chorale (cl and pf) (1976) (Seesaw, 1976)
Rhapsody arabesque (cl and pf) (1976) (Seesaw, 1976)
Sargasso (cl and pf) (1976) (Seesaw, 1976)
Fool's gold (vib) (1978) (Seesaw)
The great horned owl (mar) (1979)
Maola (hp) (1977)
Prelude and fugue (fl) (1974) (Seesaw, 1976)
Serenade, On Zander's cobweb photo (gtr) (1979)

PIANO
Antares (4 hands) (1974)
Danse Micawber (4 hands) (1976) (prize, Mu Phi Epsilon contest)
Four songs without words (1982)
Loure and rondeau (4 hands) (1979)
Sweeney among the nightingales (4 hands) (1976) (Seesaw, 1976) (prize, Mu Phi Epsilon contest)
Variations in 4/4 (4 hands)
Blending stumps (prep pf) (1976) (Seesaw, 1976)
Come To standing (1975) (Seesaw, 1976)
Dry rot (prep pf) (1977) (Seesaw)
Greycastle (prep pf) (1974) (Seesaw, 1976)
Joint geography dance (1982)
Lament (1964)
The lost river, Sevier (1978) (Seesaw)
Offering to Birdfeather (1974)
Orb (prep pf) (1976) (Seesaw, 1976)
Popo Agie (prep pf; also vib) (1979)
Seven waltzes, for Emily Dickinson (prep pf) (1980)
Six waltzes (prep pf) (1980)
Solenodon (1964)
Song in Licia for Savonarola (1974)
Spectres (prep pf) (1976) (Seesaw, 1976)
Transverse process (1977) (Seesaw)
Two sound studies (prep pf) (1983)
Variations 7 (prep pf) (1978) (Seesaw)
Teaching works

VOCAL
Hamaguchi, oratorio (Milton Miller) (2 B, A, T, cham-ch, fl, vlc, drone and prep pf) (1973) (hon mention, Mu Phi Epsilon contest)
Dendid (African folk text) (m-ch) (1975)
Jabberwocky (Lewis Carroll) (mix-ch and pf) (1980)
By the waters of Manhattan (C. Reznikoff) (speaker and pf) (1964)
Four songs (James Joyce) (Bar and pf) (1984)
Lo, how a rose e'er blooming (m-qrt) (1980)
My luv (Robert Burns) (m-qrt) (1981)
To the suicides of 1962 (W.D. Justice) (speaker and pf) (1969)

SACRED
Isaiah 40:31 (mix-ch and org ad lib) (1980)
Resurrection (mix-ch, fl and pf) (Sisra Press)
Report to God (mix-ch and pf)
Take my hands and let them move, anthem (F.R. Havergal) (mix-ch and org) (1973)
This bread is torn, hymn for the Eucharist (Roger Piece) (mix-ch and org) (1975)
THEATRE
Collage (Piece) (1965)
Episodes for intermission (1963)
Music for Buchner's Woyzeck (1969)
Music for Brecht's St. Joan of the Stockyards (1972)
FILM MUSIC
Chambered Nautilus (pf, ob and hp) (1972)
ELECTRONIC
Buffalo Bill (e.e. cummings) (vce, tape, pf and cl) (1978)
Publications
Articles relating music structure to the structure of human movement in: *The Piano Quarterly*; *In Theory Only*; *Perspectives.*
Spanning: *Essays on Music Theory, Movement and Performance.*
Ref. composer, 185, 228, 468, 474, 494, 563, 622, 625

PIERCE, Sarah Anderson
American organist, choir conductor, teacher and composer. b. Newport News, VA, December 11, 1955. She studied composition under Drs. Frederick Beyer and Arthur Hunkins at Greensboro College, receiving a B.Mus. magna cum laude (composition, theory) in 1978. She gained her M.Mus. (composition) in 1981 after studying electronic composition under Drs. Alan Leichtling and Otto Henry at East Carolina University, Greenville. She teaches the organ privately and conducts the local church choir. PHOTOGRAPH.
Compositions
CHAMBER
The marriage (10 strs and winds) (1978)
Four pieces (prep hpcd) (1977)
Lullaby (perc) (1982)
ORGAN
Opening gates (1979)
Song of the bridegroom (1978)
Theme and 8 variations (1976)
VOCAL
Variations on a theme of motherhood (S, cl and fl) (1982)
SACRED
Four psalms of exaltation (ch and orch) (1981)
Heritage of the servants of the Lord (w-ch) (1976)
Psalm 40 (m-S and pf) (1978)
Ref. composer

PIERPONT, Marie de
French organist and composer. d. March, 1896.
Compositions
CHAMBER
Organ pieces
Piano pieces
VOCAL
Songs
OPERA
Le triomphe du coeur
Van Dyck amoureux
Ref. 226, 276, 307, 433

PIERRET, Phedora
French pianist, teacher and composer. b. Paris, ca. 1810. She was a pupil of M. Zimmermann and H. Herz and received first prize for the piano from the Paris Conservatoire in 1826. She taught the piano, solfege and singing and composed piano pieces and vocal romances.
Ref. 263

PIERROT, Noélie Marie Antoinette
French organist, professor and composer. b. Paris, 1899. She studied at the Schola Cantorum and the Paris Conservatoire, where she won first prize for the organ, counterpoint and fugue. She was a professor at the Schola Cantorum from 1925 to 1931 and the Gregorian Institute from 1943 to 1946. She was organist at St. Pierre du Gros-Caillou Church, Paris from 1929 and a soloist with the ORTF after 1935. She gave recitals in Europe and made numerous recordings of Bach and French composers.
Compositions
ORGAN
Chorale on a theme by Gabriel Faure
VOCAL
Melodies (S and pf)
SACRED
Motets
Publications
New Method for the Keyboard. 4 books.
Organ Method. With Jean Bonfils.
Editions of organ works of 16th, 17th and 18th-centuries.
Editions of Padovano's works.
Ref. 94, 206

PIETSCH, Edna Frieda
American pianist, violinist, lecturer and composer. b. Milwaukee, WI, May 7, 1894. She studied the piano under Ida Schroeder for 20 years, beginning when she was eight. She studied harmony and composition under William Middelschutte, Carl Eppert, Rudolf Kopp and Bernard Dieter at Chicago Conservatory and took violin lessons with Pearl Brice. From 1942 to 1966 she taught composition at Wisconsin Conservatory. Some of her works were performed by the Chicago Symphony Orchestra in Milwaukee in 1942 and 1946. She received many composition awards.
Compositions
ORCHESTRA
Symphony
Two piano concertos
Viola concerto
Fantasy for orchestra (1942)
Five oriental impressions (small orch) (1946)
CHAMBER
Piano quintet
Suite (ww qnt) (1953)
String quartet in D-Major (1953)
Largo appassionata (vln, vlc and pf)
Woodland fantasy (fl and pf)
Other pieces
PIANO
Five poems
Sonata
VOCAL
Approx. 30 songs
Bibliography
Austin, D. *Honor for Miss Pietsch. Milwaukee Sentinel*, June 5, 1971.
Ref. composer, Working papers on women in music, 94, 142

PIGGOTT, Audrey Margaret
20th-century Canadian cellist, pianist and composer. b. London. She became an A.R.C.M. (performer) of the Royal College of Music, London. She also studied at the Ecole Normale de Musique, Paris. She made concert appearances in England and Canada with prominent orchestras and on the radio.
Compositions
VOCAL
Six Elizabethan songs (w-vces)
Song cycle: Consolation (Elizabeth Barrett Browning); Death (Thomas Hood); Friendship (Hartley Coleridge); Silence (Hood) (A and 8 vlc)
Two part songs: A boy's song; On Westminster Bridge
INCIDENTAL MUSIC
For radio and television plays
Ref. 206, 229, 622, 643

PIGNETELLI, Mariana
16th-century Italian composer. She was the patroness of Pietro Bonaventura Metastasio and composed the music for most of his dramas.
Compositions
INCIDENTAL MUSIC
Music for plays:
Achilles in Ciros
Atilio Regulo
Demonfonte
Temistocles
Titus' Clemency
Ref. 268

PIKE, Eleanor B. Franklin
English pianist, choral conductor, professor and composer. b. London, 1890; d. ca. 1973. She studied at the Tobias Matthay Piano School and later became an L.R.A.M., A.R.C.M., L.T.C.L. and M.R.S.T. She was also a professor of music.

Compositions
CHAMBER
Reverie (vln, vlc and pf) (Augener)
Idylle (vln and pf) (Swaap)
A sea song (vln and pf)
PIANO
Numerous pieces incl.:
Duets
Trios
Publications
The Easiest Tune Book. For children. Edwin Ashdown Ltd.
Ref. 63, 94, 490

PILIS, Heda

Yugoslav music editor, singer and composer. b. Osijek, June 3, 1925. She studied singing at the Vatroslav Lisinski music school in Zagreb and worked as a music editor for Radio Zagreb. Her songs were written mainly for children and inspired by folk melodies. She took part in numerous regional and children's festivals and some of her compositions won prizes. DISCOGRAPHY. PHOTOGRAPH.
Compositions
VOCAL
Popular and children's songs (vce and orch or pf) incl.:
Jeka (1960)
Jesen na morskoj obali (1962)
I'll marry you
Mary
Merry vocals
My granny
Our pussy cat
Put ljubavi (1961)
Susret na plesu (1959)
Ti, rijeka i ti (1960)
U proljetno vece (1959)
Vrtuljak (1962)
Ref. composer, 416, 563

PILLING, Dorothy

Composition
PIANO
Minuet in G (Assoc. Board, 1935)
Ref. 473

PINAR, Florencia del

15th-century Spanish poetess and composer. Her brother Pinar was also a poet. Three of her poems appeared in early 16th-century Cancioneros (song books) in the British Museum, the Cancionero Costantina and the Cancionero general of Hernando del Castillo, 1511.
Ref. 464

PINEL, Julie

18th-century French composer.
Compositions
CHAMBER
Dances of dubious authenticity (Roger)
Instrumental pieces
Lute pieces (Roger)
VOCAL
Nouveau receuil d'airs serieux et à boire (1 or 2 vces and figured bass) (Paris, 1737)
Ref. 128, 653

PINOTTINI, Maria Teresa d'. See AGNESI-PINOTTINI, Maria Teresa d'

PIO DI SAVOJA, Isabella D. (nee Scapinelli, Countess)

Italian composer. b. Carpi, ca. 1768; d. Casinalbo, Modena, April 23, 1809. She was the daughter of Count Bartolomeo Scapinelli and Maria Borghi. She married Bernardino Pio di G. Andrea in 1788.
Compositions
VOCAL
Three ariettas: Placa gli sdegni tuoi; Se lungi men'vo; Sei troppo vezzosa (hp and vce) (Estense collection) (1885)
Ref. 105, 157

PIRES DE CAMPOS, Lina

Brazilian pianist, teacher and composer. b. São Paulo, 1918. She studied the piano under E. Lubrano Franco and L. Peracchi; theory under F. Francheschini, Caldeira Filho and O. Lacerda and after 1958, composition under Camargo Guarnieri. She graduated from the João Gomes de Aruajo Conservatorio and the Instituto Musical Benedetto Marcello, São Paulo with the gold medal for the best student. After some years as a pianist and assistant to Magdalena Tagliaferro (q.v.) she founded her own music school in 1964 and in 1977 won the Teacher of the Year award from the Music Association, São Paulo. She was a member of the Music Commission for São Paulo from 1969 to 1971 and a jurist in national piano competitions. DISCOGRAPHY.
Compositions
ORCHESTRA
Ponteio No. 1 (str orch)
Toada (str orch)
CHAMBER
Sonatina (fl and pf) (1976)
Ponteio a tocatina (vla) (1970)
Preludios, nos, 1, 2 and 3 (vla) (1975)
PIANO
Acalanto (1959)
Ciclo da boneca, 5 small pieces (1961)
Cinco peças infantis (1962)
Estorietas, Nos. 1, 2, and 3 (1975)
Ponteio, No. 1 (1959)
Ponteio, No. 2 (ded Guarnieri) (1976)
Sete variacões sobre o tema Mucama Bonita (1962)
Valsa Nos. 1 and 2 (1960, 1975)
Variacões sobre tema brasileira
VOCAL
Chula (Amazonia) (mix-ch a-cap) (1962)
João Cambuete (w-ch a-cap) (1962)
Pedreiros (m-ch a-cap) (1962)
Songs incl.:
Confissão (1966)
Embolada (1961) (2nd prize, A Cancão Brasileira contest)
Eu sou como aquela fonte (hon mention, Cuidade de Santos contest, 1966)
Modinha (1961)
Retrato (1977)
Toada (1961)
Voce diz que me quer bem (1960)
Ref. Alan Pedigo (Booneville, AR), 563

PIRES DE PIRES, D. Maria Clementina

20th-century Brazilian composer.
Composition
OPERA
Folclore (Kum)
Ref. 156

PIRES DOS REIS, Hilda

Brazilian pianist, conductor, professor and composer. b. Rio de Janeiro, October 10, 1919. She gained her D.Mus. (conducting and piano) from the Federal University of Rio de Janeiro. She later became head of the composition department and a professor at the Federal University's music school. She taught the piano at the Brazilian Conservatory and researched harmony. PHOTOGRAPH.
Compositions
ORCHESTRA
Revery (1963)
Spanish fantasy (1945)
CHAMBER
Brazilian quintet (4 trb and trp) (1983)
Medieval quintet (fl, ob, cl, hn and bsn) (1982)
Brazilian quartet (4 bsn) (1983)
String quartet in B-Minor (2 vln, vla and bsn) (1940)
Trio No. 1 (vln, pf and bsn) (1938)
Brazilian fantasy (trp and pf) (1984)
Brazilian serenade (d-b and pf) (1983)
Brazilian serenade Nos. 1 and 2 (vln and pf) (1946)
Fantasy sonata (vln and pf) (1937)
Introduction and popular song (vlc and pf) (1953)
Serenade: serenade and art song (bsn and pf) (1967)
Waltz: Brazilian serenade and song (vlc and pf) (1950)
Miniature (org) (1983)
Studies Nos. 1 and 2 (gtr) (1979)
PIANO
Brazilian fantasy, serenade (1974)
Serenade waltz; Fantasy waltz (2 pf) (1971)

Batuque (1939)
Sonatina (1938)
VOCAL
Cantares (vce and pf) (1965)
Eu te quis tanto (vce and pf) (1950)
Jongo (vce and pf) (1941)
Interrupted history (vce and pf) (1983)
Song (vce, fl and pf) (1957)
Legenda (vce and pf) (1945)
Tristezas de amor (vce and pf) (1965)
Via-lactea (vce and pf) (1959)
Publications
Conceitos filosoficos e cientificos na pedagogia musical.
Genese do nacinalismo musical brasileiro. Revista do Conservatorio Brasileiro de Musica.
A Tonalidade com elemento basico do educacão formal classica.
Villa-Lobos, patrono. Revista do Ministerio da Educacão e Cultura.
Ref. composer, 333

PISTOLEKORS, Laura. See LAGO.

PITCHER, Gladys
American cellist, music editor, teacher and composer. b. Belfast, ME, 1890. She graduated from the New England Conservatory and did post-graduate work in theory, composition and the cello. She taught at Beloit College and the Work-Study-Play School, Passaic, NJ, and directed music in schools in Bennington, VT, and Manchester, NH. She worked as a music editor for C.C. Birchard Company, Boston.
Compositions
PIANO
At the bend of the road
Sun and water
VOCAL
The bugle of spring (ch)
Come spring (ch)
Pack clouds away (ch)
A story (ch)
The wood where the nightingale sings (w-ch and pf) (C. Birchard)
Dozen songs of the Americas (Belwin, 1958)
Japanesque
Vagabond song
OPERETTA
The tale of the toys
ARRANGEMENTS
Through all the world below (mix-ch and pf) (Neil A. Kjos)
Ten American songs (w-ch and pf) (Birchard)
Ref. 190, 292, 374, 622

PITMAN, Alice Locke. See PITTMAN, Alice Locke

PITOT, Genevieve
American pianist, arranger and composer. b. New Orleans, May 20, 1901. She was a pupil of Valsina Guillot, Anita Gonzales and Eugenie Wehrmann Schaffner in New Orleans and then of Alfred Cortot and Blanche Geraldy-Bascouret in Paris.
Compositions
PIANO
Sonatine (1947)
VOCAL
The morns are meeker (Emily Dickinson)
My river (T.S. Eliot)
Songs (James Joyce)
Other songs and arrangements
BALLET
The golden age
This property is condemned
Winesberg (1958)
Music for Martha Graham and Charles Weidman
Ref. 347, 488

PITT, Emma
20th-century American authoress, musician and composer.
Compositions
VOCAL
Songs incl.:
Buds and blossoms
Our royal prince
SACRED
In His name
Ref. 276, 292

PITTMAN (Pitman, Putman, Putnam), Alice Locke (Mrs. Wesley)
19th-century American composer.
Compositions
CHAMBER
Melody in B-Flat, op. 25 (vln and pf)
Violin pieces
VOCAL
Songs incl.:
Bright smiles the sun
Confession
The roe
Spinning song
MISCELLANEOUS
At rest
Ref. 226, 276, 292, 347, 433

PITTMAN, Evelyn LaRue
Black American choir conductor, teacher, writer and composer. b. McAlester, OK, January 6, 1910. At an early age she composed music for a Greek play, produced by the Morehouse-Spelman Players. She studied under Kemper Harreld at Spelman College, Atlanta and after graduating, entered Langston University. In Oklahoma City she taught and organized an orchestra and chorus, presented an operetta and a weekly radio program and founded the professional Evelyn Pittman Choir, which performed on radio and represented Oklahoma and Texas at the world fair in 1938. She moved to New York and attended the Juilliard School of Music, studying composition under Robert Ward in 1948. She later attended the University of Norman, studied under Harrison Kerr and Dean and obtained an M.M. in 1954. In 1956 she went to Paris and studied under Nadia Boulanger (q.v.).
Compositions
VOCAL
Anyhow (mix-ch a-cap) (New York: C. Fischer, 1952)
I love the springtime (mix-ch)
Joshua (soloists, mix-ch and pf) (Fischer, 1955)
Oklahoma is my home (mix-ch)
Sit down servant (A, B and ch a-cap) (Fischer, 1949)
Trampin' (mix-ch a-cap) (Stamford, CT: Jack Spratt Music Co., 1961)
We love America (mix-ch)
Rich heritage, song collection (1944)
OPERA
Cousin Esther, folk opera (composer) (1954, rev 1956)
Freedom's Child (1971)
INCIDENTAL MUSIC
Again the river (Helen Schyler)
Music for Greek play
ARRANGEMENTS
Anyhow or by'n by, spiritual (mix-ch a-cap) (ded composer's sister)
Nobody knows de trouble I see, spiritual (solo and mix-vces a-cap) (Fischer, 1954)
Rocka mah soul, spiritual (4 vces) (ded composer's mother) (Fischer, 1952)
Bibliography
Green, Mildred. *A study of the Lives and Works of Five Black Women Composers in America.* Ph. D. dissertation. University of Oklahoma. 1975.
Publications
Rich Heritage. 2 vols. White Plains, NY, 1968.
Ref. 136, 141, 335, 347, 415, 549

PIZER, Elizabeth Faw Hayden
American pianist, accompanist-coach, musicologist and composer. b. Watertown, NY, January 9, 1954. She began playing the piano at the age of two and studied privately under Lori Grief and Chandler Gregg for 16 years. She started notating musical themes from the age of eight. She studied at the Boston Conservatory, then moved to San Francisco and became an accompanist-coach, working at the San Jose State University for the opera workshop, in several performing ensembles and privately. She was a broadcast co-ordinator and producer for KCSM-FM San Mateo, CA, from 1981 and chairlady of the International League of Women Composers, 1984 to 1985. Her music is extensively performed in the United States. PHOTOGRAPH.
Compositions
ORCHESTRA
Under and overture, op. 37 (orch without strs) (1979)
BAND
Fanfare overture
CHAMBER
Piece of eight, op. 42 (2 ob, 2 cl, 2 hn and 2 bsn) (1977)
Nocturne, op. 28 (hp, cel, ob, vla and vlc) (1976)
Interfuguelude, op. 43 (str qrt; also fl, cor anglais, hn and bsn) (1977)
String quartet (1981)
Qulisoly, op. 38 (fl or vln and pf) (1976)

PIANO
A mon père, pour mon père, op. 40 (1977)
Expressions intime, op. 14-18 (1975)
Jimnobody No. 1, op. 22 (1976)
Jimnobody No. 2, op. 24 (1976)
Lyric fancies (1983)
Sonata No. 2, op. 10, in 1 mvt (1974)
Two brief pieces, op. 12 and 13 (1975)
VOCAL
Madrigals Anon, op. 51, 3 madrigals (5 part a-cap ch) (1979)
Slow, slow, fresh fount (Ben Jonson) (mix-ch and fl) (1977)
Five haiku, op. 48 (vce and cham ens) (1978)
Five haiku II, op. 50 (m-S and pf) (1979) (1st prize, Biennial National League of American Pen Women composition competition, 1982)
Look down, fair moon (Walt Whitman) (vce and pf) (1976)
When to the sessions of sweet silent thought, op. 47 (Shakespeare) (1978)
SACRED
Oratorio
Alleluia, op. 25 (2 S and mix-ch) (1976)
Holy Eucharist rite II, op. 46 (solo, mix-ch and pf or org) (1978)
Kyrie, op. 39 (mix-ch) (1976)
Kyrie eleison (mix-ch a-cap) (1983)
ELECTRONIC
In the Land of Nod (syn and tape) (1979)
Sunken flutes (syn and tape) (1979)
Ref. composer, 474, 622, 625

PLANICK, Annette Meyers
20th-century American composer of orchestral works, chamber music, piano pieces and songs (New York Music Publishers Holding Corp; Cole Music).
Ref. 40, 94, 347

PLASENCIA, Ubalda
19th-century Peruvian pianist and composer. She performed at the chamber concerts given by Mrs. Gorriti de Belzu in 1876.
Composition
PIANO
El incognito, waltz
Bibliography
Barbacci, R. *Apuntis para un diccionario biografica musical peruano.*
Fenix. *La revista de la biblioteca nacional de Lima.* No. 6, p. 486. 1949.
Ref. 403

PLATER, Marie. See CZETWERTYNSKA, Marie, Princess

PLATEROWA-BROEL-ZYBERK, Maria
19th-century Polish composer.
Compositions
VOCAL
Barcarolla (Italian text) (1885)
Ecce panis (2 vces and org) (1885)
Mgly poranne, op. 10 (vce and pf) (1885)
La notte (Italian text) (1885)
Serenata (Italian text) (1885)
SACRED
Parce Domine (2 vces) (1885)
Tantum ergo (4 vces and org) (1885)
Ref. 118

PLE-CAUSSADE, Simone
French pianist, lecturer and composer. b. Paris, August 14, 1897. She studied at the Paris Conservatoire under Cortot, H. Dallier, M. Emmanuel, Estyle, L. Capet and Georges Caussade, whom she later married. In 1928 she succeeded her husband at the Paris Conservatoire as a teacher of fugue and counterpoint. Among her pupils were Betsy Jolas (q.v.), Magne, J.E. Marie and Nikiprowetzky.
Compositions
ORCHESTRA
Concert (pf, trp, vlc and orch)
ORGAN
Communion pour la Fête de l'Assomption de la Fête de la bien heureuse Vierge Marie
Elevation pour la Fête de l'Assomption
Offertoire
Pater Noster
Regina coeli avec variations
Sonnens les matines

PIANO
Melodies
Preludes
Sonatas
VOCAL
Cantatas (ch a-cap)
Motets (equal vces)
Songs
SACRED
Psalms
Ref. 13, 17, 94, 477

PLEYEL, Camilla or Camille. See PLEYEL, Marie Felicity Denise

PLEYEL, Marie Felicity Denise (nee Mocke, Mooke or Moke)
French concert pianist, lecturer and composer. b. Paris, July 4, 1811; d. Brussels, March 30, 1875. She married Camille Pleyel, pianist, piano maker and composer, divorcing in 1844. She studied music under Jaque Hertz, Moscheles and Kalkbrenner. She made her debut as a pianist when she was 15 and later appeared in St. Petersburg and Germany and was highly praised by Schumann, Liszt, Mendelssohn and Chopin. She also played in the Paris Salon Pape in 1845 and in London in 1846. She taught at the Brussels Conservatoire from 1848 to 1872.
Compositions
CHAMBER
Piano pieces
ARRANGEMENTS
Premiers mélanges d'airs tires des opera de Rossini (pf)
Ref. 85, 103, 129, 260, 276, 332, 347

PLICQUE, Eveline
20th-century American composer. She won the Prix de Rome in 1950.
Composition
ORCHESTRA
Symphonie concertante (cham orch) (Henmar)
Ref. 280, 448

PLIEVA, Zhanna Vasilievna
20th-century Russian composer.
Composition
CHAMBER
Trio (pf and strs)
Ref. Otto Harrassowitz (Wiesbaden)

PLITT, Agathe
German concert pianist, teacher and composer. b. Thorn, 1831. In 1847 she went to Berlin, where Queen Elizabeth of Prussia recognised her talent as a pianist and financed her further musical education. Agathe made a number of successful concert tours from Berlin, where she lived and taught. She composed cantatas, choral pieces, songs, sacred motets and psalms.
Ref. 29, 226, 276, 347

PLONSEY, Jennifer
20th-century American composer.
Compositions
ORCHESTRA
Alto flute concerto (fl and orch) (1983)
CHAMBER
Stillness gives time (str qnt)
Three bypaths (ww qnt) (1984)
Floating sequence circle (vln, pf and b-cl) (1983)
Conjoint episodes (org and trp) (1984)
ELECTRONIC
The city made for people, suite (1984)
Ref. AMC newsletter

PLUMSTEAD, Mary (nee Frost)
English composer. b. 1905; d. May 4, 1980. DISCOGRAPHY.
Compositions
VOCAL
Songs incl.:
Close thine eyes (Quarles)
Four songs
A grateful heart (Hebert)

Ha'nacker mill
He was the one
Pied beauty
Sigh no more ladies (Shakespeare)
Slowly (James Reeves) (London: Boosey & Hawkes, ca. 1974)
The song of the Royal Duchy
Take, O take those lips away (Shakspeare)
SACRED
The song of the Cross
Ref. 94, 622

PODGORSKA, Ewa. See ADDENDUM

POINTON, Barbara

English lecturer and composer. b. Stoke-On-Trent, August 13, 1939. She obtained an honors degree from Birmingham University in 1960 and was a senior lecturer in music at Homerton College, Cambridge. She was awarded a Barber scholarship in 1959 and 1960.

Compositions
CHAMBER
Triptych (str qrt) (1968)
SACRED
Hymn to St. Thomas of Canterbury (1969)
TEACHING PIECES
Songs for the pictogram system for remedial readers
Ref. 206

POLAK, Nina

19th-century composer.

Compositions
CHAMBER
Arlequinade schottische (vln, fl and hn) (Noel)
Chasseurs d'Ambert, polka-mazurka (vln, fl and hn)
PIANO
Boléro
Camille, grande valse brillante
Cloches, waltz
Dans les bois, waltz
La diva, op. 1, waltz (Heugel)
Divertissement, op. 7
Fontemay-aux-roses, mazurka
Graziosa, mazurka
Louise Amelie, polka de salon
Mauresque, waltz
Pauline, redowa
Polka des oiseaux
Riyan, schottisch
Souvenir, mazurka
Sue la lac, barcarolle
Vaillance, mazurka
Zirna, op. 23, polka-mazurka (Grus)
Ref. 297

POLANOWSKA, Teofila

19th-century Polish pianist and composer. She studied the piano in Paris from 1840 to 1850.

Compositions
PIANO
Pieces incl.:
L'aurore, valse brillante, op. 18
Deux polkas, op. 15
Mélodie, op. 14 (ded Prince Adam Czartoryski)
Polonaise brillante
Ref. 35, 118

POLCZINSKA, Adolphine. See MANNKOPF, Adolphine

POLDOWSKI, Irene Regine. See WIENIAWSKA, Irene Regine

POLICARPO TEIXEIRA, Maria Margarida Fernandes

Portuguese concert pianist, violinist, teacher and composer. b. Guimaraes, 1905. She studied solfege and music theory under her father, Antonio Fernandes Policarpo; the violin under her uncle and the piano under Julia Viamonte. She gave her first piano concert at the age of ten and performed in several towns in Portugal.

Compositions
OPERETTA
Ines Pereira, farce (1938)
Juramento de amor (1936)
O Lourenço de Braga (1934)
INCIDENTAL MUSIC
Music for gymnastic classes
Ref. 268

POLIGNAC, Armande de, Countess of Chabannes

French conductor and composer. b. Paris, January 1, 1876; d. Seine-et-Oise, April, 29, 1962. She studied in Paris under Eugen Gigout Faure and Vincent d'Indy. She wrote ballet music for Loie Fuller and conducted her own work in the Chatelet. She married Count Alfred of Chabannes.

Compositions
ORCHESTRA
Les mille et une nuits, symphony (also ballet) (1914)
Aubade
CHAMBER
Quintets (Ricordi)
Le voyage, suite (str qrt)
Sonata (vln and pf)
Petite suite (pf) (1939)
VOCAL
Songs incl.:
Extraits de La Flute de Jade de F. Toussaint, 2 poems (vce and pf) (Paris: Nouvelle Revue Française)
BALLET
Chimeres, Greek ballet (1923)
La recherche de la verite, Chinese ballet (small orch) (1915)
La source loitaine, Persian ballet (1913)
Urashima, Japanese ballet
OPERA
L'hypocryte santifie (ca. 1910)
Judith de Bethulie, dramatic opera (1916)
Morgane, in 1 act
Les roses du Calife, op. 1 (1909)
Tamyris (1921)
OPERETTA
La petite sirène (1907)
Ref. 14, 105, 291, 347, 431, 622

POLIN, Claire (Mrs. Merle S. Schaff)

American flautist, musicologist, professor and composer. b. Philadelphia, January 1, 1926. She studied composition under Vincent Persichetti at the Philadelphia Conservatory and gained a B.Mus. in 1948, M.Mus. in 1950 and D.Mus. in 1955. She also studied composition under Peter Mennin at the Juilliard School of Music and Lukas Foss and Roger Sessions at Tanglewood. She attended Temple and Dropsie universities. She studied the flute privately under William Kincaid. She lectured on the flute, composition and musicology at Philadelphia Conservatory from 1949 to 1964 and from 1958 was associate professor at Rutgers University, lecturing in music history and theory, American music, the flute and history of art. She was active as a flautist in Europe and the Middle East and guest of honor of the State of Israel at the 6th international harp competition, where some of her works were performed. She was awarded the Delta Omicron prize for composition from 1954 to 1959, the Leverhulme fellowship to the University of Wales, Aberystwyth from 1963 to 1969 and two MacDowell fellowships. She won the Georgia State University Brass Symposium international award in 1970 and in 1973 was awarded a research-creative writing grant from Rutgers University. She received numerous commissions and her compositions have been widely performed by leading orchestras including the London Repertory Orchestra, the Seoul National Symphony, the New York Brass Quintet and the London Pro Musica Antiqua and in recent years in Russia, which she visited in 1980. She won ASCAP awards and received honorable mentions in Mannheim, in 1975 and Vercelli in 1974. She is a member of the Pan-Orphic Duo. DISCOGRAPHY. PHOTOGRAPH.

Compositions
ORCHESTRA
Symphony No. 1, in 2 mvts (New York: Seesaw Music, 1961)
Second symphony (Korean) (1974) (Seesaw, 1975)
Amphion (1979)
The Golden Fleece (1979)
Mythos, concerto (hp and str orch) (1983)
Three scenes from Gilgamesh (fl and str orch) (Seesaw, 1975)
CHAMBER
The Journey of Owain Madoc (on Welsh discovery of America, 1170) (brass and perc ens) (1971) (Seesaw, 1974)
Cader idris (brass qnt) (1970) (New York: G. Schirmer, 1971)
Consecutive (fl, cl, vln, vlc and pf) (1967)
Ma'alot (vla and perc qrt) (Seesaw, 1981)

Makimono I (fl, cl, vln, vlc and pf) (Seesaw, 1972)
Makimono II (brass qnt) (1973)
Pentalogue (2 trp, trb, tba and hpcd) (1967)
Res naturae (ww qnt) (1980) (Dorn, 1982)
Synaulia (fl, cl, vln, vlc and pf) (1968) (Seesaw)
Telemannicon II (brass ens) (1980)
String quartet No. 1 (1953)
String quartet No. 2 (1954)
String quartet No. 3 (The Legend of Orion) (1961)
Klockwork (a-sax, hn and bsn) (Dorn Prod.)
Salaspils (vln, vlc and pf; also vce, vln, vlc and pf) (1980)
Tower sonata (fl, cl and bsn) (Seesaw, 1975)
The walum olum (cl, vla and pf) (1984)
Dark nebulae (vla and perc; also S, fl and pf)
The death of Procis (fl and tba) (Seesaw, 1973)
Felina (hp and vln) (1980) (Seesaw, 1982)
First flute sonata (fl and pf) (Southern Music, 1954)
Kuequenaku-cambriola (perc and pf) (1982) (comm Tricentennial, Philadelphia)
Pièce d'encore (vla or vln) (Seesaw, 1976)
Second sonata (fl and hp) (Seesaw, 1975)
Sonata (fl and hp) (1968-1974)
Vigniatures (vln and hp) (Seesaw, 1981)
Eligmos archaios (hp) (Seesaw, 1974)
Georgics (fl) (1981) (Dorn, 1982)
Margoa (fl) (Seesaw, 1972)
Rainstance (gtr)
Serpentine (vla) (Seesaw, 1974)
Structures (fl) (Elkan-Vogel, 1964)
Summer settings (hp) (New York: Lyra Music, 1967)

PIANO
Laissez sonner, sonata (Seesaw, 1976)
Out of childhood (1969) (Seesaw, 1973)

VOCAL
Lorca songs (w-ch and pf) (1969)
No man is an island (mix-ch and pf) (1969)
Antigone (S and str qrt) (1964)
Hen Ganiadau Gwanwyn, music for the Prince of Wales (vce and vlc) (1972)
No-Rai, Korean song cycle (S, fl and d-b) (1964)
Welsh bardic odes (1959)
Windsongs (vce and gtr) (1978)

SACRED
Biblical madrigals (mix-ch) (1974)
De spei (mix-ch and pf) (1974)
Infinito, requiem (S, speaker, 4-part mix-ch and a-sax) (1972)
Isaiah syndrome (narr, mix-ch, vln, vlc, hp and perc) (1980)
Rosa mundi (mix-ch and pf) (1974)
Canticles from Song of Songs (m-vces) (1959)
Te Deum (m-vces) (1974)

ELECTRONIC
O, Aderyn Pur (fl, a-sax and tape) (1974) (Seesaw, 1973)
Telemannicon (solo or duo ob with tape) (1975) (Seesaw, 1973)

Publications

The Ap Huw Manuscript. Switzerland Institute of Medieval Music. 1982.
Advanced Flutist. With William Kincaid. 2 vols. Elkan Vogel. 1974.
Art and Practice of Modern Flute Technique. With William Kincaid. 3 vols. 1967.
Music of the Ancient Near East. Vantage Press, 1954. Repr. Greenwood Press, 1974.
Bible and Early Welsh Music. Tatzlil Musicological Magazine. 1980.

Bibliography

MOMA: Women Composers: Summergarden Concert. High Fidelty; Musical America, 25. December, 1975.

Ref. composer, 40, 77, 84, 137, 142, 185, 190, 228, 280, 457, 494, 563, 611, 622, 624, 625

POLK, Grace Porterfield

20th-century American soprano, lecturer, poetess and composer. b. Richmond, IN,. She was national chairlady of poetry of the National League of American Pen Women.

Compositions

VOCAL
Songs incl.:
June dawn
My garden of roses
A ray of sunshine
Springtime
Children's songs

OPERETTA
Three operettas

Ref. 292, 323, 347

POLK REED, Marlyce Rae. See REED, Marlyce Rae Polk

POLKO, Elise Vogel

German mezzo-soprano, writer and composer. b. Leipzig, January 31, 1822; d. Munich, May 15, 1899. She was the sister of the explorer Eduard Vogel. She displayed early musical talent and advised by Mendelssohn, studied under Garcia in Paris. She became well known as a singer. After her marriage she concentrated on writing and the composition of piano pieces and songs.

Publications

Die Bettler Oper.
Faustina Hasse. 3 vols.
Musical sketches.
Nicolo Paganini und die Geigenbauer.
Reminiscenes of Mendelssohn.
Unsere Musikklassiker.

Ref. 276, 347, 433

POLLACK, Muriel. See POLLOCK, Muriel

POLLET, Marie Nicole Simonin

French harpist, teacher and composer. b. Paris, May 4, 1787. She was the daughter of Jean-Baptiste Simonin, a maker of stringed instruments who invented a mechanism for the harp. Elise studied the harp for three years under Blattman and then Dalmivare. She gave several concerts in 1808 and also taught the harp. She traveled to Germany, Poland, Russia and Italy in 1815. She wrote a book on harp playing method and composed harp pieces.

Ref. 26, 119, 124, 129, 162, 276, 433

POLLOCK (Pollack), Muriel (Molly Davidson)

American organist, pianist and composer. b. Kingsbridge, NY, January 21, 1904; d. Hollywood. She began composing at the age of 11. She worked for the NBC as an organist from 1935 to 1938 and continued her career in Hollywood as an accompanist and soloist of both classics and jazz.

Compositions

ORCHESTRA
Bolero
Everglade
Hispana
Mood in blue
Reminiscence
Shadows on the Bayou
Spanish suite

PIANO
Pieces incl.:
Notions, suite (1935)
Rooster rag (1917)
Other suites

VOCAL
Songs incl.:
Do you recall Saturday?
Give me your love
In Allah's garden
Love is a dancer
Ode to a man about town
Mood in blue

THEATRE
Songs for Pleasure Bound, play

Publications

Talking books for children incl. *Cinderella*; *Jack and Jill*; *Sleeping Beauty*.

Ref. 39, 228, 292, 347, 494

POLONIO, Cinira

Brazilian actress, singer and composer. b. Rio de Janeiro, 1861; d. 1948. She studied singing and music in France and Italy and made her debut as Marguerite in *Faust* in Rio, 1878.

Composition

OPERETTA
O Relogho de Cardeal (Machado Correira) (Lisbon, 1919)

Ref. 268, 431

PONCE, Ethel

20th-century American pianist, singer, teacher and composer. b. New York. She was one of the Ponce Sisters, a singing duo. She taught music in a private school.

Compositions
ORCHESTRA
Three dialogues (pf and orch)
MISCELLANEOUS
Blue haze
Happy landing
Holiday
A light in the window
Ref. 39, 280

PONSA, Maria Luisa (pseud. M.L. D'Orsay)

Spanish pianist and composer. b. Barcelona, 1878; d. Barcelona, 1919. She studied under Albeniz and later Marmontel in Paris. She founded the Instituto Musical, Barcelona.
Compositions
ORCHESTRA
Suite española
PIANO
Salon dances (under pseud)
VOCAL
Canciones catalanas
Himne a Catalunya
Ref. 107

POOL, Arlette (Marie)

American concert pianist, accompanist, teacher and composer. b. Meridian, MS, February 5, 1926. She gained her B.M. in 1946 and M.M. in 1948 from the Louisiana State University. She did private study with Earl D. Stout at Baton Rouge from 1945 to 1948 and James Friskin and Mischakoff in New York in 1948. She made her debut as a pianist in 1946 with the Louisiana State University symphony orchestra. She was an accompanist at the Louisiana State University music school from 1948, then became head of the piano department at Perkinston Junior College.
Compositions
CHAMBER
Suite (pf and vln) (1945)
Passacaglia and fugue (org) (1946)
PIANO
Sonatina (2 pf) (1945)
Sonata (1948)
Theme and variations (1945)
VOCAL
Choral pieces (w-ch a-cap)
Ref. 496

POOL, Jeannie Gayle (Mrs. K. Barker)

American flautist, critic, lecturer, poetess, research and development consultant, writer and composer. b. Paris, IL, November 6, 1951. She studied journalism at Ohio University from 1969 to 1971; the flute at Hartford Conservatory, Connecticut from 1971 to 1973; gained a B.A. in music in 1977 from Hunter College, New York and did graduate studies at Columbia University Graduate School of Arts and Sciences, New York, 1977 to 1979. She studied the flute under Harold Bennett, New York from 1973 to 1977. She is a music research and development consultant; a visual artist and poet and currently a free lance radio producer, with a weekly radio program. She was the national director of the first National Congresses of Women in Music, 1981 and the director of the Second, Third and Fourth International Congress on Women in Music, 1982, 1984 and 1985. She received a Sigma Alpha Iota award for outstanding programming in music, 1982. She is a lecturer at Loyola Marymount University, CA., and a director of the International Institute for the Study of Women in Music at California State University Northridge. PHOTOGRAPH.
Compositions
CHAMBER
Suite (fl) (1975)
ELECTRONIC
From the nineteenth floor (tape and perc ens) (1981)
Basic piano 101 (tape) (1977)
Duet for voice and bell (tape) (1980)
Life in all (mix-ch on tape) (1981)
Rants, collection of text sound pieces (1982) (J. Gale, 1982)
MULTIMEDIA
Mudesay (1977)
For the love of mankind (1982)
Ref. composer

POOL, Marie. See POOL, Arlette

POOLE, Anna Ware (Mrs. J.T. Cook)

Early 20th-century American pianist, singer, teacher and composer. b. Buffalo, NY,. She studied under L.M. Gottschalk and Carlotta Patti, became a pianist and singer and taught for a number of years. She composed piano pieces and songs.
Ref. 226

POOLE, Caroline

18th-century English composer.
Compositions
VOCAL
The orphan that's wet with the rain, a favourite song (composer) (London: Lavenu, 1800)
The sequel to Crazy Jane, a favourite song (composer) (Lavenu, 1800)
Ref. 65, 405

POOLE, Maria (Mrs. Dickons)

English soprano and composer. b. London, ca. 1770; d. May 4, 1833. She studied singing under Rauzzini in Bath and first appeared in concert in Vauxhall, 1783. She sang at Covent Garden and in concert throughout England and after 1816 in European capitals.
Compositions
VOCAL
And say no, a favourite ballad (London: Longman & Broderip, 1792)
Six canzonets and a lullaby (vce and pf or hp) (Longman & Broderip, ca. 1794)
Dear Le Verrou, a favourite ballad (Longman & Broderip, ca. 1792)
The wandering lamb, a favourite ballad
Ref. 6, 65, 128, 405

POOLER, Marie

American teacher and composer. b. Wisconsin, April 22, 1928. She studied at St. Olaf College and obtained her B.A. and at California State College, Fullerton. She taught at Shimer College, IL, from 1949 to 1951 and in public schools, 1957 to 1967, and at Long Beach City College, CA, after 1971.
Compositions
VOCAL
Songs
SACRED
Praise the Lord, His glories show (mix-ch) (H.W. Gray)
Anthems
Hymns
Choral works
Arrangements
Ref. 142, 190

POPATENKO, Tamara Aleksandrovna

Soviet composer. b. Moscow, April 9, 1912. She graduated from the Moscow Conservatory, where she studied composition under V. Shebalin.
Compositions
ORCHESTRA
Classic suite (1938)
Suite (orch of Russian folk insts) (1944)
Three children's suites: Novo godnyaya (1946); Igrushki (1947); Gusi-lebedi (1951)
CHAMBER
Two quartets (1938)
Dreams (hn and pf) (1959)
Eleven easy pieces (vln and pf) (1948)
Four pieces (vln and pf) (1954)
Humoresque (vla and pf) (1963)
Romance (vln and pf) (1957)
Scherzo (vln and pf; also hn and pf, 1970)
Sonata (vla and pf) (1956)
Variations (vlc and pf) (1959)
Waltz, Iva (vla and pf) (1963)
Druzhba, dance suite (1970)
VOCAL
Gornii veter, cantata (Y.A. Ostrovskov) (1967)
Akvareli (L. Tatyanicheva) (mix-ch a-cap) (1972)
Liricheskii triptich (N. Nekrasov) (mix-ch a-cap) (1972)
Ydikli lydea shumyat (M. Lapirov and P. Komarov) (mix-ch a-cap) (1966)

Romances (R. Beris) (1955)
Romances (M. Lermontov) (1951)
Romances (A. Pushkin) (1949)
Selections of choruses (mix-ch a-cap; also mix-ch and pf) (Sovietski Kompozitor, 1980)
Sixteen romances (French poets) (1947)
Over 200 songs for children
BALLET
Repkal (1964)
OPERETTA
Na lesnoi opushke, for children
Pryanich ni chelovechek, for children (1971)
Zlmhaya skazka, for children
THEATRE
Lisa, Zayats i Petukh, musical tale (1971)
Lisa i Drozd, musical tale (1974)
Lyagushata i Tsaplya, musical tale (1971)
Snegurochka, play
Teremok, musical tale (1957)
INCIDENTAL MUSIC
Chudo-melnista, cartoon film (1950)
Radio plays (1944-1951)
Ref. 9, 21, 87, 94, 330

POLPINIERE, Mme. le. See DESHAYES, Marie

POPOVICI, Elise

Rumanian concert pianist, conductor, lecturer and composer. b. Suceava, May 11, 1921. In Suceava she studied the piano, theory, harmony, counterpoint and composition from 1928 to 1940 under Professor August Karnet. In Iasi she studied the piano under Elisa Ciolan from 1942 to 1948 and orchestral and choral conducting under Antonin Ciolan at the Conservatory. She also studied harmony, counterpoint and composition under Professor Constantin Georgescu and history of music under Professor George Pascu. She graduated from the conservatory in 1947 and continued her studies in Bucharest, where her teachers included Ada Nasturel (piano), Paul Constantinescu (harmony), Zeno Vancea (counterpoint), Tudor Ciortea (musical forms) and Constantin Bugeanu (instrumentation and orchestration). She began her career as a concert and chamber pianist in 1944. In 1949 she became a research worker at the Folklore Institute, Bucharest. In 1956 she returned to Iasi to be music mistress and pianist at the State Opera and then lectured in harmony, counterpoint and the piano at the George Enescu Conservatory. PHOTOGRAPH.

Compositions
ORCHESTRA
Symphonic poem (1959)
Geampara, folk dance (1956)
CHAMBER
String quintet (1970)
Wind quintet (1971)
Four miniatures (vln, vla, vlc and pf) (1969)
Adagio and burlesque (vln, vlc and pf) (1968)
Four sketches (trp, hn and trb) (1969)
Trio (cl, vlc and pf) (1971)
Trio (cl, vln and pf) (1973)
Ballad (vlc and pf) (1970)
Sonata (cl and pf) (1967)
Sonata (vla and pf) (1969)
Sonata (vlc and pf) (1967)
Pieces (vln, vlc, vla, trp and hn)
PIANO
Dance in Rumanian folk style (1950)
Five Rumanian folk dances (1955)
Little suite (1951)
Sonatine (1966)
Toccata (1953)
VOCAL
Haramoursh, suite of folk songs (2 vces and orch or pf) (1952)
Forest whistle (Eminescu) (ch a-cap) (1972)
Tie the love in white kerchief, folk song (ch a-cap) (1971)
Wedding suite (ch a-cap) (1954)
The cuckoo is singing in the riverside coppice (vce and pf) (1954)
Gold and silver (Jebeleanu) (vce and pf) (1960)
I have heard, my sweetheart, Rumanian folk song (vce and pf) (1952)
Lullaby (O. Cazimir) (m-S and pf) (1959)
Pastorale (Stefan) (vce and pf) (1959)
Seed flowers, my dear (folk words) (vce and pf) (1957)
Seven lieder (Chirai Lodreanu) (vce and pf) (1957)
Songs (Eugen Jebeleanu, Alexandru Sahighian and Aurel Baranga)
THEATRE
Numerous pieces for marionette theatre, Iasi
Ref. composer

PORCAIRAGUES, Azalais de. See AZALAIS DE PORCAIRAGUES

PORTCH, Margaret

Composition
PIANO
Titania's Court: Pease-blossom - Moth - Cobweb - Mustard seed (Anglo-French)
Ref. 473

PORTER, Debra

20th-century American gamelan player, pianist, accompanist and composer. She is currently the accompanist for Reed College Dance Department. She composes mainly for dance.

Composition
VOCAL
Butterfly waltz (Taoist tale) (2 vces) (1982) (ded Judith Massee)
Ref. V. McDermott (Portland)

PORTER, Ellen Jane. see LORENZ, Ellen Jane

PORTER, Mrs. See LORENZ, Ellen Jane

PORTER, Mrs. David. See NOYES, Edith Rowena

PORTER, Ruth. See CRAWFORD SEEGER, Ruth

POSADA Y TORRE, Ana

19th-century Cuban pianist, singer and composer. b. San Juan de los Remedios. She studied the piano under Mannel Lahoz and then S. Mendizabal. With her sister she became well known as a singer and pianist in Madrid in the 1880s. She composed piano pieces and songs.
Ref. 389

POST, Jennifer

American composer. b. 1949.

Compositions
CHAMBER
Three dances (fl and hpcd) (1970)
Ref. 346

POSTON, Elizabeth

English organist, concert pianist, authoress and composer. b. Highfield, October 24, 1905. She studied the piano from a very young age and later attended The Royal College of Music, London. She also studied the piano under Harold Samuel and the organ under Sir Stanley Marchant, organist of St. Paul's Cathedral. For a while she turned to art and toured in Italy. On her return to England in 1939 she became director of music for the European service of the BBC. She resigned in 1945 to devote herself to composition and received help from Vaughan Williams. She appeared as a pianist at the National Gallery Concerts between 1940 and 1945. She was influenced by her years in Italy to write her *Sei canzoni* with the intention of doing for Italian folk songs what Bartok had done for the Hungarian. Seven of her songs were published before she was twenty. DISCOGRAPHY.

Compositions
ORCHESTRA
Fanfare for Halle on Sir John Barbirolli's 70th-Birthday (1969)
Harlow concertante (str qrt and str orch) (1969)
CHAMBER
Concertino for ancient instruments (on theme of Martin Peerson) (rec, ob d'amore, vla da gamba and hpcd) (1950)
Trio (fl, cl or vla and hp) (1958)
Peter halfpenny's tunes (rec and pf) (1959)
Sonatina (pipes and pf) (1951)
Sonatina (vlc and pf) (1972)
Suite (fl and ob)
Serenatina (pipes) (1959)
Two pieces for psaltery

PIANO
Fiesta (Novello, 1960)
Lullaby (London: Novello, 1960)
VOCAL
A garland of laurel (T and str orch) (1950)
An English day book (ch) (1971) (comm Farnham Festival)
An English kalendar (ch) (1969) (comm Farnham Festival)
Ardan mor (1928)
Be still, my sweet sweeting (1928)
The bellman's song (1925)
Brown is my love (1925)
Call for the robin redbreast (1928)
In youth is pleasure (1928)
Maid quiet (1925)
Sei canzoni: Six Italian folk songs (1950)
Seven songs of Machiavelli (T, fl, hp and lute) (1967)
She is all so slight (1942)
Six French folk songs (1972)
Song of the season (1968)
The stockdoves (1945)
Sweet Suffolk owl (second setting with hp or pf) (1972)
Two arrangements of William Boyce: By thy banks, gentle Stour; Tell me, lovely shepherd
SACRED
The Holy Child (mix-ch, soloists and str orch or org) (1950)
The Nativity (mix-ch, soloists and str orch or org) (1951)
Benediction for the arts (ch and org) (1970)
Happy are the men (unison ch and pf or org) (1959)
Song of wisdom (w or mix-ch) (1956)
St. Cecilia festival anthem: Antiphon and psalm - Laudate Dominum (ch and org) (1955)
Three Scottish carols (mix-ch and strs or org) (1969)
Two carols in memory of Peter Warlock: O Bethlehem (mix-ch) (1956); Praise our Lord (w-ch and pf) (1956)
Welcome, Child of Mary, carol (mix-ch, soloists and cham ens or org) (1967)
In Bethlehem Town, carol (1958)
Jesus Christ and the apple tree, carol collection
Magnificat (2 vces and org) (1961)
Nativity for N-town (1962)
OPERA
The briery bush
INCIDENTAL MUSIC
Music for radio incl.:
Comus (Milton) (1946)
Elizabethans (1945)
In Parenthesis (David Jones) (1946)
Lives of the Poets (Suckling, Herrick, Donne) (1943-1947)
Paradise Lost (Milton) (1947)
The Royal Thames (1946)
The Spear of Gold (L.A.G. Strong) (1946)
Twelfth Night (Shakespeare) (1947)
A Room with a View (E.M. Forster) film
Howard's End, film (1970)
Publications
The Baby's Song Book. 1971.
The Cambridge Hymnal. 1967.
Cantata de la terre. With Paul Arma.
The Faber Book of Folk Songs. 1972.
The Penguin Book of American Folk Songs. 1964.
Schubert. Calbert Books. 1954.
Translations.
Ref. 2, 8, 14, 15, 22, 70, 84, 141, 347, 477, 563, 609, 622, 637

POTOCKA-PILAVA, Laura
Polish composer. ca. 1800.
Composition
VOCAL
Wladyslaw Lokietek (Warsaw: Spiewy historyczne, J. U. Niemcewicz, 1816)
Ref. 118

POTT, Aloyse (alt. name Winklarde Forazet, a family name)
Austrian cellist, pianist and composer. She studied the piano under Charles Czerny and composition under Gyrowetz.
Compositions
CHAMBER
String quartets
VOCAL
Lieder
SACRED
Mass (4 vces and orch)
Ref. 26, 347

POTTER, Anice. See TERHUNE, Anice

POUILLAN, Mlle. See POUILLAU, Mlle.

POUILLAU (Pouillan), Mlle.
18th-century French harpsichordist, pianist and composer. b. Paris.
Compositions
CHAMBER
Three sonatas, op. 1 (hpcd, vln and vlc) (1783)
PIANO
Pieces incl.:
Sonatas
Ref. 25, 26, 119, 226, 276, 347, 433

POULET DEFONTAINE, Madeleine
French composer. b. Lavardac Lot-en-Garonne, September 11, 1904. She studied at the Conservatory of Bordeaux and married the conductor Gaston Poulet.
Compositions
CHAMBER
Saxophone quartet
String quartet
String trio
VOCAL
Two songs (mix-ch a-cap)
SACRED
Oratorio (soloists, ch and orch)
BALLET
La boutique au oiseaux
Galaxie
ELECTRONIC
Concerto (ondes Martentot)
Ref. composer

POWELL, Maud
American violinist and composer. b. 1868; d. 1920.
Composition
CHAMBER
Plantation melodies (vln and pf)
Ref. 63, 323

POWELL, Mrs. Watkins
19th-century American composer.
Compositions
VOCAL
Songs incl.:
Answer
Cradle song
Cupid kissed me
Ref. 276, 433

POWERS, Ada Weigel
Early 20th-century American pianist and composer. b. Watertown, NY,. She composed piano and violin pieces, ballet music and songs.
Ref. 226, 347

POWNALL, Mary Ann (nee Wrighten)
English actress, singer and composer. b. February, 1751; d. August 11, 1796. She was well known as a ballad singer and actress before going to America in 1792, where she became a member of the Old American Company and organized and participated in a number of concerts in Boston and other cities. Her song *Jemmy in the Glen* was one of the first songs published by a woman in America. She died of shock eight days after the elopement of her daughter with a pantomimist.
Compositions
VOCAL
Songs incl.:
Advice by the ladies of Boston
'Bly the Colin
Cottage boy
An English air
A favourite song

The happy rencontre, or second thoughts are best (1794) (New York: I. Moller, 1798)
Jemmy of the Glen (Baltimore: Joseph Carr, 1778)
Kiss me now or never
Kisses sued for (Shakespeare) (New York: G. Gilbert, 1795)
Mrs. Pownal's address
My Henry swore at his parting
Washington

Publications

Six Songs for Harpsichord. With James Hewitt. 1794.
Second book of songs for piano or harpsichord. With James Hewitt. 1793.

Ref. 226, 228, 347, 372, 415, 633

POZZONE, Maria. See ADDENDUM

PRADELL, Leila

American pianist, teacher and composer. b. Boston, September 15, 1932. She graduated from Boston University with a B.M. and from New England Conservatory with an M.M., after studying composition under Judd Looke. After two years' study at Tanglewood she went to Paris to attend master classes given by Nadia Boulanger. She was composer and consultant for a school system in Boston, directed many musicals for adults and children and was a pianist and teacher at schools in Alaska and Massachusetts. She represented the New England Conservatory at the International Society for Contemporary Music, Bonn, Germany in 1977. She taught theory and composition in the preparatory department of the New England Conservatory. PHOTOGRAPH.

Compositions

ORCHESTRA
Fugue
Petite suite magique (1974)
Suite for children (1973)

PIANO
Diary from Athens, suite
Game of fifths
Micropatterns (Belwin, 1982)
Sonatina, in 3 movements
Suite, in 3 movements

VOCAL
Paint box, song cycle (S, chil-ch and pf)
Alaskan fall (S and pf) (1970)
Carousel (S, str qrt and hp) (1976)
Children from many lands (vce, pf and Orff insts)
Children of tomorrow (vce and pf)
June (vce and Orff insts)
My world (vce and pf)
River (S, vlc and pf)
Peace round, 3 parts
Song cycle of protest for Vietnam (S, gtr and pf)
Thoughts of Vanuschka (S, hn, fl and pf) (1976)
A tree that stands
Two short songs

SACRED
Easter vigil
Prayer, in 9 parts

OPERA
Tom Thumb, in 1 act

THEATRE
The Hobbit
Don Quixote

MULTIMEDIA
One work (tape, ch, dance and card game)

Ref. composer

PRATESI, Mira. See SULPIZI, Mira

PRATTEN, Mrs. Robert Sidney

English guitarist and composer. b. England, ca. 1840. She married the flautist and composer Robert Sidney Pratten. She composed over 250 pieces for the guitar.

Publications

A book of instruction for the gigliera, a wood and straw instrument.
Guitar School. Methods.
Learning the Guitar Simplified.

Ref. 6, 226, 276, 433

PRAVOSSUDOVITCH (Prawossudowitsch), Natalja Michajlovna

Russian pianist and composer. b. Vilna, August 14, 1899. From 1918 to 1925 she studied at the Leningrad Conservatory under Vera Skriabina (piano), S. Liapunov (counterpoint), N. Chernov (fugue and form) and M. Steinberg (instrumentation) and graduated with a diploma in composition. From 1929 to 1931 she attended the Berlin Academy of Arts where she took master classes with Arnold Schoenberg. In 1931 she moved to Merano, Italy. DISCOGRAPHY.

Compositions

ORCHESTRA
First symphony, op. 35, Vita e meditazione, in 4 mvts (1935)
Second symphony, op. 40, Simplicissima, in 3 mvts (1960)
Third symphony, op. 41, Sinfonia concertante, in 3 mvts (1961)
Suite for piano and large orchestra, op. 32, in 5 mvts (1938)
Piano Concerto, op. 16, in 1 mvt (1927)
Concerto for string quartet and chamber orchestra, op. 26 (1931)
Intermezzo No. 1, op. 29 (large orch) (1933)
Intermezzo No. 2, op. 38 (large orch) (1959)
Prelude, op. 10 (1923)
Sketches, op. 6 (1921)
Sketches, op. 8 (1922)
Tema e variazioni, op. 37 (1958)

CHAMBER
Piece for clarinet, violoncello, pianoforte and percussion, op. 19 (1928)
String quartet, op. 25 (1930)
String trio, op. 36 (1957)
Trio for two violins and violoncello, op. 33 (1937)
Trio for violoncello and pianoforte, op. 7 (1922)
Sonata, op. 28 (vlc and pf) (1932)
Variations on a theme by Schubert, op. 22 (vln and pf) (1928)
Two solo pieces for violoncello, op. 20 (1928)

PIANO
Agitato e fugato, op. 64 (1983)
Fantasia, op. 50 (1974)
Foxtrot-tempo, op. 15 (1925)
Fragmento, op. 45 (1969)
Fugue, op. 21 (1928)
Interrogando, op. 44 (1968)
Petite valse impromptu, op. 43 (1968)
Piano version of horn melody with orchestra, op. 51 (1974)
Piccolo studio e fugato, op. 61 (1982)
Prelude, op. 48 (1972)
Preludes and fugues, ops. 52, 53, 54, 56, 57, 58, 59, 60 and 63 (1976-1983)
Primitivi, 6 pieces, op. 17 (1927)
Sammlung lustiger Mollbagatellen, op. 3 (1920)
Scherzo e fugato, op. 62 (1982)
Short improvisations, op. 1 (before 1917)
Sonata, op. 13 (1925) (Helene Rubinstein prize, international composition competition, Buenos Aires, 1962).
Sonatine, op. 23 (1929)
Small pieces, op. 4
Suite No. 1, op. 46 (1969)
Suite No. 2, op. 47 (1972)
Suite No. 3, op. 55 (1978)
Tema con variazioni, op. 12 (1924)

VOCAL
Chorus a capella, op. 2 (composer) (1917)
Chorus a capella, op. 30 (German text) (1934)
Piece, op. 9 (S, vlc and pf) (1922)
Small pieces, op. 5 (vce and pf)
Songs on Russian texts, op. 18 (vce and pf) (1927)
Three German songs, op. 24 (S and pf) (1930)
Three German songs, op. 27 (composer) (S and pf) (1932)
Berceuse, op. 39 (S and pf) (1960)

SACRED
Passion und Auferstehung, op. 34, Easter music in 7 movements (mix-ch and large orch) (1940)
Fragment of Mass, op. 11 (mix-ch a-cap) (1924)

Publications

Meister Arnold Schoenberg and meine Berliner Erinnerungen. Memoirs.

Ref. 70, 105, 226

PRAWOSSUDOWITSCH, Natali(j)a. See PRAVOSSUDOVITCH, Natalja

PRAXILLA

Greek musician and poetess of Sicyon. ca. 450 B.C. She belonged to the Dorian school of lyric poetry. She was famous for her skolias or table-songs (later called drinking songs), which were sung at banquets, as a solo or by a chorus. She was also known for her dithyrambs and an epic poem entitled *Adonia*. In Athens her songs were compared to those of Alkman and Sappho (q.v.).

Ref. 264, 382

PRAY, Ada Jordan

20th-century American pianist, teacher and composer. She composed piano pieces and songs.
Ref. 347, 353

PRECIADOS Y MANESCAU, Cecilia

19th-century Spanish composer. She was the daughter of a music teacher D. Jose Preciados.
Composition
OPERETTA
El Conde de Viento Negro, zarzuela (D. Jose Preciados) (1867)
Ref. 389

PREDIC-SAPER, Branislava

Yugoslav pianist and composer. b. Zajecar, East Serbia, 1946. She studied the piano and theory at the Secondary Music School Josip Slavenski in Belgrade, from where she graduated in 1965. She attended the Music Academy in Belgrade and studied under Pedrag Milosevic. During her second year she won the first prize in the Union of Youth competition for *Sinfonijeta za gudace i timpane*. From 1966 to 1971 she was musical advisor for experimental and music drama programs and then worked as music program editor for the Students' Cultural Center. In 1973 she won first prize in the Yugoslav Competition of Belgrade Music Festival with her *Sofoson I*. PHOTOGRAPH.
Compositions
ORCHESTRA
Simfonijeta za gudace i timpane (str orch and timp) (1966-1967)
Sofoson 1 (1st prize, BEMUS, 1973)
CHAMBER
String quartet (1969-1970)
Variations (vln and pf) (1968)
PIANO
Song and dance (1964)
Suite (1965)
VOCAL
Bolna draga (mix-ch a-cap) (1965)
Rekvijem (mix-ch a-cap) (1965)
Zaljubljemost (vce and pf) (1965)
INCIDENTAL MUSIC
Zelena pijaca, childrens' radio play
Ref. Union of Yugoslav Composers

PRENTNER, Marie

20th-century Austrian composer. b. Vienna. She studied under Leschetizky.
Bibliography
Barnes, E.A. *Notable Musical Women. Etude*, November, 1929.
Ref. 323

PREOBRAJENSKA, Vera Nicolaevna

Russian-American pianist, arranger, editor, lecturer, writer and composer. b. San Francisco, April 27, 1926. She received a B.A. (1953) from San Francisco State University (1953) and an M.A. (1972) and Ph.D. (1973) from Bernadean University, Las Vegas. She studied composition under Darius Milhaud, Ernest Block, Roger Sessions, Frederick Jacobi, Ernest von Dohnanyi, Alexander Tcherepnin and Dmitri Shostakovich. She made her debut as a pianist in 1950. She was concert manager of Musical Artists of America from 1956 to 1961 and lectured at the University of California, Berkeley from 1965 to 1968. From 1972 to 1974 she served as chairlady of the department of music at Bernadean University and was then honorary director of music at Santa Cruz Academy of Music from 1974 to 1975. She contributed to various musical publications. From 1949 she was a writer, arranger and orchestrator for commercial song writing. She won two composition prizes from the National League of Pen Women. DISCOGRAPHY.
Compositions
ORCHESTRA
Blue symphony (1946)
Third symphony
Rhapsodie (pf and orch) (1952)
Concerto for piano and orchestra (pf and cham orch; also 2 pf) (1983)
American tone poem (1977)
Awakening, art song (cham orch) (1983)
Chinese tone poem (cham orch) (1982)
Classical menuetto (str orch) (1946)
Mazurka (1957)
La petite sinfonietta de Russie, in 3 mvts (cham orch) (1982)
Promenade (str orch) (1946)
September elegy (cham orch) (1982)
Slavic tone poem (1978)
Suite (str orch) (1946)
Suite for Strings II (1947)
BAND
Mazurka (1976)
Patriotic march: Spirit of 1976 (1976)
CHAMBER
Mazurka, op. 2, no. 1 (fl, 2 cl, hn, 2 vln, vla and vlc) (1947)
Chamber quintet, 3 mvts (2 vln, vla, cl and pf) (1961)
Clarinet quintet (1976)
Piano quintet (1976)
Characteristic suite (str qrt) (1945)
Petit sonatine (str qrt) (1972)
Preludium (str qnt) (1972)
String quartet, in 3 mvts (1983)
Impromptu (ob, vln and vlc) (1978)
Trio (fl, vln and vlc) (1976)
Trio variations (ob, vlc and bsn) (1983)
Concert serenade (vln and pf) (1948)
Sonata in D-Major No. 2 (vln and pf) (1957)
Two part invention I and II (vlc and pf) (1983)
Sonata, in 3 mvts (b-cl) (1983)
Sonata, in 3 mvts (fl) (1983)
Sonata, in 3 mvts (vln) (1983)
Sonatina (gtr) (1983)
Rondino (gtr)
ORGAN
Fugue in A-Minor
Preludium
PIANO
Adolescence, children's suite (1964)
Etudes I, II and III (1983)
Idyle (Pastorale) (1983)
Piano jazz-sonata, op. 1 (also orch) (hon mention, Darius Milhaud composition class)
Seven mazurkas (1947)
Sonata (1983)
Sonata, in 3 mvts (1945)
Sonata in E-Minor (1958)
Sonatine (1983)
Suite of 6 pieces (also ballet) (1956)
Suite of 6 Russian pieces (1962)
Three mazurkas (1961)
Two Chinese dances (1949)
VOCAL
A statues graveyard (mix-ch) (1983)
Ode to the Lincoln's Gettysburg address (mix-ch and pf) (1960)
Undertones of Frost, symphonic sequence in 4 mvts (L.V. Inke) (vce, fl, ob, bsn, tba, vln, vlc and brass) (1960)
Fingerflow (L.V. Inke) (med-vce, fl, man, perc- 2 players, incl. kettledrs) (1960)
Art songs, op. 1 (vce and pf) (1945)
Awakening (Ostroumov) (vce and pf) (1977)
California (also orch)
Country and Western folk songs
Cycle of English art songs (1947)
Cycle of Russian art songs (1947)
Dreams, op. 3, art song
Found (American folk song)
The things that make me care
SACRED
The Creation, cantata (mix-ch) (Berkeley: Orthodox, 1970)
Hebraic cantata (mix-ch and cham orch) (1976)
Christmas prayer (mix-ch) (Orthodox, 1962)
Easter prayer (mix-ch) (Orthodox, 1960)
Lord's prayer (mix-ch) (Orthodox, 1967)
Prayer for the Holy Communion (Russian text) (mix-ch)
Prayer to Mary (mix-ch) (Orthodox, 1965)
Prayer to the Guardian Angel (mix-ch) (Orthodox, 1966)
Russian Requiem (ch; also vce and pf) (1954)
The Creed (Orthodox, 1969)
DANCE SCORES
Concept of the egg, dance comedy (1952)
Clara Militch, ballet (pf)
Crime and Punishment, dance drama (str qrt, cl and pf) (1956)
Hebraic Rhapsody, ballet score (str orch) (1968)
OPERA
The Money Lender, chamber opera (Dostoievsky)
ARRANGEMENTS
Transcriptions:
Mazurkas, ops. 1-7 (cham orch) (1982)
Polka and valse (cham orch) (1982)
Awakening, art song (cham orch) (1982)
Four art songs: Sea shells, Parting; Two symbols; Face to face (cham orch) (1982)
Publications
Song Writers Course. Parts I and II.
Numerous poetry publications in the Letter Box, *Ram Magazine*, Brooklyn, NY. 1980.
Ref. composer, 40, 84, 137, 142, 190, 206, 228, 347, 474, 475, 563, 622

PRESCOTT, Mrs. Cyril. See LOWTHIAN, Caroline

PRESCOTT, Oliveria Louisa

English teacher and composer. b. London, September 3, 1842; d. London, September 9, 1919. She studied under Lindsay Sloper and then for seven years at the Royal Academy of Music under Sir G.A. Macfarren, Jewson, Folkes and Ralph, becaming an A.R.A.M. She taught harmony at the Church of England High School for Girls, London from 1879 to 1893 and lectured in harmony and composition for the University of Cambridge correspondence system for women. She was musical assistant to Professor Macfarren.

Compositions

ORCHESTRA

Symphony in B-Flat
Symphony in D-Minor
Concert finale in D-Minor
Concerto in A (pf and orch)
Bright October, concert piece
Golden supper, overture
Oedipus and Antigone, overture
Overture (1876)
Tithonus, overture
Woodland, overture

CHAMBER

Quartet in G (pf and strs)
String quartet in A-Minor
String quartet in C-Minor

VOCAL

Lord Ullin's daughter, cantata (ch and orch)
Hero watching for Leander (S and orch)
Love and laughter (S and orch)
Ballad of Young John
Bohemian song (4 vces and strs)
Border ballad
Cryer, part song
Douglas Raid, part song
Equestrian courtship, part song (T. Hood) (1885)
The fisherwife, song
The huntsman, 4 part song (J. Stewart) (London: Hutchings & Romer, 1883)
Song of waterspirits, four part song (C. Evans) (ca. 1874)

SACRED

Psalm 13 (S, ch and orch)
The presence, unison song (ch)
Psalm 126 (vces a-cap)
The righteous live for evermore, anthem
Say not, the struggle nought availeth, part song (A.H. Clough) (1885)
Our conversation is in Heaven, anthem

Publications

About Music. 1903.
Form or Design in Music. Part I, Instrumental; Part II, Vocal. London, 1908.

Ref. 6, 44, 70, 102, 105, 226, 361, 433

PRESSLAFF, Hilary. See TANN, Hilary

PRESTI, Ida

French guitarist, professor and composer. b. Suresnes, May 31, 1924; d. Rochester, April 24, 1967. She studied under her father, Professor Marcel Montagnon and E. Pujol. She made her debut in Paris at the age of ten and appeared as a soloist at the age of 13, with the Societe de Concerts de la Conservatoire. She played at the music festival in Strasbourg in 1949. She was professor of the guitar at the Schola Cantorum, Paris and married the guitarist A. Lagoya, with whom she performed as a duo. DISCOGRAPHY.

Compositions

GUITAR

Etude fantasque (2 gtr)
Danse d'Avila (2 gtr)
Hommage à Manuel Ponce
Etude du matin
Etude No. 2
Six etudes (Schott)

Ref. 1, 9, 44, 85, 96, 282, 347, 563

PRESTON, Matilee Loeb-Evans

20th-century American pianist and composer. b. Toledo, OH,. She composed piano pieces and songs.

Ref. 323, 347

PREZIOSI, Antonietta

20th-century Italian musician, writer and composer. b. Genoa. She studied under G. Schipa, D. De Luca, G. Napoli and C.B. Bellini among others. She was praised by the journalist Nicola Lapegna as a talented artist. She contributed articles to journals and other periodicals and composed over 100 works published in 15 volumes.

Ref. 56

PRICE, Beryl

English pianist, conductor and composer. b. London, March 7, 1912. She studied at the Royal Academy of Music, London under Charles Reddic (piano), Harry Farjeon (composition) and Ernest Read (conducting).

Compositions

ORCHESTRA

Concerto (vlc and small orch) (1948)

CHAMBER

Five bagatelles (ww qrt) (1970)
Moreton bagatelles (treble and b-vl and hpcd) (1959)
String trio (1959) (Cobbett prize)
Sonata (vla and pf) (1947)
Five pieces (clav) (Stainer & Bell, 1959)
Music for virginals (1961)
Moto perpetuo (vln) (1956)

PIANO

The sea, music for mime (2 pf) (1951)
Festival pieces
Sonata (1949)
Variations on the Literary Dustman, 11 etudes (1954)

VOCAL

A cycle of cats (w-ch and pf) (rev 1970) (OUP, 1970)
Four things exceeding wise (w-ch a-cap) (1975)
Hear Joel, choral sequence (mix-ch and org) (1972)
Puer natus est (mix-ch and org) (1976)
Sigh no more, ladies, part song (w-ch a-cap) (Robertson)
Come you makers of music, part song (1962) (Stainer & Bell)
The Duke of Wellington, unison song (1976) (Robertson)
First came the primrose, part song (1959) (Stainer & Bell)
Lubber breeze, song (vce and pf) (1933) (Curwen, 1936)
Shepherd on a hill, 3 Elizabethan songs (1940) (Curwen, 1948)
The snail, part song (1976) (Robertson)
Songs from Calvalcanti (vce and pf) (1942)
Songs of heroes, unison songs (1969) (OUP, 1969)
Sweet Afton, part song (1959) (Stainer & Bell)

SACRED

The ass's tale, Christmas cantata (w-ch and pf) (1960) (Stainer & Bell)
On song's eternity (cham ch and virs) (1976)
Shepherds and angels, Christmas suite (w-ch and pf) (1970) (OUP, 1970)
Two songs of the Nativity (2 part-ch and pf)
Wise Men's riddles (double-ch a-cap) (1977)
Piper's carol (1960) (Stainer & Bell, 1960)
We saw Him sleeping, song (vce and pf) (1932) (Curwen, 1936)

FILM MUSIC

Music for instructional films for Royal Society for Prevention of Accidents

TEACHING PIECES

Airs from seven lands (fl) (OUP, 1976)
Catriona's Scottish airs (cl) (1961) (OUP, 1961)
Emerald Isle (vlc) (OUP, 1970)
On the go (pf) (1973) (OUP, 1973)

Ref. composer

PRICE, Deon Nielsen

American harpsichordist, pianist, lecturer and composer. b. Salt Lake City, May 16, 1934. She studied under Carl Fuerstner and Leon Dallin at Brigham Young University, Provo, graduating with a B.A. (piano). At the Academia Pro Arte, Heidelberg, Germany she studied for two years under Professor Erwin Schmieder, giving recitals in the same period. She graduated from the University of Michigan, Ann Arbor, with an M.M. (piano and composition), having studied under Leslie Bassett, Benning Dexter, Gyorgy Sandor, Joseph Brinkman and Hans T. David. At the University of California she took master classes with Leonard Shure and studied for two years under Aube Tzerko. She graduated from the University of Southern California with a doctorate of musical arts (piano performance, 1977). Her teachers there were Gwendolyn Koldofsky, Daniel Pollack, Haley Stevens, Samuel Alder and Brooks Smith. She lectured at California universities, worked as an accompanist and gave recitals of her own compositions at 20 universities and colleges.

Compositions
ORCHESTRA
Epitaphs (pf and orch) (1982)
Chorale collage (cham orch) (1979)
Youthful fantasy (vlc orch) (1978)
CHAMBER
Music camp (brass and ww) (1981)
Allegro barbaro (str qrt) (1961)
Three chorales (brass qrt) (1961)
Two chorales (4 vlc) (1980)
Trio (vla, cl and pf) (1982)
Affects, sonata (cl and pf) (1979)
Big Sur triptych (a-sax and pf)
Non-Mesuree et mesuree (gtr and cl or S-sax) (1981)
Vectoral rhapsody (a-sax and pf) (1981)
Diversions (pf) (1960)
Escapade (hpcd) (1977)
Hexachord (cl) (1977)
Stile antico: Chromos, tonos, concitato (vlc) (1975)
VOCAL
I heard a mother singing (w-ch and 5-part str ens) (1961)
Cartoons 1980, song cycle (m-S and pf) (1980)
Four medieval songs (vce and hpcd) (1974)
Textures (vce, vlc and pf) (1981)
Two settings of Walt Whitman (Bar and vla) (1961)
SACRED
Five chorales (mix-ch) (1979)
Three anthems (w-ch and pf) (1980)
Publications
The Special Skills of an Accompanist. Clavier Magazine, October 1978.
Group Instruction in Piano Accompanying. Clavier Magazine, November 1981.
Ref. composer

PRICE, Florence Beatrice (nee Smith)
Black American organist, pianist, lecturer and composer. b. Little Rock, AR, April 9, 1888; d. Chicago, June 3, 1953. She received her early musical training from her mother, an accomplished musician. She later studied the piano, the organ and musical theory under Jeffrey, Klahre, Elson, Cutter and Duham; composition and counterpoint under Chadwick and Converse and at the New England Conservatory, Boston, from which she graduated with honors in 1906. She continued her studies at Chicago Musical College and the American Conservatory under Leo Sowerby. She later studied composition under Drs. Carl Bush and Wesley La Violette and orchestration and instrumental technique under Arthur Olaf Anderson. Her first teaching position was at Cotton Plant-Arkadelphia Academy. She later taught in the music department, Shorter College, North Little Rock and at Clark University, Atlanta. She was a soloist with the Chicago Symphony Orchestra, playing her own works; other performances followed. Florence was the first black woman in the United States to win recognition as a composer. Some 81 of her scores are in the library of the University of Arkansas. Her *Symphony in E-Minor* was performed by the Chicago Symphony under the direction of Frederick Stock at the Chicago World Fair; the first time a major orchestra performed a symphony by a black woman. This led to the performances of her works by other major orchestras. Her songs were sung by the foremost singers, such as Marian Anderson, Blanche Thebom and Leontyne Price. DISCOGRAPHY.
Compositions
ORCHESTRA
Symphony in D-Minor
Symphony in G-Minor
Symphony No. 1 in E-Minor (1925) (Wanamaker Prize, 1931)
Symphony No. 3 in C-Minor
Colonial dance symphony
Concert overture No. 1 (based on Negro spiritual)
Concert overture No. 2 (based on 3 Negro spirituals)
Concerto in 1 mvt (pf and orch)
Concerto in D-Major (vln and orch)
Concerto in D-Minor (pf and orch)
Concerto in F-Minor (pf and orch)
Mississippi River symphony, in 4 mvts
Rhapsody (pf and orch)
Violin concerto No. 2
Ethiopia's shadow in America (hon mention Wanamaker, 1932)
The oak, tone poem
Suite of dances
CHAMBER
Quintet (pf and strs)
Negro folksongs in counterpoint (str qrt)
Moods (fl, cl and pf)
Suite (brass and pf)
By candlelight (vln and pf) (Chicago: McKinley Pub.)
The deserted garden (vln and pf) (Bryn Mawr, PA: Theodore Presser)
Mellow twilight (vln and pf; also pf) (McKinley)
Piece (vn and pf)
Playful rondo (vln and pf) (Mckinley)
ORGAN
Adoration
Evening song (New York: Galaxy Music Corp., 1951)
In quiet mood (Galaxy Music, 1951)
Passacaglia and fugue
Sonata No. 1
Suite No. 1 (1959)
Variations on a folk song
PIANO
Annie Laurie (2 pf) (McKinley)
The goblin and the mosquito (2 or 1 pf) (Chicago: Clayton F. Summy Co., 1951)
Three little Negro dances (2 pf; also band) (Theodore Presser)
Anticipation (McKinley, 1928)
At the cotton gin (New York: G. Schirmer) (prize, G. Schirmer, 1928)
Bright eyes (Presser, 1937)
The butterfly (New York: C. Fischer, 1936)
Cabin song (Presser, 1937)
Clover blossom (McKinley, 1947)
The cotton dance (OUP, 1942) (hon mention Wanamaker, 1931)
Criss cross (McKinley, 1947)
Dances in the canebrakes (Los Angeles: Affiliated Musicians, 1953)
Doll waltz (Vals de la musica) (McKinley, 1928)
The engine (McKinley)
Fantasie No. 4 (hon mention Wanamaker, 1932)
The gnat and the bee (C. Fischer, 1935)
Here and then (McKinley, 1947)
Levee dance (Presser)
March of the beetles (McKinley, 1947)
Morning sunbeam (Presser, 1937)
Nobody knows the trouble I see (Presser)
The old boatman
Rock-a-bye (McKinley, 1947)
The rose (C. Fischer, 1936)
A sachem's pipe (C. Fischer, 1935)
The sea swallow (Clayton F. Summy, 1951)
Sonata in E-Minor (1959) (hon mention Wanamaker, 1932)
Tecumseh (C. Fischer, 1935)
The waltzing fairy (El duende valsante) (McKinley, 1928)
The waterfall (McKinley)
Zephyr, Mexican folk song (McKinley)
VOCAL
Lincoln walks at midnight (mix-ch and orch)
The wind and the sea (mix-ch and str orch)
Song of hope (composer) (vce and orch)
Spring journey (w-ch and str orch)
Sea gulls (w-ch, strs and d-bs)
Song for snow (mix-ch and pf) (C. Fischer, 1957)
The waves of Breffney (mix-ch a-cap)
Moon bridge (Mary Gamble) (w-ch; also vce and pf) (New York: Remick Music Co., 1950; Gamble Hinged Music, 1930)
Nature's Magic (w-ch and pf) (Clayton Summy, 1953)
Witch of the Meadow (Gamble) (w-ch) (Gamble Hinged, 1947)
New Moon (w-vces and opt S obb with 4 hand pf) (Gamble Hinged) Art songs incl.:
An April day (Joseph F. Cotter) (New York: Handy Bros., Music Co., 1949)
Cobbler (David Morton)
The dawn is awake
The dream ship
Dreaming town (1934)
Fantasy in purple (Langston Hughes)
In the land of cotton (2nd prize, Holstein, 1925)
Memories of Dixieland (2nd prize, Holstein, 1927)
Night (Louise C. Wallace) (New York: Edward B. Marks Music Corp., 1946)
Out of the south blew a wind (Fanny Carter Woods) (Edward B. Marks, 1946)
Song of the open road
Songs to a dark virgin (Langston Hughes) (G. Schirmer, 1941)
To my little son (Julia Johnson Davis)
Travel's end (Mary Folwell Hoisington)
Winter idyll (David Morton)
SACRED
Adoration (Dayton: Loenz Pub. Co.)
God gives me you, wedding song (mix-ch and pf; also vce and pf) (Connelly)
Offertory (Lorenz)
Silent night (McKinley)
Were you there when they crucified my Lord (C. Fischer; OUP, 1942)

ARRANGEMENTS
Heav'n bound soldier, Negro spirituals (w-vces) (Handy Bros., 1949)
I am bound for the Kingdom, 2 traditonal Negro spirituals (ded Maria Anderson) (Handy Bros., 1949)
My soul's been anchored in de Lord, spiritual (also vce and orch) (Gambled Hinged Music, 1937)
Two traditional spirituals (vce and pf) (Handy Bros., 1948)

Bibliography
Green, Mildred. *A Study of the Lives and Works of Five Black Women Composers in America*. Ph.D. dissertation, University of Oklahoma. University Microfilms International, Ann Arbor, MI. 1975.
Jackson, Barbara Garvey. *Black Perspectives in Music*, 5:1.
Ref. 26, 39, 40, 53, 136, 142, 226, 228, 285, 287, 292, 335, 347, 415, 433, 477, 496, 549, 622, 653

PRICE, Sara A.

19th-century American composer. She was a farmer's wife who lost seven of her nine children in the civil war. Her song was found in her diary.

Composition
VOCAL
The housewife's complaint
Ref. 478

PRIESING, Dorothy Jean (nee McLemore)

American pianist, assistant professor, authoress and composer. b. Nantucket, MA, July 31, 1910. She received her B.S. and M.A. from Columbia University. She studied under James Friskin, Howard Brockway and Rubin Goldmark at the Juilliard School of Music and was a pupil of Nadia Boulanger (q.v.) at Fontainebleu, France. At the Juilliard School she received the Coolidge prize for composition. She was a lecturer at Columbia University from 1936 to 1939 and at the Juilliard School of Music from 1942 to 1947 and became associate professor at Montclair State College in 1953. She gave recitals in solo and chamber performances. She was a co-author of two books on piano playing. DISCOGRAPHY.

Compositions
BAND
Invocation
CHAMBER
Violin sonata
Three piano preludes (1940)
VOCAL
Carol of the children (w-ch) (1950)
Now is the carolling season (mix-ch) (1954)
Sister awake (w-ch) (1941)
Three Elizabethan songs (mix-ch) (1975)
Wild swans (w-ch) (1941)
Wonder of the darksome night (mix-ch) (1950)
April swim (S)
Four songs on poems by James Joyce (1960)
Noel (1941)
Ref. composer, 39, 40, 137, 142, 347, 563

PRIETO (Prieto y Fernandez de la Llana), Maria Teresa

Spanish pianist and composer. b. Oviedo, 1910; d. January 24, 1982. She studied at the Instituto de Oviedo and the Academia de Bellas Artes de Oviedo, where she received five diplomas with five first places. She studied the piano under Saturnino Fresno. In 1933 she graduated in harmony from the Royal Conservatory of Madrid and studied composition under Benito Garcia de la Parra. In 1936 she settled in Mexico, where she studied composition under Manuel M. Ponce in 1937 and orchestration under Carlos Chaves. At Mills College she studied composition and orchestration under Darius Milhaud in 1948. Many of her orchestral compositions were performed by the Mexico Symphonic Orchestra.

Compositions
ORCHESTRA
Impression sinfonica, symphony (pf and orch) (1942)
Sinfonia asturiana, symphony (1943)
Sinfonia breve, symphony (1945)
Sinfonia cantabile, symphony (1956)
Sinfonia de la danza prima, symphony (1955)
Adagio y fuga (vlc and orch) (1960)
Doce miniaturas, 12 tonales y 12 en los modos autenticos gregorianos (vln and orch) (1957)
Fantasia sobre una fuga (pf and orch) (1950)
Poema sinfonico Chichem Itza, symphonic poem (1944)
Suite sinfonica, suite de ballet (1967)
Allegro orquestral (1973)
Cuatro tiempos, sonata modal (1970)
Doble fuga-do mayor (1971)
Tema variado y fuga (dodecafonico) (1968)
Variaciones y fuga (1946)
CHAMBER
Cuarteto en fa (1974)
Cuarteto en fa menor (1954)
Cuarteto modal (Samuel Ros prize, 1958)
Cuarteto para cuerda en sol major (1951)
Fuga para aliento (str qrt) (1969)
Fuga para cuerda en si B menor (str qrt) (1952)
Fuga postdodecafonica para cuerda (str qrt) (1953)
PIANO
Anada (1937)
Doce variaciones seriales (1961)
Doce variaciones tonales (1962)
Escena de ninos (1939)
Esencias (1963)
Esquema dodecafonico fugado (1939)
Marcha de los soldaditos (1937)
Preludio y fuga en do major (1938)
Tema y 3 variaciones (1939)
Tema variado y fuga (1968)
VOCAL
Excelsitud (ch and orch) (1941)
Oda celeste (vce and orch) (1947)
Oracion de quietud, symphonic poem (ch and orch) (1949)
Palabras divinas (vce and orch) (1972)
Tres canciones (Spanish and French) (vce and orch) (1948)
Songs incl.:
Camino (G. Lorca)
Canciones en Gallego (1965)
Cordoba (G. Lorca) (1970)
Six melodies in Spanish and English (1940)
SACRED
Aleluya, from the songs of David (vce and orch) (1974)
Ave Maria (vce and orch) (1966)
Dios te Otorg la Gracia (vce and pf) (1965)
MISCELLANEOUS
Cuadro de la naturaleza Asturias (1958)
Cuadro de la naturaleza Valle de Mexico (1959)
Ref. composer, 8, 44, 94, 100, 477, 609, 622

PRIETO Y FERNANDEZ DE AL LLANA, Maria Teresa. See PRIETO, Maria

PRIMA CANTATRICE DEL MONDO. See CATALANI, Angelica

PRINCE, Stella. See STOCKER, Stella

PRINCESS OF PRUSSIA. See WILHELMINA, Sophie Friederike

PRIOLI MORISINA, Marietta

17th-century Italian composer.

Composition
CHAMBER
Balleti et correnti (2 vln, vlc and spinet) (ded Dowager Empress Eleonora) (Venice: Franc. Magni detto Gardeno, 1665)
Ref. 105, 143, 216, 563

PRIOLLI, Maria Luisa de Matos

Brazilian pianist, lecturer and composer. b. Rio de Janeiro, May 24, 1915. She studied under her mother at an early age and later at the Instituto Nacional de Musica, Rio under M.A. Rumley (piano), A. Franca (harmony), P. Silva (counterpoint and fugue), J. Otaviano (composition) and F. Mignone (conducting). She studied composition in London from 1936 to 1937 under W. Chatermann and the piano and analysis under W. Bantock and obtained her teacher's diploma from the Trinity College of Music. From 1937 she taught in schools and universities. She is a member of the National Academy of Music.

Compositions
ORCHESTRA
Concerto for piano and orchestra in C-Minor (1940)
CHAMBER
String quartet in F-Major (1940)
Trio in G-Major (1938)
Fugue (org) (1969)
Tres estudios (vln) (1942)

PIANO
Capricho serenata (1942)
Fuga e posludio (1974)
Lundu carioca (1974)
Ronda infantil No. 1 (1937)
Ronda infantil No. 2 (1961)
Sonata, op. 21 (1968)
VOCAL
Songs incl.:
Inquietude (vce and pf) (1939)
Presença (vce and pf) (1973)
Saudade (vce and pf) (1939)
SACRED
Aleluia (4 vces) (1960)
Ave Maria (vce and pf) (1974)
Missa festival (2 vces) (1974)
Sanctus (4 vces) (1975)
Publications
Ornamentos, sua execução conforme a unidade ritmica. Rio de Janeiro, 1946.
Principios basicos de musica para a juventude. 2 vols. Rio de Janeiro, 1953.
Solfejos melodicos e progressivos. 2 vols. Rio de Janeiro, 1951.
Ref. 333

PRITCHARD, Gwyn
20th-century British composer.
Composition
MISCELLANEOUS
Objects in space (ens)
Ref. 422

PRITI-PAINTAL
B. 1960.
Compositions
CHAMBER
Jugalbandi (vln and pf)
PIANO
Abyas kritt
Manali fantasia
Prayrna
Ref. Frau und Musik

PROCACCINI, Teresa
Italian organist, pianist, teacher and composer. b. Cerignola, Foggia, March 23, 1934. She revealed early musical talent and composed small piano pieces at the age of eight. She studied at the Conservatorio di Foggia and graduated in the piano in 1952. At the Conservatorio of S. Cecilia in Rome she graduated in the organ and composition under the guidance of F. Germani and V. Mortari. She followed postgraduate courses in Rome under Silvestri, in Naples under Denza and in Siena at the Accademia Chigiana. Her works have been performed in Europe, Canada, Australia and North and South America and broadcast throughout Europe. She was director of the Conservatorio di Musica of Foggia from 1971 to 1973 and taught a master's course in composition at the Conservatorio L. Refice of Frosinone and directed a composition course at the Nations Festivals of Chamber Music at Citta di Castello. She was an invited observer at the Festivals of Contemporary Music in Prague and Warsaw in 1973 and represented Italy at the Komponistinnen aus drei Jahrhunderten organized by Berlin Radio. She teaches composition at the St. Cecilia Conservatory in Rome and at the Accademia Musicale 'O Respighi' in Assisi. She is also a music consultant for the publishers Armando Armando, Rome. DISCOGRAPHY. PHOTOGRAPH.
Compositions
ORCHESTRA
Concerto for harp and orchestra, op. 78 (1980)
Concerto per organo e orchestra, op. 12 (org and sym orch) (1957)
Concerto per trio e orchestra, I folletti, op. 14 (1958)
Sonata in tricromia per orchestra e pianoforte concertante, op. 11 (pf and sym orch) (1957) (Ed. Bongiovanni)
Fantasia per orchestra, op. 16 (sym orch) (1958)
Sensazioni sonore, 4 pezzi per orchestra, op. 41 (sym orch) (Milan: Ed. Sonzogno)
Tre danze, op. 24 (2 trp and str orch) (1961)
Musica barbara, op. 20 (pf and cham orch) (1959)
Concertino, op. 64 (fl and str orch) (1976)
Divagazioni. op. 21 (str orch) (1959)
Musica per archi, op. 49 (str orch) (1971)
Sinfonietta per piccola orchestra, op. 7 (small orch) (1956)
Tre danze, op. 94 (cham orch) (1984)
Un cavallino avventuroso, op. 23 (cham orch) (1960) (also pf, op. 22)
Piccolo concerto, op. 19 (15 insts) (1959)
CHAMBER
Marionette, op. 58 (pf and 10 insts) (1975) (Festival delle nazioni, chamber music, 1975)
Musica barbara, op. 80 (pf and 10 insts) (1980)
Concertino, op. 68 (bsn and 9 insts) (1977)
Un cavallino avventuroso, op. 82 (nonet) (1981)
Preludio e marcia, op. 70 (hn and 8 insts) (1977)
Ottetto per archi e fiati, op. 83 (ww and strs) (1981)
Clown music, op. 36, 4 pieces (wind qnt) (1968) (Padua: Ed. Zanibon) (Casella International Composition prize)
Divertissement, op. 79 (4 trp and 1 trb) (1980)
Invenzione, op. 9 (pf, fl, ob, cl and bsn) (1957)
Meditazione, op. 71 (hn and str qrt) (1978)
Quintetto per corno e arci, op. 46 (hn and strs) (1971)
Serenata, op. 31 (2 vln, vlc, fl and hpcd) (1967)
Nove preludi, op. 29 (3 insts and pf)
Quartetto per flauto, oboe, fagotto e pianoforte, op. 27 (1965)
String quartet, op. 42 (1969)
Andante e rondo, op. 50 (3 insts)
Improvisazioni per violino, viola e violoncello, op. 37 (1968)
Sonatina No. 2, op. 43 (3 insts)
Trio, op. 5 (1956)
Trio, op. 35 (cl, vlc and pf) (1968)
Dialoghi, op. 75 (pf and perc) (1979)
Dialogo, op. 34 (vla and pf) (1968)
Duo, op. 85 (vln and vla) (1982)
Fantasia, op. 10 (vln and pf) (1957)
Introduzione e allegro, op. 39 (fl and pf) (1969)
Lied, op. 67 (fl and hp) (1977)
Lied No. 2, op. 74 (ob and pf) (1978)
Meditazione, op. 72 (hn and pf) (1978)
Mystere, op. 63 (c-bsn and pf) (1976)
Serenata notturna, op. 69 (hn and hp) (1977)
Sonata per fagotto e pianoforte, op. 32 (1968)
Sonata per flauto e pianoforte, op. 63 (1976)
Sonata rapsodica, op. 8 (vlc and pf) (1957)
Tre pezzi facili, op. 26 (bsn and pf) op. 30 (Paris, Milan: A. Leduc)
Sonata per viola e pianoforte, op. 40 (1969)
Andante e rondo, op. 50 (fl) (1971)
Eagle, op. 90 (fl) (1983)
Sei pezzi incaici, op. 61 (gtr) (1975)
Sei studi, op. 63 (gtr) (1975)
Sonata per violoncello solo, op. 28 (1965)
ORGAN
Andante elegiaco, op. 48 (1971)
Improvviso e toccata, op. 33 (1968)
PIANO
Sensazioni sonore, op. 35, 4 pieces (2 pf) (Sonzogno)
Little horses story, op. 73 (4 hands) (1978)
Marionette, op. 51 (4 hands) (1972)
Fantasia, op. 4 (1956)
Nove preludi, op. 29 (1966)
Otto piccoli pezzi, op. 91 (1983)
Sei pezzi infantili, op. 25 (1961)
Sonata, op. 3 (1956)
Sonata in tricromia, op. 2 (1955) (Bologna: Bongiovanni)
Sonatina, op. 18 (1958)
Sonatina No. 2, op. 43 (1970)
VOCAL
Il giudizio d Salomone, op. 15, oratorio (soloists, ch and orch) (1958)
In memoriam, cantata, op. 96 (reciter, ch and orch) (1984)
La peste di Atene, op. 17, cantata (ch and orch) (1958)
Dannazione e preghiera, op. 13 (m-S and str orch) (1958) (International Festival of Music, Ravenna, 1970)
Il grilo, op. 93 (Lorca) (ch and youth orch) (1983)
Liriche, op. 57 (S and str orch) (1974)
Tre canti popolari, op. 77 (vce, ch, fl, gtr and small orch) (1979)
Piazza della musica No. 1 (reciter and 20 insts)
Il bambino di plastica, op 81 (reciter, ch and hp) (1981)
Levataccia, op. 47 (mix-ch) (1971)
Il pupazzo di neve, op. 86 (reciter and 10 insts or pf) (1982)
Sueno, op. 92 (reciter, w-ch, fl and pf) (1983)
Tre canti popolari, op. 38 (ch) (1969)
Air, op. 89 (S, cl and pf) (1983)
Canciones, op. 54 (S, cl, bsn and pf) (1972)
Cantare e giocare, 50 songs
Chanson (vce and gtr) (1975)
Elegia, op. 44 (vce, fl and pf) (1970)
Evocazione, op. 52 (vces and pf) (1972)
Memory, vocalise, op. 76 (S and pf) (1979)
Tre liriche, op. 1 (vce and pf) (1955)
BALLET
Medea, op. 84 (1981)

OPERA
Crispino de Fiumeri
Il paese ei suoni, op. 95 (1984)
La prima notte, op. 55, comic opera in 1 act (1973) (1977)
Questione di fiducia, op. 56, comic opera in 1 act (1975)
L'uomo del tamburo, op. 94 (1984)
OPERETTA
Piazza della musica No. 1, op. 54, for children (1975)
INCIDENTAL MUSIC
Annina e il sorcio Pompeo (Aceto) (1980)
Il cappello di pagla di Firenze (Labiche) (1983)
Oedipus (Seneca) (1974)
Sogno ma forse no (Pirandello) (1978)
L'uccello di fuoco (1980)
ELECTRONIC
Divertimento, op. 6 (pf, trp, musical saw, vib and perc) (1956)
Ref. composer, 474, 563, 622

PROCTOR, Alice McElroy
American pianist, conductor, lecturer and composer. b. Albany, NY, April 18, 1915. She gained her B.A. in 1935 and M.A. in 1936 from Smith College. She was the first woman to gain a Ph.D. in composition from the Eastman School of Music, Rochester University in 1940. She taught the piano, harmony and music history at Southwestern State College Weatherford, OK, from 1939 to 1943 and the piano privately from 1943 to 1978. From 1970 to 1978 she was one of the piano faculty of the Milton Academy, MA. She composed piano pieces, choral works and songs.
Publications
Fun for Two. 1955.
Fun to Play. 1955.
Panorama. Compiler and editor. Piano pieces. 1953
Ref. 40, 347, 643

PROHASKA, Bernhardine
Bohemian composer. b. 1803. Her opera was performed in Leipzig.
Composition
OPERA
Der Blick des Basilisken (1846)
Ref. 431

PROPHETESS OF THE CRUSADES. See HILDEGARD, Saint

PROSDOCIMI, Ada
Italian composer.
Compositions
VOCAL
Sei romanze: Cuore e cavallo; Fantasticheria; In fuga; Nirvana; La tua stella; Ninna-nanna (vce and pf) (Ricordi)
SACRED
Ave Maria (Ricordi)
Ref. Ricordi

PRUNEDER, Frav. See ADDENDUM

PRUNTY, Evelyn Grace Potter
American organist, pianist, teacher and composer. b. Cleghorn IA, February 11, 1916. She studied at the Morningside College from 1933 to 1934 and Cherokee Junior College from 1934 to 1935. She studied the piano privately and became a private piano teacher and a church organist.
Ref. 475

PSTROKONSKA-NAVRATIL, Grazyna Hanna
Polish musicologist and composer. b. Wroclaw, July 16, 1947. She studied composition at the State Music College, Wroclaw and received her diploma in 1971. She held various appointments in radio and television and was a research worker in the department of composition and theory at the State Music College. She was honored by the All-Polish Competition for Young Composers in 1968 and 1973 and won the International Competition for Women Composers, Mannheim in 1975.
Compositions
ORCHESTRA
Reanimacja (large orch) (1972)
Concerto (1969)
Concerto grosso (cl, hn, pf, perc and str orch) (1971)
Music for pianoforte and chamber orchestra (1973)
CHAMBER
Arabesque (str qrt) (1979)
Canon for a rhythm group (pf and perc ens)
String quartet (1968)
Three sonorous miniatures (vln, trp, cl and pf) (1967)
Ostinato (perc ens)
Eco (2 fl) (1980)
Nocturne (vlc and pf) (1973)
PIANO
Sonatina (1972)
La vetrata (1979)
VOCAL
Abecadlo (mix-ch and inst ens) (1973)
O radosci, choral triptych (W. Broniewski) (1972)
Song series (M. Jastrun) (S and pf) (1971)
SACRED
Slavic Pope, cantata
INCIDENTAL MUSIC
Dwiewczynka z zapalkami, radio symphonic tale after H.C. Anderson
ELECTRONIC
Epitaphios (tape)
Studio (vln and tape)
Ref. 77, 359, 465

PTASZYNSKA, Marta
Polish percussionist, pianist, lecturer and composer. b. Warsaw, July 29, 1943. She began studying the piano at the age of four and later studied the piano and music theory at the Music School, Warsaw and percussion under Professor J. Zgodzinski in Poznan. She received her M.A. in 1968 from the Warsaw Conservatory with distinctions in percussion, composition and music theory. She continued her composition studies in Warsaw and on a French government grant, under Nadia Boulanger (q.v.) in Paris from 1969 to 1970. At the same time she attended a course in electronic music at the Groupe des Recherches Musicales of the French radio. From 1965 to 1970 she was president of the Circle of Young Composers in Poland. At the Cleveland Institute of Music she earned the artist diploma degree in 1974, after studying percussion under Donald Erb. As a percussionist she specializes in performing avant-garde works by composers such as Serocki, Stockhausen, Cage and Boucourechliev, as well as her own compositions. She was a member of the Percussion Ensemble, Poznan and the Cleveland Institute of Music Contemporary Ensemble. She appeared several times at the Warsaw International Festival of Contemporary Music as a soloist and a member of an ensemble, playing her own and other works. She lectured in percussion at the Warsaw Conservatory, composition at Bennington College, the Universities of Berkeley and Santa Barbara and was guest lecturer at other universities. Some of her compositions won awards in Poland and awards from the Percussive Arts Society of America (1974 and 1976). DISCOGRAPHY. PHOTOGRAPH.
Compositions
ORCHESTRA
Concerto for percussion and orchestra (1974) (Poland: PWM, 1973; New York: E. Marks)
Chimes, bells, wood, stones (1977)
Conductus (wind orch) (1982) (E. Marks)
Crystallites (1974)
Improvisations (PWM, 1968; E. Marks)
Spectri sonori (PWM, 1973; E. Marks)
CHAMBER
Madrigals-In memoriam I. Stravinsky (wind and str qrt, trp, trb and gong) (1971) (Poland: Authors Agency) (prize, Union of Polish Composers, 1971)
Projections sonores (cham ens) (1970)
Music for five degrees (recs or fls and perc ens) (1979)
Classical variations (timp and str qrt) (1976)
Dream lands, magic spaces (vln and perc ens) (1979) (PWM; E. Marks)
Ornaments de bois (fl, cl, bsn and mar) (1970)
Transformations (perc ens) (1970)
Music of five steps, for children (2 fl and perc) (1979) (Authors Agency) (gold medal, International Society of Musical Education, 1980)
Synchromy (perc trio) (1978)
Candenza (fl and perc) (1972) (PWM)
Fantasy Mexican, for children (perc and pf) (PWM, 1971)
Jeu-parti (hp and vib) (1970) (New York: Paul Price, 1978)
Little mosaic, for children (perc and pf) (PWM, 1968)
Mobile (2 perc) (1975) (PWM; E. Marks)
Passacaglia and fugue (org and perc) (1967)
Preludes (vib and perc) (PWM, 1967; E. Marks)
Scherzo (xy and pf) (PWM, 1967; E. Marks)
Prelude, arioso, toccata (vln) (1968) (PWM)
Quodlibet (d-b) (1976) (PWM)
Space model (perc) (1971) (PWM)
Suite variee, for children (hp) (1972) (Paris: Leduc)
Touracou (hpcd) (1974) (PWM)
Two poems (tba) (1973) (PWM; E. Marks)
Variations (fl) (PWM, 1967; E. Marks)

PIANO
Three interludes (2 pf) (1969) (PWM: E. Marks)
Farewell souvenir (1975)
Journeys into space, in 2 parts (1979-1980) (PWM)
Miniatures for young pianists (1982) (E. Marks)
VOCAL
Two sonnets to Orpheus (vce and cham orch) (1981) (PWM)
Epigrams (20 w-vces, pf, fl, hp and perc) (1966-1967) (E. Marks)
Bajka o slowikach (K. Galczynski) (Bar and cham ens) (1969)
Chant for all people on the earth (Leslie Woolf Hedley) (S, T, Bar, mix-ch, chil-ch and orch) (1969-1970)
Un grand sommeil noir (P. Verlaine) (S, fl and hp) (1977) (PWM)
Tunes from different sides, children's songs (chil-vces and perc ens) (PWM)
OPERA
Oscar from Alva (G. Byron) (1972) (Polish radio and television award)
THEATRE
Helio-centricum-musicum, instrumental theatre (1973)
Soirée snobe chez La Princesse, instrumental theatre (1979)
ELECTRONIC
Quodlibet (d-b and tape) (1981)
Stress (perc and tape) (with E. Sokira)
MULTIMEDIA
Siderals (2 perc qnt and lights) (1974) (PWM, E. Marks)
Publications
Colorful World of Percussion. PWM, 1984.
Ref. composer, 64, 77, 142, 189, 625

PUCHE, Sofia
Spanish concert pianist, teacher and composer. b. Barcelona, 1918. She studied at the Escuela Municipal, Barcelona and received the first prize 'Maria Barrientos'. She performed as a soloist and with major orchestras and taught harmony and theory at the Escuela Municipal.
Compositions
PIANO
Three sonatas
Variaciones
VOCAL
Songs incl.:
Impresiones poeticas
Rimas, collection
Ref. 107

PUCIC-SORKOCEVIC, Yelena
Early 19th-century Croatian composer. She was the daughter of the composer and cultural historian Antun Sorkocevic and was the first known Croatian woman composer. She composed a song in 1816.
Ref. 57, 435

PUGET, Loise (Loisa, Luisa, Louise, Louisa) (married name, Lemoine)
French singer and composer. b. Paris, February 11, 1810; d Pau, November 27, 1889. Her songs, which she sang in concerts and salons, achieved extraordinary popularity during the reign of Louis Philippe and each year from 1830 to 1845 a new volume appeared. In 1842 she married the actor Gustave Lemoine, who wrote most of the texts to her songs. Encouraged by her success, she aspired to the theatre and took lessons from Adolphe Adams and wrote two operettas, the first of which was sung by Ponchard and Laure Damoreau-Cinti (q.v.). A number of her songs were also published in German.
Compositions
PIANO
Mystère de Paris, quadrille (4 hands) (Heugel, Schott)
Ave Maria (Augener)
Contradanze (Mariani)
Jeunesse, waltz (Girod)
Mauvais oeil, overture
Scherzantine (Costil)
VOCAL
Moon is up (mix-ch) (Chappell)
Musquetaire (mix-ch) (Labbe)
Songs incl.:
A la Grace de Dieu (Ashdown, Schott)
Amant le plus tendre (Heugel)
Amoureux de Bretagne (Schott)
Angelus de soir (Heugel)
Baiser de la promise (vce and pf or gtr) (Schott)
La benediction d'un père (vlce, vlc and pf) (Fromont)
Chanson andalouse, duo (Lemoine) (vce and man and pf or gtr)
Cheveux de la Bretonne (Schott)
Compliments de Normandie, duo (Eveillard)
Confession de brigand (Lemoine)
Demande en marriage, duo (Eveillard)
Enfant que Dieu garde (Schott)
Exile de France (Schott)
Fête du printemps (Schott)
It is not the gold (Brainard)
Je t'aime (vce and pf or gtr) (Williams)
Je veux t'aimer (vce and gtr or pf) (Williams)
Marche française, chant patriotique des anciens sous-officiers, comme fanfare (Evette)
Marie Stuart (Lemoine)
Mon pays (Schott)
Polka d'Auvergne (Noel)
La Quitouse ou pour les pauvres, s'il vous plait (vce and pf)
Le soleil de ma bretagne (Schott)
Ta dot (Schott)
Veritable amour (Williams) (vce, gtr and pf)
Over 250 other songs, romances, chansonettes
SACRED
Ave Maria (Ashdown, Haton, Williams)
OPERA
Beaucoup de bruit......
Drey Freier auf einmal, in one act (possibly the work of Jean Baptiste Lemoine)
OPERETTA
Mauvais oeil (Gerik, Lemoine) (1836)
Le Veilleuse, ou Les nuits de Milady (1869)
Ref. 8, 9, 26, 43, 102, 105, 107, 123, 128, 129, 163, 225, 226, 268, 276, 297, 307, 335, 347, 361, 394

PUIG-ROGET, Henriette. See ROGET, Henriette

PUKUI, Mary Abigail Kawena-'Ula-o-ka-lani-a-hi'jaka-i-ka-poli-o-pele-ka-wahine-l'Ai-honua
Hawaiian chanter, teacher, translator, writer and composer. b. Ka'u, April 20, 1895. She was recognised as the greatest authority on Hawaiian culture and language. She taught Hawaiian at a local school and composed songs, many in collaboration with well known composers. She was the recipient of many honors, including honorary L.L.D.s From the Universities of Hawaii (1960) and Brigham Young, Hawaii (1974). She composed the music to over 50 songs ranging from hula music to Christmas carols.
Compositions
VOCAL
Songs incl.:
Ku'u liko o la'ialoha
Mele ho'ala (1949)
Pua aloalo
Ref. 438

PULER, Clara P. see ADDENDUM

PURGOLD, Nadezhda Nikolayevna (Mrs. Rimsky-Korsakov)
Russian pianist, writer and composer. b. St. Petersburg, October 19, 1848; d. Petrograd, May 11, 1919. She was the sister of the singer A.P. Molas. She studied the piano under A.K. Shtang and A.A. Gerka and later Anton Rubinstein. At the St. Petersburg Conservatory she studied theoretical subjects. Her teacher of composition and instrumentation was her future husband, the composer Nikolai Andreyevich Rimsky-Korsakov. She wrote articles in Russian musical journals on Dargomyzhsky, Rimsky-Korsakov, Diaghilev and Tchaikovsky.
Compositions
ORCHESTRA
Zakoldovannoye miesto, symphonic poem based on Gogol (ded Mussorgsky)
PIANO
Scherzo in B-Major
ARRANGEMENTS
Works of Russian composers (pf)
Midsummer Night, opera in 4 acts (Rimsky-Korsakov) (vce and pf)
Ref. 70, 74, 196, 330

PUSICH, D. Antonia Gertrudes
Portuguese pianist, authoress, playwright and composer. b. S. Nicolau, Cape Verde Islands, October 1, 1805; d. Lisbon, October 6, 1883. She studied music and languages and was a talented pianist. She was a political activist, siding with her father, Admiral Antonio Pusich, in battles against injustices. In 1841 she entered journalism, wrote for the *Revista Popular* and became the first woman founder, proprietor and editor of the journals *Assembleia*, *Beneficiencia* and *A Cruzade*. Although best known for her literary achievements, her compositions were performed at the Philharmonic Academy.

Compositions
ORCHESTRA
Small Piece (1847-1848)
Ref. 104, 268, 290, 268

PUTMAN, Alice Locke. See PITTMAN, Alice Locke

PUTNAM, Alice Locke. See PITTMAN, Alice Locke

PUZZI, Fanny

Italian composer. b. ca. 1884.
Compositions
VOCAL
Songs incl.:
Days gone by (Ricordi)
Dolce un pensier (Ricordi)
Indovina, solo (Boosey)
Lily of the valley (Boosey)
Only a flower (Boosey)
Passato e avvenire, romanza (m-S) (Ricordi)
Quando al l'affao schiuso (Ricordi)
Ref. 246, 297

PYKE, Helen

English pianist and composer. d. July 13, 1954. She married the musicologist and conductor Mosco Carner. She specialized in public and radio duo-piano performances, first with Paul Hamburger and then Maurice Cole. She composed piano pieces.
Ref. 8

PYNE, Louisa Aubert (Mrs. Wilmore)

19th-century English organist and composer.
Ref. 85, 347

QAINA

According to the Syrian historian Ben Hebraeus (d. 1289) the daughters of Cain were the inventors of musical instruments. From this stems the name Qaina (plural Qainat) given to the Arabian songstresses or singing girls.

QALAM

9th-century Arabian songstress at the court of Caliph Abd al-Rahman II (822-852) in Andalusia. She was of Basque origin and when very young, was sent to study in the east, particularly in Medina. In addition to being a musician, she was a scholar, scribe, historian of poetry and literature and a raconteur. During her time Abd al-Rahman II founded a school in Andalusia, whose musicians were said to rival those of Medina. The apartments in his palace where she studied were known as the Medinese. Besides Qalam, the chief singers at the court were Fadl I (q.v.) and Alam.
Ref. 171, 244

QALAM AL-SALAHIYYA

9th-century Arabian songstress of the Court of Baghdad, ca. 840. She was a slave belonging to Salih and was taught her art by al-Zubair ibn Daman, a musician of Mecca and was called to the court of Harun al-Rashid in Baghdad (786-809). When the Caliph al-Watiq (842-847) heard her sing, he wished to acquire her. Salih demanded one hundred thousand ducats and the governorship of Egypt for her. To appease the caliph's anger at this demand, he gave her to him as a gift.
Ref. 171, 234

QAMAR (KAMAR)

9th-century Arabian songstress. She was a slave and an excellent composer, noted for her knowledge of music and her eloquence and erudition. She was owned by Abu Muhammed al'Udhri and bought from him for an immense sum by Ibrahim bin Hajaj al-Lakhmi, the Emir of Seville and Carmona.
Ref. 170, 171

QASMUNA

11th-century Spanish Jewess, poetess and composer of women's love songs; a genre dating back to the first half of the 11th-century and dealing, in Arabic or sometimes Hebrew, with love, wine, spring and nature and which can be considered the earliest discovered lyrical poetry of Romanesque literature. These poems were written and set to the lute by Arabian-Spanish women. The tradition of the same type of music has continued in North Africa to where many Arabs of Spain later fled and is still cultivated in girls' schools there.
Ref. 170, 476

QU'AD (Kaad)

Arabian songstress. ca. 610. She and Thamad (q.v.) were known as the jaradatan (the two grasshoppers) of the Emir of the Banu Amaliq, Mu'aiwiya ibn Bakr. They appear in the story of the destruction of the people of 'Ad, reputedly in South Arabia. When the land was afflicted with drought a deputation was sent to Makuraba (Mecca) to seek divine aid. The Emir entertained the supplicants with the music of the jaradatan and they neglected their mission. In anger the deity sent a storm to break over 'Ad, destroying the whole race. Qu'ad and Thamad are also referred to in the Kitab al-Agani as belonging to the Quraish chief Abdallah ibn Judan, in a period just prior to the dawn of Islam. He later gave them to his friend Umayya ibn Abil-Salt (d. 630), a pagan poet of Mecca.
Ref. 171, 234

QUANTIN-SAULNIER, Denise

French pianist and composer. b. St. Denis, June 14, 1922. She started studying music at the age of four.
Compositions
CHAMBER
Small piece, op. 16 (pf and rec) (1962)
Sonata, op. 37 (pf and vln) (1966)
PIANO
Au jardin, op. 59 (1970)
Barcarolle pour aude, op. 62 (1970)
La bergere et la prince, op. 8 (1961)
Chagrin de poupée, op. 60 (1970)
Charme des quatre saisons, op. 3 (1961)
Le chariot le cygne et le brochet, op. 5 (based on a theme by Kriloff) (1961)
Choses légères, op. 33 (1964)
Cinq pleurants du tombeau de Jean de Berry, op. 21 (1962)
Cinq variations sur un thème ecrit par des hirondelles (1968)
Deux fantaisies sur un thème grave, op. 54 (1968)
Deux dances, op. 56 (1969)
Escarmouches sur un thème sentimental
Fantaisie à propos d'arpeges op. 71 (1972)
Hommage à Couperin, op. 10, 12 pieces in 4 categories
L'idylle contrariee, puis coronée, romantic ballet (1963)
Une journée de mirmarmur, op. 20, 4 scenes (1962)
Keepsake, op. 7, 6 illustrations (1961)
Macabreries, op. 14 (Horizons funèbres) (1962)
Nocturne, op. 28 (1963) (rev as op. 47, 1967)
Nocturne Annabel Lee No. 4, op. 17 (Edgar Allan Poe) (1962)
Nocturne No. 5, op. 23 (Verlaine) (1963)
Nocturne No. 6, op. 24 (1963)
Nocturne No. 7, op. 25 (Musset) (1963)
Nocturne No. 8, op. 26 (1963)
Nocturne No. 9, op. 29 (Elegie) (1963) (also vln and pf) (1973)
Nocturne No. 10, op. 3 (1963)
Nocturne No. 11, op. 32 (1963)
Nocturne No. 12, op. 47 (1967)
Le petit musée, op. 34 (from Poussin to Picasso) (1964)
Petite suite zoologique, op. 36 (1964)
Secondes variations, op. 35 (1964)
Six romances, ops. 40, 41, 42, 43, 44 and 45 (1966)
Sonatine, op. 4, in 3 mvts (1961)
Sonatine baroque, op. 48 (1967)
Suite badine, op. 46 (1967)
Suite pastorale No. 2 (1961)
Sur le Pont-Neuf tout neuf, op. 22 (1963)
Tombeau de Scarletti, op. 6 (1961)
Toccata ragique, op. 16 (1962)
Trois vitraux, op. 9
Trois nocturnes, ops. 11, 12 and 13, based on 3 poems by Verlaine (1962)
Trois sortilèges, op. 53 (1968)
Triptyque, op. 18 (1962)
Three poetic divertissements, op. 73
Variations, op. 1 (1961)
Vignettes, op. 64 (1970)
Voyages drolatiques autant qu'imaginaires, op. 19 (1962)

Variations sur un thème vaguement russe, op. 27 (1963)
Autour d'une valse, op. 61 (left hand) (1970)
For the left hand, op. 63 (1970)
Suite capricieuse, op. 57 (left hand) (1970)
VOCAL
Four melodies, ops. 49, 50, 51 and 52 (vce and pf) (1967-1968)
Four melodies, ops. 65. 66. 67 and 68 (Dumas) (vce and pf) (1971)
Melodie, op. 69 (Offrande funèraire) (Dumas) (1972)
Melodies, ops. 38 and 39 (vce and pf) (1966)
BALLET
La masque de mort rouge, op. 69 (Edgar Allan Poe) (1972)
Ref. composer

QUEEN, Virginia

American associate professor and composer. b. Dallas, October 25, 1921. She studied at the American Conservatory and the University of Colorado. From 1946 she was associate professor at Ouachita Baptist University, AR.
Compositions
PIANO
Pieces incl.:
Adagio and scherzo
Three vagaries
SACRED
Let Thy Holy Spirit come upon us (w-vces) (1961)
Ref. 142

QUEEN OF THE KEYBOARD. See VASCONCELOS, Maria Regina

QUEEN OF SCOTS. See STUART, Mary

QUESADA, Virginia

American composer. b. Bayside, NY, February 11, 1951. She studied under Joel Chadabe at the State University of New York, Albay.
Compositions
ELECTRONIC
Roller rink (tape) (1973)
MULTIMEDIA
God commercial (tape and film) (1972)
Women's lip (tape and film) (1973)
Ref. 142

QUIEL, Hildegard

German teacher and composer. b. Berlin, April 23, 1888. She was a pupil of Humperdinck and Elizabeth Kuyper (q.v.). She taught at the music school in Wittenberge.
Compositions
CHAMBER
Trio in E (vln, vlc and pf) (Paragon Verlag, 1921)
Sonata in A (vln and pf) (Paragon Verlag, 1921)
VOCAL
Choruses
Songs
THEATRE
Rosenrot
Schneeweisschen
Ref. 41, 70, 105, 226

QUINAULT, Marie Anne

French singer and composer. b. France, 1692; d. 1793. She studied music under her father and made her debut at the Opera in 1709. In 1715 she joined the Comedie Française, from which she retired in 1722. She became the mistress of the Duke of Orleans and then of the former Duke of Nivernais. Through the favour of these influential figures she received a pension from the king and lodging at the Louvre in the Pavillon de l'infante, which she maintained for 60 years. A number of her compositions were performed at Versailles and she was decorated with the order of St. Michael by the King of France. This was the first time such a distinction was awarded to a woman. She composed sacred motets and other pieces.
Ref. 26, 226, 276, 347, 433

QUICIANI, Lucia

17th-century Italian composer. She studied under Marcantonio Negri.
Composition
VOCAL
Udite lagrimosi spiriti, madrigal (in collection Affetti Amorosi, Libro I, by M. Negri) (Venice: Ricciardo Amadino, 1711)
Ref. 105, 653

QUINLAN, Agnes Clune

Irish pianist, teacher, writer on music and composer. d. Limerick, 1949. She studied at the Royal Academy of Music, London and gave lecture recitals, specialising in Irish music. Her compositions were mainly in the Gaelic idiom and included piano pieces and songs.
Ref. 226, 347, 353

QUINN-VEES, Deborah

20th-century American composer.
Composition
ELECTRONIC
The rusted drum of insects, the crystal hairs of wind (2 fl, bsn, vlc, pf, perc, electric b-gtr and vces)
Ref. Recital CAL arts women composers program

QUINTANILLA, Alba

Venezuelan harpist, harpsichordist, pianist, conductor, lecturer and composer. b. Merida, July 11, 1944. She received musical instruction from her parents and later studied the piano, the harp, the harpsichord, composition and conducting under V.E. Sojo, R. Pereira, J.B. Plaza, Gonzalo and Evencio Castellanos, C. de Majo, E. Taborda, L. Butterini and P. Manelski at the Jose Angel Lamas Escuela Superior de Musica, Caracas. She performed as a soloist harpist and keyboard instrumentalist and premiered her *Tres Canciones* conducting the Venezuelan Symphony Orchestra; being the first woman to do so. She taught theory, solfege, harmony, counterpoint and the harp in conservatories and schools from 1963 and is an active member of the Venezuelan Symphony Orchestra. She received honors in 1976 and won national music prizes in 1964, 1966 and 1967.
Compositions
CHAMBER
Brass quintet
PIANO
Caballito de Escoba
Recordando a Teresa, waltz (ded T. Carreno q.v.)
Suite Venezuela
VOCAL
La Llanura, cantata (mix-ch and str orch) (1969)
Tres canciones (m-S and orch) (national vocal music prize, 1967)
Himno de los juegos inter-militares (ch) (1972)
Ciclo de canciones (S and pf) (1966)
Ref. Alan Pedigo (Booneville, AR)

QUINZANA, Sister Rosalba

17th-century Italian nun, singer and composer of the convent of St. Redegonda, Milan.
Ref. 502

QUIST, Pamela Layman. See LAYMAN, Pamela

RABEN-LEVETZAU, Nina

Early 20th-century Danish composer.
Compositions
VOCAL
Fire sange til tekster af Suzanne Raben-Levetzau: Den sidste gang vi var sammen:
Det ved du
Du sagde (W. Hansen) (1918)
The arrow and the song
Through valleys soft and shady
Tristesse (Alfred de Musset) (1918)
We used to sail the summer sea (Hansen) (1919)
Ref. 331

RABER DE REINDERS, Esther

Dutch pianist, teacher, writer and composer. b. Buenos Aires, February 21, 1940, now resident in South Africa. She received her theoretical teacher's diploma from the Fraccassi Conservatory, Buenos Aires in 1955 and in 1957 her piano teacher's diploma. She also spent several years studying at the Lopez Carlos Buchardo National Conservatory. Her teachers included Professor Enrique Barenboim in Israel (piano), Richard Cherry (harmony and counterpoint) and Dr. Jeanne Zaidel-Rudolph (q.v.). In 1984 she obtained her licentiate of music from the South African Academy for contemporary musicians. She taught in Argentina and Israel between 1959 and 1968 and from 1968 ran her own music studio in Israel and from 1972, in Johannesburg. PHOTOGRAPH.

Compositions
PIANO
El rio me trae recuerdos (1961) (Julio Korn)
Preludes (1985)
Six sentimental pieces (1983)
Susurrandote (1961) (Korn)
Publications
Disciplined thinking for the performer.
The theory of music.
Ref. composer, 643

RABINOF, Sylvia (Mrs. Benno)
American pianist, choral conductor, lecturer, writer and composer. b. New York, October 10. She attended New York University and studied under Simon Barere, Ignace Paderewski, Rudolf Serkin, Albert Stoessel, Bernard Wagenaar, Philip James and Georges Enesco. She received an honorary D.M. from Lincoln Memorial University. From 1942 to 1944 she conducted the Morley Singers and from 1970 to 1973 was on the piano faculty of various universities. She performed in concert, on radio and with symphony orchestras. From 1949 she toured worldwide, appearing in duo concerts with her violinist husband, Benno Rabinof. She is a member of ASCAP.
Compositions
ORCHESTRA
Suite (cham orch)
Turkey in the straw, concert variation
PIANO
Three profiles
VOCAL
Carnaval, tone poem (ch and orch)
SACRED
Deluge, cantata
OPERETTA
Hamlet, the flea, for children
TEACHING PIECES
Gastronomic suite (pf)
Publications
Musicianship through Improvisation and the Improvisor. 1969.
Ref. 39, 40, 85, 142, 347

RABORG, Rosa Ortiz de Zevallos de
19th-century Peruvian pianist and composer. She performed at the evening concerts of Mrs. Juana Manuela Gorriti de Belzu, a patron of music.
Compositions
PIANO
Tu y yo (1876)
Veinte y octo de julio, waltz (1876)
Ref. 403

RACOVITZA-FLONDOR, Florica
Rumanian pianist and composer. b. Rogojeste, Bucovina, November 27, 1897. She was the daughter of composer Tudor Flondor. She studied in Vienna at the Akademie fuer Musik und darstellende Kunst from 1916 to 1922 and theory under R. Stoehr; harmony, counterpoint and composition under Joseph Marx; history of music under Eusebie Mandicevski and the piano under Emil Sauer. In Bucharest she studied composition under Mihail Jora. PHOTOGRAPH.
Compositions
ORGAN
Chorale (1954)
Prelude (1954)
PIANO
Burlesque (1958)
Caprice (1961)
Dance
From children's life, suite (1951) (Editions Musicales, 1956)
Fugues in F-Minor and G-Major (1921, 1922)
Improvisation (1969)
Noveletta (1965)
Prelude and fugue in C-Minor (Editions Musicales, 1922)
Sonata in F-Minor (1955)
Song without words
The source in the woods (1951)
Three intermezzi (1959)
Three preludes (1938, 1955, 1960)
Three Rumanian dances (1955)
Three studies (1963, 1966, 1968) (No. 2, Editions Musicales, 1969)
Toccata (1964)
Two songs for piano (1956)
Variations on a Rumanian theme (1957)
Ref. composer, 196

RADECKI, Olga von
19th-century Russian composer.
Compositions
VOCAL
Songs incl.:
The night has a thousand eyes
Sea hath its pearls
Ref. 226, 276

RADEKE, Winifred
20th-century composer.
Composition
ORCHESTRA
Concerto in D-Major (fl, ob, continuo and str orch) (Schott)
Ref. 403

RADERMACHER, Erika
Swiss pianist, professor, singer and composer. b. Eschweiler, West Germany, April 16, 1936. She studied the piano under Else Schmitz-Gohr in Cologne and Bruno Seidlhofer in Vienna and singing under Jolanda Rodio in Berne and Sylvia Gaehwiller in Zurich. She is a member of *Ensemble Neue Horizonte Berne* and professor of the piano at the Berne Conservatory. She was the recipient of numerous piano prizes including one from the Austrian State in Lausanne in 1981 and in 1983 she and her husband, Urs Peter Schneider, won the Bernese music prize. PHOTOGRAPH.
Compositions
CHAMBER
Streichquartett (2 vlc, vla and vln) (1970)
Liebe Gott und tu, was du willst (vln, vlc and pf) (1985)
Chi oder X (vln and pf) (1983)
(Nicht) frei, aber (auch nicht) einsam (vln and pf) (1982)
Sonate, hommage an Frederik Chopin (vlc and pf) (1984)
PIANO
Alle Uhren, selbst die traegsten... (1981)
Zwei Kinderstuecke (1944)
VOCAL
Sieben Rosen spaeter (S and 8 insts) (1981)
Lust (speaker and B-cl) (1983)
THEATRE
Wer hat dich, du schoener Wald... (1984)
ELECTRONIC
Die Moldau (ww, wind and tape) (1984)
Ref. composer, 651

RADIC, Maureen
20th-century Australian composer.
Compositions
INCIDENTAL MUSIC
Plays:
Sideshow, arrangements of World War I songs (1971)
Some of my best friends are women, music and songs (1976)
Ref. 442

RADIGUE, Eliane
French composer. b. Paris, January 24. She studied at the Studio d'Essai, Paris, from 1957 to 1958 under Peter Schaeffer and Peter Henry and at the Studio Apsome under Peter Henry from 1967 to 1968. She spent 1970 at New York University, where she was artist-in-residence. She also worked at the Electronic Music Studios at Iowa University and at the California Institute of the Arts. She has her own studio in Paris where she concentrates on the arp synthesizer. Her works have been performed in the United States and Europe. PHOTOGRAPH.
Compositions
ELECTRONIC
Adnos (1974)
Arthesis (1973)
Biogenesis (1973)
Chry-ptus (1971)
Geelriandre (1971)
In memoriam ostinate (1969)
No. 17 (1970)
Ohmnt (1968)
Schlinen (1972)
Seventh birth (1971)
Stress (1970)
Transamorem-transmortem (1973)
Usral (1969)
E = a = b = a + b *Pour Farhi* (1969)
Ref. composer, 622

RADMALL, Peggy
20th-century British violinist and composer. b. Croydon. She studied at the Royal Academy of Music and privately under Carl Flesch and Max Rostal. She composed and arranged pieces for the violin and the viola.
Ref. 490

RADNOR, Helen, Countess of (Viscountess Folkestone)
Late 19th-20th-century English conductor, editor, singer and composer. She aided in the foundation of the Royal College of Music, London and organized her ladies string band and chorus, giving numerous charity concerts. She conducted concerts and was musical editor of 'An Order of Service' for children.
Compositions
VOCAL
Songs
SACRED
An order of service for children with music, occasional services and appendix
Occasional services with music (shortened carol and midnight) and appendix of psalms and hymns
An order of service for children and appendix
Occasional services with music (Novello)
General thanksgiving and simple choral communion (Novello)
Hymns
Psalms
Ref. 6, 85, 226, 276, 297, 347, 433

RADOFF, Elaine. See BARKIN, Elaine

RADZIWILL, Princess
19th-century Polish composer.
Compositions
PIANO
Cecile, op. 13, 2e valse de salon (Heugel)
Dimanche, 10 pensées musicales (Heugel)
Feu follet, op. 15, caprice (Heugel)
Idylle, op. 14 (Heugel)
Mai, valse de salon (Heugel)
Mazurka, op. 12 (Heugel)
Melodies orientales, op. 16 (Heugel)
Romance sans paroles, op. 17 (Heugel)
Ref. 297

RAFAELE. See ALEOTTI, Raffaela-Argenata

RAHMN, Elza Loethner
Swedish organist, pianist, teacher and composer. b. Koping, June 21, 1872. She studied at the Stockholm Conservatory and the Virgil Piano School in New York. She was church organist and taught music in New York and Massachusetts. She composed piano pieces and songs.
Ref. 226

RAIGORODSKY, Leda Natalia Heimsath (Mrs. Harter)
20th-century American music critic, lecturer and composer. b. Tulsa, OK. She obtained her M.A. (composition and music history) from the American University, Washington, DC, in 1963 and studied privately under Quincy Porter at Yale University, Bernard Wagenaar at the Juilliard School of Music and Stanley Hummel. She lectured, taught music theory and the piano and was programmer of classical music for radio from 1962 to 1963 and 1965 and 1966. She is a music critic, has written notes for the radio and was an announcer and interviewer for music programs.
Compositions
ORCHESTRA
Symphony No. 1 (also fl, hp and bsn) (1963)
CHAMBER
Introduction, reflection and allegro (wind qnt) (1963, rev 1967)
Dusk (fl and pf) (1963)
Preludes (pf)
SACRED
She lies asleep, requiem (ch, hn and pf) (1950, rev 1961)
Psalm 21 (I will lift up mine eyes) (1965)
Psalm 23 (1969)
Psalm 27 (1966)
Psalm 121 (1965)
Psalm of thanksgiving (1967)
Psalm 100 (Cantad alegnes a Dios) (1968)
Wake ye people and sing (new words for requiem, 1950)
Songs incl.:
Christmas love (1962)
The Lord's Prayer (1970)
Love's promise (1963)
Thanksgiving (1971)
OPERA
The Promise of Peace, sacred (large ch) (1969)
Ref. composer, 622, 625

RAIK. See RAIQ

RAKSIN, Ruby. See RASKIN, Ruby

RAINIER, Priaulx (Ivy Priaulx)
British violinist, professor and composer. b. Howick, South Africa, February 3, 1903; d. October 10, 1986. She entered the South African College of Music at the age of ten, studying harmony and the violin under the principal, W.H. Bell. In 1920 she was awarded the Cape University Scholarship for the violin and went to study at the Royal Academy of Music in London. She studied the violin under Rowsby Woof and harmony and counterpoint under J.B. McEwen. She began to concentrate on composition after receiving a grant in 1935 and in 1937 went to study under Nadia Boulanger (q.v.) in Paris. Priaulx was professor of composition at the Royal Academy of Music from 1943 to 1961. In 1953 she was elected fellow of the Royal Academy of Music and Collard fellow of the Worshipful Company of Musicians, City of London. In February 1973 the BBC broadcast a retrospective concert of some of her chamber works to celebrate the occasion of her 70th birthday. She was commissioned to compose works for the Purcell Singers, the London Philharmonic Society (to celebrate Sir Adrian Boult's ten years' directorship), the SABC and the BBC. She was the recipient of a number of grants and bursaries and in 1982 the University of Cape Town honored her with a doctorate in music. DISCOGRAPHY.
Compositions
ORCHESTRA
Celebration (vln and orch) (comm Yehudi Menuhin, 1977)
Concerto (vlc and orch) (1964) (Schott)
Concerto for two winds and orchestra (ob, cl and orch)
Due canti e finale, concerto (vln and orch) (1975) (Schott)
Incantation (cl and orch) (1933) (Schott)
Phala-phala, dance concerto (1961) (Schott)
Aequora lunae (1967) (Schott) (comm BBC)
Ballet suite (1950) (Schott)
Sinfonia da camera (str orch) (1947) (Schott)
CHAMBER
Trios and triads (10 trios and perc) (1973)
Six pieces for 5 wind instruments (fl, ob, cl, hn and bsn) (1954) (Schott)
Ploermel (winds and perc) (1973) (Schott)
Quanta (ob and str trio) (1962) (Schott)
String quartet (1924) (Schott)
String quartet No. 1 (1939) (Schott)
String quartet No. 2 (1951) (Schott)
Grand duo (vlc, vln and pf) (1983) (Schott)
String trio (1965) (Schott)
Duo (vln and pf) (1932) (Schott)
Sonata (vla and pf) (1945) (Schott)
Suite (cl and pf) (1943) (Schott)
Pastoral triptych (ob) (1960) (Schott)
Quinque (hpcd) (1971) (Schott)
Suite (vlc) (1963) (Schott)
Wild life celebration (1984)
ORGAN
Organ gloriana (1972) (Schott)
Primordial canticles (1974) (Schott)
PIANO
Barbaric dance suite (1949) (Schott)
Five keyboard pieces (1951) (Schott)
Pieces for Keyboard, 1 and 2 (1952) (Schott)
VOCAL
Two archaic songs (ch a-cap) (1927) (Schott)
The bee oracles (Edith Sitwell) (T or B, fl, ob, vln, vlc and hpcd) (1970) (Schott)
Cycle for declamation (S, T or B) (1953) (Schott)
Dance of the rain (T and gtr) (1948) (Schott)
Duo-vision and prayer (T and pf) (1974) (Schott)
Three Greek epigrams (S and pf) (1937) (Schott)
Ubunzima (Zulu text) (T or S and gtr) (1948) (Schott)

SACRED
Requiem (S or T and ch) (1955) (Schott)
Prayers from the ark (T and hp) (1974) (Schott)
FILM MUSIC
Figures in a landscape (1954) (Schott)

Bibliography

Amis, John. *Priaulx Rainier. Musical Times*, July 1955.
Baxter, Timothy. *Priaulx Rainier, a Study of Her Musical Style. Composer*, no. 60. Spring 1977.
Glock, William. *The Music of Priaulx Rainier. The Listener*, November 13, 1947.
Routh, Francis. *Contemporary British Music (1945-1970)*. London, 1972. Pp. 351-364.

Ref. 2, 8, 13, 15, 22, 68, 70, 73, 74, 77, 96, 175, 177, 184, 189, 201, 230, 377, 422, 563, 609, 612, 622, 377

RAIQ (Raik, Rayyig, Rik) (Bloom of Youth)

Arabian teacher and songstress. ca. 820. She was one of the foremost singers of the innovative, Persian-influenced romantic school of music. She was a slave in the household of Ibrahim ibn al-Mahdi who later purchased Shariyya (q.v.) and Raiq became her teacher.

Ref. 171

RAKHMANKULOVA, Mariam Mannanovna

Soviet mezzo-soprano, writer and composer. b. Kazan, November 20, 1901. She studied composition under B. Schechter at the Moscow Conservatory from 1935 to 1937 and graduated from the department of the Tatar Opera in 1939 where her teacher was Petrenko. She then sang in the Tatar State Opera and Ballet Theatre, on radio and with the Kazan Philharmonic Orchestra. She wrote numerous articles and translated the texts of songs into the Tatar language. She was awarded the title of Honored Artist of the Tatar Autonomous SSR, the Order of Lenin and other medals and was active in local government.

Compositions

ORCHESTRA
Kechkene khikaya (str orch) (1940)
Malenkaya skazka (str orch) (1940)
PIANO
Pesnya bez slov (1938)
VOCAL
Prazdnik elki (K. Nedzhmi) (ch) (1952)
Songs:
Akh, pesni moi (A. Erikeyev) (1962)
Chechek (A. Pushkin) (1937)
Devochka i babochka (G. Tukaya) (1943)
Kolybelnaya (folk words) (1944)
Kyz blen kubelek (G. Tukaya) (1937)
Nasha pesnya (Russian folk words) (1937)
Pesnya o Kube (M. Khusain) (1964)
Poteshniy uchenik (G. Tukaya) (1943)
Priezhaite v gosti (M. Khusain) (1953)
Rodina (G. Kutuya) (1942)
Tsvetok (A. Pushkin) (1942)
Two Tatar folk songs (1940-1950)
INCIDENTAL MUSIC
Plays incl.:
Elka, for radio (D. Appakov) (1944)
Tapkyr yeget (D. Appakov) (1945)
Film music

Ref. 21, 87, 330

RALPH, Kate (nee Roberts) (Mrs. Francis) (pseud. Morfida)

19th-century English pianist and composer. b. London. She studied at the London Academy of Music where she was presented with a scholarship by Clara Schumann (q.v.). She gave various chamber concerts. She married the violinist Francis Ralph.

Compositions

CHAMBER
Six pieces (vln and pf) (Leonard)
VOCAL
Arise beloved (vce and pf) (Leonard)

Ref. 6, 85, 260, 276, 297, 347, 433

RALSTON, Frances Marion (Fanny)

American pianist, lecturer and composer. b. St. Louis, MO, January 7, 1875; d. Arcadia, CA, February 5, 1952. She studied at the New England Conservatory, Boston and under Foote, Goetschius, Fannie Payne, Nellie Strong Stevenson, Richard S. Poppen and Ernest R. Kroeger. In Chicago she studied under Adolf Weidig and in Boston under Carl Faelten. She gave a recital of her own compositions at St. Louis in 1896. She was director of the music department at Central College, Lexington, MO, for two years and director of the Music School of Rockford College, IL, for nine years.

Compositions

ORCHESTRA
Rhapsodie (pf and orch, also 2 or 1 pf)
CHAMBER
Sonata spirituel (vln and pf) (New York: Breitkopf, 1927)
ORGAN
Scotch idyll (C.F. Summy, 1916)
Winter
PIANO
Etude (Breitkopf)
Fantasie impromptu
Impressions at Wellesley
Orientales
Prelude and fugue in G
Six etudes
Six pieces in the Greek modes
Six preludes
Sonate (C.F. Summy, 1921)
Sonata in C-Sharp Minor
Song without words, op. 10 (St. Louis: Balmer & Weber, 1905)
Theme and variations (C.F. Summy, 1919)
Three impressions
Three little waltzes (New York: Composers Press, 1946)
VOCAL
Songs incl.:
Greeting
Ich liebe Dich

Publications

Reflections of a Musician. R.G. Badger, 1920.

Ref. 70, 228, 266, 276, 292, 433, 460

RALSTON, Fanny. See RALSTON, Frances Marion

RAMAKERS (Vigneron-Ramakers), Christiane Josée (pseud. Jo Delande)

Belgian organist, pianist, conductor, teacher, writer and composer. b. Leopoldsburg, January 25, 1914. She studied at the Limburg Organ School in Hasselt under Arthur and Herman Meulemans. She was the founder and director of the Maasmechelen Music Academy in 1945 and the Jeugd en Muziek Eisden Maasmechelen, 1956. She was the recipient of the Koopal prize in 1961 and the Limburg Aovinciol music prize, 1978. She wrote literary works under her pseudonym.

Compositions

ORCHESTRA
Alternator, op. 17
Ballade, op. 13
Concertino, op. 5
Duo rhapsodique, op. 6
Petit cortège, op. 10
Studies (small orch) (1957)
CHAMBER
Saxophone-quartet (1959)
VOCAL
Drie zangen van liefde en dood, op. 19
THEATRE
Het daghet (Y.P. Stasse) (ch and orch)

Ref. 457

RAMANN, Lina

German pianist, teacher, music writer and composer. b. Mainstockheim, near Kitzingen, June 24, 1833; d. Munich, March 30, 1912. She studied under Franz and Brendel in Leipzig. In 1858 she founded a music institute in Glueckstadt but it closed during the German-Danish war in 1864. She moved to Gera, Thuringia and taught and performed there and then went to the United States for some years. On her return she and Ida Volkmann (q.v.) founded a music school in Nuremberg and in 1890, in Munich. Then she dedicated herself to writing about music.

Compositions

PIANO
Erste Elementarstufe des Klavierspiels (Breitkopf)
Four sonatinas, op. 9 (Kahnt)
Grundriss der Technik des Klavierspiels (Breitkopf)
Other teaching works
ARRANGEMENTS
Works by Liszt, Bach, Mosonyi and other composers, for teaching

Publications

Allgemeine Erzieh-und Unterrichtslehre der Jugend. 1869.
Aus der Gegenwart. Collection of essays.
Franz Liszt als Psalmensanger. 1886.
Liszt-Paedagogium. 5 vols.
Liszts Christus. 1880.
Die Musik als Gegenstand der Erziehung Bach und Handel.
Biography of Liszt in three parts. 1880.
Edition of Liszt's writings. 1880.

Ref. 95, 100, 105, 226, 276, 297

RAMM, Valentina Iosifovna

Soviet violinist, editor, lecturer, singer, writer and composer. b. Kharkov, Ukraine, October 22, 1888; d. Moscow, July 3, 1968. She studied the violin under K. Zitt and harmony and counterpoint under S. Krell at the Leipzig Conservatory, graduating in 1908. At the same time she studied singing under B. Heidiger. After 1908 she worked in Rostov-on-the-Don, singing and teaching singing. She returned to Moscow and attended classes in composition given by M. Gnesin. From 1928 to 1929 she was secretary of the Association of Chamber Music and taught singing at the A. Scriabin music school. From 1930 to 1932 she was an editor for Muzgiz music publishers and director of a society of young composers and from 1938 to 1940, editor of a record company. She lectured at the Kirov Music School from 1941 to 1943. She wrote articles on the history of song and song in civil strife and translated two of Bach's cantatas and over 100 songs.

Compositions

ORCHESTRA
Slavyanski marsh (wind orch) (1941)
Torzhestvennie marsh (wind orch) (1945)

CHAMBER
Quartet for wind instruments (1935)
String quartet No. 1 (1934)
String quartet No. 2 (1945)
Sonata (vln and pf) (1920)
Suite (pf) (1947)

VOCAL
Udarnitzy metalla, cantata (T. Sikorskaya) (vce and orch) (1952)
V stepnykh aulakh, cantata (Dzhambul) (vce and orch) (1939)
Nike (B. Bronevsky) (vce and orch) (1936)
Pyat dnei i pyat nochei, poems of mourning in memory of Lenin (V. Inber) (vce and orch) (1928)
Dni voiny, 5 cycles (Soviet poets) (vce and str qrt) (1943)
Four folk songs (vce, str qrt and fl) (1944)
O voine, 8 children's songs (Soviet poets) (vce and str qrt) (1963)
Songs (N. Gilyen) (vce and str qrt) (1955)
Rodina, cycle (vce and pf) (1942)
Triptych, Penthesilea (S. Parnak) (vce and pf) (1928)
Approx. 100 choruses and romances (A. Pushkin, M. Lermontov, F. Tiutchev, A. Blok and other Soviet poets)

SACRED
Santa Ursula, cantata

BALLET
Caliph-Aist, fairy tale (1943)
Skazka o mertvoi tsarevne i o semi bogatyryakh (A. Pushkin) (orch) (1954)

Publications

Schubert v massovoi auditorii. 1928.
Zapadnoyevrodeiskaya khudozhestvennaya pesnya. 1929.

Ref. 21, 87, 94, 465, 330

RAMOS, Eudocia

19th-century Peruvian pianist and composer. She performed at the concerts of the Sociedad Filarmonica, 1869 to 1870.

Compositions

PIANO
Sueno, un, melody
Las tres perlas

Ref. 403

RAMSAY, Lady Katherine, Duchess of Atholl

19th-century English composer.

Compositions

VOCAL
The blessed damozel, cantata (soli and ch) (Novello)
Songs incl.:
Green fields of England
I will make you brooches
To you, let snow and roses

Ref. 226, 276, 297, 433

RAMSEY, Catherine Gertrude. See RAMSEY, Sister Mary Anastasia

RAMSEY, Sister Mary Anastasia (Catherine Gertrude)

American organist, pianist, conductor, lecturer and composer. b. Birmingham, AL. She attended the Sacred Heart Academy at Cullman and in 1921 graduated from the St. Louis Institute of Music and in 1923 from the Cincinnati Conservatory. In 1933 she graduated with a B.A. from Loyola University and in 1942 gained her M.A. from the George Peabody College for Teachers. Her teachers included Karin Dayas and Harold Spencer (piano); G. Blackman and Ralph Odierno (voice); and Dr. Claude Almond (composition). She joined the Sacred Heart Academy in 1925 and became dean of music, organist, conductor of the orchestra and lecturer on the piano.

Compositions

ORGAN
Passacaglia in G-Minor

SACRED
Blest Father Benedict
Cantica benedicta
Lady of Fatima
Lady of Fatima, ave!

Ref. 496

RAN, Shulamit

Israeli pianist, professor and composer. b. Tel Aviv, October 21, 1949. She studied the piano under Paul Ben Haim and Alexander U. Boscovitz and made her debut in Tel Aviv at the age of 12. Her first orchestral work was performed when she was 14. She studied the piano under Dorothy Taubman in New York and Nadia Reisenberg and Maria Damont in London, before proceeding to the Mannes College of Music in New York, where she studied composition under Norman Dello Joio. She attended courses at Darmstadt and Tanglewood. She performed extensively in the United States, Europe, Argentina, Canada and Israel with leading orchestras, including the Marlboro Orchestra, the Orchestre de la Suisse Romande and the Israel Philharmonic under Zubin Mehta, as well as on radio and television. She was artist-in-residence at St. Mary's University, Canada from 1972 to 1973 and then assistant professor of composition at the University of Chicago. DISCOGRAPHY.

Compositions

ORCHESTRA
Capriccio (pf and orch)
Concert piece (pf and orch) (T. Presser, 1970)
Symphonic poem (pf and orch) (1967)

CHAMBER
Ensembles for seventeen (Presser, 1975)
Double visions (2 qnt and pf) (Presser, 1977)
A prayer (hn and insts) (1982) (Presser)
Excursions (vln, vlc and pf) (1980) (Presser)
Fantasy II (vln, pf and perc) (1973)
Private game (cl and vlc)
Three fantasy pieces (vlc and pf) (1972)
Fantasy variations (vlc) (1979) (Presser)
For an actor (cl) (1978)
Monologue (cl)
Sonata brevis (hpcd) (1977)

PIANO
Ten children's scenes (4 hands) (New York: C. Fischer, 1970)
Hyperbolae (Israeli Music, 1977)
Seven short pieces (1967)
Sonata No. 2 (1967)
Sonata waltzer (pf) (1983)
Structures (1968)
Toccata (1965) (Boosey & Hawkes)
Verticals (1983)

VOCAL
Apprehensions (vce, cl and pf) (1979) (Israeli Music)
Fanfare (S) (1981) (Presser)
Hatzvi Israel eulogy (vce and ens) (Fischer, 1972)
Seven Japanese love poems (1968)

ELECTRONIC
O, the chimneys (S, insts and tape) (Fischer, 1973)

Ref. composer, AMC newsletter, 52, 142, 184, 185, 206, 228, 415, 477, 494, 563, 622, 625

RANTA-SHIDA, Shoko

Japanese pianist, assistant professor and composer. b. Japan, January 15, 1942. She graduated from Tokyo University of Arts where she studied composition under Professors T. Ikenouchi, A. Yashiro, K. Yasukawa and K. Kanatawa. She taught composition, the piano and analysis at the Aichi Prefectural University of Arts from 1968 to 1976. Between 1976 and 1978 she was assistant professor at the College of Chinese Culture in Taiwan. She also studied electronic music. She lives in West Germany.

Compositions
CHAMBER
Chie (2 Chinese vln and perc) (1978)
Flute sonata (Japan Federation of Composers) (1968)
Yuen (perc) (1978)
ELECTRONIC MUSIC
Chatney sweet (20 syo) (1976)
Fruits in Savannah (tape and schakuhachi) (1973)
Harna (tape and pf) (1974)
Lazy garnet (vce, tape and schakuhachi) (1974)
Lonely mountain (tape and perc) (1976)
Summer talk (tape and perc) (1979)
Three words (pf, fl, vln and elec insts) (1977)
Ref. composer

RAPIN-GERBER, Eleonore
Compositions
CHAMBER
Serenade, op. 6 (2 vln and vlc)
Capriccio, op. 7 (vln and pf) (Foetisch)
Melodie, op. 5 (vln and pf) (Foetisch)
Valse, op. 8 (vln and pf)
Valse-etude, op. 4 (pf)
Ref. 297

RAPOPORT, Eda
American pianist and composer. b. Daugavpils, Latvia, December 9, 1886; d. New York, May 9, 1968. She went to the United States in 1908. She studied the piano at the Peabody Institute, Baltimore on a three year scholarship. She also studied under Gallico Lambert and Stasny. At the Institute of Musical Art she studied composition under Goetschius, Copland, Piston and Schoenberg.
Compositions
ORCHESTRA
Piano concerto (1939)
Violin concerto (1942)
Adagio (str orch) (New York, 1948)
Israfel (fl, hp and str orch) (1936)
Lamentations, based on Hebrew themes (vlc and orch or pf) (1933) (rev. 1940)
Lament: Revolt in the Warsaw Ghetto
The Mathmid, tone poem (1934)
Suite for orchestra (1943)
Three pastels (str orch; also pf)) (New York, 1947)
Three symphonic dances (1935)
CHAMBER
Indian legend (ww qnt) (New York: Associated Music Publ., 1949)
Quintet (fl and strs) (1944)
Piano quartet (1940)
Quartet (fl, vl, vlc and pf) (1933)
Quartet (vln, vlc, cl and hp) (1935)
String quartet in G, No. 2 (Weaner-Levant, 1935)
String quartet No. 1 (Hebrew themes) (Transcontinental Music, 1934)
String quartet No. 3 (1940)
Thoughts in the night (vln, vlc and pf) (Transcontinental, 1946)
Trio (cl, vlc and pf) (1933)
Trio (cl, vlc and pf) (1942)
Trio (vln, vla and vlc) (1939)
Agada (vlc and pf) (Transcontinental, 1939)
Berceuse, op. 21 (vln and pf) (1961)
Chant hebraique (vlc and pf)
Midrash (vln and pf) (Transcontinental, 1939)
Migun (vln and pf) (Transcontinental, 1939)
Poem, op. 14 (vla and pf) (1939)
Sonata (vln and pf) (1933, 1941)
Sonata (vlc and pf) (1936)
PIANO
Suite for two pianos (Independent Music, 1941)
Three etches: The old castle; Lake Louise; The grand canyon (1947)
Three impressions (1943)
Three sonatas (Assoc. Music, 1949)
VOCAL
The song of songs, cantata (S, T, fl, vlc and pf) (1937)
The raven (Edgar Allan Poe) (T or S, d-b and qrt or orch) (Weaner-Levant, 1936)
Choral suite (ch a-cap) (1939)
Welcome, Queen Sabbath (mix-ch and pf) (1944)
Pastoral string quartet with soprano (1934)
OPERA
The Fisherman and his Wife, opera-fantasy, based on Grimm
G.I. Joe, in 1 act (1945)
Ref. 40, 141, 142, 190, 191, 322, 347, 353, 477, 594

RAPP, Marguerite
German pianist and composer. b. Strasbourg, June 17, 1865; d. Rouen, November 23, 1913. She performed in recitals at the age of 13 and began composing when she was 20. Together with her sister Susanna, a violinist, she toured in concerts throughout France.
Compositions
ORCHESTRA
Symphonic poem
Diana, overture
OPERA
Opera in 3 acts (Susanna Rapp)
Ref. 105, 226

RASKIN, Ruby
20th-century American conductor and composer.
Compositions
INCIDENTAL MUSIC
The battle of the bulge, film (1966)
The brave rifles, film (1966)
Valley of the dragons, film (1961)
Music for television
Ref. 326

RASMUSSEN, Camilla. See LIEDBERGIUS, Camilla

RASSCHENAU, Marianna (Maria Anna de)
Late 17th-century composer. She was a nun who composed for the Viennese Court.
Compositions
SACRED
Le sacre visioni di Santa Teresa, oratorio (M.A. Signorini) (1703)
MISCELLANEOUS
Il consiglio di Pallade (1697)
Ref. 103, 128

RATULD, P. See ZBYSZEWSKA-OLECHNOWSKA, Maria

RAVINALE, Irma
Italian pianist, teacher and composer. b. Naples, October 1, 1937. She studied at the Conservatorio di Santa Cecilia in Rome and graduated in composition under A. de Nino and G. Petrassi; the piano under R. Rossi; choral music under C.A. Antonelli and band orchestration under G. Orsomando. She is a teacher of composition at the Conservatorio di Santa Cecilia in Rome where she was director in 1979. She received numerous prizes and awards, including four national composition prizes and an international composition prize in Trieste and in 1966 was the only woman to win the competition of the department of composition at the Conservatory of Santa Cecilia.
Compositions
ORCHESTRA
Concerto per violino e orchestra
Dialoghi per viola e chitarra e orchestra
Sinfonia concertante (gtr and orch) (1975) (ded M. Cangi)
Cangiante per clarinetto e piccola orchestra (1981)
Concerto per archi, oboe, corno e timpani
Concerto per archi da camera (1975)
CHAMBER
Invenzione concertante per 13 strumenti a fiato (1975)
Les adieux (obs and strs) (1982)
Sequentia (str qrt and gtr) (1980)
Serenata (gtr, fl and vla)
Trio notturno (vln, vla d'amore and vlc)
Jontly (2 gtr) (1982)
Improvvisazione per chitarra solo (1978)
Improvvisazione seconda (hpcd) (1982)
Invenzione (gtr)
Recherche (vln) (1981)
VOCAL
La morte meditata, cantata (Ungaretti) (B and str qrt)
Todo el amor (B, ch and orch) (P. Neruda)
Lauda (B, mix-ch and cham ens)
Canti per voce di fanciulli e undici esecutori (chil-ch and 11 insts)
Lo scorpione (Trilussa) (ch a-cap)
Ballata di amore e di guerra (S, vln, vlc and pf)
Arrangements
OPERA
Il ritratto di Dorian Grey, in 1 act (Oscar Wilde) (RAI, 1975)

MISCELLANEOUS
Ballo di fiori del male (Baudelaire)
Serenata
Spleen (1980) (international composition prize, Trieste)
Ref. composer, 228, 622

RAVISSA
Composer of six piano sonatas.
Ref. Frau und Musik

RAVIZE, Angele
French teacher and composer. b. 1887. At the Paris Conservatoire she won first prize for fugue, which she studied under Andre Gedalge and then the Lepaulle prize for young teachers. She was interested in the musical education of young children and encouraged the use of the recorder in schools. She introduced children's musical programs on the radio with pre-lschool children, often accompanied by children's orchestras.
Compositions
VOCAL
Chanson rondes et jeux, for small children (vce and pf) (Paris: Editions Bourrelier, 1950)
Arrangements of a-cappella choirs
TEACHING PIECES
Teaching works for small children, including works for the recorder
Publications
Floulege des enfants, comptines et formulettes.
Ref. composer

RAW, Vera Constance
South African choral conductor, journalist, teacher, writer and composer. b. Durban, 22 January, 1896. She studied singing under Percival Kirby at the Natal Teachers' Training College, Pietermaritzburg in 1914 and from 1917 to 1920, counterpoint, composition, conducting, music interpretation and philosophy under Edmond Schelpe. She worked as a journalist, but after being widowed, returned to music teaching and was an occasional pupil of Edmond Schelpe. In 1923 she won first prize at an Eisteddfod for her setting of a poem. She trained school choirs. Her literary works included a journal of a voyage to Persia and a short story based on Zulu customs and beliefs. She composed five piano pieces, including a gavotte, mazurka and minuet; songs and children's songs; sacred songs, three christmas carols and a setting of the Lord's Prayer in English and Afrikaans, for massed choirs.
Ref. 377

RAWLINSON, Angela
19th-century English composer.
Compositions
VOCAL
Songs incl.:
Beautiful Land of Nod (Ascherberg)
OPERETTA
Coquette (London: Boosey & Co.)
Ref. 226, 276, 433

RAY, Ruth
American violinist, teacher and composer. b. Alvin, IL, July 19, 1899. She studied at the University of Chicago and graduated from the Eastman School of Music, University of Rochester with an Mus.M. and studied with Leopold Auer for over six years, making her debut at Carnegie Hall in 1919. She appeared as a soloist with a number of major orchestras and toured extensively in America, Canada and Europe. She composed short pieces for the violin and the piano.
Ref. composer, 77

RAYMOND, Emma Marcy
American pianist and composer. b. New York, March 16, 1856; d. November, 1913. She studied the piano under Louis Moreau Gottschalk, harmony under German professors and voice under Ronconi. She composed her first song at the age of five. Several of her songs were later sung by Adelina Patti (q.v.).
Compositions
CHAMBER
Piano pieces
VOCAL
Songs incl.:
Bird of love
First love
SACRED
Ave Maria
O salutaris
OPERA
Dovetta (1889)
Ref. 226, 276, 292, 307, 433

RAYMOND, Madeleine
Canadian concert pianist and composer. b. Donnaconna, Quebec, July 5, 1919. She studied at the Ecole Superieure de Musique d' Outremont. Her teachers included Claude Champagne (composition), Jean Dansereau (interpretation), Germaine Malepart (piano) and J.J. Gagnier. She gave many piano concerts. PHOTOGRAPH.
Compositions
ORCHESTRA
Ballade sur l'eau (pf and orch)
Danse sauvage (pf and orch)
Pastorale (pf and orch)
Printemps (pf and orch)
Amours villageoises (small orch; also pf and har)
Dans les brumes du Saint-Laurent
PIANO
Berceuse pour en noel d'enfant
Danse marionelle
Deux études
Deux pastorelles
Donnaconna
Etude caprice
Idylle (1949)
Premier Noël de Louison
Scenes d'enfants
Theme and variations
Trois études
Variations sur l'automne
Ref. composer, 133, 477

RAYNAL, Germaine
20th-century French composer.
Compositions
OPERETTA
La Belle du Far-West (1920)
La Dame de Monte Carlo (1918)
Pouick! (1922)
La Reine ardente (1920)
Ref. 431

RAYYA AL-ZARQA
Arabian songstress of the Umayyad period. ca. 665. She was the sister of Sallama (q.v.) who also achieved fame as a songstress.
Ref. 171, 234

RAYYIG. See RAIQ

READ, Sarah Ferriss
19th-century American composer of songs.
Ref. 465

REBAUDI, Virginia
19th-century Italian composer.
Compositions
VOCAL
Ad Lydiam, dialogue
Inverno, romanza: Cantava gaia la capinera (M. Carcassi)
Ref. 297

REBE, Louise Christine
American concert pianist, teacher and composer of German descent. b. Philadelphia, 1900. Her father, a tenor, presented her as a piano soloist at the German Gesangverein concerts when she was ten. Her piano teachers included Giorni and Jonas and she obtained her teacher's diploma from the Sternberg School of Music in Philadelphia. She graduated with a B.S. in education from the University of Pennsylvania and studied composition at the university under Dr. Morrison Boyd. In 1928, through the encouragement of John M. Williams, she turned to the composition of piano music.

Compositions
PIANO
At the zoo, suite
Dances: Castanets; Gay Vienna waltz; In old Granada; A night in Spain
Marches: Cadet's review; Poem; The spirit of '76
Ref. 40, 292, 347, 353

REBULL, Teresa
20th-century Spanish composer. DISCOGRAPHY.
Compositions
VOCAL
Chants catalans (vce and ens)
Ref. 518, 563

RECKE, Caroline (Recke-Madsen)
Danish actress, ballerina and composer. b. 1833; d. 1901. She was the daughter of composer H.C. Lumbye and wrote the texts of most of her songs.
Compositions
VOCAL
Songs incl.:
Den forste kjaerlighed, ak ja
Han tvaer over Baenkene hang
Jeg holder fast ved dig
Naer Kysten paa Fyen
Vil du elske mig, naar Dagen lider?
Ref. 331

RECKE-MADSEN, Caroline. See RECKE, Caroline

RECLI, Giulia
Italian pianist and composer. b. Milan, December 4, 1890; d. December 19, 1970. Her mother was a pianist and Giulia grew up in a musical environment. She studied voice under G. Bonci, the piano under M. Anfossi and composition under Vittorio da Sabata and Ildebrando Pizzetti. Her works were performed in Europe and the United States and she was the first Italian woman to have her music acclaimed in Germany. She received honors and awards, including the title of Cavaliere Ufficiale della Repubblica Italiana and international composition prizes.
Compositions
ORCHESTRA
Alba dell'anima, symphonic poem (grand orch) (1914)
Tre bozzetti montanini, symphonic pieces (grand orch) (1926-1927)
Voci della foresta, symphonic poem (1932)
Aucassin et Nicolette, suite
Invocazione delle sacerdotesse (1953)
L'isla dei pastori (1953)
Other pieces
CHAMBER
Quartet in F for strings (1914) (ded Rose)
Due tempi per quartetto d'archi
Trio con pianoforte
La bambola innamorata (vln and pf) (1922)
Largamente (vln and pf) (1926)
Leggenda (vln and pf) (1922)
Sonata (vln and pf)
Penombra
Piano pieces
VOCAL
Euge Mater, cantata (S, ch and orch) (1919)
Alisa e Dafni, pastoral poem (m-S, 2 ch and small orch) (1913)
Primavera (w-ch and orch; also ch and org) (1926)
Vox clamantis in deserto (S, ch and orch) (1917)
La fede nel cielo, old legend (S; also w-ch and pf) (Ricordi, 1936)
Invocazione (mix-ch and pf) (1936) (Ricordi, 1936)
Luce e pianto (ch and org) (1918)
More than 200 songs (Spanish, Greek, Persian texts) incl.:
La sorellina dorme, duet
Bella Bellina! Anda!
Calma di mare (Goethe)
Canta il viandante nella notte
Canto di mare
Crepusculo
Fra le spiche
Fuyez l'amour
Lamento
Matutino
Nenia
Sei bozzetti popolari (Ricordi)
Tre tempi romantici (1925)
Vocavite
Duets
Arrangements and translations of Polish songs (Kurpinski and F. Brzezinska)
SACRED
Cantate Domino (mix-ch and orch) (1927)
Miserere (ch)
Per Calvarii viam, old Sicilian legend (T, S, w-ch, vln and pf) (1936) (Ricordi)
Requiem
Two masses
Choral pieces
BALLET
Piume d'oro (Grimm)
OPERA
Cento ducati e beluccia, fairy opera (B. Croce)
THEATRE
Eliduc
Villidiana
Ref. composer's sister, 14, 56, 86, 88, 94, 105, 112, 166, 226, 556, 622

RED, Virginia Stroh
American composer. b. 1935.
Compositions
ORCHESTRA
Pieces
CHAMBER
Pieces incl.:
Triad (hpcd) (1957)
VOCAL
Choral pieces (Broude Bros.; Generic Music Publ.; Broadman Press)
SACRED
Praise ye the Lord, alleluia (mix-ch)
Ref. 40, 347

REED, Florence
19th-century composer.
Compositions
ORCHESTRA
La Gascogne, waltz, op. 310 (pf and orch)
Woman's wit, gavotte (vln, pf and orch; also pf)
Chicago schottische
Heliotrope waltz
Jolly drummer's march (White)
Ma belle adorée, waltz
Moonlight and starlight, waltz on Dobrowski's song (also military orch)
Myrtle branch, gavotte (also military orch)
Peekskill military polka, op. 188
Ref. 297

REED, Ida L.
American composer. b. Barbour County, WV, November 30, 1865. She composed choral works.
Ref. 347

REED, Marlyce Rae Polk
American clarinetist, conductor, teacher and composer. b. January 14, 1955. She graduated with a B.Mus. from the University of Wisconsin in 1977 and in 1979 received her M.Mus. from the Northwestern University. In 1972 she became principal clarinetist for the American Youth in Concert Ensemble. Her teachers included Gloria Coates (q.v.), Edward Brunner and Alan Stout. She was the recipient of a number of awards and in 1976 won the Honors Concert competition at the University of Wisconsin. PHOTOGRAPH.
Compositions
ORCHESTRA
Saxophone concerto (1978)
CHAMBER
Woodwind quintet No. 1 (1982)
Brass quartet (1977)
String quartet (1978)
Three short dialogues (3 cl) (1977) (Shawnee Press)
Chromasia (a-sax and perc) (1978) (Seesaw)
Clarinet rhapsody No. 1 (cl) (1982)
Obtude (ob) (1977)

Rhapsody No. 1 (cl) (1981)
Sounds (ob) (1977)
Two autumn moods (tba) (1977)
Two poems (tba) (1977)
VOCAL
Shir kadosh (boys' ch and orch) (1979)
Art song (1975)
A dedication to my father (S) (1975)
Love come take my hand (m-S and fl)
Piper's song (m-S) (1976)
Wedding carillon (m-S and fl) (1977)
ELECTRONIC
Untitled (tape) (1978)
MISCELLANEOUS
Chromasia
In sickness
Three short dialogues
Ref. composer, 625

REED, Mrs. Wallace. See ADDENDUM

REED, Phyllis Luidens

20th-century American organist, choral conductor, singer and composer. b. Mineola, NY. She gained her B.A. from the Hope College in 1953 and diploma from Hartford Seminary in 1960. She was vesper organist for seminaries from 1957 to 1960 and organist at Bethel Methodist Church and organist and choir conductor at Redding Congregational Church, 1967 to 1968.

Compositions
MISCELLANEOUS
China trilogy (1978)
Cry for freedom (1981)
Dream variations (1974)
I have a dream (1973)
Mud-luscious (1977)
Three with Kagawa (1979)
Those who dream (1974)
Ref. 625

REEKS, Kathleen Doris

British teacher and composer. b. Hastings, 1902. She became an L.R.A.M. and an A.R.C.M. She taught music in Bournemouth from 1925 to 1931 and in Harrogate from 1931. She composed anthems and services for the school chapel.
Ref. 490

REES, Cathrine Felicie van

19th-century Dutch composer. She is the only woman to have composed a national anthem in South Africa.

Compositions
VOCAL
Kent gij dat volk vol heldenmoed, written as the Transvaal Anthem (1875)
Transvaal folksongs (mix-ch; also m-ch) (Schott; Luckhard; Belder; Eggers; Rahr)
Two Transvaal songs (m-ch) (Kiendl)
Ref. 177, 297

REES, Clara H.

19th-century American organist and composer.

Compositions
CHAMBER
Organ works
Piano works
VOCAL
Waiting for you
Other songs
Ref. 226, 260, 276, 292, 347, 433

REES, Winifred Emily

English organist, pianist, teacher and composer. b. London, May 16, 1900. She studied under Edwin Crusha, Greta Harrison and Mabel Floyd and privately for six years at the Guildhall School of Music and Drama, London, under Professor Frank Griggs. She completed a one year teacher training course at London University (singing, piano, music appreciation and advanced harmony) and is an L.G.S.M., an A.R.C.M., a M.R.S.T., an L.R.A.M. and an A.R.C.M.. She was a church organist and taught the piano for ten years in schools in Ottawa, Canada.

Compositions
ORGAN
Cavatina (Dayton, OH: Lorenz)
A toye (Chicago: Bridges)
Winds thro' the olive trees (also ch) (1952) (Lorenz)
SACRED
Blessed Jesus answers prayer (Lorenz)
Christmas nostalgia, poem (New York: Vantage Press)
God is the answer (Lorenz)
Thee we praise (Bridges)
Other anthems

Publications
Book of Theory.
Ref. composer, 490

REGAN, Anna. See SCHIMON, Anna

REGAN, Sarah Wren Love. See ADDENDUM

REHNQVIST, Karin Birgitta

Swedish teacher and composer. b. Stockholm, August 21, 1957. She studied composition at the Royal Academy of Music in Stockholm, 1976 to 1985. Her awards include one from the Royal Academy of Music.

Compositions
ORCHESTRA
Straak (1982) (Stim)
CHAMBER
Band (gtr) (1983) (Stim)
Dans (pf) (1984) (Edition Suecia)
VOCAL
Tilt (mix-ch) (1985)
Davids Nimm, version 1 and 2 (w-vce) (1984) (Suecia)
Surgeg och senapskornet (vce and insts) (1983) (Stim)
ELECTRONIC
Musik fraan vaart klimat (tape) (1982) (Stim)
Raakar (Lisbeth Hagerman) (tape and dancers)
Ref. composer

REICH, Amy

20th-century composer.

Compositions
ORCHESTRA
Three orchestral songs (1983)
HARP
Solon (1981)
MISCELLANEOUS
The one turning
Ref. AMC newsletter

REICHARDT, Bernadine Juliane (nee Benda)

German pianist, singer and composer. b. Potsdam, May 14, 1752; d. Berlin, May 11, 1783. Her family was of Bohemian origin. She was the youngest of six children of the Berlin concertmaster and virtuoso Franz Benda, who was her first music teacher. In 1777 she married Johann Friedrich Reichardt, the Prussian court conductor under whose guidance she became well known as a singer and pianist.

Compositions
PIANO
Six sonatas (Hamburg: C.E. Bohn, 1782)
VOCAL
Daphne am Bach, Brunnenlied
Das Voegelein, duettino
Sechs Lieder in Goettinger und in Voss' Musenalmanach incl.: An den Mond; Da kommt die Sonne wieder; Lied eines Maedchens (1777-1780)
Drei Lieder in Reichardt's Oden und Lieder (1781)
Ref. 12, 14, 26, 121, 128, 129, 135, 177, 197, 347, 433, 653

REICHARDT, Louise

German pianist, singer and composer. b. Berlin, April 11, 1779; d. Hamburg, November 17, 1826. She was the daughter of Johann Friedrich Reichardt, court conductor to Friedrich the Great and Bernhardine Juliane Reichardt (q.v.) and the granddaughter of the composer Franz Benda. She studied the piano and composition under her father's guidance and in 1794 appeared at the Sing Akademie in Berlin as a soprano. She accompanied her father on numerous tours in Germany and after his death in 1814 settled in Hamburg. Here she founded a singing academy with J.H. Clasing and organized a Handel Festival in 1816. She died at a young age after many unfortunate experiences, including the death of her fiance shortly before the wedding and the loss of her voice. DISCOGRAPHY.

Compositions
VOCAL
Songs incl.:
Sechs deutsche Gesaenge, op. 6 (vce and pf) (Boehme)
Sechs deutsche Lieder, op. 8 (vce and pf) (Hamburg: Cranz)
Sechs Lieder, op. 4 (Novalis) (vce and pf)
Sieben romantische Gesaenge, op. 5 (Teck) (vce and pf) (Boehme)
Zwoelf deutsche und italienische romantische Gesaenge, der Herzogin Amalie Anna von Sachsen gewidmet (vce.and pf) (Berlin, 1806)
Zwoelf Gesaenge (vce and gtr) (Breslau: Forster)
Zwoelf Gesaenge, ihrer geliebten Schwester Friederike gewidmet (Novalis, Brentano, Arim, Oelenschlaeger, Stollberg, des Knaben Wunderhorn) (Hamburg: Boehme)
Zwoelf Gesaenge, ihrer jungen Freundin und Schuelerin Louise Sillem gewidmet, op. 3 (Herder, Arnim, Novalis, Brentano, des Knaben Wunderhorn) (duet; also vce and pf) (Boehme)
SACRED
Christliche liebliche Lieder (vce and pf) (Cranz)
Sechs geistliche Lieder unserer besten Dichter (2 S and 2 Cont) (Cranz, 1823)
Bibliography
Lorenz, Franz. *Franz Benda und seine Nachkommen*. Berlin: W. de Gruyter & Co., 1967.
Ref. 14, 26, 74, 103, 105, 121, 128, 177, 210, 276, 297, 347, 563, 622, 653

REID, Lois C.
20th-century American composer. She composed piano teaching pieces, choral and sacred works.
Ref. 40, 347

REID, Sally. See REID, Sarah Johnston

REID, Sarah Johnston (Sally)
American cor anglais player, oboist, assistant professor and composer. b. East Liverpool, OH, January 30, 1948. She gained a B.M.E. at Abilene Christian University in 1971 and a Ph.D in theory and composition at the University of Texas, Austin, under Dr. M.L. Daniels and Karl Korte. Sarah is assistant professor at Abilene Christian University and director of the electronic music studio and music department. She plays the oboe and the cor anglais with the Abilene Philharmonic and is principal oboist with the San Angelo Symphony. She has written a number of papers which have been presented and published locally.
Compositions
SYMPHONIC BAND
A Wasatch symphony (1970)
Fanfare and celebration (1982)
New Manchester suite (1969)
CHAMBER
Escape wheel for five (pf, d-b and 3 cl) (1976)
Sketches (2 ob and cor anglais) (1971)
Braxton (pf and perc) (1974)
Air for horn (1973)
PIANO
Sketch based on Schumann romance (also elec) (1978)
Suite for children's ears
Three bagatelles (1969)
Waltz (1982)
VOCAL
Five haiku (vce and pf) (1973)
Haiku (m-S and pf) (in prep)
Note the silence (vce, brass qnt, pf and perc) (1975)
INCIDENTAL MUSIC
Humbledowne, play (1981)
ELECTRONIC
Ballet of the thirteen clocks (1982)
Celebration in sound and space (tape) (1981)
The eagle is born to soar (tape) (1980)
Etude for oboe and tape (1983)
Five etudes (tape)
Gyro-space 1 (1979)
Sketch No. 1 (1978)
Ten miniatures (tape) (1983)
Ref. composer, 474, 622

REID, Wendy
American teacher and composer. b. Santa Monica, CA, June 4, 1952. In 1975 she graduated from the University of Southern California, School of Performing Arts with a B.M. (composition) and then spent a year of private study with Nadia Boulanger. She graduated with her M.A. (composition) from Mills College in 1980. Her teachers included Robert Ashley, Terry Riley, James Hopkins, Halsey Stevens, David Raksin, Harris Goldman and Claire Hodgkins. She is the recipient of a number of awards including a four year California state scholarship.
Compositions
ORCHESTRA
Experiments for chamber orchestra (1975)
CHAMBER
Klee pieces (mixed ens) (1977)
Variations for violin and piano (1971)
VOCAL
Three haiku (S and pf) (1974)
Three songs (T, fl and vlc) (1972)
DANCE SCORES
Sketches for dancer and paired instruments (1973)
THEATRE
The geranium (1979)
ELECTRONIC
Glass walls (str qrt and tape) (1979)
Gungles (tape) (1980)
Three pieces (vln, perc and tape) (1980)
Tree pieces No. 4 (tape) (1981)
Ref. composer

REIFF, Lili (nee Sartorius) (Sertorius)
German pianist and composer. b. Bamberg, June 21, 1866; d. 1958. She studied at the Music Academy in Munich from 1881 until 1883 when she became a pupil of Franz Liszt in Weimar for a year. She returned to Munich to further her studies under Ludwig Thuille. In 1891 she studied under Friedrich Hegar and Conrad in Zurich. From 1885 to 1891 she toured in concert, then married and settled in Zurich. Thomas Mann dedicated a chapter of *Dr. Faustus* to her.
Compositions
ORCHESTRA
Praeludium und Walzer
Spanish procession
Three round dances (hp and str orch)
CHAMBER
Cello pieces
Piano pieces
Violin pieces
VOCAL
Pucks Liebeslied (R. Lothar)
Many songs
OPERA
Das verkaufte Lied (1926)
Maerchen Oper (1926)
Ref. Schweizer Komponistinnen, 70, 219, 226, 322

REINAGLE, Caroline. See ORGER, Caroline

REINDERS, Esther. See RABER DE REINDERS, Esther

REIS, Manuela Cancio
Portugese conductor, musicologist and composer. b. Alhanbra, 1910.
Composition
OPERETTA
Sonho ao luar (Soeiro Pereira Gomes)
Ref. 268

REISER, Violet
American organist, pianist, teacher and composer. b. New York, July 3, 1905. She studied under David Brown, Gary Sheldon, Herman Schwartzman and Dr. Clarence Adler. She was the youngest organist on the Loews Theatre circuit and later played at the Rialto and on the radio. She was solo organist at the Pythian Temple for many years. She was the winner of three awards in nationwide radio song contests. She composed more than 100 published compositions. DISCOGRAPHY. PHOTOGRAPH.
Compositions
PIANO
Arabesque, concert piece
Autumn sunrise, concert piece
Ballet pieces

Blossoms in my garden, waltz suite (John Market)
Cascades, concert piece
Cathedral chimes (Southern Music)
Etude de concert, concert piece
Gypsy village (Summy-Birchard)
Impromptu (Mercury Music; Theodore Presser)
In a gypsy tearoom (Sam Fox)
In a spanish village (Presser)
In gay Madrid
Moon mist, concert piece
Moonlight in Venice, concert piece
Morning in Manhattan (Sterling Music)
Motivation (Mercury Music; Presser)
New dawn fantasy (Musicord)
Nocturne romantique (Cherio Music)
Novelties
Plantation picnic
The prankster (Fox)
Reflections, concert piece
Reverie, concert piece
Smitten kittens
Tangoes
Valse de concert
Valse elegante (Fox)
Valse caprice, concert piece
Viennese waltzes
Waltzing ballerina
Numerous other pieces
VOCAL
Songs incl.:
Blossoms in my garden
A bouquet of violets
I won't play second fiddle
Israel, Israel
Take our love out of the shadows
ARRANGEMENTS
The glow worm (Paul Linde) (Century Music)
Melody of love (H. Engelman) (Century)
Publications
Keyboard security.
Ref. composer, 39, 40, 347, 494, 563

REISET, Maria Felicita de Reiset. See GRANDVAL, Marie Felicie

REISET E TESIER, Maria. See GRANDVAL, Marie Felicie

REISSEROVA, Julie (nee Kuhnlova)

Czech pianist, singer and composer. b. Prague, October 9, 1888; d. Prague, February 25, 1938. She came from a distinguished Prague family and began studying the piano and singing under A. Mikes. She studied composition and theory under J.B. Forster, 1919 to 1921. After her marriage to the diplomat and music writer Jan Reisser in 1921 she went to Bern and continued her studies under Hohlfeld, 1923 to 1924. In Paris she was particularly influenced by Albert Roussel, under whom she studied from 1924 to 1929 and whose opera *La testament de la tante Caroline* she translated into Czech. She attended classes given at the Ecole Normale by Nadia Boulanger (q.v.). She did much to promote Czech music in Belgrade, Vienna, Paris, Copenhagen, Rome, Bern, Lucerne and Strasbourg, where she went with her husband on his diplomatic duties.
Compositions
ORCHESTRA
Pastorale maritime (1933)
Suite (1931)
PIANO
Esquisses (1928-1932) (Skandinavisk og Borups Musikforlag, 1935)
VOCAL
Brezen (March) (vce and orch) (1925)
Pod snehem (vce and orch)
Predjari (S and orch) (1936)
Slavnostni den (w-ch) (1936)
Ref. 8, 15, 22, 44, 74, 96, 109, 197

REMER, Jan

20th-century American composer.
Composition
CHAMBER
Union (fl and hp) (1980)
Ref. AWC newsletter

REMICK, Bertha

20th-century American composer. She studied in the United States and Europe.
Compositions
ORCHESTRA
Pieces
PIANO
A fairy tale, in 5 parts (Thompson)
Romance (Thompson)
VOCAL
Songs incl.:
Im Fruehling
Irish girl's song (Thompson)
Schlummerlied der Mutter (Seeling)
Ten thousand eyes (Wood)
Ref. 226, 297

RENART, Marta Garcia

Mexican pianist, choral conductor and composer. b. Mexico City, 1942. She studied under E. Hartmann, B. Samper, P. Michaca, F. Agea and B. Flavigny in the summers of 1958 to 1962. She graduated on a scholarship from the Curtis Institute of Music, Philadelphia in 1964, where her teachers included R. Serkin and E. Sokoloff. She received a grant to continue studying composition, music analysis and conducting at Mannes College in New York, 1964 to 1967, where her teachers included C. Shachter, P. Simons and P. Bearl. She was choir-director of the 'Coro del Orfeo Catala' in Mexico, 1971 to 1977 and gave performances in both Mexico and at Carnegie Hall. She is a member of the Liga de Compositores de Musica de Concierto. She composed choral works and music for a children's play.
Ref. R. Sanz (Mexico City)

RENAUD-D'ALLEN (Mme. de Grammont)

French pianist, teacher and composer. b. Paris, 1789. She came from a noble family. She entered the Paris Conservatoire around 1802 and studied voice, the piano and harmony there. She founded a music school for which she wrote *Principes de musique* in 1817.
Compositions
PIANO
Romances
Other small pieces
VOCAL
Six ancient French airs (2 vces and pf; also hp) (Paris: Lemoine, ca. 1825)
Ref. 26, 66, 246, 347

RENE, Victor. See HALE, Irene

RENIE, Henriette

French harpist, lecturer and composer. b. Paris, September 18, 1875; d. Paris March 1, 1956. She began studying the harp under Alphonse Jean Hasselmans at the Paris Conservatoire when she was five and won the Conservatoire's first prize for the harp when she was 11 years old. She studied harmony and composition under C. Lenepveu and T. Dubois. She traveled abroad on numerous tours, appearing as a soloist with major orchestras and taught the harp at the Paris Conservatoire. She encouraged, among others, Debussy, Faure and Ravel, to compose for the harp and emphasized the harp as a solo instrument with accompaniment. After the death of Hasselmans, she became the most important harp teacher in France and one of the foremost players. Grandjany, Mme. Pignal-Regnier, Odette le Dentu (q.v.) and Bertile Robet were among her pupils. She was awarded the Prix Chartier for her chamber works. DISCOGRAPHY.
Compositions
ORCHESTRA
Caprice (hp and orch)
Elegy (hp and orch) (1907)
Harp concerto (1901)
Two symphonic pieces (hp and orch)
CHAMBER
Pieces for harp sextet
Trio (hp, fl and bsn)
Trio (vln, vlc and hp) (1909) (Rouhier)
Andante religioso (vln and hp) (1896)
Scherzo-fantaisie (vln and hp)
Sonata (vlc and pf) (Prix Chartier) (Rouhier)

HARP
Les pins de Charlannes (2 hp)
Ballade fantastique
Contemplation
Danse des gnomes
Danse des lutins
Defile lilliputien
Feuilles d'automne
Le rossignol
Légènde
VOCAL
Près d'un berceau (m-S)
Prière a la vierge (m-S)
Songs
Publications
Les classiques de la harpe. Adaptations for the harp of numerous keyboard works from the 17th to the 19th-centuries. Leduc.
Methode complete des Harfenspiels. 2 vols. Paris, 1946.
Ref. 1, 2, 13, 14, 17, 20, 22, 23, 41, 70, 74, 75, 96, 105, 172, 226, 322, 361, 433, 563

RENNES, Catharina van
Dutch pianist, choir conductor, singer, teacher and composer. b. Utrecht, August 2, 1858; d. Amsterdam, November 23, 1940. She studied composition under Richard Hol and singing under J. Messchaert. After the age of 20 she appeared frequently in oratorios and song performances. She became well-known in Holland for her 'Matinees voor kinderen en kindevrienden', in which she sang her own songs and in 1912 toured the East Indies with her pupil Hanna Verbena. She also enjoyed great success as a teacher, opening her own school of singing and eurhythmics in 1887. She directed a singing school in Hilversum and declined an offer to become head of singing at the Amsterdam Conservatory. She conducted a women's choir and for five years taught Queen Juliana at the Royal Palace at Gravenhage.
Compositions
PIANO
Heidekoninginnetje, een klaviersprookje, op. 47
Vertellingen aan 't klavier
VOCAL
De schoonste feestdag, cantata (chil-ch and pf) (Wagenaar)
Kerstcantate, op. 9 (chil-ch)
Orange-Nassau cantate, op. 33 (girls' and boys' ch)
Alt boenmisches Weihnachtslied, op. 29 (w-ch)
Avondcantate, op. 27 (A, 3-part w-ch and pf)
Levenslust, op. 15 (chil-ch and pf) (Breitkopf)
Oud nederlandsche liederen, op. 28 (1-5 vces)
Three quartets, op. 24 (2 S, 2 A and pf) (Amsterdam: Alg; Muziekhandel)
Terzette for women's voices, op. 10
Een wonderlijke nacht
Instantaneetjes uit die kinderwereld I and II, ops. 38 and 42
Kleingedichtjes, op. 52 (reprinted more than 60 times)
Kleuterdeuntjes
Lenteleven, op. 5, 2-part songs (Siegel)
Madonnakindje, op. 54
Meizoentjes I and II, op. 11, children's songs (Wagenaar)
De muizenwereld (also in German and English)
Tweestemmige miniatuurtjes, for boys and girls, op. 45
Voorjaarsbloemen
Winderflucht
Numerous other songs and collections
Ref. 2, 17, 23, 26, 44, 74, 103, 183, 276, 297, 361, 400

RENNUTET
Egyptian songstress of Amon-Ra in Karnak, New Kingdom. Her statue is in the Pelizaeus Museum, Hildesheim.
Ref. 428

RENSHAW, Rosette
Canadian organist, pianist, linguist and composer. b. Montreal, May 4, 1920. She studied music under Drs. Alfred Whitehead and Claude Champagne and gained a B.A. from McGill University and Mus.Doc. from Toronto University in 1949. She researched into French Canadian folk music, gave radio talks and was attached to the translation staff of the House of Commons, Ottawa. She won the Governor General's gold medal for the highest standing in modern languages.
Compositions
ORCHESTRA
Symphony (1948)
Madrigal (str orch) (1949)
Suite (str orch; also pf) (1950)
PIANO
Six sketches on French Canadian song Rossignolet sauvage (1950)
Sonatine (1950)
VOCAL
Cette aimable tourterelle, folk song (1946)
Je me levé à l'aurore, folk song (1946)
Lisette, folk song (1946)
Ref. 94, 133

RESNIKOFF, Miriam Levite. See LEVITE, Miriam

RESPIGHI, Elsa (nee Olivieri Sangiacomo)
Italian organist, pianist, singer, writer and composer. b. Rome, March 24, 1894. She studied the piano under Clotide Poce and Giovanni Sgambati. In 1911 she attended Accademia de Santa Cecilia in Rome and graduated in voice (Gregorian chant) after studying the organ; advanced harmony and counterpoint under Remigio Renzi and fugue and composition under the composer Ottorino Respighi, whom she later married. They toured in Europe, the United States and South America and Elsa sang their compositions. She completed the orchestration of his posthumous opera *Lucrezia* and produced his operas *Belfagor*, *Fiamma*, *Campana Sommersa* and *Maria Egiziaca*. An ardent promotor of Respighi's music, she gave up composing in order to produce his music. She founded the 'Respighi Fondo' in Venice 1969, for the propagation of musical culture in Italy.
DISCOGRAPHY. PHOTOGRAPH.
Compositions
ORCHESTRA
Serenata di maschere, symphonic poem (Milan: Ricordi)
Danza orgiastica, suite
Danza sacra, suite
Danza triste, suite
CHAMBER
Intermezzo romantico (vla, fl and hp)
VOCAL
Songs incl.:
Canzone campagnola (1921)
La mamma povera (1921)
Four songs from the Rubaiyat (Omar Khayyam) (Ricordi)
Three songs: Stati d'animo (1916)
Three songs (French text): Berceuse bretonne; dors, mon gas!; (T. Botrel); Je n'ai rien (D. Resnier) (1919) (Ricordi)
Three songs (Spanish texts): Duermete mi alma; Momento; La muerte del payador (G.O. Sangiacomo) (1918)
SACRED
Caterina da Siena, cantata (C. Guastalla) (S and cham ens) (1945)
Il pianto della Madonna, cantata (Poliziano) (S, T, mix-ch and orch) (1938)
Tre canti corali (Poliziano) (ch a-cap)(1944)
BALLET
Arrangement of Respighi's suite 'Antiche arie e danze'
OPERA
Alcesti, in 1 act (C. Guastalla) (1941)
Fior di neve, fairy opera in 3 acts
Samurai, in 3 acts (C. Guastalla) (1945)
Publications
Biografia di Ottorino Respighi. Ricordi, 1954. English and German translation.
Cinquant'anni di vita nella musica. Ed. Trevi.
Text for ballet of O. Respighi's interpretation of the Passacaglia by Bach.
Text for ballet of O. Respighi's suite for orchestra Gli uccelli.
Ref. 2, 14, 17, 22, 74, 85, 86, 94, 135, 347, 353, 361, 563, 622

REUCHSEL, Amedée
Composition
PIANO
Petite Russienne
Ref. Frau und Musik

REVIAL, Marie Pauline
19th-century French teacher and composer. d. Etretat, October 13, 1871. She taught singing at the Paris Conservatoire and was elected an officer of the Legion of Honor.

Compositions
VOCAL
Douze études pour le chant (S)
Ref. 226, 276, 433

REYNAC, Mme. de

19th-century French composer.
Composition
OPERA
Le Sorcier de Seville
Ref. 307, 431

REYNOLDS, Erma Grey Hogue

American teacher and composer. b. Laurel, MS, March 25, 1922. She studied at the California State University and obtained a B.Mus. (1970) and an M.Mus. (1973). She studied composition under Donal Michalsky. PHOTOGRAPH.
Compositions
ORCHESTRA
No dance, suite (1971)
Passacaglia (str orch) (1970)
CHAMBER
Woodwind quintet (1967)
Trio for three clarinets (1963)
Capriccio (cl and pf)
Duet (fl and a-rec) (1967)
Fantasie (bsn and pf) (1964)
March and lament (trp and trb) (1971)
Two pieces for particular people (trp and trb) (1971)
Variations (cl and pf) (1969)
Violin sonata (1965)
PIANO
Eclectic suite
Etudes (1966)
Six piano pieces for young friends
String quartet in D
Suite in five
VOCAL
Cantata for strings and chorus (1977)
Exile (soli, ch and orch) (1975)
Gloria (ch and brass ens) (1967)
Melisande's daughters (S, T and pf)
Ref. composer, 142, 625

REYNOLDS, Laura Lawton

American organist, pianist, teacher and composer. b. Allendale, SC, June 23, 1886. She graduated with a B.M. in 1903 from the Virginia Woman's College, University of Richmond and studied at the Atlanta Conservatory of Music, Georgia, from 1906 to 1907. Her teachers included Mary Harley, A.F. Unkel, Dr. Hugh Williamson, Mrs. Hugh Williamson, Edwin Hughes, Charles Seegar and Bernice Frost. She held the post of organist at the First Baptist Church of Hartsville from 1908.
Compositions
PIANO
Carolina (1930)
Slumber song (1923)
Valse in G (1905)
OPERETTA
Historical pageant (1936)
Music land (1940)
Pageant of the month (1941)
Christmas operettas
Ref. 496

REYNOLDS, Marie Hester

18th-century English composer.
Compositions
CHAMBER
Six sonatas, in 2 mvts (vln and pf) (Brighton: Henry Davey, 1785)
Ref. 128

RHEA, Lois

20th-century American composer. She married the composer Raymond Rhea. She composed choral works for treble voices.
Ref. 40, 347

RHEINGOLD, Lauma Yanovna

Latvian-Soviet concert pianist, teacher and composer. b. Riga, August 29, 1906. She studied the piano at the Petrograd Conservatory under E. Daugovet. At the Riga Conservatory she studied composition under Y. Wihtol and the piano under A. Daugul, graduating in 1926. She taught the piano and theoretical subjects in schools in Riga and was a pianist at the opera and with the Riga Philharmonic Orchestra.
Compositions
ORCHESTRA
Legend (bsn and orch) (1932)
Gory, suite
CHAMBER
Ballad (vlc and pf)
Lesa, duet (ob and cl) (1950)
Scherzo (fl and pf)
Sonata (vlc and pf)
Other pieces (vlc and pf)
PIANO
Preludes
Scherzo
Sonata (1926)
Two rhapsodies
Variations
VOCAL
Pesnya novogo rozhdenia freniksov, cantata (Go Mo-zho) (S, mix-ch and orch)
Ballada (B and orch) (1943)
Ave sil (Y. Rainis) (vocal trio)
Eight duets
More than 200 songs and romances (M. Lermontov, V. Mayakovsy)
Arrangements of Latvian songs
BALLET
Marite, for children
OPERA
Voronenok (Y. Rainis) (1945-1946)
THEATRE
Tomeliu mates vayas dienas, musical comedy (1938)
Music for plays
Ref. 87

RHENE-JAQUE (Sister Jacques-Rene) (pseud. of Marguerite Cartier)

Canadian cellist, violinist, teacher and composer. b. Beauharnois, February 4, 1918. She studied at Ecole Vincent-d'Indy in Outremont, Quebec, specializing in harmony, musical analysis, counterpoint, fugue and composition under Claude Champagne and Francois Morel. She studied orchestration under Jean Vallerand and the analysis of modern works under Marvin Duchow. She received her B.A. and licentiate diploma in music from the University of Montreal. In 1972 she studied musical composition under Tony Aubin in Nice, France. She taught the violin and the cello at Ecole Vincent-d'Indy. DISCOGRAPHY. PHOTOGRAPH.
Compositions
ORCHESTRA
Symphonie No. 1
Intermezzo rondo
Suite
CHAMBER
Allegro (vln, vla, vlc and pf)
Andante (vln, vlc and pf)
Daussila (vln and pf)
Un petit air roumain (vln and pf) (Ontario: Gordon V. Thompson, 1970)
Sonatine (cl and pf)
Spiccato e legato (vln and pf) (G.V. Thompson, 1970)
Andante sur une basse de Rameau (org)
Berceuse de Noël (org)
Deux fantaisies (vlc)
Prelude et fugue (vln)
PIANO
L'ane gris (G.V. Thompson, 1971)
Badinerie
Berceuse (Ecole Vincent-d'Indy, 1961)
Chevauchée (Vincent-d'Indy, 1970)
Danse
Deux inventions à deux voix
Escapade dans l'ile (Vincent-d'Indy, 1969)
Espieglerie (Vincent-d'Indy, 1961)
Etude No. 1
Fantaisie
Fête champêtre
Le lutin (G.V. Thompson, 1971)
Le petit jongleur (Vincent-d'Indy, 1961)

Le petit pétre (G.V. Thompson, 1971)
Scherzo (Vincent-d'Indy, 1964)
Suite No. 1
Suite No. 2
VOCAL
Les beatitudes (ch a-cap)
Ah! Si mon moins voulait danser (4 vces)
Chapelle dans les bois (vces) (Vincent-d'Indy, 1971)
Mon chateau (vces) (Vincent-d'Indy, 1968)
Il pleut, bergère (4 vces)
Le perroquet gris (Vincent-d'Indy, 1968)
Le petit elephant (Vincent-d'Indy, 1968)
Quatre poèmes d'eloi de Grandmont (vces) (Editions Maisonneuve, 1967)
Source ou coeur
La voix du golfe
SACRED
Messe breve (2 vces and org)
Cantique à Sainte Cecile
Quatre motets au S. Sacrement
Trois motets
Ref. composer, 52, 329, 347, 563

RHOADS, Mary R.
American pianist, lecturer and composer. b. Philadelphia, January 28, 1920. She studied at the Mastbaum Vocational Music School in Philadelphia and then at the University of Michigan where she graduated with a B.Mus. (theory and piano, 1962), a M.Mus. (theory and piano, 1964) and Ph.D. (theory and composition, 1969). From 1935 she taught a number of subjects both privately and at the University of Michigan and the University of Northern Colorado. She was the recipient of a number of awards and grants. PHOTOGRAPH.
Compositions
ORCHESTRA
Peace (cham orch) (1980)
BAND
Homage to Hogaku (brass ch) (1976)
CHAMBER
Fugue for strings (1965)
Join the twentieth century suite (ww, fl, sax or cl and pf) (1983)
Mai sonata (vlc and pf) (1982)
Memories of Nara (vln and pf) (1977)
PIANO
Chorale prelude (1965)
Piano sonata No. 1 (1970)
Piano sonata No. 2 (1972)
VOCAL
A child asks (ch) (1976)
Haec dies (ch) 1968)
Hosanna (ch) (1968)
Madrigale (ch) (1968)
No, No, No! (w-ch) (1975)
Four by two (S, Cont, fl and pf) (1984)
Kyoto scenes (fl, vce and pf) (1976)
Three Japanese poems (vce, hn and pf) (1980)
Voices of four women (vce, hn and pf) (1983)
THEATRE
Beauty and the Beast (1969)
Blodgett (1977)
Gigi the Gangly Goose, children's musical (1970)
Knight before Glasses, children's musical (1970)
A Man's a Man (1966)
The Mudlark, musical (1969)
Romeo and Juliet (1968)
O, what a lovely War! musical (1969)
MULTIMEDIA
Horyuji (ch, dancers and cham orch) (1981)
Ref. composer, 625

RHODEN, Natalia Naana (Natalie Claire)
American composer. b. Sacramento, CA, 1922.
Compositions
ORCHESTRA
Intermezzo (1939)
Scherzo No. 1 (1940)
Scherzo No. 3
Ref. 322

RHODES, Helen. See HARDELOT, Guy d'

RHODES, Mrs. W.L. See HARDELOT, Guy d'

RIANCO. See RAINER, Sara

RIBAS, Medina N.
19th-century Portuguese composer.
Compositions
ORCHESTRA
Caprice (Schott Freres)
CHAMBER
A la Portugaise, mazurka (vln and pf) (Fonseca)
Amizade, etude (vln and pf) (Cranz)
Carnevale d'Oporto, op. 14, burlesque variations on popular Portuguese motifs (vln and pf) (Ricordi)
Mazurka de salon, op. 41 (vln and pf) (Schott Freres)
Pene del cuore, andante espressivo (vln and pf) (Ricordi)
Saltarello, op. 21, burlesque scherzo (vln and pf) (Ricordi)
Souvenir d'amitie (vln and pf) (Durdilly)
Caprice (vln) (Fonseca)
Ref. 297

RIBONI, Liliane
20th-century French composer. DISCOGRAPHY.
Composition
THEATRE
Jeanne D'Arc

RICAU, Eugenie Katherine. See ROCHEROLLE, Eugenie Katherine

RICCI, Cesarina di Tingoli
16th-century Italian composer.
Compositions
VOCAL
Il primo libro de madrigali a cinque voci, con un dialogo a otto, 20 compositions (5 vces) (ded Cardinal S. Giorgio, di Monte Colombano, February 10, 1597) (Venice: Angelo Gardano, 1597)
Ref. 105, 128, 653

RICCIOLI FRAZZI, Eva
Italian composer. b. 1909.
Compositions
ORCHESTRA
Ricercare
Sacro mistero
CHAMBER
Quartetto
Concertino (cl and pf)
Concertino (sax and pf)
VOCAL
Cara lettera (S and pf)
Ref. Patricia Adkins Chiti (Rome), Musica Sinfonica e da Camera/27

RICH, Gladys
American teacher and composer. b. Philadelphia, April 26, 1892. She studied at the National Park Seminary in Washington, DC, the New England Conservatory in Boston, the University of Utah (B.A.) and New York University (M.A.). She studied composition under Frederick Schleider, Harvey Gaul and Edward Shippen Barnes. She was music supervisor at Newcastle, PA from 1929 to 1933 and music director of State Teachers' College at Clarion, PA, 1933 to 1938.
Compositions
VOCAL
Songs incl.:
Aloha goodnight
American lullaby
The banana man
Beneath a southern sky
Maholo nui

Nursery rhyme blues
Octavos
Partners
Sitting home
The street of little houses
SACRED
Journey of promise, cantata
Messengers of mercy, cantata
Triumph of faith, cantata
A Christmas wish, song
Sacred duets
OPERETTA
Aloha Sugar Mill
Garden Magic
The Lady Says Yes
Renting the Hive
The Toy-Shop (P. McGinley)
Walk the Plank
Ref. 39, 40, 141, 142, 292

RICHARDS, Christine-Louise
American pianist and composer. b. Radnor, PA, January 11, 1910. She studied the piano under eminent concert pianists. She was the founder, owner and director of a publishing company. She composed piano pieces.
Ref. 84

RICHARDS, Inez Day
American composer. b. Houlton, December 31, 1885.
Compositions
VOCAL
Because of thee
The faded rose
I'm drifting to heaven with you
Oh mother dear
Ref. 374

RICHARDS, Kathleen. See DALE, Kathleen

RICHARDS, Laura E.
American writer and composer. b. Boston, February 27, 1850; d. January 14, 1943.
Compositions
VOCAL
The Hottentot and other ditties (1939)
Ref. 374

RICHARDSON, Cornelia Heintzman
Canadian pianist and composer. b. Waterloo, Ontario, 1890. She studied the piano under Josef Hofmann and gave recitals.
Compositions
VOCAL
Songs incl.:
Home light (Whaley Royce)
It is not always May (Nordheimer)
Lullaby (Nordheimer)
Nuits de juin (Nordheimer)
A rain song (Nordheimer)
To victory arise (Royce)
When trees are green (Royce)
The wind in a frolic (Nordheimer)
Ref. 133, 347

RICHARDSON, Enid Dorothy
English harpsichordist, pianist, choral conductor, teacher and composer. b. Tunbridge Wells, Kent, November 25, 1905. She studied under Edward Isaacs (piano) and Georg Brandt (piano, harpsichord and composition). She is an A.R.C.M. and a L.R.A.M. She was conductor of the Censorship Madrigal Choir in Bermuda (1940 to 1943), a member of the British Council music department from 1945 to 1947, a music adviser to the British Council in the Eastern Caribbeans and conductor of the Trinidad Madrigal Choir, 1947 to 1951. She was a representative of the British Council music department in Munich and conductor of the Englisches Seminar at Munich University, 1951 to 1956. She served as music director of Manor House, Limpsfield and was conductor of the Staffhurst Wood Choir from 1957 to 1961 and music director of the Overstone School from 1963 to 1971, founder of the Orlando Singers and conductor of the group from its inception in 1968. In 1971 she became music director of the Lavenham Guildhall Concerts. She was choral conductor at European cantata festivals. Her works have been broadcast on radio in England, Europe, and the United States. Among honors bestowed upon her were prizes for piano playing in the Hastings and Buxton festivals.
Compositions
CHAMBER
Meditation rhapsodigne (fl and pf)
Classical suite in E-Minor (vln) (1929)
Rhapsodie en elegie (vla) (1940)
Sonata, in 1 mvt (vln) (1949)
Theme and variations in G-Minor (vla) (1937)
Volksweise (vla) (1940)
PIANO
Sunday morning on Mt. St. Benedict
Valse Chopinesque (1929)
Variations on a theme of Orlando (1936)
VOCAL
He came all so still (mix-ch) (1941)
Blake's cradle song (vce and pf) (1964)
Cradle carol (1969)
Death of a starling (vce and pf) (1971)
Fall on me like a silent dew (1970)
The golden bird (1969)
How sweet the moonlight sleeps (1942)
Ibo li li
O men from the fields (vce and pf) (1942)
Old Highland lullaby (1956)
Old man hobbling (vce and pf)
Requiescat (1959)
Wind through the olive trees (vce and pf) (1966)
The world's desire (1950)
SACRED
The shepherd (T, ch, fl and org) (1975)
The bells of paradise (1981)
How far is it to Bethlehem (1955)
The virgin's song (1974)
Publications
Contributions to *ISM Journal*, *Music Teachers*, *Musical Opinion*, *Musical Record* and *New Life*.
Ref. composer, 206, 359

RICHARDSON, Jennie V.
19th-century American composer. She composed piano works.
Ref. 276, 347, 433

RICHARDSON, Sharon
American composer. b. Houston, TX, August 3, 1948. She studied under Merrill Ellis at North Texas State University.
Compositions
ORCHESTRA
Serenade (vla and orch)
BAND
Fanfare and march
CHAMBER
Pieces (small ens)
Three statements for tuba
Pieces (solo insts)
Ref. 142

RICHEPIN, Eliane
French pianist and composer. b. Paris, November 23, 1919. She studied at the Paris Conservatoire and performed in Europe and North and South America.
Compositions
ORCHESTRA
Fantaisie (pf and orch) (Salabert)
CHAMBER
Pieces
VOCAL
Cantatas
Ref. 44, 280

RICHER, Janine. See RICHER, Jeannine

RICHER, Jeannine (Janine)
French lecturer and composer. b. Candebec-en-Eaux, June 6, 1924. She studied music at Rouen and the Paris Consevatoire. She studied serial music under Max Deutsch and Arnold Schoenberg and electronic music under Jean Etienne Marie at the International Center of Music Research. She was a teacher of musical analysis at the Ecole Normale de Musique in Paris until 1972.
Compositions
ORCHESTRA
Periodes (ob and str orch) (1983)
Confrontation (1981)
Traces
CHAMBER
Le lointain trottoir d'en face (brass qnt) (1982)
Epiphonies (4 d-b) (1971)
Quartet for saxophones (1958)
Quartet for trombones (1960)
Undecim (brass insts)
Memoire (pf, vln and vlc)
Alpha beta gamma (2 celtic hp) (1970)
Alchimies (2 vln) (1972)
Ligne interrompue (d-b) (1974)
Piece (fl) (1984)
GUITAR
Rite (20 gtrs) (1979)
En ce temps-la (12 gtrs)
La guitare contemporaine
Piege VI
Rives
PIANO
Triangle (2 pf) (1974)
Delta V (1971)
Entrechoquements et zones silencieuses (1971)
Hantise (1968)
Musiquemobile (1970)
Sonorite
Tremblements/derapages (1982)
VOCAL
Anonymes (large ch and 10 insts) (1973)
Vocal (ch a-cap) (1980)
OPERA
Parade cruelle (1980)
THEATRE
Les portes du chemin (comedian, visual sequences, text and music) (1972)
ELECTRONIC
Le crane (biblical text) (1973)
Oiseaux foux (1974)
Ref. composer, 76, 347

RICHINGS, Caroline
American pianist, singer, teacher and composer. b. England, 1827; d. Richmond, VA, 1882. She made her piano debut in Philadelphia in 1847 and her operatic debut in 1852. In 1867 she married the tenor, P. Barnard. She headed her own company, The Caroline Richings Old Folks Company and sang in her operetta *The Duchess* in Baltimore (1881). She taught in Richmond and died there of smallpox.
Compositions
VOCAL
Songs
SACRED
O word of God incarnate
OPERETTA
The Duchess
Ref. 53, 226, 276, 307

RICHINSE, Cecile J.
20th-century composer.
Composition
CHAMBER
Miniatures (vln and pf) (1982)
Ref. ASUC

RICHMOND, Heiress
18th-century English composer of songs.
Ref. 128

RICHMOND, Virginia
American editor, publisher, writer and composer. b. New York, January 28, 1932. She studied at the University of California, Los Angeles. She is head of a record company and producer and performer in her own television show. Her compositions received nominations for the Grammy Awards (1971).
Compositions
VOCAL
Songs incl.:
All my life I have been searching for you
At the fair
Betcha
Buffalo
Down, down, down
In my sloppy shape
It was just a moment
An old-fashioned wedding song
You made a boo-boo
THEATRE
Cheesecake and horses, musical (rev. 1969)
Elegant hill, musical
Publications
Children's books.
Medical books.
Ref. 39, 84

RICHNER-HEIM, Erika
20th-century Swiss pianist, lecturer and composer. She studied under P.O. Moeckel at the Zurich Conservatory and Lora de Micco in Palermo and Naples. After 1924 she taught the piano in schools in Zurich and at the Conservatory.
Composition
CHAMBER
Winter-und Weihnachtslieder
Ref. Hug (Zurich)

RICHTER, Ada
20th-century American lecturer and composer. b. Philadelphia. Her music teachers included Camille Zeckwer, Leo Ornstein and Alfred Richter. She ran a music school in Merchantville, NJ, with her husband and lectured in music workshops, universities, colleges and conservatories.
Compositions
VOCAL
Choral works incl.:
A child's journey
The hare and the tortoise
Jack and the beanstalk
Let's stay well
The lion and the mouse
Poems for Peter
The rag man
Three little pigs
OPERETTA
Merry Christmas
Mister Snowman
INCIDENTAL MUSIC
Cinderella
The First Christmas
The First Easter
Noah and the Ark
Peter Rabbit
Publications
Kindergarten Class Book.
My Piano Book. Series.
Stunts for Piano.
You can play Piano Series.
Ref. 39, 141, 347

RICHTER, Marga
American pianist, lecturer and composer. b. Reedsburg, WI, October 21, 1926. She studied at the McPhail School of Music and received her B.S. (1949) and M.S. (1951) from the Juilliard School, where she studied composition under William Bergsma and Vincent Persichetti and the piano under Roslyn Tureck. From 1971 to 1973 she was instructor at Nassau Community College in New York. In 1972 she and Herbert Deutsch founded the Long Island Composers' Alliance, of which she is co-director. She was commissioned to compose works performed in major cities of Europe and the United States. Among the orchestras that played her composi-

tions are the Minnesota Orchestra and the Tucson, Oakland, Madison, and Maracaibo symphonies. She received grants, awards and commissions from the National Endowment for the Arts, the Martha Baird Rockefeller Fund for Music, the National Federation of Music Clubs, Meet the Composer and ASCAP. DISCOGRAPHY. PHOTOGRAPH.

Compositions

ORCHESTRA

Music for three quintets and orchestra (1980) (T. Presser)
Landscapes of the mind 1, concerto No. 2 (pf and orch) (New York: C. Fischer, 1975)
Aria and toccata (vla and str orch; also pf) (New York: Belwin Mills, 1957)
Duesseldorf concerto (fl, vla, hp, perc and str orch) (1982) (G. Schirmer)
Blackberry vines and winter fruit (Fischer, 1976)
Eight pieces for orchestra or piano (Fischer, 1975)
Fragments (Fischer, 1975)
Lament (str orch) (New York: Broude Bros., 1958)
Variations on a sarabande (Fischer, 1975)

BAND

Country auction (1976)
One for two and two for three (2 or 3 trb) (Fischer, 1975)
Pastorale (brass) (Fischer, 1975)
Ricercare (brass or str qrt and band) (1958)

CHAMBER

Concerto (pf, vlas, vlcs and d-b) (Fischer, 1977)
Chamber piece (ww qrt, vla, vlc and d-b)
Seacliff variations (pf, vln, vla and vlc) (1984)
String quartet No. 2 (Fischer, 1975)
Landscapes of the mind III (vln, vlc and pf) (Fischer, 1975)
Sonora (2 cl and pf) (1981) (Schirmer)
Landscapes of the mind II (vln and pf) (1971)
Sonata (cl and pf) (Fischer, 1975)
Suite (vln and pf) (Fischer, 1975)
Darkening of the light (vla) (1961)
Short prelude in baroque style (hpcd) (1974)
Suite (vla) (1961)
Variations on a theme by Neithart von Reuenthal (C. Fischer)

PIANO

Landscapes III (3 pf)
Melodrama (2 pf) (1958) (Fischer, 1975)
Variations on a theme by Latimer (4 hands) (1964)
Exequy (1980)
Fragments (1963) (Fischer, 1976)
Remembrances (Fischer, 1975)
Requiem (1978)
Sonata (1954) (Fischer, 1975)
Two short pieces for young pianists

VOCAL

Do not press my hands (mix-ch) (1981)
Three songs of madness and death (mix-ch a-cap) (1955) (Fischer, 1975)
To whom? (mix-ch) (1980)
Eight songs (Chinese texts)
Fishing picture (S and pf)
The hermit (S and pf)
Into what unknown chamber (vce and pf) (1951)
Lament for Art O'Leary (vce and pf) (1983)
She at his funeral (Hardy) (vce and pf) (1954) (Fischer, 1975)
Spaeter einmal (vce and pf) (1981)
Three songs on poems of Emily Dickinson (1982)
Transmutation, song cycle (vce and pf) (1949) (Fischer, 1975)
Two Chinese songs (vce and pf) (1953) (Fischer, 1975)
Ursprung (vce and pf) (1983)

SACRED

Psalm 91 (mix-ch a-cap) (1962) (Bryn Mawr, PA: Elkan-Vogel, 1963)
Seek him (Amos 5:8) (mix-ch a-cap) (1965) (Fischer, 1975)
Three Christmas songs (chil-ch and 2 fl or pf) (1964)

BALLET

Abyss (1964) (comm Harkness Ballet) (Belwin Mills)
Bird of yearning (1967) (comm Harkness) (Fischer, 1976)
The servant (comm Harkness Ballet)
Four scores (1951-1952)

TEACHING PIECES

A farewell (1961)
Four piano pieces (1971)
The lost people, the dancers (1965)
Three violin pieces (1961)
Two short suites for young pianists (1947)

Ref. composer, 39, 40, 68, 137, 142, 146, 185, 206, 228, 280, 347, 415, 454, 474, 477, 494, 563, 611, 622, 625

RICHTER, Marion Morrey

American pianist, lecturer and composer. b. Columbus, OH, October 2, 1900. She was the daughter of Grace Hamilton Morrey, a concert pianist. She graduated from Ohio State University in 1921 with a B.A. In 1928 she graduated from the Juilliard School of Music and obtained her M.A. in 1933 and Ed.D. in 1961 from Teachers' College, Columbia University, where she taught. She toured the United States, England, Mexico, the Far East, India and Iran, giving concerts and lectures, particularly on 'Aspects of Americana' and 'Russian Soviet Music'. She was chairlady of the National Federation of Music Clubs from 1976. She appeared in and produced radio programs from 1961.

Compositions

ORCHESTRA

Band Timberjack, overture (1959)
The Waste Land, tone poem, after T.S. Eliot

CHAMBER

Sonata for trio (pf trio) (1958)
Prelude (1958)

PIANO

Capriccio
Carol suite (1956)
Prelude on a twelve tone row (1958)
Scherzo fantastique, canzona, capriccio, 3 pieces (1955)
Scherzo-intermezzo (1928)

VOCAL

Sea chant for women's voices (w-ch and pf)
Tale of a timberjack (m-ch and pf; also concert band) (1959)
A cycle of seasons (w-vces) (1950)
The daffodils (S and pf) (1950)
In winter (w-vces) (1950)
Longing (S and pf) (1950)
A ship comes in (m-vces) (1959)
Silence sings (S and pf) (1935)

SACRED

Hymn of glory, anthem (1945)
Other pieces

OPERA

Distant Drums, in 3 acts (1956)

OPERETTA

This is our Camp, for children (1950) (Boston: C.C. Birchard, 1955)

MULTIMEDIA

Choreoperette for H.S. zoo tale (soli, ch, dance, pf and perc) (1945)

Ref. composer, 40, 142, 206, 228, 347, 359, 625

RICHTER, Pauline

19th-century German composer.

Compositions

PIANO

Fruehlingswaltzer, op. 2 (Leipzig: Kahnt)
Veilchen-Polka, op. 3 (Kahnt)

VOCAL

Du bist mir nah (vce and pf) (Kahnt)
Der Pfeil und das Lied (vce and pf) (Kahnt)

Ref. 276, 297, 433

RICHTER, Rebecca

American composer.

Composition

VOCAL

Serenade (vce and pf)

Ref. 190

RICKARD, Sylvia

Canadian pianist, teacher, writer and composer. b. Toronto, May 19, 1937. She studied at the Toronto Conservatory and the Universities of British Columbia, Vancouver, Stanford-California and Grenoble, France. After living in India and Germany during the 1960s, she returned to Canada in 1972 to study under Jean Coulthard (q.v.). In 1975 she was awarded first piano prize and chamber music prize at the Okanagan Composer's Festival. PHOTOGRAPH.

Compositions

CHAMBER

String quartet (1984)
Reunion (vlc, pf and strs)
Pastoral (fl and strs)
Ile de re (vlc and pf)
Sonata (ob and org)
Suite (gtr)
Theme and variations (hp) (1981)

PIANO

Amblystoma (1981)
Sonatine

VOCAL
Four Indian songs (S and cham orch) (1984)
Three songs of autumn (B-Bar, fl and hp) (1978)
Wind quartet (S, cl and hp) (1983)
Epithalamion (S and vln) (1984)
INCIDENTAL MUSIC
A breast for beating in my hour of need, for play (vlc) (1975)
Publications
A Student's Guide to Musical Forms. Waterloo Music.
Ref. composer, Carolyn D. Lomax (Toronto)

RICKETTS, Lucy W.
20th-century American composer.
Compositions
VOCAL
Elegiac songs incl.:
Lament (vce and pf) (Composers Press)
Ref. 190

RICOTTI, Onestina
19th-century Italian pianist, teacher, writer and composer. She was the director of the National Music Institute of Turin.
Compositions
PIANO
Douce espérance, reverie
La fiancée au cheveux d'or, fantasy
Ida, barcarolle
Le rêve d'un ange, nocturne
Le sponde del Po, caprice de concert
VOCAL
Les petits tambours (ch)
Amina (vce, pf, vln or fl)
Songs incl.:
Io t'amo
Il linguaggio del cor
Ti vidi
Ref. 26, 226, 276

RIDDERSTOLPE, Caroline Johanna Lovisa, Countess (nee Kolbe)
Swedish composer. b. Berlin, 1793. Her father was the court conductor in Berlin. She studied singing under D.M. von Weber and married the Swedish governor of Esteras, Count F.L. Ridderstolpe.
Compositions
VOCAL
Songs with piano accompaniment (Stockholm: Hirsch): Nya saanger:
Den fattiga modren: Det sitter en moder paa hafvets strand
Ett barns aftonboen: Till Gud jag flyr
Hopp och minne: Ej endast hoppet plockar blommor
Nichts und Etwas: Wenn ich ein Liedchen mach'aus Nichts
Om Gud saa vill: O! skoen aer glaedjen som en dag
Schweizer-visa: Bland skogar ochh sjoear
Sju saanger:
Budskapen: Doeljen er suckan i svalkande vinden
Contemplation: An Himmels Hoehn die Sternlein gehn (also in Swedish)
Din kaerlek, aer, daa, vaarens haerold svingar
Flickan i Saetersdal: Ver still mit brost!
Ostros astiklar: Tro ej glaedjen! O jag saag ett tjaell
Sag mig ej vaelkommen naer jag kommer
Trasten: En hemlig laengtan taend af ljusets fader
Ref. 103, 297

RIDLEY, Ursula
20th-century American composer.
Compositions
OPERA
Six and Four are Ten
Ref. 141

RIESE, Helene. See LIEBMANN, Helene

RIEUNIER, Françoise
Composition
CHAMBER
Espace (perc and pf) (Leduc, Paris)

RIGGS, Mrs. George C. See WIGGINS, Kate Douglas

RIGHTON, Mary
19th-century English composer.
Composition
OPERA
Cupid and Psyche (1874)
Ref. 307

RIHOUET, Yvonne. See ROKSETH, Yvonne

RIK. See RAIQ

RILEY, Ann Marion
American organist, pianist, assistant professor and composer. b. New Richmond, WI, April 28, 1928. She gained a B.A. from Scholastica College, Duluth, MN, and M.M. from De Paul University, Chicago. In Paris she studied composition under Nadia Boulanger (q.v.), the organ under A. Marchal and the piano under J. Manchon. She was also a pupil of Jean Catoire. She won a scholarship to study at the Academie Internationale de Musique in Nice where she became a composition pupil of Alexander Tcherepnin and organ pupil of P. Cochereau. She won the academy's composition prize in 1961. She became assistant professor at Scholastica College, Duluth in 1958 and faculty member of the Music Center of Lake Country, Waukegan, IL, in 1973. PHOTOGRAPH.
Compositions
CHAMBER
Quintet (ww)
Concert for piano and brass
Piece for viola and piano
Duality (fl) (1974)
Organ pieces
PIANO
Moon suite
Patterns (1961)
VOCAL
Creation, song (S, cl and pf)
Choral works
Ref. composer, 40, 142, 347

RILEY, Myrtis F.
20th-century American pianist, lecturer and composer. b. Oak Grove, L.A. She was a pupil of Helen Gunderson and also studied under Robert Ottman in Texas. She lectured in theory and the piano at Centenary College.
Compositions
ORCHESTRA
Music for small orchestra
CHAMBER
Piano quartet
Quartet (fl, ob, vlc and pf)
Second piano quartet
Sonata (vln and pf)
Sonatine (2 pf)
VOCAL
Songs
Ref. 448

RILEY, Sister. See RILEY, Ann Marion

RINEHART, Marilyn
20th-century American composer.
Compositions
SACRED
Mary sings (mix-ch and keyboard) (Canyon Press)
Thou who cometh from above (ch)
Ref. 142, 190

RING, Claire (Clara)
19th-century American composer. She was a pupil of Hille in Philadelphia.
Compositions
PIANO
Pieces incl.:
Album leaf
Danse caprice
VOCAL
Songs
Ref. 276, 347, 433

RING, Clara. See RING, Claire

RING, Montague. See ALDRIDGE, Amanda Ira

RINGELSBERG, Mathilde
19th-century Bohemian composer. She composed dances and waltzes.
Ref. 226, 276

RISHER, Anna Priscilla
American cellist, organist, pianist, conductor, teacher and composer. b. Pittsburgh, PA, 1875. She studied the piano at the New England Conservatory under Carl Stasy, the cello under Leo Schulz, Carlo Fisher and Fritz Goener, harmony under Goetschius and composition under Chadwick. She went to California in 1918, taught music at the Cumnock School and became president of the Musician's Club. She moved to Laguna Beach to devote more time to composition.
Compositions
CHAMBER
Five instrumental trios
Cello and piano pieces
PIANO
Cinderella
Fire-fly fairies
Gnomes
In Grandmother's garden, suite
In movieland, suite
In radioland, suite
Leona, tarantella
Merry blossom time
My lady, minuet
The piper's songs
Playful winds
Rosemary
Spring is here
We will go a-maying
Ref. 40, 292, 323, 347, 353

RITTENBAND, Minna Ethel
American, organist, pianist, teacher and composer. b. Newark, NJ, June 4, 1896. She graduated from the Juilliard School of Music in 1920 and after 1942 earned teacher's certificates from the Griffith Music Foundation. She studied the piano under Abraham Nelson in 1912, Clarence Adler in 1918, Arthur Newstead in 1920 and Emil Friedberger in 1922 and completed a number of piano courses under various other teachers. She taught the piano at her studio in Newark.
Compositions
VOCAL
The golden chain (1930)
Lullaby (1940)
Mazurka (1940)
Spinning song (1932)
Ref. 496

RITTENHOUSE, Elizabeth Mae
American authoress, evangelist and composer. b. Woodlawn, AL, July 23, 1915. She was educated at the Bible Institute and joined the ministry in 1954.
Compositions
SACRED
For my sake
Memories of by-gone days
Oh halleluia Jesus lives within
Search my heart
A soldier for Christ
Ref. 39, 646

RITTER, Fanny Malone Raymond
American translator, writer and composer. b. Philadelphia, 1840; d. Poughkeepsie, NY, October 26, 1890. Her book 'Woman as a Musician' in 1876, was the first historical study on women in music to appear in the United States. She married the musician F.L. Ritter. She composed vocal trios and duets and songs for voice and the piano.
Publications
Lyre, Pen and Pencil. Essays.
Translations of Ehlert's *Letters on Music to a Lady.*
Translations of Schumann's *Essays and Criticisms: Music and Musicians.*
Ref. 85, 276, 292, 347, 433, 646

RITTER, Irene Marschand
American organist and composer. b. Philadelphia. She composed organ pieces.
Ref. 323

RITTMAN, Trude
German pianist and composer. b. September 24, 1908. She composed chamber and vocal works.
Ref. 226

RIVAY, Mlle.
19th-century French composer.
Composition
OPERA
Maitre Palma (1830)
Ref. 307

RIVE-KING, Julia (Julie)
American concert pianist, teacher and composer of French parentage. b. Cincinnati, October 30, 1854; d. Indianapolis, IN, July 24, 1937. Her mother was her first piano teacher and Julie first played in public at the age of eight. Between 1866 and 1872 she studied in New York under William Manson and Sebastian Mills and then went to Berlin where she became a pupil of Reinecke. She made her debut there in 1874 playing Beethoven's *C-Minor Concerto* and studied under Liszt in Weimar. She appeared with the New York Philharmonic Society in 1875. In 1878 she held master classes during the summer. In 1880 she formed the Rive-King Concert Company which toured widely during the 1880 to 1881 season. From 1891 to 1892 she appeared as a regular soloist with the Chicago Orchestra. She gave a series of orchestral concerts and recitals throughout the United States from 1894 to 1895 and toured with Anton Seidl's orchestra from 1896 to 1898. She played in about 4000 concerts, 500 of them with orchestras. From 1905 to 1936 she taught the piano at the Bush Conservatory in Chicago.
Compositions
PIANO
Bubbling spring (1878) (Doremi)
Concert etude in A-Flat (1877)
Concert etude in F-Sharp Minor (1887)
Gems of Scotland
Hand in hand, polka (1882)
Humoresque (1878)
Impromptu in A-Flat (1876) (Presser; Schirmer)
Knight Templar march (1882)
March of the goblins (1883)
Mazourka des graces
Mazurka caprice (1881)
On blooming meadows, concert waltz (1879)
Pensées dansantes, valse brillante (1882)
Polka caprice
Polonaise heroique (1880)
Ref. 17, 22, 74, 100, 102, 132, 276, 292, 415, 433, 617

RIVERA, Eusebia

19th-century Peruvian composer.

Composition

Polka (1856) (ded Rosa Olivieri de Luisia)

Ref. 403

RIVERA, Graciela

Puerto Rican singer, professor and composer. b. Ponce, April 17, 1921. She graduated from the Juilliard School of Music in 1943. She made her singing debut in the title role of the opera *Lucia di Lammermoor* at the Metropolitan Opera in 1952 and performed over 300 leading roles in the United States and Europe. She was assistant professor at Hostos Community College and received various honors, including the Pro Arte Musical medal, Puerto Rico and the Exemplary Citizen award, Institute of Puerto Rico.

Compositions

SACRED

Campanitas, carol
Christmas album
Padre nuestro

INCIDENTAL MUSIC

Borinquen, dance
Puerto Rican danzas

Ref. 206

RIVET, Jeanne

French composer.

Compositions

VOCAL

Aubade a l'amour (vce and pf) (H. Darsay) (Ricordi)
Le bateau rose (J. Richepin) (Ricordi)
Ciel est d'azur (Moulle)
Cloches (Chanson de la Toussaint) (Grus)
Conte foi
Je la veux, cette fleur
Mon amour est comme un oiseau (C. Gaillarde) (Ricordi)
Mort de la cigale (Choudens)
Noël (Hachette)
Two melodies: Baisers; Quand mai fleurit

Ref. 297

ROBBOY, Rosalie Smotkin

American harpist, organist, pianist, choral conductor, soprano, teacher and composer. b. Des Moines, IA, May 10, 1924. She studied at several universities in the United States receiving her B.A. from Flora Stone Mather College. From 1966 she was a harpist with various orchestras in San Diego; she directed the choirs of various schools in Cleveland, OH, from 1943 to 1954 and composed sacred music and various other pieces.

Ref. 77

ROBERSON, Ruby Lee Grubbs

American organist, pianist, teacher and composer. b. Dallas, October 5, 1921. She studied at the Chicago Conservatory Extension University and taught the piano and the organ and held the position of church organist. She composed sacred songs and anthems.

Ref. 475

ROBERT, Lucie

French organist, pianist, lecturer and composer. b. Rennes, October 3, 1936. She studied at the Paris Conservatoire and was awarded diplomas and received first prizes in her studies under Lazare-Levy and Aline Van Barentzen (piano), Henriette Puig-Roget (piano accompaniment), Pierre Pasquier (instrumental ensemble), Henri Challan (harmony), Noel Gallon (counterpoint and fugue), and Tony Aubin (composition). She won the Premier Grand Prix de Rome in 1965. She taught solfege at the Paris Conservatoire and appeared in concert from 1942 and from 1963 was a soloist with ORTF. Her works have been performed in France and abroad. DISCOGRAPHY. PHOTOGRAPH.

Compositions

ORCHESTRA

Symphonie (org and orch) (1968)
Mouvement symphonique (1974)
Double concerto for piano, alto saxophone and orchestra (comm ORTF) (1969)
Flute concerto No. 1 (1962)
Flute concerto No. 2 (1966)
Oboe concerto (1965) (comm ORTF)
Piano concerto No. 1 (1961)
Piano concerto No. 2 (1963)
Divertissement (pf and str orch) (1966)
Le grand yacht Despair, lyric poem (1962)
Triptyque (1967)

CHAMBER

San Damiano (ob and strs) (1973)
Flammes et fumées (sax qnt) (1982)
Steles (4 tba) (1984)
String quartet (1960)
Tetraphone (sax qrt) (1982) (Billaudot)
Trinome (2 sax and pf) (1982) (Billaudot)
Supplications (ob, sax and vlc) (1981)
Cadenza (a-sax and pf) (1974)
Diptyque (ob and pf) (1971)
Litanies (vlc and pf) (1981) (Billaudot)
Ostinato (pf and d-b) (1972) (Leduc)
Rythmes lyriques (2 sax) (1984)
Sonata (fl and pf) (1961)
Sonata (a-sax and pf) (Billaudot, 1975)
Strophes (sax and pf)
Variations (sax and pf)
Boites à musique (hp) (1966)
Flash (org) (1982) (Billaudot)
Lied (org) (1973)

PIANO

Sonata (2 pf) (1971)
Tokkata (2 pf) (1983)
Sonatine No. 1
Sonatine No. 2
Suite (1964)
Two preludes (1963)

VOCAL

Tout est si clair ce soir, cantata (Careme) (fl, man, S and pf) (1968)
Three waltzes (ch and orch)
Tantum ergo (ch, org, trp and trb) (1979)
La prophète de Cassandre, lyric poem (Eschyle) (1965)
Les rois mages, lyric poem (Frenaud) (1964)
Dialogue II (S and cl) (1984)
Melodies (S and cl)
Sept poèmes d'Alain Suied (vce and pf) (1984)
Sonate (vce and pf) (1980)
Sonata vocalises (S and pf) (1970)
Eight melodies (P. Souphault) (1967)
Three melodies for tenor voice (Careme) (1967)

SACRED

Fiat voluntas tua (mix-ch and org) (1973)

OPERA

L'épouse injustement soupçonnée, lyric opera (Jean Cocteau) (1963)

Ref. composer, 76, 563, 622

ROBERT-MAZEL, Helene

19th-century French pianist, teacher and composer. A writer of vocal music, she devoted her time to the practical aspects of teaching, developing a highly recommended vocal method and a collection of one and two part songs for children, which has been frequently reprinted.

Compostitions

VOCAL

A mon père, melody
L'arabe et son coursier, ballade
L'aspect des bois, ballade
Les deux captifs, duo (S and A)
Eight romances (pub as Album de Mlle. H. Robert-Mazel) (Cotelle, 1839)
La luciole, ballade
Un souvenir, melody

SACRED

Le jugement dernier, cantata

Publications

Concerts des enfants. Suite; collection of small pieces for children.
Guide musical de L'enfance. Elementary rules and a number of solfege in all major and minor keys adapted to the child's voice.

Ref. 26, 129, 226, 260, 276, 347, 433

ROBERTS, Gertrud Hermine Kuenzel

American harpsichordist, teacher and composer. b. Hastings, MN, August 23, 1906. She received her B.A. (music) in 1928 from the University of Minnesota, taught the piano privately for two years then continued her study of that instrument under Alfred Baresel in 1930 at the Conservatory of Leipzig. When she returned to Minnesota she became head of the piano department at a girls' school in St. Paul. She studied the piano privately under Julia Elbogen in Vienna from 1932 to 1933. From 1946 she lived in Hawaii and continued teaching and playing in concerts. She toured extensively, appearing as soloist of her own works as well as those of others. She was founder of a chamber group for the harpsichord. She was the recipient of a number of honors and in 1975, voted Most Distinguished Citizen in the Arts. DISCOGRAPHY. PHOTOGRAPH.

Compositions

ORCHESTRA

Concerto (hpcd and orch) (1973)
Double concerto (1976)
Elegy (pf reduction and sym orch) (1965)

CHAMBER

Sonata for flute and harpsichord (1980)
Works for piano and harpsichord

HARPSICHORD

Waltz (2 hpcd) (1962)
Chaconne in A-Minor (double-manual hpcd) (1950) (Honolulu: Island Heritage, 1972)
Charlot suite (double-manual hpcd) (1955)
Das kleine Buch der Bilder
Laendler
Passacaille in A-Minor, dance mime (double-manual hpcd) (1948)
Rondo-hommage to Couperin (double-manual hpcd) (1956) (Island Heritage, 1972)
Three bagatelles (1950)
Triptych (double-manual hpcd) (1961)

PIANO

Christmas chaconne (also hpcd) (1970)
Duo in E-Flat Major (1931)
Gavotte (also hpcd) (1933)
Twelve time gardens

VOCAL

Class graduating song, high school (1924)
Cycle (vce and pf) (1962)
In a secret garden (S and hpcd)
Love unspoken (1922) (Lady Nesta Oberman)
Yerma's lullaby (vce and hpcd) (1962)

SACRED

Fantaisie after Psalm 150 (1971) (comm 100th anniversary of St. John's Lutheran Church of Hastings, MN)

INCIDENTAL MUSIC

Alice in Wonderland (Eva Le Gallienne) (1957) (comm Honolulu Theatre for Youth)
Pineapple Country Hawaii, industrial film (1960) (comm Hawaii's Pineapple Cos.)
Tempest (Shakespeare) (1962) (comm Honolulu Community Theatre)
Thieves' Carnival (Jean Anouilh) (1959) (comm Honolulu Community Theatre)
Yerma (Lorca) (2 hpcd) (1961) (comm University of Hawaii Drama Dept.)

Bibliography

G. Roberts, harpsichordist. Reviews. Various publishers.

Ref. composer, 84, 94, 142, 228, 359, 474, 475, 477, 563, 625

ROBERTS, Jane A.

American pianist, teacher and composer. b. Chicago, October 3, 1933. She gained a B.Mus. in the piano in 1957 and B.Mus. in composition in 1980, from the American Conservatory, having studied under H. Heniot, W. Browning and W. Ferris. She taught music privately. She is a member of ASCAP.

Compositions

CHAMBER

Sonata (cl and pf) (with Jan Plantinga??) (1980)

Other chamber pieces

Piano pieces

VOCAL

Over 100 songs and song cycles

DANCE SCORES

Scores (elec)

INCIDENTAL MUSIC

Twelfth Night (Shakespeare) (1982)

MISCELLANEOUS

Bend, baby, bend (1980)

Ref. 625

ROBERTS, Mrs. Joyce O. See ROBERTS, Gertrud Hermine Kuenzel

ROBERTS, Megan L.

American pianist, violinist, director, teacher and composer. b. Hampstead, NY, October 12, 1952. She studied the theatre and music at the University of California, Santa Barbara from 1970 to 1972. She received a B.A. hons. in music from Humboldt State University, Arcata, CA, in 1976. She did postgraduate study in experimental video at the California College of Arts and Crafts from 1976 to 1977 and graduated from Mills College with an M.F.A. (film and video) in 1977. She studied composition under Robert Ashley and David Behrman, the piano under Dmitri Koovshinoff, Siegfried Schultze and Frans Marks; she also studied the violin, voice, acting and ballet. Other teachers included Emma Lou Diemer at the University of California and Charles Moon at Humboldt State University. She was choir conductor at Eureka First Congregational Church from 1973 to 1974 and worked in radio advertisement, production and sales at KXGO Radio, Arcata, CA, from 1974 to 1975. From 1975 to 1977 she did free-lance work in video and sound recording, documentation, and reproduction. She was graduate assistant at Mills College Center for Contemporary Music from 1975 to 1977. In 1976 she worked in the area of sound track composition and production sync-sound editing for an AFI film. From 1976 to 1977 she was instructor at Mills Music Training School, where she taught theory, analysis, the piano harmony and composition. She is currently involved in projects and research in the area of electronic music. She has worked extensively in areas such as audio and visual systems, film, theatre and technical collaborations with other artists. Honors include a Humboldt State University foundation grant in 1975, a Louisiana Pacific and Simpson Lumber Company grant and an award for video entries presented in the 1976 Annual CCAC Sequence Show. She also received grants for other works. She was winner of the La Mamelle Exhibition prize for video at the San Francisco Art Festival Mobius Video Show and co-winner of the Elizabeth Mills Crothers prize for composition in music from Mills College in 1977. DISCOGRAPHY. PHOTOGRAPH.

Compositions

ORCHESTRA

3-2-1 (cham orch)

CHAMBER

Chamber suite (1975) (Humboldt Arts Council grant)
Duets (vln and vlc)
Piano pieces

ELECTRONIC

Applause for small people, a pygmatic function (amp vce, pygmy-ch, amp perc and vlc) (1976)
Better homes and gardens primer for electronic music cerealized music
I could sit here all day, concert prelude (vocals, drs, moog syn, bird recordings and tape) (1976)
I had to make this tape (1976)
Music for prepared typewriter
No one cares about me anyway, from Songs for television (vocal, perc and tape) (1976)
Sorry
Split (p)ea and split p(ea) (2 speakers, 2 loudspeakers and sounds that process themselves)
Support stockings (1976)

MULTIMEDIA

As I like it-the artist explaining her art (video)
Factory
First farewell to video or I've had it with that noise boys (1976)
I never was a little boy, but I remember all the songs and WW II
In the prime time of your life action archives (video, audiotape, slides and artifacts)
Music for prepared audience (1976)
Nam June and legs in plastic
A new routine for the mills auxiliary sync squad (9 channels and 18 feet)
O.M. mix for tape and dancer
Sax and violence (1976)
Small band music of the 70's (1977)
Songs for my mother (tape, light controls, vln, large objects and dance)
Suite for a small chamber (dance triggered electronic sound environment for choreographed music produced by 4 dancers)

Ref. composer, 563, 622, 625

ROBERTS, Mrs. See RALPH, Kate

ROBERTS, Nellie Wilkinson

19th-century American composer.

Compositions

VOCAL

Songs incl.:
The old path
Sing little birds
Unawares

Ref. 276, 292, 347, 433

ROBERTS, Ruth Olive

American organist, pianist, teacher and composer. b. Fryeburg, NY, August 31, 1926. She studied the piano in Europe where her teachers included pupils of Leschetizky and Liszt. She was an organ pupil of Tobias Matthay, in London, of Heinrich Gebhardt in Boston, of Dr. John Hermann Loud and Dr. Irving J. Morgan. She returned to Europe to study at the Mozarteum, Salzburg (1955 and 1960) and the Lausanne Conservatory in 1957.

Compositions

PIANO

Longfellow Grammar School march (2 pf)
Capriccioso in F
Christmas morning
Contemplation
Ein Gebet
Eine Erinnerung
June song (with Latham True)
Song without words
To autumn

VOCAL

Songs

Ref. 40, 347, 374

ROBERTSON, Donna Lou Nagey

American harpsichordist, organist, editor, professor and composer. b. Indiana, PA, November 16, 1935. She obtained her B.S. at Indiana University of Pennsylvania and her M.Mus. at the Eastman School. She was associate professor at Mars Hill College from 1958 and in 1973, became editor of *Music Now*. She appeared in concert and received awards for her compositions.

Compositions

CHAMBER

Pantonia in C (8 fl)
Dialogues (vln, a-fl, cl, trp and trb) (1976)
Fanfare for the Prince of Darkness (tba qrt)
String quartet No. 1 (1957)
Little suite for trombone ensemble (Dorn)
Trio (ob, vln and hpcd) (1970)
Flashes in a pan (trp and mallet insts) (1975)
Five reflections (trb and pf)
Pastorale for aria and scherzo on a row (ob and pf) (1967)
Recitation with 5 reflections (trb and pf) (1973)

PIANO

Passacaglia (1963)
Prelude and fugue (1960)

VOCAL

Drop, drop slow tears (double ch) (1973)
No single thing abides (double ch) (1973)
Wachet auf (trp and mix-ch)
Beatitudes (1957)
Four Gaelic songs (vce and pf) (1962)
Love (treble vces) (1970)
Nocturne (T and trb) (1974)
Three Dylan Thomas songs (1969)

SACRED

Christ est erstanden (mix-ch, handbells and org)
Five odes to God in nature (ch) (1969)
The strife is o'er (ch) (1969)
Magnificat (1971)
Psalm 23 (fl and S) (1975)
Six psalms of Ascension (low vce) (1967)
Psalm for an academic procession (1958)
Psalm 100 (1969)
Two motets (1965)

Ref. composer, 77, 142, 347, 625

ROBERTSON, Mrs.

Early 19th-century Scottish composer of Ladykirk, Scotland.

Compositions

MISCELLANEOUS

Follow her over the border (Edinburgh: Gow & Shepherd, 1802)
Miss Johnston of Hutton's reel (Gow & Shepherd, 1802)
Rock and a wee pickle tow (Gow & Shepherd, 1802)

Ref. Philip Martin (London)

ROBERTSON, Mrs. R.E. See ROE, Gloria Ann

ROBINSON, Arthur. See ROBINSON, Fanny

ROBINSON, Berenice

American composer. b. New York, 1911.

Composition

ORCHESTRA

Overture in D, op. 13 (1940)

Ref. 322

ROBINSON, Fanny (nee Arthur)

English pianist, professor and composer. b. Southampton, September 1831; d. Dublin, October 31, 1879. She studied under Sterndale Bennet and Sigismund Thalberg. In 1849 she went to Dublin, where she made her debut. She first appeared in London in 1855 and gave her first performance in Paris in 1864. In 1856 she and her husband, conductor Joseph Robinson, joined the Royal Irish Academy of Music as professors, teaching voice and the piano.

Compositions

PIANO

Pieces

VOCAL

Songs

SACRED

God is love, cantata

Ref. 6, 177, 226, 276, 433

ROBINSON, Frances

20th-century American composer.

Compositions

PIANO

Op. 45 (4 hands)
Always merry
Ethiopian dance
Happy thoughts, waltz
Moonlight dance
Valentine, waltz

VOCAL

Butter making, action song
Daddy Long Legs
Farmer, action song
Good morning and good night
Grandfather Willow
Little maids of Japan, action song
Nutting song, action song
Sleigh song
Soldier song, action song

Ref. 297

ROBINSON, Gertrude Ina

20th-century American harpist and composer. b. Waterloo, IA. She studied in Paris under Alphonse Hasselmans and became a church harpist in New York. She composed pieces for the harp.

Ref. 75, 226, 276

ROBINSON, Margaret Mary. See BERRY, Margaret Mary Robinson

ROBITASHVILI, Lia (Liana) Georgievna

Soviet lecturer and composer. b. Tbilisi, October 26, 1930. She studied composition under A.M. Balanchivadze and S.V. Barkhudarian at the Tbilisi Conservatory from where she graduated in 1955. The previous year she commenced lecturing at music schools in Tbilisi.

Compositions

ORCHESTRA

Piano concerto, for children (1955)

CHAMBER

Pastoral song (fl and pf) (1953)

PIANO

Miniatures (1970)
Sonatina (1953)

VOCAL

Kolbelnaya (ch) (1974)
Konek (Sikharulidze) (chil-ch) (1963)
Koster v lagere (ch) (1974)
Kto vinovat (Potskhishvili) (chil-ch) (1962)
Manana i tsyplyata (K. Gugushvili) (ch) (1964)
Obidchivaya (Dzhangulashvili) (chil-ch) (1962)
Pushok i sneg (ch) (1974)
Shkhapa- shkhupi (M. Potskhishvili) (ch) (1964)

Stiralishchitsa (S. Mgvimeli) (ch) (1964)
Zub i oreshek (Potskhishvili) (chil-ch) (1962)
Ispanskaya pesna, duet (Tarkhnishvili) (1970)
Spanish duets (M. Tarkhnishvili) (1970)
Vocalise (vce, fl and pf) (1954)
Choruses for schools
Children's choruses
OPERETTA
Imeniny Fialki- Malshki, for children (1967)
Ref. 21

ROBLES, Marisa

Spanish harpist, professor and composer. b. Madrid, May 4, 1937. She made her debut in Madrid at the age of 9 and later obtained degrees in the harp, harmony and composition at the Royal Conservatory of Music, Madrid. She was appointed professor of harp at the the Royal Conservatory, Madrid, at the age of 21 and became the harp tutor to the National Youth Orchestra, England and professor of the harp at the Royal College of Music. DISCOGRAPHY.

Compositions
CHAMBER
The Narnia suite (hp, fl and picc)
VOCAL
The horse and his boy (C.S. Lewis) (narr, hp and fl)
The last battle (C.S. Lewis) (narr, hp and fl)
The lion, the witch and the wardrobe (C.S. Lewis) (narr, hp and fl)
The magician's nephew (C.S. Lewis) (narr, hp and fl)
Prince Caspian (C.S. Lewis) (narr, hp and fl)
The silver chair (C.S. Lewis) (narr, hp and fl)
The voyage of the Dawntreader (C.S. Lewis) (narr, hp and fl)
Ref. 563

ROBYN, Louise

20th-century American lecturer and composer. She was a faculty member at the American Conservatory in Chicago, teaching both children and adults. She evolved a system of musical training for children.

Publications
Keyboard Town.
Robyn-Gurlitt Album.
Technic Tales. 3 books.
Ref. 292

ROCHAT (Aeschlimann-Rochat), Andrée (pseud. Jean Durand)

Swiss pianist and composer. b. Geneva, January 12, 1900. She began her studies under Jaques-Dalcroze and received her piano diploma from the Conservatory at Geneva, then studied counterpoint under Gedalge in Paris, composition under Orefice and Bossi in Milan, Ernst Wolff in Zurich and Vladimir Vogel in Ascona. After her studies at the conservatories of Geneva and Paris she married the publisher Aeschlimann and settled in Milan. Her works have been performed on radio. PHOTOGRAPH.

Compositions
CHAMBER
Preludio, aria e finale, op. 21 (strs, cls, trp and pf) (1948) (Milan: Carisch)
Musica per archi, op. 26 (1957) (GEDOK prize, 1961) (Carisch)
Improvisation, op. 34 (pf, fl and drs) (1982) (Carisch)
Cinque pezzi brevi, op. 27 (fl and pf) (1960) (Carisch)
Duo, op. 18 (fl and hp) (1946)
Elegie, op. 23 (vlc and pf) (1952)
Sonata (vln and pf) (1932) (Carisch)
Sonata, op. 12 (vln and pf) (1938) (Carisch)
Sonata, op. 20 (fl and hp) (1947) (Carisch)
Suite, op. 25 (vln and vln) (1954) (Carisch)
Tre canzoni (cl and pf) (Carisch)
Tre intermezzi, op. 14 (cl and pf) (1940) (Carisch)
PIANO
Kaleidoscope, op. 30 (1962)
Sieben Ministuecke, op. 33 (1979)
Trois pieces, op. 32 (1970)
VOCAL
Au jardin, suite, op. 28 (M. Lacheraf) (S, m-S, fl and vln) (1961)
De musica, op. 31 (St. Augustin) (Bar, vln, trp, pf and drs) (1967)
Chants d'outre-mer, op. 22 (T and pf) (1952) (GEDOK prize)
Jeux et travaux de mes aieules (M. Gagnebin) (1962)
Sette sonetti (Dante) (S and pf) (1932)
Sette canti, op. 13 (Zavattini) (S and pf) (1940)
Tre liriche, op. 19 (A. Negri) (S and pf) (1946)
Zoographie, op. 29 (H. Maxwell) (S and pf) (1962)
SACRED
Prophet Jeremiah, cantata, op. 17 (cont, strs and 2 pf) (1946)
Drei geistliche Lieder, op. 16 (N. Bolt) (S and pf) (1946)
Publications
Journal d'un amateur de musique. Under pseud. Lausanne: Payot, 1941.
Ref. composer, 17, 59, 552, 651

ROCHEROLLE, Eugenie Katherine (nee Ricau)

American pianist and composer. b. New Orleans, LA, August 24, 1936. She graduated from Sophie Newcombe School, Tulane University, with a B.A. (music, 1958). She lived in Paris for one year, studying the piano privately under Attica Aitkens and Lucille Snyder, composition under Cardon Burnham and instrumentation under John Morrisey and Clare Grundman. Eugenie also studied under Nadia Boulanger (q.v.) and Annette Dieudonne. She won several competitions for her piano playing and her works have been performed on radio and television. DISCOGRAPHY. PHOTOGRAPH.

Compositions
ORCHESTRA
Carnival capers (1975)
Irish holiday (1973) (Marks)
Pastorale and parade (Marks, 1971)
BAND
Southern holiday (Alfred Music, San Diego)
CHAMBER
Sonatina No. 1 (fl, vln and vlc) (1977)
La danza (vln and pf) (1975)
Vignette No. 2 (vln and pf)
Three pieces for violin (1973)
PIANO
Headin' south (2 pf) (Kjos, 1981)
Tierra del Sol (2 pf) (Kjos, 1984)
American sampler (Kjos, 1980)
Autumn sky (comm Clavier Magazine, 1983)
Bayou reflections (Kjos, 1984)
Blockbuster (1984)
Christmas around the piano (Kjos, 1982)
Forest fantasy (1960)
Getting into intervals (Kjos, 1982)
Instrumental inspirations (Kjos, 1983)
Miniatures (Kjos, 1981)
Montage (Kjos, 1980)
Pages from a scrapbook (Kjos, 1984)
Patchwork, collection (General Words & Music, 1980)
Pot pourri (1971)
Seven scenes (Kjos, 1983)
Simple pleasures (1984)
Six moods (1978)
Three preludes (1966)
VOCAL
The new colossus (narr, ch and orch) (1972)
America, my home (1974) (ch and band; also ch and fl) (Warner)
Little bird (mix-ch) (Warner, 1980)
Little bitty baby (mix-ch) (Warner, 1978)
Secret of the star (ch) (Warner, 1980)
About spring (1964) (Warner)
Along the sand (1975) (Warner)
And so it was (Warner, 1971)
Baby boy, 1970 (Warner)
Continental suite (1971)
Crazy cat! (Alfred, 1978)
Crazy, man! (Warner, 1969)
He smiled at me (1977) (Warner)
How can it be? (Warner)
A joyful song (1970) (Warner)
Little baby boy (1976) (Alfred)
Little by little (1973) (Warner, 1978)
Little train (Warner)
Lookin' ahead (1971) (Warner)
No time for lookin' behind (1970) (Warner)
See the pretty baby (1969) (Warner)
Some special place (1970) (Alfred)
What'cha gonna be, my son? (1969) (Warner)
Written in the stars (1974) (Alfred)
SACRED
From the Revelation to John (2 S, mix-ch and org or pf; also wind qrt) (1976) (comm Wilton Congregational Church Choir)
Bless the little children (ch) (Alfred, 1981)
Sing Noël (ch a-cap) (Alfred, 1980)
Song of the Wise Men (ch) (Alfred, 1980)
All you peoples clap your hands (1968) (Warner)
Chariot's comin' (1977) (Warner)
Christmas child (1974) (Warner)
Christmas day is comin' (1972) (Warner)

Christmas Eve tonight (Warner, 1982)
Christmas lullaby (1976) (Warner)
Give to the Lord (1970) (Warner)
Joyous alleluia (1965) (Warner)
Little Lord (1966) (Warner)
Lord wont'cha teach me? (1977) (Warner)
Saviour child (1968) (Warner)
See baby Jesus (1965) (Warner)
Who's lookin' for glory (1967) (Warner)
THEATRE
Williamsburg, America, musical in 2 acts (1967)
Ref. composer, 142

ROCHES, Gilbert des. See LEGOUX, Julie, Baroness

ROCKEFELLER, Helen C.
20th-century American composer.
Composition
SACRED
An Easter Carol (mix-ch and pf) (H.W. Gray Co.)
Ref. 190

RODGERS, Mary.
American composer. b. New York, January 11, 1931. She is the daughter of the composer Richard Rodgers and studied at Wellesley College. She is a member of ASCAP.
Compositions
VOCAL
Ali Baba, for children
Children's introduction to jazz
Some of my best friends are children
Songs incl.:
Counter melody
In a little while
Normandy
Shy
Very soft shoes
INCIDENTAL MUSIC
Davy Jones' locker, marionettes
Feathertop, television
The Mad Show, play
Once upon a mattress, play
Selections (Shakespeare)
Three to make music, play
Ref. 39, 142

RODRIGO, Maria
Spanish pianist, conductor, teacher and composer. b. Madrid, March 20, 1868. She studied with her father, Pantaleon Rodrigo, a music teacher and at the Royal Conservatory of Madrid, under Trago (piano), Arrin (harmony) and Serrano (composition). She received a grant from the Junta de Ampliacion de Estudios to further her studies in Munich under Anto Beer-Walbrunn. She taught at the Conservatory of Music in Madrid and was assistant conductor at the Royal Opera House.
Compositions
ORCHESTRA
Symphony, 4 tempos
Alma espanola
Dos impressiones sinfonicas
Gandara, ouverture
Rimas infantiles
CHAMBER
Quinteto per pianoforte e fiatti
String quartet
Pieces for violin and piano
PIANO
Piano pieces incl.:
La copla intrusa, sonata
VOCAL
Caprichos de Goya (ch and orch)
Songs incl.:
Ayes, three songs
OPERA
Becqueriana (Alvarez Quintero Brothers)
Cancion de amor (1925)
THEATRE
Diana Cazadora, zarzuela in 1 act
La flor de la vida, zarzuela
El roble de la Jarosa
La romeria del rocio, zarzuela
MISCELLANEOUS
Tu eres la rosa, yo soy el lirio
Ref. 14, 17, 23, 60, 100, 107, 361

RODRIGUE, Nicole
Canadian pianist, teacher and composer. b. Montreal, September 29, 1943. She began studying the piano at the age of ten and proceeded to the Ecole de Musique Vincent d'Indy, graduating with a bachelor's degree and a specialist's teaching certificate. She gained a bachelor's degree in secular music from the University of Montreal, where her teachers included F. Aubut-Pratte, J.P. Couture, S. Garant, and A. Prevost. At McGill University she studied composition under Istvan Anhalt and electronic music under Paul Pedersen. Her other teachers there were Bruce Mather and Alcides Lanza. In June 1974 she became the first woman to receive an M.M.A. in composition from that university. DISCOGRAPHY.
Compositions
CHAMBER
Two atmospheres (cham ens) (1974)
Modules (hp, d-b and 7 tam-tams) (1970)
Nasca (cl, vlc, pf and vib) (1972)
Soufrière, in 6 mvts (2 fl and 2 picc) (1969)
Fission, in 6 mvts (2 perc) (1970)
SACRED
Laudes, requiem in 6 mvts (ch and cham ens) (1971)
MULTIMEDIA
Toi, of unlimited duration, in 10 mvts (hp and visual montage) (1972)
Ref. CMC, 563

RODRIGUES, Maria Joachina
18th-century Mexican composer.
Composition
SACRED
Musicos ruysenores: Cantata a duo al Nacimiento (A and T)
Ref. 178, 332

RODRIGUEZ BELLA, Catalina
20th-century Argentine pianist, lecturer, musicologist and composer. She studied the piano and composition at the National Conservatory of Buenos Aires and then lectured on composition, analysis and history of music at three different conservatories. Her particular interest was in old and modern Argentine folk music. She won the Premie Nacional de las Artes for a choral work.
Compositions
CHAMBER
Movimientos esquematicos (fl, cl and bsn)
Other pieces
VOCAL
Choral works
Ref. Donne in Musica 1980

RODRIGUEZ, Esther
Cuban composer. b. Manzanillo, November 29, 1920. She studied harmony and counterpoint at the Conservatorio Orbon under Berta Momoytio and B. Orbon and at the Conservatorio Municipal under Roldan and J. Ardevol. She is a member of the group Renovacion Musical.
Compositions
CHAMBER
Cuarteto en la Mayor (str qrt) (1943)
Sonata (vlc and pf)
PIANO
Invenciones
Preludio
VOCAL
Choral pieces
Songs
Ref. 54, 70, 94, 100

ROE, Eileen Betty
English cellist, organist, pianist, choir director, singer, teacher and composer. b. London, July 30, 1930. She studied the piano and the cello at the Royal Academy of Music, London and composition under Lennox Berkeley. She is an A.R.C.M., an F.T.C.M. and an L.R.A.M. From 1952 she was

active as a teacher and held the position of director of music at St. Helen's Church, Kensington (1958 to 1968) and at the London Academy of Music and Dramatic Art (1968 to 1978). She is currently director of music at St. Helen's Church. DISCOGRAPHY. PHOTOGRAPH.

Compositions

ORCHESTRA

Divertimento (trp and str orch; also small orch)
Burlington suite (London: Thames)

CHAMBER

Betty's bounce for wind quintet (Thames)
Galliard suite (brass qnt)
A flourish of fanfares, 4 fanfares (4 B-Flat trp) (Thames)
Seven tunes from the Cecil Harpe collection (descant rec and gtrs) (Novello)
Summer music (pf, vln, vla and vlc)
Conversation piece (recs and pf)
Alto temperaments (fl and pf)
Introduction and allegretto (hn and pf)
Sonatine (fl and pf)
Suite (2 vlc)
Temperaments (fl and gtr)
Triplice (org)

GUITAR

Omega suite (4 gtr)
Larcombe's fancy, 5 solos
Short sonata
Sonatina dolorosa
Summer suite

VOCAL

A crown of briar roses, cantata (1977)
The food fad, cantata (vce, wind, brass, vlc, perc and pf)
A quire of elements, cantata (1978)
Time takes wing (Jasper Mayne) (Bar and small str orch)
Ghouls and ghosts (mix-ch)
Goe and catche a falling starre (S and mix-ch)
The jackdaw of Theims (ch, org, pf and perc)
Mouth-music (mix-ch and pf) (Thames)
Prefabulous animiles (J. Reeves) (speaker, ch and pf) (comm Purcell Room Concert) (W. Heine-Mann, 1973)
Shadwell stair (Wilfred Owen) (mix-ch and fl) (Thames)
A song for your supper (Jacqueline Froom) (soloists, mix-ch, pf or strs, cl and fl)
Songs for the King at Whitehall (Robert Herrick) (S and wind qnt)
Song of the virtuous female spider (Ruth Pitter) (S, vln, vlc, fl, ob and hpcd or pf; also for S and 6 vlc)
Three eccentrics (ch and pf) (comm Purcell Room Concert)
Three English folk songs (mix-ch)
Burd Ellen, fable (S, A, B, fl and pf)
Two Chinese songs (S, m-S, Cont and pf)
Witches' brew (S, A, hn and pf)
All the day (vce, rec and pf)
The blacksmith and the changeling (2 m-vces and pf)
Circle beguiled (3 vces and gtr)
Daughters of Eve (2 S and pf)
Firstlings, songs (Rita Ford) (high vce, ww and gtr) (Thames)
Four Shakespeare songs (vce, fl and pf)
Folk songs for fox (vce and pf)
A garland of folk songs (vce and pf)
Hot sun, cool fire (George Peel) (vce and viol consort)
Madam's three callers (S and vlc)
Men were deceivers ever (Bar and gtr)
Musical moments (Bar and gtr)
Nine songs (various) (vce and pf) (Thames)
Noble numbers, songs (Robert Herrick) (A and pf or hpcd) (Thames)
Nursery rhymes of innocence and experience (vce and pf)
Openers and closers, 6 songs (D. Prockter and M. Holstock) (Samuel French)
Poet's corner: A pull on the heart strings; The zoo outing (M. Holstock & D. Prockter)
Ponder's songs of the seasons (Barbara Softly) (vce and pf) (Thames)
Revue songs: Bar-carol; Crusaders; Glands; Other hands; Noah calypso; Six songs from Ponder and William (Barbara Softly) (vce and pf) (Novello)
Three English folk songs
Two Chinese songs (S, m-S, Cont and pf)
Two jazz songs (S and d-b)
Two songs: Euphonium dance (J. Froom); Madam and the minister (L. Hughes) (S and d-b) (York Editions)
Verities (S and cl)

SACRED

Christ the King, cantata (A. Taylor) (mix-ch, speakers, org, pf, rec, d-b and perc)
Christus Victor, cantata-mime (J. Catterick) (Cont, B, narr, mix-ch, speaking ch, dancers and insts) (Novello)
Genesis, cantata (M. Holstock, composer and R. Ford) (ch and orch)
Away in a Manger, carol (unison vces or mix-ch and org or pf) (Thames)
Hosanna to the living Lord, anthem (Bishop Heber) (S, A, T and mix-ch)
Like as the hart (S and mix-ch)
Missa Brevis (mix-ch and org)
Out of your sleep arise and wake, carol (15th-century poem) (mix-ch, hn, trp, perc and vlc) (Thames)
Psalm 24 (soloists and mix-ch a-cap; also soloists and vces a-cap)
Sing to the Lord of Harvest, anthem (J. Monsell) (S, mix-ch and pf)
Two psalms (ch)
AD one, masque for Christmas (vces, fl and pf) (1973)
As I sat on a sunny bank, carol (2-part treble vce and pf or org) (Thames)
Behold a silly tender babe, carol (2-part vces and pf) (Oxford)
Children's song of the nativity, carol (F. Chesterton) (2-part vces, pf and ww) (Thames)
A chime of carols (vce and pf)
Christmas carols (vce and pf)
Come, all ye children, carol (Barbara Softly) (unison vces and pf or org) (Thames)
Easter eggs (S and pf)
Hark, how all the welkin rings, carol (2-part vces and pf) (Oxford)
Jubilate Deo (unison vces and org) (Weinberger)
Magnificat
Merry be man (vce and pf; also vce and org)
Nunc dimittis (unison vces and org) (Weinberger)
Rocking (vce, ww and pf)
Sing for Christmas (vce and pf)
Time to be merry (vce and pf)
Two canonic carols (vce, pf and wind)
Unto us is born a son, carol (2-part treble vce and pf or org) (Thames)
Venite, exultemus Domino (vce and org)

OPERA

Gaslight (1982) (comm Intermezzi Ensemble)

THEATRE

The Barnstormers, musical
The Family Tree
Kookoojoo and the Magic Forest, musical
Lee Street, school musical
The Miracle Masque, musical
Perseus, for children
The Trouble with Spells is ..., for children

MISCELLANEOUS

Merry be man
Pardon our rubbish, school work
Sonatina dolorosa
Women speaking

Ref. composer, 80, 563

ROE, Evelyn (Rothwell)

British composer. b. 1911.

Composition

ORCHESTRA

Concerto in C (ob and orch)

Ref. 280

ROE, Gloria Ann (nee Kliewer) (Mrs. R.E. Robertson)

American concert pianist and composer. b. Hollywood, CA, January 5, 1938. She studied at the Hollywood School of Music, the Screen Guild School of Music, Pasadena College and Trinity Conservatory, London. She made her debut as a concert pianist in 1949 appearing with Al Jolson and Eddie Cantor. She is a member of the Mennonite Church and gives concerts of sacred music in schools.

Compositions

SACRED

In the fullness of time, cantata
Abiding love
Be calm my soul
Coming home
Does it make any difference to you?
The greatest of these is Love
He is love
His grace is sufficient
How can I tell you, Father
So great salvation
Surrender
That's what He did for me
Unworthy
Why can't I say I'm sorry

Publications

Gloria Roe Choral Series.
Keyboard Favorite Series.

Ref. composer, 39, 40, 347

ROE, Helen Mary Gabrielle
English violinist and composer. b. Bournemouth, November 1, 1955. She obtained her B.A. hons. and B.Mus. (composition) from Oxford University (1977 and 1978). She studied the violin under Robert Best, 1969 to 1973, composition under David Lumsdaine, 1974 to 1976 and Peter Wiegold, 1976 to 1977. PHOTOGRAPH.
Compositions
CHAMBER
String quartet (1980)
Danse solitaire (d-b)
Notes towards a definition (vln)
PIANO
Ash Wednesday (1976)
Lightning's edge
VOCAL
Die blaue Blume (S and cham ens)
MISCELLANEOUS
Close by the place where
Paper/scissors ... rock
Ref. composer, British Info. Center, 263, 422, 457

ROE, Marion Adelle (Richards)
American organist, singer, teacher and composer. b. October 13, 1905. She studied privately under various teachers from the age of eight to 16. She studied at the American College of Music, Toledo, OH, from 1925 to 1930, and from 1930 to 1939 worked at the LaForge Music Studios in New York. In 1949 and 1958 she worked with Anton Schubel at the Opera Workshop in Cleveland, OH. She was organist at Grace Episcopal Church, Toledo from 1925 to 1930 and again from 1940 to 1946 and at the First Spiritualist Church, Toledo, from 1963 to 1971. She was the soprano soloist at St. Michael's in the Hills from 1959 to 1973. Her awards include honorary certification by the Ohio Music Teachers' Association, 1976. PHOTOGRAPH.
Compositions
ORCHESTRA
President's march (1963) (also band) (1964)
PIANO
Chinese confusion (1927)
The cuckoo clock (1928)
VOCAL
The eastern star (1939)
The golden eagle (1974)
Her little green parasol (A.V. Higgins) (1949)
Mother's evening prayer (Higgins) (1950)
My phonic singing horse (1974)
My wedding prayer (1948)
Ohio is dear to me (1967)
Pal of my memories (Higgins) (1927)
SACRED
Psalm 24
OPERETTA
Beyond the Blue (Higgins) (1947)
Publications
Golden Bel Canto. 1974.
We are Seven of Music Mansion. Edinburn, Book 1, 1952; Book 2, 1953; Book 3, 1964.
Ref. composer, 359

ROE, Richards. See ROE, Marion Adelle

ROE, Rothwell. See ROE, Evelyn

ROECKEL, Jane (nee Jackson) (Mrs. Joseph Leopold) (pseud. Jules de Sivrai)
English pianist, teacher and composer. b. 1834; d. Clifton, 1907. She studied the piano under Halle and Clara Schumann among others. She was the inventor of the 'pamphonia,' an appliance for learning the staves and clefs. She married Joseph Leopold Roeckel, a song writer.
Compositions
PIANO
Miranda, Shakespearean illustration No. 1 (Weekes)
Reverie-Mazurka (Leonard)
Taranteller Danse Russe
VOCAL
Mostyn (mix-ch)
Our King and Queen (S or T and vocal qrt; also ch) (Vincent)
Drifting on (vce and pf)
A village story (vce and pf)
Ref. 85, 276, 297, 347, 433

ROEDER, Toni
20th-century composer.
Composition
CHAMBER
Percussionsmarsch No. 1 (perc ens)
Ref. Otto Harrassowitz (Wiesbaden)

ROELOFSON, Emily B.
19th-century English composer.
Compositions
VOCAL
Songs incl.:
Christmas lullaby
Sands o' Dee
Sea shells
Ref. 276, 347

ROEMER, Hanne
Danish guitarist, pianist, saxophonist, musicologist, teacher and composer. b. 1949. After singing in the Danish Radio Girls' Choir from 1961 to 1963 she took a diploma in the piano in 1964. From 1968 until 1971 and from 1975 to 1977 she studied musicology at the University of Copenhagen. Between these periods she studied the guitar under Santiago Navasques and Karl Scheidt and at the Royal Danish Conservatory. In 1975 she began playing the saxophone and after playing in bands, founded a saxophone quartet. She taught at junior schools and music high schools in Copenhagen.
Compositions
BAND
Fodjord (1978)
Til Anaktoria (1975)
MISCELLANEOUS
Luk op for mord (1977)
Kom alle kvinder i dansen (1979)
Ref. Danish Music Info. Center

ROEPMAN, Johanna. See BORDEWIJK-ROEPMAN, Johanna

ROES, Carol
20th-century Hawaiian composer of children's songs.
Ref. 438

ROESGEN-CHAMPION, Marguerite Sara (pseud. Jean Delysse)
Swiss harpsichordist, pianist, teacher and composer. b. Geneva, January 25, 1894; d. Paris, June 30, 1976. She received her first music lessons from her mother, the singer Cecile Roesgen-Liodet. She studied the piano under Marie Panthis and composition under Ernest Bloch and Jaques-Dalcroze at the Geneva Conservatory graduating in 1913. She began a concert career as a harpsichordist, appearing with leading French orchestras, mainly in Paris, but also in Italy, Spain and Holland. In 1915 she returned to Geneva to teach at the conservatory and in 1926 moved to Paris where she devoted herself to composition. DISCOGRAPHY.
Compositions
ORCHESTRA
Aquarelles (hpcd and orch) (Paris: Senart, 1929)
Concertino (hpcd and orch) (1947)
Concerto grosso (hpcd, vln, vlc and orch) (1931)
Concerto (hp and orch) (1944)
Concerto moderne (hpcd and orch) (1931)
Concerto No. 1 (a-sax, hpcd, bsn and orch) (1938)
Concerto No. 2 (a-sax, hpcd, bsn and orch) (1945)
Introduction, sarabande et toccata (hpcd and orch) (1933)
Poème (vln and orch; also vln and pf or panpipes)
Rhapsody (pf and orch) (1944)
Three piano concertos
Faunesques, 3 symphonic poems (1929)
Overture (1970)
Fugue (hpcd ad lib and str orch) (1961)
Hymne (hpcd ad lib and str orch) (1961)
CHAMBER
Le cortège de l'arche (brass qnt) (1968)
Le'envoye de ciel (brass qnt) (1968)
Scherzo (str qrt)
String quartet (1931)
Danse rituelle (fl, hp and panpipes) (1943)

Trio (pastorale) (ob, vlc and pf) (1931)
Appassionato (vlc and pf)
Deux nocturnes (ob and org) (1948, 1953)
Liturgie (fl and hpcd) (1966)
Louanges (vln and hpcd) (1967)
Offrande mystique (fl and hp) (1967)
Sonata (fl and hpcd or pf) (1969)
Sonata (hn and pf)
Suite for two flutes
Suite française (fl and hp) (1937)
Elegie (org) (1932)
Flute sonata (1948)
Four suites (fl) (1964)
Violin sonata (1945)

HARPSICHORD
Berceuse (also pf) (Senart)
Bucoliques (Lemoine, 1937)
Etudes de sonorites (1967)
Pièces de clavecin (1934)
Pièces de clavecin en sonates
Sonatine (also pf) (1953)

PIANO
Conte bleu et or, 5 pieces (2 pf)
Sonata (2 pf) (1931)
Trois valses (2 pf) (1930)
Spoutnik (4 hands) (1971)
Etudes
Preludes
Quatre petites pièces (1937)
Suite faunesques
Three sonatas (1969-1972)

VOCAL
Cantata (T, fl and continuo) (1968)
Diane, cantata (N. Bernier)
Medee, cantata (Salabert)
La musette, cantata (Clerambault)
Three cantatas (L. Leo)
Cinq poèmes (vce and orch) (1937)
Georgiques (vce and orch) (1943)
Nymphes chasseresses (ch and orch) (Geneva, 1926)
Quatre chants arabes (fl and str orch) (1960)
Les amusements champêtres (Chedeville)
Cantique des Cantiques di re Salomone (vce and pf)
Cris (1961)
Deux melodies, genre ancien
Deux tercets (w-vces)
Herbies sentimentales (vce and pf) (1961)
Pannyre aux talons d'or (vce, fl and hp)
Six melodies (vce and pf)
Trois duos (m-S and Cont)
Trois melodies (S)
Songs

SACRED
Alleluia (vce, fl, vln, hp and continuo) (1967)
Psaume 121 (3 vces) (1961)
Motets

Ref. 14, 17, 26, 70, 76, 94, 96, 105, 193, 226, 322, 347, 552, 563

ROESSING, Helen

20th-century American composer of Pennsylvania. She composed piano pieces.
Ref. 40, 347

ROFE, Esther

Australian composer. b. 1904.

Compositions

CHAMBER
Lament for bass or alto flute (fl and pf)
Simply string pieces (with Margaret Sutherland q.v.) (Broadcast Music)

BALLET
L'amour enchantèe (orch; also 2 pf) (1950)
Mathinna (small orch) (1954)
Sea legend (1943)
Terra australis (1946)

VOCAL
London songs (Grant Volen) (1932)
Set of songs (Walter de la Mare)
The water nymph (1930)

Ref. Tasmanian Conservatory, 440, 442, 444

ROGATIS, Teresa de (Feninger)

Italian guitarist, pianist, lecturer and composer. b. Naples, October 15, 1893; d. January 8, 1979. She was considered a child prodigy and gave her first recital at the age of seven. She graduated with honors from the Conservatorio San Pietro at Majella in Naples, where she studied the piano, composition, counterpoint, harmony, conducting and voice. She embarked on a concert career and after a tour to Egypt, married and settled in Cairo. The late 1950s she helped to found the National Conservatory and taught the piano and guitar. In 1963 she went to Italy, where she continued her musical activities until late in life. Her son, the pianist Mario Feninger, founded the Teresa de Rogatis Foundation in the United States, devoted to the publication and distribution of her compositions.

Compositions

GUITAR
Balleto
Berceuse (Bologna: Venturi)
Canto arabo (1934) (Bologna: La Chitarra)
Gavotta della bambola (Milan: Il Plettro, 1920)
Mormorio della foresta (Milan: Vizzari, 1928)
Tremolo etude (ded G. Newton)
Vespro sui fiume

PIANO
Barcarola (1948)
Berceuse (1951)
The brook speaks (Ce que raconte la source) (1947) (ded M. Feninger)
Burlesca (1965)
Carillon de Noël
Colombine se plaint à pierrot
Dialogo d'amore alla fontana
Egypt Land (1946)
Elegia (1969)
Epave (1944)
Etude in C (1941)
Etude in E-Minor (1945)
Fatma danse (Milan: Curci, 1949)
Une fête au village
Feuille d'album (1944)
Gabbiani al tramonto (1971)
Gavotte et musette (1953)
The happy little horse
L'incantatore di serpenti (Curci, 1949)
Intermezzo (1961)
Je joue avec les Dieses ... les Bemols
Minuetto delle dame Gialle (Naples: L'Arte Pianistice, 1927)
Mirages (1941)
Momento capriccioso (1956)
Moonlight on the Nile
Nebbie (1950)
Octave Etude in A-Major (1943)
Octave Etude in D-Major (1941)
Oh! les gammes
Omaggio a Couperin (1948)
Ombre (1964)
Petits oiseaux, l'hiver est arrive
Piccola serenata (1961)
Pioggia (1959)
Pioggia d'autunno (1944)
Prelude and toccata (1943)
Presto (1960)
Ribellone (1960)
Racconto triste (1959)
Sonatina (1942)
Tarantella (1949)
Valse d'autrefois (1950)
Zufolata (1966)

VOCAL
M'amasti mai (Panzacchi) (vce and orch) (1912)
Aspettare (vce and orch) (1972)
Berceuse (vce and orch) (Venturi, 1953)
Canta ... (Rocco Pagliara) (vce and orch) (1918)
Chanson d'automne (Verlaine) (vce and orch) (1929)
L'eco (vce and orch) (H. Heine) (1917)
Fascino (vce and orch) (1916-1917)
Notturno (vce and orch) (Rocco Pagliara) (1918)
La rosa (vce and orch) (1913)
Senza te ... (vce and orch) (trans from Russian by G. Pagliara) (Curci, 1926)
Tes yeux (vce and orch) (H. Heine) (1959)
Vana Attesa, lyric scene (vce and orch) (1915)
Vocalise (vce and orch) (1959)

SACRED
Ave Maria (vce and pf) (1945)
O cuore divino (vce and pf) (1945)
O salutaris hostia (vce and pf) (1945)

TEACHING PIECES
Il maestro e l'allievo
Metodo per chitarra
Primi passi
Ref. Mario Feninger, 228

ROGER, Denise
French concert pianist and composer. b. Paris, January 21, 1924. She began her musical studies at the age of five. In 1933 she entered the Paris Conservatoire where she studied solfege under Mme. Massart. She received first prize (solfege) in 1934 and in that same year began to study the piano under Jeanne Chapard. She received first prize for the piano and continued her musical studies under Marguerite Long. In 1942 she won first prize in harmony and in 1948, first prizes for fugue and the piano. She studied composition under Henri Busser and continued her study of the piano under Yvonne Lefebure. In 1952 she became prize winner of the Concours International in Geneva. DISCOGRAPHY. PHOTOGRAPH.
Compositions
ORCHESTRA
Symphony for strings (1973)
Concerto (pf and orch) (1962)
Concertino (ob and orch) (1960)
Three romances (ob and orch)
Concertino (cl and str orch; also fl and str orch) (1964)
Complaintes, 5 melodies on poems by G. Apollinaire (fl, ob, cl, bsn, hp and str orch) (1957)
CHAMBER
Ballade (7 cl)
Adagio (str ens) (1981)
Diptyque (str ens) (1981)
Supplique (brass qnt) (1984)
String quartet No. 1 (1965)
String quartet No. 2 (1970)
Three movements (ob, cl, sax and bsn) (1984)
Three movements (4 cl) (1984)
Three movements (4 sax) (1984)
Three movements for reed quartet (1971)
Triptyque (4 trp) (1983)
Ciselures (pf, hn and hp) (1981)
In memoriam (3 trp) (1982)
Pieces in trio (ob, cl and bsn) (1961)
String trio (1967)
String trio No. 1 (1978)
String trio No. 2 (1979)
Trio (fl, vla and vlc) (1969)
Berceuse (cl and pf) (1981)
Cantilene (trp and pf) (1981)
Concert (vln and vla) (1966)
Concertino (cl and pf) (1979)
Concerto (sax and vlc) (1984)
Dialogues (bsn and pf) (1967)
Evocation (sax and pf) (1981)
Jardin poetique (ob and pf) (1983)
Légènde (bsn and pf) (1983)
Miniature (vln and pf) (1983)
Musique (fl and hp) (1981)
Ninna Nanna (fl and pf) (1982)
Sonata (vln and pf) (1971, 1978)
Trois romances (cl and pf) (1979)
Tableautin (vla and pf) (1983)
Contours (cl) (1979)
Etudes de concert (vlc) (1982)
Scintillements (cl) (1979)
Sonatine (fl) (1966)
Three movements for solo violin (1968)
Three pieces for clarinet (1981)
Three pieces for solo horn in F (1968)
Deux pieces (cl) (1979)
PIANO
Five pieces (1963)
Petite romance
VOCAL
Chanson de la Plus Haute Tour (mix-ch) (1982)
Offrandes (mix-ch, fl, ob, hpcd, vla and vlc) (Verlaine) (1966)
Le pont mirabeau (G. Apollinaire) (chil-ch a-cap) (1966)
Five melodies (Ronsard) (vce and fl) (1963)
A la santé, cycle of melodies (G. Apollinaire) (Bar) (1963)
Une allée du Luxembourg (Gerard de Nerval) (1964)
La blanche neige (G. Apollinaire) (1962)
Cite de Carcassonne (G. Apollinaire) (1964)
Le depart (G. Apollinaire) (1962)
Dissipabitur Capparis (P. Claudel) (1967)
Funerailles (G. Apollinaire) (1969)
Gaspard Hauser chante (P. Verlaine) (1963)
Gelée blanche (P. Claudel, according to Li Tai Pe) (1965)
Levé-toi ma compagne, ma belle, poem (extracts from Cantique des Cantiques, trans E. Dhorme) (vce, fl and hp)
Melodies on German texts, 2 poems (F. Hoelderlin) (1962)
La nuit originelle (Bar, fl, ob, vlc and pf) (1983)
Requiem (vce and str trio) (1978)
S'en est allée l'amante (G. Apollinaire) (1961)
Six melodies (H. von Hofmannsthal) (Bar) (1963)
Soleils couchants (P. Verlaine) (1963)
Three poems (Jan-Antoine de Baif) (vce, fl and hp) (1966)
Three poems (A. Rimbaud) (1966)
Two melodies (R. Rilke) (1949)
Two monodies (P. Verlaine) (Bar) (1965)
Two poems (Georg Trakl) (1962)
SACRED
Prière pour le dimanche matin, cantata (P. Claudel) (Bar, mix-ch and orch) (1967)
Liturgies intimes (Verlaine) (Bar, fl, cl and vlc) (1964)
Psalm VI (R. Brasillach) (Bar, fl, ob, vlc and hpcd) (1970)
Psaume (pour un mort) (1977)
Requiem (S, Bar and strs) (1965)
Ref. composer, Otto Harrassowitz (Wiesbaden), 649

ROGERS, Clara Kathleen (nee Barnett) (pseud. Clara Doria)
English singer, lecturer, writer and composer. b. Cheltenham, January 14, 1844; d. Boston, MA, March 8, 1931. She was the granddaughter of Robert Lindley, the song writer. She learned music from her parents at an early age. From 1856 she studied the piano at the Leipzig Conservatory under Moscheles and Plaidy; ensemble playing under David and Reitz; harmony under Papperitz and Richter; and singing under Goetze from 1858. After graduating in Leipzig she studied the piano in Berlin under Buelow and singing under Frau Zimmermann and from 1861 operatic singing in Italy under San Giovanni. In 1863 she made her debut at Turin as Isabella in *Roberto il Diavolo*, under her pseudonym and then sang in Genoa, Florence and at the San Carlo, Naples. In 1866 she went to London and in 1871 to the United States, appearing at the Academy of Music as Donna Elvira in *Don Giovanni* and in other roles. From 1902 she taught at the New England Conservatory.
Compositions
CHAMBER
String quartet
Sonata (vlc and pf)
Sonata in D-Minor, op. 25 (vln and pf) (Boston: A.P. Schmidt, 1903)
PIANO
Romanza, op. 31 (Boston: J.B. Millet, 1895)
Scherzo in A, op. 15 (1883)
VOCAL
Album of 14 songs
At break of day
Aubade, song (vln obb) (Schmidt, 1883)
Clover blossoms
Confessions
Five songs, op. 24 (1887)
The rose and the lily
Six songs (S and T) (Schmidt, 1882)
Six songs, op. 20 (Schmidt, 1884)
Six folk songs, op. 34 (Schmidt)
Three songs, op. 22 (1885) (Schmidt)
Years at the spring
Two collections of Browning songs
Publications
English Diction in Song and Speech. 1912.
Memories of a Musical Career. 1920.
My Voice and I. 1910.
The Philosophy of Singing. 1883.
The Voice in Speech. 1915.
Your Voice and You.
Ref. 102, 228, 276, 292, 297, 622

ROGERS, Emmy Brady. See ADDENDUM

0ROGERS, Ethel Tench (Mrs. Robert W.)
20th-century American organist, pianist, music director, teacher and composer. b. Newark, NJ, February 21, 1914. She studied privately under William Ichor, Arthur B. Kellsey, Howard Savage, Edward J. McGinley, Tsuyi Matsuki and Lorrene McClintock and at the Austrian-American Institute in Vienna. PHOTOGRAPH.
Compositions
ORGAN
Teaching pieces
Arrangements
PIANO
Autumn reverie
Fiesta
In olden days

Moonlit waters
Song of the night
Sparkling snowflakes
Sunset
Tarantelle
Valse romantique
Youthful dreams
Teaching pieces
Arrangements

SACRED
Jesus is born, cantata
Oh worship the King (mix-ch)
Oh Christmas day (mix-chs and opt chil-ch or soloist)
Angels from the realms of glory (vces and opt vln or fl obb)
Christmas joy, level one and level two, carols (Lillenas, 1984)
God's world is sure (vces)
Jesus calls us (vces)
Approx. 150 Anthems

Ref. composer, 40, 347, 625

ROGERS, Faith Helen

American organist, pianist, choral conductor and composer. b. Grand Junction, MI, May 10, 1886. She studied at the Oberlin Conservatory and under Adele aus der Ohe (q.v.) in Berlin. She conducted and gave recitals at Duluth, MN.

Composition

VOCAL
A ballad of trees and the master

Ref. 226

ROGERS, Melicent Joan

20th-century cellist, pianist, teacher and composer. b. Stoke Newington. She was a L.R.A.M. and taught the piano, the cello and theory from 1911 until 1935.

Compositions

CHAMBER
String quartet in E-Major
String quartet, miniature air and variations
Eltham Hill trios (vln, vlc and pf)
Lyric trio (vln, vlc and pf)
Pastoral and march (vln, vlc and pf)

VOCAL
Fifteen songs (pf)
Six songs (str grt)
Arrangements of folk songs for shepherd's pipe band

Ref. 467

ROGERS, Mrs. Robert W. See ROGERS, Ethel Tench

ROGERS, Patsy

American guitarist, pianist, recorder player, lecturer and composer. b. New York City, January 19, 1938. She studied under Henry Brant, Louis Calabro, Vivian Fine (q.v.), Iva Dee Hiatt and Lionel Nowak at Bennington College where she obtained her B.A. in 1960 and her M.A. in 1962. She has taught the piano, the guitar, the recorder and composition at a number of colleges and universities including the University of Massachusetts at Amherst, the United Nations International School in New York and the Antioch Graduate School, Keene, NH. In 1979 she was composer-in-residence at the Chamber Music Conference and Composers' Forum of the East. In 1981 she received a performance award at the First National Congress on Women in Music and in 1983 she won the Gladys Turk Song Search. PHOTOGRAPH.

Compositions

ORCHESTRA
Concerto (vla and orch) (1983)
Concerto (vln and orch) (1975)
Fanfare for chamber orchestra (ww, trp and str orch)
Bridges

CHAMBER
Dyadiastasis (fl, ob, cl, bsn, trp, trb, timp and perc)
Octet for the eight instruments of the new violin family
Ostinatia (ww, brass, perc, pf, hpcd, vln and vlc)
Wind octet
Proclamation piece (winds, brass and perc)
Fanfare for F.O.M.A.G. (ob, trp and hn)
Fortune cookies (vln, vla and vlc)
Trio (fl, vla and bsn)
Five duos (cl and vlc)
Threads - a Ssudy in percussion sonorities for two players (perc)
Wedding march: Processional; Recessional (org and perc)
Relays (vln)
Suite of short pieces for alto recorder

VOCAL
For Betty Crocker (w-ch, pf and perc or cham orch) (comm Anna Crusis Women's Choir) (1982)
In celebration (S, A, B and cham orch) (1976)
Crabbed age and youth (mix-ch and insts)
Follow thy fair sun (mix-ch and insts)
Chinese songs (S, vla and vlc)
The man with the blue guitar (S, vlc, cl and pf)
Seven macabre songs (S, T and pf)
Six French songs (S and pf) (1975)
Sonja (S and pf) (comm Wendy G. Hill) (1983)
Spaghetti: A round (mix-ch and pf) (Eve Merriam)
Three songs (S and pf) (Adrienne Rich) (1980)
Woman songs (S and pf) (1975)

SACRED
Chapel service for Iva Dee Hiatt
A Christmas overture: Festival of carols
Four choral amens (mix-ch)
Hymn (mix-ch; also vce and org)

BALLET
Crayons (cham ens) (1979)
How the elephant got its trunk (cham ens) (1978)

OPERA
Woman Alive: Conversation against Death (Eve Merriam) (1977)

THEATRE
A Husband's Notes about Her (Merriam) (1979)

INCIDENTAL MUSIC
The Tempest (Shakespeare)

ARRANGEMENTS
Adagio from Haydn's baryton trio No. 83
Das Buch der haengenden Gaerten (Schoenberg)
Requiem (Faure)

Ref. composer, 465, 474, 622, 625

ROGERS, Sharon Elery

20th-century American organist, choir conductor, teacher and composer. b. Grosse Pointe, MI, April 3. She began her studies at Detroit Conservatory in 1929. She received a B.A. from Hillsdale College and pursued graduate studies in composition and theory at Wayne State University. She was organist and choir director of several choirs at Mt. Zion Lutheran Church. She taught music in public schools.

Compositions

ORGAN
Contemporary organ settings on familiar hymns (Hope)
Festival hymn variations for the Church year (Sacred Music Press)
Preludio festivo (Flammer-Shawnee, 1965)
Solera toccata (Flammer-Shawnee, 1968)

SACRED
Over 100 published pieces incl.:
O my dearest Jesus, cantata or separate anthems (2-part or unison ch) (Sacred Music-Lorenz, 1968)
All hail that festive day of days (mix-ch and opt trps and timp) (Bourne, 1963-1964)
The Babe of Bethlehem (mix-ch and opt handbells) (Bourne, 1967)
The bells on Easter Morn (w-ch and opt handbells) (Bourne, 1968)
Blessed art thou (Benedictus ex, Domine) (mix or 2-part ch) (Flammer-Shawnee, 1968)
Born in a manger (mix and w-ch) (Flammer-Shawnee, 1962, 1976)
Celebration of Holy Eucharist (mix-ch) (Capella, 1972)
A chant of glory and praise (mix or w-ch) (Flammer-Shawnee, 1968)
Christus natus hodie (mix-ch) (Flammer-Shawnee, 1967)
Come as a child (2-part ch) (Hope, 1973)
A contemporary Noel (mix-ch) (Flammer-Shawnee, 1969)
Easter triumph (mix-ch and opt brass and timp) (Flammer-Shawnee, 1969)
Hear the sounds of the shepherds' piping (mix-ch and opt fl) (Bourne, 1970)
Mass to the glory of God (mix-ch) (Capella, 1968)
O brother man (mix or m-ch) (Flammer-Shawnee, 1964)
O be joyful in the Lord (Jubilate Deo) (mix or 2-part ch) (Flammer-Shawnee, 1967)
O come and mourn with me (mix-ch) (Hope, 1969)
The shepherds had an angel (2-part or unison ch and opt handbells) (Flammer-Shawnee, 1969)
Song of triumph (mix-ch and opt brass and timp) (Flammer-Shawnee, 1968)
Thanksgiving harvest song (mix-ch and opt trps) (Stone Chapel, 1968)
What star is this (mix-ch and opt handbells) (Stone Chapel, 1968)

Ref. composer, 395

ROGERS, Susan Whipple

American horn player, teacher and composer. b. Dallas, August 15, 1943. She won scholarships to the University of Texas, Arlington, where she studied under Lloyd Tagliaferro and for the Centenary College of Louisiana for study under Rule Beasley. She also studied privately under Edward Kozak. She taught the horn from 1960.

Compositions

CHAMBER

Trio (hn, cl and pf)
Suite (hn and pf)
Pentatonic suite (pf)

Ref. 142

ROGET (Roget-Puig, Puig-Roget), Henriette

French organist, pianist, professor and composer. b. Bastia, Corsica, January 9, 1910. She studied at the Paris Conservatoire under M. Dupre (organ) and H. Busser (composition) and won first prizes for harmony, fugue, the organ, the piano, history and accompaniment. She won the second Prix de Rome in 1933. She became organist at the Oratoire du Louvre St. Clothilde and the Great Synagogue from 1934 to 1952 and from 1957 was professor of accompaniment and score reading at the Paris Conservatoire. She frequently performed on French radio and television and was a singing mistress at the opera. DISCOGRAPHY.

Compositions

ORCHESTRA

Symphonie pour rire (1947)
Concerto classique (vlc and orch)
Concerto sicilien (pf and orch) (1943)
Montanyas del Rosello (org and orch) (1933) (Baron)
Rajoles (1955)
Rhythmes (1937)
Sinfonia andorrana (1936)

CHAMBER

Fantasia eroica (vlc and pf)
Patchwork, 5 pieces (hpcd)

ORGAN

Cortège funèbre
Deux prières (1934) (Paris: Lemoine)
Deploracion para la Semana Santa (1949)
Fantaisie sur des themes Hebraiques
Toccata severa
Triathlon, 3 pieces (1977)

PIANO

Pieces incl.:
Marine
Numerous teaching pieces for children

VOCAL

Hymnes à l'aviation (1937) (prize, Paris Exhibition)
Choral works (w-ch and chil-ch)
Nineteen poems (Tagore)
Three ballades françaises (Paul Fort)
Songs

BALLET

Catherinettes (1937)

OPERA

Master of Song (1957)

MISCELLANEOUS

Music for radio

Bibliography

Machabey, A. *Portraits de Trente Musiciens Français*. Paris, 1949.

Ref. 13, 14, 15, 17, 22, 70, 96, 193, 280, 465, 477, 563

ROGET-PUIG, Henriette. See ROGET, Henriette

ROHDE, Q'Adrianne (pseud. Dee Libbey)

20th-century American pianist and composer. b. Deland, FL, November 1. She obtained her B.Mus. from Stetson University in Florida, where she supervised students of the piano. She also studied at the American University, Fontainebleau, France. She studied composition privately under Dr. Leo Sowerby in Chicago and Nadia Boulanger (q.v.) in Paris. PHOTOGRAPH.

Compositions

ORCHESTRA

Introspect, symphony in 1 mvt (1954) (also 2 pf)
The lost forest, tone poem (1950)

BAND

Percussive positive (1974)

CHAMBER

Orange moon (fl and pf) (1954)
Essence (pf) (1958)
Flute piece
Moving tides (hp) (1956)

VOCAL

Tolling bells (Bar, A and ch) (1970) (New York: Lawson-Gould, 1973)
Cry out (vce and ch)
Wee little boy (S and w-ch) (1970) (Lawson-Gould; G. Schirmer, 1972)
Mangoes, song (1957) (Redd Evans)
Silver bird, song (1965) (Comet)
Wild horses run free

SACRED

Give honor to God

OPERETTA

Gretchen's Dream, for children

BALLET

Bee learns to dance (pf and cel) (1953)
Set free (poem as background) (1953)

MISCELLANEOUS

Impressions of a leaking faucet

Ref. composer, 39, 40, 228, 347

ROHNSTOCK, Sofie

20th-century German composer.

Composition

CHAMBER

String trio in G-Major (Munich: Grosch, 1979)

Ref. Otto Harrassowitz (Wiesbaden)

ROHRER, Gertrude Martin

20th-century American composer. She composed an opera, choral works and songs.

Ref. 40, 347, 353

ROINE BLANCE. See BLANCHE DE CASTILLE

ROKSETH, Yvonne (nee Rihouet)

French organist, violinist, violist, editor, music librarian, musicologist, professor, writer and composer. b. Maisons-Laffitte, July 17, 1890; d. Strasbourg, August 23, 1948. She studied the violin at the Paris Conservatoire, the organ under Abel Decaux and composition under Vincent d'Indy at the Schola Cantorum. She later continued her composition studies under A. Roussel and after 1920 studied music history under A. Pirro of the Sorbonne. She took degrees in both science and letters. She was organist at the Lutheran Church of the Resurrection in Paris. From 1933 she was librarian at the Paris Conservatoire and in 1937 became professor of music at Strasbourg University, where she founded a choir and orchestra in which she played the viola. During World War II she was active in the Resistance movement and awarded a medal. After the war she lectured in Switzerland and Germany and gave courses at the American Institute of Music in Florence. She edited old French music for the Société Française de Musicologie and the Montpellier manuscript of 13th-century polyphonic music. She was particularly interested in the early French polyphonists and the Burgundian school. She married Pierre Rokseth, professor of philology at Oslo University.

Compositions

ORCHESTRA

Fantasy (pf and orch)

CHAMBER

String quintet
Violin sonata
Organ and piano pieces

VOCAL

Songs

SACRED

Te Deum (soloists, ch, org and orch) (1945)
Songs

Publications

Pirro A. *Revue de Musicologie* 26. 1944. Vol. 23.
Aimer la musique ancienne. Polyphonie 3. 1949.
Antonia Bembo. Music Quarterly 23. 1937.
Le contrepoint double vers 1248. In Melanges ... L. de La Laurencie. Publications de la Société française de musicologie, vol. 2, no. 3/4. Paris, 1933.
Danses clericales du XIIIe siècle. Publications de la Faculte des lettres de Strasbourg, no. 106. Paris, 1947.
Deux Livres d'Orgue parus chez P. Attaingnant. Publications de la Société française de musicologie, vol. 1. Paris, 1925.
Les femmes musiciennes du XIIe au XVe siecle. Romania 61. 1935.
Grieg. Paris, 1933.
The Instrumental Music of the Middle Ages and Early Sixteenth Century. In New Oxford History of Music, vol. 3.

Josquin des Pres, pedagogue musical. Revue de Musicologie 11. 1927.
Lamentations de la Vièrge au pied la Croix XIIIe siècle. 1937.
Les 'Laude' et leur edition par M. Liuzzi. Romania 65. 1939.
La Liturgie de la Passion vers la fin du Xe siècle. Revue de Musicologie 31-32. 1949-1950.
Un Magnificat de M.-A Charpentier. Journal of Renaissance and Baroque Music 1. 1946-1947.
Un Motet de Moulu. Basel: Kgr. Ber., 1924.
Motets du XIIIe siècle. 1936.
La Musique d'orgue au XVe siècle et au debut du XVIe.
Note biographique sur Attaingnant. Revue de Musicologie 8. 1923-1924.
La Polyphonie parisienne du troisieme siècle. Les Cahiers techniques de l'art 1 (1947).
Polyphonies du XIIIe siecle. Le manuscript H 196 de la Faculte de Medecine de Montpellier. 4 vols. with fascimiles, transcriptions, and critical comment. Paris, 1935-1939.
Les premiers chants de l'eglise calviniste. Revue de Musicologie 36. 1954.
Reaction de la Reforme contre certains elements realistes du culte. Revue d'histoire et de philosophie religieuses, 26. 1946.
Six Motets a jouer sur le pipeau. Paris, 1934.
Une Source peu étudiée d'iconographie musicale. Revue de Musicologie 17. 1933.
Translation into French of *Einfuehrung in die Musikgeschichte*, by K. Nef. Paris, 1925, 1931; Lausanne, 1944.
Trois chansonniers français du XVe siècle. Vol. 1. 1927.
Trois motets et un prelude pour orgue parus chez P. Attaingnant et 1531. Publications de le Société française de musicologie. 1930.

Bibliography

Fedorov, V. *A. Pirro und Yvonne Rokseth*. 1950.
Fitzsimmons, Patricia Sue. *A Translation of a Commentary on La Musique d'orgue aux XVe siècle et au debut du XVIe*. University of Rochester.
Thibault, G. *Yvonne Rokseth*. Revue de Musicologie. 1948.

Ref. 2, 8, 14, 15, 17, 20, 86, 100, 112, 226, 347, 361, 391

ROLDOS FREIXES, Mercedes

Spanish pianist, teacher and composer. b. Barcelona, 1910. She studied under Maria Colbeto and Mas y Serracant (composition) and improved her playing technique under Marshall. She later taught at his academy. She gave numerous recitals from a very early age and made her public debut in 1921 at the Sala Granados. She composed piano pieces.
Ref. 107

ROMA, Caro (Carrie Northey)

American authoress, singer and composer. b. East Oakland, CA, September 10, 1886; d. East Oakland, CA, September 23, 1937. She studied at the New England Conservatory in Boston and graduated in 1890. She appeared with the Castle Square Opera Company in Boston and sang at the Tivoli Opera House in San Francisco for eight years. She toured Canada, the United States and England. In London she sang with the Turner Grand Opera and was presented with a medal by Queen Victoria.

Compositions

VOCAL
Over 1000 published songs incl.:
Can't yo' hear me calling?
The swan, song cycle
The wandering one, song cycle

OPERA
God of the Sea

Publications

June the 16th.
Other Idle Moments.
Some Idle Moments.

Ref. 74, 292, 347

ROMANA, Francesca Campana. See CAMPANA, FRANCESCA.

ROMER, Hanne. See ROEMER, Hanne

ROMERO BARBOSA, Elena

Spanish pianist, conductor and composer. b. Madrid, 1880. She studied the piano under Frank Marshall and composition under Juan Lamote de Grignon and Joaquin Turina. She gave her first piano concert when she was nine. She conducted her own orchestral compositions and performed with various Spanish symphony orchestras and for the Madrid National Radio.

Compositions

ORCHESTRA
Balada de Castilla (pf and orch)
En el cuarto de los ninos
Penibetica, small suite
Pequeña Suite

CHAMBER
Quartet (str qrt)
Cancion de cuna (vln)
Canto a Turina (pf)
Two sonatas (hpcd)

BALLET
Titres

Ref. 60, 107

ROMITELLI, Sante Maria

20th-century composer.

Compositions

FILM MUSIC
The Profiteer (1974)
A Virgin named Mary (1975)

Ref. 497

ROMM, Rosalia Davidovna

Soviet-Yakuts writer, lecturer and composer. b. Chkalov, South Urals, February 24, 1916. In 1938 she graduated from the Music School in Moscow, where she studied under V. Shebalin and in 1945 graduated from the conservatory. From 1955 to 1975 she taught at the Moscow School of Music. She married the composer Genrik Litinsky.

Compositions

ORCHESTRA
Concertino (pf and orch) (1965)
Concertino (cl and orch) (1971)
Piano concerto (1971)
Overture on Russian and Yakuts themes (1956)
Overture on Yakuts themes (1949)
Churumchuku, Yakuts legends (1962)
Four miniatures on Olonkho themes (1946-1970)
Four symphonic miniatures (1970)
Intermezzo on Yakuts themes (1955)
Poem to the memory of Gastello (1945)
Yakuts suite (1947)

CHAMBER
String quartet No. 1 (1940)
String quartet No. 2 (1946)
String quartet No. 3 (1966)
Concert suite (trp and pf) (1973)
Pieces in 24 tonalities (vln and pf; also vlc and pf, 1975; also trp and pf, 1970; also hp, 1973; also bayan, 1974)
Rhapsody on Jewish themes (cl and pf) (1942)
Tri novelli (vln and pf) (1958)
Yakuts pictures (vln and cl) (1972)
Sonatina (hp) (1955)

VOCAL
Suita igr (chil and w-ch and orch) (1971)
Yakuts tale of Lenin (Suorina Omollona) (soli, ch and orch) (1968)
Osen (Ellyai) (chil-ch) (1949)
Po zemlye shagayut deti (K. Galchinsky) (chil-ch)
Pro vysotnyi dom (A. Argo) (chil-ch) (1954)
Silnoye kino (A. Barto) (ch) (1972)
Three Yakuts songs (S. Bolotin, T. Sikorska) (ch) (1949)
Mukhi beluye letel (M. Rylski) (1955)
Zayats-belyak (M. Lapigina) (vce and pf) (1955)

Publications

Izuchenie tonalnostei v detskikh muzykalnykh shkolakh. 1970.
Muzykalnaya gramota v forme zadanii i voprosov k notnym primeram. 1966.

Ref. 21, 70, 79, 87, 94, 330

RON, Helene de

Swedish composer. b. 1840; d. 1912.

Compositions

VOCAL
Erotisk elegie, klagan: Klaga ej mera foer Muncken ...; Troest; Fritt ma sirocon kring oronen pipa, E-Minor (ded Mme. Caroline Lundewall)
Du aer min ro, in B-Minor (Z. Topelius) (2 transposed versions, G-Minor and C-Minor)
Larkroester i Maj, O du lummiga lund! (Z. Topelius) (transposed version B-Minor) (ded Augusta Hallgren)

Ref. 167

RONALDS, Belle
19th-century American composer of songs.
Ref. 276, 347, 433

RONDONNEAU, Elise
19th-century French composer.
Compositions
CHAMBER
Andante et villanelle (har and pf) (Mustel)
Chanson bretonne (har and org) (Lemoine)
Nenia, élègie (org and har) (Lemoine)
Piangera, élègie (org and har) (Lemoine)
Un rêve (org and har) (Lemoine)
Lamento (Mustel)
Nocturne (Mustel)
Two improvisations (Mustel)
PIANO
Ardennaises, valse brillante (Gallet)
Fleurs du nord (Gallet)
Jenny, valse (Gallet)
Mazurka de salon (Lebeau)
Polka-mazurka (Lebeau)
Risoluta, valse (Gallet)
Sophronie, valse (Gallet)
VOCAL
Adieu, Savoie! (Katto)
Brune fleur d'Italie (Katto)
Coulez mes jours (Kistner)
J'ai remplace frère (Katto)
J'aime mieux mon village (Katto)
Mes amours de toujours: Depuis que sous l'ombrage (Kistner; Schott)
Mon étoile d'amour (Katto)
Mon étoile d'amour: Lorsque le jour se voile (Kistner)
Mort du patre (Katto)
Notre Baronne (Unsere Graefin) (with pf in G) (Schott)
Ou tu serais (Katto)
Page de Monseigneur (Katto)
Pays de mes amours (Katto)
Prière des pecheurs (Katto; Kistner)
Yvonée (Katto)
Ref. 297

RONELL, Ann
American conductor, lyricist, singer, teacher and composer. b. Omaha, NE, December 25, ca. 1910. She studied at Radcliffe College, Cambridge and thereafter spent a short period teaching music and singing.
Compositions
VOCAL
Willow weep for me (1932)
OPERA
Oh! Susanna
BALLET
Magic of spring
FILM MUSIC
Algiers (1938)
Champagne Waltz (1937)
Commandos Strike at Dawn (1942)
The Story of G.I. Joe (1945)
Ref. 610, 622

RONSSECY, Mme. de
19th-century French harpist and composer.
Compositions
HARP
Andantino, variations (London: S. Straight, ca. 1800)
Lullaby (S. Storace, adapted by Mme. de Ronssecy) (Straight, ca. 1800)
Scotch air, variations (Straight, ca. 1800)
Scotch tune, variations (Straight, ca. 1800)
Shepherds I have lost my love, variations (Straight, ca. 1800)
Minuetto, variations
Ref. 65, 128

RONTGEN, Amanda (nee Maier)
Swedish violinist and composer. b. Landskrona, February 19, 1853; d. Amsterdam, July 15, 1894. She studied at the Stockholm Conservatory from 1869 to 1872 and then became a pupil of concertmaster Engelbert Rontgen in Leipzig, where she married his son Julius Rontgen, a pianist and composer. They moved to Amsterdam and gave many recitals together.
Compositions
CHAMBER
Piano quintet
Sonata in B-Minor (vln and pf) (1877)
Swedish dances, op. 16 (vln and pf)
Violin pieces
Ref. 44, 74, 95, 276, 433

ROOBENIAN, Amber (nee Harrington) (Mrs. W. Clark) (pseud. Jane Murdoch)
American organist and composer. b. Boston MA, May 13, 1905. She studied at the New England Conservatory under Henry Dunham, 1924 to 1925, and the Eastman School of Music, 1926 to 1927. She played the organ in churches and cinemas for three years.
Compositions
ORGAN
Samarkand
VOCAL
In an old English garden (ch)
Two red roses across the moon (ch)
The tryst (ch)
Vigil (ch)
The willow tree (ch)
Mother never told me
MISCELLANEOUS
Antique air
Concertino espagnol
Desert solitude
Long gone jublo
Reverie
Ref. 39, 142, 494

ROOT, Grace W.
19th-century American composer.
Compositions
VOCAL
Songs incl.:
For thee
The spell of the waltz
Sunset
Ref. 276, 292, 433

ROOTH, Anna-Greta
Swedish pianist and composer. b. Oxeloesund, February 8, 1901. She began her piano studies at the age of seven and from 1919 to 1920 studied the piano, voice and harmony at the Music Conservatory of Stockholm. Her songs were performed on Swedish radio. PHOTOGRAPH.
Compositions
CHAMBER
From the Dalecarlia forests (ob, fl, cl, bsn and hn; also pf, 1940)
Andante, alegretto and allegro (fl and pf) (1970)
VOCAL
Beber (Gabriela Mistra) (vce and pf) (1950)
Balacla, ballad (Mistra) (vce and pf) (1950)
Meciendo (Mistra) (vce and pf) (1950)
El corro luminoso (Mistra) (vce and pf) (1950)
Ten poems (Chinese poets of the Yang dynasty) (vce and pf) (1970-1985)
Thirty to forty songs (Swedish poets) (vce and pf) (1940-1970)
Ref. composer

ROSALES, Cecilia
19th-century Spanish lecturer, poetess and composer. b. Orense; d. Orense. She wrote articles in *La Espana Musical* and composed mainly for the violin, the flute, the harp and the double bass, plus sacred pieces for four and six voices with harp accompaniment.
Ref. 389

ROSALINA, Ana
20th-century composer.
Composition
FILM MUSIC
The Woman of Everyone (1970)
Ref. 326

ROSAS FERNANDES, Maria Helena
Brazilian pianist, choral conductor, lecturer and composer. b. Brazopolis, July 8, 1933. She studied the piano at the Brazilian Conservatory of the State of Guanabara, graduating in the higher piano course in 1964. She studied composition under O. Lacerda, receiving a bachelor's degree in composing and conducting from the Escola Superior de Musica Santa Marcelina in São Paulo in 1977. Her teachers included Noemi Perugia, Julio Medaglia and João de Souza Lima. At the University of Coampinas she studied music education, conducting, composition and vocal technique under H.J. and Margarita Koellreuter, Jose Antonio de Almeida Prado and Yulo Brandão. She taught theoretical subjects in teachers' training colleges, conservatories and schools and conducted children's choirs.
Compositions
CHAMBER
Dwawa Tsawidi (winds and perc) (1979)
Cantilena No. 1 (fl and pf) (1974)
Piece for violin and piano (1981)
Territorio e ocas (gtr and perc) (1979)
PIANO
Ciclo (1979)
Estudos (1976)
VOCAL
Marawawa (S, m-S, mix-ch, narr, 4 fl, 3 hn and perc) (1978)
Children's choruses
Ciclo do sol e dos strelas (1977)
Ref. composer

ROSATI, Elvira
Italian harpist and composer. She composed for the harp.
Ref. 86

ROSATO, Clorinda
Brazilian organist, pianist, teacher and composer. b. São Simao, December 11, 1913. She studied under Alice Ornellas and later at the Conservatorio Dramatico Musical of São Paulo under A. Candido (solfege), A. Pereira (harmony) and A.A. Gallo (elements). She gave her first recital in 1932 and graduated in 1933. She studied composition privately under F. Mignone and M. Braunwieser, the piano under F. Viana analysis under F. Frenceschini (1934 to 1935) and the organ under Ines de Campo (1950). She performed in concerts and recitals until 1965 when she retired to teach.
Compositions
CHAMBER
Quatro ensaios (str qrt) (1936)
Improviso (vln, vlc and pf) (1936)
PIANO
Anjo da guarda (1962)
Baby (1942)
Brinquedo de roda (1934)
Caximbobo (1935)
Chaconne (1943)
Dança do caboclo (1933)
Dance movement (1935)
Seresta (1939; also vce and pf, 1940)
Sonata (1942)
Valsa afetuosa (1956)
Valsinha (1938)
Waltz No. 1 (1933)
Waltz No. 2 (1939)
Waltz No. 3 (1940)
VOCAL
Engenho novo (ch) (1935)
Tatu e caboclo do sul (ch) (1937)
Quatro corais (prize, São Paulo, 1937)
Seresta (vce and pf) (1940)
SACRED
Ave Maria (ch) (1939)
Impressões sobre uma missa de Ano Santo (1950)
Natal brasileiro (1954)
Ref. 333

ROSCO, B. Jeanie (Mrs. Bumpus) (B. Jeanie Groh)
American pianist, teacher and composer. b. Wilbur, WA, November 27, 1932. She was interested in music from an early age and pursued her studies under Erwin Freundlich at the Juilliard School of Music, Constance Keene the concert pianist and Randolf Holkanson at the University of Washington. At Whitworth College she studied under Mrs. Franklin W. Ott and at Washington State University commenced composition study under Dr. Loran Olsen in 1966. She teaches the piano and concertises.
Compositions
ORCHESTRA
Piano concerto
CHAMBER
Five pieces (brass qrt) (1968)
PIANO
Capriccio two (1968)
Escapades (1975) (C. Fisher)
Spectrums (1975) (Fisher)
Three dimensions
Tone poem (1968)
Whimseys (1966) (Fisher)
SACRED
High Mass
Ref. composer, 40, 347, 494

ROSE (pseud of E. Rosenthal)
19th-century Russian composer.
Compositions
OPERA
Held Marko
Tizianello (ca. 1860)
Ref. 307

ROSE OF JESUS, Sister (pseud. of Francis Sabine Gately)
American organist, pianist, lecturer, writer and composer. b. Assinaboine, MT, April 14, 1893. She studied at Gonzaga University from 1926 to 1927, at the University of Washington where she graduated with her B.M. (1930) and her M.A. (1932) and at the University of California, Los Angeles (1947). Her piano teachers included Gendreau at Missoula, Dierke in Portland, William H. Sherwood at Chicago and Harold Bauer at Mills College. She began teaching in 1917 and continued until 1945 when she joined the faculty of Lourdes Academy in Wallace, Idaho where she held the position of supervisor of music.
Compositions
ORCHESTRA
Symphonic triptych (1932)
Suites
Eighty-four opuses
CHAMBER
String quartets
Oriental customs (1930)
VOCAL
Masses, motets and choral works
Publications
Musical Mileage 1940. Under pseud.
Ref. 496

ROSE, Sister Caroline
20th-century American composer.
Compositions
VOCAL
Songs
SACRED
Mass in honour of St. Joseph (1964)
Cantata
Ref. 465

ROSENBACH, Ulrike
20th-century West German composer.
Composition
MULTIMEDIA
Konzert im Gewaltakt Nr. 2
Ref. Frau und Musik

ROSENHOFF, Orla
Danish organist, pianist, lecturer and composer. b. October 1, 1844; d. June 4, 1905. She lived in Copenhagen and after 1859 was a pupil of Nils Gade in theory, composition and the organ. For many years she was a teacher of the piano and theory at the Copenhagen Conservatory where her pupils included Carl Nielsen and Hilda Sehested (q.v.).
Compositions
CHAMBER
String sextet
String quintet
Fantasy pieces (ob and pf)

PIANO
Hinein zum Weihnachtsbaum!, march (6 hands) (Hansen)
Pedalstudier
Smaastudier paa fem toner, op. 5 (Hansen)
Thirty smaastykker (Hansen)
Teaching pieces
VOCAL
Songs incl. 4 vols (vce and pf)
Ref. 20, 113, 297, 331

ROSENTHAL, E. See ROSE

ROSENTHAL, Pauline (nee Emanuel)
German conductor, teacher and composer. b. Aachen, 1845; d. Kassel, 1912. As a young girl she attended the Cologne Conservatory. From 1869 she lived in Hanover, Germany, where her home was frequented by the violinist Joseph Joachim and other distinguished musicians. In 1882 she went to South Africa, settled in the Cape Colony and became the leading local figure in musical affairs: She was a performer and conductor of the choral society and taught. She returned to Germany in 1907.
Compositions
VOCAL
Golden wedding (Lady Gill) (Leipzig: Breitkopf and Haertel, 1897) (ded Lord Milner)
Volkslied (Lady Gill) (Breitkopf, 1897) (ded Lord Milner)
Ref. Eric Rosenthal (Cape Town)

ROSENWEIG, Florence
Composition
VOCAL
Where the blue Danube flows (vce and pf)
Ref. 63

ROSET, Mme.
18th-century French composer. An opera of the same name and possibly hers, was performed in Moscow in 1789.
Composition
OPERA
L'Heureuse rencontre (Mme. Chaumont) (1771)
Ref. 436

ROSS, Clara
Compositions
CHAMBER
Larghetto (3 man and pf)
Sancta Maria, melody (1 or 2 vln and pf; also 1 or 2 man and pf) (Chanot)
Air de ballet (man and pf)
Andante cantabile (man and pf)
Arioso (man and pf)
Aubade (man and pf)
Automne, impromptu (man and pf)
Ballet des fées (man and pf)
Barcarolle (man and pf)
Cabaletta (man and pf)
Corona (man and pf)
Crepuscule (man and pf)
Danse pastorale (man and pf)
Dawn (man and pf)
Gioventu (man and pf)
Gracieuse (man and pf)
Hush (man and pf)
Ideal, melody (man and pf)
Marguerites (man and pf)
Memoires d'amour (man and pf)
A memory (man and pf) (Turner)
Narcisse, romance (man and pf)
On wings of song (Mendelssohn) (man and pf; also man)
Pas des cymbales (man and pf)
Poèsies musicales (man and pf)
Preghiera (man and pf)
Primavera (man and pf)
Rêve de bonheur (man and pf)
Rêve d'ete (man and pf)
Révèrie (man and pf)
Révèrie poetique (man and pf)
Serenade (man and pf; also man)
Sicilienne (man and pf)
Sonnet d'amour (man and pf)
Vie d'une fleur
Ref. 297

ROSS, Gertrude
20th-century American pianist and composer. b. Dayton, OH. She studied music in the United States and Germany.
Compositions
VOCAL
Songs incl.:
Down in the desert
Night in the desert
Ref. 292, 347

ROSSELLI-NISSIM, Mary
Italian painter, sculptor and composer. b. Florence, June 9, 1864; d. Viareggio, September 26, 1937. She studied music under her mother, Janet Nathalm Rosselli and Giuseppe Menichetti (composition). In 1896 she devoted herself to painting and sculpture and won several international prizes. In 1911 she returned to music and gained considerable fame from her songs.
Compositions
VOCAL
Canzone anacreontica (B, ch and orch)
Gran coro eroico (Garaglio) (ch and orch)
A gli Alpini d'Italia (A. Baccelli)
Avventuroso Augello, madrigal
Barcarola
Canzonetta
Casetta bianca
Cavallino, scherzetto
Dolce Aprile
Eran cinquanta (Orazio Grandi)
Gira la ruota come l'amor (Milan: Carisch & Janichen)
Le gaga
L'homme beau
Le petit homme grès
Le petit Japonais
Povero grillo, canzonetta populare fiorentina (ch ad lib)
Preghiera delle donne italiane (Federico Sanmartino)
Veneziana, barcarola: Le stele se specia ridendo nel mar (Brocco)
Voglio rubare, 17th-century madrigal (Carisch)
OPERA
Andrea del Sarto (A. Lega, from drama by A. Musset) (1931)
Fiamme, in 3 acts (G. Forzano) (1915)
Max, in 2 acts (with G. Menichetti) (G. Golisciani) (1898)
Nephta, in 1 act (1896) (hon mention, Steiner Competition, Vienna)
Ref. 86, 105, 225, 226, 297, 307

ROSSER, Annetta Hamilton
20th-century American composer.
Compositions
CHAMBER
Bagatelle (fl and pf) (Madison: Gilbert, 1977)
Bird song (fl and pf) (Gilbert, 1977)
Dialogue for flute and violin (Gilbert, 1977)
Flute in the night (fl and pf) (Gilbert, 1977)
Lullaby for an April baby (pf and vln) (Gilbert, 1977)
Meditation (ob and vln) (Gilbert, 1977)
ORGAN
Alleluia, sing and rejoice (Gilbert, 1977)
Holy innocents (Gilbert, 1977)
VOCAL
An offering of a song (S or m-S or T or Bar and fl or rec) (Gilbert, 1977)
Tears, idle tears (m-S or Bar and pf) (Gilbert, 1977)
SACRED
Meditations on the cross (S and m-S or S and Bar and org) (1977)
Ref. 228

ROSSI, Camilla de
18th-century Italian composer. b. Rome. She composed for the court of Vienna. Her works are preserved at the State Library, Vienna.
Compositions
SACRED
Il figliulo prodigo, oratorio (Rin Ciallis or composer) (1709)
Il sacrificio di Abramo, oratorio (Francesco Maria Dario) (1708)
Santa Beatrice d'Este, oratorio (1707)
Cantatas (2 vces and insts)
Sant'Alessio (petr. Ber. Palmaro) (1710)
Ref. 105, 128

ROSSI, Countess. See SONTAG, Henriette

ROSSINI, Sra. Gioacchino. See COLBRAN, Isabella Angela

ROSSO, Carol L.

American pianist, violinist, conductor, lecturer and composer. b. Santa Monica, CA, July 31, 1949. She was introduced to music at an early age by her mother, Rosann Lynette Harris Rosso, who was a pianist, organist and cellist. Carol received her early training in theory, the piano and the violin at preparatory schools in California. She studied Oriental music at Los Angeles City College and graduated from the Immaculate Heart College in Hollywood, where she specialized in theory, serial composition, the piano and conducting. She did advanced study at the California Institute of the Arts, where she taught the piano and theory and concentrated on the music of Indonesia and Africa. She taught at the Mills College Contemporary Music Center. She obtained her M.A. from Mills College, where she participated in composition and electronic music seminars and became a specialist in composition, electronic music and film production. She became familiar with North Indian raga singing and theatre lighting. She studied under Eva Naiditch Cooper and attended piano master classes with Leonid Hambro, Carol Rosenberger, Lucy Vasquez and John Ringgold; she also studied conducting under Robert Cole and voice under Dean Voorhies and Gloria Steppe. Among her composition teachers were Dorrance Stalvey, Terry Riley and David Behrman. She studied gamelan music privately under Ki Wasidipuro, Njomen Wenton and Oemartapo. She also studied African music under Nicolas M. England and Alfred Ladzekpo and Dzidogbe Lawluvi, concentrating on Ewe drumming dance and singing from Ghana.

Compositions

CHAMBER

Liberatus ad vinculas Corpus, Requiem tibiis solum (fl) (1975)

VOCAL

He wishes for the clothes of heaven (fl and w-ch)

ELECTRONIC

Overtone modulation (buchla syn) (1976)

Timbral improvisations (buchla syn) (1976)

MULTIMEDIA

Glass lights, reflections and refractions (glass sculpture, electronic music and film) (1975)

Ref. composer, 625

ROST, Emilie

Late 18th-19th-century German composer.

Compositions

VOCAL

Three songs (W. Kritzinger) (Erfurt)

Ref. 128

ROSWITHA. See HROSWITHA

ROTH-DALBERT, Anny. See DALBERT, Anny

ROTHSCHILD, Matilde, Baroness Willy de

19th-century French composer. Her songs were widely performed.

Compositions

VOCAL

Songs incl.:

Adieu (Durand; Chappell)

Ah! que son jeune coeur (Enoch)

Appelle-moi ton âme

Baechlein, dessen reine Welle

Bei Dir

Chant de la mer noire

Coquetterie

Fels und Moos

Les papillons (Durand)

Partez, cherchez un ciel plus bleu

Un rêve de bonheur (Durand)

Romance magyare

Rose de bruyère (Durand)

Si vous n'avez rien à me dire (Durand; Cranz; Chappell; Ricordi; Schirmer)

Souvenir

Tristesse

Wenn du ein Heinz

Ref. 226, 297, 347, 433

ROTHWELL, Evelyn. See ROE, Evelyn

ROTTERIN ALHEIT

13th-century German mystic and composer. Formerly a traveling professional musician of low repute. After accompanying Elisabeth of Heisen on a journey she was inspired to devote her life to religion. In Engeltal near Nuremberg she collected a group of nuns around her for whom, in spite of it being forbidden by the pope, she wrote masses and liturgies. These became so popular that even pious men disregarded the pope's prohibition to listen to them, and promptly fell into ecstacy.

Ref. 476

ROUCH, Alma

Compositions

VOCAL

Ballade du frère Panuce, carol (Noel)

Deux chansons en Langue d'Oc: Ah! si mon coeur avait des ailes; Chanson d'Estelle

Chanson romantique

Moisson des lys (Labbe)

Pommiers, chanson rustique

Twelve melodies on old and modern poems (ded M. Ambroise Thomas):

Les cerisiers

La chanson du fou

Chanson d'un vanneur de ble aux vents

Les lendemains bluette

Madrigal

Les neiges d'antan (Ballade des dames du temps jadis)

Pensées de Byron

Le premier jour de mai

Romance du XVIe siècle

Rozette

Thérèse

Vacances passées

Ref. 297

ROUSSEAU, Louise

French composer. b. Cherbourg, November 7, 1854; d. November 16, 1924.

Composition

CHAMBER

Fantaisie and variations (pf or hpcd) (Paris: Pleyel, ca. 1825)

Ref. H. Baron (London)

ROUSSEAU, Louise Genevieve. See LA HYE, Louise Genevieve

ROWAN, Barbara

American pianist and composer. b. Colorado, 1932. She studied at Mills College, Oakland, CA, in Aspen, CA, and at the the Paris Conservatoire. Her piano teachers included Petri and she studied composition under Darius Milhaud.

Compositions

ORCHESTRA

Divertimento for strings

CHAMBER

Piano quintet

Quintet (fl, ob, cl, hn and cor anglais)

Fantasie (cl and pf)

Piano pieces

VOCAL

The dove descending breaks the air (w-ch and pf)

The hollow men, cantata (soli, ch and cham ens)

Oresteian trilogy of Aeschylus (S, 8 winds and pf)

Songs

Ref. 347

ROWE, Victoria

20th-century English composer.

Composition

CHAMBER

Suite for three recorders

Ref. 263

ROWSON, Susannah

American composer.

Composition

OPERA

Slaves in Algiers

Ref. American Music, vol 1, No. 2, 1983

ROYSE, Mildred Barnes

American pianist, teacher and composer. b. Illinois, February 9, 1896. She began piano lessons at an early age with her mother. She attended the American Conservatory, Chicago, from 1918 to 1920, studied harmony, counterpoint and composition and obtained her teacher's diploma. She did advanced study in harmony, musical form and orchestration at Columbia University, New York. From 1928 to 1932 she studied privately under the composers Walter Piston and Leo Sowerby. She taught the piano and theory at Midtown Music School, New York, 1937 to 1938.

Compositions

ORCHESTRA

Suite for strings

Suite of sixteen preludes

CHAMBER

Quartets

Trio (cl, vla and pf)

Five pieces (vln and pf) (Boston: White Smith)

Haitian suite (ww and perc)

Theme and eight variations (pf)

VOCAL

Five historical songs

Choruses

SACRED

Four anthems (mix-ch) (H.W. Gray; Novello)

OPERETTA

The Gingerbread Man, for children

Naughty Ninky, for children

Ref. composer, 226

ROZET, Sonia

American pianist, teacher and composer. b. Belgium. She studied at the Hochschule fuer Musik, Berlin and the Peabody Conservatory. She composed and arranged numerous works.

Ref. 506

ROZHAVSKAYA, Yudif Grigorevna

Soviet pianist and composer. b. Kiev, November 12, 1923. In 1946 she graduated from the Kiev Conservatory with distinction in the piano. In 1947 she studied composition under M. Gozenpud and in 1950 completed postgraduate studies in the piano under E. Slivak. During World War II she was active on the war front and was awarded a medal.

Compositions

ORCHESTRA

Piano concerto (1949)

Symphonic poem Dniepr (1956)

Fantasy (orch of folk insts) (1950)

CHAMBER

Variations on Russian themes (vln, vlc and pf) (1943)

Elegy (vln and pf) (1942)

Suite (vln and pf) (1945)

Two intermezzos (vln and pf) (1936)

PIANO

Variations on Ukrainian themes (2 pf)

Ballad commemorating P. Tchaikovsky (1939)

Four etudes (1935)

Humoresque (1941)

Sonata (1976)

Sonatina (1951)

Ten pieces (1950)

Three miniatures (1966)

Two children's pieces (1945)

Two etudes (1973)

VOCAL

Moya radyanska Ukraina, collective cantata (1952)

Moya sovietskaya Ukraina, cantata (M. Stelmakh) (soli, ch and orch) (1952)

Slava zhinkam-trudivnitsyam, cantata (1950)

Snow White, suite (soloist, orator and orch) (1955)

Pieces for children's choir (Soviet authors) (1950-1955)

More than 50 romances (Pushkin, Lermontov, Shevchenko, Sosiura, Korotich, Alehmatova, Franko and other poets)

BALLET

Korolevztvo krivykh zerkal

OPERA

Skazka o poteryannom vremeni (1971)

OPERETTA

Kazka pro zagublenii chas, for children (Kiev, 1971)

INCIDENTAL MUSIC

Music for theatre, cinema, radio plays

Ref. 21, 87, 330, 420

ROZMAN, Charlotte Debaro. See ROZMAN, Sarah

ROZMAN, Sarah (Charlotte Debaro)

Israeli pianist, violinist, violist and composer. b. Hungary, 1911. She studied in Budapest and Paris and went to Israel in 1933. She performed in concerts and recitals.

Ref. Dora Sowden (Tel Aviv), 94

ROZWADOWSKI, Raffaela Contessa (nee Vitaliani)

B. Graz, ca. 1816; d. June, 1906.

Composition

OPERA

Il Corsaro (Rio de Janeiro, 1870)

Ref. 431

RUBIN, Anna Ita

American pianist, teacher, writer and composer. b. Akron, OH, May 9, 1946. She graduated with a B.A. cum laude at Pomona College, Claremont, CA, in 1968 and her B.F.A. (music, 1975) from the Californian Institute of Arts. In 1981 she was awarded her M.F.A. (composition) from the same institute having studied under Mul Powell, Mort Subotnick, Leonard Stein, Pauline Oliveros (q.v.) and Hal Budd. In 1983 she studied under Ton de Leeuw at the Sweelinck Conservatorium, Amsterdam and attended lessons with Brian Ferneyhough in Germany. Her piano teachers included Peter Hewitt, Jeannine Dowis, Eva Naiditch Cooper, Louis Goldstein and William Douglas. From 1968 until 1973 she worked as a teacher and co-ordinator of an independant high school. Among the subjects she taught was the history of women in music and theory. She was a founding member of the Independent Composers' Association, Los Angeles, and served as their president in 1980. She was the recipient of a number of awards including an award of a grant to attend the International Music Institute, Darmstadt in 1982. PHOTOGRAPH.

Compositions

ORCHESTRA

High priestess (1980)

CHAMBER

Layers (cham ens) (1981)

Marching band (6 insts) (1980)

To Kampuchea (brass qnt) (1980)

Marguerite's dance (fl, vlc and perc)

Trix ocarina (3 ocarinas)

Still and turning (vlc)

PIANO

Banana rag (1976)

Short suite (1975)

White sound/white space (1980)

VOCAL

Naming (ch) (1979)

Sappho (ch and 6 insts) (1978)

Vox, voce, voice (ch a-cap) (1981)

Die Nacht: Lament for Malcolm X (S, vln, vla, vlc, d-b, fl, cl, ob, bsn, hn and pf)

The heart (T and 6 insts) (1979)

Remember (vce and cl) (1982)

Songs to death (S, vlc and pf) (1979)

Not the usual love songs (S and m-S)

DANCE SCORES

Unpeeling (dancer, vln, cl, gtr, hn, trb and perc)

ELECTRONIC

Audible to oneself (vce, vlc and tape) (1981)

Laughing the crying and golden

Piano pieces (S, pf, tape and elec)

Reflections in a sound mirror (video)

Sneedjes

MISCELLANEOUS

Arcing, naming and echoes, 3 audience participation (1979)

Publications
Composition from a Woman's Point of View. Paid my Dues, 1978.
Curriculum and the Alternative School. New School of Education Journal, vol. 11.
The Environmentalist's Guide to the East Bay Shoreline. With Steven Fisher. 1973.
History of Women in Music. In Women's Music, Written Word Collective, 1975.
Numerous articles for professional magazines.
Ref. composer, 625

RUCHEVSKAYA, Ekaterina Alexandrovna
Soviet composer. b. 1922.
Composition
ORCHESTRA
Liutsian Prigozhin, monographic sketch (Moscow: Sovietski Kompozitor, 1977)
Ref. Otto Harrassowitz (Wiesbaden)

RUCH-TSCHIEMER, Flora
Late 19th-century Swiss composer. She composed choral works and solo songs in the Bern dialect.
Ref. 651

RUCINSKA, Lucja
Early 19th-century Polish pianist and composer. She lived in Zhitomir, Ukraine. She studied the piano under Juliusz Zarebski and accompanied the violinist Andrzej Janowicz. In 1852 she edited an Album Musical of piano compositions by selected composers, including Moniuszko, Dobrzynski, Szymanowska and Lubomirski; it was published in St. Petersburg and contains some of her own mazurkas.
Compositions
PIANO
Mazurka (Gebethner)
Mazurkas (in Album Musical) (St. Petersburg, 1852)
Polonaise, op 4 (Gebethner)
Souvenir à mes amis, mazurka (Zhitomir, Budkiewicz, 1861)
Ref. 118, 297

RUDALL, Eleonor C.
20th-century English professor and composer. She was an A.R.A.M. and an L.R.A.M. and later became professor of composition and harmony at that academy. She composed a string quartet, a sonata for the violin and the piano, a one act opera and two ballets.
Ref. 467

RUDERSDORFF, Erminie (nee Mansfield)
Ukraine singer, writer and composer. b. Ivankov, December 12, 1822; d. Boston, MA, February 26, 1882. She studied voice under Bordogni and de Micherout and toured Germany extensively. Shortly after making her debut in London in 1854 she moved to the United States.
Compositions
VOCAL
Ridolin, cantata (lib and some music with Randegger)
Maying
Publications
Einige Worte ueber das Erlernen des Gesanges.
Ref. 276, 433

RUDOLF, Anna (nee Swart)
South African singer, writer and composer. b. March 9, 1924. In 1965 her drama *Bye om 'n aster* won a special drama prize from the National Council for Adult Education.
Compositions
VOCAL
Children's songs incl.:
Mis en raak
Nog liedjies (Johannesburg: Perskor, 1971)
Nuwe liedjies vir almal (Johannesburg: Voortrekkerpers, 1965)
Sing, maats (Johannesburg: Melody Music, 1968)
Tollie Tollieman (Pretoria: Middleton and Joubert, 1969)
Vier limericks
OPERETTA
Skrikkeljanie, for children (Johannesburg: Dalro, 1968)
Van der Merwe K.o.o.s. (Dalro, 1969)
Ref. 184

RUDOLPH, Jeanne Zaidel. See ZAIDEL-RUDOLPH, Jeanne

RUDOW, Vivian Adelberg
American pianist, lecturer and composer. b. Baltimore, MD, April 1, 1936. She studied under Jean Ivey at the Peabody Conservatory where she obtained her B.M. in 1960. She was on the piano faculty of the Peabody Preparatory Department from 1958 to 1959. In 1972 she was a winner in the electronic music division of the Annapolis Fine Arts Festival contest.
Compositions
ELECTRONIC
Changing space, dance piece (1973)
Cry a thousand tears (S, a-fl or c-fl, trp and prep tape)
The lion and the hares (1972)
Music for best of friends (1974)
Music for the Trojan Women (1972)
The oak and the reed, dance (1972)
Syntheticon and lies, dance (1974)
Ref. 142, 347, 622

RUEFF, Jeanine
French pianist, lecturer and composer. b. Paris, February 5, 1922. She studied at the Paris Conservatoire under the Gallon brothers and H. Busser. In 1945 she received the Favareille-Chailley-Richez prize for her *Piano quintet* and in 1948 won the second Grand Prix de Rome. She was an accompanist at the Paris Conservatoire in 1950 and taught solfege there from 1959. DISCOGRAPHY.
Compositions
ORCHESTRA
Symphony (Leduc)
Cello concerto (1946)
Concertino (a-sax and orch or pf) (1951) (Baron; Leduc)
Concertino (cl and orch) (1950) (Baron; Leduc)
Chanson et passepied (a-sax and orch or pf) (1951) (Leduc)
Sinfonietta (1956)
CHAMBER
Piano quintet (1945)
Andante et finale (str qrt)
String quartet (1944)
Concert en quatuor (4 sax) (1955) (Leduc)
Three pieces (wind trio) (Leduc)
A la manière de ..., 5 pieces (cl and pf) (1978) (Paris: Billaudot)
Cantilene (hn and pf) (Leduc)
Melopea (a-sax and pf) (1954)
Sonata (vlc and pf)
Sonatine (trp and pf) (Leduc)
Variations (b-flat cl and pf) (1976) (Theodore Front)
Sonata (a-sax) (Leduc)
Three movements (a-sax)
Prelude and toccata (hpcd or pf) (Leduc)
Pieces (fl, bsn, cor anglais, trb, tba, d-b and cl) (Leduc)
BALLET
Gasquoilles (1949)
OPERA
La Femme d'Enu, chamber opera (1954)
MISCELLANEOUS
Trois hommages
Ref. 9, 26, 44, 76, 80, 94, 280, 563

RUEGGER, Charlotte
Swiss concert violinist, lecturer and composer. b. Lucerne, November 17, 1876; d. 1959. She studied at the Strasbourg Conservatory and Brussels Conservatory under Zajic, Colyns and Cesar Thomson. After touring Germany, Switzerland and France she went to the United States where she taught at the Conservatory at Oberlin College, OH, and later at Meredith College, Raleigh, NC. She composed a violin concerto, a sonata and other violin pieces (Elkan-Vogel), choral pieces (Gamble-Hinged) and solo songs (Canyon).
Ref. 7, 40, 226, 347

RUFFIN, Fraeulein
German composer. d. 1526.
Composition
VOCAL
Canzone
Ref. 465

RUFF-STOEHR, Herta Maria Klara
German organist, pianist, violinist, teacher and composer. b. Hanau/Main, December 3, 1904. She began her piano studies at the age of ten in Gardelegen. Three years later she began studying the violin and after 1921, singing in Leipzig-Gautzsch and Gardelegen. Between 1938 and 1939 she studied the piano in Berlin. After the war she studied at the Music Academy of Stuttgart and the University of Tuebingen. She taught the piano and the organ in Hechingen. PHOTOGRAPH.
Compositions
ORCHESTRA
Concertino (pf and str orch) (1966)
CHAMBER
Clarinet quintet (1962)
Piano quintet (1971)
First string quartet (1947)
Quartet (cl and strs) (1968)
Quartet (fl, vln, vlc and pf) (1974)
Second string quartet (1966)
Three pieces for string quartet (2 vln and 2 vlc)
Trio (fl, vln and pf) (1962)
Trio (vln, vla and vlc) (1978)
Trio (vln, vla and vlc) (1966)
Trio (2 vln and pf) (1965)
Trio (2 vln and vlc) (1967)
Allegramente (fl and pf)
Allegramente (vln and vlc) (1961, rev 1972)
Allegretto (fl and pf) (1960)
Allegretto con leggieramente (vln and vlc) (1961)
Allegro assai (vln and pf) (1949)
Andantino (fl and pf)
Cantando (vln and pf)
Con movimento (vln and pf)
Gebet und Choral (vln and pf) (1972)
Giocoso (fl and pf) (1961)
Moderato (vln and vlc) (1961, rev 1972)
Moderato alla seconda volta (vln and pf) (1948)
Mobile (vln and pf) (1960)
Perpetuum mobile (vln and vlc) (1972)
Pfingstsequenz (vln and org or pf) (1978)
Sostenuto (vlc and pf) (1973)
Sostenuto (fl and pf) (1967)
Vivace (fl and pf)
Menuet (gtr) (1950)
ORGAN
Meditation (1978)
Phantasie (1978)
Choralmaessig variiert (1978)
Schreitende Doppelfugetta (1978)
Praeludium (1979)
Maestoso e andante religioso (1979)
Choralfantasie (1979)
Hymne auf Gottes Wirken (1979)
Numerous arrangements
PIANO
Six pieces for 4 hands (1962-1964)
Adagio – allegretto (1982)
Karfreitag – Ostersonntag (1961-1962)
Maestoso e andante religioso (1954)
Metamorphoso (1980)
Sonatinensatz (1947)
Tagebuch einer Ausstellung, 5 pieces (1958)
Twenty small pieces (1942-1975)
Numerous arrangements
VOCAL
Links ein Baeumle, rechts ein Baum (G. Prager) (mix-ch) (1948)
Wir bauen eine Strasse (mix-ch) (1948)
Choral collection for small children (1950)
Musik, du holde gnadenvolle (S, m-S and Bar) (1948)
Wie an Olympes Fusse das Gestade (S, m-S and Bar) (1954)
Herbstlied (vce and 2 vln) (1948)
Fenster dicht verhangen (S, pf, vln) (1947)
Auf einem Dach ein Sperling sass (S and m-S) (1948)
Des Lebens flinke Boten (vce and fl) (1948)
Choruses
Songs (vce and pf)
SACRED
Auf leiligen Wassern schreitet einher der Herr (mix-ch) (1950)
Frisch auf nun all Ihr Seelen (ch and vln or fl) (1953)
Gebet-Andante religioso (mix-ch) (1948)
Sei Gott getreu (ch and pf) (1956)
Wer heimlich seine Wohnstatt im Schutz des Allerhoechsten hat (ch and pf) (1954)
Other choral works (ch and pf or org)
Ref. composer, 70, 77, 206

RUFF-STOHR, Herta Maria. See RUFF-STOEHR, Herta Maria

RUGELES, Ana Mercedes de
Venezuelan teacher and composer. b. Barquisimeto, State Lara, August 8, 1915. From 1953 to 1964 she organized programs for Radio Nacional de Venezuela and from 1970 was principal of the Escuela Preparatoria de Musica J.M. Olivares.
Compositions
CHAMBER
Serenata barquisimetana (double qnt and pf) (1967)
PIANO
Pequeña suite infantil (1966)
Other works
VOCAL
Children's songs
SACRED
Hymns
Ref. 17

RUNCIE, Constance Owen Faunt Le Roy (Mrs. James)
American pianist, poetess and composer. b. Indianapolis, IN, January 15, 1836; d. Winnetka, IL, May 17, 1911. She studied the piano and composition under various masters in Germany from 1852 and on her return to the United States in 1861, began to compose songs. She was one of the first American women to receive recognition as a serious composer and organized the Minerva Club at New Harmony, IN, said to be the first such women's club in America. She was possibly the first American woman who composed a romantic opera.
Compositions
ORCHESTRA
Symphony
CHAMBER
In twilight (vln and pf)
Night (vln and pf)
Remembrance (vln and pf)
Zion march (org)
PIANO
Andante
Fragment
Sonata
VOCAL
Choral works incl.:
Das Voeglein singt
The dove of peace
Invocation to love
I will arise
A merry life
SACRED
Te Deum, cantata
Easter carol
Hear, O hear us
I hold my heart so still
My spirit rests (vce and pf) (New York: W.A. Pond, 1882)
Take my soul, O Lord
There is a land of pure delight
We have sinned unto death
Anthems
OPERA
The Prince of Asturia
Publications
Dramatic and Lyric Poems. New York, 1887.
Ref. 76, 226, 228, 292, 304, 347, 353, 415, 433, 460, 477, 484

RUPAMATI, Rani
14th-century Indian composer of Malwa, Rajastan. Her compositions were in a Hindi dialect.
Ref. National Council of Women in India, 414

RUSCA, Claudia Francesca
17th-century Italian composer. She was a nun in the cloister of Santa Catarina.
Compositions
SACRED
Magnificat (1-5 vces) (ded Cardinal Borranno) (Milan, 1630)
Sacri concerti a 1-5 voci con salmi e canzoni francesi a 4 varii motetti
Ref. 128, 335

RUSCHE, Marjorie Maxine
American pianist, conductor and composer. b. Sturgeon Bay, WI, November 18, 1949. In 1972 she studied music theory and composition under Dr. Dominick Argento and Dr. Paul Fetler. She also studied voice, the piano, musicology and conducting at the University of Minnesota graduating with an M.A. (theory and composition, 1975). She is a member of the Minnesota Composers' Forum. PHOTOGRAPH.

Compositions
ORCHESTRA
Concerto (cor anglais and orch) (1974)
Synthesis: Orchestral survey (1975)
CHAMBER
Stolen hearts (3 trp, 3 trb, 1 tba, snare-dr, cmb, b-drs) (1973)
The city (brass qnt) (1971)
Quintet (fl, B-flat cl, hn in F, vln and vlc) (1974)
Woodwind trilogy (fl, ob, B-flat cl, E-flat a-cl and bsn) (1972)
Quartet for strings (1981)
String quartet No. 1 (1973)
Trio (pf, vln and vlc) (1974)
Pentagram (fl and gtr) (1973)
Sonata (fl and pf) (1974)
Sonatina (pf) (1973)
Talisman (fl) (1975)
VOCAL
This is my country? (double ch, ob, bsn, trp, cor anglais and timp) (1973)
Auld Robin Gray (S, fl, picc and pf) (1975)
Singing songs: The singer; Melody moving downstream; Love, in my wood (S, fl, B-flat cl, cor anglais, 3 vln and vlc) (1975)
A mother mourns for the death of her son (vce and pf) (1971)
SACRED
Give us peace (mix-ch) (1972)
Seek the Lord (S and pf) (1970)
THEATRE
Grandmither (S and pf) (1975)
Much madness is divinest sense (singer-actor, fl, picc, cor anglais and pf) (1975)
MULTIMEDIA
Composition (vce, kazoos, cat and fl) (1973)
Ref. composer

RUSH, Ruth
20th-century American pianist and composer. She was named Oklahoma musician of the year by the Oklahoma Federation of Music Clubs.
Ref. AMC newsletter

RUSSCHER-OVERMAN, Meta. See OVERMAN, Meta

RUSSELL, Anna
English comedienne, singer, writer and composer. b. London, December 27, 1911. She received her musical training at the Royal College of Music.
DISCOGRAPHY.
Compositions
VOCAL
Songs incl.:
I'm sitting in the bar all alone
Feeling fine
I love the spring
Ref. 39

RUSSELL, Betsy A.
20th-century American composer.
Composition
CHAMBER
String quartet
Ref. AMC newsletter

RUSSELL, Olive Nelson
20th-century American composer.
Compositions
ORGAN
Toccata on a modal theme
VOCAL
Choral works
TEACHING PIECES
Pieces for piano
Ref. 40, 347

RUTA, Gilda, Countess (Cagnazzi)
Italian concert pianist, teacher and composer. b. Naples, October 13, 1853; d. New York, October 26, 1932. The daughter and pupil of composer Michele Ruta, she studied under the opera composer Mercadante and improved her piano technique under Franz Liszt in Rome. She made her piano debut at the age of 12 at the San Carlo Theatre of Naples, playing Beethoven's *Concerto* under the baton of M. De Giosa. In 1890 she was awarded a gold medal at the International Exhibition in Florence for her vocal and orchestral compositions. In 1896 she settled in New York where she performed with major orchestras, in recitals at Madison Square Gardens and at the Metropolitan Opera House.
Compositions
ORCHESTRA
Concerto (pf and orch)
Andante rondo (pf and str orch)
Boldero (pf and str orch)
Gavotta
Other pieces
CHAMBER
Gavotta (vln and pf; also vlc and pf; also pf) (Mariani)
Romanza senza parole (vln and pf; also vlc and pf) (Mariani)
Sonata (vln and pf) (Mariani)
PIANO
Aria di danza
Andante e rondo (Mariani)
Bolero (Mariani)
Bourree
Capriccio brillante (Mariani)
Bolero (Mariani)
Danza del XVII secolo
Elegia
Elegie (Jurgensen)
Mesta serenata
Nottunto polacco
Partita: Preludio e fuga; Andantino; Gavotta e musette; I et II Sarabanda; Allegretto cromatico; Burlesca
Polacca di concerto (Mariani)
Polacca
Primavera
Soave melancolia, barcarolle
Scherzo
Siciliano (also hp)
Suite a canoni: Arietta; Bourree; Giga; Minuetto; Prelude; Sarabanda
Tempo di gavotta e musette
Tempo di minuetto
Tre Pezzi: Fantasticando, impromptu (Forlivesi); Secondo scherzo; Serenade
Zingaresca
VOCAL
Songs incl.:
Addio!, romantic melody
Alle stelle!, romantic melody
Addio dov'era la luce
Amore ho in petto
Amore v'e morto e non ritorna piu; Senti, ho l'anima stanca
Dammi un'ora d'amor
Dolci memorie
Etero pensier
Eterna idea
Fior di mia vita, baci del mio core
Fiori di campo: Fiorellini che taciti
Moro d'amore! Nella! notturno
Nevrosi (Mariani)
O fiorellin di siepe
Oh amore, amore!
Partirai!! Domani partirai
Pei tuoi bianchi capelli
Povero amore
Quando cadran le foglie, per te
Quando la patria e libera
Rugiada e sole: Vedete nel giardino
Se v'amo! Non mi chiedete
Son sola! O dolce sera
Ultima ebrezza un ultimo profumo
Un giorno senza amor giorno perduto
Vado solingo e lagrimo
Vedi il mar
Voglio guarire: Mi si spezza la testa
Voglio morir con te! Lasciali dir
OPERA
The Fire Worshipers
Ref. 70, 85, 86, 105, 226, 276, 297, 347, 622

RUTTENSTEIN, Constance, Baroness
19th-century German composer.
Compositions
VOCAL
Ich denke dein
Lebe Wohl
Letzter Traum

SACRED
Ave Maria
Ref. 276, 433

RYAN, Winifred
20th-century American organist, choir director and composer. She composed piano pieces and songs.
Ref. 347

RYBNER, Dagmar de Corval
Swiss concert pianist, lecturer and composer. b. Baden, September 9, 1890; d. Long Island, NY, July 22, 1965. She was the daughter of the Danish pianist and composer Dr. Cornelius Rybner. She studied music in Karlsruhe, Neuchatel and New York and among her teachers was Rachmaninov. She made her debut as a concert pianist in Karlsruhe in 1906 and appeared at the Metropolitan Opera House, New York in 1912. She toured Europe and the United States and from 1924 to 1932 taught at the Curtis Institute of Music, Philadelphia and after 1933 at Barnard College. She composed pieces for the violin and the piano (Breitkopf; Schirmer; Ditson) and songs.
Ref. 89, 96, 347

RYCOFF, Lalla (Ryckoff)
American pianist and composer. b. Milwaukee, WI. She made her first appearance as a pianist in Chicago at the age of nine. She was active as a program maker and recitalist, moving later to St. Louis, MO. She composed more than 200 pieces.
Compositions
PIANO
Fairy tales for fairy fingers
Juvenile scenes in foreign lands
Our American cousins
Our little cousins abroad
Street scenes
Other teaching works
VOCAL
The quarrelsome glee club (qrt for m-ch)
It's just for you
Many songs
Ref. 292, 347

RYDER, Theodora Sturkow
American pianist, music critic, teacher and composer. b. Philadelphia, PA, August 11, 1876. Her father gave her her first music lessons and she went on to study the piano at Northwestern University under Regina Watson, Louis Staab and Carl Wolfsohn. She made her debut as a concert pianist in 1907 at the City Hall in Pittsburgh. From 1906 to 1907 she was the music critic of *The Pittsburgh Dispatch* and from 1910 maintained her private piano studios in Chicago, Los Angeles and from 1947 in Oakland.
Compositions
ORCHESTRA
The Great Lakes, symphonic suite
CHAMBER
Suite for violin and piano (1925)
PIANO
From the family album incl.:
The zoo; Antics; Imps; Valse bizarre
VOCAL
Songs
Ref. 496

RYGAARD, Christine
20th-century Danish composer.
Compositions
PIANO
Jule og Nytaarsglaeder; 4 nye Danse componerede:
No. 1, Jensine polka
No. 2, Sophie polka mazurka
No. 3, Anna polka
No. 4, Bacchus galop
Ref. 331

RYLEK-STANKOVA, Blazena
Czech singer, teacher and composer. b. Slivenec, near Prague, February 10, 1888. She studied in Prague and graduated in 1907. She was particularly interested in various teaching methods of singing and eurhythmics, which she studied under Jaques-Dalcroze in Dornach, Switzerland and taught at schools and privately. She studied singing under Platen in Dresden and L. Prochazkova-Neumannova. After 1938 she took composition lessons from Alois Haba. From 1943 to 1946 she studied quarter and sixth-tone music at Prague Conservatory.
Compositions
VOCAL
Over 50 works incl.:
Jaro, song cycle
Ref. 8, 197

RYLEY, Ellen. See WRIGHT, Ellen

RYNNING, Fredrikke Holtemann. See WAALER, Fredrikke Holtemann

RYOJIN HISHO
Japanese poetess and composer. b. ca. 1179. Her songs were collected in twenty books by the Emperor Go-Shirakawa between 1127 and 1192 and consist of Buddhist hymn, Shinto chants, folk and traditional songs
Ref. 464

RZAYEVA, Agabadzhi Ishmael kyzy
Soviet lecturer and composer. b. Baku, December 25, 1912. She studied under S. Rustamov at the Baku Music School and graduated in 1940. She continued her studies of Azerbaijanian music under N. Hadjibekov at the Conservatory of Baku, graduating in 1947. After 1939 she lectured at the music school and was a member of the government of the Azerbaijanian Soviet Socialist Republic.
Compositions
ORCHESTRA
Dzhengi, war song (Azerbaijanian insts)
Lezginka
Marsh patriotov (1950)
Yally, round dance (Azerbaijanian insts)
PIANO
Dance suite
Round dance
VOCAL
Four choruses (Azerbaijanian poets) (ch and pf) (1952)
Five songs (vce and ens)
Pioneer songs
Romances and songs (Nizami, Lermontov and other Soviet poets) (vce and pf)
THEATRE
Ginnesh eshgi, musical montage for children (ch, ballet and orch) (M. Dalbazi) (1945)
Ref. 87

SAARIAHO, Kaija
Finnish composer. b. 1952. She studied composition at the Sibelius Academy under Paavo Heininen.
Compositions
CHAMBER
Yellows (hn and perc) (1980)
Canvas (fl) (1978)
VOCAL
A Finnish-language piece (mix-ch) (1979)
Bruden, song cycle (Soedergren) (S, fl, a-fl and perc) (1977)
Jing (S and vlc) (1979)
Prelude-confession-postlude (M. Waltari) (S and pf) (1980)
Ref. FMIC

SAARINEN, Gloria Edith
New Zealand pianist, assistant professor and composer. b. Dunedin, September 21, 1934, now living in Canada. She has a B.Mus. from the University of Otago, New Zealand and studied at the Academy of Music in Vienna and at the Chigiana Academy in Siena, Italy. She made her debut at Wigmore Hall in 1959 and performed in Europe, Canada, the United States and New Zealand between 1961 and 1974. She is an L.R.S.M. and was assistant professor at the University of Calgary at Alberta, Canada from 1966 to 1974. She toured Canada and the United States with the One Third Ninth piano trio between 1973 and 1975 and made appearances on radio and television and at Stratford Festivals. She teaches at Mount Royal College, Calgary. She composed cadenzas for Mozart's concertos.
Ref. 77

SABATIER-BLOT, Mme.
19th-century French composer.
Composition
OPERA
Un Mariage per Quidproquo (Paris, 1865)
Ref. 431

SABININ, Martha von
19th-century German composer.
Compositions
CHAMBER
Piano pieces
VOCAL
Ballade, op. 4
Eight songs, op. 1
Six songs, op. 2
Six songs, op. 3
Ref. 226, 433

SACCAGGIO, Adelina Luisa Nicasia
Argentine lecturer and composer. b. October 29, 1918. She studied under Carlos Lopes Buchado at the National Conservatory, and at the Institute of Sacred Music and the M. de Falla Conservatory. She was active as a teacher from 1947 and taught at the National Conservatory in 1966. In 1947 she was appointed special music teacher for the National Council of Education.
Compositions
CHAMBER
Allegro (hn and qrt)
VOCAL
Duerme (vce and pf)
Pastoril (3 vces)
SACRED
Psalm 66 (solos, ch and orch)
Ref. 359

SACHS, Carolyn
American writer and composer. b. New York, 1952. She gained a B.A. from Harvard University, an M.A. from Columbia University and is currently studying for her doctorate. She is associate producer for Composers Recordings Inc. and writes on musical topics. She composes vocal, instrumental and electronic music for theatre, film and dance.
Ref. CRI

SADERO GENI, Maria Scarpa
Italian folklorist, singer and composer. b. 1891; d. 1961. She appeared in concerts in Italy, Europe and America.
Composition
VOCAL
Canzoni popolari regionali, collection (vce and pf) (Societa Anonima Notari)
Ref. 56, 622

SADOVNIKOFF, Mary Briggs
20th-century American composer of chamber music, choral pieces and songs.
Ref. 40, 347

SADOWSKY, Reah
American pianist and composer of Russian parentage. b. Winnipeg, Canada, December 17, 1920. She studied at the Curtis Institute of Music in 1929 and the Juilliard School of Music from 1931 to 1933. She studied the piano with her mother, a pianist and Alberto Jonas, Josef Lhevine, Milan Blanchet, Harold Samuels and Heinrich Simon. She made her first public appearance at the age of six in San Francisco with the California Symphony Orchestra and gave performances throughout the world.
Compositions
MISCELLANEOUS
Cadiz (1937)
Dance espagnole (1937)
Ref. 496

SAFARIAN, Lucia Arisovna
Soviet lecturer and composer. b. Rezhta, Iran, March 27, 1903. From 1925 to 1927 she taught music at nursery schools in Iran and from 1929 to 1935 in Erivan. From 1935 to 1941 she studied at the Conservatory in Erivan. She lectured on theoretical subjects in music schools until 1948.
Compositions
PIANO
Etudes, dances (1952)
Sonata (1938)
Suite (1938)
VOCAL
Approx. 30 songs for children (Armenian poets)
Ref. 87

SAFFERY, Eliza (Mrs. Henry Shelton)
Early 19th-century English composer.
Compositions
CHAMBER
Piano pieces
VOCAL
Broken vows
Hours of melody, song collection (1836)
I love thee, native land
Old yew tree
Reminiscences of a minstrel, 10 songs (E. Ryan) (1832)
The rover's return
Sailor's grave
Ref. 6, 85, 226, 276, 347, 433

SAHLBERG, Alma
Swedish composer. d. 1888.
Composition
VOCAL
Stjernblomman, song (Edvard Baeckstroem)
Ref. 167, 297

SAIDAMINOVA, Dilorom
Soviet composer. b. 1943. DISCOGRAPHY.
Compositions
ORCHESTRA
Symphonic poem
BALLET
Gorinchii kamien
Ref. 26, 312, 433

SAINT BRIDGET of Kildare. See BRIDGET

SAINT MARGARET of Scotland. See MARGARET, Queen of Scotland

SAINT-AMANS FILS, Monsieur Leon. See LA HYE, Louise Genevieve

SAINT-CROIX, Caroline de
French composer. b. 1843. She was a harmony student of M.J. de Coninck.
Compositions
OPERETTA
Chanson du printemps, in 1 act
Madame de Rabucor (or Rabuer), in 1 act
Pygmalion, in 1 act
Rendez-vous galants, in 1 act
Ref. 26, 226, 276, 307, 433

SAINT-DIDIER, Countess
19th-century French composer.
Composition
VOCAL
Il est rendu, cantata (ca. 1820)
Ref. 26, 312, 433